# Customer Support Information

## Plunkett's Companion to the Almanac of American Employers 2009

**Please register your book immediately...**

if you did not purchase it directly from Plunkett Research, Ltd. This will enable us to fulfill your replacement request if you have a damaged product, or your requests for assistance. Also it will enable us to notify you of future editions, so that you may purchase them from the source of your choice.

**If you are an actual purchaser but did not receive a FREE CD-ROM version with your book...***

you may request it by returning this form.

____ YES, please register me as a purchaser of the book.
I did not buy it directly from Plunkett Research, Ltd.

____ YES, please send me a free CD-ROM version of the book.
I am an actual purchaser, but I did not receive one with my book.

(Proof of purchase may be required.)

Customer Name ____________________

Title ____________________

Organization ____________________

Address ____________________

City ____________ State ________ Zip ________

Country (if other than USA) ____________________

Phone ____________ Fax ____________

E-mail ____________________

**Mail or Fax to:** Plunkett Research, Ltd.
Attn: FREE CD-ROM and/or Registration
P.O. Drawer 541737, Houston, TX 77254-1737 USA
713.932.0000 · Fax 713.932.7080 · www.plunkettresearch.com

*Purchasers of used books are not eligible to register. Use of CD-ROMs is subject to the terms of their end-user license agreements.

# PLUNKETT'S COMPANION TO THE ALMANAC OF AMERICAN EMPLOYERS: Mid-Size Firms 2009

**The only guide to America's hottest, fastest-growing mid-sized employers**



**Jack W. Plunkett**

**Published by:**
**Plunkett Research, Ltd., Houston, Texas**
**www.plunkettresearch.com**

# PLUNKETT'S COMPANION TO THE ALMANAC OF AMERICAN EMPLOYERS: Mid-Size Firms 2009


**Editor and Publisher:**
Jack W. Plunkett

**Executive Editor and Database Manager:**
Martha Burgher Plunkett

**Senior Editors and Researchers:**
Brandon Brison
Addie K. FryeWeaver
Christie Manck
John Peterson

**Editors, Researchers and Assistants:**
Elizabeth Braddock
Michelle Dotter
Michael Esterheld
Austin Hansell
Kathi Mestousis
Lindsey Meyn
Holly Scarpinato
Jana Sharooni
Jill Steinberg
Kyle Wark
Suzanne Zarosky

**E-Commerce Managers:**
Mark Cassells
Emily Hurley
Lynne Zarosky

**Information Technology Manager:**
Wenping Guo

**Cover Design:**
Kim Paxson, Just Graphics
*Junction, TX*



**Special Thanks to:**
U.S. Department of Labor
*Bureau of Labor Statistics*
U.S. Department of Commerce
*Bureau of Economic Analysis, National Technical Information Service*



**Plunkett Research, Ltd.**
**P. O. Drawer 541737, Houston, Texas 77254**
**Phone: 713.932.0000 Fax: 713.932.7080**
**www.plunkettresearch.com**

**Published by:**
**Plunkett Research, Ltd.**
**P. O. Drawer 541737**
**Houston, Texas 77254-1737**

**Phone: 713.932.0000**
**Fax: 713.932.7080**
**Internet: www.plunkettresearch.com**

**ISBN10 # 1-59392-126-8**
**ISBN13 # 978-1-59392-126-2**

**Disclaimer of liability for use and results of use:**

The editors and publishers assume no responsibility for your own success in making an investment or business decision, in seeking or keeping any job, in succeeding at any firm or in obtaining any amount or type of benefits or wages. Your own results and the job stability or financial stability of any company depend on influences outside of our control. All risks are assumed by the reader. Investigate any potential employer or business relationship carefully and carefully verify past and present finances, present business conditions and the level of compensation and benefits currently paid. Each company's details are taken from sources deemed reliable; however, their accuracy is not guaranteed. The editors and publishers assume no liability, beyond the actual payment received from a reader, for any direct, indirect, incidental or consequential, special or exemplary damages, and they do not guarantee, warrant nor make any representation regarding the use of this material. Trademarks or tradenames are used without symbols and only in a descriptive sense, and this use is not authorized by, associated with or sponsored by the trademarks' owners. Ranks and ratings are presented as an introductory and general glance at corporations, based on our research and our knowledge of businesses and the industries in which they operate. The reader should use caution.

# PLUNKETT'S COMPANION TO THE ALMANAC OF AMERICAN EMPLOYERS: Mid-Size Firms 2009

## TABLE OF CONTENTS



*Continued on the next page*

*Continued from previous page*

# INTRODUCTION

As the name implies, this volume is designed to be used in conjunction with THE ALMANAC OF AMERICAN EMPLOYERS. The main volume of THE ALMANAC covers highly successful firms of 2,500 or more employees. This "companion" volume focuses on mid-size firms, from 100 to 2,500 employees.

PLUNKETT'S COMPANION TO THE ALMANAC OF AMERICAN EMPLOYERS is an easy-to-use solution to what would otherwise be a complicated problem: How can you tell, among all of America's mid-size companies, which firms are most likely to be hiring? Among those hot firms, which are the best to work for? No other source provides this book's easy-to-understand comparisons of growth, treatment of employees, salaries, benefits, pension plans, profit sharing and many other items of great importance to job seekers.

Especially helpful is the way in which PLUNKETT'S COMPANION TO THE ALMANAC OF AMERICAN EMPLOYERS enables readers with no business background to readily compare the growth potential and benefit plans of mid-size employers. You'll see the mid-term financial record of each firm, along with the impact of earnings, sales and growth plans on each company's potential to provide employment or advancement opportunities.

Information is presented in a way that addresses the differing interests of individual employees. You'll find separate rankings for dozens of categories of data that you may want to consider. While the book is aimed primarily at job seekers, it will also be of tremendous value to researchers, marketing executives and personnel professionals. PLUNKETT'S COMPANION TO THE ALMANAC OF AMERICAN EMPLOYERS is the premier guide to the most successful mid-size employers in the nation, their policies and their performance.

PLUNKETT'S COMPANION TO THE ALMANAC OF AMERICAN EMPLOYERS is your opportunity to gain valuable knowledge in a matter of minutes. Five hundred of the most successful mid-size corporate employers in America are analyzed in this book. Tens of thousands of pieces of information, gathered from a wide variety of sources, have been researched for these corporations and are presented here in a form that can be easily understood by job seekers of all types.

Thanks to PLUNKETT'S COMPANION TO THE ALMANAC OF AMERICAN EMPLOYERS' exclusive data system, potentially confusing considerations have been reduced to simple groups of focused data. By scanning the data groups and the long list of unique indexes, you can find the best employer to fit your personal needs.

The MID-SIZE EMPLOYERS 500 are among the best companies to work for in America. Which companies offer the best benefits, are the biggest employers or earn the most profits? Where are these companies operating? What firms have the highest potential salaries? All of these things and more are made easy for the reader to determine.

Thousands of observations are made that will be of great interest to prospective employees. For many of the firms, you'll find comments about such items as plans for growth, increases or decreases in the number of employees and charitable programs. You'll also find notes about special programs for the convenience of employees, such as health and recreation facilities, job training or career paths. Finally, you'll find basic information on each company, including the home office address and telephone number; regional, national and international locations; a description of the business; and a list of selected subsidiaries and trade names. In addition, you'll find fax numbers, Internet addresses and toll-free phone numbers for most of the firms.

Whether you are currently employed by one of these corporate giants or are considering applying for a job with one, you'll be able to see how each company compares with the others, even if you don't have the slightest understanding of accounting, finance or employee benefits.

Whatever your purpose for researching corporate employers, you'll find this book to be an indispensable guide. Nonetheless, as is true with all resources, this volume has limitations that the reader should be aware of:

- Financial data and other corporate information can change quickly. A book of this type can be no more current than the data that was available as of the time of editing. Consequently, the financial picture, management and ownership of the firm(s) you are studying may have changed since the publishing date of this book. For example, this almanac includes the most up-to-date sales figures and profits available to the editors as of early 2009. That means that we have typically used corporate financial data as of mid-2008.

- Corporate mergers, changes in corporate financial ratings or stability, acquisitions and downsizing are occurring at a very rapid rate. Such events may have created significant change, subsequent to the publishing of this book, within a company you are studying.

- Some of the companies in THE MID-SIZE EMPLOYERS 500 are so large in scope and in variety of business endeavors conducted within a parent organization that we have been unable to completely list all subsidiaries, affiliations, divisions and activities within a firm's corporate structure.

- This volume is intended to be a general guide to major employers in numerous industries. That means that researchers should look to this book for an overview and, when conducting in-depth research, should contact the specific corporations and related industry associations in question for the very latest changes and data. Where possible, we have listed contact names, toll-free telephone numbers and World Wide Web site addresses for the companies, government agencies and industry associations involved so that the reader may get further details without unnecessary delay.

- We have used exhaustive efforts to locate and fairly present accurate and complete data. However, when using this book or any other source for business and industry information, the reader should use caution and due diligence by conducting further research where it seems appropriate. We wish you success in your endeavors, and we trust that your experience with this book will be both satisfactory and productive.

- To obtain the best results and to best understand the fields in the company profiles, you should first read the chapter titled "How to Use This Book."

Good luck in your job search. Be patient, do your research and use this book as an important start in the right direction.

Jack W. Plunkett
Houston, Texas
March 2009

# HOW TO USE THIS BOOK

Dozens of excellent books already exist to help you choose a career, write a resume, apply for a job, dress for the office and so on. This is not the purpose of PLUNKETT'S COMPANION TO THE ALMANAC OF AMERICAN EMPLOYERS. Instead, this book's job is to help you sort through America's mid-size corporate employers to determine which may be the best for you, or to see how your current employer compares to others. Whether you are entering the job market and looking for your first position, or you are thinking about switching companies in mid-career to find more promising vistas, this book will be a valuable guide.

The two primary sections of the book are devoted first to general information for job seekers (trends analysis and advice on conducting employer research, along with resources and contacts) and then to the "Individual Data Listings" for THE MID-SIZE EMPLOYERS 500. If time permits, you should begin your research in the front chapters of this book. Also, you will find lengthy indexes in Chapter 5 and in the back of the book.

## GENERAL INFORMATION FOR JOB SEEKERS

**Chapter 1: Major Trends Affecting Job Seekers.** This chapter presents an encapsulated view of the major trends in business and the economy that are creating rapid changes in the employment picture at mid-size corporations.

**Chapter 2: Statistics.** This chapter presents in-depth statistics on employment by education level, sex, race, unemployment rates, fastest-growing industries and more.

**Chapter 3: Research–7 Keys for Job Seekers.** This chapter provides a definitive list of items that job seekers should look for when conducting research into mid-size corporate employers.

**Chapter 4: Important Contacts for Job Seekers.** This chapter covers contacts for important government agencies, organizations, job banks, reference sources and more. Included are World Wide Web sites and contact addresses for a wide variety of uses.

## THE MID-SIZE EMPLOYERS 500

**Chapter 5: THE MID-SIZE EMPLOYERS 500: Who They Are and How They Were Chosen.** The companies compared in this book were chosen from all industries, on a nationwide basis. They were individually chosen from the most successful U.S. employers, from 100 to 2,500 employees in size, based on selected types of business and industry sectors. For a complete description, see Chapter 5.

**Individual Data Listings:**

Look at one of the companies in THE MID-SIZE EMPLOYERS 500's Individual Data Listings. You'll find the following information fields:

**Company Name:**

The company profiles are in alphabetical order by company name. If you don't find the company you are seeking, it may be a subsidiary or division of one of the firms covered in this book. Try looking it up in the Index by Subsidiaries, Brand Names and Selected Affiliations in the back of the book.

**Ranks:**

Industry Group Code: An NAIC code used to group companies within like segments. (See Chapter 5 for a list of codes.)

Ranks Within This Company's Industry Group: Ranks, within this firm's segment only, for annual sales and annual profits, with 1 being the highest rank.

**Suggested Career Paths:**

A grid arranged into six major career categories and several sub-categories. A "Y" indicates that the firm is suggested for certain types of employees, by job discipline.

**Types of Business:**

A listing of the primary types of business specialties conducted by the firm.

**Brands/Divisions/Affiliations:**

Major brand names, operating divisions or subsidiaries of the firm, as well as major corporate affiliations—such as another firm that owns a significant portion of the company's stock. A complete Index by Subsidiaries, Brand Names and Selected Affiliations is in the back of the book.

**Contacts:**

The names and titles up to 27 top officers of the company are listed, including human resources contacts.

**Address:**

The firm's full headquarters address, the headquarters telephone, plus toll-free and fax numbers where available. Also provided is the World Wide Web site address.

**Financials:**

Annual Sales (2008 or the latest fiscal year available to the editors, plus up to four previous years): These are stated in thousands of dollars (add three zeros if you want the full number). This figure represents consolidated worldwide sales from all operations. 2008 figures may be estimates or may be for only part of the year—partial year figures are appropriately footnoted.

Annual Profits (2008 or the latest fiscal year available to the editors, plus up to four previous years): These are stated in thousands of dollars (add three zeros if you want the full number). This figure represents consolidated, after-tax net profit from all operations. 2008 figures may be estimates or may be for only part of the year—partial year figures are appropriately footnoted.

Stock Ticker, International Exchange, Parent Company: When available, the unique stock market symbol used to identify this firm's common stock for trading and tracking purposes is indicated. Where appropriate, this field may contain "private" or "subsidiary" rather than a ticker symbol. If the firm is a subsidiary, its parent company is listed.

Total Number of Employees: The approximate total number of employees, worldwide, as of the end of 2008 (or the latest data available to the editors).

**Apparent Salaries/Benefits:**

(The following descriptions generally apply to U.S. employers only.)

A "Y" in appropriate fields indicates "Yes."

Due to wide variations in the manner in which corporations report benefits to the U.S. Government's regulatory bodies, not all plans will have been uncovered or correctly evaluated during our effort to research this data. Also, the availability to employees of such plans will vary according to the qualifications that employees must meet to become eligible. For example, some benefit plans may be available only to salaried workers—others only to employees who work more than 1,000 hours yearly. Benefits that are available to employees of the main or parent company may not be available to employees of the subsidiaries. In addition, employers frequently alter the nature and terms of plans offered.

NOTE: Generally, employees covered by wealth-building benefit plans do not *fully* own ("vest in") funds contributed on their behalf by the employer until as many as five years of service with that employer have passed. All pension plans are voluntary—that is, employers are not obligated to offer pensions.

Pension Plan: The firm offers a pension plan to qualified employees. In this case, in order for a "Y" to appear, the editors believe that the employer offers a defined benefit or cash balance pension plan (see discussions below). The type and generosity of these plans vary widely from firm to firm. Caution: Some employers refer to plans as "pension" or "retirement" plans when they are actually 401(k) savings plans that require a contribution by the employee.

- Defined Benefit Pension Plans: Pension plans that do not require a contribution from the employee are infrequently offered. However, a few companies, particularly larger employers in high-profit-margin industries, offer defined benefit pension plans where the employee is guaranteed to receive a set pension benefit upon retirement. The amount of the benefit is determined by the years of service with the company and the employee's salary during the later years of employment. The longer a person works for the employer, the higher the retirement benefit. These defined benefit plans are funded entirely by the employer. The benefits, up to a reasonable limit, are guaranteed by the Federal Government's Pension Benefit Guaranty Corporation. These plans are not portable—if you leave the company, you cannot transfer your benefits into a different plan. Instead, upon retirement you will receive the benefits that vested during your service with the company. If your employer offers a pension plan, it must give you a summary plan description within 90 days of the date you join the plan. You can also request a summary annual report of the plan, and once every 12 months you may request an individual benefit statement accounting of your interest in the plan.

- Defined Contribution Plans: These are quite different. They do not guarantee a certain amount of pension benefit. Instead, they set out circumstances under which the employer will make a contribution to a plan on your behalf. The most common example is the 401(k) savings plan. Pension benefits are not guaranteed under these plans.
- Cash Balance Pension Plans: These plans were recently invented. These are hybrid plans—part defined benefit and part defined contribution. Many employers have converted their older defined benefit plans into cash balance plans. The employer makes deposits (or credits a given amount of money) on the employee's behalf, usually based on a percentage of pay. Employee accounts grow based on a predetermined interest benchmark, such as the interest rate on Treasury Bonds. There are some advantages to these plans, particularly for younger workers: a) The benefits, up to a reasonable limit, are guaranteed by the Pension Benefit Guaranty Corporation. b) Benefits are portable—they can be moved to another plan when the employee changes companies. c) Younger workers and those who spend a shorter number of years with an employer may receive higher benefits than they would under a traditional defined benefit plan.

ESOP Stock Plan (Employees' Stock Ownership Plan): This type of plan is in wide use. Typically, the plan borrows money from a bank and uses those funds to purchase a large block of the corporation's stock. The corporation makes contributions to the plan over a period of time, and the stock purchase loan is eventually paid off. The value of the plan grows significantly as long as the market price of the stock holds up. Qualified employees are allocated a share of the plan based on their length of service and their level of salary. Under federal regulations, participants in ESOPs are allowed to diversify their account holdings in set percentages that rise as the employee ages and gains years of service with the company. In this manner, not all of the employee's assets are tied up in the employer's stock.

Savings Plan, 401(k): Under this type of plan, employees make a tax-deferred deposit into an account. In the best plans, the company makes annual matching donations to the employees' accounts, typically in some proportion to deposits made by the employees themselves. A good plan will match one-half of employee deposits of up to 6% of wages. For example, an employee earning $30,000 yearly might deposit $1,800 (6%) into the plan. The company will match one-half of the employee's deposit, or $900. The plan grows on a tax-deferred basis, similar to an IRA. A very generous plan will match 100% of employee deposits. However, some plans do not call for the employer to make a matching deposit at all. Other plans call for a matching contribution to be made at the discretion of the firm's board of directors. Actual terms of these plans vary widely from firm to firm. Generally, these savings plans allow employees to deposit as much as 15% of salary into the plan on a tax-deferred basis. However, the portion that the company uses to calculate its matching deposit is generally limited to a maximum of 6%. Employees should take care to diversify the holdings in their 401(k) accounts, and most people should seek professional guidance or investment management for their accounts.

Stock Purchase Plan: Qualified employees may purchase the company's common stock at a price below its market value under a specific plan. Typically, the employee is limited to investing a small percentage of wages in this plan. The discount may range from 5 to 15%. Some of these plans allow for deposits to be made through regular monthly payroll deductions. However, new accounting rules for corporations, along with other factors, are leading many companies to curtail these plans—dropping the discount allowed, cutting the maximum yearly stock purchase or otherwise making the plans less generous or appealing.

Profit Sharing: Qualified employees are awarded an annual amount equal to some portion of a company's profits. In a very generous plan, the pool of money awarded to employees would be 15% of profits. Typically, this money is deposited into a long-term retirement account. Caution: Some employers refer to plans as "profit sharing" when they are actually 401(k) savings plans. True profit sharing plans are rarely offered.

Highest Executive Salary: The highest executive salary paid, typically a 2008 amount (or the latest year available to the editors) and typically paid to the Chief Executive Officer.

Highest Executive Bonus: The apparent bonus, if any, paid to the above person.

Second Highest Executive Salary: The next-highest executive salary paid, typically a 2008 amount (or the latest year available to the editors) and typically paid to the President or Chief Operating Officer.

Second Highest Executive Bonus: The apparent bonus, if any, paid to the above person.

**Other Thoughts:**

Apparent Women Officers or Directors: It is difficult to obtain this information on an exact basis, and employers generally do not disclose the data in a public way. However, we have indicated what our best efforts reveal to be the apparent number of women who either are in the posts of corporate officers or sit on the board of directors. There is a wide variance from company to company.

Hot Spot for Advancement for Women/Minorities: A "Y" in appropriate fields indicates "Yes." These are firms that appear either to have posted a substantial number of women and/or minorities to high posts or that appear to have a good record of going out of their way to recruit, train, promote and retain women or minorities. (See the Index of Hot Spots For Women and Minorities in the back of the book.) This information may change frequently and can be difficult to obtain and verify. Consequently, the reader should use caution and conduct further investigation where appropriate.

**Growth Plans/ Special Features:**

Listed here are observations regarding the firm's strategy, hiring plans, plans for growth and product development, along with general information regarding a company's business and prospects.

**Locations:**

A "Y" in the appropriate field indicates "Yes." Primary locations outside of the headquarters, categorized by regions of the United States and by international locations. A complete index by locations is also in the front of this chapter.

# Chapter 1

# MAJOR TRENDS AFFECTING JOB SEEKERS

**Major trends sweeping through business and the economy that affect job seekers of all types:**

1) U.S. Job Market Overview
2) Downsizing/Consolidation through Mergers or Acquisitions
3) Continued Growth in Outsourcing, Including Supply Chain and Logistics Services
4) Millions Working as Temps
5) Offshoring and the Globalization of Business
6) Senior Citizens Are a Hot Commodity with Selected Employers—Baby Boomers Are Retiring
7) Employment Sectors that Will Offer an Above-Average Number of Job Opportunities in 2009:

- Biotechnology, Including Agricultural Biotechnology
- Construction and Engineering Services for Infrastructure and Government Projects
- Construction—Installation of Energy-Saving Devices, Weather Stripping and Renewable Energy Components
- Consulting—Selected Fields where Consultants May Be Able to Effect Cost-Savings for Clients
- Consumer Products Manufacturers
- Cosmetics Manufacturers
- Data Processing Services Providers
- Defense Contractors—Selected Firms
- Education
- Elder Care, Home Health Care, Nursing Homes and Assisted Living Communities
- Electronic Games
- Energy Conservation Products and Services
- Guard Services, Investigation and Surveillance
- Health Care Services, Including Managed Care
- Health Foods, Organic Foods, Enhanced Foods
- Health Products
- Health Technology, Including Computerized Patient Records
- Insurance Providers—Selected Specialty Insurance Firms
- Internet Access—High Speed
- Supply Chain Services That Offer Cost-Savings to Clients
- Nanotechnology and MEMS
- Oil and Gas Exploration and Production
- Online Search Services with Advertising Revenues
- Online-based Business and Consumer Services
- Outsourcing, Including Outsourced Business and Computer Services
- Pharmaceuticals—Generics
- Radio Frequency ID Tags (RFID)
- Renewable Energy, Especially Solar and Wind Power
- Retailing—Basic, Including Drugstores and Supermarkets
- Retailing—Discount and Warehouse Clubs
- Wireless and Cellular Communications, including WiMax

## 1) U.S. Job Market Overview

Job seekers in 2009 will find the toughest hiring climate since 2002, when the economy was suffering broadly due to 9/11 and the end of the dotcom boom. Many types of employers are restructuring and downsizing thanks to the deep financial crisis of 2007-2009. Job seekers who want good positions will be forced to be better prepared and to do better research than in the boom years of the recent past. They will also have to work harder to find a good job.

The general outlook is that 2009's job market will be very poor. Employers will be cautious about hiring new people or investing in new facilities. There will be large numbers of layoffs.

Job seekers in 2009 should be prepared for the fact that nearly all industry sectors will suffer some ill effects from economic and financial market problems that originated when the housing bubble finally popped in mid-2007 and the financial meltdown accelerated in 2008. America's unemployment rate grew steadily through 2008, and unemployment will remain very high in 2009, relative to recent years.

The good news is that a select set of employers and growth companies will offer good job opportunities during 2009. In this period of challenges, a few companies will enjoy booming business. Sectors such as solar energy, education and health care are growing. Companies involved in installing renewable energy devices, weather stripping and energy-saving equipment will prosper.

Other firms will hire only limited numbers of employees, while some will downsize dramatically. Most firms that specialize in manufacturing or selling luxury items and discretionary services will find business to be very slow. Many companies will continue to wrestle with challenges such as slow sales, intense competition and tight credit.

Growing numbers of consumers will prefer firms that sell goods and services online, offering savings of time, money and car travel. This boosts companies like Amazon.com that offer low prices combined with deep selections and great customer service.

The travel industry will continue to suffer as both business and leisure travel have been cut dramatically. Travel firms that do best will be those offering all-inclusive prices that seem like bargains, such as popular cruise lines.

The automobile and banking sectors will face continued tough times. Consumers will be more likely to fix up their old cars than buy new ones—a positive sign for auto parts stores and car repair firms. Likewise, homeowners may make repairs or do light remodeling rather than move up to a larger home.

Americans who find themselves in the market for a job will need to understand the changes surging through the economy in order to determine which companies to pursue and which to avoid. The U.S. employment market is evolving quickly, and job seekers must be both knowledgeable and nimble in order to position themselves to find promising careers.

In order to create a robust job market, corporate investment, profits, productivity and revenues must align themselves correctly. These economic indicators were positive during the 2003 to mid-2007 period, and millions of new American jobs were created. As 2007 was winding down, the residential real estate crash and difficult credit markets were combining to restrain the economy and put a damper on the creation of new jobs. Unfortunately, 2008 saw these problems begin to spread throughout most U.S. business sectors and throughout the global economy as well. Eventually, a major global meltdown at banks and investment firms occurred.

During 2009, chief executives will continue to find themselves under intense pressure to maintain profitability while keeping their staffs and investment needs lean. The uncertainty created by the financial crisis will make corporate executives extremely cautious.

New grads will find it difficult to land their dream jobs. Nonetheless, there will still be good job opportunities for those who are diligent in seeking good employers in stronger business sectors.

Some employees will find their work hours cut, face temporary furloughs, or have their pay or benefits cut. Many people who would prefer to be hired as permanent employees will find work as temps instead. Other employees will find that their jobs have been eliminated because work has been outsourced to another firm.

**Economic Factors Affecting the Job Market**

*Business Productivity*: Productivity has been rising at desirable rates in recent years. That is, more business can be produced—whether it is goods or services—by utilizing fewer workers than before. This will be extremely beneficial to the U.S. economy in the long run, but it can hurt the job market over the short term. Productivity is boosted by new technologies, improved management methods and other factors. It can also receive a quick boost from restrained corporate hiring. If rising productivity occurs along with rapidly rising sales and profits, then the job market will improve.

*Corporate Sales*: For 2009, many sectors, particularly those directly affected by housing and financial markets, will find revenue growth impossible to come by. This will make many employers much less likely to hire new people, and it will lead to layoffs at many firms.

*Corporate Profits*: When profits increase sharply, companies are inclined to increase business investment and hiring. Fortunately, 2004 through 2007 saw steady growth in corporate profits as the economy rebounded. As a result, large numbers of new jobs were created during that period, and the national unemployment rate was extremely low through mid 2007. Profitability took a deep downturn in 2008, and profits will be disappointing for most business sectors in 2009. The jobs market will suffer as a result.

The employment market during most of the 1990s was exceptionally strong. In April 2000, the unemployment rate dropped to 3.9%, a 30-year record low, and 24 million new jobs had been created in the U.S. during the then nine-year-long economic boom. (Like all boom times, the boom of the '90s finally came to a close; the unprecedented job market and stock market wound down.)

By late 2001, as the tech boom tapered off, the national unemployment rate in America shot up to 6%, representing just under 9 million people seeking jobs.

The U.S. unemployment rate in August 2007 was down to 4.6%. By August 2008, the unemployment rate shot up to 6.1%, and reached 7.6% in early 2009. It will go much higher before this recession has ended. Nonetheless, over 130 million Americans are employed, and many job seekers will be able to find satisfying jobs if they apply themselves to the job hunt, make sure their resumes' self-marketing skills are in superb shape, network effectively and do thorough research. The number of people applying for each job opening will rise. Consequently, it is vital for a job seeker to understand how to best apply for a job online, how to shine during an interview and how to create an effective list of prospective employers.

Meanwhile, many of America's 78 million Baby Boomers are hoping to retire soon and leave the job market—this will eventually make prospects more promising for younger workers. However, this trend will be tempered by the weak financial markets of 2008 and 2009. Many people over the age of 60 who want to retire will be reluctant (or unable) to do so because the value of their investments in real estate, stocks, bonds and/or funds is down considerably, and they have lost confidence in financial markets at the same time that they lost retirement dollars. Some would-be retirees will be working much later in life than they had planned.

In order to compete effectively in today's job market, one of the most important things you can do is arm yourself with knowledge. It is vital for the knowledgeable job seeker to use the best reference tools possible in order to seek out employers that offer a reasonable balance of financial stability, opportunities for advancement and good pay. Excellent job opportunities always exist if you know where to look. Many of America's most successful firms currently need large numbers of new employees.

For example, the health care sector continues to create huge numbers of job openings yearly. The American health care sector gained an average of 30,000 employees each month during 2008. There is a critical shortage of nurses and other health care specialists. Leading companies in biotechnology, renewable energy, online services and education will greatly expand their businesses over the mid term. Employment in private education rose by 33,000 in the month of January 2009. Thousands of additional companies, in technical and non-technical sectors, will need large numbers of new hires. In particular, companies that offer products or services that save time and/or money will prosper—for example, many types of discount retailers, along with companies that offer services that help businesses operate more efficiently. Meanwhile, large companies that are not increasing their overall numbers of employees will be hiring on a regular basis due to normal attrition—that is, the loss of employees due to retirement, relocation or other personal circumstances. For example, a company the size of Walgreen's typically needs to hire tens of thousands of workers yearly due to normal attrition.

**2) Downsizing/Consolidation through Mergers or Acquisitions**

Mergers, consolidations, the movement of both manufacturing and office tasks to cheaper foreign locations and other factors will continue to have a major impact on the job market and, in some cases, will lead to large layoffs. Large mergers have been taking place at a steady rate in nearly all types of industries. Many mergers are initiated because of a desire to consolidate the companies involved, combining customer bases, administrative or sales offices and production facilities, while cutting thousands of employees who hold duplicated jobs, in hopes of thereby creating more efficient, more profitable firms.

Good jobs in the U.S. manufacturing sector can still be found, despite intense competition from Chinese manufacturers. Factories are running with fewer people thanks to immense investments in technology. Output per employee is up spectacularly—to the extent that millions of manufacturing jobs were cut due to the rise in productivity, while total manufacturing activity soared thanks to productivity-creating technologies. Fewer employees, as a percentage of a factory's total workers, are now needed to manage non-production functions, such as engineering, logistics, administration and marketing.

Of course, some manufacturing industries are in deep decline, particularly the automobile industry. (Meanwhile, some of the loss in manufacturing employment has been exaggerated by the fact that manufacturing firms now outsource a good deal of their non-manufacturing operations to services companies. For example, many computer departments, company cafeterias, distribution centers and engineering needs are outsourced to outside companies that specialize in such work, thus reducing the number of in-house jobs at manufacturing companies.) Another extremely important factor in the loss of U.S. manufacturing jobs is the movement of production to foreign nations where costs are lower.

Companies in both manufacturing and service sectors have caught on to management by teams, vastly enhanced supply chain technology (such as the use of the Internet for ordering and tracking components), along with networked management and manufacturing systems, which all add up to the fact that fewer mid-management, white-collar types are needed to communicate with the people doing the day-to-day work. Production workers have been encouraged to communicate among themselves. In many cases, workers are taking on unprecedented responsibilities, setting their own goals and schedules, tracking costs and output and boosting profits. Twenty-five years ago, these were the tasks of middle managers. Today, vast numbers of those management jobs have been eliminated.

Businesses without factories are also undergoing re-engineering and leaps in productivity. For example, by upgrading software and linking desktop computers to central databases, a major U.S. insurance firm was able to go from 3,000 employees issuing new policies to only 700. At the same time, it was able to reduce the time necessary to write a new policy from 15 days to only five. Today's corporations are searching hard for innovative ways to get more work done with fewer people.

Technology Continues to Create Sweeping Changes in the Workplace:

Technology has introduced vast changes throughout industries of all types, greatly boosting productivity and reallocating (or eliminating) workers. A major cause of change for employees, and therefore job seekers, is the tidal wave of new technologies revolutionizing the workplace at all levels. Prospering companies are using new technologies to communicate with customers, automate back-office tasks and industrial operations, and push ahead with research and development. There is a never-ending stream of technological innovation. For example, major companies have already harnessed the power of networked computers. Today, they are rapidly adopting the use Internet-based telephone systems and video conferencing technologies.

The trend of using new practices and technologies while cutting layers of management is largely about communication. This is true whether it is communication between the top offices and the factory floor, communication with customers, communication between the computers in one corporate office with those in another or communication from desk-to-desk in massive service businesses.

These new technologies mean continuous retraining for much of the workforce. Job seekers who want the best posts must have the training and skills that will let them utilize new technologies effectively. Jobs are remaining unfilled at many companies because of a shortage of technically qualified people. Workforce development is a critical need nationwide.

Jobs in America are shifting to new categories of work based on technologies that didn't exist 20 years ago. For example, the job title "webmaster" was coined in the 1990s to describe the employee in charge of a firm's Internet sites and intranet operations. Services firms, as well as manufacturers, are placing more and more employees in recently created technical and service positions, while many of the tasks once performed in-house are now provided by outsourced services providers. In the telecommunications industry, phone companies have migrated to digital switches that require far less manpower to operate, along with voice-recognition equipment that has eliminated much of the need for "information" operators. In the meantime, tens of thousands of jobs have been created at cellular telephone companies. Now, Internet-based telephony (Voice Over Internet Protocol, or VOIP), competition from cable providers, fiber to the premises and wireless networks such as WiMax are poised to revolutionize the telecommunications industry yet again.

Another excellent example: Retailing, shipping and warehousing are about to see a technology revolution due to the introduction of Radio Frequency Identification Tags (RFID). This breakthrough in inventory management is based on the placement of microchips in product packaging, combined with the use of special sensors in stores and warehouses that alert a central inventory management system of product purchases and the need to restock inventory. From loading docks to shelves to cash registers to parking lots, radio frequency readers will track the movement of each and every item. Many bar codes will eventually be replaced by RFIDs, with electronic product codes stored on these microchips. The chips even eliminate the need to scan each item at checkout. Checkout stations will be equipped with readers that automatically calculate purchases. No shoplifting, no manual count inventory errors. Another benefit is that manufacturers will be able to reduce overall inventory thanks to greater efficiency.

As online ordering, tracking and inventory management continue to become more sophisticated and cost-effective, purchasing executives at firms of all types and sizes will accelerate the use of Internet-based systems for management of their supply chains. There are significant opportunities here for e-commerce services and software companies. Likewise, there is great promise for third-party logistics (3PL) companies that combine the power of Internet-based information with strategically located warehouses to fulfill the inventory needs of manufacturers.

Massive Layoffs Become an Everyday Occurrence:

Very high numbers of layoffs have become commonplace. Here again, corporate restructuring, mergers and re-engineering are driving vast changes in businesses of all types. Even during an upturn in the economy, major job cuts are announced as corporate mergers and restructuring continue. Today's recession will continue to force many firms to restructure and downsize.

### 3) Continued Growth in Outsourcing, Including Supply Chain and Logistics Services

Part of the re-engineering process at employers has been a boom in "outsourcing," or the use of outside specialty firms to do chores that firms formerly performed through in-house departments. For example, Pitney Bowes takes over the mailrooms, desktop printers and copiers at major corporations. As part of a turnkey service, Pitney Bowes supplies its own copiers and desktop printers, and then buys toner and paper by the truckload at the best possible price. It trains its employees to keep track of every single copy so its clients can control costs. Copy department employees are transferred from the client firm to Pitney Bowes, the outsourcing firm. There, these employees learn that the head of a Pitney Bowes' copy department can rise to be a regional manager, a vice president or an even higher position within the company. The client firm's costs are lowered and its profits increase. The outsourcing provider makes a tidy profit through its focused expertise.

The greatest area of outsourcing growth has long been in computer departments. IBM, Accenture and Hewlett-Packard (HP) are among the global leaders in this field. However, several other business functions are commonly outsourced. For example, ServiceMaster takes over janitorial tasks, building management and maintenance functions for giant corporate office campuses and industrial facilities. Another company outsources all of the food warehousing and distribution for nationwide restaurant chains. Why? Because it can run trucks and warehouses more efficiently while its clients concentrate on running restaurants.

While the 1960s, '70s and '80s saw many firms frantically trying to do all tasks in-house, the '90s were different. As a decade noted for rising productivity and efficiency, the '90s was an era of specialization and focus. That trend continues today. Outsourcing, which rapidly gained popularity in this period, will persist in leading the way to higher efficiency and profits. Many outsourced services companies continue to grow rapidly, and they will create (and displace) large numbers of jobs.

Some companies combine outsourcing services with temporary workers. For example, Spherion, a major temporary help firm and one of America's largest employers, is also a leading outsourcing company. Spherion's outsourcing division takes over all human resources administration functions for large clients. This means that Spherion's employees do all of the recruiting, employee records management, benefits management and so on for its client companies. This is a logical extension of Spherion's human resources expertise and good cross-marketing to its roster of corporate clients.

One of the fastest-growing fields in outsourcing has been supply chain and logistics. Companies offering services in this field include giant transportation companies like UPS. "Supply chain" refers to the entire set of supplies and service providers involved in creating and delivering a component or end product. For example, for an automobile manufacturer like Ford, the supply chain includes companies that make tires, batteries, interior components and engine parts, as well as the trucks and trains that ship these parts and the warehouses that hold them (along with the engineering team that designs them). Further along Ford's supply chain lie the automobile dealers that receive completed cars and deliver them to the end customer. Another example: For a clothing store chain like The Gap, the supply chain includes clothing designers, clothing manufacturers and the warehouses and transportation systems that deliver completed clothes to the stores.

Logistics is the art of moving goods through the supply chain. Supply chains are so complex and so critical to a company's operations that there are countless ways to automate, improve efficiencies and cut costs. Many manufacturers and retailers are outsourcing all or part of their logistics needs to firms that specialize in creating efficiencies and saving costs. Logistics and supply chain companies have been growing rapidly and creating large numbers of jobs. A concept you should be familiar with is Third Party Logistics ("3PL"), a system whereby a specialist firm in logistics provides a variety of transportation, warehousing and logistics-related services to its clients. These tasks were previously performed in-house by the client. When 3PL services are provided within the client's own facilities, it can also be referred to as "Insourcing." In other words, you might find yourself working for UPS at a site within a distribution company that has no other ties to UPS.

**4) Millions Working as Temps**

More and more, major firms are using temporary workers to fill short-term needs, cutting overall employment costs since temps usually do not receive extensive benefits, bonuses or continuing training. In addition to employees who are placed in temporary jobs by agencies, there are millions of people employed as "independent contractors" and "contract workers." Temporary staffing companies operate offices throughout the U.S., in cities small and large. To a growing extent, they hire and place workers via their sophisticated Internet sites.

The largest temporary help agencies tend to have vast global operations. For example, Adecco is a Swiss firm with extensive operations in the U.S., Europe and elsewhere, employing hundreds of thousands of people. Manpower, based in the U.S., does a major part of its business in dozens of nations worldwide.

Demand for temporary workers slows dramatically during economic downturns. The use of temps enables employers to increase the workforce quickly when orders from customers increase and to reduce it rapidly when revenues decrease. Temporary workers are also an extremely efficient way to meet needs for one-time projects, to fill the slots of permanent employees who are on leave and to screen potential candidates for full-time positions by first hiring them on a temporary basis.

In addition, some Americans prefer to work as temporary employees, feeling that this gives them more flexibility in their working lives. About one-third of temp employees state that they prefer this lifestyle. Unfortunately, many people who end up working in temporary positions would greatly prefer to be employed full-time. Many of these workers hold significant skills as well as college degrees. In fact, through the years, the temp business has become increasingly technical in nature.

A large percentage of temps work in professional specialties, such as law or accounting. Interestingly, the number of information technology temps has increased dramatically in the past several years. As shortages of certain types of IT workers occurred, many highly skilled workers were able to demand very lucrative pay for temporary assignments. Some temporary workers have gotten the most out of the system by moving readily from shrinking industries to those that are expanding as the economy evolves. Others found excellent permanent work when they were introduced to new companies as temps.

***Internet Research Tip:***

For data on the temporary staffing industry and the temporary workforce in the U.S., see the American Staffing Association (www.americanstaffing.net).

**5) Offshoring and the Globalization of Business**

Competition from workers in such nations as Mexico, Indonesia, Thailand, South Korea and particularly China means that fewer pure manufacturing jobs will be available in the U.S., where pay is high and employee benefit costs are immense compared to those in competing nations. In fact, the costs of Social Security taxes, Medicare taxes, employer-sponsored health care, vacations, holidays, retirement plans and other benefits have risen so high (an amount typically equal to 38% to 45% of wages) that they provide considerable incentive for firms to hold down the number of employees working in U.S. locations. Instead, companies are utilizing workers in other nations. A typical factory worker in Mexico makes $250 to $300 monthly, while the same worker in China makes $100 to $150 monthly for a much longer work week. Employee benefit costs in such nations are nominal.

"Offshoring" is the word now used to describe the movement of jobs of all types away from industrialized nations, like America, to less developed countries, like India, the Philippines, Indonesia and China. For example, U.S. financial services companies are sending hundreds of thousands of jobs overseas, in such areas as call centers and financial analysis. Moving jobs to countries such as India, China and the Philippines pose serious job displacement problems in the U.S. (At the same time, there is a positive factor to the growth of these emerging economies: Increasing exports to these nations of U.S. goods and services of all types, thereby creating jobs and profits in America.)

Globalization has a profound effect on Americans—consumer prices become lower, while the U.S. job market changes considerably. Consumer goods are quite inexpensive due to the vast variety of items the U.S. imports from other nations, and prices for many categories of these goods are declining rapidly. For example, Americans can purchase consumer electronics like DVD players and color televisions at increasingly lower prices, and the price of many types of apparel is much lower thanks to globalization.

More than ever before, the world is one vast marketplace. Globalization of business supply and service chains is a strong trend today and will grow even stronger in the future. For example, consider the rapid globalization of the automobile industry. The entire global automobile industry is dominated by only a handful of companies, including Toyota, GM, Ford, Daimler, Honda, Nissan, Hyundai, Volkswagen and Nissan.

American companies have been merging and consolidating on a national basis at a rapid clip. That consolidation will continue and will tend to become more global in nature. In addition, U.S. firms will enter into foreign markets through acquisitions and pure expansion.

Trade is not necessarily always stable. While global economies are undeniably linked, they do not march hand-in-hand. For example, the nose-dive taken by many Asian economies in the late 1990s occurred during one of the biggest economic booms in U.S. history. The strength of America as a consumer market was a platform that helped to stabilize and regenerate Asian businesses that were having difficulties.

U.S. firms have superiority in several key product and service sectors vital to the rest of the world, including health products, computers, e-commerce, software and entertainment of all types. The message is clear: global trade and export markets are extremely vital to the health of American business and industry. A study of 2006 results showed that a U.S. corporation listed in the Standard & Poor's 500 created, on average, 49% of its revenues from foreign nations, up from 30% in 2001. Today, exports account for more than 11% of the U.S. Gross Domestic Product (GDP). You can readily see how important exporting is. Meanwhile, America remains an economic and technological giant, accounting for about 23% of the world's economic output.

A growing middle class in India and China has been creating demand for goods exported from the U.S., including consumer products bearing desirable brands as well as luxury automobiles. Also, U.S.-based firms have been enjoying great success in franchising and licensing their methods to startup businesses in China and India, in everything from hotels to fast food to services.

Meanwhile, the U.S. is also exporting its newfound expertise in the booming superstore and discount retailing sectors. For instance, hundreds of Wal-Mart's stores are in foreign locations such as Argentina, Brazil, Canada, China, Korea, Mexico, Puerto Rico and the U.K. Eventually, Wal-Mart may bring its brand of retailing to virtually all of the world's major markets.

**6) Senior Citizens Are a Hot Commodity with Selected Employers—Baby Boomers Are Retiring**

Certain large employers, particularly national retail chains, have discovered that senior citizens are a terrific pool of potential employees. This is partly because Americans of 55 years or older are the fastest-growing segment of the population. For example, nearly 20% of Home Depot's workforce consists of people over 50 years of age. This trend is powerful enough that the AARP is forming job link partnerships with national firms such as Anheuser-Busch, Barnes & Noble and Sears.

Meanwhile, 2006 marked the year that the first Baby Boomers turned 60, meaning that many will take early retirement when their finances allow them to do so. When they leave their jobs, openings will result for younger workers.

Baby boomer generally refers to people born from 1946 to 1964. The term evolved to include the children of soldiers and war industry workers who were involved in World War II. When those veterans and workers returned to civilian life, they started or added to families in large numbers. As a result, the baby boom generation is one of the largest demographic segments in the U.S. According to MetLife, the Baby Boomers make up about 27% of the U.S. population. Based on projections within the 2000 national census of the population, these people numbered 77.7 million as of 2003.

By 2011, millions will begin turning traditional retirement age (65), resulting in extremely rapid growth in the senior portion of the population. Many Baby Boomers will leave their traditional, long-term jobs and turn to part-time work.

**7) Employment Sectors that Will Offer an Above-Average Number of Job Opportunities in 2009**

Job seekers should remain keenly aware of the fact that certain industries will have an above-average likelihood to offer job openings during 2009. This is due to a number of circumstances, including shifts in consumer tastes and requirements, normal employee turnover and attrition, structural changes within industries, global economic conditions and national policies and priorities.

Below is a list of the industries on which job seekers should concentrate their efforts.

**Employment Sectors that Will Offer an Above-Average Number of Job Opportunities in 2009:**

- Biotechnology, Including Agricultural Biotechnology
- Construction and Engineering Services for Infrastructure and Government Projects
- Construction—Installation of Energy-Saving Devices, Weather Stripping and Renewable Energy Components
- Consulting—Selected Fields where Consultants May Be Able to Effect Cost-Savings for Clients
- Consumer Products Manufacturers
- Cosmetics Manufacturers
- Data Processing Services Providers
- Defense Contractors—Selected Firms
- Education
- Elder Care, Home Health Care, Nursing Homes and Assisted Living Communities
- Electronic Games
- Energy Conservation Products and Services
- Guard Services, Investigation and Surveillance
- Health Care Services, Including Managed Care
- Health Foods, Organic Foods, Enhanced Foods
- Health Products
- Health Technology, Including Computerized Patient Records
- Insurance Providers—Selected Specialty Insurance Firms
- Internet Access—High Speed
- Supply Chain Services That Offer Cost-Savings to Clients
- Nanotechnology and MEMS
- Oil and Gas Exploration and Production
- Online Search Services with Advertising Revenues
- Online-based Business and Consumer Services
- Outsourcing, Including Outsourced Business and Computer Services
- Pharmaceuticals—Generics
- Radio Frequency ID Tags (RFID)
- Renewable Energy, Especially Solar and Wind Power
- Retailing—Basic, Including Drugstores and Supermarkets
- Retailing—Discount and Warehouse Clubs
- Wireless and Cellular Communications, including WiMax

# Chapter 2

# STATISTICS

**Contents:**

## U.S. Employment Overview: January 2009

*(Labor Counts In Thousands)*

| | |
|---|---|
| Civilian Labor Force, Total | 153,716 |
| Employed* | 142,099 |
| Unemployed | 11,616 |
| Persons 16 Years of Age and Over, Not in Labor Force | 81,203 |
| Unemployment Rate | 7.6% |
| Average Hourly Earnings, Private Industry[P] | $18.46 |
| Weekly Earnings, Private Industry[P] | $614.72 |
| Average Work Week, Private Industry (Hours)[P] | 33.3 |
| Nonfarm Employment[P] | 134,580 |
| Goods-Producing | 20,245 |
| Construction | 6,742 |
| Manufacturing | 12,713 |
| Service-Providing | 114,335 |
| Retail Trade | 14,998 |
| Professional & Business Services | 17,261 |
| Education & Health Services | 19,143 |
| Leisure & Hospitality | 13,285 |
| Government | 22,539 |

P = Preliminary.

Source: U.S. Bureau of Labor Statistics
Plunkett Research, Ltd.
www.plunkettresearch.com

# U.S. Civilian Labor Force: 1997-January 2009

*(Persons 16 & Older; In Thousands)*

| Year | Civilian Workforce Level |
|---|---|
| **1997** | 136,297 |
| **1998** | 137,673 |
| **1999** | 139,368 |
| **2000** | 142,583 |
| **2001** | 143,734 |
| **2002** | 144,863 |
| **2003** | 146,510 |
| **2004** | 147,401 |
| **2005** | 149,320 |
| **2006** | 151,428 |
| **2007** | 153,124 |
| **2008** | 154,287 |
| **2009*** | 153,445 |

* As of January; seasonally adjusted.

Note: The labor force includes all persons classified as employed or unemployed. Employed persons include people 16 years and over in the civilian noninstitutional population who, during a reference week, (a) did any work at all (at least 1 hour) as paid employees, worked in their own business, profession, or on their own farm, or worked 15 hours or more as unpaid workers in an enterprise operated by a member of the family, and (b) all those who were not working but who had jobs or businesses from which they were temporarily absent because of vacation, illness, bad weather, childcare problems, maternity or paternity leave, labor-management dispute, job training, or other family or personal reasons, whether or not they were paid for the time off or were seeking other jobs. Each employed person is counted only once, even if he or she holds more than one job. Excluded are persons whose only activity consisted of work around their own house (painting, repairing, or own home housework) or volunteer work for religious, charitable, and other organizations.

Source: U.S. Bureau of Labor Statistics

Plunkett Research, Ltd.

www.plunkettresearch.com

## Number of People Employed, U.S.: January 2008 vs. January 2009

*(Persons 16 & Older; In Thousands; Not Seasonally Adjusted)*

| Occupation | Employed | | Unemployed | | Unemp. Rates | |
|---|---|---|---|---|---|---|
| | Jan-08 | Jan-09 | Jan-08 | Jan-09 | Jan-08 | Jan-09 |
| **All workers*** | **144,607** | **140,436** | **8,221** | **13,009** | **5.4** | **8.5** |
| Management, professional & related | 52,165 | 52,358 | 1,164 | 2,238 | 2.2 | 4.1 |
| Management, business & financial | 21,749 | 21,956 | 509 | 1,056 | 2.3 | 4.6 |
| Professional & related | 30,416 | 30,402 | 655 | 1,182 | 2.1 | 3.7 |
| Service | 23,366 | 23,850 | 1,767 | 2,389 | 7.0 | 9.1 |
| Sales & office | 36,187 | 34,192 | 1,807 | 2,761 | 4.8 | 7.5 |
| Sales & related | 16,594 | 15,773 | 909 | 1,323 | 5.2 | 7.7 |
| Office & administrative support | 19,592 | 18,419 | 898 | 1,438 | 4.4 | 7.2 |
| Natural resources, construction & maintenance | 14,955 | 13,587 | 1,453 | 2,497 | 8.9 | 15.5 |
| Farming, fishing & forestry | 905 | 825 | 111 | 251 | 11.0 | 23.3 |
| Construction & extraction | 8,939 | 7,673 | 1,154 | 1,824 | 11.4 | 19.2 |
| Installation, maintenance & repair | 5,112 | 5,089 | 188 | 422 | 3.5 | 7.7 |
| Production, transportation & material moving | 17,934 | 16,449 | 1,420 | 2,432 | 7.3 | 12.9 |
| Production | 9,155 | 7,974 | 633 | 1,265 | 6.5 | 13.7 |
| Transportation & material moving | 8,779 | 8,474 | 787 | 1,167 | 8.2 | 12.1 |

* Persons with no previous work experience and persons whose last job was in the Armed Forces are included in the unemployed total. Updated population controls are introduced annually with the release of January data.

Source: U.S. Bureau of Labor Statistics
Plunkett Research, Ltd.
www.plunkettresearch.com

## Unemployed Jobseekers by Sex, Reason for Unemployment & Active Job Search Methods Used: 2008

| Sex and reason | (Thousands of persons) | | Methods used as a percent of total jobseekers | | | | | | | Average number of methods used |
|---|---|---|---|---|---|---|---|---|---|---|
| | Total unem-ployed | Total job-seekers | Emp-loyer directly | Sent out resumes or filled out app-lications | Placed or ans-wered ads | Friends or relatives | Public employ-ment agency | Private employ-ment agency | Other | |
| **Total, 16 years and over** | 8,924 | 7,749 | 56.9 | 52.3 | 17.1 | 23.8 | 18.9 | 8.0 | 14.1 | 1.92 |
| Job losers and persons who completed temporary jobs* | 4,789 | 3,614 | 59.5 | 51.4 | 20.1 | 28.0 | 24.3 | 10.6 | 15.2 | 2.10 |
| Job leavers | 896 | 896 | 58.7 | 54.8 | 18.3 | 22.5 | 16.9 | 7.8 | 13.2 | 1.93 |
| Reentrants | 2,472 | 2,472 | 53.3 | 51.7 | 14.0 | 19.5 | 14.6 | 5.9 | 14.0 | 1.73 |
| New entrants | 766 | 766 | 54.5 | 55.1 | 11.2 | 19.3 | 9.9 | 3.4 | 10.8 | 1.64 |
| **Men, 16 years and over** | 5,033 | 4,234 | 58.7 | 49.8 | 17.1 | 26.1 | 19.3 | 8.1 | 14.2 | 1.94 |
| Job losers and persons who completed temporary jobs | 3,055 | 2,255 | 61.0 | 48.7 | 19.5 | 29.9 | 23.7 | 10.2 | 15.0 | 2.08 |
| Job losers and persons who completed temporary jobs[1] | 458 | 458 | 59.2 | 52.6 | 17.9 | 24.2 | 16.9 | 7.2 | 13.2 | 1.92 |
| Reentrants | 1,128 | 1,128 | 55.1 | 49.1 | 14.0 | 21.0 | 14.9 | 6.0 | 14.1 | 1.75 |
| New entrants | 393 | 393 | 55.9 | 54.9 | 11.8 | 21.4 | 9.5 | 3.0 | 10.8 | 1.67 |
| **Women, 16 years and over** | 3,891 | 3,515 | 54.7 | 55.3 | 17.0 | 21.0 | 18.4 | 8.0 | 14.1 | 1.89 |
| Job losers and persons who completed temporary jobs* | 1,735 | 1359 | 57.1 | 56.0 | 21.1 | 24.9 | 25.2 | 11.2 | 15.6 | 2.12 |
| Job leavers | 438 | 438 | 58.1 | 57.1 | 18.8 | 20.7 | 17.0 | 8.5 | 13.2 | 1.94 |
| Reentrants | 1,345 | 1,345 | 51.8 | 54.0 | 14.0 | 18.3 | 14.2 | 5.8 | 13.9 | 1.73 |
| New entrants | 374 | 374 | 53.1 | 55.2 | 10.5 | 17.1 | 10.3 | 3.7 | 10.7 | 1.61 |

Note: The jobseekers total is less than the total unemployed because it does not include persons on temporary layoff. The percent using each method will always total more than 100 because many jobseekers use more than one method.

* Data on the number of jobseekers and the jobsearch methods used exclude persons on temporary layoff.

Source: U.S. Bureau of Labor Statistics
Plunkett Research, Ltd.
www.plunkettresearch.com

# U.S. Labor Force Ages 16 to 24 Years Old by School Enrollment, Educational Attainment, Sex, Race & Ethnicity: October 2007

| *(Numbers in Thousands, Latest Year Available)* | Civilian non-institutional population | Total | Percent of Populace | Employed | | Unemployed | | Not in Labor Force |
|---|---|---|---|---|---|---|---|---|
| | | | | Total | % of Populace | Number | Rate (%) | |
| **Total, 16 to 24 years** | 37,480 | 22,243 | 59.3 | 19,921 | 53.2 | 2,322 | 10.4 | 15,237 |
| **Enrolled in school** | 21,061 | 8,979 | 42.6 | 8,181 | 38.8 | 798 | 8.9 | 12,083 |
| Enrolled in high school[1] | 9,724 | 2,855 | 29.4 | 2,421 | 24.9 | 434 | 15.2 | 6,869 |
| Men | 5,118 | 1,431 | 28.0 | 1,203 | 23.5 | 227 | 15.9 | 3,687 |
| Women | 4,607 | 1,425 | 30.9 | 1,218 | 26.4 | 206 | 14.5 | 3,182 |
| White | 7,370 | 2,371 | 32.2 | 2,053 | 27.9 | 318 | 13.4 | 4,999 |
| Black or African American | 1,590 | 294 | 18.5 | 222 | 14.0 | 72 | 24.6 | 1,296 |
| Asian | 352 | 72 | 20.3 | 58 | 16.3 | 14 | -2.0 | 281 |
| Hispanic or Latino ethnicity | 1,659 | 368 | 22.2 | 302 | 18.2 | 66 | 17.9 | 1,291 |
| Enrolled in college | 11,337 | 6,124 | 54.0 | 5,760 | 50.8 | 364 | 5.9 | 5,213 |
| Enrolled in 2-year college | 3,217 | 2,066 | 64.2 | 1,946 | 60.5 | 121 | 5.8 | 1,151 |
| Enrolled in 4-year college | 8,120 | 4,057 | 50.0 | 3,814 | 47.0 | 243 | 6.0 | 4,063 |
| Full-time students | 9,659 | 4,693 | 48.6 | 4,398 | 45.5 | 295 | 6.3 | 4,966 |
| Part-time students | 1,678 | 1,431 | 85.3 | 1,362 | 81.2 | 69 | 4.8 | 247 |
| Men | 5,226 | 2,664 | 51.0 | 2,508 | 48.0 | 156 | 5.9 | 2,563 |
| Women | 6,110 | 3,460 | 56.6 | 3,252 | 53.2 | 208 | 6.0 | 2,651 |
| White | 8,912 | 5,008 | 56.2 | 4,759 | 53.4 | 249 | 5.0 | 3,904 |
| Black or African American | 1,423 | 674 | 47.4 | 607 | 42.7 | 67 | 9.9 | 749 |
| Asian | 668 | 240 | 35.9 | 223 | 33.4 | 17 | 7.0 | 428 |
| Hispanic or Latino ethnicity | 1,414 | 836 | 59.1 | 800 | 56.6 | 36 | 4.3 | 578 |
| Not enrolled in school | 16,419 | 13,264 | 80.8 | 11,740 | 71.5 | 1,524 | 11.5 | 3,155 |
| 16 to 19 years | 3,269 | 2,356 | 72.1 | 1,905 | 58.3 | 451 | 19.1 | 914 |
| 20 to 24 years | 13,149 | 10,908 | 83.0 | 9,835 | 74.8 | 1,073 | 9.8 | 2,241 |
| **Men** | 8,595 | 7,554 | 87.9 | 6,628 | 77.1 | 926 | 12.3 | 1,042 |
| Less than a high school diploma | 1,859 | 1,496 | 80.5 | 1,261 | 67.8 | 236 | 15.7 | 362 |
| High school graduates, no college[3] | 4,073 | 3,544 | 87.0 | 3,069 | 75.3 | 475 | 13.4 | 529 |
| Some college or associate degree | 1,768 | 1,662 | 94.0 | 1,509 | 85.4 | 152 | 9.2 | 106 |
| Bachelor's degree and higher[4] | 895 | 852 | 95.1 | 789 | 88.1 | 63 | 7.4 | 44 |
| **Women** | 7,823 | 5,710 | 73.0 | 5,112 | 65.3 | 598 | 10.5 | 2,113 |
| Less than a high school diploma | 1,419 | 689 | 48.6 | 558 | 39.3 | 131 | 19.0 | 730 |
| High school graduates, no college[3] | 3,340 | 2,371 | 71.0 | 2,077 | 62.2 | 294 | 12.4 | 969 |
| Some college or associate degree | 1,884 | 1,527 | 81.1 | 1,416 | 75.1 | 112 | 7.3 | 357 |
| Bachelor's degree and higher[4] | 1,180 | 1,122 | 95.1 | 1,061 | 90.0 | 61 | 5.4 | 58 |
| **White** | 12,740 | 10,441 | 82.0 | 9,441 | 74.1 | 1,000 | 9.6 | 2,299 |
| **Black or African American** | 2,542 | 1,938 | 76.2 | 1,521 | 59.8 | 417 | 21.5 | 604 |
| **Asian** | 462 | 379 | 82.1 | 342 | 74.0 | 37 | 9.9 | 83 |
| **Hispanic or Latino ethnicity** | 3,559 | 2,655 | 74.6 | 2,349 | 66.0 | 305 | 11.5 | 904 |

Note: Detail for the above race groups do not sum to totals because data are not presented for all races. Persons whose ethnicity is identified as Hispanic or Latino may be of any race. Because of rounding, sums of individual items may not equal totals.

[1] Includes a small number of persons who are in grades below high school.

[2] Data not shown where base is less than 75,000.

[3] Includes persons with a high school diploma or equivalent.

[4] Includes persons with a bachelor's, master's, professional, and doctoral degrees.

Source: U.S. Bureau of Labor Statistics
Plunkett Research, Ltd.
www.plunkettresearch.com

## Top 20 U.S. Occupations by Numerical Change in Job Growth: 2006-2016

*(By Thousands of Employees)*

| Occupation | Employment | | Change | | Training* |
|---|---|---|---|---|---|
| | 2006 | 2016 | Number | Percent | |
| Registered nurses | 2,505 | 3,092 | **587** | 23.5 | Associate degree |
| Retail salespersons | 4,477 | 5,034 | **557** | 12.4 | Short-term on-the-job training |
| Customer service representatives | 2,202 | 2,747 | **545** | 24.8 | Moderate-term on-the-job training |
| Combined food preparation & serving workers, including fast food | 2,503 | 2,955 | **452** | 18.1 | Short-term on-the-job training |
| Office clerks, general | 3,200 | 3,604 | **404** | 12.6 | Short-term on-the-job training |
| Personal & home care aides | 767 | 1,156 | **389** | 50.6 | Short-term on-the-job training |
| Home health aides | 787 | 1,171 | **384** | 48.7 | Short-term on-the-job training |
| Postsecondary teachers | 1,672 | 2,054 | **382** | 22.9 | Doctoral degree |
| Janitors & cleaners, except maids & housekeeping cleaners | 2,387 | 2,732 | **345** | 14.5 | Short-term on-the-job training |
| Nursing aides, orderlies & attendants | 1,447 | 1,711 | **264** | 18.2 | Postsecondary vocational award |
| Bookkeeping, accounting & auditing clerks | 2,114 | 2,377 | **263** | 12.5 | Moderate-term on-the-job training |
| Waiters & waitresses | 2,361 | 2,615 | **255** | 10.8 | Short-term on-the-job training |
| Child care workers | 1,388 | 1,636 | **248** | 17.8 | Short-term on-the-job training |
| Executive secretaries & administrative assistants | 1,618 | 1,857 | **239** | 14.8 | Work experience in a related occupation |
| Computer software engineers, applications | 507 | 733 | **226** | 44.6 | Bachelor's degree |
| Accountants & auditors | 1,274 | 1,500 | **226** | 17.7 | Bachelor's degree |
| Landscaping & groundskeeping workers | 1,220 | 1,441 | **221** | 18.1 | Short-term on-the-job training |
| Elementary school teachers, except special education | 1,540 | 1,749 | **209** | 13.6 | Bachelor's degree |
| Receptionists & information clerks | 1,173 | 1,375 | **202** | 17.2 | Short-term on-the-job training |
| Truck drivers, heavy & tractor-trailer | 1,860 | 2,053 | **193** | 10.4 | Moderate-term on-the-job training |

* An occupation is placed into 1 of 11 categories that best describes the postsecondary education or training needed by most workers to become fully qualified in that occupation. For more information about the categories, see Occupational Projections and Training Data, 2006-07 edition, Bulletin 2602 (Bureau of Labor Statistics, February 2006) and Occupational Projections and Training Data, 2008-09 edition, Bulletin 2702 (Bureau of Labor Statistics, forthcoming).

Source: U.S. Bureau of Labor Statistics

Plunkett Research, Ltd.

www.plunkettresearch.com

## Top 20 U.S. Occupations by Percent Change in Job Growth: 2006-2016

*(Employment in Thousands)*

| Occupation | Employment | | Change | | Training* |
|---|---|---|---|---|---|
| | 2006 | 2016 | Number | Percent | |
| Network systems & data communications analysts | 262 | 402 | **140** | 53.4 | Bachelor's degree |
| Personal & home care aides | 767 | 1,156 | **389** | 50.6 | Short-term on-the-job training |
| Home health aids | 787 | 1,171 | **384** | 48.7 | Short-term on-the-job training |
| Computer software engineers, applications | 507 | 733 | **226** | 44.6 | Bachelor's degree |
| Veterinary technologists & technicians | 71 | 100 | **29** | 41.0 | Associate degree |
| Personal financial advisors | 176 | 248 | **72** | 41.0 | Bachelor's degree |
| Makeup artists, theatrical & performance | 2 | 3 | **1** | 39.8 | Postsecondary vocational award |
| Medical assistants | 417 | 565 | **148** | 35.4 | Moderate-term on-the-job training |
| Veterinarians | 62 | 84 | **22** | 35.0 | First professional degree |
| Substance abuse & behavioral disorder counselors | 83 | 112 | **29** | 34.3 | Bachelor's degree |
| Skin care specialists | 38 | 51 | **13** | 34.3 | Postsecondary vocational award |
| Financial analysts | 221 | 295 | **75** | 33.8 | Bachelor's degree |
| Social & human service assistants | 339 | 453 | **114** | 33.6 | Moderate-term on-the-job training |
| Gaming surveillance officers & gaming investigators | 9 | 12 | **3** | 33.6 | Moderate-term on-the-job training |
| Physical therapist assistants | 60 | 80 | **20** | 32.4 | Associate degree |
| Pharmacy technicians | 285 | 376 | **91** | 32.0 | Moderate-term on-the-job training |
| Forensic science technicians | 13 | 17 | **4** | 30.7 | Bachelor's degree |
| Dental hygienists | 167 | 217 | **50** | 30.1 | Associate degree |
| Mental health counselors | 100 | 130 | **30** | 30.0 | Master's degree |
| Mental health & substance abuse social workers | 122 | 159 | **37** | 29.9 | Master's degree |

* An occupation is placed into 1 of 11 categories that best describes the postsecondary education or training needed by most workers to become fully qualified in that occupation. For more information about the categories, see Occupational Projections and Training Data, 2006-07 edition, Bulletin 2602 (Bureau of Labor Statistics, February 2006) and Occupational Projections and Training Data, 2008-09 edition, Bulletin 2702 (Bureau of Labor Statistics, forthcoming).

Source: U.S. Bureau of Labor Statistics

Plunkett Research, Ltd.

www.plunkettresearch.com

## Jobs with the Largest Expected Employment Increases, U.S.: 2006-2016

*(By Number Employed)*

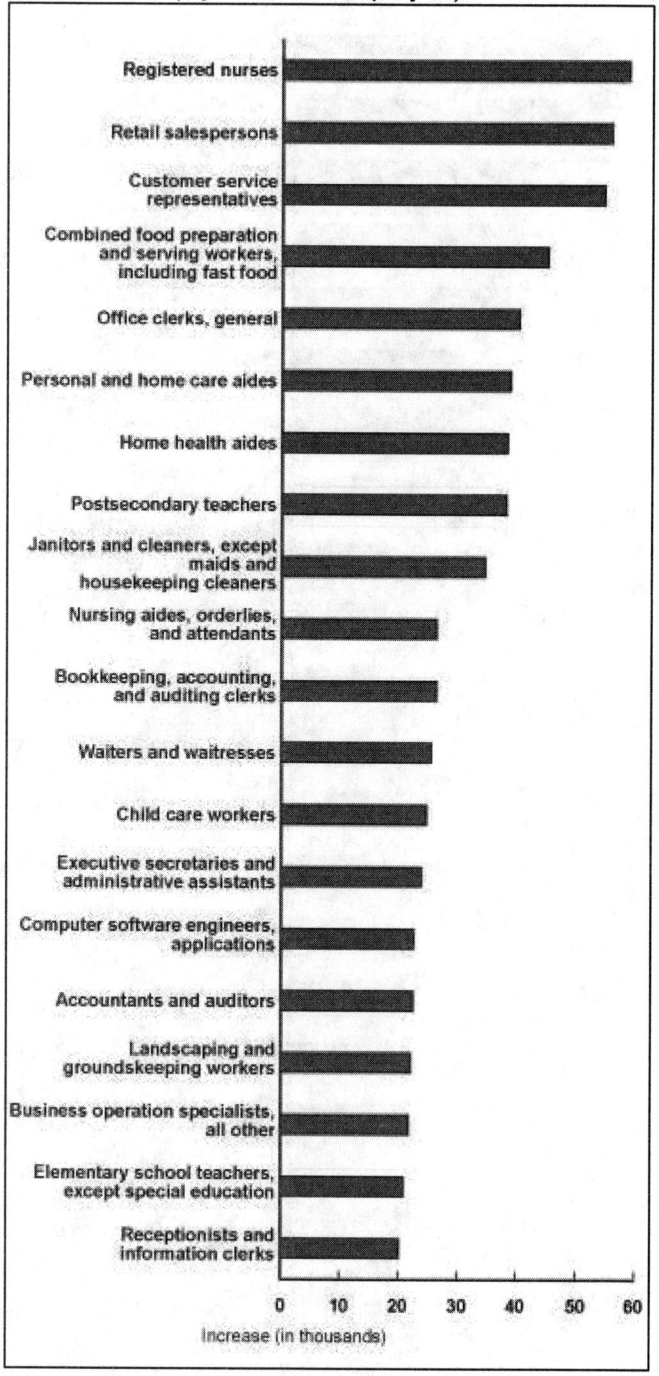


Source: U.S. Bureau of Labor Statistics
Plunkett Research, Ltd.
www.plunkettresearch.com

## Jobs with the Largest Expected Employment Decreases, U.S.: 2006-2016

*(By Number Employed)*

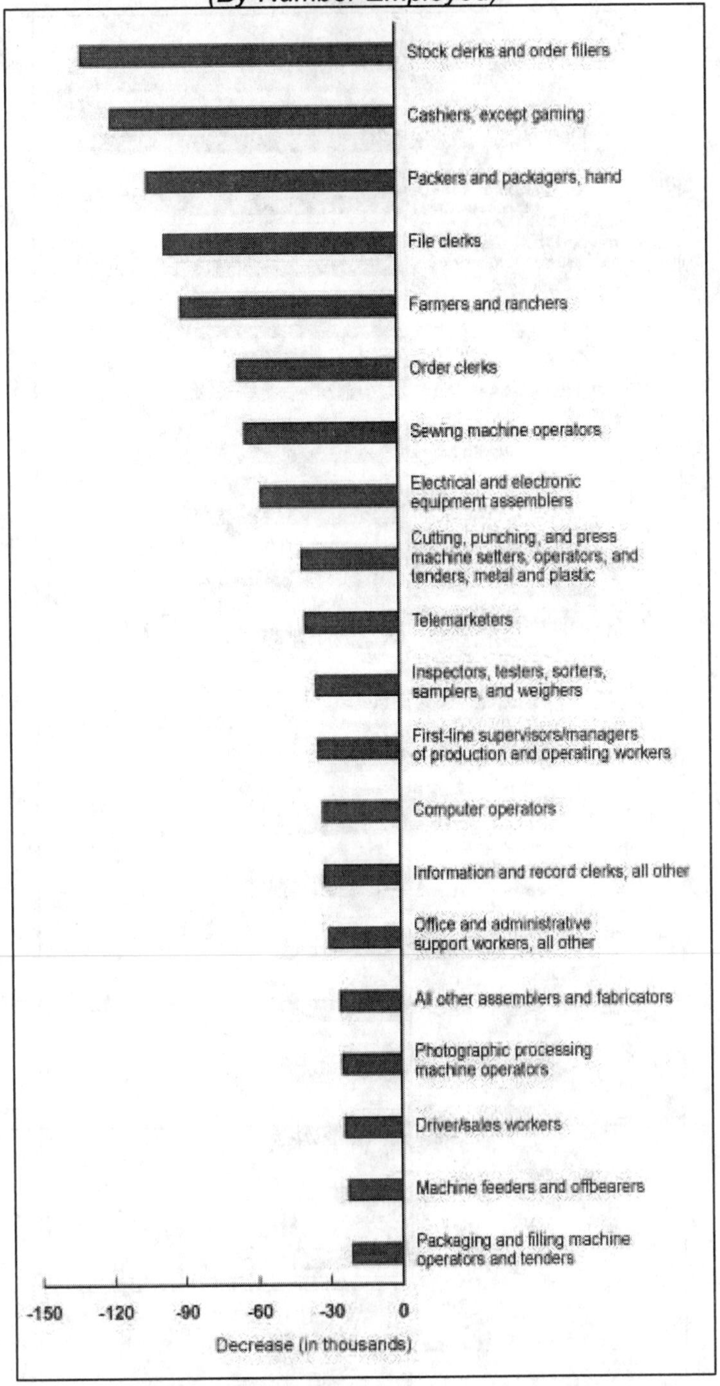


Source: U.S. Bureau of Labor Statistics
Plunkett Research, Ltd.
www.plunkettresearch.com

## Mean Hourly Earnings & Weekly Hours, Private Industry & State & Local Government: 2007

| (By Worker & Establishment Characteristics; Latest Year Available) | Civilian | | Private Industry | | State & Local Gov't | |
|---|---|---|---|---|---|---|
| | Hourly Earnings[1] | Weekly Hours[2] | Hourly Earnings[1] | Weekly Hours[2] | Hourly Earnings[1] | Weekly Hours[2] |
| **Total** | **$19.88** | **35.5** | **$19.21** | **35.4** | **$24.15** | **36.3** |
| **Worker Characteristics[3,4]** | | | | | | |
| Management, professional & related | 32.38 | 37.1 | 32.96 | 37.5 | 30.63 | 36.0 |
| Management, business & financial | 35.97 | 39.6 | 36.54 | 40.0 | 32.65 | 37.5 |
| Professional & related | 30.63 | 36.0 | 30.83 | 36.1 | 30.16 | 35.6 |
| Service | 11.36 | 31.4 | 10.06 | 30.5 | 17.77 | 36.5 |
| Sales & office | 15.98 | 34.9 | 15.97 | 34.7 | 16.17 | 36.5 |
| Sales & related | 17.27 | 32.7 | 17.29 | 32.7 | 15.62 | 34.3 |
| Office & administrative support | 15.27 | 36.2 | 15.14 | 36.1 | 16.19 | 36.6 |
| Natural resources, construction & maintenance | 20.09 | 39.4 | 20.15 | 39.4 | 19.37 | 38.8 |
| Construction & extraction | 20.14 | 39.4 | 20.27 | 39.4 | 18.69 | 38.6 |
| Installation, maintenance & repair | 20.20 | 39.5 | 20.19 | 39.6 | 20.29 | 39.2 |
| Production, transportation & material moving | 15.12 | 37.2 | 15.03 | 37.3 | 18.02 | 34.4 |
| Production | 15.44 | 38.9 | 15.38 | 38.9 | 19.96 | 39.0 |
| Transportation & material moving | 14.78 | 35.6 | 14.65 | 35.8 | 17.40 | 33.1 |
| Full time | 21.08 | 39.6 | 20.46 | 39.7 | 24.76 | 38.9 |
| Part time | 11.34 | 20.6 | 11.02 | 20.7 | 15.57 | 18.6 |
| Union | 23.96 | 36.7 | 21.90 | 36.4 | 27.17 | 37.0 |
| Nonunion | 19.14 | 35.3 | 18.89 | 35.3 | 21.73 | 35.7 |
| Time | 19.46 | 35.4 | 18.69 | 35.3 | 24.14 | 36.3 |
| Incentive | 26.94 | 38.1 | 26.90 | 38.1 | 97.34 | 25.4 |
| **Establishment Characteristics** | | | | | | |
| Goods producing | *(5)* | *(5)* | 20.79 | 39.5 | *(5)* | *(5)* |
| Service Producing | *(5)* | *(5)* | 18.74 | 34.4 | *(5)* | *(5)* |
| 1 to 49 workers | 16.84 | 34.2 | 16.80 | 34.2 | 18.02 | 33.2 |
| 50 to 99 workers | 18.06 | 34.9 | 17.99 | 34.9 | 19.24 | 35.8 |
| 100 to 499 workers | 19.46 | 36.1 | 19.09 | 36.2 | 22.51 | 36.1 |
| 500 workers or more | 24.75 | 37.0 | 24.30 | 37.1 | 25.71 | 36.7 |

Note: The survey covers all 50 states and the District of Columbia. Data were collected between December 2006 and January 2008. The average month of reference was July 2007.

[1] Earnings are the straight-time hourly wages or salaries paid to employees. They include incentive pay, cost-of-living adjustments, and hazard pay. Excluded are premium pay for overtime, vacations, holidays, nonproduction bonuses, and tips. The mean is computed by totaling the pay of all workers and dividing by the number of workers, weighted by hours.
[2] Mean weekly hours are the hours an employee is scheduled to work in a week, exclusive of overtime.
[3] Employees are classified as working either a full-time or a part-time schedule based on the definition used by each establishment. Union workers are those whose wages are determined through collective bargaining. Wages of time workers are based solely on hourly rate or salary; incentive workers are those whose wages are at least partially based on productivity payments such as piece rates, commissions, and production bonuses.
[4] A classification system including about 800 individual occupations is used to cover all workers in the civilian economy.
[5] Estimates for goods-producing and service-providing industries are published for private industry only. Industries are determined by the 2002 North American Industry Classification System (NAICS).

Source: U.S. Bureau of Labor Statistics

Plunkett Research, Ltd.

www.plunkettresearch,com

## Percent of U.S. Workers with Access to Retirement & Healthcare Benefits, Private Industry: 2007

| *(By Worker Characteristics, Establishment Characteristics & Region; Latest Year Available)* | Retirement Benefits | | | Healthcare Benefits | | | |
|---|---|---|---|---|---|---|---|
| | All Plans | Defined Benefit | Defined Contrib-ution | Medical Care | Dental Care | Vision Care | Outpatient Prescription Drug Coverage |
| **All Workers** | **61%** | **21%** | **55%** | **71%** | **46%** | **29%** | **68%** |
| Management, professional & related | 76 | 29 | 71 | 85 | 62 | 39 | 82 |
| Service | 36 | 8 | 32 | 46 | 28 | 20 | 44 |
| Sales & Office | 64 | 19 | 60 | 71 | 47 | 27 | 67 |
| Natural resources, construction & maintenance | 61 | 26 | 51 | 76 | 43 | 31 | 72 |
| Production, transportation & material moving | 65 | 26 | 56 | 78 | 49 | 30 | 75 |
| Full time | 70 | 24 | 64 | 85 | 56 | 35 | 81 |
| Part time | 31 | 10 | 27 | 24 | 16 | 11 | 23 |
| Union | 84 | 69 | 49 | 88 | 68 | 53 | 85 |
| Nonunion | 58 | 15 | 56 | 69 | 44 | 26 | 66 |
| Average wage < $15/hr. | 47 | 11 | 44 | 57 | 34 | 20 | 54 |
| Average wage > $15/hr. | 76 | 33 | 69 | 87 | 61 | 39 | 84 |
| **Establishment Characteristics** | | | | | | | |
| Goods-producing | 70 | 29 | 62 | 85 | 54 | 33 | 81 |
| Service-producing | 58 | 19 | 53 | 67 | 44 | 28 | 64 |
| 1-to-99 workers | 45 | 9 | 42 | 59 | 30 | 19 | 55 |
| 100 workers or more | 78 | 34 | 70 | 84 | 64 | 40 | 81 |
| **Region** | | | | | | | |
| Metropolitan areas | 61 | 22 | 56 | 72 | 47 | 29 | 68 |
| Nonmetropolitan areas | 57 | 14 | 53 | 66 | 41 | 26 | 64 |
| New England | 57 | 21 | 53 | 68 | 51 | 23 | 65 |
| Mid-Atlantic | 62 | 27 | 53 | 72 | 46 | 34 | 67 |
| East North Central | 64 | 25 | 56 | 72 | 45 | 25 | 70 |
| West North Central | 63 | 21 | 56 | 67 | 43 | 20 | 66 |
| South Atlantic | 62 | 17 | 59 | 72 | 44 | 27 | 69 |
| East South Central | 66 | 14 | 64 | 75 | 52 | 39 | 73 |
| West South Central | 55 | 17 | 51 | 66 | 39 | 21 | 61 |
| Mountain | 63 | 18 | 60 | 70 | 44 | 28 | 68 |
| Pacific | 57 | 21 | 49 | 72 | 54 | 39 | 68 |

Source: U.S. Bureau of Labor Statistics
Plunkett Research, Ltd.
www.plunkettresearch.com

## Percent of U.S. Private Industry Employers Offering Retirement & Healthcare Benefits: 2007

| *(By Establishment Characteristics & Region; Latest Year Available)* | Retirement Benefits | | | Healthcare Benefits[2] |
|---|---|---|---|---|
| | All plans[1] | Defined Benefit | Defined Contribution | |
| **All establishments** | **46%** | **10%** | **44%** | **60%** |
| | | | | |
| **Establishment Characteristics** | | | | |
| Goods-producing | 45 | 11 | 43 | 60 |
| Service-producing | 46 | 10 | 44 | 60 |
| 1-to-99 workers | 44 | 9 | 42 | 59 |
| 100 workers or more | 85 | 33 | 82 | 93 |
| | | | | |
| **Region** | | | | |
| Metropolitan areas | 48 | 10 | 46 | 63 |
| Nonmetropolitan areas | 37 | 10 | 37 | 51 |
| New England | 43 | 9 | 42 | 54 |
| Middle Atlantic | 49 | 12 | 47 | 63 |
| East North Central | 53 | 15 | 52 | 68 |
| West North Central | 53 | 14 | 51 | 56 |
| South Atlantic | 54 | 9 | 53 | 61 |
| East South Central | 31 | 5 | 31 | 68 |
| West South Central | 34 | 7 | 33 | 48 |
| Mountain | 38 | 10 | 35 | 56 |
| Pacific | 41 | 10 | 40 | 64 |

[1] Includes defined benefit pension plans and defined contribution retirement plans. The total is less than the sum of the individual items because many employers offer both types of plans.
[2] Healthcare plans may include a medical plan, or a separate dental, vision, or prescription drug plan.

Source: U.S. Bureau of Labor Statistics
Plunkett Research, Ltd.
www.plunkettresearch.com

# Chapter 3

# RESEARCH: 7 KEYS FOR JOB SEEKERS

**How to use your library, college placement office, the Internet and other resources to become well-informed about a company and its industry before you ask for an interview**

Research is the key to finding appropriate job openings, targeting the best possible employers and performing well when you go to job interviews. Learn what's unique about a company compared to other firms in its industry. Learn why it's prospering–or why it isn't. Where is this company going? Is it favored by stock investors? Is it privately-owned by a family, or has it been acquired by private equity investors who plan to resell it over the mid-term? What are its hottest-selling products and services? Is it investing in research and new facilities so that it may prosper in the future?

Also, as many people who have been laid off from failing startup firms have learned the hard way, determining a company's level of financial stability can be one of the most important factors in making a career decision.

The more you're willing to dig deep at the library or your college's career planning office, and the more adept you are at using the Internet for research, the better your chances of success in a job search. If you are willing to ask questions of businesspeople and of employees who currently work for your target employers, you will enhance your job search even further. The two secrets to successful job research are tenacity and focus. Know what to look for and where to find it.

Once you've landed an interview, you should research both the prospective employer and its industry even further. In this manner, you'll know what questions to ask before you agree to take the job, and you'll present yourself as a knowledgeable potential hire who is truly interested in the company and its business.

**Here are the seven keys for research that can lead you to a great employer:**

**1) Financial Stability**
Check bond ratings, credit ratings, debt level, growth in sales and growth in profits, along with the views of stock analysts and business journalists.

**2) Growth Plans**
Look for new plants, stores or offices to be opened; new technologies, products or divisions to be launched; or plans for strategic acquisitions. (See 3, 4 and 5 below.)

**3) Research and Development Programs**
How much does the firm invest in R&D? Is this research and development budget growing? For many types of companies, research is a vital investment in the future.

**4) Product Launch and Production**
Does the company have the ability to successfully launch new products and services (see 5 below) or to invest in and utilize cutting-edge technologies needed to maintain a competitive edge?

**5) Marketing and Distribution Methods**
Does the firm utilize an in-house sales force? Does it work through outside dealers and distribution partners? What are its advertising methods? Is it increasing its market share, or are competitors taking customers away? Is the company growing its international sales? Is it adept at using the Internet as a powerful sales tool? Is it successful at selling into growing international markets, such as China and India?

**6) Employee Benefits**
Are wealth-building benefit plans offered? Will the company match all or part of your deposits to a 401(k) savings plan? Check for tuition reimbursement, pension plans, profit sharing, ESOP stock ownership plans, discount stock purchase plans, stock options or performance-based bonuses.

**7) Quality-of-Work Factors**
Does the company offer continual training, wellness programs, child care, elder care support, promote-from-within policies, flexible work schedules, performance reviews, product discounts or on-site health clubs? Is it a corporate culture that fits your lifestyle?

As a serious job seeker, you should conduct in-depth research and make detailed notes about these seven key factors for each firm you are considering. Then compare each company's finances, plans and programs to others in the same industry. You'll begin to see what makes some firms outstanding and why those outstanding companies are the best places to make a career investment. For example, if you compare two discount store giants, Wal-Mart and Costco, you will find that Wal-Mart is by far the larger firm, but Costco has an outstanding record of providing superior employee pay and benefits.

Your research goal should be twofold: First, determine whether this is a firm you want to work for. Are the salaries and benefits appealing? Are layoffs likely? Is it a company with solid growth plans? A growing company will offer opportunities for you to advance when it launches new locations, services, technologies or product lines. Second, develop a personal understanding of the company and its industry so you can better sell yourself as a potential employee.

**Other Considerations:**

**Women and Minorities:**

Certain industries have a greater tendency to offer advancement opportunities for women or minorities. Historically, the banking and insurance segments have tended to promote both women and minorities, as have retailing, electric utilities, publishing and major telephone companies.

Major employers in many other industries are making serious efforts to hire, develop and promote women and minorities for top officers' positions. Some technology companies have been terrific places for women who want to advance, and a few tech companies have posted women to CEO spots, such as Anne Mulcahy at Xerox.

Black Enterprise magazine publishes an annual list of the "Most Powerful African Americans in Corporate America," (see www.blackenterprise.com).

The Executive Leadership Council, www.elcinfo.com, a Washington, D.C.-based nonprofit group that conducts programs aimed at filling more executive posts with African-Americans, has a unique statistic to report. Its membership is composed of senior-level black executives who have jobs that are no more than three levels below the CEO spot at Fortune 500 companies. When the group was founded in 1986, it had only a handful of members. Today, its membership is about 400 people employed in high-level executive jobs at 200 major corporations. Approximately one-third of them are women.

A March 2008 study released by Catalyst, a New York-based research group that focuses on women's issues in the workplace, found that 14.8% of members of boards of directors in the *Fortune 500* firms are women, up from 9.6% in 1995. (You can access the results of Catalyst studies at www.catalyst.org.) Obviously, women are making slow progress in gaining representation in the highest ranks of corporate America, and they fall far short of parity with men in that regard. The *Fortune 1000* companies recently included 23 female CEOs, according to an August 2008 study by Catalyst.

**Tips on Using Business Magazines, Newspapers and Trade Journals to Find Job Leads and Do Employer Research**

Many job seekers overlook the tremendous advantages of using industry magazines (called "trade journals") and other publications to do research.

Industry-specific trade journals frequently have classified ads in the back that list job openings. An example of a great magazine to study is *American Banker,* which can be found at major libraries. Additional information is available at www.americanbanker.com.

Journalists at trade journals and business newspapers continuously interview industry-leading executives regarding their companies' growth plans. New projects and company expansion plans described in these articles provide terrific job leads.

You can also get great contact information from these publications. Read the latest business stories about companies and industries that interest you and you will learn vital information. Best of all, you can glean from stories and interviews the names and titles of executives who lead projects, divisions and subsidiaries.

There are literally hundreds of these trade journals—at least one for each industry sector and sometimes dozens covering the largest industries.

Other great resources include local business newspapers such as the *Dallas/Ft. Worth Business Journal*, *The Wall Street Journal*, the business pages of major newspapers like *The New York Times* and publications written for major investors like *Investor's Business Daily.* At www.bizjournals.com, you can gain access to news stories from business journals from all over the U.S.

**Quality-of-Life Benefits:**

Many companies offer benefits that help employees balance their personal and professional lives. The concept is that employees who are healthy and comfortable with their personal and family lives make better, more productive employees. To that end, many companies include fitness programs and family services such as extended maternity leaves and child care or elder care, whether on-site or off-site in the form of referral services. Other popular family-friendly benefits include flextime, flexible benefits spending accounts, adoption assistance and telecommuting. In many cases, benefits are listed on employers' web sites.

Work-Life has become a popular phrase for family-friendly benefits and programs among major employers such as Intel, Abbott Laboratories, Baxter and Aramark. For additional information, you can study such organizations as the Alliance for Work-Life Progress at www.awlp.org.

**Growth Potential and Job Stability:**

A firm's growth potential should be among your top priorities. Companies are always trying to maintain or increase productivity, or the ratio of sales per employee. If a company's sales are sliding, or if it is running out of cash, the job picture starts to collapse. A little extra research into a company's finances and true potential for growth might save you from a future layoff.

Of course, employers sometimes have to resort to layoffs due to conditions outside of their control. For example, travel industry companies worldwide cut hundreds of thousands of jobs in the revenue slump following the September 11, 2001 attacks on New York City and Washington, D.C. The investment and financial services industry has been going through a period of gloom and widespread layoffs since mid-2007.

As a job seeker, you're forced to look out for your own best interests while you sort through thousands of potential employers in dozens of industries. This means that good research is vital. For example, if you put salary at the top of your list, you may have the wrong priorities. From time to time, some of the highest-paying firms have been among those cutting the largest numbers of employees. If you are looking for job stability, your biggest challenge is to pick companies that are more likely to hire now and less likely to have layoffs in the future. That's why a firm's growth outlook should be one of your guiding lights.

However, the goal is *internal* growth caused by expanding sales. Generally less appealing are firms that post a quick spike in growth through big mergers. (In many cases, merged companies lay off people who suddenly find themselves filling jobs duplicated in newly consolidated offices. Also, companies that grow excessively through acquisitions may be taking on loads of debt that can become hard to handle later. However, there are occasional exceptions to this rule, where firms are enjoying soaring demand for products or services and find it difficult to hire quickly enough to keep up.) Companies that are growing rapidly through internal expansion include those opening new stores, distribution centers or offices, developing exciting new products, moving into new markets (including international markets) and creating hot new technologies, retail formats or services. Those types of expansion frequently mean great career opportunities, including the chance for rapid job promotion.

Where can you look for growth companies? If you're tenacious, you can find opportunities where others will find only rejection. Identifying real prospects for growth takes more than a quick glance.

Here's an extremely important point for you to remember: you should look for opportunities in growing divisions that serve special niches, even when the company as a whole is cutting jobs.

**Additional key factors for strong corporate growth, and thereby the best job prospects, include:**

**1) Companies or divisions with a growing share of a promising market.**

Management's ability to anticipate or create change in the marketplace makes for a growing company with great prospects. For example, Sam Walton revolutionized the department store business by realizing that consumers want everyday low prices on name-brand merchandise. He created Wal-Mart, while competitor Sears suffered by maintaining an old-fashioned policy of special sales events on private-label goods. Wal-Mart rapidly became one of the largest creators of new jobs in the private sector. Sears was forced to slash its ranks.

Microsoft made its way to the top with unique products serving a soaring market when it developed highly functional software for personal computers. Microsoft created thousands of millionaire employees through the immense increase in the value of its stock plans. HEB, an innovative grocer in Texas, has evolved continually over the decades, constantly introducing improvements to store layouts, and even creating an exciting new HEB Marketplace concept that is a retail industry leader. HEB has large numbers of job openings of many types on a continuous basis.

The point to these stories is that you shouldn't invest your career in a company with mediocre prospects. With perseverance, you can target your own list of employers that are posting growth due to competitive advantages or growing market demand. Your best bets are companies taking reasonable risks in order to move ahead. Those risks may include investments in advertising, research and development, new technology, improved techniques on the manufacturing floor, testing of new products and the opening of new retail store formats. For example, Chico's FAS stores scored a hit by filling a niche in the women's apparel market, and Genentech became a leader in the biotechnology field by risking vast amounts on research. Also, don't overlook the potential of the export market—many American firms find much of their growth by creating products and services that enjoy demand overseas as well as in the U.S.

**2) Sales and profits: past and present.**

The companies most likely to move along at a good clip are those with an exciting mid-term history. Firms with an average annual growth in sales of 10% to 15% or more over the last three to five years are generally promising. Many small and mid-size firms grow at much faster rates and find themselves hiring continuously.

**3) Beware of fads.**

Unfortunately, a few companies post meteoric growth in businesses that turn out to be mere fads. The restaurant industry suffers from this problem on a regular basis. In recent years, companies selling bagels, frozen yogurt, rotisserie chicken and the like enjoyed impressive, nationwide growth only to collapse like a house of cards a couple of years later. Here's another example: the 1990s produced a rash of new dotcoms that were fueled by fad investors. Many of the biggest web-based busts were companies that planned to steal market share from traditional retail stores by selling items like pet food and living room furniture over the Internet. Most of these fad-based firms wasted valuable years in the careers of employees in addition to billions of dollars of venture capital—only a handful truly succeeded.

**How to Find and Use Expert Opinions:**

Superior sources used by sophisticated job researchers include reports written by: 1) stock analysts; 2) professional market research firms; and 3) journalists at business magazines and industry "trade magazines." Many major libraries have large collections of industry-specific trade magazines that can give you clues that competing job seekers will overlook. For example, *Retail Traffic Magazine*, www.retailtrafficmag.com, publishes lists of the fastest-growing retail chains. Virtually every other industry is covered by one or two trade magazines that will give you leads to growing companies. Many articles in these magazines contain the names of executives you may want to contact. Also, most industry trade magazines publish help-wanted ads in the back. The *Gale Directory of Publications and Broadcast Media* is a good index to magazines, organized by industry. You can find this directory in major libraries.

Next, move on to reports from experts. Marketing and investment professionals are looking for some of the same clues you should use as a job seeker, and reports written by full-time analysts who cover specific companies or industries can help you find firms that are growing and hiring. Reuters, www.reuters.com, is the best source for stock analysts' reports. Here, you'll find the latest business news as well as online access to industry and company coverage written by the nation's best analysts. Most of the reports have a cost, but many are free of charge, and others have prices as low as $5 to $25. Learn to use the stock research and "analyst research" features at Reuters to find exactly what you want.

Professionally written market research can be found at Marketresearch.com, www.marketresearch.com. This market research broker charges varying fees for access to the reports. However, many of the reports are reasonably priced, and the insight you gain into industries, markets and leading companies can be extremely helpful. Web sites such as this offer the ability to search for reports by a wide variety of criteria, including company name and industry.

**Other Basic Resources:**

**Annual Reports/10-Ks/S-1s**: Companies that sell their stocks to the public, including most of the firms covered in this book, publish annual reports that contain a wealth of information. Annual reports and 10-Ks cover yearly results, financial statements, management practices and other vital information for publicly held firms. S-1s provide the same type of information on companies that are selling stock to the public for the first time. You can find copies of these reports at large libraries. Online, the best place to acquire this information is at the site of the U.S. Securities and Exchange Commission. They have a user-friendly service called EDGAR that enables you to search for companies and access their financial reports at www.sec.gov. Look especially at the five-year "summary financial statement" in the back of these reports. Also, look for growth in sales and earnings. If these are falling, dig deeper to find out why. Faltering sales or profits can lead to layoffs or to a merger with another firm (which could result in deep job cuts).

Also, you can find a wealth of financial information on publicly-traded firms at Yahoo! Finance, http://finance.yahoo.com.

See Chapter 4, "Important Contacts for Job Seekers," for additional places to get basic corporate data.

**Tips on Utilizing Financial Documents Filed by Publicly Held Firms**

(Access these documents at the Securities Exchange Commission, www.sec.gov.)

**10-K (also called Annual Report on Form 10-K):**
This is an annual filing required by federal law. It follows a standard format. Information includes a complete description of the business, risk factors, historical financial data and much more. It is vital reading for job seekers. You will find that these documents are written in dry, legal language, but they contain a wealth of information.

**DEF 14A Proxy Statement:**
This is an annual document that gives shareholders certain options to consider at their annual meeting. It names the firm's board of directors and top management. It also gives the dollar value and description of salaries, bonuses, pension plans, stock options and other benefits enjoyed by the company's five highest-paid officers. Job seekers can learn a great deal about a firm's management, pay and benefits from this document. Included is a list of the people or organizations that own more than 5% of the company's stock.

**S-1:**
This is a new registration document for companies that are going public for the first time. In other words, they are creating an IPO (initial public offering). The information includes all of the data found in the 10-K and proxy statement filed annually by companies that have been public for more than one year.

**10-Q:**
This is a quarterly report detailing a company's latest sales, profits and balance sheet.

**More Ways to Research an Employer's Financial Stability and Growth Plans:**

**1) Check out its bond rating.**

There's no sense in trying to become a financial analyst on your own. Instead, go to your library and turn to the *Bond Guide* published by Standard & Poor's (New York, NY). This monthly booklet rates thousands of corporate bonds, based on a company's ability to pay principal and interest when due. If you're considering a major corporation with a bond rating of less than BB (an indicator that a company's debt is riskier than "investment grade"), you should do a lot more investigating before you continue chasing a job at that company.

**2) Talk to vendors and current employees.**

Talk to employees who work for the employer, or talk to people who do business with it. No one knows what's really going on better than people who are on the scene. If there are problems that are not yet known by the media, or if there are exciting new developments that have not yet been announced, you may find out a lot just by asking around. While you're at it, ask about corporate culture—how well are employees treated?

**Popular Job-Search Internet Sites**

| | |
|---|---|
| **HotJobs** | http://hotjobs.yahoo.com/ |
| **CareerBuilder** | www.careerbuilder.com |
| **Monster** | www.monster.com |

**Tips on Finding Information on Privately Held Employers**

Study back-issue indexes and archives to major newspapers to see what journalists are reporting about a prospective employer. Many libraries have back issues of *The Wall Street Journal, The New York Times* and other important newspapers on microfilm. At major public and university libraries, you may be able to access online databases like ProQuest and InfoTrac. These databases have excellent search engines that lead you into online archives of the best publications, including *The Wall Street Journal*, as well as many trade and local publications.

For smaller firms, go online and try American Journalism Review at www.newslink.org, where you'll be able to search news sites including hometown newspapers across the nation. Likewise, search local business newspapers at www.bizjournals.com, where you'll find links to dozens of major business weeklies like the *Houston Business Journal.*

Finally, invest in a credit report. If you really want reassurance, go to Experian SmartBusinessReports, www.smartbusinessreports.com. You can use its links to order a credit report on the employer. These reports are reasonably priced from about $20 to $45, and they can help you determine whether the company is paying its bills on time or has other problems. This could be vital in helping you determine whether to accept a job at a privately-held firm.

**3) Use Internet search engines.**

Look up your firm and industry in an Internet search engine such as Google or a portal such as Yahoo Finance, http://finance.yahoo.com. There, you may find unusual articles that were recently written about a company's product breakthroughs, treatment of women or minorities, human interest stories, training programs or stories written from other unique slants.

**4) Study other business books and guides.**

Search at a library or at an online bookseller like Amazon.com for recent books regarding major companies. For example, if you want to apply to biotech leader Genentech for a job, don't fail to read *The Billion Dollar Molecule: One Company's Quest for the Perfect Drug.* With a little research, you can turn up many other excellent books about specific companies, from banks like Bank of America to publishers like Gannett.

**Great Places for Industry Research**

**Plunkett Research,** www.plunkettresearch.com. Go to the specific industry of your choice to see an overview of trends and statistics. At our subscription service, www.plunkettresearchonline.com, subscribers have access to thousands of pages of industry analysis, statistics, contacts and company profiles, along with multiple search and export tools.

**Quintessentialcareers.com,** www.quintessentialcareers.com. Offers a "Career Resources Toolkit."

**Wetfeet.com,** www.wetfeet.com. Publishes snapshots of hundreds of employers.

**Vault.com**, www.vault.com. This site publishes insights about careers with hundreds of leading firms.

**5) Explore industry-specific web sites.**

See Chapter 4, "Important Contacts for Job Seekers," for hundreds of sites from dozens of different industry sectors. In particular, study the industry associations for the sector you want to work in.

**6) Research benefits and pension plans.**

For additional information about corporate pension plans, start with the government agency charged with protecting and regulating pensions: the Pension Benefit Guaranty Corporation, 1200 K St. NW, Washington, D.C. 20005-4026, 202-326-4000, www.pbgc.gov. They can answer certain questions over the telephone.

The U.S. Department of Labor publishes a useful book titled "Protect your Pension." They can be contacted at: U.S. Department of Labor, Employee Benefits Security Administration, 200 Constitution Ave. NW, Room N5635, Washington, D.C. 20210, 866-444-3272 or 202-219-8776, www.dol.gov/ebsa/publications/main.html.

The Social Security Administration, 800-772-1213, www.ssa.gov, can provide you with information regarding your potential Social Security benefits.

**NOTE**: Generally, employees covered by wealth-building benefit plans do not fully own ("vest in") funds contributed on their behalf by the employer until as many as five years of service with that employer have passed. All pension plans are voluntary—that is, employers are not obligated to offer pensions.

Pension Plans: The type and generosity of these plans vary widely from firm to firm. Caution: Some employers refer to plans as "pension" or "retirement" plans when they are actually 401(k) savings plans that require a contribution by the employee.

**Defined Benefit Pension Plans**: Pension plans that do not require a contribution from the employee are infrequently offered. However, a few companies, particularly larger employers in high-profit-margin industries, offer defined benefit pension plans where the employee is guaranteed to receive a set pension benefit upon retirement. The amount of the benefit is determined by the years of service with the company and the employee's salary during the later years of employment. The longer a person works for the employer, the higher the retirement benefit. These defined benefit plans are funded entirely by the employer. The benefits, up to a reasonable limit, are guaranteed by the Federal Government's Pension Benefit Guaranty Corporation. These plans are not portable—if you leave the company, you cannot transfer your benefits into a different plan. Instead, upon retirement you will receive the benefits that vested during your service with the company. If your employer offers a pension plan, it must give you a "summary plan description" within 90 days of the date you join the plan. You can also request a "summary annual report" of the plan, and once every 12 months you may request an "individual benefit statement" accounting of your interest in the plan.

**Defined Contribution Plans:** These are quite different. They do not guarantee a certain amount of pension benefit. Instead, they set out circumstances under which the employer will make a contribution to a plan on your behalf. The most common example is the 401(k) savings plan. Pension benefits are not guaranteed under these plans.

**Cash Balance Pension Plans:** These plans were recently invented. They are hybrid plans—part defined benefit and part defined contribution. Many employers have converted their older defined benefit plans into cash balance plans. The employer makes deposits (or credits a given amount of money) on the employee's behalf, usually based on a percentage of pay. Employee accounts grow based on a predetermined interest benchmark, such as the interest rate on Treasury Bonds. There are some advantages to these plans, particularly for younger workers: a) The benefits, up to a reasonable limit, are guaranteed by the Pension Benefit Guaranty Corporation. b) Benefits are portable—they can be moved to another plan when the employee changes companies. c) Younger workers and those who spend a shorter number of years with an employer may receive higher benefits than they would under a traditional defined benefit plan.

ESOP Stock Plan (Employees' Stock Ownership Plan): This type of plan is in wide use. Typically, the plan borrows money from a bank and uses those funds to purchase a large block of the corporation's stock. The corporation makes contributions to the plan over a period of time, and the stock purchase loan is eventually paid off. The value of the plan grows significantly as long as the market price of the stock holds up. Qualified employees are allocated a share of the plan based on their length of service and their level of salary. Under federal regulations, participants in ESOPs are allowed to diversify their account holdings in set percentages that rise as the employee ages and gains years of service with the company. In this manner, not all of the employee's assets are tied up in the employer's stock.

Savings Plan, 401(k): Under this type of plan, employees make a tax-deferred deposit into an account. In the best plans, the company makes annual matching donations to the employees' accounts, typically in some proportion to deposits made by the employees themselves. A good plan will match one-half of employee deposits of up to 6% of wages. For example, an employee earning $30,000 yearly might deposit $1,800 (6%) into the plan. The company will match one-half of the employee's deposit, or $900. The plan grows on a tax-deferred basis, similar to an IRA. A very generous plan will match 100% of employee deposits. However, some plans do not call for the employer to make a matching deposit at all. Other plans call for a matching contribution to be made at the discretion of the firm's board of directors. Actual terms of these plans vary widely from firm to firm. Generally, these savings plans allow employees to deposit as much as 15% of salary into the plan on a tax-deferred basis. However, the portion that the company uses to calculate its matching deposit is generally limited to a maximum of 6%. Employees should take care to diversify the holdings in their 401(k) accounts, and most people should seek professional guidance or investment management for their accounts. (Note: when profits are down, many employers exercise their right to suspend their contributions to 401(k)s. Employees may continue to make contributions, but they will not be matched by the employer in these cases.)

Stock Purchase Plan: Qualified employees may purchase the company's common stock at a price below its market value under a specific plan. Typically, the employee is limited to investing a small percentage of wages in this plan. The discount may range from 5% to 15%. Some of these plans allow for deposits to be made through regular monthly payroll deductions. However, new accounting rules for corporations, along with other factors, are leading many companies to curtail these plans—dropping the discount allowed, cutting the maximum yearly stock purchase or otherwise making the plans less generous or appealing.

Profit Sharing: Qualified employees are awarded an annual amount equal to some portion of a company's profits. In a very generous plan, the pool of money awarded to employees would be 15% of profits. Typically, this money is deposited into a long-term retirement account. Caution: Some employers refer to plans as "profit sharing" when they are actually 401(k) savings plans. True profit sharing plans are rarely offered.

**Plunkett Research Online and Plunkett's Industry Reference Books:**

1) Internet-Based Services: Plunkett Research Online is a reference service that is subscribed to by the nation's leading university placement offices, libraries and information offices. You can use it to filter prospective employers by location, industry, size and more. You can then export contact information for those companies into spreadsheets or text files. In addition, you can use the site to research the latest editions of our industry analysis. Many additional tools for job seekers are included. For an extensive online tour, see www.plunkettresearch.com.

2) Printed Almanacs: Plunkett Research also publishes industry-specific almanacs for the most important industries. These are top-notch resources for job seekers.

**Industry-Specific Books from Plunkett Research:**

- Plunkett's Advertising & Branding Industry Almanac
- Plunkett's Airline, Hotel & Travel Industry Almanac
- Plunkett's Almanac of Middle Market Companies
- Plunkett's Apparel & Textiles Industry Almanac
- Plunkett's Automobile Industry Almanac
- Plunkett's Banking, Mortgages & Credit Industry Almanac
- Plunkett's Biotech & Genetics Industry Almanac
- Plunkett's Chemicals, Coatings & Plastics Industry Almanac
- Plunkett's Consulting Industry Almanac
- Plunkett's E-Commerce & Internet Business Almanac
- Plunkett's Energy Industry Almanac
- Plunkett's Engineering & Research Industry Almanac
- Plunkett's Entertainment & Media Industry Almanac
- Plunkett's Food Industry Almanac
- Plunkett's Health Care Industry Almanac
- Plunkett's Insurance Industry Almanac
- Plunkett's InfoTech Industry Almanac
- Plunkett's Investment & Securities Industry Almanac
- Plunkett's Nanotechnology & MEMS Industry Almanac
- Plunkett's Outsourcing & Offshoring Industry Almanac
- Plunkett's Real Estate & Construction Industry Almanac
- Plunkett's Renewable, Alternative & Hydrogen Energy Industry Almanac

- Plunkett's Retail Industry Almanac
- Plunkett's Sports Industry Almanac
- Plunkett's Telecommunications Industry Almanac
- Plunkett's Transportation, Supply Chain & Logistics Industry Almanac
- Plunkett's Wireless & Cellular Telephone Industry Almanac

**Publications from Plunkett Research Written Especially for Job Seekers:**

- The Almanac of American Employers
- Plunkett's Companion to the Almanac of American Employers

Our books will give you in-depth coverage of specific industries and the leading firms in those industries, along with trends and developments in technology and services. You will find these books in public and academic libraries, college placement offices, human resources offices, corporate libraries and government agency libraries. For sample chapters and additional details, you can preview as well as purchase these books at www.plunkettresearch.com.

***Plunkett's Companion to The Almanac of American Employers*** is our book that provides profiles on 500 additional, rapidly growing corporate employers. This companion book covers smaller firms than those in the main volume of *The Almanac of American Employers*.

# Chapter 4

# IMPORTANT CONTACTS FOR JOB SEEKERS

**Contents:**

## I. Accountants & CPAs Associations

**American Institute of CPAs (AICPA)**
1211 Ave. of the Americas
New York, NY 10036-8775 US
Phone: 212-596-6200
Fax: 1-800-362-5066
Toll Free: 888-777-7077
E-mail Address: *service@aicpa.org*
Web Address: www.aicpa.org
American Institute of CPAs (AICPA) provides information and news for CPAs, news from the organization and a search for accounting firms on its web site.

## II. Advertising/Marketing Associations

**Advertising Women of New York (AWNY)**
25 W. 45th St., Ste. 403
New York, NY 10036 US
Phone: 212-221-7969
Fax: 212-221-8296
E-mail Address: *awny@awny.org*
Web Address: www.awny.org
Advertising Women of New York (AWNY) provides a forum for personal and professional growth, serves as a catalyst for the advancement of women in the communications field and promotes and supports philanthropic endeavors through the AWNY Foundation. The web site also provides content from Women Executives in Public Relations (WERP), such as its a dynamic job board.

**American Association of Advertising Agencies (AAAA)**
405 Lexington Ave., 18th Fl.
New York, NY 10174-1801 US
Phone: 212-682-2500
Fax: 212-682-8391
E-mail Address: *nhill@aaaa.org*
Web Address: www.aaaa.org
The American Association of Advertising Agencies (AAAA) is the national trade association representing the advertising agency industry in the United States.

**American Institute of Graphic Arts (AIGA)**
164 5th Ave.
New York, NY 10010 US
Phone: 212-807-1990
Fax: 212-807-1799
E-mail Address: *steve_rogenstein@aiga.org*
Web Address: www.aiga.org
The American Institute of Graphic Arts (AIGA) strives to further excellence in communication design, both as a strategic tool for business and as a cultural force.

**American Marketing Association (AMA)**
311 S. Wacker Dr., Ste. 5800
Chicago, IL 60606 US
Phone: 312-542-9000
Fax: 312-542-9001
Toll Free: 800-262-1150
E-mail Address: *info@ama.org*
Web Address: www.marketingpower.com
The American Marketing Association (AMA) serves marketing professionals in both business and education and serves all levels of marketing practitioners, educators and students.

**Cable & Telecommunications Association for Marketing (CTAM)**
201 N. Union St., Ste. 440
Alexandria, VA 22314 US
Phone: 703-549-4200
E-mail Address: *info@ctam.com*
Web Address: www.ctamnetforum.com/eweb
The Cable & Telecommunications Association for Marketing (CTAM) is dedicated to the discipline and development of consumer marketing excellence in cable television, new media and telecommunications services.

**Direct Marketing Association (DMA)**
1120 Ave. of the Americas
New York, NY 10036-6700 US
Phone: 212-768-7277
Fax: 212-302-6714
E-mail Address: *customerservice@the-dma.org*
Web Address: www.the-dma.org
The Direct Marketing Association (DMA) is the oldest and largest trade association for users and suppliers in the direct, database and interactive marketing fields.

## III. Aging

**Administration on Aging (AOA)**
1 Massachusetts Ave., Stes. 4100 & 5100
Washington, DC 20201 US
Phone: 202-619-0724
Fax: 202-357-3555
Toll Free: 800-677-1116
E-mail Address: *aoainfo@aoa.hhs.gov*
Web Address: www.aoa.gov
The Administration on Aging (AOA) is the federal focal point and advocate agency for older persons and their concerns. In this role, AOA works to heighten awareness among other federal agencies, organizations, groups and the public.

## IV. Airline & Air Cargo Industry Associations

**International Air Transport Association (IATA)**
800 Place Victoria
P.O. Box 113
Montreal, QC H4Z 1M1 Canada
Phone: 514-874-0202
Fax: 514-874-9632
E-mail Address: *corpcomms@iata.org*
Web Address: www.iata.org
The International Air Transport Association (IATA) represents about 260 airlines in order to offer the highest standards of passenger and cargo service.

## V. Alternative Energy-Ethanol

**Renewable Fuels Association (RFA)**
1 Massachusetts Ave. NW, Ste. 820
Washington, DC 20001 US
Phone: 202-289-3835
E-mail Address: *info@ethanolrfa.org*
Web Address: www.ethanolrfa.org
The Renewable Fuels Association (RFA) is a trade organization representing the ethanol industry. It publishes a wealth of useful information, including a listing of biorefineries and monthly U.S. fuel ethanol production and demand.

## VI. Alternative Energy-Solar

**Solar Energy Industries Association (SEIA)**
805 15th St. NW, Ste. 510
Washington, DC 20005 US
Phone: 202-682-0556
Fax: 202-682-7779
E-mail Address: *info@seia.org*
Web Address: www.seia.org
Solar Energy Industries Association (SEIA) operates a web site that provides news for the solar energy industry, links to related products and companies and solar energy statistics.

## VII. Alternative Energy-Wind

**American Wind Energy Association (AWEA)**
1501 M St. NW, Ste. 1000
Washington, DC 20005 US
Phone: 202-383-2500
Fax: 202-383-2505
E-mail Address: *windmail@awea.org*
Web Address: www.awea.org
The American Wind Energy Association (AWEA) promotes wind energy as a clean source of electricity worldwide. Its website provides excellent resources for research, including an online library, discussions of legislation, and descriptions of wind technologies.

## VIII. Apparel Associations

**American Apparel and Footwear Manufacturing Association (AAFA)**
1601 N. Kent St., 12th Fl.
Arlington, VA 22209 US
Phone: 703-524-1864
Fax: 703-522-6741
Toll Free: 800-520-2262
E-mail Address: *dvandyke@apparelandfootwear.org*
Web Address: www.apparelandfootwear.org
The American Apparel and Footwear Manufacturing Association (AAFA) is the national trade association for the apparel, footwear and fashion industries and their suppliers.

## IX. Banking Industry Associations

**American Bankers Association (ABA)**
1120 Connecticut Ave. NW
Washington, DC 20036 US
Fax: 202-663-7578
Toll Free: 800-226-5377
E-mail Address: *smarshall@aba.com*
Web Address: www.aba.com
The American Bankers Association (ABA) represents banks of all sizes on issues of national importance for financial institutions and their customers. The site offers financial information and solutions, financial news and member access to further advice and content.

## X. Biotechnology & Biological Industry Associations

**BioIndustry Association**
14/15 Belgrave Sq.
London, SW1X 8PS UK
Phone: 44-20-7565-7190
Fax: 44-20-7565-7191
E-mail Address: *admin@bioindustry.org*
Web Address: www.bioindustry.org
The BioIndustry Association promotes bioscience development in the U.K. The organization operates a public affairs program, a conference and seminar program, trade missions and publications for internal and external audiences.

**Biotechnology Industry Organization (BIO)**
1201 Maryland Ave. SW, Ste. 900
Washington, DC 20024 US
Phone: 202-962-9200
Fax: 202-488-6301
E-mail Address: *info@bio.org*
Web Address: www.bio.org
The Biotechnology Industry Organization (BIO) is involved in the research and development of health care, agricultural, industrial and environmental biotechnology products. BIO has both small and large member organizations.

## XI. Booksellers Associations

**American Booksellers Association, Inc.**
200 White Plains Rd., Ste. 600
Tarrytown, NY 10591 US
Fax: 914-591-2720
Toll Free: 800-637-0037
E-mail Address: *info@bookweb.org*
Web Address: www.bookweb.org
The American Booksellers Association is a nonprofit association representing independent bookstores in the United States.

## XII. Broadcasting, Cable, Radio & TV Associations

**Academy of Television Arts and Sciences**
5220 Lankershim Blvd.
North Hollywood, CA 91601-3109 US
Phone: 818-754-2800
Fax: 818-761-2827
E-mail Address: *support@emmys.org*
Web Address: www.emmys.org
The Academy of Television Arts and Sciences is a nonprofit corporation devoted to the advancement of telecommunications arts and sciences and to fostering creative leadership in the telecommunications industry. It is one of three organizations that administer the Emmy Awards. It is responsible for prime time Emmys

**American Federation of Television and Radio Artists (AFTRA)**
260 Madison Ave., 7th Fl.
New York, NY 10016-2401 US
Phone: 212-532-0800
Fax: 212-532-2242
E-mail Address: *info@aftra.org*
Web Address: www.aftra.org
The American Federation of Television and Radio Artists (AFTRA) represents actors and other professional performers and broadcasters in television, radio, sound recordings, non-broadcast/industrial programming and new technologies such as interactive programming and CD-ROMs.

**American Women in Radio and Television, Inc. (AWRT)**
1760 Old Meadow Rd., Ste. 500
McLean, VA 22102 US
Phone: 703-506-3290
Fax: 703-506-3266
E-mail Address: *info@awrt.org*
Web Address: www.awrt.org
American Women in Radio and Television (AWRT), founded in 1951, is a national nonprofit organization dedicated to advancing the role of women in electronic media and related fields.

**Association of America's Public Television Stations (APTS)**
2100 Crystal Dr., Ste. 700
Arlington, VA 22202 US
Phone: 202-654-4200
Fax: 202-654-4236
E-mail Address: *jeffrey@apts.org*
Web Address: www.apts.org
The Association of America's Public Television Stations (APTS) is a nonprofit membership organization formed to support the continued growth and development of strong and financially sound noncommercial television service for the American public.

**Broadcast Education Association (BEA)**
1771 N St. NW
Washington, DC 20036-2891 US
Phone: 202-429-3935
E-mail Address: *tbailey@nab.org*
Web Address: www.beaweb.org
The Broadcast Education Association (BEA) is the professional association for professors, industry professionals and graduate students interested in teaching and research related to electronic media and multimedia enterprises.

**National Academy of Television Arts and Sciences**
111 W. 57th St., Ste. 600
New York, NY 10019 US
Phone: 212-586-8424
Fax: 212-246-8129
E-mail Address: *info@emmyonline.tv*
Web Address: www.emmyonline.org
The National Academy of Television Arts and Sciences is dedicated to the advancement of the arts and sciences of television and the promotion of creative leadership for artistic, educational and technical achievements within the television industry. It is responsible for awarding the Emmy Awards.

**National Association of Broadcasters (NAB)**
1771 N St. NW
Washington, DC 20036 US
Phone: 202-429-5300
Fax: 202-429-4199
E-mail Address: *nab@nab.org*
Web Address: www.nab.org
The National Association of Broadcasters (NAB) represents broadcasters for radio and television. The organization also provides benefits to employees of member companies and to individuals and companies that provide products and services to the electronic media industries.

**National Association of Television Program Executives (NATPE)**
5757 Wilshire Blvd., Penthouse 10
Los Angeles, CA 90036-3681 US
Phone: 310-453-4440
Fax: 310-453-5258
E-mail Address: *info@natpe.org*
Web Address: www.natpe.org
The National Association of Television Program Executives (NATPE) is the leading association for content professionals in the global television industry.

**National Cable and Telecommunications Association (NCTA)**
25 Massachusetts Ave. NW, Ste. 100
Washington, DC 20001 US
Phone: 202-222-2300
Fax: 202-222-2514
E-mail Address: *webmaster@ncta.com*
Web Address: www.ncta.com
The National Cable and Telecommunications Association (NCTA) is the principal trade association of the cable television industry in the United States.

**Radio Television News Directors Association (RTNDA)**
1025 F Street NW, 7th Fl.
Washington, DC 20004 US
Phone: 202-659-6510
Fax: 202-223-4007
Toll Free: 800-807-8632
E-mail Address: *stefanib@rtnda.org*
Web Address: www.rtnda.org
The Radio Television News Directors Association (RTNDA) is the world's largest professional organization exclusively committed to professionals in electronic journalism.

**Satellite Broadcasting & Communications Association of America (SBCA)**
1730 M St. NW, Ste. 600
Washington, DC 20036 US
Phone: 202-349-3620
Fax: 202-349-3621
Toll Free: 800-541-5981
E-mail Address: *info@sbca.org*
Web Address: www.sbca.com
The Satellite Broadcasting & Communications Association of America (SBCA) is the national trade organization representing all segments of the satellite consumer services industry.

**Syndication Network Television Association (SNTA)**
1 Penn Plz., Ste. 5310
New York, NY 10119 US
Phone: 212-259-3740
Fax: 212-259-3770
E-mail Address: *mburg@snta.com*
Web Address: www.snta.com

The Syndication Network Television Association (SNTA) is an organization of national and independent television stations that syndicate television shows.

**Women in Cable & Telecommunications (WICT)**
14555 Avion Pkwy., Ste. 250
Chantilly, VA 20151 US
Phone: 703-234-9810
Fax: 703-817-1595
E-mail Address: *lvega@wict.org*
Web Address: www.wict.org
Women in Cable & Telecommunications (WICT) exists to advance the position and influence of women in media through leadership programs and services at both the national and local level.

## XIII. Careers-Airlines/Flying

**Aviation/Aerospace Jobs Page**
NationJob, Inc.
601 SW 9th St., Stes. J&K
Des Moines, IA 50309 US
Fax: 515-283-1223
Toll Free: 888-526-5967
E-mail Address: *customerservice@nationjob.com*
Web Address: www.nationjob.com/aviation
The Aviation/Aerospace Jobs Page, a division of NationJob, Inc., features detailed aviation and aerospace job listings and company profiles.

**Avjobs, Inc.**
P.O. Box 630830
Littleton, CO 80163 US
Phone: 303-683-2322
Fax: 888-624-8691
E-mail Address: *info@avjobs.com*
Web Address: www.avjobs.com
Avjobs, Inc. is a group of employers dedicated to helping individuals obtain aviation, airline, aerospace and airport careers.

**Flightdeck Recruitment Ltd.**
82c East Hill
Colchester, Essex CO1 2QW UK
Phone: 44-1206-383730
Web Address: www.flightdeckrecruitment.com
Flightdeck Recruitment Ltd. provides a link between aviation recruiters who are looking for flight deck crew and pilots or flight engineers who are seeking employment.

**United States Air Force**
Web Address: www.airforce.com
The web site of the United States Air Force offers information on basic training, careers, education, deployment, benefits and Air Force life.

## XIV. Careers-Banking

**National Banking & Financial Service Network (NBFSN)**
3075 Brickhouse Ct.
Virginia Beach, VA 23452-6860 US
Phone: 757-463-5766
Fax: 757-340-0826
E-mail Address: *susan@nbn-jobs.com*
Web Address: www.banking-financejobs.com
The National Banking & Financial Service Network (NBFSN) is made up of recruiting firms in the banking and financial services marketplace. The web site provides job listings.

## XV. Careers-Biotech

**Biotechemployment.com**
Phone: 561-630-5201
E-mail Address: *jobs@Biotechemployment.com*
Web Address: www.biotechemployment.com
Biotechemployment.com is an online resource for job seekers in biotechnology. The site's features includes resume posting, job search agents and employer profiles. It is part of the eJobstores.com, Inc., which includes the Health Care Job Store sites.

**Chase Group (The)**
10955 Lowell Ave., Ste. 500
Overland Park, KS 66210 US
Phone: 913-663-3100
Fax: 913-663-3131
E-mail Address: *chase@chasegroup.com*
Web Address: www.chasegroup.com
The Chase Group is an executive search firm specializing in biomedical and pharmaceutical placement.

**RPh on the Go USA, Inc.**
5510 Howard St.
Skokie, IL 60077-2620 US
Phone: 847-588-7170
Fax: 847-588-7060
Toll Free: 800-553-7359
E-mail Address: *lbalaguer@rphonthego.com*
Web Address: www.rphonthego.com
RPh on the Go USA, Inc. places temporary and permanent qualified professionals in the pharmacy community.

## XVI. Careers-Computers/Technology

**Computerjobs.com, Inc.**
280 Interstate N. Cir. SE, Ste. 300
Atlanta, GA 30339-2411 US
Toll Free: 800-850-0045
E-mail Address: *michael@marketingmax.com*
Web Address: www.computerjobs.com
Computerjobs.com, Inc. is an employment web site that offers users a link to computer-related job opportunities organized by skill and market.

**Dice**
4101 NW Urbandale Dr.
Urbandale, IA 50322 US
Phone: 515-280-1144
Fax: 515-280-1452
Toll Free: 877-386-3323
Web Address: www.dice.com
Dice provides free employment services for IT jobs. The site includes advanced job searches by geographic location and category, availability announcements and resume postings, as well as employer profiles, a recruiter's page and career links. Dice is owned by Dice Holdings, Inc., a publicly traded company.

**Institute for Electrical and Electronics Engineers (IEEE) Job Site**
IEEE
445 Hoes Ln.
Piscataway, NJ 08855-1331 US
Phone: 732-981-0060
Toll Free: 800-678-4333
E-mail Address: *candidatejobsite@ieee.org*
Web Address: careers.ieee.org
The Institute for Electrical and Electronics Engineers (IEEE) Job Site provides a host of employment services for technical professionals, employers and recruiters. The site offers job listings by geographic area, a resume bank and links to employment services.

**Pencom Systems, Inc.**
152 Remsen St.
New York, NY 11201 US
Phone: 718-923-1111
Fax: 718-923-6066
E-mail Address: *tom@pencom.com*
Web Address: www.pencom.com
Pencom Systems, Inc., an open systems recruiting company, offers a web site geared toward high-technology and scientific professionals, featuring an interactive salary survey, career advisor, job listings and technology resources.

**SearchTech Solutions**
307 Orchard City Dr., Ste. 300
Campbell, CA 95008 US
Phone: 408-540-1800
Fax: 408-540-1815
Toll Free: 888-695-4362
E-mail Address: *resumes@stecs.com*
Web Address: www.stecs.com
SearchTech Solutions is a recruiting, placement and consulting firm focused on Engineering, Product Development and Innovation, Supply Chain and IT industries. Its web site offers resume writing assistance, including editing, writing and customizing.

## XVII. Careers-First Time Jobs/New Grads

**Alumni-Network Recruitment Corporation**
Oakville, ON Canada
Phone: 905-465-2547
E-mail Address: *karen@alumni-network.com*
Web Address: www.alumni-network.com
Alumni-Network Recruitment Corporation is a professional search and recruiting firm, specializing in ERP, E-Commerce and Engineering.

**Black Collegian Online (The)**
140 Carondelet St.
New Orleans, LA 70130 US
Phone: 504-523-0154
Web Address: www.black-collegian.com
The Black Collegian Online features listings for job and internship opportunities, as well as other tools for students of color; it is the web site of The Black Collegian Magazine, published by IMDiversity, Inc. The site includes a list of the top 100 minority corporate employers and an assessment of job opportunities.

**Canadian Association of Career Educators and Employers (CACEE)**
720 Spadina Ave., Ste. 202
Toronto, ON M5S 2T9 Canada
Fax: 416-929-5256
Toll Free: 866-922-3303
E-mail Address: *janinec@cacee.com*
Web Address: www.cacee.com
The Canadian Association of Career Educators and Employers (CACEE) is a partnership of employer recruiters and career services professionals. The group provides information, advice and professional development opportunities to employers, career services professionals and students.

**Collegegrad.com, Inc.**
234 E. College Ave., Ste. 200
State College, PA 16801 US
Phone: 262-375-6700
Toll Free: 1-800-991-4642
Web Address: www.collegegrad.com
Collegegrad.com, Inc. offers in-depth resources for college students and recent grads seeking entry-level jobs.

**Job Web**
Nat'l Association of Colleges & Employers (NACE)
62 Highland Ave.
Bethlehem, PA 18017-9085 US
Phone: 610-868-1421
Fax: 610-868-0208
Toll Free: 800-544-5272
E-mail Address: *editors@jobweb.com*
Web Address: www.jobweb.com
Job Web, owned and sponsored by National Association of Colleges and Employers (NACE), displays job openings and employer descriptions. The site also offers a database of career fairs, searchable by state or keyword, with contact information.

**MBAjobs.net**
Fax: 413-556-8849
E-mail Address: *contact@mbajobs.net*
Web Address: www.mbajobs.net
MBAjobs.net is a unique international service for MBA students and graduates, employers, recruiters and business schools. The MBAjobs.net service is provided by WebInfoCo.

**MonsterTRAK**
11845 W. Olympic Blvd., Ste. 500
Los Angeles, CA 90064 US
Toll Free: 800-999-8725
E-mail Address: *trakstudent@monster.com*
Web Address: www.monstertrak.monster.com
MonsterTRAK features links to hundreds of university and college career centers across the U.S. with entry-level job listings categorized by industry. Major companies can also utilize MonsterTRAK.

**National Association of Colleges and Employers (NACE)**
62 Highland Ave.
Bethlehem, PA 18017-9085 US
Phone: 610-868-1421
Fax: 610-868-0208
Toll Free: 800-544-5272
E-mail Address: *mcollins@naceweb.org*
Web Address: www.naceweb.org

The National Association of Colleges and Employers (NACE) is a premier U.S. organization representing college placement offices and corporate recruiters who focus on hiring new grads.

## XVIII. Careers-General Job Listings

**6FigureJobs**
25 3rd St., Ste. 230
Stamford, CT 06905 US
Toll Free: 800-605-5154
Web Address: www.6figurejobs.com
6FigureJobs offers executives a database of high-level positions. Membership is free for qualified individuals.

**Career Exposure, Inc.**
805 SW Broadway, Ste. 2250
Portland, OR 97205 US
Phone: 503-221-7779
Fax: 503-221-7780
E-mail Address: *lisam@mackenzie-marketing.com*
Web Address: www.careerexposure.com
Career Exposure, Inc. is an online career center and job placement service, with resources for employers, recruiters and job seekers.

**CareerBuilder, Inc.**
200 N. LaSalle St., Ste. 1100
Chicago, IL 60601 US
Phone: 773-527-3600
Toll Free: 800-638-4212
Web Address: www.careerbuilder.com
CareerBuilder, Inc. focuses on the needs of companies and also provides a database of job openings. The site has 1.5 million jobs posted by 300,000 employers, and receives an average 23 million unique visitors monthly. The company also operates online career centers for 150 newspapers, 1,000 partners and other online portals such as America Online. Resumes are sent directly to the company, and applicants can set up a special e-mail account for job-seeking purposes. CareerBuilder is primarily a joint venture between three newspaper giants: The McClatchy Company (which recently acquired former partner Knight Ridder), Gannett Co., Inc. and Tribune Company. In 2007, Microsoft acquired a minority interest in CareerBuilder, allowing the site to ally itself with MSN.

**CareerOneStop**
Toll Free: 877-348-0502
E-mail Address: *info@careeronestop.org*
Web Address: www.careeronestop.org
CareerOneStop is operated by the employment commissions of various state agencies. It contains job listings in both the private sector and in government. CareerOneStop is sponsored by the U.S. Department of Labor. It includes a wide variety of useful career resources and workforce information.

**Careers Organization (The)**
E-mail Address: *info@Careers.Org*
Web Address: www.careers.org
The Career Organization is a job resource center with links to jobs and pointers to other career-related web sites as well as links to associations, franchising opportunities and library resources.

**Collegerecruiter.com**
3109 W 50 St., Ste. 121
Minneapolis, MN 55410-2102 US
Phone: 952-848-2211
Fax: 702-537-2227
Toll Free: 800-835-4989
E-mail Address: *Steven@CollegeRecruiter.com*
Web Address: www.collegerecruiter.com
Collegerecruiter.com provides college students with internship, part-time and summer job listings. Recent graduates can search for career opportunities by category and location. The site also provides information about student loans and loan consolidation.

**ContractJobHunter**
C. E. Publications, Inc.
P.O. Box 3006
Bothell, WA 98041-3006 US
Phone: 425-806-5200
Fax: 425-806-5585
E-mail Address: *staff@cjhunter.com*
Web Address: www.ceweekly.wa.com
ContractJobHunter is a web-based version of the magazine Contract Employment Weekly Online. It posts job listings and links to contract firms. Libraries for reference materials and resume writing guidelines are also offered. The site is a service of C. E. Publications, Inc.

**EmploymentGuide**
150 Granby St.
Norfolk, VA 23510 US
Toll Free: 877-876-4039
Web Address: www.employmentguide.com
EmploymentGuide offers general career resources along with lists of position openings, company profiles and a resume database. It also circulates a free print publication.

**EscapeArtist.com Inc.**
832-1245 World Trade Ctr.
Panama, WTC-0832 Republic of Panama
Fax: 786-513-3702
Web Address: www.escapeartist.com
EscapeArtist.com Inc.'s web site provides job searches for overseas positions, as well as international working condition resources and immigration information.

**ExecuNet, Inc.**
295 Westport Ave.
Norwalk, CT 06851 US
Toll Free: 800-637-3126
E-mail Address: *member.services@execunet.com*
Web Address: www.execunet.com
ExecuNet, Inc. is an executive career management information and contact service.

**Executiveagent.com**
Kennedy Information, Inc.
1 Phoenix Mill Ln., 3rd Fl.
Peterborough, NH 03458 US
Phone: 603-924-1006
Fax: 603-924-4034
Toll Free: 800-531-0007
Web Address: www.executiveagent.com
Executiveagent.com allows senior-level professionals to have their resumes sent to executive placement firms for a fee. The site is owned by Kennedy Information, Inc.

**Getajob**
Web Address: www.getajob.com
Getajob provides job listings, employment articles, a resume database, book titles and newsgroups for the job seeker.

**Guru.com**
5001 Baum Blvd., Ste. 760
Pittsburgh, PA 15213 US
Fax: 412-687-4466
Toll Free: 888-678-0136
E-mail Address: *pr@guru.com*
Web Address: www.guru.com
Guru.com is an excellent site for freelancers and contract workers, especially in the IT field.

**Higheredjobs.com**
328 Innovation Blvd., Ste. 300
State College, PA 16803 US
Phone: 814-861-3080
Fax: 814-861-3082
E-mail Address: *sales@HigherEdJobs.com*
Web Address: www.higheredjobs.com
Higheredjobs.com lists job vacancies in colleges and universities.

**IMDiversity, Inc.**
140 Carondelet St.
New Orleans, LA 70130 US
Phone: 504-523-0154
Fax: 504-523-9271
Web Address: www.imdiversity.com
IMDiversity, Inc. provides job listings and career development information. The web site also has divisions for particular minority groups.

**Job Search USA**
E-mail Address: *info@jobsearchusa.org*
Web Address: www.jobsearchusa.org
Job Search USA is a major job posting site that contains job opportunities classified by a variety of keywords.

**JobCentral**
DirectEmployers Association, Inc.
9002 N. Purdue Rd., Quad III, Ste. 100
Indianapolis, IN 46268 US
Phone: 317-874-9000
Fax: 317-874-9100
Toll Free: 866-268-6206
E-mail Address: *info@jobcentral.com*
Web Address: www.jobcentral.com
JobCentral, operated by the nonprofit DirectEmployers Association, Inc., links users directly to hundreds of thousands of job opportunities posted on the sites of participating employers, thus bypassing the usual job search sites. This saves employers money and allows job seekers to access many more job opportunities.

**Jobsinthemoney.com**
4101 NW Urbandale Dr.
Urbandale, IA 50322 US
Phone: 515-280-1144
Fax: 515-280-1452
Toll Free: 800-979-3423
E-mail Address: *cs@jobsinthemoney.com*
Web Address: www.jobsinthemoney.com
Jobsinthemoney.com provides employment listings in the finance industry as well as job tools, such as salary surveys, resume writing assistance and industry news. It is owned by Dice, a part of Dice Holdings, Inc.

**LaborMarketInfo**
Employment Dev. Dept., Labor Market Info. Div.
800 Capitol Mall, MIC 83
Sacramento, CA 95814 US
Phone: 916-262-2162
Fax: 916-262-2352
Toll Free: 800-480-3287
Web Address: www.labormarketinfo.edd.ca.gov
LaborMarketInfo, formerly the California Cooperative Occupational Information System, is geared to providing job seekers and employers a wide range of resources, namely the ability to find, access and use labor market information and services. It provides demographical statistics for employment on both a local and regional level, as well as career searching tools for California residents. The web site is sponsored by California's Employment Development Office.

**Mediabistro.com**
475 Park Ave. S., 4th Fl.
New York, NY 10016 US
Phone: 212-389-2000
Fax: 212-966-8984
E-mail Address: *laurelT@mediabistro.com*
Web Address: www.mediabistro.com
Mediabistro.com offers an array of employment resources, including job listings in the media industry.

**Monster Worldwide, Inc.**
622 3rd Ave., 39th Fl.
New York, NY 10017 US
Phone: 212-351-7000
Fax: 646-658-0541
Toll Free: 800-666-7837
E-mail Address: *moreinfo@monster.com*
Web Address: www.monsterworldwide.com
Monster Worldwide, Inc. primarily operates Monster.com, an electronic career center that displays hundreds of thousands of job opportunities in 36 countries worldwide. Job seekers can build and store a resume online and find job listings that match their profiles. Monster.com e-mails any resulting hits once per week. Monster Worldwide also offers some Internet advertising services.

**NationJob, Inc.**
601 SW 9th St., Ste. J&K
Des Moines, IA 50309 US
Fax: 515-283-1223
Toll Free: 888-526-5967
E-mail Address: *customerservice@nationjob.com*
Web Address: www.nationjob.com
NationJob, Inc.'s web site allows users can develop a profile of the ideal job based on the criterion of location, industry, salary; and, if they provide an e-mail address, wait for appropriate listings to be sent to them through the firm's PJScout feature.

**NETSHARE, Inc.**
83 Hamilton Dr., Ste. 202
Novato, CA 94949 US
Toll Free: 800-241-5642
E-mail Address: *netshare@netshare.com*

Web Address: www.netshare.com
Netshare provides access to exclusive listings of executive jobs that pay $70,000 and up. Job seekers pay either $37.50/month or $395/year for the service.

**Net-Temps, Inc.**
55 Middlesex St., Ste. 220
North Chelmsford, MA 01863 US
Fax: 978-251-7250
Toll Free: 800-307-0062
E-mail Address: *service@net-temps.com*
Web Address: www.net-temps.com
Net-Temps, Inc. offers a web site, operated by professional career consultants, that features job listings and job seeking tips.

**Recruiters Online Network**
947 Essex Ln.
Medina, OH 44256 US
Phone: 888-364-4667
Fax: 888-237-8686
E-mail Address: *info@recruitersonline.com*
Web Address: www.recruitersonline.com
The Recruiters Online Network provides job postings from thousands of recruiters, Careers Online Magazine, a resume database, as well as other career resources.

**True Careers, Inc.**
Web Address: www.truecareers.com
True Careers, Inc. offers job listings and provides an array of career resources. The company also offers a search of over 2 million scholarships. It is partnered with CareerBuilder.com, which powers its career information and resume posting functions.

**USAJOBS**
U.S. Office of Personnel Management
1900 E St. NW
Washington, DC 20415 US
Phone: 202-606-1800
Web Address: usajobs.opm.gov
USAJOBS, a program of the U.S. Office of Personnel Management, is the official job site for the U.S. Federal Government. It provides a comprehensive list of U.S. government jobs, allowing users to search for employment by location; agency; type of work, using the Federal Government's numerical identification code, the General Schedule (GS) Series; or by senior executive positions. It also has a special veterans' employment section; an information center, offering resume and interview tips and other useful information such as hiring trends and a glossary of Federal terms; and allows users to create a profile and post a resume.

**Wall Street Journal - CareerJournal**
Wall Street Journal
200 Liberty St.
New York, NY 10281 US
Phone: 212-416-2000
Toll Free: 800-568-7625
E-mail Address: *onelinejournal@wsj.com*
Web Address: online.wsj.com/careers
The Wall Street Journal's CareerJournal, an executive career site, features a job database with thousands of available positions; career news and employment related articles; and advice regarding resume writing, interviews, networking, office life and job hunting.

**Yahoo! HotJobs**
45 W. 18th St., 6th Fl.
New York, NY 10011 US
Phone: 646-351-5300
Web Address: hotjobs.yahoo.com
Yahoo! HotJobs, designed for experienced professionals, employers and job seekers, is a Yahoo-owned site that provides company profiles, a resume posting service and a resume workshop. The site allows posters to block resumes from being viewed by certain companies and provides a notification service of new jobs.

## XIX. Careers-Health Care

**Medicalworkers.com**
191 University Blvd., Ste. 252
Denver, CO 80206 US
Phone: 720-227-9364
E-mail Address: *cs@medicalworkers.com*
Web Address: www.medicalworkers.com
Medicalworkers.com is an employment site for medical and health care professionals.

**Medjump.com**
7119 E. Shea Blvd., Stes. 109-535
Scottsdale, AZ 85254 US
E-mail Address: *info@medjump.net*
Web Address: www.medjump.com
Medjump.com is dedicated to empowering health care and medical-related professionals with the necessary tools to market their abilities and skills.

**Medzilla, Inc.**
P.O. Box 1710
Marysville, WA 98270 US
Phone: 360-657-5681
Fax: 775-514-9440
E-mail Address: *mgroutage@medzilla.com*
Web Address: www.medzilla.com
Medzilla, Inc.'s web site offers job searches, salary surveys, a search agent and information on health care employment.

**Monster Career Advice-Healthcare**
Monster Worldwide, Inc.
622 3rd Ave.
New York, NY 10017 US
Phone: 212-351-7000
Toll Free: 800-666-7837
Web Address: career-advice.monster.com/get-the-job/healthcare/home.aspx
Monster Career Advice-Healthcare, a service of Monster Worldwide, Inc., provides job listings, job searches and search agents for the medical field.

**NationJob Network-Medical and Health Care Jobs Page**
601 SW 9th St., Stes. H&J
Des Moines, IA 50309 US
Fax: 515-243-5384
Toll Free: 800-292-7731
E-mail Address: *customerservice@nationjob.com*
Web Address: www.nationjob.com/medical
The NationJob Network-Medical and Health Care Jobs Page offers information and listings for health care employment.

**Nurse-Recruiter.com**
36 Washington St., Ste. 170
Wellesley, MA 02481 US
Toll Free: 877-562-7966
E-mail Address: *support@nurserecruiter.com*
Web Address: www.nurse-recruiter.com
Nurse-Recruiter.com is a nurse-owned, web-centric company devoted to bringing health care employers and the nursing community together.

**PracticeLink**
P.O. Box 100
415 2nd Ave.
Hinton, WV 25951 US
Toll Free: 800-776-8383
Web Address: www.practicelink.com
PracticeLink is one of the largest physician employment web sites. It is a free service used by more than 18,000 practice-seeking physicians annually to quickly search and locate potential physician practice opportunities. PracticeLink is financially supported by more than 700 hospitals, medical groups, private practices and health care systems that advertise more than 5,000 opportunities.

## XX. Careers-Job Listings for Seniors

**Dinosaur Exchange**
Dino-X Ltd., P.O. Box 100
Sydney Vane House Admiral Park
St Peter Port, Guernsey GY1 3EL Channel Islands
E-mail Address: *CustomerSupport@dinosaur-exchange.com*
Web Address: www.dinosaur-exchange.com
Dinosaur Exchange, opened in 2003, is a job forum for the elderly, which allows seniors to post resumes and be contacted by employers. Dino-X Ltd. owns and operates the web site.

**Employment Network for Retired Government Experts (ENRGE)**
Zavala, Inc.
P.O. Box 1532
N. Falmouth, MA 02556 US
Phone: 508-564-4140
Web Address: www.enrge.us
The Employment Network for Retired Government Experts (ENRGE) helps government employees to remain active in their professions after retirement. ENERGE is the business name of Zavala, Inc.

**Senior Job Bank**
NHC Group, Inc.
P.O. Box 508
Marlborough, MA 01752 US
Toll Free: 888-501-0804
Web Address: www.seniorjobbank.org
The Senior Job Bank web site offers an easy, effective and free method for senior citizens to find occasional, part-time, flexible, temporary or full-time jobs. The site is owned and managed by NHC Group, Inc.

**Seniors4Hire.org**
The Forward Group, OBO Seniors4Hire.org
7071 Warner Ave. F466
Huntington Beach, CA 92647 US
Phone: 714-848-0996
Fax: 714-848-5445
E-mail Address: *info@seniors4hire.org*
Web Address: www.seniors4hire.org
Seniors4Hire.org is an online career center with job postings, employment resources and information on community service employment programs for older workers, retirees and senior citizens. The site is owned and operated by The Forward Group.

**YourEncore**
20 N. Meridian St., Ste. 800
Indianapolis, IN 46204 US
Phone: 317-226-9301
Fax: 317-226-9312
E-mail Address: *General.Information@yourencore.com*
Web Address: www.yourencore.com
YourEncore is a program that seeks to employ retirees by matching them with member companies. The web site utilizes retirees mainly in the areas of engineering, science and product development.

## XXI. Careers-Job Reference Tools

**CareerXroads (CXR)**
Mark Mehler
P.O. Box 253
Kendall Park, NJ 08824 US
Phone: 732-821-6652
E-mail Address: *mmc@careerxroads.com*
Web Address: www.careerxroads.com
CareerXroads (CXR) publishes an annual guide on job and resume web sites. It was cofounded by Gerry Crispin and Mark Mehler.

**Job-Hunt.org**
NETability, Inc.
186 Main St.
Marlborough, MA 01752 US
Phone: 508-624-6261
E-mail Address: *info@job-hunt.org*
Web Address: www.job-hunt.org
Job-Hunt.org, rather than collecting resumes or posting job vacancies, offers a vast list of job listing web sites and links to helpful job search tools. It is owned by NETability, Inc.

**JobStar**
E-mail Address: *electrajobstar@earthlink.net*
Web Address: www.jobstar.org
JobStar has a salary info link to over 300 different salary information and salary survey sites. It also contains job listings focused on the California market.

**Joyce Lain Kennedy's Careers**
Sun Features Inc.
P.O. Box 368
Cardiff, CA 92007 US
Web Address: www.sunfeatures.com
Provides links to recommended employment sites, as well as links to Joyce Lain Kennedy's books and booklets and her well-respected career tips.

**NewsVoyager**
Newspaper Association of America
4401 Wilson Blvd., Ste. 900
Arlington, VA 22203-1867 US

Phone: 571-366-1000
Fax: 571-366-1195
E-mail Address: *sally.clarke@naa.org*
Web Address: www.newsvoyager.com
NewsVoyager, a service of the Newspaper Association of America (NAA), links individuals to local, national and international newspapers. Job seekers can search through thousands of classified sections.

**Quintessential Careers (QC)**
EmpoweringSties.com
DeLand, Fl 32720 US
Phone: 386-740-8872
Fax: 386-740-9764
E-mail Address: *randall@quintcareers.com*
Web Address: www.quintcareers.com
Quintessential Careers (QC) provides a large collection of data and links for job seekers, including advice, tools and job postings; it also offers a guide to researching companies. QC is a subsidiary of EmpoweringSties.com.

**Vault.com, Inc.**
75 Varick St., 8th Fl.
New York, NY 10013 US
Phone: 212-366-4212
E-mail Address: *feedback@staff.vault.com*
Web Address: www.vault.com
Vault.com, Inc. is a comprehensive career web site for employers and employees, with job postings and valuable information on a wide variety of industries. Vault gears many of its features toward MBAs. The site has been recognized by Forbes and Fortune Magazines.

**Wetfeet.com**
101 Howard St., Ste. 300
San Francisco, CA 94105 US
Phone: 415-284-7900
Fax: 415-284-7910
E-mail Address: *info@wetfeet.com*
Web Address: www.wetfeet.com
Wetfeet.com provides an excellent combination of links and resources for job seekers.

**What Color is Your Parachute?**
E-mail Address: *rnbolles@jobhuntersbible.com*
Web Address: www.jobhuntersbible.com
The What Color is Your Parachute? official web site, JobHuntersBible.com, is based on the "Job-Hunting on the Internet" chapter of Richard (Dick) Bolle's best-selling book. Designed to aid job hunters and career changers who want to use the Internet as part of their job search, the site provides links to job listing, resume, career counseling, contacts and research sites.

## XXII. Careers-Restaurants

**Foodservice.com**
Phone: 678-256-8014
Toll Free: 800-896-4442
E-mail Address: *customercare@Foodservice.com*
Web Address: www.foodservice.com
Foodservice.com, managed and run by Food Service Interactive, LLC, offers web site design and job search services for the food service industry.

**Resources in Food, Inc. (RIF)**
1007 N. Main St.
Columbia, IL 62236 US
Phone: 618-281-3100
Fax: 866-281-7374
Toll Free: 877-743-1100
E-mail Address: *rifchicago@rifood.com*
Web Address: www.rifood.com
Resources in Food (RIF) provides professional management placement for the hospitality industry.

## XXIII. Careers-Telecommunications

**Call Center Careers**
6525 Gunpark Dr., Ste. 570, PMB 127
Boulder, CO 80301 US
Phone: 303-527-1440
Fax: 303-530-0154
Toll Free: 877-562-8588
E-mail Address: *sales@callcentercareers.com*
Web Address: www.callcentercareers.com
Call Center Careers provides recruiting and staffing services to the call center industry.

## XXIV. Communications Professional Associations

**Association for Women In Communications (AWC)**
3337 Duke St.
Alexandria, VA 22314 US
Phone: 703-370-7436
Fax: 703-370-7437
E-mail Address: *info@womcom.org*
Web Address: www.womcom.org
The Association for Women In Communications (AWC) is a professional organization that works for the advancement of women across all communications disciplines by recognizing excellence, promoting leadership and positioning its members at the forefront of the communications industry.

**International Association of Business Communicators (IABC)**
1 Hallidie Plaza, Ste. 600
San Francisco, CA 94102 US
Phone: 415-544-4700
Fax: 415-544-4747
Toll Free: 800-776-4222
E-mail Address: *jugalde@iabc.com*
Web Address: www.iabc.com
The International Association of Business Communicators (IABC) is the leading resource for effective business communication practices.

## XXV. Computer & Electronics Industry Associations

**AeA**
5201 Great America Pkwy., Ste. 400
Santa Clara, CA 95054 US
Phone: 408-987-4200
Fax: 408-987-4298
Toll Free: 800-284-4232
E-mail Address: *csc@aeanet.org*
Web Address: www.aeanet.org
AeA, formerly the American Electronics Association, is a trade association which represents thousands of U.S. electronics firms,

including electronic systems and component manufacturers, suppliers and end users. It also publishes the annual AeA Directory with geographic and product indexes.

**Association of Electronics Industries of Singapore (AEIS)**
1010 Dover Rd. #02-03, SPGG
139658 Singapore
Phone: 65-6776-1880
Fax: 65-6776-0238
E-mail Address: *hamzah@epc.com.sg*
Web Address: www.aeis.org.sg
The Association of Electronics Industries of Singapore (AEIS) is the country's representative of electronics business, covering manufacturers of industrial electronics, electronics components and consumer electronics products as well as industrial electronics companies associated with the electronics industry.

**Association of the Computer and Multimedia Industry of Malaysia (PIKOM)**
1106 & 1107, Block B, Phileo Damansara II
No. 15, Jalan 16/11
Petaling Jaya, Selangor Darul Ehsan 46350 Malaysia
Phone: 603-7955-2922
Fax: 603-7955-2933
E-mail Address: *info@pikom.org.my*
Web Address: www.pikom.org.my
The Association of the Computer and Multimedia Industry of Malaysia, or, in Malay, Persatuan Industri Komputer dan Multimedia Malaysia (PIKOM), is the national association representing the information and communications technology (ICT) industry in Malaysia.

**Communications Industry Association of Japan (CIAJ)**
3rd Fl., JEI Hamamatsucho Bldg.
2-2-12 Hamamatsucho, Minato-ku
Tokyo, 105-0013 Japan
Phone: 81-3-5403-9363
Fax: 81-3-5463-9360
E-mail Address: *webmaster@ciaj.or.jp*
Web Address: www.ciaj.or.jp
The Communications Industry Association of Japan (CIAJ) works to help the development of the communication and information network industry in Japan through the promotion of info-communication technologies.

**Electronic Industries Association of India (ELCINA)**
ELCINA House, 422 Okhla Industrial Estate
New Delhi, 110020 India
Phone: 91-11-2692-4597
Fax: 91-11-2692-3440
E-mail Address: *elcina@vsnl.com*
Web Address: www.elcina.com
The Electronic Industries Association of India (ELCINA) is an organization for the promotion of electronic hardware manufacturing through active representation and advice to the Indian government.

**Electronics and Computer Software Export Promotion Council (ESC)**
3rd Fl., PHD House
Opp. Asiad Village
New Delhi, 110016 India
Phone: 91-11-2696-5103
Fax: 91-11-2685-3412
E-mail Address: *esc@vsnl.net*
Web Address: www.escindia.in
The Electronics and Computer Software Export Promotion Council (ESC) represents the info-communication technology industry through electronics and IT trade facilitation.

**Electronics Technicians Association (ETA)**
5 Depot St.
Greencastle, IN 46135 US
Phone: 765-653-8262
Fax: 765-653-4287
Toll Free: 800-288-3824
E-mail Address: *eta@eta-i.org*
Web Address: www.eta-i.org
The Electronics Technicians Association (ETA) is a nonprofit professional association for electronics technicians. The firm provides recognized professional credentials for electronics technicians.

**Federation of Malaysia Manufacturers (FMM)**
Wisma FMM No. 3, Persiaran Dagang, PJU 9
Bandar Sri Damansara
Kuala Lumpur, 52200 Malaysia
Phone: 603-6276-1211
Fax: 603-6274-1266
E-mail Address: *webmaster@fmm.org.my*
Web Address: www.fmm.org.my
The Federation of Malaysian Manufacturers is an economic organization for the electric and electronic industry in Malaysia.

**Federation of Thai Industries Electrical, Electronics and Allied Industries Club (FTI)**
4th Fl., Zone C Queen Sirikit National Convention Ctr.
60 New Rachadapisek Rd., Klongtoey
Bangkok, 10110 Thailand
Phone: 66-2-345-1000
Fax: 66-2-345-1296-99
E-mail Address: *information@off.fti.or.th*
Web Address: www.fti.or.th/FTI Project/GroupCallEng.aspx
The Federation of Thai Industries Electrical, Electronics and Allied Industries Club (FTI) is the organization for the Electrical, Electronics and Allied Industries in Thailand.

**Indian Electrical & Electronics Manufacturers Association (IEEMA)**
501 Kakad Chambers
132 Dr. Annie Besant Rd., Worli
Mumbai, 400018 India
Phone: 91-22-2493-0532
Fax: 91-22-2493-2705
E-mail Address: *mumbai@ieema.org*
Web Address: www.ieema.org
The Indian Electrical & Electronics Manufacturers Association (IEEMA) represents all sectors of the electrical and allied products businesses of the Indian electrical industry.

**Manufacturers' Association for Information Technology (MAIT)**
4th Fl., PHD House
Opp. Asian Games Village
New Delhi, 110-016 India
Phone: 91-11-2685-5487
Fax: 91-11-2685-1321
E-mail Address: *mait@vsnl.com*
Web Address: www.mait.com

The Manufacturers' Association for Information Technology (MAIT) is an organization that focuses on the promotion of the hardware, training, design/R&D and the associated services sectors of the Indian IT industry.

**National Electrical Manufacturers Association (NEMA)**
1300 N. 17th St., Ste. 1752
Rosslyn, VA 22209 US
Phone: 703-841-3200
Fax: 703-841-5900
E-mail Address: *communications@nema.org*
Web Address: www.nema.org
The National Electrical Manufacturers Association (NEMA) develops standards for the electrical manufacturing industry and promotes safety in the manufacture and use of electrical products.

**Semiconductor & Electronics Industries in the Philippines, Inc. (SEIPI)**
Unit 902, Tower 2, RCBC Plz., Ayala Ave.
Makati City, 1200 Philippines
Phone: 632-844-9028
Fax: 632-844-9037
E-mail Address: *philippine.electronics@seipi.org.ph*
Web Address: www.seipi.org.ph
The SEIPI Foundation is an organization of foreign and local semiconductor and electronics companies in the Philippines.

**Semiconductor Industry Association (SIA)**
181 Metro Dr., Ste. 450
San Jose, CA 95110 US
Phone: 408-436-6600
Fax: 408-436-6646
E-mail Address: *mailbox@sia-online.org*
Web Address: www.sia-online.org
The Semiconductor Industry Association (SIA) is a trade association representing the semiconductor industry in the U.S. Through its coalition of 95 companies, SIA represents more than 85% of semiconductor production in the U.S. The coalition aims to advance the competitiveness of the chip industry and shape public policy on issues particular to the industry.

**Singapore Manufacturers Association (SCa)**
2 Bukit Merah Central (#03-00)
SPRING Singapore Bldg.
159835 Singapore
Phone: 65-6826-3000
Fax: 65-6826-3008
E-mail Address: *hq@smafederation.org.sg*
Web Address: www.smafederation.org.sg
The Singapore Manufacturers Association (SCa) represents the manufacturing industry in Singapore, and helps its members deal issues such as productivity enhancement, research and development, technological upgrading and innovation and worker training.

**Taiwan Electrical and Electronic Manufacturers' Association (TEEMA)**
Prince Financial Ctr., 6F, No. 109, Sec. 6
Min Chuan E. Rd.
Taipei, 114 Taiwan
Phone: 886-2-8792-6666
Fax: 886-2-8792-6088
Web Address: www.teema.org.tw
The Taiwan Electrical and Electronic Manufacturers' Association (TEEMA) works as an intermediary between its members and the government to help the industry to succeed.

**Telecom Equipment Manufacturers Association of India (TEMA)**
PHD House, 4th Fl., Ramakrishna Dalmia Wing
Opp. Asian Games Village
New Delhi, 110 0016 India
Phone: 91-11-685-9621
Fax: 91-11-685-9620
Web Address: www.tfci.com/cni/tema.htm
The Telecom Equipment Manufacturers Association of India (TEMA) is national organization for companies in the telecommunications industry. The group disseminates and exchanges information with the Indian government, foreign agencies, embassies, trade missions, Indian missions abroad and leading international trade associations.

**Vietnam Electronic Industries Association (VEIA)**
11B Phan Huy Chu, Hoan Kiem
Ha Noi, Vietnam
Phone: 84-4-933-2845
Fax: 84-4-933-2846
E-mail Address: *veia-vn@hn.vnn.vn*
Web Address: www.VEIA.org.vn
Vietnam Electronic Industries Association (VEIA) is the representative body for the electronic businesses in Vietnam.

## XXVI. Consulting Industry Associations

**American Association of Healthcare Consultants (AAHC)**
5938 N. Drake Ave.
Chicago, IL 60659 US
Fax: 773-463-3552
Toll Free: 888-350-2242
E-mail Address: *info@aahcmail.org*
Web Address: www.aahc.net
The American Association of Healthcare Consultants (AAHC) is a professional society for credentialed consultants practicing in health care organization and delivery.

## XXVII. Corporate Information Resources

**bizjournals.com**
120 W. Morehead St., Ste. 400
Charlotte, NC 28202 US
Web Address: www.bizjournals.com
Bizjournals.com is the online media division of American City Business Journals, the publisher of dozens of leading city business journals nationwide. It provides access to research into the latest news regarding companies small and large.

**Business Wire**
44 Montgomery St., 39th Fl.
San Francisco, CA 94104 US
Phone: 415-986-4422
Fax: 415-788-5335
Toll Free: 800-227-0845
Web Address: www.businesswire.com
Business Wire offers news releases, industry- and company-specific news, top headlines, conference calls, IPOs on the Internet, media services and access to tradeshownews.com and

BW Connect On-line through its informative and continuously updated web site.

**Edgar Online, Inc.**
50 Washington St., 11th Fl.
Norwalk, CT 06854 US
Phone: 203-852-5666
Fax: 203-852-5667
Toll Free: 800-416-6651
Web Address: www.edgar-online.com
Edgar Online, Inc. is a gateway and search tool for viewing corporate documents, such as annual reports on Form 10-K, filed with the U.S. Securities and Exchange Commission.

**PR Newswire Association LLC**
810 7th Ave., 32nd Fl.
New York, NY 10019 US
Phone: 201-360-6700
Toll Free: 800-832-5522
E-mail Address: *information@prnewswire.com*
Web Address: www.prnewswire.com
PR Newswire Association LLC provides comprehensive communications services for public relations and investor relations professionals ranging from information distribution and market intelligence to the creation of online multimedia content and investor relations web sites. Users can also view recent corporate press releases. The Association is owned by United Business Media plc.

**Silicon Investor**
100 W. Main
P.O. Box 29
Freeman, MO 64746 US
E-mail Address: *admin_dave@techstocks.com*
Web Address: siliconinvestor.advfn.com
Silicon Investor is focused on providing information about technology companies. The company's web site serves as a financial discussion forum and offers quotes, profiles and charts.

## XXVIII. Disabling Conditions

**Job Accommodation Network (JAN)**
P.O. Box 6080
Morgantown, WV 26506-6080 US
Phone: 304-293-7186
Fax: 304-293-5407
Toll Free: 800-526-7234
E-mail Address: *jan@jan.wvu.edu*
Web Address: janweb.icdi.wvu.edu
The Job Accommodation Network (JAN) is a free consulting service that provides information about job accommodations, the Americans with Disabilities Act and the employability of people with disabilities.

## XXIX. Economic Data & Research

**STAT-USA/Internet**
STAT-USA, HCHB, Rm. 4885
U.S. Department of Commerce
Washington, DC 20230 US
Phone: 202-482-1986
Fax: 202-482-2164
Toll Free: 800-782-8872
E-mail Address: *statmail@esa.doc.gov*
Web Address: www.stat-usa.gov
STAT-USA/Internet offers daily economic news, statistical releases and databases relating to export and trade, as well as the domestic economy. It is provided by STAT-USA, which is an agency in the Economics & Statistics Administration of the U.S. Department of Commerce. The site mainly consists of two main databases, the State of the Nation (SOTN), which focuses on the current state of the U.S. economy; and the Global Business Opportunities (GLOBUS) & the National Trade Data Bank (NTDB), which deals with U.S. export opportunities, global political/socio-economic conditions and other world economic issues.

## XXX. Electrical Engineering Industry Associations

**International Society for Optical Engineering (SPIE)**
1000 20th St.
Bellingham, WA 98225-6705 US
Phone: 360-676-3290
Fax: 360-647-1445
Toll Free: 888-504-8171
E-mail Address: *CustomerService@SPIE.org*
Web Address: www.spie.org
The International Society for Optical Engineering (SPIE) is a nonprofit technical society aimed at the advancement and dissemination of knowledge in optics, photonics and imaging.

## XXXI. Energy Associations-Electric Power

**American Public Power Association (APPA)**
1875 Connecticut Ave. NW, Ste. 1200
Washington, DC 20009-5715 US
Phone: 202-467-2900
Fax: 202-467-2910
E-mail Address: *mrufe@appanet.org*
Web Address: www.appanet.org
The American Public Power Association (APPA) is a nonprofit service organization for the country's community-owned electric utilities, dedicated to advancing the public policy interests of its members and their consumers.

**Edison Electric Institute (EEI)**
701 Pennsylvania Ave. NW
Washington, DC 20004-2696 US
Phone: 202-508-5000
E-mail Address: *feedback@eei.org*
Web Address: www.eei.org
The Edison Electric Institute (EEI) is an association of U.S. shareholder-owned electric companies as well as worldwide affiliates and industry associates. Its web site provides energy news and a link to Electric Perspectives magazine.

**Women's International Network of Utility Professionals (WINUP)**
P.O. Box 817
Fergus Falls, MN 56538-0817 US
Phone: 218-731-1659
E-mail Address: *tdrexler@otpco.com*
Web Address: www.winup.org
The Women's International Network of Utility Professionals (WINUP) provides networking and support for women in the utility industry.

## XXXII. Energy Associations-Natural Gas

**American Gas Association (AGA)**
400 N. Capitol St. NW, Ste. 450
Washington, DC 20001 US
Phone: 202-824-7000
E-mail Address: *rshelby@aga.org*
Web Address: www.aga.org
The American Gas Association (AGA) represents a large number of natural gas providers, advocating for these companies and providing a broad range of programs and services for members.

## XXXIII. Energy Associations-Other

**American Association of Blacks in Energy**
1625 K St. NW, Ste. 450
Washington, DC 20006 US
Phone: 202-371-9530
Fax: 202-371-9218
E-mail Address: *info@aabe.org*
Web Address: www.aabe.org
The American Association of Blacks in Energy is dedicated to ensuring the input of African Americans and other minorities in discussions and developments of energy policies, regulations, research and development technologies and environmental issues.

**Council of Petroleum Accountants Societies, Inc. (COPAS)**
3900 E. Mexico Ave., Ste. 602
Denver, CO 80210 US
Phone: 303-300-1131
Fax: 303-300-3733
Toll Free: 877-992-6727
E-mail Address: *Execdir@copas.org*
Web Address: www.copas.org
The Council of Petroleum Accountants Societies, Inc. (COPAS) provides a forum for discussing and solving the variety of problems related to accounting for oil and gas. COPAS also provides valuable educational materials related to oil and gas accounting.

**Society of Energy Professionals International**
300-425 Bloor St. E
Toronto, ON M4W 3R4 Canada
Phone: 416-979-2709
Fax: 416-979-5794
E-mail Address: *society@society.on.ca*
Web Address: www.thesociety.ca
The Society of Energy Professionals International is an independent trade union representing professionals in the energy industry within Ontario, Canada.

## XXXIV. Energy Associations-Petroleum, Exploration, Production, etc.

**American Association of Professional Landmen (AAPL)**
4100 Fossil Creek Blvd.
Fort Worth, TX 76137 US
Phone: 817-847-7700
Fax: 817-847-7704
E-mail Address: *aapl@landman.org*
Web Address: www.landman.org
The American Association of Professional Landmen (AAPL) promotes the highest standards of performance for all land professionals and seeks to advance their stature and to encourage sound stewardship of energy and mineral resources.

**American Petroleum Institute (API)**
1220 L St. NW
Washington, DC 20005-4070 US
Phone: 202-682-8000
Web Address: www.api.org
American Petroleum Institute (API) represents U.S. oil and gas industries and its web site includes in-depth sections for energy consumers and energy professionals.

**Independent Petroleum Association of America (IPAA)**
1201 15th St. NW, Ste. 300
Washington, DC 20005 US
Phone: 202-857-4722
Fax: 202-857-4799
E-mail Address: *rcarter@ipaa.org*
Web Address: www.ipaa.org
The Independent Petroleum Association of America (IPAA) provides a forum for the exploration and production segment of the independent oil and natural gas business. It also provides information on the domestic exploration and production industry.

**International Association of Drilling Contractors (IADC)**
10370 Richmond Ave., Ste. 760
Houston, TX 77042 US
Phone: 713-292-1945
Fax: 713-292-1946
E-mail Address: *info@iadc.org*
Web Address: www.iadc.org
The International Association of Drilling Contractors (IADC) represents the worldwide oil and gas drilling industry and promotes commitment to safety, preservation of the environment and advances in drilling technology.

## XXXV. Engineering, Research & Scientific Associations

**American Association of Petroleum Geologists (AAPG)**
1444 S. Boulder Ave.
Tulsa, OK 74119 US
Phone: 918-584-2555
Fax: 918-560-2665
Toll Free: 800-364-2274
E-mail Address: *lnation@aapg.org*
Web Address: www.aapg.org
The American Association of Petroleum Geologists (AAPG) is an international geological organization that supports educational and scientific programs and projects related to geosciences.

**American Chemical Society (ACS)**
1155 16th St. NW
Washington, DC 20036 US
Phone: 202-872-4600
Fax: 202-776-8258
Toll Free: 800-227-5558
E-mail Address: *help@acs.org*
Web Address: portal.acs.org/portal/acs/corg/content
The American Chemical Society (ACS) is a nonprofit organization aimed at promoting the understanding of chemistry and chemical sciences. It represents a wide range of disciplines including chemistry, chemical engineering and other technical fields.

**American Institute of Aeronautics and Astronautics (AIAA)**
1801 Alexander Bell Dr., Ste. 500
Reston, VA 20191-4344 US
Phone: 703-264-7500
Fax: 703-264-7551
Toll Free: 800-639-2422
E-mail Address: *klausd@aiaa.org*
Web Address: www.aiaa.org
The American Institute of Aeronautics and Astronautics (AIAA) is a nonprofit society aimed at advancing the arts, sciences and technology of aeronautics and astronautics. The institute represents the U.S. in the International Astronautical Federation and the International Council on the Aeronautical Sciences.

**American Institute of Chemical Engineers (AIChE)**
3 Park Ave.
New York, NY 10016-5991 US
Phone: 203-702-7660
Fax: 203-775-5177
Toll Free: 800-242-4363
E-mail Address: *xpress@aiche.org*
Web Address: www.aiche.org
The American Institute of Chemical Engineers (AIChE) provides leadership in advancing the chemical engineering profession. The organization, which is comprised of 40,000 members from 93 countries, provides informational resources to chemical engineers.

**American Society for Healthcare Engineering (ASHE)**
1 N. Franklin, 28th Fl.
Chicago, IL 60606 US
Phone: 312-422-3800
Fax: 312-422-4571
E-mail Address: *ashe@aha.org*
Web Address: www.ashe.org
The American Society for Healthcare Engineering (ASHE) is the advocate and resource for continuous improvement in the health care engineering and facilities management professions.

**American Society of Agricultural and Biological Engineers (ASABE)**
2950 Niles Rd.
St. Joseph, MI 49085 US
Phone: 269-429-0300
Fax: 269-429-3852
E-mail Address: *hq@asabe.org*
Web Address: www.asabe.org
The American Society of Agricultural and Biological Engineers (ASABE) is a nonprofit professional and technical organization interested in engineering knowledge and technology for food and agriculture and associated industries.

**American Society of Civil Engineers (ASCE)**
1801 Alexander Bell Dr.
Reston, VA 20191-4400 US
Phone: 703-295-6300
Fax: 703-295-6222
Toll Free: 800-548-2723
Web Address: www.asce.org
The American Society of Civil Engineers (ASCE) is a leading professional organization serving civil engineers. It ensures safer buildings, water systems and other civil engineering works by developing technical codes and standards.

**American Society of Mechanical Engineers (ASME)**
3 Park Ave.
New York, NY 10016-5990 US
Phone: 973-882-1170
Fax: 973-882-1717
Toll Free: 800-843-2763
E-mail Address: *infocentral@asme.org*
Web Address: www.asme.org
The American Society of Mechanical Engineers (ASME) offers quality programs and activities in mechanical engineering. It also facilitates the development and application of technology in areas of interest to the mechanical engineering profession.

**American Society of Safety Engineers (ASSE)**
Customer Service
1800 E. Oakton St.
Des Plaines, IL 60018 US
Phone: 847-699-2929
Fax: 847-768-3434
E-mail Address: *customerservice@asse.org*
Web Address: www.asse.org
The American Society of Safety Engineers (ASSE) is the world's oldest and largest professional safety organization. It manages, supervises and consults on safety, health and environmental issues in industry, insurance, government and education.

**Association of Federal Communications Consulting Engineers (AFCCE)**
P.O. Box 19333
Washington, DC 20036 US
Web Address: www.afcce.org
The Association of Federal Communications Consulting Engineers (AFCCE) is a professional organization of individuals who regularly assist clients on technical issues before the Federal Communications Commission (FCC).

**Institute of Industrial Engineers (IIE)**
3577 Parkway Ln., Ste. 200
Norcross, GA 30092 US
Phone: 770-449-0460
Fax: 770-441-3295
Toll Free: 800-494-0460
E-mail Address: *execoffice@iienet.org*
Web Address: www.iienet.org
The Institute of Industrial Engineers (IIE) is dedicated to the professional needs of industrial engineers.

**Institute of Structural Engineers (IStructE)**
11 Upper Belgrave St.
London, SW1X 8BH UK
Phone: 44-(0)20-7235-4535
Fax: 44-(0)20-7235-4294
Web Address: www.istructe.org.uk
The Institute of Structural Engineers (IStructE) is a professional organization, headquartered in the U.K., that sets and maintains standards for professional structural engineers.

**National Society of Professional Engineers (NSPE)**
1420 King St.
Alexandria, VA 22314-2794 US
Phone: 703-684-2800
Fax: 703-836-4875
Toll Free: 888-285-6773
E-mail Address: *memserv@nspe.org*
Web Address: www.nspe.org

The National Society of Professional Engineers (NSPE) represents individual engineering professionals and licensed engineers across all disciplines. NSPE serves approximately 45,000 members and has more than 500 chapters.

**Society of Automotive Engineers (SAE)**
755 W. Big Beaver, Ste. 1600
Troy, MA 48084 US
Phone: 248-273-2455
Fax: 248-273-2494
Toll Free: 877-606-7323
E-mail Address: *automotive_hq@sae.org*
Web Address: www.sae.org
The Society of Automotive Engineers (SAE) is a resource for technical information and expertise used in designing, building, maintaining and operating self-propelled vehicles for use on land, sea, air or space.

**Society of Broadcast Engineers, Inc. (SBE)**
9102 N. Meridian St., Ste. 150
Indianapolis, IN 46260 US
Phone: 317-846-9000
Fax: 317-846-9120
E-mail Address: *mclappe@sbe.org*
Web Address: www.sbe.org
The Society of Broadcast Engineers (SBE) exists to increase knowledge of broadcast engineering and promote its interests, as well as to continue the education of professionals in the industry.

**Society of Cable Telecommunications Engineers (SCTE)**
140 Philips Rd.
Exton, PA 19341-1318 US
Phone: 610-363-6888
Fax: 610-363-5898
Toll Free: 800-542-5040
E-mail Address: *scte@scte.org*
Web Address: www.scte.org
The Society of Cable Telecommunications Engineers (SCTE) is a nonprofit professional association dedicated to advancing the careers and serving the industry of telecommunications professionals by providing technical training, certification and standards.

**Society of Hispanic Professional Engineers (SHPE)**
5400 E. Olympic Blvd., Ste. 210
Los Angeles, CA 90022 US
Phone: 323-725-3970
Fax: 323-725-0316
E-mail Address: *shpenational@shpe.org*
Web Address: oneshpe.shpe.org
The Society of Hispanic Professional Engineers (SHPE) is a national nonprofit organization that promotes Hispanics in science, engineering and math.

**Society of Manufacturing Engineers (SME)**
1 SME Dr.
Dearborn, MI 48121 US
Phone: 313-425-3000
Fax: 313-425-3412
Toll Free: 800-733-4763
E-mail Address: *communications@sme.org*
Web Address: www.sme.org
The Society of Manufacturing Engineers (SME) a leading professional organization serving engineers in the manufacturing industries.

**Society of Motion Picture and Television Engineers (SMPTE)**
3 Barker Ave., 5th Fl.
White Plains, NY 10601 US
Phone: 914-761-1100
Fax: 914-761-3115
Web Address: www.smpte.org
The Society of Motion Picture and Television Engineers (SMPTE) is the leading technical society for the motion imaging industry. The firm publishes recommended practice and engineering guidelines, as well the SMPTE Journal.

**Society of Petroleum Engineers (SPE)**
222 Palisades Creek Dr.
Richardson, TX 75080-2040 US
Phone: 972-952-9393
Fax: 972-952-9435
Toll Free: 800-456-6863
E-mail Address: *service@spe.org*
Web Address: www.spe.org
The Society of Petroleum Engineers (SPE) helps connect engineers in the oil and gas industry with ideas, answers, resources and technological information.

**Society of Women Engineers (SWE)**
230 E. Ohio St., Ste. 400
Chicago, IL 60611 US
Phone: 312-596-5223
Toll Free: 877-793-4636
E-mail Address: *hq@swe.org*
Web Address: www.swe.org
The Society of Women Engineers (SWE) is a nonprofit educational and service organization of female engineers.

## XXXVI. Entertainment & Amusement Associations

**International Association of Amusement Parks and Attractions (IAAPA)**
1448 Duke St.
Alexandria, VA 22314 US
Phone: 703-836-4800
Fax: 703-836-6742
E-mail Address: *dmandt@iaapa.org*
Web Address: www.iaapa.org
The International Association of Amusement Parks and Attractions (IAAPA) is dedicated to the preservation and prosperity of the amusement industry.

**International Special Events Society (ISES)**
401 N. Michigan Ave.
Chicago, IL 60611-4267 US
Phone: 312-321-6853
Fax: 312-673-6953
Toll Free: 800-688-4737
E-mail Address: *info@ises.com*
Web Address: www.ises.com
The International Special Events Society (ISES) is a society of special events professionals representing the industry's diverse disciplines.

## XXXVII. Film & Television Resources

**SCREENSite**
P.O. Box 870152
Tuscaloosa, AL 35487 US

Phone: 205-348-6350
E-mail Address: *jbutler@ua.edu*
Web Address: www.screensite.org
SCREENSite is a resource center for film and TV scholarship with an archive of course syllabi, e-mail listings of media scholars, conference information, school listings and job list.

## XXXVIII. Film & Theater Associations

**Academy of Motion Picture Arts and Sciences (AMPAS)**
8949 Wilshire Blvd.
Beverly Hills, CA 90211-1972 US
Phone: 310-247-3000
Fax: 310-859-9619
Web Address: www.oscars.org
The Academy of Motion Picture Arts and Sciences (AMPAS) is a professional honorary organization, founded to advance the arts and sciences of motion pictures. Besides hosting the Academy Awards and selecting the winners of the Oscars, AMPAS organizes smaller events highlighting the art of filmmaking, including lectures and seminars, and is currently building the Academy Museum of Motion Pictures.

**Alliance of Motion Picture and Television Producers (AMPTP)**
15301 Ventura Blvd.
Encino, CA 91403 US
Toll Free: 818-995-3600
Web Address: www.amptp.org
The Alliance of Motion Picture and Television Producers (AMPTP) is the primary trade association with respect to labor issues in the motion picture and television industry.

**American Cinema Editors, Inc. (ACE)**
100 Universal City Plz.
Verna Fields Bldg. 2282, Rm. 190
Universal City, CA 91608 US
Phone: 818-777-2900
Fax: 818-733-5023
E-mail Address: *amercinema@earthlink.net*
Web Address: www.ace-filmeditors.org
American Cinema Editors (ACE) is an honorary society of motion picture editors that seeks to advance the art and science of the editing profession.

**American Society of Cinematographers (ASC)**
1782 N. Orange Dr.
Hollywood, CA 90028 US
Phone: 323-969-4333
Fax: 323-882-6391
Toll Free: 800-448-0145
E-mail Address: *office@theasc.com*
Web Address: www.theasc.com
The American Society of Cinematographers (ASC) is a trade association for cinematographers in the motion picture industry.

**Art Directors Guild (ADG)**
11969 Ventura Blvd., 2nd Fl.
Studio City, CA 91604 US
Phone: 818-762-9995
Fax: 818-762-9997
E-mail Address: *nick@artdirectors.org*
Web Address: www.artdirectors.org
The Art Directors Guild (ADG) represents the creative talents that conceive and manage the background and settings for most films and television projects.

**Association of Cinema and Video Laboratories (ACVL)**
Chip Wilkinson, Pres., ACVL
630 9th Ave.
New York, NY 10036 US
Phone: 212-586-4822
Fax: 212-582-3744
E-mail Address: *cfw2447@rcn.com*
Web Address: www.acvl.org
The Association of Cinema and Video Laboratories (ACVL) is an international organization whose members are pledged to the highest possible standards of service to the film and video industries.

**Independent Film & Television Alliance (IFTA)**
10850 Wilshire Blvd., 9th Fl.
Los Angeles, CA 90024-4321 US
Phone: 310-446-1000
Fax: 310-446-1600
E-mail Address: *info@ifta-online.org*
Web Address: www.ifta-online.org
The Independent Film & Television Alliance (IFTA), formerly the American Film Marketing Association (AFMA), is a trade association whose mission is to provide the independent film and television industry with high-quality, market-oriented services and worldwide representation.

**International Alliance of Theatrical Stage Employees (IATSE)**
1430 Broadway, 20th Fl.
New York, NY 10018 US
Phone: 212-730-1770
Fax: 212-921-7699
E-mail Address: *webmaster@iatse-intl.org*
Web Address: www.iatse-intl.org
The International Alliance of Theatrical Stage Employees (IATSE) is the labor union representing technicians, artisans and crafts workers in the entertainment industry, including live theater, film and television production and trade shows.

**International Animated Film Society (ASIFA-Hollywood)**
2114 W. Burbank Blvd.
Burbank, CA 91506 US
Phone: 818-842-4691
E-mail Address: *info@asifa-hollywood.org*
Web Address: www.asifa-hollywood.org
International Animated Film Society (ASIFA-Hollywood) is a nonprofit organization dedicated to the advancement of the art of animation.

**International Documentary Association (IDA)**
1201 W. 5th St., Ste. M270
Los Angeles, CA 90017 US
Phone: 213-534-3600
Fax: 213-534-3610
E-mail Address: *amina@documentary.org*
Web Address: www.documentary.org
The International Documentary Association (IDA) is a nonprofit member service organization, providing publications, benefits and a public forum to its members for issues regarding nonfiction film, video and multimedia.

**Motion Picture Association of America (MPAA)**
15301 Ventura Blvd., Bldg. E
Sherman Oaks, CA 91403 US
Phone: 818-995-6600
Fax: 818-285-4403
Web Address: www.mpaa.org
The Motion Picture Association of America (MPAA) serves as the voice and advocate of the U.S. motion picture, home video and television industries.

**Motion Picture Editors Guild (MPEG)**
7715 Sunset Blvd., Ste. 200
Hollywood, CA 90046 US
Fax: 323-876-0861
Toll Free: 800-705-8700
E-mail Address: *mail@editorsguild.com*
Web Address: www.editorsguild.com
The Motion Picture Editors Guild's (MPEG) web site provides an online directory of editors, a discussion forum and links to related magazines and other organizations that serve the motion picture industry.

**Producers Guild of America, Inc. (PGA)**
8530 Wilshire Blvd., Ste. 450
Beverly Hills, CA 90211 US
Phone: 310-358-9020
Fax: 310-358-9520
E-mail Address: *info@producersguild.org*
Web Address: www.producersguild.org
The Producers Guild of America, Inc. (PGA) is a nonprofit organization for career professionals who initiate, create, coordinate, supervise and control all aspects of the motion picture and television production processes.

**Screen Actors Guild (SAG)**
5757 Wilshire Blvd., 7th Fl.
Los Angeles, CA 90036-3600 US
Phone: 323-954-1600
Fax: 323-549-6603
Toll Free: 800-724-0767
E-mail Address: *saginfo@sag.org*
Web Address: www.sag.org
The Screen Actors Guild (SAG) represents its members through negotiation and enforcement of collective bargaining agreements that establish equitable levels of compensation, benefits and working conditions for performers. Established in 1933, the guild has 20 branches that represent 120,000 actors nationwide.

**Women In Film (WIF)**
8857 W. Olympic Blvd., Ste. 201
Beverly Hills, CA 90211-3605 US
Phone: 310-657-5144
Fax: 310-657-5154
E-mail Address: *info@wif.org*
Web Address: www.wif.org
Women In Film (WIF) strives to empower, promote and mentor women in the entertainment, communication and media industries through a network of contacts, educational programs and events.

## XXXIX. Fitness

**American Fitness Professionals and Associates (AFPA)**
P.O. Box 214
Ship Bottom, NJ 08008 US
Phone: 609-978-7583
Fax: 609-978-7582
E-mail Address: *afpa@afpafitness.com*
Web Address: www.afpafitness.com
American Fitness Professionals and Associates (AFPA) offers health and fitness professionals certification programs, continuing education courses, home correspondence courses and regional conventions.

## XL. Food Industry Associations, General

**Institute of Food Technologies (IFT)**
525 W. Van Buren, Ste. 1000
Chicago, IL 60607 US
Phone: 312-782-8424
Fax: 312-782-8348
Toll Free: 800-438-3663
E-mail Address: *info@ift.org*
Web Address: www.ift.org
The Institute of Food Technologies (IFT) is devoted to the advancement of the science and technology of food through the exchange of knowledge. The site provides information and resources for job seekers in the food industry. Members work in food science, food technology and related professions in industry, academia and government.

**United Food and Commercial Workers International Union (UFCW)**
1775 K St. NW
Washington, DC 20006 US
Phone: 202-223-3111
Web Address: www.ufcw.org
The United Food and Commercial Workers International Union (UFCW) is a union for members who are employed in many different industries but are concentrated in retail food, meatpacking, poultry and other food processing industries.

## XLI. Food Processor Industry Associations

**Grocery Manufacturers Association (GMA)**
1350 I St. NW, Ste. 300
Washington, DC 20005 US
Phone: 202-639-5900
Fax: 202-639-5932
E-mail Address: *info@gmaonline.org*
Web Address: www.gmaonline.org
The Grocery Manufacturers Association (GMA), formerly the National Food Products Association (NFPA), is the voice of the food, beverage and consumer products industry on scientific and public policy issues involving food safety, food security, nutrition, technical and regulatory matters and consumer affairs.

## XLII. Grocery Industry Associations

**Food Marketing Institute (FMI)**
2345 Crystal Dr., Ste. 800
Arlington, VA 22202 US
Phone: 202-452-8444
Fax: 202-429-4519
E-mail Address: *fmi@fmi.org*
Web Address: www.fmi.org

The Food Marketing Institute (FMI) is a nonprofit association conducting programs in research, education, industry relations and public affairs on behalf of its 1,500 members.

## XLIII. Health Care Business & Professional Associations

**Advanced Medical Technology Association (AdvaMed)**
701 Pennsylvania Ave. NW, Ste. 800
Washington, DC 20004-2654 US
Phone: 202-783-8700
Fax: 202-783-8750
E-mail Address: *info@advamed.org*
Web Address: www.advamed.org
The Advanced Medical Technology Association (AdvaMed) strives to be the advocate for a legal, regulatory and economic climate that advances global health care by assuring worldwide access to the benefits of medical technology.

**American Academy of Medical Administrators (AAMA)**
701 Lee St., Ste. 600
Des Plaines, IL 60016-4516 US
Phone: 847-759-8601
Fax: 847-759-8602
E-mail Address: *info@aameda.org*
Web Address: www.aameda.org
The American Academy of Medical Administrators (AAMA) is an association for health care leaders to enhance their profession and community health.

**American Academy of Nursing (AAN)**
888 17th St. NW, Ste. 800
Washington, DC 20006 US
Phone: 202-777-1170
Fax: 202-777-0107
E-mail Address: *info@aannet.org*
Web Address: www.aannet.org
The American Academy of Nursing (AAN) works to help nursing leaders transform the health care system in order to optimize public well-being.

**American Association of Medical Assistants (AAMA)**
20 N. Wacker Dr., Ste. 1575
Chicago, IL 60606 US
Phone: 312-899-1500
Fax: 312-899-1259
Web Address: www.aama-ntl.org
The American Association of Medical Assistants (AAMA) seeks to promote the professional identity and stature of its members and the medical assisting profession through education and credentialing.

**American College of Health Care Administrators (ACHCA)**
12100 Sunset Hills Rd., Ste. 130
Reston, VA 20190 US
Phone: 703-739-7900
Fax: 866-874-1585
E-mail Address: *kbgallagher@achca.org*
Web Address: www.achca.org
The American College of Health Care Administrators (ACHCA) offers educational programming and career development for health care administrators.

**American College of Healthcare Executives (ACHE)**
1 N. Franklin, Ste. 1700
Chicago, IL 60606-3529 US
Phone: 312-424-2800
Fax: 312-424-0023
E-mail Address: *geninfo@ache.org*
Web Address: www.ache.org
The American College of Healthcare Executives (ACHE) is an international professional society of health care executives that offers certification and educational programs.

**American Dental Association (ADA)**
211 E. Chicago Ave.
Chicago, IL 60611-2678 US
Phone: 312-440-2500
E-mail Address: *online@ada.org*
Web Address: www.ada.org
The American Dental Association (ADA) is a professional association of dentists committed to the public's oral health, ethics, science and professional advancement.

**American Dietetic Association (ADA)**
120 S. Riverside Plz., Ste. 2000
Chicago, IL 60606-6995 US
Fax: 312-899-4899
Toll Free: 800-877-1600
E-mail Address: *foundation@eatright.org*
Web Address: www.eatright.org
The American Dietetic Association (ADA) is the world's largest organization of food and nutrition professionals, with nearly 65,000 members. In addition to services for its professional members, this organization's web site offers consumers a Nutrition Knowledge Center and a Healthy Lifestyle Center.

**American Health Information Management Association (AHIMA)**
233 N. Michigan Ave., 21st Fl.
Chicago, IL 60601-5800 US
Phone: 312-233-1100
Fax: 312-233-1090
E-mail Address: *info@ahima.org*
Web Address: www.ahima.org
The American Health Information Management Association (AHIMA) is a professional association that consists of specially educated health information management professionals who work throughout the health care industry.

**American Medical Informatics Association (AMIA)**
4915 St. Elmo Ave., Ste. 401
Bethesda, MD 20814 US
Phone: 301-657-1291
Fax: 301-657-1296
E-mail Address: *mail@amia.org*
Web Address: www.amia.org
The American Medical Informatics Association (AMIA) is a membership organization of individuals, institutions and corporations dedicated to developing and using information technologies to improve health care.

**American Medical Technologists (AMT)**
10700 W. Higgins Rd., Ste. 150
Rosemont, IL 60018 US
Phone: 847-823-5169
Fax: 847-823-0458
Toll Free: 800-275-1268

E-mail Address: *membership@amt1.com*
Web Address: www.amt1.com
American Medical Technologists (AMT) is a nonprofit certification agency and professional membership association representing individuals in health care.

**American Medical Women's Association (AMWA)**
100 N. 200th St., 4th Fl.
Philadelphia, PA 19103 US
Phone: 215-320-3716
Fax: 215-564-2175
Toll Free: 866-564-2483
E-mail Address: *info@amwa-doc.org*
Web Address: www.amwa-doc.org
The American Medical Women's Association (AMWA) is an organization of women physicians and medical students dedicated to serving as the unique voice for women's health and the advancement of women in medicine.

**American Occupational Therapy Association, Inc. (AOTA)**
4720 Montgomery Ln.
P.O. Box 31220
Bethesda, MD 20824-1220 US
Phone: 301-652-2682
Fax: 301-652-7711
Web Address: www.aota.org
The American Occupational Therapy Association, Inc. (AOTA) advances the quality, availability, use and support of occupational therapy through standard-setting, advocacy, education and research on behalf of its members and the public.

**American Organization of Nurse Executives (AONE)**
Liberty Place, 325 7th St. NW
Washington, DC 20004 US
Phone: 202-626-2240
Fax: 202-638-5499
E-mail Address: *aone@aha.org*
Web Address: www.aone.org
The American Organization of Nurse Executives (AONE) is a national organization of nurses who design, facilitate and manage health care.

**American Public Health Association (APHA)**
800 I St. NW
Washington, DC 20001-3710 US
Phone: 202-777-2742
Fax: 202-777-2534
E-mail Address: *comments@apha.org*
Web Address: www.apha.org
The American Public Health Association (APHA) is an association of individuals and organizations working to improve the public's health and to achieve equity in health status for all.

**American School Health Association (ASHA)**
7263 State Rte. 43
P.O. Box 708
Kent, OH 44240 US
Phone: 330-678-1601
Fax: 330-678-4526
E-mail Address: *asha@ashaweb.org*
Web Address: www.ashaweb.org
The American School Health Association (ASHA) advocates high-quality school health instruction, health services and a healthy school environment.

**College of Healthcare Information Management Executives (CHIME)**
3300 Washtenaw Ave., Ste. 225
Ann Arbor, MI 48104 US
Phone: 734-665-0000
Fax: 734-665-4922
E-mail Address: *staff@cio-chime.org*
Web Address: www.cio-chime.org
College of Healthcare Information Management Executives (CHIME) was formed with the dual objective of serving the professional development needs of health care CIOs and advocating the more effective use of information management within health care.

**Dental Trade Alliance (DTA)**
2300 Clarendon Blvd., Ste. 1003
Arlington, VA 22201 US
Phone: 703-379-7755
Fax: 703-931-9429
E-mail Address: *info@dentaltradealliance.org*
Web Address: www.dentaltradealliance.org
The Dental Trade Alliance (DTA) represents dental manufacturers, dental dealers and dental laboratories.

**Health and Science Communications Association (HeSCA)**
39 Wedgewood Dr., Ste. A
Jewett City, CT 06351 US
Phone: 860-376-5915
Fax: 860-376-6621
E-mail Address: *hesca@hesca.org*
Web Address: www.hesca.org
The Health and Science Communications Association (HeSCA) is an association of communications professionals committed to sharing knowledge and resources in the health sciences arena.

**Health Industry Business Communications Council (HIBCC)**
2525 E. Arizona Biltmore Cir., Ste. 127
Phoenix, AZ 85016 US
Phone: 602-381-1091
Fax: 602-381-1093
E-mail Address: *info@hibcc.org*
Web Address: www.hibcc.org
The Health Industry Business Communications Council (HIBCC) seeks to facilitate electronic communications by developing appropriate standards for information exchange among all health care trading partners.

**Health Industry Distributors Association (HIDA)**
310 Montgomery St.
Alexandria, VA 22314-1516 US
Phone: 703-549-4432
Fax: 703-549-6495
E-mail Address: *sandler@hida.org*
Web Address: www.hida.org
The Health Industry Distributors Association (HIDA) is the international trade association representing medical products distributors.

**Healthcare Financial Management Association (HFMA)**
2 Westbrook Corporate Ctr., Ste. 700
Westchester, IL 60154 US
Phone: 708-531-9600
Fax: 708-531-0032
Toll Free: 800-252-4362
Web Address: www.hfma.org

The Healthcare Financial Management Association (HFMA) is one of the nation's leading personal membership organizations for health care financial management executives and leaders.

**Healthcare Information and Management Systems Society (HIMSS)**
230 E. Ohio St., Ste. 500
Chicago, IL 60611-3270 US
Phone: 312-664-4467
Fax: 312-664-6143
E-mail Address: *himss@himss.org*
Web Address: www.himss.org
The Healthcare Information and Management Systems Society (HIMSS) provides leadership in the optimal use of technology, information and management systems for the betterment of health care.

**Hearing Industries Association (HIA)**
1444 I St. NW, Ste. 700
Washington, DC 20005 US
Phone: 202-449-1090
Fax: 202-216-9646
E-mail Address: *mspangler@bostrom.com*
Web Address: www.hearing.org
The Hearing Industries Association (HIA) represents and unifies the many aspects of the hearing industry.

**Medical Device Manufacturers Association (MDMA)**
1350 I St. NW, Ste. 540
Washington, DC 20005 US
Phone: 202-354-7171
Web Address: www.medicaldevices.org
The Medical Device Manufacturers Association (MDMA) is a national trade association that represents independent manufacturers of medical devices, diagnostic products and health care information systems.

**Medical Group Management Association (MGMA)**
104 Inverness Ter. E.
Englewood, CO 80112-5306 US
Phone: 303-799-1111
Fax: 303-643-4439
Toll Free: 877-275-6462
E-mail Address: *service@mgma.com*
Web Address: www.mgma.com
Medical Group Management Association (MGMA) is one of the nation's principal voices for medical group practice.

**National Association of Health Services Executives (NAHSE)**
1140 Connecticut Ave. NW, Ste. 505
Washington, DC 20036 US
Phone: 202-429-6060
Fax: 301-429-6767
E-mail Address: *nahsehq@nahse.org*
Web Address: www.nahse.org
The National Association of Health Services Executives (NAHSE) is a nonprofit association of black health care executives who promote the advancement and development of black health care leaders and elevate the quality of health care services rendered to minority and underserved communities.

**Regulatory Affairs Professionals Society (RAPS)**
5635 Fishers Ln., Ste. 550
Rockville, MD 20852 US
Phone: 301-770-2920
Fax: 301-770-2924
E-mail Address: *raps@raps.org*
Web Address: www.raps.org
The Regulatory Affairs Professionals Society (RAPS) is an international professional society representing the health care regulatory affairs profession and individual professionals worldwide.

## XLIV. Hotel/Lodging Associations

**American Hotel and Lodging Association**
1201 New York Ave. NW, Ste. 600
Washington, DC 20005-3931 US
Phone: 202-289-3100
Fax: 202-289-3199
E-mail Address: *informationcenter@ahla.com*
Web Address: www.ahla.com
The American Hotel and Lodging Association is a federation of state lodging associations throughout the U.S.

## XLV. Human Resources Industry Associations

**Society of Human Resource Management (SHRM)**
1800 Duke St.
Alexandria, VA 22314 US
Phone: 703-548-3440
Fax: 703-535-6490
Toll Free: 800-283-7476
E-mail Address: *shrm@shrm.org*
Web Address: www.shrm.org
The Society of Human Resource Management (SHRM) addresses the interests and needs of HR professionals through its resource materials.

## XLVI. Industry Research/Market Research

**Forrester Research**
400 Technology Sq.
Cambridge, MA 02139 US
Phone: 617-613-6000
Fax: 617-613-5200
Toll Free: 866-367-7378
Web Address: www.forrester.com
Forrester Research identifies and analyzes emerging trends in technology and their impact on business. Among the firm's specialties are the financial services, retail, health care, entertainment, automotive and information technology industries.

**Marketresearch.com**
11200 Rockville Pike, Ste. 504
Rockville, MD 20852 US
Phone: 240-747-3000
Fax: 240-747-3004
Toll Free: 800-298-5699
E-mail Address: *customerservice@marketresearch.com*
Web Address: www.marketresearch.com
Marketresearch.com is a leading broker for professional market research and industry analysis. Users are able to search the company's database of research publications including data on global industries, companies, products and trends.

**Plunkett Research, Ltd.**
P.O. Drawer 541737

Houston, TX 77254-1737 US
Phone: 713-932-0000
Fax: 713-932-7080
E-mail Address: *customersupport@plunkettresearch.com*
Web Address: www.plunkettresearch.com
Plunkett Research, Ltd. is a leading provider of market research, industry trends analysis and business statistics. Since 1985, it has served clients worldwide, including corporations, universities, libraries, consultants and government agencies. At the firm's web site, visitors can view product information and pricing and access a great deal of basic market information on industries such as financial services, InfoTech, e-commerce, health care and biotech.

## XLVII. Insurance Industry Associations

**America's Health Insurance Plans (AHIP)**
601 Pennsylvania Ave. NW, Ste. 500
Washington, DC 20004 US
Phone: 202-778-3200
Fax: 202-331-7487
E-mail Address: *ahip@ahip.org*
Web Address: www.ahip.org
America's Health Insurance Plans (AHIP) is a prominent trade association representing the private health care insurance system.

**American Insurance Association (AIA)**
1130 Connecticut Ave. NW, Ste. 1000
Washington, DC 20036 US
Phone: 202-828-7100
Fax: 202-293-1219
E-mail Address: *info@aiadc.org*
Web Address: www.aiadc.org
The American Insurance Association (AIA) is a leading property and casualty insurance trade organization, representing companies that offer all types of property and casualty insurance.

## XLVIII. Insurance Industry Associations-Agents & Brokers

**Council of Insurance Agents & Brokers (CIAB)**
701 Pennsylvania Ave. NW, Ste. 750
Washington, DC 20004 US
Phone: 202-783-4400
Fax: 202-783-4410
E-mail Address: *ciab@ciab.com*
Web Address: www.ciab.com
The Council of Insurance Agents & Brokers (CIAB) is an association for commercial insurance and employee benefits intermediaries in the U.S. and abroad.

**Independent Insurance Agents & Brokers of America, Inc. (IIABA)**
127 S. Peyton St.
Alexandria, VA 22314 US
Fax: 703-683-7556
Toll Free: 800-221-7917
E-mail Address: *info@iiaba.org*
Web Address: www.independentagent.com
Independent Insurance Agents & Brokers of America (IIABA) represents its over 300,000 members who are independent insurance agents and brokers.

**Professional Insurance Agents (PIA)**
25 Chamberlain St.
P.O. Box 997
Glenmont, NY 12077-0997 US
Fax: 888-225-6935
Toll Free: 800-424-4244
E-mail Address: *pia@pia.org*
Web Address: www.piaonline.org
Professional Insurance Agents (PIA) is a group of voluntary, membership-based trade associations representing professional, independent property and casualty insurance agents.

## XLIX. Magazines, Business & Financial

**BusinessWeek Online**
P.O. Box 8418
Red Oak, IA 51591-1418 US
Fax: 712-623-5229
Toll Free: 800-635-1200
E-mail Address: *bwzcustserv@cdsfulfillment.com*
Web Address: www.businessweek.com
Business Week Online offers an investor service, global business advice, technology news, small business guides, career information, business school advice, daily news briefs and more.

**Forbes Online**
90 5th Ave.
New York, NY 10011 US
Phone: 212-366-8900
E-mail Address: *dweathers@forbes.net*
Web Address: www.forbes.com
Forbes Online offers varied stock information, news and commentary on business, technology and personal finance, as well as financial calculators and advice.

**Fortune**
Time & Life Bldg.
Rockefeller Ctr.
New York, NY 10020-1393 US
Phone: 212-522-6724
Fax: 212-522-6412
Toll Free: 800-777-1444
E-mail Address: *Katy_Reitz@timeinc.com*
Web Address: money.cnn.com/magazines/fortune
Fortune, one of the world's premiere business magazines, contains news, business profiles and information on investing, careers, small business, technology and other details of U.S. and international business. Fortune is a publication of Cable News Network (CNN), a Time Warner company.

**Investor's Business Daily (IBD)**
12655 Beatrice St.
Los Angeles, CA 90066 US
Phone: 310-448-6600
Toll Free: 800-831-2525
E-mail Address: *ibdnews@investors.com*
Web Address: www.investors.com
Investor's Business Daily (IBD) offers subscribers information and articles on the stock market, educational resources, advice from analyst William O'Neil, personal portfolios and updates on events and workshops.

**Wall Street Journal Online (The)**
200 Liberty St.

New York, NY 10281 US
Phone: 212-416-2000
Toll Free: 800-568-7625
E-mail Address: *onlinejournal@wsj.com*
Web Address: www.wsj.com
The outstanding resources of The Wall Street Journal are available online for a nominal fee.

## L. MBA Resources

**MBA Depot**
Phone: 512-499-8728
Web Address: www.mbadepot.com
MBA Depot is an online community for MBA professionals.

## LI. Online Recruiting & Employment ASPs & Solutions

**Authoria, Inc.**
300 5th Ave.
Waltham, MA 02451 US
Phone: 781-530-2000
Fax: 781-530-2001
Toll Free: 877-422-1114
E-mail Address: *info@authoria.com*
Web Address: www.authoria.com
Authoria, Inc.'s web site offers companies and job seekers a variety of human resources content. The site includes recruiting management, performance management, incentive management, compensation management, succession planning and benefit and policy communication services.

**Insala**
1331 Airport Fwy., Ste. 313
Euless, TX 76040 US
Phone: 817-355-0939
Fax: 817-355-0746
E-mail Address: *info@insala.com*
Web Address: www.insala.com
Insala provides job search software solutions for the outplacement industry.

**Kenexa**
650 E. Swedesford Rd., 2nd Fl.
Wayne, PA 19087 US
Phone: 877-971-9171
Fax: 610-971-9181
Toll Free: 800-391-9557
E-mail Address: *contactus@kenexa.com*
Web Address: www.kenexa.com
Kenexa is a back-end recruiting and job-posting service that is used by many companies in building a workforce. Products and services include recruitment software solutions, talent consulting and recruitment process management.

**Workstream**
2600 Lake Lucien Dr., Ste. 410
Maitland, FL 32751 US
Phone: 407-475-5500
Fax: 407-475-5502
Toll Free: 866-953-8800
E-mail Address: *info@workstreaminc.com*
Web Address: www.workstreaminc.com
Workstream creates workforce management solutions through a combination of technology and services designed to integrate an organization.

## LII. Pensions, Benefits & 401(k)s Associations

**Profit Sharing/401(k) Council of America (PSCA)**
20 N. Wacker Dr., Ste. 3700
Chicago, IL 60606 US
Phone: 312-419-1863
Fax: 312-419-1864
E-mail Address: *psca@psca.org*
Web Address: www.psca.org
The Profit Sharing/401(k) Council of America (PSCA) is a national nonprofit association of 1,200 companies and their 6 million employees. The group expresses its members' interests to federal policymakers and offers practical, cost-effective assistance with profit sharing and 401(k) plan design, administration, investment, compliance and communication. Its web site offers a thorough glossary, statistics and educational material.

## LIII. Pensions, Benefits & 401(k)s Resources

**Employee Benefits Security Administration (EBSA)**
200 Constitution Ave. NW
Washington, DC 20210 US
Phone: 202-693-8700
Fax: 202-693-8736
Toll Free: 866-444-3272
Web Address: www.dol.gov/ebsa
The Employee Benefits Security Administration (EBSA) is a division of the U.S. Department of Labor, whose web site features a wealth of benefits information for both employers and employees. Included are the answers to such questions as to how a company's bankruptcy will affect its employees and what one should know about pension rights.

**Pension Benefit Guarantee Corporation (PBGC)**
1200 K St. NW
Washington, DC 20005-4026 US
Phone: 202-326-4000
Fax: 202-326-4344
Toll Free: 800-400-7242
E-mail Address: *participant.pro@pbgc.gov*
Web Address: www.pbgc.gov
The Pension Benefit Guarantee Corporation (PBGC) is a U.S. Government agency that guarantees a portion of the retirement incomes of about 44 million American workers in about 30,000 private defined benefit pension plans. Its web site contains information regarding this guarantee, along with information on retirement planning and links to several related organizations.

## LIV. Pharmaceutical Industry Associations (Drug Industry)

**American Pharmaceutical Association (APhA)**
1100 15th St. NW, Ste. 400
Washington, DC 20005-1707 US
Phone: 202-628-4410
Fax: 202-783-2351
Toll Free: 800-237-2742
E-mail Address: *infocenter@aphanet.org*
Web Address: www.aphanet.org

American Pharmaceutical Association (APhA) is a national professional society that provides news and information to pharmacists.

**Pharmaceutical Research and Manufacturers of America (PhRMA)**
950 F St. NW, Ste. 300
Washington, DC 20004 US
Phone: 202-835-3400
Fax: 202-835-3414
Web Address: www.phrma.org
Pharmaceutical Research and Manufacturers of America (PhRMA) represents the nation's leading research-based pharmaceutical and biotechnology companies.

## LV. Printers & Publishers Associations

**International Publishing Management Association (IPMA)**
710 Regency Dr., Ste. 6
Kearney, MO 64060 US
Phone: 816-902-4762
Fax: 816-902-4766
E-mail Address: *ipmainfo@ipma.org*
Web Address: www.ipma.org
The International Publishing Management Association (IPMA) is an exclusive not-for-profit organization dedicated to assisting in-house corporate publishing and distribution professionals.

**Magazine Publishers of America, Inc.**
810 7th Ave., 24th Fl.
New York, NY 10019 US
Phone: 212-872-3700
E-mail Address: *mpa@magazine.org*
Web Address: www.magazine.org
Magazine Publishers of America, Inc. is the industry association for consumer magazines.

**National Association of Printers & Lithographers (NAPL)**
75 W. Century Rd., Ste. 100
Paramus, NJ 07652 US
Phone: 201-634-9600
Fax: 201-634-0234
Toll Free: 800-642-6275
E-mail Address: *dlospaluto@napl.org*
Web Address: www.napl.org
The National Association of Printers & Lithographers (NAPL) focuses on helping graphic arts professionals increase their expertise.

**Newspaper Association of America (NAA)**
4401 Wilson Blvd., Ste. 900
Arlington, VA 22203-1867 US
Phone: 571-366-1000
Fax: 571-366-1195
E-mail Address: *Jeff.Sigmund@naa.org*
Web Address: www.naa.org
The Newspaper Association of America (NAA) is a nonprofit organization representing the newspaper industry.

## LVI. Real Estate Industry Associations

**Institute of Real Estate Management (IREM)**
430 N. Michigan Ave.
Chicago, IL 60611 US
Fax: 800-338-4736
Toll Free: 800-837-0706
E-mail Address: *custserv@irem.org*
Web Address: www.irem.org
The Institute of Real Estate Management (IREM) seeks to educate real estate managers, certify their competence and professionalism, serve as an advocate on issues affecting the real estate management industry and enhance its members' professional competence so they can better identify and meet the needs of those who use their services.

**National Association of Real Estate Brokers (NAREB)**
9831 Greenbelt Rd.
Ste. 309
Lanham, MD 20706 US
Phone: 301-552-9340
Fax: 301-552-9216
E-mail Address: *NAREB3@comcast.net*
Web Address: www.nareb.com
The National Association of Real Estate Brokers (NAREB) is a national trade organization dedicated to bringing together the nation's minority professionals in the real estate industry.

**National Association of Real Estate Companies (NAREC)**
216 W. Jackson Blvd., Ste. 625
Chicago, IL 60606 US
Phone: 312-263-1755
Fax: 312-750-1203
E-mail Address: *info@narec.org*
Web Address: www.narec.org
The National Association of Real Estate Companies (NAREC) is composed of representatives of publicly and privately owned real estate companies, significant subsidiaries of publicly owned companies and public accounting firms.

**National Association of Realtors (NAR)**
430 N. Michigan Ave.
Chicago, IL 60611-4087 US
Phone: 202-383-1176
Toll Free: 800-874-6500
E-mail Address: *lsalvant@realtors.org*
Web Address: www.realtor.org
The National Association of Realtors (NAR) is composed of realtors involved in residential and commercial real estate as brokers, salespeople, property managers, appraisers and counselors and in other areas of the industry. NAR also sponsors Realtor.com, operated by Move, Inc.

**Women's Council of Realtors (WCR)**
430 N. Michigan Ave.
Chicago, IL 60611 US
Toll Free: 800-245-8512
E-mail Address: *wcr@wcr.org*
Web Address: www.wcr.org
The Women's Council of Realtors (WCR) is a community of female real estate professionals.

## LVII. Recording & Music Associations

**American Federation of Musicians (AFM)**
1501 Broadway, Ste. 600
New York, NY 10036 US
Phone: 212-869-1330
Fax: 212-764-6134

E-mail Address: *sam@afm.org*
Web Address: www.afm.org
The American Federation of Musicians (AFM) is the largest union in the world for music professionals.

**American Society of Composers, Authors & Publishers (ASCAP)**
1 Lincoln Plaza
New York, NY 10023 US
Phone: 212-621-6000
Fax: 212-724-9064
E-mail Address: *info@ascap.com*
Web Address: www.ascap.com
American Society of Composers, Authors & Publishers (ASCAP) is a membership association of U.S. composers, songwriters and publishers of every kind of music with hundreds of thousands of members worldwide.

**Content Delivery & Storage Association (CDSA)**
182 Nassau St., Ste. 204
Princeton, NJ 08542-7005 US
Phone: 609-279-1700
Fax: 609-279-1999
E-mail Address: *mbevel@contentdeliveryandstorage.org*
Web Address: www.contentdeliveryandstorage.org
The Content Delivery & Storage Association (CDSA), formerly the International Recording Media Association, is a worldwide trade association encompassing organizations involved in every facet of recording media, including entertainment, information and software content storage.

**International Association of Audio Information Services (IAAIS)**
3920 Willshire Dr.
Lawrence, KS 66049 US
Toll Free: 800-280-5325
E-mail Address: *Stuart.Holland@state.mn.us*
Web Address: www.iaais.org
International Association of Audio Information Services (IAAIS) is an organization that provides audio access to information for people who are print-disabled.

**Music Publisher's Association of the United States (MPA)**
243 5th Ave., Ste. 236
New York, NY 10016 US
Phone: 212-327-4044
E-mail Address: *admin@mpa.org*
Web Address: mpa.org
The Music Publisher's Association of the United States (MPA) serves as a forum for publishers to deal with the music industry's vital issues and is actively involved in supporting and advancing compliance with copyright law, combating copyright infringement and exploring the need for further reform.

**Recording Industry Association of America (RIAA)**
1025 F St. NW, 10th Fl.
Washington, DC 20004 US
Phone: 202-775-0101
Web Address: www.riaa.com
The Recording Industry Association of America (RIAA) is the trade group that represents the U.S. recording industry.

**Society of Professional Audio Recording Services (SPARS)**
9 Music Sq. S., Ste. 222
Nashville, TN 37203 US
Fax: 615-296-0386
Toll Free: 800-771-7727
E-mail Address: *spars@spars.com*
Web Address: www.spars.com
The Society of Professional Audio Recording Services (SPARS) is an organization for members of the recording industry to share practical business information about audio and multimedia facility ownership, management and operations.

**Songwriters Guild of America**
209 10th Ave. S., Ste. 321
Nashville, TN 37203 US
Phone: 615-742-9945
Fax: 615-742-9948
E-mail Address: *corporate@songwritersguild.com*
Web Address: www.songwritersguild.com
The Songwriters Guild of America is the nation's largest and oldest songwriters' organization, serving its members with information and programs to further their careers and understanding of the music industry.

## LVIII. Retail Industry Associations

**National Retail Federation (NRF)**
325 7th St. NW, Ste. 1100
Washington, DC 20004 US
Phone: 202-783-7971
Fax: 202-737-2849
Toll Free: 800-673-4692
E-mail Address: *gattim@nrf.com*
Web Address: www.nrf.com
The National Retail Federation (NRF) is one of the world's largest retail trade organizations. Its membership includes the leading department, specialty, independent, discount and mass merchandise stores in the United States and 50 nations worldwide.

## LIX. Satellite-Related Professional Organizations

**Society of Satellite Professionals International (SSPI)**
The New York Information Technology Ctr.
55 Broad St., 14th Fl.
New York, NY 10004 US
Phone: 212-809-5199
Fax: 212-825-0075
E-mail Address: *rbell@sspi.org*
Web Address: www.sspi.org
The Society of Satellite Professionals International (SSPI) is a nonprofit member-benefit society that serves satellite professionals worldwide throughout the span of their careers.

## LX. Securities Industry Associations

**North American Securities Administrators Association, Inc. (NASAA)**
750 1st St. NE, Ste. 1140
Washington, DC 20002 US
Phone: 202-737-0900
Fax: 202-783-3571
E-mail Address: *bw@nasaa.org*
Web Address: www.nasaa.org
The North American Securities Administrators Association (NASAA) is the oldest international organization committed to

investor protection. Its web site provides information on franchising and raising capital, as well as state blue sky securities laws and resources for small investment advisors.

**Securities Industry and Financial Markets Association (SIFMA)**
120 Broadway, 35th Fl.
New York, NY 10271-0080 US
Phone: 212-313-1200
Fax: 212-313-1301
E-mail Address: *inquiries@sifma.org*
Web Address: www.sifma.org
The Securities Industry and Financial Markets Association (SIFMA), formed by the recent merger of the Securities Industry Association (SIA) and the Bond Market Association, brings together the shared interests of more than 650 securities and bond industry firms to accomplish common goals.

## LXI. Software Industry Resources

**Software Engineering Institute (SEI)-Carnegie Mellon**
Customer Relations
4500 Fifth Ave.
Pittsburgh, PA 15213-2612 US
Phone: 412-268-5800
Fax: 412-268-6257
Toll Free: 888-201-4479
E-mail Address: *customer-relations@sei.cmu.edu*
Web Address: www.sei.cmu.edu
The Software Engineering Institute (SEI) is a federally funded research and development center at Carnegie Mellon University, sponsored by the U.S. Department of Defense through the Office of the Under Secretary of Defense for Acquisition, Technology, and Logistics [OUSD (AT&L)]. The SEI's core purpose is to help users make measured improvements in their software engineering capabilities.

## LXII. Stock Market Data

**MSN Money Central**
Web Address: moneycentral.msn.com
MSN Money Central features daily announcements, special reports, highlights from financial providers and a wealth of links and other financial information.

**Reuters.com**
Thompson Reuters Headquarters
3 Times Sq.
New York, NY 10036 US
Phone: 646-223-4000
Toll Free: 800-738-8377
Web Address: www.reuters.com
Reuters.com, a service of Thompson Reuters, offers information on business and world markets, political and international news and company-specific stock information.

**Yahoo! Finance**
Yahoo! Inc.
701 1st Ave.
Sunnyvale, CA 94089 US
Phone: 408-349-5070
Web Address: finance.yahoo.com
Yahoo! Finance provides a wealth of links and a supreme search guide. Users can find just about any financial information concerning both U.S. and world markets. Tax, insurance information, financial news and community research can be conducted through this site, as can searches for other aspects of the financial world.

## LXIII. Telecommunications Industry Associations

**National Association of Telecommunications Officers and Advisors (NATOA)**
1800 Diagonal Rd., Ste. 495
Alexandria, VA 22314 US
Phone: 703-519-8035
Fax: 703-519-8036
E-mail Address: *info@natoa.org*
Web Address: www.natoa.org
The National Association of Telecommunications Officers and Advisors (NATOA) works to support and serve the telecommunications interests and needs of local governments.

## LXIV. Temporary Staffing Firms

**Adecco**
Saegereistrasse 10
Glattbrugg, CH-8152 Switzerland
Phone: 41-44-878-88-88
Fax: 41-44-829-89-24
E-mail Address: *investor.relations@adecco.com*
Web Address: www.adecco.com
Adecco maintains human resources and staffing services offices in 70 countries. It provides temporary and permanent personnel.

**Allegis Group**
7301 Parkway Dr.
Hanover, MD 21076 US
Phone: 410-579-4800
Fax: 410-540-7556
Toll Free: 877-388-3823
Web Address: www.allegisgroup.com
The Allegis Group provides technical, professional and industrial recruiting and staffing services. Allegis specializes in information technology staffing services. The firm operates in the United Kingdom, Germany and The Netherlands as Aerotek and TEKsystems, and in India as Allegis Group India. Aerotek provides staffing solutions for aviation, engineering, automotive and scientific personnel markets.

**CDI Corporation**
1717 Arch St., 35th Fl.
Philadelphia, PA 19103-2768 US
Phone: 215-569-2200
Fax: 215-569-1300
Toll Free: 800-996-7566
Web Address: www.cdicorp.com
CDI Corporation specializes in engineering and information technology staffing services. Company segments include CDI IT Solutions, specializing in information technology, CDI Engineering Solutions, specializing in engineering outsourcing services, AndersElite Limited, operating in the United Kingdom and Australia, and MRINetwork, specializing in executive recruitment.

**Express Personnel Services**
International Headquarters
8516 NW Expy.

Oklahoma, OK 73162 US
Phone: 405-840-5000
Toll Free: 800-222-4057
E-mail Address: *OnlineInfo@expresspros.com*
Web Address: www.expresspros.com
Express Personnel operates through a network of over 600 locations in the United States, Canada, South Africa and Australia. Services include temporary and flexible staffing, evaluation and direct hire, professional and contract staffing, human resource services and online payroll processing (U.S. only).

**Hudson Highland Group, Inc.**
560 Lexington Ave., 4th & 5th Fl.
New York, NY 10022 US
Phone: 212-351-7400
Fax: 917-256-8592
Web Address: www.hudson.com
Hudson Highland Group, Inc. provides permanent recruitment, contract and human resources consulting and inclusion solutions. Services range from single placements to total outsourced solutions. The company employs more than 3,300 professionals serving clients and candidates in more than 20 countries.

**Kelly Services, Inc.**
999 W. Big Beaver Rd.
Troy, MI 48084-4782 US
Phone: 248-362-4444
E-mail Address: *kfirst@kellyservices.com*
Web Address: www.kellyservices.com
Kelly Services is a staffing solutions company providing approximately 700,000 employees to more than 150,000 client companies in 26 countries.

**Kforce, Inc.**
1001 E. Palm Ave.
Tampa, FL 33605 US
Phone: 813-552-5000
Toll Free: 877-453-6723
Web Address: www.kforce.com
Kforce, Inc. is one of the country's largest, fastest-growing temporary placement firms, with more than 70 offices in 44 cities across the U.S. It specializes in employees for the following types of jobs: finance and accounting, scientific, technology, health care, clinical research, mortgages, title insurance and real estate.

**Labor Ready, Inc.**
P.O. Box 2910
Tacoma, WA 98401-2910 US
Phone: 253-383-9101
Fax: 877-733-0399
Toll Free: 877-733-0430
Web Address: www.laborready.com
Labor Ready, Inc. specializes in temporary staffing in construction, manufacturing, hospitality services, transportation, landscaping, warehousing, retail and more with almost 700 branches throughout the U.S., Canada and Puerto Rico.

**Manpower, Inc.**
100 Manpower Pl.
Milwaukee, WI 53212 US
Phone: 414-961-1000
Web Address: www.manpower.com
One of the largest temporary staffing providers in the world, Manpower places approximately 2 million workers annually in a variety of positions around the world.

**Michael Page International plc**
Page House, 1 Dashwood Lang Rd.
Addlestone, Weybridge
Surrey, KT15 2QW UK
Phone: 44-1932-264-144
Fax: 44-1932-264-297
Web Address: www.michaelpage.co.uk
Michael Page is one of the world's leading professional recruitment consultancies specializing in the placement of candidates in permanent, contract, temporary and interim positions. The Group has operations in the US, UK, Continental Europe, Asia-Pacific and a regional presence in France and Australia. In the US, the firm's focus is on the areas of financial services, supply chain, executive searches, marketing, legal and administrative support. In addition, in the UK the firm specializes in engineering and manufacturing.

**Monster Worldwide, Inc.**
622 Third Ave., 39th Fl.
New York, NY 10017 US
Phone: 212-351-7000
Fax: 646-658-0541
Toll Free: 800-666-7837
Web Address: www.monster.com
Monster Worldwide, Inc., parent company of Monster.com, provides online career and personnel services. The firm operates in 36 countries.

**MPS Group, Inc.**
1 Independent Dr.
Jacksonville, FL 32202 US
Phone: 904-360-2000
Fax: 904-360-2972
Web Address: www.mpsgroup.com
MPS Group is a leading provider of staffing, consulting, and human resource solutions with offices throughout the United States, Canada, the United Kingdom, and continental Europe. Primary brands include Accounting Principals, Badenoch, Entegee Engineering Technical Group, Soliant Health and Modis International IT solutions

**Radia Holdings, Inc.**
Roppongi Hills Mori Tower 35F
6-10-1, Roppongi, Minato-ku
Tokyo, 106-6135 Japan
Phone: 81-03-3405-9228
Fax: 81-03-3405-9449
Web Address: www.radiaholdings.com
Radia Holdings, Inc., provides integrated human resources services under multiple brands in Asia, North America, Europe and Australia. Radia is the largest staffing provider in Japan. Some brands in the United States and Canada include Technical Aid Corporation (TAC), Talent Tree, Inc., Willstaff, Inc., and Advantage Human Resourcing Inc. Europe brands include TAC Europe, Advantage and FSS. Japan brands include Ctec, HiTec, CSI and Premier Staff. Asia brands include TechnoPro and TAC China.

**Robert Half International Inc. (RHI)**
2884 Sand Hill Rd.
Menlo Park, CA 94025 US

Phone: 650-234-6000
E-mail Address: *webmaster@rhi.com*
Web Address: www.rhi.com
Robert Half International Inc. (RHI) specializes in accounting and finance positions. It also places workers in administrative, information technology, legal, advertising and marketing positions on temporary or permanent bases.

**Robert Walters plc**
55 Strand
London, WC2N 5WR UK
Phone: 44 (0) 20 7379 3333
Fax: 44 (0) 20 7509 8714
E-mail Address: *london@robertwalters.com*
Web Address: www.robertwalters.com
Robert Walters plc is a professional recruitment specialist, outsourcing and human resource consultant. The firm provides services for the temporary, contract and permanent placement of individuals in the sectors of finance, operations, legal, information technology, marketing and administration support. It has offices in 17 countries including the US.

**Spherion Corporation**
2050 Spectrum Blvd.
Fort Lauderdale, FL 33309 US
Phone: 954-308-7600
E-mail Address: *kiphavel@spherion.com*
Web Address: www.spherion.com
Spherion, which was Interim Services, provides temporary staffing, recruitment and employee consulting. The company has more than 900 offices throughout the world.

**Synergie SA (France)**
11, avenue de Colonel Bonnet
Paris, 75016 France
Phone: 33-1-44-14-90-20
Web Address: www.synergie.fr
Synergie provides human resource management services which include temporary placement, consulting and training. The firm operates primarily in France, but also operates through a network of 550 agencies in 12 European countries, UK and Canada.

**Tempstaff Co., Ltd (Japan)**
Shinjuku Maynds Tower 2-1-1
Yoyogi, Shibuya-ku
Tokyo, 151-0053 Japan
Phone: 03-5350-1212
Fax: 03-3597-6160
Web Address: www.tempstaff.co.jp
Tempstaff Co., Ltd provides temporary and permanent placement and recruiting and outsourcing services. It has 264 offices in Japan and ten overseas offices including Los Angeles, Shanghai, Suzhou, Guangzhou, Hong Kong, Taiwan, Korea, Singapore and Indonesia.

**Volt Information Sciences, Inc.**
560 Lexington Ave., 15th Fl.
New York, NY 10022 US
Phone: 212-704-2400
Web Address: www.volt.com
Volt Information Sciences, Inc. maintains 300 temporary staffing offices in North America and in the U.K.

## LXV. Testing Resources

**CPP, Inc.**
1055 Joaquin Rd., 2nd Fl.
Mountain View, CA 94043 US
Phone: 650-969-8901
Fax: 650-969-8608
Toll Free: 800-624-1765
E-mail Address: *custserv@cpp.com*
Web Address: www.cpp.com
CPP, Inc. (formerly known as Consulting Psychologists Press) publishes the Meyers-Briggs Type Indicator, Strong Inventory Test and other psychological assessment-related products. CPP also provides information about the tests and, through division Davies-Black Publishing, offers business-related books and services, including those covering career management and leadership development.

## LXVI. Textile & Fabric Associations

**International Textile and Apparel Association (ITAA)**
6060 Sunrise Vista Dr., Ste. 1300
Citrus Heights, CA 95610 US
Phone: 916-723-1628
Fax: 719-722-8149
E-mail Address: *info@itaaonline.org*
Web Address: www.itaaonline.org
The International Textile and Apparel Association (ITAA) is a nonprofit educational and scientific corporation dedicated to providing opportunities to scholars in the retail, textile and apparel industries.

## LXVII. Travel Business & Professional Associations

**American Society of Travel Agents (ASTA)**
1101 King St., Ste. 200
Alexandria, VA 22314 US
Fax: 703-739-3268
Toll Free: 800-275-2782
E-mail Address: *askasta@astahq.com*
Web Address: www.astanet.com
The American Society of Travel Agents (ASTA) is one of the world's largest associations of travel professionals.

**Association of Corporate Travel Executives (ACTE)**
515 King St., Ste. 440
Alexandria, VA 22314 US
Phone: 703-683-5322
Fax: 703-683-2720
E-mail Address: *info@acte.org*
Web Address: www.acte.org
The Association of Corporate Travel Executives (ACTE) serves the specialized travel interests of corporate purchasers and travel service suppliers from nearly 50 countries.

**Association of Retail Travel Agents (ARTA)**
c/o Travel Destinations, Inc.
4320 North Miller Rd.
Scottsdale, AZ 85251 US
Fax: 615-985-0600
Toll Free: 800-969-6069
E-mail Address: *info@artaonline.com*
Web Address: www.artaonline.com

The Association of Retail Travel Agents (ARTA) is one of the largest nonprofit associations in North America to exclusively represent travel agents.

**Association of Travel Marketing Executives (ATME)**
P.O. Box 3176
West Tisbury, MA 02575 US
Phone: 508-693-0550
Fax: 508-693-0115
E-mail Address: *admin@atme.org*
Web Address: www.atme.org
The Association of Travel Marketing Executives (ATME) is a global professional association of senior-level travel marketing executives dedicated to providing cutting-edge information, education and opportunities for meaningful networking with peers.

**National Society of Minorities in Hospitality**
107 S. West St., PMB 119
Alexandria, VA 22314 US
Phone: 703-549-9899
Fax: 703-997-7795
E-mail Address: *hq@nsmh.org*
Web Address: www.nsmh.org
The National Society of Minorities in Hospitality strives to establish a working relationship between the hospitality industry and minority students.

**Network of Executive Women in Hospitality, Inc. (NEWH)**
P.O. Box 322
Shawano, WI 54166 US
Fax: 800-693-6394
Toll Free: 800-593-6394
Web Address: www.newh.org
The Network of Executive Women in Hospitality, Inc. (NEWH) brings together professionals from all facets of the hospitality industry by providing opportunities for education, professional development and networking. Although primarily a U.S.-based organization, NEWH does have international chapters in Toronto and London.

## LXVIII. Travel Industry Associations

**Destination Marketing Association International**
2025 M St. NW, Ste. 500
Washington, DC 20036 US
Phone: 202-296-7888
Fax: 202-296-7889
Toll Free: 888-275-3140
E-mail Address: *info@destinationmarketing.org*
Web Address: www.destinationmarketing.org
The Destination Marketing Association International, formerly the International Association of Convention & Visitor Bureaus, strives to enhance the professionalism, effectiveness and image of destination management organizations worldwide.

**International Association of Conference Centers (IACC)**
243 N. Lindbergh Blvd.
St. Louis, MO 63141 US
Phone: 314-993-8575
Fax: 314-993-8919
E-mail Address: *info@iacconline.org*
Web Address: www.iacconline.com
The International Association of Conference Centers (IACC) is a nonprofit, facilities-based organization founded to promote a greater awareness and understanding of the unique features of conference centers around the world.

**National Tour Association (NTA)**
546 E. Main St.
Lexington, KY 40508 US
Phone: 859-226-4444
Fax: 859-226-4414
Toll Free: 800-682-8886
E-mail Address: *questions@ntastaff.com*
Web Address: www.ntaonline.com
The National Tour Association (NTA) is an association for travel professionals who have an interest in the packaged travel sector of the industry.

**Society of Incentive and Travel Executives**
401 N. Michigan Ave.
Chicago, IL 60611 US
Phone: 312-321-5148
Fax: 312-527-6783
E-mail Address: *Marcie_Valerio@site-intl.org*
Web Address: www.site-intl.org
The Society of Incentive and Travel Executives is a worldwide organization of business professionals dedicated to the recognition and development of motivational and performance improvement strategies in the travel industry.

**Travel Industry Association**
1100 New York Ave. NW, Ste. 450
Washington, DC 20005-3934 US
Phone: 202-408-8422
Fax: 202-408-1255
E-mail Address: *feedback@tia.org*
Web Address: www.tia.org
The Travel Industry Association is a nonprofit association that represents and speaks for the common interests and concerns of all components of the U.S. travel industry.

## LXIX. U.S. Government Agencies

**Bureau of Economic Analysis (BEA)**
1441 L St. NW
Washington, DC 20230 US
Phone: 202-606-9900
E-mail Address: *customerservice@bea.gov*
Web Address: www.bea.gov
The Bureau of Economic Analysis (BEA), an agency of the U.S. Department of Commerce, is the nation's economic accountant, preparing estimates that illuminate key national, international and regional aspects of the U.S. economy.

**Bureau of Labor Statistics (BLS)**
2 Massachusetts Ave. NE
Washington, DC 20212-0001 US
Phone: 202-691-5200
Web Address: stats.bls.gov
The Bureau of Labor Statistics (BLS) is the principal fact-finding agency for the Federal Government in the field of labor economics and statistics. It is an independent national statistical agency that collects, processes, analyzes and disseminates statistical data to the American public, U.S. Congress, other federal agencies, state and local governments, business and labor.

The BLS also serves as a statistical resource to the Department of Labor.

**Equal Employment Opportunity Commission (EEOC)**
1801 L St. NW
Washington, DC 20507 US
Phone: 202-663-4900
Toll Free: 800-669-4000
E-mail Address: *info@eeoc.gov*
Web Address: www.eeoc.gov
The Equal Employment Opportunity Commission (EEOC) is a Federal Government agency focused on practices and programs that foster equal opportunity at work and elsewhere. Its web site features details about various protective laws regarding employment. It also provides information on how to file a discrimination claim.

**FedStats**
Web Address: www.fedstats.gov
FedStats compiles information for statistics from over 100 U.S. federal agencies. Visitors can sort the information by agency, geography and topic, as well as perform searches.

**Government Printing Office (GPO)**
732 N. Capitol St. NW
Washington, DC 20401 US
Phone: 202-512-0000
Fax: 202-512-2104
Toll Free: 866.512.1800
E-mail Address: *contactcenter@gpo.gov*
Web Address: www.gpo.gov
The U.S. Government Printing Office (GPO) is the primary information source concerning the activities of Federal agencies. GPO gathers, catalogues, produces, provides, authenticates and preserves published information.

**National Labor Relations Board (NLRB)**
1099 14th St. NW
Washington, DC 20570-0001 US
Phone: 202-208-3000
Fax: 202-208-3013
Toll Free: 866-667-6572
Web Address: www.nlrb.gov
The National Labor Relations Board (NLRB) provides case reports on labor disputes, searchable by company or union.

**U.S. Census Bureau**
4600 Silver Hill Rd.
Washington, DC 20233-8800 US
Phone: 301-763-4636
Fax: 301-457-3670
Toll Free: 800-923-8282
E-mail Address: *pio@census.gov*
Web Address: www.census.gov
The U.S. Census Bureau is the official collector of data about the people and economy of the U.S. Founded in 1790, it provides official social, demographic and economic information.

**U.S. Department of Commerce (DOC)**
1401 Constitution Ave. NW
Washington, DC 20230 US
Phone: 202-482-2000
E-mail Address: *cgutierrez@doc.gov*
Web Address: www.doc.gov
The U.S. Department of Commerce (DOC) regulates trade and provides valuable economic analysis of the economy.

**U.S. Department of Labor (DOL)**
Frances Perkins Bldg.
200 Constitution Ave. NW
Washington, DC 20210 US
Toll Free: 866-487-2365
Web Address: www.dol.gov
The U.S. Department of Labor (DOL) is the government agency responsible for labor regulations. This site provides tools to help citizens find out whether companies are complying with family and medical-leave requirements.

**U.S. Securities and Exchange Commission (SEC)**
100 F St. NE
Washington, DC 20549 US
Phone: 202-551-6000
Toll Free: 888-732-6585
E-mail Address: *publicinfo@sec.gov*
Web Address: www.sec.gov
The U.S. Securities and Exchange Commission (SEC) is a nonpartisan, quasi-judicial regulatory agency responsible for administering federal securities laws. These laws are designed to protect investors in securities markets and ensure that they have access to disclosure of all material information concerning publicly traded securities. Visitors to the web site can access the EDGAR database of corporate financial and business information.

## LXX. Waste Industry Associations

**Air & Waste Management Association**
1 Gateway Ctr., 3rd Fl.
420 Fort Duquesne Blvd.
Pittsburgh, PA 15222-1435 US
Phone: 412-232-3444
Fax: 412-232-3450
Toll Free: 800-270-3444
E-mail Address: *info@awma.org*
Web Address: www.awma.org
The Air & Waste Management Association provides training, information and networking opportunities to environmental professionals worldwide.

## LXXI. Water Resources Associations

**American Water Resources Association (AWRA)**
P.O. Box 1626
Middleburg, VA 20118 US
Phone: 540-687-8390
Fax: 540-687-8395
E-mail Address: *info@awra.org*
Web Address: www.awra.org
The American Water Resources Association (AWRA) represents the interests of professionals involved in water resources.

## LXXII. Writers, Photographers & Editors Associations

**American Society of Journalists and Authors, Inc. (ASJA)**
1501 Broadway, Ste. 302
New York, NY 10036 US
Phone: 212-997-0947

Fax: 212-937-2315
E-mail Address: *director@asja.org*
Web Address: www.asja.org
The American Society of Journalists and Authors (ASJA) is of the nation's leading organizations of independent nonfiction writers.

**American Society of Magazine Editors (ASME)**
Magazine Publishers of America (MPA)
810 7th Ave., 24th Fl.
New York, NY 10019 US
Phone: 212-872-3736
E-mail Address: *asme@magazine.org*
Web Address: www.magazine.org/asme
The American Society of Magazine Editors (ASME) is a professional organization for editors of print and online magazines. ASME is part of the Magazine Publishers of America (MPA).

**American Society of Newspaper Editors (ASNE)**
11690B Sunrise Valley Dr.
Reston, VA 20191-1409 US
Phone: 703-453-1122
Fax: 703-453-1133
E-mail Address: *asne@asne.org*
Web Address: www.asne.org
The American Society of Newspaper Editors (ASNE) is an association that brings together editors of daily newspapers and people directly involved with developing content for daily newspapers.

**International Women's Writing Guild (IWWG)**
P.O. Box 810, Gracie Sta.
New York, NY 10028-0082 US
Phone: 212-737-7536
Fax: 212-737-9469
E-mail Address: *dirhahn@iwwg.org*
Web Address: www.iwwg.com
The International Women's Writing Guild (IWWG) is a network for the personal and professional empowerment of women through writing.

**Media Communications Association International (MCAI)**
2810 Crossroads Dr., Ste. 3800
Madison, WI 53718 US
Phone: 608-443-2464
Fax: 608-443-2474
E-mail Address: *execdirect@mca-i.org*
Web Address: www.mca-i.org
The Media Communications Association International (MCAI) is the leading global community for media communications professionals seeking to drive the convergence of communications and technology for the growth of the profession.

**National Association of Hispanic Journalists (NAHJ)**
1000 National Press Bldg.
529 14th St. NW
Washington, DC 20045-2001 US
Phone: 202-662-7145
Fax: 202-662-7144
Toll Free: 888-346-6245
E-mail Address: *nahj@nahj.org*
Web Address: www.nahj.org
The National Association of Hispanic Journalists (NAHJ) is dedicated to the recognition and professional advancement of Hispanics in the news industry.

**National Association of Science Writers, Inc. (NASW)**
P.O. Box 890
Hedgesville, WV 25427 US
Phone: 304-754-5077
Fax: 304-754-5076
E-mail Address: *director@nasw.org*
Web Address: www.nasw.org
The National Association of Science Writers (NASW) exists to foster the dissemination of accurate information regarding science through all media devoted to informing the public.

**National Conference of Editorial Writers (NCEW)**
3899 N. Front St.
Harrisburg, PA 17110 US
Phone: 717-703-3015
Fax: 717-703-3014
E-mail Address: *ncew@pa-news.org*
Web Address: www.ncew.org
The National Conference of Editorial Writers (NCEW) strives to stimulate the conscience and quality of editorial writing.

**National Federation of Press Women (NFPW)**
P.O. Box 5556
Arlington, VA 22205 US
Fax: 703-812-4555
Toll Free: 800-780-2715
E-mail Address: *presswomen@aol.com*
Web Address: www.nfpw.org
The National Federation of Press Women (NFPW) is an organization of professional journalists and communicators.

**National Writers Union (NWU)**
113 University Pl., 6th Fl.
New York, NY 10003 US
Phone: 212-254-0279
Fax: 212-254-0673
E-mail Address: *nwu@nwu.org*
Web Address: www.nwu.org
The National Writers Union (NWU) is a labor union that represents freelance writers in all genres, formats and media. It is committed to improving the economic and working conditions of freelance writers.

**Society of Children's Book Writers and Illustrators (SCBWI)**
8271 Beverly Blvd.
Los Angeles, CA 90048 US
Phone: 323-782-1010
Fax: 323-782-1892
E-mail Address: *scbwi@scbwi.org*
Web Address: www.scbwi.org
The Society of Children's Book Writers and Illustrators (SCBWI) serves people who write, illustrate or share a vital interest in children's literature, including publishers, librarians, booksellers and agents.

# Chapter 5

# THE MID-SIZE EMPLOYERS 500, 2009: WHO THEY ARE AND HOW THEY WERE CHOSEN

*Note: financial data given for each of the MID-SIZE EMPLOYERS 500 firms is for the year ended December 31, 2008, a fiscal year ended in 2008 or the latest figures available to the editors. Telephone numbers, addresses, contact names, Internet addresses and other vital facts were collected in late 2008.*

The companies chosen to be listed in PLUNKETT'S COMPANION TO THE ALMANAC OF AMERICAN EMPLOYERS are not the same as the "Fortune 500" or any other list of corporations. The MID-SIZE EMPLOYERS 500 (the actual count is 514 companies) were chosen specifically for their likelihood to provide new job openings to the greatest number of employees. Complete information about each firm can be found in the "Individual Data Listings," beginning about the middle of this book. They are in alphabetical order.

THE MID-SIZE EMPLOYERS 500 includes companies from all parts of the United States and from a broad range of selected industry segments: banks, retailers, service companies, wholesalers and distributors, insurance companies and others, as well as industrial companies, technology firms and manufacturers.

Simply stated, the list contains 514 of the most successful, mid-size employers in the United States today. In particular, the list contains companies that we have selected to have qualities that we feel will be of greatest interest to job seekers of today who are looking for opportunities to obtain employment with mid-size corporations.

In order to make this reference guide as useful as possible, we have altered the company selection criteria that were used in early editions. Rather than focusing largely on mid-term growth histories, we are instead focusing more on type of business and industry sector served. This is because some sectors may not be hiring in large numbers today. Consequently, we have deleted some truly outstanding companies due to the state of their particular markets. However, job seekers should bear in mind the fact that firms of many types will continue to restrain hiring. In addition, frequent layoffs have become standard in corporate America. (See Chapter 1 "Trends" for further thoughts about layoffs and other trends.)

To be included in our list, the firms generally were selected on the following criteria:

**1) U.S.-based companies.** (However, a small number of companies may be subsidiaries of foreign-based firms.)
**2) Between 100 and 2,500 employees.** This size, by employee count, is our criteria for "mid-size".
**3) Selected Type of Business and/or Industry Sector:** Companies were chosen based on our analysis of the business potential of their products, services and industrial sectors in light of today's economy.

The companies were chosen in this manner for the following reasons:

**500 COMPANIES** (the actual count is 514 companies) so there is a broad base among which to make comparisons and from which you can study potential employers.

**MID-SIZE EMPLOYERS** (between 100 and 2,500 employees) so the information can supplement the main volume of The Almanac of American Employers which focuses on employers with more than 2,500 employees.

**COMPANIES THAT OPERATE IN PROMISING BUSINESS SECTORS** because:

1) Companies that are stable or enjoying growing business are much more likely to have job openings. (See Chapter 1, "Trends.")

2) These companies may be much more likely to offer advancement opportunities. Current employees may benefit from promote-from-within policies when new plants, new stores, new product lines or new offices are opened.

A low score in any part of this book should not be taken as a slur against the company so ranked; it should be taken as evidence of the obvious: some companies are better to work for than others, depending, of course, on what you value. It is not easy to get into the MID-SIZE EMPLOYERS 500, and the mere presence of a company on the list can be taken as evidence that it has excelled in many ways. To start with, it has to have generated enough business to employ large numbers of people–never a simple task. Nonetheless, job seekers should use caution. Situations can change quickly at corporate employers, and job seekers should make certain they are armed with the latest information prior to making a final decision.

## INDUSTRY LIST, WITH CODES

**This book refers to the following list of unique industry codes, based on the 1997 NAIC code system (NAIC is used by many analysts as a replacement for older SIC codes because NAIC is more specific to today's industry sectors). Companies profiled in this book are given a primary NAIC code, reflecting the main line of business of each firm.**

### Agriculture

| | |
|---|---|
| | ***Farming*** |
| **111300** | Fruit & Tree Nut Farming |
| **112300** | Poultry Production |
| **311613** | Rendering & Meat Byproduct Processing |

### Apparel

| | |
|---|---|
| | ***Apparel & Shoe Manufacturing*** |
| **315000** | Apparel Manufacturing-General |
| **316210** | Shoe Manufacturing-General |

### Entertainment

| | |
|---|---|
| | ***Publishing*** |
| **511120** | Magazines Publishing |
| **511130** | Books, Publishing |
| | ***Film, Video & Music Recording*** |
| **512110** | TV/Video/Theatrical, Production |
| **532230** | Video Rental |
| | ***Gambling & Recreation*** |
| **713940** | Fitness Centers/Health Clubs |
| | ***Hotels & Accommodations*** |
| **721211** | RV Parks & Campgrounds |

### Energy

| | |
|---|---|
| | ***Fuel Mining & Extraction*** |
| **211111** | Oil & Natural Gas Exploration & Production |
| | ***Utilities*** |
| **221000** | Utilities-Electric & Gas |
| **221000A** | Utilities-Electric |
| **221000B** | Utilities-Gas |
| | ***Petroleum-Refining & Manufacturing*** |
| **324110** | Petroleum Refineries |
| **324190** | Other Petrochemical & Coal Products Manufacturing |
| | ***Manufacturing, Electrical*** |
| **335910** | Battery Manufacturing |
| **335929** | Superconducting Materials & Other Wire |

### Financial Services

| | |
|---|---|
| | ***Banking, Credit & Finance*** |
| **522320** | Payment & Transaction Processing Services |
| **522320A** | Payment & Transaction Processing--Benefits Management |
| | ***Stocks & Investments*** |
| **523110** | Investment Banking |

| | |
|---|---|
| **523120** | Stock Brokerage |
| **523210** | Stocks, Bonds & Commodities Exchanges |
| | ***Insurance*** |
| **524113** | Insurance-Life |
| **524114** | Insurance-Health, HMO's & PPO's |
| **524114A** | Insurance--Supplemental Health |
| **524126** | Insurance-Property & Casualty |
| **524130** | Insurance-Reinsurance |
| **524210A** | Insurance Intermediary-Online |
| | ***Benefit Plans*** |
| **525120** | Employee Benefit Plans |

## Food & Restaurants

| | |
|---|---|
| | ***Food Service*** |
| **722110** | Restaurants |
| **722213** | Food Service, Snacks & Nonalcoholic Beverage Bars |
| **722310** | Food Service Contractors |

## Health Care

| | |
|---|---|
| | ***Health Products, Manufacturing*** |
| **325411** | Medicinals & Botanicals, Manufacturing |
| **325412** | Drugs (Pharmaceuticals), Discovery & Manufacturing |
| **325412A** | Drug Delivery Systems |
| **325412B** | Veterinary Products Manufacturing |
| **325413** | Diagnostic Services and Substances Manufacturing |
| **325414** | Biological Products, Manufacturing |
| **325416** | Drugs (Pharmaceuticals), Generic Manufacturing |
| **339113** | Medical/Dental/Surgical Equipment & Supplies, Manufacturing |
| | ***Health Products, Wholesale Distribution*** |
| **421450** | Medical/Dental/Surgical Equipment & Supplies, Distribution |
| | ***Equipment Rental*** |
| **532400** | Equipment Rental |
| | ***Health Care-Clinics, Labs and Organizations*** |
| **524298** | Disease Management & Utilization Management |
| **621111** | Physician Practice Management |
| **621490** | Clinics--Outpatient Clinics & Surgery |
| **621511** | Laboratories & Diagnostic Services--Medical |
| **621610** | Home Health Care |

## InfoTech

| | |
|---|---|
| | ***Computers & Electronics Manufacturing*** |
| **334110** | Computer Networking & Related Equipment, Manufacturing |
| **334111** | Computer Hardware, Manufacturing |
| **334112** | Computer Storage Equipment & Misc Parts, Manufacturing |
| **334119** | Computer Accessories, Monitors, Printers Manufacturing |
| **334310** | Audio & Video Equipment, Consumer Electronics |
| **334413** | Semiconductors (Microchips)/Integrated Circuits/Components, Manufacturing |
| **334500** | Instrument Manufacturing, including Measurement, Control, Test & Navigational |
| | ***Computers & Electronics, Distribution*** |
| **421430** | Computer & Telecommunications Equipment Distribution |
| | ***Software*** |
| **511201** | Computer Software, Accounting, Banking & Financial |
| **511202** | Computer Software, Content & Document Management |
| **511203** | Computer Software, Sales & Customer Relationship Management |
| **511204** | Computer Software, Operating Systems, Languages & Development Tools |
| **511206** | Computer Software, Data Base & File Management |
| **511207** | Computer Software, Business Management & ERP |
| **511208** | Computer Software, Games & Entertainment |
| **511209** | Computer Software, Multimedia, Graphics & Publishing |
| **511211** | Computer Software, Security & Anti-Virus |
| **511212** | Computer Software, Healthcare & Biotechnology |
| **511213** | Computer Software, Telecom, Communications & VOIP |
| **511214** | Computer Software, Networking & Storage |
| **511215** | Computer Software, Product Lifecycle, Engineering, Design & CAD |
| **511216** | Computer Software, E-Commerce & Web Analytics |
| **511217** | Computer Software, Supply Chain & Logistics |
| **511218** | Computer Software, Educational & Training |
| | ***Information & Data Processing Services*** |
| **514199** | Online Publishing, Services & Niche Portals |
| **514199B** | Search Engine Portals |
| **514210** | Data Processing Services |
| | ***Information Services-Professional*** |
| **541512** | Consulting--Computer, Telecommunications & Internet |
| **541512A** | Consulting--Information Systems & Applications Research |

## Manufacturing

| | |
|---|---|
| | ***Food Products Manufacturing*** |
| **311000** | Food Products, Manufacturing |
| **311230** | Breakfast Cereal Manufacturing |
| **311330** | Chocolate & Confectionery Manufacturing |
| **311410** | Frozen Food Manufacturing |
| **311500** | Dairy Products, Manufacturing |
| **311823** | Dry Pasta Manufacturing |
| **311920** | Coffee & Tea Manufacturing |
| **311940** | Seasonings, Flavorings & Dressings Manufacturing |
| | ***Beverage & Tobacco Manufacturing*** |
| **312111** | Beverages--Soft Drinks & Juices Manufacturing |
| **312113** | Ice-Manufacturing |
| **312130** | Beverages--Wineries |
| | ***Chemicals*** |
| **325000** | Chemicals, Manufacturing |
| | ***Plastics & Rubber*** |
| **326100** | Plastic Products, Manufacturing |
| | ***Nonmetallic Minerals/Rock/Aggregate*** |
| **327000** | Nonmetallic Mineral, Rock & Aggregate Manufacturing |
| | ***Machinery & Manufacturing Equipment*** |
| **333295** | Semiconductor Manufacturing Equipment |
| **333298** | Fuel Cells Manufacturing |
| **333298A** | Solar Cells, Photovoltaic Cells, Manufacturing |

## Nanotechnology

***Nanotechnology***

**541710** Research and Development/Physical, Engineering and Life Sciences
**541710B** Nanotechnology-Biotech/Health

## Retailing

***Computers & Electronics Stores***

**443120A** Computers & Software-Direct Selling

***Food & Beverage Stores***

**445110** Grocery Stores/Supermarkets
**445110E** Grocery Stores/Supermarkets-Online

***Drug Stores, Beauty Supply & Health Items Stores***

**446110E** Drug Stores-Online

***Apparel & Accessories Stores***

**448210E** Shoes & Accessories Stores-Online
**448310E** Jewelry Stores-Online

***Sporting Goods, Hobbies, Books & Music Stores***

**451110** Sporting Goods Stores
**451110E** Sporting Goods Stores-Online
**451220E** Music Stores-Online

***Miscellaneous Retailers***

**453910** Pets/Pet Supplies Stores
**453990** Other Retailers, Misc. Retailers

## Services

***Agriculture***

**115112** Agricultural Crop Production Support, Seeds, Fertilizers

***Construction***

**234000** Construction, Heavy & Civil Engineering

***Consulting & Professional Services***

**541330** Engineering & Facilities Support Services
**541611** Consulting--Management & Business
**541612** Consulting-Human Resources
**541613** Consulting--Marketing
**541690** Consulting--Scientific & Technical
**541810A** Advertising/Marketing--Online
**541890** Advertising Specialties & Other Services Related to Advertising
**541910** Market Research

***Educational***

**611410** Business Training, Distance Learning

***Performing Arts. Spectator Sports and Related Industries***

**711410** Agents, Performers, Models, Athletes

***Automotive Services***

**811100** Automotive Repair & Maintenance
**811191** Automotive Oil Change & Lubrication Shops

## Telecommunications

***Telecommunications Equipment***

**334200** Communications Equipment, Manufacturing
**334210** Telecommunications Equipment Manufacturing
**334220** Radio & Wireless Communication, Manufacturing
**334290** Security, Detection & Intercom System Manufacturing

***Telecommunications***

**513300A** Telephone Service-Local Exchange Carrier & Diversified
**513300B** Telephone Service-Long Distance
**513300D** Telecommunications & Internet Services-Specialty
**513322** Telephone Service-Cellular, U.S. & Non-U.S.
**513390C** Telecommunications-Private Data Networks & Network Services
**514191** Internet Access Provider
**514191A** Internet Application Service Hosts & Co-location Providers

## Transportation

***Truck***

**488510** Freight Forwarding & Support Services

## Wholesale Distribution-Other

***Distribution-Durable Goods***

**421690** Electronic Parts & Equipment, Distribution
**422600** Chemicals & Plastics, Distribution
**423120** Automobile Parts, Wholesale Distribution

***Distribution-Nondurable Goods***

**422710** Petroleum Bulk Stations & Terminals Distribution
**422720** Petroleum Products (except Bulk Stations/Terminals) Distribution & Pipelines
**422820** Wines & Spirits, Distribution

# INDEX OF RANKINGS WITHIN INDUSTRY GROUPS

| Company | Industry Code | 2007 Sales (U.S. $ thousands) | Sales Rank | 2007 Profits (U.S. $ thousands) | Profits Rank |
|---|---|---|---|---|---|
| **Advertising Specialties & Other Services Related to Advertising** | | | | | |
| NATIONAL CINEMEDIA INC | 541890 | 331,900 | 1 | 20,600 | 1 |
| **Advertising/Marketing--Online** | | | | | |
| 24/7 REAL MEDIA INC | 541810A | | | | |
| ACXIOM DIGITAL | 541810A | | | | |
| AKQA INC | 541810A | 221,500 | 3 | | |
| CHOICESTREAM INC | 541810A | | | | |
| COUPONS INC | 541810A | | | | |
| DOUBLECLICK INC | 541810A | 346,700 | 2 | | |
| VALUECLICK INC | 541810A | 616,508 | 1 | 70,612 | 1 |
| VIBRANT MEDIA INC | 541810A | | | | |
| **Aerospace & Aircraft Related Manufacturing** | | | | | |
| AVIALL INC | 336410 | 2,000,000 | 1 | | |
| FLIR SYSTEMS | 336410 | 779,397 | 2 | 136,711 | 1 |
| **Agents, Performers, Models, Athletes** | | | | | |
| CKX INC | 711410 | 266,777 | 1 | 12,144 | 1 |
| IMG WORLDWIDE INC | 711410 | | | | |
| INTERNATIONAL CREATIVE MANAGEMENT (ICM) | 711410 | 155,000 | 2 | | |
| **Agricultural Crop Production Support, Seeds, Fertilizers** | | | | | |
| AMERICAN VANGUARD CORP | 115112 | 216,662 | 2 | 18,728 | 1 |
| SCOULAR COMPANY | 115112 | 4,300,000 | 1 | | |
| **Apparel Manufacturing & Design-General** | | | | | |
| VOLCOM INC | 315000 | 265,193 | 1 | 33,335 | 1 |
| **Apparel Manufacturing-Athletic Clothes** | | | | | |
| UNDER ARMOUR INC | 315000A | 606,561 | 1 | 52,558 | 1 |
| **Audio & Video Equipment, Consumer Electronics** | | | | | |
| DAKTRONICS INC | 334310 | 433,201 | 1 | 24,427 | 1 |
| TIVO INC | 334310 | 258,921 | 2 | -47,754 | 2 |
| **Automobile Parts Manufacturing** | | | | | |
| MOTORCAR PARTS OF AMERICA INC | 336300 | 136,323 | 1 | -2,475 | 1 |
| **Automobile Parts, Wholesale Distribution** | | | | | |
| AMERICAN TIRE DISTRIBUTORS | 423120 | 1,877,500 | 1 | | |
| HAHN AUTOMOTIVE WAREHOUSE INC | 423120 | 140,300 | 2 | | |
| **Automotive Oil Change & Lubrication Shops** | | | | | |
| LUCOR INC | 811191 | 100,500 | 1 | | |
| **Automotive Repair & Maintenance** | | | | | |
| AAMCO TRANSMISSIONS INC | 811100 | | | | |
| CALIBER HOLDINGS CORP | 811100 | | | | |
| MIDAS INC | 811100 | 180,000 | 1 | 13,300 | 1 |
| STERLING AUTOBODY CENTERS | 811100 | | | | |
| ZIEBART INTERNATIONAL CORP | 811100 | 114,000 | 2 | | |
| **Battery Manufacturing** | | | | | |
| INTERSTATE BATTERY SYSTEM OF AMERICA | 335910 | 1,500,000 | 1 | | |
| **Beverages--Soft Drinks, Bottled Water & Juices Manufacturing** | | | | | |
| HANSEN NATURAL | 312111 | 904,465 | 1 | 149,406 | 1 |

| Company | Industry Code | 2007 Sales (U.S. $ thousands) | Sales Rank | 2007 Profits (U.S. $ thousands) | Profits Rank |
|---|---|---|---|---|---|
| NATIONAL BEVERAGE CORP | 312111 | 539,030 | 2 | 24,682 | 2 |
| **Beverages--Wineries** | | | | | |
| KENDALL-JACKSON WINE ESTATES LTD | 312130 | | | | |
| **Biological Products, Manufacturing** | | | | | |
| ALPHARMA INC | 325414 | 722,425 | 1 | -13,581 | 3 |
| ANIKA THERAPEUTICS INC | 325414 | 30,830 | 4 | -6,035 | 2 |
| GENENCOR INTERNATIONAL | 325414 | 90,700 | 3 | | |
| GTC BIOTHERAPEUTICS INC | 325414 | 13,896 | 5 | -36,321 | 4 |
| LIFECELL CORPORATION | 325414 | 191,130 | 2 | 26,883 | 1 |
| **Books, Publishing** | | | | | |
| MARVEL ENTERTAINMENT INC | 511130 | 485,807 | 1 | 139,823 | 1 |
| **Breakfast Cereal Manufacturing** | | | | | |
| MALT-O-MEAL COMPANY | 311230 | 490,000 | 1 | | |
| **Business Training, Distance Learning** | | | | | |
| BLACKBOARD INC | 611410 | 239,448 | 1 | 12,865 | 1 |
| ECOLLEGE.COM | 611410 | | | | |
| HEALTHSTREAM INC | 611410 | 43,949 | 2 | 4,087 | 2 |
| **Chemicals & Plastics, Distribution** | | | | | |
| VALLEY NATIONAL GASES LLC | 422600 | | | | |
| **Chemicals, Manufacturing** | | | | | |
| ARIZONA CHEMICAL COMPANY | 325000 | | | | |
| ICO INC | 325000 | 417,917 | 2 | 21,118 | 1 |
| ISONICS CORPORATION | 325000 | 27,731 | 3 | -13,165 | 2 |
| KRONOS WORLDWIDE INC | 325000 | 1,310,300 | 1 | -66,700 | 3 |
| **Chocolate & Confectionery Manufacturing** | | | | | |
| TOOTSIE ROLL INDUSTRIES INC | 311330 | 492,742 | 1 | 51,625 | 1 |
| TOPPS COMPANY INC | 311330 | 326,700 | 2 | | |
| **Clinics--Outpatient Clinics & Surgery** | | | | | |
| AMSURG CORP | 621490 | 531,085 | 1 | 44,175 | 1 |
| CRITICAL CARE SYSTEMS | 621490 | | | | |
| DIALYSIS CORPORATION OF AMERICA | 621490 | 74,535 | 7 | 3,086 | 5 |
| DYNACQ HEALTHCARE INC | 621490 | 42,846 | 8 | 4,155 | 4 |
| HEALTHTRONICS INC | 621490 | 140,418 | 4 | -14,632 | 8 |
| HEARUSA INC | 621490 | 102,804 | 6 | -3,282 | 6 |
| LCA-VISION INC | 621490 | 292,635 | 2 | 32,504 | 2 |
| NOVAMED INC | 621490 | 128,621 | 5 | -5,594 | 7 |
| US PHYSICAL THERAPY INC | 621490 | 151,686 | 3 | 8,738 | 3 |
| **Coffee & Tea Manufacturing** | | | | | |
| FARMER BROTHERS CO | 311920 | 216,259 | 2 | 6,815 | 2 |
| GREEN MOUNTAIN COFFEE ROASTERS INC | 311920 | 341,651 | 1 | 12,843 | 1 |
| **Communications Equipment, Manufacturing** | | | | | |
| ARRIS GROUP INC | 334200 | 992,194 | 1 | 98,340 | 1 |
| COMTECH TELECOMMUNICATIONS CORP | 334200 | 445,684 | 2 | 65,213 | 2 |
| EMS TECHNOLOGIES INC | 334200 | 287,879 | 4 | 18,744 | 3 |
| SONUS NETWORKS INC | 334200 | 320,310 | 3 | -23,637 | 4 |
| **Computer & Telecommunications Equipment Distribution** | | | | | |
| SCANSOURCE INC | 421430 | 1,986,927 | 1 | 42,626 | 1 |

| Company | Industry Code | 2007 Sales (U.S. $ thousands) | Sales Rank | 2007 Profits (U.S. $ thousands) | Profits Rank |
|---|---|---|---|---|---|
| **Computer Accessories, Monitors, Printers Manufacturing** | | | | | |
| ELECTRONICS FOR IMAGING | 334119 | 620,586 | 3 | 26,843 | 2 |
| INTERMEC INC | 334119 | 849,200 | 2 | 23,100 | 4 |
| METROLOGIC INSTRUMENTS | 334119 | | | | |
| POLYCOM INC | 334119 | 929,908 | 1 | 62,881 | 1 |
| SYNAPTICS INC | 334119 | 266,787 | 4 | 26,534 | 3 |
| **Computer Hardware, Manufacturing** | | | | | |
| COGNEX CORP | 334111 | 225,737 | 5 | 26,899 | 2 |
| GERBER SCIENTIFIC INC | 334111 | 574,798 | 2 | 13,508 | 4 |
| PALM INC | 334111 | 1,560,507 | 1 | 56,383 | 1 |
| RADISYS CORP | 334111 | 325,232 | 4 | -17,552 | 5 |
| SUPER MICRO COMPUTER INC | 334111 | 420,393 | 3 | 19,339 | 3 |
| **Computer Networking & Related Equipment, Manufacturing** | | | | | |
| DIGI INTERNATIONAL INC | 334110 | 173,263 | 4 | 19,773 | 4 |
| ECHELON CORP | 334110 | 137,577 | 5 | -14,512 | 6 |
| EMULEX CORP | 334110 | 470,187 | 3 | 29,434 | 3 |
| INTERACTIVE INTELLIGENCE | 334110 | 109,901 | 6 | 17,456 | 5 |
| NETGEAR INC | 334110 | 727,787 | 1 | 45,954 | 2 |
| QLOGIC CORP | 334110 | 586,697 | 2 | 105,418 | 1 |
| **Computer Software, Accounting, Banking & Financial** | | | | | |
| ACI WORLDWIDE INC | 511201 | 366,218 | 1 | -9,131 | 7 |
| CONCUR TECHNOLOGIES INC | 511201 | 129,107 | 5 | 8,225 | 3 |
| CYBERSOURCE CORP | 511201 | 116,999 | 6 | 2,429 | 6 |
| FUNDTECH LTD | 511201 | 104,634 | 7 | 7,107 | 4 |
| ONLINE RESOURCES CORP | 511201 | 135,132 | 4 | 10,946 | 2 |
| S1 CORPORATION | 511201 | 204,925 | 3 | 19,495 | 1 |
| SS&C TECHNOLOGIES INC | 511201 | 248,168 | 2 | 6,575 | 5 |
| **Computer Software, Business Management & ERP** | | | | | |
| NETSUITE INC | 511207 | 108,541 | 3 | -23,906 | 3 |
| TIBCO SOFTWARE INC | 511207 | 577,386 | 1 | 51,888 | 1 |
| ULTIMATE SOFTWARE GROUP | 511207 | 151,464 | 2 | 33,129 | 2 |
| **Computer Software, Content & Document Management** | | | | | |
| INTERWOVEN INC | 511202 | 225,668 | 1 | 23,678 | 2 |
| VIGNETTE CORP | 511202 | 191,814 | 2 | 24,825 | 1 |
| **Computer Software, Data Base & File Management** | | | | | |
| EMBARCADERO TECHNOLOGIES INC | 511206 | | | | |
| **Computer Software, E-Commerce & Web Analytics** | | | | | |
| ART TECHNOLOGY GROUP INC | 511216 | 137,060 | 2 | -4,187 | 1 |
| OMNITURE INC | 511216 | 143,127 | 1 | -9,429 | 2 |
| **Computer Software, Educational & Training** | | | | | |
| SKILLSOFT PLC | 511218 | 225,172 | 1 | 24,153 | 1 |
| **Computer Software, Electronic Games & Entertainment** | | | | | |
| GLU MOBILE INC | 511208 | 66,867 | 2 | -3,591 | 2 |
| THQ INC | 511208 | 1,026,856 | 1 | 68,038 | 1 |
| **Computer Software, Healthcare & Biotechnology** | | | | | |
| ALLSCRIPTS HEALTHCARE SOLUTIONS INC | 511212 | 281,908 | 3 | 20,563 | 4 |
| AMICAS INC | 511212 | 49,888 | 5 | -862 | 5 |
| ECLIPSYS CORPORATION | 511212 | 477,533 | 1 | 41,141 | 1 |

| Company | Industry Code | 2007 Sales (U.S. $ thousands) | Sales Rank | 2007 Profits (U.S. $ thousands) | Profits Rank |
|---|---|---|---|---|---|
| QUALITY SYSTEMS INC | 511212 | 157,165 | 4 | 33,232 | 2 |
| TRIZETTO GROUP INC | 511212 | 451,791 | 2 | 28,230 | 3 |
| **Computer Software, Multimedia, Graphics & Publishing** | | | | | |
| CHYRON CORP | 511209 | 32,327 | 2 | 3,715 | 2 |
| REALNETWORKS INC | 511209 | 567,620 | 1 | 48,315 | 1 |
| **Computer Software, Network Management, System Testing, & Storage** | | | | | |
| ALTIRIS INC | 511214 | | | | |
| F5 NETWORKS INC | 511214 | 525,667 | 1 | 77,000 | 1 |
| NETSCOUT SYSTEMS INC | 511214 | 102,472 | 2 | 7,737 | 2 |
| **Computer Software, Operating Systems, Languages & Development Tools** | | | | | |
| PROGRESS SOFTWARE CORP | 511204 | 493,500 | 1 | 42,280 | 2 |
| RED HAT INC | 511204 | 400,624 | 2 | 59,907 | 1 |
| SERENA SOFTWARE INC | 511204 | 255,291 | 4 | -47,212 | 4 |
| WIND RIVER SYSTEMS INC | 511204 | 285,298 | 3 | 573 | 3 |
| **Computer Software, Product Lifecycle, Engineering, Design & CAD** | | | | | |
| ANSYS INC | 511215 | 385,340 | 1 | 82,392 | 1 |
| PITNEY BOWES MAPINFO | 511215 | | | | |
| **Computer Software, Sales & Customer Relationship Management** | | | | | |
| CSG SYSTEMS INTERNATIONAL | 511203 | 419,261 | 1 | 60,771 | 1 |
| ELOYALTY CORPORATION | 511203 | 102,105 | 5 | -18,738 | 6 |
| LIVEPERSON INC | 511203 | 52,228 | 6 | 5,821 | 4 |
| MICROSTRATEGY INC | 511203 | 335,373 | 2 | 58,468 | 2 |
| RIGHTNOW TECHNOLOGIES INC | 511203 | 112,077 | 4 | -18,641 | 5 |
| SPSS INC | 511203 | 291,000 | 3 | 33,725 | 3 |
| **Computer Software, Security & Anti-Virus** | | | | | |
| BLUE COAT SYSTEMS INC | 511211 | 177,700 | 3 | -7,198 | 2 |
| INTERNET SECURITY SYSTEMS | 511211 | | | | |
| RSA SECURITY INC | 511211 | | | | |
| SECURE COMPUTING CORP | 511211 | 237,905 | 1 | -35,056 | 4 |
| VASCO DATA SECURITY INTERNATIONAL INC | 511211 | 119,980 | 4 | 20,963 | 1 |
| WEBSENSE INC | 511211 | 211,665 | 2 | -14,565 | 3 |
| **Computer Software, Supply Chain & Logistics** | | | | | |
| ARIBA INC | 511217 | 301,667 | 3 | -14,977 | 3 |
| ASPEN TECHNOLOGY INC | 511217 | 341,029 | 1 | 45,518 | 1 |
| MANHATTAN ASSOCIATES INC | 511217 | 337,401 | 2 | 30,751 | 2 |
| **Computer Software, Telecom, Communications & VOIP** | | | | | |
| ARUBA NETWORKS INC | 511213 | 127,499 | 3 | -24,382 | 4 |
| INTEGRAL SYSTEMS INC | 511213 | 128,654 | 2 | 12,826 | 1 |
| OPENTV CORP | 511213 | 109,977 | 4 | -5,161 | 2 |
| SEACHANGE INTERNATIONAL | 511213 | 161,334 | 1 | -8,237 | 3 |
| TRAPEZE NETWORKS INC | 511213 | 24,500 | 5 | | |
| **Computer Storage Equipment & Misc. Parts, Manufacturing** | | | | | |
| IMATION CORP | 334112 | 2,062,000 | 1 | -50,400 | 2 |
| ISILON SYSTEMS INC | 334112 | 88,998 | 2 | -26,932 | 1 |
| **Computers & Software-Direct Selling** | | | | | |
| PC CONNECTION INC | 443120A | 1,785,379 | 1 | 22,995 | 1 |
| PC MALL INC | 443120A | 1,215,433 | 2 | 12,443 | 2 |

| Company | Industry Code | 2007 Sales (U.S. $ thousands) | Sales Rank | 2007 Profits (U.S. $ thousands) | Profits Rank |
|---|---|---|---|---|---|
| **Construction, Heavy & Civil Engineering** | | | | | |
| TDINDUSTRIES | 234000 | | | | |
| **Consulting--Computer, Telecommunications & Internet** | | | | | |
| HACKETT GROUP | 541512 | 177,008 | 2 | 8,995 | 2 |
| INTELLIGROUP INC | 541512 | 145,066 | 3 | 2,964 | 3 |
| PERFICIENT INC | 541512 | 218,148 | 1 | 16,230 | 1 |
| **Consulting-Human Resources** | | | | | |
| HEIDRICK & STRUGGLES INTERNATIONAL INC | 541612 | 648,266 | 1 | 56,463 | 1 |
| **Consulting--Information Systems & Applications Research** | | | | | |
| EPAM SYSTEMS | 541512A | | | | |
| FORRESTER RESEARCH INC | 541512A | 212,056 | 1 | 18,943 | 1 |
| SENTO | 541512A | | | | |
| **Consulting--Management & Business** | | | | | |
| CORPORATE EXECUTIVE BOARD COMPANY | 541611 | 532,716 | | 80,587 | |
| HURON CONSULTING GROUP | 541611 | 504,292 | | 41,901 | |
| **Consulting--Marketing** | | | | | |
| GALLUP ORGANIZATION | 541613 | 250,000 | 1 | | |
| **Consulting--Scientific & Technical** | | | | | |
| AMERESCO | 541690 | | | | |
| ENERNOC INC | 541690 | 60,838 | 1 | -23,582 | 1 |
| RECYCLED ENERGY DEVELOPMENT | 541690 | | | | |
| **Dairy Products, Manufacturing** | | | | | |
| DANNON COMPANY INC | 311500 | 203,100 | 2 | | |
| GREAT LAKES CHEESE CO INC | 311500 | 1,780,000 | 1 | | |
| WHITEWAVE FOODS CO | 311500 | 80,000 | 3 | | |
| **Data Processing Services** | | | | | |
| INVESTMENT TECHNOLOGY GROUP INC (ITG) | 514210 | 730,999 | 1 | 111,107 | 1 |
| TRANSCEND SERVICES INC | 514210 | 42,454 | 2 | 11,479 | 2 |
| **Diagnostic Services and Substances Manufacturing** | | | | | |
| AFFYMETRIX INC | 325413 | 371,320 | 2 | 12,593 | 4 |
| BIOSITE INC | 325413 | | | | |
| CALIPER LIFE SCIENCES | 325413 | 140,707 | 4 | -24,080 | 10 |
| CEPHEID | 325413 | 129,473 | 6 | -21,423 | 8 |
| EPIX PHARMACEUTICALS INC | 325413 | 14,960 | 13 | -62,789 | 12 |
| E-Z-EM INC | 325413 | 137,840 | 5 | 8,543 | 6 |
| GENOMIC HEALTH INC | 325413 | 64,027 | 10 | -27,292 | 11 |
| GEN-PROBE INC | 325413 | 403,014 | 1 | 86,140 | 1 |
| LUMINEX CORPORATION | 325413 | 75,010 | 9 | -2,711 | 7 |
| MERIDIAN BIOSCIENCE INC | 325413 | 122,963 | 7 | 26,721 | 3 |
| NEOGEN CORPORATION | 325413 | 86,138 | 8 | 9,125 | 5 |
| SEQUENOM INC | 325413 | 41,002 | 11 | -21,983 | 9 |
| TECHNE CORP | 325413 | 223,482 | 3 | 85,111 | 2 |
| THIRD WAVE TECHNOLOGIES | 325413 | 31,100 | 12 | | |
| **Disease Management & Utilization Management** | | | | | |
| MATRIA HEALTHCARE INC | 524298 | 352,235 | 1 | 21,428 | 1 |
| **Drug Delivery Systems** | | | | | |
| ALKERMES INC | 325412A | 240,717 | 3 | 166,979 | 1 |

| Company | Industry Code | 2007 Sales (U.S. $ thousands) | Sales Rank | 2007 Profits (U.S. $ thousands) | Profits Rank |
|---|---|---|---|---|---|
| ALZA CORP | 325412A | 198,400 | 4 | | |
| BENTLEY PHARMACEUTICALS | 325412A | 124,687 | 5 | 2,685 | 3 |
| KV PHARMACEUTICAL CO | 325412A | 443,627 | 1 | 58,090 | 2 |
| NEKTAR THERAPEUTICS | 325412A | 273,027 | 2 | -32,761 | 4 |
| NOVEN PHARMACEUTICALS | 325412A | 83,161 | 6 | -45,376 | 5 |
| **Drug Stores-Online** | | | | | |
| DRUGSTORE.COM INC | 446110E | 445,723 | 1 | -11,511 | 1 |
| **Drugs (Pharmaceuticals), Discovery & Manufacturing** | | | | | |
| ALEXION PHARMACEUTICALS | 325412 | 72,041 | 25 | -92,290 | 29 |
| AMYLIN PHARMACEUTICALS | 325412 | 780,997 | 4 | -211,136 | 36 |
| APP PHARMACEUTICALS INC | 325412 | 647,374 | 5 | 34,358 | 9 |
| AVI BIOPHARMA INC | 325412 | 10,985 | 37 | -27,168 | 20 |
| BIOMARIN PHARMACEUTICAL | 325412 | 121,581 | 19 | -15,803 | 17 |
| CAMBREX CORP | 325412 | 252,574 | 12 | 209,248 | 3 |
| CELGENE CORP | 325412 | 1,405,820 | 1 | 226,433 | 2 |
| CELL GENESYS INC | 325412 | 1,380 | 39 | -99,274 | 30 |
| CELL THERAPEUTICS INC | 325412 | 127 | 40 | -138,108 | 32 |
| COLLAGENEX PHARMACEUTICALS INC | 325412 | 63,586 | 27 | -8,794 | 13 |
| CUBIST PHARMACEUTICALS | 325412 | 294,620 | 10 | 48,147 | 7 |
| CV THERAPEUTICS INC | 325412 | 82,823 | 23 | -181,006 | 35 |
| DYAX CORP | 325412 | 26,096 | 34 | -56,309 | 26 |
| ENDO PHARMACEUTICALS HOLDINGS INC | 325412 | 1,085,608 | 3 | 227,440 | 1 |
| EXELIXIS INC | 325412 | 113,470 | 20 | -86,381 | 28 |
| GERON CORPORATION | 325412 | 7,622 | 38 | -36,697 | 23 |
| HUMAN GENOME SCIENCES | 325412 | 41,851 | 30 | -262,448 | 37 |
| INSPIRE PHARMACEUTICALS | 325412 | 48,665 | 29 | -63,740 | 27 |
| JAZZ PHARMACEUTICALS | 325412 | 65,303 | 26 | -138,778 | 33 |
| MAXYGEN INC | 325412 | 23,157 | 35 | -49,315 | 25 |
| MEDAREX INC | 325412 | 56,258 | 28 | -27,055 | 19 |
| MEDICINES CO | 325412 | 257,534 | 11 | -18,272 | 18 |
| MEDICIS PHARMACEUTICAL | 325412 | 464,651 | 7 | 75,051 | 5 |
| MILLENNIUM PHARMACEUTICALS INC | 325412 | 527,525 | 6 | 14,909 | 11 |
| MYRIAD GENETICS INC | 325412 | 157,126 | 17 | -34,962 | 22 |
| OSCIENT PHARMACEUTICALS | 325412 | 79,969 | 24 | -29,853 | 21 |
| REGENERON PHARMACEUTICALS INC | 325412 | 125,024 | 18 | -105,600 | 31 |
| SALIX PHARMACEUTICALS | 325412 | 235,792 | 13 | 8,225 | 12 |
| SCICLONE PHARMACEUTICALS | 325412 | 27,058 | 33 | -9,948 | 14 |
| SCIELE PHARMA INC | 325412 | 382,255 | 9 | 45,407 | 8 |
| SCIOS INC | 325412 | 98,600 | 21 | | |
| SEATTLE GENETICS | 325412 | 22,420 | 36 | -48,932 | 24 |
| SEPRACOR INC | 325412 | 1,225,230 | 2 | 58,333 | 6 |
| STIEFEL LABORATORIES INC | 325412 | 444,900 | 8 | | |
| UNITED THERAPEUTICS CORP | 325412 | 210,943 | 14 | 19,859 | 10 |
| VERTEX PHARMACEUTICALS | 325412 | 199,012 | 16 | -391,279 | 38 |
| VIROPHARMA INC | 325412 | 203,770 | 15 | 95,353 | 4 |
| XOMA LTD | 325412 | 84,252 | 22 | -12,326 | 15 |
| ZILA INC | 325412 | 28,801 | 32 | -13,164 | 16 |

| Company | Industry Code | 2007 Sales (U.S. $ thousands) | Sales Rank | 2007 Profits (U.S. $ thousands) | Profits Rank |
|---|---|---|---|---|---|
| ZYMOGENETICS INC | 325412 | 38,477 | 31 | -148,144 | 34 |
| **Drugs (Pharmaceuticals), Generic Manufacturing** | | | | | |
| CARACO PHARMACEUTICAL LABORATORIES | 325416 | 117,027 | 2 | 26,858 | 2 |
| HI-TECH PHARMACAL CO INC | 325416 | 58,898 | 3 | -2,036 | 3 |
| PAR PHARMACEUTICAL COMPANIES INC | 325416 | 769,666 | 1 | 49,898 | 1 |
| **Dry Pasta Manufacturing** | | | | | |
| AMERICAN ITALIAN PASTA CO | 311823 | 398,122 | 1 | 5,348 | 1 |
| **Electronic Parts & Equipment, Distribution** | | | | | |
| BRIGHTSTAR CORPORATION | 421690 | 3,660,000 | 1 | | |
| **Employee Benefit Plans** | | | | | |
| CATALYST HEALTH SOLUTIONS | 525120 | 1,857,697 | 1 | 39,268 | 1 |
| **Engineering & Facilities Support Services** | | | | | |
| ENGLOBAL CORP | 541330 | 363,227 | 2 | 12,464 | 2 |
| KIMLEY-HORN AND ASSOCIATES INC | 541330 | | | | |
| SHARED TECHNOLOGIES | 541330 | | | | |
| VSE CORP | 541330 | 653,164 | 1 | 14,102 | 1 |
| **Equipment Rental** | | | | | |
| UNIVERSAL HOSPITAL SERVICES INC | 532400 | 263,976 | 1 | -63,570 | 1 |
| **Fitness Centers/Health Clubs** | | | | | |
| CURVES INTERNATIONAL INC | 713940 | | | | |
| **Food Products, Manufacturing** | | | | | |
| HANOVER FOODS CORP | 311000 | 290,300 | 1 | | |
| **Food Service Contractors** | | | | | |
| CENTERPLATE | 722310 | 740,700 | 1 | -1,900 | 1 |
| **Food Service, Snacks & Nonalcoholic Beverage Bars** | | | | | |
| TULLY'S COFFEE CORP | 722213 | 69,000 | 1 | | |
| **Freight Forwarding & Support Services** | | | | | |
| FEDEX SUPPLY CHAIN SERVICES INC | 488510 | 98,600 | 1 | | |
| **Frozen Food Manufacturing** | | | | | |
| MICHELINAS INC | 311410 | 66,200 | 1 | | |
| **Fruit & Tree Nut Farming** | | | | | |
| DIAMOND FOODS INC | 111300 | 522,585 | 1 | 8,433 | 1 |
| **Fuel Cells Manufacturing** | | | | | |
| AROTECH CORPORATION | 333298 | 57,719 | 1 | -3,056 | 1 |
| FUELCELL ENERGY INC | 333298 | 48,234 | 2 | -68,674 | 4 |
| MEDIS TECHNOLOGIES | 333298 | 400 | 4 | -38,200 | 2 |
| PLUG POWER INC | 333298 | 16,271 | 3 | -60,571 | 3 |
| **Grocery Stores/Supermarkets** | | | | | |
| ARDEN GROUP INC | 445110 | 485,939 | 2 | 29,207 | 1 |
| ASSOCIATED WHOLESALE GROCERS INC | 445110 | 5,700,000 | 1 | | |
| FRESH BRANDS INC | 445110 | 260,100 | 4 | | |
| NUGGET MARKET | 445110 | | | | |
| SPROUTS FARMERS MARKET | 445110 | 300,000 | 3 | | |
| **Grocery Stores/Supermarkets-Online** | | | | | |
| FRESHDIRECT LLC | 445110E | 200,000 | 1 | | |
| PEAPOD LLC | 445110E | | | | |
| **Home Health Care** | | | | | |
| CONTINUCARE CORP | 621610 | 217,146 | 1 | 6,303 | 1 |

| Company | Industry Code | 2007 Sales (U.S. $ thousands) | Sales Rank | 2007 Profits (U.S. $ thousands) | Profits Rank |
|---|---|---|---|---|---|
| **Ice-Manufacturing** | | | | | |
| REDDY ICE HOLDINGS INC | 312113 | 339,038 | 1 | 10,343 | 1 |
| **Instrument Manufacturing, including Measurement, Control, Test & Navigational** | | | | | |
| AMERICAN SCIENCE & ENGINEERING INC | 334500 | 153,186 | 3 | 24,610 | 2 |
| ILLUMINA INC | 334500 | 366,799 | 2 | -278,359 | 4 |
| MTS SYSTEMS | 334500 | 410,091 | 1 | 41,996 | 1 |
| NANOMETRICS INC | 334500 | 146,290 | 4 | -4,008 | 3 |
| **Insurance Intermediary-Online** | | | | | |
| EHEALTH INC | 524210A | 87,791 | 1 | 31,595 | 1 |
| **Insurance--Health, HMO's & PPO's** | | | | | |
| BLUE CARE NETWORK OF MICHIGAN | 524114 | 2,151,857 | 3 | 49,847 | 2 |
| HARVARD PILGRIM HEALTH CARE INC | 524114 | 2,498,310 | 1 | 45,638 | 3 |
| HEALTH INSURANCE PLAN OF GREATER NEW YORK | 524114 | | | | |
| METROPOLITAN HEALTH NETWORKS | 524114 | 277,577 | 4 | 5,914 | 4 |
| MOLINA HEALTHCARE INC | 524114 | 2,492,454 | 2 | 58,330 | 1 |
| **Insurance--Life** | | | | | |
| AMERICAN FIDELITY ASSURANCE COMPANY | 524113 | 752,000 | 6 | | |
| FBL FINANCIAL GROUP | 524113 | 914,599 | 5 | 86,339 | 4 |
| GREAT AMERICAN FINANCIAL RESOURCES INC | 524113 | | | | |
| INDEPENDENCE HOLDING CO | 524113 | 402,322 | 7 | -2,328 | 6 |
| JACKSON NATIONAL LIFE INSURANCE COMPANY | 524113 | 4,110,144 | 1 | 619,279 | 1 |
| PHOENIX COMPANIES | 524113 | 2,572,800 | 4 | 123,900 | 3 |
| PROTECTIVE LIFE CORP | 524113 | 3,051,700 | 2 | 289,566 | 2 |
| UNIVERSAL AMERICAN CORP | 524113 | 3,034,623 | 3 | 84,072 | 5 |
| **Insurance--Property & Casualty** | | | | | |
| ALLEGHANY CORP | 524126 | 1,432,041 | 5 | 305,277 | 3 |
| COMMERCE GROUP INC | 524126 | 1,982,447 | 2 | 190,903 | 5 |
| CRUM & FORSTER HOLDINGS | 524126 | 1,563,647 | 3 | 293,182 | 4 |
| HCC INSURANCE HOLDINGS | 524126 | 2,388,373 | 1 | 395,429 | 1 |
| HORACE MANN EDUCATORS CORPORATION | 524126 | 887,005 | 7 | 82,788 | 8 |
| PHILADELPHIA CONSOLIDATED HOLDING CORP | 524126 | 1,529,594 | 4 | 326,813 | 2 |
| PMA CAPITAL CORPORATION | 524126 | 455,777 | 9 | -42,528 | 9 |
| PROASSURANCE CORP | 524126 | 706,068 | 8 | 168,186 | 6 |
| STATE AUTO FINANCIAL CORP | 524126 | 1,011,600 | 6 | 119,100 | 7 |
| **Insurance--Reinsurance** | | | | | |
| ODYSSEY RE HOLDINGS CORP | 524130 | 2,989,095 | 3 | 595,575 | 1 |
| REINSURANCE GROUP OF AMERICA INC | 524130 | 5,718,400 | 1 | 293,800 | 3 |
| TRANSATLANTIC HOLDINGS INC | 524130 | 4,381,830 | 2 | 487,141 | 2 |
| **Insurance--Supplemental Health** | | | | | |
| DELPHI FINANCIAL GROUP INC | 524114A | 1,570,619 | 1 | 164,512 | 1 |
| VISION SERVICE PLAN | 524114A | | | | |
| **Internet Access Provider** | | | | | |
| CLEARWIRE CORP | 514191 | 151,440 | 2 | -727,466 | 3 |
| TERREMARK WORLDWIDE INC | 514191 | 100,948 | 3 | -14,952 | 2 |

| Company | Industry Code | 2007 Sales (U.S. $ thousands) | Sales Rank | 2007 Profits (U.S. $ thousands) | Profits Rank |
|---|---|---|---|---|---|
| UNITED ONLINE INC | 514191 | 513,503 | 1 | 57,777 | 1 |
| **Internet Application Service Hosts & Co-location Providers** | | | | | |
| AKAMAI TECHNOLOGIES INC | 514191A | 636,406 | 1 | 100,967 | 1 |
| DIGITAL RIVER INC | 514191A | 349,275 | 4 | 70,814 | 2 |
| J2 GLOBAL COMMUNICATIONS | 514191A | 220,697 | 5 | 68,461 | 3 |
| NAVISITE INC | 514191A | 125,860 | 6 | -25,910 | 7 |
| NIC INC | 514191A | 85,755 | 7 | 11,955 | 6 |
| PREMIERE GLOBAL SERVICES | 514191A | 559,706 | 2 | 33,355 | 4 |
| RACKSPACE HOSTING INC | 514191A | 495,480 | 3 | 17,410 | 5 |
| **Investment Banking** | | | | | |
| EVERCORE PARTNERS INC | 523110 | 321,599 | 2 | -34,495 | 2 |
| HOULIHAN LOKEY | 523110 | | | | |
| MOELIS & COMPANY | 523110 | | | | |
| ROBERT W BAIRD & CO INC | 523110 | 729,000 | 1 | | |
| THOMAS WEISEL PARTNERS GROUP INC | 523110 | 289,049 | 3 | 20 | 1 |
| **Jewelry Stores-Online** | | | | | |
| BLUE NILE INC | 448310E | 319,264 | 1 | 17,459 | 1 |
| **Laboratories & Diagnostic Services--Medical** | | | | | |
| ALLIANCE IMAGING INC | 621511 | 444,919 | 1 | 16,232 | 1 |
| BIO REFERENCE LABORATORIES INC | 621511 | 250,431 | 3 | 13,957 | 2 |
| CRYOLIFE INC | 621511 | 94,763 | 4 | 7,201 | 3 |
| MEDTOX SCIENTIFIC INC | 621511 | 80,285 | 5 | 6,690 | 4 |
| RADNET INC | 621511 | 425,470 | 2 | -18,131 | 5 |
| **Magazines, Publishing** | | | | | |
| MARTHA STEWART LIVING OMNIMEDIA INC | 511120 | 327,890 | 1 | 10,289 | 1 |
| **Market Research** | | | | | |
| NETRATINGS INC | 541910 | | | | |
| **Medical/Dental/Surgical Equipment & Supplies, Distribution** | | | | | |
| CHINDEX INTERNATIONAL INC | 421450 | 105,921 | 1 | 2,982 | 1 |
| NYER MEDICAL GROUP INC | 421450 | 64,631 | 2 | 86 | 2 |
| **Medical/Dental/Surgical Equipment & Supplies, Manufacturing** | | | | | |
| ABAXIS INC | 339113 | 86,221 | 32 | 10,073 | 20 |
| ALIGN TECHNOLOGY INC | 339113 | 284,332 | 13 | 35,724 | 5 |
| AMERICAN MEDICAL SYSTEMS HOLDINGS INC | 339113 | 463,928 | 5 | 12,900 | 18 |
| ANALOGIC CORP | 339113 | 340,782 | 9 | 15,380 | 14 |
| ASPECT MEDICAL SYSTEMS | 339113 | 97,324 | 29 | 2,256 | 34 |
| ATRION CORPORATION | 339113 | 88,540 | 31 | 14,006 | 15 |
| ATS MEDICAL INC | 339113 | 49,587 | 42 | -23,008 | 41 |
| CANDELA CORP | 339113 | 148,557 | 23 | 6,256 | 29 |
| CANTEL MEDICAL CORP | 339113 | 219,044 | 17 | 8,446 | 24 |
| CHOLESTECH CORP | 339113 | 69,500 | 36 | 9,400 | 22 |
| COHERENT INC | 339113 | 601,153 | 2 | 15,951 | 12 |
| DATASCOPE CORP | 339113 | 378,800 | 8 | 17,465 | 10 |
| DJO INCORPORATED | 339113 | 492,134 | 4 | -82,422 | 42 |
| EXACTECH INC | 339113 | 124,209 | 24 | 8,483 | 23 |
| EXCEL TECHNOLOGY INC | 339113 | 160,023 | 22 | 17,732 | 9 |
| HAEMONETICS CORPORATION | 339113 | 449,607 | 6 | 49,109 | 3 |

| Company | Industry Code | 2007 Sales (U.S. $ thousands) | Sales Rank | 2007 Profits (U.S. $ thousands) | Profits Rank |
|---|---|---|---|---|---|
| I-FLOW CORPORATION | 339113 | 116,474 | 28 | 41,228 | 4 |
| IMMUCOR INC | 339113 | 223,678 | 16 | 60,068 | 2 |
| INAMED CORP | 339113 | | | | |
| INTEGRA LIFESCIENCES HOLDINGS CORP | 339113 | 550,459 | 3 | 33,471 | 7 |
| IRIDEX CORP | 339113 | 55,532 | 41 | -22,272 | 40 |
| IRIS INTERNATIONAL INC | 339113 | 84,306 | 33 | 7,549 | 26 |
| LIFECORE BIOMEDICAL INC | 339113 | 69,629 | 35 | 7,719 | 25 |
| MEDICAL ACTION INDUSTRIES | 339113 | 217,328 | 18 | 12,969 | 17 |
| MENTOR CORP | 339113 | 301,974 | 11 | 290,614 | 1 |
| MERIT MEDICAL SYSTEMS INC | 339113 | 207,768 | 19 | 15,588 | 13 |
| MICROTEK MEDICAL HOLDINGS | 339113 | | | | |
| NATIONAL DENTEX CORP | 339113 | 170,361 | 21 | 6,626 | 28 |
| NATUS MEDICAL | 339113 | 118,374 | 26 | 9,780 | 21 |
| POLYMEDICA CORPORATION | 339113 | 675,487 | 1 | 33,672 | 6 |
| QUIDEL CORP | 339113 | 118,065 | 27 | 13,631 | 16 |
| SCHICK TECHNOLOGIES INC | 339113 | | | | |
| SONIC INNOVATIONS INC | 339113 | 119,062 | 25 | 717 | 36 |
| SPAN AMERICA MEDICAL SYSTEMS INC | 339113 | 60,544 | 39 | 2,874 | 33 |
| SPECTRANETICS CORP | 339113 | 82,874 | 34 | 7,229 | 27 |
| SRI/SURGICAL EXPRESS INC | 339113 | 94,201 | 30 | -3,193 | 38 |
| STAAR SURGICAL CO | 339113 | 59,363 | 40 | -15,999 | 39 |
| SYMMETRY MEDICAL INC | 339113 | 290,922 | 12 | -149 | 37 |
| SYNOVIS LIFE TECHNOLOGIES | 339113 | 67,874 | 37 | 3,810 | 31 |
| THERAGENICS CORP | 339113 | 62,210 | 38 | 5,635 | 30 |
| THORATEC CORPORATION | 339113 | 234,780 | 14 | 3,235 | 32 |
| TOMOTHERAPY INC | 339113 | 232,810 | 15 | 10,662 | 19 |
| VENTANA MEDICAL SYSTEMS | 339113 | | | | |
| VITAL SIGNS INC | 339113 | 205,257 | 20 | 19,159 | 8 |
| WRIGHT MEDICAL GROUP INC | 339113 | 386,850 | 7 | 961 | 35 |
| ZOLL MEDICAL CORP | 339113 | 309,451 | 10 | 16,662 | 11 |
| **Medicinals & Botanicals, Manufacturing** | | | | | |
| CHATTEM INC | 325411 | 423,378 | 1 | 59,690 | 1 |
| MARTEK BIOSCIENCES CORP | 325411 | 306,813 | 2 | 32,013 | 2 |
| SCHIFF NUTRITION INTERNATIONAL INC | 325411 | 172,656 | 3 | 12,436 | 3 |
| **Music Stores-Online** | | | | | |
| AUDIBLE INC | 451220E | 109,968 | 1 | 2,425 | 1 |
| **Nanotechnology-Biotech/Health** | | | | | |
| AMAG PHARMACEUTICALS INC | 541710B | 2,552 | 1 | -33,894 | 1 |
| **Nonmetallic Mineral, Rock & Aggregate Manufacturing** | | | | | |
| AMCOL INTERNATIONAL CORP | 327000 | 744,334 | 1 | 56,735 | 1 |
| **Oil & Natural Gas Exploration & Production** | | | | | |
| BERRY PETROLEUM CO | 211111 | 583,457 | 16 | 129,928 | 14 |
| CNX GAS CORPORATION | 211111 | 477,308 | 19 | 135,678 | 13 |
| DENBURY RESOURCES INC | 211111 | 971,950 | 11 | 253,147 | 7 |
| ENCORE ACQUISITION CO | 211111 | 754,945 | 14 | 17,155 | 19 |
| EOG RESOURCES INC | 211111 | 4,190,791 | 2 | 1,089,918 | 2 |
| EXCO RESOURCES INC | 211111 | 906,510 | 12 | 49,656 | 15 |

| Company | Industry Code | 2007 Sales (U.S. $ thousands) | Sales Rank | 2007 Profits (U.S. $ thousands) | Profits Rank |
|---|---|---|---|---|---|
| FOREST OIL CORPORATION | 211111 | 1,083,892 | 9 | 169,306 | 11 |
| MCMORAN EXPLORATION CO | 211111 | 481,167 | 18 | -59,734 | 21 |
| NEWFIELD EXPLORATION CO | 211111 | 1,783,000 | 5 | 450,000 | 5 |
| NOBLE ENERGY INC | 211111 | 3,272,030 | 3 | 943,870 | 3 |
| PETROLEUM DEVELOPMENT CORPORATION | 211111 | 305,235 | 20 | 33,209 | 17 |
| PIONEER NATURAL RESOURCES COMPANY | 211111 | 1,830,571 | 4 | 372,728 | 6 |
| PLAINS EXPLORATION AND PRODUCTION COMPANY | 211111 | 1,272,840 | 7 | 158,751 | 12 |
| PRIMEENERGY CORPORATION | 211111 | 146,455 | 21 | 7,590 | 20 |
| QUICKSILVER RESOURCES INC | 211111 | 561,258 | 17 | 479,378 | 4 |
| RANGE RESOURCES CORP | 211111 | 862,091 | 13 | 230,569 | 8 |
| SOUTHWESTERN ENERGY CO | 211111 | 1,255,131 | 8 | 221,174 | 9 |
| ST MARY LAND & EXPLORATION | 211111 | 990,094 | 10 | 189,712 | 10 |
| SWIFT ENERGY CO | 211111 | 654,121 | 15 | 21,287 | 18 |
| TARGA RESOURCES PARTNERS | 211111 | 1,661,500 | 6 | 40,300 | 16 |
| XTO ENERGY INC | 211111 | 5,513,000 | 1 | 1,691,000 | 1 |
| **Online Publishing, Services & Niche Portals** | | | | | |
| HEALTH GRADES INC | 514199 | 32,742 | 5 | 6,748 | 4 |
| IVILLAGE INC | 514199 | | | | |
| JUPITERMEDIA CORP | 514199 | 140,334 | 3 | -82,275 | 5 |
| KNOT INC | 514199 | 98,688 | 4 | 11,869 | 2 |
| REVOLUTION HEALTH GROUP | 514199 | 28,700 | 6 | | |
| SHUTTERFLY INC | 514199 | 186,727 | 2 | 10,095 | 3 |
| WEBMD HEALTH CORP | 514199 | 331,954 | 1 | 65,884 | 1 |
| **Other Petrochemical & Coal Products Manufacturing** | | | | | |
| EVERGREEN ENERGY INC | 324190 | 48,657 | 1 | -204,676 | 1 |
| **Other Retailers, Misc. Retailers** | | | | | |
| LESLIE'S POOLMART INC | 453990 | 468,900 | 1 | | |
| **Payment & Transaction Processing Services** | | | | | |
| ATHENAHEALTH INC | 522320 | 100,773 | 7 | -3,503 | 3 |
| CARDTRONICS INC | 522320 | 378,298 | 6 | -27,090 | 5 |
| COINSTAR INC | 522320 | 546,297 | 4 | -22,253 | 4 |
| COMDATA CORP | 522320 | 411,600 | 5 | | |
| EURONET WORLDWIDE INC | 522320 | 917,574 | 2 | 53,160 | 1 |
| HEARTLAND PAYMENT SYSTEMS INC | 522320 | 1,313,846 | 1 | 35,870 | 2 |
| VERIFONE HOLDINGS INC | 522320 | 902,892 | 3 | -34,016 | 6 |
| **Payment & Transaction Processing--Benefits Management** | | | | | |
| BIOSCRIP INC | 522320A | 1,197,732 | 1 | 3,317 | 1 |
| **Petroleum Bulk Stations & Terminals Distribution** | | | | | |
| GLOBAL PARTNERS LP | 422710 | 6,757,834 | 1 | 47,013 | 2 |
| NUSTAR ENERGY LP | 422710 | 1,475,014 | 2 | 150,298 | 1 |
| **Petroleum Products (except Bulk Stations/Terminals) Distribution & Pipelines** | | | | | |
| GENESIS ENERGY LP | 422720 | 1,199,653 | 4 | -13,550 | 4 |
| MAGELLAN MIDSTREAM PARTNERS LP | 422720 | 1,318,121 | 3 | 242,790 | 3 |
| ONEOK PARTNERS LP | 422720 | 5,831,558 | 2 | 407,747 | 1 |
| TEPPCO PARTNERS LP | 422720 | 9,658,060 | 1 | 279,180 | 2 |
| **Petroleum Refineries** | | | | | |
| FRONTIER OIL CORPORATION | 324110 | 5,188,740 | 1 | 499,125 | 1 |

| Company | Industry Code | 2007 Sales (U.S. $ thousands) | Sales Rank | 2007 Profits (U.S. $ thousands) | Profits Rank |
|---|---|---|---|---|---|
| HOLLY CORP | 324110 | 4,791,742 | 2 | 334,128 | 2 |
| **Pets/Pet Supplies Stores** | | | | | |
| PETMED EXPRESS INC | 453910 | 162,246 | 1 | 14,443 | 1 |
| **Physician Practice Management** | | | | | |
| INTEGRAMED AMERICA INC | 621111 | 151,998 | 1 | 3,257 | 1 |
| LOGISTICARE INC | 621111 | | | | |
| **Plastic Products, Manufacturing** | | | | | |
| POLYPORE INTERNATIONAL | 326100 | 537,100 | 1 | 500 | 1 |
| **Poultry Production** | | | | | |
| CAL-MAINE FOODS INC | 112300 | 598,128 | 1 | 36,656 | 1 |
| **Radio & Wireless Communication, Manufacturing** | | | | | |
| ALIEN TECHNOLOGY CORP | 334220 | | | | |
| GLOBECOMM SYSTEMS INC | 334220 | 150,745 | 3 | 8,326 | 4 |
| LORAL SPACE & COMMUNICATIONS LTD | 334220 | 882,454 | 1 | 29,659 | 2 |
| RADYNE CORPORATION | 334220 | 142,054 | 4 | 10,212 | 3 |
| SPECTRALINK CORP | 334220 | | | | |
| VIASAT INC | 334220 | 516,566 | 2 | 30,166 | 1 |
| **Rendering & Meat Byproduct Processing** | | | | | |
| DARLING INTERNATIONAL INC | 311613 | 645,313 | 1 | 45,533 | 1 |
| **Research & Development--Physical, Engineering & Life Sciences** | | | | | |
| ALBANY MOLECULAR RESEARCH | 541710 | 192,511 | 1 | 8,936 | 2 |
| CELERA CORPORATION | 541710 | 43,400 | 4 | -20,600 | 5 |
| ENCORIUM GROUP INC | 541710 | 36,802 | 5 | -2,751 | 4 |
| FUEL TECH INC | 541710 | 80,297 | 3 | 7,243 | 3 |
| SYMYX TECHNOLOGIES | 541710 | 125,072 | 2 | 18,784 | 1 |
| **Restaurants** | | | | | |
| INTERNATIONAL DAIRY QUEEN | 722110 | 476,000 | 1 | | |
| **RV Parks & Campgrounds** | | | | | |
| KAMPGROUNDS OF AMERICA | 721211 | 48,300 | 1 | | |
| **Search Engine Portals** | | | | | |
| MARCHEX INC | 514199B | 139,391 | 1 | -1,505 | 1 |
| **Seasonings, Flavorings & Dressings Manufacturing** | | | | | |
| M&F WORLDWIDE CORP | 311940 | 1,472,800 | 1 | -4,200 | 1 |
| NUTRASWEET COMPANY | 311940 | | | | |
| **Security, Detection & Intercom System Manufacturing** | | | | | |
| DEI HOLDINGS INC | 334290 | 401,140 | 1 | -139,968 | 2 |
| LOJACK CORP | 334290 | 222,749 | 2 | 21,405 | 1 |
| **Semiconductor Manufacturing Equipment & Services** | | | | | |
| AMTECH SYSTEMS INC | 333295 | 45,984 | 2 | 2,417 | 2 |
| ATMI INC | 333295 | 364,088 | 1 | 40,359 | 1 |
| **Semiconductors (Microchips)/Integrated Circuits/Components, Manufacturing** | | | | | |
| ATHEROS COMMUNICATIONS | 334413 | 416,960 | 1 | 39,980 | 1 |
| DSP GROUP INC | 334413 | 248,788 | 3 | -4,753 | 4 |
| INFINERA CORP | 334413 | 245,852 | 4 | -55,342 | 5 |
| OPTELECOM-NKF INC | 334413 | 42,503 | 5 | 1,281 | 3 |
| STANDARD MICROSYSTEMS | 334413 | 370,594 | 2 | 27,015 | 2 |

| Company | Industry Code | 2007 Sales (U.S. $ thousands) | Sales Rank | 2007 Profits (U.S. $ thousands) | Profits Rank |
|---|---|---|---|---|---|
| **Shoe Manufacturing-General** | | | | | |
| STEVEN MADDEN LTD | 316210 | 431,050 | 1 | 35,690 | 1 |
| **Shoes & Accessories Stores-Online** | | | | | |
| ZAPPOS.COM INC | 448210E | 528,000 | 1 | | |
| **Solar Cells, Photovoltaic Cells, Manufacturing** | | | | | |
| EMCORE CORP | 333298A | 169,606 | 2 | -58,722 | 5 |
| ENERGY CONVERSION DEVICES | 333298A | 113,567 | 3 | -25,231 | 4 |
| EVERGREEN SOLAR INC | 333298A | 69,866 | 4 | -16,602 | 3 |
| FIRST SOLAR LLC | 333298A | 503,976 | 1 | 158,354 | 1 |
| HELIOVOLT CORP | 333298A | | | | |
| SOLAR RESERVE | 333298A | | | | |
| SOLFOCUS INC | 333298A | | | | |
| SPIRE CORPORATION | 333298A | 38,423 | 5 | -1,686 | 2 |
| **Sporting Goods Stores** | | | | | |
| SPORTSMAN'S GUIDE INC | 451110 | | | | |
| **Sporting Goods Stores-Online** | | | | | |
| GOLFSMITH INTERNATIONAL HOLDINGS INC | 451110E | 388,157 | 1 | -40,820 | 1 |
| **Stock Brokerage** | | | | | |
| INTERACTIVE BROKERS GROUP | 523120 | 2,023,400 | 1 | 300,500 | 1 |
| KNIGHT CAPITAL GROUP INC | 523120 | 896,749 | 2 | 122,240 | 2 |
| **Stocks, Bonds & Commodities Exchanges** | | | | | |
| CME GROUP | 523210 | 1,756,100 | 2 | 658,500 | 1 |
| INTERCONTINENTALEXCHANGE INC (ICE) | 523210 | 574,293 | 4 | 240,612 | 3 |
| NASDAQ OMX | 523210 | 2,436,592 | 1 | 518,401 | 2 |
| NYMEX HOLDINGS (NEW YORK MERCANTILE EXCHANGE) | 523210 | 673,604 | 3 | 224,039 | 4 |
| **Superconducting Materials & Other Wire** | | | | | |
| AMERICAN SUPERCONDUCTOR | 335929 | 52,183 | 1 | -36,675 | 1 |
| **Telecommunications & Internet Services-Specialty** | | | | | |
| ACME PACKET INC | 513300D | 113,052 | 4 | 19,561 | 2 |
| AMERICAN TOWER CORP | 513300D | 1,456,594 | 1 | 56,316 | 1 |
| CROWN CASTLE INTERNATIONAL CORP | 513300D | 1,385,486 | 2 | -222,813 | 4 |
| LCC INTERNATIONAL INC | 513300D | 145,723 | 3 | -30,767 | 3 |
| TELIRIS | 513300D | | | | |
| WEBEX COMMUNICATIONS INC | 513300D | | | | |
| **Telecommunications Equipment Manufacturing** | | | | | |
| ANAREN INC | 334210 | 128,987 | 10 | 15,350 | 4 |
| APPLIED SIGNAL TECHNOLOGY | 334210 | 170,375 | 7 | 6,812 | 5 |
| AVANEX CORPORATION | 334210 | 212,755 | 6 | -30,605 | 11 |
| C-COR INC | 334210 | 277,329 | 4 | 28,098 | 2 |
| CHANNELL COMMERCIAL CORP | 334210 | 133,163 | 9 | 273 | 7 |
| CIENA CORP | 334210 | 779,769 | 1 | 82,788 | 1 |
| HARMONIC INC | 334210 | 311,204 | 3 | 23,421 | 3 |
| HARRIS STRATEX NETWORKS | 334210 | 507,900 | 2 | -17,900 | 10 |
| OPNEXT INC | 334210 | 222,859 | 5 | 696 | 6 |
| SYCAMORE NETWORKS INC | 334210 | 156,048 | 8 | -13,205 | 9 |
| VERAZ NETWORKS INC | 334210 | 125,754 | 11 | -2,604 | 8 |

| Company | Industry Code | 2007 Sales (U.S. $ thousands) | Sales Rank | 2007 Profits (U.S. $ thousands) | Profits Rank |
|---|---|---|---|---|---|
| **Telecommunications-Private Data Networks & Network Services** | | | | | |
| EQUINIX INC | 513390C | 419,442 | 2 | -5,188 | 2 |
| INTERNAP NETWORK SERVICES | 513390C | 234,090 | 3 | -5,555 | 3 |
| SAVVIS INC | 513390C | 793,833 | 1 | 250,591 | 1 |
| **Telephone Service-Cellular, U.S. & Non-U.S.** | | | | | |
| GOAMERICA INC | 513322 | 18,625 | 3 | -3,750 | 2 |
| LEAP WIRELESS INTERNATIONAL INC | 513322 | 1,630,803 | 2 | -75,927 | 3 |
| METROPCS COMMUNICATIONS | 513322 | 2,235,734 | 1 | 100,403 | 1 |
| **Telephone Service--Local Exchange Carrier & Diversified** | | | | | |
| ALASKA COMMUNICATIONS SYSTEMS GROUP | 513300A | 385,785 | 3 | 144,136 | 1 |
| GENERAL COMMUNICATION INC (GCI) | 513300A | 520,311 | 1 | 13,504 | 4 |
| HICKORY TECH CORPORATION | 513300A | 156,649 | 4 | 8,611 | 5 |
| NTELOS HOLDING CORP | 513300A | 500,394 | 2 | 32,453 | 2 |
| SHENANDOAH TELECOMMUNICATIONS CO | 513300A | 141,183 | 5 | 18,803 | 3 |
| **Telephone Service--Long Distance** | | | | | |
| IBASIS INC | 513300B | 938,558 | 1 | 16,123 | 1 |
| **TV/Video/Theatrical, Production** | | | | | |
| DREAMWORKS ANIMATION SKG | 512110 | 767,178 | 1 | 218,364 | 1 |
| LUCASFILM LTD | 512110 | | | | |
| **Utilities-Electric** | | | | | |
| BLACK HILLS CORP | 221000A | 695,914 | 7 | 98,772 | 4 |
| CALPINE CORPORATION | 221000A | 7,970,000 | 1 | 2,693,000 | 1 |
| CENTRAL VERMONT PUBLIC SERVICE CORPORATION | 221000A | 329,107 | 8 | 15,804 | 8 |
| DPL INC | 221000A | 1,515,700 | 3 | 221,800 | 2 |
| GREEN MOUNTAIN POWER | 221000A | 247,380 | 10 | 10,142 | 9 |
| IDACORP INC | 221000A | 879,394 | 6 | 82,339 | 5 |
| ORMAT TECHNOLOGIES | 221000A | 295,919 | 9 | 27,376 | 7 |
| SACRAMENTO MUNICIPAL UTILITY DISTRICT | 221000A | 1,312,083 | 4 | | |
| TAMPA ELECTRIC COMPANY | 221000A | | | | |
| UIL HOLDINGS CORPORATION | 221000A | 981,999 | 5 | 44,697 | 6 |
| WESTAR ENERGY | 221000A | 1,726,834 | 2 | 167,384 | 3 |
| **Utilities-Electric & Gas** | | | | | |
| ATLANTIC CITY ELECTRIC CO | 221000 | 1,542,500 | 3 | 60,100 | 3 |
| AVISTA CORPORATION | 221000 | 1,417,757 | 4 | 38,475 | 6 |
| DYNEGY INC | 221000 | 3,103,000 | 1 | 264,000 | 1 |
| NORTHWESTERN CORP | 221000 | 1,200,060 | 6 | 53,191 | 5 |
| UNISOURCE ENERGY CORP | 221000 | 1,381,373 | 5 | 58,373 | 4 |
| WGL HOLDINGS INC | 221000 | 2,646,008 | 2 | 107,900 | 2 |
| **Utilities-Gas** | | | | | |
| EQUITABLE RESOURCES INC | 221000B | 1,361,406 | 5 | 257,483 | 2 |
| LACLEDE GROUP INC | 221000B | 1,855,861 | 3 | 49,771 | 5 |
| NATIONAL FUEL GAS CO | 221000B | 2,039,566 | 2 | 337,455 | 1 |
| PIEDMONT NATURAL GAS CO | 221000B | 1,711,292 | 4 | 104,387 | 4 |
| SOUTHERN UNION COMPANY | 221000B | 2,616,665 | 1 | 228,711 | 3 |
| **Veterinary Products Manufacturing** | | | | | |
| HESKA CORP | 325412B | 82,335 | 1 | 34,808 | 1 |

| Company | Industry Code | 2007 Sales (U.S. $ thousands) | Sales Rank | 2007 Profits (U.S. $ thousands) | Profits Rank |
|---|---|---|---|---|---|
| **Video Rental** | | | | | |
| NETFLIX INC | 532230 | 1,205,340 | 1 | 66,952 | 1 |
| **Wines & Spirits, Distribution** | | | | | |
| NATIONAL WINE & SPIRITS INC | 422820 | 725,000 | 2 | | |
| YOUNG'S MARKET COMPANY | 422820 | 2,100,000 | 1 | | |

## ALPHABETICAL INDEX

DATASCOPE CORP
DEI HOLDINGS INC
DELPHI FINANCIAL GROUP INC
DENBURY RESOURCES INC
DIALYSIS CORPORATION OF AMERICA
DIAMOND FOODS INC
DIGI INTERNATIONAL INC
DIGITAL RIVER INC
DJO INCORPORATED
DOUBLECLICK INC
DPL INC
DREAMWORKS ANIMATION SKG INC
DRUGSTORE.COM INC
DSP GROUP INC
DYAX CORP
DYNACQ HEALTHCARE INC
DYNEGY INC
ECHELON CORP
ECLIPSYS CORPORATION
ECOLLEGE.COM
EHEALTH INC
ELECTRONICS FOR IMAGING INC
ELOYALTY CORPORATION
EMBARCADERO TECHNOLOGIES INC
EMCORE CORP
EMS TECHNOLOGIES INC
EMULEX CORP
ENCORE ACQUISITION CO
ENCORIUM GROUP INC
ENDO PHARMACEUTICALS HOLDINGS INC
ENERGY CONVERSION DEVICES INC
ENERNOC INC
ENGLOBAL CORP
EOG RESOURCES INC
EPAM SYSTEMS
EPIX PHARMACEUTICALS INC
EQUINIX INC
EQUITABLE RESOURCES INC
EURONET WORLDWIDE INC
EVERCORE PARTNERS INC
EVERGREEN ENERGY INC
EVERGREEN SOLAR INC
EXACTECH INC
EXCEL TECHNOLOGY INC
EXCO RESOURCES INC
EXELIXIS INC
E-Z-EM INC
F5 NETWORKS INC
FARMER BROTHERS CO
FBL FINANCIAL GROUP
FEDEX SUPPLY CHAIN SERVICES INC
FIRST SOLAR LLC
FLIR SYSTEMS
FOREST OIL CORPORATION
FORRESTER RESEARCH INC
FRESH BRANDS INC
FRESHDIRECT LLC
FRONTIER OIL CORPORATION
FUEL TECH INC
FUELCELL ENERGY INC
FUNDTECH LTD
GALLUP ORGANIZATION (THE)
GENENCOR INTERNATIONAL INC
GENERAL COMMUNICATION INC (GCI)
GENESIS ENERGY LP
GENOMIC HEALTH INC
GEN-PROBE INC
GERBER SCIENTIFIC INC
GERON CORPORATION
GLOBAL PARTNERS LP
GLOBECOMM SYSTEMS INC
GLU MOBILE INC
GOAMERICA INC
GOLFSMITH INTERNATIONAL HOLDINGS INC
GREAT AMERICAN FINANCIAL RESOURCES INC
GREAT LAKES CHEESE COMPANY INC
GREEN MOUNTAIN COFFEE ROASTERS INC
GREEN MOUNTAIN POWER CORPORATION
GTC BIOTHERAPEUTICS INC
HACKETT GROUP (THE)
HAEMONETICS CORPORATION
HAHN AUTOMOTIVE WAREHOUSE INC
HANOVER FOODS CORPORATION
HANSEN NATURAL
HARMONIC INC
HARRIS STRATEX NETWORKS INC
HARVARD PILGRIM HEALTH CARE INC
HCC INSURANCE HOLDINGS INC
HEALTH GRADES INC
HEALTH INSURANCE PLAN OF GREATER NEW YORK
HEALTHSTREAM INC
HEALTHTRONICS INC
HEARTLAND PAYMENT SYSTEMS INC
HEARUSA INC
HEIDRICK & STRUGGLES INTERNATIONAL INC
HELIOVOLT CORP
HESKA CORP
HICKORY TECH CORPORATION
HI-TECH PHARMACAL CO INC
HOLLY CORP
HORACE MANN EDUCATORS CORPORATION
HOULIHAN LOKEY
HUMAN GENOME SCIENCES INC
HURON CONSULTING GROUP INC
IBASIS INC
ICO INC
IDACORP INC
I-FLOW CORPORATION
ILLUMINA INC
IMATION CORP
IMG WORLDWIDE INC
IMMUCOR INC
INAMED CORP
INDEPENDENCE HOLDING CO
INFINERA CORP
INSPIRE PHARMACEUTICALS INC
INTEGRA LIFESCIENCES HOLDINGS CORP
INTEGRAL SYSTEMS INC
INTEGRAMED AMERICA INC
INTELLIGROUP INC
INTERACTIVE BROKERS GROUP INC
INTERACTIVE INTELLIGENCE
INTERCONTINENTALEXCHANGE INC (ICE)
INTERMEC INC
INTERNAP NETWORK SERVICES CORP
INTERNATIONAL CREATIVE MANAGEMENT (ICM)
INTERNATIONAL DAIRY QUEEN
INTERNET SECURITY SYSTEMS INC
INTERSTATE BATTERY SYSTEM OF AMERICA
INTERWOVEN INC

INVESTMENT TECHNOLOGY GROUP INC (ITG)
IRIDEX CORP
IRIS INTERNATIONAL INC
ISILON SYSTEMS INC
ISONICS CORPORATION
IVILLAGE INC
J2 GLOBAL COMMUNICATIONS INC
JACKSON NATIONAL LIFE INSURANCE COMPANY
JAZZ PHARMACEUTICALS
JUPITERMEDIA CORP
KAMPGROUNDS OF AMERICA INC
KENDALL-JACKSON WINE ESTATES LTD
KIMLEY-HORN AND ASSOCIATES INC
KNIGHT CAPITAL GROUP INC
KNOT INC (THE)
KRONOS WORLDWIDE INC
KV PHARMACEUTICAL CO
LACLEDE GROUP INC (THE)
LCA-VISION INC
LCC INTERNATIONAL INC
LEAP WIRELESS INTERNATIONAL INC
LESLIE'S POOLMART INC
LIFECELL CORPORATION
LIFECORE BIOMEDICAL INC
LIVEPERSON INC
LOGISTICARE INC
LOJACK CORP
LORAL SPACE & COMMUNICATIONS LTD
LUCASFILM LTD
LUCOR INC
LUMINEX CORPORATION
M&F WORLDWIDE CORP
MAGELLAN MIDSTREAM PARTNERS LP
MALT-O-MEAL COMPANY
MANHATTAN ASSOCIATES INC
MARCHEX INC
MARTEK BIOSCIENCES CORP
MARTHA STEWART LIVING OMNIMEDIA INC
MARVEL ENTERTAINMENT INC
MATRIA HEALTHCARE INC
MAXYGEN INC
MCMORAN EXPLORATION CO
MEDAREX INC
MEDICAL ACTION INDUSTRIES INC
MEDICINES CO (THE)
MEDICIS PHARMACEUTICAL CORP
MEDIS TECHNOLOGIES
MEDTOX SCIENTIFIC INC
MENTOR CORP
MERIDIAN BIOSCIENCE INC
MERIT MEDICAL SYSTEMS INC
METROLOGIC INSTRUMENTS INC
METROPCS COMMUNICATIONS INC
METROPOLITAN HEALTH NETWORKS
MICHELINAS INC
MICROSTRATEGY INC
MICROTEK MEDICAL HOLDINGS INC
MIDAS INC
MILLENNIUM PHARMACEUTICALS INC
MOELIS & COMPANY
MOLINA HEALTHCARE INC
MOTORCAR PARTS OF AMERICA INC
MTS SYSTEMS
MYRIAD GENETICS INC
NANOMETRICS INC
NASDAQ OMX
NATIONAL BEVERAGE CORP
NATIONAL CINEMEDIA INC
NATIONAL DENTEX CORP
NATIONAL FUEL GAS CO
NATIONAL WINE & SPIRITS INC
NATUS MEDICAL
NAVISITE INC
NEKTAR THERAPEUTICS
NEOGEN CORPORATION
NETFLIX INC
NETGEAR INC
NETRATINGS INC
NETSCOUT SYSTEMS INC
NETSUITE INC
NEWFIELD EXPLORATION CO
NIC INC
NOBLE ENERGY INC
NORTHWESTERN CORPORATION
NOVAMED INC
NOVEN PHARMACEUTICALS
NTELOS HOLDING CORP
NUGGET MARKET
NUSTAR ENERGY LP
NUTRASWEET COMPANY (THE)
NYER MEDICAL GROUP INC
NYMEX HOLDINGS (NEW YORK MERCANTILE EXCHANGE)
ODYSSEY RE HOLDINGS CORP
OMNITURE INC
ONEOK PARTNERS LP
ONLINE RESOURCES CORP
OPENTV CORP
OPNEXT INC
OPTELECOM-NKF INC
ORMAT TECHNOLOGIES
OSCIENT PHARMACEUTICALS CORPORATION
PALM INC
PAR PHARMACEUTICAL COMPANIES INC
PC CONNECTION INC
PC MALL INC
PEAPOD LLC
PERFICIENT INC
PETMED EXPRESS INC
PETROLEUM DEVELOPMENT CORPORATION
PHILADELPHIA CONSOLIDATED HOLDING CORP
PHOENIX COMPANIES (THE)
PIEDMONT NATURAL GAS COMPANY INC
PIONEER NATURAL RESOURCES COMPANY
PITNEY BOWES MAPINFO
PLAINS EXPLORATION AND PRODUCTION COMPANY
PLUG POWER INC
PMA CAPITAL CORPORATION
POLYCOM INC
POLYMEDICA CORPORATION
POLYPORE INTERNATIONAL INC
PREMIERE GLOBAL SERVICES INC
PRIMEENERGY CORPORATION
PROASSURANCE CORP
PROGRESS SOFTWARE CORP
PROTECTIVE LIFE CORP
QLOGIC CORP
QUALITY SYSTEMS INC
QUICKSILVER RESOURCES INC
QUIDEL CORP

RACKSPACE HOSTING INC
RADISYS CORP
RADNET INC
RADYNE CORPORATION
RANGE RESOURCES CORP
REALNETWORKS INC
RECYCLED ENERGY DEVELOPMENT
RED HAT INC
REDDY ICE HOLDINGS INC
REGENERON PHARMACEUTICALS INC
REINSURANCE GROUP OF AMERICA INC
REVOLUTION HEALTH GROUP LLC
RIGHTNOW TECHNOLOGIES INC
ROBERT W BAIRD & CO INC
RSA SECURITY INC
S1 CORPORATION
SACRAMENTO MUNICIPAL UTILITY DISTRICT
SALIX PHARMACEUTICALS
SAVVIS INC
SCANSOURCE INC
SCHICK TECHNOLOGIES INC
SCHIFF NUTRITION INTERNATIONAL INC
SCICLONE PHARMACEUTICALS
SCIELE PHARMA INC
SCIOS INC
SCOULAR COMPANY (THE)
SEACHANGE INTERNATIONAL INC
SEATTLE GENETICS
SECURE COMPUTING CORP
SENTO
SEPRACOR INC
SEQUENOM INC
SERENA SOFTWARE INC
SHARED TECHNOLOGIES
SHENANDOAH TELECOMMUNICATIONS CO
SHUTTERFLY INC
SKILLSOFT PLC
SOLAR RESERVE
SOLFOCUS INC
SONIC INNOVATIONS INC
SONUS NETWORKS INC
SOUTHERN UNION COMPANY
SOUTHWESTERN ENERGY CO
SPAN AMERICA MEDICAL SYSTEMS INC
SPECTRALINK CORP
SPECTRANETICS CORP
SPIRE CORPORATION
SPORTSMAN'S GUIDE INC (THE)
SPROUTS FARMERS MARKET
SPSS INC
SRI/SURGICAL EXPRESS INC
SS&C TECHNOLOGIES INC
ST MARY LAND & EXPLORATION COMPANY
STAAR SURGICAL CO
STANDARD MICROSYSTEMS CORPORATION
STATE AUTO FINANCIAL CORP
STERLING AUTOBODY CENTERS
STEVEN MADDEN LTD
STIEFEL LABORATORIES INC
SUPER MICRO COMPUTER INC
SWIFT ENERGY CO
SYCAMORE NETWORKS INC
SYMMETRY MEDICAL INC
SYMYX TECHNOLOGIES
SYNAPTICS INC
SYNOVIS LIFE TECHNOLOGIES INC
TAMPA ELECTRIC COMPANY
TARGA RESOURCES PARTNERS LP
TDINDUSTRIES
TECHNE CORP
TELIRIS
TEPPCO PARTNERS LP
TERREMARK WORLDWIDE INC
THERAGENICS CORP
THIRD WAVE TECHNOLOGIES INC
THOMAS WEISEL PARTNERS GROUP INC
THORATEC CORPORATION
THQ INC
TIBCO SOFTWARE INC
TIVO INC
TOMOTHERAPY INC
TOOTSIE ROLL INDUSTRIES INC
TOPPS COMPANY INC (THE)
TRANSATLANTIC HOLDINGS INC
TRANSCEND SERVICES INC
TRAPEZE NETWORKS INC
TRIZETTO GROUP INC (THE)
TULLY'S COFFEE CORPORATION
UIL HOLDINGS CORPORATION
ULTIMATE SOFTWARE GROUP INC
UNDER ARMOUR INC
UNISOURCE ENERGY CORPORATION
UNITED ONLINE INC
UNITED THERAPEUTICS CORP
UNIVERSAL AMERICAN CORPORATION
UNIVERSAL HOSPITAL SERVICES INC
US PHYSICAL THERAPY INC
VALLEY NATIONAL GASES LLC
VALUECLICK INC
VASCO DATA SECURITY INTERNATIONAL INC
VENTANA MEDICAL SYSTEMS INC
VERAZ NETWORKS INC
VERIFONE HOLDINGS INC
VERTEX PHARMACEUTICALS INC
VIASAT INC
VIBRANT MEDIA INC
VIGNETTE CORP
VIROPHARMA INC
VISION SERVICE PLAN
VITAL SIGNS INC
VOLCOM INC
VSE CORP
WEBEX COMMUNICATIONS INC
WEBMD HEALTH CORP
WEBSENSE INC
WESTAR ENERGY
WGL HOLDINGS INC
WHITEWAVE FOODS COMPANY
WIND RIVER SYSTEMS INC
WRIGHT MEDICAL GROUP INC
XOMA LTD
XTO ENERGY INC
YOUNG'S MARKET COMPANY LLC
ZAPPOS.COM INC
ZIEBART INTERNATIONAL CORP
ZILA INC
ZOLL MEDICAL CORP
ZYMOGENETICS INC

## INDEX OF HEADQUARTERS LOCATION BY STATE

To help you locate members of THE MID-SIZE EMPLOYERS 500 geographically, the city and state of the headquarters of each company are in the following index.


**ALABAMA**
PROASSURANCE CORP; Birmingham
PROTECTIVE LIFE CORP; Birmingham

**ALASKA**
ALASKA COMMUNICATIONS SYSTEMS GROUP; Anchorage
GENERAL COMMUNICATION INC (GCI); Anchorage

**ARIZONA**
AMTECH SYSTEMS INC; Tempe
FIRST SOLAR LLC; Tempe
LESLIE'S POOLMART INC; Phoenix
MEDICIS PHARMACEUTICAL CORP; Scottsdale
RADYNE CORPORATION; Phoenix
SPROUTS FARMERS MARKET; Phoenix
UNISOURCE ENERGY CORPORATION; Tucson
VENTANA MEDICAL SYSTEMS INC; Tucson
ZILA INC; Phoenix

**CALIFORNIA**
ABAXIS INC; Union City
ACXIOM DIGITAL; Foster City
AFFYMETRIX INC; Santa Clara
AKQA INC; San Francisco
ALIEN TECHNOLOGY CORPORATION; Morgan Hill
ALIGN TECHNOLOGY INC; Santa Clara
ALLIANCE IMAGING INC; Anaheim
ALZA CORP; Mountain View
AMERICAN VANGUARD CORP; Newport Beach
AMYLIN PHARMACEUTICALS INC; San Diego
APPLIED SIGNAL TECHNOLOGY INC; Sunnyvale
ARDEN GROUP INC; Compton
ARIBA INC; Sunnyvale
ARUBA NETWORKS INC; Sunnyvale
ATHEROS COMMUNICATIONS INC; Santa Clara
AVANEX CORPORATION; Fremont
BERRY PETROLEUM CO; Bakersfield
BIOMARIN PHARMACEUTICAL INC; Novato
BIOSITE INC; San Diego
BLUE COAT SYSTEMS INC; Sunnyvale
CALIBER HOLDINGS CORP; Irvine
CALPINE CORPORATION; San Jose
CELERA CORPORATION; Alameda
CELL GENESYS INC; South San Francisco
CEPHEID; Sunnyvale
CHANNELL COMMERCIAL CORP; Temecula
CHOLESTECH CORP; Hayward
COHERENT INC; Santa Clara
COUPONS INC; Mountain View
CV THERAPEUTICS INC; Palo Alto
CYBERSOURCE CORP; Mountain View
DEI HOLDINGS INC; Vista
DIAMOND FOODS INC; Stockton
DJO INCORPORATED; Vista
DREAMWORKS ANIMATION SKG INC; Glendale
DSP GROUP INC; San Jose
ECHELON CORP; San Jose
EHEALTH INC; Mountain View
ELECTRONICS FOR IMAGING INC; Foster City
EMBARCADERO TECHNOLOGIES INC; San Francisco
EMULEX CORP; Costa Mesa
EQUINIX INC; Foster City
EXELIXIS INC; South San Francisco
FARMER BROTHERS CO; Torrance
GENOMIC HEALTH INC; Redwood City
GEN-PROBE INC; San Diego
GERON CORPORATION; Menlo Park
GLU MOBILE INC; San Mateo
HANSEN NATURAL; Corona
HARMONIC INC; Sunnyvale
HOULIHAN LOKEY; Los Angeles
I-FLOW CORPORATION; Lake Forest
ILLUMINA INC; San Diego
INAMED CORP; Santa Barbara
INFINERA CORP; Sunnyvale
INTERNATIONAL CREATIVE MANAGEMENT (ICM); Los Angeles
INTERWOVEN INC; San Jose
IRIDEX CORP; Mountain View
IRIS INTERNATIONAL INC; Chatsworth
J2 GLOBAL COMMUNICATIONS INC; Los Angeles
JAZZ PHARMACEUTICALS; Palo Alto
KENDALL-JACKSON WINE ESTATES LTD; Santa Rosa
LEAP WIRELESS INTERNATIONAL INC; San Diego
LUCASFILM LTD; San Francisco
MAXYGEN INC; Redwood City
MENTOR CORP; Santa Barbara
MOLINA HEALTHCARE INC; Long Beach
MOTORCAR PARTS OF AMERICA INC; Torrance
NANOMETRICS INC; Milpitas
NATUS MEDICAL; San Carlos
NEKTAR THERAPEUTICS; San Carlos
NETFLIX INC; Los Gatos
NETGEAR INC; Santa Clara
NETSUITE INC; San Mateo
NUGGET MARKET; Woodland
OPENTV CORP; San Francisco
PALM INC; Sunnyvale
PC MALL INC; Torrance
POLYCOM INC; Pleasanton
QLOGIC CORP; Aliso Viejo
QUALITY SYSTEMS INC; Irvine
QUIDEL CORP; San Diego
RADNET INC; Los Angeles
SACRAMENTO MUNICIPAL UTILITY DISTRICT; Sacramento
SCICLONE PHARMACEUTICALS; Foster City

SECURE COMPUTING CORP; San Jose
SEQUENOM INC; San Diego
SERENA SOFTWARE INC; Redwood City
SHUTTERFLY INC; Redwood City
SOLAR RESERVE; Santa Monica
SOLFOCUS INC; Mountain View
STAAR SURGICAL CO; Monrovia
SUPER MICRO COMPUTER INC; San Jose
SYMYX TECHNOLOGIES; Santa Clara
SYNAPTICS INC; Santa Clara
THOMAS WEISEL PARTNERS GROUP INC; San Francisco
THORATEC CORPORATION; Pleasanton
THQ INC; Aguora Hills
TIBCO SOFTWARE INC; Palo Alto
TIVO INC; Alviso
TRAPEZE NETWORKS INC; Pleasanton
TRIZETTO GROUP INC (THE); Newport Beach
UNITED ONLINE INC; Woodland Hills
VALUECLICK INC; Westlake Village
VERAZ NETWORKS INC; San Jose
VERIFONE HOLDINGS INC; San Jose
VIASAT INC; Carlsbad
VISION SERVICE PLAN; Rancho Cordova
VOLCOM INC; Costa Mesa
WEBEX COMMUNICATIONS INC; Santa Clara
WEBSENSE INC; San Diego
WIND RIVER SYSTEMS INC; Alameda
XOMA LTD; Berkeley
YOUNG'S MARKET COMPANY LLC; Orange

**COLORADO**
CSG SYSTEMS INTERNATIONAL INC; Englewood
ECOLLEGE.COM; Denver
EVERGREEN ENERGY INC; Denver
FOREST OIL CORPORATION; Denver
HEALTH GRADES INC; Golden
HESKA CORP; Loveland
ISONICS CORPORATION; Golden
NATIONAL CINEMEDIA INC; Centennial
SPECTRALINK CORP; Boulder
SPECTRANETICS CORP; Colorado Springs
ST MARY LAND & EXPLORATION COMPANY; Denver
WHITEWAVE FOODS COMPANY; Broomfield

**CONNECTICUT**
ALEXION PHARMACEUTICALS INC; Cheshire
ATMI INC; Danbury
FUELCELL ENERGY INC; Danbury
GERBER SCIENTIFIC INC; South Windsor
INDEPENDENCE HOLDING CO; Stamford
INTERACTIVE BROKERS GROUP INC; Greenwich
JUPITERMEDIA CORP; Darien
ODYSSEY RE HOLDINGS CORP; Stamford
PHOENIX COMPANIES (THE); Hartford
PRIMEENERGY CORPORATION; Stamford
SS&C TECHNOLOGIES INC; Windsor
UIL HOLDINGS CORPORATION; New Haven

**DISTRICT OF COLUMBIA**
BLACKBOARD INC; Washington
GALLUP ORGANIZATION (THE); Washington
REVOLUTION HEALTH GROUP LLC; Washington
WGL HOLDINGS INC; Washington

**DELEWARE**
DELPHI FINANCIAL GROUP INC; Wilmington

**FLORIDA**
ARIZONA CHEMICAL COMPANY; Jacksonville
BRIGHTSTAR CORPORATION; Miami
CONTINUCARE CORP; Miami
EXACTECH INC; Gainesville
HACKETT GROUP (THE); Miami
HEARUSA INC; West Palm Beach
METROPOLITAN HEALTH NETWORKS; West Palm Beach
NATIONAL BEVERAGE CORP; Ft. Lauderdale
NOVEN PHARMACEUTICALS; Miami
PETMED EXPRESS INC; Pompano Beach
SRI/SURGICAL EXPRESS INC; Tampa
STIEFEL LABORATORIES INC; Coral Gables
TAMPA ELECTRIC COMPANY; Tampa
TERREMARK WORLDWIDE INC; Miami
ULTIMATE SOFTWARE GROUP INC; Weston

**GEORGIA**
ARRIS GROUP INC; Suwanee
CRYOLIFE INC; Kennesaw
ECLIPSYS CORPORATION; Atlanta
EMS TECHNOLOGIES INC; Norcross
IMMUCOR INC; Norcross
INTERCONTINENTALEXCHANGE INC (ICE); Atlanta
INTERNAP NETWORK SERVICES CORP; Atlanta
INTERNET SECURITY SYSTEMS INC; Atlanta
LOGISTICARE INC; Atlanta
MANHATTAN ASSOCIATES INC; Atlanta
MATRIA HEALTHCARE INC; Marietta
PREMIERE GLOBAL SERVICES INC; Atlanta
S1 CORPORATION; Norcross
SCIELE PHARMA INC; Atlanta
THERAGENICS CORP; Buford
TRANSCEND SERVICES INC; Atlanta

**IDAHO**
IDACORP INC; Boise

**ILLINOIS**
ALLSCRIPTS HEALTHCARE SOLUTIONS INC; Chicago
AMCOL INTERNATIONAL CORP; Hoffman Estates
APP PHARMACEUTICALS INC; Schaumburg
CME GROUP; Chicago
ELOYALTY CORPORATION; Lake Forest
FUEL TECH INC; Batavia

HEIDRICK & STRUGGLES INTERNATIONAL INC; Chicago
HORACE MANN EDUCATORS CORPORATION; Springfield
HURON CONSULTING GROUP INC; Chicago
MIDAS INC; Itasca
NOVAMED INC; Chicago
NUTRASWEET COMPANY (THE); Chicago
PEAPOD LLC; Skokie
RECYCLED ENERGY DEVELOPMENT; Westmont
SPSS INC; Chicago
TOOTSIE ROLL INDUSTRIES INC; Chicago
VASCO DATA SECURITY INTERNATIONAL INC; Oakbrook Terrace

**INDIANA**
INTERACTIVE INTELLIGENCE; Indianapolis
NATIONAL WINE & SPIRITS INC; Indianapolis
SYMMETRY MEDICAL INC; Warsaw

**IOWA**
FBL FINANCIAL GROUP; W. Des Moines

**KANSAS**
ASSOCIATED WHOLESALE GROCERS INC; Kansas City
EURONET WORLDWIDE INC; Leawood
NIC INC; Olathe
SCOULAR COMPANY (THE); Overland Park
WESTAR ENERGY; Topeka

**LOUISIANA**
MCMORAN EXPLORATION CO; New Orleans

**MAINE**
NYER MEDICAL GROUP INC; Bangor

**MARYLAND**
CATALYST HEALTH SOLUTIONS INC; Rockville
CHINDEX INTERNATIONAL INC; Bethesda
CIENA CORP; Linthicum
DIALYSIS CORPORATION OF AMERICA; Linthicum
HUMAN GENOME SCIENCES INC; Rockville
INTEGRAL SYSTEMS INC; Lanham
MARTEK BIOSCIENCES CORP; Columbia
OPTELECOM-NKF INC; Germantown
UNDER ARMOUR INC; Baltimore
UNITED THERAPEUTICS CORP; Silver Spring

**MASSACHUSETTS**
ACME PACKET INC; Burlington
AKAMAI TECHNOLOGIES INC; Cambridge
ALKERMES INC; Cambridge
AMAG PHARMACEUTICALS INC; Cambridge
AMERESCO; Framingham
AMERICAN SCIENCE & ENGINEERING INC; Billerica
AMERICAN SUPERCONDUCTOR CORP; Devens
AMERICAN TOWER CORP; Boston
AMICAS INC; Boston
ANALOGIC CORP; Peabody
ANIKA THERAPEUTICS INC; Bedford
ART TECHNOLOGY GROUP INC; Cambridge
ASPECT MEDICAL SYSTEMS INC; Norman
ASPEN TECHNOLOGY INC; Burlington
ATHENAHEALTH INC; Watertown
CALIPER LIFE SCIENCES; Hopkinton
CANDELA CORP; Wayland
CHOICESTREAM INC; Cambridge
COGNEX CORP; Natick
COMMERCE GROUP INC (THE); Webster
CUBIST PHARMACEUTICALS INC; Lexington
DYAX CORP; Cambridge
ENERNOC INC; Boston
EPIX PHARMACEUTICALS INC; Lexington
EVERGREEN SOLAR INC; Marlboro
FORRESTER RESEARCH INC; Cambridge
GLOBAL PARTNERS LP; Waltham
GTC BIOTHERAPEUTICS INC; Framingham
HAEMONETICS CORPORATION; Braintree
HARVARD PILGRIM HEALTH CARE INC; Wellesley
IBASIS INC; Burlington
LOJACK CORP; Westwood
MILLENNIUM PHARMACEUTICALS INC; Cambridge
NATIONAL DENTEX CORP; Natick
NAVISITE INC; Andover
NETSCOUT SYSTEMS INC; Westford
OSCIENT PHARMACEUTICALS CORPORATION; Waltham
POLYMEDICA CORPORATION; Wakefield
PROGRESS SOFTWARE CORP; Bedford
RSA SECURITY INC; Bedford
SEACHANGE INTERNATIONAL INC; Acton
SEPRACOR INC; Marlborough
SONUS NETWORKS INC; Westford
SPIRE CORPORATION; Bedford
STERLING AUTOBODY CENTERS; Natick
SYCAMORE NETWORKS INC; Chelmsford
VERTEX PHARMACEUTICALS INC; Cambridge
ZOLL MEDICAL CORP; Chelmsford

**MICHIGAN**
AROTECH CORPORATION; Ann Arbor
BLUE CARE NETWORK OF MICHIGAN; Southfield
CARACO PHARMACEUTICAL LABORATORIES; Detroit
ENERGY CONVERSION DEVICES INC; Rochester Hills
JACKSON NATIONAL LIFE INSURANCE COMPANY; Lansing
NEOGEN CORPORATION; Lansing
ZIEBART INTERNATIONAL CORP; Troy

**MINNESOTA**
AMERICAN MEDICAL SYSTEMS HOLDINGS INC; Minnetonka
ATS MEDICAL INC; Minneapolis

DIGI INTERNATIONAL INC; Minnetonka
DIGITAL RIVER INC; Eden Prairie
HICKORY TECH CORPORATION; Mankato
IMATION CORP; Oakdale
INTERNATIONAL DAIRY QUEEN; Minneapolis
LIFECORE BIOMEDICAL INC; Chaska
MALT-O-MEAL COMPANY; Minneapolis
MEDTOX SCIENTIFIC INC; St. Paul
MICHELINAS INC; Duluth
MTS SYSTEMS; Eden Prairie
SPORTSMAN'S GUIDE INC (THE); St. Paul
SYNOVIS LIFE TECHNOLOGIES INC; St. Paul
TECHNE CORP; Minneapolis
UNIVERSAL HOSPITAL SERVICES INC; Edina

**MISSISSIPPI**
CAL-MAINE FOODS INC; Jackson
MICROTEK MEDICAL HOLDINGS INC; Columbus

**MISSOURI**
AMERICAN ITALIAN PASTA COMPANY; Kansas City
KV PHARMACEUTICAL CO; St. Louis
LACLEDE GROUP INC (THE); St. Louis
REINSURANCE GROUP OF AMERICA INC; Chesterfield
SAVVIS INC; Town & Country

**MONTANA**
KAMPGROUNDS OF AMERICA INC; Billings
RIGHTNOW TECHNOLOGIES INC; Bozeman

**NEVADA**
ORMAT TECHNOLOGIES; Reno
ZAPPOS.COM INC; Henderson

**NEW HAMPSHIRE**
BENTLEY PHARMACEUTICALS INC; Exeter
CRITICAL CARE SYSTEMS; Nashua
PC CONNECTION INC; Merrimack
SKILLSOFT PLC; Nashua

**NEW JERSEY**
ALPHARMA INC; Bridgewater
ATLANTIC CITY ELECTRIC COMPANY; Mays Landing
AUDIBLE INC; Newark
BIO REFERENCE LABORATORIES INC; Elmwood Park
CAMBREX CORP; East Rutherford
CANTEL MEDICAL CORP; Little Falls
CELGENE CORP; Summit
CRUM & FORSTER HOLDINGS INC; Morristown
DATASCOPE CORP; Montvale
FUNDTECH LTD; Jersey City
GOAMERICA INC; Hackensack
HEARTLAND PAYMENT SYSTEMS INC; Princeton
INTEGRA LIFESCIENCES HOLDINGS CORP; Plainsboro
INTELLIGROUP INC; Edison
KNIGHT CAPITAL GROUP INC; Jersey City
LIFECELL CORPORATION; Branchburg
MEDAREX INC; Princeton
MEDICINES CO (THE); Parsippany
METROLOGIC INSTRUMENTS INC; Blackwood
OPNEXT INC; Eatontown
PAR PHARMACEUTICAL COMPANIES INC; Woodcliff Lake
SCIOS INC; Raritan
VITAL SIGNS INC; Totowa

**NEW MEXICO**
EMCORE CORP; Albuquerque

**NEW YORK**
24/7 REAL MEDIA INC; New York
ACI WORLDWIDE INC; New York
ALBANY MOLECULAR RESEARCH; Albany
ALLEGHANY CORP; New York
ANAREN INC; E. Syracuse
BIOSCRIP INC; Elmsford
CHYRON CORP; Melville
CKX INC; New York
COMTECH TELECOMMUNICATIONS CORP; Melville
DANNON COMPANY INC (THE); White Plains
DOUBLECLICK INC; New York
EVERCORE PARTNERS INC; New York
EXCEL TECHNOLOGY INC; East Setauket
E-Z-EM INC; Lake Success
FRESHDIRECT LLC; Long Island
GENENCOR INTERNATIONAL INC; Rochester
GLOBECOMM SYSTEMS INC; Hauppauge
HAHN AUTOMOTIVE WAREHOUSE INC; Rochester
HEALTH INSURANCE PLAN OF GREATER NEW YORK; New York
HI-TECH PHARMACAL CO INC; Amityville
INTEGRAMED AMERICA INC; Purchase
INVESTMENT TECHNOLOGY GROUP INC (ITG); New York
IVILLAGE INC; New York
KNOT INC (THE); New York
LIVEPERSON INC; New York
LORAL SPACE & COMMUNICATIONS LTD; New York
M&F WORLDWIDE CORP; New York
MARTHA STEWART LIVING OMNIMEDIA INC; New York
MARVEL ENTERTAINMENT INC; New York
MEDICAL ACTION INDUSTRIES INC; Hauppauge
MEDIS TECHNOLOGIES; New York
MOELIS & COMPANY; New York
NASDAQ OMX; New York
NATIONAL FUEL GAS CO; Williamsville
NETRATINGS INC; New York
NYMEX HOLDINGS (NEW YORK MERCANTILE EXCHANGE); New York
PITNEY BOWES MAPINFO; Troy

PLUG POWER INC; Latham
REGENERON PHARMACEUTICALS INC; Tarrytown
SCHICK TECHNOLOGIES INC; Long Island City
STANDARD MICROSYSTEMS CORPORATION; Hauppauge
STEVEN MADDEN LTD; Long Island City
TELIRIS; New York
TOPPS COMPANY INC (THE); New York
TRANSATLANTIC HOLDINGS INC; New York
UNIVERSAL AMERICAN CORPORATION; Rye Brook
VIBRANT MEDIA INC; New York
WEBMD HEALTH CORP; New York

**NORTH CAROLINA**
AMERICAN TIRE DISTRIBUTORS; Huntersville
HARRIS STRATEX NETWORKS INC; Morrisville
INSPIRE PHARMACEUTICALS INC; Durham
KIMLEY-HORN AND ASSOCIATES INC; Cary
LUCOR INC; Raleigh
PIEDMONT NATURAL GAS COMPANY INC; Charlotte
POLYPORE INTERNATIONAL INC; Charlotte
RED HAT INC; Raleigh
SALIX PHARMACEUTICALS; Morrisville

**OHIO**
DPL INC; Dayton
FEDEX SUPPLY CHAIN SERVICES INC; Hudson
GREAT AMERICAN FINANCIAL RESOURCES INC; Cincinnati
GREAT LAKES CHEESE COMPANY INC; Hiram
IMG WORLDWIDE INC; Cleveland
LCA-VISION INC; Cincinnati
MERIDIAN BIOSCIENCE INC; Cincinnati
STATE AUTO FINANCIAL CORP; Columbus
VALLEY NATIONAL GASES LLC; Independence

**OKLAHOMA**
AMERICAN FIDELITY ASSURANCE COMPANY; Oklahoma City
MAGELLAN MIDSTREAM PARTNERS LP; Tulsa
ONEOK PARTNERS LP; Tulsa

**OREGON**
AVI BIOPHARMA INC; Portland
FLIR SYSTEMS; Wilsonville
RADISYS CORP; Hillsboro

**PENNSYLVANIA**
AAMCO TRANSMISSIONS INC; Horsham
ANSYS INC; Canonsburgh
C-COR INC; State College
CNX GAS CORPORATION; Pittsburgh
COLLAGENEX PHARMACEUTICALS INC; Newtown
ENCORIUM GROUP INC; Wayne
ENDO PHARMACEUTICALS HOLDINGS INC; Chadds Ford
EPAM SYSTEMS; Newtown
EQUITABLE RESOURCES INC; Pittsburgh
HANOVER FOODS CORPORATION; Hanover
PHILADELPHIA CONSOLIDATED HOLDING CORP; Bala Cynwyd
PMA CAPITAL CORPORATION; Blue Bell
VIROPHARMA INC; Exton

**SOUTH CAROLINA**
CENTERPLATE; Spartanburg
SCANSOURCE INC; Greenville
SPAN AMERICA MEDICAL SYSTEMS INC; Greenville

**SOUTH DAKOTA**
BLACK HILLS CORP; Rapid City
DAKTRONICS INC; Brookings
NORTHWESTERN CORPORATION; Sioux Falls

**TENNESSEE**
AMSURG CORP; Nashville
CHATTEM INC; Chattanooga
COMDATA CORP; Brentwood
HEALTHSTREAM INC; Nashville
WRIGHT MEDICAL GROUP INC; Arlington

**TEXAS**
ATRION CORPORATION; Allen
AVIALL INC; Dallas Fort Worth Airport
CARDTRONICS INC; Houston
CROWN CASTLE INTERNATIONAL CORP; Houston
CURVES INTERNATIONAL INC; Waco
DARLING INTERNATIONAL INC; Irving
DENBURY RESOURCES INC; Plano
DYNACQ HEALTHCARE INC; Houston
DYNEGY INC; Houston
ENCORE ACQUISITION CO; Fort Worth
ENGLOBAL CORP; Houston
EOG RESOURCES INC; Houston
EXCO RESOURCES INC; Dallas
FRONTIER OIL CORPORATION; Houston
GENESIS ENERGY LP; Houston
GOLFSMITH INTERNATIONAL HOLDINGS INC; Austin
HCC INSURANCE HOLDINGS INC; Houston
HEALTHTRONICS INC; Austin
HELIOVOLT CORP; Austin
HOLLY CORP; Dallas
ICO INC; Houston
INTERSTATE BATTERY SYSTEM OF AMERICA; Dallas
KRONOS WORLDWIDE INC; Dallas
LUMINEX CORPORATION; Austin
METROPCS COMMUNICATIONS INC; Richardson
NEWFIELD EXPLORATION CO; Houston
NOBLE ENERGY INC; Houston
NUSTAR ENERGY LP; San Antonio
PERFICIENT INC; Austin
PIONEER NATURAL RESOURCES COMPANY; Irving

PLAINS EXPLORATION AND PRODUCTION COMPANY; Houston
QUICKSILVER RESOURCES INC; Fort Worth
RACKSPACE HOSTING INC; San Antonio
RANGE RESOURCES CORP; Fort Worth
REDDY ICE HOLDINGS INC; Dallas
SHARED TECHNOLOGIES; Coppell
SOUTHERN UNION COMPANY; Houston
SOUTHWESTERN ENERGY CO; Houston
SWIFT ENERGY CO; Houston
TARGA RESOURCES PARTNERS LP; Houston
TDINDUSTRIES; Dallas
TEPPCO PARTNERS LP; Houston
US PHYSICAL THERAPY INC; Houston
VIGNETTE CORP; Austin
XTO ENERGY INC; Fort Worth

**UTAH**
ALTIRIS INC; Lindon
MERIT MEDICAL SYSTEMS INC; South Jordan
MYRIAD GENETICS INC; Salt Lake City
OMNITURE INC; Orem
SCHIFF NUTRITION INTERNATIONAL INC; Salt Lake City
SENTO; Salt Lake City
SONIC INNOVATIONS INC; Salt Lake City

**VERMONT**
CENTRAL VERMONT PUBLIC SERVICE CORPORATION; Rutland
GREEN MOUNTAIN COFFEE ROASTERS INC; Waterbury
GREEN MOUNTAIN POWER CORPORATION; Colchester

**VIRGINIA**
CORPORATE EXECUTIVE BOARD COMPANY (THE); Arlington
LCC INTERNATIONAL INC; McLean
MICROSTRATEGY INC; McLean
NTELOS HOLDING CORP; Waynesboro
ONLINE RESOURCES CORP; Chantilly
SHENANDOAH TELECOMMUNICATIONS CO; Edinburg
VSE CORP; Alexandria

**WASHINGTON**
AVISTA CORPORATION; Spokane
BLUE NILE INC; Seattle
CELL THERAPEUTICS INC; Seattle
CLEARWIRE CORP; Kirkland
COINSTAR INC; Bellevue
CONCUR TECHNOLOGIES INC; Redmond
DRUGSTORE.COM INC; Bellevue
F5 NETWORKS INC; Seattle
INTERMEC INC; Everett
ISILON SYSTEMS INC; Seattle
MARCHEX INC; Seattle
REALNETWORKS INC; Seattle
SEATTLE GENETICS; Bothell
TULLY'S COFFEE CORPORATION; Seattle
ZYMOGENETICS INC; Seattle

**WISCONSIN**
FRESH BRANDS INC; Sheboygan
ROBERT W BAIRD & CO INC; Milwaukee
THIRD WAVE TECHNOLOGIES INC; Madison
TOMOTHERAPY INC; Madison

**WEST VIRGINIA**
PETROLEUM DEVELOPMENT CORPORATION; Bridgeport

# INDEX BY REGIONS OF THE NATION WHERE THE FIRMS HAVE LOCATIONS

## WEST

GOLFSMITH INTERNATIONAL HOLDINGS INC
GREAT LAKES CHEESE COMPANY INC
HACKETT GROUP (THE)
HANOVER FOODS CORPORATION
HANSEN NATURAL
HARMONIC INC
HARRIS STRATEX NETWORKS INC
HEALTH GRADES INC
HEALTHSTREAM INC
HEARUSA INC
HEIDRICK & STRUGGLES INTERNATIONAL INC
HESKA CORP
HOLLY CORP
HORACE MANN EDUCATORS CORPORATION
HOULIHAN LOKEY
HURON CONSULTING GROUP INC
IBASIS INC
ICO INC
IDACORP INC
I-FLOW CORPORATION
ILLUMINA INC
IMATION CORP
IMG WORLDWIDE INC
INAMED CORP
INDEPENDENCE HOLDING CO
INFINERA CORP
INSPIRE PHARMACEUTICALS INC
INTEGRA LIFESCIENCES HOLDINGS CORP
INTEGRAL SYSTEMS INC
INTEGRAMED AMERICA INC
INTELLIGROUP INC
INTERACTIVE BROKERS GROUP INC
INTERACTIVE INTELLIGENCE
INTERMEC INC
INTERNAP NETWORK SERVICES CORP
INTERNATIONAL CREATIVE MANAGEMENT (ICM)
INTERNATIONAL DAIRY QUEEN
INTERSTATE BATTERY SYSTEM OF AMERICA
INTERWOVEN INC
INVESTMENT TECHNOLOGY GROUP INC (ITG)
IRIDEX CORP
IRIS INTERNATIONAL INC
ISILON SYSTEMS INC
ISONICS CORPORATION
J2 GLOBAL COMMUNICATIONS INC
JACKSON NATIONAL LIFE INSURANCE COMPANY
JAZZ PHARMACEUTICALS
JUPITERMEDIA CORP
KAMPGROUNDS OF AMERICA INC
KENDALL-JACKSON WINE ESTATES LTD
KIMLEY-HORN AND ASSOCIATES INC
KNIGHT CAPITAL GROUP INC
KNOT INC (THE)
KRONOS WORLDWIDE INC
LCA-VISION INC
LCC INTERNATIONAL INC
LEAP WIRELESS INTERNATIONAL INC
LESLIE'S POOLMART INC
LIVEPERSON INC
LOGISTICARE INC
LOJACK CORP
LORAL SPACE & COMMUNICATIONS LTD
LUCASFILM LTD
MAGELLAN MIDSTREAM PARTNERS LP
MALT-O-MEAL COMPANY
MANHATTAN ASSOCIATES INC
MARCHEX INC
MARTEK BIOSCIENCES CORP
MARVEL ENTERTAINMENT INC
MATRIA HEALTHCARE INC
MAXYGEN INC
MEDAREX INC
MEDICAL ACTION INDUSTRIES INC
MEDICIS PHARMACEUTICAL CORP
MEDIS TECHNOLOGIES
MENTOR CORP
MERIT MEDICAL SYSTEMS INC
MICROSTRATEGY INC
MIDAS INC
MOELIS & COMPANY
MOLINA HEALTHCARE INC
MOTORCAR PARTS OF AMERICA INC
MTS SYSTEMS
MYRIAD GENETICS INC
NANOMETRICS INC
NASDAQ OMX
NATIONAL BEVERAGE CORP
NATIONAL CINEMEDIA INC
NATIONAL DENTEX CORP
NATIONAL FUEL GAS CO
NATUS MEDICAL
NAVISITE INC
NEKTAR THERAPEUTICS
NETFLIX INC
NETGEAR INC
NETRATINGS INC
NETSCOUT SYSTEMS INC
NETSUITE INC
NEWFIELD EXPLORATION CO
NOBLE ENERGY INC
NORTHWESTERN CORPORATION
NOVAMED INC
NUGGET MARKET
NUSTAR ENERGY LP
NYER MEDICAL GROUP INC
ODYSSEY RE HOLDINGS CORP
OMNITURE INC
ONEOK PARTNERS LP
ONLINE RESOURCES CORP
OPENTV CORP
OPNEXT INC
ORMAT TECHNOLOGIES
PALM INC
PC MALL INC
PERFICIENT INC
PETROLEUM DEVELOPMENT CORPORATION
PHILADELPHIA CONSOLIDATED HOLDING CORP
PIONEER NATURAL RESOURCES COMPANY
PLAINS EXPLORATION AND PRODUCTION COMPANY
POLYCOM INC
PREMIERE GLOBAL SERVICES INC
PRIMEENERGY CORPORATION
PROGRESS SOFTWARE CORP
PROTECTIVE LIFE CORP
QLOGIC CORP
QUALITY SYSTEMS INC
QUICKSILVER RESOURCES INC
QUIDEL CORP
RADISYS CORP
RADNET INC

RADYNE CORPORATION
REALNETWORKS INC
RED HAT INC
REDDY ICE HOLDINGS INC
RIGHTNOW TECHNOLOGIES INC
ROBERT W BAIRD & CO INC
RSA SECURITY INC
S1 CORPORATION
SACRAMENTO MUNICIPAL UTILITY DISTRICT
SAVVIS INC
SCANSOURCE INC
SCHIFF NUTRITION INTERNATIONAL INC
SCICLONE PHARMACEUTICALS
SCOULAR COMPANY (THE)
SEACHANGE INTERNATIONAL INC
SEATTLE GENETICS
SECURE COMPUTING CORP
SENTO
SEPRACOR INC
SEQUENOM INC
SERENA SOFTWARE INC
SHARED TECHNOLOGIES
SHUTTERFLY INC
SOLAR RESERVE
SOLFOCUS INC
SONIC INNOVATIONS INC
SONUS NETWORKS INC
SPAN AMERICA MEDICAL SYSTEMS INC
SPECTRALINK CORP
SPECTRANETICS CORP
SPROUTS FARMERS MARKET
SPSS INC
SRI/SURGICAL EXPRESS INC
SS&C TECHNOLOGIES INC
ST MARY LAND & EXPLORATION COMPANY
STAAR SURGICAL CO
STANDARD MICROSYSTEMS CORPORATION
STERLING AUTOBODY CENTERS
STEVEN MADDEN LTD
STIEFEL LABORATORIES INC
SUPER MICRO COMPUTER INC
SWIFT ENERGY CO
SYMYX TECHNOLOGIES
SYNAPTICS INC
TDINDUSTRIES
TEPPCO PARTNERS LP
TERREMARK WORLDWIDE INC
THERAGENICS CORP
THOMAS WEISEL PARTNERS GROUP INC
THORATEC CORPORATION
THQ INC
TIBCO SOFTWARE INC
TIVO INC
TOPPS COMPANY INC (THE)
TRANSATLANTIC HOLDINGS INC
TRANSCEND SERVICES INC
TRAPEZE NETWORKS INC
TRIZETTO GROUP INC (THE)
TULLY'S COFFEE CORPORATION
UNDER ARMOUR INC
UNITED ONLINE INC
UNIVERSAL AMERICAN CORPORATION
UNIVERSAL HOSPITAL SERVICES INC
US PHYSICAL THERAPY INC
VALUECLICK INC
VERAZ NETWORKS INC
VERIFONE HOLDINGS INC
VERTEX PHARMACEUTICALS INC
VIASAT INC
VIBRANT MEDIA INC
VIGNETTE CORP
VISION SERVICE PLAN
VOLCOM INC
VSE CORP
WEBEX COMMUNICATIONS INC
WEBMD HEALTH CORP
WEBSENSE INC
WHITEWAVE FOODS COMPANY
WIND RIVER SYSTEMS INC
XOMA LTD
XTO ENERGY INC
YOUNG'S MARKET COMPANY LLC
ZAPPOS.COM INC
ZIEBART INTERNATIONAL CORP
ZOLL MEDICAL CORP
ZYMOGENETICS INC

## SOUTHWEST

AAMCO TRANSMISSIONS INC
ACI WORLDWIDE INC
AKAMAI TECHNOLOGIES INC
ALLIANCE IMAGING INC
ALLSCRIPTS HEALTHCARE SOLUTIONS INC
AMCOL INTERNATIONAL CORP
AMERESCO
AMERICAN FIDELITY ASSURANCE COMPANY
AMERICAN ITALIAN PASTA COMPANY
AMERICAN MEDICAL SYSTEMS HOLDINGS INC
AMERICAN TIRE DISTRIBUTORS
AMERICAN TOWER CORP
AMERICAN VANGUARD CORP
AMSURG CORP
AMTECH SYSTEMS INC
ANSYS INC
APPLIED SIGNAL TECHNOLOGY INC
ARIBA INC
ASPEN TECHNOLOGY INC
ASSOCIATED WHOLESALE GROCERS INC
ATMI INC
ATRION CORPORATION
AVIALL INC
BIOSCRIP INC
BLACK HILLS CORP
BLACKBOARD INC
BLUE COAT SYSTEMS INC
CALIBER HOLDINGS CORP
CAL-MAINE FOODS INC
CALPINE CORPORATION
CARDTRONICS INC
CATALYST HEALTH SOLUTIONS INC
CELL THERAPEUTICS INC
CENTERPLATE
CIENA CORP
CLEARWIRE CORP
COINSTAR INC
COMDATA CORP
COMTECH TELECOMMUNICATIONS CORP
CONCUR TECHNOLOGIES INC
CRITICAL CARE SYSTEMS

CROWN CASTLE INTERNATIONAL CORP
CRUM & FORSTER HOLDINGS INC
CURVES INTERNATIONAL INC
DANNON COMPANY INC (THE)
DARLING INTERNATIONAL INC
DELPHI FINANCIAL GROUP INC
DENBURY RESOURCES INC
DIGI INTERNATIONAL INC
DYNACQ HEALTHCARE INC
DYNEGY INC
ECLIPSYS CORPORATION
ELECTRONICS FOR IMAGING INC
EMCORE CORP
ENCORE ACQUISITION CO
ENGLOBAL CORP
EOG RESOURCES INC
EXCO RESOURCES INC
FARMER BROTHERS CO
FBL FINANCIAL GROUP
FEDEX SUPPLY CHAIN SERVICES INC
FIRST SOLAR LLC
FOREST OIL CORPORATION
FRONTIER OIL CORPORATION
GALLUP ORGANIZATION (THE)
GENESIS ENERGY LP
GOLFSMITH INTERNATIONAL HOLDINGS INC
GREAT AMERICAN FINANCIAL RESOURCES INC
HACKETT GROUP (THE)
HARRIS STRATEX NETWORKS INC
HCC INSURANCE HOLDINGS INC
HEALTHTRONICS INC
HEARTLAND PAYMENT SYSTEMS INC
HEIDRICK & STRUGGLES INTERNATIONAL INC
HELIOVOLT CORP
HOLLY CORP
HORACE MANN EDUCATORS CORPORATION
HOULIHAN LOKEY
HURON CONSULTING GROUP INC
ICO INC
IMATION CORP
INDEPENDENCE HOLDING CO
INTEGRAMED AMERICA INC
INTERCONTINENTALEXCHANGE INC (ICE)
INTERMEC INC
INTERNAP NETWORK SERVICES CORP
INTERNATIONAL DAIRY QUEEN
INTERSTATE BATTERY SYSTEM OF AMERICA
INTERWOVEN INC
IRIDEX CORP
IRIS INTERNATIONAL INC
JACKSON NATIONAL LIFE INSURANCE COMPANY
KAMPGROUNDS OF AMERICA INC
KIMLEY-HORN AND ASSOCIATES INC
KNIGHT CAPITAL GROUP INC
KNOT INC (THE)
KRONOS WORLDWIDE INC
LACLEDE GROUP INC (THE)
LCA-VISION INC
LCC INTERNATIONAL INC
LEAP WIRELESS INTERNATIONAL INC
LESLIE'S POOLMART INC
LIVEPERSON INC
LOGISTICARE INC
LOJACK CORP
LUMINEX CORPORATION
MAGELLAN MIDSTREAM PARTNERS LP
MALT-O-MEAL COMPANY
MATRIA HEALTHCARE INC
MCMORAN EXPLORATION CO
MEDICIS PHARMACEUTICAL CORP
MENTOR CORP
MERIT MEDICAL SYSTEMS INC
METROPCS COMMUNICATIONS INC
MICROTEK MEDICAL HOLDINGS INC
MIDAS INC
MOLINA HEALTHCARE INC
MTS SYSTEMS
NATIONAL BEVERAGE CORP
NATIONAL CINEMEDIA INC
NATIONAL DENTEX CORP
NATIONAL FUEL GAS CO
NAVISITE INC
NETSCOUT SYSTEMS INC
NEWFIELD EXPLORATION CO
NOBLE ENERGY INC
NOVAMED INC
NUSTAR ENERGY LP
NYMEX HOLDINGS (NEW YORK MERCANTILE EXCHANGE)
ONEOK PARTNERS LP
PC CONNECTION INC
PERFICIENT INC
PHILADELPHIA CONSOLIDATED HOLDING CORP
PHOENIX COMPANIES (THE)
PIONEER NATURAL RESOURCES COMPANY
PLAINS EXPLORATION AND PRODUCTION COMPANY
POLYCOM INC
POLYMEDICA CORPORATION
PRIMEENERGY CORPORATION
PROGRESS SOFTWARE CORP
PROTECTIVE LIFE CORP
QLOGIC CORP
QUALITY SYSTEMS INC
QUICKSILVER RESOURCES INC
RACKSPACE HOSTING INC
RADNET INC
RADYNE CORPORATION
RANGE RESOURCES CORP
RED HAT INC
REDDY ICE HOLDINGS INC
RIGHTNOW TECHNOLOGIES INC
ROBERT W BAIRD & CO INC
S1 CORPORATION
SAVVIS INC
SCANSOURCE INC
SCOULAR COMPANY (THE)
SENTO
SEPRACOR INC
SHARED TECHNOLOGIES
SONUS NETWORKS INC
SOUTHERN UNION COMPANY
SOUTHWESTERN ENERGY CO
SPROUTS FARMERS MARKET
SPSS INC
SRI/SURGICAL EXPRESS INC
ST MARY LAND & EXPLORATION COMPANY
STANDARD MICROSYSTEMS CORPORATION
STERLING AUTOBODY CENTERS
STEVEN MADDEN LTD
SWIFT ENERGY CO

SYCAMORE NETWORKS INC
TARGA RESOURCES PARTNERS LP
TDINDUSTRIES
TEPPCO PARTNERS LP
THERAGENICS CORP
THQ INC
TIBCO SOFTWARE INC
TRANSCEND SERVICES INC
TRIZETTO GROUP INC (THE)
UNISOURCE ENERGY CORPORATION
UNIVERSAL AMERICAN CORPORATION
UNIVERSAL HOSPITAL SERVICES INC
US PHYSICAL THERAPY INC
VENTANA MEDICAL SYSTEMS INC
VIASAT INC
VIGNETTE CORP
VISION SERVICE PLAN
VSE CORP
WEBSENSE INC
WESTAR ENERGY
WIND RIVER SYSTEMS INC
XTO ENERGY INC
YOUNG'S MARKET COMPANY LLC
ZIEBART INTERNATIONAL CORP
ZILA INC

## MIDWEST

24/7 REAL MEDIA INC
AAMCO TRANSMISSIONS INC
ACI WORLDWIDE INC
AKAMAI TECHNOLOGIES INC
ALIEN TECHNOLOGY CORPORATION
ALKERMES INC
ALLEGHANY CORP
ALLIANCE IMAGING INC
ALLSCRIPTS HEALTHCARE SOLUTIONS INC
ALPHARMA INC
ALTIRIS INC
AMCOL INTERNATIONAL CORP
AMERESCO
AMERICAN ITALIAN PASTA COMPANY
AMERICAN MEDICAL SYSTEMS HOLDINGS INC
AMERICAN SUPERCONDUCTOR CORP
AMERICAN TIRE DISTRIBUTORS
AMERICAN TOWER CORP
AMERICAN VANGUARD CORP
ANALOGIC CORP
ANSYS INC
APP PHARMACEUTICALS INC
ARIBA INC
ARIZONA CHEMICAL COMPANY
AROTECH CORPORATION
ARRIS GROUP INC
ART TECHNOLOGY GROUP INC
ASSOCIATED WHOLESALE GROCERS INC
ATMI INC
ATS MEDICAL INC
AVIALL INC
BIOSCRIP INC
BLACK HILLS CORP
BLUE CARE NETWORK OF MICHIGAN
BRIGHTSTAR CORPORATION
CAL-MAINE FOODS INC
CALPINE CORPORATION
CAMBREX CORP
CANTEL MEDICAL CORP
CARACO PHARMACEUTICAL LABORATORIES
CATALYST HEALTH SOLUTIONS INC
CENTERPLATE
CIENA CORP
CLEARWIRE CORP
CME GROUP
CNX GAS CORPORATION
COGNEX CORP
COINSTAR INC
COMMERCE GROUP INC (THE)
CONCUR TECHNOLOGIES INC
CORPORATE EXECUTIVE BOARD COMPANY (THE)
CRITICAL CARE SYSTEMS
CROWN CASTLE INTERNATIONAL CORP
CRUM & FORSTER HOLDINGS INC
CSG SYSTEMS INTERNATIONAL INC
CURVES INTERNATIONAL INC
DAKTRONICS INC
DANNON COMPANY INC (THE)
DARLING INTERNATIONAL INC
DELPHI FINANCIAL GROUP INC
DIGI INTERNATIONAL INC
DIGITAL RIVER INC
DOUBLECLICK INC
DPL INC
DYNEGY INC
ECHELON CORP
ECOLLEGE.COM
ELECTRONICS FOR IMAGING INC
ELOYALTY CORPORATION
ENCORE ACQUISITION CO
ENERGY CONVERSION DEVICES INC
EOG RESOURCES INC
EQUINIX INC
EQUITABLE RESOURCES INC
EURONET WORLDWIDE INC
EXCO RESOURCES INC
F5 NETWORKS INC
FARMER BROTHERS CO
FBL FINANCIAL GROUP
FEDEX SUPPLY CHAIN SERVICES INC
FIRST SOLAR LLC
FLIR SYSTEMS
FRESH BRANDS INC
FRONTIER OIL CORPORATION
FUEL TECH INC
GALLUP ORGANIZATION (THE)
GENENCOR INTERNATIONAL INC
GERBER SCIENTIFIC INC
GOLFSMITH INTERNATIONAL HOLDINGS INC
GREAT AMERICAN FINANCIAL RESOURCES INC
GREAT LAKES CHEESE COMPANY INC
HACKETT GROUP (THE)
HAHN AUTOMOTIVE WAREHOUSE INC
HEARTLAND PAYMENT SYSTEMS INC
HEARUSA INC
HEIDRICK & STRUGGLES INTERNATIONAL INC
HICKORY TECH CORPORATION
HORACE MANN EDUCATORS CORPORATION
HOULIHAN LOKEY
HURON CONSULTING GROUP INC
ICO INC
I-FLOW CORPORATION

IMATION CORP
IMG WORLDWIDE INC
INDEPENDENCE HOLDING CO
INTEGRA LIFESCIENCES HOLDINGS CORP
INTEGRAMED AMERICA INC
INTELLIGROUP INC
INTERACTIVE BROKERS GROUP INC
INTERACTIVE INTELLIGENCE
INTERCONTINENTALEXCHANGE INC (ICE)
INTERMEC INC
INTERNAP NETWORK SERVICES CORP
INTERNATIONAL DAIRY QUEEN
INTERSTATE BATTERY SYSTEM OF AMERICA
INTERWOVEN INC
IRIDEX CORP
JACKSON NATIONAL LIFE INSURANCE COMPANY
KAMPGROUNDS OF AMERICA INC
KIMLEY-HORN AND ASSOCIATES INC
KNIGHT CAPITAL GROUP INC
KNOT INC (THE)
KRONOS WORLDWIDE INC
KV PHARMACEUTICAL CO
LACLEDE GROUP INC (THE)
LCA-VISION INC
LCC INTERNATIONAL INC
LEAP WIRELESS INTERNATIONAL INC
LESLIE'S POOLMART INC
LIFECORE BIOMEDICAL INC
LOGISTICARE INC
LUCOR INC
MAGELLAN MIDSTREAM PARTNERS LP
MALT-O-MEAL COMPANY
MANHATTAN ASSOCIATES INC
MARTEK BIOSCIENCES CORP
MATRIA HEALTHCARE INC
MEDICIS PHARMACEUTICAL CORP
MEDTOX SCIENTIFIC INC
MENTOR CORP
MERIDIAN BIOSCIENCE INC
METROPCS COMMUNICATIONS INC
MICHELINAS INC
MICROSTRATEGY INC
MIDAS INC
MOELIS & COMPANY
MOLINA HEALTHCARE INC
MTS SYSTEMS
NASDAQ OMX
NATIONAL BEVERAGE CORP
NATIONAL CINEMEDIA INC
NATIONAL DENTEX CORP
NATIONAL WINE & SPIRITS INC
NATUS MEDICAL
NAVISITE INC
NEOGEN CORPORATION
NETSCOUT SYSTEMS INC
NEWFIELD EXPLORATION CO
NIC INC
NOBLE ENERGY INC
NORTHWESTERN CORPORATION
NOVAMED INC
NTELOS HOLDING CORP
NUSTAR ENERGY LP
NUTRASWEET COMPANY (THE)
ODYSSEY RE HOLDINGS CORP
ONEOK PARTNERS LP
ONLINE RESOURCES CORP
PC MALL INC
PEAPOD LLC
PERFICIENT INC
PETROLEUM DEVELOPMENT CORPORATION
PHILADELPHIA CONSOLIDATED HOLDING CORP
PIONEER NATURAL RESOURCES COMPANY
PITNEY BOWES MAPINFO
POLYCOM INC
POLYMEDICA CORPORATION
POLYPORE INTERNATIONAL INC
PREMIERE GLOBAL SERVICES INC
PRIMEENERGY CORPORATION
PROASSURANCE CORP
PROGRESS SOFTWARE CORP
PROTECTIVE LIFE CORP
QLOGIC CORP
QUALITY SYSTEMS INC
RADISYS CORP
RADNET INC
RECYCLED ENERGY DEVELOPMENT
RED HAT INC
REDDY ICE HOLDINGS INC
REINSURANCE GROUP OF AMERICA INC
RIGHTNOW TECHNOLOGIES INC
ROBERT W BAIRD & CO INC
SAVVIS INC
SCOULAR COMPANY (THE)
SECURE COMPUTING CORP
SEPRACOR INC
SHARED TECHNOLOGIES
SOUTHERN UNION COMPANY
SPIRE CORPORATION
SPORTSMAN'S GUIDE INC (THE)
SPSS INC
SRI/SURGICAL EXPRESS INC
SS&C TECHNOLOGIES INC
STATE AUTO FINANCIAL CORP
STERLING AUTOBODY CENTERS
STEVEN MADDEN LTD
SWIFT ENERGY CO
SYCAMORE NETWORKS INC
SYMMETRY MEDICAL INC
SYNOVIS LIFE TECHNOLOGIES INC
TDINDUSTRIES
TECHNE CORP
TEPPCO PARTNERS LP
THIRD WAVE TECHNOLOGIES INC
THORATEC CORPORATION
THQ INC
TIBCO SOFTWARE INC
TOMOTHERAPY INC
TOOTSIE ROLL INDUSTRIES INC
TRANSATLANTIC HOLDINGS INC
TRIZETTO GROUP INC (THE)
UNITED ONLINE INC
UNIVERSAL AMERICAN CORPORATION
UNIVERSAL HOSPITAL SERVICES INC
US PHYSICAL THERAPY INC
VALLEY NATIONAL GASES LLC
VALUECLICK INC
VASCO DATA SECURITY INTERNATIONAL INC
VIASAT INC
VISION SERVICE PLAN
VITAL SIGNS INC

VSE CORP
WEBMD HEALTH CORP
WESTAR ENERGY
WIND RIVER SYSTEMS INC
XTO ENERGY INC
ZIEBART INTERNATIONAL CORP

## SOUTHEAST

AAMCO TRANSMISSIONS INC
ACI WORLDWIDE INC
AKAMAI TECHNOLOGIES INC
ALLEGHANY CORP
ALLIANCE IMAGING INC
ALPHARMA INC
AMCOL INTERNATIONAL CORP
AMERESCO
AMERICAN ITALIAN PASTA COMPANY
AMERICAN TIRE DISTRIBUTORS
AMERICAN TOWER CORP
AMERICAN VANGUARD CORP
AMICAS INC
AMSURG CORP
ANSYS INC
APPLIED SIGNAL TECHNOLOGY INC
ARIBA INC
ARIZONA CHEMICAL COMPANY
AROTECH CORPORATION
ARRIS GROUP INC
ARUBA NETWORKS INC
ASSOCIATED WHOLESALE GROCERS INC
ATRION CORPORATION
AVANEX CORPORATION
AVIALL INC
AVISTA CORPORATION
BIOSCRIP INC
BLACK HILLS CORP
BRIGHTSTAR CORPORATION
CAL-MAINE FOODS INC
CALPINE CORPORATION
CANTEL MEDICAL CORP
CATALYST HEALTH SOLUTIONS INC
C-COR INC
CENTERPLATE
CHATTEM INC
CIENA CORP
CLEARWIRE CORP
COGNEX CORP
COHERENT INC
COINSTAR INC
COMDATA CORP
COMTECH TELECOMMUNICATIONS CORP
CONCUR TECHNOLOGIES INC
CONTINUCARE CORP
CRITICAL CARE SYSTEMS
CROWN CASTLE INTERNATIONAL CORP
CRUM & FORSTER HOLDINGS INC
CRYOLIFE INC
CURVES INTERNATIONAL INC
DAKTRONICS INC
DARLING INTERNATIONAL INC
DELPHI FINANCIAL GROUP INC
DENBURY RESOURCES INC
DIALYSIS CORPORATION OF AMERICA
DYNACQ HEALTHCARE INC
DYNEGY INC
ECLIPSYS CORPORATION
ELECTRONICS FOR IMAGING INC
EMS TECHNOLOGIES INC
ENGLOBAL CORP
EOG RESOURCES INC
EQUITABLE RESOURCES INC
EURONET WORLDWIDE INC
EXACTECH INC
EXCEL TECHNOLOGY INC
FEDEX SUPPLY CHAIN SERVICES INC
FLIR SYSTEMS
FOREST OIL CORPORATION
FUNDTECH LTD
GALLUP ORGANIZATION (THE)
GENESIS ENERGY LP
GOLFSMITH INTERNATIONAL HOLDINGS INC
GREAT AMERICAN FINANCIAL RESOURCES INC
HACKETT GROUP (THE)
HARRIS STRATEX NETWORKS INC
HEALTHSTREAM INC
HEALTHTRONICS INC
HEARUSA INC
HEIDRICK & STRUGGLES INTERNATIONAL INC
HORACE MANN EDUCATORS CORPORATION
HOULIHAN LOKEY
HURON CONSULTING GROUP INC
IBASIS INC
ICO INC
IMATION CORP
IMG WORLDWIDE INC
IMMUCOR INC
INDEPENDENCE HOLDING CO
INTEGRAMED AMERICA INC
INTELLIGROUP INC
INTERCONTINENTALEXCHANGE INC (ICE)
INTERMEC INC
INTERNAP NETWORK SERVICES CORP
INTERNATIONAL DAIRY QUEEN
INTERNET SECURITY SYSTEMS INC
INTERSTATE BATTERY SYSTEM OF AMERICA
INTERWOVEN INC
IRIDEX CORP
JACKSON NATIONAL LIFE INSURANCE COMPANY
KAMPGROUNDS OF AMERICA INC
KIMLEY-HORN AND ASSOCIATES INC
KNIGHT CAPITAL GROUP INC
KRONOS WORLDWIDE INC
LCA-VISION INC
LCC INTERNATIONAL INC
LEAP WIRELESS INTERNATIONAL INC
LESLIE'S POOLMART INC
LIVEPERSON INC
LOGISTICARE INC
LOJACK CORP
LUCOR INC
MAGELLAN MIDSTREAM PARTNERS LP
MALT-O-MEAL COMPANY
MANHATTAN ASSOCIATES INC
MATRIA HEALTHCARE INC
MCMORAN EXPLORATION CO
MEDICAL ACTION INDUSTRIES INC
MEDICIS PHARMACEUTICAL CORP
MERIDIAN BIOSCIENCE INC
METROPOLITAN HEALTH NETWORKS

MICROSTRATEGY INC
MICROTEK MEDICAL HOLDINGS INC
MIDAS INC
MOTORCAR PARTS OF AMERICA INC
MTS SYSTEMS
NATIONAL BEVERAGE CORP
NATIONAL CINEMEDIA INC
NATIONAL DENTEX CORP
NATIONAL FUEL GAS CO
NAVISITE INC
NEKTAR THERAPEUTICS
NEOGEN CORPORATION
NETSCOUT SYSTEMS INC
NEWFIELD EXPLORATION CO
NOVAMED INC
NOVEN PHARMACEUTICALS
NUSTAR ENERGY LP
NYER MEDICAL GROUP INC
ODYSSEY RE HOLDINGS CORP
OPNEXT INC
PC MALL INC
PERFICIENT INC
PETMED EXPRESS INC
PHILADELPHIA CONSOLIDATED HOLDING CORP
PIEDMONT NATURAL GAS COMPANY INC
PIONEER NATURAL RESOURCES COMPANY
PLAINS EXPLORATION AND PRODUCTION COMPANY
PMA CAPITAL CORPORATION
POLYCOM INC
POLYMEDICA CORPORATION
POLYPORE INTERNATIONAL INC
PREMIERE GLOBAL SERVICES INC
PRIMEENERGY CORPORATION
PROASSURANCE CORP
PROGRESS SOFTWARE CORP
PROTECTIVE LIFE CORP
QUALITY SYSTEMS INC
RADISYS CORP
RADNET INC
RANGE RESOURCES CORP
RED HAT INC
REDDY ICE HOLDINGS INC
ROBERT W BAIRD & CO INC
S1 CORPORATION
SAVVIS INC
SCIELE PHARMA INC
SCOULAR COMPANY (THE)
SECURE COMPUTING CORP
SEPRACOR INC
SERENA SOFTWARE INC
SHARED TECHNOLOGIES
SOUTHERN UNION COMPANY
SOUTHWESTERN ENERGY CO
SPAN AMERICA MEDICAL SYSTEMS INC
SPSS INC
SRI/SURGICAL EXPRESS INC
ST MARY LAND & EXPLORATION COMPANY
STATE AUTO FINANCIAL CORP
STERLING AUTOBODY CENTERS
STEVEN MADDEN LTD
STIEFEL LABORATORIES INC
SWIFT ENERGY CO
SYMMETRY MEDICAL INC
TAMPA ELECTRIC COMPANY
TARGA RESOURCES PARTNERS LP
TEPPCO PARTNERS LP
TERREMARK WORLDWIDE INC
THERAGENICS CORP
TIBCO SOFTWARE INC
TRANSATLANTIC HOLDINGS INC
TRANSCEND SERVICES INC
ULTIMATE SOFTWARE GROUP INC
UNITED THERAPEUTICS CORP
UNIVERSAL AMERICAN CORPORATION
UNIVERSAL HOSPITAL SERVICES INC
US PHYSICAL THERAPY INC
VALLEY NATIONAL GASES LLC
VERAZ NETWORKS INC
VERIFONE HOLDINGS INC
VIASAT INC
VISION SERVICE PLAN
VSE CORP
WEBMD HEALTH CORP
WIND RIVER SYSTEMS INC
WRIGHT MEDICAL GROUP INC
XTO ENERGY INC
ZIEBART INTERNATIONAL CORP
ZILA INC

## NORTHEAST

24/7 REAL MEDIA INC
AAMCO TRANSMISSIONS INC
ACI WORLDWIDE INC
ACME PACKET INC
ACXIOM DIGITAL
AKAMAI TECHNOLOGIES INC
AKQA INC
ALBANY MOLECULAR RESEARCH
ALEXION PHARMACEUTICALS INC
ALKERMES INC
ALLEGHANY CORP
ALLIANCE IMAGING INC
ALLSCRIPTS HEALTHCARE SOLUTIONS INC
ALPHARMA INC
ALTIRIS INC
AMAG PHARMACEUTICALS INC
AMCOL INTERNATIONAL CORP
AMERESCO
AMERICAN SCIENCE & ENGINEERING INC
AMERICAN SUPERCONDUCTOR CORP
AMERICAN TIRE DISTRIBUTORS
AMERICAN TOWER CORP
AMICAS INC
AMSURG CORP
AMTECH SYSTEMS INC
ANALOGIC CORP
ANAREN INC
ANIKA THERAPEUTICS INC
ANSYS INC
APP PHARMACEUTICALS INC
APPLIED SIGNAL TECHNOLOGY INC
ARIBA INC
AROTECH CORPORATION
ARRIS GROUP INC
ART TECHNOLOGY GROUP INC
ARUBA NETWORKS INC
ASPECT MEDICAL SYSTEMS INC
ASPEN TECHNOLOGY INC
ASSOCIATED WHOLESALE GROCERS INC
ATHENAHEALTH INC

ATLANTIC CITY ELECTRIC COMPANY
ATMI INC
AUDIBLE INC
AVANEX CORPORATION
AVIALL INC
BENTLEY PHARMACEUTICALS INC
BIO REFERENCE LABORATORIES INC
BIOSCRIP INC
BLACKBOARD INC
BLUE COAT SYSTEMS INC
CALIPER LIFE SCIENCES
CAL-MAINE FOODS INC
CALPINE CORPORATION
CAMBREX CORP
CANDELA CORP
CANTEL MEDICAL CORP
CARDTRONICS INC
CATALYST HEALTH SOLUTIONS INC
C-COR INC
CELERA CORPORATION
CELGENE CORP
CENTERPLATE
CENTRAL VERMONT PUBLIC SERVICE CORPORATION
CHINDEX INTERNATIONAL INC
CHOICESTREAM INC
CHYRON CORP
CIENA CORP
CKX INC
CLEARWIRE CORP
CME GROUP
CNX GAS CORPORATION
COGNEX CORP
COHERENT INC
COINSTAR INC
COLLAGENEX PHARMACEUTICALS INC
COMDATA CORP
COMMERCE GROUP INC (THE)
COMTECH TELECOMMUNICATIONS CORP
CONCUR TECHNOLOGIES INC
CORPORATE EXECUTIVE BOARD COMPANY (THE)
CRITICAL CARE SYSTEMS
CROWN CASTLE INTERNATIONAL CORP
CRUM & FORSTER HOLDINGS INC
CUBIST PHARMACEUTICALS INC
CURVES INTERNATIONAL INC
DANNON COMPANY INC (THE)
DARLING INTERNATIONAL INC
DATASCOPE CORP
DEI HOLDINGS INC
DELPHI FINANCIAL GROUP INC
DIALYSIS CORPORATION OF AMERICA
DIGI INTERNATIONAL INC
DOUBLECLICK INC
DPL INC
DRUGSTORE.COM INC
DYAX CORP
DYNEGY INC
ECLIPSYS CORPORATION
ELECTRONICS FOR IMAGING INC
EMCORE CORP
EMULEX CORP
ENCORIUM GROUP INC
ENDO PHARMACEUTICALS HOLDINGS INC
ENERNOC INC
EOG RESOURCES INC
EPAM SYSTEMS
EPIX PHARMACEUTICALS INC
EQUINIX INC
EQUITABLE RESOURCES INC
EURONET WORLDWIDE INC
EVERCORE PARTNERS INC
EVERGREEN SOLAR INC
EXACTECH INC
EXCEL TECHNOLOGY INC
EXCO RESOURCES INC
E-Z-EM INC
F5 NETWORKS INC
FEDEX SUPPLY CHAIN SERVICES INC
FIRST SOLAR LLC
FLIR SYSTEMS
FORRESTER RESEARCH INC
FRESHDIRECT LLC
FUEL TECH INC
FUELCELL ENERGY INC
FUNDTECH LTD
GALLUP ORGANIZATION (THE)
GENENCOR INTERNATIONAL INC
GERBER SCIENTIFIC INC
GLOBAL PARTNERS LP
GLOBECOMM SYSTEMS INC
GOAMERICA INC
GOLFSMITH INTERNATIONAL HOLDINGS INC
GREAT AMERICAN FINANCIAL RESOURCES INC
GREAT LAKES CHEESE COMPANY INC
GREEN MOUNTAIN COFFEE ROASTERS INC
GREEN MOUNTAIN POWER CORPORATION
GTC BIOTHERAPEUTICS INC
HACKETT GROUP (THE)
HAEMONETICS CORPORATION
HAHN AUTOMOTIVE WAREHOUSE INC
HANOVER FOODS CORPORATION
HARRIS STRATEX NETWORKS INC
HARVARD PILGRIM HEALTH CARE INC
HCC INSURANCE HOLDINGS INC
HEALTH INSURANCE PLAN OF GREATER NEW YORK
HEALTHSTREAM INC
HEARTLAND PAYMENT SYSTEMS INC
HEARUSA INC
HEIDRICK & STRUGGLES INTERNATIONAL INC
HI-TECH PHARMACAL CO INC
HORACE MANN EDUCATORS CORPORATION
HOULIHAN LOKEY
HUMAN GENOME SCIENCES INC
HURON CONSULTING GROUP INC
IBASIS INC
ICO INC
IMG WORLDWIDE INC
INDEPENDENCE HOLDING CO
INFINERA CORP
INSPIRE PHARMACEUTICALS INC
INTEGRA LIFESCIENCES HOLDINGS CORP
INTEGRAL SYSTEMS INC
INTEGRAMED AMERICA INC
INTELLIGROUP INC
INTERACTIVE BROKERS GROUP INC
INTERACTIVE INTELLIGENCE
INTERCONTINENTALEXCHANGE INC (ICE)
INTERMEC INC
INTERNAP NETWORK SERVICES CORP
INTERNATIONAL CREATIVE MANAGEMENT (ICM)

INTERNATIONAL DAIRY QUEEN
INTERNET SECURITY SYSTEMS INC
INTERSTATE BATTERY SYSTEM OF AMERICA
INTERWOVEN INC
INVESTMENT TECHNOLOGY GROUP INC (ITG)
IRIDEX CORP
IRIS INTERNATIONAL INC
ISONICS CORPORATION
IVILLAGE INC
JACKSON NATIONAL LIFE INSURANCE COMPANY
JUPITERMEDIA CORP
KAMPGROUNDS OF AMERICA INC
KIMLEY-HORN AND ASSOCIATES INC
KNIGHT CAPITAL GROUP INC
KNOT INC (THE)
KRONOS WORLDWIDE INC
LCA-VISION INC
LCC INTERNATIONAL INC
LEAP WIRELESS INTERNATIONAL INC
LESLIE'S POOLMART INC
LIFECELL CORPORATION
LIVEPERSON INC
LOGISTICARE INC
LOJACK CORP
LORAL SPACE & COMMUNICATIONS LTD
LUCOR INC
M&F WORLDWIDE CORP
MAGELLAN MIDSTREAM PARTNERS LP
MALT-O-MEAL COMPANY
MANHATTAN ASSOCIATES INC
MARCHEX INC
MARTEK BIOSCIENCES CORP
MARTHA STEWART LIVING OMNIMEDIA INC
MARVEL ENTERTAINMENT INC
MATRIA HEALTHCARE INC
MEDAREX INC
MEDICAL ACTION INDUSTRIES INC
MEDICINES CO (THE)
MEDICIS PHARMACEUTICAL CORP
MEDIS TECHNOLOGIES
MEDTOX SCIENTIFIC INC
MERIDIAN BIOSCIENCE INC
MERIT MEDICAL SYSTEMS INC
METROLOGIC INSTRUMENTS INC
MICHELINAS INC
MICROSTRATEGY INC
MIDAS INC
MILLENNIUM PHARMACEUTICALS INC
MOELIS & COMPANY
MOTORCAR PARTS OF AMERICA INC
MTS SYSTEMS
NASDAQ OMX
NATIONAL BEVERAGE CORP
NATIONAL CINEMEDIA INC
NATIONAL DENTEX CORP
NATIONAL FUEL GAS CO
NATUS MEDICAL
NAVISITE INC
NETRATINGS INC
NETSCOUT SYSTEMS INC
NOVAMED INC
NTELOS HOLDING CORP
NUSTAR ENERGY LP
NYER MEDICAL GROUP INC
NYMEX HOLDINGS (NEW YORK MERCANTILE EXCHANGE)
ODYSSEY RE HOLDINGS CORP
ONLINE RESOURCES CORP
OPENTV CORP
OPNEXT INC
OPTELECOM-NKF INC
OSCIENT PHARMACEUTICALS CORPORATION
PALM INC
PAR PHARMACEUTICAL COMPANIES INC
PC CONNECTION INC
PEAPOD LLC
PERFICIENT INC
PETROLEUM DEVELOPMENT CORPORATION
PHILADELPHIA CONSOLIDATED HOLDING CORP
PHOENIX COMPANIES (THE)
PIEDMONT NATURAL GAS COMPANY INC
PITNEY BOWES MAPINFO
PLUG POWER INC
PMA CAPITAL CORPORATION
POLYCOM INC
POLYMEDICA CORPORATION
POLYPORE INTERNATIONAL INC
PREMIERE GLOBAL SERVICES INC
PRIMEENERGY CORPORATION
PROASSURANCE CORP
PROGRESS SOFTWARE CORP
PROTECTIVE LIFE CORP
QLOGIC CORP
QUALITY SYSTEMS INC
RADISYS CORP
RADNET INC
RADYNE CORPORATION
RANGE RESOURCES CORP
RECYCLED ENERGY DEVELOPMENT
RED HAT INC
REDDY ICE HOLDINGS INC
REGENERON PHARMACEUTICALS INC
REVOLUTION HEALTH GROUP LLC
RIGHTNOW TECHNOLOGIES INC
ROBERT W BAIRD & CO INC
RSA SECURITY INC
S1 CORPORATION
SALIX PHARMACEUTICALS
SAVVIS INC
SCANSOURCE INC
SCHICK TECHNOLOGIES INC
SCIOS INC
SCOULAR COMPANY (THE)
SEACHANGE INTERNATIONAL INC
SECURE COMPUTING CORP
SENTO
SEPRACOR INC
SEQUENOM INC
SERENA SOFTWARE INC
SHARED TECHNOLOGIES
SHENANDOAH TELECOMMUNICATIONS CO
SHUTTERFLY INC
SKILLSOFT PLC
SONUS NETWORKS INC
SOUTHERN UNION COMPANY
SPAN AMERICA MEDICAL SYSTEMS INC
SPIRE CORPORATION
SPSS INC
SRI/SURGICAL EXPRESS INC

# INDEX BY FIRMS WITH INTERNATIONAL OPERATIONS

CENTRAL VERMONT PUBLIC SERVICE CORPORATION
CEPHEID
CHANNELL COMMERCIAL CORP
CHATTEM INC
CHINDEX INTERNATIONAL INC
CHYRON CORP
CIENA CORP
CKX INC
CLEARWIRE CORP
CME GROUP
COGNEX CORP
COHERENT INC
COINSTAR INC
COLLAGENEX PHARMACEUTICALS INC
COMTECH TELECOMMUNICATIONS CORP
CONCUR TECHNOLOGIES INC
CORPORATE EXECUTIVE BOARD COMPANY (THE)
CROWN CASTLE INTERNATIONAL CORP
CRYOLIFE INC
CURVES INTERNATIONAL INC
CV THERAPEUTICS INC
CYBERSOURCE CORP
DAKTRONICS INC
DARLING INTERNATIONAL INC
DATASCOPE CORP
DEI HOLDINGS INC
DELPHI FINANCIAL GROUP INC
DIAMOND FOODS INC
DIGI INTERNATIONAL INC
DIGITAL RIVER INC
DOUBLECLICK INC
DRUGSTORE.COM INC
DSP GROUP INC
DYAX CORP
DYNACQ HEALTHCARE INC
DYNEGY INC
ECHELON CORP
ECLIPSYS CORPORATION
ECOLLEGE.COM
ELECTRONICS FOR IMAGING INC
ELOYALTY CORPORATION
EMBARCADERO TECHNOLOGIES INC
EMCORE CORP
EMS TECHNOLOGIES INC
EMULEX CORP
ENCORIUM GROUP INC
ENERGY CONVERSION DEVICES INC
ENGLOBAL CORP
EOG RESOURCES INC
EPAM SYSTEMS
EPIX PHARMACEUTICALS INC
EQUINIX INC
EURONET WORLDWIDE INC
EVERCORE PARTNERS INC
EVERGREEN SOLAR INC
EXACTECH INC
EXCEL TECHNOLOGY INC
EXELIXIS INC
E-Z-EM INC
F5 NETWORKS INC
FEDEX SUPPLY CHAIN SERVICES INC
FIRST SOLAR LLC
FLIR SYSTEMS
FOREST OIL CORPORATION
FORRESTER RESEARCH INC
FUEL TECH INC
FUELCELL ENERGY INC
FUNDTECH LTD
GALLUP ORGANIZATION (THE)
GENENCOR INTERNATIONAL INC
GERBER SCIENTIFIC INC
GLOBECOMM SYSTEMS INC
GLU MOBILE INC
GOLFSMITH INTERNATIONAL HOLDINGS INC
HACKETT GROUP (THE)
HAEMONETICS CORPORATION
HARMONIC INC
HARRIS STRATEX NETWORKS INC
HCC INSURANCE HOLDINGS INC
HEALTHTRONICS INC
HEARUSA INC
HEIDRICK & STRUGGLES INTERNATIONAL INC
HESKA CORP
HOULIHAN LOKEY
HURON CONSULTING GROUP INC
IBASIS INC
ICO INC
I-FLOW CORPORATION
ILLUMINA INC
IMATION CORP
IMG WORLDWIDE INC
IMMUCOR INC
INAMED CORP
INFINERA CORP
INTEGRA LIFESCIENCES HOLDINGS CORP
INTEGRAL SYSTEMS INC
INTELLIGROUP INC
INTERACTIVE BROKERS GROUP INC
INTERACTIVE INTELLIGENCE
INTERCONTINENTALEXCHANGE INC (ICE)
INTERMEC INC
INTERNAP NETWORK SERVICES CORP
INTERNATIONAL CREATIVE MANAGEMENT (ICM)
INTERNATIONAL DAIRY QUEEN
INTERNET SECURITY SYSTEMS INC
INTERSTATE BATTERY SYSTEM OF AMERICA
INTERWOVEN INC
INVESTMENT TECHNOLOGY GROUP INC (ITG)
IRIDEX CORP
IRIS INTERNATIONAL INC
ISILON SYSTEMS INC
J2 GLOBAL COMMUNICATIONS INC
JUPITERMEDIA CORP
KAMPGROUNDS OF AMERICA INC
KNIGHT CAPITAL GROUP INC
KRONOS WORLDWIDE INC
LCA-VISION INC
LCC INTERNATIONAL INC
LIFECORE BIOMEDICAL INC
LIVEPERSON INC
LOJACK CORP
LORAL SPACE & COMMUNICATIONS LTD
LUMINEX CORPORATION
M&F WORLDWIDE CORP
MANHATTAN ASSOCIATES INC
MARVEL ENTERTAINMENT INC
MATRIA HEALTHCARE INC
MAXYGEN INC
MEDICAL ACTION INDUSTRIES INC
MEDICINES CO (THE)

MEDIS TECHNOLOGIES
MENTOR CORP
MERIDIAN BIOSCIENCE INC
MERIT MEDICAL SYSTEMS INC
METROLOGIC INSTRUMENTS INC
MICHELINAS INC
MICROSTRATEGY INC
MICROTEK MEDICAL HOLDINGS INC
MIDAS INC
MOELIS & COMPANY
MOTORCAR PARTS OF AMERICA INC
MTS SYSTEMS
NANOMETRICS INC
NASDAQ OMX
NATIONAL DENTEX CORP
NATIONAL FUEL GAS CO
NATUS MEDICAL
NAVISITE INC
NEKTAR THERAPEUTICS
NEOGEN CORPORATION
NETGEAR INC
NETRATINGS INC
NETSCOUT SYSTEMS INC
NETSUITE INC
NEWFIELD EXPLORATION CO
NOBLE ENERGY INC
NUSTAR ENERGY LP
NYMEX HOLDINGS (NEW YORK MERCANTILE EXCHANGE)
ODYSSEY RE HOLDINGS CORP
OMNITURE INC
ONEOK PARTNERS LP
OPENTV CORP
OPNEXT INC
OPTELECOM-NKF INC
ORMAT TECHNOLOGIES
PALM INC
PC MALL INC
PERFICIENT INC
PHOENIX COMPANIES (THE)
PIONEER NATURAL RESOURCES COMPANY
PITNEY BOWES MAPINFO
PLUG POWER INC
POLYCOM INC
POLYPORE INTERNATIONAL INC
PREMIERE GLOBAL SERVICES INC
PROGRESS SOFTWARE CORP
QLOGIC CORP
QUICKSILVER RESOURCES INC
RADISYS CORP
REALNETWORKS INC
RED HAT INC
REINSURANCE GROUP OF AMERICA INC
RIGHTNOW TECHNOLOGIES INC
ROBERT W BAIRD & CO INC
RSA SECURITY INC
S1 CORPORATION
SAVVIS INC
SCANSOURCE INC
SCHIFF NUTRITION INTERNATIONAL INC
SCICLONE PHARMACEUTICALS
SCOULAR COMPANY (THE)
SEACHANGE INTERNATIONAL INC
SECURE COMPUTING CORP
SENTO
SEPRACOR INC
SEQUENOM INC
SERENA SOFTWARE INC
SKILLSOFT PLC
SOLAR RESERVE
SOLFOCUS INC
SONIC INNOVATIONS INC
SONUS NETWORKS INC
SPECTRANETICS CORP
SPIRE CORPORATION
SPSS INC
SS&C TECHNOLOGIES INC
STAAR SURGICAL CO
STANDARD MICROSYSTEMS CORPORATION
STERLING AUTOBODY CENTERS
STIEFEL LABORATORIES INC
SUPER MICRO COMPUTER INC
SWIFT ENERGY CO
SYCAMORE NETWORKS INC
SYMMETRY MEDICAL INC
SYMYX TECHNOLOGIES
SYNAPTICS INC
TARGA RESOURCES PARTNERS LP
TECHNE CORP
TELIRIS
TERREMARK WORLDWIDE INC
THOMAS WEISEL PARTNERS GROUP INC
THORATEC CORPORATION
THQ INC
TIBCO SOFTWARE INC
TIVO INC
TOMOTHERAPY INC
TOOTSIE ROLL INDUSTRIES INC
TOPPS COMPANY INC (THE)
TRANSATLANTIC HOLDINGS INC
TRAPEZE NETWORKS INC
TULLY'S COFFEE CORPORATION
ULTIMATE SOFTWARE GROUP INC
UNDER ARMOUR INC
UNITED ONLINE INC
UNITED THERAPEUTICS CORP
VALUECLICK INC
VASCO DATA SECURITY INTERNATIONAL INC
VENTANA MEDICAL SYSTEMS INC
VERAZ NETWORKS INC
VERIFONE HOLDINGS INC
VERTEX PHARMACEUTICALS INC
VIASAT INC
VIBRANT MEDIA INC
VIGNETTE CORP
VISION SERVICE PLAN
VITAL SIGNS INC
VOLCOM INC
VSE CORP
WEBEX COMMUNICATIONS INC
WEBMD HEALTH CORP
WEBSENSE INC
WESTAR ENERGY
WIND RIVER SYSTEMS INC
WRIGHT MEDICAL GROUP INC
ZIEBART INTERNATIONAL CORP
ZILA INC
ZOLL MEDICAL CORP

# Individual Data Profiles On Each Of The MID-SIZE EMPLOYERS 500

# 24/7 REAL MEDIA INC

**www.247realmedia.com**

**Industry Group Code:** 541810A **Ranks within this company's industry group:** Sales: Profits:

| Management: | | Sales/Marketing: | | Liberal Arts: | | Information Systems: | | Professionals: | | Technical/Scientific: | |
|---|---|---|---|---|---|---|---|---|---|---|---|
| Mgmt. Trainees: | | Mktg. Professionals: | Y | Gen. Writing/Editing: | Y | Info. Management: | Y | Finance/Accounting: | Y | Engineers, Elec.: | |
| Experienced Mgmt.: | Y | Retail Sales: | | Technical Writing: | | Software Dev.: | Y | Law: | Y | Engineers, Other: | |
| Int'l Business: | Y | Commercial/Industrial: | | Graphic Arts/Photog.: | Y | Hardware Dev.: | | HR/Other: | Y | Health/Lab: | |
| MBA Graduates: | Y | Sales Trainees: | Y | Music: | | Systems Integration: | Y | Training: | Y | Scientists/Research: | |
| | | Advertising Pros.: | Y | Broadcasting: | | Consulting/Other: | | Health Care: | | Petroleum/Chemicals: | |
| | | | | Other: | Y | | | Consulting: | | Math/Other: | |

## TYPES OF BUSINESS:

Internet Advertising
Web Design
Software
Direct Marketing
Promotions
Data Analysis

## BRANDS/DIVISIONS/AFFILIATES:

WPP plc
24/7 Web Results
24/7 Search
Open AdStream 6 Network Edition
Decide DNA 6
Dentsu 24/7 Search Holdings
Rich Media Foundry
K.K. 24-7 Search

## CONTACTS: *Note: Officers with more than one job title may be intentionally listed here more than once.*

Jonathan Hsu, CEO
Kris Heinrichs, CFO
Ari Bluman, Sr. VP-U.S. Sales
Oleg Vishnepolsky, CTO
Mark E. Moran, General Counsel/Sr. VP
Ari Bluman, Sr. VP-U.S. Oper.
Jae Woo Chung, Pres., K.K. 24-7 Search
Ian Leuchars, Sr. VP-Search Mktg. Svcs.
David J. Moore, Chmn.

**Phone:** 212-231-7100 **Fax:** 212-760-1774
**Toll-Free:** 877-247-2477
**Address:** 132 W. 31st St., New York, NY 10001 US

## GROWTH PLANS/SPECIAL FEATURES:

24/7 Real Media, Inc. is a global provider of interactive technology and marketing solutions for web publishers, online advertisers, advertising agencies and e-marketers. The firm's services include advertising and direct marketing sales, search engine marketing services, online advertisement serving, web advertising, site representation and web analytics. The company sells its products and services in 12 countries in North America, Europe and Asia. 24/7 is organized into three solution divisions: Technology, Media and Search. The Technology segment, through its Open AdSystem platform, is designed for advertisers/agencies, web publishers and e-commerce merchants. The Media division consists of 24/7 Web Alliance, a group of web sites that allow client advertisers to place targeted ad campaigns, and 24/7 Web Results, which provides performance-based marketing services for the Internet. The Search division, 24/7 Search, provides search marketing services for the Internet. Dentsu 24/7 Search, its Japanese subsidiary, targets markets in Asia and the Pacific Rim. The firm's Rich Media Foundry creates and traffics rich media advertising. 24/7 integrated with China's largest search engine, Baidu.com, to expand its search capacity to reach Baidu's 162 million Internet users. In 2007, the firm was acquired by WPP plc for roughly $649 million. In April 2008, the company partnered with Cygnus Business Media, Nielsen Business Media, Reed Business Information and McGraw-Hill to form BBN, the largest B2B online advertising network in the U.S. In the same month, 24/7 partnered with Mindset Media, LLC, to offer Mindset Buys, a psychographic targeting program that targets consumers by personality traits. In September 2008, 24/7 introduced Lifecycle Media Management model and Open Adstream 7.0. In November 2008, the company announced that it will partner with OgilvyOne to create ITOP 24/7, a Chinese advertising network.

## FINANCIALS: **Sales and profits are in thousands of dollars—add 000 to get the full amount. 2008 Note: Financial information for 2008 was not available for all companies at press time.**

| | | |
|---|---|---|
| 2008 Sales: $ | 2008 Profits: $ | **U.S. Stock Ticker: Subsidiary** |
| 2007 Sales: $ | 2007 Profits: $ | **Int'l Ticker:** Int'l Exchange: |
| 2006 Sales: $200,243 | 2006 Profits: $-8,622 | Employees: 368 |
| 2005 Sales: $139,794 | 2005 Profits: $ 38 | Fiscal Year Ends: 12/31 |
| 2004 Sales: $85,255 | 2004 Profits: $-3,155 | Parent Company: WPP PLC |

## SALARIES/BENEFITS:

| | | | | |
|---|---|---|---|---|
| Pension Plan: | ESOP Stock Plan: Y | Profit Sharing: | Top Exec. Salary: $270,450 | Bonus: $436,025 |
| Savings Plan: | Stock Purch. Plan: | | Second Exec. Salary: $200,000 | Bonus: $167,702 |

## OTHER THOUGHTS:

**Apparent Women Officers or Directors:**
**Hot Spot for Advancement for Women/Minorities:**

## LOCATIONS: ("Y" = Yes)

| West: | Southwest: | Midwest: | Southeast: | Northeast: | International: |
|---|---|---|---|---|---|
| Y | | Y | | Y | Y |

# AAMCO TRANSMISSIONS INC

www.aamco.com

**Industry Group Code:** 811100 **Ranks within this company's industry group:** Sales: Profits:

| Management: | | Sales/Marketing: | | Liberal Arts: | | Information Systems: | | Professionals: | | Technical/Scientific: | |
|---|---|---|---|---|---|---|---|---|---|---|---|
| Mgmt. Trainees: | | Mktg. Professionals: | Y | Gen. Writing/Editing: | | Info. Management: | Y | Finance/Accounting: | Y | Engineers, Elec.: | |
| Experienced Mgmt.: | Y | Retail Sales: | | Technical Writing: | | Software Dev.: | | Law: | Y | Engineers, Other: | |
| Int'l Business: | Y | Commercial/Industrial: | | Graphic Arts/Photog.: | | Hardware Dev.: | | HR/Other: | Y | Health/Lab: | |
| MBA Graduates: | Y | Sales Trainees: | | Music: | | Systems Integration: | | Training: | Y | Scientists/Research: | |
| | | Advertising Pros.: | | Broadcasting: | | Consulting/Other: | | Health Care: | | Petroleum/Chemicals: | |
| | | | | Other: | | | | Consulting: | | Math/Other: | |

## TYPES OF BUSINESS:

Automotive Repair & Maintenance-Transmissions
Automatic Transmission Fluid
Bioethanol Conversion

## BRANDS/DIVISIONS/AFFILIATES:

AAMCO Automatic Transmission Fluid
AAMCO Synthetic Blend ATF
AAMCO ATF D/M
AAMCO ATF+3
AAMCO ATF Type F
Cottman Transmissions
Flex-Box Smart Kit

## CONTACTS: *Note: Officers with more than one job title may be intentionally listed here more than once.*

Todd P. Leff, CEO
Todd P. Leff, Pres.
Mike Sumsky, CFO
Bruce Schmidt, VP-Mktg.
Bill Larkin, VP-Tech. Svcs.
Jim Goniea, General Counsel/VP-Law
Brian O'Donnell, Sr. VP-Oper.
Mike Sumsky, VP-Finance
Kevin Gordon, VP-Brand Dev.

| | |
|---|---|
| **Phone:** 215-643-5885 | **Fax:** 215-956-0340 |
| **Toll-Free:** 800-462-2626 | |
| **Address:** 201 Gibraltar Rd., Horsham, PA 19044-2329 US | |

## GROWTH PLANS/SPECIAL FEATURES:

AAMCO Transmissions, Inc., founded in 1963, is one of the world's largest chains of auto transmission shops with more than 800 independently owned and operated franchise locations in the U.S., Canada and Puerto Rico. AAMCO's services include diagnostic, repair and maintenance services for automatic and standard transmissions in cars and trucks; free towing; external inspections; and estimates. The company guarantees its services through a selection of six warranty packages from 90-day limited contracts to lifetime coverage. AAMCO also offers a national fleet program in which more than 500 owners of large fleets of vehicles contract transmission services at discounted prices. Moreover, the firm manufactures a branded automatic transmission fluid, AAMCO Automatic Transmission Fluid (ATF), which is marketed by Exxon Superflo. The ExxonMobil subsidiary blends, packages and markets AAMCO ATF and additional transmission fluid products (AAMCO Mercon V, AAMCO Synthetic Blend ATF, AAMCO ATF D/M, AAMCO ATF+3 and AAMCO ATF Type F) through automotive product retailers across North America. AAMCO completed a merger with Cottman Transmissions in 2006 to create one of the country's largest car care companies. The merger expanded AAMCO's repertoire to include services such as electrical, brakes and complete driveline repairs and maintenance. In 2007, former NFL player Dan Wilkinson signed a development agreement to open a minimum of seven new AAMCO centers throughout Ohio. More recently, the firm launched its Eco-Green Auto Service at approximately 40 locations in the U.S. which meet eco-friendly standards such as solvent and waste fluid recycling. These locations offer, in addition to standard AAMCO services, a bioethanol fuel conversion kit called the Flex-Box Smart Kit, developed in partnership with Flex Fuel U.S.

## FINANCIALS: **Sales and profits are in thousands of dollars—add 000 to get the full amount. 2008 Note: Financial information for 2008 was not available for all companies at press time.**

| | | |
|---|---|---|
| 2008 Sales: $ | 2008 Profits: $ | **U.S. Stock Ticker: Private** |
| 2007 Sales: $ | 2007 Profits: $ | **Int'l Ticker:** Int'l Exchange: |
| 2006 Sales: $ | 2006 Profits: $ | Employees: 160 |
| 2005 Sales: $ | 2005 Profits: $ | Fiscal Year Ends: 12/31 |
| 2004 Sales: $ | 2004 Profits: $ | Parent Company: |

## SALARIES/BENEFITS:

| | | | | |
|---|---|---|---|---|
| Pension Plan: | ESOP Stock Plan: | Profit Sharing: | Top Exec. Salary: $ | Bonus: $ |
| Savings Plan: | Stock Purch. Plan: | | Second Exec. Salary: $ | Bonus: $ |

## OTHER THOUGHTS:

**Apparent Women Officers or Directors**:
**Hot Spot for Advancement for Women/Minorities**:

## LOCATIONS: ("Y" = Yes)

| West: | Southwest: | Midwest: | Southeast: | Northeast: | International: |
|---|---|---|---|---|---|
| Y | Y | Y | Y | Y | Y |

# ABAXIS INC

www.abaxis.com

**Industry Group Code:** 339113 **Ranks within this company's industry group:** Sales: 32 Profits: 20

| Management: | | Sales/Marketing: | | Liberal Arts: | | Information Systems: | | Professionals: | | Technical/Scientific: | |
|---|---|---|---|---|---|---|---|---|---|---|---|
| Mgmt. Trainees: | | Mktg. Professionals: | Y | Gen. Writing/Editing: | | Info. Management: | Y | Finance/Accounting: | Y | Engineers, Elec.: | Y |
| Experienced Mgmt.: | Y | Retail Sales: | | Technical Writing: | Y | Software Dev.: | Y | Law: | Y | Engineers, Other: | Y |
| Int'l Business: | Y | Commercial/Industrial: | Y | Graphic Arts/Photog.: | | Hardware Dev.: | Y | HR/Other: | Y | Health/Lab: | Y |
| MBA Graduates: | Y | Sales Trainees: | Y | Music: | | Systems Integration: | | Training: | Y | Scientists/Research: | Y |
| | | Advertising Pros.: | | Broadcasting: | | Consulting/Other: | | Health Care: | Y | Petroleum/Chemicals: | |
| | | | | Other: | | | | Consulting: | | Math/Other: | Y |

## TYPES OF BUSINESS:

Point-of-Care Blood Analyzer Systems Equipment
Veterinary Blood Analyzer Systems
Reagents & Supplies

## BRANDS/DIVISIONS/AFFILIATES:

VetScan VS2
VetScan Classic
Piccolo Classic
Piccolo Xpress
VetScan HM2
Orbos Discrete Lyophilization Process
VetScan HM5

## CONTACTS: *Note: Officers with more than one job title may be intentionally listed here more than once.*

Clinton H. Severson, CEO
Clinton H.Severson, Pres.
Al Santa Ines, CFO
Christopher Bernard, VP-Mktg. & Sales, Medical Market
Kenneth P. Aron, CIO
Donald Wood, VP-Oper.
Al Santa Ines, VP-Finance
Martin Mulroy, VP-Mktg. & Sales, Veterinary Market
Clinton H. Severson, Chmn.
Vladimir E. Ostoich, VP-Gov't Affairs & Mktg., Pacific Rim

| | |
|---|---|
| **Phone:** 510-675-6500 | **Fax:** 510-441-6150 |
| **Toll-Free:** | |
| **Address:** 3240 Whipple Rd., Union City, CA 94587 US | |

## GROWTH PLANS/SPECIAL FEATURES:

Abaxis, Inc. develops, manufactures and markets portable blood analysis systems for use in veterinary or human patient-care settings to provide clinicians with rapid blood constituent measurements. The medical market accounted for 23% of total revenue during 2007, and the veterinary market accounted for 71%. The analysis systems are marketed as VetScan VS2 and VetScan Classic in the veterinary market, and as the Piccolo Classic and Piccolo Xpress in the human medical market. Abaxis' blood analysis systems consist of a compact analyzer and a series of single-use plastic discs, called reagent discs, containing all the chemicals required to perform a panel of up to 27 diagnostic tests, 21 of which are also marketed for the veterinary market, with two unique to the veterinary market. In addition to blood analysis systems, Abaxis sells the VetScan HM2 (formerly VetScan HMII) hematology analyzer that provides an 18-parameter blood count analysis, including a three-part white blood cell differential. To produce the dry reagents used in the reagent disks, Abaxis uses its Orbos Discrete Lyophilization Process (Orbos process), a process which freeze dries reagents in small quantities, enabling efficient manufacturing of reagents in a convenient and stable format. Abaxis licenses its Orbos process to bioMerieux, Cepheid and GE Healthcare. In February 2007, Abaxis entered into a distribution agreement with Cardinal Health for its Piccolo Xpress and medical reagent disks. In July 2007, it signed a distribution agreement with McKesson Medical-Surgical for the same products. In September 2007, Abaxis introduced the VetScan HM5, a veterinary hematology instrument that offers a 22-parameter complete blood count analysis. In October 2007, Abaxis signed an exclusive distribution agreement with a Japanese company to distribute the firm's complete line of products.

Abaxis offers a flexible spending account plan and memberships at financial institutions, retail outlets and clubs.

## FINANCIALS: **Sales and profits are in thousands of dollars—add 000 to get the full amount. 2008 Note: Financial information for 2008 was not available for all companies at press time.**

| | | |
|---|---|---|
| 2008 Sales: $ | 2008 Profits: $ | **U.S. Stock Ticker: ABAX** |
| 2007 Sales: $86,221 | 2007 Profits: $10,073 | **Int'l Ticker:** Int'l Exchange: |
| 2006 Sales: $68,928 | 2006 Profits: $7,475 | Employees: 321 |
| 2005 Sales: $52,758 | 2005 Profits: $4,851 | Fiscal Year Ends: 3/31 |
| 2004 Sales: $46,874 | 2004 Profits: $24,033 | Parent Company: |

## SALARIES/BENEFITS:

| | | | | |
|---|---|---|---|---|
| Pension Plan: | ESOP Stock Plan: | Profit Sharing: | Top Exec. Salary: $323,000 | Bonus: $ |
| Savings Plan: Y | Stock Purch. Plan: | | Second Exec. Salary: $199,123 | Bonus: $ |

## OTHER THOUGHTS:

**Apparent Women Officers or Directors:**
**Hot Spot for Advancement for Women/Minorities:**

## LOCATIONS: ("Y" = Yes)

| West: | Southwest: | Midwest: | Southeast: | Northeast: | International: |
|---|---|---|---|---|---|
| Y | | | | | Y |

# ACI WORLDWIDE INC

www.aciworldwide.com

**Industry Group Code:** 511201 **Ranks within this company's industry group:** Sales: 1 Profits: 7

| Management: | | Sales/Marketing: | | Liberal Arts: | | Information Systems: | | Professionals: | | Technical/Scientific: | |
|---|---|---|---|---|---|---|---|---|---|---|---|
| Mgmt. Trainees: | | Mktg. Professionals: | Y | Gen. Writing/Editing: | | Info. Management: | Y | Finance/Accounting: | Y | Engineers, Elec.: | Y |
| Experienced Mgmt.: | Y | Retail Sales: | | Technical Writing: | Y | Software Dev.: | Y | Law: | Y | Engineers, Other: | |
| Int'l Business: | Y | Commercial/Industrial: | Y | Graphic Arts/Photog.: | | Hardware Dev.: | | HR/Other: | Y | Health/Lab: | |
| MBA Graduates: | Y | Sales Trainees: | Y | Music: | | Systems Integration: | | Training: | Y | Scientists/Research: | |
| | | Advertising Pros.: | | Broadcasting: | | Consulting/Other: | Y | Health Care: | | Petroleum/Chemicals: | |
| | | | | Other: | | | | Consulting: | | Math/Other: | |

## TYPES OF BUSINESS:

Computer Software-Electronic Funds Transfer
Information Management Solutions
Electronic Banking & Smart Card Solutions
International Payments & Message Processing Software

## BRANDS/DIVISIONS/AFFILIATES:

ACI Worldwide
Transaction Systems Architects, Inc.

## CONTACTS: *Note: Officers with more than one job title may be intentionally listed here more than once.*

Philip G. Heasley, CEO
Mark R. Vipond, COO
Philip G. Heasley, Pres.
Henry C. Lyons, CFO/Sr. VP
Jeffrey S. Hale, Chief Mktg. Officer
Charles H. Linberg, CTO
David N. Morem, Chief Admin. Officer
Dennis Byrnes, General Counsel/Sr. VP/Sec.
Richard N. Launder, Pres., Global Oper.
Craig A. Maki, Chief Corp. Dev. Officer
Jim Maxwell, Media Rel.
Tamar Gerber, VP-Investor Rel.
Scott W. Behrens, Chief Acct. Officer/Controller/VP
Ralph Dangelmaier, Pres., Americas Channel Service
Harlan F. Seymour, Chmn.
Jeremy Wilmot, Pres., Asia Pacific Region

**Phone:** 646-348-6700 **Fax:** 212-470-4000
**Toll-Free:**
**Address:** 120 Broadway, Ste. 3350, New York, NY 10271 US

## GROWTH PLANS/SPECIAL FEATURES:

ACI Worldwide, Inc., formerly Transaction Systems Architects, Inc., provides electronic payment software and services covering a broad range of e-commerce, e-payment and information management solutions. Offerings include consumer and corporate banking, Internet banking and smart card services. The firm's products facilitate electronic payments and electronic bill payment and presentment. Furthermore, ACI's products monitor and manage applications on a smart card and operate on several hardware platforms, including HP, IBM, Stratus, UNIX and Microsoft Windows. The company offers products in four principal industries: retail banking, retail, wholesale banking and cross industry. Retail banking software products include payment processing, which acquires, authorizes and routes electronic payments in high-volume environments; web-based banking; fraud detection and anti-money laundering; back office solutions to automate settlement, clearing, reporting and reconciliation; and customer and token management, which manages card, account and customer functions. Retail software products include payment switching to securely acquire, authorize, authenticate and route electronic transactions; check management and collection, which is designed to limit a retailer's exposure to bad check losses; card management; rewards management; and refunds management for online refunds authorization. Wholesale banking software products include payments processing and management; online banking; fraud and risk management; trade finance; and customer and token management to automate enrollments. Cross industry software products include web-enabled software that implements a secure service-oriented architecture; security and connectivity; business continuity for data replication and system monitoring; smart IT for issuing and managing chip-base identification; and tools and utilities for data application and systems management. ACI serves over 800 customers in 88 countries, including many of the world's largest financial institutions, retailers and payment processors.

The company offers its employees health and dental coverage; life insurance; short- and long-term disability; a retirement plan; flexible schedule options; a stock purchase plan; and tuition reimbursement.

## FINANCIALS: **Sales and profits are in thousands of dollars—add 000 to get the full amount. 2008 Note: Financial information for 2008 was not available for all companies at press time.**

| | | |
|---|---|---|
| 2008 Sales: $ | 2008 Profits: $ | **U.S. Stock Ticker: ACIW** |
| 2007 Sales: $366,218 | 2007 Profits: $-9,131 | **Int'l Ticker:** Int'l Exchange: |
| 2006 Sales: $347,902 | 2006 Profits: $55,365 | Employees: 2,186 |
| 2005 Sales: $313,237 | 2005 Profits: $43,246 | Fiscal Year Ends: 9/30 |
| 2004 Sales: $292,784 | 2004 Profits: $46,685 | Parent Company: |

## SALARIES/BENEFITS:

| | | | | |
|---|---|---|---|---|
| Pension Plan: | ESOP Stock Plan: | Profit Sharing: | Top Exec. Salary: $508,333 | Bonus: $217,174 |
| Savings Plan: Y | Stock Purch. Plan: Y | | Second Exec. Salary: $275,004 | Bonus: $107,326 |

## OTHER THOUGHTS:

**Apparent Women Officers or Directors**:
**Hot Spot for Advancement for Women/Minorities**:

## LOCATIONS: ("Y" = Yes)

| West: | Southwest: | Midwest: | Southeast: | Northeast: | International: |
|---|---|---|---|---|---|
| | Y | Y | Y | Y | Y |

Note: Financial information, benefits and other data can change quickly and may vary from those stated here.

# ACME PACKET INC

**www.acmepacket.com**

**Industry Group Code:** 513300D **Ranks within this company's industry group:** Sales: 4 Profits: 2

| Management: | | Sales/Marketing: | | Liberal Arts: | | Information Systems: | | Professionals: | | Technical/Scientific: | |
|---|---|---|---|---|---|---|---|---|---|---|---|
| Mgmt. Trainees: | | Mktg. Professionals: | Y | Gen. Writing/Editing: | | Info. Management: | Y | Finance/Accounting: | Y | Engineers, Elec.: | Y |
| Experienced Mgmt.: | Y | Retail Sales: | | Technical Writing: | Y | Software Dev.: | Y | Law: | Y | Engineers, Other: | Y |
| Int'l Business: | Y | Commercial/Industrial: | Y | Graphic Arts/Photog.: | | Hardware Dev.: | | HR/Other: | Y | Health/Lab: | |
| MBA Graduates: | Y | Sales Trainees: | Y | Music: | | Systems Integration: | Y | Training: | Y | Scientists/Research: | |
| | | Advertising Pros.: | | Broadcasting: | | Consulting/Other: | | Health Care: | | Petroleum/Chemicals: | |
| | | | | Other: | | | | Consulting: | | Math/Other: | |

## TYPES OF BUSINESS:

Session Border Controllers
Professional Support Services

## BRANDS/DIVISIONS/AFFILIATES:

Net-Net OS
Net-Net 4000
Net-Net 4000 PAC
Net-Net 9000
Net-Net EMS
Acme Packet Session Aware Networking

## CONTACTS:

*Note: Officers with more than one job title may be intentionally listed here more than once.*

Andy Ory, CEO
Andy Ory, Pres.
Keith Seidman, CFO
Seamus Hourihan, VP-Mktg & Product Mgmt.
Patrick MeLampy, CTO
Dino Di Palma, VP-Bus. Dev. & Sales
Brian Norris, Dir.-Investor Rel.
Erin Medeiros, VP-Professional Svcs.
David Elsbree, Chmn.

| | |
|---|---|
| **Phone:** 781-328-4400 | **Fax:** 781-425-5077 |
| **Toll-Free:** | |
| **Address:** 71 3rd Ave., Burlington, MA 01803 US | |

## GROWTH PLANS/SPECIAL FEATURES:

Acme Packet, Inc. is a provider of session border controllers (SBC) that enable interactive communications service providers to deliver secure and high quality communications such as voice, video and other real-time multimedia sessions across defined border points where Internet protocol (IP) networks connect. SBCs are the only network element currently capable of integrating the control of signaling messages and media flows. SBCs complement, rather than replace, softswitches, data firewalls and routers. Acme Packet Session Aware Networking, the firm's technology architecture, enables the delivery of secure and high-quality interactive communication sessions across IP network borders. Implemented by the integration of the Net-Net OS software and Net-Net hardware platforms, the technology combines session routing policy; session signaling service; session media control; session monitoring and reporting; and session security service. Acme Packet's Net-Net family of products includes Net-Net OS, 4000, 4000 PAC, 9000 and EMS. The Net-Net products serve as a central element in unifying the separate IP networks that include wireline, wireless and cable networks. The company also provides a broad range of professional support services through every stage of its products' deployment. The firm sells its products and support services through roughly 45 distribution partners and a direct sales force. Acme Packet sells its products to over 500 customers in 85 countries. Customers include incumbent and competitive local exchange and long distance providers; international service providers; cable operators; Internet telephony service providers; voice application service providers; and wireless service providers. Acme Packet owns 22 patents. Revenue from customers in North America represented 48% of the company's total revenue in 2007. In June 2008, the company announced that NextGen, a Japanese engineering company, had signed an agreement to distribute the firm's SBCs as part of a packaged solution, aimed at providing security and control for Japanese IP interactive communication services.

## FINANCIALS:

**Sales and profits are in thousands of dollars—add 000 to get the full amount. 2008 Note: Financial information for 2008 was not available for all companies at press time.**

| | | |
|---|---|---|
| 2008 Sales: $ | 2008 Profits: $ | **U.S. Stock Ticker: APKT** |
| 2007 Sales: $113,052 | 2007 Profits: $19,561 | **Int'l Ticker:** Int'l Exchange: |
| 2006 Sales: $84,070 | 2006 Profits: $28,864 | Employees: 327 |
| 2005 Sales: $36,120 | 2005 Profits: $- 35 | Fiscal Year Ends: 12/31 |
| 2004 Sales: $15,993 | 2004 Profits: $-6,957 | Parent Company: |

## SALARIES/BENEFITS:

| | | | | |
|---|---|---|---|---|
| Pension Plan: | ESOP Stock Plan: | Profit Sharing: | Top Exec. Salary: $325,000 | Bonus: $ |
| Savings Plan: Y | Stock Purch. Plan: | | Second Exec. Salary: $328,034 | Bonus: $ |

## OTHER THOUGHTS:

**Apparent Women Officers or Directors**: 1
**Hot Spot for Advancement for Women/Minorities**: Y

## LOCATIONS: ("Y" = Yes)

| West: | Southwest: | Midwest: | Southeast: | Northeast: | International: |
|---|---|---|---|---|---|
| | | | | Y | Y |

# ACXIOM DIGITAL

www.acxiomdigital.com

**Industry Group Code:** 541810A **Ranks within this company's industry group:** Sales: Profits:

| Management: | | Sales/Marketing: | | Liberal Arts: | | Information Systems: | | Professionals: | | Technical/Scientific: | |
|---|---|---|---|---|---|---|---|---|---|---|---|
| Mgmt. Trainees: | | Mktg. Professionals: | Y | Gen. Writing/Editing: | Y | Info. Management: | Y | Finance/Accounting: | Y | Engineers, Elec.: | |
| Experienced Mgmt.: | Y | Retail Sales: | | Technical Writing: | | Software Dev.: | Y | Law: | Y | Engineers, Other: | |
| Int'l Business: | Y | Commercial/Industrial: | | Graphic Arts/Photog.: | Y | Hardware Dev.: | | HR/Other: | Y | Health/Lab: | |
| MBA Graduates: | Y | Sales Trainees: | Y | Music: | | Systems Integration: | Y | Training: | Y | Scientists/Research: | |
| | | Advertising Pros.: | Y | Broadcasting: | | Consulting/Other: | | Health Care: | | Petroleum/Chemicals: | |
| | | | | Other: | Y | | | Consulting: | | Math/Other: | |

## TYPES OF BUSINESS:

Direct Marketing E-Mail Services
Search Engine Marketing Services
Strategy & Analysis Services
Data Management
Web Development & Creative Design

## BRANDS/DIVISIONS/AFFILIATES:

Digital Impact
Acxiom Corporation
IMPACT
Transactional E-mail
Kefta Dynamic Targeting
Feedbuilder
Field Marketing Consolidator

## CONTACTS:

*Note: Officers with more than one job title may be intentionally listed here more than once.*

Timothy J. Suther, Pres.
Michael Gorman, Sr. VP-Search & Acquisition
Joelle Werich, Leader-Finance

| **Phone:** 650-356-3400 | **Fax:** 650-356-3410 |
|---|---|
| **Toll-Free:** 800-491-9320 | |
| **Address:** 1051 Hillsdale Blvd., Ste. 400, Foster City, CA 94404 US | |

## GROWTH PLANS/SPECIAL FEATURES:

Acxiom Digital, formerly Digital Impact, is Acxiom Corporation's online direct marketing subsidiary. Acxiom Digital offers services in five areas: E-mail marketing, website personalization, customer acquisition, search engine marketing and agency services. The firm provides these services primarily through proprietary technology, including: IMPACT, which helps enterprise marketing groups to communicate and collaborate; Transactional Email, which helps clients up-sell and cross-sell to their customers automatically based on previous transactions; Kefta Dynamic Targeting for web site personalization; Feedbuilder, which helps optimize data submitted to search indexes; Search Tools, which provides analysis of a company's position on search engines; Field Marketing Consolidator, which helps manage marketing campaigns; Deliverability 1st, which helps customize e-mails to navigate spam filters; and, through a partnership with GoodMail Systems, CertifiedEmail, a premium class of trusted e-mail that provides consumers a safe and easy way to identify authentic messages from legitimate senders. Acxiom Digital serves clients in the retail, financial services, healthcare, technology, telecommunications and travel and hospitality sectors, among others. These clients include Victoria's Secret; Capital One; Hewlett-Packard; and Marriott. In addition to these solutions, the company offers professional agency services such as strategy, analysis, data management, solutions engineering, web development, creative design and customer acquisition. In January 2008, the company implemented the Domain Keys Identified Mail (DKIM) email authentication standard on its IMPACT platform in order to provide its clients and their customers increased protection against email fraud and phishing attacks.

## FINANCIALS:

**Sales and profits are in thousands of dollars—add 000 to get the full amount. 2008 Note: Financial information for 2008 was not available for all companies at press time.**

| | | |
|---|---|---|
| 2008 Sales: $ | 2008 Profits: $ | **U.S. Stock Ticker: Subsidiary** |
| 2007 Sales: $ | 2007 Profits: $ | **Int'l Ticker:** Int'l Exchange: |
| 2006 Sales: $ | 2006 Profits: $ | Employees: 280 |
| 2005 Sales: $45,000 | 2005 Profits: $ | Fiscal Year Ends: 3/31 |
| 2004 Sales: $43,700 | 2004 Profits: $- 600 | Parent Company: ACXIOM CORP |

## SALARIES/BENEFITS:

| | | | | |
|---|---|---|---|---|
| Pension Plan: | ESOP Stock Plan: | Profit Sharing: | Top Exec. Salary: $ | Bonus: $79,830 |
| Savings Plan: | Stock Purch. Plan: | | Second Exec. Salary: $233,042 | Bonus: $233,042 |

## OTHER THOUGHTS:

**Apparent Women Officers or Directors:**
**Hot Spot for Advancement for Women/Minorities:**

## LOCATIONS: ("Y" = Yes)

| West: | Southwest: | Midwest: | Southeast: | Northeast: | International: |
|---|---|---|---|---|---|
| Y | | | | Y | Y |

# AFFYMETRIX INC

www.affymetrix.com

**Industry Group Code:** 325413 **Ranks within this company's industry group:** Sales: 2 Profits: 4

| Management: | | Sales/Marketing: | | Liberal Arts: | | Information Systems: | | Professionals: | | Technical/Scientific: | |
|---|---|---|---|---|---|---|---|---|---|---|---|
| Mgmt. Trainees: | | Mktg. Professionals: | Y | Gen. Writing/Editing: | | Info. Management: | Y | Finance/Accounting: | Y | Engineers, Elec.: | Y |
| Experienced Mgmt.: | Y | Retail Sales: | | Technical Writing: | Y | Software Dev.: | Y | Law: | Y | Engineers, Other: | Y |
| Int'l Business: | Y | Commercial/Industrial: | Y | Graphic Arts/Photog.: | | Hardware Dev.: | Y | HR/Other: | Y | Health/Lab: | Y |
| MBA Graduates: | Y | Sales Trainees: | Y | Music: | | Systems Integration: | | Training: | Y | Scientists/Research: | Y |
| | | Advertising Pros.: | | Broadcasting: | | Consulting/Other: | | Health Care: | Y | Petroleum/Chemicals: | |
| | | | | Other: | | | | Consulting: | | Math/Other: | Y |

## TYPES OF BUSINESS:

Chips-Genetics
DNA Array Technology
Genomics

## BRANDS/DIVISIONS/AFFILIATES:

GeneChip
CustomExpress
CustomSeq
USB Corporation
Panomics, Inc.

## CONTACTS: *Note: Officers with more than one job title may be intentionally listed here more than once.*

Kevin M. King, CEO
Kevin M. King, Pres.
John C. Batty, CFO
Rick Runkel, General Counsel
John C. Batty, Exec. VP-Finance
Stephen P. A. Fodor, Chmn.

| | |
|---|---|
| **Phone:** 408-731-5000 | **Fax:** 408-731-5441 |
| **Toll-Free:** 888-362-2447 | |
| **Address:** 3420 Central Expwy., Santa Clara, CA 95051 US | |

## GROWTH PLANS/SPECIAL FEATURES:

Affymetrix, Inc. develops, manufactures, sells and services consumables and systems for genetic analysis in the life sciences and clinical healthcare markets. The firm sells its products directly to pharmaceutical, biotechnology, agrichemical, diagnostics and consumer products companies, as well as academic research centers, government research laboratories, private foundation laboratories and clinical reference laboratories, in North America and Europe. The company also sells its products through life science supply specialists acting as authorized distributors in Latin America, India and the Middle East and Asia Pacific regions. Affymetrix markets products for two principal applications: monitoring of gene or exon expression levels and investigation of genetic variation. Its catalogue GeneChip expression arrays are available for the study of human, rat, mouse and a range of other mammalian and model organisms. Human, mouse and rat exon analysis arrays are also available. The firm's integrated GeneChip microarray platform includes disposable DNA probe arrays consisting of nucleic acid sequences set out in an ordered, high density pattern; certain reagents for use with the probe arrays; a scanner and other instruments used to process the probe arrays; and software to analyze and manage genomic or genetic information obtained from the probe arrays. Additionally, the company markets CustomExpress and CustomSeq products, which enable its customers to design their own custom GeneChip expression arrays or a sequence of arrays for organisms of interest to them. In January 2008, Affymetrix acquired USB Corporation, an Ohio-based developer of molecular biology and biochemical reagent products. In December 2008, Affymetrix acquired Panomics, Inc., a provider of assay products for a variety of low- to mid-plex genetic, protein and cellular analysis applications.

Affymetrix offers its employees a tuition assistance plan, health fitness membership discounts, a lunch program, a family resources program, domestic partner benefits, reimbursement accounts and medical, dental, vision, life and disability insurance.

## FINANCIALS: **Sales and profits are in thousands of dollars—add 000 to get the full amount. 2008 Note: Financial information for 2008 was not available for all companies at press time.**

| | | |
|---|---|---|
| 2008 Sales: $ | 2008 Profits: $ | **U.S. Stock Ticker: AFFX** |
| 2007 Sales: $371,320 | 2007 Profits: $12,593 | **Int'l Ticker:** Int'l Exchange: |
| 2006 Sales: $355,317 | 2006 Profits: $-13,704 | Employees: 1,141 |
| 2005 Sales: $367,602 | 2005 Profits: $65,787 | Fiscal Year Ends: 12/31 |
| 2004 Sales: $345,962 | 2004 Profits: $47,608 | Parent Company: |

## SALARIES/BENEFITS:

| | | | | |
|---|---|---|---|---|
| Pension Plan: | ESOP Stock Plan: | Profit Sharing: | Top Exec. Salary: $630,673 | Bonus: $635,000 |
| Savings Plan: Y | Stock Purch. Plan: | | Second Exec. Salary: $432,692 | Bonus: $500,000 |

## OTHER THOUGHTS:

**Apparent Women Officers or Directors**: 1
**Hot Spot for Advancement for Women/Minorities**: Y

## LOCATIONS: ("Y" = Yes)

| West: | Southwest: | Midwest: | Southeast: | Northeast: | International: |
|---|---|---|---|---|---|
| Y | | | | | Y |

Note: Financial information, benefits and other data can change quickly and may vary from those stated here.

# AKAMAI TECHNOLOGIES INC

**www.akamai.com**

**Industry Group Code:** 514191A **Ranks within this company's industry group:** Sales: 1 Profits: 1

| **Management:** | | **Sales/Marketing:** | | **Liberal Arts:** | | **Information Systems:** | | **Professionals:** | | **Technical/Scientific:** | |
|---|---|---|---|---|---|---|---|---|---|---|---|
| Mgmt. Trainees: | | Mktg. Professionals: | Y | Gen. Writing/Editing: | | Info. Management: | Y | Finance/Accounting: | Y | Engineers, Elec.: | Y |
| Experienced Mgmt.: | Y | Retail Sales: | | Technical Writing: | Y | Software Dev.: | Y | Law: | Y | Engineers, Other: | |
| Int'l Business: | Y | Commercial/Industrial: | Y | Graphic Arts/Photog.: | | Hardware Dev.: | | HR/Other: | Y | Health/Lab: | |
| MBA Graduates: | Y | Sales Trainees: | Y | Music: | | Systems Integration: | Y | Training: | Y | Scientists/Research: | |
| | | Advertising Pros.: | | Broadcasting: | | Consulting/Other: | | Health Care: | | Petroleum/Chemicals: | |
| | | | | Other: | | | | Consulting: | | Math/Other: | Y |

## TYPES OF BUSINESS:

Online Information Service-Streaming Content
e-Business Software
Web Analytics
Online Content Distribution Support Services

## BRANDS/DIVISIONS/AFFILIATES:

EdgeControl
EdgeSuite
EdgeComputing
EdgePlatform
Nine Systems Corp.
Netli, Inc.
Red Swoosh, Inc.

## CONTACTS: *Note: Officers with more than one job title may be intentionally listed here more than once.*

Paul Sagan, CEO
Paul Sagan, Pres.
J. D. Sherman, CFO
Robert W. Hughes, Exec. VP-Global Sales, Svcs. & Mktg.
Cathy Welsh, Chief Human Resources Officer
Tom Leighton, Chief Scientist
Michael M. Afergan, CTO
Harald Prokop, Sr. VP-Eng.
Melanie Haratunian, General Counsel/VP/Sec.
Robert Blumofe, Sr. VP-Oper. & Networks
Robert Wood, VP/Chief Dev. Officer
Jeff Young, Dir.-Corp. Comm.
Sandy Smith, Dir.-Investor Rel.
Chris Schoettle, Exec. VP-Site Acceleration
George Conrades, Chmn.

| **Phone:** 617-444-3000 | **Fax:** 617-444-3001 |
|---|---|
| **Toll-Free:** 877-425-2624 | |
| **Address:** 8 Cambridge Ctr., Cambridge, MA 02142-1401 US | |

## GROWTH PLANS/SPECIAL FEATURES:

Akamai Technologies, Inc. is a software and Internet content company that provides enterprise and government clients with e-business infrastructure services, enabling them to deliver web content and applications such as ads, video and other high-bandwidth content at higher speeds and with greater reliability. Akamai's EdgePlatform distributing network is one of the largest in the world, consisting of 20,000 servers in 1,000 networks and more than 70 countries. The company uses this network to deliver a broad spectrum of content and applications on demand. Service offerings include content delivery; media delivery; electronic software delivery; on-demand video management; and business performance management, under such brand names as EdgeComputing and EdgeSuite. EdgeComputing enables clients to use applications such as store/dealer locators, promotional contests, search functionality and user registration by utilizing Akamai servers, reducing demands on in-house systems. EdgeSuite is a powerful, outsourced infrastructure service that simplifies IT complexity, expands infrastructure capacity and improves site performance. Recently, Akamai acquired Nine Systems Corporation, which provides tools for producing and publishing rich media content online. The company introduced a number of innovations in 2007, including live streaming for use with the Adobe Flash FLV format; HD video streaming; and StreamOS technology, a media management tool which helps companies distribute their content online. In March 2007, Akamai acquired Netli, Inc. in an effort to enhance the performance of its web-based programs. In April 2007, the company acquired Red Swoosh, Inc., a firm that provides media management and distribution technology.

Akamai offers its employees medical insurance; a prescription drug plan; long and short term disability; group home and auto insurance; a dependent care spending account; educational assistance; an employee assistance plan; maternity and paternity leave; a pre-tax commuter benefit; group entertainment discounts; fitness programs; an employee stock purchase plan; and a 401(k) savings plan.

## FINANCIALS: **Sales and profits are in thousands of dollars—add 000 to get the full amount. 2008 Note: Financial information for 2008 was not available for all companies at press time.**

| | | |
|---|---|---|
| 2008 Sales: $ | 2008 Profits: $ | **U.S. Stock Ticker: AKAM** |
| 2007 Sales: $636,406 | 2007 Profits: $100,967 | **Int'l Ticker:** Int'l Exchange: |
| 2006 Sales: $428,672 | 2006 Profits: $57,401 | Employees: 1,300 |
| 2005 Sales: $283,115 | 2005 Profits: $327,998 | Fiscal Year Ends: 12/31 |
| 2004 Sales: $210,015 | 2004 Profits: $34,364 | Parent Company: |

## SALARIES/BENEFITS:

| | | | | |
|---|---|---|---|---|
| Pension Plan: | ESOP Stock Plan: | Profit Sharing: | Top Exec. Salary: $403,651 | Bonus: $497,362 |
| Savings Plan: Y | Stock Purch. Plan: Y | | Second Exec. Salary: $355,124 | Bonus: $452,692 |

## OTHER THOUGHTS:

**Apparent Women Officers or Directors**: 3
**Hot Spot for Advancement for Women/Minorities**: Y

## LOCATIONS: ("Y" = Yes)

| West: | Southwest: | Midwest: | Southeast: | Northeast: | International: |
|---|---|---|---|---|---|
| Y | Y | Y | Y | Y | Y |

# AKQA INC

www.akqa.com

**Industry Group Code:** 541810A **Ranks within this company's industry group:** Sales: 3 Profits:

| Management: | | Sales/Marketing: | | Liberal Arts: | | Information Systems: | | Professionals: | | Technical/Scientific: | |
|---|---|---|---|---|---|---|---|---|---|---|---|
| Mgmt. Trainees: | | Mktg. Professionals: | Y | Gen. Writing/Editing: | Y | Info. Management: | Y | Finance/Accounting: | Y | Engineers, Elec.: | |
| Experienced Mgmt.: | Y | Retail Sales: | | Technical Writing: | | Software Dev.: | Y | Law: | Y | Engineers, Other: | |
| Int'l Business: | Y | Commercial/Industrial: | | Graphic Arts/Photog.: | Y | Hardware Dev.: | | HR/Other: | Y | Health/Lab: | |
| MBA Graduates: | Y | Sales Trainees: | Y | Music: | | Systems Integration: | Y | Training: | Y | Scientists/Research: | |
| | | Advertising Pros.: | Y | Broadcasting: | | Consulting/Other: | | Health Care: | | Petroleum/Chemicals: | |
| | | | | Other: | Y | | | Consulting: | | Math/Other: | |

## TYPES OF BUSINESS:

Online Marketing
E-Mail Marketing
Web Site Design
Web Site Hosting

## BRANDS/DIVISIONS/AFFILIATES:

SearchRev
AKQA. Mobile

## CONTACTS:

*Note: Officers with more than one job title may be intentionally listed here more than once.*

Tom Bedecarre, CEO
Tim Pierce, COO
Lester Fientuck, CFO
Andrew O'Dell, Pres., Interactive Advertising
Stuart Sproule, Managing Dir.-West
Jason Whiting, Managing Dir.-East
Guy Wieynk, Managing Dir.-Europe
Ajaz Ahmed, Chmn.
Ho Chee Yue, Regional Dir.-Asia

| | |
|---|---|
| **Phone:** 415-645-9400 | **Fax:** 415-645-9420 |
| **Toll-Free:** | |
| **Address:** 118 King St., 6th Fl., San Francisco, CA 94107 US | |

## GROWTH PLANS/SPECIAL FEATURES:

A.K.Q.A., Inc. is a digital advertising firm with locations in San Francisco, New York, Washington, D.C., London, Amsterdam and Shanghai. The company creates web sites, conducts e-mail marketing campaigns and produces online interactive advertising. Additionally, the firm offers web site hosting services to clients. A.K.Q.A. has worked with media such as feature films, mobile phones, kiosks, digital organizers, DVDs and interactive TV. A.K.Q.A. Mobile works with clients to create digital products, services and content for the mobile platform. A.K.Q.A. Search provides search engine optimization and marketing. Clients include ESPN, Coca-Cola, Nike, Ferrari, McDonalds, Visa; Target; and the United States Postal Service (USPS). Among the company's most notable achievements is the design of Microsoft's X-Box 360 console interface. In May 2008, the company launched AKQA Film, a distributor and creator of digital programming, aimed at independent projects.

## FINANCIALS:

**Sales and profits are in thousands of dollars—add 000 to get the full amount. 2008 Note: Financial information for 2008 was not available for all companies at press time.**

| | | |
|---|---|---|
| 2008 Sales: $ | 2008 Profits: $ | **U.S. Stock Ticker: Private** |
| 2007 Sales: $221,500 | 2007 Profits: $ | **Int'l Ticker:** Int'l Exchange: |
| 2006 Sales: $ | 2006 Profits: $ | Employees: 548 |
| 2005 Sales: $52,000 | 2005 Profits: $ | Fiscal Year Ends: |
| 2004 Sales: $42,000 | 2004 Profits: $ | Parent Company: |

## SALARIES/BENEFITS:

| | | | | |
|---|---|---|---|---|
| Pension Plan: | ESOP Stock Plan: | Profit Sharing: | Top Exec. Salary: $ | Bonus: $ |
| Savings Plan: | Stock Purch. Plan: | | Second Exec. Salary: $ | Bonus: $ |

## OTHER THOUGHTS:

**Apparent Women Officers or Directors:**
**Hot Spot for Advancement for Women/Minorities:**

## LOCATIONS: ("Y" = Yes)

| West: | Southwest: | Midwest: | Southeast: | Northeast: | International: |
|---|---|---|---|---|---|
| Y | | | | Y | Y |

Note: Financial information, benefits and other data can change quickly and may vary from those stated here.

# ALASKA COMMUNICATIONS SYSTEMS GROUP

**www.acsalaska.com**

**Industry Group Code:** 513300A **Ranks within this company's industry group:** Sales: 3 Profits: 1

| **Management:** | | **Sales/Marketing:** | | **Liberal Arts:** | | **Information Systems:** | | **Professionals:** | | **Technical/Scientific:** | |
|---|---|---|---|---|---|---|---|---|---|---|---|
| Mgmt. Trainees: | | Mktg. Professionals: | Y | Gen. Writing/Editing: | | Info. Management: | Y | Finance/Accounting: | Y | Engineers, Elec.: | Y |
| Experienced Mgmt.: | Y | Retail Sales: | | Technical Writing: | | Software Dev.: | Y | Law: | Y | Engineers, Other: | Y |
| Int'l Business: | | Commercial/Industrial: | Y | Graphic Arts/Photog.: | | Hardware Dev.: | | HR/Other: | Y | Health/Lab: | |
| MBA Graduates: | Y | Sales Trainees: | Y | Music: | | Systems Integration: | Y | Training: | Y | Scientists/Research: | |
| | | Advertising Pros.: | | Broadcasting: | | Consulting/Other: | | Health Care: | | Petroleum/Chemicals: | |
| | | | | Other: | | | | Consulting: | | Math/Other: | |

## TYPES OF BUSINESS:

Telecommunications Services
Local Exchange Carrier
Wireless Phone Service
Long-Distance Service
Internet Access
Value Added Services

## BRANDS/DIVISIONS/AFFILIATES:

ACS of Alaska, Inc.
ACS of the Northland, Inc.
ACS of Anchorage, Inc.
ACS of Fairbanks, Inc.
ACS Wireless, Inc.
ACS Long Distance, Inc.
ACS Internet, Inc.
Alaska Communications Systems Holdings, Inc.

## CONTACTS: *Note: Officers with more than one job title may be intentionally listed here more than once.*

Liane Pelletier, CEO
Liane Pelletier, Pres.
David Wilson, CFO/Sr. VP
Sheldon Fisher, Sr. VP-Sales & Service
Anand Vadapalli, Sr. VP-Network & IT
Leonard Steinberg, General Counsel/VP/Corp. Sec.
David C. Eisenberg, Sr. VP-Corp. Strategy, Dev. & Mktg.
David Wilson, Treas.
Liane Pelletier, Chmn.

| **Phone:** 907-297-3000 | **Fax:** 907-297-3100 |
|---|---|
| **Toll-Free:** | |
| **Address:** 600 Telephone Ave., Anchorage, AK 99503 US | |

## GROWTH PLANS/SPECIAL FEATURES:

Alaska Communications Systems Group, Inc. (ACS) is a provider of integrated communications services in Alaska. It provides both wireline and wireless communications services throughout Alaska. The wireless business includes the only third-generation statewide wireless network operating in Alaska today. The company operates in two segments, wireline and wireless. The wireline segment provides communications services including voice, data, broadband, multi-protocol label switching services, network access, long distance and other services to consumers, carriers, businesses and government customers throughout Alaska and to and from Alaska. Network access services are provided primarily to long distance and other competing carriers who use the firm's local exchange facilities to provide usage services to their customers. The wireless segment provides wireless voice and data service and products and other value added services and equipment sales across Alaska. ACS's properties include over 1,000 sheath miles of fiber-optic cable, over 200 switching facilities and 194 cell sites. The company's new CDMA wireless network covers over 80% of Alaska's population, and its penetration rate has experienced steadily increasing growth over the past five years, topping 137,000 subscribers in 2007. Subsidiaries include ACS of Alaska, Inc.; ACS of the Northland, Inc. (ACSN); ACS of Fairbanks, Inc.; ACS of Anchorage, Inc.; ACS Wireless, Inc.; ACS Internet, Inc.; ACS long-distance, Inc; and Alaska Communications Systems Holdings, Inc. In April 2008, ACS agreed to acquire Crest Communications Corp., owner and operator of the North Star submarine fiber-optic cable, for about $70 million.

The company offers its employees medical, dental and vision insurance; an employee assistance program; a 401(k) plan; a pension plan; life and AD&D insurance; education assistance; and an employee stock purchase plan.

## FINANCIALS: **Sales and profits are in thousands of dollars—add 000 to get the full amount. 2008 Note: Financial information for 2008 was not available for all companies at press time.**

| | | |
|---|---|---|
| 2008 Sales: $ | 2008 Profits: $ | **U.S. Stock Ticker: ALSK** |
| 2007 Sales: $385,785 | 2007 Profits: $144,136 | **Int'l Ticker:** Int'l Exchange: |
| 2006 Sales: $348,721 | 2006 Profits: $13,278 | Employees: 1,003 |
| 2005 Sales: $326,809 | 2005 Profits: $-41,635 | Fiscal Year Ends: 12/31 |
| 2004 Sales: $302,707 | 2004 Profits: $-39,294 | Parent Company: |

## SALARIES/BENEFITS:

| | | | | |
|---|---|---|---|---|
| Pension Plan: Y | ESOP Stock Plan: | Profit Sharing: | Top Exec. Salary: $500,000 | Bonus: $1,332,000 |
| Savings Plan: Y | Stock Purch. Plan: Y | | Second Exec. Salary: $250,000 | Bonus: $555,000 |

## OTHER THOUGHTS:

**Apparent Women Officers or Directors**: 2
**Hot Spot for Advancement for Women/Minorities**: Y

## LOCATIONS: ("Y" = Yes)

| West: | Southwest: | Midwest: | Southeast: | Northeast: | International: |
|---|---|---|---|---|---|
| Y | | | | | |

# ALBANY MOLECULAR RESEARCH

**www.amriglobal.com**

**Industry Group Code:** 541710 **Ranks within this company's industry group:** Sales: 1 Profits: 2

| Management: | | Sales/Marketing: | | Liberal Arts: | | Information Systems: | | Professionals: | | Technical/Scientific: | |
|---|---|---|---|---|---|---|---|---|---|---|---|
| Mgmt. Trainees: | | Mktg. Professionals: | Y | Gen. Writing/Editing: | | Info. Management: | Y | Finance/Accounting: | Y | Engineers, Elec.: | |
| Experienced Mgmt.: | Y | Retail Sales: | | Technical Writing: | Y | Software Dev.: | Y | Law: | Y | Engineers, Other: | |
| Int'l Business: | Y | Commercial/Industrial: | | Graphic Arts/Photog.: | | Hardware Dev.: | | HR/Other: | Y | Health/Lab: | Y |
| MBA Graduates: | Y | Sales Trainees: | | Music: | | Systems Integration: | | Training: | Y | Scientists/Research: | Y |
| | | Advertising Pros.: | | Broadcasting: | | Consulting/Other: | | Health Care: | Y | Petroleum/Chemicals: | |
| | | | | Other: | | | | Consulting: | Y | Math/Other: | Y |

## TYPES OF BUSINESS:

Contract Drug Discovery & Development
Custom Biotech & Genomic Research
Chemistry Research
Manufacturing Services
Consulting Services
Analytical Chemistry Services

## BRANDS/DIVISIONS/AFFILIATES:

## CONTACTS:

*Note: Officers with more than one job title may be intentionally listed here more than once.*

Thomas E. D'Ambra, CEO
Thomas E. D'Ambra, Pres.
Mark T. Frost, CFO
W. Steven (Steve) Jennings, Sr. VP-Sales & Mktg.
Brian D. Russell, VP-Human Resources
Bruce J. Sargent, VP-Discovery R&D
Harold Meckler, VP-Science & Tech.
Steven R. Hagen, VP-Pharmaceutical Dev. & Mfg.
W. Steven (Steve) Jennings, Sr. VP-Bus. Dev.
Peter Jerome, Dir.-Investor Rel.
Mark T. Frost, Treas.
Michael P. Trova, Sr. VP-Chemistry
Richard A. Saffee, Gen. Mgr.-Large Scale Mfg.
Thomas E. D'Ambra, Chmn.
Michael D. Ironside, Dir.-Global Project Mgmt.

| **Phone:** 518-464-0279 | **Fax:** 518-512-2020 |
|---|---|
| **Toll-Free:** | |
| **Address:** 21 Corporate Cir., P.O. Box 15098, Albany, NY 12212-5098 US | |

## GROWTH PLANS/SPECIAL FEATURES:

Albany Molecular Research, Inc. (AMRI) is a chemistry-based drug discovery and development company, focusing on applications for new small-molecule and prescription drugs. It derives revenue from discovering then licensing new compounds with commercial potential for service fees, milestone and royalty payments. Some of the products of this research led to the development of the active ingredient (fexofenadine HCl) for a non-sedating antihistamine marketed by Sanofi-Aventis S.A. as Allegra in the U.S. and as Telfast outside the U.S. Since its launch in 1995, AMRI has earned more than $367.3 million in royalty and milestone revenue from this product. The firm has also licensed the rights to develop and commercialize two chemicals (amine neurotransmitter reuptake inhibitors) from Bristol-Myers Squibb Company (BMS). In addition to developing its own drugs, AMRI has increasingly acted as a custom research and development source for the pharmaceutical, genomic and biotechnology industries. It provides contract services across the entire product development cycle, from lead discovery to commercial manufacturing. The company's services allow pharmaceutical companies to outsource their chemistry departments in order to pursue a greater number of drug discovery and development opportunities. An integral part of these contract operations consists of several facilities in India and Singapore, which were launched as part of a strategic move to globalize its services. The firm also has domestic research facilities in Albany, Syracuse and Rensselaer, New York as well as in Bothell, Washington. In February 2008, AMRI acquired a custom pilot scale intermediaries manufacturing firm, FineKem Laboratories Pvt. Limited, based in Aurangabad, India. In June 2008, the first BMS-licensed chemical, indicated for treating depression, entered Phase I clinical trials in Canada. In September 2008, the second chemical, a novel cancer treatment, entered preclinical trials, and subsequent positive test results moved the chemical into Phase I trials by October 2008.

## FINANCIALS:

**Sales and profits are in thousands of dollars—add 000 to get the full amount. 2008 Note: Financial information for 2008 was not available for all companies at press time.**

| | | |
|---|---|---|
| 2008 Sales: $ | 2008 Profits: $ | **U.S. Stock Ticker: AMRI** |
| 2007 Sales: $192,511 | 2007 Profits: $8,936 | **Int'l Ticker:** Int'l Exchange: |
| 2006 Sales: $179,807 | 2006 Profits: $2,183 | Employees: 1,226 |
| 2005 Sales: $183,906 | 2005 Profits: $16,321 | Fiscal Year Ends: 12/31 |
| 2004 Sales: $169,527 | 2004 Profits: $-11,691 | Parent Company: |

## SALARIES/BENEFITS:

| | | | | |
|---|---|---|---|---|
| Pension Plan: | ESOP Stock Plan: | Profit Sharing: | Top Exec. Salary: $416,514 | Bonus: $30,660 |
| Savings Plan: Y | Stock Purch. Plan: Y | | Second Exec. Salary: $293,808 | Bonus: $39,390 |

## OTHER THOUGHTS:

**Apparent Women Officers or Directors**: 2
**Hot Spot for Advancement for Women/Minorities**:

## LOCATIONS: ("Y" = Yes)

| West: | Southwest: | Midwest: | Southeast: | Northeast: | International: |
|---|---|---|---|---|---|
| Y | | | | Y | Y |

# ALEXION PHARMACEUTICALS INC

www.alexionpharm.com

**Industry Group Code:** 325412 **Ranks within this company's industry group:** Sales: 25 Profits: 29

| **Management:** | | **Sales/Marketing:** | | **Liberal Arts:** | | **Information Systems:** | | **Professionals:** | | **Technical/Scientific:** | |
|---|---|---|---|---|---|---|---|---|---|---|---|
| Mgmt. Trainees: | | Mktg. Professionals: | Y | Gen. Writing/Editing: | | Info. Management: | Y | Finance/Accounting: | Y | Engineers, Elec.: | |
| Experienced Mgmt.: | Y | Retail Sales: | | Technical Writing: | Y | Software Dev.: | Y | Law: | Y | Engineers, Other: | |
| Int'l Business: | Y | Commercial/Industrial: | Y | Graphic Arts/Photog.: | | Hardware Dev.: | | HR/Other: | Y | Health/Lab: | Y |
| MBA Graduates: | Y | Sales Trainees: | Y | Music: | | Systems Integration: | | Training: | Y | Scientists/Research: | Y |
| | | Advertising Pros.: | | Broadcasting: | | Consulting/Other: | | Health Care: | Y | Petroleum/Chemicals: | |
| | | | | Other: | | | | Consulting: | | Math/Other: | Y |

## TYPES OF BUSINESS:

Therapeutic Products

## BRANDS/DIVISIONS/AFFILIATES:

Soliris
Alexion Europe SAS

## CONTACTS:

*Note: Officers with more than one job title may be intentionally listed here more than once.*

Leonard Bell, CEO/Treas./Sec.
David W. Keiser, COO
David W. Keiser, Pres.
Vikas Sinha, CFO/Sr. VP
Glenn Melrose, VP-Human Resources
Stephen P. Squinto, Head-Research/Exec. VP
Daniel N. Caron, Exec. Dir.-Eng.
M. Stacy Hooks, VP-Mfg. & Tech. Svcs.
Thomas I.H. Dubin, General Counsel/Sr. VP
Daniel N. Caron, Exec. Dir.-Oper.
Barry P. Luke, VP-Finance/Asst. Sec.
Russel P. Rother, Sr. VP/Chief Scientific Officer
David Hallal, VP-U.S. Commercial Oper.
Max Link, Chmn.
Patrice Coissac, Gen. Mgr./Pres., Alexion Europe SAS

**Phone:** 203-272-2596 **Fax:** 203-271-8190
**Toll-Free:**
**Address:** 325 Knotter Dr., Cheshire, CT 06410 US

## GROWTH PLANS/SPECIAL FEATURES:

Alexion Pharmaceuticals, Inc. engages in the discovery, development and delivery of therapeutic products to treat patients with severe disease states, including hematologic diseases, neurologic disease, cancer and autoimmune disorders. The company devotes substantially all of its resources to drug discovery, research, and product and clinical development. The firm has one market product, Soliris (eculizumab), the first therapy approved for the treatment of paroxysmal nocturnal hemoglobinuria (PNH). PNH is a rare genetic deficiency blood disorder, in which a patient's own complement system attacks and destroys blood cells. Soliris, a genetically altered antibody known as C5 complement inhibitor, treats PNH by selectively blocking the production of inflammation-causing proteins in the complement cascade. The company's other products are currently in preclinical or phase trial stages. These products include intravenous eculizumab for the treatment of myasthenia gravis, multifocal motor neuropathy and asthma; intravitreal eculizumab for the treatment of age-related macular degeneration; CD200 Mab for the treatment of multiple myeloma; and DC-SIGN Mab, a cancer vaccine. All of the firm's products focus on anti-inflammatory therapeutics for disease in which the complement cascade is activated. Alexion also operates several subsidiaries in Europe, including Alexion Europe SAS, which supports commercial and regulatory international operations.

## FINANCIALS:

**Sales and profits are in thousands of dollars—add 000 to get the full amount. 2008 Note: Financial information for 2008 was not available for all companies at press time.**

| | | |
|---|---|---|
| 2008 Sales: $ | 2008 Profits: $ | **U.S. Stock Ticker: ALXN** |
| 2007 Sales: $72,041 | 2007 Profits: $-92,290 | **Int'l Ticker:** Int'l Exchange: |
| 2006 Sales: $1,558 | 2006 Profits: $-131,514 | Employees: 434 |
| 2005 Sales: $1,064 | 2005 Profits: $-108,750 | Fiscal Year Ends: 12/31 |
| 2004 Sales: $4,609 | 2004 Profits: $-74,095 | Parent Company: |

## SALARIES/BENEFITS:

| | | | | |
|---|---|---|---|---|
| Pension Plan: | ESOP Stock Plan: | Profit Sharing: | Top Exec. Salary: $527,437 | Bonus: $710,000 |
| Savings Plan: | Stock Purch. Plan: | | Second Exec. Salary: $379,348 | Bonus: $292,000 |

## OTHER THOUGHTS:

**Apparent Women Officers or Directors:** 1
**Hot Spot for Advancement for Women/Minorities:**

## LOCATIONS: ("Y" = Yes)

| West: | Southwest: | Midwest: | Southeast: | Northeast: | International: |
|---|---|---|---|---|---|
| | | | | Y | Y |

# ALIEN TECHNOLOGY CORPORATION

www.alientechnology.com

**Industry Group Code:** 334220 **Ranks within this company's industry group:** Sales: Profits:

| Management: | | Sales/Marketing: | | Liberal Arts: | | Information Systems: | | Professionals: | | Technical/Scientific: | |
|---|---|---|---|---|---|---|---|---|---|---|---|
| Mgmt. Trainees: | | Mktg. Professionals: | Y | Gen. Writing/Editing: | Y | Info. Management: | Y | Finance/Accounting: | Y | Engineers, Elec.: | Y |
| Experienced Mgmt.: | Y | Retail Sales: | | Technical Writing: | Y | Software Dev.: | Y | Law: | Y | Engineers, Other: | Y |
| Int'l Business: | Y | Commercial/Industrial: | Y | Graphic Arts/Photog.: | | Hardware Dev.: | Y | HR/Other: | Y | Health/Lab: | |
| MBA Graduates: | Y | Sales Trainees: | Y | Music: | | Systems Integration: | Y | Training: | Y | Scientists/Research: | |
| | | Advertising Pros.: | | Broadcasting: | | Consulting/Other: | | Health Care: | | Petroleum/Chemicals: | |
| | | | | Other: | | | | Consulting: | | Math/Other: | |

## TYPES OF BUSINESS:

RFID Equipment
RFID Training Services

## BRANDS/DIVISIONS/AFFILIATES:

Fluidic Self Assembly
RFID Academy

## CONTACTS:

*Note: Officers with more than one job title may be intentionally listed here more than once.*

George W. Everhart, CEO
Robert K. Eulau, COO
Robert K. Eulau, Acting CFO
Patrick Ervin, VP-Worldwide Sales
John S. Smith, CTO
Curt Carrender, VP-Eng. Systems
David A. Aaron, General Counsel/Sec./VP
Ronny Haraldsvik, VP-Mktg. & Industry Rel.
Natalino Camilleri, VP-IC Eng.
Susan H. Pearson, VP-Global Alliances & Gov't Solutions
Trevia Clark, Dir.-Mktg. Comm.
Duane Zitzner, Chmn.

**Phone:** 408-782-3900 **Fax:** 408-782-3910
**Toll-Free:**
**Address:** 18220 Butterfield Blvd., Ste. 150, Morgan Hill, CA 95037 US

## GROWTH PLANS/SPECIAL FEATURES:

Alien Technology Corporation, founded in 1994, is a leading provider of UHF radio frequency identification (RFID) products. Alien's patented Fluidic Self Assembly (FSATM) manufacturing process allows it to manufacture high-volume, low-cost RFID tags. The company manufactures a variety of RFID tags and upgradeable scanners compatible with next-generation technology, including electronic product code (EPC) Class I UHF tags for complex applications such as tagging liquids and metals. In addition, the firm offers battery-assisted passive RFID tags, which support additional features including increased data memory storage, increased range, secure access systems, tamper detection, shock sensors and time/temperature monitoring. The company also offers RFID readers for applications including supply chain management, security, vehicle asset tracking, logistics and anti-counterfeiting. Alien's products have been certified as Qualified Anti-Terrorism Technologies according to the standards of the Support Anti-terrorism by Fostering Effective Technologies (SAFETY) Act of 2002, allowing the products to be used in airport baggage and cargo handling situations. Under the name RFID Academy, Alien offers various instructional courses in RFID software, hardware and implementation. Many leaders in the retail industry have recently issued mandates requiring suppliers to utilize RFID technology in their supply chains. These new mandates have prompted Alien to tailor a kit to ease the transition into reliance on RFID technologies in the retail marketplace. The kit includes the basic readers, tags and other products needed to implement RFID equipment, as well as the training and consultation required to run the equipment. In April 2007, the company announced that the U.S. Navy and U.S. Marine Corps have contracted with Alien to supply RFID tags and readers to aid in the transport of military equipment from overseas back home.

## FINANCIALS:

**Sales and profits are in thousands of dollars—add 000 to get the full amount. 2008 Note: Financial information for 2008 was not available for all companies at press time.**

| | | |
|---|---|---|
| 2008 Sales: $ | 2008 Profits: $ | **U.S. Stock Ticker: Private** |
| 2007 Sales: $ | 2007 Profits: $ | **Int'l Ticker:** Int'l Exchange: |
| 2006 Sales: $ | 2006 Profits: $ | Employees: 230 |
| 2005 Sales: $19,800 | 2005 Profits: $-53,000 | Fiscal Year Ends: 9/30 |
| 2004 Sales: $9,900 | 2004 Profits: $-27,600 | Parent Company: |

## SALARIES/BENEFITS:

| | | | | |
|---|---|---|---|---|
| Pension Plan: | ESOP Stock Plan: Y | Profit Sharing: | Top Exec. Salary: $ | Bonus: $ |
| Savings Plan: Y | Stock Purch. Plan: | | Second Exec. Salary: $ | Bonus: $ |

## OTHER THOUGHTS:

**Apparent Women Officers or Directors**: 1
**Hot Spot for Advancement for Women/Minorities**: Y

## LOCATIONS: ("Y" = Yes)

| West: | Southwest: | Midwest: | Southeast: | Northeast: | International: |
|---|---|---|---|---|---|
| Y | | Y | | | Y |

# ALIGN TECHNOLOGY INC

www.aligntech.com

**Industry Group Code:** 339113 **Ranks within this company's industry group:** Sales: 13 Profits: 5

| Management: | | Sales/Marketing: | | Liberal Arts: | | Information Systems: | | Professionals: | | Technical/Scientific: | |
|---|---|---|---|---|---|---|---|---|---|---|---|
| Mgmt. Trainees: | | Mktg. Professionals: | Y | Gen. Writing/Editing: | | Info. Management: | Y | Finance/Accounting: | Y | Engineers, Elec.: | |
| Experienced Mgmt.: | Y | Retail Sales: | | Technical Writing: | Y | Software Dev.: | Y | Law: | Y | Engineers, Other: | Y |
| Int'l Business: | Y | Commercial/Industrial: | Y | Graphic Arts/Photog.: | | Hardware Dev.: | Y | HR/Other: | Y | Health/Lab: | Y |
| MBA Graduates: | Y | Sales Trainees: | Y | Music: | | Systems Integration: | | Training: | Y | Scientists/Research: | Y |
| | | Advertising Pros.: | | Broadcasting: | | Consulting/Other: | | Health Care: | Y | Petroleum/Chemicals: | |
| | | | | Other: | | | | Consulting: | | Math/Other: | Y |

## TYPES OF BUSINESS:

Orthodontic Equipment

## BRANDS/DIVISIONS/AFFILIATES:

Invisalign
ClinCheck
Invisalign Institute
Invisalign Express
ClinAdvisor
Invisalign Pty. Ltd.
Invisalign Hong Kong Pty. Ltd.
Invisalign Teen

## CONTACTS: *Note: Officers with more than one job title may be intentionally listed here more than once.*

Thomas M. Prescott, CEO
Thomas M. Prescott, Pres.
Kenneth B. Arola, CFO
Darrell Zoromski, VP-Global Mktg./Chief Mktg. Officer
Sonia Clark, VP-Human Resources
Dana C. Cambra, VP-R&D
Sunny Azadeh, CIO/VP-IT Global
Roger E. George, General Counsel/VP-Legal Affairs/Sec.
Len Hedge, Sr. VP-Bus. Oper.
Shirley Stacy, Investor Rel.
Kenneth B. Arola, VP-Finance
Dan S. Ellis, VP-North American Sales
Emory M. Wright, VP-Oper.
C. Raymond Larkin, Chmn.
Gil Laks, VP-Int'l

**Phone:** 408-470-1000 **Fax:** 408-470-1010
**Toll-Free:**
**Address:** 881 Martin Ave., Santa Clara, CA 95050 US

## GROWTH PLANS/SPECIAL FEATURES:

Align Technology, Inc. (ATI), founded in 1997, is engaged in the design, manufacture and marketing of Invisalign, a proprietary system for treating malocclusion, or the misalignment of teeth. The Invisalign system has two components: ClinCheck and Aligners. ClinCheck is an Internet-based application that allows dental professionals to simulate treatment, in three dimensions, by modeling two-week stages of tooth movement. Aligners are thin, clear plastic, removable dental appliances that are manufactured in a series to correspond to each two-week stage of the ClinCheck simulation. Aligners are customized to perform the treatment prescribed for an individual patient by dental professionals using ClinCheck. ATI also has ClinAdvisor, a software program that provides efficient treatment options for patients. The firm offers two products: the Full Invisalign Treatment, which provides as many Aligners as needed and accounts for 88% of company sales, and Invisalign Express, which provides up to 10 Aligners and accounts for 8% of company sales. The company receives approximately 140,000 new customers on an annual basis. At ATI's facility in Costa Rica, technicians use an internally developed computer modeling program to prepare electronic treatment plans, which are transmitted electronically back to the U.S. These files form the basis of ClinCheck and are used in conjunction with stereo lithography technology to manufacture Aligner molds. A third-party manufacturer in Mexico fabricates Aligners from the molds and ships the completed products to ATI's customers. Insivalign Australia Pty. Ltd. has sole distribution rights for products in Australia, and Invisalign Hong Kong Pty. Ltd. has sole rights for Hong Kong. In January 2008, ATI announced the planned release of Invisalign Teen, a program designed to meet the needs of the teenage treatment market. In January 2008, ATI also launched a new web site for AlignTech Institute, which provides scalable educational resources and programs for Invisalign providers.

## FINANCIALS: Sales and profits are in thousands of dollars—add 000 to get the full amount. 2008 Note: Financial information for 2008 was not available for all companies at press time.

| | | |
|---|---|---|
| 2008 Sales: $ | 2008 Profits: $ | **U.S. Stock Ticker: ALGN** |
| 2007 Sales: $284,332 | 2007 Profits: $35,724 | **Int'l Ticker:** Int'l Exchange: |
| 2006 Sales: $206,354 | 2006 Profits: $-34,963 | Employees: 1,307 |
| 2005 Sales: $207,125 | 2005 Profits: $1,413 | Fiscal Year Ends: 12/31 |
| 2004 Sales: $172,800 | 2004 Profits: $8,768 | Parent Company: |

## SALARIES/BENEFITS:

| | | | | |
|---|---|---|---|---|
| Pension Plan: | ESOP Stock Plan: | Profit Sharing: | Top Exec. Salary: $480,000 | Bonus: $840,000 |
| Savings Plan: Y | Stock Purch. Plan: Y | | Second Exec. Salary: $295,360 | Bonus: $324,896 |

## OTHER THOUGHTS:

**Apparent Women Officers or Directors**: 2
**Hot Spot for Advancement for Women/Minorities**:

## LOCATIONS: ("Y" = Yes)

| West: | Southwest: | Midwest: | Southeast: | Northeast: | International: |
|---|---|---|---|---|---|
| Y | | | | | Y |

# ALKERMES INC

www.alkermes.com

**Industry Group Code:** 325412A **Ranks within this company's industry group:** Sales: 3 Profits: 1

| Management: | | Sales/Marketing: | | Liberal Arts: | | Information Systems: | | Professionals: | | Technical/Scientific: | |
|---|---|---|---|---|---|---|---|---|---|---|---|
| Mgmt. Trainees: | | Mktg. Professionals: | Y | Gen. Writing/Editing: | | Info. Management: | Y | Finance/Accounting: | Y | Engineers, Elec.: | |
| Experienced Mgmt.: | Y | Retail Sales: | | Technical Writing: | Y | Software Dev.: | | Law: | Y | Engineers, Other: | |
| Int'l Business: | Y | Commercial/Industrial: | Y | Graphic Arts/Photog.: | | Hardware Dev.: | | HR/Other: | Y | Health/Lab: | Y |
| MBA Graduates: | Y | Sales Trainees: | Y | Music: | | Systems Integration: | | Training: | Y | Scientists/Research: | Y |
| | | Advertising Pros.: | | Broadcasting: | | Consulting/Other: | | Health Care: | Y | Petroleum/Chemicals: | |
| | | | | Other: | | | | Consulting: | | Math/Other: | Y |

## TYPES OF BUSINESS:

Drug Delivery Systems
Pulmonary Drug Delivery Systems
Sustained Release Injection Delivery Systems

## BRANDS/DIVISIONS/AFFILIATES:

Vivitrol
Risperdal Consta
Advanced Inhalation Research (AIR)
AIR Inhaled Insulin
Eli Lilly & Company

## CONTACTS: *Note: Officers with more than one job title may be intentionally listed here more than once.*

David A. Broecker, CEO
Gordon G. Pugh, COO/Sr. VP
David A. Broecker, Pres.
James M. Frates, CFO/Sr. VP
F. Ken Andrews, VP-Mktg. & Sales/Chief Commercial Officer
Madeline D. Coffin, VP-Human Resources
Elliot W. Ehrich, Sr. VP-R&D/Chief Medical Officer
Kathryn L. Biberstein, General Counsel/Sr. VP/Corp. Sec.
Michael J. Landine, Sr. VP-Corp. Dev.
Rebecca J. Peterson, VP-Corp. Comm.
James M. Frates, Treas.
Kathryn L. Biberstein, Chief Compliance Officer
Blair Jackson, VP-Bus. Dev.
Richard Pops, Chmn.

| **Phone:** 617-494-0171 | **Fax:** 617-494-9263 |
|---|---|
| **Toll-Free:** | |
| **Address:** 88 Sidney St., Cambridge, MA 02139 US | |

## GROWTH PLANS/SPECIAL FEATURES:

Alkermes, Inc. is a biotechnology company that specializes in the development of sophisticated drug delivery technologies. The company currently markets two commercial products: RISPERDAL CONSTA, a long-acting atypical antipsychotic medication for schizophrenia, and VIVITROL, an injectable medication for the treatment of alcohol dependence. RISPERDAL CONSTA is administered through an intramuscular injection every two weeks and is currently approved for sale in approximately 85 countries. In 2008, the company began developing a four-week formulation of RISPERDAL CONSTA in conjunction with its partner company, Janssen Pharmaceutica, Inc. VIVITROL is aimed at prolonging abstinence in patients that abstain from alcohol a week prior to treatment, and has also been shown to reduce the number of heavy drinking days in patients. In addition to its marketed products, Alkermes also develops extended-release injectable, pulmonary and oral products for the treatment of central nervous system disorders, addiction and diabetes. Additional developing products in the company's pipeline include Exenatide LAR for the treatment of type 2 diabetes; ALKS 27 for the treatment of COPD; ALKS 29 for treatment of addiction; AKLS 33, an opioid modulator that may be used to treat a broad range of diseases and medical conditions. In April 2007, the FDA approved a 12.5 mg dose of RESPERDAL CONSTA for the treatment of schizophrenia within specific patient populations, which will allow physicians more options in individualizing or adjusting treatment approaches for their patients. In December 2007, Alkermes sold its stake in Reliant Pharmaceuticals, Inc. to GlaxoSmithKline. In March 2008, Eli Lilly and Company, Alkermes' partner in the development of the Advanced Inhalation Research (AIR) drug delivery technology, terminated the AIR development and license agreement, and thereby the AIR Inhaled Insulin program.

Alkermes provides employees with tuition reimbursement, medical and dental insurance, flexible spending accounts, an employee assistance program, tuition reimbursement and transportation benefits.

## FINANCIALS: **Sales and profits are in thousands of dollars—add 000 to get the full amount. 2008 Note: Financial information for 2008 was not available for all companies at press time.**

| | | |
|---|---|---|
| 2008 Sales: $ | 2008 Profits: $ | **U.S. Stock Ticker: ALKS** |
| 2007 Sales: $240,717 | 2007 Profits: $166,979 | **Int'l Ticker:** Int'l Exchange: |
| 2006 Sales: $239,965 | 2006 Profits: $9,445 | Employees: 760 |
| 2005 Sales: $76,126 | 2005 Profits: $-73,916 | Fiscal Year Ends: 3/31 |
| 2004 Sales: $39,054 | 2004 Profits: $-102,385 | Parent Company: |

## SALARIES/BENEFITS:

| | | | | |
|---|---|---|---|---|
| Pension Plan: | ESOP Stock Plan: Y | Profit Sharing: | Top Exec. Salary: $581,513 | Bonus: $408,000 |
| Savings Plan: Y | Stock Purch. Plan: | | Second Exec. Salary: $397,878 | Bonus: $213,000 |

## OTHER THOUGHTS:

**Apparent Women Officers or Directors**: 3
**Hot Spot for Advancement for Women/Minorities**: Y

## LOCATIONS: ("Y" = Yes)

| West: | Southwest: | Midwest: | Southeast: | Northeast: | International: |
|---|---|---|---|---|---|
| | | Y | | Y | |

# ALLEGHANY CORP

www.alleghany.com

**Industry Group Code:** 524126 **Ranks within this company's industry group:** Sales: 5 Profits: 3

| Management: | | Sales/Marketing: | | Liberal Arts: | | Information Systems: | | Professionals: | | Technical/Scientific: | |
|---|---|---|---|---|---|---|---|---|---|---|---|
| Mgmt. Trainees: | | Mktg. Professionals: | Y | Gen. Writing/Editing: | Y | Info. Management: | Y | Finance/Accounting: | Y | Engineers, Elec.: | |
| Experienced Mgmt.: | Y | Retail Sales: | | Technical Writing: | Y | Software Dev.: | | Law: | Y | Engineers, Other: | |
| Int'l Business: | Y | Commercial/Industrial: | Y | Graphic Arts/Photog.: | | Hardware Dev.: | | HR/Other: | Y | Health/Lab: | |
| MBA Graduates: | Y | Sales Trainees: | Y | Music: | | Systems Integration: | | Training: | Y | Scientists/Research: | |
| | | Advertising Pros.: | | Broadcasting: | | Consulting/Other: | | Health Care: | | Petroleum/Chemicals: | |
| | | | | Other: | | | | Consulting: | | Math/Other: | Y |

## TYPES OF BUSINESS:

Direct Property & Casualty Insurance
Commercial Insurance
Reinsurance
Commercial & Contract Surety Bonds

## BRANDS/DIVISIONS/AFFILIATES:

RSUI Group, Inc.
Capitol Transamerica
Homesite Group, Inc.
Alleghany Insurance Holdings Re LLC
Alleghany Properties Holdings, LLC
Capitol Indemnity Corp.
Capitol Specialty Insurance Corp.
Employers Direct Corp.

## CONTACTS:

*Note: Officers with more than one job title may be intentionally listed here more than once.*

Weston M. Hicks, CEO
Weston M. Hicks, Pres.
Roger B. Gorham, CFO
Robert M. Hart, General Counsel/Sr. VP/Sec.
Peter R. Sismondo, Controller/VP
James P. Slattery, Sr. VP-Insurance
Jerry G. Borrelli, VP-Finance/Chief Acct. Officer
John Carr, VP/Dir.-Tax
Roger B. Gorham, Sr. VP-Finance & Investments
John J. Burns, Jr., Chmn.

| | |
|---|---|
| **Phone:** 212-752-1356 | **Fax:** 212-759-8149 |
| **Toll-Free:** | |
| **Address:** 7 Times Square Tower, New York, NY 10036 US | |

## GROWTH PLANS/SPECIAL FEATURES:

Alleghany Corp. is an investment holding company engaged in the commercial insurance and real estate business. The company conducts its business through RSUI Group, Inc.; Capitol Transamerica Corp. (CATA); Darwin Professional Underwriters, Inc.; Alleghany Insurance Holdings Re LLC (AIHL Re); and Allegany Properties Holdings, LLC. RSUI underwrites specialty insurance coverages in the property; umbrella/excess; general liability; directors and officers liability; and professional liability lines of business. RSUI writes business on ad admitted basis in 47 states and Washington, D.C. CATA operates in 50 states and Washington, D.C., and conducts its business through subsidiaries Capital Indemnity Corp., which writes property and casualty insurance and commercial and contract surety bonds; and Capitol Specialty Insurance Corp., which offers contract surety bonds in the non-construction segment of the market. Darwin is a specialty property and casualty insurance group focused on three broad professional liability market lines of business: directors and officers liability; errors and omissions; and medical malpractice liability. AIHL Re provides catastrophe reinsurance coverage for RSUI, and also owns a 32.9% stake in Homesite Group, Inc. In July 2007, the company acquired Employers Direct Corp. for roughly $192.5 million. Employers Direct is an insurance holding company based in Agoura Hills, California. In June 2008, the company sold its roughly 55% interest in Darwin, which went public in 2006, to Allied World Assurance Company Holdings, Ltd., for approximately $94 million.

## FINANCIALS:

**Sales and profits are in thousands of dollars—add 000 to get the full amount. 2008 Note: Financial information for 2008 was not available for all companies at press time.**

| | | |
|---|---|---|
| 2008 Sales: $ | 2008 Profits: $ | **U.S. Stock Ticker: Y** |
| 2007 Sales: $1,432,041 | 2007 Profits: $305,277 | **Int'l Ticker:** Int'l Exchange: |
| 2006 Sales: $1,209,165 | 2006 Profits: $251,244 | Employees: 931 |
| 2005 Sales: $1,095,956 | 2005 Profits: $52,334 | Fiscal Year Ends: 12/31 |
| 2004 Sales: $955,575 | 2004 Profits: $117,696 | Parent Company: |

## SALARIES/BENEFITS:

| | | | | |
|---|---|---|---|---|
| Pension Plan: | ESOP Stock Plan: | Profit Sharing: | Top Exec. Salary: $1,000,000 | Bonus: $1,500,000 |
| Savings Plan: | Stock Purch. Plan: | | Second Exec. Salary: $530,000 | Bonus: $477,000 |

## OTHER THOUGHTS:

**Apparent Women Officers or Directors:**
**Hot Spot for Advancement for Women/Minorities:**

## LOCATIONS: ("Y" = Yes)

| West: | Southwest: | Midwest: | Southeast: | Northeast: | International: |
|---|---|---|---|---|---|
| | | Y | Y | Y | |

# ALLIANCE IMAGING INC

www.allianceimaging.com

**Industry Group Code:** 621511 **Ranks within this company's industry group:** Sales: 1 Profits: 1

| **Management:** | | **Sales/Marketing:** | | **Liberal Arts:** | | **Information Systems:** | | **Professionals:** | | **Technical/Scientific:** | |
|---|---|---|---|---|---|---|---|---|---|---|---|
| Mgmt. Trainees: | | Mktg. Professionals: | Y | Gen. Writing/Editing: | | Info. Management: | Y | Finance/Accounting: | Y | Engineers, Elec.: | |
| Experienced Mgmt.: | Y | Retail Sales: | | Technical Writing: | Y | Software Dev.: | | Law: | Y | Engineers, Other: | |
| Int'l Business: | | Commercial/Industrial: | Y | Graphic Arts/Photog.: | | Hardware Dev.: | | HR/Other: | Y | Health/Lab: | Y |
| MBA Graduates: | Y | Sales Trainees: | Y | Music: | | Systems Integration: | Y | Training: | Y | Scientists/Research: | Y |
| | | Advertising Pros.: | | Broadcasting: | | Consulting/Other: | | Health Care: | Y | Petroleum/Chemicals: | |
| | | | | Other: | | | | Consulting: | | Math/Other: | |

## TYPES OF BUSINESS:

Diagnostic Imaging
Diagnostic Imaging Support Services
MRI Imaging
PET Imaging
CT Imaging
Radiation Therapy

## BRANDS/DIVISIONS/AFFILIATES:

Medical Outsourcing Services LLC
Alliance Radiosurgery LLC
Alliance Oncology LLC

## CONTACTS:

*Note: Officers with more than one job title may be intentionally listed here more than once.*

Paul S. Viviano, CEO
Michael F. Frisch, COO/Exec. VP
Howard K. Aihara, CFO/Exec. VP
Eli H. Glovinsky, General Counsel/Exec. VP/Sec.
Paul S. Viviano, Chmn.

**Phone:** 714-688-7100 **Fax:** 714-688-3397
**Toll-Free:** 800-544-3215
**Address:** 1900 S. State College Blvd., Ste. 600, Anaheim, CA 92806 US

## GROWTH PLANS/SPECIAL FEATURES:

Alliance Imaging, Inc. (AII) provides outpatient diagnostic imaging and therapeutic services primarily to hospitals and other healthcare providers. The firm's services normally include the use of imaging systems, technologists to operate the systems, equipment maintenance and upgrades and management of day-to-day shared-service and fixed-site diagnostic imaging operations. It serves approximately 1,000 clients in 46 states. The company generates 60% of its revenue from magnetic resonance imaging, or MRI; 31% was derived from positron emission tomography and positron emission tomography/computed tomography, or PET and PET/CT. The remaining revenue includes other modality diagnostic imaging services revenue, primarily computed tomography (CT), and management contract revenue. The firm provides imaging services primarily to hospitals and other healthcare providers on a shared and full-time service basis, in addition to operating a growing number of fixed-site imaging centers primarily in partnerships with hospitals or health systems. Alliance has 488 diagnostic imaging systems, including 310 MRI systems and 79 PET or PET/CT systems. Of these systems, 88 were located in fixed sites, which constitute systems installed in hospitals or other buildings on hospital campuses. Of these fixed sites, 72 were MRI fixed sites, three were PET or PET/CT fixed sites, eight were other modality fixed sites and five were unconsolidated joint ventures. Subsidiaries include Alliance Radiosurgery LLC and Alliance Oncology LLC. Recent acquisitions include eight radiation therapy centers in Alabama, Arkansas, Mississippi, and Missouri from Bethesda Resources, Inc.; six stereotactic radisurgery facilities in California, Maryland, New Jersey and Tennessee; and Medical Outsourcing Services, LLC.

Alliance Imaging offers its employees education assistance, a 401(k) plan, a tax deferred savings plan, health and life insurance and paid vacation time.

## FINANCIALS:

**Sales and profits are in thousands of dollars—add 000 to get the full amount. 2008 Note: Financial information for 2008 was not available for all companies at press time.**

| | | |
|---|---|---|
| 2008 Sales: $ | 2008 Profits: $ | **U.S. Stock Ticker: AIQ** |
| 2007 Sales: $444,919 | 2007 Profits: $16,232 | **Int'l Ticker:** Int'l Exchange: |
| 2006 Sales: $455,775 | 2006 Profits: $18,632 | Employees: 2,070 |
| 2005 Sales: $430,788 | 2005 Profits: $19,849 | Fiscal Year Ends: 12/31 |
| 2004 Sales: $432,080 | 2004 Profits: $- 486 | Parent Company: |

## SALARIES/BENEFITS:

| | | | | |
|---|---|---|---|---|
| Pension Plan: | ESOP Stock Plan: | Profit Sharing: | Top Exec. Salary: $500,000 | Bonus: $500,438 |
| Savings Plan: Y | Stock Purch. Plan: | | Second Exec. Salary: $275,096 | Bonus: $242,860 |

## OTHER THOUGHTS:

**Apparent Women Officers or Directors:**
**Hot Spot for Advancement for Women/Minorities:**

## LOCATIONS: ("Y" = Yes)

| West: | Southwest: | Midwest: | Southeast: | Northeast: | International: |
|---|---|---|---|---|---|
| Y | Y | Y | Y | Y | |

# ALLSCRIPTS HEALTHCARE SOLUTIONS INC

www.allscripts.com

**Industry Group Code:** 511212 **Ranks within this company's industry group:** Sales: 3 Profits: 4

| Management: | | Sales/Marketing: | | Liberal Arts: | | Information Systems: | | Professionals: | | Technical/Scientific: | |
|---|---|---|---|---|---|---|---|---|---|---|---|
| Mgmt. Trainees: | | Mktg. Professionals: | Y | Gen. Writing/Editing: | | Info. Management: | Y | Finance/Accounting: | Y | Engineers, Elec.: | Y |
| Experienced Mgmt.: | Y | Retail Sales: | | Technical Writing: | Y | Software Dev.: | Y | Law: | Y | Engineers, Other: | |
| Int'l Business: | | Commercial/Industrial: | Y | Graphic Arts/Photog.: | | Hardware Dev.: | | HR/Other: | Y | Health/Lab: | |
| MBA Graduates: | Y | Sales Trainees: | Y | Music: | | Systems Integration: | | Training: | Y | Scientists/Research: | |
| | | Advertising Pros.: | | Broadcasting: | | Consulting/Other: | | Health Care: | | Petroleum/Chemicals: | |
| | | | | Other: | | | | Consulting: | | Math/Other: | |

## TYPES OF BUSINESS:

Prescription Management Software
Point-of-Care Decision Support Solutions
Interactive Education Services

## BRANDS/DIVISIONS/AFFILIATES:

TouchWorks Professional
TouchWorks Enterprise
Allscripts Direct
Medem, Inc.
A4 Health Systems, Inc.
Extended Care Information Network
Misys Plc

## CONTACTS: *Note: Officers with more than one job title may be intentionally listed here more than once.*

Glen E. Tullman, CEO
Benjamin Bulkley, COO
Lee Shapiro, Pres.
William J. Davis, CFO
Dan Michelson, Chief Mktg. Officer
Stanley Crane, CTO
Brian Vandenberg, General Counsel/VP
Steven P. Schwartz, Sr. VP-Bus. Dev.
John G. Cull, Pres., Medication Svcs.
Douglas A. Gentile, Chief Medical Officer
Troy Moritz, Chief Security Officer
Laurie McGraw, Pres., TouchWorks
Glen E. Tullman, Chmn.

**Phone:** 312-506-1200 **Fax:** 312-506-1201
**Toll-Free:** 800-654-0889
**Address:** 222 Merchandise Mart Plaza, Ste. 2024, Chicago, IL 60654 US

## GROWTH PLANS/SPECIAL FEATURES:

Allscripts Healthcare Solutions, Inc. provides clinical software, connectivity and information solutions that physicians use to improve healthcare. Its business groups are designed to deliver timely information connecting physicians to each other and to the entire community of care, and to transform healthcare by improving both the quality and efficiency of care. The software and related services segment of the company's business provides clinical software solutions, including electronic health record, electronic prescribing and document imaging solutions. The information services segment, through the physicians interactive business unit, provides clinical education and information solutions for physicians and patients, along with physician-patient connectivity solutions through a partnership with Medem, Inc. The prepackaged medications segment provides prepackaged medication fulfillment solutions, which includes both medications and software for dispensing and inventory control. TouchWorks Professional is a point-of-care clinical solution for small to mid-size physician practices that provides e-prescribing. The TouchWorks Professional solution is delivered online via the physician's PDA (personal digital assistant) to a nearby pharmacy. TouchWorks Enterprise is a similar product used for large physician groups, academic medical centers and integrated delivery networks. Allscripts also owns a pre-packaged medications segment with its Allscripts Direct business, which provides point-of-care medication and medical supply management solutions for physicians. Companies employing Allscripts products include Integris Health, NEA Clinic, The University of Colorado Hospital, Cooper Clinic and Summit Medical Group. In January 2008, the firm acquired Extended Care Information Network, which provides hospital care management and discharge planning software, for $90 million. In March 2008, Allscripts announced a merger with Misys Healthcare LLC, a wholly-owned subsidiary of Misys Plc, an applications software and services company. Misys Healthcare will be merged with an Allscripts subsidiary. Misys Plc will receive 54.5% of shares, and contribute $330 million.

## FINANCIALS: Sales and profits are in thousands of dollars—add 000 to get the full amount. 2008 Note: Financial information for 2008 was not available for all companies at press time.

| | | |
|---|---|---|
| 2008 Sales: $ | 2008 Profits: $ | **U.S. Stock Ticker: MDRX** |
| 2007 Sales: $281,908 | 2007 Profits: $20,563 | **Int'l Ticker:** Int'l Exchange: |
| 2006 Sales: $227,969 | 2006 Profits: $11,895 | Employees: 1,155 |
| 2005 Sales: $120,564 | 2005 Profits: $9,710 | Fiscal Year Ends: 12/31 |
| 2004 Sales: $100,770 | 2004 Profits: $3,108 | Parent Company: |

## SALARIES/BENEFITS:

| | | | | |
|---|---|---|---|---|
| Pension Plan: | ESOP Stock Plan: | Profit Sharing: | Top Exec. Salary: $475,000 | Bonus: $ |
| Savings Plan: Y | Stock Purch. Plan: | | Second Exec. Salary: $400,000 | Bonus: $ |

## OTHER THOUGHTS:

**Apparent Women Officers or Directors**: 1
**Hot Spot for Advancement for Women/Minorities**:

## LOCATIONS: ("Y" = Yes)

| West: | Southwest: | Midwest: | Southeast: | Northeast: | International: |
|---|---|---|---|---|---|
| | Y | Y | | Y | |

# ALPHARMA INC

www.alpharma.com

**Industry Group Code:** 325414 **Ranks within this company's industry group:** Sales: 1 Profits: 3

| Management: | | Sales/Marketing: | | Liberal Arts: | | Information Systems: | | Professionals: | | Technical/Scientific: | |
|---|---|---|---|---|---|---|---|---|---|---|---|
| Mgmt. Trainees: | | Mktg. Professionals: | Y | Gen. Writing/Editing: | | Info. Management: | Y | Finance/Accounting: | Y | Engineers, Elec.: | Y |
| Experienced Mgmt.: | Y | Retail Sales: | | Technical Writing: | Y | Software Dev.: | Y | Law: | Y | Engineers, Other: | Y |
| Int'l Business: | Y | Commercial/Industrial: | Y | Graphic Arts/Photog.: | | Hardware Dev.: | | HR/Other: | Y | Health/Lab: | Y |
| MBA Graduates: | Y | Sales Trainees: | Y | Music: | | Systems Integration: | | Training: | Y | Scientists/Research: | Y |
| | | Advertising Pros.: | | Broadcasting: | | Consulting/Other: | | Health Care: | Y | Petroleum/Chemicals: | Y |
| | | | | Other: | | | | Consulting: | | Math/Other: | Y |

## TYPES OF BUSINESS:

Drugs-Animal Health
Human Pharmaceuticals
Animal Feed Additives

## BRANDS/DIVISIONS/AFFILIATES:

KADIAN
FLECTOR
BMD
ALBAC
3-NITRO
HISTOSTAT
BIO-COX
King Pharmaceuticals Inc

## CONTACTS: *Note: Officers with more than one job title may be intentionally listed here more than once.*

Dean J. Mitchell, CEO
Dean J. Mitchell, Pres.
Jeffrey S. Campbell, CFO/Exec. VP
Peter Watts, Exec. VP-Human Resources
Ronald N. Warner, Chief Scientific Officer/Exec. VP
Thomas J. Spellman III, General Counsel/Exec. VP/Sec.
Peter Watts, Exec. VP-Comm.
R. Scott Shively, Sr. VP-Pharmaceuticals Commercial Oper.
Carol A. Wrenn, Pres., Animal Health
Peter G. Tombros, Chmn.

**Phone:** 908-566-3800 **Fax:** 908-566-4137
**Toll-Free:** 866-322-2525
**Address:** 440 U.S. Highway 22 East, Bridgewater, NJ 08807 US

## GROWTH PLANS/SPECIAL FEATURES:

Alpharma, Inc. is a multinational pharmaceutical company that manufactures specialty and proprietary human pharmaceutical and animal health products. The company operates in two business segments, pharmaceuticals and animal health. The pharmaceuticals unit, which is focused on prescription pain management, markets two branded products: KADIAN, which is a morphine sulfate sustained release capsule, and FLECTOR, a prescription topical non-steroidal anti-inflammatory patch that delivers anti-inflammatory and analgesic effects of diclofenac epolamine and is indicated for the topical treatment of acute pain due to minor strains, sprains, and contusions. Both of these drugs are manufactured by third parties. Alpharma's animal health segment is a leading provider of animal feed additives and water soluble therapeutics for poultry and livestock. This division markets over 100 products, which are organized into three main lines: antibiotics, anticoccidials and antibacterials. Key products include BMD, a feed additive that promotes growth and feed efficiency, as well as prevents or treats diseases in poultry and swine; ALBAC, a feed additive for poultry, swine and calves; BIO-COX, which prevents coccidiosis in poultry; and 3-NITRO and HISTOSTAT feed grade antibacterials. Animal products are manufactured by the firm at several plant locations across the U.S., China and Norway as well as by third parties. In April 2008, the firm sold its active pharmaceutical division to 3i for $395 million. This division formerly produced active pharmaceutical ingredients (APIs), marketing and selling 14 APIs, including fermentation-based APIs and one chemically synthesized API. These products were used primarily by third parties in the manufacture of finished dose pharmaceuticals. In November 2008, the company agreed to be acquired by King Pharmaceuticals Inc. for roughly $1.6 billion.

Alpharma offers employees benefits including medical, dental, prescription and vision coverage; life and disability insurance; paid time off; and tuition reimbursement.

## FINANCIALS: **Sales and profits are in thousands of dollars—add 000 to get the full amount. 2008 Note: Financial information for 2008 was not available for all companies at press time.**

| | | |
|---|---|---|
| 2008 Sales: $ | 2008 Profits: $ | **U.S. Stock Ticker: ALO** |
| 2007 Sales: $722,425 | 2007 Profits: $-13,581 | **Int'l Ticker:** Int'l Exchange: |
| 2006 Sales: $653,828 | 2006 Profits: $82,544 | Employees: 2,000 |
| 2005 Sales: $553,617 | 2005 Profits: $133,769 | Fiscal Year Ends: 12/31 |
| 2004 Sales: $513,329 | 2004 Profits: $-314,737 | Parent Company: |

## SALARIES/BENEFITS:

| | | | | |
|---|---|---|---|---|
| Pension Plan: | ESOP Stock Plan: | Profit Sharing: | Top Exec. Salary: $646,923 | Bonus: $845,000 |
| Savings Plan: Y | Stock Purch. Plan: Y | | Second Exec. Salary: $436,762 | Bonus: $212,000 |

## OTHER THOUGHTS:

**Apparent Women Officers or Directors**: 1
**Hot Spot for Advancement for Women/Minorities**:

## LOCATIONS: ("Y" = Yes)

| West: | Southwest: | Midwest: | Southeast: | Northeast: | International: |
|---|---|---|---|---|---|
| Y | | Y | Y | Y | Y |

# ALTIRIS INC

www.altiris.com

**Industry Group Code:** 511214 **Ranks within this company's industry group:** Sales: Profits:

| **Management:** | | **Sales/Marketing:** | | **Liberal Arts:** | | **Information Systems:** | | **Professionals:** | | **Technical/Scientific:** | |
|---|---|---|---|---|---|---|---|---|---|---|---|
| Mgmt. Trainees: | | Mktg. Professionals: | Y | Gen. Writing/Editing: | | Info. Management: | Y | Finance/Accounting: | Y | Engineers, Elec.: | Y |
| Experienced Mgmt.: | Y | Retail Sales: | | Technical Writing: | Y | Software Dev.: | Y | Law: | Y | Engineers, Other: | |
| Int'l Business: | Y | Commercial/Industrial: | Y | Graphic Arts/Photog.: | | Hardware Dev.: | | HR/Other: | Y | Health/Lab: | |
| MBA Graduates: | Y | Sales Trainees: | Y | Music: | | Systems Integration: | Y | Training: | Y | Scientists/Research: | |
| | | Advertising Pros.: | | Broadcasting: | | Consulting/Other: | | Health Care: | | Petroleum/Chemicals: | |
| | | | | Other: | | | | Consulting: | | Math/Other: | |

## TYPES OF BUSINESS:

IT Management Software Products

## BRANDS/DIVISIONS/AFFILIATES:

Symantec Corp
Total Management Suite
Client Management Suite
Server Management Suite
License Compliance Suite
Handheld Management Suite
Client Security Managenet Suite

## CONTACTS:

*Note: Officers with more than one job title may be intentionally listed here more than once.*

Gregory S. Butterfield, CEO
Gregory S. Butterfield, Pres.
Gregory S. Butterfield, Chmn.

| **Phone:** 801-226-8500 | **Fax:** 801-226-8506 |
|---|---|
| **Toll-Free:** 888-252-5551 | |
| **Address:** 588 W. 400 S., Lindon, UT 84042 US | |

## GROWTH PLANS/SPECIAL FEATURES:

Altiris, Inc., a wholly-owned subsidiary of Symantec Corp., is a provider of information technology management software that enables businesses to easily manage and service network-based endpoints. The company's solutions are designed to address challenges in managing technology change, backing up and restoring user data and settings; provisioning and managing business-critical servers; tracking performance and diagnostic metrics for hardware and software; taking inventory of existing IT assets; assessing security compliance; remediating vulnerabilities; protecting sensitive data; and automating service support processes for the end user. The firm's products are licensed to customers according to their needs as integrated suites or as separate modules and are designed to help customers better align IT services to business initiatives through automated operations, enforceable security and lifecycle integration, depending on customer requirements. Primary product suites include the Total Management Suite, designed to help IT organizations manage, secure and support all IT assets; the Client Management Suite, an integrated lifecycle management deployment and configuration management for client and mobile devices; the Server Management Suit, an integrated and heterogeneous deployment management and monitoring functions from a centralized console; the License Compliance Suite, an automated management of software licenses through software inventory, application metering and license agreement management; the Handheld Management Suite, which discovers, manages and secures Windows Mobile, Palm OS and BlackBerry handheld assets; and the Client Security Management Suite, which delivers configuration assurance, data protection and threat prevention. Many of the firm's products are aligned with well known hardware and software companies such as Dell, IBM, Microsoft, Intel, Fujitsu Siemens Computers, Oracle and Hewlett-Packard.

## FINANCIALS:

**Sales and profits are in thousands of dollars—add 000 to get the full amount. 2008 Note: Financial information for 2008 was not available for all companies at press time.**

| | | |
|---|---|---|
| 2008 Sales: $ | 2008 Profits: $ | **U.S. Stock Ticker: Subsidiary** |
| 2007 Sales: $ | 2007 Profits: $ | **Int'l Ticker:** Int'l Exchange: |
| 2006 Sales: $229,434 | 2006 Profits: $15,520 | Employees: 992 |
| 2005 Sales: $187,640 | 2005 Profits: $3,251 | Fiscal Year Ends: 12/31 |
| 2004 Sales: $ | 2004 Profits: $ | Parent Company: SYMANTEC CORP |

## SALARIES/BENEFITS:

| | | | | |
|---|---|---|---|---|
| Pension Plan: | ESOP Stock Plan: | Profit Sharing: | Top Exec. Salary: $ | Bonus: $ |
| Savings Plan: | Stock Purch. Plan: | | Second Exec. Salary: $ | Bonus: $ |

## OTHER THOUGHTS:

**Apparent Women Officers or Directors:**
**Hot Spot for Advancement for Women/Minorities:**

## LOCATIONS: ("Y" = Yes)

| West: | Southwest: | Midwest: | Southeast: | Northeast: | International: |
|---|---|---|---|---|---|
| Y | | Y | | Y | Y |

# ALZA CORP

www.jnj.com

**Industry Group Code:** 325412A **Ranks within this company's industry group:** Sales: 4 Profits:

| Management: | | Sales/Marketing: | | Liberal Arts: | | Information Systems: | | Professionals: | | Technical/Scientific: | |
|---|---|---|---|---|---|---|---|---|---|---|---|
| Mgmt. Trainees: | | Mktg. Professionals: | Y | Gen. Writing/Editing: | | Info. Management: | Y | Finance/Accounting: | Y | Engineers, Elec.: | |
| Experienced Mgmt.: | Y | Retail Sales: | | Technical Writing: | Y | Software Dev.: | | Law: | Y | Engineers, Other: | |
| Int'l Business: | Y | Commercial/Industrial: | Y | Graphic Arts/Photog.: | | Hardware Dev.: | | HR/Other: | Y | Health/Lab: | Y |
| MBA Graduates: | Y | Sales Trainees: | Y | Music: | | Systems Integration: | | Training: | Y | Scientists/Research: | Y |
| | | Advertising Pros.: | | Broadcasting: | | Consulting/Other: | | Health Care: | Y | Petroleum/Chemicals: | |
| | | | | Other: | | | | Consulting: | | Math/Other: | Y |

## TYPES OF BUSINESS:

Drug Delivery Systems
Pharmaceutical Development & Marketing

## BRANDS/DIVISIONS/AFFILIATES:

Johnson & Johnson
OROS
L-OROS
D-TRANS
STEALTH
DUROS
E-TRANS
IONSYS

## CONTACTS: *Note: Officers with more than one job title may be intentionally listed here more than once.*

Michael R. Jackson, Pres.
Erik Wiberg, VP-Bus. Dev.
Ravi Kiron, Exec. Dir.- New Tech. Assessment & Planning

| | |
|---|---|
| **Phone:** 650-564-5000 | **Fax:** 732-342-9819 |
| **Toll-Free:** | |
| **Address:** 1900 Charleston Rd., Mountain View, CA 94039-7120 US | |

## GROWTH PLANS/SPECIAL FEATURES:

ALZA Corp., a subsidiary of Johnson & Johnson, develops and markets pharmaceutical products involving advanced drug delivery technologies. The company focuses on several therapeutic areas, including oncology, AIDS, pain management, endocrinology and urology. ALZA partners with other companies to combine new pharmaceutical compounds with its oral, transdermal, implantable and liposomal delivery systems. It has five key brand name technologies. OROS oral delivery technology, currently incorporated into 13 different products worldwide including Sudafed 24 Hour, uses osmosis to provide controlled drug delivery for up to 24 hours, with L-OROS available for liquid formulations. D-TRANS transdermal technology is a patch drug delivery system currently used for seven different products, including Nicoderm CQ. Its STEALTH liposomal technology consists of microscopic lipid particles that incorporate a polyethylene glycol coating, which allows cancer therapeutics and gene therapy vectors to evade detection by the immune system, targeting specific areas of disease within the body. DUROS implants are miniature titanium cylinders which deliver therapeutics including small drugs, proteins, DNA and other bioactive macromolecules at a continuous rate for up to one year. E-TRANS is an electron transport technology which actively transports drugs through intact skin, both locally and systemically, using low-level electrical energy. ALZA Corp.'s drug delivery technology has been incorporated in approximately 30 commercialized products sold worldwide.

ALZA provides its employees with a wide range of benefits including pre-tax accounts for health and dependant care; medical, dental, life and accident insurance; adoption assistance; tuition reimbursement; short- and long-term disability care; daycare discounts; exercise programs; and a charitable matching gift program.

## FINANCIALS: **Sales and profits are in thousands of dollars—add 000 to get the full amount. 2008 Note: Financial information for 2008 was not available for all companies at press time.**

| | | |
|---|---|---|
| 2008 Sales: $ | 2008 Profits: $ | **U.S. Stock Ticker: Subsidiary** |
| 2007 Sales: $198,400 | 2007 Profits: $ | **Int'l Ticker:** Int'l Exchange: |
| 2006 Sales: $ | 2006 Profits: $ | Employees: 1,845 |
| 2005 Sales: $ | 2005 Profits: $ | Fiscal Year Ends: 12/31 |
| 2004 Sales: $ | 2004 Profits: $ | Parent Company: JOHNSON & JOHNSON |

## SALARIES/BENEFITS:

| | | | | |
|---|---|---|---|---|
| Pension Plan: Y | ESOP Stock Plan: | Profit Sharing: | Top Exec. Salary: $ | Bonus: $ |
| Savings Plan: Y | Stock Purch. Plan: | | Second Exec. Salary: $ | Bonus: $ |

## OTHER THOUGHTS:

**Apparent Women Officers or Directors:**
**Hot Spot for Advancement for Women/Minorities:**

## LOCATIONS: ("Y" = Yes)

| West: | Southwest: | Midwest: | Southeast: | Northeast: | International: |
|---|---|---|---|---|---|
| Y | | | | | |

Note: Financial information, benefits and other data can change quickly and may vary from those stated here.

# AMAG PHARMACEUTICALS INC

www.amagpharma.com

**Industry Group Code:** 541710B **Ranks within this company's industry group:** Sales: 1 Profits: 1

| **Management:** | | **Sales/Marketing:** | | **Liberal Arts:** | | **Information Systems:** | | **Professionals:** | | **Technical/Scientific:** | |
|---|---|---|---|---|---|---|---|---|---|---|---|
| Mgmt. Trainees: | | Mktg. Professionals: | | Gen. Writing/Editing: | | Info. Management: | Y | Finance/Accounting: | Y | Engineers, Elec.: | |
| Experienced Mgmt.: | Y | Retail Sales: | | Technical Writing: | | Software Dev.: | | Law: | Y | Engineers, Other: | |
| Int'l Business: | | Commercial/Industrial: | | Graphic Arts/Photog.: | | Hardware Dev.: | | HR/Other: | Y | Health/Lab: | |
| MBA Graduates: | Y | Sales Trainees: | | Music: | | Systems Integration: | | Training: | Y | Scientists/Research: | Y |
| | | Advertising Pros.: | | Broadcasting: | | Consulting/Other: | | Health Care: | | Petroleum/Chemicals: | |
| | | | | Other: | | | | Consulting: | | Math/Other: | |

## TYPES OF BUSINESS:

Nanoparticles, Pharmaceutical
MRI Contrast Agents
Iron Replacement Therapeutics

## BRANDS/DIVISIONS/AFFILIATES:

Combidex
Feridex I.V.
GastroMARK
Ferumoxytol
3SBio, Inc.
Guerbet
Bayer Healthcare Pharmaceuticals
Taejoon Pharmaceuticals

## CONTACTS: *Note: Officers with more than one job title may be intentionally listed here more than once.*

Brian J. G. Pereira, CEO
Brian J. G. Pereira, Pres.
David A. Arkowitz, CFO/Chief Bus. Officer
Lee F. Allen, Chief Medical Officer/Sr. VP-Clinical Dev.
Joseph L. Farmer, General Counsel/Sr. VP-Legal Affairs
Timothy G. Healey, Sr. VP-Commercial Oper.
Chris White, VP-Bus. Dev. & Corp. Planning
Carol Miceli, Press Contact
Louis Brenner, Sr. VP-Ferumoxytol Program
Robert M. Brenner, Sr. VP-Nephrology Clinical Dev./Medical Affairs

| **Phone:** 617-498-3300 | **Fax:** 617-499-3361 |
|---|---|
| **Toll-Free:** | |
| **Address:** 100 Hayden Ave., Cambridge, MA 02141 US | |

## GROWTH PLANS/SPECIAL FEATURES:

AMAG Pharmaceuticals, Inc. (AMAG) develops and manufactures super-paramagnetic iron oxide nanoparticles used as therapeutic iron compound to treat anemia and novel imaging agents to aid in the diagnosis of cancer and cardiovascular disease. Its nanoparticles are composed of bio-available iron that is easily absorbed by the body. Due to its super-paramagnetic properties, the product can also become strongly polarized in magnetic fields, which makes nanoparticles ideal candidates for MRI (magnetic resonance imaging) testing. AMAG currently has two FDA approved products on the market: Feridex I.V., a liver contrast agent, and GastroMARK, an oral contrast agent used for delineating the bowel in MRI. Both products have been approved to market in the U.S., Europe and other countries. The company's lead product candidate ferumoxytol, is being developed for use as an intravenous iron replacement therapeutic agent for the treatment of iron deficiency anemia, as well as a diagnostic agent for vascular-enhanced MRI testing to assess peripheral arterial disease. In October 2008, the firm received a response to its New Drug Application (NDA) from the FDA requesting additional information about ferumoxytol prior to its approval for marketing and sale in the U.S.. Combidex, the company's other product under development, is a molecular imaging agent consisting of iron oxide nanoparticles being developed for use in differentiating cancerous and normal lymph nodes in conjunction with MRI tests. AMAG has entered into several strategic relationships with pharmaceutical companies to market and distribute its products, including 3SBio, Inc.; Bayer Healthcare Pharmaceuticals; Guerbet; Covidien, Ltd.; and TaeJoon Pharmaceuticals. In May 2008, AMAG entered a strategic partnership with 3SBio, Inc., a leading Chinese biotechnology company, for the development and commercialization of ferumoxytol. In August 2008, the FDA granted ferumoxytol Fast Track development designation as a diagnostic agent for Vascular-Enhanced Magnetic Resonance Imaging.

## FINANCIALS: **Sales and profits are in thousands of dollars—add 000 to get the full amount. 2008 Note: Financial information for 2008 was not available for all companies at press time.**

| | | |
|---|---|---|
| 2008 Sales: $ | 2008 Profits: $ | **U.S. Stock Ticker: AMAG** |
| 2007 Sales: $2,552 | 2007 Profits: $-33,894 | **Int'l Ticker:** Int'l Exchange: |
| 2006 Sales: $2,673 | 2006 Profits: $-25,365 | Employees: 88 |
| 2005 Sales: $2,445 | 2005 Profits: $-12,714 | Fiscal Year Ends: 12/31 |
| 2004 Sales: $3,756 | 2004 Profits: $-4,495 | Parent Company: |

## SALARIES/BENEFITS:

| | | | | |
|---|---|---|---|---|
| Pension Plan: | ESOP Stock Plan: | Profit Sharing: | Top Exec. Salary: $428,608 | Bonus: $337,050 |
| Savings Plan: Y | Stock Purch. Plan: | | Second Exec. Salary: $265,000 | Bonus: $113,071 |

## OTHER THOUGHTS:

**Apparent Women Officers or Directors:**
**Hot Spot for Advancement for Women/Minorities:** Y

## LOCATIONS: ("Y" = Yes)

| West: | Southwest: | Midwest: | Southeast: | Northeast: | International: |
|---|---|---|---|---|---|
| | | | | Y | |

# AMCOL INTERNATIONAL CORP

www.amcol.com

**Industry Group Code:** 327000 **Ranks within this company's industry group:** Sales: 1 Profits: 1

| Management: | | Sales/Marketing: | | Liberal Arts: | | Information Systems: | | Professionals: | | Technical/Scientific: | |
|---|---|---|---|---|---|---|---|---|---|---|---|
| Mgmt. Trainees: | | Mktg. Professionals: | Y | Gen. Writing/Editing: | | Info. Management: | Y | Finance/Accounting: | Y | Engineers, Elec.: | |
| Experienced Mgmt.: | Y | Retail Sales: | | Technical Writing: | Y | Software Dev.: | | Law: | Y | Engineers, Other: | Y |
| Int'l Business: | Y | Commercial/Industrial: | Y | Graphic Arts/Photog.: | | Hardware Dev.: | | HR/Other: | Y | Health/Lab: | |
| MBA Graduates: | Y | Sales Trainees: | Y | Music: | | Systems Integration: | | Training: | Y | Scientists/Research: | |
| | | Advertising Pros.: | | Broadcasting: | | Consulting/Other: | | Health Care: | | Petroleum/Chemicals: | Y |
| | | | | Other: | | | | Consulting: | | Math/Other: | |

## TYPES OF BUSINESS:

Minerals & Composites
Bentonite
Truck & Freight Services
Nanocomposites
Environmental Products
Mining Services
Environmental Services

## BRANDS/DIVISIONS/AFFILIATES:

Nanocor
Vorclay
Panther Creek
Premium Gel
Additrol
Volclay International
CETCO
American Colloid

## CONTACTS: *Note: Officers with more than one job title may be intentionally listed here more than once.*

Larry Washow, CEO
Larry Washow, Pres.
Donald W. Pearson, CFO/Sr. VP
Gary Morrison, VP/Pres., American Colloid
Ryan McKendrick, Sr. VP/Pres., CETCO
Gary L. Castagna, Sr. VP/Pres., Global Minerals

| **Phone:** 847-851-1500 | **Fax:** |
|---|---|
| **Toll-Free:** 800-426-5564 | |
| **Address:** 2870 Forbs Ave., Hoffman Estates, IL 60192 US | |

## GROWTH PLANS/SPECIAL FEATURES:

Amcol International Corp. produces and markets a wide range of specialty minerals to the industrial, environmental and consumer-related industries. The company operates in five segments: Minerals, environmental, oilfield services, transportation and corporate services. The Amcol minerals segment, accounting for 48% of the firm's total sales, mines, processes and distributes clays, bentonite and bentonite-related products. It includes products marketed under the trademark names Vorclay, Panther Creek, Premium Gel and Additrol. The environmental segment, accounting for 34% of revenue, processes and distributes clays and minerals as moisture barriers for commercial construction, landfill liners and other industrial applications. Amcol is particularly interested in bentonite due to its unique chemical structure, which allows it to act as a thickener, sealant, binder, lubricant and absorption agent. The oilfield services segment, accounting for 14% of revenue, offers both onshore and offshore water treatment filtration and pipeline separation. The transportation segment, making up 4% of the firm's revenue, provides trucking and freight brokerage services for domestic subsidiaries and third parties. The company's main subsidiaries include CETCO; American Colloid; Colin Stewart Michem; Volclay International; Health and Beauty Solutions, Inc.; and Ameri-Co Carriers/Logistics, Inc. The company also manufactures nanocomposites under its subsidiary Nanocor, Inc., which modifies the surface of bentonite minerals in order to improve the physical properties of manufactured polymers. Amcol is located in more than 28 countries and operates 68 facilities. Approximately 68% of revenue is generated in the Americas. In May 2008, CETCO acquired the business assets of Premium Reeled Tubing, L.L.C.

Employees are offered medical and dental insurance; life insurance; and a 401(k) savings plan.

## FINANCIALS: **Sales and profits are in thousands of dollars—add 000 to get the full amount. 2008 Note: Financial information for 2008 was not available for all companies at press time.**

| | | |
|---|---|---|
| 2008 Sales: $ | 2008 Profits: $ | **U.S. Stock Ticker: ACO** |
| 2007 Sales: $744,334 | 2007 Profits: $56,735 | **Int'l Ticker:** Int'l Exchange: |
| 2006 Sales: $611,556 | 2006 Profits: $50,248 | Employees: 2,017 |
| 2005 Sales: $535,924 | 2005 Profits: $41,045 | Fiscal Year Ends: 12/31 |
| 2004 Sales: $461,778 | 2004 Profits: $31,565 | Parent Company: |

## SALARIES/BENEFITS:

| | | | | |
|---|---|---|---|---|
| Pension Plan: | ESOP Stock Plan: | Profit Sharing: | Top Exec. Salary: $625,000 | Bonus: $405,000 |
| Savings Plan: Y | Stock Purch. Plan: | | Second Exec. Salary: $300,000 | Bonus: $223,770 |

## OTHER THOUGHTS:

**Apparent Women Officers or Directors**: 1
**Hot Spot for Advancement for Women/Minorities**:

## LOCATIONS: ("Y" = Yes)

| West: | Southwest: | Midwest: | Southeast: | Northeast: | International: |
|---|---|---|---|---|---|
| Y | Y | Y | Y | Y | Y |

# AMERESCO

**www.ameresco.com**

**Industry Group Code:** 541690 **Ranks within this company's industry group:** Sales: Profits:

| Management: | | Sales/Marketing: | | Liberal Arts: | | Information Systems: | | Professionals: | | Technical/Scientific: | |
|---|---|---|---|---|---|---|---|---|---|---|---|
| Mgmt. Trainees: | | Mktg. Professionals: | Y | Gen. Writing/Editing: | | Info. Management: | Y | Finance/Accounting: | Y | Engineers, Elec.: | |
| Experienced Mgmt.: | Y | Retail Sales: | | Technical Writing: | | Software Dev.: | | Law: | Y | Engineers, Other: | |
| Int'l Business: | Y | Commercial/Industrial: | | Graphic Arts/Photog.: | | Hardware Dev.: | | HR/Other: | Y | Health/Lab: | |
| MBA Graduates: | Y | Sales Trainees: | Y | Music: | | Systems Integration: | | Training: | Y | Scientists/Research: | |
| | | Advertising Pros.: | | Broadcasting: | | Consulting/Other: | Y | Health Care: | | Petroleum/Chemicals: | |
| | | | | Other: | | | | Consulting: | Y | Math/Other: | |

## TYPES OF BUSINESS:

Energy Consulting
Landfill Gas-to-Energy Generation
Solar Power Technology
Cogeneration

## BRANDS/DIVISIONS/AFFILIATES:

Ameresco Canada
Citizens Conservation Services
AmerescoSolutions
Ameresco Enertech
Ameresco E-Three
Southwest Photovoltaic Systems, Inc.
Global Energy
Energy Systems

## CONTACTS: *Note: Officers with more than one job title may be intentionally listed here more than once.*

George P. Sakellaris, CEO
George P. Sakellaris, Pres.
Andrew B. Spence, CFO/VP
Eric Longbottom, VP-Mktg. & Sales
Joseph P. DeManche, Exec. VP-Eng.
David J. Corrsin, General Counsel/Exec. VP
Joseph P. DeManche, Exec. VP-Oper.
David J. Anderson, Exec. VP-Bus. Dev.
Michael T. Bakas, VP-Renewable Energy
Michael R. Castonguay, VP-Planning
Paul M. Dello Iacono, VP
Peter W. Wallis, VP-Strategic Dev.
George P. Sakellaris, Chmn.

**Phone:** 508-661-2200 **Fax:** 508-661-2201
**Toll-Free:** 866-263-7372
**Address:** 111 Speen St., Ste. 410, Framingham, MA 01701 US

## GROWTH PLANS/SPECIAL FEATURES:

Ameresco, Inc., with 38 offices throughout the U.S. and Canada, is an independent efficiency consulting company that helps corporations decrease operating expenses, upgrade and maintain facilities and stabilize operating costs. The company works with corporate customers and surrounding utilities to negotiate lower electricity costs through subsidiaries that focus on particular markets. Ameresco Canada, formerly part of DukeSolutions, Inc., serves institutional, commercial and industrial energy users in Canada. Ameresco Canada has completed over 150 projects and achieved over $479 million in energy and operating cost savings for over 3,000 buildings across Canada. Citizens Conservation Services serves private and public multi-family properties. AmerescoSolutions, also formerly part of DukeSolutions, focuses on federal government clients and has national contracts with the U.S. Departments of Defense and Energy. Ameresco Enertech, formerly LG&E Enertech, focuses on primary education, higher education, industrial and commercial facilities within Tennessee and Kentucky. Ameresco E-Three, which stands for Energy Efficient Expertise, is an energy consulting and services company with offices in Nevada serving the Western States. Recently, the company implemented a landfill gas-to-energy plant at the Buena Vista Landfill located in Watsonville, California. The new facility will generate 3.2 megawatts of alternative energy, which is enough power for 3,000 average homes. In May 2007, Ameresco acquired Southwest Photovoltaic Systems, Inc., a Tomball, Texas based designer, integrator and distributor of photovoltaic, wind and other renewable energy systems. Southwest Photovoltaic Systems is now Ameresco Solar. Also in 2007, the company acquired Global Energy and rebranded it as PV Energy Systems. PV Energy Systems offers turnkey system sizing and integrates system balance.

## FINANCIALS: Sales and profits are in thousands of dollars—add 000 to get the full amount. 2008 Note: Financial information for 2008 was not available for all companies at press time.

2008 Sales: $
2007 Sales: $
2006 Sales: $
2005 Sales: $290,504
2004 Sales: $210,594

2008 Profits: $
2007 Profits: $
2006 Profits: $
2005 Profits: $
2004 Profits: $

**U.S. Stock Ticker: Private**
**Int'l Ticker:** Int'l Exchange:
Employees: 352
Fiscal Year Ends: 12/31
Parent Company:

## SALARIES/BENEFITS:

Pension Plan: ESOP Stock Plan: Profit Sharing: Top Exec. Salary: $ Bonus: $
Savings Plan: Stock Purch. Plan: Second Exec. Salary: $ Bonus: $

## OTHER THOUGHTS:

**Apparent Women Officers or Directors**:
**Hot Spot for Advancement for Women/Minorities**:

## LOCATIONS: ("Y" = Yes)

| West: | Southwest: | Midwest: | Southeast: | Northeast: | International: |
|---|---|---|---|---|---|
| Y | Y | Y | Y | Y | Y |

# AMERICAN FIDELITY ASSURANCE COMPANY www.afadvantage.com

**Industry Group Code:** 524113 **Ranks within this company's industry group:** Sales: 6 Profits:

| Management: | | Sales/Marketing: | | Liberal Arts: | | Information Systems: | | Professionals: | | Technical/Scientific: | |
|---|---|---|---|---|---|---|---|---|---|---|---|
| Mgmt. Trainees: | | Mktg. Professionals: | Y | Gen. Writing/Editing: | Y | Info. Management: | Y | Finance/Accounting: | Y | Engineers, Elec.: | |
| Experienced Mgmt.: | Y | Retail Sales: | | Technical Writing: | Y | Software Dev.: | | Law: | Y | Engineers, Other: | |
| Int'l Business: | | Commercial/Industrial: | | Graphic Arts/Photog.: | | Hardware Dev.: | | HR/Other: | Y | Health/Lab: | |
| MBA Graduates: | Y | Sales Trainees: | Y | Music: | | Systems Integration: | | Training: | Y | Scientists/Research: | |
| | | Advertising Pros.: | Y | Broadcasting: | | Consulting/Other: | | Health Care: | Y | Petroleum/Chemicals: | |
| | | | | Other: | | | | Consulting: | | Math/Other: | Y |

## TYPES OF BUSINESS:

Life Insurance
Disability Insurance
Annuities
Supplemental Health Insurance
Asset Management

## BRANDS/DIVISIONS/AFFILIATES:

American Fidelity Educational Services (AFES)
Association and Worksite Division (AWD)
American Public Life Insurance Company (APL)
AFAmeriLife (AFAL)
Latin America Life Insurance

## CONTACTS: *Note: Officers with more than one job title may be intentionally listed here more than once.*

William M. Cameron, CEO
William M. Cameron, Pres.
Robert Brearton, CFO/Sr. VP
Al Litchenburg, Exec. VP-Office of the Chair
Dave Carpenter, Exec. VP-Office of the Chair
William M. Cameron, Chmn.

| | |
|---|---|
| **Phone:** 405-523-2000 | **Fax:** 405-523-5963 |
| **Toll-Free:** 800-654-8489 | |
| **Address:** 2000 N. Classen Blvd., Oklahoma City, OK 73106 US | |

## GROWTH PLANS/SPECIAL FEATURES:

American Fidelity Assurance Company (AFA) is a private, family-owned company. Based in Oklahoma City, it serves nearly 1.5 million customers in 49 states and 20 countries and manages over $4.6 billion in consolidated assets. AFA focuses on providing insurance products and financial services to education employees, trade association members and companies. The firm's primary businesses include disability income insurance, life insurance, annuities and supplemental health insurance. AFA's specific offerings include accident only protection insurance; health savings accounts (HSAs); 403(b) tax-deferred annuities; after-tax annuities; individual retirement annuities; Roth IRAs; children's life insurance; whole life insurance; group disability income insurance; Section 125 administration; health reimbursement arrangement (HRA) services; cancer protection plans; hospital GAP Plans; and hospital indemnity. Subsidiary American Fidelity Educational Services (AFES) provides supplemental insurance products, investment products and financial services to the educational community. The Association and Worksite Division (AWD) provides employee-paid personal wealth, asset and family protection, including group disability, cancer, life, accident and hospital indemnity insurance. The recently formed Life Division is the result of a merger between AFAmeriLife (AFAL) and AFA's Latin America Life Insurance. Subsidiary American Public Life Insurance Company (APL) provides worksite brokers with life and supplemental health insurance products.

American Fidelity offers its employees an on-site fitness center; on-site training facilities; on-site banking facilities; an on-site deli; discounts on event tickets; off-site fitness and wellness reimbursements; a business casual environment; flexible reimbursement accounts for medical and dependent daycare expenses; a holiday bonus; employee events; and health, dental and vision insurance.

## FINANCIALS: **Sales and profits are in thousands of dollars—add 000 to get the full amount. 2008 Note: Financial information for 2008 was not available for all companies at press time.**

| | | |
|---|---|---|
| 2008 Sales: $ | 2008 Profits: $ | **U.S. Stock Ticker: Private** |
| 2007 Sales: $752,000 | 2007 Profits: $ | **Int'l Ticker:** Int'l Exchange: |
| 2006 Sales: $645,000 | 2006 Profits: $ | Employees: 1,509 |
| 2005 Sales: $611,000 | 2005 Profits: $ | Fiscal Year Ends: 12/31 |
| 2004 Sales: $ | 2004 Profits: $ | Parent Company: |

## SALARIES/BENEFITS:

| | | | | |
|---|---|---|---|---|
| Pension Plan: Y | ESOP Stock Plan: | Profit Sharing: | Top Exec. Salary: $ | Bonus: $ |
| Savings Plan: Y | Stock Purch. Plan: | | Second Exec. Salary: $ | Bonus: $ |

## OTHER THOUGHTS:

**Apparent Women Officers or Directors:** 2
**Hot Spot for Advancement for Women/Minorities:**

## LOCATIONS: ("Y" = Yes)

| West: | Southwest: | Midwest: | Southeast: | Northeast: | International: |
|---|---|---|---|---|---|
| | Y | | | | |

# AMERICAN ITALIAN PASTA COMPANY

www.aipc.com

**Industry Group Code:** 311823 **Ranks within this company's industry group:** Sales: 1 Profits: 1

| Management: | | Sales/Marketing: | | Liberal Arts: | | Information Systems: | | Professionals: | | Technical/Scientific: | |
|---|---|---|---|---|---|---|---|---|---|---|---|
| Mgmt. Trainees: | | Mktg. Professionals: | Y | Gen. Writing/Editing: | | Info. Management: | Y | Finance/Accounting: | Y | Engineers, Elec.: | |
| Experienced Mgmt.: | Y | Retail Sales: | | Technical Writing: | | Software Dev.: | | Law: | Y | Engineers, Other: | |
| Int'l Business: | Y | Commercial/Industrial: | Y | Graphic Arts/Photog.: | | Hardware Dev.: | | HR/Other: | Y | Health/Lab: | |
| MBA Graduates: | Y | Sales Trainees: | Y | Music: | | Systems Integration: | | Training: | Y | Scientists/Research: | |
| | | Advertising Pros.: | Y | Broadcasting: | | Consulting/Other: | | Health Care: | | Petroleum/Chemicals: | |
| | | | | Other: | | | | Consulting: | | Math/Other: | |

## TYPES OF BUSINESS:

Dry Pasta Manufacturing
Canned Pasta
Dry Soup Mix

## BRANDS/DIVISIONS/AFFILIATES:

Mueller
Golden Grain
Mrs. Grass
Ronco
Luxury
Pennsylvania Dutch

## CONTACTS: *Note: Officers with more than one job title may be intentionally listed here more than once.*

John Kelly, CEO
Walter N. George, COO
John Kelly, Pres.
Paul R. Geist, CFO/Exec. VP
Drew Lericos, VP-Mktg.
Jayne S. Hoover, VP-R&D/Quality
Chrystal L. Johnson, VP-Info. Sys.
G. Michael Willhoite, VP-Tech. Svcs.
Eric L. Johnson, VP-Eng.
Tim Lethcoe, VP-Mfg.
Kevin Hall, VP-Sales & Oper. Planning
Douglas W. Fleming, VP/Corp. Controller
Patrick D. Regan, Sr. VP-Sales Strategy
Brian Fox, VP-Food Svc.
Thomas Branich, Sr. VP-Retail Sales
Michael J. Kaczynski, Sr. VP-Retail Sales
William R. Patterson, Chmn.
John A. Griffith, VP-Global Sourcing

| Phone: 816-584-5000 | Fax: 816-584-5100 |
|---|---|
| Toll-Free: | |
| Address: 4100 N. Mulberry Dr., Ste. 200, Kansas City, MO 64116 US | |

## GROWTH PLANS/SPECIAL FEATURES:

American Italian Pasta Company (AIPC) is a leading producer of pasta products, which are distributed to retail and industrial customers in North America and Europe. The company produces more than 300 different shapes and sizes of dry pasta in multiple package configurations, including bulk packages for institutional customers and smaller, individually-wrapped packages for retail consumers. The company's products include long goods, such as spaghetti, linguine, fettuccine, angel hair and lasagna; and short goods, such as elbow macaroni, mostaccioli, rigatoni, rotini, ziti and egg noodles. In many instances, the company produces pasta to unique customer specifications. AIPC's pasta is sold under a variety of brand names, including Ronco, Golden Grain, Pennsylvania Dutch, Martha Gooch, Mueller's, Anthony's, Mrs. Grass and Heartland. AIPC operates milling, production and distribution facilities in Missouri, South Carolina, Arizona and Verolanuova, Italy. The Italy plant serves the North American, European and other international markets with branded, private label, ingredient and food service products. The firm has a long-term supply agreement with SYSCO Corporation, the nation's largest marketer and distributor of food service products. The company is also the primary supplier of pasta to Wal-Mart, Inc., as well as a supplier of private-label and branded pasta to some of the largest grocery retailers in the U.S. In 2008, retail sales, including sales to traditional grocery retailers, club stores, mass merchants, drug and discount stores, accounted for 75% of total sales. Industrial sales, including sales to food service distributors supplying restaurants, hotels, schools and hospitals and sales to food processors, accounted for the remaining 25%. In 2008, AIPC donated more than 6,000 lbs. of spaghetti to the Susan G. Komen for the Cure Breast Cancer 3-Day series.

The firm offers its employees benefits including health, dental and vision coverage, life insurance, short- and long-term disability insurance and a 401(k) plan.

## FINANCIALS: 

**Sales and profits are in thousands of dollars—add 000 to get the full amount. 2008 Note: Financial information for 2008 was not available for all companies at press time.**

| | | |
|---|---|---|
| 2008 Sales: $569,196 | 2008 Profits: $19,111 | **U.S. Stock Ticker: AIPC** |
| 2007 Sales: $398,122 | 2007 Profits: $5,348 | **Int'l Ticker:** Int'l Exchange: |
| 2006 Sales: $367,023 | 2006 Profits: $-30,413 | Employees: 665 |
| 2005 Sales: $ | 2005 Profits: $ | Fiscal Year Ends: 9/30 |
| 2004 Sales: $417,354 | 2004 Profits: $2,989 | Parent Company: |

## SALARIES/BENEFITS:

| | | | | |
|---|---|---|---|---|
| Pension Plan: | ESOP Stock Plan: | Profit Sharing: | Top Exec. Salary: $583,922 | Bonus: $ |
| Savings Plan: Y | Stock Purch. Plan: | | Second Exec. Salary: $296,671 | Bonus: $ |

## OTHER THOUGHTS:

**Apparent Women Officers or Directors**: 2
**Hot Spot for Advancement for Women/Minorities**:

## LOCATIONS: ("Y" = Yes)

| West: | Southwest: | Midwest: | Southeast: | Northeast: | International: |
|---|---|---|---|---|---|
| | Y | Y | Y | | Y |

# AMERICAN MEDICAL SYSTEMS HOLDINGS INC www.visitams.com

**Industry Group Code:** 339113 **Ranks within this company's industry group:** Sales: 5 Profits: 18

| Management: | | Sales/Marketing: | | Liberal Arts: | | Information Systems: | | Professionals: | | Technical/Scientific: | |
|---|---|---|---|---|---|---|---|---|---|---|---|
| Mgmt. Trainees: | | Mktg. Professionals: | Y | Gen. Writing/Editing: | | Info. Management: | Y | Finance/Accounting: | Y | Engineers, Elec.: | Y |
| Experienced Mgmt.: | Y | Retail Sales: | | Technical Writing: | Y | Software Dev.: | Y | Law: | Y | Engineers, Other: | Y |
| Int'l Business: | Y | Commercial/Industrial: | Y | Graphic Arts/Photog.: | | Hardware Dev.: | Y | HR/Other: | Y | Health/Lab: | Y |
| MBA Graduates: | Y | Sales Trainees: | Y | Music: | | Systems Integration: | | Training: | Y | Scientists/Research: | Y |
| | | Advertising Pros.: | | Broadcasting: | | Consulting/Other: | | Health Care: | Y | Petroleum/Chemicals: | |
| | | | | Other: | | | | Consulting: | | Math/Other: | Y |

## TYPES OF BUSINESS:

Urological Devices Manufacturing
Erectile Dysfunction Products
Incontinence Products
Prostate Disease Products

## BRANDS/DIVISIONS/AFFILIATES:

TherMatrx, Inc.
Solarant Medical, Inc.
MiniArc Single Incision Sling
AMS 700 LGX

## CONTACTS: *Note: Officers with more than one job title may be intentionally listed here more than once.*

Anthony P. Bihl, CEO
Ross A. Longhini, COO/Exec. VP
Martin J. Emerson, Pres.
Mark A. Heggestad, CFO/Exec. VP
Janet L. Dick, Sr. VP-Human Resources
Daniel R. Mans, VP-Research & Tech.
Michael J. Casey, Dir.-IT
Lawrence W. Getlin, Sr. VP-Legal, Compliance & Quality Systems
R. Scott Etlinger, Sr. VP-Global Oper.
John F. Nealon, Sr. VP-Bus. Dev.
John F. Nealon, Interim Gen. Mgr.-Women's Health
Whitney D. Erickson, VP/Gen. Mgr.-Men's Health
Thomas A. Letscher, Sec.
Douglas W. Kohrs, Chmn.

| **Phone:** 952-930-6000 | **Fax:** 952-930-6373 |
|---|---|
| **Toll-Free:** 800-328-3881 | |
| **Address:** 10700 Bren Rd. W., Minnetonka, MN 55343 US | |

## GROWTH PLANS/SPECIAL FEATURES:

American Medical Systems Holdings, Inc. (AMS) supplies medical devices for treating urological and gynecological disorders. The company manufactures and markets a broad and well-established line of proprietary products, focusing on three major urological disorders: Incontinence, erectile dysfunction and prostate disease. AMS offers a broad line of products designed to treat men and women suffering from urinary and fecal incontinence. Products include artificial sphincters; male and female sling systems; a vaginal vault prolapse system; and graft materials. Men's health products constitute 67.7% of the company's sales, while women's health products constitute 32.3% of sales. AMS provides products for the diagnosis and treatment of erectile dysfunction such as inflatable and malleable penile prostheses and accessories, including its AMS 700 inflatable prostheses. The company sells its products through 72 independent international distributors. In 2007, the firm introduced two products: the MiniArc Single Incision Sling, designed to treat female stress urinary incontinence; and the AMS 700 LGX, designed for erectile restoration. In March 2007, the company added GreenLight therapy to its lineup of pelvic health solutions in the European market.

AMS offers a benefits package that includes an educational assistance plan, an on-site fitness center, wellness programs, an on-site cafeteria, profit sharing, a 401(k) savings plan and an employee stock purchase plan.

## FINANCIALS: **Sales and profits are in thousands of dollars—add 000 to get the full amount. 2008 Note: Financial information for 2008 was not available for all companies at press time.**

| | | |
|---|---|---|
| 2008 Sales: $ | 2008 Profits: $ | **U.S. Stock Ticker: AMMD** |
| 2007 Sales: $463,928 | 2007 Profits: $12,900 | **Int'l Ticker:** Int'l Exchange: |
| 2006 Sales: $358,318 | 2006 Profits: $-49,317 | Employees: 1,239 |
| 2005 Sales: $262,591 | 2005 Profits: $39,275 | Fiscal Year Ends: 12/29 |
| 2004 Sales: $208,772 | 2004 Profits: $-3,120 | Parent Company: |

## SALARIES/BENEFITS:

| | | | | |
|---|---|---|---|---|
| Pension Plan: | ESOP Stock Plan: | Profit Sharing: Y | Top Exec. Salary: $369,327 | Bonus: $91,316 |
| Savings Plan: Y | Stock Purch. Plan: Y | | Second Exec. Salary: $319,236 | Bonus: $55,397 |

## OTHER THOUGHTS:

**Apparent Women Officers or Directors**: 2
**Hot Spot for Advancement for Women/Minorities**: Y

## LOCATIONS: ("Y" = Yes)

| West: | Southwest: | Midwest: | Southeast: | Northeast: | International: |
|---|---|---|---|---|---|
| Y | Y | Y | | | Y |

# AMERICAN SCIENCE & ENGINEERING INC

www.as-e.com

**Industry Group Code:** 334500 **Ranks within this company's industry group:** Sales: 3 Profits: 2

| Management: | | Sales/Marketing: | | Liberal Arts: | | Information Systems: | | Professionals: | | Technical/Scientific: | |
|---|---|---|---|---|---|---|---|---|---|---|---|
| Mgmt. Trainees: | | Mktg. Professionals: | Y | Gen. Writing/Editing: | | Info. Management: | Y | Finance/Accounting: | Y | Engineers, Elec.: | Y |
| Experienced Mgmt.: | Y | Retail Sales: | | Technical Writing: | Y | Software Dev.: | | Law: | Y | Engineers, Other: | Y |
| Int'l Business: | Y | Commercial/Industrial: | Y | Graphic Arts/Photog.: | | Hardware Dev.: | Y | HR/Other: | Y | Health/Lab: | |
| MBA Graduates: | Y | Sales Trainees: | Y | Music: | | Systems Integration: | Y | Training: | Y | Scientists/Research: | Y |
| | | Advertising Pros.: | | Broadcasting: | | Consulting/Other: | | Health Care: | | Petroleum/Chemicals: | |
| | | | | Other: | | | | Consulting: | | Math/Other: | Y |

## TYPES OF BUSINESS:

X-Ray Inspection Solutions
Security Systems
Radiation Detection Technology
Maintenance, Warranty & Research Services
Engineering & Training Services

## BRANDS/DIVISIONS/AFFILIATES:

Z Portal
Z Backscatter Van
Shaped Energy
Radioactive Threat Detection
CargoSearch
PalletSearch
ParcelSearch
OmniView

## CONTACTS: *Note: Officers with more than one job title may be intentionally listed here more than once.*

Anthony R. Fabiano, CEO
Anthony R. Fabiano, Pres.
Ken Galaznik, CFO
Robert Postle, VP-Worldwide Mktg. & Sales
George M. Peterman, VP-Human Resources
Joseph Callerame, VP-Science
Joseph Callerame, VP-Tech.
Kenneth Breur, VP-Prod. Mgmt.
Robert Cline, VP-Mfg. & Materials
William F. Grieco, General Counsel/VP
Paul Grazewski, VP-Strategic Planning
Ken Galaznik, Treas.
Denis R. Brown, Chmn.

**Phone:** 978-262-8700 **Fax:** 978-262-8804
**Toll-Free:** 800-225-1608
**Address:** 829 Middlesex Turnpike, Billerica, MA 01821 US

## GROWTH PLANS/SPECIAL FEATURES:

American Science & Engineering, Inc. (ASE) develops, manufactures, markets and sells X-ray inspection and other inspection solutions for homeland security and other targeted markets. The company provides maintenance, warranty, research, engineering and training services related to these solutions. The firm's X-ray imaging products utilize several technologies, including traditional transmission X-ray technology, the proprietary Z Backscatter technology, Shaped Energy technology and Radioactive Threat Detection (RTD). The Z Backscatter technology creates photo-quality X-ray images that highlight organic threats and contraband such as explosives, plastic weapons and drugs. The Shaped Energy technology allows high X-ray penetration with reduced need for shielding and radiation exclusion zones. The RTD technology detects radioactive materials in vehicles. ASE technologies are incorporated into systems such as the Shaped Energy Gantry, CargoSearch, PalletSearch, ParcelSearch, OmniView Gantry, Z Portal, Gemini and SmartCheck. The Z Backscatter Van (ZBV) is a screening system built into a commercially available delivery van, which allows operators to conduct X-ray imaging of suspect vehicles and objects while the ZBV drives past. The high-energy systems division of ASE designs and manufactures low- to high-power electron beam and X-ray systems and subcomponents. ASE sells its products in the U.S. and throughout the world to a variety of customers, including authorities for port and border security; aviation security agencies; military organizations; and high threat commercial and government facilities. Customers use ASE's products to help combat terrorism, trade fraud, drug trafficking, weapons smuggling and illegal immigrations; and for military force protection and general facility security.

The company offers its employees medical and dental insurance; disability and life insurance; a 401(k) plan; 100% tuition reimbursement; and travel accident insurance.

## FINANCIALS: **Sales and profits are in thousands of dollars—add 000 to get the full amount. 2008 Note: Financial information for 2008 was not available for all companies at press time.**

| | | |
|---|---|---|
| 2008 Sales: $166,733 | 2008 Profits: $17,478 | **U.S. Stock Ticker: ASEI** |
| 2007 Sales: $153,186 | 2007 Profits: $24,610 | **Int'l Ticker:** Int'l Exchange: |
| 2006 Sales: $163,604 | 2006 Profits: $29,786 | Employees: 346 |
| 2005 Sales: $88,314 | 2005 Profits: $11,267 | Fiscal Year Ends: 3/31 |
| 2004 Sales: $76,342 | 2004 Profits: $1,911 | Parent Company: |

## SALARIES/BENEFITS:

| | | | | |
|---|---|---|---|---|
| Pension Plan: | ESOP Stock Plan: | Profit Sharing: | Top Exec. Salary: $399,000 | Bonus: $687,000 |
| Savings Plan: Y | Stock Purch. Plan: Y | | Second Exec. Salary: $225,000 | Bonus: $241,000 |

## OTHER THOUGHTS:

**Apparent Women Officers or Directors**:
**Hot Spot for Advancement for Women/Minorities**:

## LOCATIONS: ("Y" = Yes)

| West: | Southwest: | Midwest: | Southeast: | Northeast: | International: |
|---|---|---|---|---|---|
| | | | | Y | |

# AMERICAN SUPERCONDUCTOR CORP

www.amsc.com

**Industry Group Code:** 335929 **Ranks within this company's industry group:** Sales: 1 Profits: 1

| Management: | | Sales/Marketing: | | Liberal Arts: | | Information Systems: | | Professionals: | | Technical/Scientific: | |
|---|---|---|---|---|---|---|---|---|---|---|---|
| Mgmt. Trainees: | | Mktg. Professionals: | Y | Gen. Writing/Editing: | | Info. Management: | Y | Finance/Accounting: | Y | Engineers, Elec.: | Y |
| Experienced Mgmt.: | Y | Retail Sales: | | Technical Writing: | Y | Software Dev.: | Y | Law: | Y | Engineers, Other: | Y |
| Int'l Business: | Y | Commercial/Industrial: | Y | Graphic Arts/Photog.: | Y | Hardware Dev.: | Y | HR/Other: | Y | Health/Lab: | |
| MBA Graduates: | Y | Sales Trainees: | Y | Music: | | Systems Integration: | Y | Training: | Y | Scientists/Research: | Y |
| | | Advertising Pros.: | | Broadcasting: | | Consulting/Other: | | Health Care: | | Petroleum/Chemicals: | |
| | | | | Other: | | | | Consulting: | | Math/Other: | Y |

## TYPES OF BUSINESS:

Superconductivity Products
Power Electronic Switches
SMES Systems
Electric Motors & Generators
Superconducting Materials
Electric Transmission Cables
Nanodots

## BRANDS/DIVISIONS/AFFILIATES:

Windtec WT 1650

## CONTACTS: *Note: Officers with more than one job title may be intentionally listed here more than once.*

Gregory J. Yurek, CEO
Gregory J. Yurek, Pres.
David Henry, CFO/Sr. VP
Tim Poor, VP-Global Sales
Susan DiCecco, VP-Human Resources
Alexis Malozemoff, CTO/Exec. VP
Angelo Santamaria, VP-Global Mfg. Oper.
Tim Poor, VP-Bus. Dev.
David Henry, Treas.
Charles W. Stankiewicz, Exec. VP-AMSC Power Systems
Dan McGahn, Sr. VP/Gen. Mgr.-Superconductor Projects
Gregory J. Yurek, Chmn.
Charles W. Stankiewicz, Gen. Mgr.-Americas & Europe

**Phone:** 978-842-3000 **Fax:** 978-842-3024
**Toll-Free:**
**Address:** 64 Jackson Rd., Devens, MA 01434-4020 US

## GROWTH PLANS/SPECIAL FEATURES:

American Superconductor Corp. (AMSC) is an energy technologies company, offering and array of solutions on two proprietary technologies: programmable power electronic converters and high temperature superconductors (HTS) wires. Its products, services and system-level solutions enable cleaner, more efficient and more reliable generation, delivery and use of electric power. The company's HTS wires carry 150 times the electrical current of comparably sized copper wire. The firm operates in two segments: AMSC power systems and AMSC superconductors. The AMSC power systems division produces a broad range of products to increase electrical grid capacity and reliability; supplies electrical systems used in wind turbines; sells power electronic products that regulate wind farm voltage to enable their interconnection to the power grid; licenses proprietary wind energy system designs to manufacturers of such systems; and provides consulting services to the wind industry. The AMSC superconductors division focuses on the manufacturing of HTS wire and coils; the design and development of HTS products, such as power cables, fault current limiters and motors; and the management of large-scale HTS projects, such as HTS power cable system design, manufacturing and installation. Primary markets served are the wind energy market and the power transmission and distribution market. In 2008, the company announced that it licensed its proprietary Windtec WT 1650 turbine design and manufacturing know-how to Ghodawat Industries (India) Pvt. Ltd and to Turkey's Model Enerjil A.S.

Employees are offered medical, dental and life insurance; long term care insurance; a 401(k) plan; an employee stock purchase plan; short-and long-term disability coverage; tuition reimbursement; a flexible spending plan; an employee assistance program; and discounted rates on wholesale club memberships.

## FINANCIALS: **Sales and profits are in thousands of dollars—add 000 to get the full amount. 2008 Note: Financial information for 2008 was not available for all companies at press time.**

| | | |
|---|---|---|
| 2008 Sales: $112,396 | 2008 Profits: $-25,447 | **U.S. Stock Ticker: AMSC** |
| 2007 Sales: $52,183 | 2007 Profits: $-36,675 | **Int'l Ticker:** Int'l Exchange: |
| 2006 Sales: $50,872 | 2006 Profits: $-30,876 | Employees: 382 |
| 2005 Sales: $58,283 | 2005 Profits: $-19,660 | Fiscal Year Ends: 3/31 |
| 2004 Sales: $41,308 | 2004 Profits: $-26,733 | Parent Company: |

## SALARIES/BENEFITS:

| | | | | |
|---|---|---|---|---|
| Pension Plan: | ESOP Stock Plan: | Profit Sharing: | Top Exec. Salary: $520,000 | Bonus: $405,600 |
| Savings Plan: Y | Stock Purch. Plan: Y | | Second Exec. Salary: $265,000 | Bonus: $202,800 |

## OTHER THOUGHTS:

**Apparent Women Officers or Directors**: 1
**Hot Spot for Advancement for Women/Minorities**:

## LOCATIONS: ("Y" = Yes)

| West: | Southwest: | Midwest: | Southeast: | Northeast: | International: |
|---|---|---|---|---|---|
| | | Y | | Y | Y |

# AMERICAN TIRE DISTRIBUTORS

**www.americantiredistributors.com**

**Industry Group Code:** 423120 **Ranks within this company's industry group:** Sales: 1 Profits:

| Management: | | Sales/Marketing: | | Liberal Arts: | | Information Systems: | | Professionals: | | Technical/Scientific: | |
|---|---|---|---|---|---|---|---|---|---|---|---|
| Mgmt. Trainees: | Y | Mktg. Professionals: | Y | Gen. Writing/Editing: | | Info. Management: | Y | Finance/Accounting: | Y | Engineers, Elec.: | |
| Experienced Mgmt.: | Y | Retail Sales: | Y | Technical Writing: | | Software Dev.: | | Law: | Y | Engineers, Other: | |
| Int'l Business: | | Commercial/Industrial: | | Graphic Arts/Photog.: | Y | Hardware Dev.: | | HR/Other: | Y | Health/Lab: | |
| MBA Graduates: | Y | Sales Trainees: | Y | Music: | | Systems Integration: | | Training: | Y | Scientists/Research: | |
| | | Advertising Pros.: | Y | Broadcasting: | | Consulting/Other: | | Health Care: | | Petroleum/Chemicals: | |
| | | | | Other: | | | | Consulting: | | Math/Other: | |

## TYPES OF BUSINESS:

Tires & Related Products, Distribution

## BRANDS/DIVISIONS/AFFILIATES:

Investcorp Bank B.S.C.
Monarch
Heafner Tire
ATD Service Bay
Envizio
Texas Market Tire
Silver State Tire Company
Samaritan Wholesale Tire Company

## CONTACTS: *Note: Officers with more than one job title may be intentionally listed here more than once.*

Richard P. Johnson, CEO
William E. Berry, COO
William E. Berry, Pres.
Daniel Brown, Sr. VP-Sales
Michael Gaither, General Counsel/Exec. VP
Phillip Marrett, Sr. VP-Mktg.
Richard P. Johnson, Chmn.
Phillip Marrett, Sr. VP-Procurement

**Phone:** 704-992-2000 **Fax:** 704-992-1384
**Toll-Free:** 800-222-1167
**Address:** 12200 Herbert Wayne Ct., Ste. 150, Huntersville, NC 28070 US

## GROWTH PLANS/SPECIAL FEATURES:

American Tire Distributors (ATD), formerly Heafner Tire, is one of the nation's largest suppliers of tires and wheels, as well as tools, supplies, and other automotive service equipment. ATD is owned by the private equity firm, Investcorp Bank. The company serves the replacement tire market through approximately 82 warehouse distribution centers, delivering products to 36 states, with an extensive independent dealer network. ATD offers its tire retailers and service shop clients various tires for passenger vehicles and light trucks, tractor-trailers, buses, farm machinery and specialty and recreational vehicles. The company carries brands including Michelin, Goodyear, Bridgestone/Firestone, Dunlop and BFGoodrich, as well as its Monarch house brand, which is manufactured by Goodyear. Its wheel selection ranges from 13- to 26-inch rims for passenger vehicles and light trucks. The firm runs ATD Service Bay, which provides programs, services, tools and technologies to dealers. In addition, the ATD also offers the website Envizio, which allows consumers to see what their vehicle would look like with custom wheels. ATD owns Texas Market Tire, which expanded the company's presence through the states of Texas, Oklahoma and New Mexico; Silver State Tire Company, in Nevada; Golden State Tire Distributors, which expanded its presence in northern California; and Samaritan Wholesale Tire Company, which expanded service across Minnesota and in western Wisconsin. In May 2007, ATD acquired Jim Paris Tire City of Montebello, Inc., which is located in Colorado. In December 2007, the firm acquired the distribution centers of Homann Tire Wholesale, which expanded the company's presence in Texas and provided the first service center in Louisiana.

## FINANCIALS: **Sales and profits are in thousands of dollars—add 000 to get the full amount. 2008 Note: Financial information for 2008 was not available for all companies at press time.**

| | | |
|---|---|---|
| 2008 Sales: $ | 2008 Profits: $ | **U.S. Stock Ticker: Private** |
| 2007 Sales: $1,877,500 | 2007 Profits: $ | **Int'l Ticker:** Int'l Exchange: |
| 2006 Sales: $1,578,000 | 2006 Profits: $-4,600 | Employees: 2,400 |
| 2005 Sales: $1,150,900 | 2005 Profits: $-1,600 | Fiscal Year Ends: 12/31 |
| 2004 Sales: $1,282,100 | 2004 Profits: $25,000 | Parent Company: INVESTCORP BANK BSC |

## SALARIES/BENEFITS:

| | | | | |
|---|---|---|---|---|
| Pension Plan: | ESOP Stock Plan: | Profit Sharing: | Top Exec. Salary: $ | Bonus: $ |
| Savings Plan: | Stock Purch. Plan: | | Second Exec. Salary: $ | Bonus: $ |

## OTHER THOUGHTS:

**Apparent Women Officers or Directors:**
**Hot Spot for Advancement for Women/Minorities:**

## LOCATIONS: ("Y" = Yes)

| West: | Southwest: | Midwest: | Southeast: | Northeast: | International: |
|---|---|---|---|---|---|
| Y | Y | Y | Y | Y | |

# AMERICAN TOWER CORP

www.americantower.com

**Industry Group Code:** 513300D **Ranks within this company's industry group:** Sales: 1 Profits: 4

| Management: | | Sales/Marketing: | | Liberal Arts: | | Information Systems: | | Professionals: | | Technical/Scientific: | |
|---|---|---|---|---|---|---|---|---|---|---|---|
| Mgmt. Trainees: | | Mktg. Professionals: | Y | Gen. Writing/Editing: | | Info. Management: | Y | Finance/Accounting: | Y | Engineers, Elec.: | Y |
| Experienced Mgmt.: | Y | Retail Sales: | | Technical Writing: | Y | Software Dev.: | | Law: | Y | Engineers, Other: | Y |
| Int'l Business: | Y | Commercial/Industrial: | Y | Graphic Arts/Photog.: | | Hardware Dev.: | | HR/Other: | Y | Health/Lab: | |
| MBA Graduates: | Y | Sales Trainees: | Y | Music: | | Systems Integration: | | Training: | Y | Scientists/Research: | |
| | | Advertising Pros.: | | Broadcasting: | | Consulting/Other: | | Health Care: | | Petroleum/Chemicals: | |
| | | | | Other: | | | | Consulting: | | Math/Other: | |

## TYPES OF BUSINESS:

Broadcast & Communications Towers
Cellular Telephone Towers
Radio & TV Broadcast Towers
Network Development & Consulting

## BRANDS/DIVISIONS/AFFILIATES:

American Tower Corp
SpecraSite Communications, LLC
American Tower International, Inc.
ALLTEL Corp
AT&T Inc
Sprint Nextel Corp
T-Mobile USA
Cellco Partnership (Verizon Wireless)

## CONTACTS: *Note: Officers with more than one job title may be intentionally listed here more than once.*

James D. (Jim) Taiclet, Jr., CEO
James D. (Jim) Taiclet, Jr., Pres.
Bradley E. (Brad) Singer, CFO/Treas.
Edmund (Ed) DiSanto, Chief Admin. Officer
Edmund (Ed) DiSanto, General Counsel/Exec. VP
Steven C. Marshall, Exec. VP-Int'l Bus. Dev.
Lori Philibin, Dir.-Media Rel.
Michael Powell, Investor Rel. Officer
Jean A. Bua, VP-Finance/Corp. Controller
Steven J. Moskowitz, Pres., U.S. Tower Div.
Amit Sharma, Exec. VP/Pres., Asia
James D. (Jim) Taiclet, Jr., Chmn.
William H. (Hal) Hess, Exec. VP-Int'l Oper./Pres., Latin America

**Phone:** 617-375-7500 **Fax:** 617-375-7575
**Toll-Free:** 877-282-7483
**Address:** 116 Huntington Ave., 11th Fl., Boston, MA 02116 US

## GROWTH PLANS/SPECIAL FEATURES:

American Tower Corp. (ATC) is leading wireless and broadcast communications infrastructure company with a portfolio of over 22,800 communications sites, including wireless communications towers, broadcast communications towers and distributed antenna systems. Its portfolio consists of approximately 19,500 tower sites throughout 49 states in the U.S. and approximately 3,200 in Mexico and Brazil, as well as approximately 150 in-building distributed antenna systems that it operates in malls, casinos and hotel resorts throughout the U.S. The company conducts business in the U.S. primarily through its American Towers, Inc. and SpecraSite Communications, LLC subsidiaries, while subsidiary American Tower International, Inc. conducts its international business. ATC operates in two segments, rental and management, and network development services. ATC derives over 98% of its total revenues from its rental and management segment, in which it leases antenna sites on multi-tenant towers to wireless service providers and radio and television broadcast companies. The company's major domestic wireless customers include ALLTEL, AT&T Mobility, Sprint Nextel, T-Mobile USA and Verizon Wireless. Its major international wireless customers include Grupo Iusacell, Nextel International, Telefonica Moviles, America Moviles and Telecom Italia Mobile. ATC's network development services, which generate approximately 2% of its revenues, include site acquisition, zoning, permitting services and structural analysis services. During 2007, the company acquired 293 towers for an aggregate of $36.9 million, and constructed 152 towers and installed 17 in-building distributed antenna systems for an aggregate of $30.7 million. In September 2007, ATC established an office in Delhi, India as part of its plan to expand into new international markets.

## FINANCIALS: **Sales and profits are in thousands of dollars—add 000 to get the full amount. 2008 Note: Financial information for 2008 was not available for all companies at press time.**

| | | |
|---|---|---|
| 2008 Sales: $ | 2008 Profits: $ | **U.S. Stock Ticker: AMT** |
| 2007 Sales: $1,456,594 | 2007 Profits: $56,316 | **Int'l Ticker:** Int'l Exchange: |
| 2006 Sales: $1,317,385 | 2006 Profits: $27,484 | Employees: 1,124 |
| 2005 Sales: $944,786 | 2005 Profits: $-181,359 | Fiscal Year Ends: 12/31 |
| 2004 Sales: $706,660 | 2004 Profits: $-247,587 | Parent Company: |

## SALARIES/BENEFITS:

| | | | | |
|---|---|---|---|---|
| Pension Plan: | ESOP Stock Plan: | Profit Sharing: | Top Exec. Salary: $835,000 | Bonus: $701,400 |
| Savings Plan: Y | Stock Purch. Plan: Y | | Second Exec. Salary: $600,000 | Bonus: $468,000 |

## OTHER THOUGHTS:

**Apparent Women Officers or Directors**: 2
**Hot Spot for Advancement for Women/Minorities**: Y

## LOCATIONS: ("Y" = Yes)

| West: | Southwest: | Midwest: | Southeast: | Northeast: | International: |
|---|---|---|---|---|---|
| Y | Y | Y | Y | Y | Y |

# AMERICAN VANGUARD CORP

www.amvac-chemical.com

**Industry Group Code:** 115112 **Ranks within this company's industry group:** Sales: 2 Profits: 1

| Management: | | Sales/Marketing: | | Liberal Arts: | | Information Systems: | | Professionals: | | Technical/Scientific: | |
|---|---|---|---|---|---|---|---|---|---|---|---|
| Mgmt. Trainees: | | Mktg. Professionals: | | Gen. Writing/Editing: | | Info. Management: | Y | Finance/Accounting: | Y | Engineers, Elec.: | |
| Experienced Mgmt.: | Y | Retail Sales: | | Technical Writing: | | Software Dev.: | | Law: | Y | Engineers, Other: | |
| Int'l Business: | Y | Commercial/Industrial: | | Graphic Arts/Photog.: | | Hardware Dev.: | | HR/Other: | Y | Health/Lab: | |
| MBA Graduates: | Y | Sales Trainees: | | Music: | | Systems Integration: | | Training: | Y | Scientists/Research: | |
| | | Advertising Pros.: | Y | Broadcasting: | | Consulting/Other: | | Health Care: | | Petroleum/Chemicals: | |
| | | | | Other: | | | | Consulting: | | Math/Other: | |

## TYPES OF BUSINESS:

Pesticides
Specialty Chemicals & Agricultural Products
Distribution Services
Environmental Analysis & Consulting Services

## BRANDS/DIVISIONS/AFFILIATES:

AMVAC Chemical Corporation
GemChem, Inc.
Environmental Mediation, Inc.
AMVAC Chemical UK, Ltd.
Quimica Amvac de Mexico S.A. de C.V.
AMVAC Switzerland GmbH
AMVAC do Brasil Representacoes Ltda.
2110 Davie Corporation

## CONTACTS: *Note: Officers with more than one job title may be intentionally listed here more than once.*

Eric Wintemute, CEO
Eric Wintemute, Pres.
David T. Johnson, CFO
Chris Hildreth, Sr. VP/Dir.-Sales
Bill Feiler, VP/Dir.-Tech.
John A. Immaraju, Mgr.-Int'l Prod. Dev.
Doug Ashmore, VP/Dir.-Mfg.
James A. Barry, Chief Admin. Officer/Assistant Sec.
Timothy J. Donnelly, General Counsel/VP
Glen Johnson, Sr. VP/Dir.-Bus. Dev.
William A. Kuser, Dir.-Corp. Comm.
William A. Kuser, Dir.-Investor Rel.
James A. Barry, Treas.
Ian S. Chart, VP/Dir.-Regulatory Affairs
Ted Ramirez, Dir.-Mktg.
Robert F. Gilbane, Pres., GemChem, Inc.
Brett R. Meinsen, VP/Dir.-Finance
Alfredo Pelaez, Dir-Int'l Bus.

**Phone:** 949-260-1200 **Fax:** 949-260-1201
**Toll-Free:**
**Address:** 4695 MacArthur Ct., Ste. 1250, Newport Beach, CA 92660 US

## GROWTH PLANS/SPECIAL FEATURES:

American Vanguard Corp. (AMVAC), a holding company, operates through three main subsidiaries: AMVAC Chemical Corporation; GemChem, Inc.; and Environmental Mediation, Inc. (EMI). AMVAC Chemical manufactures a line of insecticides, fungicides, molluscicides, plant-growth regulators and soil fumigants in liquid, powder and granular forms. The subsidiary also operates internationally through its four marketing subsidiaries: AMVAC Chemical UK, Ltd.; Quimica Amvac de Mexico S.A. de C.V.; AMVAC Switzerland GmbH; and AMVAC do Brasil Representacoes Ltda. GemChem purchases raw materials for the company and acts as AMVAV's sales force as well as distributing chemicals throughout the U.S. to the cosmetic, nutritional and pharmaceutical industries. EMI provides hazardous waste, air toxics, water quality and other environmental analysis and consulting services. Its services include issue analysis, strategic planning, government relations, regulatory strategy, environmental consulting and public affairs services. AMVAC also owns 2110 Davie Corporation, a subsidiary that own real estate for corporate use. In 2007, the firm made several acquisitions, including the acquisition of an insecticide plant in Missouri and the purchase of Chemtura Corporation's pentachloronitrobenzene fungicide product line, including brand names Turfcide and Terraclor. Also in 2007, the company announced plans to increase manufacturing capacity for metam sodium and metam potassium products, which are used in the Vapam and K-Pam brands, two of AMVAC's largest selling products. In 2008, the firm bought Valent's Orthene insecticide product line; acquired a production facility in Idaho from Bayer CropScience LP; and announced the acquisition of the phorate insecticide product line, mainly used on potatoes, corn, cotton, rice, sugarcane and peanuts, from Aceto Agricultural Chemicals Corporation.

## FINANCIALS: **Sales and profits are in thousands of dollars—add 000 to get the full amount. 2008 Note: Financial information for 2008 was not available for all companies at press time.**

| | | |
|---|---|---|
| 2008 Sales: $ | 2008 Profits: $ | **U.S. Stock Ticker: AVD** |
| 2007 Sales: $216,662 | 2007 Profits: $18,728 | **Int'l Ticker:** Int'l Exchange: |
| 2006 Sales: $193,771 | 2006 Profits: $15,448 | Employees: 309 |
| 2005 Sales: $189,796 | 2005 Profits: $19,002 | Fiscal Year Ends: 12/31 |
| 2004 Sales: $150,855 | 2004 Profits: $14,477 | Parent Company: |

## SALARIES/BENEFITS:

| | | | | |
|---|---|---|---|---|
| Pension Plan: | ESOP Stock Plan: | Profit Sharing: | Top Exec. Salary: $502,533 | Bonus: $275,000 |
| Savings Plan: | Stock Purch. Plan: | | Second Exec. Salary: $257,284 | Bonus: $90,000 |

## OTHER THOUGHTS:

**Apparent Women Officers or Directors:**
**Hot Spot for Advancement for Women/Minorities:**

## LOCATIONS: ("Y" = Yes)

| West: | Southwest: | Midwest: | Southeast: | Northeast: | International: |
|---|---|---|---|---|---|
| Y | Y | Y | Y | | Y |

# AMICAS INC

www.amicas.com

**Industry Group Code:** 511212 **Ranks within this company's industry group:** Sales: 5 Profits: 5

| Management: | | Sales/Marketing: | | Liberal Arts: | | Information Systems: | | Professionals: | | Technical/Scientific: | |
|---|---|---|---|---|---|---|---|---|---|---|---|
| Mgmt. Trainees: | | Mktg. Professionals: | Y | Gen. Writing/Editing: | | Info. Management: | Y | Finance/Accounting: | Y | Engineers, Elec.: | Y |
| Experienced Mgmt.: | Y | Retail Sales: | | Technical Writing: | Y | Software Dev.: | Y | Law: | Y | Engineers, Other: | |
| Int'l Business: | Y | Commercial/Industrial: | Y | Graphic Arts/Photog.: | | Hardware Dev.: | | HR/Other: | Y | Health/Lab: | |
| MBA Graduates: | Y | Sales Trainees: | Y | Music: | | Systems Integration: | | Training: | Y | Scientists/Research: | |
| | | Advertising Pros.: | | Broadcasting: | | Consulting/Other: | | Health Care: | | Petroleum/Chemicals: | |
| | | | | Other: | | | | Consulting: | | Math/Other: | |

## TYPES OF BUSINESS:

Radiology Software Solutions
Image & Information Management Solutions
Software & Hardware Support

## BRANDS/DIVISIONS/AFFILIATES:

AMICAS Insight Solutions
AMICAS Vision Series
RadStream
Vision Reach
AMICAS Insight

## CONTACTS: *Note: Officers with more than one job title may be intentionally listed here more than once.*

Stephen N. Kahane, CEO
Peter McClennen, COO
Stephen N. Kahane, Pres.
Kevin Burns, CFO/Sr. VP
Paul Merrild, VP-Mktg.
Denise Mitchell, VP-Human Resources
Kang Wang, Sr. VP-R&D
Kevin Burns, VP-Corp. Dev.
Kevin Burns, VP-Finance
Rodney Hawkins, VP-Prod. Mgmt.
John Esposito, VP-Sales & Hospital Strategy
Kurt Hammond, VP-Sales & Outpatient Strategy
Barry Gutwillig, VP-Strategic Partnerships & Initiatives
Stephen N. Kahane, Chmn.

| | |
|---|---|
| **Phone:** 617-779-7878 | **Fax:** 617-779-7879 |
| **Toll-Free:** 800-490-8465 | |
| **Address:** 20 Guest St., Boston, MA 02135 US | |

## GROWTH PLANS/SPECIAL FEATURES:

AMICAS, Inc. is a provider of radiology and medical image and information management solutions. The company offers radiology information systems, picture archiving and communication systems, document management and revenue cycle management software solutions to radiology and other specialty healthcare providers in the ambulatory setting. The firm is divided into two primary segments: Ambulatory care and acute care. The ambulatory care facilities segment sells products to radiology groups, imaging centers, multi-specialty groups and billing services. The acute care facilities segment sells products to hospitals and integrated delivery networks. The firm's AMICAS Vision Series provides web based, end-to-end information technology solutions to radiology imaging centers. Vision Series RIS is an information system designed to address the administrative functions by capturing radiology orders, detailing the patient demographic information, scheduling appointments, generating reports and coding and preparing billing and reimbursement data. Vision Series PACS is a web-based picture archiving and communications system designed to capture, store, manipulate, and distribute diagnostic images for the entire healthcare enterprise. Vision Series Document Management is a solution designed to capture, digitize and associate paper records with other digital information. Vision Reach uses the latest web-based technologies to integrate the radiology report with key images to create a single multi-media report for referring physicians and was made available in 2007. New functionality for Vision Reach was offered in the first half of 2008. Insight Dashboards, a web-based system providing business intelligence capabilities presented in a dashboard format, is planned for general availability in 2008. In 2007, the firm acquired certain ownership rights to the IMAGINEradiology practice management software platform. Also anticipated for general availability in 2008 is the firm's Vision Series Financials product which provides modules for billing.

The company offers employees 401(k) and tuition assistance.

## FINANCIALS: **Sales and profits are in thousands of dollars—add 000 to get the full amount. 2008 Note: Financial information for 2008 was not available for all companies at press time.**

| | | |
|---|---|---|
| 2008 Sales: $ | 2008 Profits: $ | **U.S. Stock Ticker: AMCS** |
| 2007 Sales: $49,888 | 2007 Profits: $- 862 | **Int'l Ticker:** Int'l Exchange: |
| 2006 Sales: $49,437 | 2006 Profits: $-1,024 | Employees: 253 |
| 2005 Sales: $52,811 | 2005 Profits: $44,215 | Fiscal Year Ends: 12/31 |
| 2004 Sales: $42,319 | 2004 Profits: $-12,457 | Parent Company: |

## SALARIES/BENEFITS:

| | | | | |
|---|---|---|---|---|
| Pension Plan: | ESOP Stock Plan: | Profit Sharing: | Top Exec. Salary: $350,000 | Bonus: $116,238 |
| Savings Plan: Y | Stock Purch. Plan: | | Second Exec. Salary: $300,000 | Bonus: $70,193 |

## OTHER THOUGHTS:

**Apparent Women Officers or Directors**: 1
**Hot Spot for Advancement for Women/Minorities**: Y

## LOCATIONS: ("Y" = Yes)

| West: | Southwest: | Midwest: | Southeast: | Northeast: | International: |
|---|---|---|---|---|---|
| | | | Y | Y | |

# AMSURG CORP

www.amsurg.com

**Industry Group Code:** 621490 **Ranks within this company's industry group:** Sales: 1 Profits: 1

| Management: | | Sales/Marketing: | | Liberal Arts: | | Information Systems: | | Professionals: | | Technical/Scientific: | |
|---|---|---|---|---|---|---|---|---|---|---|---|
| Mgmt. Trainees: | | Mktg. Professionals: | Y | Gen. Writing/Editing: | | Info. Management: | Y | Finance/Accounting: | Y | Engineers, Elec.: | |
| Experienced Mgmt.: | Y | Retail Sales: | | Technical Writing: | Y | Software Dev.: | | Law: | Y | Engineers, Other: | |
| Int'l Business: | | Commercial/Industrial: | Y | Graphic Arts/Photog.: | | Hardware Dev.: | | HR/Other: | Y | Health/Lab: | Y |
| MBA Graduates: | Y | Sales Trainees: | Y | Music: | | Systems Integration: | | Training: | Y | Scientists/Research: | |
| | | Advertising Pros.: | Y | Broadcasting: | | Consulting/Other: | | Health Care: | Y | Petroleum/Chemicals: | |
| | | | | Other: | | | | Consulting: | | Math/Other: | |

## TYPES OF BUSINESS:

Practice-Based Ambulatory Surgery Centers
Outpatient Surgery Facilities Management

## BRANDS/DIVISIONS/AFFILIATES:

## CONTACTS:
*Note: Officers with more than one job title may be intentionally listed here more than once.*

Christopher A. Holden, CEO
Christopher A. Holden, Pres.
Claire M. Gulmi, CFO/Exec. VP
David L. Manning, Chief Dev. Officer/Sr. VP
Billie A. Payne, Sr. VP-Oper.
Kevin D. Eastridge, Chief Acct. Officer/Sr. VP-Finance
Royce D. Harrell, Chief Compliance Officer/Sr. VP-Corp. Svcs.
Thomas G. Cigarran, Chmn.

**Phone:** 615-665-1283 **Fax:** 615-665-0755
**Toll-Free:** 800-945-2301
**Address:** 20 Burton Hills Blvd., Ste. 500, Nashville, TN 37215 US

## GROWTH PLANS/SPECIAL FEATURES:

AmSurg Corp. was formed in 1992 for the purpose of developing, acquiring and operating ambulatory surgery centers in partnership with physicians throughout the U.S. The ambulatory surgery centers are licensed outpatient facilities equipped and staffed for a single medical specialty. The centers are usually located in or near a physician group partner's office, as the firm's objective is to form partnerships with physicians. The company has targeted ownership in centers that perform gastrointestinal endoscopy procedures, ophthalmology, orthopedics and otolaryngology procedures. The centers perform a narrow range of high volume, lower-risk surgical procedures. These programs have been designed with a cost structure that enables the firm to generally charge fees that are less than those charged by hospitals for similar services performed on an outpatient basis. The types of procedures performed at each center depend on the specialty of the resident physicians. However, some of the more common procedures performed include laser eye surgery, carpal tunnel repair, colonoscopy and knee surgery. Approximately 65% of the company's centers are single specialty, with the remaining 35% multi-specialty. As of December 2007, AmSurg owned a majority interest in 176 surgery centers in 32 states and Washington, D.C., two centers under development and one center awaiting state regulatory approval of its development. In addition, the firm acquired a majority interest in two surgery centers in January 2008.

## FINANCIALS:
**Sales and profits are in thousands of dollars—add 000 to get the full amount. 2008 Note: Financial information for 2008 was not available for all companies at press time.**

2008 Sales: $
2007 Sales: $531,085
2006 Sales: $455,869
2005 Sales: $387,798
2004 Sales: $326,679

2008 Profits: $
2007 Profits: $44,175
2006 Profits: $37,739
2005 Profits: $35,151
2004 Profits: $39,706

**U.S. Stock Ticker: AMSG**
**Int'l Ticker:** Int'l Exchange:
Employees: 2,150
Fiscal Year Ends: 12/31
Parent Company:

## SALARIES/BENEFITS:

Pension Plan: ESOP Stock Plan: Profit Sharing: Top Exec. Salary: $174,450 Bonus: $19,615
Savings Plan: Y Stock Purch. Plan: Second Exec. Salary: $350,000 Bonus: $57,414

## OTHER THOUGHTS:

**Apparent Women Officers or Directors**: 3
**Hot Spot for Advancement for Women/Minorities**: Y

## LOCATIONS: ("Y" = Yes)

| West: | Southwest: | Midwest: | Southeast: | Northeast: | International: |
|---|---|---|---|---|---|
| | Y | | Y | Y | |

# AMTECH SYSTEMS INC

**www.amtechsystems.com**

**Industry Group Code:** 333295 **Ranks within this company's industry group:** Sales: 2 Profits: 2

| Management: | | Sales/Marketing: | | Liberal Arts: | | Information Systems: | | Professionals: | | Technical/Scientific: | |
|---|---|---|---|---|---|---|---|---|---|---|---|
| Mgmt. Trainees: | | Mktg. Professionals: | Y | Gen. Writing/Editing: | | Info. Management: | Y | Finance/Accounting: | Y | Engineers, Elec.: | Y |
| Experienced Mgmt.: | Y | Retail Sales: | | Technical Writing: | Y | Software Dev.: | Y | Law: | Y | Engineers, Other: | Y |
| Int'l Business: | Y | Commercial/Industrial: | Y | Graphic Arts/Photog.: | | Hardware Dev.: | Y | HR/Other: | Y | Health/Lab: | |
| MBA Graduates: | Y | Sales Trainees: | Y | Music: | | Systems Integration: | | Training: | Y | Scientists/Research: | Y |
| | | Advertising Pros.: | | Broadcasting: | | Consulting/Other: | | Health Care: | | Petroleum/Chemicals: | |
| | | | | Other: | | | | Consulting: | | Math/Other: | Y |

## TYPES OF BUSINESS:

Semiconductor Manufacturing Equipment
Diffusion Furnace Systems
Wafer Polishing Systems
Machinery Support & Maintenance Services

## BRANDS/DIVISIONS/AFFILIATES:

Bruce Technologies Inc
Tempress Systems, Inc.
PR Hoffman Machine Products Inc
R2D Ingeniere SAS

## CONTACTS: *Note: Officers with more than one job title may be intentionally listed here more than once.*

Jong S. Whang, CEO
Jong S. Whang, Pres.
Bradley C. Anderson, CFO
Bradley C. Anderson, Sec.
Robert T. Hass, Chief Acct. Officer
Bradley C. Anderson, VP-Finance/Treas.

**Phone:** 480-967-5146 **Fax:** 480-968-3763
**Toll-Free:**
**Address:** 131 S. Clark Dr., Tempe, AZ 85281 US

## GROWTH PLANS/SPECIAL FEATURES:

Amtech Systems, Inc. designs, manufactures and sells equipment related to the manufacture of semiconductors. The company operates in two segments: the semiconductor and solar equipment segment and the polishing supplies segment. The semiconductor and solar equipment segment, which comprises Amtech Systems and subsidiaries Tempress Systems, Inc. and Bruce Technologies, Inc., designs, manufactures and markets a line of semiconductor manufacturing equipment, including silicon wafer handling automation and semiconductor processing equipment. This segment also provides diffusion and automation equipment to solar cell manufacturers within the solar industry. Amtech is a leading supplier of horizontal diffusion furnace systems, including related parts and services. The firm's polishing supplies segment supplies double-sided precision lapping and polishing machines and other products used in the processing of manufacturing silicon wafers for the semiconductor industry. This division is composed of subsidiary P.R. Hoffman Machine Products, Inc. The firm's automation products reduce the amount of human handling of the silicon wafers, thereby reducing exposure to particle sources during the loading and unloading of the process tubes and protecting operators from heat and chemical fumes. Amtech markets these products to companies involved in semiconductor wafer manufacturing and semiconductor integrated circuit manufacturing, to manufacturers of optical components and solar cells, and to research and development facilities, as well as to universities and research institutes. The firm's products are used in end markets such as telecommunications, computers, automobiles, hand-held devices and solar industry products. Sales to the Asia-Pacific market accounted for 68% of 2008 revenues, while Europe and North America accounted for 16% each. In 2007, Amtech acquired R2D Ingenierie, a solar cell and semiconductor automation equipment manufacturing company. In January 2008, Amtech announced that subsidiary Tempress Systems had entered into a research agreement to develop an in-line, or conveyor, diffusion furnace system for the solar industry.

## FINANCIALS: **Sales and profits are in thousands of dollars—add 000 to get the full amount. 2008 Note: Financial information for 2008 was not available for all companies at press time.**

| | | |
|---|---|---|
| 2008 Sales: $80,296 | 2008 Profits: $2,857 | **U.S. Stock Ticker: ASYS** |
| 2007 Sales: $45,984 | 2007 Profits: $2,417 | **Int'l Ticker:** Int'l Exchange: |
| 2006 Sales: $40,445 | 2006 Profits: $1,318 | Employees: 210 |
| 2005 Sales: $27,899 | 2005 Profits: $- 259 | Fiscal Year Ends: 9/30 |
| 2004 Sales: $19,299 | 2004 Profits: $-3,165 | Parent Company: |

## SALARIES/BENEFITS:

| | | | | |
|---|---|---|---|---|
| Pension Plan: | ESOP Stock Plan: | Profit Sharing: | Top Exec. Salary: $240,385 | Bonus: $115,248 |
| Savings Plan: | Stock Purch. Plan: | | Second Exec. Salary: $176,154 | Bonus: $69,149 |

## OTHER THOUGHTS:

**Apparent Women Officers or Directors:**
**Hot Spot for Advancement for Women/Minorities:**

## LOCATIONS: ("Y" = Yes)

| West: | Southwest: | Midwest: | Southeast: | Northeast: | International: |
|---|---|---|---|---|---|
| | Y | | | Y | Y |

# AMYLIN PHARMACEUTICALS INC

**www.amylin.com**

**Industry Group Code:** 325412 **Ranks within this company's industry group:** Sales: 4 Profits: 36

| Management: | | Sales/Marketing: | | Liberal Arts: | | Information Systems: | | Professionals: | | Technical/Scientific: | |
|---|---|---|---|---|---|---|---|---|---|---|---|
| Mgmt. Trainees: | | Mktg. Professionals: | Y | Gen. Writing/Editing: | | Info. Management: | Y | Finance/Accounting: | Y | Engineers, Elec.: | |
| Experienced Mgmt.: | Y | Retail Sales: | | Technical Writing: | Y | Software Dev.: | Y | Law: | Y | Engineers, Other: | |
| Int'l Business: | Y | Commercial/Industrial: | Y | Graphic Arts/Photog.: | | Hardware Dev.: | | HR/Other: | Y | Health/Lab: | Y |
| MBA Graduates: | Y | Sales Trainees: | Y | Music: | | Systems Integration: | | Training: | Y | Scientists/Research: | Y |
| | | Advertising Pros.: | | Broadcasting: | | Consulting/Other: | | Health Care: | Y | Petroleum/Chemicals: | |
| | | | | Other: | | | | Consulting: | Y | Math/Other: | Y |

## TYPES OF BUSINESS:

Pharmaceutical Discovery & Development
Drugs, Obesity
Drugs, Diabetes

## BRANDS/DIVISIONS/AFFILIATES:

SYMLIN
BYETTA
Exenatide LAR
pramlintide
Integrated Neurohormonal Therapy for Obesity
SymlinPen 60
SymlinPen 120

## CONTACTS: *Note: Officers with more than one job title may be intentionally listed here more than once.*

Daniel M. Bradbury, CEO
Daniel M. Bradbury, Pres.
Mark G. Foletta, CFO
Onaiza Cadoret-Manier, VP-Mktg.
Roger Marchetti, Sr. VP-Human Resources
Orville G. Kolterman, Sr. VP-R&D
Roger Marchetti, Sr. VP-Info. Mgmt.
Marcea B. Lloyd, General Counsel/Sr. VP-Gov't
Paul Marshall, VP-Oper.
Mark J. Gergen, Sr. VP-Corp. Dev.
Marcea B. Lloyd, Sr. VP-Corp. Affairs
Mark G. Foletta, Sr. VP-Finance
Michael Hanley, Chief Scientific Officer/VP-Discovery Research
Laura M. Clague, VP/Corp. Controller
Anna E. Crivici, VP-Project Mgmt. & Bus. Process Dev.
Sarah L. Hanssen, VP-Commercial Oper. & Strategic Rel. Mgmt.
Joseph C. Cook, Jr., Chmn.

| **Phone:** 858-552-2200 | **Fax:** 858-552-2212 |
|---|---|
| **Toll-Free:** | |
| **Address:** 9360 Towne Centre Dr., San Diego, CA 92121 US | |

## GROWTH PLANS/SPECIAL FEATURES:

Amylin Pharmaceuticals, Inc. is engaged in the discovery, development and commercialization of drug candidates for the treatment of diabetes, obesity and other diseases. The Company is currently marketing two first-in-class medicines to treat diabetes: BYETTA (exenatide) injection and SYMLIN (pramlintide acetate) injection. Additionally, the company is in Phase 2 of developing exenatide once weekly, and Phase 1 in developing exenatide nasal, both drugs used to treat diabetes. Amylin's Integrated Neurohormonal Therapy for Obesity (INTO) program studies the safety and efficacy of multiple neurohormones used in combination with Pramlintide to treat obesity. The company's obesity drugs, which are primarily a part of INTO, include Pramlintide/Metreleptin in Phase 2 and Second Generation Amylinomimetic in phase 1. Amylin has strategic alliance partnerships with Alkermes, Inc. and Eli Lilly. In recent news, the U.S. Food and Drug Administration (FDA) has approved the SymlinPen 120 and the SymlinPen 60 pen-injector devices for administering SYMLIN (pramlintide acetate) injection. These two new, pre-filled pen-injector devices feature simple, fixed dosing to improve mealtime glucose control.

Amylin provides its employees with a medical, dental and voluntary vision plan; disability and life insurance; flexible spending accounts; employee assistance; education assistance programs; and discounted gym memberships and online concierge services.

## FINANCIALS: **Sales and profits are in thousands of dollars—add 000 to get the full amount. 2008 Note: Financial information for 2008 was not available for all companies at press time.**

| | | |
|---|---|---|
| 2008 Sales: $ | 2008 Profits: $ | **U.S. Stock Ticker: AMLN** |
| 2007 Sales: $780,997 | 2007 Profits: $-211,136 | **Int'l Ticker:** Int'l Exchange: |
| 2006 Sales: $510,875 | 2006 Profits: $-218,856 | Employees: 1,900 |
| 2005 Sales: $140,474 | 2005 Profits: $-206,832 | Fiscal Year Ends: 12/31 |
| 2004 Sales: $34,268 | 2004 Profits: $-157,157 | Parent Company: |

## SALARIES/BENEFITS:

| | | | | |
|---|---|---|---|---|
| Pension Plan: | ESOP Stock Plan: | Profit Sharing: | Top Exec. Salary: $559,288 | Bonus: $192,950 |
| Savings Plan: Y | Stock Purch. Plan: Y | | Second Exec. Salary: $395,265 | Bonus: $68,180 |

## OTHER THOUGHTS:

**Apparent Women Officers or Directors**: 8
**Hot Spot for Advancement for Women/Minorities**: Y

## LOCATIONS: ("Y" = Yes)

| West: | Southwest: | Midwest: | Southeast: | Northeast: | International: |
|---|---|---|---|---|---|
| Y | | | | | Y |

# ANALOGIC CORP

www.analogic.com

**Industry Group Code:** 339113 **Ranks within this company's industry group:** Sales: 9 Profits: 14

| Management: | | Sales/Marketing: | | Liberal Arts: | | Information Systems: | | Professionals: | | Technical/Scientific: | |
|---|---|---|---|---|---|---|---|---|---|---|---|
| Mgmt. Trainees: | | Mktg. Professionals: | Y | Gen. Writing/Editing: | | Info. Management: | Y | Finance/Accounting: | Y | Engineers, Elec.: | Y |
| Experienced Mgmt.: | Y | Retail Sales: | | Technical Writing: | Y | Software Dev.: | Y | Law: | Y | Engineers, Other: | Y |
| Int'l Business: | Y | Commercial/Industrial: | Y | Graphic Arts/Photog.: | | Hardware Dev.: | Y | HR/Other: | Y | Health/Lab: | Y |
| MBA Graduates: | Y | Sales Trainees: | Y | Music: | | Systems Integration: | Y | Training: | Y | Scientists/Research: | Y |
| | | Advertising Pros.: | | Broadcasting: | | Consulting/Other: | | Health Care: | Y | Petroleum/Chemicals: | |
| | | | | Other: | | | | Consulting: | | Math/Other: | Y |

## TYPES OF BUSINESS:

Equipment-Medical Image Processing
Signal Processing Equipment
Patient Monitoring Equipment
Computed Tomography Imaging Systems
Financing
Explosive Detection Security Systems

## BRANDS/DIVISIONS/AFFILIATES:

Anexa
Anrad
Sound Technology, Inc.
B-K Medical Systems ApS
LIFEGARD
FETALGARD
EXACT (EXplosive Assessment Computed Tomography)

## CONTACTS:

*Note: Officers with more than one job title may be intentionally listed here more than once.*

James W. Green, CEO
Edmund F. Becker, Jr., COO
James W. Green, Pres.
John J. Millerick, CFO
John P. O'Connor, VP-Eng.
John J. Fry, General Counsel/Corp. Sec./VP
John J. Millerick, Treas./Sr. VP
Donald B. Melson, VP/Corp. Controller
Peter Cempellin, VP-GM Security Systems
John A. Tarello, Chmn.

| | |
|---|---|
| **Phone:** 978-326-4000 | **Fax:** 978-977-6809 |
| **Toll-Free:** | |
| **Address:** 8 Centennial Dr., Peabody, MA 01960 US | |

## GROWTH PLANS/SPECIAL FEATURES:

Analogic Corporation designs, manufactures and sells standard and customized high-precision data acquisition and image-processing-based medical and security systems and subsystems. Analogic sells primarily to original equipment manufacturers. The company primarily focuses on advanced technology in the areas of automated explosives detection, computed tomography, digital radiography, ultrasound, magnetic resonance imaging, patient monitoring and advance signal processing. The company has two segments within the electronics industry: Medical technology products and security technology products. Medical imaging products accounted for approximately 58% of product revenue in 2007. This segment consists primarily of electronic systems and subsystems for medical imaging equipment and patient monitoring equipment. B-K Medical, which designs and manufactures ultrasound systems and probes for end-user markets in urology, surgery, and radiology, accounted for approximately 24% revenues in 2007. These scanners generate real-time images of the internal anatomy that are used for medical diagnosis and interventional procedures. The security technology products segment provides advanced explosives and weapons detection systems for checked luggage and carry-on luggage at checkpoints. This segment accounted for approximately 12% of revenue in 2007. The company is developing the KING COBRA to scan checked luggage at small to mid-sized airports, and the XLB1100 ultra-high-speed explosives detection system for airports requiring baggage throughput of up to 1,100 bags an hour. The XLB1100 is currently at the U.S. Transportation Security Administration (TSA) under-going Certification Readiness Testing. In August 2008, the firm reported that restructuring initiatives had been completed, which included a voluntary retirement program. In March 2008, the company acquired Copley Controls, which it continues to incorporate.

Analogic offers employees medical and dental insurance, tuition reimbursement and a 401(k) plan.

## FINANCIALS:

**Sales and profits are in thousands of dollars—add 000 to get the full amount. 2008 Note: Financial information for 2008 was not available for all companies at press time.**

| | | |
|---|---|---|
| 2008 Sales: $ | 2008 Profits: $ | **U.S. Stock Ticker: ALOG** |
| 2007 Sales: $340,782 | 2007 Profits: $15,380 | **Int'l Ticker:** Int'l Exchange: |
| 2006 Sales: $351,445 | 2006 Profits: $25,066 | Employees: 1,500 |
| 2005 Sales: $326,479 | 2005 Profits: $28,862 | Fiscal Year Ends: 7/31 |
| 2004 Sales: $304,205 | 2004 Profits: $8,354 | Parent Company: |

## SALARIES/BENEFITS:

| | | | | |
|---|---|---|---|---|
| Pension Plan: | ESOP Stock Plan: | Profit Sharing: | Top Exec. Salary: $350,000 | Bonus: $250,000 |
| Savings Plan: Y | Stock Purch. Plan: | | Second Exec. Salary: $271,247 | Bonus: $300,000 |

## OTHER THOUGHTS:

**Apparent Women Officers or Directors:**
**Hot Spot for Advancement for Women/Minorities:**

## LOCATIONS: ("Y" = Yes)

| West: | Southwest: | Midwest: | Southeast: | Northeast: | International: |
|---|---|---|---|---|---|
| | | Y | | Y | Y |

# ANAREN INC

www.anaren.com

**Industry Group Code:** 334210 **Ranks within this company's industry group:** Sales: 10 Profits: 4

| Management: | | Sales/Marketing: | | Liberal Arts: | | Information Systems: | | Professionals: | | Technical/Scientific: | |
|---|---|---|---|---|---|---|---|---|---|---|---|
| Mgmt. Trainees: | | Mktg. Professionals: | Y | Gen. Writing/Editing: | Y | Info. Management: | Y | Finance/Accounting: | Y | Engineers, Elec.: | Y |
| Experienced Mgmt.: | Y | Retail Sales: | | Technical Writing: | Y | Software Dev.: | Y | Law: | Y | Engineers, Other: | Y |
| Int'l Business: | Y | Commercial/Industrial: | Y | Graphic Arts/Photog.: | | Hardware Dev.: | Y | HR/Other: | Y | Health/Lab: | |
| MBA Graduates: | Y | Sales Trainees: | Y | Music: | | Systems Integration: | Y | Training: | Y | Scientists/Research: | |
| | | Advertising Pros.: | | Broadcasting: | | Consulting/Other: | | Health Care: | | Petroleum/Chemicals: | |
| | | | | Other: | | | | Consulting: | | Math/Other: | |

## TYPES OF BUSINESS:

Wireless Telecommunications Components
Satellite Communications Components
Defense Electronics Components
Thick-Film Ceramic Circuits
Microwave Components

## BRANDS/DIVISIONS/AFFILIATES:

Xinger
Xinger-II
AdrenaLine
RF Power
Anaren Ceramics, Inc.
M.S. Kennedy Corp.
Lockheed Martin Corp
Raytheon Co

## CONTACTS: *Note: Officers with more than one job title may be intentionally listed here more than once.*

Lawrence A. Sala, CEO
Lawrence A. Sala, Pres.
Amy B. Tewksbury, Sr. VP-Human Resources
Carl W. Gerst, Jr., CTO/Vice Chmn.
David M. Ferrara, General Counsel/Sec.
Timothy P. Ross, Sr. VP-Bus. Dev.
Joseph E. Porcello, Sr. VP-Finance/Treas.
Gert R. Thygesen, Sr. VP-Tech.
Mark P. Burdick, Sr. VP/Gen. Mgr.
Lawrence A. Sala, Chmn.

| | |
|---|---|
| **Phone:** 315-432-8909 | **Fax:** 315-432-9121 |
| **Toll-Free:** 800-544-2414 | |
| **Address:** 6635 Kirkville Rd., E. Syracuse, NY 13057 US | |

## GROWTH PLANS/SPECIAL FEATURES:

Anaren, Inc. provides integrated microwave components, assemblies and subsystems for the wireless infrastructure, satellite communications, medical, optics, automotive, consumer products and defense sectors. Anaren's product lines include passives (couplers, power dividers, baluns and splitter/combiners), actives (vector modulators and mixers), resistive components (resistors, terminations and attenuators), ferrites (circulators and isolators) and complex assemblies (switching, beamformers, antenna feed networks, DRFMs and IMAs). The firm sells these products under the Xinger, Xinger-II, AdrenaLine and RF Power brand names, using its proprietary multi-layer stripline technology to produce compact, lightweight, cost-effective products, which can all be custom manufactured to a client's particular needs. The company also designs components and subsystems that enable high-speed wireless access to the Internet and other broadband wireless applications. Subsidiary Anaren Ceramics, Inc. specializes in fabricating extremely tight-tolerance and high reliability circuits on both traditional ceramic substrates and state-of-the-art LTCC (Low Temperature Co-fired Ceramic) materials, serving medical, automotive, telephony and defense OEMs. Some of the company's major customers include Boeing, Lockheed Martin, Raytheon and Motorola. Recently, Anaren has introduced several products designed to address WLAN, cellular telephone and Bluetooth applications at 1/100th the size of its Xinger products and featuring performance and cost advantages. In April 2008, Anaren agreed to acquire M.S. Kennedy Corp., a manufacturer of analog and mixed signal hybrids for military and aerospace applications.

Anaren offers its employees tuition assistance; an employee assistance program; an on-site fitness facility; an incentive bonus plan; flexible spending accounts; and medical, dental, life and disability insurance.

## FINANCIALS: **Sales and profits are in thousands of dollars—add 000 to get the full amount. 2008 Note: Financial information for 2008 was not available for all companies at press time.**

| | | |
|---|---|---|
| 2008 Sales: $ | 2008 Profits: $ | **U.S. Stock Ticker: ANEN** |
| 2007 Sales: $128,987 | 2007 Profits: $15,350 | **Int'l Ticker:** Int'l Exchange: |
| 2006 Sales: $105,464 | 2006 Profits: $11,099 | Employees: 871 |
| 2005 Sales: $94,461 | 2005 Profits: $7,413 | Fiscal Year Ends: 6/30 |
| 2004 Sales: $85,079 | 2004 Profits: $7,957 | Parent Company: |

## SALARIES/BENEFITS:

| | | | | |
|---|---|---|---|---|
| Pension Plan: | ESOP Stock Plan: Y | Profit Sharing: | Top Exec. Salary: $370,000 | Bonus: $499,500 |
| Savings Plan: Y | Stock Purch. Plan: | | Second Exec. Salary: $184,000 | Bonus: $124,200 |

## OTHER THOUGHTS:

**Apparent Women Officers or Directors**: 1
**Hot Spot for Advancement for Women/Minorities**:

## LOCATIONS: ("Y" = Yes)

| West: | Southwest: | Midwest: | Southeast: | Northeast: | International: |
|---|---|---|---|---|---|
| Y | | | | Y | Y |

# ANIKA THERAPEUTICS INC

**www.anikatherapeutics.com**

**Industry Group Code:** 325414 **Ranks within this company's industry group:** Sales: 4 Profits: 2

| **Management:** | | **Sales/Marketing:** | | **Liberal Arts:** | | **Information Systems:** | | **Professionals:** | | **Technical/Scientific:** | |
|---|---|---|---|---|---|---|---|---|---|---|---|
| Mgmt. Trainees: | | Mktg. Professionals: | Y | Gen. Writing/Editing: | | Info. Management: | Y | Finance/Accounting: | Y | Engineers, Elec.: | |
| Experienced Mgmt.: | Y | Retail Sales: | | Technical Writing: | Y | Software Dev.: | Y | Law: | Y | Engineers, Other: | Y |
| Int'l Business: | | Commercial/Industrial: | Y | Graphic Arts/Photog.: | | Hardware Dev.: | | HR/Other: | Y | Health/Lab: | Y |
| MBA Graduates: | Y | Sales Trainees: | Y | Music: | | Systems Integration: | | Training: | Y | Scientists/Research: | Y |
| | | Advertising Pros.: | | Broadcasting: | | Consulting/Other: | | Health Care: | Y | Petroleum/Chemicals: | |
| | | | | Other: | | | | Consulting: | | Math/Other: | Y |

## TYPES OF BUSINESS:

Tissue Protection, Healing & Repair Drugs
Hyaluronic Acid Based Drugs
Tissue Augmentation Products

## BRANDS/DIVISIONS/AFFILIATES:

Orthovisc
Elevess
Amvisc
Staarvisc-II
ShellGel
Incert
Hyvisc
DePuy Mitek

## CONTACTS:

*Note: Officers with more than one job title may be intentionally listed here more than once.*

Charles H. Sherwood, CEO
Charles H. Sherwood, Pres.
Kevin W. Quinlan, CFO
William J. Mrachek, VP-Human Resources
Andrew J. Carter, CTO
Randall W. Wilhoite, VP-Oper.
Gregory T. Fulton, Chief Commercial Officer

| | |
|---|---|
| **Phone:** 781-932-6616 | **Fax:** 781-935-4120 |
| **Toll-Free:** | |
| **Address:** 32 Wiggins Ave., Bedford, MA 01730 US | |

## GROWTH PLANS/SPECIAL FEATURES:

Anika Therapeutics, Inc. develops, manufactures and commercializes therapeutic products for tissue protection, healing and repair. These products are based on hyaluronic acid (HA), a naturally occurring, biocompatible polymer found throughout the body that plays an important role in a number of physiological functions such as the protection and lubrication of soft tissues and joints; the maintenance of the structural integrity of tissues; and the transport of molecules to and within cells. The firm's currently marketed products consist of Orthovisc, an HA product which provides lubrication for the knee and helps cushion the knee joint; Amvisc, Amvisc Plus, Staarvisc-II and ShellGel, each an injectable ophthalmic viscoelastic HA product; Hyvisc, an HA product used for treatment of joint dysfunction in horses; Incert, an HA-based anti-adhesive for surgical applications; and Elevess, an HA-based injectable dermal filler used for cosmetic tissue applications and products associated with joint health. Anika is working to produce more Elevess products in the future, as there is a growing demand for soft tissue fillers for facial wrinkles, scar remediation and lip augmentation. Orthovisc is marketed in the U.S. by DePuy Mitek, a subsidiary of Johnson & Johnson, and outside the U.S. by distributors in roughly 20 countries. Hyvisc is marketed in the U.S. through Boehringer Ingelheim Vetmedica, Inc. In December 2007, Anika and Galderma S.A. terminated their joint license agreement for the Elevess family of products. Consequently, Anika acquired the worldwide rights to the marketing and ownership of Elevess products. In July 2008, the company began shipping its Monovisc product, used for treatment of osteoarthritis, to Europe.

The company offers its employees benefits that include health, dental life and disability insurance and a 401(k) plan.

## FINANCIALS:

**Sales and profits are in thousands of dollars—add 000 to get the full amount. 2008 Note: Financial information for 2008 was not available for all companies at press time.**

| | | |
|---|---|---|
| 2008 Sales: $ | 2008 Profits: $ | **U.S. Stock Ticker: ANIK** |
| 2007 Sales: $30,830 | 2007 Profits: $-6,035 | **Int'l Ticker:** Int'l Exchange: |
| 2006 Sales: $26,841 | 2006 Profits: $4,604 | Employees: 82 |
| 2005 Sales: $29,835 | 2005 Profits: $5,893 | Fiscal Year Ends: 12/31 |
| 2004 Sales: $26,466 | 2004 Profits: $11,190 | Parent Company: |

## SALARIES/BENEFITS:

| | | | | |
|---|---|---|---|---|
| Pension Plan: | ESOP Stock Plan: | Profit Sharing: | Top Exec. Salary: $412,000 | Bonus: $206,000 |
| Savings Plan: Y | Stock Purch. Plan: | | Second Exec. Salary: $232,585 | Bonus: $58,146 |

## OTHER THOUGHTS:

**Apparent Women Officers or Directors**:
**Hot Spot for Advancement for Women/Minorities**:

## LOCATIONS: ("Y" = Yes)

| West: | Southwest: | Midwest: | Southeast: | Northeast: | International: |
|---|---|---|---|---|---|
| | | | | Y | |

# ANSYS INC

www.ansys.com

**Industry Group Code:** 511215 **Ranks within this company's industry group:** Sales: 1 Profits: 1

| Management: | | Sales/Marketing: | | Liberal Arts: | | Information Systems: | | Professionals: | | Technical/Scientific: | |
|---|---|---|---|---|---|---|---|---|---|---|---|
| Mgmt. Trainees: | | Mktg. Professionals: | Y | Gen. Writing/Editing: | | Info. Management: | Y | Finance/Accounting: | Y | Engineers, Elec.: | Y |
| Experienced Mgmt.: | Y | Retail Sales: | | Technical Writing: | Y | Software Dev.: | Y | Law: | Y | Engineers, Other: | Y |
| Int'l Business: | Y | Commercial/Industrial: | Y | Graphic Arts/Photog.: | | Hardware Dev.: | | HR/Other: | Y | Health/Lab: | |
| MBA Graduates: | Y | Sales Trainees: | Y | Music: | | Systems Integration: | | Training: | Y | Scientists/Research: | |
| | | Advertising Pros.: | | Broadcasting: | | Consulting/Other: | | Health Care: | | Petroleum/Chemicals: | |
| | | | | Other: | | | | Consulting: | | Math/Other: | Y |

## TYPES OF BUSINESS:

Software-Engineering, Design & Testing
MEMS Design Software

## BRANDS/DIVISIONS/AFFILIATES:

Multiphysics Solutions
Mechanical Solutions
Fluid Dynamics Solutions
Electromagnetics Solutions
Design for Six Sigma
Explicit Dynamics Solutions
Ansoft Corporation

## CONTACTS: *Note: Officers with more than one job title may be intentionally listed here more than once.*

James E. Cashman, III, CEO
James E. Cashman, III, Pres.
Maria T. Shields, CFO
J. Christopher Reid, VP-Mktg.
Elaine V. Keim, VP-Human Resources
Maria T. Shields, VP-Admin.
Sheila S. DiNardo, General Counsel/VP/Sec.
Maria T. Shields, VP-Finance
Brian C. Drew, VP/Gen. Mgr.-Central Dev. Unit
Joseph C. Fairbanks, VP-Worldwide Sales & Support
Hasan Ferit Boysan, VP/Gen. Mgr.-Fluids Bus. Unit
Peter J. Smith, Chmn.

| | |
|---|---|
| **Phone:** 724-746-3304 | **Fax:** 724-514-9494 |
| **Toll-Free:** 866-267-9724 | |
| **Address:** 275 Technology Dr., Canonsburgh, PA 15317 US | |

## GROWTH PLANS/SPECIAL FEATURES:

ANSYS, Inc. develops, markets and supports engineering simulation software and technologies. The company's software enables users to analyze designs directly on the desktop, providing a platform for efficient product development, from design to final-stage testing and validation. ANSYS distributes its products through a network of channel partners in more than 40 countries and through its own direct sales offices in over 60 strategic locations worldwide. The company's products are used in many industries, including aerospace, automotive, manufacturing, electronics, biomedical and defense. ANSYS' software can be divided into several product lines. Multiphysics Solutions provides simulations of structural, thermal, fluid dynamics, acoustic and electromagnetic simulation and the ability to mix these forces for complex simulations. Mechanical Solutions assists engineers in prototyping new products. Fluid Dynamics Solutions simulates the motion of liquids and gasses. Electromagnetic Solutions creates simulations of electric motors, relays, magnet design, radio frequency and microwave device design. Design for Six Sigma is analysis software that determines how models will cope with unforeseen variations that they may undergo in use. Explicit Dynamics Solutions creates simulations where a model will suffer high deformations or large strains in a short period of time, such as in plane crashes or vehicle explosions. In addition, ANSYS offers consulting, implementation and training services to aid customers in the adoption of simulation technology. In July 2008, the company completed its acquisition of Ansoft Corporation, a developer of electronic design automation software, in a transaction valued at approximately $832 million.

Employee benefits include health care, flexible spending accounts, life and disability insurance, tuition reimbursement and adoption assistance, among other benefits.

## FINANCIALS: **Sales and profits are in thousands of dollars—add 000 to get the full amount. 2008 Note: Financial information for 2008 was not available for all companies at press time.**

| | | |
|---|---|---|
| 2008 Sales: $ | 2008 Profits: $ | **U.S. Stock Ticker: ANSS** |
| 2007 Sales: $385,340 | 2007 Profits: $82,392 | **Int'l Ticker:** Int'l Exchange: |
| 2006 Sales: $263,640 | 2006 Profits: $14,156 | Employees: 1,400 |
| 2005 Sales: $158,036 | 2005 Profits: $43,903 | Fiscal Year Ends: 12/31 |
| 2004 Sales: $134,539 | 2004 Profits: $34,567 | Parent Company: |

## SALARIES/BENEFITS:

| | | | | |
|---|---|---|---|---|
| Pension Plan: | ESOP Stock Plan: | Profit Sharing: | Top Exec. Salary: $470,000 | Bonus: $536,900 |
| Savings Plan: Y | Stock Purch. Plan: | | Second Exec. Salary: $272,618 | Bonus: $145,272 |

## OTHER THOUGHTS:

**Apparent Women Officers or Directors**: 4
**Hot Spot for Advancement for Women/Minorities**: Y

## LOCATIONS: ("Y" = Yes)

| West: | Southwest: | Midwest: | Southeast: | Northeast: | International: |
|---|---|---|---|---|---|
| Y | Y | Y | Y | Y | Y |

# APP PHARMACEUTICALS INC

**www.apppharma.com**

**Industry Group Code:** 325412 **Ranks within this company's industry group:** Sales: 5 Profits: 9

| Management: | | Sales/Marketing: | | Liberal Arts: | | Information Systems: | | Professionals: | | Technical/Scientific: | |
|---|---|---|---|---|---|---|---|---|---|---|---|
| Mgmt. Trainees: | | Mktg. Professionals: | Y | Gen. Writing/Editing: | | Info. Management: | Y | Finance/Accounting: | Y | Engineers, Elec.: | |
| Experienced Mgmt.: | Y | Retail Sales: | | Technical Writing: | Y | Software Dev.: | Y | Law: | Y | Engineers, Other: | |
| Int'l Business: | Y | Commercial/Industrial: | Y | Graphic Arts/Photog.: | | Hardware Dev.: | | HR/Other: | Y | Health/Lab: | Y |
| MBA Graduates: | Y | Sales Trainees: | Y | Music: | | Systems Integration: | | Training: | Y | Scientists/Research: | Y |
| | | Advertising Pros.: | | Broadcasting: | | Consulting/Other: | | Health Care: | Y | Petroleum/Chemicals: | Y |
| | | | | Other: | | | | Consulting: | | Math/Other: | Y |

## TYPES OF BUSINESS:

Pharmaceuticals Manufacturing
Injectable Oncology Drugs
Anti-Infective Drugs
Critical Care Drugs

## BRANDS/DIVISIONS/AFFILIATES:

Fresenius Kabi Pharmaceuticals Holding Inc
Cefotan

## CONTACTS: *Note: Officers with more than one job title may be intentionally listed here more than once.*

Thomas H. Silberg, CEO
Frank Harmon, COO/Exec. VP
Thomas H. Silberg, Pres.
Richard J. Tajak, CFO/Exec. VP
James W. Callanan, VP-Human Resources
Richard E. Maroun, Chief Admin. Officer
Richard E. Maroun, General Counsel/Corp. Sec.
Katherine Gregory, VP-Business Dev.
Debra Lynn Ross, Dir.-Comm.

**Phone:** 847-413-2073 **Fax:** 800-743-7082
**Toll-Free:** 888-386-1300
**Address:** 1501 E. Woodfield Rd., Ste. 300 E., Schaumburg, IL 60173-5837 US

## GROWTH PLANS/SPECIAL FEATURES:

APP Pharmaceuticals, Inc., a subsidiary of Fresenius Kabi Pharmaceuticals Holding, Inc., is a fully integrated biopharmaceutical company that develops, manufactures and markets injectable pharmaceutical products, focusing on the injectable critical care, oncology and anti-infective markets. The firm offers injectable products in each of the three basic forms: Liquid, powder and lyophilized (freeze-dried). APP manufactures and markets more than 60 injectable critical care products, including heparin, used to treat and prevent blood clotting. The firm currently manufactures 17 injectable oncology products in 38 dosages and formulations, including the recently launched fludabarine, used to treat adult B-cell chronic lymphocytic leukemia patients who have not responded to other treatments. The company also offers 21 injectable anti-infective products, including 11 classes of antimicrobials; the company's newest product, a second-generation cephalosporin called cefotetan, is used for surgical prophylaxis and has the longest half-life of any cephalosporin. APP is currently the only company marketing cefotetan in the U.S., which it does under the brand name Cefotan. APP's products are used in hospitals, long-term care facilities, alternate care sites and clinics. In March 2008, the company launched a cefepime hydrochloride injection, to be used as a treatment for treatment of urinary tract infections, skin and skin structure infections and intra-abdominal infections. In September of the same year, APP was acquired by Fresenius Kabi Pharmaceuticals Holding, Inc. In January 2009, the firm launched a rocuronium bromide injection, the generic version of the medication Zemuron, which is used as a muscle relaxant.

Employees are offered medical, dental and vision insurance; disability and life insurance; flexible spending accounts; legal assistance; dependent spouse and child life insurance; a 401(k) plan; a tuition assistance program; and an employee assistance plan.

## FINANCIALS: **Sales and profits are in thousands of dollars—add 000 to get the full amount. 2008 Note: Financial information for 2008 was not available for all companies at press time.**

2008 Sales: $
2007 Sales: $647,374
2006 Sales: $583,201
2005 Sales: $385,082
2004 Sales: $405,247

2008 Profits: $
2007 Profits: $34,358
2006 Profits: $-46,897
2005 Profits: $17,657
2004 Profits: $18,221

**U.S. Stock Ticker: Subsidiary**
**Int'l Ticker:** Int'l Exchange:
Employees: 1,375
Fiscal Year Ends: 12/31
Parent Company: FRESENIUS KABI PHARMACEUTICALS HOLDING INC

## SALARIES/BENEFITS:

Pension Plan: ESOP Stock Plan: Profit Sharing: Top Exec. Salary: $692,885 Bonus: $100,000
Savings Plan: Y Stock Purch. Plan: Second Exec. Salary: $623,077 Bonus: $275,000

## OTHER THOUGHTS:

**Apparent Women Officers or Directors**: 2
**Hot Spot for Advancement for Women/Minorities**: Y

## LOCATIONS: ("Y" = Yes)

| West: | Southwest: | Midwest: | Southeast: | Northeast: | International: |
|---|---|---|---|---|---|
| Y | | Y | | Y | Y |

# APPLIED SIGNAL TECHNOLOGY INC

www.appsig.com

**Industry Group Code:** 334210 **Ranks within this company's industry group:** Sales: 7 Profits: 5

| Management: | | Sales/Marketing: | | Liberal Arts: | | Information Systems: | | Professionals: | | Technical/Scientific: | |
|---|---|---|---|---|---|---|---|---|---|---|---|
| Mgmt. Trainees: | | Mktg. Professionals: | Y | Gen. Writing/Editing: | Y | Info. Management: | Y | Finance/Accounting: | Y | Engineers, Elec.: | Y |
| Experienced Mgmt.: | Y | Retail Sales: | | Technical Writing: | Y | Software Dev.: | Y | Law: | Y | Engineers, Other: | Y |
| Int'l Business: | Y | Commercial/Industrial: | Y | Graphic Arts/Photog.: | | Hardware Dev.: | Y | HR/Other: | Y | Health/Lab: | |
| MBA Graduates: | Y | Sales Trainees: | Y | Music: | | Systems Integration: | Y | Training: | Y | Scientists/Research: | |
| | | Advertising Pros.: | | Broadcasting: | | Consulting/Other: | | Health Care: | | Petroleum/Chemicals: | |
| | | | | Other: | | | | Consulting: | | Math/Other: | |

## TYPES OF BUSINESS:

Telecommunications Equipment-Signal Reconnaissance
Defense Communication Products
Digital Signal Processing Equipment
Analysis & System Software

## BRANDS/DIVISIONS/AFFILIATES:

ELVIRA
Pegasus
neu-VISION

## CONTACTS: *Note: Officers with more than one job title may be intentionally listed here more than once.*

Gary L. Yancey, CEO
William B. Van Vleet III, COO
Gary L. Yancey, Pres.
James E. Doyle, CFO
Michael J. Ready, Chief Mktg. Officer
John R. Treichler, CTO
Alice Delgado, Investor Rel. Contact
James Doyle, VP-Finance
Renato F. Roscher, Jr., Exec. VP-Multichannel Systems Div.
Robert Blanchard, VP-Electronic Systems Div.
Robert T. Teague, VP-National Security Systems Div.
Joseph Leonelli, VP-Wireless Comm. Systems Div.
Gary L. Yancey, Chmn.

| | |
|---|---|
| **Phone:** 408-749-1888 | **Fax:** 408-738-1928 |
| **Toll-Free:** | |
| **Address:** 400 W. California Ave., Sunnyvale, CA 94086 US | |

## GROWTH PLANS/SPECIAL FEATURES:

Applied Signal Technology, Inc. (AST) provides advanced digital signal processing products and systems that support intelligence, surveillance and reconnaissance (ISR) activities. It designs, develops and manufactures its own systems and equipment through centralized facilities, and provides training and support for its products. AST's main area of operations is signal intelligence (SIGINT), which is subdivided into manmade signals such as electronic intelligence (ELINT) and communications intelligence (COMINT). It also offers processors for naturally occurring signals, including sonar, radar, magnetic and chemical sensors. The firm's COMINT operations include software products like ELVIRA, which acquires, processes and analyzes incoming communications traffic and runs on an IBM PC, and hardware products that intercept, store and process SIGINT across hundreds of voice-grade channels (VGCs) and other bandwidths, including microwave and satellite. ELINT operations, which fall primarily under its Pegasus line of products and services, are similar to its COMINT operations, but acquire electronic signals mainly from weapon systems. ELINT products function both automatically and through manual control, supporting battlefield mapping; threat detection such as from incoming missiles; and emitter collection and analysis. The firm's neu-VISION technology is an advanced neutron imaging system that can detect and classify hazardous materials through concrete, vehicles and other barriers, including explosive and other chemical elements, as well as radiological and nuclear materials. AST's primary customer is the U.S. government, including the Department of Defense, the Intelligence community and the Department of Homeland Security. Reflecting this governmental involvement, a large percentage of its employees hold U.S. government security clearance, and some members of its staff hold positions on important government and industrial committees and panels. Additionally, seven of its 10 manufacturing sites have government approved workspaces and laboratories for classified assignments.

AST offers its employees medical, dental and vision coverage; life, disability, and AD&D insurance; paid time off; and tuition reimbursement.

## FINANCIALS: **Sales and profits are in thousands of dollars—add 000 to get the full amount. 2008 Note: Financial information for 2008 was not available for all companies at press time.**

| | | |
|---|---|---|
| 2008 Sales: $186,331 | 2008 Profits: $8,017 | **U.S. Stock Ticker: APSG** |
| 2007 Sales: $170,375 | 2007 Profits: $6,812 | **Int'l Ticker:** Int'l Exchange: |
| 2006 Sales: $161,913 | 2006 Profits: $4,327 | Employees: 672 |
| 2005 Sales: $156,061 | 2005 Profits: $9,244 | Fiscal Year Ends: 10/31 |
| 2004 Sales: $142,836 | 2004 Profits: $11,974 | Parent Company: |

## SALARIES/BENEFITS:

| | | | | |
|---|---|---|---|---|
| Pension Plan: | ESOP Stock Plan: | Profit Sharing: Y | Top Exec. Salary: $481,236 | Bonus: $111,567 |
| Savings Plan: Y | Stock Purch. Plan: Y | | Second Exec. Salary: $369,012 | Bonus: $71,290 |

## OTHER THOUGHTS:

**Apparent Women Officers or Directors**: 1
**Hot Spot for Advancement for Women/Minorities**:

## LOCATIONS: ("Y" = Yes)

| West: | Southwest: | Midwest: | Southeast: | Northeast: | International: |
|---|---|---|---|---|---|
| Y | Y | | Y | Y | |

# ARDEN GROUP INC

www.gelsons.com

**Industry Group Code:** 445110 **Ranks within this company's industry group:** Sales: 2 Profits: 1

| Management: | | Sales/Marketing: | | Liberal Arts: | | Information Systems: | | Professionals: | | Technical/Scientific: | |
|---|---|---|---|---|---|---|---|---|---|---|---|
| Mgmt. Trainees: | Y | Mktg. Professionals: | Y | Gen. Writing/Editing: | | Info. Management: | Y | Finance/Accounting: | Y | Engineers, Elec.: | |
| Experienced Mgmt.: | Y | Retail Sales: | Y | Technical Writing: | | Software Dev.: | | Law: | Y | Engineers, Other: | |
| Int'l Business: | | Commercial/Industrial: | | Graphic Arts/Photog.: | Y | Hardware Dev.: | | HR/Other: | Y | Health/Lab: | |
| MBA Graduates: | Y | Sales Trainees: | Y | Music: | | Systems Integration: | | Training: | Y | Scientists/Research: | |
| | | Advertising Pros.: | Y | Broadcasting: | | Consulting/Other: | | Health Care: | | Petroleum/Chemicals: | |
| | | | | Other: | | | | Consulting: | | Math/Other: | |

## TYPES OF BUSINESS:

Grocery Stores, Retail
Real Estate Holdings

## BRANDS/DIVISIONS/AFFILIATES:

Gelson's Markets
Arden-Mayfair, Inc.
Mayfair Realty, Inc.
Mayfair Market

## CONTACTS: *Note: Officers with more than one job title may be intentionally listed here more than once.*

Bernard Briskin, CEO
Bernard Briskin, Pres.
Laura J. Neumann, Sr. Dir.-Financial Reporting & Compliance
Robert E. Stiles, Pres., Gelson's Markets
John Vitale, Sr. VP-Perishables, Gelson's Markets
Donna Tyndall, Sr. VP-Store Oper., Gelson's Markets
Bernard Briskin, Chmn.

**Phone:** 310-638-2842 **Fax:** 310-631-0950
**Toll-Free:**
**Address:** 2020 S. Central Ave., Compton, CA 90220 US

## GROWTH PLANS/SPECIAL FEATURES:

Arden Group, Inc. is a holding company that conducts operations through its wholly-owned subsidiary Arden-Mayfair, Inc. and Arden Mayfair's wholly-owned subsidiary Gelson's Markets, which operates supermarkets in southern California. The company also owns certain real estate properties through its subsidiary, Mayfair Realty, Inc., which is wholly-owned by Arden Group and Arden-Mayfair. Gelson's operates 18 supermarkets, 17 under the name Gelson's and one under the name Mayfair. Gelson's and Mayfair are self-service, cash-and-carry markets that offer a selection of local and national brands as well as a limited number of private-label items. Gelson's stores typically carry a wide range of items, including grocery categories such as dry groceries, produce, meat, seafood, bakery, dairy, wine, liquor, floral, sushi, vitamins, natural food products and health and beauty aids. The stores also offer a selection of organic products. Gelson's merchandising emphasizes specialty items such as imported foods and unusual delicatessen products, as well as items found in service departments such as seafood, sit-down coffee areas, bakeries and service delis. Some Gelson's stores include additional service departments such as fresh pizza, coffee bars, gelato bars and carving carts offering cooked meats. Additionally, selected stores offer banking and pharmacy services through third parties. The Mayfair store, located in Hollywood, offers merchandise similar to Gelson's but with a selection that is generally less broad. The firm also operates a 127,000-square-foot warehouse with a 4,000-square-foot truck service facility in Commerce, California. The single largest supplier for the company is Unified Western Grocers, Inc., a cooperative wholesaler, which accounted for approximately 17% of Gelson's purchases in 2007.

Employees have access to health care and pension plans. The company develops employees for career advancement, and promotes from within when possible.

## FINANCIALS: **Sales and profits are in thousands of dollars—add 000 to get the full amount. 2008 Note: Financial information for 2008 was not available for all companies at press time.**

2008 Sales: $
2007 Sales: $485,939
2006 Sales: $482,737
2005 Sales: $470,354
2004 Sales: $502,898

2008 Profits: $
2007 Profits: $29,207
2006 Profits: $23,224
2005 Profits: $19,851
2004 Profits: $22,672

**U.S. Stock Ticker: ARDNA**
**Int'l Ticker:** Int'l Exchange:
Employees: 1,328
Fiscal Year Ends: 12/31
Parent Company:

## SALARIES/BENEFITS:

Pension Plan: Y
Savings Plan:
ESOP Stock Plan:
Stock Purch. Plan:
Profit Sharing:
Top Exec. Salary: $647,282
Second Exec. Salary: $141,450
Bonus: $1,737,772
Bonus: $

## OTHER THOUGHTS:

**Apparent Women Officers or Directors**: 1
**Hot Spot for Advancement for Women/Minorities**:

## LOCATIONS: ("Y" = Yes)

| West: | Southwest: | Midwest: | Southeast: | Northeast: | International: |
|---|---|---|---|---|---|
| Y | | | | | |

# ARIBA INC

www.ariba.com

**Industry Group Code:** 511217 **Ranks within this company's industry group:** Sales: 3 Profits: 3

| Management: | | Sales/Marketing: | | Liberal Arts: | | Information Systems: | | Professionals: | | Technical/Scientific: | |
|---|---|---|---|---|---|---|---|---|---|---|---|
| Mgmt. Trainees: | | Mktg. Professionals: | Y | Gen. Writing/Editing: | | Info. Management: | Y | Finance/Accounting: | Y | Engineers, Elec.: | Y |
| Experienced Mgmt.: | Y | Retail Sales: | | Technical Writing: | Y | Software Dev.: | Y | Law: | Y | Engineers, Other: | |
| Int'l Business: | Y | Commercial/Industrial: | Y | Graphic Arts/Photog.: | | Hardware Dev.: | | HR/Other: | Y | Health/Lab: | |
| MBA Graduates: | Y | Sales Trainees: | Y | Music: | | Systems Integration: | | Training: | Y | Scientists/Research: | |
| | | Advertising Pros.: | | Broadcasting: | | Consulting/Other: | | Health Care: | | Petroleum/Chemicals: | |
| | | | | Other: | | | | Consulting: | | Math/Other: | Y |

## TYPES OF BUSINESS:

Computer Software-Transaction Processing
Procurement & Logistics Solutions
Business Process Software
Consulting Services

## BRANDS/DIVISIONS/AFFILIATES:

Ariba Spend Management
Ariba Visibility Solutions
Ariba Sourcing Solutions
Ariba Procurement & Expense Solutions
Ariba Contract Management Solutions
Ariba Invoice & Payment Solutions
Ariba Supplier Management Solutions
Procuri, Inc.

## CONTACTS: *Note: Officers with more than one job title may be intentionally listed here more than once.*

Robert M. Calderoni, CEO
Kent Parker, COO
Kevin S. Costello, Pres.
Ahmed Rubaie, CFO
Tim Minahan, Chief Mktg. Officer
Bhaskar Himatsingka, CTO
Bob Solomon, Sr. VP/Gen. Mgr.-Ariba Supplier Bus. Unit.
Robert M. Calderoni, Chmn.
Daryl T. Rolley, Sr. VP/Gen. Mgr.-Ariba North America & Asia

| **Phone:** 650-390-1000 | **Fax:** 650-390-1100 |
|---|---|
| **Toll-Free:** | |
| **Address:** 807 11th Ave., Sunnyvale, CA 94089 US | |

## GROWTH PLANS/SPECIAL FEATURES:

Ariba, Inc. provides enterprise spend management software applications, services and network access that allow customers to efficiently manage the purchasing of all non-payroll goods and services required to run their business, with offices in 21 countries. The company's software applications integrate with all major business applications and provide customers with real-time access to business data and partners via the Internet. The Ariba Spend Management (ASM) applications fall into six sets. Ariba Visibility Solutions provides customers with products and services to enhance the visibility of spending activities across all of their suppliers, divisions and purchased goods or services. Ariba Sourcing Solutions enables companies to identify the top suppliers across a broad range of categories and to negotiate procurement terms, leverage and aggregate spending, and manage procurement contracts. Ariba Procurement & Expense Solutions provides applications and services for requisitioning and procurement across all kinds of spending. Ariba Contract Management Solutions allows customers to streamline and automate the entire contract process. Ariba Invoice & Payment Solutions allows enterprises to streamline and automate paper-intensive invoicing and payment processes. Finally, Ariba Supplier Management Solutions provides enterprises with products and services to optimize buyer-seller interactions. All Ariba Solutions products combine software, network access, professional services, expertise and technology. In December 2007, Ariba acquired Procuri, Inc., a privately-held provider of on-demand supply management solutions, for $93 million.

Ariba offers its employees medical, dental, life and disability insurance.

## FINANCIALS: **Sales and profits are in thousands of dollars—add 000 to get the full amount. 2008 Note: Financial information for 2008 was not available for all companies at press time.**

| | | |
|---|---|---|
| 2008 Sales: $328,060 | 2008 Profits: $-41,062 | **U.S. Stock Ticker: ARBA** |
| 2007 Sales: $301,667 | 2007 Profits: $-14,977 | **Int'l Ticker:** Int'l Exchange: |
| 2006 Sales: $296,016 | 2006 Profits: $-47,801 | Employees: 1,740 |
| 2005 Sales: $323,043 | 2005 Profits: $-349,628 | Fiscal Year Ends: 9/30 |
| 2004 Sales: $245,798 | 2004 Profits: $-25,230 | Parent Company: |

## SALARIES/BENEFITS:

| | | | | |
|---|---|---|---|---|
| Pension Plan: | ESOP Stock Plan: | Profit Sharing: | Top Exec. Salary: $600,000 | Bonus: $660,000 |
| Savings Plan: Y | Stock Purch. Plan: | | Second Exec. Salary: $450,000 | Bonus: $270,000 |

## OTHER THOUGHTS:

**Apparent Women Officers or Directors**: 1
**Hot Spot for Advancement for Women/Minorities**:

## LOCATIONS: ("Y" = Yes)

| West: | Southwest: | Midwest: | Southeast: | Northeast: | International: |
|---|---|---|---|---|---|
| Y | Y | Y | Y | Y | Y |

# ARIZONA CHEMICAL COMPANY

www.arizonachemical.com

**Industry Group Code:** 325000 **Ranks within this company's industry group:** Sales: Profits:

| Management: | | Sales/Marketing: | | Liberal Arts: | | Information Systems: | | Professionals: | | Technical/Scientific: | |
|---|---|---|---|---|---|---|---|---|---|---|---|
| Mgmt. Trainees: | | Mktg. Professionals: | Y | Gen. Writing/Editing: | | Info. Management: | Y | Finance/Accounting: | Y | Engineers, Elec.: | Y |
| Experienced Mgmt.: | Y | Retail Sales: | | Technical Writing: | Y | Software Dev.: | | Law: | Y | Engineers, Other: | |
| Int'l Business: | Y | Commercial/Industrial: | Y | Graphic Arts/Photog.: | | Hardware Dev.: | | HR/Other: | Y | Health/Lab: | |
| MBA Graduates: | Y | Sales Trainees: | Y | Music: | | Systems Integration: | | Training: | Y | Scientists/Research: | Y |
| | | Advertising Pros.: | | Broadcasting: | | Consulting/Other: | | Health Care: | | Petroleum/Chemicals: | Y |
| | | | | Other: | | | | Consulting: | | Math/Other: | |

## TYPES OF BUSINESS:

Pine-Based Chemicals
Crude Tall Oil Fractionation

## BRANDS/DIVISIONS/AFFILIATES:

Rhone Capital LLC
Arboris, LCC
SYLVARES
UNI-REZ
SYLVAGUM
Sylfat TOFA
SYLVACLEAR
Immobilized Fragrance Oil

## CONTACTS:

*Note: Officers with more than one job title may be intentionally listed here more than once.*

Gerald C. Marterer, Gen. Mgr.
Charles Nelson, CFO/VP
Dave Cowfer, Media & Community Rel. Contact

**Phone:** 904-928-8700 **Fax:** 904-928-8779
**Toll-Free:** 800-526-5294
**Address:** 4600 Touchton Rd. E., Ste. 500, Jacksonville, FL 32246 US

## GROWTH PLANS/SPECIAL FEATURES:

Arizona Chemical Company is one of the largest manufacturers and suppliers of pine-based chemicals worldwide. It operates three business groups: Adhesives; Inks and Coatings; and Oleochemicals. Adhesives group products see use in bookbinding, carpets, contact cements, labels, nonwoven fabrics, caulks, packaging and construction. Specific products include SYLVARES brand alpha methyl styrene (AMS) resins; UNI-REZ brand hot melt polyamides resins; and three brands of rosin tackifiers (used to make things stickier, or tacky), SYLVALITE, SYLVATAC and SYLVAGUM, used in everything from chewing gum to adhesive tape. The Inks and Coatings group produces various products for the printing and thermoplastic coatings markets, including ink resins and UNI-REZ brand polyamides curing agents. The Oleochemicals group has one of the firm's most diverse product lines, with product applications including flavors, fragrances, soaps, epoxy curatives, mining ore floatation, metalworking fluids, asphalt modification, tire manufacturing, synthetic lubricants and fuel additives. Specific products include terpenes (the key ingredient in turpentine), used in flavorings, fragrances and mining; three brands of tall oil products, Sylfat TOFA, Sylvatal DTO and Sylvaros Rosin, used in plastics, alkyd paints, lubricants and fuel; SYLVACLEAR resins manufactured through the firm's patented Immobilized Fragrance Oil technology, mainly used in air fresheners; and various acids, including isostearic acid, used in everything from personal care products to engine lubricants. Arboris, LCC, a joint venture with Harting Group, operates one of the largest and most modern sterols facilities in the world; sterols are a food additive. Founded in 1930, the company operates 11 manufacturing facilities; sales offices located throughout the U.S., Latin America, Europe and Asia; research centers in Savannah, Georgia and Almere, the Netherlands; and technical support facilities worldwide. In February 2007, former parent International Paper Co. sold the company to a private equity fund run by Rhone Capital, called Rhone Capital III L.P., for $485 million.

## FINANCIALS:

**Sales and profits are in thousands of dollars—add 000 to get the full amount. 2008 Note: Financial information for 2008 was not available for all companies at press time.**

| | | |
|---|---|---|
| 2008 Sales: $ | 2008 Profits: $ | **U.S. Stock Ticker: Private** |
| 2007 Sales: $ | 2007 Profits: $ | **Int'l Ticker:** Int'l Exchange: |
| 2006 Sales: $769,000 | 2006 Profits: $ | Employees: 1,400 |
| 2005 Sales: $692,000 | 2005 Profits: $ | Fiscal Year Ends: 12/31 |
| 2004 Sales: $670,000 | 2004 Profits: $ | Parent Company: RHONE CAPITAL LLC |

## SALARIES/BENEFITS:

| | | | | |
|---|---|---|---|---|
| Pension Plan: | ESOP Stock Plan: | Profit Sharing: | Top Exec. Salary: $ | Bonus: $ |
| Savings Plan: | Stock Purch. Plan: | | Second Exec. Salary: $ | Bonus: $ |

## OTHER THOUGHTS:

**Apparent Women Officers or Directors:**
**Hot Spot for Advancement for Women/Minorities:**

## LOCATIONS: ("Y" = Yes)

| West: | Southwest: | Midwest: | Southeast: | Northeast: | International: |
|---|---|---|---|---|---|
| | | Y | Y | | Y |

# AROTECH CORPORATION

www.arotech.com

**Industry Group Code:** 333298 **Ranks within this company's industry group:** Sales: 1 Profits: 1

| Management: | | Sales/Marketing: | | Liberal Arts: | | Information Systems: | | Professionals: | | Technical/Scientific: | |
|---|---|---|---|---|---|---|---|---|---|---|---|
| Mgmt. Trainees: | | Mktg. Professionals: | Y | Gen. Writing/Editing: | | Info. Management: | Y | Finance/Accounting: | Y | Engineers, Elec.: | Y |
| Experienced Mgmt.: | Y | Retail Sales: | | Technical Writing: | Y | Software Dev.: | Y | Law: | Y | Engineers, Other: | Y |
| Int'l Business: | Y | Commercial/Industrial: | Y | Graphic Arts/Photog.: | | Hardware Dev.: | Y | HR/Other: | Y | Health/Lab: | |
| MBA Graduates: | Y | Sales Trainees: | Y | Music: | | Systems Integration: | | Training: | Y | Scientists/Research: | Y |
| | | Advertising Pros.: | | Broadcasting: | | Consulting/Other: | | Health Care: | | Petroleum/Chemicals: | |
| | | | | Other: | | | | Consulting: | | Math/Other: | Y |

## TYPES OF BUSINESS:

Mobile Electric Power Technology
Zinc-Air Batteries
Armor & Armored Vehicles
Defense & Safety Products
Training & Simulation Products

## BRANDS/DIVISIONS/AFFILIATES:

MDT Protective Industries, Ltd.
MDT Armor Corporation
Armour of America
IES Interactive Training
FAAC, Inc.
Epsilor Electronic Industries, Ltd.
Electric Fuel Battery Corporation
Electric Fuel, Ltd.

## CONTACTS: *Note: Officers with more than one job title may be intentionally listed here more than once.*

Robert S. Ehrlich, CEO
Steven Esses, COO
Steven Esses, Pres.
Thomas J. Paup, CFO/VP-Finance
Jonathan Whartman, Sr. VP-Mktg.
Yaakov Har-Oz, General Counsel/VP/Corp. Sec.
Norman Johnson, Controller
William Graham, VP-Gov't Affairs
Jonathan Whartman, Sr. VP
Robert S. Ehrlich, Chmn.

| | |
|---|---|
| **Phone:** 646-645-2107 | **Fax:** 734-761-5368 |
| **Toll-Free:** 800-281-0356 | |
| **Address:** 1229 Oak Valley Dr., Ann Arbor, MI 48108 US | |

## GROWTH PLANS/SPECIAL FEATURES:

Arotech Corporation is a defense and security products and services company operating in three business areas: high-level armoring for military and nonmilitary air and ground vehicles; interactive simulation for military, law enforcement and commercial markets; and batteries and charging systems for military use. The company armors military and civilian SUVs, buses and vans through its subsidiaries MDT Protective Industries, Ltd., located in Lod, Israel, and MDT Armor Corporation, located in Auburn, Alabama. It provides ballistic armor kits for rotary and fixed wing aircraft and marine armor through Armour of America, located in Auburn, Alabama. Arotech's training and simulation division consists of two subsidiaries: IES Interactive Training, which provides training products to military and law-enforcement professionals worldwide; and FAAC, Inc., which provides training simulation products primarily to the U.S. military. Arotech's battery and power systems division manufactures and sells lithium and Zinc-Air batteries for defense and security products as well as other military applications. Through Epsilor Electronic Industries, Ltd, the company develops and sells lithium batteries and chargers to the military and private defense industry in the Middle East, Europe and Asia. Through Electric Fuel Battery Corporation, it produces primary Zinc-Air batteries, rechargeable batteries and battery chargers for the military. Zinc-Air batteries are lighter in weight and possess higher energy density than lithium-based batteries. The company also produces water-activated lifejacket lights for commercial aviation and marine applications through Electric Fuel, Ltd. Aerotech relies heavily on sales to the U.S. military, which account for approximately 52% of the company's revenues.

## FINANCIALS: **Sales and profits are in thousands of dollars—add 000 to get the full amount. 2008 Note: Financial information for 2008 was not available for all companies at press time.**

| | | |
|---|---|---|
| 2008 Sales: $ | 2008 Profits: $ | **U.S. Stock Ticker: ARTX** |
| 2007 Sales: $57,719 | 2007 Profits: $-3,056 | **Int'l Ticker:** Int'l Exchange: |
| 2006 Sales: $43,120 | 2006 Profits: $-15,569 | Employees: 407 |
| 2005 Sales: $49,045 | 2005 Profits: $-24,043 | Fiscal Year Ends: 12/31 |
| 2004 Sales: $49,954 | 2004 Profits: $-9,042 | Parent Company: |

## SALARIES/BENEFITS:

| | | | | |
|---|---|---|---|---|
| Pension Plan: | ESOP Stock Plan: | Profit Sharing: | Top Exec. Salary: $420,110 | Bonus: $180,000 |
| Savings Plan: | Stock Purch. Plan: | | Second Exec. Salary: $143,100 | Bonus: $71,550 |

## OTHER THOUGHTS:

**Apparent Women Officers or Directors**:
**Hot Spot for Advancement for Women/Minorities**:

## LOCATIONS: ("Y" = Yes)

| West: | Southwest: | Midwest: | Southeast: | Northeast: | International: |
|---|---|---|---|---|---|
| Y | | Y | Y | Y | Y |

# ARRIS GROUP INC

www.arrisi.com

**Industry Group Code:** 334200 **Ranks within this company's industry group:** Sales: 1 Profits: 1

| Management: | | Sales/Marketing: | | Liberal Arts: | | Information Systems: | | Professionals: | | Technical/Scientific: | |
|---|---|---|---|---|---|---|---|---|---|---|---|
| Mgmt. Trainees: | | Mktg. Professionals: | Y | Gen. Writing/Editing: | Y | Info. Management: | Y | Finance/Accounting: | Y | Engineers, Elec.: | Y |
| Experienced Mgmt.: | Y | Retail Sales: | | Technical Writing: | Y | Software Dev.: | Y | Law: | Y | Engineers, Other: | Y |
| Int'l Business: | Y | Commercial/Industrial: | Y | Graphic Arts/Photog.: | | Hardware Dev.: | Y | HR/Other: | Y | Health/Lab: | |
| MBA Graduates: | Y | Sales Trainees: | Y | Music: | | Systems Integration: | Y | Training: | Y | Scientists/Research: | |
| | | Advertising Pros.: | | Broadcasting: | | Consulting/Other: | | Health Care: | | Petroleum/Chemicals: | |
| | | | | Other: | | | | Consulting: | | Math/Other: | |

## TYPES OF BUSINESS:

Communications Equipment-Cable Systems
Optical & Radio Frequency Transmission Equipment
Internet Access Products
Support & Testing Products

## BRANDS/DIVISIONS/AFFILIATES:

Broadband Communications Systems
Access, Transport and Supplies
Media & Communications Systems
Madison River Communications Corp
YourBroadbandStore.com
C-COR Inc

## CONTACTS: *Note: Officers with more than one job title may be intentionally listed here more than once.*

Robert J. (Bob) Stanzione, CEO
Robert J. (Bob) Stanzione, Pres.
David B. Potts, CFO/Exec. VP
Ronald M. (Ron) Coppock, Pres., Worldwide Sales & Mktg.
David B. Potts, CIO
Lawrence Margolis, Exec. VP-Admin.
Lawrence Margolis, General Counsel/Corp. Sec.
Lawrence A. Margolis, Exec. VP-Strategic Planning
James A. Bauer, Dir.-Investor Rel.
Marc C. Geraci, Treas./VP
James D. Lakin, Pres., Broadband
Bryant K. Isaacs, Pres., New Bus. Ventures
Robert (Bob) Puccini, Pres., TeleWire Supply
Robert J. (Bob) Stanzione, Chmn.

**Phone:** 770-473-2000 **Fax:** 770-622-8750
**Toll-Free:** 800-469-6569
**Address:** 3871 Lakefield Dr., Suwanee, GA 30024 US

## GROWTH PLANS/SPECIAL FEATURES:

Arris Group, Inc. is a global telecommunications technology company specializing in integrated broadband network solutions that include products, systems and software for content and operations management and professional services. Arris develops, manufactures and supplies cable telephony, video and high-speed data equipment. In addition, the firm is a leading supplier of infrastructure products used by cable system operators to build-out and maintain hybrid fiber-coaxial (HFC) networks. It provides products and equipment principally to cable system operators and, more specifically, to multiple system operators (MSOs). Arris' products enable MSOs and other broadband service providers to deliver a full range of integrated voice, video and high-speed data services to their subscribers. The company operates in three segments: Broadband Communications Systems (BCS); Access, Transport and Supplies (ATS); and Media & Communications Systems (MCS). Its BCS product offerings include VoIP (Voice over Internet Protocol) and high speed data products; video and IP (Internet Protocol) headend products; and constant bit rate telephony products. ATS products include HFC plant equipment products and infrastructure products for fiber optic or coaxial networks built under or above ground. Arris' MCS products include content and operations management systems, operations management systems and fixed mobile convergence networks. The company maintains domestic sales offices in Colorado, Georgia and Pennsylvania and international sales offices in Argentina, Chile, Hong Kong, Japan, the Netherlands and Spain. The firm's two largest customers are Comcast and Time Warner Cable, which generated 39.8% and 10.7% of its sales for 2007, respectively. In April 2007, the company acquired Madison River Communications Corp. for approximately $830 million. In September 2007, Arris created YourBroadbandStore.com, a retail website providing professional grade telecommunications products. In December 2007, the company acquired C-COR, Inc., a provider of integrated access and management platforms, for approximately $730 million.

## FINANCIALS: **Sales and profits are in thousands of dollars—add 000 to get the full amount. 2008 Note: Financial information for 2008 was not available for all companies at press time.**

| | | |
|---|---|---|
| 2008 Sales: $ | 2008 Profits: $ | **U.S. Stock Ticker: ARRS** |
| 2007 Sales: $992,194 | 2007 Profits: $98,340 | **Int'l Ticker:** Int'l Exchange: |
| 2006 Sales: $891,551 | 2006 Profits: $142,287 | Employees: 1,992 |
| 2005 Sales: $680,417 | 2005 Profits: $51,483 | Fiscal Year Ends: 12/31 |
| 2004 Sales: $490,041 | 2004 Profits: $-28,396 | Parent Company: |

## SALARIES/BENEFITS:

| | | | | |
|---|---|---|---|---|
| Pension Plan: | ESOP Stock Plan: | Profit Sharing: | Top Exec. Salary: $687,500 | Bonus: $763,000 |
| Savings Plan: | Stock Purch. Plan: | | Second Exec. Salary: $368,125 | Bonus: $245,000 |

## OTHER THOUGHTS:

**Apparent Women Officers or Directors**:
**Hot Spot for Advancement for Women/Minorities**:

## LOCATIONS: ("Y" = Yes)

| West: | Southwest: | Midwest: | Southeast: | Northeast: | International: |
|---|---|---|---|---|---|
| Y | | Y | Y | Y | Y |

# ART TECHNOLOGY GROUP INC

www.atg.com

**Industry Group Code:** 511216 **Ranks within this company's industry group:** Sales: 2 Profits: 1

| Management: | | Sales/Marketing: | | Liberal Arts: | | Information Systems: | | Professionals: | | Technical/Scientific: | |
|---|---|---|---|---|---|---|---|---|---|---|---|
| Mgmt. Trainees: | | Mktg. Professionals: | Y | Gen. Writing/Editing: | | Info. Management: | Y | Finance/Accounting: | Y | Engineers, Elec.: | Y |
| Experienced Mgmt.: | Y | Retail Sales: | | Technical Writing: | Y | Software Dev.: | Y | Law: | Y | Engineers, Other: | |
| Int'l Business: | Y | Commercial/Industrial: | Y | Graphic Arts/Photog.: | | Hardware Dev.: | | HR/Other: | Y | Health/Lab: | |
| MBA Graduates: | Y | Sales Trainees: | | Music: | | Systems Integration: | | Training: | Y | Scientists/Research: | |
| | | Advertising Pros.: | | Broadcasting: | | Consulting/Other: | | Health Care: | | Petroleum/Chemicals: | |
| | | | | Other: | | | | Consulting: | | Math/Other: | |

## TYPES OF BUSINESS:

Software-Web Development & E-Commerce
Consulting Services
Application Development
Design Services
Training & Support Services

## BRANDS/DIVISIONS/AFFILIATES:

eStara
OnDemand
Click to Call
Click to Chat
Call Tracking
CleverSet
Amazon.com Inc

## CONTACTS: *Note: Officers with more than one job title may be intentionally listed here more than once.*

Robert D. Burke, CEO
Robert D. Burke, Pres.
Julie M. B. Bradley, CFO
Cliff J. Conneighton, Sr. VP-Mktg.
Patricia O'Neill, Sr. VP-Human Resources
Kenneth Z. Volpe, Sr. VP-Tech.
Kenneth Z. Volpe, Sr. VP-Prod.
David McEvoy, General Counsel/VP
Drew Reynolds, Sr. VP-Corp. Dev.
Lou Frio, Sr. VP-Svcs.
John Federman, Sr. VP
Daniel C. Regis, Chmn.
Barry E. Clark, Sr. VP-Worldwide Sales

**Phone:** 617-386-1000 **Fax:** 617-386-1111
**Toll-Free:**
**Address:** 1 Main St., Cambridge, MA 02142 US

## GROWTH PLANS/SPECIAL FEATURES:

Art Technology Group (ATG) provides software solutions and support services that help businesses to develop and manage personalized web sites. ATG's products capture/maintain information about customers' personal preferences, online activity and transaction history, and use this information to provide more contextual content. Through its eStara subsidiary, the company provides OnDemand services for multi-channel interaction. Its Click to Call and Click to Chat services provide online businesses with proactive conversion solutions for enhancing online sales and support. eStara solutions allow customers to converse with a sales person or customer care agent by clicking a button on a website, e-mail, banner ad or directory listing, and eStara's Call Tracking solutions allow advertisers to track the source of each in-bound call as well as information about callers. ATG also offers its Adaptive Scenario Engine (ASE), meant to improve sales by creating personal profiles for customers and determining the efficacy of online marketing strategies. ASE also provides the tools for improving web site content and presentation. ATG provides clients with related services such as support, education and professional services. The company's primary clients are medium-sized to large companies with high numbers of online customers. Prominent clients include Amazon, AOL, Best Buy, Coca-Cola, Dell, Expedia, Intuit, LL Bean, Microsoft, PayPal and Target. In February 2008, the company acquired CleverSet, an automated personalization firm, for approximately $9 million. In April 2008, ATG partnered with Publicar, a Latin American telephone directory publisher and division of Carvajal, making eStara Click to Call available to Publicar's advertisers. Also in April 2008, ATG partnered with Blast Radius, a strategic interactive agency, to promote each other's service.

ATG offers educational reimbursement; an employee assistance program; charitable contributions match; medical, dental and vision insurance; life/disability insurance; domestic partner benefits; and on-site fitness and wellness programs.

## FINANCIALS: **Sales and profits are in thousands of dollars—add 000 to get the full amount. 2008 Note: Financial information for 2008 was not available for all companies at press time.**

2008 Sales: $
2007 Sales: $137,060
2006 Sales: $103,232
2005 Sales: $90,646
2004 Sales: $69,200

2008 Profits: $
2007 Profits: $-4,187
2006 Profits: $9,695
2005 Profits: $5,769
2004 Profits: $-9,500

**U.S. Stock Ticker: ARTG**
**Int'l Ticker:** Int'l Exchange:
Employees: 442
Fiscal Year Ends: 12/31
Parent Company:

## SALARIES/BENEFITS:

Pension Plan: ESOP Stock Plan: Profit Sharing: Top Exec. Salary: $350,000 Bonus: $174,125
Savings Plan: Y Stock Purch. Plan: Y Second Exec. Salary: $240,000 Bonus: $95,938

## OTHER THOUGHTS:

**Apparent Women Officers or Directors**: 5
**Hot Spot for Advancement for Women/Minorities**: Y

## LOCATIONS: ("Y" = Yes)

| West: | Southwest: | Midwest: | Southeast: | Northeast: | International: |
|---|---|---|---|---|---|
| Y | | Y | | Y | Y |

# ARUBA NETWORKS INC

www.arubanetworks.com

**Industry Group Code:** 511213 **Ranks within this company's industry group:** Sales: 3 Profits: 4

| Management: | | Sales/Marketing: | | Liberal Arts: | | Information Systems: | | Professionals: | | Technical/Scientific: | |
|---|---|---|---|---|---|---|---|---|---|---|---|
| Mgmt. Trainees: | | Mktg. Professionals: | Y | Gen. Writing/Editing: | | Info. Management: | Y | Finance/Accounting: | Y | Engineers, Elec.: | Y |
| Experienced Mgmt.: | Y | Retail Sales: | | Technical Writing: | Y | Software Dev.: | Y | Law: | Y | Engineers, Other: | |
| Int'l Business: | Y | Commercial/Industrial: | Y | Graphic Arts/Photog.: | | Hardware Dev.: | | HR/Other: | Y | Health/Lab: | |
| MBA Graduates: | Y | Sales Trainees: | Y | Music: | | Systems Integration: | Y | Training: | Y | Scientists/Research: | |
| | | Advertising Pros.: | | Broadcasting: | | Consulting/Other: | | Health Care: | | Petroleum/Chemicals: | |
| | | | | Other: | | | | Consulting: | | Math/Other: | |

## TYPES OF BUSINESS:

WLAN Equipment
Wireless Security Systems
Mobility Software
Convergence Software & Systems

## BRANDS/DIVISIONS/AFFILIATES:

Aruba Mobile Edge Architecture
ArubaOS Secure Mobility Software
Aruba Mobility Management System
Aruba Mobility Controllers
Aruba Access Points
RFProtect
BlueScanner
AirWave Wireless, Inc.

## CONTACTS: *Note: Officers with more than one job title may be intentionally listed here more than once.*

Dominic P. Orr, CEO
Dominic P. Orr, Pres.
Steffan Tomlinson, CFO
Gary Singh, VP-Mktg.
Aaron Bean, VP-Human Resources
Merwyn Andrade, CTO
Dave Logan, VP-Prod. Mgmt.
Sriram Ramachandran, VP-Eng.
Alexa King, VP-Legal Affairs
Richard Wilmer, VP-Oper.
Peter Cellarius, VP-Bus. Dev.
Keerti Melkote, VP-Prod. & Partnerships
Andrew Harding, VP-Strategic Initiatives
Ryoji Tsuchimoto, VP-Japan Oper.
Jagdeep Singh, VP-Customer Advocacy
Don LeBeau, Chmn.
Rob Pronk, VP-EMEA Sales

**Phone:** 408-227-4500 **Fax:** 408-227-4550
**Toll-Free:** 866-552-7822
**Address:** 1322 Crossman Ave., Sunnyvale, CA 94089-1113 US

## GROWTH PLANS/SPECIAL FEATURES:

Aruba Networks, Inc. markets and manufactures unified mobility solutions including Wi-Fi networks, identity-based security, remote access, cellular services and centralized network management. The company provides its high-performance Wi-Fi-based, wireless local area networks (WLANs) and security systems for businesses that are seeking to implement mobile communications systems over existing wired infrastructures. The firm enables the provision of mobile edge, a network architecture that addresses mobility, security and convergence. Aruba's WLAN switches and grid controllers support a multitude of functions, including VPN termination, VoIP, user-aware firewalling, RF management and intrusion prevention. Aruba's primary platform is the Aruba Mobile Edge Architecture, which allows users secure and consistent access at any remote location within an enterprise campus or office building. IT departments within each location have the capacity to control network access and prioritize application delivery at a central access control site. Products that utilize this technology include ArubaOS Secure Mobility Software for mobility controllers and access points; the Aruba Mobility Management System, which provides applications for planning, monitoring, fault management, reporting and location visualizations; Aruba Mobility Controllers for high-performance wireless LAN; and Aruba Access Points, which sorts wireless user traffic on the enterprise network towards specific Aruba Mobility Controllers. The company has sold its products to over 2,850 end customers worldwide in such industries as finance, retail, hospitality, technology, manufacturing, media, healthcare, education, utilities, telecom, government, transportation, engineering and construction. In the U.S., Aruba's customers include Microsoft, the U.S. Air Force, California State University, Google and Yale. Internationally, its customers include Saudi Aramco, NTT Data Corporation and Pu Dong International Airport. In July 2007, Aruba acquired Network Chemistry's line of RFProtect and BlueScanner wireless security products. In March 2008, the company acquired AirWave Wireless, Inc., a provider of specialized tools for the central management of large, multi-vendor wireless LAN, mesh and WiMAX networks.

## FINANCIALS: Sales and profits are in thousands of dollars—add 000 to get the full amount. 2008 Note: Financial information for 2008 was not available for all companies at press time.

2008 Sales: $
2007 Sales: $127,499
2006 Sales: $72,503
2005 Sales: $12,043
2004 Sales: $

2008 Profits: $
2007 Profits: $-24,382
2006 Profits: $-12,009
2005 Profits: $-32,635
2004 Profits: $

**U.S. Stock Ticker: ARUN**
**Int'l Ticker:** Int'l Exchange:
Employees: 441
Fiscal Year Ends: 7/31
Parent Company:

## SALARIES/BENEFITS:

| | | | | |
|---|---|---|---|---|
| Pension Plan: | ESOP Stock Plan: Y | Profit Sharing: | Top Exec. Salary: $300,000 | Bonus: $ |
| Savings Plan: | Stock Purch. Plan: | | Second Exec. Salary: $213,125 | Bonus: $ |

## OTHER THOUGHTS:

**Apparent Women Officers or Directors**: 1
**Hot Spot for Advancement for Women/Minorities**:

## LOCATIONS: ("Y" = Yes)

| West: | Southwest: | Midwest: | Southeast: | Northeast: | International: |
|---|---|---|---|---|---|
| Y | | | Y | Y | Y |

# ASPECT MEDICAL SYSTEMS INC

www.aspectms.com

**Industry Group Code:** 339113 **Ranks within this company's industry group:** Sales: 29 Profits: 34

| Management: | | Sales/Marketing: | | Liberal Arts: | | Information Systems: | | Professionals: | | Technical/Scientific: | |
|---|---|---|---|---|---|---|---|---|---|---|---|
| Mgmt. Trainees: | | Mktg. Professionals: | Y | Gen. Writing/Editing: | | Info. Management: | Y | Finance/Accounting: | Y | Engineers, Elec.: | Y |
| Experienced Mgmt.: | Y | Retail Sales: | | Technical Writing: | Y | Software Dev.: | | Law: | Y | Engineers, Other: | Y |
| Int'l Business: | Y | Commercial/Industrial: | Y | Graphic Arts/Photog.: | | Hardware Dev.: | | HR/Other: | Y | Health/Lab: | Y |
| MBA Graduates: | Y | Sales Trainees: | Y | Music: | | Systems Integration: | Y | Training: | Y | Scientists/Research: | Y |
| | | Advertising Pros.: | | Broadcasting: | | Consulting/Other: | | Health Care: | Y | Petroleum/Chemicals: | |
| | | | | Other: | | | | Consulting: | | Math/Other: | Y |

## TYPES OF BUSINESS:

Equipment-Anesthesia Monitoring Systems
Patient Monitoring Systems

## BRANDS/DIVISIONS/AFFILIATES:

Bispectral Index
BIS System
BIS Module Kit
A-2000 BIS Monitoring System
BISx / BIS Ready
BIS Vista Monitoring System
Aspect Medical Systems International B.V.
BIS View

## CONTACTS:

*Note: Officers with more than one job title may be intentionally listed here more than once.*

Nassib G. Chamoun, CEO
Nassib G. Chamoun, Pres.
Michael Falvey, CFO/VP
William Floyd, VP-Worldwide Sales & Mktg.
Margery Ahearn, VP-Human Resources
Marc Davidson, VP-Eng.
John Coolidge, VP-Mfg. Oper.
Michael Falvey, Sec.
Paul J. Manberg, VP-Clinical, Regulatory & Quality Assurance
Scott D. Kelley, VP-Medical Affairs
Philip H. Devlin, VP/Gen. Mgr., Aspect Neuroscience
J. Breckenridge Eagle, Chmn.

| Phone: 617-559-7000 | Fax: 617-559-7400 |
|---|---|
| Toll-Free: | |
| Address: One Upland Road, Norman, MA 02062 US | |

## GROWTH PLANS/SPECIAL FEATURES:

Aspect Medical Systems, Inc. develops, manufactures and markets the BIS System, which is an anesthesia monitoring system. The BIS System enables anesthesia providers to assess and manage a patient's level of consciousness during surgery by placing a sensor on a patient's forehead to measure electrical activity in the brain. Patient monitoring with the BIS System provides several benefits, including a reduction in the amount of anesthetics used, a faster wake-up time from anesthesia and a decreased risk of surgical awareness, which is the unintentional regaining of consciousness during surgery. The BIS System is based on the firm's patented core technology, the Bispectral Index, commonly known as the BIS Index. BIS technology is available in 160 countries for medical professionals. The technology is incorporated into all Aspect's products. The BIS System includes the BIS Monitor or BIS Module Kit and single-use, disposable BIS Sensors. The firm has several products including the BIS Sensors, the BIS Vista Monitoring System, the A-2000 BIS Monitoring System and the BISx / BIS Ready. Aspect also has original equipment manufacturer (OEM) relationships with several patient monitoring and anesthesia equipment companies. Aspect has two international subsidiaries, including Aspect Medical Systems International B.V. In 2007, the sale of equipment accounted for approximately 17% of the company's revenues; the sale of BIS sensors, 78%; and strategic alliance revenues, 5%. The firm's BIS View monitoring system was recently cleared for use by the FDA.

Aspect offers its employees a comprehensive benefits package that includes medical, dental and life insurance, a 401k plan, long- and short-term disability, a flexible spending account, employee stock purchase plan and paid vacation.

## FINANCIALS:

**Sales and profits are in thousands of dollars—add 000 to get the full amount. 2008 Note: Financial information for 2008 was not available for all companies at press time.**

| | | |
|---|---|---|
| 2008 Sales: $ | 2008 Profits: $ | **U.S. Stock Ticker: ASPM** |
| 2007 Sales: $97,324 | 2007 Profits: $2,256 | **Int'l Ticker:** Int'l Exchange: |
| 2006 Sales: $91,334 | 2006 Profits: $37,089 | Employees: 285 |
| 2005 Sales: $76,995 | 2005 Profits: $8,475 | Fiscal Year Ends: 12/31 |
| 2004 Sales: $55,564 | 2004 Profits: $ 303 | Parent Company: |

## SALARIES/BENEFITS:

| | | | | |
|---|---|---|---|---|
| Pension Plan: | ESOP Stock Plan: | Profit Sharing: | Top Exec. Salary: $389,738 | Bonus: $238,211 |
| Savings Plan: Y | Stock Purch. Plan: Y | | Second Exec. Salary: $281,216 | Bonus: $215,603 |

## OTHER THOUGHTS:

**Apparent Women Officers or Directors**: 1
**Hot Spot for Advancement for Women/Minorities**:

## LOCATIONS: ("Y" = Yes)

| West: | Southwest: | Midwest: | Southeast: | Northeast: | International: |
|---|---|---|---|---|---|
| | | | | Y | Y |

# ASPEN TECHNOLOGY INC

**www.aspentec.com**

**Industry Group Code:** 511217 **Ranks within this company's industry group:** Sales: 1 Profits: 1

| Management: | | Sales/Marketing: | | Liberal Arts: | | Information Systems: | | Professionals: | | Technical/Scientific: | |
|---|---|---|---|---|---|---|---|---|---|---|---|
| Mgmt. Trainees: | | Mktg. Professionals: | Y | Gen. Writing/Editing: | | Info. Management: | Y | Finance/Accounting: | Y | Engineers, Elec.: | Y |
| Experienced Mgmt.: | Y | Retail Sales: | | Technical Writing: | Y | Software Dev.: | Y | Law: | Y | Engineers, Other: | |
| Int'l Business: | Y | Commercial/Industrial: | Y | Graphic Arts/Photog.: | | Hardware Dev.: | | HR/Other: | Y | Health/Lab: | |
| MBA Graduates: | Y | Sales Trainees: | Y | Music: | | Systems Integration: | | Training: | Y | Scientists/Research: | |
| | | Advertising Pros.: | | Broadcasting: | | Consulting/Other: | | Health Care: | | Petroleum/Chemicals: | |
| | | | | Other: | | | | Consulting: | | Math/Other: | Y |

## TYPES OF BUSINESS:

Computer Software-Manufacturing Automation
Decision Support Software
Support Services
Petroleum & Chemical Process Software

## BRANDS/DIVISIONS/AFFILIATES:

aspenONE
Aspen Dynamics
aspenONE V7
Aspen InfoPlus.21
Aspen DMCplus
Aspen PIMS
Aspen Plus
Aspen HYSYS

## CONTACTS: *Note: Officers with more than one job title may be intentionally listed here more than once.*

Mark E. Fusco, CEO
Mark E. Fusco, Pres.
Bradley T. Miller, CFO/Sr. VP
Blair Wheeler, Sr. VP-Mktg.
Joanna Nikka, Sr. VP-Human Resources
Willie K. Chan, Sr. VP-R&D
Frederic G. Hammond, General Counsel/Sr. VP
Antonio Pietri, Exec. VP-Field Oper.
Richard Packwood, Sr. VP-Bus. Dev.
Bradley T. Miller, Sr. VP-Finance
David (Woody) Woodruff, Sr. VP-Americas
Michele Triponey, Sr. VP-Global Customer Support
John W. Hague, Sr. VP-Global Accounts
Henry Lau, Sr. VP/Managing Dir.- Sales & Svcs., Asia Pacific
Stephen M. Jennings, Chmn.
Paul Taylor, Sr. VP-EMEA

| | |
|---|---|
| **Phone:** 781-221-6400 | **Fax:** 781-221-6410 |
| **Toll-Free:** | |
| **Address:** 200 Wheeler Rd., Burlington, MA 01803 US | |

## GROWTH PLANS/SPECIAL FEATURES:

Aspen Technology is a leading provider of software and services for process industries. The company's decision support software and services enable its customers to automate, integrate and optimize complex engineering, manufacturing and supply chain functions. Customers use Aspen's e-business products to automate and synchronize collaborations with suppliers, customers and other trading partners over the Internet. These products enable customers to increase their competitiveness and profitability by improving manufacturing efficiency, responsiveness and product quality. The firm is also active in process modeling and chemical engineering. Its products include Aspen HYSYS and Aspen Plus for process simulation and optimization; Aspen DMCplus for advanced process control; Aspen PIMS for advanced planning and scheduling; and Aspen InfoPlus.21 for plant information management. The company provides industry solutions under the aspenONE brand name for the oil and gas, petroleum, chemicals, special chemicals, pharmaceutical and consumer goods markets. The firm also provides customer support services and customer training for its products. Aspen has a customer base of over 1,500 process manufacturers in 60 countries, including some of the world's largest chemical companies, petroleum refineries, pharmaceutical companies and engineering and construction firms. In September 2008, the firm launched aspenONE V7, a software designed for process engineering.

Employees are offered medical, vision and dental insurance; dependent care and health care reimbursement programs; a 401(k) plan; tuition reimbursement; life insurance; short-and long-term disability coverage; auto and homeowner insurance group rates; and travel accident insurance.

## FINANCIALS: **Sales and profits are in thousands of dollars—add 000 to get the full amount. 2008 Note: Financial information for 2008 was not available for all companies at press time.**

| | | |
|---|---|---|
| 2008 Sales: $ | 2008 Profits: $ | **U.S. Stock Ticker: AZPN.PK** |
| 2007 Sales: $341,029 | 2007 Profits: $45,518 | **Int'l Ticker:** Int'l Exchange: |
| 2006 Sales: $293,148 | 2006 Profits: $12,823 | Employees: 1,291 |
| 2005 Sales: $269,994 | 2005 Profits: $-70,774 | Fiscal Year Ends: 6/30 |
| 2004 Sales: $332,446 | 2004 Profits: $-29,055 | Parent Company: |

## SALARIES/BENEFITS:

| | | | | |
|---|---|---|---|---|
| Pension Plan: | ESOP Stock Plan: | Profit Sharing: | Top Exec. Salary: $450,000 | Bonus: $850,000 |
| Savings Plan: Y | Stock Purch. Plan: | | Second Exec. Salary: $250,000 | Bonus: $239,015 |

## OTHER THOUGHTS:

**Apparent Women Officers or Directors**: 4
**Hot Spot for Advancement for Women/Minorities**: Y

## LOCATIONS: ("Y" = Yes)

| West: | Southwest: | Midwest: | Southeast: | Northeast: | International: |
|---|---|---|---|---|---|
| Y | Y | | | Y | Y |

# ASSOCIATED WHOLESALE GROCERS INC

www.awginc.com

**Industry Group Code:** 445110 **Ranks within this company's industry group:** Sales: 1 Profits:

| Management: | | Sales/Marketing: | | Liberal Arts: | | Information Systems: | | Professionals: | | Technical/Scientific: | |
|---|---|---|---|---|---|---|---|---|---|---|---|
| Mgmt. Trainees: | Y | Mktg. Professionals: | Y | Gen. Writing/Editing: | | Info. Management: | Y | Finance/Accounting: | Y | Engineers, Elec.: | |
| Experienced Mgmt.: | Y | Retail Sales: | Y | Technical Writing: | | Software Dev.: | | Law: | Y | Engineers, Other: | |
| Int'l Business: | | Commercial/Industrial: | | Graphic Arts/Photog.: | Y | Hardware Dev.: | | HR/Other: | Y | Health/Lab: | |
| MBA Graduates: | Y | Sales Trainees: | Y | Music: | | Systems Integration: | | Training: | Y | Scientists/Research: | |
| | | Advertising Pros.: | Y | Broadcasting: | | Consulting/Other: | | Health Care: | | Petroleum/Chemicals: | |
| | | | | Other: | | | | Consulting: | | Math/Other: | |

## TYPES OF BUSINESS:

Grocery Stores, Retail
In-Store Pharmacies
Bakeries
Delis
Wholesale Grocery Distribution
Retail Support Services

## BRANDS/DIVISIONS/AFFILIATES:

Country Mart
Price Chopper
Price Mart
Sun Fresh
Thriftway
Apple Market
ALPS
Valu Merchandisers Company

## CONTACTS: *Note: Officers with more than one job title may be intentionally listed here more than once.*

Gary A. Phillips, CEO
Gary A. Phillips, Pres.
Robert C. Walker, CFO/Exec. VP
Joe Busch, VP-Sales
Steve Dillard, VP-Corp. Sales Dev.
Bob Hufford, Chmn.

| | |
|---|---|
| **Phone:** 913-288-1000 | **Fax:** 913-288-1587 |
| **Toll-Free:** | |
| **Address:** 5000 Kansas Ave., Kansas City, KS 66106 US | |

## GROWTH PLANS/SPECIAL FEATURES:

Associated Wholesale Grocers, Inc. (AWG) is one of the largest grocery co-operatives in the country, supplying more than 2,300 stores located in 24 states, mostly in the Midwest and South. AWG has developed several different store concepts depending on which market area the store is located. Country Mart is a warehouse-oriented, low-price store designed for small towns and rural areas. Price Chopper and Price Mart stores are among the company's most successful concepts, with large amounts of floor space, low prices, wide variety and in-store pharmacies, seafood and poultry departments, salad bars, full-service bakeries and delis. Sun Fresh is an upscale store generally located in high-density residential areas and focused on providing high-quality fresh foods. Thriftway is meant to be a convenient neighborhood store located in small and medium-sized market areas. Apple Market stores focus on providing high-quality perishables in a warm atmosphere and large store format. Cash Saver stores attempt to combine savings without sacrificing quality in small to medium-sized markets. Finally ALPS, which stands for Always Low Price Store, offers generic products in a no-frills environment at prices 30-40% below national brands. The company also operates 30 Falley's and Food 4 Less stores in Kansas and Missouri. Valu Merchandisers Co., the company's wholesale distribution subsidiary, carries approximately 22,100 items that it sells to 2,100 customers in 22 states, and provides merchandising, promotional products and various other retail services. The firm's services division offers programs including advertising, training, print shop, store engineering, design and décor, electronic data exchange, real estate reclamation and retail systems support. In 2007, the company opened its first wireless warehouse, which ships dry grocery from the new Oklahoma City, and a 1.1 million square foot distribution center in Fort Worth, Texas.

The company offers its employees a benefits package that includes a cafeteria plan, pre-tax accounts for dependent care, a 401(k) plan, a defined-benefit retirement pension, tuition reimbursement and an employee assistance program.

## FINANCIALS: **Sales and profits are in thousands of dollars—add 000 to get the full amount. 2008 Note: Financial information for 2008 was not available for all companies at press time.**

| | | |
|---|---|---|
| 2008 Sales: $ | 2008 Profits: $ | **U.S. Stock Ticker: Private** |
| 2007 Sales: $5,700,000 | 2007 Profits: $ | **Int'l Ticker:** Int'l Exchange: |
| 2006 Sales: $4,950,000 | 2006 Profits: $ | Employees: 2,000 |
| 2005 Sales: $5,000,000 | 2005 Profits: $ | Fiscal Year Ends: 12/31 |
| 2004 Sales: $4,570,000 | 2004 Profits: $ | Parent Company: |

## SALARIES/BENEFITS:

| | | | | |
|---|---|---|---|---|
| Pension Plan: Y | ESOP Stock Plan: | Profit Sharing: | Top Exec. Salary: $507,000 | Bonus: $20,000 |
| Savings Plan: Y | Stock Purch. Plan: | | Second Exec. Salary: $201,000 | Bonus: $15,000 |

## OTHER THOUGHTS:

**Apparent Women Officers or Directors**:
**Hot Spot for Advancement for Women/Minorities**:

## LOCATIONS: ("Y" = Yes)

| West: | Southwest: | Midwest: | Southeast: | Northeast: | International: |
|---|---|---|---|---|---|
| | Y | Y | Y | Y | |

# ATHENAHEALTH INC

www.athenahealth.com

**Industry Group Code:** 522320 **Ranks within this company's industry group:** Sales: 7 Profits: 3

| **Management:** | | **Sales/Marketing:** | | **Liberal Arts:** | | **Information Systems:** | | **Professionals:** | | **Technical/Scientific:** | |
|---|---|---|---|---|---|---|---|---|---|---|---|
| Mgmt. Trainees: | Y | Mktg. Professionals: | Y | Gen. Writing/Editing: | | Info. Management: | Y | Finance/Accounting: | Y | Engineers, Elec.: | |
| Experienced Mgmt.: | Y | Retail Sales: | | Technical Writing: | Y | Software Dev.: | | Law: | Y | Engineers, Other: | |
| Int'l Business: | Y | Commercial/Industrial: | Y | Graphic Arts/Photog.: | | Hardware Dev.: | | HR/Other: | Y | Health/Lab: | |
| MBA Graduates: | Y | Sales Trainees: | Y | Music: | | Systems Integration: | Y | Training: | Y | Scientists/Research: | |
| | | Advertising Pros.: | Y | Broadcasting: | | Consulting/Other: | | Health Care: | | Petroleum/Chemicals: | |
| | | | | Other: | | | | Consulting: | | Math/Other: | |

## TYPES OF BUSINESS:

Outsourced Health Reimbursement Services
Patient Information Management
Billing & Collection Services for Health Care Providers

## BRANDS/DIVISIONS/AFFILIATES:

athenaCollector
athenaEnterprise
athenaClinicals

## CONTACTS:

*Note: Officers with more than one job title may be intentionally listed here more than once.*

Jonathan Bush, CEO
James M. MacDonald, COO/Exec. VP
Jonathan Bush, Pres.
Carl B. Byers, CFO/Sr. VP
Rob Cosinuke, Chief Mktg. Officer/Sr. VP
Leslie Locke, Sr. VP-People & Process
Daniel H. Orenstein, General Counsel/VP/Sec.
Nancy G. Brown, Sr. VP-Bus. Dev. & Gov't Affairs
Carl B. Byers, Treas.
Robert M. Hueber, Sr. VP-Sales
Todd Y. Park, Chief Athenista
Jonathan Bush, Chmn.

**Phone:** 617-402-1000 **Fax:** 617-402-1099
**Toll-Free:** 800-981-5084
**Address:** 311 Arsenal St., Watertown, MA 02472 US

## GROWTH PLANS/SPECIAL FEATURES:

Athenahealth, Inc. is a provider of Internet-based business services to physician practices and one of the largest firms in the health reimbursement field. The company offers its integrated business services over the Internet on a subscription basis. The firm offers several medical group office automation subscription services, as well as related services. athenahealth's flagship product, athenaCollector, is a revenue cycle management service that includes a management platform and automates and manages billing-related functions for physicians' practices. athenaCollector tracks, controls and executes claims and billing processes. athenaClinicals, aimed at providing a solution for the EMRs, provides a wholly integrated solution for managing the processes of providing the receiving pay for care. athenaEnterprise is an optional add-on overlay designed specifically for provider networks, integrated delivery systems and other physician enterprises. athenahealth is one of the largest firms in the health reimbursement field. It has over 775 clients in more than 30 states in the U.S., and its offices include operations in India. Over 10,000 providers are served nationwide, and about 54 medical specialties are covered. The firm manages over $2 billion in client revenues annually. Customers include The Methodist Hospital System; Ohio Health Practice Management Services; Centra Health, Professionals for Women's Health; TriHealth Physician Services; Columbus Regional Healthcare System; and Rockford Health Physicians. In September 2007, the company went public. In August 2008, athenahealth, Inc. agreed to acquire the assets of Crest Line Technologies, LLC, a privately held company that provides patient messaging services to medical groups.

## FINANCIALS:

**Sales and profits are in thousands of dollars—add 000 to get the full amount. 2008 Note: Financial information for 2008 was not available for all companies at press time.**

| | | |
|---|---|---|
| 2008 Sales: $ | 2008 Profits: $ | **U.S. Stock Ticker: ATHN** |
| 2007 Sales: $100,773 | 2007 Profits: $-3,503 | **Int'l Ticker:** Int'l Exchange: |
| 2006 Sales: $75,813 | 2006 Profits: $-9,224 | Employees: 610 |
| 2005 Sales: $55,000 | 2005 Profits: $ | Fiscal Year Ends: 12/31 |
| 2004 Sales: $39,500 | 2004 Profits: $ | Parent Company: |

## SALARIES/BENEFITS:

| | | | | |
|---|---|---|---|---|
| Pension Plan: | ESOP Stock Plan: | Profit Sharing: | Top Exec. Salary: $348,077 | Bonus: $335,000 |
| Savings Plan: | Stock Purch. Plan: | | Second Exec. Salary: $300,000 | Bonus: $161,336 |

## OTHER THOUGHTS:

**Apparent Women Officers or Directors:** 3
**Hot Spot for Advancement for Women/Minorities:** Y

## LOCATIONS: ("Y" = Yes)

| West: | Southwest: | Midwest: | Southeast: | Northeast: | International: |
|---|---|---|---|---|---|
| | | | | Y | Y |

# ATHEROS COMMUNICATIONS INC

www.atheros.com

**Industry Group Code:** 334413 **Ranks within this company's industry group:** Sales: 1 Profits: 1

| Management: | | Sales/Marketing: | | Liberal Arts: | | Information Systems: | | Professionals: | | Technical/Scientific: | |
|---|---|---|---|---|---|---|---|---|---|---|---|
| Mgmt. Trainees: | | Mktg. Professionals: | Y | Gen. Writing/Editing: | | Info. Management: | Y | Finance/Accounting: | Y | Engineers, Elec.: | Y |
| Experienced Mgmt.: | Y | Retail Sales: | | Technical Writing: | Y | Software Dev.: | Y | Law: | Y | Engineers, Other: | Y |
| Int'l Business: | Y | Commercial/Industrial: | Y | Graphic Arts/Photog.: | | Hardware Dev.: | Y | HR/Other: | Y | Health/Lab: | |
| MBA Graduates: | Y | Sales Trainees: | Y | Music: | | Systems Integration: | Y | Training: | Y | Scientists/Research: | Y |
| | | Advertising Pros.: | | Broadcasting: | | Consulting/Other: | | Health Care: | | Petroleum/Chemicals: | |
| | | | | Other: | | | | Consulting: | | Math/Other: | Y |

## TYPES OF BUSINESS:

Wireless Chip Manufacturing
Semiconductor Systems

## BRANDS/DIVISIONS/AFFILIATES:

Super G
Super AG
eXtended Range
VLocity Video
VLocity MIMO
MIMO-G

## CONTACTS:

*Note: Officers with more than one job title may be intentionally listed here more than once.*

Craig H. Barratt, CEO
Craig H. Barratt, Pres.
Jack R. Lazar, CFO
Todd D. Antes, VP-Mktg.
Edward L. Martin, VP-Global Human Resources
William J. McFarland, CTO
Richard G. Bahr, VP-Eng.
Adam H. Tachner, General Counsel/VP
Paul G. Franklin, VP-Oper.
Jack R. Lazar, VP-Corp. Dev.
David D. Torre, Chief Acct. Officer/VP
Sam Endy, VP/Gen. Mgr.-Mobile Wireless Bus. Unit
Ali Hariri, VP-Bus. Dev.
Ben Naskar, VP/Gen. Mgr.-Wireless Networking Bus. Unit
Gary L. Szilagyi, VP-Worldwide Sales
John L. Hennessy, Chmn.

**Phone:** 408-773-5200 **Fax:** 408-773-9940
**Toll-Free:**
**Address:** 5480 Great America Pkwy., Santa Clara, CA 95054 US

## GROWTH PLANS/SPECIAL FEATURES:

Atheros Communications, Inc. develops semiconductor system solutions for wireless communications products such as computing and networking equipment, digital entertainment, broadband access and mobile devices. It combines its wireless systems expertise with high-performance radio frequency (RF), mixed-signal and digital semiconductor design to create integrated chipsets for complementary metal-oxide semiconductor (CMOS) processes. The company also provides a portfolio of products that range from entry-level wireless networking products for homes and small offices to sophisticated wireless infrastructure systems-on-a-chip with advanced network management capabilities for the enterprise market. These wireless system solutions are used in a variety of applications in the personal computer (PC), enterprise access, small office and branch office networking, home networking, hotspot, wireless broadband, voice, mobile computing devices and consumer electronics markets. Atheros currently provides five types of semiconductors: Radio-on-a-chip, MAC + broadband, stand-alone network processing unit, wireless system-on-a-chip and single chip solutions. The company's chipsets can be incorporated into WLAN devices to provide end users extended range, longer battery life and network management tools that reduce the overall cost of operating wireless networks. The firm's trademarks include Super G, Super AG, eXtended Range, MIMO-G, MIMO-AG, VLocity MIMO and VLocity Video. Primary consumer electronic and networking equipment customers include Philips; Samsung; Sony; Cisco Systems; D-Link; Linksys; and Nortel Networks. PC OEM customers include Hewlett-Packard; IBM; NEC; and Toshiba. In December 2007, Atheros agreed to acquire certain assets of u-Nav Microelectronics, a private fabless semiconductor company.

## FINANCIALS:

**Sales and profits are in thousands of dollars—add 000 to get the full amount. 2008 Note: Financial information for 2008 was not available for all companies at press time.**

| | | |
|---|---|---|
| 2008 Sales: $ | 2008 Profits: $ | **U.S. Stock Ticker: ATHR** |
| 2007 Sales: $416,960 | 2007 Profits: $39,980 | **Int'l Ticker:** Int'l Exchange: |
| 2006 Sales: $301,691 | 2006 Profits: $18,678 | Employees: 878 |
| 2005 Sales: $183,485 | 2005 Profits: $16,688 | Fiscal Year Ends: 12/31 |
| 2004 Sales: $169,607 | 2004 Profits: $10,824 | Parent Company: |

## SALARIES/BENEFITS:

| | | | | |
|---|---|---|---|---|
| Pension Plan: | ESOP Stock Plan: | Profit Sharing: | Top Exec. Salary: $310,000 | Bonus: $297,600 |
| Savings Plan: | Stock Purch. Plan: | | Second Exec. Salary: $280,000 | Bonus: $149,800 |

## OTHER THOUGHTS:

**Apparent Women Officers or Directors**: 2
**Hot Spot for Advancement for Women/Minorities**: Y

## LOCATIONS: ("Y" = Yes)

| West: | Southwest: | Midwest: | Southeast: | Northeast: | International: |
|---|---|---|---|---|---|
| Y | | | | | Y |

# ATLANTIC CITY ELECTRIC COMPANY

www.atlanticcityelectric.com

**Industry Group Code:** 221000 **Ranks within this company's industry group:** Sales: 3 Profits: 3

| Management: | | Sales/Marketing: | | Liberal Arts: | | Information Systems: | | Professionals: | | Technical/Scientific: | |
|---|---|---|---|---|---|---|---|---|---|---|---|
| Mgmt. Trainees: | | Mktg. Professionals: | Y | Gen. Writing/Editing: | | Info. Management: | Y | Finance/Accounting: | Y | Engineers, Elec.: | Y |
| Experienced Mgmt.: | Y | Retail Sales: | | Technical Writing: | | Software Dev.: | | Law: | Y | Engineers, Other: | Y |
| Int'l Business: | | Commercial/Industrial: | Y | Graphic Arts/Photog.: | | Hardware Dev.: | | HR/Other: | Y | Health/Lab: | |
| MBA Graduates: | Y | Sales Trainees: | | Music: | | Systems Integration: | | Training: | Y | Scientists/Research: | |
| | | Advertising Pros.: | | Broadcasting: | | Consulting/Other: | | Health Care: | | Petroleum/Chemicals: | Y |
| | | | | Other: | | | | Consulting: | | Math/Other: | |

## TYPES OF BUSINESS:

Utilities-Electricity

## BRANDS/DIVISIONS/AFFILIATES:

Pepco Holdings Inc
Conectiv

## CONTACTS:

*Note: Officers with more than one job title may be intentionally listed here more than once.*

Kenneth J. Parker, Pres.
Joseph M. Rigby, Exec. VP/COO-Pepco Holdings, Inc.
Dennis R. Wraase, Pres./CEO-Pepco Holdings, Inc.

**Phone:** 202-872-2000 **Fax:** 202-283-6090
**Toll-Free:** 800-642-3780
**Address:** 5100 Harding Hwy., Mays Landing, NJ 08330 US

## GROWTH PLANS/SPECIAL FEATURES:

Atlantic City Electric Company (ACE), a subsidiary of Pepco Holdings, Inc., is an electrical utility engaged in the transmission and distribution of electricity. The firm's primary service area service area consists of Gloucester, Camden, Burlington, Ocean, Atlantic, Cape May, and Cumberland and Salem counties in southern New Jersey. This service area provides electrical service to 544,000 customers in a 2,700 square mile region. Atlantic City Electric maintains a distribution network consisting of more than 11,000 miles of transmission and distribution lines. In 2007, ACE delivered a total of 10,187,000 megawatt hours of electricity to its customers. Of this, 44% was delivered to residential customers, 44% to commercial customers and 12% to industrial customers. In February 2007, ACE sold the B.L. England generating facility to RC Cape May Holdings, LLC for $9 million. This sale completes the firm's divestiture of its own generating facilities. ACE now relies entirely on purchases from third-party electrical sources.

Atlantic City Electric offers a range of employee benefits, including medical, dental and vision packages; life and disability coverage; healthcare and dependent care reimbursement accounts; transportation reimbursement accounts; a 401(k) retirement savings plan; and tuition reimbursement.

## FINANCIALS:

**Sales and profits are in thousands of dollars—add 000 to get the full amount. 2008 Note: Financial information for 2008 was not available for all companies at press time.**

2008 Sales: $
2007 Sales: $1,542,500
2006 Sales: $1,373,300
2005 Sales: $1,350,100
2004 Sales: $

2008 Profits: $
2007 Profits: $60,100
2006 Profits: $62,700
2005 Profits: $63,200
2004 Profits: $

**U.S. Stock Ticker: Subsidiary**
**Int'l Ticker:** Int'l Exchange:
Employees: 507
Fiscal Year Ends: 12/31
Parent Company: PEPCO HOLDINGS INC

## SALARIES/BENEFITS:

Pension Plan:
Savings Plan: Y
ESOP Stock Plan:
Stock Purch. Plan:
Profit Sharing:
Top Exec. Salary: $
Second Exec. Salary: $
Bonus: $
Bonus: $

## OTHER THOUGHTS:

**Apparent Women Officers or Directors:**
**Hot Spot for Advancement for Women/Minorities:**

## LOCATIONS: ("Y" = Yes)

| West: | Southwest: | Midwest: | Southeast: | Northeast: | International: |
|---|---|---|---|---|---|
| | | | | Y | |

# ATMI INC

www.atmi.com

**Industry Group Code:** 333295 **Ranks within this company's industry group:** Sales: 1 Profits: 1

| Management: | | Sales/Marketing: | | Liberal Arts: | | Information Systems: | | Professionals: | | Technical/Scientific: | |
|---|---|---|---|---|---|---|---|---|---|---|---|
| Mgmt. Trainees: | | Mktg. Professionals: | Y | Gen. Writing/Editing: | | Info. Management: | Y | Finance/Accounting: | Y | Engineers, Elec.: | Y |
| Experienced Mgmt.: | Y | Retail Sales: | | Technical Writing: | Y | Software Dev.: | | Law: | Y | Engineers, Other: | Y |
| Int'l Business: | Y | Commercial/Industrial: | Y | Graphic Arts/Photog.: | | Hardware Dev.: | Y | HR/Other: | Y | Health/Lab: | |
| MBA Graduates: | Y | Sales Trainees: | Y | Music: | | Systems Integration: | | Training: | Y | Scientists/Research: | |
| | | Advertising Pros.: | | Broadcasting: | | Consulting/Other: | | Health Care: | | Petroleum/Chemicals: | |
| | | | | Other: | | | | Consulting: | | Math/Other: | |

## TYPES OF BUSINESS:

Equipment-Semiconductor Manufacturing
Semiconductor Materials
Materials Packaging & Delivery Systems
Outsourced Services
Research & Development

## BRANDS/DIVISIONS/AFFILIATES:

Safe Delivery Source (SDS)
AP
ST
Anji Microelectronics
LevTech Inc

## CONTACTS: *Note: Officers with more than one job title may be intentionally listed here more than once.*

Doug Neugold, CEO
Doug Neugold, Pres.
Tim Carlson, CFO/Exec. VP
Steven Curtis, Sr. VP-Sales
Tom McGowan, VP-Human Resources
Kevin Laing, CIO/VP
Larry Dubois, CTO/Sr. VP
Ellen Harmon, Chief Legal Officer/Exec. VP/Sec.
Paul Hohlstein, Sr. VP-Oper.
Dan Sharkey, Exec. VP-Bus. Dev.
Tim Carlson, Treas.
Tod Higinbotham, Exec. VP-Process Solutions
Gene Banucci, Chmn.
Paul Hohlstein, Sr. VP-Supply Chain

| | |
|---|---|
| **Phone:** 203-794-1100 | **Fax:** |
| **Toll-Free:** 800-766-2681 | |
| **Address:** 7 Commerce Dr., Danbury, CT 06810 US | |

## GROWTH PLANS/SPECIAL FEATURES:

ATMI, Inc. provides materials, materials packaging and materials delivery systems for semiconductor and flat panel manufacturing. It specifically targets the front-end semiconductor materials market, which includes the processes used to convert a bare silicon wafer into a fully functional wafer that contains many copies of a semiconductor device or chip. Products created using the firm's materials are used in the information technology, automotive, life sciences, communications and consumer products industries. The company provides a broad range of ultra-high-purity semiconductor materials and semiconductor materials packaging and delivery systems. Notable products include the Safe Delivery Source (SDS) product line, which uses absorbent materials for the transport of highly pressurized gases used in semiconductor manufacturing, and the AP and ST brands of wafer cleaning materials. ATMI also conducts venture activities and government-funded research and development. ATMI recently sold the last of its technology businesses to Applied Materials, the leading supplier of equipment and services to the global semiconductor industry. The firm holds a minority interest in Shanghai-based Anji Microelectronics, a developer of semiconductor materials; the two companies share resources and efforts in the development and marketing of their products. The company owns six facilities in the U.S., as well as locations in China, Japan, Singapore, South Korea, Taiwan, Belgium and Germany. ATMI plans to continue its growth through product line expansion and by leveraging its core technology to create new high growth product lines, including growing its leadership position in advanced interconnect applications. In January 2008, the company acquired LevTech, Inc., a provider of disposable mixing technologies to the biotechnology and pharmaceuticals market. In December of the same year, ATMI acquired assets related to Nucleo, a single-use bioreactor and jet drive, from Artelis SA.

Employees are offered medical insurance; short-and long-term disability coverage; education assistance plans; adoption assistance; and employee assistance plans.

## FINANCIALS: **Sales and profits are in thousands of dollars—add 000 to get the full amount. 2008 Note: Financial information for 2008 was not available for all companies at press time.**

| | | |
|---|---|---|
| 2008 Sales: $ | 2008 Profits: $ | **U.S. Stock Ticker: ATMI** |
| 2007 Sales: $364,088 | 2007 Profits: $40,359 | **Int'l Ticker:** Int'l Exchange: |
| 2006 Sales: $325,913 | 2006 Profits: $39,961 | Employees: 809 |
| 2005 Sales: $281,754 | 2005 Profits: $30,722 | Fiscal Year Ends: 12/31 |
| 2004 Sales: $246,291 | 2004 Profits: $31,502 | Parent Company: |

## SALARIES/BENEFITS:

| | | | | |
|---|---|---|---|---|
| Pension Plan: | ESOP Stock Plan: | Profit Sharing: Y | Top Exec. Salary: $493,269 | Bonus: $250,921 |
| Savings Plan: Y | Stock Purch. Plan: Y | | Second Exec. Salary: $302,577 | Bonus: $149,335 |

## OTHER THOUGHTS:

**Apparent Women Officers or Directors:** 2
**Hot Spot for Advancement for Women/Minorities:**

## LOCATIONS: ("Y" = Yes)

| West: | Southwest: | Midwest: | Southeast: | Northeast: | International: |
|---|---|---|---|---|---|
| | Y | Y | | Y | Y |

Note: Financial information, benefits and other data can change quickly and may vary from those stated here.

# ATRION CORPORATION

www.atrioncorp.com

**Industry Group Code:** 339113 **Ranks within this company's industry group:** Sales: 31 Profits: 15

| Management: | | Sales/Marketing: | | Liberal Arts: | | Information Systems: | | Professionals: | | Technical/Scientific: | |
|---|---|---|---|---|---|---|---|---|---|---|---|
| Mgmt. Trainees: | | Mktg. Professionals: | Y | Gen. Writing/Editing: | | Info. Management: | Y | Finance/Accounting: | Y | Engineers, Elec.: | Y |
| Experienced Mgmt.: | Y | Retail Sales: | | Technical Writing: | Y | Software Dev.: | Y | Law: | Y | Engineers, Other: | Y |
| Int'l Business: | Y | Commercial/Industrial: | Y | Graphic Arts/Photog.: | | Hardware Dev.: | Y | HR/Other: | Y | Health/Lab: | Y |
| MBA Graduates: | Y | Sales Trainees: | Y | Music: | | Systems Integration: | Y | Training: | Y | Scientists/Research: | Y |
| | | Advertising Pros.: | | Broadcasting: | | Consulting/Other: | | Health Care: | Y | Petroleum/Chemicals: | |
| | | | | Other: | | | | Consulting: | | Math/Other: | Y |

## TYPES OF BUSINESS:

Equipment-Ophthalmic, Diagnostic & Cardiovascular
Fluid Delivery Devices
Medical Device Components
Contract Manufacturing

## BRANDS/DIVISIONS/AFFILIATES:

Quest Medical, Inc.
MPS2 Myocardial Protection System
Halkey-Roberts Corporation
LacriCATH
Atrion Medical Products, Inc.
ACTester

## CONTACTS: *Note: Officers with more than one job title may be intentionally listed here more than once.*

Emile A. Battat, CEO
David A. Battat, COO
David A. Battat, Pres.
Jeffery Strickland, CFO
Jeffery Strickland, Sec./VP
Jeffery Strickland, Treas.
Emile A. Battat, Chmn.

| | |
|---|---|
| **Phone:** 972-390-9800 | **Fax:** 972-396-7581 |
| **Toll-Free:** | |
| **Address:** One Allentown Pkwy., Allen, TX 75002-4211 US | |

## GROWTH PLANS/SPECIAL FEATURES:

Atrion Corporation designs, develops, manufactures, markets, sells and distributes products for the medical and health care industries. The company sells components to other equipment manufacturers and finished products to physicians, hospitals, clinics and other treatment centers. The firm's cardiovascular products, which accounted for 27% of its 2007 revenues, are manufactured by subsidiary Quest Medical, Inc. They include cardiac surgery vacuum relief valves and other tools used in cardiac surgery, such as the MPS2 Myocardial Protection System, a proprietary system used for the delivery of solutions to the heart during open-heart surgery, mixing drugs into the bloodstream without diluting the blood. Subsidiary Halkey-Roberts Corporation is responsible for designing, developing, manufacturing and selling Atrion's fluid delivery products (32% of 2007 revenue) such as intravenous fluid delivery lines, medical tubing clamps and various valves. Atrion's ophthalmic products (20% of 2007 revenue) include soft contact lens storage and disinfection cases and the LacriCATH line of balloon catheters; and it also provides custom packaging, warehousing and inventory management as part of its pharmaceutical reselling business. The company's other medical and non-medical products, many of which are manufactured by subsidiary Atrion Medical Products, Inc.; include the manufacturing of inflation devices, right angle connectors and closures for life rafts and other inflatable structures. These accounted for 21% of 2007 revenue. Some of its non-medical valves include those for use on electronics or munitions cases; pressure vessels; transportation container cases, the ACTester line of tests, measuring blood clotting time; and safe needle and scalpel blade containment products. Atrion also owns a 22-mile pipeline in Alabama that is leased to an industrial gas producer to transport gaseous oxygen.

Atrion provides medical, dental and life insurance; prescription drug plans; retirement plans; paid holidays and vacations; and short and long-term disability benefits.

## FINANCIALS: Sales and profits are in thousands of dollars—add 000 to get the full amount. 2008 Note: Financial information for 2008 was not available for all companies at press time.

| | | |
|---|---|---|
| 2008 Sales: $ | 2008 Profits: $ | **U.S. Stock Ticker: ATRI** |
| 2007 Sales: $88,540 | 2007 Profits: $14,006 | **Int'l Ticker:** Int'l Exchange: |
| 2006 Sales: $81,020 | 2006 Profits: $10,765 | Employees: 492 |
| 2005 Sales: $72,089 | 2005 Profits: $8,958 | Fiscal Year Ends: 12/31 |
| 2004 Sales: $66,081 | 2004 Profits: $6,470 | Parent Company: |

## SALARIES/BENEFITS:

| | | | | |
|---|---|---|---|---|
| Pension Plan: Y | ESOP Stock Plan: | Profit Sharing: | Top Exec. Salary: $500,000 | Bonus: $411,195 |
| Savings Plan: | Stock Purch. Plan: | | Second Exec. Salary: $200,000 | Bonus: $100,000 |

## OTHER THOUGHTS:

**Apparent Women Officers or Directors:**
**Hot Spot for Advancement for Women/Minorities:**

## LOCATIONS: ("Y" = Yes)

| West: | Southwest: | Midwest: | Southeast: | Northeast: | International: |
|---|---|---|---|---|---|
| | Y | | Y | | |

# ATS MEDICAL INC

www.atsmedical.com

**Industry Group Code:** 339113 **Ranks within this company's industry group:** Sales: 42 Profits: 41

| Management: | | Sales/Marketing: | | Liberal Arts: | | Information Systems: | | Professionals: | | Technical/Scientific: | |
|---|---|---|---|---|---|---|---|---|---|---|---|
| Mgmt. Trainees: | | Mktg. Professionals: | Y | Gen. Writing/Editing: | | Info. Management: | Y | Finance/Accounting: | Y | Engineers, Elec.: | Y |
| Experienced Mgmt.: | Y | Retail Sales: | | Technical Writing: | Y | Software Dev.: | | Law: | Y | Engineers, Other: | Y |
| Int'l Business: | Y | Commercial/Industrial: | Y | Graphic Arts/Photog.: | | Hardware Dev.: | | HR/Other: | Y | Health/Lab: | Y |
| MBA Graduates: | Y | Sales Trainees: | Y | Music: | | Systems Integration: | Y | Training: | Y | Scientists/Research: | Y |
| | | Advertising Pros.: | | Broadcasting: | | Consulting/Other: | | Health Care: | Y | Petroleum/Chemicals: | |
| | | | | Other: | | | | Consulting: | | Math/Other: | Y |

## TYPES OF BUSINESS:

Equipment-Mechanical Heart Valves
Grafts & Prostheses
Cardiovascular Accessories
Surgical Cryotherapy Products

## BRANDS/DIVISIONS/AFFILIATES:

ATS Open Pivot
3F Therapeutics
3F Therapeutics, Inc.,
ATS CryoMaze
ATS Medical Sales Inc
ATS Medical France, SARL
ATS Simulus
ATS 3F Aortic Bioprosthesis

## CONTACTS: *Note: Officers with more than one job title may be intentionally listed here more than once.*

Michael D. Dale, CEO
Michael D. Dale, Pres.
Michael Kramer, CFO
Thad Coffindaffer, VP-Sales
David R. Elizondo, VP-R&D & Clinical Affairs
Craig Swandal, VP-Oper.
Richard A. Curtis, VP-Bus. Dev.
Marc R. Sportsman, VP-Sales
Astrid M. Berthe, VP-Regulatory Affairs & Quality Assurance
Michael D. Dale, Chmn.
Jeremy Curtis, VP-Worldwide Mktg.

**Phone:** 763-553-7736 **Fax:** 763-557-2244
**Toll-Free:** 800-399-1381
**Address:** 3905 Annapolis Ln., Ste. 105, Minneapolis, MN 55447 US

## GROWTH PLANS/SPECIAL FEATURES:

ATS Medical, Inc. develops, manufactures, and markets medical devices for the treatment of structural heart disease. Product offerings are focused on heart valve therapy and the surgical treatment of cardiac arrhythmias. The company has four product lines: mechanical heart walves, surgical treatment of atrial fibrillation, heart valve repair and tissue heart valves. Some of ATS Medical's core products include the ATS Open Pivot Heart Valve, ATS CryoMaze Surgical Ablation products, ATS Simulus Flexible annuloplasty repair rings and bands and the ATS 3F Aortic Bioprosthesis tissue heart valve. The firm sells its products through an independent distribution network in all of its international markets except France, where it has a direct sales organization. Sales of mechanical heart valves represented approximately 72% of revenue in 2007. The marketing and sales of the firm's new non-mechanical valve products have grown to roughly 28% of total revenue in 2007. In December 2007, the FDA approved the company's new heart valve product, Open Pivot AP360. In 2007, the company acquired the surgical cryoablation business of CryoCath Technologies. In August 2008, ATS Medical received authorization to market its ATS CryoMaze cardiac ablation products in the E.U.

The company offers its employees health coverage, flexible spending accounts, educational assistance and health club reimbursement.

## FINANCIALS: Sales and profits are in thousands of dollars—add 000 to get the full amount. 2008 Note: Financial information for 2008 was not available for all companies at press time.

| | | |
|---|---|---|
| 2008 Sales: $ | 2008 Profits: $ | **U.S. Stock Ticker: ATSI** |
| 2007 Sales: $49,587 | 2007 Profits: $-23,008 | **Int'l Ticker:** Int'l Exchange: |
| 2006 Sales: $40,449 | 2006 Profits: $-27,674 | Employees: 245 |
| 2005 Sales: $34,636 | 2005 Profits: $-14,394 | Fiscal Year Ends: 12/31 |
| 2004 Sales: $28,015 | 2004 Profits: $-16,643 | Parent Company: |

## SALARIES/BENEFITS:

| | | | | |
|---|---|---|---|---|
| Pension Plan: | ESOP Stock Plan: | Profit Sharing: | Top Exec. Salary: $350,000 | Bonus: $ |
| Savings Plan: Y | Stock Purch. Plan: Y | | Second Exec. Salary: $205,000 | Bonus: $ |

## OTHER THOUGHTS:

**Apparent Women Officers or Directors**: 1
**Hot Spot for Advancement for Women/Minorities**:

## LOCATIONS: ("Y" = Yes)

| West: | Southwest: | Midwest: | Southeast: | Northeast: | International: |
|---|---|---|---|---|---|
| Y | | Y | | | Y |

# AUDIBLE INC

**www.audible.com**

**Industry Group Code:** 451220E **Ranks within this company's industry group:** Sales: 1 Profits: 1

| Management: | | Sales/Marketing: | | Liberal Arts: | | Information Systems: | | Professionals: | | Technical/Scientific: | |
|---|---|---|---|---|---|---|---|---|---|---|---|
| Mgmt. Trainees: | Y | Mktg. Professionals: | Y | Gen. Writing/Editing: | Y | Info. Management: | Y | Finance/Accounting: | Y | Engineers, Elec.: | |
| Experienced Mgmt.: | Y | Retail Sales: | Y | Technical Writing: | | Software Dev.: | Y | Law: | Y | Engineers, Other: | |
| Int'l Business: | Y | Commercial/Industrial: | | Graphic Arts/Photog.: | Y | Hardware Dev.: | | HR/Other: | Y | Health/Lab: | |
| MBA Graduates: | Y | Sales Trainees: | Y | Music: | | Systems Integration: | | Training: | Y | Scientists/Research: | |
| | | Advertising Pros.: | Y | Broadcasting: | | Consulting/Other: | | Health Care: | | Petroleum/Chemicals: | |
| | | | | Other: | | | | Consulting: | | Math/Other: | |

## TYPES OF BUSINESS:

Audio Books-Online Sales
Audio Programming Software
Time-Shifted Radio Programming
Digital Audio Players
Educational Audio Materials

## BRANDS/DIVISIONS/AFFILIATES:

Amazon.com Inc
Audible.com
AudibleListener

## CONTACTS: *Note: Officers with more than one job title may be intentionally listed here more than once.*

Donald R. Katz, CEO
William H. Mitchell, CFO
Guy A. Story, Jr., Chief Scientist
Helene Godin, Corp. Counsel
Brian M. Fielding, Exec. VP-Bus. Dev.
Beth Anderson, Sr. VP/Publisher
Will Lopes, VP-Customer Experience
Foy C. Sperring, Jr., VP-Customer Acquisition
Donald R. Katz, Chmn.

| **Phone:** 973-820-0400 | **Fax:** |
|---|---|
| **Toll-Free:** | |
| **Address:** 1 Washington Park, 16th Fl., Newark, NJ 07102 US | |

## GROWTH PLANS/SPECIAL FEATURES:

Audible, Inc. provides Internet-delivered premium spoken audio content for playback on personal computers and mobile devices. The company offers a variety of software systems and audio programming software designed to download, store and play between two and 24 hours of content from its online store, audible.com. Audible sells a wide array of audio content, including educational materials, humor, periodicals, fiction, nonfiction and time-shifted radio programming comprised of 50,000 different programs and 700 content providers. The company has several AudibleListener membership plans which provide a 30% discount of individual content purchases, exposure to periodic sales and member-only free content offerings for an annual membership fee. The company also has partnerships with leading audiobook, magazine and newspaper publishers, as well as broadcasters, business information providers and educational and cultural institutions. Audible.com features daily selected audio content from The Wall Street Journal and The New York Times, both available on a subscription basis in time for the morning drive to work each day. Other publications offered include Fast Company, Forbes, Harvard Business Review and Scientific American. In addition, the site offers a large collection of audiobook bestsellers and classics by authors such as Stephen King, James Patterson, William Shakespeare and Jane Austen, as well as speeches, lectures and on-demand radio programs. Around 45,000 titles are available for purchase on U.S. and U.K. web sites and related part websites in Germany and France have 45,000 programs. In 2008, the company was acquired by Amazon.com.

Employees are offered health insurance; a 401(k) savings plan; and a stock ownership program.

## FINANCIALS: **Sales and profits are in thousands of dollars—add 000 to get the full amount. 2008 Note: Financial information for 2008 was not available for all companies at press time.**

| | | |
|---|---|---|
| 2008 Sales: $ | 2008 Profits: $ | **U.S. Stock Ticker: Subsidiary** |
| 2007 Sales: $109,968 | 2007 Profits: $2,425 | **Int'l Ticker:** Int'l Exchange: |
| 2006 Sales: $82,032 | 2006 Profits: $-8,680 | Employees: 172 |
| 2005 Sales: $63,237 | 2005 Profits: $- 653 | Fiscal Year Ends: 12/31 |
| 2004 Sales: $34,319 | 2004 Profits: $2,077 | Parent Company: AMAZON.COM INC |

## SALARIES/BENEFITS:

| | | | | |
|---|---|---|---|---|
| Pension Plan: | ESOP Stock Plan: Y | Profit Sharing: | Top Exec. Salary: $292,808 | Bonus: $222,000 |
| Savings Plan: Y | Stock Purch. Plan: | | Second Exec. Salary: $263,607 | Bonus: $135,000 |

## OTHER THOUGHTS:

**Apparent Women Officers or Directors**: 2
**Hot Spot for Advancement for Women/Minorities**: Y

## LOCATIONS: ("Y" = Yes)

| West: | Southwest: | Midwest: | Southeast: | Northeast: | International: |
|---|---|---|---|---|---|
| | | | | Y | Y |

Note: Financial information, benefits and other data can change quickly and may vary from those stated here.

# AVANEX CORPORATION

www.avanex.com

**Industry Group Code:** 334210 **Ranks within this company's industry group:** Sales: 6 Profits: 11

| Management: | | Sales/Marketing: | | Liberal Arts: | | Information Systems: | | Professionals: | | Technical/Scientific: | |
|---|---|---|---|---|---|---|---|---|---|---|---|
| Mgmt. Trainees: | | Mktg. Professionals: | Y | Gen. Writing/Editing: | Y | Info. Management: | Y | Finance/Accounting: | Y | Engineers, Elec.: | Y |
| Experienced Mgmt.: | Y | Retail Sales: | | Technical Writing: | Y | Software Dev.: | Y | Law: | Y | Engineers, Other: | Y |
| Int'l Business: | Y | Commercial/Industrial: | Y | Graphic Arts/Photog.: | | Hardware Dev.: | Y | HR/Other: | Y | Health/Lab: | |
| MBA Graduates: | Y | Sales Trainees: | Y | Music: | | Systems Integration: | Y | Training: | Y | Scientists/Research: | |
| | | Advertising Pros.: | | Broadcasting: | | Consulting/Other: | | Health Care: | | Petroleum/Chemicals: | |
| | | | | Other: | | | | Consulting: | | Math/Other: | |

## TYPES OF BUSINESS:

Fiber-Optic Systems
Photonic Processing Equipment

## BRANDS/DIVISIONS/AFFILIATES:

PowerFilter
PowerMux
PowerShaper
PowerExchanger
PowerFlex
PowerEqualizer
PowerBlocker
PowerSource

## CONTACTS: *Note: Officers with more than one job title may be intentionally listed here more than once.*

Giovanni Barbarossa, Interim CEO
Giovanni Barbarossa, Interim Pres.
Scott Parker, Sr. VP-Sales
Ken E. Johnson, VP-Human Resources
Giovanni Barbarossa, CTO/Sr. VP
Bradley Kolb, Sr. VP-Oper.
Patrick Edsell, Sr. VP/General Mgr.
Paul Smith, Chmn.

**Phone:** 510-897-4188 **Fax:** 510-897-4189
**Toll-Free:**
**Address:** 40919 Encyclopedia Cir., Fremont, CA 94538 US

## GROWTH PLANS/SPECIAL FEATURES:

Avanex Corporation is a global provider of intelligent photonic processing solutions that enable optical communications networks to achieve next-generation performance. Telecommunications system integrators and their network carrier customers use Avanex's fiber-optic products to add greater capacity, longer-distance transmissions, improved connectivity, higher speeds and lower costs. These systems increase the number of wavelengths of light that can travel on optical networks and extend the distance an optical signal can travel without electrical regeneration. Avanex's products consist of six product families: Transmission/Lithium Niobate Modulators; Multiplexing and Signal Processing/Optical Interfaces; Amplification; Network Managed Subsystems; Switching and Routing/Micro-Optics; and Integrated Modules and Dispersion Compensation. The company's transmission products include PowerFlex, PowerReach and PowerPort optical interfaces; and PowerLog analog external modulators. Avanex's optical wavelength multiplexing and signal processing products include PowerFilter thin film filters, PowerBragg fiber-based filters and stabilizers, the PowerMux NxG interleaver and PowerEqualizer dynamic gain equalizers. The firm's amplification products include PureGain amplifiers with and without integrated electronics. Avanex's network-managed subsystems products include PowerExpress network-ready EDFA; PowerWatcher network-ready optical channel monitors and PowerNode channel monitors; switching modules; and EDFA modules. The firm's switching and routing products include PowerExchanger fixed optical add/drop modules; balanced and fixed OADM; and PowerBlocker dynamic wavelength blockers. Avanex's dispersion compensation products include PowerForm fibers, bands and modules; and PowerShaper compensators and simulators. The company owns five facilities around the world, in Erwin Park, New York; Fremont, California; Nozay, France; Bangkok, Thailand and San Donato, Italy. In March 2007, Avanex sold 90% of its French subsidiary to 3S Photonics. In June 2007, Avanex acquired assets from the Essex Corporation relating to the transponder and transceiver businesses, in an effort to expand its transmission product portfolio.

Avanex offers it employees medical, dental, and vision care.

## FINANCIALS: **Sales and profits are in thousands of dollars—add 000 to get the full amount. 2008 Note: Financial information for 2008 was not available for all companies at press time.**

| | | |
|---|---|---|
| 2008 Sales: $208,094 | 2008 Profits: $4,720 | **U.S. Stock Ticker: AVNX** |
| 2007 Sales: $212,755 | 2007 Profits: $-30,605 | **Int'l Ticker:** Int'l Exchange: |
| 2006 Sales: $162,944 | 2006 Profits: $-54,692 | Employees: 576 |
| 2005 Sales: $160,695 | 2005 Profits: $-108,371 | Fiscal Year Ends: 6/30 |
| 2004 Sales: $106,900 | 2004 Profits: $-124,100 | Parent Company: |

## SALARIES/BENEFITS:

| | | | | |
|---|---|---|---|---|
| Pension Plan: | ESOP Stock Plan: | Profit Sharing: | Top Exec. Salary: $366,057 | Bonus: $ |
| Savings Plan: Y | Stock Purch. Plan: Y | | Second Exec. Salary: $283,300 | Bonus: $ |

## OTHER THOUGHTS:

**Apparent Women Officers or Directors**:
**Hot Spot for Advancement for Women/Minorities**: Y

## LOCATIONS: ("Y" = Yes)

| West: | Southwest: | Midwest: | Southeast: | Northeast: | International: |
|---|---|---|---|---|---|
| Y | | | Y | Y | Y |

Note: Financial information, benefits and other data can change quickly and may vary from those stated here.

# AVI BIOPHARMA INC

**www.avibio.com**

**Industry Group Code:** 325412 **Ranks within this company's industry group:** Sales: 37 Profits: 20

| **Management:** | | **Sales/Marketing:** | | **Liberal Arts:** | | **Information Systems:** | | **Professionals:** | | **Technical/Scientific:** | |
|---|---|---|---|---|---|---|---|---|---|---|---|
| Mgmt. Trainees: | | Mktg. Professionals: | Y | Gen. Writing/Editing: | | Info. Management: | Y | Finance/Accounting: | Y | Engineers, Elec.: | |
| Experienced Mgmt.: | Y | Retail Sales: | | Technical Writing: | Y | Software Dev.: | Y | Law: | Y | Engineers, Other: | |
| Int'l Business: | | Commercial/Industrial: | Y | Graphic Arts/Photog.: | | Hardware Dev.: | | HR/Other: | Y | Health/Lab: | Y |
| MBA Graduates: | Y | Sales Trainees: | Y | Music: | | Systems Integration: | | Training: | Y | Scientists/Research: | Y |
| | | Advertising Pros.: | | Broadcasting: | | Consulting/Other: | | Health Care: | Y | Petroleum/Chemicals: | |
| | | | | Other: | | | | Consulting: | | Math/Other: | Y |

## TYPES OF BUSINESS:

Gene-Targeted Pharmaceuticals
Drugs - Cardiovascular Disease
Drugs - Cancer
Drugs - Infectious Disease

## BRANDS/DIVISIONS/AFFILIATES:

NeuGene
Resten-NG
Resten-CP
Ercole Biotechnology Inc

## CONTACTS:

*Note: Officers with more than one job title may be intentionally listed here more than once.*

Leslie Hudson, CEO
Alan P. Timmins, COO
Alan P. Timmins, Pres.
J. David Boyle II, CFO/Sr. VP
Ryszard Kole, Sr. VP-Discovery Research
Mark M. Webber, CIO
Dwight D. Weller, Sr. VP-Mfg. & Chemistry
Mark Webber, Gen. Mgr.-Admin.
R. Ray Cummings, VP-Bus. Dev.
Michael Hubbard, Dir.-Corp. Comm.
Mark Webber, Gen. Mgr.-Finance
Peter D. O'Hanley, VP-Regulatory Affairs & Clinical Dev.
Patrick L. Iversen, Sr. VP-Strategic Alliances
Michael D. Casey, Chmn.

| | |
|---|---|
| **Phone:** 503-227-0554 | **Fax:** 503-227-0751 |
| **Toll-Free:** | |
| **Address:** 1 S.W. Columbia, Ste. 1105, Portland, OR 97258 US | |

## GROWTH PLANS/SPECIAL FEATURES:

AVI BioPharma, Inc. is a biopharmaceutical company that develops therapeutic products principally based on third-generation NeuGene antisense technology. The company's principal products in development target life-threatening diseases, including cardiovascular, genetic and infectious diseases. These products have also been tested in preclinical trials and some clinical studies for the treatment of cancer and polycystic kidney disease (PKD), as well as in regulating drug metabolism via the P450 cytochrome system. The firm owns 186 issued or licensed patent worldwide and 192 pending patent applications. The firm's cardiovascular NeuGene antisense products include Resten-NG, a drug for the treatment of cardiovascular restenosis (the re-narrowing of a coronary artery after angioplasty) and Resten-CP, a drug for treating coronary artery bypass. AVI has filed an Investigational New Drug application with the FDA for Resten-NG. The company's infectious disease program is currently focusing on single-strand RNA viruses and targeting West Nile virus, hepatitis C, dengue virus, influenza A, SARS corona virus, Ebola Zaire virus, Marburg Musoke virus, and Junin virus. The firm's genetic disease program is currently conducting studies to treat Duchenne Muscular Dystrophy. In 2008, AVI acquired Ercole Biotechnology Inc., the firm's former collaboration partner in the development of drugs which splice messenger RNA in order to treat a variety of genetic and acquired diseases.

AVI offers employees medical and dental insurance, a 401(k) savings plan and employee stock option plans.

## FINANCIALS:

**Sales and profits are in thousands of dollars—add 000 to get the full amount. 2008 Note: Financial information for 2008 was not available for all companies at press time.**

| | | |
|---|---|---|
| 2008 Sales: $ | 2008 Profits: $ | **U.S. Stock Ticker: AVII** |
| 2007 Sales: $10,985 | 2007 Profits: $-27,168 | **Int'l Ticker:** Int'l Exchange: |
| 2006 Sales: $ 115 | 2006 Profits: $-31,073 | Employees: 125 |
| 2005 Sales: $4,783 | 2005 Profits: $-16,676 | Fiscal Year Ends: 12/31 |
| 2004 Sales: $ 430 | 2004 Profits: $-24,778 | Parent Company: |

## SALARIES/BENEFITS:

| | | | | |
|---|---|---|---|---|
| Pension Plan: | ESOP Stock Plan: | Profit Sharing: | Top Exec. Salary: $310,000 | Bonus: $43,500 |
| Savings Plan: Y | Stock Purch. Plan: Y | | Second Exec. Salary: $293,192 | Bonus: $ |

## OTHER THOUGHTS:

**Apparent Women Officers or Directors:**
**Hot Spot for Advancement for Women/Minorities:**

## LOCATIONS: ("Y" = Yes)

| West: | Southwest: | Midwest: | Southeast: | Northeast: | International: |
|---|---|---|---|---|---|
| Y | | | | | |

# AVIALL INC

www.aviall.com

**Industry Group Code:** 336410 **Ranks within this company's industry group:** Sales: 1 Profits:

| Management: | | Sales/Marketing: | | Liberal Arts: | | Information Systems: | | Professionals: | | Technical/Scientific: | |
|---|---|---|---|---|---|---|---|---|---|---|---|
| Mgmt. Trainees: | | Mktg. Professionals: | Y | Gen. Writing/Editing: | | Info. Management: | Y | Finance/Accounting: | Y | Engineers, Elec.: | |
| Experienced Mgmt.: | Y | Retail Sales: | | Technical Writing: | Y | Software Dev.: | | Law: | Y | Engineers, Other: | |
| Int'l Business: | Y | Commercial/Industrial: | Y | Graphic Arts/Photog.: | | Hardware Dev.: | | HR/Other: | Y | Health/Lab: | |
| MBA Graduates: | Y | Sales Trainees: | Y | Music: | | Systems Integration: | | Training: | Y | Scientists/Research: | |
| | | Advertising Pros.: | | Broadcasting: | | Consulting/Other: | | Health Care: | | Petroleum/Chemicals: | |
| | | | | Other: | | | | Consulting: | | Math/Other: | |

## TYPES OF BUSINESS:

Aerospace Parts Distribution
E-Commerce-Aerospace Parts
E-Business Services-Aerospace, Defense, Marine
Aftermarket Services

## BRANDS/DIVISIONS/AFFILIATES:

Aviall Services
Inventory Locator Service LLC
Internet Business Applications, Inc.
Aerospace Repairable Management System

## CONTACTS: *Note: Officers with more than one job title may be intentionally listed here more than once.*

Paul E. Fulchino, CEO
Paul E. Fulchino, Pres.
Colin M. Cohen, CFO/Sr. VP
Terry Scott, Sr. VP-Sales & Mktg.
Jeffrey J. Murphy, Sr. VP-Human Resources
Joe Lacik, VP-Info. Svcs.
Jeffrey J. Murphy, General Counsel/Sr. VP-Law/Corp. Sec.
Charley Kienzle, Sr. VP-Oper.
Colin M. Cohen, Sr. VP/Treas.
Dan Komnenovich, COO/Pres., Aviall Svcs., Inc.
Bruce Langsen, Pres., Inventory Locator Svc., LLC
Jacque Collier, VP/Controller
Lou Koch, VP-Human Resources
Paul E. Fulchino, Chmn.

**Phone:** 972-586-1000 **Fax:** 972-586-1361
**Toll-Free:** 800-284-2551
**Address:** 2750 Regent Blvd., Dallas Fort Worth Airport, TX 75261-9048 US

## GROWTH PLANS/SPECIAL FEATURES:

Aviall, Inc. is a provider of aftermarket supply-chain management services for companies in the aerospace, defense and marine industries. The company manages two main business units: Aviall Services and Inventory Locator Service LLC. Aviall Services is an independent provider of new aerospace parts and aftermarket services. The unit markets and distributes products for more than 225 manufacturers and offers approximately 1,000,000 catalog items from customer service centers in North America, Europe and Asia. The subsidiary's customer service centers are served by an automated central distribution facility in Dallas, Texas. In addition, Aviall Services offers aviation batteries, hoses, wheels, brakes and oxygen. The firm's other unit, Inventory Locator Service LLC (ILS), provides information and global e-commerce services through its online marketplace. Through a subscription, users can buy and sell commercial parts, equipment and services through a database containing more than 50 million line items and more than 5 billion parts. In addition, the subsidiary provides e-business services and consulting for the aviation, marine and defense industries. The company owns Internet Business Applications, Inc. including its inventory management software, Aerospace Repairable Management System, or ARMS.

Aviall offers its employees a comprehensive benefits package that includes child and health care flexible spending accounts, a defined-benefit pension plan, a 401(k) savings plan, an educational assistance plan, internal job posting policy, credit union membership and an employee assistance program.

## FINANCIALS: **Sales and profits are in thousands of dollars—add 000 to get the full amount. 2008 Note: Financial information for 2008 was not available for all companies at press time.**

| | | |
|---|---|---|
| 2008 Sales: $2,000,000 | 2008 Profits: $ | **U.S. Stock Ticker: Subsidiary** |
| 2007 Sales: $2,000,000 | 2007 Profits: $ | **Int'l Ticker:** Int'l Exchange: |
| 2006 Sales: $1,500,000 | 2006 Profits: $ | Employees: 1,009 |
| 2005 Sales: $1,295,201 | 2005 Profits: $56,531 | Fiscal Year Ends: 12/31 |
| 2004 Sales: $1,164,003 | 2004 Profits: $43,169 | Parent Company: BOEING COMPANY (THE) |

## SALARIES/BENEFITS:

| | | | | |
|---|---|---|---|---|
| Pension Plan: Y | ESOP Stock Plan: | Profit Sharing: | Top Exec. Salary: $542,380 | Bonus: $371,234 |
| Savings Plan: Y | Stock Purch. Plan: | | Second Exec. Salary: $332,991 | Bonus: $242,578 |

## OTHER THOUGHTS:

**Apparent Women Officers or Directors**: 1
**Hot Spot for Advancement for Women/Minorities**:

## LOCATIONS: ("Y" = Yes)

| West: | Southwest: | Midwest: | Southeast: | Northeast: | International: |
|---|---|---|---|---|---|
| Y | Y | Y | Y | Y | Y |

Note: Financial information, benefits and other data can change quickly and may vary from those stated here.

# AVISTA CORPORATION

**www.avistacorp.com**

**Industry Group Code:** 221000 **Ranks within this company's industry group:** Sales: 4 Profits: 6

| Management: | | Sales/Marketing: | | Liberal Arts: | | Information Systems: | | Professionals: | | Technical/Scientific: | |
|---|---|---|---|---|---|---|---|---|---|---|---|
| Mgmt. Trainees: | | Mktg. Professionals: | Y | Gen. Writing/Editing: | | Info. Management: | Y | Finance/Accounting: | Y | Engineers, Elec.: | Y |
| Experienced Mgmt.: | Y | Retail Sales: | | Technical Writing: | | Software Dev.: | | Law: | Y | Engineers, Other: | Y |
| Int'l Business: | | Commercial/Industrial: | Y | Graphic Arts/Photog.: | | Hardware Dev.: | | HR/Other: | Y | Health/Lab: | |
| MBA Graduates: | Y | Sales Trainees: | | Music: | | Systems Integration: | | Training: | Y | Scientists/Research: | |
| | | Advertising Pros.: | | Broadcasting: | | Consulting/Other: | | Health Care: | | Petroleum/Chemicals: | Y |
| | | | | Other: | | | | Consulting: | | Math/Other: | |

## TYPES OF BUSINESS:

Utilities-Electricity & Natural Gas
Fuel Cells
e-Business & Consulting Services
Energy Marketing
Resource Management
Community Investment Management

## BRANDS/DIVISIONS/AFFILIATES:

ReliOn
Advantage IQ
Avista Energy
Avista Utilities
Avista Development

## CONTACTS: *Note: Officers with more than one job title may be intentionally listed here more than once.*

Scott L. Morris, CEO
Scott L. Morris, Pres.
Mark Thies, CFO/Sr. VP
Karen S. Feltes, Sr. VP-Human Resources/Corp. Sec.
James M. Kensok, CIO/VP
Marian Durkin, General Counsel/Sr. VP
Christy Burmeister-Smith, Controller/Principal Acct. Officer/VP
Dennis Vermillion, VP-Energy Resources, Avista Utilities
Ann Wilson, VP/Treas.
Roger D. Woodworth, VP-Sustainable Energy Solutions, Utilities
Don Kopczynski, VP-Transmission & Dist. Oper., Utilities
Scott L. Morris, Chmn.

| | |
|---|---|
| **Phone:** 509-489-0500 | **Fax:** 509-495-8725 |
| **Toll-Free:** | |
| **Address:** 1411 E. Mission Ave., Spokane, WA 99202-2600 US | |

## GROWTH PLANS/SPECIAL FEATURES:

Avista Corporation is an energy, information and technology company with utility and subsidiary operations in the U.S. Pacific Northwest. The company produces, transmits and distributes energy as well as administering related businesses. The firm operates four business segments: Avista Utilities, Energy Marketing and Resource Management, Advantage IQ and Other. Avista Utilities manages regulated utility business operations, which include generating, transmitting and delivering electricity, natural gas and related services to customer in California, Idaho, Montana, Oregon and Washington. The utility also engages in wholesale purchases and sales of electricity and natural gas. Energy Marketing and Resource Management is currently comprised of Avista Power LLC. Advantage IQ provides e-business facility intelligence through its series of patented consulting and cost management tools that include consolidated billing, resource accounting, energy analysis and load profiling services. The company's other division includes consolidated billing, resource accounting, energy analysis and load profiling services, which it manages through various indirect subsidiaries, including Advanced Manufacturing and Development. The company recently created AVA Formation Corp., a wholly-owned holding company, in order to implement the proposed transition of Avista Corporation's organization into that of a holding company. In June 2007, Avista announced its plans to construct a 3.8-mile underground natural distribution line into Glendale, Oregon. In July 2007, the company completed its sale of Avista Energy, Inc. and all of its contracts to Coral Energy Holding, L.P., a subsidiary of Shell. In July 2007, it announced plans to begin a multi-year construction project to extend natural gas service to the city of Spirit Lake, Idaho. In June 2008, Advantage IQ acquired Cadence Network, a privately-held, Ohio-based company.

## FINANCIALS: **Sales and profits are in thousands of dollars—add 000 to get the full amount. 2008 Note: Financial information for 2008 was not available for all companies at press time.**

| | | |
|---|---|---|
| 2008 Sales: $ | 2008 Profits: $ | **U.S. Stock Ticker: AVA** |
| 2007 Sales: $1,417,757 | 2007 Profits: $38,475 | **Int'l Ticker:** Int'l Exchange: |
| 2006 Sales: $1,506,311 | 2006 Profits: $72,941 | Employees: 1,985 |
| 2005 Sales: $1,359,607 | 2005 Profits: $45,168 | Fiscal Year Ends: 12/31 |
| 2004 Sales: $1,151,580 | 2004 Profits: $35,154 | Parent Company: |

## SALARIES/BENEFITS:

| | | | | |
|---|---|---|---|---|
| Pension Plan: Y | ESOP Stock Plan: | Profit Sharing: | Top Exec. Salary: $715,000 | Bonus: $98,456 |
| Savings Plan: Y | Stock Purch. Plan: | | Second Exec. Salary: $452,461 | Bonus: $43,146 |

## OTHER THOUGHTS:

**Apparent Women Officers or Directors**: 4
**Hot Spot for Advancement for Women/Minorities**: Y

## LOCATIONS: ("Y" = Yes)

| West: | Southwest: | Midwest: | Southeast: | Northeast: | International: |
|---|---|---|---|---|---|
| Y | | | Y | | |

# BENTLEY PHARMACEUTICALS INC

www.bentleypharm.com

**Industry Group Code:** 325412A **Ranks within this company's industry group:** Sales: 5 Profits: 3

| **Management:** | | **Sales/Marketing:** | | **Liberal Arts:** | | **Information Systems:** | | **Professionals:** | | **Technical/Scientific:** | |
|---|---|---|---|---|---|---|---|---|---|---|---|
| Mgmt. Trainees: | | Mktg. Professionals: | Y | Gen. Writing/Editing: | | Info. Management: | Y | Finance/Accounting: | Y | Engineers, Elec.: | |
| Experienced Mgmt.: | Y | Retail Sales: | | Technical Writing: | Y | Software Dev.: | | Law: | Y | Engineers, Other: | |
| Int'l Business: | Y | Commercial/Industrial: | Y | Graphic Arts/Photog.: | | Hardware Dev.: | | HR/Other: | Y | Health/Lab: | Y |
| MBA Graduates: | Y | Sales Trainees: | Y | Music: | | Systems Integration: | | Training: | Y | Scientists/Research: | Y |
| | | Advertising Pros.: | | Broadcasting: | | Consulting/Other: | | Health Care: | Y | Petroleum/Chemicals: | |
| | | | | Other: | | | | Consulting: | | Math/Other: | Y |

## TYPES OF BUSINESS:

Drug Delivery Systems Technologies
Drugs-Diversified
Generic Drugs
Drug Delivery Technology

## BRANDS/DIVISIONS/AFFILIATES:

Teva Pharmaceutical Industries
Laboratorios Belmac
Laboratorios Devur
Laboratorios Rimafar
Bentley Pharmaceuticals Ireland
CPEX Pharmaceuticals Inc

## CONTACTS: *Note: Officers with more than one job title may be intentionally listed here more than once.*

James R. Murphy, CEO
John A. Sedor, Pres.
Richard P. Lindsay, CFO/VP
Fred Feldman, VP-R&D
David C. Brush, VP-Bus. Dev. & Strategic Planning
Michael McGovern, Vice Chmn.
Robert M. Stote, Chief Medical Officer/Sr. VP
James R. Murphy, Chmn.
Adolfo Herrera Malaga, Managing Dir.-European Subsidiaries

| **Phone:** 603-658-6100 | **Fax:** 603-658-6101 |
|---|---|
| **Toll-Free:** | |
| **Address:** Bentley Park, 2 Holland Way, Exeter, NH 03833 US | |

## GROWTH PLANS/SPECIAL FEATURES:

Bentley Pharmaceuticals, Inc., a subsidiary of Teva Pharmaceutical Industries, manufactures and markets generic and branded generic pharmaceuticals in Europe for the treatment of cardiovascular, gastrointestinal, infectious and central nervous system diseases. Bentley manufactures and markets approximately 129 products of various dosages and strengths, including approximately 180 product presentations. The firm markets its products primarily in Spain and has developed alliances with other companies that market its products in Portugal, Greece, the U.K., Germany, Austria, Morocco, Poland and the Czech Republic. The firm markets its products to physicians, pharmacists and hospitals through its three Spanish sales and marketing organizations: Laboratorios Belmac, Laboratorios Devur and Laboratorios Rimafar. Subsidiary Bentley Pharmaceuticals Ireland conducts the firm's sales and marketing operations throughout the E.U. Bentley's branded generic pharmaceutical product line consists of 43 products represented by approximately 20 trademarked brand names. Its generic pharmaceutical product line is comprised of 86 products. The top-selling generic and branded generic pharmaceutical products for Bentley include omeprazole, simvastatin, enalapril, paroxetine and lansoprazole. In July 2008, Bentley spun-off its drug delivery business, CPEX Pharmaceuticals, Inc., and was acquired by Teva Pharmaceutical for approximately $359.7 million. Following the acquisition, Bentley became a wholly-owned subsidiary of Teva.

## FINANCIALS: **Sales and profits are in thousands of dollars—add 000 to get the full amount. 2008 Note: Financial information for 2008 was not available for all companies at press time.**

| | | |
|---|---|---|
| 2008 Sales: $ | 2008 Profits: $ | **U.S. Stock Ticker: Subsidiary** |
| 2007 Sales: $124,687 | 2007 Profits: $2,685 | **Int'l Ticker:** Int'l Exchange: |
| 2006 Sales: $109,471 | 2006 Profits: $ 974 | Employees: 470 |
| 2005 Sales: $97,730 | 2005 Profits: $10,919 | Fiscal Year Ends: 12/31 |
| 2004 Sales: $73,393 | 2004 Profits: $5,690 | Parent Company: TEVA PHARMACEUTICAL INDUSTRIES |

## SALARIES/BENEFITS:

| | | | | |
|---|---|---|---|---|
| Pension Plan: | ESOP Stock Plan: | Profit Sharing: | Top Exec. Salary: $672,719 | Bonus: $544,902 |
| Savings Plan: | Stock Purch. Plan: | | Second Exec. Salary: $566,846 | Bonus: $326,942 |

## OTHER THOUGHTS:

**Apparent Women Officers or Directors:**
**Hot Spot for Advancement for Women/Minorities:**

## LOCATIONS: ("Y" = Yes)

| West: | Southwest: | Midwest: | Southeast: | Northeast: | International: |
|---|---|---|---|---|---|
| | | | | Y | Y |

# BERRY PETROLEUM CO

www.bry.com

**Industry Group Code:** 211111 **Ranks within this company's industry group:** Sales: 16 Profits: 14

| Management: | | Sales/Marketing: | | Liberal Arts: | | Information Systems: | | Professionals: | | Technical/Scientific: | |
|---|---|---|---|---|---|---|---|---|---|---|---|
| Mgmt. Trainees: | | Mktg. Professionals: | Y | Gen. Writing/Editing: | | Info. Management: | Y | Finance/Accounting: | Y | Engineers, Elec.: | |
| Experienced Mgmt.: | Y | Retail Sales: | | Technical Writing: | | Software Dev.: | | Law: | Y | Engineers, Other: | Y |
| Int'l Business: | Y | Commercial/Industrial: | Y | Graphic Arts/Photog.: | | Hardware Dev.: | | HR/Other: | Y | Health/Lab: | |
| MBA Graduates: | Y | Sales Trainees: | | Music: | | Systems Integration: | | Training: | Y | Scientists/Research: | |
| | | Advertising Pros.: | | Broadcasting: | | Consulting/Other: | | Health Care: | | Petroleum/Chemicals: | Y |
| | | | | Other: | | | | Consulting: | | Math/Other: | |

## TYPES OF BUSINESS:

Oil & Gas Exploration & Production

## BRANDS/DIVISIONS/AFFILIATES:

## CONTACTS:

*Note: Officers with more than one job title may be intentionally listed here more than once.*

Robert F. Heinemann, CEO
Michael Duginski, COO/Exec. VP
Robert F. Heinemann, Pres.
David D. Wolf, CFO/Exec. VP
Walter B. Ayers, VP-Human Resources
Todd Crabtree, Media
Ralph Goehring, Investor Rel.
Shawn M. Canaday, Controller
Steven B. Wilsom, Treas.
George T. Crawford, VP-California Prod.
Kenneth A. Olson, Corp. Sec.
Dan G. Anderson, VP-Rocky Mountain & Mid-Continent Prod.
Martin H. Young, Jr., Chmn.

| | |
|---|---|
| **Phone:** 661-616-3900 | **Fax:** 661-616-3881 |
| **Toll-Free:** | |
| **Address:** 5201 Truxtun Ave., Ste. 300, Bakersfield, CA 93309-0640 US | |

## GROWTH PLANS/SPECIAL FEATURES:

Berry Petroleum Co. produces, develops, acquires and explores for crude oil and natural gas. The company's principal reserves and producing properties are located in the San Joaquin Valley in Los Angeles and Ventura County in California, the Uinta Basin in Utah and the Denver-Julesburg Basin in Colorado. Within these basins, Berry operates approximately a dozen oil fields. The firm owns three cogeneration facilities that supply steam, which Berry uses for thermal recovery of its oil reserves. Berry's Midway-Sunset field facility utilizes cyclic steam recovery methods to reduce oil viscosity, thus enabling the oil to flow more easily to the surface. The firm's estimated proved reserves total over 169 mmboe (million barrels of oil equivalent). Berry markets its crude oil production to competing buyers, including independent marketing, pipeline and oil refining companies. The company has identified the Rocky Mountain region as an area for growth and maintains an office in Denver, Colorado to pursue opportunities in light oil and natural gas in that region. Approximately 40% of Berry's production and proved reserves come from the Rocky Mountain region, with the balance coming from California. The company's proved reserves consist of 69% crude oil and 31% natural gas. In May 2007, Berry sold its non-core West Montalvo assets for $63 million. In June 2008, the firm announced the purchase of natural gas producing properties on 4,500 acres in the East Texas Cotton Valley for $620 million.

Berry Petroleum offers its employees a 401(k) plan; health and dental insurance; a 529 college savings plan; and a section 125 tax reduction plan.

## FINANCIALS:

**Sales and profits are in thousands of dollars—add 000 to get the full amount. 2008 Note: Financial information for 2008 was not available for all companies at press time.**

| | | |
|---|---|---|
| 2008 Sales: $ | 2008 Profits: $ | **U.S. Stock Ticker: BRY** |
| 2007 Sales: $583,457 | 2007 Profits: $129,928 | **Int'l Ticker:** Int'l Exchange: |
| 2006 Sales: $486,338 | 2006 Profits: $107,943 | Employees: 263 |
| 2005 Sales: $406,725 | 2005 Profits: $112,356 | Fiscal Year Ends: 12/31 |
| 2004 Sales: $274,946 | 2004 Profits: $69,187 | Parent Company: |

## SALARIES/BENEFITS:

| | | | | |
|---|---|---|---|---|
| Pension Plan: | ESOP Stock Plan: | Profit Sharing: | Top Exec. Salary: $583,333 | Bonus: $720,000 |
| Savings Plan: Y | Stock Purch. Plan: | | Second Exec. Salary: $288,106 | Bonus: $245,025 |

## OTHER THOUGHTS:

**Apparent Women Officers or Directors:**
**Hot Spot for Advancement for Women/Minorities:**

## LOCATIONS: ("Y" = Yes)

| West: | Southwest: | Midwest: | Southeast: | Northeast: | International: |
|---|---|---|---|---|---|
| Y | | | | | |

Note: Financial information, benefits and other data can change quickly and may vary from those stated here.

# BIO REFERENCE LABORATORIES INC

www.bioreference.com

**Industry Group Code:** 621511 **Ranks within this company's industry group:** Sales: 3 Profits: 2

| Management: | | Sales/Marketing: | | Liberal Arts: | | Information Systems: | | Professionals: | | Technical/Scientific: | |
|---|---|---|---|---|---|---|---|---|---|---|---|
| Mgmt. Trainees: | | Mktg. Professionals: | Y | Gen. Writing/Editing: | | Info. Management: | Y | Finance/Accounting: | Y | Engineers, Elec.: | |
| Experienced Mgmt.: | Y | Retail Sales: | | Technical Writing: | Y | Software Dev.: | Y | Law: | Y | Engineers, Other: | |
| Int'l Business: | | Commercial/Industrial: | Y | Graphic Arts/Photog.: | | Hardware Dev.: | | HR/Other: | Y | Health/Lab: | Y |
| MBA Graduates: | Y | Sales Trainees: | Y | Music: | | Systems Integration: | Y | Training: | Y | Scientists/Research: | Y |
| | | Advertising Pros.: | | Broadcasting: | | Consulting/Other: | | Health Care: | Y | Petroleum/Chemicals: | |
| | | | | Other: | | | | Consulting: | | Math/Other: | |

## TYPES OF BUSINESS:

Medical Laboratories & Testing
Clinical Laboratory Services
Clinical Knowledge Database
Online Practice Management Services
Drug Testing

## BRANDS/DIVISIONS/AFFILIATES:

PSIMedica
CareEvolve
GenFlow
Cancer Genetics, Inc.
GeneDx

## CONTACTS:

*Note: Officers with more than one job title may be intentionally listed here more than once.*

Marc D. Grodman, CEO
Howard Dubinett, COO/Exec. VP
Marc D. Grodman, Pres.
Sam Singer, CFO/Sr. VP
Charles T. Todd, Sr. VP-Sales & Mktg.
James Weisberger, Chief Medical Officer/VP/Laboratory Dir.
Richard L. Faherty, CIO
Warren Erdmann, Sr. VP-Oper.
Cory Fishkin, Pres., CareEvolve
Tara Mackay, Coordinator-Investor Rel.
Nicholas Papazicos, VP-Financial Oper.
Azmy Awad, Sr. VP
John W. Littleton, VP/Dir.-Sale
Scott Fein, Sr. VP
Sally Howlett, VP-Billing
Marc D. Grodman, Chmn.

**Phone:** 201-791-2600 **Fax:**
**Toll-Free:**
**Address:** 481 Edward H. Ross Dr., Elmwood Park, NJ 07407-3118 US

## GROWTH PLANS/SPECIAL FEATURES:

Bio-Reference Laboratories, Inc. (BRLI) is a regional clinical laboratory offering services to clients in the greater New York metropolitan area and New Jersey. Serving health care providers in these areas, the firm offers testing services utilized in detection, diagnosis, evaluation, monitoring and treatment of diseases. The company processes nearly 3.7 million requisitions annually for customers including doctors, employers, clinics and governmental units. BRLI operates a network of over 50 patient service centers for the collection of patient specimens. Routine tests, which account for approximately 55% of the company's clinical business, include blood cell counts, cholesterol level testing, HIV-related tests, pap smears, pregnancy tests, urinalysis and drug testing. The company also performs specialized esoteric tests, which account for approximately 45% of its net revenues, in medical fields such as endocrinology, genetics, immunology, microbiology, oncology, serology and toxicology. BRLI's PSIMedica division is based on a Clinical Knowledge Management (ACKM) System that analyzes enrollment, claims, pharmacy, laboratory results and other data, providing administrative and clinical analysis of a population. In addition, the company hosts CareEvolve (careevolve.com), a physician-based Internet health portal that seeks to provide physicians with secure messaging to patients, payers, vendors and other health care facilities. These communications include secure laboratory, pathology and radiology ordering and result delivery. In 2007, BRLI introduced the first commercially available genome-wide oligonucleotide microarray analysis testing, useful for the diagnoses of, among other conditions, developmental disorders.

## FINANCIALS:

**Sales and profits are in thousands of dollars—add 000 to get the full amount. 2008 Note: Financial information for 2008 was not available for all companies at press time.**

| | | |
|---|---|---|
| 2008 Sales: $ | 2008 Profits: $ | **U.S. Stock Ticker: BRLI** |
| 2007 Sales: $250,431 | 2007 Profits: $13,957 | **Int'l Ticker:** Int'l Exchange: |
| 2006 Sales: $193,134 | 2006 Profits: $11,291 | Employees: 1,648 |
| 2005 Sales: $163,896 | 2005 Profits: $7,621 | Fiscal Year Ends: 10/31 |
| 2004 Sales: $136,184 | 2004 Profits: $8,516 | Parent Company: |

## SALARIES/BENEFITS:

| | | | | |
|---|---|---|---|---|
| Pension Plan: | ESOP Stock Plan: | Profit Sharing: | Top Exec. Salary: $852,000 | Bonus: $ |
| Savings Plan: | Stock Purch. Plan: | | Second Exec. Salary: $438,750 | Bonus: $ |

## OTHER THOUGHTS:

**Apparent Women Officers or Directors**: 2
**Hot Spot for Advancement for Women/Minorities**: Y

## LOCATIONS: ("Y" = Yes)

| West: | Southwest: | Midwest: | Southeast: | Northeast: | International: |
|---|---|---|---|---|---|
| | | | | Y | |

# BIOMARIN PHARMACEUTICAL INC

www.biomarinpharm.com

**Industry Group Code:** 325412 **Ranks within this company's industry group:** Sales: 19 Profits: 17

| Management: | | Sales/Marketing: | | Liberal Arts: | | Information Systems: | | Professionals: | | Technical/Scientific: | |
|---|---|---|---|---|---|---|---|---|---|---|---|
| Mgmt. Trainees: | | Mktg. Professionals: | Y | Gen. Writing/Editing: | | Info. Management: | Y | Finance/Accounting: | Y | Engineers, Elec.: | |
| Experienced Mgmt.: | Y | Retail Sales: | | Technical Writing: | Y | Software Dev.: | Y | Law: | Y | Engineers, Other: | |
| Int'l Business: | Y | Commercial/Industrial: | Y | Graphic Arts/Photog.: | | Hardware Dev.: | | HR/Other: | Y | Health/Lab: | Y |
| MBA Graduates: | Y | Sales Trainees: | Y | Music: | | Systems Integration: | | Training: | Y | Scientists/Research: | Y |
| | | Advertising Pros.: | | Broadcasting: | | Consulting/Other: | | Health Care: | Y | Petroleum/Chemicals: | |
| | | | | Other: | | | | Consulting: | | Math/Other: | Y |

## TYPES OF BUSINESS:

Biopharmaceutical Product Development
Drugs-Severe Conditions
Pediatric Disease Treatments
Asthma Treatments
Drug Delivery Technologies

## BRANDS/DIVISIONS/AFFILIATES:

Naglazyme
Kuvan
Aldurazyme
Genzyme Corporation
PEG-PAL
BH4
6R-BH4

## CONTACTS: *Note: Officers with more than one job title may be intentionally listed here more than once.*

Jean-Jacques Bienaime, CEO
Jeffrey H. Cooper, CFO/VP
Lewis Chapman, VP-Global Mktg.
Mark Wood, VP-Human Resources
Emil D. Kakkis, Chief Medical Officer/Sr. VP
Robert A. Baffi, Sr. VP-Tech. Oper.
Daniel P. Maher, VP-Prod. Dev.
R. Andrew Ramelmeier, VP-Mfg. & Process Dev.
G. Eric Davis, General Counsel/VP/Corp. Sec.
Amy Waterhouse, VP-Regulatory & Gov't Affairs
Stuart J. Swiedler, Sr. VP-Clinical Affairs
Victoria Sluzky, VP-Quality & Analytical Chemistry
Charles A. O'Neill, VP-Pharmacological Sciences
Pierre Lapalme, Chmn.
William E. Aliski, Gen. Mgr.-European Oper./VP
Steven Jungles, VP-Supply Chain

**Phone:** 415-506-6700 **Fax:** 415-382-7889
**Toll-Free:**
**Address:** 105 Digital Dr., Novato, CA 94949 US

## GROWTH PLANS/SPECIAL FEATURES:

BioMarin Pharmaceutical, Inc. develops and commercializes biopharmaceutical products for serious diseases and medical conditions. BioMarin has three approved products: Naglazyme, for the treatment of mucopolysaccharidosis VI (MPS-VI); Kuvan, for which the firm was granted marketing approval in the U.S. for the treatment of phenylketonuria (PKU) in December 2007; and Aldurazyme, for the treatment of mucopolysaccharidosis I (MPS-I). MPS-VI is a debilitating life-threatening genetic disease for which no other drug treatment currently exists. Naglazyme has been granted orphan drug status in the U.S. and E.U., which confers market exclusivity for the treatment of MPS VI expiring in 2012 and 2016, respectively. BioMarin has been granted orphan drug status in the U.S. for Kuvan, the first drug treatment for PKU, an inherited metabolic disease that affects at least 50,000 diagnosed patients globally under the age of 40. The firm believes that approximately 30-50% of those with PKU could benefit from treatment with Kuvan. Aldurazyme, developed through a 50/50 joint-venture with Genzyme Corporation, has been approved for marketing in the U.S., European Union (E.U.) and other countries for patients with MPS I. Aldurazyme has been granted orphan drug status in the U.S., expiring in 2010, and in the E.U., expiring in 2013. BioMarin's PEG-PAL (formerly referred to as Phenylase) is an investigational enzyme substitution therapy being developed as a subcutaneous injection for those who do not respond to Kuvan. The firm is developing BH4 for the treatment of indications associated with endothelial dysfunction. In early 2007, BioMarin initiated Phase II clinical trials of 6R-BH4 for peripheral arterial disease and sickle cell disease.

BioMarin offers its employees an education assistance program; a flexible spending plan; medical, dental and vision insurance; an employee assistance program; Weight Watchers meetings; and bi-weekly chair massages.

## FINANCIALS: **Sales and profits are in thousands of dollars—add 000 to get the full amount. 2008 Note: Financial information for 2008 was not available for all companies at press time.**

| | | |
|---|---|---|
| 2008 Sales: $ | 2008 Profits: $ | **U.S. Stock Ticker: BMRN** |
| 2007 Sales: $121,581 | 2007 Profits: $-15,803 | **Int'l Ticker:** Int'l Exchange: |
| 2006 Sales: $84,209 | 2006 Profits: $-28,533 | Employees: 525 |
| 2005 Sales: $25,669 | 2005 Profits: $-74,270 | Fiscal Year Ends: 12/31 |
| 2004 Sales: $18,641 | 2004 Profits: $-187,443 | Parent Company: |

## SALARIES/BENEFITS:

| | | | | |
|---|---|---|---|---|
| Pension Plan: | ESOP Stock Plan: | Profit Sharing: | Top Exec. Salary: $636,933 | Bonus: $733,815 |
| Savings Plan: Y | Stock Purch. Plan: Y | | Second Exec. Salary: $299,885 | Bonus: $108,675 |

## OTHER THOUGHTS:

**Apparent Women Officers or Directors**: 4
**Hot Spot for Advancement for Women/Minorities**: Y

## LOCATIONS: ("Y" = Yes)

| West: | Southwest: | Midwest: | Southeast: | Northeast: | International: |
|---|---|---|---|---|---|
| Y | | | | | Y |

# BIOSCRIP INC

www.bioscrip.com

**Industry Group Code:** 522320A **Ranks within this company's industry group:** Sales: 1 Profits: 1

| Management: | | Sales/Marketing: | | Liberal Arts: | | Information Systems: | | Professionals: | | Technical/Scientific: | |
|---|---|---|---|---|---|---|---|---|---|---|---|
| Mgmt. Trainees: | Y | Mktg. Professionals: | Y | Gen. Writing/Editing: | | Info. Management: | Y | Finance/Accounting: | Y | Engineers, Elec.: | |
| Experienced Mgmt.: | Y | Retail Sales: | | Technical Writing: | | Software Dev.: | Y | Law: | Y | Engineers, Other: | |
| Int'l Business: | | Commercial/Industrial: | Y | Graphic Arts/Photog.: | | Hardware Dev.: | | HR/Other: | Y | Health/Lab: | |
| MBA Graduates: | Y | Sales Trainees: | Y | Music: | | Systems Integration: | | Training: | Y | Scientists/Research: | |
| | | Advertising Pros.: | | Broadcasting: | | Consulting/Other: | | Health Care: | Y | Petroleum/Chemicals: | |
| | | | | Other: | | | | Consulting: | | Math/Other: | |

## TYPES OF BUSINESS:

Pharmacy Benefits Management
Retail, Online & Mail-Order Pharmacies
Disease Management
Specialty Pharmacy Services

## BRANDS/DIVISIONS/AFFILIATES:

## CONTACTS: *Note: Officers with more than one job title may be intentionally listed here more than once.*

Richard H. Friedman, CEO
Richard M. Smith, COO
Richard M. Smith, Pres.
Stanley Rosenbaum, CFO/Exec. VP
Scott W. Friedman, Exec. VP-Mktg. & Sales
Douglas A. Lee, CIO/VP
Barry A. Posner, General Counsel/Exec. VP/Corp. Sec.
Robert Roose, Chief Strategy Officer
Stanley Rosenbaum, Treas.
Alfred Carfora, Exec. VP-Mail & PBM Svcs.
Russel J. Corvese, Exec. VP-Mail Oper.
Thomas Ordemann, Exec. VP-Community Pharmacy Oper.
Brian J. Reagan, Exec. VP-Infusion Svcs.
Richard H. Friedman, Chmn.

**Phone:** 914-460-1600 **Fax:** 914-460-1660
**Toll-Free:** 888-818-3939
**Address:** 100 Clearbrook Rd., Elmsford, NY 10523 US

## GROWTH PLANS/SPECIAL FEATURES:

BioScrip, Inc. is a specialty pharmaceutical healthcare organization that partners with patients, physicians, healthcare payors and pharmaceutical manufacturers to provide access to medications and management solutions to optimize outcomes for chronic and other complex healthcare conditions. It operates in two segments: specialty pharmaceutical services; and pharmacy benefit management (PBM) and traditional mail services. The specialty pharmaceutical services include the support, dispensing and distribution, patient care management, data reporting as well as a range of other complex management services for certain medications. These medications include orals, injectables and infusibles used to treat patients living with chronic health conditions. The medications are provided in various capacities to patients, physicians, healthcare payors and pharmaceutical manufacturers. The PBM services include pharmacy network management, claims processing, benefit design, drug utilization review, formulary management and traditional mail order pharmacy fulfillment. The division also administers prescription discount card programs on behalf of commercial plan sponsors, most typically third party administrators. Under such programs, the company derives revenue on a per claim basis from the dispensing network pharmacy. The firm owns and operates 40 specialty pharmacies comprised of community pharmacy, located in major metropolitan areas across the U.S.; mail order pharmacies; and infusion pharmacies. While all of locations are full-service pharmacies that carry both traditional and specialty medications and are able to treat people with a variety of diseases and medical conditions, they primarily focus on serving patient populations with chronic health conditions such as cancer, hepatitis C, immunity overload, multiple sclerosis, organ transplant, hemophilia and HIV/AIDS.

Employees are offered medical and dental insurance; short- and long-term disability coverage; life insurance; and a 401(k) plan.

## FINANCIALS: **Sales and profits are in thousands of dollars—add 000 to get the full amount. 2008 Note: Financial information for 2008 was not available for all companies at press time.**

2008 Sales: $
2007 Sales: $1,197,732
2006 Sales: $1,151,940
2005 Sales: $1,073,235
2004 Sales: $630,516

2008 Profits: $
2007 Profits: $3,317
2006 Profits: $-38,289
2005 Profits: $-23,847
2004 Profits: $7,033

**U.S. Stock Ticker: BIOS**
**Int'l Ticker:** Int'l Exchange:
Employees: 1,132
Fiscal Year Ends: 12/31
Parent Company:

## SALARIES/BENEFITS:

Pension Plan: ESOP Stock Plan: Profit Sharing: Top Exec. Salary: $737,812 Bonus: $819,611
Savings Plan: Y Stock Purch. Plan: Second Exec. Salary: $400,000 Bonus: $400,000

## OTHER THOUGHTS:

**Apparent Women Officers or Directors**: 1
**Hot Spot for Advancement for Women/Minorities**:

## LOCATIONS: ("Y" = Yes)

| West: | Southwest: | Midwest: | Southeast: | Northeast: | International: |
|---|---|---|---|---|---|
| Y | Y | Y | Y | Y | |

# BIOSITE INC

www.biosite.com

**Industry Group Code:** 325413 **Ranks within this company's industry group:** Sales: Profits:

| Management: | | Sales/Marketing: | | Liberal Arts: | | Information Systems: | | Professionals: | | Technical/Scientific: | |
|---|---|---|---|---|---|---|---|---|---|---|---|
| Mgmt. Trainees: | | Mktg. Professionals: | Y | Gen. Writing/Editing: | | Info. Management: | Y | Finance/Accounting: | Y | Engineers, Elec.: | |
| Experienced Mgmt.: | Y | Retail Sales: | | Technical Writing: | Y | Software Dev.: | Y | Law: | Y | Engineers, Other: | Y |
| Int'l Business: | Y | Commercial/Industrial: | Y | Graphic Arts/Photog.: | | Hardware Dev.: | Y | HR/Other: | Y | Health/Lab: | Y |
| MBA Graduates: | Y | Sales Trainees: | Y | Music: | | Systems Integration: | | Training: | Y | Scientists/Research: | Y |
| | | Advertising Pros.: | | Broadcasting: | | Consulting/Other: | | Health Care: | Y | Petroleum/Chemicals: | |
| | | | | Other: | | | | Consulting: | | Math/Other: | Y |

## TYPES OF BUSINESS:

Medical Diagnostics Products
Rapid Immunoassays
Antibody Development Services

## BRANDS/DIVISIONS/AFFILIATES:

Biosite Discovery
Triage Drugs of Abuse Panel
Triage Cardiac Panel
Triage TOX Drug Screen
Triage BNP Test
Triage Profiler Panels
Triage Parasite Panel
Biosite Encompass

## CONTACTS: *Note: Officers with more than one job title may be intentionally listed here more than once.*

Kim D. Blickenstaff, CEO
Kenneth F. Buechler, Pres./Chief Scientific Officer
Christopher J. Twomey, CFO
Robert Anacone, Sr. VP-Worldwide Mktg. & Sales
Paul H. McPherson, VP-R&D
Stephen Lesefko, VP-Eng.
David Berger, VP-Legal Affairs
Christopher R. Hibberd, Sr. VP-Corp. Dev.
Nadine E. Padilla, VP-Corp. Rel.
Nadine E. Padilla, VP-Corp. & Investor Rel.
Christopher J. Twomey, Sr. VP-Finance/Sec.
Robin G. Weiner, VP-Quality Assurance & Govt. Affairs
Gunars E. Valkirs, Sr. VP-Biosite Discovery
Thomas G. Blassey, VP-U.S. Sales
S. Elaine Walton, VP-Quality Assurance & Program Mgt.
Kim D. Blickenstaff, Chmn.
Gary A. King, VP-Int'l Oper.

| **Phone:** 858-805-8378 | **Fax:** |
|---|---|
| **Toll-Free:** 888-246-7483 | |
| **Address:** 9975 Summers Ridge Rd., San Diego, CA 92121 US | |

## GROWTH PLANS/SPECIAL FEATURES:

Biosite, Inc. is a global diagnostics company dedicated to utilizing biotechnology in the development of diagnostic products. The firm, a private subsidiary of Inverness Medical Innovations, validates and patents novel protein biomarkers and panels of biomarkers, develops and markets products, conducts strategic research on its products, and educates healthcare providers about its products. Biosite markets immunoassay diagnostics in the areas of cardiovascular disease, drug overdose and infectious disease. Cardiovascular products include the Triage BNP Test, Triage Cardiac Panel, Triage Profiler Panels, Triage D-Dimer Test and Triage Stroke Panel. The Triage BNP test is used in more than 3,000 hospitals and doctor's offices, and helps in the diagnosis, and severity assessment, of heart failure. The Triage Drugs of Abuse Panel and Triage TOX Drug Screen are rapid, qualitative urine screens that test for up to nine different illicit and prescription drugs, or drug classes, and provide results in less than 15 minutes. The firm's Biosite Discovery research business seeks to identify new protein markers of diseases that lack effective diagnostic tests. Additionally, with Biosite Discovery, the company has the capacity to offer antibody development services to companies seeking high-affinity antibodies for use in drug research. In return, Biosite seeks diagnostic licenses. The firm's Encompass program provides comprehensive education and consultation programs for all Biosite customers. These programs include training and education; evaluation support; product training; clinical training; outcomes tracking; POC reimbursement; CLIA audit reports, and audits on request; and consulting services. In June 2007, Biosite was acquired by Inverness Medical Innovations, Inc., a diagnostics developing company, for $92.50 per share. GE Healthcare Financial Services, a leading U.S. healthcare lessor, helped finance the acquisition.

Biosite offers employees a benefits package including flexible spending accounts, an employee assistance program, bereavement leave, education reimbursement, a 401(k) plan and an employee stock purchase plan.

## FINANCIALS: **Sales and profits are in thousands of dollars—add 000 to get the full amount. 2008 Note: Financial information for 2008 was not available for all companies at press time.**

| | | |
|---|---|---|
| 2008 Sales: $ | 2008 Profits: $ | **U.S. Stock Ticker: Subsidiary** |
| 2007 Sales: $ | 2007 Profits: $ | **Int'l Ticker:** Int'l Exchange: |
| 2006 Sales: $308,592 | 2006 Profits: $39,994 | Employees: 1,036 |
| 2005 Sales: $287,699 | 2005 Profits: $54,029 | Fiscal Year Ends: 12/31 |
| 2004 Sales: $244,900 | 2004 Profits: $41,400 | Parent Company: INVERNESS MEDICAL INNOVATIONS INC |

## SALARIES/BENEFITS:

| | | | | |
|---|---|---|---|---|
| Pension Plan: | ESOP Stock Plan: | Profit Sharing: | Top Exec. Salary: $553,500 | Bonus: $264,424 |
| Savings Plan: Y | Stock Purch. Plan: Y | | Second Exec. Salary: $430,961 | Bonus: $203,944 |

## OTHER THOUGHTS:

**Apparent Women Officers or Directors**: 3
**Hot Spot for Advancement for Women/Minorities**: Y

## LOCATIONS: ("Y" = Yes)

| West: | Southwest: | Midwest: | Southeast: | Northeast: | International: |
|---|---|---|---|---|---|
| Y | | | | | Y |

Note: Financial information, benefits and other data can change quickly and may vary from those stated here.

# BLACK HILLS CORP

www.blackhillscorp.com

**Industry Group Code:** 221000A **Ranks within this company's industry group:** Sales: 7 Profits: 4

| Management: | | Sales/Marketing: | | Liberal Arts: | | Information Systems: | | Professionals: | | Technical/Scientific: | |
|---|---|---|---|---|---|---|---|---|---|---|---|
| Mgmt. Trainees: | | Mktg. Professionals: | Y | Gen. Writing/Editing: | | Info. Management: | Y | Finance/Accounting: | Y | Engineers, Elec.: | Y |
| Experienced Mgmt.: | Y | Retail Sales: | | Technical Writing: | | Software Dev.: | | Law: | Y | Engineers, Other: | Y |
| Int'l Business: | | Commercial/Industrial: | Y | Graphic Arts/Photog.: | | Hardware Dev.: | | HR/Other: | Y | Health/Lab: | |
| MBA Graduates: | Y | Sales Trainees: | Y | Music: | | Systems Integration: | | Training: | Y | Scientists/Research: | |
| | | Advertising Pros.: | | Broadcasting: | | Consulting/Other: | | Health Care: | | Petroleum/Chemicals: | Y |
| | | | | Other: | | | | Consulting: | | Math/Other: | |

## TYPES OF BUSINESS:

Utilities-Electricity & Natural Gas
Coal Production
Oil & Natural Gas Exploration & Production

## BRANDS/DIVISIONS/AFFILIATES:

Black Hills Energy
Black Hills Power
Cheyenne Light
Wyodak Resources Development Corp.

## CONTACTS: *Note: Officers with more than one job title may be intentionally listed here more than once.*

David R. Emery, CEO
David R. Emery, Pres.
Anthony S. Cleberg, CFO/Exec. VP
Scott A. Buchholz, CIO/Sr. VP
James M. Mattern, Sr. VP-Corp. Admin. & Compliance
Steven J. Helmers, General Counsel/Sr. VP
Richard W. Kinzley, Sr. VP-Strategic Planning & Dev.
Lynnette K. Wilson, Sr. VP-Comm.
Lynnette K. Wilson, Sr. VP-Investor Rel.
Garner M. Anderson, Chief Risk Officer/Treas./VP
Thomas M. Ohlmacher, COO/Pres., Wholesale Bus.
Linden R. Evans, Pres./COO-Retail Bus.
Perry S. Krush, Controller/VP
Roxann R. Basham, VP-Governance/Corp. Sec.
David R. Emery, Chmn.

| | |
|---|---|
| **Phone:** 605-721-2343 | **Fax:** |
| **Toll-Free:** | |
| **Address:** 625 9th St., Rapid City, SD 57709 US | |

## GROWTH PLANS/SPECIAL FEATURES:

Black Hills Corporation is an energy company operating primarily in the U.S. The firm divides its business in two segments: utilities and non-regulated energy. The utilities group conducts business in two divisions: electric utility; and combination electric and gas utility. Through Black Hills Power, the group engages in the generation, transmission and distribution of electricity to roughly 65,100 customers in South Dakota, Wyoming and Montana. Through Cheyenne Light, the group engages in the distribution of electric and natural gas and serves approximately 39,400 electric and 33,000 natural gas customers in Cheyenne, Wyoming area. The non-regulated energy group, which operates Black Hills Energy and its subsidiaries, conducts business in four divisions: Oil and gas, which develops and produces natural gas and crude oil; power generation, which engages in the production and sale of electric capacity and energy through a diversified portfolio of generating plants; coal mining, which, through Wyodak Resources Development Corp., mines and sells coal at the company's coal mine located near Gillette, Wyoming; and energy marketing, which, through Enserco, engages in the marketing of natural gas and crude oil primarily in the Western portion of the U.S. and in Canada. Black Hills holds varying interests in independent power plants in California, New York, Massachusetts, Wyoming, Nevada and Colorado. In April 2008, the firm entered into an agreement with Hastings Funds Management and IIF BH Investment LLC to sell seven of its power plants for $840 million. In July 2008, the firm acquired five Aquila, Inc. utilities businesses. The first is an electric utility in Colorado. The remaining four are natural gas utilities located Colorado, Iowa, Kansas and Nebraska.

The company offers its employees medical, dental and vision insurance; short- and long-term disability insurance; a 401(k) plan; life and AD&D insurance; an employee assistance program; and tuition reimbursement.

## FINANCIALS: Sales and profits are in thousands of dollars—add 000 to get the full amount. 2008 Note: Financial information for 2008 was not available for all companies at press time.

| | | |
|---|---|---|
| 2008 Sales: $ | 2008 Profits: $ | **U.S. Stock Ticker: BKH** |
| 2007 Sales: $695,914 | 2007 Profits: $98,772 | **Int'l Ticker:** Int'l Exchange: |
| 2006 Sales: $656,882 | 2006 Profits: $81,019 | Employees: 998 |
| 2005 Sales: $613,541 | 2005 Profits: $33,420 | Fiscal Year Ends: 12/31 |
| 2004 Sales: $445,543 | 2004 Profits: $57,973 | Parent Company: |

## SALARIES/BENEFITS:

| | | | | |
|---|---|---|---|---|
| Pension Plan: Y | ESOP Stock Plan: | Profit Sharing: | Top Exec. Salary: $544,231 | Bonus: $763,000 |
| Savings Plan: Y | Stock Purch. Plan: | | Second Exec. Salary: $340,600 | Bonus: $340,600 |

## OTHER THOUGHTS:

**Apparent Women Officers or Directors**: 3
**Hot Spot for Advancement for Women/Minorities**: Y

## LOCATIONS: ("Y" = Yes)

| West: | Southwest: | Midwest: | Southeast: | Northeast: | International: |
|---|---|---|---|---|---|
| Y | Y | Y | Y | | |

# BLACKBOARD INC

**www.blackboard.com**

**Industry Group Code:** 611410 **Ranks within this company's industry group:** Sales: 1 Profits: 1

| Management: | | Sales/Marketing: | | Liberal Arts: | | Information Systems: | | Professionals: | | Technical/Scientific: | |
|---|---|---|---|---|---|---|---|---|---|---|---|
| Mgmt. Trainees: | Y | Mktg. Professionals: | Y | Gen. Writing/Editing: | Y | Info. Management: | Y | Finance/Accounting: | Y | Engineers, Elec.: | |
| Experienced Mgmt.: | Y | Retail Sales: | | Technical Writing: | | Software Dev.: | Y | Law: | Y | Engineers, Other: | |
| Int'l Business: | Y | Commercial/Industrial: | Y | Graphic Arts/Photog.: | Y | Hardware Dev.: | | HR/Other: | Y | Health/Lab: | |
| MBA Graduates: | Y | Sales Trainees: | Y | Music: | | Systems Integration: | Y | Training: | Y | Scientists/Research: | |
| | | Advertising Pros.: | Y | Broadcasting: | | Consulting/Other: | | Health Care: | | Petroleum/Chemicals: | |
| | | | | Other: | Y | | | Consulting: | | Math/Other: | |

## TYPES OF BUSINESS:

Online Educational Software
e-Learning Software
Content Management Software

## BRANDS/DIVISIONS/AFFILIATES:

Blackboard Academic Suite
Blackboard Learning System
Blackboard Community System
Blackboard Content System
Blackboard Portfolio System
Blackboard Connect
NTI Group Inc

## CONTACTS: *Note: Officers with more than one job title may be intentionally listed here more than once.*

Michael L. Chasen, CEO
Michael L. Chasen, Pres.
Michael Beach, CFO
Matthew Small, General Counsel/Sec.
Matthew Small, Chief Bus. Officer
John Kinzer, Sr. VP-Finance
Jessie Woolley-Wilson, Pres., K12 at Blackboard Inc.
Judy Verses, Pres./COO-Blackboard Learn
C. Russ Carlson, Pres., Blackboard Academis Bus.
David Marr, Pres./COO-Transact
Matthew Serbin Pittinsky, Chmn.
Juan Lucca, Pres., Int'l Bus.

**Phone:** 202-463-4860 **Fax:** 202-463-4863
**Toll-Free:** 800-424-9299
**Address:** 650 Massachusetts Ave. N.W., 6th Fl., Washington, DC 20001-3796 US

## GROWTH PLANS/SPECIAL FEATURES:

Blackboard, Inc. is a provider of enterprise software applications and related services to the education industry. Its product line consists of various software applications delivered in two suites, the Blackboard Academic Suite and the Blackboard Commerce Suite. The Blackboard Academic Suite provides a scalable technology platform for delivering education online, managing digital content and aggregating access to tools, information and through an integrated web portal environment. The applications that make it up are the Blackboard Learning System basic and enterprise products, which allow education providers to support an online teaching and learning environment; the Blackboard Community System; the Blackboard Content System; the Blackboard Portfolio System; and the Blackboard Outcomes System. The Blackboard Commerce Suite can be used for on- and off-campus commerce, online e-commerce, meal plan administration, vending, laundry services, copy and print management and student and staff identification. It is comprised of the Blackboard Transaction System, the Blackboard Community System and Blackboard One. Blackboard licenses its products on a renewable basis, typically for an annual term. Clients include colleges, universities, schools and other education providers, as well as textbook publishers and student-focused merchants who serve education providers and their students. These clients use the company's software to integrate technology into the education experience and campus life and to support activities such as the assignment of digital materials on a class web site; online research and collaboration between students; the management of a departmental website by an administrator; and conducting cash-free transactions with students and faculty through pre-funded debit accounts. In January 2008, Blackboard acquired NTI Group, a provider of mass messaging and notification solutions for educational and government organizations.

Blackboard offers its employees stock options, parking reimbursement, emergency backup childcare, an employee assistance program, a 529 college fund program, emergency travel assistance and medical, dental, life and AD&D insurance.

## FINANCIALS: **Sales and profits are in thousands of dollars—add 000 to get the full amount. 2008 Note: Financial information for 2008 was not available for all companies at press time.**

| | | |
|---|---|---|
| 2008 Sales: $ | 2008 Profits: $ | **U.S. Stock Ticker: BBBB** |
| 2007 Sales: $239,448 | 2007 Profits: $12,865 | **Int'l Ticker:** Int'l Exchange: |
| 2006 Sales: $183,063 | 2006 Profits: $-10,737 | Employees: 890 |
| 2005 Sales: $135,664 | 2005 Profits: $41,853 | Fiscal Year Ends: 12/31 |
| 2004 Sales: $111,403 | 2004 Profits: $10,049 | Parent Company: |

## SALARIES/BENEFITS:

| | | | | |
|---|---|---|---|---|
| Pension Plan: | ESOP Stock Plan: | Profit Sharing: | Top Exec. Salary: $487,499 | Bonus: $555,194 |
| Savings Plan: Y | Stock Purch. Plan: | | Second Exec. Salary: $319,583 | Bonus: $175,954 |

## OTHER THOUGHTS:

**Apparent Women Officers or Directors**: 3
**Hot Spot for Advancement for Women/Minorities**: Y

## LOCATIONS: ("Y" = Yes)

| West: | Southwest: | Midwest: | Southeast: | Northeast: | International: |
|---|---|---|---|---|---|
| | Y | | | Y | Y |

# BLUE CARE NETWORK OF MICHIGAN

**www.mibcn.com**

**Industry Group Code:** 524114 **Ranks within this company's industry group:** Sales: 3 Profits: 2

| Management: | | Sales/Marketing: | | Liberal Arts: | | Information Systems: | | Professionals: | | Technical/Scientific: | |
|---|---|---|---|---|---|---|---|---|---|---|---|
| Mgmt. Trainees: | | Mktg. Professionals: | Y | Gen. Writing/Editing: | Y | Info. Management: | Y | Finance/Accounting: | Y | Engineers, Elec.: | |
| Experienced Mgmt.: | Y | Retail Sales: | | Technical Writing: | Y | Software Dev.: | | Law: | Y | Engineers, Other: | |
| Int'l Business: | | Commercial/Industrial: | Y | Graphic Arts/Photog.: | | Hardware Dev.: | | HR/Other: | Y | Health/Lab: | Y |
| MBA Graduates: | Y | Sales Trainees: | | Music: | | Systems Integration: | | Training: | Y | Scientists/Research: | |
| | | Advertising Pros.: | | Broadcasting: | | Consulting/Other: | | Health Care: | Y | Petroleum/Chemicals: | |
| | | | | Other: | | | | Consulting: | | Math/Other: | Y |

## TYPES OF BUSINESS:

Insurance-Medical & Health, HMOs & PPOs
Online Resources & Information
Disease Management

## BRANDS/DIVISIONS/AFFILIATES:

Blue Cross Blue Shield of Michigan
Health e-Blue
BlueHealthConnection
Subimo
Blue Elect Self-Referral Option
Healthy Blue Living

## CONTACTS: *Note: Officers with more than one job title may be intentionally listed here more than once.*

Jeanne Carlson, CEO
Laurie Westfall, COO/Sr. VP
Jeanne Carlson, Pres.
Susan A. Kluge, CFO/Sr. VP
Douglas R. Woll, Chief Medical Officer/Sr. VP
David R. Nelson, Chief Actuarial Officer/Sr. VP
William H. Black, Chmn.

**Phone:** 248-799-6400 **Fax:** 248-799-6979
**Toll-Free:** 800-662-6667
**Address:** 20500 Civic Center Dr., Southfield, MI 48076 US

## GROWTH PLANS/SPECIAL FEATURES:

Blue Care Network of Michigan (BCN), a subsidiary of Blue Cross Blue Shield of Michigan (BCBSM), is the largest HMO network in the state with over 500,000 members. The company works together with BCBSM by sharing resources to identify and fight fraud, protect member privacy and to support each other's technology infrastructure. The BCN offers its members traditional indemnity and Medicare, as well as supplementary management and care services. BCN works closely with its physician network and provides services and tools, such as its Health e-Blue software, to support its partners. Its BlueHealthConnection service, in collaboration with Blue Cross Blue Shield of Michigan, combines diverse programs to assist members with chronic or complex illnesses. The company's products include coverage options for individuals, groups and for extending coverage after having left a group. Its individual coverage options consist of OneBlue, which is available to individuals that are impacted by automotive or large group buyouts; Personal Plus, which is designed for individuals under the age of 65; BCN Advantage for the individual, which replaces Medicare coverage with comprehensive HMO coverage; and BCN 65, which works with Medicare to cover more health care costs. The company's group coverage options include the Blue Care Network standard HMO; the Blue Elect Self-Referral Option for employer groups of two or more in size; Healthy Blue Living, which has decreased co-payment and deductibles for members who live a healthy lifestyle; the Self-funded Option, which lets the employer assume the claims cost risk; BCN Advantage for groups; and BCN 65 for groups. Also, under the federal Consolidated Omnibus Budget Reconciliation Act (COBRA), BCN allows members to extend coverage after having left a group by paying their own premiums.

## FINANCIALS: **Sales and profits are in thousands of dollars—add 000 to get the full amount. 2008 Note: Financial information for 2008 was not available for all companies at press time.**

2008 Sales: $
2007 Sales: $2,151,857
2006 Sales: $2,034,389
2005 Sales: $1,439,429
2004 Sales: $1,395,438

2008 Profits: $
2007 Profits: $49,847
2006 Profits: $81,042
2005 Profits: $78,396
2004 Profits: $80,999

**U.S. Stock Ticker: Subsidiary**
**Int'l Ticker:** Int'l Exchange:
Employees: 1,600
Fiscal Year Ends: 12/31
Parent Company: BLUE CROSS AND BLUE SHIELD OF MICHIGAN

## SALARIES/BENEFITS:

Pension Plan: ESOP Stock Plan: Profit Sharing: Top Exec. Salary: $ Bonus: $
Savings Plan: Stock Purch. Plan: Second Exec. Salary: $ Bonus: $

## OTHER THOUGHTS:

**Apparent Women Officers or Directors**: 3
**Hot Spot for Advancement for Women/Minorities**: Y

## LOCATIONS: ("Y" = Yes)

| West: | Southwest: | Midwest: | Southeast: | Northeast: | International: |
|---|---|---|---|---|---|
| | | Y | | | |

# BLUE COAT SYSTEMS INC

www.bluecoat.com

**Industry Group Code:** 511211 **Ranks within this company's industry group:** Sales: 3 Profits: 2

| Management: | | Sales/Marketing: | | Liberal Arts: | | Information Systems: | | Professionals: | | Technical/Scientific: | |
|---|---|---|---|---|---|---|---|---|---|---|---|
| Mgmt. Trainees: | | Mktg. Professionals: | Y | Gen. Writing/Editing: | | Info. Management: | Y | Finance/Accounting: | Y | Engineers, Elec.: | Y |
| Experienced Mgmt.: | Y | Retail Sales: | | Technical Writing: | Y | Software Dev.: | Y | Law: | Y | Engineers, Other: | |
| Int'l Business: | Y | Commercial/Industrial: | Y | Graphic Arts/Photog.: | | Hardware Dev.: | | HR/Other: | Y | Health/Lab: | |
| MBA Graduates: | Y | Sales Trainees: | Y | Music: | | Systems Integration: | Y | Training: | Y | Scientists/Research: | |
| | | Advertising Pros.: | | Broadcasting: | | Consulting/Other: | | Health Care: | | Petroleum/Chemicals: | |
| | | | | Other: | | | | Consulting: | | Math/Other: | |

## TYPES OF BUSINESS:

WAN & Internet Security Applications
WAN Acceleration & Optimization Technology

## BRANDS/DIVISIONS/AFFILIATES:

ProxySG Appliances
SG Client
ProxyAV Appliances
ProxyRA Appliances
Blue Coat WebFilter
Blue Coat Reporter
Packeteer, Inc.
PacketShaper

## CONTACTS: *Note: Officers with more than one job title may be intentionally listed here more than once.*

Brian NeSmith, CEO
Brian NeSmith, Pres.
Kevin S. Royal, CFO/Sr. VP
Kevin Biggs, Sr. VP-Worldwide Sales
Betsy E. Bayha, General Counsel/Sec./Sr. VP
Dave de Simone, Sr. VP-Corp. Oper.
Bethany Mayer, Sr. VP-Worldwide Mktg.

| | |
|---|---|
| **Phone:** 408-220-2200 | **Fax:** 408-220-2250 |
| **Toll-Free:** 866-302-2628 | |
| **Address:** 420 N. Mary Ave., Sunnyvale, CA 94085-4121 US | |

## GROWTH PLANS/SPECIAL FEATURES:

Blue Coat Systems, Inc. offers business applications that accelerate and secure WAN-(Wide Area Network) and Internet-based operations. It specializes in internally and externally hosted network applications where the users are spread across multiple locations. Blue Coat has installed more than 8,000 customers worldwide, primarily medium and large enterprises in fields such as finance, government, healthcare and education. In general, the firm's technology has two applications: Secure Web Gateway Solutions, which deal with web content filtering, anti-virus protection, user identification and other Internet safety applications; and WAN Application Delivery Systems, which deal with WAN optimization or acceleration applications, such as byte caching, bandwidth management and compression. The company has a variety of products. ProxySG Appliances serve as the hardware basis of both the Secure Web Gateway and WAN Application Delivery products. They are installed in corporate headquarters, directly at Internet gateways or at WAN entry or exit points. SG Client is a software application installed on desktops or laptops at remote locations that do not have a ProxySG Appliance, such as branch offices and mobile user workstations. It mainly offers WAN optimization. ProxyAV Appliances offer hardwired anti-virus protection and other security measures designed to complement the ProxySG appliance. ProxyRA Appliances mainly offers mobile users secure access to a corporate network without having to set up a Virtual Private Network (VPN). Blue Coat WebFilter works with the ProxySG appliance to block harmful or inappropriate content. Blue Coat Reporter provides IT administrators detailed network performance reports. Lastly, the Blue Coat Director offers centralized management for the ProxySG appliances. In June 2008, the firm acquired Packeteer, Inc., developer of the PacketShaper brand WAN optimization technology, which Blue Coat will combine with the ProxySG line. Although the final purchase price is not yet settled, it will include at least $264 million for Packeteer's common stock.

## FINANCIALS: **Sales and profits are in thousands of dollars—add 000 to get the full amount. 2008 Note: Financial information for 2008 was not available for all companies at press time.**

| | | |
|---|---|---|
| 2008 Sales: $305,439 | 2008 Profits: $32,568 | **U.S. Stock Ticker: BCSI** |
| 2007 Sales: $177,700 | 2007 Profits: $-7,198 | **Int'l Ticker:** Int'l Exchange: |
| 2006 Sales: $141,722 | 2006 Profits: $2,940 | Employees: 1,033 |
| 2005 Sales: $96,186 | 2005 Profits: $4,656 | Fiscal Year Ends: 4/30 |
| 2004 Sales: $ | 2004 Profits: $ | Parent Company: |

## SALARIES/BENEFITS:

| | | | | |
|---|---|---|---|---|
| Pension Plan: | ESOP Stock Plan: | Profit Sharing: | Top Exec. Salary: $ | Bonus: $ |
| Savings Plan: | Stock Purch. Plan: | | Second Exec. Salary: $ | Bonus: $ |

## OTHER THOUGHTS:

**Apparent Women Officers or Directors**: 2
**Hot Spot for Advancement for Women/Minorities**:

## LOCATIONS: ("Y" = Yes)

| West: | Southwest: | Midwest: | Southeast: | Northeast: | International: |
|---|---|---|---|---|---|
| Y | Y | | | Y | Y |

# BLUE NILE INC

www.bluenile.com

**Industry Group Code:** 448310E **Ranks within this company's industry group:** Sales: 1 Profits: 1

| Management: | | Sales/Marketing: | | Liberal Arts: | | Information Systems: | | Professionals: | | Technical/Scientific: | |
|---|---|---|---|---|---|---|---|---|---|---|---|
| Mgmt. Trainees: | Y | Mktg. Professionals: | Y | Gen. Writing/Editing: | Y | Info. Management: | Y | Finance/Accounting: | Y | Engineers, Elec.: | |
| Experienced Mgmt.: | Y | Retail Sales: | Y | Technical Writing: | | Software Dev.: | Y | Law: | Y | Engineers, Other: | |
| Int'l Business: | Y | Commercial/Industrial: | | Graphic Arts/Photog.: | Y | Hardware Dev.: | | HR/Other: | Y | Health/Lab: | |
| MBA Graduates: | Y | Sales Trainees: | Y | Music: | | Systems Integration: | Y | Training: | Y | Scientists/Research: | |
| | | Advertising Pros.: | Y | Broadcasting: | | Consulting/Other: | | Health Care: | | Petroleum/Chemicals: | |
| | | | | Other: | | | | Consulting: | | Math/Other: | |

## TYPES OF BUSINESS:

Jewelry, Online Retail

## BRANDS/DIVISIONS/AFFILIATES:

bluenile.com

## CONTACTS:

*Note: Officers with more than one job title may be intentionally listed here more than once.*

Mark Vadon, CEO
Diane Irvine, Pres.
Marc Stolzman, CFO
Eileen B. Askew, Mgr.-Investor Rel.
Terri Maupin, VP-Finance/Controller
Darrell Cavens, Sr. VP
Dwight Gaston, Sr. VP
Susan Bell, Sr. VP
Mark Vadon, Chmn.

**Phone:** 206-336-6700 **Fax:** 206-336-6750
**Toll-Free:** 800-242-2728
**Address:** 705 5th Ave. S., Ste. 900, Seattle, WA 98104 US

## GROWTH PLANS/SPECIAL FEATURES:

Blue Nile, Inc. is an online retailer offering a broad selection of diamonds and other fine jewelry through its web site at bluenile.com. The website features interactive search functionality, as well as detailed product information. The site features more than 30,000 independently certified diamonds and over 1,000 styles of jewelry, including rings, wedding bands, necklaces, pendants, earrings, bracelets and watches. In addition to loose diamonds and settings, the company offers gold, platinum and silver jewelry with pearls, emeralds, rubies and sapphires. Customers can create their own jewelry by selecting a diamond and a favorite ring, pendant or earring design. Blue Nile has developed an online cost structure and a unique supply solution that eliminates traditional layers of diamond wholesalers and brokers, which allows the company to purchase most of its products at lower prices by avoiding mark-ups imposed by those intermediaries. This in turn allows Blue Nile to offer its products to the consumer at reduced prices. The site was originally founded in 1999 as Internetdiamonds.com. The company also maintains websites in the U.K. and Canada. The firm partners with such corporations as eBags and wine.com. In February 2008, Blue Nile began offering international shipping to 12 new countries in Europe and Asia-Pacific and now serves customers in Australia, Belgium, France, Germany, Hong Kong, Japan, the Netherlands, New Zealand, Singapore, Spain, Switzerland and Taiwan. In October of the same year, the retailer launched a new search process for its 150 engagement ring settings, allowing the customer to choose from the Classic, Sidestones, Vintage and Color collections.

Blue Nile offers its employees medical, dental and vision insurance, which includes domestic partner coverage; short- and long-term disability; a stock option plan; a 401(k) plan; life insurance; health, dependant care and transportation flexible spending accounts; an employee assistance program; transportation allowance; an employee discount program; and fitness programs.

## FINANCIALS:

**Sales and profits are in thousands of dollars—add 000 to get the full amount. 2008 Note: Financial information for 2008 was not available for all companies at press time.**

| | | |
|---|---|---|
| 2008 Sales: $ | 2008 Profits: $ | **U.S. Stock Ticker: NILE** |
| 2007 Sales: $319,264 | 2007 Profits: $17,459 | **Int'l Ticker:** Int'l Exchange: |
| 2006 Sales: $251,587 | 2006 Profits: $13,064 | Employees: 198 |
| 2005 Sales: $203,169 | 2005 Profits: $13,153 | Fiscal Year Ends: 12/31 |
| 2004 Sales: $169,242 | 2004 Profits: $9,987 | Parent Company: |

## SALARIES/BENEFITS:

| | | | | |
|---|---|---|---|---|
| Pension Plan: | ESOP Stock Plan: | Profit Sharing: | Top Exec. Salary: $385,000 | Bonus: $578,000 |
| Savings Plan: Y | Stock Purch. Plan: Y | | Second Exec. Salary: $336,641 | Bonus: $467,333 |

## OTHER THOUGHTS:

**Apparent Women Officers or Directors**: 5
**Hot Spot for Advancement for Women/Minorities**: Y

## LOCATIONS: ("Y" = Yes)

| West: | Southwest: | Midwest: | Southeast: | Northeast: | International: |
|---|---|---|---|---|---|
| Y | | | | | Y |

# BRIGHTSTAR CORPORATION

www.brightstarcorp.com

**Industry Group Code:** 421690 **Ranks within this company's industry group:** Sales: 1 Profits:

| Management: | | Sales/Marketing: | | Liberal Arts: | | Information Systems: | | Professionals: | | Technical/Scientific: | |
|---|---|---|---|---|---|---|---|---|---|---|---|
| Mgmt. Trainees: | | Mktg. Professionals: | Y | Gen. Writing/Editing: | | Info. Management: | Y | Finance/Accounting: | Y | Engineers, Elec.: | |
| Experienced Mgmt.: | Y | Retail Sales: | | Technical Writing: | Y | Software Dev.: | | Law: | Y | Engineers, Other: | |
| Int'l Business: | Y | Commercial/Industrial: | Y | Graphic Arts/Photog.: | | Hardware Dev.: | | HR/Other: | Y | Health/Lab: | |
| MBA Graduates: | Y | Sales Trainees: | Y | Music: | | Systems Integration: | | Training: | Y | Scientists/Research: | |
| | | Advertising Pros.: | | Broadcasting: | | Consulting/Other: | | Health Care: | | Petroleum/Chemicals: | |
| | | | | Other: | | | | Consulting: | | Math/Other: | |

## TYPES OF BUSINESS:

Telecommunication Supply Chain & Distribution Services
Wireless Device & Accessories Distribution
Wireless Device Manufacturing
Supply Chain, Marketing and Retail Consultation

## BRANDS/DIVISIONS/AFFILIATES:

Narbitec
Brightstar Retail
WSA Distributing
Brightstar Telecom
Tech Data Corp.
Brightstar European

## CONTACTS: *Note: Officers with more than one job title may be intentionally listed here more than once.*

R. Marcelo Claure, CEO
Denise Gibson, COO
R. Marcelo Claure, Pres.
Dennis J. Strand, CFO
Oscar Fumagali, Treas.
George Appling, COO/Pres., Global Solutions
Denise Gibson, CEO-Brightstar US
Rod Millar, Pres., Brightstar Europe
Mike Cost, Pres./COO-Brightstar US
R. Marcelo Claure, Chmn.
Juan Carlos Archila, Pres., Brightstar Latin America

| **Phone:** 305-421-6000 | **Fax:** |
|---|---|
| **Toll-Free:** | |
| **Address:** 9725 N.W. 117th Ave., Ste. 300, Miami, FL 33178 US | |

## GROWTH PLANS/SPECIAL FEATURES:

Brightstar Corporation is a global distributor and provider of value added supply chain services to the wireless and telecommunications industry. It also designs and manufactures products under licensing agreements with leading manufacturers. The company's supply chain services include inventory management, supply chain management logistics, fulfillment, customized packaging and assembly services. The firm distributes handsets, accessories, wireless data, fixed wireless, wireless broadband and prepaid wireless products. Brightstar's wireless data and telecom solutions division addresses vertical market needs through products and services within cellular infrastructure, broadband infrastructure, 2.5G and 3G modems, modules and PCMCIA cards, content applications and wireless PDAs. It also consults and invests in new business ventures. The firm operates facilities in nearly 50 countries worldwide, with the majority located in Central and South America. Brightstar's customer base includes over 220 network operators and over 30,000 distributors, agents, resellers and retailers around the world, serving more than 160,000 points of sale. Through a joint venture, Narbitec, the company designs, manufactures and distributes a complete line of fixed wireless products with a focus on rural markets. In May 2007, Brightstar announced the formation of a joint venture with WSA Distributing, named Brightstar Retail, which expands its retail services and product line in Latin America. In April 2007, Brightstar's Indian subsidy, Brightstar Telecom, partnered with LG Electronics Mobile Communications Company to offer Indian distribution of devices made by LG GSM Mobiles. To expand its European market, in February 2007, the firm partnered with Tech Data Corp. to form the joint venture, Brightstar European Ltd. Each company owns 50% of the venture.

The company organizes social functions for its employees such as sporting events and charitable fund-raising.

## FINANCIALS: **Sales and profits are in thousands of dollars—add 000 to get the full amount. 2008 Note: Financial information for 2008 was not available for all companies at press time.**

| | | |
|---|---|---|
| 2008 Sales: $ | 2008 Profits: $ | **U.S. Stock Ticker: Private** |
| 2007 Sales: $3,660,000 | 2007 Profits: $ | **Int'l Ticker:** Int'l Exchange: |
| 2006 Sales: $3,590,000 | 2006 Profits: $ | Employees: 2,087 |
| 2005 Sales: $2,252,000 | 2005 Profits: $ | Fiscal Year Ends: 12/31 |
| 2004 Sales: $ | 2004 Profits: $ | Parent Company: |

## SALARIES/BENEFITS:

| | | | | |
|---|---|---|---|---|
| Pension Plan: | ESOP Stock Plan: | Profit Sharing: | Top Exec. Salary: $ | Bonus: $ |
| Savings Plan: | Stock Purch. Plan: | | Second Exec. Salary: $ | Bonus: $ |

## OTHER THOUGHTS:

**Apparent Women Officers or Directors**: 1
**Hot Spot for Advancement for Women/Minorities**: Y

## LOCATIONS: ("Y" = Yes)

| West: | Southwest: | Midwest: | Southeast: | Northeast: | International: |
|---|---|---|---|---|---|
| | | Y | Y | | Y |

# CALIBER HOLDINGS CORP

www.calibernet.com

**Industry Group Code:** 811100 **Ranks within this company's industry group:** Sales: Profits:

| Management: | | Sales/Marketing: | | Liberal Arts: | | Information Systems: | | Professionals: | | Technical/Scientific: | |
|---|---|---|---|---|---|---|---|---|---|---|---|
| Mgmt. Trainees: | | Mktg. Professionals: | Y | Gen. Writing/Editing: | | Info. Management: | Y | Finance/Accounting: | Y | Engineers, Elec.: | |
| Experienced Mgmt.: | Y | Retail Sales: | | Technical Writing: | | Software Dev.: | | Law: | Y | Engineers, Other: | |
| Int'l Business: | | Commercial/Industrial: | | Graphic Arts/Photog.: | | Hardware Dev.: | | HR/Other: | Y | Health/Lab: | |
| MBA Graduates: | Y | Sales Trainees: | | Music: | | Systems Integration: | | Training: | Y | Scientists/Research: | |
| | | Advertising Pros.: | | Broadcasting: | | Consulting/Other: | | Health Care: | | Petroleum/Chemicals: | |
| | | | | Other: | | | | Consulting: | | Math/Other: | |

## TYPES OF BUSINESS:

Automotive Repair & Maintenance
Body Shops

## BRANDS/DIVISIONS/AFFILIATES:

Caliber Collision Centers
CaliberCare Limited Lifetime Warranty

## CONTACTS:

*Note: Officers with more than one job title may be intentionally listed here more than once.*

John Hovis, CEO
John Hovis, Pres.
Ken Mason, Dir.-Mktg.
Mark Sanders, Sr. VP-Oper.
Shannon Lynard, Dir.-Corp. Comm.
Matthew Ohrnstein, Chmn.

**Phone:** 949-224-0300 **Fax:** 949-224-0313
**Toll-Free:** 888-225-4237
**Address:** 17771 Cowan Ave., Ste. 100, Irvine, CA 92614 US

## GROWTH PLANS/SPECIAL FEATURES:

Caliber Holdings Corp., one of the largest independent body shop companies in the U.S., operates a chain of 63 automotive repair shops located throughout southern California and Texas, including a large-scale, 90,000-square-foot collision repair center in Santa Monica, California. The company offers comprehensive collision repair, which includes the equipment necessary to repair composites, high-strength steel, aluminum, safety systems, on-board computers and complex finishes. Caliber Collision Centers cooperate with 24-hour-a-day towing services and rental car networks through its Customer Services Division. In addition, the firm has partnered with most insurance companies in order to expedite and simplify repair. Caliber warrantees repair work against defects in materials and workmanship with its CaliberCare Limited Lifetime Warranty for as long as the customer owns the vehicle. The company also keeps its service centers open year-round, 24-hours-a-day.

Caliber offers its employees a benefits package including flexible spending accounts, an employee credit union, technical training and paid educational opportunities for continued advancement.

## FINANCIALS:

**Sales and profits are in thousands of dollars—add 000 to get the full amount. 2008 Note: Financial information for 2008 was not available for all companies at press time.**

| | | |
|---|---|---|
| 2008 Sales: $ | 2008 Profits: $ | **U.S. Stock Ticker: Private** |
| 2007 Sales: $ | 2007 Profits: $ | **Int'l Ticker:** Int'l Exchange: |
| 2006 Sales: $ | 2006 Profits: $ | Employees: 1,500 |
| 2005 Sales: $ | 2005 Profits: $ | Fiscal Year Ends: 12/31 |
| 2004 Sales: $ | 2004 Profits: $ | Parent Company: |

## SALARIES/BENEFITS:

| | | | | |
|---|---|---|---|---|
| Pension Plan: | ESOP Stock Plan: | Profit Sharing: | Top Exec. Salary: $ | Bonus: $ |
| Savings Plan: Y | Stock Purch. Plan: | | Second Exec. Salary: $ | Bonus: $ |

## OTHER THOUGHTS:

**Apparent Women Officers or Directors**: 1
**Hot Spot for Advancement for Women/Minorities**:

## LOCATIONS: ("Y" = Yes)

| West: | Southwest: | Midwest: | Southeast: | Northeast: | International: |
|---|---|---|---|---|---|
| Y | Y | | | | |

# CALIPER LIFE SCIENCES

www.calipertech.com

**Industry Group Code:** 325413 **Ranks within this company's industry group:** Sales: 4 Profits: 10

| Management: | | Sales/Marketing: | | Liberal Arts: | | Information Systems: | | Professionals: | | Technical/Scientific: | |
|---|---|---|---|---|---|---|---|---|---|---|---|
| Mgmt. Trainees: | | Mktg. Professionals: | Y | Gen. Writing/Editing: | | Info. Management: | Y | Finance/Accounting: | Y | Engineers, Elec.: | Y |
| Experienced Mgmt.: | Y | Retail Sales: | | Technical Writing: | Y | Software Dev.: | Y | Law: | Y | Engineers, Other: | Y |
| Int'l Business: | Y | Commercial/Industrial: | Y | Graphic Arts/Photog.: | Y | Hardware Dev.: | Y | HR/Other: | Y | Health/Lab: | Y |
| MBA Graduates: | Y | Sales Trainees: | Y | Music: | | Systems Integration: | Y | Training: | Y | Scientists/Research: | Y |
| | | Advertising Pros.: | | Broadcasting: | | Consulting/Other: | | Health Care: | Y | Petroleum/Chemicals: | |
| | | | | Other: | | | | Consulting: | | Math/Other: | Y |

## TYPES OF BUSINESS:

Bioanalysis Equipment
Microfluidic Systems
High-Throughput Screening Machines
Liquid Handling Systems
Drug Discovery Platforms
Laboratory Automation Solutions
Software

## BRANDS/DIVISIONS/AFFILIATES:

Caliper Technologies
LabChip 90
Lab Chip 3000
NovaScreen Biosciences Corp.
Xenogen Corp.
Caliper Discovery Alliances & Services
Zephyr Genomics Workstation

## CONTACTS: *Note: Officers with more than one job title may be intentionally listed here more than once.*

E. Kevin Hrusovsky, CEO
E. Kevin Hrusovsky, Pres.
Peter F. McAree, CFO/Sr. VP
Paula J. Cassidy, VP-Human Resources
Bradley W. Rice, Sr. VP-R&D
Stephen E. Creager, General Counsel/Corp. Sec./Sr. VP
Bruce J. Bal, Sr. VP-Oper.
William C. Kruka, Sr. VP-Corp. Dev.
David M. Manyak, Exec. VP-Caliper Discovery Alliances & Svcs.
Enrique Bernal, Sr. VP-In Vitro Bus. Dev.
Mark T. Roskey, VP-Reagents and Applied Biology
Bob Bishop, Chmn.

**Phone:** 508-435-9500 **Fax:** 508-435-3439
**Toll-Free:** 877-522-2447
**Address:** 68 Elm St., Hopkinton, MA 01748 US

## GROWTH PLANS/SPECIAL FEATURES:

Caliper Life Sciences uses its core technologies of liquid handling, automation and LabChip microfluidics to foster developments in the life sciences industry. The company manufactures high-throughput screening machines, automated liquid handling machines, micro-plate management, pharmaceutical development and quality control systems. Caliper is best known for its LabChip systems, which are designed to accelerate laboratory experimentation with applicability in the pharmaceutical and diagnostics industries. The firm makes two types of LabChip systems: LabChip 90 and LabChip 3000. LabChip 90, which is designed to meet the high-throughput needs of laboratories, uses microfluidic technology to automate the analysis of proteins and DNA fragments. The LabChip 3000 drug discovery system miniaturizes, integrates and automates enzymatic and cell-based assays even when unattended. LabChip assays are separations-based, so the quality of results exceeds what is achievable in homogeneous, well-based assays. Other products include various plate management; pharmaceutical development; evaporation and solid phase extraction devices; software; and workstations. Caliper Discovery Alliances & Services (CDAS) is the firm's contract research division that combines the biosciences of its two subsidiaries, NovaScreen and Xenogen, both providers of in vitro discovery services. In January 2009, the company launched the Zephyr Genomics Workstation, an improved automated solution liquid handling designed to improve quality and consistency.

Employees are offered medical, dental and vision insurance; life insurance; short-and long-term disability coverage; a 401(k) plan; a stock purchase plan; tuition reimbursement; and an employee assistance plan.

## FINANCIALS: **Sales and profits are in thousands of dollars—add 000 to get the full amount. 2008 Note: Financial information for 2008 was not available for all companies at press time.**

| | | |
|---|---|---|
| 2008 Sales: $ | 2008 Profits: $ | **U.S. Stock Ticker: CALP** |
| 2007 Sales: $140,707 | 2007 Profits: $-24,080 | **Int'l Ticker:** Int'l Exchange: |
| 2006 Sales: $107,871 | 2006 Profits: $-28,934 | Employees: 543 |
| 2005 Sales: $87,009 | 2005 Profits: $-14,457 | Fiscal Year Ends: 12/31 |
| 2004 Sales: $80,127 | 2004 Profits: $-31,600 | Parent Company: |

## SALARIES/BENEFITS:

| | | | | |
|---|---|---|---|---|
| Pension Plan: | ESOP Stock Plan: | Profit Sharing: | Top Exec. Salary: $433,500 | Bonus: $238,425 |
| Savings Plan: Y | Stock Purch. Plan: Y | | Second Exec. Salary: $276,167 | Bonus: $67,064 |

## OTHER THOUGHTS:

**Apparent Women Officers or Directors**: 2
**Hot Spot for Advancement for Women/Minorities**: Y

## LOCATIONS: ("Y" = Yes)

| West: | Southwest: | Midwest: | Southeast: | Northeast: | International: |
|---|---|---|---|---|---|
| Y | | | | Y | Y |

# CAL-MAINE FOODS INC

www.calmainefoods.com

**Industry Group Code:** 112300 **Ranks within this company's industry group:** Sales: 1 Profits: 1

| Management: | | Sales/Marketing: | | Liberal Arts: | | Information Systems: | | Professionals: | | Technical/Scientific: | |
|---|---|---|---|---|---|---|---|---|---|---|---|
| Mgmt. Trainees: | | Mktg. Professionals: | Y | Gen. Writing/Editing: | | Info. Management: | Y | Finance/Accounting: | Y | Engineers, Elec.: | |
| Experienced Mgmt.: | Y | Retail Sales: | | Technical Writing: | | Software Dev.: | | Law: | Y | Engineers, Other: | |
| Int'l Business: | | Commercial/Industrial: | | Graphic Arts/Photog.: | | Hardware Dev.: | | HR/Other: | Y | Health/Lab: | |
| MBA Graduates: | Y | Sales Trainees: | | Music: | | Systems Integration: | | Training: | Y | Scientists/Research: | |
| | | Advertising Pros.: | | Broadcasting: | | Consulting/Other: | | Health Care: | | Petroleum/Chemicals: | |
| | | | | Other: | | | | Consulting: | | Math/Other: | |

## TYPES OF BUSINESS:

Food Production-Eggs
Shell Egg Production & Distribution

## BRANDS/DIVISIONS/AFFILIATES:

Egg-Land's Best
Farmhouse
Rio Grande
Sunups
Hillandale Farms, Inc.
Hillandale Farms of Florida, Inc.
Green Forest Foods, LLC

## CONTACTS: *Note: Officers with more than one job title may be intentionally listed here more than once.*

Fred R. Adams, Jr., CEO
Adolphus B. Baker, COO
Adolphus B. Baker, Pres.
Timothy A. Dawson, CFO/VP
Jeff Hardin, VP-Sales
Jack B. Self, VP-Oper., Prod.
James Neeld, III, General Counsel
David Jenkins, VP-Oper.
Timothy A. Dawson, Treas./Corp. Sec.
Richard K. Looper, Vice Chmn.
Charles F. Collins, VP/Controller
Ken Paramore, VP-Sales
Bob Scott, VP-Oper.
Fred R. Adams, Jr., Chmn.

| | |
|---|---|
| **Phone:** 601-948-6813 | **Fax:** 601-969-0905 |
| **Toll-Free:** | |
| **Address:** 3320 Woodrow Wilson Dr., Jackson, MS 39209 US | |

## GROWTH PLANS/SPECIAL FEATURES:

Cal-Maine Foods, Inc. produces, grades, packages and markets fresh shell eggs to retailers in approximately 29 states in the Southeastern, Southwestern, Midwestern and Mid-Atlantic regions of the U.S. It controls approximately 15.5% of the country's fresh egg market. Customers include national and regional grocery store chains; club stores; egg product manufacturers; and food service distributors. The company's flock is comprised of 23 million layers (mature female chickens) and 5 million pullets (young female chickens) and breeders (male or female chickens used to produce fertile eggs). Feed for the laying flocks is produced by company-owned and -operated mills located throughout the country. Cal-Maine also produces specialty shell eggs, such as reduced-cholesterol, cage-free and organic eggs. The firm has an exclusive license agreement to market and distribute Egg-Land's Best specialty shell eggs in major metropolitan areas, including New York City and a number of states in the Southeast and Southwest. Cage-free eggs are marketed under the Farmhouse brand name. Cal-Maine also produces, markets and distributes private-label specialty shell eggs. Brands under which the company's eggs are marketed include Cal-Maine, Rio Grande and Sunups. The firm currently is the majority shareholder of Hillandale Farms of Florida, Inc. and Hillandale Farms, Inc., and is under agreement to complete the purchase of all outstanding shares by 2009. In January 2007, Cal-Maine became the sole owner and operator of Green Forest Foods, LLC. The company was formed through a joint venture between Cal-Maine and Green Forest Egg Company the year before. Green Forest Foods produces, processes and markets eggs from approximately 1 million laying hens, and supplies them to retailers and food service distributors in the south-central region of the U.S. In April 2007, the firm acquired the assets of the shell egg division belonging to George's Inc., a major poultry producer.

## FINANCIALS: **Sales and profits are in thousands of dollars—add 000 to get the full amount. 2008 Note: Financial information for 2008 was not available for all companies at press time.**

| | | |
|---|---|---|
| 2008 Sales: $915,939 | 2008 Profits: $151,861 | **U.S. Stock Ticker: CALM** |
| 2007 Sales: $598,128 | 2007 Profits: $36,656 | **Int'l Ticker:** Int'l Exchange: |
| 2006 Sales: $477,555 | 2006 Profits: $-1,013 | Employees: 1,800 |
| 2005 Sales: $375,266 | 2005 Profits: $-10,358 | Fiscal Year Ends: 5/31 |
| 2004 Sales: $572,331 | 2004 Profits: $66,442 | Parent Company: |

## SALARIES/BENEFITS:

| | | | | |
|---|---|---|---|---|
| Pension Plan: | ESOP Stock Plan: Y | Profit Sharing: | Top Exec. Salary: $250,000 | Bonus: $250,000 |
| Savings Plan: Y | Stock Purch. Plan: | | Second Exec. Salary: $223,461 | Bonus: $215,000 |

## OTHER THOUGHTS:

**Apparent Women Officers or Directors**: 1
**Hot Spot for Advancement for Women/Minorities**:

## LOCATIONS: ("Y" = Yes)

| West: | Southwest: | Midwest: | Southeast: | Northeast: | International: |
|---|---|---|---|---|---|
| Y | Y | Y | Y | Y | |

# CALPINE CORPORATION

www.calpine.com

**Industry Group Code:** 221000A **Ranks within this company's industry group:** Sales: 1 Profits: 1

| Management: | | Sales/Marketing: | | Liberal Arts: | | Information Systems: | | Professionals: | | Technical/Scientific: | |
|---|---|---|---|---|---|---|---|---|---|---|---|
| Mgmt. Trainees: | | Mktg. Professionals: | Y | Gen. Writing/Editing: | | Info. Management: | Y | Finance/Accounting: | Y | Engineers, Elec.: | Y |
| Experienced Mgmt.: | Y | Retail Sales: | | Technical Writing: | | Software Dev.: | | Law: | Y | Engineers, Other: | Y |
| Int'l Business: | Y | Commercial/Industrial: | Y | Graphic Arts/Photog.: | | Hardware Dev.: | | HR/Other: | Y | Health/Lab: | |
| MBA Graduates: | Y | Sales Trainees: | Y | Music: | | Systems Integration: | | Training: | Y | Scientists/Research: | |
| | | Advertising Pros.: | | Broadcasting: | | Consulting/Other: | | Health Care: | | Petroleum/Chemicals: | Y |
| | | | | Other: | | | | Consulting: | | Math/Other: | |

## TYPES OF BUSINESS:

Utilities-Electricity
Electrical Generation
Engineering & Support Services
Power Plant Construction
Geothermal Power Generation
Turbine Support Services & Engineering
Energy Asset Management
Energy Marketing & Trading

## BRANDS/DIVISIONS/AFFILIATES:

Calpine Canada
Calpine Merchant Services
Calpine Power Company
Calpine Power Services
Calpine Construction Finance Company
NewSouth Energy, LLC

## CONTACTS: *Note: Officers with more than one job title may be intentionally listed here more than once.*

Jack A. Fusco, CEO
Jack A. Fusco, Pres.
Zamir Rauf, Interim CFO
Eric Gonzales, Sr. VP-Mktg.
John R. Moore, Sr. VP-Human Resources
Dennis Fishback, CIO/Sr. VP
W. Thaddeus Miller, Chief Legal Officer/Exec. VP/Corp. Sec.
Jeffrey P. Kinneman, Sr VP-Strategy, Structured Finance & Restructuring
Andre Walker, VP-Investor Rel.
Melissa A. Brown, Sr. VP-Financial Planning
Gary M. Germeroth, Chief Risk Officer/Exec. VP
Thad Hill, Chief Commercial Officer/Exec. VP
Michael Rogers, Sr. VP/Pres., Power Oper.
William J. Patterson, Chmn.

| **Phone:** 408-995-5115 | **Fax:** 408-995-0505 |
|---|---|
| **Toll-Free:** | |
| **Address:** 50 W. San Fernando St., San Jose, CA 95113 US | |

## GROWTH PLANS/SPECIAL FEATURES:

Calpine Corporation develops, builds, acquires and operates combined-cycle power plants, and sells electricity with a focus on natural gas-fired combustion turbine and geothermal energy production. Operating in 22 U.S. states, the U.K. and Canada, the company has approximately 82 natural gas-fired and geothermal power plants and a total capacity of over 24,000 megawatts (MW). The firm operates through multiple subsidiaries that run a variety of energy services, including: Calpine Canada, which operates power plants in three provinces and manages the Calpine Power Income Fund; Calpine Merchant Services, which manages Calpine's power generation assets; Calpine Power Company, which manages the operations of the company's fleet of power plants; Calpine Power Services, which provides program management and operating services to third parties; and Calpine Construction Finance Company, which manages the construction of power plants. The company also operates its NewSouth Energy subsidiary, which manages marketing and communications for Calpine's assets in southern states. The company has recently sold off a number of its operations, including all of the assets of its Power Systems Mfg., LLC, subsidiary to Alstom Power, Inc. for $242 million in March 2007; and the company's 50% ownership interest in Acadia Power Partners, LLC to Cajun Gas Energy, LLC for approximately $189 million. In January 2008, the company successfully emerged from Chapter 11 bankruptcy protection. In February 2008, Calpine sold a partially completed power plant, in Alabama, to a subsidiary of Constellation Energy, for $155 million. The sale was part of the company's Chapter 11 restructuring plan.

## FINANCIALS: **Sales and profits are in thousands of dollars—add 000 to get the full amount. 2008 Note: Financial information for 2008 was not available for all companies at press time.**

| | | |
|---|---|---|
| 2008 Sales: $ | 2008 Profits: $ | **U.S. Stock Ticker: CPNL.PK** |
| 2007 Sales: $7,970,000 | 2007 Profits: $2,693,000 | **Int'l Ticker:** Int'l Exchange: |
| 2006 Sales: $6,937,000 | 2006 Profits: $-1,764,907 | Employees: 2,080 |
| 2005 Sales: $10,112,658 | 2005 Profits: $-9,939,208 | Fiscal Year Ends: 12/31 |
| 2004 Sales: $8,648,382 | 2004 Profits: $-242,461 | Parent Company: |

## SALARIES/BENEFITS:

| | | | | |
|---|---|---|---|---|
| Pension Plan: | ESOP Stock Plan: | Profit Sharing: | Top Exec. Salary: $1,500,000 | Bonus: $2,430,000 |
| Savings Plan: Y | Stock Purch. Plan: Y | | Second Exec. Salary: $500,000 | Bonus: $ 720 |

## OTHER THOUGHTS:

**Apparent Women Officers or Directors**: 1
**Hot Spot for Advancement for Women/Minorities**: Y

## LOCATIONS: ("Y" = Yes)

| West: | Southwest: | Midwest: | Southeast: | Northeast: | International: |
|---|---|---|---|---|---|
| Y | Y | Y | Y | Y | Y |

# CAMBREX CORP

www.cambrex.com

**Industry Group Code:** 325412 **Ranks within this company's industry group:** Sales: 12 Profits: 3

| Management: | | Sales/Marketing: | | Liberal Arts: | | Information Systems: | | Professionals: | | Technical/Scientific: | |
|---|---|---|---|---|---|---|---|---|---|---|---|
| Mgmt. Trainees: | | Mktg. Professionals: | Y | Gen. Writing/Editing: | | Info. Management: | Y | Finance/Accounting: | Y | Engineers, Elec.: | |
| Experienced Mgmt.: | Y | Retail Sales: | | Technical Writing: | Y | Software Dev.: | Y | Law: | Y | Engineers, Other: | |
| Int'l Business: | Y | Commercial/Industrial: | Y | Graphic Arts/Photog.: | | Hardware Dev.: | | HR/Other: | Y | Health/Lab: | Y |
| MBA Graduates: | Y | Sales Trainees: | Y | Music: | | Systems Integration: | | Training: | Y | Scientists/Research: | Y |
| | | Advertising Pros.: | | Broadcasting: | | Consulting/Other: | | Health Care: | Y | Petroleum/Chemicals: | Y |
| | | | | Other: | | | | Consulting: | | Math/Other: | Y |

## TYPES OF BUSINESS:

Contract Pharmaceutical Manufacturing
Contract Research
Pharmaceutical Ingredients
Testing Products & Services
Technical Support

## BRANDS/DIVISIONS/AFFILIATES:

Cambrex Charles City Inc
Cambrex Kariskoga AB
Cambrex Profarmaco
Cambrex Tallinn AS
FlashGel Rapid Electrophoresis System
Platinum UltraPAK

## CONTACTS: *Note: Officers with more than one job title may be intentionally listed here more than once.*

Steven M. Klosk, CEO
Steven M. Klosk, Pres.
Greg Sargen, CFO/VP
Paolo Russolo, Pres., Cambrex Profarmaco
John Miller, Chmn.

| | |
|---|---|
| **Phone:** 201-804-3000 | **Fax:** 201-804-9852 |
| **Toll-Free:** | |
| **Address:** 1 Meadowlands Plz., East Rutherford, NJ 07073 US | |

## GROWTH PLANS/SPECIAL FEATURES:

Cambrex Corp. provides products and services to aid and enhance the discovery and commercialization of therapeutics. The company offers a variety of outsourcing products and services for drug discovery research and therapeutic testing. The firm manufactures products, which are sold to research organizations, pharmaceutical, biopharmaceutical and generic drug companies. Outsourcing options include bulk biologics manufacturing; development, manufacturing and commercialization services for cell-based therapeutics and pharmaceutical products; and testing services including assays for microbiology, sterility and veterinary services. Products offered for drug discovery research include bioassays; cell model systems; cell analysis stains; electrophoresis products, including the FlashGel Rapid Electrophoresis System; and protein analysis products. Cambrex offers technical support for all its research products. In addition, Cambrex offers Platinum UltraPAK, a line of flexible packaging systems that can be modified to fit specific customer needs. Therapeutic testing products include a range of endotoxin services and products, including endotoxin detection assays, removal products, testing services accessory products, instrumentation and software. The company also offers testing products using a wide range of assays. Subsidiaries of the firm include Cambrex Charles City, Inc.; Cambrex Karlskoga AB; Cambrex Profarmaco; and Cambrex Tallinn AS. In 2008, Swedish subsidiary Cambrex Kariskoga AB acquired ProSyntest AS, an Estonia-based active pharmaceutical ingredients research and development company. ProSyntest was consequently renamed Cambrex Tallinn. In January 2009, Cambrex signed a joint marketing and development agreement with Skinvisible, Inc. to develop acne products.

Employees are offered medical, dental, vision and life insurance; short-and long-term disability coverage; a 401(k) plan; and tuition reimbursement.

## FINANCIALS: **Sales and profits are in thousands of dollars—add 000 to get the full amount. 2008 Note: Financial information for 2008 was not available for all companies at press time.**

| | | |
|---|---|---|
| 2008 Sales: $ | 2008 Profits: $ | **U.S. Stock Ticker: CBM** |
| 2007 Sales: $252,574 | 2007 Profits: $209,248 | **Int'l Ticker:** Int'l Exchange: |
| 2006 Sales: $236,659 | 2006 Profits: $-30,100 | Employees: 844 |
| 2005 Sales: $223,565 | 2005 Profits: $-110,458 | Fiscal Year Ends: 12/31 |
| 2004 Sales: $395,906 | 2004 Profits: $-26,870 | Parent Company: |

## SALARIES/BENEFITS:

| | | | | |
|---|---|---|---|---|
| Pension Plan: | ESOP Stock Plan: | Profit Sharing: | Top Exec. Salary: $500,000 | Bonus: $1,750,000 |
| Savings Plan: Y | Stock Purch. Plan: | | Second Exec. Salary: $396,567 | Bonus: $1,360,600 |

## OTHER THOUGHTS:

**Apparent Women Officers or Directors**: 2
**Hot Spot for Advancement for Women/Minorities**: Y

## LOCATIONS: ("Y" = Yes)

| West: | Southwest: | Midwest: | Southeast: | Northeast: | International: |
|---|---|---|---|---|---|
| | | Y | | Y | Y |

# CANDELA CORP

www.candelalaser.com

**Industry Group Code:** 339113 **Ranks within this company's industry group:** Sales: 23 Profits: 29

| Management: | | Sales/Marketing: | | Liberal Arts: | | Information Systems: | | Professionals: | | Technical/Scientific: | |
|---|---|---|---|---|---|---|---|---|---|---|---|
| Mgmt. Trainees: | | Mktg. Professionals: | Y | Gen. Writing/Editing: | | Info. Management: | Y | Finance/Accounting: | Y | Engineers, Elec.: | Y |
| Experienced Mgmt.: | Y | Retail Sales: | | Technical Writing: | Y | Software Dev.: | Y | Law: | Y | Engineers, Other: | Y |
| Int'l Business: | Y | Commercial/Industrial: | Y | Graphic Arts/Photog.: | | Hardware Dev.: | Y | HR/Other: | Y | Health/Lab: | Y |
| MBA Graduates: | Y | Sales Trainees: | Y | Music: | | Systems Integration: | Y | Training: | Y | Scientists/Research: | Y |
| | | Advertising Pros.: | | Broadcasting: | | Consulting/Other: | | Health Care: | Y | Petroleum/Chemicals: | |
| | | | | Other: | | | | Consulting: | | Math/Other: | Y |

## TYPES OF BUSINESS:

Equipment-Laser Systems
Cosmetic Clinical Products

## BRANDS/DIVISIONS/AFFILIATES:

GentleMax
AlexTriVantage
SmoothPeel
Serenity
GentleLASE
GentleYAG
Vbeam
Smoothbeam

## CONTACTS:

*Note: Officers with more than one job title may be intentionally listed here more than once.*

Gerard E. Puorro, CEO
Jay David Caplan, COO
Gerard E. Puorro, Pres.
Robert J. Wilber, Sr. VP-Mktg.
James C. Hsia, CTO
Lewis J. Levine, VP-Eng.
Paul R. Luchese, General Counsel/Sr. VP/Corp. Sec.
Catherine Kniker, VP-Corp. Strategic Dev.
Robert E. Quinn, Treas./Corp. Controller
Dennis S. Herman, Sr. VP-North American Sales
Robert LaRoche, VP-Global Mktg.
Toshio Mori, Pres., Candela K.K./VP
Scott Blood, VP-Quality Assurance & Regulatory Affairs
Kenneth D. Roberts, Chmn.
Robert J. Wilber, Sr. VP-Int'l Sales

**Phone:** 508-358-7400 **Fax:** 508-358-5602
**Toll-Free:** 800-733-8550
**Address:** 530 Boston Post Rd., Wayland, MA 01778 US

## GROWTH PLANS/SPECIAL FEATURES:

Candela Corporation develops, manufactures and distributes aesthetic laser systems that enable physicians, surgeons and personal care practitioners to treat various cosmetic and medical conditions. The company markets and services its products in over 70 countries from offices in the U.S., Europe, Japan and other Asian locations. Candela's products include GentleMax, AlexTriVantage, SmoothPeel, Serenity, GentleLASE, GentleYAG, Vbeam and Smoothbeam. GentleMax is an integrated aesthetic treatment workstation with multiple wavelength capability, offering chilled air cooling and the patented Dynamic Cooling Device which utilizes bursts of cryogen before and after the laser pulse. AlexTriVantage is a tattoo and pigmented lesion removal device using multi-wavelength technology and a laser-pumped-laser hand piece. SmoothPeel is an Erbium: YAG laser for skin resurfacing. Serenity is a pneumatic skin flattening technology designed for reduced pain and improved efficacy and safety. The GentleLASE family of lasers is used for permanent hair reduction, vascular lesion removal, wrinkle reduction and pigmented lesion treatment. The GentleYAG family of lasers is used for hair reduction on tanned and dark skin, treatment of pseudofolliculitis barbae, removal of leg and facial veins and skin tightening. The Vbeam Perfecta, Platinum and Aesthetica family of lasers use a pulsed dye technology to eliminate pigmentation and vascular lesions including port wine stain birthmarks, rosacea and leg and facial veins as well as to reduce wrinkles, scars, warts, psoriasis and hemangiomas. The Smoothbeam diode laser is used for the treatment of acne, acne scars and sebaceous hyperplasia and non-ablative dermal remodeling of wrinkles. The firm has shipped approximately 12,000 systems worldwide.

## FINANCIALS:

**Sales and profits are in thousands of dollars—add 000 to get the full amount. 2008 Note: Financial information for 2008 was not available for all companies at press time.**

| | | |
|---|---|---|
| 2008 Sales: $ | 2008 Profits: $ | **U.S. Stock Ticker: CLZR** |
| 2007 Sales: $148,557 | 2007 Profits: $6,256 | **Int'l Ticker:** Int'l Exchange: |
| 2006 Sales: $149,466 | 2006 Profits: $14,934 | Employees: 386 |
| 2005 Sales: $123,901 | 2005 Profits: $7,323 | Fiscal Year Ends: 6/30 |
| 2004 Sales: $104,438 | 2004 Profits: $8,119 | Parent Company: |

## SALARIES/BENEFITS:

| | | | | |
|---|---|---|---|---|
| Pension Plan: | ESOP Stock Plan: | Profit Sharing: | Top Exec. Salary: $501,502 | Bonus: $ |
| Savings Plan: Y | Stock Purch. Plan: Y | | Second Exec. Salary: $242,594 | Bonus: $ |

## OTHER THOUGHTS:

**Apparent Women Officers or Directors**: 1
**Hot Spot for Advancement for Women/Minorities**: Y

## LOCATIONS: ("Y" = Yes)

| West: | Southwest: | Midwest: | Southeast: | Northeast: | International: |
|---|---|---|---|---|---|
| | | | | Y | Y |

# CANTEL MEDICAL CORP

www.cantelmedical.com

**Industry Group Code:** 339113 **Ranks within this company's industry group:** Sales: 17 Profits: 24

| Management: | | Sales/Marketing: | | Liberal Arts: | | Information Systems: | | Professionals: | | Technical/Scientific: | |
|---|---|---|---|---|---|---|---|---|---|---|---|
| Mgmt. Trainees: | | Mktg. Professionals: | Y | Gen. Writing/Editing: | | Info. Management: | Y | Finance/Accounting: | Y | Engineers, Elec.: | |
| Experienced Mgmt.: | Y | Retail Sales: | | Technical Writing: | Y | Software Dev.: | | Law: | Y | Engineers, Other: | Y |
| Int'l Business: | Y | Commercial/Industrial: | Y | Graphic Arts/Photog.: | | Hardware Dev.: | | HR/Other: | Y | Health/Lab: | Y |
| MBA Graduates: | Y | Sales Trainees: | Y | Music: | | Systems Integration: | | Training: | Y | Scientists/Research: | Y |
| | | Advertising Pros.: | | Broadcasting: | | Consulting/Other: | | Health Care: | Y | Petroleum/Chemicals: | |
| | | | | Other: | | | | Consulting: | | Math/Other: | Y |

## TYPES OF BUSINESS:

Equipment-Disinfection & Disposable Equipment
Infection Control Products
Diagnostic Medical Equipment
Precision Instruments
Industrial Equipment
Water Treatment Equipment & Services
Maintenance Services
Dental Care Products

## BRANDS/DIVISIONS/AFFILIATES:

Fluid Solutions, Inc.
Minntech Corporation
Endoscope Reprocessing System
Mar Cor Services
Biolab Group (The)
Saf-T-Pak
Crosstex
Verimetrix

## CONTACTS: *Note: Officers with more than one job title may be intentionally listed here more than once.*

Andrew A. Krakauer, Pres.
Craig A. Sheldon, CFO/Sr. VP
Eric W. Nodiff, General Counsel/Sr. VP
Seth R. Segel, Sr. VP-Corp. Dev.
Steven C. Anaya, VP/Controller
Charles M. Diker, Chmn.

| **Phone:** 973-890-7220 | **Fax:** 973-890-7270 |
|---|---|
| **Toll-Free:** | |
| **Address:** 150 Clove Rd., 9th Fl., Little Falls, NJ 07424-2139 US | |

## GROWTH PLANS/SPECIAL FEATURES:

Cantel Medical Corp. provides products and services for the control and prevention of infection. It operates through a diverse circle of subsidiaries. Minntech Corporation develops, manufactures and markets disinfection and reprocessing systems for renal dialysis, as well as filtration and separation products for medical and non-medical applications. Minntech recently acquired the state-of-the-art Endoscope Reprocessing System and accessory infection control technologies of Netherlands-based Dyped Medical BV. Cantel also owns water treatment companies Mar Cor Services, the Biolab Group and Saf-T-Pak. Mar Cor provides design, project management, installation and maintenance services for water treatment equipment, as well as deionization and mixing systems to the medical community. Mar Cor recently purchased Fluid Solutions, Inc., a water purity systems development and implementation specialist operating throughout New England. Biolab produces water purification systems for the medical, pharmaceutical, biotechnology and semiconductor industries. Saf-T-Pak, based in Alberta, produces specialty packaging and compliance training services for the transport of infectious and biological material. Cantel's subsidiaries provide technical maintenance services for their own products as well as for selected competitors' products. Cantel's newest division, Crosstex, focuses on single-use infection control products primarily for the dental care market. In April 2007, Cantel acquired GE Water & Process Technologies' water dialysis business. In July 2007, the company acquired, through its subsidiary Crosstex, Twist 2 It Inc., a firm that designs, markets, and sells a patented, disposable prophy angle for cleaning and polishing teeth. In September 2007, the firm acquired Strong Dental Products Inc., a company that designs and markets comfort cushioning and infection control covers for x-ray film and digital x-ray sensors. Also in September 2007, Cantel acquired Verimetrix LLC, a company that designs, markets, and sells the Veriscan Pro V2.2 System, an endoscope leak and fluid detection device intended to reduce scope repair costs.

## FINANCIALS: **Sales and profits are in thousands of dollars—add 000 to get the full amount. 2008 Note: Financial information for 2008 was not available for all companies at press time.**

| | | |
|---|---|---|
| 2008 Sales: $ | 2008 Profits: $ | **U.S. Stock Ticker: CMN** |
| 2007 Sales: $219,044 | 2007 Profits: $8,446 | **Int'l Ticker:** Int'l Exchange: |
| 2006 Sales: $192,179 | 2006 Profits: $23,697 | Employees: 843 |
| 2005 Sales: $137,157 | 2005 Profits: $15,505 | Fiscal Year Ends: 7/31 |
| 2004 Sales: $123,041 | 2004 Profits: $10,654 | Parent Company: |

## SALARIES/BENEFITS:

| | | | | |
|---|---|---|---|---|
| Pension Plan: | ESOP Stock Plan: | Profit Sharing: | Top Exec. Salary: $321,979 | Bonus: $28,500 |
| Savings Plan: Y | Stock Purch. Plan: Y | | Second Exec. Salary: $262,500 | Bonus: $236,250 |

## OTHER THOUGHTS:

**Apparent Women Officers or Directors:**
**Hot Spot for Advancement for Women/Minorities:**

## LOCATIONS: ("Y" = Yes)

| West: | Southwest: | Midwest: | Southeast: | Northeast: | International: |
|---|---|---|---|---|---|
| Y | | Y | Y | Y | Y |

# CARACO PHARMACEUTICAL LABORATORIES

www.caraco.com

**Industry Group Code:** 325416 **Ranks within this company's industry group:** Sales: 2 Profits: 2

| Management: | | Sales/Marketing: | | Liberal Arts: | | Information Systems: | | Professionals: | | Technical/Scientific: | |
|---|---|---|---|---|---|---|---|---|---|---|---|
| Mgmt. Trainees: | | Mktg. Professionals: | Y | Gen. Writing/Editing: | | Info. Management: | Y | Finance/Accounting: | Y | Engineers, Elec.: | |
| Experienced Mgmt.: | Y | Retail Sales: | | Technical Writing: | Y | Software Dev.: | Y | Law: | Y | Engineers, Other: | |
| Int'l Business: | | Commercial/Industrial: | Y | Graphic Arts/Photog.: | | Hardware Dev.: | | HR/Other: | Y | Health/Lab: | Y |
| MBA Graduates: | Y | Sales Trainees: | Y | Music: | | Systems Integration: | | Training: | Y | Scientists/Research: | Y |
| | | Advertising Pros.: | | Broadcasting: | | Consulting/Other: | | Health Care: | Y | Petroleum/Chemicals: | Y |
| | | | | Other: | | | | Consulting: | | Math/Other: | Y |

## TYPES OF BUSINESS:

Drugs-Generic

## BRANDS/DIVISIONS/AFFILIATES:

Sun Pharmaceutical Industries
Allopurinol
Baclofen
Carbamazepine
Fluvoxamine
Hydrochlorothiazide
Midrin

## CONTACTS: *Note: Officers with more than one job title may be intentionally listed here more than once.*

Daniel H. Movens, CEO
Mukul Rathi, Interim CFO
Thomas Larkin, Dir.-Mktg.
Tammy Bitterman, Dir.-Human Resources
Kaushikkumar Gandhi, VP-Mfg.
Gurpartap Singh, Sr. VP-Bus. Strategies
Robert Kurkiewicz, Sr. VP- Regulatory Affairs
Jayesh Shah, Dir.-Commercial
Daniel Barone, Dir.-Quality
David Risk, Dir.-Bus. Dev.
Dilip S. Shanghvi, Chmn.

**Phone:** 313-871-8400 **Fax:** 313-871-8314
**Toll-Free:** 800-818-4555
**Address:** 1150 Elijah McCoy Dr., Detroit, MI 48202 US

## GROWTH PLANS/SPECIAL FEATURES:

Caraco Pharmaceutical Laboratories, Ltd. develops, manufactures and markets generic and private-label drugs for prescription and over-the-counter markets. The company's product portfolio includes 52 products in 114 strengths and various package sizes. These drugs relate to a variety of therapeutic segments, including arthritis, pain control, epilepsy, diabetes, antipsychotic and neurological disorders. Pharmaceutical products that the company produces include Allopurinol, and anti-gout medication; Baclofen, a skeletal muscle releaxant; Carbamazepine, a chewable anticonvulsant; Fluvoxamine, an antidepressant; Hydrochlorothiazide, an antihypertensive; and Midrin, a vascular and migraine headache suppressant. The company also has several drugs awaiting FDA approval. The company has collaborative agreements with several companies, with the most prominent being Sun Pharmaceutical Industries (Sun Pharma), which is the majority stock holder of Caraco. Under these agreements, Caraco develops generic drugs for each company to market as its own brand. The firm distributes its products through wholesalers, chain drug stores, retail pharmacies, mail-order companies, managed care organizations, hospital groups and nursing homes. Some of the wholesalers that distribute Caraco's products include Amerisource-Bergen Corporation, McKesson Corporation and Cardinal Health. In 2008, Sun Pharma Global, Inc., a wholly-owned subsidiary of Sun Pharma, completed its agreement with Caraco to transfer 25 products to the firm.

Caraco offers employees benefits including, but not limited to, medical, dental, and vision care; paid time off and holiday pay; life and disability insurance; and health and dependent care accounts.

## FINANCIALS: **Sales and profits are in thousands of dollars—add 000 to get the full amount. 2008 Note: Financial information for 2008 was not available for all companies at press time.**

2008 Sales: $
2007 Sales: $117,027
2006 Sales: $82,789
2005 Sales: $64,116
2004 Sales: $60,340

2008 Profits: $
2007 Profits: $26,858
2006 Profits: $-10,423
2005 Profits: $-2,278
2004 Profits: $- 199

**U.S. Stock Ticker: CPD**
**Int'l Ticker:** Int'l Exchange:
Employees: 662
Fiscal Year Ends: 3/31
Parent Company: SUN PHARMACEUTICAL INDUSTRIES LTD

## SALARIES/BENEFITS:

Pension Plan: ESOP Stock Plan: Profit Sharing: Top Exec. Salary: $405,600 Bonus: $200,772
Savings Plan: Y Stock Purch. Plan: Second Exec. Salary: $186,030 Bonus: $36,392

## OTHER THOUGHTS:

**Apparent Women Officers or Directors**: 1
**Hot Spot for Advancement for Women/Minorities**: Y

## LOCATIONS: ("Y" = Yes)

| West: | Southwest: | Midwest: | Southeast: | Northeast: | International: |
|---|---|---|---|---|---|
| | | Y | | | |

Note: Financial information, benefits and other data can change quickly and may vary from those stated here.

# CARDTRONICS INC

www.cardtronics.com

**Industry Group Code:** 522320 **Ranks within this company's industry group:** Sales: 6 Profits: 5

| Management: | | Sales/Marketing: | | Liberal Arts: | | Information Systems: | | Professionals: | | Technical/Scientific: | |
|---|---|---|---|---|---|---|---|---|---|---|---|
| Mgmt. Trainees: | Y | Mktg. Professionals: | Y | Gen. Writing/Editing: | | Info. Management: | Y | Finance/Accounting: | Y | Engineers, Elec.: | |
| Experienced Mgmt.: | Y | Retail Sales: | | Technical Writing: | Y | Software Dev.: | Y | Law: | Y | Engineers, Other: | |
| Int'l Business: | Y | Commercial/Industrial: | Y | Graphic Arts/Photog.: | | Hardware Dev.: | | HR/Other: | Y | Health/Lab: | |
| MBA Graduates: | Y | Sales Trainees: | Y | Music: | | Systems Integration: | Y | Training: | Y | Scientists/Research: | |
| | | Advertising Pros.: | Y | Broadcasting: | | Consulting/Other: | | Health Care: | | Petroleum/Chemicals: | |
| | | | | Other: | | | | Consulting: | | Math/Other: | |

## TYPES OF BUSINESS:

ATM Network Management
ATM Process Outsourcing
Primary Branding Programs

## BRANDS/DIVISIONS/AFFILIATES:

## CONTACTS: *Note: Officers with more than one job title may be intentionally listed here more than once.*

Jack Antonini, CEO
Keith Myers, COO
J. Chris Brewster, CFO
Brian Archer, Chief Mktg. Officer
Jerry Garcia, CIO
Michael E. Keller, General Counsel/Corp. Sec.
James Bettinger, Exec. VP-Oper.
Rick Updyke, Pres., Global Dev.
Thomas Upton, Exec. VP-Acquisitions
Michael Clinard, Pres., Global Svcs.
Fred Lummis, Chmn.
Ron Delnevo, Managing Dir.-U.K. & Europe

| | |
|---|---|
| **Phone:** 281-596-9988 | **Fax:** 281-596-9984 |
| **Toll-Free:** 800-786-9666 | |
| **Address:** 3110 Hayes Rd., Ste. 300, Houston, TX 77082 US | |

## GROWTH PLANS/SPECIAL FEATURES:

Cardtronics, Inc. is a single-source provider of automated teller machine (ATM) solutions to large, nationally-known retail merchants as well as smaller retailers and operators of facilities such as shopping malls and airports. Cardtronics operates approximately 32,950 ATMs throughout the U.S., the U.K. and Mexico. Over 10,000 of the company's ATMs are under contract with banks for the placement of the banks' logos on the machines. The company also operates the Allpoint network, one of the largest surcharge-free ATM networks in the U.S. based on the number of participating ATMs. Cardtronics deploys and operates its ATMs under two types of arrangements with its merchant customers: company-owned and merchant-owned. Under company-owned arrangements, which represent roughly 64% of its ATM network, Cardtronics provides the ATM and is typically responsible for all aspects of its operation, including transaction processing, procuring cash, supplies and telecommunications as well as routine and technical maintenance. Under merchant-owned arrangements, which represent roughly 36% of its ATM network, the merchant owns the ATM and is usually responsible for providing cash and performing simple maintenance tasks, while Cardtronics provides more complex maintenance services, transaction processing and connection to electronic funds transfer networks. The company plans to focus its growth on expanding the number of company-owned ATMs in its network. Cardtronics targets convenience stores, gas stations, grocery stores, airports and major regional and national retail outlets for its ATM locations. It has merchant agreements with such retailers as Chevron, Costco, Safeway, Target and Walgreens.

Employees are offered medical, dental and vision insurance; health care and dependent care reimbursement account options; life insurance and disability coverage; a 401(k) plan; and an employee referral program.

## FINANCIALS: **Sales and profits are in thousands of dollars—add 000 to get the full amount. 2008 Note: Financial information for 2008 was not available for all companies at press time.**

| | | |
|---|---|---|
| 2008 Sales: $ | 2008 Profits: $ | **U.S. Stock Ticker: CATM** |
| 2007 Sales: $378,298 | 2007 Profits: $-27,090 | **Int'l Ticker:** Int'l Exchange: |
| 2006 Sales: $293,605 | 2006 Profits: $- 531 | Employees: 400 |
| 2005 Sales: $268,965 | 2005 Profits: $-2,418 | Fiscal Year Ends: 12/31 |
| 2004 Sales: $192,915 | 2004 Profits: $5,805 | Parent Company: |

## SALARIES/BENEFITS:

| | | | | |
|---|---|---|---|---|
| Pension Plan: | ESOP Stock Plan: | Profit Sharing: | Top Exec. Salary: $364,651 | Bonus: $206,856 |
| Savings Plan: Y | Stock Purch. Plan: | | Second Exec. Salary: $353,714 | Bonus: $138,209 |

## OTHER THOUGHTS:

**Apparent Women Officers or Directors**:
**Hot Spot for Advancement for Women/Minorities**:

## LOCATIONS: ("Y" = Yes)

| West: | Southwest: | Midwest: | Southeast: | Northeast: | International: |
|---|---|---|---|---|---|
| | Y | | | Y | Y |

# CATALYST HEALTH SOLUTIONS INC

www.healthextras.com

**Industry Group Code:** 525120 **Ranks within this company's industry group:** Sales: 1 Profits: 1

| Management: | | Sales/Marketing: | | Liberal Arts: | | Information Systems: | | Professionals: | | Technical/Scientific: | |
|---|---|---|---|---|---|---|---|---|---|---|---|
| Mgmt. Trainees: | | Mktg. Professionals: | | Gen. Writing/Editing: | | Info. Management: | Y | Finance/Accounting: | Y | Engineers, Elec.: | |
| Experienced Mgmt.: | Y | Retail Sales: | | Technical Writing: | | Software Dev.: | | Law: | Y | Engineers, Other: | |
| Int'l Business: | Y | Commercial/Industrial: | | Graphic Arts/Photog.: | | Hardware Dev.: | | HR/Other: | Y | Health/Lab: | |
| MBA Graduates: | Y | Sales Trainees: | | Music: | | Systems Integration: | | Training: | Y | Scientists/Research: | |
| | | Advertising Pros.: | | Broadcasting: | | Consulting/Other: | | Health Care: | Y | Petroleum/Chemicals: | |
| | | | | Other: | | | | Consulting: | | Math/Other: | |

## TYPES OF BUSINESS:

Pharmaceutical Benefits Manager

## BRANDS/DIVISIONS/AFFILIATES:

HealthExtras, Inc.
Catalyst Rx
HospiScript Services, LLC
Immediate Pharmaceutical Services, Inc.

## CONTACTS: *Note: Officers with more than one job title may be intentionally listed here more than once.*

David T. Blair, CEO
Nick J. Grujich, COO/Exec. VP
Hai V. Tran, CFO
Bruce Metge, General Counsel/Corp. Sec.
Hai V. Tran, Treas.
Edward S. Civera, Chmn.

| **Phone:** | **Fax:** 301-548-2991 |
|---|---|
| **Toll-Free:** 800-323-6640 | |
| **Address:** 800 King Farm Blvd., Rockville, MD 20850 US | |

## GROWTH PLANS/SPECIAL FEATURES:

Catalyst Health Solutions, Inc., formerly HealthExtras, Inc., is a full-service Pharmacy Benefit Management (PBM) company, providing benefits to approximately 5 million members throughout the U.S. Catalyst's services include the development and implementation of pharmacy benefit programs, comprehensive pharmacy network management, formulary management and drug data analysis. Clients include self-insured employers such as state and local governments, managed care organizations, unions, hospices and third-party administrators and individuals. Catalyst is based in Maryland, but also has satellite offices in Arizona, California, Florida, Georgia, Hawaii, Iowa, Louisiana, Mississippi, Nevada, New Mexico, North Carolina, Ohio, Pennsylvania, Texas and Puerto Rico. The firm's largest operating subsidiary is Catalyst Rx which accounted for substantially all of the company's revenue in 2007. Other subsidiaries include HospiScript Services, LLC, a provider of pharmacy benefit management services to the hospice industry which was acquired by the firm in 2008; and Immediate Pharmaceutical Services, Inc., a prescription mail service facility based in Ohio.

Catalyst offers its employees a 401(k) plan and a buy-or-lease American car benefit plan.

## FINANCIALS: **Sales and profits are in thousands of dollars—add 000 to get the full amount. 2008 Note: Financial information for 2008 was not available for all companies at press time.**

| | | |
|---|---|---|
| 2008 Sales: $ | 2008 Profits: $ | **U.S. Stock Ticker: CHSI** |
| 2007 Sales: $1,857,697 | 2007 Profits: $39,268 | **Int'l Ticker:** Int'l Exchange: |
| 2006 Sales: $1,271,006 | 2006 Profits: $31,574 | Employees: 524 |
| 2005 Sales: $694,519 | 2005 Profits: $22,980 | Fiscal Year Ends: 12/31 |
| 2004 Sales: $521,325 | 2004 Profits: $16,383 | Parent Company: |

## SALARIES/BENEFITS:

| | | | | |
|---|---|---|---|---|
| Pension Plan: | ESOP Stock Plan: | Profit Sharing: | Top Exec. Salary: $413,750 | Bonus: $425,000 |
| Savings Plan: Y | Stock Purch. Plan: | | Second Exec. Salary: $295,000 | Bonus: $ |

## OTHER THOUGHTS:

**Apparent Women Officers or Directors**:
**Hot Spot for Advancement for Women/Minorities**:

## LOCATIONS: ("Y" = Yes)

| West: | Southwest: | Midwest: | Southeast: | Northeast: | International: |
|---|---|---|---|---|---|
| Y | Y | Y | Y | Y | Y |

# C-COR INC

www.c-cor.com

**Industry Group Code:** 334210 **Ranks within this company's industry group:** Sales: 4 Profits: 2

| Management: | | Sales/Marketing: | | Liberal Arts: | | Information Systems: | | Professionals: | | Technical/Scientific: | |
|---|---|---|---|---|---|---|---|---|---|---|---|
| Mgmt. Trainees: | | Mktg. Professionals: | Y | Gen. Writing/Editing: | Y | Info. Management: | Y | Finance/Accounting: | Y | Engineers, Elec.: | Y |
| Experienced Mgmt.: | Y | Retail Sales: | | Technical Writing: | Y | Software Dev.: | Y | Law: | Y | Engineers, Other: | Y |
| Int'l Business: | Y | Commercial/Industrial: | Y | Graphic Arts/Photog.: | | Hardware Dev.: | Y | HR/Other: | Y | Health/Lab: | |
| MBA Graduates: | Y | Sales Trainees: | Y | Music: | | Systems Integration: | Y | Training: | Y | Scientists/Research: | |
| | | Advertising Pros.: | | Broadcasting: | | Consulting/Other: | | Health Care: | | Petroleum/Chemicals: | |
| | | | | Other: | | | | Consulting: | | Math/Other: | |

## TYPES OF BUSINESS:

Telecommunications Equipment-Broadband Network Products
Software
Network Services

## BRANDS/DIVISIONS/AFFILIATES:

C-COR Solutions
C-COR Access and Transport
C-COR Network Services
Flex Max
Opti Max
DV6000
PLEXis
CORview Suite

## CONTACTS: *Note: Officers with more than one job title may be intentionally listed here more than once.*

David A. Woodle, CEO
William T. Hanelly, CFO
Mitchell Berman, VP-Global Mktg.
Mary G. Beahm, VP-Human Resources
Kenneth A. Wright, CTO
John O. Caezza, Pres., Oper. Group
Michael J. Pohl, Pres., Global Strategies
David E. Levitan, Pres., Network Svcs.
Timothy Gropp, Sr. VP-Worldwide Sales
David A. Woodle, Chmn.

| **Phone:** 814-238-2461 | **Fax:** 814-238-4065 |
|---|---|
| **Toll-Free:** 800-233-2267 | |
| **Address:** 60 Decibel Rd., State College, PA 16801 US | |

## GROWTH PLANS/SPECIAL FEATURES:

C-COR, Inc., organized in 1953, is a global provider of integrated network solutions, including supportive products, operation software solutions and technical services. The firm operates through three business units: C-COR Solutions; C-COR Access and Transport; and C-COR Network Services. C-COR Solutions provides software and hardware which cover on-demand content delivery, content provisioning, network optimization and health, automated work force management and digital ad insertion. C-COR Access and Transport provides interoperable and modular optical and radio frequency network transmission and distribution products for hybrid fiber coax networks as well as Gigabit Ethernet optical transport systems for business services applications. Its portfolio includes the CHP Max5000 AM headend/hub optical platform, Opti Max line of optical nodes and Flex Max line of RF amplifiers. The unit's transport portfolio includes the DV6000 video transport system, as well as next-generation transport platforms such as the MPS for intelligent packet transport and the PLEXis for advanced DWDM optical networking. Additionally, the CORview Suite of management software integrates these platforms' management systems into one user application. C-COR Network Services offers network operators a comprehensive set of outsourced technical and operational services. Its services include outside plant technical services, network integration, outsourced operation services, field engineering services and network design. Some of the firm's principal customers include many of the U.S.'s largest cable operators, such as Time Warner Cable. In December 2007, C-Cor Inc. was successfully acquired by ARRIS, a company that provides internet, cable and high-definition broadband solutions, for $730 million in cash and ARRIS stock.

C-COR offers its employees a benefits package including tuition and employee assistance programs; discounted stock; a 401(k) plan; and profit sharing.

## FINANCIALS: **Sales and profits are in thousands of dollars—add 000 to get the full amount. 2008 Note: Financial information for 2008 was not available for all companies at press time.**

| | | |
|---|---|---|
| 2008 Sales: $ | 2008 Profits: $ | **U.S. Stock Ticker: CCBL** |
| 2007 Sales: $277,329 | 2007 Profits: $28,098 | **Int'l Ticker:** Int'l Exchange: |
| 2006 Sales: $213,946 | 2006 Profits: $-27,306 | Employees: 1,260 |
| 2005 Sales: $199,327 | 2005 Profits: $-25,690 | Fiscal Year Ends: 6/30 |
| 2004 Sales: $240,918 | 2004 Profits: $44,160 | Parent Company: |

## SALARIES/BENEFITS:

| | | | | |
|---|---|---|---|---|
| Pension Plan: | ESOP Stock Plan: | Profit Sharing: Y | Top Exec. Salary: $415,385 | Bonus: $ |
| Savings Plan: Y | Stock Purch. Plan: Y | | Second Exec. Salary: $311,538 | Bonus: $ |

## OTHER THOUGHTS:

**Apparent Women Officers or Directors**: 1
**Hot Spot for Advancement for Women/Minorities**: Y

## LOCATIONS: ("Y" = Yes)

| West: | Southwest: | Midwest: | Southeast: | Northeast: | International: |
|---|---|---|---|---|---|
| Y | | | Y | Y | Y |

# CELERA CORPORATION

www.celera.com

**Industry Group Code:** 541710 **Ranks within this company's industry group:** Sales: 4 Profits: 5

| Management: | | Sales/Marketing: | | Liberal Arts: | | Information Systems: | | Professionals: | | Technical/Scientific: | |
|---|---|---|---|---|---|---|---|---|---|---|---|
| Mgmt. Trainees: | | Mktg. Professionals: | Y | Gen. Writing/Editing: | | Info. Management: | Y | Finance/Accounting: | Y | Engineers, Elec.: | |
| Experienced Mgmt.: | Y | Retail Sales: | | Technical Writing: | Y | Software Dev.: | Y | Law: | Y | Engineers, Other: | |
| Int'l Business: | | Commercial/Industrial: | | Graphic Arts/Photog.: | | Hardware Dev.: | | HR/Other: | Y | Health/Lab: | Y |
| MBA Graduates: | Y | Sales Trainees: | | Music: | | Systems Integration: | | Training: | Y | Scientists/Research: | Y |
| | | Advertising Pros.: | | Broadcasting: | | Consulting/Other: | | Health Care: | Y | Petroleum/Chemicals: | |
| | | | | Other: | | | | Consulting: | Y | Math/Other: | Y |

## TYPES OF BUSINESS:

Research-Human Genome Mapping
Information Management & Analysis Software
Consulting, Research & Development Services

## BRANDS/DIVISIONS/AFFILIATES:

Applera Corporation
Applied Biosystems Group
Abbott Laboratories
ViroSeq HIV-1 Genotyping System
Berkeley HeartLab, Inc.
Atria Genetics, Inc.
4MyHeart.com

## CONTACTS: *Note: Officers with more than one job title may be intentionally listed here more than once.*

Kathy Ordonez, Pres.
Joel Jung, CFO
Paul Arata, VP-Human Resources
Thomas White, Chief Scientific Officer
Paul Arata, VP-Admin.
Scott Milsten, General Counsel/VP/Corp. Sec.
Stacey Sias, Chief Bus. Officer
David P. Speechly, VP-Corp. Affairs
Samuel Broder, Chief Medical Officer
Russell Warnick, Chief Scientific Officer-Berkeley HeartLab, Inc.
Christopher Hall, Chief Bus. Officer-Berkeley HeartLab, Inc.
Mike Zoccoli, Gen. Mgr.-Products Bus.

**Phone:** 510-749-4200 **Fax:**
**Toll-Free:**
**Address:** 1401 Harbor Bay Parkway, Alameda, CA 94502 US

## GROWTH PLANS/SPECIAL FEATURES:

Celera Corporation, formerly Celera Genomics Group, is primarily a molecular diagnostics business that uses proprietary genomics and proteomics discovery platforms to identify and validate novel diagnostic markers. In July 2008, Celera separated from Applera Corporation, becoming an independent, publicly-traded company. Celera pursues a strategy that it refers to as targeted medicine, which is based on the belief that understanding the genetic basis of biology and disease is crucial to improving the diagnosis and treatment of many common complex diseases. The company develops products that facilitate disease detection, prediction of disease predisposition, monitoring of disease progression and determination of patient responsiveness to treatments. Its subsidiary, Berkeley HeartLab, offers innovative services to predict the risk of cardiovascular disease and to optimize patient management. Through 4myheart.com, Celera offers cardiovascular patients and physicians a web-based program that makes cardiovascular health records and lab results easily accessible to physicians and patients, among other services. The company maintains a strategic alliance with Abbott Laboratories for the development and commercialization of molecular, or nucleic acid-based, diagnostic products. These products currently include ViroSeq HIV-1 Genotyping System; products used for the detection of mutations in the CFTR gene, which cause cystic fibrosis; hepatitis C virus ASRs; ASRs for the detection of mutations in the FMR-1 gene, which cause Fragile X Syndrome; and ASRs for the detection of mutations in genes known to be involved in deep vein thrombosis. Through its genomics and proteomics research efforts, Celera additionally discovers and validates therapeutic targets, and it is seeking strategic partnerships to develop therapeutic products based on these targets.

## FINANCIALS: **Sales and profits are in thousands of dollars—add 000 to get the full amount. 2008 Note: Financial information for 2008 was not available for all companies at press time.**

| | | |
|---|---|---|
| 2008 Sales: $138,700 | 2008 Profits: $-104,100 | **U.S. Stock Ticker: CRA** |
| 2007 Sales: $43,400 | 2007 Profits: $-20,600 | **Int'l Ticker:** Int'l Exchange: |
| 2006 Sales: $46,200 | 2006 Profits: $-63,600 | Employees: 554 |
| 2005 Sales: $31,000 | 2005 Profits: $-77,100 | Fiscal Year Ends: 6/30 |
| 2004 Sales: $60,100 | 2004 Profits: $-57,500 | Parent Company: |

## SALARIES/BENEFITS:

| | | | | |
|---|---|---|---|---|
| Pension Plan: | ESOP Stock Plan: | Profit Sharing: | Top Exec. Salary: $468,077 | Bonus: $451,250 |
| Savings Plan: Y | Stock Purch. Plan: Y | | Second Exec. Salary: $484,069 | Bonus: $258,851 |

## OTHER THOUGHTS:

**Apparent Women Officers or Directors**: 3
**Hot Spot for Advancement for Women/Minorities**: Y

## LOCATIONS: ("Y" = Yes)

| West: | Southwest: | Midwest: | Southeast: | Northeast: | International: |
|---|---|---|---|---|---|
| Y | | | | Y | |

Note: Financial information, benefits and other data can change quickly and may vary from those stated here.

# CELGENE CORP

www.celgene.com

**Industry Group Code:** 325412 **Ranks within this company's industry group:** Sales: 1 Profits: 2

| Management: | | Sales/Marketing: | | Liberal Arts: | | Information Systems: | | Professionals: | | Technical/Scientific: | |
|---|---|---|---|---|---|---|---|---|---|---|---|
| Mgmt. Trainees: | | Mktg. Professionals: | Y | Gen. Writing/Editing: | | Info. Management: | Y | Finance/Accounting: | Y | Engineers, Elec.: | |
| Experienced Mgmt.: | Y | Retail Sales: | | Technical Writing: | Y | Software Dev.: | Y | Law: | Y | Engineers, Other: | |
| Int'l Business: | Y | Commercial/Industrial: | Y | Graphic Arts/Photog.: | | Hardware Dev.: | | HR/Other: | Y | Health/Lab: | Y |
| MBA Graduates: | Y | Sales Trainees: | Y | Music: | | Systems Integration: | | Training: | Y | Scientists/Research: | Y |
| | | Advertising Pros.: | | Broadcasting: | | Consulting/Other: | | Health Care: | Y | Petroleum/Chemicals: | |
| | | | | Other: | | | | Consulting: | | Math/Other: | Y |

## TYPES OF BUSINESS:

Cancer & Immune-Inflammatory Related Diseases Drugs

## BRANDS/DIVISIONS/AFFILIATES:

REVLIMID
THALOMID
ALKERAN
FOCALIN
FOCALIN XR
RITALIN
IMiDs
Pharmion Corp

## CONTACTS: *Note: Officers with more than one job title may be intentionally listed here more than once.*

Sol J. Barer, CEO
Robert J. Hugin, COO
Robert J. Hugin, Pres.
David W. Gryska, CFO/Sr. VP
Graham Burton, Sr. VP-Regulatory Affairs & Pharmacovigilance
Sol J. Barer, Chmn.
Aart Brouwer, Pres., Int'l

**Phone:** 908-673-9000 **Fax:** 732-271-4184
**Toll-Free:**
**Address:** 86 Morris Ave., Summit, NJ 07901 US

## GROWTH PLANS/SPECIAL FEATURES:

Celgene Corp. is a global integrated biopharmaceutical company primarily engaged in the discovery, development and commercialization of therapies designed to treat cancer and immune-inflammatory related diseases. The company's commercial stage products are REVLIMID and THALOMID. REVLIMID has been approved by the U.S. FDA, the European Commission (EC), the Swiss Agency for Therapeutic Products (Swissmedic) and the Australian Therapeutic Goods Administration for treatment in combination with dexamethasone for multiple myeloma patients who have received at least one prior therapy. In addition, REVLIMID has been approved by the FDA and the Canadian Therapeutics Directorate for treatment of patients with transfusion-dependent anemia due to low- or intermediate-1-risk myelodysplastic syndromes (MDS) associated with a deletion 5q cytogenetic abnormality with or without additional cytogenetic abnormalities. THALOMID has been approved by the FDA for treatment in combination with dexamethasone of patients with newly diagnosed multiple myeloma and is also approved for the treatment and suppression of cutaneous manifestations of erythema nodosum leprosum (ENL), an inflammatory complication of leprosy. Celgene also sells ALKERAN, which it obtains through a supply and distribution agreement with GlaxoSmithKline (GSK), and FOCALIN, which it sells exclusively to Novartis Pharma AG. Other sources of revenue include royalties which the company receives primarily from Novartis on its sales of the entire family of RITALIN drugs and FOCALIN XR, in addition to revenues from collaborative agreements and licensing fees. Its portfolio of drug candidates includes IMiDs compounds, which are proprietary to the firm and have demonstrated certain immunomodulatory and other biologically important properties. In March 2008, Celgene acquired Pharmion Corporation for approximately $2.9 billion.

Celgene offers its employees educational assistance, travel assistance, fitness benefits, an employee assistance program, health services, lactation rooms, flexible spending accounts and medical, dental, vision, life, AD&D, business travel accident and disability insurance.

## FINANCIALS: **Sales and profits are in thousands of dollars—add 000 to get the full amount. 2008 Note: Financial information for 2008 was not available for all companies at press time.**

| | | |
|---|---|---|
| 2008 Sales: $ | 2008 Profits: $ | **U.S. Stock Ticker: CELG** |
| 2007 Sales: $1,405,820 | 2007 Profits: $226,433 | **Int'l Ticker:** Int'l Exchange: |
| 2006 Sales: $898,873 | 2006 Profits: $68,981 | Employees: 1,685 |
| 2005 Sales: $536,941 | 2005 Profits: $63,656 | Fiscal Year Ends: 12/31 |
| 2004 Sales: $377,502 | 2004 Profits: $52,756 | Parent Company: |

## SALARIES/BENEFITS:

| | | | | |
|---|---|---|---|---|
| Pension Plan: | ESOP Stock Plan: | Profit Sharing: | Top Exec. Salary: $833,333 | Bonus: $2,248,000 |
| Savings Plan: Y | Stock Purch. Plan: | | Second Exec. Salary: $675,333 | Bonus: $1,699,800 |

## OTHER THOUGHTS:

**Apparent Women Officers or Directors**: 1
**Hot Spot for Advancement for Women/Minorities**:

## LOCATIONS: ("Y" = Yes)

| West: | Southwest: | Midwest: | Southeast: | Northeast: | International: |
|---|---|---|---|---|---|
| | | | | Y | Y |

# CELL GENESYS INC

www.cellgenesys.com

**Industry Group Code:** 325412 **Ranks within this company's industry group:** Sales: 39 Profits: 30

| Management: | | Sales/Marketing: | | Liberal Arts: | | Information Systems: | | Professionals: | | Technical/Scientific: | |
|---|---|---|---|---|---|---|---|---|---|---|---|
| Mgmt. Trainees: | | Mktg. Professionals: | Y | Gen. Writing/Editing: | | Info. Management: | Y | Finance/Accounting: | Y | Engineers, Elec.: | |
| Experienced Mgmt.: | Y | Retail Sales: | | Technical Writing: | Y | Software Dev.: | Y | Law: | Y | Engineers, Other: | |
| Int'l Business: | Y | Commercial/Industrial: | Y | Graphic Arts/Photog.: | | Hardware Dev.: | | HR/Other: | Y | Health/Lab: | Y |
| MBA Graduates: | Y | Sales Trainees: | Y | Music: | | Systems Integration: | | Training: | Y | Scientists/Research: | Y |
| | | Advertising Pros.: | | Broadcasting: | | Consulting/Other: | | Health Care: | Y | Petroleum/Chemicals: | |
| | | | | Other: | | | | Consulting: | | Math/Other: | Y |

## TYPES OF BUSINESS:

Cancer Immunotherapies
Oncolytic Virus Therapy Drugs

## BRANDS/DIVISIONS/AFFILIATES:

GVAX
CG0070
CG5757

## CONTACTS:

*Note: Officers with more than one job title may be intentionally listed here more than once.*

Stephen A. Sherwin, CEO
Sharon E. Tetlow, CFO/Sr. VP
Christine B. McKinley, Sr. VP-Human Resources
Peter K. Working, Sr. VP-R&D
Michael W. Ramsay, Sr. VP-Oper.
Robert H. Tidwell, Sr. VP-Corp. Dev.
Robert J. Dow, Sr. VP-Medical Affairs/Chief Medical Officer
Carol C. Grundfest, Sr. VP-Regulatory Affairs & Portfolio Mgmt.
Kristen M. Hege, VP-Clinical Research
Stephen A. Sherwin, Chmn.

**Phone:** 650-266-3000 **Fax:** 650-266-3010
**Toll-Free:**
**Address:** 500 Forbes Blvd., South San Francisco, CA 94080 US

## GROWTH PLANS/SPECIAL FEATURES:

Cell Genesys, Inc. is a biotechnology company that focuses on the development and commercialization of biological therapies for patients with cancer. The company currently develops cell-based immunotherapies and oncolytic virus therapies to threat different types of cancer. The firm's clinical stage cancer programs involve cell- or viral-based products that have been genetically modified to impart disease-fighting characteristics. Cell Genesys' lead program is the GVAX cell-based immunotherapy for cancer. The company is conducting two Phase III clinical trials in prostrate cancer and Phase II trials in each of pancreatic cancer and leukemia. Ongoing clinical programs evaluating the company's oncolytic virus therapies focus on CG0070, a therapy for bladder cancer, which could be evaluated in multiple types of cancer in the future. In addition, Cell Genesys has preclinical oncolytic virus therapy programs, including CG5757, which the company is evaluating as potential therapies for multiple types of cancer. The company owns roughly 392 U.S. and foreign patents issued or granted to it or available based on licensing arrangements and roughly 268 U.S. and foreign applications pending in its name or available based on licensing agreements. In December 2007, Cell Genesys sold all of its assets, intellectual property and previously established licensing agreements relating to its lentiviral gene delivery technology to GDP IP, LLC for approximately $12 million.

Cell Genesys offers its employees an employee assistance program, a flexible spending plan and medical, dental, vision, life, AD&D, travel accident and disability insurance.

## FINANCIALS:

**Sales and profits are in thousands of dollars—add 000 to get the full amount. 2008 Note: Financial information for 2008 was not available for all companies at press time.**

| | | |
|---|---|---|
| 2008 Sales: $ | 2008 Profits: $ | **U.S. Stock Ticker: CEGE** |
| 2007 Sales: $1,380 | 2007 Profits: $-99,274 | **Int'l Ticker:** Int'l Exchange: |
| 2006 Sales: $1,364 | 2006 Profits: $-82,929 | Employees: 302 |
| 2005 Sales: $4,584 | 2005 Profits: $-64,939 | Fiscal Year Ends: 12/31 |
| 2004 Sales: $11,458 | 2004 Profits: $-97,411 | Parent Company: |

## SALARIES/BENEFITS:

| | | | | |
|---|---|---|---|---|
| Pension Plan: | ESOP Stock Plan: | Profit Sharing: | Top Exec. Salary: $577,500 | Bonus: $300,000 |
| Savings Plan: Y | Stock Purch. Plan: Y | | Second Exec. Salary: $425,000 | Bonus: $157,500 |

## OTHER THOUGHTS:

**Apparent Women Officers or Directors**: 5
**Hot Spot for Advancement for Women/Minorities**: Y

## LOCATIONS: ("Y" = Yes)

| West: | Southwest: | Midwest: | Southeast: | Northeast: | International: |
|---|---|---|---|---|---|
| Y | | | | | |

# CELL THERAPEUTICS INC

www.cticseattle.com

**Industry Group Code:** 325412 **Ranks within this company's industry group:** Sales: 40 Profits: 32

| Management: | | Sales/Marketing: | | Liberal Arts: | | Information Systems: | | Professionals: | | Technical/Scientific: | |
|---|---|---|---|---|---|---|---|---|---|---|---|
| Mgmt. Trainees: | | Mktg. Professionals: | Y | Gen. Writing/Editing: | | Info. Management: | Y | Finance/Accounting: | Y | Engineers, Elec.: | |
| Experienced Mgmt.: | Y | Retail Sales: | | Technical Writing: | Y | Software Dev.: | Y | Law: | Y | Engineers, Other: | |
| Int'l Business: | Y | Commercial/Industrial: | Y | Graphic Arts/Photog.: | | Hardware Dev.: | | HR/Other: | Y | Health/Lab: | Y |
| MBA Graduates: | Y | Sales Trainees: | Y | Music: | | Systems Integration: | | Training: | Y | Scientists/Research: | Y |
| | | Advertising Pros.: | | Broadcasting: | | Consulting/Other: | | Health Care: | Y | Petroleum/Chemicals: | |
| | | | | Other: | | | | Consulting: | | Math/Other: | Y |

## TYPES OF BUSINESS:

Cancer Treatment Drugs

## BRANDS/DIVISIONS/AFFILIATES:

Zevalin
Paclitaxel Poliglumex
Pixantrone
Brostallicin

## CONTACTS:

*Note: Officers with more than one job title may be intentionally listed here more than once.*

James A. Bianco, CEO
Craig W. Philips, Pres.
Louis A. Bianco, Exec. VP-Admin.
Dan Eramian, Exec. VP-Corp. Comm.
Louis A. Bianco, Exec. VP-Finance
Gabrielle Pezzoni, Scientific Dir.-Cell Therapeutics Europe
Jack W. Singer, Chief Medical Officer
Jeff Jacob, CEO-Systems Medicine
Phillip Nudelman, Chmn.
Mauro G. Premi, Managing Dir.-Cell Therapeutics Europe

| | |
|---|---|
| **Phone:** 206-282-7100 | **Fax:** 206-284-6206 |
| **Toll-Free:** 800-215-2355 | |
| **Address:** 501 Elliott Ave. W., Ste. 400, Seattle, WA 98119 US | |

## GROWTH PLANS/SPECIAL FEATURES:

Cell Therapeutics, Inc. (CTI) develops, acquires and commercializes treatments for cancer. The company's research and in-licensing activities are concentrated on identifying new, less toxic and more effective ways to treat cancer. The firm is currently developing four drugs: Zevalin, paclitaxel poliglumex, pixantrone and brostallicin. Zevalin, the first radioimmunotherapy drug to be approved by the FDA, was recently acquired by the firm from Biogen Idec Inc. It is designed to treat relapsed or refractory low-grade, follicular, or B-cell non-Hodgkin's lymphoma. Paclitaxel poliglumex, a biologically enhanced chemotherapeutic agent, links a widely used anti-cancer agent, paclitaxel, to a polyglutamate polymer for the potential treatment of ovarian and other cancers. Pixantrone is an anthracycline derivative for the treatment of non-Hodgkin's lymphoma. Lastly, brostallicin, which is a small molecule, anti-cancer drug with a unique mechanism of action and composition of matter patent coverage, is being tested for treatment of relapsed/refractory soft tissue sarcoma. CTI is also working on a number of drug targets in discovery research. Among these programs are bisplatinum agents and proteasome inhibitors with indirect inhibition properties. In addition to discovery research, preclinical activities are focused on product lifecycle management, including the development of alternative dosage forms and routes of administration for existing products in the development pipeline. The company has exclusive rights to six issued U.S. patents and 126 U.S. and foreign pending or issued patent applications relating to its polymer drug delivery technology. The firm has a research and development facility in Europe operated through its division CTI (Europe), formerly the subsidiary Cell Therapeutics Inc.-Sede Secondaria.

CTI offers employees medical, dental and vision insurance; life and disability insurance; an employee assistance program; travel assistance; an employee stock purchase plan; and an educational assistance program. Additional perks include wellness seminars, discounted health club memberships, flu shots and ice cream socials.

## FINANCIALS:

**Sales and profits are in thousands of dollars—add 000 to get the full amount. 2008 Note: Financial information for 2008 was not available for all companies at press time.**

| | | |
|---|---|---|
| 2008 Sales: $ | 2008 Profits: $ | **U.S. Stock Ticker: CTIC** |
| 2007 Sales: $ 127 | 2007 Profits: $-138,108 | **Int'l Ticker:** Int'l Exchange: |
| 2006 Sales: $ 80 | 2006 Profits: $-135,819 | Employees: 230 |
| 2005 Sales: $16,092 | 2005 Profits: $-102,505 | Fiscal Year Ends: 12/31 |
| 2004 Sales: $29,594 | 2004 Profits: $-252,298 | Parent Company: |

## SALARIES/BENEFITS:

| | | | | |
|---|---|---|---|---|
| Pension Plan: | ESOP Stock Plan: | Profit Sharing: | Top Exec. Salary: $650,000 | Bonus: $487,500 |
| Savings Plan: Y | Stock Purch. Plan: Y | | Second Exec. Salary: $350,000 | Bonus: $84,000 |

## OTHER THOUGHTS:

**Apparent Women Officers or Directors**: 2
**Hot Spot for Advancement for Women/Minorities**: Y

## LOCATIONS: ("Y" = Yes)

| West: | Southwest: | Midwest: | Southeast: | Northeast: | International: |
|---|---|---|---|---|---|
| Y | Y | | | | Y |

Note: Financial information, benefits and other data can change quickly and may vary from those stated here.

# CENTERPLATE

www.centerplate.com

**Industry Group Code:** 722310 **Ranks within this company's industry group:** Sales: 1 Profits: 1

| Management: | | Sales/Marketing: | | Liberal Arts: | | Information Systems: | | Professionals: | | Technical/Scientific: | |
|---|---|---|---|---|---|---|---|---|---|---|---|
| Mgmt. Trainees: | | Mktg. Professionals: | Y | Gen. Writing/Editing: | | Info. Management: | Y | Finance/Accounting: | Y | Engineers, Elec.: | |
| Experienced Mgmt.: | Y | Retail Sales: | | Technical Writing: | | Software Dev.: | | Law: | Y | Engineers, Other: | |
| Int'l Business: | Y | Commercial/Industrial: | | Graphic Arts/Photog.: | | Hardware Dev.: | | HR/Other: | Y | Health/Lab: | |
| MBA Graduates: | Y | Sales Trainees: | | Music: | | Systems Integration: | | Training: | Y | Scientists/Research: | |
| | | Advertising Pros.: | | Broadcasting: | | Consulting/Other: | | Health Care: | | Petroleum/Chemicals: | |
| | | | | Other: | | | | Consulting: | | Math/Other: | |

## TYPES OF BUSINESS:

Food & Beverage Concessions
Catering Services
Merchandise Services
Facility Management

## BRANDS/DIVISIONS/AFFILIATES:

Volume Services America, Inc.
Volume Services, Inc.
Service America Corporation

## CONTACTS: *Note: Officers with more than one job title may be intentionally listed here more than once.*

Janet L. Steinmayer, CEO
Janet L. Steinmayer, Pres.
Kevin F. McNamara, CFO/Exec. VP
Rina E. Teran, Corp. Sec.
William H. Peterson, Exec. VP-Oper.
Bob Pascal, Media Rel.
Gael Doar, Investor Rel.
Myles T. McGrane, VP-Facility Design & Mgmt.
John Anderle, VP-Oper., Kentucky
David M. Williams, Chmn.

**Phone:** 864-598-8600 **Fax:** 864-598-8695
**Toll-Free:** 800-698-6992
**Address:** 201 E. Broad St., Spartanburg, SC 29306 US

## GROWTH PLANS/SPECIAL FEATURES:

Centerplate, Inc. is a leading provider of food and beverage concessions, catering and merchandise services in sports facilities, convention centers and other entertainment facilities. The firm, which operates throughout the U.S. and Canada, is the largest provider to National Football League (NFL) facilities; the third-largest provider to Major League Baseball (MLB) facilities; the largest provider to minor league baseball and spring training facilities; and one of the largest providers to major convention centers. Centerplate has provided services for numerous World Series games, Super Bowls, World Cup soccer matches and Presidential Inaugural Balls. Through the operation of food courts in its facilities, Centerplate provides concession services from several different locations that sell a variety of specialty foods and beverages, including nationally branded, franchised food and beverage products. The company also provides merchandise and program sales services in many of the sports facilities. It is responsible for all personnel, inventory control, purchasing and food preparation where it provides these services. Additionally, Centerplate offers full facility management services, including event planning and marketing, maintenance, ticket distribution, program printing, advertising and licensing rights for the facility, its suites and premium seats. The company generally provides services pursuant to long-term contracts that grant it the exclusive right to provide food and beverage products and services within the facility. Centerplate presently serves 78 sports facilities, 29 convention centers and 24 other entertainment venues. Yankee Stadium accounted for nearly 10% of its net sales during 2007. Centerplate also operates several subsidiaries, including Volume Services America, Inc.; Volume Services, Inc;. and Service America Corporation. In April 2008, the firm announced it will not be the concession provider for the new Yankee Stadium, which opens in 2009. Also in 2008, the company was awarded contracts worth $12 million for three venues in Indianapolis.

The firm's employees receive medical and dental insurance.

## FINANCIALS: **Sales and profits are in thousands of dollars—add 000 to get the full amount. 2008 Note: Financial information for 2008 was not available for all companies at press time.**

| | | |
|---|---|---|
| 2008 Sales: $ | 2008 Profits: $ | **U.S. Stock Ticker: CVP** |
| 2007 Sales: $740,700 | 2007 Profits: $-1,900 | **Int'l Ticker:** Int'l Exchange: |
| 2006 Sales: $681,120 | 2006 Profits: $3,478 | Employees: 1,550 |
| 2005 Sales: $643,112 | 2005 Profits: $-4,588 | Fiscal Year Ends: 12/31 |
| 2004 Sales: $607,154 | 2004 Profits: $2,320 | Parent Company: |

## SALARIES/BENEFITS:

| | | | | |
|---|---|---|---|---|
| Pension Plan: | ESOP Stock Plan: | Profit Sharing: | Top Exec. Salary: $650,000 | Bonus: $222,300 |
| Savings Plan: Y | Stock Purch. Plan: | | Second Exec. Salary: $360,000 | Bonus: $273,120 |

## OTHER THOUGHTS:

**Apparent Women Officers or Directors**: 2
**Hot Spot for Advancement for Women/Minorities**: Y

## LOCATIONS: ("Y" = Yes)

| West: | Southwest: | Midwest: | Southeast: | Northeast: | International: |
|---|---|---|---|---|---|
| Y | Y | Y | Y | Y | Y |

# CENTRAL VERMONT PUBLIC SERVICE CORPORATION

**www.cvps.com**

**Industry Group Code:** 221000A **Ranks within this company's industry group:** Sales: 8 Profits: 8

| Management: | | Sales/Marketing: | | Liberal Arts: | | Information Systems: | | Professionals: | | Technical/Scientific: | |
|---|---|---|---|---|---|---|---|---|---|---|---|
| Mgmt. Trainees: | | Mktg. Professionals: | Y | Gen. Writing/Editing: | | Info. Management: | Y | Finance/Accounting: | Y | Engineers, Elec.: | Y |
| Experienced Mgmt.: | Y | Retail Sales: | | Technical Writing: | | Software Dev.: | | Law: | Y | Engineers, Other: | Y |
| Int'l Business: | Y | Commercial/Industrial: | Y | Graphic Arts/Photog.: | | Hardware Dev.: | | HR/Other: | Y | Health/Lab: | |
| MBA Graduates: | Y | Sales Trainees: | Y | Music: | | Systems Integration: | | Training: | Y | Scientists/Research: | |
| | | Advertising Pros.: | | Broadcasting: | | Consulting/Other: | | Health Care: | | Petroleum/Chemicals: | Y |
| | | | | Other: | | | | Consulting: | | Math/Other: | |

## TYPES OF BUSINESS:

Utilities-Electric
Real Estate Services
Wind, Biomass & Hydroelectric Power
Nuclear Power
Bovine Methane Power

## BRANDS/DIVISIONS/AFFILIATES:

Vermont Yankee Nuclear Power Company
Connecticut Yankee Atomic Power Company
C.V. Realty, Inc.
East Barnet Hydroelectric, Inc.
Custom Investment Corp.
CVPS Cow Power
Maine Yankee Atomic Power Company

## CONTACTS: *Note: Officers with more than one job title may be intentionally listed here more than once.*

Robert H. Young, CEO
Robert H. Young, Pres.
Pamela J. Keefe, CFO/VP
Joseph M. Kraus, Sr. VP-Eng.
Dale A. Rocheleau, General Counsel/Sr. VP/Corp. Sec.
Joseph M. Kraus, Sr. VP-Oper. & Customer Service
Joan F. Gamble, VP-Strategic Change & Bus. Svcs.
Brian P. Keefe, VP-Gov't & Public Affairs
Pamela J. Keefe, Treas.
William J. Deehan, VP-Power Planning & Regulatory Affairs
Mary Alice McKenzie, Chmn.

| | |
|---|---|
| **Phone:** 802-773-2711 | **Fax:** |
| **Toll-Free:** 800-649-2877 | |
| **Address:** 77 Grove St., Rutland, VT 05701 US | |

## GROWTH PLANS/SPECIAL FEATURES:

Central Vermont Public Service Corp. (CVPS) is an energy and utility business with an expanding national and international presence. The company is engaged in the purchase, production, transmission, distribution and sale of electricity. It serves approximately 159,000 customers in 152 communities. CVPS has more than 600 miles of transmission lines and nearly 130 substations throughout Vermont. Additionally, the company has 20 hydro generation stations, two gas turbines, one diesel plant and 20 dams. The company's power supply breakdown contrasts that of the average U.S. power supplier, which is typically dominated by coal and other non-renewable energy sources. CVPS energy sources include nuclear 48%; hydro 39%; oil and wood 6%; and other 7%. The firm generates revenue from two primary segments: retail and resale sales. The retail sales segment includes sales from residential, commercial and industrial customers. Retail sales in 2007 are distributed as such, residential 41%, Commercial 33%, industrial and other 11%; resale sales represent 12% of sales; and 3% of sales are derived from the other category. The resale sales segment is comprised of long-term sales to third parties in New England; sales in the energy markets administered by ISO-New England; and short-term system capacity sales. The firm's wholly owned subsidiaries include Custom Investment Corporation, which was formed for the purpose of holding passive investments; C.V. Realty, Inc., a real estate company that owns, buys, sells and leases real and personal property and interests related to the utility business; East Barnet Hydroelectric, Inc., which was created for the purpose of financing and constructing a hydroelectric facility in Vermont; Catamount Resources Corporation (CRC), which was formed for the purpose of holding its subsidiaries that invest in unregulated business opportunities; and Eversant Corporation, which engages in the sale or rental of electric water heaters in Vermont and New Hampshire.

## FINANCIALS: **Sales and profits are in thousands of dollars—add 000 to get the full amount. 2008 Note: Financial information for 2008 was not available for all companies at press time.**

| | | |
|---|---|---|
| 2008 Sales: $ | 2008 Profits: $ | **U.S. Stock Ticker: CV** |
| 2007 Sales: $329,107 | 2007 Profits: $15,804 | **Int'l Ticker:** Int'l Exchange: |
| 2006 Sales: $325,738 | 2006 Profits: $18,352 | Employees: 552 |
| 2005 Sales: $311,359 | 2005 Profits: $6,346 | Fiscal Year Ends: 12/31 |
| 2004 Sales: $302,286 | 2004 Profits: $23,755 | Parent Company: |

## SALARIES/BENEFITS:

| | | | | |
|---|---|---|---|---|
| Pension Plan: | ESOP Stock Plan: | Profit Sharing: | Top Exec. Salary: $370,981 | Bonus: $163,000 |
| Savings Plan: Y | Stock Purch. Plan: | | Second Exec. Salary: $216,789 | Bonus: $60,300 |

## OTHER THOUGHTS:

**Apparent Women Officers or Directors**: 4
**Hot Spot for Advancement for Women/Minorities**: Y

## LOCATIONS: ("Y" = Yes)

| West: | Southwest: | Midwest: | Southeast: | Northeast: | International: |
|---|---|---|---|---|---|
| | | | | Y | Y |

# CEPHEID

www.cepheid.com

**Industry Group Code:** 325413 **Ranks within this company's industry group:** Sales: 6 Profits: 8

| Management: | | Sales/Marketing: | | Liberal Arts: | | Information Systems: | | Professionals: | | Technical/Scientific: | |
|---|---|---|---|---|---|---|---|---|---|---|---|
| Mgmt. Trainees: | | Mktg. Professionals: | Y | Gen. Writing/Editing: | | Info. Management: | Y | Finance/Accounting: | Y | Engineers, Elec.: | Y |
| Experienced Mgmt.: | Y | Retail Sales: | | Technical Writing: | Y | Software Dev.: | Y | Law: | Y | Engineers, Other: | Y |
| Int'l Business: | Y | Commercial/Industrial: | Y | Graphic Arts/Photog.: | | Hardware Dev.: | Y | HR/Other: | Y | Health/Lab: | Y |
| MBA Graduates: | Y | Sales Trainees: | Y | Music: | | Systems Integration: | | Training: | Y | Scientists/Research: | Y |
| | | Advertising Pros.: | | Broadcasting: | | Consulting/Other: | | Health Care: | Y | Petroleum/Chemicals: | |
| | | | | Other: | | | | Consulting: | | Math/Other: | Y |

## TYPES OF BUSINESS:
Equipment-Biological Testing
Genetic Profiling
DNA Analysis Systems

## BRANDS/DIVISIONS/AFFILIATES:
Smart Cycler
Smart Cycler II
GeneXpert
IVD
ASR
RUO
Sangtec Molecular Diagnostics AB
Xpert HemosIL

## CONTACTS: *Note: Officers with more than one job title may be intentionally listed here more than once.*
John L. Bishop, CEO
Andrew D. Miller, CFO/Sr. VP
Robert J. Koska, Sr. VP-Sales & Mktg.
Laurie King, VP-Human Resources
Peter J. Dailey, VP-R&D
Jan Steuperaert, VP-IT
David H. Persing, CTO/Exec. VP
Nicki Bowen, VP-Eng.
Joseph H. Smith, Sr. VP-Legal
Humberto Reyes, Exec. VP-Oper.
Joseph H. Smith, Sr. VP-Bus. Dev.
Jared Tipton, Dir.-Corp. Comm.
Jared Tipton, Dir.-Investor Rel.
Michael Myhre, VP-Corp. Controller
Lee Christel, VP-Research & Systems Integration
Russel K. Enns, Sr. VP-Regulatory, Clinical & Govt. Affairs
Robert J. Koska, Sr. VP-Worldwide Commercial Oper.
Sandra Finley, VP-Mktg.
Thomas L. Gutshall, Chmn.
Rika Dutau, VP/Managing Dir.-Cepeid Europe

| | |
|---|---|
| **Phone:** 408-541-4191 | **Fax:** 408-541-4192 |
| **Toll-Free:** 888-838-3222 | |
| **Address:** 904 Caribbean Dr., Sunnyvale, CA 94089 US | |

## GROWTH PLANS/SPECIAL FEATURES:
Cepheid is a molecular diagnostics company that develops, manufactures and markets fully integrated systems for the clinical genetic assessment, life sciences, industrial and biothreat markets. Cephid systems enable rapid molecular testing for organisms and genetic-based diseases by implementing automated technology to reduce the complicated and time-intensive steps that are usually involved in molecular testing. Complex biological systems are analyzed in the company's proprietary biocartridges, which eliminates any lengthy preparation, amplification and detection of targeted genes. The company's two principal system platforms are the SmartCycler and GeneXpert systems. SmartCycles integrates DNA amplification and detection in order to rapidly analyze samples while the GeneXpert system incorporates sample preparation with DNA amplification and detection. Both systems are utilized in areas of critical infectious diseases, immunocompromised transplantations, women's health and oncology. Other products include the IVD line, ASR line, RUO products line, biothreat products and life science products. The company has sold units to a wide range of customers, including the Center for Disease Control and Prevention, the U.S. Food and Drug Administration, Johns Hopkins University, Memorial Sloan-Kettering Cancer Center, the National Institute of Health, Stanford University and the U.S. Army Medical Research Institute for Infectious Disease (USAMRIID). GeneXpert has also been incorporated into the United States Postal Service's Biohazard Detection System to identify the presence of anthrax from air samples. In February 2007, the company acquired Sangtec Molecular Diagnostics AB, which added a line of products that manages infections in immunocompromised patients to Cepheid's technologies. In February 2008, in conjunction with Instrumentation Laboratory, the firm introduced the Xpert HemosIL assay product to the European clinical testing market; the device detects genetic variations associated with thrombophilia (increased risk of blood clotting).

Cepheid offers employees flexible spending accounts, income protections plans and an employee assistance program.

## FINANCIALS: **Sales and profits are in thousands of dollars—add 000 to get the full amount. 2008 Note: Financial information for 2008 was not available for all companies at press time.**

| | | |
|---|---|---|
| 2008 Sales: $ | 2008 Profits: $ | **U.S. Stock Ticker: CPHD** |
| 2007 Sales: $129,473 | 2007 Profits: $-21,423 | **Int'l Ticker:** Int'l Exchange: |
| 2006 Sales: $87,352 | 2006 Profits: $-25,985 | Employees: 473 |
| 2005 Sales: $85,010 | 2005 Profits: $-13,594 | Fiscal Year Ends: 12/31 |
| 2004 Sales: $52,968 | 2004 Profits: $-13,800 | Parent Company: |

## SALARIES/BENEFITS:

| | | | | |
|---|---|---|---|---|
| Pension Plan: | ESOP Stock Plan: | Profit Sharing: | Top Exec. Salary: $450,000 | Bonus: $225,000 |
| Savings Plan: Y | Stock Purch. Plan: Y | | Second Exec. Salary: $365,000 | Bonus: $126,473 |

## OTHER THOUGHTS:
**Apparent Women Officers or Directors**: 7
**Hot Spot for Advancement for Women/Minorities**: Y

## LOCATIONS: ("Y" = Yes)

| West: | Southwest: | Midwest: | Southeast: | Northeast: | International: |
|---|---|---|---|---|---|
| Y | | | | | Y |

# CHANNELL COMMERCIAL CORP

www.channellcomm.com

**Industry Group Code:** 334210 **Ranks within this company's industry group:** Sales: 9 Profits: 7

| Management: | | Sales/Marketing: | | Liberal Arts: | | Information Systems: | | Professionals: | | Technical/Scientific: | |
|---|---|---|---|---|---|---|---|---|---|---|---|
| Mgmt. Trainees: | | Mktg. Professionals: | Y | Gen. Writing/Editing: | Y | Info. Management: | Y | Finance/Accounting: | Y | Engineers, Elec.: | Y |
| Experienced Mgmt.: | Y | Retail Sales: | | Technical Writing: | Y | Software Dev.: | Y | Law: | Y | Engineers, Other: | Y |
| Int'l Business: | Y | Commercial/Industrial: | Y | Graphic Arts/Photog.: | | Hardware Dev.: | Y | HR/Other: | Y | Health/Lab: | |
| MBA Graduates: | Y | Sales Trainees: | Y | Music: | | Systems Integration: | Y | Training: | Y | Scientists/Research: | |
| | | Advertising Pros.: | | Broadcasting: | | Consulting/Other: | | Health Care: | | Petroleum/Chemicals: | |
| | | | | Other: | | | | Consulting: | | Math/Other: | |

## TYPES OF BUSINESS:

Telecommunications Infrastructure Hardware
Thermoplastic & Metal Enclosures
Fiber-Optic Cable Management Systems
Termination & Connection Products
Heat Shrink Products
Water Storage Tanks

## BRANDS/DIVISIONS/AFFILIATES:

Bushman Tanks
MAH Series
Mini-Rocker
DSLink
Rhino
GLM

## CONTACTS: *Note: Officers with more than one job title may be intentionally listed here more than once.*

William H. Channell, Jr., CEO
William H. Channell, Jr., Pres.
Patrick E. McCready, CFO
Andrew M. Zogby, Chief Mktg. Officer
Edward J. Burke, CTO
Michael Perica, Investor Rel.
Jacqueline M. Channell, Sec.
Chris Glenn, Managing Dir.-Australia Oper.
Jacqueline M. Channell, Interim Chmn.

| **Phone:** 951-719-2600 | **Fax:** 951-296-2322 |
|---|---|
| **Toll-Free:** | |
| **Address:** 26040 Ynez Rd., Temecula, CA 92591-9022 US | |

## GROWTH PLANS/SPECIAL FEATURES:

Channell Commercial Corp., founded in 1922, designs, manufactures and globally supplies telecommunications equipment to broadband and telephone network providers. The company's major product lines, which in 2007 accounted for 43% of the company's sales, include thermoplastic and metal fabricated enclosures; advanced copper termination and connection products; fiber optic cable management systems for fiber to the premises (FTTP) networks; and heat shrink products. In addition to serving customers in the global telecommunications industry, Channell also operates in the Australian water storage tank industry through its subsidiary, Bushman Tanks. Channell's enclosure products provide protection against weather and vandalism, include both above- and below-ground versions, and provide advanced heat dissipation properties. Channell designs thermo-molded application-specific thermoplastic and metal fabricated enclosures for advanced telecommunications hardware such as radio frequency (RF) electronics and photonics and transmission media. Products include the MAH Series free breathing telephony enclosures, GLB subsurface enclosures and a range of Rhino metal fabricated enclosures. The company's copper connectivity products include the Mini-Rocker line of copper connectivity modules and the DSLink modular terminal block. Channell's fiber optic products include electronic enclosures, fiber optic splice cases and fiber optic cable assemblies. The company sells its telecommunications products directly to broadband operators and telephones companies principally within developed nations around the world, and sells its water storage products, which account for 45% of its net sales, in Australia directly to end users as well as to retailers, wholesalers, distributors and agents. Channell's five largest customers in the U.S. are Verizon, Comcast, Time Warner, Cox and Bright House Networks.

Channell offers a benefits plan including a 401(k) plan; life and disability insurance; relocation benefits; as well as periodically awarding stock options.

## FINANCIALS: **Sales and profits are in thousands of dollars—add 000 to get the full amount. 2008 Note: Financial information for 2008 was not available for all companies at press time.**

| | | |
|---|---|---|
| 2008 Sales: $ | 2008 Profits: $ | **U.S. Stock Ticker: CHNL** |
| 2007 Sales: $133,163 | 2007 Profits: $ 273 | **Int'l Ticker:** Int'l Exchange: |
| 2006 Sales: $109,138 | 2006 Profits: $-6,829 | Employees: 618 |
| 2005 Sales: $116,065 | 2005 Profits: $-6,880 | Fiscal Year Ends: 12/31 |
| 2004 Sales: $102,200 | 2004 Profits: $3,609 | Parent Company: |

## SALARIES/BENEFITS:

| | | | | |
|---|---|---|---|---|
| Pension Plan: | ESOP Stock Plan: | Profit Sharing: | Top Exec. Salary: $825,523 | Bonus: $341,850 |
| Savings Plan: Y | Stock Purch. Plan: Y | | Second Exec. Salary: $204,615 | Bonus: $47,000 |

## OTHER THOUGHTS:

**Apparent Women Officers or Directors**: 1
**Hot Spot for Advancement for Women/Minorities**:

## LOCATIONS: ("Y" = Yes)

| West: | Southwest: | Midwest: | Southeast: | Northeast: | International: |
|---|---|---|---|---|---|
| Y | | | | | Y |

# CHATTEM INC

www.chattem.com

**Industry Group Code:** 325411 **Ranks within this company's industry group:** Sales: 1 Profits: 1

| Management: | | Sales/Marketing: | | Liberal Arts: | | Information Systems: | | Professionals: | | Technical/Scientific: | |
|---|---|---|---|---|---|---|---|---|---|---|---|
| Mgmt. Trainees: | | Mktg. Professionals: | Y | Gen. Writing/Editing: | | Info. Management: | Y | Finance/Accounting: | Y | Engineers, Elec.: | |
| Experienced Mgmt.: | Y | Retail Sales: | | Technical Writing: | Y | Software Dev.: | | Law: | Y | Engineers, Other: | |
| Int'l Business: | Y | Commercial/Industrial: | Y | Graphic Arts/Photog.: | | Hardware Dev.: | | HR/Other: | Y | Health/Lab: | Y |
| MBA Graduates: | Y | Sales Trainees: | Y | Music: | | Systems Integration: | | Training: | Y | Scientists/Research: | Y |
| | | Advertising Pros.: | | Broadcasting: | | Consulting/Other: | | Health Care: | Y | Petroleum/Chemicals: | Y |
| | | | | Other: | | | | Consulting: | | Math/Other: | Y |

## TYPES OF BUSINESS:

Branded Consumer Products - Medicinal
Over-the-Counter Drugs
Toiletries
Skin Care Products

## BRANDS/DIVISIONS/AFFILIATES:

Chattem (U.K.), Ltd.
Sundex, LLC
Pamprin
Icy Hot
Gold Bond
Bull Frog
Selsun Blue
Dexatrim

## CONTACTS: *Note: Officers with more than one job title may be intentionally listed here more than once.*

Zan Guerry, CEO
Robert E. Bosworth, COO
Robert E. Bosworth, Pres.
Robert Long, CFO
Charles M. Stafford, VP-Sales
Joseph J. Czerwinski, VP-Prod. Dev.
Theodore K. Whitfield, Jr., General Counsel/VP/Sec.
B. Derrill Pitts, VP-Oper.
Ron Galante, VP-New Bus. Dev.
Andrea M. Crouch, VP-Brand Mgmt.
J. Blair Ramey, VP-Mktg.
John L. Stroud, VP-Mktg.
Zan Guerry, Chmn.

| | |
|---|---|
| **Phone:** 423-821-4571 | **Fax:** 423-821-0395 |
| **Toll-Free:** | |
| **Address:** 1715 W. 38th St., Chattanooga, TN 37409 US | |

## GROWTH PLANS/SPECIAL FEATURES:

Chattem, Inc., founded in 1879 as Chattanooga Medicine Corp., is a leading marketer and manufacturer of branded consumer products, including over-the-counter drugs, toiletries, topical pain care products, medicated skin care products, medicated dandruff shampoos and dietary supplements. The company's products target niche market segments, which are often overlooked by larger companies. Principally utilizing its own sales force, Chattem sells its products nationally through mass merchandisers, drug and food channels. Chattem's topical pain care brands are Icy Hot, Icy Hot Pro-Therapy, Aspercreme, Flexall, Capzasin, Sportscreme and Arthritis Hot. The firm's medicated skin care brands are Gold Bond, Cortizone and Balmex, while Selsun Blue and Selsun Salon make up its medication dandruff shampoo line. Chattem offers dietary supplement brands Dexatrim, Garlique, Melatonex, New Phase and Omnigest EZ; Pamprin, a menstrual pain reliever; Bullfrog, a waterproof sunscreen; Unisom, a sleep aid; and Mudd, a line of specialty masque products. The company also operates an international division, which represented approximately 7% of its 2007 sales and is concentrated in Canada, where brands such as Icy Hot, Selsun, Gold Bond and Pamprin are marketed through Chattem's subsidiary Chattem Canada. European business is conducted through Chattem Global Consumer Products Ltd., an Irish subsidiary of Chattem's, as well as Chattem (U.K.) Limited, a subsidiary located in England. Additionally, the firm controls three other subsidiaries: Signal Investment & Management Co.; Sundex, LLC; and HBA Indemnity Company, Ltd. In January 2007, the company acquired the U.S. rights to five Johnson & Johnson brands: ACT, a mouthwash; Unisom, an over-the-counter sleep aid; Cortizone-10, a hydrocortisone anti-itch cream; Kaopectate, an anti-diarrhea product; and Balmex, a diaper rash product. In 2007, Chattem introduced six product line extensions: Icy Hot Heat Therapy; Icy Hot Vanishing Scent Cream; Capzasin No-Mess; Bullfrog Marathon Mist; Selsun Naturals; and Dexatrin Man Evening Appetite Control.

## FINANCIALS: **Sales and profits are in thousands of dollars—add 000 to get the full amount. 2008 Note: Financial information for 2008 was not available for all companies at press time.**

| | | |
|---|---|---|
| 2008 Sales: $ | 2008 Profits: $ | **U.S. Stock Ticker: CHTT** |
| 2007 Sales: $423,378 | 2007 Profits: $59,690 | **Int'l Ticker:** Int'l Exchange: |
| 2006 Sales: $300,548 | 2006 Profits: $45,112 | Employees: 465 |
| 2005 Sales: $279,318 | 2005 Profits: $36,047 | Fiscal Year Ends: 11/30 |
| 2004 Sales: $258,155 | 2004 Profits: $1,451 | Parent Company: |

## SALARIES/BENEFITS:

| | | | | |
|---|---|---|---|---|
| Pension Plan: | ESOP Stock Plan: | Profit Sharing: | Top Exec. Salary: $591,424 | Bonus: $826,800 |
| Savings Plan: | Stock Purch. Plan: | | Second Exec. Salary: $420,800 | Bonus: $390,000 |

## OTHER THOUGHTS:

**Apparent Women Officers or Directors**: 1
**Hot Spot for Advancement for Women/Minorities**:

## LOCATIONS: ("Y" = Yes)

| West: | Southwest: | Midwest: | Southeast: | Northeast: | International: |
|---|---|---|---|---|---|
| | | | Y | | Y |

# CHINDEX INTERNATIONAL INC

www.chindex.com

**Industry Group Code:** 421450 **Ranks within this company's industry group:** Sales: 1 Profits: 1

| Management: | | Sales/Marketing: | | Liberal Arts: | | Information Systems: | | Professionals: | | Technical/Scientific: | |
|---|---|---|---|---|---|---|---|---|---|---|---|
| Mgmt. Trainees: | | Mktg. Professionals: | Y | Gen. Writing/Editing: | | Info. Management: | Y | Finance/Accounting: | Y | Engineers, Elec.: | |
| Experienced Mgmt.: | Y | Retail Sales: | | Technical Writing: | Y | Software Dev.: | | Law: | Y | Engineers, Other: | |
| Int'l Business: | Y | Commercial/Industrial: | Y | Graphic Arts/Photog.: | | Hardware Dev.: | | HR/Other: | Y | Health/Lab: | |
| MBA Graduates: | Y | Sales Trainees: | Y | Music: | | Systems Integration: | | Training: | Y | Scientists/Research: | |
| | | Advertising Pros.: | | Broadcasting: | | Consulting/Other: | | Health Care: | Y | Petroleum/Chemicals: | |
| | | | | Other: | | | | Consulting: | | Math/Other: | |

## TYPES OF BUSINESS:

Health Care Products Distribution
Technical Services

## BRANDS/DIVISIONS/AFFILIATES:

United Family Healthcare
Beijing United Family Hospital
Shanghai United Family Hospital
Wuxi United Family International Healthcare Center

## CONTACTS:

*Note: Officers with more than one job title may be intentionally listed here more than once.*

Roberta Lipson, CEO
Roberta Lipson, Pres.
Lawrence Pemble, CFO/Exec. VP
Daniel Fulton, VP-IT Svcs.
Cheryl Chartier, Controller
Elyse Beth Silverberg, Exec. VP
Judy Zakreski, VP-U.S. Oper.
Walter Xue, VP-China Finance/Controller
Zhang Pin Qing, VP-Tech. Service
A. Kenneth Nilsson, Chmn.
Walter Stryker, Sr. VP-China Admin.

**Phone:** 301-215-7777 **Fax:** 301-215-7719
**Toll-Free:**
**Address:** 4340 E. W. Highway, Ste. 1100, Bethesda, MD 20814 US

## GROWTH PLANS/SPECIAL FEATURES:

Chindex International, Inc., an American company operating in several healthcare markets in China, including Hong Kong, provides healthcare services and sells medical equipment, instruments and products. The firm operates in two segments: healthcare services and medical products. The healthcare services division, which generated 45% of revenue in 2007, operates the United Family Healthcare network of private hospitals and clinics, the Beijing United Family Hospital and the Shanghai United Family Hospital. The United Family Healthcare facilities offer a wide range of family healthcare services, including 24-hours-a-day, seven-days-a-week emergency rooms, intensive care units, neonatal intensive care units, operating rooms, clinical laboratory, radiology and blood baking services for men, women and children. The medical products division markets, which generated 55% of revenue in 2007, distributes and sells select medical capital equipment, instrumentation and other medical products for use in hospitals in China and Hong Kong. Products sold include diagnostic color ultrasound imaging devices; robotic surgical systems and instrumentation; chemistry analyzers; sterilization systems; bone densitometers; mammography; and breast biopsy devices and lasers for cosmetic surgery. The division includes a technical service department, which is responsible for the technical support of virtually all the medical equipment that the company sells. In July 2008, Chindex received permission to market the daVinci Surgical System and the AlexLaser in China.

## FINANCIALS:

**Sales and profits are in thousands of dollars—add 000 to get the full amount. 2008 Note: Financial information for 2008 was not available for all companies at press time.**

2008 Sales: $
2007 Sales: $105,921
2006 Sales: $90,836
2005 Sales: $83,159
2004 Sales: $75,419

2008 Profits: $
2007 Profits: $2,982
2006 Profits: $ 167
2005 Profits: $-3,924
2004 Profits: $- 854

**U.S. Stock Ticker: CHDX**
**Int'l Ticker:** Int'l Exchange:
Employees: 1,007
Fiscal Year Ends: 7/09
Parent Company:

## SALARIES/BENEFITS:

Pension Plan: ESOP Stock Plan: Profit Sharing: Top Exec. Salary: $238,930 Bonus: $67,500
Savings Plan: Stock Purch. Plan: Second Exec. Salary: $236,500 Bonus: $75,000

## OTHER THOUGHTS:

**Apparent Women Officers or Directors**: 7
**Hot Spot for Advancement for Women/Minorities**: Y

## LOCATIONS: ("Y" = Yes)

| West: | Southwest: | Midwest: | Southeast: | Northeast: | International: |
|---|---|---|---|---|---|
| | | | | Y | Y |

# CHOICESTREAM INC

www.choicestream.com

**Industry Group Code:** 541810A **Ranks within this company's industry group:** Sales: Profits:

| Management: | | Sales/Marketing: | | Liberal Arts: | | Information Systems: | | Professionals: | | Technical/Scientific: | |
|---|---|---|---|---|---|---|---|---|---|---|---|
| Mgmt. Trainees: | | Mktg. Professionals: | Y | Gen. Writing/Editing: | Y | Info. Management: | Y | Finance/Accounting: | Y | Engineers, Elec.: | |
| Experienced Mgmt.: | Y | Retail Sales: | | Technical Writing: | | Software Dev.: | | Law: | Y | Engineers, Other: | |
| Int'l Business: | | Commercial/Industrial: | | Graphic Arts/Photog.: | Y | Hardware Dev.: | | HR/Other: | Y | Health/Lab: | |
| MBA Graduates: | Y | Sales Trainees: | Y | Music: | | Systems Integration: | Y | Training: | Y | Scientists/Research: | |
| | | Advertising Pros.: | Y | Broadcasting: | | Consulting/Other: | | Health Care: | | Petroleum/Chemicals: | |
| | | | | Other: | Y | | | Consulting: | | Math/Other: | |

## TYPES OF BUSINESS:

Online Personalized Display Ads & Product Information

## BRANDS/DIVISIONS/AFFILIATES:

RealRelevance Advertising

## CONTACTS:

*Note: Officers with more than one job title may be intentionally listed here more than once.*

Steve Johnson, CEO
Darin Hicks, COO
Mark Gallagher, CFO
Doug May, VP-Sales
Michael Strickman, CTO
Bob Hiss, Sr. VP-Prod. Dev. & Professional Svcs.
Doug Feick, General Counsel/Exec. VP-Bus. Affairs
Dinesh Gopinath, Chief Solutions Officer
Cheryl Kellond, Sr. VP-Advertising Bus.
Aaron Kechlev, VP-Prod. Mktg. & Mgmt.

| **Phone:** 617-498-7800 | **Fax:** |
|---|---|
| **Toll-Free:** | |
| **Address:** 210 Broadway, 4th Fl., Cambridge, MA 02139 US | |

## GROWTH PLANS/SPECIAL FEATURES:

ChoiceStream, Inc. is a provider of personalization services such as online display ads and product recommendation advertising for entertainment, e-commerce, television and mobile phone companies. The firm's RealRelevance Advertising product features a landing page and ad format combination and predicts consumer demand for future products by utilizing actual consumer shopping data. The product allows the automatic generation of thousands of different ads through a single tag and produces individually target messages and product recommendation for a wide range of audience categories. RealRelevance provides an online store and personalized call center for retail stores and a customer rating system for recommendations, as well as promotions and editorial content for media and entertainment businesses. The company's aim is to streamline data, allowing consumers to find products more efficiently and to increase clients' revenue by driving consumption. ChoiceStream serves companies such as Borders; Comcast; Blockbuster; HBO; Yahoo!; Overstock.com; and Ticketmaster. In June 2008, the firm partnered with PowerReviews, a developer of customer review solutions, in order to provide customer ratings alongside product recommendations.

## FINANCIALS:

**Sales and profits are in thousands of dollars—add 000 to get the full amount. 2008 Note: Financial information for 2008 was not available for all companies at press time.**

| | | |
|---|---|---|
| 2008 Sales: $ | 2008 Profits: $ | **U.S. Stock Ticker: Private** |
| 2007 Sales: $ | 2007 Profits: $ | **Int'l Ticker:** Int'l Exchange: |
| 2006 Sales: $ | 2006 Profits: $ | Employees: |
| 2005 Sales: $ | 2005 Profits: $ | Fiscal Year Ends: |
| 2004 Sales: $ | 2004 Profits: $ | Parent Company: |

## SALARIES/BENEFITS:

| | | | | |
|---|---|---|---|---|
| Pension Plan: | ESOP Stock Plan: | Profit Sharing: | Top Exec. Salary: $ | Bonus: $ |
| Savings Plan: | Stock Purch. Plan: | | Second Exec. Salary: $ | Bonus: $ |

## OTHER THOUGHTS:

**Apparent Women Officers or Directors**: 1
**Hot Spot for Advancement for Women/Minorities**:

## LOCATIONS: ("Y" = Yes)

| West: | Southwest: | Midwest: | Southeast: | Northeast: | International: |
|---|---|---|---|---|---|
| Y | | | | Y | |

# CHOLESTECH CORP

**www.cholestech.com**

**Industry Group Code:** 339113 **Ranks within this company's industry group:** Sales: 36 Profits: 22

| **Management:** | | **Sales/Marketing:** | | **Liberal Arts:** | | **Information Systems:** | | **Professionals:** | | **Technical/Scientific:** | |
|---|---|---|---|---|---|---|---|---|---|---|---|
| Mgmt. Trainees: | | Mktg. Professionals: | Y | Gen. Writing/Editing: | | Info. Management: | Y | Finance/Accounting: | Y | Engineers, Elec.: | Y |
| Experienced Mgmt.: | Y | Retail Sales: | | Technical Writing: | Y | Software Dev.: | Y | Law: | Y | Engineers, Other: | Y |
| Int'l Business: | Y | Commercial/Industrial: | Y | Graphic Arts/Photog.: | | Hardware Dev.: | Y | HR/Other: | Y | Health/Lab: | Y |
| MBA Graduates: | Y | Sales Trainees: | Y | Music: | | Systems Integration: | Y | Training: | Y | Scientists/Research: | Y |
| | | Advertising Pros.: | | Broadcasting: | | Consulting/Other: | | Health Care: | Y | Petroleum/Chemicals: | |
| | | | | Other: | | | | Consulting: | | Math/Other: | Y |

## TYPES OF BUSINESS:

Equipment-Blood Diagnostic Test Systems
Cholesterol Tests

## BRANDS/DIVISIONS/AFFILIATES:

LDX System
GDX System
LDX Analyzer
Itamar Medical Limited
Aspartate Aminotransferase (AST) Test
Boule Diagnostic International
Inverness Medical Innovations, Inc.

## CONTACTS: *Note: Officers with more than one job title may be intentionally listed here more than once.*

Warren E. Pinckert, II, CEO
Warren E. Pinckert, II, Pres.
John F. Glenn, CFO
Kenneth F. Miller, VP-Mktg. & Sales
Terry Wassmann, VP-Human Resources
Gregory L. Bennett, VP-R&D
John F. Glenn, Corp. Sec.
Donald P. Wood, VP-Oper.
John F. Glenn, VP-Finance/Treas.
Barbara McAleer, VP-Quality Assurance & Regulatory Affairs
John H. Landon, Chmn.

**Phone:** 510-732-7200 **Fax:** 510-732-7227
**Toll-Free:** 800-733-0404
**Address:** 3347 Investment Blvd., Hayward, CA 94545-3808 US

## GROWTH PLANS/SPECIAL FEATURES:

Cholestech Corporation, a subsidiary of Inverness Medical Innovations, Inc., provides diagnostic tools for immediate risk assessment and monitoring of heart disease, inflammatory disorders and diabetes. The company manufactures the LDX System, which includes the LDX Analyzer and a variety of single-use test cassettes. Cholestech markets the LDX System in the United States, Europe, Asia, Australia and South America. The LDX System allows health care providers to perform individual tests or combinations of tests for blood cholesterol, related lipids, glucose, liver enzymes and high sensitivity C-reactive protein using a single drop of blood within five minutes. Cholestech also markets and distributes the GDX System, which measures hemoglobin A1C, an indicator of a patient's long-term glycemic control. Cholestech distributes the GDX under a multi-year global agreement with Provalis Diagnostics, Ltd. Unlike daily glucose monitoring, which only measures a patient's glucose level at the time of testing, A1C provides an average glucose level over the previous 90 days, which indicates the long-term progress of a patient's diabetes and therapy management. Cholestech specifically targets its products for markets outside of traditional hospital or clinical laboratories. The firm's primary market is the physician office laboratory market. Cholestech has a development and product distribution agreement with Itamar Medical Limited, involving a system for assessing vascular endothelial dysfunction, which is recognized as an early stage in the development of atherosclerosis. The company also provides an Aspartate Aminotransferase (AST) Test for monitoring the effects of various drugs on the liver. Cholestech is also collaborating with Boule Diagnostic International to develop and distribute a Complete Blood Count test system. In September 2007, Cholestech was acquired by Inverness Medical Innovations, Inc. and went private.

Cholestech offers its employees a flexible spending account, an employee assistance program, credit union membership, membership to a fitness club and medical and dental coverage.

## FINANCIALS: **Sales and profits are in thousands of dollars—add 000 to get the full amount. 2008 Note: Financial information for 2008 was not available for all companies at press time.**

2008 Sales: $
2007 Sales: $69,500
2006 Sales: $64,093
2005 Sales: $52,877
2004 Sales: $52,376

2008 Profits: $
2007 Profits: $9,400
2006 Profits: $5,634
2005 Profits: $4,148
2004 Profits: $8,707

**U.S. Stock Ticker: Subsidiary**
**Int'l Ticker:** Int'l Exchange:
Employees: 216
Fiscal Year Ends: 3/26
Parent Company: INVERNESS MEDICAL INNOVATIONS INC

## SALARIES/BENEFITS:

Pension Plan: ESOP Stock Plan: Profit Sharing: Top Exec. Salary: $437,077 Bonus: $111,038
Savings Plan: Y Stock Purch. Plan: Y Second Exec. Salary: $262,163 Bonus: $111,038

## OTHER THOUGHTS:

**Apparent Women Officers or Directors**: 2
**Hot Spot for Advancement for Women/Minorities**: Y

## LOCATIONS: ("Y" = Yes)

| West: | Southwest: | Midwest: | Southeast: | Northeast: | International: |
|---|---|---|---|---|---|
| Y | | | | | |

Note: Financial information, benefits and other data can change quickly and may vary from those stated here.

# CHYRON CORP

www.chyron.com

**Industry Group Code:** 511209 **Ranks within this company's industry group:** Sales: 2 Profits: 2

| Management: | | Sales/Marketing: | | Liberal Arts: | | Information Systems: | | Professionals: | | Technical/Scientific: | |
|---|---|---|---|---|---|---|---|---|---|---|---|
| Mgmt. Trainees: | | Mktg. Professionals: | Y | Gen. Writing/Editing: | Y | Info. Management: | Y | Finance/Accounting: | Y | Engineers, Elec.: | |
| Experienced Mgmt.: | Y | Retail Sales: | | Technical Writing: | Y | Software Dev.: | Y | Law: | Y | Engineers, Other: | |
| Int'l Business: | Y | Commercial/Industrial: | Y | Graphic Arts/Photog.: | | Hardware Dev.: | | HR/Other: | Y | Health/Lab: | |
| MBA Graduates: | Y | Sales Trainees: | Y | Music: | | Systems Integration: | Y | Training: | Y | Scientists/Research: | |
| | | Advertising Pros.: | | Broadcasting: | | Consulting/Other: | | Health Care: | | Petroleum/Chemicals: | |
| | | | | Other: | | | | Consulting: | | Math/Other: | |

## TYPES OF BUSINESS:

Software-Video & Audio Presentations
Graphics Systems
Video & Audio Control & Automation Systems
Content Creation Software

## BRANDS/DIVISIONS/AFFILIATES:

Duet
Lyric
Lyric Pro
CAMIO
iSQ
WAPSTR
CodiStrator
AXIS Graphics

## CONTACTS: *Note: Officers with more than one job title may be intentionally listed here more than once.*

Michael I. Wellesley-Wesley, CEO
Kevin Prince, COO/Sr. VP
Michael I. Wellesley-Wesley, Pres.
Jerry Kieliszak, CFO/Sr. VP
Robert S. Matlin, Sec.
Gordon Blau, Head-Creative Svcs.
Roger L. Ogden, Chmn.

**Phone:** 631-845-2000 **Fax:** 631-845-1267
**Toll-Free:**
**Address:** 5 Hub Dr., Melville, NY 11747 US

## GROWTH PLANS/SPECIAL FEATURES:

Chyron Corp. develops, manufactures, markets and supports hardware and software products for video and audio production and post-production. The Graphics System/CG Family comprises real-time 2D/3D serial digital video graphics-processing platforms that integrate a Windows NT or Windows 2000 front end with real-time graphics processing to provide exceptional performance for television character generator applications. Some graphics systems brand names include Duet, HyperX2, LEX2, MicroX and SOLO2. Lyric and Lyric Pro, the firm's content creation and playback software systems, can import a variety of file formats, including TIFF and TGA, and can output files for television broadcast, HTML and interactive television. Lyric drives all the firm's graphic software systems. Chyron's Newsroom Integration and Asset Management offerings help news producers create and share visual content across a number of servers as well as allowing producers to control playback in real time with intuitive control. These products include the brand names CAMIO, iSQ, interFuse, MOS2WAP, and WAPSTR. The firm also offers dedicated systems such as CodiStrator, which offers real-time illustration features, such as used by sports commentators; and DynaCrawl, offering continuous scrolling automatically updated information, such as seen during some news broadcasts. These high-performance graphics systems are used by many of the world's leading broadcast stations to display news flashes, election results, sports scores, stock market quotations, programming notes and weather information. Chyon's customers include ABC, CBS, ESPN, Fox News, CNN, Fox Sports, C-SPAN, Discovery, Weather Channel, Home Shopping Network, Comcast, DirecTV, NBA, CBC (Canada), BBC (U.K.), France 3, Korean Broadcast, YV Catalonia (Spain) and numerous local and regional stations. In January 2008, the company acquired AXIS Graphics and subsequently launched an online division allowing the firm to reach non-broadcast media including websites, newspapers, radio stations and mobile phones.

Employees are offered medical, dental, and life insurance, as well as short-and long-term disability coverage.

## FINANCIALS: **Sales and profits are in thousands of dollars—add 000 to get the full amount. 2008 Note: Financial information for 2008 was not available for all companies at press time.**

| | | |
|---|---|---|
| 2008 Sales: $ | 2008 Profits: $ | **U.S. Stock Ticker: CHRY** |
| 2007 Sales: $32,327 | 2007 Profits: $3,715 | **Int'l Ticker:** Int'l Exchange: |
| 2006 Sales: $26,246 | 2006 Profits: $3,121 | Employees: 107 |
| 2005 Sales: $25,129 | 2005 Profits: $ 706 | Fiscal Year Ends: 12/31 |
| 2004 Sales: $23,238 | 2004 Profits: $ 305 | Parent Company: |

## SALARIES/BENEFITS:

| | | | | |
|---|---|---|---|---|
| Pension Plan: Y | ESOP Stock Plan: | Profit Sharing: | Top Exec. Salary: $431,504 | Bonus: $352,882 |
| Savings Plan: Y | Stock Purch. Plan: Y | | Second Exec. Salary: $194,013 | Bonus: $135,894 |

## OTHER THOUGHTS:

**Apparent Women Officers or Directors:**
**Hot Spot for Advancement for Women/Minorities:**

## LOCATIONS: ("Y" = Yes)

| West: | Southwest: | Midwest: | Southeast: | Northeast: | International: |
|---|---|---|---|---|---|
| | | | | Y | Y |

# CIENA CORP

www.ciena.com

**Industry Group Code:** 334210 **Ranks within this company's industry group:** Sales: 1 Profits: 1

| Management: | | Sales/Marketing: | | Liberal Arts: | | Information Systems: | | Professionals: | | Technical/Scientific: | |
|---|---|---|---|---|---|---|---|---|---|---|---|
| Mgmt. Trainees: | | Mktg. Professionals: | Y | Gen. Writing/Editing: | Y | Info. Management: | Y | Finance/Accounting: | Y | Engineers, Elec.: | Y |
| Experienced Mgmt.: | Y | Retail Sales: | | Technical Writing: | Y | Software Dev.: | Y | Law: | Y | Engineers, Other: | Y |
| Int'l Business: | Y | Commercial/Industrial: | Y | Graphic Arts/Photog.: | | Hardware Dev.: | Y | HR/Other: | Y | Health/Lab: | |
| MBA Graduates: | Y | Sales Trainees: | Y | Music: | | Systems Integration: | Y | Training: | Y | Scientists/Research: | |
| | | Advertising Pros.: | | Broadcasting: | | Consulting/Other: | | Health Care: | | Petroleum/Chemicals: | |
| | | | | Other: | | | | Consulting: | | Math/Other: | |

## TYPES OF BUSINESS:

Communications Networking Equipment
Software & Support Services
Consulting Services
Switching Platforms
Packet Interworking Products
Access Products
Network & Service Management Tools

## BRANDS/DIVISIONS/AFFILIATES:

FlexSelect
World Wide Packets, Inc.

## CONTACTS: *Note: Officers with more than one job title may be intentionally listed here more than once.*

Gary B. Smith, CEO
Arthur Smith, COO/Sr. VP
Gary B. Smith, Pres.
James E. Moylan, Jr., CFO
Mike Aquino, Sr. VP-Worldwide Sales
Randall Harris, Sr. VP-Global Human Resources
James P. Donley, CIO/VP-IT
Stephen B. Alexander, CTO/Sr. VP-Prod. & Tech.
Russell B. Stevenson, Jr., General Counsel/Sr. VP/Corp. Sec.
James Frodsham, Sr. VP-Corp. Dev.
Suzanne DuLong, Chief Comm. Officer
James E. Moylan, Jr., Sr. VP-Finance
Andrew C. Petrik, Treas./Controller/VP
Jesus Leon, Chief Dev. Officer/Sr. VP
Thomas Mock, Sr. VP-Strategic Planning
David Peed, VP/Managing Dir.-Ciena Gov't Sol., Inc.
Patrick H. Nettles, Chmn.
Neeraj Gulati, VP/Managing Dir.-Ciena India

| | |
|---|---|
| **Phone:** 410-865-8500 | **Fax:** 410-694-5750 |
| **Toll-Free:** 800-921-1144 | |
| **Address:** 1201 Winterson Rd., Linthicum, MD 21090 US | |

## GROWTH PLANS/SPECIAL FEATURES:

Ciena Corp. is a supplier of communications networking equipment, software and services that support the transport, switching, aggregation and management of voice, video and data traffic. Its product portfolio includes a range of communications networking equipment and software that it utilized from the core of communications networks, to metropolitan network infrastructures to the network edge, where end users gain access to communications services. Its products are used, individually or as part of an integrated solution, in communications network infrastructures operated by telecommunications service providers, cable operators, governments and enterprises around the globe. Through the FlexSelect architecture, the company specializes in transitioning legacy communications networks to converged, next-generation architectures. Products include transport and switching platforms; packet interworking products; access products; network and service management tools; and global services such as consulting and support services. The firm sells its communications networking equipment, software and services through direct sales efforts and channel relationships. Ciena relies on contract manufacturers to perform the majority of the manufacturing of its products. In early 2008, the company acquired World Wide Packets, Inc., a provider of carrier Ethernet solutions.

The company offers its employees medical, dental and vision insurance; short- and long-term disability insurance; flexible spending accounts; business travel accident and life insurance; stock options; a 401(k) plan; an employee stock purchase plan; an employee assistance program; and educational assistance.

## FINANCIALS: **Sales and profits are in thousands of dollars—add 000 to get the full amount. 2008 Note: Financial information for 2008 was not available for all companies at press time.**

| | | |
|---|---|---|
| 2008 Sales: $902,448 | 2008 Profits: $38,894 | **U.S. Stock Ticker: CIEN** |
| 2007 Sales: $779,769 | 2007 Profits: $82,788 | **Int'l Ticker:** Int'l Exchange: |
| 2006 Sales: $564,056 | 2006 Profits: $ 595 | Employees: 2,203 |
| 2005 Sales: $427,257 | 2005 Profits: $-453,699 | Fiscal Year Ends: 10/31 |
| 2004 Sales: $298,700 | 2004 Profits: $-789,500 | Parent Company: |

## SALARIES/BENEFITS:

| | | | | |
|---|---|---|---|---|
| Pension Plan: | ESOP Stock Plan: | Profit Sharing: | Top Exec. Salary: $509,616 | Bonus: $643,750 |
| Savings Plan: Y | Stock Purch. Plan: Y | | Second Exec. Salary: $382,020 | Bonus: $362,109 |

## OTHER THOUGHTS:

**Apparent Women Officers or Directors**: 2
**Hot Spot for Advancement for Women/Minorities**: Y

## LOCATIONS: ("Y" = Yes)

| West: | Southwest: | Midwest: | Southeast: | Northeast: | International: |
|---|---|---|---|---|---|
| Y | Y | Y | Y | Y | Y |

Note: Financial information, benefits and other data can change quickly and may vary from those stated here.

# CKX INC

www.ckx.com

**Industry Group Code:** 711410 **Ranks within this company's industry group:** Sales: 1 Profits: 1

| Management: | | Sales/Marketing: | | Liberal Arts: | | Information Systems: | | Professionals: | | Technical/Scientific: | |
|---|---|---|---|---|---|---|---|---|---|---|---|
| Mgmt. Trainees: | | Mktg. Professionals: | Y | Gen. Writing/Editing: | | Info. Management: | Y | Finance/Accounting: | Y | Engineers, Elec.: | |
| Experienced Mgmt.: | Y | Retail Sales: | | Technical Writing: | | Software Dev.: | | Law: | Y | Engineers, Other: | |
| Int'l Business: | Y | Commercial/Industrial: | | Graphic Arts/Photog.: | | Hardware Dev.: | | HR/Other: | Y | Health/Lab: | |
| MBA Graduates: | Y | Sales Trainees: | Y | Music: | | Systems Integration: | | Training: | Y | Scientists/Research: | |
| | | Advertising Pros.: | | Broadcasting: | | Consulting/Other: | | Health Care: | | Petroleum/Chemicals: | |
| | | | | Other: | | | | Consulting: | | Math/Other: | |

## TYPES OF BUSINESS:

Name, Image and Likeness Licensing
Television Content
Artist Management

## BRANDS/DIVISIONS/AFFILIATES:

19 Entertainment Limited
Elvis Presley
Muhammad Ali
IDOLS
American Idol
Graceland
Elvis Presley's Heartbreak Hotel
FX Real Estate and Entertainment Inc

## CONTACTS: *Note: Officers with more than one job title may be intentionally listed here more than once.*

Robert F.X. Sillerman, CEO
Mitchell J. Slater, COO/Sr. Exec. VP
Thomas P. Benson, CFO/Exec. VP
Kraig G. Fox, Corp. Sec.
Kraig G. Fox, Chief Corp. Dev. Officer/Exec. VP
Thomas P. Benson, Treas.
Howard J. Tytel, Sr. Exec. VP/Dir.-Legal & Govt. Affairs
Simon Fuller, CEO-19 Entertainment Limited
Jack Soden, CEO-Elvis Presley Enterprises, Inc.
Robert F.X. Sillerman, Chmn.

| **Phone:** 212-838-3100 | **Fax:** |
|---|---|
| **Toll-Free:** | |
| **Address:** 650 Madison Ave., New York, NY 10022 US | |

## GROWTH PLANS/SPECIAL FEATURES:

CKX, Inc. is engaged in the ownership, development and commercial utilization of entertainment content. Its primary assets and operations include an 85% interest in the name, image and likeness of Elvis Presley and the operations of Graceland; an 80% interest in the name, image and likeness of Muhammad Ali; and proprietary rights to the IDOLS television brand, including the American Idol series in the United States along with various local adaptations of the IDOLS television show format worldwide. The firm's Elvis Presley business consists of two components: first, intellectual property, including the licensing of the name, image, likeness and trademarks associated with Elvis Presley, as well as other intellectual property and the collection of royalties from certain motion pictures, television specials and recorded musical works and music compositions; and second, the operation of the Graceland museum and related attractions, including Elvis Presley's Heartbreak Hotel. The company also owns an interest in the name, image, likeness and rights of publicity of Muhammad Ali, as well as the rights to Muhammad Ali license agreements. The primary revenue source for this business comes from licensing Muhammad Ali's name and likeness for consumer products, commercials and other uses. In addition, the company has a license agreement with FX Real Estate and Entertainment Inc., granting the latter the right to use the intellectual property and certain other assets associated with Elvis Presley and Muhammad Ali in the development of real estate and other entertainment and attraction projects. Through subsidiary 19 Entertainment Limited, CKX owns proprietary rights to the IDOLS television brand, as well as related music, sponsorship, touring and artist management activities. The company is currently working with Cirque du Soleil to develop a permanent live Las Vegas theatrical show based on the life, times and music of Elvis Presley.

## FINANCIALS: **Sales and profits are in thousands of dollars—add 000 to get the full amount. 2008 Note: Financial information for 2008 was not available for all companies at press time.**

| | | |
|---|---|---|
| 2008 Sales: $ | 2008 Profits: $ | **U.S. Stock Ticker: CKXE** |
| 2007 Sales: $266,777 | 2007 Profits: $12,144 | **Int'l Ticker:** Int'l Exchange: |
| 2006 Sales: $210,153 | 2006 Profits: $9,193 | Employees: 619 |
| 2005 Sales: $120,605 | 2005 Profits: $-5,904 | Fiscal Year Ends: 12/31 |
| 2004 Sales: $ | 2004 Profits: $ | Parent Company: |

## SALARIES/BENEFITS:

| | | | | |
|---|---|---|---|---|
| Pension Plan: | ESOP Stock Plan: | Profit Sharing: | Top Exec. Salary: $989,352 | Bonus: $ |
| Savings Plan: | Stock Purch. Plan: | | Second Exec. Salary: $716,625 | Bonus: $275,000 |

## OTHER THOUGHTS:

**Apparent Women Officers or Directors**: 1
**Hot Spot for Advancement for Women/Minorities**:

## LOCATIONS: ("Y" = Yes)

| West: | Southwest: | Midwest: | Southeast: | Northeast: | International: |
|---|---|---|---|---|---|
| | | | | Y | Y |

# CLEARWIRE CORP

www.clearwire.com

**Industry Group Code:** 514191 **Ranks within this company's industry group:** Sales: 2 Profits: 3

| Management: | | Sales/Marketing: | | Liberal Arts: | | Information Systems: | | Professionals: | | Technical/Scientific: | |
|---|---|---|---|---|---|---|---|---|---|---|---|
| Mgmt. Trainees: | | Mktg. Professionals: | Y | Gen. Writing/Editing: | | Info. Management: | Y | Finance/Accounting: | Y | Engineers, Elec.: | |
| Experienced Mgmt.: | Y | Retail Sales: | | Technical Writing: | | Software Dev.: | | Law: | Y | Engineers, Other: | |
| Int'l Business: | Y | Commercial/Industrial: | Y | Graphic Arts/Photog.: | | Hardware Dev.: | | HR/Other: | Y | Health/Lab: | |
| MBA Graduates: | Y | Sales Trainees: | Y | Music: | | Systems Integration: | | Training: | Y | Scientists/Research: | |
| | | Advertising Pros.: | Y | Broadcasting: | | Consulting/Other: | | Health Care: | | Petroleum/Chemicals: | |
| | | | | Other: | | | | Consulting: | | Math/Other: | |

## TYPES OF BUSINESS:

Wireless Broadband Service
WiMAX Wireless Networks
Voice over Internet Protocol

## BRANDS/DIVISIONS/AFFILIATES:

ClearPremium
ClearBusiness
ClearValue
ClearClassic
Comcast
Google
Intel
Time Warner Cable

## CONTACTS:

*Note: Officers with more than one job title may be intentionally listed here more than once.*

Benjamin G. Wolff, CEO
David Sach, CFO
R. Gerard Salemme, Exec. VP-Strategy, Policy & External Affairs
Craig O. McCaw, Chmn.

**Phone:** 425-216-7600 **Fax:** 425-216-7900
**Toll-Free:** 888-253-2794
**Address:** 4400 Carillon Point, Kirkland, WA 98033 US

## GROWTH PLANS/SPECIAL FEATURES:

Clearwire Corp. builds and operates next-generation wireless broadband networks. Customers connect to the Internet using licensed wireless spectrum, in this way eliminating the traditional use of cable or phone lines. Its services consist primarily of providing wireless broadband connectivity, but in some domestic markets, Clearwire offers Voice over Internet protocol (VoIP) telephony services. The company offers its services to more than 16.3 million people in the U.S. and Europe. Its network in the U.S. is deployed in 50 markets and covers over 13.5 million people. Markets range from major metropolitan areas to small, rural communities. Operations in the U.S. are conducted through subsidiary Clearwire U.S., LLC. Internationally, operations are conducted through Clearwire International, LLC, which indirectly holds investments in Europe and Mexico. In March 2007, Clearwire went public. In May 2007, the company acquired the entire 2.5 GHz wireless broadband spectrum previously owned by AT&T Inc. and the former BellSouth. In May 2008, Clearwire entered into a definitive agreement with Sprint Nextel Corporation to combine their WiMAX businesses into a new company called Clearwire. The new company has amassed $3.2 billion in funding from Intel, Google, Comcast, Time Warner Cable and Bright House Networks, and combines cutting edge WiMAX technologies to develop and deploy the first U.S. nationwide mobile WiMAX network.

The company offers its employees medical, dental and vision insurance; flexible spending accounts; life and AD&D insurance; short- and long-term disability insurance; and a college savings plan.

## FINANCIALS:

**Sales and profits are in thousands of dollars—add 000 to get the full amount. 2008 Note: Financial information for 2008 was not available for all companies at press time.**

| | | |
|---|---|---|
| 2008 Sales: $ | 2008 Profits: $ | **U.S. Stock Ticker: CLWR** |
| 2007 Sales: $151,440 | 2007 Profits: $-727,466 | **Int'l Ticker:** Int'l Exchange: |
| 2006 Sales: $100,181 | 2006 Profits: $-284,203 | Employees: 1,990 |
| 2005 Sales: $33,454 | 2005 Profits: $-319,950 | Fiscal Year Ends: 12/31 |
| 2004 Sales: $ | 2004 Profits: $ | Parent Company: |

## SALARIES/BENEFITS:

| | | | | |
|---|---|---|---|---|
| Pension Plan: | ESOP Stock Plan: | Profit Sharing: | Top Exec. Salary: $705,462 | Bonus: $630,000 |
| Savings Plan: Y | Stock Purch. Plan: | | Second Exec. Salary: $485,560 | Bonus: $420,000 |

## OTHER THOUGHTS:

**Apparent Women Officers or Directors**:
**Hot Spot for Advancement for Women/Minorities**: Y

## LOCATIONS: ("Y" = Yes)

| West: | Southwest: | Midwest: | Southeast: | Northeast: | International: |
|---|---|---|---|---|---|
| Y | Y | Y | Y | Y | Y |

# CME GROUP

**www.cme.com**

**Industry Group Code:** 523210 **Ranks within this company's industry group:** Sales: 2 Profits: 1

| Management: | | Sales/Marketing: | | Liberal Arts: | | Information Systems: | | Professionals: | | Technical/Scientific: | |
|---|---|---|---|---|---|---|---|---|---|---|---|
| Mgmt. Trainees: | | Mktg. Professionals: | Y | Gen. Writing/Editing: | | Info. Management: | Y | Finance/Accounting: | Y | Engineers, Elec.: | |
| Experienced Mgmt.: | Y | Retail Sales: | | Technical Writing: | | Software Dev.: | Y | Law: | Y | Engineers, Other: | |
| Int'l Business: | Y | Commercial/Industrial: | | Graphic Arts/Photog.: | | Hardware Dev.: | | HR/Other: | Y | Health/Lab: | |
| MBA Graduates: | Y | Sales Trainees: | | Music: | | Systems Integration: | | Training: | Y | Scientists/Research: | |
| | | Advertising Pros.: | Y | Broadcasting: | | Consulting/Other: | | Health Care: | | Petroleum/Chemicals: | |
| | | | | Other: | | | | Consulting: | | Math/Other: | Y |

## TYPES OF BUSINESS:

Futures Exchange
Futures Clearing House
Electronic Exchange
CME Group

## BRANDS/DIVISIONS/AFFILIATES:

CME Globex
OneChicago, LLC
TRAKRS Contracts
Chicago Board of Trade
NYMEX Holdings (New York Mercantile Exchange)
Chicago Mercantile Exchange, Inc.
Board of Trade of the City of Chicago, Inc.
CMEG NY, Inc.

## CONTACTS: *Note: Officers with more than one job title may be intentionally listed here more than once.*

Craig S. Donohue, CEO
Bryan T. Durkin, COO/Managing Dir.
Phupinder Gill, Pres.
James E. Parisi, CFO/Managing Dir.
Anita Liskey, Managing Dir.-Corp. Mktg & Comm.
Kevin Kometer, CIO/Managing Dir.
Kathleen Cronin, General Counsel/Managing Dir.
Julie Holzrichter, Managing Dir.-Oper.
Hilda Harris Piell, Chief Organizational Dev./Managing Dir.
Allan Schoenberg, Dir.-Corp. Comm.
Rick Redding, Managing Dir.-Prod. & Svcs.
Kimberly S. Taylor, Managing Dir./Pres., Clearing House Div.
Kathleen Cronin, Corp. Sec.
Terrence A. Duffy, Chmn.

| | |
|---|---|
| **Phone:** 312-930-1000 | **Fax:** 312-930-3187 |
| **Toll-Free:** 800-331-3332 | |
| **Address:** 20 S. Wacker Dr., Chicago, IL 60606-7499 US | |

## GROWTH PLANS/SPECIAL FEATURES:

CME Group, a company formed by the 2007 merger of Chicago Mercantile Exchange Holdings Inc. and CBOT Holdings, is the holding company of two futures exchanges: Chicago Mercantile Exchange (CME) and the Chicago Board of Trade (CBOT). The company offers a wide array of benchmark products available across all major asset classes, including futures and options on futures based on interest rates, equity indexes, foreign exchange, agricultural commodities and alternative investments such as weather and real estate. The firm's trading technologies include the CME Globex electronic trading platform, which integrates CBOT's interest rate, equity and agricultural electronic products and is accessible virtually 24-hours-a-day throughout the trading week. The company's six telecommunication hubs in key financial centers in Europe and Asia provide customers across the globe. CME Group also operates CME Clearing, a clearing house that enables the company to more quickly and efficiently bring new products to market through coordination of clearing functions with the company's product development, technology, market regulation and other risk management activities. The firm operates several subsidiaries, including Chicago Mercantile Exchange Inc.; Board of Trade of the City of Chicago, Inc.; CMEG NY Inc.; New York Mercantile Exchange, Inc.; and Commodity Exchange, Inc. In March 2008, CME Group acquired Credit Market Analysis Limited, a private company incorporated in the U.K., and its three subsidiaries. In August 2008, the company acquired NYMEX Holdings and its subsidiaries in a deal valued at $8.3 billion.

## FINANCIALS: **Sales and profits are in thousands of dollars—add 000 to get the full amount. 2008 Note: Financial information for 2008 was not available for all companies at press time.**

| | | |
|---|---|---|
| 2008 Sales: $ | 2008 Profits: $ | **U.S. Stock Ticker: CME** |
| 2007 Sales: $1,756,100 | 2007 Profits: $658,500 | **Int'l Ticker:** Int'l Exchange: |
| 2006 Sales: $1,089,900 | 2006 Profits: $407,300 | Employees: 1,970 |
| 2005 Sales: $977,300 | 2005 Profits: $306,857 | Fiscal Year Ends: 12/31 |
| 2004 Sales: $752,800 | 2004 Profits: $219,600 | Parent Company: |

## SALARIES/BENEFITS:

| | | | | |
|---|---|---|---|---|
| Pension Plan: Y | ESOP Stock Plan: | Profit Sharing: | Top Exec. Salary: $850,000 | Bonus: $1,168,257 |
| Savings Plan: Y | Stock Purch. Plan: | | Second Exec. Salary: $600,000 | Bonus: $791,160 |

## OTHER THOUGHTS:

**Apparent Women Officers or Directors**: 5
**Hot Spot for Advancement for Women/Minorities**: Y

## LOCATIONS: ("Y" = Yes)

| West: | Southwest: | Midwest: | Southeast: | Northeast: | International: |
|---|---|---|---|---|---|
| | | Y | | Y | Y |

# CNX GAS CORPORATION

www.cnxgas.com

**Industry Group Code:** 211111 **Ranks within this company's industry group:** Sales: 19 Profits: 13

| Management: | | Sales/Marketing: | | Liberal Arts: | | Information Systems: | | Professionals: | | Technical/Scientific: | |
|---|---|---|---|---|---|---|---|---|---|---|---|
| Mgmt. Trainees: | | Mktg. Professionals: | Y | Gen. Writing/Editing: | | Info. Management: | Y | Finance/Accounting: | Y | Engineers, Elec.: | |
| Experienced Mgmt.: | Y | Retail Sales: | | Technical Writing: | | Software Dev.: | | Law: | Y | Engineers, Other: | Y |
| Int'l Business: | Y | Commercial/Industrial: | Y | Graphic Arts/Photog.: | | Hardware Dev.: | | HR/Other: | Y | Health/Lab: | |
| MBA Graduates: | Y | Sales Trainees: | | Music: | | Systems Integration: | | Training: | Y | Scientists/Research: | |
| | | Advertising Pros.: | | Broadcasting: | | Consulting/Other: | | Health Care: | | Petroleum/Chemicals: | Y |
| | | | | Other: | | | | Consulting: | | Math/Other: | |

## TYPES OF BUSINESS:

Natural Gas Exploration & Production
Coalbed Methane Development
Power Generation
Gathering & Pipelines

## BRANDS/DIVISIONS/AFFILIATES:

CONSOL Energy Inc
Duke Energy Corp
Peabody Energy Corp

## CONTACTS: *Note: Officers with more than one job title may be intentionally listed here more than once.*

Nicholas J. DeIuliis, CEO
Nicholas J. DeIuliis, Pres.
Roland J. Campanelli, VP-Mktg.
Stephen W. Johnson, General Counsel/Exec. VP
Daniel J. Zajdel, VP-Public Rel.
Daniel J. Zajdel, VP-Investor Rel.
Randall M. Albert, Sr. VP-Emerging Bus. Units
DeAnn Craig, Sr. VP-Asset Assessment
J. Michael Onifer, Sr. VP-Established Bus. Units

**Phone:** 412-200-6700 **Fax:** 412-200-6761
**Toll-Free:**
**Address:** 5 Penn Ctr. W., Ste. 401, Pittsburgh, PA 15276-0102 US

## GROWTH PLANS/SPECIAL FEATURES:

CNX Gas Corporation, a majority-owned subsidiary of CONSOL Energy Inc., seeks, develops and produces coalbed methane, mostly in the Appalachian Basin. CNX has 4.5 billion tons of proved coal reserves, more than 1.343 trillion cubic feet of net proved reserves and development rights to approximately 955,000 net acres of coalbed. The company controls the estate on 3.9 million gross acres throughout the Appalachian Basin. The company's business is one of the few gas producers with a substantial portion of its production associated with mining activity in the same coal horizons from which gas could be extracted. Formerly as much of 47% of CNX's gas was produced in this way, but now only 17% of the company's gas production is attributable to mining activities performed by CONSOL. The firm has mid-stream assets that include a gas gathering system with a 50-mile pipeline capable of transporting 100 million cubic feet of gas per day and a 30-mile system capable of 250 million cubic feet per day; various processing plants in Pennsylvania and Virginia; and a 50% interest in an 88 megawatt (MW) power plant that runs on the company's methane gas. Currently all of CNX's production is transported to market through the Columbia interstate pipeline system, but it recently entered into a 15-year transportation agreement with a Duke Energy subsidiary that will provide flexibility for the company and will also allow it to market gas to the southeastern U.S. CONSOL Energy owns 81.5% of the firm's outstanding shares. In June 2007, CNX acquired Peabody Energy's coalbed methane and gas interests. In January 2008, CONSOL Energy announced its intention to offer to acquire the 18.5% of outstanding shares of CNX Gas that it does not currently own. In February 2008, the firm partnered with Huntley & Huntley Inc. to develop 26,000 acres.

## FINANCIALS: **Sales and profits are in thousands of dollars—add 000 to get the full amount. 2008 Note: Financial information for 2008 was not available for all companies at press time.**

| | | |
|---|---|---|
| 2008 Sales: $ | 2008 Profits: $ | **U.S. Stock Ticker: CXG** |
| 2007 Sales: $477,308 | 2007 Profits: $135,678 | **Int'l Ticker:** Int'l Exchange: |
| 2006 Sales: $513,859 | 2006 Profits: $159,867 | Employees: 281 |
| 2005 Sales: $613,441 | 2005 Profits: $102,168 | Fiscal Year Ends: 12/31 |
| 2004 Sales: $397,536 | 2004 Profits: $80,788 | Parent Company: CONSOL ENERGY INC |

## SALARIES/BENEFITS:

| | | | | |
|---|---|---|---|---|
| Pension Plan: | ESOP Stock Plan: | Profit Sharing: | Top Exec. Salary: $495,769 | Bonus: $755,300 |
| Savings Plan: Y | Stock Purch. Plan: | | Second Exec. Salary: $276,154 | Bonus: $248,385 |

## OTHER THOUGHTS:

**Apparent Women Officers or Directors**: 1
**Hot Spot for Advancement for Women/Minorities**:

## LOCATIONS: ("Y" = Yes)

| West: | Southwest: | Midwest: | Southeast: | Northeast: | International: |
|---|---|---|---|---|---|
| | | Y | | Y | |

# COGNEX CORP

**www.cognex.com**

**Industry Group Code:** 334111 **Ranks within this company's industry group:** Sales: 5 Profits: 2

| **Management:** | | **Sales/Marketing:** | | **Liberal Arts:** | | **Information Systems:** | | **Professionals:** | | **Technical/Scientific:** | |
|---|---|---|---|---|---|---|---|---|---|---|---|
| Mgmt. Trainees: | | Mktg. Professionals: | Y | Gen. Writing/Editing: | | Info. Management: | Y | Finance/Accounting: | Y | Engineers, Elec.: | Y |
| Experienced Mgmt.: | Y | Retail Sales: | | Technical Writing: | Y | Software Dev.: | Y | Law: | Y | Engineers, Other: | Y |
| Int'l Business: | Y | Commercial/Industrial: | Y | Graphic Arts/Photog.: | | Hardware Dev.: | Y | HR/Other: | Y | Health/Lab: | |
| MBA Graduates: | Y | Sales Trainees: | Y | Music: | | Systems Integration: | Y | Training: | Y | Scientists/Research: | |
| | | Advertising Pros.: | | Broadcasting: | | Consulting/Other: | | Health Care: | | Petroleum/Chemicals: | |
| | | | | Other: | | | | Consulting: | | Math/Other: | |

## TYPES OF BUSINESS:

Computer Hardware-Human Vision Replacement
Machine Vision Technology
Modular Vision Systems-Computers & Software
Surface Inspection Systems
Automotive Vision Technology

## BRANDS/DIVISIONS/AFFILIATES:

In-Sight
DataMan 100

## CONTACTS: *Note: Officers with more than one job title may be intentionally listed here more than once.*

Robert J. Shillman, CEO
James F. Hoffmaster, COO
James F. Hoffmaster, Pres.
Richard A. Morin, CFO
Eric Ceyrolle, Exec. VP-Worldwide Sales & Mktg.
Richard A. Morin, Sr. VP-Admin.
Richard A. Morin, Sr. VP-Finance/Treas.
Thomas F. Nash, Pres., Surface Inspection Systems Div.
Justin Testa, Exec. VP/Bus. Unit Mgr.
Brian Phillips, VP-Sales, Americas
Robert Willett, Pres., Modular Vision Systems Div.
Robert J. Shillman, Chmn.

| **Phone:** 508-650-3000 | **Fax:** 508-650-3333 |
|---|---|
| **Toll-Free:** | |
| **Address:** 1 Vision Dr., Natick, MA 01760-2059 US | |

## GROWTH PLANS/SPECIAL FEATURES:

Cognex Corp. develops, manufactures and markets systems used to automate manufacturing processes where vision is required. Machine vision is important for applications in which human vision is inadequate to meet requirements for feature size, accuracy or speed, or in instances where substantial cost savings are obtained through reduction of labor and improved quality. Cognex's systems are used in industries including semiconductors, electronics, automotive, consumer products, metals, plastics and paper. The company comprises two divisions: the modular vision systems division (MVSD) and the surface inspection systems division (SISD). MVSD develops, manufactures and markets modular vision systems that are used to automate the manufacture of discrete items, such as semiconductor chips, cellular phones and light bulbs, by locating, identifying, inspecting and measuring them during the manufacturing process. MVSD generates approximately 87% of Cognex's revenue. SISD designs, develops, manufactures and markets surface inspection vision systems that are used to inspect the surfaces of materials processed in a continuous fashion, such as paper, metals, plastics and non-wovens, to ensure there are no flaws or defects on the surfaces. Cognex machine vision systems consist of two primary elements: a computer, which serves as a machine vision engine; and software that processes and analyzes images. When connected to a video camera, the machine vision system captures images and extracts information, which determines appropriate action for other equipment in the manufacturing process. The firm's machine vision products include In-Sight vision sensors, PC vision systems, ID products, expert sensors and surface inspection systems. Cognex recently introduced the DataMan 100 fixed-mount ID reader. In July 2008, the firm sold its in-vehicle business division to Takata Corporation Group.

Cognex offers its employees tuition reimbursement; an employee assistance program; a 529 college savings plan for dependents; a flexible spending account; and medical, dental, life, accidental death, dismemberment, disability, homeowners and automobile insurance.

## FINANCIALS: **Sales and profits are in thousands of dollars—add 000 to get the full amount. 2008 Note: Financial information for 2008 was not available for all companies at press time.**

| | | |
|---|---|---|
| 2008 Sales: $ | 2008 Profits: $ | **U.S. Stock Ticker: CGNX** |
| 2007 Sales: $225,737 | 2007 Profits: $26,899 | **Int'l Ticker:** Int'l Exchange: |
| 2006 Sales: $238,424 | 2006 Profits: $39,855 | Employees: 799 |
| 2005 Sales: $216,875 | 2005 Profits: $35,702 | Fiscal Year Ends: 12/31 |
| 2004 Sales: $201,957 | 2004 Profits: $37,744 | Parent Company: |

## SALARIES/BENEFITS:

| | | | | |
|---|---|---|---|---|
| Pension Plan: | ESOP Stock Plan: | Profit Sharing: | Top Exec. Salary: $276,289 | Bonus: $35,250 |
| Savings Plan: Y | Stock Purch. Plan: Y | | Second Exec. Salary: $248,469 | Bonus: $51,250 |

## OTHER THOUGHTS:

**Apparent Women Officers or Directors**:
**Hot Spot for Advancement for Women/Minorities**:

## LOCATIONS: ("Y" = Yes)

| West: | Southwest: | Midwest: | Southeast: | Northeast: | International: |
|---|---|---|---|---|---|
| Y | | Y | Y | Y | Y |

# COHERENT INC

www.coherent.com

**Industry Group Code:** 339113 **Ranks within this company's industry group:** Sales: 2 Profits: 12

| Management: | | Sales/Marketing: | | Liberal Arts: | | Information Systems: | | Professionals: | | Technical/Scientific: | |
|---|---|---|---|---|---|---|---|---|---|---|---|
| Mgmt. Trainees: | | Mktg. Professionals: | Y | Gen. Writing/Editing: | | Info. Management: | Y | Finance/Accounting: | Y | Engineers, Elec.: | Y |
| Experienced Mgmt.: | Y | Retail Sales: | | Technical Writing: | Y | Software Dev.: | Y | Law: | Y | Engineers, Other: | Y |
| Int'l Business: | Y | Commercial/Industrial: | Y | Graphic Arts/Photog.: | | Hardware Dev.: | Y | HR/Other: | Y | Health/Lab: | Y |
| MBA Graduates: | Y | Sales Trainees: | Y | Music: | | Systems Integration: | Y | Training: | Y | Scientists/Research: | Y |
| | | Advertising Pros.: | | Broadcasting: | | Consulting/Other: | | Health Care: | Y | Petroleum/Chemicals: | |
| | | | | Other: | | | | Consulting: | | Math/Other: | Y |

## TYPES OF BUSINESS:

Equipment-Lasers & Laser Systems
Precision Optics
Laser Accessories

## BRANDS/DIVISIONS/AFFILIATES:

Specialty Lasers and Systems
Commercial Lasers and Components
Azure
Paladin
Vitesse
Verdi
WaveMaster
Innova

## CONTACTS: *Note: Officers with more than one job title may be intentionally listed here more than once.*

John R. Ambroseo, CEO
John R. Ambroseo, Pres.
Helene Simonet, CFO/Exec. VP
Ron A. Victor, Exec. VP-Human Resources
Luis Spinelli, CTO/Exec. VP
Bret M. DiMarco, General Counsel/Exec. VP
Garry W. Rogerson, Chmn.

**Phone:** 408-764-4000 **Fax:** 408-764-4800
**Toll-Free:** 800-527-3786
**Address:** 5100 Patrick Henry Dr., Santa Clara, CA 95054 US

## GROWTH PLANS/SPECIAL FEATURES:

Coherent, Inc. designs, manufactures and markets lasers, precision optics and related accessories to customers in over 90 countries. The company operates in two segments: Specialty Lasers and Systems (SLS) and Commercial Lasers and Components (CLC). SLS develops and manufactures configurable, advanced-performance products and serves the microelectronics and scientific research markets. CLC offers OEMs (original equipment manufacturers) components and instrumentation and materials processing. The firm groups its products into four primary markets: microelectronics; materials processing; OEM components and instrumentation; and scientific research and government programs. The microelectronics segment, which accounted for 34.4% of 2008 revenue, has four main operations: semiconductor front-end manufacturing, including photomask manufacturing and semiconductor inspection; semiconductor assembly, testing and advanced packaging, including wafer scribing and singulation; flat panel display manufacturing, for use in digital cameras, mobile telephones, car navigation systems, laptop computers and television monitors; and solar cell production and other emerging processes. The material processing segment's products, 15.7% of 2008 revenue, include high-power lasers for metal processing, as well as low-to-medium power lasers for nonmetals processing, precision micromachining and laser marking. Products for the OEM components and instrumentation segment, which accounted for 29% of revenue, include bio-instrumentation lasers, with applications in confocal microscopy, DNA sequencing, flow cytometry and drug discovery. Products in the scientific research and government programs segment, 20.9% of revenue, include ultrafast lasers, diode-pumped solid-state lasers, continuous-wave systems, excimer lasers and water-cooled gas lasers, with applications in biology, physics, chemistry and engineering.

Employees of Coherent receive medical and dental plans; life and AD&D insurance; educational assistance; a productivity incentive plan; reimbursement accounts; an employee computer purchase plan; an employee assistance program; credit unions; and paid holidays.

## FINANCIALS: **Sales and profits are in thousands of dollars—add 000 to get the full amount. 2008 Note: Financial information for 2008 was not available for all companies at press time.**

| | | |
|---|---|---|
| 2008 Sales: $ | 2008 Profits: $ | **U.S. Stock Ticker: COHR** |
| 2007 Sales: $601,153 | 2007 Profits: $15,951 | **Int'l Ticker:** Int'l Exchange: |
| 2006 Sales: $584,652 | 2006 Profits: $45,394 | Employees: 2,339 |
| 2005 Sales: $516,252 | 2005 Profits: $38,414 | Fiscal Year Ends: 9/30 |
| 2004 Sales: $494,954 | 2004 Profits: $17,360 | Parent Company: |

## SALARIES/BENEFITS:

| | | | | |
|---|---|---|---|---|
| Pension Plan: | ESOP Stock Plan: | Profit Sharing: Y | Top Exec. Salary: $561,312 | Bonus: $534,621 |
| Savings Plan: Y | Stock Purch. Plan: Y | | Second Exec. Salary: $359,334 | Bonus: $239,649 |

## OTHER THOUGHTS:

**Apparent Women Officers or Directors**: 2
**Hot Spot for Advancement for Women/Minorities**: Y

## LOCATIONS: ("Y" = Yes)

| West: | Southwest: | Midwest: | Southeast: | Northeast: | International: |
|---|---|---|---|---|---|
| Y | | | Y | Y | Y |

# COINSTAR INC

www.coinstar.com

**Industry Group Code:** 522320 **Ranks within this company's industry group:** Sales: 4 Profits: 4

| Management: | | Sales/Marketing: | | Liberal Arts: | | Information Systems: | | Professionals: | | Technical/Scientific: | |
|---|---|---|---|---|---|---|---|---|---|---|---|
| Mgmt. Trainees: | Y | Mktg. Professionals: | Y | Gen. Writing/Editing: | | Info. Management: | Y | Finance/Accounting: | Y | Engineers, Elec.: | |
| Experienced Mgmt.: | Y | Retail Sales: | | Technical Writing: | Y | Software Dev.: | | Law: | Y | Engineers, Other: | |
| Int'l Business: | Y | Commercial/Industrial: | Y | Graphic Arts/Photog.: | | Hardware Dev.: | | HR/Other: | Y | Health/Lab: | |
| MBA Graduates: | Y | Sales Trainees: | Y | Music: | | Systems Integration: | Y | Training: | Y | Scientists/Research: | |
| | | Advertising Pros.: | Y | Broadcasting: | | Consulting/Other: | | Health Care: | | Petroleum/Chemicals: | |
| | | | | Other: | | | | Consulting: | | Math/Other: | |

## TYPES OF BUSINESS:

Coin Exchange Machines
E-Payment Services
Entertainment Machines
Vending Machines

## BRANDS/DIVISIONS/AFFILIATES:

Redbox Automated Retail, LLC

## CONTACTS: *Note: Officers with more than one job title may be intentionally listed here more than once.*

David W. Cole, CEO
Paul D. Davis, COO
Brian Turner, CFO
Jim Blakely, Sr. VP-Sales
Christi Liebe, VP-IT
Carl Poteete, VP-Mfg.
Don Rench, General Counsel/Corp. Sec.
John Reilly, Sr. VP-Oper.
Rich Deck, Chief Acct. Officer
Steve Verleye, Sr. VP/Gen. Mgr.-E-Pay
Alex Camara, Sr. VP/Gen. Mgr.-Worldwide Coin

**Phone:** 425-943-8000 **Fax:** 425-637-8030
**Toll-Free:** 800-928-2274
**Address:** 1800 114th Ave. SE, Bellevue, WA 98004 US

## GROWTH PLANS/SPECIAL FEATURES:

Coinstar, Inc. is primarily a manufacturer and marketer of coin exchange machines. The firm also manufactures entertainment products such as skill-cranes, bulk vending machines and kiddie rides; Coinstar additionally offers e-payment services, such as money transfer services, prepaid wireless products, stored value cards, payroll cards and prepaid debit cards. The firm also offers self-service DVD kiosks where customers can rent or purchase movies. Coinstar owns approximately 15,400 coin exchange machines, of which 10,700 are e-payment enabled, and 280,000 entertainment machines, located in the U.S., Puerto Rico, Canada and the U.K. The company also has more than 17,500 point-of-sale terminals for e-payment services in the U.S. and U.K., and 30,000 locations that offer money transfer services. The company's coin and entertainment machines often appear in Kroger, Wal-Mart, Kmart and other retailers. Its coin machines, which can process up to 600 coins per minute, exchanged over $2.9 billion in coins in 2007, typically withdrawing an 8.9% processing fee per transaction. The machines usually print a voucher that must be cashed at the retail establishment housing the machine, with the firm later reimbursing the establishment. However, Coinstar has recently begun offering gift cards and eCertificates for nationally recognized brands and retailers such as iTunes, Amazon.com, DisneyShopping.com and Borders. If the customer chooses the gift card option instead of cash, there is no processing fee. Coinstar machines also have a donation option that works in partnership with the American Red Cross, World Wildlife Fund and other organizations. There is no processing fee for this service; and customers receive a receipt for the tax-deductible transaction. The company's entertainment products are installed in more than 27,000 retail locations, totaling more than 280,000 pieces of equipment. In January 2008, the company gained majority ownership of Redbox Automated Retail, LLC, the DVD kiosk rental company.

## FINANCIALS: **Sales and profits are in thousands of dollars—add 000 to get the full amount. 2008 Note: Financial information for 2008 was not available for all companies at press time.**

| | | |
|---|---|---|
| 2008 Sales: $ | 2008 Profits: $ | **U.S. Stock Ticker: CSTR** |
| 2007 Sales: $546,297 | 2007 Profits: $-22,253 | **Int'l Ticker:** Int'l Exchange: |
| 2006 Sales: $534,442 | 2006 Profits: $18,627 | Employees: 1,900 |
| 2005 Sales: $459,739 | 2005 Profits: $22,272 | Fiscal Year Ends: 12/31 |
| 2004 Sales: $307,100 | 2004 Profits: $20,368 | Parent Company: |

## SALARIES/BENEFITS:

| | | | | |
|---|---|---|---|---|
| Pension Plan: | ESOP Stock Plan: | Profit Sharing: | Top Exec. Salary: $474,653 | Bonus: $254,762 |
| Savings Plan: Y | Stock Purch. Plan: | | Second Exec. Salary: $364,000 | Bonus: $162,690 |

## OTHER THOUGHTS:

**Apparent Women Officers or Directors**: 1
**Hot Spot for Advancement for Women/Minorities**: Y

## LOCATIONS: ("Y" = Yes)

| West: | Southwest: | Midwest: | Southeast: | Northeast: | International: |
|---|---|---|---|---|---|
| Y | Y | Y | Y | Y | Y |

# COLLAGENEX PHARMACEUTICALS INC

www.collagenex.com

**Industry Group Code:** 325412 **Ranks within this company's industry group:** Sales: 27 Profits: 13

| Management: | | Sales/Marketing: | | Liberal Arts: | | Information Systems: | | Professionals: | | Technical/Scientific: | |
|---|---|---|---|---|---|---|---|---|---|---|---|
| Mgmt. Trainees: | | Mktg. Professionals: | Y | Gen. Writing/Editing: | | Info. Management: | Y | Finance/Accounting: | Y | Engineers, Elec.: | |
| Experienced Mgmt.: | Y | Retail Sales: | | Technical Writing: | Y | Software Dev.: | Y | Law: | Y | Engineers, Other: | |
| Int'l Business: | Y | Commercial/Industrial: | Y | Graphic Arts/Photog.: | | Hardware Dev.: | | HR/Other: | Y | Health/Lab: | Y |
| MBA Graduates: | Y | Sales Trainees: | Y | Music: | | Systems Integration: | | Training: | Y | Scientists/Research: | Y |
| | | Advertising Pros.: | | Broadcasting: | | Consulting/Other: | | Health Care: | Y | Petroleum/Chemicals: | |
| | | | | Other: | | | | Consulting: | Y | Math/Other: | Y |

## TYPES OF BUSINESS:

Pharmaceuticals Development
Drugs-Periodontal Disease
Drugs-Dermatology

## BRANDS/DIVISIONS/AFFILIATES:

Pandel
Alcortin
Novacort
IMPACS
Oracea
Restoraderm
Galderma Laboratories Inc
Galderma Pharma SA

## CONTACTS: *Note: Officers with more than one job title may be intentionally listed here more than once.*

Colin W. Stewart, CEO
Colin W. Stewart, Pres.
Nancy C. Broadbent, CFO
David F. Pfeiffer, Sr. VP-Sales & Mktg.
Klaus P. J. Theobald, Sr. VP/Chief Medical Officer
Andrew K. W. Powell, General Counsel/VP/Corp. Sec.
J. Gregory Ford, VP-Bus. Dev. & Strategic Planning
Nancy C. Broadbent, Treas.
James E. Daverman, Chmn.

| **Phone:** 215-579-7388 | **Fax:** 215-579-8577 |
|---|---|
| **Toll-Free:** | |
| **Address:** 41 University Dr., Newtown, PA 18940 US | |

## GROWTH PLANS/SPECIAL FEATURES:

CollaGenex Pharmaceuticals, Inc. is a specialty pharmaceutical company focused on providing innovative medical therapies to the dermatology market. Its chief products are Oracea for the treatment of inflammatory lesions of rosacea in adults; Pandel, used for the treatment of dermatitis and psoriasis; Alcortin, a mild dermatosis gel with combined anti-fungal, anti-bacterial and anti-inflammatory effects; and Novacort, a topical corticosteroid with anti-inflammatory and anesthetic treatment for certain dermatoses. CollaGenex's development products are based on its core technologies: IMPACS, Restoraderm and SansRosa. IMPACS compounds have the potential to treat diseases that cause inflammation and destruction of the connective tissues. Restoraderm delivers key ingredients to the dermal layers underlying the skin. The SansRosa technology, which was obtained in the acquisition of SansRosa Pharmaceutical Development, has shown promise in reducing redness associated with rosacea. CollaCenex has discontinued the development of periodontal products, but still continues to market the products Atridox, Atrisorb-Freeflow and Atrisorb-D, which are licensed from Tolmar, Inc., a subsidiary of Tecnofarma, S.A.; and Periostat, its own development. In May 2007, the company announced that it had signed an agreement with QuatRx Pharmaceuticals Company to develop and commercialize QuatRx's product bencocalcidiol for psoriasis. In 2008, the firm was acquired by Galderma Laboratories, Inc., the U.S. subsidiary of Galderma Pharma S.A. Galderma Pharma is currently working to combine the two companies.

## FINANCIALS: Sales and profits are in thousands of dollars—add 000 to get the full amount. 2008 Note: Financial information for 2008 was not available for all companies at press time.

| | | |
|---|---|---|
| 2008 Sales: $ | 2008 Profits: $ | **U.S. Stock Ticker: Subsidiary** |
| 2007 Sales: $63,586 | 2007 Profits: $-8,794 | **Int'l Ticker:** Int'l Exchange: |
| 2006 Sales: $26,373 | 2006 Profits: $-33,434 | Employees: 147 |
| 2005 Sales: $26,405 | 2005 Profits: $-18,805 | Fiscal Year Ends: 12/31 |
| 2004 Sales: $52,146 | 2004 Profits: $6,528 | Parent Company: GALDERMA PHARMA SA |

## SALARIES/BENEFITS:

| | | | | |
|---|---|---|---|---|
| Pension Plan: | ESOP Stock Plan: | Profit Sharing: | Top Exec. Salary: $377,000 | Bonus: $258,246 |
| Savings Plan: Y | Stock Purch. Plan: | | Second Exec. Salary: $269,100 | Bonus: $139,932 |

## OTHER THOUGHTS:

**Apparent Women Officers or Directors**: 1
**Hot Spot for Advancement for Women/Minorities**:

## LOCATIONS: ("Y" = Yes)

| West: | Southwest: | Midwest: | Southeast: | Northeast: | International: |
|---|---|---|---|---|---|
| | | | | Y | Y |

# COMDATA CORP

www.comdata.com

**Industry Group Code:** 522320 **Ranks within this company's industry group:** Sales: 5 Profits:

| Management: | | Sales/Marketing: | | Liberal Arts: | | Information Systems: | | Professionals: | | Technical/Scientific: | |
|---|---|---|---|---|---|---|---|---|---|---|---|
| Mgmt. Trainees: | Y | Mktg. Professionals: | Y | Gen. Writing/Editing: | | Info. Management: | Y | Finance/Accounting: | Y | Engineers, Elec.: | |
| Experienced Mgmt.: | Y | Retail Sales: | | Technical Writing: | Y | Software Dev.: | | Law: | Y | Engineers, Other: | |
| Int'l Business: | | Commercial/Industrial: | Y | Graphic Arts/Photog.: | | Hardware Dev.: | | HR/Other: | Y | Health/Lab: | |
| MBA Graduates: | Y | Sales Trainees: | Y | Music: | | Systems Integration: | Y | Training: | Y | Scientists/Research: | |
| | | Advertising Pros.: | Y | Broadcasting: | | Consulting/Other: | | Health Care: | | Petroleum/Chemicals: | |
| | | | | Other: | | | | Consulting: | | Math/Other: | |

## TYPES OF BUSINESS:

Electronic Funds Transfers
Transaction Processing
Stored-Value Cards
Inter-Tax, Inc
HQ Gift Cards, LLC
Stored Value Systems (SVS International)
International Retail

## BRANDS/DIVISIONS/AFFILIATES:

Ceridian Corp
Stored Value Systems
SVS International
Comdata International Retail
Inter-Tax, Inc.

## CONTACTS: *Note: Officers with more than one job title may be intentionally listed here more than once.*

Brett Rodewald, Pres.
Kedran Whitten, Sr. VP-Mktg. & Prod. Mgmt.
Tracey Power, Sr. VP-Human Resources
Todd Joseph, Sr. VP-IT
Lisa Peerman, General Counsel/Sr. VP/Corp. Sec.
Randy Pitman, Exec. VP-Finance
Scott Phillips, Exec. VP/Gen. Mgr.-Corp. Payment Solutions
Joe Daly, Sr. VP/Gen. Mgr.-Merchant Svcs.
Walt Hannabass, Sr. VP-Credit & Collections
Keela Wofford, Sr. VP-Financial Svcs.

| | |
|---|---|
| **Phone:** 615-370-7000 | **Fax:** 615-370-7209 |
| **Toll-Free:** 800-266-3282 | |
| **Address:** 5301 Maryland Way, Brentwood, TN 37027 US | |

## GROWTH PLANS/SPECIAL FEATURES:

Comdata Corp., a subsidiary of the Ceridian Corp., processes financial data transactions. It specializes in trust-enabled payment transactions, based on an individual company's business rules, which include controlled spending, purchasing, payroll, cash card and other similar transactions. Based in Brentwood, Tennessee, the company is credited with the 1981 introduction of the first electronic fund distribution system for the transportation industry. Comdata is currently separated into six divisions: Transportation, Business Fleet Services, Merchant Services, Stored Value Systems, Payment Services and International Retail. The transportation division issues the Comdata card, which allows trucking companies to deliver payroll, fuel and settlement money to professional truck drivers on the road. The card is held by over a million professional truck drivers and is used to transfer over $12 billion in funds every year. Business Fleet Services assists local fleets owned by a variety of businesses outside the transport industry, while Merchant Services connects travel centers and truck stops with Comdata's payments systems. Stored Value Systems (SVS International) and International Retail are both devoted to providing retailers with gift card, loyalty and other customer incentive programs using the company's electronic card systems. The Payment Services division helps businesses of all types reduce payroll distribution costs up to 40% through a card-based payroll system. Comdata's network has touch points in more than 30 countries worldwide. In recent news, the company acquired Inter-Tax, Inc., a provider of paperless fuel tax services. In November 2008, the firm launched IRIS fraud protection at its data centers in Kentucky and Tennessee.

The firm offers its employees medical, dental and vision insurance; a 401(k) plan; educational assistance; a scholarship program for associates' children; short- and long-term disability insurance; life insurance; discounted auto, homeowners and renters insurance; and an employee assistance program.

## FINANCIALS: **Sales and profits are in thousands of dollars—add 000 to get the full amount. 2008 Note: Financial information for 2008 was not available for all companies at press time.**

| | | |
|---|---|---|
| 2008 Sales: $ | 2008 Profits: $ | **U.S. Stock Ticker: Subsidiary** |
| 2007 Sales: $411,600 | 2007 Profits: $ | **Int'l Ticker:** Int'l Exchange: |
| 2006 Sales: $ | 2006 Profits: $ | Employees: 1,814 |
| 2005 Sales: $408,900 | 2005 Profits: $ | Fiscal Year Ends: 12/31 |
| 2004 Sales: $356,000 | 2004 Profits: $ | Parent Company: CERIDIAN CORP |

## SALARIES/BENEFITS:

| | | | | |
|---|---|---|---|---|
| Pension Plan: | ESOP Stock Plan: | Profit Sharing: | Top Exec. Salary: $ | Bonus: $ |
| Savings Plan: Y | Stock Purch. Plan: Y | | Second Exec. Salary: $ | Bonus: $ |

## OTHER THOUGHTS:

**Apparent Women Officers or Directors**: 4
**Hot Spot for Advancement for Women/Minorities**: Y

## LOCATIONS: ("Y" = Yes)

| West: | Southwest: | Midwest: | Southeast: | Northeast: | International: |
|---|---|---|---|---|---|
| | Y | | Y | Y | |

Note: Financial information, benefits and other data can change quickly and may vary from those stated here.

# COMMERCE GROUP INC (THE)

www.commerceinsurance.com

**Industry Group Code:** 524126 **Ranks within this company's industry group:** Sales: 2 Profits: 5

| **Management:** | | **Sales/Marketing:** | | **Liberal Arts:** | | **Information Systems:** | | **Professionals:** | | **Technical/Scientific:** | |
|---|---|---|---|---|---|---|---|---|---|---|---|
| Mgmt. Trainees: | | Mktg. Professionals: | Y | Gen. Writing/Editing: | Y | Info. Management: | Y | Finance/Accounting: | Y | Engineers, Elec.: | |
| Experienced Mgmt.: | Y | Retail Sales: | | Technical Writing: | Y | Software Dev.: | | Law: | Y | Engineers, Other: | |
| Int'l Business: | | Commercial/Industrial: | Y | Graphic Arts/Photog.: | | Hardware Dev.: | | HR/Other: | Y | Health/Lab: | |
| MBA Graduates: | Y | Sales Trainees: | Y | Music: | | Systems Integration: | | Training: | Y | Scientists/Research: | |
| | | Advertising Pros.: | | Broadcasting: | | Consulting/Other: | | Health Care: | | Petroleum/Chemicals: | |
| | | | | Other: | | | | Consulting: | | Math/Other: | Y |

## TYPES OF BUSINESS:

Insurance, Direct Property & Casualty
Commercial Automobile Insurance
Homeowners' Insurance
Inland Marine Insurance
Fire Insurance
General Liability Insurance
Mortgages

## BRANDS/DIVISIONS/AFFILIATES:

Commerce Insurance Co.
American Commerce Insurance Co.
Commerce West Insurance Co.
Bay Finance
SWICO Enterprises, Ltd.

## CONTACTS: *Note: Officers with more than one job title may be intentionally listed here more than once.*

Gerald Fels, CEO
Lawrence R. Pentis, COO/Exec. VP
Gerald Fels, Pres.
Randall V. Becker, CFO/Sr. VP
Peter J. Dignan, Sr. VP-Mktg.
Cathleen M. Moynihan, Sr. VP-Human Resources
James A. Ermilio, General Counsel/Exec. VP
Peter J. Dignan, Sr. VP-Premium Acct.
Arthur J. Remillard, III, Sr. VP-Policyholder Benefits
Gerald Fels, Chmn.

| **Phone:** 508-943-9000 | **Fax:** 508-949-4921 |
|---|---|
| **Toll-Free:** 800-922-8276 | |
| **Address:** 211 Main St., Webster, MA 01570 US | |

## GROWTH PLANS/SPECIAL FEATURES:

The Commerce Group, Inc. (CGI), through its subsidiaries, writes personal and commercial property, casualty, auto and homeowners' insurance policies in 15 states. The group currently has over 1.2 million policies in effect, which makes CGI one of the largest personal auto insurers in the U.S. The company services its customers with personal and commercial property and casualty insurance primarily in Massachusetts and to a lesser extent in other states. CGI consists of five companies: Commerce Insurance Co.; American Commerce Insurance Co.; Commerce West Insurance Co.; Bay Finance; and SWICO Enterprises, Ltd. With its primary offices in Massachusetts and New Hampshire, Commerce Insurance offers private passenger auto, homeowners', personal liability, earthquake, flood and business insurance. It is one of the largest writers of private passenger auto insurance in Massachusetts. American Commerce, based in Columbus, Ohio, provides auto and homeowners' insurance. Commerce West, formerly Western Pioneer Insurance Co., provides similar insurance services to customers in California, while Bay Finance owns a portfolio of loans valued at approximately $20 million in Massachusetts and Connecticut. SWICO, through its subsidiary, State Wide Insurance Company, provides property and casualty insurance. CGI markets its products primarily through a network of independent agents. In June 2008, the Spanish insurance group, MAPFRE S.A., completed its acquisition of Commerce. The company will continue under the leadership of its present management and will retain its 2,400 employees.

The company offers its employees; medical, dental and vision insurance; life insurance; a dependant care reimbursement account; a health care reimbursement account; an employee assistance program; adoption assistance; tuition assistance; and an onsite child care center at its Massachusetts location.

## FINANCIALS: **Sales and profits are in thousands of dollars—add 000 to get the full amount. 2008 Note: Financial information for 2008 was not available for all companies at press time.**

| | | |
|---|---|---|
| 2008 Sales: $ | 2008 Profits: $ | **U.S. Stock Ticker: Subsidiary** |
| 2007 Sales: $1,982,447 | 2007 Profits: $190,903 | **Int'l Ticker:** Int'l Exchange: |
| 2006 Sales: $1,949,469 | 2006 Profits: $241,535 | Employees: 2,373 |
| 2005 Sales: $1,884,381 | 2005 Profits: $243,912 | Fiscal Year Ends: 12/31 |
| 2004 Sales: $1,806,571 | 2004 Profits: $214,431 | Parent Company: MAPFRE SA |

## SALARIES/BENEFITS:

| | | | | |
|---|---|---|---|---|
| Pension Plan: Y | ESOP Stock Plan: Y | Profit Sharing: Y | Top Exec. Salary: $882,832 | Bonus: $12,147,262 |
| Savings Plan: Y | Stock Purch. Plan: | | Second Exec. Salary: $738,411 | Bonus: $4,172,232 |

## OTHER THOUGHTS:

**Apparent Women Officers or Directors**: 3
**Hot Spot for Advancement for Women/Minorities**: Y

## LOCATIONS: ("Y" = Yes)

| West: | Southwest: | Midwest: | Southeast: | Northeast: | International: |
|---|---|---|---|---|---|
| Y | | Y | | Y | |

# COMTECH TELECOMMUNICATIONS CORP

**www.comtechtel.com**

**Industry Group Code:** 334200 **Ranks within this company's industry group:** Sales: 2 Profits: 2

| Management: | | Sales/Marketing: | | Liberal Arts: | | Information Systems: | | Professionals: | | Technical/Scientific: | |
|---|---|---|---|---|---|---|---|---|---|---|---|
| Mgmt. Trainees: | | Mktg. Professionals: | Y | Gen. Writing/Editing: | Y | Info. Management: | Y | Finance/Accounting: | Y | Engineers, Elec.: | Y |
| Experienced Mgmt.: | Y | Retail Sales: | | Technical Writing: | Y | Software Dev.: | Y | Law: | Y | Engineers, Other: | Y |
| Int'l Business: | Y | Commercial/Industrial: | Y | Graphic Arts/Photog.: | | Hardware Dev.: | Y | HR/Other: | Y | Health/Lab: | |
| MBA Graduates: | Y | Sales Trainees: | Y | Music: | | Systems Integration: | Y | Training: | Y | Scientists/Research: | |
| | | Advertising Pros.: | | Broadcasting: | | Consulting/Other: | | Health Care: | | Petroleum/Chemicals: | |
| | | | | Other: | | | | Consulting: | | Math/Other: | |

## TYPES OF BUSINESS:

Communications Equipment-Microwave & RF
Satellite Equipment & Services

## BRANDS/DIVISIONS/AFFILIATES:

Radyne Corporation

## CONTACTS: *Note: Officers with more than one job title may be intentionally listed here more than once.*

Fred Kornberg, CEO
Robert G. Rouse, COO/Exec. VP
Fred Kornberg, Pres.
Michael D. Porcelain, CFO/Sr. VP
Frank W. Otto, Sr. VP-Oper.
Jerome Kapelus, Sr. VP-Strategy & Bus. Dev.
Robert L. McCollom, Sr. VP/Pres., Comtech EF Data Corp.
Richard L. Burt, Sr. VP/Pres., Comtech Systems, Inc.
Daniel S. (Dan) Wood, Sr. VP/Pres., Comtech Mobile Datacom Corp.
Larry Konopelko, Sr. VP/Pres., Comtech PST Corp.
Fred Kornberg, Chmn.

**Phone:** 631-962-7000 **Fax:**
**Toll-Free:**
**Address:** 68 S. Service Rd., Ste. 230, Melville, NY 11747 US

## GROWTH PLANS/SPECIAL FEATURES:

Comtech Telecommunications Corp. is a communications equipment manufacturer specializing in microwave and radio frequency (RF) applications. The company operates in three business segments: telecommunications transmission, mobile data communications and RF microwave amplifiers. Comtech's largest segment, telecommunications transmission, provides advanced equipment and systems that are used to enhance satellite transmission efficiency and enable wireless communications in environments where terrestrial communications are unavailable, inefficient or too expensive. Its main telecommunications transmission products include satellite earth station equipment and systems, such as modems, frequency converters, power amplifiers, transceivers, access devices and over-the-horizon microwave equipment capable of transmitting signals over unfriendly or inaccessible terrain from 20 to 600 miles. Comtech's mobile data communications segment, its fastest growing segment, provides solutions enabling global satellite-based communications for mobile, real-time, secure transmission. Products and systems in this segment include mobile satellite transceivers, satellite packet data networks, ruggedized computers and satellite earth station network gateways, as well as associated installation, training and maintenance. Comtech's RF microwave amplifiers segment provides solid-state, high-power, broadband amplifiers in the microwave and RF spectrums. Principle applications for its amplifiers include defense applications for U.S. and foreign military customers; and sophisticated commercial applications. Some of these commercial applications include oncology treatment systems; the provision of email, Internet access and video conferencing through an aircraft satellite communication system; and testing electronic systems for electromagnetic compatibility and susceptibility to interference. In May 2008, Comtech agreed to acquire Radyne Corporation, a provider of satellite, troposcatter, microwave and cable communication receivers and transmitters, for approximately $223.6 million.

Comtech offers its employees education assistance, a health club membership, flexible spending accounts and medical, dental, vision, life, AD&D and disability insurance.

## FINANCIALS: **Sales and profits are in thousands of dollars—add 000 to get the full amount. 2008 Note: Financial information for 2008 was not available for all companies at press time.**

2008 Sales: $
2007 Sales: $445,684
2006 Sales: $391,511
2005 Sales: $307,890
2004 Sales: $223,390

2008 Profits: $
2007 Profits: $65,213
2006 Profits: $45,269
2005 Profits: $36,655
2004 Profits: $21,827

**U.S. Stock Ticker: CMTL**
**Int'l Ticker:** Int'l Exchange:
Employees: 1,230
Fiscal Year Ends: 7/31
Parent Company:

## SALARIES/BENEFITS:

| | | | | |
|---|---|---|---|---|
| Pension Plan: | ESOP Stock Plan: | Profit Sharing: | Top Exec. Salary: $625,000 | Bonus: $3,766,260 |
| Savings Plan: Y | Stock Purch. Plan: Y | | Second Exec. Salary: $370,000 | Bonus: $1,289,943 |

## OTHER THOUGHTS:

**Apparent Women Officers or Directors**:
**Hot Spot for Advancement for Women/Minorities**:

## LOCATIONS: ("Y" = Yes)

| West: | Southwest: | Midwest: | Southeast: | Northeast: | International: |
|---|---|---|---|---|---|
| Y | Y | | Y | Y | Y |

Note: Financial information, benefits and other data can change quickly and may vary from those stated here.

# CONCUR TECHNOLOGIES INC

www.concur.com

**Industry Group Code:** 511201 **Ranks within this company's industry group:** Sales: 5 Profits: 3

| Management: | | Sales/Marketing: | | Liberal Arts: | | Information Systems: | | Professionals: | | Technical/Scientific: | |
|---|---|---|---|---|---|---|---|---|---|---|---|
| Mgmt. Trainees: | | Mktg. Professionals: | Y | Gen. Writing/Editing: | | Info. Management: | Y | Finance/Accounting: | Y | Engineers, Elec.: | Y |
| Experienced Mgmt.: | Y | Retail Sales: | | Technical Writing: | Y | Software Dev.: | Y | Law: | Y | Engineers, Other: | |
| Int'l Business: | Y | Commercial/Industrial: | Y | Graphic Arts/Photog.: | | Hardware Dev.: | | HR/Other: | Y | Health/Lab: | |
| MBA Graduates: | Y | Sales Trainees: | Y | Music: | | Systems Integration: | | Training: | Y | Scientists/Research: | |
| | | Advertising Pros.: | | Broadcasting: | | Consulting/Other: | | Health Care: | | Petroleum/Chemicals: | |
| | | | | Other: | | | | Consulting: | | Math/Other: | |

## TYPES OF BUSINESS:

Software Manufacturer-Expense Reporting
Corporate Expense Management Solutions
Professional Services
Travel and Entertainment Expense Reporting Software
Meeting Expense Reporting Software

## BRANDS/DIVISIONS/AFFILIATES:

Concur Expense
Concur Vendor Payment Request
Concur Imaging Service
Concur Travel & Expense
Concur Business Intelligence
Concur Offline Access
Concur Benchmarking Service
RideCharge

## CONTACTS: *Note: Officers with more than one job title may be intentionally listed here more than once.*

Steve Singh, CEO
Rajeev Singh, COO
Rajeev Singh, Pres.
John Adair, CFO
Michael Hilton, Exec. VP-Worldwide Mktg.
Tom DePasquale, Exec. VP-R&D
Kyle R. Sugamele, Chief Legal Officer/Corp. Sec.
John Torrey, Dir.-Investor Rel.
Steve Singh, Chmn.
Suzanne Fletcher, Dir.-Travel Mgmt.

| | |
|---|---|
| **Phone:** 425-702-8808 | **Fax:** 425-702-8828 |
| **Toll-Free:** 800-401-8412 | |
| **Address:** 18400 N.E. Union Hill Rd., Redmond, WA 98052 US | |

## GROWTH PLANS/SPECIAL FEATURES:

Concur Technologies, Inc. is a provider of business services and software solutions that automate processes involved in the management of travel- and meeting-related corporate expenses. Its solutions are designed to automate and streamline corporate expense reimbursement processes, reduce operating costs and improve internal controls. The firm's flagship products are its Concur Expense services, its expense reporting solution, and Cliqbook Travel, its corporate travel management software. In addition, the company offers value-added services and software that integrate with Concur Expense, such as Concur Vendor Payment Request, Concur Imaging Service, Concur Business Intelligence, Concur Offline Access, Concur Benchmarking Service and the Concur Compliance Solution. Concur Expense provides report preparation, report routing and approval, report processing and data capture. Concur Travel & Expense is a travel and expense management service that combines travel booking and expense reporting into an automated on-demand service. The company provides its solutions as a subscription service on an outsourced basis over the Internet or through a dedicated telecommunications connection. In addition, Concur offers professional services including consulting, customer support and training. Notable customers include Dell; JCPenny Case; Ocean Spray; and Texas Instruments. In early 2008, the firm opened offices in Frankfurt, Paris and Brussels, demonstrating Concur's focus on Europe and specifically on the important French and German speaking markets. In May of the same year, the company introduced RideCharge, a service that allows business travelers to book and pay for taxi, sedan and shuttle transportation electronically through Concur Travel & Expense.

Employees are offered medical, dental and vision insurance; life insurance; short-and long-term disability coverage; an employee assistance program; flexible spending accounts; a 401(k) plan; a stock purchase plan; an employee referral program; tuition reimbursement; health club memberships; and discounts on cell phones, hardware and software.

## FINANCIALS: **Sales and profits are in thousands of dollars—add 000 to get the full amount. 2008 Note: Financial information for 2008 was not available for all companies at press time.**

| | | |
|---|---|---|
| 2008 Sales: $ | 2008 Profits: $ | **U.S. Stock Ticker: CNQR** |
| 2007 Sales: $129,107 | 2007 Profits: $8,225 | **Int'l Ticker:** Int'l Exchange: |
| 2006 Sales: $97,145 | 2006 Profits: $34,156 | Employees: 575 |
| 2005 Sales: $71,831 | 2005 Profits: $5,366 | Fiscal Year Ends: 9/30 |
| 2004 Sales: $56,550 | 2004 Profits: $2,035 | Parent Company: |

## SALARIES/BENEFITS:

| | | | | |
|---|---|---|---|---|
| Pension Plan: | ESOP Stock Plan: | Profit Sharing: | Top Exec. Salary: $431,250 | Bonus: $837,500 |
| Savings Plan: Y | Stock Purch. Plan: Y | | Second Exec. Salary: $380,000 | Bonus: $770,500 |

## OTHER THOUGHTS:

**Apparent Women Officers or Directors**: 1
**Hot Spot for Advancement for Women/Minorities**: Y

## LOCATIONS: ("Y" = Yes)

| West: | Southwest: | Midwest: | Southeast: | Northeast: | International: |
|---|---|---|---|---|---|
| Y | Y | Y | Y | Y | Y |

# CONTINUCARE CORP

www.mycontinucare.com

**Industry Group Code:** 621610 **Ranks within this company's industry group:** Sales: 1 Profits: 1

| Management: | | Sales/Marketing: | | Liberal Arts: | | Information Systems: | | Professionals: | | Technical/Scientific: | |
|---|---|---|---|---|---|---|---|---|---|---|---|
| Mgmt. Trainees: | | Mktg. Professionals: | Y | Gen. Writing/Editing: | | Info. Management: | Y | Finance/Accounting: | Y | Engineers, Elec.: | |
| Experienced Mgmt.: | Y | Retail Sales: | | Technical Writing: | | Software Dev.: | | Law: | Y | Engineers, Other: | |
| Int'l Business: | | Commercial/Industrial: | | Graphic Arts/Photog.: | | Hardware Dev.: | | HR/Other: | Y | Health/Lab: | Y |
| MBA Graduates: | Y | Sales Trainees: | | Music: | | Systems Integration: | | Training: | Y | Scientists/Research: | |
| | | Advertising Pros.: | | Broadcasting: | | Consulting/Other: | | Health Care: | Y | Petroleum/Chemicals: | |
| | | | | Other: | | | | Consulting: | | Math/Other: | |

## TYPES OF BUSINESS:

Outpatient Health Care
Managed Health Care
Practice Management Services

## BRANDS/DIVISIONS/AFFILIATES:

Humana
Vista
MDHC Companies

## CONTACTS:

*Note: Officers with more than one job title may be intentionally listed here more than once.*

Richard C. Pfenniger, Jr., CEO
Richard C. Pfenniger, Jr., Pres.
Fernando Fernandez, CFO
Luis H. Izquierdo, Sr. VP-Mktg.
Gemma Rosello, Exec. VP-Oper.
Luis H. Izquierdo, Sr. VP-Bus. Dev.
Fernando Fernandez, Sr. VP-Finance/Treas./Sec.
Sadita Bustamante, Sr. VP-Center Oper.
Jose M. Garcia, Exec. VP
Holly Lopez, VP-Support Svcs.
Richard C. Pfenniger, Jr., Chmn.

**Phone:** 305-500-2000 **Fax:** 305-500-2080
**Toll-Free:**
**Address:** 7200 Corporate Center Dr., Ste. 600, Miami, FL 33126 US

## GROWTH PLANS/SPECIAL FEATURES:

Continucare Corporation is a provider of primary care physician services. Through a network of 15 medical centers the company provides primary health care services on an outpatient basis. Continucare also provides practice management services to 15 independent physician associates (IPAs). All of Continucare's medical centers and IPAs are located in Miami-Dade, Broward and Hillsborough Counties, Florida. These facilities provide services for approximately 27,900 patients on a risk basis and 11,700 patients on a limited or non-risk basis. Medicare eligible patients, under risk arrangements with Continucare, accounted for approximately 89% of the firm's revenue in 2007. The firm's medical centers provide facilities for physicians practicing in the areas of general, family and internal medicine. Services provided to independent physician associate clinics enrolled in Humana health plans include assistance with medical utilization management; pharmacy management; specialist network development; and financial reports. Continucare's affiliated IPAs provide services to approximately 2,200 patients on a full-risk basis and to nearly 3,300 on a limited- or non-risk basis. In addition to its risk agreement with Humana, which accounts for approximately 80% of its net medical services, Continucare is currently in managed care agreement with Vista, also a risk agreement, which accounts for approximately 20% of its net medical services. In December 2007, the firm opened its first Continucare ValuClinic, a retail-based health center offering treatment for common illnesses such as bronchitis, strep throat, pink eye, seasonal allergies and skin infections, in Hollywood, Florida.

## FINANCIALS:

**Sales and profits are in thousands of dollars—add 000 to get the full amount. 2008 Note: Financial information for 2008 was not available for all companies at press time.**

| | | |
|---|---|---|
| 2008 Sales: $ | 2008 Profits: $ | **U.S. Stock Ticker: CNU** |
| 2007 Sales: $217,146 | 2007 Profits: $6,303 | **Int'l Ticker:** Int'l Exchange: |
| 2006 Sales: $132,991 | 2006 Profits: $5,338 | Employees: 563 |
| 2005 Sales: $112,231 | 2005 Profits: $15,891 | Fiscal Year Ends: 6/30 |
| 2004 Sales: $101,824 | 2004 Profits: $4,652 | Parent Company: |

## SALARIES/BENEFITS:

| | | | | |
|---|---|---|---|---|
| Pension Plan: | ESOP Stock Plan: | Profit Sharing: | Top Exec. Salary: $346,077 | Bonus: $ |
| Savings Plan: | Stock Purch. Plan: Y | | Second Exec. Salary: $218,789 | Bonus: $ |

## OTHER THOUGHTS:

**Apparent Women Officers or Directors**: 3
**Hot Spot for Advancement for Women/Minorities**: Y

## LOCATIONS: ("Y" = Yes)

| West: | Southwest: | Midwest: | Southeast: | Northeast: | International: |
|---|---|---|---|---|---|
| | | | Y | | |

# CORPORATE EXECUTIVE BOARD COMPANY (THE)

**www.executiveboard.com**

**Industry Group Code:** 541611 **Ranks within this company's industry group:** Sales: Profits:

| Management: | | Sales/Marketing: | | Liberal Arts: | | Information Systems: | | Professionals: | | Technical/Scientific: | |
|---|---|---|---|---|---|---|---|---|---|---|---|
| Mgmt. Trainees: | | Mktg. Professionals: | Y | Gen. Writing/Editing: | Y | Info. Management: | Y | Finance/Accounting: | Y | Engineers, Elec.: | |
| Experienced Mgmt.: | Y | Retail Sales: | | Technical Writing: | Y | Software Dev.: | | Law: | Y | Engineers, Other: | |
| Int'l Business: | Y | Commercial/Industrial: | | Graphic Arts/Photog.: | | Hardware Dev.: | | HR/Other: | Y | Health/Lab: | |
| MBA Graduates: | Y | Sales Trainees: | Y | Music: | | Systems Integration: | | Training: | Y | Scientists/Research: | |
| | | Advertising Pros.: | | Broadcasting: | | Consulting/Other: | Y | Health Care: | | Petroleum/Chemicals: | |
| | | | | Other: | Y | | | Consulting: | Y | Math/Other: | |

## TYPES OF BUSINESS:

Consulting-Best Management Practices
Executive Conferences & Seminars
Research Reports & Databases

## BRANDS/DIVISIONS/AFFILIATES:

CEB Toolbox, Inc.
Information Technology Toolbox, Inc.

## CONTACTS: *Note: Officers with more than one job title may be intentionally listed here more than once.*

Thomas L. Monahan, III, CEO
Joyce Liu, CFO
Michael A. Archer, Pres., Mktg.
Melody L. Jones, Chief Human Resources Officer
Glenn Tobin, General Mgr.
Thomas L. Monahan, III, Chmn.

| | |
|---|---|
| **Phone:** 571-303-3000 | **Fax:** 571-303-3100 |
| **Toll-Free:** | |
| **Address:** 1919 North Lynn St, Arlington, VA 22209 US | |

## GROWTH PLANS/SPECIAL FEATURES:

The Corporate Executive Board Company (CEB), a spin-off of the Advisory Board Company, provides best practices research and analysis; decision support tools; and executive education focusing on corporate strategy, operations and general management issues. It serves over 4,700 corporate members worldwide, including Alcoa, Charles Schwab, GM, IBM, Unilever, the Coca-Cola Company and BT. CEB's membership-based model, in which all members/customers participate in research and analysis, is central to its business strategy. This model allows access to the best business practices of members and enables CEB to provide comprehensive analysis on current business issues, assessing the collective experiences and knowledge of members on leading-edge topics. The firm's services are provided primarily on an annual subscription basis and include hosted member meetings; member teleconferences; executive education seminars; customized research briefs; web-based access to the program content databases and decision support tools; and publishing best practice research studies. CEB offers 49 membership programs that cover 10 practices areas: Human resources; strategy and research and development; information technology; sales and marketing; corporate finance; legal and compliance; operations and procurement; financial services; communications; and general management. The firm's membership renewal rate is approximately 90%. Membership programs are typically one-year renewable agreements and average $32,000 in cost. It operates through offices in Virginia (serving Washington, D.C.), Chicago, San Francisco, London, New Delhi and Sydney; and it has added 11 new research programs in the last two years, with the anticipation of adding several more annually for the next 2-3 years.

Employees of CEB medical, dental and vision coverage; flexible spending accounts; an employee assistance program; emergency back-up day care; group legal benefits; a 401(k) plan; stock purchase plan; fitness club discounts; and discounts on other products and services, including Dell computers and Verizon Wireless plans.

## FINANCIALS: **Sales and profits are in thousands of dollars—add 000 to get the full amount. 2008 Note: Financial information for 2008 was not available for all companies at press time.**

| | | |
|---|---|---|
| 2008 Sales: $ | 2008 Profits: $ | **U.S. Stock Ticker: EXBD** |
| 2007 Sales: $532,716 | 2007 Profits: $80,587 | **Int'l Ticker:** Int'l Exchange: |
| 2006 Sales: $460,623 | 2006 Profits: $79,171 | Employees: 2,440 |
| 2005 Sales: $362,226 | 2005 Profits: $75,060 | Fiscal Year Ends: 12/31 |
| 2004 Sales: $280,724 | 2004 Profits: $53,656 | Parent Company: |

## SALARIES/BENEFITS:

| | | | | |
|---|---|---|---|---|
| Pension Plan: | ESOP Stock Plan: | Profit Sharing: | Top Exec. Salary: $595,932 | Bonus: $150,000 |
| Savings Plan: Y | Stock Purch. Plan: Y | | Second Exec. Salary: $296,018 | Bonus: $45,000 |

## OTHER THOUGHTS:

**Apparent Women Officers or Directors**: 2
**Hot Spot for Advancement for Women/Minorities**:

## LOCATIONS: ("Y" = Yes)

| West: | Southwest: | Midwest: | Southeast: | Northeast: | International: |
|---|---|---|---|---|---|
| Y | | Y | | Y | Y |

# COUPONS INC

**www.couponsinc.com**

**Industry Group Code:** 541810A **Ranks within this company's industry group:** Sales: Profits:

| **Management:** | | **Sales/Marketing:** | | **Liberal Arts:** | | **Information Systems:** | | **Professionals:** | | **Technical/Scientific:** | |
|---|---|---|---|---|---|---|---|---|---|---|---|
| Mgmt. Trainees: | | Mktg. Professionals: | Y | Gen. Writing/Editing: | Y | Info. Management: | Y | Finance/Accounting: | Y | Engineers, Elec.: | |
| Experienced Mgmt.: | Y | Retail Sales: | | Technical Writing: | | Software Dev.: | | Law: | Y | Engineers, Other: | |
| Int'l Business: | | Commercial/Industrial: | | Graphic Arts/Photog.: | Y | Hardware Dev.: | | HR/Other: | Y | Health/Lab: | |
| MBA Graduates: | Y | Sales Trainees: | Y | Music: | | Systems Integration: | Y | Training: | Y | Scientists/Research: | |
| | | Advertising Pros.: | Y | Broadcasting: | | Consulting/Other: | | Health Care: | | Petroleum/Chemicals: | |
| | | | | Other: | Y | | | Consulting: | | Math/Other: | |

## TYPES OF BUSINESS:

Online Coupon Advertising & Distribution

## BRANDS/DIVISIONS/AFFILIATES:

webBricks
Bricks Duet
Concordance
Digital FSI
CustomerCare CAS
CouponFit
CouponBug LLC
GroceryIQ

## CONTACTS: *Note: Officers with more than one job title may be intentionally listed here more than once.*

Steven R. Boal, CEO
Brian Weisfeld, COO
Steven R. Boal, Pres.
Jon Schwartz, VP-Sales
Michael R. Walsh, Head-R&D
Steve Horowitz, CTO
Ravi Keswani, VP-Eng.
Bob Gonzales, VP-Oper.
Michael R. Walsh, Chief Security Officer
David Schwartz, VP-Consumer Mktg.
Francis X. Garcia, VP-Mktg. Solutions

| **Phone:** 650-605-4600 | **Fax:** 650-605-4700 |
|---|---|
| **Toll-Free:** | |
| **Address:** 400 Logue Ave., Mountain View, CA 94043 US | |

## GROWTH PLANS/SPECIAL FEATURES:

Coupons, Inc. is an online promotion company that provides marketing technology solutions and printable coupon promotional opportunities. Its services can be divided into six segments: Promotion Services, Consumer Data Acquisition, Coupon Portals, Coupon Distribution, Customer Care and Family Codes. Promotion Services allow clients to market their products online. The webBricks program allows corporate web sites to offer coupons to reward customers for market survey responses, to introduce new products, and to increase loyalty programs. adBricks lets consumers print coupons directly from their personal printer by clicking on an ad banner. oneBricks provides a coupon link through e-mail campaigns. The Consumer Data Acquisition division combines coupons and promotion tools to match individual consumer requests through its Bricks Duet programs. These programs allow the consumer to complete a survey for a particular product and the consumer is offered a coupon as an incentive. The Coupon Portals segment sorts coupon offers into a single location on company web sites. The Concordance program reads text on web pages, locates keywords that match available coupon offers in the firm's system and either displays the offer in a standard ad unit or highlights the keywords and produces an offer window when the user scrolls over the word with the mouse. The Coupon Distribution segment consists of Digital FSI, a network of 2,000 coupon content sites that lets consumers find coupons on retail store web sites, newspaper, radio station and TV sites, and lifestyle sites. The Customer Care division, through the CustomerCare CAS, allows companies to look up customer information through a web-based interface and to send coupons to customer through both postal mail and e-mail. The Family Codes division, through their CouponFit programs; manage and insure accurate codes on coupons. In 2008, the company acquired CouponBug LLC and Apple iPhone's lifestyle application, GroceryIQ.

## FINANCIALS: **Sales and profits are in thousands of dollars—add 000 to get the full amount. 2008 Note: Financial information for 2008 was not available for all companies at press time.**

| | | |
|---|---|---|
| 2008 Sales: $ | 2008 Profits: $ | **U.S. Stock Ticker: Private** |
| 2007 Sales: $ | 2007 Profits: $ | **Int'l Ticker:** Int'l Exchange: |
| 2006 Sales: $ | 2006 Profits: $ | Employees: |
| 2005 Sales: $ | 2005 Profits: $ | Fiscal Year Ends: |
| 2004 Sales: $ | 2004 Profits: $ | Parent Company: |

## SALARIES/BENEFITS:

| | | | | |
|---|---|---|---|---|
| Pension Plan: | ESOP Stock Plan: | Profit Sharing: | Top Exec. Salary: $ | Bonus: $ |
| Savings Plan: | Stock Purch. Plan: | | Second Exec. Salary: $ | Bonus: $ |

## OTHER THOUGHTS:

**Apparent Women Officers or Directors:**
**Hot Spot for Advancement for Women/Minorities:**

## LOCATIONS: ("Y" = Yes)

| West: | Southwest: | Midwest: | Southeast: | Northeast: | International: |
|---|---|---|---|---|---|
| Y | | | | | |

# CRITICAL CARE SYSTEMS

www.criticalcaresystems.com

**Industry Group Code:** 621490 **Ranks within this company's industry group:** Sales: Profits:

| Management: | | Sales/Marketing: | | Liberal Arts: | | Information Systems: | | Professionals: | | Technical/Scientific: | |
|---|---|---|---|---|---|---|---|---|---|---|---|
| Mgmt. Trainees: | | Mktg. Professionals: | Y | Gen. Writing/Editing: | | Info. Management: | Y | Finance/Accounting: | Y | Engineers, Elec.: | |
| Experienced Mgmt.: | Y | Retail Sales: | | Technical Writing: | | Software Dev.: | | Law: | Y | Engineers, Other: | |
| Int'l Business: | | Commercial/Industrial: | Y | Graphic Arts/Photog.: | | Hardware Dev.: | | HR/Other: | Y | Health/Lab: | Y |
| MBA Graduates: | Y | Sales Trainees: | Y | Music: | | Systems Integration: | | Training: | Y | Scientists/Research: | |
| | | Advertising Pros.: | Y | Broadcasting: | | Consulting/Other: | | Health Care: | Y | Petroleum/Chemicals: | |
| | | | | Other: | | | | Consulting: | | Math/Other: | |

## TYPES OF BUSINESS:

Pharmacy Services

## BRANDS/DIVISIONS/AFFILIATES:

Medco Health Solutions
Curative Health Services

## CONTACTS:

*Note: Officers with more than one job title may be intentionally listed here more than once.*

Paul F. McConnell, CEO
John C. Prior, COO
Paul F. McConnell, Pres.
John C. Prior, CFO
Craig J. Vollmer, Sr. VP-Sales & Mktg.
Andrew C. Walk, Sr. VP-Oper.

**Phone:** 603-888-1500 **Fax:** 603-888-0990
**Toll-Free:**
**Address:** 61 Spit Brook Rd., Ste. 505, Nashua, NH 03060 US

## GROWTH PLANS/SPECIAL FEATURES:

Critical Care Systems, formerly Curative Health Services, Inc., provides health care products, services and support to patients with chronic medical conditions. It operates both a specialty infusion business unit and a wound care management business. The specialty infusion unit provides intravenous and injectable biopharmaceutical and compounded pharmaceutical products and comprehensive infusion services to patients with chronic and critical disease states. All such patient care services are delivered through a national footprint of community-based branches, each including a multidisciplinary team of pharmacists, nurses, reimbursement specialists and patient service representatives. The wound care management business provides wound care services specializing in chronic wound care management. It manages, on behalf of hospital clients, a nationwide network of Wound Care Center programs that offer a range of services across a continuum of care for treatment of chronic wounds. These programs consist of diagnostic and therapeutic treatment procedures designed to meet each patient's specific wound care needs. The company has approximately 485 payor contracts and provides products or services in approximately 45 states nationwide. Critical Care Systems also operates eBioCare, a specialty online pharmacy, and Apex, a company that caters to the needs of hemophiliacs. In March 2006, the predecessor company, Curative Health, and all its subsidiaries filed voluntary Chapter 11 bankruptcy petitions. This was in order to implement and affect its prepackaged reorganization plan of February 2006. Later, it acquired Critical Care Systems and subsequently changed the company name. In November 2007, Medco Health Solutions, Inc. acquired Critical Care for $218 million.

Employees of Critical Care Systems receive benefits including medical and dental coverage; life and AD&D insurance; flexible spending accounts; an employee assistance program; and paid time off.

## FINANCIALS:

**Sales and profits are in thousands of dollars—add 000 to get the full amount. 2008 Note: Financial information for 2008 was not available for all companies at press time.**

2008 Sales: $
2007 Sales: $
2006 Sales: $
2005 Sales: $261,059
2004 Sales: $224,980

2008 Profits: $
2007 Profits: $
2006 Profits: $
2005 Profits: $-101,592
2004 Profits: $-141,405

**U.S. Stock Ticker: Subsidiary**
**Int'l Ticker:** Int'l Exchange:
Employees: 1,292
Fiscal Year Ends: 12/31
Parent Company: MEDCO HEALTH SOLUTIONS

## SALARIES/BENEFITS:

Pension Plan:
Savings Plan: Y
ESOP Stock Plan:
Stock Purch. Plan:
Profit Sharing:
Top Exec. Salary: $353,077 Bonus: $
Second Exec. Salary: $291,509 Bonus: $100,000

## OTHER THOUGHTS:

**Apparent Women Officers or Directors:**
**Hot Spot for Advancement for Women/Minorities:**

## LOCATIONS: ("Y" = Yes)

| West: | Southwest: | Midwest: | Southeast: | Northeast: | International: |
|---|---|---|---|---|---|
| Y | Y | Y | Y | Y | |

# CROWN CASTLE INTERNATIONAL CORP

www.crowncastle.com

**Industry Group Code:** 513300D **Ranks within this company's industry group:** Sales: 2 Profits: 1

| Management: | | Sales/Marketing: | | Liberal Arts: | | Information Systems: | | Professionals: | | Technical/Scientific: | |
|---|---|---|---|---|---|---|---|---|---|---|---|
| Mgmt. Trainees: | | Mktg. Professionals: | Y | Gen. Writing/Editing: | | Info. Management: | Y | Finance/Accounting: | Y | Engineers, Elec.: | Y |
| Experienced Mgmt.: | Y | Retail Sales: | | Technical Writing: | Y | Software Dev.: | | Law: | Y | Engineers, Other: | Y |
| Int'l Business: | Y | Commercial/Industrial: | Y | Graphic Arts/Photog.: | | Hardware Dev.: | | HR/Other: | Y | Health/Lab: | |
| MBA Graduates: | Y | Sales Trainees: | Y | Music: | | Systems Integration: | | Training: | Y | Scientists/Research: | |
| | | Advertising Pros.: | | Broadcasting: | | Consulting/Other: | | Health Care: | | Petroleum/Chemicals: | |
| | | | | Other: | | | | Consulting: | | Math/Other: | |

## TYPES OF BUSINESS:

Wireless Communications Towers
Broadcast Infrastructure Services
Site Management Services
Construction & Engineering Services
Radio & Television Broadcast Towers
Cell Phones

## BRANDS/DIVISIONS/AFFILIATES:

Crown Castle USA, Inc.
Crown Castle Australia Pty., Ltd.
Modeo
Crown Castle Broadcast
Crown Castle Solutions

## CONTACTS: *Note: Officers with more than one job title may be intentionally listed here more than once.*

W. Benjamin (Ben) Moreland, CEO
W. Benjamin (Ben) Moreland, Pres.
Jay A. Brown, CFO/Sr. VP
Patrick Slowey, Sr. VP-Sales & Customer Rel.
Lisa Davidson, Sr. VP-Human Resources
E. Blake Hawk, General Counsel/Exec. VP
Rob A. Fisher, VP-Acct./Controller
John P. Kelly, Exec. Vice Chmn.
James D. Young, Pres., Tower Oper.
Donald J. Reid, Jr., Corp. Sec.
J. Landis Martin, Chmn.

**Phone:** 713-570-3000 **Fax:** 713-570-3100
**Toll-Free:** 877-486-9377
**Address:** 1220 Augusta Dr., Ste. 500, Houston, TX 77057-2261 US

## GROWTH PLANS/SPECIAL FEATURES:

Crown Castle International Corp. owns and operates towers and transmission networks for wireless communications. Crown Castle owns, leases or manages over 23,800 towers in the U.S. and approximately 1400 towers in Australia, and owns towers in Puerto Rico and Canada. The company has operations in a variety of wireless communications industries, including cellular, personal communications services (PCS), enhanced specialized mobile radio (ESMR), 3G, wireless data, paging, fixed point-to-point radio and point to multipoint broadcasting (such as radio and television broadcasting). Crown Castle operates under two segments: CCUSA and CCAL. Crown Castle's domestic operations are run by Crown Castle USA, Inc. (CCUSA), while Crown Castle Australia Pty. (CCAL) conducts operations in Australia. The company's major clients include Sprint Nextel; Verizon Wireless; AT&T; and T-Mobile in the U.S., and Optus; Vodafone; Telstra; and Hutchison in Australia. The company offers wireless communications coverage to 91 of the top 100 US markets and has a strategic presence in Australia's major metropolitan areas, including Sydney, Melbourne, Brisbane, Adelaide and Perth. Crown Castle leases antenna space on wireless and broadcast towers; operates analog and digital audio and television broadcast transmission networks; operates wireless networks; and also offers construction, engineering and management services for telecommunications towers. It also manages approximately 700 towers owned by third parties.

Crown Castle offers its employees a 401(k) plan; comprehensive medical, dental and vision; prescription drug coverage; short- and long-term disability insurance; tuition reimbursement; employee assistance; flexible spending accounts; and 529 college savings programs.

## FINANCIALS: **Sales and profits are in thousands of dollars—add 000 to get the full amount. 2008 Note: Financial information for 2008 was not available for all companies at press time.**

| | | |
|---|---|---|
| 2008 Sales: $ | 2008 Profits: $ | **U.S. Stock Ticker: CCI** |
| 2007 Sales: $1,385,486 | 2007 Profits: $-222,813 | **Int'l Ticker:** Int'l Exchange: |
| 2006 Sales: $788,221 | 2006 Profits: $-41,893 | Employees: 1,200 |
| 2005 Sales: $676,759 | 2005 Profits: $-401,537 | Fiscal Year Ends: 12/31 |
| 2004 Sales: $604,202 | 2004 Profits: $233,107 | Parent Company: |

## SALARIES/BENEFITS:

| | | | | |
|---|---|---|---|---|
| Pension Plan: | ESOP Stock Plan: | Profit Sharing: | Top Exec. Salary: $495,274 | Bonus: $821,965 |
| Savings Plan: Y | Stock Purch. Plan: | | Second Exec. Salary: $360,395 | Bonus: $426,731 |

## OTHER THOUGHTS:

**Apparent Women Officers or Directors:** 1
**Hot Spot for Advancement for Women/Minorities:**

## LOCATIONS: ("Y" = Yes)

| West: | Southwest: | Midwest: | Southeast: | Northeast: | International: |
|---|---|---|---|---|---|
| Y | Y | Y | Y | Y | Y |

# CRUM & FORSTER HOLDINGS INC

www.cfins.com

**Industry Group Code:** 524126 **Ranks within this company's industry group:** Sales: 3 Profits: 4

| **Management:** | | **Sales/Marketing:** | | **Liberal Arts:** | | **Information Systems:** | | **Professionals:** | | **Technical/Scientific:** | |
|---|---|---|---|---|---|---|---|---|---|---|---|
| Mgmt. Trainees: | | Mktg. Professionals: | Y | Gen. Writing/Editing: | Y | Info. Management: | Y | Finance/Accounting: | Y | Engineers, Elec.: | |
| Experienced Mgmt.: | Y | Retail Sales: | | Technical Writing: | Y | Software Dev.: | | Law: | Y | Engineers, Other: | |
| Int'l Business: | | Commercial/Industrial: | Y | Graphic Arts/Photog.: | | Hardware Dev.: | | HR/Other: | Y | Health/Lab: | |
| MBA Graduates: | Y | Sales Trainees: | Y | Music: | | Systems Integration: | | Training: | Y | Scientists/Research: | |
| | | Advertising Pros.: | | Broadcasting: | | Consulting/Other: | | Health Care: | | Petroleum/Chemicals: | |
| | | | | Other: | | | | Consulting: | | Math/Other: | Y |

## TYPES OF BUSINESS:

Insurance, Direct Property & Casualty
Workers' Compensation
Commercial Automobile Insurance
Directors & Officers Liability Insurance
Surety
Loss & Risk Control Services
Safety Consulting
Online Claims Services

## BRANDS/DIVISIONS/AFFILIATES:

Fairfax Financial Holdings Ltd
United States Fire Insurance Company
North River Insurance Company (The)
Crum & Forster Insurance Company
Crum & Forster Indemnity Company
Crum & Forster Specialty Insurance Company
Seneca Specialty Insurance Company
Seneca Insurance Company, Inc.

## CONTACTS:

*Note: Officers with more than one job title may be intentionally listed here more than once.*

Douglas M. Libby, CEO
Mary Jane Robertson, CFO/Exec. VP/Treas.
Eileen S. Currie, Chief Mktg. Officer
Nancy Tallent, VP-Human Resources
Nicole Bennett, CIO/Sr. VP
Mark L. Owens, Sr. VP-Field Oper.
David J. Ghezzi, Sr. VP-Financial Oper.
Carl W. Berntsen, Sr. VP-Specialty Brokerage & E&S Casualty
Donald R. Fischer, Sr. VP-Mgmt. Protection
Paul Kush, Sr. VP-Claims
Robert G. Himmer, Sr. VP/Controller
Douglas M. Libby, Chmn.

| | |
|---|---|
| **Phone:** 973-490-6600 | **Fax:** 973-490-6940 |
| **Toll-Free:** | |
| **Address:** 305 Madison Ave., Morristown, NJ 07962 US | |

## GROWTH PLANS/SPECIAL FEATURES:

Crum & Forster Holdings, Inc. (C&F), a subsidiary of Canadian firm Fairfax Financial Holdings, Ltd., is a national property and casualty insurance group in the U.S. Founded in 1896, C&F provides its insurance products and services through eight companies: United States Fire Insurance Company; The North River Insurance Company; Crum & Forster Insurance Company; Crum & Forster Indemnity Company; Crum & Forster Specialty Insurance Company; Seneca Specialty Insurance Company; Seneca Insurance Company, Inc.; and Fairmont Specialty. The company writes a broad range of commercial coverage including worker's compensation, property, general liability, commercial automobile, commercial multi-peril and other lines of business. The company generally conducts business on a brokerage basis through its home office and a regional branch network, allowing it to control centrally the underwriting process, respond to local market conditions and build close relationships with producers and policyholders. C&F has over 1,300 producers located throughout the U.S., including wholesale brokers, independent regional retail firms and national brokers. In addition, the company provides a range of specialized loss control services, including loss analysis, ergonomics, occupational health services, fleet safety evaluations, training, construction safety and products liability, as well as risk control services on either a consulting or contract basis. C&F's risk control services cover broad areas, including workers' safety, fleet loss control, products and public liability and property fire protection. The firm also provides its clients with online claims reporting and an anti-fraud protection program. In 2007, approximately 57% of the company's gross premiums were for casualty coverage; 30% were for property coverage; and 13% were for other coverages, including accident and health coverage.

C&F offers its employees health and dependent care flexible spending accounts; educational assistance; a qualified transportation expense plan; a legal services plan; adoption assistance; a matching gifts program; a retirement plan; and medical and dental insurance.

## FINANCIALS:

**Sales and profits are in thousands of dollars—add 000 to get the full amount. 2008 Note: Financial information for 2008 was not available for all companies at press time.**

| | | |
|---|---|---|
| 2008 Sales: $ | 2008 Profits: $ | **U.S. Stock Ticker: Subsidiary** |
| 2007 Sales: $1,563,647 | 2007 Profits: $293,182 | **Int'l Ticker:** Int'l Exchange: |
| 2006 Sales: $1,476,841 | 2006 Profits: $213,283 | Employees: 1,373 |
| 2005 Sales: $1,109,483 | 2005 Profits: $155,936 | Fiscal Year Ends: 12/31 |
| 2004 Sales: $1,072,300 | 2004 Profits: $24,200 | Parent Company: FAIRFAX FINANCIAL HOLDINGS LTD |

## SALARIES/BENEFITS:

| | | | | |
|---|---|---|---|---|
| Pension Plan: Y | ESOP Stock Plan: | Profit Sharing: | Top Exec. Salary: $ | Bonus: $ |
| Savings Plan: | Stock Purch. Plan: | | Second Exec. Salary: $ | Bonus: $ |

## OTHER THOUGHTS:

**Apparent Women Officers or Directors**: 4
**Hot Spot for Advancement for Women/Minorities**: Y

## LOCATIONS: ("Y" = Yes)

| West: | Southwest: | Midwest: | Southeast: | Northeast: | International: |
|---|---|---|---|---|---|
| Y | Y | Y | Y | Y | |

# CRYOLIFE INC

www.cryolife.com

**Industry Group Code:** 621511 **Ranks within this company's industry group:** Sales: 4 Profits: 3

| Management: | | Sales/Marketing: | | Liberal Arts: | | Information Systems: | | Professionals: | | Technical/Scientific: | |
|---|---|---|---|---|---|---|---|---|---|---|---|
| Mgmt. Trainees: | | Mktg. Professionals: | Y | Gen. Writing/Editing: | | Info. Management: | Y | Finance/Accounting: | Y | Engineers, Elec.: | |
| Experienced Mgmt.: | Y | Retail Sales: | | Technical Writing: | Y | Software Dev.: | | Law: | Y | Engineers, Other: | |
| Int'l Business: | Y | Commercial/Industrial: | Y | Graphic Arts/Photog.: | | Hardware Dev.: | | HR/Other: | Y | Health/Lab: | Y |
| MBA Graduates: | Y | Sales Trainees: | Y | Music: | | Systems Integration: | Y | Training: | Y | Scientists/Research: | Y |
| | | Advertising Pros.: | | Broadcasting: | | Consulting/Other: | | Health Care: | Y | Petroleum/Chemicals: | |
| | | | | Other: | | | | Consulting: | | Math/Other: | |

## TYPES OF BUSINESS:

Transplant Tissue Preservation & Distribution
Surgical Adhesives
Heart Valves
Medical Implants
Biomedical Research

## BRANDS/DIVISIONS/AFFILIATES:

BioGlue
SynerGraft
BioFoam
CryoValve SG Pulmonary Human Heart Valve
AuraZyme Pharmaceuticals, Inc.
CryoLife O'Brien Porcine Aortic Heart Valve
ProPatch Soft Tissue Repair Matrix
BioGlue Surgical Adhesive

## CONTACTS: *Note: Officers with more than one job title may be intentionally listed here more than once.*

Steven G. Anderson, CEO
D. Ashley Lee, COO/Exec. VP
Steven G. Anderson, Pres.
D. Ashley Lee, CFO/Treas.
Gerald B. Seery, Sr. VP-Mktg. & Sales
Albert E. Heacox, Sr. VP-R&D
Jeffrey W. Burris, General Counsel
Timothy M. Neja, VP-Laboratory Oper.
Amy D. Horton, Chief Acct. Officer
David M. Fronk, VP-Regulatory Affairs & Quality Assurance
Scott B. Capps, VP-Clinical Research
Suzanne K. Gabbert, Corp. Sec.
William F. Northrup, III, VP-Medical Rel. & Education
Steven G. Anderson, Chmn.
David N. Hollinworth, VP/Gen. Mgr.-CryoLife Europa

| | |
|---|---|
| **Phone:** 770-419-3355 | **Fax:** 770-426-0031 |
| **Toll-Free:** 800-438-8285 | |
| **Address:** 1655 Roberts Blvd. N.W., Kennesaw, GA 30144 US | |

## GROWTH PLANS/SPECIAL FEATURES:

CryoLife, Inc. develops and commercializes implantable biological devices and preserves and distributes human tissues for cardiovascular and vascular transplant applications. The firm's implantable medical devices include BioGlue surgical adhesive, porcine heart valves and vascular grafts of bovine tissue processed using the company's SynerGraft technology. BioGlue, designed for cardiovascular, vascular, pulmonary and general surgical applications, is a polymer based on bovine blood protein and an agent for cross-linking proteins. SynerGraft technology involves the removal of cells from the structure of animal tissue, leaving a collagen matrix that has the potential to repopulate in vivo with the recipient's own cells. CryoLife distributes the CryoLife O'Brien porcine aortic heart valve and the SynerGraft bovine vascular graft in Europe, the Middle East and Africa. The company maintains two separate facilities: one in Atlanta, Georgia, which consists of laboratories, warehouse space and offices; and another facility in Fareham in the United Kingdom. In 2007, the company began the exclusive distribution of CardioWrap, a bioresorbable thin film sheet used to replace the pericardium in cardiac reconstruction and other cardiac surgeries where the patient may face re-operation within six months. The company was recently awarded a patent for BioFoam, a self-expanding adhesive designed to rapidly arrest bleeding of large vessel injuries and seal wounds. Other products in pre-clinical development are BioDisc, a replacement for vertebral discs, and ProPatch Soft Tissue Repair Matrix for rotator cuff repair. In February 2008, the firm received clearance from the Food and Drug Administration (FDA) for use of its SynerGraft technology-processed CryoValve SG pulmonary human heart valve. In June 2008, CryoLife's BioGlue Surgical Adhesive, designed for reconstructive plastic surgery, was approved for use in the European Community with a CE mark.

CryoLife offers its employees a 401(k) plan, an employee stock purchase plan, tuition reimbursement and medical, prescription drug and dental coverage.

## FINANCIALS: **Sales and profits are in thousands of dollars—add 000 to get the full amount. 2008 Note: Financial information for 2008 was not available for all companies at press time.**

| | | |
|---|---|---|
| 2008 Sales: $ | 2008 Profits: $ | **U.S. Stock Ticker: CRY** |
| 2007 Sales: $94,763 | 2007 Profits: $7,201 | **Int'l Ticker:** Int'l Exchange: |
| 2006 Sales: $81,311 | 2006 Profits: $ 365 | Employees: 405 |
| 2005 Sales: $69,282 | 2005 Profits: $-19,535 | Fiscal Year Ends: 12/31 |
| 2004 Sales: $62,384 | 2004 Profits: $-18,749 | Parent Company: |

## SALARIES/BENEFITS:

| | | | | |
|---|---|---|---|---|
| Pension Plan: | ESOP Stock Plan: | Profit Sharing: | Top Exec. Salary: $600,000 | Bonus: $408,281 |
| Savings Plan: Y | Stock Purch. Plan: Y | | Second Exec. Salary: $340,000 | Bonus: $231,359 |

## OTHER THOUGHTS:

**Apparent Women Officers or Directors**: 2
**Hot Spot for Advancement for Women/Minorities**: Y

## LOCATIONS: ("Y" = Yes)

| West: | Southwest: | Midwest: | Southeast: | Northeast: | International: |
|---|---|---|---|---|---|
| | | | Y | | Y |

# CSG SYSTEMS INTERNATIONAL INC

www.csgsystems.com

**Industry Group Code:** 511203 **Ranks within this company's industry group:** Sales: 1 Profits: 1

| Management: | | Sales/Marketing: | | Liberal Arts: | | Information Systems: | | Professionals: | | Technical/Scientific: | |
|---|---|---|---|---|---|---|---|---|---|---|---|
| Mgmt. Trainees: | | Mktg. Professionals: | Y | Gen. Writing/Editing: | | Info. Management: | Y | Finance/Accounting: | Y | Engineers, Elec.: | Y |
| Experienced Mgmt.: | Y | Retail Sales: | | Technical Writing: | Y | Software Dev.: | Y | Law: | Y | Engineers, Other: | |
| Int'l Business: | | Commercial/Industrial: | Y | Graphic Arts/Photog.: | | Hardware Dev.: | | HR/Other: | Y | Health/Lab: | |
| MBA Graduates: | Y | Sales Trainees: | Y | Music: | | Systems Integration: | | Training: | Y | Scientists/Research: | |
| | | Advertising Pros.: | | Broadcasting: | | Consulting/Other: | | Health Care: | | Petroleum/Chemicals: | |
| | | | | Other: | Y | | | Consulting: | | Math/Other: | Y |

## TYPES OF BUSINESS:

Customer Care & Billing Services
Customer Relationship Management

## BRANDS/DIVISIONS/AFFILIATES:

ComTec, Inc.
Prairie Interactive Messaging Inc
Dataprose Inc
Quaero Corporation

## CONTACTS:

*Note: Officers with more than one job title may be intentionally listed here more than once.*

Peter Kalan, CEO
Robert M. Scott, COO/Exec. VP
Peter Kalan, Pres.
Randy Wiese, CFO/Exec. VP
Suzanne Broski, VP-Human Resources
Bret Griess, CIO
Joe Ruble, Chief Admin. Officer
Joe Ruble, General Counsel/Exec. VP
Jerry Baker, Sr. VP-Bus. & New Market Dev.
Karen Eckmann, VP-Corp. Comm.
Roger Metz, VP-Investor Rel.
Brett Griess, Sr. VP-Convergent Svcs. & Solutions
Pam Sellenrick, Sr. VP/Gen. Mgr.-Output Solutions
Dwayne Ruffin, Sr. VP-Prod. Mgmt.
Jay McCracken, Sr. VP-Strategic Bus. Units
Bernard W. Reznicek, Chmn.

**Phone:** 303-796-2850 **Fax:** 303-804-4088
**Toll-Free:** 800-366-2744
**Address:** 9555 Maroon Cir., Englewood, CO 80112 US

## GROWTH PLANS/SPECIAL FEATURES:

CSG Systems International, Inc. (CSG) provides customer care and billing services to the North American broadband and direct broadcast satellite markets. CSG offers its customers a range of applications and solutions in several categories: Market Solutions, which offers support to companies providing Internet and voice services; Billing and Payments, which allows business to outsource customer care and billing; Customer Care, which allows companies to improve their customer lifecycle management; Order Management, which helps companies manage customers' requests; Workforce Management, which can automatically schedule, dispatch and route technicians; and Statement and Output Services, which helps companies generate paper and electronic billing for customers. Subsidiaries include ComTec, Inc., which provides statement production, electronic statement presentation hardware and software technologies, as well as plant capacities and Prairie Interactive Messaging, Inc., which provides inbound and outbound automated voice, text/SMS, e-mail, and fax messaging services to manage workforce communications, collections, lead generation, automated order capture, service outage notifications, and other key business functions. In May 2008, the company acquired Dataprose, Inc., a privately-owned provider of direct mail services and statement presentment. In December of the same year, the company agreed to acquire Quaero Corporation, a North Carolina-based customer service, analytics and marketing services provider.

Employees are offered medical, dental and vision insurance; life insurance; business travel accident insurance; short-and long-term disability; a legal assistance plan; a long-term care plan; flexible spending accounts; a 401(k) savings plan; an employee stock purchase plan; adoption assistance; and educational assistance.

## FINANCIALS:

**Sales and profits are in thousands of dollars—add 000 to get the full amount. 2008 Note: Financial information for 2008 was not available for all companies at press time.**

| | | |
|---|---|---|
| 2008 Sales: $ | 2008 Profits: $ | **U.S. Stock Ticker: CSGS** |
| 2007 Sales: $419,261 | 2007 Profits: $60,771 | **Int'l Ticker:** Int'l Exchange: |
| 2006 Sales: $383,106 | 2006 Profits: $59,770 | Employees: 1,877 |
| 2005 Sales: $377,317 | 2005 Profits: $53,229 | Fiscal Year Ends: 12/31 |
| 2004 Sales: $351,401 | 2004 Profits: $47,184 | Parent Company: |

## SALARIES/BENEFITS:

| | | | | |
|---|---|---|---|---|
| Pension Plan: | ESOP Stock Plan: | Profit Sharing: | Top Exec. Salary: $600,000 | Bonus: $257,391 |
| Savings Plan: Y | Stock Purch. Plan: Y | | Second Exec. Salary: $425,000 | Bonus: $251,972 |

## OTHER THOUGHTS:

**Apparent Women Officers or Directors**: 4
**Hot Spot for Advancement for Women/Minorities**: Y

## LOCATIONS: ("Y" = Yes)

| West: | Southwest: | Midwest: | Southeast: | Northeast: | International: |
|---|---|---|---|---|---|
| Y | | Y | | | |

# CUBIST PHARMACEUTICALS INC

www.cubist.com

**Industry Group Code:** 325412 **Ranks within this company's industry group:** Sales: 10 Profits: 7

| Management: | | Sales/Marketing: | | Liberal Arts: | | Information Systems: | | Professionals: | | Technical/Scientific: | |
|---|---|---|---|---|---|---|---|---|---|---|---|
| Mgmt. Trainees: | | Mktg. Professionals: | Y | Gen. Writing/Editing: | | Info. Management: | Y | Finance/Accounting: | Y | Engineers, Elec.: | |
| Experienced Mgmt.: | Y | Retail Sales: | | Technical Writing: | Y | Software Dev.: | Y | Law: | Y | Engineers, Other: | |
| Int'l Business: | Y | Commercial/Industrial: | Y | Graphic Arts/Photog.: | | Hardware Dev.: | | HR/Other: | Y | Health/Lab: | Y |
| MBA Graduates: | Y | Sales Trainees: | Y | Music: | | Systems Integration: | | Training: | Y | Scientists/Research: | Y |
| | | Advertising Pros.: | | Broadcasting: | | Consulting/Other: | | Health Care: | Y | Petroleum/Chemicals: | |
| | | | | Other: | | | | Consulting: | | Math/Other: | Y |

## TYPES OF BUSINESS:

Drugs-Infectious Disease
Antimicrobial Drugs
Antiviral Drugs

## BRANDS/DIVISIONS/AFFILIATES:

CUBICIN
Novartis AG
Chiron Healthcare Ireland, Ltd.
Medison Pharma Co., Ltd.
Oryx Pharmaceuticals, Inc.
TTY BioPharma
Kuhnil Pharma Co., Ltd.

## CONTACTS: *Note: Officers with more than one job title may be intentionally listed here more than once.*

Michael W. Bonney, CEO
Robert J. (Rob) Perez, COO/Exec. VP
Michael W. Bonney, Pres.
David W.J. McGirr, CFO/Sr. VP
Gregory Stea, VP-Mktg. & Sales
Maureen H. Powers, VP-Human Resources
Anthony S. Murabito, CIO
Lindon M. Fellows, Sr. VP-Tech. Oper.
Steven Gilman, Sr. VP-Discovery & Nonclinical Dev.
Tamara L. Joseph, General Counsel/Sr. VP/Corp. Sec.
Ed Campanaro, VP-Clinical Oper.
Praveen Tipirneni, VP-Bus. Dev.
Mary C. Stack, VP-Finance
Mark Battaglini, VP-Gov't Affairs
Barry I. Eisenstein, Sr. VP-Scientific Affairs
Dennis D. Keith, VP-Chemistry
David S. Mantus, VP-Regulatory Affairs & Program Mgmt.

| | |
|---|---|
| **Phone:** 781-860-8660 | **Fax:** 781-861-0566 |
| **Toll-Free:** | |
| **Address:** 65 Hayden Ave., Lexington, MA 02421 US | |

## GROWTH PLANS/SPECIAL FEATURES:

Cubist Pharmaceuticals, Inc. is a biopharmaceutical company focused on the research, development and commercialization of pharmaceutical products that address unmet medical needs in the anti-infective marketplace. The firm's one marketed product is CUBICIN, the first in a new class of antimicrobial drugs called lipopeptides, which is approved for treatment of skin and skin structure infections. The drug is also approved in the U.S., European Union, Israel, Taiwan and Argentina. Because CUBICIN attacks bacteria through a novel mechanism and has demonstrated the unique ability in vitro to rapidly kill virtually all clinically significant Gram-positive bacteria, it may be particularly effective in treating infections caused by drug-resistant bacteria that cannot be eradicated by existing antibiotics. The firm has completed a successful Phase III trial of the drug for endocarditis (infection of the heart valves) and bacteremia (bacteria in the blood). The firm has alliances with other companies to market Cubicin outside of the U.S. Novartis AG, through its subsidiary Chiron Healthcare Ireland, Ltd., is responsible for regulatory filings, sales, marketing and distribution costs in Europe, Australia, New Zealand, India and certain Central American, South American and Middle Eastern countries. Other international partners include Medison Pharma, Ltd., in Israel; Oryx Pharmaceuticals, Inc. in Canada; TTY BioPharm in Taiwan; and Kuhnil Pharma Co., Ltd. in Korea. In December 2007, Cubist acquired Illumigen Biosciences, Inc., a developer of the IB657 protein therapeutic compound in pre-clinical development for the treatment of Hepatitis C Virus infections, for approximately $9 million.

Cubist Pharmaceuticals offers its employees tuition assistance; an employee assistance program; flexible work schedules; fitness reimbursement; an on-site workout room; an on-site massage therapist; an on-site full service cafeteria; back-up childcare; an adoption assistance program; domestic partner coverage; and medical, dental, life and disability insurance.

## FINANCIALS: **Sales and profits are in thousands of dollars—add 000 to get the full amount. 2008 Note: Financial information for 2008 was not available for all companies at press time.**

| | | |
|---|---|---|
| 2008 Sales: $ | 2008 Profits: $ | **U.S. Stock Ticker: CBST** |
| 2007 Sales: $294,620 | 2007 Profits: $48,147 | **Int'l Ticker:** Int'l Exchange: |
| 2006 Sales: $194,748 | 2006 Profits: $- 376 | Employees: 489 |
| 2005 Sales: $120,645 | 2005 Profits: $-31,852 | Fiscal Year Ends: 12/31 |
| 2004 Sales: $68,071 | 2004 Profits: $-76,512 | Parent Company: |

## SALARIES/BENEFITS:

| | | | | |
|---|---|---|---|---|
| Pension Plan: | ESOP Stock Plan: | Profit Sharing: | Top Exec. Salary: $435,000 | Bonus: $348,000 |
| Savings Plan: Y | Stock Purch. Plan: Y | | Second Exec. Salary: $390,000 | Bonus: $200,070 |

## OTHER THOUGHTS:

**Apparent Women Officers or Directors**: 5
**Hot Spot for Advancement for Women/Minorities**: Y

## LOCATIONS: ("Y" = Yes)

| West: | Southwest: | Midwest: | Southeast: | Northeast: | International: |
|---|---|---|---|---|---|
| | | | | Y | |

# CURVES INTERNATIONAL INC

www.curvesinternational.com

**Industry Group Code:** 713940 **Ranks within this company's industry group:** Sales: Profits:

| **Management:** | | **Sales/Marketing:** | | **Liberal Arts:** | | **Information Systems:** | | **Professionals:** | | **Technical/Scientific:** | |
|---|---|---|---|---|---|---|---|---|---|---|---|
| Mgmt. Trainees: | | Mktg. Professionals: | Y | Gen. Writing/Editing: | | Info. Management: | Y | Finance/Accounting: | Y | Engineers, Elec.: | |
| Experienced Mgmt.: | Y | Retail Sales: | | Technical Writing: | | Software Dev.: | | Law: | Y | Engineers, Other: | |
| Int'l Business: | Y | Commercial/Industrial: | | Graphic Arts/Photog.: | Y | Hardware Dev.: | | HR/Other: | Y | Health/Lab: | |
| MBA Graduates: | Y | Sales Trainees: | | Music: | | Systems Integration: | | Training: | Y | Scientists/Research: | |
| | | Advertising Pros.: | Y | Broadcasting: | | Consulting/Other: | | Health Care: | | Petroleum/Chemicals: | |
| | | | | Other: | | | | Consulting: | | Math/Other: | |

## TYPES OF BUSINESS:

Fitness Centers
Magazine Publishing
Health Products
Travel Services
Online Information

## BRANDS/DIVISIONS/AFFILIATES:

diane Magazine
CurvesTravel.com
Curves Travel
GlobalFit

## CONTACTS: *Note: Officers with more than one job title may be intentionally listed here more than once.*

Gary Heavin, CEO/Founder
Michael Raymond, Pres.
Michael Raymond, VP-Mktg.
Becky Frusher, Comm. Specialist
Diane Heavin, Founder/Publisher-diane magazine

| **Phone:** 254-399-9285 | **Fax:** 254-399-9731 |
|---|---|
| **Toll-Free:** 800-848-1096 | |
| **Address:** 100 Ritchie Rd., Waco, TX 76712 US | |

## GROWTH PLANS/SPECIAL FEATURES:

Curves International is one of the largest fitness franchises in the world, with approximately 10,000 franchised locations in 69 countries including the U.S., Canada, Mexico, Central America, the Caribbean, Australia, New Zealand and the U.K. The company provides fitness and weight-loss facilities specifically designed for women. Curves currently provides over 4 million women with exercise and nutritional guidance. Its program provides a 30-minute circuit training workout session where all of the machines are arranged in a circle and clients can talk to each other as they move through the circuit. In addition to 30-minute workout sessions at Curves fitness facilities, the company provides a comprehensive program to educate and train women in healthy eating patterns. This program includes books, meal planners, tracking charts, weekly progress reports and other information geared toward helping women eat healthily. Through its web site, Curves provides links to other sites dedicated to educating women about the dangers of obesity and other serious diseases related to unhealthy living. The web site also features customizable online accounts, where members can access weight loss tips and meal plans. The company is also the creator of diane magazine, a quarterly magazine which features diet success stories, celebrity interviews, fitness tips and healthy recipes. The firm offers Curves Food, with branded versions of cereal, popcorn and granola bars. Curves also offers clothing, vitamins and supplements, and books. Curves recently launched its first franchise in Japan, with 2,000 more planned to open by 2010. Subsidiary Curves Travel operates mainly from CurvesTravel.com and offers deals and free booking and planning services to Curves members. In September 2007, Curves partnered with GlobalFit, a provider of healthy living benefits, to offer millions of American women a chance to enter the Curves program at a discounted rate.

## FINANCIALS: **Sales and profits are in thousands of dollars—add 000 to get the full amount. 2008 Note: Financial information for 2008 was not available for all companies at press time.**

| | | |
|---|---|---|
| 2008 Sales: $ | 2008 Profits: $ | **U.S. Stock Ticker: Private** |
| 2007 Sales: $ | 2007 Profits: $ | **Int'l Ticker:** Int'l Exchange: |
| 2006 Sales: $ | 2006 Profits: $ | Employees: 138 |
| 2005 Sales: $145,999 | 2005 Profits: $ | Fiscal Year Ends: 12/31 |
| 2004 Sales: $ | 2004 Profits: $ | Parent Company: |

## SALARIES/BENEFITS:

| | | | | |
|---|---|---|---|---|
| Pension Plan: | ESOP Stock Plan: | Profit Sharing: | Top Exec. Salary: $ | Bonus: $ |
| Savings Plan: | Stock Purch. Plan: | | Second Exec. Salary: $ | Bonus: $ |

## OTHER THOUGHTS:

**Apparent Women Officers or Directors**: 2
**Hot Spot for Advancement for Women/Minorities**: Y

## LOCATIONS: ("Y" = Yes)

| West: | Southwest: | Midwest: | Southeast: | Northeast: | International: |
|---|---|---|---|---|---|
| Y | Y | Y | Y | Y | Y |

Note: Financial information, benefits and other data can change quickly and may vary from those stated here.

# CV THERAPEUTICS INC

www.cvt.com

**Industry Group Code:** 325412 **Ranks within this company's industry group:** Sales: 23 Profits: 35

| Management: | | Sales/Marketing: | | Liberal Arts: | | Information Systems: | | Professionals: | | Technical/Scientific: | |
|---|---|---|---|---|---|---|---|---|---|---|---|
| Mgmt. Trainees: | | Mktg. Professionals: | Y | Gen. Writing/Editing: | | Info. Management: | Y | Finance/Accounting: | Y | Engineers, Elec.: | |
| Experienced Mgmt.: | Y | Retail Sales: | | Technical Writing: | Y | Software Dev.: | Y | Law: | Y | Engineers, Other: | |
| Int'l Business: | Y | Commercial/Industrial: | Y | Graphic Arts/Photog.: | | Hardware Dev.: | | HR/Other: | Y | Health/Lab: | Y |
| MBA Graduates: | Y | Sales Trainees: | Y | Music: | | Systems Integration: | | Training: | Y | Scientists/Research: | Y |
| | | Advertising Pros.: | | Broadcasting: | | Consulting/Other: | | Health Care: | Y | Petroleum/Chemicals: | |
| | | | | Other: | | | | Consulting: | | Math/Other: | Y |

## TYPES OF BUSINESS:

Drugs-Chronic Cardiovascular Diseases

## BRANDS/DIVISIONS/AFFILIATES:

CV Therapeutics Europe, Ltd.
Ranexa
Lexiscan
Adentri
CVT-6883
CVT-3619

## CONTACTS: *Note: Officers with more than one job title may be intentionally listed here more than once.*

Louis G. Lange, CEO
Daniel K. Spiegelman, CFO/Sr. VP
Diane L. Liguori, Sr. VP-Human Resources
Tricia Borga Suvari, General Counsel/Sr. VP/Sec.
David Banks, Sr. VP-Oper.
John Mohr, Sr. VP-Bus. Dev.
Luiz Belardinelli, Sr. VP-Pharmacology & Biomedical Research
Brent K. Blackburn, Sr. VP-Drug Discovery & Dev.
Carol D. Karp, Sr. VP-Regulatory Affairs, Quality & Drug Safety
Lewis J. Stuart, Sr. VP-Commercial Oper.
Louis G. Lange, Chmn.
Diane L. Liguori, Gen. Mgr.-European Union

| | |
|---|---|
| **Phone:** 650-384-8500 | **Fax:** 650-858-0390 |
| **Toll-Free:** | |
| **Address:** 3172 Porter Dr., Palo Alto, CA 94304 US | |

## GROWTH PLANS/SPECIAL FEATURES:

CV Therapeutics, Inc. is a biopharmaceutical company focused on the discovery, development and commercialization of new small molecule drugs for the treatment of cardiovascular diseases. The company currently promotes Ranexa (ranolazine extended-release tablets) as a second-line the treatment of chronic angina. The firm is also conducting additional studies of Ranexa to support broadening its product label to a first-line treatment for chronic angina. CV's other approved and marketed product is the Lexiscan (regadenoson) injection, an A2A-adenosine receptor agonist, which is used as a pharmacologic agent in myocardial perfusion imaging. Lexiscan is marketed by Astellas Pharma U.S., Inc. The firm's products that are clinical development include tecadenoson, a selective A1-adenosine receptor agonist for the potential reduction of rapid heart rate during acute atrial arrhythmias; Adentri, for the treatment of heart failure; and CVT-6883, a selective A2B-adenosine antagonist for treating cardiopulmonary diseases including inflammation and fibrosis. Drugs in preclinical development programs include CVT-3619, for diabetes and metabolic syndrome; CVT-10,216, a treatment for alcohol addiction; SC Desaturase, for obesity and metabolic syndrome; ABCA1/ApoA-I for atherosclerosis; and late INA for coronary artery disease. The company has a wholly-owned U.K. subsidiary, CV Therapeutics Europe Limited, that promotes the firm's activities in Europe.

CV Therapeutics offers its employees a 401(k) plan; an employee stock purchase plan; flexible spending accounts; a college savings plan; medical and dental insurance; an employee assistance program; an educational reimbursement program; and organic fresh fruit at the office.

## FINANCIALS: **Sales and profits are in thousands of dollars—add 000 to get the full amount. 2008 Note: Financial information for 2008 was not available for all companies at press time.**

| | | |
|---|---|---|
| 2008 Sales: $ | 2008 Profits: $ | **U.S. Stock Ticker: CVTX** |
| 2007 Sales: $82,823 | 2007 Profits: $-181,006 | **Int'l Ticker:** Int'l Exchange: |
| 2006 Sales: $36,785 | 2006 Profits: $-274,320 | Employees: 516 |
| 2005 Sales: $18,951 | 2005 Profits: $-227,995 | Fiscal Year Ends: 12/31 |
| 2004 Sales: $20,428 | 2004 Profits: $-115,083 | Parent Company: |

## SALARIES/BENEFITS:

| | | | | |
|---|---|---|---|---|
| Pension Plan: | ESOP Stock Plan: | Profit Sharing: | Top Exec. Salary: $700,000 | Bonus: $660,000 |
| Savings Plan: Y | Stock Purch. Plan: Y | | Second Exec. Salary: $350,000 | Bonus: $115,000 |

## OTHER THOUGHTS:

**Apparent Women Officers or Directors**: 3
**Hot Spot for Advancement for Women/Minorities**: Y

## LOCATIONS: ("Y" = Yes)

| West: | Southwest: | Midwest: | Southeast: | Northeast: | International: |
|---|---|---|---|---|---|
| Y | | | | | Y |

# CYBERSOURCE CORP

www.cybersource.com

**Industry Group Code:** 511201 **Ranks within this company's industry group:** Sales: 6 Profits: 6

| Management: | | Sales/Marketing: | | Liberal Arts: | | Information Systems: | | Professionals: | | Technical/Scientific: | |
|---|---|---|---|---|---|---|---|---|---|---|---|
| Mgmt. Trainees: | | Mktg. Professionals: | Y | Gen. Writing/Editing: | | Info. Management: | Y | Finance/Accounting: | Y | Engineers, Elec.: | Y |
| Experienced Mgmt.: | Y | Retail Sales: | | Technical Writing: | Y | Software Dev.: | Y | Law: | Y | Engineers, Other: | |
| Int'l Business: | Y | Commercial/Industrial: | Y | Graphic Arts/Photog.: | | Hardware Dev.: | | HR/Other: | Y | Health/Lab: | |
| MBA Graduates: | Y | Sales Trainees: | Y | Music: | | Systems Integration: | | Training: | Y | Scientists/Research: | |
| | | Advertising Pros.: | | Broadcasting: | | Consulting/Other: | | Health Care: | | Petroleum/Chemicals: | |
| | | | | Other: | | | | Consulting: | | Math/Other: | |

## TYPES OF BUSINESS:

E-Commerce Processing Services & Systems
Risk Management Solutions
Credit Card Processing
Tax Calculation
Fraud Screening
Compliance Services
Consulting Services

## BRANDS/DIVISIONS/AFFILIATES:

CyberSource Advanced
CyberSource Essentials
CyberSource Global Acquiring
CyberSource Payment Manager
CyberSource Risk Management Solutions
CyberSource Professional Services
BidPay.com
Authorize.Net Holdings, Inc.

## CONTACTS: *Note: Officers with more than one job title may be intentionally listed here more than once.*

William S. McKiernan, CEO
Scott Cruickshank, COO
Scott Cruickshank, Pres.
Steven D. Pellizzer, CFO
Michael Walsh, Sr. VP-Worldwide Sales
Greg Pappas, VP-Human Resources
Robert Ford, CTO
Robert Ford, Exec. VP-Prod. Dev.
David J. Kim, General Counsel/VP
George Barby, VP-Worldwide Oper.
Michael Orlando, VP-Strategic Markets
Steven D. Pellizzer, VP-Finance
Carolyn Brackett, VP-Channels & Alliances
Kyle Pexton, VP-Financial Analysis & Planning
Kirsten Fry-Sanchez, VP-Prod. Mgmt.
William S. McKiernan, Chmn.

**Phone:** 650-965-6000 **Fax:** 650-625-9145
**Toll-Free:** 888-330-2300
**Address:** 1295 Charleston Rd., Mountain View, CA 94043 US

## GROWTH PLANS/SPECIAL FEATURES:

CyberSource Corp. provides secure electronic payment and risk management services to organizations that sell products and services over the Internet. The company's payment systems allow e-commerce merchants to accept a range of online payment options, including credit cards, electronic checks, and global payment options. CyberSource Payment Solutions offers four product lines. CyberSource Essentials allows businesses to accept payment, mainly major credit cards, via a web site or virtual web terminal. CyberSource Global Acquiring works directly with banks to process credit cards in the U.S. and other regional payment types worldwide, acting as an intermediary for merchants. The CyberSource Payment Manager software processing platform authorizes and settles payments originating from one or more sales channels. Finally, CyberSource Advanced provides a suite of payment products designed for larger merchants. CyberSource Risk Management Solutions range from fully managed services to individual tools designed to help merchants address the growing challenge of online fraud. CyberSource's solutions are available as single components or as fully integrated systems; and can be managed in-house, outsourced, or utilizing both options. CyberSource Professional Services provides business and technical consulting services. These include technology selection and systems installation; integrating CyberSource products and services into the merchants' existing internal systems; devising merchant-specific risk management strategies and building custom reporting tools; analyzing the impact of online business on internal processes; disaster recovery planning; and security consulting. The firm processed over 1.2 billion transactions totaling over $54 billion in 2007. Recently, CyberSource signed an agreement with PayPal Europe Ltd. allowing CyberSource merchants to offer PayPal as a payment method. In November 2007, the firm acquired Authorize.Net Holdings, Inc., which provides online payment options. In December 2007, the firm ceased operations of its subsidiary, BidPay.com. In May 2008, the firm announced plans for a development center in Northern Ireland.

## FINANCIALS: **Sales and profits are in thousands of dollars—add 000 to get the full amount. 2008 Note: Financial information for 2008 was not available for all companies at press time.**

2008 Sales: $
2007 Sales: $116,999
2006 Sales: $70,250
2005 Sales: $50,511
2004 Sales: $36,709

2008 Profits: $
2007 Profits: $2,429
2006 Profits: $14,411
2005 Profits: $9,246
2004 Profits: $4,461

**U.S. Stock Ticker: CYBS**
**Int'l Ticker:** Int'l Exchange:
Employees: 496
Fiscal Year Ends: 12/31
Parent Company:

## SALARIES/BENEFITS:

Pension Plan: ESOP Stock Plan: Profit Sharing: Top Exec. Salary: $340,000 Bonus: $100,000
Savings Plan: Y Stock Purch. Plan: Y Second Exec. Salary: $311,250 Bonus: $42,500

## OTHER THOUGHTS:

**Apparent Women Officers or Directors**: 3
**Hot Spot for Advancement for Women/Minorities**: Y

## LOCATIONS: ("Y" = Yes)

| West: | Southwest: | Midwest: | Southeast: | Northeast: | International: |
|---|---|---|---|---|---|
| Y | | | | | Y |

# DAKTRONICS INC

www.daktronics.com

**Industry Group Code:** 334310 **Ranks within this company's industry group:** Sales: 1 Profits: 1

| Management: | | Sales/Marketing: | | Liberal Arts: | | Information Systems: | | Professionals: | | Technical/Scientific: | |
|---|---|---|---|---|---|---|---|---|---|---|---|
| Mgmt. Trainees: | | Mktg. Professionals: | Y | Gen. Writing/Editing: | Y | Info. Management: | Y | Finance/Accounting: | Y | Engineers, Elec.: | Y |
| Experienced Mgmt.: | Y | Retail Sales: | | Technical Writing: | Y | Software Dev.: | Y | Law: | Y | Engineers, Other: | |
| Int'l Business: | Y | Commercial/Industrial: | Y | Graphic Arts/Photog.: | Y | Hardware Dev.: | Y | HR/Other: | Y | Health/Lab: | |
| MBA Graduates: | Y | Sales Trainees: | Y | Music: | | Systems Integration: | Y | Training: | Y | Scientists/Research: | |
| | | Advertising Pros.: | Y | Broadcasting: | | Consulting/Other: | | Health Care: | | Petroleum/Chemicals: | |
| | | | | Other: | | | | Consulting: | | Math/Other: | Y |

## TYPES OF BUSINESS:

Electronic Advertising Displays
Programmable Display Systems
Scoreboards
Support Services & Software
Content Creation
Display Rental
Research & Development
Sound Systems

## BRANDS/DIVISIONS/AFFILIATES:

ProStar
ProAd
Galaxy
Vanguard
AllSport
European Timing Systems
Dodge Electronics
Lucas Oil Stadium

## CONTACTS: *Note: Officers with more than one job title may be intentionally listed here more than once.*

James B. Morgan, CEO
James B. Morgan, COO
James B. Morgan, Pres.
William R. Retterath, CFO
Frank Kurtenbach, VP-Sales
Carla S. Gatzke, Corp. Sec.
William R. Retterath, Treas.
Bradley T. Wiemann, VP
Reece A. Kurtenbach, VP
Aelred J. Kurtenbach, Chmn.

**Phone:** 605-692-0200 **Fax:** 605-697-4700
**Toll-Free:** 800-843-5843
**Address:** 201 Daktronics Dr., Brookings, SD 57006 US

## GROWTH PLANS/SPECIAL FEATURES:

Daktronics, Inc. is a leading supplier of electronic scoreboards, computer-programmable display systems, large video display systems and related software and services for sport, business and transportation applications. Its products include a complete line of display products, from small indoor and outdoor scoreboards and electronic displays, to large, multi-million-dollar video display systems, as well as related control and timing systems and professional services. Daktronics designs, markets, manufactures, installs and services complete integrated systems that display real-time data, graphics, animation and video. Services provided by the company include project management; on-site installation and event support; content creation; product maintenance; marketing assistance; and display rentals. Daktronics invests a significant portion of its research and development resources into full-color LED-based displays and has continued to improve and further develop its AllSport, TuffSport, OmniSport, ProStar, ProTour, ProAd, Galaxy and Vanguard systems. The firm's integrated sound systems are offered under the Sportsound brand, and rigging systems and hoists, for theaters, stadiums and other facilities, are offered under the Vortek brand. Products range in cost from small scoreboards under $1,000 to large complex systems priced in excess of $10 million. The firm's installations can be found all over the world. In January 2008, the company announced that it would provide an $11 million integrated video and scoring system for Lucas Oil Stadium in Indianapolis, Indiana. The stadium, home to the NFL's Indianapolis Colts, was officially opened in August 2008. In May 2008, Daktronics announced that it would create a centralized unit to handle its field service operations, a function that was formerly organized under the firm's various business units.

The company offers its employees health and dental plans; life, accident and disability insurance; maternity leave; continuing education reimbursement; training program sabbaticals; and a discounted computer purchase plan.

## FINANCIALS: **Sales and profits are in thousands of dollars—add 000 to get the full amount. 2008 Note: Financial information for 2008 was not available for all companies at press time.**

| | | |
|---|---|---|
| 2008 Sales: $ | 2008 Profits: $ | **U.S. Stock Ticker: DAKT** |
| 2007 Sales: $433,201 | 2007 Profits: $24,427 | **Int'l Ticker:** Int'l Exchange: |
| 2006 Sales: $309,370 | 2006 Profits: $20,961 | Employees: 2,300 |
| 2005 Sales: $230,346 | 2005 Profits: $15,660 | Fiscal Year Ends: 4/30 |
| 2004 Sales: $209,907 | 2004 Profits: $17,727 | Parent Company: |

## SALARIES/BENEFITS:

| | | | | |
|---|---|---|---|---|
| Pension Plan: | ESOP Stock Plan: | Profit Sharing: | Top Exec. Salary: $301,788 | Bonus: $129,018 |
| Savings Plan: Y | Stock Purch. Plan: | | Second Exec. Salary: $188,176 | Bonus: $57,184 |

## OTHER THOUGHTS:

**Apparent Women Officers or Directors:** 2
**Hot Spot for Advancement for Women/Minorities:**

## LOCATIONS: ("Y" = Yes)

| West: | Southwest: | Midwest: | Southeast: | Northeast: | International: |
|---|---|---|---|---|---|
| | | Y | Y | | Y |

# DANNON COMPANY INC (THE)

www.dannon.com

**Industry Group Code:** 311500 **Ranks within this company's industry group:** Sales: 2 Profits:

| Management: | | Sales/Marketing: | | Liberal Arts: | | Information Systems: | | Professionals: | | Technical/Scientific: | |
|---|---|---|---|---|---|---|---|---|---|---|---|
| Mgmt. Trainees: | | Mktg. Professionals: | Y | Gen. Writing/Editing: | | Info. Management: | Y | Finance/Accounting: | Y | Engineers, Elec.: | |
| Experienced Mgmt.: | Y | Retail Sales: | | Technical Writing: | | Software Dev.: | | Law: | Y | Engineers, Other: | |
| Int'l Business: | | Commercial/Industrial: | Y | Graphic Arts/Photog.: | | Hardware Dev.: | | HR/Other: | Y | Health/Lab: | |
| MBA Graduates: | Y | Sales Trainees: | Y | Music: | | Systems Integration: | | Training: | Y | Scientists/Research: | |
| | | Advertising Pros.: | Y | Broadcasting: | | Consulting/Other: | | Health Care: | | Petroleum/Chemicals: | |
| | | | | Other: | | | | Consulting: | | Math/Other: | |

## TYPES OF BUSINESS:

Dairy Products, Manufacturing
Yogurt Products
Nutrition Education Programs
Nutrition Professionals Training Program

## BRANDS/DIVISIONS/AFFILIATES:

Groupe Danone SA
DanActive
Danimals
Frusion
La Creme
Dannon Institute
Activia
Dan-o-nino

## CONTACTS: *Note: Officers with more than one job title may be intentionally listed here more than once.*

Juan C. Dalto, CEO
Juan C. Dalto, Pres.
Antoine Remy, CFO
Mark J. Gesti, VP-Mktg.
Tony Cicio, VP-Human Resources
Albe Wendt, VP-R&D
Jeff Hutchinson, CIO
Tim Reagan, VP-Mfg.
Ken Strick, General Counsel/VP-Legal Affairs
Eric O'Toole, VP-Bus. Dev.
Philippe Caradec, VP-Regulatory & Corp. Affairs
Antoine Remy, VP-Finance
Todd Brown, VP-Quality Assurance & Food Safety
Juan C. Dalto, VP-Dairy North America
Paul Gardner, VP-Sourcing & Supplier Dev.
Philippe Domenge, VP-Industrial
Juan C. Dalto, Chmn.
Paul Messina, VP-Supply Chain

**Phone:** 914-872-8400 **Fax:** 914-872-1565
**Toll-Free:** 877-326-6668
**Address:** 100 Hillside Ave., 3rd Fl., White Plains, NY 10603 US

## GROWTH PLANS/SPECIAL FEATURES:

The Dannon Company, Inc., a subsidiary of French company Groupe Danone S.A., produces and distributes yogurt products in the U.S. Facilities in Ohio, Texas and Utah produce yogurt and light yogurt; DanActive, an immune system booster containing beneficial live cultures; Danup, a smooth-blended dairy beverage; Danimals calcium-fortified yogurt and Dan-o-nino calcium, protein and Vitamin D-fortified yogurt, both of which are marketed for kids; Frusion fruit and yogurt smoothies; La Creme dessert yogurt; Activia, the first probiotic yogurt available in America clinically proven to regulate the digestive system; and Dannon All Natural, a low-fat yogurt made without artificial ingredients. The firm has a product line of almost 100 different flavors, styles and sizes and produces roughly 6 million cups of yogurt per day, with the company's Ohio plant producing around 230,000 cups of yogurt per hour. In addition to its production operations, the company founded the Dannon Institute in 1997. The Dannon Institute is a nonprofit organization focused on promoting research, education and communication in the area of nutrition, including educating children on the importance of a well-balanced diet. The Institute also provides training to nutrition professionals through its Nutrition Leadership Institute. The Institute's board of directors and advisory council are composed of nutrition scientists, who guide the development of new programs and educational material on nutrition. Dannon has also partnered with the Alliance for a Healthier Generation in setting standards for healthy snacks, part of a venture aimed at mitigating childhood obesity in America.

## FINANCIALS: **Sales and profits are in thousands of dollars—add 000 to get the full amount. 2008 Note: Financial information for 2008 was not available for all companies at press time.**

| | | |
|---|---|---|
| 2008 Sales: $ | 2008 Profits: $ | **U.S. Stock Ticker: Subsidiary** |
| 2007 Sales: $203,100 | 2007 Profits: $ | **Int'l Ticker:** Int'l Exchange: |
| 2006 Sales: $ | 2006 Profits: $ | Employees: 900 |
| 2005 Sales: $ | 2005 Profits: $ | Fiscal Year Ends: 12/31 |
| 2004 Sales: $ | 2004 Profits: $ | Parent Company: GROUPE DANONE SA |

## SALARIES/BENEFITS:

| | | | | |
|---|---|---|---|---|
| Pension Plan: | ESOP Stock Plan: | Profit Sharing: | Top Exec. Salary: $ | Bonus: $ |
| Savings Plan: | Stock Purch. Plan: | | Second Exec. Salary: $ | Bonus: $ |

## OTHER THOUGHTS:

**Apparent Women Officers or Directors:**
**Hot Spot for Advancement for Women/Minorities:** Y

## LOCATIONS: ("Y" = Yes)

| West: | Southwest: | Midwest: | Southeast: | Northeast: | International: |
|---|---|---|---|---|---|
| Y | Y | Y | | Y | |

# DARLING INTERNATIONAL INC

**www.darlingii.com**

**Industry Group Code:** 311613 **Ranks within this company's industry group:** Sales: 1 Profits: 1

| **Management:** | | **Sales/Marketing:** | | **Liberal Arts:** | | **Information Systems:** | | **Professionals:** | | **Technical/Scientific:** | |
|---|---|---|---|---|---|---|---|---|---|---|---|
| Mgmt. Trainees: | | Mktg. Professionals: | | Gen. Writing/Editing: | | Info. Management: | Y | Finance/Accounting: | Y | Engineers, Elec.: | |
| Experienced Mgmt.: | Y | Retail Sales: | | Technical Writing: | | Software Dev.: | | Law: | Y | Engineers, Other: | |
| Int'l Business: | Y | Commercial/Industrial: | Y | Graphic Arts/Photog.: | | Hardware Dev.: | | HR/Other: | Y | Health/Lab: | |
| MBA Graduates: | Y | Sales Trainees: | Y | Music: | | Systems Integration: | | Training: | Y | Scientists/Research: | |
| | | Advertising Pros.: | | Broadcasting: | | Consulting/Other: | | Health Care: | | Petroleum/Chemicals: | |
| | | | | Other: | | | | Consulting: | | Math/Other: | |

## TYPES OF BUSINESS:

Rendering & Meat Byproduct Processing
Grease Collection Services
Grease Trap Maintenance Services

## BRANDS/DIVISIONS/AFFILIATES:

Darling National, LLC

## CONTACTS: *Note: Officers with more than one job title may be intentionally listed here more than once.*

Randall C. Stuewe, CEO
John O. Muse, CFO/Exec. VP
Robert H. Seemann, Exec. VP-Sales & Svcs.
John O. Muse, Exec. VP-Admin.
John F. Sterling, General Counsel/Exec. VP/Sec.
John O. Muse, Exec. VP-Finance
Neil Katchen, Exec. VP/COO-Retail & Svcs.
Mitchell Kilanowski, Exec. VP-Commodities
Mark A. Myers, Exec. VP/COO-Midwest Rendering
Randall C. Stuewe, Chmn.

**Phone:** 972-717-0300 **Fax:** 972-717-1588
**Toll-Free:**
**Address:** 251 O'Connor Ridge Blvd., Ste. 300, Irving, TX 75038 US

## GROWTH PLANS/SPECIAL FEATURES:

Darling International, Inc. is a provider of rendering, recycling and recovery solutions to the nation's food industry. It collects and recycles animal byproducts and used cooking oil from food service establishments and provides grease trap cleaning services to many of the same establishments. The company processes these materials at 39 facilities located throughout the U.S. into finished products such as protein (primarily meat and bone meal), tallow (primarily bleachable fancy tallow), yellow grease and hides. The firm then sells these products nationally and internationally, primarily to producers of oleo-chemicals, bio-fuels, soaps, pet foods, leather goods and livestock feed for use as ingredients in their products or for further processing. Darling International operates in two segments: rendering, the core business of turning inedible food byproducts from meat and poultry processors into ingredients and fats for other industrial applications; and restaurant services, a group focused on growing the grease collection business and grease collection equipment sales while expanding the line of services, which includes grease trap servicing and the National Service Center (NSC), offered to food service establishments and food processors. The NSC schedules services such as fat and bone and used cooking oil collection as well as trap cleaning for contracted customers using the company's resources or third party providers. The firm uses a fleet of approximately 970 trucks and tractor-trailers to collect raw materials from over 115,000 food service establishments, butcher shops, grocery stores and independent meat and poultry processors. Subsidiaries include Darling National, LLC. In August 2008, the company acquired the assets of API Recycling's used cooking oil collection business.

## FINANCIALS: **Sales and profits are in thousands of dollars—add 000 to get the full amount. 2008 Note: Financial information for 2008 was not available for all companies at press time.**

| | | |
|---|---|---|
| 2008 Sales: $ | 2008 Profits: $ | **U.S. Stock Ticker: DAR** |
| 2007 Sales: $645,313 | 2007 Profits: $45,533 | **Int'l Ticker:** Int'l Exchange: |
| 2006 Sales: $406,990 | 2006 Profits: $5,107 | Employees: 1,880 |
| 2005 Sales: $308,867 | 2005 Profits: $7,741 | Fiscal Year Ends: 12/31 |
| 2004 Sales: $320,229 | 2004 Profits: $13,892 | Parent Company: |

## SALARIES/BENEFITS:

| | | | | |
|---|---|---|---|---|
| Pension Plan: Y | ESOP Stock Plan: | Profit Sharing: | Top Exec. Salary: $600,000 | Bonus: $1,702,905 |
| Savings Plan: Y | Stock Purch. Plan: | | Second Exec. Salary: $427,215 | Bonus: $776,757 |

## OTHER THOUGHTS:

**Apparent Women Officers or Directors**: 1
**Hot Spot for Advancement for Women/Minorities**:

## LOCATIONS: ("Y" = Yes)

| West: | Southwest: | Midwest: | Southeast: | Northeast: | International: |
|---|---|---|---|---|---|
| Y | Y | Y | Y | Y | Y |

# DATASCOPE CORP

www.datascope.com

**Industry Group Code:** 339113 **Ranks within this company's industry group:** Sales: 8 Profits: 10

| Management: | | Sales/Marketing: | | Liberal Arts: | | Information Systems: | | Professionals: | | Technical/Scientific: | |
|---|---|---|---|---|---|---|---|---|---|---|---|
| Mgmt. Trainees: | | Mktg. Professionals: | Y | Gen. Writing/Editing: | | Info. Management: | Y | Finance/Accounting: | Y | Engineers, Elec.: | Y |
| Experienced Mgmt.: | Y | Retail Sales: | | Technical Writing: | Y | Software Dev.: | Y | Law: | Y | Engineers, Other: | Y |
| Int'l Business: | Y | Commercial/Industrial: | Y | Graphic Arts/Photog.: | | Hardware Dev.: | Y | HR/Other: | Y | Health/Lab: | Y |
| MBA Graduates: | Y | Sales Trainees: | Y | Music: | | Systems Integration: | Y | Training: | Y | Scientists/Research: | Y |
| | | Advertising Pros.: | | Broadcasting: | | Consulting/Other: | | Health Care: | Y | Petroleum/Chemicals: | |
| | | | | Other: | | | | Consulting: | | Math/Other: | Y |

## TYPES OF BUSINESS:

Equipment-Intra-Aortic Pumps & Catheters
Cardiac Assist Products
Patient Monitoring Systems
Collagen Products
Vascular Products

## BRANDS/DIVISIONS/AFFILIATES:

Clearglide
InterVascular, Inc.
Panorama Patient Monitoring Network
Anestar Plus Anesthesia Delivery System
Artema Medical AB
Datascope Japan K.K.

## CONTACTS: *Note: Officers with more than one job title may be intentionally listed here more than once.*

Lawrence Saper, CEO
Antonino Laudani, COO/VP
Henry M. Scaramelli, CFO/VP
James L. Cooper, VP-Human Resources
Timothy J. Krauskopf, VP-Regulatory & Clinical Affairs
Boris Leschinsky, VP-Tech.
Fred Adelman, Chief Acct. Officer/VP
Nicholas E. Barker, VP-Corp. Design
Robert O. Cathcart, VP/Pres., Interventional Prod. Div.
Lawrence Saper, Chmn.

| | |
|---|---|
| **Phone:** 201-391-8100 | **Fax:** 201-307-5400 |
| **Toll-Free:** | |
| **Address:** 14 Phillips Pkwy., Montvale, NJ 07645-9998 US | |

## GROWTH PLANS/SPECIAL FEATURES:

Datascope Corp. develops, manufactures and markets proprietary products for clinical health care markets in interventional cardiology and radiology, cardiovascular and vascular surgery, anesthesiology, emergency medicine and critical care. Cardiac assist products include intra-aortic balloon pump, used principally to treat cardiac shock, acute heart failure and irregular heart rhythms; catheter technologies; and endoscopic vessel harvesting devices, enabling less-invasive techniques for coronary artery bypass grafting. Datascope manufactures and markets physiological monitors designed to provide for patient safety and management of patient care, including the Panorama Patient Monitoring Network as well as the Anestar Plus Anesthesia Delivery System. Datascope's InterVascular, Inc. subsidiary markets and sells a proprietary line of knitted and woven polyester vascular grafts, patches and interventional products for reconstructive vascular and cardiovascular surgery. Datascope is planning to exit the vascular closure market and phase out its interventional products business. All of the company's products are sold through direct sales representatives in the U.S. and a combination of direct sales representatives and independent distributors in international markets. In February 2007, Datascope announced the sale of its ProGuide Chronic Dialysis Catheter to Merit Medical Systems, Inc. for $3 million. In June 2007, the company acquired Artema Medical AB, a Swedish manufacturer of proprietary gas analyzers. In October 2007, the firm announced the transfer of its intra-aortic balloon pump business in Japan to its subsidiary Datascope Japan K.K., at the end of the 2007. In May 2008, Datascope sold its patient monitoring division to a subsidiary of Mindray Medical International Ltd. In June 2008, the company acquired the peripheral vascular stent business of the Sorin Group.

Datascope offers its employees flexible spending accounts, an assistance program, tuition assistance, a referral program, in-house training, work life referral services, a matching gift program, a credit union membership, casual attire and medical and dental insurance.

## FINANCIALS: **Sales and profits are in thousands of dollars—add 000 to get the full amount. 2008 Note: Financial information for 2008 was not available for all companies at press time.**

| | | |
|---|---|---|
| 2008 Sales: $ | 2008 Profits: $ | **U.S. Stock Ticker: DSCP** |
| 2007 Sales: $378,800 | 2007 Profits: $17,465 | **Int'l Ticker:** Int'l Exchange: |
| 2006 Sales: $373,000 | 2006 Profits: $25,843 | Employees: 1,200 |
| 2005 Sales: $352,700 | 2005 Profits: $14,646 | Fiscal Year Ends: 6/30 |
| 2004 Sales: $343,300 | 2004 Profits: $23,908 | Parent Company: |

## SALARIES/BENEFITS:

| | | | | |
|---|---|---|---|---|
| Pension Plan: | ESOP Stock Plan: | Profit Sharing: | Top Exec. Salary: $1,000,000 | Bonus: $ |
| Savings Plan: Y | Stock Purch. Plan: Y | | Second Exec. Salary: $371,596 | Bonus: $183,165 |

## OTHER THOUGHTS:

**Apparent Women Officers or Directors**:
**Hot Spot for Advancement for Women/Minorities**:

## LOCATIONS: ("Y" = Yes)

| West: | Southwest: | Midwest: | Southeast: | Northeast: | International: |
|---|---|---|---|---|---|
| | | | | Y | Y |

# DEI HOLDINGS INC

www.directed.com

**Industry Group Code:** 334290 **Ranks within this company's industry group:** Sales: 1 Profits: 2

| Management: | | Sales/Marketing: | | Liberal Arts: | | Information Systems: | | Professionals: | | Technical/Scientific: | |
|---|---|---|---|---|---|---|---|---|---|---|---|
| Mgmt. Trainees: | | Mktg. Professionals: | Y | Gen. Writing/Editing: | | Info. Management: | Y | Finance/Accounting: | Y | Engineers, Elec.: | Y |
| Experienced Mgmt.: | Y | Retail Sales: | | Technical Writing: | Y | Software Dev.: | Y | Law: | Y | Engineers, Other: | Y |
| Int'l Business: | Y | Commercial/Industrial: | Y | Graphic Arts/Photog.: | | Hardware Dev.: | Y | HR/Other: | Y | Health/Lab: | |
| MBA Graduates: | Y | Sales Trainees: | Y | Music: | | Systems Integration: | Y | Training: | Y | Scientists/Research: | |
| | | Advertising Pros.: | Y | Broadcasting: | | Consulting/Other: | | Health Care: | | Petroleum/Chemicals: | |
| | | | | Other: | | | | Consulting: | | Math/Other: | |

## TYPES OF BUSINESS:

Electronic Equipment-Stolen Vehicle Recovery
Remote Start Systems
Car Audio Equipment
Amplifiers
Speakers
Signal Processors
Mobile Video Systems
GPS Tracking Systems

## BRANDS/DIVISIONS/AFFILIATES:

Viper
Clifford
Orion
a/d/s/
Directed Video
Automate
Polk Audio
Trilogix Electronics Systems, Inc.

## CONTACTS: *Note: Officers with more than one job title may be intentionally listed here more than once.*

Jim Minarik, CEO
Jim Minarik, Pres.
Kevin Duffy, CFO/Exec. VP
Glenn R. Busse, Sr. VP-Sales & Customer Care
Alan P.Heim, VP-Human Resources
Michael N. Smith, VP-MIS
Mark Rutledge, Sr. VP-Prod. Dev.
Mark Rutledge, Sr. VP-Eng.
K. C. Bean, General Counsel/Sec/VP
Michael N. Smith, VP-Oper.
Richard J. Hirshberg, Sr. VP-Finance & Treas.
Sanford M. Gross, Chief Strategist-Home Audio
Troy D. Templeton, Chmn.

**Phone:** 760-598-6200 **Fax:** 760-598-6400
**Toll-Free:** 800-876-0800
**Address:** 1 Viper Way, Vista, CA 92081 US

## GROWTH PLANS/SPECIAL FEATURES:

DEI Holdings, Inc. (DEI) is one of the largest aftermarket vehicle security and remote start companies in the world. The firm is also active in the GPS tracking system, satellite radio and car, home and mobile audio and video equipment markets. DEI was the first company to develop a fully customized, integrated circuit-controlled security system; a personal computer programmable system; and a keychain transmitter with a super-high-frequency quarter-mile range. The firm's security systems include Viper, Clifford, Python, Sidwinder, Avital, Rattler, Hornet, Wasp and Valet. Security system accessories include transmitters, sirens and voice modules, LEDs and sensors. The company's audio offerings include amplifiers, subwoofers, speakers, signal processors, wires and accessories, and are marketed under the Orion, Precision Power, Directed Audio, a/d/s/ and Xtreme brand names. DEI has exclusive distribution rights for certain SIRIUS-brand satellite radio receivers and products. Video equipment is sold as Directed Video and Automate. DEI has sales contracts with retail outlets Best Buy, Circuit City, Magnolia Audio Video and Audio Express. International sales, spread across 73 countries, account for over 14% of the firm's revenue. In May 2007, DEI acquired Trilogix Electronic Systems, Inc., a company that specializes in remote start systems. In April 2008, DE extended its distribution rights agreement with SIRIUS through January 2009. In June 2008, the company changed its name from Directed Electronics, Inc. to DEI Holdings, Inc., in an effort to align the company's corporate structure with its daily operations.

## FINANCIALS: **Sales and profits are in thousands of dollars—add 000 to get the full amount. 2008 Note: Financial information for 2008 was not available for all companies at press time.**

| | | |
|---|---|---|
| 2008 Sales: $ | 2008 Profits: $ | **U.S. Stock Ticker: DEIX** |
| 2007 Sales: $401,140 | 2007 Profits: $-139,968 | **Int'l Ticker:** Int'l Exchange: |
| 2006 Sales: $437,778 | 2006 Profits: $21,009 | Employees: 581 |
| 2005 Sales: $304,558 | 2005 Profits: $-5,137 | Fiscal Year Ends: 12/31 |
| 2004 Sales: $189,869 | 2004 Profits: $13,962 | Parent Company: |

## SALARIES/BENEFITS:

| | | | | |
|---|---|---|---|---|
| Pension Plan: | ESOP Stock Plan: | Profit Sharing: | Top Exec. Salary: $550,000 | Bonus: $ |
| Savings Plan: Y | Stock Purch. Plan: | | Second Exec. Salary: $243,077 | Bonus: $ |

## OTHER THOUGHTS:

**Apparent Women Officers or Directors:**
**Hot Spot for Advancement for Women/Minorities:**

## LOCATIONS: ("Y" = Yes)

| West: | Southwest: | Midwest: | Southeast: | Northeast: | International: |
|---|---|---|---|---|---|
| Y | | | | Y | Y |

# DELPHI FINANCIAL GROUP INC

www.delphifin.com

**Industry Group Code:** 524114A **Ranks within this company's industry group:** Sales: 1 Profits: 1

| Management: | | Sales/Marketing: | | Liberal Arts: | | Information Systems: | | Professionals: | | Technical/Scientific: | |
|---|---|---|---|---|---|---|---|---|---|---|---|
| Mgmt. Trainees: | | Mktg. Professionals: | Y | Gen. Writing/Editing: | Y | Info. Management: | Y | Finance/Accounting: | Y | Engineers, Elec.: | |
| Experienced Mgmt.: | Y | Retail Sales: | | Technical Writing: | | Software Dev.: | | Law: | Y | Engineers, Other: | |
| Int'l Business: | Y | Commercial/Industrial: | Y | Graphic Arts/Photog.: | | Hardware Dev.: | | HR/Other: | Y | Health/Lab: | Y |
| MBA Graduates: | Y | Sales Trainees: | | Music: | | Systems Integration: | | Training: | Y | Scientists/Research: | |
| | | Advertising Pros.: | | Broadcasting: | | Consulting/Other: | | Health Care: | Y | Petroleum/Chemicals: | |
| | | | | Other: | | | | Consulting: | | Math/Other: | Y |

## TYPES OF BUSINESS:

Insurance-Supplemental & Specialty Health
Employee Absence Management
Workers' Compensation
Life, Disability & Accident Insurance
Annuities

## BRANDS/DIVISIONS/AFFILIATES:

Reliance Standard Life Insurance Company
First Reliance Standard Life Insurance Company
Safety National Casualty Corporation
Safety First Insurance Company
Matrix Absence Management, Inc.
Matrix Absence Solutions

## CONTACTS:

*Note: Officers with more than one job title may be intentionally listed here more than once.*

Robert Rosenkranz, CEO
Donald A. Sherman, COO
Donald A. Sherman, Pres.
Chad W. Coulter, General Counsel/Sr. VP/Corp. Sec.
Thomas W. Burghart, VP/Treas.
Lawrence E. Daurelle, CEO/Pres., Reliance Standard Life Insurance
Robert M. Smith, Jr., Exec. VP
Robert Rosenkranz, Chmn.

**Phone:** 302-478-5142 **Fax:** 302-427-7663
**Toll-Free:**
**Address:** 1105 N. Market St., Ste. 1230, Wilmington, DE 19899 US

## GROWTH PLANS/SPECIAL FEATURES:

Delphi Financial Group, Inc. is a holding company whose subsidiaries provide integrated employee benefit services primarily to small - to mid-sized employers. The firm provides the following related insurance coverages: long- and short-term disability; excess and primary workers' compensation; group life; travel accident; and dental. Delphi's asset accumulation business emphasizes individual fixed annuity products. The company offers its products and services in all 50 states, Washington, D.C. and Canada. One of the group's primary operating subsidiaries is Reliance Standard Life Insurance Company and its subsidiary, First Reliance Standard Life Insurance Company. These companies underwrite a portfolio of group life, disability and accident insurance products targeted to the employee benefits market, as well as marketing fixed annuities to individuals and groups. Delphi also operates Safety National Casualty, which provides excess workers' compensation insurance, self-insurance bonds, alternative risk services to the self-insured market; and Matrix Absence Management which offers integrated disability and absence management services to the employee benefits market across the U.S. Delphi's group employee benefits products are sold to employer groups primarily through independent brokers and agents. The company's product offerings include the Integrated Employee Benefit program; a suite of elective benefits chosen by individual employees; and an employee paid coverage for hourly and part-time members.

## FINANCIALS:

**Sales and profits are in thousands of dollars—add 000 to get the full amount. 2008 Note: Financial information for 2008 was not available for all companies at press time.**

| | | |
|---|---|---|
| 2008 Sales: $ | 2008 Profits: $ | **U.S. Stock Ticker: DFG** |
| 2007 Sales: $1,570,619 | 2007 Profits: $164,512 | **Int'l Ticker:** Int'l Exchange: |
| 2006 Sales: $1,411,591 | 2006 Profits: $142,068 | Employees: 1,551 |
| 2005 Sales: $1,222,783 | 2005 Profits: $113,334 | Fiscal Year Ends: 12/31 |
| 2004 Sales: $1,055,831 | 2004 Profits: $123,543 | Parent Company: |

## SALARIES/BENEFITS:

| | | | | |
|---|---|---|---|---|
| Pension Plan: | ESOP Stock Plan: | Profit Sharing: | Top Exec. Salary: $792,750 | Bonus: $1,200,000 |
| Savings Plan: | Stock Purch. Plan: Y | | Second Exec. Salary: $792,750 | Bonus: $840,000 |

## OTHER THOUGHTS:

**Apparent Women Officers or Directors:**
**Hot Spot for Advancement for Women/Minorities:**

## LOCATIONS: ("Y" = Yes)

| West: | Southwest: | Midwest: | Southeast: | Northeast: | International: |
|---|---|---|---|---|---|
| Y | Y | Y | Y | Y | Y |

# DENBURY RESOURCES INC

www.denbury.com

**Industry Group Code:** 211111 **Ranks within this company's industry group:** Sales: 11 Profits: 7

| Management: | | Sales/Marketing: | | Liberal Arts: | | Information Systems: | | Professionals: | | Technical/Scientific: | |
|---|---|---|---|---|---|---|---|---|---|---|---|
| Mgmt. Trainees: | | Mktg. Professionals: | Y | Gen. Writing/Editing: | | Info. Management: | Y | Finance/Accounting: | Y | Engineers, Elec.: | |
| Experienced Mgmt.: | Y | Retail Sales: | | Technical Writing: | | Software Dev.: | | Law: | Y | Engineers, Other: | Y |
| Int'l Business: | Y | Commercial/Industrial: | Y | Graphic Arts/Photog.: | | Hardware Dev.: | | HR/Other: | Y | Health/Lab: | |
| MBA Graduates: | Y | Sales Trainees: | | Music: | | Systems Integration: | | Training: | Y | Scientists/Research: | |
| | | Advertising Pros.: | | Broadcasting: | | Consulting/Other: | | Health Care: | | Petroleum/Chemicals: | Y |
| | | | | Other: | | | | Consulting: | | Math/Other: | |

## TYPES OF BUSINESS:

Oil & Gas Exploration & Production
CO2 Reserves
CO2 Pipeline

## BRANDS/DIVISIONS/AFFILIATES:

## CONTACTS:

*Note: Officers with more than one job title may be intentionally listed here more than once.*

Gareth Roberts, CEO
Gareth Roberts, Pres.
Phil Rykhoek, CFO/Sr. VP
Dan E. Cole, VP-Mktg.
Jerome C. Ballard, VP-Human Resources
Phil Rykhoek, Corp. Sec.
Robert Cornelius, Sr. VP-Oper.
Bradley A. Cox, VP-Bus. Dev.
Laurie Burkes, Mgr.-Investor Rel.
Phil Rykhoek, Treas.
Ronald T. Evans, Sr. VP-Reservoir Eng.
Ray Dubuisson, VP-Land
Charlie Gibson, VP-Production
Mark Allen, Chief Acct. Officer/VP
Ronald Greene, Chmn.

**Phone:** 972-673-2000 **Fax:** 972-673-2150
**Toll-Free:**
**Address:** 5100 Tennyson Pkwy., Ste. 300, Plano, TX 75024 US

## GROWTH PLANS/SPECIAL FEATURES:

Denbury Resources, Inc., headquartered in Plano, Texas, is an oil and gas acquisition, development, operation and exploration company with operations primarily in Louisiana, Mississippi, Alabama and Texas. The company is one of the largest oil and natural gas operators in Mississippi, and owns some of the leading reserves of sequestered CO2, used for tertiary oil recovery east of the Mississippi. CO2 injection is one of the most efficient ways of extraction crude oil, although it is not often practiced due to limited supplies of CO2, which is a resource that is typically centralized in West Texas and Mississippi. The firm utilizes its reserves at the Jackson Dome field to supply CO2 to its planned projects through a network of pipelines, and seeks to achieve its returns on capital through further development of its carbon dioxide and tertiary flooding operations. The company has recently divided its operations into five phases. Phase I is in Southwest Mississippi, and includes several fields along its 183-mile CO2 pipeline, including the fields in Little Creek, Mallalieu, McComb and Brookhaven. Phase II includes Eucutta, Soso, Martinville and Heidelberg Fields, all in Eastern Mississippi. The company runs its Phase III operations in Tinsley Field, Northwest of Jackson Dome in Mississippi. Phase IV includes the Cranfield and Lake St. John Fields, located, respectively, in Mississippi and Louisiana. Phase V is Delhi Field, located in Louisiana. The firm has estimated proven reserves of 153 million barrels of oil equivalent (about 106 million barrels oil and 278,000 million cubic feet natural gas). In October 2007, the company agreed to sell its Louisiana natural gas assets to a privately held company for $180 million. In September 2008, the company agreed to purchase Hastings Field, a potential tertiary oil field near Houston, Texas, from a subsidiary of Venoco, Inc.

## FINANCIALS:

**Sales and profits are in thousands of dollars—add 000 to get the full amount. 2008 Note: Financial information for 2008 was not available for all companies at press time.**

2008 Sales: $
2007 Sales: $971,950
2006 Sales: $732,312
2005 Sales: $560,392
2004 Sales: $382,972

2008 Profits: $
2007 Profits: $253,147
2006 Profits: $202,457
2005 Profits: $166,471
2004 Profits: $82,448

**U.S. Stock Ticker: DNR**
**Int'l Ticker:** Int'l Exchange:
Employees: 686
Fiscal Year Ends: 12/31
Parent Company:

## SALARIES/BENEFITS:

Pension Plan: ESOP Stock Plan: Profit Sharing: Top Exec. Salary: $456,413 Bonus: $469,796
Savings Plan: Y Stock Purch. Plan: Y Second Exec. Salary: $311,230 Bonus: $320,356

## OTHER THOUGHTS:

**Apparent Women Officers or Directors**: 1
**Hot Spot for Advancement for Women/Minorities**:

## LOCATIONS: ("Y" = Yes)

| West: | Southwest: | Midwest: | Southeast: | Northeast: | International: |
|---|---|---|---|---|---|
| | Y | | Y | | |

# DIALYSIS CORPORATION OF AMERICA

www.dialysiscorporation.com

**Industry Group Code:** 621490 **Ranks within this company's industry group:** Sales: 7 Profits: 5

| Management: | | Sales/Marketing: | | Liberal Arts: | | Information Systems: | | Professionals: | | Technical/Scientific: | |
|---|---|---|---|---|---|---|---|---|---|---|---|
| Mgmt. Trainees: | | Mktg. Professionals: | Y | Gen. Writing/Editing: | | Info. Management: | Y | Finance/Accounting: | Y | Engineers, Elec.: | |
| Experienced Mgmt.: | Y | Retail Sales: | | Technical Writing: | Y | Software Dev.: | | Law: | Y | Engineers, Other: | |
| Int'l Business: | | Commercial/Industrial: | Y | Graphic Arts/Photog.: | | Hardware Dev.: | | HR/Other: | Y | Health/Lab: | Y |
| MBA Graduates: | Y | Sales Trainees: | Y | Music: | | Systems Integration: | | Training: | Y | Scientists/Research: | |
| | | Advertising Pros.: | Y | Broadcasting: | | Consulting/Other: | | Health Care: | Y | Petroleum/Chemicals: | |
| | | | | Other: | | | | Consulting: | | Math/Other: | |

## TYPES OF BUSINESS:

Dialysis Facilities and Services

## BRANDS/DIVISIONS/AFFILIATES:

Medicore, Inc.

## CONTACTS:

*Note: Officers with more than one job title may be intentionally listed here more than once.*

Stephen Everett, CEO
Stephen Everett, Pres.
Andrew Jeanneret, CFO/VP-Finance
Thomas P. Carey, VP-Oper.
Daniel R. Ouzts, VP-Finance
Joanne Zimmerman, VP-Clinical Svcs.
Thomas Langbein, Chmn.

**Phone:** 410-694-0500 **Fax:** 410-694-0596
**Toll-Free:** 800-694-6945
**Address:** 1302 Concourse Dr., Ste. 204, Linthicum, MD 21090 US

## GROWTH PLANS/SPECIAL FEATURES:

Dialysis Corporation of America (DCA) provides a variety of services to patients suffering from kidney failure. It owns 36 outpatient dialysis facilities, in Pennsylvania, New Jersey, Georgia, Ohio, Maryland, Virginia and South Carolina. The locations provide patients hemodialysis service. Facilities are equipped with space for dialysis treatments, a nurses' station, a patient weigh-in area, a supply room, water treatment areas, a dialyzer reprocessing room and staff offices. Most of its dialysis facilities have the capacity to provide training, monitoring, equipment and supplies, follow-up assistance and on-call support services for home care peritoneal patients. In addition to its outpatient services, DCA also provides acute care inpatient dialysis services to twelve hospitals in areas serviced by its dialysis facilities. All these services are geared generally to the treatment of end stage renal disease (ESRD), a chronic kidney failure which causes a build-up of toxins in the bloodstream, treated with options ranging from hemodialysis to peritoneal dialysis to kidney transplant, for which the company provided approximately 252,000 hemodialysis treatments in 2007 alone. The company has recently been undergoing expansion, including: the acquisition of a dialysis center in Columbus, Ohio with 21 treatment stations in February 2007; the acquisition of a dialysis center in Selinsgrove, Pennsylvania with 21 treatment stations in March 2007; the addition of a three year contract for dialysis services to patients admitted to Maryland General Hospital in July 2007; and the expansion into Indiana through the development of a 12 station new center in September 2007. This expansion continued in 2008, with the acquisition of a majority interest in a dialysis center in Hawkinsville, Georgia with 16 treatment stations in January 2008; the opening of a new center in Barnwell, South Carolina with 15 stations in February 2008; and announced plans for the eleventh Pennsylvania facility in April 2008.

## FINANCIALS:

**Sales and profits are in thousands of dollars—add 000 to get the full amount. 2008 Note: Financial information for 2008 was not available for all companies at press time.**

| | | |
|---|---|---|
| 2008 Sales: $ | 2008 Profits: $ | **U.S. Stock Ticker: DCAI** |
| 2007 Sales: $74,535 | 2007 Profits: $3,086 | **Int'l Ticker:** Int'l Exchange: |
| 2006 Sales: $62,460 | 2006 Profits: $3,049 | Employees: 496 |
| 2005 Sales: $45,392 | 2005 Profits: $1,900 | Fiscal Year Ends: 12/31 |
| 2004 Sales: $40,986 | 2004 Profits: $2,214 | Parent Company: |

## SALARIES/BENEFITS:

| | | | | |
|---|---|---|---|---|
| Pension Plan: | ESOP Stock Plan: | Profit Sharing: | Top Exec. Salary: $286,565 | Bonus: $ |
| Savings Plan: Y | Stock Purch. Plan: | | Second Exec. Salary: $150,035 | Bonus: $ |

## OTHER THOUGHTS:

**Apparent Women Officers or Directors**: 1
**Hot Spot for Advancement for Women/Minorities**:

## LOCATIONS: ("Y" = Yes)

| West: | Southwest: | Midwest: | Southeast: | Northeast: | International: |
|---|---|---|---|---|---|
| | | | Y | Y | |

# DIAMOND FOODS INC

www.diamondfoods.com

**Industry Group Code:** 111300 **Ranks within this company's industry group:** Sales: 1 Profits: 1

| Management: | | Sales/Marketing: | | Liberal Arts: | | Information Systems: | | Professionals: | | Technical/Scientific: | |
|---|---|---|---|---|---|---|---|---|---|---|---|
| Mgmt. Trainees: | | Mktg. Professionals: | Y | Gen. Writing/Editing: | | Info. Management: | Y | Finance/Accounting: | Y | Engineers, Elec.: | |
| Experienced Mgmt.: | Y | Retail Sales: | | Technical Writing: | | Software Dev.: | | Law: | Y | Engineers, Other: | |
| Int'l Business: | Y | Commercial/Industrial: | Y | Graphic Arts/Photog.: | | Hardware Dev.: | | HR/Other: | Y | Health/Lab: | |
| MBA Graduates: | Y | Sales Trainees: | | Music: | | Systems Integration: | | Training: | Y | Scientists/Research: | |
| | | Advertising Pros.: | Y | Broadcasting: | | Consulting/Other: | | Health Care: | | Petroleum/Chemicals: | |
| | | | | Other: | | | | Consulting: | | Math/Other: | |

## TYPES OF BUSINESS:

Nut Processing
Almond-Related Products
International Distribution
Popcorn Production

## BRANDS/DIVISIONS/AFFILIATES:

Harmony
Diamond of California
Emerald
Diamond International
Pop Secret

## CONTACTS:

*Note: Officers with more than one job title may be intentionally listed here more than once.*

Michael J. Mendes, CEO
Gary K. Ford, COO/Exec. VP
Michael J. Mendes, Pres.
Steven M. Neil, CFO/Exec. VP
Lloyd J. Johnson, Chief Sales Officer
Sam Keiper, VP-Human Resources
Steven M. Neil, Chief Admin. Officer
Stephen Kim, General Counsel/VP
Sam Keiper, VP-Corp. Affairs
Robert Philipps, VP-Investor Rel.
Robert Philipps, Treas.
Andrew Burke, Sr. VP-Mktg.
John J. Gilbert, Chmn.

**Phone:** 209-467-6000 **Fax:** 209-461-7309
**Toll-Free:**
**Address:** 1050 S. Diamond St., Stockton, CA 95205 US

## GROWTH PLANS/SPECIAL FEATURES:

Diamond Foods, Inc. is a branded food company specializing in processing, marketing and distributing culinary, in-shell and ingredient nuts and snack products. Its products are sold in over 60,000 retail locations in the U.S. and in more than 100 countries. The company has four product lines: culinary, snack, in-shell and ingredient/food service. The firm sells culinary nuts under the Diamond of California brand in grocery store center aisle and produce aisles and through mass merchandisers and club stores. Culinary nuts are marketed to individuals who prepare meals or baked goods at home. Snack products are sold under the Emerald and Emerald/Harmony brands. These products, which include roasted, glazed and flavored nuts, trail mixes, seeds, dried fruit and similar offerings packaged in re-sealable containers, are typically available in grocery store snack and produce aisles, mass merchandisers, club stores, convenience stores, drug stores and other places where snacks are sold . Diamond Foods sells in-shell nuts under the Diamond of California brand, primarily during the winter holiday season. The company markets ingredient and food service nuts under the Diamond of California brand to food processors, restaurants, bakeries and food service companies and their suppliers. All of the firm's walnuts, peanuts and almonds are grown in the U.S. Diamond Foods obtains all of its walnuts directly from growers in California and purchases other nuts from importers and domestic processors. Most of the hazelnuts and pecans supply is grown in the U.S. In addition, the company imports Brazil nuts from the Amazon basin; cashew nuts from India, Africa, Brazil and Southeast Asia; hazelnuts from Turkey; pecans from Mexico; and pine nuts from China. Wal-Mart Stores, Inc. accounted for roughly 22% and Costco for about 13% of net sales in 2008. In October 2008, the firm acquired Pop Secret from General Mills, Inc. for $190 million.

## FINANCIALS:

**Sales and profits are in thousands of dollars—add 000 to get the full amount. 2008 Note: Financial information for 2008 was not available for all companies at press time.**

| | | |
|---|---|---|
| 2008 Sales: $531,492 | 2008 Profits: $14,756 | **U.S. Stock Ticker: DMND** |
| 2007 Sales: $522,585 | 2007 Profits: $8,433 | **Int'l Ticker:** Int'l Exchange: |
| 2006 Sales: $477,205 | 2006 Profits: $7,336 | Employees: 628 |
| 2005 Sales: $428,297 | 2005 Profits: $182,796 | Fiscal Year Ends: 7/31 |
| 2004 Sales: $366,385 | 2004 Profits: $177,591 | Parent Company: |

## SALARIES/BENEFITS:

| | | | | |
|---|---|---|---|---|
| Pension Plan: | ESOP Stock Plan: | Profit Sharing: | Top Exec. Salary: $537,342 | Bonus: $610,000 |
| Savings Plan: Y | Stock Purch. Plan: | | Second Exec. Salary: $288,344 | Bonus: $211,120 |

## OTHER THOUGHTS:

**Apparent Women Officers or Directors:**
**Hot Spot for Advancement for Women/Minorities:**

## LOCATIONS: ("Y" = Yes)

| West: | Southwest: | Midwest: | Southeast: | Northeast: | International: |
|---|---|---|---|---|---|
| Y | | | | | Y |

# DIGI INTERNATIONAL INC

www.digi.com

**Industry Group Code:** 334110 **Ranks within this company's industry group:** Sales: 4 Profits: 4

| Management: | | Sales/Marketing: | | Liberal Arts: | | Information Systems: | | Professionals: | | Technical/Scientific: | |
|---|---|---|---|---|---|---|---|---|---|---|---|
| Mgmt. Trainees: | | Mktg. Professionals: | Y | Gen. Writing/Editing: | | Info. Management: | Y | Finance/Accounting: | Y | Engineers, Elec.: | Y |
| Experienced Mgmt.: | Y | Retail Sales: | | Technical Writing: | Y | Software Dev.: | Y | Law: | Y | Engineers, Other: | |
| Int'l Business: | Y | Commercial/Industrial: | Y | Graphic Arts/Photog.: | | Hardware Dev.: | Y | HR/Other: | Y | Health/Lab: | |
| MBA Graduates: | Y | Sales Trainees: | Y | Music: | | Systems Integration: | Y | Training: | Y | Scientists/Research: | Y |
| | | Advertising Pros.: | | Broadcasting: | | Consulting/Other: | | Health Care: | | Petroleum/Chemicals: | |
| | | | | Other: | | | | Consulting: | | Math/Other: | |

## TYPES OF BUSINESS:

Networking Equipment
Data Communications Hardware & Software
Local Area Networking Products
Wireless & Cellular Products-Backup Connectivity

## BRANDS/DIVISIONS/AFFILIATES:

Rabbit Semiconductor, Inc.
Digi Connect ME
Digi Passport
Digi CM
Edgeport
AnywhereUSB
Spectrum Design Solutions Inc
Sarian Systems Ltd

## CONTACTS: *Note: Officers with more than one job title may be intentionally listed here more than once.*

Joseph T. Dunsmore, CEO
Joseph T. Dunsmore, Pres.
Subramanian Krishnan, CFO/Sr. VP
Larry Kraft, Sr. VP-Sales & Mktg.
Tracy Roberts, VP-Human Resources
Joel Young, Sr. VP-R&D
Tracy Roberts, VP-IT
Joel Young, CTO
Jon A. Nyland, VP-Mfg. Oper.
Curt Ahart, VP-Bus. Dev.
Subramanian Krishnan, Treas./Sr. VP
Stephen E. Popovich, VP/Gen. Mgr.-Inside Out Networks
Steve Ericson, VP-Prod. Mgmt.
John Guargena, VP-Americas Sales
Joseph T. Dunsmore, Chmn.
Frederic Luu, VP-Sales & Mktg., EMEA

**Phone:** 952-912-3444 **Fax:** 952-912-4952
**Toll-Free:** 877-912-3444
**Address:** 11001 Bren Rd. E., Minnetonka, MN 55343 US

## GROWTH PLANS/SPECIAL FEATURES:

Digi International, Inc. produces connectivity hardware and software products for multi-user environments, remote access and other data communications networks. Digi's offerings include solutions for industrial automation, building automation and security, out-of-band management (enabling immediate response in the case of catastrophic network failure), medical and healthcare, retail point-of-sale and office networking. The firm's products are divided into two categories: embedded and non-embedded. An embedded product is incorporated by a product developer into an electronic device (e.g. retail scanner, medical instrument). Embedded products include modules; chips; software and development tools; network interface cards; and various services. A non-embedded product is connected externally to a device or larger system (e.g., retail checkout, building access control panels) to provide network connectivity or port expansion. Non-embedded products include cellular routers, gateways, wireless communications adapters; console servers; serial servers; USB connected products; remote display products; cameras and sensors; serial cards; and network management software. Digi's products are compatible with operating systems such as Microsoft Windows, Novell NetWare, Linux and UNIX. Its products are available through approximately 295 distributors in more than 74 countries around the world. In July 2008, the firm acquired Spectrum Design Solutions Inc., a design services organization focusing on solving a customer's wireless development challenges. In April 2008, the firm acquired Sarian Systems, Ltd. Sarian designs, develops and manufactures advanced wireless/cellular IP-based routing equipment for mission-critical applications.

Employees are offered medical, dental and vision coverage; tuition reimbursement; flexible spending accounts; employee assistance programs; 529 college savings plan; flexible work hours; and an on-site cafeteria and exercise facilities.

## FINANCIALS: **Sales and profits are in thousands of dollars—add 000 to get the full amount. 2008 Note: Financial information for 2008 was not available for all companies at press time.**

| | | |
|---|---|---|
| 2008 Sales: $ | 2008 Profits: $ | **U.S. Stock Ticker: DGII** |
| 2007 Sales: $173,263 | 2007 Profits: $19,773 | **Int'l Ticker:** Int'l Exchange: |
| 2006 Sales: $144,663 | 2006 Profits: $11,113 | Employees: 549 |
| 2005 Sales: $125,198 | 2005 Profits: $17,665 | Fiscal Year Ends: 12/31 |
| 2004 Sales: $111,226 | 2004 Profits: $8,663 | Parent Company: |

## SALARIES/BENEFITS:

| | | | | |
|---|---|---|---|---|
| Pension Plan: | ESOP Stock Plan: | Profit Sharing: | Top Exec. Salary: $390,000 | Bonus: $127,780 |
| Savings Plan: Y | Stock Purch. Plan: Y | | Second Exec. Salary: $241,500 | Bonus: $79,125 |

## OTHER THOUGHTS:

**Apparent Women Officers or Directors**: 1
**Hot Spot for Advancement for Women/Minorities**:

## LOCATIONS: ("Y" = Yes)

| West: | Southwest: | Midwest: | Southeast: | Northeast: | International: |
|---|---|---|---|---|---|
| Y | Y | Y | | Y | Y |

# DIGITAL RIVER INC

**www.digitalriver.com**

**Industry Group Code:** 514191A **Ranks within this company's industry group:** Sales: 4 Profits: 2

| Management: | | Sales/Marketing: | | Liberal Arts: | | Information Systems: | | Professionals: | | Technical/Scientific: | |
|---|---|---|---|---|---|---|---|---|---|---|---|
| Mgmt. Trainees: | | Mktg. Professionals: | Y | Gen. Writing/Editing: | | Info. Management: | Y | Finance/Accounting: | Y | Engineers, Elec.: | Y |
| Experienced Mgmt.: | Y | Retail Sales: | | Technical Writing: | Y | Software Dev.: | Y | Law: | Y | Engineers, Other: | |
| Int'l Business: | Y | Commercial/Industrial: | Y | Graphic Arts/Photog.: | | Hardware Dev.: | | HR/Other: | Y | Health/Lab: | |
| MBA Graduates: | Y | Sales Trainees: | Y | Music: | | Systems Integration: | Y | Training: | Y | Scientists/Research: | |
| | | Advertising Pros.: | | Broadcasting: | | Consulting/Other: | | Health Care: | | Petroleum/Chemicals: | |
| | | | | Other: | | | | Consulting: | | Math/Other: | |

## TYPES OF BUSINESS:

E-Commerce Software
E-Commerce Outsourcing
Digital Software Delivery
Web Development
Marketing & Merchandising Services
Fraud Screening
Transaction Processing

## BRANDS/DIVISIONS/AFFILIATES:

BlueHornet Networks, Inc.
MindVision, Inc.
Direct Response Technologies, Inc.
Fireclick
KeywordMax
globalTech
Netgiro

## CONTACTS: *Note: Officers with more than one job title may be intentionally listed here more than once.*

Joel A. Ronning, CEO
Thomas Donnelly, CFO
Kevin L. Crudden, General Counsel/VP
Joel A. Ronning, Chmn.

| | |
|---|---|
| **Phone:** 952-253-1234 | **Fax:** 952-253-8497 |
| **Toll-Free:** | |
| **Address:** 9625 W. 76th St., Ste. 150, Eden Prairie, MN 55344 US | |

## GROWTH PLANS/SPECIAL FEATURES:

Digital River, Inc. provides outsourced e-commerce solutions primarily in the software and high-tech products markets. Its primary offering is a suite of software that enables its clients to deliver software to customers digitally. Digital River also provides a host of services through its technology platform, including web commerce development and hosting, transaction processing, integration, physical fulfillment and customer service. Additionally, the firm provides targeted advertising, fraud screening, analytical marketing and merchandising services to help clients increase web page traffic and sales through their e-commerce systems. Digital River's offerings include a complete range of services needed to conduct business online: Online store design, development and hosting; store merchandising and optimization; order management; fraud prevention screening; export controls and management; tax management; digital product delivery via download; physical product fulfillment; multi-lingual customer service; e-mail marketing; web site optimization; web analytics; and reporting. The company's client list includes firms with sales of at least $200 million annually covering a wide variety of industries, such as Allume Systems, Autodesk, CompUSA, eBay, Hewlett Packard Company, Lexmark, McAfee, Microsoft Corporation, OfficeMax, Nuance Communications, Symantec Corporation, GameZone.com and Trend Micro. Subsidiary BlueHornet Networks, Inc. is a provider of e-mail marketing solutions, while wholly-owned subsidiary MindVision, Inc. is a provider of software delivery tools and outsourced e-commerce services. Direct Response Technologies, Inc. is a provider of affiliate technology and e-marketing solutions. Other Digital River companies include Fireclick, a web analytics, information gathering firm; and affiliates KeywordMax, globalTech and Netgiro.

## FINANCIALS: **Sales and profits are in thousands of dollars—add 000 to get the full amount. 2008 Note: Financial information for 2008 was not available for all companies at press time.**

| | | |
|---|---|---|
| 2008 Sales: $ | 2008 Profits: $ | **U.S. Stock Ticker: DRIV** |
| 2007 Sales: $349,275 | 2007 Profits: $70,814 | **Int'l Ticker:** Int'l Exchange: |
| 2006 Sales: $307,632 | 2006 Profits: $60,810 | Employees: 1,265 |
| 2005 Sales: $220,408 | 2005 Profits: $56,512 | Fiscal Year Ends: 12/31 |
| 2004 Sales: $154,130 | 2004 Profits: $34,507 | Parent Company: |

## SALARIES/BENEFITS:

| | | | | |
|---|---|---|---|---|
| Pension Plan: | ESOP Stock Plan: | Profit Sharing: | Top Exec. Salary: $411,538 | Bonus: $500,000 |
| Savings Plan: Y | Stock Purch. Plan: Y | | Second Exec. Salary: $288,461 | Bonus: $200,000 |

## OTHER THOUGHTS:

**Apparent Women Officers or Directors**: 1
**Hot Spot for Advancement for Women/Minorities**:

## LOCATIONS: ("Y" = Yes)

| West: | Southwest: | Midwest: | Southeast: | Northeast: | International: |
|---|---|---|---|---|---|
| Y | | Y | | | Y |

# DJO INCORPORATED

www.djoglobal.com

**Industry Group Code:** 339113 **Ranks within this company's industry group:** Sales: 4 Profits: 42

| **Management:** | | **Sales/Marketing:** | | **Liberal Arts:** | | **Information Systems:** | | **Professionals:** | | **Technical/Scientific:** | |
|---|---|---|---|---|---|---|---|---|---|---|---|
| Mgmt. Trainees: | | Mktg. Professionals: | Y | Gen. Writing/Editing: | | Info. Management: | Y | Finance/Accounting: | Y | Engineers, Elec.: | |
| Experienced Mgmt.: | Y | Retail Sales: | | Technical Writing: | Y | Software Dev.: | | Law: | Y | Engineers, Other: | Y |
| Int'l Business: | Y | Commercial/Industrial: | Y | Graphic Arts/Photog.: | | Hardware Dev.: | | HR/Other: | Y | Health/Lab: | Y |
| MBA Graduates: | Y | Sales Trainees: | Y | Music: | | Systems Integration: | | Training: | Y | Scientists/Research: | Y |
| | | Advertising Pros.: | | Broadcasting: | | Consulting/Other: | | Health Care: | Y | Petroleum/Chemicals: | |
| | | | | Other: | | | | Consulting: | | Math/Other: | Y |

## TYPES OF BUSINESS:

Clinical Orthopedic Rehabilitation Products & Devices
Electrotherapy Products
Rehabilitation Products

## BRANDS/DIVISIONS/AFFILIATES:

ReAble Therapeutics Inc
Blackstone Capital Partners
DonJoy, ProCare and Aircast
Empi
Chattanooga Group
Ormed
Cefar-Compex
DJO Finance LLC

## CONTACTS:

*Note: Officers with more than one job title may be intentionally listed here more than once.*

Leslie H. Cross, CEO
Peter W. Baird, Pres.
Vickie L. Capps, CFO/Exec. VP
Thomas A. Capizzi, VP-Global Human Resources
Donald M. Roberts, General Counsel/Sec./Exec. VP
Vickie L. Capps, Treas.
Kenneth W. Davidson, Chmn.
Luke T. Faulstick, Pres., Global Oper.

**Phone:** 760-727-1280 **Fax:** 800-936-6569
**Toll-Free:** 800-336-5690
**Address:** 1430 Decision St., Vista, CA 92081 US

## GROWTH PLANS/SPECIAL FEATURES:

DJO Incorporated (formerly ReAble Therapeutics, Inc.) designs, manufactures, markets and distributes orthopedic devices, sports medicine equipment and other related products for the orthopedic industry worldwide. A private firm primarily owned by affiliates of Blackstone Capital Partners, its products are used to treat patients with musculoskeletal conditions resulting from degenerative diseases, deformities and acute injuries. These products serve the needs of physical therapists, orthopedic surgeons and other health care professionals. The firm is divided into three operating segments: Domestic Rehabilitation, International Rehabilitation and Surgical Implant. The Domestic Rehabilitation division is subdivided into three divisions: DonJoy, ProCare and Aircast; Empi; and Chattanooga. The DonJoy, ProCare and Aircast division manufactures products including rigid knee bracing, cold therapy products and orthopedic soft goods, which include products that offer immobilization from head to toe. Empi's offerings include transcutaneous electrical nerve stimulation (TENS) devices that block pain messages through electrical stimulation; combined magnetic field (CMF) devices that encourage bone healing; and iontophoresis transdermal medical delivery devices. The Chattanooga Group manufactures clinical rehabilitation equipment for treating skeletal, muscular, neurological and soft tissue disorders. Its products include TENS and other electrotherapy products; traction devices; and dry heat therapy products. The International Rehabilitation division, operating mainly in Europe, has three main businesses. It distributes DonJoy, ProCare and Aircast products internationally; it offers Ormed brand products, including electrotherapy and bracing products, primarily in Germany; and provides Cefar-Compex electrotherapy and rehabilitation products. The Surgical Implant division, run under the name DJO Surgical (formerly Encore Medical), manufactures orthopedic reconstructive joint implants, including those for the hip, knee and shoulder. In November 2007, subsidiary ReAble Therapeutics Finance LLC acquired DJO Opco Holdings, Inc. (formerly DJO Incorporated) for $1.3 billion; ReAble then changed its name to DJO Incorporated and ReAble Therapeutics Finance changed its name to DJO Finance LLC (DJOFL), a publicly traded company.

## FINANCIALS:

**Sales and profits are in thousands of dollars—add 000 to get the full amount. 2008 Note: Financial information for 2008 was not available for all companies at press time.**

| | | |
|---|---|---|
| 2008 Sales: $ | 2008 Profits: $ | **U.S. Stock Ticker: Private** |
| 2007 Sales: $492,134 | 2007 Profits: $-82,422 | **Int'l Ticker:** Int'l Exchange: |
| 2006 Sales: $362,285 | 2006 Profits: $-88,410 | Employees: 1,300 |
| 2005 Sales: $293,726 | 2005 Profits: $12,330 | Fiscal Year Ends: 12/31 |
| 2004 Sales: $148,081 | 2004 Profits: $5,527 | Parent Company: |

## SALARIES/BENEFITS:

| | | | | |
|---|---|---|---|---|
| Pension Plan: | ESOP Stock Plan: | Profit Sharing: | Top Exec. Salary: $434,297 | Bonus: $ |
| Savings Plan: Y | Stock Purch. Plan: | | Second Exec. Salary: $334,615 | Bonus: $200,000 |

## OTHER THOUGHTS:

**Apparent Women Officers or Directors**: 2
**Hot Spot for Advancement for Women/Minorities**:

## LOCATIONS: ("Y" = Yes)

| West: | Southwest: | Midwest: | Southeast: | Northeast: | International: |
|---|---|---|---|---|---|
| Y | | | | | |

# DOUBLECLICK INC

**www.doubleclick.com**

**Industry Group Code:** 541810A **Ranks within this company's industry group:** Sales: 2 Profits:

| **Management:** | | **Sales/Marketing:** | | **Liberal Arts:** | | **Information Systems:** | | **Professionals:** | | **Technical/Scientific:** | |
|---|---|---|---|---|---|---|---|---|---|---|---|
| Mgmt. Trainees: | | Mktg. Professionals: | Y | Gen. Writing/Editing: | Y | Info. Management: | Y | Finance/Accounting: | Y | Engineers, Elec.: | |
| Experienced Mgmt.: | Y | Retail Sales: | | Technical Writing: | | Software Dev.: | Y | Law: | Y | Engineers, Other: | |
| Int'l Business: | Y | Commercial/Industrial: | | Graphic Arts/Photog.: | Y | Hardware Dev.: | | HR/Other: | Y | Health/Lab: | |
| MBA Graduates: | Y | Sales Trainees: | Y | Music: | | Systems Integration: | Y | Training: | Y | Scientists/Research: | |
| | | Advertising Pros.: | Y | Broadcasting: | | Consulting/Other: | | Health Care: | | Petroleum/Chemicals: | |
| | | | | Other: | Y | | | Consulting: | | Math/Other: | |

## TYPES OF BUSINESS:

Online Advertising Services
Outsourcing Services
Advertising Software
Consumer Database Analysis

## BRANDS/DIVISIONS/AFFILIATES:

Google Inc
DART for Advertisers
DART for Publishers
DART Enterprise
DoubleClick Rich Media & Video
DoubleClick Ad Kit
Audience Interaction Metrics

## CONTACTS: *Note: Officers with more than one job title may be intentionally listed here more than once.*

David S. Rosenblatt, CEO
Charlie Dickson, CFO
Marianne Caponnetto, Chief Sales & Mktg. Officer
Debbie Josephs, VP-Human Resources
Greg Tagaris, CIO
John M. Rehl, Sr. VP-Global Tech. Svcs.
Neal Mohan, Sr. VP-Prod. Dev.
Stephanie Abramson, General Counsel/Exec. VP
Neal Mohan, Sr. VP-Strategy
Stuart Frankel, Sr. VP/Gen. Mgr.-Performics
Chris Young, Exec. VP-Rich Media
Michael Rubenstein, VP/Gen. Mgr.-DoubleClick Advertising Exchange
Ben Regensburger, Pres., DoubleClick Int'l

**Phone:** 212-683-0001 **Fax:** 212-287-1203
**Toll-Free:** 866-459-7606
**Address:** 111 8th Ave., 10th Fl., New York, NY 10011 US

## GROWTH PLANS/SPECIAL FEATURES:

DoubleClick, Inc., a subsidiary of Google, Inc., is a leading provider of products and services that enable direct marketers, publishers and advertisers to market to consumers on the Internet. The company has 15 offices and development hubs and 14 data centers worldwide. DoubleClick's products are offered in six categories: ad serving, rich media & video, search solutions, marketplace, optimization and workflow automation. In the ad serving category, the company's products include DART for Advertisers, a web-based ad management tool; DART for Publishers, a web-based tool for monetizing a publisher's advertising inventory; and DART Enterprise, an ad management tool offering relatively detailed business management features, such as inventory management, traffic pattern analysis and real-time campaign result reporting. In the rich media & video category, the company offers DoubleClick Rich Media & Video, which includes a service team of production, creative, trafficking and research experts; the DoubleClick Ad Kit; a range of rich media formats; an Audience Interaction Metrics package; and DoubleClick's Innovation Lab. In the search solutions category, the company offers DART Search and DoubleClick Performics Search. DoubleClick Advertising Exchange is the company's marketplace offering, offering immediate access to inventory for buyers and DoubleClick's proprietary Dynamic Allocation system for sellers. DART Adapt is the company's optimization product, capable of addressing the optimization needs of multiple campaign types. In the workflow automation category, DoubleClick's products include MediaVisor, a software application for advertising campaign management; and DART Sales Manager, a proposal and finance management tool. DoubleClick manages online advertising for companies such as MySpace, Ford Motors, MTV, and CBS Sports. In early 2008, the firm was acquired by Google from Hellman & Friedman LLC for $3.1 billion.

## FINANCIALS: **Sales and profits are in thousands of dollars—add 000 to get the full amount. 2008 Note: Financial information for 2008 was not available for all companies at press time.**

| | | |
|---|---|---|
| 2008 Sales: $ | 2008 Profits: $ | **U.S. Stock Ticker: Subsidiary** |
| 2007 Sales: $346,700 | 2007 Profits: $ | **Int'l Ticker:** Int'l Exchange: |
| 2006 Sales: $ | 2006 Profits: $ | Employees: 850 |
| 2005 Sales: $ | 2005 Profits: $ | Fiscal Year Ends: 12/31 |
| 2004 Sales: $301,600 | 2004 Profits: $37,500 | Parent Company: GOOGLE INC |

## SALARIES/BENEFITS:

| | | | | |
|---|---|---|---|---|
| Pension Plan: | ESOP Stock Plan: | Profit Sharing: | Top Exec. Salary: $ | Bonus: $444,600 |
| Savings Plan: | Stock Purch. Plan: | | Second Exec. Salary: $300,000 | Bonus: $300,000 |

## OTHER THOUGHTS:

**Apparent Women Officers or Directors**: 3
**Hot Spot for Advancement for Women/Minorities**: Y

## LOCATIONS: ("Y" = Yes)

| West: | Southwest: | Midwest: | Southeast: | Northeast: | International: |
|---|---|---|---|---|---|
| Y | | Y | | Y | Y |

# DPL INC

www.dplinc.com

**Industry Group Code:** 221000A **Ranks within this company's industry group:** Sales: 3 Profits: 2

| Management: | | Sales/Marketing: | | Liberal Arts: | | Information Systems: | | Professionals: | | Technical/Scientific: | |
|---|---|---|---|---|---|---|---|---|---|---|---|
| Mgmt. Trainees: | | Mktg. Professionals: | Y | Gen. Writing/Editing: | | Info. Management: | Y | Finance/Accounting: | Y | Engineers, Elec.: | Y |
| Experienced Mgmt.: | Y | Retail Sales: | | Technical Writing: | | Software Dev.: | | Law: | Y | Engineers, Other: | Y |
| Int'l Business: | | Commercial/Industrial: | Y | Graphic Arts/Photog.: | | Hardware Dev.: | | HR/Other: | Y | Health/Lab: | |
| MBA Graduates: | Y | Sales Trainees: | Y | Music: | | Systems Integration: | | Training: | Y | Scientists/Research: | |
| | | Advertising Pros.: | | Broadcasting: | | Consulting/Other: | | Health Care: | | Petroleum/Chemicals: | Y |
| | | | | Other: | | | | Consulting: | | Math/Other: | |

## TYPES OF BUSINESS:

Utilities-Electricity & Natural Gas
Power Generation
Real Estate
Equipment Leasing
Financial Services

## BRANDS/DIVISIONS/AFFILIATES:

Dayton Power and Light Company
DPL Energy, LLC
DPL Energy Resources, Inc.
MVE, Inc.
Miami Valley Insurance Company
DPL Finance Company, Inc.

## CONTACTS: *Note: Officers with more than one job title may be intentionally listed here more than once.*

Paul M. Barbas, CEO
Paul M. Barbas, Pres.
John J. Gillen, CFO/Sr. VP
Gary G. Stephenson, Sr. VP-Mktg.
Daniel J. McCabe, Sr. VP-Human Resources
Douglas C. Taylor, General Counsel/Sr. VP
Teresa F. Marrinan, VP-Commercial Oper.
Arthur G. Meyer, Sr. VP-Corp. & Regulatory Affairs
Frederick.J. Boyle, Chief Acct. Officer/VP
John J. Gillen, Treas.
Scott J. Kelly, Sr. VP-Service Oper.
Gary G. Stephenson, Sr. VP-Generation

| Phone: 937-259-7142 | Fax: |
|---|---|
| Toll-Free: | |
| Address: 1065 Woodman Dr., Dayton, OH 45432 US | |

## GROWTH PLANS/SPECIAL FEATURES:

DPL, Inc. is a diversified regional energy company operating primarily through its subsidiary Dayton Power and Light Company (DP&L). Providing approximately 99% of DPL's total consolidated revenue and approximately 86% of DPL's total consolidated asset base, DP&L is a public utility selling electricity to residential, commercial, industrial and governmental customers in a 6,000-square-mile area of west central Ohio. Electricity for DP&L's 24 county service area is primarily generated at eight coal-fired power plants and is distributed to more than 500,000 retail customers. DP&L also purchases retail peak load requirements from another of DPL's subsidiaries, DPL Energy, LLC (DPLE). Principal industries served by DP&L include automotive, food processing, paper, plastic manufacturing and defense. DP&L sells any excess energy and capacity into the wholesale market. Other significant subsidiaries of DPL include DPL Energy Resources, Inc. (DPLER), which sells retail electric energy under contract to major industrial and commercial customers in west central Ohio; MVE, Inc., which is primarily responsible for the management of its financial asset portfolio; and Miami Valley Insurance Company (MVIC), which is DPL's captive insurance company, providing DPL and its subsidiaries with insurance sources. DP&L has one significant subsidiary, DPL Finance Company, Inc., which provides financing to DPL, DP&L and other affiliated companies. DPL's summer generating capacity, including peaking units, is approximately 3,769 megawatts (MW). Of this capacity, approximately 2,850 MW are derived from coal-fired steam generating stations, with the balance of approximately 919 MW consisting of combustion turbine and diesel peaking units.

## FINANCIALS: **Sales and profits are in thousands of dollars—add 000 to get the full amount. 2008 Note: Financial information for 2008 was not available for all companies at press time.**

| | | |
|---|---|---|
| 2008 Sales: $ | 2008 Profits: $ | **U.S. Stock Ticker: DPL** |
| 2007 Sales: $1,515,700 | 2007 Profits: $221,800 | **Int'l Ticker:** Int'l Exchange: |
| 2006 Sales: $1,393,519 | 2006 Profits: $139,600 | Employees: 1,562 |
| 2005 Sales: $1,284,900 | 2005 Profits: $174,400 | Fiscal Year Ends: 12/31 |
| 2004 Sales: $1,199,900 | 2004 Profits: $217,300 | Parent Company: |

## SALARIES/BENEFITS:

| | | | | |
|---|---|---|---|---|
| Pension Plan: Y | ESOP Stock Plan: Y | Profit Sharing: | Top Exec. Salary: $520,385 | Bonus: $492,000 |
| Savings Plan: Y | Stock Purch. Plan: | | Second Exec. Salary: $350,246 | Bonus: $368,951 |

## OTHER THOUGHTS:

**Apparent Women Officers or Directors**: 3
**Hot Spot for Advancement for Women/Minorities**: Y

## LOCATIONS: ("Y" = Yes)

| West: | Southwest: | Midwest: | Southeast: | Northeast: | International: |
|---|---|---|---|---|---|
| | | Y | | Y | |

# DREAMWORKS ANIMATION SKG INC

www.dreamworksanimation.com

**Industry Group Code:** 512110 **Ranks within this company's industry group:** Sales: 1 Profits: 1

| Management: | | Sales/Marketing: | | Liberal Arts: | | Information Systems: | | Professionals: | | Technical/Scientific: | |
|---|---|---|---|---|---|---|---|---|---|---|---|
| Mgmt. Trainees: | | Mktg. Professionals: | Y | Gen. Writing/Editing: | Y | Info. Management: | Y | Finance/Accounting: | Y | Engineers, Elec.: | |
| Experienced Mgmt.: | Y | Retail Sales: | | Technical Writing: | | Software Dev.: | Y | Law: | Y | Engineers, Other: | Y |
| Int'l Business: | | Commercial/Industrial: | | Graphic Arts/Photog.: | Y | Hardware Dev.: | | HR/Other: | Y | Health/Lab: | |
| MBA Graduates: | Y | Sales Trainees: | Y | Music: | Y | Systems Integration: | Y | Training: | Y | Scientists/Research: | |
| | | Advertising Pros.: | Y | Broadcasting: | | Consulting/Other: | | Health Care: | | Petroleum/Chemicals: | |
| | | | | Other: | Y | | | Consulting: | | Math/Other: | |

## TYPES OF BUSINESS:

Animated Film Production
Animation Software

## BRANDS/DIVISIONS/AFFILIATES:

DreamWorks Studios
Wallace & Gromit: Curse of the Were-Rabbit
Shrek
Paramount Pictures Corp
Shrek the Musical
Tatweer Dubai LLC

## CONTACTS: *Note: Officers with more than one job title may be intentionally listed here more than once.*

Jeffrey Katzenberg, CEO
Ann Daly, COO
Lew Coleman, Pres.
Lew Coleman, CFO
Anne Globe, Head-Worldwide Mktg. & Consumer Products
Katherine Kendrick, General Counsel/Corp. Sec.
Philip Cross, Chief Acct. Officer
John Batter, Co-Pres.-Production
William J Damaschke, Co-Pres.-Production/Pres.-Live Theatrical
Roger A. Enrico, Chmn.

| | |
|---|---|
| **Phone:** 818-695-5000 | **Fax:** 818-695-9944 |
| **Toll-Free:** | |
| **Address:** 1000 Flower St., Glendale, CA 91201 US | |

## GROWTH PLANS/SPECIAL FEATURES:

DreamWorks Animation SKG, Inc. develops and produces computer-generated (CG) animated feature films that are distributed and marketed by Paramount. The firm uses proprietary software to produce its films, and its operations take place at two facilities in Glendale and Redwood City, California. The company has released a total of 17 animated films, including seven that were CG-only and one direct-to-video title. Films include such box office hits as Antz, Shrek, Shrek 2, Madagascar and Shrek the Third. DreamWorks Animation has also collaborated with Aardman Animations to release Chicken Run and Wallace & Gromit: Curse of the Were-Rabbit. Recent films include Kung Fu Panda and Madagascar 2. The studio has several films in production, including Monsters vs. Aliens; How to Train Your Dragon; and Shrek Goes Fourth. The firm's distribution agreement with Paramount runs through 2012. In December 2007, DreamWorks Animation premiered Shrek the Halls, a television Christmas special which aired on ABC. In January 2008, the company announced that it would be producing Shrek the Musical, a new Broadway musical based primarily upon the original Shrek film. In October 2008, DreamWorks Animation announced plans for a sequel to Kung Fu Panda, to be released in 2011. Also in 2008, the Company announced that it had entered into a strategic alliance with Tatweer Dubai LLC. Under this agreement, the company will license certain of its characters for use in connection with a planned DreamWorks theme park in Dubai, which is scheduled to open in 2012. The agreement also grants Tatweer the right to use DreamWorks' characters in connection with themed hotels, restaurants and other tourism projects. The company has stated that, starting in 2009, all of its feature films will be produced using stereoscopic 3D technology.

Employees receive such perks as free breakfasts and lunches, movie wrap parties and free gifts.

## FINANCIALS: **Sales and profits are in thousands of dollars—add 000 to get the full amount. 2008 Note: Financial information for 2008 was not available for all companies at press time.**

| | | |
|---|---|---|
| 2008 Sales: $ | 2008 Profits: $ | **U.S. Stock Ticker: DWA** |
| 2007 Sales: $767,178 | 2007 Profits: $218,364 | **Int'l Ticker:** Int'l Exchange: |
| 2006 Sales: $394,842 | 2006 Profits: $15,125 | Employees: 1,617 |
| 2005 Sales: $462,316 | 2005 Profits: $104,585 | Fiscal Year Ends: 12/31 |
| 2004 Sales: $1,078,160 | 2004 Profits: $333,000 | Parent Company: |

## SALARIES/BENEFITS:

| | | | | |
|---|---|---|---|---|
| Pension Plan: | ESOP Stock Plan: | Profit Sharing: | Top Exec. Salary: $1,250,000 | Bonus: $1,750,000 |
| Savings Plan: | Stock Purch. Plan: | | Second Exec. Salary: $1,000,000 | Bonus: $1,350,000 |

## OTHER THOUGHTS:

**Apparent Women Officers or Directors**: 5
**Hot Spot for Advancement for Women/Minorities**: Y

## LOCATIONS: ("Y" = Yes)

| West: | Southwest: | Midwest: | Southeast: | Northeast: | International: |
|---|---|---|---|---|---|
| Y | | | | | |

# DRUGSTORE.COM INC

**www.drugstore.com**

**Industry Group Code:** 446110E **Ranks within this company's industry group:** Sales: 1 Profits: 1

| Management: | | Sales/Marketing: | | Liberal Arts: | | Information Systems: | | Professionals: | | Technical/Scientific: | |
|---|---|---|---|---|---|---|---|---|---|---|---|
| Mgmt. Trainees: | Y | Mktg. Professionals: | Y | Gen. Writing/Editing: | Y | Info. Management: | Y | Finance/Accounting: | Y | Engineers, Elec.: | |
| Experienced Mgmt.: | Y | Retail Sales: | Y | Technical Writing: | | Software Dev.: | Y | Law: | Y | Engineers, Other: | |
| Int'l Business: | Y | Commercial/Industrial: | | Graphic Arts/Photog.: | Y | Hardware Dev.: | | HR/Other: | Y | Health/Lab: | |
| MBA Graduates: | Y | Sales Trainees: | Y | Music: | | Systems Integration: | Y | Training: | Y | Scientists/Research: | |
| | | Advertising Pros.: | Y | Broadcasting: | | Consulting/Other: | | Health Care: | | Petroleum/Chemicals: | |
| | | | | Other: | | | | Consulting: | | Math/Other: | |

## TYPES OF BUSINESS:

Retail-Online Drug Store
Over-the-Counter & Prescription Drugs
Health & Beauty Products
Vision Products
Nutritional Supplements

## BRANDS/DIVISIONS/AFFILIATES:

Beauty.com
Custom Nutrition Services, Inc.
International Vision Direct Corp.
VisionDirect.com
LensMart.com
LensQuest.com

## CONTACTS: *Note: Officers with more than one job title may be intentionally listed here more than once.*

Dawn Lepore, CEO
Tracy Wright, CFO
David Lonczak, Chief Mktg. Officer/VP
Robert Hargadon, VP-Human Resources
Luke Friang, CIO/VP
Julie Johnston, VP-OTC Merch.
Yukio Morikubo, General Counsel
Yukio Morikubo, VP-Strategy
Robert Potter, Chief Acct. Officer
Ron Kelly, VP-Customer & Pharmacy Svcs.
Kathleen McNeill, VP-Beauty
Dawn Lepore, Chmn.

| | |
|---|---|
| **Phone:** 425-372-3200 | **Fax:** 425-372-3800 |
| **Toll-Free:** 800-378-4786 | |
| **Address:** 411 108th Ave. N.E., Ste. 1400, Bellevue, WA 98004 US | |

## GROWTH PLANS/SPECIAL FEATURES:

Drugstore.com, Inc. is a leading online drugstore with an international customer base of approximately10 million. The company offers health, beauty, wellness, personal care and pharmaceutical products and information. Drugstore.com operates and manages its business in four segments: Mail-order pharmacy, local pick-up pharmacy, vision and over-the-counter and non-pharmaceuticals. The company's web site offers thousands of brand-name products, including more than 40,000 non-prescription products, and sends e-mail messages to remind customers to purchase frequently used products. Features of the web site include a broad array of health-related information, buying guides, detailed customer reviews and other tools designed to assist customers in making educated purchasing decisions. Customers can review in-depth product information, interact with customer service representatives by phone or e-mail and order products for home delivery. In addition to its flagship site (www.drugstore.com), the company operates several subsidiary Internet portals. Beauty.com specializes in brand name cosmetic products. Customized nutritional supplement programs are offered through Custom Nutrition Services, Inc. Contact lenses and other vision products can be purchased through subsidiary International Vision Direct Corp. at VisionDirect.com, LensMart.com and LensQuest.com.

## FINANCIALS: **Sales and profits are in thousands of dollars—add 000 to get the full amount. 2008 Note: Financial information for 2008 was not available for all companies at press time.**

| | | |
|---|---|---|
| 2008 Sales: $ | 2008 Profits: $ | **U.S. Stock Ticker: DSCM** |
| 2007 Sales: $445,723 | 2007 Profits: $-11,511 | **Int'l Ticker:** Int'l Exchange: |
| 2006 Sales: $415,777 | 2006 Profits: $-13,026 | Employees: 850 |
| 2005 Sales: $399,430 | 2005 Profits: $-20,899 | Fiscal Year Ends: 12/31 |
| 2004 Sales: $360,099 | 2004 Profits: $-47,735 | Parent Company: |

## SALARIES/BENEFITS:

| | | | | |
|---|---|---|---|---|
| Pension Plan: | ESOP Stock Plan: | Profit Sharing: | Top Exec. Salary: $398,077 | Bonus: $415,000 |
| Savings Plan: Y | Stock Purch. Plan: Y | | Second Exec. Salary: $232,932 | Bonus: $55,000 |

## OTHER THOUGHTS:

**Apparent Women Officers or Directors**: 4
**Hot Spot for Advancement for Women/Minorities**: Y

## LOCATIONS: ("Y" = Yes)

| West: | Southwest: | Midwest: | Southeast: | Northeast: | International: |
|---|---|---|---|---|---|
| Y | | | | Y | Y |

# DSP GROUP INC

**www.dspg.com**

**Industry Group Code:** 334413 **Ranks within this company's industry group:** Sales: 3 Profits: 4

| Management: | | Sales/Marketing: | | Liberal Arts: | | Information Systems: | | Professionals: | | Technical/Scientific: | |
|---|---|---|---|---|---|---|---|---|---|---|---|
| Mgmt. Trainees: | | Mktg. Professionals: | Y | Gen. Writing/Editing: | | Info. Management: | Y | Finance/Accounting: | Y | Engineers, Elec.: | Y |
| Experienced Mgmt.: | Y | Retail Sales: | | Technical Writing: | Y | Software Dev.: | Y | Law: | Y | Engineers, Other: | Y |
| Int'l Business: | Y | Commercial/Industrial: | Y | Graphic Arts/Photog.: | | Hardware Dev.: | Y | HR/Other: | Y | Health/Lab: | |
| MBA Graduates: | Y | Sales Trainees: | Y | Music: | | Systems Integration: | Y | Training: | Y | Scientists/Research: | Y |
| | | Advertising Pros.: | | Broadcasting: | | Consulting/Other: | | Health Care: | | Petroleum/Chemicals: | |
| | | | | Other: | | | | Consulting: | | Math/Other: | Y |

## TYPES OF BUSINESS:

Integrated Circuits-Digital Signal Processors
Speech Processors
RF Devices

## BRANDS/DIVISIONS/AFFILIATES:

DECT
Bluetooth
CIPT Business
NXP Semiconductors
Alcatel USA Inc
General Electric Co (GE)
Motorola Good Technology Group
Verizon Communications

## CONTACTS: *Note: Officers with more than one job title may be intentionally listed here more than once.*

Eliyahu (Eli) Ayalon, CEO
Boaz Edan, COO/Exec. VP
Brian Neil Robertson, Pres.
Dror Levy, CFO
Ofer Shneyour, Sr. VP-Strategic Mktg.
Eli Fogel, CTO/Sr. VP
Dror Levy, Corp. Sec.
Danny Hacohen, VP-Bus. Oper.
Dror Levy, VP-Finance
Avi Barel, VP-Sales
Lior Blanka, VP/Mgr.-Cordless Div.
Eliyahu (Eli) Ayalon, Chmn.

| **Phone:** 408-986-4300 | **Fax:** 408-986-4323 |
|---|---|
| **Toll-Free:** | |
| **Address:** 2580 N. 1st St., Ste. 460, San Jose, CA 95131 US | |

## GROWTH PLANS/SPECIAL FEATURES:

DSP Group, Inc. is a fabless semiconductor company and a global leader in the short-range wireless communication market, enabling home networking convergence for voice, video and data. DSP combines digital signal processing (DSP) technology with advanced complementary metal oxide semiconductor (CMOS) radio frequency (RF) devices, communications technologies and speech-processing algorithms. The company has developed several semiconductor devices for residential, enterprise and automotive wireless communications applications. These solutions include digital 2.4GHz, DECT (1.9GHz), 5.8GHz and Bluetooth for voice, data and video communications, as well as solutions for digital voice recorders and MP3 applications. DSP Group also develops and markets embedded, integrated silicon/software solutions for digital voice recorder, hands-free car kit, Voice over DSL (VoDSL) and Voice over Internet protocol (VoIP) applications, as well as other Voice over packet applications (VoP) for integrated access device and Internet protocol telephony markets. The company targets the digital cordless telephony, multimedia access, analog telephony, VoP and digital voice recorder and multimedia markets. DSP sells its products primarily through distributors and representatives, as well as directly to original equipment manufacturers (OEMs) and original design manufacturers (ODMs). Major consumer electronics manufacturers and brands that have incorporated the company's ICs include Alcatel; AT&T; Deutsche Telekom; Global China Technologies; Giant Electronics; GE; Motorola; Panasonic; Philips; Pioneer; Sagem; Samsung; Sharp; Siemens; Sony; SunCorp; Telecom Italia; Telefonica; Verizon; and Yamaha. Export sales generate roughly 98% of DSP's total revenue. In September 2007, DSP acquired the cordless and VoIP terminals business (CIPT Business) of NXP Semiconductors for $270 million. The CIPT Business targets applications for the cordless and VoIP residential telephony market, mainly European DECT.

## FINANCIALS: **Sales and profits are in thousands of dollars—add 000 to get the full amount. 2008 Note: Financial information for 2008 was not available for all companies at press time.**

| | | |
|---|---|---|
| 2008 Sales: $ | 2008 Profits: $ | **U.S. Stock Ticker: DSPG** |
| 2007 Sales: $248,788 | 2007 Profits: $-4,753 | **Int'l Ticker:** Int'l Exchange: |
| 2006 Sales: $216,948 | 2006 Profits: $22,379 | Employees: 502 |
| 2005 Sales: $187,225 | 2005 Profits: $29,473 | Fiscal Year Ends: 12/31 |
| 2004 Sales: $157,500 | 2004 Profits: $51,100 | Parent Company: |

## SALARIES/BENEFITS:

| | | | | |
|---|---|---|---|---|
| Pension Plan: | ESOP Stock Plan: | Profit Sharing: | Top Exec. Salary: $350,000 | Bonus: $290,000 |
| Savings Plan: | Stock Purch. Plan: | | Second Exec. Salary: $220,000 | Bonus: $70,000 |

## OTHER THOUGHTS:

**Apparent Women Officers or Directors:**
**Hot Spot for Advancement for Women/Minorities:**

## LOCATIONS: ("Y" = Yes)

| West: | Southwest: | Midwest: | Southeast: | Northeast: | International: |
|---|---|---|---|---|---|
| Y | | | | | Y |

# DYAX CORP

www.dyax.com

**Industry Group Code:** 325412 **Ranks within this company's industry group:** Sales: 34 Profits: 26

| Management: | | Sales/Marketing: | | Liberal Arts: | | Information Systems: | | Professionals: | | Technical/Scientific: | |
|---|---|---|---|---|---|---|---|---|---|---|---|
| Mgmt. Trainees: | | Mktg. Professionals: | Y | Gen. Writing/Editing: | | Info. Management: | Y | Finance/Accounting: | Y | Engineers, Elec.: | |
| Experienced Mgmt.: | Y | Retail Sales: | | Technical Writing: | Y | Software Dev.: | Y | Law: | Y | Engineers, Other: | |
| Int'l Business: | Y | Commercial/Industrial: | Y | Graphic Arts/Photog.: | | Hardware Dev.: | | HR/Other: | Y | Health/Lab: | Y |
| MBA Graduates: | Y | Sales Trainees: | Y | Music: | | Systems Integration: | | Training: | Y | Scientists/Research: | Y |
| | | Advertising Pros.: | | Broadcasting: | | Consulting/Other: | | Health Care: | Y | Petroleum/Chemicals: | Y |
| | | | | Other: | | | | Consulting: | Y | Math/Other: | Y |

## TYPES OF BUSINESS:

Pharmaceuticals Discovery & Development
Proteins, Peptides & Antibodies
Drugs-Cancer
Drugs-Anti-Inflammatory

## BRANDS/DIVISIONS/AFFILIATES:

DX-88
DX-2400
WebPhage

## CONTACTS: *Note: Officers with more than one job title may be intentionally listed here more than once.*

Henry E. Blair, CEO
Henry E. Blair, Pres.
Stephen S. Galliker, CFO
Clive R. Wood, Exec. VP-Research/Chief Scientific Officer
Ivana Magovcevic-Liebisch, Exec. VP-Admin.
Ivana Magovcevic-Liebisch, General Counsel
Gustav A. Christensen, Chief Bus. Officer/Exec. VP
Nicole Jones, Dir.-Investor Rel.
Stephen S. Galliker, Exec. VP-Finance
William E. Pullman, Chief Dev. Officer/Exec. VP
Nathaniel S. Gardiner, Sec.
Henry E. Blair, Chmn.

| | |
|---|---|
| **Phone:** 617-225-2500 | **Fax:** 617-225-2501 |
| **Toll-Free:** | |
| **Address:** 300 Technology Sq., Cambridge, MA 02139 US | |

## GROWTH PLANS/SPECIAL FEATURES:

Dyax Corp. is a biopharmaceutical company principally focused on the discovery, development and commercialization of antibodies, proteins and peptides as therapeutic products, with an emphasis on cancer and inflammatory conditions. In general, the firm strives to maintain 10 active therapeutic programs in its pipeline at all times. Its lead product candidate is DX-88, a recombinant form of a small protein that is being tested for applications in hereditary angioedema, a genetic disease that causes swelling of the larynx, gastrointestinal tract and extremities. It has passed its first Phase III trial for this application, and began its second Phase III trial in April 2007. DX-88 is also being tested to treat complications, including blood loss and systemic inflammation, during on-pump cardiothoracic surgery. This application passed Phase I and II trials, and a second Phase II trial began in May 2007. After DX-88, its most advanced candidates are DX-2240 and DX-2400, both fully human monoclonal antibodies designed to attack cancerous tumors. Dyax identifies its pipeline compounds through its proprietary phage display methodology, called WebPhage. The process involves generating phage display libraries of protein variations, screening libraries to select binding compounds with high affinity and high specificity to a target and producing and evaluating the selected binding compounds. The company also allows other companies to use WebPhage display technology to discover new compounds through its Licensing and Funded Research Program. Over 70 companies licensed this technology and 12 new compounds currently undergoing clinical trials have been derived. In February 2008, Dyax signed a license agreement granting sanofi-aventis S.A. the responsibility for the future development of DX-2240.

Employees of the firm receive medical and dental benefits; short- and long-term disability coverage; life and AD&D insurance; flexible spending accounts; paid holidays; educational assistance; an employee assistance program; health club reimbursement; and a transportation subsidy.

## FINANCIALS: **Sales and profits are in thousands of dollars—add 000 to get the full amount. 2008 Note: Financial information for 2008 was not available for all companies at press time.**

| | | |
|---|---|---|
| 2008 Sales: $ | 2008 Profits: $ | **U.S. Stock Ticker: DYAX** |
| 2007 Sales: $26,096 | 2007 Profits: $-56,309 | **Int'l Ticker:** Int'l Exchange: |
| 2006 Sales: $12,776 | 2006 Profits: $-50,323 | Employees: 177 |
| 2005 Sales: $19,859 | 2005 Profits: $-30,944 | Fiscal Year Ends: 12/31 |
| 2004 Sales: $16,590 | 2004 Profits: $-33,114 | Parent Company: |

## SALARIES/BENEFITS:

| | | | | |
|---|---|---|---|---|
| Pension Plan: | ESOP Stock Plan: | Profit Sharing: Y | Top Exec. Salary: $525,000 | Bonus: $250,000 |
| Savings Plan: Y | Stock Purch. Plan: Y | | Second Exec. Salary: $321,803 | Bonus: $145,000 |

## OTHER THOUGHTS:

**Apparent Women Officers or Directors**: 3
**Hot Spot for Advancement for Women/Minorities**: Y

## LOCATIONS: ("Y" = Yes)

| West: | Southwest: | Midwest: | Southeast: | Northeast: | International: |
|---|---|---|---|---|---|
| | | | | Y | Y |

# DYNACQ HEALTHCARE INC

www.dynacq.com

**Industry Group Code:** 621490 **Ranks within this company's industry group:** Sales: 8 Profits: 4

| Management: | | Sales/Marketing: | | Liberal Arts: | | Information Systems: | | Professionals: | | Technical/Scientific: | |
|---|---|---|---|---|---|---|---|---|---|---|---|
| Mgmt. Trainees: | | Mktg. Professionals: | Y | Gen. Writing/Editing: | | Info. Management: | Y | Finance/Accounting: | Y | Engineers, Elec.: | |
| Experienced Mgmt.: | Y | Retail Sales: | | Technical Writing: | | Software Dev.: | | Law: | Y | Engineers, Other: | |
| Int'l Business: | Y | Commercial/Industrial: | | Graphic Arts/Photog.: | | Hardware Dev.: | | HR/Other: | Y | Health/Lab: | Y |
| MBA Graduates: | Y | Sales Trainees: | Y | Music: | | Systems Integration: | | Training: | Y | Scientists/Research: | |
| | | Advertising Pros.: | Y | Broadcasting: | | Consulting/Other: | | Health Care: | Y | Petroleum/Chemicals: | |
| | | | | Other: | | | | Consulting: | | Math/Other: | |

## TYPES OF BUSINESS:

Emergency & Inpatient Surgery Facilities
Outpatient Surgery Facilities
Acute Care Hospital
Fertility Treatments
Orthopedic Surgery
Bariatric Surgery

## BRANDS/DIVISIONS/AFFILIATES:

Dynacq International, Inc.
Surgery Specialty Hospitals of America
Vista Hospital of Dallas
Shanghai DeAn Hospital

## CONTACTS: *Note: Officers with more than one job title may be intentionally listed here more than once.*

Chiu M. Chan, CEO
Alan A. Beauchamp, COO/Exec. VP
Philip S. Chan, CFO/VP
Ringo Cheng, Dir.-IT
Hermant Khemka, Corp. Controller
Chiu M. Chan, Chmn.
Jian Zhou, Dir./Gen. Mgr.-China Oper.

| Phone: 713-378-2000 | Fax: 713-673-6416 |
|---|---|
| Toll-Free: | |
| Address: 10304 Interstate 10 E., Ste. 369, Houston, TX 77029 US | |

## GROWTH PLANS/SPECIAL FEATURES:

Dynacq Healthcare, Inc. is a holding company that develops and manages general acute care hospitals that provide specialized general surgeries. The company develops and operates hospitals designed to handle surgically procedures such as bariatric, orthopedic and neuro-spine surgeries. Certain of the company's facilities also provide sleep laboratory and pain management services, as well as minor emergency treatment services and ear, nose and throat services. The company's hospitals include operating rooms, pre- and post-operative space, intensive care units, nursing units and diagnostic facilities, as well as adjacent medical office buildings that lease space to physicians and other healthcare providers. The firm currently maintains two surgical facilities in the U.S., the Surgery Specialty Hospitals of America (formerly Vista Medical Center Hospital) and Vista Hospital of Dallas. Additionally, the company owns a 70% equity interest in Shanghai DeAn Hospital, a joint venture formed under the laws of China. Vista Hospital of Dallas is the largest of Dynacq's hospitals at 90,000 square feet, and specializes in orthopedic surgery, bariatric surgery, general surgery and pain management. The Company, through its affiliates, owns or leases 100% of the real estate and equipment in its facilities. The company maintains a majority ownership and controlling interest in all of its operating entities. In August 2007 the company sold its outpatient surgery center, Vista Surgical Center West. Later in the year, the firm announced the completion of the sale of the land, building and tangible assets of Vista Surgical Hospital of Baton Rouge to the state of Louisiana.

## FINANCIALS: **Sales and profits are in thousands of dollars—add 000 to get the full amount. 2008 Note: Financial information for 2008 was not available for all companies at press time.**

| | | |
|---|---|---|
| 2008 Sales: $ | 2008 Profits: $ | **U.S. Stock Ticker: DYII** |
| 2007 Sales: $42,846 | 2007 Profits: $4,155 | **Int'l Ticker:** Int'l Exchange: |
| 2006 Sales: $35,989 | 2006 Profits: $-5,936 | Employees: 303 |
| 2005 Sales: $41,618 | 2005 Profits: $-5,137 | Fiscal Year Ends: 8/31 |
| 2004 Sales: $39,234 | 2004 Profits: $-1,600 | Parent Company: |

## SALARIES/BENEFITS:

| | | | | |
|---|---|---|---|---|
| Pension Plan: | ESOP Stock Plan: | Profit Sharing: | Top Exec. Salary: $180,000 | Bonus: $ |
| Savings Plan: | Stock Purch. Plan: | | Second Exec. Salary: $180,000 | Bonus: $ |

## OTHER THOUGHTS:

**Apparent Women Officers or Directors:**
**Hot Spot for Advancement for Women/Minorities:**

## LOCATIONS: ("Y" = Yes)

| West: | Southwest: | Midwest: | Southeast: | Northeast: | International: |
|---|---|---|---|---|---|
| | Y | | Y | | Y |

# DYNEGY INC

www.dynegy.com

**Industry Group Code:** 221000 **Ranks within this company's industry group:** Sales: 1 Profits: 1

| Management: | | Sales/Marketing: | | Liberal Arts: | | Information Systems: | | Professionals: | | Technical/Scientific: | |
|---|---|---|---|---|---|---|---|---|---|---|---|
| Mgmt. Trainees: | | Mktg. Professionals: | Y | Gen. Writing/Editing: | | Info. Management: | Y | Finance/Accounting: | Y | Engineers, Elec.: | Y |
| Experienced Mgmt.: | Y | Retail Sales: | | Technical Writing: | | Software Dev.: | | Law: | Y | Engineers, Other: | Y |
| Int'l Business: | Y | Commercial/Industrial: | Y | Graphic Arts/Photog.: | | Hardware Dev.: | | HR/Other: | Y | Health/Lab: | |
| MBA Graduates: | Y | Sales Trainees: | | Music: | | Systems Integration: | | Training: | Y | Scientists/Research: | |
| | | Advertising Pros.: | | Broadcasting: | | Consulting/Other: | | Health Care: | | Petroleum/Chemicals: | Y |
| | | | | Other: | | | | Consulting: | | Math/Other: | |

## TYPES OF BUSINESS:

Utilities-Electricity
Natural Gas Distribution & Marketing
Hydroelectric Generation

## BRANDS/DIVISIONS/AFFILIATES:

Illinois Power
LS Power
ExRes SHC, Inc.

## CONTACTS: *Note: Officers with more than one job title may be intentionally listed here more than once.*

Bruce A. Williamson, CEO
Stephen A. Furbacher, COO
Stephen A. Furbacher, Pres.
Holli C. Nichols, CFO/Exec. VP
J. Kevin Blodgett, Exec. VP-Admin.
J. Kevin Blodgett, General Counsel
Richard W. Eimer, Exec. VP-Oper.
Charles C. Cook, Exec. VP-Strategic Planning & Corp. Bus. Dev.
Carolyn J. Stone, Controller/Sr. VP
Kimberly M. O'Brien, Corp. Sec.
Lynn A. Lednicky, Exec. VP-Asst Mgmt., Dev. & Regulatory Affairs
Bruce A. Williamson, Chmn.

| | |
|---|---|
| **Phone:** 713-507-6400 | **Fax:** 713-507-6808 |
| **Toll-Free:** 800-633-4704 | |
| **Address:** 1000 Louisiana St., Ste. 5800, Houston, TX 77002 US | |

## GROWTH PLANS/SPECIAL FEATURES:

Dynegy, Inc., through its subsidiaries, provides electricity, natural gas and natural gas liquids (NGL) to U.S. customers. The company's power generation operations, which are divided into the Midwest, West and Northeast segments, sell power and related products and services, including capacity, into real-time and day-ahead markets, as well as on a forward basis. Customers include independent system operators (ISOs), municipalities, electric cooperatives, integrated utilities, transmission and distribution utilities, industrial customers, power marketers, other power generators and commercial end-users. The segment operates about 29 electric power generation facilities in 13 states, the majority of which are gas-fired. In April 2008, Dynegy sold its Sulphur, Louisiana peaking plant, Calcasieu Power Generation Facility, to Entergy Gulf States Louisiana, LLC for $57 million. In June 2008, the firm, along with LS Power Group entered into agreement to sell 11% their indirect interest in the 900-megawatt Sandy Creek Power Generation Facility to the Lower Colorado River Authority. In August 2008, a subsidiary of Dynegy sold the Rolling Hills Generation Facility, a Wilkesville Ohio peaking plant, to a company managed by Tenaska Capital Management LLC for $368 million.

The company offers its employees health and dental insurance; a 401(k) savings plan; and a retirement plan.

## FINANCIALS: **Sales and profits are in thousands of dollars—add 000 to get the full amount. 2008 Note: Financial information for 2008 was not available for all companies at press time.**

| | | |
|---|---|---|
| 2008 Sales: $ | 2008 Profits: $ | **U.S. Stock Ticker: DYN** |
| 2007 Sales: $3,103,000 | 2007 Profits: $264,000 | **Int'l Ticker:** Int'l Exchange: |
| 2006 Sales: $1,770,000 | 2006 Profits: $-333,000 | Employees: 1,800 |
| 2005 Sales: $2,313,000 | 2005 Profits: $90,000 | Fiscal Year Ends: 12/31 |
| 2004 Sales: $2,451,000 | 2004 Profits: $-15,000 | Parent Company: |

## SALARIES/BENEFITS:

| | | | | |
|---|---|---|---|---|
| Pension Plan: Y | ESOP Stock Plan: | Profit Sharing: | Top Exec. Salary: $1,000,000 | Bonus: $900,000 |
| Savings Plan: Y | Stock Purch. Plan: | | Second Exec. Salary: $520,192 | Bonus: $850,000 |

## OTHER THOUGHTS:

**Apparent Women Officers or Directors**: 4
**Hot Spot for Advancement for Women/Minorities**: Y

## LOCATIONS: ("Y" = Yes)

| West: | Southwest: | Midwest: | Southeast: | Northeast: | International: |
|---|---|---|---|---|---|
| Y | Y | Y | Y | Y | Y |

# ECHELON CORP

**www.echelon.com**

**Industry Group Code:** 334110 **Ranks within this company's industry group:** Sales: 5 Profits: 6

| Management: | | Sales/Marketing: | | Liberal Arts: | | Information Systems: | | Professionals: | | Technical/Scientific: | |
|---|---|---|---|---|---|---|---|---|---|---|---|
| Mgmt. Trainees: | | Mktg. Professionals: | Y | Gen. Writing/Editing: | | Info. Management: | Y | Finance/Accounting: | Y | Engineers, Elec.: | Y |
| Experienced Mgmt.: | Y | Retail Sales: | | Technical Writing: | Y | Software Dev.: | Y | Law: | Y | Engineers, Other: | |
| Int'l Business: | Y | Commercial/Industrial: | Y | Graphic Arts/Photog.: | | Hardware Dev.: | Y | HR/Other: | Y | Health/Lab: | |
| MBA Graduates: | Y | Sales Trainees: | Y | Music: | | Systems Integration: | Y | Training: | Y | Scientists/Research: | Y |
| | | Advertising Pros.: | | Broadcasting: | | Consulting/Other: | | Health Care: | | Petroleum/Chemicals: | |
| | | | | Other: | | | | Consulting: | | Math/Other: | |

## TYPES OF BUSINESS:

Computer Networking Equipment-Energy Controls
Remote Appliance, Sensor & Equipment Controls
Remote Diagnostics
Municipal Transportation Networks
Automation Systems
Utility Grid Diagnostic Systems

## BRANDS/DIVISIONS/AFFILIATES:

LonWorks
Pyxos
i.LON
Digital Home Alliance

## CONTACTS: *Note: Officers with more than one job title may be intentionally listed here more than once.*

M. Kenneth Oshman, CEO
Oliver Stanfield, CFO/Exec. VP
Anders Axelsson, Sr. VP-Mktg. & Sales
Robert Dolin, VP-Tech.
Robert Machlin, Sr. VP-Prod.
Kathleen Bloch, General Counsel/Sr. VP
Russell Harris, Sr. VP-Oper.
Frederik Bruggink, Sr. VP-Service Provider Group
M. Kenneth Oshman, Chmn.

| | |
|---|---|
| **Phone:** 408-938-5200 | **Fax:** 408-790-3800 |
| **Toll-Free:** 888-324-3566 | |
| **Address:** 550 Meridian Ave., San Jose, CA 95126 US | |

## GROWTH PLANS/SPECIAL FEATURES:

Echelon Corporation is a provider of control network technology for automation systems. The company develops, markets and supports products and services that allow device manufacturers, integrators and end users to implement control networks in the building, industrial, transportation, utility, home and other automation markets. Services include building automation systems, system failure prediction, municipal transportation applications, remote diagnostics and home pay-per-use capabilities. Its line of over 90 products includes transceivers, concentrator products, control modules, routers, network interfaces, development tools and software tools and toolkits. Echelon devises these technologies for both Internet standards and for its LonWorks control networking platform. Each device is also capable of communicating with other devices in its control network and taking actions based on information that it receives from them as well as allowing the integration of products or subsystems from multiple vendors. In the utility sector, Echelon operates its networked energy services (NES) system, which pinpoints power outages and can reduce stress on the grid, avoiding blackouts and brownouts. The Pyxos FT chip embedded control networking platform product is intended to reduce the cost of manufacturing, installing and maintaining a machine. For system integrators serving the street lighting, remote facility monitoring, and energy management markets, the firm has developed the i.LON Internet server family of products. The Digital Home Alliance product is designed to bring together a collection of companies that market networked home control products based upon Echelon's LonWorks. The firm's transportation products also use LonWorks systems and include products for railcars, light rail, buses, motor coaches, fire trucks, naval vessels, and aircraft.

The company offers its employees stock options; a 401(k) plan; medical, dental and vision insurance; life and AD&D insurance; short- and long-term disability insurance; flexible spending accounts; and tuition reimbursement.

## FINANCIALS: **Sales and profits are in thousands of dollars—add 000 to get the full amount. 2008 Note: Financial information for 2008 was not available for all companies at press time.**

| | | |
|---|---|---|
| 2008 Sales: $ | 2008 Profits: $ | **U.S. Stock Ticker: ELON** |
| 2007 Sales: $137,577 | 2007 Profits: $-14,512 | **Int'l Ticker:** Int'l Exchange: |
| 2006 Sales: $57,276 | 2006 Profits: $-24,440 | Employees: 319 |
| 2005 Sales: $74,428 | 2005 Profits: $-19,719 | Fiscal Year Ends: 12/31 |
| 2004 Sales: $109,921 | 2004 Profits: $5,272 | Parent Company: |

## SALARIES/BENEFITS:

| | | | | |
|---|---|---|---|---|
| Pension Plan: | ESOP Stock Plan: | Profit Sharing: | Top Exec. Salary: $417,809 | Bonus: $ |
| Savings Plan: Y | Stock Purch. Plan: Y | | Second Exec. Salary: $345,000 | Bonus: $ |

## OTHER THOUGHTS:

**Apparent Women Officers or Directors**: 3
**Hot Spot for Advancement for Women/Minorities**: Y

## LOCATIONS: ("Y" = Yes)

| West: | Southwest: | Midwest: | Southeast: | Northeast: | International: |
|---|---|---|---|---|---|
| Y | | Y | | | Y |

# ECLIPSYS CORPORATION

www.eclipsys.com

**Industry Group Code:** 511212 **Ranks within this company's industry group:** Sales: 1 Profits: 1

| Management: | | Sales/Marketing: | | Liberal Arts: | | Information Systems: | | Professionals: | | Technical/Scientific: | |
|---|---|---|---|---|---|---|---|---|---|---|---|
| Mgmt. Trainees: | | Mktg. Professionals: | Y | Gen. Writing/Editing: | | Info. Management: | Y | Finance/Accounting: | Y | Engineers, Elec.: | Y |
| Experienced Mgmt.: | Y | Retail Sales: | | Technical Writing: | Y | Software Dev.: | Y | Law: | Y | Engineers, Other: | |
| Int'l Business: | Y | Commercial/Industrial: | Y | Graphic Arts/Photog.: | | Hardware Dev.: | | HR/Other: | Y | Health/Lab: | |
| MBA Graduates: | Y | Sales Trainees: | Y | Music: | | Systems Integration: | | Training: | Y | Scientists/Research: | |
| | | Advertising Pros.: | | Broadcasting: | | Consulting/Other: | | Health Care: | | Petroleum/Chemicals: | |
| | | | | Other: | | | | Consulting: | | Math/Other: | |

## TYPES OF BUSINESS:

Computer Software
Health Care IT Products & Services

## BRANDS/DIVISIONS/AFFILIATES:

Sunrise
Sunrise Clinical Manager
Sunrise Access Manager
Sunrise Patient Financial Manager
Sunrise Decision Support Manager
Sunrise eLink
Sunrise Record Manager
Sunrise Enterprise Person Identifier

## CONTACTS: *Note: Officers with more than one job title may be intentionally listed here more than once.*

R. Andrew Eckert, CEO
R. Andrew Eckert, Pres.
W. David Morgan, CFO
Jan Smith, Sr. VP-Human Resources
John Gomez, Chief Tech. Strategy Officer/Exec. VP
Joe Petro, Sr. VP-Prod. Dev.
Brian W. Copple, General Counsel/Chief Legal Officer/Corp. Sec.
W. David Morgan, Chief Acct. Officer/ Treas.
John McAuley, Sr. VP-Outsourcing
Jay Deady, Exec. VP-Client Solutions
Matt Sappern, Sr. VP-Professional Svcs.
Eugene V. Fife, Chmn.
Nitin Deshpande, Pres., Eclipsys India

| | |
|---|---|
| **Phone:** 404-847-5000 | **Fax:** 404-847-5700 |
| **Toll-Free:** 800-869-8300 | |
| **Address:** 3 Ravinia Dr., Atlanta, GA 30346 US | |

## GROWTH PLANS/SPECIAL FEATURES:

Eclipsys Corp. is a health care information technology company and a provider of advanced clinical, financial and management information software and service solutions. The company develops and licenses proprietary software and content that is designed for use in connection with many of the key clinical, administrative and financial functions that hospitals and other healthcare organizations require. The company's flagship offering is the Sunrise line of products, which includes Sunrise Clinical Manager, Integrated Access Management, Sunrise Patient Financial Manager, Sunrise Decision Support Manager, Sunrise Record Manager, Sunrise Enterprise Person Identifier, Eclipsys Diagnostic Imaging Solutions and Sunrise eLink. This software allows hospitals to automate many of the key clinical, administrative and financial functions that they require, letting them admit patients, maintain patient records, create invoices for billing, control inventories, effect cost accounting, schedule doctor's visits and understand the profitability of specific medical procedures. It also enables physicians and nurses to check on a patient's condition, order tests, review test results, monitor a patient's medications and provide alerts to changes in a patient's condition. The company's applications are available for implementation on-site or through its remote hosting service. In addition, Eclipsys offers support services to its customers, including implementation, integration, support, maintenance and training. In October 2008, the company acquired MediNotes, a provider of physician practice information solutions, for $45 million. In January 2009, the firm acquired Premise, an integrated and clinically based software solutions company, for $38.5 million. Also in January 2009, the company partnered with University of Pennsylvania School of Nursing to offer a curriculum that incorporates the firm's information technology solutions and hardware.

The company offers its employees health, dental and vision insurance; an employee assistance program; flexible spending accounts; insurance; and a 401(k) plan.

## FINANCIALS: **Sales and profits are in thousands of dollars—add 000 to get the full amount. 2008 Note: Financial information for 2008 was not available for all companies at press time.**

| | | |
|---|---|---|
| 2008 Sales: $ | 2008 Profits: $ | **U.S. Stock Ticker: ECLP** |
| 2007 Sales: $477,533 | 2007 Profits: $41,141 | **Int'l Ticker:** Int'l Exchange: |
| 2006 Sales: $427,542 | 2006 Profits: $4,093 | Employees: 2,400 |
| 2005 Sales: $383,342 | 2005 Profits: $ 269 | Fiscal Year Ends: 12/31 |
| 2004 Sales: $309,075 | 2004 Profits: $-34,029 | Parent Company: |

## SALARIES/BENEFITS:

| | | | | |
|---|---|---|---|---|
| Pension Plan: | ESOP Stock Plan: | Profit Sharing: | Top Exec. Salary: $650,000 | Bonus: $40,000 |
| Savings Plan: Y | Stock Purch. Plan: | | Second Exec. Salary: $450,000 | Bonus: $40,000 |

## OTHER THOUGHTS:

**Apparent Women Officers or Directors**: 1
**Hot Spot for Advancement for Women/Minorities**:

## LOCATIONS: ("Y" = Yes)

| West: | Southwest: | Midwest: | Southeast: | Northeast: | International: |
|---|---|---|---|---|---|
| Y | Y | | Y | Y | Y |

Note: Financial information, benefits and other data can change quickly and may vary from those stated here.

# ECOLLEGE.COM

**www.ecollege.com**

**Industry Group Code:** 611410 **Ranks within this company's industry group:** Sales: Profits:

| Management: | | Sales/Marketing: | | Liberal Arts: | | Information Systems: | | Professionals: | | Technical/Scientific: | |
|---|---|---|---|---|---|---|---|---|---|---|---|
| Mgmt. Trainees: | Y | Mktg. Professionals: | Y | Gen. Writing/Editing: | Y | Info. Management: | Y | Finance/Accounting: | Y | Engineers, Elec.: | |
| Experienced Mgmt.: | Y | Retail Sales: | | Technical Writing: | | Software Dev.: | Y | Law: | Y | Engineers, Other: | |
| Int'l Business: | Y | Commercial/Industrial: | Y | Graphic Arts/Photog.: | Y | Hardware Dev.: | | HR/Other: | Y | Health/Lab: | |
| MBA Graduates: | Y | Sales Trainees: | Y | Music: | | Systems Integration: | Y | Training: | Y | Scientists/Research: | |
| | | Advertising Pros.: | Y | Broadcasting: | | Consulting/Other: | | Health Care: | | Petroleum/Chemicals: | |
| | | | | Other: | Y | | | Consulting: | | Math/Other: | |

## TYPES OF BUSINESS:

Online Education Software
e-Learning Solutions
Enrollment Marketing Services

## BRANDS/DIVISIONS/AFFILIATES:

eLearning
eCollege System
eCollege Teaching Solutions
eCollege Program Administration Solutions
Datamark, Inc.
Pearson Education Inc

## CONTACTS:

*Note: Officers with more than one job title may be intentionally listed here more than once.*

Matthew Leavy, CEO
Anne Keough Keehn, VP-Global Sales & Mktg.
Vance Allen, CTO
Michael P. Jackson, VP-Software Dev.
Anne Keough Keehn, VP-Bus. Dev., Higher Education & K-12
Matthew Mermagen, VP-Finance
Scot Chadwick, VP-Acct. Mgmt.
Andrew Bergad, VP-Educational Partner Oper.
John Dobbertin, VP/Dir.-Product & Infrastructure
Kendrick H. McLish, VP-Product & Strategy

**Phone:** 303-873-0005 **Fax:** 312-706-1703
**Toll-Free:** 888-884-7325
**Address:** 4900 S. Monaco St., Ste. 200, Denver, CO 80237 US

## GROWTH PLANS/SPECIAL FEATURES:

ECollege.com builds and supports online learning communities for colleges, universities, K-12 school districts and corporate training organizations. It provides these services through its eLearning business segment. The company's eLearning division provides technology, products and services that enable colleges, universities and high schools to offer online and hybrid educational programs as well as on-campus courses. Selected products include the eCollege System, which uses software and services to support customers' online programs, and comprises the eCollege Teaching Solutions, eCollege Program Administration Solutions and technology infrastructure. The outsourced product incorporates a course management system, designed toward maximum efficiency and interaction; a program administration system, which helps administrators manage the online community; and a secure hosted environment, with all the hardware, security and ancillary software necessary to function well. ELearning solutions and services offered include, but are not limited to, hosting and infrastructure; a course management system; a program administration system; content manager; operational support; academic training and consulting; course development; enterprise reporting; course evaluation system; and 24/7 user support. In October 2008, the firm announced the opening of an Australian office that will concentrate on the Asian Pacific region.

Employees of the firm are offered medical, dental and vision coverage; a 401(k) plan; an employee stock purchase program; an employee assistance plan; educational assistance; flexible work arrangements; LifeCare parenting program; adoption assistance programs; life insurance; disability insurance; emergency back-up child and elder care; a commuting expense program; employee referral programs; and flexible spending accounts.

## FINANCIALS:

**Sales and profits are in thousands of dollars—add 000 to get the full amount. 2008 Note: Financial information for 2008 was not available for all companies at press time.**

| | | |
|---|---|---|
| 2008 Sales: $ | 2008 Profits: $ | **U.S. Stock Ticker: Subsidiary** |
| 2007 Sales: $ | 2007 Profits: $ | **Int'l Ticker:** Int'l Exchange: |
| 2006 Sales: $52,085 | 2006 Profits: $-2,258 | Employees: 270 |
| 2005 Sales: $41,460 | 2005 Profits: $5,928 | Fiscal Year Ends: 12/31 |
| 2004 Sales: $34,782 | 2004 Profits: $19,360 | Parent Company: PEARSON PLC |

## SALARIES/BENEFITS:

| | | | | |
|---|---|---|---|---|
| Pension Plan: | ESOP Stock Plan: | Profit Sharing: | Top Exec. Salary: $374,880 | Bonus: $127,420 |
| Savings Plan: Y | Stock Purch. Plan: | | Second Exec. Salary: $310,265 | Bonus: $89,194 |

## OTHER THOUGHTS:

**Apparent Women Officers or Directors**: 2
**Hot Spot for Advancement for Women/Minorities**:

## LOCATIONS: ("Y" = Yes)

| West: | Southwest: | Midwest: | Southeast: | Northeast: | International: |
|---|---|---|---|---|---|
| | | Y | | | Y |

# EHEALTH INC

www.ehealthinsurance.com

**Industry Group Code:** 524210A **Ranks within this company's industry group:** Sales: 1 Profits: 1

| **Management:** | | **Sales/Marketing:** | | **Liberal Arts:** | | **Information Systems:** | | **Professionals:** | | **Technical/Scientific:** | |
|---|---|---|---|---|---|---|---|---|---|---|---|
| Mgmt. Trainees: | | Mktg. Professionals: | Y | Gen. Writing/Editing: | Y | Info. Management: | Y | Finance/Accounting: | Y | Engineers, Elec.: | |
| Experienced Mgmt.: | Y | Retail Sales: | | Technical Writing: | | Software Dev.: | Y | Law: | Y | Engineers, Other: | |
| Int'l Business: | | Commercial/Industrial: | | Graphic Arts/Photog.: | | Hardware Dev.: | | HR/Other: | Y | Health/Lab: | |
| MBA Graduates: | Y | Sales Trainees: | | Music: | | Systems Integration: | | Training: | Y | Scientists/Research: | |
| | | Advertising Pros.: | Y | Broadcasting: | | Consulting/Other: | | Health Care: | Y | Petroleum/Chemicals: | |
| | | | | Other: | | | | Consulting: | | Math/Other: | |

## TYPES OF BUSINESS:

Health Insurance Brokerage-Online
Health Insurance
Student Health Insurance
Short-term Health Insurance
Health Savings Accounts
Dental Insurance
Term Life Insurance
Dental Discount Cards

## BRANDS/DIVISIONS/AFFILIATES:

eHealthInsurance Services Inc
Ubao.com

## CONTACTS: *Note: Officers with more than one job title may be intentionally listed here more than once.*

Gary Lauer, CEO
Robert L. Fahlman, COO/Sr. VP-Carrier Rel.
Gary Lauer, Pres.
Stuart M. Huizinga, CFO/Sr. VP
Samuel C. Gibbs, III, Sr. VP-Sales
Sheldon X. Wang, CTO/Exec. VP-Tech.
Bruce Telkamp, Exec. VP-Bus. Oper.
Robert S. Hurley, Sr. VP-Carrier Rel.
John D. Desser, VP-Public Policy & Gov't Affairs
Gary Lauer, Chmn.

**Phone:** 650-584-2700 **Fax:** 650-961-2153
**Toll-Free:** 877-456-7180
**Address:** 440 E. Middlefield Rd., Mountain View, CA 94043 US

## GROWTH PLANS/SPECIAL FEATURES:

eHealth, Inc. and its subsidiaries offer Internet-based insurance agency services for individuals, families and small businesses in the U.S., as well as technology licensing and Internet advertising services. The firm's services and technology enable individuals, families and small businesses to research, analyze, compare and purchase health insurance products from health insurance carriers across the nation. eHealth operates in all 50 states and Washington, D.C. Operating primarily through its eHealthInsurance Services Inc. subsidiary, the company partners with health insurance carriers to provide individuals, families and small businesses with health insurance products online. Through its e-commerce platform, the firm organizes and presents health insurance information in a user-friendly form. Consumers are able to use this platform to research, analyze, compare and purchase more than 7,000 health insurance products. eHealth partners with over 175 health insurance carriers, including Aetna, Humana, UnitedHealthcare and Wellpoint, over 40 BlueCross BlueShield carriers, and regional carriers such as Health Net, Kaiser Permanente and Unicare. In 2007, revenue from UnitedHealthcare, Wellpoint and Aetna accounted for 19%, 18% and 11% of annual totals respectively. These partnerships allow eHealth to process consumer health insurance applications online. Through these means, the company is able to simplify and streamline the health insurance sales and purchasing process. In 2007, the firm had approximately 518,400 members. In September 2007, the company launched Ubao.com, in Xiamen, China, allowing customers to purchase health, life and accident insurance in one place. In April 2008, Ubao.com expanded its services to the Shanghai area.

eHealth offers employees comprehensive benefits and compensation packages that include stock options, a 401(k) plan, paid time off, paid holidays and health insurance.

## FINANCIALS: **Sales and profits are in thousands of dollars—add 000 to get the full amount. 2008 Note: Financial information for 2008 was not available for all companies at press time.**

2008 Sales: $
2007 Sales: $87,791
2006 Sales: $61,310
2005 Sales: $41,752
2004 Sales: $30,215

2008 Profits: $
2007 Profits: $31,595
2006 Profits: $16,477
2005 Profits: $-4,114
2004 Profits: $-3,327

**U.S. Stock Ticker: EHTH**
**Int'l Ticker:** Int'l Exchange:
Employees: 437
Fiscal Year Ends: 12/31
Parent Company:

## SALARIES/BENEFITS:

Pension Plan: ESOP Stock Plan: Profit Sharing: Top Exec. Salary: $337,502 Bonus: $245,000
Savings Plan: Y Stock Purch. Plan: Y Second Exec. Salary: $242,088 Bonus: $156,250

## OTHER THOUGHTS:

**Apparent Women Officers or Directors**: 1
**Hot Spot for Advancement for Women/Minorities**:

## LOCATIONS: ("Y" = Yes)

| West: | Southwest: | Midwest: | Southeast: | Northeast: | International: |
|---|---|---|---|---|---|
| Y | | | | | |

# ELECTRONICS FOR IMAGING INC

**www.efi.com**

**Industry Group Code:** 334119 **Ranks within this company's industry group:** Sales: 3 Profits: 2

| Management: | | Sales/Marketing: | | Liberal Arts: | | Information Systems: | | Professionals: | | Technical/Scientific: | |
|---|---|---|---|---|---|---|---|---|---|---|---|
| Mgmt. Trainees: | | Mktg. Professionals: | Y | Gen. Writing/Editing: | | Info. Management: | Y | Finance/Accounting: | Y | Engineers, Elec.: | Y |
| Experienced Mgmt.: | Y | Retail Sales: | | Technical Writing: | Y | Software Dev.: | Y | Law: | Y | Engineers, Other: | Y |
| Int'l Business: | Y | Commercial/Industrial: | Y | Graphic Arts/Photog.: | Y | Hardware Dev.: | Y | HR/Other: | Y | Health/Lab: | |
| MBA Graduates: | Y | Sales Trainees: | Y | Music: | | Systems Integration: | Y | Training: | Y | Scientists/Research: | |
| | | Advertising Pros.: | | Broadcasting: | | Consulting/Other: | | Health Care: | | Petroleum/Chemicals: | |
| | | | | Other: | | | | Consulting: | | Math/Other: | |

## TYPES OF BUSINESS:

Networking Equipment-Printing & Graphics
Print Management Applications & Software
Print Servers
Super-Wide Format Inkjet Printers

## BRANDS/DIVISIONS/AFFILIATES:

Fiery
Splash
PressVu
UltraVu
MicroPress
VUTEk
Digital StoreFront
Pace Systems Group

## CONTACTS:

*Note: Officers with more than one job title may be intentionally listed here more than once.*

Guy Gecht, CEO
Fred Rosenzweig, Pres.
John Ritchie, CFO
James L. Etheridge, Sec.
Jane Cedrone, Mgr.-Public Rel.
Gill Cogan, Chmn.

| | |
|---|---|
| **Phone:** 650-357-3500 | **Fax:** 650-357-3907 |
| **Toll-Free:** 800-568-1917 | |
| **Address:** 303 Velocity Way, Foster City, CA 94404 US | |

## GROWTH PLANS/SPECIAL FEATURES:

Electronics for Imaging, Inc. (EFI) provides color digital print controllers, super-wide format printers and inks, and print management solutions for professional and enterprise printing. The company's main products include the Fiery, Splash and MicroPress brands of stand-alone print servers connected to digital copiers, which are embedded in digital copiers and desktop color laser printers. Once networked, EFI-powered printers and copiers are shared between work groups and departments to produce color and black and white documents. The firm also offers super-wide format digital inkjet printers used for billboard graphics, commercial photo labs and large sign shops. These products include the PressVu Series; UltraVu Series; VUTEk 3360; and QS Series. Additionally, the company provides software for the commercial printing and enterprise markets. Colorproof XF offers color proofing solutions that increase workflow, power, and expandability; EFI management information systems collect, organize and present critical information to improve process control and profit potential; and Digital StoreFront and PrinterSite offer a web interface to manage print transactions between customer and printer. EFI also provides enterprise solutions including EFI SendME, which transforms paper documents into electronic files for delivery or storage. The firm sells its products to OEMs such as Canon, Xerox and KonicaMinolta. In July 2008, EFI acquired print management software company, Pace Systems Group, for $21 million. In October of the same year, the company agreed to acquire the remaining interest in Raster Printers.

Employees are offered medical, dental and vision insurance; 401(k) plans; pension plans; stock purchase plans; tuition assistance; employee assistance programs; and pet insurance.

## FINANCIALS:

**Sales and profits are in thousands of dollars—add 000 to get the full amount. 2008 Note: Financial information for 2008 was not available for all companies at press time.**

| | | |
|---|---|---|
| 2008 Sales: $ | 2008 Profits: $ | **U.S. Stock Ticker: EFII** |
| 2007 Sales: $620,586 | 2007 Profits: $26,843 | **Int'l Ticker:** Int'l Exchange: |
| 2006 Sales: $564,611 | 2006 Profits: $- 183 | Employees: 2,018 |
| 2005 Sales: $468,501 | 2005 Profits: $-4,067 | Fiscal Year Ends: 12/31 |
| 2004 Sales: $394,604 | 2004 Profits: $38,019 | Parent Company: |

## SALARIES/BENEFITS:

| | | | | |
|---|---|---|---|---|
| Pension Plan: Y | ESOP Stock Plan: | Profit Sharing: | Top Exec. Salary: $570,000 | Bonus: $478,800 |
| Savings Plan: Y | Stock Purch. Plan: Y | | Second Exec. Salary: $510,000 | Bonus: $385,560 |

## OTHER THOUGHTS:

**Apparent Women Officers or Directors**: 1
**Hot Spot for Advancement for Women/Minorities**: Y

## LOCATIONS: ("Y" = Yes)

| West: | Southwest: | Midwest: | Southeast: | Northeast: | International: |
|---|---|---|---|---|---|
| Y | Y | Y | Y | Y | Y |

# ELOYALTY CORPORATION

www.eloyaltyco.com

**Industry Group Code:** 511203 **Ranks within this company's industry group:** Sales: 5 Profits: 6

| Management: | | Sales/Marketing: | | Liberal Arts: | | Information Systems: | | Professionals: | | Technical/Scientific: | |
|---|---|---|---|---|---|---|---|---|---|---|---|
| Mgmt. Trainees: | | Mktg. Professionals: | Y | Gen. Writing/Editing: | | Info. Management: | Y | Finance/Accounting: | Y | Engineers, Elec.: | Y |
| Experienced Mgmt.: | Y | Retail Sales: | | Technical Writing: | Y | Software Dev.: | Y | Law: | Y | Engineers, Other: | |
| Int'l Business: | Y | Commercial/Industrial: | Y | Graphic Arts/Photog.: | | Hardware Dev.: | | HR/Other: | Y | Health/Lab: | |
| MBA Graduates: | Y | Sales Trainees: | Y | Music: | | Systems Integration: | | Training: | Y | Scientists/Research: | |
| | | Advertising Pros.: | | Broadcasting: | | Consulting/Other: | Y | Health Care: | | Petroleum/Chemicals: | |
| | | | | Other: | Y | | | Consulting: | Y | Math/Other: | Y |

## TYPES OF BUSINESS:

Customer Relationship Management (CRM) Consulting
Managed CRM Services
IT Consulting
Management Consulting
Contact Center Services

## BRANDS/DIVISIONS/AFFILIATES:

e-PROFILE

## CONTACTS: *Note: Officers with more than one job title may be intentionally listed here more than once.*

Kelly D. Conway, CEO
Kelly D. Conway, Pres.
Christopher Min, CFO
Christopher Min, Corp. Sec.
Steven C. Pollema, VP-Integrated Contact Solutions/CRM Bus. Unit
Tench Coxe, Chmn.

**Phone:** 847-582-7000 **Fax:** 847-582-7001
**Toll-Free:** 877-235-6925
**Address:** 150 Field Dr., Ste. 250, Lake Forest, IL 60045 US

## GROWTH PLANS/SPECIAL FEATURES:

eLoyalty Corporation, formerly a subsidiary of Technology Solutions Company, is a leading management consulting, systems integration and managed services company. It focuses on optimizing customer interactions across and within marketing, sales and service, concentrating on two major service lines: Integrated Contact Solutions, which helps clients to converge their contact center environments into one network, instead of maintaining separate voice and data networks, and includes reselling third-party (primarily Cisco Systems) hardware and software; and Behavioral Analytics, which utilizes human behavioral modeling to assess and enrich customer interactions. Other services help clients employ speech-enabled self-service options to develop contact center efficiency and assist clients in developing acquisition, cross-sell and retention of customers by advancing customer data management, interaction management and campaign automation. eLoyalty offers a broad range of Customer Relationship Management (CRM) services, including evaluating and developing business strategies; designing and implementing technical architecture; and providing ongoing support for multi-vendor systems. Its major clients include Eli Lilly, Allstate Insurance and AT&T Wireless. Consulting services, generally involving integrating or building systems for clients, are billed principally on a time-and-materials basis and occasionally on a fixed-fee basis, and accounted for 51% of eLoyalty's 2007 revenue. Managed services accounted for 40%, and include contact center managed services; computer telephony integration, maintenance and support; outsourcing call center telephony networks and cross-platform monitoring; and the provision of hosting solutions and services related to e-PROFILE Internet banking products. Reselling products accounted for 9%.

Employees are offered medical, vision and dental insurance; life insurance; domestic partner benefits; short-and long-term disability coverage; a 401(k) plan; an employee stock purchase plan; and a legal plan.

## FINANCIALS: **Sales and profits are in thousands of dollars—add 000 to get the full amount. 2008 Note: Financial information for 2008 was not available for all companies at press time.**

| | | |
|---|---|---|
| 2008 Sales: $ | 2008 Profits: $ | **U.S. Stock Ticker: ELOY** |
| 2007 Sales: $102,105 | 2007 Profits: $-18,738 | **Int'l Ticker:** Int'l Exchange: |
| 2006 Sales: $89,828 | 2006 Profits: $-11,148 | Employees: 445 |
| 2005 Sales: $79,008 | 2005 Profits: $-7,647 | Fiscal Year Ends: 12/31 |
| 2004 Sales: $72,600 | 2004 Profits: $-5,900 | Parent Company: |

## SALARIES/BENEFITS:

| | | | | |
|---|---|---|---|---|
| Pension Plan: | ESOP Stock Plan: | Profit Sharing: | Top Exec. Salary: $480,000 | Bonus: $ |
| Savings Plan: Y | Stock Purch. Plan: Y | | Second Exec. Salary: $300,000 | Bonus: $ |

## OTHER THOUGHTS:

**Apparent Women Officers or Directors:** 1
**Hot Spot for Advancement for Women/Minorities:** Y

## LOCATIONS: ("Y" = Yes)

| West: | Southwest: | Midwest: | Southeast: | Northeast: | International: |
|---|---|---|---|---|---|
| | | Y | | | Y |

# EMBARCADERO TECHNOLOGIES INC

**www.embarcadero.com**

**Industry Group Code:** 511206 **Ranks within this company's industry group:** Sales: Profits:

| **Management:** | | **Sales/Marketing:** | | **Liberal Arts:** | | **Information Systems:** | | **Professionals:** | | **Technical/Scientific:** | |
|---|---|---|---|---|---|---|---|---|---|---|---|
| Mgmt. Trainees: | | Mktg. Professionals: | Y | Gen. Writing/Editing: | | Info. Management: | Y | Finance/Accounting: | Y | Engineers, Elec.: | Y |
| Experienced Mgmt.: | Y | Retail Sales: | | Technical Writing: | Y | Software Dev.: | Y | Law: | Y | Engineers, Other: | |
| Int'l Business: | Y | Commercial/Industrial: | Y | Graphic Arts/Photog.: | | Hardware Dev.: | | HR/Other: | Y | Health/Lab: | |
| MBA Graduates: | Y | Sales Trainees: | Y | Music: | | Systems Integration: | | Training: | Y | Scientists/Research: | |
| | | Advertising Pros.: | | Broadcasting: | | Consulting/Other: | | Health Care: | | Petroleum/Chemicals: | |
| | | | | Other: | | | | Consulting: | | Math/Other: | Y |

## TYPES OF BUSINESS:

Software-Application & Database Management

## BRANDS/DIVISIONS/AFFILIATES:

Thoma Cressey Bravo
DBArtisan
DSAuditor
Describe
DT/Studio
ER/Studio
Rapid SQL

## CONTACTS:

*Note: Officers with more than one job title may be intentionally listed here more than once.*

Wayne D. Williams, CEO
Jim Lines, CFO
Greg Davoll, VP-Mktg.
Lorraine C. Gnecco, VP-Human Resources
Wayne D. Williams, CTO
Greg Keller, VP-Prod. Mgmt.
Raj P. Sabhlok, Sr. VP-Oper.
Michelle Chase, Media Rel. Contact
Scott Schoonover, VP-Sales Americas
Nigel Brown, VP-Int'l

| | |
|---|---|
| **Phone:** 415-834-3131 | **Fax:** 415-434-1721 |
| **Toll-Free:** 800-247-4274 | |
| **Address:** 100 California St., Ste. 1200, San Francisco, CA 94111 US | |

## GROWTH PLANS/SPECIAL FEATURES:

Embarcadero Technologies, Inc. is a management technology company that addresses application and database lifecycle operations for leading corporations. Embarcadero designs and develops products for information transmission across databases. The products compress time frames and increase database performance and availability, which helps companies to build, optimize and manage their databases and applications. The firm offers its DatabaseGear and its newly acquired CodeGear products to approximately 3 million people in 29 countries. DatabaseGear offers professional grade tools to design, build, and secure databases and can support the leading databases including IBM DB2, InterBase, Microsoft SQL Server, MySQL, Oracle and Sybase. CodeGear offers small to medium businesses applications for use with Windows, Java, the internet and databases. International sales account for roughly 27% of revenue, and subsidiary Embarcadero Europe Ltd. manages the sales, marketing, and support of products in Europe, the Middle East and Africa. The firm also markets products through independent distributors and through its sales office in Melbourne, Australia. Additionally, the company has agreements with distributors in various countries in Central and Latin America, as well as the Asia Pacific region. Customers include 12,000 companies, financial institutions and government agencies worldwide, including over 90 of the Fortune 100, including JPMorganChase, Bank of America, Anheuser-Busch, Qwest and MetLife. Embarcadero products include Change Manager, DBArtisan, DSAuditor, Describe, DT/Studio, ER/Studio, Performance Center and Rapid SQL. Embarcadero allows its customers to submit technical support cases online. In June 2007, the firm became a private entity when private equity group Thoma Cressey Bravo acquired it in a $200 million transaction. In July 2008, the company acquired CodeGear from Borland Software Corp. for $24.5 million.

## FINANCIALS:

**Sales and profits are in thousands of dollars—add 000 to get the full amount. 2008 Note: Financial information for 2008 was not available for all companies at press time.**

| | | |
|---|---|---|
| 2008 Sales: $ | 2008 Profits: $ | **U.S. Stock Ticker: Private** |
| 2007 Sales: $ | 2007 Profits: $ | **Int'l Ticker:** Int'l Exchange: |
| 2006 Sales: $60,000 | 2006 Profits: $5,800 | Employees: 222 |
| 2005 Sales: $57,552 | 2005 Profits: $4,337 | Fiscal Year Ends: 12/31 |
| 2004 Sales: $56,294 | 2004 Profits: $1,988 | Parent Company: THOMA CRESSEY EQUITY PARTNERS INC |

## SALARIES/BENEFITS:

| | | | | |
|---|---|---|---|---|
| Pension Plan: | ESOP Stock Plan: | Profit Sharing: | Top Exec. Salary: $302,443 | Bonus: $ |
| Savings Plan: Y | Stock Purch. Plan: | | Second Exec. Salary: $240,000 | Bonus: $ |

## OTHER THOUGHTS:

**Apparent Women Officers or Directors**: 2
**Hot Spot for Advancement for Women/Minorities**: Y

## LOCATIONS: ("Y" = Yes)

| West: | Southwest: | Midwest: | Southeast: | Northeast: | International: |
|---|---|---|---|---|---|
| Y | | | | | Y |

# EMCORE CORP

www.emcore.com

**Industry Group Code:** 333298A **Ranks within this company's industry group:** Sales: 2 Profits: 5

| Management: | | Sales/Marketing: | | Liberal Arts: | | Information Systems: | | Professionals: | | Technical/Scientific: | |
|---|---|---|---|---|---|---|---|---|---|---|---|
| Mgmt. Trainees: | | Mktg. Professionals: | Y | Gen. Writing/Editing: | | Info. Management: | Y | Finance/Accounting: | Y | Engineers, Elec.: | Y |
| Experienced Mgmt.: | Y | Retail Sales: | | Technical Writing: | Y | Software Dev.: | Y | Law: | Y | Engineers, Other: | Y |
| Int'l Business: | Y | Commercial/Industrial: | Y | Graphic Arts/Photog.: | Y | Hardware Dev.: | Y | HR/Other: | Y | Health/Lab: | |
| MBA Graduates: | Y | Sales Trainees: | Y | Music: | | Systems Integration: | | Training: | Y | Scientists/Research: | Y |
| | | Advertising Pros.: | | Broadcasting: | | Consulting/Other: | | Health Care: | | Petroleum/Chemicals: | |
| | | | | Other: | | | | Consulting: | | Math/Other: | Y |

## TYPES OF BUSINESS:

Nanotechnology-Semiconductors
Telecommunications Equipment Components
Lasers
Photovoltaic Cells
Fiber Optics

## BRANDS/DIVISIONS/AFFILIATES:

EMCORE Photovoltaics
EMCORE Fiber Optics

## CONTACTS:

*Note: Officers with more than one job title may be intentionally listed here more than once.*

Hong Q. Hou, CEO
John M. Markovich, CFO
John Iannelli, CTO
Keith J. Kosco, General Counsel/Corp. Sec.
Christopher Larocca, VP/Gen. Mgr.-Broadband Fiber Optics
Stephen Krasulick, VP/Gen. Mgr.-Digital Products
David Danzilio, VP/Gen. Mgr.-Photovoltaics
Monica Van Berkel, VP-Bus. Mgmt.
Reuben F. Richards, Jr., Chmn.
Charlie Wang, VP/Gen. Mgr.-Emcore China

| **Phone:** 505-332-5000 | **Fax:** 505-332-5100 |
|---|---|
| **Toll-Free:** | |
| **Address:** 10420 Research Rd. SE, Albuquerque, NM 87123 US | |

## GROWTH PLANS/SPECIAL FEATURES:

EMCORE Corp. is a provider of compound semiconductor-based components and subsystems for the broadband, fiber optic, satellite and terrestrial solar power markets. The company operates in two segments, fiber optics and photovoltaics. The fiber optics segment offers optical components, subsystems and systems that enable the transmission of video, voice and data over high-capacity fiber optic cable for the high-speed data and telecommunications, cable television and fiber-to-the-premises networks. The segment also targets the satellite communications networks, storage area networks, video transport and defense and homeland security markets. The photovoltaics segment provides solar products for satellite and terrestrial applications. For satellite applications, EMCORE offers high-efficiency compound semiconductor-based gallium arsenide solar cells, covered interconnect cells and fully integrated solar panels. For terrestrial applications, the company offers its high-efficiency GaAs solar cells for use in solar power concentrator systems. The firm has two manufacturing facilities located in New Mexico and California. In 2008, EMCORE acquired Intel's telecom-related portion of its Optical Platform Division and also the enterprise and storage assets of its Optical Platform Division and the Intel Connects Cable business. These assets will be incorporated into Emcore's Digital Products division.

The company offers its employees medical, dental and vision insurance; life insurance; a 401(k) plan; long-term disability insurance; an employee assistance program; a tuition reimbursement program; flexible spending accounts; and an employee stock purchase plan.

## FINANCIALS:

**Sales and profits are in thousands of dollars—add 000 to get the full amount. 2008 Note: Financial information for 2008 was not available for all companies at press time.**

| | | |
|---|---|---|
| 2008 Sales: $239,303 | 2008 Profits: $-80,860 | **U.S. Stock Ticker: EMKR** |
| 2007 Sales: $169,606 | 2007 Profits: $-58,722 | **Int'l Ticker:** Int'l Exchange: |
| 2006 Sales: $143,533 | 2006 Profits: $54,923 | Employees: 1,006 |
| 2005 Sales: $115,367 | 2005 Profits: $-13,485 | Fiscal Year Ends: 9/30 |
| 2004 Sales: $93,069 | 2004 Profits: $-13,426 | Parent Company: |

## SALARIES/BENEFITS:

| | | | | |
|---|---|---|---|---|
| Pension Plan: | ESOP Stock Plan: | Profit Sharing: | Top Exec. Salary: $412,165 | Bonus: $326,536 |
| Savings Plan: Y | Stock Purch. Plan: Y | | Second Exec. Salary: $360,080 | Bonus: $313,600 |

## OTHER THOUGHTS:

**Apparent Women Officers or Directors:** 1
**Hot Spot for Advancement for Women/Minorities:**

## LOCATIONS: ("Y" = Yes)

| West: | Southwest: | Midwest: | Southeast: | Northeast: | International: |
|---|---|---|---|---|---|
| Y | Y | | | Y | Y |

# EMS TECHNOLOGIES INC

www.ems-t.com

**Industry Group Code:** 334200 **Ranks within this company's industry group:** Sales: 4 Profits: 3

| Management: | | Sales/Marketing: | | Liberal Arts: | | Information Systems: | | Professionals: | | Technical/Scientific: | |
|---|---|---|---|---|---|---|---|---|---|---|---|
| Mgmt. Trainees: | | Mktg. Professionals: | Y | Gen. Writing/Editing: | Y | Info. Management: | Y | Finance/Accounting: | Y | Engineers, Elec.: | Y |
| Experienced Mgmt.: | Y | Retail Sales: | | Technical Writing: | Y | Software Dev.: | Y | Law: | Y | Engineers, Other: | Y |
| Int'l Business: | Y | Commercial/Industrial: | Y | Graphic Arts/Photog.: | | Hardware Dev.: | Y | HR/Other: | Y | Health/Lab: | |
| MBA Graduates: | Y | Sales Trainees: | Y | Music: | | Systems Integration: | Y | Training: | Y | Scientists/Research: | |
| | | Advertising Pros.: | | Broadcasting: | | Consulting/Other: | | Health Care: | | Petroleum/Chemicals: | |
| | | | | Other: | | | | Consulting: | | Math/Other: | |

## TYPES OF BUSINESS:

Wireless Communications Equipment
Space & Technology Products
Satellite Equipment
Antennas
Wireless LAN Products
Mobile Computers
Military Communications Equipment

## BRANDS/DIVISIONS/AFFILIATES:

SATCOM
EMS Wireless
LXE, Inc.

## CONTACTS: *Note: Officers with more than one job title may be intentionally listed here more than once.*

Paul Domorski, CEO
Paul Domorski, Pres.
Gary Shell, CFO/Sr. VP
Perry D. Tanner, VP-Corp. Mktg.
Michael R. Robertson, Dir.-Human Resources
Michael R. Robertson, Dir.-Admin.
Timothy C. Reis, General Counsel/VP
Neil A. Mackay, Exec. VP-Strategy
Gary Shell, Treas.
William H. Roeder, Sr. VP/Acting Gen. Mgr.
Neil A. Mackay, Pres., EMS Satcom
Gary M. Hebb, VP/Gen. Mgr.-EMS Satcom
David Smith, VP/Gen. Mgr.-EMS Defense & Space Systems
John B. Mowell, Chmn.

| | |
|---|---|
| **Phone:** 770-263-9200 | **Fax:** 770-263-9207 |
| **Toll-Free:** | |
| **Address:** 660 Engineering Dr., Norcross, GA 30092 US | |

## GROWTH PLANS/SPECIAL FEATURES:

EMS Technologies, Inc. designs, manufactures and markets advanced wireless communications products. Its services are primarily used in supply chain management networks, satellite-based voice and data communications and defense and space applications for communications surveillance and electronic countermeasures. The company operates through three units: Defense & space systems (D&SS), SATCOM and LXE. The D&SS unit specializes in manufacturing highly engineered microwave-based hardware for satellites and defense electronics applications primarily for space and defense prime contractors or commercial communications systems integrators. The segment provides defense customers with critical subsystems and components for terrestrial, airborne and space-based communication; for radar and electronic warfare systems; and supports advanced surveillance, electronic counter-measure and secure communications capabilities. Additionally, it performs research and development services directly for the U.S. Department of Defense. SATCOM supplies a broad array of terminals and antennas to enable customers in aircraft and other mobile platforms, such as military command vehicles or over-the-road trucks, to communicate over satellite networks at a variety of data speeds. The division's products (e.g., aeronautical antennas and terminals; Inmarsat high-speed data terminals; and satellite packet data terminals) are marketed to third-parties that incorporate it with their products and services for sale and delivery to end-users, while its emergency management products are often marketed directly to end-user organizations. The LXE business unit designs, manufactures and installs rugged mobile terminals for use with wireless local area networks (WLANs). Designed to operate in harsh environments and in settings with difficult radio-connectivity characteristics, its products consist of hand-held terminals, vehicle-mounted terminals, wireless networks, host connectivity software, accessories as well as maintenance services primarily for commercial purposes.

## FINANCIALS: **Sales and profits are in thousands of dollars—add 000 to get the full amount. 2008 Note: Financial information for 2008 was not available for all companies at press time.**

| | | |
|---|---|---|
| 2008 Sales: $ | 2008 Profits: $ | **U.S. Stock Ticker: ELMG** |
| 2007 Sales: $287,879 | 2007 Profits: $18,744 | **Int'l Ticker:** Int'l Exchange: |
| 2006 Sales: $261,119 | 2006 Profits: $33,008 | Employees: 1,100 |
| 2005 Sales: $225,887 | 2005 Profits: $-11,443 | Fiscal Year Ends: 12/31 |
| 2004 Sales: $201,100 | 2004 Profits: $ 192 | Parent Company: |

## SALARIES/BENEFITS:

| | | | | |
|---|---|---|---|---|
| Pension Plan: | ESOP Stock Plan: | Profit Sharing: | Top Exec. Salary: $414,713 | Bonus: $358,561 |
| Savings Plan: | Stock Purch. Plan: | | Second Exec. Salary: $294,302 | Bonus: $204,688 |

## OTHER THOUGHTS:

**Apparent Women Officers or Directors**: 1
**Hot Spot for Advancement for Women/Minorities**:

## LOCATIONS: ("Y" = Yes)

| West: | Southwest: | Midwest: | Southeast: | Northeast: | International: |
|---|---|---|---|---|---|
| | | | Y | | Y |

Note: Financial information, benefits and other data can change quickly and may vary from those stated here.

# EMULEX CORP

www.emulex.com

**Industry Group Code:** 334110 **Ranks within this company's industry group:** Sales: 3 Profits: 3

| Management: | | Sales/Marketing: | | Liberal Arts: | | Information Systems: | | Professionals: | | Technical/Scientific: | |
|---|---|---|---|---|---|---|---|---|---|---|---|
| Mgmt. Trainees: | | Mktg. Professionals: | Y | Gen. Writing/Editing: | | Info. Management: | Y | Finance/Accounting: | Y | Engineers, Elec.: | Y |
| Experienced Mgmt.: | Y | Retail Sales: | | Technical Writing: | Y | Software Dev.: | Y | Law: | Y | Engineers, Other: | |
| Int'l Business: | Y | Commercial/Industrial: | Y | Graphic Arts/Photog.: | | Hardware Dev.: | Y | HR/Other: | Y | Health/Lab: | |
| MBA Graduates: | Y | Sales Trainees: | Y | Music: | | Systems Integration: | Y | Training: | Y | Scientists/Research: | Y |
| | | Advertising Pros.: | | Broadcasting: | | Consulting/Other: | | Health Care: | | Petroleum/Chemicals: | |
| | | | | Other: | | | | Consulting: | | Math/Other: | |

## TYPES OF BUSINESS:

Networking Equipment-High-Performance Interfaces
High-Speed Fiber-Channel Products
Networking Software

## BRANDS/DIVISIONS/AFFILIATES:

LightPulse
InSpeed
FibreSpy

## CONTACTS:

*Note: Officers with more than one job title may be intentionally listed here more than once.*

Jim McCluney, CEO
Jeff Benck, COO/Exec. VP
Jim McCluney, Pres.
Michael J. Rockenbach, CFO/Exec. VP
Steve Daheb, Chief Mktg. Officer/Exec. VP
Susan Bowman, Exec. VP-Human Resources & Facilities
Marshall Lee, Exec. VP-Eng.
Randall Wick, General Counsel/VP
John Warwick, Sr. VP-Oper.
Steve Berg, Sr. VP-Corp. Dev.
Bob Whitson, Sr. VP/Gen. Mgr.-Embedded Storage Products
Paul F. Folino, Chmn.

**Phone:** 714-662-5600 **Fax:** 714-241-0792
**Toll-Free:** 800-368-5391
**Address:** 3333 Susan St., Costa Mesa, CA 92626 US

## GROWTH PLANS/SPECIAL FEATURES:

Emulex Corporation, a leading global supplier of storage networking host bus adapters (HBAs), manufactures hardware and software network access products mostly involving fiber channel and fabric storage switches. These products are electronic component parts assembled on internally designed printed circuit boards, which are sold as board-level products. Host server products include LightPulse HBA's, custom form factor solutions for original equipment manufacturer (OEM) blade servers, and application-specific integrated circuits (ASICs). Embedded storage products include InSpeed and FibreSpy switches, and input/output controller (IOC) solutions, as well as embedded bridge and embedded router products. Intelligent network products consist of intelligent storage processors that are deployed within storage area network appliances and storage arrays. Emulex sells worldwide to OEMs and end users through its own worldwide selling organization as well as through its two tier distribution partners, who include Acal plc group; Avnet, Inc.; Bell Microproducts, Inc.; Info X Technology Solutions; Macnica Networks Corporation; Netmarks Inc.; Tech Data Corporation; and Tokyo Electron Device Ltd. In November 2008, the company opened a new international operations office in Dublin, marking the fourth Emulex office in Europe.

Employees are offered medical, dental and life insurance; disability plans; flexible spending accounts; a 401(k) plan; an employee stock purchase plan; subsidized memberships at 24 Hour Fitness; and credit union eligibility.

## FINANCIALS:

**Sales and profits are in thousands of dollars—add 000 to get the full amount. 2008 Note: Financial information for 2008 was not available for all companies at press time.**

| | | |
|---|---|---|
| 2008 Sales: $488,301 | 2008 Profits: $-7,071 | **U.S. Stock Ticker: ELX** |
| 2007 Sales: $470,187 | 2007 Profits: $29,434 | **Int'l Ticker:** Int'l Exchange: |
| 2006 Sales: $402,813 | 2006 Profits: $40,451 | Employees: 853 |
| 2005 Sales: $375,653 | 2005 Profits: $71,589 | Fiscal Year Ends: 6/30 |
| 2004 Sales: $364,422 | 2004 Profits: $-532,322 | Parent Company: |

## SALARIES/BENEFITS:

| | | | | |
|---|---|---|---|---|
| Pension Plan: | ESOP Stock Plan: | Profit Sharing: | Top Exec. Salary: $589,645 | Bonus: $375,982 |
| Savings Plan: Y | Stock Purch. Plan: Y | | Second Exec. Salary: $565,248 | Bonus: $364,471 |

## OTHER THOUGHTS:

**Apparent Women Officers or Directors**: 1
**Hot Spot for Advancement for Women/Minorities**: Y

## LOCATIONS: ("Y" = Yes)

| West: | Southwest: | Midwest: | Southeast: | Northeast: | International: |
|---|---|---|---|---|---|
| Y | | | | Y | Y |

# ENCORE ACQUISITION CO

**www.encoreacq.com**

**Industry Group Code:** 211111 **Ranks within this company's industry group:** Sales: 14 Profits: 19

| **Management:** | | **Sales/Marketing:** | | **Liberal Arts:** | | **Information Systems:** | | **Professionals:** | | **Technical/Scientific:** | |
|---|---|---|---|---|---|---|---|---|---|---|---|
| Mgmt. Trainees: | | Mktg. Professionals: | Y | Gen. Writing/Editing: | | Info. Management: | Y | Finance/Accounting: | Y | Engineers, Elec.: | |
| Experienced Mgmt.: | Y | Retail Sales: | | Technical Writing: | | Software Dev.: | | Law: | Y | Engineers, Other: | Y |
| Int'l Business: | Y | Commercial/Industrial: | Y | Graphic Arts/Photog.: | | Hardware Dev.: | | HR/Other: | Y | Health/Lab: | |
| MBA Graduates: | Y | Sales Trainees: | | Music: | | Systems Integration: | | Training: | Y | Scientists/Research: | |
| | | Advertising Pros.: | | Broadcasting: | | Consulting/Other: | | Health Care: | | Petroleum/Chemicals: | Y |
| | | | | Other: | | | | Consulting: | | Math/Other: | |

## TYPES OF BUSINESS:

Oil & Gas Exploration & Production
Strategic Acquisitions
Reservoir Management

## BRANDS/DIVISIONS/AFFILIATES:

## CONTACTS: *Note: Officers with more than one job title may be intentionally listed here more than once.*

Jon S. Brumley, CEO
L. Ben Nivens, Jr., COO/Sr. VP
Jon S. Brumley, Pres.
Robert C. Reeves, CFO
Andy R. Lowe, VP-Mktg.
Dan Lott, Dir.-Human Resources
Thomas H. Olle, VP-Strategic Solutions
Diane Weaver, VP-Investor Rel.
Robert C. Reeves, Sr. VP/Treas.
John W. Arms, Sr. VP-Acquisitions
Andrea Hunter, VP/Controller/Principal Acct. Officer
N. Kevin Treadway, VP-Land
I. Jon Brumley, Chmn.

## GROWTH PLANS/SPECIAL FEATURES:

Encore Acquisition Co. focuses on the acquisition and development of oil and natural gas reserves from onshore fields in the U.S. The company has acquired producing properties with proven reserves and leasehold acreage and grown the production and proven reserves by drilling, exploring, reengineering or expanding existing waterflood projects, and applying tertiary recovery techniques. The company's properties and its oil and natural gas reserves are located in four core areas: The Cedar Creek Anticline (CCA) in the Williston Basin of Montana and North Dakota; the Permian Basin of west Texas and southeastern New Mexico; the Rockies, which includes non-CCA assets in the Williston and Powder River Basins of Montana and North Dakota and the Paradox Basin of southeastern Utah; and the mid-continent areas, which includes the Arkoma and Anadarko Basins of Oklahoma, the North Louisiana Salt Basin and the East Texas Basin. The firm has total proved reserves of about 189 million barrels of oil equivalent and 256 billions of cubic feet equivalent of natural gas. The CCA represents about 50% of Encore Acquisition's total proved reserves. In December 2007, the firm entered into agreement to sell oil and natural gas producing land, located in the Permian and Williston Basins, to Encore Partners LP. The property being purchased has proven reserves of 10.8 million barrels of oil equivalent, 88% proved developed producing and 65% oil.

| **Phone:** 817-877-9955 | **Fax:** 817-877-1655 |
|---|---|
| **Toll-Free:** | |
| **Address:** 777 Main St., Ste. 1400, Fort Worth, TX 76102 US | |

## FINANCIALS: **Sales and profits are in thousands of dollars—add 000 to get the full amount. 2008 Note: Financial information for 2008 was not available for all companies at press time.**

| | | |
|---|---|---|
| 2008 Sales: $1,135,418 | 2008 Profits: $430,812 | **U.S. Stock Ticker: EAC** |
| 2007 Sales: $754,945 | 2007 Profits: $17,155 | **Int'l Ticker:** Int'l Exchange: |
| 2006 Sales: $640,862 | 2006 Profits: $92,398 | Employees: 364 |
| 2005 Sales: $457,324 | 2005 Profits: $103,425 | Fiscal Year Ends: 12/31 |
| 2004 Sales: $298,533 | 2004 Profits: $82,147 | Parent Company: |

## SALARIES/BENEFITS:

| | | | | |
|---|---|---|---|---|
| Pension Plan: | ESOP Stock Plan: | Profit Sharing: | Top Exec. Salary: $537,500 | Bonus: $850,000 |
| Savings Plan: | Stock Purch. Plan: | | Second Exec. Salary: $350,000 | Bonus: $700,000 |

## OTHER THOUGHTS:

**Apparent Women Officers or Directors**: 2
**Hot Spot for Advancement for Women/Minorities**:

## LOCATIONS: ("Y" = Yes)

| West: | Southwest: | Midwest: | Southeast: | Northeast: | International: |
|---|---|---|---|---|---|
| Y | Y | Y | | | |

# ENCORIUM GROUP INC

www.encorium.com

**Industry Group Code:** 541710 **Ranks within this company's industry group:** Sales: 5 Profits: 4

| **Management:** | | **Sales/Marketing:** | | **Liberal Arts:** | | **Information Systems:** | | **Professionals:** | | **Technical/Scientific:** | |
|---|---|---|---|---|---|---|---|---|---|---|---|
| Mgmt. Trainees: | | Mktg. Professionals: | Y | Gen. Writing/Editing: | | Info. Management: | Y | Finance/Accounting: | Y | Engineers, Elec.: | |
| Experienced Mgmt.: | Y | Retail Sales: | | Technical Writing: | Y | Software Dev.: | Y | Law: | Y | Engineers, Other: | |
| Int'l Business: | Y | Commercial/Industrial: | | Graphic Arts/Photog.: | | Hardware Dev.: | | HR/Other: | Y | Health/Lab: | |
| MBA Graduates: | Y | Sales Trainees: | | Music: | | Systems Integration: | | Training: | Y | Scientists/Research: | Y |
| | | Advertising Pros.: | | Broadcasting: | | Consulting/Other: | | Health Care: | | Petroleum/Chemicals: | |
| | | | | Other: | | | | Consulting: | Y | Math/Other: | |

## TYPES OF BUSINESS:

Contract Research
Clinical Trial & Data Management
Disease Assessment Software
Biostatistical Analysis
Regulatory Affairs Services

## BRANDS/DIVISIONS/AFFILIATES:

Remedium Oy
Covalent Group, Inc.

## CONTACTS:
*Note: Officers with more than one job title may be intentionally listed here more than once.*

David Ginsberg, CEO
Linda L. Nardone, COO/Exec. VP
Kenneth M. Borow, Pres.
Philip L. Calamia, Interim CFO
Eeva-Kaarina Koskelo, VP-Clinical Oper., Europe & Asia
Kai E. Lindevall, Chmn.
Kai E. Lindevall, Pres.,-Int'l Oper.

**Phone:** 610-975-9533 **Fax:** 610-975-9556
**Toll-Free:**
**Address:** 1 Glenhardie Corp Ctr., 1275 Drummers Ln. Ste. 100, Wayne, PA 19087 US

## GROWTH PLANS/SPECIAL FEATURES:

Encorium Group, Inc., formed in 2006 from a merger between Remedium Oy and Covalent Group, Inc., is a contract research organization (CRO) that designs and manages clinical trials in the pharmaceutical, biotechnology and medical device development process. Encorium offers therapeutic expertise, experienced team management and advanced technologies, with the capacity to conduct clinical trials on a global basis. The company specializes in Phase I through IV clinical trials, cost-effectiveness studies and outcomes studies for pharmaceutical companies, managed-care organizations, insurers and employers. It offers a full array of integrated services, including strategic trial planning; project management; monitoring; data management; biostatistics; pharmacovigilance; medical writing; quality assurance; outsourcing of clinical staff; and medical device certification in the European Union. The firm's clinical trials management services include assistance with case report form design, investigator recruitment, patient enrollment and study monitoring and data collection. Encorium has clinical trial experience across a wide variety of therapeutic areas, such as cardiovascular, nephrology, endocrinology/metabolism, hematology, diabetes, neurology, oncology, immunology, vaccines, infectious diseases, gastroenterology, dermatology, hepatology, rheumatology, urology, ophthalmology, women's health and respiratory medicine. Encorium's clients consist of many of the largest companies in the pharmaceutical, biotechnology and medical device industries. During 2007, it provided services to 96 different clients covering 215 separate studies, of which 77 clients and 184 studies were associated with its European operations. Roughly 37% of Encorium's revenue was generated by its operations in the U.S. during 2007 and roughly 63% by its operations in Europe. In 2007, the firm's three largest clients accounted for 38% of its net revenues. Encorium is generally awarded contracts based upon its response to requests for proposals received from pharmaceutical, biotechnology and medical device companies, and its business development and marketing strategy is based on expanding its relationships with its existing clients as well as gaining new clients.

## FINANCIALS:
**Sales and profits are in thousands of dollars—add 000 to get the full amount. 2008 Note: Financial information for 2008 was not available for all companies at press time.**

| | | |
|---|---|---|
| 2008 Sales: $ | 2008 Profits: $ | **U.S. Stock Ticker: ENCO** |
| 2007 Sales: $36,802 | 2007 Profits: $-2,751 | **Int'l Ticker:** Int'l Exchange: |
| 2006 Sales: $17,684 | 2006 Profits: $- 494 | Employees: 275 |
| 2005 Sales: $12,727 | 2005 Profits: $-1,484 | Fiscal Year Ends: 12/31 |
| 2004 Sales: $13,590 | 2004 Profits: $-4,223 | Parent Company: |

## SALARIES/BENEFITS:

| | | | | |
|---|---|---|---|---|
| Pension Plan: | ESOP Stock Plan: | Profit Sharing: | Top Exec. Salary: $373,628 | Bonus: $58,432 |
| Savings Plan: Y | Stock Purch. Plan: | | Second Exec. Salary: $322,714 | Bonus: $ |

## OTHER THOUGHTS:

**Apparent Women Officers or Directors:** 2
**Hot Spot for Advancement for Women/Minorities:** Y

## LOCATIONS: ("Y" = Yes)

| West: | Southwest: | Midwest: | Southeast: | Northeast: | International: |
|---|---|---|---|---|---|
| | | | | Y | Y |

# ENDO PHARMACEUTICALS HOLDINGS INC

www.endo.com

**Industry Group Code:** 325412 **Ranks within this company's industry group:** Sales: 3 Profits: 1

| Management: | | Sales/Marketing: | | Liberal Arts: | | Information Systems: | | Professionals: | | Technical/Scientific: | |
|---|---|---|---|---|---|---|---|---|---|---|---|
| Mgmt. Trainees: | | Mktg. Professionals: | Y | Gen. Writing/Editing: | | Info. Management: | Y | Finance/Accounting: | Y | Engineers, Elec.: | |
| Experienced Mgmt.: | Y | Retail Sales: | | Technical Writing: | Y | Software Dev.: | Y | Law: | Y | Engineers, Other: | |
| Int'l Business: | Y | Commercial/Industrial: | Y | Graphic Arts/Photog.: | | Hardware Dev.: | | HR/Other: | Y | Health/Lab: | Y |
| MBA Graduates: | Y | Sales Trainees: | Y | Music: | | Systems Integration: | | Training: | Y | Scientists/Research: | Y |
| | | Advertising Pros.: | | Broadcasting: | | Consulting/Other: | | Health Care: | Y | Petroleum/Chemicals: | Y |
| | | | | Other: | | | | Consulting: | | Math/Other: | Y |

## TYPES OF BUSINESS:

Drugs-Pain Management
Pharmaceutical Preparations

## BRANDS/DIVISIONS/AFFILIATES:

Endo Pharmaceuticals, Inc.
Lidoderm
Opana
Percocet
Frova
Novartis Consumer Health, Inc.
Teikoku Seiyaku Co., Ltd.

## CONTACTS:

*Note: Officers with more than one job title may be intentionally listed here more than once.*

David P. Holveck, CEO
Nancy J. Wysenski, COO
David P. Holveck, Pres.
Charles A. Rowland, Jr., CFO/Exec. VP
Ivan Gergel, Exec. VP-R&D
Caroline B. Manogue, Chief Legal Officer/Corp. Sec./Exec. VP
Blaine T. Davis, VP-Corp. Comm.
Blaine T. Davis, VP-Investor Rel.
Joyce N. LaViscount, Chief Acct. Officer/VP-Financial Oper.
Roger H. Kimmel, Chmn.

| | |
|---|---|
| **Phone:** 610-558-9800 | **Fax:** 610-558-7699 |
| **Toll-Free:** | |
| **Address:** 100 Endo Blvd., Chadds Ford, PA 19317 US | |

## GROWTH PLANS/SPECIAL FEATURES:

Endo Pharmaceuticals Holdings, Inc., through subsidiary Endo Pharmaceuticals, Inc., is a specialty pharmaceutical company engaged in the research, development, sale and marketing of branded and generic prescription pharmaceuticals used primarily to treat and manage pain. The company has a portfolio of branded products that includes such names as Lidoderm, a topical patch containing lidocaine; Opana and Opana ER, indicated for the relief of moderate to severe pain in patients requiring continuous opioid treatment; Percocet, indicated for the treatment of moderate to moderately severe pain; and Frova, a migraine treatment product. Branded products generate approximately 92% of Endo's net sales in 2007, with 65% of its net sales generated from Lidoderm. Its non-branded generic portfolio currently consists of products primarily focused in pain management. The firm focuses selectively on generics that have one or more barriers to market entry, such as complex formulation, regulatory or legal challenges or difficulty in raw material sourcing. Endo's branded product portfolio includes three products in Phase III clinical trials, three products in Phase II clinical trials and one product in Phase I trials. The firm's primary suppliers of contract manufacturing services are Novartis Consumer Health, Inc. and Teikoku Seiyaku Co., Ltd. It markets its branded products through a dedicated sales force of approximately 700 sales representatives in the U.S. to high-prescribing physicians in the pain management, neurology, surgery, anesthesiology, oncology and primary care, as well as retail pharmacies.

Endo offers its employees educational assistance; individual development plans; financial planning assistance; flexible time off; parenting benefits; an employee assistance program; flexible spending accounts; and medical, dental, vision, pharmacy and disability insurance.

## FINANCIALS:

**Sales and profits are in thousands of dollars—add 000 to get the full amount. 2008 Note: Financial information for 2008 was not available for all companies at press time.**

| | | |
|---|---|---|
| 2008 Sales: $ | 2008 Profits: $ | **U.S. Stock Ticker: ENDP** |
| 2007 Sales: $1,085,608 | 2007 Profits: $227,440 | **Int'l Ticker:** Int'l Exchange: |
| 2006 Sales: $909,659 | 2006 Profits: $137,839 | Employees: 1,208 |
| 2005 Sales: $820,164 | 2005 Profits: $202,295 | Fiscal Year Ends: 12/31 |
| 2004 Sales: $615,100 | 2004 Profits: $143,300 | Parent Company: |

## SALARIES/BENEFITS:

| | | | | |
|---|---|---|---|---|
| Pension Plan: | ESOP Stock Plan: | Profit Sharing: | Top Exec. Salary: $606,000 | Bonus: $300,000 |
| Savings Plan: Y | Stock Purch. Plan: Y | | Second Exec. Salary: $450,000 | Bonus: $225,000 |

## OTHER THOUGHTS:

**Apparent Women Officers or Directors**: 3
**Hot Spot for Advancement for Women/Minorities**: Y

## LOCATIONS: ("Y" = Yes)

| West: | Southwest: | Midwest: | Southeast: | Northeast: | International: |
|---|---|---|---|---|---|
| | | | | Y | |

# ENERGY CONVERSION DEVICES INC

www.ovonic.com

**Industry Group Code:** 333298A **Ranks within this company's industry group:** Sales: 3 Profits: 4

| Management: | | Sales/Marketing: | | Liberal Arts: | | Information Systems: | | Professionals: | | Technical/Scientific: | |
|---|---|---|---|---|---|---|---|---|---|---|---|
| Mgmt. Trainees: | | Mktg. Professionals: | Y | Gen. Writing/Editing: | | Info. Management: | Y | Finance/Accounting: | Y | Engineers, Elec.: | Y |
| Experienced Mgmt.: | Y | Retail Sales: | | Technical Writing: | Y | Software Dev.: | Y | Law: | Y | Engineers, Other: | Y |
| Int'l Business: | Y | Commercial/Industrial: | Y | Graphic Arts/Photog.: | Y | Hardware Dev.: | Y | HR/Other: | Y | Health/Lab: | |
| MBA Graduates: | Y | Sales Trainees: | Y | Music: | | Systems Integration: | | Training: | Y | Scientists/Research: | Y |
| | | Advertising Pros.: | | Broadcasting: | | Consulting/Other: | | Health Care: | | Petroleum/Chemicals: | |
| | | | | Other: | | | | Consulting: | | Math/Other: | Y |

## TYPES OF BUSINESS:

Solar Energy Technology
Battery Technology
Optical Memory Technology
Hydrogen Technology
Fuel Cells

## BRANDS/DIVISIONS/AFFILIATES:

United Solar Ovonic, LLC

## CONTACTS: *Note: Officers with more than one job title may be intentionally listed here more than once.*

Mark D. Morelli, CEO
Mark D. Morelli, Pres.
Harry W. Zike, CFO/VP
Marcelino Susas, VP-Strategic Mktg.
Art Rogers, VP-Human Resources
Tom Toner, VP-Sys. Eng.
Jay B. Knoll, Chief Admin. Officer
Jay B. Knoll, General Counsel/Sr. VP
Joe Conroy, Sr. VP-Oper.
Ghazaleh Koefod, Corp. Sec.
Subhendu Guha, Sr. VP/Chmn.-United Solar Ovonic
Corby C. Whitaker, VP-Global Sales

**Phone:** 248-293-0440 **Fax:** 248-844-1214
**Toll-Free:** 800-528-0617
**Address:** 2956 Waterview Dr., Rochester Hills, MI 48309 US

## GROWTH PLANS/SPECIAL FEATURES:

Energy Conversion Devices, Inc. (ECD) commercializes materials, products and production processes for the alternative energy generation, energy storage and IT markets. The company operates in two segments: United Solar Ovonic and Ovonic materials. The United Solar Ovonic segment, which operates through United Solar Ovonic, LLC, designs, develops, manufactures and sells PV modules that generate clean, renewable energy by converting sunlight into electricity. This business is based principally on the proprietary technology for thin-film amorphous silicon photovoltaic (PV) modules. The PV modules are lightweight, thin, flexible and durable and can be integrated directly with roofing materials for a seamless appearance. Conventional PV products, which currently represent over 90% of the solar modules sold globally, are made of crystalline or polycrystalline silicon and are covered in glass enclosed by a metal frame. The Ovonic materials segment invents, designs, and develops materials and products based on the firm's materials science technology, principally amorphous and disordered materials. The division currently commercializes the nickel metal hydride batteries (NiMH), which are rechargeable energy storage solutions. ECD manufactures and sells its products through joint venture companies and licensing arrangements with major companies throughout the world. The firm has over 300 U.S. patents and over 400 foreign counterparts. In 2008, ECD signed an agreement to power General Motor's assembly plant in Spain with its thin-film flexible solar laminates. United Solar Ovonic also signed an agreement to supply the European steel transformation company, Marcegaglia S.p.A with individual PV cells for their commercial roofing products.

The company offers its employees benefits that include a 401(k) plan; medical, vision and dental insurance; life and AD&D insurance; and disability benefits.

## FINANCIALS: **Sales and profits are in thousands of dollars—add 000 to get the full amount. 2008 Note: Financial information for 2008 was not available for all companies at press time.**

2008 Sales: $255,861 | 2008 Profits: $3,853
2007 Sales: $113,567 | 2007 Profits: $-25,231
2006 Sales: $102,419 | 2006 Profits: $-18,596
2005 Sales: $156,570 | 2005 Profits: $50,332
2004 Sales: $66,304 | 2004 Profits: $-51,421

**U.S. Stock Ticker: ENER**
**Int'l Ticker:** Int'l Exchange:
Employees: 1,090
Fiscal Year Ends: 6/30
Parent Company:

## SALARIES/BENEFITS:

Pension Plan: | ESOP Stock Plan: | Profit Sharing: | Top Exec. Salary: $389,430 | Bonus: $538,100
Savings Plan: Y | Stock Purch. Plan: | | Second Exec. Salary: $306,943 | Bonus: $225,000

## OTHER THOUGHTS:

**Apparent Women Officers or Directors**: 1
**Hot Spot for Advancement for Women/Minorities**:

## LOCATIONS: ("Y" = Yes)

| West: | Southwest: | Midwest: | Southeast: | Northeast: | International: |
|---|---|---|---|---|---|
| | | Y | | | Y |

# ENERNOC INC

www.enernoc.com

**Industry Group Code:** 541690 **Ranks within this company's industry group:** Sales: 1 Profits: 1

| Management: | | Sales/Marketing: | | Liberal Arts: | | Information Systems: | | Professionals: | | Technical/Scientific: | |
|---|---|---|---|---|---|---|---|---|---|---|---|
| Mgmt. Trainees: | | Mktg. Professionals: | Y | Gen. Writing/Editing: | | Info. Management: | Y | Finance/Accounting: | Y | Engineers, Elec.: | |
| Experienced Mgmt.: | Y | Retail Sales: | | Technical Writing: | | Software Dev.: | | Law: | Y | Engineers, Other: | |
| Int'l Business: | | Commercial/Industrial: | | Graphic Arts/Photog.: | | Hardware Dev.: | | HR/Other: | Y | Health/Lab: | |
| MBA Graduates: | Y | Sales Trainees: | Y | Music: | | Systems Integration: | | Training: | Y | Scientists/Research: | |
| | | Advertising Pros.: | | Broadcasting: | | Consulting/Other: | | Health Care: | | Petroleum/Chemicals: | |
| | | | | Other: | | | | Consulting: | | Math/Other: | |

## TYPES OF BUSINESS:

Energy Efficiency Technology & Services

## BRANDS/DIVISIONS/AFFILIATES:

## CONTACTS:

*Note: Officers with more than one job title may be intentionally listed here more than once.*

Tim Healy, CEO
Darren Brady, COO
David Brewster, Pres.
Neal Isaacson, CFO/Sr. VP
David Samuels, Sr. VP-Sales
Terry Sick, VP-Prod. Dev.
Terry Sick, VP-Eng.
Gregg Dixon, Sr. VP-Bus. Dev.
David Samuels, Exec. VP
Tim Healy, Chmn.

| | |
|---|---|
| **Phone:** 617-224-9900 | **Fax:** 617-224-9910 |
| **Toll-Free:** | |
| **Address:** 75 Federal St., Ste 300, Boston, MA 02110 US | |

## GROWTH PLANS/SPECIAL FEATURES:

EnerNOC is a developer and provider of clean energy solutions. The firm uses its network operations center (NOC) to remotely manage and reduce electricity consumption across a network of commercial, institutional and industrial customer sites to enable a more information-based and responsive electric power grid. Its customers are electric power grid operators and utilities, as well as commercial, institutional and industrial end-users of electricity. The company has developed a proprietary suite of technology applications and operational processes that enable us to make demand response capacity and energy available to grid operators and utilities on demand and remotely manage electricity consumption at commercial, institutional and industrial customer sites. These solutions offer several benefits including, but not limited to, reduced environment impact, value proposition to grid operators and utilities and energy management solutions for end-use customers. Additionally, the firm provides several technology-enabled energy management solutions to its commercial, institutional and industrial customers. Services offered include the following: advanced metering applications, energy analytics and control and energy procurement services. Advanced metering applications offers meter data gathering and storage services for advanced meters. Energy analytics and control offers clients a technology based energy analytics service designed to help optimize the way buildings operate, measure the impact of key energy and environmental decisions, and enhance the comfort of occupants. The firms PowerTrak application integrates data from disparate energy management systems with utility metering to gather data on a customer's overall energy usage. Its analysts then use tools, filters, and applications to monitor and review this data, and provide distilled information and recommendations designed to optimize performance; reduce energy consumption; reduce carbon emissions; prioritize maintenance needs; and enhance occupant comfort. Energy procurement services offers end-use commercial, institutional and industrial customers various services related to procuring commodity supply contracts from competitive electricity suppliers.

## FINANCIALS:

**Sales and profits are in thousands of dollars—add 000 to get the full amount. 2008 Note: Financial information for 2008 was not available for all companies at press time.**

| | | |
|---|---|---|
| 2008 Sales: $ | 2008 Profits: $ | **U.S. Stock Ticker: ENOC** |
| 2007 Sales: $60,838 | 2007 Profits: $-23,582 | **Int'l Ticker:** Int'l Exchange: |
| 2006 Sales: $26,100 | 2006 Profits: $-5,771 | Employees: 253 |
| 2005 Sales: $9,826 | 2005 Profits: $-1,706 | Fiscal Year Ends: 12/31 |
| 2004 Sales: $ | 2004 Profits: $ | Parent Company: |

## SALARIES/BENEFITS:

| | | | | |
|---|---|---|---|---|
| Pension Plan: | ESOP Stock Plan: | Profit Sharing: | Top Exec. Salary: $307,500 | Bonus: $325,000 |
| Savings Plan: | Stock Purch. Plan: | | Second Exec. Salary: $265,000 | Bonus: $265,000 |

## OTHER THOUGHTS:

**Apparent Women Officers or Directors:**
**Hot Spot for Advancement for Women/Minorities:**

## LOCATIONS: ("Y" = Yes)

| West: | Southwest: | Midwest: | Southeast: | Northeast: | International: |
|---|---|---|---|---|---|
| | | | | Y | |

# ENGLOBAL CORP

www.englobal.com

**Industry Group Code:** 541330 **Ranks within this company's industry group:** Sales: 2 Profits: 2

| Management: | | Sales/Marketing: | | Liberal Arts: | | Information Systems: | | Professionals: | | Technical/Scientific: | |
|---|---|---|---|---|---|---|---|---|---|---|---|
| Mgmt. Trainees: | | Mktg. Professionals: | Y | Gen. Writing/Editing: | | Info. Management: | Y | Finance/Accounting: | Y | Engineers, Elec.: | Y |
| Experienced Mgmt.: | Y | Retail Sales: | | Technical Writing: | Y | Software Dev.: | | Law: | Y | Engineers, Other: | Y |
| Int'l Business: | Y | Commercial/Industrial: | Y | Graphic Arts/Photog.: | | Hardware Dev.: | | HR/Other: | Y | Health/Lab: | |
| MBA Graduates: | Y | Sales Trainees: | | Music: | | Systems Integration: | | Training: | Y | Scientists/Research: | |
| | | Advertising Pros.: | | Broadcasting: | | Consulting/Other: | | Health Care: | | Petroleum/Chemicals: | |
| | | | | Other: | | | | Consulting: | Y | Math/Other: | |

## TYPES OF BUSINESS:

Engineering Services
Petrochemicals Industry Support Services
Control & Instrumentation Systems
Consulting & Inspection Services
Project Management

## BRANDS/DIVISIONS/AFFILIATES:

## CONTACTS:

*Note: Officers with more than one job title may be intentionally listed here more than once.*

William A. Coskey, CEO
William A. Coskey, Pres.
Robert W. Raiford, CFO
Robert J. Church, Corp. Mgr.-Human Resources
Alex Schroeder, Manager-Corp. IT
Natalie S. Hairston, Corp. Sec./Chief Governance Officer
Michael M. Patton, Sr. VP-Bus. Dev.
Natalie S. Hairston, VP-Investor Rel.
Robert W. Raiford, Treas.
R. David Kelley, Sr. VP-Corp. Svcs.
Don A. Johnson, Mgr.-Health, Safety & Environmental
Michael H. Lee, Pres./COO-ENGlobal Land, Inc.
David W. Smith, Pres., ENGlobal Engineering, Inc.
William A. Coskey, Chmn.

**Phone:** 281-878-1000 **Fax:** 281-878-1010
**Toll-Free:** 800-411-6040
**Address:** 654 N. Sam Houston Pkwy E., Ste. 400, Houston, TX 77060-5914 US

## GROWTH PLANS/SPECIAL FEATURES:

ENGlobal Corp. is a leading international provider of engineering services and systems to the petroleum refining, petrochemical, pipeline, production and processing industries. The firm operates in four segments: Engineering, Construction, Automation and Land. The engineering segment provides consulting services relating to the development, management and execution of projects requiring professional engineering and related project services. Services provided by this segment include feasibility studies, engineering, design, procurement and construction management. The engineering segment provides these services to the upstream, midstream and downstream energy industries and branches of the U.S. military, and in some instances it delivers its services via in-plant personnel assigned throughout the U.S. and internationally. The construction segment provides construction management personnel and services in the areas of inspection, mechanical integrity, vendor and turnaround surveillance, field support, construction, quality assurance and plant asset management. Its customers include pipeline, refining, utility, chemical, petroleum, petrochemical, oil and gas, and power industries throughout the U.S. Construction segment personnel are typically assigned to client facilities throughout the U.S. The automation segment provides services related to the design, fabrication, and implementation of process distributed control and analyzer systems, advanced automation and information technology projects. This segment's customers include members of the domestic and foreign energy related industries. Automation segment personnel assist in on-site commissioning, start-up and training for the company's specialized systems. The land segment provides land management, right-of-way, environmental compliance and governmental regulatory compliance services primarily to the pipeline, utility and telecom companies and other owner/operators of infrastructure facilities throughout the U.S. and Canada. Major customers include Chevron Phillips, ExxonMobil, Frontier Refining, Enterprise Products and Honeywell, Inc.

ENGlobal provides its employees with educational reimbursement; health, dental, vision and life insurance; disability benefits; and flexible spending accounts.

## FINANCIALS:

**Sales and profits are in thousands of dollars—add 000 to get the full amount. 2008 Note: Financial information for 2008 was not available for all companies at press time.**

| | | |
|---|---|---|
| 2008 Sales: $ | 2008 Profits: $ | **U.S. Stock Ticker: ENG** |
| 2007 Sales: $363,227 | 2007 Profits: $12,464 | **Int'l Ticker:** Int'l Exchange: |
| 2006 Sales: $303,090 | 2006 Profits: $-3,486 | Employees: 2,443 |
| 2005 Sales: $233,585 | 2005 Profits: $4,782 | Fiscal Year Ends: 12/31 |
| 2004 Sales: $148,888 | 2004 Profits: $2,364 | Parent Company: |

## SALARIES/BENEFITS:

| | | | | |
|---|---|---|---|---|
| Pension Plan: | ESOP Stock Plan: | Profit Sharing: | Top Exec. Salary: $316,250 | Bonus: $ |
| Savings Plan: Y | Stock Purch. Plan: | | Second Exec. Salary: $245,000 | Bonus: $ |

## OTHER THOUGHTS:

**Apparent Women Officers or Directors**: 2
**Hot Spot for Advancement for Women/Minorities**: Y

## LOCATIONS: ("Y" = Yes)

| West: | Southwest: | Midwest: | Southeast: | Northeast: | International: |
|---|---|---|---|---|---|
| Y | Y | | Y | | Y |

# EOG RESOURCES INC

www.eogresources.com

**Industry Group Code:** 211111 **Ranks within this company's industry group:** Sales: 2 Profits: 2

| Management: | | Sales/Marketing: | | Liberal Arts: | | Information Systems: | | Professionals: | | Technical/Scientific: | |
|---|---|---|---|---|---|---|---|---|---|---|---|
| Mgmt. Trainees: | | Mktg. Professionals: | Y | Gen. Writing/Editing: | | Info. Management: | Y | Finance/Accounting: | Y | Engineers, Elec.: | |
| Experienced Mgmt.: | Y | Retail Sales: | | Technical Writing: | | Software Dev.: | | Law: | Y | Engineers, Other: | Y |
| Int'l Business: | Y | Commercial/Industrial: | Y | Graphic Arts/Photog.: | | Hardware Dev.: | | HR/Other: | Y | Health/Lab: | |
| MBA Graduates: | Y | Sales Trainees: | | Music: | | Systems Integration: | | Training: | Y | Scientists/Research: | |
| | | Advertising Pros.: | | Broadcasting: | | Consulting/Other: | | Health Care: | | Petroleum/Chemicals: | Y |
| | | | | Other: | | | | Consulting: | | Math/Other: | |

## TYPES OF BUSINESS:

Oil & Gas Exploration & Production
Energy Marketing

## BRANDS/DIVISIONS/AFFILIATES:

Enron Oil & Gas Company
EOG Resources Canada, Inc.

## CONTACTS:

*Note: Officers with more than one job title may be intentionally listed here more than once.*

Mark G. Papa, CEO
Timothy K. Driggers, CFO/VP
Marc R. Eschenburg, VP-Mktg. & Regulatory Affairs
Patricia L. Edwards, VP-Human Resources
Sandeep Bhakhri, CIO/VP
Lloyd W. Helms, Jr., VP-Eng. & Acquisitions
Patricia L. Edwards, VP-Admin./Corp. Sec.
Frederick J. Plaeger, II, General Counsel/Sr. VP
Gary L. Thomas, Sr. Exec. VP-Oper.
Maire A. Baldwin, VP-Investor Rel.
Ann D. Jansen, VP-Acct.
Loren M. Leiker, Sr. Exec. VP-Exploration
William R. Thomas, Exec. VP/Gen. Mgr.-Fort Worth
Micheal P. Donaldson, Corp. Sec.
Edmund P. Segner, III, VP
Mark G. Papa, Chmn.
Lindell L. Looger, VP/Gen. Mgr.-Int'l/Pres., EOG Resources Int'l Inc.

**Phone:** 713-651-7000 **Fax:** 713-651-6995
**Toll-Free:** 877-363-3647
**Address:** 1111 Bagby, Sky Lobby 2, Houston, TX 77002-7361 US

## GROWTH PLANS/SPECIAL FEATURES:

EOG Resources, Inc. (EOG), formerly Enron Oil and Gas Company, is one of the largest independent oil and gas companies in the U.S. Together with its subsidiaries, EOG explores for, develops, produces and markets natural gas and crude oil primarily in the U.S., but also in Canada, Trinidad, the U.K. and other international areas. EOG's total estimated net proved reserves are 6,802 billion cubic feet, of which 6,095 billion cubic feet are natural gas reserves and 118 million barrels are crude oil, condensate and natural gas liquids (NGL) reserves. Approximately 60% of these reserves are located in the U.S., 20% in Canada and 20% in Trinidad. In the U.S., EOG produced an average of 145 million cubic feet per day (MMcfd) of natural gas and 300 barrels per day of crude oil, condensate and NGL at its Fort Worth Basin Barnett Shale play. Additional key producing areas in the U.S. include the Upper Gulf Coast, the Permian Basin, the Rocky Mountains area, the Mid-Continent area, South Texas, the Gulf of Mexico and the Appalachian Basin. In Canada, EOG conducts business through its subsidiary, EOG Resources Canada, Inc. Key producing areas in Canada are the Southeast Alberta/Southwest Saskatchewan shallow natural gas trends including the Drumheller, Twining and Halkirk areas, the Pembina/Highvale area of Central Alberta, the grand Prairie/Wapiti area of Northwest Alberta and the Waskada area in Southwest Manitoba

EOG offers employees comprehensive benefits including: Retirement plans, flex dollars, flexible work schedules, medical, dental and vision insurance, life insurance, accidental death and dismemberment insurance, long-term disability, health care and dependent daycare spending accounts, and retirement health plans.

## FINANCIALS:

**Sales and profits are in thousands of dollars—add 000 to get the full amount. 2008 Note: Financial information for 2008 was not available for all companies at press time.**

| | | |
|---|---|---|
| 2008 Sales: $6,530,000 | 2008 Profits: $2,440,000 | **U.S. Stock Ticker: EOG** |
| 2007 Sales: $4,190,791 | 2007 Profits: $1,089,918 | **Int'l Ticker:** Int'l Exchange: |
| 2006 Sales: $3,912,542 | 2006 Profits: $1,299,885 | Employees: 2,122 |
| 2005 Sales: $3,620,200 | 2005 Profits: $1,259,576 | Fiscal Year Ends: 12/31 |
| 2004 Sales: $2,271,225 | 2004 Profits: $624,855 | Parent Company: |

## SALARIES/BENEFITS:

| | | | | |
|---|---|---|---|---|
| Pension Plan: Y | ESOP Stock Plan: | Profit Sharing: | Top Exec. Salary: $940,000 | Bonus: $1,500,000 |
| Savings Plan: Y | Stock Purch. Plan: Y | | Second Exec. Salary: $520,154 | Bonus: $640,000 |

## OTHER THOUGHTS:

**Apparent Women Officers or Directors**: 5
**Hot Spot for Advancement for Women/Minorities**: Y

## LOCATIONS: ("Y" = Yes)

| West: | Southwest: | Midwest: | Southeast: | Northeast: | International: |
|---|---|---|---|---|---|
| Y | Y | Y | Y | Y | Y |

# EPAM SYSTEMS

**www.epam.com**

**Industry Group Code:** 541512A **Ranks within this company's industry group:** Sales: Profits:

| Management: | | Sales/Marketing: | | Liberal Arts: | | Information Systems: | | Professionals: | | Technical/Scientific: | |
|---|---|---|---|---|---|---|---|---|---|---|---|
| Mgmt. Trainees: | | Mktg. Professionals: | Y | Gen. Writing/Editing: | | Info. Management: | Y | Finance/Accounting: | Y | Engineers, Elec.: | |
| Experienced Mgmt.: | Y | Retail Sales: | | Technical Writing: | Y | Software Dev.: | Y | Law: | Y | Engineers, Other: | |
| Int'l Business: | Y | Commercial/Industrial: | | Graphic Arts/Photog.: | | Hardware Dev.: | | HR/Other: | Y | Health/Lab: | |
| MBA Graduates: | Y | Sales Trainees: | | Music: | | Systems Integration: | | Training: | Y | Scientists/Research: | |
| | | Advertising Pros.: | | Broadcasting: | | Consulting/Other: | Y | Health Care: | | Petroleum/Chemicals: | |
| | | | | Other: | Y | | | Consulting: | Y | Math/Other: | |

## TYPES OF BUSINESS:

IT Support Services
Customer Relationship Management
Consulting

## BRANDS/DIVISIONS/AFFILIATES:

B2BITS Corp.

## CONTACTS:

*Note: Officers with more than one job title may be intentionally listed here more than once.*

Arkadiy Dobkin, CEO
Arkadiy Dobkin, Pres.
Ilya Cantor, CFO
Balazs Fejes, CTO
David Scott, Sr. VP-Bus. Solutions
Alena Busko, Media
Max Bogretsov, Sr. VP-Global Delivery
Anatoly Gaverdovskiy, Sr. VP-CIS Oper.
David Scott, Sr. VP-Bus. Solutions
Mark Bisker, CEO-B2BITS Corp.
Karl Robb, Exec. VP/Pres., EU Oper.

| | |
|---|---|
| **Phone:** 267-759-9000 | **Fax:** 267-759-8989 |
| **Toll-Free:** | |
| **Address:** 41 University Dr., Ste. 202, Newtown, PA 18940 US | |

## GROWTH PLANS/SPECIAL FEATURES:

EPAM Systems is an IT outsourcing company that provides software services through 18 offices located across Europe, Asia and North America. The company has deployed projects in 31 countries and 13 languages. EPAM offers services including technology consulting, custom software development, software product development, application testing, application maintenance, application reengineering and offshore development center (ODC) set up services. The firm's technology consulting expertise includes IT strategy development; review of existing IT landscape; enterprise application integration strategy and consulting; application architecture review; end-to-end business scenarios elaboration; business and technical analysis; gap analysis; technology-specific support and maintenance consulting; implementation practice elaboration; and application training. EPAM's software development services include product research; prototyping; development; quality assurance and testing; deployment; performance tuning; maintenance and support; customization; porting and cross-platform migration; and component design and integration. The company's application testing services include functional testing, automated testing and continuous integration for distributed software project implementation. EPAM has client support facilities in New Jersey, London and Frankfurt, while its software development operations are conducted in Russia, Belarus and the Ukraine. Its European headquarters and delivery center is located in Budapest. The company has worked with clients in various industries, including software, technology, healthcare, insurance, travel, entertainment, financial services, retail, media, research, publishing, manufacturing, transportation and energy. EPAM's clients have included Microsoft, Oracle, Reuters, Colgate-Palmolive, Philips, the London Stock Exchange and Lufthansa Systems. In April 2008, EPAM acquired B2BITS Corp., a provider of solutions and consulting services to financial services capital markets organizations.

In December 2008, the company announced its 190th ranking in Software Magazine's Software 500 list, an annual list of the world's 500 largest software and service providers.

## FINANCIALS:

**Sales and profits are in thousands of dollars—add 000 to get the full amount. 2008 Note: Financial information for 2008 was not available for all companies at press time.**

| | | |
|---|---|---|
| 2008 Sales: $ | 2008 Profits: $ | **U.S. Stock Ticker: Private** |
| 2007 Sales: $ | 2007 Profits: $ | **Int'l Ticker:** Int'l Exchange: |
| 2006 Sales: $80,000 | 2006 Profits: $ | Employees: 1,010 |
| 2005 Sales: $39,900 | 2005 Profits: $ | Fiscal Year Ends: 12/31 |
| 2004 Sales: $30,100 | 2004 Profits: $ | Parent Company: |

## SALARIES/BENEFITS:

| | | | | |
|---|---|---|---|---|
| Pension Plan: | ESOP Stock Plan: | Profit Sharing: | Top Exec. Salary: $ | Bonus: $ |
| Savings Plan: | Stock Purch. Plan: | | Second Exec. Salary: $ | Bonus: $ |

## OTHER THOUGHTS:

**Apparent Women Officers or Directors**: 1
**Hot Spot for Advancement for Women/Minorities**:

## LOCATIONS: ("Y" = Yes)

| West: | Southwest: | Midwest: | Southeast: | Northeast: | International: |
|---|---|---|---|---|---|
| | | | | Y | Y |

Note: Financial information, benefits and other data can change quickly and may vary from those stated here.

# EPIX PHARMACEUTICALS INC

**www.epixmed.com**

**Industry Group Code:** 325413 **Ranks within this company's industry group:** Sales: 13 Profits: 12

| **Management:** | | **Sales/Marketing:** | | **Liberal Arts:** | | **Information Systems:** | | **Professionals:** | | **Technical/Scientific:** | |
|---|---|---|---|---|---|---|---|---|---|---|---|
| Mgmt. Trainees: | | Mktg. Professionals: | Y | Gen. Writing/Editing: | | Info. Management: | Y | Finance/Accounting: | Y | Engineers, Elec.: | |
| Experienced Mgmt.: | Y | Retail Sales: | | Technical Writing: | Y | Software Dev.: | Y | Law: | Y | Engineers, Other: | Y |
| Int'l Business: | Y | Commercial/Industrial: | Y | Graphic Arts/Photog.: | | Hardware Dev.: | | HR/Other: | Y | Health/Lab: | Y |
| MBA Graduates: | Y | Sales Trainees: | Y | Music: | | Systems Integration: | | Training: | Y | Scientists/Research: | Y |
| | | Advertising Pros.: | | Broadcasting: | | Consulting/Other: | | Health Care: | Y | Petroleum/Chemicals: | |
| | | | | Other: | | | | Consulting: | | Math/Other: | |

## TYPES OF BUSINESS:

Medical Diagnostics Products
MRI Contrast Agents

## BRANDS/DIVISIONS/AFFILIATES:

Vasovist

## CONTACTS:

*Note: Officers with more than one job title may be intentionally listed here more than once.*

Michael G. Kauffman, CEO
Kim C. Drapkin, CFO
Brenda Sousa, VP-Human Resources
Sharon Shacham, Sr. VP-Drug Dev.
Chen Schor, Chief Bus. Officer
Sheila DeWitt, VP-Discovery
Simon S. Jones, VP-Biology & ADMET
Yael Marantz, VP-Computational Drug Discovery
Frederick Frank, Chmn.

**Phone:** 781-761-7600 **Fax:** 781-761-7641
**Toll-Free:**
**Address:** 4 Maguire Rd., Lexington, MA 02421 US

## GROWTH PLANS/SPECIAL FEATURES:

EPIX Pharmaceuticals, Inc. develops targeted contrast agents to improve the quality of magnetic resonance imaging (MRI) as a tool for diagnosing human disease. The firm has four product candidates in clinical trials: PRX-00023, for depression, which is concluding Phase II testing; PRX-03140, for Alzheimer's Disease, which is in Phase II testing and which GSK has the exclusive option for; PRX-08056, for pulmonary hyperension in COPD, which is in Phase II testing; and PRX-07034, for cognitive impairment, which has just concluded Phase I testing. The firm's lead product, Vasovist (formerly MS-325), is an injectable intravascular contrast agent designed for multiple cardiovascular imaging applications, including peripheral vascular disease and coronary artery disease. EPIX believes that Vasovist will significantly enhance the quality of MRI images and provide physicians with a minimally-invasive and cost-effective diagnostic method. Vasovist has the potential to replace highly invasive and costly conventional X-ray angiography, over which it has a number of advantages. The agent is safer, involves no patient exposure to ionizing radiation, allows 60 minutes of arterial and venous imaging, facilitates imaging of multiple vascular areas in a single exam and provides three-dimensional data. Vasovist has been approved for marketing in more than 30 countries outside the U.S. EPIX collaborates with Schering AG for the development and commercialization of Vasovist, and also works with the three leading MRI equipment manufacturers, General Electric Medical Systems, Siemens Medical Systems and Philips Medical Systems. EPIX is also developing a contrast agent, EP-2104R, that shows detailed images of blood clots using MRI. The firm continues to maintain an Israeli headquarters in Ramat-Gan. In June 2008, EPIX resubmitted a new drug application for Vasovist, following years of negotiations with the FDA regarding its previous submission.

## FINANCIALS:

**Sales and profits are in thousands of dollars—add 000 to get the full amount. 2008 Note: Financial information for 2008 was not available for all companies at press time.**

| | | |
|---|---|---|
| 2008 Sales: $ | 2008 Profits: $ | **U.S. Stock Ticker: EPIX** |
| 2007 Sales: $14,960 | 2007 Profits: $-62,789 | **Int'l Ticker:** Int'l Exchange: |
| 2006 Sales: $6,041 | 2006 Profits: $-157,393 | Employees: 119 |
| 2005 Sales: $7,190 | 2005 Profits: $-21,269 | Fiscal Year Ends: 12/31 |
| 2004 Sales: $12,259 | 2004 Profits: $-22,621 | Parent Company: |

## SALARIES/BENEFITS:

| | | | | |
|---|---|---|---|---|
| Pension Plan: | ESOP Stock Plan: | Profit Sharing: | Top Exec. Salary: $384,786 | Bonus: $ |
| Savings Plan: Y | Stock Purch. Plan: Y | | Second Exec. Salary: $342,794 | Bonus: $ |

## OTHER THOUGHTS:

**Apparent Women Officers or Directors**: 5
**Hot Spot for Advancement for Women/Minorities**: Y

## LOCATIONS: ("Y" = Yes)

| West: | Southwest: | Midwest: | Southeast: | Northeast: | International: |
|---|---|---|---|---|---|
| | | | | Y | Y |

# EQUINIX INC

www.equinix.com

**Industry Group Code:** 513390C **Ranks within this company's industry group:** Sales: 2 Profits: 2

| Management: | | Sales/Marketing: | | Liberal Arts: | | Information Systems: | | Professionals: | | Technical/Scientific: | |
|---|---|---|---|---|---|---|---|---|---|---|---|
| Mgmt. Trainees: | | Mktg. Professionals: | Y | Gen. Writing/Editing: | | Info. Management: | Y | Finance/Accounting: | Y | Engineers, Elec.: | Y |
| Experienced Mgmt.: | Y | Retail Sales: | | Technical Writing: | Y | Software Dev.: | Y | Law: | Y | Engineers, Other: | |
| Int'l Business: | Y | Commercial/Industrial: | Y | Graphic Arts/Photog.: | | Hardware Dev.: | | HR/Other: | Y | Health/Lab: | |
| MBA Graduates: | Y | Sales Trainees: | Y | Music: | | Systems Integration: | Y | Training: | Y | Scientists/Research: | |
| | | Advertising Pros.: | | Broadcasting: | | Consulting/Other: | | Health Care: | | Petroleum/Chemicals: | |
| | | | | Other: | | | | Consulting: | | Math/Other: | |

## TYPES OF BUSINESS:

Data Networks
Internet Exchange Services

## BRANDS/DIVISIONS/AFFILIATES:

Smart Hands

## CONTACTS:

*Note: Officers with more than one job title may be intentionally listed here more than once.*

Stephen M. Smith, CEO
Sam Kapoor, COO
Stephen M. Smith, Pres.
Keith D. Taylor, CFO
Keri Crask, VP-Human Resources
Brandi Morandi, General Counsel/Corp. Sec.
Herb Kirchner, VP-Bus. Oper.
Marjorie S. Backaus, Chief Bus. Officer
Jason Starr, Dir.-Investor Rel.
Renee Lanam, Chief Dev. Officer
Peter Ferris, Pres., U.S. Oper.
Eric Schwartz, Pres., Europe Oper.
Samuel Lee, Pres., Asia-Pacific Oper.
Peter F. Van Camp, Exec. Chmn.

**Phone:** 650-513-7000 **Fax:** 650-513-7900
**Toll-Free:**
**Address:** 301 Velocity Way, 5th Fl., Foster City, CA 94404-4803 US

## GROWTH PLANS/SPECIAL FEATURES:

Equinix, Inc. provides network neutral co-location, interconnection and managed services to enterprises, content companies, systems integrators and some of the world's largest network providers. The company operates Internet Business Exchange (IBX) centers in the U.S., Australia and Asia, where customers can interconnect with the providers that serve over 90% of the world's Internet networks. These IBX hubs are located in Ashburn, Virginia; Newark and Secaucus, New Jersey; San Jose, Santa Clara and Los Angeles, California; Chicago, Illinois; Dallas, Texas; Tokyo, Japan; Hong Kong, China; Sydney, Australia; and Singapore. Because Equinix does not operate its own network, it can connect users to whichever network has the most available bandwidth. The company's products and services include co-location services, such as cabinets, AC and DC power, operations personnel and equipment; direct connection between business partners, which allows customers to easily trade network traffic without purchasing circuits, and managed IT infrastructure services, which uses the company's IBX hubs to optimize customers' infrastructure and resources. The firm's Smart Hands service provides access to IBX technical staff when a customer's own staff is unavailable. Nine of the top 10 Internet properties are Equinix customers, along with numerous other enterprise and governmental customers, including Amazon; Electronic Arts; Fox Interactive Media; Google; IBM; Sony; MSN; Yahoo!; and The Gap. In June 2008, Equinix announced a collaboration with Meebo, an Internet live communications platform, to establish operations at the company's IBX in Silicon Valley, allowing Meebo to enhance delivery of its services. In February 2008, the company announced plans to expand its Hong Kong IBX by 80% and its Singapore IBX by 12%.

Equinix offers commuter and tuition reimbursement programs; worldwide travel assistance; a 401(k) plan; and an employee assistance program.

## FINANCIALS:

**Sales and profits are in thousands of dollars—add 000 to get the full amount. 2008 Note: Financial information for 2008 was not available for all companies at press time.**

| | | |
|---|---|---|
| 2008 Sales: $ | 2008 Profits: $ | **U.S. Stock Ticker: EQIX** |
| 2007 Sales: $419,442 | 2007 Profits: $-5,188 | **Int'l Ticker:** Int'l Exchange: |
| 2006 Sales: $286,915 | 2006 Profits: $-6,397 | Employees: 911 |
| 2005 Sales: $221,057 | 2005 Profits: $42,612 | Fiscal Year Ends: 12/31 |
| 2004 Sales: $163,671 | 2004 Profits: $-68,631 | Parent Company: |

## SALARIES/BENEFITS:

| | | | | |
|---|---|---|---|---|
| Pension Plan: | ESOP Stock Plan: | Profit Sharing: | Top Exec. Salary: $337,500 | Bonus: $437,500 |
| Savings Plan: Y | Stock Purch. Plan: Y | | Second Exec. Salary: $285,000 | Bonus: $ |

## OTHER THOUGHTS:

**Apparent Women Officers or Directors**: 3
**Hot Spot for Advancement for Women/Minorities**: Y

## LOCATIONS: ("Y" = Yes)

| West: | Southwest: | Midwest: | Southeast: | Northeast: | International: |
|---|---|---|---|---|---|
| Y | | Y | | Y | Y |

# EQUITABLE RESOURCES INC

**www.eqt.com**

**Industry Group Code:** 221000B **Ranks within this company's industry group:** Sales: 5 Profits: 2

| **Management:** | | **Sales/Marketing:** | | **Liberal Arts:** | | **Information Systems:** | | **Professionals:** | | **Technical/Scientific:** | |
|---|---|---|---|---|---|---|---|---|---|---|---|
| Mgmt. Trainees: | | Mktg. Professionals: | Y | Gen. Writing/Editing: | | Info. Management: | Y | Finance/Accounting: | Y | Engineers, Elec.: | Y |
| Experienced Mgmt.: | Y | Retail Sales: | | Technical Writing: | | Software Dev.: | | Law: | Y | Engineers, Other: | Y |
| Int'l Business: | Y | Commercial/Industrial: | Y | Graphic Arts/Photog.: | | Hardware Dev.: | | HR/Other: | Y | Health/Lab: | |
| MBA Graduates: | Y | Sales Trainees: | Y | Music: | | Systems Integration: | | Training: | Y | Scientists/Research: | |
| | | Advertising Pros.: | | Broadcasting: | | Consulting/Other: | | Health Care: | | Petroleum/Chemicals: | Y |
| | | | | Other: | | | | Consulting: | | Math/Other: | |

## TYPES OF BUSINESS:

Utilities-Natural Gas
Pipelines
Well Operations
Gas Production
Plant Design, Construction & Management
Energy Marketing

## BRANDS/DIVISIONS/AFFILIATES:

Equitable Gas Company
Equitrans, L.P.
Equitable Production Company
Columbia Gas Transmission
East Tennessee Natural Gas Company
Dominion Transmission
Dominion Resources Inc

## CONTACTS: *Note: Officers with more than one job title may be intentionally listed here more than once.*

Murry S. Gerber, CEO
David L. Porges, COO
David L. Porges, Pres.
Philip P. Conti, CFO/Sr. VP
Charlene Petrelli, Chief Human Resources Officer/VP
Lewis B. Gardner, General Counsel/VP
Theresa Z. Bone, Corp. Controller/VP
Randall L. Crawford, Pres., Midstream/Distributions/Sr. VP
Joseph E. O'Brien, Sr. VP
John A. Bergonzi, VP-Finance
James E. Crockard, III, Treas.
Murry S. Gerber, Chmn.

| **Phone:** 412-553-5700 | **Fax:** 412-553-5757 |
|---|---|
| **Toll-Free:** | |
| **Address:** 225 N. Shore Dr., Pittsburgh, PA 15212-5861 US | |

## GROWTH PLANS/SPECIAL FEATURES:

Equitable Resources, Inc. is a fully integrated energy exploration, production, transmission, distribution and marketing company, focusing on Appalachian-area natural gas supply activities. Equitable Resources offers energy products, including natural gas, natural gas liquids, crude oil, and services to wholesale and retail customers. Equitable Resources reorganized in 2008 in order to create a subsidiary to consolidate its state-regulated distribution activities. It currently operates in three divisions: Equitable Production, Equitable Midstream and Equitable Distribution. The Equitable Production segment includes the company's exploration for, and development and production of, natural gas, and a limited amount of crude oil, in the Appalachian Basin. Equitable Midstream's operations include the natural gas gathering, processing, transportation and storage activities of the firm as well as sales of natural gas liquids. Equitable Distribution's operations primarily comprise the state-regulated distribution activities of the company.

## FINANCIALS: **Sales and profits are in thousands of dollars—add 000 to get the full amount. 2008 Note: Financial information for 2008 was not available for all companies at press time.**

| | | |
|---|---|---|
| 2008 Sales: $1,576,488 | 2008 Profits: $255,604 | **U.S. Stock Ticker: EQT** |
| 2007 Sales: $1,361,406 | 2007 Profits: $257,483 | **Int'l Ticker:** Int'l Exchange: |
| 2006 Sales: $1,267,910 | 2006 Profits: $220,286 | Employees: 1,400 |
| 2005 Sales: $1,253,724 | 2005 Profits: $260,055 | Fiscal Year Ends: 12/31 |
| 2004 Sales: $1,191,609 | 2004 Profits: $279,854 | Parent Company: |

## SALARIES/BENEFITS:

| | | | | |
|---|---|---|---|---|
| Pension Plan: | ESOP Stock Plan: | Profit Sharing: | Top Exec. Salary: $624,996 | Bonus: $1,000,000 |
| Savings Plan: Y | Stock Purch. Plan: | | Second Exec. Salary: $420,192 | Bonus: $725,000 |

## OTHER THOUGHTS:

**Apparent Women Officers or Directors**: 4
**Hot Spot for Advancement for Women/Minorities**: Y

## LOCATIONS: ("Y" = Yes)

| West: | Southwest: | Midwest: | Southeast: | Northeast: | International: |
|---|---|---|---|---|---|
| | | Y | Y | Y | |

# EURONET WORLDWIDE INC

www.euronetworldwide.com

**Industry Group Code:** 522320 **Ranks within this company's industry group:** Sales: 2 Profits: 1

| Management: | | Sales/Marketing: | | Liberal Arts: | | Information Systems: | | Professionals: | | Technical/Scientific: | |
|---|---|---|---|---|---|---|---|---|---|---|---|
| Mgmt. Trainees: | Y | Mktg. Professionals: | Y | Gen. Writing/Editing: | | Info. Management: | Y | Finance/Accounting: | Y | Engineers, Elec.: | |
| Experienced Mgmt.: | Y | Retail Sales: | | Technical Writing: | Y | Software Dev.: | Y | Law: | Y | Engineers, Other: | |
| Int'l Business: | Y | Commercial/Industrial: | Y | Graphic Arts/Photog.: | | Hardware Dev.: | | HR/Other: | Y | Health/Lab: | |
| MBA Graduates: | Y | Sales Trainees: | Y | Music: | | Systems Integration: | Y | Training: | Y | Scientists/Research: | |
| | | Advertising Pros.: | Y | Broadcasting: | | Consulting/Other: | | Health Care: | | Petroleum/Chemicals: | |
| | | | | Other: | | | | Consulting: | | Math/Other: | |

## TYPES OF BUSINESS:

Electronic Payments Solutions & Services
ATM & POS Operation & Management Services
Card Outsourcing Services
Software Solutions
Money Transfer & Bill Payment Services
Electronic Prepaid Top-Up Services

## BRANDS/DIVISIONS/AFFILIATES:

Euronet Payments & Remittance Inc
Ria Envia Inc
Euronet Essentis Limited

## CONTACTS: *Note: Officers with more than one job title may be intentionally listed here more than once.*

Michael J. Brown, CEO
Kevin Caponecchi, Pres.
Rick L. Weller, CFO/Exec. VP
Jeffrey B. Newman, General Counsel/Exec. VP
Paul S. Althasen, Exec. VP
David Morgan, Exec. VP/Managing Dir.-Global Money Transfer
Anthony (Tony) Grandidge, Sr. VP/Managing Dir.-Asia Pacific EFT
Timothy A. Fanning, COO-Global Money Transfer
Michael J. Brown, Chmn.

| | |
|---|---|
| **Phone:** 913-327-4200 | **Fax:** 913-327-1921 |
| **Toll-Free:** | |
| **Address:** 4601 College Blvd., Ste. 300, Leawood, KS 66211 US | |

## GROWTH PLANS/SPECIAL FEATURES:

Euronet Worldwide, Inc. is an electronic payments provider, offering ATM and point-of-sale (POS) operation and management services; card outsourcing services; software solutions; money transfer and bill payment services; and electronic prepaid top-up services to financial institutions, mobile operators and retailers. The company operates in three segments: EFT processing, prepaid processing and money transfer. The EFT processing segment provides electronic payment and transaction processing solutions consisting of ATM network participation; outsourced ATM, POS and card management solutions; and electronic recharge services for prepaid mobile airtime purchases via an ATM or directly from the handset. The division processes transactions for a network of over 10,100 ATMS and more than 53,000 POS terminals across Europe, the Middle East, Africa and Asia Pacific. The prepaid processing segment provides distribution of prepaid mobile airtime and other prepaid products and collections services. The division operates a network of over 397,000 POS terminals providing electronic processing of prepaid mobile airtime top-up services in the U.S., Europe, Africa and Asia Pacific. The segment also includes the money transfer and bill payment business, Euronet Payments & Remittance, Inc. Money transfer services are available from the U.S. to destinations in Latin America, China, India and the Philippines, as well as from the U.K. and India. Bill payment services are offered to customers in the U.S., the U.K. and Poland. The money transfer segment, created following the April 2007 acquisition of RIA Envia, Inc. and its operating subsidiaries, provides money transfer services through a sending network of agents and company-owned stores in the U.S., the Caribbean, Europe and Asia Pacific. The segment disperses money transfers through a worldwide payer network. In 2008, the firm announced its intent to sell Euronet Essentis Limited, a U.K. software entity previously included in the EFT Processing Segment, in order to narrow its focus on the transaction processing businesses.

## FINANCIALS: **Sales and profits are in thousands of dollars—add 000 to get the full amount. 2008 Note: Financial information for 2008 was not available for all companies at press time.**

| | | |
|---|---|---|
| 2008 Sales: $ | 2008 Profits: $ | **U.S. Stock Ticker: EEFT** |
| 2007 Sales: $917,574 | 2007 Profits: $53,160 | **Int'l Ticker:** Int'l Exchange: |
| 2006 Sales: $629,181 | 2006 Profits: $46,002 | Employees: 2,500 |
| 2005 Sales: $531,159 | 2005 Profits: $22,355 | Fiscal Year Ends: 12/31 |
| 2004 Sales: $381,080 | 2004 Profits: $12,852 | Parent Company: |

## SALARIES/BENEFITS:

| | | | | |
|---|---|---|---|---|
| Pension Plan: | ESOP Stock Plan: | Profit Sharing: | Top Exec. Salary: $500,000 | Bonus: $ |
| Savings Plan: | Stock Purch. Plan: | | Second Exec. Salary: $275,550 | Bonus: $ |

## OTHER THOUGHTS:

**Apparent Women Officers or Directors**: 2
**Hot Spot for Advancement for Women/Minorities**: Y

## LOCATIONS: ("Y" = Yes)

| West: | Southwest: | Midwest: | Southeast: | Northeast: | International: |
|---|---|---|---|---|---|
| Y | | Y | Y | Y | Y |

# EVERCORE PARTNERS INC

**www.evercore.com**

**Industry Group Code:** 523110 **Ranks within this company's industry group:** Sales: 2 Profits: 2

| Management: | | Sales/Marketing: | | Liberal Arts: | | Information Systems: | | Professionals: | | Technical/Scientific: | |
|---|---|---|---|---|---|---|---|---|---|---|---|
| Mgmt. Trainees: | | Mktg. Professionals: | | Gen. Writing/Editing: | | Info. Management: | Y | Finance/Accounting: | Y | Engineers, Elec.: | |
| Experienced Mgmt.: | Y | Retail Sales: | | Technical Writing: | | Software Dev.: | | Law: | Y | Engineers, Other: | |
| Int'l Business: | Y | Commercial/Industrial: | | Graphic Arts/Photog.: | | Hardware Dev.: | | HR/Other: | Y | Health/Lab: | |
| MBA Graduates: | Y | Sales Trainees: | | Music: | | Systems Integration: | | Training: | Y | Scientists/Research: | |
| | | Advertising Pros.: | | Broadcasting: | | Consulting/Other: | | Health Care: | | Petroleum/Chemicals: | |
| | | | | Other: | | | | Consulting: | | Math/Other: | |

## TYPES OF BUSINESS:

Investment Banking
Merger, Acquisition & Divestiture Advisory Services
Financing & Restructuring Advisory
Asset Management

## BRANDS/DIVISIONS/AFFILIATES:

Protego Asesores S.A. de C.V.
Discovery Capital Partners LLC
Evercore LP
Protego Casa de Bolsa
Braveheart Financial Services Limited

## CONTACTS: *Note: Officers with more than one job title may be intentionally listed here more than once.*

Roger C. Altman, CEO
Timothy LaLonde, COO-Advisory
Robert B. Walsh, CFO
Gail Landis, Head-Sales & Mktg.
Nicol Grosso, Dir.-Human Resources
Nicol Grosso, Dir.-Facilities & Admin.
Adam B. Frankel, General Counsel
Kathleen Reiland, Sr. Managing Dir./COO-Investment Mgmt.
Christopher M. Freudenreich, Dir.-External Reporting & Compliance Acct.
Pedro Aspe, Co-Chmn./CEO-Protego
Jeffrey M. Reisenberg, VP-Corp. Advisory Bus.
Joanna Hellen, Dir.-Finance, Evercore Europe
Roger C. Altman, Co-Chmn.

| **Phone:** 212-857-3100 | **Fax:** 212-857-3101 |
|---|---|
| **Toll-Free:** | |
| **Address:** 55 E. 52nd St., 43rd Fl., New York, NY 10055 US | |

## GROWTH PLANS/SPECIAL FEATURES:

Evercore Partners, Inc. is an investment banking firm providing advisory services to prominent multinational corporations on significant mergers, acquisitions, divestitures, restructurings and other strategic corporate transactions. The company's operations consist of two business segments: Advisory and investment management. The advisory segment provides confidential, strategic and tactical advice to both public and private companies, with a particular focus on large, multinational corporations. Advisory generates revenue from fees for providing advice on matters of strategic importance to its clients, including mergers, acquisitions, restructurings, divestitures, leveraged buy-outs, recapitalizations and other corporate transactions. In 2007 this segment generated 92% of the firm's net revenue and earned advisory fees from 145 clients. The investment management segment principally manages and invests capital on behalf of third parties. A broad range of institutional and high net-worth investors, including corporate and public pension funds, endowments, foundations, insurance companies and family offices, have committed capital to the funds managed by the firm. Investment management generates revenue from fees earned for managing private equity funds and the portfolio companies of the Private Equity Funds. In addition, the segment earns revenue from incentive fees, referred to as carried interest, earned when certain financial returns are achieved over the life of a fund, through net gains and losses on investments of our own capital in the funds, and from other sources. Investment management also generates revenue from managing funds invested in public securities.

## FINANCIALS: **Sales and profits are in thousands of dollars—add 000 to get the full amount. 2008 Note: Financial information for 2008 was not available for all companies at press time.**

| | | |
|---|---|---|
| 2008 Sales: $340,000 | 2008 Profits: $-9,384 | **U.S. Stock Ticker: EVR** |
| 2007 Sales: $321,599 | 2007 Profits: $-34,495 | **Int'l Ticker:** Int'l Exchange: |
| 2006 Sales: $96,089 | 2006 Profits: $3,786 | Employees: 290 |
| 2005 Sales: $125,600 | 2005 Profits: $63,152 | Fiscal Year Ends: 12/31 |
| 2004 Sales: $ | 2004 Profits: $ | Parent Company: |

## SALARIES/BENEFITS:

| | | | | |
|---|---|---|---|---|
| Pension Plan: | ESOP Stock Plan: | Profit Sharing: | Top Exec. Salary: $500,000 | Bonus: $2,116,000 |
| Savings Plan: | Stock Purch. Plan: | | Second Exec. Salary: $500,000 | Bonus: $2,116,000 |

## OTHER THOUGHTS:

**Apparent Women Officers or Directors**: 9
**Hot Spot for Advancement for Women/Minorities**: Y

## LOCATIONS: ("Y" = Yes)

| West: | Southwest: | Midwest: | Southeast: | Northeast: | International: |
|---|---|---|---|---|---|
| Y | | | | Y | Y |

# EVERGREEN ENERGY INC

www.evgenergy.com

**Industry Group Code:** 324190 **Ranks within this company's industry group:** Sales: 1 Profits: 1

| Management: | | Sales/Marketing: | | Liberal Arts: | | Information Systems: | | Professionals: | | Technical/Scientific: | |
|---|---|---|---|---|---|---|---|---|---|---|---|
| Mgmt. Trainees: | | Mktg. Professionals: | Y | Gen. Writing/Editing: | Y | Info. Management: | Y | Finance/Accounting: | Y | Engineers, Elec.: | Y |
| Experienced Mgmt.: | Y | Retail Sales: | | Technical Writing: | | Software Dev.: | | Law: | Y | Engineers, Other: | Y |
| Int'l Business: | Y | Commercial/Industrial: | Y | Graphic Arts/Photog.: | | Hardware Dev.: | | HR/Other: | Y | Health/Lab: | |
| MBA Graduates: | Y | Sales Trainees: | | Music: | | Systems Integration: | | Training: | Y | Scientists/Research: | |
| | | Advertising Pros.: | | Broadcasting: | | Consulting/Other: | | Health Care: | | Petroleum/Chemicals: | Y |
| | | | | Other: | | | | Consulting: | | Math/Other: | |

## TYPES OF BUSINESS:

Clean Coal Technology
Coal Production
Research & Engineering
Coal Bed Methane

## BRANDS/DIVISIONS/AFFILIATES:

KFx, Inc.
K-Fuel
Buckeye Industrial Mining Co.
MR&E LLC
Landrica Development Company
Bechtel Power Corporation
C-Lock Technology, Inc.

## CONTACTS: *Note: Officers with more than one job title may be intentionally listed here more than once.*

Kevin R. Collins, CEO
Kevin Collins, Pres.
Diana L. Kubik, CFO/VP
William Wolff, Exec. VP-Eng.
William G. Laughlin, General Counsel/VP/Corp. Sec.
Jimmac G. Lofton, VP-Corp. Dev.
Paul E. Jacobson, VP-Corp. Comm.
Michael J. Rosenberg, VP-Bus. Dev.
Theodore Venners, Chief Strategy Officer
William Walker, Chmn.
Scott Terhune, VP-Int'l Bus. Dev

| **Phone:** 303-293-2992 | **Fax:** 303-293-8430 |
|---|---|
| **Toll-Free:** | |
| **Address:** 1225 17th St., Ste. 1300, Denver, CO 80202-5506 US | |

## GROWTH PLANS/SPECIAL FEATURES:

Evergreen Energy Inc., formerly KFx, Inc., is a clean coal company that offers combined energy, environmental and economic solutions to coal-fired power generating facilities and industrial coal users in the U.S. and internationally. The firm's proprietary K-Fuel process uses heat and pressure to transform high moisture, low-Btu coals such as sub-bituminous coal into a more energy efficient, and a lower emission fuel. This process removes significant amounts of impurities such as mercury and reduces emissions of carbon dioxide, sulfur dioxide and nitrogen oxide. Some K-Fuel facilities are located at coal-fired power generating plants referred to as K-Direct facilities. The company's long term goals are to develop K-Fuel and K-direct facilities, and license K-Fuel to third parties through acquisitions, joint ventures and organic growth. Evergreen's subsidiaries include MR&E LLC, a research and engineering firm focused on thermal process engineering; Landrica Development Company, Evergreen Energy Asia Pacific Corp., C-Lock Technology, Inc., which provides a web-based carbon accounting and marketing tool; and Buckeye Industrial Mining Co., which mines, processes and sells coal to power generating facilities and industrial users. In January 2008, the company's subsidiary Evergreen Energy Asia Pacific Corp. entered an agreement with Sumitomo Corporation and a leading Indonesian mining group to commence development on a 1.5 million ton per year K-Fuel plant on Kalimantan, an Indonesian island. In February of the same year, the company completed a test burn of K-Fuel combined with Ohio Btu coal producing an almost 82 percent drop in mercury. The testing proves a new lower-cost option for coal fueled broilers in submission to stricter mercury emission laws.

## FINANCIALS: **Sales and profits are in thousands of dollars—add 000 to get the full amount. 2008 Note: Financial information for 2008 was not available for all companies at press time.**

| | | |
|---|---|---|
| 2008 Sales: $ | 2008 Profits: $ | **U.S. Stock Ticker: EEE** |
| 2007 Sales: $48,657 | 2007 Profits: $-204,676 | **Int'l Ticker:** Int'l Exchange: |
| 2006 Sales: $36,710 | 2006 Profits: $-51,527 | Employees: 207 |
| 2005 Sales: $ 984 | 2005 Profits: $-23,313 | Fiscal Year Ends: 12/31 |
| 2004 Sales: $ 28 | 2004 Profits: $-10,555 | Parent Company: |

## SALARIES/BENEFITS:

| | | | | |
|---|---|---|---|---|
| Pension Plan: | ESOP Stock Plan: | Profit Sharing: | Top Exec. Salary: $294,714 | Bonus: $ |
| Savings Plan: | Stock Purch. Plan: | | Second Exec. Salary: $255,796 | Bonus: $ |

## OTHER THOUGHTS:

**Apparent Women Officers or Directors**: 1
**Hot Spot for Advancement for Women/Minorities**:

## LOCATIONS: ("Y" = Yes)

| West: | Southwest: | Midwest: | Southeast: | Northeast: | International: |
|---|---|---|---|---|---|
| Y | | | | | |

# EVERGREEN SOLAR INC

**www.evergreensolar.com**

**Industry Group Code:** 333298A **Ranks within this company's industry group:** Sales: 4 Profits: 3

| Management: | | Sales/Marketing: | | Liberal Arts: | | Information Systems: | | Professionals: | | Technical/Scientific: | |
|---|---|---|---|---|---|---|---|---|---|---|---|
| Mgmt. Trainees: | | Mktg. Professionals: | Y | Gen. Writing/Editing: | | Info. Management: | Y | Finance/Accounting: | Y | Engineers, Elec.: | Y |
| Experienced Mgmt.: | Y | Retail Sales: | | Technical Writing: | Y | Software Dev.: | Y | Law: | Y | Engineers, Other: | Y |
| Int'l Business: | Y | Commercial/Industrial: | Y | Graphic Arts/Photog.: | Y | Hardware Dev.: | Y | HR/Other: | Y | Health/Lab: | |
| MBA Graduates: | Y | Sales Trainees: | Y | Music: | | Systems Integration: | | Training: | Y | Scientists/Research: | Y |
| | | Advertising Pros.: | | Broadcasting: | | Consulting/Other: | | Health Care: | | Petroleum/Chemicals: | |
| | | | | Other: | | | | Consulting: | | Math/Other: | Y |

## TYPES OF BUSINESS:

Solar Energy Technology

## BRANDS/DIVISIONS/AFFILIATES:

String Ribbon
EverQ

## CONTACTS:

*Note: Officers with more than one job title may be intentionally listed here more than once.*

Richard M. Feldt, CEO
Richard M. Feldt, Pres.
Michael El-Hillow, CFO
Terry Baily, Sr. VP-Mktg. & Sales
Gary T. Pollard, VP-Human Resources
Brown F. Williams, Exec. VP-Science & Eng.
Michael El-Hillow, Sec.
Rudolfo Archbold, VP-Oper.
Richard G. Chleboski, VP-Strategy & Bus. Dev.
Carl Stegerwald, VP-Construction Mgmt. & Facilities Eng.
Richard M. Feldt, Chmn.

| | |
|---|---|
| **Phone:** 508-357-2221 | **Fax:** 508-229-0747 |
| **Toll-Free:** | |
| **Address:** 138 Bartlett St., Marlboro, MA 01752 US | |

## GROWTH PLANS/SPECIAL FEATURES:

Evergreen Solar, Inc. develops, manufactures and markets solar power products to the worldwide solar power market. Solar power applications include wireless power for remote homes, water pumping, lighting and rural electrification, as well as complete power systems for electric utility customers that choose to generate their own environmentally benign power. Specifically, Evergreen Solar employs its patented String Ribbon technology, which is designed to use silicon efficiently, to sell solar modules. The company has global marketing operations that sell solar panels for residential, commercial and industrial use and intends to further elevate itself by initiating large-scale manufacturing. Evergreen markets its products through trade shows, on-going customer communications, promotional material, its web site, direct mail and advertising. The firm manufactures its products at a 56,000-square-foot administrative, laboratory and manufacturing facility in Marlboro, Massachusetts. Currently, the Marlboro factory has a capacity of 18 megawatts per year. The recently constructed facility in Devens, Massachusetts, is expected to reach 160 MW when it reaches its full capacity in 2009. Additionally, the firm is engaged in a joint partnership, along with Q-Cells and Renewable Energy Corporation ASA (REC). The three companies are equal partners in EverQ, a limited liability corporation that operates a facility in Thalheim, Germany to manufacture, market and sell solar products based on the String Ribbon technology. The facility has a current capacity of 180 megawatts, with plans to reach 600-megawatt capacity by 2012. In December 2007, Evergreen Solar signed a ten-year polysilicon supply agreement with the French company, Silicum de Provence S.A.S.

Employees are offered a 401(k) plan; a stock purchase plan; health and dental insurance; and life and disability insurance.

## FINANCIALS:

**Sales and profits are in thousands of dollars—add 000 to get the full amount. 2008 Note: Financial information for 2008 was not available for all companies at press time.**

| | | |
|---|---|---|
| 2008 Sales: $111,959 | 2008 Profits: $-84,935 | **U.S. Stock Ticker: ESLR** |
| 2007 Sales: $69,866 | 2007 Profits: $-16,602 | **Int'l Ticker:** Int'l Exchange: |
| 2006 Sales: $22,240 | 2006 Profits: $-22,267 | Employees: 400 |
| 2005 Sales: $44,032 | 2005 Profits: $-17,316 | Fiscal Year Ends: 12/31 |
| 2004 Sales: $23,536 | 2004 Profits: $-19,363 | Parent Company: |

## SALARIES/BENEFITS:

| | | | | |
|---|---|---|---|---|
| Pension Plan: | ESOP Stock Plan: | Profit Sharing: | Top Exec. Salary: $396,154 | Bonus: $400,000 |
| Savings Plan: Y | Stock Purch. Plan: Y | | Second Exec. Salary: $318,750 | Bonus: $268,082 |

## OTHER THOUGHTS:

**Apparent Women Officers or Directors:**
**Hot Spot for Advancement for Women/Minorities:**

## LOCATIONS: ("Y" = Yes)

| West: | Southwest: | Midwest: | Southeast: | Northeast: | International: |
|---|---|---|---|---|---|
| | | | | Y | Y |

# EXACTECH INC

www.exac.com

**Industry Group Code:** 339113 **Ranks within this company's industry group:** Sales: 24 Profits: 23

| Management: | | Sales/Marketing: | | Liberal Arts: | | Information Systems: | | Professionals: | | Technical/Scientific: | |
|---|---|---|---|---|---|---|---|---|---|---|---|
| Mgmt. Trainees: | | Mktg. Professionals: | Y | Gen. Writing/Editing: | | Info. Management: | Y | Finance/Accounting: | Y | Engineers, Elec.: | |
| Experienced Mgmt.: | Y | Retail Sales: | | Technical Writing: | Y | Software Dev.: | | Law: | Y | Engineers, Other: | Y |
| Int'l Business: | Y | Commercial/Industrial: | Y | Graphic Arts/Photog.: | | Hardware Dev.: | | HR/Other: | Y | Health/Lab: | Y |
| MBA Graduates: | Y | Sales Trainees: | Y | Music: | | Systems Integration: | | Training: | Y | Scientists/Research: | Y |
| | | Advertising Pros.: | | Broadcasting: | | Consulting/Other: | | Health Care: | Y | Petroleum/Chemicals: | |
| | | | | Other: | | | | Consulting: | | Math/Other: | Y |

## TYPES OF BUSINESS:

Equipment-Joint Replacement
Orthopedic Implant Devices
Surgical Instruments
Biologic Products
Bone Fusion Materials

## BRANDS/DIVISIONS/AFFILIATES:

Optetrak
AcuMatch
Link Saddle Prosthesis
Opteform
Optefil
Cemex
AcuDriver Automated Osteotome System
Saddle

## CONTACTS:

*Note: Officers with more than one job title may be intentionally listed here more than once.*

William Petty, CEO
David Petty, Pres.
Joel C. Phillips, CFO
Bob Purcell, VP-U.S. Sales
Betty B. Petty, VP-Human Resources
Gary J. Miller, Exec. VP-R&D
Betty B. Petty, VP-Admin.
Betty B. Petty, Corp. Sec.
Bruce Thompson, Sr. VP/Gen. Mgr.-Biologics Div.
William Petty, Chmn.
Daniel Berdat, VP-Int'l Sales & Mktg.

| | |
|---|---|
| **Phone:** 352-377-1140 | **Fax:** 352-378-2617 |
| **Toll-Free:** 800-392-2832 | |
| **Address:** 2320 NW 66th Ct., Gainesville, FL 32653 US | |

## GROWTH PLANS/SPECIAL FEATURES:

Exactech, Inc. develops, manufactures, distributes and sells orthopedic implant devices, surgical instrumentation and materials and biologic materials to hospitals and physicians. The company's orthopedic implant products repair or replace joints that have deteriorated. Products include Optetrak, a knee replacement system; and the AcuMatch integrated hip system with the C-Series cemented femoral stem, the A-series acetabular hip socket components, the P-series press-fit femoral stem, the M-Series modular femoral stem, the L-Series femoral stem system, bipolar and unipolar partial hip replacement components, femoral heads and a cemented acetabular component; the Link Saddle Prosthesis, which supports unreconstructable pelvic regions; the Link SPII hip stem; and the Link Partial Pelvis. Biologic allograft materials, such as Exactech's Opteform and Optefil, repair bone defects and provide an interface for bone growth. The company offers Cemex, a bone cement system; the AcuDriver Automated Osteotome System, an air-driven impact hand piece used by surgeons during joint implant revision procedures to remove failed prostheses and bone cement; and the Accelerate Platelet Concentration System, which improves the healing joints and tissue following orthopedic procedures. Exactech's oncology products include the Link MP, Partial Pelvis, Saddle Prosthesis, Total Femur and the M-series Modular Femoral Stem for hip implant devices; along with the Link Endo-Model Modular Rotating Hinge and the Total Femor joint knee systems. In 2007, Exactech received FDA clearance to market Equinoxe Reverse Shoulder, part of the company's shoulder arthroplasty line. In January 2008, the firm acquired the Altiva Corporation, a spinal products company. In February 2008, the firm opened a Japanese wholly-owned subsidiary. In April 2008, Exactech acquired France Medica SAS, a French importer and distributor of orthopaedic products and surgical supplies. In June 2008, the firm added Novation Crown Cup Acetabular System, with a titanium plasma-spray acetabular shell, to its hip product line.

## FINANCIALS:

**Sales and profits are in thousands of dollars—add 000 to get the full amount. 2008 Note: Financial information for 2008 was not available for all companies at press time.**

| | | |
|---|---|---|
| 2008 Sales: $ | 2008 Profits: $ | **U.S. Stock Ticker: EXAC** |
| 2007 Sales: $124,209 | 2007 Profits: $8,483 | **Int'l Ticker:** Int'l Exchange: |
| 2006 Sales: $102,430 | 2006 Profits: $7,752 | Employees: 265 |
| 2005 Sales: $91,016 | 2005 Profits: $6,604 | Fiscal Year Ends: 12/31 |
| 2004 Sales: $81,815 | 2004 Profits: $7,304 | Parent Company: |

## SALARIES/BENEFITS:

| | | | | |
|---|---|---|---|---|
| Pension Plan: | ESOP Stock Plan: | Profit Sharing: Y | Top Exec. Salary: $441,755 | Bonus: $236,281 |
| Savings Plan: Y | Stock Purch. Plan: Y | | Second Exec. Salary: $276,387 | Bonus: $111,463 |

## OTHER THOUGHTS:

**Apparent Women Officers or Directors**: 1
**Hot Spot for Advancement for Women/Minorities**:

## LOCATIONS: ("Y" = Yes)

| West: | Southwest: | Midwest: | Southeast: | Northeast: | International: |
|---|---|---|---|---|---|
| | | | Y | Y | Y |

# EXCEL TECHNOLOGY INC

www.exceltechinc.com

**Industry Group Code:** 339113 **Ranks within this company's industry group:** Sales: 22 Profits: 9

| Management: | | Sales/Marketing: | | Liberal Arts: | | Information Systems: | | Professionals: | | Technical/Scientific: | |
|---|---|---|---|---|---|---|---|---|---|---|---|
| Mgmt. Trainees: | | Mktg. Professionals: | Y | Gen. Writing/Editing: | | Info. Management: | Y | Finance/Accounting: | Y | Engineers, Elec.: | Y |
| Experienced Mgmt.: | Y | Retail Sales: | | Technical Writing: | Y | Software Dev.: | Y | Law: | Y | Engineers, Other: | Y |
| Int'l Business: | Y | Commercial/Industrial: | Y | Graphic Arts/Photog.: | | Hardware Dev.: | Y | HR/Other: | Y | Health/Lab: | Y |
| MBA Graduates: | Y | Sales Trainees: | Y | Music: | | Systems Integration: | | Training: | Y | Scientists/Research: | Y |
| | | Advertising Pros.: | | Broadcasting: | | Consulting/Other: | | Health Care: | Y | Petroleum/Chemicals: | |
| | | | | Other: | | | | Consulting: | | Math/Other: | Y |

## TYPES OF BUSINESS:

Equipment-Electro-Optical Components & Laser Systems
Optical Scanning Equipment
Photomask Repair Systems
Scientific & Industrial Lasers
Medical Lasers-Skin & Eye Treatment

## BRANDS/DIVISIONS/AFFILIATES:

Control Systemation, Inc.
Baublys
Control Laser
Synrad
Cambridge Technology
Quantronix
Photo Research

## CONTACTS: *Note: Officers with more than one job title may be intentionally listed here more than once.*

Antoine Dominic, CEO
Antoine Dominic, COO
Antoine Dominic, Pres.
Alice Varisano, CFO
Alice Varisano, Sec.
Greg Anderson, Pres., Control Systemation, Inc.
Redmond P. Aylward, Pres., Cambridge Tech., Inc.
Laurence E. Cramer, Pres., Continuum Electro-Optics, Inc.
Dave Clarke, Pres., Synrad, Inc.
J. Donald Hill, Chmn.
Reinhard Baumert, Pres., Excel Tech. Europe GmbH

**Phone:** 631-784-6175 **Fax:** 631-784-6195
**Toll-Free:**
**Address:** 41 Research Way, East Setauket, NY 11733 US

## GROWTH PLANS/SPECIAL FEATURES:

Excel Technology, Inc. designs, develops, manufactures and markets laser systems and electro-optical components for industry, science and medicine. The company's many subsidiaries include Control Systemation, Inc., which focuses on turnkey laser-based micro-machining systems and part-handling workstations for factory automation. In recent years, Excel consolidated the product lines and development efforts of subsidiaries Baublys and Control Laser to eliminate duplicative products and efforts, to increase efficiency and to create a unified market presence for the firm's laser marking and engraving operations. Current products and applications include Baublys-Control Laser marking and engraving systems; Synrad carbon dioxide lasers; Cambridge scanners; Quantronix photomask repair systems and scientific and industrial solid-state lasers; TOC optical products; and Photo Research light and color measurement products. Excel's Cambridge Technology subsidiary provides beam steering scanner-based applications, servicing a growing number of laser-based medical applications, including digital radiography, skin resurfacing and eye treatment. Through its subsidiary Continuum, Excel develops, manufactures and markets pulsed lasers and related accessories for the scientific and commercial marketplaces. Excel Europe, the company's European subsidiary, buys laser systems, spare parts and related consumable materials from Quantronix, Baublys-Control Laser and Synrad for resale to European and other foreign customers, as well as providing field repair services. Excel Japan, the firm's Japanese subsidiary, focuses on marketing, selling, distributing, integrating and servicing Quantronix and Continuum products in Japan. In 2007, the company developed Agilite, a new product based on flexible pulse-width technology, which is the first of its kind to map out pulse-width parameter space. The tool is being developed for application in materials processing and therapeutic medical markets.

## FINANCIALS: Sales and profits are in thousands of dollars—add 000 to get the full amount. 2008 Note: Financial information for 2008 was not available for all companies at press time.

| | | |
|---|---|---|
| 2008 Sales: $ | 2008 Profits: $ | **U.S. Stock Ticker: XLTC** |
| 2007 Sales: $160,023 | 2007 Profits: $17,732 | **Int'l Ticker:** Int'l Exchange: |
| 2006 Sales: $154,496 | 2006 Profits: $14,019 | Employees: 719 |
| 2005 Sales: $137,717 | 2005 Profits: $15,208 | Fiscal Year Ends: 12/31 |
| 2004 Sales: $136,631 | 2004 Profits: $14,762 | Parent Company: |

## SALARIES/BENEFITS:

| | | | | |
|---|---|---|---|---|
| Pension Plan: | ESOP Stock Plan: | Profit Sharing: | Top Exec. Salary: $542,000 | Bonus: $1,153,764 |
| Savings Plan: Y | Stock Purch. Plan: Y | | Second Exec. Salary: $275,000 | Bonus: $65,200 |

## OTHER THOUGHTS:

**Apparent Women Officers or Directors**: 1
**Hot Spot for Advancement for Women/Minorities**:

## LOCATIONS: ("Y" = Yes)

| West: | Southwest: | Midwest: | Southeast: | Northeast: | International: |
|---|---|---|---|---|---|
| Y | | | Y | Y | Y |

# EXCO RESOURCES INC

**www.excoresources.com**

**Industry Group Code:** 211111 **Ranks within this company's industry group:** Sales: 12 Profits: 15

| Management: | | Sales/Marketing: | | Liberal Arts: | | Information Systems: | | Professionals: | | Technical/Scientific: | |
|---|---|---|---|---|---|---|---|---|---|---|---|
| Mgmt. Trainees: | | Mktg. Professionals: | Y | Gen. Writing/Editing: | | Info. Management: | Y | Finance/Accounting: | Y | Engineers, Elec.: | |
| Experienced Mgmt.: | Y | Retail Sales: | | Technical Writing: | | Software Dev.: | | Law: | Y | Engineers, Other: | Y |
| Int'l Business: | Y | Commercial/Industrial: | Y | Graphic Arts/Photog.: | | Hardware Dev.: | | HR/Other: | Y | Health/Lab: | |
| MBA Graduates: | Y | Sales Trainees: | | Music: | | Systems Integration: | | Training: | Y | Scientists/Research: | |
| | | Advertising Pros.: | | Broadcasting: | | Consulting/Other: | | Health Care: | | Petroleum/Chemicals: | Y |
| | | | | Other: | | | | Consulting: | | Math/Other: | |

## TYPES OF BUSINESS:

Oil & Gas Exploration & Production

## BRANDS/DIVISIONS/AFFILIATES:

TXOK Acquisition, Inc.
Power Gas Marketing & Transmission, Inc.
Winchester Energy Co., Ltd.

## CONTACTS: *Note: Officers with more than one job title may be intentionally listed here more than once.*

Douglas H. Miller, CEO
Harold L. Hickey, COO/VP
Stephen F. Smith, Pres./Sec.
J. Douglas Ramsey, CFO/VP
John D. Jacobi, VP-Mktg.
Joe D. Ford, VP-Human Resources
Marcia Reeves Simpson, VP-Eng.
William L. Boeing, General Counsel/Sec/VP
Michael R. Chambers, VP-Oper.
John D. Jacobi, Exec. VP-Bus. Dev.
Mark E. Wilson, Controller/VP
Richard L. Hodges, VP-Land
Stephen E. Puckett, VP-Reservoir Eng.
Paul B. Rudnicki, VP-Financial Planning & Analysis
Wendy L. Straatmann, Pres., North Coast Energy Inc.
Douglas H. Miller, Chmn.

| **Phone:** 214-368-2084 | **Fax:** 214-368-2087 |
|---|---|
| **Toll-Free:** | |
| **Address:** 12377 Merit Dr., Ste. 1700, Dallas, TX 75251 US | |

## GROWTH PLANS/SPECIAL FEATURES:

EXCO Resources, Inc. is an independent oil and natural gas company engaged in the acquisition, development and exploitation of onshore North American oil and natural gas properties. The company's operations are focused in key North American oil and natural gas areas including east Texas/north Louisiana, Appalachia, Mid-Continent and Permian. The firm has proved reserves of about 1.9 trillion cubic feet equivalent, of which 93% was natural gas and 71% was proved developed reserves. EXCO owns and operates a network of natural gas gathering systems comprised of roughly 550 miles of pipeline in the east Texas/north Louisiana area of operations, which gathers and transports natural gas to larger gathering systems and intrastate, interstate and local distribution pipelines owned by third parties. Of all the natural gas gathered and transported by this system, about 76% represents products from the company's assets and about 24% represents production from the assets of third parties. The firm utilizes 3-D seismic and advanced drilling technologies when appropriate. In July 2008, EXCO acquired producing oil and natural gas properties and acreage from Gregg, Rusk, and Upshur Counties, Texas from private sellers for roughly $252 million.

The company offers its employees medical, dental, life and disability insurance and a 401(k) plan.

## FINANCIALS: **Sales and profits are in thousands of dollars—add 000 to get the full amount. 2008 Note: Financial information for 2008 was not available for all companies at press time.**

| | | |
|---|---|---|
| 2008 Sales: $ | 2008 Profits: $ | **U.S. Stock Ticker: XCO** |
| 2007 Sales: $906,510 | 2007 Profits: $49,656 | **Int'l Ticker:** Int'l Exchange: |
| 2006 Sales: $559,449 | 2006 Profits: $138,954 | Employees: 689 |
| 2005 Sales: $34,813 | 2005 Profits: $ 857 | Fiscal Year Ends: 12/31 |
| 2004 Sales: $92,791 | 2004 Profits: $6,161 | Parent Company: |

## SALARIES/BENEFITS:

| | | | | |
|---|---|---|---|---|
| Pension Plan: | ESOP Stock Plan: | Profit Sharing: | Top Exec. Salary: $750,000 | Bonus: $160,000 |
| Savings Plan: Y | Stock Purch. Plan: | | Second Exec. Salary: $550,000 | Bonus: $120,000 |

## OTHER THOUGHTS:

**Apparent Women Officers or Directors**: 2
**Hot Spot for Advancement for Women/Minorities**:

## LOCATIONS: ("Y" = Yes)

| West: | Southwest: | Midwest: | Southeast: | Northeast: | International: |
|---|---|---|---|---|---|
| Y | Y | Y | | Y | |

# EXELIXIS INC

www.exelixis.com

**Industry Group Code:** 325412 **Ranks within this company's industry group:** Sales: 20 Profits: 28

| Management: | | Sales/Marketing: | | Liberal Arts: | | Information Systems: | | Professionals: | | Technical/Scientific: | |
|---|---|---|---|---|---|---|---|---|---|---|---|
| Mgmt. Trainees: | | Mktg. Professionals: | Y | Gen. Writing/Editing: | | Info. Management: | Y | Finance/Accounting: | Y | Engineers, Elec.: | |
| Experienced Mgmt.: | Y | Retail Sales: | | Technical Writing: | Y | Software Dev.: | Y | Law: | Y | Engineers, Other: | |
| Int'l Business: | Y | Commercial/Industrial: | Y | Graphic Arts/Photog.: | | Hardware Dev.: | | HR/Other: | Y | Health/Lab: | Y |
| MBA Graduates: | Y | Sales Trainees: | Y | Music: | | Systems Integration: | | Training: | Y | Scientists/Research: | Y |
| | | Advertising Pros.: | | Broadcasting: | | Consulting/Other: | | Health Care: | Y | Petroleum/Chemicals: | |
| | | | | Other: | | | | Consulting: | Y | Math/Other: | Y |

## TYPES OF BUSINESS:

Genetic Research & Drug Development
Crop Protection Products
Genomics
Anti-Cancer Compounds

## BRANDS/DIVISIONS/AFFILIATES:

Exelixis Plant Sciences Inc

## CONTACTS:

*Note: Officers with more than one job title may be intentionally listed here more than once.*

George A. Scangos, CEO
George A. Scangos, Pres.
Frank Karbe, CFO/Exec. VP
Michael Morrissey, Pres., R&D
Pamela A. Simonton, General Counsel/Exec. VP
Lupe M. Rivera, Sr. VP-Oper.
Fran Heller, Exec. VP-Bus. Dev.
D. Ry Wagner, VP-Research, Exelixis Plant Sciences
Gisela M. Schwab, Chief Medical Officer/Exec. VP
Peter Lamb, Chief Scientific Officer/Sr. VP-Discovery Research
Stelios Papadopoulos, Chmn.

**Phone:** 650-837-7000 **Fax:** 650-837-8300
**Toll-Free:**
**Address:** 210 E. Grand Ave., South San Francisco, CA 94083 US

## GROWTH PLANS/SPECIAL FEATURES:

Exelixis, Inc. is a biotechnology company that focuses on the discovery and development of potential new drug therapies for cancer and other life-threatening diseases. The company has developed an integrated research and discovery platform utilizing proprietary technologies such as medicinal chemistry, bioinformatics, structural biology and early in vivo testing to provide an efficient and cost-effective process in gene analysis and drug development. Exelixis' translational research group employs knowledge generated in the discovery process to identify targeted patient populations for possible gene mutations or gene variants that impact response to therapy. The company's clinical program then conducts clinical trials to move candidate compounds through clinical registration phases in order to market newly discovered treatments. Exelixis Plant Sciences, a subsidiary of Exelixis, is working in collaboration with agricultural companies in plant biotechnology and crop protection. Research areas in crop protection focus on chemical products such as herbicides, insecticides and nematides designed specifically to target implicated crops. The plant biotechnology sector aims to develop crops with higher yields and improved nutritional profiles in oil content and protein composition. Exelixis has entered into research collaborations with Bristol-Myers Squibb to identify novel targets for new drugs in the fields of oncology and cardiovascular disease. The firm collaborates its research with GlaxoSmithKline in therapeutic areas such as vascular biology, inflammatory disease and oncology.

Employees are offered medical, dental and vision insurance; domestic partner benefits; health and dependent care flexible spending accounts; life and AD&D insurance; an employee assistance program; a 401(k) plan; long-term disability coverage; business travel accident insurance; a college savings plan; a group legal plan; an adoption assistance program; an infertility assistance program; onsite programs such as dry-cleaning and massage; pet insurance; back up dependent care; a tuition reimbursement program; a stock purchase plan; discounts on entertainment events; subsidized cafeteria meals; and subsidies for fitness center memberships.

## FINANCIALS:

**Sales and profits are in thousands of dollars—add 000 to get the full amount. 2008 Note: Financial information for 2008 was not available for all companies at press time.**

| | | |
|---|---|---|
| 2008 Sales: $ | 2008 Profits: $ | **U.S. Stock Ticker: EXEL** |
| 2007 Sales: $113,470 | 2007 Profits: $-86,381 | **Int'l Ticker:** Int'l Exchange: |
| 2006 Sales: $98,670 | 2006 Profits: $-101,492 | Employees: 735 |
| 2005 Sales: $75,961 | 2005 Profits: $-84,404 | Fiscal Year Ends: 12/31 |
| 2004 Sales: $52,857 | 2004 Profits: $-137,245 | Parent Company: |

## SALARIES/BENEFITS:

| | | | | |
|---|---|---|---|---|
| Pension Plan: | ESOP Stock Plan: | Profit Sharing: | Top Exec. Salary: $794,135 | Bonus: $477,000 |
| Savings Plan: Y | Stock Purch. Plan: Y | | Second Exec. Salary: $439,802 | Bonus: $220,286 |

## OTHER THOUGHTS:

**Apparent Women Officers or Directors**: 4
**Hot Spot for Advancement for Women/Minorities**: Y

## LOCATIONS: ("Y" = Yes)

| West: | Southwest: | Midwest: | Southeast: | Northeast: | International: |
|---|---|---|---|---|---|
| Y | | | | | Y |

Note: Financial information, benefits and other data can change quickly and may vary from those stated here.

# E-Z-EM INC

www.ezem.com

**Industry Group Code:** 325413 **Ranks within this company's industry group:** Sales: 5 Profits: 6

| Management: | | Sales/Marketing: | | Liberal Arts: | | Information Systems: | | Professionals: | | Technical/Scientific: | |
|---|---|---|---|---|---|---|---|---|---|---|---|
| Mgmt. Trainees: | | Mktg. Professionals: | Y | Gen. Writing/Editing: | | Info. Management: | Y | Finance/Accounting: | Y | Engineers, Elec.: | Y |
| Experienced Mgmt.: | Y | Retail Sales: | | Technical Writing: | Y | Software Dev.: | Y | Law: | Y | Engineers, Other: | Y |
| Int'l Business: | Y | Commercial/Industrial: | Y | Graphic Arts/Photog.: | | Hardware Dev.: | Y | HR/Other: | Y | Health/Lab: | Y |
| MBA Graduates: | Y | Sales Trainees: | Y | Music: | | Systems Integration: | | Training: | Y | Scientists/Research: | Y |
| | | Advertising Pros.: | | Broadcasting: | | Consulting/Other: | | Health Care: | Y | Petroleum/Chemicals: | |
| | | | | Other: | | | | Consulting: | | Math/Other: | Y |

## TYPES OF BUSINESS:

Medical Diagnostics Products
Virtual Colonoscopy Products
Diagnostic Contrast Media
Diagnostic Radiology Devices
Custom Pharmaceuticals
Gastrointestinal Diagnostic Products
Decontaminant Lotions

## BRANDS/DIVISIONS/AFFILIATES:

NutraPrep
CT Smoothies
Readi-CAT
Varibar
innerviewGI
Reactive Skin Decontaminant Lotion (RSDL)
EmpowerSync

## CONTACTS: *Note: Officers with more than one job title may be intentionally listed here more than once.*

Anthony A. Lombardo, CEO
Anthony A. Lombardo, Pres.
Joseph Cacchioli, Acting CFO
Peter J. Graham, Head-Human Resources
Jeffrey S. Peacock, Sr. VP-Global Scientific
Jeffrey S. Peacock, Sr. VP-Tech. Oper.
Peter J. Graham, General Counsel/VP/Sec.
Joseph J. Palma, Sr. VP-Corp. Rel.
Brad S. Schreck, Sr. VP-Global Mktg. Eng.
Paul S. Echenberg, Chmn.

**Phone:** 516-333-8230 **Fax:** 516-333-8278
**Toll-Free:** 800-544-4624
**Address:** 1111 Marcus Ave., Ste. LL26, Lake Success, NY 11042 US

## GROWTH PLANS/SPECIAL FEATURES:

E-Z-EM, Inc. develops, manufactures and markets diagnostic products used by physicians during image-assisted procedures to detect anatomic abnormalities and diseases. Its products and services are designed for use in the radiology, gastroenterology, speech pathology and virtual colonoscopy industries for colorectal cancer screening and testing for other gastrointestinal disorders. E-Z-EM's products coat portions of the throat or digestive tract to help targeted systems appear under imaging systems such as X-ray fluoroscopy and computed tomography (CT) imaging. The company's lead products include CT Smoothies, Readi-CAT contrast products, NutraPrep low residue pre-procedural foods, the Varibar line of swallowing evaluation agents, CT injector systems and the innerviewGI hardware and software system for conducting virtual colonoscopy. E-Z-EM provides contract manufacturing in the areas of diagnostic contrast media, pharmaceuticals and cosmetics. One of the firm's latest U.S. Food and Drug Administration-approved products include E-Z-EM's EmpowerSync system, a product based on the CAN-CiA (Controller Area Network-CAN in Automation) DSP 425 protocol. EmpowerSync permits synchronized operation of EmpowerCT and EmpowerCTA injector systems and CT scanners from all of the manufacturers who also adopt the DSP 425 standard. The company is currently working with O'Dell Engineering Ltd. to commercialize a product line of Reactive Skin Decontaminant Lotions (RSDL) for neutralizing chemical warfare agents. These RSDL products are in use in the armed forces of Canada, Australia, Ireland and the Netherlands. Recently, RSDL received Milestone C approval from the Joint Program Executive Office for Chemical Biological Defense (JPEO-CBD), clearing the way for procurement by the individual service branches of the U.S. Department of Defense.

E-Z-EM offers its employees medical, dental, life and travel insurance; long term disability; a 401(k); a stock purchase plan; employee training and development programs; tuition reimbursement; and flexible spending accounts.

## FINANCIALS: Sales and profits are in thousands of dollars—add 000 to get the full amount. 2008 Note: Financial information for 2008 was not available for all companies at press time.

| | | |
|---|---|---|
| 2008 Sales: $ | 2008 Profits: $ | **U.S. Stock Ticker: EZEM** |
| 2007 Sales: $137,840 | 2007 Profits: $8,543 | **Int'l Ticker:** Int'l Exchange: |
| 2006 Sales: $137,083 | 2006 Profits: $9,766 | Employees: 590 |
| 2005 Sales: $111,700 | 2005 Profits: $6,936 | Fiscal Year Ends: 5/31 |
| 2004 Sales: $148,771 | 2004 Profits: $6,726 | Parent Company: |

## SALARIES/BENEFITS:

| | | | | |
|---|---|---|---|---|
| Pension Plan: | ESOP Stock Plan: | Profit Sharing: Y | Top Exec. Salary: $350,784 | Bonus: $101,610 |
| Savings Plan: Y | Stock Purch. Plan: Y | | Second Exec. Salary: $224,591 | Bonus: $101,610 |

## OTHER THOUGHTS:

**Apparent Women Officers or Directors:**
**Hot Spot for Advancement for Women/Minorities:**

## LOCATIONS: ("Y" = Yes)

| West: | Southwest: | Midwest: | Southeast: | Northeast: | International: |
|---|---|---|---|---|---|
| | | | | Y | Y |

Note: Financial information, benefits and other data can change quickly and may vary from those stated here.

# F5 NETWORKS INC

**www.f5.com**

**Industry Group Code:** 511214 **Ranks within this company's industry group:** Sales: 1 Profits: 1

| Management: | | Sales/Marketing: | | Liberal Arts: | | Information Systems: | | Professionals: | | Technical/Scientific: | |
|---|---|---|---|---|---|---|---|---|---|---|---|
| Mgmt. Trainees: | | Mktg. Professionals: | Y | Gen. Writing/Editing: | | Info. Management: | Y | Finance/Accounting: | Y | Engineers, Elec.: | Y |
| Experienced Mgmt.: | Y | Retail Sales: | | Technical Writing: | Y | Software Dev.: | Y | Law: | Y | Engineers, Other: | |
| Int'l Business: | Y | Commercial/Industrial: | Y | Graphic Arts/Photog.: | | Hardware Dev.: | | HR/Other: | Y | Health/Lab: | |
| MBA Graduates: | Y | Sales Trainees: | Y | Music: | | Systems Integration: | Y | Training: | Y | Scientists/Research: | |
| | | Advertising Pros.: | | Broadcasting: | | Consulting/Other: | | Health Care: | | Petroleum/Chemicals: | |
| | | | | Other: | | | | Consulting: | | Math/Other: | |

## TYPES OF BUSINESS:

Server Software
Internet Traffic Management Solutions
Firewall Software
File Virtualization

## BRANDS/DIVISIONS/AFFILIATES:

Application Security Manager
BIG-IP Controller
FirePass Controller
iControl Software
ARX

## CONTACTS: *Note: Officers with more than one job title may be intentionally listed here more than once.*

John McAdam, CEO
John McAdam, Pres.
Andy Reinland, CFO/Sr. VP
Dan Matte, Sr. VP-Mktg.
Karl Triebes, CTO
Karl Triebes, Sr. VP-Prod. Dev.
Jess Christianson, General Counsel/Sr. VP
Edward J. Eames, Sr. VP-Bus. Oper.
John Rodriguez, Chief Acct. Officer/Sr. VP
Mark Anderson, Sr. VP-Worldwide Sales
Lori MacVittie, Manager-Tech. Mktg.
Christopher P. Lynch, Sr. VP-Data Solutions
Alan J. Higginson, Chmn.

| | |
|---|---|
| **Phone:** 206-272-5555 | **Fax:** 206-272-5556 |
| **Toll-Free:** 888-882-4447 | |
| **Address:** 401 Elliott Ave. W., Seattle, WA 98119 US | |

## GROWTH PLANS/SPECIAL FEATURES:

F5 Networks, Inc. provides application delivery networking products that improve the security, availability and performance of applications running on networks that use the Internet Protocol (IP). Its core products, the BIG-IP controller, FirePass controller, Application Security Manager firewall and iControl, help manage traffic to servers and network devices in a way that maximizes availability and throughput. BIG-IP products share a common fully-proxy operating system that enables them to inspect and modify traffic flow to and from servers and has built-in functionality to secure, optimize and ensure the availability of application traffic. The company's FirePass product provides secure SSL-VPN (Secure Socket Layer-Virtual Private Network) that allows enterprises to provide authorized users connected to the Internet with secure remote access to corporate networks and applications by leveraging standard Web browser technology. The Application Security Manager firewall provides content-based, application-level security against attacks. The iControl software interface products enable communication with one another and allow integration with third party products, including custom and commercial enterprise applications. Intelligent file virtualization manages file storage infrastructure through non-disruptive data migration, automated storage tiering, dynamic load balancing, and efficient data replication though the ARX product family. The company sells its products and services to large enterprise customers and service providers through a variety of channels, including distributors, value-added resellers and systems integrators. In 2007, F5 Networks acquired Acopia Networks, a provider of file-virtualization products.

F5 Networks offers its employees medical, dental and vision insurance as well as life and disability insurance; flexible spending accounts; a 401(k) plan; tuition assistance; an employee assistance program; and an employee stock purchase plan.

## FINANCIALS: **Sales and profits are in thousands of dollars—add 000 to get the full amount. 2008 Note: Financial information for 2008 was not available for all companies at press time.**

| | | |
|---|---|---|
| 2008 Sales: $650,173 | 2008 Profits: $74,331 | **U.S. Stock Ticker: FFIV** |
| 2007 Sales: $525,667 | 2007 Profits: $77,000 | **Int'l Ticker:** Int'l Exchange: |
| 2006 Sales: $394,049 | 2006 Profits: $66,005 | Employees: 1,694 |
| 2005 Sales: $281,410 | 2005 Profits: $46,902 | Fiscal Year Ends: 9/30 |
| 2004 Sales: $171,190 | 2004 Profits: $36,328 | Parent Company: |

## SALARIES/BENEFITS:

| | | | | |
|---|---|---|---|---|
| Pension Plan: | ESOP Stock Plan: | Profit Sharing: | Top Exec. Salary: $495,502 | Bonus: $420,283 |
| Savings Plan: Y | Stock Purch. Plan: Y | | Second Exec. Salary: $342,698 | Bonus: $185,839 |

## OTHER THOUGHTS:

**Apparent Women Officers or Directors:**
**Hot Spot for Advancement for Women/Minorities:**

## LOCATIONS: ("Y" = Yes)

| West: | Southwest: | Midwest: | Southeast: | Northeast: | International: |
|---|---|---|---|---|---|
| Y | | Y | | Y | Y |

# FARMER BROTHERS CO

www.farmerbroscousa.com

**Industry Group Code:** 311920 **Ranks within this company's industry group:** Sales: 2 Profits: 2

| Management: | | Sales/Marketing: | | Liberal Arts: | | Information Systems: | | Professionals: | | Technical/Scientific: | |
|---|---|---|---|---|---|---|---|---|---|---|---|
| Mgmt. Trainees: | Y | Mktg. Professionals: | Y | Gen. Writing/Editing: | | Info. Management: | Y | Finance/Accounting: | Y | Engineers, Elec.: | |
| Experienced Mgmt.: | Y | Retail Sales: | | Technical Writing: | | Software Dev.: | | Law: | Y | Engineers, Other: | |
| Int'l Business: | | Commercial/Industrial: | Y | Graphic Arts/Photog.: | Y | Hardware Dev.: | | HR/Other: | Y | Health/Lab: | |
| MBA Graduates: | Y | Sales Trainees: | Y | Music: | | Systems Integration: | | Training: | Y | Scientists/Research: | |
| | | Advertising Pros.: | Y | Broadcasting: | | Consulting/Other: | | Health Care: | | Petroleum/Chemicals: | |
| | | | | Other: | | | | Consulting: | | Math/Other: | |

## TYPES OF BUSINESS:

Coffee & Tea Manufacturing
Foodservice Distribution
Coffee-Related Products
Soup, Gravy and Sauce Mixes
Spices
Pancake and Biscuit Mixes

## BRANDS/DIVISIONS/AFFILIATES:

Sierra Flavored & Herb Teas
Coffee Bean International
Coffee Bean Holding Co., Inc.

## CONTACTS:

*Note: Officers with more than one job title may be intentionally listed here more than once.*

Roger M. Laverty, CEO
Drew H. Webb, COO/Exec. VP
Roger M. Laverty, Pres.
John E. Simmons, CFO
John M. Anglin, Sec.
John E. Simmons, Treas.
Michael J. King, VP-Restaurant & Institutional Sales Div.
Guenter W. Berger, Chmn.

**Phone:** 310-787-5200 **Fax:** 310-787-5246
**Toll-Free:** 800-735-2878
**Address:** 20333 S. Normandie Ave., Torrance, CA 90502 US

## GROWTH PLANS/SPECIAL FEATURES:

Farmer Brothers Co. is a manufacturer and distributor of coffee, tea, food products and spices to the institutional food service segment. The firm's product line is specifically focused on the needs of this market segment, including restaurants and institutional establishments that prepare and market meals, such as hotels, hospitals, convenience stores and grocery stores over a 31-state service area. The company's line has more than 400 items in various categories, including roasted coffees in a variety of blends and flavors, such as Kona Blend, Sierra Blend, Amaretto Flavor and Vanilla Nut; coffee-related products such as coffee machines and filters; sugar and creamers; assorted teas; cocoa; pancake and biscuit mixes; spices; soups; and beverage bases. For the past three years, the sale of roasted coffee represents 50% of the company's total sales. The firm's selling division distributes its products to foodservice customers at their places of business, and the company operates its own long-haul trucking fleet to maintain control the supply of products to its warehouses, each truck bearing the Consistently Good company logo. The firm's distribution hub is its Torrance, California facility, which houses the firm's administrative offices, roasting plant and warehouses. Distribution is supported by small branch warehouses located throughout the company's service area. Portions of the firm's products are distributed by third parties or are direct shipped via common carrier. In October 2008, the company's subsidiary, Coffee Bean International opened a new 125,000 square foot coffee roasting facility in Portland, Oregon. In December of the same year, the firm agreed to acquire the direct store delivery coffee business from Sara Lee Corp.

Employees are offered medical, dental, life and disability insurance; a pension plan; a 401(k) plan; and an employee stock ownership plan.

## FINANCIALS:

**Sales and profits are in thousands of dollars—add 000 to get the full amount. 2008 Note: Financial information for 2008 was not available for all companies at press time.**

| | | |
|---|---|---|
| 2008 Sales: $266,485 | 2008 Profits: $-7,924 | **U.S. Stock Ticker: FARM** |
| 2007 Sales: $216,259 | 2007 Profits: $6,815 | **Int'l Ticker:** Int'l Exchange: |
| 2006 Sales: $207,453 | 2006 Profits: $4,756 | Employees: 1,256 |
| 2005 Sales: $198,420 | 2005 Profits: $-5,427 | Fiscal Year Ends: 6/30 |
| 2004 Sales: $193,589 | 2004 Profits: $12,687 | Parent Company: |

## SALARIES/BENEFITS:

| | | | | |
|---|---|---|---|---|
| Pension Plan: Y | ESOP Stock Plan: Y | Profit Sharing: | Top Exec. Salary: $350,038 | Bonus: $175,000 |
| Savings Plan: Y | Stock Purch. Plan: | | Second Exec. Salary: $287,375 | Bonus: $100,000 |

## OTHER THOUGHTS:

**Apparent Women Officers or Directors**: 1
**Hot Spot for Advancement for Women/Minorities**:

## LOCATIONS: ("Y" = Yes)

| West: | Southwest: | Midwest: | Southeast: | Northeast: | International: |
|---|---|---|---|---|---|
| Y | Y | Y | | | |

# FBL FINANCIAL GROUP

**www.fblfinancial.com**

**Industry Group Code:** 524113 **Ranks within this company's industry group:** Sales: 5 Profits: 4

| **Management:** | | **Sales/Marketing:** | | **Liberal Arts:** | | **Information Systems:** | | **Professionals:** | | **Technical/Scientific:** | |
|---|---|---|---|---|---|---|---|---|---|---|---|
| Mgmt. Trainees: | | Mktg. Professionals: | Y | Gen. Writing/Editing: | Y | Info. Management: | Y | Finance/Accounting: | Y | Engineers, Elec.: | |
| Experienced Mgmt.: | Y | Retail Sales: | | Technical Writing: | Y | Software Dev.: | | Law: | Y | Engineers, Other: | |
| Int'l Business: | | Commercial/Industrial: | | Graphic Arts/Photog.: | | Hardware Dev.: | | HR/Other: | Y | Health/Lab: | |
| MBA Graduates: | Y | Sales Trainees: | Y | Music: | | Systems Integration: | | Training: | Y | Scientists/Research: | |
| | | Advertising Pros.: | Y | Broadcasting: | | Consulting/Other: | | Health Care: | Y | Petroleum/Chemicals: | |
| | | | | Other: | | | | Consulting: | | Math/Other: | Y |

## TYPES OF BUSINESS:

Insurance-Life
Property & Casualty Insurance
Financial Services
Mutual Funds
Annuities

## BRANDS/DIVISIONS/AFFILIATES:

Farm Bureau Financial Services
EquiTrust Financial Services
Farm Bureau Life Insurance Company
EquiTrust Life Insurance Company
American Equity Investment Life Insurance Company
EMC National Life Company

## CONTACTS:

*Note: Officers with more than one job title may be intentionally listed here more than once.*

James W. Noyce, CEO
James P. Brannen, CFO
John M. Paule, Chief Mktg. Officer
James P. Brannen, Chief Admin. Officer
Richard J. Kypta, General Counsel/Sec./Exec. VP-Farm Bureau Life
James P. Brannen, Treas.
John M. Paule, Exec. VP-EquiTrust Life Insurance Company
Bruce A. Trost, Exec. VP-Property Casualty Companies
Craig A. Lang, Chmn.

| | |
|---|---|
| **Phone:** 515-225-5400 | **Fax:** 515-226-6053 |
| **Toll-Free:** | |
| **Address:** 5400 University Ave., W. Des Moines, IA 50266 US | |

## GROWTH PLANS/SPECIAL FEATURES:

FBL Financial Group, Inc. sells individual life and annuity products principally under the consumer brand names Farm Bureau Financial Services and EquiTrust Financial Services, which are represented by the distribution channels of FBL's subsidiaries Farm Bureau Life Insurance Company and EquiTrust Life Insurance Company. The Farm Bureau Life distribution system consists of exclusive agents in 15 Midwestern and Western states. The agents are multi-line agents who sell both property-casualty insurance products and life insurance and investment products under the Farm Bureau name. The subsidiary's target market consists primarily of farmers, ranchers, rural and suburban residents and related individuals and businesses. Many of FBL's customers are self-employed individuals who are responsible for providing for their own insurance needs. The Farm Bureau subsidiaries sell universal life, variable universal life, traditional life and disability income insurance and traditional and variable annuity products. Several subsidiaries support various functional areas of Farm Bureau Life and other affiliates, by providing investment advisory, marketing and distribution and leasing services. EquiTrust Life has three business dimensions: the EquiTrust Life independent channel, alliances with other companies to distribute products and two closed blocks of coinsured business. The EquiTrust Life independent channel, which operates through independent agents, is focused on growth through recruitment of insurance agents to sell EquiTrust Life products. Through its variable product alliances, FBL provides its partner companies with competitive variable products, with the option of brand-labeling. FBL's two closed block coinsurance agreements are with American Equity Investment Life Insurance Company and EMC National Life Company.

FBL offers its employees tuition reimbursement, education programs, free parking, an employee assistance program, alternative work schedules, flexible spending accounts and medical, dental, life and disability insurance.

## FINANCIALS:

**Sales and profits are in thousands of dollars—add 000 to get the full amount. 2008 Note: Financial information for 2008 was not available for all companies at press time.**

| | | |
|---|---|---|
| 2008 Sales: $ | 2008 Profits: $ | **U.S. Stock Ticker: FFG** |
| 2007 Sales: $914,599 | 2007 Profits: $86,339 | **Int'l Ticker:** Int'l Exchange: |
| 2006 Sales: $887,353 | 2006 Profits: $90,129 | Employees: 1,818 |
| 2005 Sales: $728,148 | 2005 Profits: $72,842 | Fiscal Year Ends: 12/31 |
| 2004 Sales: $682,602 | 2004 Profits: $66,076 | Parent Company: |

## SALARIES/BENEFITS:

| | | | | |
|---|---|---|---|---|
| Pension Plan: Y | ESOP Stock Plan: | Profit Sharing: | Top Exec. Salary: $631,250 | Bonus: $650,945 |
| Savings Plan: Y | Stock Purch. Plan: Y | | Second Exec. Salary: $434,591 | Bonus: $196,066 |

## OTHER THOUGHTS:

**Apparent Women Officers or Directors**: 1
**Hot Spot for Advancement for Women/Minorities**:

## LOCATIONS: ("Y" = Yes)

| West: | Southwest: | Midwest: | Southeast: | Northeast: | International: |
|---|---|---|---|---|---|
| Y | Y | Y | | | |

# FEDEX SUPPLY CHAIN SERVICES INC

www.fedex.com

**Industry Group Code:** 488510 **Ranks within this company's industry group:** Sales: 1 Profits:

| Management: | | Sales/Marketing: | | Liberal Arts: | | Information Systems: | | Professionals: | | Technical/Scientific: | |
|---|---|---|---|---|---|---|---|---|---|---|---|
| Mgmt. Trainees: | | Mktg. Professionals: | | Gen. Writing/Editing: | | Info. Management: | Y | Finance/Accounting: | Y | Engineers, Elec.: | |
| Experienced Mgmt.: | Y | Retail Sales: | | Technical Writing: | | Software Dev.: | | Law: | Y | Engineers, Other: | |
| Int'l Business: | Y | Commercial/Industrial: | | Graphic Arts/Photog.: | | Hardware Dev.: | | HR/Other: | Y | Health/Lab: | |
| MBA Graduates: | Y | Sales Trainees: | | Music: | | Systems Integration: | | Training: | Y | Scientists/Research: | |
| | | Advertising Pros.: | | Broadcasting: | | Consulting/Other: | | Health Care: | | Petroleum/Chemicals: | |
| | | | | Other: | | | | Consulting: | | Math/Other: | |

## TYPES OF BUSINESS:

Supply Chain Management
Transportation Management
Warehousing
Consulting
Inventory Visibility Services

## BRANDS/DIVISIONS/AFFILIATES:

FedEx Corporation

## CONTACTS: *Note: Officers with more than one job title may be intentionally listed here more than once.*

Tom Schmitt, CEO
Tom Schmitt, Pres.

**Phone:** 330-342-3000 **Fax:**
**Toll-Free:** 800-543-7657
**Address:** 5455 Darrow Rd., Hudson, OH 44236 US

## GROWTH PLANS/SPECIAL FEATURES:

FedEx Supply Chain Services, Inc., a division of FedEx Services, itself a subsidiary of FedEx Corporation, offers an extensive range of supply chain management services, with a fleet of 600 vehicles and roughly 40 warehouses, totaling over four million square feet. The firm's portfolio of services includes transportation management, order fulfillment, orchestrated delivery and returns programs. These services are generally tailored to the apparel, automotive, healthcare, high tech, industrial machinery and retail industries. FedEx Supply Chain's transportation management programs use advanced electronic data interchange to speed communications between customers and their suppliers, which results in more cost-effective solutions and enhanced levels of customer service. Its fulfillment program provides order administration, configuring services, comprehensive visibility of inventory (including inbound, outbound and static inventory), order execution and emergency delivery (completed in 2-4 hours). Return management services include billable stamps, a package returns program and other electronically produced return labels.

FedEx Supply Chain offers its employees tuition assistance, reduced rate shipping, credit union membership, global travel opportunities and medical, dental, vision, disability and life insurance.

## FINANCIALS: **Sales and profits are in thousands of dollars—add 000 to get the full amount. 2008 Note: Financial information for 2008 was not available for all companies at press time.**

| | | |
|---|---|---|
| 2008 Sales: $ | 2008 Profits: $ | **U.S. Stock Ticker: Subsidiary** |
| 2007 Sales: $98,600 | 2007 Profits: $ | **Int'l Ticker:** Int'l Exchange: |
| 2006 Sales: $ | 2006 Profits: $ | Employees: 1,800 |
| 2005 Sales: $ | 2005 Profits: $ | Fiscal Year Ends: 12/31 |
| 2004 Sales: $ | 2004 Profits: $ | Parent Company: FEDEX CORPORATION |

## SALARIES/BENEFITS:

| | | | | |
|---|---|---|---|---|
| Pension Plan: Y | ESOP Stock Plan: | Profit Sharing: | Top Exec. Salary: $ | Bonus: $ |
| Savings Plan: Y | Stock Purch. Plan: Y | | Second Exec. Salary: $ | Bonus: $ |

## OTHER THOUGHTS:

**Apparent Women Officers or Directors:**
**Hot Spot for Advancement for Women/Minorities:**

## LOCATIONS: ("Y" = Yes)

| West: | Southwest: | Midwest: | Southeast: | Northeast: | International: |
|---|---|---|---|---|---|
| Y | Y | Y | Y | Y | Y |

# FIRST SOLAR LLC

www.firstsolar.com

**Industry Group Code:** 333298A **Ranks within this company's industry group:** Sales: 1 Profits: 1

| Management: | | Sales/Marketing: | | Liberal Arts: | | Information Systems: | | Professionals: | | Technical/Scientific: | |
|---|---|---|---|---|---|---|---|---|---|---|---|
| Mgmt. Trainees: | | Mktg. Professionals: | Y | Gen. Writing/Editing: | | Info. Management: | Y | Finance/Accounting: | Y | Engineers, Elec.: | Y |
| Experienced Mgmt.: | Y | Retail Sales: | | Technical Writing: | Y | Software Dev.: | Y | Law: | Y | Engineers, Other: | Y |
| Int'l Business: | Y | Commercial/Industrial: | Y | Graphic Arts/Photog.: | Y | Hardware Dev.: | Y | HR/Other: | Y | Health/Lab: | |
| MBA Graduates: | Y | Sales Trainees: | Y | Music: | | Systems Integration: | | Training: | Y | Scientists/Research: | Y |
| | | Advertising Pros.: | | Broadcasting: | | Consulting/Other: | | Health Care: | | Petroleum/Chemicals: | |
| | | | | Other: | | | | Consulting: | | Math/Other: | Y |

## TYPES OF BUSINESS:

Photovoltaic Equipment
Thin-Film Solar Modules
Solar Module Collection & Recycling

## BRANDS/DIVISIONS/AFFILIATES:

Turner Renewable Energy LLC
First Solar Electric LLC
Sempra Generation

## CONTACTS:
*Note: Officers with more than one job title may be intentionally listed here more than once.*

Michael J. Ahearn, CEO
Bruce Sohn, Pres.
Jens Meyerhoff, CFO
John Carrington, Exec. VP-Global Mktg.
John Gaffney, General Counsel/Exec. VP
John Carrington, Exec. VP-Bus. Dev.
Larry Polizzotto, VP-Investor Rel.
Kathy Weiss, VP-Gov't Rel.
I. Paul Kacir, Corp. Sec.
Michael J. Ahearn, Chmn.
Jim Miller, Exec. VP-Product & Global Supply Chain Mgmt.

| | |
|---|---|
| **Phone:** 602-414-9300 | **Fax:** 602-414-9400 |
| **Toll-Free:** | |
| **Address:** 350 W. Washington St., Ste. 600, Tempe, AZ 85281 US | |

## GROWTH PLANS/SPECIAL FEATURES:

First Solar, LLC develops and manufactures thin-film solar modules that are based on its proprietary thin film semiconductor technology. First Solar photovoltaic (PV) modules are optimized for use in grid-connected applications and are sold to solar project developers for use in commercial projects. First Solar's process deposits thin films of semiconductor materials quickly and uniformly. The company uses cadmium telluride as a semiconducting material, which is a byproduct of the mining and production of base metals such as zinc and copper. The firm's customers primarily develop, own and operate solar power plants or sell turnkey solar power plants to end-users that include owners of land, agricultural buildings, commercial warehouses, offices and industrial buildings; public agencies; municipal government authorities; utility companies; and financial investors that desire to own large-scale solar power plant projects. The firm maintains a collection and recycling program in which end-users can return their solar modules for collection and recycling at no cost at any time. In July 2007, the company entered into five agreements for the manufacture and sale of solar modules totaling 685 Megawatts (MW). In September 2007, First Solar approved the construction of a 120-megawatt manufacturing plant in Malaysia. The new plant will be built in conjunction with two other plants already under construction in Malaysia. In November 2007, the firm entered into new long-term module supply agreements with a subsidiary of Babcock & Brown, as well as Ecostream Switzerland GmbH. In November 2007, the company acquired Turner Renewable Energy LLC, a commercial solar project design company that will operate under the name of First Solar Electric LLC. In July 2008, the company announced plans to build a 10 MW photovoltaic power plant in Nevada for Sempra Generation. In October 2008, First Solar began construction to expand its Ohio facility and increase its annual capacity to approximately 192 MW. First Solar claimed to achieve a manufacturing cost of only $1.08 per watt during the third quarter of 2008.

## FINANCIALS:
**Sales and profits are in thousands of dollars—add 000 to get the full amount. 2008 Note: Financial information for 2008 was not available for all companies at press time.**

| | | |
|---|---|---|
| 2008 Sales: $ | 2008 Profits: $ | **U.S. Stock Ticker: FSLR** |
| 2007 Sales: $503,976 | 2007 Profits: $158,354 | **Int'l Ticker:** Int'l Exchange: |
| 2006 Sales: $134,974 | 2006 Profits: $3,974 | Employees: 1,462 |
| 2005 Sales: $48,063 | 2005 Profits: $-6,462 | Fiscal Year Ends: 12/31 |
| 2004 Sales: $ | 2004 Profits: $ | Parent Company: |

## SALARIES/BENEFITS:

| | | | | |
|---|---|---|---|---|
| Pension Plan: | ESOP Stock Plan: | Profit Sharing: | Top Exec. Salary: $450,000 | Bonus: $765,000 |
| Savings Plan: Y | Stock Purch. Plan: | | Second Exec. Salary: $330,000 | Bonus: $365,836 |

## OTHER THOUGHTS:

**Apparent Women Officers or Directors**: 1
**Hot Spot for Advancement for Women/Minorities**:

## LOCATIONS: ("Y" = Yes)

| West: | Southwest: | Midwest: | Southeast: | Northeast: | International: |
|---|---|---|---|---|---|
| | Y | Y | | Y | Y |

# FLIR SYSTEMS

www.flir.com

**Industry Group Code:** 336410 **Ranks within this company's industry group:** Sales: 2 Profits: 1

| Management: | | Sales/Marketing: | | Liberal Arts: | | Information Systems: | | Professionals: | | Technical/Scientific: | |
|---|---|---|---|---|---|---|---|---|---|---|---|
| Mgmt. Trainees: | | Mktg. Professionals: | Y | Gen. Writing/Editing: | | Info. Management: | Y | Finance/Accounting: | Y | Engineers, Elec.: | Y |
| Experienced Mgmt.: | Y | Retail Sales: | | Technical Writing: | Y | Software Dev.: | Y | Law: | Y | Engineers, Other: | |
| Int'l Business: | Y | Commercial/Industrial: | Y | Graphic Arts/Photog.: | | Hardware Dev.: | | HR/Other: | Y | Health/Lab: | |
| MBA Graduates: | Y | Sales Trainees: | Y | Music: | | Systems Integration: | | Training: | Y | Scientists/Research: | |
| | | Advertising Pros.: | | Broadcasting: | | Consulting/Other: | | Health Care: | | Petroleum/Chemicals: | |
| | | | | Other: | | | | Consulting: | | Math/Other: | |

## TYPES OF BUSINESS:

Thermal Imaging Systems
Infrared Camera Systems

## BRANDS/DIVISIONS/AFFILIATES:

Ifara Tecnologias, S.L.

## CONTACTS: *Note: Officers with more than one job title may be intentionally listed here more than once.*

Earl R. Lewis, CEO
Earl R. Lewis, Pres.
Stephen M. Bailey, CFO
William W. Davis, General Counsel/Sec./Sr. VP
Anthony L. Trunzo, Sr. VP-Corp. Strategy & Dev.
Stephen M. Bailey, Sr. VP-Finance
Arne Almerfors, Exec. VP/Pres., Thermography Div.
Andrew C. Teich, Pres., Commercial Vision Systems Div.
William A. Sundermeier, Pres., Government Systems Div.
Earl R. Lewis, Chmn.

| | |
|---|---|
| **Phone:** 503-498-3547 | **Fax:** |
| **Toll-Free:** | |
| **Address:** 27700 S.W. Pkwy. Ave., Wilsonville, OR 97070-8238 US | |

## GROWTH PLANS/SPECIAL FEATURES:

FLIR Systems (FLIR) is a global designer, manufacturer and marketer of thermal imaging systems used in commercial, industrial and government applications. FLIR operates in three business segments: thermography, commercial vision systems (CVS) and government systems (GS). The firm's thermography segment, which generated 34% of its 2007 revenue, focuses on commercial and industrial applications, typically where imaging and temperature measurement together are required. Its thermography products range in price from $5,000 for a handheld camera for building inspection to over $150,000 for its most sophisticated science cameras. The firm's CVS segment, which generated 17% of its 2007 revenue, is focused on emerging commercial markets for infrared imaging technology where the primary need is to see at night or in adverse conditions. The segment includes its infrared sensor business, which sells camera cores internally as well as to third parties on an original equipment manufacturer (OEM) basis. CVS products range in price from under $2,000 for an OEM imaging core to over $450,000 for a high definition airborne electronic news gathering broadcast system. FLIR's GS segment, which generated 49% of its 2007 revenue, is focused on governmental customers and markets where very high performance is required. Typical applications include surveillance, force protection, drug interdiction, search and rescue, special operations and target designation. GS products are often customized for specific applications and frequently incorporate additional sensors. GS products range in price from $30,000 for its handheld and fixed security systems to over $1 million for its most advanced stabilized laser designation systems. In April 2008, FLIR acquired Ifara Tecnologias, S.L., a provider of middleware and client application software used to create sensor networks, for approximately $9.7 million.

FLIR offers its employees an education assistance program, a fitness subsidy, an employee assistance program and a choice of medical plans.

## FINANCIALS: **Sales and profits are in thousands of dollars—add 000 to get the full amount. 2008 Note: Financial information for 2008 was not available for all companies at press time.**

| | | |
|---|---|---|
| 2008 Sales: $1,076,974 | 2008 Profits: $203,733 | **U.S. Stock Ticker: FLIR** |
| 2007 Sales: $779,397 | 2007 Profits: $136,711 | **Int'l Ticker:** Int'l Exchange: |
| 2006 Sales: $575,000 | 2006 Profits: $100,896 | Employees: 1,743 |
| 2005 Sales: $508,561 | 2005 Profits: $90,765 | Fiscal Year Ends: 12/31 |
| 2004 Sales: $482,651 | 2004 Profits: $71,495 | Parent Company: |

## SALARIES/BENEFITS:

| | | | | |
|---|---|---|---|---|
| Pension Plan: | ESOP Stock Plan: | Profit Sharing: | Top Exec. Salary: $750,000 | Bonus: $1,500,000 |
| Savings Plan: Y | Stock Purch. Plan: | | Second Exec. Salary: $569,943 | Bonus: $420,000 |

## OTHER THOUGHTS:

**Apparent Women Officers or Directors:**
**Hot Spot for Advancement for Women/Minorities:**

## LOCATIONS: ("Y" = Yes)

| West: | Southwest: | Midwest: | Southeast: | Northeast: | International: |
|---|---|---|---|---|---|
| Y | | Y | Y | Y | Y |

# FOREST OIL CORPORATION

www.forestoil.com

**Industry Group Code:** 211111 **Ranks within this company's industry group:** Sales: 9 Profits: 11

| Management: | | Sales/Marketing: | | Liberal Arts: | | Information Systems: | | Professionals: | | Technical/Scientific: | |
|---|---|---|---|---|---|---|---|---|---|---|---|
| Mgmt. Trainees: | | Mktg. Professionals: | Y | Gen. Writing/Editing: | | Info. Management: | Y | Finance/Accounting: | Y | Engineers, Elec.: | |
| Experienced Mgmt.: | Y | Retail Sales: | | Technical Writing: | | Software Dev.: | | Law: | Y | Engineers, Other: | Y |
| Int'l Business: | Y | Commercial/Industrial: | Y | Graphic Arts/Photog.: | | Hardware Dev.: | | HR/Other: | Y | Health/Lab: | |
| MBA Graduates: | Y | Sales Trainees: | | Music: | | Systems Integration: | | Training: | Y | Scientists/Research: | |
| | | Advertising Pros.: | | Broadcasting: | | Consulting/Other: | | Health Care: | | Petroleum/Chemicals: | Y |
| | | | | Other: | | | | Consulting: | | Math/Other: | |

## TYPES OF BUSINESS:

Oil & Gas Exploration & Production
Oil & Gas Marketing

## BRANDS/DIVISIONS/AFFILIATES:

Forest Oil Western Region
Forest Oil Southern Region
Foest Oil Canada
Forest Oil International
Forest Oil Eastern Region
Houston Exploration Company (The)

## CONTACTS: *Note: Officers with more than one job title may be intentionally listed here more than once.*

H. Craig Clark, CEO
J.C. Ridens, COO/Exec. VP
H. Craig Clark, Pres.
Dave H. Keyte, CFO/Exec. VP
Robert Wofford, VP-Oil & Gas Mktg.
Paul J. Dusha, VP-Human Resources
Rick Hatcher, CTO/VP
Glen J. Mizenko, Sr. VP-Eng.
Cyrus D. Marter, IV, General Counsel/Sec./Sr. VP
Timothy F. Savoy, VP-Oper. Support
Glen J. Mizenko, Sr. VP-Bus. Dev.
Michael Kennedy, VP-Finance/Treas.
David Anderson, Pres., Canadian Forest Oil
Ronald Nutt, VP-Southern Region
Stephen Harpham, Sr. VP-Western Region
Mark E. Bush, VP-Eastern Region
James Lightner, Chmn.
Cecil N. Colwell, Sr. VP-Worldwide Drilling

| | |
|---|---|
| **Phone:** 303-812-1400 | **Fax:** |
| **Toll-Free:** | |
| **Address:** 707 17th St., Ste. 3600, Denver, CO 80202 US | |

## GROWTH PLANS/SPECIAL FEATURES:

Forest Oil Corporation is an oil and gas company engaged in the acquisition, exploration, development and production of oil, natural gas and natural gas liquids. The company is organized into five distinct business segments: Southern, Western, Eastern, Canada and International. About 85% of the company's proved reserves are located in the U.S., 21% are in Canada and approximately 3% are in Italy. Forest Oil's southern segment has production and proved reserves located in eastern and southern Texas, and Louisiana. The western segment oversees the company's operations in western Texas and the Texas Panhandle, New Mexico, North Dakota, western Oklahoma, Colorado, Utah and Wyoming. The eastern unit's operations are located in eastern Texas, Arkansas and Louisiana. The Canada business unit's operations are located mainly in central Alberta. The international segment is primarily located in South Africa and Italy. In June 2007, Forest Oil acquired the Houston Exploration Company for $750 million in cash plus other considerations, obtaining assets in Texas and Colorado that will add about 2 trillion cubic feet of natural gas and equivalent reserves to Forest's total. In August 2007, the firm sold the totality of its assets in Alaska including subsidiary Forest Alaska Operating LLC, to Long Beach based Pacific Energy Resources, Ltd. for a closing price of approximately $485.4 million in cash and other considerations. In October 2007, the company obtained positive results in a test well in Monte Pallano area of central Italy. Forest holds a 90% working interest in approximately 8,000 net acres in the Monte Pallano Area. In May 2008, the company acquired properties located in its Ark-La-Tex core areas for $285 million. In September 2008, Forest Oil completed the acquisition of producing assets in its Greater Buffalo Wallow and East Texas/North Louisiana core areas.

## FINANCIALS: **Sales and profits are in thousands of dollars—add 000 to get the full amount. 2008 Note: Financial information for 2008 was not available for all companies at press time.**

| | | |
|---|---|---|
| 2008 Sales: $ | 2008 Profits: $ | **U.S. Stock Ticker: FST** |
| 2007 Sales: $1,083,892 | 2007 Profits: $169,306 | **Int'l Ticker:** Int'l Exchange: |
| 2006 Sales: $819,992 | 2006 Profits: $168,502 | Employees: 728 |
| 2005 Sales: $1,072,045 | 2005 Profits: $151,568 | Fiscal Year Ends: 12/31 |
| 2004 Sales: $912,898 | 2004 Profits: $122,551 | Parent Company: |

## SALARIES/BENEFITS:

| | | | | |
|---|---|---|---|---|
| Pension Plan: | ESOP Stock Plan: | Profit Sharing: | Top Exec. Salary: $563,750 | Bonus: $300,000 |
| Savings Plan: | Stock Purch. Plan: | | Second Exec. Salary: $393,750 | Bonus: $300,000 |

## OTHER THOUGHTS:

**Apparent Women Officers or Directors:**
**Hot Spot for Advancement for Women/Minorities:**

## LOCATIONS: ("Y" = Yes)

| West: | Southwest: | Midwest: | Southeast: | Northeast: | International: |
|---|---|---|---|---|---|
| Y | Y | | Y | | Y |

# FORRESTER RESEARCH INC

www.forrester.com

**Industry Group Code:** 541512A **Ranks within this company's industry group:** Sales: 1 Profits: 1

| Management: | | Sales/Marketing: | | Liberal Arts: | | Information Systems: | | Professionals: | | Technical/Scientific: | |
|---|---|---|---|---|---|---|---|---|---|---|---|
| Mgmt. Trainees: | | Mktg. Professionals: | Y | Gen. Writing/Editing: | Y | Info. Management: | Y | Finance/Accounting: | Y | Engineers, Elec.: | |
| Experienced Mgmt.: | Y | Retail Sales: | | Technical Writing: | Y | Software Dev.: | Y | Law: | Y | Engineers, Other: | |
| Int'l Business: | Y | Commercial/Industrial: | | Graphic Arts/Photog.: | | Hardware Dev.: | | HR/Other: | Y | Health/Lab: | |
| MBA Graduates: | Y | Sales Trainees: | | Music: | | Systems Integration: | | Training: | Y | Scientists/Research: | |
| | | Advertising Pros.: | | Broadcasting: | | Consulting/Other: | Y | Health Care: | Y | Petroleum/Chemicals: | |
| | | | | Other: | Y | | | Consulting: | Y | Math/Other: | |

## TYPES OF BUSINESS:

Market Research
Consulting & Advisory
Workshops & Events

## BRANDS/DIVISIONS/AFFILIATES:

RoleView
Forrester Wave (The)
Consumer Technographics Data & Services
Business Data & Services
Forrester Leadership Boards
Giga Information Group Inc
JupiterResearch LLC

## CONTACTS: *Note: Officers with more than one job title may be intentionally listed here more than once.*

George F. Colony, CEO
Charles Rutstein, COO
Michael A. Doyle, CFO
Dwight Griesman, Chief Mktg. Officer
Elizabeth Lemons, Chief People Officer
George M. Orlov, CIO
George M. Orlov, CTO
Gail S. Mann, Chief Legal Officer/Sec.
Brian E. Kardon, Chief Strategy Officer
Julie Meringer, Managing Dir.-IT Client Group
Mark R. Nemec, Managing Dir.-Tech. Industry Client Group
Dennis van Lingen, Managing Dir.-Mktg. & Strategy Client Group
George F. Colony, Chmn.
Dennis van Lingen, Chief EMEA Officer

**Phone:** 617-613-6000 **Fax:** 617-613-5200
**Toll-Free:** 866-367-7378
**Address:** 400 Technology Sq., Cambridge, MA 02139 US

## GROWTH PLANS/SPECIAL FEATURES:

Forrester Research, Inc., an Internet research firm, specializes in the analysis of technology change and its impact on business, consumers and society. The firm offers products and services in four major areas: Research, Data, Consulting and Community. The firm's Research product, renamed RoleView in 2007, consists of a library of cross-linked documents that interconnects its reports, data, product rankings, best practices, evaluation tools and research archives. RoleView access is provided through web sites that allow clients to access research and tools relevant to their professional roles. Data products and services focus on consumers' and business users' attitudes about and behavior toward technology, including ownership, future purchases, and adoption trends. These products incorporate extensive survey research designed and analyzed by the firm's staff. Consulting services leverage RoleView to deliver customized research to assist clients in executing technology and business strategy, assessing viable initiatives for competitive technology gains, and making large technology investments. Specifically, the firm assists its clients with effective use of technology, innovation and organizational design; supply and demand networks; and IT sourcing. Finally, Community offerings are designed to foster effective connections between peers in the same or similar roles, analysts, and the relevant research. Finally, Community products include Forrester Leadership Boards, participation in workshops, and attendance at Forrester events. Leadership Board members receive access to analyst teams, membership-directed research, industry-specific benchmark data and networking through event meetings and group audio-conferences. Subsidiary Giga Information Group, Inc. provides technology research, advice and personalized consulting services. In July 2008, the firm acquired JupiterResearch, LLC.

Employees of the firm are offered medical, dental and vision insurance; employee assistance programs; flexible spending accounts; a 401(k) plan; performance bonuses; stock purchase plan; discount entertainment vouchers; travel assistance; nursing/lactation care center; backup childcare; and onsite massages, gym and piano lesions.

## FINANCIALS: **Sales and profits are in thousands of dollars—add 000 to get the full amount. 2008 Note: Financial information for 2008 was not available for all companies at press time.**

| | | |
|---|---|---|
| 2008 Sales: $240,875 | 2008 Profits: $29,215 | **U.S. Stock Ticker: FORR** |
| 2007 Sales: $212,056 | 2007 Profits: $18,943 | **Int'l Ticker:** Int'l Exchange: |
| 2006 Sales: $181,473 | 2006 Profits: $16,171 | Employees: 903 |
| 2005 Sales: $151,398 | 2005 Profits: $11,348 | Fiscal Year Ends: 12/31 |
| 2004 Sales: $138,500 | 2004 Profits: $4,100 | Parent Company: |

## SALARIES/BENEFITS:

| | | | | |
|---|---|---|---|---|
| Pension Plan: | ESOP Stock Plan: | Profit Sharing: | Top Exec. Salary: $300,000 | Bonus: $116,250 |
| Savings Plan: Y | Stock Purch. Plan: | | Second Exec. Salary: $275,000 | Bonus: $97,750 |

## OTHER THOUGHTS:

**Apparent Women Officers or Directors**: 3
**Hot Spot for Advancement for Women/Minorities**: Y

## LOCATIONS: ("Y" = Yes)

| West: | Southwest: | Midwest: | Southeast: | Northeast: | International: |
|---|---|---|---|---|---|
| Y | | | | Y | Y |

Note: Financial information, benefits and other data can change quickly and may vary from those stated here.

# FRESH BRANDS INC

**www.fresh-brands.com**

**Industry Group Code:** 445110 **Ranks within this company's industry group:** Sales: 4 Profits:

| **Management:** | | **Sales/Marketing:** | | **Liberal Arts:** | | **Information Systems:** | | **Professionals:** | | **Technical/Scientific:** | |
|---|---|---|---|---|---|---|---|---|---|---|---|
| Mgmt. Trainees: | Y | Mktg. Professionals: | Y | Gen. Writing/Editing: | | Info. Management: | Y | Finance/Accounting: | Y | Engineers, Elec.: | |
| Experienced Mgmt.: | Y | Retail Sales: | Y | Technical Writing: | | Software Dev.: | | Law: | Y | Engineers, Other: | |
| Int'l Business: | | Commercial/Industrial: | | Graphic Arts/Photog.: | Y | Hardware Dev.: | | HR/Other: | Y | Health/Lab: | |
| MBA Graduates: | Y | Sales Trainees: | Y | Music: | | Systems Integration: | | Training: | Y | Scientists/Research: | |
| | | Advertising Pros.: | Y | Broadcasting: | | Consulting/Other: | | Health Care: | | Petroleum/Chemicals: | |
| | | | | Other: | | | | Consulting: | | Math/Other: | |

## TYPES OF BUSINESS:

Grocery Stores
Food Wholesaler

## BRANDS/DIVISIONS/AFFILIATES:

Dick's Supermarkets
Piggly Wiggly Supermarkets
Topco
Springtime
Piggly Wiggly Preferred Club Card
Dick's Savings Club Card
Piggly Wiggly E-Savings

## CONTACTS: *Note: Officers with more than one job title may be intentionally listed here more than once.*

John H. Dahly, CFO/Sr. VP
John H. Dahly, Corp. Sec.
John H. Dahly, Treas.
Walter G. Winding, III, Chmn.

| **Phone:** 920-457-4433 | **Fax:** 920-457-6295 |
|---|---|
| **Toll-Free:** | |
| **Address:** 2215 Union Ave., Sheboygan, WI 53081 US | |

## GROWTH PLANS/SPECIAL FEATURES:

Fresh Brands, Inc. is a wholesale distributor and retailer of groceries and other foods. The company also owns the Piggly Wiggly supermarket chain where it operates about 25 supermarkets and franchises approximately 70 stores. Fresh Brands was acquired by Certifresh Holdings, which is owned by Certified Grocers Midwest, Inc. The company converted all its supermarkets previously run under the name Dick's to the Piggly Wiggly name. The firm's supermarkets, primarily located in small and suburban communities in Wisconsin and Illinois, offer various products including groceries, frozen foods, prepared foods, fresh produce, meat, poultry, eggs and dairy products, as well as non-food items such as health and beauty aids, housewares, magazines and periodicals, video cassette rentals, flowers and plants, greeting cards, general merchandise and promotional programs traditionally found only in large metropolitan markets. Select stores also offer wine and liquor, lottery tickets, photo processing services, in-house banking and event and concert tickets. The company's private-label products include Topco fresh meats and Springtime soft drinks, fruit drinks and bottled water. The firm's coordinated merchandising and advertising efforts include weekly newspaper ad inserts, billboards, television and radio spots and sponsorship of entertainment and charitable events. Its Piggly Wiggly Preferred Club Card is designed to reward current customers and attract new customers by offering discounts on weekly and monthly store specials. The card also doubles as a check-cashing and video rental identification card. Fresh Brands has also partnered with ValuPage to launch Piggly Wiggly E-Savings, an online grocery savings program for Preferred Club Card holders

## FINANCIALS: **Sales and profits are in thousands of dollars—add 000 to get the full amount. 2008 Note: Financial information for 2008 was not available for all companies at press time.**

| | | |
|---|---|---|
| 2008 Sales: $ | 2008 Profits: $ | **U.S. Stock Ticker: Subsidiary** |
| 2007 Sales: $260,100 | 2007 Profits: $ | **Int'l Ticker:** Int'l Exchange: |
| 2006 Sales: $ | 2006 Profits: $ | Employees: 2,400 |
| 2005 Sales: $ | 2005 Profits: $ | Fiscal Year Ends: 12/31 |
| 2004 Sales: $673,100 | 2004 Profits: $-3,000 | Parent Company: CERTIFRESH HOLDINGS |

## SALARIES/BENEFITS:

| | | | | |
|---|---|---|---|---|
| Pension Plan: | ESOP Stock Plan: | Profit Sharing: | Top Exec. Salary: $329,327 | Bonus: $39,250 |
| Savings Plan: Y | Stock Purch. Plan: Y | | Second Exec. Salary: $224,231 | Bonus: $ |

## OTHER THOUGHTS:

**Apparent Women Officers or Directors**:
**Hot Spot for Advancement for Women/Minorities**:

## LOCATIONS: ("Y" = Yes)

| West: | Southwest: | Midwest: | Southeast: | Northeast: | International: |
|---|---|---|---|---|---|
| | | Y | | | |

# FRESHDIRECT LLC

www.freshdirect.com

**Industry Group Code:** 445110E **Ranks within this company's industry group:** Sales: 1 Profits:

| Management: | | Sales/Marketing: | | Liberal Arts: | | Information Systems: | | Professionals: | | Technical/Scientific: | |
|---|---|---|---|---|---|---|---|---|---|---|---|
| Mgmt. Trainees: | Y | Mktg. Professionals: | Y | Gen. Writing/Editing: | Y | Info. Management: | Y | Finance/Accounting: | Y | Engineers, Elec.: | |
| Experienced Mgmt.: | Y | Retail Sales: | Y | Technical Writing: | | Software Dev.: | Y | Law: | Y | Engineers, Other: | |
| Int'l Business: | | Commercial/Industrial: | | Graphic Arts/Photog.: | Y | Hardware Dev.: | | HR/Other: | Y | Health/Lab: | |
| MBA Graduates: | Y | Sales Trainees: | Y | Music: | | Systems Integration: | Y | Training: | Y | Scientists/Research: | |
| | | Advertising Pros.: | Y | Broadcasting: | | Consulting/Other: | | Health Care: | | Petroleum/Chemicals: | |
| | | | | Other: | | | | Consulting: | | Math/Other: | |

## TYPES OF BUSINESS:

Online Grocery Sales
Home Grocery Delivery
Catering

## BRANDS/DIVISIONS/AFFILIATES:

## CONTACTS:

*Note: Officers with more than one job title may be intentionally listed here more than once.*

Richard S. Braddock, CEO
Jason Ackerman, CFO/Vice Chmn.
Steve Druckman, Chief Mktg. Officer
Richard S. Braddock, Chmn.

| **Phone:** 718-928-1000 | **Fax:** 718-433-0648 |
|---|---|
| **Toll-Free:** | |
| **Address:** 23-30 Borden Ave., Long Island, NY 11101 US | |

## GROWTH PLANS/SPECIAL FEATURES:

FreshDirect, LLC is an online retail grocery business serving approximately 250,000 customers in New York City and the surrounding areas. It offers more than 3,000 fresh food and grocery items, including fruits and vegetables, meat, seafood, deli items, cheese, dairy, coffee, tea, bakery goods, pasta and frozen food, as well as kosher and organic produce, health and beauty items and wine. It also provides catering services and a full line of ready-to-heat meals prepared by its on-staff chef. FreshDirect owns and operates a 300,000-square-foot, state-of-the-art processing facility, which enables the company to process and ship fresh meats, produce and dairy products quickly and efficiently. FreshDirect is also able to offer lower prices, on average 25% lower than traditional retail grocers, due to the lack of intermediary distribution channels. Orders are placed via telephone or Internet and arrive at the home or office within a specified two-hour period. Orders may be placed up to seven days in advance and if placed before 11 p.m. on weekdays and before 7 p.m. on the weekends will be delivered the next day. Deliveries are made from 2-11:30 p.m. Monday through Thursday; from 2-10 p.m. on Friday; and from 7:30 a.m. to 7 p.m. on Saturday and Sunday. Minimum order amounts are $30, and each order is charged a $5.49-$6.79 delivery fee depending on location. Customers can also pick up their orders at the facility.

## FINANCIALS:

**Sales and profits are in thousands of dollars—add 000 to get the full amount. 2008 Note: Financial information for 2008 was not available for all companies at press time.**

| | | |
|---|---|---|
| 2008 Sales: $ | 2008 Profits: $ | **U.S. Stock Ticker: Private** |
| 2007 Sales: $200,000 | 2007 Profits: $ | **Int'l Ticker:** Int'l Exchange: |
| 2006 Sales: $175,000 | 2006 Profits: $ | Employees: 1,800 |
| 2005 Sales: $150,000 | 2005 Profits: $ | Fiscal Year Ends: 9/30 |
| 2004 Sales: $100,000 | 2004 Profits: $ | Parent Company: |

## SALARIES/BENEFITS:

| | | | | |
|---|---|---|---|---|
| Pension Plan: | ESOP Stock Plan: | Profit Sharing: | Top Exec. Salary: $ | Bonus: $ |
| Savings Plan: | Stock Purch. Plan: | | Second Exec. Salary: $ | Bonus: $ |

## OTHER THOUGHTS:

**Apparent Women Officers or Directors:**
**Hot Spot for Advancement for Women/Minorities:**

## LOCATIONS: ("Y" = Yes)

| West: | Southwest: | Midwest: | Southeast: | Northeast: | International: |
|---|---|---|---|---|---|
| | | | | Y | |

# FRONTIER OIL CORPORATION

www.frontieroil.com

**Industry Group Code:** 324110 **Ranks within this company's industry group:** Sales: 1 Profits: 1

| **Management:** | | **Sales/Marketing:** | | **Liberal Arts:** | | **Information Systems:** | | **Professionals:** | | **Technical/Scientific:** | |
|---|---|---|---|---|---|---|---|---|---|---|---|
| Mgmt. Trainees: | | Mktg. Professionals: | Y | Gen. Writing/Editing: | | Info. Management: | Y | Finance/Accounting: | Y | Engineers, Elec.: | Y |
| Experienced Mgmt.: | Y | Retail Sales: | | Technical Writing: | | Software Dev.: | | Law: | Y | Engineers, Other: | Y |
| Int'l Business: | | Commercial/Industrial: | Y | Graphic Arts/Photog.: | | Hardware Dev.: | | HR/Other: | Y | Health/Lab: | |
| MBA Graduates: | Y | Sales Trainees: | | Music: | | Systems Integration: | | Training: | Y | Scientists/Research: | |
| | | Advertising Pros.: | | Broadcasting: | | Consulting/Other: | | Health Care: | | Petroleum/Chemicals: | Y |
| | | | | Other: | | | | Consulting: | | Math/Other: | |

## TYPES OF BUSINESS:

Petroleum Refining

## BRANDS/DIVISIONS/AFFILIATES:

Frontier Oil and Refining Company
Shell Oil Products US
Equiva Trading Company
Shell Oil Co
Ethanol Management Company
CB&I

## CONTACTS:

*Note: Officers with more than one job title may be intentionally listed here more than once.*

James R. Gibbs, CEO
James R. Gibbs, Pres.
Michael C. Jennings, CFO/Exec. VP
Paul Eisman, Exec. VP-Mktg. Oper.
J. Currie Bechtol, General Counsel/VP
Paul Eisman, Exec. VP-Refining Oper.
Gerald B. Faudel, VP-Corp. Rel.
Doug Aron, VP-Corp. Finance
Jon D. Galvin, VP
Nancy J. Zupan, VP/Controller
Leo J. Hoonakker, VP/Treas.
James R. Gibbs, Chmn.

**Phone:** 713-688-9600 **Fax:** 713-688-0616
**Toll-Free:**
**Address:** 10000 Memorial Dr., Ste. 600, Houston, TX 77024-3411 US

## GROWTH PLANS/SPECIAL FEATURES:

Frontier Oil Corporation is an independent oil refining and marketing company with refineries located in Wyoming and Kansas and a total crude oil processing capacity of approximately 162,000 barrels per day. The firm's complex refineries can process heavier, less expensive types of crude oil while producing a high percentage of gasoline, diesel fuel and other high-margin refined products. The company's Cheyenne, Wyoming refinery has a permitted crude processing capacity of 52,000 barrels per day. The firm markets its refined products primarily in the eastern slope of the Rocky Mountain region, which encompasses eastern Colorado (including the Denver metropolitan area), eastern Wyoming and western Nebraska. The Cheyenne refinery has a coking unit that allows it to process heavy crude oil for use as a feedstock, which is less expensive. In 2007, heavy crude oil constituted approximately 72% of the Cheyenne Refinery's total crude oil charge. The Cheyenne Refinery's 2007 product yield included gasoline (42%), diesel fuel (30%) and asphalt and other refined petroleum products (28%). Frontier Oil's El Dorado refinery, Shell Oil Products US, is one of the largest refineries in the Rocky Mountain region, with a permitted crude processing capacity of 110,000 barrels per day. The El Dorado refinery's product mix includes gasoline, diesel and jet fuel, chemicals and other refined petroleum products. The refinery's products are primarily shipped via pipeline to terminals for distribution by truck or rail. In 2007, the El Dorado Refinery's product yield included gasoline (50%), diesel and jet fuel (36%) and chemicals and other refined petroleum products (14%). Other company assets include Ethanol Management Company (EMC), which was acquired in February 2007 for approximately $3.1 million.

## FINANCIALS:

**Sales and profits are in thousands of dollars—add 000 to get the full amount. 2008 Note: Financial information for 2008 was not available for all companies at press time.**

2008 Sales: $
2007 Sales: $5,188,740
2006 Sales: $4,795,953
2005 Sales: $4,001,162
2004 Sales: $2,861,716

2008 Profits: $
2007 Profits: $499,125
2006 Profits: $379,277
2005 Profits: $272,532
2004 Profits: $69,764

**U.S. Stock Ticker: FTO**
**Int'l Ticker:** Int'l Exchange:
Employees: 800
Fiscal Year Ends: 12/31
Parent Company:

## SALARIES/BENEFITS:

Pension Plan: ESOP Stock Plan: Profit Sharing: Top Exec. Salary: $885,000 Bonus: $
Savings Plan: Stock Purch. Plan: Second Exec. Salary: $430,000 Bonus: $421,400

## OTHER THOUGHTS:

**Apparent Women Officers or Directors**: 1
**Hot Spot for Advancement for Women/Minorities**:

## LOCATIONS: ("Y" = Yes)

| West: | Southwest: | Midwest: | Southeast: | Northeast: | International: |
|---|---|---|---|---|---|
| Y | Y | Y | | | |

# FUEL TECH INC

www.fuel-tech.com

**Industry Group Code:** 541710 **Ranks within this company's industry group:** Sales: 3 Profits: 3

| Management: | | Sales/Marketing: | | Liberal Arts: | | Information Systems: | | Professionals: | | Technical/Scientific: | |
|---|---|---|---|---|---|---|---|---|---|---|---|
| Mgmt. Trainees: | | Mktg. Professionals: | Y | Gen. Writing/Editing: | | Info. Management: | Y | Finance/Accounting: | Y | Engineers, Elec.: | |
| Experienced Mgmt.: | Y | Retail Sales: | | Technical Writing: | Y | Software Dev.: | Y | Law: | Y | Engineers, Other: | |
| Int'l Business: | Y | Commercial/Industrial: | | Graphic Arts/Photog.: | | Hardware Dev.: | | HR/Other: | Y | Health/Lab: | |
| MBA Graduates: | Y | Sales Trainees: | | Music: | | Systems Integration: | | Training: | Y | Scientists/Research: | |
| | | Advertising Pros.: | | Broadcasting: | | Consulting/Other: | | Health Care: | | Petroleum/Chemicals: | |
| | | | | Other: | | | | Consulting: | | Math/Other: | |

## TYPES OF BUSINESS:

Nitrogen Oxide Reduction Technology
Combustion Unit Efficiency Technology
Air Pollution Reduction Technology
Boiler Optimization Technology
Efficiency Improvement Technology

## BRANDS/DIVISIONS/AFFILIATES:

FUEL CHEM
NOxOUT
NOxOUT ULTRA
NOxOUT-SCR
TIFI Targeted In-Furnace Injection
Beijing Fuel Tech Environmental Technologies Co.
Tackticks, LLC
FlowTack, LLC

## CONTACTS: *Note: Officers with more than one job title may be intentionally listed here more than once.*

John F. Norris, Jr., CEO
John F. Norris, Jr., Pres.
John P. Graham, CFO/Treas./Sr. VP
Stephen P. Brady, Sr. VP-Sales & Mktg.
William H. Sun, VP-Air Pollution Tech.
Charles W. Grinnell, General Counsel/Corp. Sec./VP
Kevin R. Dougherty, VP-Bus. Dev. & Mktg.
Tracy H. Krumme, VP-Corp. Comm.
Tracy H. Krumme, VP-Investor Rel.
Ellen T. Albrecht, Controller/VP
Vincent M. Albanese, Sr. VP-Regulatory Affairs
M. Linda Lin, VP-China & Pacific Rim
Timothy J. Eibes, VP-Project Execution
Christopher R. Smyrniotis, VP-Fuel Chem Tech.
Ralph E. Bailey, Exec. Chmn.
Michael P. Maley, Sr. VP-Int'l Bus. Dev. & Project Execution

| | |
|---|---|
| **Phone:** 630-845-4500 | **Fax:** 630-845-4501 |
| **Toll-Free:** 800-666-9688 | |
| **Address:** 512 Kingsland Dr., Batavia, IL 60510-2299 US | |

## GROWTH PLANS/SPECIAL FEATURES:

Fuel Tech, Inc. is a fully integrated company that uses a suite of technologies to provide boiler optimization, efficiency improvement and air pollution reduction and control solutions to utility and industrial customers worldwide. Fuel Tech's special focus is the worldwide marketing of its nitrogen oxide (NOx) reduction and FUEL CHEM processes. NOx reduction technology, which includes the NOxOUT, NOxOUT ULTRA and NOxOUT-SCR processes, can reduce NOx emissions from 30%-85% in flue gas from boilers, incinerators, furnaces and other stationary combustion sources. The NOx reduction business is primarily driven by the U.S. air pollution control market, and thus depends on air pollution regulations and regulation enforcement. Outside the U.S., Fuel Tech sells NOx control systems in Europe, where the E.U. Directives require that certain waste incinerators and cement plants be in compliance with specified NOx reduction targets by 2008, while certain power plants must be in compliance by 2010. Fuel Tech is also seeking to expand its NOx control operations in China, where it recently formed Beijing Fuel Tech Environmental Technologies Co., Ltd. FUEL CHEM improves the efficiency, reliability and environmental status of plants in the electric utility, pulp and paper, industrial and waste-to-energy markets. It controls slagging, fouling, corrosion, loss on ignition, opacity and acid plume; and controls sulfur trioxide, ammonium bisulfate, particulate matter, carbon dioxide and NOx formation by adding chemicals into the fuel or via TIFI Targeted In-Furnace Injection programs. FUEL CHEM programs currently operate in over 90 combustion units, treating various solid and liquid fuels, including coal, heavy oil, biomass and municipal waste. In October 2008, Fuel Tech acquired Tackticks, LLC and its 75%-owned subsidiary FlowTack, LLC for $4 million; Tackticks focuses on catalytic-based NOx reduction systems, while FlowTack offers fluid modeling services for power plants.

Employees of the firm receive medical, dental, life, personal accident and AD&D insurance.

## FINANCIALS: **Sales and profits are in thousands of dollars—add 000 to get the full amount. 2008 Note: Financial information for 2008 was not available for all companies at press time.**

| | | |
|---|---|---|
| 2008 Sales: $ | 2008 Profits: $ | **U.S. Stock Ticker: FTEK** |
| 2007 Sales: $80,297 | 2007 Profits: $7,243 | **Int'l Ticker:** Int'l Exchange: |
| 2006 Sales: $75,115 | 2006 Profits: $6,826 | Employees: 178 |
| 2005 Sales: $52,928 | 2005 Profits: $7,588 | Fiscal Year Ends: 12/31 |
| 2004 Sales: $30,832 | 2004 Profits: $1,572 | Parent Company: |

## SALARIES/BENEFITS:

| | | | | |
|---|---|---|---|---|
| Pension Plan: | ESOP Stock Plan: | Profit Sharing: Y | Top Exec. Salary: $406,250 | Bonus: $88,504 |
| Savings Plan: Y | Stock Purch. Plan: | | Second Exec. Salary: $256,250 | Bonus: $35,445 |

## OTHER THOUGHTS:

**Apparent Women Officers or Directors**: 3
**Hot Spot for Advancement for Women/Minorities**: Y

## LOCATIONS: ("Y" = Yes)

| West: | Southwest: | Midwest: | Southeast: | Northeast: | International: |
|---|---|---|---|---|---|
| | | Y | | Y | Y |

# FUELCELL ENERGY INC

www.fuelcellenergy.com

**Industry Group Code:** 333298 **Ranks within this company's industry group:** Sales: 2 Profits: 4

| Management: | | Sales/Marketing: | | Liberal Arts: | | Information Systems: | | Professionals: | | Technical/Scientific: | |
|---|---|---|---|---|---|---|---|---|---|---|---|
| Mgmt. Trainees: | | Mktg. Professionals: | Y | Gen. Writing/Editing: | | Info. Management: | Y | Finance/Accounting: | Y | Engineers, Elec.: | Y |
| Experienced Mgmt.: | Y | Retail Sales: | | Technical Writing: | Y | Software Dev.: | Y | Law: | Y | Engineers, Other: | Y |
| Int'l Business: | Y | Commercial/Industrial: | Y | Graphic Arts/Photog.: | | Hardware Dev.: | Y | HR/Other: | Y | Health/Lab: | |
| MBA Graduates: | Y | Sales Trainees: | Y | Music: | | Systems Integration: | | Training: | Y | Scientists/Research: | Y |
| | | Advertising Pros.: | | Broadcasting: | | Consulting/Other: | | Health Care: | | Petroleum/Chemicals: | |
| | | | | Other: | | | | Consulting: | | Math/Other: | Y |

## TYPES OF BUSINESS:

Fuel Cell Technology

## BRANDS/DIVISIONS/AFFILIATES:

Direct FuelCell
DFC300
DFC1500
DFC3000
DFC-ERG

## CONTACTS: *Note: Officers with more than one job title may be intentionally listed here more than once.*

R. Daniel Brdar, CEO
R. Daniel Brdar, Pres.
Joseph G. Mahler, CFO
Bruce A. Ludemann, Sr. VP-Mktg. & Sales
Christopher R. Bentley, Exec. VP-Gov't R&D Oper.
Christopher R. Bentley, Exec. VP-Strategic Mfg. Dev.
Joseph G. Mahler, Sec.
Joseph G. Mahler, Sr. VP-Corp. Strategy
Joseph G. Mahler, Treas.
R. Daniel Brdar, Chmn.

| **Phone:** 203-825-6000 | **Fax:** 203-825-6100 |
|---|---|
| **Toll-Free:** | |
| **Address:** 3 Great Pasture Rd., Danbury, CT 06813 US | |

## GROWTH PLANS/SPECIAL FEATURES:

FuelCell Energy, Inc. develops and manufactures fuel cell power plants for ultra-clean, efficient and reliable electric power generation. To date, its products have generated over 200 million kWh of electricity and are operating at over 40 locations around the world. The firm has developed a proprietary patented carbonate fuel cell utilized for stationary power generation. Its patented fuel cell technology is known as the Direct FuelCell (DFC), because it introduces hydrocarbon fuel, such as pipeline natural gas or biogas from breweries, directly into the fuel cell without requiring external reforming for producing hydrogen. This one-step operation results in a more efficient, simpler and more cost-effective energy conversion system than other fuel cells which utilize complex external reforming equipment to convert fuel to hydrogen. It designs its products to meet the power requirements of a wide range of customers, including utilities, wastewater treatment plants, industrial facilities, hospitals, data centers, shopping centers and universities. The firm has three core power plants, the DFC300, DFC1500 and DFC3000, rated at 300 kilowatts (kW), 1.2 megawatts (MW) and 2.4 MW respectively, designed for applications up to 50 MW. Its latest product is the 2.2 MW DFC-ERG (Energy Recovery Generation) plant, which utilizes energy normally lost at pressure transformers in major natural gas lines to generate electricity. Significant funding for the organization comes from the U.S. Department of Energy, the Department of Defense and the Environmental Protection Agency, as well as other outside sources. In January 2008, FuelCell received approval from the Connecticut Department of Utility Control for 16.2 MW of projects and incorporates six of the firms DFC3000 fuel cells.

## FINANCIALS: **Sales and profits are in thousands of dollars—add 000 to get the full amount. 2008 Note: Financial information for 2008 was not available for all companies at press time.**

| | | |
|---|---|---|
| 2008 Sales: $100,735 | 2008 Profits: $-93,357 | **U.S. Stock Ticker: FCEL** |
| 2007 Sales: $48,234 | 2007 Profits: $-68,674 | **Int'l Ticker:** Int'l Exchange: |
| 2006 Sales: $33,288 | 2006 Profits: $-76,105 | Employees: 443 |
| 2005 Sales: $30,370 | 2005 Profits: $-68,186 | Fiscal Year Ends: 10/31 |
| 2004 Sales: $31,386 | 2004 Profits: $-86,443 | Parent Company: |

## SALARIES/BENEFITS:

| | | | | |
|---|---|---|---|---|
| Pension Plan: Y | ESOP Stock Plan: | Profit Sharing: | Top Exec. Salary: $364,130 | Bonus: $87,500 |
| Savings Plan: Y | Stock Purch. Plan: | | Second Exec. Salary: $263,240 | Bonus: $38,250 |

## OTHER THOUGHTS:

**Apparent Women Officers or Directors:**
**Hot Spot for Advancement for Women/Minorities:**

## LOCATIONS: ("Y" = Yes)

| West: | Southwest: | Midwest: | Southeast: | Northeast: | International: |
|---|---|---|---|---|---|
| | | | | Y | Y |

# FUNDTECH LTD

www.fundtech.com

**Industry Group Code:** 511201 **Ranks within this company's industry group:** Sales: 7 Profits: 4

| Management: | | Sales/Marketing: | | Liberal Arts: | | Information Systems: | | Professionals: | | Technical/Scientific: | |
|---|---|---|---|---|---|---|---|---|---|---|---|
| Mgmt. Trainees: | | Mktg. Professionals: | Y | Gen. Writing/Editing: | | Info. Management: | Y | Finance/Accounting: | Y | Engineers, Elec.: | Y |
| Experienced Mgmt.: | Y | Retail Sales: | | Technical Writing: | Y | Software Dev.: | Y | Law: | Y | Engineers, Other: | |
| Int'l Business: | Y | Commercial/Industrial: | Y | Graphic Arts/Photog.: | | Hardware Dev.: | | HR/Other: | Y | Health/Lab: | |
| MBA Graduates: | Y | Sales Trainees: | Y | Music: | | Systems Integration: | | Training: | Y | Scientists/Research: | |
| | | Advertising Pros.: | | Broadcasting: | | Consulting/Other: | | Health Care: | | Petroleum/Chemicals: | |
| | | | | Other: | | | | Consulting: | | Math/Other: | |

## TYPES OF BUSINESS:

Software-Financial Services
Cash & Treasury Management Software
Internet Software

## BRANDS/DIVISIONS/AFFILIATES:

ACCESS Banking
PAYplus
CASHplus
Radius Partners
TRADEplus
Prang GmbH
Accountis Ltd.
Synergy Financial Systems Ltd.

## CONTACTS: *Note: Officers with more than one job title may be intentionally listed here more than once.*

Reuven Ben Menachem, CEO
Michael Sgroe, COO
Michael Sgroe, Pres.
Yoram Bibring, CFO
Brian Jou, Exec. VP-Global Prod. Mgmt.
Joseph P. Mazzetti, Exec. VP-Corp. Dev.
Margie Petrasek, Investor Rel.
Moti Porath, Exec. VP-Bus. Dev.
Leslie Bertha, Exec. VP-Fundtech North America
Gideon Argov, Chmn.
Gil Gadot, Managing Dir.-APAC

| | |
|---|---|
| **Phone:** 201-946-1100 | **Fax:** 201-946-1313 |
| **Toll-Free:** | |
| **Address:** 30 Montgomery Street, Ste. 501, Jersey City, NJ 07302 US | |

## GROWTH PLANS/SPECIAL FEATURES:

Fundtech, Ltd., with over $128 billion in assets, provides e-commerce and e-banking software solutions enabling businesses to electronically manage cash, process payments and transfer funds. The firm offers products in five major categories: cash management, payment processing, foreign exchange settlements, financial messaging and, most recently, securities post-trade settlement. The company's client/server and Internet software products automate the process of transferring funds among corporations, banks and clearance systems, enabling businesses to manage their global cash positions efficiently in real-time. Fundtech offers services for implementing new products and technologies, maintaining systems and planning for disaster recovery. The firm is one of the largest providers of services linking banks to networks, such as the U.S. Federal Reserve System, which has approximately 7,500 banks on its FedLine system. On a global basis, Fundtech allows banks to link to the Society for Worldwide Financial Interbank Telecommunications (SWIFT) network, which facilitates cross-border transactions for approximately 7,000 banks in over 200 countries. In addition, the company offers software that link banks to the Continuous Linked Settlement System (CLS), which reduces foreign exchange settlement risk. Fundtech's ACCESS Banking, PAYplus and CASHplus lines of software are used by financial institutions around the globe, including Bank of America, Citibank, Washington Mutual, Deutsche Bank and National Australia Bank. Together with recently acquired Radius Partners, Fundtech developed its newest product, TRADEplus, a software solution aimed at achieving real time Delivery versus Payment in post-trade securities processing. In February 2007, the firm acquired Prang GmbH, a German software payment provider. In February 2008, Fundtech acquired Accountis Ltd., a Welsh supplier of electronic invoice presentment and payment systems; and acquired the Automated Clearing House (ACH) Software product line from TROY Group, Inc. In October 2008, the firm acquired Synergy Financial Systems Ltd., bringing Fundtech's SWIFT client base to over 200 financial institutions.

## FINANCIALS: **Sales and profits are in thousands of dollars—add 000 to get the full amount. 2008 Note: Financial information for 2008 was not available for all companies at press time.**

| | | |
|---|---|---|
| 2008 Sales: $ | 2008 Profits: $ | **U.S. Stock Ticker: FNDT** |
| 2007 Sales: $104,634 | 2007 Profits: $7,107 | **Int'l Ticker:** Int'l Exchange: |
| 2006 Sales: $85,509 | 2006 Profits: $3,751 | Employees: 921 |
| 2005 Sales: $74,500 | 2005 Profits: $4,300 | Fiscal Year Ends: 12/31 |
| 2004 Sales: $58,537 | 2004 Profits: $2,467 | Parent Company: |

## SALARIES/BENEFITS:

| | | | | |
|---|---|---|---|---|
| Pension Plan: | ESOP Stock Plan: | Profit Sharing: | Top Exec. Salary: $ | Bonus: $65,000 |
| Savings Plan: | Stock Purch. Plan: | | Second Exec. Salary: $160,000 | Bonus: $160,000 |

## OTHER THOUGHTS:

**Apparent Women Officers or Directors:** 2
**Hot Spot for Advancement for Women/Minorities:**

## LOCATIONS: ("Y" = Yes)

| West: | Southwest: | Midwest: | Southeast: | Northeast: | International: |
|---|---|---|---|---|---|
| Y | | | Y | Y | Y |

# GALLUP ORGANIZATION (THE)

**www.gallup.com**

**Industry Group Code:** 541613 **Ranks within this company's industry group:** Sales: 1 Profits:

| Management: | | Sales/Marketing: | | Liberal Arts: | | Information Systems: | | Professionals: | | Technical/Scientific: | |
|---|---|---|---|---|---|---|---|---|---|---|---|
| Mgmt. Trainees: | | Mktg. Professionals: | Y | Gen. Writing/Editing: | Y | Info. Management: | Y | Finance/Accounting: | Y | Engineers, Elec.: | |
| Experienced Mgmt.: | Y | Retail Sales: | | Technical Writing: | Y | Software Dev.: | Y | Law: | Y | Engineers, Other: | |
| Int'l Business: | Y | Commercial/Industrial: | | Graphic Arts/Photog.: | | Hardware Dev.: | | HR/Other: | Y | Health/Lab: | |
| MBA Graduates: | Y | Sales Trainees: | | Music: | | Systems Integration: | Y | Training: | Y | Scientists/Research: | |
| | | Advertising Pros.: | | Broadcasting: | | Consulting/Other: | Y | Health Care: | Y | Petroleum/Chemicals: | |
| | | | | Other: | Y | | | Consulting: | | Math/Other: | Y |

## TYPES OF BUSINESS:

Research & Surveys
Management Consulting
Customer Loyalty Surveys
Brand & Advertising Research
Performance Improvement Programs

## BRANDS/DIVISIONS/AFFILIATES:

Gallup Poll (The)
Gallup Path
Gallup Press
Gallup University
Invoke Solutions

## CONTACTS: *Note: Officers with more than one job title may be intentionally listed here more than once.*

James K. Clifton, CEO
Jane E. Miller, COO/Exec. VP
James Clifton, Pres.
James Krieger, CFO
James Krieger, Vice Chmn.
Frank M. Newport, Editor-In-Chief, The Gallup Poll
James K. Clifton, Chmn.

| | |
|---|---|
| **Phone:** 202-715-3030 | **Fax:** 202-715-3045 |
| **Toll-Free:** 877-242-5587 | |
| **Address:** 901 F St. NW, Washington, DC 20004 US | |

## GROWTH PLANS/SPECIAL FEATURES:

The Gallup Organization has been recognized for its Gallup Poll surveys since Dr. George Gallup founded the company in 1935. Since its beginning, the firm has diversified its business operations to include a variety of advisory services. The company offers corporate services such as management consulting; customer loyalty surveys; brand and advertising research; and performance improvement programs. Advising committees harness a variety of research-based measurement tools, development programs and strategic advisory services that help individuals and organizations maximize performance. The model that Gallup employs is known as the Gallup Path, and its step-by-step methodology is designed to leave companies with stock and profit increases. The approach is centered on effective leadership, engaged employees and the capitalization of the strength of all team members. The firm uses its vast research sources concerning human behavior to achieve these ends. The scientists and consultants at Gallup are trained to measure and improve customer and employee engagement, create performance review systems, design performance-based compensation systems and design and implement an organizational performance strategy. Gallup serves companies within industries including automotive, business services, health care, hospitality and retail, as well as education, government and nonprofit organizations. The company's expertise, whether concerning public opinion polling, societal issues, education, management or human talent, is shared with the public through the company's publishing venture, Gallup Press. Gallup University offers specialized business degree programs that center on the company's core strategies.

## FINANCIALS: **Sales and profits are in thousands of dollars—add 000 to get the full amount. 2008 Note: Financial information for 2008 was not available for all companies at press time.**

| | | |
|---|---|---|
| 2008 Sales: $ | 2008 Profits: $ | **U.S. Stock Ticker: Private** |
| 2007 Sales: $250,000 | 2007 Profits: $ | **Int'l Ticker:** Int'l Exchange: |
| 2006 Sales: $240,000 | 2006 Profits: $ | Employees: 2,000 |
| 2005 Sales: $230,000 | 2005 Profits: $ | Fiscal Year Ends: 12/31 |
| 2004 Sales: $200,000 | 2004 Profits: $ | Parent Company: |

## SALARIES/BENEFITS:

| | | | | |
|---|---|---|---|---|
| Pension Plan: | ESOP Stock Plan: | Profit Sharing: | Top Exec. Salary: $ | Bonus: $ |
| Savings Plan: | Stock Purch. Plan: | | Second Exec. Salary: $ | Bonus: $ |

## OTHER THOUGHTS:

**Apparent Women Officers or Directors**:
**Hot Spot for Advancement for Women/Minorities**:

## LOCATIONS: ("Y" = Yes)

| West: | Southwest: | Midwest: | Southeast: | Northeast: | International: |
|---|---|---|---|---|---|
| Y | Y | Y | Y | Y | Y |

# GENENCOR INTERNATIONAL INC

www.genencor.com

**Industry Group Code:** 325414 **Ranks within this company's industry group:** Sales: 3 Profits:

| Management: | | Sales/Marketing: | | Liberal Arts: | | Information Systems: | | Professionals: | | Technical/Scientific: | |
|---|---|---|---|---|---|---|---|---|---|---|---|
| Mgmt. Trainees: | | Mktg. Professionals: | Y | Gen. Writing/Editing: | | Info. Management: | Y | Finance/Accounting: | Y | Engineers, Elec.: | Y |
| Experienced Mgmt.: | Y | Retail Sales: | | Technical Writing: | Y | Software Dev.: | Y | Law: | Y | Engineers, Other: | Y |
| Int'l Business: | Y | Commercial/Industrial: | Y | Graphic Arts/Photog.: | | Hardware Dev.: | | HR/Other: | Y | Health/Lab: | Y |
| MBA Graduates: | Y | Sales Trainees: | Y | Music: | | Systems Integration: | | Training: | Y | Scientists/Research: | Y |
| | | Advertising Pros.: | | Broadcasting: | | Consulting/Other: | | Health Care: | Y | Petroleum/Chemicals: | Y |
| | | | | Other: | | | | Consulting: | Y | Math/Other: | Y |

## TYPES OF BUSINESS:

Biological Manufacturing
Biotech Research & Discovery
Enzyme-Based Products
Protein-Based Products
Bioethanol Technology Research & Development
Enzymes for Ethanol Production

## BRANDS/DIVISIONS/AFFILIATES:

Danisco A/S
Multifect Protex
Accellerase
Optimax
Gensweet
Agtech Products Inc.

## CONTACTS: *Note: Officers with more than one job title may be intentionally listed here more than once.*

Tjerk De Ruiter, CEO
Jim Sjoerdsma, VP-Human Resources
Michael V. Arbige, Exec. VP-R&D
Michael V. Arbige, Exec. VP-Tech.
Soonhee Jang, VP-Intellectual Property/Chief IP Counsel
Philippe Lavielle, Exec. VP-Bus. Dev.
Jennifer Hutchins, Media
Andrew Ashworth, VP-Finance
James Laughton, Exec. VP-Animal Nutrition/Food & Beverage Enzymes
Glenn Nedwin, Exec. VP-Technical Enzymes
Philippe Lavielle, Exec. VP-Bus. Dev., Biomass
Ken Herfert, Sr. VP-Supply

**Phone:** 585-256-5200 **Fax:** 585-256-6952
**Toll-Free:**
**Address:** 200 Meridian Centre Blvd., Rochester, NY 14618-3916 US

## GROWTH PLANS/SPECIAL FEATURES:

Genencor International, Inc., the biotechnology division of Danish firm Danisco A/S, discovers, develops and sells biocatalysts and other biochemicals. It delivers 250 products to customers in 80 countries throughout the world. The firm does so through five R&D centers located in the USA, Denmark, Finland, the Netherlands and China; and 10 manufacturing centers throughout world. Its products serve the following sectors: Agri Processing, Industrial Processing and Consumer Products. Agri Processing products serve customers who process agricultural raw materials, including plant proteins, to produce animal feeds, food, food ingredients and renewable fuels. Specific enzymes include Multifect Protex, used in rice and soybean processing; Accellerase, used to enhance the production of ethanol from biomass; Optimax, which converts starches, such as wheat, into glucose, a non-sweet sugar; and Gensweet, which coverts glucose into fructose, a sweetener. Industrial Processing products mainly include enzymes used in everything from denim finishing in the textiles industry and as processing agents in the wastewater treatment and oil and gas production sectors to medical instrument cleaning and even as decontamination agents in chemical and biological warfare attack situations. Consumer Products applications include enzymes used in fabric and household care products to remove recalcitrant stains more efficiently than soaps and detergents alone; and in personal care items such as contact lens cleaner, whitening toothpaste and diabetic test kits. The firm recently joined forces with BRAIN, a leading metagenomic enzyme and screening technology company, to produce biobased chemicals from renewable feedstock. In 2008, Genencor launched a new biosafety program that focuses on biodefense, bioremediation and prion disinfection in primarily the military, medical and dental sectors. The firm's parent company, Danisco, recently furthered its biotechnology efforts with the acquisition of Agtech Products Inc., a US-based agricultural biotechnology company dedicated to producing microbial-based products for animal nutrition.

## FINANCIALS: Sales and profits are in thousands of dollars—add 000 to get the full amount. 2008 Note: Financial information for 2008 was not available for all companies at press time.

2008 Sales: $
2007 Sales: $90,700
2006 Sales: $
2005 Sales: $
2004 Sales: $410,417

2008 Profits: $
2007 Profits: $
2006 Profits: $
2005 Profits: $
2004 Profits: $26,178

**U.S. Stock Ticker: Subsidiary**
**Int'l Ticker:** Int'l Exchange:
Employees: 1,098
Fiscal Year Ends: 12/31
Parent Company: DANISCO A/S

## SALARIES/BENEFITS:

Pension Plan: ESOP Stock Plan: Profit Sharing: Top Exec. Salary: $540,346 Bonus: $370,900
Savings Plan: Y Stock Purch. Plan: Second Exec. Salary: $337,888 Bonus: $172,800

## OTHER THOUGHTS:

**Apparent Women Officers or Directors:** 2
**Hot Spot for Advancement for Women/Minorities:**

## LOCATIONS: ("Y" = Yes)

| West: | Southwest: | Midwest: | Southeast: | Northeast: | International: |
|---|---|---|---|---|---|
| Y | | Y | | Y | Y |

# GENERAL COMMUNICATION INC (GCI)

www.gci.com

**Industry Group Code:** 513300A **Ranks within this company's industry group:** Sales: 1 Profits: 4

| Management: | | Sales/Marketing: | | Liberal Arts: | | Information Systems: | | Professionals: | | Technical/Scientific: | |
|---|---|---|---|---|---|---|---|---|---|---|---|
| Mgmt. Trainees: | | Mktg. Professionals: | Y | Gen. Writing/Editing: | | Info. Management: | Y | Finance/Accounting: | Y | Engineers, Elec.: | Y |
| Experienced Mgmt.: | Y | Retail Sales: | | Technical Writing: | | Software Dev.: | Y | Law: | Y | Engineers, Other: | Y |
| Int'l Business: | | Commercial/Industrial: | Y | Graphic Arts/Photog.: | | Hardware Dev.: | | HR/Other: | Y | Health/Lab: | |
| MBA Graduates: | Y | Sales Trainees: | Y | Music: | | Systems Integration: | Y | Training: | Y | Scientists/Research: | |
| | | Advertising Pros.: | | Broadcasting: | | Consulting/Other: | | Health Care: | | Petroleum/Chemicals: | |
| | | | | Other: | | | | Consulting: | | Math/Other: | |

## TYPES OF BUSINESS:

Local Telephone Service
Long-Distance Services
Cable Television Services
Wireless Communications Services
Video-on-Demand Services
Network Management
Satellite-Based Services
Internet Services

## BRANDS/DIVISIONS/AFFILIATES:

Alaska DigiTel
SchoolAccess
United Utilities, Inc. (UUI)
Unicom
United Companies, Inc.
Sea Lion Corporation
Togiak Natives Limited
DeltaNet

## CONTACTS: *Note: Officers with more than one job title may be intentionally listed here more than once.*

Ronald A. (Ron) Duncan, CEO
Ronald A. (Ron) Duncan, Pres.
John M. Lowber, CFO/Sr. VP
Gina Borland, VP-Prod. Mgmt., Voice & Messaging
Dana L. Tindall, Sr. VP-Legal, Gov't. & Regulatory Affairs
Richard P. Dowling, Sr. VP-Corp. Dev.
John M. Lowber, Treas./Corp. Sec.
G. Wilson Hughes, Exec. VP/Gen. Mgr.
Richard D. Westlund, Sr. VP/Gen. Mgr.-Network Access Svcs.
William C. (Bill) Behnke, Sr. VP-Strategic Initiatives
Gregory F. Chapados, Sr. VP-Federal Affairs & Bus. Dev.
Stephen M. Brett, Chmn.

**Phone:** 907-868-5600 **Fax:** 907-868-5676
**Toll-Free:** 800-770-7886
**Address:** 2550 Denali St., Ste. 1000, Anchorage, AK 99503-2781 US

## GROWTH PLANS/SPECIAL FEATURES:

General Communication, Inc. (GCI) is a leading diversified communications company in Alaska, providing facilities-based local and long distance voice, cable video, Internet and data communication services under the GCI brand and reselling wireless telephone services under the Alaska DigiTel brand. The company has 100,400 long-distance subscribers, 120,000 local access lines, 143,300 basic cable subscribers, 77,300 wireless lines and 96,500 cable modem subscribers. Through its SchoolAccess program, GCI provides satellite-delivered voice, video and data services to many of Alaska's rural communities, connecting more than 85,000 students from Alaska, Montana, New Mexico and Arizona. SchoolAccess enables students, teachers and administrators to access information, curriculum and distance-learning courses. GCI acquired a majority interest in Alaska DigiTel, LLC, an Alaskan wireless provider, in January 2007 and plans to expand Alaska DigiTel's Code Division Multiple Access (CDMA) network and construct a Global System for Mobile Communications (GSM) network by the end of 2010. The firm also agreed to acquire the remaining minority interest in Alaska DigiTel for approximately $10 million in December 2007. GCI is currently constructing an 802-mile fiber optic cable network in Southeast Alaska that will connect Ketchikan, Wrangell, Petersburg, Angoon and Sitka to the lower 48 states, which it expects to complete by November 2008. In October 2007, the company agreed to acquire the United Utilities (UUI) and Unicom telecommunications subsidiaries of United Companies, Inc., a holding company owned by Sea Lion Corporation and Togiak Natives Limited, for $40 million. The transaction is expected to be completed by late 2008. UUI provides local telephone service to 60 rural Alaska communities and Unicom operates DeltaNet, a long-haul broadband microwave network surrounding the Yukon-Kuskokwim Delta.

GCI offers its employees educational reimbursement, a wellness program, an employee assistance program and medical, dental, vision, life and disability insurance.

## FINANCIALS: **Sales and profits are in thousands of dollars—add 000 to get the full amount. 2008 Note: Financial information for 2008 was not available for all companies at press time.**

2008 Sales: $
2007 Sales: $520,311
2006 Sales: $477,482
2005 Sales: $443,026
2004 Sales: $424,826

2008 Profits: $
2007 Profits: $13,504
2006 Profits: $18,520
2005 Profits: $20,831
2004 Profits: $21,252

**U.S. Stock Ticker: GNCMA**
**Int'l Ticker:** Int'l Exchange:
Employees: 1,295
Fiscal Year Ends: 12/31
Parent Company:

## SALARIES/BENEFITS:

Pension Plan:
Savings Plan: Y
ESOP Stock Plan:
Stock Purch. Plan:
Profit Sharing:
Top Exec. Salary: $585,208 Bonus: $100,000
Second Exec. Salary: $462,500 Bonus: $77,000

## OTHER THOUGHTS:

**Apparent Women Officers or Directors**: 2
**Hot Spot for Advancement for Women/Minorities**: Y

## LOCATIONS: ("Y" = Yes)

| West: | Southwest: | Midwest: | Southeast: | Northeast: | International: |
|---|---|---|---|---|---|
| Y | | | | | |

# GENESIS ENERGY LP

www.genesiscrudeoil.com

**Industry Group Code:** 422720 **Ranks within this company's industry group:** Sales: 4 Profits: 4

| Management: | | Sales/Marketing: | | Liberal Arts: | | Information Systems: | | Professionals: | | Technical/Scientific: | |
|---|---|---|---|---|---|---|---|---|---|---|---|
| Mgmt. Trainees: | | Mktg. Professionals: | Y | Gen. Writing/Editing: | | Info. Management: | Y | Finance/Accounting: | Y | Engineers, Elec.: | Y |
| Experienced Mgmt.: | Y | Retail Sales: | | Technical Writing: | | Software Dev.: | | Law: | Y | Engineers, Other: | Y |
| Int'l Business: | | Commercial/Industrial: | Y | Graphic Arts/Photog.: | | Hardware Dev.: | | HR/Other: | Y | Health/Lab: | |
| MBA Graduates: | Y | Sales Trainees: | Y | Music: | | Systems Integration: | | Training: | Y | Scientists/Research: | |
| | | Advertising Pros.: | | Broadcasting: | | Consulting/Other: | | Health Care: | | Petroleum/Chemicals: | Y |
| | | | | Other: | | | | Consulting: | | Math/Other: | |

## TYPES OF BUSINESS:

Crude Oil Distribution
Crude Oil Gathering & Marketing
Carbon Dioxide Marketing
Pipelines
Synthetic Fuel
Road Transportation
Carbon Dioxide Processing

## BRANDS/DIVISIONS/AFFILIATES:

Denbury Resources Inc
Syngas
Praxair Inc
Sandhill Group LLC
Port Hudson Crude Oil
BP Pipelines (North America) Inc.
DG Marine Transportation, LLC

## CONTACTS: *Note: Officers with more than one job title may be intentionally listed here more than once.*

Grant E. Sims, CEO
Joseph A. Blount, Jr., COO
Joseph A. Blount, Jr., Pres.
Robert V. Deere, CFO
Ross A. Benavides, General Counsel/Corp. Sec.
Brad N. Graves, Exec. VP-Bus. Dev.
Karen N. Pape, VP/Controller
Gareth Roberts, Chmn.

| | |
|---|---|
| **Phone:** 713-860-2500 | **Fax:** 713-860-2640 |
| **Toll-Free:** | |
| **Address:** 919 Milam, Ste. 2100, Houston, TX 77002 US | |

## GROWTH PLANS/SPECIAL FEATURES:

Genesis Energy, LP's primary lines of business are crude oil gathering and marketing, crude oil pipeline transportation and industrial gases. It is an independent gatherer and marketer of crude oil, with operations concentrated in Texas, Louisiana, Alabama, Florida and Mississippi. The company is affiliated with Denbury Resources, which has proved carbon dioxide reserves of approximately 5.6 trillion cubic feet. Genesis is engaged in the purchase and aggregation of crude oil at the wellhead and the bulk purchase of oil at pipeline and terminal facilities for resale at various points along the crude oil distribution chain. The company generates revenues by transporting the relatively inexpensive crude oil along the distribution chain and marketing the oil to refineries at increased prices. The firm transports approximately 60,000 barrels of oil per day with a 235-mile pipeline system in Mississippi, a 90-mile system in Texas and a 100-mile system extending from northern Florida into southern Alabama. The company also supplies carbon dioxide to industrial customers. Genesis has a 50% interest in Syngas, a joint venture with Praxair that runs a facility producing synthetic gas and high-pressure steam. Genesis also has a 50% interest in Sandhill Group LLC through which it participates in the production and distribution of liquid carbon dioxide for use in the food, chemical and oil industries. In July 2008, the company formed an inland barge transportation joint venture with TD Marine, an entity owned by the Davison family of Ruston, Louisiana. The joint venture, named DG Marine Transportation, LLC, acquired the inland marine transportation of Grifco Transportation, Ltd.

The company offers its employees a 401(k); a profit sharing plan; and medical, dental, disability and life insurance.

## FINANCIALS: Sales and profits are in thousands of dollars—add 000 to get the full amount. 2008 Note: Financial information for 2008 was not available for all companies at press time.

| | | |
|---|---|---|
| 2008 Sales: $ | 2008 Profits: $ | **U.S. Stock Ticker: GEL** |
| 2007 Sales: $1,199,653 | 2007 Profits: $-13,550 | **Int'l Ticker:** Int'l Exchange: |
| 2006 Sales: $918,369 | 2006 Profits: $8,381 | Employees: 655 |
| 2005 Sales: $1,078,739 | 2005 Profits: $3,415 | Fiscal Year Ends: 12/31 |
| 2004 Sales: $927,143 | 2004 Profits: $-1,412 | Parent Company: |

## SALARIES/BENEFITS:

| | | | | |
|---|---|---|---|---|
| Pension Plan: | ESOP Stock Plan: | Profit Sharing: | Top Exec. Salary: $310,000 | Bonus: $111,581 |
| Savings Plan: Y | Stock Purch. Plan: | | Second Exec. Salary: $270,000 | Bonus: $94,577 |

## OTHER THOUGHTS:

**Apparent Women Officers or Directors**: 2
**Hot Spot for Advancement for Women/Minorities**:

## LOCATIONS: ("Y" = Yes)

| West: | Southwest: | Midwest: | Southeast: | Northeast: | International: |
|---|---|---|---|---|---|
| | Y | | Y | | |

# GENOMIC HEALTH INC

**www.genomichealth.com**

**Industry Group Code:** 325413 **Ranks within this company's industry group:** Sales: 10 Profits: 11

| **Management:** | | **Sales/Marketing:** | | **Liberal Arts:** | | **Information Systems:** | | **Professionals:** | | **Technical/Scientific:** | |
|---|---|---|---|---|---|---|---|---|---|---|---|
| Mgmt. Trainees: | | Mktg. Professionals: | Y | Gen. Writing/Editing: | | Info. Management: | Y | Finance/Accounting: | Y | Engineers, Elec.: | |
| Experienced Mgmt.: | Y | Retail Sales: | | Technical Writing: | Y | Software Dev.: | Y | Law: | Y | Engineers, Other: | Y |
| Int'l Business: | | Commercial/Industrial: | Y | Graphic Arts/Photog.: | | Hardware Dev.: | Y | HR/Other: | Y | Health/Lab: | Y |
| MBA Graduates: | Y | Sales Trainees: | Y | Music: | | Systems Integration: | | Training: | Y | Scientists/Research: | Y |
| | | Advertising Pros.: | | Broadcasting: | | Consulting/Other: | | Health Care: | Y | Petroleum/Chemicals: | |
| | | | | Other: | | | | Consulting: | | Math/Other: | Y |

## TYPES OF BUSINESS:

Genomic-Based Cancer Diagnostic Test Development

## BRANDS/DIVISIONS/AFFILIATES:

Oncotype DX

## CONTACTS:

*Note: Officers with more than one job title may be intentionally listed here more than once.*

Randal W. Scott, CEO
Kimberly J. (Kim) Popovits, COO
Kimberly J. (Kim) Popovits, Pres.
G. Bradley (Brad) Cole, CFO
Tricia Tomlinson, Sr. VP-Human Resources
Joffre B. Baker, Chief Scientific Officer
G. Bradley (Brad) Cole, Sec.
G. Bradley (Brad) Cole, Exec. VP-Oper.
David Logan, Sr. VP-Commercial
Steven Shak, Chief Medical Officer
Randal W. Scott, Chmn.

**Phone:** 650-556-9300 **Fax:** 650-556-1132
**Toll-Free:** 866-662-6897
**Address:** 301 Penobscot Dr., Redwood City, CA 94063 US

## GROWTH PLANS/SPECIAL FEATURES:

Genomic Health, Inc. focuses on the development and commercialization of genomic-based clinical diagnostic tests for cancer. Oncotype DX, its first and only marketed test product, is designed to help physicians determine the most effective treatment type for early stage breast cancer. Unlike comparable test assay systems that use fresh or frozen samples, Oncotype DX uses tissue samples that are chemically preserved and sealed in paraffin wax, thus allowing for easier handling and transportation. Hence, unlike other tests that may require a frozen sample shipped on dry ice, the Oncotype DX sample can be sent via regular overnight mail. All samples are processed at the firm's laboratory in Redwood City, California. Most physicians receive the results of their test within 10-14 days. Oncotype DX is offered as a laboratory service that tests 21 specific genes in a tumor sample to provide tumor-specific information (or the oncotype of the tumor), mainly to calculate the probability of recurrence and the potential efficacy of chemotherapy. This technology mainly compares the genetic makeup of the tissue sample with archived information from other cancer patients, in order to facilitate a correlation between the patient's condition and known clinical outcomes. It expresses the resulting profile as a single quantitative score, called the Recurrence Score, which ranges from 0-100. Higher Recurrence Scores indicate a more aggressive tumor, lower scores indicate less aggressive tumors. From its inception in January 2004 to December 2007, Oncotype DX has been used in over 46,500 tests administered by 7,000 physicians. The company is seeking new applications for Oncotype DX, as well as seeking new products for other cancers. In February 2008, the Oncotype DX report began including qualitative scores for the estrogen receptor (ER) and progesterone receptor (PR), which are used in calculating the Recurrence Score.

Employees of the firm receive medical, dental and vision coverage; and life and disability insurance.

## FINANCIALS:

**Sales and profits are in thousands of dollars—add 000 to get the full amount. 2008 Note: Financial information for 2008 was not available for all companies at press time.**

| | | |
|---|---|---|
| 2008 Sales: $110,579 | 2008 Profits: $-16,089 | **U.S. Stock Ticker: GHDX** |
| 2007 Sales: $64,027 | 2007 Profits: $-27,292 | **Int'l Ticker:** Int'l Exchange: |
| 2006 Sales: $29,174 | 2006 Profits: $-28,920 | Employees: 288 |
| 2005 Sales: $5,202 | 2005 Profits: $-31,361 | Fiscal Year Ends: 12/31 |
| 2004 Sales: $ | 2004 Profits: $ | Parent Company: |

## SALARIES/BENEFITS:

| | | | | |
|---|---|---|---|---|
| Pension Plan: | ESOP Stock Plan: | Profit Sharing: | Top Exec. Salary: $340,000 | Bonus: $25,000 |
| Savings Plan: Y | Stock Purch. Plan: | | Second Exec. Salary: $315,000 | Bonus: $25,000 |

## OTHER THOUGHTS:

**Apparent Women Officers or Directors**: 2
**Hot Spot for Advancement for Women/Minorities**:

## LOCATIONS: ("Y" = Yes)

| West: | Southwest: | Midwest: | Southeast: | Northeast: | International: |
|---|---|---|---|---|---|
| Y | | | | | |

# GEN-PROBE INC

www.gen-probe.com

**Industry Group Code:** 325413 **Ranks within this company's industry group:** Sales: 1 Profits: 1

| Management: | | Sales/Marketing: | | Liberal Arts: | | Information Systems: | | Professionals: | | Technical/Scientific: | |
|---|---|---|---|---|---|---|---|---|---|---|---|
| Mgmt. Trainees: | | Mktg. Professionals: | Y | Gen. Writing/Editing: | | Info. Management: | Y | Finance/Accounting: | Y | Engineers, Elec.: | Y |
| Experienced Mgmt.: | Y | Retail Sales: | | Technical Writing: | Y | Software Dev.: | Y | Law: | Y | Engineers, Other: | Y |
| Int'l Business: | Y | Commercial/Industrial: | Y | Graphic Arts/Photog.: | | Hardware Dev.: | Y | HR/Other: | Y | Health/Lab: | Y |
| MBA Graduates: | Y | Sales Trainees: | Y | Music: | | Systems Integration: | | Training: | Y | Scientists/Research: | Y |
| | | Advertising Pros.: | | Broadcasting: | | Consulting/Other: | | Health Care: | Y | Petroleum/Chemicals: | |
| | | | | Other: | | | | Consulting: | | Math/Other: | Y |

## TYPES OF BUSINESS:

Medical Diagnostics Products
Diagnostic Tests
Blood Screening Assays
Services-Commercial Physical Research
Services-Commercial Biological Research

## BRANDS/DIVISIONS/AFFILIATES:

TIGRIS
Novartis Corp.
Procleix
PROCELIEX ULTRIO

## CONTACTS: *Note: Officers with more than one job title may be intentionally listed here more than once.*

Henry L. Nordhoff, CEO
Carl W. Hull, COO
Carl W. Hull, Pres.
Herm Rosenman, CFO/Sr. VP-Finance
Stephen J. Kondor, Sr. VP-Mktg. & Sales
Diana De Walt, Sr. VP-Human Resources
Daniel L. Kacian, Exec. VP/Chief Scientist
R. William Bowen, General Counsel/VP/Secretary
Jorgine Ellerbrock, Sr. VP-Oper.
Paul Gargan, VP-Bus. Dev.
Robert B. Blake, VP-Instrument Systems
Lyle J. Arnold, VP-Research
Christina Yang, Sr. VP-Clinical/Regulatory/Quality
Tammy J. Brach, VP-Program Mgr.
Henry L. Nordhoff, Chmn.
Gurney Lashley, VP-Supply Chain Mgmt.

**Phone:** 858-410-8000 **Fax:** 800-288-3141
**Toll-Free:** 800-523-5001
**Address:** 10210 Genetic Center Dr., San Diego, CA 92121-4362 US

## GROWTH PLANS/SPECIAL FEATURES:

Gen-Probe, Inc. develops, manufactures and markets nucleic acid testing (NAT) products for clinical diagnosis of human diseases and screening of human blood donations. Gen-Probe has over 200 U.S. patents including one for its automated nucleic acid sequence isolation system, TIGRIS; and has received U.S. Food and Drug Administration (FDA) approval for over 60 products, including the company's WNV (West Nile Virus) assay on aSAS to screen donated human blood, and tests to detect microorganisms indicative of sexually transmitted diseases, tuberculosis, strep throat, pneumonia and fungal infections. The company also developed, and now manufactures, the only FDA-approved blood screening assay for the simultaneous detection of HIV-1 and HCV (hepatitis C virus), presently marketed by Novartis Corporation and used by blood collection agencies like the American Red Cross and America's Blood Centers. Products are also marketed to clinical laboratories, public health institutions and hospitals in the U.S. and Canada. Gen-Probe plans to continue developing its current market positions, while also seeking out applications for its proprietary NAT technologies, potentially to include viral load testing, cancer monitoring, pharmacogenomics, industrial uses and bioterrorism-related testing. In 2007, the FDA approved Gen-Probe's Pocleix TIGRIS system to screen blood, tissues and organs for WNV using the Procleix WNV assay; TIGRIS can now analyze 1,000 blood samples in about 14 hours.

Gen-Probe employee benefits include income protection, paid time off, an employee assistance plan, flexible spending accounts and an on-site cafeteria. In addition, the company has a tuition assistance program, many in-house training opportunities and the Gen-Probe E-Learning program, through which employees can take over 100 online courses to develop skills at their own pace.

## FINANCIALS: **Sales and profits are in thousands of dollars—add 000 to get the full amount. 2008 Note: Financial information for 2008 was not available for all companies at press time.**

| | | |
|---|---|---|
| 2008 Sales: $ | 2008 Profits: $ | **U.S. Stock Ticker: GPRO** |
| 2007 Sales: $403,014 | 2007 Profits: $86,140 | **Int'l Ticker:** Int'l Exchange: |
| 2006 Sales: $354,764 | 2006 Profits: $59,498 | Employees: 987 |
| 2005 Sales: $305,965 | 2005 Profits: $60,089 | Fiscal Year Ends: 12/31 |
| 2004 Sales: $269,707 | 2004 Profits: $54,575 | Parent Company: |

## SALARIES/BENEFITS:

| | | | | |
|---|---|---|---|---|
| Pension Plan: | ESOP Stock Plan: Y | Profit Sharing: | Top Exec. Salary: $677,389 | Bonus: $668,250 |
| Savings Plan: Y | Stock Purch. Plan: Y | | Second Exec. Salary: $384,169 | Bonus: $280,500 |

## OTHER THOUGHTS:

**Apparent Women Officers or Directors**: 4
**Hot Spot for Advancement for Women/Minorities**: Y

## LOCATIONS: ("Y" = Yes)

| West: | Southwest: | Midwest: | Southeast: | Northeast: | International: |
|---|---|---|---|---|---|
| Y | | | | | |

# GERBER SCIENTIFIC INC

**www.gerberscientific.com**

**Industry Group Code:** 334111 **Ranks within this company's industry group:** Sales: 2 Profits: 4

| **Management:** | | **Sales/Marketing:** | | **Liberal Arts:** | | **Information Systems:** | | **Professionals:** | | **Technical/Scientific:** | |
|---|---|---|---|---|---|---|---|---|---|---|---|
| Mgmt. Trainees: | | Mktg. Professionals: | Y | Gen. Writing/Editing: | | Info. Management: | Y | Finance/Accounting: | Y | Engineers, Elec.: | Y |
| Experienced Mgmt.: | Y | Retail Sales: | | Technical Writing: | Y | Software Dev.: | Y | Law: | Y | Engineers, Other: | Y |
| Int'l Business: | Y | Commercial/Industrial: | Y | Graphic Arts/Photog.: | | Hardware Dev.: | Y | HR/Other: | Y | Health/Lab: | |
| MBA Graduates: | Y | Sales Trainees: | Y | Music: | | Systems Integration: | Y | Training: | Y | Scientists/Research: | |
| | | Advertising Pros.: | | Broadcasting: | | Consulting/Other: | | Health Care: | | Petroleum/Chemicals: | |
| | | | | Other: | | | | Consulting: | | Math/Other: | |

## TYPES OF BUSINESS:

Computer Hardware-Automated Manufacturing Systems
Computer-Aided Design Systems
Ophthalmic Lens Processing Equipment
Apparel & Flexible Materials Equipment
Digital Imaging Equipment

## BRANDS/DIVISIONS/AFFILIATES:

Gerber Technology, Inc.
Gerber Scientific Products, Inc.
Gerber Coburn
Spandex Ltd.
EDGE FX
SOLARA UV2
OMEGA 2.5
Virtek Vision International Inc

## CONTACTS: *Note: Officers with more than one job title may be intentionally listed here more than once.*

Marc T. Giles, CEO
Marc T. Giles, Pres.
Michael R. Elia, CFO/Exec. VP
William V. Grikis, Jr., General Counsel/Sr. VP
Joseph R. Mele, Sr. VP-Oper.
Stephen Lovass, Sr. VP/Pres., Gerber Scientific Products
Alex Incera, Pres., Gerber Coburn
Rodney Larson, Sr. VP/Pres., Spandex, Ltd.
John R. Hancock, Sr. VP/Pres., Gerber Technology
Donald P. Aiken, Chmn.
James S. Arthurs, Sr. VP/Pres., Gerber Scientific, Asia Pacific

**Phone:** 860-644-1551 **Fax:** 860-643-7039
**Toll-Free:**
**Address:** 83 Gerber Rd. W., South Windsor, CT 06074 US

## GROWTH PLANS/SPECIAL FEATURES:

Gerber Scientific, Inc. provides integrated computerized design and manufacturing equipment, software and related services for the following industries: sign-making and specialty graphics; apparel and flexible materials; and ophthalmic lens processing. Gerber's sign making and specialty graphics products, produced through the subsidiaries Gerber Scientific Products (GSP) and Spandex Ltd., include digital imaging equipment; plotters and routers (cutting tools); digital print materials; and design software. Gerber Scientific products include, but are not limited to digital imaging equipment; inkjet printing; aftermarket supplies; distribution; and raw materials. Spandex offers highly competitive market and technical knowledge, strong supplier relationships and supply chain infrastructure and a wide array of products and support services. Gerber Technology (GT) runs the apparel and flexible materials business. Products include product lifecycle management software, plotters and single- or multi-ply cutting systems. Gerber's ophthalmic lens processing unit is run by Gerber Coburn (GC). GC designs, manufactures and services software and supplies used in all aspects of surfacing prescriptions in lenses. Products include lab management software and lens inspection systems. Sign making and specialty graphics produced 56% of the firm's revenue; apparel and flexible materials produced 33%; and ophthalmic lens processing made up 11%. In November 2008, Gerber Scientific acquired the majority holding of Virtek Vision International, a provider of laser templating, inspection, marking and engraving products.

## FINANCIALS: **Sales and profits are in thousands of dollars—add 000 to get the full amount. 2008 Note: Financial information for 2008 was not available for all companies at press time.**

| | | |
|---|---|---|
| 2008 Sales: $640,017 | 2008 Profits: $14,504 | **U.S. Stock Ticker: GRB** |
| 2007 Sales: $574,798 | 2007 Profits: $13,508 | **Int'l Ticker:** Int'l Exchange: |
| 2006 Sales: $530,418 | 2006 Profits: $2,644 | Employees: 2,200 |
| 2005 Sales: $517,322 | 2005 Profits: $-5,638 | Fiscal Year Ends: 4/30 |
| 2004 Sales: $516,816 | 2004 Profits: $4,581 | Parent Company: |

## SALARIES/BENEFITS:

| | | | | |
|---|---|---|---|---|
| Pension Plan: | ESOP Stock Plan: | Profit Sharing: | Top Exec. Salary: $561,346 | Bonus: $288,563 |
| Savings Plan: Y | Stock Purch. Plan: | | Second Exec. Salary: $254,897 | Bonus: $97,910 |

## OTHER THOUGHTS:

**Apparent Women Officers or Directors:**
**Hot Spot for Advancement for Women/Minorities:**

## LOCATIONS: ("Y" = Yes)

| West: | Southwest: | Midwest: | Southeast: | Northeast: | International: |
|---|---|---|---|---|---|
| | | Y | | Y | Y |

# GERON CORPORATION

www.geron.com

**Industry Group Code:** 325412 **Ranks within this company's industry group:** Sales: 38 Profits: 23

| Management: | | Sales/Marketing: | | Liberal Arts: | | Information Systems: | | Professionals: | | Technical/Scientific: | |
|---|---|---|---|---|---|---|---|---|---|---|---|
| Mgmt. Trainees: | | Mktg. Professionals: | Y | Gen. Writing/Editing: | | Info. Management: | Y | Finance/Accounting: | Y | Engineers, Elec.: | |
| Experienced Mgmt.: | Y | Retail Sales: | | Technical Writing: | Y | Software Dev.: | Y | Law: | Y | Engineers, Other: | |
| Int'l Business: | | Commercial/Industrial: | Y | Graphic Arts/Photog.: | | Hardware Dev.: | | HR/Other: | Y | Health/Lab: | Y |
| MBA Graduates: | Y | Sales Trainees: | Y | Music: | | Systems Integration: | | Training: | Y | Scientists/Research: | Y |
| | | Advertising Pros.: | | Broadcasting: | | Consulting/Other: | | Health Care: | Y | Petroleum/Chemicals: | |
| | | | | Other: | | | | Consulting: | | Math/Other: | Y |

## TYPES OF BUSINESS:

Drug Discovery & Development
Telomerase Technologies
Human Stem Cell Technologies

## BRANDS/DIVISIONS/AFFILIATES:

Start Licensing, Inc.

## CONTACTS: *Note: Officers with more than one job title may be intentionally listed here more than once.*

Thomas B. Okarma, CEO
Thomas B. Okarma, Pres.
David L. Greenwood, CFO/Exec. VP
Calvin B. Harley, Chief Scientific Officer
David J. Earp, Chief Patent Counsel
David J. Earp, Sr. VP-Bus. Dev.
David L. Greenwood, Treas./Sec.
Fabio M. Benedetti, Sr. VP-Oncology/Chief Medical Officer
Jane S. Lebkowski, Sr. VP-Regenerative Medicine
Melissa A. Kelly Behrs, Sr. VP-Therapeutic Dev. & Oncology
Alexander E. Barkas, Chmn.

| **Phone:** 650-473-7700 | **Fax:** 650-473-7750 |
|---|---|
| **Toll-Free:** | |
| **Address:** 230 Constitution Dr., Menlo Park, CA 94025 US | |

## GROWTH PLANS/SPECIAL FEATURES:

Geron Corp. develops biopharmaceuticals for the treatment of cancer and chronic degenerative diseases, including spinal cord injury, heart failure and diabetes. The company's therapies are based on telomerase and human embryonic stem cell technologies. The company is advancing telomerase targeted therapies, including an anti-cancer drug and a cancer vaccine, through multiple clinical trials and their spinal cord injury treatment is anticipated to be the first such product to enter clinical development. Telomeres enable cell division, protect chromosomes from degradation and act as molecular clocks for cellular aging. The enzyme telomerase restores telomere length, which shortens as cells multiply, extending a cell's ability to replicate. Geron is developing anti-cancer therapies based on telomerase inhibitors, telomerase therapeutic vaccines and telomerase-based oncolytic viruses. The company seeks to use human embryonic stem cells (hESC) as a potential source for manufacturing replacement cells and tissues for organ repair. The firm is now testing six different hESC-derived therapeutic cell types in animal models, four of which have demonstrated efficacy. The most advanced hESC-derived product, GRNOPC1, is targeted for the treatment of spinal cord injury. Geron's second hESC product, GRNCM1, is a population of cariomyocytes, the contractile cells of the heart, which is intended for the treatment of patients with myocardial disease. The firm owns or licenses over 160 U.S. and 290 foreign patents, with more than 415 pending applications worldwide. Geron formed Start Licensing, Inc., a joint-venture with Exeter Life Sciences, to manage and license a portfolio of animal reproductive and cloning technologies. In July 2007, the company announced the initiation of a clinical trial of GRN163L, a telomerase inhibitor drug, in patients with advanced non-small cell lung cancer. As of December 2007, GRNVAC1, a leukemia vaccine, is in Phase II trials.

The company offers its employees a paid winter break between Christmas and New Year's Day.

## FINANCIALS: **Sales and profits are in thousands of dollars—add 000 to get the full amount. 2008 Note: Financial information for 2008 was not available for all companies at press time.**

| | | |
|---|---|---|
| 2008 Sales: $ | 2008 Profits: $ | **U.S. Stock Ticker: GERN** |
| 2007 Sales: $7,622 | 2007 Profits: $-36,697 | **Int'l Ticker:** Int'l Exchange: |
| 2006 Sales: $3,277 | 2006 Profits: $-31,365 | Employees: 140 |
| 2005 Sales: $6,158 | 2005 Profits: $-33,689 | Fiscal Year Ends: 12/31 |
| 2004 Sales: $1,053 | 2004 Profits: $-79,558 | Parent Company: |

## SALARIES/BENEFITS:

| | | | | |
|---|---|---|---|---|
| Pension Plan: | ESOP Stock Plan: | Profit Sharing: | Top Exec. Salary: $510,000 | Bonus: $275,000 |
| Savings Plan: Y | Stock Purch. Plan: Y | | Second Exec. Salary: $425,000 | Bonus: $172,000 |

## OTHER THOUGHTS:

**Apparent Women Officers or Directors**: 2
**Hot Spot for Advancement for Women/Minorities**: Y

## LOCATIONS: ("Y" = Yes)

| West: | Southwest: | Midwest: | Southeast: | Northeast: | International: |
|---|---|---|---|---|---|
| Y | | | | | |

# GLOBAL PARTNERS LP

**www.globalp.com**

**Industry Group Code:** 422710 **Ranks within this company's industry group:** Sales: 1 Profits: 2

| Management: | | Sales/Marketing: | | Liberal Arts: | | Information Systems: | | Professionals: | | Technical/Scientific: | |
|---|---|---|---|---|---|---|---|---|---|---|---|
| Mgmt. Trainees: | | Mktg. Professionals: | Y | Gen. Writing/Editing: | | Info. Management: | Y | Finance/Accounting: | Y | Engineers, Elec.: | |
| Experienced Mgmt.: | Y | Retail Sales: | | Technical Writing: | | Software Dev.: | | Law: | Y | Engineers, Other: | |
| Int'l Business: | Y | Commercial/Industrial: | Y | Graphic Arts/Photog.: | | Hardware Dev.: | | HR/Other: | Y | Health/Lab: | |
| MBA Graduates: | Y | Sales Trainees: | Y | Music: | | Systems Integration: | | Training: | Y | Scientists/Research: | |
| | | Advertising Pros.: | | Broadcasting: | | Consulting/Other: | | Health Care: | | Petroleum/Chemicals: | |
| | | | | Other: | | | | Consulting: | | Math/Other: | |

## TYPES OF BUSINESS:

Energy Marketing
Wholesale Distillates & Gasoline
Fuel Distribution

## BRANDS/DIVISIONS/AFFILIATES:

Global Companies LLC
Glen Hes Corp.
Global Montello Group Corp.
Chelsea Sandwich LLC
Heating Oil Plus
DieselOne
Bioheat
SubZero

## CONTACTS: *Note: Officers with more than one job title may be intentionally listed here more than once.*

Eric Slifka, CEO
Thomas J. Hollister, COO
Eric Slifka, Pres.
Thomas J. Hollister, CFO
Edward J. Faneuil, General Counsel/Exec. VP/Corp. Sec.
William G. Davidson, Sr. VP-Oper. & Terminals
Scott Solomon, VP-Investor Rel.
Charles A. Rudinsky, Chief Acct. Officer/Treas./Exec. VP
Alfred A. Slifka, Chmn.

| **Phone:** 781-894-8800 | **Fax:** |
|---|---|
| **Toll-Free:** | |
| **Address:** 800 South St., Ste. 200, Waltham, MA 02454 US | |

## GROWTH PLANS/SPECIAL FEATURES:

Global Partners, LP is a wholesale and commercial distributor of gasoline, distillates (such as home heating oil, diesel and kerosene) and residual oil to wholesalers, retailers and commercial customers whose business is organized within two operating segments, wholesale and commercial. Within these segments, the company divides its products into three categories: distillates, gasoline and residual oil. In 2007, distillates accounted for 49% of the company's total volume sold, with gasoline accounting for 42% and residual oil accounting for the remaining 9%. The company is one of the leading wholesalers of distillates and gasoline throughout the northeastern U.S. Global Partners, through wholly-owned subsidiary Global Operating LLC, owns four operating subsidiaries: Global Companies LLC; Glen Hes Corp.; Global Montello Group Corp.; and Chelsea Sandwich LLC. Through a network of deepwater and inland terminals, the firm wholesales number two heating oil, premium heating oil under the name Heating Oil Plus, biofuels under the name Bioheat, kerosene and pour point depressant under the name SubZero to unbranded retail gasoline stations and other resellers of transportations fuels, home heating oil retailers and wholesale distributors. Global Partners also wholesales distillates and gasoline through 20 bulk terminals each with a storage capacity of more than 50,000 barrels. The company also has throughput or exchange agreements at 17 bulk terminals and 34 inland storage facilities. Global Montello Group is the firm's public bid respondent. It responds to bid requests from municipal, state and federal agencies, as well as public and private institutions such as hospitals, schools and private companies. The commercial segment sells unbranded gasoline, home heating oil, diesel, kerosene and residual oil to customers in the public sector and to large commercial and industrial customers, such as federal and state agencies, municipalities, large industrial companies, transportation authorities and water resource authorities, colleges and universities and small utilities.

## FINANCIALS: **Sales and profits are in thousands of dollars—add 000 to get the full amount. 2008 Note: Financial information for 2008 was not available for all companies at press time.**

| | | |
|---|---|---|
| 2008 Sales: $ | 2008 Profits: $ | **U.S. Stock Ticker: GLP** |
| 2007 Sales: $6,757,834 | 2007 Profits: $47,013 | **Int'l Ticker:** Int'l Exchange: |
| 2006 Sales: $4,472,418 | 2006 Profits: $33,416 | Employees: 230 |
| 2005 Sales: $4,045,800 | 2005 Profits: $18,100 | Fiscal Year Ends: 12/31 |
| 2004 Sales: $3,187,600 | 2004 Profits: $17,300 | Parent Company: |

## SALARIES/BENEFITS:

| | | | | |
|---|---|---|---|---|
| Pension Plan: | ESOP Stock Plan: | Profit Sharing: | Top Exec. Salary: $243,800 | Bonus: $1,486,700 |
| Savings Plan: | Stock Purch. Plan: | | Second Exec. Salary: $104,000 | Bonus: $130,000 |

## OTHER THOUGHTS:

**Apparent Women Officers or Directors:**
**Hot Spot for Advancement for Women/Minorities:**

## LOCATIONS: ("Y" = Yes)

| West: | Southwest: | Midwest: | Southeast: | Northeast: | International: |
|---|---|---|---|---|---|
| | | | | Y | |

# GLOBECOMM SYSTEMS INC

www.globecommsystems.com

**Industry Group Code:** 334220 **Ranks within this company's industry group:** Sales: 3 Profits: 4

| Management: | | Sales/Marketing: | | Liberal Arts: | | Information Systems: | | Professionals: | | Technical/Scientific: | |
|---|---|---|---|---|---|---|---|---|---|---|---|
| Mgmt. Trainees: | | Mktg. Professionals: | Y | Gen. Writing/Editing: | Y | Info. Management: | Y | Finance/Accounting: | Y | Engineers, Elec.: | Y |
| Experienced Mgmt.: | Y | Retail Sales: | | Technical Writing: | Y | Software Dev.: | Y | Law: | Y | Engineers, Other: | Y |
| Int'l Business: | Y | Commercial/Industrial: | Y | Graphic Arts/Photog.: | | Hardware Dev.: | Y | HR/Other: | Y | Health/Lab: | |
| MBA Graduates: | Y | Sales Trainees: | Y | Music: | | Systems Integration: | Y | Training: | Y | Scientists/Research: | |
| | | Advertising Pros.: | | Broadcasting: | | Consulting/Other: | | Health Care: | | Petroleum/Chemicals: | |
| | | | | Other: | | | | Consulting: | | Math/Other: | Y |

## TYPES OF BUSINESS:

Satellite Ground Systems & Networks
Satellite Data Transmission

## BRANDS/DIVISIONS/AFFILIATES:

Globecomm Network Services Corp.
Globecomm Services Maryland LLC
GlobalSat

## CONTACTS: *Note: Officers with more than one job title may be intentionally listed here more than once.*

David E. Hershberg, CEO
Kenneth A. Miller, Pres.
Andrew C. Melfi, CFO
Stephen C. Yablonski, Sr. VP-Sales & Mktg.
Paul Eterno, VP-Human Resources
Stephen C. Yablonski, Sr. VP-Prod. Dev.
Andrew C. Melfi, Treas./VP
Donald G. Woodring, VP-Network & Systems Analysis
Paul J. Johnson, Sr. VP-Customer Rel. & Contracts
David E. Hershberg, Chmn.

**Phone:** 631-231-9800 **Fax:** 631-231-1557
**Toll-Free:**
**Address:** 45 Oser Ave., Hauppauge, NY 11788 US

## GROWTH PLANS/SPECIAL FEATURES:

Globecomm Systems, Inc. (GSI) provides end-to-end value-added satellite-based communications products, services and solutions by combining its core satellite ground segment systems and network capabilities, with the satellite communication services capabilities that are provided by its wholly-owned subsidiaries Globecomm Network Service Corp. and Globecomm Services Maryland LLC. The products and services that the company offers are pre-engineered systems; systems design and integration services; managed network services; and life cycle support services. The firm engineers all the necessary satellite and terrestrial facilities and provides the integration services required to implement those facilities. The company also operates and maintains managed networks and provides life cycle support service on an ongoing basis. The company designs, engineers, integrates and installs satellite-based ground systems and network solutions, which typically consist of earth stations (integrated systems consisting of antennas, radio signal transmitting and receiving equipment, modulation/demodulation equipment, monitor and control systems, as well as voice, data and video network interface equipment) and ancillary subsystems. GSI's business is global, and it derives most of its revenue from developing countries. In May 2007, GSI acquired the GlobalSat division of Lyman Bros., Inc. In June 2007, GSI was awarded $20.7 million by General Communication, Inc. (GCI) to provide wireless phone services to 200 rural villages throughout Alaska.

The company offers its employees health, medical and dental insurance; life insurance; education assistance; and a 401(k) plan.

## FINANCIALS: **Sales and profits are in thousands of dollars—add 000 to get the full amount. 2008 Note: Financial information for 2008 was not available for all companies at press time.**

2008 Sales: $196,525 | 2008 Profits: $27,019
2007 Sales: $150,745 | 2007 Profits: $8,326
2006 Sales: $126,036 | 2006 Profits: $4,492
2005 Sales: $109,584 | 2005 Profits: $4,814
2004 Sales: $87,236 | 2004 Profits: $-1,341

**U.S. Stock Ticker: GCOM**
**Int'l Ticker:** Int'l Exchange:
Employees: 282
Fiscal Year Ends: 6/30
Parent Company:

## SALARIES/BENEFITS:

Pension Plan: | ESOP Stock Plan: | Profit Sharing: | Top Exec. Salary: $422,124 | Bonus: $424,600
Savings Plan: Y | Stock Purch. Plan: | | Second Exec. Salary: $318,985 | Bonus: $263,960

## OTHER THOUGHTS:

**Apparent Women Officers or Directors:**
**Hot Spot for Advancement for Women/Minorities:**

## LOCATIONS: ("Y" = Yes)

| West: | Southwest: | Midwest: | Southeast: | Northeast: | International: |
|---|---|---|---|---|---|
| | | | | Y | Y |

# GLU MOBILE INC

**www.glu.com**

**Industry Group Code:** 511208 **Ranks within this company's industry group:** Sales: 2 Profits: 2

| Management: | | Sales/Marketing: | | Liberal Arts: | | Information Systems: | | Professionals: | | Technical/Scientific: | |
|---|---|---|---|---|---|---|---|---|---|---|---|
| Mgmt. Trainees: | | Mktg. Professionals: | Y | Gen. Writing/Editing: | | Info. Management: | Y | Finance/Accounting: | Y | Engineers, Elec.: | Y |
| Experienced Mgmt.: | Y | Retail Sales: | | Technical Writing: | Y | Software Dev.: | Y | Law: | Y | Engineers, Other: | |
| Int'l Business: | Y | Commercial/Industrial: | Y | Graphic Arts/Photog.: | Y | Hardware Dev.: | | HR/Other: | Y | Health/Lab: | |
| MBA Graduates: | Y | Sales Trainees: | Y | Music: | Y | Systems Integration: | | Training: | Y | Scientists/Research: | |
| | | Advertising Pros.: | | Broadcasting: | | Consulting/Other: | | Health Care: | | Petroleum/Chemicals: | |
| | | | | Other: | Y | | | Consulting: | | Math/Other: | |

## TYPES OF BUSINESS:

Mobile Entertainment Applications
Mobile Phone Games

## BRANDS/DIVISIONS/AFFILIATES:

MIG Information Technology Co. Ltd.
Superscape Group plc
Warner Bros. Digital Distribution
Warner Bros. Entertainment

## CONTACTS: *Note: Officers with more than one job title may be intentionally listed here more than once.*

Greg Ballard, CEO
Greg Ballard, Pres.
Eric Ludwig, Interim CFO
Ron Sha, CIO/VP
Alex Galvagni, CTO
Alex Galvagni, Sr. VP-Global Prod. Dev.
Kevin Chou, General Counsel/VP/Corp. Sec.
Nate Jones, VP-Corp. Dev.
Eric Ludwig, Sr. VP-Finance
Jill Braff, Sr. VP-Global Publishing
Robert Hayes, Managing Dir.-Asia Pacific
Frank Keeling, Managing Dir.-EMEA
Daniel K. Skaff, Lead Dir.
David Ward, Chmn.-EMEA
Greg Suarez, VP-Licensing

**Phone:** 650-532-2400 **Fax:** 650-532-2500
**Toll-Free:**
**Address:** 2207 Bridgepointe Pkwy., Ste. 250, San Mateo, CA 94404 US

## GROWTH PLANS/SPECIAL FEATURES:

Glu Mobile, Inc. is a global publisher of mobile games. The company has developed and published a portfolio of more than 195 casual and traditional games across a number of genres, including action, board game, card/casino, puzzle, sports, strategy/role playing games and TV/movie. The company has more than 1 billion subscribers worldwide served by its more than 200 wireless carriers and other distributors. The firm creates games and related applications based on third-party licensed brands and other intellectual property, as well as on its own original brands and intellectual property. Glu Mobile's business leverages the marketing resources and distribution infrastructure of wireless carriers and the brands and other intellectual property of third-party content owners, allowing it to focus its efforts on developing and publishing mobile games. In March 2007, Glu Mobile had its initial public offering of stock (IPO) and became a public company. In May 2007, the company partnered with Warner Bros. Digital Distribution, which gives the company worldwide rights to develop, market and distribute mobile games and content based on select new film releases as well as games and content from Warner Bros. Entertainment's library. In late 2007, the firm acquired MIG Information Technology Co. Ltd., a developer and publisher of mobile games for China. In March 2008, Glu Mobile acquired about 93% of the issued share capital of Superscape Group plc. It is currently trying to acquire the rest of the shares.

## FINANCIALS: **Sales and profits are in thousands of dollars—add 000 to get the full amount. 2008 Note: Financial information for 2008 was not available for all companies at press time.**

| | | |
|---|---|---|
| 2008 Sales: $89,767 | 2008 Profits: $-107,312 | **U.S. Stock Ticker: GLUU** |
| 2007 Sales: $66,867 | 2007 Profits: $-3,591 | **Int'l Ticker:** Int'l Exchange: |
| 2006 Sales: $46,166 | 2006 Profits: $-12,310 | Employees: 287 |
| 2005 Sales: $25,651 | 2005 Profits: $-17,901 | Fiscal Year Ends: 12/31 |
| 2004 Sales: $7,022 | 2004 Profits: $-8,322 | Parent Company: |

## SALARIES/BENEFITS:

| | | | | |
|---|---|---|---|---|
| Pension Plan: | ESOP Stock Plan: | Profit Sharing: | Top Exec. Salary: $301,442 | Bonus: $ |
| Savings Plan: | Stock Purch. Plan: | | Second Exec. Salary: $250,576 | Bonus: $ |

## OTHER THOUGHTS:

**Apparent Women Officers or Directors**: 3
**Hot Spot for Advancement for Women/Minorities**: Y

## LOCATIONS: ("Y" = Yes)

| West: | Southwest: | Midwest: | Southeast: | Northeast: | International: |
|---|---|---|---|---|---|
| Y | | | | | Y |

# GOAMERICA INC

www.goamerica.com

**Industry Group Code:** 513322 **Ranks within this company's industry group:** Sales: 3 Profits: 2

| Management: | | Sales/Marketing: | | Liberal Arts: | | Information Systems: | | Professionals: | | Technical/Scientific: | |
|---|---|---|---|---|---|---|---|---|---|---|---|
| Mgmt. Trainees: | | Mktg. Professionals: | Y | Gen. Writing/Editing: | | Info. Management: | Y | Finance/Accounting: | Y | Engineers, Elec.: | Y |
| Experienced Mgmt.: | Y | Retail Sales: | | Technical Writing: | Y | Software Dev.: | Y | Law: | Y | Engineers, Other: | |
| Int'l Business: | | Commercial/Industrial: | Y | Graphic Arts/Photog.: | | Hardware Dev.: | | HR/Other: | Y | Health/Lab: | |
| MBA Graduates: | Y | Sales Trainees: | | Music: | | Systems Integration: | | Training: | Y | Scientists/Research: | |
| | | Advertising Pros.: | Y | Broadcasting: | | Consulting/Other: | | Health Care: | | Petroleum/Chemicals: | |
| | | | | Other: | | | | Consulting: | | Math/Other: | |

## TYPES OF BUSINESS:

Wireless Data Products
Deaf & Speech-Impaired Communications Systems

## BRANDS/DIVISIONS/AFFILIATES:

i711.com
Go.Web
Insight Cinema
Wireless Toolkit
T-Mobile
Verizon TRS
Hands On Video Relay Services

## CONTACTS: *Note: Officers with more than one job title may be intentionally listed here more than once.*

Dan Luis, CEO
John Ferron, COO
John Ferron, CFO
Joe Karp, VP-Mktg.
Jesse Odom, CTO
Mark Stern, VP-Product Mgmt. & Accessible Comm. Svcs.
Aaron Dobrinsky, Chmn.

**Phone:** 201-996-1717 **Fax:** 201-996-1772
**Toll-Free:**
**Address:** 433 Hackensack Ave., 3rd Fl., Hackensack, NJ 07601 US

## GROWTH PLANS/SPECIAL FEATURES:

GoAmerica, Inc. is a communications service provider, offering solutions primarily for consumers who are deaf, hard of hearing or speech-impaired. The firm's revenue is derived from wireless subscription services and from equipment and commissions associated with the sale of wireless handheld services. Its wireless subscription plans operate over the T-Mobile wireless data network and consist of two offerings, the resale of recurring monthly data-only services and the value-added Wireless Toolkit, which includes services such as AAA roadside assistance, TTY/TDD messaging and access to Insight Cinema's captioned movie information. Additionally, the firm offers wireless data products to consumer and enterprise markets through Go.Web, which allows secure wireless connections. GoAmerica also offers i711.com services, which enable people who are deaf or hard of hearing to call and 'converse' with hearing parties by using a computer, wireless handheld device or similar unit, though an operator that intercepts text to voice and vice versa. The firm sells its wireless devices directly to customers and indirectly through sub-dealers. GoAmerica has a dealer agreement with T-Mobile whereby the firm sells devices and earns a commission from T-Mobile upon activation of the device with an associated service rate plan. In 2008, GoAmerica acquired the assets of the Verizon Telecommunications Relay Services division, a leading provider of relay services; and completed a merger with Hands On Video Relay Services, a California-based provider of video relay and interpreting services. The combined company has five lines of business: Internet Text Relay Services; Video Relay Services; Community Interpreting Services; Wireless Devices and Services; and State Telecommunications Relay Services.

## FINANCIALS: **Sales and profits are in thousands of dollars—add 000 to get the full amount. 2008 Note: Financial information for 2008 was not available for all companies at press time.**

| | | |
|---|---|---|
| 2008 Sales: $ | 2008 Profits: $ | **U.S. Stock Ticker: GOAM** |
| 2007 Sales: $18,625 | 2007 Profits: $-3,750 | **Int'l Ticker:** Int'l Exchange: |
| 2006 Sales: $12,776 | 2006 Profits: $-1,960 | Employees: 393 |
| 2005 Sales: $4,931 | 2005 Profits: $-4,372 | Fiscal Year Ends: 12/31 |
| 2004 Sales: $6,029 | 2004 Profits: $-4,444 | Parent Company: |

## SALARIES/BENEFITS:

| | | | | |
|---|---|---|---|---|
| Pension Plan: | ESOP Stock Plan: | Profit Sharing: | Top Exec. Salary: $200,000 | Bonus: $ |
| Savings Plan: | Stock Purch. Plan: | | Second Exec. Salary: $165,000 | Bonus: $ |

## OTHER THOUGHTS:

**Apparent Women Officers or Directors:**
**Hot Spot for Advancement for Women/Minorities:**

## LOCATIONS: ("Y" = Yes)

| West: | Southwest: | Midwest: | Southeast: | Northeast: | International: |
|---|---|---|---|---|---|
| | | | | Y | |

# GOLFSMITH INTERNATIONAL HOLDINGS INC

**www.golfsmith.com**

**Industry Group Code:** 451110E **Ranks within this company's industry group:** Sales: 1 Profits: 1

| Management: | | Sales/Marketing: | | Liberal Arts: | | Information Systems: | | Professionals: | | Technical/Scientific: | |
|---|---|---|---|---|---|---|---|---|---|---|---|
| Mgmt. Trainees: | Y | Mktg. Professionals: | Y | Gen. Writing/Editing: | Y | Info. Management: | Y | Finance/Accounting: | Y | Engineers, Elec.: | |
| Experienced Mgmt.: | Y | Retail Sales: | Y | Technical Writing: | | Software Dev.: | Y | Law: | Y | Engineers, Other: | |
| Int'l Business: | Y | Commercial/Industrial: | | Graphic Arts/Photog.: | Y | Hardware Dev.: | | HR/Other: | Y | Health/Lab: | |
| MBA Graduates: | Y | Sales Trainees: | Y | Music: | | Systems Integration: | | Training: | Y | Scientists/Research: | |
| | | Advertising Pros.: | Y | Broadcasting: | | Consulting/Other: | | Health Care: | | Petroleum/Chemicals: | |
| | | | | Other: | | | | Consulting: | | Math/Other: | |

## TYPES OF BUSINESS:

Golf Equipment Manufacturing
Retail Sales
Catalog Publication
Tennis Equipment
Used Golf and Tennis Equipment

## BRANDS/DIVISIONS/AFFILIATES:

Golfsmith International, Inc.
Lynx
Zevo
Snake Eyes
Golfsmith
Killer Bee
Clubmaker Magazine
Don Sherwood Golf & Tennis

## CONTACTS: *Note: Officers with more than one job title may be intentionally listed here more than once.*

Martin E. Hanaka, CEO
Martin E. Hanaka, Pres.
Virginia Bunte, CFO/Sr. VP
Matthew Corey, VP-Mktg. & Brand
Gillian Felix, Sr. VP-Human Resources & Guest Experience
Jeff Sheets, VP-R&D
Andrew Spratt, VP-Info. Svcs.
Fred Quandt, Sr. VP-Merch.
R. Scott Wood, General Counsel/Sec.
Joseph J. Kester, VP-Field Oper.
Michael Polishook, VP-Sales & New Bus. Dev.
Virginia Bunte, Treas.
David Lowe, VP-Brands & Golf Instruction
Adrian Gonzalez, VP-Store Admin. & Guest Experience
Martin E. Hanaka, Chmn.

**Phone:** 512-837-8810 **Fax:** 512-821-4191
**Toll-Free:** 800-813-6897
**Address:** 11000 North IH-35, Austin, TX 78753 US

## GROWTH PLANS/SPECIAL FEATURES:

Golfsmith International Holdings, Inc. is the parent company of Golfsmith International, Inc., a specialty retailer of golf and tennis equipment, apparel and accessories. The company expanded into the tennis category through its acquisition of six Don Sherwood Golf & Tennis stores and the subsequent introduction of tennis equipment, apparel, and accessories in the majority of its stores. The firm has a 40-year history as a catalog retailer, principally publishing Golfsmith Consumer Catalog, which targets the avid golfer, and Golfsmith Clubmaking Catalog, a specialty catalog for people who build their own clubs. Originally founded as a club components and custom club making company, Golfsmith continues to design and manufacture under the various brand names of Lynx, Zevo, Snake Eyes, Golfsmith and Killer Bee. The firm founded the Golf Clubmakers Association (GCA), the largest such organization in the golf industry. Golfsmith operates as an integrated multi-channel retailer and has 74 stores across the U.S. In the U.K., the firm sells its equipment through a commissioned sales force directly to retailers. Through most of Europe and parts of Asia, it sells its products through a network of agents, distributors and through its website. The company has 31 registered domain names that link to golfsmith.com. In 52 stores, the firm has an activity-based shopping environment, called GolfTEC Learning Centers, where customers can test the performance of golf clubs, obtain precision club-fitting through its SmartFit program and benefit from PGA-certified golf instruction. The company's stores and web site offer a proprietary credit card and product selection that features national brands, Golfsmith's products and pre-owned clubs. Most revenue, 77.4%, is generated in store, and the number of stores increased from 46 to 74 between 2006 and 2008.

The company offers employees medical and dental insurance; a cafeteria plan; a 401(k) plan; and life insurance.

## FINANCIALS: **Sales and profits are in thousands of dollars—add 000 to get the full amount. 2008 Note: Financial information for 2008 was not available for all companies at press time.**

| | | |
|---|---|---|
| 2008 Sales: $ | 2008 Profits: $ | **U.S. Stock Ticker: GOLF** |
| 2007 Sales: $388,157 | 2007 Profits: $-40,820 | **Int'l Ticker:** Int'l Exchange: |
| 2006 Sales: $357,890 | 2006 Profits: $-8,109 | Employees: 1,665 |
| 2005 Sales: $323,794 | 2005 Profits: $2,957 | Fiscal Year Ends: 12/31 |
| 2004 Sales: $296,202 | 2004 Profits: $-4,756 | Parent Company: |

## SALARIES/BENEFITS:

| | | | | |
|---|---|---|---|---|
| Pension Plan: | ESOP Stock Plan: | Profit Sharing: | Top Exec. Salary: $403,580 | Bonus: $ |
| Savings Plan: Y | Stock Purch. Plan: | | Second Exec. Salary: $207,239 | Bonus: $ |

## OTHER THOUGHTS:

**Apparent Women Officers or Directors**: 2
**Hot Spot for Advancement for Women/Minorities**: G

## LOCATIONS: ("Y" = Yes)

| West: | Southwest: | Midwest: | Southeast: | Northeast: | International: |
|---|---|---|---|---|---|
| Y | Y | Y | Y | Y | Y |

# GREAT AMERICAN FINANCIAL RESOURCES INC

www.gafri.com

**Industry Group Code:** 524113 **Ranks within this company's industry group:** Sales: Profits:

| Management: | | Sales/Marketing: | | Liberal Arts: | | Information Systems: | | Professionals: | | Technical/Scientific: | |
|---|---|---|---|---|---|---|---|---|---|---|---|
| Mgmt. Trainees: | | Mktg. Professionals: | Y | Gen. Writing/Editing: | Y | Info. Management: | Y | Finance/Accounting: | Y | Engineers, Elec.: | |
| Experienced Mgmt.: | Y | Retail Sales: | | Technical Writing: | Y | Software Dev.: | | Law: | Y | Engineers, Other: | |
| Int'l Business: | | Commercial/Industrial: | | Graphic Arts/Photog.: | | Hardware Dev.: | | HR/Other: | Y | Health/Lab: | |
| MBA Graduates: | Y | Sales Trainees: | Y | Music: | | Systems Integration: | | Training: | Y | Scientists/Research: | |
| | | Advertising Pros.: | Y | Broadcasting: | | Consulting/Other: | | Health Care: | Y | Petroleum/Chemicals: | |
| | | | | Other: | | | | Consulting: | | Math/Other: | Y |

## TYPES OF BUSINESS:

Retirement Insurance
Health Insurance
Supplemental Health Insurance
Short & Long Term Disability Insurance
Life Insurance

## BRANDS/DIVISIONS/AFFILIATES:

United Teacher Associates Insurance Co.
Loyal American Life Insurance Co.
Ceres Group, Inc.
American Financial Group Inc
Marketform Group Limited
Strategic Comp Holdings, LLC

## CONTACTS: *Note: Officers with more than one job title may be intentionally listed here more than once.*

S. Craig Lindner, CEO
Charles R. Scheper, COO
S. Craig Lindner, Pres.
Christopher P. Miliano, CFO/Exec. VP/Treas.
Tom Maxey, Chief Mktg. Officer/Exec. VP
Jeffry S. Wolverton, CIO
Mark F. Muething, General Counsel/Exec. VP/Sec.
Jeffrey G. Hester, Controller
Mathew T. Dutkiewicz, Exec. VP
John B. Berding, Exec. VP-Investments
Michael J. Prager, Exec. VP/Chief Actuary

**Phone:** 513-333-5300 **Fax:** 513-412-3777
**Toll-Free:** 888-497-8556
**Address:** 525 Vine St., Cincinnati, OH 45202 US

## GROWTH PLANS/SPECIAL FEATURES:

Great American Financial Resources, Inc. (GAFRI), a wholly-owned subsidiary of American Financial Group, Inc., markets retirement products, primarily fixed, indexed and variable annuities, and various forms of supplemental insurances. The company's principal annuities products are flexible premium deferred annuities and single premium deferred annuities. Annuities are long-term retirement savings instruments that benefit from income accruing on a tax-deferred basis. In addition to traditional fixed rate annuities and indexed-annuities, the firm offers variable annuities, in which the earnings credited to the policy vary based on the investment results of the underlying investment options chosen by the policyholder, generally without any guarantee of principal except in the case of death of the insured. Subsidiary United Teacher Associates Insurance Co. (UTA) offers a variety of supplemental insurance products and annuities through independent agents. UTA's principal health products include coverage for Medicare supplement, cancer and long-term care. Loyal American Life Insurance Co. offers a variety of supplemental health and life products. The principal products sold by Loyal include cancer, accidental injury, short-term disability and hospital indemnity. In September 2007, GAFRI was acquired by American Financial Group, Inc., which purchased the remaining interest it did not hold in GAFRI for about $225 million.

The company offers its employees medical dental and vision insurance; flexible spending accounts; short- and long-term disability insurance; life insurance; a retirement and savings plan; an employee stock purchase plan; an education financial assistance program; an employee assistance program; and a wellness program.

## FINANCIALS: **Sales and profits are in thousands of dollars—add 000 to get the full amount. 2008 Note: Financial information for 2008 was not available for all companies at press time.**

2008 Sales: $
2007 Sales: $
2006 Sales: $1,044,000
2005 Sales: $934,200
2004 Sales: $924,700

2008 Profits: $
2007 Profits: $
2006 Profits: $98,900
2005 Profits: $69,900
2004 Profits: $101,800

**U.S. Stock Ticker: Subsidiary**
**Int'l Ticker:** Int'l Exchange:
Employees: 1,500
Fiscal Year Ends:
Parent Company: AMERICAN FINANCIAL GROUP INC

## SALARIES/BENEFITS:

Pension Plan: Y ESOP Stock Plan: Profit Sharing: Top Exec. Salary: $525,020 Bonus: $425,865
Savings Plan: Y Stock Purch. Plan: Y Second Exec. Salary: $525,020 Bonus: $425,865

## OTHER THOUGHTS:

**Apparent Women Officers or Directors**: 1
**Hot Spot for Advancement for Women/Minorities**:

## LOCATIONS: ("Y" = Yes)

| West: | Southwest: | Midwest: | Southeast: | Northeast: | International: |
|---|---|---|---|---|---|
| | Y | Y | Y | Y | |

# GREAT LAKES CHEESE COMPANY INC

**www.greatlakescheese.com**

**Industry Group Code:** 311500 **Ranks within this company's industry group:** Sales: 1 Profits:

| **Management:** | | **Sales/Marketing:** | | **Liberal Arts:** | | **Information Systems:** | | **Professionals:** | | **Technical/Scientific:** | |
|---|---|---|---|---|---|---|---|---|---|---|---|
| Mgmt. Trainees: | | Mktg. Professionals: | Y | Gen. Writing/Editing: | | Info. Management: | Y | Finance/Accounting: | Y | Engineers, Elec.: | |
| Experienced Mgmt.: | Y | Retail Sales: | | Technical Writing: | | Software Dev.: | | Law: | Y | Engineers, Other: | |
| Int'l Business: | | Commercial/Industrial: | Y | Graphic Arts/Photog.: | | Hardware Dev.: | | HR/Other: | Y | Health/Lab: | |
| MBA Graduates: | Y | Sales Trainees: | Y | Music: | | Systems Integration: | | Training: | Y | Scientists/Research: | |
| | | Advertising Pros.: | Y | Broadcasting: | | Consulting/Other: | | Health Care: | | Petroleum/Chemicals: | |
| | | | | Other: | | | | Consulting: | | Math/Other: | |

## TYPES OF BUSINESS:

Dairy Products, Manufacturing

## BRANDS/DIVISIONS/AFFILIATES:

Empire Cheese
Great Lakes
Adams Reserve

## CONTACTS: *Note: Officers with more than one job title may be intentionally listed here more than once.*

Gary Vanic, CEO
Gary Vanic, Pres.
Russell Mullins, CFO
Hans Epprecht, Chmn.

| | |
|---|---|
| **Phone:** 440-834-2500 | **Fax:** 440-834-1002 |
| **Toll-Free:** | |
| **Address:** 17825 Great Lakes Pkwy., Hiram, OH 44234-1806 US | |

## GROWTH PLANS/SPECIAL FEATURES:

Great Lakes Cheese Company, Inc. is a privately owned cheese producer and distributor. The company, which was founded in 1958 by current company chairman Hans Epprecht in Cleveland, has since expanded to include cheese processing and manufacturing plants in Wisconsin and New York, as well as packaging plants in Utah and its 220,000-square-foot headquarters facility in Ohio. The firm also operates a facility in Cuba, NY that operates under the Empire Cheese brand name. In total, there are seven plants including the company's three super plants which are located Ohio, Utah and Wisconsin. Great Lakes Cheese offers a wide variety of cheese, including natural, processed and imported cheese including provolone's, mozzarellas, cheddars, colby's, swiss and Jack, as well as popular imported cheeses such as Danish havarti and blue, Holland gouda, Switzerland gruyere and boursin garlic. All products can be ordered to dairy (store brand), deli or foodservice specifications. Cheeses manufactured by the company are sold under a wide variety of private label store brands plus the Great Lakes and Adams Reserve names. Primary customers include supermarket chains, club stores, national foodservice accounts and foodservice distributors.

Great Lakes Cheese provides its employees with medical, dental and life insurance; long-term disability insurance; profit sharing; a 401(k) plan; an employee stock ownership plan; and an employee assistance program.

## FINANCIALS: **Sales and profits are in thousands of dollars—add 000 to get the full amount. 2008 Note: Financial information for 2008 was not available for all companies at press time.**

| | | |
|---|---|---|
| 2008 Sales: $ | 2008 Profits: $ | **U.S. Stock Ticker: Private** |
| 2007 Sales: $1,780,000 | 2007 Profits: $ | **Int'l Ticker:** Int'l Exchange: |
| 2006 Sales: $1,700,000 | 2006 Profits: $ | Employees: 1,800 |
| 2005 Sales: $ | 2005 Profits: $ | Fiscal Year Ends: 12/31 |
| 2004 Sales: $ | 2004 Profits: $ | Parent Company: |

## SALARIES/BENEFITS:

| | | | | |
|---|---|---|---|---|
| Pension Plan: | ESOP Stock Plan: Y | Profit Sharing: | Top Exec. Salary: $ | Bonus: $ |
| Savings Plan: Y | Stock Purch. Plan: | | Second Exec. Salary: $ | Bonus: $ |

## OTHER THOUGHTS:

**Apparent Women Officers or Directors:**
**Hot Spot for Advancement for Women/Minorities:**

## LOCATIONS: ("Y" = Yes)

| West: | Southwest: | Midwest: | Southeast: | Northeast: | International: |
|---|---|---|---|---|---|
| Y | | Y | | Y | |

# GREEN MOUNTAIN COFFEE ROASTERS INC

**www.greenmountaincoffee.com**

**Industry Group Code:** 311920 **Ranks within this company's industry group:** Sales: 1 Profits: 1

| Management: | | Sales/Marketing: | | Liberal Arts: | | Information Systems: | | Professionals: | | Technical/Scientific: | |
|---|---|---|---|---|---|---|---|---|---|---|---|
| Mgmt. Trainees: | Y | Mktg. Professionals: | Y | Gen. Writing/Editing: | | Info. Management: | Y | Finance/Accounting: | Y | Engineers, Elec.: | |
| Experienced Mgmt.: | Y | Retail Sales: | | Technical Writing: | | Software Dev.: | | Law: | Y | Engineers, Other: | |
| Int'l Business: | | Commercial/Industrial: | Y | Graphic Arts/Photog.: | Y | Hardware Dev.: | | HR/Other: | Y | Health/Lab: | |
| MBA Graduates: | Y | Sales Trainees: | Y | Music: | | Systems Integration: | | Training: | Y | Scientists/Research: | |
| | | Advertising Pros.: | Y | Broadcasting: | | Consulting/Other: | | Health Care: | | Petroleum/Chemicals: | |
| | | | | Other: | | | | Consulting: | | Math/Other: | |

## TYPES OF BUSINESS:

Coffee Manufacturing
Wholesale Coffee Distribution
Online & Direct Sales
Coffee Brewing Equipment
Specialty Coffee

## BRANDS/DIVISIONS/AFFILIATES:

Green Mountain Coffee Roasters
Newman's Own Organics
Keurig, Inc.
K-Cup
Cafe EXPRESS
PBS Blend

## CONTACTS: *Note: Officers with more than one job title may be intentionally listed here more than once.*

Larry Blanford, CEO
Scott McCreary, COO
Larry Blanford, Pres.
Frances Rathke, CFO
Kathryn S. Brooks, VP-Human Resources & Organizational Dev.
Frances Rathke, Sec.
Stephen J. Sabol, VP-Dev./Chmn.-Keurig, Inc.
Sandy Yusen, Dir.-Public Rel.
Kathleen Shaffer, Investor Svcs. Coordinator
Frances Rathke, Treas.
Michelle V. Stacy, Pres., Keurig, Inc.
Robert P. Stiller, Chmn.

**Phone:** 802-244-5621 **Fax:** 802-244-5436
**Toll-Free:** 800-545-2326
**Address:** 33 Coffee Ln., Waterbury, VT 05676 US

## GROWTH PLANS/SPECIAL FEATURES:

Green Mountain Coffee Roasters, Inc. (GMCR) is a leading company in the specialty coffee industry. Following the acquisition of Keurig, Inc., the firm operates two segments: Green Mountain Coffee (GMC) and Keurig. Both segments operate mainly in domestic wholesale and retail markets. GMC sells whole bean and ground coffee; coffee, hot cocoa and tea in K-Cups; Keurig single-cup brewers; and other accessories. GMC sells its products in six markets: Office coffee service, supermarkets, convenience stores, food service, consumer direct, and resellers. The majority of its sales come from wholesale customers in the U.S. GMC usually provides brewing and grinding equipment and maintenance to wholesale customers free of charge, and also offers consumers the Cafe EXPRESS coffee club, which offers member discounts and customized account profiles. Keurig sells its single-cup brewers; coffee, hot cocoa and tea in K-Cup to distributors for offices and hotels, and select retailers including club stores and department stores. Its products are produced by various suppliers, including GMC, Celestial Seasonings and Diedrich; and related accessories. Unlike GMC, Keurig also sells directly to consumers. GMCR sells over 100 coffee varieties under the Green Mountain Coffee Roasters and Newman's Own Organics brands. It roasts high-quality Arabica coffees and offers selections including single-origins, estates, certified organics, Fair Trade Certified coffees, brand-name products, proprietary blends and flavored coffees. In September 2008, the company agreed to acquire Tully's coffee brand and wholesale business from Tully's Coffee Corporation for $40.3 million. In November of the same year, GMCR brought single-cup brewers and K-Cups to grocery stores nationwide, increasing the availability of these products to 17,000 locations. The Classic, Keurig's new single-cup brewer is sold exclusively at grocery stores.

Employees are offered medical, dental and vision insurance; life and disability insurance; an employee assistance program; discounts on merchandise, pet, home and auto insurance; flexible spending accounts; and scholarship programs.

## FINANCIALS: Sales and profits are in thousands of dollars—add 000 to get the full amount. 2008 Note: Financial information for 2008 was not available for all companies at press time.

| | | |
|---|---|---|
| 2008 Sales: $500,277 | 2008 Profits: $22,299 | **U.S. Stock Ticker: GMCR** |
| 2007 Sales: $341,651 | 2007 Profits: $12,843 | **Int'l Ticker:** Int'l Exchange: |
| 2006 Sales: $225,323 | 2006 Profits: $8,443 | Employees: 1,152 |
| 2005 Sales: $161,536 | 2005 Profits: $8,956 | Fiscal Year Ends: 9/28 |
| 2004 Sales: $137,444 | 2004 Profits: $7,825 | Parent Company: |

## SALARIES/BENEFITS:

| | | | | |
|---|---|---|---|---|
| Pension Plan: | ESOP Stock Plan: | Profit Sharing: | Top Exec. Salary: $455,577 | Bonus: $282,105 |
| Savings Plan: Y | Stock Purch. Plan: Y | | Second Exec. Salary: $316,000 | Bonus: $198,000 |

## OTHER THOUGHTS:

**Apparent Women Officers or Directors**: 6
**Hot Spot for Advancement for Women/Minorities**: Y

## LOCATIONS: ("Y" = Yes)

| West: | Southwest: | Midwest: | Southeast: | Northeast: | International: |
|---|---|---|---|---|---|
| | | | | Y | |

Note: Financial information, benefits and other data can change quickly and may vary from those stated here.

# GREEN MOUNTAIN POWER CORPORATION

**www.gmpvt.com**

**Industry Group Code:** 221000A **Ranks within this company's industry group:** Sales: 10 Profits: 9

| Management: | | Sales/Marketing: | | Liberal Arts: | | Information Systems: | | Professionals: | | Technical/Scientific: | |
|---|---|---|---|---|---|---|---|---|---|---|---|
| Mgmt. Trainees: | | Mktg. Professionals: | Y | Gen. Writing/Editing: | | Info. Management: | Y | Finance/Accounting: | Y | Engineers, Elec.: | Y |
| Experienced Mgmt.: | Y | Retail Sales: | | Technical Writing: | | Software Dev.: | | Law: | Y | Engineers, Other: | Y |
| Int'l Business: | | Commercial/Industrial: | Y | Graphic Arts/Photog.: | | Hardware Dev.: | | HR/Other: | Y | Health/Lab: | |
| MBA Graduates: | Y | Sales Trainees: | Y | Music: | | Systems Integration: | | Training: | Y | Scientists/Research: | |
| | | Advertising Pros.: | | Broadcasting: | | Consulting/Other: | | Health Care: | | Petroleum/Chemicals: | Y |
| | | | | Other: | | | | Consulting: | | Math/Other: | |

## TYPES OF BUSINESS:

Utilities-Electric & Natural Gas
Hydroelectric Power Generation
Nuclear Power Generation
Wind Power Generation
Biomass Power Generation

## BRANDS/DIVISIONS/AFFILIATES:

Northern New England Energy Corporation
Vermont Electric Power Company
Entergy Vermont Yankee Nuclear LLC
Gaz Metro Limited Partnership

## CONTACTS: *Note: Officers with more than one job title may be intentionally listed here more than once.*

Mary G. Powell, CEO
Mary G. Powell, Pres.
Dawn D. Bugbee, CFO/VP
Donald J. Rendall, Jr., General Counsel/Corp. Sec./VP
Robert J. Griffin, VP-Power Supply & Risk Mgmt.
Walter S. Oakes, VP-Field Oper.
Nordahl L. Brue, Chmn.

| **Phone:** 802-864-5731 | **Fax:** 802-655-8419 |
|---|---|
| **Toll-Free:** | |
| **Address:** 163 Acorn Ln., Colchester, VT 05446 US | |

## GROWTH PLANS/SPECIAL FEATURES:

Green Mountain Power (GMP), a wholly-owned subsidiary of Gaz Metro Limited Partnership, is a century-old utility company that provides electricity and energy services and products based primarily on renewable fuels to approximately 92,000 retail electricity customers in Vermont, with a service area covering about a quarter of Vermont's population with 4,723 miles of wire. The company also sells electricity wholesale throughout New England and markets operations services to other utility companies in Vermont. GMP's major power source comes from a 620-megawatt nuclear generating plant, owned and operated by Entergy Vermont Yankee Nuclear LLC. Its transmission system is owned by Vermont Electric Power Company, of which it owns a 30% share holding. GMP is known as one of the few environmentally progressive utility companies, owning a total of eight hydroelectric generating stations and a wind generating facility. The firm is one of the nation's leading utilities for low sulfur dioxide and carbon dioxide emissions, low nitrogen oxide emissions and for the percentage of renewable energy with respect to the total mix of energy sources. In 2006, only 2.2% of the company's fuel mix was from fossil fuels, while 50.4% was from hydro, 43% was from nuclear, 4.3% was from wood and 0.1% was from wind. Constituent sectors in its industry base include computer assembly and components manufacturing (and other electronics manufacturing); granite fabrication; service enterprises such as government, insurance and tourism; and dairy farming. In March 2007, the Vermont Public Service Board approved the acquisition of GMP by a subsidiary of Gaz Metro Limited, the Vermont-based Northern New England Energy Corporation (NNEEC). The transaction was completed in April 2007.

## FINANCIALS: **Sales and profits are in thousands of dollars—add 000 to get the full amount. 2008 Note: Financial information for 2008 was not available for all companies at press time.**

| | | |
|---|---|---|
| 2008 Sales: $ | 2008 Profits: $ | **U.S. Stock Ticker: Subsidiary** |
| 2007 Sales: $247,380 | 2007 Profits: $10,142 | **Int'l Ticker:** Int'l Exchange: |
| 2006 Sales: $240,476 | 2006 Profits: $10,123 | Employees: 192 |
| 2005 Sales: $245,860 | 2005 Profits: $11,180 | Fiscal Year Ends: 12/31 |
| 2004 Sales: $228,816 | 2004 Profits: $11,584 | Parent Company: GAZ METRO LIMITED PARTNERSHIP |

## SALARIES/BENEFITS:

| | | | | |
|---|---|---|---|---|
| Pension Plan: Y | ESOP Stock Plan: | Profit Sharing: | Top Exec. Salary: $369,931 | Bonus: $168,256 |
| Savings Plan: Y | Stock Purch. Plan: Y | | Second Exec. Salary: $262,999 | Bonus: $119,728 |

## OTHER THOUGHTS:

**Apparent Women Officers or Directors**: 4
**Hot Spot for Advancement for Women/Minorities**: Y

## LOCATIONS: ("Y" = Yes)

| West: | Southwest: | Midwest: | Southeast: | Northeast: | International: |
|---|---|---|---|---|---|
| | | | | Y | |

Note: Financial information, benefits and other data can change quickly and may vary from those stated here.

# GTC BIOTHERAPEUTICS INC

www.gtc-bio.com

**Industry Group Code:** 325414 **Ranks within this company's industry group:** Sales: 5 Profits: 4

| Management: | | Sales/Marketing: | | Liberal Arts: | | Information Systems: | | Professionals: | | Technical/Scientific: | |
|---|---|---|---|---|---|---|---|---|---|---|---|
| Mgmt. Trainees: | | Mktg. Professionals: | Y | Gen. Writing/Editing: | | Info. Management: | Y | Finance/Accounting: | Y | Engineers, Elec.: | |
| Experienced Mgmt.: | Y | Retail Sales: | | Technical Writing: | Y | Software Dev.: | Y | Law: | Y | Engineers, Other: | |
| Int'l Business: | Y | Commercial/Industrial: | Y | Graphic Arts/Photog.: | | Hardware Dev.: | | HR/Other: | Y | Health/Lab: | Y |
| MBA Graduates: | Y | Sales Trainees: | Y | Music: | | Systems Integration: | | Training: | Y | Scientists/Research: | Y |
| | | Advertising Pros.: | | Broadcasting: | | Consulting/Other: | | Health Care: | Y | Petroleum/Chemicals: | Y |
| | | | | Other: | | | | Consulting: | | Math/Other: | Y |

## TYPES OF BUSINESS:

Recombinant Proteins
Drugs-Anticoagulants
Transgenic Animals

## BRANDS/DIVISIONS/AFFILIATES:

Atryn
PharmAthene, Inc.
Merrimack Pharmaceuticals, Inc.
OVATION Pharmaceuticals, Inc.

## CONTACTS: *Note: Officers with more than one job title may be intentionally listed here more than once.*

Geoffrey F. Cox, CEO
Geoffrey F. Cox, Pres.
John B. Green, CFO
Harry M. Meade, Sr. VP-R&D
Daniel S. Woloshen, General Counsel/Sr. VP
Gregory Liposky, Sr. VP-Oper.
Ashley Lawton, VP-Bus. Dev.
Thomas E. Newberry, VP-Corp. Comm.
John B. Green, Sr. VP-Finance
Carol A. Ziomek, VP-Dev.
Suzanne Groet, VP-Therapeutic Protein Dev.
Richard A. Scotland, Sr. VP-Regulatory Affairs
Geoffrey F. Cox, Chmn.

| **Phone:** 508-620-9700 | **Fax:** 508-370-3797 |
|---|---|
| **Toll-Free:** | |
| **Address:** 175 Crossing Blvd., Framingham, MA 01702 US | |

## GROWTH PLANS/SPECIAL FEATURES:

GTC Biotherapeutics, Inc. (GTC) applies transgenic technology to develop recombinant proteins for human therapeutic uses. The company uses transgenic animals that express specific recombinant proteins in their milk. The firm generates transgenic animals through microinjection and nuclear transfer, and it expects to rely primarily on nuclear transfer techniques in new program development work. GTC uses goats in most of its commercial development programs due to the relatively short gestation times and relatively high milk production volume of the animals. The company's leading product is ATryn for patients with hereditary antithrombin deficiency undergoing surgical procedures. Antithrombin is an important protein found in the bloodstream with anticoagulant and anti-inflammatory properties. The drug is currently under application for a Biologics License for use in hereditary antithrombin deficient patients in the U.S., while it has been approved for use in the European Union. It is also in clinical trials for disseminated intravascular coagulation, which is an acquired deficiency of antithrombin that occurs in sepsis. The company is also using transgenic methods to produce monoclonal antibodies (MAbs), including potential therapeutic and follow-on biologics. Other transgenic projects currently under development include a recombinant human coagulation factor for the treatment of hemophilia; a second recombinant human coagulation factor for type B hemophilia; and an elastase inhibitor to treat emphysema and several other respiratory disorders. Through partnership programs, the firm is also developing treatments for exposure to nerve gas, with PharmAthene, Inc.; and human alpha-fetoprotein, currently being evaluated for treatment of rheumatoid arthritis and psoriasis, with Merrimack Pharmaceuticals, Inc. In June 2008, GTC entered an agreement with OVATION Pharmaceuticals, Inc. for the development and marketing of ATryn in the U.S.

GTC offers its employees tuition reimbursement, heath, dental and life insurance, stock options and a 401(k) investment plan.

## FINANCIALS: **Sales and profits are in thousands of dollars—add 000 to get the full amount. 2008 Note: Financial information for 2008 was not available for all companies at press time.**

| | | |
|---|---|---|
| 2008 Sales: $ | 2008 Profits: $ | **U.S. Stock Ticker: GTCB** |
| 2007 Sales: $13,896 | 2007 Profits: $-36,321 | **Int'l Ticker:** Int'l Exchange: |
| 2006 Sales: $6,128 | 2006 Profits: $-33,345 | Employees: 167 |
| 2005 Sales: $4,152 | 2005 Profits: $-30,112 | Fiscal Year Ends: 1/01 |
| 2004 Sales: $6,626 | 2004 Profits: $-29,493 | Parent Company: |

## SALARIES/BENEFITS:

| | | | | |
|---|---|---|---|---|
| Pension Plan: | ESOP Stock Plan: | Profit Sharing: | Top Exec. Salary: $480,000 | Bonus: $15,393 |
| Savings Plan: Y | Stock Purch. Plan: Y | | Second Exec. Salary: $306,342 | Bonus: $5,986 |

## OTHER THOUGHTS:

**Apparent Women Officers or Directors**: 2
**Hot Spot for Advancement for Women/Minorities**: Y

## LOCATIONS: ("Y" = Yes)

| West: | Southwest: | Midwest: | Southeast: | Northeast: | International: |
|---|---|---|---|---|---|
| | | | | Y | |

Note: Financial information, benefits and other data can change quickly and may vary from those stated here.

# HACKETT GROUP (THE)

**www.thehackettgroup.com**

**Industry Group Code:** 541512 **Ranks within this company's industry group:** Sales: 2 Profits: 2

| Management: | | Sales/Marketing: | | Liberal Arts: | | Information Systems: | | Professionals: | | Technical/Scientific: | |
|---|---|---|---|---|---|---|---|---|---|---|---|
| Mgmt. Trainees: | | Mktg. Professionals: | Y | Gen. Writing/Editing: | | Info. Management: | Y | Finance/Accounting: | Y | Engineers, Elec.: | |
| Experienced Mgmt.: | Y | Retail Sales: | | Technical Writing: | Y | Software Dev.: | Y | Law: | Y | Engineers, Other: | |
| Int'l Business: | Y | Commercial/Industrial: | | Graphic Arts/Photog.: | | Hardware Dev.: | | HR/Other: | Y | Health/Lab: | |
| MBA Graduates: | Y | Sales Trainees: | Y | Music: | | Systems Integration: | | Training: | Y | Scientists/Research: | |
| | | Advertising Pros.: | | Broadcasting: | | Consulting/Other: | Y | Health Care: | | Petroleum/Chemicals: | |
| | | | | Other: | Y | | | Consulting: | Y | Math/Other: | |

## TYPES OF BUSINESS:

E-Business Consulting
Strategic Planning
Database Development
Custom Applications
Performance Measurement
Technology Integration
Application Maintenance
Return On Investment

## BRANDS/DIVISIONS/AFFILIATES:

Mind~Share
Hackett Group (The)
AnswerThink Inc

## CONTACTS:

*Note: Officers with more than one job title may be intentionally listed here more than once.*

Ted A. Fernandez, CEO
David N. Dungan, COO/Vice Chmn.
Robert A. Ramirez, CFO
Gary Baker, Dir.-Comm.
Robert A. Ramirez, Exec. VP-Finance
Ted A. Fernandez, Chmn.

**Phone:** 305-375-8005 **Fax:** 305-379-8810
**Toll-Free:** 866-442-2538
**Address:** 1001 Brickell Bay Dr., 30 Floor, Miami, FL 33131 US

## GROWTH PLANS/SPECIAL FEATURES:

The Hackett Group, Inc. (HGI), formerly AnswerThink, Inc., is a leading business and technology consulting firm that focuses on providing performance measurement, business transformation, business applications, technology integration and offshore application maintenance and support. The company changed its name in January 2008 to better align itself with its subsidiary, The Hackett Group, a strategic advisory firm focusing on best practice research, benchmarking, business transformation and working capital management services. HGI is one of the world's largest end-to-end e-business solutions providers, with offices throughout the world including countries such as the U.S., France, the U.K., Germany, the Netherlands, India and Australia. The firm's services include advisory programs, benchmarking, business transformation, working capital, business applications and business intelligence implementation. With strategic and functional knowledge in finance, human resources, information technology (IT), procurement, supply chain management, corporate services, customer service and sales and marketing, HGI provides its services to industries including automotive, consumer goods, financial services, technology, life sciences, manufacturing, media, entertainment, retail, telecommunications, transportation and utilities. The company focuses on long-term client relationships with Global 2000 firms and other sophisticated strategic buyers of business and IT consulting services. Although virtually all of HGI's advisors and consultants have the ability to and are expected to contribute to new revenue opportunities, its primary internal business development resources are comprised of the leadership team and senior directors; the sales organization; business development associates; and the delivery organization. The company's management control systems are comprised of various accounting, billing, financial reporting, human resources, marketing and resource allocation systems, many of which are integrated with its knowledge management system, Mind~Share.

## FINANCIALS:

**Sales and profits are in thousands of dollars—add 000 to get the full amount. 2008 Note: Financial information for 2008 was not available for all companies at press time.**

| | | |
|---|---|---|
| 2008 Sales: $ | 2008 Profits: $ | **U.S. Stock Ticker: HCKT** |
| 2007 Sales: $177,008 | 2007 Profits: $8,995 | **Int'l Ticker:** Int'l Exchange: |
| 2006 Sales: $180,555 | 2006 Profits: $-5,048 | Employees: 800 |
| 2005 Sales: $163,318 | 2005 Profits: $ 604 | Fiscal Year Ends: 12/31 |
| 2004 Sales: $143,547 | 2004 Profits: $- 148 | Parent Company: |

## SALARIES/BENEFITS:

| | | | | |
|---|---|---|---|---|
| Pension Plan: | ESOP Stock Plan: | Profit Sharing: | Top Exec. Salary: $750,000 | Bonus: $750,000 |
| Savings Plan: Y | Stock Purch. Plan: | | Second Exec. Salary: $420,000 | Bonus: $540,280 |

## OTHER THOUGHTS:

**Apparent Women Officers or Directors**:
**Hot Spot for Advancement for Women/Minorities**:

## LOCATIONS: ("Y" = Yes)

| West: | Southwest: | Midwest: | Southeast: | Northeast: | International: |
|---|---|---|---|---|---|
| Y | Y | Y | Y | Y | Y |

# HAEMONETICS CORPORATION

www.haemonetics.com

**Industry Group Code:** 339113 **Ranks within this company's industry group:** Sales: 6 Profits: 3

| Management: | | Sales/Marketing: | | Liberal Arts: | | Information Systems: | | Professionals: | | Technical/Scientific: | |
|---|---|---|---|---|---|---|---|---|---|---|---|
| Mgmt. Trainees: | | Mktg. Professionals: | Y | Gen. Writing/Editing: | | Info. Management: | Y | Finance/Accounting: | Y | Engineers, Elec.: | Y |
| Experienced Mgmt.: | Y | Retail Sales: | | Technical Writing: | Y | Software Dev.: | Y | Law: | Y | Engineers, Other: | Y |
| Int'l Business: | Y | Commercial/Industrial: | Y | Graphic Arts/Photog.: | | Hardware Dev.: | Y | HR/Other: | Y | Health/Lab: | Y |
| MBA Graduates: | Y | Sales Trainees: | Y | Music: | | Systems Integration: | | Training: | Y | Scientists/Research: | Y |
| | | Advertising Pros.: | | Broadcasting: | | Consulting/Other: | | Health Care: | Y | Petroleum/Chemicals: | |
| | | | | Other: | | | | Consulting: | | Math/Other: | Y |

## TYPES OF BUSINESS:

Equipment-Blood-Recovery Systems
Surgical Blood Salvage Equipment
Blood Component Therapy Equipment
Automated Blood Collection Equipment

## BRANDS/DIVISIONS/AFFILIATES:

PCS System
MCS System
ACS System
Cell Saver System
OrthoPAT System
cardioPAT System
SmartSuction System
Cymbal System

## CONTACTS: *Note: Officers with more than one job title may be intentionally listed here more than once.*

Brad Nutter, CEO
Brian Concannon, COO
Christopher Lindop, CFO
Peter Allen, Chief Mktg. Officer
Joseph Forish, VP-Human Resources
Robert Ebbeling, VP-Tech. Oper.
William Granville, VP-Worldwide Mfg.
James O'Shaughnessy, General Counsel
Christopher Lindop, VP-Bus. Dev.
Lisa Lopez, VP-Corp. Affairs
Susan Hanlon, VP-Finance
Peter Allen, Pres., Donor Div.
Dottie Barr, Mgr.-ERP Program
Alec Bobroff, VP-Blood Management Solutions
Jan Conneely, VP/Gen. Mgr.-Arryx
Brad Nutter, Chmn.
Remi Corlin, Pres., APAC
Mark Beucler, VP/Gen. Mgr.-Global Distribution

**Phone:** 781-848-7100 **Fax:** 781-356-3558
**Toll-Free:** 800-225-5242
**Address:** 400 Wood Rd., Braintree, MA 02184-9114 US

## GROWTH PLANS/SPECIAL FEATURES:

Haemonetics Corporation manufactures automated systems for the collection, processing and surgical salvage of blood. Haemonetics' customers include hospitals, commercial plasma fractionators and national health organizations in 50 countries. The company's blood donor products include: PCS brand plasma systems, automating the collection of plasma from paid donors; the MCS brand blood bank system, automating the collection of platelets from volunteer donors; and the ACS brand blood bank system, automating the process used to freeze, thaw and wash red blood cells. Haemonetics' patient products include the Cell Saver, OrthoPAT and cardioPAT brand blood salvage systems, which collect blood lost during or after surgery for transfusion; and the SmartSuction family of products used to clear the surgical field. The company's software and services division principally provides support to its donor division customers. The company's subsidiary Arryx, Inc.'s proprietary technology uses light to move and manipulate small objects. In 2007, Haemonetics: announced the launch of its Cymbal system, a new mobile blood collection system; acquired Infonale, a developer of information technology software and consulting services for optimizing hospital blood use; formed a new subsidiary, Haemonetics Software Solutions, Inc., to provide information technology solutions to the blood and plasma collection industries; and acquired Haemoscope Corp.'s TEG Thrombelastograph Hemostasis Analyzer business. In January 2008, Haemonetics announced a new software module in its blood bank management suite. In February 2008, Arryx added the HOTkit Complete Holo-Tweezers Solution to its proprietary Holographic Optical Trapping product line. In March 2008, the company announced the addition of eLynx, a paperless data capture and temporary storage system, to its software suite.

Haemonetics offers its employees an on-site child care center, a flexible spending program, a tuition reimbursement/educational assistance plan, employee assistance programs, a referral bonus program, a wellness program, company sponsored events and medical, dental and vision coverage.

## FINANCIALS: **Sales and profits are in thousands of dollars—add 000 to get the full amount. 2008 Note: Financial information for 2008 was not available for all companies at press time.**

| | | |
|---|---|---|
| 2008 Sales: $516,440 | 2008 Profits: $51,980 | **U.S. Stock Ticker: HAE** |
| 2007 Sales: $449,607 | 2007 Profits: $49,109 | **Int'l Ticker:** Int'l Exchange: |
| 2006 Sales: $419,733 | 2006 Profits: $69,076 | Employees: 1,875 |
| 2005 Sales: $383,600 | 2005 Profits: $39,600 | Fiscal Year Ends: 3/31 |
| 2004 Sales: $364,229 | 2004 Profits: $29,320 | Parent Company: |

## SALARIES/BENEFITS:

| | | | | |
|---|---|---|---|---|
| Pension Plan: | ESOP Stock Plan: | Profit Sharing: | Top Exec. Salary: $520,000 | Bonus: $308,048 |
| Savings Plan: Y | Stock Purch. Plan: Y | | Second Exec. Salary: $400,105 | Bonus: $114,234 |

## OTHER THOUGHTS:

**Apparent Women Officers or Directors**: 5
**Hot Spot for Advancement for Women/Minorities**: Y

## LOCATIONS: ("Y" = Yes)

| West: | Southwest: | Midwest: | Southeast: | Northeast: | International: |
|---|---|---|---|---|---|
| | | | | Y | Y |

# HAHN AUTOMOTIVE WAREHOUSE INC

www.hahnauto.com

**Industry Group Code:** 423120 **Ranks within this company's industry group:** Sales: 2 Profits:

| Management: | | Sales/Marketing: | | Liberal Arts: | | Information Systems: | | Professionals: | | Technical/Scientific: | |
|---|---|---|---|---|---|---|---|---|---|---|---|
| Mgmt. Trainees: | Y | Mktg. Professionals: | Y | Gen. Writing/Editing: | | Info. Management: | Y | Finance/Accounting: | Y | Engineers, Elec.: | |
| Experienced Mgmt.: | Y | Retail Sales: | Y | Technical Writing: | | Software Dev.: | | Law: | Y | Engineers, Other: | |
| Int'l Business: | | Commercial/Industrial: | | Graphic Arts/Photog.: | Y | Hardware Dev.: | | HR/Other: | Y | Health/Lab: | |
| MBA Graduates: | Y | Sales Trainees: | Y | Music: | | Systems Integration: | | Training: | Y | Scientists/Research: | |
| | | Advertising Pros.: | Y | Broadcasting: | | Consulting/Other: | | Health Care: | | Petroleum/Chemicals: | |
| | | | | Other: | | | | Consulting: | | Math/Other: | |

## TYPES OF BUSINESS:

Auto Parts, Retail Stores
Auto Parts, Wholesale Distribution
Auto Repair Instruction & Publication

## BRANDS/DIVISIONS/AFFILIATES:

Advantage Auto Stores
Genuine Auto Parts
University of Auto Value Installer Training Guide
Auto Value Service Center Program
UCI Warehouse Distributors
Auto Value
Meisenzahl Auto Parts
NU-WAY Auto Parts

## CONTACTS: *Note: Officers with more than one job title may be intentionally listed here more than once.*

Eli N. Futerman, Co-CEO/Co-Pres.
Daniel J. Chessin, Co-Pres./Co-CEO
Albert J. Van Erp, CFO
Albert J. Van Erp, VP-Finance

| | |
|---|---|
| **Phone:** 585-235-1595 | **Fax:** 585-235-8615 |
| **Toll-Free:** | |
| **Address:** 415 W. Main St., Rochester, NY 14608 US | |

## GROWTH PLANS/SPECIAL FEATURES:

Hahn Automotive sells automotive aftermarket products to commercial service establishments on a regional basis. Its business is conducted through nine full-service distribution centers and 22 pick-up warehouses to 15 states in the Northeastern and Midwestern U.S. The company also operates an accessory warehouse in New York under the RAAC brand. To complement its distribution centers, Hahn Automotive also operates 80 retail locations under the Advantage Auto Stores and Genuine Auto Parts brands; these locations sell to both professional dealers and do-it-yourself individuals. The company purchases nearly 150,000 automotive aftermarket stock keeping units (SKUs), consisting predominately of nationally branded automotive hard parts, as well as maintenance items, accessories and private-label products, from manufacturers. Hahn Automotive is a member of the Auto Value group, a collection of aftermarket automotive companies, for marketing and support. As a member of the Auto Value group, the stores are affiliated with over 100 distribution centers and more than 1,700 stores throughout North America, including Canada and Mexico. Advantage Auto also supplies its customers with its University of Auto Value Installer Training Guide, which has information on hundreds of publications, clinics, videos and workshops across the country. In addition, the group offers customized marketing assistance, as well as its Auto Value Service Center Program, which provides Auto Value signage, on-hold messaging, installer uniforms, the 1-800 Service Center Locator Service and equipment leasing programs. In October 2007, the firm acquired Prime Automotive Parts Co., Inc., an automotive aftermarket warehouse distributor based in New York, New Jersey and Connecticut.

## FINANCIALS: **Sales and profits are in thousands of dollars—add 000 to get the full amount. 2008 Note: Financial information for 2008 was not available for all companies at press time.**

| | | |
|---|---|---|
| 2008 Sales: $ | 2008 Profits: $ | **U.S. Stock Ticker: Private** |
| 2007 Sales: $140,300 | 2007 Profits: $ | **Int'l Ticker:** Int'l Exchange: |
| 2006 Sales: $ | 2006 Profits: $ | Employees: 1,100 |
| 2005 Sales: $ | 2005 Profits: $ | Fiscal Year Ends: 9/30 |
| 2004 Sales: $ | 2004 Profits: $ | Parent Company: |

## SALARIES/BENEFITS:

| | | | | |
|---|---|---|---|---|
| Pension Plan: | ESOP Stock Plan: | Profit Sharing: | Top Exec. Salary: $ | Bonus: $ |
| Savings Plan: Y | Stock Purch. Plan: | | Second Exec. Salary: $ | Bonus: $ |

## OTHER THOUGHTS:

**Apparent Women Officers or Directors:**
**Hot Spot for Advancement for Women/Minorities:**

## LOCATIONS: ("Y" = Yes)

| West: | Southwest: | Midwest: | Southeast: | Northeast: | International: |
|---|---|---|---|---|---|
| | | Y | | Y | |

# HANOVER FOODS CORPORATION

www.hanoverfoods.com

**Industry Group Code:** 311000 **Ranks within this company's industry group:** Sales: 1 Profits:

| Management: | | Sales/Marketing: | | Liberal Arts: | | Information Systems: | | Professionals: | | Technical/Scientific: | |
|---|---|---|---|---|---|---|---|---|---|---|---|
| Mgmt. Trainees: | | Mktg. Professionals: | Y | Gen. Writing/Editing: | | Info. Management: | Y | Finance/Accounting: | Y | Engineers, Elec.: | |
| Experienced Mgmt.: | Y | Retail Sales: | | Technical Writing: | | Software Dev.: | | Law: | Y | Engineers, Other: | |
| Int'l Business: | Y | Commercial/Industrial: | Y | Graphic Arts/Photog.: | | Hardware Dev.: | | HR/Other: | Y | Health/Lab: | |
| MBA Graduates: | Y | Sales Trainees: | Y | Music: | | Systems Integration: | | Training: | Y | Scientists/Research: | |
| | | Advertising Pros.: | Y | Broadcasting: | | Consulting/Other: | | Health Care: | | Petroleum/Chemicals: | |
| | | | | Other: | | | | Consulting: | | Math/Other: | |

## TYPES OF BUSINESS:

Food Products-Manufacturing
Frozen Foods
Canned Vegetables
Snack Products
Agriculture

## BRANDS/DIVISIONS/AFFILIATES:

Hanover Farms
Bickel's Snack Foods
Bon Ton
Wege

## GROWTH PLANS/SPECIAL FEATURES:

Hanover Foods Corporation, founded in 1924, is a leading independent food processor. The company's products include canned and frozen vegetables; frozen meat products; frozen entrees; frozen soft pretzels; canned and frozen mushrooms; fresh foods; and snack food products. The firm distributes these items in the Eastern U.S. Hanover grows, processes and packages all of its products from start to finish, producing over 40 million cases of food per year. At the company's canning plant, located in Hanover, PA, vegetable, bean and pasta items are produced in seven- to 10-ounce sizes and are stored in cans and glass jars. Hanover produces its frozen soft pretzels and shelf-stable hard pretzels at its nearby sales building. The company recently acquired a tomato plant in California as well, which it expects to stabilize its tomato paste costs. It markets its products under the brand names Hanover, Hanover Farms, Bickel's Snack Foods, Bon Ton and Wege

## CONTACTS: *Note: Officers with more than one job title may be intentionally listed here more than once.*

John A. Warehime, CEO
John A. Warehime, Pres.
Gary T. Knisely, CFO/Exec. VP
Daniel E. Schuchart, VP-Sales
Gary T. Knisely, General Counsel/Corp. Sec.
Pietro D. Giraffa, Jr., Chief Acct. Officer/VP/Controller
Steven E. Robertson, Treas.
John A. Warehime, Chmn.
Alan T. Young, Sr. VP-Purchasing & Transportation

| | |
|---|---|
| **Phone:** 717-632-6000 | **Fax:** 717-637-2890 |
| **Toll-Free:** | |
| **Address:** 1486 York Rd., P.O. Box 334, Hanover, PA 17331 US | |

## FINANCIALS: **Sales and profits are in thousands of dollars—add 000 to get the full amount. 2008 Note: Financial information for 2008 was not available for all companies at press time.**

| | | |
|---|---|---|
| 2008 Sales: $ | 2008 Profits: $ | **U.S. Stock Ticker: Private** |
| 2007 Sales: $290,300 | 2007 Profits: $ | **Int'l Ticker:** Int'l Exchange: |
| 2006 Sales: $ | 2006 Profits: $ | Employees: 2,205 |
| 2005 Sales: $ | 2005 Profits: $ | Fiscal Year Ends: 5/31 |
| 2004 Sales: $318,028 | 2004 Profits: $11,441 | Parent Company: |

## SALARIES/BENEFITS:

| | | | | |
|---|---|---|---|---|
| Pension Plan: | ESOP Stock Plan: | Profit Sharing: | Top Exec. Salary: $773,950 | Bonus: $326,550 |
| Savings Plan: | Stock Purch. Plan: | | Second Exec. Salary: $255,256 | Bonus: $196,547 |

## OTHER THOUGHTS:

**Apparent Women Officers or Directors:**
**Hot Spot for Advancement for Women/Minorities:**

## LOCATIONS: ("Y" = Yes)

| West: | Southwest: | Midwest: | Southeast: | Northeast: | International: |
|---|---|---|---|---|---|
| Y | | | | Y | |

# HANSEN NATURAL

www.hansens.com

**Industry Group Code:** 312111 **Ranks within this company's industry group:** Sales: 1 Profits: 1

| Management: | | Sales/Marketing: | | Liberal Arts: | | Information Systems: | | Professionals: | | Technical/Scientific: | |
|---|---|---|---|---|---|---|---|---|---|---|---|
| Mgmt. Trainees: | Y | Mktg. Professionals: | Y | Gen. Writing/Editing: | | Info. Management: | Y | Finance/Accounting: | Y | Engineers, Elec.: | |
| Experienced Mgmt.: | Y | Retail Sales: | | Technical Writing: | | Software Dev.: | | Law: | Y | Engineers, Other: | |
| Int'l Business: | Y | Commercial/Industrial: | Y | Graphic Arts/Photog.: | Y | Hardware Dev.: | | HR/Other: | Y | Health/Lab: | |
| MBA Graduates: | Y | Sales Trainees: | Y | Music: | | Systems Integration: | | Training: | Y | Scientists/Research: | |
| | | Advertising Pros.: | Y | Broadcasting: | | Consulting/Other: | | Health Care: | | Petroleum/Chemicals: | |
| | | | | Other: | | | | Consulting: | | Math/Other: | |

## TYPES OF BUSINESS:

Beverages-Natural Sodas
Energy Drinks
Fruit Juice

## BRANDS/DIVISIONS/AFFILIATES:

Hansen's
Blue Sky
Java Monster
Monster Energy
Lost Energy
Fizzit
Junior Juice
Rumba

## CONTACTS: *Note: Officers with more than one job title may be intentionally listed here more than once.*

Rodney C. Sacks, CEO
Hilton H. Schlosberg, COO
Hilton H. Schlosberg, Pres.
Hilton H. Schlosberg, CFO
Linda Lopez, Dir.-Human Resources
Hilton H. Schlosberg, Corp. Sec./Vice Chmn.
Rodney C. Sacks, Chmn.

| | |
|---|---|
| **Phone:** 951-739-6200 | **Fax:** 951-739-6220 |
| **Toll-Free:** 800-426-7367 | |
| **Address:** 550 Monica Cir., Ste. 201, Corona, CA 92880 US | |

## GROWTH PLANS/SPECIAL FEATURES:

Hansen Natural is a holding company for Hansen Beverage Company (HBC), which develops, markets, sells and distributes naturally-made beverages, including natural sodas, fruit juices, juice drinks, energy drinks, dairy based coffee drinks, fruit juice smoothies, functional drinks, iced teas, lemonades, juice cocktails, children's multi-vitamin juice drinks, powdered drink mixes and non-carbonated lightly flavored energy waters. The company maintains several brands including Hansen's Natural Sodas; Energade; E2O Energy Water; Junior Juice; Monster Energy; Blue Sky; Fizzit; Lost Energy; Joker Mad Energy; Hansen's Energy Pro; Organic Juice Slam and Rumba. The firm outsources its manufacturing needs to third party bottlers and contract packers, whom Hansen supplies with juices, flavors, vitamins, minerals, nutrients, herbs, supplements, caps, labels, trays and ingredients. Bottling services are handled through contracts made with Southwest Canning and Packaging, Nor-Cal Beverage, Seven-Up Bottling and Southeast Atlantic Beverage, among others. Distribution levels vary from state to state and a limited range of products are marketed abroad in places like Japan, Korea, the Caribbean and Saudi Arabia. Domestic customers are usually retail and specialty chains, club stores, mass merchandisers, convenience chains, food service and full service beverage distributors and health food distributors. Major customers include Costco, Trader Joe's, Sam's Club, Vons, Wal-Mart, Safeway and Albertson's. In 2008, the firm signed several agreements which will allow distribution of Monster Energy Drinks in Mexico, Europe, Canada and selected U.S. territories.

## FINANCIALS: **Sales and profits are in thousands of dollars—add 000 to get the full amount. 2008 Note: Financial information for 2008 was not available for all companies at press time.**

| | | |
|---|---|---|
| 2008 Sales: $ | 2008 Profits: $ | **U.S. Stock Ticker: HANS** |
| 2007 Sales: $904,465 | 2007 Profits: $149,406 | **Int'l Ticker:** Int'l Exchange: |
| 2006 Sales: $605,774 | 2006 Profits: $97,949 | Employees: 904 |
| 2005 Sales: $348,886 | 2005 Profits: $62,776 | Fiscal Year Ends: 12/31 |
| 2004 Sales: $180,341 | 2004 Profits: $20,387 | Parent Company: |

## SALARIES/BENEFITS:

| | | | | |
|---|---|---|---|---|
| Pension Plan: | ESOP Stock Plan: | Profit Sharing: | Top Exec. Salary: $275,000 | Bonus: $125,000 |
| Savings Plan: Y | Stock Purch. Plan: | | Second Exec. Salary: $275,000 | Bonus: $125,000 |

## OTHER THOUGHTS:

**Apparent Women Officers or Directors:**
**Hot Spot for Advancement for Women/Minorities:**

## LOCATIONS: ("Y" = Yes)

| West: | Southwest: | Midwest: | Southeast: | Northeast: | International: |
|---|---|---|---|---|---|
| Y | | | | | |

# HARMONIC INC

www.harmonicinc.com

**Industry Group Code:** 334210 **Ranks within this company's industry group:** Sales: 3 Profits: 3

| Management: | | Sales/Marketing: | | Liberal Arts: | | Information Systems: | | Professionals: | | Technical/Scientific: | |
|---|---|---|---|---|---|---|---|---|---|---|---|
| Mgmt. Trainees: | | Mktg. Professionals: | Y | Gen. Writing/Editing: | Y | Info. Management: | Y | Finance/Accounting: | Y | Engineers, Elec.: | Y |
| Experienced Mgmt.: | Y | Retail Sales: | | Technical Writing: | Y | Software Dev.: | Y | Law: | Y | Engineers, Other: | Y |
| Int'l Business: | Y | Commercial/Industrial: | Y | Graphic Arts/Photog.: | | Hardware Dev.: | Y | HR/Other: | Y | Health/Lab: | |
| MBA Graduates: | Y | Sales Trainees: | Y | Music: | | Systems Integration: | Y | Training: | Y | Scientists/Research: | |
| | | Advertising Pros.: | | Broadcasting: | | Consulting/Other: | | Health Care: | | Petroleum/Chemicals: | |
| | | | | Other: | | | | Consulting: | | Math/Other: | |

## TYPES OF BUSINESS:

Networking Equipment
Video Stream Processing
Cable Edge & Access
Software

## BRANDS/DIVISIONS/AFFILIATES:

CLEARcut Studio
MAXLink
PWRLink
METROLink
GIGALight
DiviCom

## CONTACTS: *Note: Officers with more than one job title may be intentionally listed here more than once.*

Patrick Harshman, CEO
Patrick Harshman, Pres.
Robin N. Dickson, CFO
Nimrod Ben-Natan, VP-Product Mktg. Solutions & Strategy
Anne Lynch, VP-Human Resources
Neven Haltmayer, VP-R&D
Charles Bonasera, VP-Oper.
David Price, VP-Bus. Dev. & Mktg. Comm.
Mark E. Renfroe, VP-American Sales
David Trescot, VP-Rhozet Bus. Unit
Raymond Tse, VP-APAC Sales
Glen Sakata, VP-EMEA Sales
Anthony . Ley, Chmn.
Matthew Aden, VP-Worldwide Sales & Service

**Phone:** 408-542-2500 **Fax:** 408-542-2511
**Toll-Free:** 800-788-1330
**Address:** 549 Baltic Way, Sunnyvale, CA 94089 US

## GROWTH PLANS/SPECIAL FEATURES:

Harmonic, Inc. designs, manufactures and sells products and systems that enable network operators to efficiently deliver broadcast and on-demand video services that include digital video, video-on-demand (VOD), high definition television as well as high-speed Internet access and telephony. Sales of video processing solutions and edge and access systems to cable television operators account for the majority of the net sales. Harmonic provides technical support services to its customers worldwide. Its video processing solutions provide broadband operators with the ability to acquire a variety of signals from different sources, in different protocols, and to organize, manage and distribute this content to maximize use of the available bandwidth. Its edge products enable cable operators to deliver customized broadcast or narrowcast on-demand services to their subscribers. The firm's access products, which consist mainly of optical transmission products, node platforms and return path products, allow cable operators to deliver video, data and voice services over their networks. Harmonic sells its products to various broadband communication companies, which include Cablevision Systems, Charter Communications, Comcast, Cox Communications, EchoStar and Time Warner Cable in the U.S.; and Alcatel-Lucent, Astra Platform Services and Nokia-Siemens Networks internationally. In July 2007, Harmonic acquired Rhozet Corporation, which develops and markets software-based transcoding solutions that facilitate the creation of multi-format video. With this acquisition, Harmonic can deliver traditional video programming over the Internet and mobile devices. The acquisition also broadens Harmonic's customer base to encompass broadcast content creators and online video services providers.

Harmonic offers its employees a 401 (k) plan; an employee stock purchase plan; stock options; flexible spending accounts; life insurance; travel & accident insurance; a fitness center; public transportation benefits; 529 plans; employee assistance program; and health insurance, which includes medical, dental, vision and disability.

## FINANCIALS: **Sales and profits are in thousands of dollars—add 000 to get the full amount. 2008 Note: Financial information for 2008 was not available for all companies at press time.**

2008 Sales: $364,963
2007 Sales: $311,204
2006 Sales: $247,684
2005 Sales: $257,378
2004 Sales: $248,300

2008 Profits: $63,992
2007 Profits: $23,421
2006 Profits: $1,007
2005 Profits: $-5,731
2004 Profits: $1,600

**U.S. Stock Ticker: HLIT**
**Int'l Ticker:** Int'l Exchange:
Employees: 658
Fiscal Year Ends: 12/31
Parent Company:

## SALARIES/BENEFITS:

Pension Plan:
Savings Plan: Y
ESOP Stock Plan: Y
Stock Purch. Plan: Y
Profit Sharing:
Top Exec. Salary: $400,000 Bonus: $377,344
Second Exec. Salary: $330,000 Bonus: $233,482

## OTHER THOUGHTS:

**Apparent Women Officers or Directors:** 1
**Hot Spot for Advancement for Women/Minorities:**

## LOCATIONS: ("Y" = Yes)

| West: | Southwest: | Midwest: | Southeast: | Northeast: | International: |
|---|---|---|---|---|---|
| Y | | | | | Y |

# HARRIS STRATEX NETWORKS INC

www.harrisstratex.com

**Industry Group Code:** 334210 **Ranks within this company's industry group:** Sales: 2 Profits: 10

| Management: | | Sales/Marketing: | | Liberal Arts: | | Information Systems: | | Professionals: | | Technical/Scientific: | |
|---|---|---|---|---|---|---|---|---|---|---|---|
| Mgmt. Trainees: | | Mktg. Professionals: | Y | Gen. Writing/Editing: | Y | Info. Management: | Y | Finance/Accounting: | Y | Engineers, Elec.: | Y |
| Experienced Mgmt.: | Y | Retail Sales: | | Technical Writing: | Y | Software Dev.: | Y | Law: | Y | Engineers, Other: | Y |
| Int'l Business: | Y | Commercial/Industrial: | Y | Graphic Arts/Photog.: | | Hardware Dev.: | Y | HR/Other: | Y | Health/Lab: | |
| MBA Graduates: | Y | Sales Trainees: | Y | Music: | | Systems Integration: | Y | Training: | Y | Scientists/Research: | |
| | | Advertising Pros.: | | Broadcasting: | | Consulting/Other: | | Health Care: | | Petroleum/Chemicals: | |
| | | | | Other: | | | | Consulting: | | Math/Other: | |

## TYPES OF BUSINESS:

Wireless Transmission Systems

## BRANDS/DIVISIONS/AFFILIATES:

Stratex Networks, Inc.
Harris Corporation
Eclipse
TRuepoint
Constellation
Megastar
NetBoss
ProVision

## CONTACTS: *Note: Officers with more than one job title may be intentionally listed here more than once.*

Harald J. Braun, CEO
Thomas H. Waechter, COO
Harald J. Braun, Pres.
Sarah A. (Sally) Dudash, CFO/Principal Acct. Officer
Shaun McFall, VP-Mktg.
Stephen J. (Steve) Gilmore, VP-Human Resources
Richard Plane, CIO/VP-IT Svcs.
Paul A. Kennard, CTO/VP-Int'l Sales
John Koenig, VP-Prod. Line Mgmt.
Ed Hutton, VP-Eng.
Juan B. Otero, General Counsel/Corp. Sec.
Heinz Stumpe, VP-Global Oper.
Carol A. Goudey, Treas.
Meena Elliott, Associate General Counsel/Asst. Sec.
Charles D. Kissner, Chmn.
Jayne Leighton, VP-North America & Caribbean Sales & Svcs.

**Phone:** 919-767-3230 **Fax:** 919-767-3233
**Toll-Free:** 888-478-9669
**Address:** Research Triangle Park, 637 Davis Dr., Morrisville, NC 27560 US

## GROWTH PLANS/SPECIAL FEATURES:

Harris Stratex Networks, Inc. was formed through the combination of Stratex Networks, Inc. and Harris Corporation's Microwave Communications Division in January 2007, becoming a leading global independent supplier of turnkey wireless network solutions and comprehensive network management software. The firm serves all global markets, including mobile network operators, public safety agencies, private network operators, utility companies, transportation companies, government agencies and broadcasters. Harris Stratex's products include point-to-point digital microwave radio systems for mobile system access, backhaul, trunking and license-exempt applications, supporting new network deployments, network expansion and capacity upgrades. Its principal product families of licensed point-to-point microwave radios include Eclipse, a platform for nodal wireless transmission systems, and TRuepoint, a platform for high-performance point-to-point wireless communications. Constellation and Megastar are significant product families used for high-capacity trunking applications. Harris Stratex operates through three business segments: North America microwave, international microwave and network operations. The North America microwave segment, which generates roughly 43% of the firm's total revenue, delivers microwave radio products and services in North America primarily to the cellular backhaul and public safety segments. In the international microwave segment, which generates roughly 53% of its revenue, the firm primarily provides wireless systems to developing nations. Harris Stratex also sees high-capacity backhaul as another major opportunity for growth in the international microwave segment. The network operations segment, which generates roughly 4% of the company's revenue, offers a range of software-based network management solutions for network operators worldwide, from element management to turnkey, end-to-end network management and service assurance solutions for such communications and information networks as broadband, wireline, wireless and converged networks. Harris Stratex's NetBoss product line develops, designs, produces, sells and services network management systems for these applications. Other element management product families include ProVision and StarView.

## FINANCIALS: **Sales and profits are in thousands of dollars—add 000 to get the full amount. 2008 Note: Financial information for 2008 was not available for all companies at press time.**

| | | |
|---|---|---|
| 2008 Sales: $718,400 | 2008 Profits: $-11,900 | **U.S. Stock Ticker: HSTX** |
| 2007 Sales: $507,900 | 2007 Profits: $-17,900 | **Int'l Ticker:** Int'l Exchange: |
| 2006 Sales: $357,500 | 2006 Profits: $-35,800 | Employees: 1,410 |
| 2005 Sales: $310,400 | 2005 Profits: $-3,800 | Fiscal Year Ends: 6/30 |
| 2004 Sales: $157,300 | 2004 Profits: $-37,100 | Parent Company: |

## SALARIES/BENEFITS:

| | | | | |
|---|---|---|---|---|
| Pension Plan: | ESOP Stock Plan: | Profit Sharing: | Top Exec. Salary: $426,346 | Bonus: $126,000 |
| Savings Plan: | Stock Purch. Plan: | | Second Exec. Salary: $205,756 | Bonus: $45,528 |

## OTHER THOUGHTS:

**Apparent Women Officers or Directors**: 4
**Hot Spot for Advancement for Women/Minorities**: Y

## LOCATIONS: ("Y" = Yes)

| West: | Southwest: | Midwest: | Southeast: | Northeast: | International: |
|---|---|---|---|---|---|
| Y | Y | | Y | Y | Y |

# HARVARD PILGRIM HEALTH CARE INC

**www.harvardpilgrim.org**

**Industry Group Code:** 524114 **Ranks within this company's industry group:** Sales: 1 Profits: 3

| Management: | | Sales/Marketing: | | Liberal Arts: | | Information Systems: | | Professionals: | | Technical/Scientific: | |
|---|---|---|---|---|---|---|---|---|---|---|---|
| Mgmt. Trainees: | | Mktg. Professionals: | Y | Gen. Writing/Editing: | Y | Info. Management: | Y | Finance/Accounting: | Y | Engineers, Elec.: | |
| Experienced Mgmt.: | Y | Retail Sales: | | Technical Writing: | Y | Software Dev.: | | Law: | Y | Engineers, Other: | |
| Int'l Business: | | Commercial/Industrial: | Y | Graphic Arts/Photog.: | | Hardware Dev.: | | HR/Other: | Y | Health/Lab: | Y |
| MBA Graduates: | Y | Sales Trainees: | | Music: | | Systems Integration: | | Training: | Y | Scientists/Research: | |
| | | Advertising Pros.: | | Broadcasting: | | Consulting/Other: | | Health Care: | Y | Petroleum/Chemicals: | |
| | | | | Other: | | | | Consulting: | | Math/Other: | Y |

## TYPES OF BUSINESS:

Insurance-Medical & Health, HMOs & PPOs
Indemnity Insurance

## BRANDS/DIVISIONS/AFFILIATES:

Harvard Pilgrim Health Care of New England
HPHC Insurance Company
First Seniority
Medicare Enhance
HPHConnect
Health Plans, Inc.
Benefit Plan Management, Inc.

## CONTACTS: *Note: Officers with more than one job title may be intentionally listed here more than once.*

Charles D. Baker, CEO
Bruce M. Bullen, COO
Charles D. Baker, Pres.
James W. DuCharme, CFO
Vincent Capozzi, Sr. VP-Sales & Customer Svc.
Deborah A. Hicks, VP-Human Resources
Deborah A. Norton, CIO/Sr. VP-IT
Vicki Coates, VP-Benefits, Products & Market Performance
Laura S. Peabody, General Counsel/Sr. VP
Deborah A. Norton, Sr. VP-Oper.
David Cochran, Sr. VP-Strategic Dev.
Marie Montgomery, VP-Corp. Acct./Controller
Roberta Herman, Sr. VP/Chief Medical Officer
William R. Breidenbach, Pres., Health Plans, Inc.
Lynn A. Bowman, VP-Customer & Member Service
Beth-Ann Roberts, VP-Northern New England Oper.
Charles D. Baker, Chmn.

| | |
|---|---|
| **Phone:** 617-745-1000 | **Fax:** 617-509-7590 |
| **Toll-Free:** 888-888-4742 | |
| **Address:** 93 Worcester St., Wellesley, MA 02481 US | |

## GROWTH PLANS/SPECIAL FEATURES:

Harvard Pilgrim Health Care, Inc. is a not-for-profit health plan with approximately 1 million members and a network of more than 28,000 providers and 135 hospitals. The firm provides health coverage in Massachusetts and Maine, as well as in New Hampshire through its Harvard Pilgrim Health Care of New England subsidiary. In addition, the firm is the parent company of HPHC Insurance Company, an indemnity insurance company in Massachusetts and New Hampshire. The firm offers a variety of plan choices, including HMOs, PPOs and point-of-service plans. The company also enrolls Medicare beneficiaries through its First Seniority programs, as well as offering its HPHConnect web site for online benefits administration. Subsidiary Health Plans, Inc. specializes in administering customized self-insured or ASO (Administrative Services Only) plans for employers. Health Plans, Inc. is the largest third party administrator (TPA) in New England. Through a recently formed alliance with UnitedHealth Group, combining the company's network of doctors and hospitals with UnitedHealth's national network, the Harvard Pilgrim also offers a program for multi-site, multi-state employers that have a substantial number of employees in the company's region.

Harvard Pilgrim employee benefits include tuition reimbursement, an on-site fitness center, credit unions, employee discounts, adoption assistance, concierge services, mass transit subsidy, employee assistance, flexible spending accounts, medical and dental insurance, life insurance and disability coverage.

## FINANCIALS: **Sales and profits are in thousands of dollars—add 000 to get the full amount. 2008 Note: Financial information for 2008 was not available for all companies at press time.**

| | | |
|---|---|---|
| 2008 Sales: $ | 2008 Profits: $ | **U.S. Stock Ticker: Nonprofit** |
| 2007 Sales: $2,498,310 | 2007 Profits: $45,638 | **Int'l Ticker:** Int'l Exchange: |
| 2006 Sales: $2,488,095 | 2006 Profits: $70,536 | Employees: 1,400 |
| 2005 Sales: $2,235,843 | 2005 Profits: $73,807 | Fiscal Year Ends: 12/31 |
| 2004 Sales: $2,300,000 | 2004 Profits: $38,600 | Parent Company: |

## SALARIES/BENEFITS:

| | | | | |
|---|---|---|---|---|
| Pension Plan: | ESOP Stock Plan: | Profit Sharing: | Top Exec. Salary: $ | Bonus: $ |
| Savings Plan: Y | Stock Purch. Plan: | | Second Exec. Salary: $ | Bonus: $ |

## OTHER THOUGHTS:

**Apparent Women Officers or Directors**: 10
**Hot Spot for Advancement for Women/Minorities**: Y

## LOCATIONS: ("Y" = Yes)

| West: | Southwest: | Midwest: | Southeast: | Northeast: | International: |
|---|---|---|---|---|---|
| | | | | Y | |

# HCC INSURANCE HOLDINGS INC

www.hcc.com

**Industry Group Code:** 524126 **Ranks within this company's industry group:** Sales: 1 Profits: 1

| Management: | | Sales/Marketing: | | Liberal Arts: | | Information Systems: | | Professionals: | | Technical/Scientific: | |
|---|---|---|---|---|---|---|---|---|---|---|---|
| Mgmt. Trainees: | | Mktg. Professionals: | Y | Gen. Writing/Editing: | Y | Info. Management: | Y | Finance/Accounting: | Y | Engineers, Elec.: | |
| Experienced Mgmt.: | Y | Retail Sales: | | Technical Writing: | Y | Software Dev.: | | Law: | Y | Engineers, Other: | |
| Int'l Business: | Y | Commercial/Industrial: | Y | Graphic Arts/Photog.: | | Hardware Dev.: | | HR/Other: | Y | Health/Lab: | |
| MBA Graduates: | Y | Sales Trainees: | Y | Music: | | Systems Integration: | | Training: | Y | Scientists/Research: | |
| | | Advertising Pros.: | | Broadcasting: | | Consulting/Other: | | Health Care: | | Petroleum/Chemicals: | |
| | | | | Other: | | | | Consulting: | | Math/Other: | Y |

## TYPES OF BUSINESS:

Insurance, Direct Property & Casualty
Health Insurance
Offshore Energy Insurance
Aviation & Marine Insurance
Accident Insurance
Reinsurance
Consulting Services

## BRANDS/DIVISIONS/AFFILIATES:

Houston Casualty Company
HCC Insurance Company
HCC International Insurance Company
U.S. Specialty Insurance Company
HCC Life Insurance Company
Avemco Insurance Company
Professional Indemnity Agency
HCC Specialty Underwriters

## CONTACTS: *Note: Officers with more than one job title may be intentionally listed here more than once.*

Frank J. Bramanti, CEO
John N. Molbeck, Jr., COO
John N. Molbeck, Jr., Pres.
Edward H. Ellis, Jr., CFO/Exec. VP
Lisa A. Moore, VP-Human Resources
William Lukefahr, CIO/VP
Randy D. Rinicella, General Counsel/Sr. VP
Bernard H. White, VP-Investor Rel.
Annette J. Goodreau, Chief Actuary/Sr. VP
Michael J. Schell, Exec. VP/CEO-Houston Casualty Company
Craig J. Kelbel, Exec. VP/CEO/Pres., HCC Life Insurance Company
Barry J. Cook, Exec. VP/CEO/Pres., HCC Insurance Holdings Int'l
Thomas G. Kaiser, Pres., Houston Casualty Co. & USSIC
Christopher J. B. Williams, Chmn.

| | |
|---|---|
| **Phone:** 713-690-7300 | **Fax:** 713-462-2401 |
| **Toll-Free:** | |
| **Address:** 13403 N.W. Frwy., Houston, TX 77040-6094 US | |

## GROWTH PLANS/SPECIAL FEATURES:

HCC Insurance Holdings, Inc. provides specialized property and casualty, surety, and group life, accident and health insurance coverages and related agency and reinsurance brokerage services to commercial customers and individuals. With operations primarily in the U.S., the U.K., Spain, Bermuda, Belgium and Ireland, the company underwrites insurance on both a primary basis and on a reinsurance basis both directly and through a network of independent and affiliated brokers, producers and agents. HCC's principal insurance company subsidiaries are Houston Casualty Insurance Company; HCC Insurance Company; HCC International Insurance Company; U.S. Specialty Insurance Company; HCC Life Insurance Company; and Avemco Insurance Company. Additional insurance subsidiaries include HCC Europe, HCC Reinsurance Company; HCC Specialty Insurance Company; United States Surety Company; and Perico Life Insurance Company. Underwriting activities are focused on providing insurance and reinsurance in such lines of business as diversified financial products, aviation, London market account and group life, accident and health. The firm also underwrites on behalf of non-affiliated insurance companies through its managing general agency operations. These agency operations specialize in domestic general aviation insurance, medical stop-loss coverage for employer-sponsored self-insured health plans, occupational accident coverage for self-insured truckers and a variety of accident- and health-related insurance and reinsurance products. The company's principal underwriting agencies are Professional Indemnity Agency; HCC Specialty Underwriters; HCC Global Financial Products; Covenant Underwriters; and HCC Indemnity Guaranty Agency. HCC also operates several insurance intermediary subsidiaries that provide marketing, placing and consulting services for affiliated and non-affiliated clients. In January 2008, the company acquired MultiNational Underwriters, LLC.

## FINANCIALS: **Sales and profits are in thousands of dollars—add 000 to get the full amount. 2008 Note: Financial information for 2008 was not available for all companies at press time.**

| | | |
|---|---|---|
| 2008 Sales: $ | 2008 Profits: $ | **U.S. Stock Ticker: HCC** |
| 2007 Sales: $2,388,373 | 2007 Profits: $395,429 | **Int'l Ticker:** Int'l Exchange: |
| 2006 Sales: $2,075,295 | 2006 Profits: $342,285 | Employees: 1,682 |
| 2005 Sales: $1,642,688 | 2005 Profits: $191,192 | Fiscal Year Ends: 12/31 |
| 2004 Sales: $1,284,607 | 2004 Profits: $162,699 | Parent Company: |

## SALARIES/BENEFITS:

| | | | | |
|---|---|---|---|---|
| Pension Plan: | ESOP Stock Plan: | Profit Sharing: | Top Exec. Salary: $1,950,000 | Bonus: $1,950,000 |
| Savings Plan: | Stock Purch. Plan: | | Second Exec. Salary: $1,253,035 | Bonus: $2,500,000 |

## OTHER THOUGHTS:

**Apparent Women Officers or Directors**: 2
**Hot Spot for Advancement for Women/Minorities**: Y

## LOCATIONS: ("Y" = Yes)

| West: | Southwest: | Midwest: | Southeast: | Northeast: | International: |
|---|---|---|---|---|---|
| | Y | | | Y | Y |

# HEALTH GRADES INC

www.healthgrades.com

**Industry Group Code:** 514199 **Ranks within this company's industry group:** Sales: 5 Profits: 4

| Management: | | Sales/Marketing: | | Liberal Arts: | | Information Systems: | | Professionals: | | Technical/Scientific: | |
|---|---|---|---|---|---|---|---|---|---|---|---|
| Mgmt. Trainees: | | Mktg. Professionals: | Y | Gen. Writing/Editing: | Y | Info. Management: | Y | Finance/Accounting: | Y | Engineers, Elec.: | |
| Experienced Mgmt.: | Y | Retail Sales: | | Technical Writing: | | Software Dev.: | Y | Law: | Y | Engineers, Other: | |
| Int'l Business: | | Commercial/Industrial: | Y | Graphic Arts/Photog.: | Y | Hardware Dev.: | | HR/Other: | Y | Health/Lab: | |
| MBA Graduates: | Y | Sales Trainees: | Y | Music: | | Systems Integration: | Y | Training: | Y | Scientists/Research: | |
| | | Advertising Pros.: | Y | Broadcasting: | | Consulting/Other: | | Health Care: | | Petroleum/Chemicals: | |
| | | | | Other: | | | | Consulting: | | Math/Other: | |

## TYPES OF BUSINESS:

Online Health Information
Health Providers Ratings Data
Consulting Services
Marketing Assistance Services

## BRANDS/DIVISIONS/AFFILIATES:

CompareYourCare
Clinical Excellence Research & Consulting Group
Physician Quality Guide
Nursing Home Quality Guide
Home Health Quality
Internet Patient Acquisition

## CONTACTS: *Note: Officers with more than one job title may be intentionally listed here more than once.*

Kerry R. Hicks, CEO
Kerry R. Hicks, Pres.
Allen Dodge, CFO/Exec. VP
Jan Rutherford, Sr. VP-Sales
Mark Bartling, Sr. VP-IT
Bill Wosilius, Sr. VP-Oper.
Scott Shapiro, Sr. VP-Corp. Comm. & Mktg.
David G. Hicks, Exec. VP
Sarah P. Loughran, Exec. VP
Samantha Collier, Sr. VP-Medical Affairs/Chief Medical Officer
Mike Shanks, Sr. VP
Kerry R. Hicks, Chmn.

| **Phone:** 303-716-0041 | **Fax:** 303-716-1298 |
|---|---|
| **Toll-Free:** | |
| **Address:** 500 Golden Ridge Rd., Ste. 100, Golden, CO 80401 US | |

## GROWTH PLANS/SPECIAL FEATURES:

Health Grades, Inc. (HGI) is a health care ratings and consulting company that provides the means to assess and compare the quality or qualifications of health care providers including hospitals, nursing homes, home health agencies, hospice programs and fertility clinics. It currently provides ratings or profile information on over 5,800 hospitals, 750,000 physicians in over 125 specialties and 19,000 nursing homes. This information is available on the firm's web site free of charge to consumers, employers and health plans, with more detailed reports available for a fee. HGI offers hospitals with high ratings the opportunity to license its ratings and trademarks and provides marketing assistance. The company also offers consulting services to hospitals that either want to build a reputation based on quality of care or are working to identify areas to improve quality. The firm's Health Management Suite of products is available to organizations to license under the Clinical Excellence Research & Consulting Guide, Physician Quality Guide, Nursing Home Quality Guide and Home Health Quality brands. For physicians, HGI offers its Internet Patient Acquisition program, allowing physicians to sponsor their own profile, as an alternative form of marketing. HGI has an ongoing collaboration with the Leapfrog Group to analyze and report the findings of hospital patient safety surveys. Leapfrog's survey assesses the extent to which hospitals strive to implement patient safety practices and rewards for advances in safety. In addition to its other online databases, in March 2007 HGI launched the first physician malpractice database in the country that is the public. In July 2007, the company expanded and renamed its Hospital Quality consultancy group to the HealthGrades Clinical Excellence Research & Consulting group. In May 2008, HGI made its information available on Google Health. In June 2008, the firm published its first 1,100 page reference guide for consumers.

## FINANCIALS: Sales and profits are in thousands of dollars—add 000 to get the full amount. 2008 Note: Financial information for 2008 was not available for all companies at press time.

| | | |
|---|---|---|
| 2008 Sales: $ | 2008 Profits: $ | **U.S. Stock Ticker: HGRD** |
| 2007 Sales: $32,742 | 2007 Profits: $6,748 | **Int'l Ticker:** Int'l Exchange: |
| 2006 Sales: $27,764 | 2006 Profits: $3,182 | Employees: 142 |
| 2005 Sales: $20,808 | 2005 Profits: $4,140 | Fiscal Year Ends: 12/31 |
| 2004 Sales: $14,538 | 2004 Profits: $1,782 | Parent Company: |

## SALARIES/BENEFITS:

| | | | | |
|---|---|---|---|---|
| Pension Plan: | ESOP Stock Plan: | Profit Sharing: | Top Exec. Salary: $328,311 | Bonus: $140,500 |
| Savings Plan: Y | Stock Purch. Plan: Y | | Second Exec. Salary: $218,400 | Bonus: $35,000 |

## OTHER THOUGHTS:

**Apparent Women Officers or Directors**: 3
**Hot Spot for Advancement for Women/Minorities**: Y

## LOCATIONS: ("Y" = Yes)

| West: | Southwest: | Midwest: | Southeast: | Northeast: | International: |
|---|---|---|---|---|---|
| Y | | | | | |

# HEALTH INSURANCE PLAN OF GREATER NEW YORK

**www.hipusa.com**

**Industry Group Code:** 524114 **Ranks within this company's industry group:** Sales: Profits:

| **Management:** | | **Sales/Marketing:** | | **Liberal Arts:** | | **Information Systems:** | | **Professionals:** | | **Technical/Scientific:** | |
|---|---|---|---|---|---|---|---|---|---|---|---|
| Mgmt. Trainees: | | Mktg. Professionals: | Y | Gen. Writing/Editing: | Y | Info. Management: | Y | Finance/Accounting: | Y | Engineers, Elec.: | |
| Experienced Mgmt.: | Y | Retail Sales: | | Technical Writing: | Y | Software Dev.: | | Law: | Y | Engineers, Other: | |
| Int'l Business: | | Commercial/Industrial: | Y | Graphic Arts/Photog.: | | Hardware Dev.: | | HR/Other: | Y | Health/Lab: | Y |
| MBA Graduates: | Y | Sales Trainees: | | Music: | | Systems Integration: | | Training: | Y | Scientists/Research: | |
| | | Advertising Pros.: | | Broadcasting: | | Consulting/Other: | | Health Care: | Y | Petroleum/Chemicals: | |
| | | | | Other: | | | | Consulting: | | Math/Other: | Y |

## TYPES OF BUSINESS:

Insurance-Medical & Health, HMOs & PPOs
HMO

## BRANDS/DIVISIONS/AFFILIATES:

ConnectiCare Holding Company
Vytra Health Plans
HIP Integrative Wellness
Group Health, Inc. (GHI)
PerfectHealth
Medical Home High Value Network
EmblemHealth, Inc.

## CONTACTS: *Note: Officers with more than one job title may be intentionally listed here more than once.*

Anthony L. Watson, CEO
Daniel T. McGowan, COO
Daniel T. McGowan, Pres.
Michael D. Fullwood, CFO/Exec. VP
Dewitt M. Smith, Sr. VP-Mktg. & Sales
Fred Blickman, Sr. VP-Human Resources
John H. Steber, CIO
Pedro Villalba, CTO/Sr. VP-IT
Vincent Scicchitano, Sr. VP-Prod. & Customer Mgmt.
Michael D. Fullwood, General Counsel/Corp. Sec.
John H. Steber, Exec. VP-Oper.
Stephen A. Zeng, VP-Corp. Dev.
Arthur J. Byrd, VP-Investor Rel.
Dominic F. D'Adamo, Sr. VP-Finance/Corp. Controller
Arthur J. Byrd, Treas.
Dan J. Dragalin, Exec. VP-Medical Affairs/Corp. Chief Medical Off.
Arthur H. Barnes, Sr. VP-External Affairs & Corp. Contributions
Edward A. Lucy, Sr. VP-Strategy, Mgmt. & Delivery Systems
Anthony L. Watson, Chmn.

**Phone:** 212-630-5000 **Fax:** 212-630-8747
**Toll-Free:** 800-447-8255
**Address:** 55 Water St., New York, NY 10041-8190 US

## GROWTH PLANS/SPECIAL FEATURES:

Health Insurance Plan of Greater New York (HIP), owned by EmblemHealth, Inc., is a New York City based HMO. HIP maintains contracts with 160 hospitals, including acute care institutions, in New York, Connecticut and Massachusetts, to provide services to members. HIP's total network, including subsidiaries, comprises nearly 43,000 physicians and other providers in over 72,000 locations in New York, Connecticut and Massachusetts. The company has acquired several businesses in its history including Vytra Health Plans, ConnectiCare and PerfectHealth, bringing HIP's total combined membership to approximately 1.3 million. HIP was the first health insurance company in the nation to translate its web site into Chinese and Korean in addition to Spanish, as well as being rated the number-one insurance company in the U.S. for the innovative use of technology by Information Week Magazine. In addition to HIP's comprehensive heath insurance options, the company provides programs and discounts for alternative medicine such as acupuncture, massage therapy and nutritional counseling, mental health services and chemical dependency treatment, pharmacy services, dental plans and women's wellness programs. HIP Integrative Wellness is an initiative supporting the belief that the best patient care will be attentive to the patient's spiritual, emotional and mental states as well as the physical. HIP is affiliated with Group Health, Inc. (GHI) due to a shared parent company, EmblemHealth. The companies have a total of 4 million members and 92,000 providers in 142,000 northeastern locations. In January 2008, HIP, along with GHI, launched a Medical Home High Value Network project that will allow adult primary care physicians in New York to create medical home practices.

HIP offers its employees reduced-cost medical, dental, optical and life insurance; short- and long-term disability; a pension plan; a 401(k) plan; commuter benefits; college savings plans; discounted health club memberships; flexible spending accounts; and tuition assistance.

## FINANCIALS: Sales and profits are in thousands of dollars—add 000 to get the full amount. 2008 Note: Financial information for 2008 was not available for all companies at press time.

| | | |
|---|---|---|
| 2008 Sales: $ | 2008 Profits: $ | **U.S. Stock Ticker: Nonprofit** |
| 2007 Sales: $ | 2007 Profits: $ | **Int'l Ticker:** Int'l Exchange: |
| 2006 Sales: $5,039,667 | 2006 Profits: $205,106 | Employees: 1,800 |
| 2005 Sales: $4,599,802 | 2005 Profits: $115,333 | Fiscal Year Ends: 12/31 |
| 2004 Sales: $3,654,183 | 2004 Profits: $215,260 | Parent Company: EMBLEMHEALTH INC |

## SALARIES/BENEFITS:

| | | | | |
|---|---|---|---|---|
| Pension Plan: Y | ESOP Stock Plan: | Profit Sharing: | Top Exec. Salary: $ | Bonus: $ |
| Savings Plan: Y | Stock Purch. Plan: | | Second Exec. Salary: $ | Bonus: $ |

## OTHER THOUGHTS:

**Apparent Women Officers or Directors**: 11
**Hot Spot for Advancement for Women/Minorities**: Y

## LOCATIONS: ("Y" = Yes)

| West: | Southwest: | Midwest: | Southeast: | Northeast: | International: |
|---|---|---|---|---|---|
| | | | | Y | |

# HEALTHSTREAM INC

www.healthstream.com

**Industry Group Code:** 611410 **Ranks within this company's industry group:** Sales: 2 Profits: 2

| Management: | | Sales/Marketing: | | Liberal Arts: | | Information Systems: | | Professionals: | | Technical/Scientific: | |
|---|---|---|---|---|---|---|---|---|---|---|---|
| Mgmt. Trainees: | Y | Mktg. Professionals: | Y | Gen. Writing/Editing: | Y | Info. Management: | Y | Finance/Accounting: | Y | Engineers, Elec.: | |
| Experienced Mgmt.: | Y | Retail Sales: | | Technical Writing: | | Software Dev.: | Y | Law: | Y | Engineers, Other: | |
| Int'l Business: | | Commercial/Industrial: | Y | Graphic Arts/Photog.: | Y | Hardware Dev.: | | HR/Other: | Y | Health/Lab: | |
| MBA Graduates: | Y | Sales Trainees: | Y | Music: | | Systems Integration: | Y | Training: | Y | Scientists/Research: | |
| | | Advertising Pros.: | Y | Broadcasting: | | Consulting/Other: | | Health Care: | | Petroleum/Chemicals: | |
| | | | | Other: | | | | Consulting: | | Math/Other: | |

## TYPES OF BUSINESS:

Educational & Training Content
Internet-based Educational Programs

## BRANDS/DIVISIONS/AFFILIATES:

HealthStream Learning Center
Authoring Pro
A.D.A.M., Inc.
HealthStream Express
Data Management and Research, Inc.
Jackson Organization (The)
HealthStream Research
HCAHPS Preparation and Improvement Library

## CONTACTS: *Note: Officers with more than one job title may be intentionally listed here more than once.*

Robert A. Frist, Jr., CEO
Robert A. Frist, Jr., Pres.
Gerard M. Hayden, CFO/Sr. VP
Kevin P. O'Hara, Sr. VP-Mktg.
Arthur E. Newman, Exec. VP-Human Resources
J. Edward Pearson, Sr. VP-HealthStream Research
Jeffrey Doster, CTO/Sr. VP
Kevin P. O'Hara, General Counsel/Sec./Sr. VP
Mollie Condra, Sr. Dir.-Comm.
Mollie Condra, Sr. Dir.-Investor Re.
Arthur E. Newman, Exec. VP-Finance & Acct.
Arthur E. Newman, Exec. VP-Systems
Robert A. Frist, Jr., Chmn.

| | |
|---|---|
| **Phone:** 615-301-3100 | **Fax:** 615-301-3200 |
| **Toll-Free:** 800-933-9293 | |
| **Address:** 209 10th Ave. S., Ste. 450, Nashville, TN 37203 US | |

## GROWTH PLANS/SPECIAL FEATURES:

HealthStream, Inc. provides Internet-based training, information and services for the health care industry. The firm provides services to healthcare organizations (HCOs) throughout the U.S. for acute-care facilities, pharmaceutical and medical device (PMD) companies. Within its HCO business unit, HealthStream focuses on expanding its web-based application service provider, e-learning and installed learning management products. The company's flagship HealthStream Learning Center (HLC) platform provides organizations with Internet-based training and continuing education services. Training material is hosted on a central data center, eliminating the need for on-site installations. HLC enables administrators to configure and modify materials, track completion and predict training expenses. HealthStream has provided training to 2,200 healthcare organizations, and has approximately 1.705 million hospital-based subscribers currently enrolled in HLC. In addition to its standard HLC subscription, the firm also offers the Authoring Pro upgrade, with an industry leading image library, owned by A.D.A.M., Inc.; and it offers HealthStream Express, a streamlined version of HLC. Within its PMD business unit, the company focuses on providing services such as live and online educational and training activities aimed at health care professionals, as well as online training for medical industry sales representatives. HealthStream Research (HSR) is the newest branch of the company with approximately 1,100 customer hospitals. HSR formed after the acquisition of The Jackson Organization, Research Consultants, Inc. (TJO) in March 2007. TJO offers quality and satisfaction surveys, data analyses of survey results and other research-based measurement tools quality and satisfaction surveys primarily to physicians, patients, employees and community members. HSR provides hospital-based customers with patient, physician, employee, and community surveys, data analyses of survey results, and other research-based measurement tools to compliment the HLC platform. Launched in 2008, the HCAHPS Preparation and Improvement Library is online courseware to address the findings of patient survey research.

## FINANCIALS: **Sales and profits are in thousands of dollars—add 000 to get the full amount. 2008 Note: Financial information for 2008 was not available for all companies at press time.**

| | | |
|---|---|---|
| 2008 Sales: $ | 2008 Profits: $ | **U.S. Stock Ticker: HSTM** |
| 2007 Sales: $43,949 | 2007 Profits: $4,087 | **Int'l Ticker:** Int'l Exchange: |
| 2006 Sales: $31,783 | 2006 Profits: $2,500 | Employees: 420 |
| 2005 Sales: $27,400 | 2005 Profits: $1,900 | Fiscal Year Ends: 12/31 |
| 2004 Sales: $20,100 | 2004 Profits: $-1,000 | Parent Company: |

## SALARIES/BENEFITS:

| | | | | |
|---|---|---|---|---|
| Pension Plan: | ESOP Stock Plan: | Profit Sharing: | Top Exec. Salary: $200,000 | Bonus: $9,208 |
| Savings Plan: Y | Stock Purch. Plan: Y | | Second Exec. Salary: $194,167 | Bonus: $15,725 |

## OTHER THOUGHTS:

**Apparent Women Officers or Directors**: 2
**Hot Spot for Advancement for Women/Minorities**:

## LOCATIONS: ("Y" = Yes)

| West: | Southwest: | Midwest: | Southeast: | Northeast: | International: |
|---|---|---|---|---|---|
| Y | | | Y | Y | |

# HEALTHTRONICS INC

**www.healthtronics.com**

**Industry Group Code:** 621490 **Ranks within this company's industry group:** Sales: 4 Profits: 8

| Management: | | Sales/Marketing: | | Liberal Arts: | | Information Systems: | | Professionals: | | Technical/Scientific: | |
|---|---|---|---|---|---|---|---|---|---|---|---|
| Mgmt. Trainees: | | Mktg. Professionals: | Y | Gen. Writing/Editing: | | Info. Management: | Y | Finance/Accounting: | Y | Engineers, Elec.: | |
| Experienced Mgmt.: | Y | Retail Sales: | | Technical Writing: | Y | Software Dev.: | | Law: | Y | Engineers, Other: | |
| Int'l Business: | Y | Commercial/Industrial: | Y | Graphic Arts/Photog.: | | Hardware Dev.: | | HR/Other: | Y | Health/Lab: | Y |
| MBA Graduates: | Y | Sales Trainees: | Y | Music: | | Systems Integration: | | Training: | Y | Scientists/Research: | |
| | | Advertising Pros.: | Y | Broadcasting: | | Consulting/Other: | | Health Care: | Y | Petroleum/Chemicals: | |
| | | | | Other: | | | | Consulting: | | Math/Other: | |

## TYPES OF BUSINESS:

Lithotripsy Services
Orthopedics Practice Management
Urologic Staffing

## BRANDS/DIVISIONS/AFFILIATES:

Prime Medical Services, Inc.
HealthTronics Surgical Services, Inc.
LithoDiamond Ultra
MultiVantage
RevoLix
TotalRad Radiation Therapy Solutions
Keystone Mobile Partners LP
Advanced Medical Partners, Inc. (AMPI)

## CONTACTS: *Note: Officers with more than one job title may be intentionally listed here more than once.*

James B. Whittenburg, CEO
James B. Whittenburg, Pres.
Ross A. Goolsby, CFO/Sr. VP
Jeff Howell, VP-Bus. Dev.
Richard A. Rusk, VP/Controller/Treas./Sec.
Christopher B. Schneider, Pres., Medical Products
James S. B. Whittenburg, Pres., Urology Svcs.
R. Steven Hicks, Chmn.

**Phone:** 512-328-2892 **Fax:** 512-328-8510
**Toll-Free:** 888-252-6575
**Address:** 1301 Capital of Texas Hwy., Ste. B-200, Austin, TX 78746 US

## GROWTH PLANS/SPECIAL FEATURES:

HealthTronics, Inc. is a health care service provider operating in two business segments: Urological services and products; and medical devices and services. HealthTronics' urological unit focuses on lithotripsy systems, which serve a network of 3,000 physicians throughout the U.S. Lithotripsy is the non-invasive treatment of kidney stones using shockwaves to break up the stones and allow them to pass painlessly from the body with a short recovery period, usually a matter of hours. The company's lithotripsy services include scheduling, staffing, training, quality assurance, maintenance, regulatory compliance and contracting with hospitals and surgery centers. In the medical devices and service sector, HealthTronics manufactures, sells and maintains lithotripters and related equipment, including the LithoDiamond Ultra lithotriper, which combines electromagnetic and electrohydraulic therapy options. The unit also distributes intra-operative X-ray imaging systems, such as MultiVantage for multipurpose surgical suites, and other mobile patient management tables. HealthTronics also has the RevoLix, minimally invasive line of laser products for urological procedures, including the RevoLix Duo, one of the only products to combine lithotripsy and laser technologies in one. In May 2007, the medical services branch released the TotalRad Radiation Therapy Solutions, which provides cutting-edge Image Guided Radiation Therapy (IGRT) for urologists in the treatment of prostate cancer. In June 2007, the firm acquired a 35% interest in Keystone Mobile Partners, LP, a leading provider of lithotripsy services in Pennsylvania. In April 2008, HealthTronics completed the acquisition of Advanced Medical Partners, Inc., a provider of urological cryosurgery services.

## FINANCIALS: **Sales and profits are in thousands of dollars—add 000 to get the full amount. 2008 Note: Financial information for 2008 was not available for all companies at press time.**

2008 Sales: $
2007 Sales: $140,418
2006 Sales: $142,891
2005 Sales: $152,267
2004 Sales: $87,143

2008 Profits: $
2007 Profits: $-14,632
2006 Profits: $8,683
2005 Profits: $9,188
2004 Profits: $1,353

**U.S. Stock Ticker: HTRN**
**Int'l Ticker:** Int'l Exchange:
Employees: 419
Fiscal Year Ends: 12/31
Parent Company:

## SALARIES/BENEFITS:

Pension Plan: ESOP Stock Plan: Profit Sharing: Top Exec. Salary: $337,198 Bonus: $405,000
Savings Plan: Stock Purch. Plan: Second Exec. Salary: $269,791 Bonus: $330,000

## OTHER THOUGHTS:

**Apparent Women Officers or Directors**:
**Hot Spot for Advancement for Women/Minorities**:

## LOCATIONS: ("Y" = Yes)

| West: | Southwest: | Midwest: | Southeast: | Northeast: | International: |
|---|---|---|---|---|---|
| | Y | | Y | | Y |

# HEARTLAND PAYMENT SYSTEMS INC www.heartlandpaymentsystems.com

**Industry Group Code:** 522320 **Ranks within this company's industry group:** Sales: 1 Profits: 2

| Management: | | Sales/Marketing: | | Liberal Arts: | | Information Systems: | | Professionals: | | Technical/Scientific: | |
|---|---|---|---|---|---|---|---|---|---|---|---|
| Mgmt. Trainees: | Y | Mktg. Professionals: | Y | Gen. Writing/Editing: | | Info. Management: | Y | Finance/Accounting: | Y | Engineers, Elec.: | |
| Experienced Mgmt.: | Y | Retail Sales: | | Technical Writing: | Y | Software Dev.: | | Law: | Y | Engineers, Other: | |
| Int'l Business: | | Commercial/Industrial: | Y | Graphic Arts/Photog.: | | Hardware Dev.: | | HR/Other: | Y | Health/Lab: | |
| MBA Graduates: | Y | Sales Trainees: | Y | Music: | | Systems Integration: | Y | Training: | Y | Scientists/Research: | |
| | | Advertising Pros.: | Y | Broadcasting: | | Consulting/Other: | | Health Care: | | Petroleum/Chemicals: | |
| | | | | Other: | | | | Consulting: | | Math/Other: | |

## TYPES OF BUSINESS:

Financial Processing Services
Credit/Debit Processing
Payroll Processing Services
Processing Equipment Provider

## BRANDS/DIVISIONS/AFFILIATES:

HPS Exchange
Chockstone Inc

## CONTACTS: *Note: Officers with more than one job title may be intentionally listed here more than once.*

Robert O. Carr, CEO
Robert H.B. Baldwin Jr., Pres.
Robert H.B. Baldwin Jr., CFO
Stanford C. Brown, Chief Sales Officer
Brian Rubarts, CIO
Alan Sims, CTO
Charles H.N. Kallenbach, General Counsel/Chief Legal Officer
Joseph E. White, Chief Acct. Officer
Thomas M. Sheridan, Chief Portfolio Officer
Marty Moretti, Chief Service. Officer
Kris Herrin, Chief Security Officer
Robert O. Carr, Chmn.

| | |
|---|---|
| **Phone:** 609-683-3831 | **Fax:** 609-683-3815 |
| **Toll-Free:** 888-798-3131 | |
| **Address:** 90 Nassau St., Princeton, NJ 08542 US | |

## GROWTH PLANS/SPECIAL FEATURES:

Heartland Payment Systems, Inc. (HPS) is a provider of credit/debit card, payroll and other associated processing services. Heartland primarily serves restaurant, hospitality, hotel and retail merchants throughout the U.S. Headquartered in Princeton, New Jersey, the firm also maintains offices in Ohio, Indiana, Tennessee, Texas, Colorado and Ontario, Canada. The firm's services include credit/debit card processing, payroll services and the HPS Exchange, while products include gift cards (with company logos), terminals, printers and other processing equipment. HPS' credit/debit card processing services allow clients to extend a variety of payment options to customers; the firm processes all major credit cards, including Visa, MasterCard, American Express, Diners Club, JCB and Discover, 24 hours per day, 365 days a year. HPS' payroll services entail calculation of payroll checks (which includes taxes, voluntary reductions, retirement plans and direct deposit), tax returns/filing concerns and additional services, such as reimbursement checks and automated check signing. The HPS Exchange is a company-developed transaction processing platform with added features unique to HPS. The HPS Exchange features fast transaction processing, customized reports/receipts and online merchant management, which allows retailers to immediately view transaction processing details in real time. HPS' products include gift cards tailored to each of its retail clients; cards contain stored value which is read on the card's magnetic strip, as well as company logo information. Processing equipment available for clients include a PIN pad, wireless and hand-held terminals, all of which is installed by HPS' local managers. HPS additionally publishes brochures and articles related to fraud control, interchange rates and other information specific to the industries it serves. In November 2008, the company acquired Chockstone, Inc., a provider of gift card programs.

Employees are offered medical and dental coverage; flexible spending accounts; and life insurance.

## FINANCIALS: **Sales and profits are in thousands of dollars—add 000 to get the full amount. 2008 Note: Financial information for 2008 was not available for all companies at press time.**

| | | |
|---|---|---|
| 2008 Sales: $ | 2008 Profits: $ | **U.S. Stock Ticker: HPY** |
| 2007 Sales: $1,313,846 | 2007 Profits: $35,870 | **Int'l Ticker:** Int'l Exchange: |
| 2006 Sales: $1,097,041 | 2006 Profits: $28,544 | Employees: 2,406 |
| 2005 Sales: $834,824 | 2005 Profits: $19,093 | Fiscal Year Ends: 12/31 |
| 2004 Sales: $602,851 | 2004 Profits: $8,855 | Parent Company: |

## SALARIES/BENEFITS:

| | | | | |
|---|---|---|---|---|
| Pension Plan: | ESOP Stock Plan: | Profit Sharing: | Top Exec. Salary: $476,425 | Bonus: $109,197 |
| Savings Plan: Y | Stock Purch. Plan: | | Second Exec. Salary: $350,000 | Bonus: $95,000 |

## OTHER THOUGHTS:

**Apparent Women Officers or Directors**:
**Hot Spot for Advancement for Women/Minorities**:

## LOCATIONS: ("Y" = Yes)

| West: | Southwest: | Midwest: | Southeast: | Northeast: | International: |
|---|---|---|---|---|---|
| | Y | Y | | Y | |

# HEARUSA INC

www.hearusa.com

**Industry Group Code:** 621490 **Ranks within this company's industry group:** Sales: 6 Profits: 6

| Management: | | Sales/Marketing: | | Liberal Arts: | | Information Systems: | | Professionals: | | Technical/Scientific: | |
|---|---|---|---|---|---|---|---|---|---|---|---|
| Mgmt. Trainees: | | Mktg. Professionals: | Y | Gen. Writing/Editing: | | Info. Management: | Y | Finance/Accounting: | Y | Engineers, Elec.: | |
| Experienced Mgmt.: | Y | Retail Sales: | Y | Technical Writing: | | Software Dev.: | | Law: | Y | Engineers, Other: | |
| Int'l Business: | Y | Commercial/Industrial: | | Graphic Arts/Photog.: | | Hardware Dev.: | | HR/Other: | Y | Health/Lab: | Y |
| MBA Graduates: | Y | Sales Trainees: | Y | Music: | | Systems Integration: | | Training: | Y | Scientists/Research: | |
| | | Advertising Pros.: | Y | Broadcasting: | | Consulting/Other: | | Health Care: | Y | Petroleum/Chemicals: | |
| | | | | Other: | | | | Consulting: | | Math/Other: | |

## TYPES OF BUSINESS:

Hearing Care Centers
Hearing Benefits Management
Hearing Aids
Hearing Care Devices

## BRANDS/DIVISIONS/AFFILIATES:

HEARx
HearUSA Hearing Care Network
Siemens Hearing Instruments

## CONTACTS: *Note: Officers with more than one job title may be intentionally listed here more than once.*

Stephen J. Hansbrough, CEO
Kenneth Schofield, COO
Gino Chouinard, Pres.
Gino Chouinard, CFO/Exec. VP
Gene Fell, Sr. VP-Bus. Dev.
Paige Brough, Sr. VP-Corp. Comm.
Cindy Beyer, Sr. VP-Professional Svcs.
Paul A. Brown, Chmn.

**Phone:** 561-478-8770 **Fax:** 561-478-9603
**Toll-Free:**
**Address:** 1250 Northpoint Pkwy., West Palm Beach, FL 33407 US

## GROWTH PLANS/SPECIAL FEATURES:

HearUSA, Inc., formerly known as HEARx, owns and manages a network of approximately 173 HearUSA hearing care centers that provide a full range of audiological products and services for the hearing impaired. The company serves customers in Florida, New York, New Jersey, Massachusetts, Ohio, Michigan, Minnesota, Missouri, California and Ontario, Canada. HearUSA also sponsors a network of approximately 1,600 credentialed audiologist providers that participate in selected hearing benefit programs contracted by the company with employer groups, health insurers and benefit sponsors in 49 states. Through the network, the company can pursue national hearing care contracts and offer managed hearing benefits in areas outside its center markets. HearUSA services over 400 benefit programs for hearing care with various health maintenance organizations, preferred provider organizations, insurers, benefit administrators and health care providers. Each HearUSA center is staffed by a licensed audiologist or hearing instrument specialist, and most are located in shopping or medical centers. The centers offer a complete range of high quality hearing aids, with emphasis on the latest digital technology along with assessment and evaluation of hearing. In addition, HearUSA offers other products related to hearing care, such as telephone and television amplifiers, telecaptioners and decoders, pocket talkers, specially adapted telephones, alarm clocks, doorbells and fire alarms. HearUSA also offers online information about hearing loss, hearing aids, assistive listening devices and the services offered by hearing health care professionals. The company's web site also offers online purchases of hearing-related products, such as batteries, hearing aid accessories and assistive listening devices. In November 2007, HearUSA entered the North Carolina hearing care market by acquiring two private practices in Charlotte.

## FINANCIALS: **Sales and profits are in thousands of dollars—add 000 to get the full amount. 2008 Note: Financial information for 2008 was not available for all companies at press time.**

2008 Sales: $
2007 Sales: $102,804
2006 Sales: $88,786
2005 Sales: $76,672
2004 Sales: $68,750

2008 Profits: $
2007 Profits: $-3,282
2006 Profits: $-3,174
2005 Profits: $-2,264
2004 Profits: $-3,449

**U.S. Stock Ticker: EAR**
**Int'l Ticker:** Int'l Exchange:
Employees: 534
Fiscal Year Ends: 12/31
Parent Company:

## SALARIES/BENEFITS:

Pension Plan: ESOP Stock Plan: Profit Sharing: Top Exec. Salary: $341,000 Bonus: $
Savings Plan: Y Stock Purch. Plan: Second Exec. Salary: $264,000 Bonus: $

## OTHER THOUGHTS:

**Apparent Women Officers or Directors**: 2
**Hot Spot for Advancement for Women/Minorities**: Y

## LOCATIONS: ("Y" = Yes)

| West: | Southwest: | Midwest: | Southeast: | Northeast: | International: |
|---|---|---|---|---|---|
| Y | | Y | Y | Y | Y |

# HEIDRICK & STRUGGLES INTERNATIONAL INC

www.heidrick.com

**Industry Group Code:** 541612 **Ranks within this company's industry group:** Sales: 1 Profits: 1

| Management: | | Sales/Marketing: | | Liberal Arts: | | Information Systems: | | Professionals: | | Technical/Scientific: | |
|---|---|---|---|---|---|---|---|---|---|---|---|
| Mgmt. Trainees: | | Mktg. Professionals: | Y | Gen. Writing/Editing: | Y | Info. Management: | Y | Finance/Accounting: | Y | Engineers, Elec.: | |
| Experienced Mgmt.: | Y | Retail Sales: | | Technical Writing: | Y | Software Dev.: | | Law: | Y | Engineers, Other: | |
| Int'l Business: | Y | Commercial/Industrial: | | Graphic Arts/Photog.: | | Hardware Dev.: | | HR/Other: | Y | Health/Lab: | |
| MBA Graduates: | Y | Sales Trainees: | Y | Music: | | Systems Integration: | | Training: | Y | Scientists/Research: | |
| | | Advertising Pros.: | | Broadcasting: | | Consulting/Other: | Y | Health Care: | | Petroleum/Chemicals: | |
| | | | | Other: | Y | | | Consulting: | Y | Math/Other: | |

## TYPES OF BUSINESS:

Leadership Consulting & Services
Executive Search

## BRANDS/DIVISIONS/AFFILIATES:

## CONTACTS:

*Note: Officers with more than one job title may be intentionally listed here more than once.*

L. Kevin Kelly, CEO
Eileen A. Kamerick, CFO/Exec. VP
Eileen A. Kamerick, Chief Admin. Officer
Eric M. Sodorff, Dir.-Comm.
Valerie E. Germain, Managing Partner-Strategic Partnerships
Charles Moore, Managing Partner-Life Sciences, Asia Pacific
Richard I. Beattie, Chmn.
David C. Peters, Regional Managing Partner-EMEA

| | |
|---|---|
| **Phone:** 312-496-1200 | **Fax:** |
| **Toll-Free:** | |
| **Address:** 233 S. Wacker Dr., Ste. 4200, Chicago, IL 60606-6303 US | |

## GROWTH PLANS/SPECIAL FEATURES:

Heidrick & Struggles International, Inc. (H&S) is a provider of executive search and leadership consulting services, with operations in 30 countries. The firm helps its clients build leadership teams by facilitating the recruitment, management and deployment of senior executives for its clients' executive management and board positions. H&S focuses on seven industry categories: Business and professional services; consumer; education/nonprofit; financial services; health care; industrial; and technology. The company provides its executive search services on a retained basis, recruiting senior executives whose first year base salary and bonus averaged approximately $345,000 on a worldwide basis. Its strategy of focusing on top-level services offers it several advantages, including access to and influence with key decision makers; increased potential for recurring search consulting engagements; higher fees per search; enhanced brand visibility; and a global footprint. H&S's clients include Fortune 1000, major non-U.S., middle market, emerging growth, governmental, higher education and not-for profit companies. The company's search process typically consists of analyzing the client's business needs; determining the required set of skills for the position; defining the required experience; identifying other characteristics of the desired successful candidate; selecting, contacting, interviewing and evaluating candidates; presenting confidential written reports on the candidates who best fit the position specification; scheduling a mutually convenient meeting between the client and each candidate; completing references on the final candidate selected by the client; and assisting the client in structuring the compensation package and supporting the successful candidate's integration into the client team. In addition to executive search, H&S provides a range of leadership consulting services, including succession planning, top team effectiveness, executive assessment, talent management, executive development and mergers and acquisitions human capital effectiveness. In February 2009, the firm acquired Ray & Berndtson's Warsaw, Poland office. In May 2008, the firm acquired IronHill Partners. In August 2008, H&S acquired 75 Search Partners, LLC.

## FINANCIALS:

**Sales and profits are in thousands of dollars—add 000 to get the full amount. 2008 Note: Financial information for 2008 was not available for all companies at press time.**

| | | |
|---|---|---|
| 2008 Sales: $ | 2008 Profits: $ | **U.S. Stock Ticker: HSII** |
| 2007 Sales: $648,266 | 2007 Profits: $56,463 | **Int'l Ticker:** Int'l Exchange: |
| 2006 Sales: $501,994 | 2006 Profits: $34,243 | Employees: 1,647 |
| 2005 Sales: $432,850 | 2005 Profits: $39,218 | Fiscal Year Ends: 12/31 |
| 2004 Sales: $398,176 | 2004 Profits: $82,308 | Parent Company: |

## SALARIES/BENEFITS:

| | | | | |
|---|---|---|---|---|
| Pension Plan: | ESOP Stock Plan: | Profit Sharing: | Top Exec. Salary: $800,000 | Bonus: $672,000 |
| Savings Plan: Y | Stock Purch. Plan: | | Second Exec. Salary: $656,000 | Bonus: $265,440 |

## OTHER THOUGHTS:

**Apparent Women Officers or Directors**: 3
**Hot Spot for Advancement for Women/Minorities**: Y

## LOCATIONS: ("Y" = Yes)

| West: | Southwest: | Midwest: | Southeast: | Northeast: | International: |
|---|---|---|---|---|---|
| Y | Y | Y | Y | Y | Y |

# HELIOVOLT CORP

**www.heliovolt.net**

**Industry Group Code:** 333298A **Ranks within this company's industry group:** Sales: Profits:

| Management: | | Sales/Marketing: | | Liberal Arts: | | Information Systems: | | Professionals: | | Technical/Scientific: | |
|---|---|---|---|---|---|---|---|---|---|---|---|
| Mgmt. Trainees: | | Mktg. Professionals: | Y | Gen. Writing/Editing: | | Info. Management: | Y | Finance/Accounting: | Y | Engineers, Elec.: | Y |
| Experienced Mgmt.: | Y | Retail Sales: | | Technical Writing: | Y | Software Dev.: | Y | Law: | Y | Engineers, Other: | Y |
| Int'l Business: | | Commercial/Industrial: | Y | Graphic Arts/Photog.: | Y | Hardware Dev.: | Y | HR/Other: | Y | Health/Lab: | |
| MBA Graduates: | Y | Sales Trainees: | Y | Music: | | Systems Integration: | | Training: | Y | Scientists/Research: | Y |
| | | Advertising Pros.: | | Broadcasting: | | Consulting/Other: | | Health Care: | | Petroleum/Chemicals: | |
| | | | | Other: | | | | Consulting: | | Math/Other: | Y |

## TYPES OF BUSINESS:

Architectural Solar Cells

## BRANDS/DIVISIONS/AFFILIATES:

FASST Technology
Architectural Glass & Aluminum Co.

## CONTACTS: *Note: Officers with more than one job title may be intentionally listed here more than once.*

Ron Bernal, Interim CEO
Ron Bernal, Pres.
Sanjeev Kumar, CFO
David Hughen, VP-Human Resources
Cindi Albee, VP-IT Svcs.
Louay Eldado, CTO
David Bowen, VP-Mfg. Oper.
Carolyn Radabaugh, Chief Counsel
B.J. Stanberry, Chief Strategy Officer
Steve Darnell, VP-Finance
Iga Hallberg, VP-Bus. Dev.
B.J. Stanberry, Chmn.
Larry Peruffo, VP-Supply Chain

| **Phone:** 512-767-6000 | **Fax:** |
|---|---|
| **Toll-Free:** | |
| **Address:** 8201 E. Riverside Dr., Ste. 600, Austin, TX 78744-1604 US | |

## GROWTH PLANS/SPECIAL FEATURES:

Heliovolt Corporation is a producer of high-efficiency thin-film solar energy products, which develops and markets technology for applying thin-film photovoltaic coatings to conventional construction materials. The company's primary solution is its proprietary FASST process, a low-cost, flexible manufacturing process for high-performance solar thin-film photovoltaics that prints Copper Indium Gallium Selenide (CIGS), a reliable and high-performing thin film compound, directly onto a variety of substrates, such as glass, steel, metal, composites and some polymers. The firm's products can be adapted for use in architectural modules, such as sunshades, sun louvers and curtains, skylights, curtain walls, spandrels, windows and atria; and can also be used in building-integrated photovoltaic (BIPV) systems by being embedded directly into roofing materials, glass and cladding, sunshades, canopies, skylights and modules. Heliovolt also offers customized printing services for a variety of materials. In May 2008, the company announced a partnership with Architectural Glass & Aluminum Co. to develop and manufacture BIPV products. In October 2008, Heliovolt opened its first thin-film factory, located in Austin, Texas.

Heliovolt offers its employees medical, dental and vision insurance, a health savings account, long and short-term disability insurance and a 401(k) plan.

## FINANCIALS: **Sales and profits are in thousands of dollars—add 000 to get the full amount. 2008 Note: Financial information for 2008 was not available for all companies at press time.**

| | | |
|---|---|---|
| 2008 Sales: $ | 2008 Profits: $ | **U.S. Stock Ticker: Private** |
| 2007 Sales: $ | 2007 Profits: $ | **Int'l Ticker:** Int'l Exchange: |
| 2006 Sales: $ | 2006 Profits: $ | Employees: |
| 2005 Sales: $ | 2005 Profits: $ | Fiscal Year Ends: |
| 2004 Sales: $ | 2004 Profits: $ | Parent Company: |

## SALARIES/BENEFITS:

| | | | | |
|---|---|---|---|---|
| Pension Plan: | ESOP Stock Plan: | Profit Sharing: | Top Exec. Salary: $ | Bonus: $ |
| Savings Plan: Y | Stock Purch. Plan: | | Second Exec. Salary: $ | Bonus: $ |

## OTHER THOUGHTS:

**Apparent Women Officers or Directors**: 3
**Hot Spot for Advancement for Women/Minorities**:

## LOCATIONS: ("Y" = Yes)

| West: | Southwest: | Midwest: | Southeast: | Northeast: | International: |
|---|---|---|---|---|---|
| | Y | | | | |

# HESKA CORP

www.heska.com

**Industry Group Code:** 325412B **Ranks within this company's industry group:** Sales: 1 Profits: 1

| Management: | | Sales/Marketing: | | Liberal Arts: | | Information Systems: | | Professionals: | | Technical/Scientific: | |
|---|---|---|---|---|---|---|---|---|---|---|---|
| Mgmt. Trainees: | | Mktg. Professionals: | Y | Gen. Writing/Editing: | | Info. Management: | Y | Finance/Accounting: | Y | Engineers, Elec.: | |
| Experienced Mgmt.: | Y | Retail Sales: | | Technical Writing: | Y | Software Dev.: | | Law: | Y | Engineers, Other: | |
| Int'l Business: | Y | Commercial/Industrial: | | Graphic Arts/Photog.: | | Hardware Dev.: | | HR/Other: | Y | Health/Lab: | Y |
| MBA Graduates: | Y | Sales Trainees: | Y | Music: | | Systems Integration: | | Training: | Y | Scientists/Research: | Y |
| | | Advertising Pros.: | | Broadcasting: | | Consulting/Other: | | Health Care: | Y | Petroleum/Chemicals: | |
| | | | | Other: | | | | Consulting: | | Math/Other: | |

## TYPES OF BUSINESS:

Drugs-Animal Health & Pet Care
Veterinary Diagnostics Products & Services
Animal Dietary Supplements
Veterinary Vaccines

## BRANDS/DIVISIONS/AFFILIATES:

Core Companion Animal Health
HESKA Feline UltraNasal FVRCP Vaccine
i-STAT 1 Handheld Clinical Analyzer
DRI-CHEM Veterinary Chemistry Analyzer
HEMATRUE Veterinary Hematology Analyzer
VET/IV 2.2 Infusion Pump
ERD - Healthscreen Urine Test
ALLERCEPT

## CONTACTS:

*Note: Officers with more than one job title may be intentionally listed here more than once.*

Robert B. Grieve, CEO
Robert B. Grieve, Pres.
Jason A. Napolitano, CFO/Exec. VP
Amy N. Connell, VP-Mktg.
Mark D. Cicotello, VP-Human Resources
Malcolm A. Hammerton, VP-IT
Nancy Wisnewski, VP-Prod. Dev.
John R. Flanders, General Counsel/VP/Corp. Sec.
Michael J. McGinley, VP-Global Oper.
Michael A. Bent, Controller/Principle Acct. Officer
Kenneth Schrader, VP-Bus. Oper.
G. Lynn Snodgrass, VP-Sales
Nancy Wisnewski, VP-Tech. Customer Service
Donald L. Wassom, Managing Dir.-Heska AG
Robert B. Grieve, Chmn.
Donald L. Wassom, Dir.-Global Allergy

| | |
|---|---|
| **Phone:** 970-493-7272 | **Fax:** 970-619-3003 |
| **Toll-Free:** 800-464-3752 | |
| **Address:** 3760 Rocky Mountain Ave., Loveland, CO 80538 US | |

## GROWTH PLANS/SPECIAL FEATURES:

Heska Corp. focuses on the discovery, development, marketing and support of animal health care products. The company uses biotechnology to create a broad range of diagnostic, therapeutic and vaccine products for dogs, cats and other animals. The business is divided into two segments: Core Companion Animal Health (CCA) and Other Vaccines, Pharmaceuticals and Products (OVP), previously Diamond Animal Health. The CCA segment includes diagnostic and monitoring instruments and supplies, single-use diagnostic tests, vaccines, pharmaceuticals and nutritional supplements, primarily for canine and feline use. Its line of veterinary diagnostic instruments includes the i-STAT 1 Handheld Clinical Analyzer, for electrolyte, blood gas, chemistry and basic hematology analysis; the DRI-CHEM Veterinary Chemistry Analyzer, which analyzes blood chemistry and electrolytes; the HEMATRUE Veterinary Hematology Analyzer, a blood analyzer focused on white blood cell count, red blood cell count, platelet count and hemoglobin levels; and the VET/IV 2.2 infusion pump for regulated infusion of fluids, drugs or nutritional products. Heska's diagnostic tests include tests for heartworms, allergy tests and early renal damage detection products. The E.R.D.-Healthscreen Urine Tests can identify dogs and cats at risk for kidney disease before the majority of kidney function is lost. The company also sells the HESKA Feline Ultranasal FVRCP Vaccine, a three-way modified live vaccine to prevent disease caused by respiratory viruses, and more general ALLERCEPT Allergy Treatment Sets for animals with positive allergy results. The OVP business manufactures private label vaccines and pharmaceutical products that are marketed and distributed by third parties primarily for cattle, although some products are also manufactured for small mammals and fish. In addition, OVP manufactures certain companion animal health products for marketing and sale by Heska. Other products include heartworm prevention tablets, a fatty acid supplement and a chewable thyroid supplement.

## FINANCIALS:

**Sales and profits are in thousands of dollars—add 000 to get the full amount. 2008 Note: Financial information for 2008 was not available for all companies at press time.**

| | | |
|---|---|---|
| 2008 Sales: $ | 2008 Profits: $ | **U.S. Stock Ticker: HSKA** |
| 2007 Sales: $82,335 | 2007 Profits: $34,808 | **Int'l Ticker:** Int'l Exchange: |
| 2006 Sales: $75,060 | 2006 Profits: $1,828 | Employees: 311 |
| 2005 Sales: $69,437 | 2005 Profits: $ 282 | Fiscal Year Ends: 12/31 |
| 2004 Sales: $67,691 | 2004 Profits: $-4,815 | Parent Company: |

## SALARIES/BENEFITS:

| | | | | |
|---|---|---|---|---|
| Pension Plan: | ESOP Stock Plan: | Profit Sharing: | Top Exec. Salary: $377,667 | Bonus: $60,242 |
| Savings Plan: | Stock Purch. Plan: | | Second Exec. Salary: $230,729 | Bonus: $24,519 |

## OTHER THOUGHTS:

**Apparent Women Officers or Directors**: 3
**Hot Spot for Advancement for Women/Minorities**: Y

## LOCATIONS: ("Y" = Yes)

| West: | Southwest: | Midwest: | Southeast: | Northeast: | International: |
|---|---|---|---|---|---|
| Y | | | | | Y |

# HICKORY TECH CORPORATION

**www.hickorytech.com**

**Industry Group Code:** 513300A **Ranks within this company's industry group:** Sales: 4 Profits: 5

| **Management:** | | **Sales/Marketing:** | | **Liberal Arts:** | | **Information Systems:** | | **Professionals:** | | **Technical/Scientific:** | |
|---|---|---|---|---|---|---|---|---|---|---|---|
| Mgmt. Trainees: | | Mktg. Professionals: | Y | Gen. Writing/Editing: | | Info. Management: | Y | Finance/Accounting: | Y | Engineers, Elec.: | Y |
| Experienced Mgmt.: | Y | Retail Sales: | | Technical Writing: | | Software Dev.: | Y | Law: | Y | Engineers, Other: | Y |
| Int'l Business: | | Commercial/Industrial: | Y | Graphic Arts/Photog.: | | Hardware Dev.: | | HR/Other: | Y | Health/Lab: | |
| MBA Graduates: | Y | Sales Trainees: | Y | Music: | | Systems Integration: | Y | Training: | Y | Scientists/Research: | |
| | | Advertising Pros.: | | Broadcasting: | | Consulting/Other: | | Health Care: | | Petroleum/Chemicals: | |
| | | | | Other: | | | | Consulting: | | Math/Other: | |

## TYPES OF BUSINESS:

Local Exchange Carrier
Computer Data Processing
Local Telephone Service
Internet Access
Billing Services
Digital TV

## BRANDS/DIVISIONS/AFFILIATES:

National Independent Billing, Inc.
Crystal Communications, Inc.
Enventis Telecom, Inc.
Mankato Citizens Telephone Company
Mid-Communications, Inc.
Heartland Telecommunications Company of Iowa, Inc.
Cable Network, Inc.

## CONTACTS: *Note: Officers with more than one job title may be intentionally listed here more than once.*

John W. Finke, CEO
John W. Finke, Pres.
David A. Christensen, CFO/Sr. VP
Mary T. Jacobs, VP-Human Resources
David A. Christensen, Sec.
Jennifer M. Spaude, Dir.-Public Rel.
Jennifer M. Spaude, Dir.-Investor Rel.
David A. Christensen, Treas.
Lane C. Nordquist, VP/Pres., Info. Solutions Div.
John P. Morton, VP/Pres., Business Solutions Div.
Damon D. Dutz, VP/Pres., Consumer & Network Solutions Div.
Walt A. Prahl, VP/Pres., Wholesale Solutions & Bus. Dev. Div.
R. Wynn Kearney, Jr., Chmn.

**Phone:** 507-387-1151 **Fax:** 507-625-9191
**Toll-Free:** 800-326-5789
**Address:** 221 E. Hickory St., P.O. Box 3248, Mankato, MN 56002-3248 US

## GROWTH PLANS/SPECIAL FEATURES:

Hickory Tech Corporation is a telecommunications company that operates in two business segments, telecom and Enventis. The company's core business is conducted through its telecom sector, which primarily consists of the operations of three incumbent local telephone companies (Mankato Citizens Telephone Company; Mid-Communications, Inc.; and Heartland Telecommunications Company of Iowa, Inc.), one competitive local exchange carrier and the firm's subsidiary, National Independent Billing, Inc. (NIBI). The competitive local exchange carrier, Crystal Communications, Inc., provides local telephone service, long-distance, DSL and digital TV, and also connects communications networks of interexchange carriers and wireless carriers with the equipment and facilities of end users. NIBI provides data processing and related services to the company and other telecommunications firms. NIBI services include processing of long-distance telephone calls, preparation of subscriber telephone bills, customer record keeping and carrier access bills. In addition to these companies, the telecom sector owns one other subsidiary, Cable Network, Inc., and operates fiber-optic cable facilities. Hickory Tech's second segment, operating though subsidiary Eventis Telecom, Inc., provides integrated fiber network, IP (Internet protocol) telephony and data services. Enventis own or leases approximately 1,500 route miles of fiber optic table that directly connects clients to the Enventis Network.

Hickory Tech offers tuition reimbursement; employee assistance; discounts on local phone and Internet services; medical, dental and vision coverage; life and disability insurance; an employee stock purchase plan; flexible spending accounts; and a 401(k) saving plan. Employees also receive discounts on memberships to fitness facilities and tickets to local attractions and events.

## FINANCIALS: **Sales and profits are in thousands of dollars—add 000 to get the full amount. 2008 Note: Financial information for 2008 was not available for all companies at press time.**

| | | |
|---|---|---|
| 2008 Sales: $ | 2008 Profits: $ | **U.S. Stock Ticker: HTCO** |
| 2007 Sales: $156,649 | 2007 Profits: $8,611 | **Int'l Ticker:** Int'l Exchange: |
| 2006 Sales: $132,901 | 2006 Profits: $2,268 | Employees: 400 |
| 2005 Sales: $77,922 | 2005 Profits: $8,529 | Fiscal Year Ends: 12/31 |
| 2004 Sales: $78,807 | 2004 Profits: $7,590 | Parent Company: |

## SALARIES/BENEFITS:

| | | | | |
|---|---|---|---|---|
| Pension Plan: | ESOP Stock Plan: | Profit Sharing: | Top Exec. Salary: $269,808 | Bonus: $277,879 |
| Savings Plan: Y | Stock Purch. Plan: Y | | Second Exec. Salary: $167,768 | Bonus: $151,188 |

## OTHER THOUGHTS:

**Apparent Women Officers or Directors**: 3
**Hot Spot for Advancement for Women/Minorities**: Y

## LOCATIONS: ("Y" = Yes)

| West: | Southwest: | Midwest: | Southeast: | Northeast: | International: |
|---|---|---|---|---|---|
| | | Y | | | |

# HI-TECH PHARMACAL CO INC

www.hitechpharm.com

**Industry Group Code:** 325416 **Ranks within this company's industry group:** Sales: 3 Profits: 3

| Management: | | Sales/Marketing: | | Liberal Arts: | | Information Systems: | | Professionals: | | Technical/Scientific: | |
|---|---|---|---|---|---|---|---|---|---|---|---|
| Mgmt. Trainees: | | Mktg. Professionals: | Y | Gen. Writing/Editing: | | Info. Management: | Y | Finance/Accounting: | Y | Engineers, Elec.: | |
| Experienced Mgmt.: | Y | Retail Sales: | | Technical Writing: | Y | Software Dev.: | Y | Law: | Y | Engineers, Other: | |
| Int'l Business: | Y | Commercial/Industrial: | Y | Graphic Arts/Photog.: | | Hardware Dev.: | | HR/Other: | Y | Health/Lab: | Y |
| MBA Graduates: | Y | Sales Trainees: | Y | Music: | | Systems Integration: | | Training: | Y | Scientists/Research: | Y |
| | | Advertising Pros.: | | Broadcasting: | | Consulting/Other: | | Health Care: | Y | Petroleum/Chemicals: | Y |
| | | | | Other: | | | | Consulting: | | Math/Other: | Y |

## TYPES OF BUSINESS:

Drugs-Generic
Nutritional Products
Over-the-Counter Products
Ophthalmic Products
Manufacturing Contract Services
Inhalation Products
Diabetes Products
Generic Drugs

## BRANDS/DIVISIONS/AFFILIATES:

Diabetic Tussin
DiabetiSweet
DiabetDerm
Multi-Betic
Zostrix
Midlothian Laboratories, LLC

## CONTACTS: *Note: Officers with more than one job title may be intentionally listed here more than once.*

David S. Seltzer, CEO
David S. Seltzer, Pres.
William Peters, CFO/VP
Edwin A. Berrios, VP-Mktg. & Sales
Polireddy Dondeti, Sr. Dir.-R&D
James P. Tracy, VP-Info. Sys.
David S. Seltzer, Sec.
Eyal Mares, VP-Oper.
Christopher LoSardo, VP-Corp. Dev.
Margaret Santorufo, Controller/VP
Gary M. April, Pres., Health Care Prod. Div./Divisional VP-Sales
Joanne Curri, Dir.-Regulatory Affairs
Pudpong Poolsuk, Sr. Dir.-Science
Tanya Akimova, Dir.-New Bus. Dev.
David S. Seltzer, Chmn.

| **Phone:** 631-789-8228 | **Fax:** 631-789-8429 |
|---|---|
| **Toll-Free:** | |
| **Address:** 369 Bayview Ave., Amityville, NY 11701-2802 US | |

## GROWTH PLANS/SPECIAL FEATURES:

Hi-Tech Pharmacal Co., Inc. is a manufacturer and marketer prescription, over-the-counter (OTC) and nutritional products that are sold in liquid and cream forms. A wide range of products are produced for various disease states, including asthma, bronchial disorders, dermatological disorders, allergies, pain, stomach, oral care, neurological disorders and other conditions. The firm divides its products into two main lines: generic and OTC brands. The generic products division primarily includes prescription items such as oral solutions and suspensions, topical creams and ointments as well as nasal sprays. This division also manufactures ophthalmic, optic and inhalation products and provides sterile manufacturing contract services. Hi-Tech's top five selling generic products are: sulfamethoxazole and trimethoprim; promethazine products; chlorhexadine gluconate; pediatric multivitamins; and urea based creams, lotions, gels and nail sticks. The firm's OTC brands division, also named the health care products division, develops and markets a line of branded products primarily for people with diabetes, including Diabetic Tussin, a line of cough medications; DiabetiSweet, sugar substitutes that can be used for baking and cooking; Multi-betic, a daily multi-vitamin; and DiabetDerm, a diabetic skin care line. This division also sells Zostrix, a brand of capsaisin products for pain and arthritis. In 2007, sales of generic pharmaceuticals represented 81% of total sales and sales of the health care products line of over-the-counter products accounted for 19% of total sales. The company's customers consist of generic distributors, drug wholesalers, chain drug stores, mass merchandise chains, certain Federal government agencies and mail-order pharmacies. Business has mainly depended upon the following customers: McKesson Corporation, Walgreens, Cardinal Health, Inc., CVS, AmeriSourceBergen Corporation, CVS and Wal-Mart. In December 2007, the firm acquired the assets of Midlothian Laboratories, LLC, a generic pharmaceutical company specializing in cough and cold products and prescription vitamins, for $5 million.

## FINANCIALS: **Sales and profits are in thousands of dollars—add 000 to get the full amount. 2008 Note: Financial information for 2008 was not available for all companies at press time.**

| | | |
|---|---|---|
| 2008 Sales: $ | 2008 Profits: $ | **U.S. Stock Ticker: HITK** |
| 2007 Sales: $58,898 | 2007 Profits: $-2,036 | **Int'l Ticker:** Int'l Exchange: |
| 2006 Sales: $78,020 | 2006 Profits: $11,453 | Employees: 262 |
| 2005 Sales: $67,683 | 2005 Profits: $8,288 | Fiscal Year Ends: 4/30 |
| 2004 Sales: $56,366 | 2004 Profits: $6,592 | Parent Company: |

## SALARIES/BENEFITS:

| | | | | |
|---|---|---|---|---|
| Pension Plan: | ESOP Stock Plan: | Profit Sharing: | Top Exec. Salary: $401,000 | Bonus: $314,000 |
| Savings Plan: Y | Stock Purch. Plan: | | Second Exec. Salary: $285,000 | Bonus: $ |

## OTHER THOUGHTS:

**Apparent Women Officers or Directors**: 3
**Hot Spot for Advancement for Women/Minorities**: Y

## LOCATIONS: ("Y" = Yes)

| West: | Southwest: | Midwest: | Southeast: | Northeast: | International: |
|---|---|---|---|---|---|
| | | | | Y | |

# HOLLY CORP

www.hollycorp.com

**Industry Group Code:** 324110 **Ranks within this company's industry group:** Sales: 2 Profits: 2

| Management: | | Sales/Marketing: | | Liberal Arts: | | Information Systems: | | Professionals: | | Technical/Scientific: | |
|---|---|---|---|---|---|---|---|---|---|---|---|
| Mgmt. Trainees: | | Mktg. Professionals: | Y | Gen. Writing/Editing: | | Info. Management: | Y | Finance/Accounting: | Y | Engineers, Elec.: | Y |
| Experienced Mgmt.: | Y | Retail Sales: | | Technical Writing: | | Software Dev.: | | Law: | Y | Engineers, Other: | Y |
| Int'l Business: | Y | Commercial/Industrial: | Y | Graphic Arts/Photog.: | | Hardware Dev.: | | HR/Other: | Y | Health/Lab: | |
| MBA Graduates: | Y | Sales Trainees: | | Music: | | Systems Integration: | | Training: | Y | Scientists/Research: | |
| | | Advertising Pros.: | | Broadcasting: | | Consulting/Other: | | Health Care: | | Petroleum/Chemicals: | Y |
| | | | | Other: | | | | Consulting: | | Math/Other: | |

## TYPES OF BUSINESS:

Petroleum Refining
Petroleum Distribution
Pipelines & Terminals
Asphalt

## BRANDS/DIVISIONS/AFFILIATES:

Holly Asphalt Co.
Holly Energy Partners, L.P.
Rio Grande Pipeline Co.
Navajo Refining Co., L.P.
Holly Refining & Marketing Co.
Woods Cross Refinery

## CONTACTS: *Note: Officers with more than one job title may be intentionally listed here more than once.*

Matthew P. Clifton, CEO
David L. Lamp, Pres.
Bruce R. Shaw, CFO/Sr. VP
George J. Damiris, Sr. VP-Supply & Mktg.
Nancy F. Hartmann, VP-Human Resources
Nellson D. Burns, VP-IT
Denise C. McWatters, General Counsel/VP/Sec.
Mark T. Cunningham, VP-Oper.
George J. Damiris, VP-Corp. Dev.
M. Neale Hickerson, VP-Investor Rel.
P. Dean Ridenour, Chief Acct. Officer
Scott C. Surplus, Controller/VP
Gary B. Fuller, Sr. VP-Refinery Operations
Philip L. Youngblood, VP-Environmental Affairs
Matthew P. Clifton, Chmn.

| **Phone:** 214-871-3555 | **Fax:** 214-871-3560 |
|---|---|
| **Toll-Free:** | |
| **Address:** 100 Crescent Ct., Ste. 1600, Dallas, TX 75201 US | |

## GROWTH PLANS/SPECIAL FEATURES:

Holly Corporation is an independent petroleum refiner that produces high-value light products such as gasoline, diesel fuel and jet fuel. The company operates refineries in New Mexico and Utah; oversees 900 miles of crude oil pipelines located primarily in west Texas and New Mexico. It operates Holly Asphalt Co., formerly NK Asphalt Partner, which manufactures and markets asphalt products from various terminals in Arizona and New Mexico. The firm also owns a 45% interest in Holly Energy Partners, L.P., which has logistics assets including roughly 1,700 miles of petroleum pipelines in Texas, New Mexico and Oklahoma; 10 refined product terminals; two refinery truck rack facilities; a refined products tank farm facility; and a 70% interest in Rio Grande Pipeline Co. Holly's Navajo Refining Co., L.P. owns the Navajo refinery, which has a crude capacity of 85,000 barrels per day of sour and sweet crude oils; can process up to about 90% sour crude oils; and serves markets in the southwestern U.S. and northern Mexico. Subsidiary Holly Refining and Marketing Co. operates the Woods Cross refinery near Salt Lake City, Utah, which specializes in high conversion that processes regional sweet and Canadian sour crude oils (26,000 barrels per day). In February 2008, Holly Corporation agreed to acquire pipeline and tankage assets from Holly Energy Partners, L.P. In July 2008, UNEV Pipeline, L.L.C., a limited liability company whose members are Holly UNEV Pipeline Company, a subsidiary of Holly Corporation and Sinclair Transportation Company, purchased Musket Corporation terminal and rail facilities near Cedar City, Utah. The terminal will be operated by Holly Energy Partners Operating L.P.

## FINANCIALS: **Sales and profits are in thousands of dollars—add 000 to get the full amount. 2008 Note: Financial information for 2008 was not available for all companies at press time.**

| | | |
|---|---|---|
| 2008 Sales: $5,867,668 | 2008 Profits: $120,558 | **U.S. Stock Ticker: HOC** |
| 2007 Sales: $4,791,742 | 2007 Profits: $334,128 | **Int'l Ticker:** Int'l Exchange: |
| 2006 Sales: $4,023,217 | 2006 Profits: $266,566 | Employees: 909 |
| 2005 Sales: $3,046,313 | 2005 Profits: $167,658 | Fiscal Year Ends: 12/31 |
| 2004 Sales: $2,246,373 | 2004 Profits: $83,879 | Parent Company: |

## SALARIES/BENEFITS:

| | | | | |
|---|---|---|---|---|
| Pension Plan: | ESOP Stock Plan: | Profit Sharing: | Top Exec. Salary: $727,833 | Bonus: $2,008,000 |
| Savings Plan: | Stock Purch. Plan: | | Second Exec. Salary: $306,587 | Bonus: $311,000 |

## OTHER THOUGHTS:

**Apparent Women Officers or Directors**: 3
**Hot Spot for Advancement for Women/Minorities**: Y

## LOCATIONS: ("Y" = Yes)

| West: | Southwest: | Midwest: | Southeast: | Northeast: | International: |
|---|---|---|---|---|---|
| Y | Y | | | | |

# HORACE MANN EDUCATORS CORPORATION www.horacemann.com

**Industry Group Code:** 524126 **Ranks within this company's industry group:** Sales: 7 Profits: 8

| Management: | | Sales/Marketing: | | Liberal Arts: | | Information Systems: | | Professionals: | | Technical/Scientific: | |
|---|---|---|---|---|---|---|---|---|---|---|---|
| Mgmt. Trainees: | | Mktg. Professionals: | Y | Gen. Writing/Editing: | Y | Info. Management: | Y | Finance/Accounting: | Y | Engineers, Elec.: | |
| Experienced Mgmt.: | Y | Retail Sales: | | Technical Writing: | Y | Software Dev.: | | Law: | Y | Engineers, Other: | |
| Int'l Business: | | Commercial/Industrial: | Y | Graphic Arts/Photog.: | | Hardware Dev.: | | HR/Other: | Y | Health/Lab: | |
| MBA Graduates: | Y | Sales Trainees: | Y | Music: | | Systems Integration: | | Training: | Y | Scientists/Research: | |
| | | Advertising Pros.: | | Broadcasting: | | Consulting/Other: | | Health Care: | | Petroleum/Chemicals: | |
| | | | | Other: | | | | Consulting: | | Math/Other: | Y |

## TYPES OF BUSINESS:

Insurance, Direct Property & Casualty
Annuities
Life Insurance
Investment Products

## BRANDS/DIVISIONS/AFFILIATES:

Horace Mann Insurance Company
Teachers Insurance Company
Horace Mann Life Insurance Company
Horace Mann Property & Casualty Insurance Company
Horace Mann Lloyds
Experience Life

## CONTACTS: *Note: Officers with more than one job title may be intentionally listed here more than once.*

Louis G. Lower II, CEO
Louis G. Lower II, Pres.
Peter Heckman, CFO/Exec. VP
Robert (Butch) Joyner, Sr. VP-Mktg.
Ann M. Caparros, General Counsel/Corp.Sec./Chief Compliance Officer
Karen Ruffatto, Administrator-Investor Rel.
Dwayne D. Hallman, Sr. VP-Finance
Douglas W. Reynolds, Exec. VP-Insurance Oper.
Paul D. Andrews, Sr. VP-Corp. Svcs.
Frank D'Ambra III, Sr. VP-Life & Annuity Div.
Bret A. Conklin, Sr. VP/Controller
Joseph J. Melone, Chmn.

| **Phone:** 217-789-2500 | **Fax:** 217-788-5161 |
|---|---|
| **Toll-Free:** | |
| **Address:** 1 Horace Mann Plz., Springfield, IL 62715-0001 US | |

## GROWTH PLANS/SPECIAL FEATURES:

Horace Mann Educators Corporation (HMEC), with $6.3 billion in assets, underwrites and markets personal lines of property, casualty and life insurance and retirement annuities in the U.S. The firm's products are marketed primarily to educators and other employees of public schools and their families; HMEC is one of the largest national, multi-line insurance corporations to focus on the needs of the educators. It has nearly 1 million customers, typically in households with two sources of income that focus their financial planning needs on retirement, security, savings and primary insurance. HMEC employs its own insurance agents, many of whom are former teachers or have some other strong tie to the educational community. The company operates in three divisions. The property and casualty insurance division generated approximately 55% of HMEC's 2007 revenue; the annuity division, 35%; and the life insurance division, the remaining 10%. In the property and casualty division, private passenger automobile insurance accounted for approximately 68% of the division's premiums written; homeowners insurance, 31%; and educator excess professional liability insurance, approximately 1%. The annuity division has approved pay-roll reduction for its 403(b) tax-qualified annuity products for approximately one-third of the 16,000 U.S. school districts. Approximately 63% of new annuity contact deposits for 2007 were for 403(b) annuities. Its Experience Life product is a flexible, adjustable premium life insurance contract, which allows the customer to combine elements of term life insurance, interest-sensitive whole life insurance and an interest-bearing account. The firm's principal insurance subsidiaries located in Illinois are the Horace Mann Insurance Company; Teachers Insurance Company; and Horace Mann Life Insurance Company. Other subsidiaries include Horace Mann Property & Casualty Insurance Company, a California corporation; and Horace Mann Lloyds, located in Texas. Collectively, its principle subsidiaries are licensed to write business in 49 states and Washington, D.C.

## FINANCIALS: Sales and profits are in thousands of dollars—add 000 to get the full amount. 2008 Note: Financial information for 2008 was not available for all companies at press time.

| | | |
|---|---|---|
| 2008 Sales: $834,800 | 2008 Profits: $10,900 | **U.S. Stock Ticker: HMN** |
| 2007 Sales: $887,005 | 2007 Profits: $82,788 | **Int'l Ticker:** Int'l Exchange: |
| 2006 Sales: $885,842 | 2006 Profits: $98,708 | Employees: 2,300 |
| 2005 Sales: $869,412 | 2005 Profits: $77,273 | Fiscal Year Ends: 12/31 |
| 2004 Sales: $878,349 | 2004 Profits: $56,313 | Parent Company: |

## SALARIES/BENEFITS:

| | | | | |
|---|---|---|---|---|
| Pension Plan: Y | ESOP Stock Plan: | Profit Sharing: | Top Exec. Salary: $640,008 | Bonus: $719,931 |
| Savings Plan: Y | Stock Purch. Plan: | | Second Exec. Salary: $384,000 | Bonus: $328,975 |

## OTHER THOUGHTS:

**Apparent Women Officers or Directors**: 1
**Hot Spot for Advancement for Women/Minorities**:

## LOCATIONS: ("Y" = Yes)

| West: | Southwest: | Midwest: | Southeast: | Northeast: | International: |
|---|---|---|---|---|---|
| Y | Y | Y | Y | Y | |

# HOULIHAN LOKEY

www.hlhz.com

**Industry Group Code:** 523110 **Ranks within this company's industry group:** Sales: Profits:

| Management: | | Sales/Marketing: | | Liberal Arts: | | Information Systems: | | Professionals: | | Technical/Scientific: | |
|---|---|---|---|---|---|---|---|---|---|---|---|
| Mgmt. Trainees: | | Mktg. Professionals: | | Gen. Writing/Editing: | | Info. Management: | Y | Finance/Accounting: | Y | Engineers, Elec.: | |
| Experienced Mgmt.: | Y | Retail Sales: | | Technical Writing: | | Software Dev.: | | Law: | Y | Engineers, Other: | |
| Int'l Business: | Y | Commercial/Industrial: | | Graphic Arts/Photog.: | | Hardware Dev.: | | HR/Other: | Y | Health/Lab: | |
| MBA Graduates: | Y | Sales Trainees: | | Music: | | Systems Integration: | | Training: | Y | Scientists/Research: | |
| | | Advertising Pros.: | | Broadcasting: | | Consulting/Other: | | Health Care: | | Petroleum/Chemicals: | |
| | | | | Other: | | | | Consulting: | | Math/Other: | |

## TYPES OF BUSINESS:

Investment Banking
Mergers & Acquisitions
Financing
Financial Advisory Services
Financial Restructuring

## BRANDS/DIVISIONS/AFFILIATES:

Orix Corporation
Orix USA Corp.
Business Forum
BusinessForum.hlhz.com

## CONTACTS: *Note: Officers with more than one job title may be intentionally listed here more than once.*

Scott Beiser, Co-CEO
Cynthia Bush, Global Head-Recruiting
Jeff Werbalowsky, Co-CEO

| | |
|---|---|
| **Phone:** 310-553-8871 | **Fax:** 310-553-2173 |
| **Toll-Free:** 800-788-5300 | |
| **Address:** 1930 Century Park W., Los Angeles, CA 90067 US | |

## GROWTH PLANS/SPECIAL FEATURES:

Houlihan Lokey Howard & Zukin, Inc. (Houlihan Lokey) is an investment banking firm, and constitutes the investment banking arm of Orix USA Corp., which is itself a subsidiary of Orix Corporation. The company's services fall into four broad, overlapping categories: mergers and acquisitions (M&A); financing; financial opinions and advisory services; and financial restructuring. For M&A transactions, Houlihan Lokey assists clients in everything from setting up a purchase or divestiture to coordinating financial-related closure issues and most everything in between, including handling transaction negotiations and helping buyers acquire financing. It also works with firms seeking to set up equity or joint venture partnerships. For financing, the company offers financial products and services targeting mid-sized corporations, including creating employee stock ownership plans (ESOPs). It also raises public and private equity for corporate clients. For financial opinions and advisory services, Houlihan Lokey analyzes everything from transactions and financial reporting to corporate benefits such as equity incentive plans and ESOPs. Lastly, the firm's financial restructuring services focus on helping companies facing bankruptcy or other special situations. For example, the firm was involved with the bankruptcy restructuring for Enron, WorldCom and Conseco. In the past 10 years, the firm has handled over 500 restructuring transactions, valued in excess of $1.25 trillion. It has also worked extensively with M&A transactions for distressed companies, completing over 150 such transactions. Besides the above-mentioned services, the firm also hosts Business Forum, available at BusinessForum.hlhz.com, an online community for business professionals that allows members, who must meet strict requirements (including minimum salary requirements), to meet and form networks with other members, promote their businesses and discover the services offered by other members.

Employees of Orix USA receive benefits including dental, major medical and life insurance; short and long term disability benefits; flexible spending accounts; paid time off; and educational assistance.

## FINANCIALS: **Sales and profits are in thousands of dollars—add 000 to get the full amount. 2008 Note: Financial information for 2008 was not available for all companies at press time.**

| | | |
|---|---|---|
| 2008 Sales: $ | 2008 Profits: $ | **U.S. Stock Ticker: Subsidiary** |
| 2007 Sales: $ | 2007 Profits: $ | **Int'l Ticker:** Int'l Exchange: |
| 2006 Sales: $ | 2006 Profits: $ | Employees: 800 |
| 2005 Sales: $ | 2005 Profits: $ | Fiscal Year Ends: |
| 2004 Sales: $ | 2004 Profits: $ | Parent Company: ORIX CORPORATION |

## SALARIES/BENEFITS:

| | | | | |
|---|---|---|---|---|
| Pension Plan: | ESOP Stock Plan: | Profit Sharing: | Top Exec. Salary: $ | Bonus: $ |
| Savings Plan: Y | Stock Purch. Plan: | | Second Exec. Salary: $ | Bonus: $ |

## OTHER THOUGHTS:

**Apparent Women Officers or Directors:**
**Hot Spot for Advancement for Women/Minorities:**

## LOCATIONS: ("Y" = Yes)

| West: | Southwest: | Midwest: | Southeast: | Northeast: | International: |
|---|---|---|---|---|---|
| Y | Y | Y | Y | Y | Y |

# HUMAN GENOME SCIENCES INC

www.hgsi.com

**Industry Group Code:** 325412 **Ranks within this company's industry group:** Sales: 30 Profits: 37

| Management: | | Sales/Marketing: | | Liberal Arts: | | Information Systems: | | Professionals: | | Technical/Scientific: | |
|---|---|---|---|---|---|---|---|---|---|---|---|
| Mgmt. Trainees: | | Mktg. Professionals: | Y | Gen. Writing/Editing: | | Info. Management: | Y | Finance/Accounting: | Y | Engineers, Elec.: | |
| Experienced Mgmt.: | Y | Retail Sales: | | Technical Writing: | Y | Software Dev.: | Y | Law: | Y | Engineers, Other: | |
| Int'l Business: | | Commercial/Industrial: | Y | Graphic Arts/Photog.: | | Hardware Dev.: | | HR/Other: | Y | Health/Lab: | Y |
| MBA Graduates: | Y | Sales Trainees: | Y | Music: | | Systems Integration: | | Training: | Y | Scientists/Research: | Y |
| | | Advertising Pros.: | | Broadcasting: | | Consulting/Other: | | Health Care: | Y | Petroleum/Chemicals: | Y |
| | | | | Other: | | | | Consulting: | | Math/Other: | Y |

## TYPES OF BUSINESS:

Oncology, Immunology & Infectious Diseases Drugs

## BRANDS/DIVISIONS/AFFILIATES:

LymphoStat-B
Albuferon
Abthrax

## CONTACTS:

*Note: Officers with more than one job title may be intentionally listed here more than once.*

H. Thomas Watkins, CEO
H. Thomas Watkins, Pres.
Timothy C. Barabe, CFO/Sr. VP
Susan Bateson, Sr. VP-Human Resources
David C. Stump, Exec. VP-R&D
Joseph A. Morin, VP-Eng.
Randy Maddox, VP-Mfg. Oper.
James H. Davis, General Counsel/Exec. VP/Sec.
Curan M. Simpson, Sr. VP-Oper.
Sally D. Bolmer, Sr. VP-Development & Regulatory Affairs
Jerry Parrott, VP-Corp. Comm. & Public Policy
Barry A. Labinger, Chief Commercial Officer/Exec. VP
Ann L. Wong, VP-Clinical Oper.
Giles Gallant, VP-Clinical Research, Oncology
Daniel J. Odenheimer, VP-Clinical Research, General Medicine
Argeris N. Karabelas, Chmn.

| **Phone:** 301-309-8504 | **Fax:** 301-309-8512 |
|---|---|
| **Toll-Free:** | |
| **Address:** 14200 Shady Grove Rd., Rockville, MD 20850 US | |

## GROWTH PLANS/SPECIAL FEATURES:

Human Genome Sciences, Inc. (HGS) is a commercially focused drug development company with three products in late-stage clinical development: Albuferon for chronic hepatitis, LymphoStat-B for systemic lupus erythematosus and ABthrax for anthrax disease. The company also has a pipeline of novel compounds in earlier stages of clinical development in oncology, immunology and infectious disease, including rheumatoid arthritis and HIV/AIDS. The firm's partners conduct clinical trials of additional drugs to treat cardiovascular, metabolic and central nervous system diseases and advanced a number of products derived from the company's technology to clinical development. The Albuferon collaborator is Novartis and the LymphoStat-B collaborator is GlaxoSmithKline. ABthrax is being developed under a contract with the U.S.government; based on highly successfully efficacy studies, HGS has begun manufacturing on schedule to distribute to the Strategic National Stockpile by fall 2008. HGS's leading products still in early to mid development are its TRAIL receptor antibodies for cancer, for which it reacquired the rights in April, and substantial financial rights to three drugs in the GlaxoSmithKline (GSK) clinical pipeline. GlaxoSmithKline entered several small molecule drugs into clinical development including GSK480848, for the treatment of atherosclerosis; GSK462795, for the treatment of bone disease; and GSK649868, for the treatment of sleep disorders. In the areas of research and development, the company also specializes in human-antibody and albumin-fusion technology; HGS has over 500 U.S. patents covering genes and proteins. In February 2008, HGS and Xencor, Inc. announced an antibody collaboration ulilizing Xencor's XmAb technology. In May 2008, HGS instigated Phase I clinical trial of its lead AP inhibitor, HGS1029, for patients with advanced solid tumors.

The company offers its employees medical, dental and vision insurance; flexible spending accounts; life and AD&D insurance; short- and long-term disability; a 401(k) plan; an employee stock purchase plan; education assistance, and ongoing training through employee development programs.

## FINANCIALS:

**Sales and profits are in thousands of dollars—add 000 to get the full amount. 2008 Note: Financial information for 2008 was not available for all companies at press time.**

| | | |
|---|---|---|
| 2008 Sales: $ | 2008 Profits: $ | **U.S. Stock Ticker: HGSI** |
| 2007 Sales: $41,851 | 2007 Profits: $-262,448 | **Int'l Ticker:** Int'l Exchange: |
| 2006 Sales: $25,755 | 2006 Profits: $-251,173 | Employees: 850 |
| 2005 Sales: $19,113 | 2005 Profits: $-239,439 | Fiscal Year Ends: 12/31 |
| 2004 Sales: $3,831 | 2004 Profits: $-242,898 | Parent Company: |

## SALARIES/BENEFITS:

| | | | | |
|---|---|---|---|---|
| Pension Plan: | ESOP Stock Plan: Y | Profit Sharing: | Top Exec. Salary: $671,154 | Bonus: $500,000 |
| Savings Plan: Y | Stock Purch. Plan: Y | | Second Exec. Salary: $460,000 | Bonus: $205,000 |

## OTHER THOUGHTS:

**Apparent Women Officers or Directors:** 3
**Hot Spot for Advancement for Women/Minorities:** Y

## LOCATIONS: ("Y" = Yes)

| West: | Southwest: | Midwest: | Southeast: | Northeast: | International: |
|---|---|---|---|---|---|
| | | | | Y | |

# HURON CONSULTING GROUP INC

www.huronconsultinggroup.com

**Industry Group Code:** 541611 **Ranks within this company's industry group:** Sales: Profits:

| Management: | | Sales/Marketing: | | Liberal Arts: | | Information Systems: | | Professionals: | | Technical/Scientific: | |
|---|---|---|---|---|---|---|---|---|---|---|---|
| Mgmt. Trainees: | | Mktg. Professionals: | Y | Gen. Writing/Editing: | Y | Info. Management: | Y | Finance/Accounting: | Y | Engineers, Elec.: | |
| Experienced Mgmt.: | Y | Retail Sales: | | Technical Writing: | Y | Software Dev.: | | Law: | Y | Engineers, Other: | |
| Int'l Business: | Y | Commercial/Industrial: | | Graphic Arts/Photog.: | | Hardware Dev.: | | HR/Other: | Y | Health/Lab: | |
| MBA Graduates: | Y | Sales Trainees: | Y | Music: | | Systems Integration: | | Training: | Y | Scientists/Research: | |
| | | Advertising Pros.: | | Broadcasting: | | Consulting/Other: | Y | Health Care: | | Petroleum/Chemicals: | |
| | | | | Other: | Y | | | Consulting: | Y | Math/Other: | |

## TYPES OF BUSINESS:

Financial Consulting
Legal Consulting
Health and Education Consulting
Corporate Consulting

## BRANDS/DIVISIONS/AFFILIATES:

Galt & Company
Wellspring Partners Ltd.
Glass & Associates, Inc.
Callaway Partners, LLC

## CONTACTS: *Note: Officers with more than one job title may be intentionally listed here more than once.*

Gary E. Holdren, CEO
Daniel P. Broadhurst, COO/Asst. Sec.
Gary E. Holdren, Pres.
Gary L. Burge, CFO/VP/Treas.
Bruce B. Cox, VP-Mktg.
Mary M. Sawall, VP-Human Resources
Natalia Delgado, General Counsel/Corp. Sec./VP
Wayne E. Lipski, Controller
Shahzad Bashir, VP-Legal Consulting & Southwest Region
James H. Roth, VP-Healthcare & Education Consulting
Gary E. Holdren, Chmn.

| | |
|---|---|
| **Phone:** 312-583-8700 | **Fax:** 312-583-8701 |
| **Toll-Free:** | |
| **Address:** 550 W. Van Buren St., Chicago, IL 60607 US | |

## GROWTH PLANS/SPECIAL FEATURES:

Huron Consulting Group, Inc. is a financial and operational consulting services firm. Huron operates through four segments: Financial Consulting; Legal Consulting; Health and Education Consulting; and Corporate Consulting. The Financial Consulting segment offers financial analysis for disputes and investigations including business disputes, lawsuits and regulatory or internal investigations. It also provides economic consulting, offering economic and statistical analyses; valuation services for transactions, litigation and bankruptcies; corporate governance services, mainly targeting risk management, internal audit and Sarbanes-Oxley compliance needs; and tax compliance services. Legal Consulting includes legal department cost effectiveness improvement consultations and electronic discovery and records management services, such as computer forensics, document processing and records process development. Health and Education Consulting operates three practices: a pharmaceutical and health plans practice, offering medical cost containment or healthcare contract consulting for the federal government or private pharmaceutical and medical device companies; a healthcare practice, offering hospitals, physicians and others supply chain improvements, financial planning and strategic growth and planning services; and a higher education practice, offering colleges, universities and academic medical centers services covering research administration, regulatory compliance and technology planning and implementation. Lastly, Corporate Consulting covers restructuring and turnaround services for distressed companies, creditor constituencies and other stake holders. Additionally, through subsidiary Galt & Company, this segment offers strategic and organizational consulting. In January 2009, the firm acquired Nextmove, a Saudi Arabia based consulting company. In July 2008, Huron Consulting acquired a management consulting firm, Stockamp & Associates, for approximately $219 million.

Employees are offered medical, dental and vision care; work/life, health and dependant care reimbursements accounts; transportation program; stock purchase plan; and a travel recognition program.

## FINANCIALS: **Sales and profits are in thousands of dollars—add 000 to get the full amount. 2008 Note: Financial information for 2008 was not available for all companies at press time.**

| | | |
|---|---|---|
| 2008 Sales: $ | 2008 Profits: $ | **U.S. Stock Ticker: HURN** |
| 2007 Sales: $504,292 | 2007 Profits: $41,901 | **Int'l Ticker:** Int'l Exchange: |
| 2006 Sales: $288,588 | 2006 Profits: $26,689 | Employees: 1,600 |
| 2005 Sales: $225,962 | 2005 Profits: $17,769 | Fiscal Year Ends: 12/31 |
| 2004 Sales: $173,911 | 2004 Profits: $19,684 | Parent Company: |

## SALARIES/BENEFITS:

| | | | | |
|---|---|---|---|---|
| Pension Plan: | ESOP Stock Plan: | Profit Sharing: | Top Exec. Salary: $1,100,000 | Bonus: $ |
| Savings Plan: Y | Stock Purch. Plan: Y | | Second Exec. Salary: $600,000 | Bonus: $ |

## OTHER THOUGHTS:

**Apparent Women Officers or Directors**: 2
**Hot Spot for Advancement for Women/Minorities**: Y

## LOCATIONS: ("Y" = Yes)

| West: | Southwest: | Midwest: | Southeast: | Northeast: | International: |
|---|---|---|---|---|---|
| Y | Y | Y | Y | Y | Y |

# IBASIS INC

www.ibasis.com

**Industry Group Code:** 513300B **Ranks within this company's industry group:** Sales: 1 Profits: 1

| Management: | | Sales/Marketing: | | Liberal Arts: | | Information Systems: | | Professionals: | | Technical/Scientific: | |
|---|---|---|---|---|---|---|---|---|---|---|---|
| Mgmt. Trainees: | | Mktg. Professionals: | Y | Gen. Writing/Editing: | | Info. Management: | Y | Finance/Accounting: | Y | Engineers, Elec.: | Y |
| Experienced Mgmt.: | Y | Retail Sales: | | Technical Writing: | | Software Dev.: | Y | Law: | Y | Engineers, Other: | Y |
| Int'l Business: | Y | Commercial/Industrial: | Y | Graphic Arts/Photog.: | | Hardware Dev.: | | HR/Other: | Y | Health/Lab: | |
| MBA Graduates: | Y | Sales Trainees: | Y | Music: | | Systems Integration: | Y | Training: | Y | Scientists/Research: | |
| | | Advertising Pros.: | Y | Broadcasting: | | Consulting/Other: | | Health Care: | | Petroleum/Chemicals: | |
| | | | | Other: | | | | Consulting: | | Math/Other: | |

## TYPES OF BUSINESS:

International Long Distance Service
Wholesale Voice Services
Prepaid Calling Cards
VOIP Service

## BRANDS/DIVISIONS/AFFILIATES:

Mobile Matrix
DirectSIP
Pingo
KPN B.V.
Royal KPN NV
TDC A/S

## CONTACTS: *Note: Officers with more than one job title may be intentionally listed here more than once.*

Ofer Gneezy, CEO
Ofer Gneezy, Pres.
Richard G. Tennant, CFO
Edwin A. D. van Ierland, Sr. VP-Global Sales
Tamah Rosker, VP-Human Resources
Paul H. Floyd, Sr. VP-R&D
Mark Saponar, VP-Info. Sys.
Ajay T. Joseph, CTO
Gert-Jan Huizer, VP-Prod. Mktg. & Portfolio Mgmt.
Alan Bugos, VP-Advanced Eng. & Tech.
Richard G. Tennant, Sr. VP-Admin.
Mark S. Flynn, Chief Legal Officer/Corp. Sec.
Joe Essex, VP-Oper.
Jayesh Patel, VP-Bus. Dev. & Strategy
Richard G. Tennant, Sr. VP-Finance
Gordon J. VanderBrug, Exec. VP
Tony Bloom, VP-Retail Prepaid
Brad Guth, VP-Service Delivery & Analysis
Michael Crimmins, VP-North America
Ofer Gneezy, Chmn.
Louis Eslami, VP-EMEA

**Phone:** 781-505-7500 **Fax:** 781-505-7300
**Toll-Free:**
**Address:** 20 2nd Ave., Burlington, MA 01803 US

## GROWTH PLANS/SPECIAL FEATURES:

iBasis, Inc. is a carrier of international long distance telephone calls and a provider of prepaid calling cards sold online and through retail stores throughout the U.S. The company operates a wholesale trading business, in which it connects buyers and sellers of international telecommunications services, and a retail business. In its trading business, iBasis receives voice traffic from buyers, local service providers and telecommunications carriers. The firm uses proprietary technology to automate the selection of routes and termination partners based on a variety of performance, quality and business metrics. It offers its trading service on a wholesale basis to carriers, mobile operators, consumer VoIP (Voice over Internet Protocol) companies, telephony resellers and other service providers worldwide. iBasis has call termination agreements with local service providers in more than 100 countries in North America, Europe, Asia, the Middle East, Latin America, Africa and Australia. In the mobile market, the company offers its Mobile Matrix portfolio of mobile data services, which includes mobile messaging and roaming. In targeting the emerging consumer VoIP providers, iBasis has expanded its DirectVoIP IP interconnection offering with DirectSIP, which supports Session Initiation Protocol interconnection. The firm's retail business consists of retail prepaid calling cards which are marketed through distributors primarily to ethnic communities within major metropolitan markets in the U.S. and Pingo, a prepaid calling service that it sells directly to consumers through an e-commerce model. Both offerings can be private-labeled for other service providers. In October 2007, iBasis acquired KPN B.V., the international wholesale voice business of Royal KPN N.V. In April 2008, the company acquired the non-Nordic international wholesale voice business of TDC, a leading telecommunications company in Denmark, for approximately $10 million.

iBasis offers its employees a health club discount, free international calling cards and medical, dental and disability insurance.

## FINANCIALS: **Sales and profits are in thousands of dollars—add 000 to get the full amount. 2008 Note: Financial information for 2008 was not available for all companies at press time.**

| | | |
|---|---|---|
| 2008 Sales: $1,323,585 | 2008 Profits: $-16,529 | **U.S. Stock Ticker: IBAS** |
| 2007 Sales: $938,558 | 2007 Profits: $16,123 | **Int'l Ticker:** Int'l Exchange: |
| 2006 Sales: $814,189 | 2006 Profits: $42,490 | Employees: 390 |
| 2005 Sales: $385,485 | 2005 Profits: $-2,038 | Fiscal Year Ends: 12/31 |
| 2004 Sales: $263,678 | 2004 Profits: $-18,324 | Parent Company: |

## SALARIES/BENEFITS:

| | | | | |
|---|---|---|---|---|
| Pension Plan: | ESOP Stock Plan: | Profit Sharing: | Top Exec. Salary: $350,000 | Bonus: $232,234 |
| Savings Plan: Y | Stock Purch. Plan: | | Second Exec. Salary: $300,000 | Bonus: $189,058 |

## OTHER THOUGHTS:

**Apparent Women Officers or Directors**: 1
**Hot Spot for Advancement for Women/Minorities**:

## LOCATIONS: ("Y" = Yes)

| West: | Southwest: | Midwest: | Southeast: | Northeast: | International: |
|---|---|---|---|---|---|
| Y | | | Y | Y | Y |

# ICO INC

www.icopolymers.com

**Industry Group Code:** 325000 **Ranks within this company's industry group:** Sales: 2 Profits: 1

| Management: | | Sales/Marketing: | | Liberal Arts: | | Information Systems: | | Professionals: | | Technical/Scientific: | |
|---|---|---|---|---|---|---|---|---|---|---|---|
| Mgmt. Trainees: | | Mktg. Professionals: | Y | Gen. Writing/Editing: | | Info. Management: | Y | Finance/Accounting: | Y | Engineers, Elec.: | |
| Experienced Mgmt.: | Y | Retail Sales: | | Technical Writing: | Y | Software Dev.: | | Law: | Y | Engineers, Other: | Y |
| Int'l Business: | Y | Commercial/Industrial: | Y | Graphic Arts/Photog.: | | Hardware Dev.: | | HR/Other: | Y | Health/Lab: | |
| MBA Graduates: | Y | Sales Trainees: | Y | Music: | | Systems Integration: | | Training: | Y | Scientists/Research: | Y |
| | | Advertising Pros.: | | Broadcasting: | | Consulting/Other: | | Health Care: | | Petroleum/Chemicals: | Y |
| | | | | Other: | | | | Consulting: | | Math/Other: | Y |

## TYPES OF BUSINESS:

Polymers
Specialty Resins & Concentrates
Polymer Processing Services

## BRANDS/DIVISIONS/AFFILIATES:

Bayshore Industrial, LP
ICO Brazil
ICO Europe
ICO Asia Pacific
ICO North America

## CONTACTS:

*Note: Officers with more than one job title may be intentionally listed here more than once.*

A. John Knapp, Jr., CEO
A. John Knapp, Jr., Pres.
Bradley T. Leuschner, CFO
Charlotte Fischer Ewart, General Counsel/Sec.
Bradley T. Leuschner, Investor Rel.
Bradley T. Leuschner, Treas.
Stephen Barkmann, Pres., Bayshore Industrial
Eric Parsons, Pres., ICO North America
Dario Masutti, Pres., ICO Asia Pacific
Andy Ubhi, VP, Middle East and India
Gregory T. Barmore, Chmn.
Derek Bristow, Pres., ICO Europe

| | |
|---|---|
| **Phone:** 713-351-4100 | **Fax:** 713-335-2201 |
| **Toll-Free:** | |
| **Address:** 1811 Bering Dr., Ste. 200, Houston, TX 77057 US | |

## GROWTH PLANS/SPECIAL FEATURES:

ICO, Inc. and its subsidiaries manufacture specialty resins and concentrates and provide specialized polymer processing services. The firm's specialty resins are typically produced in powdered form and include polyethylene, polyester, polypropylene, nylon, fluorocarbons, cellulose acetates, vinyls, phenolics, polyurethane, acrylics, epoxies and waxes. ICO manufactures concentrates by melt blending plastics and other additives to form alloy resins. Concentrates are typically sold to resin or plastic film producers and impart characteristics such as, anti-blocking, flame-retardance, color, ultraviolet stabilization and tear resistance. Bayshore Industrial, a subsidiary of ICO and the firm's largest concentrate operation, sells concentrates primarily for the film industry. ICO also provides toll processing services, including ambient grinding, jet milling, compounding and ancillary services for polymer resins produced in pellet form, as well as other materials. ICO's manufacturing services are an intermediate step between the production of polymer resins and the manufacture of a wide variety of products such as toys, water tanks, paint, garbage bags, plastic film and other polymer products. These products and services are provided through seven facilities in the U.S., six in Europe, four in Asia Pacific, one in the U.A.E. and one in Brazil. In addition, the company's segments are ICO Europe, ICO North America, ICO Asia Pacific, ICO Brazil and Bayshore Industrial. ICO's customers include major chemical companies; polymer production affiliates of major oil exploration and production companies; and manufacturers of plastic products.

## FINANCIALS:

**Sales and profits are in thousands of dollars—add 000 to get the full amount. 2008 Note: Financial information for 2008 was not available for all companies at press time.**

| | | |
|---|---|---|
| 2008 Sales: $446,701 | 2008 Profits: $15,314 | **U.S. Stock Ticker: ICOC** |
| 2007 Sales: $417,917 | 2007 Profits: $21,118 | **Int'l Ticker:** Int'l Exchange: |
| 2006 Sales: $324,331 | 2006 Profits: $12,004 | Employees: 910 |
| 2005 Sales: $269,606 | 2005 Profits: $4,505 | Fiscal Year Ends: 9/30 |
| 2004 Sales: $257,525 | 2004 Profits: $ 257 | Parent Company: |

## SALARIES/BENEFITS:

| | | | | |
|---|---|---|---|---|
| Pension Plan: | ESOP Stock Plan: | Profit Sharing: | Top Exec. Salary: $248,419 | Bonus: $194,212 |
| Savings Plan: Y | Stock Purch. Plan: | | Second Exec. Salary: $246,907 | Bonus: $117,230 |

## OTHER THOUGHTS:

**Apparent Women Officers or Directors**: 1
**Hot Spot for Advancement for Women/Minorities**:

## LOCATIONS: ("Y" = Yes)

| West: | Southwest: | Midwest: | Southeast: | Northeast: | International: |
|---|---|---|---|---|---|
| Y | Y | Y | Y | Y | Y |

# IDACORP INC

**www.idacorpinc.com**

**Industry Group Code:** 221000A **Ranks within this company's industry group:** Sales: 6 Profits: 5

| **Management:** | | **Sales/Marketing:** | | **Liberal Arts:** | | **Information Systems:** | | **Professionals:** | | **Technical/Scientific:** | |
|---|---|---|---|---|---|---|---|---|---|---|---|
| Mgmt. Trainees: | | Mktg. Professionals: | Y | Gen. Writing/Editing: | | Info. Management: | Y | Finance/Accounting: | Y | Engineers, Elec.: | Y |
| Experienced Mgmt.: | Y | Retail Sales: | | Technical Writing: | | Software Dev.: | | Law: | Y | Engineers, Other: | Y |
| Int'l Business: | | Commercial/Industrial: | Y | Graphic Arts/Photog.: | | Hardware Dev.: | | HR/Other: | Y | Health/Lab: | |
| MBA Graduates: | Y | Sales Trainees: | Y | Music: | | Systems Integration: | | Training: | Y | Scientists/Research: | |
| | | Advertising Pros.: | | Broadcasting: | | Consulting/Other: | | Health Care: | | Petroleum/Chemicals: | Y |
| | | | | Other: | | | | Consulting: | | Math/Other: | |

## TYPES OF BUSINESS:

Utility-Electric
Hydroelectric Generation
Energy Solutions & Marketing
Housing & Real Estate Investments

## BRANDS/DIVISIONS/AFFILIATES:

Idaho Power Company
IDACORP Financial Services, Inc.
Ida-West Energy Company
Energy Resources Co.
Jim Bridger
Bridger Coal Co.

## CONTACTS:

*Note: Officers with more than one job title may be intentionally listed here more than once.*

J. LaMont Keen, CEO
J. LaMont Keen, Pres.
Darrel T. Anderson, CFO
Luci K. McDonald, VP-Human Resources
Dennis C. Gribble, CIO/VP
Darrel T. Anderson, Sr. VP-Admin. Svcs.
Tom R. Saldin, General Counsel/Sr. VP
Greg W. Panter, VP-Public Affairs
Steve R. Keen, VP/Treas.
Lori D. Smith, Chief Risk Officer/VP-Corp. Planning
Naomi C. Shankel, VP-Audit & Compliance
Patrick A. Harrington, Corp. Sec.
Jeffrey L. Malmen, VP-Public Affairs
Jon H. Miller, Chmn.

| **Phone:** 208-388-2200 | **Fax:** |
|---|---|
| **Toll-Free:** | |
| **Address:** 1221 W. Idaho St., Boise, ID 83702-5627 US | |

## GROWTH PLANS/SPECIAL FEATURES:

IDACORP, Inc. is a holding company whose principal operating subsidiary is Idaho Power Company (IPC). Other subsidiaries include Ida-West Energy (Ida-West), which has a 50% interest in nine hydroelectric plants in Idaho and California; and IDACORP Financial Services, Inc. (IFS), an investor in affordable housing developments and other real estate ventures. IPC, the firm's core business, is involved in the generation, purchase, transmission, distribution and sale of electric energy in a 24,000-square-mile area, covering 71 cities in southern Idaho and nine in eastern Oregon, serving approximately 482,000 customers. IPC owns and operates 17 hydroelectric power plants, two natural gas-fired plants and one diesel-powered generator and shares ownership in three coal-fired generating plants. In 2007, hydro accounted for 46% of generation and thermal for 54%. IPC is the parent of Energy Resources Co., a joint venture in Bridger Coal Co., which supplies coal to the Jim Bridger generating plant operates by IPC. IPC's principal commercial and industrial customers are involved in food processing, electronics and general manufacturing, lumber, beet sugar refining and the ski industry. IFS invests primarily in affordable housing developments, which provide a return principally by reducing federal and state income taxes through tax credits and accelerated tax depreciation benefits. IFS focuses on a diversified approach to its investment strategy in order to limit both geographic and operational risk.

## FINANCIALS:

**Sales and profits are in thousands of dollars—add 000 to get the full amount. 2008 Note: Financial information for 2008 was not available for all companies at press time.**

| | | |
|---|---|---|
| 2008 Sales: $ | 2008 Profits: $ | **U.S. Stock Ticker: IDA** |
| 2007 Sales: $879,394 | 2007 Profits: $82,339 | **Int'l Ticker:** Int'l Exchange: |
| 2006 Sales: $926,291 | 2006 Profits: $107,403 | Employees: 2,044 |
| 2005 Sales: $842,864 | 2005 Profits: $63,661 | Fiscal Year Ends: 12/31 |
| 2004 Sales: $841,063 | 2004 Profits: $72,983 | Parent Company: |

## SALARIES/BENEFITS:

| | | | | |
|---|---|---|---|---|
| Pension Plan: | ESOP Stock Plan: | Profit Sharing: | Top Exec. Salary: $498,077 | Bonus: $259,740 |
| Savings Plan: | Stock Purch. Plan: | | Second Exec. Salary: $308,846 | Bonus: $107,359 |

## OTHER THOUGHTS:

**Apparent Women Officers or Directors**: 2
**Hot Spot for Advancement for Women/Minorities**: Y

## LOCATIONS: ("Y" = Yes)

| West: | Southwest: | Midwest: | Southeast: | Northeast: | International: |
|---|---|---|---|---|---|
| Y | | | | | |

# I-FLOW CORPORATION

www.iflo.com

**Industry Group Code:** 339113 **Ranks within this company's industry group:** Sales: 28 Profits: 4

| Management: | | Sales/Marketing: | | Liberal Arts: | | Information Systems: | | Professionals: | | Technical/Scientific: | |
|---|---|---|---|---|---|---|---|---|---|---|---|
| Mgmt. Trainees: | | Mktg. Professionals: | Y | Gen. Writing/Editing: | | Info. Management: | Y | Finance/Accounting: | Y | Engineers, Elec.: | Y |
| Experienced Mgmt.: | Y | Retail Sales: | | Technical Writing: | Y | Software Dev.: | Y | Law: | Y | Engineers, Other: | Y |
| Int'l Business: | Y | Commercial/Industrial: | Y | Graphic Arts/Photog.: | | Hardware Dev.: | | HR/Other: | Y | Health/Lab: | Y |
| MBA Graduates: | Y | Sales Trainees: | Y | Music: | | Systems Integration: | | Training: | Y | Scientists/Research: | Y |
| | | Advertising Pros.: | | Broadcasting: | | Consulting/Other: | | Health Care: | Y | Petroleum/Chemicals: | |
| | | | | Other: | | | | Consulting: | | Math/Other: | Y |

## TYPES OF BUSINESS:

Medical Equipment-Mobile Infusion Systems
Anesthesia Kits
Rental Infusion Equipment

## BRANDS/DIVISIONS/AFFILIATES:

On-Q PainBuster Post-Operative Pain Relief System
Soaker Catheter
SilverSoaker Catheter
C-bloc Continuous Nerve Block System
Block Medical de Mexico
Homepump Eclipse
Easypump
Acrymed Incorporated

## CONTACTS: *Note: Officers with more than one job title may be intentionally listed here more than once.*

Donald M. Earhart, CEO
James J. Dal Porto, COO/Exec. VP
Donald M. Earhart, Pres.
James R. Talevich, CFO
James J. Dal Porto, Corp. Sec.
James R. Talevich, Treas.
Donald M. Earhart, Chmn.

**Phone:** 929-206-2700 **Fax:** 949-206-2600
**Toll-Free:** 800-448-3569
**Address:** 20202 Windrow Dr., Lake Forest, CA 92630 US

## GROWTH PLANS/SPECIAL FEATURES:

I-Flow Corporation designs, develops and markets technically advanced, low-cost ambulatory drug delivery systems. Its products are used in hospitals, homes and freestanding surgery centers and physicians' offices. The firm's operations are divided into two primary market segments: regional anesthesia and intravenous (IV) infusion therapy. I-Flow manufactures a line of portable infusion pumps, catheters, needles and pain kits. I-Flow's acute pain kit product line includes the On-Q PainBuster Post-Operative Pain Relief System, the Soaker Catheter, the SilverSoaker Catheter and the C-bloc Continuous Nerve Block System. The company's On-Q systems offer continuous wound site pain management, which is considered to be one of the most ideal treatments for post-operative pain because fewer narcotics are used than in traditional methods of post-operative pain management. I-Flow's product line of elastomeric pumps delivers medication from an elastic balloon that does not rely on gravity for proper delivery, making it both safe and simple enough for patients to use for self-administration. The company's elastomeric line of products, including its Homepump Eclipse and Easypump, can be used for antibiotic therapy, pain management medications, chemotherapy and other medications. I-Flow's non-electric IV bag delivery systems, including its Paragon and Sidekick ambulatory infusion pumps, consist of a reusable mechanical infuser and specially designed administration sets. I-Flow also owns a subsidiary in Mexico, Block Medical de Mexico, which manufactures a substantial portion of the company's products. In October 2007, the company sold its subsidiary, InfuSystem, Inc. to HAPC, Inc. In February 2008, I-Flow acquired Acrymed Incorporated, a developer of infection control and wound healing products.

## FINANCIALS: **Sales and profits are in thousands of dollars—add 000 to get the full amount. 2008 Note: Financial information for 2008 was not available for all companies at press time.**

| | | |
|---|---|---|
| 2008 Sales: $ | 2008 Profits: $ | **U.S. Stock Ticker: IFLO** |
| 2007 Sales: $116,474 | 2007 Profits: $41,228 | **Int'l Ticker:** Int'l Exchange: |
| 2006 Sales: $93,582 | 2006 Profits: $13,674 | Employees: 970 |
| 2005 Sales: $72,119 | 2005 Profits: $-8,405 | Fiscal Year Ends: 12/31 |
| 2004 Sales: $51,796 | 2004 Profits: $-17,110 | Parent Company: |

## SALARIES/BENEFITS:

| | | | | |
|---|---|---|---|---|
| Pension Plan: | ESOP Stock Plan: | Profit Sharing: | Top Exec. Salary: $434,199 | Bonus: $704,545 |
| Savings Plan: Y | Stock Purch. Plan: | | Second Exec. Salary: $274,118 | Bonus: $469,697 |

## OTHER THOUGHTS:

**Apparent Women Officers or Directors**:
**Hot Spot for Advancement for Women/Minorities**:

## LOCATIONS: ("Y" = Yes)

| West: | Southwest: | Midwest: | Southeast: | Northeast: | International: |
|---|---|---|---|---|---|
| Y | | Y | | | Y |

# ILLUMINA INC

www.illumina.com

**Industry Group Code:** 334500 **Ranks within this company's industry group:** Sales: 2 Profits: 4

| Management: | | Sales/Marketing: | | Liberal Arts: | | Information Systems: | | Professionals: | | Technical/Scientific: | |
|---|---|---|---|---|---|---|---|---|---|---|---|
| Mgmt. Trainees: | | Mktg. Professionals: | Y | Gen. Writing/Editing: | | Info. Management: | Y | Finance/Accounting: | Y | Engineers, Elec.: | Y |
| Experienced Mgmt.: | Y | Retail Sales: | | Technical Writing: | Y | Software Dev.: | Y | Law: | Y | Engineers, Other: | Y |
| Int'l Business: | Y | Commercial/Industrial: | Y | Graphic Arts/Photog.: | | Hardware Dev.: | Y | HR/Other: | Y | Health/Lab: | |
| MBA Graduates: | Y | Sales Trainees: | Y | Music: | | Systems Integration: | Y | Training: | Y | Scientists/Research: | Y |
| | | Advertising Pros.: | | Broadcasting: | | Consulting/Other: | | Health Care: | | Petroleum/Chemicals: | |
| | | | | Other: | | | | Consulting: | | Math/Other: | Y |

## TYPES OF BUSINESS:

Instruments-Genetic Variation Measurement
Array Technology
Digital Microbead Technology
Software
Genotyping Services

## BRANDS/DIVISIONS/AFFILIATES:

BeadArray
Sentrix Array Matrix
Sentrix BeadChip
Oligator
International HapMap Project
CyVera Corp.
BeadXpress Systen
Solexa, Inc.

## CONTACTS: *Note: Officers with more than one job title may be intentionally listed here more than once.*

Jay T. Flatley, CEO
Jay T. Flatley, Pres.
Christian Henry, CFO/Sr. VP
Christian G. Cabou, General Counsel/Sr. VP
Maurissa Bornstein, Mgr.-Public Rel.
Peter J. Fromen, Sr. Dir.-Investor Rel.
Mike Bouchard, VP-Finance
Joel McComb, Sr. VP/Gen. Mgr.-Life Sciences
John West, Sr. VP/Gen. Mgr.-DNA Sequencing
Tristan Orpin, Sr. VP-Commercial Oper.
Gregory F. Heath, Sr. VP/Gen. Mgr.-Diagnostics
William H. Rastetter, Chmn.

**Phone:** 858-202-4500 **Fax:** 858-202-4766
**Toll-Free:** 800-809-4566
**Address:** 9885 Towne Centre Dr., San Diego, CA 92121-1975 US

## GROWTH PLANS/SPECIAL FEATURES:

Illumina, Inc. develops tools for the large-scale analysis of genetic variation and function. The firm's tools provide genomic information that can be used to improve drugs and therapies, customize diagnoses and treatments and cure disease. Its patented BeadArray technology, which boasts the capability of performing multiple assays simultaneously, is deployed in two formats, both currently marketed under the Sentrix brand. These use fiber optics to achieve a level of array miniaturization that allows experimentation to be easily scaled up. Illumina arranges its arrays in patterns that match the wells of industry-standard microtiter plates, allowing higher throughput than other technologies. The company's other, complementary technology, Oligator, permits parallel synthesis of the millions of pieces of DNA necessary to perform large-scale genetic analysis. VeraCode technology, acquired from the CyVera Corporation, is similar to the BeadArray, but for lower multiplex projects, and is used in the company's BeadXpress system. The company acquired DNA sequencing technology from Solexa in 2007. Illumina additionally provides genotyping services for other companies, as well as software, benchtop and production systems, installation and certain warranty services for its products. Illumina is one of five U.S. research groups, participating in the International HapMap Project, a global consortium aimed at creating a detailed map of genetic variation. The firm is also one of three participating in the 1000 Genomes Project, which will build on HapMap. In 2008, Illumina launched several new Infinium High Density (HD) products, including new BeadChip technologies. The firm launched the Infinium BovineSNP50 BeadChip, Human610-Quad, HumanHT-12 BeadChip and the iScan System to replace the BeadStation.

Illumina offers its employees flexible spending accounts, an educational assistance program, training opportunities, referral bonuses, an incentive plan, an on-site gym, wellness benefits and many company activities.

## FINANCIALS: **Sales and profits are in thousands of dollars—add 000 to get the full amount. 2008 Note: Financial information for 2008 was not available for all companies at press time.**

| | | |
|---|---|---|
| 2008 Sales: $573,225 | 2008 Profits: $50,477 | **U.S. Stock Ticker: ILMN** |
| 2007 Sales: $366,799 | 2007 Profits: $-278,359 | **Int'l Ticker:** Int'l Exchange: |
| 2006 Sales: $184,586 | 2006 Profits: $39,968 | Employees: 1,041 |
| 2005 Sales: $73,501 | 2005 Profits: $-20,874 | Fiscal Year Ends: 12/31 |
| 2004 Sales: $50,583 | 2004 Profits: $-6,225 | Parent Company: |

## SALARIES/BENEFITS:

| | | | | |
|---|---|---|---|---|
| Pension Plan: | ESOP Stock Plan: | Profit Sharing: | Top Exec. Salary: $575,577 | Bonus: $302,250 |
| Savings Plan: Y | Stock Purch. Plan: Y | | Second Exec. Salary: $360,577 | Bonus: $4,223,030 |

## OTHER THOUGHTS:

**Apparent Women Officers or Directors**: 2
**Hot Spot for Advancement for Women/Minorities**:

## LOCATIONS: ("Y" = Yes)

| West: | Southwest: | Midwest: | Southeast: | Northeast: | International: |
|---|---|---|---|---|---|
| Y | | | | | Y |

# IMATION CORP

www.imation.com

**Industry Group Code:** 334112 **Ranks within this company's industry group:** Sales: 1 Profits: 2

| Management: | | Sales/Marketing: | | Liberal Arts: | | Information Systems: | | Professionals: | | Technical/Scientific: | |
|---|---|---|---|---|---|---|---|---|---|---|---|
| Mgmt. Trainees: | | Mktg. Professionals: | Y | Gen. Writing/Editing: | | Info. Management: | Y | Finance/Accounting: | Y | Engineers, Elec.: | Y |
| Experienced Mgmt.: | Y | Retail Sales: | | Technical Writing: | Y | Software Dev.: | Y | Law: | Y | Engineers, Other: | |
| Int'l Business: | Y | Commercial/Industrial: | Y | Graphic Arts/Photog.: | | Hardware Dev.: | Y | HR/Other: | Y | Health/Lab: | |
| MBA Graduates: | Y | Sales Trainees: | | Music: | | Systems Integration: | Y | Training: | Y | Scientists/Research: | |
| | | Advertising Pros.: | | Broadcasting: | | Consulting/Other: | | Health Care: | | Petroleum/Chemicals: | |
| | | | | Other: | | | | Consulting: | | Math/Other: | |

## TYPES OF BUSINESS:

Data Storage Products
Diskettes & Storage Tapes
Optical Storage Media
Imaging Systems
Hard Drives
Flash Memory Devices

## BRANDS/DIVISIONS/AFFILIATES:

Imation
Memorex
TDK Life on Record
Disc Stakka
Global Data Media
Memcorp
Xtreme Accessories LLC

## CONTACTS: *Note: Officers with more than one job title may be intentionally listed here more than once.*

Frank P. Russomanno, CEO
Frank P. Russomanno, Pres.
Paul R. Zellar, CFO/VP
Stephen F. Moss, Chief Mktg. Officer/VP
Jacqueline A. Chase, VP-Human Resources
Subodh Kulkarni, VP-R&D
Subodh Kulkarni, VP-Mfg.
John L. Sullivan, General Counsel/Sr. VP/Corp. Sec.
Peter A. Koehn, VP-Global Oper.
James C. Ellis, VP-Strategy & M&A
Bradley D. Allen, VP-Corp. Comm.
Bradley D. Allen, VP-Investor Rel.
Subodh Kulkarni, VP-Global Commercial Business
Linda W. Hart, Chmn.

| | |
|---|---|
| **Phone:** 651-704-4000 | **Fax:** 888-704-4200 |
| **Toll-Free:** 888-466-3456 | |
| **Address:** 1 Imation Pl., Oakdale, MN 55128-3421 US | |

## GROWTH PLANS/SPECIAL FEATURES:

Imation Corp. develops, manufactures, sources, markets and distributes removable data storage media products (both optical and magnetic) for users of a broad array of digital information technologies in approximately 100 countries worldwide. The primary brand names under which it sells its products are Imation, Memorex and TDK Life on Record. The firm offers a variety of products that capture, process, store, reproduce and distribute information and images for information-intensive markets, including enterprise computing, network servers, personal computing, graphic arts, medical imaging, photographic imaging, commercial and consumer markets. Products include 4mm and 8mm data cartridges, the Disc Stakka, USB flash devices, dictating cassettes, CD-R and CD-RW media discs, Tandberg VXA packet technology, storage accessories, Travan data cartridges, LTO/Ultrium data cartridges and the Odyssey removable HDD storage system. The company is a media supplier to the enterprise data center market, where organizations store, manage and protect mission-critical data. Imation also co-operates a global sales and marketing joint venture company, Global Data Media, with Moser Baer India, Ltd. to meet rising demand from consumers and businesses for high-capacity removable optical storage media. Through subsidiary Memcorp, the company also sells various consumer electronics products, such as flat panel displays and televisions, including LCD displays and digital picture frames; clock-radios; DVD players, karaoke systems; and MP3 players. Imation has recently been combining its global manufacturing and research & development functions into one operational unit to commercialize new products more rapidly. In June 2008, the company acquired substantially all of the assets of Xtreme Accessories, LLC (XtremeMac), a provider of consumer electronics products and accessories, for approximately $9 million.

The company offers a variety of benefits, including medical, dental and vision coverage; short-term and long-term disability coverage; life and AD&D insurance; legal services; pension and 401(k) plans; and tuition reimbursement.

## FINANCIALS: **Sales and profits are in thousands of dollars—add 000 to get the full amount. 2008 Note: Financial information for 2008 was not available for all companies at press time.**

| | | |
|---|---|---|
| 2008 Sales: $2,154,600 | 2008 Profits: $-33,300 | **U.S. Stock Ticker: IMN** |
| 2007 Sales: $2,062,000 | 2007 Profits: $-50,400 | **Int'l Ticker:** Int'l Exchange: |
| 2006 Sales: $1,584,700 | 2006 Profits: $76,400 | Employees: 1,570 |
| 2005 Sales: $1,258,100 | 2005 Profits: $87,900 | Fiscal Year Ends: 12/31 |
| 2004 Sales: $1,173,700 | 2004 Profits: $29,900 | Parent Company: |

## SALARIES/BENEFITS:

| | | | | |
|---|---|---|---|---|
| Pension Plan: Y | ESOP Stock Plan: | Profit Sharing: | Top Exec. Salary: $625,012 | Bonus: $ |
| Savings Plan: Y | Stock Purch. Plan: | | Second Exec. Salary: $365,238 | Bonus: $ |

## OTHER THOUGHTS:

**Apparent Women Officers or Directors:** 2
**Hot Spot for Advancement for Women/Minorities:** Y

## LOCATIONS: ("Y" = Yes)

| West: | Southwest: | Midwest: | Southeast: | Northeast: | International: |
|---|---|---|---|---|---|
| Y | Y | Y | Y | | Y |

# IMG WORLDWIDE INC

www.imgworld.com

**Industry Group Code:** 711410 **Ranks within this company's industry group:** Sales: Profits:

| Management: | | Sales/Marketing: | | Liberal Arts: | | Information Systems: | | Professionals: | | Technical/Scientific: | |
|---|---|---|---|---|---|---|---|---|---|---|---|
| Mgmt. Trainees: | | Mktg. Professionals: | Y | Gen. Writing/Editing: | | Info. Management: | Y | Finance/Accounting: | Y | Engineers, Elec.: | |
| Experienced Mgmt.: | Y | Retail Sales: | | Technical Writing: | | Software Dev.: | | Law: | Y | Engineers, Other: | |
| Int'l Business: | Y | Commercial/Industrial: | | Graphic Arts/Photog.: | | Hardware Dev.: | | HR/Other: | Y | Health/Lab: | |
| MBA Graduates: | Y | Sales Trainees: | Y | Music: | | Systems Integration: | | Training: | Y | Scientists/Research: | |
| | | Advertising Pros.: | | Broadcasting: | | Consulting/Other: | | Health Care: | | Petroleum/Chemicals: | |
| | | | | Other: | | | | Consulting: | | Math/Other: | |

## TYPES OF BUSINESS:

Agents-Athletes
Agents-Models
Agents-Writers, Artists & Musicians
Event Marketing
Corporate Marketing Consulting Services
Sports Television Programming
Sports Schools & Training

## BRANDS/DIVISIONS/AFFILIATES:

IMG Coaches
IMG Models
IMG Artists
IMG Consulting
Darlow Smithson Productions
Tiger Aspect Productions
Forstmann Little & Co.
Tennis Week Magazine

## CONTACTS: *Note: Officers with more than one job title may be intentionally listed here more than once.*

Theodore J. Forstmann, CEO
Jim Tucker, VP-U.S. Bus. Dev.
Chris Albrecht, Pres., IMG Global Media
Michel Masquelier, Exec. VP/Head-Acquisition & Sales Worldwide
George Pyne, Pres., IMG Sports & Entertainment
Lee Rosenbaum, VP-Publishing
Theodore J. Forstmann, Chmn.
Ian Todd, Pres., IMG Int'l

| | |
|---|---|
| **Phone:** 216-522-1200 | **Fax:** 216-522-1145 |
| **Toll-Free:** | |
| **Address:** 1360 E. 9th St., Ste. 100, Cleveland, OH 44114 US | |

## GROWTH PLANS/SPECIAL FEATURES:

IMG Worldwide, Inc. is one of largest sports and lifestyle marketing and management agencies in the world. The company represents some of the world's top athletes, broadcasters, models, classical musicians, authors and newsmakers throughout more than 60 offices in 30 countries. The agency operates three divisions: Sports, Entertainment and Media. The Sports division handles everything from events and sponsorships to client representation and training. The company owns, produces and manages several prestigious sporting events including events at Wimbledon and Nobel Prize functions. Sports clients include golfers Tiger Woods; tennis player Venus Williams; baseball player Derek Jeter; basketball player Charles Barkley; and hockey player Jaromir Jagr. The Entertainment division handles a multitude of fashion related events and personalities. This segment represents a variety of models such as Gisele and Cindy Crawford. The Media department creates, distributes, sells and represents content across every medium. IMG's Media division, along with the firm's subsidiaries TWI, Darlow Smithson Productions, CSI Sports, Tiger Aspect Productions, Tigress Productions Limited and Nunet AG, is one of the world's largest independent producers and distributors of televised sports programming. It annually produces and distributes 11,000 hours of original programming to over 220 countries. IMG is held by private equity firm Forstmann Little & Co. Recent acquisitions include Tennis Week Magazine, tennisweek.com, CSI Sports, Nunet AG, BSI Speedway, Quintus, Collegiate Licensing Company and Partners International. In 2008, the company signed a deal with Chinese national TV broadcaster CCTV to launch a joint venture aimed at increasing commercialization of sports in China

## FINANCIALS: Sales and profits are in thousands of dollars—add 000 to get the full amount. 2008 Note: Financial information for 2008 was not available for all companies at press time.

| | | |
|---|---|---|
| 2008 Sales: $ | 2008 Profits: $ | **U.S. Stock Ticker: Private** |
| 2007 Sales: $ | 2007 Profits: $ | **Int'l Ticker:** Int'l Exchange: |
| 2006 Sales: $ | 2006 Profits: $ | Employees: 2,300 |
| 2005 Sales: $ | 2005 Profits: $ | Fiscal Year Ends: 12/31 |
| 2004 Sales: $ | 2004 Profits: $ | Parent Company: FORSTMANN LITTLE & CO |

## SALARIES/BENEFITS:

| | | | | |
|---|---|---|---|---|
| Pension Plan: | ESOP Stock Plan: | Profit Sharing: | Top Exec. Salary: $ | Bonus: $ |
| Savings Plan: | Stock Purch. Plan: | | Second Exec. Salary: $ | Bonus: $ |

## OTHER THOUGHTS:

**Apparent Women Officers or Directors**:
**Hot Spot for Advancement for Women/Minorities**:

## LOCATIONS: ("Y" = Yes)

| West: | Southwest: | Midwest: | Southeast: | Northeast: | International: |
|---|---|---|---|---|---|
| Y | | Y | Y | Y | Y |

# IMMUCOR INC

www.immucor.com

**Industry Group Code:** 339113 **Ranks within this company's industry group:** Sales: 16 Profits: 2

| Management: | | Sales/Marketing: | | Liberal Arts: | | Information Systems: | | Professionals: | | Technical/Scientific: | |
|---|---|---|---|---|---|---|---|---|---|---|---|
| Mgmt. Trainees: | | Mktg. Professionals: | Y | Gen. Writing/Editing: | | Info. Management: | Y | Finance/Accounting: | Y | Engineers, Elec.: | Y |
| Experienced Mgmt.: | Y | Retail Sales: | | Technical Writing: | Y | Software Dev.: | Y | Law: | Y | Engineers, Other: | Y |
| Int'l Business: | Y | Commercial/Industrial: | Y | Graphic Arts/Photog.: | | Hardware Dev.: | Y | HR/Other: | Y | Health/Lab: | Y |
| MBA Graduates: | Y | Sales Trainees: | Y | Music: | | Systems Integration: | | Training: | Y | Scientists/Research: | Y |
| | | Advertising Pros.: | | Broadcasting: | | Consulting/Other: | | Health Care: | Y | Petroleum/Chemicals: | |
| | | | | Other: | | | | Consulting: | | Math/Other: | Y |

## TYPES OF BUSINESS:

Equipment-Blood Testing
Automated Blood Bank Instruments
Blood Reagents

## BRANDS/DIVISIONS/AFFILIATES:

ABS2000
ROSYS Plato
DIAS Plus
ImmucorGamma Inc
BeadChip
Immucor Sales Inc
IBG Immucor Limited
BioArray Solutions Ltd

## CONTACTS: *Note: Officers with more than one job title may be intentionally listed here more than once.*

Gioacchino (Nino) DeChirico, CEO
Gioacchino (Nino) De Chirico, Pres.
Richard A. Flynt, CFO/VP
Michael C. Poynter, VP-Sales
Ralph A. Eatz, Chief Scientific Officer/Sr. VP
Phil Moise, General Counsel/Sec./VP
Joseph E. Rosen, Chmn.
Jean-Jacques de Jaegher, VP-Int'l

| **Phone:** 770-441-2051 | **Fax:** 770-441-3807 |
|---|---|
| **Toll-Free:** 800-829-2553 | |
| **Address:** 3130 Gateway Dr., Norcross, GA 30091-5625 US | |

## GROWTH PLANS/SPECIAL FEATURES:

Immucor, Inc. develops, manufactures and sells a complete line of reagents and automated systems used primarily by hospitals, clinical laboratories and blood banks in a number of tests performed to detect and identify certain properties of the cell and serum components of human blood prior to blood transfusion. The company has manufacturing facilities in the United States and Canada and sells products from these facilities and through its affiliates in Germany, Italy, Belgium, Spain, Portugal, France and Japan. Immucor's automated walk-away instrument for the hospital blood bank transfusion laboratory is the Galileo and is marketed to customers worldwide, including Europe, North America, and Japan. The company launched their latest instrument, the Echo, in late 2007. Echo is geared toward the small- to medium-sized hospital market, which is the largest segment of Immucor's customers, numbering approximately 5,000 to 6,000 worldwide. In 2008, the firm decided to sell products directly in France instead of through a distributor and developed a transition plan with Bio-Rad Laboratories, Inc., a former distributor. Immucor spent approximately $1.4 million to establish the new organization in France. In June 2008, with the similar intent to sell products directly in the U.K., the firm acquired all of the outstanding shares of IBG Immucor Limited, a private U.K. company for approximately $4.4 million. In May 2008, in Japan, the firm concluded a three-year transition arrangement with Kainos related to the 2005 purchase of its distribution business. In August 2008, the firm closed its acquisition of BioArray Solutions Ltd., a privately held company based in Warren, NJ for approximately $117 million. BioArray has developed, patented and introduced its BeadChip system for molecular medicine, which uses arrays of proprietary microparticles to analyze DNA.

## FINANCIALS: **Sales and profits are in thousands of dollars—add 000 to get the full amount. 2008 Note: Financial information for 2008 was not available for all companies at press time.**

| | | |
|---|---|---|
| 2008 Sales: $261,199 | 2008 Profits: $71,454 | **U.S. Stock Ticker: BLUD** |
| 2007 Sales: $223,678 | 2007 Profits: $60,068 | **Int'l Ticker:** Int'l Exchange: |
| 2006 Sales: $183,506 | 2006 Profits: $39,843 | Employees: 610 |
| 2005 Sales: $144,786 | 2005 Profits: $23,910 | Fiscal Year Ends: 5/31 |
| 2004 Sales: $112,558 | 2004 Profits: $12,538 | Parent Company: |

## SALARIES/BENEFITS:

| | | | | |
|---|---|---|---|---|
| Pension Plan: | ESOP Stock Plan: | Profit Sharing: | Top Exec. Salary: $503,469 | Bonus: $338,000 |
| Savings Plan: Y | Stock Purch. Plan: | | Second Exec. Salary: $375,446 | Bonus: $244,400 |

## OTHER THOUGHTS:

**Apparent Women Officers or Directors**:
**Hot Spot for Advancement for Women/Minorities**:

## LOCATIONS: ("Y" = Yes)

| West: | Southwest: | Midwest: | Southeast: | Northeast: | International: |
|---|---|---|---|---|---|
| | | | Y | | Y |

# INAMED CORP

www.allerganandinamed.com

**Industry Group Code:** 339113 **Ranks within this company's industry group:** Sales: Profits:

| Management: | | Sales/Marketing: | | Liberal Arts: | | Information Systems: | | Professionals: | | Technical/Scientific: | |
|---|---|---|---|---|---|---|---|---|---|---|---|
| Mgmt. Trainees: | | Mktg. Professionals: | Y | Gen. Writing/Editing: | | Info. Management: | Y | Finance/Accounting: | Y | Engineers, Elec.: | |
| Experienced Mgmt.: | Y | Retail Sales: | | Technical Writing: | Y | Software Dev.: | | Law: | Y | Engineers, Other: | Y |
| Int'l Business: | Y | Commercial/Industrial: | Y | Graphic Arts/Photog.: | | Hardware Dev.: | | HR/Other: | Y | Health/Lab: | Y |
| MBA Graduates: | Y | Sales Trainees: | Y | Music: | | Systems Integration: | | Training: | Y | Scientists/Research: | Y |
| | | Advertising Pros.: | | Broadcasting: | | Consulting/Other: | | Health Care: | Y | Petroleum/Chemicals: | |
| | | | | Other: | | | | Consulting: | | Math/Other: | Y |

## TYPES OF BUSINESS:

Supplies-Prostheses
Breast Implants
Tissue Expanders
Facial Implants
Obesity Products

## BRANDS/DIVISIONS/AFFILIATES:

INAMED Aesthetics
INAMED Health
INAMED International
Hydra Fill
Styl 150 One Stage BioDIMENSIONAL
Lap Band
Allergan Inc

## CONTACTS: *Note: Officers with more than one job title may be intentionally listed here more than once.*

Nicholas L. Teti, CEO
Nicholas L. Teti, Pres.
Nicholas L. Teti, Chmn.

**Phone:** 805-683-6761 **Fax:** 805-692-5432
**Toll-Free:**
**Address:** 5540 Ekwill St., Santa Barbara, CA 93111 US

## GROWTH PLANS/SPECIAL FEATURES:

INAMED Corp., a subsidiary of Allergan, Inc., is a global surgical and medical device company engaged in the development, manufacturing and marketing of products for the plastic and reconstructive surgery; aesthetic medicine; and obesity markets. The company operates through two primary divisions, INAMED Aesthetics and INAMED Health, as well maintaining partnerships with Biomatrix and Genzyme Biosurgery. INAMED Aesthetics offers a line of breast implants for augmentation and reconstruction surgeries following mastectomies, as well as collagen-based facial implants to correct facial wrinkles and improve lip definition. INAMED Health develops and markets medical devices to treat obesity using minimally invasive surgery. The company also offers a physician marketing program designed to assist in increasing incremental consultations, promote practice differentiation and optimize profitability. Products include The Style 150 - One Stage BioDIMENSIONAL reconstruction system for breast reconstruction and tissue expanders; Hydra Fill, a hyaluronic acid based face implant; and Lap Band, for treatment of severe obesity. INAMED International extends the company's sales, marketing and manufacturing presence to locations in Canada, Germany, France, Spain, Italy, Ireland, the U.K., Costa Rica, Japan and Australia.

The company offers its employees medical, dental, vision and prescription drug insurance; an employee assistance plan; life and AD&D insurance; short- and long-term disability insurance; travel accident insurance; a 401(k) plan; an employee stock purchase plan; and educational assistance.

## FINANCIALS: Sales and profits are in thousands of dollars—add 000 to get the full amount. 2008 Note: Financial information for 2008 was not available for all companies at press time.

| | | |
|---|---|---|
| 2008 Sales: $ | 2008 Profits: $ | **U.S. Stock Ticker: Subsidiary** |
| 2007 Sales: $ | 2007 Profits: $ | **Int'l Ticker:** Int'l Exchange: |
| 2006 Sales: $ | 2006 Profits: $ | Employees: 1,300 |
| 2005 Sales: $437,800 | 2005 Profits: $-26,200 | Fiscal Year Ends: |
| 2004 Sales: $384,400 | 2004 Profits: $63,100 | Parent Company: ALLERGAN INC |

## SALARIES/BENEFITS:

| | | | | |
|---|---|---|---|---|
| Pension Plan: | ESOP Stock Plan: | Profit Sharing: | Top Exec. Salary: $452,698 | Bonus: $625,100 |
| Savings Plan: Y | Stock Purch. Plan: Y | | Second Exec. Salary: $296,068 | Bonus: $315,000 |

## OTHER THOUGHTS:

**Apparent Women Officers or Directors**:
**Hot Spot for Advancement for Women/Minorities**:

## LOCATIONS: ("Y" = Yes)

| West: | Southwest: | Midwest: | Southeast: | Northeast: | International: |
|---|---|---|---|---|---|
| Y | | | | | Y |

# INDEPENDENCE HOLDING CO

**www.ihcgroup.com**

**Industry Group Code:** 524113 **Ranks within this company's industry group:** Sales: 7 Profits: 6

| **Management:** | | **Sales/Marketing:** | | **Liberal Arts:** | | **Information Systems:** | | **Professionals:** | | **Technical/Scientific:** | |
|---|---|---|---|---|---|---|---|---|---|---|---|
| Mgmt. Trainees: | | Mktg. Professionals: | Y | Gen. Writing/Editing: | Y | Info. Management: | Y | Finance/Accounting: | Y | Engineers, Elec.: | |
| Experienced Mgmt.: | Y | Retail Sales: | | Technical Writing: | Y | Software Dev.: | | Law: | Y | Engineers, Other: | |
| Int'l Business: | | Commercial/Industrial: | | Graphic Arts/Photog.: | | Hardware Dev.: | | HR/Other: | Y | Health/Lab: | |
| MBA Graduates: | Y | Sales Trainees: | Y | Music: | | Systems Integration: | | Training: | Y | Scientists/Research: | |
| | | Advertising Pros.: | Y | Broadcasting: | | Consulting/Other: | | Health Care: | Y | Petroleum/Chemicals: | |
| | | | | Other: | | | | Consulting: | | Math/Other: | Y |

## TYPES OF BUSINESS:

Insurance Underwriting
Medical Stop-Loss
Group Disability & Life Insurance
Individual Life Insurance

## BRANDS/DIVISIONS/AFFILIATES:

Standard Security Life Insurance Company
Madison National Life Insurance Company, Inc.
Insurers Administrative Corporation
Majestic Underwriters, LLC
GroupLink, Inc.
IHC Health Solutions, Inc.
Community America Insurance Services, Inc.
Independence American

## CONTACTS: *Note: Officers with more than one job title may be intentionally listed here more than once.*

Roy T. K. Thung, CEO
David Kettig, Co-COO/Sr. VP
Roy T. K. Thung, Pres.
Teresa A. Herbert, CFO/Sr. VP
Jeffrey C. Smedsrud, Sr. VP/Chief Mktg. & Strategy Officer
Adam C. Vandervoort, General Counsel/VP/Sec.
Colleen P. Maggi, Controller/VP
Scott Wood, Co-COO/Sr. VP
Bernon R. Erickson, Jr., Chief Health Actuary/Sr. VP
Henry B. Spencer, VP-Investments
C. Winfield Swarr, Chief Underwriting Officer/VP
Edward Netter, Chmn.

| **Phone:** 203-358-8000 | **Fax:** 203-348-3103 |
|---|---|
| **Toll-Free:** 877-442-4267 | |
| **Address:** 96 Cummings Point Rd., Stamford, CT 06902 US | |

## GROWTH PLANS/SPECIAL FEATURES:

Independence Holding Co. (IHC) is a holding company principally engaged in the life and health insurance business. The company operates through its wholly-owned insurance companies, Standard Security Insurance Company and Madison National Life Insurance Company, Inc.; and its marketing and administrative companies, including Insurers Administrative Corporation, Health Plan Administrators, GroupLink, IHC Health Solutions, Inc. and Community America Insurance Services, Inc. The company's employer medical stop-loss is its largest product line. Medical stop-loss insurance allows self-insured employers to manage the risk of excessive health insurance exposures by limiting aggregate and specific losses to a predetermined amount. Standard Security Life markets major medical stop-loss in all 50 states, Washington D.C., the Virgin Islands and Puerto Rico. In addition, it also sells short-term statutory disability benefit product in New York State and certain life, annuity and blanket accident coverage sold primarily in New York State to volunteer emergency personnel. Madison National Life sells group life and disability, credit life and disability and individual life insurance in 49 states, Puerto Rico, the U.S. Virgin Islands and Puerto Rico. It also markets group life and disability products, primarily in the Midwest; credit life and disability; and individual life and annuities to military and civilian government employees. The firm also acquires block of life policies from other insurance companies. Independence American reinsures a significant portion of the medical stop-loss business written by Standard Security Life and Madison National Life. In 2007, IHC acquired Actuarial Management Corporation and IHC Health Solutions, a marketing company specializing in alternative distribution methods and strategic partnerships. In April 2008, IHC's subsidiary, Madison National Life, finalized the sale of its credit segment and acquired a $65 million block of life insurance policies, of which Madison National Life will assume administration in October 2008.

## FINANCIALS: **Sales and profits are in thousands of dollars—add 000 to get the full amount. 2008 Note: Financial information for 2008 was not available for all companies at press time.**

| | | |
|---|---|---|
| 2008 Sales: $ | 2008 Profits: $ | **U.S. Stock Ticker: IHC** |
| 2007 Sales: $402,322 | 2007 Profits: $-2,328 | **Int'l Ticker:** Int'l Exchange: |
| 2006 Sales: $364,688 | 2006 Profits: $14,061 | Employees: 682 |
| 2005 Sales: $296,417 | 2005 Profits: $17,301 | Fiscal Year Ends: 12/31 |
| 2004 Sales: $225,669 | 2004 Profits: $22,939 | Parent Company: |

## SALARIES/BENEFITS:

| | | | | |
|---|---|---|---|---|
| Pension Plan: | ESOP Stock Plan: | Profit Sharing: | Top Exec. Salary: $401,441 | Bonus: $316,620 |
| Savings Plan: | Stock Purch. Plan: | | Second Exec. Salary: $364,000 | Bonus: $128,121 |

## OTHER THOUGHTS:

**Apparent Women Officers or Directors**: 2
**Hot Spot for Advancement for Women/Minorities**:

## LOCATIONS: ("Y" = Yes)

| West: | Southwest: | Midwest: | Southeast: | Northeast: | International: |
|---|---|---|---|---|---|
| Y | Y | Y | Y | Y | |

# INFINERA CORP

www.infinera.com

**Industry Group Code:** 334413 **Ranks within this company's industry group:** Sales: 4 Profits: 5

| Management: | | Sales/Marketing: | | Liberal Arts: | | Information Systems: | | Professionals: | | Technical/Scientific: | |
|---|---|---|---|---|---|---|---|---|---|---|---|
| Mgmt. Trainees: | | Mktg. Professionals: | Y | Gen. Writing/Editing: | | Info. Management: | Y | Finance/Accounting: | Y | Engineers, Elec.: | Y |
| Experienced Mgmt.: | Y | Retail Sales: | | Technical Writing: | Y | Software Dev.: | Y | Law: | Y | Engineers, Other: | Y |
| Int'l Business: | Y | Commercial/Industrial: | Y | Graphic Arts/Photog.: | | Hardware Dev.: | Y | HR/Other: | Y | Health/Lab: | |
| MBA Graduates: | Y | Sales Trainees: | Y | Music: | | Systems Integration: | Y | Training: | Y | Scientists/Research: | Y |
| | | Advertising Pros.: | | Broadcasting: | | Consulting/Other: | | Health Care: | | Petroleum/Chemicals: | |
| | | | | Other: | | | | Consulting: | | Math/Other: | Y |

## TYPES OF BUSINESS:

Optical-Electronic Conversion Equipment
Optical Network Infrastructure Equipment
Network Design & Engineering

## BRANDS/DIVISIONS/AFFILIATES:

Digital Optical Network
DTN System
Infinera IQ Network Operating System
Infinera Management Suite
Little Optics

## CONTACTS:

*Note: Officers with more than one job title may be intentionally listed here more than once.*

Jagdeep Singh, CEO
Thomas J. (Tom) Fallon, COO
Jagdeep Singh, Pres.
Duston M. Williams, CFO
Howard Lukens, VP-Strategic Sales
Paul M. Whitney, VP-Human Resources
Drew Perkins, CTO
William R. (Rusty) Cumpston, VP-Sys. Eng.
Fred Kish, VP-PIC Dev. & Mfg.
Michael O. McCarthy III, General Counsel/VP
David F. Welch, Chief Strategy Officer
Lonny Orona, VP-Worldwide Customer Svcs. & Tech. Support
Minoo Mortazavi, VP-Strategic Materials
Jagdeep Singh, Chmn.
Scott A. Chandler, VP-Worldwide Sales

**Phone:** 408-572-5200 **Fax:** 408-572-5343
**Toll-Free:**
**Address:** 169 Java Dr., Sunnyvale, CA 94089 US

## GROWTH PLANS/SPECIAL FEATURES:

Infinera Corp. is a provider of solutions for optical communications networks. The company's Digital Optical Network architecture is based on one of the world's only commercially-deployed, large scale photonic integrated circuits (PICs). Its PICs transmit and receive 100 gigabit per second (Gbps) of optical capacity and incorporate the functionality of over 60 discrete optical components into a pair of indium phosphide chips approximately the size of a child's fingernail. The company has used its PIC technology to design a new digital optical communications system called the DTN System, designed to enable optical to electrical to optical conversion of communication signals; to significantly improve communications service providers' economics and service offerings as compared to traditional systems; and to provide faster service delivery and network management flexibility. The DTN System integrates the functionality of over 60 discrete optical components within a single PIC pair, reducing physical space requirements for a given amount of optical network capacity. The DTN System additionally processes traffic digitally, which ensures greater signal quality and network management flexibility. Infinera's DTN System also includes software that utilizes digital data to enable network provisioning, management, testing and control. The firm's carrier-class DTN System runs its Infinera IQ Network Operating System and is integrated with its Infinera Management Suite software, which together are designed to enhance and simplify network monitoring, management and control. The company's goal is to establish its Digital Optical Network as a leading architecture for optical communications networks. Infinera's support services include technical assistance; planning and network design services; network trial assistance; engineering; furnishing; installation testing; documentation; and training. The company has sold its DTN System to 41 customers worldwide. In February 2007, Infinera acquired Little Optics, a provider of planar lightwave circuits. In June 2007, the company went public.

## FINANCIALS:

**Sales and profits are in thousands of dollars—add 000 to get the full amount. 2008 Note: Financial information for 2008 was not available for all companies at press time.**

| | |
|---|---|
| 2008 Sales: $519,212 | 2008 Profits: $78,728 |
| 2007 Sales: $245,852 | 2007 Profits: $-55,342 |
| 2006 Sales: $58,236 | 2006 Profits: $-89,935 |
| 2005 Sales: $4,127 | 2005 Profits: $-64,826 |
| 2004 Sales: $ | 2004 Profits: $ |

**U.S. Stock Ticker: INFN**
**Int'l Ticker:** Int'l Exchange:
Employees: 711
Fiscal Year Ends: 12/31
Parent Company:

## SALARIES/BENEFITS:

| | | | | |
|---|---|---|---|---|
| Pension Plan: | ESOP Stock Plan: | Profit Sharing: | Top Exec. Salary: $250,000 | Bonus: $250,000 |
| Savings Plan: | Stock Purch. Plan: | | Second Exec. Salary: $230,962 | Bonus: $300,000 |

## OTHER THOUGHTS:

**Apparent Women Officers or Directors:**
**Hot Spot for Advancement for Women/Minorities:**

## LOCATIONS: ("Y" = Yes)

| West: | Southwest: | Midwest: | Southeast: | Northeast: | International: |
|---|---|---|---|---|---|
| Y | | | | Y | Y |

# INSPIRE PHARMACEUTICALS INC

www.inspirepharm.com

**Industry Group Code:** 325412 **Ranks within this company's industry group:** Sales: 29 Profits: 27

| Management: | | Sales/Marketing: | | Liberal Arts: | | Information Systems: | | Professionals: | | Technical/Scientific: | |
|---|---|---|---|---|---|---|---|---|---|---|---|
| Mgmt. Trainees: | | Mktg. Professionals: | Y | Gen. Writing/Editing: | | Info. Management: | Y | Finance/Accounting: | Y | Engineers, Elec.: | |
| Experienced Mgmt.: | Y | Retail Sales: | | Technical Writing: | Y | Software Dev.: | Y | Law: | Y | Engineers, Other: | |
| Int'l Business: | | Commercial/Industrial: | Y | Graphic Arts/Photog.: | | Hardware Dev.: | | HR/Other: | Y | Health/Lab: | Y |
| MBA Graduates: | Y | Sales Trainees: | Y | Music: | | Systems Integration: | | Training: | Y | Scientists/Research: | Y |
| | | Advertising Pros.: | | Broadcasting: | | Consulting/Other: | | Health Care: | Y | Petroleum/Chemicals: | |
| | | | | Other: | | | | Consulting: | | Math/Other: | Y |

## TYPES OF BUSINESS:

Drugs-Respiratory & Ocular
Cystic Fibrosis Treatment
Retinal Disease Treatment
Dry Eye Treatment
Allergic Conjunctivitis
Cardiovascular Disease Treatment

## BRANDS/DIVISIONS/AFFILIATES:

Restasis
Elestat
AzaSite
Prolacria
Bilastine
Denufosol Tetrasodium

## CONTACTS:

*Note: Officers with more than one job title may be intentionally listed here more than once.*

Christy L. Shaffer, CEO
Christy L. Shaffer, Pres.
Thomas R. Staab, II, CFO
Jeff W. Sampere, VP-Mktg.
Benjamin R. Yerxa, Chief Scientific Officer
Sean K. Blake, Dir.-IT
W.M. Mulchi, VP-Tech. Oper.
Denise M. Sheehan, VP-Prod. Planning
W.M. Mulchi, VP-Mfg.
Joseph M. Spagnardi, General Counsel/Sr. VP/Sec.
Donald J. Kellerman, Sr. VP-Dev.
Jenny R. Kobin, VP-Corp Comm.
Jenny R. Kobin, VP-Investor Rel.
Mark A. Siemek, Dir.-Financial Planning, Analysis & SEC Reports
Lynn Smiley, Chief Medical Officer
Benjamin R. Yerxa, Exec. VP-Strategic Oper.
Joseph K. Schachle, Exec. VP/Chief-Commercial Oper.
Gerald W. St. Peter, Sr. VP-Sales & Managed Markets
Kenneth B. Lee, Jr., Chmn.

**Phone:** 919-941-9777 **Fax:** 919-941-9797
**Toll-Free:** 877-800-4536
**Address:** 4222 Emperor Blvd., Ste. 200, Durham, NC 27703-8466 US

## GROWTH PLANS/SPECIAL FEATURES:

Inspire Pharmaceuticals, Inc. is a biopharmaceutical company dedicated to discovering, developing and commercializing prescription pharmaceutical products in the opthamalic and respiratory/allergies areas. The firm also focuses on the design and synthesis of P2 receptor related agonists, where it has significant expertise. Inspire's ophthalmic products and product candidates are concentrated in the allergic conjunctivitis, dry eye disease, cystic fibrosis, acute cardiac care, seasonal allergic rhinitis and glaucoma indications. The firm's product portfolio includes Elestat for allergic conjunctivitis, Restasis for dry eye disease, and AzaSite for bacterial conjunctivitis. Elestat and Restasis are licensed to Allergan and currently marketed in the U.S. AzaSite was developed, as a collaborative project, with InSite Vision. Products in clinical development include Prolacria (diquafosol tetrasodium) for dry eye, which has completed Phase III testing and has received two approvable letters from the FDA; denufosol tetrasodium (INS37217 Respiratory) for cystic fibrosis, currently in Phase III trials; Bilastine oral antihistamine for allergic rhinitis, currently in Phase III trials; Epinastine nasal spray for allergic rhinitis, currently in Phase III; and INS115644 for glaucoma, currently in Phase I. Inspire has a development and license agreement with Boehringer Ingelheim International GmbH, granting Inspire certain exclusive rights to develop and market an intranasal dosage form of Epinastine in the U.S. and Canada, for the treatment and prevention of seasonal allergic rhinitis. In April 2007, AzaSite was approved by the FDA, and in August 2007, AzaSite was launched in the U.S. In April 2008, the company discontinued development of Epinastine nasal spray due to unmet primary endpoints in Phase III trials. In June 2008, Inspire announced successful Phase III results for denufosol tetrasodium.

Inspire offers health insurance, an employee assistance program, and vacation packages. Additionally, it offers monthly on-site massage therapists, weekly yoga and Pilates classes, as well as group activities and parties.

## FINANCIALS:

**Sales and profits are in thousands of dollars—add 000 to get the full amount. 2008 Note: Financial information for 2008 was not available for all companies at press time.**

| | | |
|---|---|---|
| 2008 Sales: $ | 2008 Profits: $ | **U.S. Stock Ticker: ISPH** |
| 2007 Sales: $48,665 | 2007 Profits: $-63,740 | **Int'l Ticker:** Int'l Exchange: |
| 2006 Sales: $37,059 | 2006 Profits: $-42,115 | Employees: 250 |
| 2005 Sales: $23,266 | 2005 Profits: $-31,847 | Fiscal Year Ends: 12/31 |
| 2004 Sales: $11,068 | 2004 Profits: $-44,069 | Parent Company: |

## SALARIES/BENEFITS:

| | | | | |
|---|---|---|---|---|
| Pension Plan: | ESOP Stock Plan: | Profit Sharing: Y | Top Exec. Salary: $449,946 | Bonus: $300,000 |
| Savings Plan: Y | Stock Purch. Plan: | | Second Exec. Salary: $175,478 | Bonus: $96,000 |

## OTHER THOUGHTS:

**Apparent Women Officers or Directors**: 6
**Hot Spot for Advancement for Women/Minorities**: Y

## LOCATIONS: ("Y" = Yes)

| West: | Southwest: | Midwest: | Southeast: | Northeast: | International: |
|---|---|---|---|---|---|
| Y | | | | Y | |

# INTEGRA LIFESCIENCES HOLDINGS CORP

www.integra-ls.com

**Industry Group Code:** 339113 **Ranks within this company's industry group:** Sales: 3 Profits: 7

| Management: | | Sales/Marketing: | | Liberal Arts: | | Information Systems: | | Professionals: | | Technical/Scientific: | |
|---|---|---|---|---|---|---|---|---|---|---|---|
| Mgmt. Trainees: | | Mktg. Professionals: | Y | Gen. Writing/Editing: | | Info. Management: | Y | Finance/Accounting: | Y | Engineers, Elec.: | Y |
| Experienced Mgmt.: | Y | Retail Sales: | | Technical Writing: | Y | Software Dev.: | Y | Law: | Y | Engineers, Other: | Y |
| Int'l Business: | Y | Commercial/Industrial: | Y | Graphic Arts/Photog.: | | Hardware Dev.: | | HR/Other: | Y | Health/Lab: | Y |
| MBA Graduates: | Y | Sales Trainees: | Y | Music: | | Systems Integration: | | Training: | Y | Scientists/Research: | Y |
| | | Advertising Pros.: | | Broadcasting: | | Consulting/Other: | | Health Care: | Y | Petroleum/Chemicals: | |
| | | | | Other: | | | | Consulting: | | Math/Other: | Y |

## TYPES OF BUSINESS:

Medical Equipment Manufacturing
Implants & Biomaterials
Absorbable Medical Products
Tissue Regeneration Technology
Neurosurgery Products
Skin Replacement Products

## BRANDS/DIVISIONS/AFFILIATES:

Integra NeuroSciences
Integra Plastic and Reconstructive Surgery
JARIT Surgical Instruments, Inc.
DuraGen Dural Graft Matrix
NeuraGen Nerve Guide
CURE International
Precise Dental
Tibiaxys Plating System

## CONTACTS: *Note: Officers with more than one job title may be intentionally listed here more than once.*

Stuart M. Essig, CEO
Gerard S. Carlozzi, COO/Exec. VP
Stuart M. Essig, Pres.
John B. Henneman, CFO/Exec. VP
Deborah A. Leonetti, Chief Mktg. Officer/Sr. VP-Mktg.
Wilma J. Davis, Sr. VP-Human Resources
Simon J. Archibald, Chief Scientific Officer/VP-Clinical Affairs
Wilma Davis, Acting CIO
Linda Littlejohns, VP-Clinical Dev.
Donald R. Nociolo, Sr. VP-Mfg. Oper.
John B. Henneman, III, Exec. VP-Admin.
Richard D. Gorelick, General Counsel/VP
James A. Oti, Sr. VP-Global Oper.
Maria Platsis, VP-Corp. Dev.
John Bostjancic, VP-Investor Rel.
John B. Henneman, Exec. VP-Finance
Nora Brennan, Treas./VP
Judith E. O'Grady, Sr. VP-Quality, Regulatory & Clinical Affairs
Jerry Corbin, VP/Corp. Controller
Richard E. Caruso, Chmn.
Eric Fourcault, Pres., EMEA Div.

**Phone:** 609-275-0500 **Fax:** 609-275-5363
**Toll-Free:** 800-654-2873
**Address:** 311 C Enterprise Dr., Plainsboro, NJ 08536 US

## GROWTH PLANS/SPECIAL FEATURES:

Integra Lifesciences Holdings Corporation develops, manufactures and markets medical devices, implants and biomaterials for use in neurotrauma, neurosurgery, reconstructive surgery and general surgery. The company's two primary product lines include neurosurgical/orthopedic implants and medical/surgical implants. The Neuro/Ortho implants group provides dural grafts for the repair of dura mater, dermal regeneration and engineered wound dressing; implants for small bone and joint fixation; repair of peripheral nerves; and hydrocephalus management. The MedSurg Equipment product group produces ultrasonic surgery systems for tissue ablation, cranial stabilization and brain retraction systems as well as instrumentation for use in general, neurosurgical, spinal, plastic and reconstructive surgery. Patented products of the company include the DuraGen Dural Graft Matrix, the NeuraGen Nerve Guide, the INTEGRA Dermal Regeneration Template and the INTEGRA Bilayer Matrix Wound Dressing, which incorporates Integra's proprietary absorbable implant technology. Products principally focus on injuries that involve the brain, cranium, spine and central nervous system and the repair and reconstruction of soft tissue. Integra's products are marketed and sold through its subsidiaries, Integra NeuroSciences and Integra Reconstructive Surgery. The firm also has strategic alliances with Miltex Surgical Instruments, Inc.; Zimmer Holdings, Inc.; and others. Integra's sales teams are located throughout the U.S., Canada, Germany, the U.K., the Benelux region and France. In December 2007, Integra acquired the Precise Dental group of companies for $10 million in cash. In May 2008, the firm announced the introduction of its Tibiaxys Plating Systems, designed to treat ankle arthritis and deformity.

## FINANCIALS: **Sales and profits are in thousands of dollars—add 000 to get the full amount. 2008 Note: Financial information for 2008 was not available for all companies at press time.**

| | | |
|---|---|---|
| 2008 Sales: $ | 2008 Profits: $ | **U.S. Stock Ticker: IART** |
| 2007 Sales: $550,459 | 2007 Profits: $33,471 | **Int'l Ticker:** Int'l Exchange: |
| 2006 Sales: $419,297 | 2006 Profits: $29,407 | Employees: 2,500 |
| 2005 Sales: $277,935 | 2005 Profits: $37,194 | Fiscal Year Ends: 12/31 |
| 2004 Sales: $229,825 | 2004 Profits: $17,197 | Parent Company: |

## SALARIES/BENEFITS:

| | | | | |
|---|---|---|---|---|
| Pension Plan: | ESOP Stock Plan: | Profit Sharing: | Top Exec. Salary: $550,000 | Bonus: $550,000 |
| Savings Plan: Y | Stock Purch. Plan: Y | | Second Exec. Salary: $420,000 | Bonus: $168,000 |

## OTHER THOUGHTS:

**Apparent Women Officers or Directors**: 5
**Hot Spot for Advancement for Women/Minorities**: Y

## LOCATIONS: ("Y" = Yes)

| West: | Southwest: | Midwest: | Southeast: | Northeast: | International: |
|---|---|---|---|---|---|
| Y | | Y | | Y | Y |

# INTEGRAL SYSTEMS INC

**www.integ.com**

**Industry Group Code:** 511213 **Ranks within this company's industry group:** Sales: 2 Profits: 1

| Management: | | Sales/Marketing: | | Liberal Arts: | | Information Systems: | | Professionals: | | Technical/Scientific: | |
|---|---|---|---|---|---|---|---|---|---|---|---|
| Mgmt. Trainees: | | Mktg. Professionals: | Y | Gen. Writing/Editing: | | Info. Management: | Y | Finance/Accounting: | Y | Engineers, Elec.: | Y |
| Experienced Mgmt.: | Y | Retail Sales: | | Technical Writing: | Y | Software Dev.: | Y | Law: | Y | Engineers, Other: | |
| Int'l Business: | Y | Commercial/Industrial: | Y | Graphic Arts/Photog.: | | Hardware Dev.: | | HR/Other: | Y | Health/Lab: | |
| MBA Graduates: | Y | Sales Trainees: | Y | Music: | | Systems Integration: | | Training: | Y | Scientists/Research: | |
| | | Advertising Pros.: | | Broadcasting: | | Consulting/Other: | | Health Care: | | Petroleum/Chemicals: | |
| | | | | Other: | | | | Consulting: | | Math/Other: | |

## TYPES OF BUSINESS:

Satellite Systems & Software
Signal Monitoring Systems & Software
Telemetry Processing Systems
Systems Integration Services

## BRANDS/DIVISIONS/AFFILIATES:

Real Time Logic, Inc.
SAT Corporation
Newpoint Technologies, Inc.
EPOCH Integrated Product Suite
ABE
EPOCH Web Server
Task Initiator
EPOCH Triggers

## CONTACTS:

*Note: Officers with more than one job title may be intentionally listed here more than once.*

John Higginbotham, CEO
William M. Bambarger, Jr., CFO
Peter J. (Pete) Gaffney, Exec. VP-Tech.
Elaine M. Brown, Exec. VP-Admin.
Peter J. (Pete) Gaffney, Exec. VP-New Bus. Dev.
Stuart C. Daughtridge, Exec. VP-Commercial Div.
James G. Schuetzle, Exec. VP-Gov't. Div.
John M. (Jack) Albertine, Chmn.

**Phone:** 301-731-4233 **Fax:** 301-731-9606
**Toll-Free:** 800-295-4233
**Address:** 5000 Philadelphia Way, Lanham, MD 20706-4417 US

## GROWTH PLANS/SPECIAL FEATURES:

Integral Systems, Inc. is a Maryland-based company that builds satellite ground systems and equipment for command and control; integration and test; data processing; and simulation. Integral Systems has provided ground systems for over 200 different satellite missions for communications, science, meteorology and earth resource applications. The company's products are designed to reduce the cost and minimize the development risk associated with traditional, custom-built satellite ground systems. Integral Systems was the first company to offer a comprehensive commercial off-the-shelf (COTS) software product line for command and control. As a systems integrator, it configures its products to provide turnkey satellite control facilities that can operate multiple satellites from most manufacturers. Subsidiary Real Time Logic, Inc. designs and builds the company's satellite communications equipment and systems, which are used principally for satellite tracking stations, control centers, spacecraft factories and range facilities. Subsidiaries SAT Corporation and Newpoint Technologies, Inc. provide complimentary ground system components and systems. Most of the company's sales involve a combination of COTS software and hardware products together with development services for mission-specific requirements and system integration. The EPOCH Integrated Product Suite is designed to operate a variety of satellites with minimum personnel and features a distributed architecture consisting of a series of servers and user workstations interconnected by an ethernet local area network (LAN). Included in the product suite is the EPOCH T&C Server and EPOCH Client, its real-time satellite data processing and control software products; OASYS, its mission-planning software; ABE, its offline analysis product; and Archive Manager, which performs archive data generation, storage, storage management and retrieval. Additional products include EPOCH Web Server, which provides access to real-time and historical satellite data through the Internet; Task Initiator, which provides automation capabilities to automatically execute scheduled or event-initiated tasks; and EPOCH Triggers, which provides automatic execution of system actions based on preprogrammed conditions.

## FINANCIALS:

**Sales and profits are in thousands of dollars—add 000 to get the full amount. 2008 Note: Financial information for 2008 was not available for all companies at press time.**

| | | |
|---|---|---|
| 2008 Sales: $ | 2008 Profits: $ | **U.S. Stock Ticker: ISYS** |
| 2007 Sales: $128,654 | 2007 Profits: $12,826 | **Int'l Ticker:** Int'l Exchange: |
| 2006 Sales: $116,531 | 2006 Profits: $12,339 | Employees: 455 |
| 2005 Sales: $97,725 | 2005 Profits: $6,301 | Fiscal Year Ends: 9/30 |
| 2004 Sales: $90,311 | 2004 Profits: $6,761 | Parent Company: |

## SALARIES/BENEFITS:

| | | | | |
|---|---|---|---|---|
| Pension Plan: | ESOP Stock Plan: | Profit Sharing: | Top Exec. Salary: $272,583 | Bonus: $ |
| Savings Plan: | Stock Purch. Plan: | | Second Exec. Salary: $261,264 | Bonus: $80,000 |

## OTHER THOUGHTS:

**Apparent Women Officers or Directors:** 1
**Hot Spot for Advancement for Women/Minorities:**

## LOCATIONS: ("Y" = Yes)

| West: | Southwest: | Midwest: | Southeast: | Northeast: | International: |
|---|---|---|---|---|---|
| Y | | | | Y | Y |

# INTEGRAMED AMERICA INC

www.integramed.com

**Industry Group Code:** 621111 **Ranks within this company's industry group:** Sales: 1 Profits: 1

| Management: | | Sales/Marketing: | | Liberal Arts: | | Information Systems: | | Professionals: | | Technical/Scientific: | |
|---|---|---|---|---|---|---|---|---|---|---|---|
| Mgmt. Trainees: | | Mktg. Professionals: | Y | Gen. Writing/Editing: | | Info. Management: | Y | Finance/Accounting: | Y | Engineers, Elec.: | |
| Experienced Mgmt.: | Y | Retail Sales: | | Technical Writing: | | Software Dev.: | Y | Law: | Y | Engineers, Other: | |
| Int'l Business: | | Commercial/Industrial: | | Graphic Arts/Photog.: | | Hardware Dev.: | | HR/Other: | Y | Health/Lab: | Y |
| MBA Graduates: | Y | Sales Trainees: | Y | Music: | | Systems Integration: | | Training: | Y | Scientists/Research: | |
| | | Advertising Pros.: | | Broadcasting: | | Consulting/Other: | | Health Care: | Y | Petroleum/Chemicals: | |
| | | | | Other: | | | | Consulting: | | Math/Other: | |

## TYPES OF BUSINESS:

Fertility Treatments
Physician Practice Management-Reproductive Services
Treatment Financing Programs
Fertility-Related Pharmaceutical Distribution

## BRANDS/DIVISIONS/AFFILIATES:

FertilityWeb
IntegraMed Pharmaceutical Services, Inc.
IntegraMed Financial Services
ARTWorks Clinical Information System
ARTWorks Practice Management Information System
FertilityPartners
FertilityMarKit
Vein Clinics of America

## CONTACTS: *Note: Officers with more than one job title may be intentionally listed here more than once.*

Jay Higham, CEO
Jay Higham, Pres.
John W. Hlywak, Jr., CFO/Exec. VP
Scott Soifer, Sr. VP-Admin.
Claude White, General Counsel/VP
Scott Soifer, Sr. VP-Dev.
Pamela Schumann, Pres.-Consumer Svcs.
Joe Travia, Pres.-Fertility Centers Div.
Daniel P. Doman, Pres.-Vein Clinics Div.
Gerardo Canet, Chmn.

| **Phone:** 914-253-8000 | **Fax:** 914-253-8008 |
|---|---|
| **Toll-Free:** 800-458-0044 | |
| **Address:** 2 Manhattanville Rd., 3rd Fl., Purchase, NY 10577 US | |

## GROWTH PLANS/SPECIAL FEATURES:

IntegraMed America, Inc. offers products and services to patients and providers in the fertility industry. The company operates three segments: Fertility Centers, Consumer Services and Vein Clinics. The company provides services to a network of 96 reproductive science centers including fertility clinics, embryologic laboratories and clinical research sites, which all provide conventional fertility and assisted reproductive technology (ART) services. Through these centers, IntegraMed performs approximately 20% of all in-vitro fertilization procedures in the U.S. The company's discrete service packages include FertilityWeb, a web site development, hosting and marketing service; FertilityPurchase, a group purchasing program; FertilityMarKit marketing and sales programs; ARTWorks Clinical Information System; ARTWorks Practice Management Information System; and FertilityPartners, its turnkey fertility center operation. FertilityPartners offers administrative services such as accounting, human resources and purchasing of supplies; servicing and financing patient accounts receivable; marketing and sales; and integrated information systems. In addition, the firm distributes pharmaceutical products and services directly to patients through subsidiary IntegraMed Pharmaceutical Services, Inc., which, through a partnership with Ivpcare, Inc., has access to programs such as CycleTrack and Education Matters. CycleTrack allows the firm to limit drug distribution to only the amount required by each individual patient, minimizing the cost to third-party payers and patients. Education Matters is a comprehensive patient education program that offers videos and written materials devoted to educating patients on the proper handling and administration of complex fertility products. Recently, IntegraMed has added New York, New York; Oklahoma City, Oklahoma; and Chapel Hill, North Carolina to its fertility network. The company also opened vein clinics in Marietta, Georgia; Alexandria, Virginia; and Boca Raton, Florida to support its August 2007 acquisition of Vein Clinics of America.

## FINANCIALS: **Sales and profits are in thousands of dollars—add 000 to get the full amount. 2008 Note: Financial information for 2008 was not available for all companies at press time.**

| | | |
|---|---|---|
| 2008 Sales: $198,083 | 2008 Profits: $3,940 | **U.S. Stock Ticker: INMD** |
| 2007 Sales: $151,998 | 2007 Profits: $3,257 | **Int'l Ticker:** Int'l Exchange: |
| 2006 Sales: $126,438 | 2006 Profits: $3,224 | Employees: 1,182 |
| 2005 Sales: $128,890 | 2005 Profits: $1,723 | Fiscal Year Ends: 12/31 |
| 2004 Sales: $107,653 | 2004 Profits: $1,186 | Parent Company: |

## SALARIES/BENEFITS:

| | | | | |
|---|---|---|---|---|
| Pension Plan: | ESOP Stock Plan: | Profit Sharing: | Top Exec. Salary: $300,000 | Bonus: $195,000 |
| Savings Plan: | Stock Purch. Plan: | | Second Exec. Salary: $245,000 | Bonus: $122,500 |

## OTHER THOUGHTS:

**Apparent Women Officers or Directors**: 3
**Hot Spot for Advancement for Women/Minorities**: Y

## LOCATIONS: ("Y" = Yes)

| West: | Southwest: | Midwest: | Southeast: | Northeast: | International: |
|---|---|---|---|---|---|
| Y | Y | Y | Y | Y | |

Note: Financial information, benefits and other data can change quickly and may vary from those stated here.

# INTELLIGROUP INC

www.intelligroup.com

**Industry Group Code:** 541512 **Ranks within this company's industry group:** Sales: 3 Profits: 3

| Management: | | Sales/Marketing: | | Liberal Arts: | | Information Systems: | | Professionals: | | Technical/Scientific: | |
|---|---|---|---|---|---|---|---|---|---|---|---|
| Mgmt. Trainees: | | Mktg. Professionals: | Y | Gen. Writing/Editing: | | Info. Management: | Y | Finance/Accounting: | Y | Engineers, Elec.: | |
| Experienced Mgmt.: | Y | Retail Sales: | | Technical Writing: | Y | Software Dev.: | Y | Law: | Y | Engineers, Other: | |
| Int'l Business: | Y | Commercial/Industrial: | | Graphic Arts/Photog.: | | Hardware Dev.: | | HR/Other: | Y | Health/Lab: | |
| MBA Graduates: | Y | Sales Trainees: | | Music: | | Systems Integration: | | Training: | Y | Scientists/Research: | |
| | | Advertising Pros.: | | Broadcasting: | | Consulting/Other: | Y | Health Care: | | Petroleum/Chemicals: | |
| | | | | Other: | Y | | | Consulting: | Y | Math/Other: | |

## TYPES OF BUSINESS:

IT Consulting & Outsourcing
Logistics Software

## BRANDS/DIVISIONS/AFFILIATES:

Uptimizer
Empowered Solutions

## CONTACTS:

*Note: Officers with more than one job title may be intentionally listed here more than once.*

Vikram Gulati, CEO
Kalyan Sundaram Mahaligam, COO
Vikram Gulati, Pres.
Alok Bajpai, CFO
Alok Pant, Sr. VP-Global Mktg. & Alliances
Vikram Samant, VP-Strategic Accounts, North America
Bhalachandra Bhosale, Sr. VP-Global SAP Practice
Soren Heilskov, Managing Dir.-Intelligroup Nordic A/S
Gopal Ramasamy, VP-Outsourcing Services
Sreenivas Unnamatla, Managing Dir.-Japan
Satish Subramaniam, Managing Dir.-Europe & Middle East

| | |
|---|---|
| **Phone:** 732-590-1600 | **Fax:** 732-362-2100 |
| **Toll-Free:** 800-535-0156 | |
| **Address:** 499 Thornall St., Edison, NJ 08837 US | |

## GROWTH PLANS/SPECIAL FEATURES:

Intelligroup, Inc. is a leading global provider of strategic information technology (IT) outsourcing services. Intelligroup develops, tests, implements and supports IT solutions for global corporations and public-sector organizations. The company offers consulting services in Systems Application Products (SAP), PeopleSoft applications and Oracle applications, as well as well as providing infrastructure management services for e-businesses using Java and Microsoft.Net platforms. SAP projects, both standard and highly customized, are streamlined through Intelligroup's use of the Uptimizer, a proprietary tool that sizes and analyzes an upgrade project before it begins. Intelligroup's PeopleSoft consultants, operating out of the company's Empowered Solutions division, work with public sector and educational clients. The company partnered with Hitachi, Ltd. Information and Telecommunications Systems Group to create the Hitachi Global Solution Center. Additionally, Xerox; LSI Logic; and Century Business Services have employed the firm to implement, develop and support Oracle applications. All three consulting services utilize Intelligroup's onsite/offshore delivery method that links the client's office with Intelligroup's center in India. A secure satellite network maintains communication between onshore and offshore locations. This allows round-the-clock service, cutting costs considerably. The firm develops products for end-market segments such as consumer products, life sciences, high tech, education and banking finance securities and insurance. In January 2009, the company was selected by Almac Clinical Services to develop a Clinical Services Ordering and Supply Management Operating System (COSMOS) based on Oracle E-Business Suite.

## FINANCIALS:

**Sales and profits are in thousands of dollars—add 000 to get the full amount. 2008 Note: Financial information for 2008 was not available for all companies at press time.**

| | | |
|---|---|---|
| 2008 Sales: $ | 2008 Profits: $ | **U.S. Stock Ticker: ITIG** |
| 2007 Sales: $145,066 | 2007 Profits: $2,964 | **Int'l Ticker:** Int'l Exchange: |
| 2006 Sales: $125,309 | 2006 Profits: $-3,707 | Employees: 2,293 |
| 2005 Sales: $125,326 | 2005 Profits: $-6,591 | Fiscal Year Ends: 12/31 |
| 2004 Sales: $128,903 | 2004 Profits: $- 866 | Parent Company: |

## SALARIES/BENEFITS:

| | | | | |
|---|---|---|---|---|
| Pension Plan: | ESOP Stock Plan: | Profit Sharing: | Top Exec. Salary: $225,000 | Bonus: $216,000 |
| Savings Plan: Y | Stock Purch. Plan: | | Second Exec. Salary: $160,000 | Bonus: $76,000 |

## OTHER THOUGHTS:

**Apparent Women Officers or Directors:**
**Hot Spot for Advancement for Women/Minorities:**

## LOCATIONS: ("Y" = Yes)

| West: | Southwest: | Midwest: | Southeast: | Northeast: | International: |
|---|---|---|---|---|---|
| Y | | Y | Y | Y | Y |

# INTERACTIVE BROKERS GROUP INC

www.interactivebrokers.com

**Industry Group Code:** 523120 **Ranks within this company's industry group:** Sales: 1 Profits: 1

| Management: | | Sales/Marketing: | | Liberal Arts: | | Information Systems: | | Professionals: | | Technical/Scientific: | |
|---|---|---|---|---|---|---|---|---|---|---|---|
| Mgmt. Trainees: | | Mktg. Professionals: | Y | Gen. Writing/Editing: | | Info. Management: | Y | Finance/Accounting: | Y | Engineers, Elec.: | |
| Experienced Mgmt.: | Y | Retail Sales: | | Technical Writing: | | Software Dev.: | Y | Law: | Y | Engineers, Other: | |
| Int'l Business: | Y | Commercial/Industrial: | | Graphic Arts/Photog.: | | Hardware Dev.: | | HR/Other: | Y | Health/Lab: | |
| MBA Graduates: | Y | Sales Trainees: | | Music: | | Systems Integration: | | Training: | Y | Scientists/Research: | |
| | | Advertising Pros.: | | Broadcasting: | | Consulting/Other: | | Health Care: | | Petroleum/Chemicals: | |
| | | | | Other: | | | | Consulting: | | Math/Other: | Y |

## TYPES OF BUSINESS:

Electronic Brokerage & Trading
Electronic Trade Execution
Brokerage Software & Online Service
Market Maker
Options Exchange

## BRANDS/DIVISIONS/AFFILIATES:

Timber Hill
Interactive Brokers Group Inc
Kellogg Capital Group LLC
Future Trade Technologies
Future Trade Securities

## CONTACTS:

*Note: Officers with more than one job title may be intentionally listed here more than once.*

Thomas Peterffy, CEO
Thomas Peterffy, Pres.
Paul J. Brody, CFO
Thomas A. Frank, CIO/Exec. VP
Paul J. Brody, Sec.
Paul J. Brody, Treas.
Milan Galik, Sr. VP-Software Dev.
Thomas Peterffy, Chmn.

| | |
|---|---|
| **Phone:** 203-618-5800 | **Fax:** 203-618-5770 |
| **Toll-Free:** 877-442-2757 | |
| **Address:** 1 Pickwick Plz., Greenwich, CT 06830 US | |

## GROWTH PLANS/SPECIAL FEATURES:

Interactive Brokers Group, Inc. (IBG) is an automated global electronic market maker and broker specializing in routing orders and executing and processing trades in securities, futures and foreign exchange instruments on more than 70 electronic exchanges and trading venues around the world. The company is focused on developing proprietary software to automate broker-dealer functions, and its activities are divided into two principal business segments: market making and electronic brokerage. As a market maker, IBG provides continuous bid and offer quotations on approximately 420,000 securities and futures products listed on over 70 electronic exchanges around the world. Its quotes are derived by proprietary mathematical models that assimilate market data and reevaluate quotes each second. The company conducts its market making business through its Timber Hill subsidiaries, and this business segment represented 70% of overall revenues in 2007. As a direct market access broker, the company serves the customers of both traditional brokers and prime brokers. It provides customers with its proprietary order management, trade execution and portfolio management software platform. Through this software platform, customers can simultaneously access different financial markets worldwide and trade from a single account, based in any major currency, across multiple asset classes, including stocks, options, futures, foreign exchange and bonds. IBG serves approximately 95,000 institutional and individual brokerage customers. The company conducts it electronic brokerage business through its Interactive Brokers subsidiaries, and this business segment represented 29% of revenues in 2007. In August 2007, the company acquired the specialist operations of Kellogg Capital Group LLC on the American Stock Exchange. In November 2007, the firm acquired Future Trade Technologies (an integrated electronic equity and option trading company), along with its wholly-owned subsidiary, Future Trade Securities.

## FINANCIALS:

**Sales and profits are in thousands of dollars—add 000 to get the full amount. 2008 Note: Financial information for 2008 was not available for all companies at press time.**

| | | |
|---|---|---|
| 2008 Sales: $ | 2008 Profits: $ | **U.S. Stock Ticker: IBKR** |
| 2007 Sales: $2,023,400 | 2007 Profits: $300,500 | **Int'l Ticker:** Int'l Exchange: |
| 2006 Sales: $1,736,800 | 2006 Profits: $734,200 | Employees: 675 |
| 2005 Sales: $1,217,000 | 2005 Profits: $ | Fiscal Year Ends: 12/31 |
| 2004 Sales: $700,000 | 2004 Profits: $ | Parent Company: |

## SALARIES/BENEFITS:

| | | | | |
|---|---|---|---|---|
| Pension Plan: | ESOP Stock Plan: | Profit Sharing: | Top Exec. Salary: $1,200,000 | Bonus: $ |
| Savings Plan: | Stock Purch. Plan: | | Second Exec. Salary: $430,000 | Bonus: $ |

## OTHER THOUGHTS:

**Apparent Women Officers or Directors:**
**Hot Spot for Advancement for Women/Minorities:**

## LOCATIONS: ("Y" = Yes)

| West: | Southwest: | Midwest: | Southeast: | Northeast: | International: |
|---|---|---|---|---|---|
| Y | | Y | | Y | Y |

# INTERACTIVE INTELLIGENCE

www.inin.com

**Industry Group Code:** 334110 **Ranks within this company's industry group:** Sales: 6 Profits: 5

| Management: | | Sales/Marketing: | | Liberal Arts: | | Information Systems: | | Professionals: | | Technical/Scientific: | |
|---|---|---|---|---|---|---|---|---|---|---|---|
| Mgmt. Trainees: | | Mktg. Professionals: | Y | Gen. Writing/Editing: | | Info. Management: | Y | Finance/Accounting: | Y | Engineers, Elec.: | Y |
| Experienced Mgmt.: | Y | Retail Sales: | | Technical Writing: | Y | Software Dev.: | Y | Law: | Y | Engineers, Other: | |
| Int'l Business: | Y | Commercial/Industrial: | Y | Graphic Arts/Photog.: | | Hardware Dev.: | | HR/Other: | Y | Health/Lab: | |
| MBA Graduates: | Y | Sales Trainees: | Y | Music: | | Systems Integration: | Y | Training: | Y | Scientists/Research: | Y |
| | | Advertising Pros.: | | Broadcasting: | | Consulting/Other: | | Health Care: | | Petroleum/Chemicals: | |
| | | | | Other: | | | | Consulting: | | Math/Other: | |

## TYPES OF BUSINESS:

Business Communication Software

## BRANDS/DIVISIONS/AFFILIATES:

Customer Interaction Center
Vonexus Enterprise Interaction Center
Messaging Interaction Center

## CONTACTS:

*Note: Officers with more than one job title may be intentionally listed here more than once.*

Donald E. Brown, CEO
Donald E. Brown, Pres.
Stephen R. Head, CFO
Gary R. Blough, Exec. VP-Worldwide Sales
Michael D. Gagle, Chief Scientist
Stephen R. Head, VP-Admin.
Stephen R. Head, Corp. Sec.
William J. Gildea, VP-Bus. Dev.
Stephen R. Head, VP-Finance/Treas.
Joseph A. Staples, Sr. VP-Worldwide Mktg.
Pamela J. Hynes, VP-Customer Svcs.
Donald E. Brown, Chmn.

**Phone:** 317-872-3000 **Fax:** 317-872-3000
**Toll-Free:** 800-267-1364
**Address:** 7601 Interactive Way, Indianapolis, IN 46278 US

## GROWTH PLANS/SPECIAL FEATURES:

Interactive Intelligence, Inc., founded in 1994, develops software applications for various business communication services. Its primary markets are contact centers, enterprise IP telephony and enterprise messaging. For contact centers, the firm's products allow clients to intelligently route, monitor, record, track, and report on phone calls, as well as fax, e-mail and web interactions, whether in a single center or across multi-site contact center operations. Contact center applications also allow clients services including predictive dialing, workforce management and screen recording. The company's enterprise IP telephony solutions build off its success with contact center applications. It offers software solutions for various IP telephony applications, including multimedia queuing, mobile access and messaging, targeting enterprises with 100-1,500 users, especially those that rely on the Microsoft platform. Lastly, the enterprise messaging suite comprises solutions for voice mail; unified messaging, which combines voice mail, e-mail and fax into one inbox; and enhanced messaging, which combines features including customizable call rules, real-time presence management and Find-Me/Follow-Me (a type of call forwarding or call routing). Interactive Intelligence's primary products include the Customer Interaction Center, which serves the contact center and enterprise IP telephony markets; the Vonexus Enterprise Interaction Center, which serves the enterprise IP telephony market; and the Messaging Interaction Center. Interactive Intelligence has 2,500 customers, including Honda, Hydro-Quebec, Harrah's Entertainment, the University of California, Walgreens and Amway. It sells its products directly to end-users and through a distribution network of over 250 value-added resellers (VARs), including Hitachi and AT&T, Inc. In 2007, 65% of the firm's product orders came through its distribution partners.

Employees of the firm receive health and life insurance plans.

## FINANCIALS:

**Sales and profits are in thousands of dollars—add 000 to get the full amount. 2008 Note: Financial information for 2008 was not available for all companies at press time.**

2008 Sales: $121,406
2007 Sales: $109,901
2006 Sales: $83,044
2005 Sales: $62,937
2004 Sales: $

2008 Profits: $4,338
2007 Profits: $17,456
2006 Profits: $10,248
2005 Profits: $2,108
2004 Profits: $

**U.S. Stock Ticker: ININ**
**Int'l Ticker:** Int'l Exchange:
Employees: 595
Fiscal Year Ends: 12/31
Parent Company:

## SALARIES/BENEFITS:

Pension Plan: ESOP Stock Plan: Profit Sharing: Top Exec. Salary: $402,127 Bonus: $5,794
Savings Plan: Y Stock Purch. Plan: Y Second Exec. Salary: $325,000 Bonus: $174,486

## OTHER THOUGHTS:

**Apparent Women Officers or Directors:** 1
**Hot Spot for Advancement for Women/Minorities:**

## LOCATIONS: ("Y" = Yes)

| West: | Southwest: | Midwest: | Southeast: | Northeast: | International: |
|---|---|---|---|---|---|
| Y | | Y | | Y | Y |

# INTERCONTINENTALEXCHANGE INC (ICE)

www.theice.com

**Industry Group Code:** 523210 **Ranks within this company's industry group:** Sales: 4 Profits: 3

| Management: | | Sales/Marketing: | | Liberal Arts: | | Information Systems: | | Professionals: | | Technical/Scientific: | |
|---|---|---|---|---|---|---|---|---|---|---|---|
| Mgmt. Trainees: | | Mktg. Professionals: | Y | Gen. Writing/Editing: | | Info. Management: | Y | Finance/Accounting: | Y | Engineers, Elec.: | |
| Experienced Mgmt.: | Y | Retail Sales: | | Technical Writing: | | Software Dev.: | Y | Law: | Y | Engineers, Other: | |
| Int'l Business: | Y | Commercial/Industrial: | | Graphic Arts/Photog.: | | Hardware Dev.: | | HR/Other: | Y | Health/Lab: | |
| MBA Graduates: | Y | Sales Trainees: | | Music: | | Systems Integration: | | Training: | Y | Scientists/Research: | |
| | | Advertising Pros.: | Y | Broadcasting: | | Consulting/Other: | | Health Care: | | Petroleum/Chemicals: | |
| | | | | Other: | | | | Consulting: | | Math/Other: | Y |

## TYPES OF BUSINESS:

Commodity Futures Exchange
Energy Futures
Real-Time Market Data
OTC Clearing
Options Trading
Electronic Trade Confirmations

## BRANDS/DIVISIONS/AFFILIATES:

ICE Markets
ICE Futures
ICE Services
ICE eConfirm
WebICE
ICEMaker
ICE Data
Creditex Group Inc.

## CONTACTS: *Note: Officers with more than one job title may be intentionally listed here more than once.*

Jeffrey C. Sprecher, CEO
Charles A. Vice, COO
Charles A. Vice, Pres.
Scott A. Hill, CFO/Sr. VP
David S. Goone, Sr. VP-Sales
Edwin Marcial, CTO/Sr. VP
Johnathan H. Short, General Counsel/Sec./Sr. VP
David S. Goone, Sr. VP-Bus. Dev.
Thomas W. Farley, Pres./COO-ICE Futures, U.S.
Jeffrey C. Sprecher, Chmn.
David J. Peniket, Pres./COO-ICE Futures Europe

| **Phone:** 770-857-4700 | **Fax:** 212-643-4537 |
|---|---|
| **Toll-Free:** | |
| **Address:** 2100 RiverEdge Pkwy., Ste. 500, Atlanta, GA 30328 US | |

## GROWTH PLANS/SPECIAL FEATURES:

IntercontinentalExchange, Inc. (ICE) is one of the leading electronic marketplaces for the trading of energy and energy-related stocks and futures in the world. Direct access to ICE is available on thousands of active trading screens at over 1,500 OTC (Over-The-Counter) participant firms and over 750 energy futures participant firms. The company operates through three business segments. Through ICE Markets, the company offers bilateral and cleared OTC contracts and futures trading for such commodities as crude and refined oil products, natural gas, electricity and emissions. This segment also includes subsidiary ICE Futures, which offers online trading for futures and options in the global energy markets. Segment ICE Services offers a broad range of trading-related services including electronic trade confirmation through its ICE eConfirm and access to clearing services. It also offers several web-based trading tools: WebICE, a browser-based access to ICE's trading platform; and ICEMaker, allowing customers to link front-end trading strategies in Microsoft Excel directly to the ICE platform without having to write complex API code. ICE Data provides market information including historical prices, real-time prices, indices, tick-data, end of day settlements and market price valuations, covering markets including oil and petrochemical products; power; natural gas and coal; freight; tankers; and precious metals. In September 2008, the company acquired Creditex Group, Inc., a provider of trade execution and processing of credit default swaps in U.S., European and Asian markets.

Employees are offered a 401(k) plan, as well as medical, life and disability insurance.

## FINANCIALS: **Sales and profits are in thousands of dollars—add 000 to get the full amount. 2008 Note: Financial information for 2008 was not available for all companies at press time.**

| | | |
|---|---|---|
| 2008 Sales: $ | 2008 Profits: $ | **U.S. Stock Ticker: ICE** |
| 2007 Sales: $574,293 | 2007 Profits: $240,612 | **Int'l Ticker:** Int'l Exchange: |
| 2006 Sales: $313,799 | 2006 Profits: $143,268 | Employees: 506 |
| 2005 Sales: $155,865 | 2005 Profits: $40,410 | Fiscal Year Ends: 12/31 |
| 2004 Sales: $108,414 | 2004 Profits: $21,949 | Parent Company: |

## SALARIES/BENEFITS:

| | | | | |
|---|---|---|---|---|
| Pension Plan: | ESOP Stock Plan: | Profit Sharing: | Top Exec. Salary: $725,000 | Bonus: $1,047,625 |
| Savings Plan: Y | Stock Purch. Plan: | | Second Exec. Salary: $500,000 | Bonus: $595,000 |

## OTHER THOUGHTS:

**Apparent Women Officers or Directors**: 1
**Hot Spot for Advancement for Women/Minorities**: Y

## LOCATIONS: ("Y" = Yes)

| West: | Southwest: | Midwest: | Southeast: | Northeast: | International: |
|---|---|---|---|---|---|
| | Y | Y | Y | Y | Y |

# INTERMEC INC

www.intermec.com

**Industry Group Code:** 334119 **Ranks within this company's industry group:** Sales: 2 Profits: 4

| Management: | | Sales/Marketing: | | Liberal Arts: | | Information Systems: | | Professionals: | | Technical/Scientific: | |
|---|---|---|---|---|---|---|---|---|---|---|---|
| Mgmt. Trainees: | | Mktg. Professionals: | | Gen. Writing/Editing: | | Info. Management: | Y | Finance/Accounting: | Y | Engineers, Elec.: | Y |
| Experienced Mgmt.: | Y | Retail Sales: | | Technical Writing: | Y | Software Dev.: | Y | Law: | Y | Engineers, Other: | Y |
| Int'l Business: | Y | Commercial/Industrial: | Y | Graphic Arts/Photog.: | Y | Hardware Dev.: | Y | HR/Other: | Y | Health/Lab: | |
| MBA Graduates: | Y | Sales Trainees: | Y | Music: | | Systems Integration: | Y | Training: | Y | Scientists/Research: | |
| | | Advertising Pros.: | | Broadcasting: | | Consulting/Other: | | Health Care: | | Petroleum/Chemicals: | |
| | | | | Other: | | | | Consulting: | | Math/Other: | |

## TYPES OF BUSINESS:

Computer Hardware-Bar Code Systems
Supply Chain Software & Services
RFID Products
Software
Mobile Computing Products

## BRANDS/DIVISIONS/AFFILIATES:

UNOVA, Inc.
Intermec

## CONTACTS:

*Note: Officers with more than one job title may be intentionally listed here more than once.*

Patrick J. Byrne, CEO
Patrick J. Byrne, Pres.
Robert J. Driessnack, CFO/Sr. VP
Mike Wills, Sr. VP-Global Sales & Service
Jeanne Lyon, VP-Human Resources
Arvin Danielson, CTO
Janis L. Harwell, General Counsel/Sr. VP/Corp. Sec.
Ray Cronin, VP/General Manager-RFID
Earl Thompson, Sr. VP-Mobile Solutions Bus. Unit
Allen J. Lauer, Chmn.
Dennis Faerber, Sr. VP-Global Supply Chain Oper.

| **Phone:** 425-348-2600 | **Fax:** 425-267-2983 |
|---|---|
| **Toll-Free:** 800-755-5505 | |
| **Address:** 6001 36th Ave. W., Everett, WA 98203-1264 US | |

## GROWTH PLANS/SPECIAL FEATURES:

Intermec, Inc., formerly UNOVA, designs, develops, manufactures, integrates, sells, resells and services wired and wireless automated identification and data collection (AIDC) products, including radio frequency identification (RFID) products; mobile computing products; wired and wireless bar code printers; and label media products. The company's products are sold to customers domestically and internationally in market segments including industrial goods, consumer packaged goods, transportation, logistics, retail and the public sector, and in work applications such as manufacturing production, warehousing, field service, direct store delivery, in-transit visibility, store floor operations and RFID supply chain management. Intermec's bar code scanning products include wireless handheld computers and terminals; linear and area imagers incorporating active pixel technology; and badge and laser scanners. These products are able to read or collect data and move that data directly into standard enterprise resource planning systems, warehouse management systems and order fulfillment, transportation, logistics and other business applications. The company also manufactures rugged handheld computers for use in warehouses and industrial environments. The company's mobile computing products include handheld and vehicle-mounted mobile computers and accessories and related services that facilitate local-area and wide-area wireless and wired data communications. These products typically contain multiple wireless technologies that can operate simultaneously in a mobile computer, allowing customers to communicate remotely with their field employees. Intermec's line of bar code printers ranges from low-cost, light-duty models to higher-cost industrial models that accommodate a number of printing widths, materials and label configurations. Intermec's RFID product line is focused on passive UHF technology and consists of RFID tags, readers, software and related equipment sold under the Intermec trade name. Customers include the U.S. Army and the U.K.'s Royal Mail service, as well as 70% of Fortune 1000 companies.

Intermec offers its employees tuition reimbursement; flexible spending accounts; and medical, dental, vision, accident and life insurance.

## FINANCIALS:

**Sales and profits are in thousands of dollars—add 000 to get the full amount. 2008 Note: Financial information for 2008 was not available for all companies at press time.**

| | | |
|---|---|---|
| 2008 Sales: $890,883 | 2008 Profits: $35,462 | **U.S. Stock Ticker: IN** |
| 2007 Sales: $849,200 | 2007 Profits: $23,100 | **Int'l Ticker:** Int'l Exchange: |
| 2006 Sales: $850,000 | 2006 Profits: $32,000 | Employees: 2,308 |
| 2005 Sales: $875,500 | 2005 Profits: $61,800 | Fiscal Year Ends: 12/31 |
| 2004 Sales: $811,300 | 2004 Profits: $-49,100 | Parent Company: |

## SALARIES/BENEFITS:

| | | | | |
|---|---|---|---|---|
| Pension Plan: | ESOP Stock Plan: | Profit Sharing: | Top Exec. Salary: $643,000 | Bonus: $278,049 |
| Savings Plan: Y | Stock Purch. Plan: Y | | Second Exec. Salary: $360,577 | Bonus: $500,000 |

## OTHER THOUGHTS:

**Apparent Women Officers or Directors**: 3
**Hot Spot for Advancement for Women/Minorities**: Y

## LOCATIONS: ("Y" = Yes)

| West: | Southwest: | Midwest: | Southeast: | Northeast: | International: |
|---|---|---|---|---|---|
| Y | Y | Y | Y | Y | Y |

Note: Financial information, benefits and other data can change quickly and may vary from those stated here.

# INTERNAP NETWORK SERVICES CORP

www.internap.com

**Industry Group Code:** 513390C **Ranks within this company's industry group:** Sales: 3 Profits: 3

| Management: | | Sales/Marketing: | | Liberal Arts: | | Information Systems: | | Professionals: | | Technical/Scientific: | |
|---|---|---|---|---|---|---|---|---|---|---|---|
| Mgmt. Trainees: | | Mktg. Professionals: | Y | Gen. Writing/Editing: | | Info. Management: | Y | Finance/Accounting: | Y | Engineers, Elec.: | Y |
| Experienced Mgmt.: | Y | Retail Sales: | | Technical Writing: | Y | Software Dev.: | Y | Law: | Y | Engineers, Other: | |
| Int'l Business: | Y | Commercial/Industrial: | Y | Graphic Arts/Photog.: | | Hardware Dev.: | | HR/Other: | Y | Health/Lab: | |
| MBA Graduates: | Y | Sales Trainees: | Y | Music: | | Systems Integration: | Y | Training: | Y | Scientists/Research: | |
| | | Advertising Pros.: | | Broadcasting: | | Consulting/Other: | | Health Care: | | Petroleum/Chemicals: | |
| | | | | Other: | | | | Consulting: | | Math/Other: | |

## TYPES OF BUSINESS:

Internet Access Provider
Voice-Over-Internet Protocol
Multimedia Streaming
Virtual Private Networking
Value-Added Services

## BRANDS/DIVISIONS/AFFILIATES:

Performance IP
Flow Control Platform
Internap Japan Co., Ltd.
VitalStream Holdings, Inc.

## CONTACTS: *Note: Officers with more than one job title may be intentionally listed here more than once.*

James P. DeBlasio, CEO
James P. DeBlasio, Pres.
George E. Kilguss, III, CFO
Randal Thompson, VP-Global Sales
Tim Sullivan, CTO
Richard P. Dobb, Chief Admin. Officer
Richard P. Dobb, General Counsel/Corp. Sec./VP
Andrew McBath, Dir.-Investor Rel.
Tamara Augustyn, VP-Finance/Chief Accountant
Patricia L. Higgins, Vice Chmn.
Andrew S. Albrecht, VP-Corp. Dev.
Michael Higgins, VP/Gen. Mgr.-Data Center Solutions
Alan Hannan, VP/Gen. Mgr.-IP Svcs.
Eugene Eidenberg, Chmn.

| **Phone:** 404-302-9700 | **Fax:** 404-475-0520 |
|---|---|
| **Toll-Free:** 877-843-7627 | |
| **Address:** 250 Williams St., Ste. E-100, Atlanta, GA 30303 US | |

## GROWTH PLANS/SPECIAL FEATURES:

Internap Network Services Corp. markets products and services that optimize the performance and reliability of strategic business Internet applications. Applications served include e-commerce, customer relationship management, multimedia streaming, VoIP (Voice over Internet Protocol), virtual private networks and supply chain management. These products and services are complemented by value-added services including content delivery networks, collocation services, managed security devices and data center services. Internap's products include the Performance IP service and the Flow Control Platform (FCP). The firm delivers services through 50 network access points across North America, Europe, Asia and Australia, which feature direct high-speed connections to multiple major Internet backbones operated by firms such as Sprint, Verizon and AT&T. Internap's proprietary route optimization technology monitors the performance of Internet networks allowing its customer traffic to be routed over the optimal path in a way that maximizes performance and reliability of the transactions by minimizing loss and delays inherent across the Internet. The company offers its services to more than 3,800 customers in the U.S. and abroad. Internap Japan Co., Ltd., a joint venture with Japanese telecom giant Nippon Telegraph and Telephone Corp. (NTT), provides Internet connectivity for Japanese businesses. In February 2007, the company acquired VitalStream Holdings, Inc., a provider of products and services for storing and delivering audio and video digital media to large audiences over the Internet.

Employees of Internap receive medical, vision and dental plans; an employee assistance program; discounted auto, legal, home and renter's insurance; and subsidized coverage for spouses, domestic partners and other family members.

## FINANCIALS: **Sales and profits are in thousands of dollars—add 000 to get the full amount. 2008 Note: Financial information for 2008 was not available for all companies at press time.**

| | | |
|---|---|---|
| 2008 Sales: $ | 2008 Profits: $ | **U.S. Stock Ticker: INAP** |
| 2007 Sales: $234,090 | 2007 Profits: $-5,555 | **Int'l Ticker:** Int'l Exchange: |
| 2006 Sales: $181,375 | 2006 Profits: $3,657 | Employees: 420 |
| 2005 Sales: $153,717 | 2005 Profits: $-4,964 | Fiscal Year Ends: 12/31 |
| 2004 Sales: $144,546 | 2004 Profits: $-18,062 | Parent Company: |

## SALARIES/BENEFITS:

| | | | | |
|---|---|---|---|---|
| Pension Plan: | ESOP Stock Plan: | Profit Sharing: | Top Exec. Salary: $425,000 | Bonus: $337,663 |
| Savings Plan: Y | Stock Purch. Plan: Y | | Second Exec. Salary: $247,917 | Bonus: $88,333 |

## OTHER THOUGHTS:

**Apparent Women Officers or Directors**: 2
**Hot Spot for Advancement for Women/Minorities**:

## LOCATIONS: ("Y" = Yes)

| West: | Southwest: | Midwest: | Southeast: | Northeast: | International: |
|---|---|---|---|---|---|
| Y | Y | Y | Y | Y | Y |

# INTERNATIONAL CREATIVE MANAGEMENT (ICM) www.icmtalent.com

**Industry Group Code:** 711410 **Ranks within this company's industry group:** Sales: 2 Profits:

| Management: | | Sales/Marketing: | | Liberal Arts: | | Information Systems: | | Professionals: | | Technical/Scientific: | |
|---|---|---|---|---|---|---|---|---|---|---|---|
| Mgmt. Trainees: | | Mktg. Professionals: | Y | Gen. Writing/Editing: | | Info. Management: | Y | Finance/Accounting: | Y | Engineers, Elec.: | |
| Experienced Mgmt.: | Y | Retail Sales: | | Technical Writing: | | Software Dev.: | | Law: | Y | Engineers, Other: | |
| Int'l Business: | Y | Commercial/Industrial: | | Graphic Arts/Photog.: | | Hardware Dev.: | | HR/Other: | Y | Health/Lab: | |
| MBA Graduates: | Y | Sales Trainees: | Y | Music: | | Systems Integration: | | Training: | Y | Scientists/Research: | |
| | | Advertising Pros.: | | Broadcasting: | | Consulting/Other: | | Health Care: | | Petroleum/Chemicals: | |
| | | | | Other: | | | | Consulting: | | Math/Other: | |

## TYPES OF BUSINESS:

Agents-Actors & Directors
Agents-Writers & Musicians
Agents-Literary
Agents-Lecture

## BRANDS/DIVISIONS/AFFILIATES:

ICM Artists
ICM Foreign Rights
Life Rights
Broder Webb Chervin Silbermann Agency

## CONTACTS:

*Note: Officers with more than one job title may be intentionally listed here more than once.*

Jeffrey Berg, CEO
Chris Silbermann, Pres.
Richard B. Levy, General Counsel
Richard B. Levy, Chief Bus. Dev. Officer
Esther Newberg, Sr. VP
Jeffrey Berg, Chmn.

| **Phone:** 310-550-4000 | **Fax:** 310-550-4100 |
|---|---|
| **Toll-Free:** | |
| **Address:** 10250 Constellation Blvd., Los Angeles, CA 90067 US | |

## GROWTH PLANS/SPECIAL FEATURES:

International Creative Management, Inc. (ICM) is one of the world's largest talent and literary agencies, with offices in Los Angeles, New York and London. The company represents actors, directors, musicians and writers, as well as creative talent in theater, commercials, public speaking and new media. ICM's clients include actors Woody Allen, Christopher Walken, Charlton Heston, Ellen Degeneres, William Shatner, Chris Rock and Orlando Bloom; musicians Courtney Love, Beyonce Knowles and Nadia Turner; authors Tom Bodett and Violet Blue; and directors Roman Polanski, Danny Boyle, Doug Atchinson and Robert Rodriguez. The company's music and performance subsidiary, ICM Artists, represents classical instrumentalists, vocalists and conductors, chamber ensembles, choirs and dance and opera companies, as well as other performing groups. ICM's Foreign Rights department, based in London, sells ICM book and magazine products in the U.K. and other foreign countries and the Life Rights division secures the rights to newspaper and magazine articles as well as personal life stories of people who might serve as the basis for a television production.

## FINANCIALS:

**Sales and profits are in thousands of dollars—add 000 to get the full amount. 2008 Note: Financial information for 2008 was not available for all companies at press time.**

| | | |
|---|---|---|
| 2008 Sales: $ | 2008 Profits: $ | **U.S. Stock Ticker: Private** |
| 2007 Sales: $155,000 | 2007 Profits: $ | **Int'l Ticker:** Int'l Exchange: |
| 2006 Sales: $150,000 | 2006 Profits: $ | Employees: 393 |
| 2005 Sales: $140,000 | 2005 Profits: $ | Fiscal Year Ends: 6/30 |
| 2004 Sales: $100,000 | 2004 Profits: $ | Parent Company: |

## SALARIES/BENEFITS:

| | | | | |
|---|---|---|---|---|
| Pension Plan: | ESOP Stock Plan: | Profit Sharing: | Top Exec. Salary: $ | Bonus: $ |
| Savings Plan: | Stock Purch. Plan: | | Second Exec. Salary: $ | Bonus: $ |

## OTHER THOUGHTS:

**Apparent Women Officers or Directors:**
**Hot Spot for Advancement for Women/Minorities:**

## LOCATIONS: ("Y" = Yes)

| West: | Southwest: | Midwest: | Southeast: | Northeast: | International: |
|---|---|---|---|---|---|
| Y | | | | Y | Y |

# INTERNATIONAL DAIRY QUEEN

www.dairyqueen.com

**Industry Group Code:** 722110 **Ranks within this company's industry group:** Sales: 1 Profits:

| Management: | | Sales/Marketing: | | Liberal Arts: | | Information Systems: | | Professionals: | | Technical/Scientific: | |
|---|---|---|---|---|---|---|---|---|---|---|---|
| Mgmt. Trainees: | Y | Mktg. Professionals: | Y | Gen. Writing/Editing: | | Info. Management: | Y | Finance/Accounting: | Y | Engineers, Elec.: | |
| Experienced Mgmt.: | Y | Retail Sales: | | Technical Writing: | | Software Dev.: | | Law: | Y | Engineers, Other: | |
| Int'l Business: | Y | Commercial/Industrial: | | Graphic Arts/Photog.: | Y | Hardware Dev.: | | HR/Other: | Y | Health/Lab: | |
| MBA Graduates: | Y | Sales Trainees: | | Music: | | Systems Integration: | | Training: | Y | Scientists/Research: | |
| | | Advertising Pros.: | Y | Broadcasting: | | Consulting/Other: | | Health Care: | | Petroleum/Chemicals: | |
| | | | | Other: | | | | Consulting: | | Math/Other: | |

## TYPES OF BUSINESS:

Restaurants
Fast Food Chains
Frozen Desserts

## BRANDS/DIVISIONS/AFFILIATES:

Dairy Queen
Karmelkorn Shoppe
Orange Julius
BLIZZARD
Berkshire Hathaway Inc

## CONTACTS:

*Note: Officers with more than one job title may be intentionally listed here more than once.*

John Gainor, CEO
Charles J. Chapman, COO
John Gainor, Pres.
James S. Simpson, CFO
James S. Simpson, Chief Admin. Officer
James S. Simpson, Treas./Controller

| **Phone:** 952-830-8696 | **Fax:** 952-830-0273 |
|---|---|
| **Toll-Free:** | |
| **Address:** 7505 Metro Blvd., Minneapolis, MN 55439 US | |

## GROWTH PLANS/SPECIAL FEATURES:

International Dairy Queen, Inc., a subsidiary of Berkshire Hathaway, Inc., develops and services a system of Dairy Queen restaurants, Karmelkorn Shoppes and Orange Julius stores. There are more than 5,600 Dairy Queens located in 20 countries. Restaurant locations include the U.S., Canada, Europe, Asia, Mexico, and the Middle East. Dairy Queen's dairy dessert product line includes soft-serve ice cream cones, BLIZZARD flavor treats, shakes, malts, sundaes and specialty frozen confections. The restaurants also offer a menu of fast food items including hamburgers, hot dogs, chicken strips, barbecue and chicken sandwiches, French fries and onion rings. International Dairy Queen franchises over 280 Orange Julius stores, featuring blended drinks made from orange juice, fruits and fruit flavors; and 26 Karmelkorn Shoppes featuring popcorn and other treat items. The company is also an active sponsor of Children's Miracle Network (CMN); in the past 19 years, Dairy Queen operators in the U.S. and Canada have raised $44 million for CMN. The firm has agreements with four franchises which allow for production of 21 new restaurants in North Carolina and Florida until 2011.

The company offers its employees a benefits package including medical insurance; short- and long-term disability; life insurance; worker's compensation insurance; a 401(k); and a deferred profit sharing plan.

## FINANCIALS:

**Sales and profits are in thousands of dollars—add 000 to get the full amount. 2008 Note: Financial information for 2008 was not available for all companies at press time.**

2008 Sales: $
2007 Sales: $476,000
2006 Sales: $
2005 Sales: $
2004 Sales: $

2008 Profits: $
2007 Profits: $
2006 Profits: $
2005 Profits: $
2004 Profits: $

**U.S. Stock Ticker: Subsidiary**
**Int'l Ticker:** Int'l Exchange:
Employees: 2,055
Fiscal Year Ends: 12/31
Parent Company: BERKSHIRE HATHAWAY INC

## SALARIES/BENEFITS:

Pension Plan:
Savings Plan: Y
ESOP Stock Plan:
Stock Purch. Plan:
Profit Sharing:
Top Exec. Salary: $
Second Exec. Salary: $
Bonus: $
Bonus: $

## OTHER THOUGHTS:

**Apparent Women Officers or Directors:**
**Hot Spot for Advancement for Women/Minorities:**

## LOCATIONS: ("Y" = Yes)

| West: | Southwest: | Midwest: | Southeast: | Northeast: | International: |
|---|---|---|---|---|---|
| Y | Y | Y | Y | Y | Y |

# INTERNET SECURITY SYSTEMS INC

**www.iss.net**

**Industry Group Code:** 511211 **Ranks within this company's industry group:** Sales: Profits:

| Management: | | Sales/Marketing: | | Liberal Arts: | | Information Systems: | | Professionals: | | Technical/Scientific: | |
|---|---|---|---|---|---|---|---|---|---|---|---|
| Mgmt. Trainees: | | Mktg. Professionals: | Y | Gen. Writing/Editing: | | Info. Management: | Y | Finance/Accounting: | Y | Engineers, Elec.: | Y |
| Experienced Mgmt.: | Y | Retail Sales: | | Technical Writing: | Y | Software Dev.: | Y | Law: | Y | Engineers, Other: | |
| Int'l Business: | Y | Commercial/Industrial: | Y | Graphic Arts/Photog.: | | Hardware Dev.: | | HR/Other: | Y | Health/Lab: | |
| MBA Graduates: | Y | Sales Trainees: | Y | Music: | | Systems Integration: | Y | Training: | Y | Scientists/Research: | |
| | | Advertising Pros.: | | Broadcasting: | | Consulting/Other: | | Health Care: | | Petroleum/Chemicals: | |
| | | | | Other: | | | | Consulting: | | Math/Other: | |

## TYPES OF BUSINESS:

Software-Network Security
Outsourced Security Management Services
Consulting, Training & Research Services

## BRANDS/DIVISIONS/AFFILIATES:

ISS Professional Security Services
International Business Machines Corp (IBM)

## CONTACTS:

*Note: Officers with more than one job title may be intentionally listed here more than once.*

Thomas E. Noonan, CEO
Thomas E. Noonan, Pres.
Raghavan Rajaji, CFO
Lawrence A. Costanza, Sr. VP-Americas Sales
Helen Berg, CIO
Christopher J. Rouland, CTO
Heath Thompsons, VP-Eng.
Raghavan Rajaji, Sr. VP-Admin.
Greg Adams, VP-Product Dev.
Raghavan Rajaji, Sr. VP-Finance
Christopher Klaus, Chief Security Advisor/Founder
Jaap H. Smit, VP-EMEA Oper.
Peter Evans, VP-Corp. Mktg.
Ja Hong Lin, Pres., Asia/Pacific Oper.

**Phone:** 404-236-2600 **Fax:** 404-236-2605
**Toll-Free:** 888-901-7477
**Address:** 6303 Barfield Rd., Atlanta, GA 30328 US

## GROWTH PLANS/SPECIAL FEATURES:

Internet Security Systems, Inc. (ISS), a business unit of IBM, manufactures security and information protection software for online assets. The firm's products provide preemptive protection for all levels of the IT infrastructure, including network gateways, servers and endpoint devices such as PCs, laptops and handhelds. The company's software incorporates security technologies including intrusion prevention systems; intrusion detection systems; firewall and virtual private networking; content security; web filtering; antivirus; vulnerability assessment; and security management. The firm's security management solutions include software products, managed security services, online security research and advisory services. Services are designed to detect, prevent and respond to attacks, misuse and security policy violations. ISS Professional Security Services specializes in providing assessment, design, deployment, management and education services for organizations lacking the internal resources to implement such programs. ISS also maintains a research and development team which tests software vulnerabilities and collaborates with government agencies, industry consortiums and software developers. The company has more than 11,000 customers worldwide, with locations in North and South America, the Caribbean, Europe, Asia, Australia and the Middle East. Customers typically include large international banks, governments, public insurance companies and IT companies. In August 2007, the firm released a new virtual e-mail security platform which allows customers to block spam and viruses with minimal physical hardware. In September 2008, the firm unveiled a new initiative for smaller business' security needs, including its new Proventia Network Multi-Function Security, a Unified Threat Management solution.

ISS offers its employees benefits including medical insurance, a 401(k) plan, disability coverage, an on-site fitness center and an on-site cafeteria.

## FINANCIALS:

**Sales and profits are in thousands of dollars—add 000 to get the full amount. 2008 Note: Financial information for 2008 was not available for all companies at press time.**

2008 Sales: $
2007 Sales: $
2006 Sales: $
2005 Sales: $329,800
2004 Sales: $289,900

2008 Profits: $
2007 Profits: $
2006 Profits: $
2005 Profits: $38,500
2004 Profits: $26,300

**U.S. Stock Ticker: Subsidiary**
**Int'l Ticker:** Int'l Exchange:
Employees: 1,250
Fiscal Year Ends: 12/31
Parent Company: INTERNATIONAL BUSINESS MACHINES CORP (IBM)

## SALARIES/BENEFITS:

Pension Plan: ESOP Stock Plan: Profit Sharing: Top Exec. Salary: $400,000 Bonus: $351,764
Savings Plan: Y Stock Purch. Plan: Y Second Exec. Salary: $330,448 Bonus: $204,302

## OTHER THOUGHTS:

**Apparent Women Officers or Directors**: 1
**Hot Spot for Advancement for Women/Minorities**:

## LOCATIONS: ("Y" = Yes)

| West: | Southwest: | Midwest: | Southeast: | Northeast: | International: |
|---|---|---|---|---|---|
| | | | Y | Y | Y |

# INTERSTATE BATTERY SYSTEM OF AMERICA

**www.interstatebatteries.com**

**Industry Group Code:** 335910 **Ranks within this company's industry group:** Sales: 1 Profits:

| **Management:** | | **Sales/Marketing:** | | **Liberal Arts:** | | **Information Systems:** | | **Professionals:** | | **Technical/Scientific:** | |
|---|---|---|---|---|---|---|---|---|---|---|---|
| Mgmt. Trainees: | | Mktg. Professionals: | Y | Gen. Writing/Editing: | | Info. Management: | Y | Finance/Accounting: | Y | Engineers, Elec.: | Y |
| Experienced Mgmt.: | Y | Retail Sales: | | Technical Writing: | Y | Software Dev.: | | Law: | Y | Engineers, Other: | Y |
| Int'l Business: | Y | Commercial/Industrial: | Y | Graphic Arts/Photog.: | | Hardware Dev.: | | HR/Other: | Y | Health/Lab: | |
| MBA Graduates: | Y | Sales Trainees: | Y | Music: | | Systems Integration: | | Training: | Y | Scientists/Research: | |
| | | Advertising Pros.: | Y | Broadcasting: | | Consulting/Other: | | Health Care: | | Petroleum/Chemicals: | |
| | | | | Other: | | | | Consulting: | | Math/Other: | |

## TYPES OF BUSINESS:

Battery Manufacturing
Retail Battery Sales
Battery Distribution

## BRANDS/DIVISIONS/AFFILIATES:

All Battery Centers
Pinnacle
Mega-Tron
Workaholic
Ameritron
Canatron
Technology PowerCare
PowerVolt

## CONTACTS:

*Note: Officers with more than one job title may be intentionally listed here more than once.*

Carlos Sepulveda, CEO
Carlos Sepulveda, Pres.
Dennis Brown, VP-Mktg.
Chris Willis, VP-Human Resources/Counsel
Merv Tarde, CIO/VP-IT
Walt Holmes, General Counsel/VP-PowerCare
Mickey Elam, VP-e-Commerce
Scott Miller, VP-Advertising & Public Rel.
Lisa Huntsberry, VP-Corp. Acct. & Svcs. Team
Mickey Elam, VP-All Battery
Jeff Haddock, VP-Independent Dist. Group
Alex Louis, VP-Interstate Owned Territories
Billy Norris, VP-National Accounts
Norm Miller, Chmn.
Chris Antoniou, VP-Supply Chain Mgmt.

**Phone:** 972-991-1444 **Fax:** 972-458-8288
**Toll-Free:** 888-772-3600
**Address:** 12770 Merit Dr., Ste. 1000, Dallas, TX 75251 US

## GROWTH PLANS/SPECIAL FEATURES:

Interstate Battery System of America, Inc. (IBSA) produces and distributes batteries through its distributors, dealers, All Battery Centers stores and online. The company's batteries can be used for automotive and marine industries; motorcycles; snowmobiles; 4-wheelers; watercrafts; recreational vehicles; lawn mowers; watches; households; laptops; hearing-aids; wheelchairs and mobility scooters; foklifts; cordless and cellular phones; and backup power supplies for industrial and telecommunications industries. More than 200,000 retail dealers sell Interstate batteries throughout the U.S. and Canada. IBSA also has over 300 wholesale distributors. At its retailers, an Interstate regional manager comes at regular intervals to rotate stock and pick up old batteries for recycling in order to keep the stock fresh. The company's All Battery Centers network provides over 7,000 different types of household and business batteries. These batteries utilize NiCad, NiMH, SLA, Lithium, Alkaline, Zinc Air and Silver Oxide cell technology. The firm's proprietary Pinnacle battery technology provides significant advantages such as longer battery life, more life cycles and high heat resistance, as well as improved discharge recovery rates and shorter battery charging time. Household batteries are used for products such as flashlights and camcorders, and business batteries are used for products such as pagers and computer backup power. Consumers are also able to purchase many of the company's batteries online. The company does business with automotive manufacturers such as Toyota, Lexus, U-Haul and Subaru. Brand names include Ameritron, Workaholic, Mega-Tron, Pinnacle, Canatron, Technology PowerCare and PowerVolt. In August 2008, the firm announced it was looking for new headquarters and planned to hire 50 employees in the next year.

The company offers its employees medical, dental and vision insurance; prescription coverage; life and long-term disability insurance; flexible spending accounts; a 401(k) plan; subsidized health club memberships; free covered parking; and one free battery per year plus discounts on all batteries.

## FINANCIALS:

**Sales and profits are in thousands of dollars—add 000 to get the full amount. 2008 Note: Financial information for 2008 was not available for all companies at press time.**

| | | |
|---|---|---|
| 2008 Sales: $ | 2008 Profits: $ | **U.S. Stock Ticker: Private** |
| 2007 Sales: $1,500,000 | 2007 Profits: $ | **Int'l Ticker:** Int'l Exchange: |
| 2006 Sales: $1,000,000 | 2006 Profits: $ | Employees: 1,415 |
| 2005 Sales: $754,900 | 2005 Profits: $ | Fiscal Year Ends: |
| 2004 Sales: $700,000 | 2004 Profits: $ | Parent Company: |

## SALARIES/BENEFITS:

| | | | | |
|---|---|---|---|---|
| Pension Plan: | ESOP Stock Plan: | Profit Sharing: Y | Top Exec. Salary: $ | Bonus: $ |
| Savings Plan: Y | Stock Purch. Plan: | | Second Exec. Salary: $ | Bonus: $ |

## OTHER THOUGHTS:

**Apparent Women Officers or Directors**: 1
**Hot Spot for Advancement for Women/Minorities**:

## LOCATIONS: ("Y" = Yes)

| West: | Southwest: | Midwest: | Southeast: | Northeast: | International: |
|---|---|---|---|---|---|
| Y | Y | Y | Y | Y | Y |

# INTERWOVEN INC

**www.interwoven.com**

**Industry Group Code:** 511202 **Ranks within this company's industry group:** Sales: 1 Profits: 2

| Management: | | Sales/Marketing: | | Liberal Arts: | | Information Systems: | | Professionals: | | Technical/Scientific: | |
|---|---|---|---|---|---|---|---|---|---|---|---|
| Mgmt. Trainees: | | Mktg. Professionals: | Y | Gen. Writing/Editing: | | Info. Management: | Y | Finance/Accounting: | Y | Engineers, Elec.: | Y |
| Experienced Mgmt.: | Y | Retail Sales: | | Technical Writing: | Y | Software Dev.: | Y | Law: | Y | Engineers, Other: | |
| Int'l Business: | Y | Commercial/Industrial: | Y | Graphic Arts/Photog.: | | Hardware Dev.: | | HR/Other: | Y | Health/Lab: | |
| MBA Graduates: | Y | Sales Trainees: | Y | Music: | | Systems Integration: | | Training: | Y | Scientists/Research: | |
| | | Advertising Pros.: | | Broadcasting: | | Consulting/Other: | | Health Care: | | Petroleum/Chemicals: | |
| | | | | Other: | | | | Consulting: | | Math/Other: | |

## TYPES OF BUSINESS:

Software-Enterprise Content Management
Document Management Software
Consulting Services

## BRANDS/DIVISIONS/AFFILIATES:

TeamSite
Interwoven WorkSite
Interwoven RecordsManager
Optimost LLC
Discovery Mining, Inc.

## CONTACTS:

*Note: Officers with more than one job title may be intentionally listed here more than once.*

Joe Cowan, CEO
Max Carnecchia, Pres.
John Calonico, CFO
Ben Kiker, Chief Mktg. Officer/Sr. VP
Rafiq Mohammadi, CTO
Jeff Kissling, Sr. VP-Eng.
John Calonico, Sec.
Keren Ackerman, Dir.-Investor Rel.
John Calonico, Sr. VP-Finance
Steve Martello, Sr. VP-Client Svcs.
Bob L. Corey, Chmn.

| | |
|---|---|
| **Phone:** 408-774-2000 | **Fax:** 408-774-2002 |
| **Toll-Free:** 888-468-3796 | |
| **Address:** 160 E. Tasman Dr., San Jose, CA 95134 US | |

## GROWTH PLANS/SPECIAL FEATURES:

Interwoven, Inc. provides content management software and services that allow businesses to create, manage and distribute business content such as documents, spreadsheets, e-mails and presentations both internally and externally. Its content management platform consists of six integrated software solutions, which can be used for brand management, enterprise portals, global web content management, content distribution, corporate governance, deal management, document management and online self-service. Other products include the TeamSite server software, which enables the creation, contribution, collaboration and management of content; Interwoven WorkSite server software, which delivers storage and access to unstructured content, including documents, spreadsheets, e-mails, presentations and drawings, through either a web browser or Microsoft Office applications; and Interwoven RecordsManager server software, which allows formal records management policies and practices to be applied to electronic and non-electronic documents. The firm also offers deployment and integration consulting services for its software systems, as well as strategic consulting services. It licenses its software products through offices in 15 countries to more than 4,000 organizations worldwide, including FedEx, the Federal Reserve Bank, Microsoft, Samsung, Shell and Yamaha. The firm recently partnered with BlackBerry to introduce its first mobile product, which enhances BlackBerry mobile e-mail and document management capabilities by leveraging synchronization abilities of servers. It also partnered with Metastorm to develop a packaged integration adaptor supported by both companies. The product will combine content and process flows to gain visibility and control of the business processes. The firm recently announced that it plans to provide its Scrittura OTC Derivatives Solution, a document automation technology, to the Latin American financial services market. In November 2007, Interwoven acquired Optimost LLC, a web site optimization software pioneer, for $52 million.

Employees of Interwoven receive flexible spending accounts; life and travel insurance; medical, dental and vision benefits; and paid time off.

## FINANCIALS:

**Sales and profits are in thousands of dollars—add 000 to get the full amount. 2008 Note: Financial information for 2008 was not available for all companies at press time.**

| | | |
|---|---|---|
| 2008 Sales: $ | 2008 Profits: $ | **U.S. Stock Ticker: IWOV** |
| 2007 Sales: $225,668 | 2007 Profits: $23,678 | **Int'l Ticker:** Int'l Exchange: |
| 2006 Sales: $200,319 | 2006 Profits: $6,437 | Employees: 888 |
| 2005 Sales: $175,037 | 2005 Profits: $ 626 | Fiscal Year Ends: 12/31 |
| 2004 Sales: $160,388 | 2004 Profits: $-23,667 | Parent Company: |

## SALARIES/BENEFITS:

| | | | | |
|---|---|---|---|---|
| Pension Plan: | ESOP Stock Plan: | Profit Sharing: | Top Exec. Salary: $337,500 | Bonus: $453,430 |
| Savings Plan: Y | Stock Purch. Plan: Y | | Second Exec. Salary: $300,000 | Bonus: $350,000 |

## OTHER THOUGHTS:

**Apparent Women Officers or Directors:**
**Hot Spot for Advancement for Women/Minorities:**

## LOCATIONS: ("Y" = Yes)

| West: | Southwest: | Midwest: | Southeast: | Northeast: | International: |
|---|---|---|---|---|---|
| Y | Y | Y | Y | Y | Y |

# INVESTMENT TECHNOLOGY GROUP INC (ITG)

www.itginc.com

**Industry Group Code:** 514210 **Ranks within this company's industry group:** Sales: 1 Profits: 1

| Management: | | Sales/Marketing: | | Liberal Arts: | | Information Systems: | | Professionals: | | Technical/Scientific: | |
|---|---|---|---|---|---|---|---|---|---|---|---|
| Mgmt. Trainees: | Y | Mktg. Professionals: | Y | Gen. Writing/Editing: | | Info. Management: | Y | Finance/Accounting: | Y | Engineers, Elec.: | |
| Experienced Mgmt.: | Y | Retail Sales: | | Technical Writing: | Y | Software Dev.: | Y | Law: | Y | Engineers, Other: | |
| Int'l Business: | Y | Commercial/Industrial: | Y | Graphic Arts/Photog.: | | Hardware Dev.: | | HR/Other: | Y | Health/Lab: | |
| MBA Graduates: | Y | Sales Trainees: | Y | Music: | | Systems Integration: | Y | Training: | Y | Scientists/Research: | |
| | | Advertising Pros.: | | Broadcasting: | | Consulting/Other: | | Health Care: | | Petroleum/Chemicals: | |
| | | | | Other: | | | | Consulting: | | Math/Other: | |

## TYPES OF BUSINESS:

Online Trading Systems
Transaction Research
Data Processing Services
Hedge Fund Services & Research

## BRANDS/DIVISIONS/AFFILIATES:

AlterNet Securities, Inc.
ITG Analytics, Inc.
Triton
Radical
ITG POSIT
Blockalert
ITG Logic
RedSky Financial, LLC

## CONTACTS: *Note: Officers with more than one job title may be intentionally listed here more than once.*

Robert Gasser, CEO
Robert Gasser, Pres.
Howard C. Naphtali, CFO
Chris Heckman, Managing Dir./Co-Head-Sales & Trading
David L. Meitz, Mng. Dir.-Software Dev., Tech. & Trading Support
Mark Wright, Managing Dir.-Global Prod.
P. Mats Goebels, General Counsel/Corp. Sec.
Maureen Murphy, Dir.-Corp. Comm.
Maureen Murphy, Dir.-Investor Rel. & Mktg.
Angelo Bulone, Controller/Managing Dir.
Stephen Alepa, Managing Dir.-ITG Financial Network
Ian Domowitz, CEO-ITG Solutions Network
Alan Herzog, Managing Dir.-ITG Hedge Fund Svcs.
Nick Thadaney, CEO-ITG Canada
Maureen O'Hara, Chmn.
Alasdair Haynes, CEO-Int'l

| | |
|---|---|
| **Phone:** 212-588-4000 | **Fax:** 212-444-6295 |
| **Toll-Free:** 800-426-5523 | |
| **Address:** 380 Madison Ave., 4th Fl., New York, NY 10017 US | |

## GROWTH PLANS/SPECIAL FEATURES:

Investment Technology Group, Inc. (ITG) is a global specialized agency brokerage and technology firm, combining pre-trade analysis, order management, trade execution and post-trade evaluation to provide clients with continuous improvements in trading and cost efficiency. ITG's principal subsidiaries include AlterNet Securities, Inc.; Investment Technology Group Limited (ITG Europe); ITG Australia Limited; ITG Canada Corp.; ITG Hong Kong Limited; ITG Japan Ltd.; ITG Software Solutions, Inc., a developer of intangible property and software; ITG Analytics, Inc., a provider of pre- and post-trade analysis, fair value and trade optimization services; The Macgregor Group, Inc., a leading provider of trade order management technology for the financial community; Plexus Plan Sponsor Group, Inc., a provider of transaction cost analysis and transition consulting to the plan sponsor community; and Block Alert LLC, a 50% owned joint venture. The company's primary services include Triton, a windows-based trading platform that includes complete market access and research capabilities; Radical, a broker-neutral desktop application providing connectivity to liquidity pools and execution venues; ITG POSIT, an electronic stock crossing system; Blockalert, powered by POSIT, which seeks out crossing opportunities in the trade blotters of participating clients; ITG Logic, a pre-trading analytical platform that monitors trade performance and cost to evaluate portfolio risk; and TCA, post-trading software that assists with execution requirements. In June 2007, the company agreed to acquire RedSky Financial, LLC, a private Chicago based broker-dealer specializing in electronic multi-asset class trading with an emphasis on exchange-traded equity derivative products, for approximately $22 million. In September 2007, ITG launched ITG Net, which combines ITG's existing routing network with the Macgregor Financial Network global connectivity and client service and support model.

## FINANCIALS: **Sales and profits are in thousands of dollars—add 000 to get the full amount. 2008 Note: Financial information for 2008 was not available for all companies at press time.**

| | | |
|---|---|---|
| 2008 Sales: $ | 2008 Profits: $ | **U.S. Stock Ticker: ITG** |
| 2007 Sales: $730,999 | 2007 Profits: $111,107 | **Int'l Ticker:** Int'l Exchange: |
| 2006 Sales: $599,484 | 2006 Profits: $97,923 | Employees: 1,218 |
| 2005 Sales: $408,161 | 2005 Profits: $67,686 | Fiscal Year Ends: 12/31 |
| 2004 Sales: $334,486 | 2004 Profits: $40,983 | Parent Company: |

## SALARIES/BENEFITS:

| | | | | |
|---|---|---|---|---|
| Pension Plan: Y | ESOP Stock Plan: | Profit Sharing: | Top Exec. Salary: $750,000 | Bonus: $1,575,000 |
| Savings Plan: Y | Stock Purch. Plan: Y | | Second Exec. Salary: $500,000 | Bonus: $1,450,000 |

## OTHER THOUGHTS:

**Apparent Women Officers or Directors**: 2
**Hot Spot for Advancement for Women/Minorities**: Y

## LOCATIONS: ("Y" = Yes)

| West: | Southwest: | Midwest: | Southeast: | Northeast: | International: |
|---|---|---|---|---|---|
| Y | | | | Y | Y |

# IRIDEX CORP

www.iridex.com

**Industry Group Code:** 339113 **Ranks within this company's industry group:** Sales: 41 Profits: 40

| Management: | | Sales/Marketing: | | Liberal Arts: | | Information Systems: | | Professionals: | | Technical/Scientific: | |
|---|---|---|---|---|---|---|---|---|---|---|---|
| Mgmt. Trainees: | | Mktg. Professionals: | Y | Gen. Writing/Editing: | | Info. Management: | Y | Finance/Accounting: | Y | Engineers, Elec.: | Y |
| Experienced Mgmt.: | Y | Retail Sales: | | Technical Writing: | Y | Software Dev.: | Y | Law: | Y | Engineers, Other: | Y |
| Int'l Business: | Y | Commercial/Industrial: | Y | Graphic Arts/Photog.: | | Hardware Dev.: | Y | HR/Other: | Y | Health/Lab: | Y |
| MBA Graduates: | Y | Sales Trainees: | Y | Music: | | Systems Integration: | | Training: | Y | Scientists/Research: | Y |
| | | Advertising Pros.: | | Broadcasting: | | Consulting/Other: | | Health Care: | Y | Petroleum/Chemicals: | |
| | | | | Other: | | | | Consulting: | | Math/Other: | Y |

## TYPES OF BUSINESS:

Equipment-Laser Systems
Ophthalmological & Dermatological Laser Systems

## BRANDS/DIVISIONS/AFFILIATES:

OcuLight TX
IRIS Medical IQ810 Laser System
OcuLight Symphony
OcuLight SL
OcuLight GL
EndoProbe
Laserscope
Gemini Laser System

## CONTACTS: *Note: Officers with more than one job title may be intentionally listed here more than once.*

Theodore A. Boutacoff, CEO
Theodore A. Boutacoff, Pres.
James H. Mackaness, CFO
Donald J. Todd, Sr. VP-Mktg. & Customer Support
Timothy Powers, VP-Oper.
James L. Donovan, VP-Corp. Bus. Dev.
Theodore A. Boutacoff, Chmn.
Eduardo Arias, Sr. VP-Int'l Sales & Bus. Dev.

**Phone:** 650-940-4700 **Fax:** 650-940-4710
**Toll-Free:** 800-388-4747
**Address:** 1212 Terra Bella Ave., Mountain View, CA 94043-1824 US

## GROWTH PLANS/SPECIAL FEATURES:

IRIDEX Corporation provides therapeutic based laser systems and delivery devices used in aesthetic medicine, ophthalmology and otolaryngology. IRIDEX markets its products through a direct sales force in the U.S. and a network of 77 distributors that sells to 107 countries. IRIDEX also has two European subsidiaries in the aesthetics division, in the U.K. and France. In the aesthetic medicine division, the company's products treat skin conditions, primarily vascular and pigmented lesions. The company's dermatology laser systems include the DioLite XP and the VariLite Dual Wavelength Laser systems. IRIDEX's ophthalmologic division includes the company's family of OcuLight laser systems, which accounts for the majority of its revenues, is used for ophthalmic applications primarily in operating rooms. The OcuLight product family includes the OcuLight TX, IRIS Medical IQ810 Laser System, the OcuLight Symphony, OcuLight SL, OcuLight SLx, OcuLight GL and OcuLight GLx laser photocoagulation systems. IRIDEX's ophthalmology products are used in the treatment of serious eye diseases, including the three leading causes of irreversible blindness: diabetic retinopathy, glaucoma and age-related macular degeneration (AMD). The company's ophthalmic and dermatology laser system consists of small, portable laser consoles and delivery devices. Ophthalmologists use the company's laser with either an indirect laser ophthalmoscope or a disposable single-use EndoProbe. IRIDEX's otolaryngology division uses 532 nm laser systems, such as the OcuLight TX, OcuLight GLx and OcuProbe, to perform certain hearing loss correction procedures, such as stapedectomies and stapedotomies. In January 2007, IRIDEX acquired Laserscope's aesthetics business, including four patents, a license to an additional nine Laserscope patents and a license under Palomar hair removal patents. In August 2008, IRIDEX received FDA approval for its IRIDEX IQ Laser Systems, including the IRIDEX IQ 532, IQ 577, IQ 630-670, and IQ 810 Laser Systems and their associated delivery devices, used in ophthalmology, otolaryngology and dermatology.

## FINANCIALS: **Sales and profits are in thousands of dollars—add 000 to get the full amount. 2008 Note: Financial information for 2008 was not available for all companies at press time.**

| | | |
|---|---|---|
| 2008 Sales: $ | 2008 Profits: $ | **U.S. Stock Ticker: IRIX** |
| 2007 Sales: $55,532 | 2007 Profits: $-22,272 | **Int'l Ticker:** Int'l Exchange: |
| 2006 Sales: $35,904 | 2006 Profits: $-5,753 | Employees: 151 |
| 2005 Sales: $37,029 | 2005 Profits: $1,671 | Fiscal Year Ends: 12/31 |
| 2004 Sales: $32,810 | 2004 Profits: $- 402 | Parent Company: |

## SALARIES/BENEFITS:

| | | | | |
|---|---|---|---|---|
| Pension Plan: | ESOP Stock Plan: | Profit Sharing: | Top Exec. Salary: $257,742 | Bonus: $ 804 |
| Savings Plan: Y | Stock Purch. Plan: Y | | Second Exec. Salary: $241,831 | Bonus: $ 804 |

## OTHER THOUGHTS:

**Apparent Women Officers or Directors**:
**Hot Spot for Advancement for Women/Minorities**:

## LOCATIONS: ("Y" = Yes)

| West: | Southwest: | Midwest: | Southeast: | Northeast: | International: |
|---|---|---|---|---|---|
| Y | Y | Y | Y | Y | Y |

# IRIS INTERNATIONAL INC

www.proiris.com

**Industry Group Code:** 339113 **Ranks within this company's industry group:** Sales: 33 Profits: 26

| Management: | | Sales/Marketing: | | Liberal Arts: | | Information Systems: | | Professionals: | | Technical/Scientific: | |
|---|---|---|---|---|---|---|---|---|---|---|---|
| Mgmt. Trainees: | | Mktg. Professionals: | Y | Gen. Writing/Editing: | | Info. Management: | Y | Finance/Accounting: | Y | Engineers, Elec.: | Y |
| Experienced Mgmt.: | Y | Retail Sales: | | Technical Writing: | Y | Software Dev.: | Y | Law: | Y | Engineers, Other: | Y |
| Int'l Business: | Y | Commercial/Industrial: | Y | Graphic Arts/Photog.: | | Hardware Dev.: | Y | HR/Other: | Y | Health/Lab: | Y |
| MBA Graduates: | Y | Sales Trainees: | Y | Music: | | Systems Integration: | | Training: | Y | Scientists/Research: | Y |
| | | Advertising Pros.: | | Broadcasting: | | Consulting/Other: | | Health Care: | Y | Petroleum/Chemicals: | |
| | | | | Other: | | | | Consulting: | | Math/Other: | Y |

## TYPES OF BUSINESS:

Equipment-Body Fluid Analysis
Automated Urinalysis Workstations
Digital Imaging Software, Research & Development

## BRANDS/DIVISIONS/AFFILIATES:

Nucleic Acid Detection Immunoassay (NADiA)
iQ
IRICELL

## CONTACTS: *Note: Officers with more than one job title may be intentionally listed here more than once.*

Cesar M. Garcia, CEO
Cesar M. Garcia, Pres.
Peter L. Donato, CFO/VP
Peter L. Donato, Sec.
John U. Yi, VP-Oper.
Robert A. Mello, VP/Pres., Iris Sample Processing
Cesar M. Garcia, Chmn.

| | |
|---|---|
| **Phone:** 818-709-1244 | **Fax:** 818-700-9661 |
| **Toll-Free:** 800-776-4747 | |
| **Address:** 9172 Eton Ave., Chatsworth, CA 91311-5874 US | |

## GROWTH PLANS/SPECIAL FEATURES:

IRIS International, Inc. is a leading global in vitro diagnostics company focused on products that analyze particles and living cell forms and structures, or morphology, of a variety of bodily fluids. The initial applications for IRIS' technology have been in the urinalysis market and it is a leading worldwide provider of urine microscopy systems, with an installed base of over 1,700 systems in over 50 countries. In this market, IRIS also provides integrated solutions comprising urine microscopy and urine chemistry products as well as consumable supplies, system support services and sample preparation products. It is developing an automated urine bacteria screening instrument to provide and faster and cost-effective automated alternative to urine cultures. The firm intends to expand into related market segments that can benefit from automated morphology solutions, including the analysis of other body fluids such as blood. IRIS additionally has an active research and development platform in molecular diagnostics based on its Nucleic Acid Detection Immunoassay (NADiA) platform, which it is developing for various applications in oncology and infectious disease. The firm has historically focused on developing, manufacturing and commercializing in vitro diagnostics (IVD) instruments and consumables for urinalysis, including its iQ analyzers, a family of fully automated, image-based bench-top analyzers for urine microscopy. While IRIS' iQ analyzers are currently only available in the U.S., it plans to launch its chemistry analyzer IRICELL during 2008 internationally. In May 2007, the company announced a decision to close its ADIR subsidiary, as ADIR no longer qualifies for government funding under new Small Business Administration guidelines.

IRIS offers its employees education reimbursement, a cafeteria plan and medical, dental, vision, life and disability insurance.

## FINANCIALS: **Sales and profits are in thousands of dollars—add 000 to get the full amount. 2008 Note: Financial information for 2008 was not available for all companies at press time.**

| | | |
|---|---|---|
| 2008 Sales: $ | 2008 Profits: $ | **U.S. Stock Ticker: IRIS** |
| 2007 Sales: $84,306 | 2007 Profits: $7,549 | **Int'l Ticker:** Int'l Exchange: |
| 2006 Sales: $72,067 | 2006 Profits: $- 175 | Employees: 308 |
| 2005 Sales: $62,780 | 2005 Profits: $6,131 | Fiscal Year Ends: 12/31 |
| 2004 Sales: $43,650 | 2004 Profits: $2,280 | Parent Company: |

## SALARIES/BENEFITS:

| | | | | |
|---|---|---|---|---|
| Pension Plan: | ESOP Stock Plan: | Profit Sharing: | Top Exec. Salary: $374,582 | Bonus: $155,975 |
| Savings Plan: Y | Stock Purch. Plan: | | Second Exec. Salary: $241,458 | Bonus: $52,850 |

## OTHER THOUGHTS:

**Apparent Women Officers or Directors:**
**Hot Spot for Advancement for Women/Minorities:**

## LOCATIONS: ("Y" = Yes)

| West: | Southwest: | Midwest: | Southeast: | Northeast: | International: |
|---|---|---|---|---|---|
| Y | Y | | | Y | Y |

Note: Financial information, benefits and other data can change quickly and may vary from those stated here.

# ISILON SYSTEMS INC

**www.isilon.com**

**Industry Group Code:** 334112 **Ranks within this company's industry group:** Sales: 2 Profits: 1

| Management: | | Sales/Marketing: | | Liberal Arts: | | Information Systems: | | Professionals: | | Technical/Scientific: | |
|---|---|---|---|---|---|---|---|---|---|---|---|
| Mgmt. Trainees: | | Mktg. Professionals: | Y | Gen. Writing/Editing: | | Info. Management: | Y | Finance/Accounting: | Y | Engineers, Elec.: | Y |
| Experienced Mgmt.: | Y | Retail Sales: | | Technical Writing: | | Software Dev.: | Y | Law: | Y | Engineers, Other: | |
| Int'l Business: | Y | Commercial/Industrial: | Y | Graphic Arts/Photog.: | | Hardware Dev.: | Y | HR/Other: | Y | Health/Lab: | |
| MBA Graduates: | Y | Sales Trainees: | | Music: | | Systems Integration: | Y | Training: | Y | Scientists/Research: | |
| | | Advertising Pros.: | | Broadcasting: | | Consulting/Other: | | Health Care: | | Petroleum/Chemicals: | |
| | | | | Other: | | | | Consulting: | | Math/Other: | |

## TYPES OF BUSINESS:

Clustered Storage Systems

## BRANDS/DIVISIONS/AFFILIATES:

Isilon IQ
OneFS
Isilon IQ Accelerator
Isilon EX 6000
SyncIQ
SmartConnect
SnapshotIQ

## CONTACTS:
*Note: Officers with more than one job title may be intentionally listed here more than once.*

Sujal M. Patel, CEO
Sujal M. Patel, Pres.
Bill Richter, Interim CFO
Ram Appalaraju, Sr. VP-Worldwide Sales
Gwen Weld, VP-Human Resources & Organizational Dev.
Paul Rutherford, CTO
Brett Helsel, Sr. VP-Eng.
Keenan Conder, General Counsel/VP/Corp. Sec.
Mary Godwin, VP-Oper.
Bill Richter, VP-Finance
Steve Fitz, Sr. VP-Worldwide Field Oper.
William D. Ruckelshaus, Chmn.

**Phone:** 206-315-7500 **Fax:** 206-315-7501
**Toll-Free:** 877-247-4566
**Address:** 3101 West Ave., Seattle, WA 98121 US

## GROWTH PLANS/SPECIAL FEATURES:

Isilon Systems, Inc. is a leading provider of clustered storage systems for digital content. The company's Isilon IQ storage systems are comprised of three or more nodes, each of which is a self-contained, rack-mountable device that contains industry standard hardware, including disk drives, a central processing unit (CPU), memory chips and network interfaces, and is integrated with its proprietary OneFS operating system software, which unifies a cluster of nodes into a single shared resource. OneFS combines the three distinct layers of traditional storage architecture, which consist of a file system, a volume manager and a redundant array of independent disks, or RAID, into a single unified software layer. Consequently, Isilon IQ nodes automatically work together to aggregate their collective computing power into a single, unified storage system that is designed to withstand the failure of any piece of hardware, including disks, switches or even entire nodes. The company also provides its Isilon IQ Accelerator and Isilon EX 6000 platform extension nodes, which optimize system performance, in addition to three related software applications that extend the capabilities and functionality of its systems: SyncIQ replication software, SmartConnect load-balancing software and SnapshotIQ protection software. As of 2008, Isilon has sold its clustered storage systems to more than 675 customers across a wide range of industries both directly through its field sales force and indirectly through a channel partner program that includes more than 100 value-added resellers and distributors. Customers of Isilon include NBC Sports, Cedar-Sinai Medical Center and MySpace.

Employees are offered medical, dental, vision, life and disability insurance; flexible spending accounts; a 401(k) plan; and a discount stock purchase plan.

## FINANCIALS:
**Sales and profits are in thousands of dollars—add 000 to get the full amount. 2008 Note: Financial information for 2008 was not available for all companies at press time.**

| | | |
|---|---|---|
| 2008 Sales: $114,422 | 2008 Profits: $-25,078 | **U.S. Stock Ticker: ISLN** |
| 2007 Sales: $88,998 | 2007 Profits: $-26,932 | **Int'l Ticker:** Int'l Exchange: |
| 2006 Sales: $61,206 | 2006 Profits: $-25,988 | Employees: 321 |
| 2005 Sales: $21,083 | 2005 Profits: $-19,185 | Fiscal Year Ends: 12/31 |
| 2004 Sales: $ | 2004 Profits: $ | Parent Company: |

## SALARIES/BENEFITS:

| | | | | |
|---|---|---|---|---|
| Pension Plan: | ESOP Stock Plan: | Profit Sharing: | Top Exec. Salary: $291,865 | Bonus: $131,759 |
| Savings Plan: Y | Stock Purch. Plan: Y | | Second Exec. Salary: $234,860 | Bonus: $96,750 |

## OTHER THOUGHTS:

**Apparent Women Officers or Directors**: 2
**Hot Spot for Advancement for Women/Minorities**:

## LOCATIONS: ("Y" = Yes)

| West: | Southwest: | Midwest: | Southeast: | Northeast: | International: |
|---|---|---|---|---|---|
| Y | | | | | Y |

# ISONICS CORPORATION

www.isonics.com

**Industry Group Code:** 325000 **Ranks within this company's industry group:** Sales: 3 Profits: 2

| Management: | | Sales/Marketing: | | Liberal Arts: | | Information Systems: | | Professionals: | | Technical/Scientific: | |
|---|---|---|---|---|---|---|---|---|---|---|---|
| Mgmt. Trainees: | | Mktg. Professionals: | | Gen. Writing/Editing: | | Info. Management: | Y | Finance/Accounting: | Y | Engineers, Elec.: | Y |
| Experienced Mgmt.: | Y | Retail Sales: | | Technical Writing: | Y | Software Dev.: | | Law: | Y | Engineers, Other: | |
| Int'l Business: | | Commercial/Industrial: | Y | Graphic Arts/Photog.: | | Hardware Dev.: | | HR/Other: | Y | Health/Lab: | |
| MBA Graduates: | Y | Sales Trainees: | | Music: | | Systems Integration: | | Training: | Y | Scientists/Research: | Y |
| | | Advertising Pros.: | | Broadcasting: | | Consulting/Other: | | Health Care: | | Petroleum/Chemicals: | |
| | | | | Other: | | | | Consulting: | | Math/Other: | |

## TYPES OF BUSINESS:

Homeland Security Products & Services
Silicon Wafer Reclaim & Test Products
Wafer Thinning
Customer Wafer Products

## BRANDS/DIVISIONS/AFFILIATES:

Protection Plus Security Corp.
Isonics Vancouver, Inc.
Isonics Homeland Security and Defense Corp.
Senselt Corp.
Interpro Zinc LLC
Institute fur Umwelttechnologien GmbH

## CONTACTS: *Note: Officers with more than one job title may be intentionally listed here more than once.*

Christopher Toffales, CEO
John Sakys, COO
John Sakys, Pres.
Gregory A. Meadows, CFO/VP
Christopher Toffales, Chmn.

| **Phone:** 303-279-7900 | **Fax:** 303-279-7300 |
|---|---|
| **Toll-Free:** | |
| **Address:** 5906 McIntyre St., Golden, CO 80403 US | |

## GROWTH PLANS/SPECIAL FEATURES:

Isonics Corp., based in Colorado, focuses on the development and provision of homeland security products and services and the manufacture of 300-milimeter (and smaller diameter) test wafers and reclamation services, wafer thinning and custom wafer products and services for the silicon industry. It operates in two segments: silicon products and services; and security services. The silicon products and services division specializes in test and monitoring wafers; high quality wafer reclaim; wafer thinning; and custom wafer services. The segment performs storage simulation tests on its products to ensure prolonged shelf-life. Final cleaning processes are monitored for trace metals. The protection plus security segment operates through Protection Plus Security Corp., which works with clients to develop individual integrated security solutions. The company's other subsidiaries include Isonics Vancouver, Inc. and Isonics Homeland Security and Defense Corporation, and the firm also maintains a 90% interest in Senselt Corp. and a 25% interest in Interpro Zinc LLC, a company that conducts research and development for the recovery and recycling of zinc metal. In January 2008, Isonics sold its 30% interest in Institute fur Umwelttechnologien GmbH.

## FINANCIALS: Sales and profits are in thousands of dollars—add 000 to get the full amount. 2008 Note: Financial information for 2008 was not available for all companies at press time.

| | | |
|---|---|---|
| 2008 Sales: $ | 2008 Profits: $ | **U.S. Stock Ticker: ISON** |
| 2007 Sales: $27,731 | 2007 Profits: $-13,165 | **Int'l Ticker:** Int'l Exchange: |
| 2006 Sales: $18,580 | 2006 Profits: $-32,341 | Employees: 477 |
| 2005 Sales: $2,692 | 2005 Profits: $-15,177 | Fiscal Year Ends: 4/30 |
| 2004 Sales: $8,721 | 2004 Profits: $-4,163 | Parent Company: |

## SALARIES/BENEFITS:

| | | | | |
|---|---|---|---|---|
| Pension Plan: | ESOP Stock Plan: | Profit Sharing: | Top Exec. Salary: $2,577,500 | Bonus: $26,367 |
| Savings Plan: | Stock Purch. Plan: | | Second Exec. Salary: $232,350 | Bonus: $23,780 |

## OTHER THOUGHTS:

**Apparent Women Officers or Directors:**
**Hot Spot for Advancement for Women/Minorities:**

## LOCATIONS: ("Y" = Yes)

| West: | Southwest: | Midwest: | Southeast: | Northeast: | International: |
|---|---|---|---|---|---|
| Y | | | | Y | |

# IVILLAGE INC

**www.ivillage.com**

**Industry Group Code:** 514199 **Ranks within this company's industry group:** Sales: Profits:

| **Management:** | | **Sales/Marketing:** | | **Liberal Arts:** | | **Information Systems:** | | **Professionals:** | | **Technical/Scientific:** | |
|---|---|---|---|---|---|---|---|---|---|---|---|
| Mgmt. Trainees: | | Mktg. Professionals: | Y | Gen. Writing/Editing: | Y | Info. Management: | Y | Finance/Accounting: | Y | Engineers, Elec.: | |
| Experienced Mgmt.: | Y | Retail Sales: | | Technical Writing: | | Software Dev.: | Y | Law: | Y | Engineers, Other: | |
| Int'l Business: | | Commercial/Industrial: | Y | Graphic Arts/Photog.: | Y | Hardware Dev.: | | HR/Other: | Y | Health/Lab: | |
| MBA Graduates: | Y | Sales Trainees: | Y | Music: | | Systems Integration: | Y | Training: | Y | Scientists/Research: | |
| | | Advertising Pros.: | Y | Broadcasting: | | Consulting/Other: | | Health Care: | | Petroleum/Chemicals: | |
| | | | | Other: | Y | | | Consulting: | | Math/Other: | |

## TYPES OF BUSINESS:

Online Women's Network
Educational Publishing
Online Promotions & Direct Marketing
Consulting Services

## BRANDS/DIVISIONS/AFFILIATES:

NBC Universal
iVillage.com
iVillage UK
iVillage Total Health
Astrology.com
GardenWeb
gURL.com
Newborn Channel

## CONTACTS: *Note: Officers with more than one job title may be intentionally listed here more than once.*

Michael Gutkowski, COO
Todd Saypoff, CFO
Linda Boff, Chief Mktg. Officer
Barry S. Kresch, Sr. VP-Research
Carla Wojnaroski, Sr. VP/Editor-in-Chief
Deborah I. (Debi) Fine, Pres., iVillage Properties
Gregg Zegras, Sr. VP-iVillage Health
Peter R. Naylor, Sr. VP-Sales, NBC Universal Digital Media

| **Phone:** 212-600-6000 | **Fax:** 212-604-9133 |
|---|---|
| **Toll-Free:** | |
| **Address:** 500 7th Ave., 14th Fl., New York, NY 10018 US | |

## GROWTH PLANS/SPECIAL FEATURES:

iVillage, Inc., a subsidiary of NBC Universal, Inc., is a leading women's media company consisting of several online and offline properties offering unique content, community applications, tools and interactive features. The company's iVillage.com website, with 31.4 million unique visitors, provides information on such topics as health, parenting, pregnancy, beauty, style, fitness, relationships, food and entertainment, as well as thousands of message boards and a variety of social networking tools. iVillage's brand extensions include iVillage UK, its U.K.-oriented online information network for women; iVillage Total Health, providing information on women's health issues; owned sites Astrology.com, GardenWeb and gURL.com; and the Newborn Channel. In July 2007, iVillage launched iVillage Weddings, a website offering wedding-oriented information and support.

iVillage offers its employees subsidized child care, adoption reimbursement, back-up child care, dependent scholarships, employee discounts, an employee assistance program, leadership development programs, tuition reimbursement, educational loans, health club discounts, fitness programs, flexible spending accounts, domestic partner benefits and medical, dental, vision and prescription insurance.

## FINANCIALS: **Sales and profits are in thousands of dollars—add 000 to get the full amount. 2008 Note: Financial information for 2008 was not available for all companies at press time.**

| | | |
|---|---|---|
| 2008 Sales: $ | 2008 Profits: $ | **U.S. Stock Ticker: Subsidiary** |
| 2007 Sales: $ | 2007 Profits: $ | **Int'l Ticker:** Int'l Exchange: |
| 2006 Sales: $ | 2006 Profits: $ | Employees: 278 |
| 2005 Sales: $91,061 | 2005 Profits: $9,456 | Fiscal Year Ends: 12/31 |
| 2004 Sales: $66,903 | 2004 Profits: $2,677 | Parent Company: NBC UNIVERSAL |

## SALARIES/BENEFITS:

| | | | | |
|---|---|---|---|---|
| Pension Plan: | ESOP Stock Plan: | Profit Sharing: | Top Exec. Salary: $ | Bonus: $ |
| Savings Plan: | Stock Purch. Plan: | | Second Exec. Salary: $327,000 | Bonus: $327,000 |

## OTHER THOUGHTS:

**Apparent Women Officers or Directors**: 2
**Hot Spot for Advancement for Women/Minorities**: Y

## LOCATIONS: ("Y" = Yes)

| West: | Southwest: | Midwest: | Southeast: | Northeast: | International: |
|---|---|---|---|---|---|
| | | | | Y | |

# J2 GLOBAL COMMUNICATIONS INC

www.j2global.com

**Industry Group Code:** 514191A **Ranks within this company's industry group:** Sales: 5 Profits: 3

| Management: | | Sales/Marketing: | | Liberal Arts: | | Information Systems: | | Professionals: | | Technical/Scientific: | |
|---|---|---|---|---|---|---|---|---|---|---|---|
| Mgmt. Trainees: | | Mktg. Professionals: | Y | Gen. Writing/Editing: | | Info. Management: | Y | Finance/Accounting: | Y | Engineers, Elec.: | Y |
| Experienced Mgmt.: | Y | Retail Sales: | | Technical Writing: | Y | Software Dev.: | Y | Law: | Y | Engineers, Other: | |
| Int'l Business: | Y | Commercial/Industrial: | Y | Graphic Arts/Photog.: | | Hardware Dev.: | | HR/Other: | Y | Health/Lab: | |
| MBA Graduates: | Y | Sales Trainees: | Y | Music: | | Systems Integration: | Y | Training: | Y | Scientists/Research: | |
| | | Advertising Pros.: | | Broadcasting: | | Consulting/Other: | | Health Care: | | Petroleum/Chemicals: | |
| | | | | Other: | | | | Consulting: | | Math/Other: | |

## TYPES OF BUSINESS:

Unified Messaging & Communication Services
Internet-Based Faxing
Internet Conferencing
Web-base Voicemail

## BRANDS/DIVISIONS/AFFILIATES:

eFax
jConnect
OneBox
eVoice
jBlast
eFax Broadcast
eVoice Receptionist
OneBox Receptionist

## CONTACTS: *Note: Officers with more than one job title may be intentionally listed here more than once.*

Nehemia (Hemi) Zucker, CEO
Scott Turicchi, Pres.
Kathy Griggs, CFO
Ken Ford, VP-Mktg.
Patty Brunton, VP-Human Resources
Ken Truesdale, VP-Prod. Dev.
Vince Niedielski, VP-Eng.
Jeffery D. Adelman, General Counsel/VP/Sec.
Zohar Loshitzer, Exec. VP-Corp. Strategy
Mike Pugh, VP-Global Web Mktg.
Kathy Griggs, Chief Acct. Officer
Ken Ford, VP-Svcs. & Support
Tom Dolan, VP-Sales
Alan Alters, VP-Network Oper.
Richard S. Ressler, Chmn.
Tim McLean, VP-Int'l

**Phone:** 323-860-9200 **Fax:** 323-464-1446
**Toll-Free:** 888-438-5329
**Address:** 6922 Hollywood Blvd., Los Angeles, CA 90028 US

## GROWTH PLANS/SPECIAL FEATURES:

j2 Global Communications, Inc. is a provider of messaging and communications services to individuals and businesses in over 3,000 cities in 42 countries. The company provides faxing and voicemail services, document management services, web-initiated conference calling and unified-messaging and communications services. The firm's services are marketed primarily under the brand names: jConnect, jBlast, eFax, Onebox, Onebox Receptionist and eVoice. J2 operates in four segments: Fax Mail, Unified Communications, Voice and E-mail. The Fax Mail division, which represents the majority of the company's revenue, markets eFax, eFax Corporate, eFax Broadcast, Send2Fax, jBlast and UniFax to individuals and small businesses. Unified Communications offers jConnect Free, which assigns each subscriber a randomly selected Direct Inward Dial (DID) phone number with limited fax and voicemail space; jConnect Premier, which allows subscribers to choose either a toll-free or local number with inbound fax, voicemail, and email capabilities from any touch-tone phone; and Onebox, which adds a find-me-follow-me option for customizing incoming call prioritization and outgoing call options. eVoice delivers a subscriber's voicemail messages to their inbox via the Internet. E-mail services include Electric Mail, an outsourced hosted e-mail service that includes Electric WebMail with E-mmunity virus scanning and SpamSMART filtering. j2 has nearly 12 million DID phone numbers deployed. In July 2007, j2 acquired YAC Limited, an Ireland-based messaging services provider. In May 2008, j2's Onebox service launched a new Live Receptionist option, allowing offices to redirect their calls to alternative locations or recipients outside of business hours. Also in 2008, j2 acquired the digital faxing business of MediaBurst Limited, the enhanced voice servicer of Phone People Holdings Corporation and the RapidFax business of Easylink Services International.

j2 Global Communications, Inc. offers employees a 401(k) plan and comprehensive medical and life insurance, as well as an employee stock purchase plan.

## FINANCIALS: Sales and profits are in thousands of dollars—add 000 to get the full amount. 2008 Note: Financial information for 2008 was not available for all companies at press time.

| | | |
|---|---|---|
| 2008 Sales: $ | 2008 Profits: $ | **U.S. Stock Ticker: JCOM** |
| 2007 Sales: $220,697 | 2007 Profits: $68,461 | **Int'l Ticker:** Int'l Exchange: |
| 2006 Sales: $181,079 | 2006 Profits: $53,131 | Employees: 410 |
| 2005 Sales: $143,941 | 2005 Profits: $50,618 | Fiscal Year Ends: 12/31 |
| 2004 Sales: $106,343 | 2004 Profits: $30,616 | Parent Company: |

## SALARIES/BENEFITS:

| | | | | |
|---|---|---|---|---|
| Pension Plan: | ESOP Stock Plan: | Profit Sharing: | Top Exec. Salary: $402,789 | Bonus: $232,849 |
| Savings Plan: Y | Stock Purch. Plan: Y | | Second Exec. Salary: $349,616 | Bonus: $165,657 |

## OTHER THOUGHTS:

**Apparent Women Officers or Directors**: 2
**Hot Spot for Advancement for Women/Minorities**: Y

## LOCATIONS: ("Y" = Yes)

| West: | Southwest: | Midwest: | Southeast: | Northeast: | International: |
|---|---|---|---|---|---|
| Y | | | | | Y |

# JACKSON NATIONAL LIFE INSURANCE COMPANY www.jnl.com

**Industry Group Code:** 524113 **Ranks within this company's industry group:** Sales: 1 Profits: 1

| Management: | | Sales/Marketing: | | Liberal Arts: | | Information Systems: | | Professionals: | | Technical/Scientific: | |
|---|---|---|---|---|---|---|---|---|---|---|---|
| Mgmt. Trainees: | | Mktg. Professionals: | Y | Gen. Writing/Editing: | Y | Info. Management: | Y | Finance/Accounting: | Y | Engineers, Elec.: | |
| Experienced Mgmt.: | Y | Retail Sales: | | Technical Writing: | Y | Software Dev.: | | Law: | Y | Engineers, Other: | |
| Int'l Business: | | Commercial/Industrial: | | Graphic Arts/Photog.: | | Hardware Dev.: | | HR/Other: | Y | Health/Lab: | |
| MBA Graduates: | Y | Sales Trainees: | Y | Music: | | Systems Integration: | | Training: | Y | Scientists/Research: | |
| | | Advertising Pros.: | Y | Broadcasting: | | Consulting/Other: | | Health Care: | Y | Petroleum/Chemicals: | |
| | | | | Other: | | | | Consulting: | | Math/Other: | Y |

## TYPES OF BUSINESS:

Life Insurance
Financial Services
Annuities
Asset Management
Retail Brokerage Services

## BRANDS/DIVISIONS/AFFILIATES:

Prudential plc
Jackson National Life Distributors LLC
Curian Capital LLC
PPM America, Inc.
JNL Southeast Agency LLC
National Planning Holdings, Inc.
Jackson National Asset Management LLC
PPM America, Inc.

## CONTACTS: *Note: Officers with more than one job title may be intentionally listed here more than once.*

Clark P. Manning, CEO
Michael A. Wells, COO
Clark P. Manning, Pres.
Andy Hopping, CFO/Exec. VP/Treas.
Steve Hrapkiewicz, Sr. VP-Human Resources
George Napoles, CIO/Exec. VP
George Napoles, Chief Admin. Officer
Tom Meyer, General Counsel/Sr. VP
Jim Binder, VP-Corp. Strategy
Jim Binder, VP-Finance
Jacky Morin, VP-Institutional Prod.
John Brown, VP-Gov't Rel.
Lisa Drake, Sr. VP/Chief Actuary
Clifford Jack, Chief Dist. Officer/Exec. VP

**Phone:** 517-381-5500 **Fax:** 517-706-5517
**Toll-Free:** 800-873-5654
**Address:** 1 Corporate Way, Lansing, MI 48951 US

## GROWTH PLANS/SPECIAL FEATURES:

Jackson National Life Insurance Company, a subsidiary of U.K. firm Prudential plc, offers life insurance and financial services such as fixed, indexed and variable annuities. In addition, the company offers life insurance and institution products and, through subsidiaries and affiliated firms, asset management and retail brokerage services. The firm has more than $82 billion in total assets. Jackson National markets its products in 49 states and Washington, D.C. through wholesalers and broker/dealers. Jackson National Life Distributors LLC, a wholesale distributor subsidiary, operates in two groups: registered wholesalers, which target independent broker-dealers whose representatives are registered securities brokers; and guaranteed wholesalers, which market fixed and fixed index annuities and life insurance products. The company's Institutional Marketing Group markets annuity and life insurance products to financial institutions. The group also offers specialized education programs to financial institutions. Curian Capital LLC is the firm's asset management subsidiary providing customized investment solutions. National Planning Holdings, Inc. is Jackson's National affiliated network of independent broker-dealers. Subsidiary JNL Southeast Agency LLC, based in Atlanta, Georgia, is a career agency that sells the company's traditional life insurance and fixed annuity products. With more than 100 area sales representatives, JNL provides these products to customers in Arkansas, Florida, Georgia, North Carolina, Mississippi, Virginia, South Carolina and Tennessee. Subsidiary Jackson National Asset Management LLC provides fund account and reporting for Jackson National's variable funds. Subsidiary PPM America, Inc. and affiliate PPM Finance, Inc. manage the company's investment portfolio.

## FINANCIALS: **Sales and profits are in thousands of dollars—add 000 to get the full amount. 2008 Note: Financial information for 2008 was not available for all companies at press time.**

| | | |
|---|---|---|
| 2008 Sales: $ | 2008 Profits: $ | **U.S. Stock Ticker: Subsidiary** |
| 2007 Sales: $4,110,144 | 2007 Profits: $619,279 | **Int'l Ticker:** Int'l Exchange: |
| 2006 Sales: $3,712,167 | 2006 Profits: $541,565 | Employees: 2,300 |
| 2005 Sales: $3,809,500 | 2005 Profits: $594,100 | Fiscal Year Ends: 12/31 |
| 2004 Sales: $3,553,600 | 2004 Profits: $630,500 | Parent Company: PRUDENTIAL PLC |

## SALARIES/BENEFITS:

| | | | | |
|---|---|---|---|---|
| Pension Plan: Y | ESOP Stock Plan: | Profit Sharing: | Top Exec. Salary: $ | Bonus: $ |
| Savings Plan: Y | Stock Purch. Plan: | | Second Exec. Salary: $ | Bonus: $ |

## OTHER THOUGHTS:

**Apparent Women Officers or Directors**: 2
**Hot Spot for Advancement for Women/Minorities**:

## LOCATIONS: ("Y" = Yes)

| West: | Southwest: | Midwest: | Southeast: | Northeast: | International: |
|---|---|---|---|---|---|
| Y | Y | Y | Y | Y | |

# JAZZ PHARMACEUTICALS

www.jazzpharmaceuticals.com

**Industry Group Code:** 325412 **Ranks within this company's industry group:** Sales: 26 Profits: 33

| Management: | | Sales/Marketing: | | Liberal Arts: | | Information Systems: | | Professionals: | | Technical/Scientific: | |
|---|---|---|---|---|---|---|---|---|---|---|---|
| Mgmt. Trainees: | | Mktg. Professionals: | Y | Gen. Writing/Editing: | | Info. Management: | Y | Finance/Accounting: | Y | Engineers, Elec.: | |
| Experienced Mgmt.: | Y | Retail Sales: | | Technical Writing: | Y | Software Dev.: | Y | Law: | Y | Engineers, Other: | |
| Int'l Business: | | Commercial/Industrial: | Y | Graphic Arts/Photog.: | | Hardware Dev.: | | HR/Other: | Y | Health/Lab: | Y |
| MBA Graduates: | Y | Sales Trainees: | Y | Music: | | Systems Integration: | | Training: | Y | Scientists/Research: | Y |
| | | Advertising Pros.: | | Broadcasting: | | Consulting/Other: | | Health Care: | Y | Petroleum/Chemicals: | Y |
| | | | | Other: | | | | Consulting: | Y | Math/Other: | Y |

## TYPES OF BUSINESS:

Pharmaceuticals Discovery & Development
Neurological & Psychiatric Therapeutics

## BRANDS/DIVISIONS/AFFILIATES:

Xyrem
Antizol
Luvox CR
JZP-6

## CONTACTS: *Note: Officers with more than one job title may be intentionally listed here more than once.*

Samuel R. Saks, CEO
Robert M. Myers, Pres.
Matthew K. Fust, CFO
Edwin W. Luker, VP-Sales
Heather McGaughey, VP-Human Resources
Mark G. Eller, VP-Research
Michael DesJardin, VP-Prod. Dev.
Nandan Oza, VP-Mfg.
Carol A. Gamble, General Counsel/Sr. VP/Corp. Sec.
Jason Levin, VP-Corp. Dev.
Janne L. T. Wissel, Chief Compliance Officer/Sr. VP
Felissa H. Cagan, VP-Intellectual Property
Alan H. Cohen, Chief Medical Officer
Bruce C. Cozadd, Chmn.
Nandan Oza, VP-Supply Chain

| | |
|---|---|
| **Phone:** 650-496-3777 | **Fax:** 650-496-3781 |
| **Toll-Free:** | |
| **Address:** 3180 Porter Dr., Palo Alto, CA 94304 US | |

## GROWTH PLANS/SPECIAL FEATURES:

Jazz Pharmaceuticals, Inc. develops and commercializes products that address neurology and psychiatry. The company applies formulations and drug delivery technologies to known drug compounds to improve the efficacy and reduce adverse side effects of existing therapies. Also central to Jazz's business plan is the aggressive establishment of an innovative product portfolio through in-licensing, direct acquisition and collaboration. Jazz distributes or is developing products for the following medical issues: cataplexy, narcolepsy, obsessive compulsive disorder, social anxiety disorder, fibromyalgia, epilepsy, poison recovery and restless leg syndrome. At present the company has been approved to market three drugs: Xyrem, an oral compound for the cataplexy suffered by narcoleptics; Antizol, an antidote for ethylene glycol and methanol poisoning; and, most recently, Luvox CR, a once-a-day product approved for the treatment of obsessive compulsive disorder. Antizol is the only antidote FDA-approved for the treatment of ethylene glycol and methanol poisoning. Through the National Organization of Rare Disorders, Inc. (NORD), a non-profit organization dedicated to the identification, treatment and cure of rare orphan diseases, Jazz also provides Patient Assistance Programs on Xyrem for U.S. patients who are uninsured or underinsured. Jazz announced its initial public offering of 6,000,000 shares of common stock in May 2007, and began trading on the NASDAQ Global Market in June 2007. The firm received FDA approval for its Luvox CR in February 2008. The FDA also approved a second version of Jazz's Antizole in 2008. In June 2008, the firm announced completion of the first of two Phase III clinical trials for its JZP-6, designed for the treatment of fibromyalgia.

## FINANCIALS: **Sales and profits are in thousands of dollars—add 000 to get the full amount. 2008 Note: Financial information for 2008 was not available for all companies at press time.**

| | | |
|---|---|---|
| 2008 Sales: $ | 2008 Profits: $ | **U.S. Stock Ticker: JAZZ** |
| 2007 Sales: $65,303 | 2007 Profits: $-138,778 | **Int'l Ticker:** Int'l Exchange: |
| 2006 Sales: $44,856 | 2006 Profits: $-59,391 | Employees: 409 |
| 2005 Sales: $21,442 | 2005 Profits: $-85,156 | Fiscal Year Ends: 12/31 |
| 2004 Sales: $ | 2004 Profits: $ | Parent Company: |

## SALARIES/BENEFITS:

| | | | | |
|---|---|---|---|---|
| Pension Plan: | ESOP Stock Plan: | Profit Sharing: | Top Exec. Salary: $443,385 | Bonus: $140,000 |
| Savings Plan: | Stock Purch. Plan: | | Second Exec. Salary: $423,354 | Bonus: $140,000 |

## OTHER THOUGHTS:

**Apparent Women Officers or Directors**: 5
**Hot Spot for Advancement for Women/Minorities**: Y

## LOCATIONS: ("Y" = Yes)

| West: | Southwest: | Midwest: | Southeast: | Northeast: | International: |
|---|---|---|---|---|---|
| Y | | | | | |

# JUPITERMEDIA CORP

**www.jupitermedia.com**

**Industry Group Code:** 514199 **Ranks within this company's industry group:** Sales: 3 Profits: 5

| Management: | | Sales/Marketing: | | Liberal Arts: | | Information Systems: | | Professionals: | | Technical/Scientific: | |
|---|---|---|---|---|---|---|---|---|---|---|---|
| Mgmt. Trainees: | | Mktg. Professionals: | Y | Gen. Writing/Editing: | Y | Info. Management: | Y | Finance/Accounting: | Y | Engineers, Elec.: | |
| Experienced Mgmt.: | Y | Retail Sales: | | Technical Writing: | | Software Dev.: | Y | Law: | Y | Engineers, Other: | |
| Int'l Business: | Y | Commercial/Industrial: | Y | Graphic Arts/Photog.: | Y | Hardware Dev.: | | HR/Other: | Y | Health/Lab: | |
| MBA Graduates: | Y | Sales Trainees: | Y | Music: | | Systems Integration: | Y | Training: | Y | Scientists/Research: | |
| | | Advertising Pros.: | Y | Broadcasting: | | Consulting/Other: | | Health Care: | | Petroleum/Chemicals: | |
| | | | | Other: | Y | | | Consulting: | | Math/Other: | |

## TYPES OF BUSINESS:

Business & Technology News Portal
Online Image Library
Market Research
Trade Shows

## BRANDS/DIVISIONS/AFFILIATES:

JupiterImages
JupiterOnlineMedia
internet.com
Mediabistro.com
STEP Inside Design Magazine
Dynamic Graphics Magazine
AdsOfTheWorld.com
CreativeBits.org

## CONTACTS: *Note: Officers with more than one job title may be intentionally listed here more than once.*

Alan M. Meckler, CEO
Alan M. Meckler, COO
Alan M. Meckler, Pres.
Donald J. O'Neil, CFO/VP
Michael DeMilt, VP-Mktg.
Alan M. Meckler, Chmn.

| | |
|---|---|
| **Phone:** 203-662-2800 | **Fax:** 203-655-4686 |
| **Toll-Free:** | |
| **Address:** 23 Old Kings Hwy. S., Darien, CT 06820 US | |

## GROWTH PLANS/SPECIAL FEATURES:

Jupitermedia Corp. is a leading global provider of images, original information, job boards and events for information technology, business and creative professionals. Jupitermedia develops and disseminates original content and provides access to one of the largest online image libraries. The firm delivers its content through a number of proprietary channels, including its extensive online media networks, online image networks and its various trade shows and conferences. The company's Jupiterimages division is one of the leading paid subscription-based image companies in the world, with over 9 million online images serving creative professionals, with brands including BananaStock, Workbook Stock, FoodPix, Comstock Images, photos.com, clipart.com and others. The company's media segment consists of the JupiterOnlineMedia division, which consists of five online networks for IT professionals (Internet.com and EarthWeb.com), developers (DevX.com) and media and creative professionals (Mediabistro.com and Graphics.com). The networks include more than 150 web sites, as well as nearly 150 e-mail newsletters that are viewed by over 15 million users monthly. JupiterOnlineMedia also offers two print magazines for creative professionals, Dynamic Graphics Magazine and STEP Inside Design Magazine. Operations also include specialized career Web sites for select professional communities, which can be found online at Mediabistro.com and JustTechJobs.com. In addition, JupiterOnlineMedia includes JupiterEvents and Mediabistro's media-related events, which produce offline conference and trade shows focused on IT and business-specific topics. In June 2007, the company acquired AdsOfTheWorld.com and CreativeBits.org. In October 2008, Jupitermedia announced plans to sell its online images business, Jupiterimages, to rival Getty Images, Inc, for a purchase price of $96 million.

Jupitermedia offers its employees flexible spending accounts, tuition reimbursement and a 401(k) plan, in addition to medical, dental, life and AD&D insurance.

## FINANCIALS: **Sales and profits are in thousands of dollars—add 000 to get the full amount. 2008 Note: Financial information for 2008 was not available for all companies at press time.**

| | | |
|---|---|---|
| 2008 Sales: $ | 2008 Profits: $ | **U.S. Stock Ticker: JUPM** |
| 2007 Sales: $140,334 | 2007 Profits: $-82,275 | **Int'l Ticker:** Int'l Exchange: |
| 2006 Sales: $137,530 | 2006 Profits: $11,489 | Employees: 704 |
| 2005 Sales: $113,754 | 2005 Profits: $78,399 | Fiscal Year Ends: 12/31 |
| 2004 Sales: $52,636 | 2004 Profits: $15,737 | Parent Company: |

## SALARIES/BENEFITS:

| | | | | |
|---|---|---|---|---|
| Pension Plan: | ESOP Stock Plan: | Profit Sharing: | Top Exec. Salary: $339,577 | Bonus: $60,000 |
| Savings Plan: Y | Stock Purch. Plan: | | Second Exec. Salary: $334,077 | Bonus: $55,000 |

## OTHER THOUGHTS:

**Apparent Women Officers or Directors:**
**Hot Spot for Advancement for Women/Minorities:**

## LOCATIONS: ("Y" = Yes)

| West: | Southwest: | Midwest: | Southeast: | Northeast: | International: |
|---|---|---|---|---|---|
| Y | | | | Y | Y |

# KAMPGROUNDS OF AMERICA INC

www.koapressroom.com

**Industry Group Code:** 721211 **Ranks within this company's industry group:** Sales: 1 Profits:

| Management: | | Sales/Marketing: | | Liberal Arts: | | Information Systems: | | Professionals: | | Technical/Scientific: | |
|---|---|---|---|---|---|---|---|---|---|---|---|
| Mgmt. Trainees: | | Mktg. Professionals: | Y | Gen. Writing/Editing: | | Info. Management: | Y | Finance/Accounting: | Y | Engineers, Elec.: | |
| Experienced Mgmt.: | Y | Retail Sales: | | Technical Writing: | | Software Dev.: | | Law: | Y | Engineers, Other: | |
| Int'l Business: | Y | Commercial/Industrial: | | Graphic Arts/Photog.: | Y | Hardware Dev.: | | HR/Other: | Y | Health/Lab: | |
| MBA Graduates: | Y | Sales Trainees: | | Music: | | Systems Integration: | | Training: | Y | Scientists/Research: | |
| | | Advertising Pros.: | Y | Broadcasting: | | Consulting/Other: | | Health Care: | | Petroleum/Chemicals: | |
| | | | | Other: | | | | Consulting: | | Math/Other: | |

## TYPES OF BUSINESS:

Campgrounds
RV Camping Services

## BRANDS/DIVISIONS/AFFILIATES:

KOA
Kamping Kabins
Kamping Kottages
Kamping Lodges
Circusland RV Park
KOA Care Camps

## CONTACTS: *Note: Officers with more than one job title may be intentionally listed here more than once.*

Jim Rogers, CEO
Shane Ott, COO
Shane Ott, Pres.
John J. Burke, CFO/VP
Lorne Armer, VP-Mktg.
Lora Burrowes, VP-Human Resources
Jef Sutherland, VP-Info. Svcs.
Mike Zimmerman, General Counsel/VP
Mike Gast, VP-Comm.
John J. Burke, Treas.
Pat Hittmeier, VP-System Dev.
Louise Everett, VP-Franchisee Svcs.
Carl Fives, Regional VP-Company Owned Properties
Jim Rogers, Chmn.

**Phone:** 406-248-7444 **Fax:** 406-248-7414
**Toll-Free:**
**Address:** 550 N. 31st St., Billings, MT 59101 US

## GROWTH PLANS/SPECIAL FEATURES:

Kampgrounds of America, Inc. (KOA) operates and franchises one of the largest network of commercial campsites in North America. There are more than 500 established KOA campgrounds across North America and Japan. The company owns 15, while the rest are franchised. KOA's campgrounds offer toll-free reservations, restrooms, showers, laundry facilities, playgrounds and pools, as well as a variety of lodging options from RV sites with hookups to Kamping Kabins, Kamping Kottages and Kamping Lodges. The firm has partnered with HOTSPOTZZ to offer high-speed wireless Wi-Fi Internet access at its campgrounds, which is available at over 90 locations. KOA has a scout program that is open to Boy Scouts, Girl Scouts and Girl Guides throughout the US and Canada. The program gives special discounts to scout troops interested in using KOA facilities for camping and earning badges. The company also runs 35 KOA Care Camps in North America. The Care Camps are specifically for children with cancer, and the company has an annual fundraising event to raise money for this project. The firm has also partnered with RVTradeOnline.com so that visitors to KOA's website can buy and sell RVs via the Internet. In June 2007, KOA announced a partnership with ResearveAmerica, an online camping reservation website, to offer online reservations at select KOA campgrounds. In February 2008, the firm announced a new reward program. The company added 12 new North American properties in the first half of 2008.

KOA employees who have completed one season in the Work Kamper program receive benefits such as entrance into various cash drawings, free camping for 2-5 days while traveling to the next assignment and discounted camping, among others.

## FINANCIALS: **Sales and profits are in thousands of dollars—add 000 to get the full amount. 2008 Note: Financial information for 2008 was not available for all companies at press time.**

2008 Sales: $
2007 Sales: $48,300
2006 Sales: $
2005 Sales: $
2004 Sales: $

2008 Profits: $
2007 Profits: $
2006 Profits: $
2005 Profits: $
2004 Profits: $

**U.S. Stock Ticker: Private**
**Int'l Ticker:** Int'l Exchange:
Employees: 400
Fiscal Year Ends: 12/31
Parent Company:

## SALARIES/BENEFITS:

Pension Plan: ESOP Stock Plan: Profit Sharing: Top Exec. Salary: $ Bonus: $
Savings Plan: Stock Purch. Plan: Second Exec. Salary: $ Bonus: $

## OTHER THOUGHTS:

**Apparent Women Officers or Directors**: 2
**Hot Spot for Advancement for Women/Minorities**: Y

## LOCATIONS: ("Y" = Yes)

| West: | Southwest: | Midwest: | Southeast: | Northeast: | International: |
|---|---|---|---|---|---|
| Y | Y | Y | Y | Y | Y |

# KENDALL-JACKSON WINE ESTATES LTD

**www.kj.com**

**Industry Group Code:** 312130 **Ranks within this company's industry group:** Sales: Profits:

| Management: | | Sales/Marketing: | | Liberal Arts: | | Information Systems: | | Professionals: | | Technical/Scientific: | |
|---|---|---|---|---|---|---|---|---|---|---|---|
| Mgmt. Trainees: | | Mktg. Professionals: | Y | Gen. Writing/Editing: | | Info. Management: | Y | Finance/Accounting: | Y | Engineers, Elec.: | |
| Experienced Mgmt.: | Y | Retail Sales: | | Technical Writing: | | Software Dev.: | | Law: | Y | Engineers, Other: | |
| Int'l Business: | Y | Commercial/Industrial: | Y | Graphic Arts/Photog.: | Y | Hardware Dev.: | | HR/Other: | Y | Health/Lab: | |
| MBA Graduates: | Y | Sales Trainees: | Y | Music: | | Systems Integration: | | Training: | Y | Scientists/Research: | |
| | | Advertising Pros.: | Y | Broadcasting: | | Consulting/Other: | | Health Care: | | Petroleum/Chemicals: | |
| | | | | Other: | | | | Consulting: | | Math/Other: | |

## TYPES OF BUSINESS:

Beverages-Wineries
Barrel Manufacturing
Wine Distribution
Online Sales
Wine Club

## BRANDS/DIVISIONS/AFFILIATES:

Napa Mountain
Stature
Highland Estates
Grand Reserve
Vintner's Reserve
World Cooperage
Kendall-Jackson Wine Center
Healdsburg Tasting Room

## CONTACTS: *Note: Officers with more than one job title may be intentionally listed here more than once.*

Jess S. Jackson, Jr., Interim CEO
Randy Ullom, Winemaster
Chris Johnson, Winemaker-Bordeaux
Mark Theis, Winemaker-Whites
Jess S. Jackson, Jr., Interim Chmn.

**Phone:** 707-544-4000 **Fax:** 707-544-0105
**Toll-Free:** 800-769-3649
**Address:** 421 Aviation Blvd., Santa Rosa, CA 95403 US

## GROWTH PLANS/SPECIAL FEATURES:

Kendall-Jackson Wine Estates, Ltd., a family-owned and -operated company, is one of California's largest wineries. The company's vineyard is approximately 120 acres predominately located in Sonoma County, as well as Mendocino, Napa, Monterey and Santa Barbara counties in both Northern and Southern California. Kendall-Jackson also had two tasting rooms, one located in Fulton, California and the other located in Healdsburg, California. Kendall-Jackson centers on what are known as the eight noble grape varietals: Sauvignon blanc, chardonnay, Riesling, pinot noir, syrah, merlot, cabernet sauvignon and zinfandel. The company's wine is bottled with the labels Napa Mountain, Stature, Highland Estates, Grand Reserve and Vintner's Reserve. Together with partner World Cooperage, the company runs one of the only American-owned stave mills in France, which is where all of its white oak barrels are manufactured. Kendall-Jackson distributes its wines to grocery chains and retail liquor stores nationwide. Its products are available at many fine restaurants and other food service operations, as well as through the company website. Finally, Kendall-Jackson wine clubs offer discounts; VIP access at events and seminars; free tasting at the Kendall-Jackson Wine Center in Fulton and the Healdsburg Tasting Room in Healdsburg, both in California; newsletters; online customized boxed gift sets, wine glasses and other gifts and accessories, including cookbooks; as well as other benefits.

## FINANCIALS: **Sales and profits are in thousands of dollars—add 000 to get the full amount. 2008 Note: Financial information for 2008 was not available for all companies at press time.**

| | | |
|---|---|---|
| 2008 Sales: $ | 2008 Profits: $ | **U.S. Stock Ticker: Private** |
| 2007 Sales: $ | 2007 Profits: $ | **Int'l Ticker:** Int'l Exchange: |
| 2006 Sales: $ | 2006 Profits: $ | Employees: 1,000 |
| 2005 Sales: $ | 2005 Profits: $ | Fiscal Year Ends: 6/30 |
| 2004 Sales: $ | 2004 Profits: $ | Parent Company: |

## SALARIES/BENEFITS:

| | | | | |
|---|---|---|---|---|
| Pension Plan: | ESOP Stock Plan: | Profit Sharing: | Top Exec. Salary: $ | Bonus: $ |
| Savings Plan: | Stock Purch. Plan: | | Second Exec. Salary: $ | Bonus: $ |

## OTHER THOUGHTS:

**Apparent Women Officers or Directors**:
**Hot Spot for Advancement for Women/Minorities**:

## LOCATIONS: ("Y" = Yes)

| West: | Southwest: | Midwest: | Southeast: | Northeast: | International: |
|---|---|---|---|---|---|
| Y | | | | | |

# KIMLEY-HORN AND ASSOCIATES INC

www.kimley-horn.com

**Industry Group Code:** 541330 **Ranks within this company's industry group:** Sales: Profits:

| Management: | | Sales/Marketing: | | Liberal Arts: | | Information Systems: | | Professionals: | | Technical/Scientific: | |
|---|---|---|---|---|---|---|---|---|---|---|---|
| Mgmt. Trainees: | | Mktg. Professionals: | Y | Gen. Writing/Editing: | | Info. Management: | Y | Finance/Accounting: | Y | Engineers, Elec.: | Y |
| Experienced Mgmt.: | Y | Retail Sales: | | Technical Writing: | Y | Software Dev.: | | Law: | Y | Engineers, Other: | Y |
| Int'l Business: | | Commercial/Industrial: | Y | Graphic Arts/Photog.: | | Hardware Dev.: | | HR/Other: | Y | Health/Lab: | |
| MBA Graduates: | Y | Sales Trainees: | | Music: | | Systems Integration: | | Training: | Y | Scientists/Research: | Y |
| | | Advertising Pros.: | | Broadcasting: | | Consulting/Other: | | Health Care: | | Petroleum/Chemicals: | |
| | | | | Other: | | | | Consulting: | | Math/Other: | |

## TYPES OF BUSINESS:

Engineering
Project Consulting

## BRANDS/DIVISIONS/AFFILIATES:

## CONTACTS:

*Note: Officers with more than one job title may be intentionally listed here more than once.*

Mark S. Wilson, Pres.
Nicholas L. Ellis, CFO

| **Phone:** 919-677-2000 | **Fax:** 919-677-2050 |
|---|---|
| **Toll-Free:** | |
| **Address:** 3001 Weston Pkwy., Cary, NC 27513-2301 US | |

## GROWTH PLANS/SPECIAL FEATURES:

Kimley-Horn and Associates, Inc. is an engineering and land planning firm. The firm operates approximately 65 offices throughout the U.S. The company offers a variety of services in a wide range of industries including the aviation industry; environmental services; forensic engineering; intelligent transportation systems; land development; transit; urban planning/landscape architecture; wireless communications; water resources; and transportation. The aviation division is able to plan, design and administer various construction projects. The environmental services division offers a variety of services such as planning and feasibility studies; environmental documentation; and environmental restoration. The forensic engineering segment offers sound engineering services to better understand a specific case. Intelligent transportation services provides a multitude of services including ITS architectures; systems engineering analyses; ITS master planning; deployment plans and feasibility studies. Land Development provides clients with several services such as planning, site engineering and surveying/mapping. The transit division includes services such as bus system planning, regional operations studies, modeling and simulation, as well as financial feasibility and cost studies. Urban planning/landscape segment is able to provide clients design, redevelopment, architecture and construction services. Wireless communications maintains contractors in approximately 41 states. In turn, the division is able to compile information on 3,950 towers. Water resources offers customers alternative supplies; flood control; stormwater management; wastewater collection; treatment and disposal; water resources permitting; and water supply, treatment and distribution. The transportation segment is able to provide a wide spectrum of services for mass transit and transportation system needs.

Employees of the firm are offered medical and dental coverage; a 401(k) plan; incentive based bonuses; a vision plan; short and long term disability; a prescription drug plan; an employee assistance program; a health care and dependant care flexible spending program; professional memberships; certifications and development programs; a quit smoking program; tuition reimbursement; worker's compensation; and a survivor income benefits plan

## FINANCIALS:

**Sales and profits are in thousands of dollars—add 000 to get the full amount. 2008 Note: Financial information for 2008 was not available for all companies at press time.**

| | | |
|---|---|---|
| 2008 Sales: $ | 2008 Profits: $ | **U.S. Stock Ticker: Private** |
| 2007 Sales: $ | 2007 Profits: $ | **Int'l Ticker:** Int'l Exchange: |
| 2006 Sales: $ | 2006 Profits: $ | Employees: 2,190 |
| 2005 Sales: $ | 2005 Profits: $ | Fiscal Year Ends: 12/31 |
| 2004 Sales: $ | 2004 Profits: $ | Parent Company: |

## SALARIES/BENEFITS:

| | | | | |
|---|---|---|---|---|
| Pension Plan: | ESOP Stock Plan: | Profit Sharing: | Top Exec. Salary: $ | Bonus: $ |
| Savings Plan: | Stock Purch. Plan: | | Second Exec. Salary: $ | Bonus: $ |

## OTHER THOUGHTS:

**Apparent Women Officers or Directors:**
**Hot Spot for Advancement for Women/Minorities:**

## LOCATIONS: ("Y" = Yes)

| West: | Southwest: | Midwest: | Southeast: | Northeast: | International: |
|---|---|---|---|---|---|
| Y | Y | Y | Y | Y | |

# KNIGHT CAPITAL GROUP INC

**www.knight.com**

**Industry Group Code:** 523120 **Ranks within this company's industry group:** Sales: 2 Profits: 2

| **Management:** | | **Sales/Marketing:** | | **Liberal Arts:** | | **Information Systems:** | | **Professionals:** | | **Technical/Scientific:** | |
|---|---|---|---|---|---|---|---|---|---|---|---|
| Mgmt. Trainees: | | Mktg. Professionals: | Y | Gen. Writing/Editing: | | Info. Management: | Y | Finance/Accounting: | Y | Engineers, Elec.: | |
| Experienced Mgmt.: | Y | Retail Sales: | | Technical Writing: | | Software Dev.: | Y | Law: | Y | Engineers, Other: | |
| Int'l Business: | Y | Commercial/Industrial: | | Graphic Arts/Photog.: | | Hardware Dev.: | | HR/Other: | Y | Health/Lab: | |
| MBA Graduates: | Y | Sales Trainees: | | Music: | | Systems Integration: | | Training: | Y | Scientists/Research: | |
| | | Advertising Pros.: | | Broadcasting: | | Consulting/Other: | | Health Care: | | Petroleum/Chemicals: | |
| | | | | Other: | | | | Consulting: | | Math/Other: | Y |

## TYPES OF BUSINESS:

Equities Trade Execution
Asset Management

## BRANDS/DIVISIONS/AFFILIATES:

Knight Capital Markets
Knight Equity Markets
Knight Equity Markets International
Deephaven Capital Management
Deephaven Market Neutral Master Fund
Direct Trading Institutional
Hotspot FX
ValuBond, Inc.

## CONTACTS: *Note: Officers with more than one job title may be intentionally listed here more than once.*

Thomas M. Joyce, CEO
Steven Bisgay, CFO/Managing Dir.
Bronwen Bastone, Managing Dir.-Human Resources
Steven J. Sadoff, CIO/Sr. Managing Dir.
Leonard J. Amoruso, General Counsel/Sr. Managing Dir.
Margaret Wyrwas, Sr. Managing Dir.-Corp. Comm.
Margaret Wyrwas, Sr. Managing Dir.-Investor Rel.
Gregory C. Voetsch, Exec. VP/Head-Institutional Client Group
James P. Smyth, Exec. VP/Head of Broker-Dealer Client Group
Colin J. Smith, Chief Investment Officer/CEO-Deephaven Capital
Michael Williams, Head-Hotspot FX/Sr. Managing Dir.
Thomas M. Joyce, Chmn.

| **Phone:** 201-222-9400 | **Fax:** 201-557-6853 |
|---|---|
| **Toll-Free:** 800-544-7508 | |
| **Address:** 525 Washington Blvd., Jersey City, NJ 07310 US | |

## GROWTH PLANS/SPECIAL FEATURES:

Knight Capital Group, Inc., formerly Knight Trading Group, Inc. and before that Knight Trimark Group, Inc., provides trade execution services for stock and stock options, as well as asset management services. Knight's customers are primarily broker-dealers, institutional investors and online trading firms. It has two operating business segments: Asset management and global markets. Knight serves high net worth investors with asset management services using a variety of strategies including sophisticated arbitrage trading, including convertible, statistical, and risk arbitrage; private placement; and distressed debt. These services are provided through Deephaven Capital Management, with $3.9 billion in assets under management. The majority of these assets are in the Deephaven Market Neutral Master Fund, a fund that seeks to produce returns for investors using low-risk strategies. The firm's global markets business, acting through subsidiaries Direct Trading Institutional, Hotspot FX, Knight Capital Markets, Knight Equity Markets and Knight Equity Markets International, trades or makes a market in nearly every U.S. equity security. Knight's market share largely resides in the NASDAQ, the stock exchange preferred by leading technology companies. It also provides trade execution services in a large number of international securities, futures, options, foreign currencies and fixed income instruments. When necessary, the company uses its own capital to make a market. Besides its operating segments, the firm also has a corporate segment, which includes investment income earned on strategic investments and Knight's corporate investment in funds managed by the Asset Management segment. In January 2008, the firm acquired EdgeTrade, Inc., an execution and algorithmic software company, for $59.5 million. In April 2008, Clearbrook Financial, LLC formed a joint venture with Knight, Knight Portfolio Access, LLC, to provide products and services to retail brokerage firms and registered investment advisors. In July 2008, Knight acquired Libertas Holdings, LLC for $75 million.

## FINANCIALS: **Sales and profits are in thousands of dollars—add 000 to get the full amount. 2008 Note: Financial information for 2008 was not available for all companies at press time.**

| | | |
|---|---|---|
| 2008 Sales: $1,042,616 | 2008 Profits: $177,911 | **U.S. Stock Ticker: NITE** |
| 2007 Sales: $896,749 | 2007 Profits: $122,240 | **Int'l Ticker:** Int'l Exchange: |
| 2006 Sales: $956,289 | 2006 Profits: $158,346 | Employees: 868 |
| 2005 Sales: $634,623 | 2005 Profits: $66,361 | Fiscal Year Ends: 12/31 |
| 2004 Sales: $625,750 | 2004 Profits: $91,132 | Parent Company: |

## SALARIES/BENEFITS:

| | | | | |
|---|---|---|---|---|
| Pension Plan: | ESOP Stock Plan: | Profit Sharing: | Top Exec. Salary: $750,000 | Bonus: $4,409,885 |
| Savings Plan: Y | Stock Purch. Plan: | | Second Exec. Salary: $250,000 | Bonus: $2,832,500 |

## OTHER THOUGHTS:

**Apparent Women Officers or Directors**: 2
**Hot Spot for Advancement for Women/Minorities**: Y

## LOCATIONS: ("Y" = Yes)

| West: | Southwest: | Midwest: | Southeast: | Northeast: | International: |
|---|---|---|---|---|---|
| Y | Y | Y | Y | Y | Y |

# KNOT INC (THE)

www.theknot.com

**Industry Group Code:** 514199 **Ranks within this company's industry group:** Sales: 4 Profits: 2

| Management: | | Sales/Marketing: | | Liberal Arts: | | Information Systems: | | Professionals: | | Technical/Scientific: | |
|---|---|---|---|---|---|---|---|---|---|---|---|
| Mgmt. Trainees: | | Mktg. Professionals: | Y | Gen. Writing/Editing: | Y | Info. Management: | Y | Finance/Accounting: | Y | Engineers, Elec.: | |
| Experienced Mgmt.: | Y | Retail Sales: | | Technical Writing: | | Software Dev.: | Y | Law: | Y | Engineers, Other: | |
| Int'l Business: | | Commercial/Industrial: | Y | Graphic Arts/Photog.: | Y | Hardware Dev.: | | HR/Other: | Y | Health/Lab: | |
| MBA Graduates: | Y | Sales Trainees: | Y | Music: | | Systems Integration: | Y | Training: | Y | Scientists/Research: | |
| | | Advertising Pros.: | Y | Broadcasting: | | Consulting/Other: | | Health Care: | | Petroleum/Chemicals: | |
| | | | | Other: | Y | | | Consulting: | | Math/Other: | |

## TYPES OF BUSINESS:

Online Resource for Wedding Planning
Online Gift Registry
Wedding Books & Magazines
Online Community
Wedding Supplies

## BRANDS/DIVISIONS/AFFILIATES:

Knot Online (The)
Knot Weddings Magazine (The)
TheKnot.com
TheNest.com
LilaGuide.com
The Knot TV
The Knot Wedding Shop
TheBump.com

## CONTACTS: *Note: Officers with more than one job title may be intentionally listed here more than once.*

David Liu, CEO
Carol Koh Evans, COO
David Liu, Pres.
John Mueller, CFO
Nic Di Iorio, Exec. VP/Managing Dir.-Tech. Group
Carley Roney, Editor-in-Chief
David Liu, Chmn.

| **Phone:** 212-219-8555 | **Fax:** 212-219-1929 |
|---|---|
| **Toll-Free:** 877-843-5668 | |
| **Address:** 462 Broadway, 6th Fl., New York, NY 10013 US | |

## GROWTH PLANS/SPECIAL FEATURES:

The Knot, Inc. is one of the world's leading wedding media and services companies, providing couples with planning information, interactive tools and a vast array of online resources. The firm's web site, TheKnot.com, has 2.1 million unique visitors per month and approximately 3,600 new online members per day. Additionally, The Knot is the exclusive wedding content provider to portals including MSN, Netscape and Compuserve. The company provides over 1,000 products, including decorated disposable cameras, wedding bubbles and bells, ring pillows, toasting flutes, car decorating kits, table centerpieces, goblets and glasses, garters and unity candles. In addition, the company publishes The Knot Weddings Magazine, a national publication which features editorial content covering every major wedding planning decision. The firm also maintains regional versions of the same magazines. Both magazines are distributed to newsstands and bookstores across the country with a combined circulation of 1.4 million. The Knot also authors a book series on wedding planning and a gift-book series on wedding gowns and flowers. The Knot Wedding Shop is one of the largest online wedding retailers in the world, offering supplies, favors and attendant gifts among other things. The company's online services include gift registries, searchable databases, planning tools, a guest list manager, a budgeter and advice columns. The Knot also generates member involvement through chat rooms, message boards and personalized interactive services. The Knot owns and operates TheNest.com, for newlyweds; and LilaGuide.com, an additional site with resources for all parents. In February 2008, the company acquired The Bump Media, Inc. which was subsequently absorbed into the company under TheBump.com, providing print and online guides to fertility, pregnancy, birth and baby resources.

Employees are offered medical and dental insurance; short- and long-term disability coverage; life insurance; flexible spending accounts; an employee assistance program; a 401(k) plan; and an employee stock purchase plan.

## FINANCIALS: **Sales and profits are in thousands of dollars—add 000 to get the full amount. 2008 Note: Financial information for 2008 was not available for all companies at press time.**

| | | |
|---|---|---|
| 2008 Sales: $ | 2008 Profits: $ | **U.S. Stock Ticker: KNOT** |
| 2007 Sales: $98,688 | 2007 Profits: $11,869 | **Int'l Ticker:** Int'l Exchange: |
| 2006 Sales: $72,679 | 2006 Profits: $23,426 | Employees: 451 |
| 2005 Sales: $51,408 | 2005 Profits: $3,952 | Fiscal Year Ends: 12/31 |
| 2004 Sales: $41,397 | 2004 Profits: $1,275 | Parent Company: |

## SALARIES/BENEFITS:

| | | | | |
|---|---|---|---|---|
| Pension Plan: | ESOP Stock Plan: | Profit Sharing: | Top Exec. Salary: $367,000 | Bonus: $25,000 |
| Savings Plan: Y | Stock Purch. Plan: Y | | Second Exec. Salary: $328,125 | Bonus: $ |

## OTHER THOUGHTS:

**Apparent Women Officers or Directors**: 4
**Hot Spot for Advancement for Women/Minorities**: Y

## LOCATIONS: ("Y" = Yes)

| West: | Southwest: | Midwest: | Southeast: | Northeast: | International: |
|---|---|---|---|---|---|
| Y | Y | Y | | Y | |

# KRONOS WORLDWIDE INC

**www.kronostio2.com**

**Industry Group Code:** 325000 **Ranks within this company's industry group:** Sales: 1 Profits: 3

| Management: | | Sales/Marketing: | | Liberal Arts: | | Information Systems: | | Professionals: | | Technical/Scientific: | |
|---|---|---|---|---|---|---|---|---|---|---|---|
| Mgmt. Trainees: | | Mktg. Professionals: | Y | Gen. Writing/Editing: | | Info. Management: | Y | Finance/Accounting: | Y | Engineers, Elec.: | Y |
| Experienced Mgmt.: | Y | Retail Sales: | | Technical Writing: | Y | Software Dev.: | | Law: | Y | Engineers, Other: | |
| Int'l Business: | Y | Commercial/Industrial: | Y | Graphic Arts/Photog.: | | Hardware Dev.: | | HR/Other: | Y | Health/Lab: | |
| MBA Graduates: | Y | Sales Trainees: | | Music: | | Systems Integration: | | Training: | Y | Scientists/Research: | Y |
| | | Advertising Pros.: | | Broadcasting: | | Consulting/Other: | | Health Care: | | Petroleum/Chemicals: | Y |
| | | | | Other: | | | | Consulting: | | Math/Other: | |

## TYPES OF BUSINESS:

Titanium Dioxide Manufacturer & Distributor
Ilmenite Mining
Iron-Based Chemicals

## BRANDS/DIVISIONS/AFFILIATES:

NL Industries Inc
Valhi, Inc.
Kronos International, Inc.
Huntsman Holding LLC.
Kronos Ecochem

## CONTACTS: *Note: Officers with more than one job title may be intentionally listed here more than once.*

Harold C. Simmons, CEO
Gregory M. Swalwell, CFO
H. Joseph Maas, Pres., Sales & Mktg.
Ulfert Fiand, Pres., Tech.
Ulfert Fiand, Pres., Mfg.
Robert D. Graham, General Counsel/VP/Sec.
Douglas C. Weaver, Sr. VP-Dev.
Gregory M. Swalwell, VP-Finance
John A. St. Wrba, VP/Treas.
Tim C. Hafer, Controller
Kelly C. Luttmer, VP/Dir.-Tax
Steven L. Watson, Vice Chmn.
Harold C. Simmons, Chmn.

| **Phone:** 972-233-1700 | **Fax:** |
|---|---|
| **Toll-Free:** | |
| **Address:** 5430 LBJ Freeway, Ste. 1700, Dallas, TX 75240 US | |

## GROWTH PLANS/SPECIAL FEATURES:

Kronos Worldwide, Inc. is a global producer and marketer of titanium dioxide, or TiO2, pigments, used for products such as coatings, plastics, paper, fibers, food, ceramics and cosmetics. Titanium Oxide (TiO2), an inorganic whitening pigment imparting opacity and brightness, is manufactured with chloride and sulfate processes. The company offers over 40 different grades of TiO2, which the firm produces in two crystalline forms: Rutile and anatase. Sales of TiO2 in 2007 accounted for 90% of the company's total revenue. In addition, Kronos Worldwide provides product lines that are complementary of TiO2, including ilmenite, a raw material used directly as a feedstock by some sulfate-process TiO2 plants; iron-based chemicals, which are co-products of the TiO2 pigment production process; and titanium oxychloride and titanyl sulfate, which are side-stream products from the production of TiO2. The firm's iron-based chemicals, marketed through its Ecochem division, are used primarily as treatment and conditioning agents for industrial effluents and municipal wastewater and are used secondarily in the manufacture of iron pigments, cement and agricultural products. Titanium oxychloride is used in the production of electroceramic capacitors for cell phones and other electronic devices, while both titanium oxychloride and titanyl sulfate products are used in pearlescent pigments. The company sells and provides technical services for its products to over 4,000 customers, primarily plastic, paint and paper manufacturers, in over 100 countries with the majority of sales in Europe and North America. Kronos Worldwide maintained roughly 19% of the European TiO2 sales volume in 2007. The firm holds a 50% interest in a manufacturing joint venture with Huntsman Holding LLC. The joint venture owns and operates a chloride process TiO2 facility located in Louisiana. Valhi, Inc. owns approximately 59% of the Kronos Worldwide stock and NL Industries own 36% of the firm's stock.

## FINANCIALS: **Sales and profits are in thousands of dollars—add 000 to get the full amount. 2008 Note: Financial information for 2008 was not available for all companies at press time.**

| | | |
|---|---|---|
| 2008 Sales: $ | 2008 Profits: $ | **U.S. Stock Ticker: KRO** |
| 2007 Sales: $1,310,300 | 2007 Profits: $-66,700 | **Int'l Ticker:** Int'l Exchange: |
| 2006 Sales: $1,279,447 | 2006 Profits: $81,969 | Employees: 2,400 |
| 2005 Sales: $1,196,729 | 2005 Profits: $71,451 | Fiscal Year Ends: 12/31 |
| 2004 Sales: $1,128,600 | 2004 Profits: $314,092 | Parent Company: |

## SALARIES/BENEFITS:

| | | | | |
|---|---|---|---|---|
| Pension Plan: | ESOP Stock Plan: | Profit Sharing: | Top Exec. Salary: $1,022,000 | Bonus: $ |
| Savings Plan: Y | Stock Purch. Plan: | | Second Exec. Salary: $513,800 | Bonus: $ |

## OTHER THOUGHTS:

**Apparent Women Officers or Directors**: 1
**Hot Spot for Advancement for Women/Minorities**:

## LOCATIONS: ("Y" = Yes)

| West: | Southwest: | Midwest: | Southeast: | Northeast: | International: |
|---|---|---|---|---|---|
| Y | Y | Y | Y | Y | Y |

# KV PHARMACEUTICAL CO

**www.kvpharmaceutical.com**

**Industry Group Code:** 325412A **Ranks within this company's industry group:** Sales: 1 Profits: 2

| Management: | | Sales/Marketing: | | Liberal Arts: | | Information Systems: | | Professionals: | | Technical/Scientific: | |
|---|---|---|---|---|---|---|---|---|---|---|---|
| Mgmt. Trainees: | | Mktg. Professionals: | Y | Gen. Writing/Editing: | | Info. Management: | Y | Finance/Accounting: | Y | Engineers, Elec.: | |
| Experienced Mgmt.: | Y | Retail Sales: | | Technical Writing: | Y | Software Dev.: | | Law: | Y | Engineers, Other: | |
| Int'l Business: | Y | Commercial/Industrial: | Y | Graphic Arts/Photog.: | | Hardware Dev.: | | HR/Other: | Y | Health/Lab: | Y |
| MBA Graduates: | Y | Sales Trainees: | Y | Music: | | Systems Integration: | | Training: | Y | Scientists/Research: | Y |
| | | Advertising Pros.: | | Broadcasting: | | Consulting/Other: | | Health Care: | Y | Petroleum/Chemicals: | Y |
| | | | | Other: | | | | Consulting: | | Math/Other: | Y |

## TYPES OF BUSINESS:

Pharmaceutical Products
Drug Delivery & Formulation Technologies
Specialty Ingredients
Taste Masking Systems
Branded Prescription Pharmaceuticals

## BRANDS/DIVISIONS/AFFILIATES:

ETHEX Corporation
Ther-Rx Corporation
Particle Dynamics, Inc.
Particle and Coating Technologies, Inc.
Liquette
Gynazole-1
FlavorTech
Micromask

## CONTACTS: *Note: Officers with more than one job title may be intentionally listed here more than once.*

Marc S. Hermelin, CEO
Ronald J. Kanterman, CFO/VP
Eric D. Moyermann, Pres., Pharmaceutical Mfg.
David S. Hermelin, VP-Corp. Strategy & Oper. Analysis
Catherine Biffignani, VP-Corp. Comm.
Catherine Biffignani, VP-Investor Rel.
Richard H. Chibnall, VP-Finance
Raymond F. Chiostri, Chmn./CEO-Particle Dynamics, Inc.
Patricia K. McCullough, CEO-ETHEX Corp.
Philip J. Vogt, Pres., ETHEX Corp.
Paul T. Brady, Pres., Particle Dynamics, Inc.
Marc S. Hermelin, Chmn.

| | |
|---|---|
| **Phone:** 314-645-6600 | **Fax:** 314-644-2419 |
| **Toll-Free:** | |
| **Address:** 2503 S. Hanley Rd., St. Louis, MO 63144 US | |

## GROWTH PLANS/SPECIAL FEATURES:

KV Pharmaceutical Co. is a pharmaceutical company that develops, acquires, manufactures and markets technologically branded and generic prescription pharmaceutical products. The company develops a wide variety of drug delivery and formulation technologies, which are primarily focused in four areas: SITE RELEASE bioadhesives; taste masking; oral controlled release; and oral quick dissolving tablets. The firm incorporates these technologies in the products it markets to control and improve the absorption and utilization of active pharmaceutical compounds. KV has a broad range of dosage form capabilities including tablets, capsules, creams, liquids and ointments. The company manufactures and markets these specialty pharmaceutical products through three wholly-owned subsidiaries: ETHEX Corporation, which targets generic and non-branded market segments; Ther-Rx Corporation, featuring branded product lines; and Particle Dynamics, Inc., a specialty ingredient products company. KV's operating units currently feature some 15 drug delivery technologies. The company's site-specific treatments isolate drugs to a specific area of the body to increase their effectiveness. Taste-masking systems and quick-dissolving tablets are aimed at improving the taste of drugs and are marketed under names including Liquette, FlavorTech and Micromask. ETHEX, the company's major subsidiary, offers more than 100 products in four major categories: Cardiovascular, women's health, pain management and respiratory/cough/cold. Ther-Rx markets branded prescription pharmaceutical products, currently representing six brands in the cardiovascular, women's health and oral hematinic categories with a portfolio of 10 distinctive products. Particle Dynamics develops, manufactures and markets technically advanced, value-added specialty ingredient products to the pharmaceutical, nutritional and personal care industries. In January 2008, KV purchased the rights to Gestivia from CYTYC Prenatal Products and Hologic, Inc., a preterm birth prevention drug.

KV offers its employees health, dental, life, accidental death and dismemberment insurance; an employee stock option plan; a 401(k) plan; a profit sharing plan; short- and long-term disability; educational assistance; and an employee assistance program.

## FINANCIALS: **Sales and profits are in thousands of dollars—add 000 to get the full amount. 2008 Note: Financial information for 2008 was not available for all companies at press time.**

| | | |
|---|---|---|
| 2008 Sales: $601,896 | 2008 Profits: $88,354 | **U.S. Stock Ticker: KV** |
| 2007 Sales: $443,627 | 2007 Profits: $58,090 | **Int'l Ticker:** Int'l Exchange: |
| 2006 Sales: $367,618 | 2006 Profits: $11,416 | Employees: 1,590 |
| 2005 Sales: $303,493 | 2005 Profits: $33,269 | Fiscal Year Ends: 3/31 |
| 2004 Sales: $283,900 | 2004 Profits: $45,800 | Parent Company: |

## SALARIES/BENEFITS:

| | | | | |
|---|---|---|---|---|
| Pension Plan: | ESOP Stock Plan: | Profit Sharing: Y | Top Exec. Salary: $1,281,764 | Bonus: $2,545,857 |
| Savings Plan: Y | Stock Purch. Plan: Y | | Second Exec. Salary: $332,000 | Bonus: $116,000 |

## OTHER THOUGHTS:

**Apparent Women Officers or Directors:** 2
**Hot Spot for Advancement for Women/Minorities:** Y

## LOCATIONS: ("Y" = Yes)

| West: | Southwest: | Midwest: | Southeast: | Northeast: | International: |
|---|---|---|---|---|---|
| | | Y | | | |

# LACLEDE GROUP INC (THE)

**www.thelacledegroup.com**

**Industry Group Code:** 221000B **Ranks within this company's industry group:** Sales: 3 Profits: 5

| Management: | | Sales/Marketing: | | Liberal Arts: | | Information Systems: | | Professionals: | | Technical/Scientific: | |
|---|---|---|---|---|---|---|---|---|---|---|---|
| Mgmt. Trainees: | | Mktg. Professionals: | Y | Gen. Writing/Editing: | | Info. Management: | Y | Finance/Accounting: | Y | Engineers, Elec.: | Y |
| Experienced Mgmt.: | Y | Retail Sales: | | Technical Writing: | | Software Dev.: | | Law: | Y | Engineers, Other: | Y |
| Int'l Business: | | Commercial/Industrial: | Y | Graphic Arts/Photog.: | | Hardware Dev.: | | HR/Other: | Y | Health/Lab: | |
| MBA Graduates: | Y | Sales Trainees: | | Music: | | Systems Integration: | | Training: | Y | Scientists/Research: | |
| | | Advertising Pros.: | | Broadcasting: | | Consulting/Other: | | Health Care: | | Petroleum/Chemicals: | Y |
| | | | | Other: | | | | Consulting: | | Math/Other: | |

## TYPES OF BUSINESS:

Utilities-Natural Gas
Underground Natural Gas Storage Fields
Transportation & Storage of Liquid Propane
Underground Locating & Marking Services
Insurance Services
Real Estate Development
Natural Gas Marketing

## BRANDS/DIVISIONS/AFFILIATES:

Laclede Gas Company
SM&P Utility Resources, Inc.
Laclede Gas Family Services, Inc.
Laclede Development Company
Laclede Venture Corp.
Laclede Investment, LLC
Laclede Pipeline Company
Laclede Energy Resources, Inc.

## CONTACTS: *Note: Officers with more than one job title may be intentionally listed here more than once.*

Douglas H. Yaeger, CEO
Douglas H. Yaeger, Pres.
Mark D. Waltermire, CFO
Richard A. Skau, Sr. VP-Human Resources
Mark C. Darrell, General Counsel/Sr. VP
Michael C. Geiselhart, VP-Strategic Dev. & Planning
Lynn D. Rawlings, Treas.
Mary C. Kullman, Chief Governance Officer/Corp. Sec.
Michael R. Spotanski, Sr. VP-Oper., Laclede Gas Co.
David P. Abernathy, VP-Industrial Rel. & Claims Mgmt.
K. J. Neises, Exec. VP-Energy & Admin. Svcs., Laclede Gas Co.
Douglas H. Yaeger, Chmn.

**Phone:** 314-342-0500 **Fax:** 314-421-1979
**Toll-Free:**
**Address:** 720 Olive St., St. Louis, MO 63101 US

## GROWTH PLANS/SPECIAL FEATURES:

The Laclede Group, Inc. is a public utility holding company that operates primarily in two segments, regulated core utility operations and non-regulated activities. It provides natural gas service through its regulated core utility operations. The regulated gas distribution segment includes Laclede Gas Company, Laclede Group's largest subsidiary and core business unit. Laclede Gas is a public utility engaged in the retail distribution and sale of natural gas. Laclede Gas is one of the largest natural gas distribution utility firms in Missouri, serving more than 630,000 residential, commercial, and industrial customers in St. Louis and parts of 10 other counties in eastern Missouri. Laclede Group's non-regulated services segment includes Laclede Energy Resources, Inc. (LER), a subsidiary engaged in the non-regulated marketing of natural gas and related activities. Other non-regulated subsidiaries of the Laclede Group include Laclede Pipeline Company, which operates a propane pipeline in Missouri and Illinois; Laclede Investment, LLC, which invests in other enterprises; Laclede Energy Resources, Inc., a natural gas marketing company; Laclede Gas Family Services, Inc., a registered insurance agency in Missouri; Laclede Development Company, which participates in real estate development; and Laclede Venture Corp., which offers services for the compression of natural gas. All of Laclede Group's subsidiaries are wholly-owned. In March 2008, the firm sold its underground locating and marking subsidiary, SM&P Utility Resources, Inc., to Kohlberg and Company for $85 million.

## FINANCIALS: Sales and profits are in thousands of dollars—add 000 to get the full amount. 2008 Note: Financial information for 2008 was not available for all companies at press time.

2008 Sales: $2,208,973 — 2008 Profits: $77,922
2007 Sales: $1,855,861 — 2007 Profits: $49,771
2006 Sales: $1,835,028 — 2006 Profits: $48,989
2005 Sales: $1,455,554 — 2005 Profits: $40,125
2004 Sales: $1,250,320 — 2004 Profits: $36,118

**U.S. Stock Ticker: LG**
**Int'l Ticker:** Int'l Exchange:
Employees: 1,807
Fiscal Year Ends: 9/30
Parent Company:

## SALARIES/BENEFITS:

Pension Plan: Y ESOP Stock Plan: Profit Sharing: Top Exec. Salary: $546,667 Bonus: $403,180
Savings Plan: Stock Purch. Plan: Second Exec. Salary: $321,100 Bonus: $217,885

## OTHER THOUGHTS:

**Apparent Women Officers or Directors**: 7
**Hot Spot for Advancement for Women/Minorities**: Y

**LOCATIONS: ("Y" = Yes)**

| West: | Southwest: | Midwest: | Southeast: | Northeast: | International: |
|---|---|---|---|---|---|
| | Y | Y | | | |

# LCA-VISION INC

www.lasikplus.com

**Industry Group Code:** 621490 **Ranks within this company's industry group:** Sales: 2 Profits: 2

| Management: | | Sales/Marketing: | | Liberal Arts: | | Information Systems: | | Professionals: | | Technical/Scientific: | |
|---|---|---|---|---|---|---|---|---|---|---|---|
| Mgmt. Trainees: | | Mktg. Professionals: | Y | Gen. Writing/Editing: | | Info. Management: | Y | Finance/Accounting: | Y | Engineers, Elec.: | |
| Experienced Mgmt.: | Y | Retail Sales: | | Technical Writing: | Y | Software Dev.: | | Law: | Y | Engineers, Other: | |
| Int'l Business: | Y | Commercial/Industrial: | Y | Graphic Arts/Photog.: | | Hardware Dev.: | | HR/Other: | Y | Health/Lab: | Y |
| MBA Graduates: | Y | Sales Trainees: | Y | Music: | | Systems Integration: | | Training: | Y | Scientists/Research: | |
| | | Advertising Pros.: | Y | Broadcasting: | | Consulting/Other: | | Health Care: | Y | Petroleum/Chemicals: | |
| | | | | Other: | | | | Consulting: | | Math/Other: | |

## TYPES OF BUSINESS:

Services-Laser Vision Correction Surgery Centers
PRK (photo-refractive keratectomy)
LASIK (Laser-In-Situ Keratomileusis)

## BRANDS/DIVISIONS/AFFILIATES:

LasikPlus
IntraLase

## CONTACTS: *Note: Officers with more than one job title may be intentionally listed here more than once.*

Steven C. Straus, CEO
Alan H. Buckey, CFO
Stephen M. Jones, Sr. VP-Human Resources
David L. Thomas, Sr. VP-Oper.
Patricia Forsythe, VP-Investor Rel.
Alan H. Buckey, Exec. VP-Finance
Michael J. Celebrezze, Sr. VP-Finance/Treas.
E. Anthony Woods, Chmn.

| | |
|---|---|
| **Phone:** 513-792-9292 | **Fax:** 513-792-5620 |
| **Toll-Free:** 800-688-4550 | |
| **Address:** 7840 Montgomery Rd., Cincinnati, OH 45236 US | |

## GROWTH PLANS/SPECIAL FEATURES:

LCA-Vision, Inc. is a provider of fixed-site laser vision correction services at its LasikPlus vision centers. The company derives all of its operating revenues from laser refractive surgery and is the only reported segment. The company's vision centers help correct nearsightedness, farsightedness and astigmatism. Treatments are done by using one of two methods, PRK (photo-refractive keratectomy) and LASIK (Laser-In-Situ Keratomileusis). PRK removes the thin layer of cell covering the outer surface of the cornea (the epithelium) and treats it with excimer laser pulses. LASIK reshapes the cornea with an excimer laser by cutting a flap in the top of the cornea to expose the inner cornea. The corneal flap is then treated with excimer laser pulses according to the patient's prescription. The LASIK procedure now accounts for virtually all of the procedures performed by LCA, as recovery time is significantly shorter and patient discomfort is negligible. LCA currently uses three suppliers for fixed site excimer lasers: Bausch & Lomb, Advanced Medical Optics and Alcon. The company operates about 70 LasikPlus vision correction centers in the U.S. and also has a joint venture in Canada. The firm has performed more than 740,000 laser vision correction procedures since the company's inception. LCA has gradually transferred all of its facilities to closed-access, which means LCA maintains full operational and financial control over its business, directly employing its own ophthalmologists and taking on full responsibility for marketing and patient acquisition. The company also offers procedures using a new wavefront-guided LASIK system, a system that allows doctors to map out the exact surface of the cornea before surgery, and thus provide personalized, more accurate modifications to the cornea, with an end result of clearer vision. In 2008, the firm opened new LasikPlus vision centers in Savannah, Georgia and Woodbridge, New Jersey.

The company offers employees medical insurance and other benefits.

## FINANCIALS: **Sales and profits are in thousands of dollars—add 000 to get the full amount. 2008 Note: Financial information for 2008 was not available for all companies at press time.**

| | | |
|---|---|---|
| 2008 Sales: $205,176 | 2008 Profits: $-6,635 | **U.S. Stock Ticker: LCAV** |
| 2007 Sales: $292,635 | 2007 Profits: $32,504 | **Int'l Ticker:** Int'l Exchange: |
| 2006 Sales: $238,925 | 2006 Profits: $28,370 | Employees: 784 |
| 2005 Sales: $192,397 | 2005 Profits: $31,653 | Fiscal Year Ends: 12/31 |
| 2004 Sales: $127,122 | 2004 Profits: $32,029 | Parent Company: |

## SALARIES/BENEFITS:

| | | | | |
|---|---|---|---|---|
| Pension Plan: | ESOP Stock Plan: | Profit Sharing: | Top Exec. Salary: $350,000 | Bonus: $ |
| Savings Plan: | Stock Purch. Plan: | | Second Exec. Salary: $282,000 | Bonus: $ |

## OTHER THOUGHTS:

**Apparent Women Officers or Directors:**
**Hot Spot for Advancement for Women/Minorities:**

## LOCATIONS: ("Y" = Yes)

| West: | Southwest: | Midwest: | Southeast: | Northeast: | International: |
|---|---|---|---|---|---|
| Y | Y | Y | Y | Y | Y |

# LCC INTERNATIONAL INC

www.lcc.com

**Industry Group Code:** 513300D **Ranks within this company's industry group:** Sales: 3 Profits: 3

| Management: | | Sales/Marketing: | | Liberal Arts: | | Information Systems: | | Professionals: | | Technical/Scientific: | |
|---|---|---|---|---|---|---|---|---|---|---|---|
| Mgmt. Trainees: | | Mktg. Professionals: | Y | Gen. Writing/Editing: | | Info. Management: | Y | Finance/Accounting: | Y | Engineers, Elec.: | Y |
| Experienced Mgmt.: | Y | Retail Sales: | | Technical Writing: | Y | Software Dev.: | Y | Law: | Y | Engineers, Other: | Y |
| Int'l Business: | Y | Commercial/Industrial: | Y | Graphic Arts/Photog.: | | Hardware Dev.: | | HR/Other: | Y | Health/Lab: | |
| MBA Graduates: | Y | Sales Trainees: | Y | Music: | | Systems Integration: | | Training: | Y | Scientists/Research: | |
| | | Advertising Pros.: | | Broadcasting: | | Consulting/Other: | | Health Care: | | Petroleum/Chemicals: | |
| | | | | Other: | | | | Consulting: | Y | Math/Other: | |

## TYPES OF BUSINESS:

Radio-Frequency Engineering & Consulting
Network Design
Deployment Services
Network Operations Maintenance
Training Services

## BRANDS/DIVISIONS/AFFILIATES:

Wireless Institute, Inc.

## CONTACTS: *Note: Officers with more than one job title may be intentionally listed here more than once.*

Kenneth Young, CEO
Kenneth Young, Pres.
Louis Salamone, CFO/Exec. VP
John Buckholz, VP-IT
Brian J. Dunn, General Counsel/VP
Ananth Veluppillai, Sr. VP-Oper., Americas
Julie Dobson, Chmn.
Stan Schreuder, Sr. VP-Europe

**Phone:** 703-873-2000 **Fax:** 703-873-2100
**Toll-Free:**
**Address:** 7900 Westpark Dr., Ste. A-315, McLean, VA 22102 US

## GROWTH PLANS/SPECIAL FEATURES:

LCC International, Inc. is an independent provider of RF (radio-frequency) engineering and consulting services to the wireless telecommunications industry. LCC has serviced hundreds of cellular, PCS, paging and other two-way mobile systems throughout the world for over 20 years. The company currently provides services to more than 350 wireless systems operators in over 50 countries. The firm's goal is to help wireless operators meet their network deployment objectives and improve financial performance by using LCC's resources and capital. The company's services are broken down into four groups: LCC's technology and business consulting group solves engineering, deployment, operational and business challenges that have not been addressed before; the design and optimization group develops networks in locations spanning the globe; the deployment and turnkey group utilizes interdisciplinary teams to deploy its networks; and the operations and maintenance group provides 24-hours-a-day, seven-days-a-week management and maintenance of its outsourced wireless network operations. LCC also has its own Wireless Institute (WI-LCC) that provides multilingual premier wireless industry training to its employees. In June 2008, the company became the exclusive provider of Radio Frequency engineering to TruePosition, a deliverer of high-performance wireless location services. In September of the same year, LCC voluntarily delisted from the NASDAQ Global Market. The firm now trades on Pink Sheets.

## FINANCIALS: **Sales and profits are in thousands of dollars—add 000 to get the full amount. 2008 Note: Financial information for 2008 was not available for all companies at press time.**

| | | |
|---|---|---|
| 2008 Sales: $ | 2008 Profits: $ | **U.S. Stock Ticker: LCCI** |
| 2007 Sales: $145,723 | 2007 Profits: $-30,767 | **Int'l Ticker:** Int'l Exchange: |
| 2006 Sales: $129,953 | 2006 Profits: $-8,030 | Employees: 1,304 |
| 2005 Sales: $145,642 | 2005 Profits: $-12,527 | Fiscal Year Ends: 12/31 |
| 2004 Sales: $193,158 | 2004 Profits: $-6,311 | Parent Company: |

## SALARIES/BENEFITS:

| | | | | |
|---|---|---|---|---|
| Pension Plan: | ESOP Stock Plan: | Profit Sharing: | Top Exec. Salary: $671,642 | Bonus: $330,676 |
| Savings Plan: Y | Stock Purch. Plan: | | Second Exec. Salary: $375,000 | Bonus: $ |

## OTHER THOUGHTS:

**Apparent Women Officers or Directors**: 1
**Hot Spot for Advancement for Women/Minorities**: Y

## LOCATIONS: ("Y" = Yes)

| West: | Southwest: | Midwest: | Southeast: | Northeast: | International: |
|---|---|---|---|---|---|
| Y | Y | Y | Y | Y | Y |

# LEAP WIRELESS INTERNATIONAL INC

www.leapwireless.com

**Industry Group Code:** 513322 **Ranks within this company's industry group:** Sales: 2 Profits: 3

| Management: | | Sales/Marketing: | | Liberal Arts: | | Information Systems: | | Professionals: | | Technical/Scientific: | |
|---|---|---|---|---|---|---|---|---|---|---|---|
| Mgmt. Trainees: | | Mktg. Professionals: | Y | Gen. Writing/Editing: | | Info. Management: | Y | Finance/Accounting: | Y | Engineers, Elec.: | Y |
| Experienced Mgmt.: | Y | Retail Sales: | | Technical Writing: | Y | Software Dev.: | Y | Law: | Y | Engineers, Other: | |
| Int'l Business: | Y | Commercial/Industrial: | Y | Graphic Arts/Photog.: | | Hardware Dev.: | | HR/Other: | Y | Health/Lab: | |
| MBA Graduates: | Y | Sales Trainees: | | Music: | | Systems Integration: | Y | Training: | Y | Scientists/Research: | |
| | | Advertising Pros.: | Y | Broadcasting: | | Consulting/Other: | | Health Care: | | Petroleum/Chemicals: | |
| | | | | Other: | | | | Consulting: | | Math/Other: | |

## TYPES OF BUSINESS:

Cellular Telephone Service
Retail Sales

## BRANDS/DIVISIONS/AFFILIATES:

Cricket Communications, Inc.
Jump Mobile
Travel Time
Cricket Flex Bucket
Cricket Clicks
Cricket by Week
Alaska Native Broadband 1, LLC
CSM Wireless LLC

## CONTACTS: *Note: Officers with more than one job title may be intentionally listed here more than once.*

S. Douglas Hutcheson, CEO
Albin Moschner, COO
S. Douglas Hutcheson, Pres.
S. Douglas Hutcheson, CFO
Leonard C. Stephens, Sr. VP-Human Resources
Dave Truzinski, Sr. VP/CIO
Glenn Umetsu, Exec. VP/CTO
Collin Holland, Sr. VP-Eng. & Technical Oper.
Robert J. Irving, Jr., General Counsel/Sr. VP
David Davis, Sr. VP-Oper.
Bill Ingram, Sr. VP-Strategy
Amy Wakeham, Dir.-Investor Rel.
Jeff Nachbor, Sr. VP-Financial Oper.
Greg Lund, Dir.-Media Rel.
Linda Wokoun, Sr. VP-Field Oper. & Customer Care
Greg Post, Sr. VP-Field Oper. & Sales
T. Scott Edwards, Sr. VP-Mktg.
Mark H. Rachesky, Chmn.

| **Phone:** 858-882-6000 | **Fax:** 858-882-6010 |
|---|---|
| **Toll-Free:** | |
| **Address:** 10307 Pacific Center Ct., San Diego, CA 92121 US | |

## GROWTH PLANS/SPECIAL FEATURES:

Leap Wireless International, Inc. provides mobile wireless services targeted to meet the needs of younger and lower-income customers under-served by traditional communications companies. Leap operates under the Cricket brand, which is distributed by Cricket Communications Inc. and in Oregon by the LCW Wireless Operations, LLC. Cricket, through a variety of flat-rate service plans, offers a choice of unlimited anytime local voice minutes; unlimited anytime domestic long distance voice minutes; unlimited text, instant and picture messaging; and additional value-added services over an all digital CDMA network. Leap also offers Jump Mobile, a unique prepaid wireless service offering customers free unlimited incoming calls from anywhere, outgoing calls at 10 cents per minute and free incoming and outgoing text messaging. Both Cricket and Jump Mobile are offered without long-term commitments or credit checks. Cricket's products and services include Cricket service plans; Cricket plan upgrades; handsets; handset replacement and return; Cricket wireless Internet service; and Jump Mobile. Cricket currently operates in 23 states, has approximately 2.9 million customers and holds licenses in 35 of the top 50 markets in the U.S. Leap sells Cricket products and service through two channels: Retail locations and kiosks; and authorized dealers and distributors. Leap and LCW Operations have 152 direct locations and 2690 indirect distributors, including 790 premier dealers. In 2007, Leap increased its network footprint by approximately 6 million points of presence (POPs). In September 2007, Cricket introduced its first unlimited wireless broadband service in select markets, which allows customers to access the Internet through their laptops for one low, flat rate with no long-term commitments or credit checks.

Leap offers its employees tuition assistance; flexible spending accounts; employee assistance programs; massages; car washes and dry cleaning services; adoption assistance; domestic partner benefits; fitness reimbursement; medical, dental and vision insurance; and a 401(k).

## FINANCIALS: **Sales and profits are in thousands of dollars—add 000 to get the full amount. 2008 Note: Financial information for 2008 was not available for all companies at press time.**

| | | |
|---|---|---|
| 2008 Sales: $ | 2008 Profits: $ | **U.S. Stock Ticker: LEAP** |
| 2007 Sales: $1,630,803 | 2007 Profits: $-75,927 | **Int'l Ticker:** Int'l Exchange: |
| 2006 Sales: $1,167,187 | 2006 Profits: $-24,357 | Employees: 2,425 |
| 2005 Sales: $957,771 | 2005 Profits: $30,685 | Fiscal Year Ends: 12/31 |
| 2004 Sales: $50,317 | 2004 Profits: $- 168 | Parent Company: |

## SALARIES/BENEFITS:

| | | | | |
|---|---|---|---|---|
| Pension Plan: | ESOP Stock Plan: | Profit Sharing: | Top Exec. Salary: $610,385 | Bonus: $472,648 |
| Savings Plan: Y | Stock Purch. Plan: | | Second Exec. Salary: $361,654 | Bonus: $233,542 |

## OTHER THOUGHTS:

**Apparent Women Officers or Directors**: 2
**Hot Spot for Advancement for Women/Minorities**: Y

## LOCATIONS: ("Y" = Yes)

| West: | Southwest: | Midwest: | Southeast: | Northeast: | International: |
|---|---|---|---|---|---|
| Y | Y | Y | Y | Y | |

# LESLIE'S POOLMART INC

**www.lesliespool.com**

**Industry Group Code:** 453990 **Ranks within this company's industry group:** Sales: 1 Profits:

| **Management:** | | **Sales/Marketing:** | | **Liberal Arts:** | | **Information Systems:** | | **Professionals:** | | **Technical/Scientific:** | |
|---|---|---|---|---|---|---|---|---|---|---|---|
| Mgmt. Trainees: | Y | Mktg. Professionals: | Y | Gen. Writing/Editing: | | Info. Management: | Y | Finance/Accounting: | Y | Engineers, Elec.: | |
| Experienced Mgmt.: | Y | Retail Sales: | Y | Technical Writing: | | Software Dev.: | | Law: | Y | Engineers, Other: | |
| Int'l Business: | | Commercial/Industrial: | | Graphic Arts/Photog.: | Y | Hardware Dev.: | | HR/Other: | Y | Health/Lab: | |
| MBA Graduates: | Y | Sales Trainees: | Y | Music: | | Systems Integration: | | Training: | Y | Scientists/Research: | |
| | | Advertising Pros.: | Y | Broadcasting: | | Consulting/Other: | | Health Care: | | Petroleum/Chemicals: | |
| | | | | Other: | | | | Consulting: | | Math/Other: | |

## TYPES OF BUSINESS:

Swimming Pool Supplies, Retail
Catalog & Online Sales
Installation, Repair & Maintenance Services

## BRANDS/DIVISIONS/AFFILIATES:

Leslie's Swimming Pool Supplies
Leonard Green & Partners

## CONTACTS: *Note: Officers with more than one job title may be intentionally listed here more than once.*

Lawrence H. Hayward, CEO
Michael L. Hatch, COO
Michael L. Hatch, Pres.
Steven L. Ortega, CFO/Exec. VP
Michael L. Hatch, Sr. VP-Mktg.
Janet I. McDonald, CIO/Sr. VP
Michael L. Hatch, Sr. VP-Merch.
Brian Agnew, Sr. VP-Store Oper.
Lawrence H. Hayward, Chmn.
Rick D. Carlson, VP-Commercial, Service & Logistics

**Phone:** 602-366-3999 **Fax:** 602-366-3934
**Toll-Free:**
**Address:** 3925 E. Broadway Rd., Ste. 100, Phoenix, AZ 85040 US

## GROWTH PLANS/SPECIAL FEATURES:

Leslie's Poolmart, Inc. is a leading national specialty retailer of swimming pool supplies and related products. The company currently markets its products through over 577 Leslie's Swimming Pool Supplies retail stores in 35 states, a mail-order catalog and an e-commerce site. Leslie's major product categories are pool chemicals; major equipment; cleaning and testing equipment; pool covers, reels and lines; above-ground pools in certain stores; and recreational items, including floats, games, lounges, masks, fins and snorkels. Leslie's also manufactures chlorine tablets and repackages a variety of bulk chemicals into various containers suitable for retail sales. Additionally, the firm formulates a variety of specialty liquids, including water clarifiers, tile cleaners, algaecides and stain preventives. Leslie's focuses on customer service, with most stores supported by a service department that offers poolside equipment installation and repair; leak detection and repair; and seasonal opening and closing services. The company's commercial clients, which include apartments, hotels, resorts, water parks and golf courses, are offered free delivery within 25 miles, certified pool operator training, on-site inspections and chemical automation programs. The company has expanded its line of recreational accessories and now offers a free water analysis service. Leonard Green and Partners owns more than 80% of the company.

The company offers its employee's medical, vision and dental benefits; prescription drug coverage; basic life insurance; short- and long-term disability insurance; a 401(k); and an employee assistance program.

## FINANCIALS: **Sales and profits are in thousands of dollars—add 000 to get the full amount. 2008 Note: Financial information for 2008 was not available for all companies at press time.**

2008 Sales: $
2007 Sales: $468,900
2006 Sales: $440,600
2005 Sales: $388,500
2004 Sales: $356,000

2008 Profits: $
2007 Profits: $
2006 Profits: $20,500
2005 Profits: $-4,400
2004 Profits: $16,200

**U.S. Stock Ticker: Private**
**Int'l Ticker:** Int'l Exchange:
Employees: 2,200
Fiscal Year Ends: 9/30
Parent Company:

## SALARIES/BENEFITS:

Pension Plan:
Savings Plan: Y
ESOP Stock Plan:
Stock Purch. Plan:
Profit Sharing:
Top Exec. Salary: $400,000 Bonus: $168,000
Second Exec. Salary: $275,000 Bonus: $115,500

## OTHER THOUGHTS:

**Apparent Women Officers or Directors**: 1
**Hot Spot for Advancement for Women/Minorities**:

## LOCATIONS: ("Y" = Yes)

| West: | Southwest: | Midwest: | Southeast: | Northeast: | International: |
|---|---|---|---|---|---|
| Y | Y | Y | Y | Y | |

# LIFECELL CORPORATION

www.lifecell.com

**Industry Group Code:** 325414 **Ranks within this company's industry group:** Sales: 2 Profits: 1

| Management: | | Sales/Marketing: | | Liberal Arts: | | Information Systems: | | Professionals: | | Technical/Scientific: | |
|---|---|---|---|---|---|---|---|---|---|---|---|
| Mgmt. Trainees: | | Mktg. Professionals: | Y | Gen. Writing/Editing: | | Info. Management: | Y | Finance/Accounting: | Y | Engineers, Elec.: | |
| Experienced Mgmt.: | Y | Retail Sales: | | Technical Writing: | Y | Software Dev.: | Y | Law: | Y | Engineers, Other: | Y |
| Int'l Business: | Y | Commercial/Industrial: | Y | Graphic Arts/Photog.: | | Hardware Dev.: | | HR/Other: | Y | Health/Lab: | Y |
| MBA Graduates: | Y | Sales Trainees: | Y | Music: | | Systems Integration: | | Training: | Y | Scientists/Research: | Y |
| | | Advertising Pros.: | | Broadcasting: | | Consulting/Other: | | Health Care: | Y | Petroleum/Chemicals: | |
| | | | | Other: | | | | Consulting: | | Math/Other: | Y |

## TYPES OF BUSINESS:

Tissue Replacement Products
Skin Replacement Technology
Bone Grafting Technology
Regenerative Medicine

## BRANDS/DIVISIONS/AFFILIATES:

Kinetic Concepts Inc
AlloDerm
GraftJacket
AlloCraft DBM
Repliform
Strattice

## CONTACTS: *Note: Officers with more than one job title may be intentionally listed here more than once.*

Paul G. Thomas, CEO
Paul G. Thomas, Pres.
Steven T. Sobieski, CFO
Steven T. Sobieski, VP-Admin.
Bruce S. Lamb, Sr. VP-Regulatory Affairs
Lisa N. Colleran, Sr. VP-Commercial Oper.
Bruce S. Lamb, Sr. VP-Dev.
Steven T. Sobieski, VP-Finance
Paul G. Thomas, Chmn.

**Phone:** 908-947-1100 **Fax:** 908-947-1089
**Toll-Free:**
**Address:** 1 Millennium Way, Branchburg, NJ 08876-3876 US

## GROWTH PLANS/SPECIAL FEATURES:

LifeCell Corporation specializes in regenerative medicine, developing and manufacturing products geared toward the repair, replacement and preservation of human tissues. The company has developed and patented several proprietary technologies, including a method for producing an acellular tissue matrix, a method for cell preservation through signal transduction and a method for freeze-drying biological cells and tissues without damage. Products are used in reconstructive, orthopedic and urogynecologic surgical procedures to repair soft tissue defects. The company has many different products. AlloDerm is a tissue matrix derived from human skin. Originally used as a skin graft for deep second and third degree burns, it is now commonly used as a soft tissue replacement, including for plastic reconstructive surgery and periodontal procedures. BioHorizons Implant Systems, Inc. is the exclusive distributor in the U.S. and certain international markets for AlloDerm's periodontal applications; while the firm itself markets AlloDerm in the U.S. for plastic reconstructive, general surgical and burn applications. GraftJacket is used for orthopedic applications, including tendon reinforcement, and by podiatrists for lower extremity wounds. Wright Medical Group exclusively distributes GraftJacket in the U.S. and certain international markets. AlloCraft DBM is a putty-like material used for bone grafts. Stryker Corp. is the exclusive U.S. distributor for AlloCraft DBM. Lastly, Repliform is used for urogynecologic surgical procedures. Boston Scientific Corp. is the exclusive worldwide sales and marketing agent of Repliform for use in urogynecology. In 2007, the company introduced Strattice, a sterile reconstructive tissue matrix that supports tissue regeneration and is used in breast reconstruction and hernia repair. In May 2008, the firm was acquired by and became a wholly-owned subsidiary of Kinetic Concepts, Inc. (KCI) for $1.59 billion.

Employees of LifeCell receive medical, dental and vision insurance; life and AD&D insurance; short- and long-term disability; an employee assistance program; and a college savings plan.

## FINANCIALS: **Sales and profits are in thousands of dollars—add 000 to get the full amount. 2008 Note: Financial information for 2008 was not available for all companies at press time.**

| | | |
|---|---|---|
| 2008 Sales: $ | 2008 Profits: $ | **U.S. Stock Ticker: Subsidiary** |
| 2007 Sales: $191,130 | 2007 Profits: $26,883 | **Int'l Ticker:** Int'l Exchange: |
| 2006 Sales: $141,680 | 2006 Profits: $20,469 | Employees: 443 |
| 2005 Sales: $94,398 | 2005 Profits: $12,044 | Fiscal Year Ends: 12/31 |
| 2004 Sales: $61,127 | 2004 Profits: $7,184 | Parent Company: KINETIC CONCEPTS INC |

## SALARIES/BENEFITS:

| | | | | |
|---|---|---|---|---|
| Pension Plan: | ESOP Stock Plan: | Profit Sharing: | Top Exec. Salary: $500,000 | Bonus: $397,500 |
| Savings Plan: Y | Stock Purch. Plan: | | Second Exec. Salary: $285,850 | Bonus: $130,162 |

## OTHER THOUGHTS:

**Apparent Women Officers or Directors**: 1
**Hot Spot for Advancement for Women/Minorities**:

## LOCATIONS: ("Y" = Yes)

| West: | Southwest: | Midwest: | Southeast: | Northeast: | International: |
|---|---|---|---|---|---|
| | | | | Y | |

# LIFECORE BIOMEDICAL INC

www.lifecore.com

**Industry Group Code:** 339113 **Ranks within this company's industry group:** Sales: 35 Profits: 25

| Management: | | Sales/Marketing: | | Liberal Arts: | | Information Systems: | | Professionals: | | Technical/Scientific: | |
|---|---|---|---|---|---|---|---|---|---|---|---|
| Mgmt. Trainees: | | Mktg. Professionals: | Y | Gen. Writing/Editing: | | Info. Management: | Y | Finance/Accounting: | Y | Engineers, Elec.: | Y |
| Experienced Mgmt.: | Y | Retail Sales: | | Technical Writing: | Y | Software Dev.: | Y | Law: | Y | Engineers, Other: | Y |
| Int'l Business: | Y | Commercial/Industrial: | Y | Graphic Arts/Photog.: | | Hardware Dev.: | Y | HR/Other: | Y | Health/Lab: | Y |
| MBA Graduates: | Y | Sales Trainees: | Y | Music: | | Systems Integration: | | Training: | Y | Scientists/Research: | Y |
| | | Advertising Pros.: | | Broadcasting: | | Consulting/Other: | | Health Care: | Y | Petroleum/Chemicals: | |
| | | | | Other: | | | | Consulting: | | Math/Other: | Y |

## TYPES OF BUSINESS:

Biomaterials & Medical Device Manufacturing
Bone Regeneration Products
Surgical Devices
Dental Implants

## BRANDS/DIVISIONS/AFFILIATES:

Support Plus
Lifecore Prima Implant System
SBT Acquisition Inc.
SBT Holdings Inc.

## CONTACTS:

*Note: Officers with more than one job title may be intentionally listed here more than once.*

Dennis J. Allingham, CEO
Dennis J. Allingham, Pres.
David M. Noel, CFO
James G. Hall, VP-Technical Oper.
Kipling Thacker, VP-New Bus. Dev.
David M. Noel, VP-Finance
Larry D. Hiebert, VP/Gen. Mgr.-Hyaluronan Div.

**Phone:** 952-368-4300 **Fax:** 952-368-3411
**Toll-Free:**
**Address:** 3515 Lyman Blvd., Chaska, MN 55318 US

## GROWTH PLANS/SPECIAL FEATURES:

Lifecore Biomedical, Inc. develops and manufactures biomaterials and medical devices with applications in various surgical markets. The company operates two divisions, the hyaluronan division and the oral restorative division. Its hyaluronan division is principally involved in the development and manufacture of products utilizing hyaluronan, a naturally occurring polysaccharide that is widely distributed in the extracellar matrix of connective tissues in both animals and humans. This division sells primarily to three medical segments: Ophthalmic, orthopedic and veterinary. Lifecore also supplies hyaluronan to customers pursuing other medical applications, such as wound care, aesthetic surgery, medical device coatings, tissue engineering, drug delivery and pharmaceuticals. Lifecore's oral restorative division develops and markets precision surgical and prosthetic devices for the restoration of damaged or deteriorating dentition and associated support tissues. The company's dental implants are permanently implanted in the jaw for tooth replacement therapy as long-term support for crowns, bridges and dentures. It also offers bone regenerative products for the repair of bone defects resulting from periodontal disease and tooth loss. Additionally, the oral restorative division provides professional support services to its dental surgery clients through comprehensive education curricula, as provided in the company's various Support Plus programs and surgical courses. These professional continuing education programs are designed to train restorative clinicians and their auxiliary teams in the principles of tooth replacement therapy and practice management. Recently, the company announced the proprietary Lifecore Prima Implant System. In March 2008, private equity firm Warburg Pincus acquired Lifecore, taking the company private.

## FINANCIALS:

**Sales and profits are in thousands of dollars—add 000 to get the full amount. 2008 Note: Financial information for 2008 was not available for all companies at press time.**

| | | |
|---|---|---|
| 2008 Sales: $ | 2008 Profits: $ | **U.S. Stock Ticker: Private** |
| 2007 Sales: $69,629 | 2007 Profits: $7,719 | **Int'l Ticker:** Int'l Exchange: |
| 2006 Sales: $63,097 | 2006 Profits: $7,040 | Employees: 241 |
| 2005 Sales: $55,695 | 2005 Profits: $17,511 | Fiscal Year Ends: 6/30 |
| 2004 Sales: $47,036 | 2004 Profits: $ 707 | Parent Company: WARBURG PINCUS LLC |

## SALARIES/BENEFITS:

| | | | | |
|---|---|---|---|---|
| Pension Plan: | ESOP Stock Plan: | Profit Sharing: | Top Exec. Salary: $312,000 | Bonus: $81,120 |
| Savings Plan: Y | Stock Purch. Plan: Y | | Second Exec. Salary: $160,000 | Bonus: $27,200 |

## OTHER THOUGHTS:

**Apparent Women Officers or Directors**:
**Hot Spot for Advancement for Women/Minorities**:

## LOCATIONS: ("Y" = Yes)

| West: | Southwest: | Midwest: | Southeast: | Northeast: | International: |
|---|---|---|---|---|---|
| | | Y | | | Y |

# LIVEPERSON INC

www.liveperson.com

**Industry Group Code:** 511203 **Ranks within this company's industry group:** Sales: 6 Profits: 4

| Management: | | Sales/Marketing: | | Liberal Arts: | | Information Systems: | | Professionals: | | Technical/Scientific: | |
|---|---|---|---|---|---|---|---|---|---|---|---|
| Mgmt. Trainees: | | Mktg. Professionals: | Y | Gen. Writing/Editing: | | Info. Management: | Y | Finance/Accounting: | Y | Engineers, Elec.: | Y |
| Experienced Mgmt.: | Y | Retail Sales: | | Technical Writing: | Y | Software Dev.: | Y | Law: | Y | Engineers, Other: | |
| Int'l Business: | Y | Commercial/Industrial: | Y | Graphic Arts/Photog.: | | Hardware Dev.: | | HR/Other: | Y | Health/Lab: | |
| MBA Graduates: | Y | Sales Trainees: | Y | Music: | | Systems Integration: | Y | Training: | Y | Scientists/Research: | |
| | | Advertising Pros.: | | Broadcasting: | | Consulting/Other: | | Health Care: | | Petroleum/Chemicals: | |
| | | | | Other: | Y | | | Consulting: | | Math/Other: | Y |

## TYPES OF BUSINESS:

E-Commerce Software
Customer Service Software
Sales & Marketing Service Software
Live Chat Applications

## BRANDS/DIVISIONS/AFFILIATES:

Timpani
Timpani Sales and Marketing
Timpani Contact Center
Timpani Voice
LivePerson Pro
LivePerson Contact Center
LivePerson Enterprise
Kasamba, Inc.

## CONTACTS: *Note: Officers with more than one job title may be intentionally listed here more than once.*

Robert LoCascio, CEO
Timothy Bixby, Pres.
Timothy Bixby, CFO
Kevin Kohn, Exec. VP-Mktg.
Monica Greenberg, General Counsel/Sr. VP-Bus. Affairs
Michael Kovach, Sr. VP/Corp. Controller
Philippe Lang, Sr. VP-Small Bus.
Jim Dicso, Sr. VP-Enterprise Sales & Service
Robert LoCascio, Chmn.
Eli Campo, Exec. VP/General Mgr.-Tech. Oper., Israel

**Phone:** 212-609-4200 **Fax:**
**Toll-Free:**
**Address:** 462 7th Ave., 3rd Fl., New York, NY 10018 US

## GROWTH PLANS/SPECIAL FEATURES:

LivePerson, Inc. is a leading facilitator of online e-commerce interaction, enhancing real-time sales, customer support and personalized expert advice through more than 50 million chat interactions annually. The company offers real-time sales, marketing and customer service solutions to online businesses with the aim of improving customer relationships. Timpani, LivePerson's integrated multi-channel communication software platform, combines a variety of features help companies manage online customer sales and support. Timpani products include: Timpani Sales and Marketing, which combines online site traffic monitoring software with a sophisticated rules engine to enable LivePerson clients to proactively engage website visitors; Timpani Contact Center, which provides online customer support capability via a unified, multi-channel interface comprised of chat, voice, e-mail and self-service knowledgebase; and Timpani Voice, which bridges the gap between web-based contact channels and company call centers, combining online collaboration tools with real-time analytics and comprehensive reporting. In addition, the company offers LivePerson Pro, which enables small business clients to economically increase online sales; LivePerson Contact Center, an all-in-one platform encompassing live chat, e-mail, self-service and telephone logs; and LivePerson Enterprise, offering multi-channel engagement solutions for larger companies. The firm's professional services team offers consulting services to enterprise clients, helping to analyze their needs and implement appropriate solutions. In addition to its business services, LivePerson also hosts an online marketplace that allows experts and individual service providers to sell their information and knowledge via real-time chat with consumers. Users can seek advice in various categories including personal counseling, computers and programming, health and medicine, education, shopping, professional development, spirituality, legal services and other topics. LivePerson clients include over 7,000 companies, including the University of New Orleans; Saturn; LogicWorks; Lillian Vernon; Hoovers; Home Depot; Dodge; and EarthLink. In 2007, LivePerson acquired Kasamba, Inc., a leading online provider of live expert advice delivered to consumers via real-time chat.

## FINANCIALS: **Sales and profits are in thousands of dollars—add 000 to get the full amount. 2008 Note: Financial information for 2008 was not available for all companies at press time.**

| | | |
|---|---|---|
| 2008 Sales: $ | 2008 Profits: $ | **U.S. Stock Ticker: LPSN** |
| 2007 Sales: $52,228 | 2007 Profits: $5,821 | **Int'l Ticker:** Int'l Exchange: |
| 2006 Sales: $33,521 | 2006 Profits: $2,202 | Employees: 314 |
| 2005 Sales: $22,277 | 2005 Profits: $2,542 | Fiscal Year Ends: 12/31 |
| 2004 Sales: $17,392 | 2004 Profits: $2,092 | Parent Company: |

## SALARIES/BENEFITS:

| | | | | |
|---|---|---|---|---|
| Pension Plan: | ESOP Stock Plan: | Profit Sharing: | Top Exec. Salary: $275,000 | Bonus: $155,000 |
| Savings Plan: | Stock Purch. Plan: | | Second Exec. Salary: $275,000 | Bonus: $155,000 |

## OTHER THOUGHTS:

**Apparent Women Officers or Directors:** 1
**Hot Spot for Advancement for Women/Minorities:**

## LOCATIONS: ("Y" = Yes)

| West: | Southwest: | Midwest: | Southeast: | Northeast: | International: |
|---|---|---|---|---|---|
| Y | Y | | Y | Y | Y |

# LOGISTICARE INC

www.logisticare.com

**Industry Group Code:** 621111 **Ranks within this company's industry group:** Sales: Profits:

| Management: | | Sales/Marketing: | | Liberal Arts: | | Information Systems: | | Professionals: | | Technical/Scientific: | |
|---|---|---|---|---|---|---|---|---|---|---|---|
| Mgmt. Trainees: | | Mktg. Professionals: | Y | Gen. Writing/Editing: | | Info. Management: | Y | Finance/Accounting: | Y | Engineers, Elec.: | |
| Experienced Mgmt.: | Y | Retail Sales: | | Technical Writing: | | Software Dev.: | Y | Law: | Y | Engineers, Other: | |
| Int'l Business: | | Commercial/Industrial: | Y | Graphic Arts/Photog.: | | Hardware Dev.: | | HR/Other: | Y | Health/Lab: | |
| MBA Graduates: | Y | Sales Trainees: | Y | Music: | | Systems Integration: | | Training: | Y | Scientists/Research: | |
| | | Advertising Pros.: | | Broadcasting: | | Consulting/Other: | | Health Care: | | Petroleum/Chemicals: | |
| | | | | Other: | | | | Consulting: | | Math/Other: | |

## TYPES OF BUSINESS:

Medical Transportation Management Services
Outsourced Logistics Services

## BRANDS/DIVISIONS/AFFILIATES:

LogistiCAD
EMTrack
Providence Service Corporation

## CONTACTS: *Note: Officers with more than one job title may be intentionally listed here more than once.*

John L. Shermyen, CEO
Herman M. Schwarz, COO
John L. Shermyen, Pres.
Thomas E. Oram, CFO
Jenny Southern, Dir.-Human Resources
Rob Cornell, CIO
Albert Cortina, Chief Admin. Officer
Chinta Gaston, General Counsel
Lisa Leach, Dir.-Oper.
Kthy Ryland, VP-Bus. Dev.
Ray P. Williams, Sr. VP-Public Affairs
Windy J. Brooks, Controller
Vuong Chu Ba, Dir.-Compliance
Ken Hoggard, Dir.-Network Dev.
Lisa Leach, Dir.-State Oper.
Sandy Reifel, Dir.-Client Svcs.

**Phone:** 770-907-7596 **Fax:** 770-907-7598
**Toll-Free:** 800-486-7647
**Address:** 1800 Phoenix Blvd., Ste. 120, Atlanta, GA 30349 US

## GROWTH PLANS/SPECIAL FEATURES:

LogistiCare, Inc. is an outsourced scheduler of patient transport services for insurance companies, managed care organizations and government health agencies, with expertise in the area of non-emergency medical transportation (NEMT). Instead of owning its own vehicles, the firm manages call centers, patient eligibility screening, scheduling, dispatch, billing and quality assurance. It also manages local transportation provider networks of local, commercial, non-profit and public transportation companies. LogistiCare recruits and accredits local firms for its network of providers. In sum, the company has contracts with 1,100 transportation providers and roughly 8,000 vehicles, coordinating about 17 million trips per year. LogistiCare operates 11 network operations centers that are linked via T-1 lines in order to handle a call volume of approximately 4.1 million per year. All calls are recorded digitally and archived in the system database. The firm developed the integrated software system known as LogistiCAD in order to automatically coordinate all of this data and generate scheduling, routing, quality assurance reporting, transportation cost estimates and billing verification. It processes transportation requests and dispatches drivers through its network of carriers, using its proprietary EMTrack system that tracks all of the company's vehicles. LogistiCare is able to use its LogistiCAD system in conjunction with sophisticated GPS navigation to gain improved transportation access and service delivery in rural and remote areas. The company's government clients include state Medicaid agencies, school boards and ADA paratransit authorities. Healthcare sector clients include hospital systems and many of the nations largest managed care organizations. In August 2007, LogistiCare established a new call center in Mullins, South Carolina that will manage four regions of South Carolina's Medicaid non-emergency medical transportation and schedule a projected 1.4 million trips annually. In December 2007, LogistiCare was acquired by Providence Service Corporation for approximately $220 million.

## FINANCIALS: **Sales and profits are in thousands of dollars—add 000 to get the full amount. 2008 Note: Financial information for 2008 was not available for all companies at press time.**

2008 Sales: $
2007 Sales: $
2006 Sales: $252,000
2005 Sales: $255,000
2004 Sales: $220,000

2008 Profits: $
2007 Profits: $
2006 Profits: $
2005 Profits: $
2004 Profits: $

**U.S. Stock Ticker: Subsidiary**
**Int'l Ticker:** Int'l Exchange:
Employees: 900
Fiscal Year Ends: 12/31
Parent Company: PROVIDENCE SERVICE CORPORATION

## SALARIES/BENEFITS:

Pension Plan: ESOP Stock Plan: Profit Sharing: Top Exec. Salary: $ Bonus: $
Savings Plan: Stock Purch. Plan: Second Exec. Salary: $ Bonus: $

## OTHER THOUGHTS:

**Apparent Women Officers or Directors**: 7
**Hot Spot for Advancement for Women/Minorities**: Y

## LOCATIONS: ("Y" = Yes)

| West: | Southwest: | Midwest: | Southeast: | Northeast: | International: |
|---|---|---|---|---|---|
| Y | Y | Y | Y | Y | |

# LOJACK CORP

www.lojack.com

**Industry Group Code:** 334290 **Ranks within this company's industry group:** Sales: 2 Profits: 1

| **Management:** | | **Sales/Marketing:** | | **Liberal Arts:** | | **Information Systems:** | | **Professionals:** | | **Technical/Scientific:** | |
|---|---|---|---|---|---|---|---|---|---|---|---|
| Mgmt. Trainees: | | Mktg. Professionals: | Y | Gen. Writing/Editing: | | Info. Management: | Y | Finance/Accounting: | Y | Engineers, Elec.: | Y |
| Experienced Mgmt.: | Y | Retail Sales: | | Technical Writing: | Y | Software Dev.: | Y | Law: | Y | Engineers, Other: | Y |
| Int'l Business: | Y | Commercial/Industrial: | Y | Graphic Arts/Photog.: | | Hardware Dev.: | Y | HR/Other: | Y | Health/Lab: | |
| MBA Graduates: | Y | Sales Trainees: | Y | Music: | | Systems Integration: | Y | Training: | Y | Scientists/Research: | |
| | | Advertising Pros.: | Y | Broadcasting: | | Consulting/Other: | | Health Care: | | Petroleum/Chemicals: | |
| | | | | Other: | | | | Consulting: | | Math/Other: | |

## TYPES OF BUSINESS:

Electronic Equipment-Stolen Vehicle Recovery
Vehicle Security Devices

## BRANDS/DIVISIONS/AFFILIATES:

LoJack Stolen Vehicle Recovery System
LoJack Early Warning Recovery System
Boomerang Tracking
LoJack for Laptops
Absolute Software
Locate by LoJack

## CONTACTS: *Note: Officers with more than one job title may be intentionally listed here more than once.*

Richard T. Riley, CEO
Ronald V. Waters III, COO
Ronald V. Waters III, Pres.
Michael Umana, CFO/Sr. VP
Kevin M. Mullins, Sr. VP/Gen. Mgr.-Sales
William R. Duvall, CTO/Exec. VP
Thomas Wooters, General Counsel/Exec. VP
Paul McMahon, Dir.-Corp. Comm.
Richard T. Riley, Chmn.
Thomas M. Camp, Sr. VP/Gen. Mgr.-Int'l

**Phone:** 781-326-4700 **Fax:** 781-326-7255
**Toll-Free:** 800-456-5225
**Address:** 200 Lowder Brook Dr., Ste. 1000, Westwood, MA 02090 US

## GROWTH PLANS/SPECIAL FEATURES:

LoJack Corporation creates and markets technology products and services for the tracking and recovery of valuable mobile assets. LoJack offers two systems for vehicle recovery, the LoJack System and the Boomerang System. The LoJack System, based on radio frequency (RF) technology, is comprised of a Registration System, maintained and operated by LoJack; a Sector Activation System and Vehicle Tracking Units, both operated by law enforcement officials; and a LoJack Unit, a VHF transponder. The LoJack system is designed to be integrated into existing law enforcement computer and telecommunication systems and procedures. If a car equipped with a LoJack unit is stolen, its owner reports the theft to the local police department. A radio signal will be transmitted automatically to the unit in the stolen vehicle, activating its tracking signal. Revenue from the domestic segment of LoJack products and units comprised 67% for fiscal 2007. LoJack also offers LoJack for Construction Equipment and LoJack for Motorcycles. The Boomerang System is based on RF and cellular technology, using internationally developed tracking devices and the wireless networks of major regional telecommunications companies to locate and track stolen assets. Revenue from the Boomerang segment comprised 9% for fiscal 2007. The LoJack System is used in 26 U.S. states and Washington, D.C., as well as in 31 countries internationally. LoJack also licenses its name to Absolute Software, which markets computer theft recovery products under the brand name LoJack for Laptops. In 2008, LoJack launched Locate by LoJack for fleet managers and equipment owners, which provides key functions such as location-on-demand, geofencing, engine hours and user defined reporting.

LoJack offers its employees a 401 (k) plan, an employee stock purchase plan, a 529 plan, discounts on company products and adoption assistance.

## FINANCIALS: **Sales and profits are in thousands of dollars—add 000 to get the full amount. 2008 Note: Financial information for 2008 was not available for all companies at press time.**

| | | |
|---|---|---|
| 2008 Sales: $ | 2008 Profits: $ | **U.S. Stock Ticker: LOJN** |
| 2007 Sales: $222,749 | 2007 Profits: $21,405 | **Int'l Ticker:** Int'l Exchange: |
| 2006 Sales: $213,288 | 2006 Profits: $16,507 | Employees: 925 |
| 2005 Sales: $190,726 | 2005 Profits: $18,439 | Fiscal Year Ends: 12/31 |
| 2004 Sales: $145,691 | 2004 Profits: $10,400 | Parent Company: |

## SALARIES/BENEFITS:

| | | | | |
|---|---|---|---|---|
| Pension Plan: | ESOP Stock Plan: | Profit Sharing: | Top Exec. Salary: $486,539 | Bonus: $279,000 |
| Savings Plan: Y | Stock Purch. Plan: Y | | Second Exec. Salary: $330,769 | Bonus: $185,256 |

## OTHER THOUGHTS:

**Apparent Women Officers or Directors**:
**Hot Spot for Advancement for Women/Minorities**:

## LOCATIONS: ("Y" = Yes)

| West: | Southwest: | Midwest: | Southeast: | Northeast: | International: |
|---|---|---|---|---|---|
| Y | Y | | Y | Y | Y |

# LORAL SPACE & COMMUNICATIONS LTD

www.loral.com

**Industry Group Code:** 334220 **Ranks within this company's industry group:** Sales: 1 Profits: 2

| Management: | | Sales/Marketing: | | Liberal Arts: | | Information Systems: | | Professionals: | | Technical/Scientific: | |
|---|---|---|---|---|---|---|---|---|---|---|---|
| Mgmt. Trainees: | | Mktg. Professionals: | Y | Gen. Writing/Editing: | Y | Info. Management: | Y | Finance/Accounting: | Y | Engineers, Elec.: | Y |
| Experienced Mgmt.: | Y | Retail Sales: | | Technical Writing: | Y | Software Dev.: | Y | Law: | Y | Engineers, Other: | Y |
| Int'l Business: | Y | Commercial/Industrial: | Y | Graphic Arts/Photog.: | | Hardware Dev.: | Y | HR/Other: | Y | Health/Lab: | |
| MBA Graduates: | Y | Sales Trainees: | Y | Music: | | Systems Integration: | Y | Training: | Y | Scientists/Research: | |
| | | Advertising Pros.: | | Broadcasting: | | Consulting/Other: | | Health Care: | | Petroleum/Chemicals: | |
| | | | | Other: | | | | Consulting: | | Math/Other: | Y |

## TYPES OF BUSINESS:

Satellite Equipment
Communications & Weather Satellite Systems
Fixed Satellite & Network Services
Information Delivery Systems
Managed Communications Networks
Internet Services

## BRANDS/DIVISIONS/AFFILIATES:

Loral Skynet
Space Systems/Loral Inc
SkyReach
SkyReachSM Cellular Backhaul
XTAR LLC

## CONTACTS: *Note: Officers with more than one job title may be intentionally listed here more than once.*

Michael B. Targoff, CEO/Vice Chmn.
Michael B. Targoff, Pres.
Harvey B. Rein, CFO/Sr. VP
Avi Katz, General Counsel/Sec./Sr. VP
Russell R. Mack, VP-Bus. Ventures
Jeanette H. Clonan, VP-Comm.
Jeanette H. Clonan, VP-Investor Rel.
Richard P. Mastoloni, Sr. VP-Finance/Treas.
John Capogrossi, VP/Controller
Barry J. Sitler, VP-Tax
C. Patrick DeWitt, Sr. VP/CEO-Space Systems/Loral, Inc.
Arnold Friedman, Sr. VP-Worldwide Mktg & Sales, Space Systems/Loral
Mark H. Rachesky, Chmn.

| | |
|---|---|
| **Phone:** 212-697-1105 | **Fax:** 212-338-5662 |
| **Toll-Free:** | |
| **Address:** 600 3rd Ave., New York, NY 10016 US | |

## GROWTH PLANS/SPECIAL FEATURES:

Loral Space & Communications, Ltd. is a leader in satellite communications. Subsidiary Loral Skynet Corporation manages and operates the firm's Satellite Services business. It maintains satellites in geosynchronous orbits, approximately 22,000 miles above the equator, which provide high-bandwidth services and serve as the backbone for many forms of telecommunications. Customers lease transponder capacity for distribution of cable television programming, for direct-to-home (DTH) video transmission, live video feeds from breaking news and sporting events and broadband data distribution. Skynet Network Services' aspect, SkyReach, is a group of hub-based Internet protocol (IP) services that provides customers with secure private networks and high-speed Internet access using Skynet's established satellite/fiber structure. The SkyReachSM Cellular Backhaul for mobile and cell phone users replaces E1/T1 lines with satellite lines, allowing for better network and operator connectivity. Subsidiary Space Systems/Loral, Inc. designs and manufactures satellites and space system components for commercial and government broadcasting applications including fixed satellite services, direct to home broadcasting, broadband data distribution, wireless telephony, digital radio, military communications, weather monitoring and air traffic management. The company currently operates a fleet of four satellites and counts HBO, Disney, Global Crossing, BT North America and China Central TV as major customers. Loral also owns 56% of XTAR, LLC, a joint venture with Spanish telecommunications company HISDESAT. XTAR provides X-band services to government users in the U.S., Spain and other allied countries, including the U.S. Department of State, the Spanish Ministry of Defense and the Danish armed forces. In 2008, Space Systems/Loral was selected to provide space craft to Intelsat, an international provider of fixed satellite services.

Employees are offered health insurance; life insurance; and a pension plan.

## FINANCIALS: **Sales and profits are in thousands of dollars—add 000 to get the full amount. 2008 Note: Financial information for 2008 was not available for all companies at press time.**

| | | |
|---|---|---|
| 2008 Sales: $ | 2008 Profits: $ | **U.S. Stock Ticker: LORL** |
| 2007 Sales: $882,454 | 2007 Profits: $29,659 | **Int'l Ticker:** Int'l Exchange: |
| 2006 Sales: $797,333 | 2006 Profits: $-22,720 | Employees: 2,340 |
| 2005 Sales: $626,400 | 2005 Profits: $1,017,256 | Fiscal Year Ends: 12/31 |
| 2004 Sales: $522,100 | 2004 Profits: $-176,700 | Parent Company: |

## SALARIES/BENEFITS:

| | | | | |
|---|---|---|---|---|
| Pension Plan: Y | ESOP Stock Plan: | Profit Sharing: | Top Exec. Salary: $1,152,000 | Bonus: $1,142,375 |
| Savings Plan: | Stock Purch. Plan: | | Second Exec. Salary: $953,654 | Bonus: $441,508 |

## OTHER THOUGHTS:

**Apparent Women Officers or Directors**: 1
**Hot Spot for Advancement for Women/Minorities**:

## LOCATIONS: ("Y" = Yes)

| West: | Southwest: | Midwest: | Southeast: | Northeast: | International: |
|---|---|---|---|---|---|
| Y | | | | Y | Y |

# LUCASFILM LTD

www.lucasfilm.com

**Industry Group Code:** 512110 **Ranks within this company's industry group:** Sales: Profits:

| Management: | | Sales/Marketing: | | Liberal Arts: | | Information Systems: | | Professionals: | | Technical/Scientific: | |
|---|---|---|---|---|---|---|---|---|---|---|---|
| Mgmt. Trainees: | | Mktg. Professionals: | Y | Gen. Writing/Editing: | Y | Info. Management: | Y | Finance/Accounting: | Y | Engineers, Elec.: | Y |
| Experienced Mgmt.: | Y | Retail Sales: | | Technical Writing: | | Software Dev.: | Y | Law: | Y | Engineers, Other: | Y |
| Int'l Business: | Y | Commercial/Industrial: | | Graphic Arts/Photog.: | Y | Hardware Dev.: | | HR/Other: | Y | Health/Lab: | |
| MBA Graduates: | Y | Sales Trainees: | Y | Music: | Y | Systems Integration: | Y | Training: | Y | Scientists/Research: | |
| | | Advertising Pros.: | Y | Broadcasting: | | Consulting/Other: | | Health Care: | | Petroleum/Chemicals: | |
| | | | | Other: | Y | | | Consulting: | | Math/Other: | |

## TYPES OF BUSINESS:

Film Production
Special Effects
Sound Effects
Digital Animation
Software & Video Games
Online Publishing
Merchandising

## BRANDS/DIVISIONS/AFFILIATES:

Industrial Light & Magic
Skywalker Sound
Lucas Digital
LucasArts
Lucas Online
Indiana Jones
Star Wars
Lucasfilm Animation Singapore

## CONTACTS: *Note: Officers with more than one job title may be intentionally listed here more than once.*

Micheline Chau, COO
Micheline Chau, Pres.
Richard Kerris, CTO
Jan van der Voort, Chief Admin. Officer
Chrissie England, Pres., Industrial Light & Magic
Glenn Kiser, VP/General Mgr.-Skywalker Sound
Howard Roffman, Pres., Lucas Licensing
Darrell Rodriguiz, Sr. VP/Pres., LucasArts
George Lucas, Chmn.

| | |
|---|---|
| **Phone:** 415-662-1800 | **Fax:** |
| **Toll-Free:** | |
| **Address:** 1110 Gorgas Ave., San Francisco, CA 94129 US | |

## GROWTH PLANS/SPECIAL FEATURES:

Lucasfilm Ltd., created by filmmaker George Lucas in 1971, is one of the most successful independent production companies. It has produced some of the most popular films in history, including the original Star Wars trilogy and the more recent prequels, along with the Indiana Jones films. Star Wars Episode I: The Phantom Menace has earned approximately $920 million since its release in 1999 and claims the number five spot on the list of all-time highest grossing films. The company operates through seven divisions. Lucasfilm is responsible for production, promotion and strategic management of theatrical, television and entertainment properties. Industrial Light & Magic (ILM) creates digital and visual special effects for the entertainment industry and has received 31 Academy Award nominations and 15 awards. Skywalker Sound produces post-production digital sound effects, for which it has won 18 Academy Awards. LucasArts is a software company that develops computer games based on Lucas's movies. The firm's licensing division is responsible for licensing and merchandising Lucasfilm properties. Animation and Lucasfilm Animation Singapore are digital animation studios. Finally, Lucasfilm's online division produces entertainment, education, reference and e-commerce sites for Lucasfilm properties. Since 2005, the company has been operating out of the Letterman Digital Arts Center. This center brings the entire organization together and enables units producing games and films to collaborate more closely and share technologies. In February 2008, the company released The Adventures of Young Indiana Jones on DVD. In August 2008, Lucasfilm joined with Warner Bros. Pictures and Turner Broadcasting System, Inc., to release Star Wars: The Clone Wars, a full-length animated movie and Cartoon Network/TNT series.

The Letterman Digital Arts Center contains a 300-seat theater, a childcare center, a fitness center and an ultra-fast 1-gigabyte network hookup at every desktop.

## FINANCIALS: **Sales and profits are in thousands of dollars—add 000 to get the full amount. 2008 Note: Financial information for 2008 was not available for all companies at press time.**

| | | |
|---|---|---|
| 2008 Sales: $ | 2008 Profits: $ | **U.S. Stock Ticker: Private** |
| 2007 Sales: $ | 2007 Profits: $ | **Int'l Ticker:** Int'l Exchange: |
| 2006 Sales: $ | 2006 Profits: $ | Employees: 1,500 |
| 2005 Sales: $1,483,000 | 2005 Profits: $ | Fiscal Year Ends: 3/31 |
| 2004 Sales: $ | 2004 Profits: $ | Parent Company: |

## SALARIES/BENEFITS:

| | | | | |
|---|---|---|---|---|
| Pension Plan: | ESOP Stock Plan: | Profit Sharing: | Top Exec. Salary: $ | Bonus: $ |
| Savings Plan: Y | Stock Purch. Plan: | | Second Exec. Salary: $ | Bonus: $ |

## OTHER THOUGHTS:

**Apparent Women Officers or Directors**: 3
**Hot Spot for Advancement for Women/Minorities**: Y

## LOCATIONS: ("Y" = Yes)

| West: | Southwest: | Midwest: | Southeast: | Northeast: | International: |
|---|---|---|---|---|---|
| Y | | | | | |

# LUCOR INC

www.jiffylube.com

**Industry Group Code:** 811191 **Ranks within this company's industry group:** Sales: 1 Profits:

| Management: | | Sales/Marketing: | | Liberal Arts: | | Information Systems: | | Professionals: | | Technical/Scientific: | |
|---|---|---|---|---|---|---|---|---|---|---|---|
| Mgmt. Trainees: | | Mktg. Professionals: | Y | Gen. Writing/Editing: | | Info. Management: | Y | Finance/Accounting: | Y | Engineers, Elec.: | |
| Experienced Mgmt.: | Y | Retail Sales: | | Technical Writing: | | Software Dev.: | | Law: | Y | Engineers, Other: | |
| Int'l Business: | | Commercial/Industrial: | | Graphic Arts/Photog.: | | Hardware Dev.: | | HR/Other: | Y | Health/Lab: | |
| MBA Graduates: | Y | Sales Trainees: | | Music: | | Systems Integration: | | Training: | Y | Scientists/Research: | |
| | | Advertising Pros.: | | Broadcasting: | | Consulting/Other: | | Health Care: | | Petroleum/Chemicals: | |
| | | | | Other: | | | | Consulting: | | Math/Other: | |

## TYPES OF BUSINESS:

Automotive Oil Change & Lubrication Shops

## BRANDS/DIVISIONS/AFFILIATES:

Jiffy Lube International

## GROWTH PLANS/SPECIAL FEATURES:

Lucor, Inc. is one of largest franchisers of Jiffy Lube International in the United States. Jiffy Lube is known for its fast oil changes, which it provides across North America with more than 2,200 locations. Approximately 88% of Jiffy Lube's centers are franchised. Lucor operates a chain of about 210 of these automotive service shops, with locations in North Carolina, Tennessee, Virginia, Pennsylvania, Kentucky, Ohio, Michigan and Georgia. Lucor's service centers offer basic maintenance services including oil and oil filter changes, chassis lubrication, battery checks, air filter replacement, tire inflation, vacuuming and window washing, as well as preventative maintenance such as emissions inspections. The shops also check lights and wiper blades and replenish fluids, among other services. The private company is partially owned by Lucor's co-founders, the Conway brothers Stephen and Jerry.

## CONTACTS: *Note: Officers with more than one job title may be intentionally listed here more than once.*

Stephen P. Conway, CEO
Jerry B. Conway, COO
Jerry B. Conway, Pres.
Stephen P. Conway, Chmn.

| **Phone:** 919-828-9511 | **Fax:** 919-828-4847 |
|---|---|
| **Toll-Free:** | |
| **Address:** 790 Pershing Rd., Raleigh, NC 27608 US | |

## FINANCIALS: **Sales and profits are in thousands of dollars—add 000 to get the full amount. 2008 Note: Financial information for 2008 was not available for all companies at press time.**

| | | |
|---|---|---|
| 2008 Sales: $ | 2008 Profits: $ | **U.S. Stock Ticker: Private** |
| 2007 Sales: $100,500 | 2007 Profits: $ | **Int'l Ticker:** Int'l Exchange: |
| 2006 Sales: $ | 2006 Profits: $ | Employees: 2,011 |
| 2005 Sales: $ | 2005 Profits: $ | Fiscal Year Ends: 12/31 |
| 2004 Sales: $ | 2004 Profits: $ | Parent Company: |

## SALARIES/BENEFITS:

| | | | | |
|---|---|---|---|---|
| Pension Plan: | ESOP Stock Plan: | Profit Sharing: | Top Exec. Salary: $ | Bonus: $ |
| Savings Plan: | Stock Purch. Plan: | | Second Exec. Salary: $ | Bonus: $ |

## OTHER THOUGHTS:

**Apparent Women Officers or Directors**:
**Hot Spot for Advancement for Women/Minorities**:

## LOCATIONS: ("Y" = Yes)

| West: | Southwest: | Midwest: | Southeast: | Northeast: | International: |
|---|---|---|---|---|---|
| | | Y | Y | Y | |

# LUMINEX CORPORATION

www.luminexcorp.com

**Industry Group Code:** 325413 **Ranks within this company's industry group:** Sales: 9 Profits: 7

| Management: | | Sales/Marketing: | | Liberal Arts: | | Information Systems: | | Professionals: | | Technical/Scientific: | |
|---|---|---|---|---|---|---|---|---|---|---|---|
| Mgmt. Trainees: | | Mktg. Professionals: | Y | Gen. Writing/Editing: | | Info. Management: | Y | Finance/Accounting: | Y | Engineers, Elec.: | Y |
| Experienced Mgmt.: | Y | Retail Sales: | | Technical Writing: | Y | Software Dev.: | Y | Law: | Y | Engineers, Other: | Y |
| Int'l Business: | Y | Commercial/Industrial: | Y | Graphic Arts/Photog.: | | Hardware Dev.: | Y | HR/Other: | Y | Health/Lab: | Y |
| MBA Graduates: | Y | Sales Trainees: | Y | Music: | | Systems Integration: | | Training: | Y | Scientists/Research: | Y |
| | | Advertising Pros.: | | Broadcasting: | | Consulting/Other: | | Health Care: | Y | Petroleum/Chemicals: | |
| | | | | Other: | | | | Consulting: | | Math/Other: | Y |

## TYPES OF BUSINESS:

Medical Diagnostics
Bioassays
Software
xMAP Testing

## BRANDS/DIVISIONS/AFFILIATES:

xMAP
Luminex 100 IS System
Luminex HTS System
Luminex 200 System
xPONENT
MagPlex Magnetic Microspheres
xTAG
Luminex Molecular Diagnostics

## CONTACTS: *Note: Officers with more than one job title may be intentionally listed here more than once.*

Patrick J. Balthrop, CEO
Douglas C. Bryant, COO/Exec. VP
Patrick J. Balthrop, Pres.
Harriss T. Currie, CFO
Darin Leigh, VP-Mktg. & Sales
Steve Back, VP-Mfg.
David S. Reiter, General Counsel/VP/Corp. Sec.
Russell W. Bradley, VP-Bus. Dev. & Strategic Planning
Harriss T. Currie, VP-Finance/Treas.
Andrew D. Ewing, VP-Luminex Tech Oper.
Gregory J. Gosch, VP-Luminex Bioscience Group
Jeremy Bridge-Cook, VP-Luminex Molecular Diagnostics
Oliver H. Meek, VP-Quality Assurance & Regulatory Affairs
G. Walter Loewenbaum, Chmn.

| | |
|---|---|
| **Phone:** 512-219-8020 | **Fax:** 512-219-5195 |
| **Toll-Free:** 888-219-8020 | |
| **Address:** 12212 Technology Blvd., Austin, TX 78727 US | |

## GROWTH PLANS/SPECIAL FEATURES:

Luminex Corporation manufactures and markets biological testing technologies for the life sciences industry. The firm's technologies enable biological tests (bioassays) to detect biochemicals, proteins and genes in samples for the purpose of protein expression profiling, genomic research, genetic disease, immunodiagnostics and biodefense/environmental testing. The company's xMAP system can perform up to 100 bioassays on a single drop of fluid. The xMAP system makes use of microspheres (microscopic polystyrene beads), lasers, digital signal processing and traditional chemistry in order to run various diagnostic tests. The system is an industry-leading technology because of the rapid and precise results it produces from a relatively small sample. Products, xPONENT software and MagPlex magnetic microspheres enhance ease-of-use and automation capabilities in the xMAP technologies: The firm licenses its xMAP technology to various partners in several industries, who then develop marketable products and services for end-users. Partners include companies within the research/drug discovery fields, such as Radix BioSolutions and Cayman Chemical Company, as well as companies within clinical diagnostics fields, such as Inverness Medical and Bayer HealthCare. The firm's xTAG technology, developed by Luminex Molecular Diagnostics, consists of several components including multiplexed PCR or target identification primers, DNA Tags, xMAP microspheres and data analysis software. The technology permits the development of molecular diagnostics assays for clinical use by hospitals and reference laboratories. Products designed for use in the Luminex Systems include the Luminex 100 IS System, an analyzer based on the principles of flow chemistry; Luminex HTS System, a high-throughput screening system which performs thousands of bioassays daily; the Luminex 200 System, used by clinical and research laboratory professionals; and various microspheres.

## FINANCIALS: **Sales and profits are in thousands of dollars—add 000 to get the full amount. 2008 Note: Financial information for 2008 was not available for all companies at press time.**

| | | |
|---|---|---|
| 2008 Sales: $104,447 | 2008 Profits: $3,057 | **U.S. Stock Ticker: LMNX** |
| 2007 Sales: $75,010 | 2007 Profits: $-2,711 | **Int'l Ticker:** Int'l Exchange: |
| 2006 Sales: $52,989 | 2006 Profits: $1,507 | Employees: 344 |
| 2005 Sales: $42,313 | 2005 Profits: $-2,666 | Fiscal Year Ends: 12/31 |
| 2004 Sales: $35,880 | 2004 Profits: $-3,605 | Parent Company: |

## SALARIES/BENEFITS:

| | | | | |
|---|---|---|---|---|
| Pension Plan: | ESOP Stock Plan: | Profit Sharing: | Top Exec. Salary: $408,000 | Bonus: $524,496 |
| Savings Plan: Y | Stock Purch. Plan: | | Second Exec. Salary: $230,930 | Bonus: $210,275 |

## OTHER THOUGHTS:

**Apparent Women Officers or Directors:**
**Hot Spot for Advancement for Women/Minorities:**

## LOCATIONS: ("Y" = Yes)

| West: | Southwest: | Midwest: | Southeast: | Northeast: | International: |
|---|---|---|---|---|---|
| | Y | | | | Y |

# M&F WORLDWIDE CORP

www.mandfworldwide.com

**Industry Group Code:** 311940 **Ranks within this company's industry group:** Sales: 1 Profits: 1

| Management: | | Sales/Marketing: | | Liberal Arts: | | Information Systems: | | Professionals: | | Technical/Scientific: | |
|---|---|---|---|---|---|---|---|---|---|---|---|
| Mgmt. Trainees: | Y | Mktg. Professionals: | Y | Gen. Writing/Editing: | | Info. Management: | Y | Finance/Accounting: | Y | Engineers, Elec.: | |
| Experienced Mgmt.: | Y | Retail Sales: | | Technical Writing: | | Software Dev.: | | Law: | Y | Engineers, Other: | |
| Int'l Business: | Y | Commercial/Industrial: | Y | Graphic Arts/Photog.: | Y | Hardware Dev.: | | HR/Other: | Y | Health/Lab: | |
| MBA Graduates: | Y | Sales Trainees: | Y | Music: | | Systems Integration: | | Training: | Y | Scientists/Research: | |
| | | Advertising Pros.: | Y | Broadcasting: | | Consulting/Other: | | Health Care: | | Petroleum/Chemicals: | |
| | | | | Other: | | | | Consulting: | | Math/Other: | |

## TYPES OF BUSINESS:

Licorice Products
Flavoring Products
Tobacco Flavorings
Plant Products
Technology Products
Check-Related Products & Services
Direct Marketing Services
Testing Services

## BRANDS/DIVISIONS/AFFILIATES:

Mafco Worldwide Corp.
Harland Clarke Corp.
Magnasweet
Right Dress
Harland Financial Solutions
Scantron Corp.
Data Management I LLC

## CONTACTS: *Note: Officers with more than one job title may be intentionally listed here more than once.*

Barry F. Schwartz, CEO
Howard Gittis, Pres.
Paul G. Savas, CFO/Exec. VP
Stephen G. Taub, Pres./CEO-Mafco Worldwide
Charles T. Dawson, CEO/Pres., Harland Clarke Corp.
Jeffrey D. Hegedahl, CEO/Pres., Scantron
John O'Malley, Pres., Harland Financial Solutions
Ronald O. Perelman, Chmn.

**Phone:** 212-572-8600 **Fax:** 212-572-8650
**Toll-Free:**
**Address:** 35 E. 62nd St., New York, NY 10021 US

## GROWTH PLANS/SPECIAL FEATURES:

M&F Worldwide Corp. acts as a holding company operating through four indirect and wholly-owned subsidiaries: Mafco Worldwide; Harland Clarke Corp.; Harland Financial Solutions; and Scantron Corp. Mafco produces a variety of licorice flavors from licorice root at its facilities in New Jersey and Virginia and internationally in France and China. Approximately 67% of Mafco's licorice sales are to the worldwide tobacco industry for use as flavoring and moistening agents in the manufacture of American-blend cigarettes, moist snuff, chewing tobacco and pipe tobacco. The company's prominent brand names include Magnasweet, a flavoring, and Right Dress, a licorice root byproduct gardening mulch. The company sells licorice worldwide to confectioners, food processors, cosmetic companies and pharmaceutical manufacturers for use as flavoring and masking agents used in various brands of chewing gum, lip balm, energy bars, non-carbonated beverages, chewable vitamins, aspirin and other products. Harland Clarke Corp. provides check and check-related products, direct marketing and contact center services to financial and commercial institutions and individual consumers. Harland Financial Solutions delivers technology products and services to the financial services industry, principally targeted at commercial banks, thrifts, credit unions and mortgage companies. Scantron Corp. provides testing and assessment systems and services and data collection and analysis services to educational institutions, businesses and government. In February 2008, M&F acquired Data Management I LLC, a subsidiary of NCS Pearson, for $225 million. Data Management, a designer, manufacturer and servicer of data collection products, became a subsidiary of Scantron following the acquisition.

## FINANCIALS: **Sales and profits are in thousands of dollars—add 000 to get the full amount. 2008 Note: Financial information for 2008 was not available for all companies at press time.**

| | | |
|---|---|---|
| 2008 Sales: $ | 2008 Profits: $ | **U.S. Stock Ticker: MFW** |
| 2007 Sales: $1,472,800 | 2007 Profits: $-4,200 | **Int'l Ticker:** Int'l Exchange: |
| 2006 Sales: $722,000 | 2006 Profits: $36,200 | Employees: 212 |
| 2005 Sales: $121,400 | 2005 Profits: $24,009 | Fiscal Year Ends: 12/31 |
| 2004 Sales: $93,400 | 2004 Profits: $25,200 | Parent Company: |

## SALARIES/BENEFITS:

| | | | | |
|---|---|---|---|---|
| Pension Plan: | ESOP Stock Plan: | Profit Sharing: | Top Exec. Salary: $1,025,000 | Bonus: $1,076,250 |
| Savings Plan: | Stock Purch. Plan: | | Second Exec. Salary: $965,000 | Bonus: $965,000 |

## OTHER THOUGHTS:

**Apparent Women Officers or Directors**: 1
**Hot Spot for Advancement for Women/Minorities**: Y

## LOCATIONS: ("Y" = Yes)

| West: | Southwest: | Midwest: | Southeast: | Northeast: | International: |
|---|---|---|---|---|---|
| | | | | Y | Y |

# MAGELLAN MIDSTREAM PARTNERS LP

www.magellanlp.com

**Industry Group Code:** 422720 **Ranks within this company's industry group:** Sales: 3 Profits: 3

| Management: | | Sales/Marketing: | | Liberal Arts: | | Information Systems: | | Professionals: | | Technical/Scientific: | |
|---|---|---|---|---|---|---|---|---|---|---|---|
| Mgmt. Trainees: | | Mktg. Professionals: | Y | Gen. Writing/Editing: | | Info. Management: | Y | Finance/Accounting: | Y | Engineers, Elec.: | Y |
| Experienced Mgmt.: | Y | Retail Sales: | | Technical Writing: | | Software Dev.: | | Law: | Y | Engineers, Other: | Y |
| Int'l Business: | | Commercial/Industrial: | Y | Graphic Arts/Photog.: | | Hardware Dev.: | | HR/Other: | Y | Health/Lab: | |
| MBA Graduates: | Y | Sales Trainees: | Y | Music: | | Systems Integration: | | Training: | Y | Scientists/Research: | |
| | | Advertising Pros.: | | Broadcasting: | | Consulting/Other: | | Health Care: | | Petroleum/Chemicals: | Y |
| | | | | Other: | | | | Consulting: | | Math/Other: | |

## TYPES OF BUSINESS:

Pipelines-Petroleum Storage & Distribution Services
Petroleum Pipelines
Petroleum Products Terminal Facilities
Ammonia Pipelines

## BRANDS/DIVISIONS/AFFILIATES:

Madison Dearborn Partners
Carlyle/Riverstone Holdings

## CONTACTS: *Note: Officers with more than one job title may be intentionally listed here more than once.*

Don R. Wellendorf, CEO
Michael Mears, COO
Don R. Wellendorf, Pres.
John D. Chandler, CFO/Sr. VP
Lisa J. Korner, Sr. VP-Human Resources
Richard A. Olson, Sr. VP-Tech. Svcs.
Lisa J. Korner, Sr. VP-Admin.
Lonny E. Townsend, General Counsel/Sr. VP/Compliance & Ethics Officer
Richard A. Olson, Sr. VP-Oper.
Brett C. Riley, Sr. VP-Bus. Dev.
John D. Chandler, Treas.
Michael N. Mears, Sr. VP-Transportation & Terminals
Susan H. Costin, Sec.
Don R. Wellendorf, Chmn.

**Phone:** 918-574-7000 **Fax:** 918-573-6714
**Toll-Free:** 800-574-6671
**Address:** 1 Williams Ctr., Tulsa, OK 74172 US

## GROWTH PLANS/SPECIAL FEATURES:

Magellan Midstream Partners, LP is principally engaged in the transportation, storage and distribution of refined petroleum products, with interests in pipelines and terminal facilities. The majority of the company is owned by Madison Dearborn Partners, LLC and by a subsidiary of the Carlyle Group. Magellan owns and operates an extends 8,500 miles and covers a 13-state area, extending from the Gulf Coast refining region of Texas through the Midwest to Colorado, North Dakota, Minnesota, Wisconsin and Illinois. Its pipeline system transports petroleum products and LPGs and includes 47 terminals. The products transported on its pipeline system are largely transportation fuels, and in 2007 were comprised of 52% gasoline, 39% distillates (which include diesel fuels and heating oil) and 9% aviation fuel and LPGs. The firm's petroleum products pipeline system segment accounted for 88% of consolidated total revenues in 2007. The firm has 7 petroleum products marine terminal facilities located along the United States Gulf and East Coasts, and 27 petroleum products inland terminals located principally in the southeastern United States. The company's ammonia pipeline system provides ammonia, which is used as a nitrogen fertilizer, for ultimate distribution to end users in Iowa, Kansas, Minnesota, Missouri, Nebraska, Oklahoma and South Dakota. The system extends roughly 1,100 miles from production facilities in Texas and Oklahoma to various points in the Midwest. Magellan's customers include retailers of gasoline and other petroleum products, wholesalers that sell to retailers and large commercial and industrial end users, exchange transaction customers and traders. In May 2008, Magellan announced plans to construct an 80-mile petroleum products pipeline to connect to the Port Arthur region.

## FINANCIALS: **Sales and profits are in thousands of dollars—add 000 to get the full amount. 2008 Note: Financial information for 2008 was not available for all companies at press time.**

| | | |
|---|---|---|
| 2008 Sales: $ | 2008 Profits: $ | **U.S. Stock Ticker: MMP** |
| 2007 Sales: $1,318,121 | 2007 Profits: $242,790 | **Int'l Ticker:** Int'l Exchange: |
| 2006 Sales: $1,223,560 | 2006 Profits: $192,728 | Employees: 1,127 |
| 2005 Sales: $1,137,072 | 2005 Profits: $159,483 | Fiscal Year Ends: 12/31 |
| 2004 Sales: $695,374 | 2004 Profits: $110,203 | Parent Company: |

## SALARIES/BENEFITS:

| | | | | |
|---|---|---|---|---|
| Pension Plan: | ESOP Stock Plan: | Profit Sharing: | Top Exec. Salary: $397,115 | Bonus: $476,539 |
| Savings Plan: Y | Stock Purch. Plan: | | Second Exec. Salary: $245,384 | Bonus: $184,038 |

## OTHER THOUGHTS:

**Apparent Women Officers or Directors**: 1
**Hot Spot for Advancement for Women/Minorities**:

## LOCATIONS: ("Y" = Yes)

| West: | Southwest: | Midwest: | Southeast: | Northeast: | International: |
|---|---|---|---|---|---|
| Y | Y | Y | Y | Y | |

# MALT-O-MEAL COMPANY

www.malt-o-meal.com

**Industry Group Code:** 311230 **Ranks within this company's industry group:** Sales: 1 Profits:

| Management: | | Sales/Marketing: | | Liberal Arts: | | Information Systems: | | Professionals: | | Technical/Scientific: | |
|---|---|---|---|---|---|---|---|---|---|---|---|
| Mgmt. Trainees: | | Mktg. Professionals: | Y | Gen. Writing/Editing: | | Info. Management: | Y | Finance/Accounting: | Y | Engineers, Elec.: | |
| Experienced Mgmt.: | Y | Retail Sales: | | Technical Writing: | | Software Dev.: | | Law: | Y | Engineers, Other: | |
| Int'l Business: | | Commercial/Industrial: | Y | Graphic Arts/Photog.: | | Hardware Dev.: | | HR/Other: | Y | Health/Lab: | |
| MBA Graduates: | Y | Sales Trainees: | Y | Music: | | Systems Integration: | | Training: | Y | Scientists/Research: | |
| | | Advertising Pros.: | Y | Broadcasting: | | Consulting/Other: | | Health Care: | | Petroleum/Chemicals: | |
| | | | | Other: | | | | Consulting: | | Math/Other: | |

## TYPES OF BUSINESS:

Breakfast Cereal Manufacturing
Hot Wheat Cereals
Instant Oatmeal

## BRANDS/DIVISIONS/AFFILIATES:

Tootie Fruities
Froot Loops
Kellogg Co
Coco Roos
Raisin Bran
Cinnamon Toasters
100 Calorie Cereal Snack'ers
Strawberry Cream Mini Spooners

## CONTACTS: *Note: Officers with more than one job title may be intentionally listed here more than once.*

John Lettmann, CEO
Chris Neugent, Pres.
John A. Gappa, CFO
John Lettmann, Chmn.

**Phone:** 612-338-8551 **Fax:** 612-339-5710
**Toll-Free:** 800-743-3029
**Address:** 80 S. 8th St., Ste. 2700, Minneapolis, MN 55402 US

## GROWTH PLANS/SPECIAL FEATURES:

Malt-O-Meal Company, founded in 1919, manufactures a line of hot and cold breakfast cereals sold nationwide. Malt-O-Meal currently operates three production facilities and three distribution centers in the U.S. The company's original business was a cream of wheat cereal, but it has expanded to produce a line of approximately 22 bagged and boxed cereals that imitate popular box brands. These cereals use similar naming and color schemes but less advertising and packaging than their counterparts. For example, Malt-O-Meal's Tootie Fruities are similar to Fruit Loops, a more recognized Kellogg's brand. Other Malt-O-Meal cold cereal offerings include Coco Roos, Raisin Bran, Frosted Flakes, Golden Puffs, Puffed Wheat, Puffed Rice and Cinnamon Toasters. Malt-O-Meal offers hot wheat cereal in original, chocolate and maple and brown sugar flavors. The company's website includes nutritional and product information in both English and Spanish. Additionally, the site offers links to several blogs including the recipe blog, the news blog and the M-O-M blog.

Employees are of the firm are offered a 401(k) plan; retirement plans; bonus programs; health care programs; flexible spending accounts; 100% tuition payment including books; life insurance; career development and advancement; and an employee assistance program. Additionally, the firm encourages employees to contribute their time and talents to various philanthropic organizations.

## FINANCIALS: **Sales and profits are in thousands of dollars—add 000 to get the full amount. 2008 Note: Financial information for 2008 was not available for all companies at press time.**

| | | |
|---|---|---|
| 2008 Sales: $ | 2008 Profits: $ | **U.S. Stock Ticker: Private** |
| 2007 Sales: $490,000 | 2007 Profits: $ | **Int'l Ticker:** Int'l Exchange: |
| 2006 Sales: $ | 2006 Profits: $ | Employees: 1,100 |
| 2005 Sales: $ | 2005 Profits: $ | Fiscal Year Ends: 12/31 |
| 2004 Sales: $ | 2004 Profits: $ | Parent Company: |

## SALARIES/BENEFITS:

| | | | | |
|---|---|---|---|---|
| Pension Plan: | ESOP Stock Plan: | Profit Sharing: | Top Exec. Salary: $ | Bonus: $ |
| Savings Plan: | Stock Purch. Plan: | | Second Exec. Salary: $ | Bonus: $ |

## OTHER THOUGHTS:

**Apparent Women Officers or Directors:**
**Hot Spot for Advancement for Women/Minorities:**

## LOCATIONS: ("Y" = Yes)

| West: | Southwest: | Midwest: | Southeast: | Northeast: | International: |
|---|---|---|---|---|---|
| Y | Y | Y | Y | Y | |

# MANHATTAN ASSOCIATES INC

**www.manh.com**

**Industry Group Code:** 511217 **Ranks within this company's industry group:** Sales: 2 Profits: 2

| **Management:** | | **Sales/Marketing:** | | **Liberal Arts:** | | **Information Systems:** | | **Professionals:** | | **Technical/Scientific:** | |
|---|---|---|---|---|---|---|---|---|---|---|---|
| Mgmt. Trainees: | | Mktg. Professionals: | Y | Gen. Writing/Editing: | | Info. Management: | Y | Finance/Accounting: | Y | Engineers, Elec.: | Y |
| Experienced Mgmt.: | Y | Retail Sales: | | Technical Writing: | Y | Software Dev.: | Y | Law: | Y | Engineers, Other: | |
| Int'l Business: | Y | Commercial/Industrial: | Y | Graphic Arts/Photog.: | | Hardware Dev.: | | HR/Other: | Y | Health/Lab: | |
| MBA Graduates: | Y | Sales Trainees: | Y | Music: | | Systems Integration: | | Training: | Y | Scientists/Research: | |
| | | Advertising Pros.: | | Broadcasting: | | Consulting/Other: | | Health Care: | | Petroleum/Chemicals: | |
| | | | | Other: | | | | Consulting: | | Math/Other: | Y |

## TYPES OF BUSINESS:

Software-Supply Chain
Consulting & Support
RFID System Integration

## BRANDS/DIVISIONS/AFFILIATES:

PRISM
Manhattan Associates Europe B.V.
Manhattan Associates France SARL
Manhattan Associates GmbH
Manhattan Associates KK
Manhattan Associates Software (Shanghai), Co. Ltd.
Manhattan Associates (India) Development Centre
Manhattan Associates Pty Ltd.

## CONTACTS: *Note: Officers with more than one job title may be intentionally listed here more than once.*

Peter Sinisgalli, CEO
Peter Sinisgalli, Pres.
Dennis Story, CFO/Sr. VP
Terrie O'Hanlon, Chief Mktg. Officer/Sr. VP
Terry Geraghty, Sr. VP-Global Human Resources
Pervinder Johar, CTO/Sr. VP
David Dabbiere, Chief Legal Officer/Sr. VP
Jeff Cashman, Sr. VP-Bus. Dev.
Eddie Capel, Sr. VP-Product Mgmt. & Customer Support
Steve Smith, Sr. VP-EMEA
John J. Huntz, Jr., Chmn.
Jeff Baum, Sr. VP-Int'l

**Phone:** 770-955-7070 **Fax:** 770-955-0302
**Toll-Free:**
**Address:** 2300 Windy Ridge Pkwy., 10th Fl., Atlanta, GA 30339 US

## GROWTH PLANS/SPECIAL FEATURES:

Manhattan Associates, Inc. develops and provides technology-based supply chain software solutions. Its solutions consist of software, services and hardware and are used for both the planning and execution of supply chain activities. All of the company's solutions also include services such as design, configuration, implementation, product assessment and training, as well as customer support and software enhancement subscriptions. The firm specializes in demand forecasting and inventory replenishment; warehouse and labor management; performance analysis and event planning. Manhattan Associates' software includes PRISM (Proven Rapid Implementation Structured Methodology), designed to reduce implementation time and risk. Through several vendor partnerships, the company offers many hardware systems including bar code scanners, data collection terminals and document printers. The Educational Services Organization provides clients with a team of consultants who offer training programs concerning the use of the firm's equipment, as well as 24-hour customer support and software enhancement subscriptions. The firm serves various industries including consumer goods, food, government, high-tech/electronics, industrial/wholesale, life science, logistics service providers and retail. Manhattan Associates' partners include IBM, HP, Printronix, LXE, Ascential and Microsoft.

Employees are offered health, dental and vision insurance; life insurance; short-and long-term disability coverage; a 401(k) plan; and educational assistance.

## FINANCIALS: **Sales and profits are in thousands of dollars—add 000 to get the full amount. 2008 Note: Financial information for 2008 was not available for all companies at press time.**

| | | |
|---|---|---|
| 2008 Sales: $ | 2008 Profits: $ | **U.S. Stock Ticker: MANH** |
| 2007 Sales: $337,401 | 2007 Profits: $30,751 | **Int'l Ticker:** Int'l Exchange: |
| 2006 Sales: $288,868 | 2006 Profits: $19,331 | Employees: 2,241 |
| 2005 Sales: $246,404 | 2005 Profits: $18,637 | Fiscal Year Ends: 12/31 |
| 2004 Sales: $214,919 | 2004 Profits: $21,633 | Parent Company: |

## SALARIES/BENEFITS:

| | | | | |
|---|---|---|---|---|
| Pension Plan: | ESOP Stock Plan: | Profit Sharing: | Top Exec. Salary: $440,000 | Bonus: $447,263 |
| Savings Plan: Y | Stock Purch. Plan: | | Second Exec. Salary: $325,000 | Bonus: $436,800 |

## OTHER THOUGHTS:

**Apparent Women Officers or Directors**: 1
**Hot Spot for Advancement for Women/Minorities**: Y

## LOCATIONS: ("Y" = Yes)

| West: | Southwest: | Midwest: | Southeast: | Northeast: | International: |
|---|---|---|---|---|---|
| Y | | Y | Y | Y | Y |

# MARCHEX INC

www.marchex.com

**Industry Group Code:** 514199B **Ranks within this company's industry group:** Sales: 1 Profits: 1

| Management: | | Sales/Marketing: | | Liberal Arts: | | Information Systems: | | Professionals: | | Technical/Scientific: | |
|---|---|---|---|---|---|---|---|---|---|---|---|
| Mgmt. Trainees: | | Mktg. Professionals: | Y | Gen. Writing/Editing: | Y | Info. Management: | Y | Finance/Accounting: | Y | Engineers, Elec.: | |
| Experienced Mgmt.: | Y | Retail Sales: | | Technical Writing: | | Software Dev.: | Y | Law: | Y | Engineers, Other: | |
| Int'l Business: | | Commercial/Industrial: | Y | Graphic Arts/Photog.: | Y | Hardware Dev.: | | HR/Other: | Y | Health/Lab: | |
| MBA Graduates: | Y | Sales Trainees: | Y | Music: | | Systems Integration: | | Training: | Y | Scientists/Research: | |
| | | Advertising Pros.: | Y | Broadcasting: | | Consulting/Other: | | Health Care: | | Petroleum/Chemicals: | |
| | | | | Other: | | | | Consulting: | | Math/Other: | |

## TYPES OF BUSINESS:

Online Marketing
Search Engine Marketing

## BRANDS/DIVISIONS/AFFILIATES:

Yellow.com
OpenList.com
ChicagoDoctors.com
BostonMortgage.com
Marchex Connect 2.0

## CONTACTS: *Note: Officers with more than one job title may be intentionally listed here more than once.*

Russell C. Horowitz, CEO
John Keister, COO
John Keister, Pres.
Michael Arends, CFO
Ethan Caldwell, Chief Admin. Officer
Ethan Caldwell, General Counsel
Peter Christothoulou, Chief Strategy Officer
Russell C. Horowitz, Chmn.

| **Phone:** 206-331-3300 | **Fax:** 206-331-3695 |
|---|---|
| **Toll-Free:** | |
| **Address:** 413 Pine St., Ste. 500, Seattle, WA 98101 US | |

## GROWTH PLANS/SPECIAL FEATURES:

Marchex, Inc. is an online advertising company and publisher of local content, with over 200,000 web sites in its portfolio. Specifically, it focuses on search marketing, local search and direct navigation. The company's merchant advertiser technology services include local content network, feed management, bid management and pay-per-clicking targeting. The company's local content network includes web sites focused on helping users find and make informed decisions about where to get local products and services. It features listings from more than 15 million local businesses in the U.S. and more than 1.3 million expert and user-generated reviews on local businesses. Examples of web sites in the network include Yellow.com, OpenList.com, chicagodoctors.com and bostonmortgage.com. The feed management services crawl and extract relevant product content from merchant advertisers' databases and web sites to create product and service listings. The bid management services enable merchant advertisers to track, monitor and optimize the placement of search advertising campaigns across a number of search engines. Marchex delivers pay-per-clicking advertising listings that are reflective of the advertisers' products and services to online users in response to their keyword search queries and to their typing of specific web sites into their browser. The firm also offers search engine optimization consulting services, to help advertisers optimize their web sites for algorithmic search engine results. Through its services, the company distributes advertisements from tens of thousands of advertisers through hundreds of traffic sources, including search and shopping engines, directories and web sites. Syndication distribution partners include Ask.com; Google; Yahoo!; MSN Shopping; Shopping.com; BusinessWeek.com; The Motley Fool; and USA Today. In July 2008, the firm launched Marchex Connect 2.0, an updated version of its local advertising platform.

The company offers its employees medical, dental and vision insurance; life and disability insurance; an employee stock purchase plan; a 401(k) plan and an employee assistance program.

## FINANCIALS: **Sales and profits are in thousands of dollars—add 000 to get the full amount. 2008 Note: Financial information for 2008 was not available for all companies at press time.**

| | | |
|---|---|---|
| 2008 Sales: $ | 2008 Profits: $ | **U.S. Stock Ticker: MCHX** |
| 2007 Sales: $139,391 | 2007 Profits: $-1,505 | **Int'l Ticker:** Int'l Exchange: |
| 2006 Sales: $127,759 | 2006 Profits: $- 444 | Employees: 314 |
| 2005 Sales: $94,995 | 2005 Profits: $3,907 | Fiscal Year Ends: 12/31 |
| 2004 Sales: $43,804 | 2004 Profits: $- 733 | Parent Company: |

## SALARIES/BENEFITS:

| | | | | |
|---|---|---|---|---|
| Pension Plan: | ESOP Stock Plan: | Profit Sharing: | Top Exec. Salary: $255,000 | Bonus: $ |
| Savings Plan: Y | Stock Purch. Plan: | | Second Exec. Salary: $200,000 | Bonus: $ |

## OTHER THOUGHTS:

**Apparent Women Officers or Directors**: 1
**Hot Spot for Advancement for Women/Minorities**:

## LOCATIONS: ("Y" = Yes)

| West: | Southwest: | Midwest: | Southeast: | Northeast: | International: |
|---|---|---|---|---|---|
| Y | | | | Y | |

# MARTEK BIOSCIENCES CORP

**www.martekbio.com**

**Industry Group Code:** 325411 **Ranks within this company's industry group:** Sales: 2 Profits: 2

| **Management:** | | **Sales/Marketing:** | | **Liberal Arts:** | | **Information Systems:** | | **Professionals:** | | **Technical/Scientific:** | |
|---|---|---|---|---|---|---|---|---|---|---|---|
| Mgmt. Trainees: | | Mktg. Professionals: | Y | Gen. Writing/Editing: | | Info. Management: | Y | Finance/Accounting: | Y | Engineers, Elec.: | |
| Experienced Mgmt.: | Y | Retail Sales: | | Technical Writing: | Y | Software Dev.: | | Law: | Y | Engineers, Other: | |
| Int'l Business: | Y | Commercial/Industrial: | Y | Graphic Arts/Photog.: | | Hardware Dev.: | | HR/Other: | Y | Health/Lab: | Y |
| MBA Graduates: | Y | Sales Trainees: | Y | Music: | | Systems Integration: | | Training: | Y | Scientists/Research: | Y |
| | | Advertising Pros.: | | Broadcasting: | | Consulting/Other: | | Health Care: | Y | Petroleum/Chemicals: | Y |
| | | | | Other: | | | | Consulting: | | Math/Other: | Y |

## TYPES OF BUSINESS:

Microalgae-Based Product Manufacturing
Drugs-Nutritional Oils
Dietary Supplements
Contract Manufacturing

## BRANDS/DIVISIONS/AFFILIATES:

Martek Biosciences Kingtree
ARASCO
DHASCO
life'sDHA
life'sARA
Columbia Biosciences Corporation

## CONTACTS: *Note: Officers with more than one job title may be intentionally listed here more than once.*

Steve Dubin, CEO
Peter A. Nitze, COO/Exec. VP
David Abramson, Pres.
Peter L. Buzy, CFO
Barney Easterling, Sr. VP-Mfg.
Peter L. Buzy, Exec. VP-Admin.
David M. Feitel, General Counsel/Sr. VP/Corp. Sec.
Peter L. Buzy, Exec. VP-Finance/Treas.
Tim Fealey, Sr. VP/Chief Innovation Officer
Robert Flanagan, Chmn.

| **Phone:** 410-740-0081 | **Fax:** 410-740-2985 |
|---|---|
| **Toll-Free:** | |
| **Address:** 6480 Dobbin Rd., Columbia, MD 21045 US | |

## GROWTH PLANS/SPECIAL FEATURES:

Martek Biosciences commercially develops products that promote health and wellness through its portfolio of nutritional supplements and advanced diagnostic aids. The company's nutritional products group currently manufactures and sells two patented nutritional fatty acids, DHA (docosahexaenoic acid), under the DHASCO and life'sDHA brand names, and ARA (arachidonic acid), under the ARASCO and life'sARA brand names. life'sDHA is a vegetarian source of omega-3 fatty acids and is used in infant formula, perinatal products, foods and beverages and dietary supplements, while life'sARA is an omega-6 fatty acid that is primarily used in infant formula. These fatty acids assist in the development of the optic and central nervous systems in newborns and also promote adult mental, optical and cardiovascular health, which lowers the risk of developing cardiovascular disease, Alzheimer's disease and dementia. Martek is additionally investigating the potential benefits of DHA in breast cancer, cystic fibrosis and other visual and neurological disorders, as well as its usefulness as a supplement for nursing and pregnant women. The company's licensees and clients for DHA and ARA include Abbott Laboratories under the Similac ADVANCE brand; Mead Johnson Nutritionals, under the Enfamil LIPIL brand; PBM Products, Inc., under the Bright Beginnings brand; Nestle under the Good Start Supreme brand; and Wyeth Nutritionals, which produces enhanced infant formula for Wal-Mart under the private label Parent's Choice. In addition to nutritional products, Martek provides contract manufacturing services, which customize production processes for the synthesis of enzymes, specialty chemicals, vitamins and agricultural specialty products. Martek recently introduced four new products from Spectrum Organics, including Spectrum Prenatal DHA for Pregnant and Nursing Mothers; Spectrum Toddler DHA; Spectrum Chewable Children's DHA; and Spectrum Vegetarian DHA. In June 2007, the company sold its fluorescent detection products business to Columbia Biosciences Corporation.

## FINANCIALS: **Sales and profits are in thousands of dollars—add 000 to get the full amount. 2008 Note: Financial information for 2008 was not available for all companies at press time.**

| | | |
|---|---|---|
| 2008 Sales: $ | 2008 Profits: $ | **U.S. Stock Ticker: MATK** |
| 2007 Sales: $306,813 | 2007 Profits: $32,013 | **Int'l Ticker:** Int'l Exchange: |
| 2006 Sales: $270,654 | 2006 Profits: $14,938 | Employees: 515 |
| 2005 Sales: $217,852 | 2005 Profits: $15,284 | Fiscal Year Ends: 10/31 |
| 2004 Sales: $184,493 | 2004 Profits: $47,048 | Parent Company: |

## SALARIES/BENEFITS:

| | | | | |
|---|---|---|---|---|
| Pension Plan: | ESOP Stock Plan: | Profit Sharing: | Top Exec. Salary: $550,000 | Bonus: $137,500 |
| Savings Plan: Y | Stock Purch. Plan: | | Second Exec. Salary: $426,000 | Bonus: $106,500 |

## OTHER THOUGHTS:

**Apparent Women Officers or Directors:**
**Hot Spot for Advancement for Women/Minorities:**

## LOCATIONS: ("Y" = Yes)

| West: | Southwest: | Midwest: | Southeast: | Northeast: | International: |
|---|---|---|---|---|---|
| Y | | Y | | Y | |

# MARTHA STEWART LIVING OMNIMEDIA INC www.marthastewart.com

**Industry Group Code:** 511120 **Ranks within this company's industry group:** Sales: 1 Profits: 1

| **Management:** | | **Sales/Marketing:** | | **Liberal Arts:** | | **Information Systems:** | | **Professionals:** | | **Technical/Scientific:** | |
|---|---|---|---|---|---|---|---|---|---|---|---|
| Mgmt. Trainees: | | Mktg. Professionals: | Y | Gen. Writing/Editing: | | Info. Management: | Y | Finance/Accounting: | Y | Engineers, Elec.: | |
| Experienced Mgmt.: | Y | Retail Sales: | | Technical Writing: | | Software Dev.: | | Law: | Y | Engineers, Other: | |
| Int'l Business: | | Commercial/Industrial: | | Graphic Arts/Photog.: | | Hardware Dev.: | | HR/Other: | Y | Health/Lab: | |
| MBA Graduates: | Y | Sales Trainees: | | Music: | | Systems Integration: | | Training: | Y | Scientists/Research: | |
| | | Advertising Pros.: | Y | Broadcasting: | | Consulting/Other: | | Health Care: | | Petroleum/Chemicals: | |
| | | | | Other: | | | | Consulting: | | Math/Other: | |

## TYPES OF BUSINESS:

Magazine Publishing
Television & Video Production
Book Publishing
Home & Garden Products
Web Sites
Satellite Radio
Merchandising

## BRANDS/DIVISIONS/AFFILIATES:

Martha Stewart Living
Martha Stewart Weddings
Blueprint
Everyday Food
Martha Stewart Living Radio
Martha Stewart Crafts
Emeril Lagasse

## CONTACTS: *Note: Officers with more than one job title may be intentionally listed here more than once.*

Wenda Harris Millard, Co-CEO
Allison Jacques, Interim CFO
Robin Marino, Pres., Merch.
Allison Jacques, Controller
Robin Marino, Co-CEO
Gael Towey, Chief Creative Officer
Wenda Harris Millard, Pres., Media
Charles Koppelman, Chmn.

| **Phone:** 212-827-8000 | **Fax:** 212-827-8204 |
|---|---|
| **Toll-Free:** | |
| **Address:** 11 West 42nd St., New York, NY 10036 US | |

## GROWTH PLANS/SPECIAL FEATURES:

Martha Stewart Living Omnimedia, Inc. (MSL) is an integrated content and commerce company that creates how-to content and merchandise for homemakers and other consumers. The company is comprised of four business segments: publishing, broadcasting, merchandising and Internet. This combination of segments enables the company to cross-promote its content and products, which generally span eight core areas: home, cooking and entertaining, gardening, crafts, holidays, organizing, weddings, and whole living, which focuses on healthy living and sustainable practices. The publishing segment, accounting for 56% of 2007 revenues, currently publishes five magazines (Martha Stewart Living, Everyday Food, Martha Stewart Weddings, Body + Soul and Blueprint) and various special-interest books. In 2007, MSL secured a book deal with Clarkson-Potter Publishing to publish an additional 10 books over five years. The broadcasting segment, accounting for 12% of 2007 revenues, develops television programming, including Everyday Food, The Martha Stewart Show and Martha Stewart Crafts. The company widened its television presence in 2007 by acquiring two cable television licensing deals with The Fine Living TV Network and DIY Network to air syndicated content and segments of past shows. The company also produces a satellite radio channel, Martha Stewart Living Radio, on SIRIUS Satellite radio. Merchandise, contributing 26% of 2007 revenues, is distributed under several labels, including Martha Stewart Everyday (the firm's mass-market brand label) and Martha Stewart Collection, sold exclusively through Macy's. MSL's Internet segment, representing 6% of 2007 revenues, includes MarthaStewart.com and MarthasFlowers.com. In February 2008, the firm purchased the rights to the Emeril Lagasse franchise of cookbooks, TV shows and kitchen products for $50 million. In the spring of 2008, MSL and 1-800-FLOWERS.COM launched a co-branded floral and gift basket program. In July 2008, the company announced the expansion of its Martha Stewart Crafts line into the majority of Wal-Mart stores across the U.S. and Canada.

## FINANCIALS: **Sales and profits are in thousands of dollars—add 000 to get the full amount. 2008 Note: Financial information for 2008 was not available for all companies at press time.**

| | | |
|---|---|---|
| 2008 Sales: $ | 2008 Profits: $ | **U.S. Stock Ticker: MSO** |
| 2007 Sales: $327,890 | 2007 Profits: $10,289 | **Int'l Ticker:** Int'l Exchange: |
| 2006 Sales: $288,341 | 2006 Profits: $-16,995 | Employees: 760 |
| 2005 Sales: $212,433 | 2005 Profits: $-75,789 | Fiscal Year Ends: 12/31 |
| 2004 Sales: $187,438 | 2004 Profits: $-59,600 | Parent Company: |

## SALARIES/BENEFITS:

| | | | | |
|---|---|---|---|---|
| Pension Plan: | ESOP Stock Plan: | Profit Sharing: | Top Exec. Salary: $900,000 | Bonus: $873,000 |
| Savings Plan: | Stock Purch. Plan: | | Second Exec. Salary: $900,000 | Bonus: $ |

## OTHER THOUGHTS:

**Apparent Women Officers or Directors**: 4
**Hot Spot for Advancement for Women/Minorities**: Y

## LOCATIONS: ("Y" = Yes)

| West: | Southwest: | Midwest: | Southeast: | Northeast: | International: |
|---|---|---|---|---|---|
| | | | | Y | |

# MARVEL ENTERTAINMENT INC

**www.marvel.com**

**Industry Group Code:** 511130 **Ranks within this company's industry group:** Sales: 1 Profits: 1

| Management: | | Sales/Marketing: | | Liberal Arts: | | Information Systems: | | Professionals: | | Technical/Scientific: | |
|---|---|---|---|---|---|---|---|---|---|---|---|
| Mgmt. Trainees: | | Mktg. Professionals: | | Gen. Writing/Editing: | | Info. Management: | Y | Finance/Accounting: | Y | Engineers, Elec.: | |
| Experienced Mgmt.: | Y | Retail Sales: | | Technical Writing: | | Software Dev.: | | Law: | Y | Engineers, Other: | |
| Int'l Business: | Y | Commercial/Industrial: | | Graphic Arts/Photog.: | | Hardware Dev.: | | HR/Other: | Y | Health/Lab: | |
| MBA Graduates: | Y | Sales Trainees: | | Music: | | Systems Integration: | | Training: | Y | Scientists/Research: | |
| | | Advertising Pros.: | | Broadcasting: | | Consulting/Other: | | Health Care: | | Petroleum/Chemicals: | |
| | | | | Other: | | | | Consulting: | | Math/Other: | |

## TYPES OF BUSINESS:

Comic Book Publishing
Toys
Licensing & Merchandising
Movie Production
Online Services

## BRANDS/DIVISIONS/AFFILIATES:

Hasbro
Marvel Comics
Marvel Digital Comics Unlimited
X-Men
Incredible Hulk
Fantastic Four
Daredevil
Ghost Rider

## CONTACTS: *Note: Officers with more than one job title may be intentionally listed here more than once.*

Isaac Perlmutter, CEO/Vice Chmn.
Kenneth P. West, CFO/Exec. VP
Simon Philips, Pres., World Wide Consumer Prod.
John Turitzin, General Counsel/Exec. VP
Ira Rubenstein, Exec. VP-Global Digital Media Group
Simon Philips, CEO-Marvel Animation
Alan Fine, Chief Mktg. Officer-Marvel Characters, Inc.
Alan Fine, CEO-Publishing Div.
Morton E. Handel, Chmn.

| | |
|---|---|
| **Phone:** 212-576-4000 | **Fax:** |
| **Toll-Free:** | |
| **Address:** 417 Fifth Ave., 11th Fl., New York, NY 10016 US | |

## GROWTH PLANS/SPECIAL FEATURES:

Marvel Entertainment, Inc. and its subsidiaries constitute one of the world's most prominent character-based entertainment companies, with a proprietary library of over 5,000 characters, including Spider-Man, Iron Man, The Incredible Hulk, Captain America, Thor, Ghost Rider, The Fantastic Four, X-Men, Blade, Daredevil, The Punisher, Namor the Submariner, Nick Fury, The Avengers, Silver Surfer and Ant-Man. The company's business is divided into four divisions: licensing, publishing, toys and film production. The licensing division licenses the company's characters for use in a wide variety of products and media, including toys, electronic games, apparel, accessories and collectibles. This division also receives fees from the sale of licenses to a variety of media, including feature films, television and video games. The publishing segment creates and publishes comic books and trade paperbacks principally in North America. Comic books are distributed through three channels: comic book specialty stores, traditional retail outlets and subscription sales. The toy segment designs, develops, markets and distributes a limited line of toys worldwide. Toys are currently produced and sold exclusively by Hasbro, according to an agreement that began at the beginning of 2007 and will remain active until the end of 2011. The film production segment develops, produces and distributes films, which are financed by a company-owned $525 million film facility. The first two films produced by the film production segment, Iron Man and The Incredible Hulk, were released in 2008. In November 2007, the firm introduced Marvel Digital Comics Unlimited, an online subscription service that allows access to thousands of comic book titles from Marvel's historic comic book archive. In early 2008, the company launched a new website, marvelkids.com, featuring Marvel characters and content for children ages 6-11.

## FINANCIALS: **Sales and profits are in thousands of dollars—add 000 to get the full amount. 2008 Note: Financial information for 2008 was not available for all companies at press time.**

| | | |
|---|---|---|
| 2008 Sales: $ | 2008 Profits: $ | **U.S. Stock Ticker: MVL** |
| 2007 Sales: $485,807 | 2007 Profits: $139,823 | **Int'l Ticker:** Int'l Exchange: |
| 2006 Sales: $351,798 | 2006 Profits: $58,704 | Employees: 250 |
| 2005 Sales: $390,507 | 2005 Profits: $102,819 | Fiscal Year Ends: 12/31 |
| 2004 Sales: $513,468 | 2004 Profits: $124,877 | Parent Company: |

## SALARIES/BENEFITS:

| | | | | |
|---|---|---|---|---|
| Pension Plan: | ESOP Stock Plan: | Profit Sharing: | Top Exec. Salary: $713,200 | Bonus: $2,850,000 |
| Savings Plan: | Stock Purch. Plan: | | Second Exec. Salary: $700,000 | Bonus: $ |

## OTHER THOUGHTS:

**Apparent Women Officers or Directors:**
**Hot Spot for Advancement for Women/Minorities:**

## LOCATIONS: ("Y" = Yes)

| West: | Southwest: | Midwest: | Southeast: | Northeast: | International: |
|---|---|---|---|---|---|
| Y | | | | Y | Y |

# MATRIA HEALTHCARE INC

www.matria.com

**Industry Group Code:** 524298 **Ranks within this company's industry group:** Sales: 1 Profits: 1

| Management: | | Sales/Marketing: | | Liberal Arts: | | Information Systems: | | Professionals: | | Technical/Scientific: | |
|---|---|---|---|---|---|---|---|---|---|---|---|
| Mgmt. Trainees: | | Mktg. Professionals: | Y | Gen. Writing/Editing: | | Info. Management: | Y | Finance/Accounting: | Y | Engineers, Elec.: | |
| Experienced Mgmt.: | Y | Retail Sales: | | Technical Writing: | | Software Dev.: | | Law: | Y | Engineers, Other: | |
| Int'l Business: | Y | Commercial/Industrial: | Y | Graphic Arts/Photog.: | | Hardware Dev.: | | HR/Other: | Y | Health/Lab: | Y |
| MBA Graduates: | Y | Sales Trainees: | Y | Music: | | Systems Integration: | | Training: | Y | Scientists/Research: | |
| | | Advertising Pros.: | | Broadcasting: | | Consulting/Other: | | Health Care: | Y | Petroleum/Chemicals: | |
| | | | | Other: | | | | Consulting: | | Math/Other: | |

## TYPES OF BUSINESS:

Disease Management Services
Home Health Care-Obstetrical
Blood Sampling & Testing Devices
High-Risk Maternity Care
Women & Children's Health
Medical Diagnostics

## BRANDS/DIVISIONS/AFFILIATES:

Inverness Medical Innovations, Inc.
Health Enhancement
Miavita, LLC
WinningHabits, Inc.
CorSolutions Medical, Inc.
Quality Oncology, Inc.

## CONTACTS: *Note: Officers with more than one job title may be intentionally listed here more than once.*

Parker H. Petit, CEO
Thomas Underwood, COO
Thomas Underwood, Pres.
Jeffrey L. Hinton, CFO/Sr. VP
Thornton A. Kuntz, Jr., Chief Admin. Officer/Sr. VP
Roberta L. McCaw, General Counsel/VP-Legal/Sec.
Yvonne V. Scoggins, Sr. VP-Bus. Analysis
Richard A. Cockrell, VP-Investor Rel.
Parker H. Petit, Chmn.

| | |
|---|---|
| **Phone:** 770-767-4500 | **Fax:** 770-767-4521 |
| **Toll-Free:** 800-456-4060 | |
| **Address:** 1850 Parkway Pl., Marietta, GA 30067 US | |

## GROWTH PLANS/SPECIAL FEATURES:

Matria Healthcare, Inc. provides comprehensive, integrated programs and services focused on wellness, disease and condition management, productivity enhancement and informatics. The company calls its suite of services Health Enhancement, which has 50 service centers throughout the U.S. Matria primarily serves self-insured employers; private and government sponsored health plans; pharmaceutical companies; and patients. Approximately 54% of its 2007 revenue came from health plans, 36% from employers, 7% from government payors and 3% from administrative services only self-insured employer clients. Matria's disease management programs help patients with diabetes, emphysema, asthma, obesity, chronic pain, substance abuse, cancer, back pain, coronary artery disease, high-risk obstetrics, smoking cessation and asthma. The company also offers interactive online services, such as smoking cessation aids and exercise programs. Matria also offers women's and children's health care, with disease management services designed to assist physicians in the management of maternity patients. Services include risk assessment; patient education and management; infusion therapy; gestational diabetes management; and other monitoring and clinical services as prescribed by the patient's physician. Some of Matria's subsidiaries include Quality Oncology, Inc., a provider of cancer disease management services; Miavita, LLC, an online provider of health and wellness programs; and WinningHabits, Inc., a provider of corporate wellness programs; and CorSolutions Medical, Inc., a leading provider of disease management services. In January 2008, the company formalized an agreement to provide support, products and services for Microsoft's HealthVault, an internet-based health platform designed to help people better manage their health information. In May 2008, shareholders approved a proposed merger with Inverness Medical Innovations, Inc., which is set to make Matria a wholly-owned subsidiary of the global medical diagnostic firm.

The company offers employees educational assistance, adoption assistance and credit union membership.

## FINANCIALS: **Sales and profits are in thousands of dollars—add 000 to get the full amount. 2008 Note: Financial information for 2008 was not available for all companies at press time.**

| | | |
|---|---|---|
| 2008 Sales: $ | 2008 Profits: $ | **U.S. Stock Ticker: Subsidiary** |
| 2007 Sales: $352,235 | 2007 Profits: $21,428 | **Int'l Ticker:** Int'l Exchange: |
| 2006 Sales: $336,139 | 2006 Profits: $52,690 | Employees: 1,803 |
| 2005 Sales: $179,231 | 2005 Profits: $13,963 | Fiscal Year Ends: 12/31 |
| 2004 Sales: $145,087 | 2004 Profits: $27,066 | Parent Company: INVERNESS MEDICAL INNOVATIONS INC |

## SALARIES/BENEFITS:

| | | | | |
|---|---|---|---|---|
| Pension Plan: | ESOP Stock Plan: | Profit Sharing: | Top Exec. Salary: $572,423 | Bonus: $ |
| Savings Plan: Y | Stock Purch. Plan: Y | | Second Exec. Salary: $407,490 | Bonus: $ |

## OTHER THOUGHTS:

**Apparent Women Officers or Directors**: 2
**Hot Spot for Advancement for Women/Minorities**: Y

## LOCATIONS: ("Y" = Yes)

| West: | Southwest: | Midwest: | Southeast: | Northeast: | International: |
|---|---|---|---|---|---|
| Y | Y | Y | Y | Y | Y |

# MAXYGEN INC

www.maxygen.com

**Industry Group Code:** 325412 **Ranks within this company's industry group:** Sales: 35 Profits: 25

| Management: | | Sales/Marketing: | | Liberal Arts: | | Information Systems: | | Professionals: | | Technical/Scientific: | |
|---|---|---|---|---|---|---|---|---|---|---|---|
| Mgmt. Trainees: | | Mktg. Professionals: | Y | Gen. Writing/Editing: | | Info. Management: | Y | Finance/Accounting: | Y | Engineers, Elec.: | |
| Experienced Mgmt.: | Y | Retail Sales: | | Technical Writing: | Y | Software Dev.: | Y | Law: | Y | Engineers, Other: | |
| Int'l Business: | Y | Commercial/Industrial: | Y | Graphic Arts/Photog.: | | Hardware Dev.: | | HR/Other: | Y | Health/Lab: | Y |
| MBA Graduates: | Y | Sales Trainees: | Y | Music: | | Systems Integration: | | Training: | Y | Scientists/Research: | Y |
| | | Advertising Pros.: | | Broadcasting: | | Consulting/Other: | | Health Care: | Y | Petroleum/Chemicals: | |
| | | | | Other: | | | | Consulting: | Y | Math/Other: | Y |

## TYPES OF BUSINESS:
Drug Discovery & Development
Improved & Novel Pharmaceuticals
Research Services
Chemicals
Research & Development-Molecular Evolution

## BRANDS/DIVISIONS/AFFILIATES:
MolecularBreeding
DNAShuffling
MaxyScan
Maxy-G34
MAXY-4
Codexis

## CONTACTS:
*Note: Officers with more than one job title may be intentionally listed here more than once.*

Russell J. Howard, CEO
Elliot Goldstein, COO
Lawrence W. Briscoe, CFO/Sr. VP
Elliot Goldstein, Chief Medical Officer
John Borkholder, Chief Corp. Counsel/Corp. Sec.
Grant Yonehiro, Chief Bus. Officer/Sr. VP
Michele Boudreau, Dir.-Public Relations
Michele Boudreau, Dir.-Investor Relations
Isaac Stein, Chmn.

| **Phone:** 650-298-5300 | **Fax:** 650-364-2715 |
|---|---|
| **Toll-Free:** | |
| **Address:** 301 Galveston Dr., Redwood City, CA 94063 US | |

## GROWTH PLANS/SPECIAL FEATURES:

Maxygen, Inc. is a biotechnology company that works on the discovery and development of improved protein pharmaceuticals for the treatment of diseases and serious medical conditions. Technologies developed by Maxygen include MolecularBreeding, a process that mimics the natural events of evolution using a recombination process called DNAShuffling that generates a diverse library of DNA sequences. MolecularBreeding allows the company to rapidly move from product concept to IND (investigational new drug)-ready drug candidate, lowering costs associated with research and expanding the potential for discovery. The company's MaxyScan screening system selects individual proteins with desired characteristics from gene variants within the library for additional experimentation. Maxygen currently has two product candidates in different clinical study phases: Maxy-G34, a neutropenia treatment; and MAXY-4, a rheumatoid arthritis and other immune or autoimmune diseases treatment. Maxygen additionally has an HIV vaccine research program and a minority investment in Codexis, a biotechnology company that improves the manufacturing process of small molecular pharmaceutical products. In July 2008, the company sold its hemophilia program assets, including Maxy VII, a hemophilia and possibly an acute bleeding conditions treatment, to Bayer Healthcare for $90 million. In August of the same year, the firm received a 2 year, $3.4 million grant from the U.S. Department of Defense for the development of advanced vaccine technology. Maxygen will work in collaboration with Aldevron LLC. In September 2008, the company granted Astellas Pharma Inc. the rights to commercialize MAXY-4 lead candidates for transplant rejection and autoimmune diseases.

Employees are offered medical and dental insurance; group life and AD&D Insurance; flexible spending accounts; health club reimbursements; an on-site workout room; free flu shots; disability coverage; financial planning services; emergency child and elder care; tuition reimbursement; commuter voucher programs; concierge services; and credit union membership.

## FINANCIALS:
**Sales and profits are in thousands of dollars—add 000 to get the full amount. 2008 Note: Financial information for 2008 was not available for all companies at press time.**

| | | |
|---|---|---|
| 2008 Sales: $100,709 | 2008 Profits: $30,325 | **U.S. Stock Ticker: MAXY** |
| 2007 Sales: $23,157 | 2007 Profits: $-49,315 | **Int'l Ticker:** Int'l Exchange: |
| 2006 Sales: $25,021 | 2006 Profits: $-16,482 | Employees: 96 |
| 2005 Sales: $14,501 | 2005 Profits: $-18,436 | Fiscal Year Ends: 12/31 |
| 2004 Sales: $16,275 | 2004 Profits: $9,342 | Parent Company: |

## SALARIES/BENEFITS:

| | | | | |
|---|---|---|---|---|
| Pension Plan: | ESOP Stock Plan: | Profit Sharing: | Top Exec. Salary: $500,500 | Bonus: $236,100 |
| Savings Plan: Y | Stock Purch. Plan: Y | | Second Exec. Salary: $457,449 | Bonus: $225,225 |

## OTHER THOUGHTS:
**Apparent Women Officers or Directors:** 1
**Hot Spot for Advancement for Women/Minorities:**

## LOCATIONS: ("Y" = Yes)

| West: | Southwest: | Midwest: | Southeast: | Northeast: | International: |
|---|---|---|---|---|---|
| Y | | | | | Y |

# MCMORAN EXPLORATION CO

**www.mcmoran.com**

**Industry Group Code:** 211111 **Ranks within this company's industry group:** Sales: 18 Profits: 21

| Management: | | Sales/Marketing: | | Liberal Arts: | | Information Systems: | | Professionals: | | Technical/Scientific: | |
|---|---|---|---|---|---|---|---|---|---|---|---|
| Mgmt. Trainees: | | Mktg. Professionals: | Y | Gen. Writing/Editing: | | Info. Management: | Y | Finance/Accounting: | Y | Engineers, Elec.: | |
| Experienced Mgmt.: | Y | Retail Sales: | | Technical Writing: | | Software Dev.: | | Law: | Y | Engineers, Other: | Y |
| Int'l Business: | | Commercial/Industrial: | Y | Graphic Arts/Photog.: | | Hardware Dev.: | | HR/Other: | Y | Health/Lab: | |
| MBA Graduates: | Y | Sales Trainees: | | Music: | | Systems Integration: | | Training: | Y | Scientists/Research: | |
| | | Advertising Pros.: | | Broadcasting: | | Consulting/Other: | | Health Care: | | Petroleum/Chemicals: | Y |
| | | | | Other: | | | | Consulting: | | Math/Other: | |

## TYPES OF BUSINESS:

Oil & Gas-Exploration & Production
Liquefied Natural Gas Transportation & Storage
Pipelines

## BRANDS/DIVISIONS/AFFILIATES:

Main Pass Energy Hub
McMoRan Oil & Gas LLC
Freeport-McMoRan Energy LLC
K-McVentures I LLC
Newfield Exploration Co.

## CONTACTS: *Note: Officers with more than one job title may be intentionally listed here more than once.*

Glenn A. Kleinert, CEO
Glenn A. Kleinert, Pres.
Nancy D. Parmelee, CFO/Sr. VP
Nancy D. Parmelee, Sec.
Richard C. Adkerson, Co-Chmn.
James R. Moffet, Co-Chmn.

| | |
|---|---|
| **Phone:** 504-582-4000 | **Fax:** |
| **Toll-Free:** | |
| **Address:** 1615 Poydras St., New Orleans, LA 70112 US | |

## GROWTH PLANS/SPECIAL FEATURES:

McMoRan Exploration Co. engages in the exploration, development and production of oil and natural gas offshore in the Gulf of Mexico and onshore in the Gulf Coast region, primarily in high-risk, high-potential, deep exploration prospects. The company focuses on exploring for deeper pools of hydrocarbons below existing or previous shallow production operations. The process is advantageous because the drilling infrastructure is already available to the company in most cases, significantly decreasing development costs. Typically these operations are in shallow water, but can go to depths of 15,000 to 25,000 feet or more. McMoRan has expertise in various exploration and production technologies, including incorporating 3-D seismic interpretation capabilities with traditional structural geological techniques, offshore drilling to significant total depths and horizontal drilling. The company also owns or has rights to an extensive seismic database, including 3-D seismic data on substantially all of its acreage. McMoRan operates through two wholly-owned subsidiaries: McMoRan Oil and Gas LLC, which is the firm's principal operating subsidiary and conducts the company's oil and gas operations, and Freeport-McMoRan Energy LLC, which is currently pursuing the development of the Main Pass Energy Hub (MPEH) project. The MPEH project will include an offshore LNG regasification terminal capable of 1 billion cubic feet per day and onsite cavern storage for natural gas in the large salt dome at the site, as well as a pipeline system to deliver gas to markets in the U.S. Freeport Energy owns all of the oil operations at Main Pass through K-Mc Ventures I LLC.

## FINANCIALS: **Sales and profits are in thousands of dollars—add 000 to get the full amount. 2008 Note: Financial information for 2008 was not available for all companies at press time.**

| | | |
|---|---|---|
| 2008 Sales: $1,072,482 | 2008 Profits: $-211,292 | **U.S. Stock Ticker: MMR** |
| 2007 Sales: $481,167 | 2007 Profits: $-59,734 | **Int'l Ticker:** Int'l Exchange: |
| 2006 Sales: $209,738 | 2006 Profits: $-44,716 | Employees: 110 |
| 2005 Sales: $130,127 | 2005 Profits: $-31,470 | Fiscal Year Ends: 12/31 |
| 2004 Sales: $29,849 | 2004 Profits: $-52,032 | Parent Company: |

## SALARIES/BENEFITS:

| | | | | |
|---|---|---|---|---|
| Pension Plan: | ESOP Stock Plan: | Profit Sharing: | Top Exec. Salary: $325,000 | Bonus: $500,000 |
| Savings Plan: | Stock Purch. Plan: | | Second Exec. Salary: $300,000 | Bonus: $475,000 |

## OTHER THOUGHTS:

**Apparent Women Officers or Directors**: 1
**Hot Spot for Advancement for Women/Minorities**: Y

## LOCATIONS: ("Y" = Yes)

| West: | Southwest: | Midwest: | Southeast: | Northeast: | International: |
|---|---|---|---|---|---|
| | Y | | Y | | |

# MEDAREX INC

www.medarex.com

**Industry Group Code:** 325412 **Ranks within this company's industry group:** Sales: 28 Profits: 19

| **Management:** | | **Sales/Marketing:** | | **Liberal Arts:** | | **Information Systems:** | | **Professionals:** | | **Technical/Scientific:** | |
|---|---|---|---|---|---|---|---|---|---|---|---|
| Mgmt. Trainees: | | Mktg. Professionals: | Y | Gen. Writing/Editing: | | Info. Management: | Y | Finance/Accounting: | Y | Engineers, Elec.: | |
| Experienced Mgmt.: | Y | Retail Sales: | | Technical Writing: | Y | Software Dev.: | Y | Law: | Y | Engineers, Other: | |
| Int'l Business: | | Commercial/Industrial: | Y | Graphic Arts/Photog.: | | Hardware Dev.: | | HR/Other: | Y | Health/Lab: | Y |
| MBA Graduates: | Y | Sales Trainees: | Y | Music: | | Systems Integration: | | Training: | Y | Scientists/Research: | Y |
| | | Advertising Pros.: | | Broadcasting: | | Consulting/Other: | | Health Care: | Y | Petroleum/Chemicals: | |
| | | | | Other: | | | | Consulting: | | Math/Other: | Y |

## TYPES OF BUSINESS:

Drugs-Human Monoclonal Antibodies
Transgenic Mouse Technology
Drugs-Cancer
Drugs-Autoimmune Disease

## BRANDS/DIVISIONS/AFFILIATES:

UltiMAb Human Antibody Development System
HuMAb-Mouse
KM-Mouse
Genmab
TC-Mouse

## CONTACTS: *Note: Officers with more than one job title may be intentionally listed here more than once.*

Howard H. Pien, CEO
Howard H. Pien, Pres.
Christian S. Schade, CFO
Thomas K. Kaney, Sr. VP-Human Resources
Nils Lonberg, Sr. VP/Dir.-Scientific
Geoffrey M. Nichol, Sr. VP-Prod. Dev.
Christian S. Schade, Sr. VP-Admin.
Ursula B. Bartels, General Counsel/Sr. VP/Corp. Sec.
Ronald A. Pepin, Sr. VP-Bus. Dev.
Nichol Harber, Corp. Comm.
Christian S. Schade, Sr. VP-Finance
Howard H. Pien, Chmn.

| **Phone:** 609-430-2880 | **Fax:** 609-430-2850 |
|---|---|
| **Toll-Free:** | |
| **Address:** 707 State Rd., Princeton, NJ 08540-1437 US | |

## GROWTH PLANS/SPECIAL FEATURES:

Medarex, Inc. is a biopharmaceutical company devoted to the production of fully human antibody-based therapeutic product candidates to fight cancer, inflammation, autoimmune disorders and other diseases. The firm's UltiMAb Human Antibody Development System uses transgenic mice, specifically Medarex's HuMAb-Mouse, Kirin Brewing Co., Ltd.'s TC Mouse and the KM-Mouse, a hybrid of the former two mice. In this system, mouse-derived antibody gene expression is suppressed and effectively replaced with human antibody gene expression. With UltiMAb, the company can create fully human antibodies with no mouse proteins. Consequently, UltiMAb antibodies are less likely to be rejected by patients, have more favorable safety profiles and may be eliminated by the human body more slowly, potentially reducing the required dosing. Over 40 product candidates use UltiMAb technology, developed in-house or through collaborations, that are currently in clinical testing stages, including treatments for melanoma; lymphoma; breast, prostate, kidney and other cancers; rheumatoid arthritis; and inflammatory diseases. Eight of the most advanced candidates are in Phase III clinical trials or the subject of regulatory applications for marketing authorization. The UltiMAb technology is licensed to pharmaceutical and biotechnology companies that also pay royalties on commercial sales of their products. Over 45 pharmaceutical and biotechnology companies have collaborative or licensing agreements with Medarex to jointly develop opportunities for new antibodies and to commercialize products, including Amgen, Inc.; Bristol-Myers Squibb Company; Centocor, Inc.; Eli Lilly and Company; ImClone Systems Incorporated; MedImmune, Inc;. and Novartis Pharma AG. In May 2007, Medarex and Mitsubishi Pharma, a subsidiary of Mistubishi Chemical Holdings Corp., entered into a collaborative agreement to research and develop a potential treatment for autoimmune disorders. In February 2008, the company sold its stake in Genmab, a Danish biotechnology company that works with HuMAb-Mouse technology.

## FINANCIALS: **Sales and profits are in thousands of dollars—add 000 to get the full amount. 2008 Note: Financial information for 2008 was not available for all companies at press time.**

| | | |
|---|---|---|
| 2008 Sales: $ | 2008 Profits: $ | **U.S. Stock Ticker: MEDX** |
| 2007 Sales: $56,258 | 2007 Profits: $-27,055 | **Int'l Ticker:** Int'l Exchange: |
| 2006 Sales: $48,646 | 2006 Profits: $-181,701 | Employees: 500 |
| 2005 Sales: $51,455 | 2005 Profits: $-148,012 | Fiscal Year Ends: 12/31 |
| 2004 Sales: $12,474 | 2004 Profits: $-186,392 | Parent Company: |

## SALARIES/BENEFITS:

| | | | | |
|---|---|---|---|---|
| Pension Plan: | ESOP Stock Plan: | Profit Sharing: | Top Exec. Salary: $492,550 | Bonus: $328,000 |
| Savings Plan: Y | Stock Purch. Plan: | | Second Exec. Salary: $409,615 | Bonus: $413,250 |

## OTHER THOUGHTS:

**Apparent Women Officers or Directors**: 3
**Hot Spot for Advancement for Women/Minorities**: Y

## LOCATIONS: ("Y" = Yes)

| West: | Southwest: | Midwest: | Southeast: | Northeast: | International: |
|---|---|---|---|---|---|
| Y | | | | Y | |

# MEDICAL ACTION INDUSTRIES INC

www.medical-action.com

**Industry Group Code:** 339113 **Ranks within this company's industry group:** Sales: 18 Profits: 17

| Management: | | Sales/Marketing: | | Liberal Arts: | | Information Systems: | | Professionals: | | Technical/Scientific: | |
|---|---|---|---|---|---|---|---|---|---|---|---|
| Mgmt. Trainees: | | Mktg. Professionals: | Y | Gen. Writing/Editing: | | Info. Management: | Y | Finance/Accounting: | Y | Engineers, Elec.: | |
| Experienced Mgmt.: | Y | Retail Sales: | | Technical Writing: | Y | Software Dev.: | | Law: | Y | Engineers, Other: | Y |
| Int'l Business: | Y | Commercial/Industrial: | Y | Graphic Arts/Photog.: | | Hardware Dev.: | | HR/Other: | Y | Health/Lab: | Y |
| MBA Graduates: | Y | Sales Trainees: | Y | Music: | | Systems Integration: | | Training: | Y | Scientists/Research: | Y |
| | | Advertising Pros.: | | Broadcasting: | | Consulting/Other: | | Health Care: | Y | Petroleum/Chemicals: | |
| | | | | Other: | | | | Consulting: | | Math/Other: | Y |

## TYPES OF BUSINESS:

Supplies-Laparoscopy Sponges & Operating Room Towels
Disposable Surgical Products
Waste Containment Systems
Patient Bedside Utensils
Laboratory Products
Minor Procedure Kits & Trays
Sterilization Products
Dressings

## BRANDS/DIVISIONS/AFFILIATES:

SOF KRIMP
SePro
Tubegauz

## CONTACTS:

*Note: Officers with more than one job title may be intentionally listed here more than once.*

Paul D. Meringolo, CEO
Paul D. Meringolo, Pres.
Charles L. Kelly, Jr., CFO
Manuel B. Losada, VP-Mktg. & Sales
Laurie Darnaby, Dir.-Human Resources
Carmine Morello, VP-IT
Richard G. Satin, General Counsel/Corp. Sec.
Richard G. Satin, VP-Oper.
John Kringel, Sr. Dir.-Business Planning & Market Dev.
Adnan Syed, Dir.-E-commerce & System Dev.
Victor Bacchioni, Corp. Controller
Anthony Gadzinkski, Dir.-Corp. Accounts & Dist.
Steve Carlson, Dir.-North American Mfg. & Dist. Oper.
Vincent Colletti, Dir.-Internal Audit
Peter Meringolo, Dir.-Int'l Mktg.
Paul D. Meringolo, Chmn.
Eric Liu, VP-Int'l Oper. & Global Dev.
Tim Fullick, Dir.-Supply Chain

| | |
|---|---|
| **Phone:** 631-231-4600 | **Fax:** 631-231-3075 |
| **Toll-Free:** | |
| **Address:** 800 Prime Pl., Hauppauge, NY 11788 US | |

## GROWTH PLANS/SPECIAL FEATURES:

Medical Action Industries, Inc. (MAI) develops, manufactures, markets and distributes a variety of disposable medical products to acute care facilities in both domestic and international markets. The company recently expanded its end-user base to include physician, dental and veterinary offices, out-patient surgery centers and long-term care facilities. MAI specializes in the provision of medical products in six categories: Patient bedside utensils; minor procedure kits and trays; containment systems for medical waste; operating room disposables and sterilization products; dressings and surgical sponges; and laboratory products. Patient bedside utensils include wash basins; bedpans; pitchers; urinals; emesis basins; and soap dishes. Minor procedure kits and trays products include central line dressing trays; suture removal trays; incision and drainage trays; razor and shave prep kits; and instruments and instrument trays, among others. Containment systems products include biohazardous waste containment bags; non-infectious medical waste bags; chemotherapy waste containment bags; sterility maintenance covers; and autoclavable bags, among others. Disposables and sterilization products include needle counters; sterilization indicators; disposable operating room towels; and surgical headwear and shoe covers. Dressings and surgical sponges include burn dressings; gauze sponges; conforming bandage rolls; and specialty sponges; along with proprietary SOF KRIMP bandage rolls and Tubegauz elastic net and SePro value brand elastic nets, which are tubular bandages used for dressing retention. Laboratory products include Petri dishes; specimen containers; calculi strainers; and culture tubes, among others. These products are marketed through an extensive network of independent distributors, direct sales personnel and manufacturers' representatives. MAI's manufacturing, packaging and warehousing activities are conducted in North Carolina, Tennessee, West Virginia and Colorado.

## FINANCIALS:

**Sales and profits are in thousands of dollars—add 000 to get the full amount. 2008 Note: Financial information for 2008 was not available for all companies at press time.**

| | | |
|---|---|---|
| 2008 Sales: $290,528 | 2008 Profits: $13,225 | **U.S. Stock Ticker: MDCI** |
| 2007 Sales: $217,328 | 2007 Profits: $12,969 | **Int'l Ticker:** Int'l Exchange: |
| 2006 Sales: $150,942 | 2006 Profits: $11,461 | Employees: 385 |
| 2005 Sales: $141,423 | 2005 Profits: $10,682 | Fiscal Year Ends: 3/31 |
| 2004 Sales: $127,601 | 2004 Profits: $9,434 | Parent Company: |

## SALARIES/BENEFITS:

| | | | | |
|---|---|---|---|---|
| Pension Plan: | ESOP Stock Plan: | Profit Sharing: | Top Exec. Salary: $500,000 | Bonus: $245,000 |
| Savings Plan: Y | Stock Purch. Plan: | | Second Exec. Salary: $318,000 | Bonus: $78,000 |

## OTHER THOUGHTS:

**Apparent Women Officers or Directors**: 2
**Hot Spot for Advancement for Women/Minorities**: Y

## LOCATIONS: ("Y" = Yes)

| West: | Southwest: | Midwest: | Southeast: | Northeast: | International: |
|---|---|---|---|---|---|
| Y | | | Y | Y | Y |

# MEDICINES CO (THE)

www.themedicinescompany.com

**Industry Group Code:** 325412 **Ranks within this company's industry group:** Sales: 11 Profits: 18

| **Management:** | | **Sales/Marketing:** | | **Liberal Arts:** | | **Information Systems:** | | **Professionals:** | | **Technical/Scientific:** | |
|---|---|---|---|---|---|---|---|---|---|---|---|
| Mgmt. Trainees: | | Mktg. Professionals: | Y | Gen. Writing/Editing: | | Info. Management: | Y | Finance/Accounting: | Y | Engineers, Elec.: | |
| Experienced Mgmt.: | Y | Retail Sales: | | Technical Writing: | Y | Software Dev.: | Y | Law: | Y | Engineers, Other: | |
| Int'l Business: | Y | Commercial/Industrial: | Y | Graphic Arts/Photog.: | | Hardware Dev.: | | HR/Other: | Y | Health/Lab: | Y |
| MBA Graduates: | Y | Sales Trainees: | Y | Music: | | Systems Integration: | | Training: | Y | Scientists/Research: | Y |
| | | Advertising Pros.: | | Broadcasting: | | Consulting/Other: | | Health Care: | Y | Petroleum/Chemicals: | Y |
| | | | | Other: | | | | Consulting: | | Math/Other: | Y |

## TYPES OF BUSINESS:

Pharmaceuticals Acquisition & Development
Acute Care Hospital Products
Anticoagulants

## BRANDS/DIVISIONS/AFFILIATES:

Angiomax
Cleviprex (Clevidine)
Cangrelor
Angiox

## CONTACTS: *Note: Officers with more than one job title may be intentionally listed here more than once.*

Clive A. Meanwell, CEO
John P. Kelley, COO
John P. Kelley, Pres.
Glenn Sblendorio, CFO/Exec. VP
Catharine Newberry, Sr. VP/Chief Human Strategy Officer
Paul M. Antinori, General Counsel/VP
Kelli Watson, Sr. VP-Global Comm.
Clive A. Meanwell, Chmn.
Glyn R. Parkin, Sr. VP-Int'l. Oper.

**Phone:** 973-656-1616 **Fax:** 973-656-0746
**Toll-Free:**
**Address:** 8 Campus Dr., Parsippany, NJ 07054 US

## GROWTH PLANS/SPECIAL FEATURES:

The Medicines Co. (TMC) is a global pharmaceutical company specializing in acute care hospital products. The firm acquires, develops and commercializes pharmaceutical products in late stages of development. TMC's first product, Angiomax, is an intravenous direct thrombin inhibitor approved for use as an anticoagulant in patients undergoing coronary angioplasty. The firm is currently developing two additional late-stage pharmaceutical products as potential acute care hospital products. The first of these, Cleviprex (clevidipine), is an intravenous drug intended for the control of blood pressure in intensive care patients who require rapid and precise control of blood pressure. The company submitted a new drug application (NDA) with the FDA to market Cleviprex in late 2007. The company's second potential product, cangrelor, is an intravenous antiplatelet agent that prevents platelet activation and aggregation, which we believe has potential advantages in the treatment of vascular disease. Cangrelor is currently in two separate Phase III trials. These trials are being conducted simultaneously, in the hope that they will serve as the basis for a submission for approval in the U.S. and the European Union. Its revenue to date has been generated almost entirely from sales of Angiomax in the U.S. Angiomax is currently being sold through third-party distributors in Canada, Israel and New Zealand. The firm markets Angiomax in all 25 member states of the European Union under the European name Angiox, formerly via the Nycomed Group and Grupo Ferrer, TMC's European distribution partners. TMC is focused on developing its international infrastructure, to which end it reacquired from Nycomed the rights to Angiox; this is the first step into directly marketing the drug internationally.

## FINANCIALS: **Sales and profits are in thousands of dollars—add 000 to get the full amount. 2008 Note: Financial information for 2008 was not available for all companies at press time.**

2008 Sales: $348,157 | 2008 Profits: $-8,504
2007 Sales: $257,534 | 2007 Profits: $-18,272
2006 Sales: $213,952 | 2006 Profits: $63,726
2005 Sales: $150,207 | 2005 Profits: $-7,753
2004 Sales: $144,251 | 2004 Profits: $16,999

**U.S. Stock Ticker: MDCO**
**Int'l Ticker:** Int'l Exchange:
Employees: 305
Fiscal Year Ends: 12/31
Parent Company:

## SALARIES/BENEFITS:

Pension Plan: | ESOP Stock Plan: | Profit Sharing: | Top Exec. Salary: $566,000 | Bonus: $260,360
Savings Plan: Y | Stock Purch. Plan: Y | | Second Exec. Salary: $45,000 | Bonus: $216,000

## OTHER THOUGHTS:

**Apparent Women Officers or Directors**: 2
**Hot Spot for Advancement for Women/Minorities**:

## LOCATIONS: ("Y" = Yes)

| West: | Southwest: | Midwest: | Southeast: | Northeast: | International: |
|---|---|---|---|---|---|
| | | | | Y | Y |

# MEDICIS PHARMACEUTICAL CORP

www.medicis.com

**Industry Group Code:** 325412 **Ranks within this company's industry group:** Sales: 7 Profits: 5

| Management: | | Sales/Marketing: | | Liberal Arts: | | Information Systems: | | Professionals: | | Technical/Scientific: | |
|---|---|---|---|---|---|---|---|---|---|---|---|
| Mgmt. Trainees: | | Mktg. Professionals: | Y | Gen. Writing/Editing: | | Info. Management: | Y | Finance/Accounting: | Y | Engineers, Elec.: | |
| Experienced Mgmt.: | Y | Retail Sales: | | Technical Writing: | Y | Software Dev.: | Y | Law: | Y | Engineers, Other: | |
| Int'l Business: | Y | Commercial/Industrial: | Y | Graphic Arts/Photog.: | | Hardware Dev.: | | HR/Other: | Y | Health/Lab: | Y |
| MBA Graduates: | Y | Sales Trainees: | Y | Music: | | Systems Integration: | | Training: | Y | Scientists/Research: | Y |
| | | Advertising Pros.: | | Broadcasting: | | Consulting/Other: | | Health Care: | Y | Petroleum/Chemicals: | |
| | | | | Other: | | | | Consulting: | | Math/Other: | Y |

## TYPES OF BUSINESS:

Dermatological, Aesthetic & Podiatric Conditions Drugs
Acne Treatment
Topical Creams
Wrinkle Treatment

## BRANDS/DIVISIONS/AFFILIATES:

Perlane
Restylane
Solodyn
Triaz
Vanos
Ziana
LipoSonix, Inc.

## CONTACTS: *Note: Officers with more than one job title may be intentionally listed here more than once.*

Jonah Shacknai, CEO
Mark A. Prygocki, Sr., COO/Exec. VP
Richard D. Peterson, CFO/Exec. VP
Vincent Ippolito, Exec. VP-Sales & Mktg.
Mitchell S. Wortzman, Chief Scientific Officer/Exec. VP
Joseph P. Cooper, Exec. VP-Prod. Dev.
Jason Hanson, General Counsel/Exec. VP/Corp. Sec.
Joseph P. Cooper, Exec. VP-Corp. Dev.
Richard D. Peterson, Treas.
Jonah Shacknai, Chmn.

| | |
|---|---|
| **Phone:** 602-808-8800 | **Fax:** 602-808-0822 |
| **Toll-Free:** | |
| **Address:** 7720 North Dobson Rd., Scottsdale, AZ 85256 US | |

## GROWTH PLANS/SPECIAL FEATURES:

Medicis Pharmaceutical Corp. is a specialty pharmaceutical company that develops and markets products for treatment of dermatological, aesthetic and podiatric conditions. The company offers a range of products addressing various conditions or aesthetic improvement, including facial wrinkles; acne; fungal infections; rosacea; hyperpigmentation; photoaging; psoriasis; skin and skin-structure infections; seborrheic dermatitis; and cosmesis (improvement in the texture and appearance of skin). These products are marketed under the firm's 18 branded lines, which consist of secondary products plus six primary brands. The primary brands are Perlane, an injectable gel for implantation into the deep dermis to superficial subcutis for the correction of facial wrinkles; Restylane, an injectable gel for treatment of facial wrinkles and folds such as nasolabial folds; Solodyn, a daily dosage for the treatment of inflammatory lesions of non-nodular acne vulgaris; Triaz, a topical patented gel and cleanser and patent-pending pad treatments for acne; Vanos, a high potency topical corticosteroid indicated for the relief of inflammatory and pruritic manifestations of corticosteroid responsive dermatoses; and Ziana, a once-daily topical gel treatment for acne vulgaris. Medicis customers include wholesale pharmaceutical distributors such as Cardinal Health, Inc., McKesson Corp. and other major drug chains. McKesson, which is the company's sole distributor of Restylane and Perlane products in the U.S. and Canada, generates approximately 52.2% of revenues, while Cardinal Health generates roughly 16.9% of revenues. In 2007, the firm made a $20 million equity investment in Revance and purchased an option to acquire Revance or to license its topical botulinum toxin type A product exclusively in North America. In 2008, Medicis acquired LipoSonix, Inc., an independent company that specializes in body contouring technology.

Medicis offers its employees a 401(k) plan; medical, dental and life insurance; short- and long-term disability; educational assistance; and flexible spending accounts.

## FINANCIALS: **Sales and profits are in thousands of dollars—add 000 to get the full amount. 2008 Note: Financial information for 2008 was not available for all companies at press time.**

| | | |
|---|---|---|
| 2008 Sales: $ | 2008 Profits: $ | **U.S. Stock Ticker: MRX** |
| 2007 Sales: $464,651 | 2007 Profits: $75,051 | **Int'l Ticker:** Int'l Exchange: |
| 2006 Sales: $349,242 | 2006 Profits: $-75,849 | Employees: 472 |
| 2005 Sales: $376,899 | 2005 Profits: $64,990 | Fiscal Year Ends: 12/31 |
| 2004 Sales: $303,722 | 2004 Profits: $30,840 | Parent Company: |

## SALARIES/BENEFITS:

| | | | | |
|---|---|---|---|---|
| Pension Plan: | ESOP Stock Plan: | Profit Sharing: | Top Exec. Salary: $1,060,000 | Bonus: $1,001,700 |
| Savings Plan: Y | Stock Purch. Plan: | | Second Exec. Salary: $515,000 | Bonus: $405,563 |

## OTHER THOUGHTS:

**Apparent Women Officers or Directors**: 1
**Hot Spot for Advancement for Women/Minorities**:

## LOCATIONS: ("Y" = Yes)

| West: | Southwest: | Midwest: | Southeast: | Northeast: | International: |
|---|---|---|---|---|---|
| Y | Y | Y | Y | Y | |

# MEDIS TECHNOLOGIES

www.medistechnologies.com

**Industry Group Code:** 333298 **Ranks within this company's industry group:** Sales: 4 Profits: 2

| Management: | | Sales/Marketing: | | Liberal Arts: | | Information Systems: | | Professionals: | | Technical/Scientific: | |
|---|---|---|---|---|---|---|---|---|---|---|---|
| Mgmt. Trainees: | | Mktg. Professionals: | Y | Gen. Writing/Editing: | | Info. Management: | Y | Finance/Accounting: | Y | Engineers, Elec.: | Y |
| Experienced Mgmt.: | Y | Retail Sales: | | Technical Writing: | Y | Software Dev.: | Y | Law: | Y | Engineers, Other: | Y |
| Int'l Business: | Y | Commercial/Industrial: | Y | Graphic Arts/Photog.: | | Hardware Dev.: | Y | HR/Other: | Y | Health/Lab: | |
| MBA Graduates: | Y | Sales Trainees: | Y | Music: | | Systems Integration: | | Training: | Y | Scientists/Research: | Y |
| | | Advertising Pros.: | | Broadcasting: | | Consulting/Other: | | Health Care: | | Petroleum/Chemicals: | |
| | | | | Other: | | | | Consulting: | | Math/Other: | Y |

## TYPES OF BUSINESS:

Fuel Cells
Conductive Polymers
Biotechnology Equipment
Engine Research & Development

## BRANDS/DIVISIONS/AFFILIATES:

CellScan
Medis El, Ltd.
More Energy, Ltd.
Cell Kinetics, Ltd.
24/7 Power Pack
CKChip

## CONTACTS: *Note: Officers with more than one job title may be intentionally listed here more than once.*

Jose Mejia, CEO
Howard Weingrow, COO
Jose Mejia, Pres.
Israel Fisher, CFO/Sr. VP
Michelle Rush, Sr. VP-Mktg.
Jasmine Wagman-Negev, General Counsel
Michael S. Resnick, Chief Acct. Officer/Sr. VP
Asaf Ben-Arye, CEO-Cell Kinetics, Ltd.
Gennadi Finkelshtain, General Mgr.-More Energy, Ltd.
Robert K. Lifton, Chmn.

| | |
|---|---|
| **Phone:** 212-935-8484 | **Fax:** 212-935-9216 |
| **Toll-Free:** | |
| **Address:** 805 3rd Ave., 15th Fl., New York, NY 10022 US | |

## GROWTH PLANS/SPECIAL FEATURES:

Medis Technologies, Ltd. designs, develops and markets innovative liquid fuel cell products principally for the mobile handset and portable consumer electronics markets. The company is located in New York, with its subsidiaries Medis El, More Energy and Cell Kinetics located in Israel. The firm's products are designed to power and charge portable electronic devices such as most cellular phones, digital cameras, personal digital assistants, MP3 players, hand-held video games and other devices with similar power requirements, as well as a range of military devices. Medis Technologies' first consumer fuel cell product, called the 24/7 Power Pack, is a portable and disposable auxiliary power source capable of providing power to operate portable electronic equipment with dead batteries, while charging those batteries. The company is also working on promoting the refuelable version of the Power Pack for the U.S. Department of Defense, which is being developed by General Dynamics. In addition to portable fuel cells, the firm's indirect wholly-owned subsidiary, Medis El, Ltd., developed the CellScan, a static cytometer. The CellScan measures the fluorescence emanating from living cells when the cells are in a static state. The potential applications of the CellScan include determining the chemosensitivity of a cancer, breast cancer testing and detecting autoimmune diseases and drug allergies. Medis Techologies' indirect majority-owned subsidiary, Cell Kinetics Ltd., commercially exploits the CellScan system under the CKChip product line. Among other products in development are a more powerful refuelable fuel cell for laptop computers and a stationary fuel cell for back-up emergency power for small office and home use and for servers. In April 2008, the company signed a distribution agreement with Rikaken Co., Ltd for the marketing and distribution of CKChip in Japan. In August of the same year, Medis Technologies began offering the 24/7 Power Pack in select Best Buy and Best Buy Mobile stores.

## FINANCIALS: Sales and profits are in thousands of dollars—add 000 to get the full amount. 2008 Note: Financial information for 2008 was not available for all companies at press time.

| | | |
|---|---|---|
| 2008 Sales: $ | 2008 Profits: $ | **U.S. Stock Ticker: MDTL** |
| 2007 Sales: $ 400 | 2007 Profits: $-38,200 | **Int'l Ticker:** Int'l Exchange: |
| 2006 Sales: $ 150 | 2006 Profits: $-33,047 | Employees: 167 |
| 2005 Sales: $ 425 | 2005 Profits: $-18,550 | Fiscal Year Ends: 12/31 |
| 2004 Sales: $ | 2004 Profits: $-15,662 | Parent Company: |

## SALARIES/BENEFITS:

| | | | | |
|---|---|---|---|---|
| Pension Plan: | ESOP Stock Plan: | Profit Sharing: | Top Exec. Salary: $315,000 | Bonus: $ |
| Savings Plan: | Stock Purch. Plan: | | Second Exec. Salary: $289,000 | Bonus: $ |

## OTHER THOUGHTS:

**Apparent Women Officers or Directors**: 2
**Hot Spot for Advancement for Women/Minorities**:

## LOCATIONS: ("Y" = Yes)

| West: | Southwest: | Midwest: | Southeast: | Northeast: | International: |
|---|---|---|---|---|---|
| Y | | | | Y | Y |

# MEDTOX SCIENTIFIC INC

**www.medtox.com**

**Industry Group Code:** 621511 **Ranks within this company's industry group:** Sales: 5 Profits: 4

| Management: | | Sales/Marketing: | | Liberal Arts: | | Information Systems: | | Professionals: | | Technical/Scientific: | |
|---|---|---|---|---|---|---|---|---|---|---|---|
| Mgmt. Trainees: | | Mktg. Professionals: | Y | Gen. Writing/Editing: | | Info. Management: | Y | Finance/Accounting: | Y | Engineers, Elec.: | |
| Experienced Mgmt.: | Y | Retail Sales: | | Technical Writing: | Y | Software Dev.: | Y | Law: | Y | Engineers, Other: | |
| Int'l Business: | | Commercial/Industrial: | Y | Graphic Arts/Photog.: | | Hardware Dev.: | | HR/Other: | Y | Health/Lab: | Y |
| MBA Graduates: | Y | Sales Trainees: | Y | Music: | | Systems Integration: | Y | Training: | Y | Scientists/Research: | Y |
| | | Advertising Pros.: | | Broadcasting: | | Consulting/Other: | | Health Care: | Y | Petroleum/Chemicals: | |
| | | | | Other: | | | | Consulting: | | Math/Other: | |

## TYPES OF BUSINESS:

Diagnostic Device Manufacturing
Forensic & Clinical Lab Services
Diagnostic Drug Screening Devices

## BRANDS/DIVISIONS/AFFILIATES:

MEDTOX Diagnostics, Inc.
MEDTOX Laboratories, Inc.
PROFILE-II
VERDICT-II
ClearCourse
SURE-SCREEN
Drug Abuse Recognition System (DARS)
EZ-SCREEN

## CONTACTS: *Note: Officers with more than one job title may be intentionally listed here more than once.*

Richard J. Braun, CEO
Richard J. Braun, Pres.
Kevin J. Wiersma, CFO
James A. Schoonover, Chief Mktg. Officer/VP-Sales & Mktg.
Susan E. Puskas, VP-Human Resources
Steven J. Schmidt, VP-Finance
Susan E. Puskas, VP-Quality & Regulatory Affairs
B. Mitchell Owens, VP/COO-Diagnostics Div.
Kevin J. Wiersma, VP/COO-Laboratory Div.
Richard J. Braun, Chmn.

| | |
|---|---|
| **Phone:** 651-636-7466 | **Fax:** 651-636-5351 |
| **Toll-Free:** 800-832-3244 | |
| **Address:** 402 W. County Rd. D, St. Paul, MN 55112 US | |

## GROWTH PLANS/SPECIAL FEATURES:

MEDTOX Scientific, Inc. manufactures and distributes diagnostic devices and provides forensic and clinical laboratory services. The firm operates through two divisions, laboratory services and product sales. The laborary services division is operated by the company's subsidiary MEDTOX Laboratories, Inc., which provides laboratory drug testing services for corporations, medical facilities and the federal government. MEDTOX Laboratories derives the majority of its revenues, roughly 65%, from workplace drugs-of-abuse testing. It also offers specialty services, accounting for 35% of revenues, including clinical toxicology; medical diagnostics; general clinical testing for the pharmaceutical industry; heavy metal, trace element and solvent analysis; it also offers logistics, data and program management services. The firm's other subsidiary, MEDTOX Diagnostics, Inc., which operates the product sales division, is based in Burlington, North Carolina and manufactures on-site drug screening products for the corporate, health care, criminal justice, temporary service and drug rehabilitation markets. MEDTOX Diagnostics' point-of-collection testing (POCT) products, which account for 88% of its sales, include the PROFILE-II, which is sold to hospitals, and the VERDICT-II and SURE-SCREEN lines, which are sold within the criminal justice and drug rehabilitation markets. These products test for a variety of drugs including amphetamines, marijuana, cocaine, opiates, phencyclidine (PCP), benzoylecgonine, morphine and methamphetamine. The company also offers its ClearCourse comprehensive drug testing program, which consists of Drug Abuse Recognition System (DARS) training; SURE-SCREEN drug testing devices; WEBTOX online data management; and MEDTOX's own laboratory assistance for confirmation testing. Among this company's other products are the EZ-SCREEN breath alcohol test and agricultural diagnostics products used to detect antibiotic residues. This division also offers contract manufacturing services.

MEDTOX offers its employees medical and dental insurance; tuition reimbursement; corporate discounts; life insurance; and flexible spending accounts.

## FINANCIALS: **Sales and profits are in thousands of dollars—add 000 to get the full amount. 2008 Note: Financial information for 2008 was not available for all companies at press time.**

| | | |
|---|---|---|
| 2008 Sales: $85,813 | 2008 Profits: $5,572 | **U.S. Stock Ticker: MTOX** |
| 2007 Sales: $80,285 | 2007 Profits: $6,690 | **Int'l Ticker:** Int'l Exchange: |
| 2006 Sales: $69,804 | 2006 Profits: $4,548 | Employees: 523 |
| 2005 Sales: $63,047 | 2005 Profits: $3,318 | Fiscal Year Ends: 12/31 |
| 2004 Sales: $56,736 | 2004 Profits: $1,821 | Parent Company: |

## SALARIES/BENEFITS:

| | | | | |
|---|---|---|---|---|
| Pension Plan: | ESOP Stock Plan: | Profit Sharing: | Top Exec. Salary: $336,903 | Bonus: $906,808 |
| Savings Plan: Y | Stock Purch. Plan: | | Second Exec. Salary: $207,200 | Bonus: $275,276 |

## OTHER THOUGHTS:

**Apparent Women Officers or Directors**: 1
**Hot Spot for Advancement for Women/Minorities**:

## LOCATIONS: ("Y" = Yes)

| West: | Southwest: | Midwest: | Southeast: | Northeast: | International: |
|---|---|---|---|---|---|
| | | Y | | Y | |

# MENTOR CORP

www.mentorcorp.com

**Industry Group Code:** 339113 **Ranks within this company's industry group:** Sales: 11 Profits: 1

| Management: | | Sales/Marketing: | | Liberal Arts: | | Information Systems: | | Professionals: | | Technical/Scientific: | |
|---|---|---|---|---|---|---|---|---|---|---|---|
| Mgmt. Trainees: | | Mktg. Professionals: | Y | Gen. Writing/Editing: | | Info. Management: | Y | Finance/Accounting: | Y | Engineers, Elec.: | |
| Experienced Mgmt.: | Y | Retail Sales: | | Technical Writing: | Y | Software Dev.: | | Law: | Y | Engineers, Other: | Y |
| Int'l Business: | Y | Commercial/Industrial: | Y | Graphic Arts/Photog.: | | Hardware Dev.: | | HR/Other: | Y | Health/Lab: | Y |
| MBA Graduates: | Y | Sales Trainees: | Y | Music: | | Systems Integration: | | Training: | Y | Scientists/Research: | Y |
| | | Advertising Pros.: | | Broadcasting: | | Consulting/Other: | | Health Care: | Y | Petroleum/Chemicals: | |
| | | | | Other: | | | | Consulting: | | Math/Other: | Y |

## TYPES OF BUSINESS:

Supplies-Plastic Surgery Products
Breast Implants
Liposuction

## BRANDS/DIVISIONS/AFFILIATES:

Contour Profile Tissue Expander
Contour Profile
MemoryGel
BufferZone
Centerscope
Mentor UltraSculpt
Puragen
Prevell

## CONTACTS: *Note: Officers with more than one job title may be intentionally listed here more than once.*

Joshua H. Levine, CEO
Edward S. Northup, COO/VP
Joshua H. Levine, Pres.
Michael O'Neill, CFO/VP
Brian E. Luedtke, VP-Global Mktg. & Sales
Vicki S. Chuck, VP-Human Resources
Udo W. Graf, VP-R&D
Andrew G. Tymkiw, VP-Global Mfg. Oper.
Joseph A. Newcomb, General Counsel/VP/Corp. Sec.
Noam A. Krantz, VP-Corp. Dev.
Darl S. Moreland, VP-Compliance & Quality Assurance
Nicola A. Selley, VP-Clinical & Regulatory Submissions
AnnaMarie Daniels, VP-Mentor Biologics
Joseph E. Whitters, Chmn.

**Phone:** 805-879-6000 **Fax:** 805-964-2712
**Toll-Free:** 800-525-0245
**Address:** 201 Mentor Dr., Santa Barbara, CA 93111 US

## GROWTH PLANS/SPECIAL FEATURES:

Mentor Corporation develops, manufactures, licenses and markets a broad range of products serving the plastic and reconstructive surgical markets worldwide. The company's aesthetic products fall into three general categories: surgical breast implants; soft tissue aspiration or body contouring (liposuction); and facial rejuvenation products for skin restoration. Mentor's line of breast implant products includes Contour Profile, its saline-filled implant brand, and MemoryGel, its silicone gel-filled implant brand. MemoryGel received FDA approval for sale in November 2007, prior to which the company could only market it outside of the U.S. The company also markets: the Contour Profile Tissue Expander lines of breast expanders, which prepare the tissue to hold the implant; BufferZone, a self-sealing technology; and Centerscope, a line of injector port locators. All of these mammary prostheses are used in augmentation procedures to enhance breast size and shape, correct breast asymmetries, help restore fullness after breast-feeding and reconstruct breasts following a mastectomy. Mentor's body contouring segment markets a line of liposuction products and disposable supplies, including its Mentor UltraSculpt technology, which is more accurate and less physically traumatic than conventional liposuction. The company also offers a line of extremity tissue expanders used in growing tissue for reconstruction and skin graft procedures. Finally, Mentor supplies dermal filters, such as Puragen and Prevell, and cosmeceutical products that help plastic surgeons and dermatologists correct for wrinkles and various other skin conditions. In July 2007, Mentor acquired Perouse Plastie SAS, a French medical device company. In February 2008, the firm launched an online resource for women considering cosmetic procedures at LoveYourLook.com. In March 2008, the FDA approved Mentor's Prevelle Silk, developed with Genzyme Corporation. Prevelle Silk is part of a new line of hyaluronic acid dermal fillers for facial lines and wrinkles.

## FINANCIALS: **Sales and profits are in thousands of dollars—add 000 to get the full amount. 2008 Note: Financial information for 2008 was not available for all companies at press time.**

2008 Sales: $373,208
2007 Sales: $301,974
2006 Sales: $268,272
2005 Sales: $251,726
2004 Sales: $218,437

2008 Profits: $63,415
2007 Profits: $290,614
2006 Profits: $62,357
2005 Profits: $54,881
2004 Profits: $54,779

**U.S. Stock Ticker: MNT**
**Int'l Ticker:** Int'l Exchange:
Employees: 1,190
Fiscal Year Ends: 3/31
Parent Company:

## SALARIES/BENEFITS:

Pension Plan: ESOP Stock Plan: Profit Sharing: Top Exec. Salary: $533,846 Bonus: $658,125
Savings Plan: Y Stock Purch. Plan: Second Exec. Salary: $412,693 Bonus: $303,469

## OTHER THOUGHTS:

**Apparent Women Officers or Directors:** 5
**Hot Spot for Advancement for Women/Minorities:** Y

## LOCATIONS: ("Y" = Yes)

| West: | Southwest: | Midwest: | Southeast: | Northeast: | International: |
|---|---|---|---|---|---|
| Y | Y | Y | | | Y |

# MERIDIAN BIOSCIENCE INC

www.meridianbioscience.com

**Industry Group Code:** 325413 **Ranks within this company's industry group:** Sales: 7 Profits: 3

| Management: | | Sales/Marketing: | | Liberal Arts: | | Information Systems: | | Professionals: | | Technical/Scientific: | |
|---|---|---|---|---|---|---|---|---|---|---|---|
| Mgmt. Trainees: | | Mktg. Professionals: | Y | Gen. Writing/Editing: | | Info. Management: | Y | Finance/Accounting: | Y | Engineers, Elec.: | |
| Experienced Mgmt.: | Y | Retail Sales: | | Technical Writing: | Y | Software Dev.: | Y | Law: | Y | Engineers, Other: | Y |
| Int'l Business: | Y | Commercial/Industrial: | Y | Graphic Arts/Photog.: | | Hardware Dev.: | Y | HR/Other: | Y | Health/Lab: | Y |
| MBA Graduates: | Y | Sales Trainees: | Y | Music: | | Systems Integration: | | Training: | Y | Scientists/Research: | Y |
| | | Advertising Pros.: | | Broadcasting: | | Consulting/Other: | | Health Care: | Y | Petroleum/Chemicals: | |
| | | | | Other: | | | | Consulting: | | Math/Other: | Y |

## TYPES OF BUSINESS:

Diagnostic Test Kits
Contract Manufacturing
Bulk Antigens, Antibodies & Reagents

## BRANDS/DIVISIONS/AFFILIATES:

Biodesign
OEM Concepts
Viral Antigens
cGMP
ImmunoCard STAT EHEC

## CONTACTS: *Note: Officers with more than one job title may be intentionally listed here more than once.*

John A. Kraeutler, CEO
Melissa A. Lueke, CFO/VP
Todd W. Motto, VP-Sales & Mktg.
Grady Barnes, VP-R&D
Lawrence J. Baldini, Exec. VP-Info. Systems
Lawrence J. Baldini, Exec. VP-Oper.
Susan D. Rolih, VP-Regulatory Affairs & Quality Systems
Richard L. Eberly, Exec. VP/Pres., Meridian Life Science
William J. Motto, Chmn.
Antonio A. Interno, Sr. VP/Pres./Managing Dir.-Europe

**Phone:** 513-271-3700 **Fax:** 513-271-3762
**Toll-Free:** 888-763-6769
**Address:** 3471 River Hills Dr., Cincinnati, OH 45244 US

## GROWTH PLANS/SPECIAL FEATURES:

Meridian Biosciences, Inc. is a life science company that develops, manufactures, sells and distributes diagnostic test kits, primarily for respiratory, gastrointestinal, viral and parasitic infectious diseases; manufactures and distributes bulk antigens, antibodies and reagents; and contract manufactures proteins and other biologicals. The company operates in three segments: U.S. diagnostics, European diagnostics and life science. The U.S. diagnostics segment focuses on the development, manufacture, sale and distribution of diagnostic test kits, which utilize immunodiagnostic technologies that test samples of body fluids or tissue for the presence of antigens and antibodies of specific infectious diseases. Products also include transport media that store and preserve specimen samples from patient collection to laboratory testing. The European diagnostics segment focuses on the sale and distribution of diagnostic test kits. Its sales and distribution network consists of direct sales forces in Belgium, France, Holland and Italy, and independent distributors in other European, African and Middle Eastern countries. The life sciences segment focuses on the development, manufacture, sale and distribution of bulk antigens, antibodies and reagents, as well as contract development and manufacturing services. The segment is represented by four product-line brands: Biodesign, which represents monoclonal and polyclonal antibodies and assay reagents; OEM (original equipment manufacturer) Concepts, which represents contract ascites and antibody production services; Viral Antigens, which represents viral proteins; and cGMP biologics, which represents contract development and manufacturing services for drug and vaccine discovery and development. Meridian's core diagnostic products generated 80% of revenue in 2007. In February 2007, the company received clearance from the FDA to market ImmunoCard STAT EHEC, a test for the diagnosis of E. coli infection. In November 2007, the firm was cleared to market TRU FLU and TRU RSV, new rapid tests for influenza and respitory syncytical virus.

The company offers its employees health, dental and life insurance; tuition reimbursement; and an employee assistance plan.

## FINANCIALS: **Sales and profits are in thousands of dollars—add 000 to get the full amount. 2008 Note: Financial information for 2008 was not available for all companies at press time.**

| | | |
|---|---|---|
| 2008 Sales: $139,639 | 2008 Profits: $30,202 | **U.S. Stock Ticker: VIVO** |
| 2007 Sales: $122,963 | 2007 Profits: $26,721 | **Int'l Ticker:** Int'l Exchange: |
| 2006 Sales: $108,413 | 2006 Profits: $18,333 | Employees: 363 |
| 2005 Sales: $92,965 | 2005 Profits: $12,565 | Fiscal Year Ends: 9/30 |
| 2004 Sales: $79,606 | 2004 Profits: $9,185 | Parent Company: |

## SALARIES/BENEFITS:

| | | | | |
|---|---|---|---|---|
| Pension Plan: | ESOP Stock Plan: | Profit Sharing: Y | Top Exec. Salary: $494,904 | Bonus: $300,005 |
| Savings Plan: Y | Stock Purch. Plan: Y | | Second Exec. Salary: $391,928 | Bonus: $300,005 |

## OTHER THOUGHTS:

**Apparent Women Officers or Directors**: 2
**Hot Spot for Advancement for Women/Minorities**: Y

## LOCATIONS: ("Y" = Yes)

| West: | Southwest: | Midwest: | Southeast: | Northeast: | International: |
|---|---|---|---|---|---|
| | | Y | Y | Y | Y |

Note: Financial information, benefits and other data can change quickly and may vary from those stated here.

# MERIT MEDICAL SYSTEMS INC

**www.merit.com**

**Industry Group Code:** 339113 **Ranks within this company's industry group:** Sales: 19 Profits: 13

| **Management:** | | **Sales/Marketing:** | | **Liberal Arts:** | | **Information Systems:** | | **Professionals:** | | **Technical/Scientific:** | |
|---|---|---|---|---|---|---|---|---|---|---|---|
| Mgmt. Trainees: | | Mktg. Professionals: | Y | Gen. Writing/Editing: | | Info. Management: | Y | Finance/Accounting: | Y | Engineers, Elec.: | |
| Experienced Mgmt.: | Y | Retail Sales: | | Technical Writing: | Y | Software Dev.: | | Law: | Y | Engineers, Other: | Y |
| Int'l Business: | Y | Commercial/Industrial: | Y | Graphic Arts/Photog.: | | Hardware Dev.: | | HR/Other: | Y | Health/Lab: | Y |
| MBA Graduates: | Y | Sales Trainees: | Y | Music: | | Systems Integration: | | Training: | Y | Scientists/Research: | Y |
| | | Advertising Pros.: | | Broadcasting: | | Consulting/Other: | | Health Care: | Y | Petroleum/Chemicals: | |
| | | | | Other: | | | | Consulting: | | Math/Other: | Y |

## TYPES OF BUSINESS:

Disposable Products-Cardiology & Radiology

## BRANDS/DIVISIONS/AFFILIATES:

Futura Safety Scalpel

## CONTACTS:

*Note: Officers with more than one job title may be intentionally listed here more than once.*

Fred P. Lampropoulos, CEO
Arlin D. Nelson, COO
Fred P. Lampropoulos, Pres.
Kent W. Stanger, CFO
Martin R. Stephens, VP-Sales
Kent W. Stanger, Corp. Sec.
Kent W. Stanger, Treas.
Fred P. Lampropoulos, Chmn.

**Phone:** 801-253-1600 **Fax:** 801-253-1652
**Toll-Free:** 800-356-3748
**Address:** 1600 W. Merit Pkwy., South Jordan, UT 84095 US

## GROWTH PLANS/SPECIAL FEATURES:

Merit Medical Systems, Inc. develops, manufactures and distributes disposable proprietary medical products used in interventional diagnostic and therapeutic procedures, particularly in cardiology and radiology. Products include coronary control syringes; inflation devices; specialty syringes; waste management products; high-pressure tubing and connectors; disposable blood pressure transducer and pressure monitoring tubing and accessories; disposable hemostasis valves; guide wire torque devices and accessories; drainage catheters and accessories; diagnostic angiographic pigtail catheters; guide catheters; percutaneous sheath introducers, obturators and vessel dialators; diagnostic guide wires; pressure infusor bags; and angiography needles and accessories. Sales are made primarily to U.S. hospitals through a direct sales force. In 2007, the U.S. domestic sales force made approximately 41% of U.S. sales directly to hospitals and roughly 14% of U.S. sales through other channels such as U.S. customs packagers and distributors. Original equipment manufacturers accounted for approximately 15% of 2007 revenue. About 31% of sales in 2007 were made in international markets. Merit has subsidiaries in Ireland, Germany, France, the U.K., Belgium, the Netherlands, Denmark and Sweden. In January 2008, the firm finalized the purchase of certain assets from Micrus Endovascular. In February 2008, the firm announced it entered into an agreement with Timothy Clark, M.D., to acquire a U.S. Patent called Methods for obtaining hemostasis of percutaneous wounds.

The company offers its employees medical and dental insurance; short- and long-term disability insurance; life and AD&D insurance; a 401(k) plan; an employee stock purchase plan; and an employee assistance program.

## FINANCIALS:

**Sales and profits are in thousands of dollars—add 000 to get the full amount. 2008 Note: Financial information for 2008 was not available for all companies at press time.**

| | | |
|---|---|---|
| 2008 Sales: $227,143 | 2008 Profits: $20,727 | **U.S. Stock Ticker: MMSI** |
| 2007 Sales: $207,768 | 2007 Profits: $15,588 | **Int'l Ticker:** Int'l Exchange: |
| 2006 Sales: $190,674 | 2006 Profits: $12,301 | Employees: 1,515 |
| 2005 Sales: $166,585 | 2005 Profits: $15,778 | Fiscal Year Ends: 12/31 |
| 2004 Sales: $151,398 | 2004 Profits: $17,932 | Parent Company: |

## SALARIES/BENEFITS:

| | | | | |
|---|---|---|---|---|
| Pension Plan: | ESOP Stock Plan: | Profit Sharing: | Top Exec. Salary: $458,000 | Bonus: $ 50 |
| Savings Plan: Y | Stock Purch. Plan: | | Second Exec. Salary: $308,654 | Bonus: $ |

## OTHER THOUGHTS:

**Apparent Women Officers or Directors:**
**Hot Spot for Advancement for Women/Minorities:**

## LOCATIONS: ("Y" = Yes)

| West: | Southwest: | Midwest: | Southeast: | Northeast: | International: |
|---|---|---|---|---|---|
| Y | Y | | | Y | Y |

# METROLOGIC INSTRUMENTS INC

**www.metrologic.com**

**Industry Group Code:** 334119 **Ranks within this company's industry group:** Sales: Profits:

| Management: | | Sales/Marketing: | | Liberal Arts: | | Information Systems: | | Professionals: | | Technical/Scientific: | |
|---|---|---|---|---|---|---|---|---|---|---|---|
| Mgmt. Trainees: | | Mktg. Professionals: | Y | Gen. Writing/Editing: | | Info. Management: | Y | Finance/Accounting: | Y | Engineers, Elec.: | Y |
| Experienced Mgmt.: | Y | Retail Sales: | | Technical Writing: | Y | Software Dev.: | Y | Law: | Y | Engineers, Other: | Y |
| Int'l Business: | Y | Commercial/Industrial: | Y | Graphic Arts/Photog.: | Y | Hardware Dev.: | Y | HR/Other: | Y | Health/Lab: | |
| MBA Graduates: | Y | Sales Trainees: | Y | Music: | | Systems Integration: | Y | Training: | Y | Scientists/Research: | |
| | | Advertising Pros.: | | Broadcasting: | | Consulting/Other: | | Health Care: | | Petroleum/Chemicals: | |
| | | | | Other: | | | | Consulting: | | Math/Other: | |

## TYPES OF BUSINESS:

Computer Accessories-Bar Code Scanners
Laser Scanner Products
Wireless Scanner Interfaces
Holographic Scanners

## BRANDS/DIVISIONS/AFFILIATES:

Adaptive Optics Associates, Inc.
MS Voyager

## CONTACTS: *Note: Officers with more than one job title may be intentionally listed here more than once.*

Darius Adamczyk, CEO
Michael Coluzzi, CFO
Mark C. Schmidt, VP-Mktg. & Prod. Mgmt.
Bruce Harrison, General Counsel/VP
Joseph Sawitsky, Exec. VP-Oper.
Michael Coluzzi, Treas./VP
Mark Ryan, VP-EMEA
Greg T. DiNoia, VP-Americas
Jim Griffin, Dir.-Bus. Dev., Americas
Dale M. Fischer, VP-Asia Pacific

**Phone:** 856-228-8100 **Fax:** 856-228-0653
**Toll-Free:** 800-667-8400
**Address:** 90 Coles Rd., Blackwood, NJ 08012 US

## GROWTH PLANS/SPECIAL FEATURES:

Metrologic Instruments, Inc. designs, markets and manufactures sophisticated imaging systems using laser and holographic technologies; high-speed automated data capture hardware; and bar code scanners. Metrologic's vertically integrated operations include the design and manufacture of its own optics, optical coatings, magnetic and inductive electronic components and fabricated parts. It holds more than 350 patents worldwide and has over 100 patents pending. The firm's automatic identification products, including hand-held scanners, fixed-projection scanners, in-counter scanners and industrial scanners, serve customers in the transportation, logistics, retail, commercial, manufacturing and postal and parcel delivery industries. Traditionally, over 80% of the company's revenue has come from bar code scanner sales. The company's scanners interface with most computers, cash registers, mobile computing terminals and Internet-ready appliances. The firm's MS Voyager series of automatically triggered hand-held scanners is used in retailing, libraries, industrial warehousing, production lines and commercial applications worldwide. Metrologic products are sold in over 110 countries, with international sales and services coordinated through international headquarters in Germany and Singapore; and additional offices in India, China, Thailand, Korea, Japan, Australia, New Zealand, Russia, Poland, the U.K., France, Spain, Italy, Brazil, Mexico and other countries. Metrologic's industrial laser-and vision-based scanning systems are branded and marketed through the firm's subsidiary, Adaptive Optics Associates, Inc. (AOA). The company has two manufacturing facilities, one in Blackwood, New Jersey and one in Suzhou, China. In July 2008, Honeywell acquired Metrologic for $720 million, which will become part of the Honeywell Imaging and Mobility segment of Honeywell Security.

In addition to medical and prescription coverage, the company offers its employees a 401(k) plan and tuition reimbursement.

## FINANCIALS: **Sales and profits are in thousands of dollars—add 000 to get the full amount. 2008 Note: Financial information for 2008 was not available for all companies at press time.**

| | | |
|---|---|---|
| 2008 Sales: $ | 2008 Profits: $ | **U.S. Stock Ticker: Subsidiary** |
| 2007 Sales: $ | 2007 Profits: $ | **Int'l Ticker:** Int'l Exchange: |
| 2006 Sales: $ | 2006 Profits: $ | Employees: 1,400 |
| 2005 Sales: $210,453 | 2005 Profits: $17,813 | Fiscal Year Ends: 12/31 |
| 2004 Sales: $177,955 | 2004 Profits: $22,680 | Parent Company: HONEYWELL INTERNATIONAL INC |

## SALARIES/BENEFITS:

| | | | | |
|---|---|---|---|---|
| Pension Plan: | ESOP Stock Plan: | Profit Sharing: | Top Exec. Salary: $300,000 | Bonus: $ |
| Savings Plan: Y | Stock Purch. Plan: | | Second Exec. Salary: $188,000 | Bonus: $58,900 |

## OTHER THOUGHTS:

**Apparent Women Officers or Directors:** 1
**Hot Spot for Advancement for Women/Minorities:**

## LOCATIONS: ("Y" = Yes)

| West: | Southwest: | Midwest: | Southeast: | Northeast: | International: |
|---|---|---|---|---|---|
| | | | | Y | Y |

# METROPCS COMMUNICATIONS INC

www.metropcs.com

**Industry Group Code:** 513322 **Ranks within this company's industry group:** Sales: 1 Profits: 1

| Management: | | Sales/Marketing: | | Liberal Arts: | | Information Systems: | | Professionals: | | Technical/Scientific: | |
|---|---|---|---|---|---|---|---|---|---|---|---|
| Mgmt. Trainees: | | Mktg. Professionals: | Y | Gen. Writing/Editing: | | Info. Management: | Y | Finance/Accounting: | Y | Engineers, Elec.: | Y |
| Experienced Mgmt.: | Y | Retail Sales: | | Technical Writing: | Y | Software Dev.: | Y | Law: | Y | Engineers, Other: | |
| Int'l Business: | Y | Commercial/Industrial: | Y | Graphic Arts/Photog.: | | Hardware Dev.: | | HR/Other: | Y | Health/Lab: | |
| MBA Graduates: | Y | Sales Trainees: | | Music: | | Systems Integration: | Y | Training: | Y | Scientists/Research: | |
| | | Advertising Pros.: | Y | Broadcasting: | | Consulting/Other: | | Health Care: | | Petroleum/Chemicals: | |
| | | | | Other: | | | | Consulting: | | Math/Other: | |

## TYPES OF BUSINESS:

Mobile Phone Service

## BRANDS/DIVISIONS/AFFILIATES:

TravelTalk

## CONTACTS:

*Note: Officers with more than one job title may be intentionally listed here more than once.*

Roger D. Linquist, CEO
Thomas C. Keys, COO
Roger D. Linquist, Pres.
J. Braxton Carter, CFO/Exec. VP
Phillip R. Terry, VP-Corp. Mktg.
Thomas J. Bolger, Sr. VP-Human Resources
John J. Olsen, CIO/VP
Malcom M. Lorang, CTO/Sr. VP
Mark A. Stachiw, General Counsel/Exec. VP/Corp. Sec.
Douglas S. Glen, Sr. VP-Corp. Dev.
Christine B. Kornegay, Chief Acct. Officer/Controller/VP
Robert A. Young, Sr. VP-Market Oper.-Northeast
Herbert Graves, Sr. VP-Market Oper.-West
Keith D. Terreri, VP-Finance/Treas.
David Walker, VP-Network Oper.
Roger D. Linquist, Chmn.

| Phone: 214-570-5800 | Fax: |
|---|---|
| Toll-Free: | |
| Address: 2250 Lakeside Blvd., Richardson, TX 75082 US | |

## GROWTH PLANS/SPECIAL FEATURES:

MetroPCS Communications, Inc. (MetroPCS) is a wireless broadband personal communication services provider on a pre-paid, no long-term contract, flat rate, unlimited usage basis in selected major metropolitan markets in the U.S., including San Francisco, Miami, Los Angeles, Atlanta, Sacramento, Tampa/Sarasota/Orland, Dallas/Ft. Worth and Detroit, with a total licensed population of roughly 67 million. The company provides services to about 4 million customers. The firm's service allows its customers to place unlimited local calls from within the service area and to receive unlimited calls from any area while in the local service areas under a flat monthly rate plan. For additional fees, MetroPCS provides unlimited long distance calls from within the service area, unlimited voicemail, caller ID, call waiting, text messaging, mobile Internet browsing, ringtones, ring back tones, downloads, games, content applications, as well as international long distance and text messaging. Approximately 85% of customers choose to purchase additional services. The company offers TravelTalk, a service option that allows customers to use their MetroPCS service when traveling to major metropolitan areas within the U.S. In addition, there is no extra charge when traveling to other MetroPCS markets. Recently, the firm purchased advanced wireless services licenses covering a total population of roughly 126 million in metropolitan areas including Philadelphia and Boston and the entire states of New York, Connecticut, Massachusetts and New Jersey. In April 2007, MetroPCS went public.

The company offers its employees medical, dental and vision insurance; flexible spending accounts; life and AD&D insurance; short- and long-term disability insurance; business travel accident insurance; a 401(k) plan; and an employee phone plan.

## FINANCIALS:

**Sales and profits are in thousands of dollars—add 000 to get the full amount. 2008 Note: Financial information for 2008 was not available for all companies at press time.**

| | | |
|---|---|---|
| 2008 Sales: $ | 2008 Profits: $ | **U.S. Stock Ticker: PCS** |
| 2007 Sales: $2,235,734 | 2007 Profits: $100,403 | **Int'l Ticker:** Int'l Exchange: |
| 2006 Sales: $1,546,863 | 2006 Profits: $53,806 | Employees: 2,498 |
| 2005 Sales: $1,038,428 | 2005 Profits: $176,065 | Fiscal Year Ends: 12/31 |
| 2004 Sales: $748,250 | 2004 Profits: $43,411 | Parent Company: |

## SALARIES/BENEFITS:

| | | | | |
|---|---|---|---|---|
| Pension Plan: | ESOP Stock Plan: | Profit Sharing: | Top Exec. Salary: $586,154 | Bonus: $969,400 |
| Savings Plan: Y | Stock Purch. Plan: | | Second Exec. Salary: $357,692 | Bonus: $416,000 |

## OTHER THOUGHTS:

**Apparent Women Officers or Directors**: 1
**Hot Spot for Advancement for Women/Minorities**: Y

## LOCATIONS: ("Y" = Yes)

| West: | Southwest: | Midwest: | Southeast: | Northeast: | International: |
|---|---|---|---|---|---|
| | Y | Y | | | |

# METROPOLITAN HEALTH NETWORKS

**www.metcare.com**

**Industry Group Code:** 524114 **Ranks within this company's industry group:** Sales: 4 Profits: 4

| Management: | | Sales/Marketing: | | Liberal Arts: | | Information Systems: | | Professionals: | | Technical/Scientific: | |
|---|---|---|---|---|---|---|---|---|---|---|---|
| Mgmt. Trainees: | | Mktg. Professionals: | Y | Gen. Writing/Editing: | Y | Info. Management: | Y | Finance/Accounting: | Y | Engineers, Elec.: | |
| Experienced Mgmt.: | Y | Retail Sales: | | Technical Writing: | Y | Software Dev.: | | Law: | Y | Engineers, Other: | |
| Int'l Business: | | Commercial/Industrial: | Y | Graphic Arts/Photog.: | | Hardware Dev.: | | HR/Other: | Y | Health/Lab: | Y |
| MBA Graduates: | Y | Sales Trainees: | | Music: | | Systems Integration: | | Training: | Y | Scientists/Research: | |
| | | Advertising Pros.: | | Broadcasting: | | Consulting/Other: | | Health Care: | Y | Petroleum/Chemicals: | |
| | | | | Other: | | | | Consulting: | | Math/Other: | Y |

## TYPES OF BUSINESS:

Provider Service Network
HMO
Managed Care Risk Contracting
Disease Management
Pharmacy Benefits Management
Utilization Management

## BRANDS/DIVISIONS/AFFILIATES:

MetHealth
Metcare
Metcare RX, Inc.
Medicare Advantage HMO
METCARE Health Plans, Inc.
AdvantageCare
Humana Inc.

## CONTACTS: *Note: Officers with more than one job title may be intentionally listed here more than once.*

Michael M. Earley, CEO
Robert Sabo, CFO
Britt Travis, Sr. VP-Sales & Mktg.
Sharon Munroe, VP-Human Resources
Roman G. Fisher, CIO/Sr. VP
Roberto L. Palenzuela, General Counsel/Chief Compliance Officer
Maria A. Xirau, VP-Oper.
Jose A. Guethon, Chief Medical Officer-AdvantageCare
Brenton Hood, VP-Network Oper.
Lucille Soltesz, VP-Quality Mgmt.
Hymin Zucker, Chief Medical Officer-Metcare of Florida, Inc.
Michael M. Earley, Chmn.

**Phone:** 561-805-8500 **Fax:** 561-805-8501
**Toll-Free:** 888-663-8227
**Address:** 250 Australian Ave. S., Ste. 400, West Palm Beach, FL 33401 US

## GROWTH PLANS/SPECIAL FEATURES:

Metropolitan Health Networks, Inc. (MHN) provides comprehensive healthcare services for approximately 25,400 Medicare patients and 6,200 Medicare Advantage beneficiaries through its provider service network (PSN) and its health maintenance organization (HMO) in South and Central Florida. Both of MHN's PSN and HMO operations are focused on individuals covered by Medicare, which covers the costs of hospitalization, medical care and other related health services for U.S. citizens that are 65 years or older, qualified disabled persons and persons suffering from end-staged renal disease. In addition to its primary care practices, the PSN holds network contracts with Humana and 30 independent primary care physician practices and operates nine primary care physician practice and one medical oncology physician practice. Metropolitan's HMO operations are conducted through its wholly-owned subsidiary, Metcare Health Plans, Inc, which offers services to Medicare beneficiaries in six Florida counties under its AdvantageCare plan. The company also operates a managed care network and infrastructure of experts in disease, quality and utilization management, which involves the proper utilization of costs and care of high-risk patients, generating a standard of measurement for its overall patient care against the best medical practices and conducting a daily review of data created by encounters, referrals, hospital admissions and nursing home information. In 2008, Humana Inc. announced its plans to acquire Metcare Health Plans, Inc. for $14 million.

The firm offers employees health insurance, education assistance, supplemental health benefits, a credit union and a Costco membership.

## FINANCIALS: **Sales and profits are in thousands of dollars—add 000 to get the full amount. 2008 Note: Financial information for 2008 was not available for all companies at press time.**

| | |
|---|---|
| 2008 Sales: $ | 2008 Profits: $ |
| 2007 Sales: $277,577 | 2007 Profits: $5,914 |
| 2006 Sales: $228,216 | 2006 Profits: $ 473 |
| 2005 Sales: $183,765 | 2005 Profits: $2,382 |
| 2004 Sales: $158,070 | 2004 Profits: $18,822 |

**U.S. Stock Ticker: MDF**
**Int'l Ticker:** Int'l Exchange:
Employees: 199
Fiscal Year Ends: 12/31
Parent Company:

## SALARIES/BENEFITS:

Pension Plan: ESOP Stock Plan: Profit Sharing: Top Exec. Salary: $355,879 Bonus: $241,100
Savings Plan: Y Stock Purch. Plan: Second Exec. Salary: $300,000 Bonus: $192,200

## OTHER THOUGHTS:

**Apparent Women Officers or Directors:** 3
**Hot Spot for Advancement for Women/Minorities:** Y

## LOCATIONS: ("Y" = Yes)

| West: | Southwest: | Midwest: | Southeast: | Northeast: | International: |
|---|---|---|---|---|---|
| | | | Y | | |

# MICHELINAS INC

www.michelinas.com

**Industry Group Code:** 311410 **Ranks within this company's industry group:** Sales: 1 Profits:

| Management: | | Sales/Marketing: | | Liberal Arts: | | Information Systems: | | Professionals: | | Technical/Scientific: | |
|---|---|---|---|---|---|---|---|---|---|---|---|
| Mgmt. Trainees: | | Mktg. Professionals: | Y | Gen. Writing/Editing: | | Info. Management: | Y | Finance/Accounting: | Y | Engineers, Elec.: | |
| Experienced Mgmt.: | Y | Retail Sales: | | Technical Writing: | | Software Dev.: | | Law: | Y | Engineers, Other: | |
| Int'l Business: | Y | Commercial/Industrial: | Y | Graphic Arts/Photog.: | | Hardware Dev.: | | HR/Other: | Y | Health/Lab: | |
| MBA Graduates: | Y | Sales Trainees: | Y | Music: | | Systems Integration: | | Training: | Y | Scientists/Research: | |
| | | Advertising Pros.: | Y | Broadcasting: | | Consulting/Other: | | Health Care: | | Petroleum/Chemicals: | |
| | | | | Other: | | | | Consulting: | | Math/Other: | |

## TYPES OF BUSINESS:

Frozen Foods

## BRANDS/DIVISIONS/AFFILIATES:

Michelina's Lean Gourmet
Authentico
Michelina's Signature
Michelina's Snack Rolls
Michelina's Yu Sing
Zap'ems

## CONTACTS: *Note: Officers with more than one job title may be intentionally listed here more than once.*

Joel Conner, CEO
Joel Conner, Pres.
Danette Bucsko, CFO
Charlie Pountney, Sr. Exec. VP-Mktg. & Sales
Jeff Wilson, Sr. VP-Oper.
Maris Ehlers, VP-New Bus. Dev.
Stacey Fowler, Sr. VP/Gen. Mgr.-Fusion Culinary Center
Jeff Tuttle, Sr. VP-Mktg.
Joel Conner, Chmn.

| | |
|---|---|
| **Phone:** 218-723-5555 | **Fax:** 218-624-7019 |
| **Toll-Free:** 800-521-1281 | |
| **Address:** 525 S. Lake Ave., Duluth, MN 55802 US | |

## GROWTH PLANS/SPECIAL FEATURES:

Michelina's, Inc., formerly Luigino's, Inc., is a leading manufacturer of frozen entrees. The firm offers over 200 products under the Michelina's, Authentico, Michelina's Lean Gourmet, Michelina's Signature, Michelina's Snack Rolls, Michelina's Yu Sing and Zap'ems brands. Products include ready-to-microwave pasta, meat and sauce dishes, kids' entrees, Oriental dishes, soups and frozen pizzas. Some examples include Signature Shrimp Alfredo, Yu Sing Spicy Peanut Chicken, Zap'ems Chili-Mac and Lean Gourmet Roasted Sirloin Supreme. Luigino's founder, Jeno Paulucci, also invented Jeno's Pizza Rolls (now owned by General Mills). Michelina's products are shipped from its Jackson, OH production facility to the mass retail, wholesale club, supermarket, foodservice and drug store channels. The company's products are distributed all over the U.S., as well as internationally.

## FINANCIALS: **Sales and profits are in thousands of dollars—add 000 to get the full amount. 2008 Note: Financial information for 2008 was not available for all companies at press time.**

| | | |
|---|---|---|
| 2008 Sales: $ | 2008 Profits: $ | **U.S. Stock Ticker: Private** |
| 2007 Sales: $66,200 | 2007 Profits: $ | **Int'l Ticker:** Int'l Exchange: |
| 2006 Sales: $ | 2006 Profits: $ | Employees: 1,300 |
| 2005 Sales: $ | 2005 Profits: $ | Fiscal Year Ends: 12/31 |
| 2004 Sales: $ | 2004 Profits: $ | Parent Company: |

## SALARIES/BENEFITS:

| | | | | |
|---|---|---|---|---|
| Pension Plan: | ESOP Stock Plan: | Profit Sharing: | Top Exec. Salary: $ | Bonus: $ |
| Savings Plan: | Stock Purch. Plan: | | Second Exec. Salary: $ | Bonus: $ |

## OTHER THOUGHTS:

**Apparent Women Officers or Directors:** 2
**Hot Spot for Advancement for Women/Minorities:** Y

## LOCATIONS: ("Y" = Yes)

| West: | Southwest: | Midwest: | Southeast: | Northeast: | International: |
|---|---|---|---|---|---|
| | | Y | | Y | Y |

Note: Financial information, benefits and other data can change quickly and may vary from those stated here.

# MICROSTRATEGY INC

www.microstrategy.com

**Industry Group Code:** 511203 **Ranks within this company's industry group:** Sales: 2 Profits: 2

| Management: | | Sales/Marketing: | | Liberal Arts: | | Information Systems: | | Professionals: | | Technical/Scientific: | |
|---|---|---|---|---|---|---|---|---|---|---|---|
| Mgmt. Trainees: | | Mktg. Professionals: | Y | Gen. Writing/Editing: | | Info. Management: | Y | Finance/Accounting: | Y | Engineers, Elec.: | Y |
| Experienced Mgmt.: | Y | Retail Sales: | | Technical Writing: | Y | Software Dev.: | Y | Law: | Y | Engineers, Other: | |
| Int'l Business: | Y | Commercial/Industrial: | Y | Graphic Arts/Photog.: | | Hardware Dev.: | | HR/Other: | Y | Health/Lab: | |
| MBA Graduates: | Y | Sales Trainees: | Y | Music: | | Systems Integration: | | Training: | Y | Scientists/Research: | |
| | | Advertising Pros.: | | Broadcasting: | | Consulting/Other: | | Health Care: | | Petroleum/Chemicals: | |
| | | | | Other: | Y | | | Consulting: | | Math/Other: | Y |

## TYPES OF BUSINESS:

Software-Data Analysis
Business Intelligence & Marketing Software
Customer Relationship Management Software
Consulting Services

## BRANDS/DIVISIONS/AFFILIATES:

MicroStrategy 8
MicroStrategy Technical Support
MicroStrategy Consulting
MicroStrategy Education
Technical Advisory Services
Angel.com
Alarm.com

## CONTACTS:

*Note: Officers with more than one job title may be intentionally listed here more than once.*

Michael J. Saylor, CEO
Sanju K. Bansal, COO/Exec. VP
Michael J. Saylor, Pres.
Arthur S. Locke, III, CFO
Paul Zolfaqhari, VP-Worldwide Sales
Vincent M. Gabriele, Exec. VP-Human Resources
Peng Xiao, CIO/Exec. VP
Jeffrey A. Bedell, CTO/Exec. VP
Jonathan F. Klein, General Counsel/Exec. VP-Law
Paul Zolfaqhari, Exec. VP-Oper.
Arthur S. Locke, III, VP-Finance
Sanju K. Bansal, Vice Chmn.
Michael J. Saylor, Chmn.
Adam M. McDonald, VP-Worldwide Svcs.

| | |
|---|---|
| **Phone:** 703-848-8600 | **Fax:** 703-848-8610 |
| **Toll-Free:** 866-966-6787 | |
| **Address:** 1861 International Dr., McLean, VA 22102 US | |

## GROWTH PLANS/SPECIAL FEATURES:

MicroStrategy, Inc. provides business intelligence software that analyzes raw enterprise data to spot trends, providing companies with opportunities to make informed business decisions. The firm's primary product, MicroStrategy 8 is an integrated, enterprise-class business intelligence software platform that enables organizations to consolidate business intelligence applications for reporting, analysis and report delivery applications. The platform allows companies to comb through databases, deliver customized information and develop numerous applications such as personalized marketing efforts, customer relationship management, web analysis, supply chain efficiency and sales and marketing analysis. MicroStrategy's interactive software delivers information to workgroups, the enterprise and extranet communities via e-mail, web, fax, wireless and voice communication channels. MicroStrategy Technical Support provides a set of support options through a support team, an online support site and options to secure dedicated technical support. MicroStrategy Consulting offers a range of business intelligence and data warehousing expertise gathered from helping thousands of customers across diverse industries implement departmental, enterprise and extranet applications across various types of databases. The company's consulting staff identifies the optimal design and implementation strategy that includes detailed business requirements, user interface requirements and performance tuning. MicroStrategy Education offers goal-oriented, comprehensive education solutions for customers and partners, including self-tutorials, custom course development, joint training with customers' internal staff and standard course offerings. The company also offers Technical Advisory Services, which provides subject matter expertise, project management, strategic consulting and expedited resources to enhance the success of customer deployments. MicroStrategy also has two businesses, Angel.com and Alarm.com, which do not focus on the business intelligence market. Angel.com provides interactive voice response telephony systems. Alarm.com provides web-enabled security and activity monitoring technology. MicroStrategy serves 2,800 businesses including PetSmart, Starbucks Corporation, Wells Fargo, Cingular Wireless and the U.S. Postal Service.

## FINANCIALS:

**Sales and profits are in thousands of dollars—add 000 to get the full amount. 2008 Note: Financial information for 2008 was not available for all companies at press time.**

| | | |
|---|---|---|
| 2008 Sales: $360,393 | 2008 Profits: $41,833 | **U.S. Stock Ticker: MSTR** |
| 2007 Sales: $335,373 | 2007 Profits: $58,468 | **Int'l Ticker:** Int'l Exchange: |
| 2006 Sales: $313,823 | 2006 Profits: $70,876 | Employees: 1,582 |
| 2005 Sales: $268,662 | 2005 Profits: $64,743 | Fiscal Year Ends: 12/31 |
| 2004 Sales: $231,208 | 2004 Profits: $168,313 | Parent Company: |

## SALARIES/BENEFITS:

| | | | | |
|---|---|---|---|---|
| Pension Plan: | ESOP Stock Plan: | Profit Sharing: | Top Exec. Salary: $525,000 | Bonus: $1,819,592 |
| Savings Plan: | Stock Purch. Plan: | | Second Exec. Salary: $341,667 | Bonus: $410,305 |

## OTHER THOUGHTS:

**Apparent Women Officers or Directors**:
**Hot Spot for Advancement for Women/Minorities**:

## LOCATIONS: ("Y" = Yes)

| West: | Southwest: | Midwest: | Southeast: | Northeast: | International: |
|---|---|---|---|---|---|
| Y | | Y | Y | Y | Y |

# MICROTEK MEDICAL HOLDINGS INC

www.microtekmed.com

**Industry Group Code:** 339113 **Ranks within this company's industry group:** Sales: Profits:

| Management: | | Sales/Marketing: | | Liberal Arts: | | Information Systems: | | Professionals: | | Technical/Scientific: | |
|---|---|---|---|---|---|---|---|---|---|---|---|
| Mgmt. Trainees: | | Mktg. Professionals: | Y | Gen. Writing/Editing: | | Info. Management: | Y | Finance/Accounting: | Y | Engineers, Elec.: | |
| Experienced Mgmt.: | Y | Retail Sales: | | Technical Writing: | Y | Software Dev.: | | Law: | Y | Engineers, Other: | Y |
| Int'l Business: | Y | Commercial/Industrial: | Y | Graphic Arts/Photog.: | | Hardware Dev.: | | HR/Other: | Y | Health/Lab: | Y |
| MBA Graduates: | Y | Sales Trainees: | Y | Music: | | Systems Integration: | | Training: | Y | Scientists/Research: | Y |
| | | Advertising Pros.: | | Broadcasting: | | Consulting/Other: | | Health Care: | Y | Petroleum/Chemicals: | |
| | | | | Other: | | | | Consulting: | | Math/Other: | Y |

## TYPES OF BUSINESS:

Supplies-Assorted Health Care Products
Disposable Products
Biohazard Disposal Products
Safety & Protection Products
Fluid Management Products
Nuclear Protective & Disposal Products

## BRANDS/DIVISIONS/AFFILIATES:

Microtek Medical, Inc.
Iosorb
LTS-Plus
MediaPlast
OREX Technologies International
International Medical Products, B.V.
KMMS Holdings, Ltd.
Ecolab, Inc.

## CONTACTS: *Note: Officers with more than one job title may be intentionally listed here more than once.*

Dan R. Lee, VP/Gen. Mgr.
Mark Alvarez, VP-Mktg. & Sales
Mark Alvarez, VP-Oper.

| | |
|---|---|
| **Phone:** 662-327-1863 | **Fax:** 662-327-5921 |
| **Toll-Free:** 800-824-3027 | |
| **Address:** 512 Lehmberg Rd., Columbus, MS 39704 US | |

## GROWTH PLANS/SPECIAL FEATURES:

Microtek Medical Holdings, Inc. (MMHI), a wholly-owned subsidiary of Ecolab, Inc., is a leading manufacturer and marketer of infection control products, fluid control products and safety products to healthcare professionals. It conducts virtually all operations through Microtek Medical, Inc. (MMI), a subsidiary that develops, manufactures and sells infection control, fluid control and safety products to health care professionals for use in environments such as operating rooms and outpatient surgical centers. These consist primarily of disposable equipment drapes, specialty patient drapes, Iosorb and LTS-Plus biohazard encapsulation products, CleanOp cleaning kits, Venodyne pneumatic pumps, decanters and wound evacuation products. MMI also offers the MediaPlast line of fluid management products and ChillBuster portable patient warming system. The company, through its Innovative Services Division, engages in contract manufacturing and private labeling of specialty medical devices. MMHI's OREX Technologies International (OTI) subsidiary develops and sells protective products for the nuclear power market, such as coveralls, hoods and booties. OTI's MICROBasix processing system is used to process and dispose of contaminated OREX products. The firm licenses all manufacturing and sales of its OREX materials and processing technology to Eastern Technologies, Inc. The company also owns KMMS Holdings, Ltd. and its European manufacturing and distribution operations, which, collectively, are known as Samco. Headquartered in Malta and with distribution capabilities in Munich, Germany, Samco manufactures and sells a variety of disposable surgical products. In November 2007, Ecolab, Inc. acquired the company for approximately $227 million.

Microtek employees are offered health, dental, disability and term life insurance.

## FINANCIALS: **Sales and profits are in thousands of dollars—add 000 to get the full amount. 2008 Note: Financial information for 2008 was not available for all companies at press time.**

| | | |
|---|---|---|
| 2008 Sales: $ | 2008 Profits: $ | **U.S. Stock Ticker: Subsidiary** |
| 2007 Sales: $ | 2007 Profits: $ | **Int'l Ticker:** Int'l Exchange: |
| 2006 Sales: $141,577 | 2006 Profits: $7,915 | Employees: 1,873 |
| 2005 Sales: $134,458 | 2005 Profits: $14,504 | Fiscal Year Ends: 12/31 |
| 2004 Sales: $126,581 | 2004 Profits: $9,921 | Parent Company: ECOLAB INC |

## SALARIES/BENEFITS:

| | | | | |
|---|---|---|---|---|
| Pension Plan: | ESOP Stock Plan: | Profit Sharing: | Top Exec. Salary: $367,854 | Bonus: $85,906 |
| Savings Plan: | Stock Purch. Plan: | | Second Exec. Salary: $232,181 | Bonus: $85,906 |

## OTHER THOUGHTS:

**Apparent Women Officers or Directors**:
**Hot Spot for Advancement for Women/Minorities**:

## LOCATIONS: ("Y" = Yes)

| West: | Southwest: | Midwest: | Southeast: | Northeast: | International: |
|---|---|---|---|---|---|
| | Y | | Y | | Y |

# MIDAS INC

www.midasinc.com

**Industry Group Code:** 811100 **Ranks within this company's industry group:** Sales: 1 Profits: 1

| **Management:** | | **Sales/Marketing:** | | **Liberal Arts:** | | **Information Systems:** | | **Professionals:** | | **Technical/Scientific:** | |
|---|---|---|---|---|---|---|---|---|---|---|---|
| Mgmt. Trainees: | | Mktg. Professionals: | Y | Gen. Writing/Editing: | | Info. Management: | Y | Finance/Accounting: | Y | Engineers, Elec.: | |
| Experienced Mgmt.: | Y | Retail Sales: | | Technical Writing: | | Software Dev.: | | Law: | Y | Engineers, Other: | |
| Int'l Business: | Y | Commercial/Industrial: | | Graphic Arts/Photog.: | | Hardware Dev.: | | HR/Other: | Y | Health/Lab: | |
| MBA Graduates: | Y | Sales Trainees: | | Music: | | Systems Integration: | | Training: | Y | Scientists/Research: | |
| | | Advertising Pros.: | | Broadcasting: | | Consulting/Other: | | Health Care: | | Petroleum/Chemicals: | |
| | | | | Other: | | | | Consulting: | | Math/Other: | |

## TYPES OF BUSINESS:

Automotive Repair & Maintenance
Real Estate Operations

## BRANDS/DIVISIONS/AFFILIATES:

Midas Realty Corp.
Talleres Rapidos Centroamericanos TRC, S.A
SpeeDee
Midas International Corporation
AutoZone Inc
Uni-Select Inc

## CONTACTS:

*Note: Officers with more than one job title may be intentionally listed here more than once.*

Alan D. Feldman, CEO
Alan D. Feldman, Pres.
William M. Guzik, CFO/Exec. VP
Rick Dow, Chief Mktg. Officer/Sr. VP
Ben Parma, VP-Human Resources
Alvin K. Marr, General Counsel/Sr. VP/Corp. Sec.
Bob Troyer, Press Rel.
James M. Haeger, VP/Controller
John A. Warzecha, Sr. VP-Franchise Oper. & Sales
Alan D. Feldman, Chmn.

| **Phone:** 630-438-3000 | **Fax:** 630-438-3880 |
|---|---|
| **Toll-Free:** | |
| **Address:** 1300 Arlington Heights Rd., Itasca, IL 60143 US | |

## GROWTH PLANS/SPECIAL FEATURES:

Midas, Inc. provides auto repair and maintenance services in the U.S., Canada, Europe, Australia, the Middle East, Latin America and the Caribbean through company-operated and franchised shops. The firm operates under numerous subsidiaries including Midas International Corporation. Under the Midas brand, the company offers exhaust, brake, suspension, air conditioning and maintenance services. Midas farms out its wholesale parts distribution and quick-delivery operations through AutoZone, Inc. and Uni-Select, Inc. Subsidiary Midas Realty Corporation selects, leases and acquires sites and constructs facilities for company-operated and franchised shops throughout North America. It also enters into contingent operating lease agreements in order to ensure control of the real estate used by Midas shops. There are more than 2,500 Midas shops in 19 countries around the world. North American operations account for approximately 1,800 of these shops, with company-owned shops accounting for nearly 65 locations and franchises for approximately 1,685 locations, the remainder consisting of recently acquired SpeeDee locations. In 2007, 12% of retail business was generated by exhaust; 38% by brakes; 9% by suspension, shocks and struts; and 41% from new Midas categories, which include tires and related services, fleet maintenance services and general maintenance. In the U.S., the company uses Arvin exhaust products supplied by AutoZone. In 2007, the firm closed six company-owned stores in Florida. On February 2008, Midas signed an agreement with Talleres Rapidos Centroamericanos TRC, S.A., a subsidiary of Purdy Motor S.A., to build and operate Midas shops in Costa Rica. In April 2008, Midas acquired the assets of G.C. & K.B. Investments, Inc., which franchised 181 SpeeDee quick-lube and automotive maintenance shops in the U.S. and Mexico.

## FINANCIALS:

**Sales and profits are in thousands of dollars—add 000 to get the full amount. 2008 Note: Financial information for 2008 was not available for all companies at press time.**

| | | |
|---|---|---|
| 2008 Sales: $ | 2008 Profits: $ | **U.S. Stock Ticker: MDS** |
| 2007 Sales: $180,000 | 2007 Profits: $13,300 | **Int'l Ticker:** Int'l Exchange: |
| 2006 Sales: $176,700 | 2006 Profits: $10,500 | Employees: 700 |
| 2005 Sales: $192,500 | 2005 Profits: $2,200 | Fiscal Year Ends: 12/31 |
| 2004 Sales: $197,500 | 2004 Profits: $4,100 | Parent Company: |

## SALARIES/BENEFITS:

| | | | | |
|---|---|---|---|---|
| Pension Plan: | ESOP Stock Plan: | Profit Sharing: | Top Exec. Salary: $725,000 | Bonus: $ |
| Savings Plan: | Stock Purch. Plan: | | Second Exec. Salary: $295,000 | Bonus: $ |

## OTHER THOUGHTS:

**Apparent Women Officers or Directors**: 1
**Hot Spot for Advancement for Women/Minorities**:

## LOCATIONS: ("Y" = Yes)

| West: | Southwest: | Midwest: | Southeast: | Northeast: | International: |
|---|---|---|---|---|---|
| Y | Y | Y | Y | Y | Y |

# MILLENNIUM PHARMACEUTICALS INC

www.mlnm.com

**Industry Group Code:** 325412 **Ranks within this company's industry group:** Sales: 6 Profits: 11

| Management: | | Sales/Marketing: | | Liberal Arts: | | Information Systems: | | Professionals: | | Technical/Scientific: | |
|---|---|---|---|---|---|---|---|---|---|---|---|
| Mgmt. Trainees: | | Mktg. Professionals: | Y | Gen. Writing/Editing: | | Info. Management: | Y | Finance/Accounting: | Y | Engineers, Elec.: | |
| Experienced Mgmt.: | Y | Retail Sales: | | Technical Writing: | Y | Software Dev.: | Y | Law: | Y | Engineers, Other: | |
| Int'l Business: | Y | Commercial/Industrial: | Y | Graphic Arts/Photog.: | | Hardware Dev.: | | HR/Other: | Y | Health/Lab: | Y |
| MBA Graduates: | Y | Sales Trainees: | Y | Music: | | Systems Integration: | | Training: | Y | Scientists/Research: | Y |
| | | Advertising Pros.: | | Broadcasting: | | Consulting/Other: | | Health Care: | Y | Petroleum/Chemicals: | Y |
| | | | | Other: | | | | Consulting: | | Math/Other: | Y |

## TYPES OF BUSINESS:

Pharmaceuticals Discovery & Development
Gene-Based Drug Discovery Platform
Small-Molecule Drugs

## BRANDS/DIVISIONS/AFFILIATES:

MLN0002
VELCADE
MLN1202
MLN3897
Takeda Pharmaceutical Company Ltd

## CONTACTS: *Note: Officers with more than one job title may be intentionally listed here more than once.*

Deborah Dunsire, CEO
Deborah Dunsire, Pres.
Marsha Fanucci, CFO/Sr. VP
Stephen M. Gansler, Sr. VP-Human Resources
Joseph B. Bolen, Chief Scientific Officer
Laurie B. Keating, General Counsel/Sr. VP
Anna Protopapas, Sr. VP-Corp. Dev.
Christophe Bianchi, Exec. VP-Commercial Oper.
Peter F. Smith, Sr. VP-Non-Clinical Dev. Sciences
Nancy Simonian, Chief Medical Officer

| | |
|---|---|
| **Phone:** 617-679-7000 | **Fax:** 617-374-7788 |
| **Toll-Free:** 800-390-5663 | |
| **Address:** 40 Landsdowne St., Cambridge, MA 02139 US | |

## GROWTH PLANS/SPECIAL FEATURES:

Millennium Pharmaceuticals, a subsidiary of Takeda Pharmaceuticals Company, Ltd., researches and manufactures therapeutic products for the treatment of patients with cancer and inflammatory diseases. The company's development platform focuses on combing knowledge of genomics and protein homeostasis, a set of particular molecular pathways that affect the establishment and progression of diseases, in order to produce drug candidates. The firm currently has one marketed product called VELCADE. VELCADE is an oncology drug that is injected into patients for the treatment of multiple myeloma, a cancer of the blood, and mantle cell lymphoma. VELCADE is also being tested in Phase II and III trials for the treatment of follicular B-cell non-Hodgkin's lymphoma, hematologic malignancies and solid tumors including lung, breast, prostate and ovarian cancers. The firm also receives a considerable share of its revenue from royalties culled from INTEGRILIN, a drug used to treat acute coronary syndrome, marketed by Schering-Plough. In addition to its marketed drug, the company has several drug candidates in preclinical and clinical development for the treatment of advanced malignancies and various inflammatory diseases. Inflammatory disease drug candidates include MLN0002, a humanized monoclonal antibody which is in Phase II trials for inflammatory bowel diseases, such as Crohn's disease and ulcerative colitis; MLN3897, an orally active, small molecule antagonist that the firm is developing in collaboration with Sanofi-aventis, and MLN1202, which is in Phase II trials for the treatment of patients at high risk for atherosclerosis. In January 2008, the firm signed an agreement to collaborate with Harvard Medical School's Office of Technology Development on a research program in the area of protein homeostasis. In May 2008, Millennium was acquired by Takeda Pharmaceutical Company, Ltd. and became its wholly-owned subsidiary.

Millennium offers employees medical, dental and vision coverage; flexible spending accounts; life and disability insurance; and education and transportation assistance.

## FINANCIALS: **Sales and profits are in thousands of dollars—add 000 to get the full amount. 2008 Note: Financial information for 2008 was not available for all companies at press time.**

| | | |
|---|---|---|
| 2008 Sales: $ | 2008 Profits: $ | **U.S. Stock Ticker: Subsidiary** |
| 2007 Sales: $527,525 | 2007 Profits: $14,909 | **Int'l Ticker:** Int'l Exchange: |
| 2006 Sales: $486,830 | 2006 Profits: $-43,953 | Employees: 966 |
| 2005 Sales: $558,308 | 2005 Profits: $-198,249 | Fiscal Year Ends: 12/31 |
| 2004 Sales: $448,206 | 2004 Profits: $-252,297 | Parent Company: TAKEDA PHARMACEUTICAL COMPANY LTD |

## SALARIES/BENEFITS:

| | | | | |
|---|---|---|---|---|
| Pension Plan: | ESOP Stock Plan: | Profit Sharing: | Top Exec. Salary: $871,667 | Bonus: $1,540,000 |
| Savings Plan: Y | Stock Purch. Plan: Y | | Second Exec. Salary: $450,224 | Bonus: $315,000 |

## OTHER THOUGHTS:

**Apparent Women Officers or Directors**: 5
**Hot Spot for Advancement for Women/Minorities**: Y

## LOCATIONS: ("Y" = Yes)

| West: | Southwest: | Midwest: | Southeast: | Northeast: | International: |
|---|---|---|---|---|---|
| | | | | Y | |

# MOELIS & COMPANY

www.moelis.com

**Industry Group Code:** 523110 **Ranks within this company's industry group:** Sales: Profits:

| **Management:** | | **Sales/Marketing:** | | **Liberal Arts:** | | **Information Systems:** | | **Professionals:** | | **Technical/Scientific:** | |
|---|---|---|---|---|---|---|---|---|---|---|---|
| Mgmt. Trainees: | | Mktg. Professionals: | | Gen. Writing/Editing: | | Info. Management: | Y | Finance/Accounting: | Y | Engineers, Elec.: | |
| Experienced Mgmt.: | Y | Retail Sales: | | Technical Writing: | | Software Dev.: | | Law: | Y | Engineers, Other: | |
| Int'l Business: | Y | Commercial/Industrial: | | Graphic Arts/Photog.: | | Hardware Dev.: | | HR/Other: | Y | Health/Lab: | |
| MBA Graduates: | Y | Sales Trainees: | | Music: | | Systems Integration: | | Training: | Y | Scientists/Research: | |
| | | Advertising Pros.: | | Broadcasting: | | Consulting/Other: | | Health Care: | | Petroleum/Chemicals: | |
| | | | | Other: | | | | Consulting: | | Math/Other: | |

## TYPES OF BUSINESS:

Investment Banking
Private Equity
Investment Advisory Services

## BRANDS/DIVISIONS/AFFILIATES:

## CONTACTS:

*Note: Officers with more than one job title may be intentionally listed here more than once.*

Kenneth D. Moelis, CEO
Elizabeth Crain, COO
Peter Vogelsang, General Counsel
Christopher Stehling, Head-Finance & Acct.
Elizabeth Crain, Chief Compliance Officer
Steve Bloom, Sr. VP
Todd Bomberg, Sr. VP
Timothy W. Dahms, Sr. VP

**Phone:** 212-880-7300 **Fax:** 212-880-4260
**Toll-Free:**
**Address:** 245 Park Ave. 32nd Fl., New York, NY 10167 US

## GROWTH PLANS/SPECIAL FEATURES:

Moelis & Company is an investment bank that offers advisory and investment fund management services. With offices in New York, Boston, Chicago, London and Los Angeles, the firm operates in two business divisions: Advisory and merchant banking. The advisory segment focuses on providing strategic and financial alternatives involving buy-side and sell-side mergers and acquisitions and accessing potential buyers, negotiating transactions relating to exclusive sales; and offering advice on restructuring(particularly on transactions, structuring, pricing, timing, and financing) and capital raising. Select transactions within this division include Yahoo! and Hilton. The merchant banking division creates investments and strategic transactions for a variety of industries and asset-classes. The company has more than 150 professionals, including over 100 investment bankers and utilizes a team approach to its services. Moelis plans to add companies in the healthcare and energy business sectors to its portfolio in the near future and also plans to expand its restructuring services.

## FINANCIALS:

**Sales and profits are in thousands of dollars—add 000 to get the full amount. 2008 Note: Financial information for 2008 was not available for all companies at press time.**

2008 Sales: $
2007 Sales: $
2006 Sales: $
2005 Sales: $
2004 Sales: $

2008 Profits: $
2007 Profits: $
2006 Profits: $
2005 Profits: $
2004 Profits: $

**U.S. Stock Ticker: Private**
**Int'l Ticker:** Int'l Exchange:
Employees:
Fiscal Year Ends:
Parent Company:

## SALARIES/BENEFITS:

Pension Plan: ESOP Stock Plan: Profit Sharing: Top Exec. Salary: $ Bonus: $
Savings Plan: Stock Purch. Plan: Second Exec. Salary: $ Bonus: $

## OTHER THOUGHTS:

**Apparent Women Officers or Directors**: 4
**Hot Spot for Advancement for Women/Minorities**: Y

## LOCATIONS: ("Y" = Yes)

| West: | Southwest: | Midwest: | Southeast: | Northeast: | International: |
|---|---|---|---|---|---|
| Y | | Y | | Y | Y |

# MOLINA HEALTHCARE INC

www.molinahealthcare.com

**Industry Group Code:** 524114 **Ranks within this company's industry group:** Sales: 2 Profits: 1

| Management: | | Sales/Marketing: | | Liberal Arts: | | Information Systems: | | Professionals: | | Technical/Scientific: | |
|---|---|---|---|---|---|---|---|---|---|---|---|
| Mgmt. Trainees: | | Mktg. Professionals: | Y | Gen. Writing/Editing: | Y | Info. Management: | Y | Finance/Accounting: | Y | Engineers, Elec.: | |
| Experienced Mgmt.: | Y | Retail Sales: | | Technical Writing: | Y | Software Dev.: | | Law: | Y | Engineers, Other: | |
| Int'l Business: | | Commercial/Industrial: | Y | Graphic Arts/Photog.: | | Hardware Dev.: | | HR/Other: | Y | Health/Lab: | Y |
| MBA Graduates: | Y | Sales Trainees: | | Music: | | Systems Integration: | | Training: | Y | Scientists/Research: | |
| | | Advertising Pros.: | | Broadcasting: | | Consulting/Other: | | Health Care: | Y | Petroleum/Chemicals: | |
| | | | | Other: | | | | Consulting: | | Math/Other: | Y |

## TYPES OF BUSINESS:

HMO-Low Income Patients
Medicaid HMO
SCHIP HMO

## BRANDS/DIVISIONS/AFFILIATES:

Mercy CarePlus
Molina Healthcare of Virginia
Florida NetPASS, LLC

## CONTACTS: *Note: Officers with more than one job title may be intentionally listed here more than once.*

J. Mario Molina, CEO
Terry Bayer, COO
J. Mario Molina, Pres.
John C. Molina, CFO
Martha (Molina) Bernadett, Exec. VP-R&D
Mark L. Andrews, Chief Legal Officer/Corp. Sec.
James Howatt, Chief Medical Officer

**Phone:** 562-435-3666 **Fax:**
**Toll-Free:** 888-562-5442
**Address:** 200 Oceangate, Ste. 100, Long Beach, CA 90802 US

## GROWTH PLANS/SPECIAL FEATURES:

Molina Healthcare, Inc. is a multi-stage managed care organization participating in government-sponsored health care programs for low-income persons, such as the Medicaid program and the State Children's Health Insurance Program (SCHIP), as well as a small number of persons who are dually eligible under the Medicaid and Medicare programs. Molina conducts its business primarily through nine licensed and locally operated health plans, each a wholly-owned subsidiary licensed as a health maintenance organization, in the states of California, Michigan, Missouri, Nevada, New Mexico, Ohio, Texas, Utah and Washington. (HMO). Approximately 1.2 million members are enrolled. Molina's revenues primarily derive from premium revenues paid by the relevant state Medicaid authority, which are generally an fixed amount per member per month whether the member utilizes no medical services in that month or whether they utilize services in excess of that amount. Each HMO contracts with health care providers in the relevant communities or states, including primary care physicians, specialist physicians, physician groups and hospitals. Molina's California HMO operates 19 of its own primary care community clinics. Molina is developing a predictive modeling capability for a more proactive case and health management approach as well as a provider profiling capability for network physicians. The company also develops specialized disease management programs, educational programs and pharmacy management programs. In November 2007, Molina acquired Mercy CarePlus, a Medicaid managed care organization based in St. Louis, Missouri for approximately $80 million. In July 2008, the firm announced Molina Healthcare of Virginia will operate Fairfax County Community Health Care Network, which has three county primary care clinics. In August 2008, Molina announced expansion into Florida with the acquisition of Florida NetPASS, LLC. Also in August, the firm announced the transfer of its IT center from California to New Mexico.

## FINANCIALS: **Sales and profits are in thousands of dollars—add 000 to get the full amount. 2008 Note: Financial information for 2008 was not available for all companies at press time.**

| | | |
|---|---|---|
| 2008 Sales: $ | 2008 Profits: $ | **U.S. Stock Ticker: MOH** |
| 2007 Sales: $2,492,454 | 2007 Profits: $58,330 | **Int'l Ticker:** Int'l Exchange: |
| 2006 Sales: $2,004,995 | 2006 Profits: $45,727 | Employees: 2,300 |
| 2005 Sales: $1,650,058 | 2005 Profits: $27,596 | Fiscal Year Ends: 12/31 |
| 2004 Sales: $1,175,268 | 2004 Profits: $55,773 | Parent Company: |

## SALARIES/BENEFITS:

| | | | | |
|---|---|---|---|---|
| Pension Plan: | ESOP Stock Plan: | Profit Sharing: | Top Exec. Salary: $775,000 | Bonus: $726,335 |
| Savings Plan: Y | Stock Purch. Plan: Y | | Second Exec. Salary: $700,000 | Bonus: $492,034 |

## OTHER THOUGHTS:

**Apparent Women Officers or Directors**: 4
**Hot Spot for Advancement for Women/Minorities**: Y

## LOCATIONS: ("Y" = Yes)

| West: | Southwest: | Midwest: | Southeast: | Northeast: | International: |
|---|---|---|---|---|---|
| Y | Y | Y | | | |

# MOTORCAR PARTS OF AMERICA INC

www.motorcarparts.com

**Industry Group Code:** 336300 **Ranks within this company's industry group:** Sales: 1 Profits: 1

| **Management:** | | **Sales/Marketing:** | | **Liberal Arts:** | | **Information Systems:** | | **Professionals:** | | **Technical/Scientific:** | |
|---|---|---|---|---|---|---|---|---|---|---|---|
| Mgmt. Trainees: | | Mktg. Professionals: | Y | Gen. Writing/Editing: | | Info. Management: | Y | Finance/Accounting: | Y | Engineers, Elec.: | Y |
| Experienced Mgmt.: | Y | Retail Sales: | | Technical Writing: | | Software Dev.: | | Law: | Y | Engineers, Other: | Y |
| Int'l Business: | Y | Commercial/Industrial: | Y | Graphic Arts/Photog.: | | Hardware Dev.: | | HR/Other: | Y | Health/Lab: | |
| MBA Graduates: | Y | Sales Trainees: | Y | Music: | | Systems Integration: | | Training: | Y | Scientists/Research: | |
| | | Advertising Pros.: | | Broadcasting: | | Consulting/Other: | | Health Care: | | Petroleum/Chemicals: | |
| | | | | Other: | | | | Consulting: | | Math/Other: | |

## TYPES OF BUSINESS:

Replacement Alternators & Starters

## BRANDS/DIVISIONS/AFFILIATES:

Quality Built to Last
Automotive Importing Manufacturing, Inc.

## CONTACTS:

*Note: Officers with more than one job title may be intentionally listed here more than once.*

Selwyn Joffe, CEO
Steven Kratz, COO
Selwyn Joffe, Pres.
David Lee, CFO
Tom Stricker, VP-Sales
Michael Umansky, General Counsel/VP/Corp. Sec.
Kevin Daly, Chief Acct. Officer
Meryvn McCulloch, VP-Acquisitions
Larry Fedoruk, VP-Heavy Duty Div.
Selwyn Joffe, Chmn.

**Phone:** 310-212-7910 **Fax:** 310-212-6315
**Toll-Free:** 800-890-9988
**Address:** 2929 California St., Torrance, CA 90503 US

## GROWTH PLANS/SPECIAL FEATURES:

Motorcar Parts of America, Inc. (MPA) remanufactures and distributes replacement alternators and starters for import and domestic cars and light trucks, including leading brands from companies such as General Motors, Ford, Daimler, Chrysler, Toyota, Honda, Nissan, Mitsubishi, Hyundai and Volkswagen. MPA's product line features approximately 940 starter models and 1,560 alternator models, as well as starter ignition wire sets. The firm's products are sold throughout the U.S. to more than 5,500 automotive parts stores, including some of the largest chains of retail automotive stores such as AutoZone, CSK Automotive and O'Reilly Automotive. MPA also gears its marketing and sales efforts toward traditional warehouse distributors and supplies remanufactured alternators and starters to General Motors. Approximately 96% of the firm's products are sold for resale under customer private labels, with the remaining 4% sold under its own brand name, Quality Built to Last. The company has remanufacturing, warehousing and shipping operations in California, Singapore and Malaysia, as well as a sales office in Charlotte, North Carolina. In May 2008, MPA acquired the operating assets of Automotive Importing Manufacturing, Inc., a privately-held company based in Rancho Cordova, California.

## FINANCIALS:

**Sales and profits are in thousands of dollars—add 000 to get the full amount. 2008 Note: Financial information for 2008 was not available for all companies at press time.**

| | | |
|---|---|---|
| 2008 Sales: $133,337 | 2008 Profits: $4,607 | **U.S. Stock Ticker: MPAA** |
| 2007 Sales: $136,323 | 2007 Profits: $-2,475 | **Int'l Ticker:** Int'l Exchange: |
| 2006 Sales: $108,397 | 2006 Profits: $6,298 | Employees: 311 |
| 2005 Sales: $95,785 | 2005 Profits: $6,288 | Fiscal Year Ends: 3/31 |
| 2004 Sales: $80,548 | 2004 Profits: $5,811 | Parent Company: |

## SALARIES/BENEFITS:

| | | | | |
|---|---|---|---|---|
| Pension Plan: | ESOP Stock Plan: | Profit Sharing: | Top Exec. Salary: $542,000 | Bonus: $600,000 |
| Savings Plan: | Stock Purch. Plan: | | Second Exec. Salary: $400,000 | Bonus: $40,000 |

## OTHER THOUGHTS:

**Apparent Women Officers or Directors:**
**Hot Spot for Advancement for Women/Minorities:**

## LOCATIONS: ("Y" = Yes)

| West: | Southwest: | Midwest: | Southeast: | Northeast: | International: |
|---|---|---|---|---|---|
| Y | | | Y | Y | Y |

# MTS SYSTEMS

www.mts.com

**Industry Group Code:** 334500 **Ranks within this company's industry group:** Sales: 1 Profits: 1

| Management: | | Sales/Marketing: | | Liberal Arts: | | Information Systems: | | Professionals: | | Technical/Scientific: | |
|---|---|---|---|---|---|---|---|---|---|---|---|
| Mgmt. Trainees: | | Mktg. Professionals: | Y | Gen. Writing/Editing: | | Info. Management: | Y | Finance/Accounting: | Y | Engineers, Elec.: | Y |
| Experienced Mgmt.: | Y | Retail Sales: | | Technical Writing: | Y | Software Dev.: | | Law: | Y | Engineers, Other: | Y |
| Int'l Business: | Y | Commercial/Industrial: | Y | Graphic Arts/Photog.: | | Hardware Dev.: | Y | HR/Other: | Y | Health/Lab: | |
| MBA Graduates: | Y | Sales Trainees: | Y | Music: | | Systems Integration: | Y | Training: | Y | Scientists/Research: | |
| | | Advertising Pros.: | | Broadcasting: | | Consulting/Other: | | Health Care: | | Petroleum/Chemicals: | |
| | | | | Other: | | | | Consulting: | | Math/Other: | Y |

## TYPES OF BUSINESS:

Mechanical Testing Equipment
Modeling & Testing Software
Consulting Services
Industrial Position Sensors

## BRANDS/DIVISIONS/AFFILIATES:

Insight
Temposonics
SWIFT 50 GLP
Series 201 Actuators
MAST
Bionix
AeroPro 5.0
SANS Group

## CONTACTS: *Note: Officers with more than one job title may be intentionally listed here more than once.*

Laura B. Hamilton, CEO
Susan E. Knight, CFO/VP
Kathleen M. Staby, VP-Human Resources
Joachim Hellwig, VP-Sensors Div.
Laura B. Hamilton, Chmn.

| | |
|---|---|
| **Phone:** 952-937-4000 | **Fax:** 952-937-4515 |
| **Toll-Free:** 800-328-2255 | |
| **Address:** 14000 Technology Dr., Eden Prairie, MN 55344 US | |

## GROWTH PLANS/SPECIAL FEATURES:

MTS Systems Corporation is a global supplier of mechanical test systems and industrial position sensors that are designed to aid customers in improving the design, development and manufacturing process of its products. MTS is organized into two business segments, the test segment and the sensors segment. The test segment, accounting for 80% of the firm's revenue, offers customers services research and product development to determine the properties and performance of materials within the transportation, aerospace, nano, bio and electromechanical markets. Products include rolling road simulators, friction stir welding machines and earthquake simulation systems. Additional nanomechanical tests are designed for highly precise applications within the semiconductor, consumer electronics, thin films and coating industries while biomechanical tests can be performed on implants, prostheses and other medical and dental devices and materials. The sensors segment, accounting for 20% of the firm's revenue, implements MTS sensors, sensing systems and other accessories to measure process variables or to automate production processes. This segment's products utilize a specific implementation of magnetostriction technology known as Temposonics, and include displacement position sensors, which measure the positioning, durability and continuous control of manufacturing machinery, mobile equipment and continuous measurement devices, and liquid level sensors, which measure the level of liquids in tanks and vessels. The industrial division typically caters to manufacturers of mobile equipment, steel-making equipment, plastic molding machines, pulp and paper processing equipment, semiconductor equipment and surgical room equipment. In October 2008, the company acquired the privately held, China based company, SANS Group.

Employees are offered medical, vision and dental insurance; short-and long-term disability; life and AD&D insurance; spouse and child life insurance; a 401(k) plan; an employee stock purchase plan; health care and dependent care flexible spending accounts; and tuition reimbursement.

## FINANCIALS: Sales and profits are in thousands of dollars—add 000 to get the full amount. 2008 Note: Financial information for 2008 was not available for all companies at press time.

| | | |
|---|---|---|
| 2008 Sales: $460,515 | 2008 Profits: $49,191 | **U.S. Stock Ticker: MTSC** |
| 2007 Sales: $410,091 | 2007 Profits: $41,996 | **Int'l Ticker:** Int'l Exchange: |
| 2006 Sales: $387,924 | 2006 Profits: $39,323 | Employees: 1,660 |
| 2005 Sales: $367,950 | 2005 Profits: $37,058 | Fiscal Year Ends: 9/30 |
| 2004 Sales: $338,204 | 2004 Profits: $28,983 | Parent Company: |

## SALARIES/BENEFITS:

| | | | | |
|---|---|---|---|---|
| Pension Plan: | ESOP Stock Plan: | Profit Sharing: | Top Exec. Salary: $543,119 | Bonus: $518,614 |
| Savings Plan: Y | Stock Purch. Plan: Y | | Second Exec. Salary: $374,042 | Bonus: $306,141 |

## OTHER THOUGHTS:

**Apparent Women Officers or Directors**: 3
**Hot Spot for Advancement for Women/Minorities**: Y

## LOCATIONS: ("Y" = Yes)

| West: | Southwest: | Midwest: | Southeast: | Northeast: | International: |
|---|---|---|---|---|---|
| Y | Y | Y | Y | Y | Y |

# MYRIAD GENETICS INC

**www.myriad.com**

**Industry Group Code:** 325412 **Ranks within this company's industry group:** Sales: 17 Profits: 22

| Management: | | Sales/Marketing: | | Liberal Arts: | | Information Systems: | | Professionals: | | Technical/Scientific: | |
|---|---|---|---|---|---|---|---|---|---|---|---|
| Mgmt. Trainees: | | Mktg. Professionals: | Y | Gen. Writing/Editing: | | Info. Management: | Y | Finance/Accounting: | Y | Engineers, Elec.: | |
| Experienced Mgmt.: | Y | Retail Sales: | | Technical Writing: | Y | Software Dev.: | Y | Law: | Y | Engineers, Other: | |
| Int'l Business: | | Commercial/Industrial: | Y | Graphic Arts/Photog.: | | Hardware Dev.: | | HR/Other: | Y | Health/Lab: | Y |
| MBA Graduates: | Y | Sales Trainees: | Y | Music: | | Systems Integration: | | Training: | Y | Scientists/Research: | Y |
| | | Advertising Pros.: | | Broadcasting: | | Consulting/Other: | | Health Care: | Y | Petroleum/Chemicals: | Y |
| | | | | Other: | | | | Consulting: | | Math/Other: | Y |

## TYPES OF BUSINESS:

Pharmaceuticals Discovery & Development
Cancer Treatments
Alzheimer's Treatment
Cancer Diagnostics

## BRANDS/DIVISIONS/AFFILIATES:

Myriad Genetic Laboratories, Inc.
Myriad Pharmaceuticals, Inc.
Flurizan
BRACAnalysis
COLARIS
MELARIS
COLARIS AP
Azixa

## CONTACTS:

*Note: Officers with more than one job title may be intentionally listed here more than once.*

Peter D. Meldrum, CEO
Peter D. Meldrum, Pres.
James S. Evans, CFO
Jerry Lanchbury, Exec. VP-Research
Robert G. Harrison, CIO
Richard Marsh, General Counsel/Exec. VP/Corp. Sec.
William A. Hockett, III, Exec. VP-Corp. Comm.
Gregory C. Critchfield, Pres., Myriad Genetic Laboratories, Inc.
Adrian N. Hobden, Pres., Myriad Pharmaceuticals, Inc.
Mark H. Skolnick, Chief Scientific Officer
Mark C. Capone, COO-Myriad Genetic Laboratories, Inc.
John T. Henderson, Chmn.

**Phone:** 801-584-3600 **Fax:** 801-584-3640
**Toll-Free:**
**Address:** 320 Wakara Way, Salt Lake City, UT 84108 US

## GROWTH PLANS/SPECIAL FEATURES:

Myriad Genetics, Inc. is a biopharmaceutical company that develops and markets novel therapeutic and molecular diagnostic products. The company develops a number of proprietary technologies that are aimed at understanding the genetic basis of human disease in order to effectively treat diseases. Myriad's molecular diagnostic business is focused on both predictive medicine and personalized medicine. Predictive medicine analyzes genes to assess an individual's potential risk of developing while personalized medicine analyzes genes to assess a patient's risk in disease progression and recurrence and drug response. The company currently owns four commercial predictive medicine products: BRACAnalysis for breast and ovarian cancer; COLARIS for colon and uterine cancer; COLARIS AP for polyp-forming syndromes of colon cancer; and MELARIS for melanoma. In addition, the company owns TheraGuide 5-FU, which helps predict whether cancer patients are likely to suffer serious toxic reactions to the drug 5-Fluorouracil. Myriad researchers have also made progressive discoveries in the fields of cancer, Alzheimer's disease and infectious diseases. The lead product pipeline includes Azixa for the treatment of solid cancer tumors and brain metastases; MPC-2130 for the treatment of hematologic cancers; MPC-0920 for the treatment of thrombosis; and Vivecon (formerly MPI-49839) for the treatment of AIDS. Myriad has a variety of partnerships to discover genes and proteins associated with human disease to elucidate protein networks, screen small molecule libraries against drug target assays, develop novel drug candidates and sequence the entire genomes. In December 2007, the firm applied to begin human trials for Vivecon. In June 2008, the company ceased research of Flurizan, for Alzheimer's disease, after failing to reach statistical significance in Phase III trials.

Myriad offers employees tax free reimbursement accounts, incentive stock options and medical and dental insurance programs.

## FINANCIALS:

**Sales and profits are in thousands of dollars—add 000 to get the full amount. 2008 Note: Financial information for 2008 was not available for all companies at press time.**

| | | |
|---|---|---|
| 2008 Sales: $334,000 | 2008 Profits: $47,845 | **U.S. Stock Ticker: MYGN** |
| 2007 Sales: $157,126 | 2007 Profits: $-34,962 | **Int'l Ticker:** Int'l Exchange: |
| 2006 Sales: $114,279 | 2006 Profits: $-38,189 | Employees: 994 |
| 2005 Sales: $82,406 | 2005 Profits: $-39,978 | Fiscal Year Ends: 6/30 |
| 2004 Sales: $56,648 | 2004 Profits: $-40,620 | Parent Company: |

## SALARIES/BENEFITS:

| | | | | |
|---|---|---|---|---|
| Pension Plan: | ESOP Stock Plan: | Profit Sharing: | Top Exec. Salary: $676,978 | Bonus: $550,761 |
| Savings Plan: Y | Stock Purch. Plan: Y | | Second Exec. Salary: $465,478 | Bonus: $350,761 |

## OTHER THOUGHTS:

**Apparent Women Officers or Directors**: 1
**Hot Spot for Advancement for Women/Minorities**:

## LOCATIONS: ("Y" = Yes)

| West: | Southwest: | Midwest: | Southeast: | Northeast: | International: |
|---|---|---|---|---|---|
| Y | | | | | |

# NANOMETRICS INC

www.nanometrics.com

**Industry Group Code:** 334500 **Ranks within this company's industry group:** Sales: 4 Profits: 3

| Management: | | Sales/Marketing: | | Liberal Arts: | | Information Systems: | | Professionals: | | Technical/Scientific: | |
|---|---|---|---|---|---|---|---|---|---|---|---|
| Mgmt. Trainees: | | Mktg. Professionals: | Y | Gen. Writing/Editing: | | Info. Management: | Y | Finance/Accounting: | Y | Engineers, Elec.: | Y |
| Experienced Mgmt.: | Y | Retail Sales: | | Technical Writing: | Y | Software Dev.: | | Law: | Y | Engineers, Other: | Y |
| Int'l Business: | Y | Commercial/Industrial: | Y | Graphic Arts/Photog.: | | Hardware Dev.: | Y | HR/Other: | Y | Health/Lab: | |
| MBA Graduates: | Y | Sales Trainees: | Y | Music: | | Systems Integration: | Y | Training: | Y | Scientists/Research: | Y |
| | | Advertising Pros.: | | Broadcasting: | | Consulting/Other: | | Health Care: | | Petroleum/Chemicals: | |
| | | | | Other: | | | | Consulting: | | Math/Other: | Y |

## TYPES OF BUSINESS:

Research & Development-Nanotechnology
Process Control Metrology Systems

## BRANDS/DIVISIONS/AFFILIATES:

Tevet Process Control Technologies, Ltd.

## CONTACTS:

*Note: Officers with more than one job title may be intentionally listed here more than once.*

Timothy J. Stultz, CEO
Bruce Crawford, COO
Timothy J. Stultz, Pres.
Bruce Crawford, Interim CFO
Bruce C. Rhine, Chmn.

**Phone:** 408-545-6000 **Fax:** 408-232-5910
**Toll-Free:**
**Address:** 1550 Buckeye Dr., Milpitas, CA 95035 US

## GROWTH PLANS/SPECIAL FEATURES:

Nanometrics, Inc. designs, manufactures and markets process control metrology systems used in the manufacture of silicon and compound semiconductor substrates, devices and integrated circuits. Metrology systems measure thin film properties, critical dimensions, overlay control and optical, electrical and material properties, including the structural composition of silicon and compound semiconductor devices, during the manufacturing process. The company divides its metrology systems into three categories: standalone, fully automated systems, which are used for high-volume manufacturing process control; integrated systems built into semiconductor processing equipment, which provide real-time measurements to improve process control and increase throughput; and standalone, manual and semi-automatic systems for manufacturing process characterization and for engineering and low-volume production environments. Nanometrics' metrology systems particularly facilitate the manufacturing process in three major semiconductor process areas: Chemical mechanical planarization (CMP); chemical vapor deposition (CVD); and lithography/etch. Nanometrics offers products with such diverse applications as film analysis, Fourier Transform Infrared (FTIR), inspection, mask metrology, overlay metrology and scatterometry, as well as providing contamination and defect process control and carrier concentration solutions. The company is headquartered in Milpitas, California, with additional offices in Bend, Oregon as well as Europe, China, Japan, Taiwan, Israel, Korea and Singapore. In May 2008, Nanometrics acquired Tevet Process Control Technologies, Ltd., an integrated metrology company focused on the worldwide semiconductor and solar manufacturing industry.

The company offers its employees a 401(k) plan; profit sharing; an employee stock purchasing plan; tuition reimbursement; a flex spending plan for health care and child care expenses; and an employee referral bonus.

## FINANCIALS:

**Sales and profits are in thousands of dollars—add 000 to get the full amount. 2008 Note: Financial information for 2008 was not available for all companies at press time.**

| | | |
|---|---|---|
| 2008 Sales: $ | 2008 Profits: $ | **U.S. Stock Ticker: NANO** |
| 2007 Sales: $146,290 | 2007 Profits: $-4,008 | **Int'l Ticker:** Int'l Exchange: |
| 2006 Sales: $96,374 | 2006 Profits: $-22,127 | Employees: 523 |
| 2005 Sales: $70,543 | 2005 Profits: $1,511 | Fiscal Year Ends: 12/31 |
| 2004 Sales: $69,931 | 2004 Profits: $3,699 | Parent Company: |

## SALARIES/BENEFITS:

| | | | | |
|---|---|---|---|---|
| Pension Plan: | ESOP Stock Plan: | Profit Sharing: Y | Top Exec. Salary: $341,800 | Bonus: $79,314 |
| Savings Plan: Y | Stock Purch. Plan: Y | | Second Exec. Salary: $204,800 | Bonus: $29,864 |

## OTHER THOUGHTS:

**Apparent Women Officers or Directors:**
**Hot Spot for Advancement for Women/Minorities:**

## LOCATIONS: ("Y" = Yes)

| West: | Southwest: | Midwest: | Southeast: | Northeast: | International: |
|---|---|---|---|---|---|
| Y | | | | | Y |

# NASDAQ OMX

www.nasdaqomx.com

**Industry Group Code:** 523210 **Ranks within this company's industry group:** Sales: 1 Profits: 2

| Management: | | Sales/Marketing: | | Liberal Arts: | | Information Systems: | | Professionals: | | Technical/Scientific: | |
|---|---|---|---|---|---|---|---|---|---|---|---|
| Mgmt. Trainees: | | Mktg. Professionals: | Y | Gen. Writing/Editing: | | Info. Management: | Y | Finance/Accounting: | Y | Engineers, Elec.: | |
| Experienced Mgmt.: | Y | Retail Sales: | | Technical Writing: | | Software Dev.: | Y | Law: | Y | Engineers, Other: | |
| Int'l Business: | Y | Commercial/Industrial: | | Graphic Arts/Photog.: | | Hardware Dev.: | | HR/Other: | Y | Health/Lab: | |
| MBA Graduates: | Y | Sales Trainees: | | Music: | | Systems Integration: | | Training: | Y | Scientists/Research: | |
| | | Advertising Pros.: | Y | Broadcasting: | | Consulting/Other: | | Health Care: | | Petroleum/Chemicals: | |
| | | | | Other: | | | | Consulting: | | Math/Other: | Y |

## TYPES OF BUSINESS:

Stock Exchange
Exchange Software
Market Data
Insurance Agency
Newswire & Multimedia Services

## BRANDS/DIVISIONS/AFFILIATES:

Nasdaq Stock Market, LLC (The)
Nasdaq Market Center
Nasdaq Biotechnology Index
Nasdaq Composite Index
OMX Pan European Market

## CONTACTS: *Note: Officers with more than one job title may be intentionally listed here more than once.*

Robert Greifeld, CEO
Magnus Bocker, Pres.
David P. Warren, CFO/Exec. VP
John Jacobs, Chief Mktg. Officer
Anna M. Ewing, CIO/Exec. VP
Edward S. Knight, General Counsel/Exec. VP
Anna M. Ewing, Exec. VP-Oper.
Adena T. Friendman, Exec. VP-Corp. Strategy & Global Data Products
John L. Jacobs, Exec. VP-Worldwide Mktg. & Financial Products
Bruce E. Aust, Exec. VP-Corp. Client Group
Christopher R. Concannon, Exec. VP-Transaction Svcs.
Carl-Magnus Hallberg, Sr. VP-Global IT Svcs.

| Phone: 212-401-8700 | Fax: |
|---|---|
| Toll-Free: | |
| Address: 1 Liberty Plz., 165 Broadway, New York, NY 10006 US | |

## GROWTH PLANS/SPECIAL FEATURES:

NASDAQ OMX, the holding company that operates the NASDAQ stock exchange as well as the OMX exchange in Europe, is a provider of securities listing, trading and information products and services. The stock exchange lists over 3,100 companies with a combined market capitalization of over $4.2 trillion. The firm operates in two segments: market services and issuer services. The market services segment includes the transaction-based business and the market information services business. The NASDAQ Market Center is a transaction-based platform that provides the ability to access, process, display and integrate orders and quotes, enabling customers to execute trades in over 7,400 equity securities. The NASDAQ Market Center allows the firm to route and execute buy and sell orders as well as report transactions for NASDAQ-listed securities and those securities listed on other national securities exchanges, providing fee-based revenues. NASDAQ also generates revenues by providing varying levels of quote and trade information to market participants and data vendors, who in turn sell subscriptions for this information to the public. The company's systems enable vendors to gain direct access to detailed order data, index information, mutual fund pricing information and corporate action information on NASDAQ-listed securities. The issuer services business segment includes the securities listings business; insurance business; shareholder and newswire services; and the financial products business. It also develops and licenses financial products and associated derivatives based on NASDAQ indexes, such as the NASDAQ Composite Index and the NASDAQ Biotechnology Index. In late 2007, NASDAQ agreed to sell nearly all of its 31% stake in the London Stock Exchange (LSE). In 2008, NASDAQ's parent company acquired OMX, an exchange based in Europe. In September 2008, the newly merged company launched the OMX Pan European Market, a trading platform designed to electronically match buyers and sellers of stocks listed on various exchanges throughout Europe.

## FINANCIALS: **Sales and profits are in thousands of dollars—add 000 to get the full amount. 2008 Note: Financial information for 2008 was not available for all companies at press time.**

| | | |
|---|---|---|
| 2008 Sales: $ | 2008 Profits: $ | **U.S. Stock Ticker: NDAQ** |
| 2007 Sales: $2,436,592 | 2007 Profits: $518,401 | **Int'l Ticker:** Int'l Exchange: |
| 2006 Sales: $1,657,776 | 2006 Profits: $127,893 | Employees: 891 |
| 2005 Sales: $879,919 | 2005 Profits: $61,690 | Fiscal Year Ends: 12/31 |
| 2004 Sales: $540,400 | 2004 Profits: $11,400 | Parent Company: |

## SALARIES/BENEFITS:

| | | | | |
|---|---|---|---|---|
| Pension Plan: | ESOP Stock Plan: | Profit Sharing: | Top Exec. Salary: $1,000,000 | Bonus: $3,800,000 |
| Savings Plan: | Stock Purch. Plan: | | Second Exec. Salary: $425,000 | Bonus: $950,000 |

## OTHER THOUGHTS:

**Apparent Women Officers or Directors**: 4
**Hot Spot for Advancement for Women/Minorities**: Y

## LOCATIONS: ("Y" = Yes)

| West: | Southwest: | Midwest: | Southeast: | Northeast: | International: |
|---|---|---|---|---|---|
| Y | | Y | | Y | Y |

# NATIONAL BEVERAGE CORP

www.nbcfiz.com

**Industry Group Code:** 312111 **Ranks within this company's industry group:** Sales: 2 Profits: 2

| Management: | | Sales/Marketing: | | Liberal Arts: | | Information Systems: | | Professionals: | | Technical/Scientific: | |
|---|---|---|---|---|---|---|---|---|---|---|---|
| Mgmt. Trainees: | Y | Mktg. Professionals: | Y | Gen. Writing/Editing: | | Info. Management: | Y | Finance/Accounting: | Y | Engineers, Elec.: | |
| Experienced Mgmt.: | Y | Retail Sales: | | Technical Writing: | | Software Dev.: | | Law: | Y | Engineers, Other: | |
| Int'l Business: | | Commercial/Industrial: | Y | Graphic Arts/Photog.: | Y | Hardware Dev.: | | HR/Other: | Y | Health/Lab: | |
| MBA Graduates: | Y | Sales Trainees: | Y | Music: | | Systems Integration: | | Training: | Y | Scientists/Research: | |
| | | Advertising Pros.: | Y | Broadcasting: | | Consulting/Other: | | Health Care: | | Petroleum/Chemicals: | |
| | | | | Other: | | | | Consulting: | | Math/Other: | |

## TYPES OF BUSINESS:

Beverages-Soft Drinks Manufacturing
Juice Drinks
Bottled Water
Energy Drinks

## BRANDS/DIVISIONS/AFFILIATES:

Shasta
Faygo
Everfresh
LaCROIX
VooDoo Rain
Ohana
Rip It
Double Hit

## CONTACTS: *Note: Officers with more than one job title may be intentionally listed here more than once.*

Nick A. Caporella, CEO
Joseph G. Caporella, Pres.
Dean A. McCoy, Sr. VP/Chief Acct. Officer
George R. Bracken, Sr. VP-Finance
Nick A. Caporella, Chmn.
Edward F. Knecht, Exec. VP-Procurement

**Phone:** 954-581-0922 **Fax:** 954-475-8780
**Toll-Free:** 877-622-3499
**Address:** 8100 S.W. 10th St., Ste. 4000, Ft. Lauderdale, FL 33324 US

## GROWTH PLANS/SPECIAL FEATURES:

National Beverage Corp. develops, manufactures, markets and distributes carbonated and non-carbonated beverage products throughout the U.S. The company's products emphasize distinctive flavor variety and include its flagship brands Shasta and Faygo, which encompass complete lines of multi-flavored and cola soft drinks. Shasta is the largest of the company's brands and includes multiple flavors as well as bottled spring and drinking waters. Established 95 years ago, Faygo products are primarily distributed east of the Mississippi River and include a multi-flavored product line. Additionally, National Beverage offers an assortment of premium beverages geared toward health-conscious consumers, including Everfresh, Home Juice and Mr. Pure 100% juice and juice-based products; and LaCROIX, Mt. Shasta, Crystal Bay and ClearFruit flavored and spring water products. The company also produces specialty products, including VooDoo Rain, a line of alternative beverages geared toward young consumers; Ohana fruit-flavored drinks; Rip It and PowerBlast, energy drinks available in both liquid and powdered form; Double Hit coffee energy drinks; and St. Nick's holiday soft drinks. Substantially all of National Beverage's brands are produced in its 13 manufacturing facilities, which are located in major metropolitan markets throughout the continental U.S. The company also develops and produces soft drinks for retail grocery chains, warehouse clubs, mass-merchandisers and wholesalers, as well as soft drinks for other beverage companies. National Beverage distributes products to convenience stores, gas stations and other small establishments through its own direct-store delivery fleets, along with those of independent distributors, and distributes to hospitals, schools, military bases, airlines and hotels primarily through independent distributors.

Employees are offered health, dental, life and disability insurance, as well as a 401(k) plan.

## FINANCIALS: **Sales and profits are in thousands of dollars—add 000 to get the full amount. 2008 Note: Financial information for 2008 was not available for all companies at press time.**

2008 Sales: $566,001
2007 Sales: $539,030
2006 Sales: $516,802
2005 Sales: $495,572
2004 Sales: $512,061

2008 Profits: $22,480
2007 Profits: $24,682
2006 Profits: $22,226
2005 Profits: $16,886
2004 Profits: $18,691

**U.S. Stock Ticker: FIZZ**
**Int'l Ticker:** Int'l Exchange:
Employees: 1,300
Fiscal Year Ends: 4/30
Parent Company:

## SALARIES/BENEFITS:

Pension Plan: ESOP Stock Plan: Profit Sharing: Top Exec. Salary: $400,000 Bonus: $301,226
Savings Plan: Y Stock Purch. Plan: Second Exec. Salary: $170,000 Bonus: $47,000

## OTHER THOUGHTS:

**Apparent Women Officers or Directors:**
**Hot Spot for Advancement for Women/Minorities:**

## LOCATIONS: ("Y" = Yes)

| West: | Southwest: | Midwest: | Southeast: | Northeast: | International: |
|---|---|---|---|---|---|
| Y | Y | Y | Y | Y | |

# NATIONAL CINEMEDIA INC

www.ncm.com

**Industry Group Code:** 541890 **Ranks within this company's industry group:** Sales: 1 Profits: 1

| Management: | | Sales/Marketing: | | Liberal Arts: | | Information Systems: | | Professionals: | | Technical/Scientific: | |
|---|---|---|---|---|---|---|---|---|---|---|---|
| Mgmt. Trainees: | | Mktg. Professionals: | Y | Gen. Writing/Editing: | | Info. Management: | Y | Finance/Accounting: | Y | Engineers, Elec.: | |
| Experienced Mgmt.: | Y | Retail Sales: | | Technical Writing: | | Software Dev.: | | Law: | Y | Engineers, Other: | |
| Int'l Business: | | Commercial/Industrial: | | Graphic Arts/Photog.: | | Hardware Dev.: | | HR/Other: | Y | Health/Lab: | |
| MBA Graduates: | Y | Sales Trainees: | Y | Music: | | Systems Integration: | | Training: | Y | Scientists/Research: | |
| | | Advertising Pros.: | | Broadcasting: | | Consulting/Other: | | Health Care: | | Petroleum/Chemicals: | |
| | | | | Other: | | | | Consulting: | | Math/Other: | |

## TYPES OF BUSINESS:

In-Theater Advertisement
Event Hosting
Theater-Based Networked Events

## BRANDS/DIVISIONS/AFFILIATES:

National CineMedia LLC
FirstLook
CineMeetings
NCM Fathom
AMC Entertainment Inc
Cinemark Inc
Regal Entertainment Group

## CONTACTS: *Note: Officers with more than one job title may be intentionally listed here more than once.*

Kurt C. Hall, CEO
Thomas C. Galley, COO/Exec. VP
Kurt C. Hall, Pres.
Gary W. Ferrera, CFO/Exec. VP
Clifford E. Marks, Chief Mktg. Officer/Pres., Sales
Thomas C. Galley, CTO
Ralph E. Hardy, General Counsel
Kurt C. Hall, Chmn.

**Phone:** 303-792-3600 **Fax:** 303-792-8800
**Toll-Free:** 800-828-2828
**Address:** 9110 E. Nichols Ave., Ste. 200, Centennial, CO 80112-3405 US

## GROWTH PLANS/SPECIAL FEATURES:

National CineMedia, Inc. (NCM) is a holding company for National CineMedia LLC, which operates 17,000 screens in 1,350 theaters across 47 states, serving approximately 700 million patrons annually. It has long-term exhibitor services agreements with its founding members, three of the largest motion picture exhibition companies in the U.S.: AMC Entertainment, Inc.; Cinemark USA, Inc.; and Regal Entertainment Group. NCM operates the Digital Content Network (DCN), one of the largest digital in-theatre networks in North America, broadcasting branded entertainment to approximately 15,000 of its theatres via satellite, including HD (High-Definition) commercials in their lobbies and auditoriums through the company's Lobby Entertainment Network (LEN). The firm derives revenue mainly from advertising, CineMeetings and Fathom Events. Advertising activities include the development, production, sale and distribution of branded, pre-feature entertainment and advertising programming along with an advertising programming (through First Look) for theater lobbies. FirstLook is comprised of up to four segments, each approximately four to seven minutes in length. Segment four, the first section of FirstLook, begins approximately 20 minutes prior to the advertised show time and generally includes local and regional advertising. CineMeetings facilitates live and pre-recorded networked and single-site meetings, corporate events and church services movie theatres throughout the firm's network. NCM provides centralized event management including booking, event coordination and execution, technical support, promotional tools, advanced audio/visual technologies and catering services. Fathom Events distribute live and pre-recorded concerts, sporting events and other entertainment programming content to theatres across its digital network. NCMs network is able to deliver live high-definition content to nearly 350 theatres; live up-converted standard definition content to nearly 350 theatres; and high-definition pre-recorded content to virtually all its in-network digital screens. Revenue produced by these three divisions account for approximately 91.6%, 5.6% and 2.8%, respectively.

## FINANCIALS: **Sales and profits are in thousands of dollars—add 000 to get the full amount. 2008 Note: Financial information for 2008 was not available for all companies at press time.**

| | | |
|---|---|---|
| 2008 Sales: $ | 2008 Profits: $ | **U.S. Stock Ticker: NCMI** |
| 2007 Sales: $331,900 | 2007 Profits: $20,600 | **Int'l Ticker:** Int'l Exchange: |
| 2006 Sales: $219,300 | 2006 Profits: $-10,500 | Employees: 535 |
| 2005 Sales: $116,600 | 2005 Profits: $-5,200 | Fiscal Year Ends: 12/31 |
| 2004 Sales: $ | 2004 Profits: $ | Parent Company: |

## SALARIES/BENEFITS:

| | | | | |
|---|---|---|---|---|
| Pension Plan: | ESOP Stock Plan: | Profit Sharing: | Top Exec. Salary: $700,000 | Bonus: $1,065,146 |
| Savings Plan: | Stock Purch. Plan: | | Second Exec. Salary: $675,000 | Bonus: $775,000 |

## OTHER THOUGHTS:

**Apparent Women Officers or Directors**: 1
**Hot Spot for Advancement for Women/Minorities**:

## LOCATIONS: ("Y" = Yes)

| West: | Southwest: | Midwest: | Southeast: | Northeast: | International: |
|---|---|---|---|---|---|
| Y | Y | Y | Y | Y | |

# NATIONAL DENTEX CORP

www.nationaldentex.com

**Industry Group Code:** 339113 **Ranks within this company's industry group:** Sales: 21 Profits: 28

| Management: | | Sales/Marketing: | | Liberal Arts: | | Information Systems: | | Professionals: | | Technical/Scientific: | |
|---|---|---|---|---|---|---|---|---|---|---|---|
| Mgmt. Trainees: | | Mktg. Professionals: | Y | Gen. Writing/Editing: | | Info. Management: | Y | Finance/Accounting: | Y | Engineers, Elec.: | |
| Experienced Mgmt.: | Y | Retail Sales: | | Technical Writing: | Y | Software Dev.: | | Law: | Y | Engineers, Other: | Y |
| Int'l Business: | Y | Commercial/Industrial: | Y | Graphic Arts/Photog.: | | Hardware Dev.: | | HR/Other: | Y | Health/Lab: | Y |
| MBA Graduates: | Y | Sales Trainees: | Y | Music: | | Systems Integration: | | Training: | Y | Scientists/Research: | Y |
| | | Advertising Pros.: | | Broadcasting: | | Consulting/Other: | | Health Care: | Y | Petroleum/Chemicals: | |
| | | | | Other: | | | | Consulting: | | Math/Other: | Y |

## TYPES OF BUSINESS:

Dental Prosthetic Appliances
Dental Laboratories

## BRANDS/DIVISIONS/AFFILIATES:

Green Dental Laboratories, Inc.
Keller Group, Inc.
Impact Dental Laboratory, Ltd.
NTI-tss

## CONTACTS:

*Note: Officers with more than one job title may be intentionally listed here more than once.*

David L. Brown, CEO
David L. Brown, Pres.
Wayne M. Coll, CFO/VP
Lynn D. Dine, VP-R&D
Richard G. Mariacher, VP-Tech. Svcs.
Donald H. Siegel, Sec.
Doug Baker, VP-Oper.
Richard F. Becker, Jr., Treas./Exec. VP
Richard G. Mariacher, VP-Industry Rel.
Arthur B. Champagne, Sr. VP
Dean Ribeiro, VP-Client Rel.
Josh Green, Exec. VP-Laboratory Oper.
David V. Harkins, Chmn.

| | |
|---|---|
| **Phone:** 508-907-7800 | **Fax:** |
| **Toll-Free:** | |
| **Address:** 2 Vision Dr., Natick, MA 01760 US | |

## GROWTH PLANS/SPECIAL FEATURES:

National Dentex Corp. designs, manufactures, markets and sells custom dental prosthetic appliances such as crowns, bridges and dentures. The company owns and operates 41 full-service dental laboratories and seven branch laboratories located throughout 31 states and one Canadian province. The firm operates in three segments: Green Dental, representing the operations of Green Dental Laboratories, Inc. located in Arkansas; Keller, representing the operations of Keller Group, Inc.; and NDX Laboratories, which represents the company's remaining laboratories. National Dentex's products are groups in three main categories: restorative, which consist primarily of crowns and bridges; reconstructive, which consist primarily of partial dentures and full dentures; and cosmetic products, which consist primarily of porcelain veneers and ceramic crowns. The products are manufactured from materials such as high noble, noble and predominantly base alloys, dental resins, composites and porcelain. The company's products are produced by trained technicians working primarily with work orders and cases, such as impressions, models and occlusal registrations of a patient's teeth, provided by the dentists in the company's customer base. Each of the company's local dental laboratories markets and sells its products through its own direct sales force. The branch laboratories are smaller than the main laboratories and thus offer fewer products. When one of the branches is unable to fill an order, it sends it on to one of the full-service laboratories. In April 2008, National Dentex announced the extension of an agreement for manufacturing and distribution rights of the NTI-tss, a small dental mouthpiece for the prevention of migraine pain from tension.

The company offers its employees medical and dental insurance; educational assistance; an employee stock purchase plan; a profit sharing plan; stock options; and life insurance.

## FINANCIALS:

**Sales and profits are in thousands of dollars—add 000 to get the full amount. 2008 Note: Financial information for 2008 was not available for all companies at press time.**

| | | |
|---|---|---|
| 2008 Sales: $ | 2008 Profits: $ | **U.S. Stock Ticker: NADX** |
| 2007 Sales: $170,361 | 2007 Profits: $6,626 | **Int'l Ticker:** Int'l Exchange: |
| 2006 Sales: $150,107 | 2006 Profits: $5,763 | Employees: 2,027 |
| 2005 Sales: $135,843 | 2005 Profits: $7,089 | Fiscal Year Ends: 12/31 |
| 2004 Sales: $111,753 | 2004 Profits: $5,159 | Parent Company: |

## SALARIES/BENEFITS:

| | | | | |
|---|---|---|---|---|
| Pension Plan: | ESOP Stock Plan: | Profit Sharing: Y | Top Exec. Salary: $350,000 | Bonus: $92,750 |
| Savings Plan: Y | Stock Purch. Plan: Y | | Second Exec. Salary: $350,000 | Bonus: $56,000 |

## OTHER THOUGHTS:

**Apparent Women Officers or Directors**: 1
**Hot Spot for Advancement for Women/Minorities**:

## LOCATIONS: ("Y" = Yes)

| West: | Southwest: | Midwest: | Southeast: | Northeast: | International: |
|---|---|---|---|---|---|
| Y | Y | Y | Y | Y | Y |

# NATIONAL FUEL GAS CO

**www.natfuel.com**

**Industry Group Code:** 221000B **Ranks within this company's industry group:** Sales: 2 Profits: 1

| **Management:** | | **Sales/Marketing:** | | **Liberal Arts:** | | **Information Systems:** | | **Professionals:** | | **Technical/Scientific:** | |
|---|---|---|---|---|---|---|---|---|---|---|---|
| Mgmt. Trainees: | | Mktg. Professionals: | Y | Gen. Writing/Editing: | | Info. Management: | Y | Finance/Accounting: | Y | Engineers, Elec.: | Y |
| Experienced Mgmt.: | Y | Retail Sales: | | Technical Writing: | | Software Dev.: | | Law: | Y | Engineers, Other: | Y |
| Int'l Business: | Y | Commercial/Industrial: | Y | Graphic Arts/Photog.: | | Hardware Dev.: | | HR/Other: | Y | Health/Lab: | |
| MBA Graduates: | Y | Sales Trainees: | | Music: | | Systems Integration: | | Training: | Y | Scientists/Research: | |
| | | Advertising Pros.: | | Broadcasting: | | Consulting/Other: | | Health Care: | | Petroleum/Chemicals: | Y |
| | | | | Other: | | | | Consulting: | | Math/Other: | |

## TYPES OF BUSINESS:

Oil & Gas Exploration & Production
Natural Gas Utility
Pipelines & Storage
Sawmills & Timber Marketing
Energy Marketing
Energy Management Services

## BRANDS/DIVISIONS/AFFILIATES:

National Fuel Gas Distribution Corp.
National Fuel Gas Supply Corp.
Seneca Energy Canada, Inc.
Seneca Reources Corp.
Horizon Energy Development, Inc.
National Fuel Resources, Inc.
Highland Forest Resources, Inc.
Empire State Pipeline

## CONTACTS: *Note: Officers with more than one job title may be intentionally listed here more than once.*

David F. Smith, CEO
David F. Smith, COO
David F. Smith, Pres.
Ronald J. Tanski, Principal Financial Officer/Treas.
Paula M. Ciprich, General Counsel/Sec.
Donna L. DeCarolis, VP-Bus. Dev.
Karen M. Camiolo, Controller/Principal Acct. Officer
Anna Marie Cellino, Pres., National Fuel Gas Distribution Corporation
Ronald J. Tanski, Pres., Empire State Pipeline
Matthew D. Cabell, Pres., Seneca Resources Corporation
Duane A. Wassum, Pres., Highland Forest Resources, Inc.
Philip C. Ackerman, Chmn.

| | |
|---|---|
| **Phone:** 716-857-7000 | **Fax:** |
| **Toll-Free:** 800-365-3234 | |
| **Address:** 6363 Main St., Williamsville, NY 14221 US | |

## GROWTH PLANS/SPECIAL FEATURES:

National Fuel Gas Co. is a holding company with operations in five business segments: utility; pipeline and storage; exploration and production; energy marketing; and timber. The utility operations are carried out by National Fuel Gas Distribution Corp., which sells or transports natural gas to approximately 725,000 customers in New York and Pennsylvania. The pipeline and storage operations are carried out by National Fuel Gas Supply Corp. and Empire State Pipeline. It provides interstate natural gas transmission and storage for affiliated and nonaffiliated companies from southwestern Pennsylvania to the New York-Canadian border at the Niagara River. Seneca Resources Corp., Inc. conducts the company's exploration and production activities. They explore for, develop and purchase oil and natural gas reserves in California; the Appalachian region of the U.S.; Wyoming; and the Gulf Coast regions of Texas, Louisiana, and Alabama. The energy marketing operations, carried out by National Fuel Resources, Inc., markets natural gas to industrial, commercial, public authority and residential end users in New York and Pennsylvania. The timber division, through Highland Forest Resources, Inc., operates two sawmills and processes hardwoods residing in about 103,700 acres of timber property in Pennsylvania and New York. Other subsidiaries include Horizon Energy Development, Inc., which engages in foreign and domestic energy projects; Horizon LFG, Inc., is engaged in the purchase, sale and transportation of landfill gas in Ohio, Michigan, Kentucky, Missouri, Maryland and Indiana; Leidy Hub, Inc., provides various natural gas hub services to customers in the eastern U.S.; Data-Track Account Services, Inc., which offers collection services primarily for the company's subsidiaries; and Horizon Power, Inc., which develops and operates mid-range independent power production facilities and landfill gas electric generation facilities.

## FINANCIALS: **Sales and profits are in thousands of dollars—add 000 to get the full amount. 2008 Note: Financial information for 2008 was not available for all companies at press time.**

| | | |
|---|---|---|
| 2008 Sales: $2,400,361 | 2008 Profits: $268,728 | **U.S. Stock Ticker: NFG** |
| 2007 Sales: $2,039,566 | 2007 Profits: $337,455 | **Int'l Ticker:** Int'l Exchange: |
| 2006 Sales: $2,239,675 | 2006 Profits: $138,091 | Employees: 1,943 |
| 2005 Sales: $1,923,500 | 2005 Profits: $189,500 | Fiscal Year Ends: 9/30 |
| 2004 Sales: $2,031,393 | 2004 Profits: $166,586 | Parent Company: |

## SALARIES/BENEFITS:

| | | | | |
|---|---|---|---|---|
| Pension Plan: | ESOP Stock Plan: | Profit Sharing: | Top Exec. Salary: $825,000 | Bonus: $ |
| Savings Plan: | Stock Purch. Plan: | | Second Exec. Salary: $496,875 | Bonus: $ |

## OTHER THOUGHTS:

**Apparent Women Officers or Directors**: 6
**Hot Spot for Advancement for Women/Minorities**: Y

## LOCATIONS: ("Y" = Yes)

| West: | Southwest: | Midwest: | Southeast: | Northeast: | International: |
|---|---|---|---|---|---|
| Y | Y | | Y | Y | Y |

# NATIONAL WINE & SPIRITS INC

**www.nwscorp.com**

**Industry Group Code:** 422820 **Ranks within this company's industry group:** Sales: 2 Profits:

| Management: | | Sales/Marketing: | | Liberal Arts: | | Information Systems: | | Professionals: | | Technical/Scientific: | |
|---|---|---|---|---|---|---|---|---|---|---|---|
| Mgmt. Trainees: | Y | Mktg. Professionals: | Y | Gen. Writing/Editing: | | Info. Management: | Y | Finance/Accounting: | Y | Engineers, Elec.: | |
| Experienced Mgmt.: | Y | Retail Sales: | | Technical Writing: | | Software Dev.: | | Law: | Y | Engineers, Other: | |
| Int'l Business: | | Commercial/Industrial: | Y | Graphic Arts/Photog.: | | Hardware Dev.: | | HR/Other: | Y | Health/Lab: | |
| MBA Graduates: | Y | Sales Trainees: | Y | Music: | | Systems Integration: | | Training: | Y | Scientists/Research: | |
| | | Advertising Pros.: | Y | Broadcasting: | | Consulting/Other: | | Health Care: | | Petroleum/Chemicals: | |
| | | | | Other: | | | | Consulting: | | Math/Other: | |

## TYPES OF BUSINESS:

Wine & Spirits Distribution

## BRANDS/DIVISIONS/AFFILIATES:

NWS Corp.
NWS Michigan
NWS Wine World
Michigan Wine Merchants

## CONTACTS: *Note: Officers with more than one job title may be intentionally listed here more than once.*

James E. LaCrosse, CEO
John J. Baker, COO/Exec. VP
James E. LaCrosse, Pres.
James E. LaCrosse, CFO
Gregory J. Mauloff, Exec. VP-Sales & Mktg.
Karin L. Matura, Corp. VP-Human Resources
Dwight P. Deming, CIO
John J. Baker, Corp. Sec.
Steven A. Null, VP-Corp. Oper.
Karin L. Matura, Corp. VP-Dev.
Patrick A. Trefun, Corp. Controller/Treas.
James E. LaCrosse, Chmn.

**Phone:** 317-636-6092 **Fax:** 317-685-8810
**Toll-Free:**
**Address:** 700 W. Morris St., Indianapolis, IN 46206-1602 US

## GROWTH PLANS/SPECIAL FEATURES:

National Wine & Spirits, Inc. (NWS) is a distributor of wine and spirits predominantly in the Midwest. The company distributes to 22,000 locations including restaurants, liquor stores and retailers. Suppliers include brand names such as Absolut, Bailey's, Jim Beam, Johnnie Walker and Smirnoff. The firm serves Midwestern markets through its wholly-owned subsidiaries NWS Corporation and NWS Michigan. NWS Corporation, headquartered in Indianapolis, Indiana, is the firm's flagship operation. The subsidiary maintains a hyper-terminal and office in South Bend and branch offices in Crown Point, Fort Wayne and Evansville. NWS Michigan is headquartered in Brownstone, where the main warehouse is located, and also maintains wine sale offices in Madison Heights; a hyper-terminal and office in Grand Rapids; and a warehouse and office in Escanaba. NWS Michigan purchased L&L Wine World and acquired the rights to the majority of the AHD Wine Vintner's portfolio. The subsidiary sells wine through two divisions: NWS Wine World and Michigan Wine Merchants, the latter of which focuses on the fine wine segment of the market. The firm utilizes a distribution network consisting of master warehouses, hyper-terminals and cross-docking facilities located throughout Indiana, Kentucky and Michigan. A fleet of 350 delivery vehicles provides shipping services for the firm.

## FINANCIALS: **Sales and profits are in thousands of dollars—add 000 to get the full amount. 2008 Note: Financial information for 2008 was not available for all companies at press time.**

| | | |
|---|---|---|
| 2008 Sales: $ | 2008 Profits: $ | **U.S. Stock Ticker: Private** |
| 2007 Sales: $725,000 | 2007 Profits: $ | **Int'l Ticker:** Int'l Exchange: |
| 2006 Sales: $717,600 | 2006 Profits: $ | Employees: 1,725 |
| 2005 Sales: $553,700 | 2005 Profits: $5,400 | Fiscal Year Ends: 3/31 |
| 2004 Sales: $540,700 | 2004 Profits: $-9,100 | Parent Company: |

## SALARIES/BENEFITS:

| | | | | |
|---|---|---|---|---|
| Pension Plan: | ESOP Stock Plan: | Profit Sharing: | Top Exec. Salary: $409,700 | Bonus: $ |
| Savings Plan: | Stock Purch. Plan: | | Second Exec. Salary: $350,000 | Bonus: $25,000 |

## OTHER THOUGHTS:

**Apparent Women Officers or Directors**: 2
**Hot Spot for Advancement for Women/Minorities**: Y

## LOCATIONS: ("Y" = Yes)

| West: | Southwest: | Midwest: | Southeast: | Northeast: | International: |
|---|---|---|---|---|---|
| | | Y | | | |

# NATUS MEDICAL

**www.natus.com**

**Industry Group Code:** 339113 **Ranks within this company's industry group:** Sales: 26 Profits: 21

| Management: | | Sales/Marketing: | | Liberal Arts: | | Information Systems: | | Professionals: | | Technical/Scientific: | |
|---|---|---|---|---|---|---|---|---|---|---|---|
| Mgmt. Trainees: | | Mktg. Professionals: | Y | Gen. Writing/Editing: | | Info. Management: | Y | Finance/Accounting: | Y | Engineers, Elec.: | Y |
| Experienced Mgmt.: | Y | Retail Sales: | | Technical Writing: | Y | Software Dev.: | Y | Law: | Y | Engineers, Other: | Y |
| Int'l Business: | Y | Commercial/Industrial: | Y | Graphic Arts/Photog.: | | Hardware Dev.: | Y | HR/Other: | Y | Health/Lab: | Y |
| MBA Graduates: | Y | Sales Trainees: | Y | Music: | | Systems Integration: | | Training: | Y | Scientists/Research: | Y |
| | | Advertising Pros.: | | Broadcasting: | | Consulting/Other: | | Health Care: | Y | Petroleum/Chemicals: | |
| | | | | Other: | | | | Consulting: | | Math/Other: | Y |

## TYPES OF BUSINESS:

Medical Diagnostics Manufacturer
Newborn Care Products
Software

## BRANDS/DIVISIONS/AFFILIATES:

Excel-Tech Ltd.
NeuroCom International
Schwarzer GmbH
Sonamed Corporation
Xltek
Bio-logic
Olympic Medical
Fischer-Zoth

## CONTACTS: *Note: Officers with more than one job title may be intentionally listed here more than once.*

James B. Hawkins, CEO
James B. Hawkins, Pres.
Steven J. Murphy, CFO
Kenneth M. Traverso, VP-Mktg. & Sales
D. Christopher Chung, VP-R&D
D. Christopher Chung, VP-Eng. & Med. Affairs
William L. Mince, VP-Oper.
Steven J. Murphy, VP-Finance
Robert A. Gunst, Chmn.

| **Phone:** 650-802-0400 | **Fax:** 650-802-0401 |
|---|---|
| **Toll-Free:** 800-255-3901 | |
| **Address:** 1501 Industrial Rd., San Carlos, CA 94070 US | |

## GROWTH PLANS/SPECIAL FEATURES:

Natus is a provider of healthcare products used for the screening, detection, treatment, monitoring and tracking of common medical ailments such as hearing impairment, neurological dysfunction, epilepsy, sleep disorders and newborn care. Product offerings include computerized neurodiagnostic systems for audiology, neurology, polysomnography and neonatology, as well as newborn care products such as hearing screening systems, phototherapy devices for the treatment of newborn jaundice, head-cooling products for the treatment of brain injury in newborns and software systems for managing and tracking disorders and diseases for public health laboratories. Natus has facilities in California, Illinois, New York, Washington, Germany, France and Canada; and has four wholly-owned subsidiaries: Bio-logic, Olympic Medical, Fischer-Zoth and Xltek. The firm has completed a number of acquisitions, including purchase of neurologic diagnostics manufacturer Excel-Tech Ltd. in late 2007. In September 2008, Natus announced that it had agreed to acquire privately held NeuroCom International, Inc. for $18 million. NeuroCom, based in Clackamas, Oregon, develops and markets computerized systems for the assessment and rehabilitation of balance and mobility disorders. Also in 2008, Natus acquired the neurology business of privately held Schwarzer GmbH in a cash transaction and Sonamed Corporation, a private manufacturer of disposable supplies for screening newborns for hearing loss, for $9 million in cash. That same year, the company underwent a restructuring in which activities were consolidated as follows: North American diagnostic neurology product lines at the Xltek facility in Canada; newborn hearing screening and diagnostic hearing product lines at the Bio-logic facility in Illinois; and newborn care products at the Olympic Medical facility in Washington State.

## FINANCIALS: **Sales and profits are in thousands of dollars—add 000 to get the full amount. 2008 Note: Financial information for 2008 was not available for all companies at press time.**

| | | |
|---|---|---|
| 2008 Sales: $ | 2008 Profits: $ | **U.S. Stock Ticker: BABY** |
| 2007 Sales: $118,374 | 2007 Profits: $9,780 | **Int'l Ticker:** Int'l Exchange: |
| 2006 Sales: $89,915 | 2006 Profits: $- 927 | Employees: 435 |
| 2005 Sales: $43,045 | 2005 Profits: $6,152 | Fiscal Year Ends: 12/31 |
| 2004 Sales: $36,506 | 2004 Profits: $-2,407 | Parent Company: |

## SALARIES/BENEFITS:

| | | | | |
|---|---|---|---|---|
| Pension Plan: | ESOP Stock Plan: | Profit Sharing: | Top Exec. Salary: $375,000 | Bonus: $ |
| Savings Plan: | Stock Purch. Plan: | | Second Exec. Salary: $299,000 | Bonus: $ |

## OTHER THOUGHTS:

**Apparent Women Officers or Directors**: 1
**Hot Spot for Advancement for Women/Minorities**:

## LOCATIONS: ("Y" = Yes)

| West: | Southwest: | Midwest: | Southeast: | Northeast: | International: |
|---|---|---|---|---|---|
| Y | | Y | | Y | Y |

# NAVISITE INC

www.navisite.com

**Industry Group Code:** 514191A **Ranks within this company's industry group:** Sales: 6 Profits: 7

| Management: | | Sales/Marketing: | | Liberal Arts: | | Information Systems: | | Professionals: | | Technical/Scientific: | |
|---|---|---|---|---|---|---|---|---|---|---|---|
| Mgmt. Trainees: | | Mktg. Professionals: | Y | Gen. Writing/Editing: | | Info. Management: | Y | Finance/Accounting: | Y | Engineers, Elec.: | |
| Experienced Mgmt.: | Y | Retail Sales: | | Technical Writing: | Y | Software Dev.: | Y | Law: | Y | Engineers, Other: | |
| Int'l Business: | Y | Commercial/Industrial: | Y | Graphic Arts/Photog.: | | Hardware Dev.: | | HR/Other: | Y | Health/Lab: | |
| MBA Graduates: | Y | Sales Trainees: | Y | Music: | | Systems Integration: | Y | Training: | Y | Scientists/Research: | |
| | | Advertising Pros.: | | Broadcasting: | | Consulting/Other: | | Health Care: | | Petroleum/Chemicals: | |
| | | | | Other: | | | | Consulting: | | Math/Other: | |

## TYPES OF BUSINESS:

Web Site Hosting
Application Services Provider
Server & Application Management
Internet Application Solutions
e-Business Services
Electronic Software Distribution
Outsourcing Services

## BRANDS/DIVISIONS/AFFILIATES:

NaviView
Avasta Inc
Conxion Corp
Surebridge Inc

## CONTACTS: *Note: Officers with more than one job title may be intentionally listed here more than once.*

Arthur Becker, CEO
Jim Pluntze, CFO
Rathin Sinha, Chief Mktg. Officer
Denis Martin, CTO/Exec. VP
Mark Clayman, Sr. VP-Hosting Svcs.
Sumeet Sabharwal, Sr. VP-Global Delivery
Andrew Ruhan, Chmn.

| | |
|---|---|
| **Phone:** 978-682-8300 | **Fax:** 978-688-8100 |
| **Toll-Free:** 877-485-9251 | |
| **Address:** 400 Minuteman Rd., Andover, MA 01810 US | |

## GROWTH PLANS/SPECIAL FEATURES:

NaviSite, Inc. is an application services provider offering e-business-based Internet outsourcing, web hosting, server management, application management and Internet application services. Its clients are middle-market organizations, such as mid-sized companies, divisions of large multinational companies and government agencies. The firm's services allow customers to outsource the hosting and management operations of their information technology infrastructure and applications, such as commerce systems, enterprise software applications and e-mail. Services include application management, application hosting and professional services. The application management aspect encompasses monitoring, diagnosing and resolving problems, enabling software, eBusiness and Web Solutions, content management and custom application management. Application hosting involves managed services, content delivery and co-location. The firm's professional services include the delivery of software electronically using NaviSite technology and physical space, environmental support and specified power with back-up power generation and network connectivity options. Navisite's NaviView platform delivers services to customers and includes an event detection system, synthetic transaction monitoring, automated remediation, a component information manager, and an escalation manager. The company offers hosting services in 16 state-of-the-art data centers in the U.S. and the U.K. It also offers infrastructure outsourcing, application management and other outsourcing services to customers ranging from Fortune 500 companies to new businesses. Subsidiaries include Avasta, Inc.; Conexion Corp; and Surebridge, Inc. Customers include the U.S. Department of State; America's Job Bank; the Denver Broncos; Johns Hopkins University; Dresser-Rand Company; and McGlinchy Stafford; as well as Telstra, Coverpoint, Parks Hotel Management, Global Marine and United Utilities in the U.K. Atlantic Investors LLC owns approximately 31% of NaviSite.

Employees are offered medical and dental insurance; vision hardware reimbursement; life and AD&D insurance; short- and long term disability; flexible spending accounts; a 401(k) plan; an employee assistance program; and education assistance.

## FINANCIALS: **Sales and profits are in thousands of dollars—add 000 to get the full amount. 2008 Note: Financial information for 2008 was not available for all companies at press time.**

| | | |
|---|---|---|
| 2008 Sales: $154,194 | 2008 Profits: $-8,684 | **U.S. Stock Ticker: NAVI** |
| 2007 Sales: $125,860 | 2007 Profits: $-25,910 | **Int'l Ticker:** Int'l Exchange: |
| 2006 Sales: $108,844 | 2006 Profits: $-13,931 | Employees: 694 |
| 2005 Sales: $109,863 | 2005 Profits: $-16,084 | Fiscal Year Ends: 7/31 |
| 2004 Sales: $91,172 | 2004 Profits: $-21,354 | Parent Company: |

## SALARIES/BENEFITS:

| | | | | |
|---|---|---|---|---|
| Pension Plan: | ESOP Stock Plan: | Profit Sharing: | Top Exec. Salary: $350,000 | Bonus: $138,944 |
| Savings Plan: Y | Stock Purch. Plan: | | Second Exec. Salary: $243,000 | Bonus: $50,000 |

## OTHER THOUGHTS:

**Apparent Women Officers or Directors**:
**Hot Spot for Advancement for Women/Minorities**:

## LOCATIONS: ("Y" = Yes)

| West: | Southwest: | Midwest: | Southeast: | Northeast: | International: |
|---|---|---|---|---|---|
| Y | Y | Y | Y | Y | Y |

Note: Financial information, benefits and other data can change quickly and may vary from those stated here.

# NEKTAR THERAPEUTICS

**www.nektar.com**

**Industry Group Code:** 325412A **Ranks within this company's industry group:** Sales: 2 Profits: 4

| Management: | | Sales/Marketing: | | Liberal Arts: | | Information Systems: | | Professionals: | | Technical/Scientific: | |
|---|---|---|---|---|---|---|---|---|---|---|---|
| Mgmt. Trainees: | | Mktg. Professionals: | Y | Gen. Writing/Editing: | | Info. Management: | Y | Finance/Accounting: | Y | Engineers, Elec.: | |
| Experienced Mgmt.: | Y | Retail Sales: | | Technical Writing: | Y | Software Dev.: | | Law: | Y | Engineers, Other: | |
| Int'l Business: | Y | Commercial/Industrial: | Y | Graphic Arts/Photog.: | | Hardware Dev.: | | HR/Other: | Y | Health/Lab: | Y |
| MBA Graduates: | Y | Sales Trainees: | Y | Music: | | Systems Integration: | | Training: | Y | Scientists/Research: | Y |
| | | Advertising Pros.: | | Broadcasting: | | Consulting/Other: | | Health Care: | Y | Petroleum/Chemicals: | |
| | | | | Other: | | | | Consulting: | | Math/Other: | Y |

## TYPES OF BUSINESS:

Drug Delivery Systems
PEG-Based Delivery Systems
Molecular & Particle Engineering
Equipment-Inhalers

## BRANDS/DIVISIONS/AFFILIATES:

Nektar PEGylation Technology
Nektar Pulmonary Technology
Macugen
PEGASYS
Exubera
Neulasta
Somavert
PEG-INTRON

## CONTACTS: *Note: Officers with more than one job title may be intentionally listed here more than once.*

Howard W. Robin, CEO
Bharatt Chowrira, COO
Howard W. Robin, Pres.
John Nicholson, CFO/Sr. VP
Dorian Rinella, VP-Human Resources & Facilities
Gil M. Labrucherie, General Counsel/Sec.
Rinko Ghosh, Sr. VP-Bus. Dev./Alliance Mgmt.
John Nicholson, Sr. VP-Finance
Nevan Elam, Sr. VP/Head-Pulmonary Bus. Unit
John S. Patton, Chief Research Fellow
Bharatt Chowrira, Head-Pegylation Bus. Unit
Robert B. Chess, Chmn.

| | |
|---|---|
| **Phone:** 650-631-3100 | **Fax:** 650-631-3150 |
| **Toll-Free:** | |
| **Address:** 201 Industrial Rd., San Carlos, CA 94070 US | |

## GROWTH PLANS/SPECIAL FEATURES:

Nektar Therapeutics is a biopharmaceutical company focused on developing technology for unmet medical needs. The company, which recently restructured to focus on its therapeutic drug development operations, develops and enables differentiated therapeutics through its technology platforms. The firm aims to create differentiated, innovative products by applying its platform technologies to established or novel medicine. Nektar Therapeutics creates potential breakthrough products in two ways: by developing products in collaboration with pharmaceutical and biotechnology companies that seek to improve and differentiate their products; and by applying its technologies to already approved drugs. The company's leading technology platforms are Pulmonary Technology and PEGylation Technology. Pulmonary Technology makes drugs inhaleable to deliver them to and through the lungs for both systemic and local lung applications. PEGylation Technology is a chemical process designed to enhance the performance of most drug classes with the potential to improve solubility and stability; increase drug half-life; reduce immune responses to an active drug; and improve the efficacy and/or safety of a molecule in certain instances. Leading products approved by the U.S. Food and Drug Administration (FDA) include Macugen treatment for macular degeneration; PEGASYS for chronic Hepatitis C; Somavert human growth hormone receptor antagonist; Exubera inhaleable insulin; PEG-INTRON for treating Hepatitis C; and Neulasta for the treatment of neutropenia, a condition where the body produces too few white blood cells. Most of these have been developed in collaboration with other pharmaceutical companies, including Amgen; Novartis Pharma; Bayer; Pfizer; and Schering-Plough. In May 2008, Nektar was awarded a patent covering compositions and methods for delivering pulmonary-targeted antibiotics such as tobramycin and other aminoglycosides using the company's Dry Powder Inhaled Technology.

Nektar offers its employees medical, dental and vision plans; accident and life insurance; retirement and investment plans; and life enrichment programs, including tuition reimbursement and fitness membership discounts.

## FINANCIALS: **Sales and profits are in thousands of dollars—add 000 to get the full amount. 2008 Note: Financial information for 2008 was not available for all companies at press time.**

| | | |
|---|---|---|
| 2008 Sales: $ | 2008 Profits: $ | **U.S. Stock Ticker: NKTR** |
| 2007 Sales: $273,027 | 2007 Profits: $-32,761 | **Int'l Ticker:** Int'l Exchange: |
| 2006 Sales: $217,718 | 2006 Profits: $-154,761 | Employees: 575 |
| 2005 Sales: $126,279 | 2005 Profits: $-185,111 | Fiscal Year Ends: 12/31 |
| 2004 Sales: $114,270 | 2004 Profits: $-101,886 | Parent Company: |

## SALARIES/BENEFITS:

| | | | | |
|---|---|---|---|---|
| Pension Plan: | ESOP Stock Plan: | Profit Sharing: | Top Exec. Salary: $654,243 | Bonus: $601,800 |
| Savings Plan: Y | Stock Purch. Plan: | | Second Exec. Salary: $451,153 | Bonus: $344,000 |

## OTHER THOUGHTS:

**Apparent Women Officers or Directors**: 1
**Hot Spot for Advancement for Women/Minorities**: Y

## LOCATIONS: ("Y" = Yes)

| West: | Southwest: | Midwest: | Southeast: | Northeast: | International: |
|---|---|---|---|---|---|
| Y | | | Y | | Y |

Note: Financial information, benefits and other data can change quickly and may vary from those stated here.

# NEOGEN CORPORATION

www.neogen.com

**Industry Group Code:** 325413 **Ranks within this company's industry group:** Sales: 8 Profits: 5

| Management: | | Sales/Marketing: | | Liberal Arts: | | Information Systems: | | Professionals: | | Technical/Scientific: | |
|---|---|---|---|---|---|---|---|---|---|---|---|
| Mgmt. Trainees: | | Mktg. Professionals: | Y | Gen. Writing/Editing: | | Info. Management: | Y | Finance/Accounting: | Y | Engineers, Elec.: | Y |
| Experienced Mgmt.: | Y | Retail Sales: | | Technical Writing: | Y | Software Dev.: | Y | Law: | Y | Engineers, Other: | Y |
| Int'l Business: | Y | Commercial/Industrial: | Y | Graphic Arts/Photog.: | | Hardware Dev.: | Y | HR/Other: | Y | Health/Lab: | Y |
| MBA Graduates: | Y | Sales Trainees: | Y | Music: | | Systems Integration: | | Training: | Y | Scientists/Research: | Y |
| | | Advertising Pros.: | | Broadcasting: | | Consulting/Other: | | Health Care: | Y | Petroleum/Chemicals: | Y |
| | | | | Other: | | | | Consulting: | | Math/Other: | Y |

## TYPES OF BUSINESS:

Sanitary & Livestock Diagnostic Products
Food Safety Test Kits
Animal Health Test Kits
Pharmacology Test Kits
Agricultural Test Kits
Veterinary Instruments
Veterinary Pharmaceuticals

## BRANDS/DIVISIONS/AFFILIATES:

Agri-Scan
Acumedia
Dr. Frank's
Triple Heat
Triple Cast
Triple Block
Triple Crown
UriCon

## CONTACTS: *Note: Officers with more than one job title may be intentionally listed here more than once.*

James L. Herbert, CEO
Lon M. Bohannon, COO
Lon M. Bohannon, Pres.
Richard R. Current, CFO/VP
Mark A. Mozola, VP-R&D
Kenneth V. Kodilla, VP-Mfg.
Richard R. Current, Sec.
Anthony E. Maltese, VP-Corp. Dev.
Edward L. Bradley, VP-Food Safety
Terri A. Morrical, VP-Animal Safety
Paul S. Satoh, VP-Basic & Exploratory Research
Joseph Madden, VP-Scientific Affairs
James L. Herbert, Chmn.

**Phone:** 517-372-9200 **Fax:** 517-372-2006
**Toll-Free:** 800-234-5333
**Address:** 620 Lesher Pl., Lansing, MI 48912 US

## GROWTH PLANS/SPECIAL FEATURES:

Neogen Corporation and its subsidiaries develop, manufacture and market a diverse line of products for food and animal safety. The company's food safety segment consists primarily of diagnostic kits and complementary products (e.g., dehydrated culture media). The products are marketed by company sales personnel in the U.S., Canada, the U.K. and parts of Europe and by distributors elsewhere to food producers and processors to detect dangerous and/or unintended substances in human and animal food, such as food-born pathogens, natural toxins, food allergens, genetic modifications, ruminant by-products, drug residues, pesticide residues and general sanitation concerns. Neogen's animal safety segment is engaged in the development, manufacture and marketing of pharmaceuticals, rodenticides, disinfectants, vaccines, veterinary instruments, topicals and diagnostic products for the worldwide animal safety market. The majority of these consumable products are marketed through a network of national and international distributors, as well as a number of large farm supply retail chains in the U.S. and Canada. The company's U.S. Department of Agriculture (USDA)-licensed facility in Tampa, Florida produces immunostimulant products for horses and dogs and its unique equine botulism vaccine. Neogen's BotVax B vaccine protects horses and foals against type B botulism, commonly known as Shaker Foal Syndrome and is the only USDA-approved vaccine for the prevention of Type B botulism in horses. Trademarks include Neogen flask; AccuScan; AccuPoint; Acumedia; Agri-Scan; Agri-Screen; Alert; BetaStar; Centrus; D3 Needles; CD&R; Dr. Frank's; ElectroJac; ELISA Technologies; Fura-Zone; Gold Nugget; Paddock&Pasture; Triple Heat; Triple Crown; Triple Cast; Triple Block; TopHoof; UriKare; UriCon; and Vita-15, among many others. In June 2008, Neogen formed a new subsidiary, Neogen Latino America SPA, headquartered in Mexico City, which will distribute the company's products throughout Mexico. In July 2008, Neogen acquired a product line of 14 different product formulations from DuPont Animal Health Solutions.

## FINANCIALS: **Sales and profits are in thousands of dollars—add 000 to get the full amount. 2008 Note: Financial information for 2008 was not available for all companies at press time.**

| | | |
|---|---|---|
| 2008 Sales: $102,418 | 2008 Profits: $12,098 | **U.S. Stock Ticker: NEOG** |
| 2007 Sales: $86,138 | 2007 Profits: $9,125 | **Int'l Ticker:** Int'l Exchange: |
| 2006 Sales: $72,433 | 2006 Profits: $7,941 | Employees: 447 |
| 2005 Sales: $62,756 | 2005 Profits: $5,916 | Fiscal Year Ends: 5/31 |
| 2004 Sales: $55,498 | 2004 Profits: $5,099 | Parent Company: |

## SALARIES/BENEFITS:

| | | | | |
|---|---|---|---|---|
| Pension Plan: | ESOP Stock Plan: | Profit Sharing: | Top Exec. Salary: $275,000 | Bonus: $150,000 |
| Savings Plan: Y | Stock Purch. Plan: Y | | Second Exec. Salary: $195,000 | Bonus: $70,000 |

## OTHER THOUGHTS:

**Apparent Women Officers or Directors**: 1
**Hot Spot for Advancement for Women/Minorities**:

## LOCATIONS: ("Y" = Yes)

| West: | Southwest: | Midwest: | Southeast: | Northeast: | International: |
|---|---|---|---|---|---|
| | | Y | Y | | Y |

Note: Financial information, benefits and other data can change quickly and may vary from those stated here.

# NETFLIX INC

www.netflix.com

**Industry Group Code:** 532230 **Ranks within this company's industry group:** Sales: 1 Profits: 1

| Management: | | Sales/Marketing: | | Liberal Arts: | | Information Systems: | | Professionals: | | Technical/Scientific: | |
|---|---|---|---|---|---|---|---|---|---|---|---|
| Mgmt. Trainees: | Y | Mktg. Professionals: | Y | Gen. Writing/Editing: | | Info. Management: | Y | Finance/Accounting: | Y | Engineers, Elec.: | |
| Experienced Mgmt.: | Y | Retail Sales: | | Technical Writing: | | Software Dev.: | Y | Law: | Y | Engineers, Other: | |
| Int'l Business: | | Commercial/Industrial: | | Graphic Arts/Photog.: | | Hardware Dev.: | | HR/Other: | Y | Health/Lab: | |
| MBA Graduates: | Y | Sales Trainees: | | Music: | | Systems Integration: | | Training: | Y | Scientists/Research: | |
| | | Advertising Pros.: | Y | Broadcasting: | | Consulting/Other: | | Health Care: | | Petroleum/Chemicals: | |
| | | | | Other: | Y | | | Consulting: | | Math/Other: | |

## TYPES OF BUSINESS:

Online DVD Rental
Video on Demand

## BRANDS/DIVISIONS/AFFILIATES:

## CONTACTS:

*Note: Officers with more than one job title may be intentionally listed here more than once.*

Reed Hastings, CEO
Barry McCarthy, CFO
Leslie Kilgore, Chief Mktg. Officer
Patty McCord, Chief Talent Officer
Neil Hunt, Chief Prod. Officer
Ted Sarandos, Chief Content Officer
Greg Peters, VP-Partner Prod. Dev.
Reed Hastings, Chmn.

**Phone:** 408-540-3700 **Fax:**
**Toll-Free:**
**Address:** 100 Winchester Cir., Los Gatos, CA 95032 US

## GROWTH PLANS/SPECIAL FEATURES:

Netflix, Inc. is one of the largest online movie rental subscription services, providing approximately 7.5 million subscribers access to a library of more than 100,000 movie, television and other filmed entertainment titles on DVD. The company offers nine subscription plans, starting at $4.99 a month. There are no due dates, late fees or shipping costs. Subscribers select titles at Netflix's web site, receive the movies by mail and return them at their convenience using prepaid mailers. Netflix then mails the next available DVD in a subscriber's queue. In 2007, the company introduced its Watch Instantly feature, allowing subscribers to view a growing library of movies and television episodes over the Internet. Currently, Netflix has more than 12,000 titles available for instant viewing. The service comes with the normal subscription packages, and does not affect the number of DVDs customers receive through the mail. The firm's proprietary recommendation service enables it to create a customized store for each subscriber and to generate personalized recommendations. Netflix purchases titles directly from studios, distributors and independent producers, and operates more than 55 distribution centers nationwide, allowing it to provide fast delivery service to subscribers. The company promotes its service to consumers through various marketing programs, including online promotions, television and radio advertising, package inserts, direct mail and other promotions with third parties. In September 2008, the company announced an agreement with the CBS Television Network and Disney-ABC Television Group allowing current episodes of a number of popular TV shows to be available through Watch Instantly. Over the course of 2008, Netflix also partnered with several consumer electronics companies to develop methods to stream movies and TV episodes via the Internet to subscribers' TV sets through such devices as TiVo DVRs and the Xbox 360 video game system.

## FINANCIALS:

**Sales and profits are in thousands of dollars—add 000 to get the full amount. 2008 Note: Financial information for 2008 was not available for all companies at press time.**

| | | |
|---|---|---|
| 2008 Sales: $ | 2008 Profits: $ | **U.S. Stock Ticker: NFLX** |
| 2007 Sales: $1,205,340 | 2007 Profits: $66,952 | **Int'l Ticker:** Int'l Exchange: |
| 2006 Sales: $996,660 | 2006 Profits: $49,082 | Employees: 1,542 |
| 2005 Sales: $682,213 | 2005 Profits: $42,027 | Fiscal Year Ends: 12/31 |
| 2004 Sales: $506,228 | 2004 Profits: $20,838 | Parent Company: |

## SALARIES/BENEFITS:

| | | | | |
|---|---|---|---|---|
| Pension Plan: | ESOP Stock Plan: | Profit Sharing: | Top Exec. Salary: $850,000 | Bonus: $ |
| Savings Plan: Y | Stock Purch. Plan: Y | | Second Exec. Salary: $810,000 | Bonus: $ |

## OTHER THOUGHTS:

**Apparent Women Officers or Directors**: 2
**Hot Spot for Advancement for Women/Minorities**: Y

## LOCATIONS: ("Y" = Yes)

| West: | Southwest: | Midwest: | Southeast: | Northeast: | International: |
|---|---|---|---|---|---|
| Y | | | | | |

# NETGEAR INC

www.netgear.com

**Industry Group Code:** 334110 **Ranks within this company's industry group:** Sales: 1 Profits: 2

| Management: | | Sales/Marketing: | | Liberal Arts: | | Information Systems: | | Professionals: | | Technical/Scientific: | |
|---|---|---|---|---|---|---|---|---|---|---|---|
| Mgmt. Trainees: | | Mktg. Professionals: | Y | Gen. Writing/Editing: | | Info. Management: | Y | Finance/Accounting: | Y | Engineers, Elec.: | Y |
| Experienced Mgmt.: | Y | Retail Sales: | | Technical Writing: | Y | Software Dev.: | Y | Law: | Y | Engineers, Other: | |
| Int'l Business: | Y | Commercial/Industrial: | Y | Graphic Arts/Photog.: | | Hardware Dev.: | Y | HR/Other: | Y | Health/Lab: | |
| MBA Graduates: | Y | Sales Trainees: | Y | Music: | | Systems Integration: | Y | Training: | Y | Scientists/Research: | Y |
| | | Advertising Pros.: | | Broadcasting: | | Consulting/Other: | | Health Care: | | Petroleum/Chemicals: | |
| | | | | Other: | | | | Consulting: | | Math/Other: | |

## TYPES OF BUSINESS:

Networking Equipment
Wireless Networking Products
Broadband Products
Antennas & Accessories
Security Products
Software
Wi-Fi Phones
Entertainment Management Software

## BRANDS/DIVISIONS/AFFILIATES:

SkipJam Corp.
Infrant Technologies, Inc.

## CONTACTS: *Note: Officers with more than one job title may be intentionally listed here more than once.*

Patrick C.S. Lo, CEO
Christine M. Gorjanc, CFO
Michael Werdann, VP-Americas Sales
Mark Merrill, CTO
Charles T. Olson, Sr. VP-Eng.
Albert Liu, General Counsel/Corp. Sec.
Michael Falcon, Sr. VP-Oper.
Patrick C.S. Lo, Chmn.
David Soares, Sr. VP-Worldwide Sales & Support

**Phone:** 408-907-8000 **Fax:** 408-907-8097
**Toll-Free:** 888-638-4327
**Address:** 4500 Great America Pkwy., Santa Clara, CA 95054 US

## GROWTH PLANS/SPECIAL FEATURES:

NETGEAR, Inc. designs, develops and markets networking products for home users and small businesses, defined as fewer than 250 employees. NETGEAR has offices in California in the U.S. and 18 countries around the world. The firm's products allow users to share Internet access, peripherals, files, digital multimedia content and applications among multiple personal computers and other Internet-enabled devices. NETGEAR's products are grouped into three major lines: Ethernet networking products, broadband products and network connectivity products. Ethernet products include switches, network interface cards, peripheral servers and VPN firewalls; broadband products include routers, gateways, IP telephony products and products that include an integrated wireless access point, such as a wireless gateway; and networking connectivity products include access points, wireless network interface cards, Wi-Fi phones and adapters, and media adapters and bridges. The company also offers security products, antennas, accessories and software. NETGEAR sells its products through multiple sales channels worldwide, including traditional retailers, online retailers, wholesale distributors, direct marketing resellers, value-added resellers and broadband service providers. International sales make up the majority of the company's net revenue, contributing 62% in 2007. Two of its significant customers include Ingram Micro, Inc. and Tech Data Corporation. NETGEAR's net revenue grew 26.9% in 2007, in part through the sales of Ready NAS products that were acquired with the May purchase of Infrant Technologies, Inc.

## FINANCIALS: **Sales and profits are in thousands of dollars—add 000 to get the full amount. 2008 Note: Financial information for 2008 was not available for all companies at press time.**

2008 Sales: $743,344
2007 Sales: $727,787
2006 Sales: $573,570
2005 Sales: $449,610
2004 Sales: $383,139

2008 Profits: $17,719
2007 Profits: $45,954
2006 Profits: $41,132
2005 Profits: $33,623
2004 Profits: $23,465

**U.S. Stock Ticker: NTGR**
**Int'l Ticker:** Int'l Exchange:
Employees: 518
Fiscal Year Ends: 12/31
Parent Company:

## SALARIES/BENEFITS:

Pension Plan: ESOP Stock Plan: Profit Sharing: Top Exec. Salary: $574,038 Bonus: $57,500
Savings Plan: Y Stock Purch. Plan: Y Second Exec. Salary: $291,864 Bonus: $

## OTHER THOUGHTS:

**Apparent Women Officers or Directors**: 1
**Hot Spot for Advancement for Women/Minorities**: Y

## LOCATIONS: ("Y" = Yes)

| West: | Southwest: | Midwest: | Southeast: | Northeast: | International: |
|---|---|---|---|---|---|
| Y | | | | | Y |

# NETRATINGS INC

**www.nielsen-netratings.com**

**Industry Group Code:** 541910 **Ranks within this company's industry group:** Sales: Profits:

| Management: | | Sales/Marketing: | | Liberal Arts: | | Information Systems: | | Professionals: | | Technical/Scientific: | |
|---|---|---|---|---|---|---|---|---|---|---|---|
| Mgmt. Trainees: | | Mktg. Professionals: | Y | Gen. Writing/Editing: | Y | Info. Management: | Y | Finance/Accounting: | Y | Engineers, Elec.: | |
| Experienced Mgmt.: | Y | Retail Sales: | | Technical Writing: | | Software Dev.: | Y | Law: | Y | Engineers, Other: | |
| Int'l Business: | Y | Commercial/Industrial: | Y | Graphic Arts/Photog.: | | Hardware Dev.: | | HR/Other: | Y | Health/Lab: | |
| MBA Graduates: | Y | Sales Trainees: | Y | Music: | | Systems Integration: | | Training: | Y | Scientists/Research: | |
| | | Advertising Pros.: | | Broadcasting: | | Consulting/Other: | | Health Care: | | Petroleum/Chemicals: | |
| | | | | Other: | Y | | | Consulting: | | Math/Other: | Y |

## TYPES OF BUSINESS:

Internet Audience Information & Analysis
Marketing Services
Market Research

## BRANDS/DIVISIONS/AFFILIATES:

Nielsen/NetRatings
Nielsen Company BV (The)
VNU NV
NetView
AdRelevance
@Plan
MegaPanel
SiteCensus

## CONTACTS: *Note: Officers with more than one job title may be intentionally listed here more than once.*

Shankar Iyer, CTO
Manish Bhatia, Exec. VP-Global Oper.
John A. Dimling, Chmn.

| | |
|---|---|
| **Phone:** 646-654-7990 | **Fax:** 212-703-5901 |
| **Toll-Free:** 888-634-1222 | |
| **Address:** 770 Broadway,13th Fl., New York, NY 10003 US | |

## GROWTH PLANS/SPECIAL FEATURES:

NetRatings, Inc., operating under the Nielsen/NetRatings brand, is a subsidiary of The Nielsen Company (formerly VNU Group) providing Internet audience measurement and analysis. NetRatings is a wholly-owned subsidiary of Nielsen. The company's products and services are designed to aid companies in making critical business decisions regarding Internet strategies and initiatives. The firm's primary products and services include NetView, AdRelevance, @Plan, MegaPanel, SiteCensus, WebRF, Web Intercept and Homescan Online. NetView, NetRatings' original product, provides in-depth measurement of audience behavior online and in digital media, including instant messaging and media players. AdRelevance offers comprehensive information on online advertising. @Plan is a resource for demographic, lifestyle and product preferences that guides advertisers, agencies and web publishers in online marketing and media strategies. MegaPanel provides increased depth of Internet behavior and activity for the market research industry, including e-commerce transaction information. SiteCensus offers extensive web analytical services based on traffic flows and visitor behaviors. WebRF offers advertisers and web publishers the ability to plan and evaluate the impact of Internet advertising. WebIntercept allows clients to survey Internet users based on their real-time online behavior. Homescan Online improves the effectiveness of online marketing for the consumer packaged goods industry and web publishers. In February 2008, the company launched VideoCensus, the first syndicated online video measurement that combines panel and server research methods. In May 2008, the company extended @Plan by making it accessible to mobile web users. Also in May 2008, the company launched a new Digital Strategic Services Group to assist clients in managing online reputations, controlling Consumer-Generated Media, and growing brand support. In October 2008, the company partnered with Beijing Zhonggian Wangrun Information Technology Co., Ltd., the only authorized internet firm in China to create and publish web site rankings, to develop and deliver internet measurement and analysis services in China.

## FINANCIALS: **Sales and profits are in thousands of dollars—add 000 to get the full amount. 2008 Note: Financial information for 2008 was not available for all companies at press time.**

| | | |
|---|---|---|
| 2008 Sales: $ | 2008 Profits: $ | **U.S. Stock Ticker: Subsidiary** |
| 2007 Sales: $ | 2007 Profits: $ | **Int'l Ticker:** Int'l Exchange: |
| 2006 Sales: $81,769 | 2006 Profits: $2,829 | Employees: 397 |
| 2005 Sales: $68,017 | 2005 Profits: $-8,395 | Fiscal Year Ends: 12/31 |
| 2004 Sales: $59,300 | 2004 Profits: $-17,419 | Parent Company: NIELSEN COMPANY BV (THE) |

## SALARIES/BENEFITS:

| | | | | |
|---|---|---|---|---|
| Pension Plan: | ESOP Stock Plan: | Profit Sharing: | Top Exec. Salary: $358,333 | Bonus: $280,000 |
| Savings Plan: | Stock Purch. Plan: | | Second Exec. Salary: $256,250 | Bonus: $128,750 |

## OTHER THOUGHTS:

**Apparent Women Officers or Directors:**
**Hot Spot for Advancement for Women/Minorities:**

## LOCATIONS: ("Y" = Yes)

| West: | Southwest: | Midwest: | Southeast: | Northeast: | International: |
|---|---|---|---|---|---|
| Y | | | | Y | Y |

# NETSCOUT SYSTEMS INC

www.netscout.com

**Industry Group Code:** 511214 **Ranks within this company's industry group:** Sales: 2 Profits: 2

| Management: | | Sales/Marketing: | | Liberal Arts: | | Information Systems: | | Professionals: | | Technical/Scientific: | |
|---|---|---|---|---|---|---|---|---|---|---|---|
| Mgmt. Trainees: | | Mktg. Professionals: | Y | Gen. Writing/Editing: | | Info. Management: | Y | Finance/Accounting: | Y | Engineers, Elec.: | Y |
| Experienced Mgmt.: | Y | Retail Sales: | | Technical Writing: | Y | Software Dev.: | Y | Law: | Y | Engineers, Other: | |
| Int'l Business: | Y | Commercial/Industrial: | Y | Graphic Arts/Photog.: | | Hardware Dev.: | | HR/Other: | Y | Health/Lab: | |
| MBA Graduates: | Y | Sales Trainees: | Y | Music: | | Systems Integration: | Y | Training: | Y | Scientists/Research: | |
| | | Advertising Pros.: | | Broadcasting: | | Consulting/Other: | | Health Care: | | Petroleum/Chemicals: | |
| | | | | Other: | | | | Consulting: | | Math/Other: | |

## TYPES OF BUSINESS:

Performance Management Systems
Application Management Solutions

## BRANDS/DIVISIONS/AFFILIATES:

nGenius
nGenius Application Fabric Monitor (AFMon)
nGenius Analytics
NextPoint Networks, Inc.
Network General Corporation
Sniffer
nGenius K2

## CONTACTS:

*Note: Officers with more than one job title may be intentionally listed here more than once.*

Anil Singhal, CEO
Michael Szabados, COO
Anil Singhal, Pres.
David Sommers, CFO
John Downing, Sr. VP-Worldwide Sales Oper.
Victor Becker, VP-Human Resources
Ashwani Singhal, Sr. VP-R&D
Ken Boyd, CIO/Sr. VP-Svcs.
Bruce Kelley, Jr., CTO/VP
Tracy Steele, VP-Mfg. & Bus. Oper.
David Sommers, Sr. VP-General Oper.
Bruce Sweet, VP-Bus. Dev.
Christine Johansen, Mgr.-Public Rel.
Jeff Wakely, VP-Finance/Chief Acct. Officer
Jim Frey, VP-Mktg.
Anil Singhal, Chmn.

**Phone:** 978-614-4000 **Fax:** 978-614-4004
**Toll-Free:** 888-999-5946
**Address:** 310 Littleton Rd., Westford, MA 01886 US

## GROWTH PLANS/SPECIAL FEATURES:

NetScout Systems, Inc. designs, develops, manufactures, markets, sells and supports a family of products that assures the performance and availability of critical business applications and services in complex, high-speed networks. The company manufactures and markets these products as an integrated hardware and software solution that is used by enterprises, governmental agencies and service providers worldwide. The company's nGenius Performance Management System software product is a multi-function performance management solution implemented in a single, integrated application that monitors and reports on network, service and application traffic; troubleshoots performance problems; and provides precise information for capacity planning. It integrates real-time and historical information in a single management application. The system collects data from nGenius Probes, routers, switches and other flow-based information sources, such as NetFlow, and provides in-depth system-wide views of all applications on the network infrastructure. Other nGenius products include the Application Fabric Monitor (AFMon), offering improved and extended features for packet analysis, a tight user interface and workflow integration with nGenius Performance Manager; and nGenius Analytics, one of the first intelligent early warning systems in the performance management marketplace. NetScout sells its products to corporations, government agencies, other non-profit entities and other organizations with large- and medium-sized high-speed computer networks. The company's products have been sold to customers operating in industries such as financial services, technology, telecommunications, manufacturing, service provider, healthcare and retail. Subsidiary NextPoint Networks, Inc. develops performance and service-level management systems. In November 2007, the firm acquired Network General Corporation for $213 million. Network General develops network analysis and data mining products under the Sniffer brand; Network General is being integrated into NetScout's other business. In April 2008, NetScout launched the nGenius K2, which principally offers IT professionals an at-a-glace overview of their network's health and overall performance, as well as improving the nGenius Analytics' early warning system.

## FINANCIALS:

**Sales and profits are in thousands of dollars—add 000 to get the full amount. 2008 Note: Financial information for 2008 was not available for all companies at press time.**

2008 Sales: $168,956
2007 Sales: $102,472
2006 Sales: $97,876
2005 Sales: $85,214
2004 Sales: $71,534

2008 Profits: $-2,088
2007 Profits: $7,737
2006 Profits: $5,797
2005 Profits: $2,870
2004 Profits: $- 545

**U.S. Stock Ticker: NTCT**
**Int'l Ticker:** Int'l Exchange:
Employees: 790
Fiscal Year Ends: 3/31
Parent Company:

## SALARIES/BENEFITS:

Pension Plan: ESOP Stock Plan: Profit Sharing: Top Exec. Salary: $261,154 Bonus: $162,500
Savings Plan: Stock Purch. Plan: Second Exec. Salary: $226,261 Bonus: $162,500

## OTHER THOUGHTS:

**Apparent Women Officers or Directors**: 2
**Hot Spot for Advancement for Women/Minorities**: Y

## LOCATIONS: ("Y" = Yes)

| West: | Southwest: | Midwest: | Southeast: | Northeast: | International: |
|---|---|---|---|---|---|
| Y | Y | Y | Y | Y | Y |

# NETSUITE INC

www.netsuite.com

**Industry Group Code:** 511207 **Ranks within this company's industry group:** Sales: 3 Profits: 3

| Management: | | Sales/Marketing: | | Liberal Arts: | | Information Systems: | | Professionals: | | Technical/Scientific: | |
|---|---|---|---|---|---|---|---|---|---|---|---|
| Mgmt. Trainees: | | Mktg. Professionals: | Y | Gen. Writing/Editing: | | Info. Management: | Y | Finance/Accounting: | Y | Engineers, Elec.: | Y |
| Experienced Mgmt.: | Y | Retail Sales: | | Technical Writing: | Y | Software Dev.: | Y | Law: | Y | Engineers, Other: | |
| Int'l Business: | Y | Commercial/Industrial: | Y | Graphic Arts/Photog.: | | Hardware Dev.: | | HR/Other: | Y | Health/Lab: | |
| MBA Graduates: | Y | Sales Trainees: | | Music: | | Systems Integration: | | Training: | Y | Scientists/Research: | |
| | | Advertising Pros.: | | Broadcasting: | | Consulting/Other: | | Health Care: | | Petroleum/Chemicals: | |
| | | | | Other: | | | | Consulting: | | Math/Other: | Y |

## TYPES OF BUSINESS:

Business Management Application Suites
Enterprise Resource Planning
Customer Relationship Management
E-Commerce Capabilities

## BRANDS/DIVISIONS/AFFILIATES:

NetSuite
NetSuite CRM+
NetSuite Small Business
OpenAir Inc

## CONTACTS:

*Note: Officers with more than one job title may be intentionally listed here more than once.*

Zach Nelson, CEO
Zach Nelson, Pres.
Jim McGeever, CFO
David Downing, Chief Mktg. Officer
Evan Goldberg, CTO
Tim Dilley, Exec. VP-Professional Svcs.
Evan Goldberg, Chmn.
Dean Mansfield, Pres., Worldwide Sales & Dist.

**Phone:** 650-627-1000 **Fax:** 650-627-1001
**Toll-Free:**
**Address:** 2955 Campus Dr., Ste. 100, San Mateo, CA 94403-2511 US

## GROWTH PLANS/SPECIAL FEATURES:

NetSuite, Inc. is a leading vendor of on-demand, integrated business management application suites for small and medium-sized businesses. It provides a suite of enterprise resource planning (ERP), customer relationship management (CRM) and e-commerce capabilities that enables customers to manage their back-office, front-office and web operations in a single application. The company's main offering is NetSuite, which is designed to provide the core business management capabilities that most of its customers require. NetSuite, NetSuite CRM+ and NetSuite Small Business are designed for use by most types of businesses. In addition, the firm offers industry-specific configurations for use by wholesale/distribution, services and software companies. Finally, NetSuite sells additional on-demand application modules that customers can purchase to obtain additional functionality required for their specific business needs. NetSuite's suite serves as a single system for running business operations and is targeted at small and medium-sized businesses, as well as divisions of large companies. All elements of the company's application suite share the same customer and transaction data, enabling cross-departmental business process automation and real-time monitoring of core business metrics. In addition, the integrated ERP, CRM and e-commerce capabilities provide users with real-time visibility and appropriate functionality through dashboards tailored to their particular job function and access rights. The firm delivers its suite over the Internet as a subscription service using the software-as-a-service or on-demand model. It is available wherever a user has Internet access, whether on a personal computer or a mobile device. NetSuite has over 5,600 customers, and derived approximately 18% of 2007 revenues from sales outside of North America. The company went public in late 2007. In June 2008, NetSuite announced plans to acquire OpenAir, Inc., a provider of professional services automation software. In August 2008, the company announced the opening of a new sales and services facility near Denver, Colorado.

## FINANCIALS:

**Sales and profits are in thousands of dollars—add 000 to get the full amount. 2008 Note: Financial information for 2008 was not available for all companies at press time.**

| | | |
|---|---|---|
| 2008 Sales: $152,476 | 2008 Profits: $-15,864 | **U.S. Stock Ticker: N** |
| 2007 Sales: $108,541 | 2007 Profits: $-23,906 | **Int'l Ticker:** Int'l Exchange: |
| 2006 Sales: $67,202 | 2006 Profits: $-35,722 | Employees: 675 |
| 2005 Sales: $60,000 | 2005 Profits: $ | Fiscal Year Ends: 12/31 |
| 2004 Sales: $ | 2004 Profits: $ | Parent Company: |

## SALARIES/BENEFITS:

| | | | | |
|---|---|---|---|---|
| Pension Plan: | ESOP Stock Plan: | Profit Sharing: | Top Exec. Salary: $362,500 | Bonus: $163,849 |
| Savings Plan: | Stock Purch. Plan: | | Second Exec. Salary: $337,500 | Bonus: $294,954 |

## OTHER THOUGHTS:

**Apparent Women Officers or Directors**: 1
**Hot Spot for Advancement for Women/Minorities**:

## LOCATIONS: ("Y" = Yes)

| West: | Southwest: | Midwest: | Southeast: | Northeast: | International: |
|---|---|---|---|---|---|
| Y | | | | | Y |

# NEWFIELD EXPLORATION CO

www.newfld.com

**Industry Group Code:** 211111 **Ranks within this company's industry group:** Sales: 5 Profits: 5

| Management: | | Sales/Marketing: | | Liberal Arts: | | Information Systems: | | Professionals: | | Technical/Scientific: | |
|---|---|---|---|---|---|---|---|---|---|---|---|
| Mgmt. Trainees: | | Mktg. Professionals: | Y | Gen. Writing/Editing: | | Info. Management: | Y | Finance/Accounting: | Y | Engineers, Elec.: | |
| Experienced Mgmt.: | Y | Retail Sales: | | Technical Writing: | | Software Dev.: | | Law: | Y | Engineers, Other: | Y |
| Int'l Business: | Y | Commercial/Industrial: | Y | Graphic Arts/Photog.: | | Hardware Dev.: | | HR/Other: | Y | Health/Lab: | |
| MBA Graduates: | Y | Sales Trainees: | | Music: | | Systems Integration: | | Training: | Y | Scientists/Research: | |
| | | Advertising Pros.: | | Broadcasting: | | Consulting/Other: | | Health Care: | | Petroleum/Chemicals: | Y |
| | | | | Other: | | | | Consulting: | | Math/Other: | |

## TYPES OF BUSINESS:

Oil & Gas Exploration & Production

## BRANDS/DIVISIONS/AFFILIATES:

Woodford Shale
Mountain Front Wash
Stone Energy Corp.
Monument Butte Field
McMoRan Exploration Co.
Constellation Energy Partners
Centrica plc

## CONTACTS: *Note: Officers with more than one job title may be intentionally listed here more than once.*

David A. Trice, CEO
David A. Trice, Pres.
Terry W. Rathert, CFO/Sr. VP/Sec.
Mona L. Bernhardt, VP-Human Resources
Mark Spicer, VP-IT
John D. Marziotti, General Counsel
Lee K. Boothby, Sr. VP-Bus. Dev. & Acquisitions
Stephen C. Campbell, VP-Investor Rel.
W. Mark Blumenshine, VP-Land
John H. Jasek, VP-Gulf Coast
Michael D. Van Horn, Sr. VP-Exploration
George T. Dunn, VP-Mid-Continent
David A. Trice, Chmn.
William D. Schneider, VP-Int'l

**Phone:** 281-847-6000 **Fax:** 281-405-4242
**Toll-Free:**
**Address:** 363 N. Sam Houston Pkwy. E., Ste. 2020, Houston, TX 77060 US

## GROWTH PLANS/SPECIAL FEATURES:

Newfield Exploration Co. (NEC) independently explores, develops and acquires crude oil and natural gas properties both domestically and internationally. Approximately 70% of Newfield's 2.3 trillion cubic feet equivalent of proved reserves is natural gas and 65% is proved developed. Representing 35% of its 2006 reserves, the firm's main Mid-Continent plays are Woodford Shale and Mountain Front Wash. Approximately 20% of its reserves, Newfield's Gulf Coast operations are concentrated in Texas. Acquired from Stone Energy Corp. for $577.9 million, the firm's main Rocky Mountain development, holding 20% of Newfield's reserves, is the Monument Butte Field in the Uinta Basin of Utah. Its producing Gulf of Mexico operations, with 15% of reserves, are mainly located in shallow water. Finally, 10% of its reserves are located internationally, mainly offshore China and Malaysia. The company's business strategy is largely based on growing its reserves through a balanced risk/reward drilling portfolio and maintaining a quality workforce through equity ownership. Newfield relies heavily on 3-D seismic data to determine the best prospects for exploration and development. In August 2007, McMoRan Exploration Co. purchased Newfield's producing shallow water Gulf of Mexico portfolio for $1.1 billion. Also in August 2007, Newfield signed two new production sharing contracts for the South China Sea. In October 2007, Newfield sold its interests in the U.K. region of the North Sea to Centrica plc for $486.4 million. In May 2008, NEC entered an agreement with ExxonMobil to jointly explore and develop approximately 87,000 gross acres in South Texas.

Newfield employees participate directly in the company's decision-making process through an employee forum, where, based on their technical experience and knowledge of the prospect, employees cast shareholder votes on whether to drill or not. A significant portion of employee compensation is dependent on the profitability of the company.

## FINANCIALS: Sales and profits are in thousands of dollars—add 000 to get the full amount. 2008 Note: Financial information for 2008 was not available for all companies at press time.

2008 Sales: $2,225,000
2007 Sales: $1,783,000
2006 Sales: $1,673,000
2005 Sales: $1,762,000
2004 Sales: $1,352,700

2008 Profits: $-373,000
2007 Profits: $450,000
2006 Profits: $591,000
2005 Profits: $348,000
2004 Profits: $312,100

**U.S. Stock Ticker: NFX**
**Int'l Ticker:** Int'l Exchange:
Employees: 927
Fiscal Year Ends: 12/31
Parent Company:

## SALARIES/BENEFITS:

Pension Plan:
Savings Plan: Y
ESOP Stock Plan: Y
Stock Purch. Plan:
Profit Sharing: Y
Top Exec. Salary: $520,833 Bonus: $2,700,000
Second Exec. Salary: $291,667 Bonus: $1,250,000

## OTHER THOUGHTS:

**Apparent Women Officers or Directors:** 2
**Hot Spot for Advancement for Women/Minorities:** Y

## LOCATIONS: ("Y" = Yes)

| West: | Southwest: | Midwest: | Southeast: | Northeast: | International: |
|---|---|---|---|---|---|
| Y | Y | Y | Y | | Y |

# NIC INC

www.nicusa.com

**Industry Group Code:** 514191A **Ranks within this company's industry group:** Sales: 7 Profits: 6

| Management: | | Sales/Marketing: | | Liberal Arts: | | Information Systems: | | Professionals: | | Technical/Scientific: | |
|---|---|---|---|---|---|---|---|---|---|---|---|
| Mgmt. Trainees: | | Mktg. Professionals: | Y | Gen. Writing/Editing: | | Info. Management: | Y | Finance/Accounting: | Y | Engineers, Elec.: | Y |
| Experienced Mgmt.: | Y | Retail Sales: | | Technical Writing: | Y | Software Dev.: | Y | Law: | Y | Engineers, Other: | |
| Int'l Business: | | Commercial/Industrial: | Y | Graphic Arts/Photog.: | | Hardware Dev.: | | HR/Other: | Y | Health/Lab: | |
| MBA Graduates: | Y | Sales Trainees: | Y | Music: | | Systems Integration: | Y | Training: | Y | Scientists/Research: | |
| | | Advertising Pros.: | | Broadcasting: | | Consulting/Other: | | Health Care: | | Petroleum/Chemicals: | |
| | | | | Other: | | | | Consulting: | | Math/Other: | |

## TYPES OF BUSINESS:

E-Government Services
Internet Portal Services
Electronic Filing Software
Application Development
Online Campaign Expenditure Development

## BRANDS/DIVISIONS/AFFILIATES:

NIC Technologies
NIC Conquest
Kansas.gov
Alabama.gov
IN.gov
Virginia.gov
Tennessee.gov

## CONTACTS: *Note: Officers with more than one job title may be intentionally listed here more than once.*

Harry H. Herington, CEO
William F. Bradley, Jr., COO
Stephen M. Kovzan, CFO
Chris Neff, VP-Mktg.
William F. Bradley, Jr., General Counsel
Elizabeth Proudfit, VP-Bus. Dev.
Nancy Beaton, Dir.-Comm.
Nancy Beaton, Dir.-Investor Rel.
Candy Irven, Dir.-Partnerships & Alliances
Harry H. Herington, Chmn.

**Phone:** **Fax:** 913-498-3472
**Toll-Free:** 877-234-3468
**Address:** 25501 W. Valley Pkwy., Ste. 300, Olathe, KS 66061 US

## GROWTH PLANS/SPECIAL FEATURES:

NIC, Inc. is a provider of eGovernment services that help governments use the Internet to increase internal efficiencies and provide a higher level of service to businesses and citizens. It operates in two divisions: portal outsourcing businesses and software & services businesses. The portal outsourcing business enters into long-term contracts with governments to design, build and operate web-based portals on their behalf. These portals consist of web sites and applications that allow businesses and citizens to access government information online and complete transactions, including applying for a permit, retrieving driver's license records or filing a government-mandated form or report. The self-funding business model allows the firm to generate revenues by sharing in the fees its collects from eGovernment transactions. NIC currently has contracts to provide portal outsourcing services to 21 states. The company typically enters into three- to five-year contracts with government partners and manages operations for each contractual relationship through separate local subsidiaries. The software and services businesses primarily include the company's Uniform Commercial Code (UCC) and corporate filings software development, as well as its ethics and elections businesses. The UCC and corporate filings software development business, NIC Conquest, is a provider of software applications and services for electronic filings and document management solutions for governments. This business is primarily engaged in servicing its contract with the California Secretary of State and is not actively marketing its applications and services in respect of new engagements. The ethics and elections business, NIC Technologies, designs and develops online campaign expenditure and ethics compliance systems for federal and state government agencies. This business is primarily engaged in servicing its contracts with the Federal Election Commission and the State of Michigan.

The company offers its employees medical and dental insurance; life and disability insurance; a 401(k) plan; an employee stock purchase plan; and tuition reimbursement.

## FINANCIALS: **Sales and profits are in thousands of dollars—add 000 to get the full amount. 2008 Note: Financial information for 2008 was not available for all companies at press time.**

| | | |
|---|---|---|
| 2008 Sales: $100,575 | 2008 Profits: $11,921 | **U.S. Stock Ticker: EGOV** |
| 2007 Sales: $85,755 | 2007 Profits: $11,955 | **Int'l Ticker:** Int'l Exchange: |
| 2006 Sales: $71,376 | 2006 Profits: $10,739 | Employees: 418 |
| 2005 Sales: $59,243 | 2005 Profits: $6,363 | Fiscal Year Ends: 12/31 |
| 2004 Sales: $55,762 | 2004 Profits: $7,105 | Parent Company: |

## SALARIES/BENEFITS:

| | | | | |
|---|---|---|---|---|
| Pension Plan: | ESOP Stock Plan: | Profit Sharing: | Top Exec. Salary: $325,000 | Bonus: $113,750 |
| Savings Plan: Y | Stock Purch. Plan: | | Second Exec. Salary: $315,000 | Bonus: $110,250 |

## OTHER THOUGHTS:

**Apparent Women Officers or Directors**: 3
**Hot Spot for Advancement for Women/Minorities**: Y

## LOCATIONS: ("Y" = Yes)

| West: | Southwest: | Midwest: | Southeast: | Northeast: | International: |
|---|---|---|---|---|---|
| | | Y | | | |

Note: Financial information, benefits and other data can change quickly and may vary from those stated here.

# NOBLE ENERGY INC

**www.nobleenergyinc.com**

**Industry Group Code:** 211111 **Ranks within this company's industry group:** Sales: 3 Profits: 3

| Management: | | Sales/Marketing: | | Liberal Arts: | | Information Systems: | | Professionals: | | Technical/Scientific: | |
|---|---|---|---|---|---|---|---|---|---|---|---|
| Mgmt. Trainees: | | Mktg. Professionals: | Y | Gen. Writing/Editing: | | Info. Management: | Y | Finance/Accounting: | Y | Engineers, Elec.: | |
| Experienced Mgmt.: | Y | Retail Sales: | | Technical Writing: | | Software Dev.: | | Law: | Y | Engineers, Other: | Y |
| Int'l Business: | Y | Commercial/Industrial: | Y | Graphic Arts/Photog.: | | Hardware Dev.: | | HR/Other: | Y | Health/Lab: | |
| MBA Graduates: | Y | Sales Trainees: | | Music: | | Systems Integration: | | Training: | Y | Scientists/Research: | |
| | | Advertising Pros.: | | Broadcasting: | | Consulting/Other: | | Health Care: | | Petroleum/Chemicals: | Y |
| | | | | Other: | | | | Consulting: | | Math/Other: | |

## TYPES OF BUSINESS:

Oil & Gas Exploration & Production
Oil & Gas Marketing
Methanol Production

## BRANDS/DIVISIONS/AFFILIATES:

Noble Energy Marketing, Inc.
Atlantic Methanol Production Company, LLC

## CONTACTS: *Note: Officers with more than one job title may be intentionally listed here more than once.*

Charles D. Davidson, CEO
David L. Stover, COO/Exec. VP
Charles D. Davidson, Pres.
Chris Tong, CFO/Sr. VP
Andrea Lee Robison, VP-Human Resources
Robert K. Burleson, VP-Bus. Admin.
Arnold J. Johnson, General Counsel/Sec./VP
Fredrick B. Bruning, Chief Acct. Officer/VP
Susan M. Cunningham, Sr. VP-Exploration & Corp. Reserves
Ted D. Brown, Sr. VP-North America Northern Region
Gerald M. Stevenson, Treas./VP
Charles (Chip) Rimer, VP-Drilling
Charles D. Davidson, Chmn.
Rodney D. Cook, Sr. VP-Int'l Div.

**Phone:** 281-872-3100 **Fax:** 281-872-3111
**Toll-Free:**
**Address:** 100 Glenborough Dr., Ste. 100, Houston, TX 77067 US

## GROWTH PLANS/SPECIAL FEATURES:

Noble Energy, Inc. is an independent energy company whose activities include the exploration, development, production and marketing of crude oil and natural gas. The firm's areas of operations are divided into three segments: domestic onshore, domestic offshore and international. Domestic onshore operations are conducted on the Gulf Coast; in the mid-continent area of Oklahoma, Texas and New Mexico; and in the Rocky Mountain region of Colorado. Domestic offshore activities are located in the Gulf of Mexico. International operations are conducted in Ecuador, Argentina, the North Sea, the Mediterranean Sea, Equatorial Guinea, Israel, China and Cameroon. The most significant international projects are located in Ecuador, Equatorial Guinea and Israel. In Ecuador, the company owns a natural gas fired power plant capable of providing 10% of the country's electric requirements. In Equatorial Guinea, the majority of the firm's production is sold to a methanol plant, which is owned by Atlantic Methanol Production Company (AMPCO), in which Noble Energy has a 45% interest. In Israel, the firm has discovered over 1 trillion cubic feet of natural gas, and has a long-term contract to provide natural gas to Israel Electric Company. The marketing of Noble Energy's domestic resources is conducted by wholly-owned subsidiary Noble Energy Marketing, Inc. (NEMI). NEMI markets the company's oil and natural gas directly to end-users through other natural gas marketers' pipelines. International resources are marketed through short- and long-term contracts. In 2007, the firm made discoveries of new crude oil and natural gas resources in Cameroon, Equatorial Guinea and the Gulf of Mexico. In October 2008, Nobel Energy announced an oil discovery at the Gunflint/Freedom prospect in Mississippi Canyon Block 948. In July 2008, Nobel Energy confirmed the discovery of multiple hydro-carbon bearing reservoirs.

## FINANCIALS: **Sales and profits are in thousands of dollars—add 000 to get the full amount. 2008 Note: Financial information for 2008 was not available for all companies at press time.**

2008 Sales: $3,901,000 | 2008 Profits: $1,350,000
2007 Sales: $3,272,030 | 2007 Profits: $943,870
2006 Sales: $2,940,082 | 2006 Profits: $678,428
2005 Sales: $2,186,723 | 2005 Profits: $645,720
2004 Sales: $1,351,051 | 2004 Profits: $328,710

**U.S. Stock Ticker: NBL**
**Int'l Ticker:** Int'l Exchange:
Employees: 1,398
Fiscal Year Ends: 12/31
Parent Company:

## SALARIES/BENEFITS:

Pension Plan: | ESOP Stock Plan: | Profit Sharing: | Top Exec. Salary: $1,025,000 | Bonus: $3,793,400
Savings Plan: | Stock Purch. Plan: | | Second Exec. Salary: $495,836 | Bonus: $1,326,575

## OTHER THOUGHTS:

**Apparent Women Officers or Directors**: 2
**Hot Spot for Advancement for Women/Minorities**:

## LOCATIONS: ("Y" = Yes)

| West: | Southwest: | Midwest: | Southeast: | Northeast: | International: |
|---|---|---|---|---|---|
| Y | Y | Y | | | Y |

# NORTHWESTERN CORPORATION

www.northwesternenergy.com

**Industry Group Code:** 221000 **Ranks within this company's industry group:** Sales: 6 Profits: 5

| Management: | | Sales/Marketing: | | Liberal Arts: | | Information Systems: | | Professionals: | | Technical/Scientific: | |
|---|---|---|---|---|---|---|---|---|---|---|---|
| Mgmt. Trainees: | | Mktg. Professionals: | Y | Gen. Writing/Editing: | | Info. Management: | Y | Finance/Accounting: | Y | Engineers, Elec.: | Y |
| Experienced Mgmt.: | Y | Retail Sales: | | Technical Writing: | | Software Dev.: | | Law: | Y | Engineers, Other: | Y |
| Int'l Business: | | Commercial/Industrial: | Y | Graphic Arts/Photog.: | | Hardware Dev.: | | HR/Other: | Y | Health/Lab: | |
| MBA Graduates: | Y | Sales Trainees: | | Music: | | Systems Integration: | | Training: | Y | Scientists/Research: | |
| | | Advertising Pros.: | | Broadcasting: | | Consulting/Other: | | Health Care: | | Petroleum/Chemicals: | Y |
| | | | | Other: | | | | Consulting: | | Math/Other: | |

## TYPES OF BUSINESS:

Utilities-Electricity & Natural Gas
Energy Transmission & Distribution
Natural Gas Transmission & Distribution
Pipelines
Electrical Generation

## BRANDS/DIVISIONS/AFFILIATES:

Northwestern Energy
NorthWestern Services, LLC
Nekota Resources, LLC

## CONTACTS:

*Note: Officers with more than one job title may be intentionally listed here more than once.*

Robert C. Rowe, CEO
Robert C. Rowe, Pres.
Brian B. Bird, CFO/VP
Gregory G.A. Trandem, VP-Admin. Svcs.
Miggie E. Cramblit, General Counsel/Corp. Sec./VP
Bobbi L. Schroeppel, VP-Customer Care & Comm.
Paul J. Evans, Treas.
David G. Gates, VP-Wholesale Oper.
Curtis T. Pohl, VP-Retail Oper.
Patrick R. Corcoran, VP-Gov't & Regulatory Affairs
Kendall G. Kliewer, Controller/VP
E. Linn Draper, Jr., Chmn.
John D. Hines, Chief Supply Officer

| Phone: 605-978-2900 | Fax: 605-978-2840 |
|---|---|
| Toll-Free: | |
| Address: 3010 W. 69th St., Sioux Falls, SD 57108 US | |

## GROWTH PLANS/SPECIAL FEATURES:

NorthWestern Corp., doing business as Northwestern Energy, is one of the largest providers of electricity and natural gas in the upper Midwest and Northwest, serving roughly 650,000 customers in Montana, South Dakota and Nebraska. The company operates in five segments: regulated electric operations; unregulated electric operations; regulated natural gas operations; and other, which primarily consists of miscellaneous service activities not included in the other segments. Through the regulated electric operations, the firm delivers electricity to about 328,000 customers in 187 communities in Montana; the Yellowstone National Park in Wyoming; and more than 60,100 customers in 110 communities in South Dakota. The unregulated electric operations segment leases a 30% share of Colstrip Unit 4, a 740-megawatt demonstrated-capacity coal-fired power plant located in southeastern Montana. Northwestern sells the majority of its generation from Colstrip Unit 4 to Puget Sound Energy and DB Energy Trading, LLC. Through the regulated natural gas operations, the company distributes natural gas to 177,000 customers in 105 Montana communities and 84,500 customers in South Dakota and Nebraska. In November 2007, the firm began seeking bids to supply locally produced wind energy to its South Dakota electric customers. In June 2008, Northwestern agreed to sell its ownership in Colstrip Unit 4 to Bicent (Montana) Power Company, LLC for $404 million.

The company offers its employees medical, dental and vision insurance; flexible spending accounts; a 401(k) plan; life and accident insurance; short- and long-term disability insurance; a pension plan; an employee assistance program; tuition reimbursement; and adoption benefits.

## FINANCIALS:

**Sales and profits are in thousands of dollars—add 000 to get the full amount. 2008 Note: Financial information for 2008 was not available for all companies at press time.**

| | | |
|---|---|---|
| 2008 Sales: $1,260,793 | 2008 Profits: $67,601 | **U.S. Stock Ticker: NWEC** |
| 2007 Sales: $1,200,060 | 2007 Profits: $53,191 | **Int'l Ticker:** Int'l Exchange: |
| 2006 Sales: $1,132,653 | 2006 Profits: $37,900 | Employees: 1,351 |
| 2005 Sales: $1,165,750 | 2005 Profits: $59,467 | Fiscal Year Ends: 12/31 |
| 2004 Sales: $1,038,989 | 2004 Profits: $544,433 | Parent Company: |

## SALARIES/BENEFITS:

| | | | | |
|---|---|---|---|---|
| Pension Plan: Y | ESOP Stock Plan: | Profit Sharing: | Top Exec. Salary: $521,635 | Bonus: $169,014 |
| Savings Plan: Y | Stock Purch. Plan: | | Second Exec. Salary: $301,846 | Bonus: $109,411 |

## OTHER THOUGHTS:

**Apparent Women Officers or Directors**: 3
**Hot Spot for Advancement for Women/Minorities**: Y

## LOCATIONS: ("Y" = Yes)

| West: | Southwest: | Midwest: | Southeast: | Northeast: | International: |
|---|---|---|---|---|---|
| Y | | Y | | | |

# NOVAMED INC

www.novamed.com

**Industry Group Code:** 621490 **Ranks within this company's industry group:** Sales: 5 Profits: 7

| Management: | | Sales/Marketing: | | Liberal Arts: | | Information Systems: | | Professionals: | | Technical/Scientific: | |
|---|---|---|---|---|---|---|---|---|---|---|---|
| Mgmt. Trainees: | | Mktg. Professionals: | Y | Gen. Writing/Editing: | | Info. Management: | Y | Finance/Accounting: | Y | Engineers, Elec.: | |
| Experienced Mgmt.: | Y | Retail Sales: | | Technical Writing: | | Software Dev.: | | Law: | Y | Engineers, Other: | |
| Int'l Business: | | Commercial/Industrial: | | Graphic Arts/Photog.: | | Hardware Dev.: | | HR/Other: | Y | Health/Lab: | Y |
| MBA Graduates: | Y | Sales Trainees: | Y | Music: | | Systems Integration: | | Training: | Y | Scientists/Research: | |
| | | Advertising Pros.: | Y | Broadcasting: | | Consulting/Other: | | Health Care: | Y | Petroleum/Chemicals: | |
| | | | | Other: | | | | Consulting: | | Math/Other: | |

## TYPES OF BUSINESS:

Outpatient Surgery
Eye-Care Services
Laser Vision Correction
Corrective Lenses Labs
Eye-Care Products Distribution
Purchasing and Supply Chain Services
Marketing Services

## BRANDS/DIVISIONS/AFFILIATES:

Buying Group (The)

## CONTACTS: *Note: Officers with more than one job title may be intentionally listed here more than once.*

Thomas S. Hall, CEO
Thomas S. Hall, Pres.
Scott T. Macomber, CFO/Exec. VP
Robert D. Watson, VP-Mktg. Svcs. Group
John W. Lawrence, Jr., General Counsel/Sr. VP
Cassandra T. Speier, Sr. VP-Oper.
Thomas J. Chirillo, Sr. VP-Corp. Dev.
John P. Hart, Corp. Controller/VP
William J. Kennedy, Sr. VP-Bus. Dev.
Graham B. Cherrington, Sr. VP
Frank L. Soppa, VP-Optical Svcs. Group
Thomas S. Hall, Chmn.

**Phone:** 312-664-4100 **Fax:** 312-664-4250
**Toll-Free:** 800-388-4133
**Address:** 980 N. Michigan Ave., Ste. 1620, Chicago, IL 60611 US

## GROWTH PLANS/SPECIAL FEATURES:

NovaMed, Inc. is a health care services company that strives to acquire, develop and operate ambulatory surgery centers (ASCs) in joint ownership with physicians throughout the U.S. Its facilities consist of 34 primarily practice-based ASCs in 17 states. All but 10 of the locations are single-specialty ophthalmic surgical facilities where eye-care professionals perform surgical procedures, such as cataract and laser vision correction. NovaMed provides excimer lasers to eye-care professionals for use in laser vision correction surgery through fixed-site laser service agreements. The company continues to expand its ASC services into specialties such as orthopedics, gastroenterology, urology, pain management, plastic surgery and gynecology. In addition to its ASCs, NovaMed also owns and operates an optical products purchasing organization; a marketing products and services business, which provides eye clinics with brochures, videos and advertising design services; and an optical laboratory business that specializes in surfacing and finishing corrective eyeglass lenses, and selling them to ophthalmologists, optometrists, opticians and optical retail chains. The firm offers its management services to two eye care practices by providing business, information technology, administrative and financial services in exchange for a management fee. NovaMed is constantly expanding its operations through new ASC acquisitions: in January 2007, it acquired an ASC located in St. Peters, Missouri; in June 2007, it acquired an ASC in Portage, Michigan; and in July 2008, it acquired an ASC in Baton Rouge, Louisiana. In December 2007, NovaMed announced plans to sell or close three ASCs located in Laredo, Texas; Thibodaux, Louisiana; and Columbus, Georgia. In January 2008, the firm acquired The Buying Group, an optical products purchasing company, for approximately $7 million.

## FINANCIALS: **Sales and profits are in thousands of dollars—add 000 to get the full amount. 2008 Note: Financial information for 2008 was not available for all companies at press time.**

| | | |
|---|---|---|
| 2008 Sales: $141,220 | 2008 Profits: $9,577 | **U.S. Stock Ticker: NOVA** |
| 2007 Sales: $128,621 | 2007 Profits: $-5,594 | **Int'l Ticker:** Int'l Exchange: |
| 2006 Sales: $104,256 | 2006 Profits: $5,737 | Employees: 691 |
| 2005 Sales: $81,226 | 2005 Profits: $5,589 | Fiscal Year Ends: 12/31 |
| 2004 Sales: $63,648 | 2004 Profits: $4,459 | Parent Company: |

## SALARIES/BENEFITS:

| | | | | |
|---|---|---|---|---|
| Pension Plan: | ESOP Stock Plan: | Profit Sharing: | Top Exec. Salary: $525,577 | Bonus: $ |
| Savings Plan: | Stock Purch. Plan: | | Second Exec. Salary: $279,866 | Bonus: $ |

## OTHER THOUGHTS:

**Apparent Women Officers or Directors:** 1
**Hot Spot for Advancement for Women/Minorities:** Y

## LOCATIONS: ("Y" = Yes)

| West: | Southwest: | Midwest: | Southeast: | Northeast: | International: |
|---|---|---|---|---|---|
| Y | Y | Y | Y | Y | |

# NOVEN PHARMACEUTICALS

www.noven.com

**Industry Group Code:** 325412A **Ranks within this company's industry group:** Sales: 6 Profits: 5

| Management: | | Sales/Marketing: | | Liberal Arts: | | Information Systems: | | Professionals: | | Technical/Scientific: | |
|---|---|---|---|---|---|---|---|---|---|---|---|
| Mgmt. Trainees: | | Mktg. Professionals: | Y | Gen. Writing/Editing: | | Info. Management: | Y | Finance/Accounting: | Y | Engineers, Elec.: | |
| Experienced Mgmt.: | Y | Retail Sales: | | Technical Writing: | Y | Software Dev.: | | Law: | Y | Engineers, Other: | |
| Int'l Business: | Y | Commercial/Industrial: | Y | Graphic Arts/Photog.: | | Hardware Dev.: | | HR/Other: | Y | Health/Lab: | Y |
| MBA Graduates: | Y | Sales Trainees: | Y | Music: | | Systems Integration: | | Training: | Y | Scientists/Research: | Y |
| | | Advertising Pros.: | | Broadcasting: | | Consulting/Other: | | Health Care: | Y | Petroleum/Chemicals: | |
| | | | | Other: | | | | Consulting: | | Math/Other: | Y |

## TYPES OF BUSINESS:

Drug Delivery Systems
Hormone Replacement Products
Pain Management Products
Central Nervous System Products
Transdermal Drug Delivery Systems

## BRANDS/DIVISIONS/AFFILIATES:

Vivelle
Menorest
Daytrana
Novartis AG
Estalis
Noven Therapeutics
Estradot
Novogyne Pharmaceuticals

## CONTACTS: *Note: Officers with more than one job title may be intentionally listed here more than once.*

Peter C. Brandt, CEO
Peter C. Brandt, Pres.
Michael D. Price, CFO/VP
Anthony Venditti, VP-Mktg. & Sales
Carolyn Donaldson, VP-Human Resources
Steven F. Dinh, Chief Scientific Officer/VP
Juan A. Mantelle, CTO/VP
Jeff T. Mihm, General Counsel/VP
Richard Gilbert, VP-Oper.
Paven Handa, VP-Bus. Dev.
Joseph C. Jones, VP-Corp. Affairs
Wayne P. Yetter, Chmn.

| Phone: 305-253-5099 | Fax: 305-251-1887 |
|---|---|
| Toll-Free: | |
| Address: 11960 SW 144th St., Miami, FL 33186 US | |

## GROWTH PLANS/SPECIAL FEATURES:

Noven Pharmaceuticals, Inc. develops and manufactures advanced transdermal drug delivery systems and prescription transdermal products. Its principal commercialized products are transdermal drug delivery systems designed with its DOT Matrix technology for use in hormone replacement therapy. The firm's first product was an estrogen patch for the treatment of menopausal symptoms, marketed under the name Vivelle in the U.S. and Canada, and under the name Menorest in Europe and other markets. The company also launched the smallest transdermal estrogen patch ever approved by the Food and Drug Administration (FDA), Vivelle-Dot. Noven markets the product in several foreign countries under the name Estradot. Noven also produces a combination estrogen/progestin transdermal patch for the treatment of menopausal symptoms, marketed under the name CombiPatch in the U.S., and Estalis in Europe and other markets. The company markets a daily methylphenidate patch called Daytrana for the treatment of ADHD through an agreement with Shire. The company also specializes in treatments for central nervous system conditions and pain. Noven has partial ownership of a joint venture, Vivelle Ventures, formed in partnership with Novartis Pharmaceuticals doing business under the name Novogyne Pharmaceuticals. Novogyne markets Vivelle, Vivelle-Dot and CombiPatch in the U.S. The firm also markets its Lidocaine/DentiPatch for dental pain associated with dental procedures. In August 2007, Noven acquired JDS Pharmaceuticals LLC for $125 million. The company was recently Noven Therapeutics Inc., selling two prescription psychiatry products, Lithobid and Pexeva, for bipolar disporder and depression, respectively. Noven Therapeutics also has Mesafem in Phase III of the development pipeline, a non-hormonal therapy for the treatment of vasomotor symptoms associated with menopause. In December 2007, the FDA granted tentative approval for Stavzor, a product developed for Noven Therapeutics, meant to treat manic episodes associated with bipolar disorder, monotherapy and adjunctive therapy in multiple seizure types, and prophylaxis of migraine headaches.

## FINANCIALS: **Sales and profits are in thousands of dollars—add 000 to get the full amount. 2008 Note: Financial information for 2008 was not available for all companies at press time.**

| | | |
|---|---|---|
| 2008 Sales: $ | 2008 Profits: $ | **U.S. Stock Ticker: NOVN** |
| 2007 Sales: $83,161 | 2007 Profits: $-45,376 | **Int'l Ticker:** Int'l Exchange: |
| 2006 Sales: $60,689 | 2006 Profits: $15,988 | Employees: 586 |
| 2005 Sales: $52,532 | 2005 Profits: $9,972 | Fiscal Year Ends: 12/31 |
| 2004 Sales: $45,891 | 2004 Profits: $11,224 | Parent Company: |

## SALARIES/BENEFITS:

| | | | | |
|---|---|---|---|---|
| Pension Plan: | ESOP Stock Plan: | Profit Sharing: | Top Exec. Salary: $611,251 | Bonus: $ |
| Savings Plan: Y | Stock Purch. Plan: | | Second Exec. Salary: $314,810 | Bonus: $ |

## OTHER THOUGHTS:

**Apparent Women Officers or Directors**: 1
**Hot Spot for Advancement for Women/Minorities**: Y

## LOCATIONS: ("Y" = Yes)

| West: | Southwest: | Midwest: | Southeast: | Northeast: | International: |
|---|---|---|---|---|---|
| | | | Y | | |

# NTELOS HOLDING CORP

**www.ntelos.com**

**Industry Group Code:** 513300A **Ranks within this company's industry group:** Sales: 2 Profits: 2

| **Management:** | | **Sales/Marketing:** | | **Liberal Arts:** | | **Information Systems:** | | **Professionals:** | | **Technical/Scientific:** | |
|---|---|---|---|---|---|---|---|---|---|---|---|
| Mgmt. Trainees: | | Mktg. Professionals: | Y | Gen. Writing/Editing: | | Info. Management: | Y | Finance/Accounting: | Y | Engineers, Elec.: | Y |
| Experienced Mgmt.: | Y | Retail Sales: | | Technical Writing: | | Software Dev.: | Y | Law: | Y | Engineers, Other: | Y |
| Int'l Business: | | Commercial/Industrial: | Y | Graphic Arts/Photog.: | | Hardware Dev.: | | HR/Other: | Y | Health/Lab: | |
| MBA Graduates: | Y | Sales Trainees: | Y | Music: | | Systems Integration: | Y | Training: | Y | Scientists/Research: | |
| | | Advertising Pros.: | | Broadcasting: | | Consulting/Other: | | Health Care: | | Petroleum/Chemicals: | |
| | | | | Other: | | | | Consulting: | | Math/Other: | |

## TYPES OF BUSINESS:

Wireless & Wireline Services
Digital PCS Services
Paging Services
Internet Services

## BRANDS/DIVISIONS/AFFILIATES:

Sprint Spectrum L.P.
Sprint Nextel Corp
Clifton Forge-Waynesboro Telephone Company

## CONTACTS: *Note: Officers with more than one job title may be intentionally listed here more than once.*

James S. Quarforth, CEO
James S. Quarforth, Pres.
Michael B. Moneymaker, CFO/Exec. VP
Mary McDermott, Sr. VP-Legal & Regulatory Affairs
Michael B. Moneymaker, Treas./Corp. Sec.
Carl A. Rosberg, Exec. VP/Pres., Wireless Oper.
David R. Maccarelli, Exec. VP/Pres., Wireline Oper.
James S. Quarforth, Chmn.

| | |
|---|---|
| **Phone:** 540-946-3500 | **Fax:** 540-946-3595 |
| **Toll-Free:** 877-468-3567 | |
| **Address:** 401 Spring Ln., Ste. 300, Waynesboro, VA 22980 US | |

## GROWTH PLANS/SPECIAL FEATURES:

nTelos Holding Corp. is a leading provider of wireless and wireline communications services to consumers and businesses primarily in Virginia and West Virginia. The company's wireless operations are composed of its nTelos-branded retail and wholesale businesses that it operates under an exclusive contract with Sprint Spectrum L.P., a subsidiary of Sprint Nextel Corporation. Its wireless business operates a 100% code division multiple access (CDMA) digital PCS (personal communications service) network in Virginia, West Virginia and portions of Kentucky, Maryland, Ohio and North Carolina. nTelos has approximately 407,000 wireless subscribers, representing 7.8% of its total covered population. During 2007, the company added 186 new wireless cell sites, increasing its total cell sites to 1,023. It also amended its agreement with Sprint Spectrum during 2007 to act as its exclusive wholesale provider of network services through 2015. The company's wireline business, which was founded in 1897 as the Clifton Forge-Waynesboro Telephone Company, is supported by a 2,110-mile regional fiber optic network. nTelos conducts its wireline business through two subsidiaries that qualify as rural local exchange carriers (RLEC). The company operates approximately 44,000 RLEC telephone access lines and participates in partnerships that directly connect its networks with many of the largest markets in the mid-Atlantic region. nTelos markets and sells voice, data and local and long distance services almost exclusively to business customers through its competitive local exchange carrier (CLEC) and Internet service provider (ISP) operation, with approximately 49,000 CLEC access line connections. It also offers DSL services in over 95% of its RLEC service area and operates approximately 20,000 broadband access connections in its markets. In late 2007, the company introduced nTelos video in selected neighborhoods within its two RLEC service areas, providing an alternative to cable and satellite television with more than 200 all-digital channels and 18 high-definition channels.

## FINANCIALS: **Sales and profits are in thousands of dollars—add 000 to get the full amount. 2008 Note: Financial information for 2008 was not available for all companies at press time.**

| | | |
|---|---|---|
| 2008 Sales: $ | 2008 Profits: $ | **U.S. Stock Ticker: NTLS** |
| 2007 Sales: $500,394 | 2007 Profits: $32,453 | **Int'l Ticker:** Int'l Exchange: |
| 2006 Sales: $440,076 | 2006 Profits: $-7,185 | Employees: 1,408 |
| 2005 Sales: $265,859 | 2005 Profits: $1,098 | Fiscal Year Ends: 12/31 |
| 2004 Sales: $343,310 | 2004 Profits: $38,312 | Parent Company: |

## SALARIES/BENEFITS:

| | | | | |
|---|---|---|---|---|
| Pension Plan: | ESOP Stock Plan: | Profit Sharing: | Top Exec. Salary: $445,813 | Bonus: $704,696 |
| Savings Plan: | Stock Purch. Plan: | | Second Exec. Salary: $298,039 | Bonus: $376,886 |

## OTHER THOUGHTS:

**Apparent Women Officers or Directors**: 1
**Hot Spot for Advancement for Women/Minorities**:

## LOCATIONS: ("Y" = Yes)

| West: | Southwest: | Midwest: | Southeast: | Northeast: | International: |
|---|---|---|---|---|---|
| | | Y | | Y | |

# NUGGET MARKET

www.nuggetmarket.com

**Industry Group Code:** 445110 **Ranks within this company's industry group:** Sales: Profits:

| Management: | | Sales/Marketing: | | Liberal Arts: | | Information Systems: | | Professionals: | | Technical/Scientific: | |
|---|---|---|---|---|---|---|---|---|---|---|---|
| Mgmt. Trainees: | Y | Mktg. Professionals: | Y | Gen. Writing/Editing: | | Info. Management: | Y | Finance/Accounting: | Y | Engineers, Elec.: | |
| Experienced Mgmt.: | Y | Retail Sales: | Y | Technical Writing: | | Software Dev.: | | Law: | Y | Engineers, Other: | |
| Int'l Business: | | Commercial/Industrial: | | Graphic Arts/Photog.: | Y | Hardware Dev.: | | HR/Other: | Y | Health/Lab: | |
| MBA Graduates: | Y | Sales Trainees: | Y | Music: | | Systems Integration: | | Training: | Y | Scientists/Research: | |
| | | Advertising Pros.: | Y | Broadcasting: | | Consulting/Other: | | Health Care: | | Petroleum/Chemicals: | |
| | | | | Other: | | | | Consulting: | | Math/Other: | |

## TYPES OF BUSINESS:

Supermarket

## BRANDS/DIVISIONS/AFFILIATES:

FishWise
PriceSurvey

## CONTACTS:

*Note: Officers with more than one job title may be intentionally listed here more than once.*

Eric Stille, Pres.
Kate Stille, Dir.-Mktg.
Gregory J. Stille, VP
Eugene N. Stille, Chmn.

| | |
|---|---|
| **Phone:** 530-669-3300 | **Fax:** 530-662-0929 |
| **Toll-Free:** | |
| **Address:** 168 Court St., Woodland, CA 95695 US | |

## GROWTH PLANS/SPECIAL FEATURES:

Nugget Market is a family-owned chain of nine full service grocery stores located in the Sacramento area. The stores offer conventional and organic produce; meat and seafood, including Harris Ranch beef, Foster Farms chicken, and Nugget's own sausage; specialty grocery items; specialty cheese; bakery products; adult beverages; eco-friendly bath, body and hair-care products; and vitamins, herbs and supplements. The company's FishWise system is a color-coded labeling program designed to make customers aware of the sustainability and population health of particular seafood items sold. The stores also maintain kitchens with different prepared meals inspired by international cuisines, as well as staples such as sandwiches and salads. Additionally, coffee and juice bars are located in each establishment. The company aims to offer the lowest prices in the area and provides a PriceSurvey for customers to compare Nugget prices to those of other stores. The number of people who believe nugget provides the lowest prices are then posted above the front entrance. The firm provides recipes for various types of dishes, as well as a calendar of store events on nuggetmarket.com. Such events include wine tastings, gift card drawings, and talks with health professionals.

Nugget Market is rated number 10 in Fortune Magazine's 2009 list of the country's 100 Best Companies to Work For. Employees are offered medical, dental and vision insurance; a 401(k) plan; life insurance; and long-term disability coverage.

## FINANCIALS:

**Sales and profits are in thousands of dollars—add 000 to get the full amount. 2008 Note: Financial information for 2008 was not available for all companies at press time.**

| | | |
|---|---|---|
| 2008 Sales: $ | 2008 Profits: $ | **U.S. Stock Ticker: Private** |
| 2007 Sales: $ | 2007 Profits: $ | **Int'l Ticker:** Int'l Exchange: |
| 2006 Sales: $ | 2006 Profits: $ | Employees: 1,536 |
| 2005 Sales: $ | 2005 Profits: $ | Fiscal Year Ends: |
| 2004 Sales: $ | 2004 Profits: $ | Parent Company: |

## SALARIES/BENEFITS:

| | | | | |
|---|---|---|---|---|
| Pension Plan: | ESOP Stock Plan: | Profit Sharing: | Top Exec. Salary: $ | Bonus: $ |
| Savings Plan: Y | Stock Purch. Plan: | | Second Exec. Salary: $ | Bonus: $ |

## OTHER THOUGHTS:

**Apparent Women Officers or Directors**: 1
**Hot Spot for Advancement for Women/Minorities**:

## LOCATIONS: ("Y" = Yes)

| West: | Southwest: | Midwest: | Southeast: | Northeast: | International: |
|---|---|---|---|---|---|
| Y | | | | | |

# NUSTAR ENERGY LP

www.nustarenergy.com

**Industry Group Code:** 422710 **Ranks within this company's industry group:** Sales: 2 Profits: 1

| Management: | | Sales/Marketing: | | Liberal Arts: | | Information Systems: | | Professionals: | | Technical/Scientific: | |
|---|---|---|---|---|---|---|---|---|---|---|---|
| Mgmt. Trainees: | | Mktg. Professionals: | Y | Gen. Writing/Editing: | | Info. Management: | Y | Finance/Accounting: | Y | Engineers, Elec.: | Y |
| Experienced Mgmt.: | Y | Retail Sales: | | Technical Writing: | | Software Dev.: | | Law: | Y | Engineers, Other: | Y |
| Int'l Business: | Y | Commercial/Industrial: | Y | Graphic Arts/Photog.: | | Hardware Dev.: | | HR/Other: | Y | Health/Lab: | |
| MBA Graduates: | Y | Sales Trainees: | Y | Music: | | Systems Integration: | | Training: | Y | Scientists/Research: | |
| | | Advertising Pros.: | | Broadcasting: | | Consulting/Other: | | Health Care: | | Petroleum/Chemicals: | Y |
| | | | | Other: | | | | Consulting: | | Math/Other: | |

## TYPES OF BUSINESS:

Petroleum Pipeline Transportation
Anhydrous Ammonia Transportation
Refined Products Transportation

## BRANDS/DIVISIONS/AFFILIATES:

Valero Energy Corp.
Kaneb Services LLC
Kaneb Pipe Line Partners, L.P.
NuStar Logistics L.P.
Kaneb Pipe Line Operating Partnership, L.P.
CITGO

## CONTACTS: *Note: Officers with more than one job title may be intentionally listed here more than once.*

Curtis Anastasio, CEO
Curtis Anastasio, Pres.
Steve Blank, CFO/Sr. VP
Paul Brattlof, Sr. VP-Mktg.
Brad Ramsey, VP-Eng.
Brad Barron, General Counsel/Sr. VP/Sec.
Rick Bluntzer, VP-Oper.
Mary Morgan, Sr. VP-Bus. Dev. & Mktg.
Mary Rose Brown, Sr. VP-Corp. Comm.
Tom Shoaf, VP/Controller
Steve Blank, Treas.
Mike Hoeltzel, Sr. VP-Strategic Planning
Bill Greehey, Chmn.
Paul Brattlof, VP-Supply Chain

**Phone:** 210-918-2000 **Fax:** 210-918-5057
**Toll-Free:** 800-866-9060
**Address:** 2330 Loop 1604 W., San Antonio, TX 78248 US

## GROWTH PLANS/SPECIAL FEATURES:

NuStar Energy L.P., formerly Valero L.P., is one of the largest terminal and independent petroleum liquids pipeline operators in the U.S. The company's principal services include providing pipeline transportation services, terminalling services, storage lease services and crude oil storage handling services. NuStar's product sales primarily consist of the sale of bunker fuel to marine vessels. The company conducts its operations through its subsidiaries, primarily NuStar Logistics L.P. and Kaneb Pipe Line Operating Partnership, L.P. NuStar has five business segments: refined product terminals, refined product pipelines, crude oil pipelines, crude oil storage tanks and marketing. The refined product terminals segment owns 52 terminals in the U.S. providing storage and handling services on a fee basis for petroleum products, specialty chemicals and other liquids, including crude oil and other feedstocks. The refined product pipelines segment owns common carrier pipelines in Texas, Oklahoma, Colorado, New Mexico, Kansas, Nebraska, Iowa, South Dakota, North Dakota and Minnesota covering approximately 6,251 miles. In addition, NuStar owns a 2,000-mile anhydrous ammonia pipeline. The crude oil pipelines segment owns 812 miles of crude oil pipelines transporting crude oil and other feedstocks from various points in Texas, Oklahoma, Kansas and Colorado to the company's refineries as well as associated crude oil storage facilities in Texas and Oklahoma that are located along the crude oil pipelines. NuStar also own 57 miles of crude oil pipeline in Illinois, which serves ConocoPhillips' Wood River refinery. The crude oil storage tanks segment owns 60 crude oil and intermediate feedstock storage tanks and related assets. The marketing segment involves the sales activities of bunker fuel and other petroleum products. In March 2008, NuStar acquired CITGO Asphalt Refining Company's asphalt operations and assets.

The company offers its employees a health and wellness program; adoption assistance; and tuition reimbursement.

## FINANCIALS: Sales and profits are in thousands of dollars—add 000 to get the full amount. 2008 Note: Financial information for 2008 was not available for all companies at press time.

2008 Sales: $
2007 Sales: $1,475,014
2006 Sales: $1,137,261
2005 Sales: $659,557
2004 Sales: $220,792

2008 Profits: $
2007 Profits: $150,298
2006 Profits: $149,530
2005 Profits: $111,073
2004 Profits: $78,418

**U.S. Stock Ticker: NS**
**Int'l Ticker:** Int'l Exchange:
Employees: 1,663
Fiscal Year Ends: 12/31
Parent Company:

## SALARIES/BENEFITS:

Pension Plan: Y
Savings Plan: Y
ESOP Stock Plan:
Stock Purch. Plan:
Profit Sharing:
Top Exec. Salary: $428,400 Bonus: $393,120
Second Exec. Salary: $311,916 Bonus: $238,524

## OTHER THOUGHTS:

**Apparent Women Officers or Directors:** 2
**Hot Spot for Advancement for Women/Minorities:**

## LOCATIONS: ("Y" = Yes)

| West: | Southwest: | Midwest: | Southeast: | Northeast: | International: |
|---|---|---|---|---|---|
| Y | Y | Y | Y | Y | Y |

# NUTRASWEET COMPANY (THE)

www.nutrasweet.com

**Industry Group Code:** 311940 **Ranks within this company's industry group:** Sales: Profits:

| Management: | | Sales/Marketing: | | Liberal Arts: | | Information Systems: | | Professionals: | | Technical/Scientific: | |
|---|---|---|---|---|---|---|---|---|---|---|---|
| Mgmt. Trainees: | | Mktg. Professionals: | Y | Gen. Writing/Editing: | | Info. Management: | Y | Finance/Accounting: | Y | Engineers, Elec.: | |
| Experienced Mgmt.: | Y | Retail Sales: | | Technical Writing: | | Software Dev.: | | Law: | Y | Engineers, Other: | |
| Int'l Business: | | Commercial/Industrial: | Y | Graphic Arts/Photog.: | Y | Hardware Dev.: | | HR/Other: | Y | Health/Lab: | |
| MBA Graduates: | Y | Sales Trainees: | Y | Music: | | Systems Integration: | | Training: | Y | Scientists/Research: | |
| | | Advertising Pros.: | Y | Broadcasting: | | Consulting/Other: | | Health Care: | | Petroleum/Chemicals: | |
| | | | | Other: | | | | Consulting: | | Math/Other: | |

## TYPES OF BUSINESS:

Artificial Sweeteners

## BRANDS/DIVISIONS/AFFILIATES:

NutraSweet
J.W. Childs Equity Patners II LP
Neotame
American Sugar Refining Inc

## CONTACTS:

*Note: Officers with more than one job title may be intentionally listed here more than once.*

Craig Petray, CEO
William DeFer, COO
William DeFer, Pres.
Kevin Bauer, Sr. VP-Sales & Marketing

**Phone:** 312-873-5000 **Fax:** 312-873-5050
**Toll-Free:** 800-323-5321
**Address:** 10 S. Wacker Dr., Chicago, IL 60606 US

## GROWTH PLANS/SPECIAL FEATURES:

The NutraSweet Company, headquartered in Chicago, Illinois, is one of the world's largest producers of the artificial sweetener aspartame, which is roughly 200 times sweeter than table sugar. J.W. Childs Equity Partners II, L.P., NutraSweet's owner, is a private investment firm in Boston specializing in acquiring and growing mid-market companies. The firm's NutraSweet-brand sweetener is sold in over 100 countries and used by roughly 250 million consumers every year. Additionally, the sweetener is used in more than 5,000 consumer food and beverage products throughout the world such as breath mints; chewing gum; ice cream; yogurts; juices; pie and bakery fillings, toppings and syrups; over-the-counter pharmaceuticals; sauces; and ready-to-eat refrigerated desserts. The company sells its sweetener in the retail, food service and restaurant markets. In addition, through agreements with some of the world's largest food producers, the sweetener can be found in many foods and beverages including bakery products, carbonated drinks, tea, fruit juices, coffee, ice cream, yogurt, pie and bakery fillings, ready-to-eat desserts, dry mixes, cough lozenges, chewable vitamins, barbecue sauce and assorted syrups. The firm is heavily invested in research and development for enhancement and formulation to ensure the safety and quality of its product. NutraSweet's sweetener and flavor enhancer, Neotame, is between 8,000 and 13,000 times sweeter than table sugar. Although it was approved for general use by the FDA in 2002, Neotame has not become widely used.

## FINANCIALS:

**Sales and profits are in thousands of dollars—add 000 to get the full amount. 2008 Note: Financial information for 2008 was not available for all companies at press time.**

| | | |
|---|---|---|
| 2008 Sales: $ | 2008 Profits: $ | **U.S. Stock Ticker: Private** |
| 2007 Sales: $ | 2007 Profits: $ | **Int'l Ticker:** Int'l Exchange: |
| 2006 Sales: $ | 2006 Profits: $ | Employees: 417 |
| 2005 Sales: $162,500 | 2005 Profits: $ | Fiscal Year Ends: 12/31 |
| 2004 Sales: $130,000 | 2004 Profits: $ | Parent Company: JW CHILDS EQUITY PARTNERS II LP |

## SALARIES/BENEFITS:

| | | | | |
|---|---|---|---|---|
| Pension Plan: | ESOP Stock Plan: | Profit Sharing: | Top Exec. Salary: $ | Bonus: $ |
| Savings Plan: | Stock Purch. Plan: | | Second Exec. Salary: $ | Bonus: $ |

## OTHER THOUGHTS:

**Apparent Women Officers or Directors:**
**Hot Spot for Advancement for Women/Minorities:**

## LOCATIONS: ("Y" = Yes)

| West: | Southwest: | Midwest: | Southeast: | Northeast: | International: |
|---|---|---|---|---|---|
| | | Y | | | |

# NYER MEDICAL GROUP INC

www.nyermedicalgroup.com

**Industry Group Code:** 421450 **Ranks within this company's industry group:** Sales: 2 Profits: 2

| Management: | | Sales/Marketing: | | Liberal Arts: | | Information Systems: | | Professionals: | | Technical/Scientific: | |
|---|---|---|---|---|---|---|---|---|---|---|---|
| Mgmt. Trainees: | | Mktg. Professionals: | Y | Gen. Writing/Editing: | | Info. Management: | Y | Finance/Accounting: | Y | Engineers, Elec.: | |
| Experienced Mgmt.: | Y | Retail Sales: | | Technical Writing: | Y | Software Dev.: | | Law: | Y | Engineers, Other: | |
| Int'l Business: | Y | Commercial/Industrial: | Y | Graphic Arts/Photog.: | | Hardware Dev.: | | HR/Other: | Y | Health/Lab: | |
| MBA Graduates: | Y | Sales Trainees: | Y | Music: | | Systems Integration: | | Training: | Y | Scientists/Research: | |
| | | Advertising Pros.: | | Broadcasting: | | Consulting/Other: | | Health Care: | Y | Petroleum/Chemicals: | |
| | | | | Other: | | | | Consulting: | | Math/Other: | |

## TYPES OF BUSINESS:

Distribution-Medical Equipment
Home Health Supplies
Surgical/Laboratory Supplies
Fire, Police & Rescue Equipment
Drug Stores
Online Medical Supply Sales
Emergency Medical Services Supplies

## BRANDS/DIVISIONS/AFFILIATES:

ADCO Surgical Supply, Inc.
ADCO South Medical Supplies, Inc.
Eaton Apothecary
D.A.W., Inc.
MedicalMailOrder.com
Medicine-On-Time

## CONTACTS: *Note: Officers with more than one job title may be intentionally listed here more than once.*

Mark Dumouchel, CEO
Mark Dumouchel, Pres.
Karen L. Wright, Sec.
Karen L. Wright, VP-Oper.
Karen L. Wright, Treas./VP-Finance
Mark Dumouchel, Pres., D.A.W., Inc.
David Dumouchel, VP
Michael Curry, VP/Sec.-D.A.W., Inc.
Wayne Gunter, VP

| | |
|---|---|
| **Phone:** 207-942-5273 | **Fax:** 207-941-9392 |
| **Toll-Free:** | |
| **Address:** 1292 Hammond St., Bangor, ME 04401 US | |

## GROWTH PLANS/SPECIAL FEATURES:

Nyer Medical Group, Inc. (NMG) is a holding company that operates medical supply subsidiaries and a chain of pharmacies. It operates through three wholly-owned subsidiaries: ADCO Surgical Supply, Inc.; ADCO South Medical Supplies, Inc.; and D.A.W., Inc. The firm's ADCO Surgical Supply and ADCO South Medical Supplies subsidiaries sell surgical and medical equipment and supplies, wholesale and retail, to health care facilities throughout New England, Florida and worldwide through its website medicalmailorder.com. ADCO derives 90% of its revenues from sales to institutional customers (primarily nursing homes and physician offices), while the balance comes from its retail and home health centers. ADCO and ADCO South provide over 4,500 combined stock items and special orders for non stock items. Doing business as Eaton Apothecary, subsidiary D.A.W., Inc. operates a chain of 15 pharmacy drug stores located in the greater Boston area and has contracts to manage three pharmacies owned by federally qualified health centers. Eaton additionally has contracts to provide pharmacy services to patients of three other federally qualified health centers. Pursuant to the contracts, Eaton maintains an inventory owned by the health centers for the purpose of dispensing prescriptions to health center patients. The vast majority of the prescriptions dispensed are dispensed to uninsured patients. The health centers then bill the Massachusetts Uncompensated Care Pool for the dispensed prescriptions. Eaton also operates three Medicine-On-Time medication management systems, which cater to elderly clients who are unable to manage their medication regimens and yet are not frail enough for nursing homes. In July 2007, Nyer announced that Eaton had added three new pharmacies, bringing its total number of pharmacies to 18. In February 2008, Nyer acquired the remaining 20% interest in Eaton.

## FINANCIALS: **Sales and profits are in thousands of dollars—add 000 to get the full amount. 2008 Note: Financial information for 2008 was not available for all companies at press time.**

| | | |
|---|---|---|
| 2008 Sales: $71,240 | 2008 Profits: $- 4 | **U.S. Stock Ticker: NYER** |
| 2007 Sales: $64,631 | 2007 Profits: $ 86 | **Int'l Ticker:** Int'l Exchange: |
| 2006 Sales: $63,597 | 2006 Profits: $ 858 | Employees: 351 |
| 2005 Sales: $61,184 | 2005 Profits: $ 224 | Fiscal Year Ends: 6/30 |
| 2004 Sales: $61,687 | 2004 Profits: $- 425 | Parent Company: |

## SALARIES/BENEFITS:

| | | | | |
|---|---|---|---|---|
| Pension Plan: | ESOP Stock Plan: | Profit Sharing: | Top Exec. Salary: $143,788 | Bonus: $14,976 |
| Savings Plan: | Stock Purch. Plan: | | Second Exec. Salary: $143,788 | Bonus: $14,976 |

## OTHER THOUGHTS:

**Apparent Women Officers or Directors**: 1
**Hot Spot for Advancement for Women/Minorities**:

## LOCATIONS: ("Y" = Yes)

| West: | Southwest: | Midwest: | Southeast: | Northeast: | International: |
|---|---|---|---|---|---|
| Y | | | Y | Y | |

# NYMEX HOLDINGS (NEW YORK MERCANTILE EXCHANGE)

**www.nymex.com**

**Industry Group Code:** 523210 **Ranks within this company's industry group:** Sales: 3 Profits: 4

| Management: | | Sales/Marketing: | | Liberal Arts: | | Information Systems: | | Professionals: | | Technical/Scientific: | |
|---|---|---|---|---|---|---|---|---|---|---|---|
| Mgmt. Trainees: | | Mktg. Professionals: | Y | Gen. Writing/Editing: | | Info. Management: | Y | Finance/Accounting: | Y | Engineers, Elec.: | |
| Experienced Mgmt.: | Y | Retail Sales: | | Technical Writing: | | Software Dev.: | Y | Law: | Y | Engineers, Other: | |
| Int'l Business: | Y | Commercial/Industrial: | | Graphic Arts/Photog.: | | Hardware Dev.: | | HR/Other: | Y | Health/Lab: | |
| MBA Graduates: | Y | Sales Trainees: | | Music: | | Systems Integration: | | Training: | Y | Scientists/Research: | |
| | | Advertising Pros.: | Y | Broadcasting: | | Consulting/Other: | | Health Care: | | Petroleum/Chemicals: | |
| | | | | Other: | | | | Consulting: | | Math/Other: | Y |

## TYPES OF BUSINESS:

Futures Exchange
Clearing & Settlement Services
Electronic Trading
Market Data

## BRANDS/DIVISIONS/AFFILIATES:

New York Mercantile Exchange, Inc.
NYMEX Exchange
Commodity Exchange, Inc.
COMEX
NYMEX ClearPort Trading
NYMEX ClearPort Clearing
NYMEX ACCESS
CME Group Inc

## CONTACTS: *Note: Officers with more than one job title may be intentionally listed here more than once.*

James Newsome, CEO
James Newsome, Pres.
Kenneth Shifrin, CFO
Joseph Raia, Sr. VP-Mktg.
Robert A. Levin, Sr. VP-Research
Samuel H. Gaer, CIO/Exec. VP
Ian Wall, Sr. VP-Tech.
Benjamin Chesir, Sr. VP-New Prod. Dev.
Christopher K. Bowen, Chief Admin. Officer
Richard Kerschner, General Counsel
Christopher Rodriguez, Sr. VP-Corp. Dev. & Strategic Planning
Thomas F. LaSala, Chief Regulatory Officer
Sean Keating, Sr. VP-Clearing Svcs.
Richard Kerschner, Sr. VP-Corp. Governance & Strategic Initiatives
Brian Regan, Sr. VP
Richard Schaeffer, Chmn.

**Phone:** 212-299-2000 **Fax:**
**Toll-Free:**
**Address:** 1 N. End Ave., World Financial Ctr., New York, NY 10282-1101 US

## GROWTH PLANS/SPECIAL FEATURES:

NYMEX Holdings, Inc. is the holding company of two exchanges: New York Mercantile Exchange, Inc. (NYMEX Exchange) and Commodity Exchange, Inc. (COMEX), a wholly-owned subsidiary of NYMEX Exchange. NYMEX Exchange is one of the largest exchanges in the world for the trading of energy futures and options contracts, including contracts for crude oil, natural gas, heating oil, gasoline, propane and electricity, and is a leading exchange for trading platinum group metals contracts, including platinum futures and options contracts and palladium futures contracts. COMEX is the one of the largest marketplaces for gold and silver futures and options contracts as well as one of North America's largest exchanges for futures and options contracts for copper and aluminum. Collectively, the exchanges also trade soft commodities futures, such as coffee, sugar, cocoa and cotton. NYMEX Exchange and COMEX provide physical facilities necessary for an open-outcry auction market, electronic trading systems and systems for matching and clearing all trades executed on the exchanges. NYMEX derives significant revenues from the sale of market data. The company is also a major provider of financial services to the energy and metals industries. Another core component of the business is the revenue derived from the exchanges' NYMEX ClearPort Trading facilities and from providing clearing and settlement services through its clearinghouse, the NYMEX ClearPort Clearing system. In December 2007, the company announced the formation of The Green Exchange, which offers a range of environmental futures, options and swap contracts for markets focused on solutions to climate change and renewable energy. In August 2008, NYMEX was acquired by CME Group, formerly Chicago Mercantile Exchange Holdings, in a deal valued at $8.3 billion.

## FINANCIALS: **Sales and profits are in thousands of dollars—add 000 to get the full amount. 2008 Note: Financial information for 2008 was not available for all companies at press time.**

| | | |
|---|---|---|
| 2008 Sales: $ | 2008 Profits: $ | **U.S. Stock Ticker: Subsidiary** |
| 2007 Sales: $673,604 | 2007 Profits: $224,039 | **Int'l Ticker:** Int'l Exchange: |
| 2006 Sales: $497,249 | 2006 Profits: $154,801 | Employees: 400 |
| 2005 Sales: $334,108 | 2005 Profits: $71,128 | Fiscal Year Ends: 12/31 |
| 2004 Sales: $241,325 | 2004 Profits: $27,367 | Parent Company: CME GROUP |

## SALARIES/BENEFITS:

| | | | | |
|---|---|---|---|---|
| Pension Plan: | ESOP Stock Plan: | Profit Sharing: | Top Exec. Salary: $900,000 | Bonus: $3,600,000 |
| Savings Plan: | Stock Purch. Plan: | | Second Exec. Salary: $900,000 | Bonus: $2,600,000 |

## OTHER THOUGHTS:

**Apparent Women Officers or Directors:**
**Hot Spot for Advancement for Women/Minorities:** Y

## LOCATIONS: ("Y" = Yes)

| West: | Southwest: | Midwest: | Southeast: | Northeast: | International: |
|---|---|---|---|---|---|
| | Y | | | Y | Y |

# ODYSSEY RE HOLDINGS CORP

**www.odysseyre.com**

**Industry Group Code:** 524130 **Ranks within this company's industry group:** Sales: 3 Profits: 1

| Management: | | Sales/Marketing: | | Liberal Arts: | | Information Systems: | | Professionals: | | Technical/Scientific: | |
|---|---|---|---|---|---|---|---|---|---|---|---|
| Mgmt. Trainees: | | Mktg. Professionals: | Y | Gen. Writing/Editing: | Y | Info. Management: | Y | Finance/Accounting: | Y | Engineers, Elec.: | |
| Experienced Mgmt.: | Y | Retail Sales: | | Technical Writing: | Y | Software Dev.: | | Law: | Y | Engineers, Other: | |
| Int'l Business: | Y | Commercial/Industrial: | Y | Graphic Arts/Photog.: | | Hardware Dev.: | | HR/Other: | Y | Health/Lab: | |
| MBA Graduates: | Y | Sales Trainees: | Y | Music: | | Systems Integration: | | Training: | Y | Scientists/Research: | |
| | | Advertising Pros.: | | Broadcasting: | | Consulting/Other: | | Health Care: | | Petroleum/Chemicals: | |
| | | | | Other: | | | | Consulting: | | Math/Other: | Y |

## TYPES OF BUSINESS:

Insurance-Reinsurance
Property & Casualty
Treaty Reinsurance
Facultative Reinsurance
Business Liability

## BRANDS/DIVISIONS/AFFILIATES:

Hudson Insurance Company
Newline Underwriting Management Limited
Odyssey America Reinsurance Corporation
Odyssey UK Holdings Corp.
Clearwater Insurance Company
Fairfax Financial Holdings Ltd
Clearwater Select Insurance Company
Hooghuis Group LLC

## CONTACTS: *Note: Officers with more than one job title may be intentionally listed here more than once.*

Andrew A. Barnard, CEO
Charles D. Troiano, COO/Exec. VP
Andrew A. Barnard, Pres.
R. Scott Donovan, CFO/Exec. VP
Mark W. Hinkley, Exec. VP-Mktg.
Donald L. Smith, General Counsel/Sr. VP/Corp. Sec.
Mark W. Hinkley, Exec. VP-Comm.
Anthony J. Narciso, Jr., Sr. VP/Controller
James E. Migliorini, CEO-U.S. Insurance Div.
Michael G. Wacek, CEO-Americas Div.
Brian D. Young CEO, CEO-London Market Oper. & Global Insurance
Carl A. Overy, CEO-London Market Div.
V. Prem Watsa, Chmn.
Lucien Pietropoli, CEO-EuroAsia Div.

| | |
|---|---|
| **Phone:** 203-977-8000 | **Fax:** 203-356-0196 |
| **Toll-Free:** | |
| **Address:** 300 First Stamford Pl., Stamford, CT 06902 US | |

## GROWTH PLANS/SPECIAL FEATURES:

Odyssey Re Holdings Corp., operating through several subsidiaries, is a leading underwriter of reinsurance, providing a full range of property and casualty products on a worldwide basis. The company offers a range of both treaty and facultative reinsurance to property and casualty insurers and reinsurers and writes specialty and non-traditional lines of reinsurance, including professional liability, marine and aerospace. The firm's operations are managed through four divisions: Americas, EuroAsia, London market and U.S. insurance. The Americas division includes U.S. and Canadian treaty property, general casualty, specialty casualty, surety and facultative casualty reinsurance, as well as Latin American treaty and facultative businesses. The EuroAsia division is composed of offices in Paris, Stockholm, Singapore and Tokyo and writes primarily treaty and facultative property policies. Odyssey's London market division operates through its London branch, which provides worldwide property and casualty reinsurance, and Newline at Lloyd's, which focuses on casualty insurance. In addition, its health care unit underwrites medical malpractice and hospital professional liability insurance, primarily through subsidiary Hudson Specialty Insurance Company. In premiums, 67.7% written are reinsurance, with 32.3% coming from primary insurance. In reinsurance, 27.5% of premiums written are from casualty, 30.3% from property and 67.7% from the specialty class, which includes marine, aviation, surety and credit. The U.S. market represented 51.8% of premiums written in 2007. The company's main subsidiaries include Odyssey America Reinsurance Corporation, a property and casualty reinsurance company; Odyssey UK Holdings Corp., a Europe-based operation controlling the firm's Newline operation; and the Clearwater Insurance Company, a firm which holds insurance licenses in 43 states. Odyssey Re Holdings is majority-owned by Fairfax Financial Holdings, Ltd. In 2007, Newline opened an office in Singapore, marking its first international office, referred to as Newline Asia. In June 2008, the firm acquired Hooghuis Group LLC, an underwriting agency.

## FINANCIALS: **Sales and profits are in thousands of dollars—add 000 to get the full amount. 2008 Note: Financial information for 2008 was not available for all companies at press time.**

| | | |
|---|---|---|
| 2008 Sales: $ | 2008 Profits: $ | **U.S. Stock Ticker: ORH** |
| 2007 Sales: $2,989,095 | 2007 Profits: $595,575 | **Int'l Ticker:** Int'l Exchange: |
| 2006 Sales: $2,902,074 | 2006 Profits: $499,649 | Employees: 635 |
| 2005 Sales: $2,556,778 | 2005 Profits: $-117,666 | Fiscal Year Ends: 12/31 |
| 2004 Sales: $2,619,783 | 2004 Profits: $205,201 | Parent Company: |

## SALARIES/BENEFITS:

| | | | | |
|---|---|---|---|---|
| Pension Plan: | ESOP Stock Plan: | Profit Sharing: | Top Exec. Salary: $1,000,000 | Bonus: $1,250,000 |
| Savings Plan: | Stock Purch. Plan: | | Second Exec. Salary: $500,000 | Bonus: $400,000 |

## OTHER THOUGHTS:

**Apparent Women Officers or Directors:**
**Hot Spot for Advancement for Women/Minorities:**

## LOCATIONS: ("Y" = Yes)

| West: | Southwest: | Midwest: | Southeast: | Northeast: | International: |
|---|---|---|---|---|---|
| Y | | Y | Y | Y | Y |

# OMNITURE INC

www.omniture.com

**Industry Group Code:** 511216 **Ranks within this company's industry group:** Sales: 1 Profits: 2

| Management: | | Sales/Marketing: | | Liberal Arts: | | Information Systems: | | Professionals: | | Technical/Scientific: | |
|---|---|---|---|---|---|---|---|---|---|---|---|
| Mgmt. Trainees: | | Mktg. Professionals: | Y | Gen. Writing/Editing: | | Info. Management: | Y | Finance/Accounting: | Y | Engineers, Elec.: | Y |
| Experienced Mgmt.: | Y | Retail Sales: | | Technical Writing: | Y | Software Dev.: | Y | Law: | Y | Engineers, Other: | |
| Int'l Business: | Y | Commercial/Industrial: | Y | Graphic Arts/Photog.: | | Hardware Dev.: | | HR/Other: | Y | Health/Lab: | |
| MBA Graduates: | Y | Sales Trainees: | | Music: | | Systems Integration: | | Training: | Y | Scientists/Research: | |
| | | Advertising Pros.: | | Broadcasting: | | Consulting/Other: | | Health Care: | | Petroleum/Chemicals: | |
| | | | | Other: | | | | Consulting: | | Math/Other: | |

## TYPES OF BUSINESS:

Web Analytics Software
Online Marketing Consulting
Training Services

## BRANDS/DIVISIONS/AFFILIATES:

SiteCatalyst
Omniture Data Warehouse
Omniture SearchCenter
Omniture University
Omniture Best Practices
Omniture Client Services & Support
Omniture Merchandizing
Visual Sciences Inc

## CONTACTS:

*Note: Officers with more than one job title may be intentionally listed here more than once.*

Josh James, CEO
Josh James, Pres.
Michael S. Herring, CFO/Exec. VP
Gail M. Ennis, Sr. VP-Mktg.
Eric A. McAllister, Chief Human Resources Officer/VP-Human Resources
Brett M. Error, CTO/Exec. VP-Prod.
Shawn J. Lindquist, Chief Legal Officer/Sr. VP/Sec.
John F. Mellor, Exec. VP-Bus. Dev. & Corp. Strategy
Michael Look, VP-Investor Rel.
Christopher C. Harrington, Pres., Worldwide Sales & Client Svcs.
D. Fraser Bullock, Chmn.
Neil M. Weston, Sr. VP/General Mgr.-EMEA

**Phone:** 801-722-7000 **Fax:** 801-722-7001
**Toll-Free:** 877-722-7088
**Address:** 550 E. Timpanogos Cir., Bldg. G, Orem, UT 84097 US

## GROWTH PLANS/SPECIAL FEATURES:

Omniture, Inc. is a provider of hosted web analysis tools and services for corporations. The firm's services aid clients in measuring the effectiveness of their web sites and marketing initiatives. Omniture focuses on providing high-volume, complex web sites with comprehensive and adaptable solutions for evaluating site traffic, effectiveness of advertising, sale sources and e-commerce transactions to approximately 5,000 clients across 86 countries. The company's main product, the SiteCatalyst Suite, consists of four separate applications that have been integrated into one platform. SiteCatalyst is a remotely hosted, subscription-based reporting software platform that provides real-time web site analysis, offering opinions on effectiveness of marketing initiatives. Omniture Discover allows more in-depth analysis, giving users the option to optimize processes based on more specific information regarding customer traffic, needs and preferences. Omniture Data Warehouse both organizes and produces reports on data aggregation systems. Finally, Omniture SearchCenter helps clients develop keyword-marketing programs. The company also offers an assortment of other services related to Internet marketing. Omniture University is an online marketing education program, with training available on the web, in the classroom, through video or through Internet seminar. The Omniture Best Practices team is a customer service group trained to assist in implementing new market initiatives. The Client Services and Support division provides 24-hour, worldwide client support in-person, over the phone or in chat rooms. In January 2008, the company acquired Visual Sciences, Inc. In November 2008, Omniture acquired certain business assets of privately held company, Mercado including Mercado Ignition, which was subsequently re-launched as Omniture Merchandizing. Omniture Merchandizing provides a suite of solutions that include intuitive shopping interfaces, built-in shopper vocabulary, metrics driven merchandising and social merchandising.

Employees are offered health, dental and vision insurance; life insurance; short-and long-term disability insurance; new baby bonuses; an employee assistance program; adoption assistance; employee discounts; and onsite gaming rooms.

## FINANCIALS:

**Sales and profits are in thousands of dollars—add 000 to get the full amount. 2008 Note: Financial information for 2008 was not available for all companies at press time.**

| | | |
|---|---|---|
| 2008 Sales: $ | 2008 Profits: $ | **U.S. Stock Ticker: OMTR** |
| 2007 Sales: $143,127 | 2007 Profits: $-9,429 | **Int'l Ticker:** Int'l Exchange: |
| 2006 Sales: $79,749 | 2006 Profits: $-7,725 | Employees: 713 |
| 2005 Sales: $42,804 | 2005 Profits: $-17,441 | Fiscal Year Ends: 12/31 |
| 2004 Sales: $20,565 | 2004 Profits: $ | Parent Company: |

## SALARIES/BENEFITS:

| | | | | |
|---|---|---|---|---|
| Pension Plan: | ESOP Stock Plan: | Profit Sharing: | Top Exec. Salary: $340,000 | Bonus: $416,288 |
| Savings Plan: Y | Stock Purch. Plan: | | Second Exec. Salary: $227,500 | Bonus: $300,295 |

## OTHER THOUGHTS:

**Apparent Women Officers or Directors**: 2
**Hot Spot for Advancement for Women/Minorities**:

## LOCATIONS: ("Y" = Yes)

| West: | Southwest: | Midwest: | Southeast: | Northeast: | International: |
|---|---|---|---|---|---|
| Y | | | | | Y |

Note: Financial information, benefits and other data can change quickly and may vary from those stated here.

# ONEOK PARTNERS LP

www.oneok.com

**Industry Group Code:** 422720 **Ranks within this company's industry group:** Sales: 2 Profits: 1

| Management: | | Sales/Marketing: | | Liberal Arts: | | Information Systems: | | Professionals: | | Technical/Scientific: | |
|---|---|---|---|---|---|---|---|---|---|---|---|
| Mgmt. Trainees: | | Mktg. Professionals: | Y | Gen. Writing/Editing: | | Info. Management: | Y | Finance/Accounting: | Y | Engineers, Elec.: | Y |
| Experienced Mgmt.: | Y | Retail Sales: | | Technical Writing: | | Software Dev.: | | Law: | Y | Engineers, Other: | Y |
| Int'l Business: | Y | Commercial/Industrial: | Y | Graphic Arts/Photog.: | | Hardware Dev.: | | HR/Other: | Y | Health/Lab: | |
| MBA Graduates: | Y | Sales Trainees: | Y | Music: | | Systems Integration: | | Training: | Y | Scientists/Research: | |
| | | Advertising Pros.: | | Broadcasting: | | Consulting/Other: | | Health Care: | | Petroleum/Chemicals: | Y |
| | | | | Other: | | | | Consulting: | | Math/Other: | |

## TYPES OF BUSINESS:

Pipelines-Natural Gas
Natural Gas Processing

## BRANDS/DIVISIONS/AFFILIATES:

Midwestern Gas Transmission Company
Northwest Border Pipeline Company
ONEOK, Inc.
OkTex
Viking Gas Transmission Company
Guardian Pipeline

## CONTACTS: *Note: Officers with more than one job title may be intentionally listed here more than once.*

John W. Gibson, CEO
James C. Kneale, COO
James C. Kneale, Pres.
Curtis L. Dinan, CFO/Sr. VP
John Barker, General Counsel/Exec. VP/Sec.
Caron A. Lawhorn, Chief Acct. Officer/Sr. VP
Curtis L. Dinan, Treas.
Pierce Norton, Exec. VP-Natural Gas
Terry Spencer, Exec. VP-Natural Gas Liquids
Wes Christensen, Sr. VP-Natural Gas Liquids Oper.
John W. Gibson, Chmn.

| | |
|---|---|
| **Phone:** 918-588-7000 | **Fax:** 918-588-7971 |
| **Toll-Free:** 877-208-7318 | |
| **Address:** 100 W. 5th St., Tulsa, OK 74103 US | |

## GROWTH PLANS/SPECIAL FEATURES:

ONEOK Partners, LP owns and manages natural gas gathering, processing and intrastate pipeline assets and natural gas liquids (NGL) gathering and distribution pipelines, storage and fractionators, connecting much of the natural gas and NGL supply in the mid-continent region. The company also owns a 50% equity interest in a transporter of natural gas imported from Canada and the U.S. The firm operates in four segments: natural gas gathering and processing, which primarily gathers and processes raw natural gas; natural gas pipelines, which operates regulated interstate and intrastate natural gas transmission pipelines and storage facilities; natural gas liquids gathering and fractionation, which gathers, treats and fractionates, stores and markets NGLs; and natural gas liquids pipelines, which operates interstate natural gas liquids gathering and distribution pipelines. The company owns a 50% interest in Northern Border Pipeline Company, which owns and operates a 1,249-mile natural gas pipeline system that transports over approximately 18% of all natural gas imported from Canada to the U.S. The firm also owns Midwestern Gas Transmission Company, which owns a 350-mile interstate natural gas pipeline system that runs from Tennessee to Illinois; and Viking Gas Transmission Company, which serves markets in Minnesota, Wisconsin and North Dakota. Other pipeline properties include OkTex Pipeline, operating in Oklahoma, Texas, New Mexico and Mexico; and Guardian Pipeline, operating in Illinois and Wisconsin.

## FINANCIALS: **Sales and profits are in thousands of dollars—add 000 to get the full amount. 2008 Note: Financial information for 2008 was not available for all companies at press time.**

| | | |
|---|---|---|
| 2008 Sales: $ | 2008 Profits: $ | **U.S. Stock Ticker: OKS** |
| 2007 Sales: $5,831,558 | 2007 Profits: $407,747 | **Int'l Ticker:** Int'l Exchange: |
| 2006 Sales: $4,738,248 | 2006 Profits: $445,186 | Employees: 1,136 |
| 2005 Sales: $678,560 | 2005 Profits: $147,013 | Fiscal Year Ends: 12/31 |
| 2004 Sales: $590,383 | 2004 Profits: $144,720 | Parent Company: |

## SALARIES/BENEFITS:

| | | | | |
|---|---|---|---|---|
| Pension Plan: | ESOP Stock Plan: | Profit Sharing: | Top Exec. Salary: $405,705 | Bonus: $536,963 |
| Savings Plan: | Stock Purch. Plan: | | Second Exec. Salary: $295,926 | Bonus: $389,000 |

## OTHER THOUGHTS:

**Apparent Women Officers or Directors:** 1
**Hot Spot for Advancement for Women/Minorities:**

## LOCATIONS: ("Y" = Yes)

| West: | Southwest: | Midwest: | Southeast: | Northeast: | International: |
|---|---|---|---|---|---|
| Y | Y | Y | | | Y |

# ONLINE RESOURCES CORP

www.orcc.com

**Industry Group Code:** 511201 **Ranks within this company's industry group:** Sales: 4 Profits: 2

| **Management:** | | **Sales/Marketing:** | | **Liberal Arts:** | | **Information Systems:** | | **Professionals:** | | **Technical/Scientific:** | |
|---|---|---|---|---|---|---|---|---|---|---|---|
| Mgmt. Trainees: | | Mktg. Professionals: | Y | Gen. Writing/Editing: | | Info. Management: | Y | Finance/Accounting: | Y | Engineers, Elec.: | Y |
| Experienced Mgmt.: | Y | Retail Sales: | | Technical Writing: | Y | Software Dev.: | Y | Law: | Y | Engineers, Other: | |
| Int'l Business: | | Commercial/Industrial: | Y | Graphic Arts/Photog.: | | Hardware Dev.: | | HR/Other: | Y | Health/Lab: | |
| MBA Graduates: | Y | Sales Trainees: | Y | Music: | | Systems Integration: | | Training: | Y | Scientists/Research: | |
| | | Advertising Pros.: | | Broadcasting: | | Consulting/Other: | | Health Care: | | Petroleum/Chemicals: | |
| | | | | Other: | | | | Consulting: | | Math/Other: | |

## TYPES OF BUSINESS:

Software-Electronic Banking
Online Banking Services
Web Design & Hosting Services

## BRANDS/DIVISIONS/AFFILIATES:

Quotien
Incurrent
CertnFunds
Princeton eCom Corp.
Internet Transaction Solutions, Inc.

## CONTACTS: *Note: Officers with more than one job title may be intentionally listed here more than once.*

Matthew P. Lawlor, CEO
Raymond T. Crosier, COO
Raymond T. Crosier, Pres.
Catherine A. Graham, CFO/Exec. VP
Paul Franko, Corp. CTO/Sr. VP-Banking Tech. Svcs.
Daniel M. Thomas, Sr. VP-Strategic Dev.
Robert E. Craig, Exec. VP/Gen. Mgr.-e-Commerce Svcs.
Beth Halloran, Sr. Dir.-Corp. Comm.
Ronald J. Bergamesca, Exec. VP/Gen. Mgr.-Credit Union Svcs.
Stephanie Chaufournier, Exec. VP/General Manager-Banking CSP Payments
Sheila Narayan, Exec. VP/Gen. Mgr.-Banking CSP Payments
Ronald J. Bergamesca, Gen. Mgr.-Community Bank
Matthew P. Lawlor, Chmn.

**Phone:** 703-653-3100 **Fax:** 703-653-3105
**Toll-Free:**
**Address:** 4795 Meadow Wood Ln., Ste. 300, Chantilly, VA 20151 US

## GROWTH PLANS/SPECIAL FEATURES:

Online Resources Corp. provides outsourced, web-based financial technology services branded to over 1,900 financial institutions, biller, card issuer and creditor clients. The company services over 12 million billable consumer and business end-users. End-users may access and view their accounts online and perform various web-based, self-service functions. They may also make electronic bill payments and fund transfers, utilizing the firm's debit architecture and other payment methods. Additionally, Online Resources offers professional services, including software solutions, which enable various deployment options, a broad range of customization and other value-added services. Multi-year service contracts with its clients provide the firm with a recurring and predictable revenue stream that grows with increases in users and transactions. In 2007 the company derived approximately 13% of its revenues from account presentation and relationship management, 77% from payments and 10% from professional services, custom software solutions and other revenues. The company operates in two segments: banking services and e-commerce services. Both segments provide a suite of web-based account presentation, payment, relationship management and professional services. The company's Quotien product integrates customer and financial data, electronic funds transfer and service gateways. The Incurrent product line is designed for credit card issuers and processors. Through Incurrent, cardholders may access their account information, view transactions, set up payments and perform other self-service functions. The CertnFunds product line is designed for e-commerce providers, primarily payment acquirers and large online billers. In 2008, Online Resources entered into several multi-year agreements with various organizations for use of the firm's online services. Services obtained include, online collections, retail and business banking services, and bill payment services.

The company offers employees medical, dental and vision insurance; flexible spending accounts; 401(k) and employee stock purchase plans; tuition reimbursement; credit union membership; a college savings plan; and an employee assistance program.

## FINANCIALS: **Sales and profits are in thousands of dollars—add 000 to get the full amount. 2008 Note: Financial information for 2008 was not available for all companies at press time.**

| | | |
|---|---|---|
| 2008 Sales: $ | 2008 Profits: $ | **U.S. Stock Ticker: ORCC** |
| 2007 Sales: $135,132 | 2007 Profits: $10,946 | **Int'l Ticker:** Int'l Exchange: |
| 2006 Sales: $91,736 | 2006 Profits: $ 321 | Employees: 626 |
| 2005 Sales: $60,501 | 2005 Profits: $22,663 | Fiscal Year Ends: 12/31 |
| 2004 Sales: $42,285 | 2004 Profits: $3,947 | Parent Company: |

## SALARIES/BENEFITS:

| | | | | |
|---|---|---|---|---|
| Pension Plan: | ESOP Stock Plan: | Profit Sharing: | Top Exec. Salary: $332,807 | Bonus: $ |
| Savings Plan: Y | Stock Purch. Plan: Y | | Second Exec. Salary: $252,417 | Bonus: $ |

## OTHER THOUGHTS:

**Apparent Women Officers or Directors**: 3
**Hot Spot for Advancement for Women/Minorities**: Y

## LOCATIONS: ("Y" = Yes)

| West: | Southwest: | Midwest: | Southeast: | Northeast: | International: |
|---|---|---|---|---|---|
| Y | | Y | | Y | |

# OPENTV CORP

www.opentv.com

**Industry Group Code:** 511213 **Ranks within this company's industry group:** Sales: 4 Profits: 2

| Management: | | Sales/Marketing: | | Liberal Arts: | | Information Systems: | | Professionals: | | Technical/Scientific: | |
|---|---|---|---|---|---|---|---|---|---|---|---|
| Mgmt. Trainees: | | Mktg. Professionals: | Y | Gen. Writing/Editing: | | Info. Management: | Y | Finance/Accounting: | Y | Engineers, Elec.: | Y |
| Experienced Mgmt.: | Y | Retail Sales: | | Technical Writing: | Y | Software Dev.: | Y | Law: | Y | Engineers, Other: | |
| Int'l Business: | Y | Commercial/Industrial: | Y | Graphic Arts/Photog.: | | Hardware Dev.: | | HR/Other: | Y | Health/Lab: | |
| MBA Graduates: | Y | Sales Trainees: | Y | Music: | | Systems Integration: | Y | Training: | Y | Scientists/Research: | |
| | | Advertising Pros.: | | Broadcasting: | | Consulting/Other: | | Health Care: | | Petroleum/Chemicals: | |
| | | | | Other: | | | | Consulting: | | Math/Other: | |

## TYPES OF BUSINESS:

Software-Interactive Television

## BRANDS/DIVISIONS/AFFILIATES:

Kudelski Group
Ruzz TV Pty

## CONTACTS:

*Note: Officers with more than one job title may be intentionally listed here more than once.*

Ben Bennett, CEO
Shum Mukherjee, CFO
Michael Ivanchenko, Sr. VP-Worldwide Sales
Tony Webster, Sr. VP-Human Resources
Mark Beariault, General Counsel
Tracy Geist, Sr. VP-Market Dev.
Christine Oury, Dir.-Comm.
Joel Zdepski, Sr. VP/Gen. Mgr.-Middleware
Paul Woidke, Sr. VP-Advanced Advertising
Andre Kudelski, Chmn.

**Phone:** 415-962-5000 **Fax:** 415-962-5300
**Toll-Free:**
**Address:** 275 Sacramento St., San Francisco, CA 94111 US

## GROWTH PLANS/SPECIAL FEATURES:

OpenTV Corp. provides software, services and applications for digital interactive television (iTV). The company's software has been shipped with or installed in more than 115 million set-top boxes worldwide and has been selected by over 45 network operators worldwide, including BskyB in the U.K.; TPS and Noos in France; Shanghai Cable in China; Via Digital in Spain; GLA, the exclusive provider of DIRECTV in Latin America; and EchoStar's DISH Network in the U.S. OpenTV licenses its set-top box software to more than 40 digital set-top box manufacturers and licenses its authoring tools to hundreds of independent developers and content and service providers. The firm operates in two segments: middleware solutions and advertising solutions. The middleware solutions segment is composed of set-top box middleware and embedded browser technologies, as well as software components that are deployed at the network operator's headend. The advertising solutions segment provides software solutions for the creation and delivery of advertising for digital television systems. The company offers products including information applications such as music, news, weather and sports; communications applications including e-mail, chat rooms and instant messaging; e-commerce applications such as online retailing and banking; and gaming applications such as fantasy sports, games and quizzes. Kudelski Group, a provider of content protection and related digital television technologies, has voting control of OpenTV. In September 2008, OpenTV acquired Ruzz TV Pty, a privately-held Australian company that provides turnkey software solutions for television broadcasters.

Employees are offered health, life, and disability insurance, as well as a 401(k) plan and a stock purchase plan.

## FINANCIALS:

**Sales and profits are in thousands of dollars—add 000 to get the full amount. 2008 Note: Financial information for 2008 was not available for all companies at press time.**

| | | |
|---|---|---|
| 2008 Sales: $ | 2008 Profits: $ | **U.S. Stock Ticker: OPTV** |
| 2007 Sales: $109,977 | 2007 Profits: $-5,161 | **Int'l Ticker:** Int'l Exchange: |
| 2006 Sales: $95,210 | 2006 Profits: $-10,818 | Employees: 497 |
| 2005 Sales: $87,380 | 2005 Profits: $-8,473 | Fiscal Year Ends: 12/31 |
| 2004 Sales: $77,169 | 2004 Profits: $-21,962 | Parent Company: |

## SALARIES/BENEFITS:

| | | | | |
|---|---|---|---|---|
| Pension Plan: | ESOP Stock Plan: | Profit Sharing: | Top Exec. Salary: $489,995 | Bonus: $106,000 |
| Savings Plan: Y | Stock Purch. Plan: Y | | Second Exec. Salary: $337,257 | Bonus: $ |

## OTHER THOUGHTS:

**Apparent Women Officers or Directors**: 2
**Hot Spot for Advancement for Women/Minorities**:

## LOCATIONS: ("Y" = Yes)

| West: | Southwest: | Midwest: | Southeast: | Northeast: | International: |
|---|---|---|---|---|---|
| Y | | | | Y | Y |

# OPNEXT INC

www.opnext.com

**Industry Group Code:** 334210 **Ranks within this company's industry group:** Sales: 5 Profits: 6

| Management: | | Sales/Marketing: | | Liberal Arts: | | Information Systems: | | Professionals: | | Technical/Scientific: | |
|---|---|---|---|---|---|---|---|---|---|---|---|
| Mgmt. Trainees: | | Mktg. Professionals: | Y | Gen. Writing/Editing: | Y | Info. Management: | Y | Finance/Accounting: | Y | Engineers, Elec.: | Y |
| Experienced Mgmt.: | Y | Retail Sales: | | Technical Writing: | Y | Software Dev.: | Y | Law: | Y | Engineers, Other: | Y |
| Int'l Business: | Y | Commercial/Industrial: | Y | Graphic Arts/Photog.: | | Hardware Dev.: | Y | HR/Other: | Y | Health/Lab: | |
| MBA Graduates: | Y | Sales Trainees: | Y | Music: | | Systems Integration: | Y | Training: | Y | Scientists/Research: | |
| | | Advertising Pros.: | | Broadcasting: | | Consulting/Other: | | Health Care: | | Petroleum/Chemicals: | |
| | | | | Other: | | | | Consulting: | | Math/Other: | |

## TYPES OF BUSINESS:

Optical Modules & Components

## BRANDS/DIVISIONS/AFFILIATES:

XENPAK
X2
XPAK
XFP
XMD
SFP
SFP+

## CONTACTS:

*Note: Officers with more than one job title may be intentionally listed here more than once.*

Harry L. Bosco, CEO
Gilles Bouchard, COO
Harry L. Bosco, Pres.
Robert J. Nobile, CFO/Sr. VP
Atsushi (James) Horiuchi, Sr. VP-Global Sales
Larry Dooling, CIO
Michael Chan, Exec. VP-Bus. Dev. & Product Portfolio Mgmt.
Tadayuki Kanno, Sr. VP-Modules & Devices
Tammy L. Wedemeyer, VP-Bus. Mgmt.
Richard Zoccolillo, VP-Pluggables & Subsystems
Naoya Takahashi, Chmn.
Kei Oki, Pres., Opnext Japan, Inc./Exec. VP-Opnext, Inc.
Thi La, VP-Procurement

| **Phone:** 732-544-3400 | **Fax:** 732-544-3540 |
|---|---|
| **Toll-Free:** | |
| **Address:** 1 Christopher Way, Eatontown, NJ 07724 US | |

## GROWTH PLANS/SPECIAL FEATURES:

Opnext, Inc. is a designer and manufacturer of optical modules and components, which enable high-speed telecommunications and data communications networks globally. The company's transceiver modules, which typically utilize the firm's lasers and detectors, convert signals between electrical and optical for transmitting and receiving data over fiber optic networks. Opnext provides telecommunications and data communications applications primarily at the 10 gigabits per second (Gbps) and 40Gbps data rates. The company has a broad portfolio of industry-defined product types, including tunable and fixed wavelength 300 pin, XENPAK, X2, XPAK, XFP, XMD, SFP and SFP+. These products include switches, routers, transports, transceivers, servers and hubs. The firm also manufactures a complete line of red laser diodes and infrared laser diodes for industrial and commercial applications. Additional firm services include outsourcing subsystem development services. The firm has a global customer base for both the telecommunications and data communications markets that include Alcatel-Lucent; Ciena Corp.; Cisco Systems, Inc.; ECI Telecom LTD; Extreme Networks, Inc.; Fujitsu, Ltd.; Hitachi, Ltd.; Huawei Technologies Co., Ltd.; Juniper Networks, Inc.; and Mitsubishi Electric corp. Cisco and Alcatel Lucent are the company's largest customers, generating roughly 40% and 20% of the firm's revenues respectively. In 2008, the firm agreed to acquire StrataLight Communications, Inc., a leading designer and manufacturer of 40Gbps line-side optical subsystems and advanced dispersion compensation modules.

## FINANCIALS:

**Sales and profits are in thousands of dollars—add 000 to get the full amount. 2008 Note: Financial information for 2008 was not available for all companies at press time.**

| | | |
|---|---|---|
| 2008 Sales: $283,498 | 2008 Profits: $17,048 | **U.S. Stock Ticker: OPXT** |
| 2007 Sales: $222,859 | 2007 Profits: $ 696 | **Int'l Ticker:** Int'l Exchange: |
| 2006 Sales: $151,691 | 2006 Profits: $-31,493 | Employees: 438 |
| 2005 Sales: $138,432 | 2005 Profits: $-32,744 | Fiscal Year Ends: 3/31 |
| 2004 Sales: $79,390 | 2004 Profits: $-80,490 | Parent Company: |

## SALARIES/BENEFITS:

| | | | | |
|---|---|---|---|---|
| Pension Plan: | ESOP Stock Plan: | Profit Sharing: | Top Exec. Salary: $400,000 | Bonus: $240,000 |
| Savings Plan: Y | Stock Purch. Plan: | | Second Exec. Salary: $325,000 | Bonus: $120,000 |

## OTHER THOUGHTS:

**Apparent Women Officers or Directors**: 2
**Hot Spot for Advancement for Women/Minorities**:

## LOCATIONS: ("Y" = Yes)

| West: | Southwest: | Midwest: | Southeast: | Northeast: | International: |
|---|---|---|---|---|---|
| Y | | | Y | Y | Y |

# OPTELECOM-NKF INC

www.optelecom.com

**Industry Group Code:** 334413 **Ranks within this company's industry group:** Sales: 5 Profits: 3

| Management: | | Sales/Marketing: | | Liberal Arts: | | Information Systems: | | Professionals: | | Technical/Scientific: | |
|---|---|---|---|---|---|---|---|---|---|---|---|
| Mgmt. Trainees: | | Mktg. Professionals: | Y | Gen. Writing/Editing: | | Info. Management: | Y | Finance/Accounting: | Y | Engineers, Elec.: | Y |
| Experienced Mgmt.: | Y | Retail Sales: | | Technical Writing: | Y | Software Dev.: | Y | Law: | Y | Engineers, Other: | Y |
| Int'l Business: | Y | Commercial/Industrial: | Y | Graphic Arts/Photog.: | | Hardware Dev.: | Y | HR/Other: | Y | Health/Lab: | |
| MBA Graduates: | Y | Sales Trainees: | Y | Music: | | Systems Integration: | Y | Training: | Y | Scientists/Research: | Y |
| | | Advertising Pros.: | | Broadcasting: | | Consulting/Other: | | Health Care: | | Petroleum/Chemicals: | |
| | | | | Other: | | | | Consulting: | | Math/Other: | Y |

## TYPES OF BUSINESS:

Fiber-Optic Communications Products
Fiber Optic Products
Video Surveillance Equipment

## BRANDS/DIVISIONS/AFFILIATES:

Optelecom-NKF Holding B.V.
Siqura

## CONTACTS: *Note: Officers with more than one job title may be intentionally listed here more than once.*

Edmund D. Ludwig, CEO
Thomas Overwijn, COO/Exec. VP
Edmund D. Ludwig, Pres.
Steven Tamburo, CFO
Roland Hooghiemstra, VP-Mktg. & Sales
Coen Hooghiemstra, VP-Eng.
Greg Hall, VP-Mfg.
James Armstrong, Corp. Sec.
James Armstrong, Exec. VP-Bus. Dev. & U.S. Federal Systems
Edmund D. Ludwig, Chmn.

| | |
|---|---|
| **Phone:** 301-444-2200 | **Fax:** 301-444-2299 |
| **Toll-Free:** 800-293-4237 | |
| **Address:** 12920 Cloverleaf Center Dr., Germantown, MD 20874 US | |

## GROWTH PLANS/SPECIAL FEATURES:

Optelecom-NKF, Inc. is a leading global supplier of Internet Protocol (IP) video and fiber transmission equipment, including video servers, IP cameras, network video recorders and video management and video analytics software. These products are used for traffic management and security surveillance in airports, seaports, prisons, public areas and buildings. Optelecom splits its products into two primary business segments: IP video products and fiber optic products. The firm's IP products, which generate 24% of sales, are designed for small- to large-size closed circuit TV applications. These products digitize and compress video signal sources, enabling the transmission of video using Ethernet and IP. IP hardware products (video codecs, Ethernet switches and recording and storage equipment) and IP software products (Operator Office and the Optelecom-NKF Software Development Kit) are sold under the Siqura brand name. The firm's fiber optic products include data communications products, such as modems and Ethernet media converters; digital video transmission products; coarse wavelength division multiplexer systems, which transmit and receive multiple channels of light operating at different wavelengths; and high resolution video transmission products. These offerings, which generate 73% of sales, consist of the MC series and the 9000 series. In addition to these two segments, the firm also sells small amounts of electro optics products. The electro optics unit, which generates 3% of sales, focuses on manufacturing interferometric fiber optic gyro coils. Optelecom sells its products through direct sales, commercial integrators and resellers. In 2008, the company opened a new regional sales office in Dubai in the United Arab Emirates. Also in 2008, the firm formed a new European holding company called Optelecom-NKF Holding B.V. It will hold all of the company's international subsidiaries.

Optelecom offers employees medical, vision and dental coverage; disability and life insurance; tuition reimbursement; and flexible spending accounts.

## FINANCIALS: **Sales and profits are in thousands of dollars—add 000 to get the full amount. 2008 Note: Financial information for 2008 was not available for all companies at press time.**

| | | |
|---|---|---|
| 2008 Sales: $ | 2008 Profits: $ | **U.S. Stock Ticker: OPTC** |
| 2007 Sales: $42,503 | 2007 Profits: $1,281 | **Int'l Ticker:** Int'l Exchange: |
| 2006 Sales: $39,484 | 2006 Profits: $1,554 | Employees: 177 |
| 2005 Sales: $33,865 | 2005 Profits: $2,681 | Fiscal Year Ends: 12/31 |
| 2004 Sales: $19,395 | 2004 Profits: $1,594 | Parent Company: |

## SALARIES/BENEFITS:

| | | | | |
|---|---|---|---|---|
| Pension Plan: | ESOP Stock Plan: | Profit Sharing: | Top Exec. Salary: $242,000 | Bonus: $126,550 |
| Savings Plan: Y | Stock Purch. Plan: Y | | Second Exec. Salary: $190,000 | Bonus: $36,100 |

## OTHER THOUGHTS:

**Apparent Women Officers or Directors**:
**Hot Spot for Advancement for Women/Minorities**:

## LOCATIONS: ("Y" = Yes)

| West: | Southwest: | Midwest: | Southeast: | Northeast: | International: |
|---|---|---|---|---|---|
| | | | | Y | Y |

# ORMAT TECHNOLOGIES

www.ormat.com

**Industry Group Code:** 221000A **Ranks within this company's industry group:** Sales: 9 Profits: 7

| Management: | | Sales/Marketing: | | Liberal Arts: | | Information Systems: | | Professionals: | | Technical/Scientific: | |
|---|---|---|---|---|---|---|---|---|---|---|---|
| Mgmt. Trainees: | | Mktg. Professionals: | Y | Gen. Writing/Editing: | | Info. Management: | Y | Finance/Accounting: | Y | Engineers, Elec.: | Y |
| Experienced Mgmt.: | Y | Retail Sales: | | Technical Writing: | | Software Dev.: | | Law: | Y | Engineers, Other: | Y |
| Int'l Business: | Y | Commercial/Industrial: | Y | Graphic Arts/Photog.: | | Hardware Dev.: | | HR/Other: | Y | Health/Lab: | |
| MBA Graduates: | Y | Sales Trainees: | Y | Music: | | Systems Integration: | | Training: | Y | Scientists/Research: | |
| | | Advertising Pros.: | | Broadcasting: | | Consulting/Other: | | Health Care: | | Petroleum/Chemicals: | Y |
| | | | | Other: | | | | Consulting: | | Math/Other: | |

## TYPES OF BUSINESS:

Electricity Generation-Geothermal
Geothermal Plant Design & Construction
Small Electric Generators
Procurement Services
Maintenance Services
Construction Services
Engineering Services
Recovered Energy, Biomass & Solar Plants

## BRANDS/DIVISIONS/AFFILIATES:

Ormat Energy Converter

## CONTACTS: *Note: Officers with more than one job title may be intentionally listed here more than once.*

Yehudit (Dita) Bronicki, CEO
Yoram Bronicki, COO
Yoram Bronicki, Pres.
Joseph Tenne, CFO
Joseph Shiloah, Exec. VP-Mktg. & Sales
Lucien Y. Bronicki, CTO
Nadav Amir, Exec. VP-Eng.
Etty Rosner, VP-Contract Admin.
Zvi Reiss, VP-Project Mgmt.
Lucien Y. Bronicki, Chmn.

| **Phone:** 775-356-9029 | **Fax:** 775-356-9039 |
|---|---|
| **Toll-Free:** | |
| **Address:** 6225 Neil Road, Ste. 300, Reno, NV 89511 US | |

## GROWTH PLANS/SPECIAL FEATURES:

Ormat Technologies is engaged in the geothermal and recovered energy power business. The company designs, develops, builds, owns and operates geothermal and recovered energy plants, using equipment that it designs and manufactures. It also designs products related to remote power units and other power generating units, as well as offering services related to the engineering, procurement, construction, operation and maintenance of geothermal and recovered energy power plants. The proprietary Ormat Energy Converter is the basis for the company's recovered energy and geothermal plants. This is a Closed Cycle Vapor Turbogenerator that uses an organic motive fluid and operates following the Organic Rankine Cycle. The firm also produces modular power units for use in unattended, remote applications ranging from 200 to 5,000 watts. Ormat owns (or controls) and operates a total of 11 geothermal power plants the U.S., Guatemala, Kenya and Nicaragua. The firm also owns and operates four recovered energy plans in the U.S. In 2007, the company entered 20-year power purchase agreements with Nevada Power Company (NPC) and Southern California Edison. In August 2007, the company won a bid for roughly 68,900 acres of geothermal leases in Nevada. In the same month, the firm entered a $5.7 million agreement to sell an Ormat Energy Converter to Italcementi Group for use in a Martinsburg, West Virginia cement plant. In April 2008, the firm's Heber South geothermal project reached commercial operation. In May 2008, the company partnered with Montana-Dakota Utilities Co. to design and construct a new 5.3 megawatt recovered energy generation facility. In June 2008, Ormat secured a $16 million contract for geothermal power plants in Turkey. The following month, the company secured a $42 million contract in New Zealand. In September 2008, the firm secured geothermal rights near Anchorage, Alaska

## FINANCIALS: **Sales and profits are in thousands of dollars—add 000 to get the full amount. 2008 Note: Financial information for 2008 was not available for all companies at press time.**

| | | |
|---|---|---|
| 2008 Sales: $ | 2008 Profits: $ | **U.S. Stock Ticker: ORA** |
| 2007 Sales: $295,919 | 2007 Profits: $27,376 | **Int'l Ticker:** Int'l Exchange: |
| 2006 Sales: $268,937 | 2006 Profits: $34,447 | Employees: 899 |
| 2005 Sales: $237,992 | 2005 Profits: $15,177 | Fiscal Year Ends: 12/31 |
| 2004 Sales: $219,230 | 2004 Profits: $17,791 | Parent Company: |

## SALARIES/BENEFITS:

| | | | | |
|---|---|---|---|---|
| Pension Plan: | ESOP Stock Plan: | Profit Sharing: | Top Exec. Salary: $234,418 | Bonus: $91,151 |
| Savings Plan: | Stock Purch. Plan: | | Second Exec. Salary: $204,810 | Bonus: $159,847 |

## OTHER THOUGHTS:

**Apparent Women Officers or Directors**: 2
**Hot Spot for Advancement for Women/Minorities**: Y

## LOCATIONS: ("Y" = Yes)

| West: | Southwest: | Midwest: | Southeast: | Northeast: | International: |
|---|---|---|---|---|---|
| Y | | | | | Y |

# OSCIENT PHARMACEUTICALS CORPORATION

www.oscient.com

**Industry Group Code:** 325412 **Ranks within this company's industry group:** Sales: 24 Profits: 21

| Management: | | Sales/Marketing: | | Liberal Arts: | | Information Systems: | | Professionals: | | Technical/Scientific: | |
|---|---|---|---|---|---|---|---|---|---|---|---|
| Mgmt. Trainees: | | Mktg. Professionals: | Y | Gen. Writing/Editing: | | Info. Management: | Y | Finance/Accounting: | Y | Engineers, Elec.: | |
| Experienced Mgmt.: | Y | Retail Sales: | | Technical Writing: | Y | Software Dev.: | Y | Law: | Y | Engineers, Other: | |
| Int'l Business: | | Commercial/Industrial: | Y | Graphic Arts/Photog.: | | Hardware Dev.: | | HR/Other: | Y | Health/Lab: | Y |
| MBA Graduates: | Y | Sales Trainees: | Y | Music: | | Systems Integration: | | Training: | Y | Scientists/Research: | Y |
| | | Advertising Pros.: | | Broadcasting: | | Consulting/Other: | | Health Care: | Y | Petroleum/Chemicals: | |
| | | | | Other: | | | | Consulting: | Y | Math/Other: | Y |

## TYPES OF BUSINESS:

Pharmaceuticals Commercialization
Pharmaceuticals Development
Antibiotics

## BRANDS/DIVISIONS/AFFILIATES:

FACTIVE
ANTARA
Ramoplanin

## CONTACTS:

*Note: Officers with more than one job title may be intentionally listed here more than once.*

Steven M. Rauscher, CEO
Steven M. Rauscher, Pres.
Philippe M. Maitre, CFO/Exec. VP
Mark A. Glickman, VP-Sales
Joseph A. Pane, VP-Human Resources
Inder Kaul, VP-Clinical Dev., Medical & Regulatory Affairs
Robert Spadafora, VP-Legal Affairs
Nick Colangelo, Exec. VP-Oper.
Nick Colangelo, Exec. VP-Corp. Dev.
Christopher J.M. Taylor, VP-Corp. Comm.
Christopher J.M. Taylor, VP-Investor Rel.
Anthony Watkins, VP-Corp. Dev.
Diane McGuire, VP-Oper.
Aaron D. Berg, VP-Mktg.
David K. Stone, Chmn.

| | |
|---|---|
| **Phone:** 781-398-2300 | **Fax:** 781-893-9535 |
| **Toll-Free:** | |
| **Address:** 1000 Winter St., Ste. 2200, Waltham, MA 02451 US | |

## GROWTH PLANS/SPECIAL FEATURES:

Oscient Pharmaceuticals Corporation primarily engages in the commercialization of FDA approved products, which the firm obtains through drug acquisitions, in-licensing and co-promotion. It markets pharmaceuticals through a national sales force that targets primary care physicians, cardiologists, endocrinologists and pulmonologists. The company currently sells two approved products: FACTIVE and ANTARA. FACTIVE (gemifloxacin mesylate) is a fluoroquinolone antibiotic that has been approved in tablet formulation for two indications: community-acquired pneumonia of mild to moderate severity and acute bacterial exacerbations of chronic bronchitis. It works by inhibiting bacterial DNA synthesis through the blocking of both DNA gyrase and topoisomerase IV, enzymes needed for bacterial growth and survival. The firm licenses the rights to gemifloxacin (FACTIVE's active ingredient) from LG Life Sciences and has in turn sublicensed the rights to market FACTIVE tablets to several other companies: Pfizer, S.A. de C.V. in Mexico; Abbott Laboratories Ltd. in Canada; and Menarini International Operation Luxembourg SA. in areas of Europe. ANTARA (fenofibrate) is indicated for the adjunct treatment of hypercholesterolemia (high blood cholesterol) and hypertriglyceridemia (high triglycerides) in combination with diet. It works by activating lipoprotein lipase and reducing lipoprotein lipase inhibitors in order to eliminate triglyceride-rich particles from plasma. In addition to its marketed drugs, the company is engaged in advanced clinical development of a novel antibiotic candidate, Ramoplanin, for the treatment of Clostridium difficile-associated disease.

Oscient offers employees medical, dental, vision, and life insurance; a 401(k) plan; short and long-term disability; flexible spending accounts; tuition reimbursement; travel assistance; an on-site health club; and adoption assistance.

## FINANCIALS:

**Sales and profits are in thousands of dollars—add 000 to get the full amount. 2008 Note: Financial information for 2008 was not available for all companies at press time.**

| | | |
|---|---|---|
| 2008 Sales: $ | 2008 Profits: $ | **U.S. Stock Ticker: OSCI** |
| 2007 Sales: $79,969 | 2007 Profits: $-29,853 | **Int'l Ticker:** Int'l Exchange: |
| 2006 Sales: $46,152 | 2006 Profits: $-78,477 | Employees: 322 |
| 2005 Sales: $23,609 | 2005 Profits: $-88,593 | Fiscal Year Ends: 12/31 |
| 2004 Sales: $6,613 | 2004 Profits: $-93,271 | Parent Company: |

## SALARIES/BENEFITS:

| | | | | |
|---|---|---|---|---|
| Pension Plan: | ESOP Stock Plan: | Profit Sharing: | Top Exec. Salary: $432,600 | Bonus: $196,253 |
| Savings Plan: Y | Stock Purch. Plan: | | Second Exec. Salary: $340,000 | Bonus: $128,537 |

## OTHER THOUGHTS:

**Apparent Women Officers or Directors**: 1
**Hot Spot for Advancement for Women/Minorities**:

## LOCATIONS: ("Y" = Yes)

| West: | Southwest: | Midwest: | Southeast: | Northeast: | International: |
|---|---|---|---|---|---|
| | | | | Y | |

# PALM INC

www.palm.com

**Industry Group Code:** 334111 **Ranks within this company's industry group:** Sales: 1 Profits: 1

| Management: | | Sales/Marketing: | | Liberal Arts: | | Information Systems: | | Professionals: | | Technical/Scientific: | |
|---|---|---|---|---|---|---|---|---|---|---|---|
| Mgmt. Trainees: | | Mktg. Professionals: | Y | Gen. Writing/Editing: | | Info. Management: | Y | Finance/Accounting: | Y | Engineers, Elec.: | Y |
| Experienced Mgmt.: | Y | Retail Sales: | | Technical Writing: | Y | Software Dev.: | Y | Law: | Y | Engineers, Other: | Y |
| Int'l Business: | Y | Commercial/Industrial: | Y | Graphic Arts/Photog.: | | Hardware Dev.: | Y | HR/Other: | Y | Health/Lab: | |
| MBA Graduates: | Y | Sales Trainees: | Y | Music: | | Systems Integration: | Y | Training: | Y | Scientists/Research: | |
| | | Advertising Pros.: | | Broadcasting: | | Consulting/Other: | | Health Care: | | Petroleum/Chemicals: | |
| | | | | Other: | | | | Consulting: | | Math/Other: | |

## TYPES OF BUSINESS:

Computer Hardware-Handheld Organizers
PDAs
Handheld Computer Accessories & Software

## BRANDS/DIVISIONS/AFFILIATES:

PalmOne, Inc.
Palm
Treo Smartphones
Tungsten
Zire
Foleo

## CONTACTS: *Note: Officers with more than one job title may be intentionally listed here more than once.*

Ed Colligan, CEO
Ed Colligan, Pres.
Andrew (Andy) J. Brown, CFO
Brodie Keast, Sr. VP-Mktg.
Rena Lane, Sr. VP-Human Resources
Mike Bell, Sr. VP-Prod. Dev.
Mary E. Doyle, General Counsel/Corp. Sec./Sr. VP
Jeff Devine, Sr. VP-Global Oper.
Mark Bercow, Sr. VP-Bus. Dev.
Michael Abbott, Sr. VP-Application Software & Svcs.
Way Ting, Sr. VP-System Software
Jon Rubinstein, Exec. Chmn.

**Phone:** 408-617-7000 **Fax:** 408-617-0100
**Toll-Free:** 800-881-7256
**Address:** 950 W. Maude Ave., Sunnyvale, CA 94085 US

## GROWTH PLANS/SPECIAL FEATURES:

Palm, Inc. is a leading global provider of handheld computing devices, or personal digital assistants (PDAs), add-ons and accessories as well as related services and software. The company develops, designs and markets its Palm-branded handheld devices in two areas: smartphones and handheld computers. Its product lines provide a wide range of business productivity tools and personal and entertainment applications designed for mobile professionals and business customers as well as entry-level consumers. Palm offers its smartphones, handheld computers and accessories through a network of wireless carriers, as well as retail and business outlets worldwide. In the U.S. wireless carriers offering Palm products include Sprint, Verizon Wireless and AT&T. Sprint represents approximately 41% of the firm's 2008 revenue; Verizon represents 13%; and AT&T represents 11%. Some products and services offered include the Treo and Centro Smartphones; Palm OS Platform; Windows Mobile OS Platform; and the Tungsten and Palm handheld computers. Palm's products are differentiated in terms of price, design, functionality and software applications that are delivered with the device. All products offer features such as instant-on one-touch access to the most frequently used applications and non-volatile flash memory that protects stored data even if the charge and power run out. Additional features found in some of the firms products include wireless communication capabilities, such as Bluetooth and wireless fidelity, or Wi-Fi; messaging capabilities, e-mail, web browsing, wireless synchronization and telephone communications; multimedia features; a slot for stamp-sized expansion cards for storage, content and input/output devices; and productivity software. All products run on the Palm systems platform or Windows Mobile OS platform. However, the firm is currently developing a new OS and related next-generation systems software. Palm expects this new OS and software to be completed in time to ship products based on this platform in 2009.

## FINANCIALS: **Sales and profits are in thousands of dollars—add 000 to get the full amount. 2008 Note: Financial information for 2008 was not available for all companies at press time.**

| | | |
|---|---|---|
| 2008 Sales: $1,318,691 | 2008 Profits: $-105,419 | **U.S. Stock Ticker: PALM** |
| 2007 Sales: $1,560,507 | 2007 Profits: $56,383 | **Int'l Ticker:** Int'l Exchange: |
| 2006 Sales: $1,578,509 | 2006 Profits: $336,170 | Employees: 1,050 |
| 2005 Sales: $1,270,410 | 2005 Profits: $66,387 | Fiscal Year Ends: 5/31 |
| 2004 Sales: $949,654 | 2004 Profits: $-21,849 | Parent Company: |

## SALARIES/BENEFITS:

| | | | | |
|---|---|---|---|---|
| Pension Plan: | ESOP Stock Plan: | Profit Sharing: | Top Exec. Salary: $757,500 | Bonus: $ |
| Savings Plan: Y | Stock Purch. Plan: | | Second Exec. Salary: $427,500 | Bonus: $ |

## OTHER THOUGHTS:

**Apparent Women Officers or Directors**: 2
**Hot Spot for Advancement for Women/Minorities**: Y

## LOCATIONS: ("Y" = Yes)

| West: | Southwest: | Midwest: | Southeast: | Northeast: | International: |
|---|---|---|---|---|---|
| Y | | | | Y | Y |

# PAR PHARMACEUTICAL COMPANIES INC

www.parpharm.com

**Industry Group Code:** 325416 **Ranks within this company's industry group:** Sales: 1 Profits: 1

| Management: | | Sales/Marketing: | | Liberal Arts: | | Information Systems: | | Professionals: | | Technical/Scientific: | |
|---|---|---|---|---|---|---|---|---|---|---|---|
| Mgmt. Trainees: | | Mktg. Professionals: | Y | Gen. Writing/Editing: | | Info. Management: | Y | Finance/Accounting: | Y | Engineers, Elec.: | |
| Experienced Mgmt.: | Y | Retail Sales: | | Technical Writing: | Y | Software Dev.: | Y | Law: | Y | Engineers, Other: | |
| Int'l Business: | Y | Commercial/Industrial: | Y | Graphic Arts/Photog.: | | Hardware Dev.: | | HR/Other: | Y | Health/Lab: | Y |
| MBA Graduates: | Y | Sales Trainees: | Y | Music: | | Systems Integration: | | Training: | Y | Scientists/Research: | Y |
| | | Advertising Pros.: | | Broadcasting: | | Consulting/Other: | | Health Care: | Y | Petroleum/Chemicals: | Y |
| | | | | Other: | | | | Consulting: | | Math/Other: | Y |

## TYPES OF BUSINESS:

Drugs-Generic & Branded
Pharmaceutical Intermediates

## BRANDS/DIVISIONS/AFFILIATES:

Pharmaceutical Resources, Inc.
Par Pharmaceutical, Inc.
Megace ES
Kali Laboratories, Inc.
FineTech Laboratories Ltd.
Optimer Pharmaceutials, Inc.

## CONTACTS: *Note: Officers with more than one job title may be intentionally listed here more than once.*

Patrick G. LePore, CEO
Gerard A. Martino, COO/Exec. VP
Patrick G. LePore, Pres.
Veronica A. Lubatkin, CFO/Exec. VP
Thomas Haughey, General Counsel/Sec./Exec. VP
Paul V. Campanelli, Exec. VP/Pres., Generic Products Div.
John A. MacPhee, Pres., Branded Products Div.
Patrick G. LePore, Chmn.

| | |
|---|---|
| **Phone:** 201-802-4000 | **Fax:** 201-802-4600 |
| **Toll-Free:** | |
| **Address:** 300 Tice Blvd., Woodcliff Lake, NJ 07677 US | |

## GROWTH PLANS/SPECIAL FEATURES:

Par Pharmaceutical Companies, Inc. (formerly Pharmaceutical Resources, Inc.) develops, manufactures and markets branded and generic pharmaceuticals through its principal subsidiary, Par Pharmaceutical, Inc. Products include treatments for central nervous system disorders, cardiovascular drugs, analgesics, anti-inflammatory products, anti-bacterials, anti-diabetics, antihistamines, anti-virals, cholesterol-lowering drugs and ovulation stimulants. Par operates in two segments, generic pharmaceuticals and branded pharmaceuticals. In the generic segment, the company's product line includes generic prescription drugs consisting of 180 products representing various dosage strengths for 80 separate drugs. These are manufactured principally in the solid oral dosage form (tablet, caplet and two-piece hard shell capsule). Some products are the result of license agreements with the branded drug's manufacturer, including generics of Glucophage and Glucovance through Bristol-Meyers Squibb Company; Flonase and Zantac through GlaxoSmithKline plc; and Toprol XL through AstraZeneca. Par shifted its branded industry to a new subsidiary, Strativa Pharmaceuticals, in 2007. Par's only product in the branded segment is Megace ES, which is approved for the treatment of anorexia, cachexia, or an unexplained, significant weight loss in patients with a diagnosis of AIDS. With the recent acquisition of Kali Laboratories, Inc., Par more than doubled the size of its research and development capabilities. The company recently received FDA approval to market generic versions of Isotopin SR and Ultracet, for hypertension and pain respectively. The firm recently divested former subsidiary FineTech Laboratories Ltd. In 2007, Par announced the commencement of shipping of metoprolol succinate extended release 100mg and 200mg tablets, as well as the shipment of generic Zantac syrup. Also in 2007, Par acquired the North American rights to Zensana, an oral spray to prevent nausea after radiation treatments.

Par offers employees a 529 college savings plan, career growth opportunities, annual incentive programs and a flexible spending plan, along with health, dental and life insurance.

## FINANCIALS: **Sales and profits are in thousands of dollars—add 000 to get the full amount. 2008 Note: Financial information for 2008 was not available for all companies at press time.**

| | | |
|---|---|---|
| 2008 Sales: $ | 2008 Profits: $ | **U.S. Stock Ticker: PRX** |
| 2007 Sales: $769,666 | 2007 Profits: $49,898 | **Int'l Ticker:** Int'l Exchange: |
| 2006 Sales: $725,168 | 2006 Profits: $5,847 | Employees: 716 |
| 2005 Sales: $432,256 | 2005 Profits: $-15,309 | Fiscal Year Ends: 9/30 |
| 2004 Sales: $647,975 | 2004 Profits: $7,558 | Parent Company: |

## SALARIES/BENEFITS:

| | | | | |
|---|---|---|---|---|
| Pension Plan: | ESOP Stock Plan: | Profit Sharing: | Top Exec. Salary: $715,726 | Bonus: $350,000 |
| Savings Plan: Y | Stock Purch. Plan: Y | | Second Exec. Salary: $436,635 | Bonus: $350,000 |

## OTHER THOUGHTS:

**Apparent Women Officers or Directors**: 1
**Hot Spot for Advancement for Women/Minorities**:

## LOCATIONS: ("Y" = Yes)

| West: | Southwest: | Midwest: | Southeast: | Northeast: | International: |
|---|---|---|---|---|---|
| | | | | Y | |

# PC CONNECTION INC

www.pcconnection.com

**Industry Group Code:** 443120A **Ranks within this company's industry group:** Sales: 1 Profits: 1

| Management: | | Sales/Marketing: | | Liberal Arts: | | Information Systems: | | Professionals: | | Technical/Scientific: | |
|---|---|---|---|---|---|---|---|---|---|---|---|
| Mgmt. Trainees: | Y | Mktg. Professionals: | Y | Gen. Writing/Editing: | Y | Info. Management: | Y | Finance/Accounting: | Y | Engineers, Elec.: | |
| Experienced Mgmt.: | Y | Retail Sales: | Y | Technical Writing: | | Software Dev.: | | Law: | Y | Engineers, Other: | |
| Int'l Business: | | Commercial/Industrial: | Y | Graphic Arts/Photog.: | Y | Hardware Dev.: | | HR/Other: | Y | Health/Lab: | |
| MBA Graduates: | Y | Sales Trainees: | Y | Music: | | Systems Integration: | | Training: | Y | Scientists/Research: | |
| | | Advertising Pros.: | Y | Broadcasting: | | Consulting/Other: | | Health Care: | | Petroleum/Chemicals: | |
| | | | | Other: | | | | Consulting: | | Math/Other: | |

## TYPES OF BUSINESS:

Computer Products, Direct Selling
Computer Accessories
Software
IT Services
Online Sales
Catalog Sales

## BRANDS/DIVISIONS/AFFILIATES:

PC Connection Inc
GovConnection Inc
MoreDirect Inc
Traxx
MacConnection
HealthConnection

## CONTACTS:

*Note: Officers with more than one job title may be intentionally listed here more than once.*

Patricia Gallup, CEO
Patricia Gallup, Pres.
Jack Ferguson, CFO/Exec. VP
David Beffa-Negrini, Sr. VP-Corp. Mktg.
Bradley Mousseau, VP-Human Resources
Jack Ferguson, Treas.
Timothy McGrath, Exec. VP-Enterprise Group
David Beffa-Negrini, Sr. VP-Creative Svcs.
Patricia Gallup, Chmn.

**Phone:** 603-683-2000 **Fax:** 603-423-5748
**Toll-Free:** 800-800-0009
**Address:** 730 Milford Rd., Merrimack, NH 03054-4631 US

## GROWTH PLANS/SPECIAL FEATURES:

PC Connection, Inc. is a national direct marketer of information technology (IT) products and services, including computer systems, software and peripheral equipment, networking communications and others. PC Connection offers a selection of over 150,000 products targeted for business use. Its most frequently ordered products are carried in inventory and are typically shipped to customers the same day the order is received. The company operates through three primary business segments: SMB, which serves consumers and small- to medium-sized businesses (SMBs, which are companies with 20 to 1,000 employees) through the PC Connection Sales subsidiaries; Public Sector, serving federal, state, and local government and educational institutions through the GovConnection subsidiary; and Large Account, which handles large corporate accounts through the MoreDirect subsidiary. MoreDirect's Traxx Internet-based system is an integrated application with sales order processing, integrated supply chain visibility and full EDI links. The firm's MacConnection subsidiary is dedicated to selling Apple products. PC Connection sells products through a combination of outbound telemarketing, field sales, targeted direct mail catalogs, web sites, Internet advertising and through selected computer magazines. Approximately 87% of sales are made to return customers. Internet sales make up roughly 29.6% of the company's net sales, while about 68% was made up by outbound telemarketing and field sales. Approximately 54% of total sales are generated through the SMB market. In addition, the company recently launched HealthConnection, a fivefold service that provides IT infrastructure, document management, capture of health data at Point-Of-Care; HIPAA compliance and mobility.

PC Connection offers its employees medical, vision, dental, life and disability coverage; tuition reimbursement; adoption assistance; fitness reimbursement; legal services; computer loans; various product discounts; chair massages; and on-site dry cleaning services.

## FINANCIALS:

**Sales and profits are in thousands of dollars—add 000 to get the full amount. 2008 Note: Financial information for 2008 was not available for all companies at press time.**

| | | |
|---|---|---|
| 2008 Sales: $ | 2008 Profits: $ | **U.S. Stock Ticker: PCCC** |
| 2007 Sales: $1,785,379 | 2007 Profits: $22,995 | **Int'l Ticker:** Int'l Exchange: |
| 2006 Sales: $1,635,651 | 2006 Profits: $13,776 | Employees: 1,616 |
| 2005 Sales: $1,444,297 | 2005 Profits: $4,447 | Fiscal Year Ends: 12/31 |
| 2004 Sales: $1,353,800 | 2004 Profits: $8,300 | Parent Company: |

## SALARIES/BENEFITS:

| | | | | |
|---|---|---|---|---|
| Pension Plan: | ESOP Stock Plan: | Profit Sharing: | Top Exec. Salary: $500,000 | Bonus: $524,000 |
| Savings Plan: Y | Stock Purch. Plan: Y | | Second Exec. Salary: $423,846 | Bonus: $461,100 |

## OTHER THOUGHTS:

**Apparent Women Officers or Directors**: 1
**Hot Spot for Advancement for Women/Minorities**: Y

## LOCATIONS: ("Y" = Yes)

| West: | Southwest: | Midwest: | Southeast: | Northeast: | International: |
|---|---|---|---|---|---|
| | Y | | | Y | |

# PC MALL INC

www.pcmall.com

**Industry Group Code:** 443120A **Ranks within this company's industry group:** Sales: 2 Profits: 2

| Management: | | Sales/Marketing: | | Liberal Arts: | | Information Systems: | | Professionals: | | Technical/Scientific: | |
|---|---|---|---|---|---|---|---|---|---|---|---|
| Mgmt. Trainees: | Y | Mktg. Professionals: | Y | Gen. Writing/Editing: | Y | Info. Management: | Y | Finance/Accounting: | Y | Engineers, Elec.: | |
| Experienced Mgmt.: | Y | Retail Sales: | Y | Technical Writing: | | Software Dev.: | | Law: | Y | Engineers, Other: | |
| Int'l Business: | Y | Commercial/Industrial: | Y | Graphic Arts/Photog.: | Y | Hardware Dev.: | | HR/Other: | Y | Health/Lab: | |
| MBA Graduates: | Y | Sales Trainees: | Y | Music: | | Systems Integration: | | Training: | Y | Scientists/Research: | |
| | | Advertising Pros.: | Y | Broadcasting: | | Consulting/Other: | | Health Care: | | Petroleum/Chemicals: | |
| | | | | Other: | | | | Consulting: | | Math/Other: | |

## TYPES OF BUSINESS:

Computer & Software Products Retailer
Accessories & Supplies
Direct Marketing & Telemarketing
Catalog Sales
Online Sales

## BRANDS/DIVISIONS/AFFILIATES:

PC Mall Gov, Inc.
MacMall
MacMall.com
PCMall.com
PCMallGov.com
GMRI.com
WareForce.com
OnSale.com

## CONTACTS: *Note: Officers with more than one job title may be intentionally listed here more than once.*

Frank Khulusi, CEO
Frank Khulusi, Pres.
Brandon H. LaVerne, CFO
Kristin M. Rogers, Exec. VP-Sales & Mktg.
Robert I. Newton, General Counsel
Joseph B. Hayek, Exec. VP-Corp. Dev.
Joseph B. Hayek, Exec. VP-Investor Rel.
Daniel J. DeVries, Exec. VP-Consumer
Frank Khulusi, Chmn.

**Phone:** 310-354-5600 **Fax:** 310-225-6903
**Toll-Free:** 800-555-6255
**Address:** 2555 W. 190th St., Ste. 201, Torrance, CA 90504 US

## GROWTH PLANS/SPECIAL FEATURES:

PC Mall, Inc. is a rapid response direct marketer of computer hardware, software, peripherals, electronics and other consumer products and services. It operates in two segments: a value added direct marketer of technology solutions for businesses, government and education institutions, as well as consumers; and an online retailer of computer and consumer electronic products under the OnSale.com brand. The company sells more than 100,000 different products relating to systems needs, networking, software, software licensing, storage, audio/video, electronics and printers. PC Mall sells software packages in the business and personal productivity, utility, language, educational and entertainment categories, including spreadsheet and database software. The products sold are authorized through leading manufacturers such as 3Com, Microsoft, Apple and Cisco. The firm also offers customers value-added services, such as the ability to purchase systems that have been specifically configured to meet the customer's requirements. PC Mall offers its products and services through outbound and inbound telemarketing account executives, the Internet, direct marketing techniques, direct response catalogs, a direct sales force and three retail showrooms. In addition, it offers a broad selection of products through its distinctive full-color catalogs under the PC Mall, Mac Mall, and PC Mall Gov brands; its web sites, PCMall.com, MacMall.com, PCMallGov.com, GMRI.com, WareForce.com and OnSale.com; and other promotional materials. Through contracts, open market and procurement card purchases, the company's PC Mall Gov subsidiary makes products available to federal agencies, state and local governments and educational customers. Customer orders are filled by PC Mall's distribution center located near Memphis, Tennessee or through the firm's extensive network of distributors. The firm also offers call-center activities including customer service, technical support and inbound sales to its Philippines office.

Employees are offered a 401(k) plan; medical and dental insurance; and products at a discounted price.

## FINANCIALS: **Sales and profits are in thousands of dollars—add 000 to get the full amount. 2008 Note: Financial information for 2008 was not available for all companies at press time.**

| | | |
|---|---|---|
| 2008 Sales: $ | 2008 Profits: $ | **U.S. Stock Ticker: MALL** |
| 2007 Sales: $1,215,433 | 2007 Profits: $12,443 | **Int'l Ticker:** Int'l Exchange: |
| 2006 Sales: $1,005,820 | 2006 Profits: $3,956 | Employees: 2,410 |
| 2005 Sales: $997,232 | 2005 Profits: $-3,713 | Fiscal Year Ends: 12/31 |
| 2004 Sales: $978,320 | 2004 Profits: $1,013 | Parent Company: |

## SALARIES/BENEFITS:

| | | | | |
|---|---|---|---|---|
| Pension Plan: | ESOP Stock Plan: | Profit Sharing: | Top Exec. Salary: $800,000 | Bonus: $355,491 |
| Savings Plan: Y | Stock Purch. Plan: | | Second Exec. Salary: $312,000 | Bonus: $135,000 |

## OTHER THOUGHTS:

**Apparent Women Officers or Directors**: 1
**Hot Spot for Advancement for Women/Minorities**:

## LOCATIONS: ("Y" = Yes)

| West: | Southwest: | Midwest: | Southeast: | Northeast: | International: |
|---|---|---|---|---|---|
| Y | | Y | Y | | Y |

Note: Financial information, benefits and other data can change quickly and may vary from those stated here.

# PEAPOD LLC

**www.peapod.com**

**Industry Group Code:** 445110E **Ranks within this company's industry group:** Sales: Profits:

| **Management:** | | **Sales/Marketing:** | | **Liberal Arts:** | | **Information Systems:** | | **Professionals:** | | **Technical/Scientific:** | |
|---|---|---|---|---|---|---|---|---|---|---|---|
| Mgmt. Trainees: | Y | Mktg. Professionals: | Y | Gen. Writing/Editing: | Y | Info. Management: | Y | Finance/Accounting: | Y | Engineers, Elec.: | |
| Experienced Mgmt.: | Y | Retail Sales: | Y | Technical Writing: | | Software Dev.: | Y | Law: | Y | Engineers, Other: | |
| Int'l Business: | | Commercial/Industrial: | | Graphic Arts/Photog.: | Y | Hardware Dev.: | | HR/Other: | Y | Health/Lab: | |
| MBA Graduates: | Y | Sales Trainees: | Y | Music: | | Systems Integration: | Y | Training: | Y | Scientists/Research: | |
| | | Advertising Pros.: | Y | Broadcasting: | | Consulting/Other: | | Health Care: | | Petroleum/Chemicals: | |
| | | | | Other: | | | | Consulting: | | Math/Other: | |

## TYPES OF BUSINESS:

Groceries, Online Retail
Grocery Delivery Services
Media & Research Services

## BRANDS/DIVISIONS/AFFILIATES:

Ahold USA Inc
Royal Ahold NV
Peapod by Giant
Peapod by Stop & Shop

## CONTACTS:

*Note: Officers with more than one job title may be intentionally listed here more than once.*

Andrew B. Parkinson, Pres.
Mike Brennan, Sr. VP-Mktg. & Customer Svc.
John Burchard, CIO/Sr. VP
Thomas L. Parkinson, CTO/Sr. VP
Elana Margolis, Media Contact
Scott DeGraeve, Sr. VP/Gen. Mgr.-Chicago & Peapod by Giant
Dave McHugh, VP/Gen. Mgr.-Peapod by Stop & Shop

**Phone:** 847-583-9400 **Fax:** 847-583-9494
**Toll-Free:**
**Address:** 9933 Woods Dr., Ste. 375, Skokie, IL 60077 US

## GROWTH PLANS/SPECIAL FEATURES:

Peapod, LLC, a subsidiary of Royal Ahold, delivers groceries that consumers order over the Internet. The company's grocery delivery service, which costs between $6.95 and $9.95 per order (the cost is dependant on the dollar value of the order), provides consumers with a virtual supermarket, personalized shopping and delivery and responsive telephone and e-mail support. A typical order totals $150, with customers shopping on average twice a month. Peapod provides more than 8,000 products in produce; meat and seafood; deli items; prepared foods; natural and organic foods; Kosher foods; office and school supplies; seasonal items; video products; pet items; health and beauty aids; wine, beer and spirits; and private-label products from Peapod by Stop & Shop and Peapod by Giant. The firm has partnerships with Stop & Shop and Giant Food stores. Peapod also provides consumer goods companies with a forum for targeted interactive advertising, electronic coupons and extensive product research. The company operates through centralized distribution from its two warehouses in Chicago and Washington, D.C., which together total 75,000 square feet. It also owns 7,000 square-foot warerooms adjacent to its partner stores in Connecticut, Massachusetts, New York, New Jersey and Rhode Island. Peapod delivers to 1,500 zip codes and more than 12.7 million households. The firm has a supermarket presence in major cities and suburban areas in Massachusetts, Virginia, Maryland, Wisconsin, Washington, D.C., Connecticut, New York, Rhode Island, Illinois and New Jersey. Peapod has delivered more than 10 million orders since its inception.

## FINANCIALS:

**Sales and profits are in thousands of dollars—add 000 to get the full amount. 2008 Note: Financial information for 2008 was not available for all companies at press time.**

| | | |
|---|---|---|
| 2008 Sales: $ | 2008 Profits: $ | **U.S. Stock Ticker: Subsidiary** |
| 2007 Sales: $ | 2007 Profits: $ | **Int'l Ticker:** Int'l Exchange: |
| 2006 Sales: $ | 2006 Profits: $ | Employees: 130 |
| 2005 Sales: $ | 2005 Profits: $ | Fiscal Year Ends: 12/31 |
| 2004 Sales: $ | 2004 Profits: $ | Parent Company: ROYAL AHOLD NV |

## SALARIES/BENEFITS:

| | | | | |
|---|---|---|---|---|
| Pension Plan: | ESOP Stock Plan: | Profit Sharing: | Top Exec. Salary: $ | Bonus: $9,039 |
| Savings Plan: | Stock Purch. Plan: | | Second Exec. Salary: $146,903 | Bonus: $146,903 |

## OTHER THOUGHTS:

**Apparent Women Officers or Directors**:
**Hot Spot for Advancement for Women/Minorities**:

## LOCATIONS: ("Y" = Yes)

| West: | Southwest: | Midwest: | Southeast: | Northeast: | International: |
|---|---|---|---|---|---|
| | | Y | | Y | |

# PERFICIENT INC

www.perficient.com

**Industry Group Code:** 541512 **Ranks within this company's industry group:** Sales: 1 Profits: 1

| Management: | | Sales/Marketing: | | Liberal Arts: | | Information Systems: | | Professionals: | | Technical/Scientific: | |
|---|---|---|---|---|---|---|---|---|---|---|---|
| Mgmt. Trainees: | | Mktg. Professionals: | Y | Gen. Writing/Editing: | | Info. Management: | Y | Finance/Accounting: | Y | Engineers, Elec.: | Y |
| Experienced Mgmt.: | Y | Retail Sales: | | Technical Writing: | Y | Software Dev.: | Y | Law: | Y | Engineers, Other: | |
| Int'l Business: | Y | Commercial/Industrial: | | Graphic Arts/Photog.: | | Hardware Dev.: | | HR/Other: | Y | Health/Lab: | |
| MBA Graduates: | Y | Sales Trainees: | | Music: | | Systems Integration: | | Training: | Y | Scientists/Research: | |
| | | Advertising Pros.: | | Broadcasting: | | Consulting/Other: | Y | Health Care: | | Petroleum/Chemicals: | |
| | | | | Other: | Y | | | Consulting: | Y | Math/Other: | |

## TYPES OF BUSINESS:

Consulting-On-Site Technical Services
Middleware
Web Services
Content Management Software
Enterprise Portal Services
IT Outsourcing

## BRANDS/DIVISIONS/AFFILIATES:

## CONTACTS: *Note: Officers with more than one job title may be intentionally listed here more than once.*

John T. (Jack) McDonald, CEO
Jeffrey S. Davis, COO
Jeffrey S. Davis, Pres.
Paul E. Martin, CFO
Richard T. Kalbfleish, VP-Admin.
Paul E. Martin, Corp. Sec.
Kathy Henely, VP-Corp. Oper.
Richard T. Kalbfleish, VP-Finance
Chris Gianattasio, VP-Field Oper.
John Jenkins, VP-Field Oper.
Thomas Pash, VP-Field Oper.
Tim Thompson, VP-Client Dev.
John T. (Jack) McDonald, Chmn.

| | |
|---|---|
| **Phone:** 512-531-6000 | **Fax:** 512-306-7331 |
| **Toll-Free:** | |
| **Address:** 1120 S. Capital of Texas Hwy., Ste. 220, Bldg. 3, Austin, TX 78746 US | |

## GROWTH PLANS/SPECIAL FEATURES:

Perficient, Inc. is an information technology (IT) consulting firm providing large enterprise companies primarily throughout the U.S. with Internet-based technology solutions using third party software products developed by its partners. Its solutions include custom applications; portals and collaboration; e-commerce; online customer management (CRM); enterprise customer management (ECM); business intelligence; business integration; mobile technology; technology platform implementations; and service oriented architectures. Perficient's experience with platforms including J2EE, .Net and open-source enables it to design, develop, implement and integrate custom application solutions that provide enterprise-specific functionality. The firm provides secure and scalable enterprise portals, including searchable data systems; collaborative systems for process improvement; transaction processing; unified and extended reporting; and content management and personalization. Its e-commerce infrastructures dynamically integrate with back-end systems and complementary applications that provide for transaction volume scalability and content management. Perficient conducts interviews, facilitated requirements gathering sessions and call center analysis in designing its CRM solutions. The firm's ECM solutions include enterprise imaging and document management; web content management; digital asset management; enterprise records management; compliance and control; business process management and collaboration; and enterprise search. The company's mobile technology solutions include mobile content delivery systems; wireless value-added services such as SIP, IMS, SMS, MMS and Push-to-Talk; custom developed applications to pervasive devices such as Symbian, WML, J2ME, MIDP and Linux; and customer care solutions such as provisioning, mediation, rating and billing. Perficient's platform services include application server selection; architecture planning, installation and configuration; clustering for availability, performance assessment and issue remediation; security services; and technology migrations. The firm also offers education and mentoring services to its clients. Perficient serves its customers from a network of 19 locations throughout the U.S. and international locations in Canada, China, Macedonia and India.

## FINANCIALS: **Sales and profits are in thousands of dollars—add 000 to get the full amount. 2008 Note: Financial information for 2008 was not available for all companies at press time.**

| | | |
|---|---|---|
| 2008 Sales: $ | 2008 Profits: $ | **U.S. Stock Ticker: PRFT** |
| 2007 Sales: $218,148 | 2007 Profits: $16,230 | **Int'l Ticker:** Int'l Exchange: |
| 2006 Sales: $160,926 | 2006 Profits: $9,567 | Employees: 1,427 |
| 2005 Sales: $96,997 | 2005 Profits: $7,177 | Fiscal Year Ends: 12/31 |
| 2004 Sales: $58,848 | 2004 Profits: $3,913 | Parent Company: |

## SALARIES/BENEFITS:

| | | | | |
|---|---|---|---|---|
| Pension Plan: | ESOP Stock Plan: | Profit Sharing: | Top Exec. Salary: $276,250 | Bonus: $532,408 |
| Savings Plan: Y | Stock Purch. Plan: | | Second Exec. Salary: $276,250 | Bonus: $532,408 |

## OTHER THOUGHTS:

**Apparent Women Officers or Directors**: 3
**Hot Spot for Advancement for Women/Minorities**: Y

## LOCATIONS: ("Y" = Yes)

| West: | Southwest: | Midwest: | Southeast: | Northeast: | International: |
|---|---|---|---|---|---|
| Y | Y | Y | Y | Y | Y |

# PETMED EXPRESS INC

www.1800petmeds.com

**Industry Group Code:** 453910 **Ranks within this company's industry group:** Sales: 1 Profits: 1

| Management: | | Sales/Marketing: | | Liberal Arts: | | Information Systems: | | Professionals: | | Technical/Scientific: | |
|---|---|---|---|---|---|---|---|---|---|---|---|
| Mgmt. Trainees: | Y | Mktg. Professionals: | Y | Gen. Writing/Editing: | Y | Info. Management: | Y | Finance/Accounting: | Y | Engineers, Elec.: | |
| Experienced Mgmt.: | Y | Retail Sales: | Y | Technical Writing: | | Software Dev.: | Y | Law: | Y | Engineers, Other: | |
| Int'l Business: | | Commercial/Industrial: | | Graphic Arts/Photog.: | Y | Hardware Dev.: | | HR/Other: | Y | Health/Lab: | |
| MBA Graduates: | Y | Sales Trainees: | Y | Music: | | Systems Integration: | | Training: | Y | Scientists/Research: | |
| | | Advertising Pros.: | Y | Broadcasting: | | Consulting/Other: | | Health Care: | | Petroleum/Chemicals: | |
| | | | | Other: | | | | Consulting: | | Math/Other: | |

## TYPES OF BUSINESS:

Prescription & Non-Prescription Pet Drugs
Mail Order Pet Pharmacy
Veterinary Medications
Animal Vitamins & Nutraceuticals
Pet Care Products

## BRANDS/DIVISIONS/AFFILIATES:

1-800-PetMeds
PetHealth101.com

## CONTACTS: *Note: Officers with more than one job title may be intentionally listed here more than once.*

Menderes Akdag, CEO
Menderes Akdag, Pres.
Bruce S. Rosenbloom, CFO
Robert C. Schweitzer, Chmn.

**Phone:** 954-979-5995 **Fax:** 954-971-0544
**Toll-Free:**
**Address:** 1441 SW 29th Ave., Pompano Beach, FL 33069 US

## GROWTH PLANS/SPECIAL FEATURES:

PetMed Express, Inc. (doing business as 1-800-PetMeds) is a nationwide pet pharmacy that markets prescription and non-prescription pet medications and other health products for dogs, cats and horses. PetMed markets its products through national television, online and direct mail/print advertising campaigns. The 1-800-PetMeds catalog is a full-color catalog featuring the firm's most popular products and produced by a combination of in-house writers, production artists and independent contractors. The firm offers over 750 products, including such brands as Frontline Plus, K9 Advantix, Advantage, Heartgard Plus, Sentinel, Interceptor, Program, Revolution, Deramaxx and Rimadyl. Non-prescription medications include flea and tick control products; bone and joint care products; vitamins and nutritional supplements; and hygiene products. Prescription medications offered by the company include heartworm preventatives; thyroid and arthritis medications; antibiotics; and other specialty medications, as well as generic substitutes. Sales of non-prescription medications compose approximately 69% of PetMed's total sales, while prescription medications generate 30% and shipping and handling charges generate approximately 1%. The company attracts approximately 17 million visitors to its website per year, of whom approximately 10% place an order. Internet sales generate approximately 65% of the company's total sales. PetMed additionally sponsors PetHealth101.com, which provides information regarding pet behavior, illness and natural and pharmaceutical remedies for pet problems. Approximately 50% of the firm's customers reside in California, Florida, Texas, New York, Pennsylvania, Georgia, Virginia and New Jersey. While its primary focus has been on retail customers, PetMed also sells various non-prescription medications wholesale to a variety of businesses, with such sales generating less than 1% of its total sales. The company's average retail purchase is approximately $80. In addition to pet medications, the firm also produces grooming tools, odor controllers, beds, bowls, leashes, training aids and treats.

## FINANCIALS: **Sales and profits are in thousands of dollars—add 000 to get the full amount. 2008 Note: Financial information for 2008 was not available for all companies at press time.**

2008 Sales: $188,336
2007 Sales: $162,246
2006 Sales: $137,583
2005 Sales: $108,358
2004 Sales: $93,994

2008 Profits: $20,022
2007 Profits: $14,443
2006 Profits: $12,063
2005 Profits: $8,010
2004 Profits: $5,813

**U.S. Stock Ticker: PETS**
**Int'l Ticker:** Int'l Exchange:
Employees: 256
Fiscal Year Ends: 3/31
Parent Company:

## SALARIES/BENEFITS:

Pension Plan: ESOP Stock Plan: Profit Sharing: Top Exec. Salary: $254,615 Bonus: $
Savings Plan: Stock Purch. Plan: Second Exec. Salary: $146,060 Bonus: $1,000

## OTHER THOUGHTS:

**Apparent Women Officers or Directors:**
**Hot Spot for Advancement for Women/Minorities:**

## LOCATIONS: ("Y" = Yes)

| West: | Southwest: | Midwest: | Southeast: | Northeast: | International: |
|---|---|---|---|---|---|
| | | | Y | | |

# PETROLEUM DEVELOPMENT CORPORATION

www.petd.com

**Industry Group Code:** 211111 **Ranks within this company's industry group:** Sales: 20 Profits: 17

| Management: | | Sales/Marketing: | | Liberal Arts: | | Information Systems: | | Professionals: | | Technical/Scientific: | |
|---|---|---|---|---|---|---|---|---|---|---|---|
| Mgmt. Trainees: | | Mktg. Professionals: | Y | Gen. Writing/Editing: | | Info. Management: | Y | Finance/Accounting: | Y | Engineers, Elec.: | |
| Experienced Mgmt.: | Y | Retail Sales: | | Technical Writing: | | Software Dev.: | | Law: | Y | Engineers, Other: | Y |
| Int'l Business: | Y | Commercial/Industrial: | Y | Graphic Arts/Photog.: | | Hardware Dev.: | | HR/Other: | Y | Health/Lab: | |
| MBA Graduates: | Y | Sales Trainees: | | Music: | | Systems Integration: | | Training: | Y | Scientists/Research: | |
| | | Advertising Pros.: | | Broadcasting: | | Consulting/Other: | | Health Care: | | Petroleum/Chemicals: | Y |
| | | | | Other: | | | | Consulting: | | Math/Other: | |

## TYPES OF BUSINESS:

Oil & Gas Production
Oil & Gas Sales
Well Operations
Gas Marketing

## BRANDS/DIVISIONS/AFFILIATES:

Riley Natural Gas

## CONTACTS:

*Note: Officers with more than one job title may be intentionally listed here more than once.*

Richard W. McCullough, CEO
Richard W. McCullough, Pres.
Richard W. McCullough, CFO
John A. DeLawder, Dir.-Human Resources
Karen Griffin, Dir.-IT
Susan A. Foster, Dir.-Reserve Eng.
Dan Amidon, General Counsel
Scott J. Reasoner, VP-Oper.
Celesta M. Miracle, VP-Strategic Planning
Celesta M. Miracle, VP-Investor Rel.
Darwin L. Stump, Chief Acct. Officer
James R. Schaff, VP-Land
Eric R. Stearns, Exec. VP-Exploration & Production
Tom W. Carpenter, Dir.-Geosciences
Steven R. Williams, Chmn.

**Phone:** 304-842-3597 **Fax:** 304-842-0913
**Toll-Free:** 800-624-3821
**Address:** 120 Genesis Blvd., Bridgeport, WV 26330 US

## GROWTH PLANS/SPECIAL FEATURES:

Petroleum Development Corp. is an independent energy company engaged primarily in the development, production and marketing of natural gas and oil. During 2007, approximately 84.1% of the firm's production came from Rocky Mountain Region wells, 9.8% from Appalachian Basin wells and 6.1% from Michigan Basin wells. Production operations have not commenced in the Fort Worth Basin. Petroleum Development operates in four segments: drilling and development; natural gas marketing; oil and gas sales; and well operations and pipeline. The drilling and development segment drills wells for itself and for investor partners. The natural gas marketing segment operates through Riley Natural Gas (RNG), which purchases, aggregates and resells natural gas developed by the firm and other producers. In addition, RNG has experience in the use of risk management strategies and also manages the marketing of oil and gas for the wells outside the Appalachian Basin. The oil and gas segment manages the income from the sale of oil and gas produced by the company's wells, which are mainly located in the Rocky Mountain Region. The well operations and pipeline segment represents the revenue generated by the operation of the company's wells. On average, Petroleum Development owns about 20% to 37% working interest in the wells but, as the well operator, charges a fee for its services to the other owner to cover operating, accounting and insurance costs. The firm has not sponsored new drilling partnerships in 2008 in order to focus efforts on maximizing the value of existing partnerships and continuing growth through drilling and exploration. In December 2007, the firm announced it sold a portion of its North Dakota properties. In 2009, the firm is moving its corporate headquarters to Denver Colorado.

## FINANCIALS:

**Sales and profits are in thousands of dollars—add 000 to get the full amount. 2008 Note: Financial information for 2008 was not available for all companies at press time.**

| | | |
|---|---|---|
| 2008 Sales: $ | 2008 Profits: $ | **U.S. Stock Ticker: PETD** |
| 2007 Sales: $305,235 | 2007 Profits: $33,209 | **Int'l Ticker:** Int'l Exchange: |
| 2006 Sales: $286,503 | 2006 Profits: $237,772 | Employees: 256 |
| 2005 Sales: $325,198 | 2005 Profits: $41,452 | Fiscal Year Ends: 12/31 |
| 2004 Sales: $264,483 | 2004 Profits: $33,228 | Parent Company: |

## SALARIES/BENEFITS:

| | | | | |
|---|---|---|---|---|
| Pension Plan: | ESOP Stock Plan: | Profit Sharing: | Top Exec. Salary: $370,000 | Bonus: $471,750 |
| Savings Plan: | Stock Purch. Plan: | | Second Exec. Salary: $292,500 | Bonus: $310,781 |

## OTHER THOUGHTS:

**Apparent Women Officers or Directors:** 4
**Hot Spot for Advancement for Women/Minorities:** Y

## LOCATIONS: ("Y" = Yes)

| West: | Southwest: | Midwest: | Southeast: | Northeast: | International: |
|---|---|---|---|---|---|
| Y | | Y | | Y | |

# PHILADELPHIA CONSOLIDATED HOLDING CORP

www.phly.com

**Industry Group Code:** 524126 **Ranks within this company's industry group:** Sales: 4 Profits: 2

| Management: | | Sales/Marketing: | | Liberal Arts: | | Information Systems: | | Professionals: | | Technical/Scientific: | |
|---|---|---|---|---|---|---|---|---|---|---|---|
| Mgmt. Trainees: | | Mktg. Professionals: | Y | Gen. Writing/Editing: | Y | Info. Management: | Y | Finance/Accounting: | Y | Engineers, Elec.: | |
| Experienced Mgmt.: | Y | Retail Sales: | | Technical Writing: | Y | Software Dev.: | | Law: | Y | Engineers, Other: | |
| Int'l Business: | | Commercial/Industrial: | Y | Graphic Arts/Photog.: | | Hardware Dev.: | | HR/Other: | Y | Health/Lab: | |
| MBA Graduates: | Y | Sales Trainees: | Y | Music: | | Systems Integration: | | Training: | Y | Scientists/Research: | |
| | | Advertising Pros.: | | Broadcasting: | | Consulting/Other: | | Health Care: | | Petroleum/Chemicals: | |
| | | | | Other: | | | | Consulting: | | Math/Other: | Y |

## TYPES OF BUSINESS:

Direct Property & Casualty Insurance
Commercial, Personal & Specialty Lines
Auto Insurance

## BRANDS/DIVISIONS/AFFILIATES:

Philadelphia Indemnity Insurance Company
Philadelphia Insurance Company
PCHC Investment Corp.
Liberty American Insurance Company
Maguire Insurance Agency, Inc.
Liberty American Premium Finance Company
Liberty American Insurance Group, Inc.
Liberty American Select Insurance Company

## CONTACTS: *Note: Officers with more than one job title may be intentionally listed here more than once.*

James J. Maguire, Jr., CEO
Christopher J. Maguire, COO/Exec. VP
James J. Maguire, Jr., Pres.
Craig P. Keller, CFO/Exec. VP
Sean S. Sweeney, Chief Mktg. Officer/Exec. VP
Craig P. Keller, Corp. Sec.
Craig P. Keller, Treas.
William J. Benecke, Exec. VP/Chief Claims Officer
T. Bruce Meyer, Pres./CEO-Liberty American Insurance Group, Inc.
James J. Maguire, Chmn.

**Phone:** 610-617-7900 **Fax:** 610-617-7940
**Toll-Free:** 800-873-4552
**Address:** 1 Bala Plaza, Ste. 100, Bala Cynwyd, PA 19004 US

## GROWTH PLANS/SPECIAL FEATURES:

Philadelphia Consolidated Holdings Corp. designs, markets and underwrites specialty commercial and personal property and casualty insurance products incorporating value-added coverages and services for select target markets or niches. The company operates in three segments: commercial, specialty and personal lines underwriting. The commercial lines underwriting segment, which accounted for about 82% of 2007 revenue, provides commercial multi-peril package; commercial automobile; specialty property and inland marine; and antique/collector care insurance products. The specialty lines underwriting group, responsible for roughly 14.5%, offers professional and management liability insurance products. The personal lines underwriting segment, which generated approximately 3.5%, provides personal property insurance products, targeted at homeowners and the manufactured housing market in Florida, and the National Flood Insurance Program, serving personal and commercial policyholders. Philadelphia Consolidated operates primarily through subsidiaries Philadelphia Indemnity Insurance Company; Philadelphia Insurance Company; PCHC Investment Corp.; Liberty American Insurance Company; Maguire Insurance Agency, Inc.; Liberty American Premium Finance Company; Liberty American Insurance Services, Inc; Liberty American Insurance Group, Inc.; and Liberty American Select Insurance Company. Philadelphia Indemnity Insurance Company, Philadelphia Insurance Company, Liberty American Select Insurance Company, Inc. and Liberty American Insurance Company are licensed to issue insurance policies. Maguire Insurance Agency is a captive underwriting manager and Liberty American Insurance Services markets, underwrites and services homeowners and mobile homeowners insurance policies. A group of 210 preferred agents and a network of about 11,300 independent producers supplement the production underwriting organization, which consists of 330 professionals located in 45 regional offices across the U.S. In July 2008, the firm agreed to be acquired by Tokio Marine Holdings, Inc. for $4.7 billion.

The company offers its employees medical and vision insurance; life and AD&D insurance; disability insurance; employee assistance; and tuition reimbursement.

## FINANCIALS: **Sales and profits are in thousands of dollars—add 000 to get the full amount. 2008 Note: Financial information for 2008 was not available for all companies at press time.**

| | | |
|---|---|---|
| 2008 Sales: $ | 2008 Profits: $ | **U.S. Stock Ticker: PHLY** |
| 2007 Sales: $1,529,594 | 2007 Profits: $326,813 | **Int'l Ticker:** Int'l Exchange: |
| 2006 Sales: $1,253,770 | 2006 Profits: $288,849 | Employees: 1,324 |
| 2005 Sales: $1,051,429 | 2005 Profits: $156,688 | Fiscal Year Ends: 12/31 |
| 2004 Sales: $818,856 | 2004 Profits: $83,683 | Parent Company: |

## SALARIES/BENEFITS:

| | | | | |
|---|---|---|---|---|
| Pension Plan: | ESOP Stock Plan: | Profit Sharing: Y | Top Exec. Salary: $1,000,000 | Bonus: $ |
| Savings Plan: Y | Stock Purch. Plan: Y | | Second Exec. Salary: $550,000 | Bonus: $600,000 |

## OTHER THOUGHTS:

**Apparent Women Officers or Directors**: 2
**Hot Spot for Advancement for Women/Minorities**: Y

## LOCATIONS: ("Y" = Yes)

| West: | Southwest: | Midwest: | Southeast: | Northeast: | International: |
|---|---|---|---|---|---|
| Y | Y | Y | Y | Y | |

Note: Financial information, benefits and other data can change quickly and may vary from those stated here.

# PHOENIX COMPANIES (THE)

**www.phoenixwm.com**

**Industry Group Code:** 524113 **Ranks within this company's industry group:** Sales: 4 Profits: 3

| Management: | | Sales/Marketing: | | Liberal Arts: | | Information Systems: | | Professionals: | | Technical/Scientific: | |
|---|---|---|---|---|---|---|---|---|---|---|---|
| Mgmt. Trainees: | | Mktg. Professionals: | Y | Gen. Writing/Editing: | Y | Info. Management: | Y | Finance/Accounting: | Y | Engineers, Elec.: | |
| Experienced Mgmt.: | Y | Retail Sales: | | Technical Writing: | Y | Software Dev.: | | Law: | Y | Engineers, Other: | |
| Int'l Business: | Y | Commercial/Industrial: | | Graphic Arts/Photog.: | | Hardware Dev.: | | HR/Other: | Y | Health/Lab: | |
| MBA Graduates: | Y | Sales Trainees: | Y | Music: | | Systems Integration: | | Training: | Y | Scientists/Research: | |
| | | Advertising Pros.: | Y | Broadcasting: | | Consulting/Other: | | Health Care: | Y | Petroleum/Chemicals: | |
| | | | | Other: | | | | Consulting: | | Math/Other: | Y |

## TYPES OF BUSINESS:

Insurance-Life
Mutual Funds
Annuities
Brokerage Services
Wealth Management
Trust Services
Investment

## BRANDS/DIVISIONS/AFFILIATES:

Philadelphia Financial Group
Phoenix Investment Partners, Ltd.
Phoenix Life Insurance Company
Phoenix Charter Trust Company
Virtus Investment Partners, Inc.

## CONTACTS: *Note: Officers with more than one job title may be intentionally listed here more than once.*

Dona D. Young, CEO
Dona D. Young, Pres.
Peter A. Hofmann, CFO/Sr. Exec. VP
Edward W. Cassidy, Exec. VP-Life & Annuity Sales
Bonnie J. Malley, Exec. VP-Human Resources
Walter H. Zultowski, Sr. VP-Research & Concept Dev.
John V. LaGrasse, CIO/Exec. VP
Deborah M. Zawisza, CTO/Sr. VP-IT
Thomas Buckingham, Sr. VP-Prod. Dev.
Tracy L. Rich, General Counsel/Exec. VP
Edward W. Cassidy, Exec. VP-Oper.
Michele U. Farley, Sr. VP-Corp. Comm.
David R. Pellerin, Chief Acct. Officer/Sr. VP
Daniel T. Geraci, Exec. VP-Asset Mgmt.
Phillip K. Polkinghorn, Exec. VP-Life & Annuity
George R. Aylward, Sr. Exec. VP/Pres., Asset Mgmt.
James D. Wehr, Chief Investment Officer/Sr. VP
Dona D. Young, Chmn.

| **Phone:** 860-403-5000 | **Fax:** 860-403-5855 |
|---|---|
| **Toll-Free:** | |
| **Address:** 1 American Row, Hartford, CT 06102-5056 US | |

## GROWTH PLANS/SPECIAL FEATURES:

The Phoenix Companies, Inc. is a provider of wealth management products and services designed specifically for affluent and high-net-worth clients. Through a variety of select advisors and financial services firms, the company serves the accumulation, preservation and wealth transfer needs of individuals and families, business owners, senior corporate executives and institutions. Phoenix's primary subsidiaries include Phoenix Investment Partners, Ltd., Phoenix Life Insurance Company and Phoenix Charter Trust Company. In addition, the company offers life insurance, annuities, asset management, trust services and private placement through the Philadelphia Financial Group. Phoenix Investment Partners, an asset management company, also operates through 10 subsidiaries and affiliates. Its services range from maintaining mutual funds, closed-end funds and alternative financial products to offering institutional management services and disciplined money management. Phoenix acquired the remaining minority interest in Kayne Anderson Rudnick, a portfolio management firm, increasing its stake to 100%. The company recently raised its stock market price target following a rapid rise in shares and introduced a concierge service to their life insurance underwriting services. In February 2008, Phoenix announced its intention to spin off Phoenix Investment Partners to shareholders. In July 2008, the firm announced that Phoenix Investment Partners will be renamed Virtus Investment Partners, Inc. when the spin off is complete.

The firm provides a choice of benefits designed to meet associates' differing needs and budgets, including flexible spending accounts and transportation reimbursement.

## FINANCIALS: **Sales and profits are in thousands of dollars—add 000 to get the full amount. 2008 Note: Financial information for 2008 was not available for all companies at press time.**

| | | |
|---|---|---|
| 2008 Sales: $ | 2008 Profits: $ | **U.S. Stock Ticker: PNX** |
| 2007 Sales: $2,572,800 | 2007 Profits: $123,900 | **Int'l Ticker:** Int'l Exchange: |
| 2006 Sales: $2,578,000 | 2006 Profits: $99,900 | Employees: 1,600 |
| 2005 Sales: $2,608,900 | 2005 Profits: $108,400 | Fiscal Year Ends: 12/31 |
| 2004 Sales: $2,743,200 | 2004 Profits: $86,400 | Parent Company: |

## SALARIES/BENEFITS:

| | | | | |
|---|---|---|---|---|
| Pension Plan: Y | ESOP Stock Plan: | Profit Sharing: | Top Exec. Salary: $950,000 | Bonus: $1,923,000 |
| Savings Plan: Y | Stock Purch. Plan: | | Second Exec. Salary: $450,000 | Bonus: $885,200 |

## OTHER THOUGHTS:

**Apparent Women Officers or Directors**: 8
**Hot Spot for Advancement for Women/Minorities**: Y

## LOCATIONS: ("Y" = Yes)

| West: | Southwest: | Midwest: | Southeast: | Northeast: | International: |
|---|---|---|---|---|---|
| | Y | | | Y | Y |

# PIEDMONT NATURAL GAS COMPANY INC

**www.piedmontng.com**

**Industry Group Code:** 221000B **Ranks within this company's industry group:** Sales: 4 Profits: 4

| Management: | | Sales/Marketing: | | Liberal Arts: | | Information Systems: | | Professionals: | | Technical/Scientific: | |
|---|---|---|---|---|---|---|---|---|---|---|---|
| Mgmt. Trainees: | | Mktg. Professionals: | Y | Gen. Writing/Editing: | | Info. Management: | Y | Finance/Accounting: | Y | Engineers, Elec.: | Y |
| Experienced Mgmt.: | Y | Retail Sales: | | Technical Writing: | | Software Dev.: | | Law: | Y | Engineers, Other: | Y |
| Int'l Business: | | Commercial/Industrial: | Y | Graphic Arts/Photog.: | | Hardware Dev.: | | HR/Other: | Y | Health/Lab: | |
| MBA Graduates: | Y | Sales Trainees: | | Music: | | Systems Integration: | | Training: | Y | Scientists/Research: | |
| | | Advertising Pros.: | | Broadcasting: | | Consulting/Other: | | Health Care: | | Petroleum/Chemicals: | Y |
| | | | | Other: | | | | Consulting: | | Math/Other: | |

## TYPES OF BUSINESS:

Utilities-Natural Gas
Pipelines
Gas Transportation & Storage
Natural Gas Marketing

## BRANDS/DIVISIONS/AFFILIATES:

Cardinal Pipeline Co., LLC
Pine Needle LNG Co., LLC
SouthStar Energy Services
Hardy Storage Co., LLC

## CONTACTS: *Note: Officers with more than one job title may be intentionally listed here more than once.*

Thomas E. Skains, CEO
Thomas E. Skains, Pres.
David J. Dzuricky, CFO/Sr. VP
Ranelle Q. Warfield, VP-Sales & Mktg.
Lesli Ennis, VP-Info. Svcs.
Jane R. Lewis-Raymond, General Counsel/VP/Sec./Chief Compliance Officer
Robert O. Pritchard, Treas./VP/Chief Risk Officer
Kevin M. O'Hara, Sr. VP-Corp. & Community Affairs
Michael H. Yount, Sr. VP-Utility Oper.
Franklin H. Yoho, Sr. VP-Commercial Oper.
Jose M. Simon, Controller/VP
Thomas E. Skains, Chmn.

| **Phone:** 704-364-3120 | **Fax:** 704-365-8515 |
|---|---|
| **Toll-Free:** | |
| **Address:** 4720 Piedmont Row Dr., Charlotte, NC 28210 US | |

## GROWTH PLANS/SPECIAL FEATURES:

Piedmont Natural Gas Co., Inc. is an energy services company primarily engaged in the distribution of natural gas to residential, commercial and industrial customers in North Carolina, South Carolina and Tennessee. The company is one of the largest natural gas utilities in the Southeast, with over 1,000,000 customers, including 62,000 customers served by municipalities who are wholesale customers. Piedmont owns approximately 3,100 miles of lateral pipeline and 23,900 miles of distribution mains. The company is also invested in several of non-utility, energy related businesses including unregulated retail natural gas marketing and interstate and intrastate natural gas storage and transportation. The firm owns about a 21% membership in the Cardinal Pipeline Co., LLC, which owns and operates an intrastate gas pipeline in North Carolina. It also owns 40% of Pine Needle LNG Company, LLC, which owns an interstate liquefied natural gas storage facility in North Carolina. Piedmont has a 30% equity interest in SouthStar Energy Services, which offers a combination of unregulated energy products and services to industrial, commercial and residential customers in the southeastern U.S. Business strategies for Piedmont include focusing on core-utility businesses, pursuing new construction markets and converting existing homes and businesses to natural gas.

The company offers its employees a pension plan, a 401(k) match, stock purchase options, medical insurance, flexible spending accounts, short-and long-term disability and tuition-refund plans.

## FINANCIALS: **Sales and profits are in thousands of dollars—add 000 to get the full amount. 2008 Note: Financial information for 2008 was not available for all companies at press time.**

| | | |
|---|---|---|
| 2008 Sales: $ | 2008 Profits: $ | **U.S. Stock Ticker: PNY** |
| 2007 Sales: $1,711,292 | 2007 Profits: $104,387 | **Int'l Ticker:** Int'l Exchange: |
| 2006 Sales: $1,924,628 | 2006 Profits: $97,189 | Employees: 1,876 |
| 2005 Sales: $1,761,091 | 2005 Profits: $101,270 | Fiscal Year Ends: 10/31 |
| 2004 Sales: $1,529,739 | 2004 Profits: $95,188 | Parent Company: |

## SALARIES/BENEFITS:

| | | | | |
|---|---|---|---|---|
| Pension Plan: Y | ESOP Stock Plan: Y | Profit Sharing: | Top Exec. Salary: $642,308 | Bonus: $278,329 |
| Savings Plan: Y | Stock Purch. Plan: | | Second Exec. Salary: $347,115 | Bonus: $117,477 |

## OTHER THOUGHTS:

**Apparent Women Officers or Directors**: 4
**Hot Spot for Advancement for Women/Minorities**: Y

## LOCATIONS: ("Y" = Yes)

| West: | Southwest: | Midwest: | Southeast: | Northeast: | International: |
|---|---|---|---|---|---|
| | | | Y | Y | |

# PIONEER NATURAL RESOURCES COMPANY

www.pioneernrc.com

**Industry Group Code:** 211111 **Ranks within this company's industry group:** Sales: 4 Profits: 6

| Management: | | Sales/Marketing: | | Liberal Arts: | | Information Systems: | | Professionals: | | Technical/Scientific: | |
|---|---|---|---|---|---|---|---|---|---|---|---|
| Mgmt. Trainees: | | Mktg. Professionals: | Y | Gen. Writing/Editing: | | Info. Management: | Y | Finance/Accounting: | Y | Engineers, Elec.: | |
| Experienced Mgmt.: | Y | Retail Sales: | | Technical Writing: | | Software Dev.: | | Law: | Y | Engineers, Other: | Y |
| Int'l Business: | Y | Commercial/Industrial: | Y | Graphic Arts/Photog.: | | Hardware Dev.: | | HR/Other: | Y | Health/Lab: | |
| MBA Graduates: | Y | Sales Trainees: | | Music: | | Systems Integration: | | Training: | Y | Scientists/Research: | |
| | | Advertising Pros.: | | Broadcasting: | | Consulting/Other: | | Health Care: | | Petroleum/Chemicals: | Y |
| | | | | Other: | | | | Consulting: | | Math/Other: | |

## TYPES OF BUSINESS:

Oil & Gas Exploration & Production

## BRANDS/DIVISIONS/AFFILIATES:

Pioneer Natural Resources USA, Inc.
Westpan Resources Company
Mesa Environmental Ventures Co.
Lorencito Gas Gathering, LLC
Long Canyon Gas Company, LLC
Petroleum South Cape (Pty) Ltd.
Midkiff Development Drilling Program, Ltd.

## CONTACTS:

*Note: Officers with more than one job title may be intentionally listed here more than once.*

Scott D. Sheffield, CEO
Timothy L. Dove, COO
Timothy L. Dove, Pres.
Richard P. Dealy, CFO/Exec. VP
Thomas C. Halbouty, CIO/VP
Larry N. Paulsen, VP-Admin. & Risk Mgmt.
Mark S. Berg, General Counsel/Exec. VP
Danny L. Kellum, Exec. VP-Domestic Oper.
William F. Hannes, Exec. VP- Bus. Dev.
Susan A. Spratlen, VP-Corp. Comm. & Public Affairs
Frank E. Hopkins, VP-Investor Rel.
Chris J. Cheatwood, Exec. VP-Geoscience
Jay P. Still, Exec. VP-Domestic Division
Roger W. Wallace, VP- Gov't Affairs
Mark H. Kleinman, Corp. Sec./Chief Compliance Officer/VP
Scott D. Sheffield, Chmn.
David McManus, VP-Int'l Oper.

| | |
|---|---|
| **Phone:** 972-444-9001 | **Fax:** 972-969-3576 |
| **Toll-Free:** | |
| **Address:** 5205 N. O'Connor Blvd., Ste. 200, Irving, TX 75039 US | |

## GROWTH PLANS/SPECIAL FEATURES:

Pioneer Natural Resources Company is one of the largest independent exploration and production companies in the U.S. The company owns interests in oil, NGL and gas properties located in the U.S., Canada, Equatorial Guinea, Nigeria, South Africa and Tunisia. The firm has total proved reserves of about 1 billion barrels of oil equivalent. Pioneer's operations are spread between domestic and international divisions. The domestic division includes the Spraberry field in west Texas; the Hugoton gas field in southwest Kansas and Oklahoma; the West Panhandle gas field in Texas; the Raton field gas operations in southern Colorado; tests and pilot programs in the Rocky Mountains; testing of unconventional gas plays in northern Louisiana and Mississippi; the Pawnee gas field production and exploration wells in the Edwards Reef expansion in southern Texas; and a 70% interest in the Oooguruk project on Alaska's north slope. The firm's international operations are centered in Canada, with gas production at Chinchaga and coal bed methane production at Horseshoe Canyon; and Africa, with exploration projects in Tunisia and offshore South Africa. The company focuses its production efforts toward increasing its average daily production of oil and gas through development drilling, production enhancement activities and acquisitions of producing properties. Pioneer's drilling activities seek to increase its oil and gas reserves, production and cash flow by concentrating on drilling low-risk development wells and by conducting additional development activities such as well recompletions. In August 2007, the company agreed to sell its Canadian subsidiary, Pioneer Natural Resources Canada, Inc., to Abu Dhabi National Energy Company PJSC for $540 million.

## FINANCIALS:

**Sales and profits are in thousands of dollars—add 000 to get the full amount. 2008 Note: Financial information for 2008 was not available for all companies at press time.**

| | | |
|---|---|---|
| 2008 Sales: $2,338,287 | 2008 Profits: $220,063 | **U.S. Stock Ticker: PXD** |
| 2007 Sales: $1,830,571 | 2007 Profits: $372,728 | **Int'l Ticker:** Int'l Exchange: |
| 2006 Sales: $1,500,871 | 2006 Profits: $739,700 | Employees: 1,702 |
| 2005 Sales: $1,544,600 | 2005 Profits: $534,568 | Fiscal Year Ends: 12/31 |
| 2004 Sales: $1,014,800 | 2004 Profits: $312,854 | Parent Company: |

## SALARIES/BENEFITS:

| | | | | |
|---|---|---|---|---|
| Pension Plan: | ESOP Stock Plan: | Profit Sharing: | Top Exec. Salary: $850,000 | Bonus: $1,147,500 |
| Savings Plan: Y | Stock Purch. Plan: | | Second Exec. Salary: $360,000 | Bonus: $850,000 |

## OTHER THOUGHTS:

**Apparent Women Officers or Directors**: 2
**Hot Spot for Advancement for Women/Minorities**: Y

## LOCATIONS: ("Y" = Yes)

| West: | Southwest: | Midwest: | Southeast: | Northeast: | International: |
|---|---|---|---|---|---|
| Y | Y | Y | Y | | Y |

# PITNEY BOWES MAPINFO

**www.mapinfo.com**

**Industry Group Code:** 511215 **Ranks within this company's industry group:** Sales: Profits:

| Management: | | Sales/Marketing: | | Liberal Arts: | | Information Systems: | | Professionals: | | Technical/Scientific: | |
|---|---|---|---|---|---|---|---|---|---|---|---|
| Mgmt. Trainees: | | Mktg. Professionals: | Y | Gen. Writing/Editing: | | Info. Management: | Y | Finance/Accounting: | Y | Engineers, Elec.: | Y |
| Experienced Mgmt.: | Y | Retail Sales: | | Technical Writing: | Y | Software Dev.: | Y | Law: | Y | Engineers, Other: | Y |
| Int'l Business: | Y | Commercial/Industrial: | Y | Graphic Arts/Photog.: | | Hardware Dev.: | | HR/Other: | Y | Health/Lab: | |
| MBA Graduates: | Y | Sales Trainees: | Y | Music: | | Systems Integration: | | Training: | Y | Scientists/Research: | |
| | | Advertising Pros.: | | Broadcasting: | | Consulting/Other: | | Health Care: | | Petroleum/Chemicals: | |
| | | | | Other: | | | | Consulting: | | Math/Other: | Y |

## TYPES OF BUSINESS:

Computer Software-Mapping & Geography
GIS Geographic Information Systems
Municipal Resource Planning
Consulting Services
Software Support Services
Data Analytics
Computer Network Planning

## BRANDS/DIVISIONS/AFFILIATES:

ExchangeInfo Plus
PSAP Pro
AnySite Financial
Envinsa
MapXtreme
MapInfo Professional
MarkeTech Systems, Inc.

## CONTACTS:

*Note: Officers with more than one job title may be intentionally listed here more than once.*

Michael J. Hickey, Pres.
Reid Hislop, VP-Corp. Mktg.
James Scott, VP-Eng.
Doug Gordon, Dir.-Strategy
Scott Landers, VP-Finance
Ben Semmes, VP-Global Svcs.
John C. Cavalier, Chmn.
John O'Hara, Exec. VP-Int'l

| | |
|---|---|
| **Phone:** 518-285-6000 | **Fax:** 518-285-6070 |
| **Toll-Free:** 800-327-8627 | |
| **Address:** 1 Global View, Troy, NY 12180 US | |

## GROWTH PLANS/SPECIAL FEATURES:

Pitney Bowes MapInfo (MapInfo) designs, develops, markets, licenses and supports mapping software products (GIS Geographic Information Systems) that use geography to solve problems relating to sales and marketing analysis, site selection, asset management, risk analysis, routing and logistics. MapInfo's business strategy emphasizes the development of software products for business mapping and spatial analysis, marketed through multiple channels of distribution. Products range from stand-alone software for the desktop PC to development tools for creating custom applications for PC, client/server, Internet and other networked environments. The firm's standards-based Envinsa enterprise location intelligence platform allows organizations to build location-based applications. MapInfo's regularly updated street and boundary data is available for key markets around the world. This data is designed for use in MapInfo applications for routing, drivetime studies, background information analysis and visualization. Boundary data maps are available for postal, political and industry-specific areas. MapInfo also offers worldwide demographic data products containing information such as population, income, expenditure, retail activity, employment, consumer trends, business and Internet summary data and lifestyle segmentation data. The company also offers custom modeling/profiling, data analytics and industry-specific data sets. The ExchangeInfo Plus product provides communications infrastructure data that enables service providers analyze the U.S. local telephone exchange system. The PSAP Pro product enables providers to plan routing of 911 calls to appropriate public safety departments. Customers include BT Group, Nortel Network, the NYPD and the FBI. MapInfo added James River Insurance, Steak n' Shake and several municipalities. In April 2007, the firm was acquired for $408 million by Pitney Bowes, Inc. In 2007, the firm acquired Graphical Data Capture, Ltd., a U.K. location intelligence provider, and Encom, which provides software and services for mineral and petroleum exploration.

## FINANCIALS:

**Sales and profits are in thousands of dollars—add 000 to get the full amount. 2008 Note: Financial information for 2008 was not available for all companies at press time.**

| | | |
|---|---|---|
| 2008 Sales: $ | 2008 Profits: $ | **U.S. Stock Ticker: Subsidiary** |
| 2007 Sales: $ | 2007 Profits: $ | **Int'l Ticker:** Int'l Exchange: |
| 2006 Sales: $165,495 | 2006 Profits: $9,661 | Employees: 900 |
| 2005 Sales: $149,424 | 2005 Profits: $10,235 | Fiscal Year Ends: 9/30 |
| 2004 Sales: $124,673 | 2004 Profits: $5,123 | Parent Company: PITNEY BOWES INC |

## SALARIES/BENEFITS:

| | | | | |
|---|---|---|---|---|
| Pension Plan: | ESOP Stock Plan: | Profit Sharing: | Top Exec. Salary: $450,000 | Bonus: $282,150 |
| Savings Plan: Y | Stock Purch. Plan: Y | | Second Exec. Salary: $283,640 | Bonus: $80,622 |

## OTHER THOUGHTS:

**Apparent Women Officers or Directors**: 1
**Hot Spot for Advancement for Women/Minorities**:

## LOCATIONS: ("Y" = Yes)

| West: | Southwest: | Midwest: | Southeast: | Northeast: | International: |
|---|---|---|---|---|---|
| | | Y | | Y | Y |

# PLAINS EXPLORATION AND PRODUCTION COMPANY

**www.plainsxp.com**

**Industry Group Code:** 211111 **Ranks within this company's industry group:** Sales: 7 Profits: 12

| **Management:** | | **Sales/Marketing:** | | **Liberal Arts:** | | **Information Systems:** | | **Professionals:** | | **Technical/Scientific:** | |
|---|---|---|---|---|---|---|---|---|---|---|---|
| Mgmt. Trainees: | | Mktg. Professionals: | Y | Gen. Writing/Editing: | | Info. Management: | Y | Finance/Accounting: | Y | Engineers, Elec.: | |
| Experienced Mgmt.: | Y | Retail Sales: | | Technical Writing: | | Software Dev.: | | Law: | Y | Engineers, Other: | Y |
| Int'l Business: | | Commercial/Industrial: | Y | Graphic Arts/Photog.: | | Hardware Dev.: | | HR/Other: | Y | Health/Lab: | |
| MBA Graduates: | Y | Sales Trainees: | | Music: | | Systems Integration: | | Training: | Y | Scientists/Research: | |
| | | Advertising Pros.: | | Broadcasting: | | Consulting/Other: | | Health Care: | | Petroleum/Chemicals: | Y |
| | | | | Other: | | | | Consulting: | | Math/Other: | |

## TYPES OF BUSINESS:

Oil & Gas Exploration & Production

## BRANDS/DIVISIONS/AFFILIATES:

Pogo Producing Co.

## CONTACTS: *Note: Officers with more than one job title may be intentionally listed here more than once.*

James C. Flores, CEO
James C. Flores, Pres.
Winston M. Talbert, CFO/Exec. VP
John F. Wombwell, General Counsel/Exec. VP/Sec.
Doss R. Bourgeois, Exec. VP-Exploration & Production
James C. Flores, Chmn.

| | |
|---|---|
| **Phone:** 713-579-6000 | **Fax:** 713-579-6500 |
| **Toll-Free:** 800-934-6083 | |
| **Address:** 700 Milam St., Ste. 3100, Houston, TX 77002 US | |

## GROWTH PLANS/SPECIAL FEATURES:

Plains Exploration and Production Company (PXP) acquires, develops, exploits, explores and produces oil and gas in the U.S. It owns properties in six states and has principal operations in the Los Angeles and San Joaquin Basins in California; the Santa Maria Basin offshore California; the Gulf Coast Basin onshore and offshore Louisiana, including the Gulf of Mexico; and the Piceance Basin in Colorado. The company's principal focus areas include mature properties with long-lived reserves as well as newer properties with development, exploitation and exploration potential. The firm has estimated proven reserves of approximately 352 million barrels of oil equivalent. About 63% of the company's production is in the form of heavy crude oil. The heavy crude is primarily sold to ConocoPhilips under a 15-year contract expiring in December 2014. Approximately 35% of the company's crude oil is sold through Plains All American Pipeline, L.P. In March 2008, one of PXP's subsidiaries agreed to acquire, from a private company, oil and gas producing properties in South Texas for $335 million. In June 2008, PXP agreed to acquire a 20% interest in Chesapeake's Haynesville Shale leasehold for $1.65 billion. In addition, PXP has agreed to fund 50% of Chesapeake's 80% share of drilling and completion costs for future Haynesville Shale JV wells over a several year period until an additional $1.65 billion has been paid. Also in June 2008, PXP announced it acquired crude oil put option contracts on 40,000 barrels of oil per day in 2009 and 2010. In September 2008, PXP agreed to sell its interests in oil and gas properties located in the Permian and Piceance Basins for $1.25 billion to Occidental Petroleum Corp.

## FINANCIALS: **Sales and profits are in thousands of dollars—add 000 to get the full amount. 2008 Note: Financial information for 2008 was not available for all companies at press time.**

| | | |
|---|---|---|
| 2008 Sales: $ | 2008 Profits: $ | **U.S. Stock Ticker: PXP** |
| 2007 Sales: $1,272,840 | 2007 Profits: $158,751 | **Int'l Ticker:** Int'l Exchange: |
| 2006 Sales: $1,018,503 | 2006 Profits: $597,528 | Employees: 775 |
| 2005 Sales: $944,420 | 2005 Profits: $-214,012 | Fiscal Year Ends: 12/31 |
| 2004 Sales: $671,706 | 2004 Profits: $8,840 | Parent Company: |

## SALARIES/BENEFITS:

| | | | | |
|---|---|---|---|---|
| Pension Plan: | ESOP Stock Plan: | Profit Sharing: | Top Exec. Salary: $966,667 | Bonus: $1,200,000 |
| Savings Plan: Y | Stock Purch. Plan: | | Second Exec. Salary: $500,000 | Bonus: $650,000 |

## OTHER THOUGHTS:

**Apparent Women Officers or Directors**:
**Hot Spot for Advancement for Women/Minorities**:

## LOCATIONS: ("Y" = Yes)

| West: | Southwest: | Midwest: | Southeast: | Northeast: | International: |
|---|---|---|---|---|---|
| Y | Y | | Y | | |

# PLUG POWER INC

www.plugpower.com

**Industry Group Code:** 333298 **Ranks within this company's industry group:** Sales: 3 Profits: 3

| Management: | | Sales/Marketing: | | Liberal Arts: | | Information Systems: | | Professionals: | | Technical/Scientific: | |
|---|---|---|---|---|---|---|---|---|---|---|---|
| Mgmt. Trainees: | | Mktg. Professionals: | Y | Gen. Writing/Editing: | | Info. Management: | Y | Finance/Accounting: | Y | Engineers, Elec.: | Y |
| Experienced Mgmt.: | Y | Retail Sales: | | Technical Writing: | Y | Software Dev.: | Y | Law: | Y | Engineers, Other: | Y |
| Int'l Business: | Y | Commercial/Industrial: | Y | Graphic Arts/Photog.: | | Hardware Dev.: | Y | HR/Other: | Y | Health/Lab: | |
| MBA Graduates: | Y | Sales Trainees: | Y | Music: | | Systems Integration: | | Training: | Y | Scientists/Research: | Y |
| | | Advertising Pros.: | | Broadcasting: | | Consulting/Other: | | Health Care: | | Petroleum/Chemicals: | |
| | | | | Other: | | | | Consulting: | | Math/Other: | Y |

## TYPES OF BUSINESS:

Fuel Cell Technology
Onsite Generation Systems
Proton Exchange Membrane Technology
Back-Up Power Systems

## BRANDS/DIVISIONS/AFFILIATES:

GenCore
GenSys On-site Power Systems
Gencore Power Back-up
Honda R&D Co., Ltd.
Cellex Power Products, Inc.
General Hydrogen Corp.

## CONTACTS: *Note: Officers with more than one job title may be intentionally listed here more than once.*

Andrew Marsh, CEO
Andrew Marsh, Pres.
Gerry A. Anderson, CFO
Mark A. Sperry, Chief Mktg. Officer/VP
Tammy Kimble, VP-Human Resources
Thomas M. Hutchison, VP-Eng.
Gerard L. Conway, Jr., General Counsel/Corp. Sec.
John Gartner, VP-Oper.
Katrina Fritz Intwala, VP-Gov't Rel./Mktg. Comm.
Allan Greenberg, VP-Sales
George C. McNamee, Chmn.

| | |
|---|---|
| **Phone:** 518-782-7700 | **Fax:** 518-782-9060 |
| **Toll-Free:** | |
| **Address:** 968 Albany-Shaker Rd., Latham, NY 12110 US | |

## GROWTH PLANS/SPECIAL FEATURES:

Plug Power, Inc. designs, develops and manufactures on-site electrical power generation systems incorporating proton exchange membrane (PEM) fuel cells for stationary applications. The company has established an extended enterprise through strategic relationships with marketing, technology, supply chain and government partners. The firm's initial product was a fully integrated, grid-parallel 5-kilowatt fuel cell system that operates on natural gas. It is being marketed to a select number of customers, including utilities, government entities and its distribution partners, GE Fuel Cell Systems and DTE Energy Technologies, Inc. The company currently has three major product offerings: on-site hydrogen generating systems, which provide pure, compressed hydrogen without the necessity of transporting hydrogen gas cylinders; GenCore Power Back-up systems, used to prevent gaps in electricity flow in industrial plant controls and telecommunications; and Gensys On-site Power Systems, which are designed, often for residential homes, to generate continuous power by converting available fuels into electricity and heat. The firm is also developing technology in support of the automotive fuel cell market under a series of agreements with Honda R&D Co., Ltd. of Japan. More than 650 Plug Power fuel cell systems have been delivered to customers worldwide in commercial, public sector, telecommunications, utility and uninterruptible power supply markets. The company's power backup systems have been installed for power and telecom utilities in Venezuela and South Africa. In October 2008, the company entered a supply agreement with Rittal, a supplier of housing and enclosure technology, to integrate GenCore fuel cell technology with Rittal enclosures to create RitCell5000, the first available hydrogen fuel cell solution.

The company offers its employees health and dental insurance; a 401(k) plan; life and disability insurance; an employee stock purchase plan; stock options; and education assistance.

## FINANCIALS: **Sales and profits are in thousands of dollars—add 000 to get the full amount. 2008 Note: Financial information for 2008 was not available for all companies at press time.**

| | | |
|---|---|---|
| 2008 Sales: $ | 2008 Profits: $ | **U.S. Stock Ticker: PLUG** |
| 2007 Sales: $16,271 | 2007 Profits: $-60,571 | **Int'l Ticker:** Int'l Exchange: |
| 2006 Sales: $7,836 | 2006 Profits: $-50,310 | Employees: 390 |
| 2005 Sales: $13,487 | 2005 Profits: $-51,743 | Fiscal Year Ends: 12/31 |
| 2004 Sales: $16,141 | 2004 Profits: $-46,739 | Parent Company: |

## SALARIES/BENEFITS:

| | | | | |
|---|---|---|---|---|
| Pension Plan: | ESOP Stock Plan: | Profit Sharing: | Top Exec. Salary: $325,000 | Bonus: $57,539 |
| Savings Plan: Y | Stock Purch. Plan: Y | | Second Exec. Salary: $249,616 | Bonus: $62,500 |

## OTHER THOUGHTS:

**Apparent Women Officers or Directors**: 2
**Hot Spot for Advancement for Women/Minorities**:

## LOCATIONS: ("Y" = Yes)

| West: | Southwest: | Midwest: | Southeast: | Northeast: | International: |
|---|---|---|---|---|---|
| | | | | Y | Y |

Note: Financial information, benefits and other data can change quickly and may vary from those stated here.

# PMA CAPITAL CORPORATION

www.pmacapital.com

**Industry Group Code:** 524126 **Ranks within this company's industry group:** Sales: 9 Profits: 9

| Management: | | Sales/Marketing: | | Liberal Arts: | | Information Systems: | | Professionals: | | Technical/Scientific: | |
|---|---|---|---|---|---|---|---|---|---|---|---|
| Mgmt. Trainees: | | Mktg. Professionals: | Y | Gen. Writing/Editing: | Y | Info. Management: | Y | Finance/Accounting: | Y | Engineers, Elec.: | |
| Experienced Mgmt.: | Y | Retail Sales: | | Technical Writing: | Y | Software Dev.: | | Law: | Y | Engineers, Other: | |
| Int'l Business: | | Commercial/Industrial: | Y | Graphic Arts/Photog.: | | Hardware Dev.: | | HR/Other: | Y | Health/Lab: | |
| MBA Graduates: | Y | Sales Trainees: | Y | Music: | | Systems Integration: | | Training: | Y | Scientists/Research: | |
| | | Advertising Pros.: | | Broadcasting: | | Consulting/Other: | | Health Care: | | Petroleum/Chemicals: | |
| | | | | Other: | | | | Consulting: | | Math/Other: | Y |

## TYPES OF BUSINESS:

Insurance, Direct Property & Casualty
Workers' Compensation Insurance
Auto Insurance
Specialty Insurance

## BRANDS/DIVISIONS/AFFILIATES:

PMA Insurance Group
MedRisk, Inc.
PMA Re Management Co.
Midlands Management Corporation
PMA Management Corp. of New England, Inc.

## CONTACTS: *Note: Officers with more than one job title may be intentionally listed here more than once.*

Vincent T. Donnelly, CEO
Vincent T. Donnelly, Pres.
William E. Hitselberger, CFO/Exec. VP
Jennifer Johnston, Sr. VP/Chief Strategic Mktg. Officer
Stephen Kibblehouse, General Counsel/Exec. VP
Neal C. Schneider, Chmn.

| | |
|---|---|
| **Phone:** 610-397-5298 | **Fax:** 610-397-5422 |
| **Toll-Free:** | |
| **Address:** 380 Sentry Pkwy., Blue Bell, PA 19422-0754 US | |

## GROWTH PLANS/SPECIAL FEATURES:

PMA Capital Corporation is an insurance holding company. PMA conducts business in the property and casualty insurance industry as PMA Insurance Group. The firm writes workers' compensation and other standard lines of commercial insurance, including commercial general liability, commercial automobile and commercial multi-peril, as well as related services to entities located in its 10-state marketing territory, concentrated in the mid-Atlantic and southern regions of the U.S. Customers currently include mid-sized and large manufacturing companies and banks, as well as construction entities, hospitality organizations and business services. The group focuses primarily on workers' compensation, only expanding into other types of coverage if it relates to that primary concern. Recently, the firm announced an alliance with MedRisk, Inc., in the hope that this partnership will reduce the costs associated with offering workers' compensation by giving their clients access to MedRisk's network of physical and occupational therapists. PMA Re Management Co., which is currently a run-off operation, used to write a broad range of property and casualty reinsurance products with an emphasis on risk-exposed casualty excess-of-loss reinsurance within the brokered market. Now PMA Re provides the firm with accounting, actuarial, administrative, claims-handling, legal, human resources and underwriting services. In October 2007, the company acquired Midlands Management Corporation for a price ranging from $22.8 million to $44.5 million, depending on Midlands performance over the next four years. Midlands is a managing general agent as well as being engaged in program administration and providing third party administrator services. In June 2008, the firm acquired Webster Risk Services for $5.9 million; Webster will be renamed PMA Management Corp. of New England, Inc.

Employees of PMA receive tuition assistance; group term life insurance as well as medical, dental and vision insurance coverage; a bonus for referring qualified potential team members to PMA; and $150 health club reimbursement.

## FINANCIALS: **Sales and profits are in thousands of dollars—add 000 to get the full amount. 2008 Note: Financial information for 2008 was not available for all companies at press time.**

| | | |
|---|---|---|
| 2008 Sales: $494,157 | 2008 Profits: $5,689 | **U.S. Stock Ticker: PMACA** |
| 2007 Sales: $455,777 | 2007 Profits: $-42,528 | **Int'l Ticker:** Int'l Exchange: |
| 2006 Sales: $432,590 | 2006 Profits: $4,051 | Employees: 1,221 |
| 2005 Sales: $443,096 | 2005 Profits: $-21,020 | Fiscal Year Ends: 12/31 |
| 2004 Sales: $612,724 | 2004 Profits: $1,830 | Parent Company: |

## SALARIES/BENEFITS:

| | | | | |
|---|---|---|---|---|
| Pension Plan: | ESOP Stock Plan: | Profit Sharing: Y | Top Exec. Salary: $696,250 | Bonus: $212,692 |
| Savings Plan: Y | Stock Purch. Plan: | | Second Exec. Salary: $425,000 | Bonus: $81,812 |

## OTHER THOUGHTS:

**Apparent Women Officers or Directors:** 2
**Hot Spot for Advancement for Women/Minorities:**

## LOCATIONS: ("Y" = Yes)

| West: | Southwest: | Midwest: | Southeast: | Northeast: | International: |
|---|---|---|---|---|---|
| | | | Y | Y | |

# POLYCOM INC

www.polycom.com

**Industry Group Code:** 334119 **Ranks within this company's industry group:** Sales: 1 Profits: 1

| Management: | | Sales/Marketing: | | Liberal Arts: | | Information Systems: | | Professionals: | | Technical/Scientific: | |
|---|---|---|---|---|---|---|---|---|---|---|---|
| Mgmt. Trainees: | | Mktg. Professionals: | Y | Gen. Writing/Editing: | | Info. Management: | Y | Finance/Accounting: | Y | Engineers, Elec.: | Y |
| Experienced Mgmt.: | Y | Retail Sales: | | Technical Writing: | Y | Software Dev.: | Y | Law: | Y | Engineers, Other: | Y |
| Int'l Business: | Y | Commercial/Industrial: | Y | Graphic Arts/Photog.: | Y | Hardware Dev.: | Y | HR/Other: | Y | Health/Lab: | |
| MBA Graduates: | Y | Sales Trainees: | Y | Music: | | Systems Integration: | Y | Training: | Y | Scientists/Research: | |
| | | Advertising Pros.: | | Broadcasting: | | Consulting/Other: | | Health Care: | | Petroleum/Chemicals: | |
| | | | | Other: | | | | Consulting: | | Math/Other: | |

## TYPES OF BUSINESS:

Communications Equipment & Software
Network Management Software
Professional Service & Support

## BRANDS/DIVISIONS/AFFILIATES:

Polycom RMX 2000
ReadiVoice
InnoVox 480
Acoustic Clarity Technology
SoundStructure
Vortex
Polycom Communicator Speakerphone
SpectraLink Corp

## CONTACTS:

*Note: Officers with more than one job title may be intentionally listed here more than once.*

Robert C. Hagerty, CEO
Robert C. Hagerty, Pres.
Michael R. Kourey, CFO/Sr. VP-Finance & Admin.
Heidi M. Melin, Chief Mktg. Officer/Sr. VP
Gary M. Zieses, Sr. VP-Human Resources
Sayed M. Darwish, Chief Admin. Officer
Sayed M. Darwish, General Counsel/VP/Corp. Sec.
Robert B. Steele, Sr. VP-Worldwide Oper.
Laura J. Durr, Principal Acct. Officer/Worldwide Controller/VP
Sunil K. Bhalla, Sr. VP/Gen. Mgr.-Voice Comm.
Joseph A. Sigrist, Sr. VP/Gen. Mgr.-Video Solutions Bus.
David R. Phillips, Sr. VP-Worldwide Sales
Donald J. Floyd, VP-Internal Audit
Robert C. Hagerty, Chmn.
Geno J. Alissi, Sr. VP/Gen. Mgr.-Global Svcs.

**Phone:** 925-924-6000 **Fax:** 925-924-6100
**Toll-Free:** 800-765-9266
**Address:** 4750 Willow Rd., Pleasanton, CA 94588-2708 US

## GROWTH PLANS/SPECIAL FEATURES:

Polycom, Inc. is a global provider of communications equipment that enables enterprise users to conduct video, voice, data and web communications. The company operates in four segments: Video solutions, which generated 53% of its revenue in 2007 and includes video communications products and network systems products; voice communications, which accounted for 34% of revenue and includes its conference phone, wired desktop voice products and wireless handset voice products; and services, which accounted for 13% of revenue and includes professional service and support offerings. Polycom's family of high definition (HD) and standard definition video conferencing products and HD telepresence solutions encompasses a range of offerings from entry level to professional high definition products. Its Polycom HDX, VSX and V-series product lines consist of a suite of high-performance group and desktop video conferencing systems. The firm's Polycom PVX desktop video software application extends professional-grade video conferencing to the desktop or laptop computer. The Polycom RMX 2000 HD unified conferencing platform is a real-time media conferencing platform that provides conferencing infrastructure to support emerging video applications such as desktop collaboration, video over cellular networks, high definition and telepresence. Polycom's ReadiVoice conferencing solution is a reservationless voice conferencing system operating on the InnoVox 480 and 4000 media servers. Most of the company's voice products feature its patented Acoustic Clarity Technology, which allows simultaneous conversations and minimizes background noise, echoes, word clipping and distortion. Its SoundStructure and Vortex series of installed voice conferencing products provide solutions for larger, high-end conference rooms, training rooms, auditoriums, courtrooms, classrooms and other permanent installations. The Polycom Communicator Speakerphone is the firm's initial entry into the PC-based Voice and Video over Internet Protocol (V2oIP) and Voice over Instant Messaging (VoIM) markets. In March 2007, the firm acquired SpectraLink Corp., a manufacturer of on-premises wireless telephone systems, for roughly $220 million.

## FINANCIALS:

**Sales and profits are in thousands of dollars—add 000 to get the full amount. 2008 Note: Financial information for 2008 was not available for all companies at press time.**

| | | |
|---|---|---|
| 2008 Sales: $ | 2008 Profits: $ | **U.S. Stock Ticker: PLCM** |
| 2007 Sales: $929,908 | 2007 Profits: $62,881 | **Int'l Ticker:** Int'l Exchange: |
| 2006 Sales: $682,385 | 2006 Profits: $71,924 | Employees: 2,478 |
| 2005 Sales: $580,659 | 2005 Profits: $62,745 | Fiscal Year Ends: 12/31 |
| 2004 Sales: $540,252 | 2004 Profits: $35,349 | Parent Company: |

## SALARIES/BENEFITS:

| | | | | |
|---|---|---|---|---|
| Pension Plan: | ESOP Stock Plan: | Profit Sharing: | Top Exec. Salary: $575,000 | Bonus: $564,075 |
| Savings Plan: | Stock Purch. Plan: | | Second Exec. Salary: $399,700 | Bonus: $274,474 |

## OTHER THOUGHTS:

**Apparent Women Officers or Directors**: 3
**Hot Spot for Advancement for Women/Minorities**: Y

## LOCATIONS: ("Y" = Yes)

| West: | Southwest: | Midwest: | Southeast: | Northeast: | International: |
|---|---|---|---|---|---|
| Y | Y | Y | Y | Y | Y |

Note: Financial information, benefits and other data can change quickly and may vary from those stated here.

# POLYMEDICA CORPORATION

www.polymedica.com

**Industry Group Code:** 339113 **Ranks within this company's industry group:** Sales: 1 Profits: 6

| Management: | | Sales/Marketing: | | Liberal Arts: | | Information Systems: | | Professionals: | | Technical/Scientific: | |
|---|---|---|---|---|---|---|---|---|---|---|---|
| Mgmt. Trainees: | | Mktg. Professionals: | Y | Gen. Writing/Editing: | | Info. Management: | Y | Finance/Accounting: | Y | Engineers, Elec.: | |
| Experienced Mgmt.: | Y | Retail Sales: | | Technical Writing: | Y | Software Dev.: | Y | Law: | Y | Engineers, Other: | Y |
| Int'l Business: | Y | Commercial/Industrial: | Y | Graphic Arts/Photog.: | | Hardware Dev.: | | HR/Other: | Y | Health/Lab: | Y |
| MBA Graduates: | Y | Sales Trainees: | Y | Music: | | Systems Integration: | | Training: | Y | Scientists/Research: | Y |
| | | Advertising Pros.: | | Broadcasting: | | Consulting/Other: | | Health Care: | Y | Petroleum/Chemicals: | |
| | | | | Other: | | | | Consulting: | | Math/Other: | Y |

## TYPES OF BUSINESS:

Equipment-Insulin & Related Products
Diabetes Testing Supplies
Prescription Respiratory Products
Prescription Oral Medications
Urology & Suppository Products
Home Diagnostic Kits

## BRANDS/DIVISIONS/AFFILIATES:

Liberty Diabetes
National Diabetic Pharmacies, LLC
IntelliCare, Inc.

## CONTACTS: *Note: Officers with more than one job title may be intentionally listed here more than once.*

Patrick T. Ryan, CEO
Keith W. Jones, COO
Stephen C. Farrell, Pres.
Jonathan A. Starr, CFO
Devin J. Anderson, General Counsel/Sec.
Thomas O. Pyle, Chmn.

| **Phone:** 781-486-8111 | **Fax:** 781-938-6950 |
|---|---|
| **Toll-Free:** | |
| **Address:** 701 Edgewater Dr., Ste. 360, Wakefield, MA 01880 US | |

## GROWTH PLANS/SPECIAL FEATURES:

PolyMedica Corporation is a leading provider of direct-to-consumer medical products, conducting business through two segments: Diabetes and Pharmacy. The larger segment, Diabetes, sells insulin, syringes and other products primarily to Medicare-eligible customers suffering from diabetes and related chronic diseases. These products are sold under the brand name Liberty. Also, the company began distribution of a second private-label AgaMatrix/Liberty brand blood glucose monitor in 2007 to complement its private label relationship with Abbott Diabetes Care. The pharmaceuticals segment provides prescription oral medications not covered by Medicare and sells prescription urology and suppository products, over-the-counter female urinary discomfort products and AZO home medical diagnostic kits. The company offers its pharmaceuticals through both prescription drug plans and Medicare Advantage prescription plans to approximately 943,000 existing Diabetes patients and their spouses. PolyMedica attracts new patients through direct mail and targeted television, Internet and print advertising, in addition to physician referrals, business partner relationships, and the acquisition of competitors and by acting as a service provider to members of commercial health plans. PolyMedica's direct-mail program serves approximately 875,000 customers throughout the country. Following its recent acquisition of IntelliCare, Inc., PolyMedica provides healthcare communication services and technology solutions that enhance patient care communications by offering medical call and contact center services and technology solutions focused on electronic patient relationship management. In October 2007, PolyMedica was acquired by Medco Health Solutions, Inc. for approximately $1.5 billion.

## FINANCIALS: **Sales and profits are in thousands of dollars—add 000 to get the full amount. 2008 Note: Financial information for 2008 was not available for all companies at press time.**

| | | |
|---|---|---|
| 2008 Sales: $ | 2008 Profits: $ | **U.S. Stock Ticker: Subsidiary** |
| 2007 Sales: $675,487 | 2007 Profits: $33,672 | **Int'l Ticker:** Int'l Exchange: |
| 2006 Sales: $491,515 | 2006 Profits: $60,398 | Employees: 2,180 |
| 2005 Sales: $451,467 | 2005 Profits: $32,434 | Fiscal Year Ends: 3/31 |
| 2004 Sales: $419,694 | 2004 Profits: $37,932 | Parent Company: MEDCO HEALTH SOLUTIONS |

## SALARIES/BENEFITS:

| | | | | |
|---|---|---|---|---|
| Pension Plan: | ESOP Stock Plan: | Profit Sharing: | Top Exec. Salary: $696,713 | Bonus: $ |
| Savings Plan: Y | Stock Purch. Plan: | | Second Exec. Salary: $395,299 | Bonus: $ |

## OTHER THOUGHTS:

**Apparent Women Officers or Directors:**
**Hot Spot for Advancement for Women/Minorities:**

## LOCATIONS: ("Y" = Yes)

| West: | Southwest: | Midwest: | Southeast: | Northeast: | International: |
|---|---|---|---|---|---|
| | Y | Y | Y | Y | |

# POLYPORE INTERNATIONAL INC

www.polypore.net

**Industry Group Code:** 326100 **Ranks within this company's industry group:** Sales: 1 Profits: 1

| Management: | | Sales/Marketing: | | Liberal Arts: | | Information Systems: | | Professionals: | | Technical/Scientific: | |
|---|---|---|---|---|---|---|---|---|---|---|---|
| Mgmt. Trainees: | | Mktg. Professionals: | | Gen. Writing/Editing: | | Info. Management: | Y | Finance/Accounting: | Y | Engineers, Elec.: | |
| Experienced Mgmt.: | Y | Retail Sales: | | Technical Writing: | Y | Software Dev.: | | Law: | Y | Engineers, Other: | |
| Int'l Business: | Y | Commercial/Industrial: | | Graphic Arts/Photog.: | | Hardware Dev.: | | HR/Other: | Y | Health/Lab: | |
| MBA Graduates: | Y | Sales Trainees: | | Music: | | Systems Integration: | | Training: | Y | Scientists/Research: | |
| | | Advertising Pros.: | | Broadcasting: | | Consulting/Other: | | Health Care: | | Petroleum/Chemicals: | |
| | | | | Other: | | | | Consulting: | | Math/Other: | |

## TYPES OF BUSINESS:

Polymer-Based Membranes
Battery Separators
Medical Equipment
Filtration Membranes

## BRANDS/DIVISIONS/AFFILIATES:

Celgard LLC
Daramic LLC
Membrana GmbH
Liqui-Cel
SuperPhobic
Accurel
MicroPes
DuraPes

## CONTACTS:

*Note: Officers with more than one job title may be intentionally listed here more than once.*

Robert B. Toth, CEO
Robert B. Toth, Pres.
Lynn Amos, CFO
John O'Malley, Sr. VP-Human Resources
Phillip Bryson, General Counsel
Lynn Amos, Investor Rel.
Lynn Amos, Treas.
Mitch Pulwer, VP/Gen. Mgr.-Celgard, LLC
Pierre Hauswald, VP/Gen Mgr.-Daramic, LLC
Josef Sauer, VP/Gen Mgr.-Membrana GmbH
Michael Graff, Chmn.

| **Phone:** 704-587-8409 | **Fax:** 704-587-8796 |
|---|---|
| **Toll-Free:** | |
| **Address:** 11430 N. Community House Rd., Ste. 350, Charlotte, NC 28277-1591 US | |

## GROWTH PLANS/SPECIAL FEATURES:

Polypore International, Inc. is a leading developer, manufacturer and marketer of polymer-based microporous membranes used in separation and filtration processes. The company operates in two business segments: energy storage and separations media. The energy storage segment makes membranes for use as separators in lead-acid and lithium batteries, accounting for approximately 71% of the firm's total sales. These products are manufactured and distributed by two subsidiaries: Celgard LLC and Daramic LLC, the global leader in battery separators. Polypore's separations media segment includes subsidiary Membrana GmbH and the Liqui-Cel brand. Liqui-Cel makes degassing membranes and modules used for de-aeration of liquids in the microelectronics, pharmaceutical, power, food and beverage, industrial, photographic, ink and analytical chemistry markets. Membrana makes membranes for use in medical and industrial filtration systems and is a leading provider of medical membranes for applications such as dialysis, oxygenation and plasma separation. Other Polypore brand names include Accurel polypropylene membranes for potable water filtration; SuperPhobic membrane contactors that eliminate microbubbles in liquids; and MicroPes and DuraPes sulphonated polyethersulfone flat sheet membranes used in ultrapure water and chemical filtration. The separations media segment accounts for 29% of sales. Polypore operates 11 manufacturing sites and 13 sales offices in the Americas, Europe and Asia. In March 2008, the company's subsidiary, Daramic, acquired Microporous Holding Corporation for approximately $76 million. In May 2008, the firm, through its subsidiary Celgard, acquired the South Korean company Yurie-Wide Corporation for roughly $23 million.

## FINANCIALS:

**Sales and profits are in thousands of dollars—add 000 to get the full amount. 2008 Note: Financial information for 2008 was not available for all companies at press time.**

| | | |
|---|---|---|
| 2008 Sales: $ | 2008 Profits: $ | **U.S. Stock Ticker: PPO** |
| 2007 Sales: $537,100 | 2007 Profits: $ 500 | **Int'l Ticker:** Int'l Exchange: |
| 2006 Sales: $479,700 | 2006 Profits: $-29,600 | Employees: 1,800 |
| 2005 Sales: $432,500 | 2005 Profits: $-2,900 | Fiscal Year Ends: 12/31 |
| 2004 Sales: $ | 2004 Profits: $ | Parent Company: |

## SALARIES/BENEFITS:

| | | | | |
|---|---|---|---|---|
| Pension Plan: Y | ESOP Stock Plan: | Profit Sharing: | Top Exec. Salary: $525,000 | Bonus: $703,500 |
| Savings Plan: Y | Stock Purch. Plan: | | Second Exec. Salary: $281,549 | Bonus: $270,000 |

## OTHER THOUGHTS:

**Apparent Women Officers or Directors**: 1
**Hot Spot for Advancement for Women/Minorities**:

## LOCATIONS: ("Y" = Yes)

| West: | Southwest: | Midwest: | Southeast: | Northeast: | International: |
|---|---|---|---|---|---|
| | | Y | Y | Y | Y |

# PREMIERE GLOBAL SERVICES INC

**www.premiereglobal.com**

**Industry Group Code:** 514191A **Ranks within this company's industry group:** Sales: 2 Profits: 4

| Management: | | Sales/Marketing: | | Liberal Arts: | | Information Systems: | | Professionals: | | Technical/Scientific: | |
|---|---|---|---|---|---|---|---|---|---|---|---|
| Mgmt. Trainees: | | Mktg. Professionals: | Y | Gen. Writing/Editing: | | Info. Management: | Y | Finance/Accounting: | Y | Engineers, Elec.: | Y |
| Experienced Mgmt.: | Y | Retail Sales: | | Technical Writing: | Y | Software Dev.: | Y | Law: | Y | Engineers, Other: | |
| Int'l Business: | Y | Commercial/Industrial: | Y | Graphic Arts/Photog.: | | Hardware Dev.: | | HR/Other: | Y | Health/Lab: | |
| MBA Graduates: | Y | Sales Trainees: | Y | Music: | | Systems Integration: | Y | Training: | Y | Scientists/Research: | |
| | | Advertising Pros.: | | Broadcasting: | | Consulting/Other: | | Health Care: | | Petroleum/Chemicals: | |
| | | | | Other: | | | | Consulting: | | Math/Other: | |

## TYPES OF BUSINESS:

Message Management & Distribution Services
Conferencing Services
Document Management
Automated Marketing

## BRANDS/DIVISIONS/AFFILIATES:

Premiere Global Communications Operating System
Fax2Mail
PGiConnect.com

## CONTACTS: *Note: Officers with more than one job title may be intentionally listed here more than once.*

Boland T. Jones, CEO
Theodore P. Schrafft, Pres.
Michael E. Havener, CFO
Mark Alexander, Exec. VP-Sales & Mktg.
Erik Petrik, Chief People Officer
David M. Guthrie, CTO/Exec. VP
Scott Askins Leonard, General Counsel/Sec./Sr. VP-Legal
Michele Dobnikar, Exec. VP-Global Service Oper. & Delivery
Joel Hughey, Sr. VP-Mergers & Acquisitions
Randolph W. Salisbury, Chief Comm. Officer
Sean O'Brien, Sr. VP-Investor Rel. & Strategic Planning
Debbie McSheffrey, Treas.
John Stone, Managing Dir.-Europe
Michael Dickerson, Sr. VP/Gen. Mgr.-eMarketing Solutions
Randy Leigh, Sr. VP/CTO-Conferencing Solutions
Frank Gorkis, Sr. VP-Sales Oper. & Dev.
Boland T. Jones, Chmn.
Dennis Choo, Managing Dir.-Asia Pacific

**Phone:** 404-262-8400 **Fax:** 404-262-8525
**Toll-Free:**
**Address:** The Terminus Bldg, 3280 Peachtree Rd. NW, Ste 1000, Atlanta, GA 30305 US

## GROWTH PLANS/SPECIAL FEATURES:

Premiere Global Services, Inc. (PGS) provides integrated communications systems to 50,000 corporate customers in 23 countries. It recently restructured, changing from its former organization consisting of two business segments, Data Communications and Conferencing & Collaboration, into a new structure that is organized geographically. All of the firm's offerings are grouped under the Premiere Global Communications Operating System (PGiCOS), which is subdivided into five solutions sets. These solution sets comprise Conferencing and Collaboration Solutions, especially VoIP (Voice over Internet Protocol) and web collaboration services for large audio conferences; Desktop Document Solutions, including e-mail-based application Fax2Mail; Enterprise Document Solutions, including an automated application for digitizing paper documents; Notifications & Reminder Solutions, a tool for businesses to send voice, e-mail, fax and other updates and alerts to customers, such as regarding flight delays; and eMarketing Solutions, an e-mail marketing campaign tool. In April 2007, PGS launched pgiconnect.com, a self-service Web portal to access and utilize the PGiCOS. In May 2007, the PGi Netspoke Web conferencing product was upgraded by integrating the international calling capabilities of ReadyConference GlobalMeet and enabling customers with a unique, self-service conferencing management tool. In July 2007, PGS acquired Budget Conferencing, a Canadian-based audio and web conferencing services provider, for $19.8 million. In November 2007, the firm acquired Meet24, a Nordic-based conferencing and web collaboration provider, for $26.3 million.

## FINANCIALS: **Sales and profits are in thousands of dollars—add 000 to get the full amount. 2008 Note: Financial information for 2008 was not available for all companies at press time.**

| | | |
|---|---|---|
| 2008 Sales: $624,228 | 2008 Profits: $36,103 | **U.S. Stock Ticker: PGI** |
| 2007 Sales: $559,706 | 2007 Profits: $33,355 | **Int'l Ticker:** Int'l Exchange: |
| 2006 Sales: $496,472 | 2006 Profits: $25,509 | Employees: 2,430 |
| 2005 Sales: $497,473 | 2005 Profits: $47,417 | Fiscal Year Ends: 12/31 |
| 2004 Sales: $449,371 | 2004 Profits: $41,880 | Parent Company: |

## SALARIES/BENEFITS:

| | | | | |
|---|---|---|---|---|
| Pension Plan: | ESOP Stock Plan: | Profit Sharing: | Top Exec. Salary: $900,000 | Bonus: $1,035,000 |
| Savings Plan: Y | Stock Purch. Plan: | | Second Exec. Salary: $450,000 | Bonus: $330,030 |

## OTHER THOUGHTS:

**Apparent Women Officers or Directors**: 7
**Hot Spot for Advancement for Women/Minorities**: Y

## LOCATIONS: ("Y" = Yes)

| West: | Southwest: | Midwest: | Southeast: | Northeast: | International: |
|---|---|---|---|---|---|
| Y | | Y | Y | Y | Y |

# PRIMEENERGY CORPORATION

www.primeenergy.com

**Industry Group Code:** 211111 **Ranks within this company's industry group:** Sales: 21 Profits: 20

| Management: | | Sales/Marketing: | | Liberal Arts: | | Information Systems: | | Professionals: | | Technical/Scientific: | |
|---|---|---|---|---|---|---|---|---|---|---|---|
| Mgmt. Trainees: | | Mktg. Professionals: | Y | Gen. Writing/Editing: | | Info. Management: | Y | Finance/Accounting: | Y | Engineers, Elec.: | |
| Experienced Mgmt.: | Y | Retail Sales: | | Technical Writing: | | Software Dev.: | | Law: | Y | Engineers, Other: | Y |
| Int'l Business: | Y | Commercial/Industrial: | Y | Graphic Arts/Photog.: | | Hardware Dev.: | | HR/Other: | Y | Health/Lab: | |
| MBA Graduates: | Y | Sales Trainees: | | Music: | | Systems Integration: | | Training: | Y | Scientists/Research: | |
| | | Advertising Pros.: | | Broadcasting: | | Consulting/Other: | | Health Care: | | Petroleum/Chemicals: | Y |
| | | | | Other: | | | | Consulting: | | Math/Other: | |

## TYPES OF BUSINESS:

Oil & Gas Exploration & Production
Oil Field Services & Construction

## BRANDS/DIVISIONS/AFFILIATES:

PrimeEnergy Management Corporation
Prime Operating Company
Southwest Oilfield Construction Company
EOWS Midland Company
Eastern Oil Well Service Company

## CONTACTS: *Note: Officers with more than one job title may be intentionally listed here more than once.*

Charles E. Drimal, Jr., CEO
Charles E. Drimal, Jr., Pres.
Beverly A. Cummings, CFO
James F. Gilbert, Corp. Sec.
Beverly A. Cummings, Treas./Exec. VP

| **Phone:** 203-358-5700 | **Fax:** 203-358-5786 |
|---|---|
| **Toll-Free:** | |
| **Address:** 1 Landmark Sq., Stamford, CT 06901 US | |

## GROWTH PLANS/SPECIAL FEATURES:

PrimeEnergy Corporation is engaged in the acquisition, exploration, development and production of crude oil and natural gas. The company currently operates oil and gas wells primarily located in Texas, Oklahoma, the Gulf of Mexico, New Mexico, Colorado, Louisiana and West Virginia. Subsidiary PrimeEnergy Management Corporation (PEMC) acts as the managing general partner in 18 oil and gas limited partnerships and as the managing trustee of two asset and income business trusts. As such, PEMC is responsible for all partnership and trust activities, including the review and analysis of oil and gas properties for acquisition, the drilling of development wells and the production and sale of oil and gas from producing wells. Through its wholly-owned subsidiaries, Prime Operating Company; Southwest Oilfield Construction Company; EOWS Midland Company; and Eastern Oil Well Service Company, PrimeEnergy provides well servicing support operations and acts as operator for many of the onshore oil and gas wells in which the company has an interest, as well as for third parties. The firm also acquires producing oil and gas properties through joint ventures with industry partners and private investors. Southwest Oilfield Construction Company serves both PrimeEnergy and third parties with site preparation and construction services for oil and gas drilling and re-working operations. The firm has proved reserves of approximately 66 billion cubic feet equivalent of gas, 97% of which was developed, while 3% was still undeveloped. At present, the company does not own any refineries or marketing or bulk storage facilities and the only owned pipelines are those used in connection with producing wells and the interests in certain gas gathering systems.

## FINANCIALS: **Sales and profits are in thousands of dollars—add 000 to get the full amount. 2008 Note: Financial information for 2008 was not available for all companies at press time.**

| | | |
|---|---|---|
| 2008 Sales: $ | 2008 Profits: $ | **U.S. Stock Ticker: PNRG** |
| 2007 Sales: $146,455 | 2007 Profits: $7,590 | **Int'l Ticker:** Int'l Exchange: |
| 2006 Sales: $92,059 | 2006 Profits: $18,300 | Employees: 233 |
| 2005 Sales: $75,946 | 2005 Profits: $25,955 | Fiscal Year Ends: 12/31 |
| 2004 Sales: $62,428 | 2004 Profits: $7,275 | Parent Company: |

## SALARIES/BENEFITS:

| | | | | |
|---|---|---|---|---|
| Pension Plan: | ESOP Stock Plan: | Profit Sharing: | Top Exec. Salary: $279,753 | Bonus: $1,100,000 |
| Savings Plan: Y | Stock Purch. Plan: | | Second Exec. Salary: $279,753 | Bonus: $440,000 |

## OTHER THOUGHTS:

**Apparent Women Officers or Directors**: 1
**Hot Spot for Advancement for Women/Minorities**:

## LOCATIONS: ("Y" = Yes)

| West: | Southwest: | Midwest: | Southeast: | Northeast: | International: |
|---|---|---|---|---|---|
| Y | Y | Y | Y | Y | |

# PROASSURANCE CORP

www.proassurance.com

**Industry Group Code:** 524126 **Ranks within this company's industry group:** Sales: 8 Profits: 6

| Management: | | Sales/Marketing: | | Liberal Arts: | | Information Systems: | | Professionals: | | Technical/Scientific: | |
|---|---|---|---|---|---|---|---|---|---|---|---|
| Mgmt. Trainees: | | Mktg. Professionals: | Y | Gen. Writing/Editing: | Y | Info. Management: | Y | Finance/Accounting: | Y | Engineers, Elec.: | |
| Experienced Mgmt.: | Y | Retail Sales: | | Technical Writing: | Y | Software Dev.: | | Law: | Y | Engineers, Other: | |
| Int'l Business: | | Commercial/Industrial: | Y | Graphic Arts/Photog.: | | Hardware Dev.: | | HR/Other: | Y | Health/Lab: | |
| MBA Graduates: | Y | Sales Trainees: | Y | Music: | | Systems Integration: | | Training: | Y | Scientists/Research: | |
| | | Advertising Pros.: | | Broadcasting: | | Consulting/Other: | | Health Care: | | Petroleum/Chemicals: | |
| | | | | Other: | | | | Consulting: | | Math/Other: | Y |

## TYPES OF BUSINESS:

Professional Liability Insurance
Medical Liability Insurance

## BRANDS/DIVISIONS/AFFILIATES:

Medical Assurance, Inc.
ProNational Insurance Company
NRIC Insurance Company, Inc.
Physicians Insurance Company of Wisconsin, Inc.
Red Mountain Casualty Insurance Company, Inc.
WoodBrook Casualty Insurance, Inc.

## CONTACTS: *Note: Officers with more than one job title may be intentionally listed here more than once.*

W. Stancil Starnes, CEO
Victor T. Adamo, Pres.
Edward L. Rand, Jr., CFO/Sr. VP
Jeffrey L. Bowlby, Chief Mktg. Officer/Sr. VP
Jeffrey P. Lisenby, Legal Counsel/Corp. Sec./VP
Frank B. O'Neil, Sr. VP-Corp. Comm.
Frank B. O'Neil, Sr. VP-Investor Rel.
James J. Morello, Treas./Chief Acct. Officer/Sr. VP
Howard H. Friedman, Chief Underwriting Officer/Chief Actuary/Sr. VP
Hayes V. Whiteside, Sr. VP/Medical Dir.
Darryl K. Thoman, Chief Claims Officer/Sr. VP

**Phone:** 205-877-4400 **Fax:** 205-868-4073
**Toll-Free:** 800-282-6242
**Address:** 100 Brookwood Pl., Birmingham, AL 35209 US

## GROWTH PLANS/SPECIAL FEATURES:

ProAssurance Corp. is a holding firm for property and casualty insurance companies focused on professional liability insurance. The company sells professional liability insurance primarily to physicians, dentists, other healthcare providers and healthcare facilities, mainly in the mid-Atlantic, Midwest and Southeast. The firm also has a small book of legal professional liability business in the Midwest. ProAssurance generates the majority of its premiums from individual and small group practices, but also insures major physician groups as well as hospitals. The company's top five states (Ohio, Alabama, Florida, Michigan and Wisconsin) represented 55% of its gross premiums for 2007. The company maintains 15 local claims and underwriting offices throughout the country, in order to keep a local market presence. ProAssurance's subsidiaries include Medical Assurance, Inc.; ProNational Insurance Company; NRIC Insurance Company, Inc.; Physicians Insurance Company of Wisconsin, Inc.; and Red Mountain Casualty Insurance Company, Inc. While most of the firm's business is written in the standard market, subsidiary Red Mountain offers medical professional liability insurance on an excess and surplus lines basis. The company also writes a limited amount of medical professional liability insurance through non-core subsidiary Woodbrook Casualty Insurance, Inc. (formerly Medical Assurance of West Virginia, Inc.). The firm offers professional office package and workers' compensation insurance products in connection with its medical professional liability products. ProAssurance is licensed to do business in every state but Connecticut, Maine, New Hampshire, New York and Vermont.

## FINANCIALS: **Sales and profits are in thousands of dollars—add 000 to get the full amount. 2008 Note: Financial information for 2008 was not available for all companies at press time.**

2008 Sales: $
2007 Sales: $706,068
2006 Sales: $737,598
2005 Sales: $647,950
2004 Sales: $607,557

2008 Profits: $
2007 Profits: $168,186
2006 Profits: $236,425
2005 Profits: $113,457
2004 Profits: $72,811

**U.S. Stock Ticker: PRA**
**Int'l Ticker:** Int'l Exchange:
Employees: 587
Fiscal Year Ends: 12/31
Parent Company:

## SALARIES/BENEFITS:

Pension Plan: ESOP Stock Plan: Profit Sharing: Top Exec. Salary: $713,200 Bonus: $407,371
Savings Plan: Stock Purch. Plan: Second Exec. Salary: $498,846 Bonus: $398,825

## OTHER THOUGHTS:

**Apparent Women Officers or Directors:**
**Hot Spot for Advancement for Women/Minorities:**

## LOCATIONS: ("Y" = Yes)

| West: | Southwest: | Midwest: | Southeast: | Northeast: | International: |
|---|---|---|---|---|---|
| | | Y | Y | Y | |

# PROGRESS SOFTWARE CORP

www.progress.com

**Industry Group Code:** 511204 **Ranks within this company's industry group:** Sales: 1 Profits: 2

| Management: | | Sales/Marketing: | | Liberal Arts: | | Information Systems: | | Professionals: | | Technical/Scientific: | |
|---|---|---|---|---|---|---|---|---|---|---|---|
| Mgmt. Trainees: | | Mktg. Professionals: | Y | Gen. Writing/Editing: | | Info. Management: | Y | Finance/Accounting: | Y | Engineers, Elec.: | Y |
| Experienced Mgmt.: | Y | Retail Sales: | | Technical Writing: | Y | Software Dev.: | Y | Law: | Y | Engineers, Other: | |
| Int'l Business: | Y | Commercial/Industrial: | | Graphic Arts/Photog.: | | Hardware Dev.: | | HR/Other: | Y | Health/Lab: | |
| MBA Graduates: | Y | Sales Trainees: | Y | Music: | | Systems Integration: | | Training: | Y | Scientists/Research: | |
| | | Advertising Pros.: | | Broadcasting: | | Consulting/Other: | | Health Care: | | Petroleum/Chemicals: | |
| | | | | Other: | | | | Consulting: | | Math/Other: | Y |

## TYPES OF BUSINESS:

Software-Application Development & Integration
Application Management Software
Consulting & Technical Support Services
Data Connectivity Products
Data Management Software
Research & Development

## BRANDS/DIVISIONS/AFFILIATES:

Progress OpenEdge
Progress Apama
Progress Sonic
Progress Actional
DataDirect Shadow
DataDirect Connect
Progress EasyAsk
Project ObjectStore

## CONTACTS: *Note: Officers with more than one job title may be intentionally listed here more than once.*

Joseph W. Alsop, CEO
Richard D. Reidy, COO
Norman R. Robertson, CFO
Gary Conway, Chief Mktg. Officer/Sr. VP
Joseph A. Andrews, VP-Human Resources
Gordon Van Huizen, CTO
Norman R. Robertson, Sr. VP-Admin.
James D. Freedman, General Counsel/Sr. VP
Jeffrey Stamen, Sr. VP-Corp. Dev. & Strategy
Norman R. Robertson, Sr. VP-Finance
Larry R. Harris, VP/Gen. Mgr.-EasyAsk Prod.
David Ireland, Exec. VP, Progress Software Corp.
Peter Sliwkowski, VP-Product & Support Oper.
Michael L. Mark, Chmn.

| Phone: 781-280-4000 | Fax: |
|---|---|
| Toll-Free: 800-477-6473 | |
| Address: 14 Oak Park Dr., Bedford, MA 01730 US | |

## GROWTH PLANS/SPECIAL FEATURES:

Progress Software Corp. develops, markets and distributes application infrastructure software for the development, deployment, integration and management of business applications. The company has three reportable segments: the OpenEdge segment, which consists primarily of the OpenEdge Division and the EasyAsk Division; the Enterprise Infrastructure segment, which consists primarily of the Enterprise Infrastructure Division and the Apama Division; and the DataDirect segment, which consists primarily of the DataDirect Technologies operating unit. Within the three segments, the firm has nine principal product lines: Progress OpenEdge, Progress Apama, Progress Sonic, Progress Actional, DataDirect Shadow, DataDirect Connect, Progress EasyAsk, Progress DataXtend and Progress ObjectStore. The Progress OpenEdge platform is used for the development and deployment of business applications that are standards-based and service-oriented. The Progress Apama Event Processing platform can monitor rapidly moving event streams, detect sophisticated patterns and take action at fast speeds. Progress Sonic products help IT organizations achieve broad-scale interoperability of IT systems. The Progress Actional product line delivers service-oriented architecture and web services management products that provide visibility, security and control of the activities of services and end-to-end business processes. DataDirect Shadow is a multi-threaded, native runtime architecture and consolidated development environment providing real-time foundation architecture for standards based mainframe integration. DataDirect Connect products provide data connectivity components that use industry-standard interfaces to connect applications running on various platforms to any major database. Progress EasyAsk provides product search, navigation and merchandising for retailers' web sites. ProgressXtend products provide data integration for distributed applications. The Progress ObjectStore object data management system enables users to store C++ and Java data at a faster rate.

The company offers its employees an employee stock purchase plan; a 401(k) plan; an employee stock options program; medical and dental insurance; flexible spending account; computer discount purchase; an employee assistance program; and tuition reimbursement.

## FINANCIALS: **Sales and profits are in thousands of dollars—add 000 to get the full amount. 2008 Note: Financial information for 2008 was not available for all companies at press time.**

| | | |
|---|---|---|
| 2008 Sales: $515,560 | 2008 Profits: $46,296 | **U.S. Stock Ticker: PRGS** |
| 2007 Sales: $493,500 | 2007 Profits: $42,280 | **Int'l Ticker:** Int'l Exchange: |
| 2006 Sales: $447,063 | 2006 Profits: $29,401 | Employees: 1,926 |
| 2005 Sales: $405,376 | 2005 Profits: $46,257 | Fiscal Year Ends: 11/30 |
| 2004 Sales: $405,376 | 2004 Profits: $32,101 | Parent Company: |

## SALARIES/BENEFITS:

| | | | | |
|---|---|---|---|---|
| Pension Plan: | ESOP Stock Plan: | Profit Sharing: | Top Exec. Salary: $350,000 | Bonus: $334,750 |
| Savings Plan: Y | Stock Purch. Plan: Y | | Second Exec. Salary: $308,333 | Bonus: $245,490 |

## OTHER THOUGHTS:

**Apparent Women Officers or Directors**:
**Hot Spot for Advancement for Women/Minorities**:

## LOCATIONS: ("Y" = Yes)

| West: | Southwest: | Midwest: | Southeast: | Northeast: | International: |
|---|---|---|---|---|---|
| Y | Y | Y | Y | Y | Y |

# PROTECTIVE LIFE CORP

**www.protective.com**

**Industry Group Code:** 524113 **Ranks within this company's industry group:** Sales: 2 Profits: 2

| Management: | | Sales/Marketing: | | Liberal Arts: | | Information Systems: | | Professionals: | | Technical/Scientific: | |
|---|---|---|---|---|---|---|---|---|---|---|---|
| Mgmt. Trainees: | | Mktg. Professionals: | Y | Gen. Writing/Editing: | Y | Info. Management: | Y | Finance/Accounting: | Y | Engineers, Elec.: | |
| Experienced Mgmt.: | Y | Retail Sales: | | Technical Writing: | Y | Software Dev.: | | Law: | Y | Engineers, Other: | |
| Int'l Business: | | Commercial/Industrial: | | Graphic Arts/Photog.: | | Hardware Dev.: | | HR/Other: | Y | Health/Lab: | |
| MBA Graduates: | Y | Sales Trainees: | Y | Music: | | Systems Integration: | | Training: | Y | Scientists/Research: | |
| | | Advertising Pros.: | Y | Broadcasting: | | Consulting/Other: | | Health Care: | Y | Petroleum/Chemicals: | |
| | | | | Other: | | | | Consulting: | | Math/Other: | Y |

## TYPES OF BUSINESS:

Insurance-Life
Credit & Disability Insurance
Vehicle & Marine Insurance
Retirement Products
Annuity Products
Guaranteed Investment Contracts

## BRANDS/DIVISIONS/AFFILIATES:

Protective Life Insurance Company
First Protective Insurance Group, Inc.
Protective Life & Annuity Insurance Company
ProEquities, Inc.
West Coast Life Insurance Company

## CONTACTS: *Note: Officers with more than one job title may be intentionally listed here more than once.*

John D. Johns, CEO
Carolyn M. Johnson, COO/Exec. VP
John D. Johns, Pres.
Richard J. Beilen, CFO/Vice Chmn.
Eric Miller, VP/Dir.-Nat'l Mktg.
D. Scott Adams, Chief Human Resources Officer/Sr. VP
Deborah J. Long, General Counsel/Exec. VP/Sec.
Carolyn King, Sr. VP-Acquisitions & Corp. Dev.
Rob Shirley, VP-Investor Rel.
Steven G. Walker, Controller/Chief Acct. Officer/Sr. VP
Carl S. Thigpen, Exec. VP/Chief Investment Officer
Brent E. Griggs, Sr. VP-Asset Protection
Judy Wilson, Sr. VP-Stable Value Products
John Sawyer, VP-Bus. Dev.
John D. Johns, Chmn.

| | |
|---|---|
| **Phone:** 205-268-1000 | **Fax:** 205-268-3196 |
| **Toll-Free:** 800-866-3555 | |
| **Address:** 2801 Hwy. 280 S., Birmingham, AL 35223 US | |

## GROWTH PLANS/SPECIAL FEATURES:

Protective Life Corp. offers an array of insurance and investment products through subsidiaries Protective Life Insurance Company; West Coast Life Insurance Company; Empire General Life Assurance Corporation; Protective Life and Annuity Insurance Company; and Lyndon Property Insurance. The company operates through six segments: life marketing; acquisitions; annuities; stable value products; asset protection; and corporate and other. Its life marketing segment markets level premium term insurance, universal life, variable universal life and bank-owned life insurance products through a network of independent insurance agents, brokerage general agencies, regional stockbrokers and banks. Protective Life's acquisitions segment acquires, converts and services policies, primarily individual life insurance, from other companies. Its annuities segment manufactures, sells and supports fixed and variable annuity products. The firm's stable-value products segment markets guaranteed funding agreements, and also markets fixed and floating rate funding agreements directly to the trustees of municipal bond proceeds, institutional investors, bank trust departments and money market funds. The asset protection segment markets credit life and disability insurance, and vehicle and marine extended service contracts. This segment also sells inventory protection and guaranteed asset protection products. The company's corporate and other segment consists of earnings from lines of business that the company is not actively marketing, such as cancer insurance. In July 2008, Protective's Asset Protection Division introduced Select, an extended service contract program consisting of coverage for pre-owned and new vehicles that includes roadside assistance and substitute transportation. In the same month, the company also launched the Protective Centennial G II Universal Life Series and the West Coast LifeTime Platinum III Universal Life Series, which offer life insurance with flexible lapse protection options and guaranteed death benefit coverage.

The company offers employees an employee assistance program; tuition reimbursement; medical and dental insurance; adoption assistance; and scholarships for dependents.

## FINANCIALS: **Sales and profits are in thousands of dollars—add 000 to get the full amount. 2008 Note: Financial information for 2008 was not available for all companies at press time.**

| | | |
|---|---|---|
| 2008 Sales: $ | 2008 Profits: $ | **U.S. Stock Ticker: PL** |
| 2007 Sales: $3,051,700 | 2007 Profits: $289,566 | **Int'l Ticker:** Int'l Exchange: |
| 2006 Sales: $2,679,133 | 2006 Profits: $281,561 | Employees: 2,406 |
| 2005 Sales: $2,109,204 | 2005 Profits: $246,567 | Fiscal Year Ends: 12/31 |
| 2004 Sales: $1,988,600 | 2004 Profits: $234,600 | Parent Company: |

## SALARIES/BENEFITS:

| | | | | |
|---|---|---|---|---|
| Pension Plan: Y | ESOP Stock Plan: Y | Profit Sharing: | Top Exec. Salary: $820,833 | Bonus: $1,105,500 |
| Savings Plan: Y | Stock Purch. Plan: | | Second Exec. Salary: $417,500 | Bonus: $370,200 |

## OTHER THOUGHTS:

**Apparent Women Officers or Directors**: 6
**Hot Spot for Advancement for Women/Minorities**: Y

## LOCATIONS: ("Y" = Yes)

| West: | Southwest: | Midwest: | Southeast: | Northeast: | International: |
|---|---|---|---|---|---|
| Y | Y | Y | Y | Y | |

# QLOGIC CORP

**www.qlogic.com**

**Industry Group Code:** 334110 **Ranks within this company's industry group:** Sales: 2 Profits: 1

| Management: | | Sales/Marketing: | | Liberal Arts: | | Information Systems: | | Professionals: | | Technical/Scientific: | |
|---|---|---|---|---|---|---|---|---|---|---|---|
| Mgmt. Trainees: | | Mktg. Professionals: | Y | Gen. Writing/Editing: | | Info. Management: | Y | Finance/Accounting: | Y | Engineers, Elec.: | Y |
| Experienced Mgmt.: | Y | Retail Sales: | | Technical Writing: | Y | Software Dev.: | Y | Law: | Y | Engineers, Other: | |
| Int'l Business: | Y | Commercial/Industrial: | Y | Graphic Arts/Photog.: | | Hardware Dev.: | Y | HR/Other: | Y | Health/Lab: | |
| MBA Graduates: | Y | Sales Trainees: | Y | Music: | | Systems Integration: | Y | Training: | Y | Scientists/Research: | Y |
| | | Advertising Pros.: | | Broadcasting: | | Consulting/Other: | | Health Care: | | Petroleum/Chemicals: | |
| | | | | Other: | | | | Consulting: | | Math/Other: | |

## TYPES OF BUSINESS:

Computer Networking Equipment
Storage Area Network Products
Controller Chips

## BRANDS/DIVISIONS/AFFILIATES:

SANsurfer
SANblade
SANbox

## CONTACTS: *Note: Officers with more than one job title may be intentionally listed here more than once.*

H. K. Desai, CEO
Jeff W. Benck, COO
Jeff W. Benck, Pres.
Simon Biddiscombe, CFO/Sr. VP
Todd V. Jones, VP-Mktg. Oper. & Global Service
Phil A. Felando, VP-Human Resources
Michael L. Hawkins, General Counsel/VP/Sec.
Perry M. Mulligan, Sr. VP-Oper.
Roger J. Klein, VP/Gen. Mgr.-Host Solutions Group
Jesse L. Parker, VP/Gen. Mgr.-Network Solutions Group
Shishir Shah, VP/Gen. Mgr.-Storage Solutions Group
H. K. Desai, Chmn.

**Phone:** 949-389-6000 **Fax:** 949-389-6126
**Toll-Free:** 800-662-4471
**Address:** 26650 Aliso Viejo Pkwy., Aliso Viejo, CA 92656 US

## GROWTH PLANS/SPECIAL FEATURES:

QLogic Corp. is a supplier of storage networking solutions and network infrastructure solutions, which are sold primarily to original equipment manufacturers (OEMs) and distributors. It produces host bus adapters and Fibre Channel switches, including core, blade and stackable switches. In addition, the company designs and develops storage routers for bridging Fibre Channel and Internet Small Computer Systems Interface (iSCSI), networking and storage services platforms that provide performance improvements to third-party and OEM storage management software that has been ported to the platform. The firm is also a supplier of InfiniBand switches, including edge fabric switches and multi-protocol fabric directors; and InfiniBand host channel adapters for emerging high performance computer cluster (HPCC) environments. Finally, QLogic supplies enclosure management and baseboard management products. All of these solutions address the storage area network (SAN) or server fabric connectivity infrastructure requirements of small, medium and large enterprises. The company serves customers with solutions based on various connectivity technologies including Fibre Channel, InfiniBand and iSCSI. To ensure interoperability within the SAN, the firm works with independent hardware and software vendors, including Cisco Systems and Microsoft. Company products include SANblade HBAs, SANbox Fibre Channel Switches, SANsurfer Management Suite HBA and switch management software. Clients include major OEMs such as Cisco, Dell, Hewlett Packard, Intel, IBM, Sony and Sun Microsystems.

The company offers employees medical and dental plans; life and AD&D insurance; flexible spending accounts; a 401(k) plan; an employee stock purchase plan; short and long term disability; an incentive program; employee discounts; a patent program; education assistance; access to a credit union and a wellness program.

## FINANCIALS: **Sales and profits are in thousands of dollars—add 000 to get the full amount. 2008 Note: Financial information for 2008 was not available for all companies at press time.**

| | | |
|---|---|---|
| 2008 Sales: $597,866 | 2008 Profits: $96,210 | **U.S. Stock Ticker: QLGC** |
| 2007 Sales: $586,697 | 2007 Profits: $105,418 | **Int'l Ticker:** Int'l Exchange: |
| 2006 Sales: $494,077 | 2006 Profits: $283,588 | Employees: 933 |
| 2005 Sales: $428,719 | 2005 Profits: $157,596 | Fiscal Year Ends: 3/31 |
| 2004 Sales: $387,156 | 2004 Profits: $133,673 | Parent Company: |

## SALARIES/BENEFITS:

| | | | | |
|---|---|---|---|---|
| Pension Plan: | ESOP Stock Plan: | Profit Sharing: Y | Top Exec. Salary: $694,234 | Bonus: $651,675 |
| Savings Plan: Y | Stock Purch. Plan: Y | | Second Exec. Salary: $352,312 | Bonus: $260,000 |

## OTHER THOUGHTS:

**Apparent Women Officers or Directors:**
**Hot Spot for Advancement for Women/Minorities:**

## LOCATIONS: ("Y" = Yes)

| West: | Southwest: | Midwest: | Southeast: | Northeast: | International: |
|---|---|---|---|---|---|
| Y | Y | Y | | Y | Y |

# QUALITY SYSTEMS INC

www.qsii.com

**Industry Group Code:** 511212 **Ranks within this company's industry group:** Sales: 4 Profits: 2

| Management: | | Sales/Marketing: | | Liberal Arts: | | Information Systems: | | Professionals: | | Technical/Scientific: | |
|---|---|---|---|---|---|---|---|---|---|---|---|
| Mgmt. Trainees: | | Mktg. Professionals: | Y | Gen. Writing/Editing: | | Info. Management: | Y | Finance/Accounting: | Y | Engineers, Elec.: | Y |
| Experienced Mgmt.: | Y | Retail Sales: | | Technical Writing: | Y | Software Dev.: | Y | Law: | Y | Engineers, Other: | |
| Int'l Business: | Y | Commercial/Industrial: | Y | Graphic Arts/Photog.: | | Hardware Dev.: | | HR/Other: | Y | Health/Lab: | |
| MBA Graduates: | Y | Sales Trainees: | Y | Music: | | Systems Integration: | | Training: | Y | Scientists/Research: | |
| | | Advertising Pros.: | | Broadcasting: | | Consulting/Other: | | Health Care: | | Petroleum/Chemicals: | |
| | | | | Other: | | | | Consulting: | | Math/Other: | |

## TYPES OF BUSINESS:

Software-Practice Management

## BRANDS/DIVISIONS/AFFILIATES:

Clinical Product Suite
NextGen Healthcare Information Systems, Inc.
Electronic Medical Records
Enterprise Practice Management
Enterprise Appointment Scheduling
Enterprise Master Patient Index
Image Control System
Managed Care Server

## CONTACTS: *Note: Officers with more than one job title may be intentionally listed here more than once.*

Steven Plochocki, CEO
Steven Plochocki, Pres.
Paul Holt, CFO
Patrick B. Cline, Pres., NextGen Healthcare Information Systems
Sheldon Razin, Chmn.

| | |
|---|---|
| **Phone:** 949-255-2600 | **Fax:** 949-255-2605 |
| **Toll-Free:** 800-888-7955 | |
| **Address:** 18111 Von Karman, Ste. 600, Irvine, CA 92612 US | |

## GROWTH PLANS/SPECIAL FEATURES:

Quality Systems, Inc. develops and provides computer-based practice management, medical records, and e-business applications for medical and dental group practices, practice networks, management service organizations, ambulatory care centers, community health centers and medical and dental schools. The company is headquartered in Irvine, California and has major facilities in Horsham, Pennsylvania and Atlanta, Georgia, and additional facilities in Minnesota, Missouri, Texas, Utah, Wisconsin and Washington. Quality Systems operates through two divisions, QSI and the NextGen Healthcare Information, which both develop and market products designed to streamline patient records and administrative functions such as billing and scheduling. The company's QSI division focuses on developing, marketing and supporting software suites for dental and niche medical practices. Its Clinical Product Suite is a UNIX-based medical practice management software suite that incorporates clinical tools including periodontal charting and digital imaging of x-ray and inter-oral camera images. NextGen, the company's other operating division, develops and sells proprietary electronic medical records software and practice management systems. Its NextGen product line includes Electronic Medical Records, Enterprise Practice Management, Enterprise Appointment Scheduling, Enterprise Master Patient Index, Image Control System, Managed Care Server, Electronic Data Interchange (EDI), System Interfaces, Internet Operability, patient-centric and provider-centric web portal solutions and a handheld product. The group's EDI/Connectivity products automate a number of manual, often paper-based or telephony intensive communications between patients and providers, like as insurance claim forwards. NextGen products utilize Microsoft Windows technology and can operate in a client-server environment as well as via private intranet, the Internet or in an ASP environment. In May 2008, the firm acquired Lackland Acquisition II, LLC, which does business as Healthcare Strategic Initiatives (HSI), a full-service healthcare revenue management company servicing healthcare clients. HSI became a wholly-owned subsidiary.

## FINANCIALS: **Sales and profits are in thousands of dollars—add 000 to get the full amount. 2008 Note: Financial information for 2008 was not available for all companies at press time.**

| | | |
|---|---|---|
| 2008 Sales: $186,500 | 2008 Profits: $40,078 | **U.S. Stock Ticker: QSII** |
| 2007 Sales: $157,165 | 2007 Profits: $33,232 | **Int'l Ticker:** Int'l Exchange: |
| 2006 Sales: $119,287 | 2006 Profits: $23,322 | Employees: 704 |
| 2005 Sales: $89,000 | 2005 Profits: $16,100 | Fiscal Year Ends: 3/31 |
| 2004 Sales: $70,934 | 2004 Profits: $10,400 | Parent Company: |

## SALARIES/BENEFITS:

| | | | | |
|---|---|---|---|---|
| Pension Plan: | ESOP Stock Plan: | Profit Sharing: | Top Exec. Salary: $420,833 | Bonus: $320,000 |
| Savings Plan: Y | Stock Purch. Plan: | | Second Exec. Salary: $400,000 | Bonus: $228,000 |

## OTHER THOUGHTS:

**Apparent Women Officers or Directors:**
**Hot Spot for Advancement for Women/Minorities:**

## LOCATIONS: ("Y" = Yes)

| West: | Southwest: | Midwest: | Southeast: | Northeast: | International: |
|---|---|---|---|---|---|
| Y | Y | Y | Y | Y | |

# QUICKSILVER RESOURCES INC

**www.qrinc.com**

**Industry Group Code:** 211111 **Ranks within this company's industry group:** Sales: 17 Profits: 4

| Management: | | Sales/Marketing: | | Liberal Arts: | | Information Systems: | | Professionals: | | Technical/Scientific: | |
|---|---|---|---|---|---|---|---|---|---|---|---|
| Mgmt. Trainees: | | Mktg. Professionals: | Y | Gen. Writing/Editing: | | Info. Management: | Y | Finance/Accounting: | Y | Engineers, Elec.: | |
| Experienced Mgmt.: | Y | Retail Sales: | | Technical Writing: | | Software Dev.: | | Law: | Y | Engineers, Other: | Y |
| Int'l Business: | Y | Commercial/Industrial: | Y | Graphic Arts/Photog.: | | Hardware Dev.: | | HR/Other: | Y | Health/Lab: | |
| MBA Graduates: | Y | Sales Trainees: | | Music: | | Systems Integration: | | Training: | Y | Scientists/Research: | |
| | | Advertising Pros.: | | Broadcasting: | | Consulting/Other: | | Health Care: | | Petroleum/Chemicals: | Y |
| | | | | Other: | | | | Consulting: | | Math/Other: | |

## TYPES OF BUSINESS:

Oil & Gas Exploration & Production
Fractured Shale Gas
Coal Bed Methane
Tight Sand Gas

## BRANDS/DIVISIONS/AFFILIATES:

Cowtown Pipeline
Cowtown Plant
Quicksilver Resources Canada, Inc.
MGV Energy, Inc.
BreitBurn Energy Partners LP

## CONTACTS: *Note: Officers with more than one job title may be intentionally listed here more than once.*

Glenn Darden, CEO
Glenn Darden, Pres.
Philip W. Cook, CFO/Sr. VP
Anne D. Self, VP-Human Resources
Thomas Duncan, VP-Tech.
William S. Buckler, III, VP-Eng.
John C. Cirone, General Counsel/Corp. Sec./Sr. VP
Jeff Cook, Exec. VP-Oper.
Richard C. Buterbaugh, VP-Corp. Planning
Richard C. Buterbaugh, VP-Investor Rel.
John C. Regan, Chief Acct. Officer/Controller/VP
D. Wayne Blair, VP-Finance
C. Clay Blum, VP-Land
MarLu S. Hiller, VP-Treas.
Robert N. Wagner, VP-Reservoir Eng.
Thomas F. (Toby) Darden, Chmn.

| **Phone:** 817-665-5000 | **Fax:** 817-665-5005 |
|---|---|
| **Toll-Free:** | |
| **Address:** 777 W. Rosedale St., Fort Worth, TX 76104 US | |

## GROWTH PLANS/SPECIAL FEATURES:

Quicksilver Resources, Inc. is an oil and gas company engaged in the development and production of natural gas, natural gas liquids (NGLs) and crude oil, which it attains through a combination of developmental drilling, exploitation and property acquisitions. The company's efforts are principally focused in unconventional reservoirs found in fractured shales, coal seams and tight sands. Quicksilver's operations are concentrated in the Texas, Michigan and Western Canadian Sedimentary Basins. The company has estimated proved reserves of 1.5 trillion cubic feet equivalent, of which approximately 99% is natural gas and NGLs and approximately 62% is proved developed. Approximately 78% of Quicksilver's reserves are in Texas, 21% are in Canada and 1% is in other locations. The company's operations in Texas are located in the Fort Worth Basin, where it drilled 219 net wells during 2007, substantially all of which have been horizontal wells. The company has approximately 200 miles of natural gas gathering lines, ranging from 2-20 inches, which it refers to as the Cowtown Pipeline. The Cowtown Pipeline transports natural gas produced from Quicksilver and third party wells to its natural gas processing plant in Hood County, Texas (Cowtown Plant). The company also owns a 25-mile NGL pipeline that runs from its Cowtown Plant to a third party pipeline interconnect. Quicksilver conducts its Canadian operations through subsidiary Quicksilver Resources Canada, Inc. (QRCI), formerly known as MGV Energy, Inc. In Michigan, the company produces gas from the Antrim Shale as well as non-Antrim reservoirs. In November 2007, Quicksilver completed the divestiture of its Michigan, Indiana and Kentucky properties to BreitBurn Energy Partners L.P. for approximately $750 million. In 2008, the firm acquired 19 license in the Horn River Basin of British Columbia and 13,000 net acres in the Fort Worth Basin Barnett shale assets.

## FINANCIALS: **Sales and profits are in thousands of dollars—add 000 to get the full amount. 2008 Note: Financial information for 2008 was not available for all companies at press time.**

| | | |
|---|---|---|
| 2008 Sales: $ | 2008 Profits: $ | **U.S. Stock Ticker: KWK** |
| 2007 Sales: $561,258 | 2007 Profits: $479,378 | **Int'l Ticker:** Int'l Exchange: |
| 2006 Sales: $390,362 | 2006 Profits: $93,719 | Employees: 496 |
| 2005 Sales: $310,448 | 2005 Profits: $87,434 | Fiscal Year Ends: 12/31 |
| 2004 Sales: $179,729 | 2004 Profits: $31,272 | Parent Company: |

## SALARIES/BENEFITS:

| | | | | |
|---|---|---|---|---|
| Pension Plan: | ESOP Stock Plan: | Profit Sharing: | Top Exec. Salary: $331,770 | Bonus: $975,924 |
| Savings Plan: Y | Stock Purch. Plan: | | Second Exec. Salary: $331,770 | Bonus: $975,924 |

## OTHER THOUGHTS:

**Apparent Women Officers or Directors**: 1
**Hot Spot for Advancement for Women/Minorities**: Y

## LOCATIONS: ("Y" = Yes)

| West: | Southwest: | Midwest: | Southeast: | Northeast: | International: |
|---|---|---|---|---|---|
| Y | Y | | | | Y |

# QUIDEL CORP

www.quidel.com

**Industry Group Code:** 339113 **Ranks within this company's industry group:** Sales: 27 Profits: 16

| Management: | | Sales/Marketing: | | Liberal Arts: | | Information Systems: | | Professionals: | | Technical/Scientific: | |
|---|---|---|---|---|---|---|---|---|---|---|---|
| Mgmt. Trainees: | | Mktg. Professionals: | Y | Gen. Writing/Editing: | | Info. Management: | Y | Finance/Accounting: | Y | Engineers, Elec.: | Y |
| Experienced Mgmt.: | Y | Retail Sales: | | Technical Writing: | Y | Software Dev.: | Y | Law: | Y | Engineers, Other: | Y |
| Int'l Business: | Y | Commercial/Industrial: | Y | Graphic Arts/Photog.: | | Hardware Dev.: | | HR/Other: | Y | Health/Lab: | Y |
| MBA Graduates: | Y | Sales Trainees: | Y | Music: | | Systems Integration: | | Training: | Y | Scientists/Research: | Y |
| | | Advertising Pros.: | | Broadcasting: | | Consulting/Other: | | Health Care: | Y | Petroleum/Chemicals: | |
| | | | | Other: | | | | Consulting: | | Math/Other: | Y |

## TYPES OF BUSINESS:

Rapid Diagnosis Solutions
Point-of-Care Diagnostic Tests
Research Products

## BRANDS/DIVISIONS/AFFILIATES:

QuickVue
QuickVue Advance
RapidVue
Metra
Roche Pharma AG
Prodesse, Inc.

## CONTACTS:

*Note: Officers with more than one job title may be intentionally listed here more than once.*

Caren L. Mason, CEO
Caren L. Mason, Pres.
John M. Radak, CFO
Thomas J. Foley, CTO
Robert J. Bujarski, General Counsel/Sr. VP/Sec.
Scott M. McLeod, Sr. VP-Oper.
Richard Tarbox, III, Sr. VP/Corp. Dev. Officer
Mark A. Pulido, Chmn.

**Phone:** 858-552-1100 **Fax:** 858-546-8955
**Toll-Free:** 800-874-1517
**Address:** 10165 McKellar Ct., San Diego, CA 92121 US

## GROWTH PLANS/SPECIAL FEATURES:

Quidel Corp. develops, manufactures and markets rapid diagnostic solutions at the professional point-of-care in infectious diseases and reproductive health. The firm's products detect and manage medical conditions and illnesses such as pregnancy, infectious diseases, autoimmune disorders and osteoporosis. Quidel sells its products to professionals for use in physician offices, hospitals, clinical laboratories and wellness screening centers. In 2007, about 81% of revenue was generated from sales of the influenza, Group A Strep and pregnancy tests. The company also develops research products through its Specialty Products Group. The segment is currently responsible for more than 100 of the company's clinical and research products used worldwide in reference laboratories and in research applications at universities and biotechnology companies. The division's revenues, earnings and assets represent less than 10% of the overall operations. Brand names include QuickVue, RapidVue, QuickVue Advance and Metra. Quidel markets its products in the U.S. through a network of national and regional distributors, supported by a direct sales force. Internationally, the company sells and markets primarily in Japan and Europe by channeling products through distributor organizations and sales agents. In September 2007, Quidel partnered with Roche Pharma AG to market and sell its QuickVue Influenza A+B rapid diagnostic test in Germany. In January 2008, the company agreed to a long-term global alliance in the area of rapid clinical diagnostics for the point-of-care. In February 2008, the FDA granted a Clinical Laboratory Improvement Amendments (CLIA) waver to the QuickVue RSV test for the qualitative detection of respiratory syncytial virus (RSV). In May 2008, the firm partnered with Prodesse, Inc. to mutually promote Prodesse's ProFlu+ multiplex molecular diagnostic test within the United States.

The company offers its employees benefits including medical, dental and vision insurance; life insurance; flexible spending accounts; tuition reimbursement; discounted gym membership; discount programs; and an employee assistance program.

## FINANCIALS:

**Sales and profits are in thousands of dollars—add 000 to get the full amount. 2008 Note: Financial information for 2008 was not available for all companies at press time.**

| | | |
|---|---|---|
| 2008 Sales: $ | 2008 Profits: $ | **U.S. Stock Ticker: QDEL** |
| 2007 Sales: $118,065 | 2007 Profits: $13,631 | **Int'l Ticker:** Int'l Exchange: |
| 2006 Sales: $106,015 | 2006 Profits: $21,718 | Employees: 278 |
| 2005 Sales: $92,299 | 2005 Profits: $-9,259 | Fiscal Year Ends: 12/31 |
| 2004 Sales: $78,691 | 2004 Profits: $-6,287 | Parent Company: |

## SALARIES/BENEFITS:

| | | | | |
|---|---|---|---|---|
| Pension Plan: | ESOP Stock Plan: | Profit Sharing: | Top Exec. Salary: $464,538 | Bonus: $643,800 |
| Savings Plan: Y | Stock Purch. Plan: Y | | Second Exec. Salary: $283,647 | Bonus: $ |

## OTHER THOUGHTS:

**Apparent Women Officers or Directors**: 2
**Hot Spot for Advancement for Women/Minorities**: Y

## LOCATIONS: ("Y" = Yes)

| West: | Southwest: | Midwest: | Southeast: | Northeast: | International: |
|---|---|---|---|---|---|
| Y | | | | | |

# RACKSPACE HOSTING INC

**www.rackspace.com**

**Industry Group Code:** 514191A **Ranks within this company's industry group:** Sales: 3 Profits: 5

| Management: | | Sales/Marketing: | | Liberal Arts: | | Information Systems: | | Professionals: | | Technical/Scientific: | |
|---|---|---|---|---|---|---|---|---|---|---|---|
| Mgmt. Trainees: | | Mktg. Professionals: | Y | Gen. Writing/Editing: | | Info. Management: | Y | Finance/Accounting: | Y | Engineers, Elec.: | Y |
| Experienced Mgmt.: | Y | Retail Sales: | | Technical Writing: | Y | Software Dev.: | Y | Law: | Y | Engineers, Other: | |
| Int'l Business: | | Commercial/Industrial: | Y | Graphic Arts/Photog.: | | Hardware Dev.: | | HR/Other: | Y | Health/Lab: | |
| MBA Graduates: | Y | Sales Trainees: | Y | Music: | | Systems Integration: | Y | Training: | Y | Scientists/Research: | |
| | | Advertising Pros.: | | Broadcasting: | | Consulting/Other: | | Health Care: | | Petroleum/Chemicals: | |
| | | | | Other: | | | | Consulting: | | Math/Other: | |

## TYPES OF BUSINESS:

Web Hosting Services

## BRANDS/DIVISIONS/AFFILIATES:

Mailtrust
Noteworthy Hosted Email
Hosted Microsoft Exchange
Mosso
Rackspace US, Inc.
Rackspace Limited
Slicehost, LLC
Jungle Disk, Inc.

## CONTACTS: *Note: Officers with more than one job title may be intentionally listed here more than once.*

Lanham Napier, CEO
Lanham Napier, Pres.
Bruce R. Knooihuizen, CFO/Sr. VP/Treas.
Jim Lewandowski, Sr. VP-Worldwide Sales
Kiprian (Kip) Miles, VP-IT
John Engates, CTO
Klee Kleber, VP-Prod. & Mktg.
Alan Schoenbaum, General Counsel/Sr. VP
Troy Toman, VP-Oper. & Customer Care
Lew Moorman, Chief Strategy Officer/Sr. VP
Annalie Drusch, Media Rel. Contact
Karl Pichler, Investor Rel. Contact
Karl Pichler, VP-Finance
John Lionato, Sr. VP-Customer Support
Frederick Mendler, VP-Fanatical Support, Managed
Graham Weston, Chmn.

**Phone:** 210-312-4000 **Fax:** 210-312-4300
**Toll-Free:** 800-961-2888
**Address:** 5000 Walzem Rd., San Antonio, TX 78218 US

## GROWTH PLANS/SPECIAL FEATURES:

Rackspace Hosting Inc. specializes in hosting services for businesses, delivering web sites, web-based information technology (IT) systems and computing-as-a-service. It actively offers four service categories: Dedicated Hosting, Managed Hosting, Email Hosting and Cloud Hosting; it also has one other service category, Platform Hosting, which is still in development. Dedicated Hosting offers clients a dedicated server located in one of the firm's data centers. The customer has full administrative access to their contracted server and is responsible for its management, although management tools and customer portals are available. Managed Hosting offers clients a dedicated server in one of Rackspace's data centers that is managed by Rackspace staff. Email Hosting, offered through Mailtrust, offers business grade e-mail hosting powered by the company's data centers. Its primary e-mail offerings are Noteworthy Hosted Email and Hosted Microsoft Exchange. Following the acquisitions noted below, Cloud Hosting, operated by Mosso, consists of Cloud Sites (formerly The Hosting Cloud), a scalable platform for handling huge traffic spikes and a pay-as-you-grow pricing model; Cloud Files (formerly CloudFS), an online cloud storage service; and Cloud Servers, which offers on-demand server capacity. Platform Hosting, designed for large enterprises with significant in-house IT support, will offer an even more autonomous server hosting than either Dedicated or Managed hosting. In all, Rackspace serves 33,000 customers running on 42,000 servers in the U.S. and U.K. Its subsidiaries include Rackspace US, Inc. in the U.S.; and Rackspace Limited in the U.K. In September 2008, the firm expanded into Asia, opening a new combined headquarters and data center in Hong Kong. In October 2008, Rackspace completed two acquisitions for a combined price of $11.5 million; the two companies, Slicehost, LLC, which offers on-demand virtualized servers, and Jungle Disk, Inc., a provider of online cloud storage software and services, will operate under the Cloud Hosting Division.

## FINANCIALS: **Sales and profits are in thousands of dollars—add 000 to get the full amount. 2008 Note: Financial information for 2008 was not available for all companies at press time.**

| | | |
|---|---|---|
| 2008 Sales: $ | 2008 Profits: $ | **U.S. Stock Ticker: RAX** |
| 2007 Sales: $495,480 | 2007 Profits: $17,410 | **Int'l Ticker:** Int'l Exchange: |
| 2006 Sales: $ | 2006 Profits: $ | Employees: 2,452 |
| 2005 Sales: $ | 2005 Profits: $ | Fiscal Year Ends: 12/31 |
| 2004 Sales: $ | 2004 Profits: $ | Parent Company: |

## SALARIES/BENEFITS:

| | | | | |
|---|---|---|---|---|
| Pension Plan: | ESOP Stock Plan: | Profit Sharing: | Top Exec. Salary: $264,986 | Bonus: $119,568 |
| Savings Plan: Y | Stock Purch. Plan: | | Second Exec. Salary: $202,251 | Bonus: $126,224 |

## OTHER THOUGHTS:

**Apparent Women Officers or Directors**: 2
**Hot Spot for Advancement for Women/Minorities**:

## LOCATIONS: ("Y" = Yes)

| West: | Southwest: | Midwest: | Southeast: | Northeast: | International: |
|---|---|---|---|---|---|
| | Y | | | | |

# RADISYS CORP

www.radisys.com

**Industry Group Code:** 334111 **Ranks within this company's industry group:** Sales: 4 Profits: 5

| Management: | | Sales/Marketing: | | Liberal Arts: | | Information Systems: | | Professionals: | | Technical/Scientific: | |
|---|---|---|---|---|---|---|---|---|---|---|---|
| Mgmt. Trainees: | | Mktg. Professionals: | Y | Gen. Writing/Editing: | | Info. Management: | Y | Finance/Accounting: | Y | Engineers, Elec.: | Y |
| Experienced Mgmt.: | Y | Retail Sales: | | Technical Writing: | Y | Software Dev.: | Y | Law: | Y | Engineers, Other: | Y |
| Int'l Business: | Y | Commercial/Industrial: | Y | Graphic Arts/Photog.: | | Hardware Dev.: | Y | HR/Other: | Y | Health/Lab: | |
| MBA Graduates: | Y | Sales Trainees: | Y | Music: | | Systems Integration: | Y | Training: | Y | Scientists/Research: | |
| | | Advertising Pros.: | | Broadcasting: | | Consulting/Other: | | Health Care: | | Petroleum/Chemicals: | |
| | | | | Other: | | | | Consulting: | | Math/Other: | |

## TYPES OF BUSINESS:

Computer Hardware-Intel-Based Embedded Computers
DSP Modules & Algorithms
Network Interfaces & Protocols
Systems Platforms
Embedded Software
Systems Engineering
Integration Services

## BRANDS/DIVISIONS/AFFILIATES:

Intel Corp

## CONTACTS: *Note: Officers with more than one job title may be intentionally listed here more than once.*

Scott C. Grout, CEO
Scott C. Grout, Pres.
Brian Bronson, CFO
Christian Lepiane, VP-Global Sales, Service & Corp. Mktg.
George Shenoda, CTO
Julia Harper, VP-Corp. Oper.
Todd Etchieson, VP-Strategy & Bus. Dev.
Wade Clowes, VP/Gen. Mgr.-Commercial Market
Anthony Ambrose, VP/Gen. Mgr.-Comm. Networks
C. Scott Gibson, Chmn.

**Phone:** 503-615-1100 **Fax:** 503-615-1115
**Toll-Free:** 800-950-0044
**Address:** 5445 NE Dawson Creek Dr., Hillsboro, OR 97124 US

## GROWTH PLANS/SPECIAL FEATURES:

RadiSys Corp. is a leading provider of advanced embedded solutions for the communications networking and commercial systems markets. Its products include embedded boards, application enabling platforms and turn-key systems, which are used in complex computing, processing and network intensive applications. The company primarily markets its products to Original Equipment Manufacturers (OEMs). RadiSys' Communications Networking products includes two divisions: Wireless infrastructure and IP Networking and Messaging. Wireless infrastructure provides voice, video and data systems deployed into public networks, and includes 2, 2.5 and 3G wireless infrastructure products, packet-based switches and unified messaging products for wireless networks. IP Networking and Messaging offers products such as voice messaging, data centers, IP-based Private Branch Exchange systems, network access and security and switching applications for solutions in embedded computer, processing and networking systems applications. RadiSys also serves the Commercial Systems market, which includes medical systems, test and measurement equipment, transaction terminals and industrial automation equipment, and offers embedded solutions for products such as ultrasound equipment, immunodiagnostics and hematology systems, CAT Scan imaging equipment, ATMs, point of sale terminals, semiconductor manufacturing equipment, electronics assembly equipment and high-end network test equipment. This variety of products is offered in two categories: Standards-based Solutions, which can be used across a variety of applications; and Perfect Fit Solutions, which are custom designed for one customer on a single use basis. Customers include Agilent Technologies, Alcatel Lucent, Avaya, Fujitsu, Hewlett Packard, IBM, Nokia Siemens Networks, Nortel Networks and Philips Healthcare. During 2007, RadiSys completed its acquisition of certain assets of Intel's modular communications platforms business, including ATCA, CPCI and other legacy systems products.

RadiSys provides its employees with a benefits package that includes a 401(k) plan, financial planning assistance, flexible spending accounts, subsidized health club membership, a 24-hour nurse line and a telecommuting program, among other benefits.

## FINANCIALS: **Sales and profits are in thousands of dollars—add 000 to get the full amount. 2008 Note: Financial information for 2008 was not available for all companies at press time.**

| | | |
|---|---|---|
| 2008 Sales: $ | 2008 Profits: $ | **U.S. Stock Ticker: RSYS** |
| 2007 Sales: $325,232 | 2007 Profits: $-17,552 | **Int'l Ticker:** Int'l Exchange: |
| 2006 Sales: $292,481 | 2006 Profits: $-13,016 | Employees: 776 |
| 2005 Sales: $260,234 | 2005 Profits: $15,958 | Fiscal Year Ends: 12/31 |
| 2004 Sales: $245,824 | 2004 Profits: $13,011 | Parent Company: |

## SALARIES/BENEFITS:

| | | | | |
|---|---|---|---|---|
| Pension Plan: | ESOP Stock Plan: | Profit Sharing: | Top Exec. Salary: $452,413 | Bonus: $176,600 |
| Savings Plan: Y | Stock Purch. Plan: | | Second Exec. Salary: $273,844 | Bonus: $112,900 |

## OTHER THOUGHTS:

**Apparent Women Officers or Directors**: 2
**Hot Spot for Advancement for Women/Minorities**:

## LOCATIONS: ("Y" = Yes)

| West: | Southwest: | Midwest: | Southeast: | Northeast: | International: |
|---|---|---|---|---|---|
| Y | | Y | Y | Y | Y |

# RADNET INC

www.radnet.com

**Industry Group Code:** 621511 **Ranks within this company's industry group:** Sales: 2 Profits: 5

| Management: | | Sales/Marketing: | | Liberal Arts: | | Information Systems: | | Professionals: | | Technical/Scientific: | |
|---|---|---|---|---|---|---|---|---|---|---|---|
| Mgmt. Trainees: | | Mktg. Professionals: | Y | Gen. Writing/Editing: | | Info. Management: | Y | Finance/Accounting: | Y | Engineers, Elec.: | |
| Experienced Mgmt.: | Y | Retail Sales: | | Technical Writing: | Y | Software Dev.: | | Law: | Y | Engineers, Other: | |
| Int'l Business: | | Commercial/Industrial: | Y | Graphic Arts/Photog.: | | Hardware Dev.: | | HR/Other: | Y | Health/Lab: | Y |
| MBA Graduates: | Y | Sales Trainees: | Y | Music: | | Systems Integration: | Y | Training: | Y | Scientists/Research: | Y |
| | | Advertising Pros.: | | Broadcasting: | | Consulting/Other: | | Health Care: | Y | Petroleum/Chemicals: | |
| | | | | Other: | | | | Consulting: | | Math/Other: | |

## TYPES OF BUSINESS:

Diagnostics Services
Medical Imaging Centers

## BRANDS/DIVISIONS/AFFILIATES:

Primedex Health Systems, Inc.
RadNet Management, Inc.

## CONTACTS: *Note: Officers with more than one job title may be intentionally listed here more than once.*

Howard G. Berger, CEO
Howard G. Berger, Pres.
Mark D. Stolper, CFO/Exec. VP
Jeffrey L. Linden, General Counsel/Exec. VP
Michael N. Murdock, Chief Dev. Officer/Exec. VP
Stephen M. Forthuber, Exec. VP/COO-Eastern Oper.
Norman R. Hames, Exec. VP/COO-Western Oper.
John V. Crues, III, VP/Medical Dir.

| **Phone:** 310-445-2800 | **Fax:** 310-445-2980 |
|---|---|
| **Toll-Free:** | |
| **Address:** 1510 Cotner Ave., Los Angeles, CA 90024 US | |

## GROWTH PLANS/SPECIAL FEATURES:

RadNet, Inc., formerly known as Primedex Health Systems, Inc., operates a network of 167 diagnostic imaging centers in seven states. These centers, which are primarily located in California, Maryland, Florida, Kansas and New York, performed over 2.7 million procedures during 2007. The centers offer medical imaging services to the public, including MRI, CT, PET, ultrasound, mammography, nuclear medicine and general diagnostic radiology (or X-rays). A small percentage of the firm's facilities are single-modality sites, offering only X-ray or MRI service. These facilities are usually located near its multi-modality sites to help accommodate overflow in target demographic areas. The most common imaging procedures are X-ray, fluoroscopy, endoscopy and modalities such as CT scans and digital image processing. The centers also offer open MRI, allowing studies with patients not typically compatible with conventional MRI, such as pediatric, claustrophobic or obese patients. Patients are generally referred to the centers by their treating physicians and may be affiliated with an IPA, HMO, PPO or similar organizations. RadNet Management, Inc. manages the centers. It supplies the equipment as well as non-medical operational, management, financial and administrative services for the centers, with the medical services provided by affiliates such as Beverly Radiology Medical Group III (BRMG). BRMG is 99%-owned by Howard Berger. In July 2007, the firm acquired the assets and business of Borg Imaging Group for $11.7 million. The acquisition added six Borg imaging facilities to the firm's portfolio.

## FINANCIALS: **Sales and profits are in thousands of dollars—add 000 to get the full amount. 2008 Note: Financial information for 2008 was not available for all companies at press time.**

| | | |
|---|---|---|
| 2008 Sales: $ | 2008 Profits: $ | **U.S. Stock Ticker: RDNT** |
| 2007 Sales: $425,470 | 2007 Profits: $-18,131 | **Int'l Ticker:** Int'l Exchange: |
| 2006 Sales: $161,005 | 2006 Profits: $-6,894 | Employees: 1,237 |
| 2005 Sales: $145,573 | 2005 Profits: $-3,570 | Fiscal Year Ends: 10/31 |
| 2004 Sales: $137,277 | 2004 Profits: $-14,731 | Parent Company: |

## SALARIES/BENEFITS:

| | | | | |
|---|---|---|---|---|
| Pension Plan: | ESOP Stock Plan: | Profit Sharing: | Top Exec. Salary: $558,000 | Bonus: $ |
| Savings Plan: Y | Stock Purch. Plan: | | Second Exec. Salary: $415,000 | Bonus: $ |

## OTHER THOUGHTS:

**Apparent Women Officers or Directors**:
**Hot Spot for Advancement for Women/Minorities**:

## LOCATIONS: ("Y" = Yes)

| West: | Southwest: | Midwest: | Southeast: | Northeast: | International: |
|---|---|---|---|---|---|
| Y | Y | Y | Y | Y | |

# RADYNE CORPORATION

www.radn.com

**Industry Group Code:** 334220 **Ranks within this company's industry group:** Sales: 4 Profits: 3

| Management: | | Sales/Marketing: | | Liberal Arts: | | Information Systems: | | Professionals: | | Technical/Scientific: | |
|---|---|---|---|---|---|---|---|---|---|---|---|
| Mgmt. Trainees: | | Mktg. Professionals: | Y | Gen. Writing/Editing: | Y | Info. Management: | Y | Finance/Accounting: | Y | Engineers, Elec.: | Y |
| Experienced Mgmt.: | Y | Retail Sales: | | Technical Writing: | Y | Software Dev.: | Y | Law: | Y | Engineers, Other: | Y |
| Int'l Business: | Y | Commercial/Industrial: | Y | Graphic Arts/Photog.: | | Hardware Dev.: | Y | HR/Other: | Y | Health/Lab: | |
| MBA Graduates: | Y | Sales Trainees: | Y | Music: | | Systems Integration: | Y | Training: | Y | Scientists/Research: | |
| | | Advertising Pros.: | | Broadcasting: | | Consulting/Other: | | Health Care: | | Petroleum/Chemicals: | |
| | | | | Other: | | | | Consulting: | | Math/Other: | |

## TYPES OF BUSINESS:

Telecommunications Equipment-Satellite
Amplifiers
Modems
Converters
Receivers

## BRANDS/DIVISIONS/AFFILIATES:

Xicom Technology
Tiernan
AeroAstro
Radyne

## CONTACTS:

*Note: Officers with more than one job title may be intentionally listed here more than once.*

Myron Wagner, CEO
Malcom C. Persen, CFO/VP-Finance
Steven W. Eymann, CTO/Exec. VP
Malcom C. Persen, Corp. Sec.
Gary D. Kline, VP-Finance
Walt Wood, Pres., Xicom Technology
Louis Dubin, Pres./Gen. Mgr.-Radyne
Brian Duggan, Pres./Gen. Mgr.-Tiernan
Rick Fleeter, Pres., AeroAstro
C.J. Waylan, Chmn.

| | |
|---|---|
| **Phone:** 602-437-9620 | **Fax:** 602-437-4811 |
| **Toll-Free:** | |
| **Address:** 3138 E. Elwood St., Phoenix, AZ 85034 US | |

## GROWTH PLANS/SPECIAL FEATURES:

Radyne Corporation designs, manufactures and sells products and systems used for the operation of satellite, troposcatter, microwave and cable communication networks. Customers use products for applications for telephone (landline and mobile), data, video and audio broadcast communication, national and homeland defense, private and corporate data networks, Internet applications and digital television for cable and network broadcast. The company sells four brands: Radyne builds satellite modems, converters and switches; Xicom Technology produces high power amplifiers; AeroAstro designs and constructs microsatellite systems, components and advanced communication technologies; and Tiernan supplies HDTV and SDTV encoding and transmission equipment. The firm's products are used worldwide, including satellite modems, high power Ka band amplifiers and HD encoders for expanded direct-to-home (DTH) distribution of HDTV from satellite; HDTV encoders and decoders for major American television networks for use during their coverage of the 2008 Olympics in China and the National Basketball Association (NBA); microsatellite buses used for missions sponsored by the U.S. Department of Denfense and NASA; satellite backhaul systems for GSM mobile phone providers in India and China; major expansion of U.S. government satellite monitoring network; and satellite modems and high power amplifiers used as the backbone for major U.S. Department of Defense and Homeland Security communications systems. Radyne serves customers in over 120 countries, including customers in the television broadcast industry, international telecommunications companies, Internet service providers, private communication networks, network and cable television and the U.S. government. In 2007, the company received orders for over $6.7 million for Kaband power amplifiers and DM-240 satellite modulators to be used in DirecTV's high definition TV expansion. In May 2008, the firm agreed to be acquired by Comtech Telecommunications Corp. for nearly $225 million.

## FINANCIALS:

**Sales and profits are in thousands of dollars—add 000 to get the full amount. 2008 Note: Financial information for 2008 was not available for all companies at press time.**

| | | |
|---|---|---|
| 2008 Sales: $ | 2008 Profits: $ | **U.S. Stock Ticker: RADN** |
| 2007 Sales: $142,054 | 2007 Profits: $10,212 | **Int'l Ticker:** Int'l Exchange: |
| 2006 Sales: $134,209 | 2006 Profits: $11,865 | Employees: 412 |
| 2005 Sales: $103,263 | 2005 Profits: $10,686 | Fiscal Year Ends: 12/31 |
| 2004 Sales: $56,578 | 2004 Profits: $13,500 | Parent Company: |

## SALARIES/BENEFITS:

| | | | | |
|---|---|---|---|---|
| Pension Plan: | ESOP Stock Plan: | Profit Sharing: | Top Exec. Salary: $317,607 | Bonus: $726,884 |
| Savings Plan: | Stock Purch. Plan: | | Second Exec. Salary: $280,192 | Bonus: $292,992 |

## OTHER THOUGHTS:

**Apparent Women Officers or Directors:**
**Hot Spot for Advancement for Women/Minorities:**

## LOCATIONS: ("Y" = Yes)

| West: | Southwest: | Midwest: | Southeast: | Northeast: | International: |
|---|---|---|---|---|---|
| Y | Y | | | Y | |

# RANGE RESOURCES CORP

**www.rangeresources.com**

**Industry Group Code:** 211111 **Ranks within this company's industry group:** Sales: 13 Profits: 8

| Management: | | Sales/Marketing: | | Liberal Arts: | | Information Systems: | | Professionals: | | Technical/Scientific: | |
|---|---|---|---|---|---|---|---|---|---|---|---|
| Mgmt. Trainees: | | Mktg. Professionals: | Y | Gen. Writing/Editing: | | Info. Management: | Y | Finance/Accounting: | Y | Engineers, Elec.: | |
| Experienced Mgmt.: | Y | Retail Sales: | | Technical Writing: | | Software Dev.: | | Law: | Y | Engineers, Other: | Y |
| Int'l Business: | Y | Commercial/Industrial: | Y | Graphic Arts/Photog.: | | Hardware Dev.: | | HR/Other: | Y | Health/Lab: | |
| MBA Graduates: | Y | Sales Trainees: | | Music: | | Systems Integration: | | Training: | Y | Scientists/Research: | |
| | | Advertising Pros.: | | Broadcasting: | | Consulting/Other: | | Health Care: | | Petroleum/Chemicals: | Y |
| | | | | Other: | | | | Consulting: | | Math/Other: | |

## TYPES OF BUSINESS:

Oil & Gas Exploration & Production
Gas Processing & Transportation
Pipelines

## BRANDS/DIVISIONS/AFFILIATES:

Stroud Energy, Inc.

## CONTACTS: *Note: Officers with more than one job title may be intentionally listed here more than once.*

John H. Pinkerton, CEO
Jeff L. Ventura, COO/Exec. VP
John H. Pinkerton, Pres.
Roger S. Manny, CFO/Sr. VP
Mark D. Whitley, Sr. VP-Permian & Eng. Tech.
Alan W. Farquharson, Sr. VP-Reservoir Eng.
David P. Poole, General Counsel/Corp. Sec./Sr. VP
Chad L. Stevens, Sr. VP-Corp. Dev.
Steven L. Grose, Sr. VP-Appalachia
Charles L. Blackburn, Chmn.

| **Phone:** 817-870-2601 | **Fax:** 817-870-9100 |
|---|---|
| **Toll-Free:** | |
| **Address:** 100 Throckmorton St., Ste. 1200, Fort Worth, TX 76102 US | |

## GROWTH PLANS/SPECIAL FEATURES:

Range Resources Corporation is engaged in the exploration, development and acquisition of oil and gas properties, primarily in the Southwestern (including the Permian Basin in eastern New Mexico, East Texas Basin, Texas Panhandle and Anadarko Basin in Oklahoma), Appalachian and Gulf Coast regions of the U.S. The company operates development drilling and exploitation projects as well as exploration ventures on its extensive acreage, limiting risk by utilizing extensive geologic and engineering project analysis. Development projects include recompletions of existing wells, infill drilling and the installation of secondary recovery projects. Range Resources' drilling prospects are geographically diverse, ranging from the shallow waters of the Gulf of Mexico to the Appalachian Mountains, and target a mix of oil and gas. The firm's proven reserves at the end of 2007 were 2.2 trillion cubic feet of proved reserves, 82% of which was natural gas. It produces over 245,000 million cubic feet of natural gas and over 9,205 barrels of oil daily. Range Resources also owns 5,100 miles of gas pipeline in the Appalachian region as well as a number of smaller gathering systems in conjunction with the company's producing properties. The gathering systems transport the majority of Range Resources' gas production and third-party gas to major trunk lines and directly to end-users. Gas is sold primarily to utilities, marketing companies and industrial users. In 2007, the company sold its Austin Chalk properties in Central Texas for about $80 million and the Gulf of Mexico properties for proceeds of $155 million. In June 2008, the firm enlisted MarkWest Energy Partners to construct and operate gathering pipelines and processing facilities on Range's Marcellus Shale acreage in the Appalachian Basin.

## FINANCIALS: **Sales and profits are in thousands of dollars—add 000 to get the full amount. 2008 Note: Financial information for 2008 was not available for all companies at press time.**

| | | |
|---|---|---|
| 2008 Sales: $ | 2008 Profits: $ | **U.S. Stock Ticker: RRC** |
| 2007 Sales: $862,091 | 2007 Profits: $230,569 | **Int'l Ticker:** Int'l Exchange: |
| 2006 Sales: $744,812 | 2006 Profits: $158,702 | Employees: 733 |
| 2005 Sales: $535,840 | 2005 Profits: $111,011 | Fiscal Year Ends: 12/31 |
| 2004 Sales: $320,707 | 2004 Profits: $42,231 | Parent Company: |

## SALARIES/BENEFITS:

| | | | | |
|---|---|---|---|---|
| Pension Plan: | ESOP Stock Plan: | Profit Sharing: | Top Exec. Salary: $503,077 | Bonus: $950,000 |
| Savings Plan: Y | Stock Purch. Plan: | | Second Exec. Salary: $383,077 | Bonus: $730,000 |

## OTHER THOUGHTS:

**Apparent Women Officers or Directors:**
**Hot Spot for Advancement for Women/Minorities:**

## LOCATIONS: ("Y" = Yes)

| West: | Southwest: | Midwest: | Southeast: | Northeast: | International: |
|---|---|---|---|---|---|
| | Y | | Y | Y | |

# REALNETWORKS INC

www.realnetworks.com

**Industry Group Code:** 511209 **Ranks within this company's industry group:** Sales: 1 Profits: 1

| Management: | | Sales/Marketing: | | Liberal Arts: | | Information Systems: | | Professionals: | | Technical/Scientific: | |
|---|---|---|---|---|---|---|---|---|---|---|---|
| Mgmt. Trainees: | | Mktg. Professionals: | Y | Gen. Writing/Editing: | | Info. Management: | Y | Finance/Accounting: | Y | Engineers, Elec.: | Y |
| Experienced Mgmt.: | Y | Retail Sales: | | Technical Writing: | Y | Software Dev.: | Y | Law: | Y | Engineers, Other: | |
| Int'l Business: | Y | Commercial/Industrial: | Y | Graphic Arts/Photog.: | | Hardware Dev.: | | HR/Other: | Y | Health/Lab: | |
| MBA Graduates: | Y | Sales Trainees: | Y | Music: | | Systems Integration: | Y | Training: | Y | Scientists/Research: | |
| | | Advertising Pros.: | | Broadcasting: | | Consulting/Other: | | Health Care: | | Petroleum/Chemicals: | |
| | | | | Other: | | | | Consulting: | | Math/Other: | |

## TYPES OF BUSINESS:

Digital Media Services
Computer Software-Streaming Audio & Video
Online Retail-Digital Media
Mobile Games
Mobile Music
Mobile Video

## BRANDS/DIVISIONS/AFFILIATES:

RealPlayer
RadioPass
Rhapsody
RealMusic
RealPlayer Music Store
SonyNetservices
Atrativa

## CONTACTS: *Note: Officers with more than one job title may be intentionally listed here more than once.*

Robert Glaser, CEO
Michael Eggers, CFO/Sr. VP
Savino R. Ferrales, Sr. VP-Human Resources
Robert Kimball, General Counsel/Sec./Sr. VP-Legal & Bus. Affairs
Dan Sheeran, Sr. VP-Bus. Dev. & Corp. Partnerships
John Barbour, Pres., Game Div.
Harold Zeitz, Sr. VP-Media Software & Svcs., Games Div.
Robert Glaser, Chmn.

| | |
|---|---|
| **Phone:** 206-674-2700 | **Fax:** 206-674-2699 |
| **Toll-Free:** | |
| **Address:** 2601 Elliott Ave., Seattle, WA 98121 US | |

## GROWTH PLANS/SPECIAL FEATURES:

RealNetworks, Inc. is a creator of digital media services and software. The company operates in three segments: music; consumer; and technology products and solutions. The music segment owns and manages a set of digital music products and services designed to provide consumers with broad access to digital music. Music services include Rhapsody, a membership based music service offering unlimited access to a catalog of millions of tracks; RadioPass, an Internet radio subscription services; and RealMusic, an offering to consumers outside the U.S. of Internet radio, music downloads, music news and other music content. The consumer segment consists of media software and services and games. The division provides technology that facilitates the delivery and consumption of digital media over the Internet. Products include RealPlayer, which enables consumers to discover, play and manage audio and video programming on the Internet; and SuperPass, a subscription service that offers video and digital music and games content, commercial-free Internet radio stations, advanced CD burning and expanded features for the RealPlayer. The games subdivision owns and operates a casual digital games service that includes downloadable and online games products and subscription services focused primarily on gamers for personal computers (PCs) and mobile wireless platforms. RealNetworks develops original content for these services through the game studios Gamehouse, Mr. Goodliving, Ltd. and Zylom. The technology products and solutions segment develops and markets software products and services that enable media and communications companies to distribute digital media content to PCs, mobile phones and other non-PC devices. Through WiderThan Co., Ltd., the firm develops digital entertainment services for wireless carriers, such as ringback tones, music-on-demand and video-on-demand services. In February 2008, RealNetworks acquired Trymedia, a Casual Games syndicator from Macrovision.

## FINANCIALS: **Sales and profits are in thousands of dollars—add 000 to get the full amount. 2008 Note: Financial information for 2008 was not available for all companies at press time.**

| | | |
|---|---|---|
| 2008 Sales: $ | 2008 Profits: $ | **U.S. Stock Ticker: RNWK** |
| 2007 Sales: $567,620 | 2007 Profits: $48,315 | **Int'l Ticker:** Int'l Exchange: |
| 2006 Sales: $395,261 | 2006 Profits: $145,216 | Employees: 1,722 |
| 2005 Sales: $325,059 | 2005 Profits: $312,345 | Fiscal Year Ends: 12/31 |
| 2004 Sales: $266,719 | 2004 Profits: $-23,000 | Parent Company: |

## SALARIES/BENEFITS:

| | | | | |
|---|---|---|---|---|
| Pension Plan: | ESOP Stock Plan: | Profit Sharing: | Top Exec. Salary: $444,384 | Bonus: $1,079,200 |
| Savings Plan: Y | Stock Purch. Plan: | | Second Exec. Salary: $372,865 | Bonus: $1,042,600 |

## OTHER THOUGHTS:

**Apparent Women Officers or Directors:** 1
**Hot Spot for Advancement for Women/Minorities:**

## LOCATIONS: ("Y" = Yes)

| West: | Southwest: | Midwest: | Southeast: | Northeast: | International: |
|---|---|---|---|---|---|
| Y | | | | | Y |

Note: Financial information, benefits and other data can change quickly and may vary from those stated here.

# RECYCLED ENERGY DEVELOPMENT

www.recycled-energy.com

**Industry Group Code:** 541690 **Ranks within this company's industry group:** Sales: Profits:

| Management: | | Sales/Marketing: | | Liberal Arts: | | Information Systems: | | Professionals: | | Technical/Scientific: | |
|---|---|---|---|---|---|---|---|---|---|---|---|
| Mgmt. Trainees: | | Mktg. Professionals: | Y | Gen. Writing/Editing: | | Info. Management: | Y | Finance/Accounting: | Y | Engineers, Elec.: | Y |
| Experienced Mgmt.: | Y | Retail Sales: | | Technical Writing: | | Software Dev.: | | Law: | Y | Engineers, Other: | |
| Int'l Business: | | Commercial/Industrial: | | Graphic Arts/Photog.: | | Hardware Dev.: | | HR/Other: | Y | Health/Lab: | |
| MBA Graduates: | Y | Sales Trainees: | Y | Music: | | Systems Integration: | | Training: | Y | Scientists/Research: | |
| | | Advertising Pros.: | | Broadcasting: | | Consulting/Other: | | Health Care: | | Petroleum/Chemicals: | |
| | | | | Other: | | | | Consulting: | | Math/Other: | |

## TYPES OF BUSINESS:

Co-Generation Technology
Waste Heat-to-Energy

## BRANDS/DIVISIONS/AFFILIATES:

Turbostream

## CONTACTS:

*Note: Officers with more than one job title may be intentionally listed here more than once.*

Sean Casten, CEO
Sean Casten, Pres.
Aaron Walters, CFO
Gary Hoppenrath, VP-Eng. & Construction
Myra Karegianes, General Counsel/Sr. VP
Leif Bergquist, VP-Bus. Dev.
Dick Munson, Sr. VP-Public Affairs
Scott Kerrigan, VP-Controller
Dick Munson, Sr. VP-Strategic Planning
Thomas P. O'Brien, Sr. VP-Bus. Dev.
Leif Berqquist, VP-Bus. Dev.
John Whitehouse, VP-Bus. Dev.
Thomas R. Casten, Chmn.

| | |
|---|---|
| **Phone:** 630-590-6030 | **Fax:** 630-590-6037 |
| **Toll-Free:** | |
| **Address:** 640 Quail Ridge Dr., Westmont, IL 60559 US | |

## GROWTH PLANS/SPECIAL FEATURES:

Recycled Energy Development (RED) is a clean energy provider focused on owning and developing combined heat and power (cogeneration) facilities. The firm aims to reduce greenhouse-gas emissions, as well as reduce energy costs and increase power reliability by recycling waste heat and producing thermal power and electricity. The company also aims to create increased profits for industrial partners by providing the possibility of emission credits. It plans to decrease energy costs by at least 20% and to buy energy plants at book value for single digit 20-year mortgage payments. RED's activities revolve around developing various recycling projects that collectively are equal to 7% of U.S. energy recycling capacity and are predicted to produce high returns on capital. Turbostream, the company's wholly-owned subsidiary, is a converter of waste energy into electricity. It has currently installed more than 180 systems in 32 states and 18 countries, and has consequently saved customers $200 million and lowered global CO2 emissions by 4 million tons. Turbostream's services include detailed site engineering; design optimization; and capital equipment and turnkey installations. RED's current project is West Virginia Alloys, a subsidiary of Globe Metallurgical Inc. and includes the generation of 40-44 megawatts of cheaper power from a new coal plant without emitting carbon dioxide and without using fossil fuel.

## FINANCIALS:

**Sales and profits are in thousands of dollars—add 000 to get the full amount. 2008 Note: Financial information for 2008 was not available for all companies at press time.**

| | | |
|---|---|---|
| 2008 Sales: $ | 2008 Profits: $ | **U.S. Stock Ticker: Private** |
| 2007 Sales: $ | 2007 Profits: $ | **Int'l Ticker:** Int'l Exchange: |
| 2006 Sales: $ | 2006 Profits: $ | Employees: |
| 2005 Sales: $ | 2005 Profits: $ | Fiscal Year Ends: |
| 2004 Sales: $ | 2004 Profits: $ | Parent Company: |

## SALARIES/BENEFITS:

| | | | | |
|---|---|---|---|---|
| Pension Plan: | ESOP Stock Plan: | Profit Sharing: | Top Exec. Salary: $ | Bonus: $ |
| Savings Plan: | Stock Purch. Plan: | | Second Exec. Salary: $ | Bonus: $ |

## OTHER THOUGHTS:

**Apparent Women Officers or Directors**: 1
**Hot Spot for Advancement for Women/Minorities**:

## LOCATIONS: ("Y" = Yes)

| West: | Southwest: | Midwest: | Southeast: | Northeast: | International: |
|---|---|---|---|---|---|
| | | Y | | Y | |

# RED HAT INC

www.redhat.com

**Industry Group Code:** 511204 **Ranks within this company's industry group:** Sales: 2 Profits: 1

| Management: | | Sales/Marketing: | | Liberal Arts: | | Information Systems: | | Professionals: | | Technical/Scientific: | |
|---|---|---|---|---|---|---|---|---|---|---|---|
| Mgmt. Trainees: | | Mktg. Professionals: | Y | Gen. Writing/Editing: | | Info. Management: | Y | Finance/Accounting: | Y | Engineers, Elec.: | Y |
| Experienced Mgmt.: | Y | Retail Sales: | | Technical Writing: | Y | Software Dev.: | Y | Law: | Y | Engineers, Other: | |
| Int'l Business: | Y | Commercial/Industrial: | Y | Graphic Arts/Photog.: | | Hardware Dev.: | | HR/Other: | Y | Health/Lab: | |
| MBA Graduates: | Y | Sales Trainees: | Y | Music: | | Systems Integration: | | Training: | Y | Scientists/Research: | |
| | | Advertising Pros.: | | Broadcasting: | | Consulting/Other: | | Health Care: | | Petroleum/Chemicals: | |
| | | | | Other: | | | | Consulting: | | Math/Other: | Y |

## TYPES OF BUSINESS:

Computer Software-Linux Operating Systems
Open-Source Software

## BRANDS/DIVISIONS/AFFILIATES:

Red Hat Linux RHEL 5
JBoss Enterprise Middleware Suite
Red Hat Network
JBoss Operations Network

## CONTACTS: *Note: Officers with more than one job title may be intentionally listed here more than once.*

Jim Whitehurst, CEO
Jim Whitehurst, Pres.
Charlie Peters, CFO/Exec. VP
DeLisa Alexander, Sr. VP-People
Lee Congdon, CIO
Brian Stevens, CTO
Brian Stevens, VP-Eng.
Michael Cunningham, General Counsel/Exec. VP
Nick Van Wyk, VP-Oper./Sr. Transformation Exec.
Alex Pinchev, Exec. VP/Pres., Global Sales, Svcs. & Field Mktg.
DeLisa Alexander, Sr. VP-Brand
Paul Cormier, Exec. VP/Pres., Products & Technologies
Matthew J. Szulik, Chmn./CEO

| | |
|---|---|
| **Phone:** 919-754-3700 | **Fax:** 919-754-3701 |
| **Toll-Free:** | |
| **Address:** 1801 Varsity Dr., Raleigh, NC 27606 US | |

## GROWTH PLANS/SPECIAL FEATURES:

Red Hat, Inc. is a provider of open source software solutions, including its core enterprise operating system platform Red Hat Enterprise Linux, the enterprise middleware platform JBoss Enterprise Middleware Suite and other Red Hat enterprise technologies. The company offers a choice of operating system platforms for servers, work stations and desktops that support multiple application areas, including the data center, edge-of-the-network applications, IT infrastructure, corporate desktop and technical/developer workstation. The most recent version of Red Hat Enterprise Linux, RHEL 5, offers additional technology enhancements, including integrated virtualization. The enterprise middleware platform, JBoss Enterprise Middleware, delivers a suite of middleware products for service-oriented architectures, permitting web-enabled applications to run on open source and other platforms. JBoss Enterprise Middleware provides an application infrastructure for building and deploying distributed applications that are accessible via the Internet, corporate intranets, extranets and virtual private networks. Examples of applications deployed on JBoss include online e-business, hotel and airline reservations, online banking, credit card processing, securities trading, healthcare systems, customer and partner portals, retail and point of sale systems, telecommunications network infrastructure and grid-based systems. The integrated management services, Red Hat Network and JBoss Operations Network, permit Red Hat enterprise technologies to be updated and configured and the performance of these and other technologies to be monitored and managed in an automated fashion. The firm's suite of training and other professional service offerings enable enterprise customers to adapt Red Hat's technologies to their needs. Additionally, Red Hat provides other infrastructure enterprise technologies, including technologies for assisting software development, providing higher availability clustering of systems and services, scalable authentication and directory services. In September 2008, the company acquired Qumranet, Inc., for approximately $107 million.

Red Hat offers its employees medical, dental and vision insurance; life and disability insurance; tuition reimbursement; a 401(k) plan; and an employee assistance program.

## FINANCIALS: **Sales and profits are in thousands of dollars—add 000 to get the full amount. 2008 Note: Financial information for 2008 was not available for all companies at press time.**

| | | |
|---|---|---|
| 2008 Sales: $523,016 | 2008 Profits: $76,667 | **U.S. Stock Ticker: RHT** |
| 2007 Sales: $400,624 | 2007 Profits: $59,907 | **Int'l Ticker:** Int'l Exchange: |
| 2006 Sales: $278,330 | 2006 Profits: $79,685 | Employees: 2,200 |
| 2005 Sales: $196,466 | 2005 Profits: $45,426 | Fiscal Year Ends: 2/28 |
| 2004 Sales: $124,737 | 2004 Profits: $13,732 | Parent Company: |

## SALARIES/BENEFITS:

| | | | | |
|---|---|---|---|---|
| Pension Plan: | ESOP Stock Plan: | Profit Sharing: | Top Exec. Salary: $558,332 | Bonus: $589,363 |
| Savings Plan: Y | Stock Purch. Plan: | | Second Exec. Salary: $375,000 | Bonus: $324,149 |

## OTHER THOUGHTS:

**Apparent Women Officers or Directors**: 3
**Hot Spot for Advancement for Women/Minorities**: Y

## LOCATIONS: ("Y" = Yes)

| West: | Southwest: | Midwest: | Southeast: | Northeast: | International: |
|---|---|---|---|---|---|
| Y | Y | Y | Y | Y | Y |

Note: Financial information, benefits and other data can change quickly and may vary from those stated here.

# REDDY ICE HOLDINGS INC

**www.reddyice.com**

**Industry Group Code:** 312113 **Ranks within this company's industry group:** Sales: 1 Profits: 1

| Management: | | Sales/Marketing: | | Liberal Arts: | | Information Systems: | | Professionals: | | Technical/Scientific: | |
|---|---|---|---|---|---|---|---|---|---|---|---|
| Mgmt. Trainees: | Y | Mktg. Professionals: | Y | Gen. Writing/Editing: | | Info. Management: | Y | Finance/Accounting: | Y | Engineers, Elec.: | Y |
| Experienced Mgmt.: | Y | Retail Sales: | | Technical Writing: | | Software Dev.: | | Law: | Y | Engineers, Other: | |
| Int'l Business: | | Commercial/Industrial: | Y | Graphic Arts/Photog.: | Y | Hardware Dev.: | | HR/Other: | Y | Health/Lab: | |
| MBA Graduates: | Y | Sales Trainees: | Y | Music: | | Systems Integration: | | Training: | Y | Scientists/Research: | |
| | | Advertising Pros.: | Y | Broadcasting: | | Consulting/Other: | | Health Care: | | Petroleum/Chemicals: | |
| | | | | Other: | | | | Consulting: | | Math/Other: | |

## TYPES OF BUSINESS:

Ice Manufacturing
Bottled Water
Ice Production Equipment
Refrigerated Warehousing

## BRANDS/DIVISIONS/AFFILIATES:

Reddyice
Ice Factory (The)
Trimaran Capital Partners
Bear Stearns Merchant Banking

## CONTACTS: *Note: Officers with more than one job title may be intentionally listed here more than once.*

Gilbert M. Cassagne, CEO
Paul D. Smith, COO/Exec. VP
Gilbert M. Cassagne, Pres.
Steven J. Janusek, CFO/Exec. VP
Steven J. Janusek, Sec.
Mark A. Steffek, VP-Finance/Treas.
Thomas L. Dann, Sr. VP-Western Oper.
Graham D. Davis, Sr. VP-Central Oper.
Joseph A. Geloso, Sr. VP-Eastern Oper.
Steven D. Waters, Sr. VP-Mid-Atlantic Oper.
William P. Brick, Chmn.

| | |
|---|---|
| **Phone:** 214-526-6740 | **Fax:** 214-443-5357 |
| **Toll-Free:** 800-683-4423 | |
| **Address:** 8750 N. Central Expwy., Ste. 1800, Dallas, TX 75231 US | |

## GROWTH PLANS/SPECIAL FEATURES:

Reddy Ice Holdings, Inc. is one of the largest manufacturers and distributors of packaged ice in the U.S., servicing approximately 82,000 customer locations in 31 states and Washington, D.C. The company owns or leases 62 manufacturing facilities, 65 distribution centers and one bottled water plant. It has a production capacity of more than 18,000 tons of ice per day. Reddy Ice distributes 1.9 million tons of ice annually. The firm's two main ice products are Reddyice traditional packaged ice and The Ice Factory, the company's primary proprietary technology. The Ice Factory is a stand-alone system that produces, packages and displays ice products. It is most frequently used in high-volume supermarkets and other commercial locations, such as construction staging areas and large manufacturing plants. The company markets its ice products (shaped in cubes, half-moons, cylindrical, crushed and block forms) primarily under the Reddyice brand name, to a broad range of customers, including supermarket chains, convenience stores, wholesale ice and food distributors, commercial users, resorts, restaurants and agricultural buyers. Trimaran Capital Partners and Bear Stearns Merchant Banking each own 20% of Reddy Ice.

## FINANCIALS: **Sales and profits are in thousands of dollars—add 000 to get the full amount. 2008 Note: Financial information for 2008 was not available for all companies at press time.**

| | | |
|---|---|---|
| 2008 Sales: $ | 2008 Profits: $ | **U.S. Stock Ticker: FRZ** |
| 2007 Sales: $339,038 | 2007 Profits: $10,343 | **Int'l Ticker:** Int'l Exchange: |
| 2006 Sales: $334,950 | 2006 Profits: $14,661 | Employees: 2,100 |
| 2005 Sales: $319,772 | 2005 Profits: $-12,116 | Fiscal Year Ends: 12/31 |
| 2004 Sales: $285,727 | 2004 Profits: $16,551 | Parent Company: |

## SALARIES/BENEFITS:

| | | | | |
|---|---|---|---|---|
| Pension Plan: | ESOP Stock Plan: | Profit Sharing: | Top Exec. Salary: $675,423 | Bonus: $ |
| Savings Plan: | Stock Purch. Plan: | | Second Exec. Salary: $444,709 | Bonus: $ |

## OTHER THOUGHTS:

**Apparent Women Officers or Directors**:
**Hot Spot for Advancement for Women/Minorities**:

## LOCATIONS: ("Y" = Yes)

| West: | Southwest: | Midwest: | Southeast: | Northeast: | International: |
|---|---|---|---|---|---|
| Y | Y | Y | Y | Y | |

# REGENERON PHARMACEUTICALS INC

www.regeneron.com

**Industry Group Code:** 325412 **Ranks within this company's industry group:** Sales: 18 Profits: 31

| Management: | | Sales/Marketing: | | Liberal Arts: | | Information Systems: | | Professionals: | | Technical/Scientific: | |
|---|---|---|---|---|---|---|---|---|---|---|---|
| Mgmt. Trainees: | | Mktg. Professionals: | Y | Gen. Writing/Editing: | | Info. Management: | Y | Finance/Accounting: | Y | Engineers, Elec.: | |
| Experienced Mgmt.: | Y | Retail Sales: | | Technical Writing: | Y | Software Dev.: | Y | Law: | Y | Engineers, Other: | |
| Int'l Business: | | Commercial/Industrial: | Y | Graphic Arts/Photog.: | | Hardware Dev.: | | HR/Other: | Y | Health/Lab: | Y |
| MBA Graduates: | Y | Sales Trainees: | Y | Music: | | Systems Integration: | | Training: | Y | Scientists/Research: | Y |
| | | Advertising Pros.: | | Broadcasting: | | Consulting/Other: | | Health Care: | Y | Petroleum/Chemicals: | Y |
| | | | | Other: | | | | Consulting: | | Math/Other: | Y |

## TYPES OF BUSINESS:

Drugs-Diversified
Protein-Based Drugs
Small-Molecule Drugs
Genetics & Transgenic Mouse Technologies

## BRANDS/DIVISIONS/AFFILIATES:

VelocImmune
VelociGene
VelociMouse
VEGF Trap
VEGF Trap-Eye
IL-1 Trap
ARCALYST
REGN88

## CONTACTS: *Note: Officers with more than one job title may be intentionally listed here more than once.*

Leonard S. Schleifer, CEO
Leonard S. Schleifer, Pres.
Murray A. Goldberg, CFO
George D. Yancopoulos, Exec. VP/Chief Scientific Officer
Murray A. Goldberg, Sr. VP-Admin.
Stuart A. Kolinski, General Counsel/Sr. VP/Sec.
Murray A. Goldberg, Sr. VP-Finance/Treas.
George D. Yancopoulos, Pres., Regeneron Research Laboratories
Neil Stahl, Sr. VP-R&D Sciences
Peter Powchik, Sr. VP-Clinical Dev.
Robert J. Terifay, Sr. VP-Commercial
P. Roy Vagelos, Chmn.

**Phone:** 914-345-7400 **Fax:** 914-347-2847
**Toll-Free:**
**Address:** 777 Old Saw Mill River Rd., Tarrytown, NY 10591-6707 US

## GROWTH PLANS/SPECIAL FEATURES:

Regeneron Pharmaceuticals, Inc. is a biopharmaceutical company that discovers, develops and commercializes pharmaceutical drugs for the treatment of serious medical conditions. The firm is currently has three late-stage clinical development programs: aflibercept (VEGF Trap) in oncology; VEGF Trap eye formulation (VEGF Trap-Eye) in eye diseases using intraocular delivery; and ARCALYST (rilonacept; also known as IL-1Trap) in gout related illnesses. The VEGF Trap oncology development program is being developed jointly with the sanofi-aventis Group through a 2003 agreement. Also in collaboration with sanofi-aventis is REGN88, an antibody to the Interleukin-6 receptor (IL-6R) for treatment of rheumatoid arthritis, developed using VelocImmune technologies. ARCALYST, as an injection for the treatment of a rare, inherited, inflammatory condition, is currently on the market. Regeneron's preclinical research programs are in the areas of oncology and angiogenesis, ophthalmology, metabolic and related diseases, muscle diseases and disorders, inflammation and immune diseases, bone and cartilage, pain and cardiovascular diseases. The company expects that its next generation of product candidates will be based on its proprietary technologies for developing Traps and Human Monoclonal Antibodies. Regeneron's proprietary technologies include VelociGene, VelociMouse and VelocImmune, among others. The VelociGene technology allows precise DNA manipulation and gene staining, helping to identify where a particular gene is active in the body. VelociMouse technology allows for the direct and immediate generation of genetically altered mice from ES cells, avoiding the lengthy process involved in generating and breeding knock-out mice from chimeras. VelocImmune is a novel mouse technology platform for producing fully human monoclonal antibodies. In 2007, the company announced its entry into a licensing agreement with AstraZeneca for Regeneron's VelocImmune technology in its internal research programs to discover human monoclonal antibodies. In March 2008, ARCALYST in injection form went on the U.S. market.

Regeneron employee benefits include flexible spending accounts, financial counseling and tuition reimbursement.

## FINANCIALS: **Sales and profits are in thousands of dollars—add 000 to get the full amount. 2008 Note: Financial information for 2008 was not available for all companies at press time.**

| | | |
|---|---|---|
| 2008 Sales: $ | 2008 Profits: $ | **U.S. Stock Ticker: REGN** |
| 2007 Sales: $125,024 | 2007 Profits: $-105,600 | **Int'l Ticker:** Int'l Exchange: |
| 2006 Sales: $63,447 | 2006 Profits: $-102,337 | Employees: 682 |
| 2005 Sales: $66,193 | 2005 Profits: $-95,446 | Fiscal Year Ends: 12/31 |
| 2004 Sales: $174,017 | 2004 Profits: $41,699 | Parent Company: |

## SALARIES/BENEFITS:

| | | | | |
|---|---|---|---|---|
| Pension Plan: | ESOP Stock Plan: | Profit Sharing: | Top Exec. Salary: $685,000 | Bonus: $569,000 |
| Savings Plan: Y | Stock Purch. Plan: | | Second Exec. Salary: $568,800 | Bonus: $569,000 |

## OTHER THOUGHTS:

**Apparent Women Officers or Directors**:
**Hot Spot for Advancement for Women/Minorities**:

## LOCATIONS: ("Y" = Yes)

| West: | Southwest: | Midwest: | Southeast: | Northeast: | International: |
|---|---|---|---|---|---|
| | | | | Y | |

# REINSURANCE GROUP OF AMERICA INC

www.rgare.com

**Industry Group Code:** 524130 **Ranks within this company's industry group:** Sales: 1 Profits: 3

| Management: | | Sales/Marketing: | | Liberal Arts: | | Information Systems: | | Professionals: | | Technical/Scientific: | |
|---|---|---|---|---|---|---|---|---|---|---|---|
| Mgmt. Trainees: | | Mktg. Professionals: | Y | Gen. Writing/Editing: | Y | Info. Management: | Y | Finance/Accounting: | Y | Engineers, Elec.: | |
| Experienced Mgmt.: | Y | Retail Sales: | | Technical Writing: | Y | Software Dev.: | | Law: | Y | Engineers, Other: | |
| Int'l Business: | Y | Commercial/Industrial: | Y | Graphic Arts/Photog.: | | Hardware Dev.: | | HR/Other: | Y | Health/Lab: | |
| MBA Graduates: | Y | Sales Trainees: | Y | Music: | | Systems Integration: | | Training: | Y | Scientists/Research: | |
| | | Advertising Pros.: | | Broadcasting: | | Consulting/Other: | | Health Care: | | Petroleum/Chemicals: | |
| | | | | Other: | | | | Consulting: | | Math/Other: | Y |

## TYPES OF BUSINESS:

Reinsurance
Life Reinsurance
International Life & Disability

## BRANDS/DIVISIONS/AFFILIATES:

Reinsurance Company of Missouri, Inc.
RGA Barbados
RGA Canada
RGA Americas
RGA Reinsurance
MetLife Inc
Equity Intermediary Company

## CONTACTS: *Note: Officers with more than one job title may be intentionally listed here more than once.*

A. Greig Woodring, CEO
David B. Atkinson, COO/Exec. VP
A. Greig Woodring, Pres.
Jack B. Lay, CFO/Exec. VP
Graham S. Watson, Chief Mktg. Officer/Sr. Exec. VP
James E. Sherman, General Counsel/Exec. VP/Sec.
David B. Atkinson, Pres./CEO-RGA Reinsurance Company
Alain Neemeh, Pres./CEO-RGA Life Reinsurance Co. Canada
John Laughlin, Exec. VP-RGA Financial Markets
Brendan J. Galligan, Exec. VP-Asia Pacific Oper.
Steven A. Kandarian, Chmn.
Paul Nitsou, Exec. VP/Pres., RGA Int'l

**Phone:** 636-736-7000 **Fax:** 636-736-7100
**Toll-Free:**
**Address:** 1370 Timberlake Manor Pkwy., Chesterfield, MO 63017-6039 US

## GROWTH PLANS/SPECIAL FEATURES:

Reinsurance Group of America, Inc. (RGA) is an insurance holding company that is engaged primarily in traditional life, asset-intensive, critical illness and financial reinsurance. The company's principal assets are the Reinsurance Company of Missouri, Inc.; RGA Barbados; RGA Canada; and RGA Americas. Additionally, the firm has investments in several other wholly-owned subsidiaries. RGA's international operations include subsidiaries, branch operations and 24 representative offices in 21 countries in the Americas, Europe, Asia-Pacific and Africa. RGA is one of the largest life reinsurers in the world, with approximately $2.2 trillion of life insurance in force. The U.S. operations of the company market life reinsurance, reinsurance of asset-intensive products and financial reinsurance to the largest life insurance companies in the U.S. The Canadian operations assist clients with capital management activity and mortality risk management and provide traditional individual life reinsurance, including preferred underwriting products, as well as creditor and critical illness products. Combined, the U.S. and Canadian operations contributed to approximately 68.5% of RGA's net premiums during 2007. The company's European and South African operations provide life and critical illness reinsurance to clients throughout Europe and South Africa through yearly renewable term and coinsurance agreements. The company's Asia-Pacific operations conduct reinsurance business in the Asia-Pacific region through branch operations in Hong Kong and representative offices in Japan, Taiwan and South Korea. The company conducts reinsurance business in the Latin American region through RGA Reinsurance. Approximately 52% of RGA's outstanding stock is owned by General American Life Insurance Company, a wholly-owned subsidiary of MetLife, Inc. Under license agreements with MetLife, the company provides electronic underwriting and Internet hosting services to MetLife through its RDA Reinsurance subsidiary. In March 2007, the company began operating a licensed life reinsurance branch in Taiwan. In 2008, the firm opened a new office in Germany.

## FINANCIALS: **Sales and profits are in thousands of dollars—add 000 to get the full amount. 2008 Note: Financial information for 2008 was not available for all companies at press time.**

| | | |
|---|---|---|
| 2008 Sales: $ | 2008 Profits: $ | **U.S. Stock Ticker: RGA** |
| 2007 Sales: $5,718,400 | 2007 Profits: $293,800 | **Int'l Ticker:** Int'l Exchange: |
| 2006 Sales: $5,193,700 | 2006 Profits: $288,200 | Employees: 1,066 |
| 2005 Sales: $4,584,700 | 2005 Profits: $224,200 | Fiscal Year Ends: 12/31 |
| 2004 Sales: $4,038,900 | 2004 Profits: $221,900 | Parent Company: |

## SALARIES/BENEFITS:

| | | | | |
|---|---|---|---|---|
| Pension Plan: | ESOP Stock Plan: | Profit Sharing: Y | Top Exec. Salary: $788,462 | Bonus: $1,368,825 |
| Savings Plan: Y | Stock Purch. Plan: | | Second Exec. Salary: $475,000 | Bonus: $703,005 |

## OTHER THOUGHTS:

**Apparent Women Officers or Directors**: 1
**Hot Spot for Advancement for Women/Minorities**:

## LOCATIONS: ("Y" = Yes)

| West: | Southwest: | Midwest: | Southeast: | Northeast: | International: |
|---|---|---|---|---|---|
| | | Y | | | Y |

# REVOLUTION HEALTH GROUP LLC

www.revolutionhealth.com

**Industry Group Code:** 514199 **Ranks within this company's industry group:** Sales: 6 Profits:

| Management: | | Sales/Marketing: | | Liberal Arts: | | Information Systems: | | Professionals: | | Technical/Scientific: | |
|---|---|---|---|---|---|---|---|---|---|---|---|
| Mgmt. Trainees: | | Mktg. Professionals: | Y | Gen. Writing/Editing: | Y | Info. Management: | Y | Finance/Accounting: | Y | Engineers, Elec.: | |
| Experienced Mgmt.: | Y | Retail Sales: | | Technical Writing: | | Software Dev.: | Y | Law: | Y | Engineers, Other: | |
| Int'l Business: | | Commercial/Industrial: | Y | Graphic Arts/Photog.: | Y | Hardware Dev.: | | HR/Other: | Y | Health/Lab: | |
| MBA Graduates: | Y | Sales Trainees: | Y | Music: | | Systems Integration: | Y | Training: | Y | Scientists/Research: | |
| | | Advertising Pros.: | Y | Broadcasting: | | Consulting/Other: | | Health Care: | | Petroleum/Chemicals: | |
| | | | | Other: | Y | | | Consulting: | | Math/Other: | |

## TYPES OF BUSINESS:

Healthcare & Medical Information Provider

## BRANDS/DIVISIONS/AFFILIATES:

Revolution LLC
RevolutionHealth.com
MayoClinic.com
RHG Insurance Services, LLC
Extended Health
TLContact, Inc.
CarePages.com
HealthTalk

## CONTACTS:

*Note: Officers with more than one job title may be intentionally listed here more than once.*

Steve Case, CEO
Tim Davenport, Pres.
Ron Peele, CFO
Noel Obourn, Chief Sales Officer
Martin R. Fisher, CTO
James Bramson, General Counsel
Michael Singer, Exec. VP-Corp. Dev.
Jay Silverstein, Chief Imagineer
Jeffrey Gruen, Chief Medical Officer
Melanie Bowen, Gen. Manager-RevolutionHealth.com
Anna Slomovic, Chief Privacy Officer
Steve Case, Chmn.

| **Phone:** 202-776-1407 | **Fax:** |
|---|---|
| **Toll-Free:** | |
| **Address:** 1250 Connecticut Ave. NW, Ste. 600, Washington, DC 20036-2651 US | |

## GROWTH PLANS/SPECIAL FEATURES:

Revolution Health Group, LLC, part of the Revolution LLC group of companies founded by AOL co-founder Steve Case, seeks to allow consumers to make more informed healthcare choices. For instance, the company's web site, RevolutionHealth.com, offers a symptom checker, powered by MayoClinic.com, allowing users to input symptoms and receive feedback suggesting whether or not their condition is likely to need medical treatment. In all, the web site offers 125 similar online tools as well as other healthcare information. Additionally, Revolution Health offers membership, primarily targeting businesses, offering telephone based assistance ranging from answering health questions to helping settle health insurance claims and scheduling appointments. Furthermore, affiliate RHG Insurance Services, LLC, a licensed insurance agency, provides health insurance through insurance companies they work with (since it is not itself an insurance company), receiving a commission from any insurance purchased through it. Revolution Health, working through affiliate Extended Health, allows consumers to browse and compare health insurance products, and even helps consumers contact trusted brokers. Many of the company's services are offered free of charge; and the company makes money primarily by offering advertising on its web site, through its membership options and through RHG Insurance Services. Some of the company's partnerships include Alternative Medicine Magazine; Psychology Today; Rodale Inc., publisher of Men's Health, Women's Health, Prevention, Runner's World and other magazines; and Harvard Health Publications, a division of Harvard Medical School. In April 2007, the firm acquired TLContact, Inc., operator of CarePages.com, a leading Internet service providing family and friends the opportunity to develop online communities to support communication when someone close to them is receiving care. In December 2007, the firm acquired HealthTalk, which provides online chronic care information.

Revolution offers its employees medical and dental plans; stock options; a 401(k) plan; and a casual work environment with flexible hours.

## FINANCIALS:

**Sales and profits are in thousands of dollars—add 000 to get the full amount. 2008 Note: Financial information for 2008 was not available for all companies at press time.**

| | | |
|---|---|---|
| 2008 Sales: $ | 2008 Profits: $ | **U.S. Stock Ticker: Private** |
| 2007 Sales: $28,700 | 2007 Profits: $ | **Int'l Ticker:** Int'l Exchange: |
| 2006 Sales: $ | 2006 Profits: $ | Employees: 300 |
| 2005 Sales: $ | 2005 Profits: $ | Fiscal Year Ends: 12/31 |
| 2004 Sales: $ | 2004 Profits: $ | Parent Company: |

## SALARIES/BENEFITS:

| | | | | |
|---|---|---|---|---|
| Pension Plan: | ESOP Stock Plan: | Profit Sharing: | Top Exec. Salary: $ | Bonus: $ |
| Savings Plan: Y | Stock Purch. Plan: Y | | Second Exec. Salary: $ | Bonus: $ |

## OTHER THOUGHTS:

**Apparent Women Officers or Directors**: 4
**Hot Spot for Advancement for Women/Minorities**: Y

## LOCATIONS: ("Y" = Yes)

| West: | Southwest: | Midwest: | Southeast: | Northeast: | International: |
|---|---|---|---|---|---|
| | | | | Y | |

# RIGHTNOW TECHNOLOGIES INC

**www.rightnow.com**

**Industry Group Code:** 511203 **Ranks within this company's industry group:** Sales: 4 Profits: 5

| Management: | | Sales/Marketing: | | Liberal Arts: | | Information Systems: | | Professionals: | | Technical/Scientific: | |
|---|---|---|---|---|---|---|---|---|---|---|---|
| Mgmt. Trainees: | | Mktg. Professionals: | Y | Gen. Writing/Editing: | | Info. Management: | Y | Finance/Accounting: | Y | Engineers, Elec.: | Y |
| Experienced Mgmt.: | Y | Retail Sales: | | Technical Writing: | Y | Software Dev.: | Y | Law: | Y | Engineers, Other: | |
| Int'l Business: | Y | Commercial/Industrial: | Y | Graphic Arts/Photog.: | | Hardware Dev.: | | HR/Other: | Y | Health/Lab: | |
| MBA Graduates: | Y | Sales Trainees: | Y | Music: | | Systems Integration: | | Training: | Y | Scientists/Research: | |
| | | Advertising Pros.: | | Broadcasting: | | Consulting/Other: | | Health Care: | | Petroleum/Chemicals: | |
| | | | | Other: | Y | | | Consulting: | | Math/Other: | Y |

## TYPES OF BUSINESS:

Software-Customer Relationship Management
Sales & Marketing Software
Professional Services

## BRANDS/DIVISIONS/AFFILIATES:

RightNow Service
RightNow Sales
RightNow Marketing
RightNow Feedback
RightNow Voice
RightNow Analytics

## CONTACTS:

*Note: Officers with more than one job title may be intentionally listed here more than once.*

Greg R. Gianforte, CEO
Susan Carstensen, COO
Jeff Davison, CFO
Jason Mittelstaedt, Chief Mktg. Officer
Laef Olson, CIO
Mike A. Myer, CTO
Mike A. Myer, VP-Prod. Dev.
Alan A. Rassaby, General Counsel/VP-Legal & Risk Mgmt.
Jeff Davison, Treas.
Steve Daines, VP/Gen. Mgr.-Asia/Pacific
Greg R. Gianforte, Chmn.
Joseph Brown, VP/Gen. Mgr.-EMEA

**Phone:** 406-522-4200 **Fax:** 406-522-4227
**Toll-Free:** 877-363-5678
**Address:** 136 Enterprise Blvd., Bozeman, MT 59718-9300 US

## GROWTH PLANS/SPECIAL FEATURES:

RightNow Technologies, Inc. is a major provider of on-demand customer relationship management (CRM) products and professional services that help organizations of all sizes build customer-focused businesses. RightNow's technology enables an organization's service, marketing and sales personnel to leverage a common application platform for phone, e-mail and chat functions. Additionally, through its on-demand delivery approach, RightNow's is able to reduce the complexity associated with traditional on-premise solutions and offer its products at lower prices than competitors. Products are designed to integrate with traditional enterprise applications, and are available in 33 languages and dialects. The firm's CRM products include six RightNow branded lines. RightNow Service, which typically generates approximately 80% of the firm's revenues, is a multi-channel product that handles customer interactions in both traditional and online channels. RightNow Sales, a sales automation solution, maximizes sales efficiency and productivity. RightNow Marketing reduces the complexity of marketing campaign administration. RightNow Feedback increases a firm's real-time customer feedback capture and response options. RightNow Voice offers businesses voice automation services such as call routing, survey tools and customer self-service options. Lastly, RightNow Analytics offers service, sales, marketing and feedback analytics tools. RightNow's professional services consist of business process optimization, integration services, customer development consultations and customer relations training for contact center staff. The firm serves approximately 1,800 corporate customers worldwide, including firms in the following industries and sectors: travel and hospitality; telecommunications; retail and consumer goods; hi-tech; finance; education; civilian and defense agencies of the U.S. Federal Government; and U.S. and foreign state and local governments. Besides its Montana headquarters, RightNow has U.S. offices in New York, New Jersey, Illinois, Texas, Washington D.C. and California, as well as international locations in Australia, Japan, Canada, the U.K., Holland and Germany.

## FINANCIALS:

**Sales and profits are in thousands of dollars—add 000 to get the full amount. 2008 Note: Financial information for 2008 was not available for all companies at press time.**

| | | |
|---|---|---|
| 2008 Sales: $140,400 | 2008 Profits: $-7,300 | **U.S. Stock Ticker: RNOW** |
| 2007 Sales: $112,077 | 2007 Profits: $-18,641 | **Int'l Ticker:** Int'l Exchange: |
| 2006 Sales: $110,388 | 2006 Profits: $-5,008 | Employees: 686 |
| 2005 Sales: $87,148 | 2005 Profits: $7,693 | Fiscal Year Ends: 12/31 |
| 2004 Sales: $61,800 | 2004 Profits: $3,400 | Parent Company: |

## SALARIES/BENEFITS:

| | | | | |
|---|---|---|---|---|
| Pension Plan: | ESOP Stock Plan: | Profit Sharing: | Top Exec. Salary: $300,000 | Bonus: $88,864 |
| Savings Plan: Y | Stock Purch. Plan: | | Second Exec. Salary: $245,000 | Bonus: $109,098 |

## OTHER THOUGHTS:

**Apparent Women Officers or Directors**: 1
**Hot Spot for Advancement for Women/Minorities**: Y

## LOCATIONS: ("Y" = Yes)

| West: | Southwest: | Midwest: | Southeast: | Northeast: | International: |
|---|---|---|---|---|---|
| Y | Y | Y | | Y | Y |

# ROBERT W BAIRD & CO INC

www.rwbaird.com

**Industry Group Code:** 523110 **Ranks within this company's industry group:** Sales: 1 Profits:

| Management: | | Sales/Marketing: | | Liberal Arts: | | Information Systems: | | Professionals: | | Technical/Scientific: | |
|---|---|---|---|---|---|---|---|---|---|---|---|
| Mgmt. Trainees: | | Mktg. Professionals: | | Gen. Writing/Editing: | | Info. Management: | Y | Finance/Accounting: | Y | Engineers, Elec.: | |
| Experienced Mgmt.: | Y | Retail Sales: | | Technical Writing: | | Software Dev.: | | Law: | Y | Engineers, Other: | |
| Int'l Business: | Y | Commercial/Industrial: | | Graphic Arts/Photog.: | | Hardware Dev.: | | HR/Other: | Y | Health/Lab: | |
| MBA Graduates: | Y | Sales Trainees: | | Music: | | Systems Integration: | | Training: | Y | Scientists/Research: | |
| | | Advertising Pros.: | | Broadcasting: | | Consulting/Other: | | Health Care: | | Petroleum/Chemicals: | |
| | | | | Other: | | | | Consulting: | | Math/Other: | |

## TYPES OF BUSINESS:

Investment Banking
Investment Management
Stock Brokerage
Research
Financial Advising
Private Equity
Venture Capital

## BRANDS/DIVISIONS/AFFILIATES:

Baird
Robert W. Baird Group, Ltd.
Baird Financial Advisors
Baird Capital Partners
Baird Venture Partners
Baird Advisors
Baird Investment Management
Granville Baird

## CONTACTS: *Note: Officers with more than one job title may be intentionally listed here more than once.*

Paul E. Purcell, CEO
Russell P. Schwei, COO
Paul E. Purcell, Pres.
Leonard M. Rush, CFO
Leslie H. Dixon, Chief Human Resources Officer
Robert J. Venable, Dir.-Research
Russell P. Schwei, CIO
Glen F. Hackmann, General Counsel/Corp. Sec.
John D. Rumpf, Dir.-Comm.
Keith A. Kolb, Dir.-Public Finance
Mary Ellen Stanek, Chief Investment Officer
Laura H. Gough, Managing Dir.-Corp. & Exec. Svcs.
Steven G. Booth, Managing Dir.-Investment Banking
Paul J. Carbone, Dir.-Private Equity Group/Managing Partner
Paul E. Purcell, Chmn.
John A. Fordham, Chmn.-European Investment Banking

| | |
|---|---|
| **Phone:** 414-765-3500 | **Fax:** 414-765-3912 |
| **Toll-Free:** 800-792-2473 | |
| **Address:** 777 E. Wisconsin Ave., Milwaukee, WI 53201-0672 US | |

## GROWTH PLANS/SPECIAL FEATURES:

Robert W. Baird & Co., Inc., doing business as Baird, is a Wisconsin-based wealth management, capital markets, private equity and asset management firm that serves corporate, institutional and high-net-worth clients in the U.S., Europe, and Asia. It is one of the largest U.S. securities firms with headquarters outside New York. The employee-owned firm specializes in the areas of public finance and equity research. Baird's primary subsidiaries are Robert W. Baird & Co. in the U.S. and Robert W. Baird Group, Ltd. in Europe. Baird operates in five segments: private wealth management, equity capital markets; private equity, fixed income capital markets and asset management. The company's private wealth management group, Baird Financial Advisors, provides personalized financial advice to help corporate and individual investors grow and preserve their wealth and address client concerns such as wealth transfer, tax management, financial planning and asset allocation. Baird's equity capital markets group offers research, institutional equity services and investment banking. The private equity division, operating through Baird Capital Partners, Baird Venture Partners, Granville Baird and Baird Capital Partners Europe, focuses on smaller, high-potential firms and strives to maximize the value creation opportunities of its portfolio companies. The fixed income capital markets group provides fixed income sales and trading and houses a public finance division. Baird provides asset management through Baird Advisors and Baird Investment Management.

Employee benefits include medical, dental, vision, life and disability coverage; flexible spending accounts; profit sharing plan; 401(k) with company match; adoption assistance; and tuition reimbursement.

## FINANCIALS: **Sales and profits are in thousands of dollars—add 000 to get the full amount. 2008 Note: Financial information for 2008 was not available for all companies at press time.**

| | | |
|---|---|---|
| 2008 Sales: $ | 2008 Profits: $ | **U.S. Stock Ticker: Private** |
| 2007 Sales: $729,000 | 2007 Profits: $ | **Int'l Ticker:** Int'l Exchange: |
| 2006 Sales: $656,000 | 2006 Profits: $ | Employees: 2,184 |
| 2005 Sales: $ | 2005 Profits: $ | Fiscal Year Ends: 12/31 |
| 2004 Sales: $623,000 | 2004 Profits: $ | Parent Company: |

## SALARIES/BENEFITS:

| | | | | |
|---|---|---|---|---|
| Pension Plan: | ESOP Stock Plan: | Profit Sharing: Y | Top Exec. Salary: $ | Bonus: $ |
| Savings Plan: Y | Stock Purch. Plan: | | Second Exec. Salary: $ | Bonus: $ |

## OTHER THOUGHTS:

**Apparent Women Officers or Directors**: 3
**Hot Spot for Advancement for Women/Minorities**: Y

## LOCATIONS: ("Y" = Yes)

| West: | Southwest: | Midwest: | Southeast: | Northeast: | International: |
|---|---|---|---|---|---|
| Y | Y | Y | Y | Y | Y |

# RSA SECURITY INC

**www.rsasecurity.com**

**Industry Group Code:** 511211 **Ranks within this company's industry group:** Sales: Profits:

| Management: | | Sales/Marketing: | | Liberal Arts: | | Information Systems: | | Professionals: | | Technical/Scientific: | |
|---|---|---|---|---|---|---|---|---|---|---|---|
| Mgmt. Trainees: | | Mktg. Professionals: | Y | Gen. Writing/Editing: | | Info. Management: | Y | Finance/Accounting: | Y | Engineers, Elec.: | Y |
| Experienced Mgmt.: | Y | Retail Sales: | | Technical Writing: | Y | Software Dev.: | Y | Law: | Y | Engineers, Other: | |
| Int'l Business: | Y | Commercial/Industrial: | Y | Graphic Arts/Photog.: | | Hardware Dev.: | | HR/Other: | Y | Health/Lab: | |
| MBA Graduates: | Y | Sales Trainees: | Y | Music: | | Systems Integration: | Y | Training: | Y | Scientists/Research: | |
| | | Advertising Pros.: | | Broadcasting: | | Consulting/Other: | | Health Care: | | Petroleum/Chemicals: | |
| | | | | Other: | | | | Consulting: | | Math/Other: | |

## TYPES OF BUSINESS:

Computer Software-Security
Data Encryption Tools
Web Access Management Products

## BRANDS/DIVISIONS/AFFILIATES:

EMC Corporation
RSA Authentication Manager
RSA Sign-on Manager
RSA Certificate Manager
RSA Access Manager
RSA SecureID SmartCard
RSA Data Security System
RSA SecurID Token

## CONTACTS: *Note: Officers with more than one job title may be intentionally listed here more than once.*

Arthur W. Coviello, Jr., Pres.
Charles F. Kane, CFO
James Bandanza, VP-Worldwide Sales
Bret Hartman, CTO
James Bandanza, VP-Field Oper.
Dennis Hoffman, Chief Strategy Officer
James Bandanza, Sr. VP-Worldwide Sales & Field Oper.
Arthur W. Coviello, Jr., Exec. VP-EMC
Dennis Hoffman, VP/Gen. Mgr.-Data Security Group
Christopher Young, VP/Gen. Mgr.-Identity & Access Assurance Group
Edward Maggio, VP-Global Oper.

| | |
|---|---|
| **Phone:** 781-515-5000 | **Fax:** 781-515-5010 |
| **Toll-Free:** 800-495-1095 | |
| **Address:** 174 Middlesex Turnpike, Bedford, MA 01730 US | |

## GROWTH PLANS/SPECIAL FEATURES:

RSA Security, Inc., a subsidiary of EMC Corporation, is a provider of e-business security solutions in the telecommunications, pharmaceutical, financial and health care industries, as well as academic institutions, research laboratories and government organizations. The firm's secure mobile and remote access products include RSA SecureID authenticators and RSA Card Manager server software. They provide centrally managed two-factor user authentication systems for enterprise networks, operating systems, e-business web sites and other information technology infrastructures. RSA's secure enterprise access products manage and secure access to business-critical information resources within the enterprise. These products include RSA SecureID for Microsoft Windows and RSA SecureID Smart Card. SecureID software protects network resources by ensuring that only authorized users are granted access to information resources. Other products include SecurID two-factor authentication, a sign-on solution that manages passwords for enterprise applications and web sites, and RSA Certificate Manager, which enables organizations to issue, validate and manage digital certificates. The company provides identity and access management capabilities through its RSA Access Manager, which provides a secure environment for web-based resources and centrally controls user access privileges to web-based resources. The firm also uses its products to provide consumer identity protection and authentication services to the customers of online merchants and financial institutions. Recent developments include new capabilities in the RSA Data Security System's encryption and key management suite, designed to secure sensitive data in file systems, and the RSA SecurID Token for BlackBerry smartphones.

## FINANCIALS: **Sales and profits are in thousands of dollars—add 000 to get the full amount. 2008 Note: Financial information for 2008 was not available for all companies at press time.**

| | | |
|---|---|---|
| 2008 Sales: $ | 2008 Profits: $ | **U.S. Stock Ticker: Subsidiary** |
| 2007 Sales: $ | 2007 Profits: $ | **Int'l Ticker:** Int'l Exchange: |
| 2006 Sales: $ | 2006 Profits: $ | Employees: 1,319 |
| 2005 Sales: $310,100 | 2005 Profits: $42,400 | Fiscal Year Ends: 12/31 |
| 2004 Sales: $307,500 | 2004 Profits: $35,000 | Parent Company: EMC CORP |

## SALARIES/BENEFITS:

| | | | | |
|---|---|---|---|---|
| Pension Plan: | ESOP Stock Plan: | Profit Sharing: Y | Top Exec. Salary: $340,000 | Bonus: $100,000 |
| Savings Plan: Y | Stock Purch. Plan: Y | | Second Exec. Salary: $247,500 | Bonus: $171,131 |

## OTHER THOUGHTS:

**Apparent Women Officers or Directors**:
**Hot Spot for Advancement for Women/Minorities**:

## LOCATIONS: ("Y" = Yes)

| West: | Southwest: | Midwest: | Southeast: | Northeast: | International: |
|---|---|---|---|---|---|
| Y | | | | Y | Y |

# S1 CORPORATION

www.s1.com

**Industry Group Code:** 511201 **Ranks within this company's industry group:** Sales: 3 Profits: 1

| Management: | | Sales/Marketing: | | Liberal Arts: | | Information Systems: | | Professionals: | | Technical/Scientific: | |
|---|---|---|---|---|---|---|---|---|---|---|---|
| Mgmt. Trainees: | | Mktg. Professionals: | Y | Gen. Writing/Editing: | | Info. Management: | Y | Finance/Accounting: | Y | Engineers, Elec.: | Y |
| Experienced Mgmt.: | Y | Retail Sales: | | Technical Writing: | Y | Software Dev.: | Y | Law: | Y | Engineers, Other: | |
| Int'l Business: | Y | Commercial/Industrial: | Y | Graphic Arts/Photog.: | | Hardware Dev.: | | HR/Other: | Y | Health/Lab: | |
| MBA Graduates: | Y | Sales Trainees: | Y | Music: | | Systems Integration: | | Training: | Y | Scientists/Research: | |
| | | Advertising Pros.: | | Broadcasting: | | Consulting/Other: | | Health Care: | | Petroleum/Chemicals: | |
| | | | | Other: | | | | Consulting: | | Math/Other: | |

## TYPES OF BUSINESS:

Software-Financial Services
Internet Banking Applications

## BRANDS/DIVISIONS/AFFILIATES:

Enterprise
Postilion
FSB Solutions

## CONTACTS: *Note: Officers with more than one job title may be intentionally listed here more than once.*

Johann Dreyer, CEO
Johann Dreyer, Pres./Acting Pres., Postilion
Greg Orenstein, Chief Legal Officer
Greg Orenstein, Sr. VP-Corp. Dev.
Steve Dexter, Principal Acct. Officer/VP
Jan Kruger, Pres., S1 Enterprise
John W. Spiegel, Chmn.

| | |
|---|---|
| **Phone:** 404-923-3500 | **Fax:** 404-923-6727 |
| **Toll-Free:** 888-457-2237 | |
| **Address:** 705 Westech Dr., Norcross, GA 30092 US | |

## GROWTH PLANS/SPECIAL FEATURES:

S1 Corporation is a global provider of software and related services that automate the processing of financial transactions. The firm's solutions are designed for financial organizations including banks, credit unions, insurance companies, transaction processors, payment card associations and retailers. S1 operates in two segments: Enterprise and Postilion. The Enterprise segment represents global banking and insurance solutions primarily targeting larger financial institutions. It supports channels that a bank uses to interact with its customers, including self-service channels like the Internet for personal, business and corporate banking, trade finance, mobile banking, and full service channels such as teller, branch, sales and service and call center. The Postilion segment represents the community financial, full service banking and lending businesses in North America and global payment processing and management solutions. It provides Internet personal and business banking, voice banking and mobile banking solutions to community banks and credit unions, as well as payment processing and management solutions which drive ATMs (automated teller machines) and point-of-sale (POS) devices, to financial institutions, retailers, third-party processors, payments associations and other transaction generating endpoints. In addition, through its FSB Solutions brand, the segment offers full service banking and lending applications including teller sales and service activities and solutions for the call center agent's desktop. S1 licenses its Postilion suite of online, telephone and mobile banking applications primarily on a subscription only basis. Postilion's payment processing and management and full service banking solutions are primarily licensed on a perpetual basis. In October 2007, Postilion partnered with VAS Consultoria Empresarial to jointly market its integrated banking and payments solutions in Brazil.

S1 offers its employees educational reimbursement, an employee assistance program, an employee referral program, flexible spending accounts and medical, dental, vision, life, AD&D, business travel and disability insurance.

## FINANCIALS: **Sales and profits are in thousands of dollars—add 000 to get the full amount. 2008 Note: Financial information for 2008 was not available for all companies at press time.**

| | | |
|---|---|---|
| 2008 Sales: $ | 2008 Profits: $ | **U.S. Stock Ticker: SONE** |
| 2007 Sales: $204,925 | 2007 Profits: $19,495 | **Int'l Ticker:** Int'l Exchange: |
| 2006 Sales: $192,310 | 2006 Profits: $17,902 | Employees: 1,400 |
| 2005 Sales: $179,140 | 2005 Profits: $-1,057 | Fiscal Year Ends: 12/31 |
| 2004 Sales: $185,156 | 2004 Profits: $15,570 | Parent Company: |

## SALARIES/BENEFITS:

| | | | | |
|---|---|---|---|---|
| Pension Plan: | ESOP Stock Plan: | Profit Sharing: | Top Exec. Salary: $375,000 | Bonus: $307,132 |
| Savings Plan: Y | Stock Purch. Plan: | | Second Exec. Salary: $280,081 | Bonus: $156,890 |

## OTHER THOUGHTS:

**Apparent Women Officers or Directors:**
**Hot Spot for Advancement for Women/Minorities:**

## LOCATIONS: ("Y" = Yes)

| West: | Southwest: | Midwest: | Southeast: | Northeast: | International: |
|---|---|---|---|---|---|
| Y | Y | | Y | Y | Y |

# SACRAMENTO MUNICIPAL UTILITY DISTRICT

**www.smud.org**

**Industry Group Code:** 221000A **Ranks within this company's industry group:** Sales: 4 Profits:

| **Management:** | | **Sales/Marketing:** | | **Liberal Arts:** | | **Information Systems:** | | **Professionals:** | | **Technical/Scientific:** | |
|---|---|---|---|---|---|---|---|---|---|---|---|
| Mgmt. Trainees: | | Mktg. Professionals: | Y | Gen. Writing/Editing: | | Info. Management: | Y | Finance/Accounting: | Y | Engineers, Elec.: | Y |
| Experienced Mgmt.: | Y | Retail Sales: | | Technical Writing: | | Software Dev.: | | Law: | Y | Engineers, Other: | Y |
| Int'l Business: | | Commercial/Industrial: | Y | Graphic Arts/Photog.: | | Hardware Dev.: | | HR/Other: | Y | Health/Lab: | |
| MBA Graduates: | Y | Sales Trainees: | Y | Music: | | Systems Integration: | | Training: | Y | Scientists/Research: | |
| | | Advertising Pros.: | | Broadcasting: | | Consulting/Other: | | Health Care: | | Petroleum/Chemicals: | Y |
| | | | | Other: | | | | Consulting: | | Math/Other: | |

## TYPES OF BUSINESS:

Electric Utility
Hydroelectric Generation
Solar Generation
Wind Generation

## BRANDS/DIVISIONS/AFFILIATES:

## CONTACTS: *Note: Officers with more than one job title may be intentionally listed here more than once.*

John DiStasio, CEO/Gen. Mgr.
James Tracy, CFO
Gary King, Dir.-Workforce
Linda Johnson, CIO
Linda Johnson, Dir.-Bus. Tech.
Betty Masuoka, Asst. Gen. Mgr.-Admin. Svcs.
Arlen Orchard, General Counsel/Sec.
Linda Johnson, Dir.-Change Mgmt.
Elisabeth Brinton, Dir.-Comm. & Community Rel.
Jim Shelter, Asst. Gen. Mgr.-Energy Supply
Michael Gianunzio, Dir.-Legislative & Regulatory
Phil West, Dir.-Customer Svcs.
Larry Carr, Board Pres.

| **Phone:** 916-452-3211 | **Fax:** 916-732-5835 |
|---|---|
| **Toll-Free:** | |
| **Address:** 6201 S St., Sacramento, CA 95817 US | |

## GROWTH PLANS/SPECIAL FEATURES:

Sacramento Municipal Utility District (SMUD) is one of the largest electric utilities in the U.S. that is owned by a local government. The company serves a 900,000-square-mile area in the counties of Sacramento and Placer, California and has more approximately 589,599 customers. The firm, with 688 total megawatts of power generating capacity, uses hydroelectric and cogeneration power plants to create more than half of its electricity and purchases the remainder from alternative energy generation plants. SMUD has one of the largest solar energy distribution systems in the U.S. and recently constructed a solar energy plant with a 3.2-megawatt capacity. The company has increased generation capacity and created its own transmission control area in order to decrease dependence on third-party energy generators and compete in California's deregulated power market. The firm also has been selected to test hydrogen fuel vehicles. SMUD plans on investing money in methane-generated electricity. In April 2008, the company opened a solar-powered hydrogen fueling station to serve fuel-cell electric vehicles.

The company offers its employees benefits that include health insurance; the California Public Employees Retirement System defined benefit retirement plan; 401(k) and 457 savings plans; on-site child care and fitness center; credit union membership; the CalPERS long-term care program; a paid education and employee development program; employee discounts; a personal computer purchase program; an employee social and recreational association; camping privileges in the Sierra Nevada; an employee assistance program; and a rideshare program with commuter vans.

## FINANCIALS: **Sales and profits are in thousands of dollars—add 000 to get the full amount. 2008 Note: Financial information for 2008 was not available for all companies at press time.**

| | | |
|---|---|---|
| 2008 Sales: $ | 2008 Profits: $ | **U.S. Stock Ticker: Government-Owned** |
| 2007 Sales: $1,312,083 | 2007 Profits: $ | **Int'l Ticker:** Int'l Exchange: |
| 2006 Sales: $1,354,427 | 2006 Profits: $ | Employees: 2,226 |
| 2005 Sales: $1,225,193 | 2005 Profits: $ | Fiscal Year Ends: 12/31 |
| 2004 Sales: $1,068,727 | 2004 Profits: $ | Parent Company: |

## SALARIES/BENEFITS:

| | | | | |
|---|---|---|---|---|
| Pension Plan: Y | ESOP Stock Plan: | Profit Sharing: | Top Exec. Salary: $ | Bonus: $ |
| Savings Plan: Y | Stock Purch. Plan: | | Second Exec. Salary: $ | Bonus: $ |

## OTHER THOUGHTS:

**Apparent Women Officers or Directors**: 6
**Hot Spot for Advancement for Women/Minorities**: Y

## LOCATIONS: ("Y" = Yes)

| West: | Southwest: | Midwest: | Southeast: | Northeast: | International: |
|---|---|---|---|---|---|
| Y | | | | | |

# SALIX PHARMACEUTICALS

www.salix.com

**Industry Group Code:** 325412 **Ranks within this company's industry group:** Sales: 13 Profits: 12

| Management: | | Sales/Marketing: | | Liberal Arts: | | Information Systems: | | Professionals: | | Technical/Scientific: | |
|---|---|---|---|---|---|---|---|---|---|---|---|
| Mgmt. Trainees: | | Mktg. Professionals: | Y | Gen. Writing/Editing: | | Info. Management: | Y | Finance/Accounting: | Y | Engineers, Elec.: | |
| Experienced Mgmt.: | Y | Retail Sales: | | Technical Writing: | Y | Software Dev.: | Y | Law: | Y | Engineers, Other: | |
| Int'l Business: | Y | Commercial/Industrial: | Y | Graphic Arts/Photog.: | | Hardware Dev.: | | HR/Other: | Y | Health/Lab: | Y |
| MBA Graduates: | Y | Sales Trainees: | Y | Music: | | Systems Integration: | | Training: | Y | Scientists/Research: | Y |
| | | Advertising Pros.: | | Broadcasting: | | Consulting/Other: | | Health Care: | Y | Petroleum/Chemicals: | Y |
| | | | | Other: | | | | Consulting: | Y | Math/Other: | Y |

## TYPES OF BUSINESS:

Pharmaceuticals Development & Manufacturing
Drugs-Gastroenterology

## BRANDS/DIVISIONS/AFFILIATES:

Colazal
Azasan
Proctocort
Anusol-HC
OsmoPrep
Xifaxan
Visicol
DIACOL

## CONTACTS: *Note: Officers with more than one job title may be intentionally listed here more than once.*

Carolyn J. Logan, CEO
Carolyn J. Logan, Pres.
Adam C. Derbyshire, CFO
William P. Forbes, VP-R&D
Adam C. Derbyshire, Sr. VP-Admin.
William P. Forbes, Chief Dev. Officer
Adam C. Derbyshire, Sr. VP-Finance
John F. Chappell, Chmn.

**Phone:** 919-862-1000 **Fax:** 919-862-1095
**Toll-Free:** 888-802-9956
**Address:** 1700 Perimeter Park Dr., Morrisville, NC 27560 US

## GROWTH PLANS/SPECIAL FEATURES:

Salix Pharmaceuticals is a specialty pharmaceutical company dedicated to acquiring, developing and commercializing prescription drugs used in the treatment of a variety of gastrointestinal diseases. The company seeks to identify late-stage or approved proprietary therapeutics for in-licensing, which subsequently advances the new drugs through regulatory procedures and final product development stages. The firm's Colazal (balsalazide disodium) treats ulcerative colitis. Azasan (azathioprine tablets), initially intended to suppress immune response in organ transplant recipients, is also marketed by Salix as a treatment for rheumatoid arthritis. The company also sells Xifaxam (rifaximin), a gastrointestinal-specific oral antibiotic; Visicol, a product indicated for cleansing of the bowel as a preparation for colonoscopy; OsmoPrep tablets; MoviPrep oral solution; Anusol-HC rectal suppositories; and Proctocort, which is available in a cream form that is indicated for the relief of the inflammatory and pruritic manifestations of corticosteroid-responsive dermatoses, and in a suppository form, which is indicated for use in inflamed hemorrhoids and postirradiation proclitis. Salix recently added Pepcid Oral Suspension and Diuril Oral Suspension to its line of products by acquiring the rights to them from Merck & Co., Inc. The primary product candidates Salix is developing are balsalazide disodium tablets, which the company intends to sell for the treatment of ulcerative colitis; a patented, granulated formula of mesalamine, which it intends to sell for the treatment of ulcerative colitis; rifaximin for various additional gastrointestinal issues; Metoclopramide, for short-term therapy following gastroesophageal reflux; and Vapreotide Acetate Powder, for the treatment of acute esophageal variceal bleeding. In 2008, the firm announced positive results concerning the Phase IIb clinical trials for Rifaximin for the treatment of patients with diarrhea associated with Irritable Bowel Syndrome (IBS).

## FINANCIALS: **Sales and profits are in thousands of dollars—add 000 to get the full amount. 2008 Note: Financial information for 2008 was not available for all companies at press time.**

| | | |
|---|---|---|
| 2008 Sales: $ | 2008 Profits: $ | **U.S. Stock Ticker: SLXP** |
| 2007 Sales: $235,792 | 2007 Profits: $8,225 | **Int'l Ticker:** Int'l Exchange: |
| 2006 Sales: $208,533 | 2006 Profits: $31,510 | Employees: 270 |
| 2005 Sales: $154,903 | 2005 Profits: $-60,585 | Fiscal Year Ends: 12/31 |
| 2004 Sales: $105,496 | 2004 Profits: $6,839 | Parent Company: |

## SALARIES/BENEFITS:

| | | | | |
|---|---|---|---|---|
| Pension Plan: Y | ESOP Stock Plan: | Profit Sharing: | Top Exec. Salary: $685,000 | Bonus: $342,500 |
| Savings Plan: Y | Stock Purch. Plan: | | Second Exec. Salary: $338,000 | Bonus: $88,100 |

## OTHER THOUGHTS:

**Apparent Women Officers or Directors:** 1
**Hot Spot for Advancement for Women/Minorities:**

## LOCATIONS: ("Y" = Yes)

| West: | Southwest: | Midwest: | Southeast: | Northeast: | International: |
|---|---|---|---|---|---|
| | | | | Y | |

# SAVVIS INC

www.savvis.net

**Industry Group Code:** 513390C **Ranks within this company's industry group:** Sales: 1 Profits: 1

| Management: | | Sales/Marketing: | | Liberal Arts: | | Information Systems: | | Professionals: | | Technical/Scientific: | |
|---|---|---|---|---|---|---|---|---|---|---|---|
| Mgmt. Trainees: | | Mktg. Professionals: | Y | Gen. Writing/Editing: | | Info. Management: | Y | Finance/Accounting: | Y | Engineers, Elec.: | Y |
| Experienced Mgmt.: | Y | Retail Sales: | | Technical Writing: | Y | Software Dev.: | Y | Law: | Y | Engineers, Other: | |
| Int'l Business: | Y | Commercial/Industrial: | Y | Graphic Arts/Photog.: | | Hardware Dev.: | | HR/Other: | Y | Health/Lab: | |
| MBA Graduates: | Y | Sales Trainees: | Y | Music: | | Systems Integration: | Y | Training: | Y | Scientists/Research: | |
| | | Advertising Pros.: | | Broadcasting: | | Consulting/Other: | | Health Care: | | Petroleum/Chemicals: | |
| | | | | Other: | | | | Consulting: | | Math/Other: | |

## TYPES OF BUSINESS:

Internet Service Provider
Virtual Private Networks
Managed Hosting Services
Networking Services
Government-Related IT Services

## BRANDS/DIVISIONS/AFFILIATES:

Wam!Net

## CONTACTS: *Note: Officers with more than one job title may be intentionally listed here more than once.*

Philip J. Koen, CEO
Jeffrey Von Deylen, CFO
James Whitemore, Chief Mktg. Officer
Bryan Doerr, CTO
Bill Fathers, Sr. VP-Eng. & Dev.
Eugene DeFelice, General Counsel/Sr. VP/Sec.
Timothy Caulfield, Sr. VP-Oper.
Matthew Fanning, Managing Dir.-Bus. Dev.
Paul Goetz, Sr. VP-Sales, Americas
Mary Ann Altergott, Sr. VP-Corp. Svcs.
Bill Fathers, Sr. VP/Managing Dir.-U.S.
James Mori, Sr. VP-Client Svcs.
Richard S. Warley, Sr. VP/Managing Dir.-Int'l

| **Phone:** 314-628-7000 | **Fax:** 703-716-1164 |
|---|---|
| **Toll-Free:** 800-728-8471 | |
| **Address:** 1 Savvis Pkwy., Town & Country, MO 63017 US | |

## GROWTH PLANS/SPECIAL FEATURES:

SAVVIS, Inc. provides integrated hosting, network, digital content and professional services through its end-to-end global information technology (IT) infrastructure to approximately 4,200 businesses in 45 countries and to U.S. federal government agencies. The company's primary products and services include hosting services, managed Internet protocol virtual private network (managed IP VPN) services, other network services and digital content services. SAVVIS's hosting services provide the core facilities and network infrastructure to run business applications and provide data storage and redundancy services, and include collocation, managed hosting, utility computing and professional services. Colocation is designed for customers seeking data center space and power for their server and networking equipment needs. SAVVIS manages 29 data centers located in the U.S., Europe and Asia with roughly 1.43 million square feet of gross floor space. Managed hosting services provide an outsourced solution for a customer's server and network equipment needs. Utility computing provides customers with an applications platform that delivers on-demand scalability of an entire range of IT infrastructure at lower total cost that found with traditional service provider models. SAVVIS offers assistance and consulting in security, web-based applications, business recovery, program management, infrastructure and migration. The company's managed IP VPN service is a fully managed, end-to-end solution that includes all hardware, management systems and operations to transport an enterprise's video and data applications. Its trademark, WAM!NET, provides a shared infrastructure tied to applications that streamline process and workflow around the production of digital media and marketing content. SAVVIS's other network services include Internet access and private line services to enterprises and wholesale carrier customers. In July 2008, the firm opened a new data center in Singapore.

## FINANCIALS: **Sales and profits are in thousands of dollars—add 000 to get the full amount. 2008 Note: Financial information for 2008 was not available for all companies at press time.**

| | | |
|---|---|---|
| 2008 Sales: $857,000 | 2008 Profits: $-9,200 | **U.S. Stock Ticker: SVVS** |
| 2007 Sales: $793,833 | 2007 Profits: $250,591 | **Int'l Ticker:** Int'l Exchange: |
| 2006 Sales: $763,971 | 2006 Profits: $-43,958 | Employees: 2,233 |
| 2005 Sales: $667,012 | 2005 Profits: $-69,069 | Fiscal Year Ends: 12/31 |
| 2004 Sales: $616,823 | 2004 Profits: $-148,798 | Parent Company: |

## SALARIES/BENEFITS:

| | | | | |
|---|---|---|---|---|
| Pension Plan: | ESOP Stock Plan: | Profit Sharing: | Top Exec. Salary: $475,000 | Bonus: $391,875 |
| Savings Plan: Y | Stock Purch. Plan: | | Second Exec. Salary: $425,000 | Bonus: $235,521 |

## OTHER THOUGHTS:

**Apparent Women Officers or Directors**: 2
**Hot Spot for Advancement for Women/Minorities**:

## LOCATIONS: ("Y" = Yes)

| West: | Southwest: | Midwest: | Southeast: | Northeast: | International: |
|---|---|---|---|---|---|
| Y | Y | Y | Y | Y | Y |

# SCANSOURCE INC

www.scansource.com

**Industry Group Code:** 421430 **Ranks within this company's industry group:** Sales: 1 Profits: 1

| Management: | | Sales/Marketing: | | Liberal Arts: | | Information Systems: | | Professionals: | | Technical/Scientific: | |
|---|---|---|---|---|---|---|---|---|---|---|---|
| Mgmt. Trainees: | | Mktg. Professionals: | Y | Gen. Writing/Editing: | | Info. Management: | Y | Finance/Accounting: | Y | Engineers, Elec.: | Y |
| Experienced Mgmt.: | Y | Retail Sales: | | Technical Writing: | Y | Software Dev.: | Y | Law: | Y | Engineers, Other: | |
| Int'l Business: | Y | Commercial/Industrial: | Y | Graphic Arts/Photog.: | | Hardware Dev.: | Y | HR/Other: | Y | Health/Lab: | |
| MBA Graduates: | Y | Sales Trainees: | Y | Music: | | Systems Integration: | Y | Training: | Y | Scientists/Research: | |
| | | Advertising Pros.: | | Broadcasting: | | Consulting/Other: | | Health Care: | | Petroleum/Chemicals: | |
| | | | | Other: | | | | Consulting: | | Math/Other: | |

## TYPES OF BUSINESS:

Data Capture Products, Distribution
Bar Code & Point-of-Sale Products
Telephony Products Distribution
Business Communications Systems

## BRANDS/DIVISIONS/AFFILIATES:

Catalyst Telecom
Paracon
ScanSource Security Distribution
MTV Telecom Distribution plc

## CONTACTS: *Note: Officers with more than one job title may be intentionally listed here more than once.*

Michael L. Baur, CEO
Michael L. Baur, Pres.
Richard P. Cleys, CFO/VP
Robert S. McLain, Jr., VP-Mktg.
R. Scott Benbenek, Pres., Worldwide Oper.
Andrea D. Meade, Exec. VP-Corp. Dev. & Oper.
James G. Foody, Chmn.

**Phone:** 864-288-2432 **Fax:** 864-288-1165
**Toll-Free:**
**Address:** 6 Logue Ct., Greenville, SC 29615 US

## GROWTH PLANS/SPECIAL FEATURES:

ScanSource, Inc. is a wholesale distributor of specialty technology products, providing value-added distribution sales to resellers in the specialty technology markets. The company has two geographic distribution segments, one segment serving North America from a Tennessee distribution center, the other serving Latin America (from distribution centers located in Florida and Mexico) and Europe (from Belgium). The North American distribution segment markets automatic identification and data capture (AIDC) and point-of-sale (POS) products through its ScanSource sales unit; voice, data and converged communications equipment through its Catalyst Telecom sales unit; voice, data and converged communications products through its Paracon sales unit; and electronic security products through its ScanSource Security Distribution unit. The international distribution segment markets AIDC and POS products through its ScanSource sales unit. AIDC and POS products interface with computer systems used to automate the collection, processing and communication of information for commercial and industrial applications, including retail sales, distribution, shipping, inventory control, materials handling and warehouse management. POS products are PC-based products that have largely replaced electronic cash registers in retail and hospitality environments. The Catalyst Telecom sales unit is a distributor of Avaya communications products, including Avaya Enterprise Communications Group, Small Market Business Solutions and Internet protocol (IP) products. The Paracon sales unit markets business communications systems, specifically converged communications and computer communication integration products from manufacturers including Intel and Vertical Communications. Converged communications products combine traditional voice technologies with data technologies to deliver business communications solutions that combine computers, telecommunications and the Internet. In April 2008, ScanSource acquired U.K.-based MTV Telecom Distribution plc, a distributor of voice and data solutions.

The company offers its employees medical, dental and vision insurance; life and accident insurance; an employee assistance program; short- and long-term disability insurance; tuition assistance; and flexible spending accounts.

## FINANCIALS: **Sales and profits are in thousands of dollars—add 000 to get the full amount. 2008 Note: Financial information for 2008 was not available for all companies at press time.**

| | | |
|---|---|---|
| 2008 Sales: $2,175,485 | 2008 Profits: $55,632 | **U.S. Stock Ticker: SCSC** |
| 2007 Sales: $1,986,927 | 2007 Profits: $42,626 | **Int'l Ticker:** Int'l Exchange: |
| 2006 Sales: $1,665,600 | 2006 Profits: $39,816 | Employees: 1,000 |
| 2005 Sales: $1,469,094 | 2005 Profits: $35,604 | Fiscal Year Ends: 6/30 |
| 2004 Sales: $1,192,090 | 2004 Profits: $29,982 | Parent Company: |

## SALARIES/BENEFITS:

| | | | | |
|---|---|---|---|---|
| Pension Plan: | ESOP Stock Plan: | Profit Sharing: | Top Exec. Salary: $700,000 | Bonus: $1,184,625 |
| Savings Plan: Y | Stock Purch. Plan: Y | | Second Exec. Salary: $250,000 | Bonus: $80,376 |

## OTHER THOUGHTS:

**Apparent Women Officers or Directors**: 1
**Hot Spot for Advancement for Women/Minorities**:

## LOCATIONS: ("Y" = Yes)

| West: | Southwest: | Midwest: | Southeast: | Northeast: | International: |
|---|---|---|---|---|---|
| Y | Y | | | Y | Y |

Note: Financial information, benefits and other data can change quickly and may vary from those stated here.

# SCHICK TECHNOLOGIES INC

www.schicktech.com

**Industry Group Code:** 339113 **Ranks within this company's industry group:** Sales: Profits:

| Management: | | Sales/Marketing: | | Liberal Arts: | | Information Systems: | | Professionals: | | Technical/Scientific: | |
|---|---|---|---|---|---|---|---|---|---|---|---|
| Mgmt. Trainees: | | Mktg. Professionals: | Y | Gen. Writing/Editing: | | Info. Management: | Y | Finance/Accounting: | Y | Engineers, Elec.: | Y |
| Experienced Mgmt.: | Y | Retail Sales: | | Technical Writing: | Y | Software Dev.: | Y | Law: | Y | Engineers, Other: | Y |
| Int'l Business: | Y | Commercial/Industrial: | Y | Graphic Arts/Photog.: | | Hardware Dev.: | Y | HR/Other: | Y | Health/Lab: | Y |
| MBA Graduates: | Y | Sales Trainees: | Y | Music: | | Systems Integration: | | Training: | Y | Scientists/Research: | Y |
| | | Advertising Pros.: | | Broadcasting: | | Consulting/Other: | | Health Care: | Y | Petroleum/Chemicals: | |
| | | | | Other: | | | | Consulting: | | Math/Other: | Y |

## TYPES OF BUSINESS:

Equipment-Medical & Dental Digital Imaging Products
Dental X-Ray Devices

## BRANDS/DIVISIONS/AFFILIATES:

Sirona Dental Systems, Inc.
CDR
CDR Wireless
CDRPan
accuDEXA

## CONTACTS: *Note: Officers with more than one job title may be intentionally listed here more than once.*

Michael Stone, Pres.
Pio Cervi, VP-Int'l Sales
Ari Neugroschl, VP-Mgmt. Info. Sys.
Stan Manelkern, VP-Eng.
Will Autz, VP-Mfg.
Ronald Rosner, VP-Admin.
Ronald Rosner, VP-Finance

| **Phone:** 718-937-5765 | **Fax:** 718-937-5962 |
|---|---|
| **Toll-Free:** | |
| **Address:** 30-30 47th Ave., Long Island City, NY 11101 US | |

## GROWTH PLANS/SPECIAL FEATURES:

Schick Technologies, Inc. designs, develops and manufactures digital radiographic imaging systems and devices for the dental and medical markets. It is a wholly-owned subsidiary of German firm Sirona Dental Systems, Inc. operating in Sirona's Imaging Systems division. Schick's products, which are based on proprietary digital imaging technologies, create instant high-resolution radiographs with reduced levels of radiation. Specific products include the following. The CDR system, which has slowly become the firm's leading product, uses an intra-oral sensor to produce instant, full-size, high-resolution dental x-ray images on a color computer monitor without the use of film or the need for chemical development, while reducing the radiation dose by up to 80% compared to conventional x-rays. The firm also manufactures and sells CDR Wireless, a wireless radiography sensor for use with an existing CDR system; and CDRPan, a digital panoramic imaging device. In the field of medical radiography, the company manufactures and sells the accuDEXA bone densitometer, which assesses bone mineral density and fracture risk. Core products are based primarily on proprietary active-pixel sensor imaging technology, in addition to enhanced charged coupled device technology.

Employees of Schick receive paid time off; medical, dental and disability coverage; life insurance; and educational reimbursement.

## FINANCIALS: **Sales and profits are in thousands of dollars—add 000 to get the full amount. 2008 Note: Financial information for 2008 was not available for all companies at press time.**

| | | |
|---|---|---|
| 2008 Sales: $ | 2008 Profits: $ | **U.S. Stock Ticker: Subsidiary** |
| 2007 Sales: $ | 2007 Profits: $ | **Int'l Ticker:** Int'l Exchange: |
| 2006 Sales: $ | 2006 Profits: $ | Employees: 139 |
| 2005 Sales: $52,418 | 2005 Profits: $12,072 | Fiscal Year Ends: 9/30 |
| 2004 Sales: $39,393 | 2004 Profits: $18,109 | Parent Company: SIRONA DENTAL SYSTEMS INC |

## SALARIES/BENEFITS:

| | | | | |
|---|---|---|---|---|
| Pension Plan: | ESOP Stock Plan: | Profit Sharing: | Top Exec. Salary: $313,561 | Bonus: $243,750 |
| Savings Plan: Y | Stock Purch. Plan: | | Second Exec. Salary: $243,578 | Bonus: $187,500 |

## OTHER THOUGHTS:

**Apparent Women Officers or Directors:**
**Hot Spot for Advancement for Women/Minorities:**

## LOCATIONS: ("Y" = Yes)

| West: | Southwest: | Midwest: | Southeast: | Northeast: | International: |
|---|---|---|---|---|---|
| | | | | Y | |

# SCHIFF NUTRITION INTERNATIONAL INC

**www.schiffnutrition.com**

**Industry Group Code:** 325411 **Ranks within this company's industry group:** Sales: 3 Profits: 3

| Management: | | Sales/Marketing: | | Liberal Arts: | | Information Systems: | | Professionals: | | Technical/Scientific: | |
|---|---|---|---|---|---|---|---|---|---|---|---|
| Mgmt. Trainees: | | Mktg. Professionals: | Y | Gen. Writing/Editing: | | Info. Management: | Y | Finance/Accounting: | Y | Engineers, Elec.: | |
| Experienced Mgmt.: | Y | Retail Sales: | | Technical Writing: | Y | Software Dev.: | | Law: | Y | Engineers, Other: | |
| Int'l Business: | Y | Commercial/Industrial: | Y | Graphic Arts/Photog.: | | Hardware Dev.: | | HR/Other: | Y | Health/Lab: | Y |
| MBA Graduates: | Y | Sales Trainees: | Y | Music: | | Systems Integration: | | Training: | Y | Scientists/Research: | Y |
| | | Advertising Pros.: | Y | Broadcasting: | | Consulting/Other: | | Health Care: | Y | Petroleum/Chemicals: | |
| | | | | Other: | | | | Consulting: | | Math/Other: | |

## TYPES OF BUSINESS:

Vitamins/Nutrition Manufacturing & Specialty Retailing
Sports Nutrition Products
Weight Management Products
Nutrition Bars

## BRANDS/DIVISIONS/AFFILIATES:

Tiger's Milk
Schiff
Fi-Bar
Melatonin Plus
Move Free
Weider Nutrition International, Inc.
Single Day

## CONTACTS: *Note: Officers with more than one job title may be intentionally listed here more than once.*

Bruce J. Wood, CEO
Bruce J. Wood, Pres.
Joseph W. Baty, CFO/Exec. VP
Daniel A. Thomson, General Counsel/Exec. VP/Corp. Sec.
Thomas H. Elitharp, Exec. VP-Oper. & Support Svcs.
Daniel A. Thomson, Exec. VP-Bus. Dev.
Eric Weider, Chmn.

| | |
|---|---|
| **Phone:** 801-975-5000 | **Fax:** 801-972-2223 |
| **Toll-Free:** | |
| **Address:** 2002 S. 5070 W., Salt Lake City, UT 84104 US | |

## GROWTH PLANS/SPECIAL FEATURES:

Schiff Nutrition International, Inc., formerly Weider Nutrition International, Inc., develops, manufactures, markets, distributes and sells vitamins, nutritional supplements, weight management and sports nutrition products in the form of capsules, tablets and nutritional bars. Schiff sells and distributes its products through mass volume retailers, health food stores and distributors, drug stores, supermarkets, health clubs and gyms. Its leading domestic product brands are Schiff, Tiger's Milk Move Free and Fi-Bar. Schiff brand vitamin products include multivitamins, such as Single Day; individual vitamins, such as Vitamin B and Vitamin C; minerals, such as calcium; specialty formulas for men and women, such as Prostate Health and Folic Acid; and other specialty formulas, such as Melatonin Plus, Niacin and Lutein. Manufactured private label products are sold to key retailers for distribution under their store brand names. Private label products include vitamins and minerals; specialty supplements, such as joint care products; Vitamin B; and calcium. Manufactured private label products are sold to retailers for distribution under their store brand names. Schiff Nutrition's two largest customers are Costco and Wal-Mart, which combined accounted for 74% of the firm's sales in 2008.

Employees are offered medical, dental and vision insurance; life and disability coverage; a 401(k) plan; and stock options.

## FINANCIALS: **Sales and profits are in thousands of dollars—add 000 to get the full amount. 2008 Note: Financial information for 2008 was not available for all companies at press time.**

| | | |
|---|---|---|
| 2008 Sales: $176,914 | 2008 Profits: $11,302 | **U.S. Stock Ticker: WNI** |
| 2007 Sales: $172,656 | 2007 Profits: $12,436 | **Int'l Ticker:** Int'l Exchange: |
| 2006 Sales: $178,372 | 2006 Profits: $15,839 | Employees: 431 |
| 2005 Sales: $173,095 | 2005 Profits: $6,569 | Fiscal Year Ends: 5/31 |
| 2004 Sales: $168,127 | 2004 Profits: $8,887 | Parent Company: |

## SALARIES/BENEFITS:

| | | | | |
|---|---|---|---|---|
| Pension Plan: | ESOP Stock Plan: | Profit Sharing: | Top Exec. Salary: $493,833 | Bonus: $349,272 |
| Savings Plan: Y | Stock Purch. Plan: Y | | Second Exec. Salary: $269,000 | Bonus: $199,688 |

## OTHER THOUGHTS:

**Apparent Women Officers or Directors:**
**Hot Spot for Advancement for Women/Minorities:**

## LOCATIONS: ("Y" = Yes)

| West: | Southwest: | Midwest: | Southeast: | Northeast: | International: |
|---|---|---|---|---|---|
| Y | | | | | Y |

# SCICLONE PHARMACEUTICALS

www.sciclone.com

**Industry Group Code:** 325412 **Ranks within this company's industry group:** Sales: 33 Profits: 14

| Management: | | Sales/Marketing: | | Liberal Arts: | | Information Systems: | | Professionals: | | Technical/Scientific: | |
|---|---|---|---|---|---|---|---|---|---|---|---|
| Mgmt. Trainees: | | Mktg. Professionals: | Y | Gen. Writing/Editing: | | Info. Management: | Y | Finance/Accounting: | Y | Engineers, Elec.: | |
| Experienced Mgmt.: | Y | Retail Sales: | | Technical Writing: | Y | Software Dev.: | Y | Law: | Y | Engineers, Other: | |
| Int'l Business: | Y | Commercial/Industrial: | Y | Graphic Arts/Photog.: | | Hardware Dev.: | | HR/Other: | Y | Health/Lab: | Y |
| MBA Graduates: | Y | Sales Trainees: | Y | Music: | | Systems Integration: | | Training: | Y | Scientists/Research: | Y |
| | | Advertising Pros.: | | Broadcasting: | | Consulting/Other: | | Health Care: | Y | Petroleum/Chemicals: | Y |
| | | | | Other: | | | | Consulting: | | Math/Other: | Y |

## TYPES OF BUSINESS:

Pharmaceuticals Acquisition & Development
Immune System Enhancers
Hepatitis Therapies
Drug Manufacturing
Cancer Therapies

## BRANDS/DIVISIONS/AFFILIATES:

SciClone Pharmaceuticals International, Ltd.
ZADAXIN
SCV-07
RP101

## CONTACTS: *Note: Officers with more than one job title may be intentionally listed here more than once.*

Friedhelm Blobel, CEO
Friedhelm Blobel, Pres.
Randy McBeath, VP-Mktg.
Cynthia W. Tuthill, VP-Scientific Affairs/Chief Science Officer
Israel Rios, Chief Medical Officer
Craig Halverson, VP-Regulatory Affairs& Quality Assurance
Eric Hoechstetter, VP-Legal Affairs
Dean Woodman, Chmn.
Hans P. Schmid, Managing Dir.-SciClone Pharmaceuticals Int'l Ltd.

| | |
|---|---|
| **Phone:** 650-358-3456 | **Fax:** 650-358-3469 |
| **Toll-Free:** | |
| **Address:** 950 Tower Ln., Ste. 900, Foster City, CA 94404 US | |

## GROWTH PLANS/SPECIAL FEATURES:

SciClone Pharmaceuticals, Inc. develops and commercializes pharmaceutical and biological therapeutic compounds that are acquired or in-licensed at the late pre-clinical or early clinical development stage. The firm's lead product ZADAXIN is being evaluated in two Phase III hepatitis C virus (HCV) clinical trials in the U.S. The company is also planning a Phase III clinical trial to evaluate the drug in treating malignant melanoma. ZADAXIN is also being evaluated in late-stage clinical trials for the treatment of hepatitis B virus and certain cancers. The drug is a pure synthetic preparation of thymosin alpha 1, a natural substance that circulates in the body and is instrumental in the immune response to viral infections and certain cancers. ZADAXIN is approved for sale in over 34 countries, primarily in Asia, the Middle East and Latin America, with 92% of the company's sales of ZADAXIN coming from China through SciClone China. SciClone's other proprietary drug development candidates are SCV-07, which is in proof-of-concept Phase II testing for the treatment of Hepatitis C, and RP101, currently in an ongoing Phase II pancreatic cancer clinical trial. SCV-07 is a synthetic dipeptide that has demonstrated immunomodulatory activity by increasing T-cell differentiation and function, biological processes that are necessary for the body to fight infection. The company acquired exclusive worldwide rights, outside of Russia, to SCV-07 from Verta, Ltd. RP101 is a nucleoside analog which may enhance the effectiveness of chemotherapy, and has been granted Orphan Drug Designation by the FDA for the adjunct treatment of pancreatic cancer. SciClone acquired development rights for RP101 in the U.S. and Canada from Resistys, Inc. Subsidiary SciClone Pharmaceuticals International, Ltd., markets the firm's drugs.

SciClone offers employees medical, dental, vision and life insurance; short and long-term disability coverage; flexible spending accounts; a 401(k) plan; and an employee stock purchase program.

## FINANCIALS: **Sales and profits are in thousands of dollars—add 000 to get the full amount. 2008 Note: Financial information for 2008 was not available for all companies at press time.**

| | | |
|---|---|---|
| 2008 Sales: $ | 2008 Profits: $ | **U.S. Stock Ticker: SCLN** |
| 2007 Sales: $27,058 | 2007 Profits: $-9,948 | **Int'l Ticker:** Int'l Exchange: |
| 2006 Sales: $32,662 | 2006 Profits: $ 727 | Employees: 200 |
| 2005 Sales: $28,334 | 2005 Profits: $-7,713 | Fiscal Year Ends: 12/31 |
| 2004 Sales: $24,396 | 2004 Profits: $-13,278 | Parent Company: |

## SALARIES/BENEFITS:

| | | | | |
|---|---|---|---|---|
| Pension Plan: | ESOP Stock Plan: | Profit Sharing: | Top Exec. Salary: $425,000 | Bonus: $156,400 |
| Savings Plan: Y | Stock Purch. Plan: Y | | Second Exec. Salary: $345,000 | Bonus: $15,000 |

## OTHER THOUGHTS:

**Apparent Women Officers or Directors**: 1
**Hot Spot for Advancement for Women/Minorities**:

## LOCATIONS: ("Y" = Yes)

| West: | Southwest: | Midwest: | Southeast: | Northeast: | International: |
|---|---|---|---|---|---|
| Y | | | | | Y |

# SCIELE PHARMA INC

www.sciele.com

**Industry Group Code:** 325412 **Ranks within this company's industry group:** Sales: 9 Profits: 8

| **Management:** | | **Sales/Marketing:** | | **Liberal Arts:** | | **Information Systems:** | | **Professionals:** | | **Technical/Scientific:** | |
|---|---|---|---|---|---|---|---|---|---|---|---|
| Mgmt. Trainees: | | Mktg. Professionals: | Y | Gen. Writing/Editing: | | Info. Management: | Y | Finance/Accounting: | Y | Engineers, Elec.: | |
| Experienced Mgmt.: | Y | Retail Sales: | | Technical Writing: | Y | Software Dev.: | Y | Law: | Y | Engineers, Other: | |
| Int'l Business: | Y | Commercial/Industrial: | Y | Graphic Arts/Photog.: | | Hardware Dev.: | | HR/Other: | Y | Health/Lab: | Y |
| MBA Graduates: | Y | Sales Trainees: | Y | Music: | | Systems Integration: | | Training: | Y | Scientists/Research: | Y |
| | | Advertising Pros.: | | Broadcasting: | | Consulting/Other: | | Health Care: | Y | Petroleum/Chemicals: | |
| | | | | Other: | | | | Consulting: | | Math/Other: | Y |

## TYPES OF BUSINESS:

Drugs-Acquisition & Licensing
Prescription Drug Sales & Marketing

## BRANDS/DIVISIONS/AFFILIATES:

Shionogi & Co., Ltd.
Prenatal Elite
Fortamet
Altoprev
Triglide
Nitrolingual
Prenate DHA
Allegra

## CONTACTS:

*Note: Officers with more than one job title may be intentionally listed here more than once.*

Patrick P. Fourteau, CEO
Edward Schutter, COO
Edward Schutter, Pres.
Darrell Borne, CFO/Exec. VP
Leslie Zacks, Chief Legal & Compliance Officer/Exec. VP
Darrell Borne, Treas.
Joseph J. Ciaffoni, Chief Commercial Officer
Larry M. Dillaha, Exec. VP/Chief Medical Officer
Darrell Borne, Sec.
Pierre Lapalme, Chmn.

| **Phone:** 770-442-9707 | **Fax:** |
|---|---|
| **Toll-Free:** 800-461-3696 | |
| **Address:** 5 Concourse Pkwy., Ste. 1800, Atlanta, GA 30328 US | |

## GROWTH PLANS/SPECIAL FEATURES:

Sciele Pharma Inc. develops, markets and sells brand-name prescription products, focusing on cardiology, diabetes, women's health, and pediatric treatment. It both develops drug candidates and acquires or licenses pharmaceutical products that have high sales growth potential and complement its existing products. All total, the company sells 21 products, 11 of which it promotes through a nationwide sales and marketing force, generating 87% of its total sales. The sales force targets high-prescribing physicians and pharmaceutical wholesalers, such as McKesson Corporation and Cardinal Health, Inc. The firm's promoted products are Sular for hypertension; Fortamet, an adjunct to diet and exercise that lowers blood glucose in type 2 Diabetes patients; Altoprev, for cholesterol reduction and coronary heart disease; Triglide, for hyperchlesterolemia and hypertriglyceridemia; Nitrolingual, a pumpspray that provides acute relief during attacks of angina pectoris due to coronary artery disease; Prenate Elite and Prenate DHA, prenatal vitamins; Zovirax, a topical herpes medication; Allegra, a pediatric allergy and chronic idiopathic urticaria treatment; Methylin chewable tablets, for attention deficit/hyperactivity disorder; and Orapred, whose applications include severe allergy relief for patients with asthma. Sciele's non-promoted products include treatments for swimmer's ear infection, tension headaches, peptic ulcers, dementia, urinary tract infections and seasonal allergies. In addition to its marketed drugs, the company has products under development for a range of indications including chronic drooling, premature ejaculation, head lice, diabetes and hypertension. The firm enlists third-party manufacturers to manufacture all its products. In 2008, the firm plans to launch six new products, including a new formulation of Sular, treatments for type II diabetes and treatments for head lice. Also in 2008, the company acquired the Twinject epinephrine auto-injector, for the treatment of severe allergic reactions and anaphylaxis, from Verus Pharmaceuticals, Inc. In September 2008, the firm signed an agreement to be acquired by Japanese drug maker Shionogi & Co., Ltd.

Sciele offers employees medical, dental and vision coverage; flexible spending accounts; and life and disability insurance.

## FINANCIALS:

**Sales and profits are in thousands of dollars—add 000 to get the full amount. 2008 Note: Financial information for 2008 was not available for all companies at press time.**

| | | |
|---|---|---|
| 2008 Sales: $ | 2008 Profits: $ | **U.S. Stock Ticker: SCRX** |
| 2007 Sales: $382,255 | 2007 Profits: $45,407 | **Int'l Ticker:** Int'l Exchange: |
| 2006 Sales: $293,181 | 2006 Profits: $45,244 | Employees: 920 |
| 2005 Sales: $216,358 | 2005 Profits: $39,209 | Fiscal Year Ends: 12/31 |
| 2004 Sales: $151,967 | 2004 Profits: $26,554 | Parent Company: |

## SALARIES/BENEFITS:

| | | | | |
|---|---|---|---|---|
| Pension Plan: | ESOP Stock Plan: Y | Profit Sharing: | Top Exec. Salary: $375,000 | Bonus: $562,500 |
| Savings Plan: Y | Stock Purch. Plan: | | Second Exec. Salary: $280,000 | Bonus: $294,000 |

## OTHER THOUGHTS:

**Apparent Women Officers or Directors**:
**Hot Spot for Advancement for Women/Minorities**:

## LOCATIONS: ("Y" = Yes)

| West: | Southwest: | Midwest: | Southeast: | Northeast: | International: |
|---|---|---|---|---|---|
| | | | Y | | |

# SCIOS INC

www.sciosinc.com

**Industry Group Code:** 325412 **Ranks within this company's industry group:** Sales: 21 Profits:

| Management: | | Sales/Marketing: | | Liberal Arts: | | Information Systems: | | Professionals: | | Technical/Scientific: | |
|---|---|---|---|---|---|---|---|---|---|---|---|
| Mgmt. Trainees: | | Mktg. Professionals: | Y | Gen. Writing/Editing: | | Info. Management: | Y | Finance/Accounting: | Y | Engineers, Elec.: | |
| Experienced Mgmt.: | Y | Retail Sales: | | Technical Writing: | Y | Software Dev.: | Y | Law: | Y | Engineers, Other: | |
| Int'l Business: | | Commercial/Industrial: | Y | Graphic Arts/Photog.: | | Hardware Dev.: | | HR/Other: | Y | Health/Lab: | Y |
| MBA Graduates: | Y | Sales Trainees: | Y | Music: | | Systems Integration: | | Training: | Y | Scientists/Research: | Y |
| | | Advertising Pros.: | | Broadcasting: | | Consulting/Other: | | Health Care: | Y | Petroleum/Chemicals: | |
| | | | | Other: | | | | Consulting: | | Math/Other: | Y |

## TYPES OF BUSINESS:

Cardiovascular Drugs

## BRANDS/DIVISIONS/AFFILIATES:

Natrecor
ADHERE

## CONTACTS:

*Note: Officers with more than one job title may be intentionally listed here more than once.*

Roger Mills, VP-Medical Affairs
William C. Weldon, CEO-Johnson & Johnson

**Phone:** 650-564-5000 **Fax:**
**Toll-Free:**
**Address:** 1000 US Route 202 S., Raritan, NJ 08869 US

## GROWTH PLANS/SPECIAL FEATURES:

Scios, Inc., a subsidiary of Johnson & Johnson, is a biopharmaceutical company developing treatments for cardiovascular diseases. The firm's technology platform fuses classical medicinal chemistry with the most recent advances in disease-based gene array, bioinformatics and computational chemistry. The company's lead product, Natrecor, is an intravenous cardiovascular drug approved to treat acutely decompensated congestive heart failure (ADHF) for patients who have dyspnea (shortness of breath) at rest or with minimal activity, such as talking, eating or bathing. Natrecor is a recombinant form of the human B-type natriuretic peptide (hBNP), which is normally produced by the heart. The firm's current research and development program focuses on the discovery of new therapeutics for other cardiovascular diseases. Scios also has a program call ADHERE, Acute Decompensated Heart Failure National Registry, which is an observational registry that lists data on heart failure patient treatment and associated outcomes.

The company offers its employees medical coverage; life and disability insurance; health and wellness services; and savings and pension plans.

## FINANCIALS:

**Sales and profits are in thousands of dollars—add 000 to get the full amount. 2008 Note: Financial information for 2008 was not available for all companies at press time.**

2008 Sales: $
2007 Sales: $98,600
2006 Sales: $
2005 Sales: $
2004 Sales: $

2008 Profits: $
2007 Profits: $
2006 Profits: $
2005 Profits: $
2004 Profits: $

**U.S. Stock Ticker: Subsidiary**
**Int'l Ticker:** Int'l Exchange:
Employees: 777
Fiscal Year Ends: 12/31
Parent Company: JOHNSON & JOHNSON

## SALARIES/BENEFITS:

Pension Plan: Y
Savings Plan: Y
ESOP Stock Plan:
Stock Purch. Plan:
Profit Sharing:
Top Exec. Salary: $460,000 Bonus: $500,000
Second Exec. Salary: $267,750 Bonus: $180,000

## OTHER THOUGHTS:

**Apparent Women Officers or Directors**:
**Hot Spot for Advancement for Women/Minorities**:

## LOCATIONS: ("Y" = Yes)

| West: | Southwest: | Midwest: | Southeast: | Northeast: | International: |
|---|---|---|---|---|---|
| | | | | Y | |

# SCOULAR COMPANY (THE)

www.scoular.com

**Industry Group Code:** 115112 **Ranks within this company's industry group:** Sales: 1 Profits:

| Management: | | Sales/Marketing: | | Liberal Arts: | | Information Systems: | | Professionals: | | Technical/Scientific: | |
|---|---|---|---|---|---|---|---|---|---|---|---|
| Mgmt. Trainees: | | Mktg. Professionals: | | Gen. Writing/Editing: | | Info. Management: | Y | Finance/Accounting: | Y | Engineers, Elec.: | |
| Experienced Mgmt.: | Y | Retail Sales: | | Technical Writing: | | Software Dev.: | | Law: | Y | Engineers, Other: | |
| Int'l Business: | Y | Commercial/Industrial: | | Graphic Arts/Photog.: | | Hardware Dev.: | | HR/Other: | Y | Health/Lab: | |
| MBA Graduates: | Y | Sales Trainees: | | Music: | | Systems Integration: | | Training: | Y | Scientists/Research: | |
| | | Advertising Pros.: | | Broadcasting: | | Consulting/Other: | | Health Care: | | Petroleum/Chemicals: | |
| | | | | Other: | | | | Consulting: | | Math/Other: | |

## TYPES OF BUSINESS:

Grain Trade & Transport
Livestock Marketing
Ingredients
Animal Feed
Ethanol Production
Grain Elevators Operations
Transportation Services

## BRANDS/DIVISIONS/AFFILIATES:

## CONTACTS:

*Note: Officers with more than one job title may be intentionally listed here more than once.*

Randal Linville, CEO
Bob Ludington, COO
Randal Linville, Pres.
Theresa Ruby, VP-Human Resources & Performance Mgmt.
Jim Konz, VP-IT
Joan Maclin, General Counsel/Corp. Sec./Sr. VP
Chuck Elsea, Sr. VP-Oper.
David Faith, Sr. VP-Enterprise Dev.
Joan Maclin, Sr. VP-Comm.
Roger Barber, VP-Finance/Treas.
John Heck, Sr. VP-Asset Mgmt. & Bus. Dev.
Todd McQueen, Sr. VP-Oper.
Tom DiGiorgio, VP-Asset Mgmt. & Loss Control
Randall Foster, VP-Acct. & Control
Marshall Faith, Chmn.

| **Phone:** 913-338-1474 | **Fax:** 913-338-2999 |
|---|---|
| **Toll-Free:** 800-487-1474 | |
| **Address:** 9401 Indian Creek Pkwy., Bldg. 40, Ste. 850, Overland Park, KS 66210 US | |

## GROWTH PLANS/SPECIAL FEATURES:

The Scoular Company, founded in 1892, provides worldwide marketing and procurement services related to trading, transporting, handling and storing of grain, feed and food ingredients. With 52 grain handling facilities, the company has an annual handling capacity of 230 million bushels and a licensed storage capacity of more than 75 million bushels. Markets served by Scoular include aquaculture; flour milling; food manufacturing and processing; grain production; identity-preserved (IP) grain; industrial agricultural marketing; livestock feeding and feed manufacturing; pet food manufacturing; renewable fuels; container and vessel transportation; and rail, truck and barge transportation. In the aquaculture market, the company supplies aqua feed producers with all types of marine proteins and fats; non-marine proteins and fats; grains and grain by-products; and specialized spray-dried ingredients, which act as attractants and palatability enhancers. The company sources and supplies a range of ingredients for food manufacturers, including starches, proteins, lactates, fibers, textured proteins, specialty flours and trans-fat reductions. In the grain production market, Scoular buys, stores, handles and transports corn, hay, millet, rice, sorghum, soybean and wheat. The company supplies IP corn, white corn, soybeans, wheat and other grains for the IP grain market. Scoular provides industrial agricultural processors with grain; end-use markets for by-products and co-products; and risk management strategies. For pet food manufacturing, Scoular identifies, buys, sells and ships pet food ingredients, as well as providing blending and secondary manufacturing, packaging and logistics. The company provides risk management, grain origination, logistics and marketing in the renewable fuels market, and also invests in plants and serves as the lead developer for new plant projects. In September 2008, the firm acquired four grain-handling facilities from McAlister Grain Company. In June 2008, Scoular acquired 14 grain-handling facilities from Hancock Elevator, Inc.

Scoular offers employees medical and dental coverage; educational assistance; employee events; and health club reimbursement.

## FINANCIALS:

**Sales and profits are in thousands of dollars—add 000 to get the full amount. 2008 Note: Financial information for 2008 was not available for all companies at press time.**

| | | |
|---|---|---|
| 2008 Sales: $ | 2008 Profits: $ | **U.S. Stock Ticker: Private** |
| 2007 Sales: $4,300,000 | 2007 Profits: $ | **Int'l Ticker:** Int'l Exchange: |
| 2006 Sales: $2,770,000 | 2006 Profits: $ | Employees: 530 |
| 2005 Sales: $2,000,000 | 2005 Profits: $ | Fiscal Year Ends: 5/31 |
| 2004 Sales: $2,000,000 | 2004 Profits: $ | Parent Company: |

## SALARIES/BENEFITS:

| | | | | |
|---|---|---|---|---|
| Pension Plan: | ESOP Stock Plan: | Profit Sharing: Y | Top Exec. Salary: $ | Bonus: $ |
| Savings Plan: Y | Stock Purch. Plan: | | Second Exec. Salary: $ | Bonus: $ |

## OTHER THOUGHTS:

**Apparent Women Officers or Directors**: 2
**Hot Spot for Advancement for Women/Minorities**: Y

## LOCATIONS: ("Y" = Yes)

| West: | Southwest: | Midwest: | Southeast: | Northeast: | International: |
|---|---|---|---|---|---|
| Y | Y | Y | Y | Y | Y |

# SEACHANGE INTERNATIONAL INC

**www.schange.com**

**Industry Group Code:** 511213 **Ranks within this company's industry group:** Sales: 1 Profits: 3

| **Management:** | | **Sales/Marketing:** | | **Liberal Arts:** | | **Information Systems:** | | **Professionals:** | | **Technical/Scientific:** | |
|---|---|---|---|---|---|---|---|---|---|---|---|
| Mgmt. Trainees: | | Mktg. Professionals: | Y | Gen. Writing/Editing: | | Info. Management: | Y | Finance/Accounting: | Y | Engineers, Elec.: | Y |
| Experienced Mgmt.: | Y | Retail Sales: | | Technical Writing: | Y | Software Dev.: | Y | Law: | Y | Engineers, Other: | |
| Int'l Business: | Y | Commercial/Industrial: | Y | Graphic Arts/Photog.: | | Hardware Dev.: | | HR/Other: | Y | Health/Lab: | |
| MBA Graduates: | Y | Sales Trainees: | Y | Music: | | Systems Integration: | Y | Training: | Y | Scientists/Research: | |
| | | Advertising Pros.: | | Broadcasting: | | Consulting/Other: | | Health Care: | | Petroleum/Chemicals: | |
| | | | | Other: | | | | Consulting: | | Math/Other: | |

## TYPES OF BUSINESS:

On Demand Video Systems & Services
Broadband & Broadcast Products
Media Content Services
Technical Support & Other Services

## BRANDS/DIVISIONS/AFFILIATES:

Broadcast MediaCluster System
SPOT System
Axiom
On Demand Group Ltd.

## CONTACTS: *Note: Officers with more than one job title may be intentionally listed here more than once.*

Bill Styslinger, CEO
Bill Styslinger, Pres.
Kevin Bisson, CFO
Simon McGrath, Chief Mktg. Officer
Steve Davi, Sr. VP-Software Eng.
Kevin Bisson, Sr. VP-Admin.
Yvette M. Kanouff, Chief Strategy Officer
Martha Schaefer, Dir.-Investor Rel.
Kevin Bisson, Sr. VP-Finance/Treas.
Thomas Kracz, VP-Professional Svcs.
Ira Goldfarb, Sr. VP-Worldwide Sales
Maria Duquette, VP-Customer Svcs.
Bill Styslinger, Chmn.
Zheng Gao, Pres., SeaChange China & ZQ Interactive

**Phone:** 978-897-0100 **Fax:** 978-897-0132
**Toll-Free:**
**Address:** 50 Nagog Pk., Acton, MA 01720 US

## GROWTH PLANS/SPECIAL FEATURES:

SeaChange International, Inc. is a developer, manufacturer and marketer of digital video systems and services. The company operates in three segments: Broadband, Broadcast and Services. The broadband segment includes the video-on-demand (VOD) system, which digitally manages, stores and distributes digital video. The system allows cable system operators and telecommunications companies to offer VOD and other interactive television services, including interactive electronic advertising and retrieval of Internet content. The VOD platform is comprised of hardware in the form of servers that store and deliver video content; and software that manages the video assets, the network and the back-office functions of the service. The division sells Axiom, its VOD software, independent of the hardware and offers subscription services for the software. The segment also includes the SPOT System for the insertion of advertisements and other short-form video into television network streams. The broadcast segment includes the Broadcast MediaCluster System, which allows broadcast television companies to directly transmit content, such as commercials and other programming, to viewers through either single, multichannel or satellite delivery systems. The services segment, through subsidiary On Demand Group Ltd. (ODG), offers development and interactive media services in Europe. ODG specializes in aggregating content for VOD and network VOD platforms and provides services to cable operators in several European countries. In addition to media content services, the division installs, maintains and supports its hardware and software products in North America, Asia, South America and Europe. Customers include cable system operators, such as Comcast and Cox Communications; telecommunications companies, such as Verizon Communications; and broadcast television companies, such as ABC Disney, Clear Channel and China Central Television. In December 2007, ODG sold its 33% share of Filmflex Movies Ltd., a U.K. VOD service, for approximately $18 million.

SeaChange offers its U.S. employees medical, dental and life insurance, among other benefits.

## FINANCIALS: **Sales and profits are in thousands of dollars—add 000 to get the full amount. 2008 Note: Financial information for 2008 was not available for all companies at press time.**

2008 Sales: $179,893
2007 Sales: $161,334
2006 Sales: $126,264
2005 Sales: $157,303
2004 Sales: $148,166

2008 Profits: $2,902
2007 Profits: $-8,237
2006 Profits: $-12,199
2005 Profits: $9,866
2004 Profits: $5,561

**U.S. Stock Ticker: SEAC**
**Int'l Ticker:** Int'l Exchange:
Employees: 861
Fiscal Year Ends: 1/31
Parent Company:

## SALARIES/BENEFITS:

Pension Plan: ESOP Stock Plan: Profit Sharing: Top Exec. Salary: $401,250 Bonus: $653,761
Savings Plan: Y Stock Purch. Plan: Y Second Exec. Salary: $313,298 Bonus: $

## OTHER THOUGHTS:

**Apparent Women Officers or Directors**: 3
**Hot Spot for Advancement for Women/Minorities**: Y

## LOCATIONS: ("Y" = Yes)

| West: | Southwest: | Midwest: | Southeast: | Northeast: | International: |
|---|---|---|---|---|---|
| Y | | | | Y | Y |

# SEATTLE GENETICS

www.seattlegenetics.com

**Industry Group Code:** 325412 **Ranks within this company's industry group:** Sales: 36 Profits: 24

| Management: | | Sales/Marketing: | | Liberal Arts: | | Information Systems: | | Professionals: | | Technical/Scientific: | |
|---|---|---|---|---|---|---|---|---|---|---|---|
| Mgmt. Trainees: | | Mktg. Professionals: | Y | Gen. Writing/Editing: | | Info. Management: | Y | Finance/Accounting: | Y | Engineers, Elec.: | |
| Experienced Mgmt.: | Y | Retail Sales: | | Technical Writing: | Y | Software Dev.: | Y | Law: | Y | Engineers, Other: | |
| Int'l Business: | | Commercial/Industrial: | Y | Graphic Arts/Photog.: | | Hardware Dev.: | | HR/Other: | Y | Health/Lab: | Y |
| MBA Graduates: | Y | Sales Trainees: | Y | Music: | | Systems Integration: | | Training: | Y | Scientists/Research: | Y |
| | | Advertising Pros.: | | Broadcasting: | | Consulting/Other: | | Health Care: | Y | Petroleum/Chemicals: | Y |
| | | | | Other: | | | | Consulting: | Y | Math/Other: | Y |

## TYPES OF BUSINESS:

Biopharmaceuticals Development
Cancer Treatments
Monoclonal Antibodies

## BRANDS/DIVISIONS/AFFILIATES:

SGN-40
SGN-30
SGN-33
SGN-35
SGN-70
SGN-75
Antibody-Drug Conjugates (ADCs)

## CONTACTS: *Note: Officers with more than one job title may be intentionally listed here more than once.*

Clay B. Siegall, CEO
Clay B. Siegall, Pres.
Todd Simpson, CFO
Morris Z. Rosenberg, Sr. VP-Dev.
Thomas C. Reynolds, Chief Medical Officer
Iqbal S. Grewal, VP-Preclincal Therapeutics
Eric L. Dobmeier, Chief Bus. Officer
Peter D. Senter, VP-Chemistry
Felix J. Baker, Chmn.

| **Phone:** 425-527-4000 | **Fax:** 425-527-4001 |
|---|---|
| **Toll-Free:** | |
| **Address:** 21823 30th Dr. S.E., Bothell, WA 98021 US | |

## GROWTH PLANS/SPECIAL FEATURES:

Seattle Genetics develops monoclonal antibody (mAb)-based therapies for the treatment of cancer and autoimmune diseases. The company has an exclusive, worldwide license agreement with Genentech to develop and commercialize its lead product candidate SGN-40. Its research and development activities focus on mAb-based therapies for human cancers including lung, renal cell, Hodgkin's disease, non-Hodgkin's lymphoma, multiple myeloma and melanoma. Products in the developmental stage include SGN-33, in Phase II testing for acute myeloid leukemia (AML); SGN-40, which is in Phase II testing for multiple myeloma and non-Hodgkin's lymphoma; SGN-35, which is in Phase I for treatment of relapsed Hodgkin's lymphona; SGN-70, which is an IND for hematologic malignancies, renal cancer and immunologic diseases; and SGN-75, which is a preclinical candidate to treat renal cancer, hematologic malignancies and immunologic diseases. These product candidates represent applications of Seattle Genetics' primary platform technologies: genetically engineered monoclonal antibodies and antibody-drug conjugates (ADC). Each of these platforms is designed to support therapies that are able to identify and kill cancer cells while limiting damage to normal tissue. Seattle Genetics currently has license agreements for its proprietary ADC technology with Genentech, Bayer Pharmaceuticals, Inc. and MedImmune Inc. and Agensys Inc. In 2008, the firm licensed tumor-fighting technology to Daiichi Sankyo Co., based in Japan, for $4 million plus future milestone payments.

## FINANCIALS: **Sales and profits are in thousands of dollars—add 000 to get the full amount. 2008 Note: Financial information for 2008 was not available for all companies at press time.**

| | | |
|---|---|---|
| 2008 Sales: $35,236 | 2008 Profits: $-85,501 | **U.S. Stock Ticker: SGEN** |
| 2007 Sales: $22,420 | 2007 Profits: $-48,932 | **Int'l Ticker:** Int'l Exchange: |
| 2006 Sales: $10,005 | 2006 Profits: $-36,015 | Employees: 189 |
| 2005 Sales: $9,757 | 2005 Profits: $-29,433 | Fiscal Year Ends: 12/31 |
| 2004 Sales: $6,701 | 2004 Profits: $-35,439 | Parent Company: |

## SALARIES/BENEFITS:

| | | | | |
|---|---|---|---|---|
| Pension Plan: | ESOP Stock Plan: | Profit Sharing: | Top Exec. Salary: $486,025 | Bonus: $264,870 |
| Savings Plan: Y | Stock Purch. Plan: Y | | Second Exec. Salary: $325,446 | Bonus: $124,418 |

## OTHER THOUGHTS:

**Apparent Women Officers or Directors:**
**Hot Spot for Advancement for Women/Minorities:**

## LOCATIONS: ("Y" = Yes)

| West: | Southwest: | Midwest: | Southeast: | Northeast: | International: |
|---|---|---|---|---|---|
| Y | | | | | |

# SECURE COMPUTING CORP

**www.securecomputing.com**

**Industry Group Code:** 511211 **Ranks within this company's industry group:** Sales: 1 Profits: 4

| **Management:** | | **Sales/Marketing:** | | **Liberal Arts:** | | **Information Systems:** | | **Professionals:** | | **Technical/Scientific:** | |
|---|---|---|---|---|---|---|---|---|---|---|---|
| Mgmt. Trainees: | | Mktg. Professionals: | Y | Gen. Writing/Editing: | | Info. Management: | Y | Finance/Accounting: | Y | Engineers, Elec.: | Y |
| Experienced Mgmt.: | Y | Retail Sales: | | Technical Writing: | Y | Software Dev.: | Y | Law: | Y | Engineers, Other: | |
| Int'l Business: | Y | Commercial/Industrial: | Y | Graphic Arts/Photog.: | | Hardware Dev.: | | HR/Other: | Y | Health/Lab: | |
| MBA Graduates: | Y | Sales Trainees: | Y | Music: | | Systems Integration: | | Training: | Y | Scientists/Research: | |
| | | Advertising Pros.: | | Broadcasting: | | Consulting/Other: | | Health Care: | | Petroleum/Chemicals: | |
| | | | | Other: | | | | Consulting: | | Math/Other: | |

## TYPES OF BUSINESS:

Security Software

## BRANDS/DIVISIONS/AFFILIATES:

TrustedSource
Secure Firewall
Secure Safeword
SmartFilter
Secure Mail
Domain Health Check

## CONTACTS:

*Note: Officers with more than one job title may be intentionally listed here more than once.*

Daniel P. Ryan, CEO
Daniel P. Ryan, Pres.
Timothy J. Steinkopf, CFO
Atri Chatterjee, Sr. VP-Mktg.
Phyllis Schneck, VP-Research Integration
Michael Gallager, Sr. VP-Prod. Dev. & Support
Steve Kozachok, General Counsel/Sec./Sr. VP
Timothy J. Steinkopf, Sr. VP-Oper.
Ally Zwahlen, Sr. Mgr.-Public Rel.
Glenn Cross, Sr. VP-Worldwide Sales
Richard L. Scott, Chmn.

**Phone:** 408-979-6100 **Fax:** 408-979-6501
**Toll-Free:** 800-692-5625
**Address:** 4810 Harwood Rd., San Jose, CA 95124-5206 US

## GROWTH PLANS/SPECIAL FEATURES:

Secure Computing Corp. (SCC) is a global network security software company. The firm markets a comprehensive selection of interoperable, standards-compatible products for every segment of the networks market, including firewalls, web filters, authentication, access control and security-related professional services. SCC produces product lines for web gateway, messaging gateway and network gateway security, as well as identity and access management. Specific products include the following. The Secure Firewall (formerly Sidewinder) features embedded anti-virus, anti-spam, web filtering and traffic anomaly detection. Secure SafeWord products authenticate users when they connect at secure gateways and point them to authorized applications. SmartFilter products monitor and manage outbound web access to keep the workplace free from offensive content, limit legal liability, manage bandwidth, and protect against security risks like spyware and malware. Lastly, Secure Mail (formerly IronMail) neutralizes inbound threats such as spam, viruses and hacker attacks; and protects organizations from data leaks by preventing violations of corporate policy or regulatory compliance in outbound mail. Its products are used by over 22,000 customers in markets such as banking, financial services, health care, telecommunications, manufacturing and public utilities, as well as federal and local government agencies. TrustedSource, the company's cornerstone technology, accumulates data from over 7,000 sensors located in 51 countries, to create a profile of all sender activity on the Internet and watch for deviations from expected behavior. In May 2007, SCC launched Domain Health Check, a first-of-its-kind service that provides users with a free report about the security of their domain as seen and correlated from thousands of points around the globe. In March 2008, the firm rebranded all its products with the Secure name.

Secure Computing offers its employees medical, dental and vision care; life insurance; short- and long-term disability insurance; an employee assistance program; pre-tax reimbursement accounts; tuition reimbursement; and international travel insurance.

## FINANCIALS:

**Sales and profits are in thousands of dollars—add 000 to get the full amount. 2008 Note: Financial information for 2008 was not available for all companies at press time.**

| | | |
|---|---|---|
| 2008 Sales: $ | 2008 Profits: $ | **U.S. Stock Ticker: SCUR** |
| 2007 Sales: $237,905 | 2007 Profits: $-35,056 | **Int'l Ticker:** Int'l Exchange: |
| 2006 Sales: $176,697 | 2006 Profits: $-27,398 | Employees: 971 |
| 2005 Sales: $109,175 | 2005 Profits: $21,374 | Fiscal Year Ends: 12/31 |
| 2004 Sales: $93,378 | 2004 Profits: $12,835 | Parent Company: |

## SALARIES/BENEFITS:

| | | | | |
|---|---|---|---|---|
| Pension Plan: | ESOP Stock Plan: | Profit Sharing: Y | Top Exec. Salary: $425,833 | Bonus: $98,055 |
| Savings Plan: Y | Stock Purch. Plan: Y | | Second Exec. Salary: $297,578 | Bonus: $51,393 |

## OTHER THOUGHTS:

**Apparent Women Officers or Directors**: 2
**Hot Spot for Advancement for Women/Minorities**:

## LOCATIONS: ("Y" = Yes)

| West: | Southwest: | Midwest: | Southeast: | Northeast: | International: |
|---|---|---|---|---|---|
| Y | | Y | Y | Y | Y |

# SENTO

www.sento.com

**Industry Group Code:** 541512A **Ranks within this company's industry group:** Sales: Profits:

| Management: | | Sales/Marketing: | | Liberal Arts: | | Information Systems: | | Professionals: | | Technical/Scientific: | |
|---|---|---|---|---|---|---|---|---|---|---|---|
| Mgmt. Trainees: | | Mktg. Professionals: | Y | Gen. Writing/Editing: | | Info. Management: | Y | Finance/Accounting: | Y | Engineers, Elec.: | |
| Experienced Mgmt.: | Y | Retail Sales: | | Technical Writing: | Y | Software Dev.: | Y | Law: | Y | Engineers, Other: | |
| Int'l Business: | Y | Commercial/Industrial: | | Graphic Arts/Photog.: | | Hardware Dev.: | | HR/Other: | Y | Health/Lab: | |
| MBA Graduates: | Y | Sales Trainees: | | Music: | | Systems Integration: | | Training: | Y | Scientists/Research: | |
| | | Advertising Pros.: | | Broadcasting: | | Consulting/Other: | Y | Health Care: | | Petroleum/Chemicals: | |
| | | | | Other: | Y | | | Consulting: | Y | Math/Other: | |

## TYPES OF BUSINESS:

Customer Support Outsourcing
Call Centers

## BRANDS/DIVISIONS/AFFILIATES:

Sento Technical Services Corporation
Xtrasource Acquisition, Inc.
Right Channeling
Customer Choice Platform
Sento Business Intelligence
Recite CRM

## CONTACTS: *Note: Officers with more than one job title may be intentionally listed here more than once.*

Joseph Jacoboni, CEO
John Archdeacon, COO
Joseph Jacoboni, Pres.
Tom Tyler, Sr. VP-Mktg. & Sales
Stephen W. Fulling, CIO/Sr. VP
Stephen W. Fulling, CTO/Sr. VP
Stephen W. Fulling, Corp. Sec.
Richard Steiner, VP-Quality & Training
Bart van Eunen, VP-European Bus. Dev.
C. Lloyd Mahaffey, Chmn.
Emile Koolstra, VP-European Oper.

**Phone:** 801-431-9200 **Fax:** 801-492-2100
**Toll-Free:** 800-868-8448
**Address:** 420 E. South Temple, Ste. 400, Salt Lake City, UT 84111 US

## GROWTH PLANS/SPECIAL FEATURES:

Sento Corporation is a global provider of outsourced customer contact services to mid-market companies and significant divisions of larger companies. The firm specializes in Right Channeling, a methodology designed to optimize customer contact to enhance brand loyalty, improve customer satisfaction, drive business initiatives and reduce service costs. Sento offers comprehensive professional services and customer interaction tools to improve a company's customer acquisition, customer service and technical support through its proprietary Customer Choice Platform. The platform offering gives clients access to its Recite CRM tools, Assist agent interaction tools, outsourced Customer Contact Centers and Sento Business Intelligence (SBI) tools that report statistics that track customer and agent behavior. Companies can select communication channels from a range of integrated live support and web-enabled self-help applications that combine voice, chat, e-mail and web forums. Company operations are carried out by its two wholly-owned subsidiaries, Sento Technical Services Corporation and Xtrasource Acquisition, Inc. Sento also has contractual relations with a third-party provider in India. The firm has contact center facilities in the U.S., France and The Netherlands, providing customer contact service in 19 languages.

## FINANCIALS: **Sales and profits are in thousands of dollars—add 000 to get the full amount. 2008 Note: Financial information for 2008 was not available for all companies at press time.**

| | | |
|---|---|---|
| 2008 Sales: $ | 2008 Profits: $ | **U.S. Stock Ticker: SNTO** |
| 2007 Sales: $ | 2007 Profits: $ | **Int'l Ticker:** Int'l Exchange: |
| 2006 Sales: $51,129 | 2006 Profits: $- 154 | Employees: 1,840 |
| 2005 Sales: $31,786 | 2005 Profits: $-1,798 | Fiscal Year Ends: 3/31 |
| 2004 Sales: $21,396 | 2004 Profits: $-1,465 | Parent Company: |

## SALARIES/BENEFITS:

| | | | | |
|---|---|---|---|---|
| Pension Plan: | ESOP Stock Plan: | Profit Sharing: | Top Exec. Salary: $220,000 | Bonus: $73,592 |
| Savings Plan: | Stock Purch. Plan: | | Second Exec. Salary: $150,000 | Bonus: $30,383 |

## OTHER THOUGHTS:

**Apparent Women Officers or Directors:**
**Hot Spot for Advancement for Women/Minorities:**

## LOCATIONS: ("Y" = Yes)

| West: | Southwest: | Midwest: | Southeast: | Northeast: | International: |
|---|---|---|---|---|---|
| Y | Y | | | Y | Y |

# SEPRACOR INC

www.sepracor.com

**Industry Group Code:** 325412 **Ranks within this company's industry group:** Sales: 2 Profits: 6

| Management: | | Sales/Marketing: | | Liberal Arts: | | Information Systems: | | Professionals: | | Technical/Scientific: | |
|---|---|---|---|---|---|---|---|---|---|---|---|
| Mgmt. Trainees: | | Mktg. Professionals: | Y | Gen. Writing/Editing: | | Info. Management: | Y | Finance/Accounting: | Y | Engineers, Elec.: | |
| Experienced Mgmt.: | Y | Retail Sales: | | Technical Writing: | Y | Software Dev.: | Y | Law: | Y | Engineers, Other: | |
| Int'l Business: | Y | Commercial/Industrial: | Y | Graphic Arts/Photog.: | | Hardware Dev.: | | HR/Other: | Y | Health/Lab: | Y |
| MBA Graduates: | Y | Sales Trainees: | Y | Music: | | Systems Integration: | | Training: | Y | Scientists/Research: | Y |
| | | Advertising Pros.: | | Broadcasting: | | Consulting/Other: | | Health Care: | Y | Petroleum/Chemicals: | Y |
| | | | | Other: | | | | Consulting: | | Math/Other: | Y |

## TYPES OF BUSINESS:

Pharmaceuticals Discovery & Development
Respiratory Treatments
Central Nervous System Disorder Treatments

## BRANDS/DIVISIONS/AFFILIATES:

LUNESTA
XOPENEX
Desloratadine
Fexofenadine
Levocetirizine
BROVANA

## CONTACTS: *Note: Officers with more than one job title may be intentionally listed here more than once.*

Adrian Adams, CEO
Adrian Adams, Pres.
Robert F. Scumaci, CFO/Exec. VP
Mark H. N. Corrigan, Exec. VP-R&D
Andrew I. Koven, General Counsel/Corp. Sec./Exec. VP
Mark Iwicki, Chief Commercial Officer/Exec. VP
Timothy J. Barberich, Exec. Chmn.

| | |
|---|---|
| **Phone:** 508-481-6700 | **Fax:** 508-357-7499 |
| **Toll-Free:** 800-245-5961 | |
| **Address:** 84 Waterford Dr., Marlborough, MA 01752 US | |

## GROWTH PLANS/SPECIAL FEATURES:

Sepracor, Inc. is a research-based pharmaceutical company whose goal is to discover, develop and market products that are directed toward the treatment of respiratory and central nervous system (CNS) disorders. It also develops and markets improved versions of widely prescribed drugs, including treatments for asthma, depression and restless legs syndrome. These versions, known as improved chemical entities, feature enhancements such as reduced side effects, increased therapeutic efficacy, improved dosage forms and, in some cases, additional indications. Serpacor's lead product is adult insomnia treatment LUNESTA (eszopiclone), which generated 51% of 2007 product sales. It also markets XOPENEX Inhalation Solution, 41.4% of product sales, for use in nebulizer machines, which turn liquids into fine sprays; it is indicated for patients with asthma or chronic obstructive pulmonary disease (COPD). Sepracor markets its own and other companies' products through its sales force, co-promotion agreements and out-licensing partnerships. Due to its patents relating to the chemicals desloratadine, fexofenadine and levocetirizine, the company has out-licensing agreements for various allergy medications, including Schering-Plough for CLARINEX (desloratadine); sanofi-aventis for ALLEGRA (fexofenadine); and UCB Farchim SA for its XUSAL/XYZAL products (levocetirizine). In April 2007, the company commercially launched BROVANA (arformoterol tartrate), administered by nebulizer, which is indicated as a long-term, twice-daily treatment for COPD. In July 2007, Sepracor entered into a license agreement granting Eisai Co. Ltd. responsibility for the Japanese testing and distribution of LUNESTA, which is scheduled to finish clinical trials in Japan by 2010. Sepracor would still manufacture the tablets and active ingredient. In September 2007, GlaxoSmithKline plc (GSK) signed a license agreement allowing it to develop and commercialize LUNESTA, under the brand name LUNIVIA, outside the U.S., Canada, Mexico and Japan.

Employees of Sepracor receive health, dental, life and disability insurance; tuition reimbursement; adoption reimbursement; and back-up childcare.

## FINANCIALS: **Sales and profits are in thousands of dollars—add 000 to get the full amount. 2008 Note: Financial information for 2008 was not available for all companies at press time.**

| | | |
|---|---|---|
| 2008 Sales: $1,292,289 | 2008 Profits: $515,110 | **U.S. Stock Ticker: SEPR** |
| 2007 Sales: $1,225,230 | 2007 Profits: $58,333 | **Int'l Ticker:** Int'l Exchange: |
| 2006 Sales: $1,183,133 | 2006 Profits: $171,161 | Employees: 2,277 |
| 2005 Sales: $820,928 | 2005 Profits: $3,927 | Fiscal Year Ends: 12/31 |
| 2004 Sales: $380,877 | 2004 Profits: $-296,910 | Parent Company: |

## SALARIES/BENEFITS:

| | | | | |
|---|---|---|---|---|
| Pension Plan: | ESOP Stock Plan: | Profit Sharing: | Top Exec. Salary: $914,375 | Bonus: $660,000 |
| Savings Plan: Y | Stock Purch. Plan: Y | | Second Exec. Salary: $636,923 | Bonus: $666,640 |

## OTHER THOUGHTS:

**Apparent Women Officers or Directors**: 1
**Hot Spot for Advancement for Women/Minorities**:

## LOCATIONS: ("Y" = Yes)

| West: | Southwest: | Midwest: | Southeast: | Northeast: | International: |
|---|---|---|---|---|---|
| Y | Y | Y | Y | Y | Y |

# SEQUENOM INC

**www.sequenom.com**

**Industry Group Code:** 325413 **Ranks within this company's industry group:** Sales: 11 Profits: 9

| Management: | | Sales/Marketing: | | Liberal Arts: | | Information Systems: | | Professionals: | | Technical/Scientific: | |
|---|---|---|---|---|---|---|---|---|---|---|---|
| Mgmt. Trainees: | | Mktg. Professionals: | Y | Gen. Writing/Editing: | | Info. Management: | Y | Finance/Accounting: | Y | Engineers, Elec.: | |
| Experienced Mgmt.: | Y | Retail Sales: | | Technical Writing: | Y | Software Dev.: | Y | Law: | Y | Engineers, Other: | Y |
| Int'l Business: | Y | Commercial/Industrial: | Y | Graphic Arts/Photog.: | | Hardware Dev.: | Y | HR/Other: | Y | Health/Lab: | Y |
| MBA Graduates: | Y | Sales Trainees: | Y | Music: | | Systems Integration: | | Training: | Y | Scientists/Research: | Y |
| | | Advertising Pros.: | | Broadcasting: | | Consulting/Other: | | Health Care: | Y | Petroleum/Chemicals: | |
| | | | | Other: | | | | Consulting: | | Math/Other: | Y |

## TYPES OF BUSINESS:

Chips-DNA Arrays
Genotype Analysis Software
Cell Research Database

## BRANDS/DIVISIONS/AFFILIATES:

MassARRAY
iPLEX Gold
SEQureDx
Center for Molecular Medicine
AttoSense
SensiGen LLC

## CONTACTS: *Note: Officers with more than one job title may be intentionally listed here more than once.*

Harry Stylli, CEO
Harry Stylli, Pres.
Paul W. Hawran, CFO
Michael Monko, Sr. VP-Sales & Mktg.
Alisa Judge, VP-Human Resources
Charles R. Cantor, Chief Scientific Officer
Clarke Neumann, General Counsel/VP
Larry Myres, VP-Oper.
Elizabeth Dragon, Sr. VP-R&D
Steven Owings, VP-Commercial Dev., Prenatal Diagnostics
Robert M. Di Tullio, VP-Regulatory Affairs/Quality Sequenom Inc.
Allan T. Lombard, Chief Medical Officer

| **Phone:** 858-202-9000 | **Fax:** 858-202-9001 |
|---|---|
| **Toll-Free:** | |
| **Address:** 3595 John Hopkins Ct., San Diego, CA 92121-1331 US | |

## GROWTH PLANS/SPECIAL FEATURES:

Sequenom, Inc. is a genetics and molecular diagnostic company providing genetic analysis products, services and diagnostic applications for the development of noninvasive diagnostics in prenatal, oncology and infectious diseases and other disorders. The company's main source of revenue is derived from MassARRAY, a hardware and software application with consumable chips and reagents that analyzes high performance nucleic acids and quantitatively measures genetic target material and variations. The MassARRAY system offers cost-effective methods for numerous types of DNA analysis applications, which can range from SNP genotyping and allelotyping; quantitative gene expression analysis; quantitative methylation marker analysis; epigenomics; and pathogen typing. Sequenom's iPLEX Gold assay provides for multiplexed DNA sample analysis that enables the user to perform multiple sample genotyping analyses using a similar amount of reagents and chip surface area as used for a single DNA sample analysis. Customers of MassARRAY include clinical research laboratories, biotechnology companies, academic institutions and government agencies in North America, Europe, India, Australia, France, South Korea, New Zealand, Singapore, Taiwan and Turkey. Sequenom is developing various molecular diagnostic tests in prenatal genetic disorders, oncology and infectious diseases under the brand name SEQureDx. In the agricultural market, MassARRAY is utilized to provide farm-of-origin verification, country-of-origin verification, age verification and national ID programs for traceability analysis of livestock. In July 2008, Sequenom formed a global alliance with SensiGen LLC to develop and market advanced diagnostic tests and systems. In November 2008, the company acquired the Center for Molecular Medicine in Grand Rapids, Michigan, a Clinical Laboratory Improvement Act (CLIA) certified clinical diagnostics laboratory. In January 2009, Sequenom agreed to acquire the complete AttoSense portfolio of tests from privately held biotechnology company SensiGen LLC.

Sequenom offers its employees a Section 529 College Savings Plan; an employee assistance program; flexible spending accounts; and medical, dental, vision and disability insurance.

## FINANCIALS: Sales and profits are in thousands of dollars—add 000 to get the full amount. 2008 Note: Financial information for 2008 was not available for all companies at press time.

| | | |
|---|---|---|
| 2008 Sales: $47,149 | 2008 Profits: $-44,154 | **U.S. Stock Ticker: SQNM** |
| 2007 Sales: $41,002 | 2007 Profits: $-21,983 | **Int'l Ticker:** Int'l Exchange: |
| 2006 Sales: $28,496 | 2006 Profits: $-17,577 | Employees: 192 |
| 2005 Sales: $19,421 | 2005 Profits: $-26,537 | Fiscal Year Ends: 12/31 |
| 2004 Sales: $22,449 | 2004 Profits: $-34,625 | Parent Company: |

## SALARIES/BENEFITS:

| | | | | |
|---|---|---|---|---|
| Pension Plan: | ESOP Stock Plan: Y | Profit Sharing: | Top Exec. Salary: $420,000 | Bonus: $210,000 |
| Savings Plan: Y | Stock Purch. Plan: | | Second Exec. Salary: $294,480 | Bonus: $74,160 |

## OTHER THOUGHTS:

**Apparent Women Officers or Directors**: 2
**Hot Spot for Advancement for Women/Minorities**: Y

## LOCATIONS: ("Y" = Yes)

| West: | Southwest: | Midwest: | Southeast: | Northeast: | International: |
|---|---|---|---|---|---|
| Y | | | | Y | Y |

Note: Financial information, benefits and other data can change quickly and may vary from those stated here.

# SERENA SOFTWARE INC

www.serena.com

**Industry Group Code:** 511204 **Ranks within this company's industry group:** Sales: 4 Profits: 4

| Management: | | Sales/Marketing: | | Liberal Arts: | | Information Systems: | | Professionals: | | Technical/Scientific: | |
|---|---|---|---|---|---|---|---|---|---|---|---|
| Mgmt. Trainees: | | Mktg. Professionals: | Y | Gen. Writing/Editing: | | Info. Management: | Y | Finance/Accounting: | Y | Engineers, Elec.: | Y |
| Experienced Mgmt.: | Y | Retail Sales: | | Technical Writing: | Y | Software Dev.: | Y | Law: | Y | Engineers, Other: | |
| Int'l Business: | Y | Commercial/Industrial: | Y | Graphic Arts/Photog.: | | Hardware Dev.: | | HR/Other: | Y | Health/Lab: | |
| MBA Graduates: | Y | Sales Trainees: | Y | Music: | | Systems Integration: | | Training: | Y | Scientists/Research: | |
| | | Advertising Pros.: | | Broadcasting: | | Consulting/Other: | | Health Care: | | Petroleum/Chemicals: | |
| | | | | Other: | | | | Consulting: | | Math/Other: | Y |

## TYPES OF BUSINESS:

Software-Systems Management
Web Content Management Software

## BRANDS/DIVISIONS/AFFILIATES:

Application Lifecycle Management
IT Process Management
Project and Portfolio Management
Serena Mariner
Application Development
Compliance Solutions
ChangeMan ZMF
PVCS Professional Suite

## CONTACTS: *Note: Officers with more than one job title may be intentionally listed here more than once.*

Jeremy Burton, CEO
Jeremy Burton, Pres.
Robert I. Pender, Jr., CFO
Rene Bonvanie, Sr. VP-Mktg.
Carl Theobald, Sr. VP-Prod.
Robert I. Pender, Jr., Sr. VP-Admin.
Ed Malysz, General Counsel/Sr. VP
Robert I. Pender, Jr., Sr. VP-Finance
Peter Sianchuk, VP-Worldwide Customer Support
Rene Bonvanie, Sr. VP-Partner Programs
David Roux, Chmn.

**Phone:** 650-481-3400 **Fax:** 650-481-3700
**Toll-Free:**
**Address:** 1900 Seaport Blvd., Redwood City, CA 94063-5587 US

## GROWTH PLANS/SPECIAL FEATURES:

Serena Software, Inc. provides infrastructure software used to manage and control application change for organizations whose business operations are dependent on managing information technology. Its products are divided into five groups: Application Lifecycle Management software, which integrates multiple roles, existing tool investments, global locations and multiple platforms to optimize enterprise software development; IT Process Management, which streamline and more effectively coordinate project processes and communication; Project and Portfolio Management, which focuses on Serena Mariner, software that encompasses portfolio, project, resource, financial and demand management; Application Development; and Compliance Solutions, which allows companies to align and improve their software development processes with IT best practice methodologies. Other applications include ChangeMan ZMF mainframe development software and PVCS Professional Suite, a software configuration management tool. The firm also provides clients with advisory and technical services, education and customer support. The company has more than 15,000 clients around the world in industry sectors such as finance, manufacturing, government, healthcare, technology and telecommunications. Serena has 29 offices in 14 countries worldwide. Banco Bilbao Vizcaya Argentaria, with operations in 32 countries, standardized on Serena Software across all of its global operations for mainframe and distributed development and global business process management. In April 2008, the company released Serena Mashup Exchange, an online marketplace that accelerates the creation/use of Business Mashups. In August 2008, Serena partnered with Valtec, a firm which specializes in strategic software consultation and engineering. In September 2008, the company acquired Projity for OpenProj and Project-ON-Demand, management softwares that significantly boost the capacities of the Serena Mariner Project and Portfolio Management program.

SERENA offers its employees benefits including flexible spending accounts, educational reimbursement, discounted auto and homeowners insurance and an employee assistance program. In addition, employees enjoy a fully stocked kitchen and a referral bonus plan.

## FINANCIALS: **Sales and profits are in thousands of dollars—add 000 to get the full amount. 2008 Note: Financial information for 2008 was not available for all companies at press time.**

| | | |
|---|---|---|
| 2008 Sales: $270,195 | 2008 Profits: $-27,110 | **U.S. Stock Ticker: Private** |
| 2007 Sales: $255,291 | 2007 Profits: $-47,212 | **Int'l Ticker:** Int'l Exchange: |
| 2006 Sales: $255,772 | 2006 Profits: $35,267 | Employees: 795 |
| 2005 Sales: $208,105 | 2005 Profits: $9,486 | Fiscal Year Ends: 1/31 |
| 2004 Sales: $105,556 | 2004 Profits: $21,351 | Parent Company: |

## SALARIES/BENEFITS:

| | | | | |
|---|---|---|---|---|
| Pension Plan: | ESOP Stock Plan: | Profit Sharing: | Top Exec. Salary: $357,955 | Bonus: $504,438 |
| Savings Plan: Y | Stock Purch. Plan: | | Second Exec. Salary: $263,636 | Bonus: $364,825 |

## OTHER THOUGHTS:

**Apparent Women Officers or Directors**: 2
**Hot Spot for Advancement for Women/Minorities**: Y

## LOCATIONS: ("Y" = Yes)

| West: | Southwest: | Midwest: | Southeast: | Northeast: | International: |
|---|---|---|---|---|---|
| Y | | | Y | Y | Y |

Note: Financial information, benefits and other data can change quickly and may vary from those stated here.

# SHARED TECHNOLOGIES

www.sharedtechnologies.com

**Industry Group Code:** 541330 **Ranks within this company's industry group:** Sales: Profits:

| Management: | | Sales/Marketing: | | Liberal Arts: | | Information Systems: | | Professionals: | | Technical/Scientific: | |
|---|---|---|---|---|---|---|---|---|---|---|---|
| Mgmt. Trainees: | | Mktg. Professionals: | Y | Gen. Writing/Editing: | | Info. Management: | Y | Finance/Accounting: | Y | Engineers, Elec.: | |
| Experienced Mgmt.: | Y | Retail Sales: | | Technical Writing: | Y | Software Dev.: | Y | Law: | Y | Engineers, Other: | Y |
| Int'l Business: | | Commercial/Industrial: | Y | Graphic Arts/Photog.: | | Hardware Dev.: | | HR/Other: | Y | Health/Lab: | |
| MBA Graduates: | Y | Sales Trainees: | | Music: | | Systems Integration: | | Training: | Y | Scientists/Research: | |
| | | Advertising Pros.: | | Broadcasting: | | Consulting/Other: | Y | Health Care: | | Petroleum/Chemicals: | |
| | | | | Other: | | | | Consulting: | | Math/Other: | |

## TYPES OF BUSINESS:

Telecommunications Systems Services
Systems Installation
Unified Communications Systems

## BRANDS/DIVISIONS/AFFILIATES:

KTWare
ST EYE Real-Time Monitoring System
ST Eye SYS
ST EYE Secure & Restore

## CONTACTS: *Note: Officers with more than one job title may be intentionally listed here more than once.*

Anthony J. Parella, CEO
Glenn Means, COO
Anthony J. Parella, Pres.
Renee Hornbaker, CFO
Tom Boyhan, Pres., Sales
Eileen Quilici, VP-Human Resources
Jon M. Baird, CIO
Jeff Graham, CTO
Kelleye Martin Chube, General Counsel
Denise Crane, VP-Bus. Oper.
Helen Cetrulo, VP-Customer Care

**Phone:** 972-462-5800 **Fax:**
**Toll-Free:** 888-835-4444
**Address:** 1405 S. Beltline Road, Coppell, TX 75019 US

## GROWTH PLANS/SPECIAL FEATURES:

Shared Technologies is a technology and enterprise solutions provider within the U.S. The firm focuses on two primary divisions: system maintenance and customer care. The system maintenance segment offers installation and maintenance services to its clients. The customer care division offers local office technical support, a national technical support call center, as well as several online applications that enable customers to access real-time account information and activity. Additionally, Shared Technologies offers its clients a multitude of solutions such as voice networking, converged networking, data networking, unified communications, unified messaging, custom developed applications, disaster recovery and security management. The firm has developed working several partnerships with industry leaders such as Nortel, Microsoft, Avaya, NEC, Mitel, Tandberg and AVST. These partnerships enable Shared Technologies a means to provide a variety of solutions to best meet the client's needs.

## FINANCIALS: **Sales and profits are in thousands of dollars—add 000 to get the full amount. 2008 Note: Financial information for 2008 was not available for all companies at press time.**

| | | |
|---|---|---|
| 2008 Sales: $ | 2008 Profits: $ | **U.S. Stock Ticker: Private** |
| 2007 Sales: $ | 2007 Profits: $ | **Int'l Ticker:** Int'l Exchange: |
| 2006 Sales: $ | 2006 Profits: $ | Employees: 1,568 |
| 2005 Sales: $ | 2005 Profits: $ | Fiscal Year Ends: 1/31 |
| 2004 Sales: $ | 2004 Profits: $ | Parent Company: |

## SALARIES/BENEFITS:

| | | | | |
|---|---|---|---|---|
| Pension Plan: | ESOP Stock Plan: | Profit Sharing: | Top Exec. Salary: $ | Bonus: $ |
| Savings Plan: Y | Stock Purch. Plan: | | Second Exec. Salary: $ | Bonus: $ |

## OTHER THOUGHTS:

**Apparent Women Officers or Directors**: 5
**Hot Spot for Advancement for Women/Minorities**: Y

## LOCATIONS: ("Y" = Yes)

| West: | Southwest: | Midwest: | Southeast: | Northeast: | International: |
|---|---|---|---|---|---|
| Y | Y | Y | Y | Y | |

# SHENANDOAH TELECOMMUNICATIONS CO

www.shentel.com

**Industry Group Code:** 513300A **Ranks within this company's industry group:** Sales: 5 Profits: 3

| Management: | | Sales/Marketing: | | Liberal Arts: | | Information Systems: | | Professionals: | | Technical/Scientific: | |
|---|---|---|---|---|---|---|---|---|---|---|---|
| Mgmt. Trainees: | | Mktg. Professionals: | Y | Gen. Writing/Editing: | | Info. Management: | Y | Finance/Accounting: | Y | Engineers, Elec.: | Y |
| Experienced Mgmt.: | Y | Retail Sales: | | Technical Writing: | | Software Dev.: | Y | Law: | Y | Engineers, Other: | Y |
| Int'l Business: | | Commercial/Industrial: | Y | Graphic Arts/Photog.: | | Hardware Dev.: | | HR/Other: | Y | Health/Lab: | |
| MBA Graduates: | Y | Sales Trainees: | Y | Music: | | Systems Integration: | Y | Training: | Y | Scientists/Research: | |
| | | Advertising Pros.: | | Broadcasting: | | Consulting/Other: | | Health Care: | | Petroleum/Chemicals: | |
| | | | | Other: | | | | Consulting: | | Math/Other: | |

## TYPES OF BUSINESS:

Local Exchange Carrier
Long-Distance Service
Paging Services
Cellular Services
Equipment Leasing
Internet Access
Cable Television Service
Equipment Sales

## BRANDS/DIVISIONS/AFFILIATES:

Shenandoah Telecommunications Company
Shenandoah Telephone company
Shenandoah Cable Television Company
ShenTel Service Company
Shenandoah Mobile Company
Shenandoah Long Distance Company
Shenandoah Network Company
ShenTel Communications Company

## CONTACTS: *Note: Officers with more than one job title may be intentionally listed here more than once.*

Christopher E. French, CEO
Earle A. MacKenzie, COO/Exec. VP
Christopher E. French, Pres.
Adele M. Skolits, CFO
William L. Pirtle, VP-Sales
Jonathan R. Spencer, General Counsel/Corp. Sec./VP
Adele M. Skolits, VP-Finance
Christopher E. French, Chmn.

| **Phone:** 540-984-4141 | **Fax:** 540-984-8192 |
|---|---|
| **Toll-Free:** 800-743-6835 | |
| **Address:** 500 Shentel Way, Edinburg, VA 22824 US | |

## GROWTH PLANS/SPECIAL FEATURES:

Shenandoah Telecommunications Company (STC) is a diversified telecommunications holding company that, through its operating subsidiaries, provides both regulated and unregulated telecommunications services to end-user customers and other communications providers. The company offers a comprehensive suite of voice, video and data communications services. STC operates in six business segments: PCS; Telephone; Converged Services; Mobile; Cable TV; and Other. The firm's primary market is the northern Shenandoah Valley of Virginia and surrounding areas, including parts of Maryland, West Virginia and Pennsylvania. STC is the exclusive personal communications service (PCS) affiliate of Sprint Nextel in the four-state area from Harrisonburg, Virginia to Harrisburg, York and Altoona, Pennsylvania, providing mobility communications network products and services. In 2007, approximately 62% of STC's operating revenue was generated through Sprint Nextel and its customers using the company's portion of Sprint Nextel's nationwide PCS network. The company provides high-speed Internet, video and local and long distance services to multi-dwelling unit (MDU) communities, primarily off-campus student housing, in Virginia, Maryland, North Carolina, South Carolina, Georgia, Florida, Tennessee and Mississippi. In 2007, STC served 112 MDU housing complexes. STC offers many of its services over its own 647-mile fiber-optic network. STC's subsidiaries include Shenandoah Telecommunications Company; Shenandoah Telephone Company; Shenandoah Cable Television Company; ShenTel Service Company; Shenandoah Mobile Company; Shenandoah Long Distance Company; Shenandoah Network Company; ShenTel Communication Company; Shenandoah Personal Communication Company; Shentel Converged Services, Inc.; Shentel Converged Services of West Virginia; and Shentel Management.

Shenandoah offers its employees medical, vision, life and AD&D insurance; a 401(k) plan; short- and long-term disability insurance; and education assistance.

## FINANCIALS: **Sales and profits are in thousands of dollars—add 000 to get the full amount. 2008 Note: Financial information for 2008 was not available for all companies at press time.**

| | | |
|---|---|---|
| 2008 Sales: $ | 2008 Profits: $ | **U.S. Stock Ticker: SHEN** |
| 2007 Sales: $141,183 | 2007 Profits: $18,803 | **Int'l Ticker:** Int'l Exchange: |
| 2006 Sales: $169,195 | 2006 Profits: $17,922 | Employees: 416 |
| 2005 Sales: $146,391 | 2005 Profits: $10,735 | Fiscal Year Ends: 12/31 |
| 2004 Sales: $120,994 | 2004 Profits: $10,038 | Parent Company: |

## SALARIES/BENEFITS:

| | | | | |
|---|---|---|---|---|
| Pension Plan: | ESOP Stock Plan: | Profit Sharing: | Top Exec. Salary: $314,154 | Bonus: $107,427 |
| Savings Plan: Y | Stock Purch. Plan: | | Second Exec. Salary: $280,523 | Bonus: $75,665 |

## OTHER THOUGHTS:

**Apparent Women Officers or Directors**: 2
**Hot Spot for Advancement for Women/Minorities**: Y

## LOCATIONS: ("Y" = Yes)

| West: | Southwest: | Midwest: | Southeast: | Northeast: | International: |
|---|---|---|---|---|---|
| | | | | Y | |

# SHUTTERFLY INC

www.shutterfly.com

**Industry Group Code:** 514199 **Ranks within this company's industry group:** Sales: 2 Profits: 3

| Management: | | Sales/Marketing: | | Liberal Arts: | | Information Systems: | | Professionals: | | Technical/Scientific: | |
|---|---|---|---|---|---|---|---|---|---|---|---|
| Mgmt. Trainees: | | Mktg. Professionals: | Y | Gen. Writing/Editing: | Y | Info. Management: | Y | Finance/Accounting: | Y | Engineers, Elec.: | |
| Experienced Mgmt.: | Y | Retail Sales: | | Technical Writing: | | Software Dev.: | Y | Law: | Y | Engineers, Other: | |
| Int'l Business: | | Commercial/Industrial: | Y | Graphic Arts/Photog.: | Y | Hardware Dev.: | | HR/Other: | Y | Health/Lab: | |
| MBA Graduates: | Y | Sales Trainees: | Y | Music: | | Systems Integration: | Y | Training: | Y | Scientists/Research: | |
| | | Advertising Pros.: | Y | Broadcasting: | | Consulting/Other: | | Health Care: | | Petroleum/Chemicals: | |
| | | | | Other: | Y | | | Consulting: | | Math/Other: | |

## TYPES OF BUSINESS:

Online Photographic Service
Photo Printing
Gifts-Retail

## BRANDS/DIVISIONS/AFFILIATES:

Delta Airlines SkyMiles
Nexo Systems, Inc.
Storyboard Tool

## CONTACTS: *Note: Officers with more than one job title may be intentionally listed here more than once.*

Jeffrey T. Housenbold, CEO
Jeffrey T. Housenbold, Pres.
Mark J. Rubash, CFO/Sr. VP
Kathryn E. Olson, Chief Mktg. Officer
Peter Navin, VP-Human Resources
Ishantha Lokuge, VP-Prod. Mgmt. & User Experience
Jerry Ko, VP-Product Eng.
Bjorn Hansen, VP-Mfg. Oper.
Doug Appleton, VP-Legal
Dwayne A. Black, Sr. VP-Oper.
Douglas J. Galen, Sr. VP-Bus. & Corp. Dev.
Geoffrey Weber, VP-Internet Oper.
John A. Kaelle, VP-Finance
Peter Elarde, VP-Svcs. Bus.
Dan McCormick, VP-Prod. Bus.
Katie Ho, VP-Consumer Mktg. & E-Commerce
T. Bernie Blegen, VP/Controller
Philip A. Marineau, Chmn.

| **Phone:** 650-610-5200 | **Fax:** 650-654-1299 |
|---|---|
| **Toll-Free:** | |
| **Address:** 2800 Bridge Pkwy., Ste. 101, Redwood City, CA 94065 US | |

## GROWTH PLANS/SPECIAL FEATURES:

Shutterfly, Inc., established in 1999, is a leading Internet-based photograph publishing service. Through Shutterfly, consumers can upload, edit, share and print their photos. Allowing its customers to store their pictures online and send them to friends and family forms a large part of the company's marketing scheme. Customers may also choose to print pictures in a range of sizes from wallet-sized prints to jumbo 20x30-inch enlargements, as well as on a number of consumer goods, including calendars, greeting cards, mugs, mouse pads, tote bags, coasters, desk organizers, puzzles, playing cards, multi-media DVDs, magnets, keepsake boxes and ancillary products such as frames, photo albums and scrap-booking accessories. It has licensed content for some of its children's products, and now offers items such as a Dora the Explorer photo books and a Sesame Street adventure book. During 2007, the company completed more than 7 million orders to 2 million customers, with an average value of $26 per order. Shutterfly generated approximately 82% of its 2007 revenue from products manufactured at its facilities in Hayward, California; and Charlotte, North Carolina. Besides the manufacturing facilities, the firm also has customer support centers in Redwood City, California; and Phoenix, Arizona. The company has partnered with numerous other firms, including the Delta Airlines SkyMiles program, allowing SkyMiles members to register through a special page and earn 10 miles for every dollar spent at Shutterfly. In January 2008, Shutterfly acquired Palo Alto, California-based Nexo Systems, Inc., an online sharing and group services company, for approximately $14 million. In September 2008, the firm launched its Storyboard Tool, which allows users to publish professional-looking photo books. The user selects the photos they want in the book, and the Storyboard Tool automatically organizes them into a book format.

Employees of Shutterfly receive medical, dental, vision, short- and long-term disability, life and AD&D insurance; and an employee assistance program.

## FINANCIALS: **Sales and profits are in thousands of dollars—add 000 to get the full amount. 2008 Note: Financial information for 2008 was not available for all companies at press time.**

| | | |
|---|---|---|
| 2008 Sales: $ | 2008 Profits: $ | **U.S. Stock Ticker: SFLY** |
| 2007 Sales: $186,727 | 2007 Profits: $10,095 | **Int'l Ticker:** Int'l Exchange: |
| 2006 Sales: $123,353 | 2006 Profits: $5,798 | Employees: 431 |
| 2005 Sales: $83,902 | 2005 Profits: $38,932 | Fiscal Year Ends: 12/31 |
| 2004 Sales: $ | 2004 Profits: $ | Parent Company: |

## SALARIES/BENEFITS:

| | | | | |
|---|---|---|---|---|
| Pension Plan: | ESOP Stock Plan: | Profit Sharing: | Top Exec. Salary: $297,917 | Bonus: $150,000 |
| Savings Plan: Y | Stock Purch. Plan: | | Second Exec. Salary: $248,750 | Bonus: $41,446 |

## OTHER THOUGHTS:

**Apparent Women Officers or Directors**: 5
**Hot Spot for Advancement for Women/Minorities**: Y

## LOCATIONS: ("Y" = Yes)

| West: | Southwest: | Midwest: | Southeast: | Northeast: | International: |
|---|---|---|---|---|---|
| Y | | | | Y | |

# SKILLSOFT PLC

www.skillsoft.com

**Industry Group Code:** 511218 **Ranks within this company's industry group:** Sales: 1 Profits: 1

| Management: | | Sales/Marketing: | | Liberal Arts: | | Information Systems: | | Professionals: | | Technical/Scientific: | |
|---|---|---|---|---|---|---|---|---|---|---|---|
| Mgmt. Trainees: | | Mktg. Professionals: | Y | Gen. Writing/Editing: | Y | Info. Management: | Y | Finance/Accounting: | Y | Engineers, Elec.: | Y |
| Experienced Mgmt.: | Y | Retail Sales: | | Technical Writing: | Y | Software Dev.: | Y | Law: | Y | Engineers, Other: | |
| Int'l Business: | Y | Commercial/Industrial: | | Graphic Arts/Photog.: | | Hardware Dev.: | | HR/Other: | Y | Health/Lab: | |
| MBA Graduates: | Y | Sales Trainees: | Y | Music: | | Systems Integration: | | Training: | Y | Scientists/Research: | |
| | | Advertising Pros.: | | Broadcasting: | | Consulting/Other: | | Health Care: | | Petroleum/Chemicals: | |
| | | | | Other: | | | | Consulting: | | Math/Other: | |

## TYPES OF BUSINESS:

Software-Educational
Online Courses & Seminars
Online Mentoring Program

## BRANDS/DIVISIONS/AFFILIATES:

Books24x7, Inc.
GoTrain Corp.
Referenceware
SkillPort
Roleplay
Search-and-Learn
NetUniversity
Accelerated Path

## CONTACTS:

*Note: Officers with more than one job title may be intentionally listed here more than once.*

Charles (Chuck) Moran, CEO
Jerry Nine, Jr., COO
Charles (Chuck) Moran, Pres.
Thomas McDonald, CFO
Lee Ritze, Sr. VP-Mktg.
Mark Townsend, Exec. VP-Tech.
Tom McDonald, Exec. VP-Oper.
John Ambrose, Sr. VP-Corp. Dev., Strategy & Emerging Bus.
Donna Keenan, Manager-Public Rel.
Colm Darcy, Exec. VP-Content Dev.
Kevin Young, VP/Managing Dir.-EMEA
Glenn Nott, VP/Managing Dir.-Asia Pacific

| | |
|---|---|
| **Phone:** 603-324-3000 | **Fax:** 603-324-3009 |
| **Toll-Free:** 877-545-5763 | |
| **Address:** 107 Northeastern Blvd., Nashua, NH 03062 US | |

## GROWTH PLANS/SPECIAL FEATURES:

SkillSoft Corp. provides comprehensive, integrated e-learning software and services which help businesses deploy knowledge across their extended enterprise of employees, customers, suppliers, distributors and other business partners. SkillSoft offers courseware, simulations, online books, reference materials and online test preparation. It focuses on a variety of professional effectiveness, IT and business topics representing the critical skills required of employees in differing work environments. The company's platform allows organizations to customize their e-learning environment to meet corporate objectives and to efficiently train their employees and business partners. SkillSoft's products include Business Skill Library and IT Skills and Certification Library; subsidiary Books24x7, Inc. offers ITPro, BusinessPro and FinancePro Referenceware; and subsidiary GoTrain Corp. offers health and safety compliance courseware. Additional offerings include the Referenceware brand, a service-mark of Books24x7, as are SkillPort, Roleplay, Search-and-Learn, e-Learning for the Knowledge Economy, NetUniversity and Accelerated Path, all which are trademarked by SkillSoft. Lastly, the firm's SkillSoft Dialogue is a virtual classroom solution for creating and delivering effective live and on-demand learning. SkillSoft has partnered with leaders in learning management, such as Oracle, Plateau and SumTotal, to insure that SkillSoft can be integrated with those systems for joint customers. SkillSoft's customers include Northrop Grumman, Honda, International Business Machines (IBM), Symantec, Subway, Shell, ING, the U.S. Air Force, CIGNA, the University of Iowa, Hilton, Merck and Manpower.

Employees are offered medical, dental and vision insurance; flexible spending accounts; an employee assistance program; short-and long-term disability coverage; life insurance; a 401(k) plan; an employee stock purchase program; and tuition reimbursement.

## FINANCIALS:

**Sales and profits are in thousands of dollars—add 000 to get the full amount. 2008 Note: Financial information for 2008 was not available for all companies at press time.**

| | | |
|---|---|---|
| 2008 Sales: $281,223 | 2008 Profits: $59,998 | **U.S. Stock Ticker: SKIL** |
| 2007 Sales: $225,172 | 2007 Profits: $24,153 | **Int'l Ticker:** Int'l Exchange: |
| 2006 Sales: $215,567 | 2006 Profits: $35,215 | Employees: 1,133 |
| 2005 Sales: $212,300 | 2005 Profits: $-20,113 | Fiscal Year Ends: 1/31 |
| 2004 Sales: $193,475 | 2004 Profits: $-113,274 | Parent Company: |

## SALARIES/BENEFITS:

| | | | | |
|---|---|---|---|---|
| Pension Plan: | ESOP Stock Plan: | Profit Sharing: | Top Exec. Salary: $335,146 | Bonus: $653,901 |
| Savings Plan: Y | Stock Purch. Plan: Y | | Second Exec. Salary: $264,781 | Bonus: $338,354 |

## OTHER THOUGHTS:

**Apparent Women Officers or Directors**: 1
**Hot Spot for Advancement for Women/Minorities**:

## LOCATIONS: ("Y" = Yes)

| West: | Southwest: | Midwest: | Southeast: | Northeast: | International: |
|---|---|---|---|---|---|
| | | | | Y | Y |

# SOLAR RESERVE

www.solar-reserve.com

**Industry Group Code:** 333298A **Ranks within this company's industry group:** Sales: Profits:

| Management: | | Sales/Marketing: | | Liberal Arts: | | Information Systems: | | Professionals: | | Technical/Scientific: | |
|---|---|---|---|---|---|---|---|---|---|---|---|
| Mgmt. Trainees: | | Mktg. Professionals: | Y | Gen. Writing/Editing: | | Info. Management: | Y | Finance/Accounting: | Y | Engineers, Elec.: | Y |
| Experienced Mgmt.: | Y | Retail Sales: | | Technical Writing: | Y | Software Dev.: | Y | Law: | Y | Engineers, Other: | Y |
| Int'l Business: | Y | Commercial/Industrial: | Y | Graphic Arts/Photog.: | Y | Hardware Dev.: | Y | HR/Other: | Y | Health/Lab: | |
| MBA Graduates: | Y | Sales Trainees: | Y | Music: | | Systems Integration: | | Training: | Y | Scientists/Research: | Y |
| | | Advertising Pros.: | | Broadcasting: | | Consulting/Other: | | Health Care: | | Petroleum/Chemicals: | |
| | | | | Other: | | | | Consulting: | | Math/Other: | Y |

## TYPES OF BUSINESS:

Concentrated Solar Power Technology
Energy Storage Technology

## BRANDS/DIVISIONS/AFFILIATES:

United Technologies Corp.
US Renewables Group
Rocketdyne
Hamilton Sundstrand
Solar Power Tower
Good Energies
Nazarian Enterprises
Argonaut Private Equity

## CONTACTS: *Note: Officers with more than one job title may be intentionally listed here more than once.*

Kevin Smith, CEO
Terry Smith, Pres.
Michael Whalen, CFO
William R. Gould, Jr., CTO
Tim J. Connor, VP-Eng.
Jennifer Pountain,
Tom Georgis, VP-Dev.
Alistair Jessop, VP
Julie Way, Dir.-Dev.
Lance Hagenbuch, Program Dir.
Lee Bailey, Chmn.

| **Phone:** 310-315-2200 | **Fax:** 310-315-2201 |
|---|---|
| **Toll-Free:** 866-622-2778 | |
| **Address:** 2425 Olympic Blvd., Ste. E. 500, Santa Monica, CA 90404 US | |

## GROWTH PLANS/SPECIAL FEATURES:

SolarReserve develops solar energy power plants that generate and store electricity using molten salt Solar Power Tower technology. The company's founding partners are United Technologies, a leading advanced technology company, and US Renewables Group, an investment firm dedicated to renewable power and clean fuel ventures. Molten salt technology, originally developed by the Rocketdyne division of Hamilton Sundstrand, a wholly-owned subsidiary of United Technologies Corporation, uses thousands of tracking mirrors (called heliostats) to focus solar energy onto the top of a Power Tower. Within the receiver, the concentrated sunlight heats molten salt, a mixture of sodium and potassium nitrate, to over 1000 degrees Fahrenheit. Because molten salt maintains 98% thermal efficiency, the energy stored within it can be used 24 hours per day, without needing constant sunlight. No fossil fuels are required to operate the molten salt plants. SolarReserve holds the exclusive worldwide license to build Concentrated Solar Power (CSP) plants using molten salt technology. The company's target regions for CSP development include the Southwest U.S., southern Europe, Australia and Africa. The firm's other partners include Citi's Sustainable Development Investors, Good Energies, Nazarian Enterprises, Argonaut Private Equity and the PCG Clean Energy Fund.

## FINANCIALS: Sales and profits are in thousands of dollars—add 000 to get the full amount. 2008 Note: Financial information for 2008 was not available for all companies at press time.

| | | |
|---|---|---|
| 2008 Sales: $ | 2008 Profits: $ | **U.S. Stock Ticker: Private** |
| 2007 Sales: $ | 2007 Profits: $ | **Int'l Ticker:** Int'l Exchange: |
| 2006 Sales: $ | 2006 Profits: $ | Employees: |
| 2005 Sales: $ | 2005 Profits: $ | Fiscal Year Ends: 12/31 |
| 2004 Sales: $ | 2004 Profits: $ | Parent Company: |

## SALARIES/BENEFITS:

| | | | | |
|---|---|---|---|---|
| Pension Plan: | ESOP Stock Plan: | Profit Sharing: | Top Exec. Salary: $ | Bonus: $ |
| Savings Plan: | Stock Purch. Plan: | | Second Exec. Salary: $ | Bonus: $ |

## OTHER THOUGHTS:

**Apparent Women Officers or Directors:** 1
**Hot Spot for Advancement for Women/Minorities:**

## LOCATIONS: ("Y" = Yes)

| West: | Southwest: | Midwest: | Southeast: | Northeast: | International: |
|---|---|---|---|---|---|
| Y | | | | | Y |

# SOLFOCUS INC

**www.solfocus.com**

**Industry Group Code:** 333298A **Ranks within this company's industry group:** Sales: Profits:

| Management: | | Sales/Marketing: | | Liberal Arts: | | Information Systems: | | Professionals: | | Technical/Scientific: | |
|---|---|---|---|---|---|---|---|---|---|---|---|
| Mgmt. Trainees: | | Mktg. Professionals: | Y | Gen. Writing/Editing: | | Info. Management: | Y | Finance/Accounting: | Y | Engineers, Elec.: | Y |
| Experienced Mgmt.: | Y | Retail Sales: | | Technical Writing: | Y | Software Dev.: | Y | Law: | Y | Engineers, Other: | Y |
| Int'l Business: | Y | Commercial/Industrial: | Y | Graphic Arts/Photog.: | Y | Hardware Dev.: | Y | HR/Other: | Y | Health/Lab: | |
| MBA Graduates: | Y | Sales Trainees: | Y | Music: | | Systems Integration: | | Training: | Y | Scientists/Research: | Y |
| | | Advertising Pros.: | | Broadcasting: | | Consulting/Other: | | Health Care: | | Petroleum/Chemicals: | |
| | | | | Other: | | | | Consulting: | | Math/Other: | Y |

## TYPES OF BUSINESS:

Concentrated Solar Power Technology

## BRANDS/DIVISIONS/AFFILIATES:

Concept

## CONTACTS:

*Note: Officers with more than one job title may be intentionally listed here more than once.*

Mark Crowley, CEO
Robert Legendre, COO
Mark Crowley, Pres.
Nancy Hartsoch, VP-Mktg.
Steve Horne, CTO
Bob Raybuck, VP-Admin.
Ty Jagerson, VP-Corp. Dev.
Bob Raybuck, VP-Finance
Roberto de Diego Arozamena, Pres., SolFocus Europe
Jason Ellsworth, VP/Gen. Mgr.-Glass Works
Christian Herrero de Egana Y Daucik, VP-Sales, SolFocus Europe

| **Phone:** 650-623-7100 | **Fax:** 650-623-7101 |
|---|---|
| **Toll-Free:** | |
| **Address:** 510 Logue Ave., Mountain View, CA 94043 US | |

## GROWTH PLANS/SPECIAL FEATURES:

SolFocus, Inc. is a solar energy company that works to generate solar energy at a cost competitive to traditional fossil fuel sources. The firm's concentrator photovoltaic (CPV) technology combines high-efficiency solar cells and advanced optics to offer a solar energy alternative that is capable of delivering clean, renewable and affordable energy. Based in Mountain View, California, the firm maintains European operations in Madrid, Spain and has a manufacturing facility in Mesa, Arizona with manufacturing partnerships in India and China. Late in 2008, the company announced plans to expand its European operations with a new subsidiary in Greece, which will be partly owned by Concept, a subsidiary of the Greek renewable energy firm, Samaras. The joint venture will employ SolFocus' new 1100S system which generates remarkable panel efficiencies of 25%, offering the highest energy yield of PV systems to date. Deployment of this power will begin in the summer of 2009.

## FINANCIALS:

**Sales and profits are in thousands of dollars—add 000 to get the full amount. 2008 Note: Financial information for 2008 was not available for all companies at press time.**

| | | |
|---|---|---|
| 2008 Sales: $ | 2008 Profits: $ | **U.S. Stock Ticker: Private** |
| 2007 Sales: $ | 2007 Profits: $ | **Int'l Ticker:** Int'l Exchange: |
| 2006 Sales: $ | 2006 Profits: $ | Employees: |
| 2005 Sales: $ | 2005 Profits: $ | Fiscal Year Ends: 12/31 |
| 2004 Sales: $ | 2004 Profits: $ | Parent Company: |

## SALARIES/BENEFITS:

| | | | | |
|---|---|---|---|---|
| Pension Plan: | ESOP Stock Plan: | Profit Sharing: | Top Exec. Salary: $ | Bonus: $ |
| Savings Plan: | Stock Purch. Plan: | | Second Exec. Salary: $ | Bonus: $ |

## OTHER THOUGHTS:

**Apparent Women Officers or Directors**: 1
**Hot Spot for Advancement for Women/Minorities**:

## LOCATIONS: ("Y" = Yes)

| West: | Southwest: | Midwest: | Southeast: | Northeast: | International: |
|---|---|---|---|---|---|
| Y | | | | | Y |

# SONIC INNOVATIONS INC

www.sonici.com

**Industry Group Code:** 339113 **Ranks within this company's industry group:** Sales: 25 Profits: 36

| Management: | | Sales/Marketing: | | Liberal Arts: | | Information Systems: | | Professionals: | | Technical/Scientific: | |
|---|---|---|---|---|---|---|---|---|---|---|---|
| Mgmt. Trainees: | | Mktg. Professionals: | Y | Gen. Writing/Editing: | | Info. Management: | Y | Finance/Accounting: | Y | Engineers, Elec.: | Y |
| Experienced Mgmt.: | Y | Retail Sales: | | Technical Writing: | Y | Software Dev.: | Y | Law: | Y | Engineers, Other: | Y |
| Int'l Business: | Y | Commercial/Industrial: | Y | Graphic Arts/Photog.: | | Hardware Dev.: | Y | HR/Other: | Y | Health/Lab: | Y |
| MBA Graduates: | Y | Sales Trainees: | Y | Music: | | Systems Integration: | | Training: | Y | Scientists/Research: | Y |
| | | Advertising Pros.: | | Broadcasting: | | Consulting/Other: | | Health Care: | Y | Petroleum/Chemicals: | |
| | | | | Other: | | | | Consulting: | | Math/Other: | Y |

## TYPES OF BUSINESS:

Hearing Aids
Diagnostic Equipment

## BRANDS/DIVISIONS/AFFILIATES:

Digital Signal Processing
Natura Pro
Natura 2
Tribute
Quartet
Innova
Balance
Velocity 4

## CONTACTS:

*Note: Officers with more than one job title may be intentionally listed here more than once.*

Samuel L. (Sam) Westover, CEO
Paul R. Wennerholm, COO
Paul R. Wennerholm, Pres.
Michael Halloran, CFO/VP
Jerry DaBell, VP-R&D
Christie R. Mitchell, VP-Mfg. Oper.
Brent H. Shimada, VP-Admin.
Brent H. Shimada, General Counsel
Michael Nilsson, VP-Auditory Research
Michael Nilsson, Dir-Center for Amplification & Hearing Research
David R. Whittle, VP-Worldwide Quality
Samuel L. (Sam) Westover, Exec. Chmn.

**Phone:** 801-365-2800 **Fax:** 801-365-3000
**Toll-Free:** 888-678-4327
**Address:** 2795 E. Cottonwood Pkwy., Ste. 660, Salt Lake City, UT 84121 US

## GROWTH PLANS/SPECIAL FEATURES:

Sonic Innovations, Inc. designs, develops, manufactures and markets digital hearing aids. Its patented digital signal processing (DSP) platform is one of the smallest single-chip platforms ever installed in a hearing aid. The DSP platform contains a set of algorithms that pre-process incoming sound and present it to the impaired cochlea (inner ear) in a way that helps to restore natural loudness perception and preserves cues necessary for speech understanding. It also processes sound at a faster rate than other digital hearing aids; has the ability to filter out unnecessary background noise; and can isolate the direction of sound in such a way that sound in front of the listener is emphasized. The DSP chip contains up to 16 independent compression channels programmable with one-decibel accuracy, enhancing the naturalness of sound and allowing for a personalized product. Sonic's Balance, Innova, Natura Pro, Natura 2, Tribute and Quartet product lines conform to the six common models for hearing aids: behind-the-ear, in-the-ear, in-the-canal, half-shell, mini-canal and completely-in-the-canal. Besides hearing aids, the firm produces diagnostic equipment such as audiometers, tympanometers and otoacoustic emission devices. These can test patients in under 30 minutes, with an Otogram report summing up the patient's hearing requirements. Sonic operates in three segments: North America, which includes owned operations in the U.S. and Canada; Europe, which includes owned operations in Germany, Denmark, the Netherlands, Austria, Switzerland and England; and rest-of-world, which includes an owned operation in Australia. Outside the U.S., Sonic sells finished hearing aids and hearing aid kits primarily to distributors. Its Danish subsidiary distributes hearing aids and tinnitus products in Europe. In August 2008, Sonic launched the Velocity line of hearing aids with features including Bluetooth capability and data logging: the Velocity 24 and Velocity 12, designed for medium to high background noise environments, and the Velocity 4, for less noisy environments.

## FINANCIALS:

**Sales and profits are in thousands of dollars—add 000 to get the full amount. 2008 Note: Financial information for 2008 was not available for all companies at press time.**

| | | |
|---|---|---|
| 2008 Sales: $124,878 | 2008 Profits: $-7,484 | **U.S. Stock Ticker: SNCI** |
| 2007 Sales: $119,062 | 2007 Profits: $ 717 | **Int'l Ticker:** Int'l Exchange: |
| 2006 Sales: $105,492 | 2006 Profits: $-1,580 | Employees: 664 |
| 2005 Sales: $99,126 | 2005 Profits: $-19,608 | Fiscal Year Ends: 12/31 |
| 2004 Sales: $97,688 | 2004 Profits: $ 411 | Parent Company: |

## SALARIES/BENEFITS:

| | | | | |
|---|---|---|---|---|
| Pension Plan: | ESOP Stock Plan: | Profit Sharing: | Top Exec. Salary: $437,269 | Bonus: $261,450 |
| Savings Plan: | Stock Purch. Plan: | | Second Exec. Salary: $238,385 | Bonus: $72,955 |

## OTHER THOUGHTS:

**Apparent Women Officers or Directors**: 2
**Hot Spot for Advancement for Women/Minorities**: Y

## LOCATIONS: ("Y" = Yes)

| West: | Southwest: | Midwest: | Southeast: | Northeast: | International: |
|---|---|---|---|---|---|
| Y | | | | | Y |

# SONUS NETWORKS INC

**www.sonusnet.com**

**Industry Group Code:** 334200 **Ranks within this company's industry group:** Sales: 3 Profits: 4

| Management: | | Sales/Marketing: | | Liberal Arts: | | Information Systems: | | Professionals: | | Technical/Scientific: | |
|---|---|---|---|---|---|---|---|---|---|---|---|
| Mgmt. Trainees: | | Mktg. Professionals: | Y | Gen. Writing/Editing: | Y | Info. Management: | Y | Finance/Accounting: | Y | Engineers, Elec.: | Y |
| Experienced Mgmt.: | Y | Retail Sales: | | Technical Writing: | Y | Software Dev.: | Y | Law: | Y | Engineers, Other: | Y |
| Int'l Business: | Y | Commercial/Industrial: | Y | Graphic Arts/Photog.: | | Hardware Dev.: | Y | HR/Other: | Y | Health/Lab: | |
| MBA Graduates: | Y | Sales Trainees: | Y | Music: | | Systems Integration: | Y | Training: | Y | Scientists/Research: | |
| | | Advertising Pros.: | | Broadcasting: | | Consulting/Other: | | Health Care: | | Petroleum/Chemicals: | |
| | | | | Other: | | | | Consulting: | | Math/Other: | |

## TYPES OF BUSINESS:

Manufacturing-Networking Equipment
Voice Infrastructure Products
Switching Equipment & Software

## BRANDS/DIVISIONS/AFFILIATES:

GSX9000 Open Services Switch
GSX4000 Open Services Switch
SGX Signaling Gateway
PSX Call Routing Server
ASX Call Feature Server
NBS Network Border Switch
Sonus Insight Management System
IMX Application Platform

## CONTACTS:

*Note: Officers with more than one job title may be intentionally listed here more than once.*

Richard N. Nottenburg, CEO
Richard N. Nottenburg, Pres.
Richard J. Gaynor, CFO
Shailing Sehgal, VP-Mktg. & Prod. Mgmt.
Kathy Harris, VP-Human Resources
Gale England, VP-Prod. Oper.
Guru Pai, Sr. VP-Bus. Dev., Corp. Strategy, Sales & Svc.
Mohammed Shanableh, VP-Worldwide Sales
Matt Dillon, VP-Global Svcs.

**Phone:** 978-614-8100 **Fax:** 978-614-8101
**Toll-Free:**
**Address:** 7 Technology Park Dr., Westford, MA 01886 US

## GROWTH PLANS/SPECIAL FEATURES:

Sonus Networks, Inc. is a leading provider of voice infrastructure products for wireline and wireless service providers. Its products are a new generation of carrier-class switching equipment and software that enable voice services to be delivered over Internet Protocol (IP) packet-based networks. The company's target customers include communications service providers such as long-distance carriers, local exchange carriers, Internet service providers, wireless operators, cable operators, international telephone companies and carriers that provide service to other carriers. Sonus' suite of voice infrastructure solutions allows wireline and wireless operators to build converged voice over IP (VoIP) networks. Its products are built on the same distributed, IP-based principles embraced by the IP Multimedia Subsystem (IMS) architecture, as defined by the Third Generation Partnership Project (3GPP). This IMS architecture is being accepted by network operators globally as the common approach for building converged voice, data, wireline and wireless networks. Sonus' IMS-based solution product suite includes the GSX9000 Open Services Switch, GSX4000 Open Services Switch, SGX Signaling Gateway, the PSX Call Routing Server, the ASX Call Feature Server, the NBS Network Border Switch, the Sonus Insight Management System, the IMX Application Platform and the mobilEdge Wireless Access Node. These products, designed for deployment as the platform of a service provider's voice network, can reduce the cost to build and operate voice services compared to traditional alternatives. They offer an open platform for providers to increase their revenues through the creation and delivery of new voice and data services. Sonus also offers support and professional services including installation, systems integration and testing, technical support and educational services. In April 2008, Sonus acquired Atreus Systems, a supplier of IP voice and advanced IP service provisioning software. In December 2008, the firm announced a restructuring initiative to reduce its workforce by approximately 50 people.

## FINANCIALS:

**Sales and profits are in thousands of dollars—add 000 to get the full amount. 2008 Note: Financial information for 2008 was not available for all companies at press time.**

| | | |
|---|---|---|
| 2008 Sales: $ | 2008 Profits: $ | **U.S. Stock Ticker: SONS** |
| 2007 Sales: $320,310 | 2007 Profits: $-23,637 | **Int'l Ticker:** Int'l Exchange: |
| 2006 Sales: $279,483 | 2006 Profits: $102,854 | Employees: 926 |
| 2005 Sales: $195,362 | 2005 Profits: $4,785 | Fiscal Year Ends: 12/31 |
| 2004 Sales: $170,738 | 2004 Profits: $24,477 | Parent Company: |

## SALARIES/BENEFITS:

| | | | | |
|---|---|---|---|---|
| Pension Plan: | ESOP Stock Plan: | Profit Sharing: | Top Exec. Salary: $425,000 | Bonus: $272,000 |
| Savings Plan: Y | Stock Purch. Plan: Y | | Second Exec. Salary: $250,000 | Bonus: $96,000 |

## OTHER THOUGHTS:

**Apparent Women Officers or Directors**: 2
**Hot Spot for Advancement for Women/Minorities**:

## LOCATIONS: ("Y" = Yes)

| West: | Southwest: | Midwest: | Southeast: | Northeast: | International: |
|---|---|---|---|---|---|
| Y | Y | | | Y | Y |

Note: Financial information, benefits and other data can change quickly and may vary from those stated here.

# SOUTHERN UNION COMPANY

**www.southernunionco.com**

**Industry Group Code:** 221000B **Ranks within this company's industry group:** Sales: 1 Profits: 3

| **Management:** | | **Sales/Marketing:** | | **Liberal Arts:** | | **Information Systems:** | | **Professionals:** | | **Technical/Scientific:** | |
|---|---|---|---|---|---|---|---|---|---|---|---|
| Mgmt. Trainees: | | Mktg. Professionals: | Y | Gen. Writing/Editing: | | Info. Management: | Y | Finance/Accounting: | Y | Engineers, Elec.: | Y |
| Experienced Mgmt.: | Y | Retail Sales: | | Technical Writing: | | Software Dev.: | | Law: | Y | Engineers, Other: | Y |
| Int'l Business: | | Commercial/Industrial: | Y | Graphic Arts/Photog.: | | Hardware Dev.: | | HR/Other: | Y | Health/Lab: | |
| MBA Graduates: | Y | Sales Trainees: | | Music: | | Systems Integration: | | Training: | Y | Scientists/Research: | |
| | | Advertising Pros.: | | Broadcasting: | | Consulting/Other: | | Health Care: | | Petroleum/Chemicals: | Y |
| | | | | Other: | | | | Consulting: | | Math/Other: | |

## TYPES OF BUSINESS:

Utilities-Electricity & Natural Gas
Natural Gas Pipelines
Gas Appliances & Appliance Service
Electricity Generation

## BRANDS/DIVISIONS/AFFILIATES:

Panhandle Eastern Pipeline Co.
Trunkline LNG Co.
Florida Gas Transmission Co., LLC
Missouri Gas Energy
New England Gas Co.
Sid Richardson Energy Services, Ltd.
Southern Union Gas Services
PEI Power Corporation

## CONTACTS: *Note: Officers with more than one job title may be intentionally listed here more than once.*

George L. Lindemann, CEO
Eric D. Herschmann, COO
Eric D. Herschmann, Pres.
Richard N. Marshall, CFO/Sr. VP
Monica M. Gaudiosi, General Counsel/Sr. VP
Robert O. Bond, Sr. VP-Pipeline Oper.
John Barnett, Dir.-External Affairs
Jack Walsh, VP-Investor Rel.
George E. Aldrich, Chief Acct. Officer/Controller/VP
Robert O. Bond, Pres./COO-Panhandle Energy & CrossCountry Energy
Robert J. Hack, COO-Missouri Gas Energy
George L. Lindemann, Chmn.

| | |
|---|---|
| **Phone:** 713-989-2000 | **Fax:** |
| **Toll-Free:** | |
| **Address:** 5444 Westheimer Rd., Houston, TX 77056 US | |

## GROWTH PLANS/SPECIAL FEATURES:

Southern Union Company owns and operates assets in the regulated and unregulated natural gas industry and is primarily engaged in the gathering, processing, transportation, storage and distribution of natural gas in the U.S. The company operates in three reportable segments: transportation and storage; gathering and processing; and distribution. The transportation and storage segment is primarily engaged in the interstate transportation and storage of natural gas from gas producing areas and liquefied natural gas terminalling and regasification services. Its operations are currently conducted through Panhandle Eastern Pipe Line Company, LP and its subsidiaries (Panhandle) and its 50% interest in Florida Gas Transmission Company, LLC through Citrus Corp. The gathering and processing segment is primarily engaged in the gathering, treating, processing and redelivery of natural gas and natural gas liquids (NGLs) in Texas and New Mexico. Its operations are conducted through Southern Union Gas Services (SUGS). SUGS' operations consist of a network of approximately 4,800 miles of natural gas and NGL pipelines; four active cryogenic processing plants, with a combined capacity of 410 million cubic feet per day (MMcf/d); and five active natural gas treating plant. The distribution segment is primarily engaged in the local distribution of natural gas in Missouri and Massachusetts. The utilities serve over 550,000 residential, commercial and industrial customers through local distribution systems consisting of 9,068 miles of mains, 6,096 miles of service lines and 45 miles of transmission lines. Its operations are conducted through Missouri Gas Energy and New England Gas Company. In January 2008, the firm announced the completion of the Trunkline Gas Company's Field Zone Expansion project. The project added approximately 625 MMcf/d of capacity to the pipeline system.

## FINANCIALS: **Sales and profits are in thousands of dollars—add 000 to get the full amount. 2008 Note: Financial information for 2008 was not available for all companies at press time.**

| | | |
|---|---|---|
| 2008 Sales: $ | 2008 Profits: $ | **U.S. Stock Ticker: SUG** |
| 2007 Sales: $2,616,665 | 2007 Profits: $228,711 | **Int'l Ticker:** Int'l Exchange: |
| 2006 Sales: $2,340,144 | 2006 Profits: $64,131 | Employees: 2,337 |
| 2005 Sales: $2,019,430 | 2005 Profits: $20,683 | Fiscal Year Ends: 12/31 |
| 2004 Sales: $1,799,974 | 2004 Profits: $114,025 | Parent Company: |

## SALARIES/BENEFITS:

| | | | | |
|---|---|---|---|---|
| Pension Plan: | ESOP Stock Plan: | Profit Sharing: | Top Exec. Salary: $999,999 | Bonus: $750,000 |
| Savings Plan: Y | Stock Purch. Plan: | | Second Exec. Salary: $949,999 | Bonus: $1,900,000 |

## OTHER THOUGHTS:

**Apparent Women Officers or Directors**: 1
**Hot Spot for Advancement for Women/Minorities**:

## LOCATIONS: ("Y" = Yes)

| West: | Southwest: | Midwest: | Southeast: | Northeast: | International: |
|---|---|---|---|---|---|
| | Y | Y | Y | Y | |

# SOUTHWESTERN ENERGY CO

www.swn.com

**Industry Group Code:** 211111 **Ranks within this company's industry group:** Sales: 8 Profits: 9

| Management: | | Sales/Marketing: | | Liberal Arts: | | Information Systems: | | Professionals: | | Technical/Scientific: | |
|---|---|---|---|---|---|---|---|---|---|---|---|
| Mgmt. Trainees: | | Mktg. Professionals: | Y | Gen. Writing/Editing: | | Info. Management: | Y | Finance/Accounting: | Y | Engineers, Elec.: | |
| Experienced Mgmt.: | Y | Retail Sales: | | Technical Writing: | | Software Dev.: | | Law: | Y | Engineers, Other: | Y |
| Int'l Business: | Y | Commercial/Industrial: | Y | Graphic Arts/Photog.: | | Hardware Dev.: | | HR/Other: | Y | Health/Lab: | |
| MBA Graduates: | Y | Sales Trainees: | | Music: | | Systems Integration: | | Training: | Y | Scientists/Research: | |
| | | Advertising Pros.: | | Broadcasting: | | Consulting/Other: | | Health Care: | | Petroleum/Chemicals: | Y |
| | | | | Other: | | | | Consulting: | | Math/Other: | |

## TYPES OF BUSINESS:

Oil & Gas Exploration & Production
Gas Utility

## BRANDS/DIVISIONS/AFFILIATES:

SEECO, Inc.
Southwestern Energy Production Co.
Southwestern Energies Services Co.
DeSoto Gathering Co., LLC
DeSoto Drilling, Inc.
Diamond Production Co.

## CONTACTS: *Note: Officers with more than one job title may be intentionally listed here more than once.*

Harold M. Korell, CEO
Steven L. Mueller, COO
Steven L. Mueller, Pres.
Greg D. Kerley, CFO/Exec. VP
Mark K. Boling, General Counsel/Sec/Ex. VP.
Gene A. Hammons, Pres., Southwestern Midstream Services Co.
Harold M. Korell, Chmn.

**Phone:** 281-618-4700 **Fax:** 281-618-4818
**Toll-Free:**
**Address:** 2350 N. Sam Houston Pkwy. E., Ste. 125, Houston, TX 77032 US

## GROWTH PLANS/SPECIAL FEATURES:

Southwestern Energy Co. is an integrated energy company primarily engaged in exploring for and producing natural gas. The firm conducts the majority of its exploration and production operations in four general regions: The Arkoma Basin, East Texas, the Permian Basin and the onshore Gulf Coast. The company also focuses on creating and capturing additional value through its drilling and gathering businesses. Southwestern Energy operates in two segments: exploration and production and midstream services. The exploration and production segment engages in natural gas and oil exploration and production through its wholly-owned subsidiaries SEECO, Inc.; Southwestern Energy Production Co. (SEPCO); and Diamond Production Co. SEECO operates exclusively in Arkansas, holds a large base of both developed and undeveloped gas reserves and conducts both the ongoing conventional drilling program in the Arkansas part of the Arkoma Basin and the drilling program for the Fayetteville Shale play. SEPCO conducts development drilling and exploration programs in the Arkoma basin, Texas and New Mexico. Diamond Production has interests in properties in the Permian Basin of Texas. DeSoto Drilling, Inc., a wholly-owned subsidiary of SEPCO, operates drilling rigs in East Texas and in the Fayetteville Shale play. The midstream services segment markets and transports the firm's gas production and some third-party natural gas. The segment operates through Southwestern Energies Services, Co., a marketing subsidiary; and DeSoto Gathering Co., LLC, a gathering subsidiary. In April 2008, Southwestern Energy agreed to sell certain oil and gas leases, wells and gathering equipment in its Fayetteville Shale play to XTO Energy Inc. In July 2008, the company sold its utility, Arkansas Western Gas Company to SourceGas, LLC for $230 million, ending its natural gas distribution operations.

## FINANCIALS: **Sales and profits are in thousands of dollars—add 000 to get the full amount. 2008 Note: Financial information for 2008 was not available for all companies at press time.**

| | | |
|---|---|---|
| 2008 Sales: $ | 2008 Profits: $ | **U.S. Stock Ticker: SWN** |
| 2007 Sales: $1,255,131 | 2007 Profits: $221,174 | **Int'l Ticker:** Int'l Exchange: |
| 2006 Sales: $763,112 | 2006 Profits: $162,636 | Employees: 1,521 |
| 2005 Sales: $676,329 | 2005 Profits: $147,760 | Fiscal Year Ends: 12/31 |
| 2004 Sales: $477,137 | 2004 Profits: $103,576 | Parent Company: |

## SALARIES/BENEFITS:

| | | | | |
|---|---|---|---|---|
| Pension Plan: | ESOP Stock Plan: | Profit Sharing: | Top Exec. Salary: $550,000 | Bonus: $2,784,000 |
| Savings Plan: | Stock Purch. Plan: | | Second Exec. Salary: $335,000 | Bonus: $1,140,000 |

## OTHER THOUGHTS:

**Apparent Women Officers or Directors:**
**Hot Spot for Advancement for Women/Minorities:**

## LOCATIONS: ("Y" = Yes)

| West: | Southwest: | Midwest: | Southeast: | Northeast: | International: |
|---|---|---|---|---|---|
| | Y | | Y | | |

# SPAN AMERICA MEDICAL SYSTEMS INC

www.spanamerica.com

**Industry Group Code:** 339113 **Ranks within this company's industry group:** Sales: 39 Profits: 33

| Management: | | Sales/Marketing: | | Liberal Arts: | | Information Systems: | | Professionals: | | Technical/Scientific: | |
|---|---|---|---|---|---|---|---|---|---|---|---|
| Mgmt. Trainees: | | Mktg. Professionals: | Y | Gen. Writing/Editing: | | Info. Management: | Y | Finance/Accounting: | Y | Engineers, Elec.: | |
| Experienced Mgmt.: | Y | Retail Sales: | | Technical Writing: | Y | Software Dev.: | | Law: | Y | Engineers, Other: | Y |
| Int'l Business: | | Commercial/Industrial: | Y | Graphic Arts/Photog.: | | Hardware Dev.: | | HR/Other: | Y | Health/Lab: | Y |
| MBA Graduates: | Y | Sales Trainees: | Y | Music: | | Systems Integration: | | Training: | Y | Scientists/Research: | Y |
| | | Advertising Pros.: | | Broadcasting: | | Consulting/Other: | | Health Care: | Y | Petroleum/Chemicals: | |
| | | | | Other: | | | | Consulting: | | Math/Other: | Y |

## TYPES OF BUSINESS:

Supplies-Therapeutic Mattresses
Polyurethane Foam Products
Wound Management Products
Intravenous Catheters
Skin Care Products

## BRANDS/DIVISIONS/AFFILIATES:

Geo-Matt
Geo-Mattress
PressureGuard
Span-Aids
Isch-Dish
Sacral Dish
Selan
PJ Noyes Company

## CONTACTS: *Note: Officers with more than one job title may be intentionally listed here more than once.*

James D. Ferguson, CEO
James D. Ferguson, Pres.
Richard C. Coggins, CFO
Clyde A. Shew, VP-Medical Sales & Mktg.
James R. O'Reagan, VP-R&D
James R. O'Reagan, VP-Eng.
Richard C. Coggins, Corp. Sec.
Robert E. Ackley, VP-Oper.
Richard C. Coggins, Treas.
Wanda J. Totton, VP-Quality Control
Thomas D. Henrion, Chmn.

**Phone:** 864-288-8877 **Fax:** 864-288-8692
**Toll-Free:** 800-888-6752
**Address:** 70 Commerce Dr., Greenville, SC 29615 US

## GROWTH PLANS/SPECIAL FEATURES:

Span-America Medical Systems, Inc. manufactures and distributes polyurethane foam products for the medical and custom products markets, including polyurethane foam mattress overlays, powered and non-powered therapeutic replacement mattresses and patient positioning and seating products. Span-America markets its products to acute care hospitals, long-term care facilities and home health care providers, primarily in North America. The company produces various foam mattress overlays, including convoluted foam pads and its patented Geo-Matt overlay. The Geo-Matt design includes individual foam cells cut to exacting tolerances on computer-controlled equipment to create a clinically effective mattress surface. These products provide patients with greater comfort and treat patients who have or are susceptible to developing pressure ulcers. Span-America's overlay products are mattress pads rather than complete mattresses and are marketed as less expensive alternatives to more complex replacement mattresses. The company's Geo-Mattress products are single-density or multi-layered foam mattresses topped with the same patented Geo-Matt surface used in its overlays. Span-America's more complex non-powered replacement mattresses consist of products from the PressureGuard series and combine a polyurethane foam shell and static air cylinders. The company's specialty line of positioners is sold primarily under the trademark Span-Aids and consists of over 300 different foam items that aid in relieving the basic patient positioning problems of elevation, immobilization, muscle contracture, foot drop and foot or leg rotation. Seating products made specifically as an aid to wound healing include the Isch-Dish and Sacral Dish pressure relief cushions. Span-America also markets the Selan line of skin care creams and lotions under a license agreement with PJ Noyes Company as well as custom bedding and foam products and the Secure I.V. line of short peripheral intravenous safety catheters. The firm is currently in the process of selling its afety catheter business, including the Secure I.V. line.

## FINANCIALS: **Sales and profits are in thousands of dollars—add 000 to get the full amount. 2008 Note: Financial information for 2008 was not available for all companies at press time.**

2008 Sales: $59,265
2007 Sales: $60,544
2006 Sales: $51,557
2005 Sales: $48,439
2004 Sales: $49,929

2008 Profits: $4,869
2007 Profits: $2,874
2006 Profits: $3,055
2005 Profits: $2,439
2004 Profits: $1,985

**U.S. Stock Ticker: SPAN**
**Int'l Ticker:** Int'l Exchange:
Employees: 253
Fiscal Year Ends: 9/30
Parent Company:

## SALARIES/BENEFITS:

Pension Plan: ESOP Stock Plan: Profit Sharing: Top Exec. Salary: $263,377 Bonus: $168,935
Savings Plan: Y Stock Purch. Plan: Second Exec. Salary: $179,792 Bonus: $114,980

## OTHER THOUGHTS:

**Apparent Women Officers or Directors**: 2
**Hot Spot for Advancement for Women/Minorities**:

## LOCATIONS: ("Y" = Yes)

| West: | Southwest: | Midwest: | Southeast: | Northeast: | International: |
|---|---|---|---|---|---|
| Y | | | Y | Y | |

# SPECTRALINK CORP

www.spectralink.com

**Industry Group Code:** 334220 **Ranks within this company's industry group:** Sales: Profits:

| **Management:** | | **Sales/Marketing:** | | **Liberal Arts:** | | **Information Systems:** | | **Professionals:** | | **Technical/Scientific:** | |
|---|---|---|---|---|---|---|---|---|---|---|---|
| Mgmt. Trainees: | | Mktg. Professionals: | Y | Gen. Writing/Editing: | Y | Info. Management: | Y | Finance/Accounting: | Y | Engineers, Elec.: | Y |
| Experienced Mgmt.: | Y | Retail Sales: | | Technical Writing: | Y | Software Dev.: | Y | Law: | Y | Engineers, Other: | Y |
| Int'l Business: | Y | Commercial/Industrial: | Y | Graphic Arts/Photog.: | | Hardware Dev.: | Y | HR/Other: | Y | Health/Lab: | |
| MBA Graduates: | Y | Sales Trainees: | Y | Music: | | Systems Integration: | Y | Training: | Y | Scientists/Research: | |
| | | Advertising Pros.: | | Broadcasting: | | Consulting/Other: | | Health Care: | | Petroleum/Chemicals: | |
| | | | | Other: | | | | Consulting: | | Math/Other: | |

## TYPES OF BUSINESS:

Wireless On-Site Telephone Systems
Consulting Services

## BRANDS/DIVISIONS/AFFILIATES:

Polycom, Inc.
Link
NetLink
Kirk Telecom A/S
KIRK Scanted A/S
KIRK Telecom, Inc.
KIRK DECT

## CONTACTS: *Note: Officers with more than one job title may be intentionally listed here more than once.*

| | |
|---|---|
| **Phone:** 303-440-5330 | **Fax:** 303-440-5331 |
| **Toll-Free:** 800-676-5465 | |
| **Address:** 5755 Central Ave., Boulder, CO 80301 US | |

## GROWTH PLANS/SPECIAL FEATURES:

SpectraLink Corp., a wholly-owned subsidiary of Polycom, Inc., manufactures and sells workplace wireless telephone systems that complement existing telephone systems by providing mobile communications in a building or campus environment. The company's wireless telephone systems increase the efficiency of employees by enabling them to remain in telephone contact while moving throughout the workplace. The firm's wireless telephone systems use a micro-cellular design and interface directly with a telephone system, such as a public branch exchange, Centrex or key/hybrid systems. There are no airtime charges incurred when the customers use the company's wireless telephones system because all calls are routed through the corporate phone system. SpectraLink's product portfolio consists of three types of product categories: Link wireless telephone system, which uses a proprietary radio infrastructure in the 902-928 MHz radio band targeted to organizations that require a dedicated wireless voice solution for on-premises mobile workforce; NetLink wireless telephone products, which operate over IEEE 802.11-compliant wireless local are networks in the 2.4 GHz and 5 GHz unlicensed frequency bands using standards-based Internet protocol technology; and the KIRK DECT system, built on international Digital Enhanced Cordless Telecommunications (DECT) standards. The KIRK DECT system interfaces with existing systems through analog, T1 or IP connections, and allows users to expand the system's coverage, voice traffic and number of users easily. SpectraLink's products serve the retail, education, healthcare, industrial services, corporate offices, distribution centers, financial services and hospitality sectors. In March 2007, SpectraLink Corp. was acquired by Polycom, Inc. for $220 million.

## FINANCIALS: **Sales and profits are in thousands of dollars—add 000 to get the full amount. 2008 Note: Financial information for 2008 was not available for all companies at press time.**

| | | |
|---|---|---|
| 2008 Sales: $ | 2008 Profits: $ | **U.S. Stock Ticker: Subsidiary** |
| 2007 Sales: $ | 2007 Profits: $ | **Int'l Ticker:** Int'l Exchange: |
| 2006 Sales: $144,800 | 2006 Profits: $ | Employees: 650 |
| 2005 Sales: $97,774 | 2005 Profits: $12,024 | Fiscal Year Ends: 12/31 |
| 2004 Sales: $90,010 | 2004 Profits: $10,954 | Parent Company: POLYCOM INC |

## SALARIES/BENEFITS:

| | | | | |
|---|---|---|---|---|
| Pension Plan: | ESOP Stock Plan: | Profit Sharing: | Top Exec. Salary: $297,275 | Bonus: $187,837 |
| Savings Plan: | Stock Purch. Plan: | | Second Exec. Salary: $250,079 | Bonus: $78,719 |

## OTHER THOUGHTS:

**Apparent Women Officers or Directors:**
**Hot Spot for Advancement for Women/Minorities:**

## LOCATIONS: ("Y" = Yes)

| West: | Southwest: | Midwest: | Southeast: | Northeast: | International: |
|---|---|---|---|---|---|
| Y | | | | | |

# SPECTRANETICS CORP

www.spectranetics.com

**Industry Group Code:** 339113 **Ranks within this company's industry group:** Sales: 34 Profits: 27

| Management: | | Sales/Marketing: | | Liberal Arts: | | Information Systems: | | Professionals: | | Technical/Scientific: | |
|---|---|---|---|---|---|---|---|---|---|---|---|
| Mgmt. Trainees: | | Mktg. Professionals: | Y | Gen. Writing/Editing: | | Info. Management: | Y | Finance/Accounting: | Y | Engineers, Elec.: | Y |
| Experienced Mgmt.: | Y | Retail Sales: | | Technical Writing: | Y | Software Dev.: | Y | Law: | Y | Engineers, Other: | Y |
| Int'l Business: | Y | Commercial/Industrial: | Y | Graphic Arts/Photog.: | | Hardware Dev.: | Y | HR/Other: | Y | Health/Lab: | Y |
| MBA Graduates: | Y | Sales Trainees: | Y | Music: | | Systems Integration: | | Training: | Y | Scientists/Research: | Y |
| | | Advertising Pros.: | | Broadcasting: | | Consulting/Other: | | Health Care: | Y | Petroleum/Chemicals: | |
| | | | | Other: | | | | Consulting: | | Math/Other: | Y |

## TYPES OF BUSINESS:

Equipment-Laser Systems
Coronary & Vascular Blockage Treatments

## BRANDS/DIVISIONS/AFFILIATES:

LACI
CLiRpath 2.5 Turbo Catheter
CLeaRS
Spectranetics Laser Sheath
Lead Locking Device
FAMILI
QuickCat
ThromCat

## CONTACTS: *Note: Officers with more than one job title may be intentionally listed here more than once.*

John G. Schulte, CEO
Jonathan W. McGuire, COO
John G. Schulte, Pres.
Guy A. Childs, CFO/VP
Sandra Guenette, Dir.-Human Resources
Lawrence E. Martel, Jr., VP-Oper.
Larry O. Adighije, VP-Bus. Dev. & Strategy
Donald Fletcher, VP-Quality Assurance & Regulatory Compliance
Michael Voss, VP/Gen. Mgr.-Vascular Intervention Bus.
Thomas Rasmussen, VP-Clinical Affairs
Emile J. Geisenheimer, Chmn.
Shar Matin, VP/Managing Dir.-Spectranetics, BV

| | |
|---|---|
| **Phone:** 719-633-8333 | **Fax:** 719-633-2248 |
| **Toll-Free:** 800-633-0960 | |
| **Address:** 96 Talamine Ct., Colorado Springs, CO 80907-5186 US | |

## GROWTH PLANS/SPECIAL FEATURES:

Spectranetics Corp. develops, manufactures, markets and distributes a proprietary excimer laser system that treats coronary and vascular conditions. Spectranetics' excimer laser system is approved in the U.S., Canada, Japan and Europe for use in multiple, minimally invasive cardiovascular procedures. The system includes a CVX-300 laser unit and disposable laser catheters for use with the laser. Its laser catheters contain hundreds of fiber-optic strands that can access difficult to reach peripheral and coronary anatomy and produce evenly distributed laser energy at the tip of the catheter. Excimer lasers deliver a relatively cool ultraviolet light in short, controlled energy pulses to remove tissue. The system is used in atherectomy procedures that open clogged or obstructed arteries; and removing infected, defective or abandoned lead wires from patients with pacemakers or implantable cardiac defibrillators (ICD). It currently has 743 installed laser systems, of which 587 are located in the U.S. Spectranetics also markets the Laser Angioplasty for Critical Limb Ischemia (LACI) system, which treats total blockages in leg arteries; the CLeaRS pacemaker or ICD lead removal product line, which includes the Spectranetics Laser Sheath and Lead Locking Device; and the CLiRpath 2.5 Turbo Catheter for treatment of total occlusions of the superior femoral artery. Approximately 96% of its 2007 worldwide revenue came from disposable catheter sales, service and laser rental; 83% came from disposable catheter sales alone. The company is engaged in the FDA-approved extended Flow in Acute Myocardial Infarction after Laser Intervention (FAMILI) trial, a feasibility test aiming to rapidly restore blood flow in heart attack patients. In June 2008, the firm acquired the endovascular business of Kensey Nash, including the QuickCat thrombus aspiration catheter, ThromCat thrombectomy device and SafeCross line for chronic total occlusions.

Spectranetics offers its employees bereavement leave, flexible spending accounts and an employee assistance program.

## FINANCIALS: Sales and profits are in thousands of dollars—add 000 to get the full amount. 2008 Note: Financial information for 2008 was not available for all companies at press time.

| | | |
|---|---|---|
| 2008 Sales: $ | 2008 Profits: $ | **U.S. Stock Ticker: SPNC** |
| 2007 Sales: $82,874 | 2007 Profits: $7,229 | **Int'l Ticker:** Int'l Exchange: |
| 2006 Sales: $63,490 | 2006 Profits: $-1,447 | Employees: 374 |
| 2005 Sales: $43,212 | 2005 Profits: $1,038 | Fiscal Year Ends: 12/31 |
| 2004 Sales: $34,708 | 2004 Profits: $2,952 | Parent Company: |

## SALARIES/BENEFITS:

| | | | | |
|---|---|---|---|---|
| Pension Plan: | ESOP Stock Plan: | Profit Sharing: | Top Exec. Salary: $384,231 | Bonus: $172,850 |
| Savings Plan: Y | Stock Purch. Plan: Y | | Second Exec. Salary: $234,231 | Bonus: $106,369 |

## OTHER THOUGHTS:

**Apparent Women Officers or Directors**: 1
**Hot Spot for Advancement for Women/Minorities**:

## LOCATIONS: ("Y" = Yes)

| West: | Southwest: | Midwest: | Southeast: | Northeast: | International: |
|---|---|---|---|---|---|
| Y | | | | | Y |

# SPIRE CORPORATION

www.spirecorp.com

**Industry Group Code:** 333298A **Ranks within this company's industry group:** Sales: 5 Profits: 2

| Management: | | Sales/Marketing: | | Liberal Arts: | | Information Systems: | | Professionals: | | Technical/Scientific: | |
|---|---|---|---|---|---|---|---|---|---|---|---|
| Mgmt. Trainees: | | Mktg. Professionals: | Y | Gen. Writing/Editing: | | Info. Management: | Y | Finance/Accounting: | Y | Engineers, Elec.: | Y |
| Experienced Mgmt.: | Y | Retail Sales: | | Technical Writing: | Y | Software Dev.: | Y | Law: | Y | Engineers, Other: | Y |
| Int'l Business: | Y | Commercial/Industrial: | Y | Graphic Arts/Photog.: | Y | Hardware Dev.: | Y | HR/Other: | Y | Health/Lab: | |
| MBA Graduates: | Y | Sales Trainees: | Y | Music: | | Systems Integration: | | Training: | Y | Scientists/Research: | Y |
| | | Advertising Pros.: | | Broadcasting: | | Consulting/Other: | | Health Care: | | Petroleum/Chemicals: | |
| | | | | Other: | | | | Consulting: | | Math/Other: | Y |

## TYPES OF BUSINESS:

Photovoltaic Module Manufacturing
Biomedical Products & Technologies
Electric Utility
Solar Power Generation
Optoelectronics
Thermophotovoltaic Power Cells

## BRANDS/DIVISIONS/AFFILIATES:

Gloria Spire Solar
Spire Biomedical, Inc.
Gloria Solar Co., Ltd.
Spire Semiconductor

## CONTACTS: *Note: Officers with more than one job title may be intentionally listed here more than once.*

Roger G. Little, CEO
Rodger W. LaFavre, COO
Roger G. Little, Pres.
Christian Dufresne, CFO
Christian Dufresne, Treas.
Stephen J. Hogan, Exec. VP/Gen. Mgr.-Spire Solar
Mark C. Little, CEO-Spire Biomedical
Roger G. Little, Chmn.

| | |
|---|---|
| **Phone:** 781-275-6000 | **Fax:** 781-275-7470 |
| **Toll-Free:** 800-510-4815 | |
| **Address:** 1 Patriots Park, Bedford, MA 01730 US | |

## GROWTH PLANS/SPECIAL FEATURES:

Spire Corp. develops, manufactures and markets highly engineered products and services in three principal business areas: biomedical, solar and optoelectronics. The company operates primarily through its subsidiary Spire Semiconductor and joint venture Gloria Spire Solar. In the biomedical area, the firm provides value-added surface treatments to manufacturers of orthopedic and other medical devices that enhance the durability, antimicrobial characteristics or other material characteristics of their products; develops and markets hemodialysis catheters and related devices for the treatment of chronic kidney disease; and performs sponsored research programs into applications of advanced biomedical and biophotonic technologies. In the solar equipment area, Spire is a supplier of specialized equipment for the production of terrestrial photovoltaic modules from solar cells. The solar systems division provides custom and building-integrated photovoltaic modules, stand-alone emergency power back up and electric power grid-connected distributed power generation systems that employ photovoltaic technology. In the optoelectronics area, the company provides custom compound semiconductor foundry and fabrication services on a merchant basis to customers involved in biomedical/biophotonics instruments, telecommunications and defense applications. The firm has a device fabrication facility where it produces, under contract with customers, gallium arsenide concentrator cells (GaAs). This facility is the foundation of the Spire's solar cell process technology for silicon, polysilicon, thin film and GaAs concentrator cells, high performance LEDs and other customer semiconductor foundry services for customers. In December 2008, Spire Corp. recieved a $54 million contract with the Federal Prison Industries, Inc., known as UNICOR, to supply solar cells for the Spire-installed Turnkey Photovoltaic Module Factory within the Otisville, New York-based Federal Correctional Institution (FCI). Other recent clients include the U.S. Department of Energy (DOE), Spain-based Solaria Energia Y Medio Ambiente, S.A., and Korean-based Hanwha Chemical Corporation.

## FINANCIALS: **Sales and profits are in thousands of dollars—add 000 to get the full amount. 2008 Note: Financial information for 2008 was not available for all companies at press time.**

| | | |
|---|---|---|
| 2008 Sales: $ | 2008 Profits: $ | **U.S. Stock Ticker: SPIR** |
| 2007 Sales: $38,423 | 2007 Profits: $-1,686 | **Int'l Ticker:** Int'l Exchange: |
| 2006 Sales: $20,125 | 2006 Profits: $-8,151 | Employees: 188 |
| 2005 Sales: $22,422 | 2005 Profits: $ 44 | Fiscal Year Ends: 12/31 |
| 2004 Sales: $17,278 | 2004 Profits: $-4,120 | Parent Company: |

## SALARIES/BENEFITS:

| | | | | |
|---|---|---|---|---|
| Pension Plan: | ESOP Stock Plan: | Profit Sharing: | Top Exec. Salary: $487,000 | Bonus: $59,250 |
| Savings Plan: | Stock Purch. Plan: | | Second Exec. Salary: $150,000 | Bonus: $6,000 |

## OTHER THOUGHTS:

**Apparent Women Officers or Directors**:
**Hot Spot for Advancement for Women/Minorities**:

## LOCATIONS: ("Y" = Yes)

| West: | Southwest: | Midwest: | Southeast: | Northeast: | International: |
|---|---|---|---|---|---|
| | | Y | | Y | Y |

# SPORTSMAN'S GUIDE INC (THE)

www.sportsmansguide.com

**Industry Group Code:** 451110 **Ranks within this company's industry group:** Sales: Profits:

| Management: | | Sales/Marketing: | | Liberal Arts: | | Information Systems: | | Professionals: | | Technical/Scientific: | |
|---|---|---|---|---|---|---|---|---|---|---|---|
| Mgmt. Trainees: | Y | Mktg. Professionals: | Y | Gen. Writing/Editing: | Y | Info. Management: | Y | Finance/Accounting: | Y | Engineers, Elec.: | |
| Experienced Mgmt.: | Y | Retail Sales: | Y | Technical Writing: | | Software Dev.: | | Law: | Y | Engineers, Other: | |
| Int'l Business: | | Commercial/Industrial: | | Graphic Arts/Photog.: | Y | Hardware Dev.: | | HR/Other: | Y | Health/Lab: | |
| MBA Graduates: | Y | Sales Trainees: | Y | Music: | | Systems Integration: | | Training: | Y | Scientists/Research: | |
| | | Advertising Pros.: | Y | Broadcasting: | | Consulting/Other: | | Health Care: | | Petroleum/Chemicals: | |
| | | | | Other: | | | | Consulting: | | Math/Other: | |

## TYPES OF BUSINESS:

Outdoor & Hunting Products
Online & Catalog Sales
Outdoor Apparel & Footwear
Golf Equipment

## BRANDS/DIVISIONS/AFFILIATES:

Redcats USA
sportsmansguide.com
tgw.com
bargainoutfitters.com
boatingsavings.com
Buyer's Club

## CONTACTS:

*Note: Officers with more than one job title may be intentionally listed here more than once.*

Gregory R. Binkley, CEO
Gregory R. Binkley, Pres.
John M. Casler, Exec. VP-Mktg. & Creative Svcs.
Dale D. Monson, CIO/Sr. VP
John M. Casler, Exec. VP-Merch.
Dale D. Monson, Sr. VP-Oper.
Charles B. Lingen, Exec. VP-Finance/Treas.

**Phone:** 651-451-3030 **Fax:** 651-450-6130
**Toll-Free:** 888-844-0667
**Address:** 411 Farwell Ave. S., St. Paul, MN 55075 US

## GROWTH PLANS/SPECIAL FEATURES:

The Sportsman's Guide, Inc., a subsidiary of Redcats USA, is a multi-channel direct marketer of value-priced outdoor gear and clothing, golf equipment and general merchandise. The company sells its products through main and specialty catalogs and several e-commerce sites, including sportsmansguide.com; tgw.com, which focuses on golf products; and bargainoutfitters.com, a liquidation outlet. The firm's main catalog is mailed monthly, and offers merchandise across a broad range of categories. Additional specialized catalogs are also offered during the course of each year and focus on individual categories such as camping, government surplus, ammunition and shooting supplies, gifts and hunting. The Buyer's Club, which customers can join for an annual fee, offers 10% discounts on most merchandise (5% on ammunition), a monthly Buyer's Advantage Catalog and exclusive special offers. The Sportsman's Guide e-commerce site offers a selection similar to its print catalog in addition to certain specialty catalogs available exclusively online, such as Truck/SUV and ATV. More than 60% of the company's sales come through its web site. An online resource center features a variety of articles, advice columns and information about outdoor lifestyles and pursuits, including a section specifically aimed at women outdoor enthusiasts. In addition, customers can find maps, fish and game forecasts, local guide and outfitter listings, ballistics charts, useful links and other information on the web site. Orders can be placed 24-hours-a-day by phone or online, and the company ships all orders directly from its 330,000-square-foot warehouse. In 2008, Sportsmen's Guide launched the boatingsavings.com e-commerce site, which aims to be a one-stop shop for fishing and boating enthusiasts.

## FINANCIALS:

**Sales and profits are in thousands of dollars—add 000 to get the full amount. 2008 Note: Financial information for 2008 was not available for all companies at press time.**

2008 Sales: $
2007 Sales: $
2006 Sales: $
2005 Sales: $285,120
2004 Sales: $232,465

2008 Profits: $
2007 Profits: $
2006 Profits: $
2005 Profits: $11,453
2004 Profits: $7,593

**U.S. Stock Ticker: Subsidiary**
**Int'l Ticker:** Int'l Exchange:
Employees: 754
Fiscal Year Ends: 12/31
Parent Company: REDCATS USA

## SALARIES/BENEFITS:

Pension Plan: ESOP Stock Plan: Profit Sharing: Top Exec. Salary: $296,923 Bonus: $655,000
Savings Plan: Stock Purch. Plan: Second Exec. Salary: $234,615 Bonus: $330,000

## OTHER THOUGHTS:

**Apparent Women Officers or Directors**:
**Hot Spot for Advancement for Women/Minorities**:

## LOCATIONS: ("Y" = Yes)

| West: | Southwest: | Midwest: | Southeast: | Northeast: | International: |
|---|---|---|---|---|---|
| | | Y | | | |

# SPROUTS FARMERS MARKET

**www.sprouts.com**

**Industry Group Code:** 445110 **Ranks within this company's industry group:** Sales: 3 Profits:

| Management: | | Sales/Marketing: | | Liberal Arts: | | Information Systems: | | Professionals: | | Technical/Scientific: | |
|---|---|---|---|---|---|---|---|---|---|---|---|
| Mgmt. Trainees: | Y | Mktg. Professionals: | Y | Gen. Writing/Editing: | | Info. Management: | Y | Finance/Accounting: | Y | Engineers, Elec.: | |
| Experienced Mgmt.: | Y | Retail Sales: | Y | Technical Writing: | | Software Dev.: | | Law: | Y | Engineers, Other: | |
| Int'l Business: | | Commercial/Industrial: | | Graphic Arts/Photog.: | Y | Hardware Dev.: | | HR/Other: | Y | Health/Lab: | |
| MBA Graduates: | Y | Sales Trainees: | Y | Music: | | Systems Integration: | | Training: | Y | Scientists/Research: | |
| | | Advertising Pros.: | Y | Broadcasting: | | Consulting/Other: | | Health Care: | | Petroleum/Chemicals: | |
| | | | | Other: | | | | Consulting: | | Math/Other: | |

## TYPES OF BUSINESS:

Supermarkets

## BRANDS/DIVISIONS/AFFILIATES:

Sprouts Magazine

## GROWTH PLANS/SPECIAL FEATURES:

Sprouts Farmers Market, LLC is an independent natural foods retailer operating from 31 locations in California, Arizona, Texas and Colorado. The company's stores stock products including baked goods, beer and wine, bulk foods, dairy products, meat, poultry, produce, seafood and vitamins. Sprouts acquires these products primarily from U.S. suppliers, emphasizing local buying practices, but purchases certain seasonal fruits and vegetables from growers around the world. The firm's stores host a variety of events, such as cooking classes, health screenings and health information sessions, and the company's web site offers recipes, nutritional information and a health guide. Sprouts also publishes a bimonthly magazine featuring articles on health, recipes and items of seasonal interest. The firm's most recent store openings were in Murphy, Texas and Westminster, Colorado.

The company offers employees health, dental, vision and life insurance; a 401(k) plan; a discount on all store purchases; short-term disability insurance; and pre-paid legal services.

## CONTACTS:

*Note: Officers with more than one job title may be intentionally listed here more than once.*

Shon Boney, CEO
Doug Sanders, COO
Doug Sanders, Pres.
Brad Denton, CFO/Sr. VP
Stan Boney, Chmn.

| | |
|---|---|
| **Phone:** 480-814-8016 | **Fax:** 480-814-8017 |
| **Toll-Free:** | |
| **Address:** 11811 N. Tatum Blvd., Ste. 2400, Phoenix, AZ 85028 US | |

## FINANCIALS:

**Sales and profits are in thousands of dollars—add 000 to get the full amount. 2008 Note: Financial information for 2008 was not available for all companies at press time.**

| | | |
|---|---|---|
| 2008 Sales: $ | 2008 Profits: $ | **U.S. Stock Ticker: Private** |
| 2007 Sales: $300,000 | 2007 Profits: $ | **Int'l Ticker:** Int'l Exchange: |
| 2006 Sales: $ | 2006 Profits: $ | Employees: 2,100 |
| 2005 Sales: $ | 2005 Profits: $ | Fiscal Year Ends: |
| 2004 Sales: $ | 2004 Profits: $ | Parent Company: |

## SALARIES/BENEFITS:

| | | | | |
|---|---|---|---|---|
| Pension Plan: | ESOP Stock Plan: | Profit Sharing: | Top Exec. Salary: $ | Bonus: $ |
| Savings Plan: Y | Stock Purch. Plan: | | Second Exec. Salary: $ | Bonus: $ |

## OTHER THOUGHTS:

**Apparent Women Officers or Directors:**
**Hot Spot for Advancement for Women/Minorities:**

## LOCATIONS: ("Y" = Yes)

| West: | Southwest: | Midwest: | Southeast: | Northeast: | International: |
|---|---|---|---|---|---|
| Y | Y | | | | |

# SPSS INC

www.spss.com

**Industry Group Code:** 511203 **Ranks within this company's industry group:** Sales: 3 Profits: 3

| **Management:** | | **Sales/Marketing:** | | **Liberal Arts:** | | **Information Systems:** | | **Professionals:** | | **Technical/Scientific:** | |
|---|---|---|---|---|---|---|---|---|---|---|---|
| Mgmt. Trainees: | | Mktg. Professionals: | Y | Gen. Writing/Editing: | | Info. Management: | Y | Finance/Accounting: | Y | Engineers, Elec.: | Y |
| Experienced Mgmt.: | Y | Retail Sales: | | Technical Writing: | Y | Software Dev.: | Y | Law: | Y | Engineers, Other: | |
| Int'l Business: | Y | Commercial/Industrial: | Y | Graphic Arts/Photog.: | | Hardware Dev.: | | HR/Other: | Y | Health/Lab: | |
| MBA Graduates: | Y | Sales Trainees: | Y | Music: | | Systems Integration: | | Training: | Y | Scientists/Research: | |
| | | Advertising Pros.: | | Broadcasting: | | Consulting/Other: | | Health Care: | | Petroleum/Chemicals: | |
| | | | | Other: | Y | | | Consulting: | Y | Math/Other: | Y |

## TYPES OF BUSINESS:

Software-Statistics
Business Performance Management Software
Data Mining Software
Fraud Detection Software
Sales Forecasting
Market Research

## BRANDS/DIVISIONS/AFFILIATES:

ShowCase Corp.
Clementine
LexiQuest
Quantime, Ltd.
Integral Solutions, Ltd.
Vento Software
Net Genesis Corp.

## CONTACTS: *Note: Officers with more than one job title may be intentionally listed here more than once.*

Jack Noonan, CEO
Jack Noonan, Pres.
Raymond Panza, CFO
Jack Noonan, Chmn.

| **Phone:** 312-651-3000 | **Fax:** |
|---|---|
| **Toll-Free:** | |
| **Address:** 233 S. Wacker Dr., 11th Fl., Chicago, IL 60606 US | |

## GROWTH PLANS/SPECIAL FEATURES:

SPSS, Inc. is a major global provider of predictive analytics technology and services. Its software products provide statistical analysis, data mining, performance measurement and fraud detection. The company's business intelligence products enable organizations to develop more profitable customer relationships by using statistics to provide analytical solutions that discover what customers want and predict what they will do, especially in such areas as sales and targeted marketing. SPSS' analytical solutions integrate and analyze market, customer and operational data in key vertical markets worldwide, including the telecommunications, finance, insurance, manufacturing and retail markets. The firm's customers include research analysts, software vendors and banking, telecom, health care, education and retail firms. SPSS revenues from operations outside of the U.S. accounted for approximately 59% of total revenues. SPSS' ShowCase Corp. subsidiary offers data warehousing and content management software, which allows customers to store the data they generated, further analyze it and distribute or use it to generate reports. The company's LexiQuest products offer language-based search and categorization tools, while the firm's Clementine package provides a platform for data mining. Its Clementine 11, the newest version of its Clementine data-mining workbench, is designed for use in customer relations management, marketing, fraud detection and revenue assurance. It features dramatically enhanced solutions through the use of data analytic techniques and innovative graphic capabilities. SPSS has solidified its place in the analytical market by acquiring companies like Quantime, Ltd.; Integral Solutions, Ltd.; Vento Software; and Net Genesis Corp. The company serves over 250,000 customers in 60 countries. Its customer list includes New York University, Credit Suisse, Lloyds TSB, Corona Direct, Yamaha Motor Europe, the Gallup Organization, British Telecom, NOP World, GE Aircraft Engines, Infinity Insurance and IBM.

## FINANCIALS: **Sales and profits are in thousands of dollars—add 000 to get the full amount. 2008 Note: Financial information for 2008 was not available for all companies at press time.**

| | | |
|---|---|---|
| 2008 Sales: $ | 2008 Profits: $ | **U.S. Stock Ticker: SPSS** |
| 2007 Sales: $291,000 | 2007 Profits: $33,725 | **Int'l Ticker:** Int'l Exchange: |
| 2006 Sales: $261,532 | 2006 Profits: $15,140 | Employees: 1,246 |
| 2005 Sales: $236,063 | 2005 Profits: $16,092 | Fiscal Year Ends: 12/31 |
| 2004 Sales: $224,074 | 2004 Profits: $5,543 | Parent Company: |

## SALARIES/BENEFITS:

| | | | | |
|---|---|---|---|---|
| Pension Plan: | ESOP Stock Plan: | Profit Sharing: | Top Exec. Salary: $500,000 | Bonus: $1,638,222 |
| Savings Plan: Y | Stock Purch. Plan: Y | | Second Exec. Salary: $420,000 | Bonus: $851,876 |

## OTHER THOUGHTS:

**Apparent Women Officers or Directors:**
**Hot Spot for Advancement for Women/Minorities:**

## LOCATIONS: ("Y" = Yes)

| West: | Southwest: | Midwest: | Southeast: | Northeast: | International: |
|---|---|---|---|---|---|
| Y | Y | Y | Y | Y | Y |

Note: Financial information, benefits and other data can change quickly and may vary from those stated here.

# SRI/SURGICAL EXPRESS INC

**www.surgicalexpress.com**

**Industry Group Code:** 339113 **Ranks within this company's industry group:** Sales: 30 Profits: 38

| Management: | | Sales/Marketing: | | Liberal Arts: | | Information Systems: | | Professionals: | | Technical/Scientific: | |
|---|---|---|---|---|---|---|---|---|---|---|---|
| Mgmt. Trainees: | Y | Mktg. Professionals: | Y | Gen. Writing/Editing: | | Info. Management: | Y | Finance/Accounting: | Y | Engineers, Elec.: | Y |
| Experienced Mgmt.: | Y | Retail Sales: | | Technical Writing: | Y | Software Dev.: | | Law: | Y | Engineers, Other: | Y |
| Int'l Business: | | Commercial/Industrial: | Y | Graphic Arts/Photog.: | | Hardware Dev.: | | HR/Other: | Y | Health/Lab: | Y |
| MBA Graduates: | Y | Sales Trainees: | Y | Music: | | Systems Integration: | | Training: | Y | Scientists/Research: | Y |
| | | Advertising Pros.: | | Broadcasting: | | Consulting/Other: | | Health Care: | Y | Petroleum/Chemicals: | |
| | | | | Other: | | | | Consulting: | | Math/Other: | Y |

## TYPES OF BUSINESS:

Supplies-Surgery
Surgical Delivery Services

## BRANDS/DIVISIONS/AFFILIATES:

ComfortSure
Owens & Minor, Inc.
Premier Purchasing Partners L.P.

## CONTACTS: *Note: Officers with more than one job title may be intentionally listed here more than once.*

Gerald Woodard, CEO
Wallace D. Ruiz, CFO/Sr. VP
Jon McGuire, Sr. VP-Sales
Jack A. Hamilton, Sr. VP-Process Eng. & Quality Assurance
Charles W. Federico, Chmn.

| | |
|---|---|
| **Phone:** 813-891-9550 | **Fax:** 813-818-9076 |
| **Toll-Free:** | |
| **Address:** 12425 Race Track Rd., Tampa, FL 33626 US | |

## GROWTH PLANS/SPECIAL FEATURES:

SRI Surgical Express, Inc. provides daily processing, assembly and delivery of reusable and disposable products and instruments that hospital customers require for surgery. Reusable products include ComfortSure brand gowns; back table and Mayo stand covers; towels; procedure and patient drapes; and basin sets. The company provides daily delivery, retrieval, processing, inspection, assembly and sterilization of reusable textiles from 10 processing service facilities located across the U.S. The firm also offers off-site and on-site instrument processing. This service provides customized surgical instrument sets on a per-procedure fee basis. SRI's integrated closed-loop process starts with daily delivery of reusable and disposable surgical supplies and instruments to the healthcare provider. At the same time, the company picks up the reusable textiles, basins and instruments used in surgery and returns them to the processing facility. Used products arriving at its processing facility are sorted, cleaned, inspected, packaged, sterilized and subsequently, shipped back to the healthcare providers. This service uses two of the most technologically advanced reusable textiles for gowns and drapes: a Gore surgical barrier fabric, which is breathable yet liquid-proof and provides a viral and bacterial barrier; and an advanced microfiber polyester surgical fabric, which is liquid- and bacteria-resistant. The firm serves approximately 350 hospitals and surgery centers. SRI has a multi-year exclusive agreement to distribute Owens & Minor's Implant Tracking System to the tissue banking industry. Using barcode technology, Owens & Minor's Implant Tracking System enables clinicians to track bone and tissue implants, monitor expiration dates on implants and rapidly identify implant recipients in case of recalls. In January 2008, the company signed a three-year agreement with Premier Purchasing Partners L.P. to offer its reprocessing services and products to Premier's 1,500 hospitals and 47,000 other healthcare locations.

## FINANCIALS: **Sales and profits are in thousands of dollars—add 000 to get the full amount. 2008 Note: Financial information for 2008 was not available for all companies at press time.**

| | | |
|---|---|---|
| 2008 Sales: $ | 2008 Profits: $ | **U.S. Stock Ticker: STRC** |
| 2007 Sales: $94,201 | 2007 Profits: $-3,193 | **Int'l Ticker:** Int'l Exchange: |
| 2006 Sales: $98,831 | 2006 Profits: $-1,953 | Employees: 860 |
| 2005 Sales: $91,734 | 2005 Profits: $ 393 | Fiscal Year Ends: 12/31 |
| 2004 Sales: $91,310 | 2004 Profits: $-4,998 | Parent Company: |

## SALARIES/BENEFITS:

| | | | | |
|---|---|---|---|---|
| Pension Plan: | ESOP Stock Plan: | Profit Sharing: | Top Exec. Salary: $268,558 | Bonus: $13,000 |
| Savings Plan: | Stock Purch. Plan: | | Second Exec. Salary: $193,568 | Bonus: $20,000 |

## OTHER THOUGHTS:

**Apparent Women Officers or Directors:**
**Hot Spot for Advancement for Women/Minorities:**

## LOCATIONS: ("Y" = Yes)

| West: | Southwest: | Midwest: | Southeast: | Northeast: | International: |
|---|---|---|---|---|---|
| Y | Y | Y | Y | Y | |

# SS&C TECHNOLOGIES INC

**www.ssctech.com**

**Industry Group Code:** 511201 **Ranks within this company's industry group:** Sales: 2 Profits: 5

| Management: | | Sales/Marketing: | | Liberal Arts: | | Information Systems: | | Professionals: | | Technical/Scientific: | |
|---|---|---|---|---|---|---|---|---|---|---|---|
| Mgmt. Trainees: | | Mktg. Professionals: | Y | Gen. Writing/Editing: | | Info. Management: | Y | Finance/Accounting: | Y | Engineers, Elec.: | Y |
| Experienced Mgmt.: | Y | Retail Sales: | | Technical Writing: | Y | Software Dev.: | Y | Law: | Y | Engineers, Other: | |
| Int'l Business: | Y | Commercial/Industrial: | Y | Graphic Arts/Photog.: | | Hardware Dev.: | | HR/Other: | Y | Health/Lab: | |
| MBA Graduates: | Y | Sales Trainees: | Y | Music: | | Systems Integration: | | Training: | Y | Scientists/Research: | |
| | | Advertising Pros.: | | Broadcasting: | | Consulting/Other: | | Health Care: | | Petroleum/Chemicals: | |
| | | | | Other: | | | | Consulting: | | Math/Other: | |

## TYPES OF BUSINESS:

Financial Software
Business Process Outsourcing Services
Application Service Provider Solutions
Financial Education & Simulation Products
Hedge Fund Management Services

## BRANDS/DIVISIONS/AFFILIATES:

AdvisorWare
BANC Mall
Antares
Cogent Management, Inc.
Zoologic
Northport, LLC

## CONTACTS:

*Note: Officers with more than one job title may be intentionally listed here more than once.*

William Stone, CEO
Normand A. Boulanger, COO
Normand A. Boulanger, Pres.
Patrick J.Pedonti, CFO/Sr. VP
John Sharpe, CIO/Sr. VP
Stephen V.R. Whitman, General Counsel/Sr. VP
Steve H. Kremidas, Sr. VP-Chief Dev. Officer
Michele Rebiere, VP-Corp. Rel. & Resources
Suresh Thekkenmar, Sr. VP-Professional Svcs.
Sean Egan, Sr. VP-Real Estate
Doug Benedetto, VP-Strategic Accounts
William Stone, Chmn.

| **Phone:** 860-298-4500 | **Fax:** 860-298-4900 |
|---|---|
| **Toll-Free:** 800-234-0556 | |
| **Address:** 80 Lamberton Rd., Windsor, CT 06095 US | |

## GROWTH PLANS/SPECIAL FEATURES:

SS&C Technologies, Inc. is an international company offering a family of highly specialized, mission-critical software and services that help automate and simplify information management, analysis, accounting, reporting and compliance for investment professionals in a broad range of financial services segments. The products allow clients to rapidly access, manage and analyze large amounts of transactions-based data both in the aggregate and in detail. The company's product and services offerings are specialized to serve eight main industry segments: alternative investments; asset management; insurance and pension funds; commercial lending; financial institutions; municipal finance; real estate property management; and corporate treasury. Various branded products/services within the SS&C product lines include AdvisorWare, a software that supports hedge funds, funds of funds and family offices with sophisticated global investment, trading and management concerns; BANC Mall, an Internet-based research and lending tools for loan administration; and Antares, a real-time, event-driven trading and profit and loss reporting system designed to integrate trade modeling with trade order management. As the financial services industry continues to grow, SS&C believes that the corresponding IT budgets will grow similarly. The needs of the financial services industry lead the company to believe that strong client relationships, along with leading technology and outsourced solutions, will allow the company to grow. In October 2008, the company acquired Micro Design Services, LLC, a firm that designs and develops real-time, mission-critical order routing and execution services. In November 2008, the firm launched Gloval Debt Manager, a web site for global corporate trustees and paying agents.

Employees of the firm are offered health benefits; flexible spending accounts; life insurance; a 401(k) plan; disability insurance; and tuition reimbursement.

## FINANCIALS:

**Sales and profits are in thousands of dollars—add 000 to get the full amount. 2008 Note: Financial information for 2008 was not available for all companies at press time.**

| | | |
|---|---|---|
| 2008 Sales: $ | 2008 Profits: $ | **U.S. Stock Ticker: Private** |
| 2007 Sales: $248,168 | 2007 Profits: $6,575 | **Int'l Ticker:** Int'l Exchange: |
| 2006 Sales: $205,469 | 2006 Profits: $1,075 | Employees: 1,059 |
| 2005 Sales: $161,600 | 2005 Profits: $ | Fiscal Year Ends: 12/31 |
| 2004 Sales: $95,900 | 2004 Profits: $19,000 | Parent Company: |

## SALARIES/BENEFITS:

| | | | | |
|---|---|---|---|---|
| Pension Plan: | ESOP Stock Plan: | Profit Sharing: | Top Exec. Salary: $490,110 | Bonus: $700,000 |
| Savings Plan: Y | Stock Purch. Plan: | | Second Exec. Salary: $290,480 | Bonus: $250,000 |

## OTHER THOUGHTS:

**Apparent Women Officers or Directors:** 2
**Hot Spot for Advancement for Women/Minorities:**

## LOCATIONS: ("Y" = Yes)

| West: | Southwest: | Midwest: | Southeast: | Northeast: | International: |
|---|---|---|---|---|---|
| Y | | Y | | Y | Y |

# ST MARY LAND & EXPLORATION COMPANY

www.stmaryland.com

**Industry Group Code:** 211111 **Ranks within this company's industry group:** Sales: 10 Profits: 10

| Management: | | Sales/Marketing: | | Liberal Arts: | | Information Systems: | | Professionals: | | Technical/Scientific: | |
|---|---|---|---|---|---|---|---|---|---|---|---|
| Mgmt. Trainees: | | Mktg. Professionals: | Y | Gen. Writing/Editing: | | Info. Management: | Y | Finance/Accounting: | Y | Engineers, Elec.: | |
| Experienced Mgmt.: | Y | Retail Sales: | | Technical Writing: | | Software Dev.: | | Law: | Y | Engineers, Other: | Y |
| Int'l Business: | Y | Commercial/Industrial: | Y | Graphic Arts/Photog.: | | Hardware Dev.: | | HR/Other: | Y | Health/Lab: | |
| MBA Graduates: | Y | Sales Trainees: | | Music: | | Systems Integration: | | Training: | Y | Scientists/Research: | |
| | | Advertising Pros.: | | Broadcasting: | | Consulting/Other: | | Health Care: | | Petroleum/Chemicals: | Y |
| | | | | Other: | | | | Consulting: | | Math/Other: | |

## TYPES OF BUSINESS:

Oil & Gas Exploration & Production
Coalbed Methane
Seismic Surveys

## BRANDS/DIVISIONS/AFFILIATES:

Nance Petroleum Corp.

## CONTACTS:

*Note: Officers with more than one job title may be intentionally listed here more than once.*

Anthony J. Best, CEO
Javan D. Ottoson, COO/Exec. VP
Anthony J. Best, Pres.
Wade Pursell, CFO/Exec. VP
David J. Whitcomb, VP-Mktg.
John Monark, VP-Human Resources
Dennis A. Zubieta, VP-Eng. & Evaluation
Garry A. Wilkening, VP-Admin.
Milam Randolph Pharo, General Counsel/Sr. VP
Kenneth Knott, VP-Bus. Dev. & Land
Matthew J. Purchase, Treas.
Mark T. Solomon, Controller
Michael F. Roach, Dir.-Taxation
Mark D. Mueller, Sr. VP-Regional Mgr.
Paul M. Veatch, Sr. VP-Regional Mgr.
Mark A. Hellerstein, Chmn.

| | |
|---|---|
| **Phone:** 303-861-8140 | **Fax:** 303-861-0934 |
| **Toll-Free:** | |
| **Address:** 1776 Lincoln St., Ste. 700, Denver, CO 80203 US | |

## GROWTH PLANS/SPECIAL FEATURES:

St. Mary Land & Exploration Co. is an independent oil and gas company engaged in the exploration, exploitation, development, acquisition and production of natural gas and crude oil. The firm is based in Denver, Colorado with regional offices in Montana, Oklahoma, Texas and Louisiana. It has diversified exploration, development and production holdings in the Anadarko and Arkoma basins in Oklahoma and Arkansas; the tri-state area of southern Arkansas, northern Louisiana and eastern Texas; Louisiana and the Gulf Coast region; the Rocky Mountain region, which includes the Williston, Powder River, Green River and Wind River basins in Wyoming, North Dakota and Montana; and the Permian Basin of New Mexico and Texas. Subsidiary Nance Petroleum Corp. manages St. Mary's Rocky Mountain operations. The firm's assets include proved reserves of 74.2 millions of barrels of oil and 482.5 billion of cubic feet equivalents of natural gas. St. Mary has also begun developing its coal bed methane reserves in the Hanging Woman Basin of Wyoming. St. Mary's techniques include utilizing detailed geologic studies, 3-D seismic imaging, hydraulic fracturing, and reservoir stimulation and advanced logging techniques. In October 2007, the firm acquired oil and gas properties in south Texas from Rockford Energy Partners II, LLC for roughly $153 million.

## FINANCIALS:

**Sales and profits are in thousands of dollars—add 000 to get the full amount. 2008 Note: Financial information for 2008 was not available for all companies at press time.**

| | | |
|---|---|---|
| 2008 Sales: $ | 2008 Profits: $ | **U.S. Stock Ticker: SM** |
| 2007 Sales: $990,094 | 2007 Profits: $189,712 | **Int'l Ticker:** Int'l Exchange: |
| 2006 Sales: $787,701 | 2006 Profits: $190,015 | Employees: 438 |
| 2005 Sales: $739,590 | 2005 Profits: $151,936 | Fiscal Year Ends: 12/31 |
| 2004 Sales: $433,099 | 2004 Profits: $92,479 | Parent Company: |

## SALARIES/BENEFITS:

| | | | | |
|---|---|---|---|---|
| Pension Plan: | ESOP Stock Plan: | Profit Sharing: | Top Exec. Salary: $417,483 | Bonus: $41,748 |
| Savings Plan: | Stock Purch. Plan: | | Second Exec. Salary: $258,029 | Bonus: $25,803 |

## OTHER THOUGHTS:

**Apparent Women Officers or Directors**: 1
**Hot Spot for Advancement for Women/Minorities**: Y

## LOCATIONS: ("Y" = Yes)

| West: | Southwest: | Midwest: | Southeast: | Northeast: | International: |
|---|---|---|---|---|---|
| Y | Y | | Y | | |

Note: Financial information, benefits and other data can change quickly and may vary from those stated here.

# STAAR SURGICAL CO

www.staar.com

**Industry Group Code:** 339113 **Ranks within this company's industry group:** Sales: 40 Profits: 39

| Management: | | Sales/Marketing: | | Liberal Arts: | | Information Systems: | | Professionals: | | Technical/Scientific: | |
|---|---|---|---|---|---|---|---|---|---|---|---|
| Mgmt. Trainees: | | Mktg. Professionals: | Y | Gen. Writing/Editing: | | Info. Management: | Y | Finance/Accounting: | Y | Engineers, Elec.: | Y |
| Experienced Mgmt.: | Y | Retail Sales: | | Technical Writing: | Y | Software Dev.: | Y | Law: | Y | Engineers, Other: | Y |
| Int'l Business: | Y | Commercial/Industrial: | Y | Graphic Arts/Photog.: | | Hardware Dev.: | | HR/Other: | Y | Health/Lab: | Y |
| MBA Graduates: | Y | Sales Trainees: | Y | Music: | | Systems Integration: | | Training: | Y | Scientists/Research: | Y |
| | | Advertising Pros.: | | Broadcasting: | | Consulting/Other: | | Health Care: | Y | Petroleum/Chemicals: | |
| | | | | Other: | | | | Consulting: | | Math/Other: | Y |

## TYPES OF BUSINESS:

Equipment-Ophthalmic Surgery
Intraocular Lenses

## BRANDS/DIVISIONS/AFFILIATES:

Collamer
Visian ICL
Visian Toric ICL
Canon Staar
Preloaded Injector
SonicWAVE Phacoemulsification System
Cruise Control
AquaFlow

## CONTACTS:

*Note: Officers with more than one job title may be intentionally listed here more than once.*

Barry Caldwell, CEO
Barry Caldwell, Pres.
Deborah Andrews, CFO/VP
Nick Curtis, Sr. VP-Sales
Craig Felberg, VP-R&D and Clinical
Charles S. Kaufman, General Counsel/VP/Corp. Sec.
Paul Hambrick, VP-Oper.
Robin Hughes, VP-Mktg.
Rob Lally, VP-Quality Assurance & Regulatory Affairs
Don M. Bailey, Chmn.
David Bailey, Pres., Int'l Oper.

| | |
|---|---|
| **Phone:** 626-303-7902 | **Fax:** 626-303-2962 |
| **Toll-Free:** 800-352-7842 | |
| **Address:** 1911 Walker Ave., Monrovia, CA 91016 US | |

## GROWTH PLANS/SPECIAL FEATURES:

STAAR Surgical Co. develops, produces and markets medical devices used to improve or correct vision in patients with refractive conditions, cataracts and glaucoma. The company's main product line consists of one-piece and three-piece foldable silicone and Collamer intraocular lenses (IOLs), used after cataract extraction. The lens is folded and implanted into the eye behind the iris and in front of the natural lens using minimally invasive techniques. This procedure is performed with topical anesthesia on an outpatient basis, with visual recovery within one to 24 hours. It has developed two implantable Collamer lenses (ICLs), the Visian ICL and Visian Toric ICL, to treat astigmatic abnormalities, myopia (near-sightedness) and hypermyopia (far-sightedness). These products are sold to ophthalmologists, surgical centers, hospitals, managed care providers, health maintenance organizations and group purchasing organizations in over 40 countries. Through its Japanese joint venture company, Canon Staar, the firm has released the Preloaded Injector system for deploying intraocular lenses in the eye in international markets. Sales of IOLs accounted for approximately 39% of STAAR's 2007 revenues, while ICLs accounted for 26%. The SonicWAVE Phacoemulsification System is an alternative to surgery, using ultrasound for cataract removal. Its Cruise Control filter enables faster, cleaner phacoemulsification procedures. STAARVISC II is a viscoelastic material that maintains the shape of the eye during surgery. AquaFlow is collagen glaucoma drainage device. Sales of these other cataract products accounted for 33% of 2007 sales. These products are designed to improve patient outcomes, minimize patient risk and discomfort and simplify ophthalmic procedures and post-operative care. In January 2008, the firm purchased the interests of all other shareholders in Canon Staar; it has been rebranded as STAAR Japan, Inc. In February 2008, the company received clearance to market its Visian Toric ICL in China.

The company offers medical, dental, life, long-term disability and vision insurance.

## FINANCIALS:

**Sales and profits are in thousands of dollars—add 000 to get the full amount. 2008 Note: Financial information for 2008 was not available for all companies at press time.**

| | | |
|---|---|---|
| 2008 Sales: $ | 2008 Profits: $ | **U.S. Stock Ticker: STAA** |
| 2007 Sales: $59,363 | 2007 Profits: $-15,999 | **Int'l Ticker:** Int'l Exchange: |
| 2006 Sales: $56,951 | 2006 Profits: $-15,044 | Employees: 408 |
| 2005 Sales: $51,303 | 2005 Profits: $-11,175 | Fiscal Year Ends: 12/31 |
| 2004 Sales: $51,685 | 2004 Profits: $-11,332 | Parent Company: |

## SALARIES/BENEFITS:

| | | | | |
|---|---|---|---|---|
| Pension Plan: | ESOP Stock Plan: | Profit Sharing: | Top Exec. Salary: $415,246 | Bonus: $80,000 |
| Savings Plan: Y | Stock Purch. Plan: | | Second Exec. Salary: $304,669 | Bonus: $58,458 |

## OTHER THOUGHTS:

**Apparent Women Officers or Directors:** 1
**Hot Spot for Advancement for Women/Minorities:**

## LOCATIONS: ("Y" = Yes)

| West: | Southwest: | Midwest: | Southeast: | Northeast: | International: |
|---|---|---|---|---|---|
| Y | | | | | Y |

# STANDARD MICROSYSTEMS CORPORATION

**www.smsc.com**

**Industry Group Code:** 334413 **Ranks within this company's industry group:** Sales: 2 Profits: 2

| Management: | | Sales/Marketing: | | Liberal Arts: | | Information Systems: | | Professionals: | | Technical/Scientific: | |
|---|---|---|---|---|---|---|---|---|---|---|---|
| Mgmt. Trainees: | | Mktg. Professionals: | Y | Gen. Writing/Editing: | | Info. Management: | Y | Finance/Accounting: | Y | Engineers, Elec.: | Y |
| Experienced Mgmt.: | Y | Retail Sales: | | Technical Writing: | Y | Software Dev.: | Y | Law: | Y | Engineers, Other: | Y |
| Int'l Business: | Y | Commercial/Industrial: | Y | Graphic Arts/Photog.: | | Hardware Dev.: | Y | HR/Other: | Y | Health/Lab: | |
| MBA Graduates: | Y | Sales Trainees: | Y | Music: | | Systems Integration: | Y | Training: | Y | Scientists/Research: | Y |
| | | Advertising Pros.: | | Broadcasting: | | Consulting/Other: | | Health Care: | | Petroleum/Chemicals: | |
| | | | | Other: | | | | Consulting: | | Math/Other: | Y |

## TYPES OF BUSINESS:

Integrated Circuits-Input/Output
Networking Products

## BRANDS/DIVISIONS/AFFILIATES:

ARCNET
CircLink
Chartered Semiconductor Manufacturing, Ltd.
Taiwan Semiconductor Manufacturing Co Ltd
STMicroelectronics NV

## CONTACTS: *Note: Officers with more than one job title may be intentionally listed here more than once.*

Steven J. Bilodeau, CEO
Steven J. Bilodeau, Pres.
Kris Sennesael, CFO/VP
Mitchell Statham, VP-Worldwide Sales
Douglas Smith, CTO/VP
Aaron L. Fisher, Sr. VP-Prod. & Tech.
Walter Siegal, General Counsel/Sec./VP
Peter Byrnes, VP-Oper.
Joseph Durko, Chief Acct. Officer/Controller/VP
Robert E. Hollingsworth, Sr. VP
Johnson Tan, VP/Gen. Manager-Connected Home Media
Christian Thiel, VP
Steven J. Bilodeau, Chmn.
Yasuo Suzuki, Pres., SMSC Japan

| | |
|---|---|
| **Phone:** 631-435-6000 | **Fax:** 631-273-5550 |
| **Toll-Free:** | |
| **Address:** 80 Arkay Dr., Hauppauge, NY 11788-8847 US | |

## GROWTH PLANS/SPECIAL FEATURES:

Standard Microsystems Corporation (SMSC) designs advanced digital, mixed-signal and analog semiconductor products for a broad range of high-speed communications and computing applications. The firm follows what is commonly known as a fabless business model, meaning SMSC does not own semiconductor wafer manufacturing facilities; rather it contracts with other firms to have its products manufactured according to its design specifications. Its primary wafer suppliers are Chartered Semiconductor Manufacturing, Ltd.; Taiwan Semiconductor Manufacturing Co., Ltd.; and STMicroelectronics NV. SMSC has product offerings in three markets: Mobile and Desktop PCs, which generated 42% of SMSC's 2008 revenue; Consumer Electronics and Infotainment, 39%; and Industrial & Other, 19%. It sells its products to an international customer base that includes most of the world's leading PC and motherboard manufacturers and their subcontractors. The firm's advanced I/O circuits reside on the motherboards of PC products sold by Dell, Fujitsu, Gateway, Hewlett-Packard, IBM, Intel, NEC, Sony, Toshiba and most other leading manufacturers. SMSC products are also sold through electronics distributors, who provide value-added access to a broad base of smaller personal computer suppliers and to customers who use the company's products in diverse networking, connectivity and embedded systems applications. The firm's ARCNET line of products provide versatile networking solutions which interconnect portions of an embedded system to create a more flexible and modular design. Its CircLink hardware-based communications protocol allows networks to be planned and constructed with reduced wiring costs and more efficient design. Besides its U.S. offices, in New York, North Carolina, Arizona, Texas and California, the firm has operations in Japan, Korea, China, Taiwan, Singapore, Germany and Sweden.

Employees of SMSC receive medical, dental and vision plans; life and long-term disability coverage; tuition reimbursement; intramural sports; employee assistance; and corporate discounts.

## FINANCIALS: **Sales and profits are in thousands of dollars—add 000 to get the full amount. 2008 Note: Financial information for 2008 was not available for all companies at press time.**

| | | |
|---|---|---|
| 2008 Sales: $377,849 | 2008 Profits: $32,906 | **U.S. Stock Ticker: SMSC** |
| 2007 Sales: $370,594 | 2007 Profits: $27,015 | **Int'l Ticker:** Int'l Exchange: |
| 2006 Sales: $319,118 | 2006 Profits: $12,030 | Employees: 888 |
| 2005 Sales: $208,815 | 2005 Profits: $1,602 | Fiscal Year Ends: 2/28 |
| 2004 Sales: $215,873 | 2004 Profits: $21,518 | Parent Company: |

## SALARIES/BENEFITS:

| | | | | |
|---|---|---|---|---|
| Pension Plan: | ESOP Stock Plan: | Profit Sharing: | Top Exec. Salary: $580,962 | Bonus: $411,782 |
| Savings Plan: Y | Stock Purch. Plan: Y | | Second Exec. Salary: $331,250 | Bonus: $143,470 |

## OTHER THOUGHTS:

**Apparent Women Officers or Directors:**
**Hot Spot for Advancement for Women/Minorities:**

## LOCATIONS: ("Y" = Yes)

| West: | Southwest: | Midwest: | Southeast: | Northeast: | International: |
|---|---|---|---|---|---|
| Y | Y | | | Y | Y |

Note: Financial information, benefits and other data can change quickly and may vary from those stated here.

# STATE AUTO FINANCIAL CORP

www.stateauto.com

**Industry Group Code:** 524126 **Ranks within this company's industry group:** Sales: 6 Profits: 7

| **Management:** | | **Sales/Marketing:** | | **Liberal Arts:** | | **Information Systems:** | | **Professionals:** | | **Technical/Scientific:** | |
|---|---|---|---|---|---|---|---|---|---|---|---|
| Mgmt. Trainees: | | Mktg. Professionals: | Y | Gen. Writing/Editing: | Y | Info. Management: | Y | Finance/Accounting: | Y | Engineers, Elec.: | |
| Experienced Mgmt.: | Y | Retail Sales: | | Technical Writing: | Y | Software Dev.: | | Law: | Y | Engineers, Other: | |
| Int'l Business: | | Commercial/Industrial: | Y | Graphic Arts/Photog.: | | Hardware Dev.: | | HR/Other: | Y | Health/Lab: | |
| MBA Graduates: | Y | Sales Trainees: | Y | Music: | | Systems Integration: | | Training: | Y | Scientists/Research: | |
| | | Advertising Pros.: | | Broadcasting: | | Consulting/Other: | | Health Care: | | Petroleum/Chemicals: | |
| | | | | Other: | | | | Consulting: | | Math/Other: | Y |

## TYPES OF BUSINESS:

Direct Property & Casualty Insurance
Investment Management
Insurance Processing Software
Financial Services
Real Estate

## BRANDS/DIVISIONS/AFFILIATES:

Strategic Insurance Software
State Auto Property & Casualty Insurance
State Auto National Insurance
State Automobile Mutual Insurance Co.
Milbank Insurance Co.
Stateco Financial Services
518 Property Management & Leasing, LLC
Farmers Casualty Insurance Co.

## CONTACTS: *Note: Officers with more than one job title may be intentionally listed here more than once.*

Robert P. Restrepo Jr., CEO
Mark A. Blackburn, COO/Exec. VP
Robert P. Restrepo Jr., Pres.
Steven E. English, CFO/VP
Clyde H. Fitch Jr., Chief Sales Officer
Doug E. Allen, VP/Dir.-IT
Noreen W. Johnson, VP/Dir.-Admin.
James A. Yano, General Counsel/VP/Sec.
Lyle D. Rhodebeck, VP-Oper. Effectiveness
Cathy B. Miley, VP-Dir. of Corp. Dev.
Terrence L. Bowshier, VP/Dir.-Investor Rel.
Cynthia A. Powell, Chief Acct. Officer/VP/Treas.
Joel E. Brown, VP/Dir.-Personal Insurance
James E. Duemey, VP-Investment Officer
Larry D. Williams, VP/Dir.-Middle Market Oper.
Robert P. Restrepo Jr., Chmn.

| | |
|---|---|
| **Phone:** 614-464-5000 | **Fax:** 614-464-5325 |
| **Toll-Free:** 800-444-9950 | |
| **Address:** 518 E. Broad St., Columbus, OH 43215 US | |

## GROWTH PLANS/SPECIAL FEATURES:

State Auto Financial Corp. (STFC) is a super-regional property and casualty insurance holding company. The firm is primarily engaged in writing personal and business lines of insurance. It has three significant reportable segments: personal insurance, business insurance and investment operations. The insurance segments are managed separately because of the differences in types of customers served, products provided or services offered. The personal insurance segment provides primarily personal auto (standard and nonstandard) and homeowners to the personal insurance market. The business insurance segment provides primarily commercial auto, commercial multi-peril, fire and allied lines, other and product liability and workers' compensation insurance to small to mid-sized businesses within the commercial insurance market. The investment operations segment, managed by Stateco, provides investment services for company's invested assets. The State Auto companies market their insurance products through independent agents in 33 states. These operations are carried out by five subsidiaries: State Auto Property and Casualty Insurance; State Auto National Insurance; Milbank Insurance Co.; Farmers Casualty Insurance Co.; and State Auto Insurance Co. of Ohio. The firm and its subsidiaries are affiliated with State Automobile Mutual Insurance Co., which owns approximately 65% of the firm's outstanding common shares. State Auto also has three non-insurance subsidiaries: Stateco Financial Services, which provides investment management services to company affiliates and customers; Strategic Insurance Software, which develops insurance-processing software; and 518 Property Management and Leasing, LLC, which owns and leases real estate and personal property to the company and its affiliates. In 2008, STFC announced it will invest approximately $18.4 million in a 22,000-square-foot high-tech data center in Ohio. Through its recent acquisition of Beacon Insurance Group of Wichita Falls, the firm offers personal insurance products in Texas.

## FINANCIALS: **Sales and profits are in thousands of dollars—add 000 to get the full amount. 2008 Note: Financial information for 2008 was not available for all companies at press time.**

| | | |
|---|---|---|
| 2008 Sales: $ | 2008 Profits: $ | **U.S. Stock Ticker: STFC** |
| 2007 Sales: $1,011,600 | 2007 Profits: $119,100 | **Int'l Ticker:** Int'l Exchange: |
| 2006 Sales: $1,023,800 | 2006 Profits: $120,400 | Employees: 2,185 |
| 2005 Sales: $1,139,500 | 2005 Profits: $125,900 | Fiscal Year Ends: 12/31 |
| 2004 Sales: $1,092,400 | 2004 Profits: $110,000 | Parent Company: |

## SALARIES/BENEFITS:

| | | | | |
|---|---|---|---|---|
| Pension Plan: Y | ESOP Stock Plan: | Profit Sharing: | Top Exec. Salary: $673,558 | Bonus: $497,391 |
| Savings Plan: Y | Stock Purch. Plan: Y | | Second Exec. Salary: $425,000 | Bonus: $333,094 |

## OTHER THOUGHTS:

**Apparent Women Officers or Directors**: 7
**Hot Spot for Advancement for Women/Minorities**: Y

## LOCATIONS: ("Y" = Yes)

| West: | Southwest: | Midwest: | Southeast: | Northeast: | International: |
|---|---|---|---|---|---|
| | | Y | Y | Y | |

# STERLING AUTOBODY CENTERS

**www.sterlingautobody.com**

**Industry Group Code:** 811100 **Ranks within this company's industry group:** Sales: Profits:

| Management: | | Sales/Marketing: | | Liberal Arts: | | Information Systems: | | Professionals: | | Technical/Scientific: | |
|---|---|---|---|---|---|---|---|---|---|---|---|
| Mgmt. Trainees: | | Mktg. Professionals: | Y | Gen. Writing/Editing: | | Info. Management: | Y | Finance/Accounting: | Y | Engineers, Elec.: | |
| Experienced Mgmt.: | Y | Retail Sales: | | Technical Writing: | | Software Dev.: | | Law: | Y | Engineers, Other: | |
| Int'l Business: | Y | Commercial/Industrial: | | Graphic Arts/Photog.: | | Hardware Dev.: | | HR/Other: | Y | Health/Lab: | |
| MBA Graduates: | Y | Sales Trainees: | | Music: | | Systems Integration: | | Training: | Y | Scientists/Research: | |
| | | Advertising Pros.: | | Broadcasting: | | Consulting/Other: | | Health Care: | | Petroleum/Chemicals: | |
| | | | | Other: | | | | Consulting: | | Math/Other: | |

## TYPES OF BUSINESS:

Automotive Repair & Maintenance
Collision Repair

## BRANDS/DIVISIONS/AFFILIATES:

Allstate Insurance Corporation (The)

## CONTACTS:

*Note: Officers with more than one job title may be intentionally listed here more than once.*

Allan Robinson, Pres.
Sharon Mazanec, VP-Mktg. & Sales
Mike Nuxoll, VP-Human Resources
John Donohue, VP-IT
Tony Giannola, VP-Admin.
Bob Benjamin, VP-Oper., Eastern Territory
Tony Giannola, VP-Finance
Bob Thompson, VP-New Bus. Dev.
Russ Slocum, VP-Oper., Western Territory
Tim Swift, VP-Field Support

| | |
|---|---|
| **Phone:** 508-653-9115 | **Fax:** 508-653-9538 |
| **Toll-Free:** 800-653-5310 | |
| **Address:** 9 Tech Cir., Natick, MA 01760 US | |

## GROWTH PLANS/SPECIAL FEATURES:

Sterling Autobody Centers, operates a line of automobile collision repair centers. It operates over 60 such centers across 16 U.S. states, in California, Nevada, Arizona, Utah, Colorado, Texas, Illinois, Michigan, Ohio, Pennsylvania, New York, Maryland, Virginia, North Carolina, Georgia and Florida. Sterling operates as a subsidiary of Allstate Insurance Corp., and it only repairs vehicles involved in Allstate claims. Known for its customer service, the company picks up the damaged car, delivers the repaired car, has all cars professionally cleaned, provides a guaranteed completion date of the repair and offers a limited lifetime warranty on all parts and services. Through a partnership with Enterprise Rent-a-Car, the firm will also deliver and return a rental car for its customers. Sterling works exclusively with Sherman-Williams Automotive Finishers for paint and finish and Enterprise Rent-A-Car for replacement cars during repair.

Sterling offers its employees medical, dental, and vision care; a 401(k) plan; short and long-term disability; life insurance; and Sterling University, a company-wide program that teaches a variety of technical and managerial skills, to train and advance its employees.

## FINANCIALS:

**Sales and profits are in thousands of dollars—add 000 to get the full amount. 2008 Note: Financial information for 2008 was not available for all companies at press time.**

| | | |
|---|---|---|
| 2008 Sales: $ | 2008 Profits: $ | **U.S. Stock Ticker: Subsidiary** |
| 2007 Sales: $ | 2007 Profits: $ | **Int'l Ticker:** Int'l Exchange: |
| 2006 Sales: $ | 2006 Profits: $ | Employees: 300 |
| 2005 Sales: $ | 2005 Profits: $ | Fiscal Year Ends: |
| 2004 Sales: $ | 2004 Profits: $ | Parent Company: ALLSTATE CORPORATION (THE) |

## SALARIES/BENEFITS:

| | | | | |
|---|---|---|---|---|
| Pension Plan: | ESOP Stock Plan: | Profit Sharing: | Top Exec. Salary: $ | Bonus: $ |
| Savings Plan: Y | Stock Purch. Plan: | | Second Exec. Salary: $ | Bonus: $ |

## OTHER THOUGHTS:

**Apparent Women Officers or Directors**: 1
**Hot Spot for Advancement for Women/Minorities**:

## LOCATIONS: ("Y" = Yes)

| West: | Southwest: | Midwest: | Southeast: | Northeast: | International: |
|---|---|---|---|---|---|
| Y | Y | Y | Y | Y | Y |

# STEVEN MADDEN LTD

www.stevemadden.com

**Industry Group Code:** 316210 **Ranks within this company's industry group:** Sales: 1 Profits: 1

| Management: | | Sales/Marketing: | | Liberal Arts: | | Information Systems: | | Professionals: | | Technical/Scientific: | |
|---|---|---|---|---|---|---|---|---|---|---|---|
| Mgmt. Trainees: | | Mktg. Professionals: | Y | Gen. Writing/Editing: | | Info. Management: | Y | Finance/Accounting: | Y | Engineers, Elec.: | |
| Experienced Mgmt.: | Y | Retail Sales: | | Technical Writing: | | Software Dev.: | | Law: | Y | Engineers, Other: | |
| Int'l Business: | Y | Commercial/Industrial: | Y | Graphic Arts/Photog.: | Y | Hardware Dev.: | | HR/Other: | Y | Health/Lab: | |
| MBA Graduates: | Y | Sales Trainees: | Y | Music: | | Systems Integration: | | Training: | Y | Scientists/Research: | |
| | | Advertising Pros.: | Y | Broadcasting: | | Consulting/Other: | | Health Care: | | Petroleum/Chemicals: | |
| | | | | Other: | Y | | | Consulting: | | Math/Other: | |

## TYPES OF BUSINESS:

Shoes, Manufacturing
Retail Stores
Online Sales

## BRANDS/DIVISIONS/AFFILIATES:

Adesso-Madden, Inc.
Steve Madden
Daniel M. Friedman
Stevies
Steve Madden Mens
Steven Maddden Retail, Inc.
SM New York/Madden Girl
Compo Enhancements

## CONTACTS: *Note: Officers with more than one job title may be intentionally listed here more than once.*

Jamieson A. Karson, CEO
Awadesh Sinha, COO
Arvind Dharia, CFO
Amelia N. Varela, Exec. VP-Wholesale Sales
Robert Schmertz, Dir.-Brand
Walter Yetnikoff, Chmn.

| | |
|---|---|
| **Phone:** 718-446-1800 | **Fax:** |
| **Toll-Free:** | |
| **Address:** 52-16 Barnett Ave., Long Island City, NY 11104 US | |

## GROWTH PLANS/SPECIAL FEATURES:

Steven Madden, Ltd. designs, sources, markets and sells shoes for men, women and children. Headquartered in New York, it distributes products through its retail stores, its e-commerce website and department and specialty stores throughout the U.S. and Canada, as well as through special arrangements in Europe, Central and South America, Australia and Indonesia. The company is composed of three segments: wholesale, retail and first cost. The wholesale division is run through seven segments: Women's, Men's, Candie's, Madden Girl, Steve Madden's Fix; Steven; Stevies; and Daniel Friedman. Madden Women's wholesale, the company's largest division, designs, sources and markets the Steve Madden brand to a variety of stores and boutiques. This division produces approximately 30% of the firm's net sales. Madden men's wholesale designs, sources and markets a full collection of men's casual and athletic shoes. Candies designs, sources and markets a variety of women's and kids shoes under the Candies brand. Madden Girl designs, sources and markets a collection of young women's shoes geared for females ages 13 to 20 years of age. Fix designs, sources and markets a line of athletic sneakers geared for women ages 16 to 35. Steven designs, sources and markets footwear through the Diva Acquisition Corp. under the Steven brand. Steven offers a multitude of shoes that are styled to appeal to fashion conscious women ages 26 to 45. Stevies designs, sources and markets footwear for young girls. Daniel Friedman designs, sources and markets name brand and private label fashion handbags and accessories. The retail segment operates through Steven Madden Retail, Inc., which operates approximately 100 retail stores, 94 of which operate under the Steve Madden name. The first cost division operates through Adesso-Madden, Inc., a private-label subsidiary, that designs and sources footwear products under private labels for mass merchandisers.

## FINANCIALS: **Sales and profits are in thousands of dollars—add 000 to get the full amount. 2008 Note: Financial information for 2008 was not available for all companies at press time.**

| | | |
|---|---|---|
| 2008 Sales: $ | 2008 Profits: $ | **U.S. Stock Ticker: SHOO** |
| 2007 Sales: $431,050 | 2007 Profits: $35,690 | **Int'l Ticker:** Int'l Exchange: |
| 2006 Sales: $475,163 | 2006 Profits: $46,250 | Employees: 1,510 |
| 2005 Sales: $375,786 | 2005 Profits: $19,200 | Fiscal Year Ends: 12/31 |
| 2004 Sales: $338,144 | 2004 Profits: $12,275 | Parent Company: |

## SALARIES/BENEFITS:

| | | | | |
|---|---|---|---|---|
| Pension Plan: | ESOP Stock Plan: | Profit Sharing: | Top Exec. Salary: $500,000 | Bonus: $ |
| Savings Plan: | Stock Purch. Plan: | | Second Exec. Salary: $578,907 | Bonus: $ |

## OTHER THOUGHTS:

**Apparent Women Officers or Directors:**
**Hot Spot for Advancement for Women/Minorities:**

## LOCATIONS: ("Y" = Yes)

| West: | Southwest: | Midwest: | Southeast: | Northeast: | International: |
|---|---|---|---|---|---|
| Y | Y | Y | Y | Y | |

# STIEFEL LABORATORIES INC

**www.stiefel.com**

**Industry Group Code:** 325412 **Ranks within this company's industry group:** Sales: 8 Profits:

| **Management:** | | **Sales/Marketing:** | | **Liberal Arts:** | | **Information Systems:** | | **Professionals:** | | **Technical/Scientific:** | |
|---|---|---|---|---|---|---|---|---|---|---|---|
| Mgmt. Trainees: | | Mktg. Professionals: | Y | Gen. Writing/Editing: | | Info. Management: | Y | Finance/Accounting: | Y | Engineers, Elec.: | |
| Experienced Mgmt.: | Y | Retail Sales: | | Technical Writing: | Y | Software Dev.: | Y | Law: | Y | Engineers, Other: | |
| Int'l Business: | Y | Commercial/Industrial: | Y | Graphic Arts/Photog.: | | Hardware Dev.: | | HR/Other: | Y | Health/Lab: | Y |
| MBA Graduates: | Y | Sales Trainees: | Y | Music: | | Systems Integration: | | Training: | Y | Scientists/Research: | Y |
| | | Advertising Pros.: | | Broadcasting: | | Consulting/Other: | | Health Care: | Y | Petroleum/Chemicals: | Y |
| | | | | Other: | | | | Consulting: | | Math/Other: | Y |

## TYPES OF BUSINESS:

Dermatological & Skin Care Products

## BRANDS/DIVISIONS/AFFILIATES:

Evoclin
Duac
Revaleskin
MimyX
LUXIQ Foam
Verdeso
Olux
ABR Development

## CONTACTS: *Note: Officers with more than one job title may be intentionally listed here more than once.*

Charles W. Stiefel, CEO
Bill Humphries, Pres.
Alfonso Ugarte, VP-Global Mktg.
Steve Karasick, Sr. VP-People
Gavin Corcoran, Chief Scientific Officer
Steve Karasick, Sr. VP-IT
Brent Stiefel, Exec. VP-Global Corp. Dev. & Prod. Portfolio
Erin Bacher, Associate Dir.-Global Public Rel.
Todd Stiefel, Exec. VP-Global Strategy
Wayne Wilson, VP-U.S. Sales
Jim Hartman, Sr. VP-U.S. Commercial Oper.
Jeff Klimaski, VP/Global Corp. Compliance Officer
Charles W. Stiefel, Chmn.
Richard MacKay, Pres., Stiefel Canada, Inc.

**Phone:** 305-443-3800 **Fax:** 305-443-3467
**Toll-Free:**
**Address:** 255 Alhambra Cir., Coral Gables, FL 33134-7412 US

## GROWTH PLANS/SPECIAL FEATURES:

Stiefel Laboratories, Inc. is a specialized pharmaceutical company that focuses on the advancement of dermatology and skin care. The company's sells hundreds of products that treat a wide range of dermatological ailments including acne, psoriasis, fungal infections, eczema, dry skin, oily skin, rosacea, seborrhea, pruritus and sun damaged and aging skin. Leading products include Evoclin and Duac, acne skin care products; Revaleskin, for younger and smoother skin; MimyX, a cream that relieves dry and waxy skin for a variety of dermatoses; LUXIQ Foam, which reduces the signs of scalp dermatoses, such as scaling, redness, and plaques; Olux, also used for scalp treatment; and Verdeso, a treatment for eczema. The firm also offers pharmaceutical contract manufacturing of gels, creams, ointments, topical solutions and liquid orals, both prescription and over-the-counter. The company has subsidiaries in more than 30 countries and its products are available in more than 100 countries. In August 2007, The Blackstone Group agreed to make a $500 million minority investment in Stiefel Laboratories. In November 2007, Stiefel agreed to collaborate with Allergan, Inc., in order to develop, manufacture, distribute and market dermatological products containing tazarotene. In May 2008, the firm acquired ABR Invent and ABR Development, developers of the dermal filler Atlean. In July 2008, Stiefel agreed to acquired Barrier Therapeutics, a marketer of three pharmaceutical products, through a two-step transaction totaling roughly $148 million.

## FINANCIALS: **Sales and profits are in thousands of dollars—add 000 to get the full amount. 2008 Note: Financial information for 2008 was not available for all companies at press time.**

| | | |
|---|---|---|
| 2008 Sales: $ | 2008 Profits: $ | **U.S. Stock Ticker: Private** |
| 2007 Sales: $444,900 | 2007 Profits: $ | **Int'l Ticker:** Int'l Exchange: |
| 2006 Sales: $ | 2006 Profits: $ | Employees: 2,000 |
| 2005 Sales: $184,264 | 2005 Profits: $33,958 | Fiscal Year Ends: |
| 2004 Sales: $144,355 | 2004 Profits: $19,015 | Parent Company: |

## SALARIES/BENEFITS:

| | | | | |
|---|---|---|---|---|
| Pension Plan: | ESOP Stock Plan: | Profit Sharing: | Top Exec. Salary: $530,000 | Bonus: $325,000 |
| Savings Plan: | Stock Purch. Plan: | | Second Exec. Salary: $393,083 | Bonus: $190,000 |

## OTHER THOUGHTS:

**Apparent Women Officers or Directors**: 3
**Hot Spot for Advancement for Women/Minorities**: Y

## LOCATIONS: ("Y" = Yes)

| West: | Southwest: | Midwest: | Southeast: | Northeast: | International: |
|---|---|---|---|---|---|
| Y | | | Y | Y | Y |

# SUPER MICRO COMPUTER INC

www.supermicro.com

**Industry Group Code:** 334111 **Ranks within this company's industry group:** Sales: 3 Profits: 3

| Management: | | Sales/Marketing: | | Liberal Arts: | | Information Systems: | | Professionals: | | Technical/Scientific: | |
|---|---|---|---|---|---|---|---|---|---|---|---|
| Mgmt. Trainees: | | Mktg. Professionals: | Y | Gen. Writing/Editing: | | Info. Management: | Y | Finance/Accounting: | Y | Engineers, Elec.: | Y |
| Experienced Mgmt.: | Y | Retail Sales: | | Technical Writing: | Y | Software Dev.: | Y | Law: | Y | Engineers, Other: | Y |
| Int'l Business: | Y | Commercial/Industrial: | Y | Graphic Arts/Photog.: | | Hardware Dev.: | Y | HR/Other: | Y | Health/Lab: | |
| MBA Graduates: | Y | Sales Trainees: | Y | Music: | | Systems Integration: | Y | Training: | Y | Scientists/Research: | |
| | | Advertising Pros.: | | Broadcasting: | | Consulting/Other: | | Health Care: | | Petroleum/Chemicals: | |
| | | | | Other: | | | | Consulting: | | Math/Other: | |

## TYPES OF BUSINESS:

Server Systems & Components

## BRANDS/DIVISIONS/AFFILIATES:

## CONTACTS:

*Note: Officers with more than one job title may be intentionally listed here more than once.*

Charles Liang, CEO
Charles Liang, Pres.
Howard Hideshima, CFO
Alex Hsu, Chief Sales & Mktg. Officer
Wally Liaw, Sec.
Sara Liu, VP-Oper.
Sara Liu, Treas.
Charles Liang, Chmn.
Wally Liaw, VP-Int'l Sales

| **Phone:** 408-503-8000 | **Fax:** 408-503-8008 |
|---|---|
| **Toll-Free:** | |
| **Address:** 980 Rock Ave., San Jose, CA 95131 US | |

## GROWTH PLANS/SPECIAL FEATURES:

Super Micro Computer, Inc. designs, develops, manufactures and sells application optimized, high performance server solutions based on modular and open-standard x86 architecture. Its solutions include a range of complete rackmount and blade server systems as well as components. The firm offers its clients a high degree of flexibility and customization by providing a broad array of server components, which are interoperable and can be configured to create complete server systems. The company bases its solutions on open standard components, such as processors from Intel and AMD, and the solutions can run on Linux and Windows operating systems. The firm sells server systems in rack-mounted, standalone tower and blade form factors. It currently offers a complete range of server options with single, dual and quad CPU capability supporting Intel Pentium D and Xeon architectures in 1U, 2U, 3U and 4U, tower and blade form factors. Additionally, the firm offers complete server systems for AMD dual and quad Opteron in 1U, 2U, 4U and blade form factors. Super Micro Computer offers over 550 different server systems, and for each system it provides multiple chassis designs and power supply options. The company also offers Supermicro Intelligent Management (SIM) card solutions. Components include serverboards, designed and optimized to adhere to specific physical, electrical and design requirements in order to work with certain combinations of chassis and power supplies; chassis and power supplies; and system accessories such as microprocessors and memory and disk drives. Super Micro Computer sells its server systems and components primarily through distributors, which include value added resellers and systems integrators, and to a lesser extent original equipment manufacturers as well as a direct sales force.

The company offers its employees benefits that include health, dental and vision insurance; and a 401(k) plan.

## FINANCIALS:

**Sales and profits are in thousands of dollars—add 000 to get the full amount. 2008 Note: Financial information for 2008 was not available for all companies at press time.**

| | | |
|---|---|---|
| 2008 Sales: $540,503 | 2008 Profits: $25,419 | **U.S. Stock Ticker: SMCI** |
| 2007 Sales: $420,393 | 2007 Profits: $19,339 | **Int'l Ticker:** Int'l Exchange: |
| 2006 Sales: $302,541 | 2006 Profits: $16,947 | Employees: 803 |
| 2005 Sales: $211,763 | 2005 Profits: $7,090 | Fiscal Year Ends: 6/30 |
| 2004 Sales: $ | 2004 Profits: $ | Parent Company: |

## SALARIES/BENEFITS:

| | | | | |
|---|---|---|---|---|
| Pension Plan: | ESOP Stock Plan: | Profit Sharing: | Top Exec. Salary: $257,188 | Bonus: $21,046 |
| Savings Plan: Y | Stock Purch. Plan: | | Second Exec. Salary: $ | Bonus: $ |

## OTHER THOUGHTS:

**Apparent Women Officers or Directors:** 1
**Hot Spot for Advancement for Women/Minorities:**

## LOCATIONS: ("Y" = Yes)

| West: | Southwest: | Midwest: | Southeast: | Northeast: | International: |
|---|---|---|---|---|---|
| Y | | | | | Y |

Note: Financial information, benefits and other data can change quickly and may vary from those stated here.

# SWIFT ENERGY CO

**www.swiftenergy.com**

**Industry Group Code:** 211111 **Ranks within this company's industry group:** Sales: 15 Profits: 18

| Management: | | Sales/Marketing: | | Liberal Arts: | | Information Systems: | | Professionals: | | Technical/Scientific: | |
|---|---|---|---|---|---|---|---|---|---|---|---|
| Mgmt. Trainees: | | Mktg. Professionals: | Y | Gen. Writing/Editing: | | Info. Management: | Y | Finance/Accounting: | Y | Engineers, Elec.: | |
| Experienced Mgmt.: | Y | Retail Sales: | | Technical Writing: | | Software Dev.: | | Law: | Y | Engineers, Other: | Y |
| Int'l Business: | Y | Commercial/Industrial: | Y | Graphic Arts/Photog.: | | Hardware Dev.: | | HR/Other: | Y | Health/Lab: | |
| MBA Graduates: | Y | Sales Trainees: | | Music: | | Systems Integration: | | Training: | Y | Scientists/Research: | |
| | | Advertising Pros.: | | Broadcasting: | | Consulting/Other: | | Health Care: | | Petroleum/Chemicals: | Y |
| | | | | Other: | | | | Consulting: | | Math/Other: | |

## TYPES OF BUSINESS:

Oil & Gas Exploration & Production

## BRANDS/DIVISIONS/AFFILIATES:

## CONTACTS:

*Note: Officers with more than one job title may be intentionally listed here more than once.*

Terry E. Swift, CEO
Robert J. Banks, COO/Exec. VP
Bruce H. Vincent, Pres.
Alton D. Heckaman, Jr., CFO/Exec. VP
David P. Coatney, VP-Prod.
Steven B. Yakle, VP-Admin.
Laurent A. Baillargeon, Chief General Counsel
James M. Kitterman, Sr. VP-Oper.
Robert J. Banks, VP-Strategic Ventures
Paul Vincent, Mgr.-Investor Rel.
Adrian D. Shelley, Treas.
James P. Mitchell, Sr. VP-Commercial Transactions & Land
David W. Wesson, Controller
Tara L. Seaman, VP-Reserves & Evaluations
John C. Branca, VP-Exploration & Dev.
Terry E. Swift, Chmn.
Robert J. Banks, VP-Int'l Oper.

**Phone:** 281-874-2700 **Fax:** 281-874-2726
**Toll-Free:** 800-777-2412
**Address:** 16825 Northchase Dr., Ste. 400, Houston, TX 77060 US

## GROWTH PLANS/SPECIAL FEATURES:

Swift Energy Co., headquartered in Houston, Texas, is an independent exploration company engaged in developing, exploring, acquiring and operating oil and gas properties, with a focus on oil and natural gas reserves onshore and in the inland waters of Louisiana and Texas and onshore in New Zealand. The company has interests in domestic wells that are divided between major sites such as the Lake Washington and Masters Creek sites in Louisiana and the AWP Olmos and Brookland sites in Texas; and to smaller sites residing in Wyoming, Nebraska, Oklahoma, Arkansas, Mississippi and Alabama. The firm also has assets in New Zealand, which include drilling properties in the Rimu/Kauri and TAWN areas, both in the Taranaki Basin. The TAWN area features extensive associated processing facilities and pipelines, providing increased access to export terminals and markets and additional processing capacity for oil and natural gas. The firm has estimated proved reserves from domestic continuing operations of 133.8 million barrels of oil equivalent (mmboe), and 150.1 mmboe both domestically and in New Zealand. The total proved reserves at year end consisted of approximately 44% is natural gas, 43% is crude oil and 13% are natural gas liquids and 45% of total reserves were proved developed. The company's proved reserves are concentrated in Louisiana (59%), Texas (1%), New Zealand (11%) and areas (1%). In June 2008, the firm sold the majority of its New Zealand assets to subsidiaries of Origin Energy Limited. In May 2008, Swift Energy Co. acquired property interests from Crimson Energy Partners, L.P.

## FINANCIALS:

**Sales and profits are in thousands of dollars—add 000 to get the full amount. 2008 Note: Financial information for 2008 was not available for all companies at press time.**

| | | |
|---|---|---|
| 2008 Sales: $820,815 | 2008 Profits: $-260,490 | **U.S. Stock Ticker: SFY** |
| 2007 Sales: $654,121 | 2007 Profits: $21,287 | **Int'l Ticker:** Int'l Exchange: |
| 2006 Sales: $550,836 | 2006 Profits: $161,565 | Employees: 360 |
| 2005 Sales: $423,226 | 2005 Profits: $115,778 | Fiscal Year Ends: 12/31 |
| 2004 Sales: $310,276 | 2004 Profits: $68,450 | Parent Company: |

## SALARIES/BENEFITS:

| | | | | |
|---|---|---|---|---|
| Pension Plan: | ESOP Stock Plan: | Profit Sharing: | Top Exec. Salary: $580,000 | Bonus: $724,249 |
| Savings Plan: Y | Stock Purch. Plan: | | Second Exec. Salary: $454,000 | Bonus: $472,921 |

## OTHER THOUGHTS:

**Apparent Women Officers or Directors**: 3
**Hot Spot for Advancement for Women/Minorities**: Y

## LOCATIONS: ("Y" = Yes)

| West: | Southwest: | Midwest: | Southeast: | Northeast: | International: |
|---|---|---|---|---|---|
| Y | Y | Y | Y | | Y |

Note: Financial information, benefits and other data can change quickly and may vary from those stated here.

# SYCAMORE NETWORKS INC

www.sycamorenet.com

**Industry Group Code:** 334210 **Ranks within this company's industry group:** Sales: 8 Profits: 9

| Management: | | Sales/Marketing: | | Liberal Arts: | | Information Systems: | | Professionals: | | Technical/Scientific: | |
|---|---|---|---|---|---|---|---|---|---|---|---|
| Mgmt. Trainees: | | Mktg. Professionals: | Y | Gen. Writing/Editing: | Y | Info. Management: | Y | Finance/Accounting: | Y | Engineers, Elec.: | Y |
| Experienced Mgmt.: | Y | Retail Sales: | | Technical Writing: | Y | Software Dev.: | Y | Law: | Y | Engineers, Other: | Y |
| Int'l Business: | Y | Commercial/Industrial: | Y | Graphic Arts/Photog.: | | Hardware Dev.: | Y | HR/Other: | Y | Health/Lab: | |
| MBA Graduates: | Y | Sales Trainees: | Y | Music: | | Systems Integration: | Y | Training: | Y | Scientists/Research: | |
| | | Advertising Pros.: | | Broadcasting: | | Consulting/Other: | | Health Care: | | Petroleum/Chemicals: | |
| | | | | Other: | | | | Consulting: | | Math/Other: | Y |

## TYPES OF BUSINESS:

Optical Switching Products
Optical Network Management Products
Engineering & Support Services
Design & Planning Tools

## BRANDS/DIVISIONS/AFFILIATES:

SILVX
SILVX InSight
SN 3000
SN 16000 SC
SN 16000 MC
Eastern Research, Inc.

## CONTACTS:

*Note: Officers with more than one job title may be intentionally listed here more than once.*

Daniel E. Smith, CEO
Daniel E. Smith, Pres.
Paul F. Brauneis, CFO
John Scully, VP-Worldwide Sales & Support
Kevin J. Oye, VP-Systems & Tech.
Paul F. Brauneis, VP-Admin.
Alan R. Cormier, General Counsel/Sec.
John E. Dowling, VP-Oper.
Paul F. Brauneis, VP-Finance
Gururaj Deshpande, Chmn.

**Phone:** 978-250-2900 **Fax:** 978-256-3434
**Toll-Free:** 877-792-2667
**Address:** 220 Mill Rd., Chelmsford, MA 01824 US

## GROWTH PLANS/SPECIAL FEATURES:

Sycamore Networks, Inc. develops and markets optical networking products and provides services associated with such products for telecommunications service providers worldwide. The company's product portfolio includes optical switching products, network management products and design and planning tools that enable network operators to manage optical network capacity to support a wide range of voice, video and data services. In addition, the firm offers complete network engineering, furnishing, installation and testing services. Sycamore's optical switches, including the SN 3000, the SN 16000 SC and the SN 16000 MC, combine multiple functions in a single, highly compact system and address different capacity requirements within various segments of the network. The SILVX optical network management system provides network management, planning and administration tools that communicate with existing network management systems through common standards. The combination of SILVX and the company's networking software allows its optical switches to exchange real-time information about network traffic, enabling service providers to efficiently manage network capacity. In addition, SILVX allows service providers to model a broad range of optical network architectures, forecast and plan for capacity expansion and analyze network traffic. Customers include domestic and international wireline and wireless network service providers; and government entities with private fiber networks. During fiscal 2007, Sprint Corporation and Vodafone Group PLC accounted for 53% and 16% of revenue. In March 2008, Sycamore introduced new SILVX enhancements, SilvxManager for Windows and Layered Services Management. These new updates offer such features as partitioned views of pertinent multi-layer service information; proactive alarming through intelligent correlation of network and service layer information; simplified troubleshooting; and improved visibility and control.

Sycamore offers its employees medical, dental and vision insurance; employee assistance programs; tuition reimbursement; and a 401(k) plan.

## FINANCIALS:

**Sales and profits are in thousands of dollars—add 000 to get the full amount. 2008 Note: Financial information for 2008 was not available for all companies at press time.**

2008 Sales: $115,496
2007 Sales: $156,048
2006 Sales: $87,395
2005 Sales: $65,434
2004 Sales: $44,547

2008 Profits: $- 114
2007 Profits: $-13,205
2006 Profits: $19,388
2005 Profits: $-29,916
2004 Profits: $-68,290

**U.S. Stock Ticker: SCMR**
**Int'l Ticker:** Int'l Exchange:
Employees: 492
Fiscal Year Ends: 7/31
Parent Company:

## SALARIES/BENEFITS:

Pension Plan: ESOP Stock Plan: Y Profit Sharing: Top Exec. Salary: $263,019 Bonus: $130,797
Savings Plan: Y Stock Purch. Plan: Second Exec. Salary: $252,750 Bonus: $136,647

## OTHER THOUGHTS:

**Apparent Women Officers or Directors:**
**Hot Spot for Advancement for Women/Minorities:**

## LOCATIONS: ("Y" = Yes)

| West: | Southwest: | Midwest: | Southeast: | Northeast: | International: |
|---|---|---|---|---|---|
| | Y | Y | | Y | Y |

# SYMMETRY MEDICAL INC

**www.symmetrymedical.com**

**Industry Group Code:** 339113 **Ranks within this company's industry group:** Sales: 12 Profits: 37

| Management: | | Sales/Marketing: | | Liberal Arts: | | Information Systems: | | Professionals: | | Technical/Scientific: | |
|---|---|---|---|---|---|---|---|---|---|---|---|
| Mgmt. Trainees: | | Mktg. Professionals: | Y | Gen. Writing/Editing: | | Info. Management: | Y | Finance/Accounting: | Y | Engineers, Elec.: | |
| Experienced Mgmt.: | Y | Retail Sales: | | Technical Writing: | Y | Software Dev.: | Y | Law: | Y | Engineers, Other: | Y |
| Int'l Business: | Y | Commercial/Industrial: | Y | Graphic Arts/Photog.: | | Hardware Dev.: | | HR/Other: | Y | Health/Lab: | Y |
| MBA Graduates: | Y | Sales Trainees: | Y | Music: | | Systems Integration: | | Training: | Y | Scientists/Research: | Y |
| | | Advertising Pros.: | | Broadcasting: | | Consulting/Other: | | Health Care: | Y | Petroleum/Chemicals: | |
| | | | | Other: | | | | Consulting: | | Math/Other: | Y |

## TYPES OF BUSINESS:

Orthopedic Implants
Aerospace Market Products & Services
Medical Cases

## BRANDS/DIVISIONS/AFFILIATES:

Jet Engineering, Inc.
Symmetry Medical PolyVac
Thornton Precision Components Ltd.
UltreXX, Inc.
Total Solutions
Specialty Surgical Instruments, Inc. (SSI)
Ultra Containers of America, LLC (UCA)

## CONTACTS: *Note: Officers with more than one job title may be intentionally listed here more than once.*

Brian S. Moore, CEO
Michael W. Curtis, COO-USA
Brian S. Moore, Pres.
Fred L. Hite, CFO/Sr. VP
D. Darin Martin, Compliance Officer/Sr. VP-Regulatory Affairs
D. Darin Martin, Sr. VP-Quality Assurance
Frank Turner, Chmn.
John Hynes, Sr. VP/COO-Europe

| | |
|---|---|
| **Phone:** 574-268-2252 | **Fax:** 574-267-4551 |
| **Toll-Free:** | |
| **Address:** 3724 N. State Rd. 15, Warsaw, IN 46580 US | |

## GROWTH PLANS/SPECIAL FEATURES:

Symmetry Medical, Inc. is an independent provider of implants and related instruments and cases to global orthopedic device manufacturers. It designs, develops and produces these products for companies in other segments of the medical device market, including the dental, osteobiologic and endoscopy segments. The firm offers the following products and services: Implants, which generated 33.3% of 2007 revenues; instruments, 27.7%; cases, 26.5%; and other, 13%. Implants comprise forged, cast and machined products for the global orthopedic device market. Symmetry's instruments are used in various surgical procedures, including the placement and removal of orthopedic implants. It cases include plastic, metal and hybrid models used to organize, secure and transport medical devices for orthopedic, endoscopy, dental and other surgical procedures. Lastly, the firm's other category comprises limited specialized products and services for other non-healthcare markets, primarily the aerospace industry. The company has a variety of subsidiaries. Jet Engineering, Inc. forges, creates and fully finishes orthopedic implants. Symmetry Medical PolyVac manufactures metal, plastic and hybrid medical cases in New Hampshire and France. Thornton Precision Components Ltd., based in Sheffield, England, has supplied orthopedic components for over 100 years, specializing in precision forging, casting, rapid prototyping, machining and full finishing for implants. Lastly, UltreXX, Inc. manufacturers and supplies precision spinal and trauma instruments and implants to original equipment manufacturers internationally. The firm offers most of its products under the Total Solutions brand. In September 2007, Symmetry acquired Specialty Surgical Instruments, Inc. (SSI) and Ultra Containers of America, LLC (UCA), for $15 million. UCA has historically sold its containers through SSI's sales network, and Symmetry plans to maintain that arrangement. In January 2008, the firm acquired an orthopedic instrument manufacturing facility in New Bedford, Massachusetts, from DePuy Orthpaedics, Inc. for $45 million.

## FINANCIALS: **Sales and profits are in thousands of dollars—add 000 to get the full amount. 2008 Note: Financial information for 2008 was not available for all companies at press time.**

| | | |
|---|---|---|
| 2008 Sales: $ | 2008 Profits: $ | **U.S. Stock Ticker: SMA** |
| 2007 Sales: $290,922 | 2007 Profits: $- 149 | **Int'l Ticker:** Int'l Exchange: |
| 2006 Sales: $245,017 | 2006 Profits: $18,514 | Employees: 2,449 |
| 2005 Sales: $263,766 | 2005 Profits: $31,800 | Fiscal Year Ends: 12/31 |
| 2004 Sales: $205,391 | 2004 Profits: $11,695 | Parent Company: |

## SALARIES/BENEFITS:

| | | | | |
|---|---|---|---|---|
| Pension Plan: | ESOP Stock Plan: | Profit Sharing: | Top Exec. Salary: $430,000 | Bonus: $60,000 |
| Savings Plan: | Stock Purch. Plan: | | Second Exec. Salary: $278,591 | Bonus: $ |

## OTHER THOUGHTS:

**Apparent Women Officers or Directors:**
**Hot Spot for Advancement for Women/Minorities:**

## LOCATIONS: ("Y" = Yes)

| West: | Southwest: | Midwest: | Southeast: | Northeast: | International: |
|---|---|---|---|---|---|
| | | Y | Y | Y | Y |

# SYMYX TECHNOLOGIES

www.symyx.com

**Industry Group Code:** 541710 **Ranks within this company's industry group:** Sales: 2 Profits: 1

| Management: | | Sales/Marketing: | | Liberal Arts: | | Information Systems: | | Professionals: | | Technical/Scientific: | |
|---|---|---|---|---|---|---|---|---|---|---|---|
| Mgmt. Trainees: | | Mktg. Professionals: | Y | Gen. Writing/Editing: | | Info. Management: | Y | Finance/Accounting: | Y | Engineers, Elec.: | |
| Experienced Mgmt.: | Y | Retail Sales: | | Technical Writing: | Y | Software Dev.: | Y | Law: | Y | Engineers, Other: | |
| Int'l Business: | Y | Commercial/Industrial: | | Graphic Arts/Photog.: | | Hardware Dev.: | | HR/Other: | Y | Health/Lab: | |
| MBA Graduates: | Y | Sales Trainees: | | Music: | | Systems Integration: | | Training: | Y | Scientists/Research: | Y |
| | | Advertising Pros.: | | Broadcasting: | | Consulting/Other: | | Health Care: | | Petroleum/Chemicals: | |
| | | | | Other: | | | | Consulting: | Y | Math/Other: | |

## TYPES OF BUSINESS:

Research & Development Services
Materials Research
Nanotechnology Research
Research Software

## BRANDS/DIVISIONS/AFFILIATES:

Symyx Tools
Symyx Software
Symyx Therapeutics, Inc.
Symyx Research Collaborations
Symyx Sensors
Excipient Compatibility
Forced Degradation
Visyx Technologies, Inc.

## CONTACTS: *Note: Officers with more than one job title may be intentionally listed here more than once.*

Isy Goldwasser, CEO
Rex S. Jackson, CFO/Exec. VP
W. Henry Weinberg, Chief Tech. Officer/Exec. VP
Richard Boehner, Pres., Symyx High Productivity Research
Trevor Heritage, Pres., Symyx Software
Steven D. Goldby, Chmn.

| **Phone:** 408-764-2000 | **Fax:** 408-748-0175 |
|---|---|
| **Toll-Free:** | |
| **Address:** 3100 Central Expressway, Santa Clara, CA 95051 US | |

## GROWTH PLANS/SPECIAL FEATURES:

Symyx Technologies, Inc. develops and applies high-throughput research technologies and research software for the chemical, energy, pharmaceutical, electronics and other industries. Symyx performs research for customers using proprietary technologies to discover new and innovative materials, sell automated high-throughput instrumentation, license software for use in customers' laboratories and license discovered materials, sensors and intellectual property. Symyx primarily serves customers in two broad categories: life sciences; and chemicals and energy. Both categories focus on creating returns on investments for clients through scientific data management, microscale parallel experimentation and contract research. Among the company's discovered materials are catalysts for the manufacture of plastics and chemicals, polymers for a range of consumer and industrial applications and x-ray storage phosphors used in computed radiography. The firm usually receives royalty payments for products it helps discover along with its service fees. Symyx offers services through Symyx Research Collaborations; Symyx Tools; Symyx Software; Symyx Sensors; and Materials and Intellectual Property Licensing. A few products and services available through the firm include the Lab notebooks; lab execution and analysis software; lab operational informatics, which is a suite of software used to define, manage, track, procure and audit various materials, intellectual property and other workflows; decision support software, which can design, execute, analyze and report on data and experiments; and cheminformatics, which offers chemistry engine and chemical drawing and presentation tools. Visyx Technologies, Inc. commercializes the company's proprietary sensor technologies. Symyx has several widely known clients including ExxonMobil, Merck and the Dow Chemical Company. In August 2008, the firm acquired Integrity Biosolutions.

Employees of the firm are offered medical, dental and vision coverage; a 401(k) plan; flexible spending accounts; transportation benefits; life insurance; an employee assistance program; athletic club memberships; an employee stock purchase plan; and stock grants. Additionally, the firm offers an on-site cafeteria at the corporate headquarters.

## FINANCIALS: Sales and profits are in thousands of dollars—add 000 to get the full amount. 2008 Note: Financial information for 2008 was not available for all companies at press time.

| | | |
|---|---|---|
| 2008 Sales: $159,045 | 2008 Profits: $-106,615 | **U.S. Stock Ticker: SMMX** |
| 2007 Sales: $125,072 | 2007 Profits: $18,784 | **Int'l Ticker:** Int'l Exchange: |
| 2006 Sales: $124,900 | 2006 Profits: $8,284 | Employees: 600 |
| 2005 Sales: $108,137 | 2005 Profits: $12,002 | Fiscal Year Ends: 12/31 |
| 2004 Sales: $83,185 | 2004 Profits: $12,882 | Parent Company: |

## SALARIES/BENEFITS:

| | | | | |
|---|---|---|---|---|
| Pension Plan: | ESOP Stock Plan: | Profit Sharing: | Top Exec. Salary: $420,000 | Bonus: $136,500 |
| Savings Plan: Y | Stock Purch. Plan: Y | | Second Exec. Salary: $420,000 | Bonus: $210,000 |

## OTHER THOUGHTS:

**Apparent Women Officers or Directors:**
**Hot Spot for Advancement for Women/Minorities:**

## LOCATIONS: ("Y" = Yes)

| West: | Southwest: | Midwest: | Southeast: | Northeast: | International: |
|---|---|---|---|---|---|
| Y | | | | Y | Y |

Note: Financial information, benefits and other data can change quickly and may vary from those stated here.

# SYNAPTICS INC

www.synaptics.com

**Industry Group Code:** 334119 **Ranks within this company's industry group:** Sales: 4 Profits: 3

| Management: | | Sales/Marketing: | | Liberal Arts: | | Information Systems: | | Professionals: | | Technical/Scientific: | |
|---|---|---|---|---|---|---|---|---|---|---|---|
| Mgmt. Trainees: | | Mktg. Professionals: | | Gen. Writing/Editing: | | Info. Management: | Y | Finance/Accounting: | Y | Engineers, Elec.: | Y |
| Experienced Mgmt.: | Y | Retail Sales: | | Technical Writing: | Y | Software Dev.: | Y | Law: | Y | Engineers, Other: | Y |
| Int'l Business: | Y | Commercial/Industrial: | Y | Graphic Arts/Photog.: | Y | Hardware Dev.: | Y | HR/Other: | Y | Health/Lab: | |
| MBA Graduates: | Y | Sales Trainees: | Y | Music: | | Systems Integration: | Y | Training: | Y | Scientists/Research: | |
| | | Advertising Pros.: | | Broadcasting: | | Consulting/Other: | | Health Care: | | Petroleum/Chemicals: | |
| | | | | Other: | | | | Consulting: | | Math/Other: | |

## TYPES OF BUSINESS:

Electronic Components
User Interface Systems

## BRANDS/DIVISIONS/AFFILIATES:

TouchPad
TouchStyk
LuxPad
LightTouch
QuickStroke
FingerPrint TouchPad
ScrollStrip
NavPoint

## CONTACTS: *Note: Officers with more than one job title may be intentionally listed here more than once.*

Francis F. Lee, CEO
Francis F. Lee, Pres.
Russ Knittel, CFO/Exec. VP
Dave Long, VP-Worldwide Sales
James Harrington, VP-Global Human Resources
Shawn Day, CTO
Kin Cheung, VP-Prod. Dev.
Joe Montalbo, Sr. VP-Eng.
Russ Knittel, Chief Admin. Officer
Russ Knittel, Sec.
Alex Wong, VP-Worldwide Oper.
Russ Knittel, Treas.
Ruth Lutes, VP-Customer Care & Quality
Tom Tiernan, Exec. VP/Gen. Mgr.
Mark Vena, VP-Notebook Bus.
Federico Faggin, Chmn.
Wen-Shone Shiau, VP-Synaptics Taiwan
Doug Kahn, VP-Supply Chain Mgmt.

**Phone:** 408-454-5100 **Fax:** 408-454-5200
**Toll-Free:**
**Address:** 3120 Scott Blvd., Ste. 130, Santa Clara, CA 95054 US

## GROWTH PLANS/SPECIAL FEATURES:

Synaptics, Inc. (SYNA) is a worldwide developer of custom-designed user interface solutions for mobile computing, communications, entertainment and other electronic devices. The company's products emphasize ease of use, small size, low power consumption, advanced functionality, durability and reliability, making them applicable to a multitude of markets, including notebook computers, PC peripherals, mobile phones and portable entertainment devices such as MP3 players. SYNA's original equipment manufacturer (OEM) customers include the world's 10 largest PC OEMs and many of the world's largest hard-disk drive portable digital music player OEMs. Products for the PC market include the TouchPad, a touch-sensitive pad that senses movement of a person's finger on its surface; TouchStyk, a self contained pointing stick module; and dual pointing solutions, a combination of a TouchPad and a pointing stick into a single notebook computer. Additional products include LuxPad, Dual Mode TouchPad and QuickStroke. The company also addresses the growing market of new mobile computing and communications devices, called information appliances (or iAppliances), as well as other electronic devices. Products in this market sector include the ScrollStrip and TouchRing, which are scrolling solutions allowing users to navigate efficiently through menus and content; LightTouch capacitive buttons, which provide illuminated button functionality; as well as MobileTouch, NavPoint, ClearPad and TouchScreen products. In June 2007, Synaptics announced the second generation of its SecurePad, a biometric TouchPad solution created for notebooks. With an exclusive partnership with Validity Sensors, Inc., the latest SecurePad will incorporate Validity's LiveFlex fingerprint sensing technology for biometric security in the notebook market. In April 2008, Synaptics ClearPad and ClearArray, which provide touch screen capabilities, were chosen for the LG Secret.

Synaptics offers its employees health, dental and vision insurance; life and disability insurance; a 401(k) plan; flexible spending accounts; and an educational assistance program.

## FINANCIALS: Sales and profits are in thousands of dollars—add 000 to get the full amount. 2008 Note: Financial information for 2008 was not available for all companies at press time.

| | | |
|---|---|---|
| 2008 Sales: $361,057 | 2008 Profits: $31,000 | **U.S. Stock Ticker: SYNA** |
| 2007 Sales: $266,787 | 2007 Profits: $26,534 | **Int'l Ticker:** Int'l Exchange: |
| 2006 Sales: $184,557 | 2006 Profits: $13,701 | Employees: 420 |
| 2005 Sales: $208,139 | 2005 Profits: $37,985 | Fiscal Year Ends: 6/30 |
| 2004 Sales: $133,276 | 2004 Profits: $12,992 | Parent Company: |

## SALARIES/BENEFITS:

| | | | | |
|---|---|---|---|---|
| Pension Plan: | ESOP Stock Plan: | Profit Sharing: Y | Top Exec. Salary: $350,000 | Bonus: $470,000 |
| Savings Plan: Y | Stock Purch. Plan: Y | | Second Exec. Salary: $300,000 | Bonus: $248,000 |

## OTHER THOUGHTS:

**Apparent Women Officers or Directors:** 1
**Hot Spot for Advancement for Women/Minorities:**

## LOCATIONS: ("Y" = Yes)

| West: | Southwest: | Midwest: | Southeast: | Northeast: | International: |
|---|---|---|---|---|---|
| Y | | | | | Y |

# SYNOVIS LIFE TECHNOLOGIES INC

www.synovislife.com

**Industry Group Code:** 339113 **Ranks within this company's industry group:** Sales: 37 Profits: 31

| Management: | | Sales/Marketing: | | Liberal Arts: | | Information Systems: | | Professionals: | | Technical/Scientific: | |
|---|---|---|---|---|---|---|---|---|---|---|---|
| Mgmt. Trainees: | | Mktg. Professionals: | Y | Gen. Writing/Editing: | | Info. Management: | Y | Finance/Accounting: | Y | Engineers, Elec.: | Y |
| Experienced Mgmt.: | Y | Retail Sales: | | Technical Writing: | Y | Software Dev.: | Y | Law: | Y | Engineers, Other: | Y |
| Int'l Business: | | Commercial/Industrial: | Y | Graphic Arts/Photog.: | | Hardware Dev.: | | HR/Other: | Y | Health/Lab: | Y |
| MBA Graduates: | Y | Sales Trainees: | Y | Music: | | Systems Integration: | | Training: | Y | Scientists/Research: | Y |
| | | Advertising Pros.: | | Broadcasting: | | Consulting/Other: | | Health Care: | Y | Petroleum/Chemicals: | |
| | | | | Other: | | | | Consulting: | | Math/Other: | Y |

## TYPES OF BUSINESS:

Surgical & Interventional Treatment Products
Implantable Biomaterials

## BRANDS/DIVISIONS/AFFILIATES:

Synovis Surgical Innovations
Synovis Micro Companies Alliance
Synovis Interventional Solutions
Microvascular Anastomotis Coupler
Peri-Strips
Veritas
Tissue-Guard
4Closure Surgical Fascia Closure System

## CONTACTS: *Note: Officers with more than one job title may be intentionally listed here more than once.*

Richard W. Kramp, CEO
Richard W. Kramp, Pres.
Brett A. Reynolds, CFO
B. Nicholas Oray, VP-R&D
Brett A. Reynolds, Corp. Sec.
Tim Floeder, VP-Corp. Dev.
Brett A. Reynolds, VP-Finance
Michael K. Campbell, Pres., Micro Companies Alliance, Inc.
Mary L. Frick, VP-Regulatory Affairs & Quality Assurance
Mary L. Frick, VP-Clinical Affairs
David Buche, VP/COO-Synovis Surgical Innovations
Timothy M. Scanlan, Chmn.

| **Phone:** 651-796-7300 | **Fax:** 651-642-9018 |
|---|---|
| **Toll-Free:** 800-255-4018 | |
| **Address:** 2575 University Ave. W., St. Paul, MN 55114 US | |

## GROWTH PLANS/SPECIAL FEATURES:

Synovis Life Technologies, Inc. is a diversified medical device company engaged in developing, manufacturing and bringing to market products for the surgical treatment of disease. The company formerly operated in two business segments, the surgical business and the interventional business. The firm now operates solely through its surgical business, as its interventional business was sold in 2008 to Heraeus Vadnais Inc. The surgical business is composed of subsidiaries Synovis Innovations and Synovis Micro Companies Alliance, through which it provides implantable biomaterial products, devices for microsurgery and surgical tools. Biometrical products include Peri-Strips, a biomaterial stapling buttress used as reinforcement at the surgical stable line to reduce the risk of potentially fatal leaks; Tissue-Guard, used to repair and replace damaged tissue in cardiac, vascular, thoracic, abdominal and neuron surgeries; and Veritas, for use in pelvic floor reconstruction, stress urinary incontinence treatment, vaginal and rectal prolapse repair, hernia repair as well as soft tissue repair. Synovis Micro Companies Alliance also provides devices and products used in specialty surgeries in the microsurgery market. As stated previously, the firm sold its interventional business to Hereaus Vadnais, located in Minnesota, for $29.5 million in cash.

## FINANCIALS: **Sales and profits are in thousands of dollars—add 000 to get the full amount. 2008 Note: Financial information for 2008 was not available for all companies at press time.**

| | | |
|---|---|---|
| 2008 Sales: $ | 2008 Profits: $ | **U.S. Stock Ticker: SYNO** |
| 2007 Sales: $67,874 | 2007 Profits: $3,810 | **Int'l Ticker:** Int'l Exchange: |
| 2006 Sales: $55,835 | 2006 Profits: $-1,481 | Employees: 440 |
| 2005 Sales: $60,256 | 2005 Profits: $ 883 | Fiscal Year Ends: 10/31 |
| 2004 Sales: $55,044 | 2004 Profits: $1,278 | Parent Company: |

## SALARIES/BENEFITS:

| | | | | |
|---|---|---|---|---|
| Pension Plan: | ESOP Stock Plan: | Profit Sharing: | Top Exec. Salary: $290,000 | Bonus: $97,150 |
| Savings Plan: Y | Stock Purch. Plan: | | Second Exec. Salary: $194,480 | Bonus: $33,753 |

## OTHER THOUGHTS:

**Apparent Women Officers or Directors**: 2
**Hot Spot for Advancement for Women/Minorities**: Y

## LOCATIONS: ("Y" = Yes)

| West: | Southwest: | Midwest: | Southeast: | Northeast: | International: |
|---|---|---|---|---|---|
| | | Y | | | |

# TAMPA ELECTRIC COMPANY

**www.tampaelectric.com**

**Industry Group Code:** 221000A **Ranks within this company's industry group:** Sales: Profits:

| Management: | | Sales/Marketing: | | Liberal Arts: | | Information Systems: | | Professionals: | | Technical/Scientific: | |
|---|---|---|---|---|---|---|---|---|---|---|---|
| Mgmt. Trainees: | | Mktg. Professionals: | Y | Gen. Writing/Editing: | | Info. Management: | Y | Finance/Accounting: | Y | Engineers, Elec.: | Y |
| Experienced Mgmt.: | Y | Retail Sales: | | Technical Writing: | | Software Dev.: | | Law: | Y | Engineers, Other: | Y |
| Int'l Business: | | Commercial/Industrial: | Y | Graphic Arts/Photog.: | | Hardware Dev.: | | HR/Other: | Y | Health/Lab: | |
| MBA Graduates: | Y | Sales Trainees: | Y | Music: | | Systems Integration: | | Training: | Y | Scientists/Research: | |
| | | Advertising Pros.: | | Broadcasting: | | Consulting/Other: | | Health Care: | | Petroleum/Chemicals: | Y |
| | | | | Other: | | | | Consulting: | | Math/Other: | |

## TYPES OF BUSINESS:

Utilities-Electricity & Natural Gas
Electric Generation
Solar Power
Coal Mining & Preparation
Synthetic Fuel
Ocean & River Shipping

## BRANDS/DIVISIONS/AFFILIATES:

TECO Energy Inc
Energy Plus Homes
Metro-Link
Peoples Gas System

## CONTACTS:

*Note: Officers with more than one job title may be intentionally listed here more than once.*

Charles R. Black, Pres.
Deirdre A. Brown, VP-Customer Svc. & Regulatory Affairs
Thomas L. Hernandez, VP-Energy Supply
William T. Whale, VP-Energy Delivery

| | |
|---|---|
| **Phone:** 813-228-4111 | **Fax:** 813-228-1670 |
| **Toll-Free:** | |
| **Address:** 702 N. Franklin St., TECO Plaza, Tampa, FL 33602 US | |

## GROWTH PLANS/SPECIAL FEATURES:

Tampa Electric Company, the principal subsidiary of TECO Energy, Inc., is a public utility that generates, purchases, transmits, distributes, markets and sells electric energy and natural gas in Florida. Founded in 1899, the company operates through two divisions, electric and natural gas. Tampa Electric, with a total generating capacity of 4,400 megawatts generates, transmits and distributes electric energy. The company serves over 668,000 customers in a 2,000 square mile operating service territory including all of Hillsborough County and parts of Polk, Pasco and Pinellas counties in Florida. The company operates five plants with approximately 58% of energy produced coming from its coal fired plants, approximately 41% coming from its gas fired plants and approximately 1% coming from its oil fired plant. Other services include surge protection, tree trimming, energy systems analysis services, an Energy Plus Homes program that provides incentives to energy efficient equipment users, outdoor lighting systems, a malfunctioning streetlight reporting service and a renewable energy program, providing customers with the option to purchase a portion of their energy from renewable resources such as sunlight, landfill gas and biomass. In addition, Tampa Electric's Metro-Link department provides a fiber-optic network and related services to certain clients. Business customers that are intending to relocate can also take advantage of the firm's economic development segment, which maintains relationships with a number of resources nationwide to assist with relocation planning. Peoples Gas System, the natural gas division of Tampa Electric, operates fossil-fueled power plants and distributes natural gas for more than 320,000 residential, commercial and industrial customers. In April 2007, the company completed construction on Polk units 4 and 5, two new 160 megawatt simple-cycle combustion turbine natural gas units. In February 2008, the firm announced it would install five 60 megawatt peaking units to serve during peak periods.

## FINANCIALS:

**Sales and profits are in thousands of dollars—add 000 to get the full amount. 2008 Note: Financial information for 2008 was not available for all companies at press time.**

| | | |
|---|---|---|
| 2008 Sales: $ | 2008 Profits: $ | **U.S. Stock Ticker: Subsidiary** |
| 2007 Sales: $ | 2007 Profits: $ | **Int'l Ticker:** Int'l Exchange: |
| 2006 Sales: $2,661,900 | 2006 Profits: $165,600 | Employees: 2,452 |
| 2005 Sales: $2,295,700 | 2005 Profits: $176,700 | Fiscal Year Ends: 12/31 |
| 2004 Sales: $2,034,300 | 2004 Profits: $173,700 | Parent Company: TECO ENERGY INC |

## SALARIES/BENEFITS:

| | | | | |
|---|---|---|---|---|
| Pension Plan: Y | ESOP Stock Plan: | Profit Sharing: | Top Exec. Salary: $ | Bonus: $ |
| Savings Plan: Y | Stock Purch. Plan: | | Second Exec. Salary: $ | Bonus: $ |

## OTHER THOUGHTS:

**Apparent Women Officers or Directors**: 1
**Hot Spot for Advancement for Women/Minorities**:

## LOCATIONS: ("Y" = Yes)

| West: | Southwest: | Midwest: | Southeast: | Northeast: | International: |
|---|---|---|---|---|---|
| | | | Y | | |

Note: Financial information, benefits and other data can change quickly and may vary from those stated here.

# TARGA RESOURCES PARTNERS LP

www.targaresources.com

**Industry Group Code:** 211111 **Ranks within this company's industry group:** Sales: 6 Profits: 16

| Management: | | Sales/Marketing: | | Liberal Arts: | | Information Systems: | | Professionals: | | Technical/Scientific: | |
|---|---|---|---|---|---|---|---|---|---|---|---|
| Mgmt. Trainees: | | Mktg. Professionals: | Y | Gen. Writing/Editing: | | Info. Management: | Y | Finance/Accounting: | Y | Engineers, Elec.: | |
| Experienced Mgmt.: | Y | Retail Sales: | | Technical Writing: | | Software Dev.: | | Law: | Y | Engineers, Other: | Y |
| Int'l Business: | Y | Commercial/Industrial: | Y | Graphic Arts/Photog.: | | Hardware Dev.: | | HR/Other: | Y | Health/Lab: | |
| MBA Graduates: | Y | Sales Trainees: | | Music: | | Systems Integration: | | Training: | Y | Scientists/Research: | |
| | | Advertising Pros.: | | Broadcasting: | | Consulting/Other: | | Health Care: | | Petroleum/Chemicals: | Y |
| | | | | Other: | | | | Consulting: | | Math/Other: | |

## TYPES OF BUSINESS:

Natural Gas Gathering & Compression
Natural & Gas Liquids Processing & Selling

## BRANDS/DIVISIONS/AFFILIATES:

Targa Resources, Inc.

## CONTACTS:

*Note: Officers with more than one job title may be intentionally listed here more than once.*

Rene R. Joyce, CEO
Michael A. Heim, COO/Exec. VP
Joe Bob Perkins, Pres.
Jeffrey J. McParland, CFO/Exec. VP
James W. Whalen, Pres., Admin.
Paul W. Chung, General Counsel/Exec. VP/Sec.
John Robert Sparger, Chief Acct. Officer
Roy E. Johnson, Exec. VP
Matt Meloy, VP-Finance/Treas.

| **Phone:** 713-584-1000 | **Fax:** 713-584-1100 |
|---|---|
| **Toll-Free:** | |
| **Address:** 1000 Louisiana St., Ste. 4300, Houston, TX 77002 US | |

## GROWTH PLANS/SPECIAL FEATURES:

Targa Resources Partners LP owns, operates, acquires and develops a diversified portfolio of complementary midstream energy assets. The company currently operates in the Fort Worth Basin in north Texas and is engaged in the business of gathering, compressing, treating, processing and selling natural gas and fractioning and selling natural gas liquids (NGL) and NGL products. The firm has two divisions, natural gas gathering and processing division and the NGL logistics and marketing division. The firm's operations consist of an extensive network of roughly 11,000 miles of integrated gathering pipelines that gather and compress natural gas received from about 2,700 receipt point in the Fort Worth Basin; two natural gas processing plants that compress, treat and process the natural gas; and a fractionate portion of raw NGLs produced in the company's processing operations into NGL products. Targa Resources serves a 14-county natural gas producing region in the Fort Worth Basin that includes production from the Barnett Shale formation and other shallower formations, including the Bend Conglomerate, Caddo, Atoka, Marble Falls and other Pennsylvanian and upper Mississippi formations. The company's assets consist of the Chico system, located in the northeast part of the Fort Worth Basin; the Shackelford system, located on the western side of the Fort Worth Basin; and a 320 mile, 10-inch diameter natural gas pipeline connecting the Shackelford and Chico systems that is used primarily to send natural gas gathered in excess of the Shackelford system's processing capacity to the Chico plant. Targa Resources, Inc. owns about 40% of the firm.

## FINANCIALS:

**Sales and profits are in thousands of dollars—add 000 to get the full amount. 2008 Note: Financial information for 2008 was not available for all companies at press time.**

| | | |
|---|---|---|
| 2008 Sales: $ | 2008 Profits: $ | **U.S. Stock Ticker: NGLS** |
| 2007 Sales: $1,661,500 | 2007 Profits: $40,300 | **Int'l Ticker:** Int'l Exchange: |
| 2006 Sales: $1,738,500 | 2006 Profits: $11,600 | Employees: 920 |
| 2005 Sales: $ | 2005 Profits: $ | Fiscal Year Ends: 12/31 |
| 2004 Sales: $ | 2004 Profits: $ | Parent Company: |

## SALARIES/BENEFITS:

| | | | | |
|---|---|---|---|---|
| Pension Plan: | ESOP Stock Plan: | Profit Sharing: | Top Exec. Salary: $293,750 | Bonus: $759,769 |
| Savings Plan: | Stock Purch. Plan: | | Second Exec. Salary: $265,000 | Bonus: $636,318 |

## OTHER THOUGHTS:

**Apparent Women Officers or Directors:**
**Hot Spot for Advancement for Women/Minorities:**

## LOCATIONS: ("Y" = Yes)

| West: | Southwest: | Midwest: | Southeast: | Northeast: | International: |
|---|---|---|---|---|---|
| | Y | | Y | Y | Y |

# TDINDUSTRIES

**www.tdindustries.com**

**Industry Group Code:** 234000 **Ranks within this company's industry group:** Sales: Profits:

| Management: | | Sales/Marketing: | | Liberal Arts: | | Information Systems: | | Professionals: | | Technical/Scientific: | |
|---|---|---|---|---|---|---|---|---|---|---|---|
| Mgmt. Trainees: | | Mktg. Professionals: | | Gen. Writing/Editing: | | Info. Management: | Y | Finance/Accounting: | Y | Engineers, Elec.: | Y |
| Experienced Mgmt.: | Y | Retail Sales: | | Technical Writing: | | Software Dev.: | | Law: | Y | Engineers, Other: | Y |
| Int'l Business: | | Commercial/Industrial: | Y | Graphic Arts/Photog.: | | Hardware Dev.: | | HR/Other: | Y | Health/Lab: | |
| MBA Graduates: | Y | Sales Trainees: | | Music: | | Systems Integration: | | Training: | Y | Scientists/Research: | |
| | | Advertising Pros.: | | Broadcasting: | | Consulting/Other: | | Health Care: | | Petroleum/Chemicals: | |
| | | | | Other: | | | | Consulting: | | Math/Other: | |

## TYPES OF BUSINESS:

Construction
Facilities Services

## BRANDS/DIVISIONS/AFFILIATES:

## CONTACTS:

*Note: Officers with more than one job title may be intentionally listed here more than once.*

Harold MacDowell, CEO
Mike Fitzpatrick, CFO
Jim Bivins, VP-IT
Todd F. Lokash, VP-Mfg.
John B. Lowe Jr, Chmn.

| | |
|---|---|
| **Phone:** 972-888-9500 | **Fax:** 972-888-9482 |
| **Toll-Free:** | |
| **Address:** 13850 Diplomat Dr., Dallas, TX 75234 US | |

## GROWTH PLANS/SPECIAL FEATURES:

TDIndustries is a leading facilities service and specialty construction company. The Dallas, Texas-based firm offers construction, installation and operations services for commercial, industrial and institutional buildings. The company offers its services in nine key areas: heating ventilation, air conditioning, electrical, life safety, facilities management, plumbing, process and high purity piping, and building automation refrigeration. TDIndustries is 100%-owned by its over 900 employees and retirees with no one employee controlling more than 3% of the company's stock. It has regional offices in Fort Worth, Austin, Houston, San Antonio, Denver and Phoenix. Prominent clients include Dallas Cowboys Stadium, the Texas Governor's Mansion and Tyson Foods.

TDIndustries was ranked 37 on FORTUNE magazine's 100 Best Companies to Work For list. The firm has consistently earned placement on the prestigious list since its inception in 1998 and as a result holds Fortune's All Star distinction, an honor only held by 13 companies.

## FINANCIALS:

**Sales and profits are in thousands of dollars—add 000 to get the full amount. 2008 Note: Financial information for 2008 was not available for all companies at press time.**

| | | |
|---|---|---|
| 2008 Sales: $ | 2008 Profits: $ | **U.S. Stock Ticker: Private** |
| 2007 Sales: $ | 2007 Profits: $ | **Int'l Ticker:** Int'l Exchange: |
| 2006 Sales: $ | 2006 Profits: $ | Employees: 1,713 |
| 2005 Sales: $ | 2005 Profits: $ | Fiscal Year Ends: 12/31 |
| 2004 Sales: $ | 2004 Profits: $ | Parent Company: |

## SALARIES/BENEFITS:

| | | | | |
|---|---|---|---|---|
| Pension Plan: | ESOP Stock Plan: Y | Profit Sharing: | Top Exec. Salary: $ | Bonus: $ |
| Savings Plan: | Stock Purch. Plan: | | Second Exec. Salary: $ | Bonus: $ |

## OTHER THOUGHTS:

**Apparent Women Officers or Directors**: 1
**Hot Spot for Advancement for Women/Minorities**:

## LOCATIONS: ("Y" = Yes)

| West: | Southwest: | Midwest: | Southeast: | Northeast: | International: |
|---|---|---|---|---|---|
| Y | Y | Y | | | |

# TECHNE CORP

www.techne-corp.com

**Industry Group Code:** 325413 **Ranks within this company's industry group:** Sales: 3 Profits: 2

| Management: | | Sales/Marketing: | | Liberal Arts: | | Information Systems: | | Professionals: | | Technical/Scientific: | |
|---|---|---|---|---|---|---|---|---|---|---|---|
| Mgmt. Trainees: | | Mktg. Professionals: | Y | Gen. Writing/Editing: | | Info. Management: | Y | Finance/Accounting: | Y | Engineers, Elec.: | |
| Experienced Mgmt.: | Y | Retail Sales: | | Technical Writing: | Y | Software Dev.: | Y | Law: | Y | Engineers, Other: | Y |
| Int'l Business: | Y | Commercial/Industrial: | Y | Graphic Arts/Photog.: | | Hardware Dev.: | Y | HR/Other: | Y | Health/Lab: | Y |
| MBA Graduates: | Y | Sales Trainees: | Y | Music: | | Systems Integration: | | Training: | Y | Scientists/Research: | Y |
| | | Advertising Pros.: | | Broadcasting: | | Consulting/Other: | | Health Care: | Y | Petroleum/Chemicals: | |
| | | | | Other: | | | | Consulting: | | Math/Other: | Y |

## TYPES OF BUSINESS:

Biotechnology Products
Reagents, Antibodies & Assay Kits
Hematology Products

## BRANDS/DIVISIONS/AFFILIATES:

Research and Diagnostic Systems, Inc.
R&D Systems Europe, Ltd.
R&D Systems GmbH
Whole Blood Flow Cytometry Control
Whole Blood Glucose/Hemoglobin Control
Fortron Bio Science, Inc.
BiosPacific, Inc.
R&D Systems China Co. Ltd.

## CONTACTS: *Note: Officers with more than one job title may be intentionally listed here more than once.*

Thomas E. Oland, CEO
Thomas E. Oland, Pres.
Gergory J. Melson, CFO
Lea Simoane, Dir.-Human Resources
Richard A. Krzyzek, VP-Research
Gregory J. Melson, VP-Finance
Marcel Veronneau, VP-Hematology Oper.
Roger C. Lucas, Vice Chmn.
Wendy Shao, Gen. Mgr.-R&D Systems China Co. Ltd.,
Thomas E. Oland, Chmn.

| **Phone:** 612-379-8854 | **Fax:** 612-379-6580 |
|---|---|
| **Toll-Free:** 800-343-7475 | |
| **Address:** 614 McKinley Pl. N.E., Minneapolis, MN 55413-2610 US | |

## GROWTH PLANS/SPECIAL FEATURES:

Techne Corp. is a holding company that operates via two subsidiaries: Research and Diagnostic Systems, Inc. (R&D Systems) and R&D Systems Europe, Ltd. (R&D Europe). R&D Systems manufactures biological products in two major segments hematology controls, which are used in clinical and hospital laboratories to monitor the accuracy of blood analysis instruments; and biotechnology products, which including purified proteins and antibodies that are sold exclusively to the research market and assay kits that are sold to the research and clinical diagnostic markets. R&D Europe distributes biotechnology products throughout Europe and also operates a sales office in France and in Germany via its German subsidiary, R&D Systems GmbH. In recent years, R&D Systems has also expanded its product portfolio to include enzymes and intracellular cell signaling reagents such as proteases, kinases and phosphatases for diseases such as cancer, Alzheimer's, arthritic, autoimmunity, diabetes, hypertension, obesity, AIDS and SARS. Techne also produces controls and calibrators for a variety of medical brands such as Abbott Diagnostics, Beckman Coulter, Bayer Technicon and Sysmex. In the hematology sector, the company's Whole Blood Flow Cytometry Control is used to identify and quantify white blood cells by their surface antigens while linearity and reportable range controls assess the linearity of hematology analyzers for white blood cells, red blood ells, platelets and reticulocytes. Late in 2007, R&D Systems, Inc. opened R&D Systems China Co. Ltd., a wholly-owned subsidiary established to improve the level of service offered to R&D Systems' distributors and customers in China. The company and its new facility will operate as a warehouse/distribution hub for R&D Systems' cell biology research products and will also provide technical services and marketing support for the Chinese market.

## FINANCIALS: **Sales and profits are in thousands of dollars—add 000 to get the full amount. 2008 Note: Financial information for 2008 was not available for all companies at press time.**

| | | |
|---|---|---|
| 2008 Sales: $257,420 | 2008 Profits: $103,558 | **U.S. Stock Ticker: TECH** |
| 2007 Sales: $223,482 | 2007 Profits: $85,111 | **Int'l Ticker:** Int'l Exchange: |
| 2006 Sales: $202,617 | 2006 Profits: $73,351 | Employees: 719 |
| 2005 Sales: $178,700 | 2005 Profits: $66,100 | Fiscal Year Ends: 6/30 |
| 2004 Sales: $161,257 | 2004 Profits: $52,928 | Parent Company: |

## SALARIES/BENEFITS:

| | | | | |
|---|---|---|---|---|
| Pension Plan: | ESOP Stock Plan: | Profit Sharing: Y | Top Exec. Salary: $263,000 | Bonus: $52,547 |
| Savings Plan: Y | Stock Purch. Plan: Y | | Second Exec. Salary: $254,100 | Bonus: $ |

## OTHER THOUGHTS:

**Apparent Women Officers or Directors**: 1
**Hot Spot for Advancement for Women/Minorities**: Y

## LOCATIONS: ("Y" = Yes)

| West: | Southwest: | Midwest: | Southeast: | Northeast: | International: |
|---|---|---|---|---|---|
| | | Y | | | Y |

# TELIRIS

www.teliris.com

**Industry Group Code:** 513300D **Ranks within this company's industry group:** Sales: Profits:

| Management: | | Sales/Marketing: | | Liberal Arts: | | Information Systems: | | Professionals: | | Technical/Scientific: | |
|---|---|---|---|---|---|---|---|---|---|---|---|
| Mgmt. Trainees: | | Mktg. Professionals: | Y | Gen. Writing/Editing: | | Info. Management: | Y | Finance/Accounting: | Y | Engineers, Elec.: | Y |
| Experienced Mgmt.: | Y | Retail Sales: | | Technical Writing: | Y | Software Dev.: | | Law: | Y | Engineers, Other: | Y |
| Int'l Business: | Y | Commercial/Industrial: | Y | Graphic Arts/Photog.: | | Hardware Dev.: | | HR/Other: | Y | Health/Lab: | |
| MBA Graduates: | Y | Sales Trainees: | Y | Music: | | Systems Integration: | Y | Training: | Y | Scientists/Research: | |
| | | Advertising Pros.: | | Broadcasting: | | Consulting/Other: | | Health Care: | | Petroleum/Chemicals: | |
| | | | | Other: | | | | Consulting: | | Math/Other: | |

## TYPES OF BUSINESS:

Video Conferencing Products & Services

## BRANDS/DIVISIONS/AFFILIATES:

Teliris VirtuaLive Telepresence
Teliris Custom Telepresence
Teliris Express Telepresence
Teliris Personal Telepresence
Teliris Telepresence Gateway
Teliris InterACT TouchTable
Teliris InterACT TouchWall
Teliris InterACT Easel

## CONTACTS:

*Note: Officers with more than one job title may be intentionally listed here more than once.*

Marc Trachtenberg, CEO
Bob Johnson, Sr. VP-Mktg.
Steve Gage, Exec. VP-R&D
Bob Johnson, Sr. VP-Prod. Mgmt.
Shanley Stern Gravel, Media Contact
Martyn Lewis, Chmn.-European Union
Jim Kaufold, Sr. VP-Global Sales
Jim Oldham, VP-North American Sales
Rodney Rogers, Exec. Chmn.
Tony Smith, Managing Dir.-European Union

**Phone:** 212-490-1065 **Fax:**
**Toll-Free:**
**Address:** 55 Broadway, 14th Fl., New York, NY 10006 US

## GROWTH PLANS/SPECIAL FEATURES:

Teliris offers corporate video conferencing services. It has four core products comprising Teliris VirtuaLive Telepresence, its core technology, and three other products launched in May 2008: Teliris Custom Telepresence, Teliris Express Telepresence and Teliris Personal Telepresence. VirtuaLive comprises a suite of installed technologies incorporated into a corporate meeting room. It includes anywhere from 3-6 screens, either 52-inches or 65-inches in size, and can accommodate up to 28 persons per room. Its broadcast is 720p high definition (HD) quality images at 60 frames per second (fps). The Custom offering allows clients to install Teliris' telepresence offerings in non-traditional settings, such as oil rigs, factory floors, R&D labs and large conference rooms. The Express telepresence offering is a small-scale offering that offers two to three 46-inch screens that can accommodate 4-6 people. The broadcast is HD quality, but only 30 fps. Lastly, the Personal offering is a single 40-inch HD display offering 30 fps for one on one communication. All of the firm's products feature the Teliris Telepresence Gateway, making them compatible with other standards-based telepresence and videoconferencing systems. Besides products, Teliris offers managed telepresence services; Teliris Working Practices, a compilation of best telepresence practices; and Teliris Telepresence Design & Implementation Services. Co-headquartered in New York and London, the firm operates as Teliris, Inc. in the U.S. and as Teliris Ltd. in the U.K. It has deployments in 30 countries, serving clients including the Royal Bank of Scotland, GlaxoSmithKline and Merck. In June 2008, the company launched three new interactive technologies for its telepresence products. Teliris InterACT TouchTable and Teliris InterACT TouchWall allow users to display documents, audiovisual materials and presentations that viewers in all locations can share and manipulate freely. Additionally, Teliris InterACT Easel offers users a shareable virtual whiteboard or flip-board that allows all viewers to create and edit content.

## FINANCIALS:

**Sales and profits are in thousands of dollars—add 000 to get the full amount. 2008 Note: Financial information for 2008 was not available for all companies at press time.**

| | | |
|---|---|---|
| 2008 Sales: $ | 2008 Profits: $ | **U.S. Stock Ticker: Private** |
| 2007 Sales: $ | 2007 Profits: $ | **Int'l Ticker:** Int'l Exchange: |
| 2006 Sales: $ | 2006 Profits: $ | Employees: |
| 2005 Sales: $ | 2005 Profits: $ | Fiscal Year Ends: |
| 2004 Sales: $ | 2004 Profits: $ | Parent Company: |

## SALARIES/BENEFITS:

| | | | | |
|---|---|---|---|---|
| Pension Plan: | ESOP Stock Plan: | Profit Sharing: | Top Exec. Salary: $ | Bonus: $ |
| Savings Plan: | Stock Purch. Plan: | | Second Exec. Salary: $ | Bonus: $ |

## OTHER THOUGHTS:

**Apparent Women Officers or Directors**: 1
**Hot Spot for Advancement for Women/Minorities**:

## LOCATIONS: ("Y" = Yes)

| West: | Southwest: | Midwest: | Southeast: | Northeast: | International: |
|---|---|---|---|---|---|
| | | | | Y | Y |

# TEPPCO PARTNERS LP

www.teppco.com

**Industry Group Code:** 422720 **Ranks within this company's industry group:** Sales: 1 Profits: 2

| **Management:** | | **Sales/Marketing:** | | **Liberal Arts:** | | **Information Systems:** | | **Professionals:** | | **Technical/Scientific:** | |
|---|---|---|---|---|---|---|---|---|---|---|---|
| Mgmt. Trainees: | | Mktg. Professionals: | Y | Gen. Writing/Editing: | | Info. Management: | Y | Finance/Accounting: | Y | Engineers, Elec.: | Y |
| Experienced Mgmt.: | Y | Retail Sales: | | Technical Writing: | | Software Dev.: | | Law: | Y | Engineers, Other: | Y |
| Int'l Business: | | Commercial/Industrial: | Y | Graphic Arts/Photog.: | | Hardware Dev.: | | HR/Other: | Y | Health/Lab: | |
| MBA Graduates: | Y | Sales Trainees: | Y | Music: | | Systems Integration: | | Training: | Y | Scientists/Research: | |
| | | Advertising Pros.: | | Broadcasting: | | Consulting/Other: | | Health Care: | | Petroleum/Chemicals: | Y |
| | | | | Other: | | | | Consulting: | | Math/Other: | |

## TYPES OF BUSINESS:

Pipelines
Crude Oil Storage, Gathering & Marketing
LPG Transportation & Storage
Lubricant & Chemical Distribution
Natural Gas Gathering & Transportation
Marine Import Terminals

## BRANDS/DIVISIONS/AFFILIATES:

TE Products
TCTM
TEPPCO Midstream
Seaway Crude Pipeline Co.
Centennial Pipeline, LLC
Mont Belvieu Storage Partners, LP
Jonah Gas Gathering Co.
Texas Eastern Products Pipeline Co., LLC

## CONTACTS: *Note: Officers with more than one job title may be intentionally listed here more than once.*

Jerry E. Thompson, CEO
Jerry E. Thompson, Pres.
William G. Manias, CFO/VP
Patricia A. Totten, General Counsel/VP/Sec.
John N. Goodpasture, VP-Corp. Dev.
Samuel N. Brown, VP-Commercial Downstream
J. Michael Cockrell, Sr. VP-Commercial Upstream
Murray H. Hutchison, Chmn.

**Phone:** 713-381-3636 **Fax:** 713-759-3957
**Toll-Free:** 800-877-3636
**Address:** 1100 Louisiana St., Houston, TX 77002 US

## GROWTH PLANS/SPECIAL FEATURES:

TEPPCO Partners, LP is one of the largest common carriers of refined products and liquefied petroleum gases (LPGs) in the U.S., with over 11,600 miles of pipeline. The company also owns and operates petrochemical and natural gas liquids (NGLs) pipelines; engages in crude oil transportation, storage, gathering and marketing; and owns and operates natural gas gathering systems. The firm operates in four segments: downstream, upstream, midstream and marine services segment. The downstream segment engages in the transportation, marketing and storage of refined products, LPGs and petrochemicals. The upstream segment gathers, transports, markets and stores crude oil; and distributes lubrication oil and specialty chemicals. The midstream segment gathers natural gas and fractions and transports NGLs. The marine services segment consists of the marine transportation of crude oil, asphalt and other heated oil products by tow boats and barges. TEPPCO's 4,700-mile products pipeline system includes 35 storage facilities and 63 delivery locations. The company's facilities also include marine import terminals at Texas City and Beaumont, Texas and Providence, Rhode Island, as well as two fractionation facilities in Weld County, Colorado. The firm owns a 50% interest in Seaway Crude Pipeline Co., which includes a 500-mile pipeline and 3.3 million barrels of storage; Centennial Pipeline, LLC; Mont Belvieu Storage Partners, LP; Jonah Gas Gathering Co.; and an undivided ownership interests in the Basin Pipeline. The company operates through subsidiaries TE Products; TCTM; and TEPPCO Midstream. Texas Eastern Products Pipeline Co., LLC serves as the firm's general partner. Recent acquisitions include seven push boats and 17 barges from Horizon Maritime, L.L.C. and 42 push boats and 89 barges from Houma, Louisiana-based Cenac Towing, Inc. and Cenac Offshore, LLC.

The company offers its employees medical and dental insurance; a retirement savings plan; life and accident insurance; short- and long-term disability insurance; and an employee assistance program.

## FINANCIALS: **Sales and profits are in thousands of dollars—add 000 to get the full amount. 2008 Note: Financial information for 2008 was not available for all companies at press time.**

| | | |
|---|---|---|
| 2008 Sales: $13,532,900 | 2008 Profits: $193,600 | **U.S. Stock Ticker: TPP** |
| 2007 Sales: $9,658,060 | 2007 Profits: $279,180 | **Int'l Ticker:** Int'l Exchange: |
| 2006 Sales: $9,607,485 | 2006 Profits: $202,051 | Employees: 2,250 |
| 2005 Sales: $8,605,034 | 2005 Profits: $162,551 | Fiscal Year Ends: 12/31 |
| 2004 Sales: $5,948,090 | 2004 Profits: $138,548 | Parent Company: |

## SALARIES/BENEFITS:

| | | | | |
|---|---|---|---|---|
| Pension Plan: | ESOP Stock Plan: | Profit Sharing: | Top Exec. Salary: $463,500 | Bonus: $281,000 |
| Savings Plan: Y | Stock Purch. Plan: | | Second Exec. Salary: $267,750 | Bonus: $105,500 |

## OTHER THOUGHTS:

**Apparent Women Officers or Directors**: 1
**Hot Spot for Advancement for Women/Minorities**:

## LOCATIONS: ("Y" = Yes)

| West: | Southwest: | Midwest: | Southeast: | Northeast: | International: |
|---|---|---|---|---|---|
| Y | Y | Y | Y | Y | |

# TERREMARK WORLDWIDE INC

www.terremark.com

**Industry Group Code:** 514191 **Ranks within this company's industry group:** Sales: 3 Profits: 2

| Management: | | Sales/Marketing: | | Liberal Arts: | | Information Systems: | | Professionals: | | Technical/Scientific: | |
|---|---|---|---|---|---|---|---|---|---|---|---|
| Mgmt. Trainees: | | Mktg. Professionals: | Y | Gen. Writing/Editing: | | Info. Management: | Y | Finance/Accounting: | Y | Engineers, Elec.: | |
| Experienced Mgmt.: | Y | Retail Sales: | | Technical Writing: | | Software Dev.: | | Law: | Y | Engineers, Other: | |
| Int'l Business: | Y | Commercial/Industrial: | Y | Graphic Arts/Photog.: | | Hardware Dev.: | | HR/Other: | Y | Health/Lab: | |
| MBA Graduates: | Y | Sales Trainees: | Y | Music: | | Systems Integration: | | Training: | Y | Scientists/Research: | |
| | | Advertising Pros.: | Y | Broadcasting: | | Consulting/Other: | | Health Care: | | Petroleum/Chemicals: | |
| | | | | Other: | | | | Consulting: | | Math/Other: | |

## TYPES OF BUSINESS:

Internet Exchange Points
Managed Services

## BRANDS/DIVISIONS/AFFILIATES:

Infinistructure
Enterprise Cloud
Peering Service
Cross-Connect Service
Exchange Point Services Platform
Data Return, LLC

## CONTACTS: *Note: Officers with more than one job title may be intentionally listed here more than once.*

Manuel D. Medina, CEO
Manuel D. Medina, Pres.
Jose A. Segrera, CFO
Barry Field, Sr. VP-U.S. Commercial Sales
Adam T. Smith, Chief Legal Officer
Joseph R. Wright, Jr., Vice Chmn.
Jamie Dos Santos, CEO-Terremark Federal Group
Marvin Wheeler, Pres., U.S. Commercial Bus. Unit
Agustin Abalo, Pres., Latin American Bus. Unit
Manuel D. Medina, Chmn.
Herman Oggel, Pres., European Bus. Unit

| **Phone:** 305-856-3200 | **Fax:** 305-856-8190 |
|---|---|
| **Toll-Free:** | |
| **Address:** 2 S. Biscayne Blvd., Ste. 2900, Miami, FL 33131 US | |

## GROWTH PLANS/SPECIAL FEATURES:

Terremark Worldwide, Inc. is a global provider of managed IT infrastructure services leveraging data centers throughout the U.S., Europe and Latin America and access to carrier-neutral network connectivity. Terremark provides managed hosting, collocation, connectivity, disaster recovery, security and cloud computing services. As a carrier-neutral provider, the company does not own or operate its own network and consequently its interconnection services enable its customers to exchange network traffic through direct connection with each other or through peering connections with multiple parties. Terremark's managed services are designed to support complex, transaction-intensive, mission-critical, line-of-business and Internet facing applications. It provides managed hosting services on dedicated servers located within its facilities or virtualized servers through its Infinistructure and Enterprise Cloud platforms. Additionally, the company provides managed storage and tape backup services. Terremark's managed services include device management; operating system and application platform management; patch management; monitoring services; problem and incident management; data storage; backup and restoration; security services, such as managed firewalls, intrusion detection, anti-virus services and DDoS (distributed denial of service attack) protection and mitigation; database administration; application performance tuning; software installation and configuration; application testing; and deployment services. The firm has more than 385,000 square feet of total data center space. Terremark's Peering Services enable the secure exchange of data, deliver Internet Protocol- (IP) based services and provide content between networks. Its Cross-Connect Service enables customers to share data with any other client connected to its Exchange Point Services Platform. In May 2007, Terremark acquired Data Return, LLC, a provider of enterprise-class technology hosting solutions, for $85 million.

Terremark offers its employees an educational reimbursement program; a transit discount program; an employee assistance program; credit union membership; an employee referral program; flexible spending accounts; domestic partner benefits; and medical, dental, vision, life and disability insurance.

## FINANCIALS: **Sales and profits are in thousands of dollars—add 000 to get the full amount. 2008 Note: Financial information for 2008 was not available for all companies at press time.**

| | | |
|---|---|---|
| 2008 Sales: $187,414 | 2008 Profits: $-42,228 | **U.S. Stock Ticker: TMRK** |
| 2007 Sales: $100,948 | 2007 Profits: $-14,952 | **Int'l Ticker:** Int'l Exchange: |
| 2006 Sales: $62,529 | 2006 Profits: $-37,149 | Employees: 604 |
| 2005 Sales: $48,148 | 2005 Profits: $-9,859 | Fiscal Year Ends: 3/31 |
| 2004 Sales: $18,200 | 2004 Profits: $-22,500 | Parent Company: |

## SALARIES/BENEFITS:

| | | | | |
|---|---|---|---|---|
| Pension Plan: | ESOP Stock Plan: | Profit Sharing: | Top Exec. Salary: $358,519 | Bonus: $ |
| Savings Plan: Y | Stock Purch. Plan: | | Second Exec. Salary: $350,000 | Bonus: $103,637 |

## OTHER THOUGHTS:

**Apparent Women Officers or Directors**: 1
**Hot Spot for Advancement for Women/Minorities**:

## LOCATIONS: ("Y" = Yes)

| West: | Southwest: | Midwest: | Southeast: | Northeast: | International: |
|---|---|---|---|---|---|
| Y | | | Y | Y | Y |

# THERAGENICS CORP

www.theragenics.com

**Industry Group Code:** 339113 **Ranks within this company's industry group:** Sales: 38 Profits: 30

| Management: | | Sales/Marketing: | | Liberal Arts: | | Information Systems: | | Professionals: | | Technical/Scientific: | |
|---|---|---|---|---|---|---|---|---|---|---|---|
| Mgmt. Trainees: | | Mktg. Professionals: | Y | Gen. Writing/Editing: | | Info. Management: | Y | Finance/Accounting: | Y | Engineers, Elec.: | Y |
| Experienced Mgmt.: | Y | Retail Sales: | | Technical Writing: | Y | Software Dev.: | | Law: | Y | Engineers, Other: | Y |
| Int'l Business: | Y | Commercial/Industrial: | Y | Graphic Arts/Photog.: | | Hardware Dev.: | | HR/Other: | Y | Health/Lab: | Y |
| MBA Graduates: | Y | Sales Trainees: | Y | Music: | | Systems Integration: | | Training: | Y | Scientists/Research: | Y |
| | | Advertising Pros.: | | Broadcasting: | | Consulting/Other: | | Health Care: | Y | Petroleum/Chemicals: | |
| | | | | Other: | | | | Consulting: | | Math/Other: | Y |

## TYPES OF BUSINESS:

Medical Devices
Surgical Products

## BRANDS/DIVISIONS/AFFILIATES:

TheraSeed
Galt Medical Corp.
CP Medical Corp.
I-seed
NeedleTech Products, Inc.

## CONTACTS:
*Note: Officers with more than one job title may be intentionally listed here more than once.*

M. Christine Jacobs, CEO
M. Christine Jacobs, Pres.
Frank J. Tarallo, CFO
Bruce W. Smith, Corp. Sec.
Bruce W. Smith, Exec. VP-Strategy & Bus. Dev.
Frank J. Tarallo, Treas.
Michael Lang, Pres., Galt Medical
Patrick J. Ferguson, Pres., CP Medical
R. Michael O'Bannon, Exec. VP-Organizational Dev.
M. Christine Jacobs, Chmn.

| Phone: 770-271-0233 | Fax: |
|---|---|
| Toll-Free: | |
| Address: 5203 Bristol Industrial Way, Buford, GA 30518 US | |

## GROWTH PLANS/SPECIAL FEATURES:

Theragenics Corp. is a medical device company serving the cancer treatment and surgical markets. The company operates in two segments, the brachytherapy seed business and the surgical products business. The brachytherapy seed business segment produces, markets and sells TheraSeed, the firm's premier palladium-103 prostate cancer treatment device; I-seed, its iodone-125 based prostrate cancer treatment device; and other related products and services. Theragenics is the world's largest producer of palladium-103, the radioactive isotope that supplies the therapeutic radiation for its TheraSeed device. TheraSeed is an implant the size of a grain of rice that is used primarily in treating localized prostate cancer with a one-time, minimally invasive procedure. The implant emits radiation within the immediate prostate area, killing the tumor while sparing surrounding organs from significant radiation exposure. Physicians, hospitals and other healthcare providers, primarily located in the U.S., utilize the TheraSeed device. The majority of TheraSeed sales are channeled through one third-party distributor. The surgical products business segment consists of wound closure and vascular access products. Wound closure include sutures, needles and other surgical products with applications in, among other areas, urology, veterinary, cardiology, orthopedics, plastic surgery and dental. Vascular access includes introducers and guidewires used in the interventional radiology, interventional cardiology and vascular surgery markets. The surgical products business sells its devices and components primarily to original equipment manufacturers (OEM) and a network of distributors. Theragenics' subsidiaries, CP Medical Corp. and Galt Medical Corp., accounted for roughly 46% of revenue in 2007. In July 2008, the company acquired NeedleTech Products, Inc., a manufacturer of specialty needles and related medical devices, for $48.7 million.

The company offers its employees medical, dental and life insurance; short- and long-term disability protection; a 401(k) plan; an employee stock purchase plan; and an on-site wellness center.

## FINANCIALS:
**Sales and profits are in thousands of dollars—add 000 to get the full amount. 2008 Note: Financial information for 2008 was not available for all companies at press time.**

| | | |
|---|---|---|
| 2008 Sales: $67,358 | 2008 Profits: $-58,540 | **U.S. Stock Ticker: TGX** |
| 2007 Sales: $62,210 | 2007 Profits: $5,635 | **Int'l Ticker:** Int'l Exchange: |
| 2006 Sales: $54,096 | 2006 Profits: $6,865 | Employees: 338 |
| 2005 Sales: $44,270 | 2005 Profits: $-29,006 | Fiscal Year Ends: 12/31 |
| 2004 Sales: $33,338 | 2004 Profits: $-4,310 | Parent Company: |

## SALARIES/BENEFITS:

| | | | | |
|---|---|---|---|---|
| Pension Plan: | ESOP Stock Plan: | Profit Sharing: | Top Exec. Salary: $511,500 | Bonus: $35,000 |
| Savings Plan: Y | Stock Purch. Plan: Y | | Second Exec. Salary: $270,000 | Bonus: $20,000 |

## OTHER THOUGHTS:

**Apparent Women Officers or Directors**: 1
**Hot Spot for Advancement for Women/Minorities**: Y

## LOCATIONS: ("Y" = Yes)

| West: | Southwest: | Midwest: | Southeast: | Northeast: | International: |
|---|---|---|---|---|---|
| Y | Y | | Y | | |

# THIRD WAVE TECHNOLOGIES INC

**www.twt.com**

**Industry Group Code:** 325413 **Ranks within this company's industry group:** Sales: 12 Profits:

| Management: | | Sales/Marketing: | | Liberal Arts: | | Information Systems: | | Professionals: | | Technical/Scientific: | |
|---|---|---|---|---|---|---|---|---|---|---|---|
| Mgmt. Trainees: | | Mktg. Professionals: | Y | Gen. Writing/Editing: | | Info. Management: | Y | Finance/Accounting: | Y | Engineers, Elec.: | |
| Experienced Mgmt.: | Y | Retail Sales: | | Technical Writing: | Y | Software Dev.: | Y | Law: | Y | Engineers, Other: | Y |
| Int'l Business: | | Commercial/Industrial: | Y | Graphic Arts/Photog.: | | Hardware Dev.: | Y | HR/Other: | Y | Health/Lab: | Y |
| MBA Graduates: | Y | Sales Trainees: | Y | Music: | | Systems Integration: | | Training: | Y | Scientists/Research: | Y |
| | | Advertising Pros.: | | Broadcasting: | | Consulting/Other: | | Health Care: | Y | Petroleum/Chemicals: | |
| | | | | Other: | | | | Consulting: | | Math/Other: | Y |

## TYPES OF BUSINESS:

Genetic Analysis Products
Assays

## BRANDS/DIVISIONS/AFFILIATES:

Invader
Cleavase
Invader InPlex
Invader Plus
Universal Invader Program
qInvader

## CONTACTS:

*Note: Officers with more than one job title may be intentionally listed here more than once.*

Kevin T. Conroy, CEO

**Phone:** 608-273-8933 **Fax:** 608-273-8618
**Toll-Free:** 888-898-2357
**Address:** 502 S. Rosa Rd., Madison, WI 53719 US

## GROWTH PLANS/SPECIAL FEATURES:

Third Wave Technologies, Inc., a subsidiary of Hologic, Inc., develops, manufactures and markets genetic analysis products for clinical diagnostics and studies. Its patented genetic analysis platform, Invader, offers several advantages over conventional genetic analysis technologies. Invader relies upon the company's proprietary Cleavase enzyme for testing rather than using a complex copying technique known as a polymerase chain reaction (PCR). Available in ready-to-use formats, Third Wave's products are compatible with existing automation processes and detection platforms. These advantages make the Invader platform a convenient solution for genetic analysis, with applications ranging from disease discovery to patient care, including large-scale disease association studies, drug response marker profiling and molecular diagnostics. The company's Invader Plus product relies on a combination of the Invader platform with traditional PCR amplification. Developed in collaboration with 3M, the Invader InPlex product combines Invader chemistry with 3M's microfluidic technology, which helps to improve speed, efficiency and ease of use. Finally, qInvader detects and quantifies nucleic acids as a tool to understanding the development of cancer and other diseases. In addition to Invader products, Third Wave offers assays for cardiovascular disease and deep-vein thrombosis detection, as well as tests relating to animal and plant genetics. The company's headquarters are located in Madison, Wisconsin. In July 2008, the company became a wholly-owned subsidiary of Hologic, Inc. In 2008, the company acquired Agilent Technologies Inc.'s Full Velocity portfolio of patents, which cover nucleic acid amplification technology, for an undisclosed amount.

Third Wave employees receive incentive compensation bonuses or commissions, medical and dental insurance, life insurance, flexible benefits, on-site dry cleaning pickup, casual attire and free popcorn.

## FINANCIALS:

**Sales and profits are in thousands of dollars—add 000 to get the full amount. 2008 Note: Financial information for 2008 was not available for all companies at press time.**

| | | |
|---|---|---|
| 2008 Sales: $ | 2008 Profits: $ | **U.S. Stock Ticker: Subsidiary** |
| 2007 Sales: $31,100 | 2007 Profits: $ | **Int'l Ticker:** Int'l Exchange: |
| 2006 Sales: $28,027 | 2006 Profits: $-18,887 | Employees: 154 |
| 2005 Sales: $23,906 | 2005 Profits: $-22,346 | Fiscal Year Ends: 12/31 |
| 2004 Sales: $46,493 | 2004 Profits: $-1,942 | Parent Company: HOLOGIC INC |

## SALARIES/BENEFITS:

| | | | | |
|---|---|---|---|---|
| Pension Plan: | ESOP Stock Plan: | Profit Sharing: | Top Exec. Salary: $422,917 | Bonus: $671,241 |
| Savings Plan: Y | Stock Purch. Plan: | | Second Exec. Salary: $274,583 | Bonus: $360,666 |

## OTHER THOUGHTS:

**Apparent Women Officers or Directors**: 1
**Hot Spot for Advancement for Women/Minorities**:

## LOCATIONS: ("Y" = Yes)

| West: | Southwest: | Midwest: | Southeast: | Northeast: | International: |
|---|---|---|---|---|---|
| | | Y | | | |

# THOMAS WEISEL PARTNERS GROUP INC

www.tweisel.com

**Industry Group Code:** 523110 **Ranks within this company's industry group:** Sales: 3 Profits: 1

| Management: | | Sales/Marketing: | | Liberal Arts: | | Information Systems: | | Professionals: | | Technical/Scientific: | |
|---|---|---|---|---|---|---|---|---|---|---|---|
| Mgmt. Trainees: | | Mktg. Professionals: | | Gen. Writing/Editing: | | Info. Management: | Y | Finance/Accounting: | Y | Engineers, Elec.: | |
| Experienced Mgmt.: | Y | Retail Sales: | | Technical Writing: | | Software Dev.: | | Law: | Y | Engineers, Other: | |
| Int'l Business: | Y | Commercial/Industrial: | | Graphic Arts/Photog.: | | Hardware Dev.: | | HR/Other: | Y | Health/Lab: | |
| MBA Graduates: | Y | Sales Trainees: | | Music: | | Systems Integration: | | Training: | Y | Scientists/Research: | |
| | | Advertising Pros.: | | Broadcasting: | | Consulting/Other: | | Health Care: | | Petroleum/Chemicals: | |
| | | | | Other: | | | | Consulting: | | Math/Other: | |

## TYPES OF BUSINESS:

Investment Banking
Securities Brokerage
Equity Research
Asset Management
Strategic Advisory Services

## BRANDS/DIVISIONS/AFFILIATES:

Thomas Weisel Capital Management LLC
Thomas Weisel Healthcare Venture Partners LLC
Thomas Weisel Global Growth Partners LLC
Thomas Weisel Venture Partners LLC
Thomas Weisel Asset Management
Q Street Management LLC
Thomas Weisel Partners Insurance Services LLC
Westwind Partners

## CONTACTS: *Note: Officers with more than one job title may be intentionally listed here more than once.*

Thomas Weisel, CEO
Lionel F. Conacher, COO
Lionel F. Conacher, Pres.
Shaugn Stanley, CFO
Tom Carbeau, Head-Institutional Sales
R. Keith Gay, Head-Research
Mark Fisher, General Counsel
Anthony Stais, Head-Trading
William McLeod, Co-Head-Investment Banking
Brad Raymond, Co-Head-Investment Banking
Amy Freedman, COO-Investment Banking
Thomas Weisel, Chmn.

| | |
|---|---|
| **Phone:** 415-364-2500 | **Fax:** 415-364-2695 |
| **Toll-Free:** 800-933-3445 | |
| **Address:** 1 Montgomery St., San Francisco, CA 94101 US | |

## GROWTH PLANS/SPECIAL FEATURES:

Thomas Weisel Partners Group, Inc. (TWPG), headquartered in San Francisco, is an investment banking firm specializing in growth sectors including the technology, healthcare and consumer sectors. The group specifically focuses on servicing U.S. and international emerging growth companies and institutional investors. The firm has offices in Baltimore, Boston, Chicago, Cleveland, New York, Portland, Silicon Valley, Toronto, Montreal, Zurich, London and Mumbai. TWPG operates through the following channels: Investment Banking, Institutional Brokerage, Equity Research and Asset Management. The Banking group provides advisory services for companies in the technology, healthcare, consumer and alternative energy sectors. The Brokerage sector serves institutional and high-net-worth investors with trading advice and customized services focusing on capital preservation. Asset Management, operated primarily by Thomas Weisel Capital Management LLC, is composed of private equity investing, growth portfolios and distribution management. Additionally, the firm oversees a research department with approximately 40 analysts, focusing primarily on equity research and publicly traded companies. In January 2008, the company acquired Westwind Partners, an investment bank focused on energy and mining markets.

Employees are offered medical, dental and vision insurance; life and disability insurance; a 401(k) plan; an employee assistance program; and 529 college savings plan.

## FINANCIALS: **Sales and profits are in thousands of dollars—add 000 to get the full amount. 2008 Note: Financial information for 2008 was not available for all companies at press time.**

| | | |
|---|---|---|
| 2008 Sales: $195,465 | 2008 Profits: $-158,569 | **U.S. Stock Ticker: TWPG** |
| 2007 Sales: $289,049 | 2007 Profits: $ 20 | **Int'l Ticker:** Int'l Exchange: |
| 2006 Sales: $276,317 | 2006 Profits: $34,921 | Employees: 650 |
| 2005 Sales: $250,886 | 2005 Profits: $-7,058 | Fiscal Year Ends: 12/31 |
| 2004 Sales: $283,410 | 2004 Profits: $22,682 | Parent Company: |

## SALARIES/BENEFITS:

| | | | | |
|---|---|---|---|---|
| Pension Plan: | ESOP Stock Plan: | Profit Sharing: | Top Exec. Salary: $200,000 | Bonus: $750,000 |
| Savings Plan: Y | Stock Purch. Plan: | | Second Exec. Salary: $200,000 | Bonus: $700,000 |

## OTHER THOUGHTS:

**Apparent Women Officers or Directors**: 1
**Hot Spot for Advancement for Women/Minorities**:

## LOCATIONS: ("Y" = Yes)

| West: | Southwest: | Midwest: | Southeast: | Northeast: | International: |
|---|---|---|---|---|---|
| Y | | | | Y | Y |

# THORATEC CORPORATION

www.thoratec.com

**Industry Group Code:** 339113 **Ranks within this company's industry group:** Sales: 14 Profits: 32

| Management: | | Sales/Marketing: | | Liberal Arts: | | Information Systems: | | Professionals: | | Technical/Scientific: | |
|---|---|---|---|---|---|---|---|---|---|---|---|
| Mgmt. Trainees: | | Mktg. Professionals: | Y | Gen. Writing/Editing: | | Info. Management: | Y | Finance/Accounting: | Y | Engineers, Elec.: | Y |
| Experienced Mgmt.: | Y | Retail Sales: | | Technical Writing: | Y | Software Dev.: | Y | Law: | Y | Engineers, Other: | Y |
| Int'l Business: | Y | Commercial/Industrial: | Y | Graphic Arts/Photog.: | | Hardware Dev.: | Y | HR/Other: | Y | Health/Lab: | Y |
| MBA Graduates: | Y | Sales Trainees: | Y | Music: | | Systems Integration: | | Training: | Y | Scientists/Research: | Y |
| | | Advertising Pros.: | | Broadcasting: | | Consulting/Other: | | Health Care: | Y | Petroleum/Chemicals: | |
| | | | | Other: | | | | Consulting: | | Math/Other: | Y |

## TYPES OF BUSINESS:

Medical Equipment-Ventricular Assistance Devices
Circulatory Support Products
Vascular Graft Products
Point-of-Care Diagnostic Products

## BRANDS/DIVISIONS/AFFILIATES:

Thoratec Paracorporeal Ventricular Assist Device
Thoratec Implantable Ventricular Assist Device
HeartMate Left Ventricular Assist System
HeartMate II Left Ventricular Assist System
CentriMag Blood Pumping System
International Technidyne Corporation

## CONTACTS: *Note: Officers with more than one job title may be intentionally listed here more than once.*

Gerhard F. (Gary) Burbach, CEO
Gerhard F. (Gary) Burbach, Pres.
David V. Smith, CFO/Exec. VP
David A. Lehman, General Counsel/VP
J. Donald Hill, Vice Chmn.
Lawrence Cohen, Pres., International Technidyne Corporation
Neil F. Dimick, Chmn.

| | |
|---|---|
| **Phone:** 925-847-8600 | **Fax:** 925-847-8574 |
| **Toll-Free:** 800-528-2577 | |
| **Address:** 6035 Stoneridge Dr., Pleasanton, CA 94588 US | |

## GROWTH PLANS/SPECIAL FEATURES:

Thoratec Corporation is a leading global manufacturer of circulatory support products for the treatment of heart failure (HF). The company operates through two divisions: Cardiovascular and International Technidyne Corporation (ITC). Thoratec's primary Cardiovascular product lines are its ventricular assist devices (VADs), comprised of the Thoratec Paracorporeal Ventricular Assist Device (PVAD), the Thoratec Implantable Ventricular Assist Device (IVAD), the HeartMate Left Ventricular Assist System (HeartMate XVE) and the HeartMate II Left Ventricular Assist System (HeartMate II). The PVAD, IVAD and the HeartMate XVE are approved by the U.S. Food and Drug Administration (FDA) and CE Mark approved in Europe. The HeartMate II is CE Mark approved in Europe and is in a Phase II trial in the U.S. Thoratec additionally markets the CentriMag Blood Pumping System for acute HF and a vascular access graft for renal dialysis. Collectively, the firm's mechanical circulatory support devices are FDA-approved for bridge-to-transplant, long-term support for patients suffering from advanced stage HF who are not eligible for heart transplantation, post-cardiotomy myocardial recovery and support during cardiac surgery. It currently markets VADs that may be placed inside or outside the body; that can be used for left, right or biventricular support; and that are suitable for patients of varying sizes and ages. Thoratec estimates that doctors have implanted more than 11,000 of its devices, primarily for patients awaiting a heart transplant or those who require permanent support. The company's ITC division develops, manufactures and markets two product lines: Point-of-care diagnostic test systems for hospital point-of-care and alternate site point-of-care markets, including diagnostic test systems that monitor blood coagulation, blood gas/electrolytes, oxygenation and chemistry status; and incision products, including devices used to obtain a patient's blood sample.

Thoratec offers its employees education assistance; employee wellness education; fitness facility discounts; and medical, dental, vision, disability, AD&D and life insurance.

## FINANCIALS: **Sales and profits are in thousands of dollars—add 000 to get the full amount. 2008 Note: Financial information for 2008 was not available for all companies at press time.**

| | | |
|---|---|---|
| 2008 Sales: $313,564 | 2008 Profits: $22,532 | **U.S. Stock Ticker: THOR** |
| 2007 Sales: $234,780 | 2007 Profits: $3,235 | **Int'l Ticker:** Int'l Exchange: |
| 2006 Sales: $214,133 | 2006 Profits: $3,973 | Employees: 1,164 |
| 2005 Sales: $201,712 | 2005 Profits: $13,198 | Fiscal Year Ends: 12/31 |
| 2004 Sales: $172,341 | 2004 Profits: $3,564 | Parent Company: |

## SALARIES/BENEFITS:

| | | | | |
|---|---|---|---|---|
| Pension Plan: | ESOP Stock Plan: | Profit Sharing: | Top Exec. Salary: $400,000 | Bonus: $195,760 |
| Savings Plan: Y | Stock Purch. Plan: Y | | Second Exec. Salary: $340,000 | Bonus: $161,126 |

## OTHER THOUGHTS:

**Apparent Women Officers or Directors**: 1
**Hot Spot for Advancement for Women/Minorities**: Y

## LOCATIONS: ("Y" = Yes)

| West: | Southwest: | Midwest: | Southeast: | Northeast: | International: |
|---|---|---|---|---|---|
| Y | | Y | | Y | Y |

# THQ INC

www.thq.com

**Industry Group Code:** 511208 **Ranks within this company's industry group:** Sales: 1 Profits: 1

| Management: | | Sales/Marketing: | | Liberal Arts: | | Information Systems: | | Professionals: | | Technical/Scientific: | |
|---|---|---|---|---|---|---|---|---|---|---|---|
| Mgmt. Trainees: | | Mktg. Professionals: | Y | Gen. Writing/Editing: | Y | Info. Management: | Y | Finance/Accounting: | Y | Engineers, Elec.: | Y |
| Experienced Mgmt.: | Y | Retail Sales: | | Technical Writing: | Y | Software Dev.: | Y | Law: | Y | Engineers, Other: | |
| Int'l Business: | Y | Commercial/Industrial: | Y | Graphic Arts/Photog.: | Y | Hardware Dev.: | | HR/Other: | Y | Health/Lab: | |
| MBA Graduates: | Y | Sales Trainees: | Y | Music: | Y | Systems Integration: | | Training: | Y | Scientists/Research: | |
| | | Advertising Pros.: | | Broadcasting: | | Consulting/Other: | | Health Care: | | Petroleum/Chemicals: | |
| | | | | Other: | Y | | | Consulting: | | Math/Other: | |

## TYPES OF BUSINESS:

Software-Video Games
Mobile Gaming Software

## BRANDS/DIVISIONS/AFFILIATES:

Relic Entertainment
Vigil Games
Paradigm Entertainment
Kaos Studios
Destroy All Humans!
THQ Wireless Inc
Big Huge Games
ICE Entertainment

## CONTACTS: *Note: Officers with more than one job title may be intentionally listed here more than once.*

Brian J. Farrell, CEO
Brian J. Farrell, Pres.
Colin Slade, CFO/Exec. VP
Bob Aniello, Sr. VP-Worldwide Mktg.
Bill Goodmen, Exec. VP-Human Resources
Bill Goodmen, Exec. VP-Admin.
James M. Kennedy, Sec./Exec. VP-Bus. & Legal Affairs
Liz Pieri, VP-Mktg. Comm.
Julie MacMedan, VP-Investor Rel.
Jack Sorensen, Exec. VP-Worldwide Studios
Doug Clemmer, Pres., THQ Wireless, Inc.
Marko Hein, Gen. Manager-THQ Int'l GmbH
Brian J. Farrell, Chmn.
Ian Curran, Exec. VP-Int'l

| | |
|---|---|
| **Phone:** 818-871-5000 | **Fax:** 818-871-7590 |
| **Toll-Free:** | |
| **Address:** 29903 Agoura Rd., Aguora Hills, CA 91301 US | |

## GROWTH PLANS/SPECIAL FEATURES:

THQ, Inc. is a worldwide publisher, marketer and developer of proprietary and licensed video game software for Sony PSP, PlayStation 2 and PlayStation 3; Microsoft Xbox and Xbox 360;, Nintendo GameCube, Game Boy Advance, DS and Wii; PCs; and mobile devices. It develops titles through 16 development studios under a new strategy called Studio located in the U.S., Australia, Canada and the U.K. The strategy is designed to leverage resources across the entire organization to benefit each of the separate studios. Its studios include Relic Entertainment; Sandblast Games; Locomotive Games; Mass Media; Heavy Iron Studios; Incinerator Studios; Concrete Games; Rainbow Studios; Vigil Games; Paradigm Entertainment; Volition, Inc.; Kaos Studios; Helixe; Juice Games; THQ Studio Australia; and Blue Tongue Entertainment. Games based on the company's own intellectual property include Company of Heroes, Destroy All Humans!, Juiced, MX vs. ATV, Red Faction and Saints Row. Its games based on properties it licenses from third parties include Hot Wheels, Scooby-Doo, Sonic the Hedgehog, SpongeBob SquarePants, World Wrestling Entertainment, Bratz, Warhammer 40,000 and several Disney/Pixar properties, including Finding Nemo, Cars and Ratatouille. The firm also has software and artwork developed for it by third parties. Subsidiary THQ Wireless, Inc. produces ringtones and videogames for mobile phones, including products related to the Star Wars franchise, which the firm only develops for wireless applications. The company's corporate strategy focuses on improving its internal development capabilities and technology base, increasing its international presence and exploring the potential of the mobile interactive entertainment segment. In 2008, THQ acquired Big Huge Games, a development studio focused on Role-Playing-Games. In the same year, the firm announced a joint venture with ICE Entertainment, an operator of online games based in Shanghai. The venture plans to launch Dragonica, a multiplayer online casual game, in North America in 2009.

## FINANCIALS: **Sales and profits are in thousands of dollars—add 000 to get the full amount. 2008 Note: Financial information for 2008 was not available for all companies at press time.**

| | | |
|---|---|---|
| 2008 Sales: $1,030,467 | 2008 Profits: $-35,337 | **U.S. Stock Ticker: THQI** |
| 2007 Sales: $1,026,856 | 2007 Profits: $68,038 | **Int'l Ticker:** Int'l Exchange: |
| 2006 Sales: $806,560 | 2006 Profits: $32,106 | Employees: 2,400 |
| 2005 Sales: $756,731 | 2005 Profits: $34,072 | Fiscal Year Ends: 3/31 |
| 2004 Sales: $640,846 | 2004 Profits: $35,839 | Parent Company: |

## SALARIES/BENEFITS:

| | | | | |
|---|---|---|---|---|
| Pension Plan: | ESOP Stock Plan: | Profit Sharing: | Top Exec. Salary: $651,087 | Bonus: $165,000 |
| Savings Plan: Y | Stock Purch. Plan: | | Second Exec. Salary: $432,539 | Bonus: $156,261 |

## OTHER THOUGHTS:

**Apparent Women Officers or Directors**: 2
**Hot Spot for Advancement for Women/Minorities**: Y

## LOCATIONS: ("Y" = Yes)

| West: | Southwest: | Midwest: | Southeast: | Northeast: | International: |
|---|---|---|---|---|---|
| Y | Y | Y | | Y | Y |

# TIBCO SOFTWARE INC

www.tibco.com

**Industry Group Code:** 511207 **Ranks within this company's industry group:** Sales: 1 Profits: 1

| Management: | | Sales/Marketing: | | Liberal Arts: | | Information Systems: | | Professionals: | | Technical/Scientific: | |
|---|---|---|---|---|---|---|---|---|---|---|---|
| Mgmt. Trainees: | | Mktg. Professionals: | Y | Gen. Writing/Editing: | | Info. Management: | Y | Finance/Accounting: | Y | Engineers, Elec.: | Y |
| Experienced Mgmt.: | Y | Retail Sales: | | Technical Writing: | Y | Software Dev.: | Y | Law: | Y | Engineers, Other: | |
| Int'l Business: | Y | Commercial/Industrial: | Y | Graphic Arts/Photog.: | | Hardware Dev.: | | HR/Other: | Y | Health/Lab: | |
| MBA Graduates: | Y | Sales Trainees: | Y | Music: | | Systems Integration: | | Training: | Y | Scientists/Research: | |
| | | Advertising Pros.: | | Broadcasting: | | Consulting/Other: | | Health Care: | | Petroleum/Chemicals: | |
| | | | | Other: | | | | Consulting: | | Math/Other: | Y |

## TYPES OF BUSINESS:

Software-Business Process
Data Management Software
Consulting & Support Services

## BRANDS/DIVISIONS/AFFILIATES:

TIBCO ActiveMatrix
TIBCO BusinessConnect
TIBCO BusinessFactor
TIBCO Spotfire
Insightful Corporation

## CONTACTS: *Note: Officers with more than one job title may be intentionally listed here more than once.*

Vivek Y. Ranadive, CEO
Murray Rode, CFO
Ram Menon, Exec. VP-Worldwide Mktg.
Tom Laffey, Exec. VP-Prod. & Tech.
William Hughes, General Counsel/Exec. VP/Corp. Sec.
Murray Rode, Exec. VP-Strategic Oper.
Murat Sonmez, Exec. VP-Global Field Oper.
Christopher Ahlberg, Pres., Spotfire Div.
Vivek Y. Ranadive, Chmn.

**Phone:** 650-846-1000 **Fax:** 650-846-1005
**Toll-Free:**
**Address:** 3303 Hillview Ave., Palo Alto, CA 94304 US

## GROWTH PLANS/SPECIAL FEATURES:

TIBCO Software, Inc. is a provider of infrastructure software, focused on creating and marketing software solutions for use in the integration of business information, processes and applications. The company offers a range of standards-based infrastructure software products that help customers to streamline business process management through reliable real-time access to information. TIBCO's software products are capable of instantly correlating information about an organization's operations and performance with information about expected behavior and business rules, allowing customers to anticipate and respond to business developments. While its products can be sold individually to address specific technical challenges, the overall emphasis of the firm's development and sales efforts is to create products that interoperate and can be sold together as a suite. TIBCO's products are designed to address three primary areas of operational efficiency: Service Oriented Architecture (SOA), Business Process Management (BPM) and Business Optimization. The firm's SOA offerings enable organizations to migrate their IT infrastructure to a common framework by turning information and functions into discrete and reusable components that can be invoked from across the business and aggregated with other such services to create composite applications. BPM products enable the automation and coordination of the assets and tasks that make up business processes. The firm's Business Optimization software automatically converts and analyzes data, and can also initiate appropriate notifications or adaptation of business processes. The firm also offers professional services, including consulting, planning, maintenance and support of information systems. In September 2008, the company acquired Insightful Corporation, a provider of statistical data analysis and data mining solutions, in a transaction valued at approximately $25 million.

The company offers its U.S. employees such benefits as life and AD&D insurance; short- and long-term disability benefits; medical, dental and vision plans; tuition reimbursement; credit union membership; a 401(k) plan and an employee assistance program.

## FINANCIALS: **Sales and profits are in thousands of dollars—add 000 to get the full amount. 2008 Note: Financial information for 2008 was not available for all companies at press time.**

| | | |
|---|---|---|
| 2008 Sales: $644,471 | 2008 Profits: $52,411 | **U.S. Stock Ticker: TIBX** |
| 2007 Sales: $577,386 | 2007 Profits: $51,888 | **Int'l Ticker:** Int'l Exchange: |
| 2006 Sales: $517,279 | 2006 Profits: $72,864 | Employees: 2,070 |
| 2005 Sales: $445,910 | 2005 Profits: $72,555 | Fiscal Year Ends: 11/30 |
| 2004 Sales: $387,220 | 2004 Profits: $44,920 | Parent Company: |

## SALARIES/BENEFITS:

| | | | | |
|---|---|---|---|---|
| Pension Plan: | ESOP Stock Plan: | Profit Sharing: | Top Exec. Salary: $500,000 | Bonus: $50,000 |
| Savings Plan: Y | Stock Purch. Plan: | | Second Exec. Salary: $344,000 | Bonus: $35,000 |

## OTHER THOUGHTS:

**Apparent Women Officers or Directors:**
**Hot Spot for Advancement for Women/Minorities:**

## LOCATIONS: ("Y" = Yes)

| West: | Southwest: | Midwest: | Southeast: | Northeast: | International: |
|---|---|---|---|---|---|
| Y | Y | Y | Y | Y | Y |

Note: Financial information, benefits and other data can change quickly and may vary from those stated here.

# TIVO INC

www.tivo.com

**Industry Group Code:** 334310 **Ranks within this company's industry group:** Sales: 2 Profits: 2

| Management: | | Sales/Marketing: | | Liberal Arts: | | Information Systems: | | Professionals: | | Technical/Scientific: | |
|---|---|---|---|---|---|---|---|---|---|---|---|
| Mgmt. Trainees: | | Mktg. Professionals: | Y | Gen. Writing/Editing: | | Info. Management: | Y | Finance/Accounting: | Y | Engineers, Elec.: | Y |
| Experienced Mgmt.: | Y | Retail Sales: | | Technical Writing: | Y | Software Dev.: | Y | Law: | Y | Engineers, Other: | Y |
| Int'l Business: | Y | Commercial/Industrial: | Y | Graphic Arts/Photog.: | Y | Hardware Dev.: | Y | HR/Other: | Y | Health/Lab: | |
| MBA Graduates: | Y | Sales Trainees: | Y | Music: | | Systems Integration: | Y | Training: | Y | Scientists/Research: | |
| | | Advertising Pros.: | Y | Broadcasting: | | Consulting/Other: | | Health Care: | | Petroleum/Chemicals: | |
| | | | | Other: | | | | Consulting: | | Math/Other: | |

## TYPES OF BUSINESS:

Television Home Recording Technology
Digital Video Recorders
Advertising Services

## BRANDS/DIVISIONS/AFFILIATES:

TiVoToGo
TiVo KidZone
TiVo Online
Season Pass
WishList
Gemstar-TV Guide International, Inc.
Seven Media Group

## CONTACTS: *Note: Officers with more than one job title may be intentionally listed here more than once.*

Tom Rogers, CEO
Tom Rogers, Pres.
Anna Brunelle, CFO
Nancy Kato, Sr. VP-Human Resources
James Barton, CTO/Sr. VP
Matthew Zinn, General Counsel/Sr. VP/Sec.
Mark Roberts, Sr. VP-Oper. & Consumer Prod.
Matthew Zinn, Chief Privacy Officer
Joe Miller, Sr. VP-Consumer Sales & Dist.
Jeff Klugman, Sr. VP/Gen. Mgr.-Advertising Eng. Div.

**Phone:** 408-519-9100 **Fax:** 408-519-5330
**Toll-Free:**
**Address:** 2160 Gold St., PO Box 2160, Alviso, CA 95002 US

## GROWTH PLANS/SPECIAL FEATURES:

TiVo, Inc. is a provider of technology and services for digital video recorders. The subscription-based TiVo provides consumers with an easy way to record, watch and control television and receive videos, pictures and movies from cable, broadcast and broadband sources. TiVo offers such features as Season Pass recordings, WishList searches, TiVoToGo transfers, TiVo KidZone (which offers parental controls) and TiVo Online Scheduling. The company has roughly 3.6 million subscribers. It distributes the TiVo service through consumer electronics retailers and through its online store. Additionally, the firm provides the service through agreements with television service providers such as satellite and cable providers, including DIRECTV, Comcast and Cox. TiVo's technology portfolio for enabling the TiVo services includes the TiVo service client software platform, the TiVo service infrastructure and TiVo-enabled digital video recorder (DVR) hardware design. The TiVo service infrastructure enables the ongoing operation of the TiVo service, managing the distribution of propriety services and specialized content such as program guide data, showcases and TiVo client software upgrades. TiVo-enabled DVRs can support analog cable, digital cable, satellite and or over-the-air broadcast television, including standard definition and high definition television. TiVo also provides marketing products for the television industry, including a unique platform for advertisers and audience research measurement. In July 2008, TiVo and Seven Media Group announced plans to launch TiVo service in Australia.

The company offers its employees a 401(k) plan; an employee stock purchase plan; health insurance; an employee assistance program; life and AD&D insurance; a college savings plan; and flexible spending accounts. Other corporate benefits include on-site workout programs, commuter options, on-site car wash and dry cleaning and wellness reimbursements.

## FINANCIALS: **Sales and profits are in thousands of dollars—add 000 to get the full amount. 2008 Note: Financial information for 2008 was not available for all companies at press time.**

| | | |
|---|---|---|
| 2008 Sales: $272,676 | 2008 Profits: $-31,457 | **U.S. Stock Ticker: TIVO** |
| 2007 Sales: $258,921 | 2007 Profits: $-47,754 | **Int'l Ticker:** Int'l Exchange: |
| 2006 Sales: $198,129 | 2006 Profits: $-34,398 | Employees: 495 |
| 2005 Sales: $173,011 | 2005 Profits: $-79,842 | Fiscal Year Ends: 1/31 |
| 2004 Sales: $141,080 | 2004 Profits: $-32,018 | Parent Company: |

## SALARIES/BENEFITS:

| | | | | |
|---|---|---|---|---|
| Pension Plan: | ESOP Stock Plan: | Profit Sharing: | Top Exec. Salary: $800,000 | Bonus: $495,075 |
| Savings Plan: Y | Stock Purch. Plan: Y | | Second Exec. Salary: $355,469 | Bonus: $ |

## OTHER THOUGHTS:

**Apparent Women Officers or Directors**: 2
**Hot Spot for Advancement for Women/Minorities**: Y

## LOCATIONS: ("Y" = Yes)

| West: | Southwest: | Midwest: | Southeast: | Northeast: | International: |
|---|---|---|---|---|---|
| Y | | | | Y | Y |

# TOMOTHERAPY INC

www.tomotherapy.com

**Industry Group Code:** 339113 **Ranks within this company's industry group:** Sales: 15 Profits: 19

| Management: | | Sales/Marketing: | | Liberal Arts: | | Information Systems: | | Professionals: | | Technical/Scientific: | |
|---|---|---|---|---|---|---|---|---|---|---|---|
| Mgmt. Trainees: | | Mktg. Professionals: | Y | Gen. Writing/Editing: | | Info. Management: | Y | Finance/Accounting: | Y | Engineers, Elec.: | Y |
| Experienced Mgmt.: | Y | Retail Sales: | | Technical Writing: | Y | Software Dev.: | Y | Law: | Y | Engineers, Other: | Y |
| Int'l Business: | Y | Commercial/Industrial: | Y | Graphic Arts/Photog.: | | Hardware Dev.: | Y | HR/Other: | Y | Health/Lab: | Y |
| MBA Graduates: | Y | Sales Trainees: | Y | Music: | | Systems Integration: | | Training: | Y | Scientists/Research: | Y |
| | | Advertising Pros.: | | Broadcasting: | | Consulting/Other: | | Health Care: | Y | Petroleum/Chemicals: | |
| | | | | Other: | | | | Consulting: | | Math/Other: | Y |

## TYPES OF BUSINESS:

Radiation Oncology Equipment

## BRANDS/DIVISIONS/AFFILIATES:

Hi Art
Chengdu Twin Peak Accelerator Technology, Inc.
Hi Art Co., Ltd.

## CONTACTS:

*Note: Officers with more than one job title may be intentionally listed here more than once.*

Frederick A. Robertson, CEO
Steven G. Books, COO
Paul J. Reckwerdt, Pres.
Stephen C. Hathaway, CFO
Delwin T. Coufal, VP-Mktg.
Alison Sparks, VP-Human Resources
Gustavo Hugo Olivera, VP-Research
Paul J. Pienkowski, VP-Prod. Dev.
Brenda S. Furlow, General Counsel/Sec./VP
Eric A. Schloesser, VP-Bus. Dev.
Stephen C. Hathaway, Treas.
Kenneth D. Buroker, VP-Regulatory Affairs & Quality
Richard Springer, VP-Customer Support
Thomas Rockwell Mackie, Chmn.
Shawn D. Guse, VP-Global Sales

**Phone:** 608-824-2800 **Fax:** 608-824-2996
**Toll-Free:**
**Address:** 1240 Deming Way, Madison, WI 53717-1954 US

## GROWTH PLANS/SPECIAL FEATURES:

TomoTherapy, Inc. manufactures the Hi Art radiation therapy system for the treatment of a range of cancer types. The Hi Art system combines integrated CT (computed tomography) imaging with radiation therapy to deliver radiation treatment with speed and precision while reducing radiation exposure to surrounding healthy tissue. The system contains a linear accelerator, a device that generates external beam radiation that is used both to capture high quality, quantitative images and to deliver therapeutic radiation to selected targets in a spiral delivery pattern 360 degrees around the body. The linear accelerator rotates around a rigid circular frame, or ring gantry, that is housed in a protective closing. This design contrasts with traditional radiation therapy systems, which utilize a single, rotating arm that can deliver radiation from only a limited number of angles. Another unique feature of the Hi Art system is its ability to provide daily quantitative imaging and to incorporate adaptive radiation therapy easily and efficiently into the regular clinical workflow of clinicians. The typical workflow process of the Hi Art system consists of patient imaging; treatment planning and optimization, in which the dose is repeatedly calculated and the radiation beam shape and intensity is updated; patient positioning and treatment delivery; and dosage verification. TomoTherapy markets its system to hospitals and cancer treatment centers in North America, Europe, the Middle East and Asia-Pacific. Since its inception, the firm has installed over 150 of its systems in more than 16 countries. Sales to North America generated 56% of TomoTherapy's revenue during 2007, while sales to Europe generated 26% and sales to Asia-Pacific generated 18%. In April 2008, the firm agreed to acquire linear accelerator manufacturer Chengdu Twin Peak Accelerator Technology, Inc. In July 2008, the company agreed to acquire its Japanese sales and service assets from Hi Art Co., Ltd.

## FINANCIALS:

**Sales and profits are in thousands of dollars—add 000 to get the full amount. 2008 Note: Financial information for 2008 was not available for all companies at press time.**

2008 Sales: $204,589 — 2008 Profits: $-37,510
2007 Sales: $232,810 — 2007 Profits: $10,662
2006 Sales: $156,102 — 2006 Profits: $14,915
2005 Sales: $75,754 — 2005 Profits: $ 239
2004 Sales: $ — 2004 Profits: $

**U.S. Stock Ticker: TOMO**
**Int'l Ticker:** Int'l Exchange:
Employees: 665
Fiscal Year Ends: 12/31
Parent Company:

## SALARIES/BENEFITS:

Pension Plan: ESOP Stock Plan: Profit Sharing:
Savings Plan: Y Stock Purch. Plan:
Top Exec. Salary: $401,250 Bonus: $476,625
Second Exec. Salary: $287,500 Bonus: $245,625

## OTHER THOUGHTS:

**Apparent Women Officers or Directors**: 3
**Hot Spot for Advancement for Women/Minorities**: Y

## LOCATIONS: ("Y" = Yes)

| West: | Southwest: | Midwest: | Southeast: | Northeast: | International: |
|---|---|---|---|---|---|
| | | Y | | | Y |

# TOOTSIE ROLL INDUSTRIES INC

**www.tootsie.com**

**Industry Group Code:** 311330 **Ranks within this company's industry group:** Sales: 1 Profits: 1

| Management: | | Sales/Marketing: | | Liberal Arts: | | Information Systems: | | Professionals: | | Technical/Scientific: | |
|---|---|---|---|---|---|---|---|---|---|---|---|
| Mgmt. Trainees: | Y | Mktg. Professionals: | Y | Gen. Writing/Editing: | | Info. Management: | Y | Finance/Accounting: | Y | Engineers, Elec.: | |
| Experienced Mgmt.: | Y | Retail Sales: | | Technical Writing: | | Software Dev.: | | Law: | Y | Engineers, Other: | |
| Int'l Business: | Y | Commercial/Industrial: | Y | Graphic Arts/Photog.: | | Hardware Dev.: | | HR/Other: | Y | Health/Lab: | |
| MBA Graduates: | Y | Sales Trainees: | Y | Music: | | Systems Integration: | | Training: | Y | Scientists/Research: | |
| | | Advertising Pros.: | Y | Broadcasting: | | Consulting/Other: | | Health Care: | | Petroleum/Chemicals: | |
| | | | | Other: | | | | Consulting: | | Math/Other: | |

## TYPES OF BUSINESS:

Confectionery Product Manufacturing

## BRANDS/DIVISIONS/AFFILIATES:

Tootsie Roll Pops
Caramel Apple Pops
Charms
Blow-Pop
Blue Razz
Cella's
Andes
Sugar Daddy

## CONTACTS:

*Note: Officers with more than one job title may be intentionally listed here more than once.*

Melvin J. Gordon, CEO
Ellen R. Gordon, COO
Ellen R. Gordon, Pres.
Thomas E. Corr, VP-Mktg. & Sales
John W. Newlin, Jr., VP-Mfg.
G. Howard Ember, Jr., VP-Finance
Barry P. Bowen, Treas.
Melvin J. Gordon, Chmn.
John P. Majors, VP-Dist.

| | |
|---|---|
| **Phone:** 773-838-3400 | **Fax:** 773-838-3534 |
| **Toll-Free:** | |
| **Address:** 7401 S. Cicero Ave., Chicago, IL 60629 US | |

## GROWTH PLANS/SPECIAL FEATURES:

Tootsie Roll Industries, Inc. is engaged in the manufacture and sale of confectionary products. It is famous for its round piece of chewy, chocolate-like candy that still sells for one penny, the original price, even though the company now offers candy packages priced up to more than seven dollars. The majority of its products are sold under trademarks such as Tootsie Roll, Tootsie Roll Pop, Child's Play, Caramel Apple Pops, Charms, Blow-Pop, Blue Razz, Zip-a-Dee Pops, Cella's, Mason Dots, Mason Crows, Junior Mint, Charleston Chew, Sugar Daddy, Sugar Babies, Andes, Fluffy Stuff, Wack-O-Wax, Dubble Bubble, Razzles, Frooties, Cry Baby and Nik-l-Nip. The company's products are marketed in a variety of packages designed to be suitable for display and sale in different types of retail outlets. They are distributed through roughly 100 candy and grocery brokers and by the firm itself to about 15,000 customers throughout the U.S. These customers include wholesale distributors of candy and groceries, supermarkets, variety stores, dollar stores, chain grocers, drug chains, discount chains, cooperative grocery associations, warehouse and membership club stores, convenience stores, vending machine operators, the U. S. military and fund-raising charitable organizations. Tootsie Roll Industries' principal markets are in the U.S., Canada and Mexico, although the company maintains distribution channels in more than 75 countries. The Mexican plant supplies a small percentage of the products marketed in the U.S. and Canada. The majority of production from the Canadian plant is sold in the U.S. Revenues from Wal-Mart Stores, Inc. aggregated roughly 22.4% of total net sales in 2007. In January 2009, Tootsie Roll announced plans to open a new 240,000 square foot distribution center in the Humboldt Industrial Park in Hazle Township, Pennsylvania. This center will handle the company's distribution operations to the Northeast and the Atlantic Seaboard.

## FINANCIALS:

**Sales and profits are in thousands of dollars—add 000 to get the full amount. 2008 Note: Financial information for 2008 was not available for all companies at press time.**

2008 Sales: $
2007 Sales: $492,742
2006 Sales: $495,990
2005 Sales: $487,739
2004 Sales: $420,110

2008 Profits: $
2007 Profits: $51,625
2006 Profits: $65,919
2005 Profits: $77,227
2004 Profits: $64,174

**U.S. Stock Ticker: TR**
**Int'l Ticker:** Int'l Exchange:
Employees: 2,200
Fiscal Year Ends: 12/31
Parent Company:

## SALARIES/BENEFITS:

Pension Plan: ESOP Stock Plan: Profit Sharing:
Savings Plan: Stock Purch. Plan:

Top Exec. Salary: $999,000 Bonus: $1,512,000
Second Exec. Salary: $952,000 Bonus: $318,000

## OTHER THOUGHTS:

**Apparent Women Officers or Directors**: 2
**Hot Spot for Advancement for Women/Minorities**: Y

## LOCATIONS: ("Y" = Yes)

| West: | Southwest: | Midwest: | Southeast: | Northeast: | International: |
|---|---|---|---|---|---|
| | | Y | | | Y |

# TOPPS COMPANY INC (THE)

www.topps.com

**Industry Group Code:** 311330 **Ranks within this company's industry group:** Sales: 2 Profits:

| Management: | | Sales/Marketing: | | Liberal Arts: | | Information Systems: | | Professionals: | | Technical/Scientific: | |
|---|---|---|---|---|---|---|---|---|---|---|---|
| Mgmt. Trainees: | Y | Mktg. Professionals: | Y | Gen. Writing/Editing: | | Info. Management: | Y | Finance/Accounting: | Y | Engineers, Elec.: | |
| Experienced Mgmt.: | Y | Retail Sales: | | Technical Writing: | | Software Dev.: | | Law: | Y | Engineers, Other: | |
| Int'l Business: | Y | Commercial/Industrial: | Y | Graphic Arts/Photog.: | | Hardware Dev.: | | HR/Other: | Y | Health/Lab: | |
| MBA Graduates: | Y | Sales Trainees: | Y | Music: | | Systems Integration: | | Training: | Y | Scientists/Research: | |
| | | Advertising Pros.: | Y | Broadcasting: | | Consulting/Other: | | Health Care: | | Petroleum/Chemicals: | |
| | | | | Other: | | | | Consulting: | | Math/Other: | |

## TYPES OF BUSINESS:

Candy & Gum Manufacturing
Collectibles
Trading Cards
Collectible Strategy Games

## BRANDS/DIVISIONS/AFFILIATES:

Bazooka
Ring Pop
Push Pop
Football Flix
Topps Heritage
WizKids

## CONTACTS:

*Note: Officers with more than one job title may be intentionally listed here more than once.*

Scott Silverstein, CEO
Scott Silverstein, Pres.
Joseph Del Toro, CFO/VP
John S. Budd, VP-Mktg., Confectionary
Ira Friedman, VP-New Product Dev. & Publishing
Warren Friss, VP/Gen. Mgr.-Entertainment
John C. Buscaglia, VP-Sales, Entertainment
Christopher Rodman, VP-Topps Europe
Sherry L. Schultz, VP/Gen. Mgr.-Confectionery
Michael P. Clancy, VP-Int'l

**Phone:** 212-376-0300 **Fax:** 212-376-0573
**Toll-Free:**
**Address:** 1 Whitehall St., New York, NY 10004 US

## GROWTH PLANS/SPECIAL FEATURES:

The Topps Company, Inc. is a marketer of premium-branded confectionery products and collectible entertainment products. The firm markets a variety of products such as lollipops, including the Ring Pop, Push Pop and Baby Bottle Pop; Bazooka-brand bubble gum; and certain licensed candy items. In addition to candies and gum, the company markets products such as comic books; trading cards; sticker album collections featuring professional athletes, popular television shows, movies and other licensed characters; and collectible strategy games. The firm has subsidiaries in the U.K., Canada, Italy and Argentina, as well as its U.S. headquarters located in New York City and operations center located in Duryea, Pennsylvania. The firm also operates an extensive web site that offers feature stories on various athletes and national sports teams; the Card Connect Message board for card trading; the Topps Spokesmen link; and the Topps Direct link, which allows access to the Topps Online Store (to purchase candy), eTopps (an interactive trading card site), and the Topps Vault (a link that allows customers to bid on rare and limited items). The firms corporate partners includes Alex Rodriquez; Barry Bonds; Beckett Magazine; Major League Baseball; Major League Baseball Association; National Basketball Association; National Basketball Players Association; National Football League; Sporting News; National Football League Players Association; Take 2 Interactive; and Mickey Mantle.

## FINANCIALS:

**Sales and profits are in thousands of dollars—add 000 to get the full amount. 2008 Note: Financial information for 2008 was not available for all companies at press time.**

| | | |
|---|---|---|
| 2008 Sales: $ | 2008 Profits: $ | **U.S. Stock Ticker: Private** |
| 2007 Sales: $326,700 | 2007 Profits: $ | **Int'l Ticker:** Int'l Exchange: |
| 2006 Sales: $293,838 | 2006 Profits: $1,239 | Employees: 422 |
| 2005 Sales: $294,231 | 2005 Profits: $10,915 | Fiscal Year Ends: 2/28 |
| 2004 Sales: $294,917 | 2004 Profits: $12,884 | Parent Company: |

## SALARIES/BENEFITS:

| | | | | |
|---|---|---|---|---|
| Pension Plan: | ESOP Stock Plan: | Profit Sharing: | Top Exec. Salary: $985,000 | Bonus: $197,000 |
| Savings Plan: Y | Stock Purch. Plan: | | Second Exec. Salary: $376,654 | Bonus: $90,850 |

## OTHER THOUGHTS:

**Apparent Women Officers or Directors:** 1
**Hot Spot for Advancement for Women/Minorities:**

## LOCATIONS: ("Y" = Yes)

| West: | Southwest: | Midwest: | Southeast: | Northeast: | International: |
|---|---|---|---|---|---|
| Y | | | | Y | Y |

Note: Financial information, benefits and other data can change quickly and may vary from those stated here.

# TRANSATLANTIC HOLDINGS INC

**www.transre.com**

**Industry Group Code:** 524130 **Ranks within this company's industry group:** Sales: 2 Profits: 2

| **Management:** | | **Sales/Marketing:** | | **Liberal Arts:** | | **Information Systems:** | | **Professionals:** | | **Technical/Scientific:** | |
|---|---|---|---|---|---|---|---|---|---|---|---|
| Mgmt. Trainees: | | Mktg. Professionals: | Y | Gen. Writing/Editing: | Y | Info. Management: | Y | Finance/Accounting: | Y | Engineers, Elec.: | |
| Experienced Mgmt.: | Y | Retail Sales: | | Technical Writing: | Y | Software Dev.: | | Law: | Y | Engineers, Other: | |
| Int'l Business: | Y | Commercial/Industrial: | Y | Graphic Arts/Photog.: | | Hardware Dev.: | | HR/Other: | Y | Health/Lab: | |
| MBA Graduates: | Y | Sales Trainees: | Y | Music: | | Systems Integration: | | Training: | Y | Scientists/Research: | |
| | | Advertising Pros.: | | Broadcasting: | | Consulting/Other: | | Health Care: | | Petroleum/Chemicals: | |
| | | | | Other: | | | | Consulting: | | Math/Other: | Y |

## TYPES OF BUSINESS:

Property & Casualty Reinsurance
Life Reinsurance
Marine & Aerospace Reinsurance
Surety & Credit Reinsurance

## BRANDS/DIVISIONS/AFFILIATES:

American International Group (AIG)
Transatlantic Reinsurance Co
Trans Re Zurich
Putnam Reinsurance Co
RAM Holdings Ltd
Kuwait Reinsurance Co

## CONTACTS: *Note: Officers with more than one job title may be intentionally listed here more than once.*

Robert F. Orlich, CEO
Robert F. Orlich, Pres.
Steven F. Skalicky, CFO
George DiMartino, CIO/Sr. VP
Gary A. Schwartz, General Counsel/Sr. VP
Beth Levene, Sr. VP-Claims Mgr.
Kenneth Apfel, Sr. VP/Chief Actuary
Mike Sapnar, Exec. VP/Chief Underwriting Officer-Domestic Oper.
Elizabeth M. Tuck, Sec.
Robert F. Orlich, Chmn.
Paul Bonny, Pres., Int'l Oper.

| **Phone:** 212-770-2000 | **Fax:** 212-269-6801 |
|---|---|
| **Toll-Free:** | |
| **Address:** 80 Pine St., New York, NY 10005 US | |

## GROWTH PLANS/SPECIAL FEATURES:

Transatlantic Holdings, Inc., a partially-owned subsidiary of American International Group, Inc. (AIG), offers reinsurance capacity for property and casualty products on both a treaty and facultative basis through subsidiaries Transatlantic Reinsurance Co., Trans Re Zurich and Putnam Reinsurance Co. The firm offers reinsurance on both a treaty and facultative basis for a broad spectrum of property and casualty products. The company's principal lines of reinsurance include other liability, including directors' and officers' liability and errors and omissions coverages; ocean marine and aviation; medical malpractice; auto liability, including non-standard risks; accident, health, surety and credit in the casualty lines; and fire, allied lines, auto physical damage and homeowners multiple peril lines in the property lines. Reinsurance is provided for most major lines of insurance on both excess-of-loss and pro rata bases. These products are provided directly and through brokers to insurance and reinsurance companies in both domestic and international markets. Transatlantic and its subsidiaries are licensed, accredited, authorized or can serve as a reinsurer in North America, Puerto Rico, Europe and Latin America and are authorized to maintain a representative office in Shanghai, China. The company supplements its traditional revenues with investments in diversified taxable bonds and tax-exempt municipal bonds. The firm holds a 40% interest in Kuwait Reinsurance Co., which provides property, casualty and life reinsurance products to clients in the Middle Eastern and North African markets. AIG owns roughly 60% of Transatlantic's shares. In July 2008, Transatlantic Reinsurance Company (TRC) announced the opening of a representative office in Munich, Germany. TRC recently applied to act as an admitted reinsurer in the Brazilian reinsurance market.

## FINANCIALS: **Sales and profits are in thousands of dollars—add 000 to get the full amount. 2008 Note: Financial information for 2008 was not available for all companies at press time.**

2008 Sales: $4,082,549
2007 Sales: $4,381,830
2006 Sales: $4,049,496
2005 Sales: $3,768,125
2004 Sales: $3,990,057

2008 Profits: $102,254
2007 Profits: $487,141
2006 Profits: $428,152
2005 Profits: $37,910
2004 Profits: $254,584

**U.S. Stock Ticker: TRH**
**Int'l Ticker:** Int'l Exchange:
Employees: 570
Fiscal Year Ends: 12/31
Parent Company: AMERICAN INTERNATIONAL GROUP (AIG)

## SALARIES/BENEFITS:

Pension Plan: ESOP Stock Plan: Profit Sharing: Top Exec. Salary: $800,000 Bonus: $1,214,000
Savings Plan: Stock Purch. Plan: Second Exec. Salary: $687,254 Bonus: $467,680

## OTHER THOUGHTS:

**Apparent Women Officers or Directors**: 2
**Hot Spot for Advancement for Women/Minorities**: Y

## LOCATIONS: ("Y" = Yes)

| West: | Southwest: | Midwest: | Southeast: | Northeast: | International: |
|---|---|---|---|---|---|
| Y | | Y | Y | Y | Y |

# TRANSCEND SERVICES INC

www.transcendservices.com

**Industry Group Code:** 514210 **Ranks within this company's industry group:** Sales: 2 Profits: 2

| Management: | | Sales/Marketing: | | Liberal Arts: | | Information Systems: | | Professionals: | | Technical/Scientific: | |
|---|---|---|---|---|---|---|---|---|---|---|---|
| Mgmt. Trainees: | | Mktg. Professionals: | Y | Gen. Writing/Editing: | | Info. Management: | Y | Finance/Accounting: | Y | Engineers, Elec.: | |
| Experienced Mgmt.: | Y | Retail Sales: | | Technical Writing: | Y | Software Dev.: | Y | Law: | Y | Engineers, Other: | |
| Int'l Business: | | Commercial/Industrial: | Y | Graphic Arts/Photog.: | | Hardware Dev.: | | HR/Other: | Y | Health/Lab: | |
| MBA Graduates: | Y | Sales Trainees: | Y | Music: | | Systems Integration: | Y | Training: | Y | Scientists/Research: | |
| | | Advertising Pros.: | | Broadcasting: | | Consulting/Other: | | Health Care: | | Petroleum/Chemicals: | |
| | | | | Other: | | | | Consulting: | | Math/Other: | |

## TYPES OF BUSINESS:

Data Processing Services
Internet-Based Medical Transcription Services

## BRANDS/DIVISIONS/AFFILIATES:

BeyondTXT
OTP Technologies, Inc.

## CONTACTS: *Note: Officers with more than one job title may be intentionally listed here more than once.*

Larry G. Gerdes, CEO
Susan McGrogan, COO
Larry G. Gerdes, Pres.
Lance Cornell, CFO
Leo Cooper, Exec. VP-Sales & Mktg.
Lance Cornell, Corp. Sec.
Lance Cornell, Treas.
Larry G. Gerdes, Chmn.

| | |
|---|---|
| **Phone:** 678-808-0600 | **Fax:** 678-808-0601 |
| **Toll-Free:** 800-555-8727 | |
| **Address:** One Glenlake Parkway, Ste. 1325, Atlanta, GA 30328 US | |

## GROWTH PLANS/SPECIAL FEATURES:

Transcend Services, Inc. provides medical transcription services to the healthcare industry. Customers include hospitals, hospital systems, multi-specialty clinics and physician group practices. Transcend provides services to over 160 hospitals and clinics, with typical customers providing an average annual revenue of about $265,000, and several larger customers contributing annual revenues exceeding $1.3 million. The company offers two primary options to its customers: for customers without transcription technology available, Transcend offers BeyondTXT; alternatively, Transcend can access a customer's existing system to provide transcription services. BeyondTXT is a web-enabled voice and data distribution technology that allows a physician to dictate reports into several dictation products on the market, including handheld devices, hospital- or clinic-based transcription stations, and home phones or cell phones. This information is captured digitally by Transcend' central voice hub in Atlanta, Georgia, where the digital files are compressed, encrypted and stored. The audio recordings are then accessed by home-based medical transcription professionals through the Internet, who either transcribe the physicians' voice recordings directly or edit an electronic document created by BeyondTXT's voice recognition tool. After transcription, documents are returned to the Atlanta hub over the Internet, and are then distributed securely to hospital information systems via fax, printers or the Internet. Documents are generally produced and delivered within 24 hours, but may be delivered in as little as four hours for premium prices. The company's operations run 24 hours a day, 365 days a year. In January 2007, the company acquired some assets of OTP Technologies, Inc., a Chicago-area medical transcription company. In August 2007, the company joined the Medical Transcription Services Organization (MTSO) Alliance sponsored by eScription, Inc., a leading medical transcription services company, in an effort to increase customer satisfaction and company efficiency.

Transcend Services offers medical, dental and vision plans; life insurance; and paid time off.

## FINANCIALS: **Sales and profits are in thousands of dollars—add 000 to get the full amount. 2008 Note: Financial information for 2008 was not available for all companies at press time.**

| | | |
|---|---|---|
| 2008 Sales: $ | 2008 Profits: $ | **U.S. Stock Ticker: TRCR** |
| 2007 Sales: $42,454 | 2007 Profits: $11,479 | **Int'l Ticker:** Int'l Exchange: |
| 2006 Sales: $32,912 | 2006 Profits: $1,457 | Employees: 1,005 |
| 2005 Sales: $25,817 | 2005 Profits: $- 817 | Fiscal Year Ends: 12/31 |
| 2004 Sales: $15,197 | 2004 Profits: $ 299 | Parent Company: |

## SALARIES/BENEFITS:

| | | | | |
|---|---|---|---|---|
| Pension Plan: | ESOP Stock Plan: | Profit Sharing: | Top Exec. Salary: $250,000 | Bonus: $87,500 |
| Savings Plan: Y | Stock Purch. Plan: Y | | Second Exec. Salary: $170,000 | Bonus: $59,500 |

## OTHER THOUGHTS:

**Apparent Women Officers or Directors**: 1
**Hot Spot for Advancement for Women/Minorities**:

## LOCATIONS: ("Y" = Yes)

| West: | Southwest: | Midwest: | Southeast: | Northeast: | International: |
|---|---|---|---|---|---|
| Y | Y | | Y | | |

# TRAPEZE NETWORKS INC

www.trapezenetworks.com

**Industry Group Code:** 511213 **Ranks within this company's industry group:** Sales: 5 Profits:

| Management: | | Sales/Marketing: | | Liberal Arts: | | Information Systems: | | Professionals: | | Technical/Scientific: | |
|---|---|---|---|---|---|---|---|---|---|---|---|
| Mgmt. Trainees: | | Mktg. Professionals: | Y | Gen. Writing/Editing: | | Info. Management: | Y | Finance/Accounting: | Y | Engineers, Elec.: | Y |
| Experienced Mgmt.: | Y | Retail Sales: | | Technical Writing: | Y | Software Dev.: | Y | Law: | Y | Engineers, Other: | |
| Int'l Business: | Y | Commercial/Industrial: | Y | Graphic Arts/Photog.: | | Hardware Dev.: | | HR/Other: | Y | Health/Lab: | |
| MBA Graduates: | Y | Sales Trainees: | Y | Music: | | Systems Integration: | Y | Training: | Y | Scientists/Research: | |
| | | Advertising Pros.: | | Broadcasting: | | Consulting/Other: | | Health Care: | | Petroleum/Chemicals: | |
| | | | | Other: | | | | Consulting: | | Math/Other: | |

## TYPES OF BUSINESS:

Wi-Fi Systems Software
WLAN Products & Services
Wi-Fi System Design

## BRANDS/DIVISIONS/AFFILIATES:

Trapeze Mobility System
Mobility Exchange
Mobility Point
Mobility System Software
RingMaster
Smart Mobile
Virtual Private Groups
CommHub

## CONTACTS: *Note: Officers with more than one job title may be intentionally listed here more than once.*

James W. (Jim) Vogt, CEO
James W. (Jim) Vogt, Pres.
Kees van Veenendaal, VP-Worldwide Sales
James Reeves, VP-R&D & Worldwide Customer Support
Dan Simone, CTO/VP
Ahmet Tuncay, VP-Prod. Mgmt. & Mktg.
James W. (Jim) Vogt, Chmn.

**Phone:** 925-474-2200 **Fax:** 925-251-0642
**Toll-Free:** 877-359-8779
**Address:** 5753 W. Las Positas Blvd., Pleasanton, CA 94588 US

## GROWTH PLANS/SPECIAL FEATURES:

Trapeze Networks, Inc. develops and provides software to implement scalable wireless local area network (WLAN) infrastructures enterprise headquarters, campuses, multi-tenant facilities and branch offices. The company focuses on systems that demonstrate high levels of security by means of user identification; further, the systems typically integrate wireless mobile technology with existing wired infrastructure while still maintaining such security. The company supports services like high quality voice and data from any 802.11 wireless devices: personal digital assistants (PDAs), tablet PCs, laptops, handheld terminals and other such devices. The company's main product is the Trapeze Mobility System, which is composed of four elements: Mobility Exchange WLAN switch; Mobility Point wireless access point; Mobility System Software; and the RingMaster tool suite, which allows IT managers to perform pre- and post-deployment planning, configuration verification, management and optimization of the WLAN infrastructure. Trapeze's built-in security services detect intrusions, offer strong encryption and create Virtual Private Groups to protect trusted users and their guests. The company has supplied its networking products to CommHub, the Experience Music Project, Hella Behr, Independent Television News, Logitech, Ohlone College, San Antonio Community Hospital and the Tameside Metropolitan Borough Council.

## FINANCIALS: **Sales and profits are in thousands of dollars—add 000 to get the full amount. 2008 Note: Financial information for 2008 was not available for all companies at press time.**

2008 Sales: $
2007 Sales: $24,500
2006 Sales: $
2005 Sales: $
2004 Sales: $

2008 Profits: $
2007 Profits: $
2006 Profits: $
2005 Profits: $
2004 Profits: $

**U.S. Stock Ticker: Private**
**Int'l Ticker:** Int'l Exchange:
Employees: 92
Fiscal Year Ends: 12/31
Parent Company:

## SALARIES/BENEFITS:

Pension Plan: ESOP Stock Plan: Profit Sharing: Top Exec. Salary: $ Bonus: $
Savings Plan: Stock Purch. Plan: Second Exec. Salary: $ Bonus: $

## OTHER THOUGHTS:

**Apparent Women Officers or Directors**:
**Hot Spot for Advancement for Women/Minorities**:

## LOCATIONS: ("Y" = Yes)

| West: | Southwest: | Midwest: | Southeast: | Northeast: | International: |
|---|---|---|---|---|---|
| Y | | | | | Y |

# TRIZETTO GROUP INC (THE)

**www.trizetto.com**

**Industry Group Code:** 511212 **Ranks within this company's industry group:** Sales: 2 Profits: 3

| Management: | | Sales/Marketing: | | Liberal Arts: | | Information Systems: | | Professionals: | | Technical/Scientific: | |
|---|---|---|---|---|---|---|---|---|---|---|---|
| Mgmt. Trainees: | | Mktg. Professionals: | Y | Gen. Writing/Editing: | | Info. Management: | Y | Finance/Accounting: | Y | Engineers, Elec.: | Y |
| Experienced Mgmt.: | Y | Retail Sales: | | Technical Writing: | Y | Software Dev.: | Y | Law: | Y | Engineers, Other: | |
| Int'l Business: | Y | Commercial/Industrial: | Y | Graphic Arts/Photog.: | | Hardware Dev.: | | HR/Other: | Y | Health/Lab: | |
| MBA Graduates: | Y | Sales Trainees: | Y | Music: | | Systems Integration: | Y | Training: | Y | Scientists/Research: | |
| | | Advertising Pros.: | | Broadcasting: | | Consulting/Other: | Y | Health Care: | | Petroleum/Chemicals: | |
| | | | | Other: | | | | Consulting: | | Math/Other: | |

## TYPES OF BUSINESS:

Software-Medical Billing & Administration
Health Care Internet Portal
IT Staffing & Consulting Services
Hosted Services
Consulting Services

## BRANDS/DIVISIONS/AFFILIATES:

Facets
QicLink
CareAdvance
QNXT Case Management

## CONTACTS: *Note: Officers with more than one job title may be intentionally listed here more than once.*

Jeffrey H. Margolis, CEO
Tony Bellomo, Pres.
Dan Spirek, Exec. VP/Chief Mktg. Officer
Alan Ross, Sr. VP-Human Capital Mgmt.
Patricia Gorman, CIO/Quality Officer-Corp. Info. Svcs.
Jim Sullivan, General Counsel/Sr. VP/Sec.
Dan Spirek, Exec. VP/Chief Strategy Officer
Tim Hascall, Exec. VP-Professional Svcs.
Joseph Manheim, Sr. VP-Benefits Admin. & Cage Mgmt.
John Jordan, Exec. VP-Sales
Mark Tomaino, Sr. VP-Corp. Dev.
Jeffrey H. Margolis, Chmn.

**Phone:** 949-719-2200 **Fax:** 949-219-2197
**Toll-Free:** 800-569-1222
**Address:** 567 San Nicolas Dr., Ste. 360, Newport Beach, CA 92660 US

## GROWTH PLANS/SPECIAL FEATURES:

The TriZetto Group, Inc. provides software application services to the health care industry, enabling payors and other constituents in the healthcare supply chain to improve the coordination of benefits and care for healthcare consumers. The company's software solutions include enterprise core administration, care management, network management, consumer retail healthcare and government programs. Software packages include the Facets, QicLink and CareAdvance applications. Facets is a scalable, enterprise-wide core administration product for healthcare payors, allowing them to meet various business requirements, including claims processing, claims re-pricing, risk fund accounting, referral management and customer service. QicLink is one of the most widely-used automated claims administration technologies in the U.S. It allows benefits administrators to handle enrollment, customer service, claims adjudication, billing, accounts receivable, re-pricing and payment processes. The CareAdvance suite of applications allows health plans to automate various aspects of care management, including member identification and assessment, guideline-based care planning, member and provider communications, task and team management, ongoing member monitoring and personalized health content. TriZetto also offers applications focused on Medicare Advantage and managed Medicaid plans. Through its hosting services, the company can host and manage customer applications from its own data center or remotely manage on-site applications. In addition, the firm offers business process outsourcing services allowing customers to outsource non-critical functions, including claims administration, enrollment and rules configuration. Moreover, TriZetto's consulting staff provides project management, technology consulting and other customer-specific solutions to health plans and benefits administrators. In 2008, the company was acquired and taken private by Apax Partners, in a transaction valued at approximately $1.4 billion.

TriZetto offers its employees such benefits as medical, dental and vision care; life and disability insurance; tuition reimbursement; a group legal plan; and an employee assistance program.

## FINANCIALS: **Sales and profits are in thousands of dollars—add 000 to get the full amount. 2008 Note: Financial information for 2008 was not available for all companies at press time.**

2008 Sales: $
2007 Sales: $451,791
2006 Sales: $347,937
2005 Sales: $292,219
2004 Sales: $274,600

2008 Profits: $
2007 Profits: $28,230
2006 Profits: $15,115
2005 Profits: $22,021
2004 Profits: $8,458

**U.S. Stock Ticker: Private**
**Int'l Ticker:** Int'l Exchange:
Employees: 2,000
Fiscal Year Ends: 12/31
Parent Company: APAX PARTNERS INC

## SALARIES/BENEFITS:

Pension Plan: ESOP Stock Plan: Profit Sharing: Top Exec. Salary: $573,408 Bonus: $621,853
Savings Plan: Y Stock Purch. Plan: Second Exec. Salary: $425,251 Bonus: $430,000

## OTHER THOUGHTS:

**Apparent Women Officers or Directors**: 2
**Hot Spot for Advancement for Women/Minorities**: Y

## LOCATIONS: ("Y" = Yes)

| West: | Southwest: | Midwest: | Southeast: | Northeast: | International: |
|---|---|---|---|---|---|
| Y | Y | Y | | Y | |

# TULLY'S COFFEE CORPORATION

www.tullys.com

**Industry Group Code:** 722213 **Ranks within this company's industry group:** Sales: 1 Profits:

| Management: | | Sales/Marketing: | | Liberal Arts: | | Information Systems: | | Professionals: | | Technical/Scientific: | |
|---|---|---|---|---|---|---|---|---|---|---|---|
| Mgmt. Trainees: | Y | Mktg. Professionals: | Y | Gen. Writing/Editing: | | Info. Management: | Y | Finance/Accounting: | Y | Engineers, Elec.: | |
| Experienced Mgmt.: | Y | Retail Sales: | Y | Technical Writing: | | Software Dev.: | | Law: | Y | Engineers, Other: | |
| Int'l Business: | Y | Commercial/Industrial: | | Graphic Arts/Photog.: | Y | Hardware Dev.: | | HR/Other: | Y | Health/Lab: | |
| MBA Graduates: | Y | Sales Trainees: | Y | Music: | | Systems Integration: | | Training: | Y | Scientists/Research: | |
| | | Advertising Pros.: | Y | Broadcasting: | | Consulting/Other: | | Health Care: | | Petroleum/Chemicals: | |
| | | | | Other: | | | | Consulting: | | Math/Other: | |

## TYPES OF BUSINESS:

Coffee Stores
Coffee Roasting
Coffee & Tea Products & Accessories
Catalog & Online Sales
Wholesale Distribution
Yerba Mate Beverages
Franchising

## BRANDS/DIVISIONS/AFFILIATES:

Ghiradelli Chocolate
Guyaki
Tully's Coffe Asia Pacific, Inc.
Asia Food Culture Management Pte, Ltd.
Tully's Coffee Asia Pacific Partners, LP

## CONTACTS:

*Note: Officers with more than one job title may be intentionally listed here more than once.*

Carl Pennington, Sr., Pres.
Andy Wynne, CFO/VP
Martin Walker, VP-Mktg. & Merch.
Ron Gai, VP-Wholesale
Mark DaCosta, VP-Wholesale Logistics & Oper.
Sid Williams, VP-Retail Oper.
Tom T. O'Keefe, Chmn.
John Rader, VP/Gen. Mgr.-Supply Chain

**Phone:** 206-233-2070 **Fax:** 206-233-2077
**Toll-Free:** 800-968-8559
**Address:** 3100 Airport Way S., Seattle, WA 98134 US

## GROWTH PLANS/SPECIAL FEATURES:

Tully's Coffee Corp., a subsidiary of Green Mountain Coffee Roasters Inc., is a fully handcrafted coffee roaster and distributor in the western U.S. The company produces a wide range of coffees as well as brewing machines, serving ware, tea and fine foods such as mints and chocolate. Tully's is committed to sourcing select Arabica beans, which it roasts by hand in small batches using vintage cast iron roasters from the 1950s. Customers can purchase Tully's products at store locations throughout Washington, Idaho, California, Arizona and Oregon or through its online store. Selected Tully's products can be purchased at most popular grocery chains located in the western U.S. The firm has licensed Tully's Coffee Japan to operate and franchise retail locations throughout Japan. The company's wholesale operation delivers its products, either directly or through a distribution partner, to foodservice, hotel, airline, campus dining, office service and grocery operations. Due to a partnership with Ghirardelli Chocolate, one of America's oldest premium chocolate manufacturers, Tully's offers drinks made with Ghirardelli's white chocolate, dark chocolate and caramel gourmet sauces. The company also offers a line of healthy and energizing beverages through its partnership with Guyaki, a provider of certified organic yerba mate beverages. In January 2008, wholly-owned subsidiary Tully's Coffee Asia Pacific, Inc. and Asia Food Culture Management Pte, Ltd. established a joint venture called Tully's Coffee Asia Pacific Partners, LP. The venture seeks to develop the Tully's brand in Asia, Australia and New Zealand. In September 2008, the company was acquired by Green Mountain Coffee Roasters, Inc. for $40.3 million. The company will remain independent and maintain existing management.

The company offers its employees discounted auto and home insurance, a 401(k) plan, medical and dental insurance, short- and long-term disability insurance, an employee assistance plan, life insurance, legal services, and flexible spending accounts.

## FINANCIALS:

**Sales and profits are in thousands of dollars—add 000 to get the full amount. 2008 Note: Financial information for 2008 was not available for all companies at press time.**

| | | |
|---|---|---|
| 2008 Sales: $69,100 | 2008 Profits: $ | **U.S. Stock Ticker: Private** |
| 2007 Sales: $69,000 | 2007 Profits: $ | **Int'l Ticker:** Int'l Exchange: |
| 2006 Sales: $58,245 | 2006 Profits: $15,423 | Employees: 975 |
| 2005 Sales: $53,980 | 2005 Profits: $-4,625 | Fiscal Year Ends: 3/31 |
| 2004 Sales: $50,800 | 2004 Profits: $-2,700 | Parent Company: |

## SALARIES/BENEFITS:

| | | | | |
|---|---|---|---|---|
| Pension Plan: | ESOP Stock Plan: | Profit Sharing: | Top Exec. Salary: $ | Bonus: $ |
| Savings Plan: Y | Stock Purch. Plan: | | Second Exec. Salary: $ | Bonus: $ |

## OTHER THOUGHTS:

**Apparent Women Officers or Directors:**
**Hot Spot for Advancement for Women/Minorities:**

## LOCATIONS: ("Y" = Yes)

| West: | Southwest: | Midwest: | Southeast: | Northeast: | International: |
|---|---|---|---|---|---|
| Y | | | | | Y |

# UIL HOLDINGS CORPORATION

www.uil.com

**Industry Group Code:** 221000A **Ranks within this company's industry group:** Sales: 5 Profits: 6

| Management: | | Sales/Marketing: | | Liberal Arts: | | Information Systems: | | Professionals: | | Technical/Scientific: | |
|---|---|---|---|---|---|---|---|---|---|---|---|
| Mgmt. Trainees: | | Mktg. Professionals: | Y | Gen. Writing/Editing: | | Info. Management: | Y | Finance/Accounting: | Y | Engineers, Elec.: | Y |
| Experienced Mgmt.: | Y | Retail Sales: | | Technical Writing: | | Software Dev.: | | Law: | Y | Engineers, Other: | Y |
| Int'l Business: | | Commercial/Industrial: | Y | Graphic Arts/Photog.: | | Hardware Dev.: | | HR/Other: | Y | Health/Lab: | |
| MBA Graduates: | Y | Sales Trainees: | Y | Music: | | Systems Integration: | | Training: | Y | Scientists/Research: | |
| | | Advertising Pros.: | | Broadcasting: | | Consulting/Other: | | Health Care: | | Petroleum/Chemicals: | Y |
| | | | | Other: | | | | Consulting: | | Math/Other: | |

## TYPES OF BUSINESS:

Utilities-Electricity
Electricity Generation & Distribution
Electrical Systems Design

## BRANDS/DIVISIONS/AFFILIATES:

United Illuminating Co.
Xcelecom, Inc.
United Capital Investments, Inc.
United Bridgeport Energy, Inc.
Zero Stage Capital
Ironbridge Mezzanine Fund

## CONTACTS: *Note: Officers with more than one job title may be intentionally listed here more than once.*

James P. Torgerson, CEO
James P. Torgerson, Pres.
Richard J. Nicholas, CFO/Exec. VP
Linda Randell, General Counsel/Sr. VP/Corp. Sec.
Susan Allen, VP-Investor Rel.
Steven P. Favuzza, Controller/VP
Richard J. Reed, VP-Electric System, The United Illuminating Co.
Deborah C. Hoffman, VP-Audit Svcs./Chief Compliance Officer
Anthony J. Vallillo, COO/Pres., United Illuminating Co.
F. Patrick McFadden, Jr., Chmn.

| **Phone:** 203-499-2000 | **Fax:** 1-203-4993626 |
|---|---|
| **Toll-Free:** | |
| **Address:** 157 Church St., New Haven, CT 06506 US | |

## GROWTH PLANS/SPECIAL FEATURES:

UIL Holdings Corporation (UIL) is a holding company that primarily operates in the regulated utility business. The utility business consists of the electric transmission and distribution operations of The United Illuminating Company (UI). UIL Holdings also has non-utility businesses consisting of an operating lease and passive minority ownership interests in two investment funds, collectively held at United Capital Investments, Inc. (UCI), a heating and cooling facility and a mechanical contracting business. The United Illuminating Company is a regional distribution utility that provides electricity to a 355-square-mile area in the greater New Haven and Bridgeport areas of Connecticut. It is engaged principally in the purchase, transmission, distribution and sale of electricity for residential, commercial and industrial purposes. As of December 2007, UI had approximately 323,000 customers. Of UI's 2007 retail electric revenues, approximately 53.7% were derived from residential sales, 38.9% from commercial sales, 6.3% from industrial sales and 1.1% from street lighting and other sales. The non-utility businesses include United Capital Investments. UCI invests in projects that earn above-average returns and form logical extensions to its current energy and subsidiary businesses. Investments also include Zero Stage Capital and Ironwood Mezzanine Fund. Other non-utility businesses include Thermal Energies, a district heating and cooling facility in Connecticut and Xcel Services Inc., a mechanical contracting division. In October 2008, UIL was awarded a 50% partnership between UI and NRG Energy, Inc. The partnership will build a 200 megawatts peaking generation site in Connecticut.

## FINANCIALS: **Sales and profits are in thousands of dollars—add 000 to get the full amount. 2008 Note: Financial information for 2008 was not available for all companies at press time.**

| | | |
|---|---|---|
| 2008 Sales: $948,720 | 2008 Profits: $48,148 | **U.S. Stock Ticker: UIL** |
| 2007 Sales: $981,999 | 2007 Profits: $44,697 | **Int'l Ticker:** Int'l Exchange: |
| 2006 Sales: $845,950 | 2006 Profits: $-65,164 | Employees: 981 |
| 2005 Sales: $812,414 | 2005 Profits: $31,254 | Fiscal Year Ends: 12/31 |
| 2004 Sales: $764,095 | 2004 Profits: $86,945 | Parent Company: |

## SALARIES/BENEFITS:

| | | | | |
|---|---|---|---|---|
| Pension Plan: | ESOP Stock Plan: | Profit Sharing: | Top Exec. Salary: $503,750 | Bonus: $933,810 |
| Savings Plan: | Stock Purch. Plan: | | Second Exec. Salary: $481,250 | Bonus: $433,125 |

## OTHER THOUGHTS:

**Apparent Women Officers or Directors**: 5
**Hot Spot for Advancement for Women/Minorities**: Y

## LOCATIONS: ("Y" = Yes)

| West: | Southwest: | Midwest: | Southeast: | Northeast: | International: |
|---|---|---|---|---|---|
| | | | | Y | |

# ULTIMATE SOFTWARE GROUP INC

www.ultimatesoftware.com

**Industry Group Code:** 511207 **Ranks within this company's industry group:** Sales: 2 Profits: 2

| Management: | | Sales/Marketing: | | Liberal Arts: | | Information Systems: | | Professionals: | | Technical/Scientific: | |
|---|---|---|---|---|---|---|---|---|---|---|---|
| Mgmt. Trainees: | | Mktg. Professionals: | Y | Gen. Writing/Editing: | | Info. Management: | Y | Finance/Accounting: | Y | Engineers, Elec.: | Y |
| Experienced Mgmt.: | Y | Retail Sales: | | Technical Writing: | Y | Software Dev.: | Y | Law: | Y | Engineers, Other: | |
| Int'l Business: | Y | Commercial/Industrial: | Y | Graphic Arts/Photog.: | | Hardware Dev.: | | HR/Other: | Y | Health/Lab: | |
| MBA Graduates: | Y | Sales Trainees: | | Music: | | Systems Integration: | | Training: | Y | Scientists/Research: | |
| | | Advertising Pros.: | | Broadcasting: | | Consulting/Other: | | Health Care: | | Petroleum/Chemicals: | |
| | | | | Other: | | | | Consulting: | | Math/Other: | Y |

## TYPES OF BUSINESS:

Employee Management Software

## BRANDS/DIVISIONS/AFFILIATES:

UltiPro
Intersourcing
Workplace
Ultimate Software Group of Canada, Inc. (The)
Ultimate Software Group UK Limited (The)
RTIX Americas, Inc.

## CONTACTS: *Note: Officers with more than one job title may be intentionally listed here more than once.*

Scott Scherr, CEO
Marc D. Scherr, COO/Vice Chmn.
Scott Scherr, Pres.
Mitchell K. Dauerman, CFO/Exec. VP
Vivian Maza, Sec.
Darlene Marcroft, Media Contact
Mitchell K. Dauerman, Treas.
Scott Scherr, Chmn.

| | |
|---|---|
| **Phone:** 954-331-7000 | **Fax:** |
| **Toll-Free:** 800-432-1729 | |
| **Address:** 2000 Ultimate Way, Weston, FL 33326 US | |

## GROWTH PLANS/SPECIAL FEATURES:

The Ultimate Software Group, Inc. designs, markets, implements and supports human resources (HR), payroll and talent management software primarily in the U.S. It has two key products: UltiPro, a web-based employee management program; and Intersourcing, a software-as-a-service (SaaS) version of UltiPro, meaning it is available on-demand as a subscription service, rather than being purchased outright. Intersourcing is generally offered to larger enterprises; that is, those with more than 700 employees. To manage Intersourcing, the company contracts two data centers, in Miami and Atlanta. The Atlanta data center is owned Quality Technology Services (QTS) by while the Miami center is owned by AT&T, Inc. Since November 2007, both data centers have been operated by QTS. Both UltiPro and Intersourcing run on the Microsoft technology platform. The firm serves 1,600 businesses representing 3 million employees. Company customers have included Playboy Enterprises, Inc.; Nikon, Inc.; Popeyes Chicken & Biscuits; the Phoenix Suns and Arizona Diamondbacks professional sports teams; the San Diego Convention Center; the City of Ann Arbor; and Bryant University. The firm has two wholly-owned subsidiaries: The Ultimate Software Group of Canada, Inc., which does not conduct any operations, and The Ultimate Software Group UK Limited (formerly RTIX Limited), which has its own wholly-owned subsidiary, RTIX Americas, Inc. During 2007, Ultimate began offering Workplace, a version of Intersourcing that offers UltiPro to small and mid-sized companies with 200-700 employees.

Employees of Ultimate receive benefits including medical and dental coverage; and life and disability insurance.

## FINANCIALS: **Sales and profits are in thousands of dollars—add 000 to get the full amount. 2008 Note: Financial information for 2008 was not available for all companies at press time.**

| | | |
|---|---|---|
| 2008 Sales: $ | 2008 Profits: $ | **U.S. Stock Ticker: ULTI** |
| 2007 Sales: $151,464 | 2007 Profits: $33,129 | **Int'l Ticker:** Int'l Exchange: |
| 2006 Sales: $114,811 | 2006 Profits: $4,133 | Employees: 747 |
| 2005 Sales: $88,603 | 2005 Profits: $3,425 | Fiscal Year Ends: 12/31 |
| 2004 Sales: $ | 2004 Profits: $ | Parent Company: |

## SALARIES/BENEFITS:

| | | | | |
|---|---|---|---|---|
| Pension Plan: | ESOP Stock Plan: | Profit Sharing: | Top Exec. Salary: $600,000 | Bonus: $ |
| Savings Plan: Y | Stock Purch. Plan: | | Second Exec. Salary: $550,000 | Bonus: $ |

## OTHER THOUGHTS:

**Apparent Women Officers or Directors:** 1
**Hot Spot for Advancement for Women/Minorities:**

## LOCATIONS: ("Y" = Yes)

| West: | Southwest: | Midwest: | Southeast: | Northeast: | International: |
|---|---|---|---|---|---|
| | | | Y | | Y |

# UNDER ARMOUR INC

www.underarmour.com

**Industry Group Code:** 315000A **Ranks within this company's industry group:** Sales: 1 Profits: 1

| **Management:** | | **Sales/Marketing:** | | **Liberal Arts:** | | **Information Systems:** | | **Professionals:** | | **Technical/Scientific:** | |
|---|---|---|---|---|---|---|---|---|---|---|---|
| Mgmt. Trainees: | Y | Mktg. Professionals: | Y | Gen. Writing/Editing: | Y | Info. Management: | Y | Finance/Accounting: | Y | Engineers, Elec.: | |
| Experienced Mgmt.: | Y | Retail Sales: | | Technical Writing: | | Software Dev.: | | Law: | Y | Engineers, Other: | |
| Int'l Business: | Y | Commercial/Industrial: | Y | Graphic Arts/Photog.: | Y | Hardware Dev.: | | HR/Other: | Y | Health/Lab: | |
| MBA Graduates: | Y | Sales Trainees: | Y | Music: | | Systems Integration: | | Training: | Y | Scientists/Research: | |
| | | Advertising Pros.: | Y | Broadcasting: | | Consulting/Other: | | Health Care: | | Petroleum/Chemicals: | |
| | | | | Other: | | | | Consulting: | | Math/Other: | |

## TYPES OF BUSINESS:

Compression Performance Apparel
Outdoor and Sports Apparel
Shirts

## BRANDS/DIVISIONS/AFFILIATES:

HeatGear
ColdGear
AllSeasonGear

## CONTACTS: *Note: Officers with more than one job title may be intentionally listed here more than once.*

Kevin Plank, CEO
Wayne Marino, COO
David W. McCreight, Pres.
Brad Dickerson, CFO
William J. Kraus, Sr. VP-Mktg.
Melissa A. Wallace, VP-Human Resources
Kip J. Fulks, Sr. VP-Prod. Dev., Sourcing & Quality Assurance
Kevin M. Haley, House Counsel/Sec./VP
Matthew C. Mirchin, VP-North American Sales
Suzanne Karkus, Sr. VP-Apparel
J. Scott Plank, Sr. VP-Retail
Stephen J. Battista, Sr.VP-Brand
Kevin Plank, Chmn.
Peter Mahrer, Pres./Managing Dir.-Under Armour Europe, B.V.
James E. Calo, Chief Supply Chain Officer

| **Phone:** 410-454-6428 | **Fax:** 410-468-2516 |
|---|---|
| **Toll-Free:** | |
| **Address:** 1020 Hull St., 3rd Fl., Baltimore, MD 21230 US | |

## GROWTH PLANS/SPECIAL FEATURES:

Under Armour, Inc. (UA) designs, developments, markets and distributes technologically advanced, branded performance products for men, women and youth. It offers several lines of apparel and accessories that utilize a variety of synthetic microfiber fabrications engineered to replace cotton in the world of athletics and fitness with performance alternatives. UA's active wear and sports apparel accessories are designed to wick perspiration away from the skin; help regulate body temperature; enhance comfort and mobility; and improve performance regardless of weather condition. Its products are designed and merchandised along three gearlines: HEATGEAR, for when it is hot; COLDGEAR, for cold weather; and ALLSEASONGEAR, for times between the extremes. Within each gearline, Under Armour's garments come in three fit types: compression (tight fitting), fitted (athletic cut) and loose (relaxed). Products primarily consist of t-shirts designed to be worn under uniforms, ski vests or protective gear; athletic shoes; and batting, football, golf and running gloves. UA markets its products at multiple price levels to compete with cotton and other traditional products.The firm's products are offered worldwide in over 15,000 retail stores and can currently be purchased across the U.S., Canada, Japan and Western Europe through large national and regional chains of retailers, as well as smaller, independent and specialty retailers. Unaffiliated manufacturers operating in 19 countries manufacture virtually all of the company's products. International professional football, baseball, basketball, hockey, rugby and soccer players, as well as athletes in major collegiate and Olympic sports, wear its products. The company is the official supplier of footwear to the NFL (National Football League).

## FINANCIALS: **Sales and profits are in thousands of dollars—add 000 to get the full amount. 2008 Note: Financial information for 2008 was not available for all companies at press time.**

| | | |
|---|---|---|
| 2008 Sales: $725,244 | 2008 Profits: $38,229 | **U.S. Stock Ticker: UA** |
| 2007 Sales: $606,561 | 2007 Profits: $52,558 | **Int'l Ticker:** Int'l Exchange: |
| 2006 Sales: $430,689 | 2006 Profits: $38,979 | Employees: 1,400 |
| 2005 Sales: $281,053 | 2005 Profits: $19,719 | Fiscal Year Ends: 12/31 |
| 2004 Sales: $205,181 | 2004 Profits: $16,322 | Parent Company: |

## SALARIES/BENEFITS:

| | | | | |
|---|---|---|---|---|
| Pension Plan: | ESOP Stock Plan: | Profit Sharing: | Top Exec. Salary: $500,000 | Bonus: $1,000,000 |
| Savings Plan: Y | Stock Purch. Plan: | | Second Exec. Salary: $300,000 | Bonus: $225,000 |

## OTHER THOUGHTS:

**Apparent Women Officers or Directors**: 2
**Hot Spot for Advancement for Women/Minorities**: Y

## LOCATIONS: ("Y" = Yes)

| West: | Southwest: | Midwest: | Southeast: | Northeast: | International: |
|---|---|---|---|---|---|
| Y | | | | Y | Y |

# UNISOURCE ENERGY CORPORATION

www.uns.com

**Industry Group Code:** 221000 **Ranks within this company's industry group:** Sales: 5 Profits: 4

| Management: | | Sales/Marketing: | | Liberal Arts: | | Information Systems: | | Professionals: | | Technical/Scientific: | |
|---|---|---|---|---|---|---|---|---|---|---|---|
| Mgmt. Trainees: | | Mktg. Professionals: | Y | Gen. Writing/Editing: | | Info. Management: | Y | Finance/Accounting: | Y | Engineers, Elec.: | Y |
| Experienced Mgmt.: | Y | Retail Sales: | | Technical Writing: | | Software Dev.: | | Law: | Y | Engineers, Other: | Y |
| Int'l Business: | Y | Commercial/Industrial: | Y | Graphic Arts/Photog.: | | Hardware Dev.: | | HR/Other: | Y | Health/Lab: | |
| MBA Graduates: | Y | Sales Trainees: | | Music: | | Systems Integration: | | Training: | Y | Scientists/Research: | |
| | | Advertising Pros.: | | Broadcasting: | | Consulting/Other: | | Health Care: | | Petroleum/Chemicals: | Y |
| | | | | Other: | | | | Consulting: | | Math/Other: | |

## TYPES OF BUSINESS:

Utilities-Electricity & Natural Gas
Investments

## BRANDS/DIVISIONS/AFFILIATES:

Tucson Electric Power Co.
UniSource Energy Services, Inc.
Millennium Energy Holdings, Inc.
UniSource Energy Development Co.
Southwest Energy Solutions, Inc.
Luna Energy Facility (The)

## CONTACTS: *Note: Officers with more than one job title may be intentionally listed here more than once.*

James S. Pignatelli, CEO
Michael J. DeConcini, COO
James S. Pignatelli, Pres.
Kevin P. Larson, CFO/Sr. VP/Treas.
Catherine E. Ries, VP-Human Resources
Thomas A. McKenna, VP-Eng.
Raymond S. Heyman, General Counsel/Sr. VP
Steven W. Lynn, VP-Comm. & Gov't Rel.
Karen G. Kissinger, Controller/VP/Chief Compliance Officer
Philip J. Dion III, VP-Legal & Environmental Svcs.
David G. Hutchens, VP-Wholesale Energy
Herlinda H. Kennedy, Corp. Sec.
Kentton C. Grant, VP-Finance & Rates
James S. Pignatelli, Chmn.

| | |
|---|---|
| **Phone:** 520-571-4000 | **Fax:** 520-884-3602 |
| **Toll-Free:** | |
| **Address:** 1 S. Church Ave., Ste. 100, Tucson, AZ 85702 US | |

## GROWTH PLANS/SPECIAL FEATURES:

UniSource Energy Corp. is a diverse energy company. It is the holding company for Tucson Electric Power Co. (TEP); UniSource Energy Services, Inc. (UES); Millennium Energy Holdings, Inc.; and UniSource Energy Development Co. (UED). The firm conducts its business in three primary business segments, TEP, UNS Gas and UNS Electric. TEP, which generated 77% of the revenue in 2007, is an electric utility that provides electric service to more than 397,000 customers in the Tucson, Arizona metropolitan area. Its principal fuel for electric generation is low-sulfur, bituminous or sub-bituminous coal from mines in Arizona, New Mexico and Colorado. The majority of the coal supplies are purchased under long-term contracts. TEP also holds a franchise to provide electric distribution service to customers in the city of Tucson and south Tucson. UES, through its two operating subsidiaries, UNS Gas, Inc. and UNS Electric, Inc., provides gas and electric service to 30 communities in Northern and Southern Arizona. In 2007, UNS Gas had approximately 146,000 retail customers and UNS Electric had approximately 90,000 retail customers. Millennium invests in unregulated businesses and emerging technology companies. UED develops generating resources and other project development activities, including the expansion of the Springerville Generating Station. Southwest Energy Solutions, Inc., a subsidiary of Millennium, provides electrical contracting services in Arizona to commercial, industrial and governmental customers in both high voltage and inside wiring capacities, and meter reading services to TEP.

## FINANCIALS: **Sales and profits are in thousands of dollars—add 000 to get the full amount. 2008 Note: Financial information for 2008 was not available for all companies at press time.**

| | | |
|---|---|---|
| 2008 Sales: $ | 2008 Profits: $ | **U.S. Stock Ticker: UNS** |
| 2007 Sales: $1,381,373 | 2007 Profits: $58,373 | **Int'l Ticker:** Int'l Exchange: |
| 2006 Sales: $1,308,141 | 2006 Profits: $67,447 | Employees: 1,306 |
| 2005 Sales: $1,229,535 | 2005 Profits: $46,144 | Fiscal Year Ends: 12/31 |
| 2004 Sales: $1,168,978 | 2004 Profits: $45,919 | Parent Company: |

## SALARIES/BENEFITS:

| | | | | |
|---|---|---|---|---|
| Pension Plan: | ESOP Stock Plan: | Profit Sharing: | Top Exec. Salary: $694,438 | Bonus: $791,000 |
| Savings Plan: | Stock Purch. Plan: | | Second Exec. Salary: $304,077 | Bonus: $146,000 |

## OTHER THOUGHTS:

**Apparent Women Officers or Directors**: 6
**Hot Spot for Advancement for Women/Minorities**: Y

## LOCATIONS: ("Y" = Yes)

| West: | Southwest: | Midwest: | Southeast: | Northeast: | International: |
|---|---|---|---|---|---|
| | Y | | | | |

# UNITED ONLINE INC

www.unitedonline.net

**Industry Group Code:** 514191 **Ranks within this company's industry group:** Sales: 1 Profits: 1

| Management: | | Sales/Marketing: | | Liberal Arts: | | Information Systems: | | Professionals: | | Technical/Scientific: | |
|---|---|---|---|---|---|---|---|---|---|---|---|
| Mgmt. Trainees: | | Mktg. Professionals: | Y | Gen. Writing/Editing: | | Info. Management: | Y | Finance/Accounting: | Y | Engineers, Elec.: | |
| Experienced Mgmt.: | Y | Retail Sales: | | Technical Writing: | | Software Dev.: | Y | Law: | Y | Engineers, Other: | |
| Int'l Business: | Y | Commercial/Industrial: | Y | Graphic Arts/Photog.: | | Hardware Dev.: | | HR/Other: | Y | Health/Lab: | |
| MBA Graduates: | Y | Sales Trainees: | Y | Music: | | Systems Integration: | | Training: | Y | Scientists/Research: | |
| | | Advertising Pros.: | Y | Broadcasting: | | Consulting/Other: | | Health Care: | | Petroleum/Chemicals: | |
| | | | | Other: | | | | Consulting: | | Math/Other: | |

## TYPES OF BUSINESS:

Internet Service Provider
Social Networking Web Sites
Online Loyalty Marketing

## BRANDS/DIVISIONS/AFFILIATES:

Juno
NetZero
Classmates.com
MyPoints.com
Trombi
StayFriends
FTD Group, Inc.

## CONTACTS: *Note: Officers with more than one job title may be intentionally listed here more than once.*

Mark R. Goldston, CEO
Mark R. Goldston, Pres.
Scott H. Ray, CFO/Exec. VP
Jeremy Helfand, Chief Sales Officer/Exec. VP
Paul E. Jordan, Chief Personnel Officer/Exec. VP
Gerald J. Popek, CTO/Exec. VP
Frederic A. Randall, Jr., General Counsel/Exec. VP
Robert Taragan, Exec. VP-Oper.
Erik Randerson, VP-Investor Rel.
Robert Taragan, Gen. Mgr.-CyberTarget
Matt Wisk, Chief Marketing Officer/Exec. VP
Mark R. Goldston, Chmn.

**Phone:** 818-287-3000 **Fax:** 818-287-3001
**Toll-Free:**
**Address:** 21301 Burbank Blvd., Woodland Hills, CA 91367 US

## GROWTH PLANS/SPECIAL FEATURES:

United Online, Inc. is a nationwide provider of consumer Internet and media services formed from the merger of NetZero, Inc. and Juno Online Services, Inc. The company divides its business into two primary services: Classmates media and communications. The Classmates media segment offers online social networking through its website ClassMates.com and through four international social networking services including StayFriends websites in Austria, Germany and Sweden and the Trombi website in France Through the social networking websites, the company serves 50 million registered accounts, including 3.5 million pay accounts. This segment also provides online loyalty marketing through MyPoints.com. The MyPoints program provides consumers with points-based rewards for responding to e-mail offers, completing online surveys, shopping online and completing other online activities. The rewards points can be traded in for third-party gift cards and benefits from over 60 merchants. The communications segment is primarily comprised of dial-up Internet and e-mail access through NetZero and Juno. The company's dial-up services, which are available in more than 10,000 cities nationwide, consist in accelerated dial-up Internet access, standard dial-up Internet access and a free dial-up Internet access service that is subject to hourly limitations. This segment also offers minimal DSL services, which are purchased from third-parties. In addition to billable accounts, United Online derives revenues from selling online advertising space and services on its websites and in e-mails. In 2007, the firm launched its first video mail services, which allow NetZero and Juno customers to add and view personal videos as part of their e-mail without downloading the video. In 2008, United Online agreed to acquire FTD Group, Inc., a leading provider of floral products and services in the U.S., Canada, the U.K. and Ireland.

United Online offers employees health and welfare benefits and a 401(k) savings plan.

## FINANCIALS: **Sales and profits are in thousands of dollars—add 000 to get the full amount. 2008 Note: Financial information for 2008 was not available for all companies at press time.**

| | | |
|---|---|---|
| 2008 Sales: $669,403 | 2008 Profits: $-94,657 | **U.S. Stock Ticker: UNTD** |
| 2007 Sales: $513,503 | 2007 Profits: $57,777 | **Int'l Ticker:** Int'l Exchange: |
| 2006 Sales: $522,654 | 2006 Profits: $42,272 | Employees: 928 |
| 2005 Sales: $525,061 | 2005 Profits: $47,127 | Fiscal Year Ends: 12/31 |
| 2004 Sales: $448,617 | 2004 Profits: $117,480 | Parent Company: |

## SALARIES/BENEFITS:

| | | | | |
|---|---|---|---|---|
| Pension Plan: | ESOP Stock Plan: | Profit Sharing: | Top Exec. Salary: $925,000 | Bonus: $1,143,049 |
| Savings Plan: Y | Stock Purch. Plan: | | Second Exec. Salary: $427,000 | Bonus: $427,000 |

## OTHER THOUGHTS:

**Apparent Women Officers or Directors:**
**Hot Spot for Advancement for Women/Minorities:**

## LOCATIONS: ("Y" = Yes)

| West: | Southwest: | Midwest: | Southeast: | Northeast: | International: |
|---|---|---|---|---|---|
| Y | | Y | | Y | Y |

# UNITED THERAPEUTICS CORP

www.unither.com

**Industry Group Code:** 325412 **Ranks within this company's industry group:** Sales: 14 Profits: 10

| Management: | | Sales/Marketing: | | Liberal Arts: | | Information Systems: | | Professionals: | | Technical/Scientific: | |
|---|---|---|---|---|---|---|---|---|---|---|---|
| Mgmt. Trainees: | | Mktg. Professionals: | Y | Gen. Writing/Editing: | | Info. Management: | Y | Finance/Accounting: | Y | Engineers, Elec.: | |
| Experienced Mgmt.: | Y | Retail Sales: | | Technical Writing: | Y | Software Dev.: | Y | Law: | Y | Engineers, Other: | |
| Int'l Business: | Y | Commercial/Industrial: | Y | Graphic Arts/Photog.: | | Hardware Dev.: | | HR/Other: | Y | Health/Lab: | Y |
| MBA Graduates: | Y | Sales Trainees: | Y | Music: | | Systems Integration: | | Training: | Y | Scientists/Research: | Y |
| | | Advertising Pros.: | | Broadcasting: | | Consulting/Other: | | Health Care: | Y | Petroleum/Chemicals: | |
| | | | | Other: | | | | Consulting: | | Math/Other: | Y |

## TYPES OF BUSINESS:

Cardiovascular, Cancer & Infectious Diseases Therapeutics
Dietary Supplements
Telecardiology Products

## BRANDS/DIVISIONS/AFFILIATES:

Unither Pharma, Inc.
Medicomp, Inc.
HeartBar
Remodulin
OvaRex
Lung Rx

## CONTACTS: *Note: Officers with more than one job title may be intentionally listed here more than once.*

Martine Rothblatt, CEO
Roger Jeffs, COO
Roger Jeffs, Pres.
John Ferrari, CFO
Shola Oyewole, CIO
Paul A. Mahon, General Counsel
Paul A. Mahon, Exec. VP-Strategic Planning
John Ferrari, Treas.
Dan Balda, Pres./COO-Medicomp, Inc.
David Walsh, Exec. VP/COO-Production
Martine Rothblatt, Chmn.

| | |
|---|---|
| **Phone:** 301-608-9292 | **Fax:** 301-608-9291 |
| **Toll-Free:** | |
| **Address:** 1110 Spring St., Silver Spring, MD 20910 US | |

## GROWTH PLANS/SPECIAL FEATURES:

United Therapeutics Corp. (UTC) is a biotechnology company focused on the development and commercialization of therapeutic products for patients with cancer, cardiovascular diseases, and other infectious diseases. The company's key therapeutic platforms include: prostacyclin analogs, which are stable synthetic forms of prostacyclin, a molecule produced by the body that affects blood-vessel health and function; immunotherapeutic monoclonal antibodies, which are antibodies that activate patients' immune systems to treat cancer; and glycobiology antiviral agents, which are a class of small molecules that have shows preclinical indications of efficacy against a broad range of viruses. Remodulin, the company's lead product, is an FDA-approved, treprostinil-based compound designed for the treatment of pulmonary arterial hypertension (PAH), for patients with negative symptoms associated with exercise. UTC has commercial rights for Remodulin in most European Union countries, Israel, Australia, Mexico, Argentina, and Peru. The firm is developing inhaled and oral formulations of treprostinil-based products, in addition to Beraprost-MR, a prostacyclin analog designed to treat cardiovascular diseases. One of the firm's subsidiaries, Unither Pharma, Inc., markets the HeartBar line of products, which are arginine-enriched dietary supplements designed to help maintaining healthy circulatory function. Medicomp, Inc., a wholly owned subsidiary, manufactures and markets a variety of telecardiology services, including cardiac Holter monitoring, event monitoring and analysis, and pacemaker monitoring. Medicomp's services are delivered through its proprietary Digital Decipher Holter recorder/analyzer and its CardioPAL family of event monitors. In June 2008, Lung Rx, w holly owned subsidiary focused on pulmonary medicine and pulmonary therapeutic products, submitted a New Drug Application to the FDA for marketing approval of an inhaled form of treprostinil, for the treatment of pulmonary arterial hypertension.

UTC offers its employees medical, vision, dental and prescription insurance; life and AD&D insurance; short- and long-term disability; flexible spending accounts; educational assistance; and an employee assistance program.

## FINANCIALS: **Sales and profits are in thousands of dollars—add 000 to get the full amount. 2008 Note: Financial information for 2008 was not available for all companies at press time.**

| | | |
|---|---|---|
| 2008 Sales: $281,497 | 2008 Profits: $-42,789 | **U.S. Stock Ticker: UTHR** |
| 2007 Sales: $210,943 | 2007 Profits: $19,859 | **Int'l Ticker:** Int'l Exchange: |
| 2006 Sales: $159,632 | 2006 Profits: $73,965 | Employees: 320 |
| 2005 Sales: $115,915 | 2005 Profits: $65,016 | Fiscal Year Ends: 12/31 |
| 2004 Sales: $73,590 | 2004 Profits: $15,449 | Parent Company: |

## SALARIES/BENEFITS:

| | | | | |
|---|---|---|---|---|
| Pension Plan: | ESOP Stock Plan: | Profit Sharing: | Top Exec. Salary: $767,100 | Bonus: $12,000 |
| Savings Plan: Y | Stock Purch. Plan: | | Second Exec. Salary: $668,800 | Bonus: $8,400 |

## OTHER THOUGHTS:

**Apparent Women Officers or Directors:** 1
**Hot Spot for Advancement for Women/Minorities:**

## LOCATIONS: ("Y" = Yes)

| West: | Southwest: | Midwest: | Southeast: | Northeast: | International: |
|---|---|---|---|---|---|
| | | | Y | Y | Y |

Note: Financial information, benefits and other data can change quickly and may vary from those stated here.

# UNIVERSAL AMERICAN CORPORATION

www.uafc.com

**Industry Group Code:** 524113 **Ranks within this company's industry group:** Sales: 3 Profits: 5

| Management: | | Sales/Marketing: | | Liberal Arts: | | Information Systems: | | Professionals: | | Technical/Scientific: | |
|---|---|---|---|---|---|---|---|---|---|---|---|
| Mgmt. Trainees: | | Mktg. Professionals: | Y | Gen. Writing/Editing: | Y | Info. Management: | Y | Finance/Accounting: | Y | Engineers, Elec.: | |
| Experienced Mgmt.: | Y | Retail Sales: | | Technical Writing: | Y | Software Dev.: | | Law: | Y | Engineers, Other: | |
| Int'l Business: | | Commercial/Industrial: | | Graphic Arts/Photog.: | | Hardware Dev.: | | HR/Other: | Y | Health/Lab: | |
| MBA Graduates: | Y | Sales Trainees: | Y | Music: | | Systems Integration: | | Training: | Y | Scientists/Research: | |
| | | Advertising Pros.: | Y | Broadcasting: | | Consulting/Other: | | Health Care: | Y | Petroleum/Chemicals: | |
| | | | | Other: | | | | Consulting: | | Math/Other: | Y |

## TYPES OF BUSINESS:

Health Insurance
Life Insurance
Medicare Supplement Insurance
Annuity Products
Administrative Services

## BRANDS/DIVISIONS/AFFILIATES:

CHCS Services, Inc.
Nurse Navigator
Harmony Health, Inc.
MemberHealth, Inc.

## CONTACTS: *Note: Officers with more than one job title may be intentionally listed here more than once.*

Richard A. Barasch, CEO
Gary W. Bryant, COO/Exec. VP
Robert A. Waegelein, CFO/Exec. VP
Mitchell J. Stier, General Counsel/Sr. VP
Gary Jacobs, Sr. VP-Corp. Dev.
Theodore M. Carpenter, Jr., Pres./CEO-Medicare Advantage Division
Jason J. Israel, COO-CHCS Services, Inc.
Richard A. Barasch, Chmn.

**Phone:** 914-934-5200 **Fax:** 914-934-0700
**Toll-Free:**
**Address:** 6 International Dr., Ste. 190, Rye Brook, NY 10573-1068 US

## GROWTH PLANS/SPECIAL FEATURES:

Universal American Corp. (formerly known as Universal American Financial Corp.) is a health insurance holding company with an emphasis on providing an array of health insurance and managed care products and services to the senior population. The company operates in five segments. The senior managed care/Medicare Advantage segment operates Medicare Advantage coordinated care plans in Texas, Oklahoma and Florida, and Medicare Advantage PFFS plans in 35 states. The senior market health insurance segment sells health insurance products designed for the senior market through its Senior Solutions career agency force and through a network of independent general agencies. The division's primary product is Medicare supplement and also offers a stand-alone prescription drug benefit. The specialty health insurance segment's products include fixed benefit accident and sickness disability; and other health insurance products sold to the self-employed market in the U.S. The life insurance and annuity segment includes all of the life insurance and annuity business that the firm sells in the U.S. Products include final expense life insurance and asset accumulation life insurance. The senior administrative services segment provides, through subsidiary CHCS Services, Inc., outsourcing services that support insurance and non-insurance products. The division's services include policy underwriting and issuance; policy billing and collection; telephone verification; policyholder services; claims adjudication and payment; clinical case management; case assessment; and referral to health care facilities. The Nurse Navigator is a non-insurance elder care service product that includes health related information and referrals and access to nationwide networks of geriatric care nurses and long-term care providers available on a discounted basis. In September 2007, the company acquired MemberHealth, Inc. for roughly $630 million.

## FINANCIALS: Sales and profits are in thousands of dollars—add 000 to get the full amount. 2008 Note: Financial information for 2008 was not available for all companies at press time.

2008 Sales: $4,665,100
2007 Sales: $3,034,623
2006 Sales: $1,305,064
2005 Sales: $856,748
2004 Sales: $661,457

2008 Profits: $95,100
2007 Profits: $84,072
2006 Profits: $119,306
2005 Profits: $53,876
2004 Profits: $63,871

**U.S. Stock Ticker: UAM**
**Int'l Ticker:** Int'l Exchange:
Employees: 2,000
Fiscal Year Ends: 12/31
Parent Company:

## SALARIES/BENEFITS:

Pension Plan: ESOP Stock Plan: Profit Sharing: Top Exec. Salary: $798,340 Bonus: $150,750
Savings Plan: Stock Purch. Plan: Second Exec. Salary: $442,632 Bonus: $90,450

## OTHER THOUGHTS:

**Apparent Women Officers or Directors**: 1
**Hot Spot for Advancement for Women/Minorities**:

## LOCATIONS: ("Y" = Yes)

| West: | Southwest: | Midwest: | Southeast: | Northeast: | International: |
|---|---|---|---|---|---|
| Y | Y | Y | Y | Y | |

# UNIVERSAL HOSPITAL SERVICES INC

www.uhs.com

**Industry Group Code:** 532400 **Ranks within this company's industry group:** Sales: 1 Profits: 1

| Management: | | Sales/Marketing: | | Liberal Arts: | | Information Systems: | | Professionals: | | Technical/Scientific: | |
|---|---|---|---|---|---|---|---|---|---|---|---|
| Mgmt. Trainees: | | Mktg. Professionals: | Y | Gen. Writing/Editing: | | Info. Management: | Y | Finance/Accounting: | Y | Engineers, Elec.: | |
| Experienced Mgmt.: | Y | Retail Sales: | | Technical Writing: | | Software Dev.: | | Law: | Y | Engineers, Other: | |
| Int'l Business: | | Commercial/Industrial: | Y | Graphic Arts/Photog.: | | Hardware Dev.: | | HR/Other: | Y | Health/Lab: | |
| MBA Graduates: | Y | Sales Trainees: | Y | Music: | | Systems Integration: | | Training: | Y | Scientists/Research: | |
| | | Advertising Pros.: | | Broadcasting: | | Consulting/Other: | | Health Care: | Y | Petroleum/Chemicals: | |
| | | | | Other: | | | | Consulting: | | Math/Other: | |

## TYPES OF BUSINESS:

Medical Equipment Outsourcing & Services
Technical & Professional Services
Medical Equipment Sales & Remarketing

## BRANDS/DIVISIONS/AFFILIATES:

Bear Stearns Cos Inc (The)

## CONTACTS: *Note: Officers with more than one job title may be intentionally listed here more than once.*

Gary D. Blackford, CEO
Timothy W. Kuck, COO/Exec. VP
Gary D. Blackford, Pres.
Rex T. Clevenger, CFO/Exec. VP
Jeffrey L. Singer, Exec. VP-Sales & Mktg.
Walter T. Chesley, Sr. VP-Human Resources
David G. Lawson, Sr. VP-Info. & Strategic Resources
Diana Vance-Bryan, General Counsel/Sr. VP
Walter T. Chesley, Sr. VP-Dev.
Scott M. Madson, Controller/Chief Acct. Officer
Steve Heintze, Sr. VP-Nat'l Acct.
Phil Zeller, VP-Asset Optimization
Susan Ellington, VP-Oper. (East Region)
Robert Zdon, VP-Oper. (Central Region)
Gary D. Blackford, Chmn.

| | |
|---|---|
| **Phone:** 952-893-3200 | **Fax:** 952-893-0704 |
| **Toll-Free:** 800-847-7368 | |
| **Address:** 7700 France Ave. S., Ste. 275, Edina, MN 55435 US | |

## GROWTH PLANS/SPECIAL FEATURES:

Universal Hospital Services, Inc. (UHS) is a provider of medical equipment outsourcing and services to the healthcare industry. The firm services over 7,000 customers throughout the U.S. UHS customers include national, regional and local acute care hospitals, alternate site providers (such as nursing homes and home care providers) and medical equipment manufacturers. Its medical equipment outsourcing customer base includes more than 3,875 acute care hospitals and approximately 3,575 alternate site providers. The company operates in three segments: medical equipment outsourcing; technical and professional services; and medical equipment sales and remarketing. The medical equipment outsourcing segment accounted for 76.6% of the company's revenue. The company offers various programs designed to provide patient care while meeting the facility's financial goals. Programs offered are the Asset Management Partnership Program (AMPP) and the Moveable Medical Equipment Outsourcing program, among several others. AMPP focuses on reducing capital expenditures; increasing equipment productivity; and improving quality of care and nursing satisfaction, while Moveable Medical Equipment Outsourcing offers solutions that maximize utilization, increase productivity and support patient care and safety. The firm owns and manages over 500,000 pieces of medical equipment and partners with over 200 manufactures. UHS equipment rentals for hospitals include several products such as bariatric equipment and suites; critical care products; patient-monitoring products; newborn care equipment; respiratory infusion therapy products; orthopedics equipment; and support surfaces equipment. In 2007, UHS entered into an agreement to purchase the biomedical services division of Intellamed, Inc. Later that same year, UHS was acquired by an affiliate of Bear Stearns for approximately $712 million.

The company offers employees medical, dental and vision insurance; educational assistance; flexible spending accounts; and a 401(k) plan.

## FINANCIALS: **Sales and profits are in thousands of dollars—add 000 to get the full amount. 2008 Note: Financial information for 2008 was not available for all companies at press time.**

| | | |
|---|---|---|
| 2008 Sales: $ | 2008 Profits: $ | **U.S. Stock Ticker: Private** |
| 2007 Sales: $263,976 | 2007 Profits: $-63,570 | **Int'l Ticker:** Int'l Exchange: |
| 2006 Sales: $225,100 | 2006 Profits: $ 100 | Employees: 1,318 |
| 2005 Sales: $215,900 | 2005 Profits: $-1,600 | Fiscal Year Ends: 12/31 |
| 2004 Sales: $199,600 | 2004 Profits: $-3,600 | Parent Company: |

## SALARIES/BENEFITS:

| | | | | |
|---|---|---|---|---|
| Pension Plan: | ESOP Stock Plan: | Profit Sharing: | Top Exec. Salary: $234,862 | Bonus: $151,600 |
| Savings Plan: | Stock Purch. Plan: | | Second Exec. Salary: $175,784 | Bonus: $118,000 |

## OTHER THOUGHTS:

**Apparent Women Officers or Directors**: 2
**Hot Spot for Advancement for Women/Minorities**:

## LOCATIONS: ("Y" = Yes)

| West: | Southwest: | Midwest: | Southeast: | Northeast: | International: |
|---|---|---|---|---|---|
| Y | Y | Y | Y | Y | |

# US PHYSICAL THERAPY INC

www.usph.com

**Industry Group Code:** 621490 **Ranks within this company's industry group:** Sales: 3 Profits: 3

| Management: | | Sales/Marketing: | | Liberal Arts: | | Information Systems: | | Professionals: | | Technical/Scientific: | |
|---|---|---|---|---|---|---|---|---|---|---|---|
| Mgmt. Trainees: | | Mktg. Professionals: | Y | Gen. Writing/Editing: | | Info. Management: | Y | Finance/Accounting: | Y | Engineers, Elec.: | |
| Experienced Mgmt.: | Y | Retail Sales: | | Technical Writing: | | Software Dev.: | | Law: | Y | Engineers, Other: | |
| Int'l Business: | | Commercial/Industrial: | Y | Graphic Arts/Photog.: | | Hardware Dev.: | | HR/Other: | Y | Health/Lab: | Y |
| MBA Graduates: | Y | Sales Trainees: | Y | Music: | | Systems Integration: | | Training: | Y | Scientists/Research: | |
| | | Advertising Pros.: | Y | Broadcasting: | | Consulting/Other: | | Health Care: | Y | Petroleum/Chemicals: | |
| | | | | Other: | | | | Consulting: | | Math/Other: | |

## TYPES OF BUSINESS:

Occupational & Physical Therapy Clinics

## BRANDS/DIVISIONS/AFFILIATES:

STAR Physical Therapy

## CONTACTS:

*Note: Officers with more than one job title may be intentionally listed here more than once.*

Chris Reading, CEO
Chris Reading, Pres.
Larry McAfee, CFO/Exec. VP
Trey Domann, Mgr.-Bus. Dev.

**Phone:** 713-297-7000 **Fax:** 713-297-7090
**Toll-Free:** 800-580-6285
**Address:** 1300 W. Sam Houston Pkwy. S., Ste. 300, Houston, TX 77042 US

## GROWTH PLANS/SPECIAL FEATURES:

U.S. Physical Therapy, Inc. (UPT) operates outpatient physical therapy and occupational therapy clinics that provide pre- and post-operative care and treatment or orthopedic-related disorders, sports-injuries, preventive care, rehabilitation of injured workers and neurological-related injuries. The company operates through subsidiary clinic partnerships, in which the firm generally owns a 1% general partnership interest and 64% limited partnership interest. The managing therapists of the clinics own the remaining limited partnership interest in the majority of the clinics. To a lesser extent, UPT operates some clinics, through wholly-owned subsidiaries, under profit sharing arrangements with therapists. The company operates over some 350 outpatient physical and occupational therapy clinics in 42 states. Each clinic's staff typically includes one or more licensed physical or occupational therapists along with assistants, aides, exercise physiologists and athletic trainers. The clinics initially perform an evaluation of each patient, which is then followed by a treatment plan specific to the injury as prescribed by the patient's physician. The treatment plan may include a number of procedures, including therapeutic exercise, manual therapy techniques, ultrasound, electrical stimulation, hot packs, iontophoresis, education on management of daily life skills and home exercise programs. A clinic's business primarily comes from referrals by local physicians. In September 2007, the company acquired a majority interest in STAR Physical Therapy, a multi-partner outpatient rehabilitation practice with operations in southeastern U.S. In June 2008, the firm acquired 65% of a multi-partner outpatient rehabilitation practice with 9 clinics located in the Mid-Atlantic region.

The company offers its employees medical, dental and vision insurance; life and accidental death and dismemberment insurance, paid time off, disability insurance and education assistance.

## FINANCIALS:

**Sales and profits are in thousands of dollars—add 000 to get the full amount. 2008 Note: Financial information for 2008 was not available for all companies at press time.**

| | |
|---|---|
| 2008 Sales: $ | 2008 Profits: $ |
| 2007 Sales: $151,686 | 2007 Profits: $8,738 |
| 2006 Sales: $135,194 | 2006 Profits: $6,296 |
| 2005 Sales: $126,256 | 2005 Profits: $8,791 |
| 2004 Sales: $111,709 | 2004 Profits: $6,678 |

**U.S. Stock Ticker: USPH**
**Int'l Ticker:** Int'l Exchange:
Employees: 1,957
Fiscal Year Ends: 12/31
Parent Company:

## SALARIES/BENEFITS:

| | | | | |
|---|---|---|---|---|
| Pension Plan: | ESOP Stock Plan: | Profit Sharing: | Top Exec. Salary: $354,471 | Bonus: $177,500 |
| Savings Plan: Y | Stock Purch. Plan: | | Second Exec. Salary: $344,856 | Bonus: $344,664 |

## OTHER THOUGHTS:

**Apparent Women Officers or Directors:**
**Hot Spot for Advancement for Women/Minorities:**

## LOCATIONS: ("Y" = Yes)

| West: | Southwest: | Midwest: | Southeast: | Northeast: | International: |
|---|---|---|---|---|---|
| Y | Y | Y | Y | Y | |

# VALLEY NATIONAL GASES LLC

www.vngas.com

**Industry Group Code:** 422600 **Ranks within this company's industry group:** Sales: Profits:

| Management: | | Sales/Marketing: | | Liberal Arts: | | Information Systems: | | Professionals: | | Technical/Scientific: | |
|---|---|---|---|---|---|---|---|---|---|---|---|
| Mgmt. Trainees: | | Mktg. Professionals: | Y | Gen. Writing/Editing: | | Info. Management: | Y | Finance/Accounting: | Y | Engineers, Elec.: | |
| Experienced Mgmt.: | Y | Retail Sales: | | Technical Writing: | | Software Dev.: | | Law: | Y | Engineers, Other: | |
| Int'l Business: | | Commercial/Industrial: | Y | Graphic Arts/Photog.: | | Hardware Dev.: | | HR/Other: | Y | Health/Lab: | |
| MBA Graduates: | Y | Sales Trainees: | Y | Music: | | Systems Integration: | | Training: | Y | Scientists/Research: | |
| | | Advertising Pros.: | | Broadcasting: | | Consulting/Other: | | Health Care: | | Petroleum/Chemicals: | |
| | | | | Other: | | | | Consulting: | | Math/Other: | |

## TYPES OF BUSINESS:

Bulk Industrial, Medical & Specialty Gases
Welding Equipment & Supplies
Fire Protection Equipment
Propane Distribution

## BRANDS/DIVISIONS/AFFILIATES:

CI Capital Partners, LLC
N. H. Bragg & Sons

## CONTACTS: *Note: Officers with more than one job title may be intentionally listed here more than once.*

Michael J. Ziegler, CEO
Howard Hubert, COO
Howard Hubert, Pres.

**Phone:** 216-573-9909 **Fax:** 216-573-9969
**Toll-Free:** 800-380-1300
**Address:** Metro Office Ctr. Bldg, 6500 Rockside Rd, Ste. 200, Independence, OH 44131 US

## GROWTH PLANS/SPECIAL FEATURES:

Valley National Gases, LLC (VNG) mainly produces and supplies industrial and specialty gasses, including fuel, as well as supplying a range of other industrial products such as welding equipment. The firm has 92 locations in 18 states, serving over 225,000 industrial, commercial and residential customers. VNG's gas operations consist primarily of packaging and mixing industrial, medical and specialty gases, including oxygen, nitrogen, carbon dioxide (primarily for carbonated beverages) and argon, in pressurized cylinders and transporting these cylinders to customers. The firm's industrial and specialty gas customers include those involved in the metal fabrication, construction, research and laboratory, medical, commercial, agricultural and residential consumer markets. VNG's bulk gas operations include supplying helium, medical oxygen and other gases in cryogenic transports; storing gases in supplier-provided cryogenic and propane tanks; and supplying bulk gas storage and transportation related equipment. The firm also builds and installs cryogenic delivery systems. Its bulk propane operations consist of distributing the fuel to industrial, agricultural, residential and other customers. Its welding and cutting operations consist of distributing equipment and supplies including welding machines, wire, fluxes and electrodes. The firm also offers safety equipment, especially fire equipment such as hand-held fire extinguishers and large-scale fire suppression systems, and a range of personal safety equipment including respirators, dust masks and eye protection products. Services of the company include general engineering and laser system support. In February 2007, VNG was acquired by CI Capital Partners, LLC (formerly Caxton-Iseman Capital) for roughly $304 million and subsequently taken private. Since July 2007, the firm has made five acquisitions, including the gas and welding business of N. H. Bragg & Sons, acquired in May 2008.

Employees of VNG receive prescription drug, medical, dental, vision and life insurance coverage; tuition reimbursement; and paid vacations.

## FINANCIALS: **Sales and profits are in thousands of dollars—add 000 to get the full amount. 2008 Note: Financial information for 2008 was not available for all companies at press time.**

| | | |
|---|---|---|
| 2008 Sales: $ | 2008 Profits: $ | **U.S. Stock Ticker: Private** |
| 2007 Sales: $ | 2007 Profits: $ | **Int'l Ticker:** Int'l Exchange: |
| 2006 Sales: $210,531 | 2006 Profits: $15,210 | Employees: 748 |
| 2005 Sales: $167,699 | 2005 Profits: $12,371 | Fiscal Year Ends: 6/30 |
| 2004 Sales: $154,456 | 2004 Profits: $7,680 | Parent Company: CI CAPITAL PARTNERS LLC |

## SALARIES/BENEFITS:

| | | | | |
|---|---|---|---|---|
| Pension Plan: | ESOP Stock Plan: | Profit Sharing: | Top Exec. Salary: $180,000 | Bonus: $128,000 |
| Savings Plan: Y | Stock Purch. Plan: | | Second Exec. Salary: $150,000 | Bonus: $80,000 |

## OTHER THOUGHTS:

**Apparent Women Officers or Directors:**
**Hot Spot for Advancement for Women/Minorities:**

## LOCATIONS: ("Y" = Yes)

| West: | Southwest: | Midwest: | Southeast: | Northeast: | International: |
|---|---|---|---|---|---|
| | | Y | Y | Y | |

# VALUECLICK INC

**www.valueclick.com**

**Industry Group Code:** 541810A **Ranks within this company's industry group:** Sales: 1 Profits: 1

| Management: | | Sales/Marketing: | | Liberal Arts: | | Information Systems: | | Professionals: | | Technical/Scientific: | |
|---|---|---|---|---|---|---|---|---|---|---|---|
| Mgmt. Trainees: | | Mktg. Professionals: | Y | Gen. Writing/Editing: | Y | Info. Management: | Y | Finance/Accounting: | Y | Engineers, Elec.: | |
| Experienced Mgmt.: | Y | Retail Sales: | | Technical Writing: | | Software Dev.: | Y | Law: | Y | Engineers, Other: | |
| Int'l Business: | Y | Commercial/Industrial: | | Graphic Arts/Photog.: | Y | Hardware Dev.: | | HR/Other: | Y | Health/Lab: | |
| MBA Graduates: | Y | Sales Trainees: | Y | Music: | | Systems Integration: | Y | Training: | Y | Scientists/Research: | |
| | | Advertising Pros.: | Y | Broadcasting: | | Consulting/Other: | | Health Care: | | Petroleum/Chemicals: | |
| | | | | Other: | Y | | | Consulting: | | Math/Other: | |

## TYPES OF BUSINESS:

Internet-Based Advertising Services
Direct Marketing
E-Mail Marketing
Affiliate Marketing
Software & Technical Services
Application Service Provider

## BRANDS/DIVISIONS/AFFILIATES:

Mediaplex
Be Free
Commission Junction
CJ Marketplace
MOJO
PriceRunner
Search123.com
MeziMedia

## CONTACTS: *Note: Officers with more than one job title may be intentionally listed here more than once.*

Tom A. Vadnais, CEO
John P. Pitstick, CFO
Peter J. Wolfert, CTO
Scott P. Barlow, General Counsel/VP
John Ardis, VP-Corp. Strategy
Bill Todd, Gen. Mgr.-ValueClick Media
G. Scott Piotroski, Gen. Mgr.-Lead Generation
Ann Hoey, Gen. Mgr.-Mediaplex
Kerri Pollard, Gen. Mgr.-Commission Junction
James R. Zarley, Exec. Chmn.
Carl J. White, CEO-Europe

**Phone:** 818-575-4500 **Fax:** 818-575-4501
**Toll-Free:** 877-825-8323
**Address:** 30699 Russell Ranch Rd., Ste. 250, Westlake Village, CA 91362 US

## GROWTH PLANS/SPECIAL FEATURES:

ValueClick, Inc. is one of the world's largest online marketing services companies. It sells targeted and measurable online advertising campaigns and programs for advertisers and advertising agency customers, generating qualified customer leads, online sales and increased brand recognition on their behalf with large numbers of online consumers. The company operates in four segments: Media, affiliate marketing, comparison shopping and technology. The media segment provides a suite of online marketing services and tailored programs that help marketers create and increase awareness for their products and brands, attract visitors and generate leads and sales through the Internet. The division offers products in categories such as display advertising, which reaches 132 million unique Internet users in the U.S. through a network of 16,000 active online publisher relationships in the U.S. and 21,000 worldwide; lead generation marketing, which manages online campaigns that generate customer inquiries for an advertiser's product or service; e-mail marketing, which allows advertisers to target customers on a large scale with opt-in e-mail lists; and e-commerce. The affiliate marketing segment enables an advertiser to develop its own online sales force comprised of third-party affiliate publishers. Through subsidiaries Be Free, search123.com and Commission Junction, the segment offers CJ Marketplace, an advertising network where advertisers upload their offers, making them available for placement by affiliates; and search marketing, which allows advertisers to find customers who are engaged in researching and buying products and services online. The comparison shopping segment, consisting primarily of the Pricerunner, Shopping.net and MeziMedia destination web sites, enables consumers to research and compare products from among thousands of online and offline merchants. The technology segment provides advertisers, advertising agencies, web site publishers and other companies with tools to manage their business operations and marketing program. The Mediaplex subsidiary offers MOJO technology-based products.

Employees are offered medical, dental, and vision insurance; flexible spending accounts; and an employee assistance program.

## FINANCIALS: **Sales and profits are in thousands of dollars—add 000 to get the full amount. 2008 Note: Financial information for 2008 was not available for all companies at press time.**

| | | |
|---|---|---|
| 2008 Sales: $625,806 | 2008 Profits: $-218,636 | **U.S. Stock Ticker: VCLK** |
| 2007 Sales: $616,508 | 2007 Profits: $70,612 | **Int'l Ticker:** Int'l Exchange: |
| 2006 Sales: $545,616 | 2006 Profits: $63,129 | Employees: 922 |
| 2005 Sales: $304,007 | 2005 Profits: $40,644 | Fiscal Year Ends: 12/31 |
| 2004 Sales: $169,178 | 2004 Profits: $87,887 | Parent Company: |

## SALARIES/BENEFITS:

| | | | | |
|---|---|---|---|---|
| Pension Plan: | ESOP Stock Plan: | Profit Sharing: | Top Exec. Salary: $440,625 | Bonus: $337,500 |
| Savings Plan: Y | Stock Purch. Plan: Y | | Second Exec. Salary: $397,917 | Bonus: $200,000 |

## OTHER THOUGHTS:

**Apparent Women Officers or Directors**: 2
**Hot Spot for Advancement for Women/Minorities**:

## LOCATIONS: ("Y" = Yes)

| West: | Southwest: | Midwest: | Southeast: | Northeast: | International: |
|---|---|---|---|---|---|
| Y | | Y | | Y | Y |

Note: Financial information, benefits and other data can change quickly and may vary from those stated here.

# VASCO DATA SECURITY INTERNATIONAL INC

www.vasco.com

**Industry Group Code:** 511211 **Ranks within this company's industry group:** Sales: 4 Profits: 1

| Management: | | Sales/Marketing: | | Liberal Arts: | | Information Systems: | | Professionals: | | Technical/Scientific: | |
|---|---|---|---|---|---|---|---|---|---|---|---|
| Mgmt. Trainees: | | Mktg. Professionals: | Y | Gen. Writing/Editing: | | Info. Management: | Y | Finance/Accounting: | Y | Engineers, Elec.: | Y |
| Experienced Mgmt.: | Y | Retail Sales: | | Technical Writing: | Y | Software Dev.: | Y | Law: | Y | Engineers, Other: | |
| Int'l Business: | Y | Commercial/Industrial: | Y | Graphic Arts/Photog.: | | Hardware Dev.: | | HR/Other: | Y | Health/Lab: | |
| MBA Graduates: | Y | Sales Trainees: | Y | Music: | | Systems Integration: | Y | Training: | Y | Scientists/Research: | |
| | | Advertising Pros.: | | Broadcasting: | | Consulting/Other: | | Health Care: | | Petroleum/Chemicals: | |
| | | | | Other: | | | | Consulting: | | Math/Other: | |

## TYPES OF BUSINESS:

Security Software
Authentication Devices
Banking Transaction Support Products
Credit Card Verification Products
Remote Verification Products
Anti-Fraud Services

## BRANDS/DIVISIONS/AFFILIATES:

Digipass
VACMAN Controller
Cryptech
VACMAN
Identikey
VACMAN RADIUS Middleware

## CONTACTS: *Note: Officers with more than one job title may be intentionally listed here more than once.*

T. Kendall Hunt, CEO
Jan Valcke, COO
Jan Valcke, Pres.
Clifford K. Bown, CFO/Exec. VP
T. Kendall Hunt, Chmn.

**Phone:** 630-932-8844 **Fax:** 630-932-8852
**Toll-Free:**
**Address:** 1901 S. Meyers Rd., Ste. 210, Oakbrook Terrace, IL 60180 US

## GROWTH PLANS/SPECIAL FEATURES:

VASCO Data Security International, Inc. designs, develops, markets and supports open-standards-based hardware and software security systems that manage and secure access to information assets. The company's products provide mission-critical security to corporate customers' internal and external infrastructures. The firm also secures financial transactions made over private enterprise networks and public networks such as the Internet. VASCO's primary product line is the VACMAN Controller, which supports all VASCO authentication technologies including passwords, dynamic password technology (Digipass), certificates and biometrics. VASCO's product line includes VACMAN, which includes VACMAN Controller and VACMAN Middleware security software; aXs GUARD; Digipass, a suite of over 50 multi-application client e-signature software products based on the world's most widely spread electronic client platforms; DigipassPlus, an authentication service that combines all VASCO products in an outsourced service offering; and IdentiKey. With IdentiKey, a credit card customer is given a small token on which a password constantly changes. The password can be used to securely authorize ATM transactions or credit card purchases, including online purchases. Targeted markets are the applications that use fixed passwords as security. Digipass is used in a wide variety of applications, the largest of which is banking, both corporate and retail banking. Another application of the Digipass is to secure access to corporate networks for home-based, traveling and other remote users. VASCO has major financial institution customers globally, such as HSBC and ING. In 2007, the company's top 10 customers accounted for 45% of worldwide revenue. In January 2008, VASCO launched Digipass 110, the zero-footprint e-signature solution aimed at the large volume e-commerce and retail e-banking markets. In April 2008, VASCO launched Digipass 905, allowing consumers to protect themselves from attempted Internet fraud when conducting online transactions by connecting the Digipass to a PC via USB.

## FINANCIALS: **Sales and profits are in thousands of dollars—add 000 to get the full amount. 2008 Note: Financial information for 2008 was not available for all companies at press time.**

| | | |
|---|---|---|
| 2008 Sales: $132,977 | 2008 Profits: $24,291 | **U.S. Stock Ticker: VDSI** |
| 2007 Sales: $119,980 | 2007 Profits: $20,963 | **Int'l Ticker:** Int'l Exchange: |
| 2006 Sales: $76,062 | 2006 Profits: $12,587 | Employees: 240 |
| 2005 Sales: $54,579 | 2005 Profits: $7,701 | Fiscal Year Ends: 12/31 |
| 2004 Sales: $29,893 | 2004 Profits: $3,253 | Parent Company: |

## SALARIES/BENEFITS:

| | | | | |
|---|---|---|---|---|
| Pension Plan: | ESOP Stock Plan: | Profit Sharing: | Top Exec. Salary: $411,743 | Bonus: $451,160 |
| Savings Plan: | Stock Purch. Plan: Y | | Second Exec. Salary: $300,000 | Bonus: $284,890 |

## OTHER THOUGHTS:

**Apparent Women Officers or Directors:**
**Hot Spot for Advancement for Women/Minorities:**

## LOCATIONS: ("Y" = Yes)

| West: | Southwest: | Midwest: | Southeast: | Northeast: | International: |
|---|---|---|---|---|---|
| | | Y | | Y | Y |

# VENTANA MEDICAL SYSTEMS INC

www.ventanamed.com

**Industry Group Code:** 339113 **Ranks within this company's industry group:** Sales: Profits:

| Management: | | Sales/Marketing: | | Liberal Arts: | | Information Systems: | | Professionals: | | Technical/Scientific: | |
|---|---|---|---|---|---|---|---|---|---|---|---|
| Mgmt. Trainees: | | Mktg. Professionals: | Y | Gen. Writing/Editing: | | Info. Management: | Y | Finance/Accounting: | Y | Engineers, Elec.: | Y |
| Experienced Mgmt.: | Y | Retail Sales: | | Technical Writing: | Y | Software Dev.: | Y | Law: | Y | Engineers, Other: | Y |
| Int'l Business: | Y | Commercial/Industrial: | Y | Graphic Arts/Photog.: | | Hardware Dev.: | Y | HR/Other: | Y | Health/Lab: | Y |
| MBA Graduates: | Y | Sales Trainees: | Y | Music: | | Systems Integration: | | Training: | Y | Scientists/Research: | Y |
| | | Advertising Pros.: | | Broadcasting: | | Consulting/Other: | | Health Care: | Y | Petroleum/Chemicals: | |
| | | | | Other: | | | | Consulting: | | Math/Other: | Y |

## TYPES OF BUSINESS:

Instrument-Reagent Systems
Discovery Systems
Clinical Systems
Consumable Products

## BRANDS/DIVISIONS/AFFILIATES:

SYMPHONY
VIAS
Discovery
BenchMark
NexES
EBAR

## CONTACTS: *Note: Officers with more than one job title may be intentionally listed here more than once.*

Christopher Gleeson, CEO

| | |
|---|---|
| **Phone:** 520-887-2155 | **Fax:** 520-229-4207 |
| **Toll-Free:** 800-227-2155 | |
| **Address:** 1910 Innovation Park Dr., Tucson, AZ 85755 US | |

## GROWTH PLANS/SPECIAL FEATURES:

Ventana Medical Systems, Inc. develops, manufactures and markets medical diagnostic instruments and reagent systems, and provides technology for use in the slide-based diagnosis of cancer and infectious disease. The firm's products are sold to pharmaceutical and biotechnology companies with the aim of speeding the discovery of new drug targets and automating diagnostic and drug discovery procedures in clinical histology. Its products are split into two main categories, instruments and reagents. The company's instruments consist of equipment intended to standardize the preparation and staining of human tissue or cells mounted on a microscope slide. Instruments such as the SYMPHONY system, a one touch slide preparation machine, help pathologists interpret patient samples. The company also sells instruments under the VIAS, BenchMark, NexES, EBAR and Discovery brand names. In addition to instruments, Ventana markets reagents and other consumable accessories required to operate its instruments. Reagent products include high definition slides that improve diagnostic visualization; immunoenzymatic reaction systems, which use monoclonal or polyclonal antibodies to detect cells or tissue antigens; blocking reagents, which give excellent color separation and elimination of non-specific staining; oligonucleotide probes; and specialty stains. Ventana also collaborates with pharmaceutical companies to identify, develop and commercialize new diagnostic tests through its PharmaServices division. The company's customers include hospital-based anatomical pathology labs, independent reference labs, drug discovery labs of pharmaceutical companies, biotechnology companies, government labs, medical research centers and reseller serving these units. In January 2008, the firm was acquired by The Roche Group for $3.4 billion, becoming a subsidiary of the Swiss healthcare company.

Ventana offers its employees medical, dental, vision, life and accident insurance; an employee assistance plan; short- and long-term disability coverage; a 401(k) plan; a retirement plan; an education assistance program; an employee assistance program; and a 529 CollegeBound fund.

## FINANCIALS: **Sales and profits are in thousands of dollars—add 000 to get the full amount. 2008 Note: Financial information for 2008 was not available for all companies at press time.**

| | | |
|---|---|---|
| 2008 Sales: $ | 2008 Profits: $ | **U.S. Stock Ticker: Subsidiary** |
| 2007 Sales: $ | 2007 Profits: $ | **Int'l Ticker:** Int'l Exchange: |
| 2006 Sales: $238,223 | 2006 Profits: $31,578 | Employees: 952 |
| 2005 Sales: $199,132 | 2005 Profits: $25,488 | Fiscal Year Ends: 12/31 |
| 2004 Sales: $166,102 | 2004 Profits: $21,289 | Parent Company: ROCHE GROUP (THE) |

## SALARIES/BENEFITS:

| | | | | |
|---|---|---|---|---|
| Pension Plan: | ESOP Stock Plan: | Profit Sharing: | Top Exec. Salary: $367,500 | Bonus: $58,800 |
| Savings Plan: | Stock Purch. Plan: | | Second Exec. Salary: $273,269 | Bonus: $58,800 |

## OTHER THOUGHTS:

**Apparent Women Officers or Directors:**
**Hot Spot for Advancement for Women/Minorities:**

## LOCATIONS: ("Y" = Yes)

| West: | Southwest: | Midwest: | Southeast: | Northeast: | International: |
|---|---|---|---|---|---|
| | Y | | | | Y |

# VERAZ NETWORKS INC

www.veraznetworks.com

**Industry Group Code:** 334210 **Ranks within this company's industry group:** Sales: 11 Profits: 8

| Management: | | Sales/Marketing: | | Liberal Arts: | | Information Systems: | | Professionals: | | Technical/Scientific: | |
|---|---|---|---|---|---|---|---|---|---|---|---|
| Mgmt. Trainees: | | Mktg. Professionals: | Y | Gen. Writing/Editing: | Y | Info. Management: | Y | Finance/Accounting: | Y | Engineers, Elec.: | Y |
| Experienced Mgmt.: | Y | Retail Sales: | | Technical Writing: | Y | Software Dev.: | Y | Law: | Y | Engineers, Other: | Y |
| Int'l Business: | Y | Commercial/Industrial: | Y | Graphic Arts/Photog.: | | Hardware Dev.: | Y | HR/Other: | Y | Health/Lab: | |
| MBA Graduates: | Y | Sales Trainees: | Y | Music: | | Systems Integration: | Y | Training: | Y | Scientists/Research: | |
| | | Advertising Pros.: | | Broadcasting: | | Consulting/Other: | | Health Care: | | Petroleum/Chemicals: | |
| | | | | Other: | | | | Consulting: | | Math/Other: | |

## TYPES OF BUSINESS:

Internet Protocol Products
Digital Circuit Multiplication Equipment Products

## BRANDS/DIVISIONS/AFFILIATES:

ControlSwitch
I-Gate 4000
iMN Multimedia Delivery Platform

## CONTACTS: *Note: Officers with more than one job title may be intentionally listed here more than once.*

Douglas A. Sabella, CEO
Douglas A. Sabella, Pres.
Albert J. Wood, CFO
Dawn Hogh, VP-Mktg.
Denise Pierre, VP-Global Human Resources
Israel Zohar, CIO
W.R. Rohrbach, VP-Strategy & Bus. Dev.
David Dial, VP-Global Svcs.
Amit Chawla, Exec. VP-Global Bus. Units
Promod Haque, Chmn.
Pinhas Reich, VP-Global Sales
Israel Zohar, VP-Supply Chain Mgmt.

| **Phone:** 408-750-9400 | **Fax:** 408-546-0081 |
|---|---|
| **Toll-Free:** | |
| **Address:** 926 Rock Ave., Ste. 20, San Jose, CA 95131 US | |

## GROWTH PLANS/SPECIAL FEATURES:

Veraz Networks, Inc. is a global provider of voice infrastructure solutions for established and emerging wireline and wireless service providers. Veraz Network's products and services include DTX-600 DCME (Digital Circuit Multiplication Equipment); the I-Gate 4000 family of media gateways; and the ControlSwitch solution. DTX-600 DCME is used to compress voice, fax, data and signaling traffic between any two legacy networks and serves as a bandwidth optimization platform. I-Gate 4000 PRO and I-Gate 4000 EDGE media gateways are hardware devices that transport and convert the voice traffic between public switched telephone networks (PSTN) and Internet protocol (IP) networks. I-Gate 4000 PRO is designed for medium and large-scale Central Office or co-location points of presence deployments used by service providers. The I-Gate 4000 EDGE is designed for low-density applications to extend the reach of service providers' networks to low density markets and enterprises. ControlSwitch provides call control, call policy/routing, signaling gateway and media device control, in addition to back office functions in support of provisioning, billing, and network operations. Veraz Networks sells its products through a direct sales force, distributors, systems integrators and resellers. The company's customers include over 400 service providers that deploy DCME products in over 90 countries. In June 2008, Veraz launched iMN Multimedia Delivery Platform, a compact switch that enables service providers to deliver advanced time-division multiplexing (TDM), Voice over Internet Protocol (VoIP) and web services.

## FINANCIALS: **Sales and profits are in thousands of dollars—add 000 to get the full amount. 2008 Note: Financial information for 2008 was not available for all companies at press time.**

| | | |
|---|---|---|
| 2008 Sales: $ | 2008 Profits: $ | **U.S. Stock Ticker: VRAZ** |
| 2007 Sales: $125,754 | 2007 Profits: $-2,604 | **Int'l Ticker:** Int'l Exchange: |
| 2006 Sales: $99,646 | 2006 Profits: $-13,670 | Employees: 503 |
| 2005 Sales: $76,200 | 2005 Profits: $-14,300 | Fiscal Year Ends: 12/31 |
| 2004 Sales: $69,100 | 2004 Profits: $-5,800 | Parent Company: |

## SALARIES/BENEFITS:

| | | | | |
|---|---|---|---|---|
| Pension Plan: | ESOP Stock Plan: | Profit Sharing: | Top Exec. Salary: $290,000 | Bonus: $25,000 |
| Savings Plan: | Stock Purch. Plan: | | Second Exec. Salary: $231,000 | Bonus: $ |

## OTHER THOUGHTS:

**Apparent Women Officers or Directors**: 2
**Hot Spot for Advancement for Women/Minorities**:

## LOCATIONS: ("Y" = Yes)

| West: | Southwest: | Midwest: | Southeast: | Northeast: | International: |
|---|---|---|---|---|---|
| Y | | | Y | Y | Y |

# VERIFONE HOLDINGS INC

www.verifone.com

**Industry Group Code:** 522320 **Ranks within this company's industry group:** Sales: 3 Profits: 6

| Management: | | Sales/Marketing: | | Liberal Arts: | | Information Systems: | | Professionals: | | Technical/Scientific: | |
|---|---|---|---|---|---|---|---|---|---|---|---|
| Mgmt. Trainees: | Y | Mktg. Professionals: | Y | Gen. Writing/Editing: | | Info. Management: | Y | Finance/Accounting: | Y | Engineers, Elec.: | |
| Experienced Mgmt.: | Y | Retail Sales: | | Technical Writing: | Y | Software Dev.: | Y | Law: | Y | Engineers, Other: | |
| Int'l Business: | Y | Commercial/Industrial: | Y | Graphic Arts/Photog.: | | Hardware Dev.: | | HR/Other: | Y | Health/Lab: | |
| MBA Graduates: | Y | Sales Trainees: | Y | Music: | | Systems Integration: | Y | Training: | Y | Scientists/Research: | |
| | | Advertising Pros.: | Y | Broadcasting: | | Consulting/Other: | | Health Care: | | Petroleum/Chemicals: | |
| | | | | Other: | | | | Consulting: | | Math/Other: | |

## TYPES OF BUSINESS:

Payment & Transaction Processing
Electronic Payment Devices
Wireless Payment Systems
Specialty Payment Services

## BRANDS/DIVISIONS/AFFILIATES:

MX Solutions
Vx Solutions
Verix Operating Environment
SoftPay Software
VeriShield
iOrder Food Service Kiosk
POSitouch Hospitality Systems
Peripheral Computer Industries

## CONTACTS: *Note: Officers with more than one job title may be intentionally listed here more than once.*

Douglas G. Bergeron, CEO
Robert Dykes, CFO/Sr. VP
Paul Rasory, Sr. VP-Mktg.
Dawn LaPlante, VP-Human Resources
Dave Turnbull, Sr. VP-R&D
Patrick McGivern, Sr. VP-Oper.
Lazy Yanay, Managing Dir.-VeriFone Middle East
Elmore Waller, Exec. VP-Integrated Solutions
Dan Yienger, VP-Petroleum Sales
Jennifer Miles, VP & Gen. Mgr.-Integrated Systems Retail
Charles R. Rinehart, Chmn.
William C. Nichols, Sr. VP & Gen. Mgr.-Asia Pacific
Patrick McGivern, Sr. VP-Global Supply Chain

**Phone:** 408-232-7800 **Fax:** 408-232-7811
**Toll-Free:**
**Address:** 2099 Gateway Pl., Ste. 600, San Jose, CA 95110 US

## GROWTH PLANS/SPECIAL FEATURES:

VeriFone Holdings, Inc. is a designer and marketer of electronic payment technologies and services that holds the long term goal of facilitating the global shift toward electronic payment transactions and away from cash and checks. The company focuses on point of sale payment systems for global financial institutions, payment processors, petroleum companies, large retailers, government organizations and healthcare companies, as well as independent sales organizations. VeriFone's payment system consists of point of sale electronic payment devices that run the firm's proprietary and third party operating systems, security and encryption software and certified payment software as well as third party, value-added applications. The payment systems are able to process a wide range of payment types including signature and PIN-based debit cards, credit cards, radio frequency identification (RFID) cards and tokens, smart cards, pre-paid gift and other stored-value cards, electronic bill payment, check authorization and conversion, signature capture and electronic benefits transfer. The electronic payment systems are available in several distinctive modular configurations, including wireline, wireless, countertop, integrated and stand-alone payment terminals models. Customers are also offered support for installed systems, consulting and project management services for system deployment and customization of integrated software solutions. In November 2007, VeriFone, introduced VeriFone Access, a product designed to manage electronic payments, to Mexico. In December of the same year, the company purchased the EFTPOS Services Business from the Australian firm, Peripheral Computer Industries (PCI). Among the new products introduced in 2008 are an EMV certified integrated transportation payment system that is used on buses in Kahramanmaras, Turkey and the Vx 700, an electronic payments module to be used in kiosk, vending machines and ticketing devices.

Employees of the company are offered medical, dental and vision insurance; life insurance; AD&D insurance; financial protection benefits; disability coverage; flexible spending accounts; a 401(k); an employee assistance program; and education reimbursement.

## FINANCIALS: **Sales and profits are in thousands of dollars—add 000 to get the full amount. 2008 Note: Financial information for 2008 was not available for all companies at press time.**

| | | |
|---|---|---|
| 2008 Sales: $921,931 | 2008 Profits: $-421,180 | **U.S. Stock Ticker: PAY** |
| 2007 Sales: $902,892 | 2007 Profits: $-34,016 | **Int'l Ticker:** Int'l Exchange: |
| 2006 Sales: $581,070 | 2006 Profits: $59,511 | Employees: 2,224 |
| 2005 Sales: $485,367 | 2005 Profits: $33,239 | Fiscal Year Ends: 10/31 |
| 2004 Sales: $390,088 | 2004 Profits: $5,606 | Parent Company: |

## SALARIES/BENEFITS:

| | | | | |
|---|---|---|---|---|
| Pension Plan: | ESOP Stock Plan: | Profit Sharing: | Top Exec. Salary: $695,833 | Bonus: $192,284 |
| Savings Plan: Y | Stock Purch. Plan: | | Second Exec. Salary: $396,667 | Bonus: $150,000 |

## OTHER THOUGHTS:

**Apparent Women Officers or Directors**: 4
**Hot Spot for Advancement for Women/Minorities**: Y

## LOCATIONS: ("Y" = Yes)

| West: | Southwest: | Midwest: | Southeast: | Northeast: | International: |
|---|---|---|---|---|---|
| Y | | | Y | | Y |

# VERTEX PHARMACEUTICALS INC

**www.vpharm.com**

**Industry Group Code:** 325412 **Ranks within this company's industry group:** Sales: 16 Profits: 38

| **Management:** | | **Sales/Marketing:** | | **Liberal Arts:** | | **Information Systems:** | | **Professionals:** | | **Technical/Scientific:** | |
|---|---|---|---|---|---|---|---|---|---|---|---|
| Mgmt. Trainees: | | Mktg. Professionals: | Y | Gen. Writing/Editing: | | Info. Management: | Y | Finance/Accounting: | Y | Engineers, Elec.: | |
| Experienced Mgmt.: | Y | Retail Sales: | | Technical Writing: | Y | Software Dev.: | Y | Law: | Y | Engineers, Other: | |
| Int'l Business: | Y | Commercial/Industrial: | Y | Graphic Arts/Photog.: | | Hardware Dev.: | | HR/Other: | Y | Health/Lab: | Y |
| MBA Graduates: | Y | Sales Trainees: | Y | Music: | | Systems Integration: | | Training: | Y | Scientists/Research: | Y |
| | | Advertising Pros.: | | Broadcasting: | | Consulting/Other: | | Health Care: | Y | Petroleum/Chemicals: | Y |
| | | | | Other: | | | | Consulting: | | Math/Other: | Y |

## TYPES OF BUSINESS:

Small Molecule Drugs

## BRANDS/DIVISIONS/AFFILIATES:

Telaprevir
Lexiva
Telzir
MK-0457
VX-702
VX-770
VX-883
VX-409

## CONTACTS: *Note: Officers with more than one job title may be intentionally listed here more than once.*

Joshua Boger, CEO
Joshua Boger, Pres.
Ian F. Smith, CFO/Exec. VP
Lisa Kelly-Croswell, Sr. VP-Human Resources
Peter Mueller, Chief Scientific Officer
Kenneth S. Boger, General Counsel/Sr. VP
Kurt C. Graves, Head-Strategic Dev./Exec. VP/Chief Commercial Off.
Peter Mueller, Exec. VP-Drug Innovation & Realization
Richard C. Garrison, Sr. VP/Catalyst
John J. Alam, Exec. VP-Medicine Dev./Chief Medical Officer
Amit K. Sachdev, Sr. VP-Public Policy & Gov't Affairs
Charles A. Sanders, Chmn.

| **Phone:** 617-444-6100 | **Fax:** 617-444-6680 |
|---|---|
| **Toll-Free:** | |
| **Address:** 130 Waverly St., Cambridge, MA 02139 US | |

## GROWTH PLANS/SPECIAL FEATURES:

Vertex Pharmaceuticals, Inc. discovers, develops and commercializes small molecule drugs for the treatment of serious diseases. The company concentrates most of its drug development resources on four drug candidates: Telaprevir, for the treatment of hepatitis C virus infection; VX-702, for the treatment of rheumatoid arthritis and other inflammatory diseases; VX-770, for the treatment of cystic fibrosis; and VX-883, for the treatment of bacterial infection. The firm's lead product, telaprevir, is an oral hepatitis C protease inhibitor in Phase III clinical trials. The U.S. Food and Drug Administration (FDA) granted fast track designation to telaprevir. Vertex's pipeline includes several drug candidates that are being developed by its collaborators. The most advanced of these drug candidates is MK-0457, an Aurora kinase inhibitor developed by Merck & Co., Inc. for the treatment of cancer. Other collaborations include Cystic Fibrosis Foundation Therapeutics, Inc., with which it is developing VX-770; GlaxoSmithKline, for the development and commercialization of VX-409; and Kissei Pharmaceutical Co., Ltd., for the development and commercialization of VX-702. Forsamprenavir calcium, a company-discovered compound for the treatment of HIV infection, is marketed by the firm's collaborator GlaxoSmithKlein plc as Lexiva in the U.S. and Telzir in Europe. The firm began Phase III clinical trials for telaprevir in March 2008.

Employee benefits at Vertex include medical, dental and vision insurance; flexible benefits; educational assistance; commuter benefits; employee assistance; child and elder care; banking and mortgage discounts; and discount entertainment passes.

## FINANCIALS: **Sales and profits are in thousands of dollars—add 000 to get the full amount. 2008 Note: Financial information for 2008 was not available for all companies at press time.**

| | | |
|---|---|---|
| 2008 Sales: $175,504 | 2008 Profits: $-459,851 | **U.S. Stock Ticker: VRTX** |
| 2007 Sales: $199,012 | 2007 Profits: $-391,279 | **Int'l Ticker:** Int'l Exchange: |
| 2006 Sales: $216,356 | 2006 Profits: $-206,891 | Employees: 1,150 |
| 2005 Sales: $160,890 | 2005 Profits: $-203,417 | Fiscal Year Ends: 12/31 |
| 2004 Sales: $102,717 | 2004 Profits: $-166,247 | Parent Company: |

## SALARIES/BENEFITS:

| | | | | |
|---|---|---|---|---|
| Pension Plan: | ESOP Stock Plan: | Profit Sharing: | Top Exec. Salary: $616,615 | Bonus: $318,888 |
| Savings Plan: Y | Stock Purch. Plan: Y | | Second Exec. Salary: $444,361 | Bonus: $229,804 |

## OTHER THOUGHTS:

**Apparent Women Officers or Directors**: 2
**Hot Spot for Advancement for Women/Minorities**: Y

## LOCATIONS: ("Y" = Yes)

| West: | Southwest: | Midwest: | Southeast: | Northeast: | International: |
|---|---|---|---|---|---|
| Y | | | | Y | Y |

# VIASAT INC

www.viasat.com

**Industry Group Code:** 334220 **Ranks within this company's industry group:** Sales: 2 Profits: 1

| Management: | | Sales/Marketing: | | Liberal Arts: | | Information Systems: | | Professionals: | | Technical/Scientific: | |
|---|---|---|---|---|---|---|---|---|---|---|---|
| Mgmt. Trainees: | | Mktg. Professionals: | Y | Gen. Writing/Editing: | Y | Info. Management: | Y | Finance/Accounting: | Y | Engineers, Elec.: | Y |
| Experienced Mgmt.: | Y | Retail Sales: | | Technical Writing: | Y | Software Dev.: | Y | Law: | Y | Engineers, Other: | Y |
| Int'l Business: | Y | Commercial/Industrial: | Y | Graphic Arts/Photog.: | | Hardware Dev.: | Y | HR/Other: | Y | Health/Lab: | |
| MBA Graduates: | Y | Sales Trainees: | Y | Music: | | Systems Integration: | Y | Training: | Y | Scientists/Research: | |
| | | Advertising Pros.: | | Broadcasting: | | Consulting/Other: | | Health Care: | | Petroleum/Chemicals: | |
| | | | | Other: | | | | Consulting: | | Math/Other: | |

## TYPES OF BUSINESS:

Telecommunications Equipment-Digital Satellite
Networking & Wireless Signal Processing

## BRANDS/DIVISIONS/AFFILIATES:

SurfBeam
Intelligent Compression Technologies, Inc.
ViaSat-1

## CONTACTS:

*Note: Officers with more than one job title may be intentionally listed here more than once.*

Mark D. Dankberg, CEO
Richard A. Baldridge, COO
Richard A. Baldridge, Pres.
Ron Wangerin, CFO/VP
H. Steve Estes, VP-Human Resources
Mark J. Miller, Co-CTO/VP/Mgr.-Eng.
Steven R. Hart, VP/Mgr.-Eng./Co-CTO
Gregory D. Monahan, VP-Admin. & New Facilities Acquisition
Keven K. Lippert, General Counsel/Sec./VP
Kevin J. Harkenrider, VP-Oper.
Tom Moore, Sr. VP/Pres, ViaSat-1 Ka-band Broadband Initiative
Mark D. Dankberg, Chmn.

**Phone:** 760-476-2200 **Fax:** 760-929-3941
**Toll-Free:**
**Address:** 6155 El Camino Real, Carlsbad, CA 92009-1699 US

## GROWTH PLANS/SPECIAL FEATURES:

ViaSat, Inc. provides digital satellite communications and other wireless networking and signal processing equipment and services. Its sales generally consist of two parts: Project contracts to study, research, develop, test, support and manufacture customized communication systems, which are often turned into off-the-shelf products; and selling, deploying and supporting its off-the-shelf products. ViaSat operates in three segments: Government Systems, Commercial Networks and Satellite Services. The Government Systems segment encompasses products serving defense customers, including its tactical data link product line; tactical networking and information assurance, enabling the government and military to secure information up to Top Secret levels; and mobile satellite communication systems. Current defense products include a multifunction information distribution system (MIDS); simulation and test equipment for airborne radio systems; and UHF DAMA satellite communications products, such as modems, terminals and network control systems. The Commercial Networks segment includes consumer satellite broadband systems, powered by ViaSat's SurfBeam; mobile broadband systems, including the design and development of airborne, maritime and ground mobile terminals and systems; enterprise VSAT (Very Small Aperture Terminal) networks; satellite communications, MMIC (monolithic microwave integrated circuit) and enterprise network technology design and development; and antenna systems. Lastly, the Satellite Services segment, similar to the Commercial Networks segment, offers mobile satellite communications services to airborne- and marine-based customers in the U.S., North Atlantic and Europe; and managed broadband wireless networking services. In February 2007, ViaSat acquired Intelligent Compression Technologies, Inc., which provides patented data compression techniques, advanced transport protocols and application optimization, for $20 million. In February 2008, the firm commissioned a subsidiary of Loral Space & Communications, Inc., called Space Systems/Loral, to build ViaSat-1, a Ka-band broadband satellite. ViaSat-1, scheduled to launch in 2011, will increase the current satellite broadband Internet access available to customers in the U.S., Canada, the Caribbean and Europe by a factor of 10.

## FINANCIALS:

**Sales and profits are in thousands of dollars—add 000 to get the full amount. 2008 Note: Financial information for 2008 was not available for all companies at press time.**

| | | |
|---|---|---|
| 2008 Sales: $574,650 | 2008 Profits: $33,513 | **U.S. Stock Ticker: VSAT** |
| 2007 Sales: $516,566 | 2007 Profits: $30,166 | **Int'l Ticker:** Int'l Exchange: |
| 2006 Sales: $433,823 | 2006 Profits: $23,515 | Employees: 1,680 |
| 2005 Sales: $345,939 | 2005 Profits: $19,267 | Fiscal Year Ends: 3/31 |
| 2004 Sales: $278,600 | 2004 Profits: $13,200 | Parent Company: |

## SALARIES/BENEFITS:

| | | | | |
|---|---|---|---|---|
| Pension Plan: | ESOP Stock Plan: | Profit Sharing: | Top Exec. Salary: $545,000 | Bonus: $640,000 |
| Savings Plan: Y | Stock Purch. Plan: Y | | Second Exec. Salary: $420,000 | Bonus: $390,000 |

## OTHER THOUGHTS:

**Apparent Women Officers or Directors:**
**Hot Spot for Advancement for Women/Minorities:**

## LOCATIONS: ("Y" = Yes)

| West: | Southwest: | Midwest: | Southeast: | Northeast: | International: |
|---|---|---|---|---|---|
| Y | Y | Y | Y | Y | Y |

Note: Financial information, benefits and other data can change quickly and may vary from those stated here.

# VIBRANT MEDIA INC

www.vibrantmedia.com

**Industry Group Code:** 541810A **Ranks within this company's industry group:** Sales: Profits:

| **Management:** | | **Sales/Marketing:** | | **Liberal Arts:** | | **Information Systems:** | | **Professionals:** | | **Technical/Scientific:** | |
|---|---|---|---|---|---|---|---|---|---|---|---|
| Mgmt. Trainees: | | Mktg. Professionals: | Y | Gen. Writing/Editing: | | Info. Management: | Y | Finance/Accounting: | Y | Engineers, Elec.: | |
| Experienced Mgmt.: | Y | Retail Sales: | | Technical Writing: | | Software Dev.: | | Law: | Y | Engineers, Other: | |
| Int'l Business: | Y | Commercial/Industrial: | | Graphic Arts/Photog.: | Y | Hardware Dev.: | | HR/Other: | Y | Health/Lab: | |
| MBA Graduates: | Y | Sales Trainees: | Y | Music: | | Systems Integration: | Y | Training: | Y | Scientists/Research: | |
| | | Advertising Pros.: | Y | Broadcasting: | | Consulting/Other: | | Health Care: | | Petroleum/Chemicals: | |
| | | | | Other: | Y | | | Consulting: | | Math/Other: | |

## TYPES OF BUSINESS:

Online Advertising

## BRANDS/DIVISIONS/AFFILIATES:

Vibrant In-Text Solutions
Vibrant Video
Vibrant Interactive Ads
SmartAD
IntelliTXT
Vibrant Video (Expandable)

## CONTACTS: *Note: Officers with more than one job title may be intentionally listed here more than once.*

Doug Stevenson, CEO
Dennis Morgan, CFO
Anna Kassoway, VP-Mktg.
Denise Garcia, Sr. VP-Research
Richard Brindley, CTO
Gavin McCloskey, Sr. VP-Oper.
Denise Garcia, Sr. VP-Corp. Strategy
Laura Colona, Dir.-Public Rel.
Gavin McCloskey, Sr. VP-Finance
Paul K. Joachim, Sr. VP-Sales, North America
Craig Gooding, Chief Commercial Officer, Bus. Dev. & Sales
Anna Kassoway, VP-Creative Solutions
Doug Stevenson, Chmn.
Henry Clifford-Jones, Gen. Mgr.-Europe

**Phone:** 646-312-6100 **Fax:** 212-867-4925
**Toll-Free:** 888-321-8427
**Address:** 565 5th Ave., 15th Fl., New York, NY 10017 US

## GROWTH PLANS/SPECIAL FEATURES:

Vibrant Media, Inc. offers video and contextual advertising services. The firm's core offering consists of Vibrant In-Text Solutions, which includes Vibrant Video and Vibrant Interactive Ads. The firm's SmartAD software uses Vibrant's IntelliTXT technology to scan and double-underline web page key words, and customer advertisements appear when moved over with a cursor. Vibrant Video allows customers to deliver video, movie trailers, TV ads or music videos through the In-Text link, while Vibrant Interactive Ads allows customers to deliver static images, flash animation, MPU (Message Plus Unit) or animated .gif files. The In-Text ads usually provide a link that users may follow to learn more about, or in some cases actually purchase a customer's product. Vibrant has a creative department, media account planners and an optimization team to assist customers in designing their In-Text ad, including converting flash to video and choosing key words. After a customer has purchased and installed an In-Text service, Vibrant provides continuous, web-based reports on the campaign's performance. The firm's Vibrant Video (Expandable), which expands a video advertisement when a user moves their mouse cursor over the image. The firm only serves customers with sites receiving over 500,000 page views per month and has strict content standards, refusing to offer In-Text ads for sites containing, promoting or linking directly to gambling, violent content, drugs or pornography, for example. Customers include Sun Microsystems; Sony; Microsoft; and NEC. It currently provides ads only in the U.S., Canada, U.K., Sweden, Germany, France, Spain, the Netherlands, Denmark and Belgium. In September 2008, Vibrant Media released a new advanced editorial application for web publishers, Vibrant Related Content. In December 2008 the company partnered with ITV, a U.K. commercial television network; as a result of the year-long contract, Vibrant will provide in-text solutions to all of ITV's online properties.

## FINANCIALS: **Sales and profits are in thousands of dollars—add 000 to get the full amount. 2008 Note: Financial information for 2008 was not available for all companies at press time.**

| | | |
|---|---|---|
| 2008 Sales: $ | 2008 Profits: $ | **U.S. Stock Ticker: Private** |
| 2007 Sales: $ | 2007 Profits: $ | **Int'l Ticker:** Int'l Exchange: |
| 2006 Sales: $ | 2006 Profits: $ | Employees: |
| 2005 Sales: $ | 2005 Profits: $ | Fiscal Year Ends: 12/31 |
| 2004 Sales: $ | 2004 Profits: $ | Parent Company: |

## SALARIES/BENEFITS:

| | | | | |
|---|---|---|---|---|
| Pension Plan: | ESOP Stock Plan: | Profit Sharing: | Top Exec. Salary: $ | Bonus: $ |
| Savings Plan: | Stock Purch. Plan: | | Second Exec. Salary: $ | Bonus: $ |

## OTHER THOUGHTS:

**Apparent Women Officers or Directors**: 1
**Hot Spot for Advancement for Women/Minorities**:

## LOCATIONS: ("Y" = Yes)

| West: | Southwest: | Midwest: | Southeast: | Northeast: | International: |
|---|---|---|---|---|---|
| Y | | | | Y | Y |

# VIGNETTE CORP

www.vignette.com

**Industry Group Code:** 511202 **Ranks within this company's industry group:** Sales: 2 Profits: 1

| Management: | | Sales/Marketing: | | Liberal Arts: | | Information Systems: | | Professionals: | | Technical/Scientific: | |
|---|---|---|---|---|---|---|---|---|---|---|---|
| Mgmt. Trainees: | | Mktg. Professionals: | Y | Gen. Writing/Editing: | | Info. Management: | Y | Finance/Accounting: | Y | Engineers, Elec.: | Y |
| Experienced Mgmt.: | Y | Retail Sales: | | Technical Writing: | Y | Software Dev.: | Y | Law: | Y | Engineers, Other: | |
| Int'l Business: | Y | Commercial/Industrial: | Y | Graphic Arts/Photog.: | | Hardware Dev.: | | HR/Other: | Y | Health/Lab: | |
| MBA Graduates: | Y | Sales Trainees: | Y | Music: | | Systems Integration: | | Training: | Y | Scientists/Research: | |
| | | Advertising Pros.: | | Broadcasting: | | Consulting/Other: | | Health Care: | | Petroleum/Chemicals: | |
| | | | | Other: | | | | Consulting: | | Math/Other: | |

## TYPES OF BUSINESS:

Computer Software-Content Management
Consulting & Support Services

## BRANDS/DIVISIONS/AFFILIATES:

Vidavee
Vignette Content Management

## CONTACTS: *Note: Officers with more than one job title may be intentionally listed here more than once.*

Mike Aviles, CEO
Mike Aviles, Pres.
Pat Kelly, CFO
Dave Dutch, Sr. VP-Products & Mktg.
Gayle Wiley, Sr. VP-Global Human Resources
Somesh Singh, Sr. VP-R&D
Conleth O'Connell, CTO
Bryce M. Johnson, General Counsel/Sr. VP
Somesh Singh, Sr. VP-Tech. Oper.
Jan H Lindelow, Chmn.
Dick Cahill, Gen. Mgr.-EMEA

| | |
|---|---|
| **Phone:** 512-741-4300 | **Fax:** 512-741-1537 |
| **Toll-Free:** 888-608-9900 | |
| **Address:** 1301 S. MoPac Expy., Ste. 100, Austin, TX 78746 US | |

## GROWTH PLANS/SPECIAL FEATURES:

Vignette Corp. provides content management applications used by organizations to create and maintain online relationships with customers, employees, business partners and suppliers. The firm's family of software products enables companies to manage and deliver content from virtually any source. Vignette products include offerings in eleven categories: Web content management, which supports Web site creation, management, process automation, publishing and analytics; portals, which enable the development and delivery of customizable Web applications; collaboration products, link employees, customers, prospects and partners with shared, Web-based workspaces; document and records management products, which enable capture, authoring, versioning, retention and disposition management, security, auditing, discovery and litigation management; imaging and workflow products, which support high-performance document capture, processing, storage, management and retrieval; media solutions for digital content, offering a management solution for content from a variety of sources; social media solutions, facilitating the creation of online communities; personalization products; accelerated delivery solutions; interaction management products; and enterprise content integration products, which provide graphical integration links to many applications, platforms and protocols. The firm's content management software is designed to manage and share information, optimize business processes, integrate systems and information, manage the lifecycle of enterprise information and facilitate collaboration by supporting information sharing. The company also offers support and consulting services. The firm also maintains strategic alliances with hardware platform manufacturers, operating systems vendors, software and database developers, resellers, system integrators and service organizations. Vignette markets its products and services throughout the Americas, Europe, Asia and Australia. In late 2007, the firm launched Rich Media Services, an addition to its latest Vignette Content Management helps in the creation and management of rich media assets. Recent client sites include USA.gov, IRS.gov, NASA.gov and MarthaStewart.com among others. In April 2008, Vignette agreed to acquire Vidavee, a video Web services company.

## FINANCIALS: **Sales and profits are in thousands of dollars—add 000 to get the full amount. 2008 Note: Financial information for 2008 was not available for all companies at press time.**

| | | |
|---|---|---|
| 2008 Sales: $169,546 | 2008 Profits: $-6,276 | **U.S. Stock Ticker: VIGN** |
| 2007 Sales: $191,814 | 2007 Profits: $24,825 | **Int'l Ticker:** Int'l Exchange: |
| 2006 Sales: $197,574 | 2006 Profits: $12,319 | Employees: 667 |
| 2005 Sales: $190,675 | 2005 Profits: $20,394 | Fiscal Year Ends: 12/31 |
| 2004 Sales: $177,927 | 2004 Profits: $-52,855 | Parent Company: |

## SALARIES/BENEFITS:

| | | | | |
|---|---|---|---|---|
| Pension Plan: | ESOP Stock Plan: | Profit Sharing: | Top Exec. Salary: $390,000 | Bonus: $283,500 |
| Savings Plan: | Stock Purch. Plan: | | Second Exec. Salary: $275,000 | Bonus: $116,900 |

## OTHER THOUGHTS:

**Apparent Women Officers or Directors**: 3
**Hot Spot for Advancement for Women/Minorities**: Y

## LOCATIONS: ("Y" = Yes)

| West: | Southwest: | Midwest: | Southeast: | Northeast: | International: |
|---|---|---|---|---|---|
| Y | Y | | | Y | Y |

Note: Financial information, benefits and other data can change quickly and may vary from those stated here.

# VIROPHARMA INC

www.viropharma.com

**Industry Group Code:** 325412 **Ranks within this company's industry group:** Sales: 15 Profits: 4

| Management: | | Sales/Marketing: | | Liberal Arts: | | Information Systems: | | Professionals: | | Technical/Scientific: | |
|---|---|---|---|---|---|---|---|---|---|---|---|
| Mgmt. Trainees: | | Mktg. Professionals: | Y | Gen. Writing/Editing: | | Info. Management: | Y | Finance/Accounting: | Y | Engineers, Elec.: | |
| Experienced Mgmt.: | Y | Retail Sales: | | Technical Writing: | Y | Software Dev.: | Y | Law: | Y | Engineers, Other: | |
| Int'l Business: | | Commercial/Industrial: | Y | Graphic Arts/Photog.: | | Hardware Dev.: | | HR/Other: | Y | Health/Lab: | Y |
| MBA Graduates: | Y | Sales Trainees: | Y | Music: | | Systems Integration: | | Training: | Y | Scientists/Research: | Y |
| | | Advertising Pros.: | | Broadcasting: | | Consulting/Other: | | Health Care: | Y | Petroleum/Chemicals: | |
| | | | | Other: | | | | Consulting: | | Math/Other: | Y |

## TYPES OF BUSINESS:

Oral Antibiotics
Hepatitis C Drugs
Infectious Diseases Drugs

## BRANDS/DIVISIONS/AFFILIATES:

Vanococin HCl Capsules
Maribavir
HCV-796
Camvia
Cinryze
NTCD

## CONTACTS: *Note: Officers with more than one job title may be intentionally listed here more than once.*

Vincent J. Milano, CEO
Daniel B. Soland, COO/VP
Vincent J. Milano, Pres.
Colin Broom, Chief Scientific Officer/VP
Thomas F. Doyle, VP-Strategic Initiatives
Michel de Rosen, Chmn.
Robert G. Pietrusko, VP-Global Regulatory Affairs & Quality

| **Phone:** 610-458-7300 | **Fax:** 610-458-7380 |
|---|---|
| **Toll-Free:** | |
| **Address:** 397 Eagleview Blvd., Exton, PA 19341 US | |

## GROWTH PLANS/SPECIAL FEATURES:

ViroPharma, Inc. is a biopharmaceutical company that develops and commercializes products that address serious infectious diseases, with a focus on products used by physician specialists or in hospital settings. The company's only marketed product is Vancocin HC1 capsules, an oral antibiotic for the treatment of antibiotic-associated pseudomembranous colitis and enterocolitis, including methicilin-resistant strains. The firm is developing Camvia (formerly maribavir), currently in Phase III, for the prevention and treatment of cytomegalovirus diseases and HCV-796, currently in Phase II, for the treatment of hepatitis C virus. ViroPharma has a licensing agreement for the rights to develop non-toxigenic strains of C. difficile (NTCD) for the treatment and prevention of CDI. The firm has licensed the U.S. and Canadian rights for an intranasal formulation of pleconaril, to Schering-Plough for the treatment of picornavirus infections. Customers of Vancocin include wholesalers, who then distribute the drug to pharmacies, hospitals and long term care facilities. In May 2007, the company announced the decision to establish a European subsidiary that would be in charge of developing and commercializing Camvia in Europe. In June 2007, the firm announced that U.S. Food and Drug Administration (FDA) granted fast track designation for HCV-796 for treatment of hepatitis C virus infection. In July 2007, ViroPharma announced that it had initiated a Phase III clinical trial for Camvia for patients undergoing a liver transplant procedure. In July 2008 the firm agreed to acquire Lev Pharmaceuticals for $442.9 million; this transaction includes Lev's lead product Cinryze, currently under review as a treatment for hereditary angioedema.

The company offers its employees medical and dental benefits; a 401(k) plan; and stock options.

## FINANCIALS: **Sales and profits are in thousands of dollars—add 000 to get the full amount. 2008 Note: Financial information for 2008 was not available for all companies at press time.**

| | | |
|---|---|---|
| 2008 Sales: $ | 2008 Profits: $ | **U.S. Stock Ticker: VPHM** |
| 2007 Sales: $203,770 | 2007 Profits: $95,353 | **Int'l Ticker:** Int'l Exchange: |
| 2006 Sales: $167,181 | 2006 Profits: $66,666 | Employees: 115 |
| 2005 Sales: $132,417 | 2005 Profits: $113,705 | Fiscal Year Ends: 12/31 |
| 2004 Sales: $22,389 | 2004 Profits: $-19,534 | Parent Company: |

## SALARIES/BENEFITS:

| | | | | |
|---|---|---|---|---|
| Pension Plan: | ESOP Stock Plan: | Profit Sharing: | Top Exec. Salary: $392,000 | Bonus: $168,168 |
| Savings Plan: Y | Stock Purch. Plan: Y | | Second Exec. Salary: $327,000 | Bonus: $142,245 |

## OTHER THOUGHTS:

**Apparent Women Officers or Directors:**
**Hot Spot for Advancement for Women/Minorities:**

## LOCATIONS: ("Y" = Yes)

| West: | Southwest: | Midwest: | Southeast: | Northeast: | International: |
|---|---|---|---|---|---|
| | | | | Y | |

# VISION SERVICE PLAN

**www.vsp.com**

**Industry Group Code:** 524114A **Ranks within this company's industry group:** Sales: Profits:

| Management: | | Sales/Marketing: | | Liberal Arts: | | Information Systems: | | Professionals: | | Technical/Scientific: | |
|---|---|---|---|---|---|---|---|---|---|---|---|
| Mgmt. Trainees: | | Mktg. Professionals: | Y | Gen. Writing/Editing: | Y | Info. Management: | Y | Finance/Accounting: | Y | Engineers, Elec.: | |
| Experienced Mgmt.: | Y | Retail Sales: | | Technical Writing: | | Software Dev.: | | Law: | Y | Engineers, Other: | |
| Int'l Business: | Y | Commercial/Industrial: | Y | Graphic Arts/Photog.: | | Hardware Dev.: | | HR/Other: | Y | Health/Lab: | Y |
| MBA Graduates: | Y | Sales Trainees: | | Music: | | Systems Integration: | | Training: | Y | Scientists/Research: | |
| | | Advertising Pros.: | | Broadcasting: | | Consulting/Other: | | Health Care: | Y | Petroleum/Chemicals: | |
| | | | | Other: | | | | Consulting: | | Math/Other: | Y |

## TYPES OF BUSINESS:

Insurance-Supplemental and Specialty Health
Vision Insurance
Optical Frames
Laboratory Products & Materials, Optometry

## BRANDS/DIVISIONS/AFFILIATES:

Sight for Students
Get Focused
VSP Optical Laboratories
Altair
Eyefinity
Marchon Eyewear, Inc.

## CONTACTS: *Note: Officers with more than one job title may be intentionally listed here more than once.*

Rob Lynch, CEO
Rob Lynch, Pres.
Patricia Cochran, CFO/VP
Ric Steere, VP-Sales
Elaine Leuchars, VP-Human Resources
Steve Scott, VP-IT
Thomas Fessler, General Counsel/VP-Legal Div.
Gary Brooks, Sr. VP-Oper.
Terri Wilson, VP-Strategic Accounts & Sales Oper.
Robert Bass, Treas.
Kate Renwick-Espinosa, VP-Mktg.
Don Price, VP-Provider Rel.
Cheryl Johnson, VP-Health Care Svcs.
Bill Conner, Pres., VSP Optical Laboratories
James L. Short, Chmn.
Don Oakley, VP-Ophthalmic Supply Chain & Svcs.

| | |
|---|---|
| **Phone:** 916-851-5000 | **Fax:** 916-851-4858 |
| **Toll-Free:** 800-852-7600 | |
| **Address:** 3333 Quality Dr., Rancho Cordova, CA 95670 US | |

## GROWTH PLANS/SPECIAL FEATURES:

Vision Service Plan (VSP) provides eye care benefits in the United States and Canada. The plan boasts over 55 million members served by more than 25,000 private practice doctors, in both rural and metropolitan areas. VSP offers general eye care and eye glasses as well as laser vision correction. The firm has over 29,000 clients, including 228 Fortune 500 companies and approximately 100 health plans. The firm has offices throughout the nation, as well as three wholly owned optical laboratories. VSP has assisted 250,000 children through its Sight for Students program, which provides vision exams and glasses to low-income and uninsured children. The program has a $40 million budget to support low-income and uninsured children. The Get Focused program is VSP's national eye care awareness campaign, designed to promote eye education and regular eye exams. VSP also offers loans to assist eye doctors to buy existing practices, buy into partnerships or make down payments on private practices in California, Ohio, Texas and Colorado, through its VSP Optical Laboratories subsidiary. The VSP family of companies also consists of Altair Eyewear, which is a private label optical frame company that that sells exclusively to VSP eyecare professionals; and Eyefinity, which is an independent e-commerce business that offers professionals products and lab materials, and that has relationships with over 18,000 private eyecare practices. In 2007, VSP expanded its service into Canada, with VSP Canada. In September 2007, VSP entered into a joint venture with Perfect Optics, an optical laboratory near San Diego, California. In July 2008, the firm purchased its fourth optical lab, Ultra Lens in Florida. In August 2008, the company acquired Marchon Eyewear, Inc., which will become a wholly-owned subsidiary of VSP.

VSP offers its employees benefits including a bonus program, an employee assistance program and credit union membership.

## FINANCIALS: **Sales and profits are in thousands of dollars—add 000 to get the full amount. 2008 Note: Financial information for 2008 was not available for all companies at press time.**

| | | |
|---|---|---|
| 2008 Sales: $ | 2008 Profits: $ | **U.S. Stock Ticker: Private** |
| 2007 Sales: $ | 2007 Profits: $ | **Int'l Ticker:** Int'l Exchange: |
| 2006 Sales: $ | 2006 Profits: $ | Employees: 1,900 |
| 2005 Sales: $2,200,000 | 2005 Profits: $ | Fiscal Year Ends: 12/31 |
| 2004 Sales: $ | 2004 Profits: $ | Parent Company: |

## SALARIES/BENEFITS:

| | | | | |
|---|---|---|---|---|
| Pension Plan: | ESOP Stock Plan: | Profit Sharing: | Top Exec. Salary: $ | Bonus: $ |
| Savings Plan: Y | Stock Purch. Plan: | | Second Exec. Salary: $ | Bonus: $ |

## OTHER THOUGHTS:

**Apparent Women Officers or Directors**: 6
**Hot Spot for Advancement for Women/Minorities**: Y

## LOCATIONS: ("Y" = Yes)

| West: | Southwest: | Midwest: | Southeast: | Northeast: | International: |
|---|---|---|---|---|---|
| Y | Y | Y | Y | Y | Y |

# VITAL SIGNS INC

www.vital-signs.com

**Industry Group Code:** 339113 **Ranks within this company's industry group:** Sales: 20 Profits: 8

| Management: | | Sales/Marketing: | | Liberal Arts: | | Information Systems: | | Professionals: | | Technical/Scientific: | |
|---|---|---|---|---|---|---|---|---|---|---|---|
| Mgmt. Trainees: | | Mktg. Professionals: | Y | Gen. Writing/Editing: | | Info. Management: | Y | Finance/Accounting: | Y | Engineers, Elec.: | Y |
| Experienced Mgmt.: | Y | Retail Sales: | | Technical Writing: | Y | Software Dev.: | Y | Law: | Y | Engineers, Other: | Y |
| Int'l Business: | Y | Commercial/Industrial: | Y | Graphic Arts/Photog.: | | Hardware Dev.: | | HR/Other: | Y | Health/Lab: | Y |
| MBA Graduates: | Y | Sales Trainees: | Y | Music: | | Systems Integration: | | Training: | Y | Scientists/Research: | Y |
| | | Advertising Pros.: | | Broadcasting: | | Consulting/Other: | | Health Care: | Y | Petroleum/Chemicals: | |
| | | | | Other: | | | | Consulting: | | Math/Other: | Y |

## TYPES OF BUSINESS:

Supplies-Respiratory & Critical Care
Single-Patient-Use Medical Products
Anesthesia Products
Home Care Products

## BRANDS/DIVISIONS/AFFILIATES:

Futall AB
Vital Signs Sweden AB
Disposa-View
Sleep Services of America, Inc.
Greenlight II
Do You Snore, LLC
Southern Medical Equipment, Inc.
Advanced Sleep Technologies of Georgia, Inc.

## CONTACTS: *Note: Officers with more than one job title may be intentionally listed here more than once.*

Terence D. Wall, CEO
Alex Chanin, COO
Terence D. Wall, Pres.
Mark D. Mishler, CFO/Exec. VP
Mark Jefferson, VP-Mktg. & Sales
Jay Sturm, VP-Human Resources
Alan Furler, VP-R&D
Benn Vennesland, VP-Mfg. Oper.
Jay Sturm, General Counsel
John Easom, VP-Global Bus. Dev. & Planning
Anthony Martino, VP-Quality & Regulatory Affairs
Terence D. Wall, Chmn.

| | |
|---|---|
| **Phone:** 973-790-1330 | **Fax:** 973-790-3307 |
| **Toll-Free:** 800-932-0760 | |
| **Address:** 20 Campus Rd., Totowa, NJ 07512 US | |

## GROWTH PLANS/SPECIAL FEATURES:

Vital Signs, Inc. designs, manufactures and markets disposable medical products in its five business segments: Anesthesia, respiratory/critical care, sleep disorder, interventional cardiology/radiology and emergency markets. Vital Signs's subsidiaries include Breas, Sleep Services of America, Thomas Medical, Stelex, Vloworks, Vital Path and Vital Signs U.K. The company's anesthesia products include facemasks, breathing circuits, general anesthesia systems, disposable pressure infusers and single-use fiber-optic laryngoscope systems. Respiratory and critical care products include manual resuscitators, blood pressure cuffs, disposable arterial blood gas syringes and collection systems, heated humidification systems, continuous positive airway pressure systems, humidifiers, nebulizers and pediatric emergency systems. Vital Signs operates 56 sleep laboratories and centers to diagnose obstructive sleep apnea and also manufactures and sells products to treat these sleeping conditions. The cardiology/radiology business operates through subsidiary Thomas Medical Products, which develops and manufactures precision devices such as percutaneous valved introducers, peelaway valved introducers, guiding sheaths and delivery sheaths to facilitate access to the cardiovascular system. The firm sells its products through national distributors and its own sales offices to over 73 countries worldwide. In April 2007, the firm's subsidiary, Sleep Services of America, Inc., acquired the assets of Do You Snore, LLC; Southern Medical Equipment, Inc.; and Advanced Sleep Technologies of Georgia, Inc.

## FINANCIALS: **Sales and profits are in thousands of dollars—add 000 to get the full amount. 2008 Note: Financial information for 2008 was not available for all companies at press time.**

| | | |
|---|---|---|
| 2008 Sales: $ | 2008 Profits: $ | **U.S. Stock Ticker: VITL** |
| 2007 Sales: $205,257 | 2007 Profits: $19,159 | **Int'l Ticker:** Int'l Exchange: |
| 2006 Sales: $202,124 | 2006 Profits: $30,117 | Employees: 1,257 |
| 2005 Sales: $194,037 | 2005 Profits: $26,389 | Fiscal Year Ends: 9/30 |
| 2004 Sales: $183,991 | 2004 Profits: $22,053 | Parent Company: |

## SALARIES/BENEFITS:

| | | | | |
|---|---|---|---|---|
| Pension Plan: | ESOP Stock Plan: | Profit Sharing: | Top Exec. Salary: $380,000 | Bonus: $73,500 |
| Savings Plan: Y | Stock Purch. Plan: | | Second Exec. Salary: $200,000 | Bonus: $42,000 |

## OTHER THOUGHTS:

**Apparent Women Officers or Directors:**
**Hot Spot for Advancement for Women/Minorities:**

## LOCATIONS: ("Y" = Yes)

| West: | Southwest: | Midwest: | Southeast: | Northeast: | International: |
|---|---|---|---|---|---|
| | | Y | | Y | Y |

Note: Financial information, benefits and other data can change quickly and may vary from those stated here.

# VOLCOM INC

www.volcom.com

**Industry Group Code:** 315000 **Ranks within this company's industry group:** Sales: 1 Profits: 1

| Management: | | Sales/Marketing: | | Liberal Arts: | | Information Systems: | | Professionals: | | Technical/Scientific: | |
|---|---|---|---|---|---|---|---|---|---|---|---|
| Mgmt. Trainees: | | Mktg. Professionals: | Y | Gen. Writing/Editing: | | Info. Management: | Y | Finance/Accounting: | Y | Engineers, Elec.: | |
| Experienced Mgmt.: | Y | Retail Sales: | | Technical Writing: | | Software Dev.: | | Law: | Y | Engineers, Other: | |
| Int'l Business: | Y | Commercial/Industrial: | Y | Graphic Arts/Photog.: | Y | Hardware Dev.: | | HR/Other: | Y | Health/Lab: | |
| MBA Graduates: | Y | Sales Trainees: | Y | Music: | | Systems Integration: | | Training: | Y | Scientists/Research: | |
| | | Advertising Pros.: | Y | Broadcasting: | | Consulting/Other: | | Health Care: | | Petroleum/Chemicals: | |
| | | | | Other: | | | | Consulting: | | Math/Other: | |

## TYPES OF BUSINESS:

Activewear
Sports-Specific Apparel

## BRANDS/DIVISIONS/AFFILIATES:

Volcom
Volcasts

## CONTACTS:

*Note: Officers with more than one job title may be intentionally listed here more than once.*

Richard Woolcott, CEO
Jason W. Steris, COO
Richard Woolcot, Pres.
Douglas P. Collier, CFO
Tom Ruiz, VP-Sales
Douglas Ingram, General Counsel/Exec. VP
Douglas P. Collier, Treas./Sec.
Troy Eckert, VP-Mktg.
Kip Arnette, Chief Design Officer/Co-Pres., Electric Visual
Bruce Beach, CEO/Co-Pres., Electric Visual
Rene Woolcott, Chmn.

| **Phone:** 949-646-2175 | **Fax:** 949-646-5247 |
|---|---|
| **Toll-Free:** | |
| **Address:** 1740 Monrovia Ave., Costa Mesa, CA 92627 US | |

## GROWTH PLANS/SPECIAL FEATURES:

Volcom, Inc. is a designer, marketer and distributor of clothing and accessories for young men and women. Its products are sold in over 40 countries worldwide. Richard Woolcott and Tucker Hall, two snowboard enthusiasts who created the firm in 1991, incorporated their anti-establishment philosophy into the company's original ideals. Volcom products, marketed under the Volcom brand name, are created for participants of boardsports, including skateboarding, snowboarding and surfing; they are inspired by a fusion of fashion, functionality and athletic performance. The firm manages an online store, where consumers can view and purchase most of the firm's product line. Products are organized into five groups: young boy's clothing, men's clothing, men's accessories, girl's clothing and girl's accessories. The product line includes t-shirts, fleece, swimwear, denim, boardshorts, bottoms, jackets, tops, slip-on footwear, sandles and outerwear. Accessories include headwear, underwear, socks, belts, wallets and luggage. Volcom's web site has a variety of interactive features beyond the online store. Visitors can view and submit art; download wallpapers for PCs or Macs (featuring art, advertisements and sports-inspired photos); download Volcasts (podcasts featuring stories and interviews with athletes); buy movies and music; and view upcoming concert tours which the Volcom demographic is likely to be interested in. The firm's executive, warehousing and distribution offices are located in Costa Mesa, California. Volcom positions itself as a club for young snowboarders and skateboarders in addition to its being a vendor for sports-specific apparel and products. In January 2008, the firm acquired Electric Visual Evolution LLC (Electric), for approximately $25.3 million. Electric's products include eyewear, clothing and accessories. In July 2008, the company acquired Laguna Surf & Sport, a retail partner in Southern California; details of the transaction were not disclosed. In September 2008, the firm acquired its distributor in Japan; details of the transaction were not disclosed.

## FINANCIALS:

**Sales and profits are in thousands of dollars—add 000 to get the full amount. 2008 Note: Financial information for 2008 was not available for all companies at press time.**

| | | |
|---|---|---|
| 2008 Sales: $ | 2008 Profits: $ | **U.S. Stock Ticker: VLCM** |
| 2007 Sales: $265,193 | 2007 Profits: $33,335 | **Int'l Ticker:** Int'l Exchange: |
| 2006 Sales: $201,186 | 2006 Profits: $28,753 | Employees: 337 |
| 2005 Sales: $159,951 | 2005 Profits: $29,337 | Fiscal Year Ends: 12/31 |
| 2004 Sales: $113,175 | 2004 Profits: $24,593 | Parent Company: |

## SALARIES/BENEFITS:

| | | | | |
|---|---|---|---|---|
| Pension Plan: | ESOP Stock Plan: | Profit Sharing: | Top Exec. Salary: $400,000 | Bonus: $120,000 |
| Savings Plan: | Stock Purch. Plan: | | Second Exec. Salary: $375,000 | Bonus: $281,500 |

## OTHER THOUGHTS:

**Apparent Women Officers or Directors**: 1
**Hot Spot for Advancement for Women/Minorities**:

## LOCATIONS: ("Y" = Yes)

| West: | Southwest: | Midwest: | Southeast: | Northeast: | International: |
|---|---|---|---|---|---|
| Y | | | | | Y |

# VSE CORP

www.vsecorp.com

**Industry Group Code:** 541330 **Ranks within this company's industry group:** Sales: 1 Profits: 1

| Management: | | Sales/Marketing: | | Liberal Arts: | | Information Systems: | | Professionals: | | Technical/Scientific: | |
|---|---|---|---|---|---|---|---|---|---|---|---|
| Mgmt. Trainees: | | Mktg. Professionals: | Y | Gen. Writing/Editing: | | Info. Management: | Y | Finance/Accounting: | Y | Engineers, Elec.: | Y |
| Experienced Mgmt.: | Y | Retail Sales: | | Technical Writing: | Y | Software Dev.: | | Law: | Y | Engineers, Other: | Y |
| Int'l Business: | Y | Commercial/Industrial: | Y | Graphic Arts/Photog.: | | Hardware Dev.: | | HR/Other: | Y | Health/Lab: | |
| MBA Graduates: | Y | Sales Trainees: | | Music: | | Systems Integration: | | Training: | Y | Scientists/Research: | Y |
| | | Advertising Pros.: | | Broadcasting: | | Consulting/Other: | | Health Care: | | Petroleum/Chemicals: | |
| | | | | Other: | | | | Consulting: | | Math/Other: | |

## TYPES OF BUSINESS:

Technical Services to Government
Engineering Services
Logistics Services
Technology Research & Development
Equipment Maintenance, Refurbishment & Implementation
Information Technology Support

## BRANDS/DIVISIONS/AFFILIATES:

Energetics, Inc.
BAV
Communications and Electronics
Coast Guard
Engineering and Logistics
Fleet Maintenance
G&B Solutions, Inc.
Integrated Concepts and Research Corporation

## CONTACTS: *Note: Officers with more than one job title may be intentionally listed here more than once.*

Maurice Gauthier, CEO
Maurice Gauthier, Pres.
Thomas R. Loftus, CFO/Exec. VP
Randy Hollstein, VP-Mktg.
Elizabeth M. Price, Dir.-Human Resources
Carl Williams, Pres., Integrated Concepts & Research Corp.
David Chivers, CIO
Randy Hollstein, Dir.-Prod. Dev. & New Bus.
Thomas M. Kerinan, General Counsel/VP/Asst. Sec.
James W. Lexo, Jr., Exec. VP-Strategic Planning & Bus. Initiatives
Sylvia Gethicker, Dir.-Public Rel., Advertising & Mass Comm.
Craig S. Weber, Investor Rel./Corp. Sec.
Thomas G. Dacus, Exec. VP/Pres., Federal Group
James E. Reed, Pres., Energy & Environment Group
Carl M. Williams, Pres., ICRC
Linda Berdine, Pres., G&B Solutions, Inc.
Donald M. Ervine, Chmn.
James M. Knowlton, Exec. VP/Pres., Int'l Group
A.J. Rose, Dir.-Purchasing

**Phone:** 703-960-4600 **Fax:** 703-960-2688
**Toll-Free:**
**Address:** 2550 Huntington Ave., Alexandria, VA 22303-1499 US

## GROWTH PLANS/SPECIAL FEATURES:

VSE Corp. is a contract provider of diversified engineering, logistics, management, and technical services mostly to the U.S. government. The firm provides these services through its wholly-owned subsidiaries Energetics, Inc., Integrated Concepts and Research Corporation (ICRC) and G&B Solutions, Inc. and the following divisions: BAV, providing assistance to the U.S. Navy in executing its Foreign Military Sales Program; Communications and Electronics; Coast Guard; Engineering and Logistics; Fleet Support Services; Fleet Maintenance; Management Sciences; and Systems Engineering. The company also divides its business operations into four segments: the Federal Group; the International Group; the IT, Energy and Management Consulting Group (formerly the Energy and Environmental Group); and the Infrastructure Group (formerly the Infrastructure and Information Technology Group). The Federal Group provides engineering, technical, management, integrated logistics support and information technology services to all U.S. military branches and to other government agencies. The International Group provides engineering, industrial, logistics and foreign military sales services to similar groups. The IT, Energy and Management Consulting Group, which includes Energetics, Inc. and G&B Solutions, Inc., provides technical and consulting services primarily to various civilian government agencies. Energetics, Inc. provides technical and management support in the areas of nuclear energy, technology research, development and demonstration, and consulting services in the energy and environmental management fields. The Infrastructure Group encompasses ICRC and is engaged in providing technical and management services to the U.S. government, including transportation infrastructure services, advanced vehicle technology, aerospace services and engineering and information technology. In 2007, VSE acquired Integrated Concepts and Research Corporation, a technical and management services company principally serving the U.S. government. In April 2008, the company acquired G&B Solutions, Inc., an information technology and management consulting provider. In September 2008, the firm opened an operations center in Pennsylvania.

## FINANCIALS: **Sales and profits are in thousands of dollars—add 000 to get the full amount. 2008 Note: Financial information for 2008 was not available for all companies at press time.**

| | | |
|---|---|---|
| 2008 Sales: $ | 2008 Profits: $ | **U.S. Stock Ticker: VSEC** |
| 2007 Sales: $653,164 | 2007 Profits: $14,102 | **Int'l Ticker:** Int'l Exchange: |
| 2006 Sales: $363,734 | 2006 Profits: $7,789 | Employees: 1,223 |
| 2005 Sales: $280,139 | 2005 Profits: $6,169 | Fiscal Year Ends: 12/31 |
| 2004 Sales: $216,011 | 2004 Profits: $3,444 | Parent Company: |

## SALARIES/BENEFITS:

| | | | | |
|---|---|---|---|---|
| Pension Plan: | ESOP Stock Plan: | Profit Sharing: | Top Exec. Salary: $337,000 | Bonus: $337,000 |
| Savings Plan: | Stock Purch. Plan: | | Second Exec. Salary: $208,000 | Bonus: $208,000 |

## OTHER THOUGHTS:

**Apparent Women Officers or Directors:** 4
**Hot Spot for Advancement for Women/Minorities:** Y

## LOCATIONS: ("Y" = Yes)

| West: | Southwest: | Midwest: | Southeast: | Northeast: | International: |
|---|---|---|---|---|---|
| Y | Y | Y | Y | Y | Y |

# WEBEX COMMUNICATIONS INC

**www.webex.com**

**Industry Group Code:** 513300D **Ranks within this company's industry group:** Sales: Profits:

| Management: | | Sales/Marketing: | | Liberal Arts: | | Information Systems: | | Professionals: | | Technical/Scientific: | |
|---|---|---|---|---|---|---|---|---|---|---|---|
| Mgmt. Trainees: | | Mktg. Professionals: | Y | Gen. Writing/Editing: | | Info. Management: | Y | Finance/Accounting: | Y | Engineers, Elec.: | Y |
| Experienced Mgmt.: | Y | Retail Sales: | | Technical Writing: | Y | Software Dev.: | Y | Law: | Y | Engineers, Other: | Y |
| Int'l Business: | Y | Commercial/Industrial: | Y | Graphic Arts/Photog.: | | Hardware Dev.: | | HR/Other: | Y | Health/Lab: | |
| MBA Graduates: | Y | Sales Trainees: | Y | Music: | | Systems Integration: | Y | Training: | Y | Scientists/Research: | |
| | | Advertising Pros.: | | Broadcasting: | | Consulting/Other: | | Health Care: | | Petroleum/Chemicals: | |
| | | | | Other: | | | | Consulting: | | Math/Other: | |

## TYPES OF BUSINESS:

Online Collaboration Services
Online Conferencing Services & Software

## BRANDS/DIVISIONS/AFFILIATES:

WebExOne Inc
WebEx WebOffice
WebEx Meeting Center
WebEx Enterprise Edition
MyWebEx
WebEx MediaTone Network
MyWebExPCNow
Cisco Systems Inc

## CONTACTS: *Note: Officers with more than one job title may be intentionally listed here more than once.*

Subrah S. Iyar, CEO
Bill Heil, COO
Bill Heil, Pres.
Michael T. Everett, CFO
Van M. Diamandakis, VP-Corp. Mktg.
Shawn Farshchi, CIO
Shawn Farshchi, VP-Tech. Oper.
Jeff Tonkel, Prod. Mgmt.
David Farrington, General Counsel/VP
Ray Villareal, VP-Worldwide Field Oper. & Mktg.
Peter Carson, VP-Bus. Dev.
Praful Shah, VP-Strategic Comm.
Dean Macintosh, VP-Finance
David Farrington, VP-Corp. Dev.
David Berman, VP- Worldwide Corp. Sales
Subrah S. Iyar, Chmn.
Jeffrey Schmidt, VP-Int'l Sales & Worldwide Channels

**Phone:** 408-435-7000 **Fax:** 408-496-4353
**Toll-Free:** 877-509-3239
**Address:** 3979 Freedom Cir., Santa Clara, CA 95054 US

## GROWTH PLANS/SPECIAL FEATURES:

WebEx Communications, Inc., a subsidiary of Cisco Systems, Inc., provides conferencing services that allow businesses to conduct meetings, provide interactive demonstrations and view documents and other content on the Internet using a web browser. It also provides integrated telephone and web-based audio and video with the addition of such basic equipment as telephones, web cameras and microphones. In addition, the firm's wholly-owned subsidiary WebExOne's software suite WebEx WebOffice provides collaboration capabilities including reviewing and modifying documents, posting additional documents, sending and responding to task assignments, scheduling meetings and events, and updating database entries. The company's flagship product is WebEx Meeting Center, a multimedia communications service. Enterprise Edition allows users to integrate MyWebEx with Microsoft Outlook and to conduct a secure meeting on the web where the content or application resides in an unattended remote computer. The WebEx MediaTone Network is a private, switched, web-based network that is designed to deliver scalable, secure, web collaboration services to its customers worldwide. MyWebExPCNow is a service that allows the user to access a remote computer from any location in the world, with the user needing only a web browser and Internet access. MeetMeNow is a different version of its web meeting service for individual professionals that adds personal video conferencing capabilities from within the Microsoft Office suite. Some of the firm's partners include AT&T, Oracle, Verizon, GeoLearning, LifeScape Technologies, Mindjet, Face Time, Parature, Xerox, Bell Canada, AOL and Jabber, Inc.

## FINANCIALS: **Sales and profits are in thousands of dollars—add 000 to get the full amount. 2008 Note: Financial information for 2008 was not available for all companies at press time.**

| | | |
|---|---|---|
| 2008 Sales: $ | 2008 Profits: $ | **U.S. Stock Ticker: Subsidiary** |
| 2007 Sales: $ | 2007 Profits: $ | **Int'l Ticker:** Int'l Exchange: |
| 2006 Sales: $380,012 | 2006 Profits: $48,574 | Employees: 2,189 |
| 2005 Sales: $308,422 | 2005 Profits: $53,002 | Fiscal Year Ends: 12/31 |
| 2004 Sales: $249,133 | 2004 Profits: $47,880 | Parent Company: CISCO SYSTEMS INC |

## SALARIES/BENEFITS:

| | | | | |
|---|---|---|---|---|
| Pension Plan: | ESOP Stock Plan: | Profit Sharing: | Top Exec. Salary: $284,000 | Bonus: $142,402 |
| Savings Plan: | Stock Purch. Plan: | | Second Exec. Salary: $250,000 | Bonus: $240,180 |

## OTHER THOUGHTS:

**Apparent Women Officers or Directors**: 1
**Hot Spot for Advancement for Women/Minorities**: Y

## LOCATIONS: ("Y" = Yes)

| West: | Southwest: | Midwest: | Southeast: | Northeast: | International: |
|---|---|---|---|---|---|
| Y | | | | | Y |

# WEBMD HEALTH CORP

www.webmd.com

**Industry Group Code:** 514199 **Ranks within this company's industry group:** Sales: 1 Profits: 1

| Management: | | Sales/Marketing: | | Liberal Arts: | | Information Systems: | | Professionals: | | Technical/Scientific: | |
|---|---|---|---|---|---|---|---|---|---|---|---|
| Mgmt. Trainees: | | Mktg. Professionals: | Y | Gen. Writing/Editing: | Y | Info. Management: | Y | Finance/Accounting: | Y | Engineers, Elec.: | |
| Experienced Mgmt.: | Y | Retail Sales: | | Technical Writing: | Y | Software Dev.: | Y | Law: | Y | Engineers, Other: | |
| Int'l Business: | Y | Commercial/Industrial: | Y | Graphic Arts/Photog.: | Y | Hardware Dev.: | | HR/Other: | Y | Health/Lab: | |
| MBA Graduates: | Y | Sales Trainees: | Y | Music: | | Systems Integration: | Y | Training: | Y | Scientists/Research: | |
| | | Advertising Pros.: | Y | Broadcasting: | | Consulting/Other: | | Health Care: | | Petroleum/Chemicals: | |
| | | | | Other: | Y | | | Consulting: | | Math/Other: | |

## TYPES OF BUSINESS:

Health Care Internet Portals
Publishing

## BRANDS/DIVISIONS/AFFILIATES:

WebMD Health Holdings, Inc.
WebMD Health Network
Medscape
Little Blue Book (The)
WebMD Magazine
Subimo, LLC
HLTH Corp.
ViPS

## CONTACTS: *Note: Officers with more than one job title may be intentionally listed here more than once.*

Wayne T. Gattinella, CEO
Anthony Vuolo, COO
Wayne T. Gattinella, Pres.
Mark D. Funston, CFO/Exec. VP
William Pence, CTO/Exec. VP
Douglas W. Wamsley, General Counsel/Exec. VP/Corp. Sec.
Nan-Kirsten Forte, Exec. VP-Consumer Svcs.
Steven Zatz, Exec. VP-Professional Svcs.
Craig Froude, Exec. VP-WebMD Health Svcs.
Martin J. Wygood, Chmn.

**Phone:** 212-624-3700 **Fax:** 212-624-3800
**Toll-Free:**
**Address:** 111 8th Ave., New York, NY 10011 US

## GROWTH PLANS/SPECIAL FEATURES:

WebMD Health Corp., formerly a unit of Emdeon Corp. known as WebMD Health Holdings, Inc., provides health information services to consumers; physicians and healthcare professionals; employers; and health plans. The public online service, the WebMD Health Network, offers WebMD Health, the company's primary public portal, and Medscape from WebMD, a public portal for physicians and health care professionals. WebMD Health provides health and wellness articles and features, and decision-support services to help consumers make informed decisions about health care providers, health risks and treatment options. Available information and interactive tools include detailed data on specific diseases or conditions, symptom analysis, physician location and individual health care data storage. Medscape from WebMD assists physicians and health care professionals in improving clinical knowledge with original content such as daily news, commentary, conference coverage and continuing medical education. The WebMD Health Network has an approximate monthly average of 41.8 million unique users per month. The firm generates revenue from its public offerings primarily through advertising sales and sponsorships. Private portals offered by WebMD enable employees and health plan members to learn about benefits, providers and treatment decisions, customized to a user's health insurance plan. Revenue is generated from the private side though content and technology licensed to employers such as American Airlines, Microsoft, PepsiCo, Cigna and Empire Blue Cross and Blue Shield. In addition, the company has a publishing segment that produces publications such as The Little Blue Book, a physician directory; and WebMD the Magazine, a consumer magazine distributed free of charge to physician office waiting rooms. In July 2008, the company sold ViPS for $225,000.

## FINANCIALS: **Sales and profits are in thousands of dollars—add 000 to get the full amount. 2008 Note: Financial information for 2008 was not available for all companies at press time.**

2008 Sales: $382,777 | 2008 Profits: $26,702
2007 Sales: $331,954 | 2007 Profits: $65,884
2006 Sales: $248,776 | 2006 Profits: $2,536
2005 Sales: $168,938 | 2005 Profits: $7,745
2004 Sales: $134,148 | 2004 Profits: $6,461

**U.S. Stock Ticker: WBMD**
**Int'l Ticker:** Int'l Exchange:
Employees: 1,175
Fiscal Year Ends: 12/31
Parent Company:

## SALARIES/BENEFITS:

Pension Plan: | ESOP Stock Plan: | Profit Sharing: | Top Exec. Salary: $975,000 | Bonus: $520,000
Savings Plan: | Stock Purch. Plan: | | Second Exec. Salary: $560,000 | Bonus: $270,000

## OTHER THOUGHTS:

**Apparent Women Officers or Directors:** 1
**Hot Spot for Advancement for Women/Minorities:**

## LOCATIONS: ("Y" = Yes)

| West: | Southwest: | Midwest: | Southeast: | Northeast: | International: |
|---|---|---|---|---|---|
| Y | | Y | Y | Y | Y |

# WEBSENSE INC

**www.websense.com**

**Industry Group Code:** 511211 **Ranks within this company's industry group:** Sales: 2 Profits: 3

| Management: | | Sales/Marketing: | | Liberal Arts: | | Information Systems: | | Professionals: | | Technical/Scientific: | |
|---|---|---|---|---|---|---|---|---|---|---|---|
| Mgmt. Trainees: | | Mktg. Professionals: | Y | Gen. Writing/Editing: | | Info. Management: | Y | Finance/Accounting: | Y | Engineers, Elec.: | Y |
| Experienced Mgmt.: | Y | Retail Sales: | | Technical Writing: | Y | Software Dev.: | Y | Law: | Y | Engineers, Other: | |
| Int'l Business: | Y | Commercial/Industrial: | Y | Graphic Arts/Photog.: | | Hardware Dev.: | | HR/Other: | Y | Health/Lab: | |
| MBA Graduates: | Y | Sales Trainees: | Y | Music: | | Systems Integration: | | Training: | Y | Scientists/Research: | |
| | | Advertising Pros.: | | Broadcasting: | | Consulting/Other: | | Health Care: | | Petroleum/Chemicals: | |
| | | | | Other: | | | | Consulting: | | Math/Other: | |

## TYPES OF BUSINESS:

Software-Employee Internet Management

## BRANDS/DIVISIONS/AFFILIATES:

Websense Web Security Gateway
Websense Data Security Suite
Websense Hosted Email Security
PortAuthority Technologies, Inc.
SurfControl plc

## CONTACTS: *Note: Officers with more than one job title may be intentionally listed here more than once.*

Gene Hodges, CEO
Douglas C. Wride, Pres.
Dudley Mendenhall, CFO/Sr. VP
Leo Cole, VP-Mktg.
Susan Brown, VP-Human Resources
Jim Haskin, CIO/Sr. VP
Dan Hubbard, CTO
John McCormack, Sr. VP-Prod. Dev.
Michael Newman, General Counsel/Sr. VP
Devin Redmond, VP-Bus. Dev.
Kate Patterson, VP-Corp. Comm.
Kate Patterson, VP-Investor Rel.
Mike Bouchard, VP-Finance
David Roberts, Sr. VP-Americas
Kian Saneii, Gen. Mgr.-Websense Wireless/VP-Websense
John B. Carrington, Chmn.
Geoff Haggart, VP-EMEA & APAC

| | |
|---|---|
| **Phone:** 858-320-8000 | **Fax:** 858-458-2950 |
| **Toll-Free:** 800-723-1166 | |
| **Address:** 10240 Sorrento Valley Rd., San Diego, CA 92121 US | |

## GROWTH PLANS/SPECIAL FEATURES:

Websense, Inc. is a leading provider of integrated content security software solutions, including Web security, e-mail and messaging security and data loss prevention (DLP) solutions, to over 43 million employees at more than 50,000 organizations worldwide. The company offers suites of Web, e-mail and data security products, available as layered software or hosted (on-demand) solutions. The company's products are designed to provide Web, data and e-mail security by preventing employee access to unwanted and dangerous Web elements, such as sites that contain inappropriate content or sites that download malicious code; filtering unwanted e-mails out of incoming traffic; filtering viruses and other malicious attachments out of e-mails and instant messages; managing the use of non-Web Internet traffic, such as peer-to-peer communications and instant messaging; restricting the unauthorized use and loss of sensitive data, such as customer or employee information; controlling misuse of computing resources, including the unauthorized download of high-bandwidth content. Some of the company's products include Websense Web Security Gateway, which secures Web traffic while enabling Web-based applications; the Websense Data Security Suite, which discovers, protects and monitors information on a network; and Websense Hosted Email Security, which blocks inbound and outbound e-mail threats. Websense maintains research and development facilities in San Diego and Los Gatos, California; Reading, England; Beijing, China; Sydney, Australia and Ra'anana, Israel. As a result of acquiring PortAuthority Technologies, Inc. in early 2007, Websense now offers DLP software, which helps prevent the loss of confidential information from internal threats. Later in 2007, the company acquired SurfControl plc for $407 million.

## FINANCIALS: **Sales and profits are in thousands of dollars—add 000 to get the full amount. 2008 Note: Financial information for 2008 was not available for all companies at press time.**

| | | |
|---|---|---|
| 2008 Sales: $ | 2008 Profits: $ | **U.S. Stock Ticker: WBSN** |
| 2007 Sales: $211,665 | 2007 Profits: $-14,565 | **Int'l Ticker:** Int'l Exchange: |
| 2006 Sales: $178,814 | 2006 Profits: $32,093 | Employees: 1,180 |
| 2005 Sales: $148,636 | 2005 Profits: $38,768 | Fiscal Year Ends: 12/31 |
| 2004 Sales: $111,859 | 2004 Profits: $26,176 | Parent Company: |

## SALARIES/BENEFITS:

| | | | | |
|---|---|---|---|---|
| Pension Plan: | ESOP Stock Plan: | Profit Sharing: | Top Exec. Salary: $541,962 | Bonus: $601,577 |
| Savings Plan: | Stock Purch. Plan: Y | | Second Exec. Salary: $356,146 | Bonus: $206,124 |

## OTHER THOUGHTS:

**Apparent Women Officers or Directors**: 2
**Hot Spot for Advancement for Women/Minorities**: Y

## LOCATIONS: ("Y" = Yes)

| West: | Southwest: | Midwest: | Southeast: | Northeast: | International: |
|---|---|---|---|---|---|
| Y | Y | | | | Y |

# WESTAR ENERGY

www.westarenergy.com

**Industry Group Code:** 221000A **Ranks within this company's industry group:** Sales: 2 Profits: 3

| Management: | | Sales/Marketing: | | Liberal Arts: | | Information Systems: | | Professionals: | | Technical/Scientific: | |
|---|---|---|---|---|---|---|---|---|---|---|---|
| Mgmt. Trainees: | | Mktg. Professionals: | Y | Gen. Writing/Editing: | | Info. Management: | Y | Finance/Accounting: | Y | Engineers, Elec.: | Y |
| Experienced Mgmt.: | Y | Retail Sales: | | Technical Writing: | | Software Dev.: | | Law: | Y | Engineers, Other: | Y |
| Int'l Business: | Y | Commercial/Industrial: | Y | Graphic Arts/Photog.: | | Hardware Dev.: | | HR/Other: | Y | Health/Lab: | |
| MBA Graduates: | Y | Sales Trainees: | Y | Music: | | Systems Integration: | | Training: | Y | Scientists/Research: | |
| | | Advertising Pros.: | | Broadcasting: | | Consulting/Other: | | Health Care: | | Petroleum/Chemicals: | Y |
| | | | | Other: | | | | Consulting: | | Math/Other: | |

## TYPES OF BUSINESS:

Utilities-Electricity & Natural Gas
Nuclear Power Plants

## BRANDS/DIVISIONS/AFFILIATES:

Kansas Gas and Electric Co.
Wolf Creek Generating Station
Wolf Creek Nuclear Operating Corp.

## CONTACTS: *Note: Officers with more than one job title may be intentionally listed here more than once.*

William B. Moore, CEO
Doug Sterbenz, COO/Exec. VP
William B. Moore, Pres.
Mark A. Ruelle, CFO/Exec. VP
Larry Irick, General Counsel/VP/Corp. Sec.
Bruce Akin, VP-Oper. Strategy & Support
James Ludwig, Exec. VP-Public Affairs & Consumer Svcs.
Tony Somma, Treas.
Kelly B. Harrison, VP-Transmission Oper. & Environmental Svcs.
Jeff Beasley, VP-Corp. Compliance & Internal Audit
Greg A. Greenwood, VP-Generation Construction
Charles Q. Chandler, IV, Chmn.

**Phone:** 785-575-6300 **Fax:** 785-575-1796
**Toll-Free:**
**Address:** 818 Kansas Ave., Topeka, KS 66612 US

## GROWTH PLANS/SPECIAL FEATURES:

Westar Energy, Inc. is an electric utility in Kansas, providing electric generation, transmission and distribution services to approximately 674,000 customers. The company provides these services in central and northeastern Kansas, including the cities of Topeka, Lawrence, Manhattan, Salina and Hutchinson. Wholly-owned subsidiary Kansas Gas and Electric Co. (KGE) provides the same services for south-central and southeastern Kansas areas, including the Wichita metropolitan area. Both Westar Energy and KGE conduct business under the Westar Energy name. Westar also supplies electric energy at wholesale to electric distribution systems in 55 Kansas cities and four rural electric cooperatives and has contracts for the sale, purchase or exchange of wholesale electricity with other utilities. Along with utility supplies, KGE owns a 47% interest in the Wolf Creek Generating Station, a nuclear power plant located near Burlington, Kansas, and a 47% interest in Wolf Creek Nuclear Operating Corp., the operating company for the generating station. Westar owns an 84% interest in three coal-fired units at Jeffrey Energy Center and a 50% interest in the two coal-fired units at LaCygne Generating Station. Approximately 56% of the company's total energy capacity comes from coal, and 40% from natural gas or oil. The firm also provides energy generating capacity to other companies, including four energy businesses in Oklahoma and Kansas. In January 2008, the company reached agreements with developers to begin building three wind farms in Kansas, which are expected to generate approximately 200 megawatts (MW) of energy. Westar plans to initially own half of the wind generators, and to purchase energy produced by the other half of the wind farms under twenty year supply contracts.

The company offers its employees medical and dental insurance; flexible spending accounts; life and disability insurance; a retirement plant; a 401(k) plan; tuition reimbursement; and an employee assistance program.

## FINANCIALS: Sales and profits are in thousands of dollars—add 000 to get the full amount. 2008 Note: Financial information for 2008 was not available for all companies at press time.

| | | |
|---|---|---|
| 2008 Sales: $ | 2008 Profits: $ | **U.S. Stock Ticker: WR** |
| 2007 Sales: $1,726,834 | 2007 Profits: $167,384 | **Int'l Ticker:** Int'l Exchange: |
| 2006 Sales: $1,605,743 | 2006 Profits: $164,339 | Employees: 2,323 |
| 2005 Sales: $1,583,278 | 2005 Profits: $134,640 | Fiscal Year Ends: 12/31 |
| 2004 Sales: $1,464,489 | 2004 Profits: $177,900 | Parent Company: |

## SALARIES/BENEFITS:

| | | | | |
|---|---|---|---|---|
| Pension Plan: Y | ESOP Stock Plan: | Profit Sharing: | Top Exec. Salary: $525,000 | Bonus: $ |
| Savings Plan: Y | Stock Purch. Plan: | | Second Exec. Salary: $453,365 | Bonus: $ |

## OTHER THOUGHTS:

**Apparent Women Officers or Directors**: 3
**Hot Spot for Advancement for Women/Minorities**: Y

## LOCATIONS: ("Y" = Yes)

| West: | Southwest: | Midwest: | Southeast: | Northeast: | International: |
|---|---|---|---|---|---|
| | Y | Y | | | Y |

Note: Financial information, benefits and other data can change quickly and may vary from those stated here.

# WGL HOLDINGS INC

**www.wglholdings.com**

**Industry Group Code:** 221000 **Ranks within this company's industry group:** Sales: 2 Profits: 2

| Management: | | Sales/Marketing: | | Liberal Arts: | | Information Systems: | | Professionals: | | Technical/Scientific: | |
|---|---|---|---|---|---|---|---|---|---|---|---|
| Mgmt. Trainees: | | Mktg. Professionals: | Y | Gen. Writing/Editing: | | Info. Management: | Y | Finance/Accounting: | Y | Engineers, Elec.: | Y |
| Experienced Mgmt.: | Y | Retail Sales: | | Technical Writing: | | Software Dev.: | | Law: | Y | Engineers, Other: | Y |
| Int'l Business: | | Commercial/Industrial: | Y | Graphic Arts/Photog.: | | Hardware Dev.: | | HR/Other: | Y | Health/Lab: | |
| MBA Graduates: | Y | Sales Trainees: | | Music: | | Systems Integration: | | Training: | Y | Scientists/Research: | |
| | | Advertising Pros.: | | Broadcasting: | | Consulting/Other: | | Health Care: | | Petroleum/Chemicals: | Y |
| | | | | Other: | | | | Consulting: | | Math/Other: | |

## TYPES OF BUSINESS:

Natural Gas Utility
Energy Marketing
Consumer Financing
Energy Systems Design & Engineering
Residential & Light Commercial Services

## BRANDS/DIVISIONS/AFFILIATES:

Washington Gas Light Co.
Hampshire Gas Co.
Crab Run Gas Co.
Washington Gas Resources Corp.
Washington Gas Energy Services, Inc.
Washington Gas Energy Systems, Inc.
Washington Gas Credit Corp.

## CONTACTS: *Note: Officers with more than one job title may be intentionally listed here more than once.*

James H. DeGraffenreidt, Jr., CEO
Terry McCallister, COO
Terry McCallister, Pres.
Vincent L. Ammann, Jr., CFO/VP
William Zeigler Jr., VP-Human Resources
Beverly J. Burke, General Counsel/VP
Elizabeth M. Arnold, VP-Strategy
Roberta W. Sims, VP-Corp. Comm.
Mark P. O'Flynn, Controller
Gautam Chandra, VP-Bus. Process Outsourcing & Non-Utility Oper.
Wilma Kumar-Robock, VP-Support Svcs.
Douglas V. Pope, Sec./Corp. Governance. Officer
Adrian P. Chapman, VP-Washington Gas
James H. DeGraffenreidt, Jr., Chmn.

**Phone:** 703-750-2000 **Fax:** 703-750-4574
**Toll-Free:**
**Address:** 101 Constitution Ave. NW, Washington, DC 20080 US

## GROWTH PLANS/SPECIAL FEATURES:

WGL Holdings, Inc. is a holding company that sells and delivers natural gas and provides a variety of energy-related products and services to customers primarily in Washington, D.C. and the surrounding metropolitan areas in Maryland and Virginia. The firm operates in three business segments: regulated utility, retail energy marketing and commercial HVAC products and services through subsidiaries Washington Gas Light Co.; Washing Gas Resources Corp.; Hampshire Gas Co.; and Crab Run Gas Co. Washington Gas is a regulated public utility that delivers and sells natural gas in Washington, D.C., Maryland and Virginia. Washington Gas Resources owns most of the company's unregulated subsidiaries including Washington Gas Energy Services, Inc. (WGE Services); Washington Gas Energy Systems, Inc. (WGE Systems); and Washington Gas Credit Corp. (Credit Corp.). WGE Services is engaged in the sale of natural gas and electricity to residential, commercial and industrial customers in Maryland, Virginia, Delaware and Washington, D.C. It purchases natural gas and electricity for resale and does not own or operate any natural gas or electric generation, production, transmission or distribution assets. WGE Systems is a provider of commercial energy services including the design, construction, and renovation of mechanical HVAC systems, electrical distribution systems, control and security systems, energy conservation measures and alternative energy technologies to institutional and commercial customers. Hampshire Gas is a regulated utility that operates an underground natural gas storage facility in West Virginia. Crab Run is an exploration and production company whose assets are managed by an Oklahoma-based firm in which Crab Run is a limited partner. In 2008, Washington Gas opened a training facility in Springfield, Virginia.

## FINANCIALS: **Sales and profits are in thousands of dollars—add 000 to get the full amount. 2008 Note: Financial information for 2008 was not available for all companies at press time.**

| | | |
|---|---|---|
| 2008 Sales: $2,628,194 | 2008 Profits: $116,523 | **U.S. Stock Ticker: WGL** |
| 2007 Sales: $2,646,008 | 2007 Profits: $107,900 | **Int'l Ticker:** Int'l Exchange: |
| 2006 Sales: $2,637,883 | 2006 Profits: $87,578 | Employees: 1,448 |
| 2005 Sales: $2,163,343 | 2005 Profits: $103,493 | Fiscal Year Ends: 9/30 |
| 2004 Sales: $2,066,443 | 2004 Profits: $96,637 | Parent Company: |

## SALARIES/BENEFITS:

| | | | | |
|---|---|---|---|---|
| Pension Plan: | ESOP Stock Plan: | Profit Sharing: | Top Exec. Salary: $730,000 | Bonus: $638,750 |
| Savings Plan: Y | Stock Purch. Plan: | | Second Exec. Salary: $455,000 | Bonus: $341,250 |

## OTHER THOUGHTS:

**Apparent Women Officers or Directors**: 5
**Hot Spot for Advancement for Women/Minorities**: Y

## LOCATIONS: ("Y" = Yes)

| West: | Southwest: | Midwest: | Southeast: | Northeast: | International: |
|---|---|---|---|---|---|
| | | | | Y | |

# WHITEWAVE FOODS COMPANY

www.whitewave.com

**Industry Group Code:** 311500 **Ranks within this company's industry group:** Sales: 3 Profits:

| Management: | | Sales/Marketing: | | Liberal Arts: | | Information Systems: | | Professionals: | | Technical/Scientific: | |
|---|---|---|---|---|---|---|---|---|---|---|---|
| Mgmt. Trainees: | | Mktg. Professionals: | Y | Gen. Writing/Editing: | | Info. Management: | Y | Finance/Accounting: | Y | Engineers, Elec.: | |
| Experienced Mgmt.: | Y | Retail Sales: | | Technical Writing: | | Software Dev.: | | Law: | Y | Engineers, Other: | |
| Int'l Business: | | Commercial/Industrial: | Y | Graphic Arts/Photog.: | | Hardware Dev.: | | HR/Other: | Y | Health/Lab: | |
| MBA Graduates: | Y | Sales Trainees: | Y | Music: | | Systems Integration: | | Training: | Y | Scientists/Research: | |
| | | Advertising Pros.: | Y | Broadcasting: | | Consulting/Other: | | Health Care: | | Petroleum/Chemicals: | |
| | | | | Other: | | | | Consulting: | | Math/Other: | |

## TYPES OF BUSINESS:

Soymilk & Soy-Based Products
Dairy Products

## BRANDS/DIVISIONS/AFFILIATES:

Dean Foods Company
Silk
International Delight
Land O' Lakes
Rachel's
Horizon Organic
STOK

## CONTACTS: *Note: Officers with more than one job title may be intentionally listed here more than once.*

Joseph E. Scalzo, CEO
Joseph E. Scalzo, Pres.
Kelly Haecker, CFO
Thomas N. Zanetich, Sr. VP-Human Resources
Bill Luttrell, VP-R&D
Roger Theodoredis, General Counsel/Sr. VP
J. Scott Toth, Sr. VP-Oper.
Greg McKelvey, VP-Strategic Planning
Kelly Shea, Sr. VP-Industry Rel. & Organic Stewardship
Debbie Carosella, Sr. VP-Innovation
Hank Provost, VP-Organizational Dev. & Talent Mgmt.
Mike Keown, Pres., Indulgent Brands
Chris Sliva, Sr. VP-Sales/Chief Customer Officer

| | |
|---|---|
| **Phone:** 303-635-4000 | **Fax:** 303-635-5504 |
| **Toll-Free:** | |
| **Address:** 12002 Airport Way, Broomfield, CO 80021 US | |

## GROWTH PLANS/SPECIAL FEATURES:

WhiteWave Foods Company, a division of Dean Foods Co., manufactures and sells soy-based products and dairy throughout the U.S. The company's most popular brand is Silk, a line of soymilks. Additional products include Horizon Organic certified milk, dairy products, eggs and juices; International Delight flavored creamers; Land O' Lakes products; Silk cultured soy yogurt substitute; soy-based smoothies; Hershey's Milks and Milkshakes; and Rachel's yogurt. All of WhiteWave's soy products are made from certified organic soybeans and are certified Kosher. Silk and Horizon use renewable wind powered energy sources in their production and supply chain. WhiteWave operates a website detailing its products, ingredients, organic certification requirements and issues, green power news, soy-based recipes and cooking tips. In 2007, the firm introduced STOK, a black coffee shot with the caffeine of an extra shot of espresso. STOK is available in regular or sweet, and is sold at convenience stores.

## FINANCIALS: **Sales and profits are in thousands of dollars—add 000 to get the full amount. 2008 Note: Financial information for 2008 was not available for all companies at press time.**

| | | |
|---|---|---|
| 2008 Sales: $ | 2008 Profits: $ | **U.S. Stock Ticker: Subsidiary** |
| 2007 Sales: $80,000 | 2007 Profits: $ | **Int'l Ticker:** Int'l Exchange: |
| 2006 Sales: $ | 2006 Profits: $ | Employees: 1,200 |
| 2005 Sales: $ | 2005 Profits: $ | Fiscal Year Ends: 12/31 |
| 2004 Sales: $ | 2004 Profits: $ | Parent Company: DEAN FOODS CO |

## SALARIES/BENEFITS:

| | | | | |
|---|---|---|---|---|
| Pension Plan: | ESOP Stock Plan: | Profit Sharing: | Top Exec. Salary: $ | Bonus: $ |
| Savings Plan: | Stock Purch. Plan: | | Second Exec. Salary: $ | Bonus: $ |

## OTHER THOUGHTS:

**Apparent Women Officers or Directors**: 2
**Hot Spot for Advancement for Women/Minorities**: Y

## LOCATIONS: ("Y" = Yes)

| West: | Southwest: | Midwest: | Southeast: | Northeast: | International: |
|---|---|---|---|---|---|
| Y | | | | | |

# WIND RIVER SYSTEMS INC

**www.windriver.com**

**Industry Group Code:** 511204 **Ranks within this company's industry group:** Sales: 3 Profits: 3

| Management: | | Sales/Marketing: | | Liberal Arts: | | Information Systems: | | Professionals: | | Technical/Scientific: | |
|---|---|---|---|---|---|---|---|---|---|---|---|
| Mgmt. Trainees: | | Mktg. Professionals: | Y | Gen. Writing/Editing: | | Info. Management: | Y | Finance/Accounting: | Y | Engineers, Elec.: | Y |
| Experienced Mgmt.: | Y | Retail Sales: | | Technical Writing: | Y | Software Dev.: | Y | Law: | Y | Engineers, Other: | |
| Int'l Business: | Y | Commercial/Industrial: | Y | Graphic Arts/Photog.: | | Hardware Dev.: | | HR/Other: | Y | Health/Lab: | |
| MBA Graduates: | Y | Sales Trainees: | Y | Music: | | Systems Integration: | | Training: | Y | Scientists/Research: | |
| | | Advertising Pros.: | | Broadcasting: | | Consulting/Other: | | Health Care: | | Petroleum/Chemicals: | |
| | | | | Other: | | | | Consulting: | | Math/Other: | Y |

## TYPES OF BUSINESS:

Computer Software-Embedded Systems
Consulting Services
Operating Systems
Device Software Optimization

## BRANDS/DIVISIONS/AFFILIATES:

pSOS
Wind River Platform
VxWorks
RTLinux
S.C. Comsys S.R.L.
MIZI Research, Inc.
NASA

## CONTACTS:

*Note: Officers with more than one job title may be intentionally listed here more than once.*

Ken Klein, CEO
Barry Mainz, COO
Ken Klein, Pres.
Ian Halifax, CFO
John Bruggeman, Chief Mktg. Officer
Jeff Loehr, VP-Human Resources
Tomas Evensen, CTO/General Mgr.-Common Tech. Prod. Div.
Ian Halifax, Sr. VP-Admin.
Ian Halifax, Sr. VP-Finance/Sec.
Scot Morrison, Sr. VP/General Mgr.-VxWorks Prod. Div.
Damian Artt, VP-Worldwide Sales & Svcs.
Tomas Evensen, VP/General Mgr.-Wind River Tools
Vincent Rerolle, Sr. VP/General Mgr.-Linux Prod. Div.
Ken Klein, Chmn.

| | |
|---|---|
| **Phone:** 510-748-4100 | **Fax:** 510-749-2010 |
| **Toll-Free:** 800-545-9463 | |
| **Address:** 500 Wind River Way, Alameda, CA 94501 US | |

## GROWTH PLANS/SPECIAL FEATURES:

Wind River Systems, Inc., a leader in device software optimization (DSO), develops, markets and sells operating systems, middleware and software development tools for embedded systems to be used in a diverse range of products, including set-top boxes, automobile braking and navigation systems, mobile handsets, Internet routers, avionics control panels and coronary pacemakers. The company operates in four segments: VxWorks, which consists of the firm's proprietary VxWorks real-time operating system and related products; Linux, which comprises Wind River's open-source-based, commercial-grade Linux operating systems and related products; Non-Core Products and Design Services, which comprises the company's pSOS real-time operating system, other non-core products and turn-key product design services; and Other, which includes development tools, device management products and related services. Wind River also offers an Eclipse-based Workbench software development suite, which allows customers to manage the design, development, debugging and testing of their device software systems. Wind River technology is worldwide deployed in more than 300 million devices, and the company's major customers include Apple, Hewlett-Packard, Boeing, Motorola, NASA, and Mitsubishi. The company offers solutions to the aerospace and defense, automotive, consumer, industrial and network equipment industries. Wind River has provided technology to NASA's Jet Propulsion Lab for space exploration and the Stardust Project. In 2007, the firm acquired the intellectual property which includes patents, copyrights, trademarks and associated product rights for RTLinux, a hard real-time Linux technology developed by Finite State Machine Labs, Inc., (FSMLabs). It also recently acquired S.C. Comsys S.R.L., an embedded software professional services organization based in Romania, for $1.4 million. In October 2008, the firm acquired MIZI Research, Inc., a developer of mobile application platforms based on embedded Linux.

Wind River offers its employees tuition reimbursement, a stock purchase plan, credit union membership, health club membership discounts, flexible spending accounts and an employee assistance program.

## FINANCIALS:

**Sales and profits are in thousands of dollars—add 000 to get the full amount. 2008 Note: Financial information for 2008 was not available for all companies at press time.**

| | | |
|---|---|---|
| 2008 Sales: $328,631 | 2008 Profits: $-2,358 | **U.S. Stock Ticker: WIND** |
| 2007 Sales: $285,298 | 2007 Profits: $ 573 | **Int'l Ticker:** Int'l Exchange: |
| 2006 Sales: $266,323 | 2006 Profits: $29,295 | Employees: 1,507 |
| 2005 Sales: $235,400 | 2005 Profits: $8,165 | Fiscal Year Ends: 1/31 |
| 2004 Sales: $204,119 | 2004 Profits: $-24,564 | Parent Company: |

## SALARIES/BENEFITS:

| | | | | |
|---|---|---|---|---|
| Pension Plan: | ESOP Stock Plan: | Profit Sharing: | Top Exec. Salary: $650,000 | Bonus: $280,000 |
| Savings Plan: Y | Stock Purch. Plan: Y | | Second Exec. Salary: $350,000 | Bonus: $98,000 |

## OTHER THOUGHTS:

**Apparent Women Officers or Directors:**
**Hot Spot for Advancement for Women/Minorities:**

## LOCATIONS: ("Y" = Yes)

| West: | Southwest: | Midwest: | Southeast: | Northeast: | International: |
|---|---|---|---|---|---|
| Y | Y | Y | Y | Y | Y |

# WRIGHT MEDICAL GROUP INC

www.wmt.com

**Industry Group Code:** 339113 **Ranks within this company's industry group:** Sales: 7 Profits: 35

| Management: | | Sales/Marketing: | | Liberal Arts: | | Information Systems: | | Professionals: | | Technical/Scientific: | |
|---|---|---|---|---|---|---|---|---|---|---|---|
| Mgmt. Trainees: | | Mktg. Professionals: | Y | Gen. Writing/Editing: | | Info. Management: | Y | Finance/Accounting: | Y | Engineers, Elec.: | |
| Experienced Mgmt.: | Y | Retail Sales: | | Technical Writing: | Y | Software Dev.: | Y | Law: | Y | Engineers, Other: | Y |
| Int'l Business: | Y | Commercial/Industrial: | Y | Graphic Arts/Photog.: | | Hardware Dev.: | | HR/Other: | Y | Health/Lab: | Y |
| MBA Graduates: | Y | Sales Trainees: | Y | Music: | | Systems Integration: | | Training: | Y | Scientists/Research: | Y |
| | | Advertising Pros.: | | Broadcasting: | | Consulting/Other: | | Health Care: | Y | Petroleum/Chemicals: | |
| | | | | Other: | | | | Consulting: | | Math/Other: | Y |

## TYPES OF BUSINESS:

Orthopedic Implants
Reconstructive Joint Devices
Biologics Materials

## BRANDS/DIVISIONS/AFFILIATES:

Wright Medical Technology, Inc.
ADVANCE
CONSERVE
A-CLASS
CHARLOTTE
MICRONAIL
ORTHOSPHERE
GRAFTJACKET

## CONTACTS: *Note: Officers with more than one job title may be intentionally listed here more than once.*

Gary D. Henley, CEO
Gary D. Henley, Pres.
John K. Bakewell, CFO/Exec. VP
Eric A. Stookey, VP-North American Sales
Frank S. Bono, Sr. VP-R&D
Kyle M. Joines, VP-Mfg.
Jason P. Hood, General Counsel/VP/Corp. Sec.
William L. Griffin, Jr., Sr. VP-Global Oper.
Timothy E. Davis, Jr., VP-Bus. Dev.
Lance A. Berry, Controller/VP
Paul A. Arrendell, VP-Global Quality Systems
Rhonda L. Fellows, Sr. VP-Gov't Affairs & Reimbursement
Alicia M. Napoli, VP-Clinical & Regulatory Affairs
John T. Treace, VP-Biologics & Extremity Mktg.
F. Barry Bays, Chmn.
Paul R. Kosters, Pres., EMEA
William J. Flannery, VP-Logistics & Materials

**Phone:** 901-867-9971 **Fax:** 901-867-9534
**Toll-Free:** 800-238-7117
**Address:** 5677 Airline Rd., Arlington, TN 38002 US

## GROWTH PLANS/SPECIAL FEATURES:

Wright Medical Group, Inc., primarily through its Wright Medical Technology, Inc. subsidiary, is a global orthopedic medical device company specializing in the design, manufacture and marketing of reconstructive joint devices and biologics products. Wright offers products in four primary market sectors: knee reconstruction, hip reconstruction, extremity reconstruction and biologics. The company's knee reconstruction portfolio includes total knee reconstruction products, revision replacement implants and limb preservation products. The ADVANCE knee system is its primary knee product line offering, featuring the ADVANCE medial pivot knee, designed to approximate the movement and function of a healthy knee by using a unique spherical medial feature. Wright's hip joint reconstruction portfolio provides offerings in the areas of bone-conserving implants, total hip reconstruction, revision replacement implants and limb preservation. The CONSERVE family of products incorporates anatomically-replicating large diameter bearings and its patent-pending A-CLASS advanced metal technology, which is designed to result in significantly less wear than traditional metal-on-metal hip implants. Wright's extremity products include its CHARLOTTE foot and ankle system; MICRONAIL intramedullary wrist fracture repair system; and ORTHOSPHERE carpometacarpal implant for the repair of the basal thumb joint. The company offers biologics products used to replace and repair damaged or diseased bone, tendons and soft tissues utilizing synthetic and human tissue-based materials. Products include its GRAFTJACKET soft tissue graft designed for augmentation of tendon and ligament repairs; OSTEOSET bone graft substitute; and ALLOMATRIX injectable putty. In April 2007, the company acquired the reconstructive foot surgery business of Darco International, Inc. for approximately $17 million. In October 2007, Wright acquired the BIO-ARCH foot and ankle implant from Metasurg for approximately $2.5 million. In April 2008, the company acquired INBONE Technologies, Inc. for approximately $24 million. In June 2008, Wright acquired the foot and ankle product line of A.M. Surgical, Inc. for approximately $2.1 million.

## FINANCIALS: **Sales and profits are in thousands of dollars—add 000 to get the full amount. 2008 Note: Financial information for 2008 was not available for all companies at press time.**

2008 Sales: $465,547
2007 Sales: $386,850
2006 Sales: $338,938
2005 Sales: $319,137
2004 Sales: $297,539

2008 Profits: $3,197
2007 Profits: $ 961
2006 Profits: $14,411
2005 Profits: $21,065
2004 Profits: $24,022

**U.S. Stock Ticker: WMGI**
**Int'l Ticker:** Int'l Exchange:
Employees: 1,050
Fiscal Year Ends: 12/31
Parent Company:

## SALARIES/BENEFITS:

Pension Plan: ESOP Stock Plan: Profit Sharing: Top Exec. Salary: $416,250 Bonus: $202,530
Savings Plan: Stock Purch. Plan: Second Exec. Salary: $322,784 Bonus: $87,318

## OTHER THOUGHTS:

**Apparent Women Officers or Directors**: 5
**Hot Spot for Advancement for Women/Minorities**: Y

## LOCATIONS: ("Y" = Yes)

| West: | Southwest: | Midwest: | Southeast: | Northeast: | International: |
|---|---|---|---|---|---|
| | | | Y | | Y |

# XOMA LTD

**www.xoma.com**

**Industry Group Code:** 325412 **Ranks within this company's industry group:** Sales: 22 Profits: 15

| **Management:** | | **Sales/Marketing:** | | **Liberal Arts:** | | **Information Systems:** | | **Professionals:** | | **Technical/Scientific:** | |
|---|---|---|---|---|---|---|---|---|---|---|---|
| Mgmt. Trainees: | | Mktg. Professionals: | Y | Gen. Writing/Editing: | | Info. Management: | Y | Finance/Accounting: | Y | Engineers, Elec.: | |
| Experienced Mgmt.: | Y | Retail Sales: | | Technical Writing: | Y | Software Dev.: | Y | Law: | Y | Engineers, Other: | |
| Int'l Business: | | Commercial/Industrial: | Y | Graphic Arts/Photog.: | | Hardware Dev.: | | HR/Other: | Y | Health/Lab: | Y |
| MBA Graduates: | Y | Sales Trainees: | Y | Music: | | Systems Integration: | | Training: | Y | Scientists/Research: | Y |
| | | Advertising Pros.: | | Broadcasting: | | Consulting/Other: | | Health Care: | Y | Petroleum/Chemicals: | |
| | | | | Other: | | | | Consulting: | | Math/Other: | Y |

## TYPES OF BUSINESS:

Therapeutic Antibodies

## BRANDS/DIVISIONS/AFFILIATES:

Raptiva
Lucentis
HCD122
Genetech, Inc.
Millenium
XOMA 052
XOMA 629
Triton

## CONTACTS:

*Note: Officers with more than one job title may be intentionally listed here more than once.*

Steven B. Engle, CEO
Steven B. Engle, Pres.
J. David Boyle II, CFO
Charles C. Wells, VP-Human Resources
Charles C. Wells, VP-IT
Christopher J. Margolin, General Counsel/VP/Sec.
Robert S. Tenerowicz, VP-Oper.
Mary L. Anderson, VP-Bus. Dev.
J. David Boyle II, VP-Finance
Patrick J. Scannon, Chief Biotechnology Officer/Exec. VP
Daniel P. Cafaro, VP-Regulatory Affairs & Compliance
Patricai Donahue, VP-Collaborations Bus.
Calvin L. McGoogan, VP-Quality & Facilities
Steven B. Engle, Chmn.

| | |
|---|---|
| **Phone:** 510-214-7200 | **Fax:** 510-644-2011 |
| **Toll-Free:** | |
| **Address:** 2910 7th St., Berkeley, CA 94710 US | |

## GROWTH PLANS/SPECIAL FEATURES:

Xoma, Ltd. is a biopharmaceutical company that discovers and develops therapeutic antibodies, primarily directed toward treatments for cancer and immune disorders. The company has a royalty interest in one marketed antibody product, Raptiva (efalizumab), as well as interests in additional therapeutic antibody candidates being developed by others as a result of licensing technologies. Raptiva, marketed by Genetech, Inc., is a humanized therapeutic monoclonal antibody developed to treat immune system disorders. The drug is approved in the U.S. for the treatment of moderate-to-severe plaque psoriasis and marketed in over 50 countries. Xoma's product development pipeline includes proprietary products and collaborative programs at various stages of preclinical and clinical development, which are for the most part directed toward treating cancer and immune disorders. Lucentis, by Genentech, is an antibody fragment against vascular endothelial growth factor for the treatment of age-related macular degeneration. The drug is marketed in the U.S. and the E.U., where it is distributed by Novartis AG. The drug uses the company's bacterial cell expression technology. Other drugs undergoing clinical trials include HCD122 (formerly CHIR-12.12), a fully human anti-CD40 antagonist antibody intended as a treatment for B-cell mediated diseases; XOMA 052 (formerly XMA005.2), a monoclonal antibody designed to be used as an injectable therapeutic for treating multiple inflammatory indications; and XOMA 629 (a reformulation of XMP.629), a topical anti-bacterial formulation of a BPI-derived peptide under development as a possible treatment for acne. The firm possesses a broad technology platform for the discovery, optimization and manufacture of therapeutic antibodies as well as a fully integrated product development infrastructure for antibodies and other biologics. Xoma has collaborations with several companies, including Genetech, Inc.; Takeda; Schering-Plough; Millenium; and Triton.

## FINANCIALS:

**Sales and profits are in thousands of dollars—add 000 to get the full amount. 2008 Note: Financial information for 2008 was not available for all companies at press time.**

| | | |
|---|---|---|
| 2008 Sales: $ | 2008 Profits: $ | **U.S. Stock Ticker: XOMA** |
| 2007 Sales: $84,252 | 2007 Profits: $-12,326 | **Int'l Ticker:** Int'l Exchange: |
| 2006 Sales: $29,498 | 2006 Profits: $-51,841 | Employees: 311 |
| 2005 Sales: $18,669 | 2005 Profits: $2,779 | Fiscal Year Ends: 12/31 |
| 2004 Sales: $3,665 | 2004 Profits: $-78,942 | Parent Company: |

## SALARIES/BENEFITS:

| | | | | |
|---|---|---|---|---|
| Pension Plan: | ESOP Stock Plan: | Profit Sharing: | Top Exec. Salary: $360,000 | Bonus: $115,631 |
| Savings Plan: Y | Stock Purch. Plan: Y | | Second Exec. Salary: $310,000 | Bonus: $110,033 |

## OTHER THOUGHTS:

**Apparent Women Officers or Directors**: 2
**Hot Spot for Advancement for Women/Minorities**:

## LOCATIONS: ("Y" = Yes)

| West: | Southwest: | Midwest: | Southeast: | Northeast: | International: |
|---|---|---|---|---|---|
| Y | | | | | |

# XTO ENERGY INC

www.xtoenergy.com

**Industry Group Code:** 211111 **Ranks within this company's industry group:** Sales: 1 Profits: 1

| Management: | | Sales/Marketing: | | Liberal Arts: | | Information Systems: | | Professionals: | | Technical/Scientific: | |
|---|---|---|---|---|---|---|---|---|---|---|---|
| Mgmt. Trainees: | | Mktg. Professionals: | Y | Gen. Writing/Editing: | | Info. Management: | Y | Finance/Accounting: | Y | Engineers, Elec.: | |
| Experienced Mgmt.: | Y | Retail Sales: | | Technical Writing: | | Software Dev.: | | Law: | Y | Engineers, Other: | Y |
| Int'l Business: | Y | Commercial/Industrial: | Y | Graphic Arts/Photog.: | | Hardware Dev.: | | HR/Other: | Y | Health/Lab: | |
| MBA Graduates: | Y | Sales Trainees: | | Music: | | Systems Integration: | | Training: | Y | Scientists/Research: | |
| | | Advertising Pros.: | | Broadcasting: | | Consulting/Other: | | Health Care: | | Petroleum/Chemicals: | Y |
| | | | | Other: | | | | Consulting: | | Math/Other: | |

## TYPES OF BUSINESS:

Oil & Gas Exploration & Production

## BRANDS/DIVISIONS/AFFILIATES:

Hunt Petroleum Corp.

## CONTACTS:

*Note: Officers with more than one job title may be intentionally listed here more than once.*

Bob R. Simpson, CEO
Keith A. Hutton, Pres.
Louis G. Baldwin, CFO/Exec. VP
Terry L. Schultz, Sr. VP-Mktg.
Vaughn O. Vennerberg, II, Chief of Staff/Sr. Exec. VP
L. Frank Thomas, III, VP-IT
Kenneth F. Staab, Sr. VP-Eng.
Frank G. McDonald, General Counsel/Sr. VP
Gary D. Simpson, Sr. VP-Investor Rel. & Finance
Brent W. Clum, Treas./Sr. VP
Karen Wilson, VP-Human Resources
Timorhy Petrus, VP-Acquisitions
Nick Dungey, Sr. VP-Natural Gas Oper.
Bennie G. Kniffen, Controller/Sr. VP
Bob R. Simpson, Chmn.

| | |
|---|---|
| **Phone:** 817-870-2800 | **Fax:** 817-870-1671 |
| **Toll-Free:** 800-299-2800 | |
| **Address:** 810 Houston St., Fort Worth, TX 76102 US | |

## GROWTH PLANS/SPECIAL FEATURES:

XTO Energy, Inc. is engaged in the acquisition, development, exploitation and exploration of producing oil and gas properties and in the production, processing, marketing and transportation of oil and natural gas. The firm's proved reserves are predominantly in the eastern region, including the east Texas basin, northwestern Louisiana and Mississippi; the north Texas region, including the Barnett Shale; the San Juan region; the Permian and south Texas region; and the mid-continent and Rocky Mountain region, including the Fayetteville and Woodford Shales. As of 2007, the firm's estimated proven reserves were 241 million barrels of oil, 9.44 trillion cubic feet of natural gas and 67 million barrels of natural gas liquids. The company has an inventory of between 9,500 and 10,300 potential development drilling locations. In addition, XTO Energy employs a disciplined acquisition program to augment its core properties and expand its reserve base. The company also operates gas gathering systems in areas where it has production. Recent acquisitions by the company include natural gas and oil properties from Dominion Resources, Inc.; more than 16,000 acres in the Barnett Shale for $550 million; producing properties, leasehold acreage and gathering infrastructure from Southwestern Energy Company; and producing properties from Linn Energy LLC and Headington Oil Company. In September 2008, XTO Energy completed its acquisition of Hunt Petroleum Corporation and other associated entities for approximately $4.2 billion.

The company offers its employees medical, dental and vision insurance; life and AD&D insurance; a 401(k) plan; and retirement plans.

## FINANCIALS:

**Sales and profits are in thousands of dollars—add 000 to get the full amount. 2008 Note: Financial information for 2008 was not available for all companies at press time.**

| | | |
|---|---|---|
| 2008 Sales: $7,695,000 | 2008 Profits: $1,912,000 | **U.S. Stock Ticker: XTO** |
| 2007 Sales: $5,513,000 | 2007 Profits: $1,691,000 | **Int'l Ticker:** Int'l Exchange: |
| 2006 Sales: $4,576,000 | 2006 Profits: $1,860,000 | Employees: 2,361 |
| 2005 Sales: $3,519,000 | 2005 Profits: $1,152,000 | Fiscal Year Ends: 12/31 |
| 2004 Sales: $1,947,601 | 2004 Profits: $507,882 | Parent Company: |

## SALARIES/BENEFITS:

| | | | | |
|---|---|---|---|---|
| Pension Plan: Y | ESOP Stock Plan: | Profit Sharing: | Top Exec. Salary: $1,312,508 | Bonus: $35,500,000 |
| Savings Plan: Y | Stock Purch. Plan: | | Second Exec. Salary: $762,506 | Bonus: $5,400,000 |

## OTHER THOUGHTS:

**Apparent Women Officers or Directors:** 6
**Hot Spot for Advancement for Women/Minorities:** Y

## LOCATIONS: ("Y" = Yes)

| West: | Southwest: | Midwest: | Southeast: | Northeast: | International: |
|---|---|---|---|---|---|
| Y | Y | Y | Y | Y | |

# YOUNG'S MARKET COMPANY LLC

www.youngsmarket.com

**Industry Group Code:** 422820 **Ranks within this company's industry group:** Sales: 1 Profits:

| Management: | | Sales/Marketing: | | Liberal Arts: | | Information Systems: | | Professionals: | | Technical/Scientific: | |
|---|---|---|---|---|---|---|---|---|---|---|---|
| Mgmt. Trainees: | Y | Mktg. Professionals: | Y | Gen. Writing/Editing: | | Info. Management: | Y | Finance/Accounting: | Y | Engineers, Elec.: | |
| Experienced Mgmt.: | Y | Retail Sales: | Y | Technical Writing: | | Software Dev.: | | Law: | Y | Engineers, Other: | |
| Int'l Business: | | Commercial/Industrial: | | Graphic Arts/Photog.: | Y | Hardware Dev.: | | HR/Other: | Y | Health/Lab: | |
| MBA Graduates: | Y | Sales Trainees: | Y | Music: | | Systems Integration: | | Training: | Y | Scientists/Research: | |
| | | Advertising Pros.: | Y | Broadcasting: | | Consulting/Other: | | Health Care: | | Petroleum/Chemicals: | |
| | | | | Other: | | | | Consulting: | | Math/Other: | |

## TYPES OF BUSINESS:

Alcohol Distribution

## BRANDS/DIVISIONS/AFFILIATES:

Better Brands

## CONTACTS:

*Note: Officers with more than one job title may be intentionally listed here more than once.*

Vernon O. Underwood, CEO
Jeffrey Underwood, Co-COO/Co-Pres.
Chris Underwood, Co-Pres./Co-COO
Dennis Hamann, CFO/Exec. VP
Valerie Gart, Sr. VP-Strategic Human Resources
Karen Eaton, Sr. VP/CIO
Don Robbins, General Counsel/Exec. VP
Paul A. Vert, Exec. VP
Janet Smith, Sec./Exec. VP
Vernon O. Underwood, Chmn.

**Phone:** 714-283-4933 **Fax:** 714-283-6175
**Toll-Free:** 800-317-6150
**Address:** 2164 N. Batavia St., Orange, CA 92865 US

## GROWTH PLANS/SPECIAL FEATURES:

Young's Market Company, LLC, based in California, is one of the largest distributors of beer, wine and distilled spirits in the U.S., with operations in California, Hawaii, Arizona, Oregon, Washington, Alaska, Idaho, Utah, Montana and Wyoming. The firm was founded in 1888 as a grocery and specialty food shop in California. Young's distributes products for Bacardi, Beck's, Brown-Forman (including its Sonoma-Cutrer Vineyards and Foster's Group Australian Wines) and many other wineries and distilleries on the U.S. west coast and abroad. It also markets mixers and chasers that go along with the alcoholic products. The firm conducts inventories, manages merchandising displays and performs other vital sales-related tasks, along with taking orders for stores and supplying stock. The company's sales campaigns average nearly 10,000 store visits each week. Young's also operates in Hawaii through its Better Brands subsidiary. Customers include liquor stores, grocery stores, bars and other retail outlets. Young's has been owned by the Underwood family, relatives of the Young family, since 1990. Recently, the company completed its transition to a new state-of-the-art warehouse and distribution facility in Chino, California. In August 2008, the firm initiated a new recycling program.

Employees of Young's are offered benefits including a 401(k) plan. Certain positions are also offered a car allowance.

## FINANCIALS:

**Sales and profits are in thousands of dollars—add 000 to get the full amount. 2008 Note: Financial information for 2008 was not available for all companies at press time.**

2008 Sales: $
2007 Sales: $2,100,000
2006 Sales: $2,060,000
2005 Sales: $1,500,000
2004 Sales: $1,400,000

2008 Profits: $
2007 Profits: $
2006 Profits: $
2005 Profits: $
2004 Profits: $

**U.S. Stock Ticker: Private**
**Int'l Ticker:** Int'l Exchange:
Employees: 2,130
Fiscal Year Ends: 2/28
Parent Company:

## SALARIES/BENEFITS:

Pension Plan: ESOP Stock Plan: Profit Sharing: Top Exec. Salary: $ Bonus: $
Savings Plan: Y Stock Purch. Plan: Second Exec. Salary: $ Bonus: $

## OTHER THOUGHTS:

**Apparent Women Officers or Directors**: 3
**Hot Spot for Advancement for Women/Minorities**: Y

## LOCATIONS: ("Y" = Yes)

| West: | Southwest: | Midwest: | Southeast: | Northeast: | International: |
|---|---|---|---|---|---|
| Y | Y | | | | |

# ZAPPOS.COM INC

www.zappos.com

**Industry Group Code:** 448210E **Ranks within this company's industry group:** Sales: 1 Profits:

| Management: | | Sales/Marketing: | | Liberal Arts: | | Information Systems: | | Professionals: | | Technical/Scientific: | |
|---|---|---|---|---|---|---|---|---|---|---|---|
| Mgmt. Trainees: | Y | Mktg. Professionals: | Y | Gen. Writing/Editing: | Y | Info. Management: | Y | Finance/Accounting: | Y | Engineers, Elec.: | |
| Experienced Mgmt.: | Y | Retail Sales: | Y | Technical Writing: | | Software Dev.: | Y | Law: | Y | Engineers, Other: | |
| Int'l Business: | | Commercial/Industrial: | | Graphic Arts/Photog.: | Y | Hardware Dev.: | | HR/Other: | Y | Health/Lab: | |
| MBA Graduates: | Y | Sales Trainees: | Y | Music: | | Systems Integration: | Y | Training: | Y | Scientists/Research: | |
| | | Advertising Pros.: | Y | Broadcasting: | | Consulting/Other: | | Health Care: | | Petroleum/Chemicals: | |
| | | | | Other: | | | | Consulting: | | Math/Other: | |

## TYPES OF BUSINESS:

Online Shoe Retail
Online Handbags & Accessories Retail
Online Consumer Products Sales

## BRANDS/DIVISIONS/AFFILIATES:

Zappos Life

## CONTACTS: *Note: Officers with more than one job title may be intentionally listed here more than once.*

Tony Hsieh, CEO
Alfred Lin, COO
Alfred Lin, CFO
Fred Mossler, VP-Mktg.
Fred Mossler, VP-Merch.
Fred Mossler, VP-Outlet Oper.
Fred Mossler, VP-Creative Svcs./Product Presentation/Help Desk
Alfred Lin, Chmn.

**Phone:** 702-943-7777 **Fax:** 702-943-7778
**Toll-Free:** 800-927-7671
**Address:** 2280 Corporate Cir., Ste. 100, Henderson, NV 89074 US

## GROWTH PLANS/SPECIAL FEATURES:

Zappos.com, Inc. is an online retailer of shoes and handbags. As of 2008, the firm carried more than 3 million pairs of shoes, handbags, clothing items and accessories in inventory, including 1,136 brands that are difficult to find in mainstream shopping malls. Zappos sells a wide variety of moderately-priced to high end footwear, including shoes with wide, narrow, athletic, couture and designer specifications. The two company warehouses are continually stocked with about 2 million items and total more than 1 million square feet of storage space, which guarantees that anything listed for sale is in stock. Shipping and return shipping are offered free of charge. In addition to shoes, Zappos also stocks a wide variety of backpacks and an assortment of other accessories, such as socks, belts, leather goods, luggage, eyewear, watches and shoe paraphernalia. The company also has an eco-friendly line of men's and women's clothing and shoes. Although the company's current business focuses mainly on shoes, Zappos plans to expand product offerings in many areas. An integral part of Zappos' business plan is insuring that orders are delivered as quickly as possible. In conjunction with free return shipping, this makes shopping online nearly as convenient as shopping in a physical store. The company ships Zappos Life, a so-called maglog (magazine and catalog) with many orders. Roughly 60% of sales are generated by repeat customers.

## FINANCIALS: **Sales and profits are in thousands of dollars—add 000 to get the full amount. 2008 Note: Financial information for 2008 was not available for all companies at press time.**

2008 Sales: $
2007 Sales: $528,000
2006 Sales: $400,000
2005 Sales: $200,000
2004 Sales: $

2008 Profits: $
2007 Profits: $
2006 Profits: $
2005 Profits: $
2004 Profits: $

**U.S. Stock Ticker: Private**
**Int'l Ticker:** Int'l Exchange:
Employees: 1,600
Fiscal Year Ends: 12/31
Parent Company:

## SALARIES/BENEFITS:

Pension Plan: ESOP Stock Plan: Profit Sharing: Top Exec. Salary: $ Bonus: $
Savings Plan: Stock Purch. Plan: Second Exec. Salary: $ Bonus: $

## OTHER THOUGHTS:

**Apparent Women Officers or Directors**:
**Hot Spot for Advancement for Women/Minorities**:

## LOCATIONS: ("Y" = Yes)

| West: | Southwest: | Midwest: | Southeast: | Northeast: | International: |
|---|---|---|---|---|---|
| Y | | | | | |

# ZIEBART INTERNATIONAL CORP

**www.ziebart.com**

**Industry Group Code:** 811100 **Ranks within this company's industry group:** Sales: 2 Profits:

| Management: | | Sales/Marketing: | | Liberal Arts: | | Information Systems: | | Professionals: | | Technical/Scientific: | |
|---|---|---|---|---|---|---|---|---|---|---|---|
| Mgmt. Trainees: | | Mktg. Professionals: | Y | Gen. Writing/Editing: | | Info. Management: | Y | Finance/Accounting: | Y | Engineers, Elec.: | |
| Experienced Mgmt.: | Y | Retail Sales: | | Technical Writing: | | Software Dev.: | | Law: | Y | Engineers, Other: | |
| Int'l Business: | Y | Commercial/Industrial: | | Graphic Arts/Photog.: | | Hardware Dev.: | | HR/Other: | Y | Health/Lab: | |
| MBA Graduates: | Y | Sales Trainees: | | Music: | | Systems Integration: | | Training: | Y | Scientists/Research: | |
| | | Advertising Pros.: | | Broadcasting: | | Consulting/Other: | | Health Care: | | Petroleum/Chemicals: | |
| | | | | Other: | | | | Consulting: | | Math/Other: | |

## TYPES OF BUSINESS:

Automotive Repair & Maintenance
Aftermarket Accessories Installation
Detailing
Paint & Fabric Protection
Window Tinting
Rust Protection

## BRANDS/DIVISIONS/AFFILIATES:

Renu-A-Shine
Inner-Clean
Protect-A-Shine
Diamond Gloss
Inner Guard

## CONTACTS: *Note: Officers with more than one job title may be intentionally listed here more than once.*

Thomas E. Wolfe, CEO
Thomas E. Wolfe, Pres.
Sue Spriet, Dir.-Admin.
William Patterson, VP-Finance
Michael Riley, Sr. VP
Michael Pino, Sr. VP
James L. Levagood, Dir.-Computer Oper.
Daniel C. Baker, Sr. VP
Thomas E. Wolfe, Chmn.

**Phone:** 248-588-4100 **Fax:** 248-588-1444
**Toll-Free:** 800-877-1312
**Address:** 1290 E. Maple Rd., Troy, MI 48083 US

## GROWTH PLANS/SPECIAL FEATURES:

Ziebart International Corp. is the largest installer of aftermarket accessories in North America and has been a leader in car care products and services since 1959. The company's services include detailing, paint and fabric protection, window tinting, rust protection and installation of electronic systems, sunroofs, alarm systems and a range of other accessories. The company specializes in truck accessories, such as bed liners and scratch and scuff paint repair. The firm's proprietary services include Renu-A-Shine and Inner-Clean for both interior and exterior detailing and Protect-A-Shine, Diamond Gloss and Inner Guard protection services. Ziebart operates a network of approximately 400 locations in more than 40 countries around the world. The firm maintains strategic business partnerships with groups including Speedy Auto Glass and Rhino Linings. Ziebart also offers management and technical training for its franchisees. The company has been named to Entrepreneur's list of the Top 500 Franchisers for 15 consecutive years; Success magazine's Franchise Gold 100 for four consecutive years; Income Opportunities' Platinum 200 list; and as one of Franchise Times magazine's Top 200.

## FINANCIALS: **Sales and profits are in thousands of dollars—add 000 to get the full amount. 2008 Note: Financial information for 2008 was not available for all companies at press time.**

2008 Sales: $
2007 Sales: $114,000
2006 Sales: $
2005 Sales: $
2004 Sales: $

2008 Profits: $
2007 Profits: $
2006 Profits: $
2005 Profits: $
2004 Profits: $

**U.S. Stock Ticker: Private**
**Int'l Ticker:** Int'l Exchange:
Employees: 230
Fiscal Year Ends:
Parent Company:

## SALARIES/BENEFITS:

Pension Plan: ESOP Stock Plan: Profit Sharing: Top Exec. Salary: $ Bonus: $
Savings Plan: Stock Purch. Plan: Second Exec. Salary: $ Bonus: $

## OTHER THOUGHTS:

**Apparent Women Officers or Directors**:
**Hot Spot for Advancement for Women/Minorities**:

## LOCATIONS: ("Y" = Yes)

| West: | Southwest: | Midwest: | Southeast: | Northeast: | International: |
|---|---|---|---|---|---|
| Y | Y | Y | Y | Y | Y |

# ZILA INC

**www.zila.com**

**Industry Group Code:** 325412 **Ranks within this company's industry group:** Sales: 32 Profits: 16

| **Management:** | | **Sales/Marketing:** | | **Liberal Arts:** | | **Information Systems:** | | **Professionals:** | | **Technical/Scientific:** | |
|---|---|---|---|---|---|---|---|---|---|---|---|
| Mgmt. Trainees: | | Mktg. Professionals: | Y | Gen. Writing/Editing: | | Info. Management: | Y | Finance/Accounting: | Y | Engineers, Elec.: | |
| Experienced Mgmt.: | Y | Retail Sales: | | Technical Writing: | Y | Software Dev.: | Y | Law: | Y | Engineers, Other: | |
| Int'l Business: | Y | Commercial/Industrial: | Y | Graphic Arts/Photog.: | | Hardware Dev.: | | HR/Other: | Y | Health/Lab: | Y |
| MBA Graduates: | Y | Sales Trainees: | Y | Music: | | Systems Integration: | | Training: | Y | Scientists/Research: | Y |
| | | Advertising Pros.: | | Broadcasting: | | Consulting/Other: | | Health Care: | Y | Petroleum/Chemicals: | Y |
| | | | | Other: | | | | Consulting: | | Math/Other: | Y |

## TYPES OF BUSINESS:

Cancer Detection Products
Dental Products

## BRANDS/DIVISIONS/AFFILIATES:

ViziLite Plus
OraTest
Professional Dental Technologies, Inc.
Zila Pharmaceuticals, Inc.
Zila, Ltd.
Zila Technical, Inc.
Zila Biotechnology, Inc.
TBlue360

## CONTACTS: *Note: Officers with more than one job title may be intentionally listed here more than once.*

David R. Bethune, Interim CEO
Gary Klinefelter, General Counsel/VP
Diane Klein, Treas./VP-Finance
David Barshis, Sr. VP/Gen. Mgr.-Zila Pharmaceuticals, Inc.
David R. Bethune, Chmn.

| **Phone:** 602-266-6700 | **Fax:** |
|---|---|
| **Toll-Free:** | |
| **Address:** 5227 N. 7th St., Phoenix, AZ 85014 US | |

## GROWTH PLANS/SPECIAL FEATURES:

Zila, Inc. is a specialty pharmaceutical company dedicated to the prevention, detection and treatment of oral diseases, with a primary focus on oral cancer. Zila was formerly a provider of preventative healthcare technologies and products, which made the transition, with the acquisition of Professional Dental Technologies, Inc., into a cancer detection company. Zila is a holding company that conducts its operations through several wholly-owned subsidiaries, including Zila Pharmaceuticals, Inc., Professional Dental Technologies, Inc. (Pro-Dentec), Zila Biotechnology, Inc., Zila Technical, Inc. and Zila Limited (in the U.K.). The company's flagship product is ViziLite Plus with TBlue630, a chemiluminescent disposable light used for the illumination and marking of oral mucosal abnormalities. The firm also designs, manufactures and markets a suite of periodontal products sold directly to dental professionals, which includes the Rota-dent Professional Powered Brush, the Pro-Select Platinum ultrasonic scaler and a variety of oral pharmaceutical products approved for both in-office and home use. The company also maintains a research and development segment to investigate pre-cancer/cancer detection using Zila's patented ZTC and OraTest oral cancer detection technologies. Most recently, Zila has gained approval to launch ViziLite Plus in Canada, the U.K. and Greece. In May 2007, Zila sold its Peridex brand of prescription periodontal rinse products for approximately $9.5 million.

The company offers its employees health insurance; flexible spending accounts; retirement and savings benefits; and stock options.

## FINANCIALS: **Sales and profits are in thousands of dollars—add 000 to get the full amount. 2008 Note: Financial information for 2008 was not available for all companies at press time.**

| | | |
|---|---|---|
| 2008 Sales: $45,061 | 2008 Profits: $-16,378 | **U.S. Stock Ticker: ZILA** |
| 2007 Sales: $28,801 | 2007 Profits: $-13,164 | **Int'l Ticker:** Int'l Exchange: |
| 2006 Sales: $2,822 | 2006 Profits: $-29,346 | Employees: 367 |
| 2005 Sales: $1,199 | 2005 Profits: $1,099 | Fiscal Year Ends: 7/31 |
| 2004 Sales: $36,682 | 2004 Profits: $-4,375 | Parent Company: |

## SALARIES/BENEFITS:

| | | | | |
|---|---|---|---|---|
| Pension Plan: Y | ESOP Stock Plan: | Profit Sharing: | Top Exec. Salary: $347,524 | Bonus: $ |
| Savings Plan: Y | Stock Purch. Plan: Y | | Second Exec. Salary: $334,600 | Bonus: $ |

## OTHER THOUGHTS:

**Apparent Women Officers or Directors**: 2
**Hot Spot for Advancement for Women/Minorities**: Y

## LOCATIONS: ("Y" = Yes)

| West: | Southwest: | Midwest: | Southeast: | Northeast: | International: |
|---|---|---|---|---|---|
| | Y | | Y | | Y |

# ZOLL MEDICAL CORP

www.zoll.com

**Industry Group Code:** 339113 **Ranks within this company's industry group:** Sales: 10 Profits: 11

| Management: | | Sales/Marketing: | | Liberal Arts: | | Information Systems: | | Professionals: | | Technical/Scientific: | |
|---|---|---|---|---|---|---|---|---|---|---|---|
| Mgmt. Trainees: | | Mktg. Professionals: | Y | Gen. Writing/Editing: | | Info. Management: | Y | Finance/Accounting: | Y | Engineers, Elec.: | Y |
| Experienced Mgmt.: | Y | Retail Sales: | | Technical Writing: | Y | Software Dev.: | Y | Law: | Y | Engineers, Other: | Y |
| Int'l Business: | Y | Commercial/Industrial: | Y | Graphic Arts/Photog.: | | Hardware Dev.: | Y | HR/Other: | Y | Health/Lab: | Y |
| MBA Graduates: | Y | Sales Trainees: | Y | Music: | | Systems Integration: | | Training: | Y | Scientists/Research: | Y |
| | | Advertising Pros.: | | Broadcasting: | | Consulting/Other: | | Health Care: | Y | Petroleum/Chemicals: | |
| | | | | Other: | | | | Consulting: | | Math/Other: | Y |

## TYPES OF BUSINESS:

Cardiac Resuscitation Devices
Disposable Electrodes
Data Management Systems

## BRANDS/DIVISIONS/AFFILIATES:

Rectilinear Biphasic
Real CPR Help
LifeVest
AED Pro
AED Plus
AutoPulse Automated Chest Compression System
RescueNet
ZOLL Infuser

## CONTACTS: *Note: Officers with more than one job title may be intentionally listed here more than once.*

Richard A. Packer, CEO
Jonathan Rennert, Pres.
A. Ernest Whiton, CFO
Ward M. Hamilton, VP-Mktg.
E. Jane Wilson, VP-R&D
A. Ernest Whiton, VP-Admin.
Stephen Korn, General Counsel/VP/Corp. Sec.
Edward T. Dunn, VP-Oper.
John P. Bergeron, Treas./VP
Steven K. Flora, Sr. VP-North American Sales
Richard A. Packer, Chmn.
Alex N. Moghadam, VP-Int'l Oper.

| | |
|---|---|
| **Phone:** 978-421-9655 | **Fax:** 978-421-0025 |
| **Toll-Free:** 800-348-9011 | |
| **Address:** 269 Mill Rd., Chelmsford, MA 01824 US | |

## GROWTH PLANS/SPECIAL FEATURES:

Zoll Medical Corp. develops technologies and software to help clinicians, emergency medical services (EMS) personnel and lay rescuers advance and improve the practice of resuscitation. Zoll's line of resuscitation products include three core technologies that are implemented throughout the product line: Rectilinear Biphasic waveform, which is utilized in its line of professional defibrillators and automated external defibrillators (AEDs); external pacing technology, which is used in its professional defibrillators; and Real CPR Help technology, which is used in its professional defibrillators and AEDs. The company has developed a uniquely shaped biphasic waveform that achieves higher efficacy at lower current levels than monophasic waveforms, reducing the heart's exposure to high peak current. In addition, Zoll's biphasic waveform keeps the waveform shape and duration constant over a wide range of patients whose differing physiologies affect the conduction of current. The company's products include professional defibrillators, such as the M Series, E Series, R Series and the LifeVest wearable defibrillator, which is prescribed by cardiologists; AEDs that assist with manual CPR efforts, including the AED Pro and the AED Plus; disposable electrodes used with its defibrillators; the AutoPulse Automated Chest Compression System, used to automate the process of delivering chest compressions; documentation and information management, including RescueNet for EMS and fire personnel and CodeNet for hospitals; device and technology designed for endovascular hypothermia; and fluid replacement utilizing the ZOLL Infuser, also known as the Power Infuser, in trauma. The company and its subsidiaries currently hold over 120 U.S. and 70 foreign patents, which relate to pacing, defibrillation, CPR and other resuscitation therapies.

## FINANCIALS: **Sales and profits are in thousands of dollars—add 000 to get the full amount. 2008 Note: Financial information for 2008 was not available for all companies at press time.**

| | | |
|---|---|---|
| 2008 Sales: $398,018 | 2008 Profits: $23,441 | **U.S. Stock Ticker: ZOLL** |
| 2007 Sales: $309,451 | 2007 Profits: $16,662 | **Int'l Ticker:** Int'l Exchange: |
| 2006 Sales: $255,633 | 2006 Profits: $11,140 | Employees: 1,431 |
| 2005 Sales: $211,340 | 2005 Profits: $1,963 | Fiscal Year Ends: 9/30 |
| 2004 Sales: $211,785 | 2004 Profits: $8,956 | Parent Company: |

## SALARIES/BENEFITS:

| | | | | |
|---|---|---|---|---|
| Pension Plan: | ESOP Stock Plan: | Profit Sharing: | Top Exec. Salary: $375,000 | Bonus: $425,000 |
| Savings Plan: | Stock Purch. Plan: | | Second Exec. Salary: $250,000 | Bonus: $177,000 |

## OTHER THOUGHTS:

**Apparent Women Officers or Directors**: 1
**Hot Spot for Advancement for Women/Minorities**:

## LOCATIONS: ("Y" = Yes)

| West: | Southwest: | Midwest: | Southeast: | Northeast: | International: |
|---|---|---|---|---|---|
| Y | | | | Y | Y |

# ZYMOGENETICS INC

www.zymogenetics.com

**Industry Group Code:** 325412 **Ranks within this company's industry group:** Sales: 31 Profits: 34

| Management: | | Sales/Marketing: | | Liberal Arts: | | Information Systems: | | Professionals: | | Technical/Scientific: | |
|---|---|---|---|---|---|---|---|---|---|---|---|
| Mgmt. Trainees: | | Mktg. Professionals: | Y | Gen. Writing/Editing: | | Info. Management: | Y | Finance/Accounting: | Y | Engineers, Elec.: | |
| Experienced Mgmt.: | Y | Retail Sales: | | Technical Writing: | Y | Software Dev.: | Y | Law: | Y | Engineers, Other: | |
| Int'l Business: | | Commercial/Industrial: | Y | Graphic Arts/Photog.: | | Hardware Dev.: | | HR/Other: | Y | Health/Lab: | Y |
| MBA Graduates: | Y | Sales Trainees: | Y | Music: | | Systems Integration: | | Training: | Y | Scientists/Research: | Y |
| | | Advertising Pros.: | | Broadcasting: | | Consulting/Other: | | Health Care: | Y | Petroleum/Chemicals: | Y |
| | | | | Other: | | | | Consulting: | | Math/Other: | Y |

## TYPES OF BUSINESS:

Therapeutic Proteins
Hemostasis, Inflammatory & Autoimmune Diseases Drugs
Cancer & Viral Infections Drugs

## BRANDS/DIVISIONS/AFFILIATES:

rhThrombin
Interleukin-21
PEG-IFN
Atacicept
Merck Serono
Novo Nordisk
Bayer Schering Pharma AG
RECOTHROM

## CONTACTS: *Note: Officers with more than one job title may be intentionally listed here more than once.*

Bruce L. A. Carter, CEO
Douglas E. Williams, Pres.
James A. Johnson, CFO/Exec. VP
Michael J. Dwyer, Sr. VP-Sales & Mktg.
Darren R. Hamby, Sr. VP-Human Resources
Douglas E. Williams, Chief Scientific Officer
Vaughn B. Himes, Sr. VP-Tech. Oper.
Suzanne M. Shema, General Counsel/Sr. VP
Heather Franklin, Sr. VP-Bus. Dev.
James A. Johnson, Treas.
Nicole Onetto, Sr. VP/Chief Medical Officer
Suzanne M. Shema, Sr. VP-Law & Compliance
Bruce L. A. Carter, Chmn.

**Phone:** 206-442-6600 **Fax:** 206-442-6608
**Toll-Free:** 800-775-6686
**Address:** 1201 Eastlake Ave. E., Seattle, WA 98102 US

## GROWTH PLANS/SPECIAL FEATURES:

ZymoGenetics, Inc. discovers, develops, manufactures and commercializes therapeutic proteins for the treatment of human diseases. The company's current therapeutic focus is in the areas of hemostasis; inflammatory and autoimmune diseases; cancer; and viral infections. The firm's first internally developed product candidate, RECOTHROM Thrombin (also referred to as rThrombin or recombinant thrombin), was approved by the FDA in January 2008 as a topical hemostat to control moderate bleeding during surgical procedures and is now being marketed in the U.S. Outside of the U.S., the company has partnered with Bayer Schering Pharma AG to develop and commercialize RECOTHROM. Other products include atacicept (formerly known as TACI-Ig), a soluble receptor with potential applications for the treatment of cancer and autoimmune diseases; Interleukin-21 (IL-21), a cytokine with potential applications for the treatment of cancer; and PEG-IFN (formerly known as IL-29), a cytokine with potential applications for the treatment of viral infections. ZymoGenetics collaborates with Merck Serono for atacicept and with Novo Nordisk for Interleukin-21. ZymoGenetics contributed to the discovery or development of six recombinant protein products currently on the market: Novolin, NovoSeven, Regranex, GEM 21S, GlucanGen and Cleactor. The company holds more than 300 unexpired issued or allowed U.S. patents and over 370 U.S. patent application pending. In addition, the firm has more than 660 issued or allowed foreign patents. In March 2007, the company received FDA approval for rhThrombin administered by spray device as an aid to controlling bleeding during surgery. In June 2008, the company received a $100 million funding commitment from Deerfield Management, a healthcare investment organization.

The company offers its employees medical, dental and vision insurance; a 401(k) plan; stock options; an employee assistance program; short- and long-term disability; life and AD&D insurance; a volunteer program; employee discounts; and tuition reimbursement.

## FINANCIALS: **Sales and profits are in thousands of dollars—add 000 to get the full amount. 2008 Note: Financial information for 2008 was not available for all companies at press time.**

2008 Sales: $73,989
2007 Sales: $38,477
2006 Sales: $25,380
2005 Sales: $42,909
2004 Sales: $35,694

2008 Profits: $-116,241
2007 Profits: $-148,144
2006 Profits: $-130,002
2005 Profits: $-78,027
2004 Profits: $-88,756

**U.S. Stock Ticker: ZGEN**
**Int'l Ticker:** Int'l Exchange:
Employees: 570
Fiscal Year Ends: 12/31
Parent Company:

## SALARIES/BENEFITS:

Pension Plan: ESOP Stock Plan: Profit Sharing: Top Exec. Salary: $612,551 Bonus: $276,373
Savings Plan: Y Stock Purch. Plan: Y Second Exec. Salary: $437,917 Bonus: $209,250

## OTHER THOUGHTS:

**Apparent Women Officers or Directors**: 3
**Hot Spot for Advancement for Women/Minorities**: Y

## LOCATIONS: ("Y" = Yes)

| West: | Southwest: | Midwest: | Southeast: | Northeast: | International: |
|---|---|---|---|---|---|
| Y | | | | | |

# ADDITIONAL INDEXES

## CONTENTS:

# INDEX OF FIRMS NOTED AS HOT SPOTS FOR ADVANCEMENT FOR WOMEN & MINORITIES

ACME PACKET INC
AFFYMETRIX INC
AKAMAI TECHNOLOGIES INC
ALASKA COMMUNICATIONS SYSTEMS GROUP
ALIEN TECHNOLOGY CORPORATION
ALKERMES INC
AMAG PHARMACEUTICALS INC
AMERICAN MEDICAL SYSTEMS HOLDINGS INC
AMERICAN TOWER CORP
AMICAS INC
AMSURG CORP
AMYLIN PHARMACEUTICALS INC
ANSYS INC
APP PHARMACEUTICALS INC
ART TECHNOLOGY GROUP INC
ASPEN TECHNOLOGY INC
ATHENAHEALTH INC
ATHEROS COMMUNICATIONS INC
AUDIBLE INC
AVANEX CORPORATION
AVISTA CORPORATION
BIO REFERENCE LABORATORIES INC
BIOMARIN PHARMACEUTICAL INC
BIOSITE INC
BLACK HILLS CORP
BLACKBOARD INC
BLUE CARE NETWORK OF MICHIGAN
BLUE NILE INC
BRIGHTSTAR CORPORATION
CALIPER LIFE SCIENCES
CALPINE CORPORATION
CAMBREX CORP
CANDELA CORP
CARACO PHARMACEUTICAL LABORATORIES
C-COR INC
CELERA CORPORATION
CELL GENESYS INC
CELL THERAPEUTICS INC
CENTERPLATE
CENTRAL VERMONT PUBLIC SERVICE CORPORATION
CEPHEID
CHINDEX INTERNATIONAL INC
CHOLESTECH CORP
CIENA CORP
CLEARWIRE CORP
CME GROUP
COHERENT INC
COINSTAR INC
COMDATA CORP
COMMERCE GROUP INC (THE)
CONCUR TECHNOLOGIES INC
CONTINUCARE CORP
CRUM & FORSTER HOLDINGS INC
CRYOLIFE INC
CSG SYSTEMS INTERNATIONAL INC
CUBIST PHARMACEUTICALS INC
CURVES INTERNATIONAL INC
CV THERAPEUTICS INC
CYBERSOURCE CORP
DANNON COMPANY INC (THE)
DOUBLECLICK INC
DPL INC
DREAMWORKS ANIMATION SKG INC
DRUGSTORE.COM INC
DYAX CORP
DYNEGY INC
ECHELON CORP
ELECTRONICS FOR IMAGING INC
ELOYALTY CORPORATION
EMBARCADERO TECHNOLOGIES INC
EMULEX CORP
ENCORIUM GROUP INC
ENDO PHARMACEUTICALS HOLDINGS INC
ENGLOBAL CORP
EOG RESOURCES INC
EPIX PHARMACEUTICALS INC
EQUINIX INC
EQUITABLE RESOURCES INC
EURONET WORLDWIDE INC
EVERCORE PARTNERS INC
EXELIXIS INC
FORRESTER RESEARCH INC
FUEL TECH INC
GENERAL COMMUNICATION INC (GCI)
GEN-PROBE INC
GERON CORPORATION
GLU MOBILE INC
GREEN MOUNTAIN COFFEE ROASTERS INC
GREEN MOUNTAIN POWER CORPORATION
GTC BIOTHERAPEUTICS INC
HAEMONETICS CORPORATION
HARRIS STRATEX NETWORKS INC
HARVARD PILGRIM HEALTH CARE INC
HCC INSURANCE HOLDINGS INC
HEALTH GRADES INC
HEALTH INSURANCE PLAN OF GREATER NEW YORK
HEARUSA INC
HEIDRICK & STRUGGLES INTERNATIONAL INC
HESKA CORP
HICKORY TECH CORPORATION
HI-TECH PHARMACAL CO INC
HOLLY CORP
HUMAN GENOME SCIENCES INC
HURON CONSULTING GROUP INC
IDACORP INC
IMATION CORP
INSPIRE PHARMACEUTICALS INC
INTEGRA LIFESCIENCES HOLDINGS CORP
INTEGRAMED AMERICA INC
INTERCONTINENTALEXCHANGE INC (ICE)
INTERMEC INC
INVESTMENT TECHNOLOGY GROUP INC (ITG)
IVILLAGE INC
J2 GLOBAL COMMUNICATIONS INC
JAZZ PHARMACEUTICALS
KAMPGROUNDS OF AMERICA INC
KNIGHT CAPITAL GROUP INC
KNOT INC (THE)
KV PHARMACEUTICAL CO
LACLEDE GROUP INC (THE)
LCC INTERNATIONAL INC
LEAP WIRELESS INTERNATIONAL INC
LOGISTICARE INC
LUCASFILM LTD
M&F WORLDWIDE CORP
MANHATTAN ASSOCIATES INC
MARTHA STEWART LIVING OMNIMEDIA INC
MATRIA HEALTHCARE INC
MCMORAN EXPLORATION CO
MEDAREX INC
MEDICAL ACTION INDUSTRIES INC
MENTOR CORP
MERIDIAN BIOSCIENCE INC
METROPCS COMMUNICATIONS INC
METROPOLITAN HEALTH NETWORKS
MICHELINAS INC
MILLENNIUM PHARMACEUTICALS INC
MOELIS & COMPANY
MOLINA HEALTHCARE INC
MTS SYSTEMS
NASDAQ OMX
NATIONAL FUEL GAS CO
NATIONAL WINE & SPIRITS INC
NEKTAR THERAPEUTICS
NETFLIX INC
NETGEAR INC
NETSCOUT SYSTEMS INC
NEWFIELD EXPLORATION CO
NIC INC
NORTHWESTERN CORPORATION
NOVAMED INC
NOVEN PHARMACEUTICALS
NYMEX HOLDINGS (NEW YORK MERCANTILE EXCHANGE)
ONLINE RESOURCES CORP
ORMAT TECHNOLOGIES
PALM INC
PC CONNECTION INC
PERFICIENT INC
PETROLEUM DEVELOPMENT CORPORATION
PHILADELPHIA CONSOLIDATED HOLDING CORP
PHOENIX COMPANIES (THE)
PIEDMONT NATURAL GAS COMPANY INC
PIONEER NATURAL RESOURCES COMPANY

POLYCOM INC
PREMIERE GLOBAL SERVICES INC
PROTECTIVE LIFE CORP
QUICKSILVER RESOURCES INC
QUIDEL CORP
RED HAT INC
REVOLUTION HEALTH GROUP LLC
RIGHTNOW TECHNOLOGIES INC
ROBERT W BAIRD & CO INC
SACRAMENTO MUNICIPAL UTILITY DISTRICT
SCOULAR COMPANY (THE)
SEACHANGE INTERNATIONAL INC
SEQUENOM INC
SERENA SOFTWARE INC
SHARED TECHNOLOGIES
SHENANDOAH TELECOMMUNICATIONS CO
SHUTTERFLY INC
SONIC INNOVATIONS INC
ST MARY LAND & EXPLORATION COMPANY
STATE AUTO FINANCIAL CORP
STIEFEL LABORATORIES INC
SWIFT ENERGY CO
SYNOVIS LIFE TECHNOLOGIES INC
TECHNE CORP
THERAGENICS CORP
THORATEC CORPORATION
THQ INC
TIVO INC
TOMOTHERAPY INC
TOOTSIE ROLL INDUSTRIES INC
TRANSATLANTIC HOLDINGS INC
TRIZETTO GROUP INC (THE)
UIL HOLDINGS CORPORATION
UNDER ARMOUR INC
UNISOURCE ENERGY CORPORATION
VERIFONE HOLDINGS INC
VERTEX PHARMACEUTICALS INC
VIGNETTE CORP
VISION SERVICE PLAN
VSE CORP
WEBEX COMMUNICATIONS INC
WEBSENSE INC
WESTAR ENERGY
WGL HOLDINGS INC
WHITEWAVE FOODS COMPANY
WRIGHT MEDICAL GROUP INC
XTO ENERGY INC
YOUNG'S MARKET COMPANY LLC
ZILA INC
ZYMOGENETICS INC

# INDEX OF SUBSIDIARIES, BRAND NAMES AND AFFILIATIONS

**Brand or subsidiary, followed by the name of the related corporation**

@Plan; **NETRATINGS INC**
100 Calorie Cereal Snack'ers; **MALT-O-MEAL COMPANY**
1-800-PetMeds; **PETMED EXPRESS INC**
19 Entertainment Limited; **CKX INC**
2110 Davie Corporation; **AMERICAN VANGUARD CORP**
24/7 Power Pack; **MEDIS TECHNOLOGIES**
24/7 Search; **24/7 REAL MEDIA INC**
24/7 Web Results; **24/7 REAL MEDIA INC**
3F Therapeutics; **ATS MEDICAL INC**
3F Therapeutics, Inc.,; **ATS MEDICAL INC**
3-NITRO; **ALPHARMA INC**
3SBio, Inc.; **AMAG PHARMACEUTICALS INC**
4Closure Surgical Fascia Closure System; **SYNOVIS LIFE TECHNOLOGIES INC**
4MyHeart.com; **CELERA CORPORATION**
518 Property Management & Leasing, LLC; **STATE AUTO FINANCIAL CORP**
6R-BH4; **BIOMARIN PHARMACEUTICAL INC**
A.D.A.M., Inc.; **HEALTHSTREAM INC**
a/d/s/; **DEI HOLDINGS INC**
A-2000 BIS Monitoring System; **ASPECT MEDICAL SYSTEMS INC**
A4 Health Systems, Inc.; **ALLSCRIPTS HEALTHCARE SOLUTIONS INC**
AAMCO ATF D/M; **AAMCO TRANSMISSIONS INC**
AAMCO ATF Type F; **AAMCO TRANSMISSIONS INC**
AAMCO ATF+3; **AAMCO TRANSMISSIONS INC**
AAMCO Automatic Transmission Fluid; **AAMCO TRANSMISSIONS INC**
AAMCO Synthetic Blend ATF; **AAMCO TRANSMISSIONS INC**
Abbott Laboratories; **CELERA CORPORATION**
ABE; **INTEGRAL SYSTEMS INC**
ABR Development; **STIEFEL LABORATORIES INC**
ABS2000; **IMMUCOR INC**
Absolute Software; **LOJACK CORP**
Abthrax; **HUMAN GENOME SCIENCES INC**
Accelerated Path; **SKILLSOFT PLC**
Accellerase; **GENENCOR INTERNATIONAL INC**
ACCESS Banking; **FUNDTECH LTD**
Access, Transport and Supplies; **ARRIS GROUP INC**
Accountis Ltd.; **FUNDTECH LTD**
accuDEXA; **SCHICK TECHNOLOGIES INC**
Accurel; **POLYPORE INTERNATIONAL INC**
ACI Worldwide; **ACI WORLDWIDE INC**
A-CLASS; **WRIGHT MEDICAL GROUP INC**
Acme Packet Session Aware Networking; **ACME PACKET INC**
Acoustic Clarity Technology; **POLYCOM INC**
Acrymed Incorporated; **I-FLOW CORPORATION**
ACS Internet, Inc.; **ALASKA COMMUNICATIONS SYSTEMS GROUP**
ACS Long Distance, Inc.; **ALASKA COMMUNICATIONS SYSTEMS GROUP**
ACS of Alaska, Inc.; **ALASKA COMMUNICATIONS SYSTEMS GROUP**
ACS of Anchorage, Inc.; **ALASKA COMMUNICATIONS SYSTEMS GROUP**
ACS of Fairbanks, Inc.; **ALASKA COMMUNICATIONS SYSTEMS GROUP**
ACS of the Northland, Inc.; **ALASKA COMMUNICATIONS SYSTEMS GROUP**
ACS System; **HAEMONETICS CORPORATION**
ACS Wireless, Inc.; **ALASKA COMMUNICATIONS SYSTEMS GROUP**
ACTester; **ATRION CORPORATION**
Activia; **DANNON COMPANY INC (THE)**
AcuDriver Automated Osteotome System; **EXACTECH INC**
AcuMatch; **EXACTECH INC**
Acumedia; **NEOGEN CORPORATION**
Acxiom Corporation; **ACXIOM DIGITAL**
Adams Reserve; **GREAT LAKES CHEESE COMPANY INC**
Adaptive Optics Associates, Inc.; **METROLOGIC INSTRUMENTS INC**
ADCO South Medical Supplies, Inc.; **NYER MEDICAL GROUP INC**
ADCO Surgical Supply, Inc.; **NYER MEDICAL GROUP INC**
Additrol; **AMCOL INTERNATIONAL CORP**
Adentri; **CV THERAPEUTICS INC**
Adesso-Madden, Inc.; **STEVEN MADDEN LTD**
ADHERE; **SCIOS INC**
AdRelevance; **NETRATINGS INC**
AdrenaLine; **ANAREN INC**
AdsOfTheWorld.com; **JUPITERMEDIA CORP**
ADVANCE; **WRIGHT MEDICAL GROUP INC**
Advanced Inhalation Research (AIR); **ALKERMES INC**
Advanced Medical Partners, Inc. (AMPI); **HEALTHTRONICS INC**
Advanced Sleep Technologies of Georgia, Inc.; **VITAL SIGNS INC**
Advantage Auto Stores; **HAHN AUTOMOTIVE WAREHOUSE INC**
Advantage IQ; **AVISTA CORPORATION**
AdvantageCare; **METROPOLITAN HEALTH NETWORKS**
AdvisorWare; **SS&C TECHNOLOGIES INC**
AED Plus; **ZOLL MEDICAL CORP**
AED Pro; **ZOLL MEDICAL CORP**
AeroAstro; **RADYNE CORPORATION**
AeroPro 5.0; **MTS SYSTEMS**
Aerospace Repairable Management System; **AVIALL INC**
AFAmeriLife (AFAL); **AMERICAN FIDELITY ASSURANCE COMPANY**
Agri-Scan; **NEOGEN CORPORATION**
Agtech Products Inc.; **GENENCOR INTERNATIONAL INC**
Ahold USA Inc; **PEAPOD LLC**
AIR Inhaled Insulin; **ALKERMES INC**
AirWave Wireless, Inc.; **ARUBA NETWORKS INC**
AKQA. Mobile; **AKQA INC**
Alabama.gov; **NIC INC**
Alarm.com; **MICROSTRATEGY INC**
Alaska Communications Systems Holdings, Inc.; **ALASKA COMMUNICATIONS SYSTEMS GROUP**
Alaska DigiTel; **GENERAL COMMUNICATION INC (GCI)**
Alaska Native Broadband 1, LLC; **LEAP WIRELESS INTERNATIONAL INC**
ALBAC; **ALPHARMA INC**
Albuferon; **HUMAN GENOME SCIENCES INC**
Alcatel USA Inc; **DSP GROUP INC**
Alcortin; **COLLAGENEX PHARMACEUTICALS INC**
Aldurazyme; **BIOMARIN PHARMACEUTICAL INC**
Alexion Europe SAS; **ALEXION PHARMACEUTICALS INC**
AlexTriVantage; **CANDELA CORP**
ALKERAN; **CELGENE CORP**
All Battery Centers; **INTERSTATE BATTERY SYSTEM OF AMERICA**
Alleghany Insurance Holdings Re LLC; **ALLEGHANY CORP**
Alleghany Properties Holdings, LLC; **ALLEGHANY CORP**

## INDEX OF SUBSIDIARIES, BRAND NAMES AND AFFILIATIONS, CONT.

Allegra; **SCIELE PHARMA INC**
ALLERCEPT; **HESKA CORP**
Allergan Inc; **INAMED CORP**
Alliance Oncology LLC; **ALLIANCE IMAGING INC**
Alliance Radiosurgery LLC; **ALLIANCE IMAGING INC**
AlloCraft DBM; **LIFECELL CORPORATION**
AlloDerm; **LIFECELL CORPORATION**
Allopurinol; **CARACO PHARMACEUTICAL LABORATORIES**
Allscripts Direct; **ALLSCRIPTS HEALTHCARE SOLUTIONS INC**
AllSeasonGear; **UNDER ARMOUR INC**
AllSport; **DAKTRONICS INC**
Allstate Insurance Corporation (The); **STERLING AUTOBODY CENTERS**
ALLTEL Corp; **AMERICAN TOWER CORP**
ALPS; **ASSOCIATED WHOLESALE GROCERS INC**
Altair; **VISION SERVICE PLAN**
AlterNet Securities, Inc.; **INVESTMENT TECHNOLOGY GROUP INC (ITG)**
Altoprev; **SCIELE PHARMA INC**
Amazon.com Inc; **AUDIBLE INC**
Amazon.com Inc; **ART TECHNOLOGY GROUP INC**
AMC Entertainment Inc; **NATIONAL CINEMEDIA INC**
Ameresco Canada; **AMERESCO**
Ameresco Enertech; **AMERESCO**
Ameresco E-Three; **AMERESCO**
AmerescoSolutions; **AMERESCO**
American Colloid; **AMCOL INTERNATIONAL CORP**
American Commerce Insurance Co.; **COMMERCE GROUP INC (THE)**
American Equity Investment Life Insurance Company; **FBL FINANCIAL GROUP**
American Fidelity Educational Services (AFES); **AMERICAN FIDELITY ASSURANCE COMPANY**
American Financial Group Inc; **GREAT AMERICAN FINANCIAL RESOURCES INC**
American Idol; **CKX INC**
American International Group (AIG); **TRANSATLANTIC HOLDINGS INC**
American Public Life Insurance Company (APL); **AMERICAN FIDELITY ASSURANCE COMPANY**
American Sugar Refining Inc; **NUTRASWEET COMPANY (THE)**
American Tower Corp; **AMERICAN TOWER CORP**
American Tower International, Inc.; **AMERICAN TOWER CORP**
Ameritron; **INTERSTATE BATTERY SYSTEM OF AMERICA**
AMICAS Insight; **AMICAS INC**
AMICAS Insight Solutions; **AMICAS INC**
AMICAS Vision Series; **AMICAS INC**
AMS 700 LGX; **AMERICAN MEDICAL SYSTEMS HOLDINGS INC**
AMVAC Chemical Corporation; **AMERICAN VANGUARD CORP**
AMVAC Chemical UK, Ltd.; **AMERICAN VANGUARD CORP**
AMVAC do Brasil Representacoes Ltda.; **AMERICAN VANGUARD CORP**
AMVAC Switzerland GmbH; **AMERICAN VANGUARD CORP**
Amvisc; **ANIKA THERAPEUTICS INC**
Anaren Ceramics, Inc.; **ANAREN INC**
Andes; **TOOTSIE ROLL INDUSTRIES INC**
Anestar Plus Anesthesia Delivery System; **DATASCOPE CORP**
Anexa; **ANALOGIC CORP**
Angel.com; **MICROSTRATEGY INC**
Angiomax; **MEDICINES CO (THE)**
Angiox; **MEDICINES CO (THE)**
Anji Microelectronics; **ATMI INC**
Anrad; **ANALOGIC CORP**
Ansoft Corporation; **ANSYS INC**
AnswerThink Inc; **HACKETT GROUP (THE)**
ANTARA; **OSCIENT PHARMACEUTICALS CORPORATION**
Antares; **SS&C TECHNOLOGIES INC**
Antibody-Drug Conjugates (ADCs); **SEATTLE GENETICS**
Antizol; **JAZZ PHARMACEUTICALS**
Anusol-HC; **SALIX PHARMACEUTICALS**
AnySite Financial; **PITNEY BOWES MAPINFO**
AnywhereUSB; **DIGI INTERNATIONAL INC**
AP; **ATMI INC**
Apple Market; **ASSOCIATED WHOLESALE GROCERS INC**
Applera Corporation; **CELERA CORPORATION**
Application Development; **SERENA SOFTWARE INC**
Application Lifecycle Management; **SERENA SOFTWARE INC**
Application Security Manager; **F5 NETWORKS INC**
Applied Biosystems Group; **CELERA CORPORATION**
AquaFlow; **STAAR SURGICAL CO**
ARASCO; **MARTEK BIOSCIENCES CORP**
Arboris, LCC; **ARIZONA CHEMICAL COMPANY**
ARCALYST; **REGENERON PHARMACEUTICALS INC**
Architectural Glass & Aluminum Co.; **HELIOVOLT CORP**
ARCNET; **STANDARD MICROSYSTEMS CORPORATION**
Arden-Mayfair, Inc.; **ARDEN GROUP INC**
Argonaut Private Equity; **SOLAR RESERVE**
Ariba Contract Management Solutions; **ARIBA INC**
Ariba Invoice & Payment Solutions; **ARIBA INC**
Ariba Procurement & Expense Solutions; **ARIBA INC**
Ariba Sourcing Solutions; **ARIBA INC**
Ariba Spend Management; **ARIBA INC**
Ariba Supplier Management Solutions; **ARIBA INC**
Ariba Visibility Solutions; **ARIBA INC**
Armour of America; **AROTECH CORPORATION**
Artema Medical AB; **DATASCOPE CORP**
ARTWorks Clinical Information System; **INTEGRAMED AMERICA INC**
ARTWorks Practice Management Information System; **INTEGRAMED AMERICA INC**
Aruba Access Points; **ARUBA NETWORKS INC**
Aruba Mobile Edge Architecture; **ARUBA NETWORKS INC**
Aruba Mobility Controllers; **ARUBA NETWORKS INC**
Aruba Mobility Management System; **ARUBA NETWORKS INC**
ArubaOS Secure Mobility Software; **ARUBA NETWORKS INC**
ARX; **F5 NETWORKS INC**
Asia Food Culture Management Pte, Ltd.; **TULLY'S COFFEE CORPORATION**
Aspartate Aminotransferase (AST) Test; **CHOLESTECH CORP**
Aspect Medical Systems International B.V.; **ASPECT MEDICAL SYSTEMS INC**
Aspen DMCplus; **ASPEN TECHNOLOGY INC**
Aspen Dynamics; **ASPEN TECHNOLOGY INC**
Aspen HYSYS; **ASPEN TECHNOLOGY INC**
Aspen InfoPlus.21; **ASPEN TECHNOLOGY INC**
Aspen PIMS; **ASPEN TECHNOLOGY INC**
Aspen Plus; **ASPEN TECHNOLOGY INC**
aspenONE; **ASPEN TECHNOLOGY INC**

## INDEX OF SUBSIDIARIES, BRAND NAMES AND AFFILIATIONS, CONT.

## INDEX OF SUBSIDIARIES, BRAND NAMES AND AFFILIATIONS, CONT.

## INDEX OF SUBSIDIARIES, BRAND NAMES AND AFFILIATIONS, CONT.

## INDEX OF SUBSIDIARIES, BRAND NAMES AND AFFILIATIONS, CONT.

## INDEX OF SUBSIDIARIES, BRAND NAMES AND AFFILIATIONS, CONT.

## INDEX OF SUBSIDIARIES, BRAND NAMES AND AFFILIATIONS, CONT.

## INDEX OF SUBSIDIARIES, BRAND NAMES AND AFFILIATIONS, CONT.

## INDEX OF SUBSIDIARIES, BRAND NAMES AND AFFILIATIONS, CONT.

## INDEX OF SUBSIDIARIES, BRAND NAMES AND AFFILIATIONS, CONT.

## INDEX OF SUBSIDIARIES, BRAND NAMES AND AFFILIATIONS, CONT.

## INDEX OF SUBSIDIARIES, BRAND NAMES AND AFFILIATIONS, CONT.

## INDEX OF SUBSIDIARIES, BRAND NAMES AND AFFILIATIONS, CONT.

## INDEX OF SUBSIDIARIES, BRAND NAMES AND AFFILIATIONS, CONT.

## INDEX OF SUBSIDIARIES, BRAND NAMES AND AFFILIATIONS, CONT.

## INDEX OF SUBSIDIARIES, BRAND NAMES AND AFFILIATIONS, CONT.

## INDEX OF SUBSIDIARIES, BRAND NAMES AND AFFILIATIONS, CONT.

## INDEX OF SUBSIDIARIES, BRAND NAMES AND AFFILIATIONS, CONT.

## INDEX OF SUBSIDIARIES, BRAND NAMES AND AFFILIATIONS, CONT.

## INDEX OF SUBSIDIARIES, BRAND NAMES AND AFFILIATIONS, CONT.

## INDEX OF SUBSIDIARIES, BRAND NAMES AND AFFILIATIONS, CONT.

## INDEX OF SUBSIDIARIES, BRAND NAMES AND AFFILIATIONS, CONT.

## INDEX OF SUBSIDIARIES, BRAND NAMES AND AFFILIATIONS, CONT.

## INDEX OF SUBSIDIARIES, BRAND NAMES AND AFFILIATIONS, CONT.

## INDEX OF SUBSIDIARIES, BRAND NAMES AND AFFILIATIONS, CONT.

# INDEX BY COMPANIES FOR SPECIFIC TYPES OF JOB SEEKERS

**Indexed by the following categories:**



## Information Systems

| Consulting/Other |
|---|
| ACI WORLDWIDE INC |
| AMERESCO |
| CORPORATE EXECUTIVE BOARD COMPANY (THE) |
| ELOYALTY CORPORATION |
| EPAM SYSTEMS |
| FORRESTER RESEARCH INC |
| GALLUP ORGANIZATION (THE) |
| HACKETT GROUP (THE) |
| HEIDRICK & STRUGGLES INTERNATIONAL INC |
| HURON CONSULTING GROUP INC |
| INTELLIGROUP INC |
| PERFICIENT INC |
| SENTO |
| SHARED TECHNOLOGIES |
| TRIZETTO GROUP INC (THE) |

| Hardware Development |
|---|
| ABAXIS INC |
| AFFYMETRIX INC |
| ALIEN TECHNOLOGY CORPORATION |
| ALIGN TECHNOLOGY INC |
| AMERICAN MEDICAL SYSTEMS HOLDINGS INC |
| AMERICAN SCIENCE & ENGINEERING INC |
| AMERICAN SUPERCONDUCTOR CORP |
| AMTECH SYSTEMS INC |
| ANALOGIC CORP |
| ANAREN INC |
| APPLIED SIGNAL TECHNOLOGY INC |
| AROTECH CORPORATION |
| ARRIS GROUP INC |
| ATHEROS COMMUNICATIONS INC |
| ATMI INC |
| ATRION CORPORATION |
| AVANEX CORPORATION |
| BIOSITE INC |
| CALIPER LIFE SCIENCES |
| CANDELA CORP |
| C-COR INC |
| CEPHEID |
| CHANNELL COMMERCIAL CORP |
| CHOLESTECH CORP |
| CIENA CORP |
| COGNEX CORP |
| COHERENT INC |
| COMTECH TELECOMMUNICATIONS CORP |
| DAKTRONICS INC |
| DATASCOPE CORP |
| DEI HOLDINGS INC |
| DIGI INTERNATIONAL INC |
| DSP GROUP INC |
| ECHELON CORP |
| ELECTRONICS FOR IMAGING INC |
| EMCORE CORP |
| EMS TECHNOLOGIES INC |
| EMULEX CORP |
| ENERGY CONVERSION DEVICES INC |
| EVERGREEN SOLAR INC |
| EXCEL TECHNOLOGY INC |
| E-Z-EM INC |
| FIRST SOLAR LLC |
| FUELCELL ENERGY INC |
| GENOMIC HEALTH INC |
| GEN-PROBE INC |
| GERBER SCIENTIFIC INC |
| GLOBECOMM SYSTEMS INC |
| HAEMONETICS CORPORATION |
| HARMONIC INC |
| HARRIS STRATEX NETWORKS INC |
| HELIOVOLT CORP |
| ILLUMINA INC |
| IMATION CORP |
| IMMUCOR INC |
| INFINERA CORP |
| INTERMEC INC |
| IRIDEX CORP |
| IRIS INTERNATIONAL INC |
| ISILON SYSTEMS INC |
| LIFECORE BIOMEDICAL INC |
| LOJACK CORP |
| LORAL SPACE & COMMUNICATIONS LTD |
| LUMINEX CORPORATION |
| MEDIS TECHNOLOGIES |
| MERIDIAN BIOSCIENCE INC |
| METROLOGIC INSTRUMENTS INC |
| MTS SYSTEMS |
| NANOMETRICS INC |
| NATUS MEDICAL |
| NEOGEN CORPORATION |
| NETGEAR INC |
| OPNEXT INC |
| OPTELECOM-NKF INC |
| PALM INC |
| PLUG POWER INC |
| POLYCOM INC |
| QLOGIC CORP |
| RADISYS CORP |
| RADYNE CORPORATION |
| SCANSOURCE INC |
| SCHICK TECHNOLOGIES INC |
| SEQUENOM INC |
| SOLAR RESERVE |
| SOLFOCUS INC |
| SONIC INNOVATIONS INC |
| SONUS NETWORKS INC |
| SPECTRALINK CORP |
| SPECTRANETICS CORP |
| SPIRE CORPORATION |
| STANDARD MICROSYSTEMS CORPORATION |
| SUPER MICRO COMPUTER INC |
| SYCAMORE NETWORKS INC |
| SYNAPTICS INC |
| TECHNE CORP |
| THIRD WAVE TECHNOLOGIES INC |
| THORATEC CORPORATION |
| TIVO INC |
| TOMOTHERAPY INC |
| VENTANA MEDICAL SYSTEMS INC |
| VERAZ NETWORKS INC |
| VIASAT INC |
| ZOLL MEDICAL CORP |

| Information Management |
|---|
| 24/7 REAL MEDIA INC |
| AAMCO TRANSMISSIONS INC |
| ABAXIS INC |
| ACI WORLDWIDE INC |

| |
|---|
| ACME PACKET INC |
| ACXIOM DIGITAL |
| AFFYMETRIX INC |
| AKAMAI TECHNOLOGIES INC |
| AKQA INC |
| ALASKA COMMUNICATIONS SYSTEMS GROUP |
| ALBANY MOLECULAR RESEARCH |
| ALEXION PHARMACEUTICALS INC |
| ALIEN TECHNOLOGY CORPORATION |
| ALIGN TECHNOLOGY INC |
| ALKERMES INC |
| ALLEGHANY CORP |
| ALLIANCE IMAGING INC |
| ALLSCRIPTS HEALTHCARE SOLUTIONS INC |
| ALPHARMA INC |
| ALTIRIS INC |
| ALZA CORP |
| AMAG PHARMACEUTICALS INC |
| AMCOL INTERNATIONAL CORP |
| AMERESCO |
| AMERICAN FIDELITY ASSURANCE COMPANY |
| AMERICAN ITALIAN PASTA COMPANY |
| AMERICAN MEDICAL SYSTEMS HOLDINGS INC |
| AMERICAN SCIENCE & ENGINEERING INC |
| AMERICAN SUPERCONDUCTOR CORP |
| AMERICAN TIRE DISTRIBUTORS |
| AMERICAN TOWER CORP |
| AMERICAN VANGUARD CORP |
| AMICAS INC |
| AMSURG CORP |
| AMTECH SYSTEMS INC |
| AMYLIN PHARMACEUTICALS INC |
| ANALOGIC CORP |
| ANAREN INC |
| ANIKA THERAPEUTICS INC |
| ANSYS INC |
| APP PHARMACEUTICALS INC |
| APPLIED SIGNAL TECHNOLOGY INC |
| ARDEN GROUP INC |
| ARIBA INC |
| ARIZONA CHEMICAL COMPANY |
| AROTECH CORPORATION |
| ARRIS GROUP INC |
| ART TECHNOLOGY GROUP INC |
| ARUBA NETWORKS INC |
| ASPECT MEDICAL SYSTEMS INC |
| ASPEN TECHNOLOGY INC |
| ASSOCIATED WHOLESALE GROCERS INC |
| ATHENAHEALTH INC |
| ATHEROS COMMUNICATIONS INC |
| ATLANTIC CITY ELECTRIC COMPANY |
| ATMI INC |
| ATRION CORPORATION |
| ATS MEDICAL INC |
| AUDIBLE INC |
| AVANEX CORPORATION |
| AVI BIOPHARMA INC |
| AVIALL INC |
| AVISTA CORPORATION |
| BENTLEY PHARMACEUTICALS INC |
| BERRY PETROLEUM CO |
| BIO REFERENCE LABORATORIES INC |
| BIOMARIN PHARMACEUTICAL INC |
| BIOSCRIP INC |
| BIOSITE INC |
| BLACK HILLS CORP |
| BLACKBOARD INC |
| BLUE CARE NETWORK OF MICHIGAN |
| BLUE COAT SYSTEMS INC |
| BLUE NILE INC |
| BRIGHTSTAR CORPORATION |
| CALIBER HOLDINGS CORP |
| CALIPER LIFE SCIENCES |
| CAL-MAINE FOODS INC |
| CALPINE CORPORATION |
| CAMBREX CORP |
| CANDELA CORP |
| CANTEL MEDICAL CORP |
| CARACO PHARMACEUTICAL LABORATORIES |
| CARDTRONICS INC |
| CATALYST HEALTH SOLUTIONS INC |
| C-COR INC |
| CELERA CORPORATION |
| CELGENE CORP |
| CELL GENESYS INC |
| CELL THERAPEUTICS INC |
| CENTERPLATE |
| CENTRAL VERMONT PUBLIC SERVICE CORPORATION |
| CEPHEID |
| CHANNELL COMMERCIAL CORP |
| CHATTEM INC |
| CHINDEX INTERNATIONAL INC |
| CHOICESTREAM INC |
| CHOLESTECH CORP |
| CHYRON CORP |
| CIENA CORP |
| CKX INC |
| CLEARWIRE CORP |
| CME GROUP |
| CNX GAS CORPORATION |
| COGNEX CORP |
| COHERENT INC |
| COINSTAR INC |
| COLLAGENEX PHARMACEUTICALS INC |
| COMDATA CORP |
| COMMERCE GROUP INC (THE) |
| COMTECH TELECOMMUNICATIONS CORP |
| CONCUR TECHNOLOGIES INC |
| CONTINUCARE CORP |
| CORPORATE EXECUTIVE BOARD COMPANY (THE) |
| COUPONS INC |
| CRITICAL CARE SYSTEMS |
| CROWN CASTLE INTERNATIONAL CORP |
| CRUM & FORSTER HOLDINGS INC |
| CRYOLIFE INC |
| CSG SYSTEMS INTERNATIONAL INC |
| CUBIST PHARMACEUTICALS INC |
| CURVES INTERNATIONAL INC |
| CV THERAPEUTICS INC |
| CYBERSOURCE CORP |
| DAKTRONICS INC |
| DANNON COMPANY INC (THE) |
| DARLING INTERNATIONAL INC |
| DATASCOPE CORP |
| DEI HOLDINGS INC |
| DELPHI FINANCIAL GROUP INC |
| DENBURY RESOURCES INC |
| DIALYSIS CORPORATION OF AMERICA |
| DIAMOND FOODS INC |
| DIGI INTERNATIONAL INC |
| DIGITAL RIVER INC |
| DJO INCORPORATED |
| DOUBLECLICK INC |
| DPL INC |
| DREAMWORKS ANIMATION SKG |

| |
|---|
| INC |
| DRUGSTORE.COM INC |
| DSP GROUP INC |
| DYAX CORP |
| DYNACQ HEALTHCARE INC |
| DYNEGY INC |
| ECHELON CORP |
| ECLIPSYS CORPORATION |
| ECOLLEGE.COM |
| EHEALTH INC |
| ELECTRONICS FOR IMAGING INC |
| ELOYALTY CORPORATION |
| EMBARCADERO TECHNOLOGIES INC |
| EMCORE CORP |
| EMS TECHNOLOGIES INC |
| EMULEX CORP |
| ENCORE ACQUISITION CO |
| ENCORIUM GROUP INC |
| ENDO PHARMACEUTICALS HOLDINGS INC |
| ENERGY CONVERSION DEVICES INC |
| ENERNOC INC |
| ENGLOBAL CORP |
| EOG RESOURCES INC |
| EPAM SYSTEMS |
| EPIX PHARMACEUTICALS INC |
| EQUINIX INC |
| EQUITABLE RESOURCES INC |
| EURONET WORLDWIDE INC |
| EVERCORE PARTNERS INC |
| EVERGREEN ENERGY INC |
| EVERGREEN SOLAR INC |
| EXACTECH INC |
| EXCEL TECHNOLOGY INC |
| EXCO RESOURCES INC |
| EXELIXIS INC |
| E-Z-EM INC |
| F5 NETWORKS INC |
| FARMER BROTHERS CO |
| FBL FINANCIAL GROUP |
| FEDEX SUPPLY CHAIN SERVICES INC |
| FIRST SOLAR LLC |
| FLIR SYSTEMS |
| FOREST OIL CORPORATION |
| FORRESTER RESEARCH INC |
| FRESH BRANDS INC |
| FRESHDIRECT LLC |
| FRONTIER OIL CORPORATION |
| FUEL TECH INC |
| FUELCELL ENERGY INC |
| FUNDTECH LTD |
| GALLUP ORGANIZATION (THE) |
| GENENCOR INTERNATIONAL INC |
| GENERAL COMMUNICATION INC (GCI) |
| GENESIS ENERGY LP |
| GENOMIC HEALTH INC |
| GEN-PROBE INC |
| GERBER SCIENTIFIC INC |
| GERON CORPORATION |
| GLOBAL PARTNERS LP |
| GLOBECOMM SYSTEMS INC |
| GLU MOBILE INC |
| GOAMERICA INC |
| GOLFSMITH INTERNATIONAL HOLDINGS INC |
| GREAT AMERICAN FINANCIAL RESOURCES INC |
| GREAT LAKES CHEESE COMPANY INC |
| GREEN MOUNTAIN COFFEE ROASTERS INC |
| GREEN MOUNTAIN POWER CORPORATION |
| GTC BIOTHERAPEUTICS INC |
| HACKETT GROUP (THE) |
| HAEMONETICS CORPORATION |
| HAHN AUTOMOTIVE WAREHOUSE INC |
| HANOVER FOODS CORPORATION |
| HANSEN NATURAL |
| HARMONIC INC |
| HARRIS STRATEX NETWORKS INC |
| HARVARD PILGRIM HEALTH CARE INC |
| HCC INSURANCE HOLDINGS INC |
| HEALTH GRADES INC |
| HEALTH INSURANCE PLAN OF GREATER NEW YORK |
| HEALTHSTREAM INC |
| HEALTHTRONICS INC |
| HEARTLAND PAYMENT SYSTEMS INC |
| HEARUSA INC |
| HEIDRICK & STRUGGLES INTERNATIONAL INC |
| HELIOVOLT CORP |
| HESKA CORP |
| HICKORY TECH CORPORATION |
| HI-TECH PHARMACAL CO INC |
| HOLLY CORP |
| HORACE MANN EDUCATORS CORPORATION |
| HOULIHAN LOKEY |
| HUMAN GENOME SCIENCES INC |
| HURON CONSULTING GROUP INC |
| IBASIS INC |
| ICO INC |
| IDACORP INC |
| I-FLOW CORPORATION |
| ILLUMINA INC |
| IMATION CORP |
| IMG WORLDWIDE INC |
| IMMUCOR INC |
| INAMED CORP |
| INDEPENDENCE HOLDING CO |
| INFINERA CORP |
| INSPIRE PHARMACEUTICALS INC |
| INTEGRA LIFESCIENCES HOLDINGS CORP |
| INTEGRAL SYSTEMS INC |
| INTEGRAMED AMERICA INC |
| INTELLIGROUP INC |
| INTERACTIVE BROKERS GROUP INC |
| INTERACTIVE INTELLIGENCE |
| INTERCONTINENTALEXCHANGE INC (ICE) |
| INTERMEC INC |
| INTERNAP NETWORK SERVICES CORP |
| INTERNATIONAL CREATIVE MANAGEMENT (ICM) |
| INTERNATIONAL DAIRY QUEEN |
| INTERNET SECURITY SYSTEMS INC |
| INTERSTATE BATTERY SYSTEM OF AMERICA |
| INTERWOVEN INC |
| INVESTMENT TECHNOLOGY GROUP INC (ITG) |
| IRIDEX CORP |
| IRIS INTERNATIONAL INC |
| ISILON SYSTEMS INC |
| ISONICS CORPORATION |
| IVILLAGE INC |
| J2 GLOBAL COMMUNICATIONS INC |
| JACKSON NATIONAL LIFE INSURANCE COMPANY |
| JAZZ PHARMACEUTICALS |
| JUPITERMEDIA CORP |
| KAMPGROUNDS OF AMERICA INC |
| KENDALL-JACKSON WINE ESTATES LTD |

| |
|---|
| KIMLEY-HORN AND ASSOCIATES INC |
| KNIGHT CAPITAL GROUP INC |
| KNOT INC (THE) |
| KRONOS WORLDWIDE INC |
| KV PHARMACEUTICAL CO |
| LACLEDE GROUP INC (THE) |
| LCA-VISION INC |
| LCC INTERNATIONAL INC |
| LEAP WIRELESS INTERNATIONAL INC |
| LESLIE'S POOLMART INC |
| LIFECELL CORPORATION |
| LIFECORE BIOMEDICAL INC |
| LIVEPERSON INC |
| LOGISTICARE INC |
| LOJACK CORP |
| LORAL SPACE & COMMUNICATIONS LTD |
| LUCASFILM LTD |
| LUCOR INC |
| LUMINEX CORPORATION |
| M&F WORLDWIDE CORP |
| MAGELLAN MIDSTREAM PARTNERS LP |
| MALT-O-MEAL COMPANY |
| MANHATTAN ASSOCIATES INC |
| MARCHEX INC |
| MARTEK BIOSCIENCES CORP |
| MARTHA STEWART LIVING OMNIMEDIA INC |
| MARVEL ENTERTAINMENT INC |
| MATRIA HEALTHCARE INC |
| MAXYGEN INC |
| MCMORAN EXPLORATION CO |
| MEDAREX INC |
| MEDICAL ACTION INDUSTRIES INC |
| MEDICINES CO (THE) |
| MEDICIS PHARMACEUTICAL CORP |
| MEDIS TECHNOLOGIES |
| MEDTOX SCIENTIFIC INC |
| MENTOR CORP |
| MERIDIAN BIOSCIENCE INC |
| MERIT MEDICAL SYSTEMS INC |
| METROLOGIC INSTRUMENTS INC |
| METROPCS COMMUNICATIONS INC |
| METROPOLITAN HEALTH NETWORKS |
| MICHELINAS INC |
| MICROSTRATEGY INC |
| MICROTEK MEDICAL HOLDINGS INC |

| |
|---|
| MIDAS INC |
| MILLENNIUM PHARMACEUTICALS INC |
| MOELIS & COMPANY |
| MOLINA HEALTHCARE INC |
| MOTORCAR PARTS OF AMERICA INC |
| MTS SYSTEMS |
| MYRIAD GENETICS INC |
| NANOMETRICS INC |
| NASDAQ OMX |
| NATIONAL BEVERAGE CORP |
| NATIONAL CINEMEDIA INC |
| NATIONAL DENTEX CORP |
| NATIONAL FUEL GAS CO |
| NATIONAL WINE & SPIRITS INC |
| NATUS MEDICAL |
| NAVISITE INC |
| NEKTAR THERAPEUTICS |
| NEOGEN CORPORATION |
| NETFLIX INC |
| NETGEAR INC |
| NETRATINGS INC |
| NETSCOUT SYSTEMS INC |
| NETSUITE INC |
| NEWFIELD EXPLORATION CO |
| NIC INC |
| NOBLE ENERGY INC |
| NORTHWESTERN CORPORATION |
| NOVAMED INC |
| NOVEN PHARMACEUTICALS |
| NTELOS HOLDING CORP |
| NUGGET MARKET |
| NUSTAR ENERGY LP |
| NUTRASWEET COMPANY (THE) |
| NYER MEDICAL GROUP INC |
| NYMEX HOLDINGS (NEW YORK MERCANTILE EXCHANGE) |
| ODYSSEY RE HOLDINGS CORP |
| OMNITURE INC |
| ONEOK PARTNERS LP |
| ONLINE RESOURCES CORP |
| OPENTV CORP |
| OPNEXT INC |
| OPTELECOM-NKF INC |
| ORMAT TECHNOLOGIES |
| OSCIENT PHARMACEUTICALS CORPORATION |
| PALM INC |
| PAR PHARMACEUTICAL COMPANIES INC |

| |
|---|
| PC CONNECTION INC |
| PC MALL INC |
| PEAPOD LLC |
| PERFICIENT INC |
| PETMED EXPRESS INC |
| PETROLEUM DEVELOPMENT CORPORATION |
| PHILADELPHIA CONSOLIDATED HOLDING CORP |
| PHOENIX COMPANIES (THE) |
| PIEDMONT NATURAL GAS COMPANY INC |
| PIONEER NATURAL RESOURCES COMPANY |
| PITNEY BOWES MAPINFO |
| PLAINS EXPLORATION AND PRODUCTION COMPANY |
| PLUG POWER INC |
| PMA CAPITAL CORPORATION |
| POLYCOM INC |
| POLYMEDICA CORPORATION |
| POLYPORE INTERNATIONAL INC |
| PREMIERE GLOBAL SERVICES INC |
| PRIMEENERGY CORPORATION |
| PROASSURANCE CORP |
| PROGRESS SOFTWARE CORP |
| PROTECTIVE LIFE CORP |
| QLOGIC CORP |
| QUALITY SYSTEMS INC |
| QUICKSILVER RESOURCES INC |
| QUIDEL CORP |
| RACKSPACE HOSTING INC |
| RADISYS CORP |
| RADNET INC |
| RADYNE CORPORATION |
| RANGE RESOURCES CORP |
| REALNETWORKS INC |
| RECYCLED ENERGY DEVELOPMENT |
| RED HAT INC |
| REDDY ICE HOLDINGS INC |
| REGENERON PHARMACEUTICALS INC |
| REINSURANCE GROUP OF AMERICA INC |
| REVOLUTION HEALTH GROUP LLC |
| RIGHTNOW TECHNOLOGIES INC |
| ROBERT W BAIRD & CO INC |
| RSA SECURITY INC |
| S1 CORPORATION |
| SACRAMENTO MUNICIPAL UTILITY DISTRICT |

| |
|---|
| SALIX PHARMACEUTICALS |
| SAVVIS INC |
| SCANSOURCE INC |
| SCHICK TECHNOLOGIES INC |
| SCHIFF NUTRITION INTERNATIONAL INC |
| SCICLONE PHARMACEUTICALS |
| SCIELE PHARMA INC |
| SCIOS INC |
| SCOULAR COMPANY (THE) |
| SEACHANGE INTERNATIONAL INC |
| SEATTLE GENETICS |
| SECURE COMPUTING CORP |
| SENTO |
| SEPRACOR INC |
| SEQUENOM INC |
| SERENA SOFTWARE INC |
| SHARED TECHNOLOGIES |
| SHENANDOAH TELECOMMUNICATIONS CO |
| SHUTTERFLY INC |
| SKILLSOFT PLC |
| SOLAR RESERVE |
| SOLFOCUS INC |
| SONIC INNOVATIONS INC |
| SONUS NETWORKS INC |
| SOUTHERN UNION COMPANY |
| SOUTHWESTERN ENERGY CO |
| SPAN AMERICA MEDICAL SYSTEMS INC |
| SPECTRALINK CORP |
| SPECTRANETICS CORP |
| SPIRE CORPORATION |
| SPORTSMAN'S GUIDE INC (THE) |
| SPROUTS FARMERS MARKET |
| SPSS INC |
| SRI/SURGICAL EXPRESS INC |
| SS&C TECHNOLOGIES INC |
| ST MARY LAND & EXPLORATION COMPANY |
| STAAR SURGICAL CO |
| STANDARD MICROSYSTEMS CORPORATION |
| STATE AUTO FINANCIAL CORP |
| STERLING AUTOBODY CENTERS |
| STEVEN MADDEN LTD |
| STIEFEL LABORATORIES INC |
| SUPER MICRO COMPUTER INC |
| SWIFT ENERGY CO |
| SYCAMORE NETWORKS INC |
| SYMMETRY MEDICAL INC |

| |
|---|
| SYMYX TECHNOLOGIES |
| SYNAPTICS INC |
| SYNOVIS LIFE TECHNOLOGIES INC |
| TAMPA ELECTRIC COMPANY |
| TARGA RESOURCES PARTNERS LP |
| TDINDUSTRIES |
| TECHNE CORP |
| TELIRIS |
| TEPPCO PARTNERS LP |
| TERREMARK WORLDWIDE INC |
| THERAGENICS CORP |
| THIRD WAVE TECHNOLOGIES INC |
| THOMAS WEISEL PARTNERS GROUP INC |
| THORATEC CORPORATION |
| THQ INC |
| TIBCO SOFTWARE INC |
| TIVO INC |
| TOMOTHERAPY INC |
| TOOTSIE ROLL INDUSTRIES INC |
| TOPPS COMPANY INC (THE) |
| TRANSATLANTIC HOLDINGS INC |
| TRANSCEND SERVICES INC |
| TRAPEZE NETWORKS INC |
| TRIZETTO GROUP INC (THE) |
| TULLY'S COFFEE CORPORATION |
| UIL HOLDINGS CORPORATION |
| ULTIMATE SOFTWARE GROUP INC |
| UNDER ARMOUR INC |
| UNISOURCE ENERGY CORPORATION |
| UNITED ONLINE INC |
| UNITED THERAPEUTICS CORP |
| UNIVERSAL AMERICAN CORPORATION |
| UNIVERSAL HOSPITAL SERVICES INC |
| US PHYSICAL THERAPY INC |
| VALLEY NATIONAL GASES LLC |
| VALUECLICK INC |
| VASCO DATA SECURITY INTERNATIONAL INC |
| VENTANA MEDICAL SYSTEMS INC |
| VERAZ NETWORKS INC |
| VERIFONE HOLDINGS INC |
| VERTEX PHARMACEUTICALS INC |
| VIASAT INC |
| VIBRANT MEDIA INC |
| VIGNETTE CORP |
| VIROPHARMA INC |
| VISION SERVICE PLAN |

| |
|---|
| VITAL SIGNS INC |
| VOLCOM INC |
| VSE CORP |
| WEBEX COMMUNICATIONS INC |
| WEBMD HEALTH CORP |
| WEBSENSE INC |
| WESTAR ENERGY |
| WGL HOLDINGS INC |
| WHITEWAVE FOODS COMPANY |
| WIND RIVER SYSTEMS INC |
| WRIGHT MEDICAL GROUP INC |
| XOMA LTD |
| XTO ENERGY INC |
| YOUNG'S MARKET COMPANY LLC |
| ZAPPOS.COM INC |
| ZIEBART INTERNATIONAL CORP |
| ZILA INC |
| ZOLL MEDICAL CORP |
| ZYMOGENETICS INC |

| Software Development |
|---|
| 24/7 REAL MEDIA INC |
| ABAXIS INC |
| ACI WORLDWIDE INC |
| ACME PACKET INC |
| ACXIOM DIGITAL |
| AFFYMETRIX INC |
| AKAMAI TECHNOLOGIES INC |
| AKQA INC |
| ALASKA COMMUNICATIONS SYSTEMS GROUP |
| ALBANY MOLECULAR RESEARCH |
| ALEXION PHARMACEUTICALS INC |
| ALIEN TECHNOLOGY CORPORATION |
| ALIGN TECHNOLOGY INC |
| ALLSCRIPTS HEALTHCARE SOLUTIONS INC |
| ALPHARMA INC |
| ALTIRIS INC |
| AMERICAN MEDICAL SYSTEMS HOLDINGS INC |
| AMERICAN SUPERCONDUCTOR CORP |
| AMICAS INC |
| AMTECH SYSTEMS INC |
| AMYLIN PHARMACEUTICALS INC |
| ANALOGIC CORP |
| ANAREN INC |
| ANIKA THERAPEUTICS INC |
| ANSYS INC |

| |
|---|
| APP PHARMACEUTICALS INC |
| APPLIED SIGNAL TECHNOLOGY INC |
| ARIBA INC |
| AROTECH CORPORATION |
| ARRIS GROUP INC |
| ART TECHNOLOGY GROUP INC |
| ARUBA NETWORKS INC |
| ASPEN TECHNOLOGY INC |
| ATHEROS COMMUNICATIONS INC |
| ATRION CORPORATION |
| AUDIBLE INC |
| AVANEX CORPORATION |
| AVI BIOPHARMA INC |
| BIO REFERENCE LABORATORIES INC |
| BIOMARIN PHARMACEUTICAL INC |
| BIOSCRIP INC |
| BIOSITE INC |
| BLACKBOARD INC |
| BLUE COAT SYSTEMS INC |
| BLUE NILE INC |
| CALIPER LIFE SCIENCES |
| CAMBREX CORP |
| CANDELA CORP |
| CARACO PHARMACEUTICAL LABORATORIES |
| CARDTRONICS INC |
| C-COR INC |
| CELERA CORPORATION |
| CELGENE CORP |
| CELL GENESYS INC |
| CELL THERAPEUTICS INC |
| CEPHEID |
| CHANNELL COMMERCIAL CORP |
| CHOLESTECH CORP |
| CHYRON CORP |
| CIENA CORP |
| CME GROUP |
| COGNEX CORP |
| COHERENT INC |
| COLLAGENEX PHARMACEUTICALS INC |
| COMTECH TELECOMMUNICATIONS CORP |
| CONCUR TECHNOLOGIES INC |
| CSG SYSTEMS INTERNATIONAL INC |
| CUBIST PHARMACEUTICALS INC |
| CV THERAPEUTICS INC |
| CYBERSOURCE CORP |
| DAKTRONICS INC |
| DATASCOPE CORP |

| |
|---|
| DEI HOLDINGS INC |
| DIGI INTERNATIONAL INC |
| DIGITAL RIVER INC |
| DOUBLECLICK INC |
| DREAMWORKS ANIMATION SKG INC |
| DRUGSTORE.COM INC |
| DSP GROUP INC |
| DYAX CORP |
| ECHELON CORP |
| ECLIPSYS CORPORATION |
| ECOLLEGE.COM |
| EHEALTH INC |
| ELECTRONICS FOR IMAGING INC |
| ELOYALTY CORPORATION |
| EMBARCADERO TECHNOLOGIES INC |
| EMCORE CORP |
| EMS TECHNOLOGIES INC |
| EMULEX CORP |
| ENCORIUM GROUP INC |
| ENDO PHARMACEUTICALS HOLDINGS INC |
| ENERGY CONVERSION DEVICES INC |
| EPAM SYSTEMS |
| EPIX PHARMACEUTICALS INC |
| EQUINIX INC |
| EURONET WORLDWIDE INC |
| EVERGREEN SOLAR INC |
| EXCEL TECHNOLOGY INC |
| EXELIXIS INC |
| E-Z-EM INC |
| F5 NETWORKS INC |
| FIRST SOLAR LLC |
| FLIR SYSTEMS |
| FORRESTER RESEARCH INC |
| FRESHDIRECT LLC |
| FUEL TECH INC |
| FUELCELL ENERGY INC |
| FUNDTECH LTD |
| GALLUP ORGANIZATION (THE) |
| GENENCOR INTERNATIONAL INC |
| GENERAL COMMUNICATION INC (GCI) |
| GENOMIC HEALTH INC |
| GEN-PROBE INC |
| GERBER SCIENTIFIC INC |
| GERON CORPORATION |
| GLOBECOMM SYSTEMS INC |
| GLU MOBILE INC |

| |
|---|
| GOAMERICA INC |
| GOLFSMITH INTERNATIONAL HOLDINGS INC |
| GTC BIOTHERAPEUTICS INC |
| HACKETT GROUP (THE) |
| HAEMONETICS CORPORATION |
| HARMONIC INC |
| HARRIS STRATEX NETWORKS INC |
| HEALTH GRADES INC |
| HEALTHSTREAM INC |
| HELIOVOLT CORP |
| HICKORY TECH CORPORATION |
| HI-TECH PHARMACAL CO INC |
| HUMAN GENOME SCIENCES INC |
| IBASIS INC |
| I-FLOW CORPORATION |
| ILLUMINA INC |
| IMATION CORP |
| IMMUCOR INC |
| INFINERA CORP |
| INSPIRE PHARMACEUTICALS INC |
| INTEGRA LIFESCIENCES HOLDINGS CORP |
| INTEGRAL SYSTEMS INC |
| INTEGRAMED AMERICA INC |
| INTELLIGROUP INC |
| INTERACTIVE BROKERS GROUP INC |
| INTERACTIVE INTELLIGENCE |
| INTERCONTINENTALEXCHANGE INC (ICE) |
| INTERMEC INC |
| INTERNAP NETWORK SERVICES CORP |
| INTERNET SECURITY SYSTEMS INC |
| INTERWOVEN INC |
| INVESTMENT TECHNOLOGY GROUP INC (ITG) |
| IRIDEX CORP |
| IRIS INTERNATIONAL INC |
| ISILON SYSTEMS INC |
| IVILLAGE INC |
| J2 GLOBAL COMMUNICATIONS INC |
| JAZZ PHARMACEUTICALS |
| JUPITERMEDIA CORP |
| KNIGHT CAPITAL GROUP INC |
| KNOT INC (THE) |
| LCC INTERNATIONAL INC |
| LEAP WIRELESS INTERNATIONAL INC |
| LIFECELL CORPORATION |
| LIFECORE BIOMEDICAL INC |

| |
|---|
| LIVEPERSON INC |
| LOGISTICARE INC |
| LOJACK CORP |
| LORAL SPACE & COMMUNICATIONS LTD |
| LUCASFILM LTD |
| LUMINEX CORPORATION |
| MANHATTAN ASSOCIATES INC |
| MARCHEX INC |
| MAXYGEN INC |
| MEDAREX INC |
| MEDICINES CO (THE) |
| MEDICIS PHARMACEUTICAL CORP |
| MEDIS TECHNOLOGIES |
| MEDTOX SCIENTIFIC INC |
| MERIDIAN BIOSCIENCE INC |
| METROLOGIC INSTRUMENTS INC |
| METROPCS COMMUNICATIONS INC |
| MICROSTRATEGY INC |
| MILLENNIUM PHARMACEUTICALS INC |
| MYRIAD GENETICS INC |
| NASDAQ OMX |
| NATUS MEDICAL |
| NAVISITE INC |
| NEOGEN CORPORATION |
| NETFLIX INC |
| NETGEAR INC |
| NETRATINGS INC |
| NETSCOUT SYSTEMS INC |
| NETSUITE INC |
| NIC INC |
| NTELOS HOLDING CORP |
| NYMEX HOLDINGS (NEW YORK MERCANTILE EXCHANGE) |
| OMNITURE INC |
| ONLINE RESOURCES CORP |
| OPENTV CORP |
| OPNEXT INC |
| OPTELECOM-NKF INC |
| OSCIENT PHARMACEUTICALS CORPORATION |
| PALM INC |
| PAR PHARMACEUTICAL COMPANIES INC |
| PEAPOD LLC |
| PERFICIENT INC |
| PETMED EXPRESS INC |
| PITNEY BOWES MAPINFO |
| PLUG POWER INC |
| POLYCOM INC |
| POLYMEDICA CORPORATION |
| PREMIERE GLOBAL SERVICES INC |
| PROGRESS SOFTWARE CORP |
| QLOGIC CORP |
| QUALITY SYSTEMS INC |
| QUIDEL CORP |
| RACKSPACE HOSTING INC |
| RADISYS CORP |
| RADYNE CORPORATION |
| REALNETWORKS INC |
| RED HAT INC |
| REGENERON PHARMACEUTICALS INC |
| REVOLUTION HEALTH GROUP LLC |
| RIGHTNOW TECHNOLOGIES INC |
| RSA SECURITY INC |
| S1 CORPORATION |
| SALIX PHARMACEUTICALS |
| SAVVIS INC |
| SCANSOURCE INC |
| SCHICK TECHNOLOGIES INC |
| SCICLONE PHARMACEUTICALS |
| SCIELE PHARMA INC |
| SCIOS INC |
| SEACHANGE INTERNATIONAL INC |
| SEATTLE GENETICS |
| SECURE COMPUTING CORP |
| SENTO |
| SEPRACOR INC |
| SEQUENOM INC |
| SERENA SOFTWARE INC |
| SHARED TECHNOLOGIES |
| SHENANDOAH TELECOMMUNICATIONS CO |
| SHUTTERFLY INC |
| SKILLSOFT PLC |
| SOLAR RESERVE |
| SOLFOCUS INC |
| SONIC INNOVATIONS INC |
| SONUS NETWORKS INC |
| SPECTRALINK CORP |
| SPECTRANETICS CORP |
| SPIRE CORPORATION |
| SPSS INC |
| SS&C TECHNOLOGIES INC |
| STAAR SURGICAL CO |
| STANDARD MICROSYSTEMS CORPORATION |
| STIEFEL LABORATORIES INC |
| SUPER MICRO COMPUTER INC |
| SYCAMORE NETWORKS INC |
| SYMMETRY MEDICAL INC |
| SYMYX TECHNOLOGIES |
| SYNAPTICS INC |
| SYNOVIS LIFE TECHNOLOGIES INC |
| TECHNE CORP |
| THIRD WAVE TECHNOLOGIES INC |
| THORATEC CORPORATION |
| THQ INC |
| TIBCO SOFTWARE INC |
| TIVO INC |
| TOMOTHERAPY INC |
| TRANSCEND SERVICES INC |
| TRAPEZE NETWORKS INC |
| TRIZETTO GROUP INC (THE) |
| ULTIMATE SOFTWARE GROUP INC |
| UNITED ONLINE INC |
| UNITED THERAPEUTICS CORP |
| VALUECLICK INC |
| VASCO DATA SECURITY INTERNATIONAL INC |
| VENTANA MEDICAL SYSTEMS INC |
| VERAZ NETWORKS INC |
| VERIFONE HOLDINGS INC |
| VERTEX PHARMACEUTICALS INC |
| VIASAT INC |
| VIGNETTE CORP |
| VIROPHARMA INC |
| VITAL SIGNS INC |
| WEBEX COMMUNICATIONS INC |
| WEBMD HEALTH CORP |
| WEBSENSE INC |
| WIND RIVER SYSTEMS INC |
| WRIGHT MEDICAL GROUP INC |
| XOMA LTD |
| ZAPPOS.COM INC |
| ZILA INC |
| ZOLL MEDICAL CORP |
| ZYMOGENETICS INC |

| Systems Integration |
|---|
| 24/7 REAL MEDIA INC |
| ACME PACKET INC |
| ACXIOM DIGITAL |
| AKAMAI TECHNOLOGIES INC |
| AKQA INC |
| ALASKA COMMUNICATIONS SYSTEMS GROUP |
| ALIEN TECHNOLOGY CORPORATION |
| ALLIANCE IMAGING INC |
| ALTIRIS INC |

| |
|---|
| AMERICAN SCIENCE & ENGINEERING INC |
| AMERICAN SUPERCONDUCTOR CORP |
| ANALOGIC CORP |
| ANAREN INC |
| APPLIED SIGNAL TECHNOLOGY INC |
| ARRIS GROUP INC |
| ARUBA NETWORKS INC |
| ASPECT MEDICAL SYSTEMS INC |
| ATHENAHEALTH INC |
| ATHEROS COMMUNICATIONS INC |
| ATRION CORPORATION |
| ATS MEDICAL INC |
| AVANEX CORPORATION |
| BIO REFERENCE LABORATORIES INC |
| BLACKBOARD INC |
| BLUE COAT SYSTEMS INC |
| BLUE NILE INC |
| CALIPER LIFE SCIENCES |
| CANDELA CORP |
| CARDTRONICS INC |
| C-COR INC |
| CHANNELL COMMERCIAL CORP |
| CHOICESTREAM INC |
| CHOLESTECH CORP |
| CHYRON CORP |
| CIENA CORP |
| COGNEX CORP |
| COHERENT INC |
| COINSTAR INC |
| COMDATA CORP |
| COMTECH TELECOMMUNICATIONS CORP |
| COUPONS INC |
| CRYOLIFE INC |
| DAKTRONICS INC |
| DATASCOPE CORP |
| DEI HOLDINGS INC |
| DIGI INTERNATIONAL INC |
| DIGITAL RIVER INC |
| DOUBLECLICK INC |
| DREAMWORKS ANIMATION SKG INC |
| DRUGSTORE.COM INC |
| DSP GROUP INC |
| ECHELON CORP |
| ECOLLEGE.COM |
| ELECTRONICS FOR IMAGING INC |
| EMS TECHNOLOGIES INC |
| EMULEX CORP |
| EQUINIX INC |
| EURONET WORLDWIDE INC |
| F5 NETWORKS INC |
| FRESHDIRECT LLC |
| GALLUP ORGANIZATION (THE) |
| GENERAL COMMUNICATION INC (GCI) |
| GERBER SCIENTIFIC INC |
| GLOBECOMM SYSTEMS INC |
| HARMONIC INC |
| HARRIS STRATEX NETWORKS INC |
| HEALTH GRADES INC |
| HEALTHSTREAM INC |
| HEARTLAND PAYMENT SYSTEMS INC |
| HICKORY TECH CORPORATION |
| IBASIS INC |
| ILLUMINA INC |
| IMATION CORP |
| INFINERA CORP |
| INTERACTIVE INTELLIGENCE |
| INTERMEC INC |
| INTERNAP NETWORK SERVICES CORP |
| INTERNET SECURITY SYSTEMS INC |
| INVESTMENT TECHNOLOGY GROUP INC (ITG) |
| ISILON SYSTEMS INC |
| IVILLAGE INC |
| J2 GLOBAL COMMUNICATIONS INC |
| JUPITERMEDIA CORP |
| KNOT INC (THE) |
| LEAP WIRELESS INTERNATIONAL INC |
| LIVEPERSON INC |
| LOJACK CORP |
| LORAL SPACE & COMMUNICATIONS LTD |
| LUCASFILM LTD |
| MEDTOX SCIENTIFIC INC |
| METROLOGIC INSTRUMENTS INC |
| METROPCS COMMUNICATIONS INC |
| MTS SYSTEMS |
| NANOMETRICS INC |
| NAVISITE INC |
| NETGEAR INC |
| NETSCOUT SYSTEMS INC |
| NIC INC |
| NTELOS HOLDING CORP |
| OPENTV CORP |
| OPNEXT INC |
| OPTELECOM-NKF INC |
| PALM INC |
| PEAPOD LLC |
| POLYCOM INC |
| PREMIERE GLOBAL SERVICES INC |
| QLOGIC CORP |
| RACKSPACE HOSTING INC |
| RADISYS CORP |
| RADNET INC |
| RADYNE CORPORATION |
| REALNETWORKS INC |
| REVOLUTION HEALTH GROUP LLC |
| RSA SECURITY INC |
| SAVVIS INC |
| SCANSOURCE INC |
| SEACHANGE INTERNATIONAL INC |
| SHENANDOAH TELECOMMUNICATIONS CO |
| SHUTTERFLY INC |
| SONUS NETWORKS INC |
| SPECTRALINK CORP |
| STANDARD MICROSYSTEMS CORPORATION |
| SUPER MICRO COMPUTER INC |
| SYCAMORE NETWORKS INC |
| SYNAPTICS INC |
| TELIRIS |
| TIVO INC |
| TRANSCEND SERVICES INC |
| TRAPEZE NETWORKS INC |
| TRIZETTO GROUP INC (THE) |
| VALUECLICK INC |
| VASCO DATA SECURITY INTERNATIONAL INC |
| VERAZ NETWORKS INC |
| VERIFONE HOLDINGS INC |
| VIASAT INC |
| VIBRANT MEDIA INC |
| WEBEX COMMUNICATIONS INC |
| WEBMD HEALTH CORP |
| ZAPPOS.COM INC |

## Liberal Arts

| General Writing |
|---|
| 24/7 REAL MEDIA INC |
| ACXIOM DIGITAL |
| AKQA INC |
| ALIEN TECHNOLOGY CORPORATION |

| |
|---|
| ALLEGHANY CORP |
| AMERICAN FIDELITY ASSURANCE COMPANY |
| ANAREN INC |
| APPLIED SIGNAL TECHNOLOGY INC |
| ARRIS GROUP INC |
| AUDIBLE INC |
| AVANEX CORPORATION |
| BLACKBOARD INC |
| BLUE CARE NETWORK OF MICHIGAN |
| BLUE NILE INC |
| C-COR INC |
| CHANNELL COMMERCIAL CORP |
| CHOICESTREAM INC |
| CHYRON CORP |
| CIENA CORP |
| COMMERCE GROUP INC (THE) |
| COMTECH TELECOMMUNICATIONS CORP |
| CORPORATE EXECUTIVE BOARD COMPANY (THE) |
| COUPONS INC |
| CRUM & FORSTER HOLDINGS INC |
| DAKTRONICS INC |
| DELPHI FINANCIAL GROUP INC |
| DOUBLECLICK INC |
| DREAMWORKS ANIMATION SKG INC |
| DRUGSTORE.COM INC |
| ECOLLEGE.COM |
| EHEALTH INC |
| EMS TECHNOLOGIES INC |
| EVERGREEN ENERGY INC |
| FBL FINANCIAL GROUP |
| FORRESTER RESEARCH INC |
| FRESHDIRECT LLC |
| GALLUP ORGANIZATION (THE) |
| GLOBECOMM SYSTEMS INC |
| GOLFSMITH INTERNATIONAL HOLDINGS INC |
| GREAT AMERICAN FINANCIAL RESOURCES INC |
| HARMONIC INC |
| HARRIS STRATEX NETWORKS INC |
| HARVARD PILGRIM HEALTH CARE INC |
| HCC INSURANCE HOLDINGS INC |
| HEALTH GRADES INC |
| HEALTH INSURANCE PLAN OF GREATER NEW YORK |
| HEALTHSTREAM INC |
| HEIDRICK & STRUGGLES INTERNATIONAL INC |
| HORACE MANN EDUCATORS CORPORATION |
| HURON CONSULTING GROUP INC |
| INDEPENDENCE HOLDING CO |
| IVILLAGE INC |
| JACKSON NATIONAL LIFE INSURANCE COMPANY |
| JUPITERMEDIA CORP |
| KNOT INC (THE) |
| LORAL SPACE & COMMUNICATIONS LTD |
| LUCASFILM LTD |
| MARCHEX INC |
| METROPOLITAN HEALTH NETWORKS |
| MOLINA HEALTHCARE INC |
| NETRATINGS INC |
| ODYSSEY RE HOLDINGS CORP |
| OPNEXT INC |
| PC CONNECTION INC |
| PC MALL INC |
| PEAPOD LLC |
| PETMED EXPRESS INC |
| PHILADELPHIA CONSOLIDATED HOLDING CORP |
| PHOENIX COMPANIES (THE) |
| PMA CAPITAL CORPORATION |
| PROASSURANCE CORP |
| PROTECTIVE LIFE CORP |
| RADYNE CORPORATION |
| REINSURANCE GROUP OF AMERICA INC |
| REVOLUTION HEALTH GROUP LLC |
| SHUTTERFLY INC |
| SKILLSOFT PLC |
| SONUS NETWORKS INC |
| SPECTRALINK CORP |
| SPORTSMAN'S GUIDE INC (THE) |
| STATE AUTO FINANCIAL CORP |
| SYCAMORE NETWORKS INC |
| THQ INC |
| TRANSATLANTIC HOLDINGS INC |
| UNDER ARMOUR INC |
| UNIVERSAL AMERICAN CORPORATION |
| VALUECLICK INC |
| VERAZ NETWORKS INC |
| VIASAT INC |
| VISION SERVICE PLAN |
| WEBMD HEALTH CORP |
| ZAPPOS.COM INC |

| Graphic Arts |
|---|
| 24/7 REAL MEDIA INC |
| ACXIOM DIGITAL |
| AKQA INC |
| AMERICAN SUPERCONDUCTOR CORP |
| AMERICAN TIRE DISTRIBUTORS |
| ARDEN GROUP INC |
| ASSOCIATED WHOLESALE GROCERS INC |
| AUDIBLE INC |
| BLACKBOARD INC |
| BLUE NILE INC |
| CALIPER LIFE SCIENCES |
| CHOICESTREAM INC |
| COUPONS INC |
| CURVES INTERNATIONAL INC |
| DAKTRONICS INC |
| DOUBLECLICK INC |
| DREAMWORKS ANIMATION SKG INC |
| DRUGSTORE.COM INC |
| ECOLLEGE.COM |
| ELECTRONICS FOR IMAGING INC |
| EMCORE CORP |
| ENERGY CONVERSION DEVICES INC |
| EVERGREEN SOLAR INC |
| FARMER BROTHERS CO |
| FIRST SOLAR LLC |
| FRESH BRANDS INC |
| FRESHDIRECT LLC |
| GLU MOBILE INC |
| GOLFSMITH INTERNATIONAL HOLDINGS INC |
| GREEN MOUNTAIN COFFEE ROASTERS INC |
| HAHN AUTOMOTIVE WAREHOUSE INC |
| HANSEN NATURAL |
| HEALTH GRADES INC |
| HEALTHSTREAM INC |
| HELIOVOLT CORP |
| INTERMEC INC |
| INTERNATIONAL DAIRY QUEEN |
| IVILLAGE INC |
| JUPITERMEDIA CORP |
| KAMPGROUNDS OF AMERICA INC |
| KENDALL-JACKSON WINE ESTATES LTD |

| |
|---|
| KNOT INC (THE) |
| LESLIE'S POOLMART INC |
| LUCASFILM LTD |
| M&F WORLDWIDE CORP |
| MARCHEX INC |
| METROLOGIC INSTRUMENTS INC |
| NATIONAL BEVERAGE CORP |
| NUGGET MARKET |
| NUTRASWEET COMPANY (THE) |
| PC CONNECTION INC |
| PC MALL INC |
| PEAPOD LLC |
| PETMED EXPRESS INC |
| POLYCOM INC |
| REDDY ICE HOLDINGS INC |
| REVOLUTION HEALTH GROUP LLC |
| SHUTTERFLY INC |
| SOLAR RESERVE |
| SOLFOCUS INC |
| SPIRE CORPORATION |
| SPORTSMAN'S GUIDE INC (THE) |
| SPROUTS FARMERS MARKET |
| STEVEN MADDEN LTD |
| SYNAPTICS INC |
| THQ INC |
| TIVO INC |
| TULLY'S COFFEE CORPORATION |
| UNDER ARMOUR INC |
| VALUECLICK INC |
| VIBRANT MEDIA INC |
| VOLCOM INC |
| WEBMD HEALTH CORP |
| YOUNG'S MARKET COMPANY LLC |
| ZAPPOS.COM INC |

| Music |
|---|
| DREAMWORKS ANIMATION SKG INC |
| GLU MOBILE INC |
| LUCASFILM LTD |
| THQ INC |

| Other |
|---|
| 24/7 REAL MEDIA INC |
| ACXIOM DIGITAL |
| AKQA INC |
| BLACKBOARD INC |
| CHOICESTREAM INC |
| CORPORATE EXECUTIVE BOARD COMPANY (THE) |
| COUPONS INC |
| CSG SYSTEMS INTERNATIONAL INC |
| DOUBLECLICK INC |
| DREAMWORKS ANIMATION SKG INC |
| ECOLLEGE.COM |
| ELOYALTY CORPORATION |
| EPAM SYSTEMS |
| FORRESTER RESEARCH INC |
| GALLUP ORGANIZATION (THE) |
| GLU MOBILE INC |
| HACKETT GROUP (THE) |
| HEIDRICK & STRUGGLES INTERNATIONAL INC |
| HURON CONSULTING GROUP INC |
| INTELLIGROUP INC |
| IVILLAGE INC |
| JUPITERMEDIA CORP |
| KNOT INC (THE) |
| LIVEPERSON INC |
| LUCASFILM LTD |
| MICROSTRATEGY INC |
| NETFLIX INC |
| NETRATINGS INC |
| PERFICIENT INC |
| REVOLUTION HEALTH GROUP LLC |
| RIGHTNOW TECHNOLOGIES INC |
| SENTO |
| SHUTTERFLY INC |
| SPSS INC |
| STEVEN MADDEN LTD |
| THQ INC |
| VALUECLICK INC |
| VIBRANT MEDIA INC |
| WEBMD HEALTH CORP |

| Technical Writing |
|---|
| ABAXIS INC |
| ACI WORLDWIDE INC |
| ACME PACKET INC |
| AFFYMETRIX INC |
| AKAMAI TECHNOLOGIES INC |
| ALBANY MOLECULAR RESEARCH |
| ALEXION PHARMACEUTICALS INC |
| ALIEN TECHNOLOGY CORPORATION |
| ALIGN TECHNOLOGY INC |
| ALKERMES INC |
| ALLEGHANY CORP |
| ALLIANCE IMAGING INC |
| ALLSCRIPTS HEALTHCARE SOLUTIONS INC |
| ALPHARMA INC |
| ALTIRIS INC |
| ALZA CORP |
| AMCOL INTERNATIONAL CORP |
| AMERICAN FIDELITY ASSURANCE COMPANY |
| AMERICAN MEDICAL SYSTEMS HOLDINGS INC |
| AMERICAN SCIENCE & ENGINEERING INC |
| AMERICAN SUPERCONDUCTOR CORP |
| AMERICAN TOWER CORP |
| AMICAS INC |
| AMSURG CORP |
| AMTECH SYSTEMS INC |
| AMYLIN PHARMACEUTICALS INC |
| ANALOGIC CORP |
| ANAREN INC |
| ANIKA THERAPEUTICS INC |
| ANSYS INC |
| APP PHARMACEUTICALS INC |
| APPLIED SIGNAL TECHNOLOGY INC |
| ARIBA INC |
| ARIZONA CHEMICAL COMPANY |
| AROTECH CORPORATION |
| ARRIS GROUP INC |
| ART TECHNOLOGY GROUP INC |
| ARUBA NETWORKS INC |
| ASPECT MEDICAL SYSTEMS INC |
| ASPEN TECHNOLOGY INC |
| ATHENAHEALTH INC |
| ATHEROS COMMUNICATIONS INC |
| ATMI INC |
| ATRION CORPORATION |
| ATS MEDICAL INC |
| AVANEX CORPORATION |
| AVI BIOPHARMA INC |
| AVIALL INC |
| BENTLEY PHARMACEUTICALS INC |
| BIO REFERENCE LABORATORIES INC |
| BIOMARIN PHARMACEUTICAL INC |
| BIOSITE INC |
| BLUE CARE NETWORK OF MICHIGAN |
| BLUE COAT SYSTEMS INC |
| BRIGHTSTAR CORPORATION |
| CALIPER LIFE SCIENCES |
| CAMBREX CORP |

| |
|---|
| CANDELA CORP |
| CANTEL MEDICAL CORP |
| CARACO PHARMACEUTICAL LABORATORIES |
| CARDTRONICS INC |
| C-COR INC |
| CELERA CORPORATION |
| CELGENE CORP |
| CELL GENESYS INC |
| CELL THERAPEUTICS INC |
| CEPHEID |
| CHANNELL COMMERCIAL CORP |
| CHATTEM INC |
| CHINDEX INTERNATIONAL INC |
| CHOLESTECH CORP |
| CHYRON CORP |
| CIENA CORP |
| COGNEX CORP |
| COHERENT INC |
| COINSTAR INC |
| COLLAGENEX PHARMACEUTICALS INC |
| COMDATA CORP |
| COMMERCE GROUP INC (THE) |
| COMTECH TELECOMMUNICATIONS CORP |
| CONCUR TECHNOLOGIES INC |
| CORPORATE EXECUTIVE BOARD COMPANY (THE) |
| CROWN CASTLE INTERNATIONAL CORP |
| CRUM & FORSTER HOLDINGS INC |
| CRYOLIFE INC |
| CSG SYSTEMS INTERNATIONAL INC |
| CUBIST PHARMACEUTICALS INC |
| CV THERAPEUTICS INC |
| CYBERSOURCE CORP |
| DAKTRONICS INC |
| DATASCOPE CORP |
| DEI HOLDINGS INC |
| DIALYSIS CORPORATION OF AMERICA |
| DIGI INTERNATIONAL INC |
| DIGITAL RIVER INC |
| DJO INCORPORATED |
| DSP GROUP INC |
| DYAX CORP |
| ECHELON CORP |
| ECLIPSYS CORPORATION |
| ELECTRONICS FOR IMAGING INC |
| ELOYALTY CORPORATION |
| EMBARCADERO TECHNOLOGIES INC |
| EMCORE CORP |
| EMS TECHNOLOGIES INC |
| EMULEX CORP |
| ENCORIUM GROUP INC |
| ENDO PHARMACEUTICALS HOLDINGS INC |
| ENERGY CONVERSION DEVICES INC |
| ENGLOBAL CORP |
| EPAM SYSTEMS |
| EPIX PHARMACEUTICALS INC |
| EQUINIX INC |
| EURONET WORLDWIDE INC |
| EVERGREEN SOLAR INC |
| EXACTECH INC |
| EXCEL TECHNOLOGY INC |
| EXELIXIS INC |
| E-Z-EM INC |
| F5 NETWORKS INC |
| FBL FINANCIAL GROUP |
| FIRST SOLAR LLC |
| FLIR SYSTEMS |
| FORRESTER RESEARCH INC |
| FUEL TECH INC |
| FUELCELL ENERGY INC |
| FUNDTECH LTD |
| GALLUP ORGANIZATION (THE) |
| GENENCOR INTERNATIONAL INC |
| GENOMIC HEALTH INC |
| GEN-PROBE INC |
| GERBER SCIENTIFIC INC |
| GERON CORPORATION |
| GLOBECOMM SYSTEMS INC |
| GLU MOBILE INC |
| GOAMERICA INC |
| GREAT AMERICAN FINANCIAL RESOURCES INC |
| GTC BIOTHERAPEUTICS INC |
| HACKETT GROUP (THE) |
| HAEMONETICS CORPORATION |
| HARMONIC INC |
| HARRIS STRATEX NETWORKS INC |
| HARVARD PILGRIM HEALTH CARE INC |
| HCC INSURANCE HOLDINGS INC |
| HEALTH INSURANCE PLAN OF GREATER NEW YORK |
| HEALTHTRONICS INC |
| HEARTLAND PAYMENT SYSTEMS INC |
| HEIDRICK & STRUGGLES INTERNATIONAL INC |
| HELIOVOLT CORP |
| HESKA CORP |
| HI-TECH PHARMACAL CO INC |
| HORACE MANN EDUCATORS CORPORATION |
| HUMAN GENOME SCIENCES INC |
| HURON CONSULTING GROUP INC |
| ICO INC |
| I-FLOW CORPORATION |
| ILLUMINA INC |
| IMATION CORP |
| IMMUCOR INC |
| INAMED CORP |
| INDEPENDENCE HOLDING CO |
| INFINERA CORP |
| INSPIRE PHARMACEUTICALS INC |
| INTEGRA LIFESCIENCES HOLDINGS CORP |
| INTEGRAL SYSTEMS INC |
| INTELLIGROUP INC |
| INTERACTIVE INTELLIGENCE |
| INTERMEC INC |
| INTERNAP NETWORK SERVICES CORP |
| INTERNET SECURITY SYSTEMS INC |
| INTERSTATE BATTERY SYSTEM OF AMERICA |
| INTERWOVEN INC |
| INVESTMENT TECHNOLOGY GROUP INC (ITG) |
| IRIDEX CORP |
| IRIS INTERNATIONAL INC |
| ISONICS CORPORATION |
| J2 GLOBAL COMMUNICATIONS INC |
| JACKSON NATIONAL LIFE INSURANCE COMPANY |
| JAZZ PHARMACEUTICALS |
| KIMLEY-HORN AND ASSOCIATES INC |
| KRONOS WORLDWIDE INC |
| KV PHARMACEUTICAL CO |
| LCA-VISION INC |
| LCC INTERNATIONAL INC |
| LEAP WIRELESS INTERNATIONAL INC |
| LIFECELL CORPORATION |
| LIFECORE BIOMEDICAL INC |
| LIVEPERSON INC |
| LOJACK CORP |
| LORAL SPACE & COMMUNICATIONS |

| |
|---|
| LTD |
| LUMINEX CORPORATION |
| MANHATTAN ASSOCIATES INC |
| MARTEK BIOSCIENCES CORP |
| MAXYGEN INC |
| MEDAREX INC |
| MEDICAL ACTION INDUSTRIES INC |
| MEDICINES CO (THE) |
| MEDICIS PHARMACEUTICAL CORP |
| MEDIS TECHNOLOGIES |
| MEDTOX SCIENTIFIC INC |
| MENTOR CORP |
| MERIDIAN BIOSCIENCE INC |
| MERIT MEDICAL SYSTEMS INC |
| METROLOGIC INSTRUMENTS INC |
| METROPCS COMMUNICATIONS INC |
| METROPOLITAN HEALTH NETWORKS |
| MICROSTRATEGY INC |
| MICROTEK MEDICAL HOLDINGS INC |
| MILLENNIUM PHARMACEUTICALS INC |
| MOLINA HEALTHCARE INC |
| MTS SYSTEMS |
| MYRIAD GENETICS INC |
| NANOMETRICS INC |
| NATIONAL DENTEX CORP |
| NATUS MEDICAL |
| NAVISITE INC |
| NEKTAR THERAPEUTICS |
| NEOGEN CORPORATION |
| NETGEAR INC |
| NETSCOUT SYSTEMS INC |
| NETSUITE INC |
| NIC INC |
| NOVEN PHARMACEUTICALS |
| NYER MEDICAL GROUP INC |
| ODYSSEY RE HOLDINGS CORP |
| OMNITURE INC |
| ONLINE RESOURCES CORP |
| OPENTV CORP |
| OPNEXT INC |
| OPTELECOM-NKF INC |
| OSCIENT PHARMACEUTICALS CORPORATION |
| PALM INC |
| PAR PHARMACEUTICAL COMPANIES INC |
| PERFICIENT INC |
| PHILADELPHIA CONSOLIDATED HOLDING CORP |
| PHOENIX COMPANIES (THE) |
| PITNEY BOWES MAPINFO |
| PLUG POWER INC |
| PMA CAPITAL CORPORATION |
| POLYCOM INC |
| POLYMEDICA CORPORATION |
| POLYPORE INTERNATIONAL INC |
| PREMIERE GLOBAL SERVICES INC |
| PROASSURANCE CORP |
| PROGRESS SOFTWARE CORP |
| PROTECTIVE LIFE CORP |
| QLOGIC CORP |
| QUALITY SYSTEMS INC |
| QUIDEL CORP |
| RACKSPACE HOSTING INC |
| RADISYS CORP |
| RADNET INC |
| RADYNE CORPORATION |
| REALNETWORKS INC |
| RED HAT INC |
| REGENERON PHARMACEUTICALS INC |
| REINSURANCE GROUP OF AMERICA INC |
| RIGHTNOW TECHNOLOGIES INC |
| RSA SECURITY INC |
| S1 CORPORATION |
| SALIX PHARMACEUTICALS |
| SAVVIS INC |
| SCANSOURCE INC |
| SCHICK TECHNOLOGIES INC |
| SCHIFF NUTRITION INTERNATIONAL INC |
| SCICLONE PHARMACEUTICALS |
| SCIELE PHARMA INC |
| SCIOS INC |
| SEACHANGE INTERNATIONAL INC |
| SEATTLE GENETICS |
| SECURE COMPUTING CORP |
| SENTO |
| SEPRACOR INC |
| SEQUENOM INC |
| SERENA SOFTWARE INC |
| SHARED TECHNOLOGIES |
| SKILLSOFT PLC |
| SOLAR RESERVE |
| SOLFOCUS INC |
| SONIC INNOVATIONS INC |
| SONUS NETWORKS INC |
| SPAN AMERICA MEDICAL SYSTEMS INC |
| SPECTRALINK CORP |
| SPECTRANETICS CORP |
| SPIRE CORPORATION |
| SPSS INC |
| SRI/SURGICAL EXPRESS INC |
| SS&C TECHNOLOGIES INC |
| STAAR SURGICAL CO |
| STANDARD MICROSYSTEMS CORPORATION |
| STATE AUTO FINANCIAL CORP |
| STIEFEL LABORATORIES INC |
| SUPER MICRO COMPUTER INC |
| SYCAMORE NETWORKS INC |
| SYMMETRY MEDICAL INC |
| SYMYX TECHNOLOGIES |
| SYNAPTICS INC |
| SYNOVIS LIFE TECHNOLOGIES INC |
| TECHNE CORP |
| TELIRIS |
| THERAGENICS CORP |
| THIRD WAVE TECHNOLOGIES INC |
| THORATEC CORPORATION |
| THQ INC |
| TIBCO SOFTWARE INC |
| TIVO INC |
| TOMOTHERAPY INC |
| TRANSATLANTIC HOLDINGS INC |
| TRANSCEND SERVICES INC |
| TRAPEZE NETWORKS INC |
| TRIZETTO GROUP INC (THE) |
| ULTIMATE SOFTWARE GROUP INC |
| UNITED THERAPEUTICS CORP |
| UNIVERSAL AMERICAN CORPORATION |
| VASCO DATA SECURITY INTERNATIONAL INC |
| VENTANA MEDICAL SYSTEMS INC |
| VERAZ NETWORKS INC |
| VERIFONE HOLDINGS INC |
| VERTEX PHARMACEUTICALS INC |
| VIASAT INC |
| VIGNETTE CORP |
| VIROPHARMA INC |
| VITAL SIGNS INC |
| VSE CORP |
| WEBEX COMMUNICATIONS INC |
| WEBMD HEALTH CORP |
| WEBSENSE INC |
| WIND RIVER SYSTEMS INC |
| WRIGHT MEDICAL GROUP INC |
| XOMA LTD |

| |
|---|
| ZILA INC |
| ZOLL MEDICAL CORP |
| ZYMOGENETICS INC |

## Management

| Experienced Management |
|---|
| 24/7 REAL MEDIA INC |
| AAMCO TRANSMISSIONS INC |
| ABAXIS INC |
| ACI WORLDWIDE INC |
| ACME PACKET INC |
| ACXIOM DIGITAL |
| AFFYMETRIX INC |
| AKAMAI TECHNOLOGIES INC |
| AKQA INC |
| ALASKA COMMUNICATIONS SYSTEMS GROUP |
| ALBANY MOLECULAR RESEARCH |
| ALEXION PHARMACEUTICALS INC |
| ALIEN TECHNOLOGY CORPORATION |
| ALIGN TECHNOLOGY INC |
| ALKERMES INC |
| ALLEGHANY CORP |
| ALLIANCE IMAGING INC |
| ALLSCRIPTS HEALTHCARE SOLUTIONS INC |
| ALPHARMA INC |
| ALTIRIS INC |
| ALZA CORP |
| AMAG PHARMACEUTICALS INC |
| AMCOL INTERNATIONAL CORP |
| AMERESCO |
| AMERICAN FIDELITY ASSURANCE COMPANY |
| AMERICAN ITALIAN PASTA COMPANY |
| AMERICAN MEDICAL SYSTEMS HOLDINGS INC |
| AMERICAN SCIENCE & ENGINEERING INC |
| AMERICAN SUPERCONDUCTOR CORP |
| AMERICAN TIRE DISTRIBUTORS |
| AMERICAN TOWER CORP |
| AMERICAN VANGUARD CORP |
| AMICAS INC |
| AMSURG CORP |
| AMTECH SYSTEMS INC |
| AMYLIN PHARMACEUTICALS INC |
| ANALOGIC CORP |
| ANAREN INC |
| ANIKA THERAPEUTICS INC |
| ANSYS INC |
| APP PHARMACEUTICALS INC |
| APPLIED SIGNAL TECHNOLOGY INC |
| ARDEN GROUP INC |
| ARIBA INC |
| ARIZONA CHEMICAL COMPANY |
| AROTECH CORPORATION |
| ARRIS GROUP INC |
| ART TECHNOLOGY GROUP INC |
| ARUBA NETWORKS INC |
| ASPECT MEDICAL SYSTEMS INC |
| ASPEN TECHNOLOGY INC |
| ASSOCIATED WHOLESALE GROCERS INC |
| ATHENAHEALTH INC |
| ATHEROS COMMUNICATIONS INC |
| ATLANTIC CITY ELECTRIC COMPANY |
| ATMI INC |
| ATRION CORPORATION |
| ATS MEDICAL INC |
| AUDIBLE INC |
| AVANEX CORPORATION |
| AVI BIOPHARMA INC |
| AVIALL INC |
| AVISTA CORPORATION |
| BENTLEY PHARMACEUTICALS INC |
| BERRY PETROLEUM CO |
| BIO REFERENCE LABORATORIES INC |
| BIOMARIN PHARMACEUTICAL INC |
| BIOSCRIP INC |
| BIOSITE INC |
| BLACK HILLS CORP |
| BLACKBOARD INC |
| BLUE CARE NETWORK OF MICHIGAN |
| BLUE COAT SYSTEMS INC |
| BLUE NILE INC |
| BRIGHTSTAR CORPORATION |
| CALIBER HOLDINGS CORP |
| CALIPER LIFE SCIENCES |
| CAL-MAINE FOODS INC |
| CALPINE CORPORATION |
| CAMBREX CORP |
| CANDELA CORP |
| CANTEL MEDICAL CORP |
| CARACO PHARMACEUTICAL LABORATORIES |
| CARDTRONICS INC |
| CATALYST HEALTH SOLUTIONS INC |
| C-COR INC |
| CELERA CORPORATION |
| CELGENE CORP |
| CELL GENESYS INC |
| CELL THERAPEUTICS INC |
| CENTERPLATE |
| CENTRAL VERMONT PUBLIC SERVICE CORPORATION |
| CEPHEID |
| CHANNELL COMMERCIAL CORP |
| CHATTEM INC |
| CHINDEX INTERNATIONAL INC |
| CHOICESTREAM INC |
| CHOLESTECH CORP |
| CHYRON CORP |
| CIENA CORP |
| CKX INC |
| CLEARWIRE CORP |
| CME GROUP |
| CNX GAS CORPORATION |
| COGNEX CORP |
| COHERENT INC |
| COINSTAR INC |
| COLLAGENEX PHARMACEUTICALS INC |
| COMDATA CORP |
| COMMERCE GROUP INC (THE) |
| COMTECH TELECOMMUNICATIONS CORP |
| CONCUR TECHNOLOGIES INC |
| CONTINUCARE CORP |
| CORPORATE EXECUTIVE BOARD COMPANY (THE) |
| COUPONS INC |
| CRITICAL CARE SYSTEMS |
| CROWN CASTLE INTERNATIONAL CORP |
| CRUM & FORSTER HOLDINGS INC |
| CRYOLIFE INC |
| CSG SYSTEMS INTERNATIONAL INC |
| CUBIST PHARMACEUTICALS INC |
| CURVES INTERNATIONAL INC |
| CV THERAPEUTICS INC |
| CYBERSOURCE CORP |
| DAKTRONICS INC |
| DANNON COMPANY INC (THE) |
| DARLING INTERNATIONAL INC |
| DATASCOPE CORP |
| DEI HOLDINGS INC |

| |
|---|
| DELPHI FINANCIAL GROUP INC |
| DENBURY RESOURCES INC |
| DIALYSIS CORPORATION OF AMERICA |
| DIAMOND FOODS INC |
| DIGI INTERNATIONAL INC |
| DIGITAL RIVER INC |
| DJO INCORPORATED |
| DOUBLECLICK INC |
| DPL INC |
| DREAMWORKS ANIMATION SKG INC |
| DRUGSTORE.COM INC |
| DSP GROUP INC |
| DYAX CORP |
| DYNACQ HEALTHCARE INC |
| DYNEGY INC |
| ECHELON CORP |
| ECLIPSYS CORPORATION |
| ECOLLEGE.COM |
| EHEALTH INC |
| ELECTRONICS FOR IMAGING INC |
| ELOYALTY CORPORATION |
| EMBARCADERO TECHNOLOGIES INC |
| EMCORE CORP |
| EMS TECHNOLOGIES INC |
| EMULEX CORP |
| ENCORE ACQUISITION CO |
| ENCORIUM GROUP INC |
| ENDO PHARMACEUTICALS HOLDINGS INC |
| ENERGY CONVERSION DEVICES INC |
| ENERNOC INC |
| ENGLOBAL CORP |
| EOG RESOURCES INC |
| EPAM SYSTEMS |
| EPIX PHARMACEUTICALS INC |
| EQUINIX INC |
| EQUITABLE RESOURCES INC |
| EURONET WORLDWIDE INC |
| EVERCORE PARTNERS INC |
| EVERGREEN ENERGY INC |
| EVERGREEN SOLAR INC |
| EXACTECH INC |
| EXCEL TECHNOLOGY INC |
| EXCO RESOURCES INC |
| EXELIXIS INC |
| E-Z-EM INC |
| F5 NETWORKS INC |

| |
|---|
| FARMER BROTHERS CO |
| FBL FINANCIAL GROUP |
| FEDEX SUPPLY CHAIN SERVICES INC |
| FIRST SOLAR LLC |
| FLIR SYSTEMS |
| FOREST OIL CORPORATION |
| FORRESTER RESEARCH INC |
| FRESH BRANDS INC |
| FRESHDIRECT LLC |
| FRONTIER OIL CORPORATION |
| FUEL TECH INC |
| FUELCELL ENERGY INC |
| FUNDTECH LTD |
| GALLUP ORGANIZATION (THE) |
| GENENCOR INTERNATIONAL INC |
| GENERAL COMMUNICATION INC (GCI) |
| GENESIS ENERGY LP |
| GENOMIC HEALTH INC |
| GEN-PROBE INC |
| GERBER SCIENTIFIC INC |
| GERON CORPORATION |
| GLOBAL PARTNERS LP |
| GLOBECOMM SYSTEMS INC |
| GLU MOBILE INC |
| GOAMERICA INC |
| GOLFSMITH INTERNATIONAL HOLDINGS INC |
| GREAT AMERICAN FINANCIAL RESOURCES INC |
| GREAT LAKES CHEESE COMPANY INC |
| GREEN MOUNTAIN COFFEE ROASTERS INC |
| GREEN MOUNTAIN POWER CORPORATION |
| GTC BIOTHERAPEUTICS INC |
| HACKETT GROUP (THE) |
| HAEMONETICS CORPORATION |
| HAHN AUTOMOTIVE WAREHOUSE INC |
| HANOVER FOODS CORPORATION |
| HANSEN NATURAL |
| HARMONIC INC |
| HARRIS STRATEX NETWORKS INC |
| HARVARD PILGRIM HEALTH CARE INC |
| HCC INSURANCE HOLDINGS INC |
| HEALTH GRADES INC |
| HEALTH INSURANCE PLAN OF GREATER NEW YORK |

| |
|---|
| HEALTHSTREAM INC |
| HEALTHTRONICS INC |
| HEARTLAND PAYMENT SYSTEMS INC |
| HEARUSA INC |
| HEIDRICK & STRUGGLES INTERNATIONAL INC |
| HELIOVOLT CORP |
| HESKA CORP |
| HICKORY TECH CORPORATION |
| HI-TECH PHARMACAL CO INC |
| HOLLY CORP |
| HORACE MANN EDUCATORS CORPORATION |
| HOULIHAN LOKEY |
| HUMAN GENOME SCIENCES INC |
| HURON CONSULTING GROUP INC |
| IBASIS INC |
| ICO INC |
| IDACORP INC |
| I-FLOW CORPORATION |
| ILLUMINA INC |
| IMATION CORP |
| IMG WORLDWIDE INC |
| IMMUCOR INC |
| INAMED CORP |
| INDEPENDENCE HOLDING CO |
| INFINERA CORP |
| INSPIRE PHARMACEUTICALS INC |
| INTEGRA LIFESCIENCES HOLDINGS CORP |
| INTEGRAL SYSTEMS INC |
| INTEGRAMED AMERICA INC |
| INTELLIGROUP INC |
| INTERACTIVE BROKERS GROUP INC |
| INTERACTIVE INTELLIGENCE |
| INTERCONTINENTALEXCHANGE INC (ICE) |
| INTERMEC INC |
| INTERNAP NETWORK SERVICES CORP |
| INTERNATIONAL CREATIVE MANAGEMENT (ICM) |
| INTERNATIONAL DAIRY QUEEN |
| INTERNET SECURITY SYSTEMS INC |
| INTERSTATE BATTERY SYSTEM OF AMERICA |
| INTERWOVEN INC |
| INVESTMENT TECHNOLOGY GROUP INC (ITG) |
| IRIDEX CORP |

IRIS INTERNATIONAL INC
ISILON SYSTEMS INC
ISONICS CORPORATION
IVILLAGE INC
J2 GLOBAL COMMUNICATIONS INC
JACKSON NATIONAL LIFE INSURANCE COMPANY
JAZZ PHARMACEUTICALS
JUPITERMEDIA CORP
KAMPGROUNDS OF AMERICA INC
KENDALL-JACKSON WINE ESTATES LTD
KIMLEY-HORN AND ASSOCIATES INC
KNIGHT CAPITAL GROUP INC
KNOT INC (THE)
KRONOS WORLDWIDE INC
KV PHARMACEUTICAL CO
LACLEDE GROUP INC (THE)
LCA-VISION INC
LCC INTERNATIONAL INC
LEAP WIRELESS INTERNATIONAL INC
LESLIE'S POOLMART INC
LIFECELL CORPORATION
LIFECORE BIOMEDICAL INC
LIVEPERSON INC
LOGISTICARE INC
LOJACK CORP
LORAL SPACE & COMMUNICATIONS LTD
LUCASFILM LTD
LUCOR INC
LUMINEX CORPORATION
M&F WORLDWIDE CORP
MAGELLAN MIDSTREAM PARTNERS LP
MALT-O-MEAL COMPANY
MANHATTAN ASSOCIATES INC
MARCHEX INC
MARTEK BIOSCIENCES CORP
MARTHA STEWART LIVING OMNIMEDIA INC
MARVEL ENTERTAINMENT INC
MATRIA HEALTHCARE INC
MAXYGEN INC
MCMORAN EXPLORATION CO
MEDAREX INC
MEDICAL ACTION INDUSTRIES INC
MEDICINES CO (THE)
MEDICIS PHARMACEUTICAL CORP
MEDIS TECHNOLOGIES

MEDTOX SCIENTIFIC INC
MENTOR CORP
MERIDIAN BIOSCIENCE INC
MERIT MEDICAL SYSTEMS INC
METROLOGIC INSTRUMENTS INC
METROPCS COMMUNICATIONS INC
METROPOLITAN HEALTH NETWORKS
MICHELINAS INC
MICROSTRATEGY INC
MICROTEK MEDICAL HOLDINGS INC
MIDAS INC
MILLENNIUM PHARMACEUTICALS INC
MOELIS & COMPANY
MOLINA HEALTHCARE INC
MOTORCAR PARTS OF AMERICA INC
MTS SYSTEMS
MYRIAD GENETICS INC
NANOMETRICS INC
NASDAQ OMX
NATIONAL BEVERAGE CORP
NATIONAL CINEMEDIA INC
NATIONAL DENTEX CORP
NATIONAL FUEL GAS CO
NATIONAL WINE & SPIRITS INC
NATUS MEDICAL
NAVISITE INC
NEKTAR THERAPEUTICS
NEOGEN CORPORATION
NETFLIX INC
NETGEAR INC
NETRATINGS INC
NETSCOUT SYSTEMS INC
NETSUITE INC
NEWFIELD EXPLORATION CO
NIC INC
NOBLE ENERGY INC
NORTHWESTERN CORPORATION
NOVAMED INC
NOVEN PHARMACEUTICALS
NTELOS HOLDING CORP
NUGGET MARKET
NUSTAR ENERGY LP
NUTRASWEET COMPANY (THE)
NYER MEDICAL GROUP INC
NYMEX HOLDINGS (NEW YORK MERCANTILE EXCHANGE)
ODYSSEY RE HOLDINGS CORP
OMNITURE INC

ONEOK PARTNERS LP
ONLINE RESOURCES CORP
OPENTV CORP
OPNEXT INC
OPTELECOM-NKF INC
ORMAT TECHNOLOGIES
OSCIENT PHARMACEUTICALS CORPORATION
PALM INC
PAR PHARMACEUTICAL COMPANIES INC
PC CONNECTION INC
PC MALL INC
PEAPOD LLC
PERFICIENT INC
PETMED EXPRESS INC
PETROLEUM DEVELOPMENT CORPORATION
PHILADELPHIA CONSOLIDATED HOLDING CORP
PHOENIX COMPANIES (THE)
PIEDMONT NATURAL GAS COMPANY INC
PIONEER NATURAL RESOURCES COMPANY
PITNEY BOWES MAPINFO
PLAINS EXPLORATION AND PRODUCTION COMPANY
PLUG POWER INC
PMA CAPITAL CORPORATION
POLYCOM INC
POLYMEDICA CORPORATION
POLYPORE INTERNATIONAL INC
PREMIERE GLOBAL SERVICES INC
PRIMEENERGY CORPORATION
PROASSURANCE CORP
PROGRESS SOFTWARE CORP
PROTECTIVE LIFE CORP
QLOGIC CORP
QUALITY SYSTEMS INC
QUICKSILVER RESOURCES INC
QUIDEL CORP
RACKSPACE HOSTING INC
RADISYS CORP
RADNET INC
RADYNE CORPORATION
RANGE RESOURCES CORP
REALNETWORKS INC
RECYCLED ENERGY DEVELOPMENT
RED HAT INC
REDDY ICE HOLDINGS INC

| |
|---|
| REGENERON PHARMACEUTICALS INC |
| REINSURANCE GROUP OF AMERICA INC |
| REVOLUTION HEALTH GROUP LLC |
| RIGHTNOW TECHNOLOGIES INC |
| ROBERT W BAIRD & CO INC |
| RSA SECURITY INC |
| S1 CORPORATION |
| SACRAMENTO MUNICIPAL UTILITY DISTRICT |
| SALIX PHARMACEUTICALS |
| SAVVIS INC |
| SCANSOURCE INC |
| SCHICK TECHNOLOGIES INC |
| SCHIFF NUTRITION INTERNATIONAL INC |
| SCICLONE PHARMACEUTICALS |
| SCIELE PHARMA INC |
| SCIOS INC |
| SCOULAR COMPANY (THE) |
| SEACHANGE INTERNATIONAL INC |
| SEATTLE GENETICS |
| SECURE COMPUTING CORP |
| SENTO |
| SEPRACOR INC |
| SEQUENOM INC |
| SERENA SOFTWARE INC |
| SHARED TECHNOLOGIES |
| SHENANDOAH TELECOMMUNICATIONS CO |
| SHUTTERFLY INC |
| SKILLSOFT PLC |
| SOLAR RESERVE |
| SOLFOCUS INC |
| SONIC INNOVATIONS INC |
| SONUS NETWORKS INC |
| SOUTHERN UNION COMPANY |
| SOUTHWESTERN ENERGY CO |
| SPAN AMERICA MEDICAL SYSTEMS INC |
| SPECTRALINK CORP |
| SPECTRANETICS CORP |
| SPIRE CORPORATION |
| SPORTSMAN'S GUIDE INC (THE) |
| SPROUTS FARMERS MARKET |
| SPSS INC |
| SRI/SURGICAL EXPRESS INC |
| SS&C TECHNOLOGIES INC |
| ST MARY LAND & EXPLORATION COMPANY |
| STAAR SURGICAL CO |

| |
|---|
| STANDARD MICROSYSTEMS CORPORATION |
| STATE AUTO FINANCIAL CORP |
| STERLING AUTOBODY CENTERS |
| STEVEN MADDEN LTD |
| STIEFEL LABORATORIES INC |
| SUPER MICRO COMPUTER INC |
| SWIFT ENERGY CO |
| SYCAMORE NETWORKS INC |
| SYMMETRY MEDICAL INC |
| SYMYX TECHNOLOGIES |
| SYNAPTICS INC |
| SYNOVIS LIFE TECHNOLOGIES INC |
| TAMPA ELECTRIC COMPANY |
| TARGA RESOURCES PARTNERS LP |
| TDINDUSTRIES |
| TECHNE CORP |
| TELIRIS |
| TEPPCO PARTNERS LP |
| TERREMARK WORLDWIDE INC |
| THERAGENICS CORP |
| THIRD WAVE TECHNOLOGIES INC |
| THOMAS WEISEL PARTNERS GROUP INC |
| THORATEC CORPORATION |
| THQ INC |
| TIBCO SOFTWARE INC |
| TIVO INC |
| TOMOTHERAPY INC |
| TOOTSIE ROLL INDUSTRIES INC |
| TOPPS COMPANY INC (THE) |
| TRANSATLANTIC HOLDINGS INC |
| TRANSCEND SERVICES INC |
| TRAPEZE NETWORKS INC |
| TRIZETTO GROUP INC (THE) |
| TULLY'S COFFEE CORPORATION |
| UIL HOLDINGS CORPORATION |
| ULTIMATE SOFTWARE GROUP INC |
| UNDER ARMOUR INC |
| UNISOURCE ENERGY CORPORATION |
| UNITED ONLINE INC |
| UNITED THERAPEUTICS CORP |
| UNIVERSAL AMERICAN CORPORATION |
| UNIVERSAL HOSPITAL SERVICES INC |
| US PHYSICAL THERAPY INC |
| VALLEY NATIONAL GASES LLC |
| VALUECLICK INC |
| VASCO DATA SECURITY |

| |
|---|
| INTERNATIONAL INC |
| VENTANA MEDICAL SYSTEMS INC |
| VERAZ NETWORKS INC |
| VERIFONE HOLDINGS INC |
| VERTEX PHARMACEUTICALS INC |
| VIASAT INC |
| VIBRANT MEDIA INC |
| VIGNETTE CORP |
| VIROPHARMA INC |
| VISION SERVICE PLAN |
| VITAL SIGNS INC |
| VOLCOM INC |
| VSE CORP |
| WEBEX COMMUNICATIONS INC |
| WEBMD HEALTH CORP |
| WEBSENSE INC |
| WESTAR ENERGY |
| WGL HOLDINGS INC |
| WHITEWAVE FOODS COMPANY |
| WIND RIVER SYSTEMS INC |
| WRIGHT MEDICAL GROUP INC |
| XOMA LTD |
| XTO ENERGY INC |
| YOUNG'S MARKET COMPANY LLC |
| ZAPPOS.COM INC |
| ZIEBART INTERNATIONAL CORP |
| ZILA INC |
| ZOLL MEDICAL CORP |
| ZYMOGENETICS INC |

| International Business |
|---|
| 24/7 REAL MEDIA INC |
| AAMCO TRANSMISSIONS INC |
| ABAXIS INC |
| ACI WORLDWIDE INC |
| ACME PACKET INC |
| ACXIOM DIGITAL |
| AFFYMETRIX INC |
| AKAMAI TECHNOLOGIES INC |
| AKQA INC |
| ALBANY MOLECULAR RESEARCH |
| ALEXION PHARMACEUTICALS INC |
| ALIEN TECHNOLOGY CORPORATION |
| ALIGN TECHNOLOGY INC |
| ALKERMES INC |
| ALLEGHANY CORP |
| ALPHARMA INC |
| ALTIRIS INC |
| ALZA CORP |

| |
|---|
| AMCOL INTERNATIONAL CORP |
| AMERESCO |
| AMERICAN ITALIAN PASTA COMPANY |
| AMERICAN MEDICAL SYSTEMS HOLDINGS INC |
| AMERICAN SCIENCE & ENGINEERING INC |
| AMERICAN SUPERCONDUCTOR CORP |
| AMERICAN TOWER CORP |
| AMERICAN VANGUARD CORP |
| AMICAS INC |
| AMTECH SYSTEMS INC |
| AMYLIN PHARMACEUTICALS INC |
| ANALOGIC CORP |
| ANAREN INC |
| ANSYS INC |
| APP PHARMACEUTICALS INC |
| APPLIED SIGNAL TECHNOLOGY INC |
| ARIBA INC |
| ARIZONA CHEMICAL COMPANY |
| AROTECH CORPORATION |
| ARRIS GROUP INC |
| ART TECHNOLOGY GROUP INC |
| ARUBA NETWORKS INC |
| ASPECT MEDICAL SYSTEMS INC |
| ASPEN TECHNOLOGY INC |
| ATHENAHEALTH INC |
| ATHEROS COMMUNICATIONS INC |
| ATMI INC |
| ATRION CORPORATION |
| ATS MEDICAL INC |
| AUDIBLE INC |
| AVANEX CORPORATION |
| AVIALL INC |
| BENTLEY PHARMACEUTICALS INC |
| BERRY PETROLEUM CO |
| BIOMARIN PHARMACEUTICAL INC |
| BIOSITE INC |
| BLACKBOARD INC |
| BLUE COAT SYSTEMS INC |
| BLUE NILE INC |
| BRIGHTSTAR CORPORATION |
| CALIPER LIFE SCIENCES |
| CALPINE CORPORATION |
| CAMBREX CORP |
| CANDELA CORP |
| CANTEL MEDICAL CORP |
| CARDTRONICS INC |
| CATALYST HEALTH SOLUTIONS INC |

| |
|---|
| C-COR INC |
| CELGENE CORP |
| CELL GENESYS INC |
| CELL THERAPEUTICS INC |
| CENTERPLATE |
| CENTRAL VERMONT PUBLIC SERVICE CORPORATION |
| CEPHEID |
| CHANNELL COMMERCIAL CORP |
| CHATTEM INC |
| CHINDEX INTERNATIONAL INC |
| CHOLESTECH CORP |
| CHYRON CORP |
| CIENA CORP |
| CKX INC |
| CLEARWIRE CORP |
| CME GROUP |
| CNX GAS CORPORATION |
| COGNEX CORP |
| COHERENT INC |
| COINSTAR INC |
| COLLAGENEX PHARMACEUTICALS INC |
| COMTECH TELECOMMUNICATIONS CORP |
| CONCUR TECHNOLOGIES INC |
| CORPORATE EXECUTIVE BOARD COMPANY (THE) |
| CROWN CASTLE INTERNATIONAL CORP |
| CRYOLIFE INC |
| CUBIST PHARMACEUTICALS INC |
| CURVES INTERNATIONAL INC |
| CV THERAPEUTICS INC |
| CYBERSOURCE CORP |
| DAKTRONICS INC |
| DARLING INTERNATIONAL INC |
| DATASCOPE CORP |
| DEI HOLDINGS INC |
| DELPHI FINANCIAL GROUP INC |
| DENBURY RESOURCES INC |
| DIAMOND FOODS INC |
| DIGI INTERNATIONAL INC |
| DIGITAL RIVER INC |
| DJO INCORPORATED |
| DOUBLECLICK INC |
| DRUGSTORE.COM INC |
| DSP GROUP INC |
| DYAX CORP |
| DYNACQ HEALTHCARE INC |
| DYNEGY INC |

| |
|---|
| ECHELON CORP |
| ECLIPSYS CORPORATION |
| ECOLLEGE.COM |
| ELECTRONICS FOR IMAGING INC |
| ELOYALTY CORPORATION |
| EMBARCADERO TECHNOLOGIES INC |
| EMCORE CORP |
| EMS TECHNOLOGIES INC |
| EMULEX CORP |
| ENCORE ACQUISITION CO |
| ENCORIUM GROUP INC |
| ENDO PHARMACEUTICALS HOLDINGS INC |
| ENERGY CONVERSION DEVICES INC |
| ENGLOBAL CORP |
| EOG RESOURCES INC |
| EPAM SYSTEMS |
| EPIX PHARMACEUTICALS INC |
| EQUINIX INC |
| EQUITABLE RESOURCES INC |
| EURONET WORLDWIDE INC |
| EVERCORE PARTNERS INC |
| EVERGREEN ENERGY INC |
| EVERGREEN SOLAR INC |
| EXACTECH INC |
| EXCEL TECHNOLOGY INC |
| EXCO RESOURCES INC |
| EXELIXIS INC |
| E-Z-EM INC |
| F5 NETWORKS INC |
| FEDEX SUPPLY CHAIN SERVICES INC |
| FIRST SOLAR LLC |
| FLIR SYSTEMS |
| FOREST OIL CORPORATION |
| FORRESTER RESEARCH INC |
| FUEL TECH INC |
| FUELCELL ENERGY INC |
| FUNDTECH LTD |
| GALLUP ORGANIZATION (THE) |
| GENENCOR INTERNATIONAL INC |
| GEN-PROBE INC |
| GERBER SCIENTIFIC INC |
| GLOBAL PARTNERS LP |
| GLOBECOMM SYSTEMS INC |
| GLU MOBILE INC |
| GOLFSMITH INTERNATIONAL HOLDINGS INC |
| GTC BIOTHERAPEUTICS INC |

| |
|---|
| HACKETT GROUP (THE) |
| HAEMONETICS CORPORATION |
| HANOVER FOODS CORPORATION |
| HANSEN NATURAL |
| HARMONIC INC |
| HARRIS STRATEX NETWORKS INC |
| HCC INSURANCE HOLDINGS INC |
| HEALTHTRONICS INC |
| HEARUSA INC |
| HEIDRICK & STRUGGLES INTERNATIONAL INC |
| HESKA CORP |
| HI-TECH PHARMACAL CO INC |
| HOLLY CORP |
| HOULIHAN LOKEY |
| HURON CONSULTING GROUP INC |
| IBASIS INC |
| ICO INC |
| I-FLOW CORPORATION |
| ILLUMINA INC |
| IMATION CORP |
| IMG WORLDWIDE INC |
| IMMUCOR INC |
| INAMED CORP |
| INFINERA CORP |
| INTEGRA LIFESCIENCES HOLDINGS CORP |
| INTEGRAL SYSTEMS INC |
| INTELLIGROUP INC |
| INTERACTIVE BROKERS GROUP INC |
| INTERACTIVE INTELLIGENCE |
| INTERCONTINENTALEXCHANGE INC (ICE) |
| INTERMEC INC |
| INTERNAP NETWORK SERVICES CORP |
| INTERNATIONAL CREATIVE MANAGEMENT (ICM) |
| INTERNATIONAL DAIRY QUEEN |
| INTERNET SECURITY SYSTEMS INC |
| INTERSTATE BATTERY SYSTEM OF AMERICA |
| INTERWOVEN INC |
| INVESTMENT TECHNOLOGY GROUP INC (ITG) |
| IRIDEX CORP |
| IRIS INTERNATIONAL INC |
| ISILON SYSTEMS INC |
| J2 GLOBAL COMMUNICATIONS INC |
| JUPITERMEDIA CORP |
| KAMPGROUNDS OF AMERICA INC |

| |
|---|
| KENDALL-JACKSON WINE ESTATES LTD |
| KNIGHT CAPITAL GROUP INC |
| KRONOS WORLDWIDE INC |
| KV PHARMACEUTICAL CO |
| LCA-VISION INC |
| LCC INTERNATIONAL INC |
| LEAP WIRELESS INTERNATIONAL INC |
| LIFECELL CORPORATION |
| LIFECORE BIOMEDICAL INC |
| LIVEPERSON INC |
| LOJACK CORP |
| LORAL SPACE & COMMUNICATIONS LTD |
| LUCASFILM LTD |
| LUMINEX CORPORATION |
| M&F WORLDWIDE CORP |
| MANHATTAN ASSOCIATES INC |
| MARTEK BIOSCIENCES CORP |
| MARVEL ENTERTAINMENT INC |
| MATRIA HEALTHCARE INC |
| MAXYGEN INC |
| MEDICAL ACTION INDUSTRIES INC |
| MEDICINES CO (THE) |
| MEDICIS PHARMACEUTICAL CORP |
| MEDIS TECHNOLOGIES |
| MENTOR CORP |
| MERIDIAN BIOSCIENCE INC |
| MERIT MEDICAL SYSTEMS INC |
| METROLOGIC INSTRUMENTS INC |
| METROPCS COMMUNICATIONS INC |
| MICHELINAS INC |
| MICROSTRATEGY INC |
| MICROTEK MEDICAL HOLDINGS INC |
| MIDAS INC |
| MILLENNIUM PHARMACEUTICALS INC |
| MOELIS & COMPANY |
| MOTORCAR PARTS OF AMERICA INC |
| MTS SYSTEMS |
| NANOMETRICS INC |
| NASDAQ OMX |
| NATIONAL DENTEX CORP |
| NATIONAL FUEL GAS CO |
| NATUS MEDICAL |
| NAVISITE INC |
| NEKTAR THERAPEUTICS |
| NEOGEN CORPORATION |
| NETGEAR INC |

| |
|---|
| NETRATINGS INC |
| NETSCOUT SYSTEMS INC |
| NETSUITE INC |
| NEWFIELD EXPLORATION CO |
| NOBLE ENERGY INC |
| NOVEN PHARMACEUTICALS |
| NUSTAR ENERGY LP |
| NYER MEDICAL GROUP INC |
| NYMEX HOLDINGS (NEW YORK MERCANTILE EXCHANGE) |
| ODYSSEY RE HOLDINGS CORP |
| OMNITURE INC |
| ONEOK PARTNERS LP |
| OPENTV CORP |
| OPNEXT INC |
| OPTELECOM-NKF INC |
| ORMAT TECHNOLOGIES |
| PALM INC |
| PAR PHARMACEUTICAL COMPANIES INC |
| PC MALL INC |
| PERFICIENT INC |
| PETROLEUM DEVELOPMENT CORPORATION |
| PHOENIX COMPANIES (THE) |
| PIONEER NATURAL RESOURCES COMPANY |
| PITNEY BOWES MAPINFO |
| PLUG POWER INC |
| POLYCOM INC |
| POLYMEDICA CORPORATION |
| POLYPORE INTERNATIONAL INC |
| PREMIERE GLOBAL SERVICES INC |
| PRIMEENERGY CORPORATION |
| PROGRESS SOFTWARE CORP |
| QLOGIC CORP |
| QUALITY SYSTEMS INC |
| QUICKSILVER RESOURCES INC |
| QUIDEL CORP |
| RADISYS CORP |
| RADYNE CORPORATION |
| RANGE RESOURCES CORP |
| REALNETWORKS INC |
| RED HAT INC |
| REINSURANCE GROUP OF AMERICA INC |
| RIGHTNOW TECHNOLOGIES INC |
| ROBERT W BAIRD & CO INC |
| RSA SECURITY INC |
| S1 CORPORATION |
| SALIX PHARMACEUTICALS |

| |
|---|
| SAVVIS INC |
| SCANSOURCE INC |
| SCHICK TECHNOLOGIES INC |
| SCHIFF NUTRITION INTERNATIONAL INC |
| SCICLONE PHARMACEUTICALS |
| SCIELE PHARMA INC |
| SCOULAR COMPANY (THE) |
| SEACHANGE INTERNATIONAL INC |
| SECURE COMPUTING CORP |
| SENTO |
| SEPRACOR INC |
| SEQUENOM INC |
| SERENA SOFTWARE INC |
| SKILLSOFT PLC |
| SOLAR RESERVE |
| SOLFOCUS INC |
| SONIC INNOVATIONS INC |
| SONUS NETWORKS INC |
| SOUTHWESTERN ENERGY CO |
| SPECTRALINK CORP |
| SPECTRANETICS CORP |
| SPIRE CORPORATION |
| SPSS INC |
| SS&C TECHNOLOGIES INC |
| ST MARY LAND & EXPLORATION COMPANY |
| STAAR SURGICAL CO |
| STANDARD MICROSYSTEMS CORPORATION |
| STERLING AUTOBODY CENTERS |
| STEVEN MADDEN LTD |
| STIEFEL LABORATORIES INC |
| SUPER MICRO COMPUTER INC |
| SWIFT ENERGY CO |
| SYCAMORE NETWORKS INC |
| SYMMETRY MEDICAL INC |
| SYMYX TECHNOLOGIES |
| SYNAPTICS INC |
| TARGA RESOURCES PARTNERS LP |
| TECHNE CORP |
| TELIRIS |
| TERREMARK WORLDWIDE INC |
| THERAGENICS CORP |
| THOMAS WEISEL PARTNERS GROUP INC |
| THORATEC CORPORATION |
| THQ INC |
| TIBCO SOFTWARE INC |
| TIVO INC |
| TOMOTHERAPY INC |
| TOOTSIE ROLL INDUSTRIES INC |
| TOPPS COMPANY INC (THE) |
| TRANSATLANTIC HOLDINGS INC |
| TRAPEZE NETWORKS INC |
| TRIZETTO GROUP INC (THE) |
| TULLY'S COFFEE CORPORATION |
| ULTIMATE SOFTWARE GROUP INC |
| UNDER ARMOUR INC |
| UNISOURCE ENERGY CORPORATION |
| UNITED ONLINE INC |
| UNITED THERAPEUTICS CORP |
| VALUECLICK INC |
| VASCO DATA SECURITY INTERNATIONAL INC |
| VENTANA MEDICAL SYSTEMS INC |
| VERAZ NETWORKS INC |
| VERIFONE HOLDINGS INC |
| VERTEX PHARMACEUTICALS INC |
| VIASAT INC |
| VIBRANT MEDIA INC |
| VIGNETTE CORP |
| VISION SERVICE PLAN |
| VITAL SIGNS INC |
| VOLCOM INC |
| VSE CORP |
| WEBEX COMMUNICATIONS INC |
| WEBMD HEALTH CORP |
| WEBSENSE INC |
| WESTAR ENERGY |
| WIND RIVER SYSTEMS INC |
| WRIGHT MEDICAL GROUP INC |
| XTO ENERGY INC |
| ZIEBART INTERNATIONAL CORP |
| ZILA INC |
| ZOLL MEDICAL CORP |

| Management Trainees |
|---|
| AMERICAN TIRE DISTRIBUTORS |
| ARDEN GROUP INC |
| ASSOCIATED WHOLESALE GROCERS INC |
| ATHENAHEALTH INC |
| AUDIBLE INC |
| BIOSCRIP INC |
| BLACKBOARD INC |
| BLUE NILE INC |
| CARDTRONICS INC |
| COINSTAR INC |
| COMDATA CORP |
| DRUGSTORE.COM INC |
| ECOLLEGE.COM |
| EURONET WORLDWIDE INC |
| FARMER BROTHERS CO |
| FRESH BRANDS INC |
| FRESHDIRECT LLC |
| GOLFSMITH INTERNATIONAL HOLDINGS INC |
| GREEN MOUNTAIN COFFEE ROASTERS INC |
| HAHN AUTOMOTIVE WAREHOUSE INC |
| HANSEN NATURAL |
| HEALTHSTREAM INC |
| HEARTLAND PAYMENT SYSTEMS INC |
| INTERNATIONAL DAIRY QUEEN |
| INVESTMENT TECHNOLOGY GROUP INC (ITG) |
| LESLIE'S POOLMART INC |
| M&F WORLDWIDE CORP |
| NATIONAL BEVERAGE CORP |
| NATIONAL WINE & SPIRITS INC |
| NETFLIX INC |
| NUGGET MARKET |
| PC CONNECTION INC |
| PC MALL INC |
| PEAPOD LLC |
| PETMED EXPRESS INC |
| REDDY ICE HOLDINGS INC |
| SPORTSMAN'S GUIDE INC (THE) |
| SPROUTS FARMERS MARKET |
| SRI/SURGICAL EXPRESS INC |
| TOOTSIE ROLL INDUSTRIES INC |
| TOPPS COMPANY INC (THE) |
| TULLY'S COFFEE CORPORATION |
| UNDER ARMOUR INC |
| VERIFONE HOLDINGS INC |
| YOUNG'S MARKET COMPANY LLC |
| ZAPPOS.COM INC |

| MBA Graduates |
|---|
| 24/7 REAL MEDIA INC |
| AAMCO TRANSMISSIONS INC |
| ABAXIS INC |
| ACI WORLDWIDE INC |
| ACME PACKET INC |
| ACXIOM DIGITAL |
| AFFYMETRIX INC |
| AKAMAI TECHNOLOGIES INC |
| AKQA INC |
| ALASKA COMMUNICATIONS |

| |
|---|
| SYSTEMS GROUP |
| ALBANY MOLECULAR RESEARCH |
| ALEXION PHARMACEUTICALS INC |
| ALIEN TECHNOLOGY CORPORATION |
| ALIGN TECHNOLOGY INC |
| ALKERMES INC |
| ALLEGHANY CORP |
| ALLIANCE IMAGING INC |
| ALLSCRIPTS HEALTHCARE SOLUTIONS INC |
| ALPHARMA INC |
| ALTIRIS INC |
| ALZA CORP |
| AMAG PHARMACEUTICALS INC |
| AMCOL INTERNATIONAL CORP |
| AMERESCO |
| AMERICAN FIDELITY ASSURANCE COMPANY |
| AMERICAN ITALIAN PASTA COMPANY |
| AMERICAN MEDICAL SYSTEMS HOLDINGS INC |
| AMERICAN SCIENCE & ENGINEERING INC |
| AMERICAN SUPERCONDUCTOR CORP |
| AMERICAN TIRE DISTRIBUTORS |
| AMERICAN TOWER CORP |
| AMERICAN VANGUARD CORP |
| AMICAS INC |
| AMSURG CORP |
| AMTECH SYSTEMS INC |
| AMYLIN PHARMACEUTICALS INC |
| ANALOGIC CORP |
| ANAREN INC |
| ANIKA THERAPEUTICS INC |
| ANSYS INC |
| APP PHARMACEUTICALS INC |
| APPLIED SIGNAL TECHNOLOGY INC |
| ARDEN GROUP INC |
| ARIBA INC |
| ARIZONA CHEMICAL COMPANY |
| AROTECH CORPORATION |
| ARRIS GROUP INC |
| ART TECHNOLOGY GROUP INC |
| ARUBA NETWORKS INC |
| ASPECT MEDICAL SYSTEMS INC |
| ASPEN TECHNOLOGY INC |
| ASSOCIATED WHOLESALE GROCERS INC |
| ATHENAHEALTH INC |
| ATHEROS COMMUNICATIONS INC |
| ATLANTIC CITY ELECTRIC COMPANY |
| ATMI INC |
| ATRION CORPORATION |
| ATS MEDICAL INC |
| AUDIBLE INC |
| AVANEX CORPORATION |
| AVI BIOPHARMA INC |
| AVIALL INC |
| AVISTA CORPORATION |
| BENTLEY PHARMACEUTICALS INC |
| BERRY PETROLEUM CO |
| BIO REFERENCE LABORATORIES INC |
| BIOMARIN PHARMACEUTICAL INC |
| BIOSCRIP INC |
| BIOSITE INC |
| BLACK HILLS CORP |
| BLACKBOARD INC |
| BLUE CARE NETWORK OF MICHIGAN |
| BLUE COAT SYSTEMS INC |
| BLUE NILE INC |
| BRIGHTSTAR CORPORATION |
| CALIBER HOLDINGS CORP |
| CALIPER LIFE SCIENCES |
| CAL-MAINE FOODS INC |
| CALPINE CORPORATION |
| CAMBREX CORP |
| CANDELA CORP |
| CANTEL MEDICAL CORP |
| CARACO PHARMACEUTICAL LABORATORIES |
| CARDTRONICS INC |
| CATALYST HEALTH SOLUTIONS INC |
| C-COR INC |
| CELERA CORPORATION |
| CELGENE CORP |
| CELL GENESYS INC |
| CELL THERAPEUTICS INC |
| CENTERPLATE |
| CENTRAL VERMONT PUBLIC SERVICE CORPORATION |
| CEPHEID |
| CHANNELL COMMERCIAL CORP |
| CHATTEM INC |
| CHINDEX INTERNATIONAL INC |
| CHOICESTREAM INC |
| CHOLESTECH CORP |
| CHYRON CORP |
| CIENA CORP |
| CKX INC |
| CLEARWIRE CORP |
| CME GROUP |
| CNX GAS CORPORATION |
| COGNEX CORP |
| COHERENT INC |
| COINSTAR INC |
| COLLAGENEX PHARMACEUTICALS INC |
| COMDATA CORP |
| COMMERCE GROUP INC (THE) |
| COMTECH TELECOMMUNICATIONS CORP |
| CONCUR TECHNOLOGIES INC |
| CONTINUCARE CORP |
| CORPORATE EXECUTIVE BOARD COMPANY (THE) |
| COUPONS INC |
| CRITICAL CARE SYSTEMS |
| CROWN CASTLE INTERNATIONAL CORP |
| CRUM & FORSTER HOLDINGS INC |
| CRYOLIFE INC |
| CSG SYSTEMS INTERNATIONAL INC |
| CUBIST PHARMACEUTICALS INC |
| CURVES INTERNATIONAL INC |
| CV THERAPEUTICS INC |
| CYBERSOURCE CORP |
| DAKTRONICS INC |
| DANNON COMPANY INC (THE) |
| DARLING INTERNATIONAL INC |
| DATASCOPE CORP |
| DEI HOLDINGS INC |
| DELPHI FINANCIAL GROUP INC |
| DENBURY RESOURCES INC |
| DIALYSIS CORPORATION OF AMERICA |
| DIAMOND FOODS INC |
| DIGI INTERNATIONAL INC |
| DIGITAL RIVER INC |
| DJO INCORPORATED |
| DOUBLECLICK INC |
| DPL INC |
| DREAMWORKS ANIMATION SKG INC |
| DRUGSTORE.COM INC |
| DSP GROUP INC |
| DYAX CORP |
| DYNACQ HEALTHCARE INC |
| DYNEGY INC |

| |
|---|
| ECHELON CORP |
| ECLIPSYS CORPORATION |
| ECOLLEGE.COM |
| EHEALTH INC |
| ELECTRONICS FOR IMAGING INC |
| ELOYALTY CORPORATION |
| EMBARCADERO TECHNOLOGIES INC |
| EMCORE CORP |
| EMS TECHNOLOGIES INC |
| EMULEX CORP |
| ENCORE ACQUISITION CO |
| ENCORIUM GROUP INC |
| ENDO PHARMACEUTICALS HOLDINGS INC |
| ENERGY CONVERSION DEVICES INC |
| ENERNOC INC |
| ENGLOBAL CORP |
| EOG RESOURCES INC |
| EPAM SYSTEMS |
| EPIX PHARMACEUTICALS INC |
| EQUINIX INC |
| EQUITABLE RESOURCES INC |
| EURONET WORLDWIDE INC |
| EVERCORE PARTNERS INC |
| EVERGREEN ENERGY INC |
| EVERGREEN SOLAR INC |
| EXACTECH INC |
| EXCEL TECHNOLOGY INC |
| EXCO RESOURCES INC |
| EXELIXIS INC |
| E-Z-EM INC |
| F5 NETWORKS INC |
| FARMER BROTHERS CO |
| FBL FINANCIAL GROUP |
| FEDEX SUPPLY CHAIN SERVICES INC |
| FIRST SOLAR LLC |
| FLIR SYSTEMS |
| FOREST OIL CORPORATION |
| FORRESTER RESEARCH INC |
| FRESH BRANDS INC |
| FRESHDIRECT LLC |
| FRONTIER OIL CORPORATION |
| FUEL TECH INC |
| FUELCELL ENERGY INC |
| FUNDTECH LTD |
| GALLUP ORGANIZATION (THE) |
| GENENCOR INTERNATIONAL INC |
| GENERAL COMMUNICATION INC |

| |
|---|
| (GCI) |
| GENESIS ENERGY LP |
| GENOMIC HEALTH INC |
| GEN-PROBE INC |
| GERBER SCIENTIFIC INC |
| GERON CORPORATION |
| GLOBAL PARTNERS LP |
| GLOBECOMM SYSTEMS INC |
| GLU MOBILE INC |
| GOAMERICA INC |
| GOLFSMITH INTERNATIONAL HOLDINGS INC |
| GREAT AMERICAN FINANCIAL RESOURCES INC |
| GREAT LAKES CHEESE COMPANY INC |
| GREEN MOUNTAIN COFFEE ROASTERS INC |
| GREEN MOUNTAIN POWER CORPORATION |
| GTC BIOTHERAPEUTICS INC |
| HACKETT GROUP (THE) |
| HAEMONETICS CORPORATION |
| HAHN AUTOMOTIVE WAREHOUSE INC |
| HANOVER FOODS CORPORATION |
| HANSEN NATURAL |
| HARMONIC INC |
| HARRIS STRATEX NETWORKS INC |
| HARVARD PILGRIM HEALTH CARE INC |
| HCC INSURANCE HOLDINGS INC |
| HEALTH GRADES INC |
| HEALTH INSURANCE PLAN OF GREATER NEW YORK |
| HEALTHSTREAM INC |
| HEALTHTRONICS INC |
| HEARTLAND PAYMENT SYSTEMS INC |
| HEARUSA INC |
| HEIDRICK & STRUGGLES INTERNATIONAL INC |
| HELIOVOLT CORP |
| HESKA CORP |
| HICKORY TECH CORPORATION |
| HI-TECH PHARMACAL CO INC |
| HOLLY CORP |
| HORACE MANN EDUCATORS CORPORATION |
| HOULIHAN LOKEY |
| HUMAN GENOME SCIENCES INC |
| HURON CONSULTING GROUP INC |
| IBASIS INC |

| |
|---|
| ICO INC |
| IDACORP INC |
| I-FLOW CORPORATION |
| ILLUMINA INC |
| IMATION CORP |
| IMG WORLDWIDE INC |
| IMMUCOR INC |
| INAMED CORP |
| INDEPENDENCE HOLDING CO |
| INFINERA CORP |
| INSPIRE PHARMACEUTICALS INC |
| INTEGRA LIFESCIENCES HOLDINGS CORP |
| INTEGRAL SYSTEMS INC |
| INTEGRAMED AMERICA INC |
| INTELLIGROUP INC |
| INTERACTIVE BROKERS GROUP INC |
| INTERACTIVE INTELLIGENCE |
| INTERCONTINENTALEXCHANGE INC (ICE) |
| INTERMEC INC |
| INTERNAP NETWORK SERVICES CORP |
| INTERNATIONAL CREATIVE MANAGEMENT (ICM) |
| INTERNATIONAL DAIRY QUEEN |
| INTERNET SECURITY SYSTEMS INC |
| INTERSTATE BATTERY SYSTEM OF AMERICA |
| INTERWOVEN INC |
| INVESTMENT TECHNOLOGY GROUP INC (ITG) |
| IRIDEX CORP |
| IRIS INTERNATIONAL INC |
| ISILON SYSTEMS INC |
| ISONICS CORPORATION |
| IVILLAGE INC |
| J2 GLOBAL COMMUNICATIONS INC |
| JACKSON NATIONAL LIFE INSURANCE COMPANY |
| JAZZ PHARMACEUTICALS |
| JUPITERMEDIA CORP |
| KAMPGROUNDS OF AMERICA INC |
| KENDALL-JACKSON WINE ESTATES LTD |
| KIMLEY-HORN AND ASSOCIATES INC |
| KNIGHT CAPITAL GROUP INC |
| KNOT INC (THE) |
| KRONOS WORLDWIDE INC |
| KV PHARMACEUTICAL CO |

| |
|---|
| LACLEDE GROUP INC (THE) |
| LCA-VISION INC |
| LCC INTERNATIONAL INC |
| LEAP WIRELESS INTERNATIONAL INC |
| LESLIE'S POOLMART INC |
| LIFECELL CORPORATION |
| LIFECORE BIOMEDICAL INC |
| LIVEPERSON INC |
| LOGISTICARE INC |
| LOJACK CORP |
| LORAL SPACE & COMMUNICATIONS LTD |
| LUCASFILM LTD |
| LUCOR INC |
| LUMINEX CORPORATION |
| M&F WORLDWIDE CORP |
| MAGELLAN MIDSTREAM PARTNERS LP |
| MALT-O-MEAL COMPANY |
| MANHATTAN ASSOCIATES INC |
| MARCHEX INC |
| MARTEK BIOSCIENCES CORP |
| MARTHA STEWART LIVING OMNIMEDIA INC |
| MARVEL ENTERTAINMENT INC |
| MATRIA HEALTHCARE INC |
| MAXYGEN INC |
| MCMORAN EXPLORATION CO |
| MEDAREX INC |
| MEDICAL ACTION INDUSTRIES INC |
| MEDICINES CO (THE) |
| MEDICIS PHARMACEUTICAL CORP |
| MEDIS TECHNOLOGIES |
| MEDTOX SCIENTIFIC INC |
| MENTOR CORP |
| MERIDIAN BIOSCIENCE INC |
| MERIT MEDICAL SYSTEMS INC |
| METROLOGIC INSTRUMENTS INC |
| METROPCS COMMUNICATIONS INC |
| METROPOLITAN HEALTH NETWORKS |
| MICHELINAS INC |
| MICROSTRATEGY INC |
| MICROTEK MEDICAL HOLDINGS INC |
| MIDAS INC |
| MILLENNIUM PHARMACEUTICALS INC |
| MOELIS & COMPANY |
| MOLINA HEALTHCARE INC |
| MOTORCAR PARTS OF AMERICA INC |

| |
|---|
| MTS SYSTEMS |
| MYRIAD GENETICS INC |
| NANOMETRICS INC |
| NASDAQ OMX |
| NATIONAL BEVERAGE CORP |
| NATIONAL CINEMEDIA INC |
| NATIONAL DENTEX CORP |
| NATIONAL FUEL GAS CO |
| NATIONAL WINE & SPIRITS INC |
| NATUS MEDICAL |
| NAVISITE INC |
| NEKTAR THERAPEUTICS |
| NEOGEN CORPORATION |
| NETFLIX INC |
| NETGEAR INC |
| NETRATINGS INC |
| NETSCOUT SYSTEMS INC |
| NETSUITE INC |
| NEWFIELD EXPLORATION CO |
| NIC INC |
| NOBLE ENERGY INC |
| NORTHWESTERN CORPORATION |
| NOVAMED INC |
| NOVEN PHARMACEUTICALS |
| NTELOS HOLDING CORP |
| NUGGET MARKET |
| NUSTAR ENERGY LP |
| NUTRASWEET COMPANY (THE) |
| NYER MEDICAL GROUP INC |
| NYMEX HOLDINGS (NEW YORK MERCANTILE EXCHANGE) |
| ODYSSEY RE HOLDINGS CORP |
| OMNITURE INC |
| ONEOK PARTNERS LP |
| ONLINE RESOURCES CORP |
| OPENTV CORP |
| OPNEXT INC |
| OPTELECOM-NKF INC |
| ORMAT TECHNOLOGIES |
| OSCIENT PHARMACEUTICALS CORPORATION |
| PALM INC |
| PAR PHARMACEUTICAL COMPANIES INC |
| PC CONNECTION INC |
| PC MALL INC |
| PEAPOD LLC |
| PERFICIENT INC |
| PETMED EXPRESS INC |
| PETROLEUM DEVELOPMENT CORPORATION |

| |
|---|
| PHILADELPHIA CONSOLIDATED HOLDING CORP |
| PHOENIX COMPANIES (THE) |
| PIEDMONT NATURAL GAS COMPANY INC |
| PIONEER NATURAL RESOURCES COMPANY |
| PITNEY BOWES MAPINFO |
| PLAINS EXPLORATION AND PRODUCTION COMPANY |
| PLUG POWER INC |
| PMA CAPITAL CORPORATION |
| POLYCOM INC |
| POLYMEDICA CORPORATION |
| POLYPORE INTERNATIONAL INC |
| PREMIERE GLOBAL SERVICES INC |
| PRIMEENERGY CORPORATION |
| PROASSURANCE CORP |
| PROGRESS SOFTWARE CORP |
| PROTECTIVE LIFE CORP |
| QLOGIC CORP |
| QUALITY SYSTEMS INC |
| QUICKSILVER RESOURCES INC |
| QUIDEL CORP |
| RACKSPACE HOSTING INC |
| RADISYS CORP |
| RADNET INC |
| RADYNE CORPORATION |
| RANGE RESOURCES CORP |
| REALNETWORKS INC |
| RECYCLED ENERGY DEVELOPMENT |
| RED HAT INC |
| REDDY ICE HOLDINGS INC |
| REGENERON PHARMACEUTICALS INC |
| REINSURANCE GROUP OF AMERICA INC |
| REVOLUTION HEALTH GROUP LLC |
| RIGHTNOW TECHNOLOGIES INC |
| ROBERT W BAIRD & CO INC |
| RSA SECURITY INC |
| S1 CORPORATION |
| SACRAMENTO MUNICIPAL UTILITY DISTRICT |
| SALIX PHARMACEUTICALS |
| SAVVIS INC |
| SCANSOURCE INC |
| SCHICK TECHNOLOGIES INC |
| SCHIFF NUTRITION INTERNATIONAL INC |
| SCICLONE PHARMACEUTICALS |

| |
|---|
| SCIELE PHARMA INC |
| SCIOS INC |
| SCOULAR COMPANY (THE) |
| SEACHANGE INTERNATIONAL INC |
| SEATTLE GENETICS |
| SECURE COMPUTING CORP |
| SENTO |
| SEPRACOR INC |
| SEQUENOM INC |
| SERENA SOFTWARE INC |
| SHARED TECHNOLOGIES |
| SHENANDOAH TELECOMMUNICATIONS CO |
| SHUTTERFLY INC |
| SKILLSOFT PLC |
| SOLAR RESERVE |
| SOLFOCUS INC |
| SONIC INNOVATIONS INC |
| SONUS NETWORKS INC |
| SOUTHERN UNION COMPANY |
| SOUTHWESTERN ENERGY CO |
| SPAN AMERICA MEDICAL SYSTEMS INC |
| SPECTRALINK CORP |
| SPECTRANETICS CORP |
| SPIRE CORPORATION |
| SPORTSMAN'S GUIDE INC (THE) |
| SPROUTS FARMERS MARKET |
| SPSS INC |
| SRI/SURGICAL EXPRESS INC |
| SS&C TECHNOLOGIES INC |
| ST MARY LAND & EXPLORATION COMPANY |
| STAAR SURGICAL CO |
| STANDARD MICROSYSTEMS CORPORATION |
| STATE AUTO FINANCIAL CORP |
| STERLING AUTOBODY CENTERS |
| STEVEN MADDEN LTD |
| STIEFEL LABORATORIES INC |
| SUPER MICRO COMPUTER INC |
| SWIFT ENERGY CO |
| SYCAMORE NETWORKS INC |
| SYMMETRY MEDICAL INC |
| SYMYX TECHNOLOGIES |
| SYNAPTICS INC |
| SYNOVIS LIFE TECHNOLOGIES INC |
| TAMPA ELECTRIC COMPANY |
| TARGA RESOURCES PARTNERS LP |
| TDINDUSTRIES |
| TECHNE CORP |
| TELIRIS |
| TEPPCO PARTNERS LP |
| TERREMARK WORLDWIDE INC |
| THERAGENICS CORP |
| THIRD WAVE TECHNOLOGIES INC |
| THOMAS WEISEL PARTNERS GROUP INC |
| THORATEC CORPORATION |
| THQ INC |
| TIBCO SOFTWARE INC |
| TIVO INC |
| TOMOTHERAPY INC |
| TOOTSIE ROLL INDUSTRIES INC |
| TOPPS COMPANY INC (THE) |
| TRANSATLANTIC HOLDINGS INC |
| TRANSCEND SERVICES INC |
| TRAPEZE NETWORKS INC |
| TRIZETTO GROUP INC (THE) |
| TULLY'S COFFEE CORPORATION |
| UIL HOLDINGS CORPORATION |
| ULTIMATE SOFTWARE GROUP INC |
| UNDER ARMOUR INC |
| UNISOURCE ENERGY CORPORATION |
| UNITED ONLINE INC |
| UNITED THERAPEUTICS CORP |
| UNIVERSAL AMERICAN CORPORATION |
| UNIVERSAL HOSPITAL SERVICES INC |
| US PHYSICAL THERAPY INC |
| VALLEY NATIONAL GASES LLC |
| VALUECLICK INC |
| VASCO DATA SECURITY INTERNATIONAL INC |
| VENTANA MEDICAL SYSTEMS INC |
| VERAZ NETWORKS INC |
| VERIFONE HOLDINGS INC |
| VERTEX PHARMACEUTICALS INC |
| VIASAT INC |
| VIBRANT MEDIA INC |
| VIGNETTE CORP |
| VIROPHARMA INC |
| VISION SERVICE PLAN |
| VITAL SIGNS INC |
| VOLCOM INC |
| VSE CORP |
| WEBEX COMMUNICATIONS INC |
| WEBMD HEALTH CORP |
| WEBSENSE INC |
| WESTAR ENERGY |
| WGL HOLDINGS INC |
| WHITEWAVE FOODS COMPANY |
| WIND RIVER SYSTEMS INC |
| WRIGHT MEDICAL GROUP INC |
| XOMA LTD |
| XTO ENERGY INC |
| YOUNG'S MARKET COMPANY LLC |
| ZAPPOS.COM INC |
| ZIEBART INTERNATIONAL CORP |
| ZILA INC |
| ZOLL MEDICAL CORP |
| ZYMOGENETICS INC |

## Professionals

| Consulting |
|---|
| ALBANY MOLECULAR RESEARCH |
| AMERESCO |
| AMYLIN PHARMACEUTICALS INC |
| CELERA CORPORATION |
| COLLAGENEX PHARMACEUTICALS INC |
| CORPORATE EXECUTIVE BOARD COMPANY (THE) |
| DYAX CORP |
| ELOYALTY CORPORATION |
| ENCORIUM GROUP INC |
| ENGLOBAL CORP |
| EPAM SYSTEMS |
| EXELIXIS INC |
| FORRESTER RESEARCH INC |
| GENENCOR INTERNATIONAL INC |
| HACKETT GROUP (THE) |
| HEIDRICK & STRUGGLES INTERNATIONAL INC |
| HURON CONSULTING GROUP INC |
| INTELLIGROUP INC |
| JAZZ PHARMACEUTICALS |
| LCC INTERNATIONAL INC |
| MAXYGEN INC |
| OSCIENT PHARMACEUTICALS CORPORATION |
| PERFICIENT INC |
| SALIX PHARMACEUTICALS |
| SEATTLE GENETICS |
| SENTO |
| SPSS INC |
| SYMYX TECHNOLOGIES |

| Finance/Accounting |
|---|
| 24/7 REAL MEDIA INC |

| |
|---|
| AAMCO TRANSMISSIONS INC |
| ABAXIS INC |
| ACI WORLDWIDE INC |
| ACME PACKET INC |
| ACXIOM DIGITAL |
| AFFYMETRIX INC |
| AKAMAI TECHNOLOGIES INC |
| AKQA INC |
| ALASKA COMMUNICATIONS SYSTEMS GROUP |
| ALBANY MOLECULAR RESEARCH |
| ALEXION PHARMACEUTICALS INC |
| ALIEN TECHNOLOGY CORPORATION |
| ALIGN TECHNOLOGY INC |
| ALKERMES INC |
| ALLEGHANY CORP |
| ALLIANCE IMAGING INC |
| ALLSCRIPTS HEALTHCARE SOLUTIONS INC |
| ALPHARMA INC |
| ALTIRIS INC |
| ALZA CORP |
| AMAG PHARMACEUTICALS INC |
| AMCOL INTERNATIONAL CORP |
| AMERESCO |
| AMERICAN FIDELITY ASSURANCE COMPANY |
| AMERICAN ITALIAN PASTA COMPANY |
| AMERICAN MEDICAL SYSTEMS HOLDINGS INC |
| AMERICAN SCIENCE & ENGINEERING INC |
| AMERICAN SUPERCONDUCTOR CORP |
| AMERICAN TIRE DISTRIBUTORS |
| AMERICAN TOWER CORP |
| AMERICAN VANGUARD CORP |
| AMICAS INC |
| AMSURG CORP |
| AMTECH SYSTEMS INC |
| AMYLIN PHARMACEUTICALS INC |
| ANALOGIC CORP |
| ANAREN INC |
| ANIKA THERAPEUTICS INC |
| ANSYS INC |
| APP PHARMACEUTICALS INC |
| APPLIED SIGNAL TECHNOLOGY INC |
| ARDEN GROUP INC |
| ARIBA INC |
| ARIZONA CHEMICAL COMPANY |

| |
|---|
| AROTECH CORPORATION |
| ARRIS GROUP INC |
| ART TECHNOLOGY GROUP INC |
| ARUBA NETWORKS INC |
| ASPECT MEDICAL SYSTEMS INC |
| ASPEN TECHNOLOGY INC |
| ASSOCIATED WHOLESALE GROCERS INC |
| ATHENAHEALTH INC |
| ATHEROS COMMUNICATIONS INC |
| ATLANTIC CITY ELECTRIC COMPANY |
| ATMI INC |
| ATRION CORPORATION |
| ATS MEDICAL INC |
| AUDIBLE INC |
| AVANEX CORPORATION |
| AVI BIOPHARMA INC |
| AVIALL INC |
| AVISTA CORPORATION |
| BENTLEY PHARMACEUTICALS INC |
| BERRY PETROLEUM CO |
| BIO REFERENCE LABORATORIES INC |
| BIOMARIN PHARMACEUTICAL INC |
| BIOSCRIP INC |
| BIOSITE INC |
| BLACK HILLS CORP |
| BLACKBOARD INC |
| BLUE CARE NETWORK OF MICHIGAN |
| BLUE COAT SYSTEMS INC |
| BLUE NILE INC |
| BRIGHTSTAR CORPORATION |
| CALIBER HOLDINGS CORP |
| CALIPER LIFE SCIENCES |
| CAL-MAINE FOODS INC |
| CALPINE CORPORATION |
| CAMBREX CORP |
| CANDELA CORP |
| CANTEL MEDICAL CORP |
| CARACO PHARMACEUTICAL LABORATORIES |
| CARDTRONICS INC |
| CATALYST HEALTH SOLUTIONS INC |
| C-COR INC |
| CELERA CORPORATION |
| CELGENE CORP |
| CELL GENESYS INC |
| CELL THERAPEUTICS INC |
| CENTERPLATE |

| |
|---|
| CENTRAL VERMONT PUBLIC SERVICE CORPORATION |
| CEPHEID |
| CHANNELL COMMERCIAL CORP |
| CHATTEM INC |
| CHINDEX INTERNATIONAL INC |
| CHOICESTREAM INC |
| CHOLESTECH CORP |
| CHYRON CORP |
| CIENA CORP |
| CKX INC |
| CLEARWIRE CORP |
| CME GROUP |
| CNX GAS CORPORATION |
| COGNEX CORP |
| COHERENT INC |
| COINSTAR INC |
| COLLAGENEX PHARMACEUTICALS INC |
| COMDATA CORP |
| COMMERCE GROUP INC (THE) |
| COMTECH TELECOMMUNICATIONS CORP |
| CONCUR TECHNOLOGIES INC |
| CONTINUCARE CORP |
| CORPORATE EXECUTIVE BOARD COMPANY (THE) |
| COUPONS INC |
| CRITICAL CARE SYSTEMS |
| CROWN CASTLE INTERNATIONAL CORP |
| CRUM & FORSTER HOLDINGS INC |
| CRYOLIFE INC |
| CSG SYSTEMS INTERNATIONAL INC |
| CUBIST PHARMACEUTICALS INC |
| CURVES INTERNATIONAL INC |
| CV THERAPEUTICS INC |
| CYBERSOURCE CORP |
| DAKTRONICS INC |
| DANNON COMPANY INC (THE) |
| DARLING INTERNATIONAL INC |
| DATASCOPE CORP |
| DEI HOLDINGS INC |
| DELPHI FINANCIAL GROUP INC |
| DENBURY RESOURCES INC |
| DIALYSIS CORPORATION OF AMERICA |
| DIAMOND FOODS INC |
| DIGI INTERNATIONAL INC |
| DIGITAL RIVER INC |
| DJO INCORPORATED |

| |
|---|
| DOUBLECLICK INC |
| DPL INC |
| DREAMWORKS ANIMATION SKG INC |
| DRUGSTORE.COM INC |
| DSP GROUP INC |
| DYAX CORP |
| DYNACQ HEALTHCARE INC |
| DYNEGY INC |
| ECHELON CORP |
| ECLIPSYS CORPORATION |
| ECOLLEGE.COM |
| EHEALTH INC |
| ELECTRONICS FOR IMAGING INC |
| ELOYALTY CORPORATION |
| EMBARCADERO TECHNOLOGIES INC |
| EMCORE CORP |
| EMS TECHNOLOGIES INC |
| EMULEX CORP |
| ENCORE ACQUISITION CO |
| ENCORIUM GROUP INC |
| ENDO PHARMACEUTICALS HOLDINGS INC |
| ENERGY CONVERSION DEVICES INC |
| ENERNOC INC |
| ENGLOBAL CORP |
| EOG RESOURCES INC |
| EPAM SYSTEMS |
| EPIX PHARMACEUTICALS INC |
| EQUINIX INC |
| EQUITABLE RESOURCES INC |
| EURONET WORLDWIDE INC |
| EVERCORE PARTNERS INC |
| EVERGREEN ENERGY INC |
| EVERGREEN SOLAR INC |
| EXACTECH INC |
| EXCEL TECHNOLOGY INC |
| EXCO RESOURCES INC |
| EXELIXIS INC |
| E-Z-EM INC |
| F5 NETWORKS INC |
| FARMER BROTHERS CO |
| FBL FINANCIAL GROUP |
| FEDEX SUPPLY CHAIN SERVICES INC |
| FIRST SOLAR LLC |
| FLIR SYSTEMS |
| FOREST OIL CORPORATION |
| FORRESTER RESEARCH INC |

| |
|---|
| FRESH BRANDS INC |
| FRESHDIRECT LLC |
| FRONTIER OIL CORPORATION |
| FUEL TECH INC |
| FUELCELL ENERGY INC |
| FUNDTECH LTD |
| GALLUP ORGANIZATION (THE) |
| GENENCOR INTERNATIONAL INC |
| GENERAL COMMUNICATION INC (GCI) |
| GENESIS ENERGY LP |
| GENOMIC HEALTH INC |
| GEN-PROBE INC |
| GERBER SCIENTIFIC INC |
| GERON CORPORATION |
| GLOBAL PARTNERS LP |
| GLOBECOMM SYSTEMS INC |
| GLU MOBILE INC |
| GOAMERICA INC |
| GOLFSMITH INTERNATIONAL HOLDINGS INC |
| GREAT AMERICAN FINANCIAL RESOURCES INC |
| GREAT LAKES CHEESE COMPANY INC |
| GREEN MOUNTAIN COFFEE ROASTERS INC |
| GREEN MOUNTAIN POWER CORPORATION |
| GTC BIOTHERAPEUTICS INC |
| HACKETT GROUP (THE) |
| HAEMONETICS CORPORATION |
| HAHN AUTOMOTIVE WAREHOUSE INC |
| HANOVER FOODS CORPORATION |
| HANSEN NATURAL |
| HARMONIC INC |
| HARRIS STRATEX NETWORKS INC |
| HARVARD PILGRIM HEALTH CARE INC |
| HCC INSURANCE HOLDINGS INC |
| HEALTH GRADES INC |
| HEALTH INSURANCE PLAN OF GREATER NEW YORK |
| HEALTHSTREAM INC |
| HEALTHTRONICS INC |
| HEARTLAND PAYMENT SYSTEMS INC |
| HEARUSA INC |
| HEIDRICK & STRUGGLES INTERNATIONAL INC |
| HELIOVOLT CORP |
| HESKA CORP |

| |
|---|
| HICKORY TECH CORPORATION |
| HI-TECH PHARMACAL CO INC |
| HOLLY CORP |
| HORACE MANN EDUCATORS CORPORATION |
| HOULIHAN LOKEY |
| HUMAN GENOME SCIENCES INC |
| HURON CONSULTING GROUP INC |
| IBASIS INC |
| ICO INC |
| IDACORP INC |
| I-FLOW CORPORATION |
| ILLUMINA INC |
| IMATION CORP |
| IMG WORLDWIDE INC |
| IMMUCOR INC |
| INAMED CORP |
| INDEPENDENCE HOLDING CO |
| INFINERA CORP |
| INSPIRE PHARMACEUTICALS INC |
| INTEGRA LIFESCIENCES HOLDINGS CORP |
| INTEGRAL SYSTEMS INC |
| INTEGRAMED AMERICA INC |
| INTELLIGROUP INC |
| INTERACTIVE BROKERS GROUP INC |
| INTERACTIVE INTELLIGENCE |
| INTERCONTINENTALEXCHANGE INC (ICE) |
| INTERMEC INC |
| INTERNAP NETWORK SERVICES CORP |
| INTERNATIONAL CREATIVE MANAGEMENT (ICM) |
| INTERNATIONAL DAIRY QUEEN |
| INTERNET SECURITY SYSTEMS INC |
| INTERSTATE BATTERY SYSTEM OF AMERICA |
| INTERWOVEN INC |
| INVESTMENT TECHNOLOGY GROUP INC (ITG) |
| IRIDEX CORP |
| IRIS INTERNATIONAL INC |
| ISILON SYSTEMS INC |
| ISONICS CORPORATION |
| IVILLAGE INC |
| J2 GLOBAL COMMUNICATIONS INC |
| JACKSON NATIONAL LIFE INSURANCE COMPANY |
| JAZZ PHARMACEUTICALS |
| JUPITERMEDIA CORP |

KAMPGROUNDS OF AMERICA INC
KENDALL-JACKSON WINE ESTATES LTD
KIMLEY-HORN AND ASSOCIATES INC
KNIGHT CAPITAL GROUP INC
KNOT INC (THE)
KRONOS WORLDWIDE INC
KV PHARMACEUTICAL CO
LACLEDE GROUP INC (THE)
LCA-VISION INC
LCC INTERNATIONAL INC
LEAP WIRELESS INTERNATIONAL INC
LESLIE'S POOLMART INC
LIFECELL CORPORATION
LIFECORE BIOMEDICAL INC
LIVEPERSON INC
LOGISTICARE INC
LOJACK CORP
LORAL SPACE & COMMUNICATIONS LTD
LUCASFILM LTD
LUCOR INC
LUMINEX CORPORATION
M&F WORLDWIDE CORP
MAGELLAN MIDSTREAM PARTNERS LP
MALT-O-MEAL COMPANY
MANHATTAN ASSOCIATES INC
MARCHEX INC
MARTEK BIOSCIENCES CORP
MARTHA STEWART LIVING OMNIMEDIA INC
MARVEL ENTERTAINMENT INC
MATRIA HEALTHCARE INC
MAXYGEN INC
MCMORAN EXPLORATION CO
MEDAREX INC
MEDICAL ACTION INDUSTRIES INC
MEDICINES CO (THE)
MEDICIS PHARMACEUTICAL CORP
MEDIS TECHNOLOGIES
MEDTOX SCIENTIFIC INC
MENTOR CORP
MERIDIAN BIOSCIENCE INC
MERIT MEDICAL SYSTEMS INC
METROLOGIC INSTRUMENTS INC
METROPCS COMMUNICATIONS INC
METROPOLITAN HEALTH NETWORKS
MICHELINAS INC

MICROSTRATEGY INC
MICROTEK MEDICAL HOLDINGS INC
MIDAS INC
MILLENNIUM PHARMACEUTICALS INC
MOELIS & COMPANY
MOLINA HEALTHCARE INC
MOTORCAR PARTS OF AMERICA INC
MTS SYSTEMS
MYRIAD GENETICS INC
NANOMETRICS INC
NASDAQ OMX
NATIONAL BEVERAGE CORP
NATIONAL CINEMEDIA INC
NATIONAL DENTEX CORP
NATIONAL FUEL GAS CO
NATIONAL WINE & SPIRITS INC
NATUS MEDICAL
NAVISITE INC
NEKTAR THERAPEUTICS
NEOGEN CORPORATION
NETFLIX INC
NETGEAR INC
NETRATINGS INC
NETSCOUT SYSTEMS INC
NETSUITE INC
NEWFIELD EXPLORATION CO
NIC INC
NOBLE ENERGY INC
NORTHWESTERN CORPORATION
NOVAMED INC
NOVEN PHARMACEUTICALS
NTELOS HOLDING CORP
NUGGET MARKET
NUSTAR ENERGY LP
NUTRASWEET COMPANY (THE)
NYER MEDICAL GROUP INC
NYMEX HOLDINGS (NEW YORK MERCANTILE EXCHANGE)
ODYSSEY RE HOLDINGS CORP
OMNITURE INC
ONEOK PARTNERS LP
ONLINE RESOURCES CORP
OPENTV CORP
OPNEXT INC
OPTELECOM-NKF INC
ORMAT TECHNOLOGIES
OSCIENT PHARMACEUTICALS CORPORATION
PALM INC

PAR PHARMACEUTICAL COMPANIES INC
PC CONNECTION INC
PC MALL INC
PEAPOD LLC
PERFICIENT INC
PETMED EXPRESS INC
PETROLEUM DEVELOPMENT CORPORATION
PHILADELPHIA CONSOLIDATED HOLDING CORP
PHOENIX COMPANIES (THE)
PIEDMONT NATURAL GAS COMPANY INC
PIONEER NATURAL RESOURCES COMPANY
PITNEY BOWES MAPINFO
PLAINS EXPLORATION AND PRODUCTION COMPANY
PLUG POWER INC
PMA CAPITAL CORPORATION
POLYCOM INC
POLYMEDICA CORPORATION
POLYPORE INTERNATIONAL INC
PREMIERE GLOBAL SERVICES INC
PRIMEENERGY CORPORATION
PROASSURANCE CORP
PROGRESS SOFTWARE CORP
PROTECTIVE LIFE CORP
QLOGIC CORP
QUALITY SYSTEMS INC
QUICKSILVER RESOURCES INC
QUIDEL CORP
RACKSPACE HOSTING INC
RADISYS CORP
RADNET INC
RADYNE CORPORATION
RANGE RESOURCES CORP
REALNETWORKS INC
RECYCLED ENERGY DEVELOPMENT
RED HAT INC
REDDY ICE HOLDINGS INC
REGENERON PHARMACEUTICALS INC
REINSURANCE GROUP OF AMERICA INC
REVOLUTION HEALTH GROUP LLC
RIGHTNOW TECHNOLOGIES INC
ROBERT W BAIRD & CO INC
RSA SECURITY INC
S1 CORPORATION

| |
|---|
| SACRAMENTO MUNICIPAL UTILITY DISTRICT |
| SALIX PHARMACEUTICALS |
| SAVVIS INC |
| SCANSOURCE INC |
| SCHICK TECHNOLOGIES INC |
| SCHIFF NUTRITION INTERNATIONAL INC |
| SCICLONE PHARMACEUTICALS |
| SCIELE PHARMA INC |
| SCIOS INC |
| SCOULAR COMPANY (THE) |
| SEACHANGE INTERNATIONAL INC |
| SEATTLE GENETICS |
| SECURE COMPUTING CORP |
| SENTO |
| SEPRACOR INC |
| SEQUENOM INC |
| SERENA SOFTWARE INC |
| SHARED TECHNOLOGIES |
| SHENANDOAH TELECOMMUNICATIONS CO |
| SHUTTERFLY INC |
| SKILLSOFT PLC |
| SOLAR RESERVE |
| SOLFOCUS INC |
| SONIC INNOVATIONS INC |
| SONUS NETWORKS INC |
| SOUTHERN UNION COMPANY |
| SOUTHWESTERN ENERGY CO |
| SPAN AMERICA MEDICAL SYSTEMS INC |
| SPECTRALINK CORP |
| SPECTRANETICS CORP |
| SPIRE CORPORATION |
| SPORTSMAN'S GUIDE INC (THE) |
| SPROUTS FARMERS MARKET |
| SPSS INC |
| SRI/SURGICAL EXPRESS INC |
| SS&C TECHNOLOGIES INC |
| ST MARY LAND & EXPLORATION COMPANY |
| STAAR SURGICAL CO |
| STANDARD MICROSYSTEMS CORPORATION |
| STATE AUTO FINANCIAL CORP |
| STERLING AUTOBODY CENTERS |
| STEVEN MADDEN LTD |
| STIEFEL LABORATORIES INC |
| SUPER MICRO COMPUTER INC |
| SWIFT ENERGY CO |

| |
|---|
| SYCAMORE NETWORKS INC |
| SYMMETRY MEDICAL INC |
| SYMYX TECHNOLOGIES |
| SYNAPTICS INC |
| SYNOVIS LIFE TECHNOLOGIES INC |
| TAMPA ELECTRIC COMPANY |
| TARGA RESOURCES PARTNERS LP |
| TDINDUSTRIES |
| TECHNE CORP |
| TELIRIS |
| TEPPCO PARTNERS LP |
| TERREMARK WORLDWIDE INC |
| THERAGENICS CORP |
| THIRD WAVE TECHNOLOGIES INC |
| THOMAS WEISEL PARTNERS GROUP INC |
| THORATEC CORPORATION |
| THQ INC |
| TIBCO SOFTWARE INC |
| TIVO INC |
| TOMOTHERAPY INC |
| TOOTSIE ROLL INDUSTRIES INC |
| TOPPS COMPANY INC (THE) |
| TRANSATLANTIC HOLDINGS INC |
| TRANSCEND SERVICES INC |
| TRAPEZE NETWORKS INC |
| TRIZETTO GROUP INC (THE) |
| TULLY'S COFFEE CORPORATION |
| UIL HOLDINGS CORPORATION |
| ULTIMATE SOFTWARE GROUP INC |
| UNDER ARMOUR INC |
| UNISOURCE ENERGY CORPORATION |
| UNITED ONLINE INC |
| UNITED THERAPEUTICS CORP |
| UNIVERSAL AMERICAN CORPORATION |
| UNIVERSAL HOSPITAL SERVICES INC |
| US PHYSICAL THERAPY INC |
| VALLEY NATIONAL GASES LLC |
| VALUECLICK INC |
| VASCO DATA SECURITY INTERNATIONAL INC |
| VENTANA MEDICAL SYSTEMS INC |
| VERAZ NETWORKS INC |
| VERIFONE HOLDINGS INC |
| VERTEX PHARMACEUTICALS INC |
| VIASAT INC |
| VIBRANT MEDIA INC |
| VIGNETTE CORP |

| |
|---|
| VIROPHARMA INC |
| VISION SERVICE PLAN |
| VITAL SIGNS INC |
| VOLCOM INC |
| VSE CORP |
| WEBEX COMMUNICATIONS INC |
| WEBMD HEALTH CORP |
| WEBSENSE INC |
| WESTAR ENERGY |
| WGL HOLDINGS INC |
| WHITEWAVE FOODS COMPANY |
| WIND RIVER SYSTEMS INC |
| WRIGHT MEDICAL GROUP INC |
| XOMA LTD |
| XTO ENERGY INC |
| YOUNG'S MARKET COMPANY LLC |
| ZAPPOS.COM INC |
| ZIEBART INTERNATIONAL CORP |
| ZILA INC |
| ZOLL MEDICAL CORP |
| ZYMOGENETICS INC |

| **Health Care** |
|---|
| ABAXIS INC |
| AFFYMETRIX INC |
| ALBANY MOLECULAR RESEARCH |
| ALEXION PHARMACEUTICALS INC |
| ALIGN TECHNOLOGY INC |
| ALKERMES INC |
| ALLIANCE IMAGING INC |
| ALPHARMA INC |
| ALZA CORP |
| AMERICAN FIDELITY ASSURANCE COMPANY |
| AMERICAN MEDICAL SYSTEMS HOLDINGS INC |
| AMSURG CORP |
| AMYLIN PHARMACEUTICALS INC |
| ANALOGIC CORP |
| ANIKA THERAPEUTICS INC |
| APP PHARMACEUTICALS INC |
| ASPECT MEDICAL SYSTEMS INC |
| ATRION CORPORATION |
| ATS MEDICAL INC |
| AVI BIOPHARMA INC |
| BENTLEY PHARMACEUTICALS INC |
| BIO REFERENCE LABORATORIES INC |
| BIOMARIN PHARMACEUTICAL INC |
| BIOSCRIP INC |
| BIOSITE INC |

| |
|---|
| BLUE CARE NETWORK OF MICHIGAN |
| CALIPER LIFE SCIENCES |
| CAMBREX CORP |
| CANDELA CORP |
| CANTEL MEDICAL CORP |
| CARACO PHARMACEUTICAL LABORATORIES |
| CATALYST HEALTH SOLUTIONS INC |
| CELERA CORPORATION |
| CELGENE CORP |
| CELL GENESYS INC |
| CELL THERAPEUTICS INC |
| CEPHEID |
| CHATTEM INC |
| CHINDEX INTERNATIONAL INC |
| CHOLESTECH CORP |
| COHERENT INC |
| COLLAGENEX PHARMACEUTICALS INC |
| CONTINUCARE CORP |
| CRITICAL CARE SYSTEMS |
| CRYOLIFE INC |
| CUBIST PHARMACEUTICALS INC |
| CV THERAPEUTICS INC |
| DATASCOPE CORP |
| DELPHI FINANCIAL GROUP INC |
| DIALYSIS CORPORATION OF AMERICA |
| DJO INCORPORATED |
| DYAX CORP |
| DYNACQ HEALTHCARE INC |
| EHEALTH INC |
| ENDO PHARMACEUTICALS HOLDINGS INC |
| EPIX PHARMACEUTICALS INC |
| EXACTECH INC |
| EXCEL TECHNOLOGY INC |
| EXELIXIS INC |
| E-Z-EM INC |
| FBL FINANCIAL GROUP |
| FORRESTER RESEARCH INC |
| GALLUP ORGANIZATION (THE) |
| GENENCOR INTERNATIONAL INC |
| GENOMIC HEALTH INC |
| GEN-PROBE INC |
| GERON CORPORATION |
| GREAT AMERICAN FINANCIAL RESOURCES INC |
| GTC BIOTHERAPEUTICS INC |
| HAEMONETICS CORPORATION |
| HARVARD PILGRIM HEALTH CARE INC |
| HEALTH INSURANCE PLAN OF GREATER NEW YORK |
| HEALTHTRONICS INC |
| HEARUSA INC |
| HESKA CORP |
| HI-TECH PHARMACAL CO INC |
| HUMAN GENOME SCIENCES INC |
| I-FLOW CORPORATION |
| IMMUCOR INC |
| INAMED CORP |
| INDEPENDENCE HOLDING CO |
| INSPIRE PHARMACEUTICALS INC |
| INTEGRA LIFESCIENCES HOLDINGS CORP |
| INTEGRAMED AMERICA INC |
| IRIDEX CORP |
| IRIS INTERNATIONAL INC |
| JACKSON NATIONAL LIFE INSURANCE COMPANY |
| JAZZ PHARMACEUTICALS |
| KV PHARMACEUTICAL CO |
| LCA-VISION INC |
| LIFECELL CORPORATION |
| LIFECORE BIOMEDICAL INC |
| LUMINEX CORPORATION |
| MARTEK BIOSCIENCES CORP |
| MATRIA HEALTHCARE INC |
| MAXYGEN INC |
| MEDAREX INC |
| MEDICAL ACTION INDUSTRIES INC |
| MEDICINES CO (THE) |
| MEDICIS PHARMACEUTICAL CORP |
| MEDTOX SCIENTIFIC INC |
| MENTOR CORP |
| MERIDIAN BIOSCIENCE INC |
| MERIT MEDICAL SYSTEMS INC |
| METROPOLITAN HEALTH NETWORKS |
| MICROTEK MEDICAL HOLDINGS INC |
| MILLENNIUM PHARMACEUTICALS INC |
| MOLINA HEALTHCARE INC |
| MYRIAD GENETICS INC |
| NATIONAL DENTEX CORP |
| NATUS MEDICAL |
| NEKTAR THERAPEUTICS |
| NEOGEN CORPORATION |
| NOVAMED INC |
| NOVEN PHARMACEUTICALS |
| NYER MEDICAL GROUP INC |
| OSCIENT PHARMACEUTICALS CORPORATION |
| PAR PHARMACEUTICAL COMPANIES INC |
| PHOENIX COMPANIES (THE) |
| POLYMEDICA CORPORATION |
| PROTECTIVE LIFE CORP |
| QUIDEL CORP |
| RADNET INC |
| REGENERON PHARMACEUTICALS INC |
| SALIX PHARMACEUTICALS |
| SCHICK TECHNOLOGIES INC |
| SCHIFF NUTRITION INTERNATIONAL INC |
| SCICLONE PHARMACEUTICALS |
| SCIELE PHARMA INC |
| SCIOS INC |
| SEATTLE GENETICS |
| SEPRACOR INC |
| SEQUENOM INC |
| SONIC INNOVATIONS INC |
| SPAN AMERICA MEDICAL SYSTEMS INC |
| SPECTRANETICS CORP |
| SRI/SURGICAL EXPRESS INC |
| STAAR SURGICAL CO |
| STIEFEL LABORATORIES INC |
| SYMMETRY MEDICAL INC |
| SYNOVIS LIFE TECHNOLOGIES INC |
| TECHNE CORP |
| THERAGENICS CORP |
| THIRD WAVE TECHNOLOGIES INC |
| THORATEC CORPORATION |
| TOMOTHERAPY INC |
| UNITED THERAPEUTICS CORP |
| UNIVERSAL AMERICAN CORPORATION |
| UNIVERSAL HOSPITAL SERVICES INC |
| US PHYSICAL THERAPY INC |
| VENTANA MEDICAL SYSTEMS INC |
| VERTEX PHARMACEUTICALS INC |
| VIROPHARMA INC |
| VISION SERVICE PLAN |
| VITAL SIGNS INC |
| WRIGHT MEDICAL GROUP INC |
| XOMA LTD |
| ZILA INC |
| ZOLL MEDICAL CORP |
| ZYMOGENETICS INC |

| Human Resources/Other |
|---|
| 24/7 REAL MEDIA INC |
| AAMCO TRANSMISSIONS INC |
| ABAXIS INC |
| ACI WORLDWIDE INC |
| ACME PACKET INC |
| ACXIOM DIGITAL |
| AFFYMETRIX INC |
| AKAMAI TECHNOLOGIES INC |
| AKQA INC |
| ALASKA COMMUNICATIONS SYSTEMS GROUP |
| ALBANY MOLECULAR RESEARCH |
| ALEXION PHARMACEUTICALS INC |
| ALIEN TECHNOLOGY CORPORATION |
| ALIGN TECHNOLOGY INC |
| ALKERMES INC |
| ALLEGHANY CORP |
| ALLIANCE IMAGING INC |
| ALLSCRIPTS HEALTHCARE SOLUTIONS INC |
| ALPHARMA INC |
| ALTIRIS INC |
| ALZA CORP |
| AMAG PHARMACEUTICALS INC |
| AMCOL INTERNATIONAL CORP |
| AMERESCO |
| AMERICAN FIDELITY ASSURANCE COMPANY |
| AMERICAN ITALIAN PASTA COMPANY |
| AMERICAN MEDICAL SYSTEMS HOLDINGS INC |
| AMERICAN SCIENCE & ENGINEERING INC |
| AMERICAN SUPERCONDUCTOR CORP |
| AMERICAN TIRE DISTRIBUTORS |
| AMERICAN TOWER CORP |
| AMERICAN VANGUARD CORP |
| AMICAS INC |
| AMSURG CORP |
| AMTECH SYSTEMS INC |
| AMYLIN PHARMACEUTICALS INC |
| ANALOGIC CORP |
| ANAREN INC |
| ANIKA THERAPEUTICS INC |
| ANSYS INC |
| APP PHARMACEUTICALS INC |
| APPLIED SIGNAL TECHNOLOGY INC |
| ARDEN GROUP INC |
| ARIBA INC |
| ARIZONA CHEMICAL COMPANY |
| AROTECH CORPORATION |
| ARRIS GROUP INC |
| ART TECHNOLOGY GROUP INC |
| ARUBA NETWORKS INC |
| ASPECT MEDICAL SYSTEMS INC |
| ASPEN TECHNOLOGY INC |
| ASSOCIATED WHOLESALE GROCERS INC |
| ATHENAHEALTH INC |
| ATHEROS COMMUNICATIONS INC |
| ATLANTIC CITY ELECTRIC COMPANY |
| ATMI INC |
| ATRION CORPORATION |
| ATS MEDICAL INC |
| AUDIBLE INC |
| AVANEX CORPORATION |
| AVI BIOPHARMA INC |
| AVIALL INC |
| AVISTA CORPORATION |
| BENTLEY PHARMACEUTICALS INC |
| BERRY PETROLEUM CO |
| BIO REFERENCE LABORATORIES INC |
| BIOMARIN PHARMACEUTICAL INC |
| BIOSCRIP INC |
| BIOSITE INC |
| BLACK HILLS CORP |
| BLACKBOARD INC |
| BLUE CARE NETWORK OF MICHIGAN |
| BLUE COAT SYSTEMS INC |
| BLUE NILE INC |
| BRIGHTSTAR CORPORATION |
| CALIBER HOLDINGS CORP |
| CALIPER LIFE SCIENCES |
| CAL-MAINE FOODS INC |
| CALPINE CORPORATION |
| CAMBREX CORP |
| CANDELA CORP |
| CANTEL MEDICAL CORP |
| CARACO PHARMACEUTICAL LABORATORIES |
| CARDTRONICS INC |
| CATALYST HEALTH SOLUTIONS INC |
| C-COR INC |
| CELERA CORPORATION |
| CELGENE CORP |
| CELL GENESYS INC |
| CELL THERAPEUTICS INC |
| CENTERPLATE |
| CENTRAL VERMONT PUBLIC SERVICE CORPORATION |
| CEPHEID |
| CHANNELL COMMERCIAL CORP |
| CHATTEM INC |
| CHINDEX INTERNATIONAL INC |
| CHOICESTREAM INC |
| CHOLESTECH CORP |
| CHYRON CORP |
| CIENA CORP |
| CKX INC |
| CLEARWIRE CORP |
| CME GROUP |
| CNX GAS CORPORATION |
| COGNEX CORP |
| COHERENT INC |
| COINSTAR INC |
| COLLAGENEX PHARMACEUTICALS INC |
| COMDATA CORP |
| COMMERCE GROUP INC (THE) |
| COMTECH TELECOMMUNICATIONS CORP |
| CONCUR TECHNOLOGIES INC |
| CONTINUCARE CORP |
| CORPORATE EXECUTIVE BOARD COMPANY (THE) |
| COUPONS INC |
| CRITICAL CARE SYSTEMS |
| CROWN CASTLE INTERNATIONAL CORP |
| CRUM & FORSTER HOLDINGS INC |
| CRYOLIFE INC |
| CSG SYSTEMS INTERNATIONAL INC |
| CUBIST PHARMACEUTICALS INC |
| CURVES INTERNATIONAL INC |
| CV THERAPEUTICS INC |
| CYBERSOURCE CORP |
| DAKTRONICS INC |
| DANNON COMPANY INC (THE) |
| DARLING INTERNATIONAL INC |
| DATASCOPE CORP |
| DEI HOLDINGS INC |
| DELPHI FINANCIAL GROUP INC |
| DENBURY RESOURCES INC |
| DIALYSIS CORPORATION OF AMERICA |
| DIAMOND FOODS INC |
| DIGI INTERNATIONAL INC |

| |
|---|
| DIGITAL RIVER INC |
| DJO INCORPORATED |
| DOUBLECLICK INC |
| DPL INC |
| DREAMWORKS ANIMATION SKG INC |
| DRUGSTORE.COM INC |
| DSP GROUP INC |
| DYAX CORP |
| DYNACQ HEALTHCARE INC |
| DYNEGY INC |
| ECHELON CORP |
| ECLIPSYS CORPORATION |
| ECOLLEGE.COM |
| EHEALTH INC |
| ELECTRONICS FOR IMAGING INC |
| ELOYALTY CORPORATION |
| EMBARCADERO TECHNOLOGIES INC |
| EMCORE CORP |
| EMS TECHNOLOGIES INC |
| EMULEX CORP |
| ENCORE ACQUISITION CO |
| ENCORIUM GROUP INC |
| ENDO PHARMACEUTICALS HOLDINGS INC |
| ENERGY CONVERSION DEVICES INC |
| ENERNOC INC |
| ENGLOBAL CORP |
| EOG RESOURCES INC |
| EPAM SYSTEMS |
| EPIX PHARMACEUTICALS INC |
| EQUINIX INC |
| EQUITABLE RESOURCES INC |
| EURONET WORLDWIDE INC |
| EVERCORE PARTNERS INC |
| EVERGREEN ENERGY INC |
| EVERGREEN SOLAR INC |
| EXACTECH INC |
| EXCEL TECHNOLOGY INC |
| EXCO RESOURCES INC |
| EXELIXIS INC |
| E-Z-EM INC |
| F5 NETWORKS INC |
| FARMER BROTHERS CO |
| FBL FINANCIAL GROUP |
| FEDEX SUPPLY CHAIN SERVICES INC |
| FIRST SOLAR LLC |
| FLIR SYSTEMS |

| |
|---|
| FOREST OIL CORPORATION |
| FORRESTER RESEARCH INC |
| FRESH BRANDS INC |
| FRESHDIRECT LLC |
| FRONTIER OIL CORPORATION |
| FUEL TECH INC |
| FUELCELL ENERGY INC |
| FUNDTECH LTD |
| GALLUP ORGANIZATION (THE) |
| GENENCOR INTERNATIONAL INC |
| GENERAL COMMUNICATION INC (GCI) |
| GENESIS ENERGY LP |
| GENOMIC HEALTH INC |
| GEN-PROBE INC |
| GERBER SCIENTIFIC INC |
| GERON CORPORATION |
| GLOBAL PARTNERS LP |
| GLOBECOMM SYSTEMS INC |
| GLU MOBILE INC |
| GOAMERICA INC |
| GOLFSMITH INTERNATIONAL HOLDINGS INC |
| GREAT AMERICAN FINANCIAL RESOURCES INC |
| GREAT LAKES CHEESE COMPANY INC |
| GREEN MOUNTAIN COFFEE ROASTERS INC |
| GREEN MOUNTAIN POWER CORPORATION |
| GTC BIOTHERAPEUTICS INC |
| HACKETT GROUP (THE) |
| HAEMONETICS CORPORATION |
| HAHN AUTOMOTIVE WAREHOUSE INC |
| HANOVER FOODS CORPORATION |
| HANSEN NATURAL |
| HARMONIC INC |
| HARRIS STRATEX NETWORKS INC |
| HARVARD PILGRIM HEALTH CARE INC |
| HCC INSURANCE HOLDINGS INC |
| HEALTH GRADES INC |
| HEALTH INSURANCE PLAN OF GREATER NEW YORK |
| HEALTHSTREAM INC |
| HEALTHTRONICS INC |
| HEARTLAND PAYMENT SYSTEMS INC |
| HEARUSA INC |
| HEIDRICK & STRUGGLES INTERNATIONAL INC |

| |
|---|
| HELIOVOLT CORP |
| HESKA CORP |
| HICKORY TECH CORPORATION |
| HI-TECH PHARMACAL CO INC |
| HOLLY CORP |
| HORACE MANN EDUCATORS CORPORATION |
| HOULIHAN LOKEY |
| HUMAN GENOME SCIENCES INC |
| HURON CONSULTING GROUP INC |
| IBASIS INC |
| ICO INC |
| IDACORP INC |
| I-FLOW CORPORATION |
| ILLUMINA INC |
| IMATION CORP |
| IMG WORLDWIDE INC |
| IMMUCOR INC |
| INAMED CORP |
| INDEPENDENCE HOLDING CO |
| INFINERA CORP |
| INSPIRE PHARMACEUTICALS INC |
| INTEGRA LIFESCIENCES HOLDINGS CORP |
| INTEGRAL SYSTEMS INC |
| INTEGRAMED AMERICA INC |
| INTELLIGROUP INC |
| INTERACTIVE BROKERS GROUP INC |
| INTERACTIVE INTELLIGENCE |
| INTERCONTINENTALEXCHANGE INC (ICE) |
| INTERMEC INC |
| INTERNAP NETWORK SERVICES CORP |
| INTERNATIONAL CREATIVE MANAGEMENT (ICM) |
| INTERNATIONAL DAIRY QUEEN |
| INTERNET SECURITY SYSTEMS INC |
| INTERSTATE BATTERY SYSTEM OF AMERICA |
| INTERWOVEN INC |
| INVESTMENT TECHNOLOGY GROUP INC (ITG) |
| IRIDEX CORP |
| IRIS INTERNATIONAL INC |
| ISILON SYSTEMS INC |
| ISONICS CORPORATION |
| IVILLAGE INC |
| J2 GLOBAL COMMUNICATIONS INC |
| JACKSON NATIONAL LIFE INSURANCE COMPANY |

- JAZZ PHARMACEUTICALS
- JUPITERMEDIA CORP
- KAMPGROUNDS OF AMERICA INC
- KENDALL-JACKSON WINE ESTATES LTD
- KIMLEY-HORN AND ASSOCIATES INC
- KNIGHT CAPITAL GROUP INC
- KNOT INC (THE)
- KRONOS WORLDWIDE INC
- KV PHARMACEUTICAL CO
- LACLEDE GROUP INC (THE)
- LCA-VISION INC
- LCC INTERNATIONAL INC
- LEAP WIRELESS INTERNATIONAL INC
- LESLIE'S POOLMART INC
- LIFECELL CORPORATION
- LIFECORE BIOMEDICAL INC
- LIVEPERSON INC
- LOGISTICARE INC
- LOJACK CORP
- LORAL SPACE & COMMUNICATIONS LTD
- LUCASFILM LTD
- LUCOR INC
- LUMINEX CORPORATION
- M&F WORLDWIDE CORP
- MAGELLAN MIDSTREAM PARTNERS LP
- MALT-O-MEAL COMPANY
- MANHATTAN ASSOCIATES INC
- MARCHEX INC
- MARTEK BIOSCIENCES CORP
- MARTHA STEWART LIVING OMNIMEDIA INC
- MARVEL ENTERTAINMENT INC
- MATRIA HEALTHCARE INC
- MAXYGEN INC
- MCMORAN EXPLORATION CO
- MEDAREX INC
- MEDICAL ACTION INDUSTRIES INC
- MEDICINES CO (THE)
- MEDICIS PHARMACEUTICAL CORP
- MEDIS TECHNOLOGIES
- MEDTOX SCIENTIFIC INC
- MENTOR CORP
- MERIDIAN BIOSCIENCE INC
- MERIT MEDICAL SYSTEMS INC
- METROLOGIC INSTRUMENTS INC
- METROPCS COMMUNICATIONS INC
- METROPOLITAN HEALTH NETWORKS
- MICHELINAS INC
- MICROSTRATEGY INC
- MICROTEK MEDICAL HOLDINGS INC
- MIDAS INC
- MILLENNIUM PHARMACEUTICALS INC
- MOELIS & COMPANY
- MOLINA HEALTHCARE INC
- MOTORCAR PARTS OF AMERICA INC
- MTS SYSTEMS
- MYRIAD GENETICS INC
- NANOMETRICS INC
- NASDAQ OMX
- NATIONAL BEVERAGE CORP
- NATIONAL CINEMEDIA INC
- NATIONAL DENTEX CORP
- NATIONAL FUEL GAS CO
- NATIONAL WINE & SPIRITS INC
- NATUS MEDICAL
- NAVISITE INC
- NEKTAR THERAPEUTICS
- NEOGEN CORPORATION
- NETFLIX INC
- NETGEAR INC
- NETRATINGS INC
- NETSCOUT SYSTEMS INC
- NETSUITE INC
- NEWFIELD EXPLORATION CO
- NIC INC
- NOBLE ENERGY INC
- NORTHWESTERN CORPORATION
- NOVAMED INC
- NOVEN PHARMACEUTICALS
- NTELOS HOLDING CORP
- NUGGET MARKET
- NUSTAR ENERGY LP
- NUTRASWEET COMPANY (THE)
- NYER MEDICAL GROUP INC
- NYMEX HOLDINGS (NEW YORK MERCANTILE EXCHANGE)
- ODYSSEY RE HOLDINGS CORP
- OMNITURE INC
- ONEOK PARTNERS LP
- ONLINE RESOURCES CORP
- OPENTV CORP
- OPNEXT INC
- OPTELECOM-NKF INC
- ORMAT TECHNOLOGIES
- OSCIENT PHARMACEUTICALS CORPORATION
- PALM INC
- PAR PHARMACEUTICAL COMPANIES INC
- PC CONNECTION INC
- PC MALL INC
- PEAPOD LLC
- PERFICIENT INC
- PETMED EXPRESS INC
- PETROLEUM DEVELOPMENT CORPORATION
- PHILADELPHIA CONSOLIDATED HOLDING CORP
- PHOENIX COMPANIES (THE)
- PIEDMONT NATURAL GAS COMPANY INC
- PIONEER NATURAL RESOURCES COMPANY
- PITNEY BOWES MAPINFO
- PLAINS EXPLORATION AND PRODUCTION COMPANY
- PLUG POWER INC
- PMA CAPITAL CORPORATION
- POLYCOM INC
- POLYMEDICA CORPORATION
- POLYPORE INTERNATIONAL INC
- PREMIERE GLOBAL SERVICES INC
- PRIMEENERGY CORPORATION
- PROASSURANCE CORP
- PROGRESS SOFTWARE CORP
- PROTECTIVE LIFE CORP
- QLOGIC CORP
- QUALITY SYSTEMS INC
- QUICKSILVER RESOURCES INC
- QUIDEL CORP
- RACKSPACE HOSTING INC
- RADISYS CORP
- RADNET INC
- RADYNE CORPORATION
- RANGE RESOURCES CORP
- REALNETWORKS INC
- RECYCLED ENERGY DEVELOPMENT
- RED HAT INC
- REDDY ICE HOLDINGS INC
- REGENERON PHARMACEUTICALS INC
- REINSURANCE GROUP OF AMERICA INC
- REVOLUTION HEALTH GROUP LLC
- RIGHTNOW TECHNOLOGIES INC

| |
|---|
| ROBERT W BAIRD & CO INC |
| RSA SECURITY INC |
| S1 CORPORATION |
| SACRAMENTO MUNICIPAL UTILITY DISTRICT |
| SALIX PHARMACEUTICALS |
| SAVVIS INC |
| SCANSOURCE INC |
| SCHICK TECHNOLOGIES INC |
| SCHIFF NUTRITION INTERNATIONAL INC |
| SCICLONE PHARMACEUTICALS |
| SCIELE PHARMA INC |
| SCIOS INC |
| SCOULAR COMPANY (THE) |
| SEACHANGE INTERNATIONAL INC |
| SEATTLE GENETICS |
| SECURE COMPUTING CORP |
| SENTO |
| SEPRACOR INC |
| SEQUENOM INC |
| SERENA SOFTWARE INC |
| SHARED TECHNOLOGIES |
| SHENANDOAH TELECOMMUNICATIONS CO |
| SHUTTERFLY INC |
| SKILLSOFT PLC |
| SOLAR RESERVE |
| SOLFOCUS INC |
| SONIC INNOVATIONS INC |
| SONUS NETWORKS INC |
| SOUTHERN UNION COMPANY |
| SOUTHWESTERN ENERGY CO |
| SPAN AMERICA MEDICAL SYSTEMS INC |
| SPECTRALINK CORP |
| SPECTRANETICS CORP |
| SPIRE CORPORATION |
| SPORTSMAN'S GUIDE INC (THE) |
| SPROUTS FARMERS MARKET |
| SPSS INC |
| SRI/SURGICAL EXPRESS INC |
| SS&C TECHNOLOGIES INC |
| ST MARY LAND & EXPLORATION COMPANY |
| STAAR SURGICAL CO |
| STANDARD MICROSYSTEMS CORPORATION |
| STATE AUTO FINANCIAL CORP |
| STERLING AUTOBODY CENTERS |
| STEVEN MADDEN LTD |

| |
|---|
| STIEFEL LABORATORIES INC |
| SUPER MICRO COMPUTER INC |
| SWIFT ENERGY CO |
| SYCAMORE NETWORKS INC |
| SYMMETRY MEDICAL INC |
| SYMYX TECHNOLOGIES |
| SYNAPTICS INC |
| SYNOVIS LIFE TECHNOLOGIES INC |
| TAMPA ELECTRIC COMPANY |
| TARGA RESOURCES PARTNERS LP |
| TDINDUSTRIES |
| TECHNE CORP |
| TELIRIS |
| TEPPCO PARTNERS LP |
| TERREMARK WORLDWIDE INC |
| THERAGENICS CORP |
| THIRD WAVE TECHNOLOGIES INC |
| THOMAS WEISEL PARTNERS GROUP INC |
| THORATEC CORPORATION |
| THQ INC |
| TIBCO SOFTWARE INC |
| TIVO INC |
| TOMOTHERAPY INC |
| TOOTSIE ROLL INDUSTRIES INC |
| TOPPS COMPANY INC (THE) |
| TRANSATLANTIC HOLDINGS INC |
| TRANSCEND SERVICES INC |
| TRAPEZE NETWORKS INC |
| TRIZETTO GROUP INC (THE) |
| TULLY'S COFFEE CORPORATION |
| UIL HOLDINGS CORPORATION |
| ULTIMATE SOFTWARE GROUP INC |
| UNDER ARMOUR INC |
| UNISOURCE ENERGY CORPORATION |
| UNITED ONLINE INC |
| UNITED THERAPEUTICS CORP |
| UNIVERSAL AMERICAN CORPORATION |
| UNIVERSAL HOSPITAL SERVICES INC |
| US PHYSICAL THERAPY INC |
| VALLEY NATIONAL GASES LLC |
| VALUECLICK INC |
| VASCO DATA SECURITY INTERNATIONAL INC |
| VENTANA MEDICAL SYSTEMS INC |
| VERAZ NETWORKS INC |
| VERIFONE HOLDINGS INC |
| VERTEX PHARMACEUTICALS INC |

| |
|---|
| VIASAT INC |
| VIBRANT MEDIA INC |
| VIGNETTE CORP |
| VIROPHARMA INC |
| VISION SERVICE PLAN |
| VITAL SIGNS INC |
| VOLCOM INC |
| VSE CORP |
| WEBEX COMMUNICATIONS INC |
| WEBMD HEALTH CORP |
| WEBSENSE INC |
| WESTAR ENERGY |
| WGL HOLDINGS INC |
| WHITEWAVE FOODS COMPANY |
| WIND RIVER SYSTEMS INC |
| WRIGHT MEDICAL GROUP INC |
| XOMA LTD |
| XTO ENERGY INC |
| YOUNG'S MARKET COMPANY LLC |
| ZAPPOS.COM INC |
| ZIEBART INTERNATIONAL CORP |
| ZILA INC |
| ZOLL MEDICAL CORP |
| ZYMOGENETICS INC |

| Law |
|---|
| 24/7 REAL MEDIA INC |
| AAMCO TRANSMISSIONS INC |
| ABAXIS INC |
| ACI WORLDWIDE INC |
| ACME PACKET INC |
| ACXIOM DIGITAL |
| AFFYMETRIX INC |
| AKAMAI TECHNOLOGIES INC |
| AKQA INC |
| ALASKA COMMUNICATIONS SYSTEMS GROUP |
| ALBANY MOLECULAR RESEARCH |
| ALEXION PHARMACEUTICALS INC |
| ALIEN TECHNOLOGY CORPORATION |
| ALIGN TECHNOLOGY INC |
| ALKERMES INC |
| ALLEGHANY CORP |
| ALLIANCE IMAGING INC |
| ALLSCRIPTS HEALTHCARE SOLUTIONS INC |
| ALPHARMA INC |
| ALTIRIS INC |
| ALZA CORP |
| AMAG PHARMACEUTICALS INC |

| |
|---|
| AMCOL INTERNATIONAL CORP |
| AMERESCO |
| AMERICAN FIDELITY ASSURANCE COMPANY |
| AMERICAN ITALIAN PASTA COMPANY |
| AMERICAN MEDICAL SYSTEMS HOLDINGS INC |
| AMERICAN SCIENCE & ENGINEERING INC |
| AMERICAN SUPERCONDUCTOR CORP |
| AMERICAN TIRE DISTRIBUTORS |
| AMERICAN TOWER CORP |
| AMERICAN VANGUARD CORP |
| AMICAS INC |
| AMSURG CORP |
| AMTECH SYSTEMS INC |
| AMYLIN PHARMACEUTICALS INC |
| ANALOGIC CORP |
| ANAREN INC |
| ANIKA THERAPEUTICS INC |
| ANSYS INC |
| APP PHARMACEUTICALS INC |
| APPLIED SIGNAL TECHNOLOGY INC |
| ARDEN GROUP INC |
| ARIBA INC |
| ARIZONA CHEMICAL COMPANY |
| AROTECH CORPORATION |
| ARRIS GROUP INC |
| ART TECHNOLOGY GROUP INC |
| ARUBA NETWORKS INC |
| ASPECT MEDICAL SYSTEMS INC |
| ASPEN TECHNOLOGY INC |
| ASSOCIATED WHOLESALE GROCERS INC |
| ATHENAHEALTH INC |
| ATHEROS COMMUNICATIONS INC |
| ATLANTIC CITY ELECTRIC COMPANY |
| ATMI INC |
| ATRION CORPORATION |
| ATS MEDICAL INC |
| AUDIBLE INC |
| AVANEX CORPORATION |
| AVI BIOPHARMA INC |
| AVIALL INC |
| AVISTA CORPORATION |
| BENTLEY PHARMACEUTICALS INC |
| BERRY PETROLEUM CO |
| BIO REFERENCE LABORATORIES INC |

| |
|---|
| BIOMARIN PHARMACEUTICAL INC |
| BIOSCRIP INC |
| BIOSITE INC |
| BLACK HILLS CORP |
| BLACKBOARD INC |
| BLUE CARE NETWORK OF MICHIGAN |
| BLUE COAT SYSTEMS INC |
| BLUE NILE INC |
| BRIGHTSTAR CORPORATION |
| CALIBER HOLDINGS CORP |
| CALIPER LIFE SCIENCES |
| CAL-MAINE FOODS INC |
| CALPINE CORPORATION |
| CAMBREX CORP |
| CANDELA CORP |
| CANTEL MEDICAL CORP |
| CARACO PHARMACEUTICAL LABORATORIES |
| CARDTRONICS INC |
| CATALYST HEALTH SOLUTIONS INC |
| C-COR INC |
| CELERA CORPORATION |
| CELGENE CORP |
| CELL GENESYS INC |
| CELL THERAPEUTICS INC |
| CENTERPLATE |
| CENTRAL VERMONT PUBLIC SERVICE CORPORATION |
| CEPHEID |
| CHANNELL COMMERCIAL CORP |
| CHATTEM INC |
| CHINDEX INTERNATIONAL INC |
| CHOICESTREAM INC |
| CHOLESTECH CORP |
| CHYRON CORP |
| CIENA CORP |
| CKX INC |
| CLEARWIRE CORP |
| CME GROUP |
| CNX GAS CORPORATION |
| COGNEX CORP |
| COHERENT INC |
| COINSTAR INC |
| COLLAGENEX PHARMACEUTICALS INC |
| COMDATA CORP |
| COMMERCE GROUP INC (THE) |
| COMTECH TELECOMMUNICATIONS CORP |
| CONCUR TECHNOLOGIES INC |

| |
|---|
| CONTINUCARE CORP |
| CORPORATE EXECUTIVE BOARD COMPANY (THE) |
| COUPONS INC |
| CRITICAL CARE SYSTEMS |
| CROWN CASTLE INTERNATIONAL CORP |
| CRUM & FORSTER HOLDINGS INC |
| CRYOLIFE INC |
| CSG SYSTEMS INTERNATIONAL INC |
| CUBIST PHARMACEUTICALS INC |
| CURVES INTERNATIONAL INC |
| CV THERAPEUTICS INC |
| CYBERSOURCE CORP |
| DAKTRONICS INC |
| DANNON COMPANY INC (THE) |
| DARLING INTERNATIONAL INC |
| DATASCOPE CORP |
| DEI HOLDINGS INC |
| DELPHI FINANCIAL GROUP INC |
| DENBURY RESOURCES INC |
| DIALYSIS CORPORATION OF AMERICA |
| DIAMOND FOODS INC |
| DIGI INTERNATIONAL INC |
| DIGITAL RIVER INC |
| DJO INCORPORATED |
| DOUBLECLICK INC |
| DPL INC |
| DREAMWORKS ANIMATION SKG INC |
| DRUGSTORE.COM INC |
| DSP GROUP INC |
| DYAX CORP |
| DYNACQ HEALTHCARE INC |
| DYNEGY INC |
| ECHELON CORP |
| ECLIPSYS CORPORATION |
| ECOLLEGE.COM |
| EHEALTH INC |
| ELECTRONICS FOR IMAGING INC |
| ELOYALTY CORPORATION |
| EMBARCADERO TECHNOLOGIES INC |
| EMCORE CORP |
| EMS TECHNOLOGIES INC |
| EMULEX CORP |
| ENCORE ACQUISITION CO |
| ENCORIUM GROUP INC |
| ENDO PHARMACEUTICALS HOLDINGS INC |

| |
|---|
| ENERGY CONVERSION DEVICES INC |
| ENERNOC INC |
| ENGLOBAL CORP |
| EOG RESOURCES INC |
| EPAM SYSTEMS |
| EPIX PHARMACEUTICALS INC |
| EQUINIX INC |
| EQUITABLE RESOURCES INC |
| EURONET WORLDWIDE INC |
| EVERCORE PARTNERS INC |
| EVERGREEN ENERGY INC |
| EVERGREEN SOLAR INC |
| EXACTECH INC |
| EXCEL TECHNOLOGY INC |
| EXCO RESOURCES INC |
| EXELIXIS INC |
| E-Z-EM INC |
| F5 NETWORKS INC |
| FARMER BROTHERS CO |
| FBL FINANCIAL GROUP |
| FEDEX SUPPLY CHAIN SERVICES INC |
| FIRST SOLAR LLC |
| FLIR SYSTEMS |
| FOREST OIL CORPORATION |
| FORRESTER RESEARCH INC |
| FRESH BRANDS INC |
| FRESHDIRECT LLC |
| FRONTIER OIL CORPORATION |
| FUEL TECH INC |
| FUELCELL ENERGY INC |
| FUNDTECH LTD |
| GALLUP ORGANIZATION (THE) |
| GENENCOR INTERNATIONAL INC |
| GENERAL COMMUNICATION INC (GCI) |
| GENESIS ENERGY LP |
| GENOMIC HEALTH INC |
| GEN-PROBE INC |
| GERBER SCIENTIFIC INC |
| GERON CORPORATION |
| GLOBAL PARTNERS LP |
| GLOBECOMM SYSTEMS INC |
| GLU MOBILE INC |
| GOAMERICA INC |
| GOLFSMITH INTERNATIONAL HOLDINGS INC |
| GREAT AMERICAN FINANCIAL RESOURCES INC |
| GREAT LAKES CHEESE COMPANY |
| INC |
| GREEN MOUNTAIN COFFEE ROASTERS INC |
| GREEN MOUNTAIN POWER CORPORATION |
| GTC BIOTHERAPEUTICS INC |
| HACKETT GROUP (THE) |
| HAEMONETICS CORPORATION |
| HAHN AUTOMOTIVE WAREHOUSE INC |
| HANOVER FOODS CORPORATION |
| HANSEN NATURAL |
| HARMONIC INC |
| HARRIS STRATEX NETWORKS INC |
| HARVARD PILGRIM HEALTH CARE INC |
| HCC INSURANCE HOLDINGS INC |
| HEALTH GRADES INC |
| HEALTH INSURANCE PLAN OF GREATER NEW YORK |
| HEALTHSTREAM INC |
| HEALTHTRONICS INC |
| HEARTLAND PAYMENT SYSTEMS INC |
| HEARUSA INC |
| HEIDRICK & STRUGGLES INTERNATIONAL INC |
| HELIOVOLT CORP |
| HESKA CORP |
| HICKORY TECH CORPORATION |
| HI-TECH PHARMACAL CO INC |
| HOLLY CORP |
| HORACE MANN EDUCATORS CORPORATION |
| HOULIHAN LOKEY |
| HUMAN GENOME SCIENCES INC |
| HURON CONSULTING GROUP INC |
| IBASIS INC |
| ICO INC |
| IDACORP INC |
| I-FLOW CORPORATION |
| ILLUMINA INC |
| IMATION CORP |
| IMG WORLDWIDE INC |
| IMMUCOR INC |
| INAMED CORP |
| INDEPENDENCE HOLDING CO |
| INFINERA CORP |
| INSPIRE PHARMACEUTICALS INC |
| INTEGRA LIFESCIENCES HOLDINGS CORP |
| INTEGRAL SYSTEMS INC |
| INTEGRAMED AMERICA INC |
| INTELLIGROUP INC |
| INTERACTIVE BROKERS GROUP INC |
| INTERACTIVE INTELLIGENCE |
| INTERCONTINENTALEXCHANGE INC (ICE) |
| INTERMEC INC |
| INTERNAP NETWORK SERVICES CORP |
| INTERNATIONAL CREATIVE MANAGEMENT (ICM) |
| INTERNATIONAL DAIRY QUEEN |
| INTERNET SECURITY SYSTEMS INC |
| INTERSTATE BATTERY SYSTEM OF AMERICA |
| INTERWOVEN INC |
| INVESTMENT TECHNOLOGY GROUP INC (ITG) |
| IRIDEX CORP |
| IRIS INTERNATIONAL INC |
| ISILON SYSTEMS INC |
| ISONICS CORPORATION |
| IVILLAGE INC |
| J2 GLOBAL COMMUNICATIONS INC |
| JACKSON NATIONAL LIFE INSURANCE COMPANY |
| JAZZ PHARMACEUTICALS |
| JUPITERMEDIA CORP |
| KAMPGROUNDS OF AMERICA INC |
| KENDALL-JACKSON WINE ESTATES LTD |
| KIMLEY-HORN AND ASSOCIATES INC |
| KNIGHT CAPITAL GROUP INC |
| KNOT INC (THE) |
| KRONOS WORLDWIDE INC |
| KV PHARMACEUTICAL CO |
| LACLEDE GROUP INC (THE) |
| LCA-VISION INC |
| LCC INTERNATIONAL INC |
| LEAP WIRELESS INTERNATIONAL INC |
| LESLIE'S POOLMART INC |
| LIFECELL CORPORATION |
| LIFECORE BIOMEDICAL INC |
| LIVEPERSON INC |
| LOGISTICARE INC |
| LOJACK CORP |
| LORAL SPACE & COMMUNICATIONS LTD |
| LUCASFILM LTD |
| LUCOR INC |

| |
|---|
| LUMINEX CORPORATION |
| M&F WORLDWIDE CORP |
| MAGELLAN MIDSTREAM PARTNERS LP |
| MALT-O-MEAL COMPANY |
| MANHATTAN ASSOCIATES INC |
| MARCHEX INC |
| MARTEK BIOSCIENCES CORP |
| MARTHA STEWART LIVING OMNIMEDIA INC |
| MARVEL ENTERTAINMENT INC |
| MATRIA HEALTHCARE INC |
| MAXYGEN INC |
| MCMORAN EXPLORATION CO |
| MEDAREX INC |
| MEDICAL ACTION INDUSTRIES INC |
| MEDICINES CO (THE) |
| MEDICIS PHARMACEUTICAL CORP |
| MEDIS TECHNOLOGIES |
| MEDTOX SCIENTIFIC INC |
| MENTOR CORP |
| MERIDIAN BIOSCIENCE INC |
| MERIT MEDICAL SYSTEMS INC |
| METROLOGIC INSTRUMENTS INC |
| METROPCS COMMUNICATIONS INC |
| METROPOLITAN HEALTH NETWORKS |
| MICHELINAS INC |
| MICROSTRATEGY INC |
| MICROTEK MEDICAL HOLDINGS INC |
| MIDAS INC |
| MILLENNIUM PHARMACEUTICALS INC |
| MOELIS & COMPANY |
| MOLINA HEALTHCARE INC |
| MOTORCAR PARTS OF AMERICA INC |
| MTS SYSTEMS |
| MYRIAD GENETICS INC |
| NANOMETRICS INC |
| NASDAQ OMX |
| NATIONAL BEVERAGE CORP |
| NATIONAL CINEMEDIA INC |
| NATIONAL DENTEX CORP |
| NATIONAL FUEL GAS CO |
| NATIONAL WINE & SPIRITS INC |
| NATUS MEDICAL |
| NAVISITE INC |
| NEKTAR THERAPEUTICS |
| NEOGEN CORPORATION |
| NETFLIX INC |
| NETGEAR INC |
| NETRATINGS INC |
| NETSCOUT SYSTEMS INC |
| NETSUITE INC |
| NEWFIELD EXPLORATION CO |
| NIC INC |
| NOBLE ENERGY INC |
| NORTHWESTERN CORPORATION |
| NOVAMED INC |
| NOVEN PHARMACEUTICALS |
| NTELOS HOLDING CORP |
| NUGGET MARKET |
| NUSTAR ENERGY LP |
| NUTRASWEET COMPANY (THE) |
| NYER MEDICAL GROUP INC |
| NYMEX HOLDINGS (NEW YORK MERCANTILE EXCHANGE) |
| ODYSSEY RE HOLDINGS CORP |
| OMNITURE INC |
| ONEOK PARTNERS LP |
| ONLINE RESOURCES CORP |
| OPENTV CORP |
| OPNEXT INC |
| OPTELECOM-NKF INC |
| ORMAT TECHNOLOGIES |
| OSCIENT PHARMACEUTICALS CORPORATION |
| PALM INC |
| PAR PHARMACEUTICAL COMPANIES INC |
| PC CONNECTION INC |
| PC MALL INC |
| PEAPOD LLC |
| PERFICIENT INC |
| PETMED EXPRESS INC |
| PETROLEUM DEVELOPMENT CORPORATION |
| PHILADELPHIA CONSOLIDATED HOLDING CORP |
| PHOENIX COMPANIES (THE) |
| PIEDMONT NATURAL GAS COMPANY INC |
| PIONEER NATURAL RESOURCES COMPANY |
| PITNEY BOWES MAPINFO |
| PLAINS EXPLORATION AND PRODUCTION COMPANY |
| PLUG POWER INC |
| PMA CAPITAL CORPORATION |
| POLYCOM INC |
| POLYMEDICA CORPORATION |
| POLYPORE INTERNATIONAL INC |
| PREMIERE GLOBAL SERVICES INC |
| PRIMEENERGY CORPORATION |
| PROASSURANCE CORP |
| PROGRESS SOFTWARE CORP |
| PROTECTIVE LIFE CORP |
| QLOGIC CORP |
| QUALITY SYSTEMS INC |
| QUICKSILVER RESOURCES INC |
| QUIDEL CORP |
| RACKSPACE HOSTING INC |
| RADISYS CORP |
| RADNET INC |
| RADYNE CORPORATION |
| RANGE RESOURCES CORP |
| REALNETWORKS INC |
| RECYCLED ENERGY DEVELOPMENT |
| RED HAT INC |
| REDDY ICE HOLDINGS INC |
| REGENERON PHARMACEUTICALS INC |
| REINSURANCE GROUP OF AMERICA INC |
| REVOLUTION HEALTH GROUP LLC |
| RIGHTNOW TECHNOLOGIES INC |
| ROBERT W BAIRD & CO INC |
| RSA SECURITY INC |
| S1 CORPORATION |
| SACRAMENTO MUNICIPAL UTILITY DISTRICT |
| SALIX PHARMACEUTICALS |
| SAVVIS INC |
| SCANSOURCE INC |
| SCHICK TECHNOLOGIES INC |
| SCHIFF NUTRITION INTERNATIONAL INC |
| SCICLONE PHARMACEUTICALS |
| SCIELE PHARMA INC |
| SCIOS INC |
| SCOULAR COMPANY (THE) |
| SEACHANGE INTERNATIONAL INC |
| SEATTLE GENETICS |
| SECURE COMPUTING CORP |
| SENTO |
| SEPRACOR INC |
| SEQUENOM INC |
| SERENA SOFTWARE INC |
| SHARED TECHNOLOGIES |
| SHENANDOAH TELECOMMUNICATIONS CO |
| SHUTTERFLY INC |

| |
|---|
| SKILLSOFT PLC |
| SOLAR RESERVE |
| SOLFOCUS INC |
| SONIC INNOVATIONS INC |
| SONUS NETWORKS INC |
| SOUTHERN UNION COMPANY |
| SOUTHWESTERN ENERGY CO |
| SPAN AMERICA MEDICAL SYSTEMS INC |
| SPECTRALINK CORP |
| SPECTRANETICS CORP |
| SPIRE CORPORATION |
| SPORTSMAN'S GUIDE INC (THE) |
| SPROUTS FARMERS MARKET |
| SPSS INC |
| SRI/SURGICAL EXPRESS INC |
| SS&C TECHNOLOGIES INC |
| ST MARY LAND & EXPLORATION COMPANY |
| STAAR SURGICAL CO |
| STANDARD MICROSYSTEMS CORPORATION |
| STATE AUTO FINANCIAL CORP |
| STERLING AUTOBODY CENTERS |
| STEVEN MADDEN LTD |
| STIEFEL LABORATORIES INC |
| SUPER MICRO COMPUTER INC |
| SWIFT ENERGY CO |
| SYCAMORE NETWORKS INC |
| SYMMETRY MEDICAL INC |
| SYMYX TECHNOLOGIES |
| SYNAPTICS INC |
| SYNOVIS LIFE TECHNOLOGIES INC |
| TAMPA ELECTRIC COMPANY |
| TARGA RESOURCES PARTNERS LP |
| TDINDUSTRIES |
| TECHNE CORP |
| TELIRIS |
| TEPPCO PARTNERS LP |
| TERREMARK WORLDWIDE INC |
| THERAGENICS CORP |
| THIRD WAVE TECHNOLOGIES INC |
| THOMAS WEISEL PARTNERS GROUP INC |
| THORATEC CORPORATION |
| THQ INC |
| TIBCO SOFTWARE INC |
| TIVO INC |
| TOMOTHERAPY INC |
| TOOTSIE ROLL INDUSTRIES INC |
| TOPPS COMPANY INC (THE) |

| |
|---|
| TRANSATLANTIC HOLDINGS INC |
| TRANSCEND SERVICES INC |
| TRAPEZE NETWORKS INC |
| TRIZETTO GROUP INC (THE) |
| TULLY'S COFFEE CORPORATION |
| UIL HOLDINGS CORPORATION |
| ULTIMATE SOFTWARE GROUP INC |
| UNDER ARMOUR INC |
| UNISOURCE ENERGY CORPORATION |
| UNITED ONLINE INC |
| UNITED THERAPEUTICS CORP |
| UNIVERSAL AMERICAN CORPORATION |
| UNIVERSAL HOSPITAL SERVICES INC |
| US PHYSICAL THERAPY INC |
| VALLEY NATIONAL GASES LLC |
| VALUECLICK INC |
| VASCO DATA SECURITY INTERNATIONAL INC |
| VENTANA MEDICAL SYSTEMS INC |
| VERAZ NETWORKS INC |
| VERIFONE HOLDINGS INC |
| VERTEX PHARMACEUTICALS INC |
| VIASAT INC |
| VIBRANT MEDIA INC |
| VIGNETTE CORP |
| VIROPHARMA INC |
| VISION SERVICE PLAN |
| VITAL SIGNS INC |
| VOLCOM INC |
| VSE CORP |
| WEBEX COMMUNICATIONS INC |
| WEBMD HEALTH CORP |
| WEBSENSE INC |
| WESTAR ENERGY |
| WGL HOLDINGS INC |
| WHITEWAVE FOODS COMPANY |
| WIND RIVER SYSTEMS INC |
| WRIGHT MEDICAL GROUP INC |
| XOMA LTD |
| XTO ENERGY INC |
| YOUNG'S MARKET COMPANY LLC |
| ZAPPOS.COM INC |
| ZIEBART INTERNATIONAL CORP |
| ZILA INC |
| ZOLL MEDICAL CORP |
| ZYMOGENETICS INC |

| Training |
|---|
| 24/7 REAL MEDIA INC |
| AAMCO TRANSMISSIONS INC |
| ABAXIS INC |
| ACI WORLDWIDE INC |
| ACME PACKET INC |
| ACXIOM DIGITAL |
| AFFYMETRIX INC |
| AKAMAI TECHNOLOGIES INC |
| AKQA INC |
| ALASKA COMMUNICATIONS SYSTEMS GROUP |
| ALBANY MOLECULAR RESEARCH |
| ALEXION PHARMACEUTICALS INC |
| ALIEN TECHNOLOGY CORPORATION |
| ALIGN TECHNOLOGY INC |
| ALKERMES INC |
| ALLEGHANY CORP |
| ALLIANCE IMAGING INC |
| ALLSCRIPTS HEALTHCARE SOLUTIONS INC |
| ALPHARMA INC |
| ALTIRIS INC |
| ALZA CORP |
| AMAG PHARMACEUTICALS INC |
| AMCOL INTERNATIONAL CORP |
| AMERESCO |
| AMERICAN FIDELITY ASSURANCE COMPANY |
| AMERICAN ITALIAN PASTA COMPANY |
| AMERICAN MEDICAL SYSTEMS HOLDINGS INC |
| AMERICAN SCIENCE & ENGINEERING INC |
| AMERICAN SUPERCONDUCTOR CORP |
| AMERICAN TIRE DISTRIBUTORS |
| AMERICAN TOWER CORP |
| AMERICAN VANGUARD CORP |
| AMICAS INC |
| AMSURG CORP |
| AMTECH SYSTEMS INC |
| AMYLIN PHARMACEUTICALS INC |
| ANALOGIC CORP |
| ANAREN INC |
| ANIKA THERAPEUTICS INC |
| ANSYS INC |
| APP PHARMACEUTICALS INC |
| APPLIED SIGNAL TECHNOLOGY INC |
| ARDEN GROUP INC |

| |
|---|
| ARIBA INC |
| ARIZONA CHEMICAL COMPANY |
| AROTECH CORPORATION |
| ARRIS GROUP INC |
| ART TECHNOLOGY GROUP INC |
| ARUBA NETWORKS INC |
| ASPECT MEDICAL SYSTEMS INC |
| ASPEN TECHNOLOGY INC |
| ASSOCIATED WHOLESALE GROCERS INC |
| ATHENAHEALTH INC |
| ATHEROS COMMUNICATIONS INC |
| ATLANTIC CITY ELECTRIC COMPANY |
| ATMI INC |
| ATRION CORPORATION |
| ATS MEDICAL INC |
| AUDIBLE INC |
| AVANEX CORPORATION |
| AVI BIOPHARMA INC |
| AVIALL INC |
| AVISTA CORPORATION |
| BENTLEY PHARMACEUTICALS INC |
| BERRY PETROLEUM CO |
| BIO REFERENCE LABORATORIES INC |
| BIOMARIN PHARMACEUTICAL INC |
| BIOSCRIP INC |
| BIOSITE INC |
| BLACK HILLS CORP |
| BLACKBOARD INC |
| BLUE CARE NETWORK OF MICHIGAN |
| BLUE COAT SYSTEMS INC |
| BLUE NILE INC |
| BRIGHTSTAR CORPORATION |
| CALIBER HOLDINGS CORP |
| CALIPER LIFE SCIENCES |
| CAL-MAINE FOODS INC |
| CALPINE CORPORATION |
| CAMBREX CORP |
| CANDELA CORP |
| CANTEL MEDICAL CORP |
| CARACO PHARMACEUTICAL LABORATORIES |
| CARDTRONICS INC |
| CATALYST HEALTH SOLUTIONS INC |
| C-COR INC |
| CELERA CORPORATION |
| CELGENE CORP |
| CELL GENESYS INC |

| |
|---|
| CELL THERAPEUTICS INC |
| CENTERPLATE |
| CENTRAL VERMONT PUBLIC SERVICE CORPORATION |
| CEPHEID |
| CHANNELL COMMERCIAL CORP |
| CHATTEM INC |
| CHINDEX INTERNATIONAL INC |
| CHOICESTREAM INC |
| CHOLESTECH CORP |
| CHYRON CORP |
| CIENA CORP |
| CKX INC |
| CLEARWIRE CORP |
| CME GROUP |
| CNX GAS CORPORATION |
| COGNEX CORP |
| COHERENT INC |
| COINSTAR INC |
| COLLAGENEX PHARMACEUTICALS INC |
| COMDATA CORP |
| COMMERCE GROUP INC (THE) |
| COMTECH TELECOMMUNICATIONS CORP |
| CONCUR TECHNOLOGIES INC |
| CONTINUCARE CORP |
| CORPORATE EXECUTIVE BOARD COMPANY (THE) |
| COUPONS INC |
| CRITICAL CARE SYSTEMS |
| CROWN CASTLE INTERNATIONAL CORP |
| CRUM & FORSTER HOLDINGS INC |
| CRYOLIFE INC |
| CSG SYSTEMS INTERNATIONAL INC |
| CUBIST PHARMACEUTICALS INC |
| CURVES INTERNATIONAL INC |
| CV THERAPEUTICS INC |
| CYBERSOURCE CORP |
| DAKTRONICS INC |
| DANNON COMPANY INC (THE) |
| DARLING INTERNATIONAL INC |
| DATASCOPE CORP |
| DEI HOLDINGS INC |
| DELPHI FINANCIAL GROUP INC |
| DENBURY RESOURCES INC |
| DIALYSIS CORPORATION OF AMERICA |
| DIAMOND FOODS INC |
| DIGI INTERNATIONAL INC |

| |
|---|
| DIGITAL RIVER INC |
| DJO INCORPORATED |
| DOUBLECLICK INC |
| DPL INC |
| DREAMWORKS ANIMATION SKG INC |
| DRUGSTORE.COM INC |
| DSP GROUP INC |
| DYAX CORP |
| DYNACQ HEALTHCARE INC |
| DYNEGY INC |
| ECHELON CORP |
| ECLIPSYS CORPORATION |
| ECOLLEGE.COM |
| EHEALTH INC |
| ELECTRONICS FOR IMAGING INC |
| ELOYALTY CORPORATION |
| EMBARCADERO TECHNOLOGIES INC |
| EMCORE CORP |
| EMS TECHNOLOGIES INC |
| EMULEX CORP |
| ENCORE ACQUISITION CO |
| ENCORIUM GROUP INC |
| ENDO PHARMACEUTICALS HOLDINGS INC |
| ENERGY CONVERSION DEVICES INC |
| ENERNOC INC |
| ENGLOBAL CORP |
| EOG RESOURCES INC |
| EPAM SYSTEMS |
| EPIX PHARMACEUTICALS INC |
| EQUINIX INC |
| EQUITABLE RESOURCES INC |
| EURONET WORLDWIDE INC |
| EVERCORE PARTNERS INC |
| EVERGREEN ENERGY INC |
| EVERGREEN SOLAR INC |
| EXACTECH INC |
| EXCEL TECHNOLOGY INC |
| EXCO RESOURCES INC |
| EXELIXIS INC |
| E-Z-EM INC |
| F5 NETWORKS INC |
| FARMER BROTHERS CO |
| FBL FINANCIAL GROUP |
| FEDEX SUPPLY CHAIN SERVICES INC |
| FIRST SOLAR LLC |
| FLIR SYSTEMS |

| |
|---|
| FOREST OIL CORPORATION |
| FORRESTER RESEARCH INC |
| FRESH BRANDS INC |
| FRESHDIRECT LLC |
| FRONTIER OIL CORPORATION |
| FUEL TECH INC |
| FUELCELL ENERGY INC |
| FUNDTECH LTD |
| GALLUP ORGANIZATION (THE) |
| GENENCOR INTERNATIONAL INC |
| GENERAL COMMUNICATION INC (GCI) |
| GENESIS ENERGY LP |
| GENOMIC HEALTH INC |
| GEN-PROBE INC |
| GERBER SCIENTIFIC INC |
| GERON CORPORATION |
| GLOBAL PARTNERS LP |
| GLOBECOMM SYSTEMS INC |
| GLU MOBILE INC |
| GOAMERICA INC |
| GOLFSMITH INTERNATIONAL HOLDINGS INC |
| GREAT AMERICAN FINANCIAL RESOURCES INC |
| GREAT LAKES CHEESE COMPANY INC |
| GREEN MOUNTAIN COFFEE ROASTERS INC |
| GREEN MOUNTAIN POWER CORPORATION |
| GTC BIOTHERAPEUTICS INC |
| HACKETT GROUP (THE) |
| HAEMONETICS CORPORATION |
| HAHN AUTOMOTIVE WAREHOUSE INC |
| HANOVER FOODS CORPORATION |
| HANSEN NATURAL |
| HARMONIC INC |
| HARRIS STRATEX NETWORKS INC |
| HARVARD PILGRIM HEALTH CARE INC |
| HCC INSURANCE HOLDINGS INC |
| HEALTH GRADES INC |
| HEALTH INSURANCE PLAN OF GREATER NEW YORK |
| HEALTHSTREAM INC |
| HEALTHTRONICS INC |
| HEARTLAND PAYMENT SYSTEMS INC |
| HEARUSA INC |
| HEIDRICK & STRUGGLES INTERNATIONAL INC |
| HELIOVOLT CORP |
| HESKA CORP |
| HICKORY TECH CORPORATION |
| HI-TECH PHARMACAL CO INC |
| HOLLY CORP |
| HORACE MANN EDUCATORS CORPORATION |
| HOULIHAN LOKEY |
| HUMAN GENOME SCIENCES INC |
| HURON CONSULTING GROUP INC |
| IBASIS INC |
| ICO INC |
| IDACORP INC |
| I-FLOW CORPORATION |
| ILLUMINA INC |
| IMATION CORP |
| IMG WORLDWIDE INC |
| IMMUCOR INC |
| INAMED CORP |
| INDEPENDENCE HOLDING CO |
| INFINERA CORP |
| INSPIRE PHARMACEUTICALS INC |
| INTEGRA LIFESCIENCES HOLDINGS CORP |
| INTEGRAL SYSTEMS INC |
| INTEGRAMED AMERICA INC |
| INTELLIGROUP INC |
| INTERACTIVE BROKERS GROUP INC |
| INTERACTIVE INTELLIGENCE |
| INTERCONTINENTALEXCHANGE INC (ICE) |
| INTERMEC INC |
| INTERNAP NETWORK SERVICES CORP |
| INTERNATIONAL CREATIVE MANAGEMENT (ICM) |
| INTERNATIONAL DAIRY QUEEN |
| INTERNET SECURITY SYSTEMS INC |
| INTERSTATE BATTERY SYSTEM OF AMERICA |
| INTERWOVEN INC |
| INVESTMENT TECHNOLOGY GROUP INC (ITG) |
| IRIDEX CORP |
| IRIS INTERNATIONAL INC |
| ISILON SYSTEMS INC |
| ISONICS CORPORATION |
| IVILLAGE INC |
| J2 GLOBAL COMMUNICATIONS INC |
| JACKSON NATIONAL LIFE INSURANCE COMPANY |
| JAZZ PHARMACEUTICALS |
| JUPITERMEDIA CORP |
| KAMPGROUNDS OF AMERICA INC |
| KENDALL-JACKSON WINE ESTATES LTD |
| KIMLEY-HORN AND ASSOCIATES INC |
| KNIGHT CAPITAL GROUP INC |
| KNOT INC (THE) |
| KRONOS WORLDWIDE INC |
| KV PHARMACEUTICAL CO |
| LACLEDE GROUP INC (THE) |
| LCA-VISION INC |
| LCC INTERNATIONAL INC |
| LEAP WIRELESS INTERNATIONAL INC |
| LESLIE'S POOLMART INC |
| LIFECELL CORPORATION |
| LIFECORE BIOMEDICAL INC |
| LIVEPERSON INC |
| LOGISTICARE INC |
| LOJACK CORP |
| LORAL SPACE & COMMUNICATIONS LTD |
| LUCASFILM LTD |
| LUCOR INC |
| LUMINEX CORPORATION |
| M&F WORLDWIDE CORP |
| MAGELLAN MIDSTREAM PARTNERS LP |
| MALT-O-MEAL COMPANY |
| MANHATTAN ASSOCIATES INC |
| MARCHEX INC |
| MARTEK BIOSCIENCES CORP |
| MARTHA STEWART LIVING OMNIMEDIA INC |
| MARVEL ENTERTAINMENT INC |
| MATRIA HEALTHCARE INC |
| MAXYGEN INC |
| MCMORAN EXPLORATION CO |
| MEDAREX INC |
| MEDICAL ACTION INDUSTRIES INC |
| MEDICINES CO (THE) |
| MEDICIS PHARMACEUTICAL CORP |
| MEDIS TECHNOLOGIES |
| MEDTOX SCIENTIFIC INC |
| MENTOR CORP |
| MERIDIAN BIOSCIENCE INC |
| MERIT MEDICAL SYSTEMS INC |
| METROLOGIC INSTRUMENTS INC |
| METROPCS COMMUNICATIONS INC |

| | | |
|---|---|---|
| METROPOLITAN HEALTH NETWORKS | OSCIENT PHARMACEUTICALS CORPORATION | ROBERT W BAIRD & CO INC |
| MICHELINAS INC | PALM INC | RSA SECURITY INC |
| MICROSTRATEGY INC | PAR PHARMACEUTICAL COMPANIES INC | S1 CORPORATION |
| MICROTEK MEDICAL HOLDINGS INC | PC CONNECTION INC | SACRAMENTO MUNICIPAL UTILITY DISTRICT |
| MIDAS INC | PC MALL INC | SALIX PHARMACEUTICALS |
| MILLENNIUM PHARMACEUTICALS INC | PEAPOD LLC | SAVVIS INC |
| MOELIS & COMPANY | PERFICIENT INC | SCANSOURCE INC |
| MOLINA HEALTHCARE INC | PETMED EXPRESS INC | SCHICK TECHNOLOGIES INC |
| MOTORCAR PARTS OF AMERICA INC | PETROLEUM DEVELOPMENT CORPORATION | SCHIFF NUTRITION INTERNATIONAL INC |
| MTS SYSTEMS | PHILADELPHIA CONSOLIDATED HOLDING CORP | SCICLONE PHARMACEUTICALS |
| MYRIAD GENETICS INC | PHOENIX COMPANIES (THE) | SCIELE PHARMA INC |
| NANOMETRICS INC | PIEDMONT NATURAL GAS COMPANY INC | SCIOS INC |
| NASDAQ OMX | PIONEER NATURAL RESOURCES COMPANY | SCOULAR COMPANY (THE) |
| NATIONAL BEVERAGE CORP | PITNEY BOWES MAPINFO | SEACHANGE INTERNATIONAL INC |
| NATIONAL CINEMEDIA INC | PLAINS EXPLORATION AND PRODUCTION COMPANY | SEATTLE GENETICS |
| NATIONAL DENTEX CORP | PLUG POWER INC | SECURE COMPUTING CORP |
| NATIONAL FUEL GAS CO | PMA CAPITAL CORPORATION | SENTO |
| NATIONAL WINE & SPIRITS INC | POLYCOM INC | SEPRACOR INC |
| NATUS MEDICAL | POLYMEDICA CORPORATION | SEQUENOM INC |
| NAVISITE INC | POLYPORE INTERNATIONAL INC | SERENA SOFTWARE INC |
| NEKTAR THERAPEUTICS | PREMIERE GLOBAL SERVICES INC | SHARED TECHNOLOGIES |
| NEOGEN CORPORATION | PRIMEENERGY CORPORATION | SHENANDOAH TELECOMMUNICATIONS CO |
| NETFLIX INC | PROASSURANCE CORP | SHUTTERFLY INC |
| NETGEAR INC | PROGRESS SOFTWARE CORP | SKILLSOFT PLC |
| NETRATINGS INC | PROTECTIVE LIFE CORP | SOLAR RESERVE |
| NETSCOUT SYSTEMS INC | QLOGIC CORP | SOLFOCUS INC |
| NETSUITE INC | QUALITY SYSTEMS INC | SONIC INNOVATIONS INC |
| NEWFIELD EXPLORATION CO | QUICKSILVER RESOURCES INC | SONUS NETWORKS INC |
| NIC INC | QUIDEL CORP | SOUTHERN UNION COMPANY |
| NOBLE ENERGY INC | RACKSPACE HOSTING INC | SOUTHWESTERN ENERGY CO |
| NORTHWESTERN CORPORATION | RADISYS CORP | SPAN AMERICA MEDICAL SYSTEMS INC |
| NOVAMED INC | RADNET INC | SPECTRALINK CORP |
| NOVEN PHARMACEUTICALS | RADYNE CORPORATION | SPECTRANETICS CORP |
| NTELOS HOLDING CORP | RANGE RESOURCES CORP | SPIRE CORPORATION |
| NUGGET MARKET | REALNETWORKS INC | SPORTSMAN'S GUIDE INC (THE) |
| NUSTAR ENERGY LP | RECYCLED ENERGY DEVELOPMENT | SPROUTS FARMERS MARKET |
| NUTRASWEET COMPANY (THE) | RED HAT INC | SPSS INC |
| NYER MEDICAL GROUP INC | REDDY ICE HOLDINGS INC | SRI/SURGICAL EXPRESS INC |
| NYMEX HOLDINGS (NEW YORK MERCANTILE EXCHANGE) | REGENERON PHARMACEUTICALS INC | SS&C TECHNOLOGIES INC |
| ODYSSEY RE HOLDINGS CORP | REINSURANCE GROUP OF AMERICA INC | ST MARY LAND & EXPLORATION COMPANY |
| OMNITURE INC | REVOLUTION HEALTH GROUP LLC | STAAR SURGICAL CO |
| ONEOK PARTNERS LP | RIGHTNOW TECHNOLOGIES INC | STANDARD MICROSYSTEMS CORPORATION |
| ONLINE RESOURCES CORP | | STATE AUTO FINANCIAL CORP |
| OPENTV CORP | | STERLING AUTOBODY CENTERS |
| OPNEXT INC | | STEVEN MADDEN LTD |
| OPTELECOM-NKF INC | | |
| ORMAT TECHNOLOGIES | | |

| |
|---|
| STIEFEL LABORATORIES INC |
| SUPER MICRO COMPUTER INC |
| SWIFT ENERGY CO |
| SYCAMORE NETWORKS INC |
| SYMMETRY MEDICAL INC |
| SYMYX TECHNOLOGIES |
| SYNAPTICS INC |
| SYNOVIS LIFE TECHNOLOGIES INC |
| TAMPA ELECTRIC COMPANY |
| TARGA RESOURCES PARTNERS LP |
| TDINDUSTRIES |
| TECHNE CORP |
| TELIRIS |
| TEPPCO PARTNERS LP |
| TERREMARK WORLDWIDE INC |
| THERAGENICS CORP |
| THIRD WAVE TECHNOLOGIES INC |
| THOMAS WEISEL PARTNERS GROUP INC |
| THORATEC CORPORATION |
| THQ INC |
| TIBCO SOFTWARE INC |
| TIVO INC |
| TOMOTHERAPY INC |
| TOOTSIE ROLL INDUSTRIES INC |
| TOPPS COMPANY INC (THE) |
| TRANSATLANTIC HOLDINGS INC |
| TRANSCEND SERVICES INC |
| TRAPEZE NETWORKS INC |
| TRIZETTO GROUP INC (THE) |
| TULLY'S COFFEE CORPORATION |
| UIL HOLDINGS CORPORATION |
| ULTIMATE SOFTWARE GROUP INC |
| UNDER ARMOUR INC |
| UNISOURCE ENERGY CORPORATION |
| UNITED ONLINE INC |
| UNITED THERAPEUTICS CORP |
| UNIVERSAL AMERICAN CORPORATION |
| UNIVERSAL HOSPITAL SERVICES INC |
| US PHYSICAL THERAPY INC |
| VALLEY NATIONAL GASES LLC |
| VALUECLICK INC |
| VASCO DATA SECURITY INTERNATIONAL INC |
| VENTANA MEDICAL SYSTEMS INC |
| VERAZ NETWORKS INC |
| VERIFONE HOLDINGS INC |
| VERTEX PHARMACEUTICALS INC |
| VIASAT INC |
| VIBRANT MEDIA INC |
| VIGNETTE CORP |
| VIROPHARMA INC |
| VISION SERVICE PLAN |
| VITAL SIGNS INC |
| VOLCOM INC |
| VSE CORP |
| WEBEX COMMUNICATIONS INC |
| WEBMD HEALTH CORP |
| WEBSENSE INC |
| WESTAR ENERGY |
| WGL HOLDINGS INC |
| WHITEWAVE FOODS COMPANY |
| WIND RIVER SYSTEMS INC |
| WRIGHT MEDICAL GROUP INC |
| XOMA LTD |
| XTO ENERGY INC |
| YOUNG'S MARKET COMPANY LLC |
| ZAPPOS.COM INC |
| ZIEBART INTERNATIONAL CORP |
| ZILA INC |
| ZOLL MEDICAL CORP |
| ZYMOGENETICS INC |

## Sales/Marketing

| Advertising Professionals |
|---|
| 24/7 REAL MEDIA INC |
| ACXIOM DIGITAL |
| AKQA INC |
| AMERICAN FIDELITY ASSURANCE COMPANY |
| AMERICAN ITALIAN PASTA COMPANY |
| AMERICAN TIRE DISTRIBUTORS |
| AMERICAN VANGUARD CORP |
| AMSURG CORP |
| ARDEN GROUP INC |
| ASSOCIATED WHOLESALE GROCERS INC |
| ATHENAHEALTH INC |
| AUDIBLE INC |
| BLACKBOARD INC |
| BLUE NILE INC |
| CARDTRONICS INC |
| CHOICESTREAM INC |
| CLEARWIRE CORP |
| CME GROUP |
| COINSTAR INC |
| COMDATA CORP |
| COUPONS INC |
| CRITICAL CARE SYSTEMS |
| CURVES INTERNATIONAL INC |
| DAKTRONICS INC |
| DANNON COMPANY INC (THE) |
| DEI HOLDINGS INC |
| DIALYSIS CORPORATION OF AMERICA |
| DIAMOND FOODS INC |
| DOUBLECLICK INC |
| DREAMWORKS ANIMATION SKG INC |
| DRUGSTORE.COM INC |
| DYNACQ HEALTHCARE INC |
| ECOLLEGE.COM |
| EHEALTH INC |
| EURONET WORLDWIDE INC |
| FARMER BROTHERS CO |
| FBL FINANCIAL GROUP |
| FRESH BRANDS INC |
| FRESHDIRECT LLC |
| GOAMERICA INC |
| GOLFSMITH INTERNATIONAL HOLDINGS INC |
| GREAT AMERICAN FINANCIAL RESOURCES INC |
| GREAT LAKES CHEESE COMPANY INC |
| GREEN MOUNTAIN COFFEE ROASTERS INC |
| HAHN AUTOMOTIVE WAREHOUSE INC |
| HANOVER FOODS CORPORATION |
| HANSEN NATURAL |
| HEALTH GRADES INC |
| HEALTHSTREAM INC |
| HEALTHTRONICS INC |
| HEARTLAND PAYMENT SYSTEMS INC |
| HEARUSA INC |
| IBASIS INC |
| INDEPENDENCE HOLDING CO |
| INTERCONTINENTALEXCHANGE INC (ICE) |
| INTERNATIONAL DAIRY QUEEN |
| INTERSTATE BATTERY SYSTEM OF AMERICA |
| IVILLAGE INC |
| JACKSON NATIONAL LIFE INSURANCE COMPANY |
| JUPITERMEDIA CORP |
| KAMPGROUNDS OF AMERICA INC |
| KENDALL-JACKSON WINE ESTATES |

| |
|---|
| LTD |
| KNOT INC (THE) |
| LCA-VISION INC |
| LEAP WIRELESS INTERNATIONAL INC |
| LESLIE'S POOLMART INC |
| LOJACK CORP |
| LUCASFILM LTD |
| M&F WORLDWIDE CORP |
| MALT-O-MEAL COMPANY |
| MARCHEX INC |
| MARTHA STEWART LIVING OMNIMEDIA INC |
| METROPCS COMMUNICATIONS INC |
| MICHELINAS INC |
| NASDAQ OMX |
| NATIONAL BEVERAGE CORP |
| NATIONAL WINE & SPIRITS INC |
| NETFLIX INC |
| NOVAMED INC |
| NUGGET MARKET |
| NUTRASWEET COMPANY (THE) |
| NYMEX HOLDINGS (NEW YORK MERCANTILE EXCHANGE) |
| PC CONNECTION INC |
| PC MALL INC |
| PEAPOD LLC |
| PETMED EXPRESS INC |
| PHOENIX COMPANIES (THE) |
| PROTECTIVE LIFE CORP |
| REDDY ICE HOLDINGS INC |
| REVOLUTION HEALTH GROUP LLC |
| SCHIFF NUTRITION INTERNATIONAL INC |
| SHUTTERFLY INC |
| SPORTSMAN'S GUIDE INC (THE) |
| SPROUTS FARMERS MARKET |
| STEVEN MADDEN LTD |
| TERREMARK WORLDWIDE INC |
| TIVO INC |
| TOOTSIE ROLL INDUSTRIES INC |
| TOPPS COMPANY INC (THE) |
| TULLY'S COFFEE CORPORATION |
| UNDER ARMOUR INC |
| UNITED ONLINE INC |
| UNIVERSAL AMERICAN CORPORATION |
| US PHYSICAL THERAPY INC |
| VALUECLICK INC |
| VERIFONE HOLDINGS INC |
| VIBRANT MEDIA INC |
| VOLCOM INC |
| WEBMD HEALTH CORP |
| WHITEWAVE FOODS COMPANY |
| YOUNG'S MARKET COMPANY LLC |
| ZAPPOS.COM INC |

| **Commercial/Industrial** |
|---|
| ABAXIS INC |
| ACI WORLDWIDE INC |
| ACME PACKET INC |
| AFFYMETRIX INC |
| AKAMAI TECHNOLOGIES INC |
| ALASKA COMMUNICATIONS SYSTEMS GROUP |
| ALEXION PHARMACEUTICALS INC |
| ALIEN TECHNOLOGY CORPORATION |
| ALIGN TECHNOLOGY INC |
| ALKERMES INC |
| ALLEGHANY CORP |
| ALLIANCE IMAGING INC |
| ALLSCRIPTS HEALTHCARE SOLUTIONS INC |
| ALPHARMA INC |
| ALTIRIS INC |
| ALZA CORP |
| AMCOL INTERNATIONAL CORP |
| AMERICAN ITALIAN PASTA COMPANY |
| AMERICAN MEDICAL SYSTEMS HOLDINGS INC |
| AMERICAN SCIENCE & ENGINEERING INC |
| AMERICAN SUPERCONDUCTOR CORP |
| AMERICAN TOWER CORP |
| AMICAS INC |
| AMSURG CORP |
| AMTECH SYSTEMS INC |
| AMYLIN PHARMACEUTICALS INC |
| ANALOGIC CORP |
| ANAREN INC |
| ANIKA THERAPEUTICS INC |
| ANSYS INC |
| APP PHARMACEUTICALS INC |
| APPLIED SIGNAL TECHNOLOGY INC |
| ARIBA INC |
| ARIZONA CHEMICAL COMPANY |
| AROTECH CORPORATION |
| ARRIS GROUP INC |
| ART TECHNOLOGY GROUP INC |
| ARUBA NETWORKS INC |
| ASPECT MEDICAL SYSTEMS INC |
| ASPEN TECHNOLOGY INC |
| ATHENAHEALTH INC |
| ATHEROS COMMUNICATIONS INC |
| ATLANTIC CITY ELECTRIC COMPANY |
| ATMI INC |
| ATRION CORPORATION |
| ATS MEDICAL INC |
| AVANEX CORPORATION |
| AVI BIOPHARMA INC |
| AVIALL INC |
| AVISTA CORPORATION |
| BENTLEY PHARMACEUTICALS INC |
| BERRY PETROLEUM CO |
| BIO REFERENCE LABORATORIES INC |
| BIOMARIN PHARMACEUTICAL INC |
| BIOSCRIP INC |
| BIOSITE INC |
| BLACK HILLS CORP |
| BLACKBOARD INC |
| BLUE CARE NETWORK OF MICHIGAN |
| BLUE COAT SYSTEMS INC |
| BRIGHTSTAR CORPORATION |
| CALIPER LIFE SCIENCES |
| CALPINE CORPORATION |
| CAMBREX CORP |
| CANDELA CORP |
| CANTEL MEDICAL CORP |
| CARACO PHARMACEUTICAL LABORATORIES |
| CARDTRONICS INC |
| C-COR INC |
| CELGENE CORP |
| CELL GENESYS INC |
| CELL THERAPEUTICS INC |
| CENTRAL VERMONT PUBLIC SERVICE CORPORATION |
| CEPHEID |
| CHANNELL COMMERCIAL CORP |
| CHATTEM INC |
| CHINDEX INTERNATIONAL INC |
| CHOLESTECH CORP |
| CHYRON CORP |
| CIENA CORP |
| CLEARWIRE CORP |
| CNX GAS CORPORATION |
| COGNEX CORP |
| COHERENT INC |

| |
|---|
| COINSTAR INC |
| COLLAGENEX PHARMACEUTICALS INC |
| COMDATA CORP |
| COMMERCE GROUP INC (THE) |
| COMTECH TELECOMMUNICATIONS CORP |
| CONCUR TECHNOLOGIES INC |
| CRITICAL CARE SYSTEMS |
| CROWN CASTLE INTERNATIONAL CORP |
| CRUM & FORSTER HOLDINGS INC |
| CRYOLIFE INC |
| CSG SYSTEMS INTERNATIONAL INC |
| CUBIST PHARMACEUTICALS INC |
| CV THERAPEUTICS INC |
| CYBERSOURCE CORP |
| DAKTRONICS INC |
| DANNON COMPANY INC (THE) |
| DARLING INTERNATIONAL INC |
| DATASCOPE CORP |
| DEI HOLDINGS INC |
| DELPHI FINANCIAL GROUP INC |
| DENBURY RESOURCES INC |
| DIALYSIS CORPORATION OF AMERICA |
| DIAMOND FOODS INC |
| DIGI INTERNATIONAL INC |
| DIGITAL RIVER INC |
| DJO INCORPORATED |
| DPL INC |
| DSP GROUP INC |
| DYAX CORP |
| DYNEGY INC |
| ECHELON CORP |
| ECLIPSYS CORPORATION |
| ECOLLEGE.COM |
| ELECTRONICS FOR IMAGING INC |
| ELOYALTY CORPORATION |
| EMBARCADERO TECHNOLOGIES INC |
| EMCORE CORP |
| EMS TECHNOLOGIES INC |
| EMULEX CORP |
| ENCORE ACQUISITION CO |
| ENDO PHARMACEUTICALS HOLDINGS INC |
| ENERGY CONVERSION DEVICES INC |
| ENGLOBAL CORP |
| EOG RESOURCES INC |
| EPIX PHARMACEUTICALS INC |

| |
|---|
| EQUINIX INC |
| EQUITABLE RESOURCES INC |
| EURONET WORLDWIDE INC |
| EVERGREEN ENERGY INC |
| EVERGREEN SOLAR INC |
| EXACTECH INC |
| EXCEL TECHNOLOGY INC |
| EXCO RESOURCES INC |
| EXELIXIS INC |
| E-Z-EM INC |
| F5 NETWORKS INC |
| FARMER BROTHERS CO |
| FIRST SOLAR LLC |
| FLIR SYSTEMS |
| FOREST OIL CORPORATION |
| FRONTIER OIL CORPORATION |
| FUELCELL ENERGY INC |
| FUNDTECH LTD |
| GENENCOR INTERNATIONAL INC |
| GENERAL COMMUNICATION INC (GCI) |
| GENESIS ENERGY LP |
| GENOMIC HEALTH INC |
| GEN-PROBE INC |
| GERBER SCIENTIFIC INC |
| GERON CORPORATION |
| GLOBAL PARTNERS LP |
| GLOBECOMM SYSTEMS INC |
| GLU MOBILE INC |
| GOAMERICA INC |
| GREAT LAKES CHEESE COMPANY INC |
| GREEN MOUNTAIN COFFEE ROASTERS INC |
| GREEN MOUNTAIN POWER CORPORATION |
| GTC BIOTHERAPEUTICS INC |
| HAEMONETICS CORPORATION |
| HANOVER FOODS CORPORATION |
| HANSEN NATURAL |
| HARMONIC INC |
| HARRIS STRATEX NETWORKS INC |
| HARVARD PILGRIM HEALTH CARE INC |
| HCC INSURANCE HOLDINGS INC |
| HEALTH GRADES INC |
| HEALTH INSURANCE PLAN OF GREATER NEW YORK |
| HEALTHSTREAM INC |
| HEALTHTRONICS INC |
| HEARTLAND PAYMENT SYSTEMS INC |

| |
|---|
| HELIOVOLT CORP |
| HICKORY TECH CORPORATION |
| HI-TECH PHARMACAL CO INC |
| HOLLY CORP |
| HORACE MANN EDUCATORS CORPORATION |
| HUMAN GENOME SCIENCES INC |
| IBASIS INC |
| ICO INC |
| IDACORP INC |
| I-FLOW CORPORATION |
| ILLUMINA INC |
| IMATION CORP |
| IMMUCOR INC |
| INAMED CORP |
| INFINERA CORP |
| INSPIRE PHARMACEUTICALS INC |
| INTEGRA LIFESCIENCES HOLDINGS CORP |
| INTEGRAL SYSTEMS INC |
| INTERACTIVE INTELLIGENCE |
| INTERMEC INC |
| INTERNAP NETWORK SERVICES CORP |
| INTERNET SECURITY SYSTEMS INC |
| INTERSTATE BATTERY SYSTEM OF AMERICA |
| INTERWOVEN INC |
| INVESTMENT TECHNOLOGY GROUP INC (ITG) |
| IRIDEX CORP |
| IRIS INTERNATIONAL INC |
| ISILON SYSTEMS INC |
| ISONICS CORPORATION |
| IVILLAGE INC |
| J2 GLOBAL COMMUNICATIONS INC |
| JAZZ PHARMACEUTICALS |
| JUPITERMEDIA CORP |
| KENDALL-JACKSON WINE ESTATES LTD |
| KIMLEY-HORN AND ASSOCIATES INC |
| KNOT INC (THE) |
| KRONOS WORLDWIDE INC |
| KV PHARMACEUTICAL CO |
| LACLEDE GROUP INC (THE) |
| LCA-VISION INC |
| LCC INTERNATIONAL INC |
| LEAP WIRELESS INTERNATIONAL INC |
| LIFECELL CORPORATION |
| LIFECORE BIOMEDICAL INC |

| |
|---|
| LIVEPERSON INC |
| LOGISTICARE INC |
| LOJACK CORP |
| LORAL SPACE & COMMUNICATIONS LTD |
| LUMINEX CORPORATION |
| M&F WORLDWIDE CORP |
| MAGELLAN MIDSTREAM PARTNERS LP |
| MALT-O-MEAL COMPANY |
| MANHATTAN ASSOCIATES INC |
| MARCHEX INC |
| MARTEK BIOSCIENCES CORP |
| MATRIA HEALTHCARE INC |
| MAXYGEN INC |
| MCMORAN EXPLORATION CO |
| MEDAREX INC |
| MEDICAL ACTION INDUSTRIES INC |
| MEDICINES CO (THE) |
| MEDICIS PHARMACEUTICAL CORP |
| MEDIS TECHNOLOGIES |
| MEDTOX SCIENTIFIC INC |
| MENTOR CORP |
| MERIDIAN BIOSCIENCE INC |
| MERIT MEDICAL SYSTEMS INC |
| METROLOGIC INSTRUMENTS INC |
| METROPCS COMMUNICATIONS INC |
| METROPOLITAN HEALTH NETWORKS |
| MICHELINAS INC |
| MICROSTRATEGY INC |
| MICROTEK MEDICAL HOLDINGS INC |
| MILLENNIUM PHARMACEUTICALS INC |
| MOLINA HEALTHCARE INC |
| MOTORCAR PARTS OF AMERICA INC |
| MTS SYSTEMS |
| MYRIAD GENETICS INC |
| NANOMETRICS INC |
| NATIONAL BEVERAGE CORP |
| NATIONAL DENTEX CORP |
| NATIONAL FUEL GAS CO |
| NATIONAL WINE & SPIRITS INC |
| NATUS MEDICAL |
| NAVISITE INC |
| NEKTAR THERAPEUTICS |
| NEOGEN CORPORATION |
| NETGEAR INC |
| NETRATINGS INC |
| NETSCOUT SYSTEMS INC |

| |
|---|
| NETSUITE INC |
| NEWFIELD EXPLORATION CO |
| NIC INC |
| NOBLE ENERGY INC |
| NORTHWESTERN CORPORATION |
| NOVEN PHARMACEUTICALS |
| NTELOS HOLDING CORP |
| NUSTAR ENERGY LP |
| NUTRASWEET COMPANY (THE) |
| NYER MEDICAL GROUP INC |
| ODYSSEY RE HOLDINGS CORP |
| OMNITURE INC |
| ONEOK PARTNERS LP |
| ONLINE RESOURCES CORP |
| OPENTV CORP |
| OPNEXT INC |
| OPTELECOM-NKF INC |
| ORMAT TECHNOLOGIES |
| OSCIENT PHARMACEUTICALS CORPORATION |
| PALM INC |
| PAR PHARMACEUTICAL COMPANIES INC |
| PC CONNECTION INC |
| PC MALL INC |
| PETROLEUM DEVELOPMENT CORPORATION |
| PHILADELPHIA CONSOLIDATED HOLDING CORP |
| PIEDMONT NATURAL GAS COMPANY INC |
| PIONEER NATURAL RESOURCES COMPANY |
| PITNEY BOWES MAPINFO |
| PLAINS EXPLORATION AND PRODUCTION COMPANY |
| PLUG POWER INC |
| PMA CAPITAL CORPORATION |
| POLYCOM INC |
| POLYMEDICA CORPORATION |
| PREMIERE GLOBAL SERVICES INC |
| PRIMEENERGY CORPORATION |
| PROASSURANCE CORP |
| QLOGIC CORP |
| QUALITY SYSTEMS INC |
| QUICKSILVER RESOURCES INC |
| QUIDEL CORP |
| RACKSPACE HOSTING INC |
| RADISYS CORP |
| RADNET INC |
| RADYNE CORPORATION |
| RANGE RESOURCES CORP |

| |
|---|
| REALNETWORKS INC |
| RED HAT INC |
| REDDY ICE HOLDINGS INC |
| REGENERON PHARMACEUTICALS INC |
| REINSURANCE GROUP OF AMERICA INC |
| REVOLUTION HEALTH GROUP LLC |
| RIGHTNOW TECHNOLOGIES INC |
| RSA SECURITY INC |
| S1 CORPORATION |
| SACRAMENTO MUNICIPAL UTILITY DISTRICT |
| SALIX PHARMACEUTICALS |
| SAVVIS INC |
| SCANSOURCE INC |
| SCHICK TECHNOLOGIES INC |
| SCHIFF NUTRITION INTERNATIONAL INC |
| SCICLONE PHARMACEUTICALS |
| SCIELE PHARMA INC |
| SCIOS INC |
| SEACHANGE INTERNATIONAL INC |
| SEATTLE GENETICS |
| SECURE COMPUTING CORP |
| SEPRACOR INC |
| SEQUENOM INC |
| SERENA SOFTWARE INC |
| SHARED TECHNOLOGIES |
| SHENANDOAH TELECOMMUNICATIONS CO |
| SHUTTERFLY INC |
| SOLAR RESERVE |
| SOLFOCUS INC |
| SONIC INNOVATIONS INC |
| SONUS NETWORKS INC |
| SOUTHERN UNION COMPANY |
| SOUTHWESTERN ENERGY CO |
| SPAN AMERICA MEDICAL SYSTEMS INC |
| SPECTRALINK CORP |
| SPECTRANETICS CORP |
| SPIRE CORPORATION |
| SPSS INC |
| SRI/SURGICAL EXPRESS INC |
| SS&C TECHNOLOGIES INC |
| ST MARY LAND & EXPLORATION COMPANY |
| STAAR SURGICAL CO |
| STANDARD MICROSYSTEMS CORPORATION |
| STATE AUTO FINANCIAL CORP |

| |
|---|
| STEVEN MADDEN LTD |
| STIEFEL LABORATORIES INC |
| SUPER MICRO COMPUTER INC |
| SWIFT ENERGY CO |
| SYCAMORE NETWORKS INC |
| SYMMETRY MEDICAL INC |
| SYNAPTICS INC |
| SYNOVIS LIFE TECHNOLOGIES INC |
| TAMPA ELECTRIC COMPANY |
| TARGA RESOURCES PARTNERS LP |
| TDINDUSTRIES |
| TECHNE CORP |
| TELIRIS |
| TEPPCO PARTNERS LP |
| TERREMARK WORLDWIDE INC |
| THERAGENICS CORP |
| THIRD WAVE TECHNOLOGIES INC |
| THORATEC CORPORATION |
| THQ INC |
| TIBCO SOFTWARE INC |
| TIVO INC |
| TOMOTHERAPY INC |
| TOOTSIE ROLL INDUSTRIES INC |
| TOPPS COMPANY INC (THE) |
| TRANSATLANTIC HOLDINGS INC |
| TRANSCEND SERVICES INC |
| TRAPEZE NETWORKS INC |
| TRIZETTO GROUP INC (THE) |
| UIL HOLDINGS CORPORATION |
| ULTIMATE SOFTWARE GROUP INC |
| UNDER ARMOUR INC |
| UNISOURCE ENERGY CORPORATION |
| UNITED ONLINE INC |
| UNITED THERAPEUTICS CORP |
| UNIVERSAL HOSPITAL SERVICES INC |
| US PHYSICAL THERAPY INC |
| VALLEY NATIONAL GASES LLC |
| VASCO DATA SECURITY INTERNATIONAL INC |
| VENTANA MEDICAL SYSTEMS INC |
| VERAZ NETWORKS INC |
| VERIFONE HOLDINGS INC |
| VERTEX PHARMACEUTICALS INC |
| VIASAT INC |
| VIGNETTE CORP |
| VIROPHARMA INC |
| VISION SERVICE PLAN |
| VITAL SIGNS INC |
| VOLCOM INC |
| VSE CORP |
| WEBEX COMMUNICATIONS INC |
| WEBMD HEALTH CORP |
| WEBSENSE INC |
| WESTAR ENERGY |
| WGL HOLDINGS INC |
| WHITEWAVE FOODS COMPANY |
| WIND RIVER SYSTEMS INC |
| WRIGHT MEDICAL GROUP INC |
| XOMA LTD |
| XTO ENERGY INC |
| ZILA INC |
| ZOLL MEDICAL CORP |
| ZYMOGENETICS INC |

| Marketing Professionals |
|---|
| 24/7 REAL MEDIA INC |
| AAMCO TRANSMISSIONS INC |
| ABAXIS INC |
| ACI WORLDWIDE INC |
| ACME PACKET INC |
| ACXIOM DIGITAL |
| AFFYMETRIX INC |
| AKAMAI TECHNOLOGIES INC |
| AKQA INC |
| ALASKA COMMUNICATIONS SYSTEMS GROUP |
| ALBANY MOLECULAR RESEARCH |
| ALEXION PHARMACEUTICALS INC |
| ALIEN TECHNOLOGY CORPORATION |
| ALIGN TECHNOLOGY INC |
| ALKERMES INC |
| ALLEGHANY CORP |
| ALLIANCE IMAGING INC |
| ALLSCRIPTS HEALTHCARE SOLUTIONS INC |
| ALPHARMA INC |
| ALTIRIS INC |
| ALZA CORP |
| AMCOL INTERNATIONAL CORP |
| AMERESCO |
| AMERICAN FIDELITY ASSURANCE COMPANY |
| AMERICAN ITALIAN PASTA COMPANY |
| AMERICAN MEDICAL SYSTEMS HOLDINGS INC |
| AMERICAN SCIENCE & ENGINEERING INC |
| AMERICAN SUPERCONDUCTOR CORP |
| AMERICAN TIRE DISTRIBUTORS |
| AMERICAN TOWER CORP |
| AMICAS INC |
| AMSURG CORP |
| AMTECH SYSTEMS INC |
| AMYLIN PHARMACEUTICALS INC |
| ANALOGIC CORP |
| ANAREN INC |
| ANIKA THERAPEUTICS INC |
| ANSYS INC |
| APP PHARMACEUTICALS INC |
| APPLIED SIGNAL TECHNOLOGY INC |
| ARDEN GROUP INC |
| ARIBA INC |
| ARIZONA CHEMICAL COMPANY |
| AROTECH CORPORATION |
| ARRIS GROUP INC |
| ART TECHNOLOGY GROUP INC |
| ARUBA NETWORKS INC |
| ASPECT MEDICAL SYSTEMS INC |
| ASPEN TECHNOLOGY INC |
| ASSOCIATED WHOLESALE GROCERS INC |
| ATHENAHEALTH INC |
| ATHEROS COMMUNICATIONS INC |
| ATLANTIC CITY ELECTRIC COMPANY |
| ATMI INC |
| ATRION CORPORATION |
| ATS MEDICAL INC |
| AUDIBLE INC |
| AVANEX CORPORATION |
| AVI BIOPHARMA INC |
| AVIALL INC |
| AVISTA CORPORATION |
| BENTLEY PHARMACEUTICALS INC |
| BERRY PETROLEUM CO |
| BIO REFERENCE LABORATORIES INC |
| BIOMARIN PHARMACEUTICAL INC |
| BIOSCRIP INC |
| BIOSITE INC |
| BLACK HILLS CORP |
| BLACKBOARD INC |
| BLUE CARE NETWORK OF MICHIGAN |
| BLUE COAT SYSTEMS INC |
| BLUE NILE INC |
| BRIGHTSTAR CORPORATION |
| CALIBER HOLDINGS CORP |
| CALIPER LIFE SCIENCES |

| |
|---|
| CAL-MAINE FOODS INC |
| CALPINE CORPORATION |
| CAMBREX CORP |
| CANDELA CORP |
| CANTEL MEDICAL CORP |
| CARACO PHARMACEUTICAL LABORATORIES |
| CARDTRONICS INC |
| C-COR INC |
| CELERA CORPORATION |
| CELGENE CORP |
| CELL GENESYS INC |
| CELL THERAPEUTICS INC |
| CENTERPLATE |
| CENTRAL VERMONT PUBLIC SERVICE CORPORATION |
| CEPHEID |
| CHANNELL COMMERCIAL CORP |
| CHATTEM INC |
| CHINDEX INTERNATIONAL INC |
| CHOICESTREAM INC |
| CHOLESTECH CORP |
| CHYRON CORP |
| CIENA CORP |
| CKX INC |
| CLEARWIRE CORP |
| CME GROUP |
| CNX GAS CORPORATION |
| COGNEX CORP |
| COHERENT INC |
| COINSTAR INC |
| COLLAGENEX PHARMACEUTICALS INC |
| COMDATA CORP |
| COMMERCE GROUP INC (THE) |
| COMTECH TELECOMMUNICATIONS CORP |
| CONCUR TECHNOLOGIES INC |
| CONTINUCARE CORP |
| CORPORATE EXECUTIVE BOARD COMPANY (THE) |
| COUPONS INC |
| CRITICAL CARE SYSTEMS |
| CROWN CASTLE INTERNATIONAL CORP |
| CRUM & FORSTER HOLDINGS INC |
| CRYOLIFE INC |
| CSG SYSTEMS INTERNATIONAL INC |
| CUBIST PHARMACEUTICALS INC |
| CURVES INTERNATIONAL INC |
| CV THERAPEUTICS INC |

| |
|---|
| CYBERSOURCE CORP |
| DAKTRONICS INC |
| DANNON COMPANY INC (THE) |
| DATASCOPE CORP |
| DEI HOLDINGS INC |
| DELPHI FINANCIAL GROUP INC |
| DENBURY RESOURCES INC |
| DIALYSIS CORPORATION OF AMERICA |
| DIAMOND FOODS INC |
| DIGI INTERNATIONAL INC |
| DIGITAL RIVER INC |
| DJO INCORPORATED |
| DOUBLECLICK INC |
| DPL INC |
| DREAMWORKS ANIMATION SKG INC |
| DRUGSTORE.COM INC |
| DSP GROUP INC |
| DYAX CORP |
| DYNACQ HEALTHCARE INC |
| DYNEGY INC |
| ECHELON CORP |
| ECLIPSYS CORPORATION |
| ECOLLEGE.COM |
| EHEALTH INC |
| ELECTRONICS FOR IMAGING INC |
| ELOYALTY CORPORATION |
| EMBARCADERO TECHNOLOGIES INC |
| EMCORE CORP |
| EMS TECHNOLOGIES INC |
| EMULEX CORP |
| ENCORE ACQUISITION CO |
| ENCORIUM GROUP INC |
| ENDO PHARMACEUTICALS HOLDINGS INC |
| ENERGY CONVERSION DEVICES INC |
| ENERNOC INC |
| ENGLOBAL CORP |
| EOG RESOURCES INC |
| EPAM SYSTEMS |
| EPIX PHARMACEUTICALS INC |
| EQUINIX INC |
| EQUITABLE RESOURCES INC |
| EURONET WORLDWIDE INC |
| EVERGREEN ENERGY INC |
| EVERGREEN SOLAR INC |
| EXACTECH INC |
| EXCEL TECHNOLOGY INC |

| |
|---|
| EXCO RESOURCES INC |
| EXELIXIS INC |
| E-Z-EM INC |
| F5 NETWORKS INC |
| FARMER BROTHERS CO |
| FBL FINANCIAL GROUP |
| FIRST SOLAR LLC |
| FLIR SYSTEMS |
| FOREST OIL CORPORATION |
| FORRESTER RESEARCH INC |
| FRESH BRANDS INC |
| FRESHDIRECT LLC |
| FRONTIER OIL CORPORATION |
| FUEL TECH INC |
| FUELCELL ENERGY INC |
| FUNDTECH LTD |
| GALLUP ORGANIZATION (THE) |
| GENENCOR INTERNATIONAL INC |
| GENERAL COMMUNICATION INC (GCI) |
| GENESIS ENERGY LP |
| GENOMIC HEALTH INC |
| GEN-PROBE INC |
| GERBER SCIENTIFIC INC |
| GERON CORPORATION |
| GLOBAL PARTNERS LP |
| GLOBECOMM SYSTEMS INC |
| GLU MOBILE INC |
| GOAMERICA INC |
| GOLFSMITH INTERNATIONAL HOLDINGS INC |
| GREAT AMERICAN FINANCIAL RESOURCES INC |
| GREAT LAKES CHEESE COMPANY INC |
| GREEN MOUNTAIN COFFEE ROASTERS INC |
| GREEN MOUNTAIN POWER CORPORATION |
| GTC BIOTHERAPEUTICS INC |
| HACKETT GROUP (THE) |
| HAEMONETICS CORPORATION |
| HAHN AUTOMOTIVE WAREHOUSE INC |
| HANOVER FOODS CORPORATION |
| HANSEN NATURAL |
| HARMONIC INC |
| HARRIS STRATEX NETWORKS INC |
| HARVARD PILGRIM HEALTH CARE INC |
| HCC INSURANCE HOLDINGS INC |
| HEALTH GRADES INC |

| |
|---|
| HEALTH INSURANCE PLAN OF GREATER NEW YORK |
| HEALTHSTREAM INC |
| HEALTHTRONICS INC |
| HEARTLAND PAYMENT SYSTEMS INC |
| HEARUSA INC |
| HEIDRICK & STRUGGLES INTERNATIONAL INC |
| HELIOVOLT CORP |
| HESKA CORP |
| HICKORY TECH CORPORATION |
| HI-TECH PHARMACAL CO INC |
| HOLLY CORP |
| HORACE MANN EDUCATORS CORPORATION |
| HUMAN GENOME SCIENCES INC |
| HURON CONSULTING GROUP INC |
| IBASIS INC |
| ICO INC |
| IDACORP INC |
| I-FLOW CORPORATION |
| ILLUMINA INC |
| IMATION CORP |
| IMG WORLDWIDE INC |
| IMMUCOR INC |
| INAMED CORP |
| INDEPENDENCE HOLDING CO |
| INFINERA CORP |
| INSPIRE PHARMACEUTICALS INC |
| INTEGRA LIFESCIENCES HOLDINGS CORP |
| INTEGRAL SYSTEMS INC |
| INTEGRAMED AMERICA INC |
| INTELLIGROUP INC |
| INTERACTIVE BROKERS GROUP INC |
| INTERACTIVE INTELLIGENCE |
| INTERCONTINENTALEXCHANGE INC (ICE) |
| INTERNAP NETWORK SERVICES CORP |
| INTERNATIONAL CREATIVE MANAGEMENT (ICM) |
| INTERNATIONAL DAIRY QUEEN |
| INTERNET SECURITY SYSTEMS INC |
| INTERSTATE BATTERY SYSTEM OF AMERICA |
| INTERWOVEN INC |
| INVESTMENT TECHNOLOGY GROUP INC (ITG) |
| IRIDEX CORP |
| IRIS INTERNATIONAL INC |

| |
|---|
| ISILON SYSTEMS INC |
| IVILLAGE INC |
| J2 GLOBAL COMMUNICATIONS INC |
| JACKSON NATIONAL LIFE INSURANCE COMPANY |
| JAZZ PHARMACEUTICALS |
| JUPITERMEDIA CORP |
| KAMPGROUNDS OF AMERICA INC |
| KENDALL-JACKSON WINE ESTATES LTD |
| KIMLEY-HORN AND ASSOCIATES INC |
| KNIGHT CAPITAL GROUP INC |
| KNOT INC (THE) |
| KRONOS WORLDWIDE INC |
| KV PHARMACEUTICAL CO |
| LACLEDE GROUP INC (THE) |
| LCA-VISION INC |
| LCC INTERNATIONAL INC |
| LEAP WIRELESS INTERNATIONAL INC |
| LESLIE'S POOLMART INC |
| LIFECELL CORPORATION |
| LIFECORE BIOMEDICAL INC |
| LIVEPERSON INC |
| LOGISTICARE INC |
| LOJACK CORP |
| LORAL SPACE & COMMUNICATIONS LTD |
| LUCASFILM LTD |
| LUCOR INC |
| LUMINEX CORPORATION |
| M&F WORLDWIDE CORP |
| MAGELLAN MIDSTREAM PARTNERS LP |
| MALT-O-MEAL COMPANY |
| MANHATTAN ASSOCIATES INC |
| MARCHEX INC |
| MARTEK BIOSCIENCES CORP |
| MARTHA STEWART LIVING OMNIMEDIA INC |
| MATRIA HEALTHCARE INC |
| MAXYGEN INC |
| MCMORAN EXPLORATION CO |
| MEDAREX INC |
| MEDICAL ACTION INDUSTRIES INC |
| MEDICINES CO (THE) |
| MEDICIS PHARMACEUTICAL CORP |
| MEDIS TECHNOLOGIES |
| MEDTOX SCIENTIFIC INC |
| MENTOR CORP |
| MERIDIAN BIOSCIENCE INC |

| |
|---|
| MERIT MEDICAL SYSTEMS INC |
| METROLOGIC INSTRUMENTS INC |
| METROPCS COMMUNICATIONS INC |
| METROPOLITAN HEALTH NETWORKS |
| MICHELINAS INC |
| MICROSTRATEGY INC |
| MICROTEK MEDICAL HOLDINGS INC |
| MIDAS INC |
| MILLENNIUM PHARMACEUTICALS INC |
| MOLINA HEALTHCARE INC |
| MOTORCAR PARTS OF AMERICA INC |
| MTS SYSTEMS |
| MYRIAD GENETICS INC |
| NANOMETRICS INC |
| NASDAQ OMX |
| NATIONAL BEVERAGE CORP |
| NATIONAL CINEMEDIA INC |
| NATIONAL DENTEX CORP |
| NATIONAL FUEL GAS CO |
| NATIONAL WINE & SPIRITS INC |
| NATUS MEDICAL |
| NAVISITE INC |
| NEKTAR THERAPEUTICS |
| NEOGEN CORPORATION |
| NETFLIX INC |
| NETGEAR INC |
| NETRATINGS INC |
| NETSCOUT SYSTEMS INC |
| NETSUITE INC |
| NEWFIELD EXPLORATION CO |
| NIC INC |
| NOBLE ENERGY INC |
| NORTHWESTERN CORPORATION |
| NOVAMED INC |
| NOVEN PHARMACEUTICALS |
| NTELOS HOLDING CORP |
| NUGGET MARKET |
| NUSTAR ENERGY LP |
| NUTRASWEET COMPANY (THE) |
| NYER MEDICAL GROUP INC |
| NYMEX HOLDINGS (NEW YORK MERCANTILE EXCHANGE) |
| ODYSSEY RE HOLDINGS CORP |
| OMNITURE INC |
| ONEOK PARTNERS LP |
| ONLINE RESOURCES CORP |
| OPENTV CORP |
| OPNEXT INC |

| |
|---|
| OPTELECOM-NKF INC |
| ORMAT TECHNOLOGIES |
| OSCIENT PHARMACEUTICALS CORPORATION |
| PALM INC |
| PAR PHARMACEUTICAL COMPANIES INC |
| PC CONNECTION INC |
| PC MALL INC |
| PEAPOD LLC |
| PERFICIENT INC |
| PETMED EXPRESS INC |
| PETROLEUM DEVELOPMENT CORPORATION |
| PHILADELPHIA CONSOLIDATED HOLDING CORP |
| PHOENIX COMPANIES (THE) |
| PIEDMONT NATURAL GAS COMPANY INC |
| PIONEER NATURAL RESOURCES COMPANY |
| PITNEY BOWES MAPINFO |
| PLAINS EXPLORATION AND PRODUCTION COMPANY |
| PLUG POWER INC |
| PMA CAPITAL CORPORATION |
| POLYCOM INC |
| POLYMEDICA CORPORATION |
| PREMIERE GLOBAL SERVICES INC |
| PRIMEENERGY CORPORATION |
| PROASSURANCE CORP |
| PROGRESS SOFTWARE CORP |
| PROTECTIVE LIFE CORP |
| QLOGIC CORP |
| QUALITY SYSTEMS INC |
| QUICKSILVER RESOURCES INC |
| QUIDEL CORP |
| RACKSPACE HOSTING INC |
| RADISYS CORP |
| RADNET INC |
| RADYNE CORPORATION |
| RANGE RESOURCES CORP |
| REALNETWORKS INC |
| RECYCLED ENERGY DEVELOPMENT |
| RED HAT INC |
| REDDY ICE HOLDINGS INC |
| REGENERON PHARMACEUTICALS INC |
| REINSURANCE GROUP OF AMERICA INC |
| REVOLUTION HEALTH GROUP LLC |
| RIGHTNOW TECHNOLOGIES INC |
| RSA SECURITY INC |
| S1 CORPORATION |
| SACRAMENTO MUNICIPAL UTILITY DISTRICT |
| SALIX PHARMACEUTICALS |
| SAVVIS INC |
| SCANSOURCE INC |
| SCHICK TECHNOLOGIES INC |
| SCHIFF NUTRITION INTERNATIONAL INC |
| SCICLONE PHARMACEUTICALS |
| SCIELE PHARMA INC |
| SCIOS INC |
| SEACHANGE INTERNATIONAL INC |
| SEATTLE GENETICS |
| SECURE COMPUTING CORP |
| SENTO |
| SEPRACOR INC |
| SEQUENOM INC |
| SERENA SOFTWARE INC |
| SHARED TECHNOLOGIES |
| SHENANDOAH TELECOMMUNICATIONS CO |
| SHUTTERFLY INC |
| SKILLSOFT PLC |
| SOLAR RESERVE |
| SOLFOCUS INC |
| SONIC INNOVATIONS INC |
| SONUS NETWORKS INC |
| SOUTHERN UNION COMPANY |
| SOUTHWESTERN ENERGY CO |
| SPAN AMERICA MEDICAL SYSTEMS INC |
| SPECTRALINK CORP |
| SPECTRANETICS CORP |
| SPIRE CORPORATION |
| SPORTSMAN'S GUIDE INC (THE) |
| SPROUTS FARMERS MARKET |
| SPSS INC |
| SRI/SURGICAL EXPRESS INC |
| SS&C TECHNOLOGIES INC |
| ST MARY LAND & EXPLORATION COMPANY |
| STAAR SURGICAL CO |
| STANDARD MICROSYSTEMS CORPORATION |
| STATE AUTO FINANCIAL CORP |
| STERLING AUTOBODY CENTERS |
| STEVEN MADDEN LTD |
| STIEFEL LABORATORIES INC |
| SUPER MICRO COMPUTER INC |
| SWIFT ENERGY CO |
| SYCAMORE NETWORKS INC |
| SYMMETRY MEDICAL INC |
| SYMYX TECHNOLOGIES |
| SYNOVIS LIFE TECHNOLOGIES INC |
| TAMPA ELECTRIC COMPANY |
| TARGA RESOURCES PARTNERS LP |
| TECHNE CORP |
| TELIRIS |
| TEPPCO PARTNERS LP |
| TERREMARK WORLDWIDE INC |
| THERAGENICS CORP |
| THIRD WAVE TECHNOLOGIES INC |
| THORATEC CORPORATION |
| THQ INC |
| TIBCO SOFTWARE INC |
| TIVO INC |
| TOMOTHERAPY INC |
| TOOTSIE ROLL INDUSTRIES INC |
| TOPPS COMPANY INC (THE) |
| TRANSATLANTIC HOLDINGS INC |
| TRANSCEND SERVICES INC |
| TRAPEZE NETWORKS INC |
| TRIZETTO GROUP INC (THE) |
| TULLY'S COFFEE CORPORATION |
| UIL HOLDINGS CORPORATION |
| ULTIMATE SOFTWARE GROUP INC |
| UNDER ARMOUR INC |
| UNISOURCE ENERGY CORPORATION |
| UNITED ONLINE INC |
| UNITED THERAPEUTICS CORP |
| UNIVERSAL AMERICAN CORPORATION |
| UNIVERSAL HOSPITAL SERVICES INC |
| US PHYSICAL THERAPY INC |
| VALLEY NATIONAL GASES LLC |
| VALUECLICK INC |
| VASCO DATA SECURITY INTERNATIONAL INC |
| VENTANA MEDICAL SYSTEMS INC |
| VERAZ NETWORKS INC |
| VERIFONE HOLDINGS INC |
| VERTEX PHARMACEUTICALS INC |
| VIASAT INC |
| VIBRANT MEDIA INC |
| VIGNETTE CORP |
| VIROPHARMA INC |
| VISION SERVICE PLAN |

| |
|---|
| VITAL SIGNS INC |
| VOLCOM INC |
| VSE CORP |
| WEBEX COMMUNICATIONS INC |
| WEBMD HEALTH CORP |
| WEBSENSE INC |
| WESTAR ENERGY |
| WGL HOLDINGS INC |
| WHITEWAVE FOODS COMPANY |
| WIND RIVER SYSTEMS INC |
| WRIGHT MEDICAL GROUP INC |
| XOMA LTD |
| XTO ENERGY INC |
| YOUNG'S MARKET COMPANY LLC |
| ZAPPOS.COM INC |
| ZIEBART INTERNATIONAL CORP |
| ZILA INC |
| ZOLL MEDICAL CORP |
| ZYMOGENETICS INC |

| Retail Sales |
|---|
| AMERICAN TIRE DISTRIBUTORS |
| ARDEN GROUP INC |
| ASSOCIATED WHOLESALE GROCERS INC |
| AUDIBLE INC |
| BLUE NILE INC |
| DRUGSTORE.COM INC |
| FRESH BRANDS INC |
| FRESHDIRECT LLC |
| GOLFSMITH INTERNATIONAL HOLDINGS INC |
| HAHN AUTOMOTIVE WAREHOUSE INC |
| HEARUSA INC |
| LESLIE'S POOLMART INC |
| NUGGET MARKET |
| PC CONNECTION INC |
| PC MALL INC |
| PEAPOD LLC |
| PETMED EXPRESS INC |
| SPORTSMAN'S GUIDE INC (THE) |
| SPROUTS FARMERS MARKET |
| TULLY'S COFFEE CORPORATION |
| YOUNG'S MARKET COMPANY LLC |
| ZAPPOS.COM INC |

| Sales Trainees |
|---|
| 24/7 REAL MEDIA INC |
| ABAXIS INC |
| ACI WORLDWIDE INC |
| ACME PACKET INC |
| ACXIOM DIGITAL |
| AFFYMETRIX INC |
| AKAMAI TECHNOLOGIES INC |
| AKQA INC |
| ALASKA COMMUNICATIONS SYSTEMS GROUP |
| ALEXION PHARMACEUTICALS INC |
| ALIEN TECHNOLOGY CORPORATION |
| ALIGN TECHNOLOGY INC |
| ALKERMES INC |
| ALLEGHANY CORP |
| ALLIANCE IMAGING INC |
| ALLSCRIPTS HEALTHCARE SOLUTIONS INC |
| ALPHARMA INC |
| ALTIRIS INC |
| ALZA CORP |
| AMCOL INTERNATIONAL CORP |
| AMERESCO |
| AMERICAN FIDELITY ASSURANCE COMPANY |
| AMERICAN ITALIAN PASTA COMPANY |
| AMERICAN MEDICAL SYSTEMS HOLDINGS INC |
| AMERICAN SCIENCE & ENGINEERING INC |
| AMERICAN SUPERCONDUCTOR CORP |
| AMERICAN TIRE DISTRIBUTORS |
| AMERICAN TOWER CORP |
| AMICAS INC |
| AMSURG CORP |
| AMTECH SYSTEMS INC |
| AMYLIN PHARMACEUTICALS INC |
| ANALOGIC CORP |
| ANAREN INC |
| ANIKA THERAPEUTICS INC |
| ANSYS INC |
| APP PHARMACEUTICALS INC |
| APPLIED SIGNAL TECHNOLOGY INC |
| ARDEN GROUP INC |
| ARIBA INC |
| ARIZONA CHEMICAL COMPANY |
| AROTECH CORPORATION |
| ARRIS GROUP INC |
| ARUBA NETWORKS INC |
| ASPECT MEDICAL SYSTEMS INC |
| ASPEN TECHNOLOGY INC |
| ASSOCIATED WHOLESALE GROCERS INC |
| ATHENAHEALTH INC |
| ATHEROS COMMUNICATIONS INC |
| ATMI INC |
| ATRION CORPORATION |
| ATS MEDICAL INC |
| AUDIBLE INC |
| AVANEX CORPORATION |
| AVI BIOPHARMA INC |
| AVIALL INC |
| BENTLEY PHARMACEUTICALS INC |
| BIO REFERENCE LABORATORIES INC |
| BIOMARIN PHARMACEUTICAL INC |
| BIOSCRIP INC |
| BIOSITE INC |
| BLACK HILLS CORP |
| BLACKBOARD INC |
| BLUE COAT SYSTEMS INC |
| BLUE NILE INC |
| BRIGHTSTAR CORPORATION |
| CALIPER LIFE SCIENCES |
| CALPINE CORPORATION |
| CAMBREX CORP |
| CANDELA CORP |
| CANTEL MEDICAL CORP |
| CARACO PHARMACEUTICAL LABORATORIES |
| CARDTRONICS INC |
| C-COR INC |
| CELGENE CORP |
| CELL GENESYS INC |
| CELL THERAPEUTICS INC |
| CENTRAL VERMONT PUBLIC SERVICE CORPORATION |
| CEPHEID |
| CHANNELL COMMERCIAL CORP |
| CHATTEM INC |
| CHINDEX INTERNATIONAL INC |
| CHOICESTREAM INC |
| CHOLESTECH CORP |
| CHYRON CORP |
| CIENA CORP |
| CKX INC |
| CLEARWIRE CORP |
| COGNEX CORP |
| COHERENT INC |
| COINSTAR INC |
| COLLAGENEX PHARMACEUTICALS INC |
| COMDATA CORP |

COMMERCE GROUP INC (THE)
COMTECH TELECOMMUNICATIONS CORP
CONCUR TECHNOLOGIES INC
CORPORATE EXECUTIVE BOARD COMPANY (THE)
COUPONS INC
CRITICAL CARE SYSTEMS
CROWN CASTLE INTERNATIONAL CORP
CRUM & FORSTER HOLDINGS INC
CRYOLIFE INC
CSG SYSTEMS INTERNATIONAL INC
CUBIST PHARMACEUTICALS INC
CV THERAPEUTICS INC
CYBERSOURCE CORP
DAKTRONICS INC
DANNON COMPANY INC (THE)
DARLING INTERNATIONAL INC
DATASCOPE CORP
DEI HOLDINGS INC
DIALYSIS CORPORATION OF AMERICA
DIGI INTERNATIONAL INC
DIGITAL RIVER INC
DJO INCORPORATED
DOUBLECLICK INC
DPL INC
DREAMWORKS ANIMATION SKG INC
DRUGSTORE.COM INC
DSP GROUP INC
DYAX CORP
DYNACQ HEALTHCARE INC
ECHELON CORP
ECLIPSYS CORPORATION
ECOLLEGE.COM
ELECTRONICS FOR IMAGING INC
ELOYALTY CORPORATION
EMBARCADERO TECHNOLOGIES INC
EMCORE CORP
EMS TECHNOLOGIES INC
EMULEX CORP
ENDO PHARMACEUTICALS HOLDINGS INC
ENERGY CONVERSION DEVICES INC
ENERNOC INC
EPIX PHARMACEUTICALS INC
EQUINIX INC
EQUITABLE RESOURCES INC
EURONET WORLDWIDE INC
EVERGREEN SOLAR INC
EXACTECH INC
EXCEL TECHNOLOGY INC
EXELIXIS INC
E-Z-EM INC
F5 NETWORKS INC
FARMER BROTHERS CO
FBL FINANCIAL GROUP
FIRST SOLAR LLC
FLIR SYSTEMS
FRESH BRANDS INC
FRESHDIRECT LLC
FUELCELL ENERGY INC
FUNDTECH LTD
GENENCOR INTERNATIONAL INC
GENERAL COMMUNICATION INC (GCI)
GENESIS ENERGY LP
GENOMIC HEALTH INC
GEN-PROBE INC
GERBER SCIENTIFIC INC
GERON CORPORATION
GLOBAL PARTNERS LP
GLOBECOMM SYSTEMS INC
GLU MOBILE INC
GOLFSMITH INTERNATIONAL HOLDINGS INC
GREAT AMERICAN FINANCIAL RESOURCES INC
GREAT LAKES CHEESE COMPANY INC
GREEN MOUNTAIN COFFEE ROASTERS INC
GREEN MOUNTAIN POWER CORPORATION
GTC BIOTHERAPEUTICS INC
HACKETT GROUP (THE)
HAEMONETICS CORPORATION
HAHN AUTOMOTIVE WAREHOUSE INC
HANOVER FOODS CORPORATION
HANSEN NATURAL
HARMONIC INC
HARRIS STRATEX NETWORKS INC
HCC INSURANCE HOLDINGS INC
HEALTH GRADES INC
HEALTHSTREAM INC
HEALTHTRONICS INC
HEARTLAND PAYMENT SYSTEMS INC
HEARUSA INC
HEIDRICK & STRUGGLES INTERNATIONAL INC
HELIOVOLT CORP
HESKA CORP
HICKORY TECH CORPORATION
HI-TECH PHARMACAL CO INC
HORACE MANN EDUCATORS CORPORATION
HUMAN GENOME SCIENCES INC
HURON CONSULTING GROUP INC
IBASIS INC
ICO INC
IDACORP INC
I-FLOW CORPORATION
ILLUMINA INC
IMG WORLDWIDE INC
IMMUCOR INC
INAMED CORP
INDEPENDENCE HOLDING CO
INFINERA CORP
INSPIRE PHARMACEUTICALS INC
INTEGRA LIFESCIENCES HOLDINGS CORP
INTEGRAL SYSTEMS INC
INTEGRAMED AMERICA INC
INTERACTIVE INTELLIGENCE
INTERMEC INC
INTERNAP NETWORK SERVICES CORP
INTERNATIONAL CREATIVE MANAGEMENT (ICM)
INTERNET SECURITY SYSTEMS INC
INTERSTATE BATTERY SYSTEM OF AMERICA
INTERWOVEN INC
INVESTMENT TECHNOLOGY GROUP INC (ITG)
IRIDEX CORP
IRIS INTERNATIONAL INC
IVILLAGE INC
J2 GLOBAL COMMUNICATIONS INC
JACKSON NATIONAL LIFE INSURANCE COMPANY
JAZZ PHARMACEUTICALS
JUPITERMEDIA CORP
KENDALL-JACKSON WINE ESTATES LTD
KNOT INC (THE)
KV PHARMACEUTICAL CO
LCA-VISION INC
LCC INTERNATIONAL INC
LESLIE'S POOLMART INC

LIFECELL CORPORATION
LIFECORE BIOMEDICAL INC
LIVEPERSON INC
LOGISTICARE INC
LOJACK CORP
LORAL SPACE & COMMUNICATIONS LTD
LUCASFILM LTD
LUMINEX CORPORATION
M&F WORLDWIDE CORP
MAGELLAN MIDSTREAM PARTNERS LP
MALT-O-MEAL COMPANY
MANHATTAN ASSOCIATES INC
MARCHEX INC
MARTEK BIOSCIENCES CORP
MATRIA HEALTHCARE INC
MAXYGEN INC
MEDAREX INC
MEDICAL ACTION INDUSTRIES INC
MEDICINES CO (THE)
MEDICIS PHARMACEUTICAL CORP
MEDIS TECHNOLOGIES
MEDTOX SCIENTIFIC INC
MENTOR CORP
MERIDIAN BIOSCIENCE INC
MERIT MEDICAL SYSTEMS INC
METROLOGIC INSTRUMENTS INC
MICHELINAS INC
MICROSTRATEGY INC
MICROTEK MEDICAL HOLDINGS INC
MILLENNIUM PHARMACEUTICALS INC
MOTORCAR PARTS OF AMERICA INC
MTS SYSTEMS
MYRIAD GENETICS INC
NANOMETRICS INC
NATIONAL BEVERAGE CORP
NATIONAL CINEMEDIA INC
NATIONAL DENTEX CORP
NATIONAL WINE & SPIRITS INC
NATUS MEDICAL
NAVISITE INC
NEKTAR THERAPEUTICS
NEOGEN CORPORATION
NETGEAR INC
NETRATINGS INC
NETSCOUT SYSTEMS INC
NIC INC
NOVAMED INC
NOVEN PHARMACEUTICALS
NTELOS HOLDING CORP
NUGGET MARKET
NUSTAR ENERGY LP
NUTRASWEET COMPANY (THE)
NYER MEDICAL GROUP INC
ODYSSEY RE HOLDINGS CORP
ONEOK PARTNERS LP
ONLINE RESOURCES CORP
OPENTV CORP
OPNEXT INC
OPTELECOM-NKF INC
ORMAT TECHNOLOGIES
OSCIENT PHARMACEUTICALS CORPORATION
PALM INC
PAR PHARMACEUTICAL COMPANIES INC
PC CONNECTION INC
PC MALL INC
PEAPOD LLC
PETMED EXPRESS INC
PHILADELPHIA CONSOLIDATED HOLDING CORP
PHOENIX COMPANIES (THE)
PITNEY BOWES MAPINFO
PLUG POWER INC
PMA CAPITAL CORPORATION
POLYCOM INC
POLYMEDICA CORPORATION
PREMIERE GLOBAL SERVICES INC
PROASSURANCE CORP
PROGRESS SOFTWARE CORP
PROTECTIVE LIFE CORP
QLOGIC CORP
QUALITY SYSTEMS INC
QUIDEL CORP
RACKSPACE HOSTING INC
RADISYS CORP
RADNET INC
RADYNE CORPORATION
REALNETWORKS INC
RECYCLED ENERGY DEVELOPMENT
RED HAT INC
REDDY ICE HOLDINGS INC
REGENERON PHARMACEUTICALS INC
REINSURANCE GROUP OF AMERICA INC
REVOLUTION HEALTH GROUP LLC
RIGHTNOW TECHNOLOGIES INC
RSA SECURITY INC
S1 CORPORATION
SACRAMENTO MUNICIPAL UTILITY DISTRICT
SALIX PHARMACEUTICALS
SAVVIS INC
SCANSOURCE INC
SCHICK TECHNOLOGIES INC
SCHIFF NUTRITION INTERNATIONAL INC
SCICLONE PHARMACEUTICALS
SCIELE PHARMA INC
SCIOS INC
SEACHANGE INTERNATIONAL INC
SEATTLE GENETICS
SECURE COMPUTING CORP
SEPRACOR INC
SEQUENOM INC
SERENA SOFTWARE INC
SHENANDOAH TELECOMMUNICATIONS CO
SHUTTERFLY INC
SKILLSOFT PLC
SOLAR RESERVE
SOLFOCUS INC
SONIC INNOVATIONS INC
SONUS NETWORKS INC
SPAN AMERICA MEDICAL SYSTEMS INC
SPECTRALINK CORP
SPECTRANETICS CORP
SPIRE CORPORATION
SPORTSMAN'S GUIDE INC (THE)
SPROUTS FARMERS MARKET
SPSS INC
SRI/SURGICAL EXPRESS INC
SS&C TECHNOLOGIES INC
STAAR SURGICAL CO
STANDARD MICROSYSTEMS CORPORATION
STATE AUTO FINANCIAL CORP
STEVEN MADDEN LTD
STIEFEL LABORATORIES INC
SUPER MICRO COMPUTER INC
SYCAMORE NETWORKS INC
SYMMETRY MEDICAL INC
SYNAPTICS INC
SYNOVIS LIFE TECHNOLOGIES INC
TAMPA ELECTRIC COMPANY
TECHNE CORP

| |
|---|
| TELIRIS |
| TEPPCO PARTNERS LP |
| TERREMARK WORLDWIDE INC |
| THERAGENICS CORP |
| THIRD WAVE TECHNOLOGIES INC |
| THORATEC CORPORATION |
| THQ INC |
| TIBCO SOFTWARE INC |
| TIVO INC |
| TOMOTHERAPY INC |
| TOOTSIE ROLL INDUSTRIES INC |
| TOPPS COMPANY INC (THE) |
| TRANSATLANTIC HOLDINGS INC |
| TRANSCEND SERVICES INC |
| TRAPEZE NETWORKS INC |
| TRIZETTO GROUP INC (THE) |
| TULLY'S COFFEE CORPORATION |
| UIL HOLDINGS CORPORATION |
| UNDER ARMOUR INC |
| UNITED ONLINE INC |
| UNITED THERAPEUTICS CORP |
| UNIVERSAL AMERICAN CORPORATION |
| UNIVERSAL HOSPITAL SERVICES INC |
| US PHYSICAL THERAPY INC |
| VALLEY NATIONAL GASES LLC |
| VALUECLICK INC |
| VASCO DATA SECURITY INTERNATIONAL INC |
| VENTANA MEDICAL SYSTEMS INC |
| VERAZ NETWORKS INC |
| VERIFONE HOLDINGS INC |
| VERTEX PHARMACEUTICALS INC |
| VIASAT INC |
| VIBRANT MEDIA INC |
| VIGNETTE CORP |
| VIROPHARMA INC |
| VITAL SIGNS INC |
| VOLCOM INC |
| WEBEX COMMUNICATIONS INC |
| WEBMD HEALTH CORP |
| WEBSENSE INC |
| WESTAR ENERGY |
| WHITEWAVE FOODS COMPANY |
| WIND RIVER SYSTEMS INC |
| WRIGHT MEDICAL GROUP INC |
| XOMA LTD |
| YOUNG'S MARKET COMPANY LLC |
| ZAPPOS.COM INC |
| ZILA INC |
| ZOLL MEDICAL CORP |
| ZYMOGENETICS INC |

## Technical/Scientific

| Engineers, Electrical |
|---|
| ABAXIS INC |
| ACI WORLDWIDE INC |
| ACME PACKET INC |
| AFFYMETRIX INC |
| AKAMAI TECHNOLOGIES INC |
| ALASKA COMMUNICATIONS SYSTEMS GROUP |
| ALIEN TECHNOLOGY CORPORATION |
| ALLSCRIPTS HEALTHCARE SOLUTIONS INC |
| ALPHARMA INC |
| ALTIRIS INC |
| AMERICAN MEDICAL SYSTEMS HOLDINGS INC |
| AMERICAN SCIENCE & ENGINEERING INC |
| AMERICAN SUPERCONDUCTOR CORP |
| AMERICAN TOWER CORP |
| AMICAS INC |
| AMTECH SYSTEMS INC |
| ANALOGIC CORP |
| ANAREN INC |
| ANSYS INC |
| APPLIED SIGNAL TECHNOLOGY INC |
| ARIBA INC |
| ARIZONA CHEMICAL COMPANY |
| AROTECH CORPORATION |
| ARRIS GROUP INC |
| ART TECHNOLOGY GROUP INC |
| ARUBA NETWORKS INC |
| ASPECT MEDICAL SYSTEMS INC |
| ASPEN TECHNOLOGY INC |
| ATHEROS COMMUNICATIONS INC |
| ATLANTIC CITY ELECTRIC COMPANY |
| ATMI INC |
| ATRION CORPORATION |
| ATS MEDICAL INC |
| AVANEX CORPORATION |
| AVISTA CORPORATION |
| BLACK HILLS CORP |
| BLUE COAT SYSTEMS INC |
| CALIPER LIFE SCIENCES |
| CALPINE CORPORATION |
| CANDELA CORP |
| C-COR INC |
| CENTRAL VERMONT PUBLIC SERVICE CORPORATION |
| CEPHEID |
| CHANNELL COMMERCIAL CORP |
| CHOLESTECH CORP |
| CIENA CORP |
| COGNEX CORP |
| COHERENT INC |
| COMTECH TELECOMMUNICATIONS CORP |
| CONCUR TECHNOLOGIES INC |
| CROWN CASTLE INTERNATIONAL CORP |
| CSG SYSTEMS INTERNATIONAL INC |
| CYBERSOURCE CORP |
| DAKTRONICS INC |
| DATASCOPE CORP |
| DEI HOLDINGS INC |
| DIGI INTERNATIONAL INC |
| DIGITAL RIVER INC |
| DPL INC |
| DSP GROUP INC |
| DYNEGY INC |
| ECHELON CORP |
| ECLIPSYS CORPORATION |
| ELECTRONICS FOR IMAGING INC |
| ELOYALTY CORPORATION |
| EMBARCADERO TECHNOLOGIES INC |
| EMCORE CORP |
| EMS TECHNOLOGIES INC |
| EMULEX CORP |
| ENERGY CONVERSION DEVICES INC |
| ENGLOBAL CORP |
| EQUINIX INC |
| EQUITABLE RESOURCES INC |
| EVERGREEN ENERGY INC |
| EVERGREEN SOLAR INC |
| EXCEL TECHNOLOGY INC |
| E-Z-EM INC |
| F5 NETWORKS INC |
| FIRST SOLAR LLC |
| FLIR SYSTEMS |
| FRONTIER OIL CORPORATION |
| FUELCELL ENERGY INC |
| FUNDTECH LTD |
| GENENCOR INTERNATIONAL INC |
| GENERAL COMMUNICATION INC |

| |
|---|
| (GCI) |
| GENESIS ENERGY LP |
| GEN-PROBE INC |
| GERBER SCIENTIFIC INC |
| GLOBECOMM SYSTEMS INC |
| GLU MOBILE INC |
| GOAMERICA INC |
| GREEN MOUNTAIN POWER CORPORATION |
| HAEMONETICS CORPORATION |
| HARMONIC INC |
| HARRIS STRATEX NETWORKS INC |
| HELIOVOLT CORP |
| HICKORY TECH CORPORATION |
| HOLLY CORP |
| IBASIS INC |
| IDACORP INC |
| I-FLOW CORPORATION |
| ILLUMINA INC |
| IMATION CORP |
| IMMUCOR INC |
| INFINERA CORP |
| INTEGRA LIFESCIENCES HOLDINGS CORP |
| INTEGRAL SYSTEMS INC |
| INTERACTIVE INTELLIGENCE |
| INTERMEC INC |
| INTERNAP NETWORK SERVICES CORP |
| INTERNET SECURITY SYSTEMS INC |
| INTERSTATE BATTERY SYSTEM OF AMERICA |
| INTERWOVEN INC |
| IRIDEX CORP |
| IRIS INTERNATIONAL INC |
| ISILON SYSTEMS INC |
| ISONICS CORPORATION |
| J2 GLOBAL COMMUNICATIONS INC |
| KIMLEY-HORN AND ASSOCIATES INC |
| KRONOS WORLDWIDE INC |
| LACLEDE GROUP INC (THE) |
| LCC INTERNATIONAL INC |
| LEAP WIRELESS INTERNATIONAL INC |
| LIFECORE BIOMEDICAL INC |
| LIVEPERSON INC |
| LOJACK CORP |
| LORAL SPACE & COMMUNICATIONS LTD |
| LUCASFILM LTD |
| LUMINEX CORPORATION |

| |
|---|
| MAGELLAN MIDSTREAM PARTNERS LP |
| MANHATTAN ASSOCIATES INC |
| MEDIS TECHNOLOGIES |
| METROLOGIC INSTRUMENTS INC |
| METROPCS COMMUNICATIONS INC |
| MICROSTRATEGY INC |
| MOTORCAR PARTS OF AMERICA INC |
| MTS SYSTEMS |
| NANOMETRICS INC |
| NATIONAL FUEL GAS CO |
| NATUS MEDICAL |
| NEOGEN CORPORATION |
| NETGEAR INC |
| NETSCOUT SYSTEMS INC |
| NETSUITE INC |
| NIC INC |
| NORTHWESTERN CORPORATION |
| NTELOS HOLDING CORP |
| NUSTAR ENERGY LP |
| OMNITURE INC |
| ONEOK PARTNERS LP |
| ONLINE RESOURCES CORP |
| OPENTV CORP |
| OPNEXT INC |
| OPTELECOM-NKF INC |
| ORMAT TECHNOLOGIES |
| PALM INC |
| PERFICIENT INC |
| PIEDMONT NATURAL GAS COMPANY INC |
| PITNEY BOWES MAPINFO |
| PLUG POWER INC |
| POLYCOM INC |
| PREMIERE GLOBAL SERVICES INC |
| PROGRESS SOFTWARE CORP |
| QLOGIC CORP |
| QUALITY SYSTEMS INC |
| QUIDEL CORP |
| RACKSPACE HOSTING INC |
| RADISYS CORP |
| RADYNE CORPORATION |
| REALNETWORKS INC |
| RECYCLED ENERGY DEVELOPMENT |
| RED HAT INC |
| REDDY ICE HOLDINGS INC |
| RIGHTNOW TECHNOLOGIES INC |
| RSA SECURITY INC |
| S1 CORPORATION |

| |
|---|
| SACRAMENTO MUNICIPAL UTILITY DISTRICT |
| SAVVIS INC |
| SCANSOURCE INC |
| SCHICK TECHNOLOGIES INC |
| SEACHANGE INTERNATIONAL INC |
| SECURE COMPUTING CORP |
| SERENA SOFTWARE INC |
| SHENANDOAH TELECOMMUNICATIONS CO |
| SKILLSOFT PLC |
| SOLAR RESERVE |
| SOLFOCUS INC |
| SONIC INNOVATIONS INC |
| SONUS NETWORKS INC |
| SOUTHERN UNION COMPANY |
| SPECTRALINK CORP |
| SPECTRANETICS CORP |
| SPIRE CORPORATION |
| SPSS INC |
| SRI/SURGICAL EXPRESS INC |
| SS&C TECHNOLOGIES INC |
| STAAR SURGICAL CO |
| STANDARD MICROSYSTEMS CORPORATION |
| SUPER MICRO COMPUTER INC |
| SYCAMORE NETWORKS INC |
| SYNAPTICS INC |
| SYNOVIS LIFE TECHNOLOGIES INC |
| TAMPA ELECTRIC COMPANY |
| TDINDUSTRIES |
| TELIRIS |
| TEPPCO PARTNERS LP |
| THERAGENICS CORP |
| THORATEC CORPORATION |
| THQ INC |
| TIBCO SOFTWARE INC |
| TIVO INC |
| TOMOTHERAPY INC |
| TRAPEZE NETWORKS INC |
| TRIZETTO GROUP INC (THE) |
| UIL HOLDINGS CORPORATION |
| ULTIMATE SOFTWARE GROUP INC |
| UNISOURCE ENERGY CORPORATION |
| VASCO DATA SECURITY INTERNATIONAL INC |
| VENTANA MEDICAL SYSTEMS INC |
| VERAZ NETWORKS INC |
| VIASAT INC |
| VIGNETTE CORP |

| |
|---|
| VITAL SIGNS INC |
| VSE CORP |
| WEBEX COMMUNICATIONS INC |
| WEBSENSE INC |
| WESTAR ENERGY |
| WGL HOLDINGS INC |
| WIND RIVER SYSTEMS INC |
| ZOLL MEDICAL CORP |

| Engineers, Other |
|---|
| ABAXIS INC |
| ACME PACKET INC |
| AFFYMETRIX INC |
| ALASKA COMMUNICATIONS SYSTEMS GROUP |
| ALIEN TECHNOLOGY CORPORATION |
| ALIGN TECHNOLOGY INC |
| ALPHARMA INC |
| AMCOL INTERNATIONAL CORP |
| AMERICAN MEDICAL SYSTEMS HOLDINGS INC |
| AMERICAN SCIENCE & ENGINEERING INC |
| AMERICAN SUPERCONDUCTOR CORP |
| AMERICAN TOWER CORP |
| AMTECH SYSTEMS INC |
| ANALOGIC CORP |
| ANAREN INC |
| ANIKA THERAPEUTICS INC |
| ANSYS INC |
| APPLIED SIGNAL TECHNOLOGY INC |
| AROTECH CORPORATION |
| ARRIS GROUP INC |
| ASPECT MEDICAL SYSTEMS INC |
| ATHEROS COMMUNICATIONS INC |
| ATLANTIC CITY ELECTRIC COMPANY |
| ATMI INC |
| ATRION CORPORATION |
| ATS MEDICAL INC |
| AVANEX CORPORATION |
| AVISTA CORPORATION |
| BERRY PETROLEUM CO |
| BIOSITE INC |
| BLACK HILLS CORP |
| CALIPER LIFE SCIENCES |
| CALPINE CORPORATION |
| CANDELA CORP |
| CANTEL MEDICAL CORP |
| C-COR INC |
| CENTRAL VERMONT PUBLIC SERVICE CORPORATION |
| CEPHEID |
| CHANNELL COMMERCIAL CORP |
| CHOLESTECH CORP |
| CIENA CORP |
| CNX GAS CORPORATION |
| COGNEX CORP |
| COHERENT INC |
| COMTECH TELECOMMUNICATIONS CORP |
| CROWN CASTLE INTERNATIONAL CORP |
| DATASCOPE CORP |
| DEI HOLDINGS INC |
| DENBURY RESOURCES INC |
| DJO INCORPORATED |
| DPL INC |
| DREAMWORKS ANIMATION SKG INC |
| DSP GROUP INC |
| DYNEGY INC |
| ELECTRONICS FOR IMAGING INC |
| EMCORE CORP |
| EMS TECHNOLOGIES INC |
| ENCORE ACQUISITION CO |
| ENERGY CONVERSION DEVICES INC |
| ENGLOBAL CORP |
| EOG RESOURCES INC |
| EPIX PHARMACEUTICALS INC |
| EQUITABLE RESOURCES INC |
| EVERGREEN ENERGY INC |
| EVERGREEN SOLAR INC |
| EXACTECH INC |
| EXCEL TECHNOLOGY INC |
| EXCO RESOURCES INC |
| E-Z-EM INC |
| FIRST SOLAR LLC |
| FOREST OIL CORPORATION |
| FRONTIER OIL CORPORATION |
| FUELCELL ENERGY INC |
| GENENCOR INTERNATIONAL INC |
| GENERAL COMMUNICATION INC (GCI) |
| GENESIS ENERGY LP |
| GENOMIC HEALTH INC |
| GEN-PROBE INC |
| GERBER SCIENTIFIC INC |
| GLOBECOMM SYSTEMS INC |
| GREEN MOUNTAIN POWER CORPORATION |
| HAEMONETICS CORPORATION |
| HARMONIC INC |
| HARRIS STRATEX NETWORKS INC |
| HELIOVOLT CORP |
| HICKORY TECH CORPORATION |
| HOLLY CORP |
| IBASIS INC |
| ICO INC |
| IDACORP INC |
| I-FLOW CORPORATION |
| ILLUMINA INC |
| IMMUCOR INC |
| INAMED CORP |
| INFINERA CORP |
| INTEGRA LIFESCIENCES HOLDINGS CORP |
| INTERMEC INC |
| INTERSTATE BATTERY SYSTEM OF AMERICA |
| IRIDEX CORP |
| IRIS INTERNATIONAL INC |
| KIMLEY-HORN AND ASSOCIATES INC |
| LACLEDE GROUP INC (THE) |
| LCC INTERNATIONAL INC |
| LIFECELL CORPORATION |
| LIFECORE BIOMEDICAL INC |
| LOJACK CORP |
| LORAL SPACE & COMMUNICATIONS LTD |
| LUCASFILM LTD |
| LUMINEX CORPORATION |
| MAGELLAN MIDSTREAM PARTNERS LP |
| MCMORAN EXPLORATION CO |
| MEDICAL ACTION INDUSTRIES INC |
| MEDIS TECHNOLOGIES |
| MENTOR CORP |
| MERIDIAN BIOSCIENCE INC |
| MERIT MEDICAL SYSTEMS INC |
| METROLOGIC INSTRUMENTS INC |
| MICROTEK MEDICAL HOLDINGS INC |
| MOTORCAR PARTS OF AMERICA INC |
| MTS SYSTEMS |
| NANOMETRICS INC |
| NATIONAL DENTEX CORP |
| NATIONAL FUEL GAS CO |
| NATUS MEDICAL |
| NEOGEN CORPORATION |

| |
|---|
| NEWFIELD EXPLORATION CO |
| NOBLE ENERGY INC |
| NORTHWESTERN CORPORATION |
| NTELOS HOLDING CORP |
| NUSTAR ENERGY LP |
| ONEOK PARTNERS LP |
| OPNEXT INC |
| OPTELECOM-NKF INC |
| ORMAT TECHNOLOGIES |
| PALM INC |
| PETROLEUM DEVELOPMENT CORPORATION |
| PIEDMONT NATURAL GAS COMPANY INC |
| PIONEER NATURAL RESOURCES COMPANY |
| PITNEY BOWES MAPINFO |
| PLAINS EXPLORATION AND PRODUCTION COMPANY |
| PLUG POWER INC |
| POLYCOM INC |
| POLYMEDICA CORPORATION |
| PRIMEENERGY CORPORATION |
| QUICKSILVER RESOURCES INC |
| QUIDEL CORP |
| RADISYS CORP |
| RADYNE CORPORATION |
| RANGE RESOURCES CORP |
| SACRAMENTO MUNICIPAL UTILITY DISTRICT |
| SCHICK TECHNOLOGIES INC |
| SEQUENOM INC |
| SHARED TECHNOLOGIES |
| SHENANDOAH TELECOMMUNICATIONS CO |
| SOLAR RESERVE |
| SOLFOCUS INC |
| SONIC INNOVATIONS INC |
| SONUS NETWORKS INC |
| SOUTHERN UNION COMPANY |
| SOUTHWESTERN ENERGY CO |
| SPAN AMERICA MEDICAL SYSTEMS INC |
| SPECTRALINK CORP |
| SPECTRANETICS CORP |
| SPIRE CORPORATION |
| SRI/SURGICAL EXPRESS INC |
| ST MARY LAND & EXPLORATION COMPANY |
| STAAR SURGICAL CO |
| STANDARD MICROSYSTEMS CORPORATION |
| SUPER MICRO COMPUTER INC |
| SWIFT ENERGY CO |
| SYCAMORE NETWORKS INC |
| SYMMETRY MEDICAL INC |
| SYNAPTICS INC |
| SYNOVIS LIFE TECHNOLOGIES INC |
| TAMPA ELECTRIC COMPANY |
| TARGA RESOURCES PARTNERS LP |
| TDINDUSTRIES |
| TECHNE CORP |
| TELIRIS |
| TEPPCO PARTNERS LP |
| THERAGENICS CORP |
| THIRD WAVE TECHNOLOGIES INC |
| THORATEC CORPORATION |
| TIVO INC |
| TOMOTHERAPY INC |
| UIL HOLDINGS CORPORATION |
| UNISOURCE ENERGY CORPORATION |
| VENTANA MEDICAL SYSTEMS INC |
| VERAZ NETWORKS INC |
| VIASAT INC |
| VITAL SIGNS INC |
| VSE CORP |
| WEBEX COMMUNICATIONS INC |
| WESTAR ENERGY |
| WGL HOLDINGS INC |
| WRIGHT MEDICAL GROUP INC |
| XTO ENERGY INC |
| ZOLL MEDICAL CORP |

| Health/Laboratory |
|---|
| ABAXIS INC |
| AFFYMETRIX INC |
| ALBANY MOLECULAR RESEARCH |
| ALEXION PHARMACEUTICALS INC |
| ALIGN TECHNOLOGY INC |
| ALKERMES INC |
| ALLIANCE IMAGING INC |
| ALPHARMA INC |
| ALZA CORP |
| AMERICAN MEDICAL SYSTEMS HOLDINGS INC |
| AMSURG CORP |
| AMYLIN PHARMACEUTICALS INC |
| ANALOGIC CORP |
| ANIKA THERAPEUTICS INC |
| APP PHARMACEUTICALS INC |
| ASPECT MEDICAL SYSTEMS INC |
| ATRION CORPORATION |
| ATS MEDICAL INC |
| AVI BIOPHARMA INC |
| BENTLEY PHARMACEUTICALS INC |
| BIO REFERENCE LABORATORIES INC |
| BIOMARIN PHARMACEUTICAL INC |
| BIOSITE INC |
| BLUE CARE NETWORK OF MICHIGAN |
| CALIPER LIFE SCIENCES |
| CAMBREX CORP |
| CANDELA CORP |
| CANTEL MEDICAL CORP |
| CARACO PHARMACEUTICAL LABORATORIES |
| CELERA CORPORATION |
| CELGENE CORP |
| CELL GENESYS INC |
| CELL THERAPEUTICS INC |
| CEPHEID |
| CHATTEM INC |
| CHOLESTECH CORP |
| COHERENT INC |
| COLLAGENEX PHARMACEUTICALS INC |
| CONTINUCARE CORP |
| CRITICAL CARE SYSTEMS |
| CRYOLIFE INC |
| CUBIST PHARMACEUTICALS INC |
| CV THERAPEUTICS INC |
| DATASCOPE CORP |
| DELPHI FINANCIAL GROUP INC |
| DIALYSIS CORPORATION OF AMERICA |
| DJO INCORPORATED |
| DYAX CORP |
| DYNACQ HEALTHCARE INC |
| ENDO PHARMACEUTICALS HOLDINGS INC |
| EPIX PHARMACEUTICALS INC |
| EXACTECH INC |
| EXCEL TECHNOLOGY INC |
| EXELIXIS INC |
| E-Z-EM INC |
| GENENCOR INTERNATIONAL INC |
| GENOMIC HEALTH INC |
| GEN-PROBE INC |
| GERON CORPORATION |
| GTC BIOTHERAPEUTICS INC |
| HAEMONETICS CORPORATION |

| |
|---|
| HARVARD PILGRIM HEALTH CARE INC |
| HEALTH INSURANCE PLAN OF GREATER NEW YORK |
| HEALTHTRONICS INC |
| HEARUSA INC |
| HESKA CORP |
| HI-TECH PHARMACAL CO INC |
| HUMAN GENOME SCIENCES INC |
| I-FLOW CORPORATION |
| IMMUCOR INC |
| INAMED CORP |
| INSPIRE PHARMACEUTICALS INC |
| INTEGRA LIFESCIENCES HOLDINGS CORP |
| INTEGRAMED AMERICA INC |
| IRIDEX CORP |
| IRIS INTERNATIONAL INC |
| JAZZ PHARMACEUTICALS |
| KV PHARMACEUTICAL CO |
| LCA-VISION INC |
| LIFECELL CORPORATION |
| LIFECORE BIOMEDICAL INC |
| LUMINEX CORPORATION |
| MARTEK BIOSCIENCES CORP |
| MATRIA HEALTHCARE INC |
| MAXYGEN INC |
| MEDAREX INC |
| MEDICAL ACTION INDUSTRIES INC |
| MEDICINES CO (THE) |
| MEDICIS PHARMACEUTICAL CORP |
| MEDTOX SCIENTIFIC INC |
| MENTOR CORP |
| MERIDIAN BIOSCIENCE INC |
| MERIT MEDICAL SYSTEMS INC |
| METROPOLITAN HEALTH NETWORKS |
| MICROTEK MEDICAL HOLDINGS INC |
| MILLENNIUM PHARMACEUTICALS INC |
| MOLINA HEALTHCARE INC |
| MYRIAD GENETICS INC |
| NATIONAL DENTEX CORP |
| NATUS MEDICAL |
| NEKTAR THERAPEUTICS |
| NEOGEN CORPORATION |
| NOVAMED INC |
| NOVEN PHARMACEUTICALS |
| OSCIENT PHARMACEUTICALS CORPORATION |
| PAR PHARMACEUTICAL COMPANIES INC |
| POLYMEDICA CORPORATION |
| QUIDEL CORP |
| RADNET INC |
| REGENERON PHARMACEUTICALS INC |
| SALIX PHARMACEUTICALS |
| SCHICK TECHNOLOGIES INC |
| SCHIFF NUTRITION INTERNATIONAL INC |
| SCICLONE PHARMACEUTICALS |
| SCIELE PHARMA INC |
| SCIOS INC |
| SEATTLE GENETICS |
| SEPRACOR INC |
| SEQUENOM INC |
| SONIC INNOVATIONS INC |
| SPAN AMERICA MEDICAL SYSTEMS INC |
| SPECTRANETICS CORP |
| SRI/SURGICAL EXPRESS INC |
| STAAR SURGICAL CO |
| STIEFEL LABORATORIES INC |
| SYMMETRY MEDICAL INC |
| SYNOVIS LIFE TECHNOLOGIES INC |
| TECHNE CORP |
| THERAGENICS CORP |
| THIRD WAVE TECHNOLOGIES INC |
| THORATEC CORPORATION |
| TOMOTHERAPY INC |
| UNITED THERAPEUTICS CORP |
| US PHYSICAL THERAPY INC |
| VENTANA MEDICAL SYSTEMS INC |
| VERTEX PHARMACEUTICALS INC |
| VIROPHARMA INC |
| VISION SERVICE PLAN |
| VITAL SIGNS INC |
| WRIGHT MEDICAL GROUP INC |
| XOMA LTD |
| ZILA INC |
| ZOLL MEDICAL CORP |
| ZYMOGENETICS INC |

| Math/Other |
|---|
| ABAXIS INC |
| AFFYMETRIX INC |
| AKAMAI TECHNOLOGIES INC |
| ALBANY MOLECULAR RESEARCH |
| ALEXION PHARMACEUTICALS INC |
| ALIGN TECHNOLOGY INC |
| ALKERMES INC |
| ALLEGHANY CORP |
| ALPHARMA INC |
| ALZA CORP |
| AMERICAN FIDELITY ASSURANCE COMPANY |
| AMERICAN MEDICAL SYSTEMS HOLDINGS INC |
| AMERICAN SCIENCE & ENGINEERING INC |
| AMERICAN SUPERCONDUCTOR CORP |
| AMTECH SYSTEMS INC |
| AMYLIN PHARMACEUTICALS INC |
| ANALOGIC CORP |
| ANIKA THERAPEUTICS INC |
| ANSYS INC |
| APP PHARMACEUTICALS INC |
| ARIBA INC |
| AROTECH CORPORATION |
| ASPECT MEDICAL SYSTEMS INC |
| ASPEN TECHNOLOGY INC |
| ATHEROS COMMUNICATIONS INC |
| ATRION CORPORATION |
| ATS MEDICAL INC |
| AVI BIOPHARMA INC |
| BENTLEY PHARMACEUTICALS INC |
| BIOMARIN PHARMACEUTICAL INC |
| BIOSITE INC |
| BLUE CARE NETWORK OF MICHIGAN |
| CALIPER LIFE SCIENCES |
| CAMBREX CORP |
| CANDELA CORP |
| CANTEL MEDICAL CORP |
| CARACO PHARMACEUTICAL LABORATORIES |
| CELERA CORPORATION |
| CELGENE CORP |
| CELL GENESYS INC |
| CELL THERAPEUTICS INC |
| CEPHEID |
| CHATTEM INC |
| CHOLESTECH CORP |
| CME GROUP |
| COHERENT INC |
| COLLAGENEX PHARMACEUTICALS INC |
| COMMERCE GROUP INC (THE) |
| CRUM & FORSTER HOLDINGS INC |
| CSG SYSTEMS INTERNATIONAL INC |
| CUBIST PHARMACEUTICALS INC |
| CV THERAPEUTICS INC |
| DAKTRONICS INC |

| |
|---|
| DATASCOPE CORP |
| DELPHI FINANCIAL GROUP INC |
| DJO INCORPORATED |
| DSP GROUP INC |
| DYAX CORP |
| ELOYALTY CORPORATION |
| EMBARCADERO TECHNOLOGIES INC |
| EMCORE CORP |
| ENDO PHARMACEUTICALS HOLDINGS INC |
| ENERGY CONVERSION DEVICES INC |
| EVERGREEN SOLAR INC |
| EXACTECH INC |
| EXCEL TECHNOLOGY INC |
| EXELIXIS INC |
| E-Z-EM INC |
| FBL FINANCIAL GROUP |
| FIRST SOLAR LLC |
| FUELCELL ENERGY INC |
| GALLUP ORGANIZATION (THE) |
| GENENCOR INTERNATIONAL INC |
| GENOMIC HEALTH INC |
| GEN-PROBE INC |
| GERON CORPORATION |
| GLOBECOMM SYSTEMS INC |
| GREAT AMERICAN FINANCIAL RESOURCES INC |
| GTC BIOTHERAPEUTICS INC |
| HAEMONETICS CORPORATION |
| HARVARD PILGRIM HEALTH CARE INC |
| HCC INSURANCE HOLDINGS INC |
| HEALTH INSURANCE PLAN OF GREATER NEW YORK |
| HELIOVOLT CORP |
| HI-TECH PHARMACAL CO INC |
| HORACE MANN EDUCATORS CORPORATION |
| HUMAN GENOME SCIENCES INC |
| ICO INC |
| I-FLOW CORPORATION |
| ILLUMINA INC |
| IMMUCOR INC |
| INAMED CORP |
| INDEPENDENCE HOLDING CO |
| INFINERA CORP |
| INSPIRE PHARMACEUTICALS INC |
| INTEGRA LIFESCIENCES HOLDINGS CORP |
| INTERACTIVE BROKERS GROUP INC |
| INTERCONTINENTALEXCHANGE INC (ICE) |
| IRIDEX CORP |
| IRIS INTERNATIONAL INC |
| JACKSON NATIONAL LIFE INSURANCE COMPANY |
| JAZZ PHARMACEUTICALS |
| KNIGHT CAPITAL GROUP INC |
| KV PHARMACEUTICAL CO |
| LIFECELL CORPORATION |
| LIFECORE BIOMEDICAL INC |
| LIVEPERSON INC |
| LORAL SPACE & COMMUNICATIONS LTD |
| LUMINEX CORPORATION |
| MANHATTAN ASSOCIATES INC |
| MARTEK BIOSCIENCES CORP |
| MAXYGEN INC |
| MEDAREX INC |
| MEDICAL ACTION INDUSTRIES INC |
| MEDICINES CO (THE) |
| MEDICIS PHARMACEUTICAL CORP |
| MEDIS TECHNOLOGIES |
| MENTOR CORP |
| MERIDIAN BIOSCIENCE INC |
| MERIT MEDICAL SYSTEMS INC |
| METROPOLITAN HEALTH NETWORKS |
| MICROSTRATEGY INC |
| MICROTEK MEDICAL HOLDINGS INC |
| MILLENNIUM PHARMACEUTICALS INC |
| MOLINA HEALTHCARE INC |
| MTS SYSTEMS |
| MYRIAD GENETICS INC |
| NANOMETRICS INC |
| NASDAQ OMX |
| NATIONAL DENTEX CORP |
| NATUS MEDICAL |
| NEKTAR THERAPEUTICS |
| NEOGEN CORPORATION |
| NETRATINGS INC |
| NETSUITE INC |
| NOVEN PHARMACEUTICALS |
| NYMEX HOLDINGS (NEW YORK MERCANTILE EXCHANGE) |
| ODYSSEY RE HOLDINGS CORP |
| OPTELECOM-NKF INC |
| OSCIENT PHARMACEUTICALS CORPORATION |
| PAR PHARMACEUTICAL COMPANIES INC |
| PHILADELPHIA CONSOLIDATED HOLDING CORP |
| PHOENIX COMPANIES (THE) |
| PITNEY BOWES MAPINFO |
| PLUG POWER INC |
| PMA CAPITAL CORPORATION |
| POLYMEDICA CORPORATION |
| PROASSURANCE CORP |
| PROGRESS SOFTWARE CORP |
| PROTECTIVE LIFE CORP |
| QUIDEL CORP |
| RED HAT INC |
| REGENERON PHARMACEUTICALS INC |
| REINSURANCE GROUP OF AMERICA INC |
| RIGHTNOW TECHNOLOGIES INC |
| SALIX PHARMACEUTICALS |
| SCHICK TECHNOLOGIES INC |
| SCICLONE PHARMACEUTICALS |
| SCIELE PHARMA INC |
| SCIOS INC |
| SEATTLE GENETICS |
| SEPRACOR INC |
| SEQUENOM INC |
| SERENA SOFTWARE INC |
| SOLAR RESERVE |
| SOLFOCUS INC |
| SONIC INNOVATIONS INC |
| SPAN AMERICA MEDICAL SYSTEMS INC |
| SPECTRANETICS CORP |
| SPIRE CORPORATION |
| SPSS INC |
| SRI/SURGICAL EXPRESS INC |
| STAAR SURGICAL CO |
| STANDARD MICROSYSTEMS CORPORATION |
| STATE AUTO FINANCIAL CORP |
| STIEFEL LABORATORIES INC |
| SYCAMORE NETWORKS INC |
| SYMMETRY MEDICAL INC |
| SYNOVIS LIFE TECHNOLOGIES INC |
| TECHNE CORP |
| THERAGENICS CORP |
| THIRD WAVE TECHNOLOGIES INC |
| THORATEC CORPORATION |
| TIBCO SOFTWARE INC |
| TOMOTHERAPY INC |
| TRANSATLANTIC HOLDINGS INC |

| |
|---|
| ULTIMATE SOFTWARE GROUP INC |
| UNITED THERAPEUTICS CORP |
| UNIVERSAL AMERICAN CORPORATION |
| VENTANA MEDICAL SYSTEMS INC |
| VERTEX PHARMACEUTICALS INC |
| VIROPHARMA INC |
| VISION SERVICE PLAN |
| VITAL SIGNS INC |
| WIND RIVER SYSTEMS INC |
| WRIGHT MEDICAL GROUP INC |
| XOMA LTD |
| ZILA INC |
| ZOLL MEDICAL CORP |
| ZYMOGENETICS INC |

| Petroleum/Chemical |
|---|
| ALPHARMA INC |
| AMCOL INTERNATIONAL CORP |
| APP PHARMACEUTICALS INC |
| ARIZONA CHEMICAL COMPANY |
| ATLANTIC CITY ELECTRIC COMPANY |
| AVISTA CORPORATION |
| BERRY PETROLEUM CO |
| BLACK HILLS CORP |
| CALPINE CORPORATION |
| CAMBREX CORP |
| CARACO PHARMACEUTICAL LABORATORIES |
| CENTRAL VERMONT PUBLIC SERVICE CORPORATION |
| CHATTEM INC |
| CNX GAS CORPORATION |
| DENBURY RESOURCES INC |
| DPL INC |
| DYAX CORP |
| DYNEGY INC |
| ENCORE ACQUISITION CO |
| ENDO PHARMACEUTICALS HOLDINGS INC |
| EOG RESOURCES INC |
| EQUITABLE RESOURCES INC |
| EVERGREEN ENERGY INC |
| EXCO RESOURCES INC |
| FOREST OIL CORPORATION |
| FRONTIER OIL CORPORATION |
| GENENCOR INTERNATIONAL INC |
| GENESIS ENERGY LP |
| GREEN MOUNTAIN POWER CORPORATION |
| GTC BIOTHERAPEUTICS INC |
| HI-TECH PHARMACAL CO INC |
| HOLLY CORP |
| HUMAN GENOME SCIENCES INC |
| ICO INC |
| IDACORP INC |
| JAZZ PHARMACEUTICALS |
| KRONOS WORLDWIDE INC |
| KV PHARMACEUTICAL CO |
| LACLEDE GROUP INC (THE) |
| MAGELLAN MIDSTREAM PARTNERS LP |
| MARTEK BIOSCIENCES CORP |
| MCMORAN EXPLORATION CO |
| MEDICINES CO (THE) |
| MILLENNIUM PHARMACEUTICALS INC |
| MYRIAD GENETICS INC |
| NATIONAL FUEL GAS CO |
| NEOGEN CORPORATION |
| NEWFIELD EXPLORATION CO |
| NOBLE ENERGY INC |
| NORTHWESTERN CORPORATION |
| NUSTAR ENERGY LP |
| ONEOK PARTNERS LP |
| ORMAT TECHNOLOGIES |
| PAR PHARMACEUTICAL COMPANIES INC |
| PETROLEUM DEVELOPMENT CORPORATION |
| PIEDMONT NATURAL GAS COMPANY INC |
| PIONEER NATURAL RESOURCES COMPANY |
| PLAINS EXPLORATION AND PRODUCTION COMPANY |
| PRIMEENERGY CORPORATION |
| QUICKSILVER RESOURCES INC |
| RANGE RESOURCES CORP |
| REGENERON PHARMACEUTICALS INC |
| SACRAMENTO MUNICIPAL UTILITY DISTRICT |
| SALIX PHARMACEUTICALS |
| SCICLONE PHARMACEUTICALS |
| SEATTLE GENETICS |
| SEPRACOR INC |
| SOUTHERN UNION COMPANY |
| SOUTHWESTERN ENERGY CO |
| ST MARY LAND & EXPLORATION COMPANY |
| STIEFEL LABORATORIES INC |
| SWIFT ENERGY CO |
| TAMPA ELECTRIC COMPANY |
| TARGA RESOURCES PARTNERS LP |
| TEPPCO PARTNERS LP |
| UIL HOLDINGS CORPORATION |
| UNISOURCE ENERGY CORPORATION |
| VERTEX PHARMACEUTICALS INC |
| WESTAR ENERGY |
| WGL HOLDINGS INC |
| XTO ENERGY INC |
| ZILA INC |
| ZYMOGENETICS INC |

| Scientists/Research |
|---|
| ABAXIS INC |
| AFFYMETRIX INC |
| ALBANY MOLECULAR RESEARCH |
| ALEXION PHARMACEUTICALS INC |
| ALIGN TECHNOLOGY INC |
| ALKERMES INC |
| ALLIANCE IMAGING INC |
| ALPHARMA INC |
| ALZA CORP |
| AMAG PHARMACEUTICALS INC |
| AMERICAN MEDICAL SYSTEMS HOLDINGS INC |
| AMERICAN SCIENCE & ENGINEERING INC |
| AMERICAN SUPERCONDUCTOR CORP |
| AMTECH SYSTEMS INC |
| AMYLIN PHARMACEUTICALS INC |
| ANALOGIC CORP |
| ANIKA THERAPEUTICS INC |
| APP PHARMACEUTICALS INC |
| ARIZONA CHEMICAL COMPANY |
| AROTECH CORPORATION |
| ASPECT MEDICAL SYSTEMS INC |
| ATHEROS COMMUNICATIONS INC |
| ATRION CORPORATION |
| ATS MEDICAL INC |
| AVI BIOPHARMA INC |
| BENTLEY PHARMACEUTICALS INC |
| BIO REFERENCE LABORATORIES INC |
| BIOMARIN PHARMACEUTICAL INC |
| BIOSITE INC |
| CALIPER LIFE SCIENCES |
| CAMBREX CORP |
| CANDELA CORP |

| |
|---|
| CANTEL MEDICAL CORP |
| CARACO PHARMACEUTICAL LABORATORIES |
| CELERA CORPORATION |
| CELGENE CORP |
| CELL GENESYS INC |
| CELL THERAPEUTICS INC |
| CEPHEID |
| CHATTEM INC |
| CHOLESTECH CORP |
| COHERENT INC |
| COLLAGENEX PHARMACEUTICALS INC |
| CRYOLIFE INC |
| CUBIST PHARMACEUTICALS INC |
| CV THERAPEUTICS INC |
| DATASCOPE CORP |
| DIGI INTERNATIONAL INC |
| DJO INCORPORATED |
| DSP GROUP INC |
| DYAX CORP |
| ECHELON CORP |
| EMCORE CORP |
| EMULEX CORP |
| ENCORIUM GROUP INC |
| ENDO PHARMACEUTICALS HOLDINGS INC |
| ENERGY CONVERSION DEVICES INC |
| EPIX PHARMACEUTICALS INC |
| EVERGREEN SOLAR INC |
| EXACTECH INC |
| EXCEL TECHNOLOGY INC |
| EXELIXIS INC |
| E-Z-EM INC |
| FIRST SOLAR LLC |
| FUELCELL ENERGY INC |
| GENENCOR INTERNATIONAL INC |
| GENOMIC HEALTH INC |
| GEN-PROBE INC |
| GERON CORPORATION |
| GTC BIOTHERAPEUTICS INC |
| HAEMONETICS CORPORATION |
| HELIOVOLT CORP |
| HESKA CORP |
| HI-TECH PHARMACAL CO INC |
| HUMAN GENOME SCIENCES INC |
| ICO INC |
| I-FLOW CORPORATION |
| ILLUMINA INC |
| IMMUCOR INC |

| |
|---|
| INAMED CORP |
| INFINERA CORP |
| INSPIRE PHARMACEUTICALS INC |
| INTEGRA LIFESCIENCES HOLDINGS CORP |
| INTERACTIVE INTELLIGENCE |
| IRIDEX CORP |
| IRIS INTERNATIONAL INC |
| ISONICS CORPORATION |
| JAZZ PHARMACEUTICALS |
| KIMLEY-HORN AND ASSOCIATES INC |
| KRONOS WORLDWIDE INC |
| KV PHARMACEUTICAL CO |
| LIFECELL CORPORATION |
| LIFECORE BIOMEDICAL INC |
| LUMINEX CORPORATION |
| MARTEK BIOSCIENCES CORP |
| MAXYGEN INC |
| MEDAREX INC |
| MEDICAL ACTION INDUSTRIES INC |
| MEDICINES CO (THE) |
| MEDICIS PHARMACEUTICAL CORP |
| MEDIS TECHNOLOGIES |
| MEDTOX SCIENTIFIC INC |
| MENTOR CORP |
| MERIDIAN BIOSCIENCE INC |
| MERIT MEDICAL SYSTEMS INC |
| MICROTEK MEDICAL HOLDINGS INC |
| MILLENNIUM PHARMACEUTICALS INC |
| MYRIAD GENETICS INC |
| NANOMETRICS INC |
| NATIONAL DENTEX CORP |
| NATUS MEDICAL |
| NEKTAR THERAPEUTICS |
| NEOGEN CORPORATION |
| NETGEAR INC |
| NOVEN PHARMACEUTICALS |
| OPTELECOM-NKF INC |
| OSCIENT PHARMACEUTICALS CORPORATION |
| PAR PHARMACEUTICAL COMPANIES INC |
| PLUG POWER INC |
| POLYMEDICA CORPORATION |
| QLOGIC CORP |
| QUIDEL CORP |
| RADNET INC |
| REGENERON PHARMACEUTICALS INC |

| |
|---|
| SALIX PHARMACEUTICALS |
| SCHICK TECHNOLOGIES INC |
| SCHIFF NUTRITION INTERNATIONAL INC |
| SCICLONE PHARMACEUTICALS |
| SCIELE PHARMA INC |
| SCIOS INC |
| SEATTLE GENETICS |
| SEPRACOR INC |
| SEQUENOM INC |
| SOLAR RESERVE |
| SOLFOCUS INC |
| SONIC INNOVATIONS INC |
| SPAN AMERICA MEDICAL SYSTEMS INC |
| SPECTRANETICS CORP |
| SPIRE CORPORATION |
| SRI/SURGICAL EXPRESS INC |
| STAAR SURGICAL CO |
| STANDARD MICROSYSTEMS CORPORATION |
| STIEFEL LABORATORIES INC |
| SYMMETRY MEDICAL INC |
| SYMYX TECHNOLOGIES |
| SYNOVIS LIFE TECHNOLOGIES INC |
| TECHNE CORP |
| THERAGENICS CORP |
| THIRD WAVE TECHNOLOGIES INC |
| THORATEC CORPORATION |
| TOMOTHERAPY INC |
| UNITED THERAPEUTICS CORP |
| VENTANA MEDICAL SYSTEMS INC |
| VERTEX PHARMACEUTICALS INC |
| VIROPHARMA INC |
| VITAL SIGNS INC |
| VSE CORP |
| WRIGHT MEDICAL GROUP INC |
| XOMA LTD |
| ZILA INC |
| ZOLL MEDICAL CORP |
| ZYMOGENETICS INC |